Features

Visit us on the web at
http://www.census.gov/statab/www/

Statistical Abstract of the United States

119th edition

1999

The National Data Book

Issued October 1999

U.S. Department of Commerce
William M. Daley,
Secretary

**Economics and Statistics
Administration
Robert J. Shapiro**,
Under Secretary for Economic Affairs

**U.S. CENSUS BUREAU
Kenneth Prewitt**,
Director

ECONOMICS
AND STATISTICS
ADMINISTRATION

U.S. CENSUS BUREAU

Economics and Statistics Administration

Robert J. Shapiro, Under Secretary for Economic Affairs

Kenneth Prewitt, Director
William G. Barron, Deputy Director
Nancy A. Potok, Principal Associate Director and Chief Financial Officer
Michael S. McKay, Associate Director for Finance and Administration

ADMINISTRATIVE AND CUSTOMER SERVICES DIVISION

Walter C. Odom, Chief

Acknowledgments

Lars B. Johanson was responsible for the technical supervision and coordination of this volume under the general direction of **Glenn W. King**, Chief, Statistical Compendia Branch. Assisting in the research and analytical phases of assigned sections and in the developmental aspects of new tables were **Rosemary E. Clark**, **Edward C. Jagers**, and **David J. Fleck**. **Geraldine W. Blackburn** provided primary editorial assistance. Other editorial assistance was rendered by **Patricia S. Lancaster**, **Catherine Lavender**, **Joyce Mori**, and **Barbara Shugart**.

The staff of the Administrative and Customer Services Division, under the general supervision of **Walter C. Odom,** Chief, and direct supervision of **Michael G. Garland**, Assistant Chief, performed planning, design, composition, editorial review, and printing planning and procurement for publications, Internet products, and report forms. **Penny Heiston**, assisted by **Gloria Davis** and **Elizabeth J. Williams**, provided publication coordination and editing. **Janet Sweeney** provided design and graphics services, and **Arlene Duckett** provided printing services.

The cooperation of many contributors to this volume is gratefully acknowledged. The source note below each table credits the various government and private agencies which have collaborated in furnishing information for the *Statistical Abstract*. In a few instances, contributors have requested that their data be designated as subject to copyright restrictions, as indicated in the source notes to the tables affected. Permission to use copyright material should be obtained directly from the copyright owner.

Library of Congress Card No. 4-18089

Suggested Citation

U.S. Census Bureau, *Statistical Abstract of the United States: 1999* (119th edition) Washington, DC, 1999

Reprinted without alteration on acid-free paper
National Technical Information Service (NTIS), Springfield, VA,
November 1999
ISBN (case) 0-934213-72-0   (paper) 0-934213-73-9

Preface

The *Statistical Abstract of the United States*, published since 1878, is the standard summary of statistics on the social, political, and economic organization of the United States. It is designed to serve as a convenient volume for statistical reference and as a guide to other statistical publications and sources. The latter function is served by the introductory text to each section, the source note appearing below each table, and Appendix I, which comprises the Guide to Sources of Statistics, the Guide to State Statistical Abstracts, and the Guide to Foreign Statistical Abstracts.

This volume includes a selection of data from many statistical publications, both government and private. Publications cited as sources usually contain additional statistical detail and more comprehensive discussions of definitions and concepts than can be presented here. Data not available in publications issued by the contributing agency but obtained from unpublished records are identified in the source notes as "unpublished data." More information on the subjects covered in the tables so noted may generally be obtained from the source.

Except as indicated, figures are for the United States as presently constituted. Although emphasis in the *Statistical Abstract* is primarily given to national data, many tables present data for regions and individual states and a smaller number for metropolitan areas and cities. Appendix II, Metropolitan Area Concepts and Components, presents explanatory text, a complete current listing and population data for metropolitan statistical areas (MSAs), the primary metropolitan statistical areas (PMSAs), and the consolidated metropolitan statistical areas (CMSAs) defined as of June 30, 1999. Table 43 in Section 1 presents selected population characteristics for MSAs with population of 250,000 or more. Statistics for the Commonwealth of Puerto Rico and for outlying areas of the United States are included in many state tables and are supplemented by information in Section 29. Additional information for states, cities, counties, metropolitan areas, and other small units, as well as more historical data are available in various supplements to the *Abstract* (see inside back cover).

Statistics in this edition are generally for the most recent year or period available by spring 1999. Each year almost 1,500 tables and charts are reviewed and evaluated; new tables and charts of current interest are added, continuing series are updated, and less timely data are condensed or eliminated. Text notes and appendices are revised as appropriate.

USA Statistics in Brief, 1999, a pocket-size pamphlet highlighting many statistical series in the *Abstract*, is available separately. Single copies can be obtained free from U.S. Census Bureau, Customer Services, Washington, DC 20233 (telephone 301-457-4100). We attempt to update the pamphlet several times during the year. The latest data can be found on our web site: <http://www.census.gov/statab/www/brief.html>

Changes in this edition—This year we have introduced 140 new tables covering a wide range of subject area. Several sections have preliminary data from the 1997 Economic Census, which presents industry statistics for the first time based on the North American Industry Classification System (NAICS). Comparative data for 1992 and 1997, based on the Standard Industrial Classification (SIC), are also presented. Tables 872 and 873 in Section 17, Business, present summary data for industries. Other new tables cover such topics as the foreign-born population, health care expenditures, the medicare trust fund, violence in schools, presale handgun checks, recycling programs, defense-related employment and spending, workplace violence, ownership of mutual funds, computer use, results of the 1997 Census of Agriculture, and mail order catalogue sales.

In addition to the above new tables, we have also developed a new section, 20th Century Statistics, presenting data beginning in 1900

v

where available on a broad range of subjects, including population, vital statistics, health, education, income, labor force, communications, agriculture, defense, and other areas. See Section 31. The industrial outlook tables, previously in Section 31, have been deleted since we were unable to update them. For a complete list of new tables, see Appendix VI, pp. 947.

We have also slightly modified our headnotes to provide table-specific examples of how unit indicators are interpreted.

Statistical Abstract on other media— The Abstract is available in its entirety on the Internet and, an enhanced version, on CD-ROM (except for a few copyrighted tables deleted by the request of source organizations). Our Internet site, <http://www.census.gov/statab/www>, contains this 1999 edition and earlier editions of the book, as well as summary items—Statistics in Brief, Frequently Requested Tables, and State Rankings, which will be updated as time allows. State and County Profiles is also on the site.

The CD-ROM version of the *Abstract* is enriched with links from tables to the Internet sites of appropriate government agencies. In addition, links are provided to the underlying spreadsheets (both .WK1 and .XLS) from which the data in the tables are based. Ordering information for the CD-ROM is located in the inside back cover.

Statistics for states and metropolitan areas— Extensive data for the states and metropolitan areas of the United States can be found in the *State and Metropolitan Area Data Book: 1997-98*. It features 859 data items covering everything from age and agriculture to wages and welfare for the 50 states and the District of Columbia with United States totals for comparison. Also included are over 150 data items for metropolitan areas (MAs), 43 items for component counties of MAs, and 3 population items for central cities of MAs.

This publication, as well as selected rankings of the states and metropolitan areas, is available on our Internet site at <http://www.census.gov/statab/www/smadb.html>. Some data items that appear in the book from private sources are not available on the Internet or CD-ROM versions because we did not receive copyright permission to release the data items in these formats. The CD-ROM version also includes links from the data tables to spreadsheets (both .WK1 and .XLS) with the data and pertinent geographic information, to contributing government agency Internet sites, and to related source notes and explanations. See the inside back cover for ordering information.

Limitations of the data— The contents of this volume were taken from many sources. All data from either censuses and surveys or from administrative records are subject to error arising from a number of factors: Sampling variability (for statistics based on samples), reporting errors in the data for individual units, incomplete coverage, nonresponse, imputations, and processing error. (See also Appendix III, pp. 924-942.) The Census Bureau cannot accept the responsibility for the accuracy or limitations of the data presented here, other than those for which it collects. The responsibility for selection of the material and for proper presentation, however, rests with the Bureau.

For additional information on data presented— Please consult the source publications available in local libraries or write to the agency indicated in the source notes. Write to the Census Bureau only if it is cited as the source.

Suggestions and comments— Users of the *Statistical Abstract* and its supplements (see inside back cover) are urged to make their data needs known for consideration in planning future editions. Suggestions and comments for improving coverage and presentation of data should be sent to the Director, U.S. Census Bureau, Washington, DC 20233.

Statistical Abstract User Survey— Inserted in this edition is the eighth user survey taken periodically to ask for your suggestions on various aspects of the *Abstract* and related publications. Your input will help us to maintain the usefulness of the Compendia program. If the questionnaire is missing and you would like to participate in the survey, you may obtain one by writing to us: U.S. Census Bureau, Statistical Compendia Staff, ACSD, FOB 4, Room 1109, Washington DC 20233 or e-mail us at compendia@census.gov.

Contents

[Numbers following subjects are page numbers]

Example of Table Structure

No. 1093. Private Shipyards—Summary: 1980 to 1999

[For calendar year, unless noted. (178.0 represents 178,000)]

Item	Unit	1980	1985	1990	1994	1995	1996	1997	1998	1999 [1]
Employment [2]	1,000.	178.0	138.3	130.8	107.2	105.0	100.4	98.6	99.6	99.9
Production workers	1,000.	138.8	101.2	93.6	79.7	77.8	73.5	70.8	71.6	70.3
Building activity:										
Merchant vessels: [3]										
Under construction [4]	Number.	69	10	-	1	3	10	14	12	5
Ordered	Number.	7	-	3	3	8	5	6	1	2
Delivered	Number.	23	3	-	1	1	1	4	5	1
Cancelled	Number.	4	-	-	-	-	-	4	3	
Under contract [5]	Number.	49	7	3	3	10	14	12	5	6
Naval vessels: [3]										
Under construction [4]	Number.	99	100	95	60	57	46	46	42	46
Ordered	Number.	11	11	7	12	6	11	4	17	-
Delivered	Number.	19	26	15	15	17	11	8	13	4
Under contract [5]	Number.	91	85	87	57	46	46	42	46	42
Unfinished work: [4]										
Commercial ships	Mil. dol.	2,070	450	-	58.3	93.4	365.4	572.1	746.5	596.6
Naval ships	Mil. dol.	7,107	12,091	24,495	19,679	20,768	17,734	20,116	19,097	18,079

- Represents zero. [1] As of June 1. [2] Annual average of monthly data. [3] Vessels of 1,000 tons or larger. [4] As of Jan. 1.
[5] As of Dec. 31.

Source: 1980 and 1985, Shipbuilders Council of America, Arlington, VA., unpublished data; beginning 1990, U.S. Maritime Administration, unpublished data.

Headnotes immediately below table titles provide information important for correct interpretation or evaluation of the table as a whole or for a major segment of it.

Footnotes below the bottom rule of tables give information relating to specific items or figures within the table.

Unit indicators show the *specified quantities* in which data items are presented. They are used for two primary reasons. Sometimes data are not available in absolute form and are estimates (as in the case of many surveys). In other cases we round the numbers in order to save space to show more data, as in the case above.

EXAMPLES OF UNIT INDICATOR INTERPRETATION FROM TABLE

Year	Item	Unit Indicator	Number shown	Multiplier
1980	Employment	Thousands	178.0	1,000
1980	Unfinished work	$ Millions	2,070	1,000,000

To Determine the Figure It Is Necessary to Multiply the Number Shown by the Unit Indicator:

Employment - 178.0 x 1,000 = 178,000 (Almost 180 thousand)
Unfinished work - 2,070 x 1,000,000 - $2,070,000,000 (over $2 billion).

When a table presents data with more than one unit indicator, they are found in the headnotes and column headings (Tables 2 and 4), spanner (Table 52), stub (Table 82), or unit column (shown above). When the data in a table are shown in the same unit indicator, it is shown in boldface as the first part of the headnote (Table 2). If no unit indicator is shown, data presented are in absolute form (Table 1).

Vertical rules are used to separate independent sections of a table, (Table 1), or in tables where the stub is continued into one or more additional columns (Table 2).

Averages—An average is a single number or value that is often used to represent the "typical value" of a group of numbers. It is regarded as a measure of "location" or "central tendency" of a group of numbers.

The *arithmetic mean* is the type of average used most frequently. It is derived by summing the individual item values of a particular group and dividing the total by the number of items. The arithmetic mean is often referred to as simply the "mean" or "average."

The *median* of a group of numbers is the middle number or value when each item in the group is arranged according to size (lowest to highest or visa versa); it generally has the same number of items above it as well as below it. If there is an even number if items in the group, the median is taken to be the average of the two middle numbers.

Per capita (or per person) quantities. A per capita figure represents an average computed for every person in a specified group (or population). It is derived by taking the total for an item (such as income, taxes,or retail sales) and dividing it by the number of persons in the specified population.

Guide to Tabular Presentation ix

Index numbers—An index number is the measure of difference or change, usually expressed as a percent, relating one quantity (the variable) of a specified kind to another quantity of the same kind. Index numbers are widely used to express changes in prices over periods of time but may also be used to express differences between related subjects for a single point in time.

To compute a price index, a base year or period is selected. The base year price (of the commodity or service) is then designated as the base or reference price to which the prices for other years or periods are related. Many price indexes use the year 1982 as the base year; in tables this is shown as "1982=100." A method of expressing the price relationship is: The price of a set of one or more items for a related year (e.g. 1990) **divided by** the price of the same set of items for the base year (e.g. 1982). The result multiplied by 100 provides the index number. When 100 is subtracted from the index number, the result equals the percent change in price from the base year.

Average annual percent change— Unless otherwise stated in the *Abstract* (as in Section 1, Population), average annual percent change is computed by use of a *compound interest formula.* This formula assumes that the rate of change is constant throughout a specified compounding period (1 year for average annual rates of change). The formula is similar to that used to compute the balance of a savings account which receives compound interest. According to this formula, at the end of a compounding period the amount of accrued change (e.g. school enrollment or bank interest) is added to the amount which existed at the beginning the period. As a result, over time (e.g., with each year or quarter), the same rate of change is applied to a larger and larger figure.

The *exponential formula,* which is based on continuous compounding, is often used to measure population change. It is preferred by population experts because they view population and population-related subjects as changing without interruption, ever ongoing. Both exponential and compound interest formulas assume a constant rate of change. The former, however, applies the amount of change continuously to the base rather than at the end of each compounding period. When the average annual rates are small (e.g., less than 5 percent) both formulas give virtually the same results. For an explanation of these two formulas as

they relate to population, see U.S. Census Bureau, *The Methods and Materials of Demography,* Vol. 2, 3d printing (rev.), 1975, pp. 372-381.

Current and constant dollars— Statistics in some tables in a number of sections are expressed in both current and constant dollars (see, for example, Table 733 in Section 14, Income). Current dollar figures reflect actual prices or costs prevailing during the specified year(s). Constant dollar figures are estimates representing an effort to remove the effects of price changes from statistical series reported in dollar terms. In general, constant dollar series are derived by dividing current dollar estimates by the appropriate price index for the appropriate period (for example, the Consumer Price Index). The result is a series as it would presumably exist if prices were the same throughout, as in the base year—in other words as if the dollar had constant purchasing power. Any changes in this constant dollar series would reflect only changes in real volume of output, income, expenditures, or other measure.

Explanation of Symbols

The following symbols, used in the tables throughout this book, are explained in condensed form in footnotes to the tables where they appear:

- Represents zero or rounds to less than half the unit of measurement shown.

B Base figure too small to meet statistical standards for reliability of a derived figure.

D Figure withheld to avoid disclosure pertaining to a specific organization or individual.

NA Data not enumerated, tabulated, or otherwise available separately.

NS Percent change irrelevant or insignificant.

S Figure does not meet publication standards for reasons other than that covered by symbol B, above.

X Figure not applicable because column heading and stub line make entry impossible, absurd, or meaningless.

Z Entry would amount to less than half the unit of measurement shown.

In many tables, details will not add to the totals shown because of rounding.

Telephone Contacts

To help *Abstract* users find more data and information about statistical publications, we are issuing this list of contacts for Federal agencies with major statistical programs. The intent is to give a single, first-contact point-of-entry for users of statistics. These agencies will provide general information on their statistical programs and publications, as well as specific information on how to order their publications. We are also including the Internet (World-Wide-Web) addresses for many of these agencies. These URLs were current in early August 1999.

Executive Office of the President

Office of Management and Budget
Administrator
Office of Information and Regulatory Affairs
Office of Management and Budget
Washington, DC 20503
Information: 202-395-3080
Publications: 202-395-7332
Internet address:
  http://www.whitehouse. gov/omb

Department of Agriculture

Economic Research Service
Information Center
U.S. Department of Agriculture
Room 3100
1800 M St. N.W.
Washington, DC 20036-5831
Information and Publications:
  202-694-5050
Internet address:
  http://www.econ.ag.gov/

National Agricultural Statistics Service
National Agricultural Statistics Service
U.S. Department of Agriculture
1400 Independence Ave., S.W., Room 5805
Washington, DC 20250
Information hotline:
  1-800-727-9540
Internet address:
  http://www.usda.gov/nass/

Department of Commerce

U.S. Census Bureau
Customer Services Branch
U.S. Census Bureau
U.S. Department of Commerce
Washington, DC 20233
Information and Publications:
  301-457-4100
Internet address:
  http://www.census.gov/

Bureau of Economic Analysis
Current Business Analysis Division, BE-53
Bureau of Economic Analysis
U.S. Department of Commerce
Washington, DC 20230
Information and Publications:
  202-606-9900
Internet address:
  http://www.bea.doc.gov/

International Trade Administration
Trade Statistics Division
Office of Trade and Economic Analysis
International Trade Administration
Room 2814 B
U.S. Department of Commerce
Washington, DC 20230
Information and Publications:
  202-482-2185
Internet address:
  http://www.ita.doc.gov/tradestats/

National Oceanic and Atmospheric Administration
National Oceanic and Atmospheric Administration Central Library
U.S. Department of Commerce
1315 East-West Highway
2nd Floor
Silver Spring MD 20910
Library: 301-713-2600
Internet address:
  http://www.lib.noaa.gov/

Department of Defense

Office of the Assistant Secretary of Defense (Public Affairs)
Room 1E757
Attention: Directorate for Public Communications
1400 Defense Pentagon
Washington, DC 20301-1400
Information: 703-697-5737
Internet address:
  http://web1.whs. osd.mil/diorhome.htm

U.S. Census Bureau, Statistical Abstract of the United States: 1999

Department of Education

U.S. Department of Education
400 Maryland Avenue, S.W.
Washington, DC 20202-5621
Education Information and Statistics:
1-800-424-1616
Education Publications: 1-877-433-7827
Internet address: http://www.ed.gov/

Department of Energy

Energy Information Administration
National Energy Information Center
U.S. Department of Energy
1000 Independence Ave., SW
1E248-EI-30
Washington, DC 20585
Information and Publications:
202-586-8800
Internet address:
http://www.eia.doe.gov/

Department of Health and Human Services

Health Resources and Services Administration
HRSA Office of Communications
5600 Fishers Lane, Room 14-45
Rockville, MD 20857
Publications: 301-443-3376
Internet address:
http://www.hrsa.dhhs.gov/

Substance Abuse Mental Health Services Administration
U.S. Department of Health and Human Services
5600 Fishers Lane
Room 12-105
Rockville, MD 20857
Information: 301-443-4795
Publications: 1-800-729-6686
Internet address:
http://www.samhsa.gov/

Centers for Disease Control and Prevention
Office of Information
Centers for Disease Control
1600 Clifton Road, N.E.
Atlanta, GA 30333
Public Inquiries: 1-800-311-3435
Internet address: http://www.cdc.gov/

Health Care Financing Administration
Office of Public Affairs
Health Care Financing Administration
U.S. Department of Health and Human Services
Room 303D, Humphrey Building
200 Independence Ave., S.W.
Washington, DC 20201
Media Relations: 202-690-6145
Internet address: http://www.hcfa.gov/

National Center for Health Statistics
Scientific and Technical Information Branch
National Center for Health Statistics
U.S. Department of Health and Human Services
6525 Belcrest Rd. Rm. 1064
Hyattsville, MD 20782
Information and Publications:
301-436-8500
Internet address:
http://www.cdc.gov/nchswww

Social Security Administration
Office of Research Evaluation and Statistics
Division of Publications
500 E. Street S.W. 9th Floor ITC
Washington, DC 20254
Information and Publications:
1-800-772-1213
Internet address:
http://www.ssa.gov/statistics/
orespubs.htm

Department of Housing and Urban Development

Assistant Secretary for Community Planning and Development
Office of the Assistant Secretary for Community Planning and Development
U.S. Department of Housing and Urban Development
451 7th St., S.W.
Washington, DC 20410-0555
Information: 202-708-2690
Publications: 1-800-998-9999
Internet address:
http://www.huduser.org/

Department of the Interior

Geological Survey
Earth Science Information Center
Geological Survey
U.S. Department of the Interior
507 National Center
Reston, VA 20192
Information and Publications:
703-648-5953
Internet address for minerals:
http://minerals.usgs.gov/
Internet address for other USGS materials: http://www.usgs.gov/

Department of Justice

Bureau of Justice Statistics
Statistics Division
810 7th St., N.W. 2nd Floor
Washington, DC 20531
Information and Publications:
202-307-0765
Internet address:
http://www.ojp.usdoj.gov/bjs/

National Criminal Justice Reference Service
Box 6000
Rockville, MD 20849-6000
Information and Publications:
301-519-5500
Publications: 1-800-732-3277
Internet address: http://www.ncjrs.org/

Federal Bureau of Investigation
National Crime Information Center
Federal Bureau of Investigation
U.S. Department of Justice
935 Pennsylvania Ave., N.W.
Washington, DC 20535
Information and Publications:
202-324-3691
Publications: 202-324-5611
Internet address: http://www.fbi.gov/

Immigration and Naturalization Service
Statistics Branch
Immigration and Naturalization Service
U.S. Department of Justice
425 I St., NW, Rm. 5309
Washington, DC 20536
Information and Publications:
202-305-1613
Internet address:
http://www.usdoj.gov/ins/index.html

Department of Labor

Bureau of Labor Statistics
Office of Publications and Information
Services
Bureau of Labor Statistics
U.S. Department of Labor
2 Mass. Ave., N.E., Room 2860
Washington, DC 20212
Information and Publications:
202-606-5886
Internet address: http://stats.bls.gov/

Employment and Training Administration
Office of Public Affairs
Employment and Training Administration
U.S. Department of Labor
200 Constitution Ave., N.W.,
Room S4206
Washington, DC 20210
Information and Publications:
202-219-6871
Internet address: http://www.doleta.gov/

Department of Transportation

Federal Aviation Administration
Public Inquiry Center
APA 200
Federal Aviation Administration
U.S. Department of Transportation
800 Independence Ave., S.W.
Washington, DC 20591
Information and Publications:
202-267-3484
Internet address: http://www.faa.gov/

Bureau of Transportation Statistics
400 7th St., SW
Washington, DC 20590
Products: 202-554-3564
Statistical information: 800-853-1351
Internet address: http://www.bts.gov/

Federal Highway Administration
Office of Public Affairs
Federal Highway Administration
U.S. Department of Transportation
400 7th St., S.W.
Washington, DC 20590
Information: 202-366-0660
Internet address:
http://www.fhwa.dot.gov/

National Highway Traffic Safety Administration
Office of Public & Consumer Affairs
National Highway Traffic Safety
Administration
U.S. Department of Transportation
400 7th St., S.W.
Washington, DC 20590
Information: 202-366-9550
Publications: 202-366-2587
Internet address:
http://www.nhtsa.dot.gov/

Department of the Treasury

Internal Revenue Service
Statistics of Income Division
Internal Revenue Service
P.O. Box 2608
Washington, DC 20013-2608
Information and Publications:
202-874-0410
Internet address:
http://www.irs.ustreas.gov/cover.html

Department of Veterans Affairs

Department of Veterans Affairs
Office of Public Affairs
Department of Veterans Affairs
810 Vermont Ave., N.W.
Washington, DC 20420
Information: 202-273-5400
Internet address: http://www.va.gov/

Independent Agencies

Administrative Office of the U.S. Courts
Statistics Division
Columbus Circle, N.E.
Washington, DC 20544
Information: 202-502-1455
Internet address:
http://www.uscourts.gov/

Environmental Protection Agency
Information Resource Center, Rm. M2904
Environmental Protection Agency
401 M St., S.W.
Washington, DC 20460
Information: 202-260-5922
Internet address: http://www.epa.gov/

Federal Reserve Board
Division of Research and Statistics
Federal Reserve Board
Washington, DC 20551
Information: 202-452-3301
Publications: 202-452-3245
Internet address:
http://www.bog.frb.fed.us/

National Science Foundation
Office of Legislation and Public Affairs
National Science Foundation
4201 Wilson Boulevard
Arlington Virginia 22230
Information: 703-306-1234
Publications: 301-947-2722
Internet address:
http://www.nsf.gov:80/sbe/srs/stats.htm

Securities and Exchange Commission
Office of Public Affairs
Securities and Exchange Commission
450 5th St., N.W.
Washington, DC 20549
Information: 202-942-0020
Publications: 202-942-4040
Internet address: http://www.sec.gov/

Population

This section presents statistics on the growth, distribution, and characteristics of the U.S. population. The principal source of these data is the U.S. Census Bureau, which conducts a decennial census of population, a monthly population survey, a program of population estimates and projections, and a number of other periodic surveys relating to population characteristics. For a list of relevant publications, see the Guide to Sources of Statistics in Appendix I.

Decennial censuses—The U.S. Constitution provides for a census of the population every 10 years, primarily to establish a basis for apportionment of members of the House of Representatives among the states. For over a century after the first census in 1790, the census organization was a temporary one, created only for each decennial census. In 1902, the Census Bureau was established as a permanent Federal agency, responsible for enumerating the population and also for compiling statistics on other subjects.

Historically the census of population has been a complete count. That is, an attempt is made to account for every person, for each person's residence, and for other characteristics (sex, age, family relationships, etc.). Since the 1940 census, in addition to the complete count information, some data have been obtained from representative samples of the population. In the 1990 census, variable sampling rates were employed. For most of the country, 1 in every 6 households (about 17 percent) received the long form or sample questionnaire; in governmental units estimated to have fewer than 2,500 inhabitants, every other household (50 percent) received the sample questionnaire to enhance the reliability of sample data for small areas. Exact agreement is not to be expected between sample data and the complete census

count. Sample data may be used with confidence where large numbers are involved and assumed to indicate trends and relationships where small numbers are involved.

Census Bureau data presented here have not been adjusted for underenumeration. Results from the evaluation program for the 1990 census indicate that the overall national undercount was between 1 and 2 percent. The estimate from the Post Enumeration Survey (PES) was 1.6 percent, and the estimate from Demographic Analysis (DA) was 1.8 percent. Both the PES and DA estimates show disproportionately high undercounts for some demographic groups. For example, the PES estimates of percent net undercount for Blacks (4.4 percent), Hispanics (5.0 percent), and American Indians (4.5 percent) were higher than the estimated undercount of non-Hispanic Whites (0.7 percent). Historical DA estimates demonstrate that the overall undercount rate in the census has declined significantly over the past 50 years (from an estimated 5.4 percent in 1940 to 1.8 percent in 1990), yet the undercount of Blacks has remained disproportionately high.

Current Population Survey (CPS)—This is a monthly nationwide survey of a scientifically selected sample representing the noninstitutional civilian population. The sample is located in 754 areas comprising 2,121 counties, independent cities, and minor civil divisions with coverage in every state and the District of Columbia and is subject to sampling error. At the present time, about 50,000 occupied households are eligible for interview every month; of these between 4 and 5 percent are, for various reasons, unavailable for interview.

While the primary purpose of the CPS is to obtain monthly statistics on the labor

U.S. Census Bureau, Statistical Abstract of the United States: 1999

force, it also serves as a vehicle for inquiries on other subjects. Using CPS data, the Bureau issues a series of publications under the general title of *Current Population Reports*, which cover population characteristics (P20), consumer income (P60), special studies (P23), and other topics.

Estimates of population characteristics based on the CPS will not agree with the counts from the census because the CPS and the census use different procedures for collecting and processing the data for racial groups, the Hispanic population, and other topics. Caution should also be used when comparing estimates for various years because of the periodic introduction of changes into the CPS. Beginning in January 1994, a number of changes were introduced into the CPS that effect all data comparisons with prior years. These changes include the results of a major redesign of the survey questionnaire and collection methodology and the introduction of 1990 census population controls, adjusted for the estimated undercount. This change in population controls had relatively little impact on derived measures such as means, medians, and percent distribution, but did have a significant impact on levels.

Population estimates and projections— National population estimates start with decennial census data as benchmarks and add annual population component of change data. Component of change data comes from various agencies, as follows: National Center for Health Statistics (births and deaths), Immigration and Naturalization Service (legal immigrants), Office of Refugee Resettlement (refugees), U.S. Census Bureau's International Programs Center (net movement between Puerto Rico and the U.S. mainland), Armed Forces, Department of Defense, and Office of Personnel Management (movement of military and civilian citizens abroad). Emigration and net undocumented immigration are projected based on research using census data. Estimates for states, counties, and smaller areas are based on the same component of change data, and sources as the

national estimates. School statistics from state departments of education and parochial school systems, Federal income tax returns from the Internal Revenue Service, group quarters from the Federal-State Cooperative program and the Veterans Administration, and medicare data from the Health Care Financing Administration are also included.

Data for the population by age for April 1, 1990, (shown in Tables 14, 21, and 23) are modified counts. The review of detailed 1990 information indicated that respondents tended to provide their age as of the date of completion of the questionnaire, not their age as of April 1, 1990. In addition, there may have been a tendency for respondents to round up their age if they were close to having a birthday. A detailed explanation of the age modification procedure appears in 1990 Census of Population and Housing Data Paper Listing (CPH-L-74).

Population estimates and projections are published in the P25 series of *Current Population Reports* and as *Population Paper Listings* (PPLs). These estimates and projections are generally consistent with official decennial census figures and do not reflect the amount of estimated census underenumeration. However, these estimates and projections by race have been modified and are not comparable to the census race categories (see section below under "race"). For details on methodology, see the sources cited below the individual tables.

The state population projections, by single year of age, sex, race, and Hispanic origin, prepared for 1995 to 2025 use a cohort-component methodology to generate the projected populations. This method requires separate assumptions for each population component of change: births, deaths, internal migration, and international migration. Data for population components of change derive from various governmental administrative records and census distributions. The 1994 state population estimates serve as the starting point for these projections, which are consistent with the national population projections listed in *Current Population Reports*, Series P25-1130. The two series of projections (see Table 35) are based on different internal migration assumptions: Series A, the preferred series model, which uses state-to-state migration observed from 1975-76 through 1993-94; and Series B, the economic model, which uses the Bureau of Economic Analysis employment projections.

Immigration—The principal source of immigration data is the *Statistical Yearbook of the Immigration and Naturalization Service*, published annually by the Immigration and Naturalization Service (INS), a unit of the Department of Justice. Immigration statistics are prepared from entry visas and change of immigration status forms. Immigrants are aliens admitted for legal permanent residence in the United States. The procedures for admission depend on whether the alien is residing inside or outside the United States at the time of application for permanent residence. Eligible aliens residing outside the United States are issued immigrant visas by the U.S. Department of State. Eligible aliens residing in the United States are allowed to change their status from temporary to permanent residence at INS district offices. The category, immigrant, includes persons who may have entered the United States as nonimmigrants or refugees, but who subsequently changed their status to that of a permanent resident. Nonresident aliens admitted to the United States for a temporary period are nonimmigrants (Tables 7 and 461). Refugees are considered nonimmigrants when initially admitted into the United States but are not included in nonimmigrant admission data. A refugee is any person who is outside his or her country of nationality who is unable or unwilling to return to that country because of persecution or a well-founded fear of persecution.

U.S. immigration law gives preferential immigration status to aliens who are related to certain U.S. citizens or legal permanent residents, aliens with needed job skills, or aliens who qualify as refugees. Immigration to the United States can be divided into two general categories: (1) those subject to the annual worldwide limitation, and (2) those exempt from it. The Immigration Act of 1990 established major revisions in the numerical limits and preference system regulating legal immigration. The numerical limits are imposed on visas issued and not on admissions. The maximum number of visas allowed to be issued under the preference categories in 1997 was 366,000 — 226,000 for family-sponsored immigrants and 140,000 for employment-based immigrants. There are nine categories among which the family-sponsored and employment-based immigrant visas are distributed, beginning in fiscal year 1992. The family-sponsored preferences are based on the alien's relationship with a U.S. citizen or legal permanent resident (see Table 6). The employment-based preferences are 1) priority workers (persons of extraordinary ability, outstanding professors and researchers, and certain multinational executives and managers); 2) professionals with advanced degrees or aliens with exceptional ability; 3) skilled workers, professionals without advanced degrees, and needed unskilled workers; 4) special immigrants; and 5) employment creation immigrants (investors). Within the overall limitations the per-country limit for independent countries is set to 7 percent of the total family-sponsored and employment-based limits, while dependent areas are limited to 2 percent of the total. The 1997 limit allowed no more than 25,620 preference visas for any independent country and 7,320 for any dependency. Those exempt from the worldwide limitation include immediate relatives of U.S. citizens, refugees and asylees adjusting to permanent residence, and other various classes of special immigrants (see Table 6).

The Refugee Act of 1980, effective April 1, 1980, provides for a uniform admission procedure for refugees of all countries, based on the United Nations' definition of refugees. Authorized admission ceilings are set annually by the President in consultation with Congress. After 1 year of residence in the United States, refugees are eligible for immigrant status.

Population 3

The Immigration Reform and Control Act of 1986 (IRCA) allows two groups of illegal aliens to become temporary and then permanent residents of the United States: aliens who have been in the United States unlawfully since January 1, 1982 (legalization applicants), and aliens who were employed in seasonal agricultural work for a minimum period of time (Special Agricultural Worker (SAW) applicants). The application period for temporary residency for legalization applicants began on May 5, 1987, and ended on May 4, 1988, while the application period for SAW applicants began on June 1, 1987, and ended on November 30, 1988. Legalization applicants became eligible for permanent residence beginning in fiscal year 1989. Beginning 1989 immigrant data include temporary residents who were granted permanent residence under the legalization program of IRCA.

Metropolitan Areas (MAs)—The general concept of a metropolitan area is one of a core area containing a large population nucleus, together with adjacent communities that have a high degree of social and economic integration with that core. Metropolitan statistical areas (MSAs), consolidated metropolitan statistical areas (CMSAs), and primary metropolitan statistical areas (PMSAs) are defined by the Office of Management and Budget (OMB) as a standard for Federal agencies in the preparation and publication of statistics relating to metropolitan areas. The entire territory of the United States is classified as metropolitan (inside MSAs or CMSAs—PMSAs are components of CMSAs) or nonmetropolitan (outside MSAs or CMSAs). MSAs, CMSAs, and PMSAs are defined in terms of entire counties except in New England, where the definitions are in terms of cities and towns. The OMB also defines New England County Metropolitan Areas (NECMAs) which are county-based alternatives to the MSAs and CMSAs in the six New England states. Over time, new MAs are created and the boundaries of others change. The analysis of historical trends, therefore, must be made cautiously. For descriptive details and a listing of titles and components of MAs, see Appendix II.

Urban and rural—According to the 1990 census definition, the urban population comprises all persons living in (a) places of 2,500 or more inhabitants incorporated as cities, villages, boroughs (except in Alaska and New York), and towns (except in the New England states, New York, and Wisconsin), but excluding those persons living in the rural portions of extended cities (places with low population density in one or more large parts of their area); (b) census designated places (previously termed unincorporated) of 2,500 or more inhabitants; and (c) other territory, incorporated or unincorporated, included in urbanized areas. An urbanized area comprises one or more places and the adjacent densely settled surrounding territory that together have a minimum population of 50,000 persons. In all definitions, the population not classified as urban constitutes the rural population.

Residence—In determining residence, the Census Bureau counts each person as an inhabitant of a usual place of residence (i.e., the place where one usually lives and sleeps). While this place is not necessarily a person's legal residence or voting residence, the use of these different bases of classification would produce the same results in the vast majority of cases.

Race—The Census Bureau collects and publishes racial statistics as outlined in Statistical Policy Directive No. 15 issued by the U.S. Office of Management and Budget. This directive provides standards on ethnic and racial categories for statistical reporting to be used by all Federal agencies. According to the directive, the basic racial categories are American Indian or Alaska Native, Asian or Pacific Islander, Black, and White. (The directive identifies Hispanic origin as an ethnicity.) The concept of race the Census Bureau uses reflects self-identification by respondents; that is the individual's perception of his/her racial identity. The concept is not intended to reflect any biological or anthropological definition. Although the Census Bureau

U.S. Census Bureau, Statistical Abstract of the United States: 1999

adheres to the overall guidelines of Directive No. 15, it recognizes that there are persons who do not identify with a specific racial group. The 1990 census race question included an "Other race" category with provisions for a write-in entry. Furthermore, the Census Bureau recognizes that the categories of the race item include both racial and national origin or socio-cultural groups.

Differences between the 1990 census and earlier censuses affect the comparability of data for certain racial groups and American Indian tribes. The lack of comparability is due to changes in the way some respondents reported their race as well as changes in 1990 census procedures related to the racial classification. (For a fuller explanation, see *1990 Census of Population, Volume I, General Population Characteristics* (1990 CP-1).)

Data for the population by race for April 1, 1990 (shown in Tables 12, 13, 18, 19, 21, and 23) are modified counts and are not comparable to the 1990 census race categories. These numbers were computed using 1990 census data by race which had been modified to be consistent with the guidelines in Federal Statistical Policy Directive No. 15 issued by the Office of Management and Budget. A detailed explanation of the race modification procedure appears in 1990 Census of Population and Housing Data Paper Listing (CPH-L-74).

In the CPS and other household sample surveys in which data are obtained through personal interview, respondents are asked to classify their race as: (1) White; (2) Black; (3) American Indian, Aleut, or Eskimo; or (4) Asian or Pacific Islander. The procedures for classifying persons of mixed races who could not provide a single response to the race question are generally similar to those used in the census.

Hispanic population—In the 1990 census, the Census Bureau collected data on the Hispanic origin population in the United States by using a self-identification question. Persons of Spanish/Hispanic origin are those who classified themselves in one of the specific Hispanic origin categories listed on the questionnaire—Mexican, Puerto Rican, Cuban, as well as those who indicated that they were of Other Spanish/Hispanic origin. Persons of "Other Spanish/Hispanic" origin are those whose origins are from Spain, the Spanish-speaking countries of Central or South America, or the Dominican Republic. Both in 1980 and 1990, the Hispanic origin question contained prelisted categories for the largest Hispanic-origin groups—Mexican, Puerto Rican, Cuban, and Other Spanish/Hispanic. The 1990 Hispanic origin question differed from the 1980 question in that in 1990, unlike in 1980, the question contained a write-in line for the Other Spanish/Hispanic category which were coded only for sample data. Another difference between the 1980 and 1990 Hispanic-origin question is that in 1980 the wording of the Hispanic origin question read: "Is this person of Spanish/Hispanic origin or descent?" while in 1990 the word "descent" was dropped from the question. Persons of Hispanic-origin may be of any race.

In the CPS information on Hispanic persons is gathered by using a self-identification question. Persons classify themselves in one of the Hispanic categories in response to the question: "What is the origin or descent of each person in this household?" Hispanic persons in the CPS are persons who report themselves as Mexican-American, Chicano, Mexican, Puerto Rican, Cuban, Central or South American (Spanish countries), or other Hispanic origin.

Nativity—The native population consists of all persons born in the United States, Puerto Rico, or an outlying area of the United States. It also includes persons born in a foreign country who had at least one parent who was a U.S. citizen. All other persons are classified as "foreign born."

Mobility status—The U.S. population is classified according to mobility status on the basis of a comparison between the place of residence of each individual at the time of the survey or census and the place of residence at a specified earlier date. Nonmovers are all persons who were living

U.S. Census Bureau, Statistical Abstract of the United States: 1999

in the same house or apartment at the end of the period as at the beginning of the period. Movers are all persons who were living in a different house or apartment at the end of the period than at the beginning of the period. Movers are further classified as to whether they were living in the same or different county, state, or region or were movers from abroad. Movers from abroad include all persons, either U.S. citizens or noncitizens, whose place of residence was outside the United States at the beginning of the period; that is, in Puerto Rico, an outlying area under the jurisdiction of the United States, or a foreign country.

Living arrangements—Living arrangements refer to residency in households or in group quarters. A "household" comprises all persons who occupy a "housing unit," that is, a house, an apartment or other group of rooms, or a single room that constitutes "separate living quarters." A household includes the related family members and all the unrelated persons, if any, such as lodgers, foster children, wards, or employees who share the housing unit. A person living alone or a group of unrelated persons sharing the same housing unit is also counted as a household. See text, Section 25, Construction and Housing, for definition of housing unit.

All persons not living in housing units are classified as living in group quarters. These individuals may be institutionalized, e.g., under care or custody in juvenile facilities, jails, correctional centers, hospitals, or nursing homes; or they may be residents in noninstitutional group quarters such as college dormitories, group homes, or military barracks.

Householder—The householder is the first adult household member listed on the questionnaire. The instructions call for listing first the person (or one of the persons) in whose name the home is owned or rented. If a home is owned or rented jointly by a married couple, either the husband or the wife may be listed first. Prior to 1980, the husband was always considered the household head (householder) in married-couple households.

Family—The term "family" refers to a group of two or more persons related by birth, marriage, or adoption and residing together in a household. A family includes among its members the householder.

Subfamily—A subfamily consists of a married couple and their children, if any, or one parent with one or more never-married children under 18 years old living in a household. Subfamilies are divided into "related" and "unrelated" subfamilies. A related subfamily is related to, but does not include, the householder. Members of a related subfamily are also members of the family with whom they live. The number of related subfamilies, therefore, is not included in the count of families. An unrelated subfamily may include persons such as guests, lodgers, or resident employees and their spouses and/or children; none of whom is related to the householder.

Married couple—A "married couple" is defined as a husband and wife living together in the same household, with or without children and other relatives.

Statistical reliability—For a discussion of statistical collection and estimation, sampling procedures, and measures of statistical reliability applicable to Census Bureau data, see Appendix III.

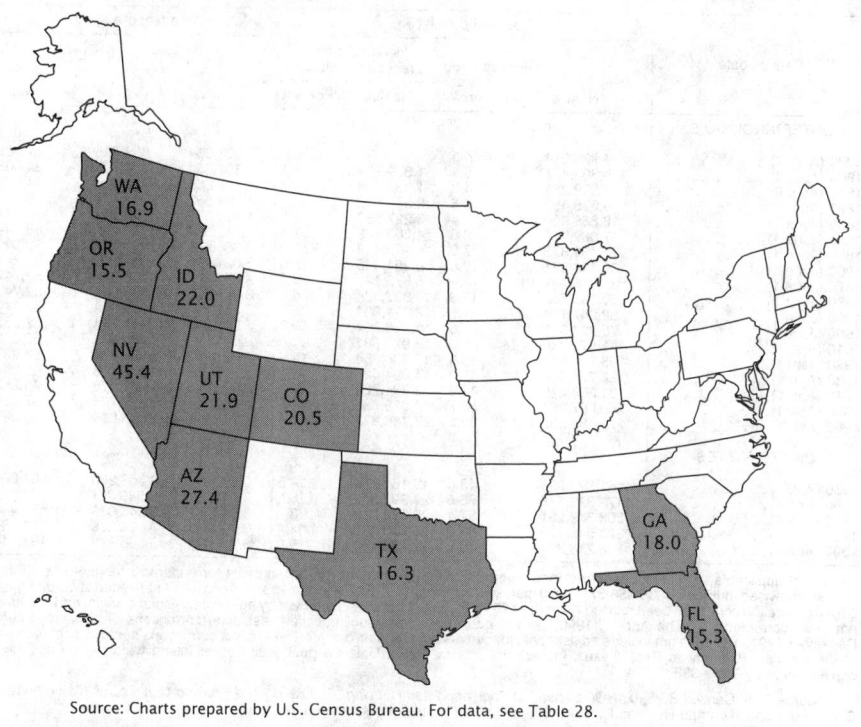

Figure 1.1
**Ten Fastest Growing States,
Percent Population Change: 1990 to 1998**

Source: Charts prepared by U.S. Census Bureau. For data, see Table 28.

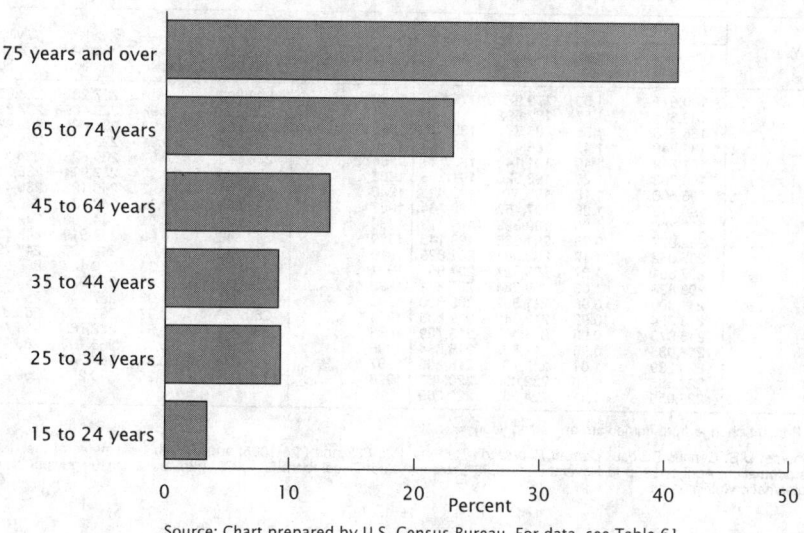

Figure 1.2
Percent of Adults Living Alone, by Age: 1998

Source: Chart prepared by U.S. Census Bureau. For data, see Table 61.

U.S. Census Bureau, Statistical Abstract of the United States: 1999

No. 1. Population and Area: 1790 to 1990

[Area figures represent area on indicated date including in some cases considerable areas not then organized or settled and not covered by the census. Total area figures for 1790 to 1970 have been recalculated on the basis of the remeasurement of states and counties for the 1980 census, but not on the basis of the 1990 census. The land and water area figures for past censuses have not been adjusted and are not strictly comparable with the total area data for comparable dates because the land areas were derived from different base data, and these values are known to have changed with the construction of reservoirs, draining of lakes, etc. Density figures are based on land area measurements as reported in earlier censuses]

Census date	Resident population		Increase over preceding census		Area (square miles)		
	Number	Per square mile of land area	Number	Percent	Total	Land	Water
CONTERMINOUS U.S. [1]							
1790 (Aug. 2)	3,929,214	4.5	(X)	(X)	891,364	864,746	24,065
1800 (Aug. 4)	5,308,483	6.1	1,379,269	35.1	891,364	864,746	24,065
1810 (Aug. 6)	7,239,881	4.3	1,931,398	36.4	1,722,685	1,681,828	34,175
1820 (Aug. 7)	9,638,453	5.5	2,398,572	33.1	1,792,552	1,749,462	38,544
1830 (June 1)	12,866,020	7.4	3,227,567	33.5	1,792,552	1,749,462	38,544
1840 (June 1)	17,069,453	9.8	4,203,433	32.7	1,792,552	1,749,462	38,544
1850 (June 1)	23,191,876	7.9	6,122,423	35.9	2,991,655	2,940,042	52,705
1860 (June 1)	31,443,321	10.6	8,251,445	35.6	3,021,295	2,969,640	52,747
1870 (June 1)	[2]39,818,449	[2]13.4	8,375,128	26.6	3,021,295	2,969,640	52,747
1880 (June 1)	50,155,783	16.9	10,337,334	26.0	3,021,295	2,969,640	52,747
1890 (June 1)	62,947,714	21.2	12,791,931	25.5	3,021,295	2,969,640	52,747
1900 (June 1)	75,994,575	25.6	13,046,861	20.7	3,021,295	2,969,834	52,553
1910 (Apr. 15)	91,972,266	31.0	15,977,691	21.0	3,021,295	2,969,565	52,822
1920 (Jan. 1)	105,710,620	35.6	13,738,354	14.9	3,021,295	2,969,451	52,936
1930 (Apr. 1)	122,775,046	41.2	17,064,426	16.1	3,021,295	2,977,128	45,259
1940 (Apr. 1)	131,669,275	44.2	8,894,229	7.2	3,021,295	2,977,128	45,259
1950 (Apr. 1)	150,697,361	50.7	19,028,086	14.5	3,021,295	2,974,726	47,661
1960 (Apr. 1)	178,464,236	60.1	27,766,875	18.4	3,021,295	2,968,054	54,207
UNITED STATES							
1950 (Apr. 1)	151,325,798	42.6	19,161,229	14.5	3,618,770	3,552,206	63,005
1960 (Apr. 1)	179,323,175	50.6	27,997,377	18.5	3,618,770	3,540,911	74,212
1970 (Apr. 1)	[3]203,302,031	[3]57.4	23,978,856	13.4	3,618,770	[3]3,540,023	[3]78,444
1980 (Apr. 1)	[4]226,542,199	64.0	23,240,168	11.4	3,618,770	3,539,289	79,481
1990 (Apr. 1)	[5]248,718,301	70.3	22,176,102	9.8	[6]3,717,796	[6]3,536,278	[6][7]181,518

X Not applicable.   [1] Excludes Alaska and Hawaii.   [2] Revised to include adjustments for underenumeration in southern states; unrevised number is 38,558,371 (13.0 per square mile).   [3] Figures corrected after 1970 final reports were issued.   [4] Total population count has been revised since the 1980 census publications. Numbers by age, race, Hispanic origin, and sex have not been corrected.   [5] The April 1, 1990, census count includes count question resolution corrections processed through December 1997, and does not include adjustments for census coverage errors.   [6] Data reflect corrections made after publication of the results.   [7] Comprises Great Lakes, inland, and coastal water. Data for prior years cover inland water only. For further explanation, see Table 393.

Source: U.S. Census Bureau, *1990 Census of Population and Housing, Population and Housing Unit Counts* (CPH-2); 1990 Census of Population and Housing Listing (1990 CPH-L-157); and unpublished data.

No. 2. Population: 1960 to 1998

[In thousands, except percent (180,671 represents 180,671,000). Estimates as of **July 1**. Total population includes Armed Forces abroad; civilian population excludes Armed Forces. For basis of estimates, see text of this section]

Year	Total		Resident population	Civilian population	Year	Total		Resident population	Civilian population
	Population	Percent change [1]				Population	Percent change [1]		
1960	180,671	1.60	179,979	178,140	1980	227,726	1.19	227,225	225,621
1961	183,691	1.67	182,992	181,143	1981	229,966	0.98	229,466	227,818
1962	186,538	1.55	185,771	183,677	1982	232,188	0.97	231,664	229,995
1963	189,242	1.45	188,483	186,493	1983	234,307	0.91	233,792	232,097
1964	191,889	1.40	191,141	189,141	1984	236,348	0.87	235,825	234,110
1965	194,303	1.26	193,526	191,605	1985	238,466	0.90	237,924	236,219
1966	196,560	1.16	195,576	193,420	1986	240,651	0.92	240,133	238,412
1967	198,712	1.09	197,457	195,264	1987	242,804	0.89	242,289	240,550
1968	200,706	1.00	199,399	197,113	1988	245,021	0.91	244,499	242,817
1969	202,677	0.98	201,385	199,145	1989	247,342	0.95	246,819	245,131
1970	205,052	1.17	203,984	201,895	1990	249,948	1.05	249,439	247,798
1971	207,661	1.27	206,827	204,866	1991	252,639	1.08	252,127	250,517
1972	209,896	1.08	209,284	207,511	1992	255,374	1.08	254,995	253,410
1973	211,909	0.96	211,357	209,600	1993	258,083	1.06	257,746	256,273
1974	213,854	0.92	213,342	211,636	1994	260,599	0.97	260,289	258,877
1975	215,973	0.99	215,465	213,789	1995	263,044	0.94	262,765	261,414
1976	218,035	0.95	217,563	215,894	1996	265,463	0.92	265,190	263,904
1977	220,239	1.01	219,760	218,106	1997	268,008	0.96	267,744	266,491
1978	222,585	1.06	222,095	220,467	1998	270,561	0.95	270,299	269,078
1979	225,055	1.11	224,567	222,969					

[1] Percent change from immediate preceding year.

Source: U.S. Census Bureau, *Current Population Reports*, P25-802 and P25-1095; and "Monthly estimates of the United States population: April 1, 1980 to November 1, 1998"; release date: December 28, 1998; <http://www.census.gov/population/estimates/nation/intfile1-1.txt>.

No. 3. Resident Population Projections: 1999 to 2050

[In thousands (272,330 represents 272,330,000). As of **July 1**. Each series shown assumes middle levels of fertility, life expectancy, and net immigration unless otherwise specified. Middle level components are shown in footnote 1]

Year	Middle series[1]	Lowest series[2]	Highest series[3]	Fertility Low	Fertility High	Life expectancy Low	Life expectancy High	Net immigration Low	Net immigration High
1999	272,330	269,861	274,865	271,678	272,915	272,006	272,697	270,835	273,910
2000	274,634	271,237	278,129	273,731	275,448	274,185	275,141	272,581	276,802
2005	285,981	276,990	295,318	283,299	288,471	284,647	287,467	280,949	291,287
2010	297,716	281,468	314,571	292,303	302,893	294,986	300,482	289,423	306,444
2015	310,134	285,472	335,597	301,444	318,595	305,539	314,376	298,356	322,508
2020	322,742	288,807	357,702	310,429	334,889	315,885	328,698	307,290	338,955
2025	335,050	290,789	380,781	318,575	351,554	325,530	343,023	315,709	355,318
2030	346,899	291,070	405,089	325,517	368,732	334,331	357,227	323,414	371,480
2040	369,980	287,685	458,444	336,407	405,660	350,592	385,898	337,416	403,986
2050	393,931	282,524	518,903	345,352	447,502	367,913	415,908	351,354	438,299

[1] Total fertility rate in 2050 = 2,245; life expectancy in 2050 = 82.0 years; and annual net immigration = 820,000. These are middle level assumptions. For explanation of total fertility rate; see headnote, Table 96. [2] Total fertility rate in 2050 = 1,910; life expectancy in 2050 = 74.8 years; and annual net immigration = 300,000. These are lowest level assumptions. [3] Total fertility rate in 2050 = 2,580; life expectancy in 2050 = 89.4 years; and annual net immigration = 1,370,000. These are highest level assumptions.

Source: U.S. Census Bureau, *Current Population Reports*, P25-1130.

No. 4. Components of Population Change, 1980 to 1998, and Projections, 1999 to 2050

[226,546 represents 226,546,000. Resident population. The estimates prior to 1990 are consistent with the original 1990 census count of 248,709,873. Starting with 1990, estimates reflect the revised April 1, 1990, census count of 248,765,170 which includes count resolution corrections processed through August 1997, and does not include adjustments for census coverage errors except for adjustments estimated for the 1995 Census Test in Oakland, California; Patterson, New Jersey; and six Louisiana parishes. These adjustments amounted to a total of 55,297 persons]

Year	Population as of Jan. 1 (1,000)	Net increase[1] Total (1,000)	Net increase Per-cent[2]	Births (1,000)	Deaths (1,000)	Net migration[3] (1,000)	Net growth rate[1]	Birth rate	Death rate	Net migration rate[3]
1980[4]	226,546	1,900	0.8	2,743	1,463	724	11.1	16.0	8.6	4.2
1981	228,446	2,200	1.0	3,629	1,978	690	9.6	15.8	8.6	3.0
1982	230,645	2,157	0.9	3,681	1,975	595	9.3	15.9	8.5	2.6
1983	232,803	2,066	0.9	3,639	2,019	592	8.8	15.6	8.6	2.5
1984	234,868	2,070	0.9	3,669	2,039	589	8.8	15.6	8.6	2.5
1985	236,938	2,171	0.9	3,761	2,086	649	9.1	15.8	8.8	2.7
1986	239,109	2,158	0.9	3,757	2,105	661	9.0	15.6	8.8	2.8
1987	241,267	2,195	0.9	3,809	2,123	666	9.1	15.7	8.8	2.7
1988	243,462	2,243	0.9	3,910	2,168	662	9.2	16.0	8.9	2.7
1989	245,705	2,438	1.0	4,041	2,150	712	9.9	16.4	8.7	2.9
1990[5]	248,143	2,535	1.0	4,148	2,155	[6]542	10.2	16.6	8.6	[6]2.2
1991	250,693	2,901	1.2	4,111	2,170	[6]960	11.5	16.3	8.6	[6]3.8
1992	253,594	2,886	1.1	4,065	2,176	997	11.3	15.9	8.5	3.9
1993	256,480	2,614	1.0	4,000	2,269	882	10.1	15.5	8.8	3.4
1994	259,094	2,483	1.0	3,953	2,279	810	9.5	15.2	8.8	3.1
1995	261,577	2,443	0.9	3,900	2,312	856	9.3	14.8	8.8	3.3
1996	264,021	2,482	0.9	3,891	2,315	905	9.4	14.7	8.7	3.4
1997	266,503	2,564	1.0	3,895	2,315	984	9.6	14.5	8.6	3.7
1998	269,067	2,559	1.0	3,888	2,308	979	9.5	14.4	8.5	3.6
PROJECTIONS[7]										
1999	271,166	2,316	0.9	3,896	2,401	820	8.5	14.3	8.8	3.0
2000	273,482	2,294	0.8	3,899	2,425	820	8.4	14.2	8.8	3.0
2005	284,847	2,278	0.8	4,001	2,543	820	8.0	14.0	8.9	2.9
2010	296,511	2,426	0.8	4,243	2,638	820	8.1	14.0	8.9	2.8
2015	308,875	2,521	0.8	4,450	2,749	820	8.1	14.3	8.9	2.6
2020	321,487	2,504	0.8	4,579	2,895	820	7.8	14.3	9.0	2.5
2025	333,838	2,414	0.7	4,679	3,085	820	7.2	14.2	9.2	2.4
2030	345,730	2,333	0.7	4,822	3,309	820	6.7	14.0	9.5	2.4
2040	368,823	2,319	0.6	5,248	3,749	820	6.3	13.9	10.1	2.2
2050	392,681	2,517	0.6	5,672	3,975	820	6.4	14.2	10.1	2.1

[1] Prior to April 1, 1990, includes "error of closure" (the amount necessary to make the components of change add to the net change between censuses), for which figures are not shown separately. [2] Percent of population at beginning of period. [3] Covers net international migration and movement of Armed Forces, federally affiliated civilian citizens, and their dependents. [4] Data are for period April 1 to December 31. [5] Net change for 1990 excludes "error of closure" for the three months prior to the April 1 census date. Therefore, it may not equal the difference between the populations at the beginning of 1990 and 1991. [6] Data reflect movement of Armed Forces due to the Gulf War. [7] Based on middle series of assumptions. See footnote 1, Table 3.

Source: U.S. Census Bureau, *Current Population Reports*, P25-1095 and P25-1130; and unpublished data.

No. 5. Immigration: 1901 to 1997

[In thousands, except rate (8,795 represents 8,795,000). **For fiscal years ending in year shown;** see text, Section 9, State and Local Government. For definition of immigrants, see text of this section. Data represent immigrants admitted. Rates based on U.S. Census Bureau estimates as of July 1 for resident population through 1929, and for total population thereafter (excluding Alaska and Hawaii prior to 1959)]

Period	Number	Rate [1]	Year	Number	Rate [1]
1901 to 1910	8,795	10.4	1980	531	2.3
1911 to 1920	5,736	5.7	1985	570	2.4
1921 to 1930	4,107	3.5	1990	1,536	6.1
1931 to 1940	528	0.4	1991	1,827	7.2
1941 to 1950	1,035	0.7	1992	974	3.8
1951 to 1960	2,515	1.5	1993	904	3.5
1961 to 1970	3,322	1.7	1994	804	3.1
1971 to 1980	4,493	2.1	1995	720	2.7
1981 to 1990	7,338	3.1	1996	916	3.5
1991 to 1997	6,945	3.8	1997	798	3.0

[1] Annual rate per 1,000 U.S. population. Rate computed by dividing sum of annual immigration totals by sum of annual U.S. population totals for same number of years.

Source: U.S. Immigration and Naturalization Service, *Statistical Yearbook*, annual.

No. 6. Immigrants Admitted, by Class of Admission: 1990 to 1997

[For fiscal year ending September 30. For definition of immigrants, see text of this section]

Class of admission	1990	1993	1994	1995	1996	1997
Immigrants, total	1,536,483	904,292	804,416	720,461	915,900	798,378
New arrivals	435,729	536,294	490,429	380,291	421,405	380,718
Adjustments	1,100,754	367,998	313,987	340,170	494,495	417,660
Preference immigrants, total	272,742	373,788	335,252	323,458	411,673	303,938
Family-sponsored immigrants, total	214,550	226,776	211,961	238,122	294,174	213,331
Unmarried sons/daughters of U.S. citizens and their children	15,861	12,819	13,181	15,182	20,909	22,536
Spouses, unmarried sons/daughters of alien residents, and their children	107,686	128,308	115,000	144,535	182,834	113,681
Married sons/daughters of U.S. citizens [1]	26,751	23,385	22,191	20,876	25,452	21,943
Brothers or sisters of U.S. citizens [1]	64,252	62,264	61,589	57,529	64,979	55,171
Employment-based immigrants, total	58,192	147,012	123,291	85,336	117,499	90,607
Priority workers [1]	(X)	21,114	21,053	17,339	27,501	21,810
Professionals with advanced degrees [1]	(X)	29,468	14,432	10,475	18,462	17,059
Skilled workers, professionals, unskilled workers [1]	(X)	87,689	76,956	50,245	62,756	42,596
Special immigrants [1]	4,463	8,158	10,406	6,737	7,844	7,781
Employment creation [1]	(X)	583	444	540	936	1,361
Professional or highly skilled immigrants [1][2]	26,546	(X)	(X)	(X)	(X)	(X)
Needed skilled or unskilled workers [1][2]	27,183	(X)	(X)	(X)	(X)	(X)
Immediate relatives	231,680	255,059	249,764	220,360	300,430	321,008
Spouses of U.S. citizens	125,426	145,843	145,247	123,238	169,760	170,263
Children of U.S. citizens	46,065	46,788	48,147	48,740	63,971	76,631
Orphans	7,088	7,348	8,200	9,384	11,366	(NA)
Parents of U.S. citizens	60,189	62,428	56,370	48,382	66,699	74,114
Refugees and asylees	97,364	127,343	121,434	114,664	128,565	112,158
Cuban Refugee Act, Nov. 1966	5,730	6,976	8,316	9,579	20,131	(NA)
Indochinese Refugee Act, Oct. 1977	33	24	11	10	5	(NA)
Refugee-Parolee Act, Oct. 1978	153	53	20	22	9	(NA)
Asylees, Refugee Act of 1980	4,937	11,804	5,983	7,837	10,037	10,106
Refugees, Refugee Act of 1980	86,511	108,486	107,104	97,169	98,383	(NA)
Other refugees	-	-	-	47	-	(NA)
Other immigrants	934,697	148,102	97,966	61,979	75,232	61,274
Children born abroad to resident aliens	2,410	2,030	1,883	1,894	1,660	1,432
Diversity Programs [3]	29,161	33,480	41,056	47,245	58,790	49,374
Amerasians (P.L. 100-202) [4]	13,059	11,116	2,822	939	956	738
Immigration Reform and Control Act of 1986 legalization adjustments	880,372	24,278	6,022	4,267	4,635	2,548
Legalization dependents [5]	(X)	55,344	34,074	277	184	64
Other	9,695	21,854	12,109	7,357	9,007	7,118

- Represents zero.   NA Not available.   X Not applicable.   [1] Includes spouses and children.   [2] Category was eliminated in 1992 by the Immigration Act of 1990.   [3] Includes categories of immigrants admitted under three laws intended to diversify immigration: P.L. 99-603, P.L. 100-658, and P.L. 101-649.   [4] Under Public Law 100-202, Amerasians are aliens born in Vietnam between January 1, 1962, and January 1, 1976, who were fathered by U.S. citizens.   [5] Spouses and children of persons granted permanent resident status under provisions of the Immigration Reform and Control Act of 1986.

Source: U.S. Immigration and Naturalization Service, *Statistical Yearbook*, annual.

No. 7. Nonimmigrants Admitted, by Class of Admission: 1985 to 1996

[In thousands, except as noted (9,540 represents 9,540,000). For fiscal years ending Sept. 30. Nonimmigrants are nonresident aliens (non-U.S. citizens) admitted to the United States for a temporary period. Excluded are border crossers, crewmen, and insular travelers]

Class of admission	1985	1990	1991	1992	1993	1994	1995	1996
Nonimmigrants [1]	9,540	17,574	18,963	20,794	21,566	22,119	22,641	24,843
Temporary visitors, total	8,405	16,080	17,386	19,238	19,879	20,319	20,887	22,880
For pleasure	6,609	13,418	14,734	16,450	16,918	17,155	17,612	19,110
For business	1,797	2,661	2,652	2,788	2,961	3,164	3,275	3,770
Transit aliens [2]	237	306	364	346	331	331	320	326
Foreign government officials [3]	90	97	98	103	102	105	104	118
Treaty traders and investors [3]	97	148	155	152	145	141	132	139
Students [3]	286	355	314	275	403	428	395	459
Representatives to international organizations [3]	57	61	64	70	73	75	72	80
Temporary workers and trainees [4]	75	140	161	163	163	186	197	227
Registered nurses [5]	(X)	(X)	1	7	7	6	7	2
Specialty occupations [6]	(X)	(X)	117	110	93	106	118	144
Workers of distinguished merit or ability [7]	47	100	(X)	(X)	(X)	(X)	(X)	(X)
Performing services unavailable in U.S.	25	36	40	34	29	29	26	24
North America Free-Trade Agreement [8]	(X)	5	8	13	17	25	24	27
Spouses and children of workers and trainees [9]	13	29	35	41	42	49	54	61
Representatives of foreign information media [3]	17	20	21	22	21	28	24	34
Exchange visitors [3]	141	215	224	232	239	259	240	257
NATO officials [3]	8	8	9	9	9	9	9	11
Fiances(ees) of U.S. citizens [10]	8	7	8	9	9	9	9	10
Intracompany transferees [3]	107	103	113	121	132	154	174	214
Parolees [11]	64	90	127	137	124	111	114	(NA)
Refugees	68	110	100	123	113	114	96	(NA)

NA Not available. X Not applicable. [1] Includes nonimmigrants whose class of admission is unknown. [2] Includes foreign government officials and their spouses and (unmarried minor or dependent) children, in transit. [3] Includes spouses and children. [4] Includes other classes of admission, not shown separately. [5] Entries began October 1, 1990 (fiscal year 1991). Data for fiscal year 1991 are underreported; an unknown number of H1A entries were counted as H1B entries. [6] Prior to October 1, 1991 (fiscal year 1992), H1B entries were termed "Distinguished merit or ability." Data for fiscal year 1991 are overreported; an unknown number of H1A entries were counted as H1B entries. [7] Beginning 1992, as a result of the Immigration Act of 1990, the existing temporary worker and trainee classes of admission have been revised and new worker classes have been created. [8] Entries under the U.S.-Canada Free Trade Agreement began in January 1989 and under the North American Free Trade Agreement (NAFTA) in January 1994. [9] Includes spouses and children under NAFTA. [10] Includes children of fiances(ees) of U.S. citizens. [11] Aliens allowed to enter the United States for a temporary period of time on emergency conditions or when the entry is determined to be in the public interest (e.g., witness in court).
Source: U.S. Immigration and Naturalization Service, *Statistical Yearbook*, annual.

No. 8. Immigrants, by Country of Birth: 1981 to 1997

[In thousands (7,338.1 represents 7,338,100). For fiscal years ending Sept. 30. For definition of immigrants, see text of this section]

Country of birth	1981-90, total	1991-95, total	1996	1997	Country of birth	1981-90, total	1991-95, total	1996	1997
All countries	7,338.1	5,230.3	915.9	798.4	Syria	20.6	13.5	3.1	(NA)
Europe [1]	705.6	728.0	147.6	119.9	Taiwan	[4]	63.4	13.4	(NA)
France	23.1	13.8	3.1	(NA)	Thailand	64.4	31.8	4.3	(NA)
Germany	70.1	36.9	6.7	(NA)	Turkey	20.9	12.0	3.7	(NA)
Greece	29.1	8.6	1.5	(NA)	Vietnam	401.4	275.8	42.1	38.5
Ireland	32.8	53.2	1.7	(NA)	North America [1]	3,125.0	2,400.2	340.5	307.5
Italy	32.9	12.2	2.5	(NA)	Canada	119.2	74.9	15.8	11.6
Poland	97.4	114.4	15.8	12.0	Mexico	1,653.3	1,487.9	163.6	146.9
Portugal	40.0	14.1	3.0	(NA)	Caribbean [1]	892.7	538.6	116.8	105.3
Romania	38.9	28.5	5.8	(NA)	Cuba	159.2	68.5	26.5	33.6
Soviet Union, former [2]	84.0	277.1	62.8	(NA)	Dominican Republic	251.8	218.5	39.6	27.1
Armenia	(NA)	[3]18.4	2.4	(NA)	Haiti	140.2	96.0	18.4	15.1
Azerbaijan	(NA)	[3]10.3	2.0	(NA)	Jamaica	213.8	90.7	19.1	17.8
Belarus	(NA)	[3]17.1	4.3	(NA)	Trinidad and Tobago	39.5	33.7	7.3	(NA)
Moldova	(NA)	[3]8.5	1.8	(NA)	Central America [1]	458.7	298.5	44.3	43.7
Russia	(NA)	[3]50.7	19.7	16.6	El Salvador	214.6	129.7	17.9	18.0
Ukraine	(NA)	[3]71.1	21.1	15.7	Guatemala	87.9	61.5	8.8	(NA)
Uzbekistan	(NA)	[3]11.5	4.7	(NA)	Honduras	49.5	36.1	5.9	(NA)
United Kingdom	142.1	81.4	13.6	10.7	Nicaragua	44.1	43.5	6.9	(NA)
Yugoslavia	19.2	19.8	11.9	(NA)	Panama	29.0	14.4	2.6	(NA)
Asia [1]	2,817.4	1,634.1	307.8	265.8	South America [1]	455.9	282.2	61.8	52.9
Afghanistan	26.6	12.3	1.3	(NA)	Argentina	25.7	14.7	2.5	(NA)
Bangladesh	15.2	27.2	8.2	(NA)	Brazil	23.7	26.5	5.9	(NA)
Cambodia	116.6	10.4	1.6	(NA)	Chile	23.4	9.7	1.7	(NA)
China	[3]388.8	227.0	41.7	41.1	Colombia	124.4	67.4	14.3	13.0
Hong Kong	63.0	45.0	7.8	(NA)	Ecuador	56.0	36.9	8.3	(NA)
India	261.9	191.6	44.9	38.1	Guyana	95.4	44.1	9.5	(NA)
Iran	154.8	68.3	11.1	9.6	Peru	64.4	53.8	12.9	10.9
Iraq	19.6	21.3	5.5	(NA)	Venezuela	17.9	12.8	3.5	(NA)
Israel	36.3	19.7	3.1	(NA)	Africa [1]	192.3	160.2	52.9	47.8
Japan	43.2	33.9	6.0	(NA)	Egypt	31.4	21.8	6.2	(NA)
Jordan	32.6	20.7	4.4	(NA)	Ethiopia	27.2	25.8	6.1	(NA)
Korea	338.8	96.0	18.2	14.2	Ghana	14.9	11.4	6.6	(NA)
Laos	145.6	35.0	2.8	(NA)	Nigeria	35.3	27.7	10.2	(NA)
Lebanon	41.6	25.5	4.4	(NA)	Other countries [5]	41.9	25.7	5.3	4.5
Pakistan	61.3	58.0	12.5	13.0					
Philippines	495.3	292.6	55.9	49.1					

NA Not available. [1] Includes countries not shown separately. [2] Includes other republics and unknown republics, not shown separately. [3] Covers years 1992-1995. [4] Data for Taiwan included with China. [5] Includes Australia, New Zealand, and unknown countries.
Source: U.S. Immigration and Naturalization Service, *Statistical Yearbook*, annual; and releases.

No. 9. Immigrants Admitted as Permanent Residents Under Refugee Acts, by Country of Birth: 1981 to 1996

[For fiscal years ending September 30. Covers immigrants who were allowed to enter the United States under 1953 Refugee Relief Act and later acts; Hungarian parolees under July 1958 Act; refugee-escapee parolees under July 1960 Act; conditional entries by refugees under Oct. 1965 Act; Cuban parolees under Nov. 1966 Act; Indochina refugees under Act of Oct. 1977; refugee-parolees under the Act of Oct. 1978, and asylees under the Act of March 1980; and refugees under the Act of March 1980]

Country of birth	1981-90, total	1991-94, total	1995	1996	Country of birth	1981-90, total	1991-94, total	1995	1996
Total	**1,013,620**	**504,893**	**114,664**	**128,565**	China [3]	7,928	3,431	803	845
Europe [1]	**155,512**	**213,840**	**46,998**	**51,977**	Hong Kong	1,916	440	48	47
Albania	353	2,545	314	154	Iran	46,773	17,669	1,245	1,212
Bulgaria	1,197	1,314	105	100	Iraq	7,540	6,814	3,848	3,802
Czechoslovakia	8,204	1,138	38	25	Laos	142,964	28,182	3,364	2,155
Hungary	4,942	1,163	28	40	Philippines	3,403	695	80	80
Poland	33,889	6,782	245	183	Syria	2,145	497	258	208
Romania	29,798	14,100	592	447	Thailand	30,259	14,451	2,932	1,940
Soviet Union, former [2]	72,306	181,711	40,120	42,356	Turkey	1,896	360	58	42
Armenia	(NA)	(NA)	214	182	Vietnam	324,453	111,265	28,595	29,700
Azerbaijan	(NA)	(NA)	1,594	1,446	**North America** [1]	**121,840**	**67,409**	**16,265**	**28,070**
Belarus	(NA)	(NA)	3,421	3,480	Cuba	113,367	41,473	12,355	22,542
Moldova	(NA)	(NA)	1,597	1,415	El Salvador	1,383	3,078	283	262
Russia	(NA)	(NA)	8,176	9,745	Guatemala	(NA)	806	158	234
Ukraine	(NA)	(NA)	14,937	16,636	Nicaragua	5,590	19,759	727	766
Uzbekistan	(NA)	(NA)	3,258	4,144	**South America** [1]	**1,976**	**1,606**	**497**	**922**
Yugoslavia	324	707	4,744	7,820	**Africa** [1]	**22,149**	**21,233**	**7,527**	**5,464**
Asia [1]	**712,092**	**200,735**	**43,314**	**42,076**	Ethiopia	18,542	13,062	1,802	985
Afghanistan	22,946	8,080	616	369	Sudan	(NA)	1,398	935	1,089
Cambodia	114,064	5,610	268	210	Other	51	70	63	56

NA Not available. [1] Includes other countries, not shown separately. [2] Includes other republics and unknown republics, not shown separately. [3] Includes Taiwan.

Source: U.S. Immigration and Naturalization Service, *Statistical Yearbook*, annual; and releases.

No. 10. Estimated Undocumented Immigrants, by Selected States and Countries of Origin: 1996

[As of October (5,000 represents 5,000,000). Based on estimates of illegal immigrant population who established residence in the United States before 1982 and did not legalize under the Immigration Reform and Control Act (IRCA) and annual estimates of the number of persons who enter surreptitiously across land borders and nonimmigrant overstays who established residence here during the 1982 to 1996 period. The estimates for each country were distributed to states by INS based on U.S. residence pattern of each country's total number of applicants for legalization under IRCA]

State	Number (1,000)	Country	Number (1,000)
United States, total [1]	**5,000**	**Total** [1]	**5,000**
California	2,000	Mexico	2,700
Texas	700	El Salvador	335
New York	540	Guatemala	165
Florida	350	Canada	120
Illinois	290	Haiti	105
New Jersey	135	Philippines	95
Arizona	115	Honduras	90
Massachusetts	85	Bahamas, The	70
Virginia	55	Nicaragua	70
Washington	52	Poland	70
Colorado	45	Colombia	65
Maryland	44	Ecuador	55
New Mexico	37	Jamaica	50
Pennsylvania	37	Dominican Republic	50
Michigan	37	Trinidad & Tobago	50
Oregon	33	Pakistan	41
Georgia	32	India	33
District of Columbia	30	Dominica	32
Connecticut	29	Peru	30
Nevada	24	Korea	30

[1] Includes other states and countries not shown separately.

Source: U.S. Immigration and Naturalization Service, "Illegal Alien Resident Population;" published 22 June 1998; <http://www.ins.usdoj.gov/stats/illegalalien/index.html>.

12   Population

[For year ending September 30. For definition of immigrants, see text of this section]

State and other area	Total		By selected country, 1996						
	1996	1997	Mexico	Philip-pines	India	Vietnam	China	Domini-can Republic	Cuba
Total	915,900	798,378	163,572	55,876	44,859	42,067	41,728	39,604	26,466
Alabama.............	1,782	1,613	162	74	234	74	112	2	3
Alaska.............	1,280	(NA)	111	385	28	24	29	24	5
Arizona.............	8,900	8,632	5,051	316	273	265	251	9	8
Arkansas............	1,494	(NA)	446	96	105	138	45	5	-
California	201,529	203,305	64,238	23,438	7,757	13,549	10,864	83	346
Colorado............	8,895	7,506	3,138	185	203	753	430	7	6
Connecticut..........	10,874	9,528	207	262	681	249	454	278	69
Delaware	1,377	(NA)	130	60	143	40	66	9	7
District of Columbia	3,784	3,373	40	108	60	350	209	95	3
Florida.............	79,461	82,318	3,155	1,796	1,393	977	773	2,050	22,217
Georgia	12,608	12,623	1,399	252	1,127	1,961	455	46	57
Hawaii.............	8,436	6,867	70	5,208	24	328	555	-	1
Idaho.............	1,825	(NA)	839	37	42	88	50	-	2
Illinois.............	42,517	38,128	11,715	2,516	3,829	777	1,164	66	109
Indiana.............	4,692	3,892	877	219	364	150	282	15	16
Iowa.............	3,037	2,766	620	95	153	447	106	4	-
Kansas.............	4,303	2,829	1,470	131	166	683	160	3	8
Kentucky	2,019	1,939	98	90	162	150	123	4	16
Louisiana	4,092	3,319	178	158	336	899	216	28	79
Maine.............	1,028	(NA)	14	39	32	69	74	3	7
Maryland	20,732	19,090	319	942	1,421	633	1,095	171	26
Massachusetts........	23,085	17,317	141	288	1,075	1,452	1,630	2,051	64
Michigan............	17,253	14,727	828	391	1,745	455	768	52	24
Minnesota..........	8,977	8,233	496	195	376	820	344	10	20
Mississippi	1,073	(NA)	61	117	122	124	72	2	26
Missouri............	5,690	4,190	451	261	397	710	326	3	56
Montana	449	(NA)	15	30	15	-	29	-	-
Nebraska	2,150	2,270	893	62	69	236	53	2	-
Nevada	5,874	6,541	2,263	806	136	83	166	15	255
New Hampshire	1,512	(NA)	40	52	90	199	95	38	-
New Jersey	63,303	41,184	1,125	3,544	6,185	630	2,140	5,006	1,593
New Mexico	5,780	2,610	4,254	91	123	99	69	3	179
New York	154,095	123,716	1,553	3,719	5,611	971	11,409	20,579	452
North Carolina	7,011	5,935	661	298	682	582	334	40	53
North Dakota........	606	(NA)	16	19	42	53	10	1	4
Ohio	10,237	8,189	320	343	1,122	294	801	29	19
Oklahoma..........	3,511	3,157	931	136	216	580	132	5	7
Oregon............	7,554	7,699	1,942	338	207	888	434	10	27
Pennsylvania........	16,938	14,553	692	440	1,785	961	1,056	296	62
Rhode Island.........	3,098	2,543	49	65	53	25	102	560	9
South Carolina........	2,151	2,446	148	166	222	121	141	2	-
South Dakota	519	(NA)	15	23	20	20	23	2	9
Tennessee	4,343	4,357	261	175	384	400	197	3	30
Texas.............	83,385	57,897	46,403	2,064	3,295	5,793	1,701	108	258
Utah	4,250	2,840	1,036	79	134	280	190	13	7
Vermont	654	(NA)	19	12	19	81	42	2	-
Virginia.............	21,375	19,277	531	1,446	1,208	1,437	743	50	47
Washington...........	18,833	18,656	3,482	1,688	577	2,105	774	7	9
West Virginia.........	583	(NA)	18	57	78	2	40	-	2
Wisconsin............	3,607	3,175	474	112	287	44	215	16	10
Wyoming	280	(NA)	94	11	10	3	12	-	2
Guam	2,820	2,083	-	2,220	13	14	81	-	-
Northern Mariana Islands	176	(NA)	-	149	-	-	14	-	-
Puerto Rico..........	8,560	4,884	73	7	9	-	66	7,354	-
Virgin Islands.........	1,384	(NA)	3	5	15	1	5	442	257
Armed services posts ...	109	(NA)	-	60	4	-	1	1	-
Other.............	10	(NA)	7	-	-	-	-	-	-

- Represents zero.   NA Not available.

Source: U.S. Immigration and Naturalization Service, Statistical Yearbook, annual.

Population 13

[In thousands (3,172 represents 3,172,000)]

Date	Sex		Race					
					Other			
						American Indian, Eskimo, Aleut	Asian, Pacific Islander	Hispanic origin [1]
	Male	Female	White	Black	Total			
1790 (Aug. 2) [2]	(NA)	(NA)	3,172	757	(NA)	(NA)	(NA)	(NA)
1800 (Aug. 4) [2]	(NA)	(NA)	4,306	1,002	(NA)	(NA)	(NA)	(NA)
1850 (June 1) [2]	11,838	11,354	19,553	3,639	(NA)	(NA)	(NA)	(NA)
1900 (June 1) [2]	38,816	37,178	66,809	8,834	351	(NA)	(NA)	(NA)
1910 (Apr. 15) [2]	47,332	44,640	81,732	9,828	413	(NA)	(NA)	(NA)
1920 (Jan. 1) [2]	53,900	51,810	94,821	10,463	427	(NA)	(NA)	(NA)
1930 (Apr. 1) [2]	62,137	60,638	110,287	11,891	597	(NA)	(NA)	(NA)
1940 (Apr. 1) [2]	66,062	65,608	118,215	12,866	589	(NA)	(NA)	(NA)
1950 (Apr. 1) [2]	74,833	75,864	134,942	15,042	713	(NA)	(NA)	(NA)
1950 (Apr. 1)......	75,187	76,139	135,150	15,045	1,131	(NA)	(NA)	(NA)
1960 (Apr. 1)......	88,331	90,992	158,832	18,872	1,620	(NA)	(NA)	(NA)
1970 (Apr. 1) [3] ...	98,926	104,309	178,098	22,581	2,557	(NA)	(NA)	(NA)
1980 (Apr. 1) [4] [5] ...	110,053	116,493	194,713	26,683	5,150	1,420	3,729	14,609
1990 (Apr. 1) [4] [6] ...	121,271	127,494	208,727	30,511	9,527	2,065	7,462	22,372
1991 (July 1) [7] ...	122,943	129,184	210,961	31,131	10,035	2,110	7,925	23,384
1992 (July 1) [7] ...	124,404	130,590	212,860	31,667	10,467	2,148	8,319	24,275
1993 (July 1) [7] ...	125,767	131,979	214,677	32,179	10,890	2,185	8,705	25,214
1994 (July 1) [7] ...	127,028	133,261	216,365	32,654	11,271	2,221	9,050	26,152
1995 (July 1) [7] ...	128,272	134,493	218,010	33,098	11,657	2,254	9,403	27,099
1996 (July 1) [7] ...	129,483	135,707	219,623	33,518	12,050	2,289	9,761	28,092
1997 (July 1) [7] ...	130,760	136,984	221,317	33,973	12,454	2,324	10,130	29,160
1998 (July 1) [7] ...	132,046	138,252	223,001	34,431	12,867	2,360	10,507	30,250
2000 (July 1) [8]	134,181	140,453	225,532	35,454	13,647	2,402	11,245	31,366
2005 (July 1) [8]	139,785	146,196	232,463	37,734	15,784	2,572	13,212	36,057
2010 (July 1) [8]	145,584	152,132	239,588	40,109	18,019	2,754	15,265	41,139
2015 (July 1) [8]	151,750	158,383	247,193	42,586	20,355	2,941	17,413	46,705
2020 (July 1) [8]	158,021	164,721	254,887	45,075	22,780	3,129	19,651	52,652
2025 (July 1) [8]	164,119	170,931	262,227	47,539	25,284	3,319	21,965	58,930
2050 (July 1) [8]	193,234	200,696	294,615	60,592	38,724	4,371	34,352	96,508

NA Not available. [1] Persons of Hispanic origin may be of any race. [2] Excludes Alaska and Hawaii. [3] The revised 1970 resident population count is 203,302,031; which incorporates changes due to errors found after tabulations were completed. The race and sex data shown here reflect the official 1970 census count. [4] The race data shown have been modified; see text of this section for explanation. [5] See footnote 4, Table 1. [6] The April 1, 1990, census count (248,765,170) includes count resolution corrections processed through August 1997 and does not include adjustments for census coverage errors except for adjustments estimated for the 1995 Census Test in Oakland, California; Patterson, New Jersey; and six Louisiana parishes. These adjustments amounted to a total of 55,297 persons. [7] Estimated. [8] Middle series projection; see Table 3.

No. 13. Resident Population Characteristics—Percent Distribution and Median Age, 1850 to 1998, and Projections, 2000 to 2050

[In percent, except as indicated. For definition of median, see Guide to Tabular Presentation]

Date	Sex		Race					Median age (years)
					American Indian, Eskimo, Aleut	Asian, Pacific Islander	Hispanic origin [1]	
	Male	Female	White	Black				
1850 (June 1) [2]	51.0	49.0	84.3	15.7	(NA)	(NA)	(NA)	18.9
1900 (June 1) [2]	51.1	48.9	87.9	11.6	(NA)	(NA)	(NA)	22.9
1910 (Apr. 15) [2]	51.5	48.5	88.9	10.7	(NA)	(NA)	(NA)	24.1
1920 (Jan. 1) [2]	51.0	49.0	89.7	9.9	(NA)	(NA)	(NA)	25.3
1930 (Apr. 1) [2]	50.6	49.4	89.8	9.7	(NA)	(NA)	(NA)	26.4
1940 (Apr. 1) [2]	50.2	49.8	89.8	9.8	(NA)	(NA)	(NA)	29.0
1950 (Apr. 1)......	49.7	50.3	89.3	9.9	(NA)	(NA)	(NA)	30.2
1960 (Apr. 1)......	49.3	50.7	88.6	10.5	(NA)	(NA)	(NA)	29.5
1970 (Apr. 1)......	48.7	51.3	87.6	11.1	(NA)	(NA)	(NA)	28.0
1980 (Apr. 1) [3] [4] ...	48.6	51.4	85.9	11.8	0.6	1.6	6.4	30.0
1990 (Apr. 1) [3] [5] ...	48.7	51.3	83.9	12.3	0.8	3.0	9.0	32.8
1995 (July 1) [6]	48.8	51.2	83.0	12.6	0.9	3.6	10.3	34.4
1998 (July 1) [6]	48.9	51.2	82.5	12.7	0.9	3.9	11.2	35.2
2000 (July 1) [7]	48.9	51.1	82.1	12.9	0.9	4.1	11.4	35.7
2025 (July 1) [7]	49.0	51.0	78.3	14.2	1.0	6.6	17.6	38.0
2050 (July 1) [7]	49.1	50.9	74.8	15.4	1.1	8.7	24.5	38.1

NA Not available. [1] Persons of Hispanic origin may be of any race. [2] Excludes Alaska and Hawaii. [3] The race data shown have been modified; see text of this section for explanation. [4] See footnote 4, Table 1. [5] See footnote 6, Table 12. [6] Estimated. [7] Middle series projection; see Table 3.

Source of Tables 12 and 13: U.S. Census Bureau, *U.S. Census of Population: 1940*, Vol. II, Part 1, and Vol. IV, Part 1; *1950*, Vol. II, Part 1; *1960*, Vol. I, Part 1; *1970*, Vol. I, Part B; *Current Population Reports*, P25-1095 and P25-1130; and "Resident Population of the United States: Estimates, by Sex, Race, and Hispanic Origin, with Median Age"; release date: December 28, 1998; <http://www.census.gov/population/estimates/nation/intfile3-1.txt>.

No. 14. Resident Population, by Age and Sex: 1980 to 1998

[In thousands, except as indicated (226,546 represents 226,546,000). 1980 and 1990 data are enumerated population as of **April 1**; data for **other years** are estimated population as of **July 1**. Excludes Armed Forces overseas. For definition of median, see Guide to Tabular Presentation]

Year and sex	Total, all years	Under 5 years	5-9 years	10-14 years	15-19 years	20-24 years	25-29 years	30-34 years	35-39 years	40-44 years	45-49 years	50-54 years	55-59 years	60-64 years	65-74 years	75-84 years	85 years and over	5-13 years	14-17 years	18-24 years	Median age (yr.)
1980, total [1]	**226,546**	**16,348**	**16,700**	**18,242**	**21,168**	**21,319**	**19,521**	**17,561**	**13,965**	**11,669**	**11,090**	**11,710**	**11,615**	**10,088**	**15,581**	**7,729**	**2,240**	**31,159**	**16,247**	**30,022**	**30.0**
Male	110,053	8,362	8,539	9,316	10,755	10,663	9,705	8,677	6,862	5,708	5,388	5,621	5,482	4,670	6,757	2,867	682	15,923	8,298	15,054	28.8
Female	116,493	7,986	8,161	8,926	10,413	10,655	9,816	8,884	7,104	5,961	5,702	6,089	6,133	5,418	8,824	4,862	1,559	15,237	7,950	14,969	31.3
1981, total	229,466	16,893	16,060	18,300	20,541	21,663	20,169	18,731	14,366	12,028	10,985	11,595	11,554	10,359	15,890	7,982	2,349	30,711	15,609	30,245	30.3
1982, total	231,664	17,228	15,958	18,145	19,962	21,682	20,704	18,714	15,566	12,464	11,011	11,414	11,463	10,567	16,147	8,203	2,437	30,528	15,057	30,162	30.5
1983, total	233,792	17,547	16,053	17,869	19,388	21,632	21,141	19,067	16,117	13,150	11,201	11,155	11,457	10,655	16,414	8,429	2,518	30,279	14,740	29,922	30.8
1984, total	235,825	17,695	16,338	17,450	18,931	21,529	21,459	19,503	16,867	13,636	11,429	10,957	11,352	10,803	16,626	8,656	2,595	30,062	14,725	29,461	31.1
1985, total	237,924	17,842	16,665	16,926	18,727	21,265	21,671	20,025	17,604	14,398	11,606	10,854	11,229	10,906	16,858	8,890	2,667	29,893	14,888	28,902	31.4
1986, total	240,133	17,963	17,098	16,474	18,813	21,287	21,893	20,479	18,611	15,608	11,878	10,781	11,135	10,859	17,137	9,129	2,742	30,078	14,824	28,287	31.7
1987, total	242,289	18,052	17,430	16,474	18,698	20,192	21,857	20,984	18,619	16,188	12,294	10,802	10,968	10,783	17,426	9,376	2,823	30,502	14,502	27,694	32.0
1988, total	244,499	18,195	17,759	16,496	18,496	19,655	21,739	21,391	18,993	16,960	12,954	10,995	10,722	10,791	17,626	9,612	2,885	31,028	14,023	27,356	32.3
1989, total	246,819	18,508	17,917	16,797	18,133	19,258	21,560	21,676	19,455	16,960	13,421	11,212	10,534	10,707	17,864	9,850	2,968	31,413	13,536	27,156	32.6
1990, total [2]	**248,765**	**18,763**	**18,040**	**17,065**	**17,890**	**19,139**	**21,333**	**21,837**	**19,849**	**17,592**	**13,746**	**11,314**	**10,489**	**10,626**	**18,047**	**10,012**	**3,022**	**31,835**	**13,344**	**26,955**	**32.8**
Male	121,271	9,602	9,234	8,741	9,177	9,747	10,706	10,865	9,836	8,679	6,741	5,494	5,009	4,947	7,908	3,745	841	16,298	6,860	13,742	31.6
Female	127,494	9,161	8,805	8,324	8,713	9,393	10,627	10,972	10,014	8,914	7,005	5,820	5,479	5,679	10,140	6,267	2,180	15,536	6,484	13,215	34.0
1991, total	252,127	19,186	18,203	17,676	17,232	19,153	20,709	22,156	20,528	18,760	14,098	11,648	10,421	10,580	18,270	10,319	3,189	32,465	13,451	26,348	33.1
1992, total	254,995	19,488	18,290	18,099	17,178	19,042	20,134	22,237	21,096	18,805	15,357	12,054	10,483	10,437	18,442	10,537	3,315	32,937	13,701	25,970	33.4
1993, total	257,746	19,670	18,439	18,505	17,373	18,781	19,564	22,224	21,602	19,207	15,929	12,728	10,677	10,235	18,629	10,737	3,446	33,376	13,987	25,734	33.7
1994, total	260,289	19,697	18,749	18,713	17,740	18,385	19,101	22,130	21,975	19,714	16,677	13,194	10,931	10,076	18,702	10,944	3,562	33,707	14,489	25,391	34.1
1995, total	262,765	19,529	19,092	18,849	18,200	17,978	18,899	21,821	22,293	20,257	17,456	13,641	11,085	10,046	18,756	11,178	3,684	34,188	14,826	25,107	34.3
1996, total	265,190	19,289	19,435	19,091	18,704	17,504	18,927	21,309	22,549	20,809	18,428	13,927	11,356	9,996	18,689	11,466	3,800	34,597	15,210	24,837	34.6
1997, total	267,744	19,097	19,749	19,091	19,140	17,483	18,812	20,732	22,629	21,376	18,465	15,157	11,755	10,062	18,528	11,751	3,919	34,996	15,495	24,973	34.9
1998, total	**270,299**	**18,966**	**19,921**	**19,242**	**19,539**	**17,674**	**18,588**	**20,186**	**22,626**	**21,894**	**18,859**	**15,726**	**12,407**	**10,269**	**18,395**	**11,952**	**4,054**	**35,389**	**15,517**	**25,470**	**35.2**
Male	132,046	9,696	10,195	9,855	10,046	8,996	9,247	10,007	11,256	10,845	9,252	7,648	5,956	4,849	8,250	4,761	1,187	18,114	7,985	12,993	34.1
Female	138,252	9,270	9,726	9,387	9,494	8,678	9,341	10,179	11,370	11,049	9,607	8,078	6,451	5,420	10,146	7,191	2,866	17,275	7,532	12,478	36.3
Percent:																					
1980 [1]	100.0	7.2	7.4	8.1	9.3	9.4	8.6	7.8	6.2	5.2	4.9	5.2	5.1	4.5	6.9	3.4	1.0	13.8	7.2	13.3	(X)
1990 [2]	100.0	7.5	7.3	6.9	7.2	7.7	8.6	8.8	8.0	7.1	5.5	4.5	4.2	4.3	7.3	4.0	1.2	12.8	5.4	10.8	(X)
1998.	100.0	7.0	7.4	7.1	7.6	6.5	6.9	7.5	8.4	8.1	7.0	5.8	4.6	3.8	6.8	4.4	1.5	13.1	5.7	9.4	(X)
Male	100.0	7.3	7.7	7.5	7.6	6.8	7.0	7.6	8.5	8.2	7.0	5.8	4.5	3.7	6.2	3.6	0.9	13.1	6.0	9.8	(X)
Female	100.0	6.7	7.0	6.8	6.9	6.3	7.0	7.4	8.2	8.0	6.9	5.8	4.7	3.9	7.3	5.2	2.1	12.5	5.4	9.0	(X)

X Not applicable. [1] Total population count has been revised since the 1980 census counts. See text of this section for explanation. The April 1, 1990, census count (248,765,170) includes count resolution corrections processed through August 1997, and does not include adjustments for census coverage errors except for adjustments estimated for the 1995 Census Test in Oakland, California; Patterson, New Jersey; and six Louisiana parishes. These adjustments amounted to a total of 55,297 persons. [2] The data shown have been modified from the official 1990 census counts. Numbers by age, race, Hispanic origin, and sex have not been corrected.

Source: U.S. Census Bureau, *Current Population Reports,* P25-1095; and unpublished data.

U.S. Census Bureau, Statistical Abstract of the United States: 1999

No. 15. Ratio of Males to Females, by Age Group, 1980 to 1998, and Projections, 2000 and 2025

[Number of males per 100 females. Total resident population]

Age	1980 (Apr. 1)	1990 [1] (Apr. 1)	1995 (July 1)	1997 (July 1)	1998 (July 1)	Projections [2] 2000 (July 1)	2025 (July 1)
All ages.	94.5	95.1	95.4	95.5	95.5	95.5	96.0
Under 14 years	104.6	104.9	104.8	104.8	104.8	104.8	105.1
14 to 24 years	101.9	104.6	104.7	104.8	104.8	104.1	104.2
25 to 44 years	97.4	98.9	98.8	98.7	98.6	98.9	97.7
45 to 64 years	90.7	92.5	93.5	93.7	93.7	93.8	93.5
65 years and over.	67.6	67.2	69.1	69.9	70.3	70.4	82.9

[1] The April 1, 1990, census count (248,765,170) includes count resolution corrections processed through August 1997, and does not include adjustments for census coverage errors except for adjustments estimated for the 1995 Census Test in Oakland, California; Patterson, New Jersey; and six Louisiana parishes. These adjustments amounted to a total of 55,297 persons.
[2] Middle series projections; see Table 3.

Source: U.S. Census Bureau, Current Population Reports, P25-1095 and P25-1130; and unpublished data.

No. 16. Resident Population, by Sex and Age: 1998

[In thousands, except as indicated (270,299 represents 270,299,000). As of July 1. For derivation of estimates, see text of this section]

Age	Total	Male	Female
Total	270,299	132,046	138,252
Under 5 yrs. old	18,966	9,696	9,270
Under 1 yr. old	3,776	1,929	1,847
1 yr. old	3,748	1,914	1,834
2 yrs. old	3,750	1,918	1,832
3 yrs. old	3,797	1,942	1,855
4 yrs. old	3,895	1,993	1,902
5 to 9 yrs. old.	19,921	10,195	9,726
5 yrs. old	3,948	2,023	1,925
6 yrs. old	4,020	2,054	1,966
7 yrs. old	4,058	2,075	1,983
8 yrs. old	3,884	1,987	1,896
9 yrs. old	4,010	2,055	1,955
10 to 14 yrs. old	19,242	9,855	9,387
10 yrs. old	3,940	2,019	1,921
11 yrs. old	3,837	1,964	1,873
12 yrs. old	3,832	1,961	1,871
13 yrs. old	3,859	1,975	1,884
14 yrs. old	3,774	1,936	1,838
15 to 19 yrs. old	19,539	10,046	9,494
15 yrs. old	3,893	2,000	1,894
16 yrs. old	3,920	2,020	1,900
17 yrs. old	3,930	2,030	1,900
18 yrs. old	3,879	1,991	1,888
19 yrs. old	3,917	2,006	1,912
20 to 24 yrs. old	17,674	8,996	8,678
20 yrs. old	3,782	1,937	1,845
21 yrs. old	3,669	1,877	1,792
22 yrs. old	3,413	1,740	1,673
23 yrs. old	3,411	1,729	1,682
24 yrs. old	3,400	1,713	1,687
25 to 29 yrs. old	18,588	9,247	9,341
25 yrs. old	3,435	1,721	1,714
26 yrs. old	3,615	1,798	1,816
27 yrs. old	3,898	1,935	1,964
28 yrs. old	3,687	1,828	1,859
29 yrs. old	3,953	1,964	1,989
30 to 34 yrs. old	20,186	10,007	10,179
30 yrs. old	3,816	1,891	1,925
31 yrs. old	3,816	1,889	1,927
32 yrs. old	3,935	1,949	1,987
33 yrs. old	4,153	2,052	2,101
34 yrs. old	4,465	2,226	2,239
35 to 39 yrs. old	22,626	11,256	11,370
35 yrs. old	4,504	2,242	2,263
36 yrs. old	4,494	2,234	2,259
37 yrs. old	4,557	2,264	2,293
38 yrs. old	4,326	2,149	2,177
39 yrs. old	4,745	2,367	2,378
40 to 44 yrs. old	21,894	10,845	11,049
40 yrs. old	4,613	2,291	2,321
41 yrs. old	4,493	2,227	2,266
42 yrs. old	4,307	2,130	2,177

Age	Total	Male	Female
43 yrs. old	4,224	2,083	2,141
44 yrs. old	4,258	2,113	2,144
45 to 49 yrs. old	18,859	9,252	9,607
45 yrs. old	4,042	1,992	2,049
46 yrs. old	3,845	1,890	1,955
47 yrs. old	3,718	1,819	1,899
48 yrs. old	3,500	1,710	1,789
49 yrs. old	3,755	1,841	1,914
50 to 54 yrs. old	15,726	7,648	8,078
50 yrs. old	3,637	1,777	1,861
51 yrs. old	3,750	1,833	1,917
52 yrs. old	2,711	1,315	1,396
53 yrs. old	2,793	1,353	1,440
54 yrs. old	2,833	1,370	1,463
55 to 59 yrs. old	12,407	5,956	6,451
55 yrs. old	2,893	1,395	1,497
56 yrs. old	2,569	1,234	1,336
57 yrs. old	2,453	1,176	1,277
58 yrs. old	2,196	1,051	1,145
59 yrs. old	2,296	1,100	1,196
60 to 64 yrs. old	10,269	4,849	5,420
60 yrs. old	2,198	1,038	1,160
61 yrs. old	2,042	969	1,073
62 yrs. old	2,020	953	1,067
63 yrs. old	2,053	973	1,081
64 yrs. old	1,956	916	1,039
65 to 69 yrs. old	9,593	4,393	5,201
65 yrs. old	1,925	892	1,033
66 yrs. old	1,905	877	1,028
67 yrs. old	1,968	902	1,065
68 yrs. old	1,900	869	1,032
69 yrs. old	1,895	852	1,043
70 to 74 yrs. old	8,802	3,857	4,945
70 yrs. old	1,895	849	1,047
71 yrs. old	1,808	798	1,010
72 yrs. old	1,756	772	984
73 yrs. old	1,696	733	964
74 yrs. old	1,647	705	941
75 to 79 yrs. old	7,218	2,997	4,221
75 yrs. old	1,581	671	910
76 yrs. old	1,550	655	895
77 yrs. old	1,472	615	858
78 yrs. old	1,359	554	805
79 yrs. old	1,256	503	753
80 to 84 yrs. old	4,734	1,764	2,970
80 yrs. old	1,112	432	680
81 yrs. old	1,022	391	631
82 yrs. old	941	351	589
83 yrs. old	878	317	561
84 yrs. old	781	273	508
85 to 89 yrs. old	2,556	814	1,742
90 to 94 yrs. old	1,117	294	823
95 to 99 yrs. old	324	70	254
100 yrs. old and over. . .	57	10	47
Median age (yr.)	35.2	34.1	36.3

Source: U.S. Census Bureau, unpublished data.

No. 17. Resident Population Projections, by Age and Sex: 1999 to 2050

[In thousands (269,861 represents 269,861,000). As of July. See headnote, Table 3]

Year	Total	Under 5 years	5 to 13 years	14 to 17 years	18 to 24 years	25 to 34 years	35 to 44 years	45 to 54 years	55 to 64 years	65 to 74 years	75 to 84 years	85 years and over
TOTAL												
Lowest series:												
1999......	269,861	18,295	35,658	15,547	25,423	37,518	44,450	35,580	23,260	18,068	12,019	4,044
2000......	271,237	17,943	35,790	15,602	25,876	36,740	44,364	36,840	23,798	17,974	12,162	4,148
2005......	276,990	16,896	34,366	16,667	27,491	35,095	41,365	40,992	29,145	17,943	12,465	4,566
2010......	281,468	16,563	31,950	16,319	29,050	36,393	37,049	42,589	34,393	20,245	11,912	5,005
2015......	285,472	16,941	30,832	15,026	28,899	38,644	35,351	39,630	38,217	24,843	11,962	5,128
2020......	288,807	17,168	30,998	14,331	26,671	40,067	36,640	35,487	39,642	29,219	13,598	4,987
2025......	290,789	16,901	31,576	14,234	25,368	38,969	38,834	33,847	36,821	32,395	16,748	5,094
2030......	291,070	16,450	31,454	14,631	25,111	36,312	40,222	35,075	32,948	33,483	19,610	5,776
2040......	287,685	16,200	30,164	14,405	25,849	35,018	36,489	38,475	32,631	27,827	22,376	8,250
2050......	282,524	16,330	30,124	13,925	24,810	35,604	35,185	34,868	35,747	27,700	18,588	9,642
Middle series:												
1999......	272,330	19,041	35,846	15,661	25,710	37,876	44,661	35,717	23,378	18,186	12,129	4,124
2000......	274,634	18,987	36,043	15,752	26,258	37,233	44,659	37,030	23,962	18,136	12,315	4,259
2005......	285,981	19,127	35,850	16,986	28,268	36,306	42,165	41,507	29,606	18,369	12,898	4,899
2010......	297,716	20,012	35,605	16,894	30,138	38,292	38,521	43,564	35,283	21,057	12,680	5,671
2015......	310,134	21,174	36,698	16,651	30,516	41,084	37,598	41,196	39,650	26,243	13,130	6,193
2020......	322,742	21,979	38,660	16,965	29,919	42,934	39,612	37,740	41,714	31,385	15,375	6,460
2025......	335,050	22,498	40,413	17,872	30,372	43,119	42,391	36,890	39,542	35,425	19,481	7,046
2030......	346,899	23,066	41,589	18,788	31,826	42,744	44,263	38,897	36,348	37,406	23,517	8,455
2040......	369,980	24,980	43,993	19,844	34,570	45,932	44,159	43,530	37,739	33,013	28,668	13,552
2050......	393,931	27,106	47,804	21,207	36,333	49,365	47,393	43,494	42,368	34,731	25,905	18,223
Highest series:												
1999......	274,865	19,726	36,039	15,780	26,004	38,264	44,932	35,868	23,482	18,290	12,257	4,225
2000......	278,129	19,955	36,300	15,909	26,651	37,766	45,038	37,241	24,105	18,276	12,490	4,399
2005......	295,318	21,350	37,266	17,318	29,064	37,599	43,197	42,119	29,997	18,723	13,367	5,317
2010......	314,571	23,649	39,195	17,467	31,248	40,275	40,302	44,738	36,018	21,696	13,465	6,518
2015......	335,597	25,757	42,763	18,228	32,120	43,587	40,161	43,020	40,839	27,278	14,260	7,583
2020......	357,702	27,273	46,855	19,641	33,084	45,836	42,878	40,263	43,473	32,937	17,007	8,456
2025......	380,781	28,828	50,036	21,737	35,428	47,204	46,208	40,172	41,925	37,593	21,882	9,768
2030......	405,089	30,818	52,876	23,276	38,886	49,091	48,519	42,895	39,398	40,270	26,861	12,198
2040......	458,444	35,901	60,446	26,000	44,069	57,362	51,925	48,560	42,258	37,096	33,907	20,920
2050......	518,903	41,213	70,000	30,005	49,683	64,279	60,324	51,967	47,950	40,319	32,070	31,093
MALE												
Middle series:												
1999......	133,039	9,740	18,355	8,042	13,063	18,869	22,184	17,446	11,150	8,171	4,839	1,179
2000......	134,181	9,712	18,454	8,090	13,338	18,535	22,181	18,092	11,433	8,180	4,937	1,228
2005......	139,785	9,786	18,353	8,724	14,359	18,014	20,891	20,304	14,166	8,408	5,306	1,473
2010......	145,584	10,243	18,232	8,679	15,313	18,990	18,993	21,325	16,922	9,752	5,363	1,771
2015......	151,750	10,844	18,801	8,554	15,505	20,393	18,479	20,119	19,077	12,273	5,711	1,995
2020......	158,021	11,259	19,813	8,718	15,201	21,319	19,466	18,347	20,120	14,791	6,845	2,141
2025......	164,119	11,525	20,712	9,184	15,432	21,405	20,848	17,878	19,048	16,826	8,839	2,422
2030......	169,950	11,813	21,311	9,653	16,171	21,214	21,775	18,854	17,441	17,878	10,819	3,021
2040......	181,261	12,788	22,534	10,192	17,563	22,808	21,723	21,139	18,093	15,796	13,522	5,103
2050......	193,234	13,877	24,488	10,893	18,462	24,533	23,352	21,150	20,403	16,699	12,342	7,036
FEMALE												
Middle series:												
1999......	139,291	9,302	17,492	7,619	12,647	19,007	22,476	18,271	12,228	10,015	7,290	2,945
2000......	140,453	9,274	17,589	7,662	12,920	18,699	22,478	18,938	12,529	9,956	7,377	3,031
2005......	146,196	9,341	17,498	8,262	13,909	18,291	21,273	21,203	15,440	9,961	7,592	3,426
2010......	152,132	9,768	17,373	8,215	14,824	19,301	19,527	22,240	18,362	11,305	7,317	3,899
2015......	158,383	10,330	17,897	8,097	15,010	20,691	19,119	21,078	20,572	13,971	7,419	4,199
2020......	164,721	10,719	18,847	8,247	14,717	21,615	20,146	19,393	21,594	16,594	8,530	4,319
2025......	170,931	10,973	19,701	8,688	14,939	21,715	21,543	19,011	20,495	18,599	10,643	4,624
2030......	176,949	11,253	20,278	9,135	15,655	21,529	22,488	20,044	18,907	19,529	12,699	5,433
2040......	188,719	12,192	21,459	9,652	17,006	23,125	22,436	22,391	19,646	17,216	15,146	8,449
2050......	200,696	13,229	23,316	10,314	17,871	24,832	24,041	22,344	21,965	18,032	13,563	11,188
PERCENT DISTRIBUTION												
Middle series:												
2000......	100.0	6.9	13.1	5.7	9.6	13.6	16.3	13.5	8.7	6.6	4.5	1.6
2010......	100.0	6.7	12.0	5.7	10.1	12.9	12.9	14.6	11.9	7.1	4.3	1.9
2020......	100.0	6.8	12.0	5.3	9.3	13.3	12.3	11.7	12.9	9.7	4.8	2.0
2030......	100.0	6.6	12.0	5.4	9.2	12.3	12.8	11.2	10.5	10.8	6.8	2.4
2040......	100.0	6.8	11.9	5.4	9.3	12.4	11.9	11.8	10.2	8.9	7.7	3.7
2050......	100.0	6.9	12.1	5.4	9.2	12.5	12.0	11.0	10.8	8.8	6.6	4.6

Source: U.S. Census Bureau, *Current Population Reports*, P25-1130.

Population 17

No. 18. Resident Population, by Race, 1980 to 1998, and Projections, 1999 to 2050

[In thousands, except as indicated (226,546 represents 226,546,000). As of **July**, except as indicated. These data are consistent with the 1980 and 1990 decennial enumerations and have been modified from the official census counts; see text of this section for explanation. See headnote, Table 3]

Year	Total	White	Black	American Indian, Eskimo, Aleut	Asian, Pacific Islander
1980 (April) [1]	226,546	194,713	26,683	1,420	3,729
1981	229,466	196,635	27,133	1,483	4,214
1982	231,664	198,037	27,508	1,537	4,581
1983	233,792	199,420	27,867	1,596	4,909
1984	235,825	200,708	28,212	1,656	5,249
1985	237,924	202,031	28,569	1,718	5,606
1986	240,133	203,430	28,942	1,783	5,978
1987	242,289	204,770	29,325	1,851	6,343
1988	244,499	206,129	29,723	1,923	6,724
1989	246,819	207,540	30,143	2,001	7,134
1990 (April) [2]	248,765	208,727	30,511	2,065	7,462
1991	252,127	210,961	31,131	2,110	7,925
1992	254,995	212,860	31,667	2,148	8,319
1993	257,746	214,677	32,179	2,185	8,705
1994	260,289	216,365	32,654	2,221	9,050
1995	262,765	218,010	33,098	2,254	9,403
1996	265,190	219,623	33,518	2,289	9,761
1997	267,744	221,317	33,973	2,324	10,130
1998	270,299	223,001	34,431	2,360	10,507
PROJECTIONS					
Lowest series:					
1999	269,861	222,346	34,721	2,355	10,440
2000	271,237	223,114	35,074	2,382	10,667
2005	276,990	226,006	36,695	2,514	11,774
2010	281,468	227,841	38,139	2,642	12,845
2015	285,472	229,295	39,491	2,766	13,920
2020	288,807	230,202	40,709	2,881	15,015
2030	291,070	228,310	42,519	3,080	17,161
2040	287,685	221,671	43,674	3,247	19,092
2050	282,524	213,782	44,477	3,383	20,882
Middle series:					
1999	272,330	224,103	34,997	2,369	10,861
2000	274,634	225,532	35,454	2,402	11,245
2005	285,981	232,463	37,734	2,572	13,212
2010	297,716	239,588	40,109	2,754	15,265
2015	310,134	247,193	42,586	2,941	17,413
2020	322,742	254,887	45,075	3,129	19,651
2030	346,899	269,046	50,001	3,515	24,337
2040	369,980	281,720	55,094	3,932	29,235
2050	393,931	294,615	60,592	4,371	34,352
Highest series:					
1999	274,865	225,848	35,332	2,383	11,302
2000	278,129	227,937	35,919	2,421	11,851
2005	295,318	238,906	39,050	2,627	14,735
2010	314,571	251,262	42,590	2,860	17,859
2015	335,597	264,859	46,435	3,108	21,195
2020	357,702	279,139	50,490	3,365	24,709
2030	405,089	309,404	59,449	3,934	32,302
2040	458,444	343,201	69,844	4,609	40,790
2050	518,903	381,505	81,815	5,384	50,199
PERCENT DISTRIBUTION					
Middle series:					
2000	100.0	82.1	12.9	0.9	4.1
2010	100.0	80.5	13.5	0.9	5.1
2020	100.0	79.0	14.0	1.0	6.1
2030	100.0	77.6	14.4	1.0	7.0
2040	100.0	76.1	14.9	1.1	7.9
2050	100.0	74.8	15.4	1.1	8.7
PERCENT CHANGE					
Middle series:					
2000-2010	8.4	6.2	13.1	14.6	35.8
2010-2020	8.4	6.4	12.4	13.6	28.7
2020-2030	7.5	5.6	10.9	12.3	23.8
2030-2040	6.7	4.7	10.2	11.8	20.1
2040-2050	6.5	4.6	10.0	11.2	17.5

[1] See footnote 4, Table 1.   [2] The April 1, 1990, census count (248,765,170) includes count resolution corrections processed through August 1997, and does not include adjustments for census coverage errors except for adjustments estimated for the 1995 Census Test in Oakland, California; Patterson, New Jersey; and six Louisiana parishes. These adjustments amounted to a total of 55,297 persons.

Source: U.S. Census Bureau, *Current Population Reports*, P25-1095 and P25-1130; and unpublished data.

No. 19. Resident Population, by Hispanic Origin Status, 1980 to 1998, and Projections, 1999 to 2050

[In thousands, except as indicated (226,546 represents 226,546,000). As of July, except as indicated. These data are consistent with the 1980 and 1990 decennial enumerations and have been modified from the official census counts; see text, of this section for explanation. See headnote, Table 3. Minus sign (-) indicates decrease]

Year	Total	Hispanic origin [1]	Not of Hispanic origin			
			White	Black	American Indian, Eskimo, Aleut	Asian, Pacific Islander
1980 (April) [2]	226,546	14,609	180,906	26,142	1,326	3,563
1981	229,466	15,560	181,974	26,532	1,377	4,022
1982	231,664	16,240	182,782	26,856	1,420	4,367
1983	233,792	16,935	183,561	27,159	1,466	4,671
1984	235,825	17,640	184,243	27,444	1,512	4,986
1985	237,924	18,368	184,945	27,738	1,558	5,315
1986	240,133	19,154	185,678	28,040	1,606	5,655
1987	242,289	19,946	186,353	28,351	1,654	5,985
1988	244,499	20,786	187,012	28,669	1,703	6,329
1989	246,819	21,648	187,713	29,005	1,755	6,698
1990 (April) [3]	248,765	22,372	188,307	29,299	1,796	6,992
1991	252,127	23,384	189,626	29,853	1,829	7,435
1992	254,995	24,275	190,718	30,332	1,857	7,812
1993	257,746	25,214	191,689	30,780	1,883	8,180
1994	260,289	26,152	192,530	31,193	1,908	8,506
1995	262,765	27,099	193,320	31,573	1,931	8,842
1996	265,190	28,092	194,029	31,933	1,954	9,181
1997	267,744	29,160	194,751	32,324	1,977	9,532
1998	270,299	30,250	195,440	32,718	2,001	9,890
PROJECTIONS						
Lowest series:						
1999	269,861	29,757	195,307	32,962	2,020	9,815
2000	271,237	30,393	195,505	33,267	2,041	10,030
2005	276,990	33,527	195,589	34,652	2,145	11,077
2010	281,468	36,652	194,628	35,856	2,243	12,088
2015	285,472	39,927	193,150	36,956	2,337	13,102
2020	288,807	43,287	191,047	37,913	2,424	14,136
2030	291,070	49,834	183,295	39,202	2,573	16,166
2040	287,685	56,104	171,054	39,841	2,695	17,991
2050	282,524	62,230	157,701	40,118	2,793	19,683
Middle series:						
1999	272,330	30,461	196,441	33,180	2,029	10,219
2000	274,634	31,366	197,061	33,568	2,054	10,584
2005	285,981	36,057	199,802	35,485	2,183	12,454
2010	297,716	41,139	202,390	37,466	2,320	14,402
2015	310,134	46,705	205,019	39,512	2,461	16,437
2020	322,742	52,652	207,393	41,538	2,601	18,557
2030	346,899	65,570	209,998	45,448	2,891	22,993
2040	369,980	80,164	209,621	49,379	3,203	27,614
2050	393,931	96,508	207,901	53,555	3,534	32,432
Highest series:						
1999	274,865	31,172	197,556	33,457	2,038	10,642
2000	278,129	32,350	198,594	33,952	2,066	11,166
2005	295,318	38,648	203,949	36,589	2,218	13,914
2010	314,571	45,760	209,963	39,572	2,391	16,885
2015	335,597	53,686	216,482	42,800	2,575	20,055
2020	357,702	62,279	223,082	46,183	2,765	23,392
2030	405,089	81,803	235,898	53,604	3,192	30,593
2040	458,444	105,274	248,715	62,132	3,703	38,620
2050	518,903	133,106	262,140	71,863	4,295	47,498
PERCENT DISTRIBUTION						
Middle series:						
2000	100.0	11.4	71.8	12.2	0.7	3.9
2010	100.0	13.8	68.0	12.6	0.8	4.8
2020	100.0	16.3	64.3	12.9	0.8	5.7
2030	100.0	18.9	60.5	13.1	0.8	6.6
2040	100.0	21.7	56.7	13.3	0.9	7.5
2050	100.0	24.5	52.8	13.6	0.9	8.2
PERCENT CHANGE						
Middle series:						
2000-2010	8.4	31.2	2.7	11.6	12.9	36.1
2010-2020	8.4	28.0	2.5	10.9	12.1	28.9
2020-2030	7.5	24.5	1.3	9.4	11.1	23.9
2030-2040	6.7	22.3	-0.2	8.6	10.8	20.1
2040-2050	6.5	20.4	-0.8	8.5	10.3	17.4

[1] Persons of Hispanic origin may be of any race. [2] See footnote 4, Table 1. [3] The April 1, 1990, census count (248,765,170) includes count resolution corrections processed through August 1997, and does not include adjustments for census coverage errors except for adjustments estimated for the 1995 Census Test in Oakland, California; Patterson, New Jersey; and six Louisiana parishes. These adjustments amounted to a total of 55,297 persons.

Source: U.S. Census Bureau, Current Population Reports, P25-1095 and P25-1130; and unpublished data.

No. 20. Components of Population Change, by Race and Hispanic Origin, 1990 to 1998, and Projections, 2000

[208,376 represents 208,376,000. The April 1, 1990, census count (248,765,170) includes count resolution corrections processed through August 1997, and does not include adjustments for census coverage errors except for adjustments estimated for the 1995 Census Test in Oakland, California; Patterson, New Jersey; and six Louisiana parishes. These adjustments amounted to a total of 55,297 persons. Minus sign (-) indicates net outmigration]

Year	Popula-tion as of Jan. 1 (1,000)	Calendar year					Rate per 1,000 midyear population			
		Net increase [1]		Births (1,000)	Deaths (1,000)	Net migra-tion [3] (1,000)	Net growth rate [1]	Birth rate	Death rate	Net migra-tion rate [3]
		Total (1,000)	Percent [2]							
WHITE										
1990	208,376	1,673	0.8	3,265	1,860	[4]268	8.0	15.6	8.9	[4]1.3
1994	215,572	1,654	0.8	3,121	1,960	493	7.6	14.4	9.1	2.3
1995	217,226	1,624	0.7	3,099	1,987	513	7.5	14.2	9.1	2.4
1996	218,850	1,649	0.8	3,093	1,993	549	7.5	14.1	9.1	2.5
1997	220,499	1,704	0.8	3,085	2,001	619	7.7	13.9	9.0	2.8
1998	222,203	1,682	0.8	3,069	1,998	611	7.5	13.8	9.0	2.7
2000, proj. [5]	224,818	1,419	0.6	2,986	2,058	491	6.3	13.2	9.1	2.2
BLACK										
1990	30,377	448	1.5	692	266	[4]22	14.6	22.6	8.7	[4]0.7
1994	32,432	456	1.4	636	282	102	14.0	19.5	8.6	3.1
1995	32,889	427	1.3	603	286	110	12.9	18.2	8.7	3.3
1996	33,316	439	1.3	595	282	126	13.1	17.7	8.4	3.8
1997	33,754	455	1.3	601	273	127	13.4	17.7	8.0	3.7
1998	34,209	462	1.3	605	268	125	13.4	17.6	7.8	3.6
2000, proj. [5]	35,225	457	1.3	685	319	90	12.9	19.3	9.0	2.6
AMERICAN INDIAN, ESKIMO, ALEUT										
1990	2,044	36	1.8	42	8	[4]3	17.3	20.1	4.1	[4]1.3
1994	2,203	34	1.6	38	10	6	15.5	17.0	4.3	2.8
1995	2,238	34	1.5	37	10	7	15.0	16.5	4.4	2.9
1996	2,272	35	1.5	38	10	7	15.3	16.6	4.4	3.2
1997	2,307	36	1.5	38	11	8	15.3	16.6	4.6	3.3
1998	2,342	36	1.5	39	11	8	15.2	16.6	4.6	3.2
2000, proj. [5]	2,386	33	1.4	42	13	4	13.7	17.3	5.2	1.6
ASIAN, PACIFIC ISLANDER										
1990	7,345	375	5.1	149	21	[4]246	49.6	19.8	2.7	[4]32.6
1994	8,886	338	3.8	158	27	208	37.4	17.4	3.0	23.0
1995	9,225	358	3.9	160	28	226	38.1	17.0	3.0	24.1
1996	9,583	359	3.7	166	30	223	36.8	17.0	3.0	22.8
1997	9,942	370	3.7	170	30	230	36.5	16.8	3.0	22.7
1998	10,312	380	3.7	175	32	236	36.2	16.7	3.0	22.5
2000, proj. [5]	11,053	386	3.5	186	36	235	34.3	16.6	3.2	20.9
HISPANIC ORIGIN [6]										
1990	22,122	822	3.7	595	84	[4]311	36.4	26.4	3.7	[4]13.8
1994	25,676	934	3.6	672	92	354	35.7	25.7	3.5	13.5
1995	26,610	993	3.7	680	96	409	36.7	25.1	3.5	15.1
1996	27,603	1,016	3.7	701	100	415	36.2	25.0	3.6	14.8
1997	28,619	1,088	3.8	712	97	473	37.3	24.4	3.3	16.2
1998	29,707	1,096	3.7	730	101	467	36.2	24.1	3.4	15.5
2000, proj. [5]	30,913	910	2.9	683	123	350	29.0	21.8	3.9	11.2
WHITE, NON-HISPANIC										
1990	188,160	927	0.5	2,720	1,782	[4]-11	4.9	14.4	9.5	[4]-0.1
1994	192,166	813	0.4	2,508	1,875	180	4.2	13.0	9.7	0.9
1995	192,980	722	0.4	2,478	1,899	143	3.7	12.8	9.8	0.7
1996	193,702	724	0.4	2,452	1,901	173	3.7	12.6	9.8	0.9
1997	194,426	711	0.4	2,435	1,911	188	3.7	12.5	9.8	1.0
1998	195,138	681	0.3	2,401	1,905	185	3.5	12.3	9.7	0.9
2000, proj. [5]	196,751	605	0.3	2,365	1,946	186	3.1	12.0	9.9	0.9
BLACK, NON-HISPANIC										
1990	29,191	397	1.4	659	262	[4]-	13.5	22.4	8.9	[4]-
1994	31,004	392	1.3	597	278	73	12.6	19.1	8.9	2.3
1995	31,395	365	1.2	564	281	83	11.6	17.9	8.9	2.6
1996	31,760	377	1.2	554	277	100	11.8	17.4	8.7	3.1
1997	32,137	391	1.2	560	268	99	12.1	17.3	8.3	3.1
1998	32,528	398	1.2	563	262	97	12.2	17.2	8.0	3.0
2000, proj. [5]	33,374	387	1.2	641	312	57	11.5	19.1	9.3	1.7

- Represents or rounds to zero.   [1] Net change for 1990 excludes "error of closure" for the three months prior to the April 1 census date.   [2] Percent of population at beginning of period.   [3] Covers net international migration and movement of Armed Forces, federally affiliated civilian citizens, and their dependents.   [4] Data reflect movement of Armed Forces due to the Gulf War.   [5] Based on middle series of assumptions. See footnote 1, Table 3.   [6] Persons of Hispanic origin may be of any race.

Source: U.S. Census Bureau, *Current Population Reports*, P25-1130; and unpublished data.

[In thousands, except percent (248,765 represents 248,765,000). As of July, except 1990 as of April. See headnote, Table 18]

Year, sex, and race	Total, all years	Under 5 years	5-9 years	10-14 years	15-19 years	20-24 years	25-29 years	30-34 years	35-39 years	40-44 years	45-49 years	50-54 years	55-59 years	60-64 years	65-74 years	75-84 years	85 years and over	5-13 years	14-17 years	18-24 years
ALL RACES																				
1990 [1]	248,765	18,763	18,040	17,065	17,890	19,139	21,333	21,837	19,849	17,592	13,746	11,314	10,489	10,626	18,047	10,012	3,022	31,835	13,344	26,955
1995	262,765	19,529	19,092	18,849	18,200	17,978	18,899	21,821	22,293	20,257	17,456	13,641	11,085	10,046	18,756	11,178	3,684	34,187	14,826	25,107
1998	270,299	18,966	19,921	19,242	19,539	17,674	18,588	20,186	22,626	21,894	18,859	15,726	12,407	10,269	18,395	11,952	4,054	35,389	15,517	25,470
Male	132,046	9,696	10,195	9,855	10,046	8,996	9,247	10,007	11,256	10,845	9,252	7,648	5,956	4,849	8,250	4,761	1,187	18,114	7,985	12,993
Female	138,252	9,270	9,726	9,387	9,494	8,678	9,341	10,179	11,370	11,049	9,607	8,078	6,451	5,420	10,146	7,191	2,866	17,275	7,532	12,478
WHITE																				
1990 [1]	208,727	14,962	14,504	13,671	14,355	15,642	17,640	18,191	16,653	15,002	11,827	9,745	9,131	9,381	16,175	9,085	2,761	25,560	10,665	21,949
1995	218,010	15,451	15,136	14,992	14,480	14,367	15,301	17,938	18,475	16,944	14,854	11,723	9,533	8,718	16,631	10,123	3,344	27,148	11,769	20,058
1998	223,001	15,052	15,687	15,202	15,492	14,094	14,868	16,347	18,626	18,178	15,831	13,474	10,673	8,853	16,163	10,796	3,666	27,907	12,284	20,284
Male	109,489	7,712	8,038	7,799	7,944	7,225	7,473	8,202	9,364	9,098	7,859	6,624	5,181	4,232	7,309	4,316	1,066	14,304	6,336	10,413
Female	113,511	7,340	7,649	7,403	7,501	6,869	7,395	8,145	9,262	9,079	7,972	6,850	5,492	4,622	8,853	6,481	2,600	13,603	5,948	9,871
BLACK																				
1990 [1]	30,511	2,942	2,714	2,632	2,717	2,657	2,782	2,720	2,361	1,883	1,415	1,178	1,042	972	1,499	772	223	4,842	2,059	3,819
1995	33,098	3,037	3,015	2,871	2,830	2,653	2,593	2,822	2,789	2,392	1,854	1,382	1,139	989	1,620	832	278	5,312	2,305	3,751
1998	34,431	2,828	3,170	2,993	3,024	2,633	2,623	2,728	2,884	2,676	2,154	1,587	1,249	1,028	1,666	881	306	5,585	2,382	3,854
Male	16,340	1,433	1,610	1,520	1,537	1,300	1,254	1,279	1,354	1,252	984	712	547	440	699	329	90	2,836	1,217	1,915
Female	18,090	1,394	1,561	1,473	1,487	1,333	1,369	1,449	1,530	1,424	1,170	876	702	588	966	552	216	2,750	1,165	1,939
AMERICAN INDIAN, ESKIMO, ALEUT																				
1990 [1]	2,065	220	209	197	191	179	188	181	157	132	99	79	64	53	73	34	9	368	151	256
1995	2,254	204	227	234	204	188	182	187	179	157	126	94	72	58	85	42	15	414	176	263
1998	2,360	200	224	243	229	189	193	181	185	170	138	108	81	63	89	49	19	418	193	274
Male	1,168	101	114	123	115	95	99	92	92	83	67	52	38	29	40	20	6	213	97	138
Female	1,192	99	110	120	114	94	93	89	93	87	71	56	42	33	49	28	13	206	95	136
ASIAN, PACIFIC ISLANDER																				
1990 [1]	2,065	220	209	197	191	179	188	181	157	132	99	79	64	53	73	34	9	368	151	256
1990 [1]	7,462	638	612	565	626	661	722	745	678	574	405	312	252	220	300	122	29	1,064	470	931
1995	9,403	837	714	752	687	770	823	874	850	764	622	441	341	280	419	181	47	1,313	575	1,035
1998	10,507	887	840	804	794	758	905	930	931	870	736	556	405	325	477	227	63	1,479	659	1,059
Male	5,049	450	433	412	402	376	421	434	445	412	342	260	190	149	201	97	26	761	335	526
Female	5,459	437	406	392	392	383	484	496	486	459	394	296	214	176	277	130	37	717	324	532
PERCENT																				
Total, 1998	100.0	7.0	7.4	7.1	7.2	6.5	6.9	7.5	8.4	8.1	7.0	5.8	4.6	3.8	6.8	4.4	1.5	13.1	5.7	9.4
White	100.0	6.7	7.0	6.8	6.9	6.3	6.7	7.3	8.4	8.2	7.1	6.0	4.8	4.0	7.2	4.8	1.6	12.5	5.5	9.1
Black	100.0	8.2	9.2	8.7	8.8	7.6	7.6	7.9	8.4	7.8	6.3	4.6	3.6	3.0	4.8	2.6	0.9	16.2	6.9	11.2
American Indian, Aleut	100.0	8.5	9.5	10.3	9.7	8.0	8.2	7.7	7.8	7.2	5.8	4.6	3.4	2.7	3.8	2.1	0.8	17.7	8.2	11.6
Asian, Pacific Islander	100.0	8.4	8.0	7.7	7.6	7.2	8.6	8.9	8.9	8.3	7.0	5.3	3.9	3.1	4.5	2.2	0.6	14.1	6.3	10.1

[1] The April 1, 1990, census count (248,765,170) includes count resolution corrections processed through August 1997, and does not include adjustments for census coverage errors except for adjustments estimated for the 1995 Census Test in Oakland, CA; Patterson, NJ; and six parishes in LA. These adjustments amounted to a total of 55,297 persons.

Source: U.S. Census Bureau, Current Population Reports, P25-1095; and unpublished data.

[In thousands, except as indicated (270,299 represents 270,299,000). As of **July 1**. Resident population. For derivation of estimates, see text of this section]

Age	Race						Not of Hispanic origin			
	Total	White	Black	American Indian, Eskimo, Aleut	Asian, Pacific Islander	Hispanic origin [1]	White	Black	American Indian, Eskimo, Aleut	Asian, Pacific Islander
Total	**270,299**	**223,001**	**34,431**	**2,360**	**10,507**	**30,250**	**195,440**	**32,718**	**2,001**	**9,890**
Under 5 yrs. old ..	18,966	15,052	2,828	200	887	3,393	11,950	2,638	164	821
Under 1 yr. old .	3,776	2,993	561	41	181	700	2,353	522	33	168
1 yr. old	3,748	2,982	551	39	175	692	2,348	513	32	163
2 yrs. old	3,750	2,991	542	39	178	664	2,384	505	32	165
3 yrs. old	3,797	3,016	566	39	176	667	2,406	529	32	163
4 yrs. old	3,895	3,070	608	41	176	670	2,459	569	34	163
5-9 yrs. old..	19,921	15,687	3,170	224	840	3,097	12,867	2,992	188	776
5 yrs. old	3,948	3,105	625	43	175	662	2,501	587	36	162
6 yrs. old	4,020	3,174	628	43	176	663	2,567	591	36	163
7 yrs. old	4,058	3,201	639	43	175	634	2,621	604	36	163
8 yrs. old	3,884	3,067	616	47	154	570	2,550	582	39	143
9 yrs. old	4,010	3,139	663	50	159	567	2,628	628	41	146
10-14 yrs. old....	19,242	15,202	2,993	243	804	2,634	12,821	2,839	203	745
10 yrs. old	3,940	3,099	632	49	161	556	2,597	598	41	148
11 yrs. old	3,837	3,036	602	47	153	527	2,559	570	39	141
12 yrs. old	3,832	3,027	595	49	161	522	2,555	564	41	149
13 yrs. old	3,859	3,059	587	49	165	517	2,590	557	41	153
14 yrs. old	3,774	2,982	578	49	165	511	2,520	549	41	153
15-19 yrs. old....	19,539	15,492	3,024	229	794	2,704	13,031	2,875	191	738
15 yrs. old	3,893	3,073	601	50	169	529	2,594	571	42	157
16 yrs. old	3,920	3,109	603	47	161	531	2,627	573	39	150
17 yrs. old	3,930	3,119	600	47	163	551	2,618	570	39	152
18 yrs. old	3,879	3,081	608	42	147	539	2,589	578	35	137
19 yrs. old	3,917	3,109	613	42	153	554	2,603	582	35	142
20-24 yrs. old....	17,674	14,094	2,633	189	758	2,595	11,716	2,498	157	709
20 yrs. old	3,782	3,018	575	40	149	552	2,512	546	33	139
21 yrs. old	3,669	2,919	560	39	152	534	2,429	531	32	142
22 yrs. old	3,413	2,726	501	37	149	510	2,258	475	31	139
23 yrs. old	3,411	2,724	500	37	150	500	2,265	475	30	140
24 yrs. old	3,400	2,707	497	37	158	498	2,250	472	31	149
25-29 yrs. old....	18,588	14,868	2,623	193	905	2,538	12,556	2,485	159	850
25 yrs. old	3,435	2,721	508	38	168	502	2,261	482	32	158
26 yrs. old	3,615	2,873	526	39	177	496	2,420	500	32	166
27 yrs. old	3,898	3,118	550	41	190	520	2,645	521	34	179
28 yrs. old	3,687	2,979	497	36	175	487	2,535	470	30	164
29 yrs. old	3,953	3,177	542	39	195	532	2,694	511	32	183
30-34 yrs. old....	20,186	16,347	2,728	181	930	2,638	13,950	2,574	149	875
30 yrs. old	3,816	3,072	526	36	183	521	2,599	496	29	172
31 yrs. old	3,816	3,084	517	36	180	517	2,614	487	29	169
32 yrs. old	3,935	3,174	540	36	186	528	2,694	509	29	175
33 yrs. old	4,153	3,380	553	36	184	529	2,899	522	30	173
34 yrs. old	4,465	3,637	593	39	196	543	3,144	560	32	185
35-39 yrs. old....	22,626	18,626	2,884	185	931	2,487	16,369	2,735	156	879
35 yrs. old	4,504	3,686	584	38	196	537	3,199	552	32	185
36 yrs. old	4,494	3,707	570	37	180	501	3,252	541	31	170
37 yrs. old	4,557	3,755	576	37	189	510	3,292	546	31	179
38 yrs. old	4,326	3,573	544	35	174	459	3,157	517	29	164
39 yrs. old	4,745	3,905	610	38	192	481	3,470	580	32	181
40-44 yrs. old....	21,894	18,178	2,676	170	870	2,061	16,312	2,551	145	826
40 yrs. old	4,613	3,820	572	37	185	457	3,406	544	31	175
41 yrs. old	4,493	3,726	553	35	179	425	3,341	527	30	169
42 yrs. old	4,307	3,574	526	33	174	413	3,199	501	28	165
43 yrs. old	4,224	3,497	516	34	177	390	3,145	492	29	168
44 yrs. old	4,258	3,562	509	31	156	376	3,221	486	26	148

See footnotes at end of table.

No. 22. Resident Population, by Race, Hispanic Origin, and Single Years of Age: 1998—Continued

[See headnote, page 22]

Age		Race					Not of Hispanic origin			
	Total	White	Black	American Indian, Eskimo, Aleut	Asian, Pacific Islander	Hispanic origin [1]	White	Black	American Indian, Eskimo, Aleut	Asian, Pacific Islander
45-49 yrs. old	18,859	15,831	2,154	138	736	1,568	14,408	2,060	121	702
45 yrs. old	4,042	3,389	465	30	158	354	3,067	444	26	150
46 yrs. old	3,845	3,241	433	28	143	321	2,950	414	24	136
47 yrs. old	3,718	3,095	441	28	153	317	2,809	422	25	146
48 yrs. old	3,500	2,952	388	25	135	285	2,693	371	22	129
49 yrs. old	3,755	3,154	427	27	147	292	2,889	409	24	141
50-54 yrs. old	15,726	13,474	1,587	108	556	1,177	12,401	1,520	96	531
50 yrs. old	3,637	3,098	380	26	134	272	2,851	364	23	128
51 yrs. old	3,750	3,256	351	24	120	259	3,020	336	21	115
52 yrs. old	2,711	2,309	277	20	105	224	2,105	264	18	100
53 yrs. old	2,793	2,385	290	19	100	216	2,188	278	17	95
54 yrs. old	2,833	2,425	290	20	98	206	2,238	279	17	93
55-59 yrs. old	12,407	10,673	1,249	81	405	886	9,864	1,198	72	387
55 yrs. old	2,893	2,496	286	19	92	199	2,315	274	17	88
56 yrs. old	2,569	2,207	264	16	82	182	2,041	253	15	78
57 yrs. old	2,453	2,103	251	16	82	180	1,939	241	14	79
58 yrs. old	2,196	1,894	217	14	71	161	1,747	208	12	68
59 yrs. old	2,296	1,972	232	15	77	164	1,822	222	14	74
60-64 yrs. old	10,269	8,853	1,028	63	325	711	8,201	988	56	312
60 yrs. old	2,198	1,888	224	14	72	154	1,747	215	13	69
61 yrs. old	2,042	1,762	202	13	66	143	1,631	194	11	63
62 yrs. old	2,020	1,735	207	13	65	142	1,606	199	11	63
63 yrs. old	2,053	1,785	196	12	61	142	1,655	188	11	58
64 yrs. old	1,956	1,683	200	12	62	131	1,563	192	10	59
65-69 yrs. old	9,593	8,341	936	49	267	597	7,793	902	44	257
65 yrs. old	1,925	1,650	205	11	59	126	1,535	198	10	57
66 yrs. old	1,905	1,650	192	10	53	120	1,540	185	9	51
67 yrs. old	1,968	1,712	192	10	53	124	1,599	185	9	51
68 yrs. old	1,900	1,665	175	9	51	116	1,558	169	8	49
69 yrs. old	1,895	1,665	171	9	50	112	1,561	165	8	48
70-74 yrs. old	8,802	7,822	730	40	210	467	7,390	706	36	202
70 yrs. old	1,895	1,669	170	9	48	107	1,570	164	8	46
71 yrs. old	1,808	1,601	155	8	44	98	1,511	150	7	42
72 yrs. old	1,756	1,558	145	8	44	94	1,472	141	7	42
73 yrs. old	1,696	1,518	132	8	38	87	1,438	128	7	37
74 yrs. old	1,647	1,476	127	7	37	82	1,399	123	7	35
75-79 yrs. old	7,218	6,488	554	30	147	327	6,184	538	28	141
75 yrs. old	1,581	1,414	125	7	35	77	1,342	122	6	34
76 yrs. old	1,550	1,400	113	6	31	71	1,334	110	6	30
77 yrs. old	1,472	1,327	110	6	30	67	1,265	107	6	29
78 yrs. old	1,359	1,221	106	5	27	60	1,165	103	5	26
79 yrs. old	1,256	1,126	100	5	24	53	1,077	98	5	23
80-84 yrs. old	4,734	4,308	327	18	80	194	4,128	318	17	77
80 yrs. old	1,112	1,011	78	4	19	45	968	76	4	18
81 yrs. old	1,022	931	70	4	17	41	893	68	3	16
82 yrs. old	941	859	62	4	16	38	823	60	3	15
83 yrs. old	878	801	59	3	15	36	767	57	3	14
84 yrs. old	781	706	58	3	14	33	676	56	3	13
85-89 yrs. old	2,556	2,328	178	11	39	111	2,224	173	10	38
90-94 yrs. old	1,117	1,006	89	6	17	50	960	87	5	16
95-99 yrs. old	324	284	33	2	5	14	270	32	2	5
100 yrs. old and over	57	48	7	1	1	3	46	7	-	1
Median age (yr.) . .	35.2	36.3	29.9	27.5	31.5	26.4	37.7	30.1	28.0	31.8

- Represents or rounds to zero. [1] Persons of Hispanic origin may be of any race.

Source: U.S. Census Bureau, unpublished data.

U.S. Census Bureau, Statistical Abstract of the United States: 1999

No. 23. Resident Population, by Age and Hispanic Origin: 1990 to 1998

[In thousands, except percent (22,372 represents 22,372,000). As of July, except 1990 as of April. See headnote, Table 18. Hispanic persons may be of any race]

Year and sex	Total, all years	Under 5 years	5-9 years	10-14 years	15-19 years	20-24 years	25-29 years	30-34 years	35-39 years	40-44 years	45-49 years	50-54 years	55-59 years	60-64 years	65-74 years	75-84 years	85 yrs and over	5-13 years	14-17 years	18-24 years
HISPANIC ORIGIN																				
1990	22,372	2,469	2,180	1,991	2,086	2,322	2,340	2,046	1,643	1,277	937	750	634	550	715	340	91	3,786	1,575	3,217
1995	27,099	3,205	2,608	2,417	2,401	2,393	2,445	2,519	2,176	1,739	1,314	964	762	634	947	434	141	4,537	1,921	3,359
1998	30,250	3,393	3,097	2,634	2,704	2,595	2,538	2,638	2,487	2,061	1,568	1,177	886	711	1,065	521	177	5,219	2,122	3,688
Male	15,233	1,733	1,579	1,347	1,407	1,344	1,314	1,367	1,279	1,041	773	566	415	326	470	211	59	2,663	1,099	1,915
Female	15,017	1,660	1,518	1,287	1,296	1,251	1,223	1,271	1,208	1,020	795	611	471	385	595	310	118	2,556	1,023	1,773
NON-HISPANIC																				
WHITE																				
1990 [1]	188,307	12,721	12,516	11,854	12,450	13,524	15,508	16,332	15,162	13,839	10,971	9,058	8,548	8,872	15,511	8,767	2,675	22,106	9,225	19,014
1995	193,320	12,523	12,774	12,801	12,290	12,178	13,078	15,647	16,502	15,368	13,659	10,844	8,836	8,136	15,756	9,719	3,211	23,037	10,022	16,984
1998	195,440	11,950	12,867	12,821	13,031	11,716	12,556	13,950	16,369	16,312	14,408	12,401	9,864	8,201	15,183	10,311	3,499	23,168	10,358	16,908
Male	95,601	6,128	6,601	6,582	6,709	5,990	6,273	6,957	8,202	8,156	7,157	6,108	4,801	3,932	6,876	4,118	1,010	11,888	5,338	8,656
Female	99,839	5,823	6,266	6,239	6,322	5,725	6,283	6,993	8,167	8,155	7,251	6,293	5,063	4,269	8,307	6,193	2,489	11,280	5,020	8,252
BLACK																				
1990 [1]	29,299	2,801	2,599	2,528	2,608	2,530	2,651	2,602	2,267	1,812	1,364	1,138	1,009	946	1,465	759	219	4,643	1,977	3,644
1995	31,573	2,857	2,861	2,736	2,699	2,527	2,456	2,676	2,659	2,288	1,779	1,328	1,096	955	1,572	812	273	5,050	2,199	3,574
1998	32,718	2,638	2,992	2,839	2,875	2,498	2,485	2,574	2,735	2,551	2,060	1,520	1,198	988	1,608	856	299	5,282	2,264	3,658
Male	15,485	1,336	1,518	1,441	1,460	1,233	1,185	1,201	1,278	1,188	938	680	523	422	675	319	88	2,680	1,155	1,817
Female	17,233	1,302	1,474	1,398	1,415	1,265	1,300	1,373	1,457	1,363	1,123	841	675	566	933	537	212	2,602	1,109	1,842
AMERICAN INDIAN, ESKIMO, ALEUT																				
1990 [1]	1,796	185	179	170	165	151	160	156	138	117	90	72	58	48	68	31	9	316	131	217
1995	1,931	171	191	198	172	159	151	158	153	136	111	84	65	53	77	39	14	349	149	221
1998	2,001	164	188	203	191	157	159	149	156	145	121	96	72	56	81	45	18	350	161	227
Male	983	82	95	103	96	79	81	75	77	70	58	46	34	26	36	19	6	178	81	114
Female	1,017	81	93	100	95	78	78	75	79	75	63	50	38	30	44	26	12	172	80	114
ASIAN, PACIFIC ISLANDER																				
1990 [1]	6,992	586	566	523	582	612	673	701	640	546	385	297	240	210	287	116	27	984	436	863
1995	8,842	773	659	698	639	722	769	822	803	725	593	421	326	269	403	174	45	1,215	534	969
1998	9,890	821	776	745	738	709	850	875	879	826	702	531	387	312	459	219	60	1,368	612	989
Male	4,744	417	401	382	373	351	393	407	420	390	326	248	182	143	193	94	25	705	312	491
Female	5,147	404	375	363	365	359	457	468	460	436	376	283	204	169	266	125	35	663	301	498
1998, PERCENT																				
Hispanic origin	100.0	11.2	10.2	8.7	8.9	8.6	8.4	8.7	8.2	6.8	5.2	3.9	2.9	2.4	3.5	1.7	0.6	17.3	7.0	12.2
Non-Hispanic:																				
White	100.0	6.1	6.6	6.6	6.7	6.0	6.4	7.1	8.4	8.3	7.4	6.3	5.0	4.2	7.8	5.3	1.8	11.9	5.3	8.7
Black	100.0	8.1	9.1	8.7	8.8	7.6	7.9	7.9	8.4	7.8	6.3	4.6	3.7	3.0	4.9	2.6	0.9	16.1	6.9	11.2
American Indian, Eskimo, Aleut	100.0	8.2	9.4	10.1	9.5	7.8	7.9	7.4	7.8	7.2	6.0	4.8	3.6	2.8	4.0	2.2	0.9	17.5	8.0	11.3
Asian, Pacific Islander	100.0	8.3	7.8	7.5	7.5	7.2	8.6	8.8	8.9	8.4	7.1	5.4	3.9	3.2	4.6	2.2	0.6	13.8	6.2	10.0

[1] The April 1, 1990, census count (248,765,170) includes count resolution corrections processed through August 1997, and does not include adjustments for census coverage errors except for adjustments estimated for the 1995 Census Test in Oakland, CA; Patterson, NJ; and six parishes in LA. These adjustments amounted to a total of 55,297 persons.

Source: U.S. Census Bureau, *Current Population Reports*, P25-1095; and unpublished data.

No. 24. Projections of Resident Population, by Age, Sex, and Race: 2000 to 2025

[As of July 1 (274,634 represents 274,634,000). Data are for middle series; for assumptions, see Table 3]

Age, sex, and race	Population (1,000)				Percent distribution			
	2000	2005	2010	2025	2000	2005	2010	2025
Total	274,634	285,981	297,716	335,050	100.0	100.0	100.0	100.0
Under 5 years old	18,987	19,127	20,012	22,498	6.9	6.7	6.7	6.7
5 to 13 years old	36,043	35,850	35,605	40,413	13.1	12.5	12.0	12.1
14 to 17 years old	15,752	16,986	16,894	17,872	5.7	5.9	5.7	5.3
18 to 24 years old	26,258	28,268	30,138	30,372	9.6	9.9	10.1	9.1
25 to 34 years old	37,233	36,306	38,292	43,119	13.6	12.7	12.9	12.9
35 to 44 years old	44,659	42,165	38,521	42,391	16.3	14.7	12.9	12.7
45 to 54 years old	37,030	41,507	43,564	36,890	13.5	14.5	14.6	11.0
55 to 64 years old	23,962	29,606	35,283	39,542	8.7	10.4	11.9	11.8
65 to 74 years old	18,136	18,369	21,057	35,425	6.6	6.4	7.1	10.6
75 to 84 years old	12,315	12,898	12,680	19,481	4.5	4.5	4.3	5.8
85 years old and over	4,259	4,899	5,671	7,046	1.6	1.7	1.9	2.1
Male	134,181	139,785	145,584	164,119	48.9	48.9	48.9	49.0
Female	140,453	146,196	152,132	170,931	51.1	51.1	51.1	51.0
White, total	225,532	232,463	239,588	262,227	100.0	100.0	100.0	100.0
Under 5 years old	14,724	14,618	15,142	16,630	6.5	6.3	6.3	6.3
5 to 13 years old	28,254	27,716	27,087	29,949	12.5	11.9	11.3	11.4
14 to 17 years old	12,412	13,177	12,951	13,166	5.5	5.7	5.4	5.0
18 to 24 years old	20,852	22,306	23,489	22,702	9.2	9.6	9.8	8.7
25 to 34 years old	29,837	28,705	30,099	32,831	13.2	12.3	12.6	12.5
35 to 44 years old	36,762	34,201	30,646	32,869	16.3	14.7	12.8	12.5
45 to 54 years old	31,247	34,574	35,911	29,010	13.9	14.9	15.0	11.1
55 to 64 years old	20,600	25,334	29,845	32,246	9.1	10.9	12.5	12.3
65 to 74 years old	15,846	15,844	18,101	29,733	7.0	6.8	7.6	11.3
75 to 84 years old	11,131	11,553	11,208	16,969	4.9	5.0	4.7	6.5
85 years old and over	3,866	4,434	5,108	6,122	1.7	1.9	2.1	2.3
Male	110,799	114,350	118,000	129,596	49.1	49.2	49.3	49.4
Female	114,734	118,113	121,588	132,631	50.9	50.8	50.7	50.6
Black, total	35,454	37,734	40,109	47,539	100.0	100.0	100.0	100.0
Under 5 years old	3,127	3,244	3,454	3,964	8.8	8.6	8.6	8.3
5 to 13 years old	5,727	5,813	5,962	6,990	16.2	15.4	14.9	14.7
14 to 17 years old	2,414	2,735	2,737	3,104	6.8	7.2	6.8	6.5
18 to 24 years old	3,966	4,233	4,674	5,053	11.2	11.2	11.7	10.6
25 to 34 years old	5,172	5,212	5,489	6,514	14.6	13.8	13.7	13.7
35 to 44 years old	5,649	5,499	5,236	6,017	15.9	14.6	13.1	12.7
45 to 54 years old	4,111	4,909	5,326	5,007	11.6	13.0	13.3	10.5
55 to 64 years old	2,406	2,995	3,801	4,865	6.8	7.9	9.5	10.2
65 to 74 years old	1,675	1,781	2,033	3,901	4.7	4.7	5.1	8.2
75 to 84 years old	890	959	1,002	1,582	2.5	2.5	2.5	3.3
85 years old and over	317	354	396	541	0.9	0.9	1.0	1.1
Male	16,811	17,874	18,981	22,473	47.4	47.4	47.3	47.3
Female	18,643	19,860	21,129	25,066	52.6	52.6	52.7	52.7
American Indian, Eskimo, Aleut, total	2,402	2,572	2,754	3,319	100.0	100.0	100.0	100.0
Under 5 years old	210	226	245	275	8.7	8.8	8.9	8.3
5 to 13 years old	418	409	429	516	17.4	15.9	15.6	15.5
14 to 17 years old	196	210	197	240	8.2	8.2	7.2	7.2
18 to 24 years old	283	323	342	368	11.8	12.6	12.4	11.1
25 to 34 years old	361	376	421	475	15.0	14.6	15.3	14.3
35 to 44 years old	354	351	349	459	14.7	13.6	12.7	13.8
45 to 54 years old	263	300	321	333	10.9	11.7	11.7	10.0
55 to 64 years old	152	186	225	276	6.3	7.2	8.2	8.3
65 to 74 years old	93	104	122	210	3.9	4.0	4.4	6.3
75 to 84 years old	51	59	65	109	2.1	2.3	2.4	3.3
85 years old and over	22	28	36	59	0.9	1.1	1.3	1.8
Male	1,185	1,266	1,354	1,629	49.3	49.2	49.2	49.1
Female	1,217	1,306	1,400	1,690	50.7	50.8	50.8	50.9
Asian, Pacific Islander, total	11,245	13,212	15,265	21,965	100.0	100.0	100.0	100.0
Under 5 years old	926	1,040	1,170	1,628	8.2	7.9	7.7	7.4
5 to 13 years old	1,644	1,912	2,126	2,958	14.6	14.5	13.9	13.5
14 to 17 years old	729	864	1,008	1,362	6.5	6.5	6.6	6.2
18 to 24 years old	1,158	1,405	1,633	2,250	10.3	10.6	10.7	10.2
25 to 34 years old	1,863	2,012	2,283	3,300	16.6	15.2	15.0	15.0
35 to 44 years old	1,894	2,114	2,290	3,046	16.8	16.0	15.0	13.9
45 to 54 years old	1,409	1,724	2,006	2,539	12.5	13.0	13.1	11.6
55 to 64 years old	804	1,091	1,412	2,155	7.1	8.3	9.2	9.8
65 to 74 years old	522	640	802	1,581	4.6	4.8	5.3	7.2
75 to 84 years old	242	327	406	821	2.2	2.5	2.7	3.7
85 years old and over	55	83	130	324	0.5	0.6	0.9	1.5
Male	5,386	6,295	7,250	10,421	47.9	47.6	47.5	47.4
Female	5,859	6,918	8,015	11,543	52.1	52.4	52.5	52.6

Source: U.S. Census Bureau, Current Population Reports, P25-1130.

Population 25

[As of July 1 (31,366 represents 31,366,000). Resident population. Data are for middle series; for assumptions, see Table 3]

Age, sex, and race	Population (1,000)				Percent distribution			
	2000	2005	2010	2025	2000	2005	2010	2025
Hispanic origin, total [1]	31,366	36,057	41,139	58,930	100.0	100.0	100.0	100.0
Under 5 years old	3,203	3,580	4,080	5,662	10.2	9.9	9.9	9.6
5 to 13 years old	5,651	6,215	6,654	9,479	18.0	17.2	16.2	16.1
14 to 17 years old	2,179	2,672	3,007	3,944	6.9	7.4	7.3	6.7
18 to 24 years old	3,679	4,270	5,101	6,560	11.7	11.8	12.4	11.1
25 to 34 years old	5,181	5,414	6,059	8,748	16.5	15.0	14.7	14.8
35 to 44 years old	4,836	5,421	5,562	7,345	15.4	15.0	13.5	12.5
45 to 54 years old	3,049	3,927	4,833	5,791	9.7	10.9	11.7	9.8
55 to 64 years old	1,717	2,260	2,997	5,272	5.5	6.3	7.3	8.9
65 to 74 years old	1,120	1,308	1,606	3,595	3.6	3.6	3.9	6.1
75 to 84 years old	568	748	896	1,771	1.8	2.1	2.2	3.0
85 years old and over	183	242	345	763	0.6	0.7	0.8	1.3
Male	15,799	18,082	20,557	29,276	50.4	50.1	50.0	49.7
Female	15,566	17,975	20,582	29,654	49.6	49.9	50.0	50.3
Non-Hispanic White, total	197,061	199,802	202,390	209,117	100.0	100.0	100.0	100.0
Under 5 years old	11,807	11,367	11,445	11,510	6.0	5.7	5.7	5.5
5 to 13 years old	23,125	22,072	21,063	21,396	11.7	11.0	10.4	10.2
14 to 17 years old	10,444	10,769	10,230	9,622	5.3	5.4	5.1	4.6
18 to 24 years old	17,510	18,443	18,880	16,785	8.9	9.2	9.3	8.0
25 to 34 years old	25,144	23,806	24,631	24,935	12.8	11.9	12.2	11.9
35 to 44 years old	32,382	29,299	25,628	26,278	16.4	14.7	12.7	12.6
45 to 54 years old	28,485	31,024	31,541	23,797	14.5	15.5	15.6	11.4
55 to 64 years old	19,039	23,285	27,137	27,490	9.7	11.7	13.4	13.1
65 to 74 years old	14,825	14,660	16,653	26,504	7.5	7.3	8.2	12.7
75 to 84 years old	10,607	10,868	10,394	15,373	5.4	5.4	5.1	7.4
85 years old and over	3,694	4,209	4,788	5,428	1.9	2.1	2.4	2.6
Male	96,438	97,946	99,381	103,169	48.9	49.0	49.1	49.3
Female	100,624	101,856	103,009	105,948	51.1	51.0	50.9	50.7
Non-Hispanic Black, total	33,568	35,485	37,466	43,511	100.0	100.0	100.0	100.0
Under 5 years old	2,929	3,016	3,187	3,571	8.7	8.5	8.5	8.2
5 to 13 years old	5,391	5,430	5,531	6,339	16.1	15.3	14.8	14.6
14 to 17 years old	2,285	2,568	2,547	2,831	6.8	7.2	6.8	6.5
18 to 24 years old	3,751	3,975	4,354	4,609	11.2	11.2	11.6	10.6
25 to 34 years old	4,863	4,883	5,111	5,942	14.5	13.8	13.6	13.7
35 to 44 years old	5,347	5,154	4,877	5,521	15.9	14.5	13.0	12.7
45 to 54 years old	3,922	4,654	5,008	4,613	11.7	13.1	13.4	10.6
55 to 64 years old	2,301	2,850	3,601	4,498	6.9	8.0	9.6	10.3
65 to 74 years old	1,608	1,695	1,921	3,634	4.8	4.8	5.1	8.4
75 to 84 years old	862	919	947	1,457	2.6	2.6	2.5	3.3
85 years old and over	310	344	381	496	0.9	1.0	1.0	1.1
Male	15,871	16,760	17,676	20,494	47.3	47.2	47.2	47.1
Female	17,697	18,725	19,790	23,017	52.7	52.8	52.8	52.9
Non-Hispanic American Indian, Eskimo, Aleut, total	2,054	2,183	2,320	2,744	100.0	100.0	100.0	100.0
Under 5 years old	180	192	206	229	8.8	8.8	8.9	8.4
5 to 13 years old	352	347	364	429	17.1	15.9	15.7	15.6
14 to 17 years old	165	175	166	198	8.0	8.0	7.1	7.2
18 to 24 years old	239	268	282	304	11.6	12.3	12.1	11.1
25 to 34 years old	303	316	349	390	14.7	14.5	15.0	14.2
35 to 44 years old	301	293	290	372	14.7	13.4	12.5	13.6
45 to 54 years old	231	259	272	275	11.2	11.8	11.7	10.0
55 to 64 years old	136	164	195	227	6.6	7.5	8.4	8.3
65 to 74 years old	82	91	106	176	4.0	4.2	4.6	6.4
75 to 84 years old	46	52	57	92	2.2	2.4	2.4	3.4
85 years old and over	21	27	34	52	1.0	1.2	1.4	1.9
Male	1,008	1,070	1,136	1,342	49.1	49.0	48.9	48.9
Female	1,046	1,113	1,184	1,401	50.9	51.0	51.1	51.1
Non-Hispanic Asian, Pacific Islander, total	10,584	12,454	14,402	20,748	100.0	100.0	100.0	100.0
Under 5 years old	867	973	1,093	1,526	8.2	7.8	7.6	7.4
5 to 13 years old	1,524	1,787	1,993	2,770	14.4	14.4	13.8	13.4
14 to 17 years old	680	803	944	1,277	6.4	6.4	6.6	6.2
18 to 24 years old	1,080	1,311	1,521	2,114	10.2	10.5	10.6	10.2
25 to 34 years old	1,744	1,887	2,141	3,104	16.5	15.2	14.9	15.0
35 to 44 years old	1,793	1,998	2,165	2,876	16.9	16.0	15.0	13.9
45 to 54 years old	1,344	1,644	1,910	2,415	12.7	13.2	13.3	11.6
55 to 64 years old	770	1,046	1,354	2,055	7.3	8.4	9.4	9.9
65 to 74 years old	500	615	771	1,516	4.7	4.9	5.4	7.3
75 to 84 years old	231	311	387	787	2.2	2.5	2.7	3.8
85 years old and over	51	78	123	308	0.5	0.6	0.9	1.5
Male	5,065	5,928	6,835	9,838	47.9	47.6	47.5	47.4
Female	5,520	6,526	7,567	10,910	52.1	52.4	52.5	52.6

[1] Persons of Hispanic origin may be of any race.

Source: U.S. Census Bureau, Current Population Reports, P25-1130.

Figure 1.3
Center of Population: 1970 to 1990

[Prior to 1960, excludes Alaska and Hawaii. The median center is located at the intersection of two median lines, a north-south line constructed so that half of the Nation's population lives east and half lives west of it, and an east-west line selected so that half of the Nation's population lives north and half lives south of it. The mean center of population is that point at which an imaginary, flat, weightless, and rigid map of the United States would balance if weights of identical value were placed on it so that each weight represented the location of one person on the date of the census]

Year	Median center		Mean center		
	Latitude-N	Longitude	Latitude-N	Longitude-W	Approximate location
1790 (August 2)	(NA)	(NA)	39 16 30	76 11 12	In Kent County, MD, 23 miles E of Baltimore MD
1850 (June 1)..	(NA)	(NA)	38 59 00	81 19 00	In Wirt County, WV, 23 miles SE of Parkersburg, WV[1]
1900 (June 1)..	40 03 32	84 49 01	39 09 36	85 48 54	In Bartholomew County, IN, 6 miles SE of Columbus, IN
1950 (April 1)..	40 00 12	84 56 51	38 50 21	88 09 33	In Richland County, IL, 8 miles NNW of Olney, IL
1960 (April 1)..	39 56 25	85 16 60	38 35 58	89 12 35	In Clinton County, IL, 6.5 miles NW of Centralia, IL
1970 (April 1)	39 47 43	85 31 43	38 27 47	89 42 22	In St. Clair County, IL, 5.3 miles ESE of Mascoutah, IL
1980 (April 1)..	39 18 60	86 08 15	38 08 13	90 34 26	In Jefferson County, MO, .25 mile W of DeSoto, MO
1990 (April 1)..	38 57 55	86 31 53	37 52 20	91 12 55	In Crawford County, MO, 10 miles SE of Steelville, MO

NA Not available.   [1]West Virginia was set off from Virginia, Dec. 31, 1862, and admitted as a state, June 19, 1863.

▲ Median Center of Population

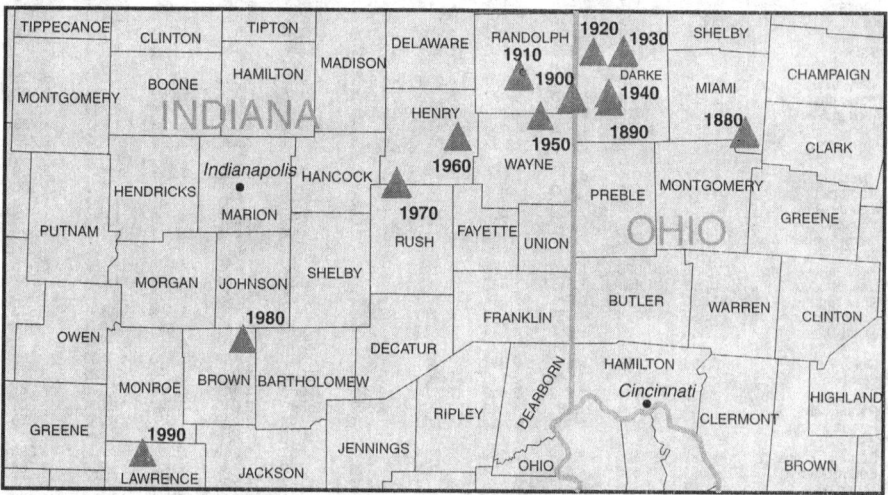

▲ Mean Center of Population

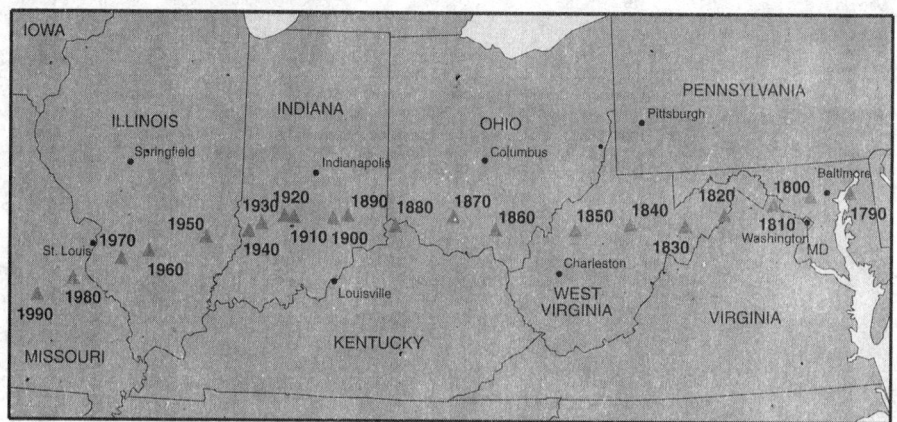

Source: Chart prepared by U.S. Census Bureau.

U.S. Census Bureau, Statistical Abstract of the United States: 1999

No. 26. Resident Population—States: 1980 to 1998

[In thousands (226,546 represents 226,546,000). As of **July 1**; except **1980** and **1990**, as of **April 1**. Insofar as possible, population shown for all years is that of present area of state]

State	1980 [1]	1985	1990 [2]	1991	1992	1993	1994	1995	1996	1997	1998
United States..	226,546	237,924	248,765	252,127	254,995	257,746	260,289	262,765	265,190	267,744	270,299
Alabama	3,894	3,973	4,040	4,090	4,138	4,192	4,239	4,270	4,291	4,322	4,352
Alaska	402	532	550	569	587	597	601	602	605	610	614
Arizona	2,718	3,184	3,665	3,762	3,867	3,994	4,148	4,307	4,432	4,553	4,669
Arkansas.	2,286	2,327	2,351	2,370	2,394	2,424	2,451	2,480	2,505	2,523	2,538
California.	23,668	26,441	29,786	30,393	30,854	31,124	31,295	31,472	31,762	32,182	32,667
Colorado	2,890	3,209	3,294	3,368	3,461	3,562	3,654	3,738	3,814	3,892	3,971
Connecticut	3,108	3,201	3,287	3,287	3,272	3,270	3,265	3,262	3,264	3,267	3,274
Delaware.	594	618	666	680	690	700	709	719	727	735	744
District of Columbia.	638	635	607	594	585	577	566	552	540	530	523
Florida	9,746	11,351	12,938	13,290	13,502	13,712	13,954	14,180	14,425	14,677	14,916
Georgia	5,463	5,963	6,478	6,623	6,760	6,895	7,046	7,189	7,334	7,490	7,642
Hawaii	965	1,040	1,108	1,132	1,151	1,164	1,176	1,183	1,187	1,192	1,193
Idaho	944	994	1,007	1,039	1,066	1,100	1,134	1,164	1,186	1,209	1,229
Illinois.	11,427	11,400	11,431	11,533	11,630	11,718	11,794	11,866	11,934	11,989	12,045
Indiana	5,490	5,459	5,544	5,601	5,648	5,701	5,741	5,787	5,827	5,865	5,899
Iowa	2,914	2,830	2,777	2,791	2,807	2,821	2,829	2,841	2,849	2,854	2,862
Kansas	2,364	2,427	2,478	2,494	2,518	2,538	2,558	2,575	2,585	2,601	2,629
Kentucky	3,661	3,695	3,687	3,716	3,758	3,794	3,824	3,856	3,883	3,910	3,936
Louisiana	4,206	4,408	4,222	4,241	4,272	4,286	4,307	4,328	4,340	4,354	4,369
Maine	1,125	1,163	1,228	1,235	1,234	1,236	1,235	1,233	1,238	1,242	1,244
Maryland	4,217	4,413	4,781	4,856	4,903	4,943	4,985	5,023	5,058	5,095	5,135
Massachusetts . . .	5,737	5,881	6,016	5,997	5,992	6,008	6,027	6,058	6,083	6,114	6,147
Michigan	9,262	9,076	9,295	9,390	9,465	9,523	9,586	9,663	9,734	9,780	9,817
Minnesota	4,076	4,184	4,376	4,428	4,472	4,524	4,566	4,605	4,648	4,687	4,725
Mississippi.	2,521	2,588	2,575	2,591	2,610	2,636	2,663	2,690	2,710	2,732	2,752
Missouri	4,917	5,000	5,117	5,158	5,194	5,238	5,291	5,337	5,369	5,408	5,439
Montana	787	822	799	808	822	840	855	868	877	879	880
Nebraska	1,570	1,585	1,578	1,591	1,602	1,612	1,622	1,635	1,648	1,657	1,663
Nevada	800	951	1,202	1,285	1,333	1,382	1,458	1,528	1,600	1,679	1,747
New Hampshire . .	921	997	1,109	1,107	1,114	1,122	1,133	1,146	1,160	1,172	1,185
New Jersey	7,365	7,566	7,748	7,784	7,826	7,873	7,916	7,962	8,008	8,058	8,115
New Mexico	1,303	1,438	1,515	1,547	1,581	1,615	1,654	1,684	1,708	1,724	1,737
New York	17,558	17,792	17,991	18,028	18,079	18,139	18,152	18,145	18,142	18,146	18,175
North Carolina . . .	5,882	6,254	6,632	6,748	6,833	6,949	7,061	7,186	7,309	7,431	7,546
North Dakota	653	677	639	634	635	637	640	641	643	641	638
Ohio	10,798	10,735	10,847	10,931	11,003	11,063	11,100	11,138	11,170	11,193	11,209
Oklahoma	3,025	3,271	3,146	3,166	3,204	3,229	3,248	3,271	3,296	3,322	3,347
Oregon	2,633	2,673	2,842	2,919	2,974	3,035	3,087	3,141	3,195	3,243	3,282
Pennsylvania	11,864	11,771	11,883	11,943	11,981	12,022	12,040	12,040	12,034	12,011	12,001
Rhode Island	947	969	1,003	1,004	1,000	998	993	989	988	987	988
South Carolina . . .	3,122	3,303	3,486	3,559	3,599	3,635	3,667	3,699	3,737	3,788	3,836
South Dakota	691	698	696	708	715	723	729	735	737	738	738
Tennessee.	4,591	4,715	4,877	4,946	5,012	5,082	5,158	5,235	5,307	5,372	5,431
Texas	14,229	16,273	16,986	17,349	17,662	18,009	18,348	18,694	19,033	19,386	19,760
Utah	1,461	1,643	1,723	1,771	1,819	1,872	1,942	1,991	2,022	2,065	2,100
Vermont	511	530	563	567	570	574	579	582	586	589	591
Virginia	5,347	5,715	6,189	6,284	6,384	6,467	6,539	6,602	6,667	6,737	6,791
Washington	4,132	4,400	4,867	5,015	5,143	5,249	5,336	5,433	5,519	5,614	5,689
West Virginia	1,950	1,907	1,793	1,798	1,806	1,817	1,819	1,822	1,820	1,815	1,811
Wisconsin	4,706	4,748	4,892	4,953	5,005	5,056	5,095	5,137	5,174	5,201	5,224
Wyoming.	470	500	454	458	464	469	475	478	480	480	481

[1] See footnote 4, Table 1.   [2] The April 1, 1990, census counts include corrections processed through August 1997, results of special censuses and test censuses, and do not include adjustments for census coverage errors.

Source: U.S. Census Bureau, *1990 Census of Population and Housing, Population and Housing Unit Counts* (CPH-2); and "ST-98-7 State Population Estimates and Demographic Components of Change: Annual Time Series, July 1, 1990 to July 1, 1998"; release date: February 5, 1999; <http://www.census.gov/population/estimates/state/st-98-7.txt>.

No. 27. State Population—Rank, Percent Change, and Population Density: 1980 to 1998

[As of **April 1**, except **1998**, as of **July 1**. For area figures of states, see Table 393. Minus sign (-) indicates decrease]

State	Rank			Percent change			Population per sq. mile of land area [1]		
	1980	1990	1998	1980-90	1990-95	1995-98	1980	1990	1998
United States	(X)	(X)	(X)	9.8	5.6	2.9	64.1	70.3	76.4
Alabama.	22	22	23	3.8	5.7	1.9	76.7	79.6	85.8
Alaska	50	49	48	36.9	9.4	2.1	0.7	1.0	1.1
Arizona.	29	24	21	34.9	17.5	8.4	23.9	32.3	41.1
Arkansas	33	33	33	2.8	5.5	2.3	43.9	45.1	48.7
California	1	1	1	25.8	5.7	3.8	151.7	191.0	209.4
Colorado.	28	26	24	14.0	13.5	6.2	27.9	31.8	38.3
Connecticut.	25	27	29	5.8	-0.8	0.4	641.4	678.5	675.7
Delaware	47	46	45	12.1	7.9	3.5	304.0	340.8	380.4
District of Columbia	(X)	(X)	(X)	-4.9	-9.0	-5.3	10,397.9	9,884.4	8,519.9
Florida	7	4	4	32.7	9.6	5.2	180.7	239.9	276.2
Georgia	13	11	10	18.6	11.0	6.3	94.3	111.8	131.9
Hawaii	39	41	41	14.9	6.8	0.8	150.2	172.5	185.7
Idaho	41	42	40	6.6	15.6	5.6	11.4	12.2	14.8
Illinois	5	6	5	(Z)	3.8	1.5	205.6	205.6	216.7
Indiana.	12	14	14	1.0	4.4	1.9	153.1	154.6	164.5
Iowa	27	30	30	-4.7	2.3	0.8	52.1	49.7	51.2
Kansas.	32	32	32	4.8	3.9	2.1	28.9	30.3	32.1
Kentucky	23	23	25	0.7	4.6	2.1	92.1	92.8	99.1
Louisiana	19	21	22	0.4	2.5	0.9	96.5	96.9	100.3
Maine.	38	38	39	9.1	0.4	0.9	36.5	39.8	40.3
Maryland	18	19	19	13.4	5.1	2.2	431.4	489.1	525.3
Massachusetts.	11	13	13	4.9	0.7	1.5	732.0	767.6	784.3
Michigan.	8	8	8	0.4	4.0	1.6	163.0	163.6	172.8
Minnesota.	21	20	20	7.4	5.2	2.6	51.2	55.0	59.4
Mississippi	31	31	31	2.2	4.5	2.3	53.7	54.9	58.7
Missouri	15	15	16	4.1	4.3	1.9	71.4	74.3	78.9
Montana	44	44	44	1.6	8.7	1.4	5.4	5.5	6.0
Nebraska	35	36	38	0.5	3.6	1.7	20.4	20.5	21.6
Nevada	43	39	36	50.1	27.2	14.3	7.3	10.9	15.9
New Hampshire	42	40	42	20.5	3.3	3.4	102.6	123.7	132.1
New Jersey.	9	9	9	5.2	2.8	1.9	992.7	1,044.3	1,093.8
New Mexico	37	37	37	16.2	11.1	3.2	10.7	12.5	14.3
New York	2	2	3	2.5	0.9	0.2	371.8	381.0	384.9
North Carolina	10	10	11	12.8	8.3	5.0	120.7	136.1	154.9
North Dakota.	46	47	47	-2.1	0.4	-0.5	9.5	9.3	9.3
Ohio	6	7	7	0.5	2.7	0.6	263.7	264.9	273.7
Oklahoma.	26	28	27	4.0	4.0	2.3	44.1	45.8	48.7
Oregon.	30	29	28	7.9	10.5	4.5	27.4	29.6	34.2
Pennsylvania.	4	5	6	0.2	1.3	-0.3	264.7	265.1	267.8
Rhode Island.	40	43	43	5.9	-1.4	-0.1	906.4	960.3	945.9
South Carolina.	24	25	26	11.7	6.1	3.7	103.6	115.8	127.4
South Dakota	45	45	46	0.8	5.5	0.5	9.1	9.2	9.7
Tennessee	17	17	17	6.2	7.3	3.7	111.4	118.3	131.7
Texas.	3	3	2	19.4	10.1	5.7	54.3	64.9	75.4
Utah	36	35	34	17.9	15.6	5.4	17.8	21.0	25.6
Vermont	48	48	49	10.0	3.5	1.4	55.3	60.8	63.9
Virginia.	14	12	12	15.8	6.7	2.9	135.0	156.3	171.5
Washington.	20	18	15	17.8	11.6	4.7	62.1	73.1	85.4
West Virginia.	34	34	35	-8.0	1.6	-0.6	81.0	74.5	75.2
Wisconsin.	16	16	18	4.0	5.0	1.7	86.6	90.1	96.2
Wyoming	49	50	50	-3.4	5.5	0.5	4.8	4.7	5.0

X Not applicable.   Z Less than 0.05 percent.   [1] Persons per square mile were calculated on the basis of land area data from the 1990 census.

Source: U.S. Census Bureau, *1990 Census of Population and Housing, Population and Housing Unit Counts* (CPH-2); and "ST-98-3 State Population Estimates: Annual Time Series, July 1, 1990 to July 1, 1998"; release date: December 31, 1998; <http://www.census.gov/population/estimates/state/st-98-3.txt>.

Population   29

[In thousands, except percent (21,533 represents 21,533,000). Covers period April 1, 1990 to July 1,1998]

| State | Net change [1] | | Births | Deaths | Net movement from abroad | | Net domestic migration |
	Number	Percent			International migration	Net federal movement	
United States	21,533	8.7	32,867	18,568	6,697	537	-
Alabama.	312	7.7	507	343	13	7	114
Alaska	64	11.6	89	20	8	9	-21
Arizona.	1,003	27.4	592	278	96	8	519
Arkansas	188	8.0	293	217	9	2	106
California	2,881	9.7	4,709	1,811	2,019	88	-2,082
Colorado.	676	20.5	453	198	58	14	359
Connecticut.	-13	-0.4	380	239	68	4	-217
Delaware	77	11.6	87	51	8	2	29
District of Columbia	-84	-13.8	80	54	28	3	-139
Florida	1,978	15.3	1,585	1,209	553	33	1,035
Georgia	1,164	18.0	930	464	90	25	598
Hawaii	85	7.6	156	59	51	19	-80
Idaho.	222	22.0	147	69	15	2	129
Illinois	615	5.4	1,553	865	337	10	-516
Indiana.	355	6.4	694	429	25	1	76
Iowa	86	3.1	312	228	19	(Z)	-13
Kansas.	151	6.1	309	191	24	8	-13
Kentucky	250	6.8	439	302	14	10	90
Louisiana	147	3.5	563	321	25	9	-117
Maine.	16	1.3	124	95	3	2	-15
Maryland	354	7.4	615	333	118	15	-49
Massachusetts.	131	2.2	697	452	135	3	-237
Michigan.	522	5.6	1,154	676	87	2	-190
Minnesota.	350	8.0	538	300	47	1	71
Mississippi	177	6.9	346	218	6	6	43
Missouri	322	6.3	621	436	34	5	94
Montana.	81	10.2	93	61	3	2	48
Nebraska	84	5.3	194	124	14	4	2
Nevada	545	45.4	198	95	45	3	397
New Hampshire	76	6.8	128	74	6	(Z)	19
New Jersey.	367	4.7	965	596	360	5	-350
New Mexico	222	14.6	227	98	36	6	55
New York	185	1.0	2,286	1,369	1,021	11	-1,722
North Carolina.	914	13.8	854	517	49	38	501
North Dakota.	-1	-0.1	71	48	4	3	-30
Ohio	362	3.3	1,302	850	48	4	-144
Oklahoma.	201	6.4	388	264	26	10	48
Oregon.	440	15.5	353	225	58	1	260
Pennsylvania.	119	1.0	1,292	1,037	104	3	-219
Rhode Island.	-15	-1.5	113	79	16	2	-64
South Carolina.	350	10.0	444	265	16	17	119
South Dakota	42	6.1	88	56	4	2	6
Tennessee	553	11.3	609	409	27	7	338
Texas.	2,773	16.3	2,680	1,107	656	44	541
Utah	377	21.9	323	86	27	2	86
Vermont	28	5.0	61	40	4	(Z)	5
Virginia.	602	9.7	778	422	131	62	68
Washington.	823	16.9	649	329	121	20	374
West Virginia.	18	1.0	176	165	3	(Z)	8
Wisconsin	332	6.8	571	365	21	(Z)	84
Wyoming	27	6.0	54	29	2	2	(-Z)

- Represents zero.   Z Less than 500.   [1] Includes residual change, not shown separately. The residual is the effect of national controls on subnational estimates. It is the difference between the implementation of the national estimates model and the county/state estimates model.

Source: U.S. Census Bureau, "ST-98-2 State Population Estimates and Demographic Components of Population Change: April 1, 1990 to July 1, 1998", and "ST-98-7 State Population Estimates and Demographic Components of Population Change: Annual Time Series, July 1, 1990 to July 1, 1998"; release date: February 5, 1999; <http://www.census.gov/population/estimates/state/st-98-2.txt> and <http://www.census.gov/population/estimates/state/st-98-7.txt>.

No. 29. Annual Inmigration, Outmigration, and Net Migration for Regions: 1980 to 1998

[In thousands (464 represents 464,000). As of **March.** For persons 1 year old and over. Excludes members of the Armed Forces except those living off post or with their families on post. Based on Current Population Survey; see text of this section and Appendix III. For composition of regions, see map, inside front cover. Minus sign (-) indicates net outmigration]

Period	North-east	Mid-west	South	West	Period	North-east	Mid-west	South	West
1980-81:					**1995-96:**				
Immigrants	464	650	1,377	871	Inmigrants	441	842	1,284	792
Outmigrants	706	1,056	890	710	Outmigrants	675	775	1,134	775
Net internal migration	-242	-406	487	161	Net internal migration	-234	68	150	16
Movers from abroad	207	180	412	514	Movers from abroad	285	130	470	476
Net migration	-35	-226	899	675	Net migration	51	198	620	492
1985-86:					**1996-97:**				
Immigrants	502	1,011	1,355	910	Inmigrants	481	661	1,338	688
Outmigrants	752	996	1,320	710	Outmigrants	600	814	947	806
Net internal migration	-250	15	35	200	Net internal migration	-119	-154	391	-118
Movers from abroad	198	158	342	502	Movers from abroad	239	169	445	450
Net migration	-52	173	377	702	Net migration	120	15	836	332
1990-91:					**1997-98:**				
Immigrants	346	782	1,421	835	Total inmigrants	504	873	1,335	660
Outmigrants	932	797	987	668	From Northeast	(X)	112	471	125
Net internal migration	-585	-15	433	167	From Midwest	71	(X)	481	201
Movers from abroad	209	208	351	617	From South	320	450	(X)	334
Net migration	-376	193	784	784	From West	113	310	383	(X)
1993-94:					Total outmigrants	708	753	1,105	806
Immigrants	348	706	1,336	746	To Northeast	(X)	71	320	113
Outmigrants	676	737	960	763	To Midwest	112	(X)	450	310
Net internal migration	-328	-31	376	-17	To South	471	481	(X)	383
Movers from abroad	267	132	451	396	To West	125	201	334	(X)
Net migration	-61	101	827	379	Net internal migration	-203	120	230	-146
					Movers from abroad	247	170	416	370
					Net migration	44	290	646	224

X Not applicable.

Source: U.S. Census Bureau, *Current Population Reports*, P20-520, and earlier reports.

No. 30. Mobility Status of the Population, by Selected Characteristics: 1980 to 1998

[As of **March (221,641 represents 221,641,000).** For persons 1 year old and over. Excludes members of the Armed Forces except those living off post or with their families on post. Based on Current Population Survey; see text of this section and Appendix III. For composition of regions, see map, inside front cover]

Mobility period and characteristic	Total (1,000)	Non-movers	Percent distribution						Movers from abroad
			Movers (different house in United States)						
			Total	Same county	Different county				
					Total	Same state	Different state		
1980-81	221,641	83	17	10	6	3	3	1	
1985-86	232,998	82	18	11	7	4	3	1	
1990-91	244,884	83	16	10	6	3	3	1	
1995-96	260,406	84	16	10	6	3	3	1	
1997-98, total persons	**265,209**	**84**	**16**	**10**	**5**	**3**	**2**	**(Z)**	
1 to 4 years old	15,802	77	23	16	7	4	3	(Z)	
5 to 9 years old	20,453	82	18	12	5	3	2	(Z)	
10 to 14 years old	19,663	85	14	10	5	2	2	(Z)	
15 to 19 years old	19,466	84	15	11	5	3	2	1	
20 to 24 years old	17,613	66	33	22	11	7	5	1	
25 to 29 years old	18,996	69	30	19	11	6	5	1	
30 to 44 years old	64,820	83	16	11	6	3	3	(Z)	
45 to 64 years old	56,312	91	8	5	3	2	2	(Z)	
65 to 74 years old	17,874	95	5	3	2	1	1	(Z)	
75 to 84 years old	11,281	96	4	3	2	1	1	(Z)	
85 years old and over	2,928	95	5	3	1	1	1	(Z)	
Northeast	50,703	89	11	7	4	2	2	(Z)	
Midwest	61,646	85	14	9	5	3	2	(Z)	
South	93,064	83	17	10	6	4	3	(Z)	
West	59,796	81	19	14	5	2	2	1	
Tenure:									
Owner-occupied units	183,157	92	8	5	3	2	1	(Z)	
Renter-occupied units	82,052	67	32	22	11	6	5	1	

Z Less than 0.5 percent.

Source: U.S. Census Bureau, *Current Population Reports*, P20-520.

U.S. Census Bureau, Statistical Abstract of the United States: 1999

No. 31. Mobility Status of Households, by Household Income: 1997-98

[As of **March** (**102,584** represents 102,584,000). See headnote, Table 30]

Household income	Total (1,000)	Non-movers	Movers (different house in United States) Total	Same county	Different county Total	Same state	Different state	Movers from abroad
Householders, 15 years and over...	**102,584**	**84**	**15**	**10**	**5**	**3**	**2**	**(Z)**
Less than $5,000	3,539	74	23	15	8	5	3	2
$5,000 to $9,999	7,776	80	19	14	5	3	2	1
$10,000 to $14,999	8,339	82	17	12	5	3	2	(Z)
$15,000 to $24,999	15,252	81	18	13	6	3	3	(Z)
$25,000 to $34,999	13,596	82	17	11	6	3	3	(Z)
$35,000 to $49,999	16,699	85	15	10	5	3	2	(Z)
$50,000 to $74,999	18,531	87	12	8	5	3	2	(Z)
$75,000 and over	18,853	90	10	5	4	2	2	(Z)

Z Less than 0.5 percent.

Source: U.S. Census Bureau, *Current Population Reports*, P20-520.

No. 32. Resident Population, by Region, Race, and Hispanic Origin: 1990

[As of **April 1** (**248,710** represents 248,710,000). For composition of regions, see map, inside front cover]

Race and Hispanic origin	Population (1,000) United States	North-east	Midwest	South	West	Percent distribution United States	North-east	Midwest	South	West
Total...........	**248,710**	**50,809**	**59,669**	**85,446**	**52,786**	**100.0**	**20.4**	**24.0**	**34.4**	**21.2**
White.............	199,686	42,069	52,018	65,582	40,017	100.0	21.1	26.0	32.8	20.0
Black.............	29,986	5,613	5,716	15,829	2,828	100.0	18.7	19.1	52.8	9.4
American Indian, Eskimo, Aleut.............	1,959	125	338	563	933	100.0	6.4	17.2	28.7	47.6
American Indian......	1,878	122	334	557	866	100.0	6.5	17.8	29.7	46.1
Eskimo...........	57	2	2	3	51	100.0	2.9	3.5	4.9	88.8
Aleut............	24	2	2	3	17	100.0	8.1	8.1	11.5	72.3
Asian and Pacific Islander.	7,274	1,335	768	1,122	4,048	100.0	18.4	10.6	15.4	55.7
Chinese..........	1,645	445	133	204	863	100.0	27.0	8.1	12.4	52.4
Filipino..........	1,407	143	113	159	991	100.0	10.2	8.1	11.3	70.5
Japanese.........	848	74	63	67	643	100.0	8.8	7.5	7.9	75.9
Asian Indian........	815	285	146	196	189	100.0	35.0	17.9	24.0	23.1
Korean...........	799	182	109	153	355	100.0	22.8	13.7	19.2	44.4
Vietnamese........	615	61	52	169	334	100.0	9.8	8.5	27.4	54.3
Laotian...........	149	16	28	29	76	100.0	10.7	18.6	19.6	51.0
Cambodian........	147	30	13	19	85	100.0	20.5	8.8	13.1	57.7
Thai.............	91	12	13	24	43	100.0	12.9	14.2	26.0	46.8
Hmong...........	90	2	37	2	50	100.0	1.9	41.3	1.8	55.0
Pakistani..........	81	28	15	22	17	100.0	34.3	18.9	26.5	20.4
Hawaiian..........	211	4	6	12	189	100.0	2.0	2.6	5.8	89.6
Samoan..........	63	2	2	4	55	100.0	2.4	3.6	6.4	87.6
Guamanian........	49	4	3	8	34	100.0	7.3	6.4	16.8	69.5
Other Asian or Pacific Islander........	263	49	34	54	126	100.0	18.6	12.9	20.5	48.0
Other races	9,805	1,667	829	2,350	4,960	100.0	17.0	8.5	24.0	50.6
Hispanic origin [1]......	22,354	3,754	1,727	6,767	10,106	100.0	16.8	7.7	30.3	45.2
Mexican.........	13,496	175	1,153	4,344	7,824	100.0	1.3	8.5	32.2	58.0
Puerto Rican.......	2,728	1,872	258	406	192	100.0	68.6	9.4	14.9	7.0
Cuban	1,044	184	37	735	88	100.0	17.6	3.5	70.5	8.5
Other Hispanic.......	5,086	1,524	279	1,282	2,002	100.0	30.0	5.5	25.2	39.4
Not of Hispanic origin....	226,356	47,055	57,942	78,679	42,680	100.0	20.8	25.6	34.8	18.9

[1] Persons of Hispanic origin may be of any race.

Source: U.S. Census Bureau, *1990 Census of Population, General Population Characteristics, United States* (CP-1-1).

No. 33. Resident Population, by Age and State: 1998

[In thousands, except percent (270,299 represents 270,299,000). As of July 1. Includes Armed Forces stationed in area. See text of this section for basis of estimates]

State	Total	Under 5 years	5 to 17 years	18 to 24 years	25 to 34 years	35 to 44 years	45 to 54 years	55 to 64 years	65 to 74 years	75 to 84 years	85 years and over	Percent 65 years and over
U.S.	270,299	18,966	50,906	25,470	38,774	44,520	34,585	22,676	18,395	11,952	4,054	12.7
AL.	4,352	295	789	436	620	687	561	395	313	191	64	13.1
AK.	614	49	143	69	76	110	88	45	22	10	2	5.5
AZ.	4,669	368	895	449	648	732	568	389	340	215	63	13.2
AR.	2,538	175	479	251	333	378	319	240	193	125	44	14.3
CA.	32,667	2,564	6,347	3,167	5,203	5,492	3,930	2,349	1,935	1,267	412	11.1
CO	3,971	279	762	377	534	701	577	340	221	135	46	10.1
CT.	3,274	211	579	258	473	570	434	279	236	171	62	14.3
DE.	744	49	130	67	117	128	94	62	54	32	10	13.0
DC	523	31	72	43	100	88	69	47	39	25	9	13.9
FL.	14,916	953	2,587	1,206	1,926	2,318	1,816	1,377	1,448	976	310	18.3
GA.	7,642	568	1,454	755	1,214	1,308	985	603	422	251	82	9.9
HI	1,193	84	214	119	155	200	161	100	88	53	16	13.3
ID	1,229	91	260	139	151	187	156	105	72	50	17	11.3
IL	12,045	891	2,297	1,121	1,737	1,985	1,514	1,005	781	529	186	12.4
IN	5,899	411	1,107	572	839	961	761	510	396	256	88	12.5
IA	2,862	182	540	277	365	443	367	257	212	156	64	15.1
KS.	2,629	182	515	262	347	426	329	213	178	126	51	13.5
KY.	3,936	264	725	398	547	631	519	360	270	166	57	12.5
LA.	4,369	313	878	475	589	683	551	376	280	168	56	11.5
ME	1,244	67	224	110	169	218	174	107	93	60	22	14.1
MD	5,135	344	943	434	792	930	685	416	324	204	64	11.5
MA	6,147	393	1,064	505	980	1,045	801	498	439	309	113	14.0
MI	9,817	657	1,895	921	1,392	1,633	1,277	820	658	426	139	12.5
MN	4,725	317	942	439	648	811	604	381	293	207	83	12.3
MS	2,752	202	555	300	381	415	330	234	184	112	40	12.2
MO	5,439	364	1,043	509	737	883	682	476	390	257	98	13.7
MT	880	53	172	89	96	141	127	86	61	42	15	13.3
NE.	1,663	115	331	167	212	263	208	138	115	80	34	13.8
NV.	1,747	136	331	148	252	290	230	159	122	63	15	11.5
NH	1,185	73	225	96	182	222	155	89	76	49	18	12.0
NJ.	8,115	547	1,443	672	1,144	1,415	1,078	710	587	390	128	13.6
NM	1,737	133	371	174	216	279	221	145	111	66	22	11.4
NY.	18,175	1,253	3,249	1,598	2,698	2,993	2,366	1,595	1,289	834	301	13.3
NC	7,546	527	1,393	700	1,127	1,221	971	661	528	317	101	12.5
ND	638	40	122	68	81	100	80	55	45	33	14	14.4
OH	11,209	742	2,102	1,053	1,562	1,828	1,447	975	805	526	171	13.4
OK	3,347	228	651	338	427	513	428	312	240	152	57	13.4
OR	3,282	217	608	303	427	535	471	288	221	158	53	13.2
PA.	12,001	720	2,140	1,022	1,619	1,955	1,572	1,070	994	688	221	15.9
RI	988	62	176	83	150	164	122	77	77	57	20	15.6
SC.	3,836	253	706	384	565	618	505	336	266	156	46	12.2
SD.	738	50	151	77	89	115	90	61	53	37	16	14.3
TN.	5,431	362	969	515	788	888	730	499	374	228	77	12.5
TX.	19,760	1,615	4,014	2,049	2,829	3,242	2,451	1,560	1,113	661	227	10.1
UT.	2,100	204	498	290	292	282	214	136	100	64	21	8.8
VT.	591	33	109	52	85	105	86	49	39	24	9	12.3
VA.	6,791	447	1,198	657	1,072	1,178	906	567	426	260	82	11.3
WA	5,689	387	1,086	540	803	989	777	456	339	235	79	11.5
WV	1,811	99	305	183	229	276	259	186	150	94	31	15.2
WI	5,224	333	1,018	498	707	867	672	438	354	244	93	13.2
WY	481	31	99	53	53	77	69	44	31	18	6	11.5

Source: U.S. Census Bureau, "Population Estimates for the U.S., Regions, Divisions, and States by 5-year Age Groups and Sex: Annual Time Series Estimates, July 1, 1990 to July 1, 1998"; published 15 June 1999; <http://www.census. gov/population/ estimates/ state/ 5age9890.txt>; and "Population Estimates for the U.S., Regions, and States by Selected Age Groups and Sex: Annual Time series, July 1, 1990 to July 1, 1998"; published 15 June 1999; <http://www.census.gov/population/estimates/ state/sage9890.txt>.

U.S. Census Bureau, Statistical Abstract of the United States: 1999

No. 34. Resident Population by Race, Hispanic Origin, and State: 1998

[In thousands (270,299 represents 270,299,000). As of July 1. These estimates are developed using a cohort-component method whereby each component of population change - births, deaths, domestic migration, and international migration is estimated separately for each birth cohort by sex and race]

State		Race						Hispanic origin [1]
	Total	White			Black	American Indian, Eskimo, Aleut	Asian, Pacific Islander	
		Total	Hispanic	Non-Hispanic				
U.S.	270,299	223,001	27,561	195,440	34,431	2,360	10,507	30,250
AL.	4,352	3,177	36	3,141	1,132	15	28	43
AK.	614	463	19	444	24	100	28	24
AZ.	4,669	4,145	963	3,182	169	256	98	1,034
AR.	2,538	2,098	44	2,055	408	14	19	49
CA.	32,667	25,965	9,454	16,511	2,456	309	3,938	10,113
CO	3,971	3,666	541	3,125	172	37	96	578
CT.	3,274	2,882	238	2,644	304	8	80	268
DE.	744	582	22	560	144	2	15	26
DC	523	180	30	149	326	2	16	38
FL.	14,916	12,319	2,080	10,239	2,268	58	271	2,243
GA	7,642	5,293	193	5,100	2,181	18	149	220
HI	1,193	395	51	344	35	7	757	96
ID	1,229	1,191	82	1,109	7	17	14	88
IL	12,045	9,775	1,145	8,630	1,840	27	403	1,224
IN	5,899	5,338	132	5,206	491	15	56	145
IA	2,862	2,761	52	2,709	57	8	36	57
KS	2,629	2,405	127	2,278	155	23	46	140
KY	3,936	3,619	28	3,591	285	6	27	33
LA	4,369	2,887	100	2,787	1,407	19	55	117
ME	1,244	1,223	8	1,215	6	6	9	9
MD	5,135	3,487	158	3,329	1,428	16	204	188
MA	6,147	5,514	298	5,217	395	15	223	377
MI	9,817	8,195	234	7,961	1,405	60	158	264
MN	4,725	4,403	76	4,327	141	58	124	87
MS	2,752	1,719	18	1,701	1,003	10	19	23
MO	5,439	4,745	77	4,668	613	21	60	87
MT	880	816	13	803	3	56	5	16
NE.	1,663	1,559	66	1,493	67	15	22	73
NV.	1,747	1,501	253	1,248	133	31	81	278
NH	1,185	1,160	16	1,144	9	2	14	18
NJ.	8,115	6,452	866	5,586	1,188	22	453	1,004
NM.	1,737	1,503	669	834	45	163	26	700
NY.	18,175	13,885	1,990	11,895	3,220	76	995	2,625
NC	7,546	5,684	139	5,545	1,665	98	100	161
ND	638	599	6	593	4	30	5	7
OH	11,209	9,768	158	9,610	1,290	23	129	179
OK	3,347	2,777	109	2,668	262	263	45	130
OR	3,282	3,070	182	2,888	61	45	106	199
PA.	12,001	10,619	265	10,354	1,166	18	198	315
RI	988	911	52	859	49	5	23	65
SC.	3,836	2,645	42	2,603	1,147	9	34	50
SD.	738	669	7	662	5	59	5	9
TN.	5,431	4,466	54	4,413	900	12	53	62
TX.	19,760	16,678	5,640	11,038	2,430	96	556	5,863
UT.	2,100	1,998	132	1,866	19	30	53	142
VT.	591	581	5	577	3	2	5	5
VA.	6,791	5,163	220	4,943	1,363	19	247	251
WA	5,689	5,058	315	4,743	198	103	330	355
WV	1,811	1,741	9	1,732	58	3	9	10
WI	5,224	4,807	120	4,687	291	46	80	134
WY	481	462	27	435	4	11	4	29

[1] Persons of Hispanic origin may be of any race.

Source: U.S. Census Bureau, "Population Estimates for States by Race and Hispanic Origin: July 1, 1998"; published 15 September 1999; <http://www.census.gov/population/estimates/state/srh/srhus98.txt>.

No. 35. State Population Projections: 2000 to 2025

[In thousands (274,634 represents 274,634,000). As of July 1. The two series of projections are based on different internal migration assumptions: 1) Series A, is the preferred series model and uses state-to-state migration observed from 1975-76 through 1993-94; and 2) Series B, the economic model, uses the Bureau of Economic Analysis employment projections. For explanation of methodology, see text of this section]

State	Series A						Series B					
	2000	2005	2010	2015	2020	2025	2000	2005	2010	2015	2020	2025
U.S	274,634	285,981	297,716	310,133	322,742	335,050	274,634	285,981	297,716	310,134	322,742	335,050
AL.......	4,451	4,631	4,798	4,956	5,100	5,224	4,436	4,617	4,802	4,986	5,162	5,319
AK.......	653	700	745	791	838	885	632	659	690	728	773	825
AZ.......	4,798	5,230	5,522	5,808	6,111	6,412	4,838	5,432	6,025	6,620	7,193	7,729
AR.......	2,631	2,750	2,840	2,922	2,997	3,055	2,623	2,757	2,887	3,008	3,109	3,184
CA.......	32,521	34,441	37,644	41,373	45,278	49,285	32,423	33,511	34,968	36,838	39,034	41,480
CO.......	4,168	4,468	4,658	4,833	5,012	5,188	4,154	4,510	4,837	5,152	5,454	5,743
CT.......	3,284	3,317	3,400	3,506	3,621	3,739	3,286	3,291	3,303	3,332	3,376	3,428
DE.......	768	800	817	832	847	861	758	793	823	851	877	899
DC.......	523	529	560	594	625	655	530	542	572	611	654	702
FL.......	15,233	16,279	17,363	18,497	19,634	20,710	15,250	16,273	17,299	18,318	19,262	20,066
GA.......	7,875	8,413	8,824	9,200	9,552	9,869	7,893	8,540	9,167	9,785	10,386	10,962
HI.......	1,257	1,342	1,440	1,553	1,677	1,812	1,238	1,297	1,367	1,447	1,537	1,634
ID.......	1,347	1,480	1,557	1,622	1,683	1,739	1,332	1,489	1,637	1,775	1,900	2,008
IL.......	12,051	12,266	12,515	12,808	13,121	13,440	12,069	12,314	12,601	12,945	13,323	13,717
IN.......	6,045	6,215	6,318	6,404	6,481	6,546	6,060	6,301	6,532	6,758	6,969	7,158
IA.......	2,900	2,941	2,968	2,994	3,019	3,040	2,891	2,939	2,992	3,047	3,095	3,133
KS.......	2,668	2,761	2,849	2,939	3,026	3,108	2,675	2,788	2,908	3,034	3,158	3,273
KY.......	3,995	4,098	4,170	4,231	4,281	4,314	3,990	4,109	4,220	4,322	4,411	4,480
LA.......	4,425	4,535	4,683	4,840	4,991	5,133	4,445	4,558	4,687	4,828	4,972	5,111
ME.......	1,259	1,285	1,323	1,362	1,396	1,423	1,250	1,259	1,268	1,276	1,282	1,282
MD.......	5,275	5,467	5,657	5,862	6,071	6,274	5,261	5,426	5,577	5,736	5,904	6,072
MA.......	6,199	6,310	6,431	6,574	6,734	6,902	6,224	6,361	6,498	6,653	6,824	7,001
MI.......	9,679	9,763	9,836	9,917	10,002	10,078	9,711	9,835	9,966	10,115	10,272	10,423
MN.......	4,830	5,005	5,147	5,283	5,406	5,510	4,822	5,014	5,212	5,414	5,606	5,778
MS.......	2,816	2,908	2,974	3,035	3,093	3,142	2,826	2,949	3,072	3,195	3,310	3,413
MO.......	5,540	5,718	5,864	6,005	6,137	6,250	5,547	5,750	5,953	6,153	6,336	6,492
MT.......	950	1,006	1,040	1,069	1,097	1,121	937	998	1,056	1,108	1,152	1,187
NE.......	1,705	1,761	1,806	1,850	1,892	1,930	1,700	1,766	1,837	1,912	1,984	2,050
NV.......	1,871	2,070	2,131	2,179	2,241	2,312	1,863	2,130	2,355	2,547	2,712	2,854
NH.......	1,224	1,281	1,329	1,372	1,410	1,439	1,217	1,267	1,307	1,344	1,377	1,402
NJ.......	8,178	8,392	8,638	8,924	9,238	9,558	8,185	8,387	8,594	8,832	9,096	9,369
NM.......	1,860	2,016	2,155	2,300	2,454	2,612	1,858	2,035	2,223	2,425	2,636	2,850
NY.......	18,146	18,250	18,530	18,916	19,359	19,830	18,174	18,227	18,363	18,616	18,969	19,396
NC.......	7,777	8,227	8,552	8,840	9,111	9,349	7,789	8,312	8,780	9,206	9,588	9,916
ND.......	662	677	690	704	717	729	657	677	701	727	754	778
OH.......	11,319	11,428	11,505	11,588	11,671	11,744	11,352	11,534	11,726	11,937	12,148	12,343
OK.......	3,373	3,491	3,639	3,789	3,930	4,057	3,370	3,471	3,578	3,684	3,784	3,871
OR.......	3,397	3,613	3,803	3,992	4,177	4,349	3,397	3,625	3,837	4,036	4,213	4,361
PA.......	12,202	12,281	12,352	12,449	12,567	12,683	12,220	12,329	12,443	12,580	12,727	12,854
RI.......	998	1,012	1,038	1,070	1,105	1,141	989	986	986	989	998	1,007
SC.......	3,858	4,033	4,205	4,369	4,517	4,645	3,852	4,015	4,169	4,318	4,455	4,574
SD.......	777	810	826	840	853	866	770	811	853	893	930	962
TN.......	5,657	5,966	6,180	6,365	6,529	6,665	5,668	6,039	6,385	6,707	6,998	7,249
TX.......	20,119	21,487	22,857	24,280	25,729	27,183	20,178	21,635	23,158	24,775	26,453	28,170
UT.......	2,207	2,411	2,551	2,670	2,781	2,883	2,216	2,477	2,738	2,995	3,246	3,487
VT.......	617	638	651	662	671	678	607	623	636	646	655	661
VA.......	6,997	7,324	7,627	7,921	8,204	8,466	6,965	7,234	7,474	7,708	7,939	8,165
WA.......	5,858	6,258	6,658	7,058	7,446	7,808	5,829	6,184	6,524	6,857	7,179	7,480
WV.......	1,841	1,849	1,851	1,851	1,850	1,845	1,833	1,842	1,852	1,861	1,864	1,864
WI.......	5,326	5,479	5,590	5,693	5,788	5,867	5,324	5,502	5,682	5,864	6,035	6,185
WY.......	525	568	607	641	670	694	519	559	598	636	671	702

Source: U.S. Census Bureau, Population Paper Listings PPL-47.

U.S. Census Bureau, Statistical Abstract of the United States: 1999

No. 36. Population Projections, by Age—States: 2000 to 2010

[In thousands (70,782 represents 70,782,000). As of July 1. The projections shown here are based on certain internal migration assumptions: Series A, is the preferred series model and uses state-to-state migration observed from 1975-76 through 1993-94]

State	Under 18 years			18 to 44 years			45 to 64 years			65 years and over		
	2000	2005	2010	2000	2005	2010	2000	2005	2010	2000	2005	2010
U.S.	70,782	71,964	72,510	108,151	106,738	106,951	60,991	71,113	78,847	34,710	36,166	39,408
AL......	1,105	1,119	1,110	1,731	1,696	1,676	1,033	1,203	1,338	582	613	674
AK......	200	213	225	278	286	301	137	155	164	38	46	55
AZ......	1,313	1,375	1,387	1,812	1,859	1,863	1,038	1,289	1,465	635	707	807
AR......	653	651	636	977	958	929	624	739	824	377	402	451
CA......	9,350	9,946	10,689	13,260	13,412	14,407	6,524	7,629	8,759	3,387	3,454	3,789
CO	1,049	1,078	1,080	1,694	1,714	1,707	973	1,153	1,260	452	523	611
CT......	791	777	767	1,283	1,234	1,232	749	850	924	461	456	477
DE......	191	191	185	311	307	298	169	201	225	97	101	109
DC......	125	130	136	215	212	226	114	122	133	69	65	65
FL......	3,507	3,563	3,573	5,425	5,443	5,483	3,546	4,362	5,072	2,755	2,911	3,235
GA	2,070	2,155	2,164	3,301	3,326	3,318	1,725	2,080	2,368	779	852	974
HI	328	354	379	495	505	528	277	319	351	157	164	182
ID	378	400	404	516	537	538	296	361	402	157	182	213
IL	3,141	3,151	3,142	4,807	4,665	4,604	2,619	2,956	3,204	1,484	1,494	1,565
IN	1,518	1,524	1,499	2,396	2,330	2,270	1,368	1,567	1,697	763	794	852
IA	706	691	678	1,091	1,052	1,018	661	746	796	442	452	476
KS	698	700	704	1,036	1,026	1,018	575	669	736	359	366	391
KY	963	951	923	1,577	1,516	1,461	946	1,093	1,197	509	538	589
LA	1,214	1,204	1,207	1,722	1,678	1,676	966	1,098	1,190	523	555	610
ME	293	284	281	485	462	449	309	366	407	172	173	186
MD	1,319	1,333	1,330	2,174	2,131	2,106	1,193	1,392	1,557	589	611	664
MA	1,496	1,488	1,452	2,499	2,429	2,393	1,361	1,566	1,723	843	827	863
MI	2,495	2,455	2,400	3,817	3,641	3,540	2,170	2,456	2,620	1,197	1,211	1,276
MN	1,236	1,216	1,212	1,935	1,906	1,858	1,063	1,256	1,391	596	627	686
MS	767	769	751	1,096	1,068	1,048	609	708	782	344	363	393
MO	1,392	1,390	1,378	2,146	2,099	2,053	1,247	1,455	1,603	755	774	830
MT	240	242	242	348	345	337	234	276	297	128	143	164
NE	443	442	443	654	646	636	369	425	462	239	248	265
NV	450	468	456	738	754	718	464	591	662	219	257	295
NH	304	303	300	503	494	486	275	336	380	142	148	163
NJ	2,004	2,024	2,009	3,216	3,136	3,131	1,868	2,139	2,348	1,090	1,093	1,150
NM	534	568	594	717	737	757	403	483	545	206	228	259
NY	4,620	4,610	4,535	7,101	6,817	6,763	4,067	4,502	4,833	2,358	2,321	2,399
NC	1,908	1,934	1,885	3,083	3,065	3,029	1,795	2,147	2,420	991	1,081	1,218
ND	168	163	163	253	249	243	142	162	173	99	103	111
OH	2,817	2,766	2,702	4,411	4,214	4,082	2,566	2,894	3,097	1,525	1,554	1,624
OK	861	852	856	1,265	1,242	1,242	775	893	980	472	504	561
OR	810	821	828	1,277	1,273	1,270	839	997	1,100	471	522	605
PA	2,902	2,845	2,762	4,582	4,363	4,236	2,819	3,206	3,446	1,899	1,867	1,908
RI	245	244	242	390	374	374	215	251	276	148	143	146
SC	970	980	968	1,513	1,479	1,470	897	1,057	1,183	478	517	584
SD	210	211	210	293	292	283	164	193	212	110	114	121
TN	1,376	1,408	1,390	2,238	2,225	2,191	1,336	1,573	1,755	707	760	844
TX	5,708	5,976	6,210	8,122	8,251	8,471	4,188	4,963	5,575	2,101	2,297	2,601
UT	719	759	776	896	941	958	390	477	541	202	234	276
VT	152	150	145	245	238	232	147	173	188	73	77	86
VA	1,697	1,728	1,725	2,912	2,876	2,861	1,600	1,875	2,096	788	845	945
WA	1,459	1,496	1,534	2,346	2,351	2,378	1,368	1,654	1,866	685	757	880
WV	404	394	379	679	636	607	471	523	549	287	296	316
WI	1,344	1,322	1,308	2,090	2,045	1,987	1,187	1,382	1,512	705	730	783
WY	139	146	153	201	205	212	123	146	160	62	71	82

Source: U.S. Census Bureau, Population Paper Listings PPL-47.

U.S. Census Bureau, Statistical Abstract of the United States: 1999

No. 37. Population Projections, by Race—States: 2000 to 2010

[In thousands (225,533 represents 225,533,000). As of July 1. The projections shown here are based on certain internal migration assumptions: Series A, is the preferred series model and uses state-to-state migration observed from 1975-76 through 1993-94]

State	White			Black			American Indian, Eskimo, Aleut			Asian, Pacific Islander		
	2000	2005	2010	2000	2005	2010	2000	2005	2010	2000	2005	2010
U.S.	225,533	232,462	239,588	35,456	37,735	40,110	2,402	2,573	2,754	11,246	13,212	15,265
AL.......	3,262	3,391	3,509	1,137	1,183	1,227	18	18	20	34	40	44
AK.......	486	508	524	29	31	33	93	92	91	46	69	96
AZ.......	4,252	4,623	4,867	177	203	222	262	277	290	107	129	143
AR.......	2,186	2,286	2,363	409	423	434	15	16	18	19	22	24
CA.......	25,517	26,583	28,655	2,425	2,511	2,702	292	296	318	4,289	5,051	5,969
CO	3,823	4,068	4,216	196	224	246	41	46	51	108	129	147
CT.......	2,873	2,862	2,893	324	350	384	8	8	8	80	96	115
DE......	603	621	626	147	158	169	2	2	2	15	17	19
DC	184	194	209	321	316	329	-	-	-	15	18	21
FL.......	12,588	13,332	14,113	2,326	2,573	2,820	51	58	64	267	316	366
GA	5,436	5,713	5,893	2,279	2,515	2,724	17	18	18	142	168	187
HI	423	449	478	31	33	35	6	6	7	796	853	920
ID	1,300	1,425	1,497	8	11	12	21	25	27	17	19	22
IL	9,736	9,839	9,968	1,865	1,914	1,971	26	28	31	423	484	543
IN	5,466	5,599	5,671	502	530	551	16	16	17	60	72	78
IA	2,786	2,810	2,825	62	69	76	9	11	12	43	52	58
KS......	2,419	2,487	2,550	173	188	203	27	29	30	50	59	64
KY......	3,671	3,760	3,817	287	298	310	6	6	8	29	33	37
LA......	2,895	2,923	2,979	1,448	1,521	1,600	20	20	22	62	72	83
ME	1,238	1,261	1,296	5	5	7	6	6	6	9	11	13
MD	3,546	3,580	3,621	1,489	1,609	1,724	16	16	16	223	260	296
MA	5,523	5,534	5,549	417	461	508	14	14	15	246	303	361
MI	8,021	8,024	8,016	1,435	1,486	1,539	61	63	65	163	190	215
MN	4,469	4,580	4,662	158	185	210	64	71	80	139	170	196
MS	1,774	1,826	1,861	1,012	1,049	1,078	8	8	8	19	23	25
MO	4,825	4,957	5,061	628	662	696	24	26	28	63	72	80
MT	879	926	952	3	6	6	61	67	72	7	9	9
NE.	1,595	1,636	1,668	72	82	88	16	18	20	23	29	31
NV.	1,619	1,777	1,817	138	159	171	31	32	32	85	103	111
NH	1,199	1,251	1,293	9	10	10	2	2	2	14	17	21
NJ.	6,442	6,465	6,512	1,239	1,328	1,422	20	23	23	475	578	681
NM	1,615	1,737	1,843	48	56	63	169	186	209	29	35	41
NY.	13,747	13,567	13,529	3,299	3,416	3,563	73	76	79	1,028	1,191	1,359
NC	5,851	6,160	6,367	1,738	1,857	1,957	94	98	101	96	113	128
ND	617	628	635	5	5	5	32	37	43	6	6	7
OH	9,835	9,852	9,842	1,320	1,386	1,452	22	24	24	140	166	186
OK	2,759	2,825	2,917	282	311	341	281	295	315	51	58	65
OR	3,167	3,350	3,508	65	74	80	51	55	59	116	135	155
PA......	10,741	10,725	10,700	1,224	1,279	1,334	18	22	22	218	258	296
RI	911	911	922	54	60	68	4	6	8	28	35	41
SC.	2,660	2,781	2,898	1,156	1,205	1,255	8	8	9	33	38	42
SD.	706	730	739	5	5	6	60	66	72	5	6	7
TN.	4,658	4,887	5,036	929	999	1,057	12	14	14	57	66	72
TX.	16,920	17,916	18,917	2,543	2,797	3,058	95	107	120	562	667	762
UT.	2,087	2,267	2,390	22	27	29	37	43	47	62	75	85
VT.	606	625	638	2	4	4	2	2	2	6	7	8
VA.	5,295	5,457	5,599	1,416	1,526	1,637	19	19	21	267	320	370
WA	5,200	5,506	5,811	192	208	224	107	115	126	358	427	496
WV	1,769	1,774	1,772	58	60	60	2	2	2	11	13	15
WI	4,853	4,937	4,988	326	366	400	49	52	55	100	126	147
WY	501	539	573	6	7	8	13	16	19	4	6	7

- Represents or rounds to zero.

Source: U.S. Census Bureau, Population Paper Listings PPL-47.

Population 37

No. 38. Population Projections, by Hispanic-Origin Status—States: 2000 to 2010

[In thousands (31,366 represents 31,366,000). As of **July 1**. The projections shown here are based on certain internal migration assumptions: Series A, is the preferred series model and uses state-to-state migration observed from 1975-76 through 1993-94. Persons of Hispanic origin may be of any race]

State	Hispanic origin			Not of Hispanic origin								
				White			Black		American Indian, Eskimo, Aleut		Asian, Pacific Islander	
	2000	2005	2010	2000	2005	2010	2000	2010	2000	2010	2000	2010
U.S	31,366	36,057	41,138	197,062	199,802	202,390	33,569	37,466	2,055	2,321	10,585	14,402
AL.......	37	42	47	3,231	3,355	3,468	1,133	1,223	18	20	32	42
AK.......	31	37	41	461	476	487	27	31	91	91	44	94
AZ.......	1,071	1,269	1,450	3,254	3,441	3,518	150	179	232	256	91	119
AR.......	33	40	46	2,155	2,249	2,320	407	432	15	18	19	23
CA.......	10,647	12,268	14,214	15,562	15,123	15,394	2,138	2,268	170	165	4,006	5,603
CO.......	594	682	770	3,268	3,434	3,505	178	216	30	37	98	132
CT.......	288	332	386	2,622	2,574	2,561	293	338	6	6	76	109
DE.......	25	29	33	582	596	597	143	165	2	2	15	19
DC.......	40	46	55	152	156	163	315	322	-	-	13	19
FL.......	2,390	2,845	3,319	10,405	10,764	11,145	2,159	2,536	39	44	239	319
GA.......	189	226	252	5,270	5,515	5,671	2,262	2,702	15	16	138	181
HI.......	107	119	132	363	372	383	27	29	4	5	755	891
ID.......	96	121	140	1,211	1,314	1,368	6	8	18	23	15	19
IL.......	1,267	1,450	1,637	8,553	8,487	8,445	1,813	1,900	18	19	399	512
IN.......	140	162	179	5,338	5,453	5,509	494	540	14	15	58	74
IA.......	54	61	71	2,737	2,755	2,762	60	72	8	10	41	56
KS.......	138	166	191	2,293	2,337	2,377	167	193	23	26	48	60
KY.......	32	38	42	3,643	3,727	3,781	285	306	6	8	27	35
LA.......	119	138	156	2,792	2,803	2,841	1,438	1,588	18	20	58	79
ME.......	8	10	14	1,230	1,251	1,284	5	5	6	6	9	13
MD.....	214	258	300	3,371	3,368	3,372	1,462	1,687	14	14	213	284
MA.....	437	524	619	5,182	5,123	5,063	332	391	10	10	239	350
MI.....	261	289	319	7,790	7,767	7,732	1,417	1,517	55	59	157	208
MN.....	95	114	132	4,387	4,480	4,546	152	202	61	76	135	192
MS	21	24	27	1,755	1,804	1,836	1,010	1,076	8	8	19	25
MO	90	105	121	4,745	4,863	4,953	622	689	22	26	61	76
MT.	20	26	28	861	904	926	3	4	59	72	7	9
NE.	61	72	80	1,540	1,572	1,596	70	84	14	18	21	29
NV.	277	350	403	1,366	1,456	1,445	128	156	25	26	77	101
NH	17	20	22	1,184	1,233	1,273	7	8	2	2	14	21
NJ.	1,044	1,196	1,348	5,558	5,462	5,387	1,104	1,232	14	15	456	656
NM	736	821	912	912	958	984	34	37	157	195	22	28
NY.	2,805	3,071	3,357	11,640	11,271	11,023	2,668	2,790	53	56	981	1,304
NC	121	139	154	5,748	6,040	6,233	1,726	1,943	92	99	92	124
ND	6	8	10	611	620	625	5	5	32	43	6	7
OH	183	206	230	9,672	9,669	9,638	1,306	1,433	20	22	136	181
OK	124	143	167	2,653	2,700	2,769	276	332	273	309	47	61
OR	195	237	278	2,990	3,133	3,253	59	71	45	53	110	147
PA	334	391	448	10,460	10,398	10,325	1,181	1,276	16	18	210	285
RI	76	92	112	851	838	834	40	48	4	6	26	39
SC......	42	50	58	2,624	2,738	2,848	1,152	1,249	8	9	31	40
SD......	8	9	10	698	721	729	5	6	60	72	5	7
TN......	57	67	75	4,607	4,828	4,969	925	1,051	12	14	55	70
TX......	5,875	6,624	7,421	11,273	11,587	11,866	2,406	2,833	60	66	506	671
UT......	138	164	185	1,961	2,117	2,219	18	23	33	43	58	81
VT......	6	6	8	600	619	630	2	4	2	2	6	8
VA......	269	322	376	5,061	5,175	5,270	1,394	1,606	16	17	257	358
WA	360	437	519	4,881	5,115	5,346	179	203	95	112	342	477
WV	11	15	17	1,758	1,761	1,757	58	58	2	2	11	15
WI	136	156	173	4,732	4,799	4,833	318	390	45	51	97	143
WY	35	42	48	469	501	529	4	6	12	17	4	7

- Represents or rounds to zero.

Source: U.S. Census Bureau, Population Paper Listings PPL-47.

U.S. Census Bureau, Statistical Abstract of the United States: 1999

No. 39. Population in Coastal Counties: 1970 to 1998

[Enumerated population as of **April 1**, except as indicated (**3,536 represents 3,536,000**). Areas as defined by U.S. National Oceanic and Atmospheric Agency, 1992. Covers 673 counties and equivalent areas with at least 15 percent of their land area either in a coastal watershed (drainage area) or in a coastal cataloging unit (a coastal area between watersheds)]

Year	Total	Counties in coastal regions					Balance of United States
		Total	Atlantic	Gulf of Mexico	Great Lakes	Pacific	
Land area, 1990 (1,000 sq. mi.)	3,536	888	148	114	115	510	2,649
POPULATION							
1970 (mil.)	203.3	110.0	51.1	10.0	26.0	22.8	93.3
1980 (mil.)	226.5	119.8	53.7	13.1	26.0	27.0	106.7
1990 (mil.)	248.7	133.4	59.0	15.2	25.9	33.2	115.3
1995 (July 1) (mil.)	262.8	139.3	61.0	16.5	26.6	35.2	123.5
1998 (July 1) (mil.)	270.2	142.7	62.3	17.1	26.8	36.5	127.5
1970 (percent)	100	54	25	5	13	11	46
1980 (percent)	100	53	24	6	11	12	47
1990 (percent)	100	54	24	6	10	13	46
1995 (July 1) (percent)	100	53	23	6	10	13	47
1998 (July 1) (percent)	100	53	23	6	10	14	47

Source: U.S. Census Bureau, *U.S. Census of Population: 1970; 1980 Census of Population*, Vol. 1, Chapter A (PC80-1-A-1), *U.S. Summary; 1990 Census of Population and Housing* (CPH1); and unpublished data.

No. 40. Metropolitan and Nonmetropolitan Area Population: 1970 to 1996

[As of **April 1**, except **1996**, as of **July 1 (139,480 represents 139,480,000)**. Data exclude Puerto Rico. Metropolitan areas are defined by U.S. Office of Management and Budget as of year shown, except as noted]

Item	1970	1980 [1] (SMSAs)	MSAs and CMSAs [2]		
			1980	1990	1996
Metropolitan areas: Number of areas	243	318	274	274	274
Population (1,000)	139,480	169,431	177,361	198,249	211,874
Percent change over previous year shown . .	[3]23.6	21.5	(X)	11.8	6.9
Percent of total U.S. population	68.6	74.8	78.3	79.7	79.9
Land area, percent of U.S. land area	10.9	16.0	19.9	19.9	19.9
Nonmetropolitan areas, population (1,000)	63,822	57,115	49,180	50,465	53,410

X Not applicable.   [1] SMSA=standard metropolitan statistical area. Areas are as defined June 30, 1981.   [2] Areas are as defined June 30, 1998.   [3] Percent change from 1960.

Source: U.S. Census Bureau, *U.S. Census of Population: 1970; 1990 Census of Population and Housing, Supplementary Reports, Metropolitan Areas as Defined by the Office of Management and Budget, June 30, 1993* (1990 CPH-S-1-1); *1990 Census of Population and Housing, Population and Housing Unit Counts* (CPH-2-1); "MA-96-5 Estimates of the Population of Metropolitan Areas: Annual Time Series, July 1, 1991 to July 1, 1996"; published: December 1997; <http://www.census.gov/population/estimates/metro-city/ma96-05.txt>; and unpublished data.

No. 41. Number and Population of Metropolitan Areas, by Population Size of Area in 1996: 1990 and 1996

[As of **April 1** for **1990** and as of **July** for **1996 (198.3 represents 198,300,000)**. Data exclude Puerto Rico. CMSA=consolidated metropolitan statistical area. MSA=metropolitan statistical area. PMSA=primary metropolitan statistical area. Areas are as defined by U.S. Office of Management and Budget, June 30, 1998. For area definitions, see Appendix II]

Population size of metropolitan area in 1996	CMSAs and MSAs				MSAs and PMSAs		
	Number	Population, 1990 (mil.)	Population, 1996		Number	Population, 1996	
			Total (mil.)	Percent in each class		Total (mil.)	Percent in each class
Total, all metropolitan areas . . .	274	198.2	211.9	100	329	211.9	100
1,000,000 or more	47	139.2	148.6	70	59	134.7	63
2,500,000 or more	18	101.3	107.4	51	17	72.0	34
1,000,000 to 2,499,999	29	37.9	41.2	19	42	62.7	29
250,000 to 999,999	93	40.9	43.9	21	116	54.2	26
500,000 to 999,999	29	19.4	20.7	10	37	25.5	12
250,000 to 499,999	64	21.5	23.2	11	79	28.7	14
100,000 to 249,999	114	16.4	17.6	8	134	21.3	10
Less than 100,000	20	1.6	1.7	1	20	1.7	1

Source: U.S. Census Bureau, *1990 Census of Population and Housing, Supplementary Reports, Metropolitan Areas as Defined by the Office of Management and Budget, June 30, 1993*, (1990 CPH-S-1-1); and *1990 Census of Population and Housing, Population and Housing Unit Counts* (CPH-2-1); and "MA-96-7 Estimates of the Population of Metropolitan Areas (alphabetical list): July 1, 1996"; published: December 1997; <http://www.census.gov/population/estimates/metro-city/ma96-07.txt>.

U.S. Census Bureau, Statistical Abstract of the United States: 1999

No. 42. Metropolitan and Nonmetropolitan Area Population by State: 1980 to 1996

[As of **April 1**, except **1996**, as of **July (177,361 represents 177,361,000)**. Metropolitan refers to 256 metropolitan statistical areas and 18 consolidated metropolitan statistical areas as defined by U.S. Office of Management and Budget, June 30, 1998; nonmetropolitan is the area outside metropolitan areas; see Appendix II. Minus sign (-) indicates decrease]

State	Metropolitan population						Nonmetropolitan population					
	Total (1,000)			Percent change, 1990-96	Percent of state		Total (1,000)			Percent change, 1990-96	Percent of state	
	1980	1990	1996		1990	1996	1980	1990	1996		1990	1996
U.S.	177,361	198,249	211,874	6.9	79.7	79.9	49,180	50,465	53,410	5.8	20.3	20.1
AL.......	2,560	2,710	2,894	6.8	67.1	67.7	1,334	1,331	1,379	3.6	32.9	32.3
AK.......	174	226	251	11.1	41.1	41.3	227	324	357	10.2	58.9	58.7
AZ.......	2,339	3,202	3,878	21.1	87.4	87.6	378	463	550	18.8	12.6	12.4
AR.......	1,026	1,109	1,212	9.3	47.2	48.3	1,260	1,242	1,298	4.5	52.8	51.7
CA.......	22,907	28,797	30,809	7.0	96.8	96.6	760	961	1,069	11.2	3.2	3.4
CO	2,408	2,779	3,212	15.6	84.4	84.0	482	515	611	18.6	15.6	16.0
CT......	2,982	3,148	3,130	-0.6	95.8	95.6	126	140	144	2.9	4.2	4.4
DE......	496	553	594	7.4	83.0	81.9	98	113	131	15.9	17.0	18.1
DC	638	607	543	-10.5	100.0	100.0	(X)	(X)	(X)	(X)	(X)	(X)
FL......	9,039	12,024	13,381	11.3	92.9	92.9	708	915	1,019	11.4	7.1	7.1
GA	3,507	4,351	5,037	15.8	67.2	68.5	1,956	2,127	2,316	8.9	32.8	31.5
HI......	763	836	872	4.3	75.5	73.6	202	272	312	14.7	24.5	26.4
ID......	322	362	446	23.2	35.9	37.5	622	645	743	15.2	64.1	62.5
IL	9,461	9,574	9,964	4.1	83.8	84.1	1,967	1,857	1,883	1.4	16.2	15.9
IN	3,885	3,962	4,187	5.7	71.5	71.7	1,605	1,582	1,653	4.5	28.5	28.3
IA	1,198	1,200	1,264	5.3	43.2	44.3	1,716	1,577	1,587	0.6	56.8	55.7
KS......	1,184	1,333	1,425	6.9	53.8	55.4	1,180	1,145	1,147	0.2	46.2	44.6
KY......	1,735	1,780	1,873	5.2	48.3	48.2	1,925	1,907	2,010	5.4	51.7	51.8
LA......	3,125	3,160	3,271	3.5	74.9	75.2	1,082	1,061	1,080	1.8	25.1	24.8
ME	405	443	445	0.5	36.1	35.8	721	785	798	1.7	63.9	64.2
MD	3,920	4,438	4,704	6.0	92.8	92.8	297	343	367	7.0	7.2	7.2
MA	5,530	5,788	5,855	1.2	96.2	96.1	207	229	237	3.5	3.8	3.9
MI	7,719	7,698	7,911	2.8	82.8	82.4	1,543	1,598	1,684	5.4	17.2	17.6
MN	2,674	3,011	3,247	7.8	68.8	69.7	1,402	1,364	1,410	3.4	31.2	30.3
MS	806	874	960	9.8	34.0	35.3	1,715	1,701	1,756	3.2	66.0	64.7
MO	3,314	3,491	3,644	4.4	68.2	68.0	1,603	1,626	1,715	5.5	31.8	32.0
MT......	265	270	296	9.6	33.8	33.7	522	529	583	10.2	66.2	66.3
NE......	728	787	847	7.6	49.9	51.3	842	791	805	1.8	50.1	48.7
NV......	666	1,014	1,374	35.5	84.4	85.7	135	188	230	22.3	15.6	14.3
NH	535	659	695	5.5	59.4	59.8	386	450	467	3.8	40.6	40.2
NJ......	7,365	7,730	7,988	3.3	100.0	100.0	(X)	(X)	(X)	(X)	(X)	(X)
NM......	675	842	971	15.3	55.6	56.7	628	673	742	10.3	44.4	43.3
NY......	16,144	16,516	16,691	1.1	91.8	91.8	1,414	1,475	1,494	1.3	8.2	8.2
NC	3,749	4,380	4,893	11.7	66.0	66.8	2,131	2,253	2,430	7.9	34.0	33.2
ND	234	257	275	7.0	40.3	42.7	418	381	369	-3.1	59.7	57.3
OH	8,791	8,826	9,056	2.6	81.4	81.1	2,007	2,021	2,117	4.8	18.6	18.9
OK	1,724	1,870	1,988	6.3	59.4	60.2	1,301	1,276	1,313	2.9	40.6	39.8
OR	1,799	1,985	2,249	13.3	69.8	70.2	834	858	955	11.3	30.2	29.8
PA......	10,067	10,084	10,194	1.1	84.9	84.6	1,798	1,799	1,862	3.5	15.1	15.4
RI......	886	938	929	-1.0	93.5	93.8	61	65	61	-6.2	6.5	6.2
SC......	2,114	2,422	2,574	6.3	69.5	69.6	1,006	1,064	1,125	5.7	30.5	30.4
SD......	194	221	244	10.4	31.7	33.3	497	475	489	2.9	68.3	66.7
TN......	3,058	3,311	3,617	9.2	67.9	68.0	1,533	1,567	1,702	8.6	32.1	32.0
TX......	11,539	14,166	16,099	13.6	83.4	84.2	2,686	2,821	3,029	7.4	16.6	15.8
UT......	1,132	1,341	1,543	15.1	77.8	77.1	329	382	457	19.6	22.2	22.9
VT......	133	152	163	7.2	26.9	27.7	378	411	426	3.6	73.1	72.3
VA......	3,966	4,775	5,198	8.9	77.2	77.9	1,381	1,414	1,477	4.5	22.8	22.1
WA	3,366	4,036	4,580	13.5	82.9	82.8	766	830	953	14.8	17.1	17.2
WV	796	748	764	2.1	41.7	41.8	1,155	1,045	1,062	1.6	58.3	58.2
WI......	3,176	3,331	3,495	4.9	68.1	67.7	1,530	1,561	1,665	6.7	31.9	32.3
WY	141	134	143	6.7	29.6	29.7	329	319	338	6.0	70.4	70.3

X Not applicable.

Source: U.S. Census Bureau, *1990 Census of Population and Housing, Supplementary Reports, Metropolitan Areas as Defined by the Office of Management and Budget, June 30, 1993*, (1990 CPH-S-1-1); *1990 Census of Population and Housing, Population and Housing Unit Counts* (CPH-2-1); and unpublished data.

No. 43. Large Metropolitan Areas—Population: 1980 to 1996

[In thousands, except percent (825 represents 825,000). As of April 1, except as noted. Covers 18 consolidated metropolitan statistical areas (CMSAs), their 73 component primary metropolitan statistical areas (PMSAs), and the remaining 122 MSAs with 250,000 and over population in 1996 as defined by the U.S. Office of Management and Budget as of June 30, 1998. For definitions and components of all metropolitan areas and population of NECMAs (New England County Metropolitan Areas), see Appendix II. Minus sign (-) indicates decrease]

Metropolitan area	Number (1,000)					Rank, 1996	Percent change	
	1980	1990 [1]	1994 (July)	1995 (July)	1996 (July)		1980-90	1990-96
Albany-Schenectady-Troy, NY MSA	825	862	882	881	879	54	4.5	2.0
Albuquerque, NM MSA	485	589	647	661	670	62	21.4	13.7
Allentown-Bethlehem-Easton, PA MSA	551	595	612	613	614	67	8.0	3.2
Anchorage, AK MSA	174	226	252	251	251	140	29.8	10.7
Appleton-Oshkosh-Neenah, WI MSA	291	315	332	336	341	114	8.2	8.1
Atlanta, GA MSA	2,233	2,960	3,338	3,441	3,541	11	32.5	19.7
Augusta-Aiken, GA-SC MSA	363	415	449	453	454	85	14.2	9.2
Austin-San Marcos, TX MSA	585	846	969	1,007	1,041	43	44.6	23.1
Bakersfield, CA MSA	403	545	611	616	623	65	35.2	14.3
Baton Rouge, LA MSA	494	528	558	563	567	71	6.9	7.4
Beaumont-Port Arthur, TX MSA	373	361	374	376	376	104	-3.2	4.0
Biloxi-Gulfport-Pascagoula, MS MSA	300	312	338	342	343	113	4.1	9.9
Binghamton, NY MSA	263	264	262	258	254	139	0.4	-3.9
Birmingham, AL MSA	815	840	880	888	895	53	3.0	6.5
Boise City, ID MSA	257	296	349	361	373	105	15.2	25.9
Boston-Worcester-Lawrence, MA-NH-ME-CT CMSA	5,122	5,455	5,497	5,534	5,563	7	6.5	2.0
Boston, MA-NH PMSA	3,149	3,228	3,231	3,252	3,263	(X)	2.5	1.1
Brockton, MA PMSA	225	236	242	244	246	(X)	5.1	4.1
Fitchburg-Leominster, MA PMSA	125	138	139	139	139	(X)	10.5	0.9
Lawrence, MA-NH PMSA	298	353	363	368	373	(X)	18.4	5.5
Lowell, MA-NH PMSA	249	281	286	288	291	(X)	12.5	3.6
Manchester, NH PMSA	146	174	178	180	182	(X)	18.9	4.8
Nashua, NH PMSA	134	168	174	176	178	(X)	25.4	6.0
New Bedford, MA PMSA	167	176	175	175	175	(X)	5.4	-0.3
Portsmouth-Rochester, NH-ME PMSA	189	223	226	228	231	(X)	18.0	3.3
Worcester, MA-CT PMSA	439	478	483	483	485	(X)	8.9	1.4
Brownsville-Harlingen-San Benito, TX MSA	210	260	299	308	315	119	24.0	21.1
Buffalo-Niagara Falls, NY MSA	1,243	1,189	1,188	1,182	1,175	36	-4.3	-1.2
Canton-Massillon, OH MSA	404	394	402	402	403	97	-2.6	2.2
Charleston-North Charleston, SC MSA	430	507	516	501	495	78	17.8	-2.3
Charleston, WV MSA	270	250	255	255	255	138	-7.1	1.6
Charlotte-Gastonia-Rock Hill, NC-SC MSA	971	1,162	1,261	1,290	1,321	32	19.6	13.7
Chattanooga, TN-GA MSA	418	424	439	443	446	88	1.6	5.1
Chicago-Gary-Kenosha, IL-IN-WI CMSA	8,115	8,240	8,501	8,547	8,600	3	1.5	4.4
Chicago, IL PMSA	7,246	7,411	7,644	7,686	7,734	(X)	2.3	4.4
Gary, IN PMSA	643	605	618	621	622	(X)	-5.9	2.9
Kankakee, IL PMSA	103	96	101	101	102	(X)	-6.5	5.9
Kenosha, WI PMSA	123	128	138	140	142	(X)	4.1	10.5
Cincinnati-Hamilton, OH-KY-IN CMSA	1,726	1,818	1,895	1,908	1,921	23	5.3	5.7
Cincinnati, OH-KY-IN PMSA	1,468	1,526	1,579	1,588	1,597	(X)	4.0	4.7
Hamilton-Middletown, OH PMSA	259	291	316	320	324	(X)	12.6	11.0
Cleveland-Akron, OH CMSA	2,938	2,860	2,905	2,908	2,913	14	-2.7	1.9
Akron, OH PMSA	660	658	673	676	680	(X)	-0.4	3.4
Cleveland-Lorain-Elyria, OH PMSA	2,278	2,202	2,232	2,232	2,233	(X)	-3.3	1.4
Colorado Springs, CO MSA	309	397	454	465	473	81	28.3	19.1
Columbia, SC MSA	410	454	474	481	488	79	10.7	7.6
Columbus, GA-AL MSA	255	261	273	272	272	134	2.4	4.4
Columbus, OH MSA	1,214	1,345	1,421	1,434	1,448	30	10.8	7.6
Corpus Christi, TX MSA	326	350	376	380	384	101	7.3	9.8
Dallas-Fort Worth, TX CMSA	3,046	4,037	4,378	4,470	4,575	9	32.5	13.3
Dallas, TX PMSA	2,055	2,676	2,911	2,975	3,048	(X)	30.2	13.9
Fort Worth-Arlington, TX PMSA	991	1,361	1,467	1,496	1,527	(X)	37.4	12.2
Davenport-Moline-Rock Island, IA-IL MSA	385	351	357	358	358	108	-8.8	2.0
Dayton-Springfield, OH MSA	942	951	954	952	951	50	1.0	-0.1
Daytona Beach, FL MSA	270	399	443	450	456	83	48.1	14.3
Denver-Boulder-Greeley, CO CMSA	1,742	1,980	2,190	2,233	2,277	20	13.7	15.0
Boulder-Longmont, CO PMSA	190	225	250	254	258	(X)	18.8	14.6
Denver, CO PMSA	1,429	1,623	1,795	1,830	1,867	(X)	13.6	15.0
Greeley, CO PMSA	123	132	145	149	152	(X)	6.8	15.5
Des Moines, IA MSA	368	393	417	423	427	92	6.9	8.8
Detroit-Ann Arbor-Flint, MI CMSA	5,293	5,187	5,239	5,260	5,284	8	-2.0	1.9
Ann Arbor, MI PMSA	455	490	513	521	530	(X)	7.7	8.1
Detroit, MI PMSA	4,388	4,267	4,293	4,305	4,318	(X)	-2.8	1.2
Flint, MI PMSA	450	430	432	434	436	(X)	-4.4	1.3
El Paso, TX MSA	480	592	667	679	684	60	23.3	15.7
Erie, PA MSA	280	276	281	281	281	133	-1.5	1.8
Eugene-Springfield, OR MSA	275	283	299	303	307	123	2.8	8.5
Evansville-Henderson, IN-KY MSA	276	279	287	287	289	128	1.0	3.5
Fayetteville, NC MSA	247	275	284	285	285	131	11.1	3.7
Fayetteville-Springdale-Rogers, AR MSA	179	211	243	253	261	135	18.1	23.7
Fort Myers-Cape Coral, FL MSA	205	335	368	375	380	102	63.3	13.4
Fort Pierce-Port St. Lucie, FL MSA	151	251	278	282	287	129	66.1	14.4
Fort Wayne, IN MSA	445	456	469	472	475	80	2.6	4.2
Fresno, CA MSA	578	756	839	848	862	56	30.8	14.1

See footnotes at end of table.

Population 41

[See headnote, page 41]

Metropolitan area	Number (1,000)					Rank, 1996	Percent change	
	1980	1990 [1]	1994 (July)	1995 (July)	1996 (July)		1980-90	1990-96
Grand Rapids-Muskegon-Holland, MI MSA	841	938	990	1,003	1,015	46	11.5	8.2
Greensboro—Winston-Salem—High Point, NC MSA .	951	1,050	1,109	1,125	1,141	38	10.5	8.7
Greenville-Spartanburg-Anderson, SC MSA	744	831	873	884	897	52	11.6	8.0
Harrisburg-Lebanon-Carlisle, PA MSA	556	588	610	612	615	66	5.7	4.6
Hartford, CT MSA	1,081	1,158	1,149	1,145	1,145	37	7.1	-1.1
Hickory-Morganton, NC MSA	270	292	306	311	315	120	8.1	7.7
Honolulu, HI MSA	763	836	869	871	872	55	9.7	4.2
Houston-Galveston-Brazoria, TX CMSA	3,118	3,731	4,108	4,178	4,253	10	19.6	14.0
Brazoria, TX PMSA	170	192	213	216	221	(X)	13.0	15.2
Galveston-Texas City, TX PMSA	196	217	235	238	241	(X)	11.1	10.7
Houston, TX PMSA	2,753	3,322	3,660	3,724	3,792	(X)	20.7	14.1
Huntington-Ashland, WV-KY-OH MSA	336	313	317	317	317	118	-7.1	1.3
Huntsville, AL MSA	243	293	328	328	330	116	20.6	12.7
Indianapolis, IN MSA	1,306	1,380	1,460	1,476	1,492	28	5.7	8.1
Jackson, MS MSA	362	395	412	416	421	93	9.2	6.5
Jacksonville, FL MSA	722	907	972	982	1,009	47	25.5	11.2
Johnson City-Kingsport-Bristol, TN-VA MSA	434	436	450	454	458	82	0.6	5.1
Kalamazoo-Battle Creek, MI MSA	421	429	440	442	444	89	2.1	3.5
Kansas City, MO-KS MSA	1,449	1,583	1,658	1,673	1,690	24	9.2	6.8
Killeen-Temple, TX MSA	215	255	289	292	297	126	19.0	16.3
Knoxville, TN MSA	546	586	630	641	649	63	7.2	10.8
Lafayette, LA MSA	331	345	361	365	369	106	4.3	6.8
Lakeland-Winter Haven, FL MSA	322	405	430	436	441	91	26.0	8.8
Lancaster, PA MSA	362	423	443	448	451	86	16.7	6.6
Lansing-East Lansing, MI MSA	420	433	445	446	448	87	3.1	3.4
Las Vegas, NV-AZ MSA	528	853	1,082	1,143	1,201	35	61.5	40.9
Lexington, KY MSA	371	406	431	435	441	90	9.4	8.7
Little Rock-North Little Rock, AR MSA	474	513	538	543	548	72	8.1	6.9
Los Angeles-Riverside-Orange County, CA CMSA . .	11,498	14,532	15,266	15,353	15,495	2	26.4	6.6
Los Angeles-Long Beach, CA PMSA	7,477	8,863	9,081	9,078	9,128	(X)	18.5	3.0
Orange County, CA PMSA	1,933	2,411	2,564	2,599	2,637	(X)	24.7	9.4
Riverside-San Bernardino, CA PMSA	1,558	2,589	2,920	2,969	3,016	(X)	66.1	16.5
Ventura, CA PMSA	529	669	701	707	715	(X)	26.4	6.8
Louisville, KY-IN MSA	954	949	981	986	992	49	-0.5	4.5
Macon, GA MSA	273	291	307	309	313	122	6.6	7.4
Madison, WI MSA	324	367	390	393	395	98	13.5	7.7
McAllen-Edinburg-Mission, TX MSA	283	384	465	482	496	77	35.4	29.2
Melbourne-Titusville-Palm Bay, FL MSA	273	399	443	450	454	84	46.2	13.8
Memphis, TN-AR-MS MSA	939	1,007	1,055	1,067	1,078	42	7.3	7.0
Miami-Fort Lauderdale, FL CMSA	2,644	3,193	3,397	3,459	3,514	12	20.8	10.1
Fort Lauderdale, FL PMSA	1,018	1,256	1,386	1,413	1,438	(X)	23.3	14.6
Miami, FL PMSA	1,626	1,937	2,012	2,046	2,076	(X)	19.2	7.2
Milwaukee-Racine, WI CMSA	1,570	1,607	1,637	1,639	1,643	25	2.4	2.2
Milwaukee-Waukesha, WI PMSA	1,397	1,432	1,454	1,455	1,458	(X)	2.5	1.8
Racine, WI PMSA	173	175	183	184	185	(X)	1.1	5.7
Minneapolis-St. Paul, MN-WI MSA	2,198	2,539	2,693	2,730	2,765	15	15.5	8.9
Mobile, AL MSA	444	477	509	514	519	75	7.5	8.8
Modesto, CA MSA	266	371	407	411	416	94	39.3	12.2
Montgomery, AL MSA	273	293	309	312	315	121	7.3	7.7
Nashville, TN MSA	851	985	1,071	1,095	1,117	40	15.8	13.4
New London-Norwich, CT-RI MSA	273	291	285	286	287	130	6.5	-1.4
New Orleans, LA MSA	1,304	1,285	1,310	1,314	1,313	33	-1.5	2.1
New York-Northern New Jersey-Long Island, NY-NJ-CT-PA CMSA	18,906	19,550	19,820	19,881	19,938	1	3.4	2.0
Bergen-Passaic, NJ PMSA	1,293	1,279	1,301	1,307	1,311	(X)	-1.1	2.6
Bridgeport, CT PMSA	439	444	442	443	444	(X)	1.2	0.0
Danbury, CT PMSA	175	194	196	198	199	(X)	10.3	3.0
Dutchess County, NY PMSA	245	259	261	262	263	(X)	5.9	1.2
Jersey City, NJ PMSA	557	553	551	551	551	(X)	-0.7	-0.4
Middlesex-Somerset-Hunterdon, NJ PMSA . .	886	1,020	1,068	1,079	1,091	(X)	15.1	7.0
Monmouth-Ocean, NJ PMSA	849	986	1,036	1,051	1,065	(X)	16.1	8.0
Nassau-Suffolk, NY PMSA	2,606	2,609	2,649	2,655	2,660	(X)	0.1	2.0
New Haven-Meriden, CT PMSA	500	530	527	524	524	(X)	5.9	-1.2
New York, NY PMSA	8,275	8,547	8,616	8,631	8,643	(X)	3.3	1.1
Newark, NJ PMSA	1,964	1,916	1,935	1,938	1,940	(X)	-2.4	1.3
Newburgh, NY-PA PMSA	278	336	355	359	363	(X)	20.8	8.0
Stamford-Norwalk, CT PMSA	326	330	330	331	332	(X)	1.3	0.6
Trenton, NJ PMSA	308	326	329	330	330	(X)	5.8	1.4
Waterbury, CT PMSA	205	222	222	222	222	(X)	8.1	0.1
Norfolk-Virginia Beach-Newport News, VA-NC MSA .	1,201	1,445	1,528	1,535	1,540	27	20.3	6.6
Oklahoma City, OK MSA	861	959	1,009	1,017	1,027	44	11.4	7.1
Omaha, NE-IA MSA	605	640	664	671	682	61	5.6	6.6
Orlando, FL MSA	805	1,225	1,363	1,386	1,417	31	52.2	15.7
Pensacola, FL MSA	290	344	373	378	386	99	18.9	12.0
Peoria-Pekin, IL MSA	366	339	344	346	347	112	-7.3	2.2

See footnotes at end of table.

U.S. Census Bureau, Statistical Abstract of the United States: 1999

No. 43. Metropolitan Areas—Population: 1980 to 1996—Continued

[See headnote, page 41]

Metropolitan area	Number (1,000)					Rank, 1996	Percent change	
	1980	1990 [1]	1994 (July)	1995 (July)	1996 (July)		1980-90	1990-96
Philadelphia-Wilmington-Atlantic City, PA-NJ-DE-MD CMSA	5,649	5,893	5,960	5,969	5,973	6	4.3	1.4
Atlantic-Cape May, NJ PMSA	276	319	330	332	334	(X)	15.6	4.5
Philadelphia, PA-NJ PMSA	4,781	4,922	4,951	4,953	4,953	(X)	2.9	0.6
Vineland-Millville-Bridgeton, NJ PMSA	133	138	139	138	136	(X)	3.9	-1.5
Wilmington-Newark, DE-MD PMSA	459	513	540	546	551	(X)	11.9	7.3
Phoenix-Mesa, AZ MSA	1,600	2,238	2,485	2,657	2,747	16	39.9	22.7
Pittsburgh, PA MSA	2,571	2,395	2,400	2,389	2,379	19	-6.9	-0.6
Portland-Salem, OR-WA CMSA	1,584	1,793	1,990	2,031	2,078	22	13.3	15.9
Portland-Vancouver, OR-WA PMSA	1,334	1,515	1,682	1,717	1,759	(X)	13.6	16.1
Salem, OR PMSA	250	278	308	314	319	(X)	11.3	14.9
Providence-Fall River-Warwick, RI-MA MSA	1,077	1,134	1,130	1,126	1,124	39	5.4	-0.9
Provo-Orem, UT MSA	218	264	302	311	320	117	20.9	21.3
Raleigh-Durham-Chapel Hill, NC MSA	665	858	968	997	1,025	45	29.1	19.4
Reading, PA MSA	313	337	349	350	352	110	7.7	4.7
Reno, NV MSA	194	255	284	291	299	125	31.5	17.3
Richmond-Petersburg, VA MSA	761	866	917	926	935	51	13.7	8.0
Rochester, NY MSA	1,031	1,062	1,088	1,087	1,088	41	3.1	2.4
Rockford, IL MSA	326	330	346	349	352	109	1.2	6.9
Sacramento-Yolo, CA CMSA	1,100	1,481	1,588	1,609	1,632	26	34.7	10.2
Sacramento, CA PMSA	986	1,340	1,441	1,460	1,482	(X)	35.8	10.6
Yolo, CA PMSA	113	141	146	148	150	(X)	24.6	6.2
Saginaw-Bay City-Midland, MI MSA	422	399	403	403	403	96	-5.3	1.0
St. Louis, MO-IL MSA	2,414	2,492	2,531	2,540	2,548	18	3.2	2.2
Salinas, CA MSA	290	356	333	334	339	115	22.5	-4.7
Salt Lake City-Ogden, UT MSA	910	1,072	1,178	1,197	1,218	34	17.8	13.6
San Antonio, TX MSA	1,089	1,325	1,433	1,463	1,490	29	21.7	12.5
San Diego, CA MSA	1,862	2,498	2,615	2,627	2,655	17	34.2	6.3
San Francisco-Oakland-San Jose, CA CMSA	5,368	6,250	6,502	6,543	6,605	5	16.4	5.7
Oakland, CA PMSA	1,762	2,080	2,180	2,193	2,210	(X)	18.1	6.2
San Francisco, CA PMSA	1,489	1,604	1,639	1,645	1,655	(X)	7.7	3.2
San Jose, CA PMSA	1,295	1,498	1,555	1,574	1,600	(X)	15.6	6.8
Santa Cruz-Watsonville, CA PMSA	188	230	235	236	238	(X)	22.1	3.5
Santa Rosa, CA PMSA	300	388	412	416	421	(X)	29.5	8.4
Vallejo-Fairfield-Napa, CA PMSA	334	450	480	479	482	(X)	34.6	7.1
Santa Barbara-Santa Maria-Lompoc, CA MSA	299	370	384	384	386	100	23.7	4.3
Sarasota-Bradenton, FL MSA	351	489	519	525	529	74	39.6	8.0
Savannah, GA MSA	231	258	276	280	283	132	11.8	9.6
Scranton—Wilkes-Barre—Hazleton, PA MSA	659	639	636	632	628	64	-3.2	-1.6
Seattle-Tacoma-Bremerton, WA CMSA	2,409	2,970	3,222	3,272	3,321	13	23.3	11.8
Bremerton, WA PMSA	147	190	217	226	232	(X)	28.9	22.1
Olympia, WA PMSA	124	161	188	193	197	(X)	29.8	22.2
Seattle-Bellevue-Everett, WA PMSA	1,652	2,033	2,179	2,204	2,235	(X)	23.1	9.9
Tacoma, WA PMSA	486	586	639	649	657	(X)	20.7	12.1
Shreveport-Bossier City, LA MSA	377	376	378	379	380	103	-0.1	0.9
South Bend, IN MSA	242	247	255	257	258	137	2.2	4.3
Spokane, WA MSA	342	361	397	402	405	95	5.7	12.1
Springfield, MO MSA	228	264	288	294	296	127	15.9	12.1
Springfield, MA MSA	570	588	581	578	577	70	3.2	-1.9
Stockton-Lodi, CA MSA	347	481	519	526	533	73	38.4	11.0
Syracuse, NY MSA	723	742	752	749	746	59	2.7	0.5
Tallahassee, FL MSA	190	234	255	257	259	136	22.7	11.0
Tampa-St. Petersburg-Clearwater, FL MSA	1,614	2,068	2,159	2,181	2,199	21	28.2	6.3
Toledo, OH MSA	617	614	612	611	611	68	-0.4	-0.4
Tucson, AZ MSA	531	667	735	755	768	57	25.5	15.1
Tulsa, OK MSA	657	709	743	747	756	58	7.9	6.7
Utica-Rome, NY MSA	320	317	315	308	302	124	-1.1	-4.5
Visalia-Tulare-Porterville, CA MSA	246	312	346	348	350	111	26.9	12.2
Washington-Baltimore, DC-MD-VA-WV CMSA	5,791	6,726	7,050	7,107	7,165	4	16.2	6.5
Baltimore, MD PMSA	2,199	2,382	2,458	2,468	2,474	(X)	8.3	3.9
Hagerstown, MD PMSA	113	121	126	127	127	(X)	7.3	4.8
Washington, DC-MD-VA-WV PMSA	3,478	4,223	4,465	4,512	4,563	(X)	21.4	8.1
West Palm Beach-Boca Raton, FL MSA	577	864	958	976	993	48	49.7	15.0
Wichita, KS MSA	442	485	507	509	513	76	9.7	5.7
York, PA MSA	313	340	360	365	368	107	8.5	8.5
Youngstown-Warren, OH MSA	645	601	603	600	599	69	-6.8	-0.4

X Not applicable. [1] The April 1, 1990, census count includes resolution corrections processed through March 1996, and does not include adjustments for census coverage errors.

Source: U.S. Census Bureau, *1990 Census of Population and Housing, Supplementary Reports, Metropolitan Areas as Defined by the Office of Management and Budget, June 30, 1993* (CPH-S-1-1); *1990 Census of Population and Housing, Population and Housing Unit Counts* (CPH-2-1); "MA-96-5 Estimates of the Population of Metropolitan Areas: Annual Time Series, July 1, 1991 to July 1, 1996"; published: December 1997; <http://www.census.gov/population/estimates/metro-city/ma96-05.txt>; and unpublished data.

Population   43

No. 44. 75 Largest Metropolitan Areas—Racial and Hispanic Origin Populations: 1997

[As of July 1 (19,876 represents 19,876,000). Areas as defined by U.S. Office of Management and Budget, June 30, 1996. Covers 273 metropolitan areas: 17 consolidated metropolitan statistical area (CMSAs) and 245 metropolitan statistical areas (MSAs) located outside of New England as well as 11 New England county metropolitan areas (NECMAs) in New England. For area definitions, see Appendix II]

Metropolitan area [1]	Total population (1,000)	Percent of total metropolitan population			
		Black	American Indian, Eskimo, Aleut	Asian and Pacific Islander	Hispanic origin [2]
New York-Northern New Jersey-Long Island, NY-NJ-CT-PA CMSA/NECMA [3]	19,876	19.4	0.3	6.4	17.1
Los Angeles-Riverside-Orange County, CA CMSA	15,609	8.3	0.7	11.1	38.5
Chicago-Gary-Kenosha, IL-IN-WI CMSA	8,642	19.2	0.2	4.0	13.5
Washington-Baltimore, DC-MD-VA-WV CMSA	7,207	25.8	0.3	4.9	5.1
San Francisco-Oakland-San Jose, CA CMSA	6,701	8.8	0.7	18.2	19.1
Philadelphia-Wilmington-Atlantic City, PA-NJ-DE-MD CMSA	5,972	19.4	0.2	2.8	4.8
Boston-Worcester-Lawrence-Lowell-Brockton, MA-NH NECMA	5,828	5.8	0.2	3.5	5.3
Detroit-Ann Arbor-Flint, MI CMSA	5,439	20.8	0.4	1.9	2.4
Dallas-Fort Worth, TX CMSA	4,683	14.2	0.6	3.5	15.5
Houston-Galveston-Brazoria, TX CMSA	4,320	18.3	0.4	5.0	24.3
Atlanta, GA MSA	3,627	25.8	0.2	2.6	3.2
Miami-Fort Lauderdale, FL CMSA	3,515	19.7	0.3	1.8	37.2
Seattle-Tacoma-Bremerton, WA CMSA	3,368	5.1	1.3	7.8	4.2
Cleveland-Akron, OH CMSA	2,908	16.6	0.2	1.3	2.3
Phoenix-Mesa, AZ MSA	2,840	4.1	2.4	2.2	20.2
Minneapolis-St. Paul, MN-WI MSA	2,792	4.5	1.0	3.6	2.1
San Diego, CA MSA	2,723	6.4	0.9	10.3	25.6
St. Louis, MO-IL MSA	2,558	17.6	0.2	1.2	1.4
Pittsburgh, PA MSA	2,361	8.4	0.1	1.0	0.8
Denver-Boulder-Greeley, CO CMSA	2,318	5.3	0.8	2.8	14.3
Tampa-St. Petersburg-Clearwater, FL MSA	2,227	10.5	0.3	1.6	9.1
Portland-Salem, OR-WA CMSA	2,113	2.7	1.0	4.1	5.9
Cincinnati-Hamilton, OH-KY-IN CMSA	1,934	11.6	0.1	1.0	0.7
Kansas City, MO-KS MSA	1,709	13.3	0.5	1.5	3.7
Sacramento-Yolo, CA CMSA	1,656	7.0	1.3	9.9	14.8
Milwaukee-Racine, WI CMSA	1,637	14.9	0.6	1.6	4.8
Norfolk-Virginia Beach-Newport News, VA-NC MSA	1,545	30.1	0.4	3.3	3.0
San Antonio, TX MSA	1,511	6.5	0.4	1.7	53.2
Indianapolis, IN MSA	1,503	13.6	0.2	1.0	1.2
Orlando, FL MSA	1,467	14.1	0.4	2.5	11.1
Columbus, OH MSA	1,460	13.2	0.2	2.0	1.0
Charlotte-Gastonia-Rock Hill, NC-SC MSA	1,350	20.5	0.4	1.5	1.7
New Orleans, LA MSA	1,308	34.9	0.3	2.1	4.9
Las Vegas, NV-AZ MSA	1,262	9.1	1.2	4.3	15.1
Salt Lake City-Ogden, UT MSA	1,248	1.3	0.8	3.1	7.7
Buffalo-Niagara Falls, NY MSA	1,165	11.6	0.7	1.3	2.6
Greensboro—Winston-Salem—High Point, NC MSA	1,153	19.6	0.4	1.0	1.4
Nashville, TN MSA	1,135	15.7	0.2	1.4	1.2
Hartford, CT NECMA	1,105	9.4	0.2	2.3	8.3
Rochester, NY MSA	1,086	10.1	0.4	1.9	3.8
Memphis, TN-AR-MS MSA	1,083	42.1	0.2	1.1	1.2
Austin-San Marcos, TX MSA	1,071	10.0	0.5	3.0	25.1
Raleigh-Durham-Chapel Hill, NC MSA	1,050	24.1	0.3	2.5	2.3
Jacksonville, FL MSA	1,035	22.6	0.4	2.5	3.5
Oklahoma City, OK MSA	1,031	10.8	4.7	2.2	4.8
Grand Rapids-Muskegon-Holland, MI MSA	1,026	7.3	0.6	1.3	3.8
West Palm Beach-Boca Raton, FL MSA	1,019	14.7	0.2	1.5	10.3
Louisville, KY-IN MSA	993	13.0	0.2	0.8	0.8
Dayton-Springfield, OH MSA	945	14.5	0.2	1.3	0.9
Richmond-Petersburg, VA MSA	943	29.9	0.3	1.8	1.5
Providence-Warwick-Pawtucket, RI NECMA	905	4.9	0.5	2.3	6.6
Greenville-Spartanburg-Anderson, SC MSA	905	17.9	0.2	0.8	1.1
Birmingham, AL MSA	900	29.0	0.2	0.5	0.7
Albany-Schenectady-Troy, NY MSA	876	5.1	0.2	1.8	2.2
Honolulu, HI MSA	870	3.8	0.5	64.3	7.4
Fresno, CA MSA	869	4.9	1.3	9.3	42.0
Tucson, AZ MSA	780	3.8	3.5	2.4	28.7
Tulsa, OK MSA	764	8.6	6.6	1.1	2.8
Syracuse, NY MSA	741	6.3	0.6	1.5	1.7
El Paso, TX MSA	702	3.5	0.5	1.5	74.4
Omaha, NE-IA MSA	687	8.6	0.6	1.6	4.6
Albuquerque, NM MSA	675	3.4	5.7	2.0	38.9
Knoxville, TN MSA	654	6.4	0.3	1.1	0.9
Bakersfield, CA MSA	629	6.4	1.7	4.4	34.5
Scranton—Wilkes-Barre—Hazleton, PA MSA	622	1.0	0.1	0.7	0.8
Harrisburg-Lebanon-Carlisle, PA MSA	615	7.7	0.1	1.5	2.3
Allentown-Bethlehem-Easton, PA MSA	614	2.5	0.1	1.5	6.0
Toledo, OH MSA	612	12.3	0.3	1.3	4.0
Youngstown-Warren, OH MSA	595	10.3	0.2	0.5	1.6
Springfield, MA NECMA	591	7.8	0.2	2.0	10.0
Baton Rouge, LA MSA	570	31.2	0.2	1.3	1.7
Little Rock-North Little Rock, AR MSA	552	20.9	0.3	0.8	1.7
Stockton-Lodi, CA MSA	543	5.7	1.1	15.3	28.4
Sarasota-Bradenton, FL MSA	539	7.0	0.3	0.8	4.4
Wichita, KS MSA	531	8.1	1.1	2.4	5.6

[1] Metropolitan areas are shown in rank order of total population. [2] Persons of Hispanic origin may be of any race. [3] Includes data for New Haven-Bridgeport-Stamford-Waterbury-Danbury, CT NECMA.

Source: U.S. Census Bureau, unpublished data.

U.S. Census Bureau, Statistical Abstract of the United States: 1999

No. 45. Metropolitan Areas With Large Numbers of Selected Racial Groups and of Hispanic Origin Population: 1997

[As of July 1 (3,856 represents 3,856,000). For Black, Hispanic origin, and Asian and Pacific Islander populations, areas selected had 100,000 or more of specified group; for American Indian, Eskimo, and Aleut population, areas selected are ten areas with largest number of that group. See headnote, Table 44]

BLACK

Metropolitan area	Number of specified group (1,000)	Percent of total metro. area
New York-Northern New Jersey-Long Island, NY-NJ-CT-PA CMSA/NECMA [2]	3,856	19.4
Washington-Baltimore, DC-MD-VA-WV CMSA	1,858	25.8
Chicago-Gary-Kenosha, IL-IN-WI CMSA	1,662	19.2
Los Angeles-Riverside-Orange County, CA CMSA	1,301	8.3
Philadelphia-Wilmington-Atlantic City, PA-NJ-DE-MD CMSA	1,162	19.4
Detroit-Ann Arbor-Flint, MI CMSA	1,133	20.8
Atlanta, GA MSA	937	25.8
Houston-Galveston-Brazoria, TX CMSA	790	18.3
Miami-Fort Lauderdale, FL CMSA	691	19.7
Dallas-Fort Worth, TX CMSA	664	14.2
San Francisco-Oakland-San Jose, CA CMSA	591	8.8
Cleveland-Akron, OH CMSA	484	16.6
Norfolk-Virginia Beach-Newport News, VA-NC MSA	465	30.1
New Orleans, LA MSA	456	34.9
Memphis, TN-AR-MS MSA	456	42.1
St. Louis, MO-IL MSA	451	17.6
Boston-Worcester-Lawrence-Lowell-Brockton, MA-NH NECMA	336	5.8
Richmond-Petersburg, VA MSA	282	29.9
Charlotte-Gastonia-Rock Hill, NC-SC MSA	276	20.5
Birmingham, AL MSA	261	29.0
Raleigh-Durham-Chapel Hill, NC MSA	253	24.1
Milwaukee-Racine, WI CMSA	245	14.9
Jacksonville, FL MSA	233	22.6
Tampa-St. Petersburg-Clearwater, FL MSA	233	10.5
Kansas City, MO-KS MSA	228	13.3
Greensboro—Winston-Salem—High Point, NC MSA	226	19.6
Cincinnati-Hamilton, OH-KY-IN CMSA	224	11.6
Orlando, FL MSA	207	14.1
Indianapolis, IN MSA	205	13.6
Pittsburgh, PA MSA	198	8.4
Columbus, OH MSA	193	13.2
Jackson, MS MSA	184	43.3
Nashville, TN MSA	178	15.7
Baton Rouge, LA MSA	178	31.2
San Diego, CA MSA	175	6.4
Seattle-Tacoma-Bremerton, WA CMSA	171	5.1
Greenville-Spartanburg-Anderson, SC MSA	162	17.9
Charleston-North Charleston, SC MSA	158	30.9
Columbia, SC MSA	152	30.1
Augusta-Aiken, GA-SC MSA	151	33.1
West Palm Beach-Boca Raton, FL MSA	150	14.7
Mobile, AL MSA	148	28.0
Shreveport-Bossier City, LA MSA	138	36.4
Dayton-Springfield, OH MSA	137	14.5
Buffalo-Niagara Falls, NY MSA	135	11.6
Louisville, KY-IN MSA	129	13.0
Minneapolis-St. Paul, MN-WI MSA	126	4.5
Macon, GA MSA	122	38.6
Denver-Boulder-Greeley, CO CMSA	122	5.3
Montgomery, AL MSA	117	36.7
Sacramento-Yolo, CA CMSA	115	7.0
Phoenix-Mesa, AZ MSA	115	4.1
Little Rock-North Little Rock, AR MSA	115	20.9
Las Vegas, NV-AZ MSA	115	9.1
Oklahoma City, OK MSA	112	10.8
Rochester, NY MSA	109	10.1
Columbus, GA-AL MSA	109	40.0
Lafayette, LA MSA	109	29.2
Austin-San Marcos, TX MSA	107	10.0
Savannah, GA MSA	105	37.1
Hartford, CT NECMA	104	9.4

HISPANIC ORIGIN [1]

Metropolitan area	Number of specified group (1,000)	Percent of total metro. area
Los Angeles-Riverside-Orange County, CA CMSA	6,002	38.5
New York-Northern New Jersey-Long Island, NY-NJ-CT-PA CMSA/NECMA [2]	3,392	17.1
Miami-Fort Lauderdale, FL CMSA	1,308	37.2
San Francisco-Oakland-San Jose, CA CMSA	1,283	19.1
Chicago-Gary-Kenosha, IL-IN-WI CMSA	1,169	13.5
Houston-Galveston-Brazoria, TX CMSA	1,050	24.3
San Antonio, TX MSA	804	53.2
Dallas-Fort Worth, TX CMSA	727	15.5
San Diego, CA MSA	697	25.6
Phoenix-Mesa, AZ MSA	575	20.2
El Paso, TX MSA	522	74.4
McAllen-Edinburg-Mission, TX MSA	449	87.8
Washington-Baltimore, DC-MD-VA-WV CMSA	370	5.1
Fresno, CA MSA	365	42.0
Denver-Boulder-Greeley, CO CMSA	331	14.3
Boston-Worcester-Lawrence-Lowell-Brockton, MA-NH NECMA	306	5.3
Philadelphia-Wilmington-Atlantic City, PA-NJ-DE-MD CMSA	287	4.8
Brownsville-Harlingen-San Benito, TX MSA	273	85.0
Austin-San Marcos, TX MSA	269	25.1
Albuquerque, NM MSA	262	38.9
Sacramento-Yolo, CA CMSA	246	14.8
Tucson, AZ MSA	224	28.7
Corpus Christi, TX MSA	223	57.7
Bakersfield, CA MSA	217	34.5
Tampa-St. Petersburg-Clearwater, FL MSA	203	9.1
Las Vegas, NV-AZ MSA	190	15.1
Laredo, TX MSA	174	95.1
Orlando, FL MSA	163	11.1
Visalia-Tulare-Porterville, CA MSA	162	45.8
Stockton-Lodi, CA MSA	154	28.4
Salinas, CA MSA	146	40.4
Seattle-Tacoma-Bremerton, WA CMSA	140	4.2
Detroit-Ann Arbor-Flint, MI CMSA	132	2.4
Santa Barbara-Santa Maria-Lompoc, CA MSA	128	32.8
Portland-Salem, OR-WA CMSA	124	5.9
Atlanta, GA MSA	117	3.2
Modesto, CA MSA	116	27.4
West Palm Beach-Boca Raton, FL MSA	105	10.3

ASIAN AND PACIFIC ISLANDER

Metropolitan area	Number of specified group (1,000)	Percent of total metro. area
Los Angeles-Riverside-Orange County, CA CMSA	1,733	11.1
New York-Northern New Jersey-Long Island, NY-NJ-CT-PA CMSA/NECMA [2]	1,276	6.4
San Francisco-Oakland-San Jose, CA CMSA	1,222	18.2
Honolulu, HI MSA	560	64.3
Washington-Baltimore, DC-MD-VA-WV CMSA	354	4.9
Chicago-Gary-Kenosha, IL-IN-WI CMSA	347	4.0
San Diego, CA MSA	280	10.3
Seattle-Tacoma-Bremerton, WA CMSA	264	7.8
Houston-Galveston-Brazoria, TX CMSA	216	5.0
Boston-Worcester-Lawrence-Lowell-Brockton, MA-NH NECMA	204	3.5
Philadelphia-Wilmington-Atlantic City, PA-NJ-DE-MD CMSA	170	2.8
Dallas-Fort Worth, TX CMSA	164	3.5
Sacramento-Yolo, CA CMSA	163	9.9
Detroit-Ann Arbor-Flint, MI CMSA	105	1.9

AMERICAN INDIAN, ESKIMO, ALEUT

Metropolitan area	Number of specified group (1,000)	Percent of total metro. area
Los Angeles-Riverside-Orange County, CA CMSA	113	0.7
Phoenix-Mesa, AZ MSA	67	2.4
New York-Northern New Jersey-Long Island, NY-NJ-CT-PA CMSA/NECMA [2]	62	0.3
Tulsa, OK MSA	51	6.6
San Francisco-Oakland-San Jose, CA CMSA	49	0.7
Oklahoma City, OK MSA	48	4.7
Seattle-Tacoma-Bremerton, WA CMSA	45	1.3
Albuquerque, NM MSA	39	5.7
Flagstaff, AZ-UT MSA	34	28.4
Dallas-Fort Worth, TX CMSA	28	0.6

[1] Persons of Hispanic origin may be of any race. [2] Includes data for New Haven-Bridgeport-Stamford-Waterbury-Danbury, CT NECMA.

Source: U.S. Census Bureau, unpublished data.

Population 45

No. 46. Urban and Rural Population, 1960 to 1990, and by State, 1990

[In thousands, except percent (179,323 represents 179,323,000). As of April 1. Resident population]

State	Urban Total	Urban Number	Urban Percent	Rural	State	Urban Total	Urban Number	Urban Percent	Rural
1960	179,323	125,269	69.9	54,054	MN	4,375	3,056	69.9	1,319
1970	¹203,212	149,647	73.6	53,565	MS	2,573	1,211	47.1	1,362
1980	²226,546	167,051	73.7	59,495					
1990, total	²248,710	187,053	75.2	61,656	MO	5,117	3,516	68.7	1,601
					MT	799	420	52.5	379
AL	4,041	2,440	60.4	1,601	NE	1,578	1,044	66.1	534
AK	550	371	67.5	179	NV	1,202	1,061	88.3	140
AZ	3,665	3,207	87.5	458	NH	1,109	566	51.0	544
AR	2,351	1,258	53.5	1,093					
CA	29,760	27,571	92.6	2,189	NJ	7,730	6,910	89.4	820
					NM	1,515	1,106	73.0	409
CO	3,294	2,716	82.4	579	NY	17,990	15,164	84.3	2,826
CT	3,287	2,602	79.1	686	NC	6,629	3,338	50.4	3,291
DE	666	487	73.0	180	ND	639	340	53.3	298
DC	607	607	100.0	-					
FL	12,938	10,967	84.8	1,971	OH	10,847	8,039	74.1	2,808
					OK	3,146	2,130	67.7	1,015
GA	6,478	4,097	63.2	2,381	OR	2,842	2,003	70.5	839
HI	1,108	986	89.0	122	PA	11,882	8,188	68.9	3,693
ID	1,007	578	57.4	429	RI	1,003	863	86.0	140
IL	11,431	9,669	84.6	1,762					
IN	5,544	3,598	64.9	1,946	SC	3,487	1,905	54.6	1,581
					SD	696	348	50.0	348
IA	2,777	1,683	60.6	1,094	TN	4,877	2,970	60.9	1,907
KS	2,478	1,713	69.1	765	TX	16,987	13,635	80.3	3,352
KY	3,685	1,910	51.8	1,775	UT	1,723	1,499	87.0	224
LA	4,220	2,872	68.1	1,348					
ME	1,228	548	44.6	680	VT	563	181	32.2	382
					VA	6,187	4,293	69.4	1,894
MD	4,781	3,888	81.3	893	WA	4,867	3,718	76.4	1,149
MA	6,016	5,070	84.3	947	WV	1,793	648	36.1	1,145
MI	9,295	6,556	70.5	2,739	WI	4,892	3,212	65.7	1,680
					WY	454	295	65.0	159

- Represents zero.   ¹ The revised 1970 resident population count is 203,302,031; which incorporates changes due to errors found after tabulations were completed.   ² Total population count has been revised since the 1980 and 1990 census publications to 226,542,199 and 248,718,301, respectively.

Source: U.S. Census Bureau, *1990 Census of Population and Housing, Population and Housing Unit Counts* (1990 CPH-2).

No. 47. Incorporated Places, by Population Size: 1970 to 1996

[131.9 represents 131,900,000]

Population size	Number of incorporated places 1970	1980	1990	1996	Population (mil.) 1970	1980	1990	1996	Percent of total 1970	1980	1990	1996
Total	18,666	19,097	19,262	19,335	131.9	140.3	152.9	162.6	100.0	100.0	100.0	100.0
1,000,000 or more	6	6	8	10	18.8	17.5	20.0	22.3	14.2	12.5	13.0	13.7
500,000 to 999,999	20	16	15	14	13.0	10.9	10.1	8.8	9.8	7.8	6.6	5.4
250,000 to 499,999	30	33	41	42	10.5	11.8	14.2	15.3	7.9	8.4	9.3	9.4
100,000 to 249,999	97	114	131	153	13.9	16.6	19.1	22.2	10.5	11.8	12.5	13.7
50,000 to 99,999	232	250	309	347	16.2	17.6	21.2	23.4	12.2	12.3	13.9	14.4
25,000 to 49,999	455	526	567	597	15.7	18.4	20.0	20.7	11.9	13.1	13.0	12.7
10,000 to 24,999	1,127	1,260	1,290	1,366	17.6	19.8	20.3	21.4	13.3	14.1	13.3	13.2
Under 10,000	16,699	16,892	16,901	16,806	26.4	28.0	28.2	28.5	20.0	20.0	18.4	17.5

Source: U.S. Census Bureau, *Census of Population: 1970* and *1980*, vol. I; *1990 Census of Population and Housing, Population and Housing Unit Counts* (CPH-2-1); computer diskette PE-59; and unpublished data.

No. 48. Cities With 100,000 or More Inhabitants in 1998—Population, 1980 to 1998, and Land Area, 1990

[**Population**: As of **April 1**; except **1998**, as of **July 1 (98 represents 98,000)**. Data refer to boundaries in effect December 1994. Minus sign (-) indicates decrease]

City	1980, total (1,000)	1990 Total (1,000)	1990 Percent Black	1990 Percent American Indian, Eskimo, Aleut	1990 Percent Asian, Pacific Islander	1990 Percent Hispanic[1]	1998 Total (1,000)	1998 Rank	Percent change 1990-98	Land area, 1990 (square miles)
Abilene, TX	98	107	7.0	0.4	1.3	15.5	108	203	1.5	103.1
Akron, OH	237	223	24.5	0.3	1.2	0.7	216	74	-3.3	62.2
Albuquerque, NM	332	385	3.0	3.0	1.7	34.5	419	36	8.9	132.2
Alexandria, VA	103	111	21.9	0.3	4.2	9.7	118	173	6.4	15.3
Allentown, PA	104	105	5.0	0.2	1.3	11.7	101	215	-4.3	17.7
Amarillo, TX	149	158	6.0	0.8	1.9	14.7	171	113	8.7	87.9
Anaheim, CA	219	266	2.5	0.5	9.4	31.4	295	57	10.8	44.3
Anchorage, AK	174	226	6.4	6.4	4.8	4.1	255	65	12.7	1,697.6
Ann Arbor, MI	108	110	9.0	0.4	7.7	2.6	110	197	0.3	25.9
Arlington, TX	160	262	8.4	0.5	3.9	8.9	306	54	17.1	93.0
Arlington, VA [2]	153	171	10.5	0.3	6.8	13.5	177	108	3.7	25.9
Atlanta, GA	425	394	67.1	0.1	0.9	1.9	404	39	2.5	131.8
Augusta-Richmond County, GA [3]	(NA)	187	(NA)	(NA)	(NA)	(NA)	188	96	0.6	(NA)
Aurora, CO	159	222	11.4	0.6	3.8	6.6	251	67	12.8	132.5
Aurora, IL	81	100	11.9	0.2	1.3	23.0	125	162	25.1	33.5
Austin, TX	346	472	12.4	0.4	3.0	23.0	552	21	17.0	217.8
Bakersfield, CA	106	176	9.4	1.1	3.6	20.5	210	79	19.3	91.8
Baltimore, MD	787	736	59.2	0.3	1.1	1.0	646	16	-12.3	80.8
Baton Rouge, LA	220	220	43.9	0.1	1.7	1.6	212	77	-3.6	73.9
Beaumont, TX	118	114	41.3	0.2	1.7	4.3	110	198	-3.9	80.1
Bellevue, WA	(NA)	95	(NA)	(NA)	(NA)	(NA)	104	208	9.3	(NA)
Berkeley, CA	103	103	18.8	0.6	14.8	8.4	108	204	5.2	10.5
Birmingham, AL	284	265	63.3	0.1	0.6	(Z)	253	66	-4.7	148.5
Boise City, ID	102	127	0.6	0.6	1.6	2.7	157	122	24.3	46.1
Boston, MA	563	574	25.6	0.3	5.3	10.8	555	20	-3.3	48.4
Bridgeport, CT	143	142	26.6	0.3	2.3	26.5	137	143	-3.0	16.0
Brownsville, TX	85	107	0.2	0.1	0.3	90.1	138	141	28.8	27.9
Buffalo, NY	358	328	30.7	0.8	1.0	4.9	301	56	-8.4	40.6
Carrollton, TX	41	82	4.9	0.4	6.8	10.2	100	216	22.3	34.8
Cedar Rapids, IA	110	109	2.9	0.2	1.0	1.1	115	182	5.3	53.5
Chandler, AZ	30	90	2.6	1.2	2.4	17.3	160	121	78.4	47.6
Charlotte, NC	315	420	31.8	0.4	1.8	1.4	505	25	20.3	174.3
Chattanooga, TN	170	152	33.7	0.2	1.0	0.6	148	133	-3.0	118.4
Chesapeake, VA	114	152	27.4	0.3	1.2	1.3	200	83	31.3	340.7
Chicago, IL	3,005	2,784	39.1	0.3	3.7	19.6	2,802	3	0.7	227.2
Chula Vista, CA	84	135	4.6	0.6	8.9	37.3	161	120	18.8	29.0
Cincinnati, OH	385	364	37.9	0.2	1.1	0.7	336	51	-7.6	77.2
Clearwater, FL	85	99	9.0	0.2	1.0	2.9	101	212	2.8	24.9
Cleveland, OH	574	506	46.6	0.3	1.0	4.6	496	28	-1.9	77.0
Colorado Springs, CO	215	280	7.0	0.8	2.4	9.1	345	48	23.0	183.2
Columbia, SC [3]	101	111	43.7	0.3	1.4	2.0	111	192	0.1	117.1
Columbus, GA [3]	169	179	38.1	0.3	1.4	3.0	182	102	2.0	216.1
Columbus, OH	565	633	22.6	0.2	2.4	1.1	670	15	5.9	190.9
Concord, CA	104	111	2.4	0.7	8.7	11.5	118	174	5.7	29.5
Coral Springs, FL	37	79	3.5	0.2	2.1	7.1	112	187	41.7	23.5
Corona, CA	38	76	2.8	0.8	7.1	30.4	113	186	48.6	28.5
Corpus Christi, TX	232	257	4.8	0.4	0.9	50.4	281	59	9.3	135.0
Costa Mesa, CA	83	96	1.3	0.5	6.6	20.0	102	211	6.2	15.6
Dallas, TX	905	1,008	29.5	0.5	2.2	20.9	1,076	9	6.8	342.4
Dayton, OH	194	182	40.4	0.2	0.6	0.7	167	115	-8.0	55.0
Denver, CO	493	468	12.8	1.2	2.4	23.0	499	27	6.7	153.3
Des Moines, IA	191	193	7.1	0.4	2.4	2.4	191	91	-1.0	75.3
Detroit, MI	1,203	1,028	75.7	0.4	0.8	2.8	970	10	-5.6	138.7
Durham, NC	101	139	45.7	0.2	2.0	1.2	154	125	10.5	69.3
Elizabeth, NJ	106	110	19.8	0.3	2.7	39.1	111	194	0.6	12.3
El Monte, CA	79	106	1.0	0.6	11.8	72.5	112	188	5.2	9.5
El Paso, TX	425	515	3.4	0.4	1.2	69.0	615	17	19.3	245.4
Erie, PA	119	109	12.0	0.2	0.5	2.4	103	209	-5.6	22.0
Escondido, CA	64	109	1.5	0.8	3.7	23.4	121	169	11.0	35.6
Eugene, OR	106	113	1.3	0.9	3.5	2.7	128	156	13.8	38.0
Evansville, IN	130	126	9.5	0.2	0.6	0.6	123	166	-2.8	40.7
Flint, MI	160	141	47.9	0.7	0.5	2.9	132	152	-6.6	33.8
Fontana, CA	37	88	8.7	0.9	4.5	36.1	110	199	25.4	35.6
Fort Collins, CO	65	87	1.0	0.5	2.4	7.1	109	200	24.5	41.2
Fort Lauderdale, FL	153	149	28.1	0.2	0.9	7.2	154	124	3.0	31.4
Fort Wayne, IN	172	196	16.7	0.3	1.0	2.7	186	98	-5.1	62.7
Fort Worth, TX	385	448	22.0	0.4	2.0	19.5	492	29	9.9	281.1
Fremont, CA	132	173	3.8	0.7	19.4	13.3	204	81	17.9	77.0
Fresno, CA	217	354	8.3	1.1	12.5	29.9	398	40	12.4	99.1
Fullerton, CA	102	114	2.2	0.5	12.2	21.3	122	167	6.8	22.1
Garden Grove, CA	123	143	1.5	0.6	20.5	23.5	151	129	5.8	17.9
Garland, TX	139	181	8.9	0.5	4.5	11.6	193	90	7.1	57.3
Gary, IN	152	117	80.6	0.2	0.2	5.7	108	201	-7.0	50.2
Glendale, AZ	97	147	3.0	0.9	2.1	15.5	193	89	31.6	52.2
Glendale, CA	139	180	1.3	0.3	14.1	21.0	185	100	2.8	30.6
Grand Prairie, TX	71	100	9.7	0.8	3.0	20.5	113	185	13.8	68.5
Grand Rapids, MI	182	189	18.5	0.8	1.1	5.0	185	99	-2.0	44.3

See footnotes at end of table.

Population 47

U.S. Census Bureau, Statistical Abstract of the United States: 1999

No. 48. Cities With 100,000 or More Inhabitants in 1998—Population, 1980 to 1998, and Land Area, 1990—Continued

[See headnote, p. 47]

City	1980, total (1,000)	Population 1990 Total (1,000)	Percent— Black	Percent— American Indian, Eskimo, Aleut	Percent— Asian, Pacific Islander	Percent— Hispanic[1]	Population 1998 Total (1,000)	Rank	Percent change, 1990-98	Land area, 1990 (square miles)
Greensboro, NC	156	184	33.9	0.5	1.4	1.0	198	84	7.6	79.8
Hampton, VA	123	134	38.9	0.3	1.7	2.0	137	144	2.4	51.8
Hartford, CT	136	140	38.9	0.3	1.4	31.6	132	153	-5.9	17.3
Hayward, CA	94	115	9.8	1.0	15.5	23.9	129	155	12.4	43.5
Henderson, NV	24	65	2.7	1.0	2.0	8.1	153	126	135.1	71.5
Hialeah, FL	145	188	1.9	0.1	0.5	87.6	211	78	12.4	19.2
Hollywood, FL[4]	121	122	8.5	0.2	1.3	11.9	130	154	6.8	27.3
Honolulu, HI[4]	365	377	1.3	0.3	70.5	4.6	396	41	5.0	85.7
Houston, TX	1,595	1,638	28.1	0.3	4.1	27.6	1,787	4	9.1	539.9
Huntington Beach, CA	171	182	0.9	0.6	8.3	11.2	195	87	7.6	26.4
Huntsville, AL	143	160	24.4	0.5	2.1	1.2	176	109	10.1	164.4
Independence, MO	112	112	1.4	0.6	1.0	2.0	117	178	4.0	78.2
Indianapolis, IN[3]	701	731	22.6	0.2	0.9	1.1	741	13	1.4	361.7
Inglewood, CA	94	110	51.9	0.4	2.5	38.5	112	189	1.8	9.2
Irvine, CA	62	110	1.8	0.2	18.1	6.3	136	147	23.7	42.3
Irving, TX	110	155	7.5	0.6	4.6	16.3	178	107	15.0	67.6
Jackson, MS[3]	203	202	55.7	0.1	0.5	0.4	188	94	-6.8	109.0
Jacksonville, FL[3]	541	635	25.2	0.3	1.9	2.6	694	14	9.2	758.7
Jersey City, NJ	224	229	29.7	0.3	11.4	24.2	232	71	1.7	14.9
Kansas City, KS	161	152	29.3	0.7	1.2	7.1	141	139	-6.7	107.8
Kansas City, MO	448	435	29.6	0.5	1.2	3.9	442	33	1.6	311.5
Knoxville, TN	175	170	15.8	0.2	1.0	0.7	166	117	-2.5	77.2
Lafayette, LA	81	102	27.2	0.2	1.3	1.7	114	184	11.5	40.9
Lakewood, CO	114	126	1.0	0.7	1.9	9.1	137	145	8.2	40.8
Lancaster, CA	48	97	7.4	0.9	3.7	15.2	119	172	21.8	88.8
Lansing, MI	130	127	18.6	1.0	1.8	7.9	128	157	0.4	33.9
Laredo, TX	91	123	0.1	0.2	0.4	93.9	176	110	43.0	32.9
Las Vegas, NV	165	258	11.4	0.9	3.6	12.5	404	37	56.6	83.3
Lexington-Fayette, KY	204	225	13.4	0.2	1.6	1.1	242	68	7.3	284.5
Lincoln, NE	172	192	2.4	0.6	1.7	2.0	213	76	11.0	63.3
Little Rock, AR	159	176	34.0	0.3	0.9	0.8	175	111	-0.2	102.9
Livonia, MI	105	101	0.3	0.2	1.3	1.3	101	213	0.5	50.0
Long Beach, CA	361	429	13.7	0.6	13.6	23.6	431	35	0.4	469.3
Los Angeles, CA	2,969	3,486	14.0	0.5	9.8	39.9	3,598	2	3.2	62.1
Louisville, KY	299	270	29.7	0.2	0.7	0.7	255	64	-5.4	13.8
Lowell, MA	92	103	2.4	0.2	11.1	10.1	101	214	-2.3	104.1
Lubbock, TX	174	186	8.6	0.3	1.4	22.5	191	92	2.6	47.9
Macon, GA	117	107	52.2	0.1	0.4	0.6	114	183	6.5	57.8
Madison, WI	171	191	4.2	0.4	3.9	2.0	209	80	9.7	33.0
Manchester, NH	91	99	1.0	0.2	1.1	2.1	103	210	3.2	32.4
McAllen, TX	66	84	0.3	0.2	0.7	77.0	107	206	27.1	256.0
Memphis, TN	646	619	54.8	0.2	0.8	0.7	604	18	-2.4	108.6
Mesa, AZ	152	289	1.9	1.0	1.5	10.9	360	46	24.5	42.8
Mesquite, TX	67	101	5.8	0.5	2.6	8.8	115	181	13.0	35.6
Miami, FL	347	359	27.4	0.2	0.6	62.5	369	44	2.8	96.1
Milwaukee, WI	636	628	30.5	0.9	1.9	6.3	578	19	-7.9	54.9
Minneapolis, MN	371	368	13.0	3.3	4.3	2.1	352	47	-4.5	118.0
Mobile, AL	200	196	38.9	0.2	1.0	1.0	202	82	3.0	30.2
Modesto, CA	107	165	2.7	1.0	7.9	16.3	182	103	10.5	135.0
Montgomery, AL	178	190	42.3	0.2	0.7	0.8	197	85	3.5	49.1
Moreno Valley, CA	(5)	119	13.8	0.7	6.6	22.9	145	135	21.7	27.9
Naperville, IL	43	86	2.1	0.1	4.8	1.8	117	177	36.5	473.3
Nashville-Davidson, TN[3]	456	488	24.3	0.2	1.4	0.9	510	24	4.5	23.8
Newark, NJ	329	275	58.5	0.2	1.2	26.1	268	60	-2.7	18.9
New Haven, CT	126	130	36.1	0.3	2.4	13.2	123	165	-5.6	180.6
New Orleans, LA	558	497	61.9	0.2	1.9	3.5	466	31	-6.3	68.3
Newport News, VA	145	171	33.6	0.3	2.3	2.8	179	106	4.2	308.9
New York, NY	7,072	7,323	28.7	0.4	7.0	24.4	7,420	1	1.3	53.8
Norfolk, VA	267	261	39.1	0.4	2.6	2.9	215	75	-17.6	56.1
Oakland, CA	339	372	43.9	0.6	14.8	13.9	366	45	-1.7	40.7
Oceanside, CA	77	128	7.9	0.7	6.1	22.6	152	127	19.0	608.2
Oklahoma City, OK	404	445	16.0	4.2	2.4	5.0	472	30	6.2	100.6
Omaha, NE	314	343	13.1	0.7	1.0	3.1	371	43	8.3	36.7
Ontario, CA	89	133	7.3	0.7	3.9	41.7	147	134	10.5	23.3
Orange, CA	91	111	1.4	0.5	7.9	22.8	124	164	11.9	67.3
Orlando, FL	128	165	26.9	0.3	1.6	8.7	181	104	10.0	55.7
Overland Park, KS	82	112	1.8	0.3	1.9	2.0	140	140	25.0	24.4
Oxnard, CA	108	143	5.2	0.8	8.6	54.4	155	123	8.5	77.6
Palmdale, CA	12	70	6.4	0.9	4.4	22.0	100	218	42.5	23.0
Pasadena, CA	118	132	19.0	0.4	8.1	27.3	135	149	2.3	43.8
Pasadena, TX	113	120	1.0	0.5	1.6	28.8	134	150	12.0	8.4
Paterson, NJ	138	141	36.0	0.3	1.4	41.0	148	131	5.2	31.9
Pembroke Pines, FL	36	66	5.3	0.2	2.0	11.5	115	180	75.9	40.9
Peoria, IL	124	114	20.9	0.2	1.7	1.6	111	191	-2.1	135.1
Philadelphia, PA	1,688	1,586	39.9	0.2	2.7	5.6	1,436	5	-9.4	419.9
Phoenix, AZ	790	984	5.2	1.9	1.7	20.0	1,198	7	21.7	55.6
Pittsburgh, PA	424	370	25.8	0.2	1.6	0.9	341	49	-7.9	

See footnotes at end of table.

U.S. Census Bureau, Statistical Abstract of the United States: 1999

[See headnote, p. 47]

City	1980, total (1,000)	Population 1990					1998			Land area, 1990 (square miles)
		Total (1,000)	Percent— Black	American Indian, Eskimo, Aleut	Asian, Pacific Islander	Hispanic[1]	Total (1,000)	Rank	Percent change, 1990-98	
Plano, TX	72	128	4.1	0.3	4.0	6.2	219	72	71.6	66.2
Pomona, CA	93	132	14.4	0.6	6.7	51.3	136	148	3.0	22.8
Portland, OR	368	464	7.7	1.2	5.3	3.2	504	26	8.7	124.7
Providence, RI	157	161	14.8	0.9	5.9	15.5	151	130	-6.1	18.5
Provo, UT	74	87	0.3	1.1	2.7	4.2	110	196	27.2	38.6
Pueblo, CO	102	99	2.2	0.8	0.6	39.5	107	205	8.8	35.9
Raleigh, NC	150	212	27.6	0.3	2.5	1.4	259	62	22.3	88.1
Rancho Cucamonga, CA	55	101	5.9	0.6	5.4	20.0	120	170	18.4	37.8
Reno, NV	101	134	2.9	1.4	4.9	11.1	163	119	22.0	57.5
Richmond, VA	219	203	55.2	0.2	0.9	0.9	194	88	-4.3	60.1
Riverside, CA	171	227	7.4	0.8	5.2	26.0	262	61	15.7	77.7
Rochester, NY	242	230	31.5	0.5	1.8	8.7	217	73	-5.8	35.8
Rockford, IL	140	142	15.0	0.3	1.5	4.2	144	136	1.3	45.0
Sacramento, CA	276	369	15.3	1.2	15.0	16.2	404	38	9.4	96.3
St. Louis, MO	453	397	47.5	0.2	0.9	1.3	339	50	-14.5	61.9
St. Paul, MN	270	272	7.4	1.4	7.1	4.2	257	63	-5.5	52.8
St. Petersburg, FL	239	240	19.6	0.2	1.7	2.6	236	70	-1.8	59.2
Salem, OR	89	108	1.5	1.6	2.4	6.1	127	161	17.5	41.5
Salinas, CA	80	109	3.0	0.9	8.1	50.6	121	168	11.7	18.6
Salt Lake City, UT	163	160	1.7	1.6	4.7	9.7	174	112	9.0	109.0
San Antonio, TX	786	959	7.0	0.4	1.1	55.6	1,114	8	16.1	333.0
San Bernardino, CA	119	170	16.0	1.0	4.0	34.6	186	97	9.6	55.1
San Diego, CA	876	1,111	9.4	0.6	11.8	20.7	1,221	6	9.9	324.0
San Francisco, CA	679	724	10.9	0.5	29.1	13.9	746	12	3.0	46.7
San Jose, CA	629	782	4.7	0.7	19.5	26.6	861	11	10.1	171.3
Santa Ana, CA	204	294	2.6	0.5	9.7	65.2	306	55	4.1	27.1
Santa Clara, CA	88	94	2.6	0.5	18.6	15.2	100	217	7.2	18.3
Santa Clarita, CA	(5)	120	1.5	0.6	4.2	13.4	127	159	5.8	40.5
Santa Rosa, CA	83	113	1.8	1.2	3.4	9.5	127	160	12.0	33.7
Savannah, GA	142	138	51.3	0.2	1.1	1.4	132	151	-4.5	62.6
Scottsdale, AZ	89	130	0.8	0.6	1.2	4.8	195	86	50.2	184.4
Seattle, WA	494	516	10.1	1.4	11.8	3.6	537	22	4.0	83.9
Shreveport, LA	206	199	44.8	0.2	0.5	1.1	188	95	-5.1	98.6
Simi Valley, CA	78	100	1.5	0.6	5.5	12.7	110	195	10.2	33.0
Sioux Falls, SD	81	101	0.7	1.6	0.7	0.6	117	179	15.8	45.1
Spokane, WA	171	177	1.9	2.0	2.1	2.1	184	101	3.9	55.9
Springfield, IL	100	105	13.0	0.2	1.0	0.8	117	176	11.1	42.5
Springfield, MA	152	157	19.2	0.2	1.0	16.9	148	132	-5.6	32.1
Springfield, MO	133	140	2.5	0.7	0.9	1.0	143	137	1.7	68.0
Stamford, CT	102	108	17.8	0.1	2.6	9.8	111	193	2.4	37.7
Sterling Heights, MI	109	118	0.4	0.2	2.9	1.1	124	163	5.5	36.6
Stockton, CA	150	211	9.6	1.0	22.8	25.0	240	69	13.8	52.6
Sunnyvale, CA	107	117	3.4	0.5	19.3	13.2	127	158	8.6	21.9
Syracuse, NY	170	164	20.3	1.3	2.2	2.9	152	128	-7.1	25.1
Tacoma, WA	159	177	11.4	2.0	6.9	3.8	180	105	1.8	48.0
Tallahassee, FL	82	125	29.1	0.2	1.8	3.0	137	146	9.5	63.3
Tampa, FL	272	280	25.0	0.3	1.4	15.0	289	58	3.3	108.7
Tempe, AZ	107	142	3.2	1.3	4.1	10.9	168	114	18.0	39.5
Thousand Oaks, CA	77	104	1.2	0.4	4.8	9.6	117	175	12.3	49.6
Toledo, OH	355	333	19.7	0.3	1.0	4.0	312	53	-6.2	80.6
Topeka, KS	119	120	10.6	1.3	0.8	5.8	119	171	-0.8	55.2
Torrance, CA	130	133	1.5	0.4	21.9	10.1	138	142	3.3	20.5
Tucson, AZ	331	411	4.3	1.6	2.2	29.3	460	32	11.9	156.3
Tulsa, OK	361	367	13.6	4.7	1.4	2.6	381	42	3.8	183.5
Vallejo, CA	80	109	21.2	0.7	23.0	10.8	112	190	2.1	30.2
Virginia Beach, VA	262	393	13.9	0.4	4.3	3.1	432	34	10.0	248.3
Waco, TX	101	104	23.1	0.3	0.9	16.3	108	202	4.5	75.8
Warren, MI	161	145	0.7	0.5	1.3	1.1	142	138	-1.7	34.3
Washington, DC	638	607	65.8	0.2	1.8	5.4	523	23	-13.8	61.4
Waterbury, CT	103	109	13.0	0.3	0.7	13.4	105	207	-3.3	28.6
Wichita, KS	280	304	11.3	1.2	2.6	5.0	329	52	8.3	115.1
Winston-Salem, NC	132	151	39.3	0.2	0.8	0.9	164	118	8.8	71.1
Worcester, MA	162	170	4.5	0.3	2.8	9.6	167	116	-1.9	37.6
Yonkers, NY	195	188	14.1	0.2	3.0	16.7	190	93	1.1	18.1

NA Not available.   Z Less than .05 percent.   [1] Hispanic persons may be of any race.   [2] Data are for Arlington CDP (census designated place) which is not incorporated as a city but is recognized for census purposes as a large urban place. Arlington CDP is coextensive with Arlington County.   [3] Represents the portion of a consolidated city that is not within one or more separately incorporated places.   [4] The population shown in this table is for the CDP; the 1990 census population for the City and County of Honolulu is 836,231.   [5] Not incorporated.

Source: U.S. Census Bureau, *1980 Census of Population*, Vol. 1, chapters A and B; *1990 Census of Population and Housing, Population and Housing Unit Counts*, (CPH-2) and *General Population Characteristics*, (CP-1); and "Population Estimates for Places: Annual Time Series, July 1, 1990 to July 1, 1998;" published 30 June 1999; <http://www.census.gov/population/estimates/metro-city/scts/SC98TS-DR.txt>.

No. 49. Population 65 Years Old and Over, by Age Group and Sex, 1980 to 1998, and Projections, 2000

[As of April, except 1998 and 2000, as of July (25,549 represents 25,549,000). Projection based on middle series, see Table 3]

Age group and sex	Number (1,000)				Percent distribution			
	1980	1990 [1]	1998	2000, proj.	1980	1990 [1]	1998	2000, proj.
Persons 65 yrs. and over	25,549	31,082	34,401	34,709	100	100	100	100
65 to 69 years old	8,782	10,067	9,593	9,410	34	32	28	27
70 to 74 years old	6,798	7,980	8,802	8,726	27	26	26	25
75 to 79 years old	4,794	6,103	7,218	7,415	19	20	21	21
80 to 84 years old	2,935	3,909	4,734	4,900	12	13	14	14
85 years old and over	2,240	3,022	4,054	4,259	9	10	12	12
Males, 65 yrs. and over	10,305	12,494	14,198	14,346	100	100	100	100
65 to 69 years old	3,903	4,508	4,393	4,321	38	36	31	30
70 to 74 years old	2,854	3,400	3,857	3,859	28	27	27	27
75 to 79 years old	1,848	2,389	2,997	3,092	18	19	21	22
80 to 84 years old	1,019	1,356	1,764	1,846	10	11	12	13
85 years old and over	682	841	1,187	1,228	7	7	8	9
Females, 65 yrs. and over	15,245	18,587	20,203	20,364	100	100	100	100
65 to 69 years old	4,880	5,559	5,201	5,089	32	30	26	25
70 to 74 years old	3,945	4,581	4,945	4,867	26	25	24	24
75 to 79 years old	2,946	3,714	4,221	4,323	19	20	21	21
80 to 84 years old	1,916	2,553	2,970	3,055	13	14	15	15
85 years old and over	1,559	2,180	2,866	3,031	10	12	14	15

[1] The April 1, 1990, census count (248,765,170) includes count resolution corrections processed through August 1997 and does not include adjustments for census coverage errors except for adjustments estimated for the 1995 Census Test in Oakland, CA; Patterson, NJ, and six parishes in LA. These adjustments amounted to a total of 55,297 persons.

Source: U.S. Census Bureau, Current Population Reports, P25-1095 and P25-1130; and unpublished data.

No. 50. Persons 65 Years Old and Over—Characteristics, by Sex: 1980 to 1998

[As of March, except as noted (24.2 represents 24,200,000). Covers civilian noninstitutional population. See headnote, Table 51]

Characteristic	Total				Male				Female			
	1980	1990	1995	1998	1980	1990	1995	1998	1980	1990	1995	1998
Total (million)	24.2	29.6	31.7	32.1	9.9	12.3	13.2	13.5	14.2	17.2	18.5	18.6
PERCENT DISTRIBUTION												
Marital status:												
Single	5.5	4.6	4.2	4.3	4.9	4.2	4.2	3.8	5.9	4.9	4.2	4.7
Married	55.4	56.1	56.9	56.6	78.0	76.5	77.0	75.1	39.5	41.4	42.5	42.9
Spouse present	53.6	54.1	54.7	54.2	76.1	74.2	74.5	72.6	37.9	39.7	40.6	40.7
Spouse absent	1.8	2.0	2.2	2.4	1.9	2.3	2.5	2.5	1.7	1.7	1.9	2.2
Widowed	35.7	34.2	33.2	32.5	13.5	14.2	13.5	14.9	51.2	48.6	47.3	45.2
Divorced	3.5	5.0	5.7	6.7	3.6	5.0	5.2	6.1	3.4	5.1	6.0	7.1
Family status:												
In families [1]	67.6	66.7	66.6	66.8	83.0	81.9	80.6	79.6	56.8	55.8	56.7	57.5
Nonfamily householders	31.2	31.9	32.4	31.9	15.7	16.6	18.4	18.4	42.0	42.8	42.4	41.7
Secondary individuals	1.2	1.4	1.0	1.3	1.3	1.5	1.0	2.0	1.1	1.4	0.9	0.7
Living arrangements:												
Living in household	99.8	99.7	99.9	100.0	99.9	99.9	100.0	100.0	99.7	99.5	99.9	100.0
Living alone	30.3	31.0	31.5	30.9	14.9	15.7	17.3	17.3	41.0	42.0	41.7	40.8
Spouse present	53.6	54.1	54.7	54.2	76.1	74.3	74.5	72.6	37.9	39.7	40.6	40.7
Living with someone else	15.9	14.6	13.7	14.9	8.9	9.9	8.1	10.0	20.8	17.8	17.6	18.4
Not in household [2]	0.2	0.3	0.1	-	0.1	0.1	-	-	0.3	0.5	0.1	-
Years of school completed:												
8 years or less	43.1	28.5	21.0	18.1	45.3	30.0	22.0	18.3	41.6	27.5	20.3	17.9
1 to 3 years of high school	16.2	16.1	[3]15.2	[3]14.9	15.5	15.7	[3]14.5	[3]14.1	16.7	16.4	[3]15.6	[3]15.4
4 years of high school	24.0	32.9	[4]33.8	[4]35.0	21.4	29.0	[4]29.2	[4]30.2	25.8	35.6	[4]37.1	[4]38.4
1 to 3 years of college	8.2	10.9	[5]17.1	[5]17.2	7.5	10.8	[5]17.1	[5]17.6	8.6	11.0	[5]17.0	[5]17.0
4 years or more of college	8.6	11.6	[6]13.0	[6]14.8	10.3	14.5	[6]17.2	[6]19.8	7.4	9.5	[6]9.9	[6]11.2
Labor force participation: [7]												
Employed	12.2	11.5	11.7	11.6	18.4	15.9	16.1	15.9	7.8	8.4	8.5	8.3
Unemployed	0.4	0.4	0.5	0.4	0.6	0.5	0.7	0.5	0.3	0.3	0.3	0.3
Not in labor force	87.5	88.1	87.9	88.1	81.0	83.6	83.2	83.5	91.9	91.3	91.2	91.4
Percent below poverty level [8]	15.2	11.4	11.7	10.5	11.1	7.8	7.2	7.0	17.9	13.9	14.9	13.1

- Represents zero. [1] Excludes those living in unrelated subfamilies. [2] In group quarters other than institutions. [3] Represents those who completed 9th to 12th grade, but have no high school diploma. [4] High school graduate. [5] Some college or associate degree. [6] Bachelor's or advanced degree. [7] Annual averages of monthly figures. Source: U.S. Bureau of Labor Statistics, Employment and Earnings, January issues. See footnote 2, Table 649. [8] Poverty status based on income in preceding year.

Source: Except as noted, U.S. Census Bureau, Current Population Reports, P20-514, and earlier reports; P60-201; and unpublished data.

No. 51. Social and Economic Characteristics of the White and Black Populations: 1990 to 1998

[As of **March, except labor force status, annual average (206,983 represents 206,983,000)**. Excludes members of Armed Forces except those living off post or with their families on post. Data for 1990 are based on 1980 census population controls; 1995 and 1998 data based on 1990 census population controls. Based on Current Population Survey; see text, this section, and Appendix III]

Characteristic	Number (1,000)						Percent distribution			
	White			Black			White		Black	
	1990	1995	1998	1990	1995	1998	1990	1998	1990	1998
Total persons	206,983	216,751	221,650	30,392	33,531	34,598	100.0	100.0	100.0	100.0
Under 5 years old	15,161	15,915	15,547	2,932	3,342	3,023	7.3	7.0	9.6	8.7
5 to 14 years old	28,405	30,786	31,394	5,546	6,268	6,577	13.7	14.2	18.2	19.0
15 to 44 years old	96,656	97,876	98,144	14,660	16,101	16,420	46.6	44.3	48.2	47.4
45 to 64 years old	40,282	44,189	48,011	4,766	5,264	5,887	19.5	21.7	15.7	17.0
65 years old and over	26,479	27,985	28,553	2,487	2,557	2,691	12.8	12.9	8.2	7.8
EDUCATIONAL ATTAINMENT										
Persons 25 years old and over	134,687	141,113	145,078	16,751	18,457	19,376	100.0	100.0	100.0	100.0
Elementary: 0 to 8 years	14,131	11,101	10,547	2,701	1,800	1,564	10.5	7.3	16.1	8.1
High school: 1 to 3 years	14,080	[1]12,882	[1]13,094	2,969	[1]3,041	[1]3,078	10.5	[1]9.0	17.7	[1]15.9
4 years	52,449	[2]47,986	[2]49,221	6,239	[2]6,686	[2]6,972	38.9	[2]33.9	37.2	[2]36.0
College: 1 to 3 years	24,350	[3]35,321	[3]36,013	2,952	[3]4,486	[3]4,906	18.1	[3]24.8	17.6	[3]25.3
4 years or more.	29,677	[4]33,824	[4]36,204	1,890	[4]2,444	[4]2,857	22.0	[4]25.0	11.3	[4]14.7
LABOR FORCE STATUS [5]										
Civilians 16 years old and over	160,625	166,914	171,478	21,477	23,246	24,373	100.0	100.0	100.0	100.0
Civilian labor force	107,447	111,950	115,415	13,740	14,817	15,982	66.9	67.3	64.0	65.6
Employed	102,261	106,490	110,931	12,175	13,279	14,556	63.7	64.7	56.7	59.7
Unemployed	5,186	5,459	4,484	1,565	1,538	1,426	3.2	2.6	7.3	5.9
Unemployment rate [6]	4.8	4.9	3.9	11.4	10.4	8.9	(X)	(X)	(X)	(X)
Not in labor force.	53,178	54,965	56,064	7,737	8,429	8,391	33.1	32.7	36.0	34.4
FAMILY TYPE										
Total families . . . . . . [7] . . .	56,590	58,437	59,511	7,470	8,093	8,408	100.0	100.0	100.0	100.0
With own children [7] . . .	26,718	27,951	28,336	4,378	4,682	4,848	47.2	47.6	58.6	57.7
Married couple . . . . [7]. . . .	46,981	47,899	48,066	3,750	3,842	3,921	83.0	80.8	50.2	46.6
With own children [7].	21,579	22,005	21,910	1,972	1,926	2,055	38.1	36.8	26.4	24.4
Female householder, no spouse present . .	7,306	8,031	8,308	3,275	3,716	3,926	12.9	14.0	43.8	46.7
With own children [7].	4,199	4,841	4,912	2,232	2,489	2,569	7.4	8.3	29.9	30.6
Male householder, no spouse present . . .[7].	2,303	2,507	3,137	446	536	562	4.1	5.3	6.0	6.7
With own children [7].	939	1,105	1,514	173	267	223	1.7	2.5	2.3	2.6
FAMILY INCOME IN PREVIOUS YEAR IN CONSTANT (1997) DOLLARS										
Total families	56,590	58,444	59,515	7,470	8,093	8,408	100.0	100.0	100.0	100.0
Less than $5,000.	1,019	1,227	1,250	568	615	580	1.8	2.1	7.6	6.9
$5,000 to $9,999	1,867	2,338	1,904	911	971	849	3.3	3.2	12.2	10.1
$10,000 to $14,999	2,773	3,156	3,035	740	834	824	4.9	5.1	9.9	9.8
$15,000 to $24,999	6,961	7,773	7,439	1,389	1,424	1,488	12.3	12.5	18.6	17.7
$25,000 to $34,999	7,470	8,007	7,558	994	1,117	1,194	13.2	12.7	13.3	14.2
$35,000 to $49,999	10,639	10,754	10,534	1,150	1,190	1,303	18.8	17.7	15.4	15.5
$50,000 or more	25,862	25,248	27,734	1,726	1,942	2,178	45.7	46.6	23.1	25.9
Median income (dol.) [8]	46,564	44,277	46,754	26,158	26,748	28,602	(X)	(X)	(X)	(X)
POVERTY										
Families below poverty level [9] .	4,409	5,312	4,990	2,077	2,212	1,986	7.8	8.4	27.8	23.6
Persons below poverty level [9] .	20,785	25,379	24,396	9,302	10,196	9,116	10.0	11.0	30.7	26.5
HOUSING TENURE										
Total occupied units	80,163	83,737	86,106	10,486	11,655	12,474	100.0	100.0	100.0	100.0
Owner-occupied	54,094	57,449	60,050	4,445	4,888	5,735	67.5	69.7	42.4	46.0
Renter-occupied	24,685	24,793	24,635	5,862	6,547	6,529	30.8	28.6	55.9	52.3
No cash rent.	1,384	1,494	1,421	178	220	210	1.7	1.7	1.7	1.7

X Not applicable.   [1] Represents those who completed 9th to 12th grade, but have no high school diploma.   [2] High school graduate.   [3] Some college or associate degree.   [4] Bachelor's or advanced degree.   [5] Source: U.S. Bureau of Labor Statistics, *Employment and Earnings*, January issues. See footnote 2, Table 649.   [6] Total unemployment as percent of civilian labor force.   [7] Children under 18 years old.   [8] For definition of median, see Guide to Tabular Presentation.   [9] For explanation of poverty level, see text, Section 14, Income.

Source: Except as noted, U.S. Census Bureau, *Current Population Reports*, P20-509, and earlier reports; P60-200; P60-201; and unpublished data.

Population   51

No. 52. Social and Economic Characteristics of the Asian and Pacific Islander Population: 1990 and 1998

[As of **March (6,679 represents 6,679,000)**. Excludes members of Armed Forces except those living off post or with their families on post. Data for 1990 are based on 1980 census population controls; 1998 data are based on 1990 census population controls. Based on Current Population Survey; see text, this section, and Appendix III]

Characteristic	Number (1,000)		Percent distribution	
	1990	1998	1990	1998
Total persons	**6,679**	**10,492**	**100.0**	**100.0**
Under 5 years old	602	882	9.0	8.4
5 to 14 years old	1,112	1,727	16.6	16.4
15 to 44 years old	3,345	5,230	50.1	49.8
45 to 64 years old	1,155	1,950	17.3	18.5
65 years old and over	465	705	7.0	6.7
EDUCATIONAL ATTAINMENT				
Persons 25 years old and over	**3,961**	**6,381**	**100.0**	**100.0**
Elementary: 0 to 8 years	543	570	13.7	8.9
High school: 1 to 3 years	234	[1]397	5.9	[1]6.2
4 years	1,038	[2]1,466	26.2	[2]23.0
College: 1 to 3 years	568	[3]1,264	14.3	[3]19.8
4 years or more	1,578	[4]2,684	39.9	[4]42.1
LABOR FORCE STATUS [5]				
Civilians 16 years old and over	**4,849**	**7,689**	**100.0**	**100.0**
Civilian labor force	3,216	5,263	66.3	68.5
Employed	3,079	5,023	63.5	65.3
Unemployed	136	240	2.8	3.1
Unemployment rate [6]	4.2	4.6	(X)	(X)
Not in labor force	1,634	2,425	33.7	31.5
FAMILY TYPE				
Total families	**1,531**	**2,381**	**100.0**	**100.0**
Married couple	1,256	1,946	82.1	81.7
Female householder, no spouse present	188	278	12.3	11.7
Male householder, no spouse present	86	157	5.6	6.6
FAMILY INCOME IN PREVIOUS YEAR IN CONSTANT (1997) DOLLARS				
Total families	**1,531**	**2,381**	**100.0**	**100.0**
Less than $5,000	(NA)	69	(NA)	2.9
$5,000 to $9,999	(NA)	64	(NA)	2.7
$10,000 to $14,999	(NA)	126	(NA)	5.3
$15,000 to $24,999	(NA)	219	(NA)	9.2
$25,000 to $34,999	(NA)	233	(NA)	9.8
$35,000 to $49,999	(NA)	424	(NA)	17.8
$50,000 or more	(NA)	1,243	(NA)	52.2
Median income [7]	52,229	51,850	(X)	(X)
POVERTY				
Families below poverty level [8]	182	244	11.9	10.2
Persons below poverty level [8]	938	1,468	14.1	14.0
HOUSING TENURE				
Total occupied units	**1,988**	**3,125**	**100.0**	**100.0**
Owner-occupied	977	1,650	49.1	52.8
Renter-occupied	982	1,438	49.4	46.0
No cash rent	30	37	1.5	1.2

NA Not available. X Not applicable. [1] Represents those who completed 9th to 12th grade but have no high school diploma. [2] High school graduate. [3] Some college or associate degree. [4] Bachelor's or advanced degree. [5] Data beginning 1994 not directly comparable with earlier years. See text, Section 13, Labor Force. [6] Total unemployment as percent of civilian labor force. [7] For definition of median, see Guide to Tabular Presentation. [8] For explanation of poverty level, see text, Section 14, Income.

Source: U.S. Census Bureau, *Current Population Reports*, P20-459; and unpublished data.

No. 53. Population Living on Selected Reservations and Trust Lands and American Indian Tribes With 10,000 or More American Indians: 1990

[As of **April**]

Reservation and trust lands with 5,000 or more American Indians, Eskimos, and Aleuts	American Indians, Eskimos, Aleuts			American Indian tribe		
	Total population	Number	Percent of total		Number	Percent distribution
All reservation and trust lands	**808,163**	**437,431**	**54.1**	**American Indian population, total** [2]	**1,878,285**	**100.0**
Navajo and Trust Lands, AZ-NM-UT.	148,451	143,405	96.6	Cherokee	308,132	16.4
Pine Ridge and Trust Lands, NE-SD	12,215	11,182	91.5	Navajo	219,198	11.7
				Chippewa	103,826	5.5
Fort Apache, AZ.	10,394	9,825	94.5	Sioux [3]	103,255	5.5
Gila River, AZ	9,540	9,116	95.6	Choctaw	82,299	4.4
Papago, AZ.	8,730	8,480	97.1	Pueblo	52,939	2.8
Rosebud and Trust Lands, SD.	9,696	8,043	83.0	Apache	50,051	2.7
				Iroquois [4]	49,038	2.6
San Carlos, AZ	7,294	7,110	97.5	Lumbee	48,444	2.6
				Creek.	43,550	2.3
Zuni Pueblo, AZ-NM	7,412	7,073	95.4	Blackfoot	32,234	1.7
Hopi and Trust Lands, AZ . . .	7,360	7,061	95.9	Canadian and Latin American. .	22,379	1.2
Blackfeet, MT	8,549	7,025	82.2	Chickasaw	20,631	1.1
Turtle Mountain and Trust Lands, ND-SD	7,106	6,772	95.3	Potawatomi [4]	16,763	0.9
Yakima and Trust Lands, WA .	27,668	6,307	22.8	Tohono O'Odham	16,041	0.9
				Pima	14,431	0.8
				Tlingit.	13,925	0.7
Osage, OK [1]	41,645	6,161	14.8	Seminole	13,797	0.7
Fort Peck, MT	10,595	5,782	54.6	Alaskan Athabaskans	13,738	0.7
Wind River, WY	21,851	5,676	26.0	Cheyenne	11,456	0.6
Eastern Cherokee, NC	6,527	5,388	82.5	Comanche	11,322	0.6
Flathead, MT.	21,259	5,130	24.1	Paiute	11,142	0.6
Cheyenne River, SD	7,743	5,100	65.9	Puget Sound Salish	10,246	0.5

[1] The Osage Reservation is coextensive with Osage County. Data shown for the reservation are for the entire reservation. [2] Includes other American Indian tribes, not shown separately. [3] Any entry with the spelling "Siouan" was miscoded to Sioux in North Carolina. [4] Reporting and/or processing problems have affected the data for this tribe.

Source: U.S. Census Bureau, *1990 Census of Population, General Population Characteristics, American Indian and Alaska Native Areas* (CP-1-1A); and press releases CB91-232 and CB92-244.

No. 54. Social and Economic Characteristics of the American Indian Population: 1990

[As of **April**. Based on a sample and subject to sampling variability]

Characteristic	American Indian, total [1]	Chero-kee	Navajo	Sioux [2]	Chip-pewa	Choc-taw	Pueblo	Apache	Iro-quois [3]	Lum-bee
Total persons	**1,937,391**	**369,035**	**225,298**	**107,321**	**105,988**	**86,231**	**55,330**	**53,330**	**52,557**	**50,888**
Percent under 5 years old	9.7	6.3	13.6	12.3	10.3	8.2	10.3	10.2	8.1	8.3
Percent 18 years old and over .	65.8	73.3	57.7	60.0	64.0	68.8	64.2	64.7	71.1	66.2
Percent 65 years old and over .	5.9	7.2	4.6	4.4	4.7	8.0	5.8	3.4	6.7	5.6
EDUCATIONAL ATTAINMENT										
Persons 25 years old and over	1,040,955	229,231	100,594	51,014	54,804	49,128	28,597	27,717	30,882	27,343
Percent high school graduates or higher.	65.6	68.2	51.0	69.7	69.7	70.3	71.5	63.8	71.9	51.6
Percent bachelor's degree or higher	9.4	11.1	4.5	8.9	8.2	13.3	7.3	6.9	11.3	9.4
FAMILY TYPE										
Total families	449,281	98,610	44,845	22,669	25,077	21,856	11,825	12,314	12,988	12,650
Percent distribution:										
Married couple.	65.8	73.1	61.1	54.2	58.4	75.2	61.2	66.9	67.5	68.5
Female householder, no spouse present	26.2	20.8	28.6	36.0	33.1	20.0	29.2	24.7	25.5	23.9
Male householder, no spouse present	8.0	6.1	10.3	9.8	8.5	4.8	9.6	8.4	7.0	7.6
INCOME IN 1989										
Median family (dol.) [4]	21,619	24,907	13,940	16,525	20,249	24,467	19,845	19,690	27,025	23,934
Median household (dol.) [4] . . .	19,900	21,922	12,817	15,611	18,801	21,640	19,097	18,484	23,460	21,708
Per capita (dol.).	8,284	10,469	4,788	6,508	7,777	9,463	6,679	7,271	10,568	8,625
Families below poverty level [5] .	122,237	19,100	21,204	8,939	7,814	4,347	3,691	3,913	2,249	2,554
Percent below poverty level .	27.2	19.4	47.3	39.4	31.2	19.9	31.2	31.8	17.3	20.2
Persons below poverty level [5]	585,273	79,271	107,526	45,658	35,231	19,453	17,981	19,246	10,253	10,966
Percent below poverty level .	31.2	22.0	48.8	44.4	34.3	23.0	33.2	37.5	20.1	22.1

[1] Includes other American Indian tribes not shown separately. [2] Any entry with the spelling "Siouan" was miscoded to Sioux in North Carolina. [3] Reporting and/or processing problems have affected the data for this tribe. [4] For definition of median, see Guide to Tabular Presentation. [5] For explanation of poverty level, see text, Section 14, Income.

Source: U.S. Census Bureau, *1990 Census of Population, Characteristics of American Indians by Tribe and Language,* 1990 CP-3-7.

No. 55. Social and Economic Characteristics of the Hispanic Population: 1998

[As of **March, except labor force status, annual average (30,773 represents 30,773,000).** Excludes members of the Armed Forces except those living off post or with their families on post. Based on Current Population Survey; see text of this section and Appendix III]

Characteristic	Number (1,000)						Percent distribution					
	His-panic, total	Mexi-can	Puerto Rican	Cuban	Central and South Ameri-can	Other His-panic	His-panic, total	Mexi-can	Puerto Rican	Cuban	Central and South Ameri-can	Other His-panic
Total persons........	30,773	19,834	3,117	1,307	4,437	2,079	100.0	100.0	100.0	100.0	100.0	100.0
Under 5 years old........	3,482	2,464	347	93	383	196	11.3	12.4	11.1	7.1	8.6	9.4
5 to 14 years old	5,862	4,106	569	141	665	382	19.0	20.7	18.2	10.8	15.0	18.4
15 to 44 years old	15,479	9,935	1,487	548	2,516	993	50.3	50.1	47.7	41.9	56.7	47.8
45 to 64 years old	4,333	2,475	516	270	702	370	14.1	12.5	16.6	20.7	15.8	17.8
65 years old and over	1,617	854	199	255	172	138	5.3	4.3	6.4	19.5	3.9	6.6
EDUCATIONAL ATTAINMENT												
Persons 25 years old and over	16,044	9,649	1,682	952	2,599	1,163	100.0	100.0	100.0	100.0	100.0	100.0
High school graduate or higher.............	8,901	4,657	1,074	645	1,686	840	55.5	48.3	63.8	67.8	64.9	72.2
Bachelor's degree or higher ..	1,768	719	201	211	452	186	11.0	7.5	11.9	22.2	17.4	16.0
LABOR FORCE STATUS [1]												
Civilians 16 years old and over	21,070	13,216	2,080	1,062	3,215	1,497	100.0	100.0	100.0	100.0	100.0	100.0
Civilian labor force	14,317	9,096	1,249	651	2,343	978	67.9	68.8	60.0	61.3	72.9	65.3
Employed	13,291	8,431	1,145	612	2,201	902	63.1	63.8	55.0	57.6	68.5	60.3
Unemployed...........	1,026	664	104	39	143	76	4.9	5.0	5.0	3.7	4.4	5.1
Unemployment rate [2] ...	7.2	7.3	8.3	6.0	6.1	7.8	(X)	(X)	(X)	(X)	(X)	(X)
Male...............	6.4	6.5	8.5	4.1	5.4	7.2	(X)	(X)	(X)	(X)	(X)	(X)
Female.............	8.2	8.6	8.2	8.6	7.0	7.9	(X)	(X)	(X)	(X)	(X)	(X)
Not in labor force	6,753	4,121	832	411	872	517	32.1	31.2	40.0	38.7	27.1	34.5
FAMILY TYPE												
Total families	6,961	4,292	770	383	1,018	498	100.0	100.0	100.0	100.0	100.0	100.0
Married couple...........	4,804	3,093	415	309	688	298	69.0	72.1	53.9	80.8	67.6	59.8
Female householder, no spouse present	1,612	858	290	58	236	169	23.2	20.0	37.7	15.1	23.2	34.0
Male householder, no spouse present	545	341	65	16	93	31	7.8	7.9	8.4	4.1	9.2	6.2
FAMILY INCOME IN 1997												
Total families	6,961	4,292	770	383	1,018	498	100.0	100.0	100.0	100.0	100.0	100.0
Less than $5,000	352	219	52	8	45	27	5.1	5.1	6.8	2.2	4.4	5.5
$5,000 to $9,999	604	347	119	28	54	55	8.7	8.1	15.5	7.4	5.3	11.1
$10,000 to $14,999.......	759	500	81	44	89	44	10.9	11.7	10.5	11.5	8.8	8.9
$15,000 to $24,999.......	1,397	921	153	58	193	72	20.1	21.5	19.9	15.2	18.9	14.5
$25,000 to $34,999.......	1,066	688	92	44	164	77	15.3	16.0	11.9	11.5	16.1	15.6
$35,000 to $49,999.......	1,199	735	107	57	207	93	17.2	17.1	13.9	15.0	20.3	18.7
$50,000 or more	1,584	882	165	143	266	129	22.8	20.5	21.4	37.2	26.2	25.8
Median income (dol.) [3]	28,141	27,088	23,729	37,537	32,030	30,130	(X)	(X)	(X)	(X)	(X)	(X)
Families below poverty level [4].	1,721	1,106	243	60	188	124	24.7	25.8	31.5	15.6	18.4	25.0
Persons below poverty level [4].	8,308	5,509	1,059	257	949	534	27.1	27.9	34.2	19.6	21.5	25.7
HOUSING TENURE												
Total occupied units ...	8,590	5,091	1,053	498	1,272	677	100.0	100.0	100.0	100.0	100.0	100.0
Owner-occupied..........	3,857	2,495	355	279	404	326	44.9	49.0	33.7	55.9	31.8	48.1
Renter-occupied [5]........	4,733	2,597	698	220	868	351	55.1	51.0	66.3	44.1	68.2	51.9

X Not applicable. [1] Source: U.S. Bureau of Labor Statistics, *Employment and Earnings*, January 1999. [2] Total unemployment as percent of civilian labor force. [3] For definition of median, see Guide to Tabular Presentation. [4] For explanation of poverty level, see text, Section 14, Income. [5] Includes no cash rent.

Source: Except as noted, U.S. Census Bureau, unpublished data.

U.S. Census Bureau, Statistical Abstract of the United States: 1999

No. 56. Native and Foreign-Born Population, by Place of Birth: 1950 to 1990

[In thousands, except percent (150,216 represents 150,216,000). Data are based on a sample from the census; for details, see text, this section. See source for sampling variability]

Year	Total population	Native population						Foreign born	
		Total	Born in state of residence	Born in other states	State of birth not reported	Born in outlying areas [1]	Born abroad or at sea of American parents	Number	Percent of total population
1950	150,216	139,869	102,788	35,284	1,370	330	96	10,347	6.9
1960	178,467	168,806	118,802	44,264	4,526	817	397	9,661	5.4
1970	203,194	193,454	131,296	51,659	8,882	873	744	9,740	4.8
1980	226,546	212,466	144,871	65,452	(NA)	1,088	1,055	14,080	6.2
1990	248,710	228,943	153,685	72,011	(NA)	1,382	1,864	19,767	7.9

NA Not available.   [1] 1950, includes Alaska and Hawaii. Includes Puerto Rico.

Source: U.S. Census Bureau, *1970 Census of Population*, Vol. II, PC(2)-2A; and *1990 Census of Population Listing* (1990CPH-L-121).

No. 57. Native and Foreign-Born Populations by Selected Characteristics: 1997

[In thousands (241,014 represents 241,014,000). As of March. The foreign-born population includes some undocumented immigrants, refugees, and temporary residents such as students and temporary workers as well as legally-admitted immigrants. Based on Current Population Survey; see text, this section, and Appendix III]

Characteristic	Native population	Foreign-born population				
		Total	Year of entry			
			Before 1970	1970 to 1979	1980 to 1989	1990 to 1997
Total	**241,014**	**25,779**	**4,749**	**4,936**	**8,555**	**7,539**
Under 5 years old................	19,482	299	(X)	(X)	(X)	299
5 to 17 years old................	49,124	2,319	(X)	13	810	1,498
18 to 24 years old................	22,047	2,940	(X)	395	990	1,555
25 to 29 years old................	16,489	2,770	25	408	1,149	1,190
30 to 34 years old................	17,843	3,154	146	514	1,499	995
35 to 44 years old................	38,664	5,296	526	1,477	2,209	1,084
45 to 64 years old................	48,276	6,211	2,226	1,778	1,490	716
65 years old and over	29,088	2,789	1,827	350	408	203
Male..........................	117,690	12,946	2,081	2,453	4,476	3,937
Female........................	123,324	12,832	2,669	2,482	4,080	3,601
White..........................	202,566	17,504	4,060	3,195	5,362	4,887
Black..........................	32,190	2,028	233	413	833	550
American Indian/Eskimo/Aleut.............	2,291	142	13	17	43	69
Asian or Pacific Islander	3,967	6,105	444	1,310	2,318	2,032
Hispanic origin [1]	18,311	11,393	1,550	2,276	4,236	3,331
EDUCATIONAL ATTAINMENT						
Persons 25 years old and over	150,361	20,220	4,749	4,528	6,755	4,188
Not high school graduate................	23,515	7,009	1,499	1,548	2,526	1,436
High school grad/some college	91,098	8,261	2,299	1,823	2,612	1,526
Bachelor's degree..................	24,185	3,172	571	747	1,079	776
Graduate or professional degree	11,563	1,778	380	410	538	450
LABOR FORCE STATUS						
Persons 16 years old and over [2]	179,733	23,649	4,749	4,935	7,991	5,971
In the civilian labor force	119,635	15,593	2,299	3,717	5,769	3,806
Employed	113,156	14,524	2,197	3,496	5,383	3,447
Unemployed....................	6,479	1,069	102	221	386	359
Not in the labor force.	59,275	8,013	2,447	1,195	2,209	2,162
INCOME IN 1996						
Persons 16 years old and over	179,733	23,649	4,749	4,935	7,991	5,971
Without income	11,310	3,376	313	434	1,171	1,455
With income	168,423	20,273	4,436	4,501	6,820	4,516
$1 to $9,999 or loss................	50,469	7,036	1,494	1,257	2,317	1,970
$10,000 to $19,999	39,068	5,565	1,072	1,135	2,009	1,349
$20,000 to $34,999	39,380	4,023	857	1,051	1,456	658
$35,000 to $49,999	19,773	1,728	474	495	500	259
$50,000 or more	19,733	1,921	539	563	538	280
POVERTY STATUS [3]						
In poverty	31,117	5,412	497	651	1,943	2,320
Not in poverty	209,342	20,347	4,252	4,284	6,611	5,201
HOMEOWNERSHIP						
In owner-occupied unit..................	169,581	12,442	3,602	3,109	3,756	1,975
In renter-occupied unit..................	71,433	13,336	1,147	1,826	4,799	5,564

X Not applicable.   [1] Persons of Hispanic origin may be of any race.   [2] Includes persons in Armed Forces, not shown separately.   [3] Persons for whom poverty status is determined.

Source: U.S. Census Bureau, *Current Population Reports*, P20-507 and Population Paper Listing PPL-92.

U.S. Census Bureau, Statistical Abstract of the United States: 1999

No. 58. Foreign-Born Population, by Country of Origin and Citizenship Status: 1997

[In thousands, except percent (25,779 represents 25,779,000). See headnote, Table 57]

Country of origin	Foreign born, total		Naturalized citizen		Not U.S. citizen	
	Number	Percent	Number	Percent	Number	Percent
All countries	25,779	100.0	9,043	100.0	16,736	100.0
Mexico	7,017	27.2	1,044	11.5	5,973	35.7
Cuba	913	3.5	474	5.2	440	2.6
Dominican Republic	632	2.5	195	2.2	437	2.6
El Salvador	607	2.4	110	1.2	497	3.0
Great Britain	606	2.4	237	2.6	369	2.2
China and Hong Kong.	1,107	4.3	536	5.9	570	3.4
India	748	2.9	263	2.9	485	2.9
Korea	591	2.3	220	2.4	372	2.2
Philippines	1,132	4.4	657	7.3	475	2.8
Vietnam	770	3.0	385	4.3	385	2.3
Elsewhere	11,655	45.2	4,921	54.4	6,734	40.2

Source: U.S. Census Bureau, "CPS Publication—Country of Origin and Year of Entry into the U.S. of the Foreign Born: March 1997"; published 29 September 1997; <http://www.bls.census.gov/cps/pub/1997/forborn.htm>.

No. 59. Population, by Selected Ancestry Group and Region: 1990

[As of April 1 (1,119 represents 1,119,000). Covers persons who reported single and multiple ancestry groups. Persons who reported a multiple ancestry group may be included in more than one category. Major classifications of ancestry groups do not represent strict geographic or cultural definitions. Based on a sample and subject to sampling variability; see text, this section. For composition of regions, see map, see front cover]

Ancestry group	Total (1,000)	Percent distribution, by region				Ancestry group	Total (1,000)	Percent distribution, by region			
		North-east	Mid-west	South	West			North-east	Mid-west	South	West
European: [1]						Swiss	1,045	16	36	17	30
British	1,119	17	18	39	26	Welsh	2,034	22	24	27	27
Czech	1,296	10	52	22	16	Central & South					
Danish	1,635	9	34	12	45	America [3]					
Dutch	6,227	16	34	29	21	and Spain:					
English [2]	32,652	18	22	35	25	Hispanic [4]	1,113	13	6	31	50
French [2]	10,321	26	26	29	20	Mexican.	11,587	1	9	33	57
German	57,947	17	39	25	19	Puerto Rican . . .	1,955	66	11	15	8
Greek	1,110	37	23	21	19	Spanish	2,024	16	8	30	45
Hungarian	1,582	36	32	17	16	Asia:					
Irish	38,736	24	25	33	17	Chinese	1,505	25	8	12	55
Italian	14,665	51	17	17	15	Filipino	1,451	10	9	13	68
Norwegian	3,869	6	52	10	33	Japanese.	1,005	9	8	11	72
Polish	9,366	37	37	15	11	North America:					
Portuguese	1,153	49	3	8	41	Afro-American. . .	23,777	15	21	54	10
Russian	2,953	44	16	18	22	American Indian .	8,708	9	22	47	23
Scotch-Irish	5,618	14	19	47	20	American.	12,396	10	18	61	11
Scottish	5,394	20	21	33	26	French Canadian.	2,167	45	20	20	15
Slovak.	1,883	40	34	14	11	White	1,800	7	13	53	28
Swedish	4,681	14	40	14	32						

[1] Non-Hispanic groups. [2] Excludes French Basque. [3] Hispanic groups. [4] A general type of response which may encompass several ancestry groups.

Source: U.S. Census Bureau, *1990 Census of Population, Supplementary Reports, Detailed Ancestry Groups for States* (1990 CP-S-1-2).

No. 60. Persons 5 Years Old and Over Speaking a Language Other Than English at Home, by Language: 1990

[As of April (198,601 represent 198,601,000). Based on a sample and subject to sampling variability]

Language spoken at home	Persons who speak language (1,000)	Language spoken at home	Persons who speak language (1,000)
Speak only English	198,601	Hindi (Urdu)	331
Spanish	17,339	Russian	242
French	1,702	Yiddish	213
German	1,547	Thai (Laotian).	206
Italian	1,309	Persian	202
Chinese	1,249	French Creole	188
Tagalog.	843	Armenian	150
Polish	723	Navaho	149
Korean	626	Hungarian	148
Vietnamese	507	Hebrew.	144
Portuguese	430	Dutch	143
Japanese	428	Mon-Khmer (Cambodian) . . .	127
Greek	388	Gujarathi	102
Arabic	355		

Source: U.S. Census Bureau, *1990 Census of Population and Housing Data Paper Listing* (CPH-L-133); and Summary Tape File 3C.

56 Population

No. 61. Living Arrangements of Persons 15 Years Old and Over, by Selected Characteristics: 1998

[In thousands (209,291 represents 209,291,000). As of **March**. Based on Current Population Survey which includes members of Armed Forces living off post or with families on post, but excludes other Armed Forces; see text, this section, and Appendix III]

Living arrangement	Total	15 to 19 years old	20 to 24 years old	25 to 34 years old	35 to 44 years old	45 to 54 years old	55 to 64 years old	65 to 74 years old	75 years old and over
Total [1]	209,291	19,466	17,613	39,354	44,462	34,057	22,255	17,874	14,209
Alone	26,327	139	1,112	3,679	4,054	4,120	3,301	4,098	5,825
With spouse	110,619	298	3,313	21,267	29,181	23,564	15,613	11,328	6,054
With other persons	72,345	19,029	13,188	14,408	11,227	6,373	3,341	2,448	2,330
White	174,708	15,462	14,168	31,779	36,736	28,871	19,140	15,760	12,793
Alone	21,998	113	860	2,881	3,292	3,280	2,717	3,527	5,330
With spouse	97,415	268	2,937	18,342	25,315	20,631	13,972	10,350	5,600
With other persons	55,295	15,081	10,371	10,556	8,129	4,960	2,451	1,883	1,863
Black	24,998	3,058	2,563	5,300	5,499	3,663	2,224	1,613	1,078
Alone	3,576	17	185	580	633	721	511	501	428
With spouse	8,051	19	249	1,789	2,281	1,762	986	680	286
With other persons	13,371	3,022	2,129	2,931	2,585	1,180	727	432	364
Hispanic origin [2]	21,430	2,722	2,663	5,488	4,606	2,700	1,633	1,015	603
Alone	1,240	15	63	232	230	169	180	182	169
With spouse	10,221	103	648	3,027	2,894	1,711	1,036	563	240
With other persons	9,969	2,604	1,952	2,229	1,482	820	417	270	194

[1] Includes other races and persons not of Hispanic origin, not shown separately.   [2] Persons of Hispanic origin may be of any race.

No. 62. Marital Status of the Population, by Sex, Race, and Hispanic Origin: 1980 to 1998

[In millions, except percent (159.5 represents 159,500,000). As of **March. Persons 18 years old and over**. Excludes members of Armed Forces except those living off post or with their families on post. Based on Current Population Survey, see text, this section, and Appendix III]

Marital status, race, and Hispanic origin	Total				Male				Female			
	1980	1990	1995	1998	1980	1990	1995	1998	1980	1990	1995	1998
Total [1]	159.5	181.8	191.6	197.4	75.7	86.9	92.0	95.0	83.8	95.0	99.6	102.4
Never married	32.3	40.4	43.9	46.6	18.0	22.4	24.6	25.5	14.3	17.9	19.3	21.0
Married	104.6	112.6	116.7	117.9	51.8	55.8	57.7	58.6	52.8	56.7	58.9	59.3
Widowed	12.7	13.8	13.4	13.6	2.0	2.3	2.3	2.6	10.8	11.5	11.1	11.0
Divorced	9.9	15.1	17.6	19.4	3.9	6.3	7.4	8.3	6.0	8.8	10.3	11.1
Percent of total	100.0	100.0	100.0	100.0	100.0	100.0	100.0	100.0	100.0	100.0	100.0	100.0
Never married	20.3	22.2	22.9	23.6	23.8	25.8	26.8	26.9	17.1	18.9	19.4	20.5
Married	65.5	61.9	60.9	59.7	68.4	64.3	62.7	61.7	63.0	59.7	59.2	57.9
Widowed	8.0	7.6	7.0	6.9	2.6	2.7	2.5	2.7	12.8	12.1	11.1	10.8
Divorced	6.2	8.3	9.2	9.8	5.2	7.2	8.0	8.8	7.1	9.3	10.3	10.8
White, total	139.5	155.5	161.3	165.3	66.7	74.8	78.1	80.4	72.8	80.6	83.2	85.0
Never married	26.4	31.6	33.2	35.1	15.0	18.0	19.2	20.0	11.4	13.6	14.0	15.2
Married	93.8	99.5	102.0	102.6	46.7	49.5	50.6	51.3	47.1	49.9	51.3	51.3
Widowed	10.9	11.7	11.3	11.5	1.6	1.9	1.9	2.1	9.3	9.8	9.4	9.3
Divorced	8.3	12.6	14.8	16.1	3.4	5.4	6.3	7.0	5.0	7.3	8.4	9.1
Percent of total	100.0	100.0	100.0	100.0	100.0	100.0	100.0	100.0	100.0	100.0	100.0	100.0
Never married	18.9	20.3	20.6	21.2	22.5	24.1	24.6	24.8	15.7	16.9	16.9	17.8
Married	67.2	64.0	63.2	62.1	70.0	66.2	64.9	63.8	64.7	61.9	61.7	60.4
Widowed	7.8	7.5	7.0	6.9	2.5	2.6	2.5	2.6	12.8	12.2	11.3	11.0
Divorced	6.0	8.1	9.1	9.8	5.0	7.2	8.1	8.7	6.8	9.0	10.1	10.7
Black, total	16.6	20.3	22.1	23.1	7.4	9.1	9.9	10.3	9.2	11.2	12.2	12.8
Never married	5.1	7.1	8.5	9.0	2.5	3.5	4.1	4.2	2.5	3.6	4.4	4.8
Married	8.5	9.3	9.6	9.6	4.1	4.5	4.6	4.7	4.5	4.8	4.9	5.0
Widowed	1.6	1.7	1.7	1.8	0.3	0.3	0.3	0.4	1.3	1.4	1.4	1.4
Divorced	1.4	2.1	2.4	2.7	0.5	0.8	0.8	1.0	0.9	1.3	1.5	1.7
Percent of total	100.0	100.0	100.0	100.0	100.0	100.0	100.0	100.0	100.0	100.0	100.0	100.0
Never married	30.5	35.1	38.4	38.9	34.3	38.4	41.7	40.9	27.4	32.5	35.8	37.3
Married	51.4	45.8	43.2	41.8	54.6	49.2	46.7	45.3	48.7	43.0	40.4	38.9
Widowed	9.8	8.5	7.6	7.6	4.2	3.7	3.1	3.7	14.3	12.4	11.3	10.7
Divorced	8.4	10.6	10.7	11.7	7.0	8.8	8.5	10.1	9.5	12.0	12.5	13.1
Hispanic, [2] **total**	7.9	13.6	17.6	19.8	3.8	6.7	8.8	10.1	4.1	6.8	8.8	9.8
Never married	1.9	3.7	5.0	5.9	1.0	2.2	3.0	3.5	0.9	1.5	2.1	2.4
Married	5.2	8.4	10.4	11.7	2.5	4.1	5.1	5.8	2.6	4.3	5.3	5.9
Widowed	0.4	0.5	0.7	0.7	0.1	0.1	0.2	0.1	0.3	0.4	0.6	0.6
Divorced	0.5	1.0	1.4	1.5	0.2	0.4	0.6	0.6	0.3	0.6	0.8	0.9
Percent of total	100.0	100.0	100.0	100.0	100.0	100.0	100.0	100.0	100.0	100.0	100.0	100.0
Never married	24.1	27.2	28.6	29.7	27.3	32.1	33.8	34.8	21.1	22.5	23.5	24.3
Married	65.6	61.7	59.3	58.9	67.1	60.9	57.9	57.5	64.3	62.4	60.7	60.3
Widowed	4.4	4.0	4.2	3.8	1.6	1.5	1.8	1.3	7.1	6.5	6.6	6.3
Divorced	5.8	7.0	7.9	7.7	4.0	5.5	6.6	6.4	7.6	8.5	9.2	9.1

[1] Includes persons of other races, not shown separately.   [2] Hispanic persons may be of any race.
Source of Tables 61 and 62: U.S. Census Bureau, *Current Population Reports*, P20-514, and earlier reports; and unpublished data.

No. 63. Marital Status of the Population, by Sex and Age: 1998

[As of **March** (95,009 represents 95,009,000). **Persons 18 years old and over.** Excludes members of Armed Forces except those living off post or with their families on post. Based on Current Population Survey; see text, this section, and Appendix III]

Sex and age	Number of persons (1,000)					Percent distribution				
	Total	Never married	Married	Wid-owed	Divorced	Total	Never married	Married	Wid-owed	Divorced
Male	**95,009**	**25,518**	**58,601**	**2,567**	**8,322**	**100.0**	**26.9**	**61.7**	**2.7**	**8.8**
18 to 19 years old........	3,807	3,706	91	-	10	100.0	97.3	2.4	-	0.3
20 to 24 years old.......	8,826	7,360	1,332	-	133	100.0	83.4	15.1	-	1.5
25 to 29 years old.......	9,450	4,822	4,219	10	398	100.0	51.0	44.6	0.1	4.2
30 to 34 years old.......	10,076	2,939	6,345	20	773	100.0	29.2	63.0	0.2	7.7
35 to 39 years old.......	11,299	2,444	7,598	44	1,213	100.0	21.6	67.2	0.4	10.7
40 to 44 years old.......	10,756	1,676	7,633	50	1,397	100.0	15.6	71.0	0.5	13.0
45 to 54 years old.......	16,598	1,481	12,665	150	2,303	100.0	8.9	76.3	0.9	13.9
55 to 64 years old.......	10,673	572	8,559	275	1,266	100.0	5.4	80.2	2.6	11.9
65 to 74 years old.......	7,992	328	6,331	707	626	100.0	4.1	79.2	8.8	7.8
75 years old and over	5,533	190	3,829	1,311	202	100.0	3.4	69.2	23.7	3.7
Female.	**102,403**	**21,043**	**59,255**	**11,027**	**11,078**	**100.0**	**20.5**	**57.9**	**10.8**	**10.8**
18 to 19 years old.......	3,780	3,565	211	-	5	100.0	94.3	5.6	-	0.1
20 to 24 years old.......	8,788	6,178	2,372	17	222	100.0	70.3	27.0	0.2	2.5
25 to 29 years old.......	9,546	3,689	5,298	35	525	100.0	38.6	55.5	0.4	5.5
30 to 34 years old.......	10,282	2,219	7,044	55	964	100.0	21.6	68.6	0.5	9.4
35 to 39 years old.......	11,392	1,626	8,145	138	1,484	100.0	14.3	71.5	1.2	13.0
40 to 44 years old.......	11,015	1,095	8,016	166	1,738	100.0	9.9	72.8	1.5	15.8
45 to 54 years old.......	17,459	1,263	12,345	697	3,154	100.0	7.2	70.8	4.0	18.1
55 to 64 years old.......	11,582	538	7,847	1,526	1,671	100.0	4.6	67.8	13.2	14.4
65 to 74 years old.......	9,882	425	5,420	3,155	882	100.0	4.3	54.8	31.9	8.9
75 years old and over	8,677	446	2,558	5,239	433	100.0	5.1	29.5	60.4	5.0

- Represents or rounds to zero.

Source: U.S. Census Bureau, *Current Population Reports*, P20-514.

No. 64. Married Couples, by Age of Husband and Age of Wife: 1998

[In thousands (55,305 represents 55,305,000). As of **March. Persons 15 years old and over.** Excludes members of Armed Forces except those living off post or with their families on post. Based on Current Population Survey; see text, this section, and Appendix III]

Age of husband	Total	Age of wife						
		15 to 24 years	25 to 34 years	35 to 44 years	45 to 54 years	55 to 64 years	65 to 74 years	75 years and over
Total.	**55,305**	**2,366**	**11,428**	**14,950**	**11,549**	**7,452**	**5,181**	**2,380**
15 to 24 years.............	1,246	982	223	24	12	-	2	3
25 to 34 years.............	9,840	1,270	7,497	1,000	55	9	6	2
35 to 44 years.............	14,230	80	3,377	9,741	982	41	4	4
45 to 54 years.............	12,014	20	258	3,737	7,487	465	37	8
55 to 64 years.............	8,154	10	57	383	2,668	4,719	296	21
65 to 74 years.............	6,147	3	9	44	303	2,070	3,467	250
75 years and over	3,674	-	7	20	42	147	1,368	2,092

- Represents or rounds to zero.

Source: U.S. Census Bureau, *Current Population Reports*, P20-515.

No. 65. Married Couples of Same or Mixed Races and Origins: 1980 to 1998

[In thousands (49,714 represents 49,714,000). As of **March. Persons 15 years old and over.** Persons of Hispanic origin may be of any race. Except as noted, based on Current Population Survey; see headnote, Table 70]

Race and origin of spouses	1980	1990	1995	1998
Married couples, total	**49,714**	**53,256**	**54,937**	**55,305**
RACE				
White/White	44,910	47,202	48,030	48,050
Black/Black.	3,354	3,687	3,703	3,839
Black/White	167	211	328	330
Black husband/White wife	122	150	206	210
White husband/Black wife	45	61	122	120
White/other race [1]	450	720	988	975
Black/other race [1]	34	33	76	43
All other couples [1]	799	1,401	1,811	2,068
HISPANIC ORIGIN				
Hispanic/Hispanic	1,906	3,085	3,857	4,279
Hispanic/other origin (not Hispanic).........	891	1,193	1,434	1,662
All other couples (not of Hispanic origin)	46,917	48,979	49,646	49,363

[1] Excluding White and Black.

Source: U.S. Census Bureau, *Current Population Reports*, P20-515, and earlier reports; and unpublished data.

No. 66. Marriage and Cohabitation Experience of Women 15 to 44 Years of Age, by Selected Characteristics: 1995

[In percent, except as indicated (60,201 represents 60,201,000). Based on the National Survey of Family Growth, a sample survey of women 15 to 44 years of age in the civilian noninstitutionalized population; for details, see source]

Characteristic	Number (1,000)	Ever married or cohabited	Ever married	Ever cohabited Total	Never married	Before first marriage	After first marriage	Never cohabited	Currently cohabiting
Total women.......	60,201	72.5	62.3	41.1	10.2	23.6	7.3	58.9	7.0
15 to 19 years old......	8,961	11.4	4.5	8.9	7.0	1.8	0.1	91.1	4.1
20 to 24 years old......	9,041	54.5	34.3	38.4	20.2	17.2	0.9	61.6	11.2
25 to 29 years old......	9,693	79.7	64.3	49.3	15.4	30.1	3.8	50.7	9.8
30 to 34 years old......	11,065	89.2	79.9	51.4	9.3	33.8	8.3	48.6	7.5
35 to 39 years old......	11,211	92.9	86.5	50.0	6.4	31.0	12.6	50.0	5.2
40 to 44 years old......	10,230	94.5	90.4	43.0	4.1	23.0	15.9	57.0	4.4
Hispanic	6,702	71.8	61.4	36.7	10.4	19.2	7.1	63.3	8.2
Non-Hispanic White......	42,522	75.3	66.4	42.6	8.9	25.6	8.1	57.4	7.0
Non-Hispanic Black......	8,210	60.3	43.1	40.1	17.3	17.9	5.0	59.9	6.9
Non-Hispanic other	2,767	66.8	58.5	31.7	8.3	19.8	3.6	68.3	4.6
Never married.	22,679	27.0	(X)	27.0	27.0	(X)	(X)	73.0	11.4
Currently married	29,673	100.0	100.0	45.4	(X)	36.8	8.6	54.6	(X)
Formerly married.	7,849	100.0	100.0	65.4	(X)	41.8	23.7	34.6	20.7
Education: [1]									
No high school diploma or GED [2]	5,424	91.4	76.8	60.1	14.6	31.1	14.5	39.9	11.6
High school diploma or GED [2]	18,169	91.3	81.9	52.0	9.4	30.1	12.5	48.0	8.0
Some college, no bachelor's degree.	12,399	82.9	72.8	46.3	10.1	28.7	7.5	53.7	6.8
Bachelor's degree or higher	11,748	79.8	70.5	37.8	9.2	25.1	3.5	62.2	5.1

X Not applicable.   [1] Covers only women 22 to 44 years old at time of interview.   [2] GED is general equivalency diploma.

Source: U.S. National Center for Health Statistics, "Fertility, Family Planning, and Women's Health: New data from the 1995 National Survey of Family Growth," Vital and Health Statistics, Series 23, No. 19, 1997.

No. 67. Percent Distribution of Women 15 to 44 Years of Age by Number of Husbands or Cohabiting Partners: 1995

[In percent, except as indicated (60,201 represents 60,201,000). Based on the National Survey of Family Growth, a sample survey of women 15 to 44 years of age in the civilian noninstitutionalized population; for details, see source]

Characteristic	Number (1,000)	Total	Never married and never cohabited	One	Two	Three	Four or more
Total women	60,201	100.0	27.5	49.8	16.0	4.8	1.9
15 to 19 years old	8,961	100.0	88.6	10.8	0.4	0.2	0.1
20 to 24 years old	9,041	100.0	45.5	46.1	6.9	1.3	0.2
25 to 29 years old	9,693	100.0	20.3	60.2	16.0	2.8	0.7
30 to 34 years old	11,065	100.0	10.8	59.0	21.6	6.0	2.6
35 to 39 years old	11,211	100.0	7.1	59.1	21.6	8.6	3.6
40 to 44 years old	10,230	100.0	5.5	57.5	25.2	8.3	3.5
Hispanic	6,702	100.0	28.2	51.8	16.0	3.1	0.9
Non-Hispanic White	42,522	100.0	24.7	50.9	16.7	5.4	2.2
Non-Hispanic Black.	8,210	100.0	39.7	42.3	13.1	3.6	1.3
Non-Hispanic other.	2,767	100.0	33.2	51.7	12.1	2.3	0.7
Never married	22,679	100.0	73.0	19.4	5.5	1.5	0.5
Currently married	29,673	100.0	(X)	74.2	19.4	5.0	1.5
Formerly married	7,849	100.0	(X)	45.7	33.5	13.5	7.3
Education: [2]							
No high school diploma or GED [3]	5,424	100.0	8.6	52.8	25.9	8.9	3.8
High school diploma or GED [3]	18,169	100.0	8.7	58.4	22.7	7.1	3.0
Some college, no bachelor's degree.	12,399	100.0	17.1	56.8	18.2	5.9	2.0
Bachelor's degree or higher	11,748	100.0	20.2	61.9	14.0	2.9	1.0

X Not applicable.   [1] Husbands with whom a woman also cohabited (outside of marriage) are counted only once.   [2] Covers only women 22 to 44 years old at time of interview.   [3] GED is general equivalency diploma.

Source: U.S. National Center for Health Statistics, "Fertility, Family Planning, and Women's Health: New data from the 1995 National Survey of Family Growth," Vital and Health Statistics, Series 23, No. 19, 1997.

Population   59

No. 68. Unmarried Couples, by Selected Characteristics: 1980 to 1998

[In thousands (1,589 represents 1,589,000). As of **March**. An "unmarried couple" is two unrelated adults of the opposite sex sharing the same household. See headnote, Table 70]

Presence of children and age of householder	1980	1985	1990	1995	1998
Unmarried couples, total.	1,589	1,983	2,856	3,668	4,236
No children under 15 years old.	1,159	1,380	1,966	2,349	2,716
Some children under 15 years old.	431	603	891	1,319	1,520
Under 25 years old.	411	425	596	742	776
25 to 44 years old	837	1,203	1,775	2,188	2,475
45 to 64 years old	221	239	358	558	797
65 years old and over	119	116	127	180	188

No. 69. Householder and Marital Status of Population, 15 Years Old and Over: 1998

[In thousands (209,291 represents 209,291,000). As of **March**. See headnote, Table 70]

Householder and marital status	Total, 15 yrs. and over	Male					Female				
		Total [1]	20 to 24 years	25 to 44 years	45 to 64 years	65 yrs. and over	Total [1]	20 to 24 years	25 to 44 years	45 to 64 years	65 yrs. and over
Total persons	209,291	101,123	8,826	41,581	27,271	13,525	108,168	8,788	42,235	29,041	18,559
Householder.	102,528	59,903	2,338	26,149	20,444	10,622	42,625	2,392	16,828	12,175	10,876
Never married	17,622	8,585	1,455	5,141	1,310	363	9,037	1,706	5,070	1,276	690
Married, spouse present .	54,317	41,859	771	17,694	15,611	7,753	12,457	516	6,371	4,059	1,455
Married, spouse absent. .	4,814	1,913	62	943	669	234	2,900	64	1,564	928	340
Widowed	11,509	2,026	-	78	309	1,638	9,483	5	306	1,905	7,267
Divorced	14,267	5,519	49	2,293	2,545	632	8,748	101	3,515	4,008	1,124
Not householder	106,763	41,220	6,487	15,433	6,827	2,902	65,542	6,396	25,408	16,866	7,683
Never married	40,681	23,005	5,905	6,740	743	155	17,676	4,472	3,560	524	181
Married, spouse present .	56,302	13,450	407	6,376	4,562	2,068	42,852	1,619	20,008	14,946	6,106
Married, spouse absent. .	2,532	1,410	91	782	382	105	1,123	173	560	259	77
Widowed	2,090	543	-	47	116	379	1,546	12	87	319	1,127
Divorced	5,157	2,812	84	1,488	1,024	196	2,345	120	1,194	819	192

- Represents or rounds to zero. [1] Includes 15 to 19 year olds.

Source of Tables 68 and 69: U.S. Census Bureau, *Current Population Reports*, P20-514, and earlier reports.

No. 70. Households, Families, Subfamilies, and Married Couples: 1970 to 1998

[In thousands, except as indicated (63,401 represents 63,401,000). As of **March**. Based on Current Population Survey; includes members of Armed Forces living off post or with their families on post, but excludes all other members of Armed Forces; see text, this section, and Appendix III. For definition of terms, see text, this section. Minus sign (-) indicates decrease]

Type of unit	1970	1975	1980	1985	1990	1995	1997	1998	Percent change		
									1970-80	1980-90	1990-98
Households	63,401	71,120	80,776	86,789	93,347	98,990	101,018	102,528	27	16	10
Average size.	3.14	2.94	2.76	2.69	2.63	2.65	2.64	2.62	(X)	(X)	(X)
Family households.	51,456	55,563	59,550	62,706	66,090	69,305	70,241	70,880	16	11	7
Married couple	44,728	46,951	49,112	50,350	52,317	53,858	53,604	54,317	10	7	4
Male householder [1].	1,228	1,485	1,733	2,228	2,884	3,226	3,847	3,911	41	66	36
Female householder [1].	5,500	7,127	8,705	10,129	10,890	12,220	12,790	12,652	58	25	16
Nonfamily households . .	11,945	15,557	21,226	24,082	27,257	29,686	30,777	31,648	78	28	16
Male householder . . .	4,063	5,912	8,807	10,114	11,606	13,190	13,707	14,133	117	32	22
Female householder. .	7,882	9,645	12,419	13,968	15,651	16,496	17,070	17,516	58	26	12
One person.	10,851	13,939	18,296	20,602	22,999	24,732	25,402	26,327	69	26	14
Families	51,586	55,712	59,550	62,706	66,090	69,305	70,241	70,880	15	11	7
Average size.	3.58	3.42	3.29	3.23	3.17	3.19	3.19	3.18	(X)	(X)	(X)
Married couple	44,755	46,971	49,112	50,350	52,317	53,858	53,604	54,317	10	7	4
Male householder [1] .	1,239	1,499	1,733	2,228	2,884	3,226	3,847	3,911	40	66	36
Female householder [1] .	5,591	7,242	8,705	10,129	10,890	12,220	12,790	12,652	56	25	16
Unrelated subfamilies	130	149	360	526	534	674	615	575	177	48	8
Married couple	27	20	20	46	68	64	50	41	(B)	(B)	(B)
Male reference persons [1]	11	14	36	85	45	59	77	72	(B)	(B)	(B)
Female reference persons [1]	91	115	304	395	421	550	487	463	234	39	10
Related subfamilies.	1,150	1,349	1,150	2,228	2,403	2,878	2,907	2,870	-	109	19
Married couple	617	576	582	719	871	1,015	1,012	947	-6	50	9
Father-child [1]	48	69	54	116	153	195	244	250	(B)	(B)	63
Mother-child [1]	484	705	512	1,392	1,378	1,668	1,651	1,673	6	169	21
Married couples	45,373	47,547	49,714	51,114	53,256	54,937	54,666	55,305	10	7	4
With own household . . .	44,728	46,951	49,112	50,350	52,317	53,858	53,604	54,317	10	7	4
Without own household .	645	596	602	764	939	1,079	1,062	988	-7	56	5
Percent without	1.4	1.3	1.2	1.5	1.8	2.0	1.9	1.8	(X)	(X)	(X)

- Represents or rounds to zero.   B Not shown; base less than 75,000.   X Not applicable.   [1] No spouse present.

Source: U.S. Census Bureau, *Current Population Reports*, P20-515, and unpublished data.

U.S. Census Bureau, Statistical Abstract of the United States: 1999

No. 71. Households, by Age of Householder and Size of Household: 1980 to 1998

[In millions (80.8 represents 80,800,000). As of **March**. Based on Current Population Survey; see headnote, Table 70]

Age of householder and size of household	1980	1985	1990	1995	1997	1998 Total [1]	1998 White	1998 Black	1998 Hispanic [2]
Total	80.8	86.8	93.3	99.0	101.0	102.5	86.1	12.5	8.6
Age of householder:									
15 to 24 years old	6.6	5.4	5.1	5.4	5.2	5.4	4.2	0.9	0.8
25 to 29 years old	9.3	9.6	9.4	8.4	8.6	8.5	6.9	1.2	1.0
30 to 34 years old	9.3	10.4	11.0	11.1	10.7	10.6	8.5	1.6	1.3
35 to 44 years old	14.0	17.5	20.6	22.9	23.8	23.9	19.8	3.1	2.3
45 to 54 years old	12.7	12.6	14.5	17.6	18.8	19.5	16.4	2.4	1.4
55 to 64 years old	12.5	13.1	12.5	12.2	12.5	13.1	11.2	1.4	0.9
65 to 74 years old	10.1	10.9	11.7	11.8	11.7	11.3	9.9	1.1	0.6
75 years old and over.	6.4	7.3	8.4	9.6	9.7	10.2	9.3	0.8	0.4
One person	18.3	20.6	23.0	24.7	25.4	26.3	22.0	3.6	1.2
Male	7.0	7.9	9.0	10.1	10.4	11.0	9.0	1.6	0.6
Female	11.3	12.7	14.0	14.6	15.0	15.3	13.0	2.0	0.6
Two persons	25.3	27.4	30.1	31.8	32.7	33.0	28.8	3.1	1.8
Three persons	14.1	15.5	16.1	16.8	17.1	17.3	14.2	2.3	1.7
Four persons	12.7	13.6	14.5	15.3	15.4	15.4	12.7	1.9	1.8
Five persons	6.1	6.1	6.2	6.6	6.8	7.0	5.8	0.9	1.2
Six persons	2.5	2.3	2.1	2.3	2.3	2.2	1.7	0.3	0.5
Seven persons or more . . .	1.8	1.3	1.3	1.4	1.3	1.3	0.9	0.3	0.4

[1] Includes other races, not shown separately. [2] Hispanic persons may be of any race.

Source: U.S. Census Bureau, *Current Population Reports*, P20-515, and earlier reports; and unpublished data.

No. 72. Household Characteristics, by Type of Household: 1998

[As of **March** (102,528 represents 102,528,000). Based on Current Population Survey; see headnote, Table 70]

Characteristic	Number of households (1,000) Total	Family households Total [1]	Family households Married couple	Family households Female house-holder [2]	Non-family house-holds	Percent distribution Total	Family households Total [1]	Family households Married couple	Family households Female house-holder [2]	Non-family house-holds
Total.	102,528	70,880	54,317	12,652	31,648	100	100	100	100	100
Age of householder:										
15 to 24 years old.	5,435	3,019	1,373	1,095	2,417	5	4	3	9	8
25 to 29 years old.	8,463	5,734	3,967	1,305	2,729	8	8	7	10	9
30 to 34 years old.	10,570	7,905	5,919	1,582	2,665	10	11	11	13	8
35 to 44 years old.	23,943	18,872	14,180	3,637	5,072	23	27	26	29	16
45 to 54 years old.	19,547	14,694	11,734	2,260	4,853	19	21	22	18	15
55 to 64 years old.	13,072	9,387	7,936	1,099	3,685	13	13	15	9	12
65 to 74 years old.	11,272	6,989	5,841	938	4,283	11	10	11	7	14
75 years old and over	10,225	4,282	3,368	738	5,944	10	6	6	6	19
Size of household:										
One person	26,327	(X)	(X)	(X)	26,327	26	(X)	(X)	(X)	83
Two persons	32,965	28,722	21,833	5,290	4,243	32	41	40	42	13
Three persons	17,331	16,640	11,595	3,858	691	17	23	21	30	2
Four persons	15,358	15,090	12,427	2,008	268	15	21	23	16	1
Five persons	7,048	6,972	5,743	924	76	7	10	11	7	(Z)
Six persons	2,232	2,195	1,807	293	37	2	3	3	2	(Z)
Seven persons or more . . .	1,267	1,260	911	278	7	1	2	2	2	(Z)
Marital status of householder:										
Never married (single)	17,622	5,449	(X)	3,831	12,173	17	8	(X)	30	38
Married, spouse present. . .	54,317	54,317	54,317	(X)	(X)	53	77	100	(X)	(X)
Married, spouse absent . . .	4,814	2,506	(X)	1,977	2,307	5	4	(X)	16	7
Widowed.	11,509	2,698	(X)	2,325	8,811	11	4	(X)	18	28
Divorced	14,267	5,910	(X)	4,518	8,357	14	8	(X)	36	26

X Not applicable.   Z Less than 0.5 percent.   [1] Includes male householder, no spouse present.   [2] No spouse present.

Source: U.S. Census Bureau, *Current Population Reports*, P20-515.

U.S. Census Bureau, Statistical Abstract of the United States: 1999

No. 73. Households, 1980 to 1998, and Persons in Households, 1998, by Type of Household and Presence of Children

[As of **March** (80,776 represents 80,776,000). Based on Current Population Survey; see headnote, Table 70]

Type of household and presence of children	Households					Persons in households, 1998		Persons per house-hold, 1998
	Number (1,000)			Percent distribution		Number (1,000)	Percent distribu-tion	
	1980	1990	1998	1990	1998			
Total households	80,776	93,347	102,528	100	100	268,984	100	2.62
Family households	59,550	66,090	70,880	71	69	229,690	85	3.24
With own children under 18 yrs. old . . .	31,022	32,289	34,760	35	34	(NA)	(NA)	(NA)
Without own children under 18 yrs. old .	28,528	33,801	36,120	36	35	(NA)	(NA)	(NA)
Married couple family	49,112	52,317	54,317	56	53	176,827	66	3.26
With own children under 18 yrs. old . . .	24,961	24,537	25,269	26	25	(NA)	(NA)	(NA)
Without own children under 18 yrs. old .	24,151	27,780	29,048	30	28	(NA)	(NA)	(NA)
Male householder, no spouse present. . . .	1,733	2,884	3,911	3	4	12,590	5	3.22
With own children under 18 yrs. old . . .	616	1,153	1,798	1	2	(NA)	(NA)	(NA)
Without own children under 18 yrs. old .	1,117	1,731	2,113	2	2	(NA)	(NA)	(NA)
Female householder, no spouse present . .	8,705	10,890	12,652	12	12	40,274	15	3.18
With own children under 18 yrs. old . . .	5,445	6,599	7,693	7	8	(NA)	(NA)	(NA)
Without own children under 18 yrs. old .	3,261	4,290	4,960	5	5	(NA)	(NA)	(NA)
Nonfamily households.	21,226	27,257	31,648	29	31	39,294	15	1.24
Living alone	18,296	22,999	26,327	25	26	26,327	10	1.00
Male householder	8,807	11,606	14,133	12	14	18,784	7	1.33
Living alone	6,966	9,049	11,010	10	11	11,010	4	1.00
Female householder	12,419	15,651	17,516	17	17	20,510	8	1.17
Living alone	11,330	13,950	15,317	15	15	15,317	6	1.00

NA Not available.

Source: U.S. Census Bureau, *Current Population Reports*, P20-515, and earlier reports; and unpublished data.

No. 74. Family and Nonfamily Households, by Race, Hispanic Origin, and Type: 1980 to 1998

[As of **March**, except as noted **(80,776 represents 80,776,000)**. Based on Current Population Survey, except as noted; see headnote, Table 70]

Race, Hispanic origin, and type	Number (1,000)					Percent distribution				
	1980	1985	1990	1995	1998	1980	1985	1990	1995	1998
TOTAL HOUSEHOLDS										
Total [1]	80,776	86,789	93,347	98,990	102,528	100	100	100	100	100
White	70,766	75,328	80,163	83,737	86,106	88	87	86	85	84
Black	8,586	9,480	10,486	11,655	12,474	11	11	11	12	12
Hispanic [2]	3,684	4,883	5,933	7,735	8,590	5	6	6	8	8
FAMILY HOUSEHOLDS										
White, total	52,243	54,400	56,590	58,437	59,511	100	100	100	100	100
Married couple	44,751	45,643	46,981	47,899	48,066	86	84	83	82	81
Male householder [3]	1,441	1,816	2,303	2,507	3,137	3	3	4	4	5
Female householder [3]	6,052	6,941	7,306	8,031	8,308	12	13	13	14	14
Black, total	6,184	6,778	7,470	8,093	8,408	100	100	100	100	100
Married couple	3,433	3,469	3,750	3,842	3,921	56	51	50	47	47
Male householder [3]	256	344	446	536	562	4	5	6	7	7
Female householder [3]	2,495	2,964	3,275	3,716	3,926	40	44	44	46	47
Asian or Pacific Islander, total [4] .	818	(NA)	1,531	1,588	2,381	100	(NA)	100	100	100
Married couple	691	(NA)	1,256	1,290	1,946	84	(NA)	82	81	82
Male householder [3]	39	(NA)	86	98	157	5	(NA)	6	6	7
Female householder [3]	88	(NA)	188	200	278	11	(NA)	12	13	12
Hispanic, total [2]	3,029	3,939	4,840	6,200	6,961	100	100	100	100	100
Married couple	2,282	2,824	3,395	4,235	4,804	75	72	70	68	69
Male householder [3]	138	210	329	479	545	5	5	7	8	8
Female householder [3]	610	905	1,116	1,485	1,612	20	23	23	24	23
NONFAMILY HOUSEHOLDS										
White, total	18,522	20,928	23,573	25,300	26,596	100	100	100	100	100
Male householder	7,499	8,608	9,951	11,093	11,725	40	41	42	44	44
Female householder	11,023	12,320	13,622	14,207	14,871	60	59	58	56	56
Black, total	2,402	2,703	3,015	3,562	4,066	100	100	100	100	100
Male householder	1,146	1,244	1,313	1,653	1,876	48	46	44	46	46
Female householder	1,256	1,459	1,702	1,909	2,190	52	54	56	54	54
Hispanic, total [2]	654	944	1,093	1,535	1,630	100	100	100	100	100
Male householder	365	509	587	790	875	56	54	54	51	54
Female householder	289	435	506	745	754	44	46	46	49	46

NA Not available. [1] Includes other races not shown separately. [2] Hispanic persons may be of any race. [3] No spouse present. [4] 1980 data as of April and are from 1980 Census of Population. When comparing 1995 estimates of number of households with other years, caution should be used.

Source: U.S. Census Bureau, *Current Population Reports*, P20-515, and earlier reports; and unpublished data.

No. 75. Households—States: 1980 to 1996

[As of **April 1**, except **beginning 1993**, as of **July 1** (80,390 represents 80,390,000). Minus sign (-) indicates decrease]

State	Number (1,000)					1996		Percent change		Persons per household		
						Total	Householder 65 yrs. and over					
	1980	1990	1993	1994	1995			1980-90	1990-96	1980	1990	1996
U.S.	80,390	91,946	95,358	95,988	97,386	98,751	21,381	14.4	7.4	2.75	2.63	2.62
AL.	1,342	1,507	1,574	1,582	1,603	1,624	367	12.3	7.8	2.84	2.62	2.58
AK.	131	189	206	207	210	214	20	43.7	13.4	2.93	2.80	2.75
AZ.	957	1,369	1,466	1,518	1,624	1,687	366	43.0	23.3	2.79	2.62	2.57
AR.	816	891	919	925	938	951	236	9.2	6.7	2.74	2.57	2.58
CA.	8,630	10,381	10,812	10,829	10,941	11,101	2,153	20.3	6.9	2.68	2.79	2.81
CO	1,061	1,282	1,388	1,424	1,466	1,502	246	20.8	17.1	2.65	2.51	2.49
CT.	1,094	1,230	1,227	1,222	1,225	1,231	287	12.5	-	2.76	2.59	2.59
DE.	207	247	262	264	270	276	58	19.5	11.4	2.79	2.61	2.56
DC	253	250	243	238	233	231	50	-1.4	-7.3	2.40	2.26	2.17
FL.	3,744	5,135	5,379	5,451	5,551	5,648	1,640	37.1	10.0	2.55	2.46	2.50
GA	1,872	2,366	2,533	2,587	2,654	2,723	465	26.4	15.1	2.84	2.66	2.64
HI	294	356	376	380	384	389	87	21.2	9.0	3.15	3.01	2.96
ID	324	361	395	405	419	430	86	11.3	19.1	2.85	2.73	2.72
IL	4,045	4,202	4,294	4,295	4,322	4,352	942	3.9	3.6	2.76	2.65	2.66
IN	1,927	2,065	2,149	2,156	2,182	2,209	472	7.2	6.9	2.77	2.61	2.57
IA	1,053	1,064	1,084	1,084	1,093	1,103	275	1.1	3.6	2.68	2.52	2.50
KS.	872	945	962	965	975	982	224	8.3	3.9	2.62	2.53	2.54
KY.	1,263	1,380	1,430	1,437	1,457	1,478	322	9.2	7.1	2.82	2.60	2.56
LA.	1,412	1,499	1,539	1,543	1,559	1,572	324	6.2	4.8	2.91	2.74	2.69
ME	395	465	474	473	477	483	109	17.7	3.8	2.75	2.56	2.50
MD	1,461	1,749	1,816	1,830	1,853	1,871	356	19.7	7.0	2.82	2.67	2.65
MA	2,033	2,247	2,264	2,269	2,297	2,322	536	10.5	3.3	2.72	2.58	2.53
MI	3,195	3,419	3,494	3,500	3,534	3,576	765	7.0	4.6	2.84	2.66	2.62
MN	1,445	1,648	1,702	1,716	1,740	1,763	366	14.0	7.0	2.74	2.58	2.58
MS	827	911	941	948	964	979	222	10.2	7.4	2.97	2.75	2.70
MO	1,793	1,961	2,001	2,009	2,031	2,052	478	9.4	4.6	2.67	2.53	2.54
MT	284	306	321	326	335	341	75	7.9	11.3	2.70	2.53	2.51
NE.	571	602	615	616	624	631	147	5.4	4.8	2.66	2.54	2.54
NV.	304	466	535	562	591	619	115	53.2	32.8	2.59	2.53	2.54
NH	323	411	419	423	431	439	85	27.1	6.7	2.75	2.62	2.58
NJ.	2,549	2,795	2,839	2,841	2,866	2,889	674	9.7	3.4	2.84	2.70	2.71
NM	441	543	578	592	607	619	122	22.9	14.1	2.90	2.74	2.72
NY.	6,340	6,639	6,702	6,684	6,709	6,737	1,524	4.7	1.5	2.70	2.63	2.62
NC	2,043	2,517	2,646	2,680	2,738	2,796	589	23.2	11.1	2.78	2.54	2.54
ND	228	241	242	242	244	247	60	5.8	2.4	2.75	2.55	2.51
OH	3,834	4,088	4,187	4,187	4,223	4,260	956	6.6	4.2	2.76	2.59	2.56
OK	1,119	1,206	1,235	1,238	1,250	1,265	291	7.8	4.9	2.62	2.53	2.54
OR	992	1,103	1,180	1,197	1,223	1,249	273	11.3	13.2	2.60	2.52	2.51
PA.	4,220	4,496	4,559	4,552	4,575	4,594	1,211	6.6	2.2	2.74	2.57	2.55
RI	339	378	378	376	376	378	96	11.6	-0.1	2.70	2.55	2.53
SC.	1,030	1,258	1,328	1,331	1,352	1,376	289	22.1	9.4	2.93	2.68	2.62
SD.	243	259	265	267	270	273	68	6.8	5.4	2.74	2.59	2.59
TN.	1,619	1,854	1,941	1,965	2,002	2,041	431	14.5	10.1	2.77	2.56	2.54
TX.	4,929	6,071	6,458	6,570	6,741	6,894	1,240	23.2	13.6	2.82	2.73	2.71
UT.	449	537	586	600	621	639	112	19.8	19.0	3.20	3.15	3.08
VT.	178	211	218	220	223	227	45	18.1	7.5	2.75	2.57	2.50
VA.	1,863	2,292	2,414	2,439	2,476	2,511	469	23.0	9.6	2.77	2.61	2.58
WA	1,541	1,872	2,019	2,049	2,097	2,139	406	21.5	14.2	2.61	2.53	2.53
WV	686	689	705	705	709	714	187	0.3	3.7	2.79	2.55	2.50
WI	1,652	1,822	1,883	1,891	1,917	1,943	432	10.3	6.6	2.77	2.61	2.58
WY	166	169	176	178	181	184	35	1.9	8.8	2.78	2.63	2.56

- Represents or rounds to zero.

Source: U.S. Census Bureau, *1980 Census of Population*, Vol. 1, Chapter B; *1990 Census of Population, General Population Characteristics, United States* (1990 CP-1-1); "ST-96-20R Estimates of Housing Units, Households, Households by Age of Householder, and Persons Per Household: July 1, 1996"; published 21 August 1997; <http://www.census.gov/population/estimates/housing/prhuhht1.txt>; and unpublished data.

Population 63

No. 76. Family Groups With Children Under 18 Years Old, by Race and Hispanic Origin: 1980 to 1998

[As of **March (32,150 represents 32,150,000)**. Family groups comprise family households, related subfamilies, and unrelated subfamilies. Excludes members of Armed Forces except those living off post or with their families on post. Based on Current Population Survey; see text, this section, and Appendix III]

Race and Hispanic origin of householder or reference person	Number (1,000)				Percent distribution			
	1980	1990	1995	1998	1980	1990	1995	1998
All races, total [1]	32,150	34,670	37,168	37,657	100	100	100	100
Two-parent family groups	25,231	24,921	25,640	25,709	79	72	69	68
One-parent family groups	6,920	9,749	11,528	11,948	22	28	31	32
Maintained by mother	6,230	8,398	9,834	9,828	19	24	26	26
Maintained by father	690	1,351	1,694	2,120	2	4	5	6
White, total	27,294	28,294	29,846	30,314	100	100	100	100
Two-parent family groups	22,628	21,905	22,320	22,237	83	77	75	73
One-parent family groups	4,664	6,389	7,525	8,077	17	23	25	27
Maintained by mother	4,122	5,310	6,239	6,328	15	19	21	21
Maintained by father	542	1,079	1,286	1,749	2	4	4	6
Black, total	4,074	5,087	5,491	5,604	100	100	100	100
Two-parent family groups	1,961	2,006	1,962	2,111	48	39	36	38
One-parent family groups	2,114	3,081	3,529	3,493	52	61	64	62
Maintained by mother	1,984	2,860	3,197	3,211	49	56	58	57
Maintained by father	129	221	332	282	3	4	6	5
Hispanic, total [2]	2,194	3,429	4,527	5,021	100	100	100	100
Two-parent family groups	1,626	2,289	2,879	3,233	74	67	64	64
One-parent family groups	568	1,140	1,647	1,789	26	33	36	36
Maintained by mother	526	1,003	1,404	1,500	24	29	31	30
Maintained by father	42	138	243	289	2	4	5	6

[1] Includes other races, not shown separately.   [2] Hispanic persons may be of any race.

Source: U.S. Census Bureau, *Current Population Reports*, P20-515, and earlier reports; and unpublished data.

No. 77. Family Groups With Children Under 18 Years Old, by Type, Race, and Hispanic Origin: 1998

[As of **March (37,657 represents 37,657,000)**. Excludes members of Armed Forces except those living off post or with their families on post. Based on Current Population Survey; see text, this section, and Appendix III]

Race and Hispanic origin of householder or reference person	Number (1,000)					Percent distribution				
	Total	Family house-holds	Subfamilies Total	Related	Unre-lated	Total	Family house-holds	Subfamilies Total	Related	Unre-lated
All races, total [1]	37,657	34,760	2,897	2,348	549	100	100	100	100	100
Two-parent family groups	25,709	25,269	439	425	14	68	73	15	18	3
One-parent family groups	11,948	9,491	2,458	1,923	535	32	27	85	82	97
Maintained by mother	9,828	7,693	2,136	1,673	463	26	22	74	71	84
Maintained by father	2,120	1,798	322	250	72	6	5	11	11	13
White, total	30,314	28,336	1,978	1,531	447	100	100	100	100	100
Two-parent family groups	22,237	21,910	326	313	13	73	77	16	20	3
One-parent family groups	8,077	6,426	1,651	1,218	433	27	23	83	80	97
Maintained by mother	6,328	4,912	1,416	1,045	371	21	17	72	68	83
Maintained by father	1,749	1,514	235	173	62	6	5	12	11	14
Black, total	5,604	4,847	757	680	77	100	100	100	100	100
Two-parent family groups	2,111	2,055	55	55	-	38	42	7	8	-
One-parent family groups	3,493	2,792	702	625	77	62	58	93	92	100
Maintained by mother	3,211	2,569	643	572	71	57	53	85	84	92
Maintained by father	282	223	59	53	6	5	5	8	8	8
Hispanic, total [2]	5,021	4,475	546	483	63	100	100	100	100	100
Two-parent family groups	3,233	3,121	112	100	12	64	70	21	21	19
One-parent family groups	1,789	1,354	435	384	51	36	30	80	80	81
Maintained by mother	1,500	1,121	379	342	37	30	25	69	71	59
Maintained by father	289	233	56	42	14	6	5	10	9	22

- Represents or rounds to zero.   [1] Includes other races, not shown separately.   [2] Hispanic persons may be of any race.

Source: U.S. Census Bureau, *Current Population Reports*, P20-515.

No. 78. Families, by Size and Presence of Children: 1980 to 1998

[In thousands, except as indicated (59,550 represents 59,550,000). As of March. Excludes members of Armed Forces except those living off post or with their families on post. Based on Current Population Survey; see text, this section, and Appendix III. For definition of families, see text, this section]

Characteristic	Number					Percent distribution				
	1980	1985	1990	1995	1998	1980	1985	1990	1995	1998
Total..............	59,550	62,706	66,090	69,305	70,880	100	100	100	100	100
Size of family:										
Two persons	23,461	25,349	27,606	29,176	30,282	39	40	42	42	43
Three persons	13,603	14,804	15,353	15,903	16,231	23	24	23	23	23
Four persons	12,372	13,259	14,026	14,624	14,633	21	21	21	21	21
Five persons	5,930	5,894	5,938	6,283	6,555	10	9	9	9	9
Six persons..........	2,461	2,175	1,997	2,106	2,047	4	4	3	3	3
Seven or more persons ..	1,723	1,225	1,170	1,213	1,130	3	2	2	2	2
Average per family	3.29	3.23	3.17	3.19	3.18	(X)	(X)	(X)	(X)	(X)
Own children under age 18:										
None	28,528	31,594	33,801	35,009	36,120	48	50	51	51	51
One.............	12,443	13,108	13,530	14,088	14,363	21	21	20	20	20
Two	11,470	11,645	12,263	13,213	13,122	19	19	19	19	19
Three.............	4,674	4,486	4,650	5,044	5,353	8	7	7	7	8
Four or more	2,435	1,873	1,846	1,951	1,921	4	3	3	3	3
Own children under age 6:										
None	46,063	48,505	50,905	53,695	55,348	77	77	77	77	78
One	9,441	9,677	10,304	10,733	10,742	16	15	16	15	15
Two or more	4,047	4,525	4,882	4,876	4,791	7	7	7	7	7

X Not applicable.

Source: U.S. Census Bureau, *Current Population Reports*, P20-515, and earlier reports; and unpublished data.

No. 79. Families, by Number of Own Children Under 18 Years Old: 1980 to 1998

[As of March (59,550 represents 59,550,000) and based on Current Population Survey; see headnote, Table 78]

Race, Hispanic origin, and year	Number of families (1,000)					Percent distribution				
	Total	No children	One child	Two children	Three or more children	Total	No children	One child	Two children	Three or more children
ALL FAMILIES [1]										
1980	59,550	28,528	12,443	11,470	7,109	100	48	21	19	12
1985	62,706	31,594	13,108	11,645	6,359	100	50	21	19	10
1990	66,090	33,801	13,530	12,263	6,496	100	51	20	19	10
1995	69,305	35,009	14,088	13,213	6,995	100	51	20	19	10
1997	70,241	35,575	14,334	13,295	7,037	100	51	20	19	10
Married couple	53,604	28,521	9,510	10,152	5,420	100	53	18	19	10
Male householder [2] ..	3,847	2,138	1,003	513	192	100	56	26	13	5
Female householder [2]	12,790	4,916	3,821	2,629	1,423	100	38	30	21	11
1998	70,880	36,120	14,363	13,122	7,275	100	51	20	19	10
Married couple	54,317	29,048	9,507	10,241	5,521	100	53	18	19	10
Male householder [2] ..	3,911	2,113	1,117	456	225	100	54	29	12	6
Female householder [2]	12,652	4,960	3,739	2,425	1,529	100	39	30	19	12
WHITE FAMILIES										
1980	52,243	25,769	10,727	9,977	5,769	100	49	21	19	11
1985	54,400	28,169	11,174	9,937	5,120	100	52	21	18	9
1990	56,590	29,872	11,186	10,342	5,191	100	53	20	18	9
1995	58,437	30,486	11,491	10,983	5,478	100	52	20	19	9
1997	58,934	30,698	11,594	11,046	5,595	100	52	20	19	10
1998	59,511	31,175	11,716	10,796	5,824	100	52	20	18	10
BLACK FAMILIES										
1980	6,184	2,364	1,449	1,235	1,136	100	38	23	20	18
1985	6,778	2,887	1,579	1,330	982	100	43	23	20	15
1990	7,470	3,093	1,894	1,433	1,049	100	41	25	19	14
1995	8,093	3,411	1,971	1,593	1,117	100	42	24	20	14
1997	8,455	3,569	2,071	1,654	1,162	100	42	25	20	14
1998	8,408	3,561	1,961	1,749	1,138	100	42	23	21	14
HISPANIC FAMILIES [3]										
1980	3,029	946	680	698	706	100	31	22	23	23
1985	3,939	1,337	904	865	833	100	34	23	22	21
1990	4,840	1,790	1,095	1,036	919	100	37	23	21	19
1995	6,200	2,216	1,408	1,406	1,171	100	36	23	23	19
1997	6,631	2,326	1,589	1,516	1,200	100	35	24	23	18
1998	6,961	2,486	1,585	1,616	1,273	100	36	23	23	18

[1] Includes other races, not shown separately.   [2] No spouse present.   [3] Hispanic persons may be of any race.

Source: U.S. Census Bureau, *Current Population Reports*, P20-515, and earlier reports; and unpublished data.

U.S. Census Bureau, Statistical Abstract of the United States: 1999

No. 80. Families by Type, Race and Hispanic Origin: 1998

[In thousands, except as indicated (70,880 represents 70,880,000). As of **March**. Excludes members of Armed Forces except those living off post or with their families on post. Based on Current Population Survey; see text of this section and Appendix III. For definition of families, see text of this section]

Characteristic	All families	Married couple families				Female family householder [3]				Male family house- holder, [3] all races
		All races [1]	White	Black	His- panic [2]	All races [1]	White	Black	His- panic [2]	
All families	70,880	54,317	48,066	3,921	4,804	12,652	8,308	3,926	1,612	3,911
Age of householder:										
Under 25 years old	3,019	1,373	1,221	111	300	1,095	612	429	180	551
25 to 34 years old	13,639	9,886	8,557	858	1,345	2,887	1,725	1,085	435	866
35 to 44 years old	18,872	14,180	12,382	1,066	1,427	3,637	2,371	1,146	461	1,055
45 to 54 years old	14,694	11,734	10,324	884	812	2,260	1,551	607	284	701
55 to 64 years old	9,387	7,936	7,125	485	507	1,099	748	314	135	352
65 to 74 years old	6,989	5,841	5,338	369	282	938	710	214	78	210
75 years old and over	4,282	3,368	3,118	149	130	738	591	132	39	176
Without own children under 18	36,120	29,048	26,156	1,865	1,683	4,960	3,396	1,357	491	2,113
With own children under 18	34,760	25,269	21,910	2,055	3,121	7,693	4,912	2,569	1,121	1,798
One own child under 18	14,363	9,507	8,231	723	1,001	3,739	2,539	1,104	445	1,117
Two own children under 18	13,122	10,241	8,913	830	1,174	2,425	1,498	865	384	456
Three or more own children under 18	7,275	5,521	4,766	502	946	1,529	875	600	292	225
Average per family with own children under 18	1.85	1.90	1.88	1.94	2.19	1.78	1.72	1.85	2.10	1.52
Marital status of householder:										
Married, spouse present	54,317	54,317	48,066	3,921	4,804	(X)	(X)	(X)	(X)	(X)
Married, spouse absent	2,506	(X)	(X)	(X)	(X)	1,977	1,269	617	399	529
Widowed	2,698	(X)	(X)	(X)	(X)	2,325	1,767	493	200	373
Divorced	5,910	(X)	(X)	(X)	(X)	4,518	3,486	914	457	1,391
Never married	5,449	(X)	(X)	(X)	(X)	3,831	1,787	1,901	557	1,618

X Not applicable.   [1] Includes other races not shown separately.   [2] Persons of Hispanic origin may be of any race.   [3] No spouse present.

Source: U.S. Census Bureau, *Current Population Reports*, P20-515.

No. 81. Family Households With Own Children Under Age 18, by Type of Family, 1980 to 1998, and by Age of Householder, 1998

[As of March (31,022 represents 31,022,000). Excludes members of Armed Forces except those living off post or with their families on post. Based on Current Population Survey; see text of this section and Appendix III]

Family type	1980	1990	1998							
			Total	15 to 24 years old	25 to 34 years old	35 to 44 years old	45 to 54 years old	55 to 64 years old	65 years old and over	
NUMBER (1,000)										
Family households with children	31,022	32,289	34,760	1,862	10,419	15,329	6,249	760	139	
Married couple	24,961	24,537	25,269	811	7,237	11,592	4,935	591	104	
Male householder [1]	616	1,153	1,798	186	489	694	349	65	14	
Female householder [1]	5,445	6,599	7,693	866	2,693	3,041	966	104	22	
PERCENT DISTRIBUTION										
Family households with children	100	100	100	100	100	100	100	100	100	
Married couple	81	76	73	44	69	76	79	78	75	
Male householder [1]	2	4	5	10	5	5	6	9	10	
Female householder [1]	18	20	22	47	26	20	15	14	16	
HOUSEHOLDS WITH CHILDREN, AS A PERCENT OF ALL FAMILY HOUSEHOLDS, BY TYPE										
Family households with children, total	52	49	49	62	76	81	43	8	1	
Married couple	51	47	47	59	73	82	42	7	1	
Male householder [1]	36	40	46	34	56	66	50	18	4	
Female householder [1]	63	61	61	79	93	84	43	9	1	

[1] No spouse present.

Source: U.S. Census Bureau, *Current Population Reports*, P20-515, and earlier reports; and unpublished data.

No. 82. Female Family Householders With No Spouse Present—Characteristics, by Race and Hispanic Origin: 1980 to 1998

[As of **March (6,052 represents 6,052,000)**. Covers persons 15 years old and over. Based on Current Population Survey; see headnote, Table 78]

Characteristic	Unit	White			Black			Hispanic origin [1]		
		1980	1990	1998	1980	1990	1998	1980	1990	1998
Female family householder.	1,000	**6,052**	**7,306**	**8,308**	**2,495**	**3,275**	**3,926**	**610**	**1,116**	**1,612**
Marital status:										
Never married (single)	Percent ...	11	15	22	27	39	48	23	27	35
Married, spouse absent	Percent ...	17	16	15	29	21	16	32	29	25
Widowed	Percent ...	33	26	21	22	17	13	15	16	12
Divorced	Percent ...	40	43	42	22	23	23	30	29	28
Presence of children under age 18:										
No own children	Percent ...	41	43	41	28	32	35	25	33	30
With own children	Percent ...	59	58	59	72	68	65	75	67	70
One child	Percent ...	28	30	31	26	30	28	28	25	28
Two children	Percent ...	20	19	18	23	22	22	23	22	24
Three children	Percent ...	7	7	7	11	9	10	15	13	11
Four or more children......	Percent ...	3	2	3	11	7	5	9	6	7
Children per family	Number ...	1.03	0.95	1.02	1.51	1.26	1.21	1.56	1.37	1.46

[1] Persons of Hispanic origin may be of any race.

Source: U.S. Census Bureau, *Current Population Reports*, P20-515, and earlier reports; and unpublished data.

No. 83. Children Under 18 Years Old, by Presence of Parents: 1980 to 1998

[As of **March (63,427 represents 63,427,000)**. Excludes persons under 18 years old who maintained households or family groups. Based on Current Population Survey; see headnote, Table 78]

Race, Hispanic origin, and year	Number (1,000)	Both parents	Percent living with—						Father only	Neither parent
			Mother only							
			Total	Divorced	Married, spouse absent	Never married	Widowed			
ALL RACES [1]										
1980	63,427	77	18	8	6	3	2		2	4
1985	62,475	74	21	9	5	6	2		2	4
1990	64,137	73	22	8	5	7	2		3	3
1995	70,254	69	23	9	6	7	1		3	3
1998	71,377	68	23	8	5	9	1		4	4
WHITE										
1980	52,242	83	14	7	4	1	2		2	2
1985	50,836	80	16	8	4	2	1		2	2
1990	51,390	79	16	8	4	3	1		3	2
1995	55,327	76	18	8	5	4	1		3	3
1998	56,124	74	18	8	4	5	1		3	3
BLACK										
1980	9,375	42	44	11	16	13	4		2	12
1985	9,479	40	51	11	12	25	3		3	7
1990	10,018	38	51	10	12	27	2		4	8
1995	11,301	33	52	11	11	29	2		4	11
1998	11,414	36	51	9	9	32	1		4	9
HISPANIC [2]										
1980	5,459	75	20	6	8	4	2		2	4
1985	6,057	68	27	7	11	7	2		2	3
1990	7,174	67	27	7	10	8	2		3	3
1995	9,843	63	28	8	9	10	1		4	4
1998	10,863	64	27	6	8	12	1		4	5

[1] Includes other races not shown separately. [2] Hispanic persons may be of any race.

Source: U.S. Census Bureau, *Current Population Reports*, P20-514, and earlier reports; and unpublished data.

Population 67

Living Arrangements of Children Under 18 Years Old Living With One or Both Parents: 1998

[In thousands (68,418 represents 68,418,000). As of March. Covers only those persons under 18 years old who are living with one or both parents. Characteristics are shown for the householder or reference person in married-couple situations. See also headnote, Table 78]

Characteristic of parent	All races[1]				White				Black				Hispanic[2]			
		Living with—				Living with—				Living with—				Living with—		
	Total	Both parents	Mother only	Father only	Total	Both parents	Mother only	Father only	Total	Both parents	Mother only	Father only	Total	Both parents	Mother only	Father only
Children under 18 years old	68,418	48,642	16,634	3,143	54,319	41,547	10,210	2,562	10,392	4,137	5,830	424	10,306	6,909	2,915	482
Age:																
15 to 24 years old	3,869	1,309	2,250	310	2,588	1,142	1,220	226	1,155	128	968	59	977	387	512	77
25 to 29 years old	7,871	4,694	2,746	432	5,878	3,962	1,552	364	1,699	549	1,098	52	1,553	939	511	103
30 to 34 years old	13,978	9,653	3,861	464	10,817	8,178	2,275	363	2,464	935	1,464	64	2,453	1,651	709	93
35 to 39 years old	17,035	12,721	3,656	658	13,823	11,011	2,278	533	2,352	1,005	1,275	72	2,275	1,635	574	66
40 to 44 years old	14,189	11,093	2,452	644	11,941	9,622	1,755	564	1,421	762	587	72	1,731	1,307	346	78
45 to 54 years old	10,247	8,209	1,498	540	8,336	6,863	1,030	444	1,108	656	374	79	1,127	834	237	56
55 to 64 years old	1,019	811	136	74	811	663	87	60	120	64	44	13	172	136	27	8
65 years old and over	208	152	33	23	127	107	12	8	72	38	21	13	20	19	-	2
Educational attainment:																
Less than 9th grade	4,061	2,719	1,180	162	3,428	2,415	868	144	323	110	200	13	2,790	1,937	764	89
9th to 12th grade, no diploma	7,527	3,999	2,980	547	5,345	3,332	1,581	433	1,829	449	1,300	80	2,207	1,306	770	132
High school graduate[3]	22,101	14,693	6,079	1,329	17,126	12,454	3,589	1,083	4,041	1,508	2,314	220	2,701	1,848	678	175
Some college, no degree or associate degree	18,901	13,265	4,881	755	14,938	11,280	3,067	591	3,092	1,322	1,669	101	1,827	1,212	554	61
Bachelor's degree	10,489	9,125	1,126	237	8,966	7,947	810	208	846	567	269	10	591	456	118	17
Graduate or professional degree	5,340	4,840	388	112	4,517	4,118	295	104	261	182	79	-	189	150	31	8
Employment status:[4]																
In the civilian labor force	57,277	42,160	12,282	2,835	46,045	36,076	7,634	2,335	8,190	3,542	4,289	360	8,111	5,806	1,876	429
Employed	54,220	40,706	10,888	2,626	44,088	34,948	6,967	2,174	7,264	3,358	3,584	322	7,539	5,502	1,641	396
Both parents employed	28,961	28,961	(X)	(X)	24,784	24,784	(X)	(X)	2,617	2,617	(X)	(X)	3,174	3,174	(X)	(X)
Unemployed	3,058	1,454	1,395	210	1,957	1,128	668	162	927	183	705	38	572	304	235	33
Not in the labor force	10,386	5,761	4,345	280	7,637	4,858	2,569	211	2,113	517	1,541	54	2,144	1,052	1,039	53
Family income:																
Under $5,000	3,030	562	2,267	201	1,771	415	1,194	162	1,067	72	965	30	637	175	421	40
$5,000 to $9,999	3,987	692	3,113	182	2,423	520	1,771	132	1,374	89	1,243	41	1,112	314	755	44
$10,000 to $14,999	4,394	1,698	2,419	278	3,037	1,405	1,389	244	1,053	123	902	27	1,226	690	454	82
$15,000 to $24,999	8,433	4,372	3,465	596	6,245	3,574	2,185	485	1,853	552	1,202	99	2,199	1,477	632	90
$25,000 to $29,999	4,203	2,670	1,183	350	3,275	2,229	771	275	697	283	352	62	867	679	133	54
$30,000 to $39,999	8,041	5,971	1,583	487	6,547	5,159	1,008	380	1,100	483	545	73	1,397	1,112	210	75
$40,000 to $49,999	7,678	6,444	915	319	6,318	5,388	657	272	977	713	237	26	997	836	125	36
$50,000 and over	28,653	26,233	1,690	730	24,704	22,857	1,234	613	2,270	1,821	384	65	1,871	1,626	184	61
Tenure:[5]																
Owned	44,750	36,875	6,216	1,658	38,292	32,401	4,503	1,388	4,211	2,534	1,502	175	4,564	3,672	733	159
Rented	23,669	11,766	10,418	1,485	16,028	9,146	5,707	1,175	6,181	1,603	4,329	250	5,742	3,237	2,182	323

- Represents or rounds to zero. X Not applicable. [1] Includes other races, not shown separately. [2] Persons of Hispanic origin may be of any race. [3] Includes equivalency. [4] Excludes children whose parent is in the Armed Forces. [5] Refers to the tenure of the householder (who may or may not be the child's parent).

Source: U.S. Census Bureau, Current Population Reports, P20-514; and unpublished data.

No. 85. Grandchildren Living in the Home of Their Grandparents: 1980 to 1998

[In thousands (63,369 represents 63,369,000). Except as noted, based on Current Population Survey; see headnote, Table 78]

Living arrangements	1980 [1]	1990	1993	1994	1995	1996	1997	1998
Total children under 18 years old...	63,369	64,137	66,893	69,508	70,254	70,908	70,983	71,377
Children living in home of grandparents	**2,306**	**3,155**	**3,368**	**3,735**	**3,965**	**4,060**	**3,894**	**3,989**
With parent(s) present	1,318	2,221	2,351	2,375	2,498	2,629	2,585	2,571
Both parents present	310	467	475	436	427	467	554	503
Mother only present	922	1,563	1,647	1,764	1,876	1,943	1,785	1,827
Father only present	86	191	229	175	195	220	247	241
Without parent(s) present	988	935	1,017	1,359	1,466	1,431	1,309	1,417

[1] Based on census of population.

Source: U.S. Census Bureau, *1980 Census of Population, PC80-2-4B, Living Arrangements of Children and Adults*, and *Current Population Reports*, P20-514, and earlier reports.

No. 86. Nonfamily Households, by Sex and Age of Householder: 1990 and 1998

[In thousands (11,606 represents 11,606,000). As of **March**. See headnote, Table 78]

Item	Male householder					Female householder				
	Total	15 to 24 yr. old	25 to 44 yr. old	45 to 64 yr. old	65 yr. old and over	Total	15 to 24 yr. old	25 to 44 yr. old	45 to 64 yr. old	65 yr. old and over
1990, total	**11,606**	**1,236**	**5,780**	**2,536**	**2,053**	**15,651**	**1,032**	**3,697**	**3,545**	**7,377**
One person (living alone) ..	9,049	674	4,231	2,203	1,943	13,950	536	2,881	3,300	7,233
Nonrelatives present	2,557	560	1,551	334	112	1,701	497	817	245	143
Never married.	5,844	1,175	3,689	696	285	4,382	976	2,406	510	491
Married [1]	1,117	28	513	391	187	794	15	261	320	198
Widowed	1,417	-	29	221	1,166	7,428	4	52	1,333	6,038
Divorced	3,228	33	1,550	1,229	416	3,046	37	977	1,382	649
1998, total	**14,133**	**1,336**	**6,533**	**3,780**	**2,483**	**17,516**	**1,080**	**3,933**	**4,758**	**7,744**
One person (living alone) ..	11,010	722	4,777	3,164	2,345	15,317	528	2,955	4,257	7,577
Nonrelatives present	3,122	614	1,754	616	137	2,199	553	979	502	168
Never married.	6,967	1,250	4,286	1,112	318	5,206	1,046	2,631	921	608
Married [1]	1,385	51	644	484	203	923	9	271	386	258
Widowed	1,653	-	36	217	1,400	7,158	3	59	1,111	5,983
Divorced	4,128	35	1,565	1,967	560	4,229	22	971	2,339	896

- Represents or rounds to zero.   [1] No spouse present.

Source: U.S. Census Bureau, *Current Population Reports*, P20-515, and unpublished data.

No. 87. Persons Living Alone, by Sex and Age: 1980 to 1998

[As of **March** (18,296 represents 18,296,000). Based on Current Population Survey; see headnote, Table 78]

Sex and age	Number of persons (1,000)					Percent distribution				
	1980	1985	1990	1995	1998	1980	1985	1990	1995	1998
Both sexes	**18,296**	**20,602**	**22,999**	**24,732**	**26,327**	**100**	**100**	**100**	**100**	**100**
15 to 24 years old	1,726	1,324	1,210	1,196	1,251	9	6	5	5	5
25 to 34 years old	4,729	3,905	3,972	3,653	3,679	[1]26	19	17	15	14
35 to 44 years old	([1])	2,322	3,138	3,663	4,054	([1])	11	14	15	15
45 to 64 years old	4,514	4,939	5,502	6,377	7,421	25	24	24	26	28
65 to 74 years old	3,851	4,130	4,350	4,374	4,098	21	20	19	18	16
75 years old and over ...	3,477	3,982	4,825	5,470	5,825	19	19	21	22	22
Male.	**6,966**	**7,922**	**9,049**	**10,140**	**11,010**	**38**	**39**	**39**	**41**	**42**
15 to 24 years old	947	750	674	623	722	5	4	3	3	3
25 to 34 years old	2,920	2,307	2,395	2,213	2,222	[1]16	11	10	9	8
35 to 44 years old	([1])	1,406	1,836	2,263	2,555	([1])	7	8	9	10
45 to 64 years old	1,613	1,845	2,203	2,787	3,164	9	9	10	11	12
65 to 74 years old	775	868	1,042	1,134	1,111	4	4	5	5	4
75 years old and over ...	711	746	901	1,120	1,234	4	4	4	5	5
Female.	**11,330**	**12,680**	**13,950**	**14,592**	**15,317**	**62**	**62**	**61**	**59**	**58**
15 to 24 years old	779	573	536	572	528	4	3	2	2	2
25 to 34 years old	1,809	1,598	1,578	1,440	1,456	[1]10	8	7	6	6
35 to 44 years old	([1])	916	1,303	1,399	1,499	([1])	4	6	6	6
45 to 64 years old	2,901	3,095	3,300	3,589	4,257	16	15	14	15	16
65 to 74 years old	3,076	3,262	3,309	3,240	2,987	17	16	14	13	11
75 years old and over ...	2,766	3,236	3,924	4,351	4,590	15	16	17	18	17

[1] Data for persons 35 to 44 years old included with persons 25 to 34 years old.

Source: U.S. Census Bureau, *Current Population Reports*, P20-514, and earlier reports; and unpublished data.

Population 69

No. 88. Religious Bodies—Selected Data

[Membership data: 3,500 represents 3,500,000. Includes the self-reported membership of religious bodies with 60,000 or more as reported to the *Yearbook of American and Canadian Churches*. Groups may be excluded if they do not supply information. The data are not standardized so comparisons between groups are difficult. The definition of "church member" is determined by the religious body]

Religious body	Year reported	Churches reported	Membership (1,000)	Pastors serving parishes [1]
African Methodist Episcopal Church [2]	1991	8,000	3,500	(NA)
African Methodist Episcopal Zion Church	1998	3,098	1,252	2,571
American Baptist Association	1986	1,705	250	1,740
American Baptist Churches in the U.S.A.	1997	5,830	[3]1,503	4,145
Armenian Apostolic Church of America	1997	28	200	22
Assemblies of God	1997	11,920	2,495	18,221
Baptist Bible Fellowship International	1997	4,500	1,200	(NA)
Baptist General Conference	1997	879	135	(NA)
Baptist Missionary Association of America	1997	1,342	234	1,500
Buddhist [4]	1990	(NA)	401	(NA)
Christian and Missionary Alliance, The	1997	1,964	328	1,654
Christian Brethren (Plymouth Brethren)	1997	1,150	100	(NA)
Christian Church (Disciples of Christ)	1997	3,818	879	3,419
Christian Churches and Churches of Christ	1988	5,579	1,072	5,525
Christian Congregation, Inc., The	1997	1,438	116	1,436
Christian Methodist Episcopal Church	1983	2,340	719	(NA)
Christian Reformed Church in North America	1997	723	196	642
Church of God in Christ	1991	15,300	5,500	28,988
Church of God of Prophecy	1997	1,908	77	2,000
Church of God (Anderson, Ind.)	1997	2,347	229	2,920
Church of God (Cleveland, Tenn.)	1995	6,060	753	3,121
Church of Jesus Christ of Latter-Day Saints, The	1997	10,811	4,923	32,433
Church of the Brethren	1997	1,095	141	827
Church of the Nazarene	1997	5,118	620	4,581
Churches of Christ	1997	14,400	1,800	14,000
Conservative Baptist Association of America	1992	1,084	200	(NA)
Coptic Orthodox Church	1992	85	180	65
Cumberland Presbyterian Church	1997	771	88	634
Diocese of America, Armenian Church	1991	72	414	49
Episcopal Church	1996	7,390	2,365	8,131
Evangelical Covenant Church, The	1997	622	93	565
Evangelical Free Church of America, The	1995	1,224	243	1,936
Evangelical Lutheran Church in America	1997	10,889	5,185	9,695
Free Methodist Church of North America	1997	1,029	73	(NA)
Full Gospel Fellowship of Churches and Ministers International	1995	650	195	725
General Association of General Baptists	1997	790	72	1,085
General Association of Regular Baptist Churches	1996	1,440	116	(NA)
General Conference Mennonite Brethren Churches	1996	368	82	590
Grace Gospel Fellowship	1992	128	60	160
Greek Orthodox Archdiocese of America	1998	523	1,955	596
Hindu [4]	1990	(NA)	227	(NA)
Independent Fundamental Churches of America	1995	670	70	(NA)
International Church of the Foursquare Gospel	1997	1,832	232	2,421
International Council of Community Churches	1995	517	250	491
International Pentecostal Holiness Church	1997	1,681	170	1,472
Jehovah's Witnesses	1997	10,883	975	(NA)
Jewish [4]	1990	(NA)	3,137	(NA)
Lutheran Church—Missouri Synod, The	1997	6,215	2,603	5,276
Mennonite Church	1996	1,004	91	1,525
Muslim / Islamic [4]	1990	(NA)	527	(NA)
National Association of Congregational Christian Churches	1998	435	69	534
National Association of Free Will Baptists	1997	2,320	210	2,800
National Baptist Convention of America, Inc.	1987	2,500	3,500	8,000
National Baptist Convention, USA,Inc.	1992	33,000	8,200	32,832
National Missionary Baptist Convention of America	1992	(NA)	2,500	(NA)
Old Order Amish Church	1993	898	81	3,592
Orthodox Church in America	1995	600	2,000	650
Pentecostal Assemblies of the World, Inc.	1997	1,600	1,000	(NA)
Pentecostal Church of God	1996	1,230	112	(NA)
Pentecostal Church in America	1997	1,340	280	1,642
Presbyterian Church (U.S.A.)	1997	11,295	3,611	9,385
Progressive National Baptist Convention, Inc.	1995	2,000	2,500	(NA)
Reformed Church in America	1997	949	305	905
Religious Society of Friends (Conservative)	1994	1,200	104	(NA)
Reorganized Church of Jesus Christ of Latter-Day Saints	1997	1,237	249	(NA)
Roman Catholic Church, The	1996	22,728	61,208	(NA)
Romanian Orthodox Episcopate of America, The	1996	37	65	37
Salvation Army, The	1995	1,264	453	3,645
Serbian Orthodox Church in the U.S.A. and Canada	1986	68	67	60
Seventh-Day Adventist Church	1997	4,348	826	2,401
Southern Baptist Convention	1997	40,887	15,892	57,300
Unitarian Universalist [4]	1990	(NA)	502	(NA)
United Church of Christ	1997	6,061	1,438	4,379
United Methodist Church, The	1996	36,170	8,496	19,580
Wesleyan Church, The	1997	1,578	119	1,524
Wisconsin Evangelical Lutheran Synod	1997	1,240	411	1,222

NA Not available.   [1] Does not include retired clergy or clergy not working with congregations.   [2] Figures obtained from the *Directory of African American Religious Bodies, 1991.*   [3] Data for 1996.   [4] Figures obtained from the National Survey of Religious Identification, a survey conducted by the City University of New York in 1990 and published in *One Nation Under God: Religion in Contemporary American Society,* by Barry Kosmin and Seymour Lachman (1993).

Source: National Council of the Churches of Christ in the USA, New York, NY, *1999 Yearbook of American and Canadian Churches,* annual (copyright). (For more info visit www.ncccusa.org).

No. 89. Religious Preference, Church Membership, and Attendance: 1980 to 1998

[In percent. Covers civilian noninstitutional population, 18 years old and over. Data represent averages of the combined results of several surveys during year or period indicated. Data are subject to sampling variability, see source]

Year	Religious preference					Church/synagogue members	Persons attending church/synagogue[1]	Age and region	Church/synagogue members, 1997
	Protestant	Catholic	Jewish	Other	None				
1980	61	28	2	2	7	69	40	18-29 years old....	63
1985	57	28	2	4	9	71	42	30-49 years old....	66
1990	56	25	2	6	11	65	40	50-64 years old....	71
1994	60	24	2	6	[2]8	68	42	65 years and over..	75
1995	58	25	2	(NA)	(NA)	69	43	East[3]	70
1996	58	25	3	5	[2]9	65	38	Midwest[4]	73
1997	58	26	2	6	[2]8	67	40	South[5]	73
1998, June	59	27	2	5	[2]7	70	40	West[6]	51

NA Not available.   [1] Persons who attended a church or synagogue in the last 7 days.   [2] Includes those respondents who did not designate.   [3] ME, NH, RI, NY, CT, VT, MA, NJ, PA, WV, DE, MD, and DC.   [4] OH, IN, IL, MI, MN, WI, IA, ND, SD, KS, NE, and MO.   [5] KY, TN, VA, NC, SC, GA, FL, AL, MS, TX, AR, OK, and LA.   [6] AZ, NM, CO, NV, MT, ID, WY, UT, CA, WA, OR, AK, and HI.

Source: Princeton Religion Research Center, Princeton, NJ, *Religion in America*, annual. Based on surveys conducted by The Gallup Organization, Inc.

No. 90. Christian Church Adherents, 1990, and Jewish Population, 1997—States

[Christian church adherents were defined as "all members, including full members, their children and the estimated number of other regular participants who are not considered as communicant, confirmed or full members." Data on Christian church adherents are based on reports of 133 church groupings and exclude 34 church bodies that reported more than 100,000 members to the *Yearbook of American and Canadian Churches*. The Jewish population includes Jews who define themselves as Jewish by religion as well as those who define themselves as Jewish in cultural terms. Data on Jewish population are based primarily on a compilation of individual estimates made by local Jewish federations. Additionally, most large communities have completed Jewish demographic surveys from which the Jewish population can be determined]

State	Christian adherents, 1990		Jewish population, 1997		State	Christian adherents, 1990		Jewish population, 1997	
	Number (1,000)	Percent of population[1]	Number (1,000)	Percent of population[1]		Number (1,000)	Percent of population[1]	Number (1,000)	Percent of population[1]
U.S.	131,084	52.7	6,005	2.3	MO	2,892	56.6	62	1.2
AL	2,858	70.7	9	0.2	MT	341	42.7	1	0.1
AK	175	31.8	3	0.5	NE	1,000	63.4	7	0.4
AZ	1,505	41.1	72	1.6	NV	366	29.6	57	3.6
AR	1,423	60.5	2	0.1	NH	431	38.9	10	0.8
CA	11,665	39.2	956	3.0	NJ	4,305	55.7	461	5.8
CO	1,244	37.8	68	1.8	NM	883	58.3	10	0.6
CT	1,933	58.9	97	3.0	NY	9,970	55.5	1,653	9.1
DE	297	44.6	14	1.9	NC	3,949	59.6	24	0.3
DC	349	57.5	25	4.7	ND	485	75.9	1	0.1
FL	5,106	39.5	620	4.3	OH	5,313	48.9	145	1.3
GA	3,659	56.5	84	1.1	OK	2,097	66.5	5	0.2
HI	391	35.3	7	0.6	OR	904	31.8	20	0.6
ID	507	50.4	(Z)	0.1	PA	6,960	58.6	282	2.3
IL	6,579	57.5	269	2.3	RI	754	75.1	16	1.6
IN	2,615	47.1	18	0.3	SC	2,149	61.7	9	0.2
IA	1,674	60.3	6	0.2	SD	474	68.1	(Z)	0.1
KS	1,346	54.3	15	0.6	TN	2,968	60.8	18	0.3
KY	2,213	60.1	11	0.3	TX	10,788	63.5	124	0.6
LA	2,959	70.1	17	0.4	UT	1,371	79.6	4	0.2
ME	439	36.1	8	0.6	VT	233	40.4	6	1.0
MD	2,101	43.9	214	4.2	VA	2,898	46.8	75	1.1
MA	3,666	60.9	279	4.6	WA	1,579	32.4	34	0.6
MI	4,580	49.2	107	1.1	WV	740	41.3	2	0.1
MN	2,807	64.2	42	0.9	WI	3,125	63.9	32	0.6
MS	1,804	70.1	1	0.1	WY	216	47.6	(Z)	0.1

Z Fewer than 500.   [1] Based on U.S. Census Bureau data for resident population enumerated as of April 1, 1990, and estimated as of July 1, 1997.

Source: Christian church adherents—M. Bradley; N. Green, Jr.; D. Jones; M. Lynn; and L. McNeil; *Churches and Church Membership in the United States 1990*, Glenmary Research Center, Atlanta, GA, 1992 (copyright); Jewish population—American Jewish Committee, New York, NY, *American Jewish Year Book, 1997* (copyright).

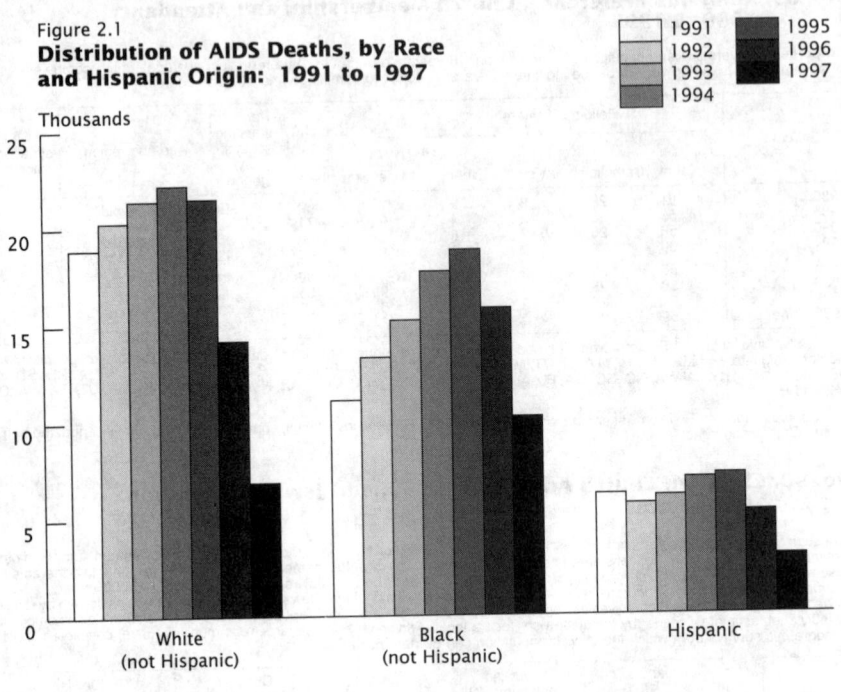

Figure 2.1
Distribution of AIDS Deaths, by Race and Hispanic Origin: 1991 to 1997

Source: Chart prepared by U.S. Census Bureau. For data, see Table 142.

Figure 2.2
Male Homicide Rates, by Race and Age: 1996

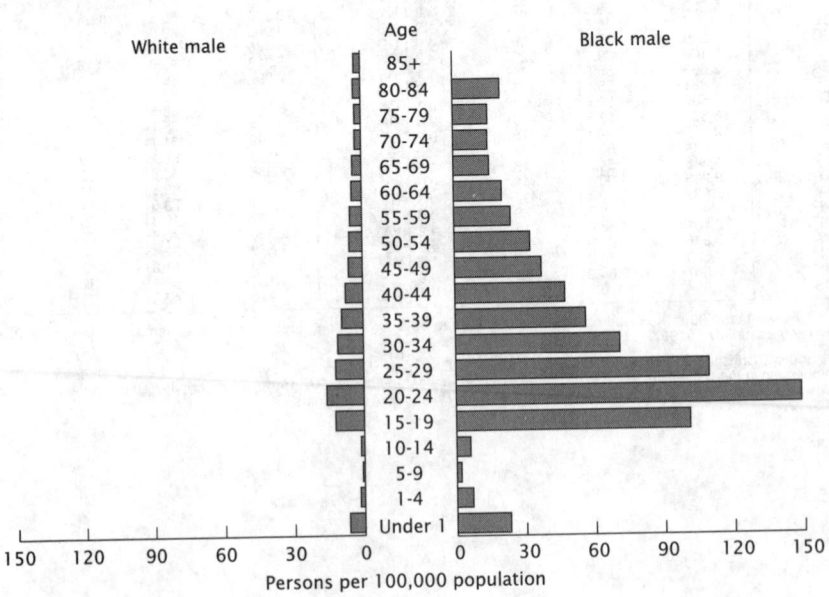

Source: Chart prepared by U.S. Census Bureau. For data, see Table 150.

72 Vital Statistics

Section 2

Vital Statistics

This section presents vital statistics data on births, deaths, abortions, fetal deaths, fertility, life expectancy, marriages, and divorces. Vital statistics are compiled for the country as a whole by the National Center for Health Statistics (NCHS) and published in its annual report, *Vital Statistics of the United States*, in certain reports of the *Vital and Health Statistics* series, and in the *National Vital Statistics Reports* (formerly *Monthly Vital Statistics Report*). Reports in this field are also issued by the various state bureaus of vital statistics. Data on fertility, on age of persons at first marriage, and on marital status and marital history are compiled by the U.S. Census Bureau from its Current Population Survey (CPS; see text, Section 1) and published in *Current Population Reports*, P20 Series. Data on abortions are published by the Alan Guttmacher Institute, New York, NY, in selected issues of *Family Planning Perspectives*.

Registration of vital events—The registration of births, deaths, fetal deaths, and other vital events in the United States is primarily a state and local function. The civil laws of every state provide for a continuous and permanent birth- and death-registration system. Many states also provide for marriage- and divorce-registration systems. Vital events occurring to U.S. residents outside the United States are not included in the data.

Births and deaths—The live-birth, death, and fetal-death statistics prepared by NCHS are based on vital records filed in the registration offices of all states, of New York City, and of the District of Columbia. The annual collection of death statistics on a national basis began in 1900 with a national death-registration area of 10 states and the District of Columbia; a similar annual collection of birth statistics for a national birth-registration area began in

1915, also with 10 reporting states and the District of Columbia. Since 1933, the birth- and death-registration areas have comprised the entire United States, including Alaska (beginning 1959) and Hawaii (beginning 1960). National statistics on fetal deaths were first compiled for 1918 and annually since 1922.

Prior to 1951, birth statistics came from a complete count of records received in the Public Health Service (now received in NCHS). From 1951 through 1971, they were based on a 50-percent sample of all registered births (except for a complete count in 1955 and a 20- to 50-percent sample in 1967). Beginning in 1972, they have been based on a complete count for states participating in the Vital Statistics Cooperative Program (VSCP) (for details, see the technical appendix in *Vital Statistics of the United States*) and on a 50-percent sample of all other areas. Beginning 1986, all reporting areas participated in the VSCP. Mortality data have been based on a complete count of records for each area (except for a 50-percent sample in 1972). Beginning in 1970, births to and deaths of nonresident aliens of the United States and U.S. citizens outside the United States have been excluded from the data. Fetal deaths and deaths among Armed Forces abroad are excluded. Data based on samples are subject to sampling error; for details, see annual issues of *Vital Statistics of the United States*.

Mortality statistics by cause of death are compiled in accordance with World Health Organization regulations according to the *International Classification of Diseases* (ICD). The ICD is revised approximately every 10 years. The ninth revision of the ICD was employed beginning in 1979. Deaths for prior years were classified according to the revision of the ICD in use at the time. Each revision of the ICD

U.S. Census Bureau, Statistical Abstract of the United States: 1999

introduces a number of discontinuities in mortality statistics; for a discussion of those between the eighth and ninth revisions of the ICD, see *Monthly Vital Statistics Report* (renamed, *National Vital Statistics Report*), Vol. 28, No. 11, supplement.

Some of the tables present age-adjusted death rates in addition to crude death rates. Age adjusted death rates shown in this section were prepared using the direct method, in which age-specific death rates for a population of interest are applied to a standard population distributed by age. Age adjustment eliminates the differences in observed rates between points in time or among compared population groups that result from age differences in population composition.

Fertility and life expectancy—The total fertility rate, defined as the number of births that 1,000 women would have in their lifetime if, at each year of age, they experienced the birth rates occurring in the specified year, is compiled and published by NCHS. Other data relating to social and medical factors which affect fertility rates, such as contraceptive use and birth expectations, are collected and made available by both NCHS and the Census Bureau. NCHS figures are based on information in birth and fetal death certificates and on the periodic National Surveys of Family Growth; Census Bureau data are based on decennial censuses and the CPS.

Data on life expectancy, the average remaining lifetime in years for persons who attain a given age, are computed and published by NCHS. For details, see the technical appendix in *Vital Statistics of the United States*.

Marriage and divorce—The compilation of nationwide statistics on marriages and divorces in the United States began in 1887-88 when the National Office of Vital Statistics prepared estimates for the years 1867-86. Although periodic updates took place after 1888, marriage and divorce statistics were not collected and published annually until 1944 by that office. In 1957 and 1958, respectively, the same office

established marriage- and divorce-registration areas. Beginning in 1957, the marriage-registration area comprised 30 states, plus Alaska, Hawaii, Puerto Rico, and the Virgin Islands; it currently includes 42 states and the District of Columbia. The divorce-registration area, starting in 1958 with 14 states, Alaska, Hawaii, and the Virgin Islands, it currently includes a total of 31 states and the Virgin Islands. Procedures for estimating the number of marriages and divorces in the registration states are discussed in *Vital Statistics of the United States*, Vol. III—Marriage and Divorce. Total counts of events for registration and nonregistration states are gathered by collecting already summarized data on marriages and divorces reported by state offices of vital statistics and by county offices of registration.

Vital statistics rates—Except as noted, vital statistics rates computed by NCHS are based on decennial census population figures as of April 1 for 1940, 1950, 1960, 1970, 1980, and 1990; and on midyear population figures for other years, as estimated by the Census Bureau (see text, Section 1).

Race—Data by race for births, deaths, marriages, and divorces from NCHS are based on information contained in the certificates of registration. The Census Bureau's Current Population Survey obtains information on race by asking respondents to classify their race as (1) White, (2) Black, (3) American Indian, Eskimo, or Aleut, or (4) Asian or Pacific Islander.

Beginning with the 1989 data year, NCHS is tabulating its birth data primarily by race of the mother. In 1988 and prior years, births were tabulated by race of the child, which was determined from the race of the parents as entered on the birth certificate.

Trend data by race shown in this section are by race of mother beginning with the 1980 data. Hispanic origin of the mother is reported and tabulated independently of race. Thus persons of Hispanic origin maybe of any race. In 1994, 91 percent of women of Hispanic origin were reported as White.

No. 91. Live Births, Deaths, Marriages, and Divorces: 1950 to 1997

[3,632 represents 3,632,000. Prior to 1960, excludes Alaska and Hawaii. Beginning 1970, excludes births to and deaths of non-residents of the United States. See Appendix III]

Year	Number (1,000) Births [1]	Deaths Total	Deaths Infant [2]	Mar-riages [3]	Divor-ces [4]	Rate per 1,000 population Births [1]	Deaths Total	Deaths Infant [2]	Mar-riages [3]	Divor-ces [4]
1950	3,632	1,452	104	1,667	385	24.1	9.6	29.2	11.1	2.6
1955	4,097	1,529	107	1,531	377	25.0	9.3	26.4	9.3	2.3
1957	4,300	1,633	112	1,518	381	25.3	9.6	26.3	8.9	2.2
1960	4,258	1,712	111	1,523	393	23.7	9.5	26.0	8.5	2.2
1965	3,760	1,828	93	1,800	479	19.4	9.4	24.7	9.3	2.5
1970	3,731	1,921	75	2,159	708	18.4	9.5	20.0	10.6	3.5
1971	3,556	1,928	68	2,190	773	17.2	9.3	19.1	10.6	3.7
1972	3,258	1,964	60	2,282	845	15.6	9.4	18.5	10.9	4.0
1973	3,137	1,973	56	2,284	915	14.8	9.3	17.7	10.8	4.3
1974	3,160	1,934	53	2,230	977	14.8	9.1	16.7	10.5	4.6
1975	3,144	1,893	51	2,153	1,036	14.6	8.8	16.1	10.0	4.8
1976	3,168	1,909	48	2,155	1,083	14.6	8.8	15.2	9.9	5.0
1977	3,327	1,900	47	2,178	1,091	15.1	8.6	14.1	9.9	5.0
1978	3,333	1,928	46	2,282	1,130	15.0	8.7	13.8	10.3	5.1
1979	3,494	1,914	46	2,331	1,181	15.6	8.5	13.1	10.4	5.3
1980	3,612	1,990	46	2,390	1,189	15.9	8.8	12.6	10.6	5.2
1981	3,629	1,978	43	2,422	1,213	15.8	8.6	11.9	10.6	5.3
1982	3,681	1,975	42	2,456	1,170	15.9	8.5	11.5	10.6	5.1
1983	3,639	2,019	41	2,446	1,158	15.6	8.6	11.2	10.5	5.0
1984	3,669	2,039	40	2,477	1,169	15.6	8.6	10.8	10.5	5.0
1985	3,761	2,086	40	2,413	1,190	15.8	8.8	10.6	10.1	5.0
1986	3,757	2,105	39	2,407	1,178	15.6	8.8	10.4	10.0	4.9
1987	3,809	2,123	38	2,403	1,166	15.7	8.8	10.1	9.9	4.8
1988	3,910	2,168	39	2,396	1,167	16.0	8.8	10.0	9.8	4.8
1989	4,041	2,150	40	2,403	1,157	16.4	8.7	9.8	9.7	4.7
1990	4,158	2,148	38	2,443	1,182	16.7	8.6	9.2	9.8	4.7
1991	4,111	2,170	37	2,371	1,187	16.3	8.6	8.9	9.4	4.7
1992	4,065	2,176	35	2,362	1,215	15.9	8.5	8.5	9.3	4.8
1993	4,000	2,269	33	2,334	1,187	15.5	8.8	8.4	9.0	4.6
1994	3,979	2,286	31	2,362	1,191	15.0	8.8	7.9	9.1	4.6
1995	3,900	2,312	30	2,336	1,169	14.8	8.8	7.6	8.9	4.4
1996 prel.	3,891	2,315	28	1,954	973	14.7	8.7	7.3	7.6	4.1
1997 prel.	3,895	2,315	28	2,344	(NA)	14.6	8.6	7.1	8.8	4.3

NA Not available. [1] Prior to 1960, data adjusted for underregistration. [2] Infants under 1 year, excluding fetal deaths; rates per 1,000 registered live births. [3] Includes estimates for some states through 1965 and also for 1976 and 1977 and marriage licenses for some states for all years except 1973 and 1975. Beginning 1978, includes nonlicensed marriages in California. [4] Includes reported annulments and some estimated state figures for all years.

Source: U.S. National Center for Health Statistics, *Vital Statistics of the United States*, annual; and *National Vital Statistics Reports (NVSR)* (formerly *Monthly Vital Statistics Report*); and unpublished data.

No. 92. Live Births, by Race and Type of Hispanic Origin—Selected Characteristics: 1990 and 1997

[4,158 represents 4,158,000. Represents registered births. Excludes births to nonresidents of the United States. Data are based on Hispanic origin of mother and race of mother. Hispanic origin data are available from only 48 states and the District of Columbia in 1990]

Race and Hispanic origin	Number of births (1,000) 1990	1997	Births to teen-age mothers, percent of total 1990	1997	Births to unmarried mothers, per-cent of total 1990	1997	Percent of mothers beginning prenatal care during— First trimester 1990	1997	Third trimester or no care 1990	1997	Percent of births with low birth weight [1] 1990	1997
Total	4,158	3,895	12.8	12.8	26.6	32.4	74.2	82.5	6.0	3.9	7.0	7.5
White	3,290	3,085	10.9	11.3	16.9	25.8	77.7	84.7	4.9	3.2	5.7	6.5
Black	684	601	23.1	22.5	66.7	69.1	60.7	72.3	10.9	7.3	13.3	13.1
American Indian, Eskimo, Aleut	39	38	19.5	(NA)	53.6	(NA)	57.9	(NA)	12.9	(NA)	6.1	6.8
Asian and Pacific Islander [2]	142	170	5.7	(NA)	15.9	(NA)	75.1	(NA)	4.5	(NA)	6.5	6.8
Filipino	26	(NA)	6.1	(NA)	(NA)	(NA)	77.1	(NA)	4.5	(NA)	7.3	7.2
Chinese	23	(NA)	1.2	(NA)	5.0	(NA)	81.3	(NA)	3.4	(NA)	4.7	8.3
Japanese	9	(NA)	2.9	(NA)	9.6	(NA)	87.0	(NA)	2.9	(NA)	6.2	5.1
Hawaiian	6	(NA)	18.4	(NA)	45.0	(NA)	65.8	(NA)	2.9	(NA)	7.2	6.8
Hispanic origin [3]	595	712	16.8	17.3	36.7	40.9	60.2	73.7	12.0	6.2	6.1	7.2
Mexican	386	(NA)	17.7	(NA)	33.3	(NA)	57.8	(NA)	13.2	(NA)	5.5	6.4
Puerto Rican	59	(NA)	21.7	(NA)	55.9	(NA)	63.5	(NA)	10.6	(NA)	9.0	8.0
Cuban	11	(NA)	7.7	(NA)	18.2	(NA)	84.8	(NA)	2.8	(NA)	5.7	9.4
Central and South American	83	(NA)	9.0	(NA)	41.2	(NA)	61.5	(NA)	10.9	(NA)	5.7	6.8
Other and unknown Hispanic	(NA)	(NA)	(NA)	(NA)	(NA)	(NA)	(NA)	(NA)	(NA)	(NA)	5.8	6.3
												7.9

NA Not available. [1] Births less than 2,500 grams (5 lb.-8 oz.). [2] Includes other races not shown separately. [3] Hispanic persons may be of any race. Includes other types, not shown separately.

Source: U.S. National Center for Health Statistics; *Vital Statistics of the United States*, annual; *National Vital Statistics Report (NVSR)* (formerly *Monthly Vital Statistics Report*); and unpublished data.

No. 93. Births and Birth Rates, by Race, Sex, and Age: 1980 to 1997

[Births in thousands (3,612 represents 3,612,000). Births by race of child. Excludes births to nonresidents of the United States. For population bases used to derive these data, see text, this section, and Appendix III]

Item	1980	1985	1989	1990	1991	1992	1993	1994	1995	1996	1997
Live births [1]	3,612	3,761	4,041	4,158	4,111	4,065	4,000	3,953	3,900	3,891	3,895
White	2,936	3,038	3,192	3,290	3,241	3,202	3,126	3,121	2,753	3,093	3,085
Black	568	582	673	684	683	674	695	636	394	595	601
American Indian	29	34	39	39	39	39	39	38	26	38	38
Asian or Pacific Islander	74	105	133	142	145	150	153	158	135	166	170
Male	1,853	1,928	2,069	2,129	2,102	2,082	2,049	2,023	1,996	1,990	(NA)
Female	1,760	1,833	1,971	2,029	2,009	1,983	1,951	1,930	1,903	1,901	(NA)
Males per 100 females	105	105	105	105	105	105	105	105	105	105	(NA)
Age of mother:											
Under 20 years old	562	478	518	533	532	518	514	518	512	503	500
20 to 24 years old	1,226	1,141	1,078	1,094	1,090	1,070	1,038	1,001	966	945	946
25 to 29 years old	1,108	1,201	1,263	1,277	1,220	1,179	1,129	1,089	1,064	1,071	1,075
30 to 34 years old	550	696	842	886	885	895	901	906	905	898	888
35 to 39 years old	141	214	294	318	331	345	357	372	384	400	408
40 years old or more	24	29	46	50	54	58	61	66	70	75	78
Birth rate per 1,000 population	15.9	15.8	16.4	16.7	16.3	15.9	15.5	15.2	14.8	14.7	14.6
White	15.1	15.0	15.4	15.8	15.4	15.0	14.7	14.4	14.2	14.1	(NA)
Black	21.3	20.4	22.3	22.4	21.9	21.3	20.5	19.5	18.2	17.8	(NA)
American Indian	20.7	19.8	19.7	18.9	18.3	18.4	17.8	17.1	16.6	16.6	(NA)
Asian or Pacific Islander	19.9	18.7	18.7	19.0	18.2	18.0	17.7	17.5	17.3	17.0	(NA)
Male	16.8	16.7	17.2	17.6	17.1	16.7	(NA)	(NA)	(NA)	(NA)	(NA)
Female	15.1	15.0	15.6	15.9	15.6	15.2	(NA)	(NA)	(NA)	(NA)	(NA)
Plural birth ratio [2]	19.3	21.0	23.0	23.3	23.9	24.4	25.2	25.7	26.1	27.4	(NA)
White	18.5	20.4	22.5	22.9	23.4	24.0	24.9	25.5	26.0	27.5	(NA)
Black	24.1	25.3	26.9	27.0	27.8	28.2	28.7	28.7	29.4	28.8	29.8	(NA)
Fertility rate per 1,000 women [3]	68.4	66.2	69.2	70.9	69.6	68.9	67.6	66.7	65.6	65.3	65.3
White [3]	64.8	64.1	66.4	68.3	67.0	66.5	65.4	64.9	64.4	64.3	64.2
Black [3]	84.7	78.8	86.2	86.8	85.2	83.2	80.5	76.9	72.3	70.7	70.8
American Indian [3]	82.7	78.6	79.0	76.2	75.1	75.4	73.4	70.9	69.1	68.7	68.9
Asian or Pacific Islander [3]	73.2	68.4	68.2	69.6	67.6	67.2	66.7	66.8	66.4	65.9	66.5
Age of mother:											
10 to 14 years old	1.1	1.2	1.4	1.4	1.4	1.4	1.4	1.4	1.3	1.2	1.2
15 to 19 years old	53.0	51.0	57.3	59.9	62.1	60.7	59.6	58.9	56.8	54.4	52.9
20 to 24 years old	115.1	108.3	113.8	116.5	115.7	114.6	112.6	111.1	109.8	110.4	110.9
25 to 29 years old	112.9	111.0	117.6	120.2	118.2	117.4	115.5	113.9	111.2	113.1	114.3
30 to 34 years old	61.9	69.1	77.4	80.8	79.5	80.2	80.8	81.5	82.5	83.9	85.4
35 to 39 years old	19.8	24.0	29.9	31.7	32.0	32.5	32.9	33.7	34.3	35.3	36.0
40 to 44 years old	3.9	4.0	5.2	5.5	5.5	5.9	6.1	6.4	6.6	6.8	6.9
45 to 49 years old	0.2	0.2	0.2	0.2	0.2	0.3	0.3	0.3	0.3	0.3	0.3

NA Not available. [1] Includes other races not shown separately. [2] Number of multiple births per 1,000 live births. [3] Per 1,000 women, 15 to 44 years old in specified group. The rate for age of mother 45 to 49 years old computed by relating births to mothers 45 years old and over to women 45 to 49 years old.

Source: U.S. National Center for Health Statistics, Vital Statistics of the United States, annual; National Vital Statistics Report (NVSR) (formerly Monthly Vital Statistics Report); and unpublished data.

No. 94. Teenagers—Births and Birth Rates, by Race and Age: 1980 to 1997

[Birth rates per 1,000 women in specified group, see text, this section]

Item	1980	1985	1989	1990	1991	1992	1993	1994	1995	1996	1997
NUMBER OF BIRTHS											
All races, total [1]	552,161	467,485	506,503	521,826	519,577	505,415	501,093	505,488	(NA)	491,577	489,211
15-17 years	198,222	167,789	181,044	183,327	188,226	187,549	190,535	195,169	(NA)	185,721	183,324
18-19 years	353,939	299,696	325,459	338,499	331,351	317,866	310,558	310,319	(NA)	305,856	305,886
White	393,564	324,590	340,472	354,482	352,359	342,739	341,817	348,081	(NA)	(NA)	121,864
15-17 years	129,341	107,993	111,736	114,934	118,809	118,786	121,309	126,388	(NA)	(NA)	220,164
18-19 years	264,223	216,597	228,736	239,548	233,550	223,953	220,508	221,693	(NA)	(NA)	130,401
Black	147,378	130,857	150,699	151,613	150,956	146,800	143,153	140,968	(NA)	(NA)	54,883
15-17 years	65,069	55,656	63,832	62,881	63,571	63,002	63,156	62,563	(NA)	(NA)	75,518
18-19 years	82,309	75,201	86,867	88,732	87,385	83,798	79,997	78,405	(NA)	(NA)	
BIRTH RATE											
All races, total [1]	53.0	51.0	57.3	59.9	62.1	60.7	59.6	58.9	56.8	54.4	52.9
15-17 years	32.5	31.0	36.4	37.5	38.7	37.8	37.8	37.6	36.0	33.8	32.6
18-19 years	82.1	79.6	84.2	88.6	94.4	94.5	92.1	91.5	89.1	86.0	84.4
White	45.4	43.3	47.9	50.8	52.8	51.8	51.1	51.1	50.1	48.1	46.8
15-17 years	25.5	24.4	28.1	29.5	30.7	30.1	30.3	30.7	30.0	28.4	27.4
18-19 years	73.2	70.4	72.9	78.0	83.5	83.8	82.1	82.1	81.2	78.4	76.6
Black	97.8	95.4	111.5	112.8	115.5	112.4	108.6	104.5	96.1	91.4	89.5
15-17 years	72.5	69.3	81.9	82.3	84.1	81.3	79.8	76.3	69.7	64.7	62.3
18-19 years	135.1	132.4	151.9	152.9	158.6	157.9	151.9	148.3	137.1	132.5	131.2

NA Not available. [1] Includes races other than White and Black.

Source: U.S. National Center for Health Statistics, Monthly Vital Statistics Report, Vol. 45, No. 5, Supplement.

No. 95. Live Births, by State: 1997

[Number of births, except rate. Registered births. Excludes births to nonresidents of the United States. By race of mother. See Appendix III]

State	All races [1]	White		Black		Hispanic [2]	Birth rate [3]	Fertility rate [4]
		Total	Non-Hispanic	Total	Non-Hispanic			
United States.	3,880,894	3,072,640	2,333,363	599,913	581,431	709,767	14.5	65.0
Alabama.	60,914	40,437	39,402	19,830	19,798	1,056	14.1	62.1
Alaska	9,947	6,592	6,110	457	444	609	16.3	72.4
Arizona.	75,699	66,266	37,860	2,500	2,375	28,472	16.6	78.1
Arkansas	36,478	28,073	26,506	7,822	7,799	1,542	14.5	67.3
California	524,840	426,231	177,863	37,320	36,109	248,948	16.3	72.3
Colorado.	56,533	51,714	38,685	2,584	2,487	13,217	14.5	64.2
Connecticut.	43,109	36,197	28,433	5,370	4,896	5,709	13.2	60.3
Delaware	10,253	7,528	6,864	2,490	2,462	637	14.0	60.3
Dist of Columbia	7,927	1,977	1,274	5,813	5,677	694	15.0	61.7
Florida	192,383	144,047	107,757	43,536	42,546	37,369	13.1	64.9
Georgia	118,221	75,602	67,874	39,715	39,404	7,164	15.8	66.1
Hawaii	17,393	4,481	3,766	578	550	2,147	14.7	69.0
Idaho	18,582	18,000	15,387	67	63	2,365	15.4	70.3
Illinois	180,803	138,517	105,487	35,466	35,256	33,171	15.2	68.4
Indiana.	83,436	73,556	69,840	8,780	8,749	3,409	14.2	62.9
Iowa	36,659	34,572	32,685	1,100	1,049	1,603	12.9	60.4
Kansas.	37,289	33,265	29,430	2,803	2,766	3,553	14.4	65.7
Kentucky	53,203	47,929	47,230	4,648	4,630	727	13.6	59.9
Louisiana	66,025	37,648	36,445	27,134	27,097	1,263	15.2	65.7
Maine.	13,669	13,323	12,656	81	68	121	11.0	49.5
'Maryland	70,215	44,471	40,890	22,933	22,490	3,274	13.8	58.9
Massachusetts.	80,364	68,623	61,446	7,716	6,208	8,235	13.1	57.8
Michigan.	133,714	105,805	93,875	24,286	23,957	5,454	13.7	60.0
Minnesota.	64,499	57,127	51,234	3,330	3,284	2,625	13.8	61.4
Mississippi	41,533	22,024	21,663	18,967	18,961	328	15.2	66.3
Missouri	74,037	61,561	59,788	11,033	10,999	1,758	13.7	62.2
Montana.	10,849	9,429	8,818	31	18	302	12.3	59.1
Nebraska	23,319	21,308	18,817	1,253	1,236	1,978	14.1	64.6
Nevada	26,911	22,857	15,121	2,129	2,064	7,713	16.0	75.4
New Hampshire	14,313	14,000	13,350	104	96	228	12.2	52.4
New Jersey.	113,279	84,539	66,168	21,034	19,302	19,635	14.1	64.1
New Mexico	26,871	22,730	9,545	506	477	13,322	15.5	70.4
New York	257,238	184,613	117,641	55,214	47,172	50,720	14.2	63.9
North Carolina.	107,015	75,880	69,102	27,477	27,376	6,906	14.4	64.3
North Dakota.	8,353	7,396	7,100	84	80	170	13.0	61.0
Ohio	152,033	127,036	123,489	22,623	22,120	3,432	13.6	60.7
Oklahoma.	48,269	38,013	34,750	4,746	4,676	3,226	14.6	67.8
Oregon.	43,809	40,235	34,369	936	914	5,854	13.5	62.7
Pennsylvania.	144,224	120,215	113,297	20,407	19,947	6,623	12.0	55.9
Rhode Island.	12,455	10,908	7,742	946	777	1,780	12.6	56.6
South Carolina.	52,214	33,074	31,971	18,408	18,382	1,129	13.9	60.4
South Dakota	10,173	8,426	8,284	91	89	141	13.8	63.6
Tennessee	74,478	57,006	55,288	16,322	16,297	1,721	13.9	61.2
Texas.	333,974	284,321	137,580	39,484	38,928	146,580	17.2	75.3
Utah	43,059	40,893	36,534	260	242	4,298	20.9	88.5
Vermont	6,607	6,523	6,305	22	22	22	11.2	49.6
Virginia.	91,862	66,726	61,428	21,073	20,956	5,374	13.6	58.0
Washington.	78,190	67,635	56,617	3,181	2,968	9,336	13.9	61.8
West Virginia.	20,730	19,851	19,778	747	744	82	11.4	53.1
Wisconsin.	66,557	57,400	54,292	6,414	6,366	3,207	12.9	58.1
Wyoming	6,387	6,060	5,527	62	58	538	13.3	61.8

[1] Includes other races not shown separately. [2] Persons of Hispanic origin may be of any race. Births by Hispanic origin of mother. [3] Per 1,000 estimated population. [4] Per 1,000 women aged 15-44 years estimated.

Source: U.S. National Center for Health Statistics, *Vital Statistics of the United States*, annual; and *National Vital Statistics Reports (NVSR)* (formerly *Monthly Vital Statistics Report*).

Vital Statistics   77

No. 96. Total Fertility Rate and Intrinsic Rate of Natural Increase: 1960 to 1997

[Based on race of child and registered births only, thru 1979. Beginning 1980, based on race of mother. Beginning 1970, excludes births to nonresidents of United States. The *total fertility rate* is the number of births that 1,000 women would have in their lifetime if, at each year of age, they experienced the birth rates occurring in the specified year. A total fertility rate of 2,110 represents "replacement level" fertility for the total population under current mortality conditions (assuming no net immigration). The *intrinsic rate of natural increase* is the rate that would eventually prevail if a population were to experience, at each year of age, the birth rates and death rates occurring in the specified year and if those rates remained unchanged over a long period of time. Minus sign (-) indicates decrease. See also Appendix III]

Annual average and year	Total fertility rate			Intrinsic rate of natural increase			Annual average and year	Total fertility rate			Intrinsic rate of natural increase		
	Total	White	Black and other	Total	White	Black and other		Total	White	Black and other	Total	White	Black and other
1960-64 . . .	3,449	3,326	4,326	18.6	17.1	27.7	1981	1,812	1,748	2,118	-5.6	-7.4	3.0
1965-69 . . .	2,622	2,512	3,362	8.2	6.4	18.6	1982	1,828	1,767	2,107	-5.2	-7.0	3.0
1970-74 . . .	2,094	1,997	2,680	-0.7	-2.5	9.1	1983	1,799	1,741	2,066	-5.8	-7.5	2.2
1975-79 . . .	1,774	1,685	2,270	-6.6	-8.5	3.0	1984	1,807	1,749	2,071	-5.6	-7.3	2.1
1980-84 . . .	1,819	1,731	2,262	-5.4	-7.3	3.0	1985	1,844	1,787	2,109	-4.8	-6.5	2.7
1985-88 . . .	1,870	1,769	2,339	-4.2	-6.3	4.3	1986	1,838	1,776	2,136	-4.9	-6.7	2.8
1970	2,480	2,385	3,067	6.0	4.5	14.4	1987	1,872	1,805	2,198	-4.1	-6.1	4.0
1971	2,267	2,161	2,920	2.6	0.8	12.6	1988	1,934	1,857	2,298	-2.9	-5.1	5.7
1972	2,010	1,907	2,628	-2.0	-3.9	8.6	1989	2,014	1,931	2,433	-1.4	-3.6	7.4
1973	1,879	1,783	2,443	-4.5	-6.5	5.7	1990	2,081	2,003	2,480	-0.1	-2.3	8.3
1974	1,835	1,749	2,339	-5.4	-7.2	4.0	1991	2,073	1,996	2,480	-0.2	-2.4	8.2
1975	1,774	1,686	2,276	-6.7	-8.6	3.0	1992	2,065	1,994	2,442	-0.4	-2.5	7.5
1976	1,738	1,652	2,223	-7.4	-9.3	2.1	1993	2,046	1,982	2,385	-0.7	-1.9	3.7
1977	1,790	1,703	2,279	-6.2	-8.1	3.2	1994	2,036	1,985	2,300	(NA)	(NA)	(NA)
1978	1,760	1,668	2,265	-6.8	-8.8	2.9	1995	2,019	1,989	2,175	(NA)	(NA)	(NA)
1979	1,808	1,716	2,310	-5.7	-7.7	3.8	1996	2,040	2,019	2,149	(NA)	(NA)	(NA)
1980	1,840	1,773	2,177	-5.1	-7.0	4.0	1997	2,040	2,017	2,158	(NA)	(NA)	(NA)

NA Not available.

Source: U.S. National Center for Health Statistics, *Vital Statistics of the United States,* annual; and unpublished data.

No. 97. Projected Fertility Rates, by Race and Age Group: 1998 and 2010

[For definition of total fertility rate, see headnote, Table 96. Birth rates represent live births per 1,000 women in age group indicated. Projections are based on middle fertility assumptions. For explanations of methodology, see text, Section 1, Population]

Age group	All races [1]		White		Black		American Indian, Eskimo, Aleut		Asian and Pacific Islanders		Hispanic [2]	
	1998	2010	1998	2010	1998	2010	1998	2010	1998	2010	1998	2010
Total fertility rate . .	2,066	2,108	1,996	2,046	2,429	2,438	2,153	2,159	1,952	1,954	2,977	2,977
Birth rates:												
10 to 14 years old. . . .	1.4	1.6	0.8	0.9	4.7	4.8	1.7	1.7	0.9	0.8	2.6	2.6
15 to 19 years old. . . .	59.8	63.6	51.3	56.0	110.5	111.5	78.9	81.8	28.2	28.7	103.7	103.7
20 to 24 years old. . . .	116.0	118.2	109.6	112.6	158.0	158.7	143.4	143.7	79.7	79.5	184.7	184.1
25 to 29 years old. . . .	118.2	119.5	119.1	120.7	112.5	113.1	108.7	109.0	121.8	121.7	152.4	152.4
30 to 34 years old. . . .	78.8	81.0	79.9	82.0	66.4	67.8	61.7	62.9	100.7	101.1	96.7	96.7
35 to 39 years old. . . .	31.6	32.1	31.5	31.7	27.7	27.7	27.4	27.4	47.9	47.3	45.3	45.3
40 to 44 years old. . . .	5.7	5.9	5.4	5.6	5.4	5.3	6.0	6.0	10.3	10.3	10.8	10.8
45 to 49 years old. . . .	0.3	0.3	0.2	0.2	0.3	0.2	0.3	0.3	1.0	1.0	0.6	0.6

[1] Includes other races not shown separately.   [2] Persons of Hispanic origin may be of any race.

Source: U.S. Census Bureau, *Current Population Reports,* P25-1130.

No. 98. Birth Rates, by Live-Birth Order and Race: 1980 to 1997

[Births per 1,000 women 15 to 44 years old in specified racial group. Live-birth order refers to number of children born alive. Figures for births of order not stated are distributed. See also headnote, Table 93]

Live-birth order	All races [1]					White					Black				
	1980	1990	1995	1996	1997	1980	1990	1995	1996	1997	1980	1990	1995	1996	1997
Total	68.4	70.9	65.6	65.7	65.3	65.6	68.3	64.4	64.7	64.2	84.9	86.8	72.3	70.8	70.8
First birth	29.5	29.0	27.3	27.0	26.6	28.8	28.4	26.9	26.7	26.3	33.7	32.4	28.7	27.6	27.4
Second birth	21.8	22.8	21.1	21.3	21.2	21.3	22.4	21.1	21.4	21.3	24.7	25.6	20.7	20.6	20.7
Third birth	10.3	11.7	10.5	10.6	10.6	9.6	11.1	10.3	10.4	10.5	14.0	15.6	12.0	12.0	12.1
Fourth birth [2]	3.9	4.5	4.0	6.8	6.8	3.4	4.0	3.8	6.1	6.2	6.5	7.4	5.7	10.6	10.6
Fifth birth	1.5	1.7	1.5	(NA)	(NA)	1.3	1.4	1.3	(NA)	(NA)	2.9	3.2	2.6	(NA)	(NA)
Sixth and seventh	1.0	1.0	0.9	(NA)	(NA)	0.8	0.8	0.7	(NA)	(NA)	2.1	2.0	1.8	(NA)	(NA)
Eighth and over	0.4	0.3	0.3	(NA)	(NA)	0.3	0.2	0.2	(NA)	(NA)	0.9	0.5	0.6	(NA)	(NA)

NA Not available.   [1] Includes other races not shown separately.   [2] 1996 data represents "fourth child and over."

Source: U.S. National Center for Health Statistics, *Vital Statistics of the United States,* annual; and *National Vital Statistics Reports (NVSR)* (formerly *Monthly Vital Statistics Report*).

No. 99. Births to Teens, Unmarried Mothers, and Prenatal Care: 1985 to 1997

[In percent. Represents registered births. See headnote, Table 92]

Characteristics	1985	1990	1993	1994	1995	1996	1997
Percent of births to teenage mothers	12.7	12.8	12.8	13.1	13.1	12.9	12.8
White	10.8	10.9	11.0	11.3	11.5	11.3	11.3
Black	23.0	23.1	22.7	23.2	23.1	22.8	22.5
American Indian, Eskimo, Aleut	19.1	19.5	20.3	21.0	21.4	20.9	(NA)
Asian and Pacific Islander [1]	5.5	5.7	5.7	5.7	5.6	5.3	(NA)
Filipino	5.8	6.1	5.8	6.0	6.2	6.1	(NA)
Chinese	1.1	1.2	1.0	1.0	0.9	0.9	(NA)
Japanese	2.9	2.9	2.7	2.8	2.5	2.5	(NA)
Hawaiian	15.9	18.4	18.5	19.6	19.1	18.4	(NA)
Other	(NA)	(NA)	6.5	6.4	6.3	5.8	(NA)
Hispanic origin [2]	16.5	16.8	17.4	17.8	17.9	17.4	(NA)
Mexican	17.5	17.7	18.2	18.6	18.8	18.1	17.3
Puerto Rican	20.9	21.7	22.3	23.2	23.5	23.1	(NA)
Cuban	7.1	7.7	6.8	7.3	7.7	7.6	(NA)
Central and South American	8.2	9.0	9.9	10.4	10.6	10.5	(NA)
Other and unknown Hispanic	(NA)	(NA)	21.0	20.8	20.1	19.8	(NA)
Percent births to unmarried mothers	22.0	26.6	31.0	32.6	32.2	32.4	32.4
White	14.5	16.9	23.6	25.4	25.3	25.7	25.8
Black	60.1	66.7	68.7	70.4	69.9	69.8	69.1
American Indian, Eskimo, Aleut	40.7	53.6	55.8	57.0	57.2	58.0	(NA)
Asian and Pacific Islander [1]	10.1	(NA)	15.7	16.2	16.3	16.7	(NA)
Filipino	12.1	15.9	17.7	18.5	19.5	19.4	(NA)
Chinese	3.7	5.0	6.7	7.2	7.9	9.2	(NA)
Japanese	7.9	9.6	10.0	11.2	10.8	11.4	(NA)
Hawaiian	(NA)	45.0	47.8	48.6	49.0	49.9	(NA)
Hispanic origin [2]	29.5	36.7	40.0	43.1	40.8	40.7	40.9
Mexican	25.7	33.3	37.0	40.8	40.8	37.9	(NA)
Puerto Rican	51.1	55.9	59.4	60.2	60.0	60.7	(NA)
Cuban	16.1	18.2	21.0	22.9	23.8	24.7	(NA)
Central and South American	34.9	41.2	45.2	45.9	44.1	44.7	(NA)
Percent of mothers beginning prenatal care 1st trimester	76.2	74.2	78.9	80.2	81.3	81.9	82.5
White	79.4	77.7	81.8	82.8	83.6	84.0	84.7
Black	61.8	60.7	66.0	68.3	70.4	71.4	72.3
American Indian, Eskimo, Aleut	60.3	57.9	63.4	65.2	66.7	67.7	(NA)
Asian and Pacific Islander [1]	75.0	(NA)	77.6	79.7	79.9	81.2	(NA)
Filipino	77.2	77.1	79.3	81.3	80.9	82.5	(NA)
Chinese	82.4	81.3	84.6	86.2	85.7	86.8	(NA)
Japanese	85.8	87.0	87.2	89.2	89.7	89.3	(NA)
Hawaiian	(NA)	65.8	70.6	77.0	75.9	78.5	(NA)
Hispanic origin [2]	61.2	60.2	66.6	68.9	70.8	72.2	73.7
Mexican	59.9	57.8	64.8	67.3	69.1	70.7	(NA)
Puerto Rican	58.3	63.5	70.0	71.7	74.0	75.0	(NA)
Cuban	82.5	84.8	88.9	90.1	89.2	89.2	(NA)
Central and South American	60.6	61.5	68.7	71.2	73.2	75.0	(NA)
Percent of mothers beginning prenatal care 3d trimester or no care	5.7	6.0	4.8	4.4	4.2	4.0	(NA)
White	4.7	4.9	3.9	3.6	3.5	3.3	(NA)
Black	10.0	10.9	9.0	8.2	7.6	7.3	(NA)
American Indian, Eskimo, Aleut	11.5	12.9	10.3	9.8	9.5	8.6	(NA)
Asian and Pacific Islander [1]	6.1	(NA)	4.6	4.1	4.3	3.9	(NA)
Filipino	4.6	4.5	4.0	3.6	4.1	3.3	(NA)
Chinese	4.2	3.4	2.9	2.7	3.0	2.5	(NA)
Japanese	2.6	2.9	2.8	1.9	2.3	2.2	(NA)
Hawaiian	(NA)	8.7	6.7	4.7	5.1	5.0	(NA)
Hispanic origin [2]	12.5	12.0	8.8	7.6	7.4	6.7	(NA)
Mexican	12.9	13.2	9.7	8.3	8.1	7.2	(NA)
Puerto Rican	15.5	10.6	7.1	6.5	5.5	5.7	(NA)
Cuban	3.7	2.8	1.8	1.6	2.1	1.6	(NA)
Central and South American	12.5	10.9	7.3	6.5	6.1	5.5	(NA)
Percent of births with low birth weight [3]	6.8	7.0	7.2	7.3	7.3	7.4	7.5
White	5.6	5.7	6.0	6.1	6.2	6.3	6.5
Black	12.4	13.3	13.3	13.2	13.1	13.0	13.0
American Indian, Eskimo, Aleut	5.9	6.1	6.4	6.4	6.6	6.5	(NA)
Asian and Pacific Islander [1]	6.1	(NA)	6.6	6.8	6.9	7.1	(NA)
Filipino	6.9	7.3	7.0	7.8	7.8	7.9	(NA)
Chinese	5.0	4.7	4.9	4.8	5.3	5.0	(NA)
Japanese	5.9	6.2	6.5	6.9	7.3	7.3	(NA)
Hawaiian	6.4	7.2	6.8	7.2	6.8	6.8	(NA)
Hispanic origin [2]	6.2	6.1	6.2	6.2	6.3	7.4	6.4
Mexican	5.8	5.5	5.8	5.8	5.8	5.9	(NA)
Puerto Rican	8.7	9.0	9.2	9.1	9.4	9.2	(NA)
Cuban	6.0	5.7	6.2	6.3	6.5	6.5	(NA)
Central and South American	5.7	5.8	5.9	6.0	6.2	6.0	(NA)

NA Not available.   [1] Includes other races not shown separately.   [2] Hispanic persons may be of any race. Includes other types, not shown separately.   [3] Births less than 2,500 grams (5 lb.-8 oz.).

Source: U.S. National Center for Health Statistics, Vital Statistics of the United States, annual; and National Vital Statistics Reports (NVSR) (formerly Monthly Vital Statistics Report).

U.S. Census Bureau, Statistical Abstract of the United States: 1999

No. 100. Births to Unmarried Women, by Race of Child and Age of Mother: 1980 to 1996

[Excludes births to nonresidents of United States. Marital status is inferred from a comparison of the child's and parents' surnames on the birth certificate for those States that do not report on marital status. No estimates included for misstatements on birth records or failures to register births. See also Appendix III]

Race of child and age of mother	1980	1990	1994	1995	1996	Race of child and age of mother	1980	1990	1994	1995	1996
NUMBER (1,000)						25 to 29 years	15.0	19.7	18.4	18.2	18.7
						30 to 34 years	6.2	10.1	10.6	10.6	10.6
Total live births [1] .	666	1,165	1,290	1,254	1,260	35 years and over.	2.4	4.5	5.6	5.8	4.9
White	320	647	794	785	965						
Black	326	473	448	421	415	**AS PERCENT OF ALL BIRTHS IN RACIAL GROUPS**					
Under 15 years	9	11	12	11	10						
15 to 19 years	263	350	381	376	373						
20 to 24 years	237	404	449	432	431	**Total** [1]	18.4	28.0	32.6	32.2	32.4
25 to 29 years	100	230	238	229	235	White	11.0	20.1	25.4	25.3	25.7
30 to 34 years	41	118	137	133	133	Black	55.2	65.2	70.4	69.9	69.8
35 years and over.	16	53	72	73	62						
						BIRTH RATE [2]					
PERCENT DISTRIBUTION											
						Total [1][3]	29.4	43.8	46.9	45.1	44.8
						White [3]	17.6	31.8	38.3	37.5	37.6
Total [1]	100.0	100.0	100.0	100.0	100.0	Black [3]	82.9	93.9	82.1	75.9	74.4
White	48.1	55.6	61.6	62.6	76.6	15 to 19 years	27.6	42.5	46.4	44.4	42.9
Black	48.9	40.6	34.8	33.6	32.9	20 to 24 years	40.9	65.1	72.2	70.3	70.7
Under 15 years	1.4	0.9	0.9	0.9	0.8	25 to 29 years	34.0	56.0	59.0	56.1	56.8
15 to 19 years	39.5	30.0	29.6	30.0	29.6	30 to 34 years	21.1	37.6	40.1	39.6	41.1
20 to 24 years	35.6	34.7	34.8	34.5	34.2						

[1] Includes other races not shown separately.   [2] Rate per 1,000 unmarried women (never-married, widowed, and divorced) estimated as of July 1.   [3] Covers women aged 15 to 44 years.

Source: U.S. National Center for Health Statistics, *Vital Statistics of the United States*, annual; and *National Vital Statistics Reports (NVSR)* (formerly *Monthly Vital Statistics Report*).

No. 101. Live Births by Plurality of Birth and Ratios, and Race of Mother: 1995 and 1996

Plurality and race of mother	1995	1996—Age of mother								
		All ages	Under 15 yrs. old	15 to 19 yrs. old	20 to 24 yrs. old	25 to 29 yrs. old	30 to 34 yrs. old	35 to 39 yrs. old	40 to 44 yrs. old	45 to 49 yrs. old
NUMBER										
Live births, total [1] . . .	3,899,589	3,891,494	11,148	491,577	945,210	1,071,287	897,913	399,510	71,804	3,045
White	3,098,885	3,093,057	5,526	344,685	726,669	878,449	747,436	329,782	58,062	2,448
Black	603,139	594,781	5,193	130,596	179,361	133,204	94,295	43,716	8,124	292
Live births in single deliveries [1]	3,797,880	3,784,805	11,006	484,339	925,704	1,042,220	866,404	383,310	69,127	2,695
White	3,018,184	3,007,997	5,463	340,201	712,980	855,027	720,655	315,836	55,712	2,123
Black	585,787	577,057	5,122	128,049	174,193	128,606	90,800	42,106	7,900	281
Live births in twin deliveries [1]	96,736	100,750	139	7,161	19,134	27,612	28,963	14,958	2,467	316
White	76,196	79,677	63	4,448	13,400	22,120	24,390	12,813	2,152	291
Black	17,000	17,285	68	2,510	5,088	4,470	3,388	1,538	212	11
Live births in higher-order multiple deliveries [1]	4,973	5,939	3	77	372	1,455	2,546	1,242	210	34
White	4,505	5,383	-	36	289	1,302	2,391	1,133	198	34
Black	352	439	3	37	80	128	107	72	12	-
RATIO PER 1,000 LIVE BIRTHS										
All multiple births [1]	26.1	27.4	12.7	14.7	20.6	27.1	35.1	40.5	37.3	114.9
White	26.0	27.5	11.4	13.0	18.8	26.7	35.8	42.3	40.5	132.8
Black	28.8	29.8	13.7	19.5	28.8	34.5	37.1	36.8	27.6	(B)
Twin births [1]	24.8	25.9	12.5	14.6	20.2	25.8	32.3	37.4	34.4	103.8
White	24.6	25.8	11.4	12.9	18.4	25.2	32.6	38.9	37.1	118.9
Black	28.2	29.1	13.1	19.2	28.4	33.6	35.9	35.2	26.1	(B)
RATIO PER 100,000 LIVE BIRTHS										
Higher-order multiple births [1]	127.5	152.6	(B)	15.7	39.4	135.8	283.5	310.9	292.5	1,116.6
White	145.4	174.0	(B)	10.4	39.8	148.2	319.9	343.6	341.0	1,388.9
Black	58.4	73.8	(B)	28.3	44.6	96.1	113.5	164.7	(B)	(B)

- Represents or rounds to zero.   B Does not meet standard of reliability or precision.   [1] Includes races other than White and Black.

Source: U.S. National Center for Health Statistics, Advance report of Final Natality Statistics, and *National Vital Statistics Reports (NVSR)* (formerly *Monthly Vital Statistics Report*).

U.S. Census Bureau, Statistical Abstract of the United States: 1999

No. 102. Low Birth Weight and Births to Teenage Mothers and to Unmarried Women—States: 1990 to 1997

[Represents registered births. Excludes births to nonresidents of the United States. Based on 100 percent of births in all states and the District of Columbia. See Appendix III]

State	Percent of births with low birth weight[1]			Births to teenage mothers percent of total			Births to unmarried women percent of total		
	1990	1995	1997	1990	1995	1997	1990	1995	1997
U.S. ...	7.0	7.3	7.5	12.8	13.1	12.8	28.0	32.2	32.4
AL.	8.4	9.0	9.3	18.2	18.5	17.6	30.1	34.5	33.9
AK.	4.8	5.3	5.9	9.7	11.2	11.1	26.2	29.9	30.3
AZ.	6.4	6.8	6.9	14.2	15.1	14.9	32.7	38.2	37.7
AR.	8.2	8.2	8.3	19.7	19.6	19.2	29.4	32.9	34.2
CA.	5.8	6.1	6.2	11.6	12.4	11.7	[2]31.6	32.1	32.8
CO	8.0	8.4	8.8	11.3	12.1	11.9	21.2	24.9	25.2
CT.	6.6	7.1	7.1	8.2	8.6	8.2	[2]26.6	30.6	32.4
DE.	7.6	8.4	8.8	11.9	13.2	13.4	29.0	34.9	36.0
DC	15.1	13.4	13.3	17.8	16.3	15.6	64.9	65.8	63.6
FL.	7.4	7.7	8.0	13.9	13.7	13.4	31.7	35.8	36.0
GA	8.7	8.8	8.8	16.7	16.3	15.5	32.8	35.2	35.4
HI	7.1	7.0	7.0	10.5	10.1	11.0	24.8	29.2	29.8
ID	5.7	5.9	6.3	12.3	14.0	12.7	16.7	19.9	20.7
IL	7.6	7.9	7.9	13.1	12.9	12.5	31.7	33.8	33.4
IN	6.6	7.5	7.3	14.5	14.7	14.2	26.2	31.9	32.2
IA	5.4	6.0	6.4	10.2	11.0	10.7	21.0	25.2	26.2
KS.	6.2	6.4	6.9	12.3	13.1	13.0	21.5	25.9	27.6
KY.	7.1	7.6	7.8	17.5	17.2	16.3	23.6	28.5	29.5
LA.	9.2	9.7	10.1	17.6	19.1	18.6	36.8	42.4	43.9
ME	5.1	6.1	5.9	10.8	10.3	10.1	22.6	27.8	29.7
MD	7.8	8.5	8.8	10.5	10.3	10.3	[2]29.6	33.3	33.5
MA	5.9	6.3	7.0	8.0	7.5	7.4	24.7	25.6	26.0
MI	7.6	7.7	7.7	13.5	12.5	11.7	[2]26.2	34.3	33.3
MN	5.1	5.9	5.8	8.0	8.4	8.7	20.9	23.9	24.7
MS	9.6	9.8	10.1	21.3	22.2	20.7	40.5	45.3	45.5
MO	7.1	7.6	7.7	14.4	14.4	13.9	28.6	32.1	33.1
MT	6.2	5.8	6.3	11.5	12.6	12.2	[2]23.7	26.5	28.8
NE.	5.3	6.3	7.0	9.8	10.0	10.5	20.7	24.3	25.8
NV.	7.2	7.4	7.7	12.6	13.7	13.5	[2]25.4	42.0	35.5
NH	4.9	5.5	5.8	7.2	7.6	7.8	16.9	22.2	23.8
NJ.	7.0	7.6	7.8	8.4	8.2	7.8	24.3	27.6	27.8
NM	7.4	7.5	7.8	16.3	18.4	17.9	35.4	42.6	43.5
NY.	7.6	7.6	7.8	9.1	9.3	10.7	[2]33.0	37.9	35.0
NC	8.0	8.7	8.8	16.2	15.2	14.3	29.4	31.4	32.2
ND	5.5	5.3	6.2	8.6	9.6	9.1	18.4	23.5	26.0
OH	7.1	7.6	7.7	13.8	13.7	13.3	[2]28.9	33.0	33.9
OK	6.6	7.0	7.3	16.2	17.1	16.9	25.2	30.5	32.3
OR	5.0	5.5	5.5	12.0	13.0	12.5	25.7	28.9	28.8
PA.	7.1	7.4	7.6	10.9	10.8	10.4	28.6	32.4	32.8
RI.	6.2	6.8	7.4	10.5	10.1	10.7	26.3	31.1	33.0
SC.	8.7	9.3	9.1	17.1	17.3	16.4	32.7	37.4	38.0
SD.	5.1	5.6	5.5	10.8	11.4	12.2	22.9	28.0	31.1
TN.	8.2	8.7	8.8	17.6	16.9	16.3	30.2	33.1	34.1
TX.	6.9	7.1	7.3	15.6	16.6	16.1	[2]17.5	30.0	30.7
UT.	5.7	6.3	6.6	10.3	10.8	10.5	13.5	15.7	16.5
VT.	5.3	5.4	6.3	8.5	8.2	8.4	20.1	24.9	26.1
VA.	7.2	7.7	7.7	11.7	11.4	11.0	26.0	29.3	29.3
WA	5.3	5.5	5.6	10.8	11.5	11.0	23.7	26.7	27.1
WV	7.1	7.9	8.3	17.8	17.2	15.9	25.4	30.5	31.3
WI.	5.9	6.0	6.4	10.2	10.5	10.7	24.2	27.4	28.1
WY	7.4	7.4	9.0	13.6	15.2	14.1	19.8	26.4	27.3

[1] Less than 2,500 grams (5 pounds-8 ounces).   [2] Marital status of mother is inferred.

Source: U.S. National Center for Health Statistics, Vital Statistics of the United States, annual; and National Vital Statistics Reports (NVSR) (formerly Monthly Vital Statistics Report).

U.S. Census Bureau, Statistical Abstract of the United States: 1999

No. 103. Live Births, by Place of Delivery, Median and Low Birth Weight, and Prenatal Care: 1980 to 1996

[Represents registered births. Excludes births to nonresidents of the United States. For total number of births, see Table 93. See Appendix III]

Item	1980	1985	1990	1993	1994	1995	1996
Births attended (1,000):							
In hospital [1]	3,576	3,722	4,110	3,959	3,912	3,861	3,891
By physician, not in hospital	12	10	14	8	7	6	6
By midwife and other, not in hospital [2]	24	29	21	20	21	21	20
Median birth weight [3]	7 lb.-7 oz.	7 lb.-7 oz.	7 lb.-7 oz.	7 lb.-7 oz.	(NA)	(NA)	7 lb.-7 oz.
Percent of births with low birth weight	6.8	6.8	7.0	7.2	7.3	7.3	7.4
White	5.7	5.6	5.7	6.0	6.1	6.2	6.3
Black	12.5	12.4	13.3	13.3	13.2	13.1	13.0
Percent of births by period in which prenatal care began:							
1st trimester	76.3	76.2	74.2	78.9	80.2	81.3	81.9
3d trimester or no prenatal care	5.1	5.7	6.0	4.8	4.4	4.2	4.0

NA Not available. [1] Includes all births in hospitals or institutions and in clinics. [2] Includes births with attendant not specified. [3] Beginning 1990, median birth weight based on race of mother; prior to 1990, based on race of child.

No. 104. Cesarean Section Deliveries, by Age of Mother: 1990 to 1996

[In thousands (4,111 represents 4,111,000), except rate. 1990 excludes data for Oklahoma, which did not report method of delivery on the birth certificate]

Age of mother	1990	1995	1996	Age of mother	1990	1995	1996
Births by method of delivery	4,111	3,900	3,891	Cesarean deliveries	733	640	631
Vaginal	3,111	3,064	3,061	Black births by method of delivery	679	603	595
After previous cesarean	84	112	116	Vaginal	517	469	462
Cesarean deliveries	914	807	797	Cesarean deliveries	146	130	128
Primary	575	510	504	Cesarean delivery rate [1]	22.7	21.0	21.0
Repeat	339	297	293	Primary [2]	16.0	15.0	15.0
White births by method of delivery	3,252	3,099	3,093	Rate of vaginal cesarean birth after previous cesarean [3]	19.0	28.0	28.0
Vaginal	2,215	2,435	2,434				

[1] Percent of all live births by cesarean delivery. [2] Number of primary cesareans per 100 live births to women who have not had a previous cesarean. [3] Number of vaginal births after previous cesarean delivery per 100 live births to women with a previous cesarean delivery.

No. 105. Live Births and Births to Teen Mothers—20 Largest Metropolitan Areas: 1993

[Excludes births to nonresidents of the United States. Data are by place of residence. Metropolitan statistical areas (MSAs), consolidated metropolitan statistical areas (CMSAs), and New England County Metropolitan Areas (NECMAs) are defined by the U.S. Office of Management and Budget as of June 30,1990. See Appendix II for definitions and components]

Metropolitan area	All births		Births to teens	
	Number	Rate per 1,000 population	Number of teen births	Percent of total births
New York-Northern New Jersey-Long Island, NY-NJ-CT-PA CMSA/NECMA	290,532	16	22,950	8
Los Angeles-Anaheim-Riverside, CA CMSA	310,792	20	36,390	12
Chicago-Gary-Lake County, IL-IN-WI CMSA	146,678	18	17,688	12
Washington, DC-MD-VA MSA	66,625	16	5,262	8
San Francisco-Oakland-San Jose, CA CMSA	101,011	16	8,753	9
Philadelphia-Wilmington-Trenton, PA-NJ-DE-MD CMSA	89,732	15	9,609	11
Boston-Lawrence-Salem-Lowell-Brockton, MA NECMA	54,291	14	3,402	6
Detroit-Ann Arbor, MI CMSA	72,354	15	8,347	12
Dallas-Fort Worth, TX CMSA	73,565	18	9,788	13
Houston-Galveston-Brazoria, TX CMSA	74,277	19	10,226	14
Miami-Fort Lauderdale, FL CMSA	52,393	16	5,476	10
Seattle-Tacoma, WA CMSA	40,565	15	3,458	9
Atlanta, GA MSA	51,280	17	5,955	12
Cleveland-Akron-Lorain, OH CMSA	40,822	15	4,891	12
Minneapolis-St. Paul, MN-WI MSA	40,314	16	2,972	7
San Diego, CA MSA	48,935	19	5,207	11
St. Louis, MO-IL MSA	38,042	15	4,953	13
Pittsburgh-Beaver Valley, PA CMSA	27,177	12	2,548	9
Phoenix, AZ MSA	40,406	18	5,643	14
Tampa-St. Petersburg-Clearwater, FL MSA	27,658	13	3,653	13
Baltimore, MD MSA	36,237	15	4,028	11
Denver-Boulder, CO CMSA	31,139	16	3,330	11
Cincinnati-Hamilton, OH-KY-IN CMSA	27,104	15	3,611	13
Milwaukee-Racine, WI CMSA	25,099	15	3,235	13
Kansas City, MO-KS MSA	24,787	15	3,011	12

Source of Tables 103-105: U.S. National Center for Health Statistics, Vital Statistics of the United States, annual; and unpublished data.

U.S. Census Bureau, Statistical Abstract of the United States: 1999

No. 106. Women Who Have Had a Child in the Last Year, by Age: 1980 to 1998

[3,247 represents 3,247,000. See headnote, Table 107]

Age of mother	Women who had a child in last year (1,000)			Total births per 1,000 women			First births per 1,000 women		
	1980	1990	1998	1980	1990	1998	1980	1990	1998
Total	**3,247**	**3,913**	**3,671**	**71.1**	**67.0**	**60.7**	**28.5**	**26.4**	**24.6**
15 to 29 years old [1] ..	2,476	2,568	2,274	103.7	90.8	81.7	48.6	43.2	40.2
15 to 19 years old ..	(NA)	338	460	(NA)	39.8	48.0	(NA)	30.1	29.3
25 to 29 years old ..	1,081	1,192	950	114.8	112.1	100.5	(NA)	46.2	41.8
30 to 44 years old	770	1,346	1,397	35.4	44.7	42.7	6.3	10.6	11.3
30 to 34 years old ..	519	892	843	60.0	80.4	82.4	(NA)	21.9	23.8
35 to 39 years old ..	192	377	437	26.9	37.3	38.5	(NA)	6.5	8.7
40 to 44 years old ..	59	77	117	9.9	8.6	10.5	(NA)	1.2	2.6

NA Not available. [1] For 1980, 18 to 29 years old.

Source: U.S. Census Bureau, *Current Population Reports*, P20-375, P20-454, P20-470, and P20-499.

No. 107. Characteristics of Women Who Have Had a Child in the Last Year: 1995 and 1998

[As of **June. (60,225 represents 60,225,000.) Women, ages 15 to 44 years old.** Covers civilian noninstitutional population. Since the number of women who had a birth during the 12-month period was tabulated and not the actual numbers of births, some small underestimation of fertility for this period may exist due to the omission of: (1) Multiple births, (2) Two or more live births spaced within the 12-month period (the woman is counted only once), (3) Women who had births in the period and who did not survive to the survey date, (4) Women who were in institutions and therefore not in the survey universe. These losses may be somewhat offset by the inclusion in the CPS of births to immigrants who did not have their children born in the United States and births to nonresident women. These births would not have been recorded in the vital registration system. Based on Current Population Survey (CPS); see text, Section 1, Population, and Appendix III]

Characteristic	1995			1998		
	Women who have had a child in the last year			Women who have had a child in the last year		
	Number of women (1,000)	Total births per 1,000 women	First births per 1,000 women	Number of women (1,000)	Total births per 1,000 women	First births per 1,000 women
Total [1]	**60,225**	**61.4**	**23.2**	**60,519**	**60.7**	**24.6**
White.	48,603	59.2	22.6	48,487	60.8	24.2
Black.	8,617	70.6	26.4	8,809	62.9	27.8
Hispanic [2]	6,632	79.6	25.0	7,359	84.0	36.1
Currently married.	31,616	85.5	30.3	30,903	81.8	29.7
Married, spouse present	29,202	87.2	31.4	28,344	85.5	31.4
Married, spouse absent [3]	2,414	64.5	17.4	2,559	40.7	11.8
Widowed or divorced	5,762	28.4	4.1	5,430	26.4	6.4
Never married	22,846	36.3	18.0	24,185	41.3	22.1
Educational attainment:						
Less than high school	12,629	57.3	19.6	13,048	60.8	23.5
High school, 4 years	18,404	67.4	25.5	17,536	59.0	21.9
College:						
1 or more years	29,192	59.3	23.2	29,935	61.6	26.7
No degree	12,724	56.1	21.2	12,626	54.6	21.7
Associate degree	4,663	56.9	19.2	4,413	65.3	28.6
Bachelor's degree	8,884	65.3	27.0	9,762	64.2	29.1
Grad. or prof. degree	2,921	59.2	26.8	3,134	76.2	36.6
Labor force status:						
Employed	39,989	46.5	20.9	40,957	47.6	19.8
Unemployed	3,287	53.5	22.8	2,808	73.6	33.5
Not in labor force	16,949	98.1	28.5	16,754	90.5	34.8
Occupation of employed women:						
Managerial-professional.	11,059	46.2	22.3	12,044	55.3	23.2
Tech., sales, admin. support.	16,997	48.6	21.5	16,801	45.9	21.7
Service workers	7,612	44.0	16.6	7,796	42.0	14.5
Farming, forestry, and fishing	501	41.0	27.9	467	30.1	4.0
Precision prod., craft, repair	813	56.6	37.5	784	36.9	15.6
Operators, fabricators, laborers	3,007	39.5	17.8	3,064	46.0	13.4
Family income:						
Under $10,000.	6,957	91.0	32.8	5,631	73.3	29.5
$10,000 to $19,999.	8,159	64.3	25.8	6,917	74.3	30.6
$20,000 to $24,999.	4,542	60.6	20.3	3,902	77.3	36.4
$25,000 to $29,999.	4,364	57.0	18.9	3,848	61.4	20.8
$30,000 to $34,999.	4,076	60.6	24.3	3,928	58.6	21.6
$35,000 to $49,999.	9,949	59.1	20.8	9,478	55.1	21.9
$50,000 to $74,999.	9,720	52.5	23.3	11,003	60.3	24.1
$75,000 and over	7,088	53.1	19.2	9,627	50.2	21.7

[1] Includes women of other races and women with family income not reported, not shown separately. [2] Persons of Hispanic origin may be of any race. [3] Includes separated women.

Source: U.S. Census Bureau, *Current Population Reports*, P20-375, P20-454, and P20-482.

Vital Statistics 83

No. 108. Women Who Have Had a Child in the Last Year, by Age and Labor Force Status: 1980 to 1998

[3,247 represents 3,247,000. See headnote, Table 107]

Year	Total, 18 to 44 years old			18 to 29 years old			30 to 44 years old		
	Number (1,000)	In the labor force		Number (1,000)	In the labor force		Number (1,000)	In the labor force	
		Number (1,000)	Percent		Number (1,000)	Percent		Number (1,000)	Percent
1980	3,247	1,233	38	2,476	947	38	770	287	37
1981	3,381	1,411	42	2,499	1,004	40	881	407	46
1982	3,433	1,508	44	2,445	1,040	43	988	469	48
1983	3,625	1,563	43	2,682	1,138	42	942	425	45
1984	3,311	1,547	47	2,375	1,058	45	984	488	50
1985	3,497	1,691	48	2,512	1,204	48	1,174	620	53
1986	3,625	1,805	50	2,452	1,185	48	1,180	623	53
1987	3,701	1,881	51	2,521	1,258	50	1,283	688	54
1988 1	3,667	1,866	51	2,384	1,177	49	1,346	793	59
1990 1	3,913	2,068	53	2,568	1,275	50	1,342	802	60
1992 1	3,688	1,985	54	2,346	1,182	50	1,501	857	57
1994 1	3,890	2,066	53	2,389	1,209	51	1,444	884	61
1995 1	3,696	2,034	55	2,252	1,150	51	(X)	(X)	(X)
1998 1	3,671	2,155	59	(X)	(X)	(X)	(X)	(X)	(X)

X Not applicable.   1 Lower age limit is 15 years old.

Source: U.S. Census Bureau, Current Population Reports, P20-482; and unpublished data.

No. 109. Childless Women and Children Ever Born, by Race, Age, and Marital Status: 1998

[36,334 represents 36,334,000. See headnote, Table 102]

Characteristics	Total number of women (1,000)	Women by number of children ever born (percent)				Children ever born	
		Total	None	One	Two or more	Total number (1,000)	Per 1,000 women
ALL RACES 1							
Women ever married	36,334	100	18.7	21.7	59.7	64,305	1,770
15 to 19 years old	372	100	49.8	32.2	18.1	254	683
20 to 24 years old	2,485	100	34.3	36.3	29.4	2,576	1,037
25 to 29 years old	5,846	100	29.6	28.5	42.0	7,728	1,322
30 to 34 years old	7,952	100	18.0	21.7	60.3	13,879	1,745
35 to 39 years old	9,685	100	12.8	17.1	70.0	19,858	2,050
40 to 44 years old	9,995	100	13.7	18.1	68.3	20,011	2,002
Women never married	24,185	100	77.5	11.6	11.0	9,926	410
15 to 19 years old	9,204	100	91.8	5.7	2.6	1,071	116
20 to 24 years old	6,315	100	75.7	15.6	8.8	2,311	366
25 to 29 years old	3,606	100	66.1	15.4	18.5	2,315	642
30 to 34 years old	2,277	100	60.2	16.3	23.6	1,931	848
35 to 39 years old	1,666	100	60.5	15.2	24.4	1,451	871
40 to 44 years old	1,118	100	66.8	10.9	22.3	847	758
WHITE							
Women ever married	30,664	100	19.3	21.9	58.8	53,274	1,737
15 to 19 years old	324	100	48.7	35.0	16.3	219	676
20 to 24 years old	2,190	100	34.0	37.4	28.7	2,249	1,027
25 to 29 years old	4,978	100	30.7	28.8	40.5	6,356	1,277
30 to 34 years old	6,668	100	18.6	21.9	59.4	11,444	1,716
35 to 39 years old	8,184	100	13.0	17.0	70.1	16,662	2,036
40 to 44 years old	8,320	100	14.0	18.1	68.0	16,344	1,964
Women never married	17,823	100	84.1	9.2	6.7	4,738	266
15 to 19 years old	7,233	100	93.5	4.3	2.2	713	99
20 to 24 years old	4,772	100	81.1	12.8	6.1	1,320	277
25 to 29 years old	2,534	100	74.8	13.6	11.7	1,078	425
30 to 34 years old	1,484	100	71.4	12.2	16.3	859	579
35 to 39 years old	1,066	100	75.9	12.4	11.7	465	436
40 to 44 years old	735	100	80.9	7.5	11.6	303	412
BLACK							
Women ever married	3,710	100	13.6	19.9	66.4	7,600	2,049
15 to 19 years old	29	(B)	(B)	(B)	(B)	30	(B)
20 to 24 years old	199	100	36.2	24.9	38.9	233	1,172
25 to 29 years old	573	100	17.5	25.6	56.8	1,023	1,778
30 to 34 years old	801	100	10.9	19.1	70.0	1,634	2,040
35 to 39 years old	1,002	100	10.5	17.6	72.0	2,253	2,248
40 to 44 years old	1,107	100	11.7	19.0	69.2	2,427	2,193
Women never married	5,099	100	52.4	21.1	26.6	4,835	948
15 to 19 years old	1,525	100	83.2	13.1	3.7	312	205
20 to 24 years old	1,178	100	49.7	29.2	21.0	920	782
25 to 29 years old	849	100	37.4	21.2	30.5	1,153	1,358
30 to 34 years old	666	100	33.1	26.4	40.4	989	1,485
35 to 39 years old	545	100	29.5	20.8	49.6	941	1,728
40 to 44 years old	336	100	34.4	18.1	47.4	519	1,545

B Base figure too small to meet statistical standards for reliability.   1 Includes other races, not shown separately.

Source: U.S. Census Bureau, Current Population Reports, Series P20-526.

No. 110. Number of Male Sexual Partners in Lifetime, by Selected Characteristics: 1995

[60,201 represents 60,201,000. Based on responses from the National Survey of Family Growth (NSFG) sponsored by the National Center for Health Statistics. Based on interview conducted in person in homes of 10,847 women between January and October 1995, using computer-assisted personal interviewing. A small part of the NSFG was conducted with self-administered technique called Audio-Assisted Self Interviewing. See source for details]

Women 15-44 years of age	Number (1,000)	Number of partners in lifetime by percent distribution							
		0 [1]	1	2	3	4	5	6-9	10 or more
All women..............	60,201	10.5	23.5	12.3	9.6	8.4	8.1	12.1	15.5
Age:									
15-19 years old...........	8,961	45.8	19.4	11.0	7.9	3.6	2.9	5.7	3.7
20-24 years old...........	9,041	11.0	21.6	13.4	11.5	9.0	7.7	11.9	13.9
25-29 years old...........	9,693	4.3	22.0	13.5	10.1	9.2	10.1	13.8	16.9
30-34 years old...........	11,065	2.8	23.4	11.8	9.1	11.5	9.7	13.8	16.9
35-39 years old...........	11,211	1.8	24.3	11.7	9.4	8.5	9.3	14.5	20.5
40-44 years old...........	10,230	2.4	29.4	12.6	9.7	8.0	8.4	11.7	17.7
Married.................	29,673	0.5	34.5	13.8	9.9	8.9	8.0	11.2	13.2
Unmarried...............	30,528	20.2	12.8	10.9	9.4	7.9	8.2	12.8	17.7
First intercourse:									
Under 16 years old........	13,944	(X)	11.3	11.2	10.2	8.6	10.6	18.5	29.0
16 years old.............	8,750	(X)	18.6	12.6	12.9	10.9	9.4	16.5	18.8
17 years old.............	8,754	(X)	17.3	14.4	11.4	12.3	12.5	13.1	18.8
18 years old.............	6,941	(X)	26.0	14.3	11.0	11.0	9.0	13.1	14.9
19 years old.............	4,759	(X)	37.6	14.7	11.6	8.0	7.2	11.0	9.2
20 years old and over	10,653	(X)	52.2	16.5	8.6	6.3	4.7	5.9	4.6
Education: [2]									
No high school diploma or GED [3]..	5,424	1.3	27.7	15.8	10.1	7.6	10.1	11.7	15.8
High school diploma or GED	18,169	2.5	23.5	13.0	10.8	9.8	9.6	13.7	17.1
Some college, no bachelor's degree...	12,399	4.6	22.3	10.3	9.6	9.1	10.2	14.1	19.9
Bachelor's degree or higher......	11,748	4.7	26.1	11.7	8.6	9.5	7.1	13.5	18.9
Poverty level income: [2]									
0-149 percent...........	10,072	3.8	21.8	13.7	9.9	9.4	10.1	13.6	17.7
Race and Hispanic origin:									
Hispanic................	6,702	12.1	37.1	15.8	8.9	5.1	5.7	6.9	8.5

X Not applicable.   [1] Never had intercourse, or never had voluntary intercourse if first intercourse was not voluntary.
[2] Limited to women 22-44 years of age at time of interview.   [3] GED = general equivalency diploma.

No. 111. Unmarried Women Who Have Had Intercourse in the 12 Months Prior to Interview: 1995

[12,708 represents 12,708,000. Represents women 15-44 years of age. See headnote, Table 110]

Women 15-44 years of age	Number (1,000)	Partners used condoms for disease prevention— percent distribution				
		Every time	More than half the time	Half the time	Less than half the time	Not at all
Total [1]	12,708	31.3	13.9	8.4	13.9	32.5
Age and number of partners: [2]						
1 partner................	8,197	31.6	9.0	6.1	10.9	42.3
2 or more partners..........	4,504	30.9	22.7	12.6	19.4	14.5
15-29 years old............	8,570	32.2	15.1	9.6	13.8	29.3
1 partner...............	5,315	32.7	10.1	7.3	10.4	39.5
2 or more partners..........	3,252	31.4	23.2	13.4	19.4	12.5
30-44 years old............	4,139	29.5	11.4	5.9	14.1	39.2
1 partner...............	2,882	29.6	7.0	3.9	11.8	47.6
2 or more partners..........	1,251	29.5	21.4	10.4	19.4	19.4
Race and Hispanic origin of partners: [2]						
Hispanic................	1,077	30.9	15.4	11.3	13.7	28.7
1 partner...............	707	29.8	12.5	9.4	11.5	36.8
2 or more partners..........	370	33.1	21.0	14.9	17.8	13.2
Non-Hispanic White	8,202	27.7	13.0	8.1	14.7	36.5
1 partner...............	5,341	28.6	7.7	5.9	10.5	47.4
2 or more partners..........	2,861	26.2	23.0	12.1	22.5	16.3
Non-Hispanic Black	3,042	39.2	15.4	9.2	12.8	23.4
1 partner...............	1,890	38.4	12.0	6.4	12.3	30.8
2 or more partners..........	1,153	40.5	21.0	13.8	13.6	11.2
Education: [3]						
No high school diploma or GED [4]....	2,128	26.6	13.9	7.6	10.8	41.1
High school diploma or GED	5,247	26.2	12.5	7.6	14.5	39.1
Some college, no bachelor's degree ..	3,779	29.7	10.6	7.6	13.9	39.7
Bachelor's degree or higher........	3,111	32.4	13.6	6.1	12.0	35.1

[1] Includes women with missing information on number of partners in the 12 months prior to interview.   [2] Number of male partners in the 12 months prior to interview.   [3] Limited to women 22-44 years of age at time of interview.   [4] GED is general equivalency diploma.

Source of Tables 110 and 111: U.S. National Center for Health Statistics, Fertility, Family Planning, and Women's Health: New data from the 1995 National Survey of Family Growth, Vital and Health Statistics, Series 23, No. 19, 1997.

No. 112. Ever Received Any Infertility Services, by Women 15-44 Years of Age, by Selected Characteristics: 1995

[60,201 represents 60,201,000. In percents, except as indicated]

Characteristics	Number (1,000)	Any services [1]	Advice	Tests on woman or man	Ovulation drugs	Surgery or treatment for blocked tubes	Assisted reproductive technology [2]
Total	60,201	15.4	6.4	4.2	3.0	1.5	1.0
AGE							
15-24 years old	18,002	4.4	1.1	0.2	0.3	0.1	(Z)
25-34 years old	20,758	17.1	6.3	3.7	3.1	1.2	0.8
35-44 years old	21,440	22.9	10.9	8.1	5.2	2.9	2.1
PARITY, AGE, AND MARITAL STATUS							
One or more births	34,958	21.8	7.7	4.6	3.6	1.8	0.9
15-24 years old.	3,889	16.1	3.3	0.3	0.6	0.5	-
25-34 years old.	13,620	21.5	6.2	3.1	3.1	1.3	0.6
35-44 years old.	17,449	23.4	9.8	6.7	4.6	2.4	1.4
Married	23,988	24.1	9.2	6.0	4.6	2.1	1.1
Unmarried	10,970	16.8	4.3	1.6	1.3	0.9	0.5
EDUCATION [3]							
No high school diploma or GED [4]	5,424	14.9	3.3	2.0	1.2	0.7	0.2
High school diploma or GED	18,169	20.0	7.8	4.9	3.9	2.0	1.1
Some college, no bachelor's degree	12,399	19.4	7.8	5.6	3.3	2.0	1.2
Bachelor's degree or higher	11,748	18.0	10.3	7.1	5.3	1.9	2.2
POVERTY LEVEL INCOME [3]							
0-149 percent	10,072	16.6	4.8	2.1	1.5	0.9	0.2

- Rounds to zero. Z Less than 0.5 percent. [1] Includes services to help get pregnant as well as to help prevent miscarriage. [2] Includes artificial insemination, in vitro fertilization (IVF, gamete intrafallopian transfer (GIFT), and other techniques not shown separately. [3] Limited to women 22-44 years of age at time of interiew. The poverty index ratio was calculated by dividing the total family income by the weighted average threshold income of families whose head of household was under 65 years of age, based on the 1994 poverty levels defined by the U.S. Census Bureau. [4] GED = General equivalency diploma.

Source: U.S. National Center for Health Statistics, *Fertility, Family Planning, and Women's Health: New data from the 1995 National Survey of Family Growth, Vital and Health Statistics,*

No. 113. Pregnancies Ending in Live Birth to Women 15-44 Years Old, and Months Pregnant When Prenatal Care Began: 1991-95

[17,052 represents 17,052,000]

Characteristic	Number (1,000)	Percent distribution			
		Total	Months pregnant when prenatal care began		
			Less than 3 months	3-4 months	5 months or more or no prenatal care
All pregnancies [1]	17,052	100.0	88.1	5.4	6.6
AGE AT TIME OF BIRTH					
Under 20 years old.	2,023	100.0	75.3	10.7	14.0
20-24 years old	4,388	100.0	84.5	7.3	8.2
25-29 years old	5,088	100.0	91.3	4.0	4.7
30-44 years old	5,553	100.0	92.5	3.1	4.3
MARITAL STATUS AT TIME OF BIRTH					
Never married	3,940	100.0	77.3	9.6	13.1
Married.	12,171	100.0	91.5	4.0	4.5
Formerly married	942	100.0	88.6	5.3	6.1
WANTEDNESS STATUS AT CONCEPTION [2]					
Intended.	11,833	100.0	91.2	3.9	4.9
Mistimed.	3,715	100.0	82.2	9.1	8.7
Unwanted.	1,485	100.0	78.0	8.2	13.8
EDUCATION [3]					
No high school diploma or GED [4]	2,368	100.0	78.9	6.9	14.3
High school diploma or GED	6,076	100.0	88.5	6.3	5.2
Some college, no bachelor's degree	3,582	100.0	94.5	3.0	2.5
Bachelor's degree or higher	3,144	100.0	93.8	2.3	3.9

[1] Includes pregnancies with missing information on prenatal care or wantedness status. [2] Based on new questions in Cycle 5. See source "Definitions of Terms." [3] Limited to women 22-44 years of age at time of interview. [4] GED is general equivalency diploma.

Source: U.S. National Center for Health Statistics, *Fertility, Family Planning, and Women's Health: New data from the 1995 National Survey of Family Growth, Vital and Health Statistics,* Series 23, No. 19, 1997.

No. 114. Pregnancies, Number and Outcome: 1976 to 1997

[5,002 represents 5,002,000. **Live births:** source of data is statistics of registered births published annually by National Center for Health Statistics (NCHS). **Induced abortions:** derived from published reports by the Alan Guttmacher Institute. **Fetal losses:** based on the National Survey of Family Growth conducted by NCHS]

Year	Number (1,000)				Rate per 1,000 women, 15 to 44 years of age			
	Total	Live births	Induced abortions	Fetal losses	Total	Live births	Induced abortions	Fetal losses
1976	5,002	3,168	1,179	655	102.7	65.0	24.2	13.4
1977	5,331	3,327	1,317	687	107.0	66.8	26.4	13.8
1978	5,433	3,333	1,410	690	106.7	65.5	27.7	13.5
1979	5,714	3,494	1,498	722	109.9	67.2	28.8	13.9
1980	5,912	3,612	1,554	746	111.9	68.4	29.4	14.1
1981	5,958	3,629	1,577	751	110.5	67.3	29.3	13.9
1982	6,024	3,681	1,574	769	110.1	67.3	28.8	14.1
1983	5,977	3,639	1,575	763	108.0	65.7	28.5	13.8
1984	6,019	3,669	1,577	773	107.4	65.5	28.1	13.8
1985	6,144	3,761	1,589	795	108.3	66.3	28.0	14.0
1986	6,129	3,757	1,574	798	106.7	65.4	27.4	13.9
1987	6,183	3,809	1,559	815	106.8	65.8	26.9	14.1
1988	6,341	3,910	1,591	840	109.1	67.3	27.4	14.5
1989	6,480	4,041	1,567	873	111.0	69.2	26.8	15.0
1990	6,668	4,158	1,609	902	113.8	70.9	27.4	15.4
1991	6,563	4,111	1,557	896	111.1	69.6	26.3	15.2
1992	6,484	4,065	1,529	890	109.9	68.9	25.9	15.1
1993	(NA)	4,000	1,500	(NA)	(NA)	67.6	25.4	(NA)
1994	(NA)	3,953	1,431	(NA)	(NA)	66.7	24.1	(NA)
1995	(NA)	3,900	1,364	(NA)	(NA)	65.6	22.9	(NA)
1996	(NA)	3,891	1,366	(NA)	(NA)	65.3	22.9	(NA)
1997	(NA)	3,881	(NA)	(NA)	(NA)	65.0	(NA)	(NA)

NA Not available.

Source: U.S. National Center for Health Statistics, *National Vital Statistics Report (NVSP)* (formerly *Monthly Vital Statistics Report*, Vol. 41, No. 6, Supplement).

No. 115. Pregnancies, by Outcome, Age of Woman, and Race: 1991

[See headnote, Table 114]

Item	Total	Under 15 years old	15 to 19 years old	20 to 24 years old	25 to 29 years old	30 to 34 years old	35 to 39 years old	40 years old and over
PREGNANCIES								
Non-Hispanic:								
White, pregnancies	3,964	8	489	1,007	1,145	884	368	63
Live births	2,635	3	250	637	834	640	235	36
Induced abortions	774	4	164	264	163	106	58	16
Fetal losses	556	1	75	107	148	138	76	11
Black, pregnancies	1,344	14	272	439	320	202	81	15
Live births	673	6	149	216	160	98	37	6
Induced abortions	507	7	101	178	119	67	29	7
Fetal losses	164	1	22	45	41	37	15	3
Hispanic:								
Pregnancies	965	5	177	306	250	149	64	14
Live births	623	2	105	199	170	100	39	8
Induced abortions	208	1	40	73	50	28	13	4
Fetal losses	134	1	32	33	30	22	12	2
RATE PER 1,000 WOMEN								
Non-Hispanic:								
White, pregnancies	91.8	1.3	84.7	151.4	154.7	107.6	47.3	8.6
Live births	61.0	0.5	43.4	95.7	112.7	77.9	30.2	4.8
Induced abortions	17.9	0.7	28.4	39.6	22.0	12.9	7.4	2.2
Fetal losses	12.9	0.2	13.0	16.0	20.0	16.8	9.7	1.6
Black, pregnancies	174.8	11.0	216.7	337.2	232.3	142.7	63.9	14.4
Live births	87.6	4.9	118.9	166.1	116.3	69.3	28.9	5.7
Induced abortions	65.9	5.1	80.5	136.4	86.3	47.1	23.0	6.2
Fetal losses	21.3	0.9	17.2	34.7	29.7	26.3	12.1	2.4
Hispanic:								
Pregnancies	167.4	4.8	180.2	285.6	224.3	143.9	74.8	19.8
Live births	108.1	2.4	106.7	186.3	152.8	96.1	44.9	11.1
Induced abortions	36.2	1.4	40.4	68.1	44.4	27.1	15.5	5.2
Fetal losses	23.2	1.0	33.1	31.2	27.1	20.7	14.4	3.6

Source: U.S. National Center for Health Statistics, *National Vital Statistics Report (NVSR)* (formerly *Monthly Vital Statistics Report*, Vol. 43, No. 12).

Vital Statistics 87

No. 116. Unintended Birth Whether Mistimed or Unwanted, by Women 15-44 Years of Age: 1995

[See headnote, Table 110]

Characteristics	Number of women, total	Women who had an unintended birth [1]		
		Number (1,000)	First birth unintended	
			Percent mistimed	Percent unwanted
Total	**60,201**	**17,077**	**80.4**	**19.6**
AGE AT BIRTH				
Under 20 years	8,961	7,666	83.4	16.6
20-24 years	9,041	5,674	84.7	15.3
25-29 years	9,693	2,440	73.6	26.4
30-44 years	11,065	1,292	56.8	43.2
BIRTH ORDER				
First birth	(NA)	12,540	84.9	15.1
Second birth	(NA)	2,926	77.5	22.5
Third or higher birth	(NA)	1,611	51.1	48.9
POVERTY LEVEL [2]				
0-149 percent	10,072	5,386	75.5	24.5
0-99 percent	5,992	3,417	73.2	26.8
RACE, HISPANIC ORIGIN AND AGE AT BIRTH				
Hispanic	6,702	2,293	74.8	25.2
Non-Hispanic White	45,522	10,641	84.4	15.6
Non-Hispanic Black	8,210	3,469	72.9	27.1
Non-Hispanic other	2,767	674	74.8	25.2

NA Not available. [1] Based on "traditional" version (comparable to Cycle 4 and previous cycles) of wantedness status. See source "Definition of Terms." [2] Limited to women 22-44 years of age at time of interview.

Source: U.S. National Center for Health Statistics, *Fertility, Family Planning, and Women's Health: New data from the 1995 National Survey of Family Growth, Vital and Health Statistics*, Series 23, No. 19, 1997.

No. 117. Single Babies Born in 1990-93 Who Were Ever Breastfed, Duration and Mean Duration of Breastfeeding in Weeks, by Selected Characteristics: 1995

Characteristics	Percent breastfed at all	Percent distribution				Mean duration in weeks
		Total	Duration of breastfeeding			
			0-2 months	3-4 months	5 or more months	
All babies [1]	**55.2**	**100.0**	**40.3**	**8.6**	**51.1**	**28.7**
Under 20 years	36.0	100.0	69.7	4.5	25.8	17.5
20-24 years	46.4	100.0	46.6	12.4	41.0	24.1
25 years and over	63.0	100.0	35.0	7.8	57.3	31.5
25-29 years	56.4	100.0	39.8	8.7	51.5	28.2
30-44 years	69.1	100.0	31.3	7.1	61.6	34.0
MARITAL STATUS AT TIME OF BIRTH						
Never married	31.4	100.0	54.8	8.3	36.8	20.8
Married	63.4	100.0	37.7	8.5	53.8	30.1
Formerly married	50.2	100.0	45.3	11.3	43.4	26.4
WANTEDNESS STATUS AT CONCEPTION						
Intended	60.4	100.0	38.1	9.4	52.6	29.7
Mistimed	46.3	100.0	50.7	6.7	42.6	23.3
Unwanted	36.9	100.0	38.1	4.7	57.3	31.6
EDUCATION [2]						
No high school diploma or GED [3]	38.9	100.0	44.9	8.8	46.4	26.8
High school diploma or GED	49.0	100.0	44.0	9.8	46.2	27.2
Some college, no bachelor's degree	63.0	100.0	43.9	7.1	49.1	26.5
Bachelor's degree or higher	81.1	100.0	28.7	8.5	62.8	35.2
POVERTY LEVEL INCOME [2]						
0-149 percent	42.6	100.0	42.4	8.3	49.2	30.2
150-299 percent	58.1	100.0	39.5	9.6	50.8	29.4
300 percent or higher	68.2	100.0	38.8	8.1	53.1	28.3
RACE AND HISPANIC ORIGIN						
Hispanic	62.2	100.0	42.7	7.1	50.2	26.7
Non-Hispanic White	59.1	100.0	38.5	8.1	53.3	29.8
Non-Hispanic Black	25.1	100.0	45.0	14.0	40.9	22.9

[1] Includes babies born to women of other race and origin groups not shown separately. [2] The poverty index ratio was calculated by dividing the total family income by the weighted average threshold income of families whose head of household was under 65 years of age, based on the U.S. Census Bureau. Limited to women 22-44 years of age at time of interview. [3] GED = general equivalence diploma.

Source: U.S. National Center for Health Statistics, *Fertility, Family Planning, and Women's Health: New data from the 1995 National Survey of Family Growth, Vital and Health Statistics*, Series 23, No. 19, 1997.

No. 118. Contraceptive Use by Women, 15 to 44 Years of Age: 1995

[60,201 represents 60,201,000. Based on samples of the female population of of the United States; see source for details. See Appendix III]

Contraceptive status and method	All women [1]	Age			Race			Marital status		
		15-24 years	25-34 years	35-44 years	Non-Hispanic		His-panic	Never married	Cur-rently married	For-merly married
					White	Black				
All women (1,000)	60,201	18,002	20,758	21,440	42,522	8,210	6,702	22,679	29,673	7,849
PERCENT DISTRIBUTION										
Sterile [2]	29.7	2.6	25.0	57.0	30.2	31.5	28.4	6.9	43.2	45.1
Surgically sterile	27.9	1.8	23.6	54.0	28.5	29.7	26.3	5.7	41.1	42.5
Noncontraceptively sterile [3] . .	3.1	0.1	1.2	7.4	3.2	3.7	2.3	0.9	4.1	5.8
Contraceptively sterile [4]	24.8	1.7	22.4	46.6	25.3	26.0	24.0	4.8	37.0	36.7
Nonsurgically sterile [5]	1.7	0.7	1.3	2.8	1.6	1.8	2.0	1.1	2.0	2.2
Pregnant, postpartum	4.6	5.9	6.9	1.3	4.3	4.5	6.3	3.1	6.4	2.2
Seeking pregnancy	4.0	2.1	6.2	3.5	3.7	4.6	4.0	1.5	6.4	1.9
Other nonusers	22.3	44.4	13.3	12.6	21.1	23.1	26.3	46.8	4.7	2.1
Never had intercourse	10.9	30.8	3.4	1.4	10.4	8.9	12.1	28.9	-	18.4
No intercourse in last month [6] .	6.2	7.0	5.3	6.5	5.7	7.2	8.6	11.5	0.5	12.7
Had intercourse in last month [6] .	5.2	6.6	4.6	4.7	5.0	7.0	5.6	6.4	4.2	5.7
Nonsurgical contraceptors	39.7	45.0	49.1	26.1	41.2	36.1	35.1	41.8	39.7	32.4
Pill	17.3	23.1	23.7	6.3	18.8	14.8	13.6	20.4	15.6	14.6
IUD	0.5	0.1	0.6	0.8	0.5	0.5	0.9	0.3	0.7	0.4
Diaphragm.	1.2	0.2	1.2	2.0	1.5	0.5	0.4	0.5	1.8	0.9
Condom	13.1	13.9	15.0	10.7	13.0	12.5	12.1	13.9	13.3	10.1
Periodic abstinence	1.5	0.5	1.8	2.0	1.6	0.7	1.3	0.6	2.3	0.7
Natural family planning	0.2	-	0.3	0.3	0.3	-	0.1	-	0.4	-
Withdrawal. . . . , ...	2.0	1.6	2.3	1.9	2.1	0.9	2.0	1.5	2.3	1.8
Other methods [7]	3.9	5.6	4.2	2.1	3.4	6.2	4.7	4.6	3.3	3.9

- Represents or rounds to zero. [1] Includes other races, not shown separately. [2] Total sterile includes male sterile for unknown reasons. [3] Persons who had sterilizing operation and who gave as one reason that they had medical problems with their female organs. [4] Includes all other sterilization operations, and sterilization of the husband or current partner. [5] Persons sterile from illness, accident, or congenital conditions. [6] Data refer to no intercourse in the 3 months prior to interview. [7] Includes implants, injectables, morning-after-pill, suppository, Today™ sponge and less frequently used methods.
Source: U.S. National Center for Health Statistics, *Advance Data From Vital and Health Statistics*, No. 182.

No. 119. Women 15-44 Years of Age Who Have Ever Had a Live Birth and Use of Maternity Leave for the Most Recent Birth: 1995

[34,958 represents 34,958,000]

Characteristics of the mother	Number (1,000)	Percent distribution						
		Total	Not em-ployed	Em-ployed	Took mater-nity leave	Did not take leave [1]		
						Not needed	Not offered	Other reasons
All women	34,958	100.0	48.0	52.0	37.3	2.3	0.9	11.6
AGE AT TIME OF BIRTH								
15-19 years old.	3,436	100.0	71.9	28.1	14.8	0.7	0.1	12.5
20-24 years old.	10,094	100.0	52.8	47.2	29.8	1.3	1.3	14.9
25-29 years old.	11,629	100.0	44.8	55.2	41.1	2.7	0.8	10.5
30-44 years old.	9,799	100.0	38.3	61.7	48.3	3.5	0.8	9.1
YEAR OF CHILD's BIRTH								
1991-95.	13,999	100.0	43.2	56.8	43.5	2.2	0.9	10.3
1981-90.	15,344	100.0	47.4	52.6	37.2	2.7	0.8	11.8
1980 and before	5,616	100.0	61.5	38.5	22.0	1.6	0.9	14.0
MARITAL STATUS AT TIME OF BIRTH								
Never married.	6,379	100.0	58.4	41.6	26.8	0.8	1.0	13.0
Married	26,439	100.0	44.9	55.1	40.3	2.8	0.8	11.1
Formerly married.	2,140	100.0	54.3	45.7	31.1	0.8	1.3	12.5
BIRTH ORDER OF CHILD								
First	10,901	100.0	35.8	64.2	46.9	1.8	1.1	14.4
Second	13,965	100.0	47.7	52.3	38.1	2.6	1.0	10.7
Third or higher	10,092	100.0	61.5	38.5	25.8	2.5	0.4	9.7
EDUCATION AT INTERVIEW [2]								
No high school diploma or GED [3].	4,961	100.0	69.6	30.4	16.5	0.7	0.4	12.8
High school diploma or GED	14,295	100.0	48.8	51.2	36.2	1.6	1.0	12.4
Some college, no bachelor's degree	7,967	100.0	40.1	59.9	44.4	2.6	1.1	11.8
Bachelor's degree or higher	5,929	100.0	32.8	67.2	52.8	5.6	0.9	7.9
RACE AND HISPANIC ORIGIN								
Hispanic	4,372	100.0	57.8	42.2	28.9	1.1	0.8	11.4

[1] The group labeled "not needed" includes women who did not need to take maternity leave: (1) Due to the timing of their birth relative to their job schedule (for example, teachers who delivered during summer break. (2) Due to the nature of their jobs (for example, worked out of their homes, self-employed). (3) Because they decided to quit their jobs after delivery. The group labeled "not offered" includes: (1) Woman whose employers did not offer (or denied) maternity leave at all (for example, woman would be fired if she took leave. (2) woman whose job benefits did not include maternity leave. The final group labeled "other reasons" includes women who decided to quit their jobs before delivery, who could not afford to take maternity leave for personal or financial reasons, and who continued to work right after delivery. [2] Women 22-44 years of age at time of interview. [3] GED is general equivalency diploma.
Source: U.S. National Center for Health Statistics, *Fertility, Family Planning, and Women's Health: New data from the 1995 National Survey of Family Growth, Vital and Health Statistics*, Series 23, No. 19, 1997.

Vital Statistics 89

No. 120. Live Births—Mothers Who Smoked During Pregnancy: 1995

[In thousands 3,117,068 represents 3,117,068,000, except percents. Excludes California, Indiana, New York, and South Dakota, which did not require reporting of tobacco use during pregnancy]

Smoking measure and race of mother	Total	\multicolumn{7}{c}{Years of school completed by mother}
		0-8 years	9-11 years	12 years	13-15 years	16 years or more	Not stated
All races [1]	3,117,068	150,203	493,234	1,048,303	686,019	693,982	45,327
White	2,449,057	125,544	342,760	800,506	544,491	604,043	31,713
Black	532,866	17,495	132,675	205,683	115,484	51,564	9,965
PERCENT							
Smoker [1]	13.6	12.3	26.0	17.5	10.3	2.6	13.1
White	14.7	13.0	30.1	19.8	11.3	2.7	13.6
Black	10.2	9.8	16.1	10.1	6.7	2.6	14.2
PERCENT DISTRIBUTION							
All races smoker	100.0	100.0	100.0	100.0	100.0	100.0	100.0
10 cigarettes or less	66.7	61.5	66.2	66.0	68.7	74.0	67.5
11-20 cigarettes	29.1	31.6	29.1	29.9	27.8	23.3	27.6
21 cigarettes or more	4.3	7.0	4.7	4.0	3.5	2.7	4.9
White smoker	100.0	100.0	100.0	100.0	100.0	100.0	100.0
10 cigarettes or less	64.2	59.3	62.8	63.7	66.8	73.2	64.1
11-20 cigarettes	31.2	33.2	31.9	31.9	29.4	23.9	30.3
21 cigarettes or more	4.6	7.5	5.3	4.4	3.8	2.9	5.6
Black smoker	100.0	100.0	100.0	100.0	100.0	100.0	100.0
10 cigarettes or less	81.2	78.3	80.7	81.7	82.7	82.4	76.4
11-20 cigarettes	16.7	18.6	16.9	16.4	15.7	16.3	20.4
21 cigarettes or more	2.1	3.1	2.4	1.9	1.6	(B)	3.2

B Base data too small to meet statistical standards for reliability of a derived figure.   [1] Includes races other than White and Black.

No. 121. Percent Low Birthweight, by Smoking Status, Age, and Race of Mother: 1996

[Low birthweight is defined as weight of less than 2,500 grams (5 lb. 8 oz.). Excludes California, Indiana, New York, and South Dakota, which did not require reporting of tobacco use during pregnancy]

Smoking status and race of mother	All ages	Under 15 years	\multicolumn{3}{c}{15-19 years}	20-24 years	25-29 years	30-34 years	35-39 years	40-49 years
			Total	15-17 years	18-19 years					
All races [1]	7.6	13.5	9.7	10.4	9.2	7.7	6.7	7.0	8.4	9.8
Smoker	12.1	16.7	11.2	11.6	10.9	10.4	11.6	13.6	17.0	19.2
Nonsmoker	6.9	13.2	9.3	10.2	8.7	7.1	6.0	6.2	7.2	8.7
White	6.5	11.1	8.2	8.9	7.8	6.5	5.8	6.1	7.2	8.5
Smoker	10.7	16.4	10.6	11.0	10.5	9.7	10.2	11.4	14.3	16.5
Nonsmoker	5.7	10.3	7.4	8.2	6.9	5.7	5.1	5.4	6.3	7.6
Black	13.1	15.8	13.2	13.6	12.9	12.0	12.4	13.9	16.3	18.2
Smoker	21.9	19.9	16.1	16.6	15.8	17.1	22.0	25.8	29.3	31.7
Nonsmoker	12.0	15.6	13.0	13.4	12.7	11.5	11.1	11.8	13.6	15.7

[1] Includes races other than White and Black.

No. 122. Live Births—Drinking Status of Mother: 1996

[In absolutes, except percents. Excludes California, New York, and South Dakota, which did not require reporting of alcohol use during pregnancy]

Drinking status, drinking measure, and race of mother	All ages	\multicolumn{7}{c}{Age of mother}
		Under 15 years	15-19 years	20-24 years	25-29 years	30-34 years	35-39 years	40-49 years
All races [1]	3,891,494	11,148	491,577	945,210	1,071,287	897,913	399,510	74,849
Drinker	45,853	62	3,690	8,425	11,367	13,301	7,546	1,462
Nondrinker	3,246,335	9,449	417,456	794,607	897,392	745,439	323,660	58,332
White	3,093,057	5,526	344,685	726,669	878,449	747,436	329,782	60,510
Drinker	33,155	42	2,776	5,957	7,885	9,731	5,672	1,092
Nondrinker	2,572,680	4,246	284,021	601,819	737,821	627,098	269,970	47,705
Black	594,781	5,193	130,596	179,361	133,204	94,295	43,716	8,416
Drinker	10,971	15	680	2,033	3,049	3,190	1,681	323
Nondrinker	537,959	4,913	121,669	164,957	119,019	82,343	37,820	7,238
PERCENT								
Drinker [1]	1.2	0.6	0.8	0.9	1.1	1.5	1.9	2.0
White	0.9	0.4	0.6	0.6	0.7	1.1	1.4	1.5
Black	0.3	0.1	0.1	0.2	0.3	0.4	0.4	0.4

[1] Includes races other than White or Black.

Source of Tables 120-122: U.S. National Center for Health Statistics, *National Vital Statistics Reports (NVSR)* (formerly *Monthly Vital Statistics Reports*).

Year	All races Women 15-44 years old (1,000)	All races Abortions Number (1,000)	All races Rate per 1,000 women	All races Ratio per 1,000 live births [1]	White Women 15-44 years old (1,000)	White Abortions Number (1,000)	White Rate per 1,000 women	White Ratio per 1,000 live births [1]	Black and other Women 15-44 years old (1,000)	Black and other Abortions Number (1,000)	Black and other Rate per 1,000 women	Black and other Ratio per 1,000 live births [1]
1975	47,606	1,034	21.7	331	40,857	701	17.2	276	6,749	333	49.3	565
1979	52,016	1,498	28.8	420	44,266	1,062	24.0	373	7,750	435	56.2	625
1980	53,048	1,554	29.3	428	44,942	1,094	24.3	376	8,106	460	56.5	642
1981	53,901	1,577	29.3	430	45,494	1,108	24.3	377	8,407	470	55.9	645
1982	54,679	1,574	28.8	428	46,049	1,095	23.8	373	8,630	479	55.9	646
1983 [2]	55,340	1,575	28.5	436	46,506	1,084	23.3	376	8,834	491	55.5	670
1984	56,061	1,577	28.1	423	47,023	1,087	23.1	366	9,038	491	54.3	646
1985	56,754	1,589	28.0	422	47,512	1,076	22.6	360	9,242	513	55.5	659
1986 [2]	57,483	1,574	27.4	416	48,010	1,045	21.8	350	9,473	529	55.9	661
1987	57,964	1,559	27.1	405	48,288	1,017	21.1	338	9,676	542	56.0	648
1988	58,192	1,591	27.3	401	48,325	1,026	21.2	333	9,867	565	57.3	638
1989 [2]	58,365	1,567	26.8	380	48,104	1,006	20.9	309	10,261	561	54.7	650
1990 [2]	58,700	1,609	27.4	389	48,224	1,039	21.5	318	10,476	570	54.4	655
1991	59,080	1,557	26.3	379	48,406	982	20.3	303	10,674	574	53.8	661
1992	59,020	1,529	25.9	380	48161	943	19.6	298	10,674	585	53.9	661
1993 [2]	59,143	1,500	25.4	378	48,137	911	18.9	291	10859	585	53.9	681
1994 [2]	59,284	1,431	24.1	364	48,121	861	17.9	277	11,007	589	53.5	700
1995	59,442	1,364	22.9	351	48,140	820	17.0	265	11,163	570	51.1	699
1996	59,606	1,366	22.9	351	48,120	800	16.6	259	11,302	544	48.1	686
									11,486	566	49.2	701

[1] Live births are those which occurred from July 1 of year shown through June 30 of the following year (to match time of conception with abortions). Births are classified by race of child 1972-1988, and by race of mother after 1988. [2] Total numbers of abortions in 1983 and 1986 have been estimated by interpolation; 1989, 1990, 1993, and 1994 have been estimated using trends in CDC data.

No. 124. Abortions, by Selected Characteristics: 1990 to 1996

[Number of abortions from surveys conducted by source; characteristics from the U.S. Centers for Disease Control's (CDC) annual abortion surveillance summaries, with adjustments for changes in States reporting data to the CDC each year. Total number of abortions in 1990 have been estimated using trends in CDC data]

Characteristic	Number (1,000) 1990	Number (1,000) 1995	Number (1,000) 1996	Percent distribution 1990	Percent distribution 1995	Percent distribution 1996	Abortion ratio [1] 1990	Abortion ratio [1] 1995	Abortion ratio [1] 1996
Total abortions	1,609	1,364	1,366	100	100	100	280	260	260
Age of woman:									
Less than 15 years old	13	11	10	1	1	1	515	480	494
15 to 19 years old	351	264	264	22	19	19	403	348	351
20 to 24 years old	532	442	434	33	32	32	328	317	315
25 to 29 years old	360	308	318	22	23	23	224	225	228
30 to 34 years old	216	196	195	13	14	14	196	179	179
35 to 39 years old	108	110	112	7	8	8	249	220	216
40 years old and over	29	32	33	2	2	2	354	310	301
Race of woman:									
White	1,039	820	800	65	60	59	241	210	206
Black and other	570	544	566	35	40	41	396	409	412
Marital status of woman: [2]									
Married	341	269	272	21	20	20	102	93	94
Unmarried	1,268	1,095	1,094	79	80	80	521	466	466
Number of prior live births:									
None	780	614	599	49	45	44	316	277	273
One	396	359	369	25	26	27	230	223	226
Two	280	248	250	17	18	18	292	285	284
Three	102	95	96	6	7	7	279	284	284
Four or more	50	48	50	3	4	4	223	228	236
Number of prior induced abortions:									
None	891	721	744	55	53	55	(NA)	(NA)	(NA)
One	443	383	365	28	28	27	(NA)	(NA)	(NA)
Two or more	275	260	256	17	19	19	(NA)	(NA)	(NA)
Weeks of gestation: [3]									
Less than 9 weeks	817	728	(NA)	51	53	(NA)	(NA)	(NA)	(NA)
9 to 10 weeks	418	317	(NA)	26	23	(NA)	(NA)	(NA)	(NA)
11 to 12 weeks	199	153	(NA)	12	11	(NA)	(NA)	(NA)	(NA)
13 weeks or more	175	166	(NA)	11	12	(NA)	(NA)	(NA)	(NA)

NA Not available. [1] Number of abortions per 1,000 abortions and live births. Live births are those which occurred from July 1 of year shown through June 30 of the following year (to match time of conception with abortions). [2] Separated women included with unmarried. [3] Data not exactly comparable with prior years because of a change in the method of calculation.

Source of Tables 123 and 124: 1975-1988 S.K. Henshaw and J. Van Vort, eds., *Abortion Factbook, 1992 Edition: Readings, Trends, and State and Local Data to 1988,* The Alan Guttmacher Institute, New York, NY, 1992 (copyright); S.K. Henshaw and J. Van Vort, *Abortion Services in the United States, 1991 and 1992; Family Perspectives, 26:100, 1994;* and unpublished data.

U.S. Census Bureau, Statistical Abstract of the United States: 1999

No. 125. Abortions—Number and Rate, by State: 1992 and 1995

[Number of abortions from surveys of hospitals, clinics, and physicians identified as providers of abortion services conducted by The Alan Guttmacher Institute. Abortion rates are computed per 1,000 women 15 to 44 years of age on July 1 of specified year]

State	Abortions (1,000)		Rate [1]		State	Abortions (1,000)		Rate [1]	
	1992	1995	1992	1995		1992	1995	1992	1995
U.S..	1,529	1,364	25.9	22.9	MO	14	11	11.6	8.9
AL.	17	15	18.2	15.0	MT.	3	3	18.2	16.2
AK.	2	2	16.5	14.2	NE.	6	4	15.7	12.1
AZ.	21	18	24.1	19.1	NV.	13	16	44.2	46.7
AR.	7	6	13.5	11.1	NH.	4	3	14.6	12.0
CA.	304	240	42.1	33.4	NJ.	55	61	31.0	34.5
CO.	20	16	23.6	18.0	NM.	6	5	17.7	14.4
CT.	20	17	26.2	23.0	NY.	195	176	46.2	42.8
DE.	6	6	35.2	34.4	NC.	36	35	22.4	21.0
DC.	21	21	138.4	151.7	ND.	1	1	10.7	9.6
FL.	85	88	30.0	30.0	OH.	50	41	19.5	16.2
GA.	40	37	24.0	21.2	OK.	9	9	12.5	12.9
HI.	12	8	46.0	29.3	OR.	16	16	23.9	22.6
ID.	2	2	7.2	5.8	PA.	50	41	18.6	15.5
IL.	68	68	25.4	25.6	RI.	7	6	30.0	25.5
IN.	16	14	12.0	10.6	SC.	12	11	14.2	12.9
IA.	7	6	11.4	9.8	SD.	1	1	6.8	6.6
KS.	13	10	22.4	18.3	TN.	19	18	16.2	15.2
KY.	10	8	11.4	8.8	TX.	97	89	23.1	20.5
LA.	14	15	13.4	14.7	UT.	4	4	9.3	8.1
ME.	4	3	14.7	9.6	VT.	3	2	21.2	17.9
MD.	31	31	26.4	25.6	VA.	35	31	22.7	20.0
MA.	41	41	28.4	29.2	WA.	33	25	27.7	20.2
MI.	56	49	25.2	22.6	WV.	3	3	7.7	7.6
MN.	16	15	15.6	14.2	WI.	15	13	13.6	11.6
MS.	8	3	12.4	5.5	WY.	-	-	4.3	2.7

- Represents or rounds to zero. [1] Rate per 1,000 women, 15 to 44 years old.

Source: S.K. Henshaw and J. Van Vort, eds., *Abortion Factb Edition: Readings, Trends, and State and Local Data to 1988,* The Alan Guttmacher Institute, New York, NY, 1992 (copyright); and S.K. Henshaw and J. Van Vort, *Abortion Services in the United States, 1991 and 1992, Family Planning Perspectives,* 26:100, 1994; and unpublished data.

No. 126. Average Lifetime in Years by Race, by State: 1989-91

State	Total	White	Black	State	Total	White	Black
U.S..	75.37	76.13	69.16	MO	75.25	76.02	68.81
				MT.	76.23	76.72	(S)
AL	73.64	75.01	69.23	NE.	76.92	77.21	(S)
AZ	76.10	76.42	70.84	NV.	74.18	74.44	(S)
AR	74.33	75.20	68.93	NH.	76.72	76.68	(S)
CA	75.86	75.92	69.65	NJ	75.42	76.46	68.47
				NM.	75.74	76.08	(S)
CO	76.96	77.06	72.41	NY.	74.68	75.61	69.33
CT	76.91	77.44	70.84	NC.	74.48	75.89	69.38
DE	74.76	75.76	69.26	ND.	77.62	77.99	(S)
DC	67.99	76.09	64.44	OH.	75.32	75.93	70.15
FL	75.84	76.82	68.77	OK.	75.10	75.21	70.85
GA	73.61	75.24	68.79	OR.	76.44	76.51	(S)
HI	78.21	77.92	(S)	PA.	75.38	76.15	68.27
ID	76.88	76.89	(S)	RI	76.54	76.80	(S)
IL	74.90	76.16	67.46	SC.	73.51	75.33	68.82
IN	75.39	75.82	69.80	SD.	76.91	77.91	(S)
IA	77.29	77.38	(S)	TN.	74.32	75.27	68.97
KS	76.76	77.06	71.22	TX.	75.14	75.75	69.79
KY	74.37	74.65	70.16	UT.	77.70	77.77	(S)
LA	73.05	74.87	68.62	VT.	76.54	76.50	(S)
ME	76.35	76.35	(S)	VA.	75.22	76.34	70.05
MD	74.79	76.30	69.69	WA.	76.82	76.92	71.34
MA	76.72	76.90	72.45	WV.	74.26	74.37	69.75
MI	75.04	76.18	68.49	WI	76.87	77.18	70.96
MN	77.76	77.97	(S)	WY.	76.21	76.34	(S)
MS	73.03	74.78	69.41				

S Does not meet standards of reliability and precision.

Source: U.S. National Center for Health Statistics, *U.S. Decennial Life Tables for 1989-91*, Volume II.

No. 127. Expectation of Life at Birth, 1970 to 1997, and Projections, 1995 to 2010

[In years. Excludes deaths of nonresidents of the United States]

Year	Total			White			Black and other			Black		
	Total	Male	Female	Total	Male	Female	Total	Male	Female	Total	Male	Female
1970	70.8	67.1	74.7	71.7	68.0	75.6	65.3	61.3	69.4	64.1	60.0	68.3
1975	72.6	68.8	76.6	73.4	69.5	77.3	68.0	63.7	72.4	66.8	62.4	71.3
1980	73.7	70.0	77.4	74.4	70.7	78.1	69.5	65.3	73.6	68.1	63.8	72.5
1982	74.5	70.8	78.1	75.1	71.5	78.7	70.9	66.8	74.9	69.4	65.1	73.6
1983	74.6	71.0	78.1	75.2	71.6	78.7	70.9	67.0	74.7	69.4	65.2	73.5
1984	74.7	71.1	78.2	75.3	71.8	78.7	71.1	67.2	74.9	69.5	65.3	73.6
1985	74.7	71.1	78.2	75.3	71.8	78.7	71.0	67.0	74.8	69.3	65.0	73.4
1986	74.7	71.2	78.2	75.4	71.9	78.8	70.9	66.8	74.9	69.1	64.8	73.4
1987	74.9	71.4	78.3	75.6	72.1	78.9	71.0	66.9	75.0	69.1	64.7	73.4
1988	74.9	71.4	78.3	75.6	72.2	78.9	70.8	66.7	74.8	68.9	64.4	73.2
1989	75.1	71.7	78.5	75.9	72.5	79.2	70.9	66.7	74.9	68.8	64.3	73.3
1990	75.4	71.8	78.8	76.1	72.7	79.4	71.2	67.0	75.2	69.1	64.5	73.6
1991	75.5	72.0	78.9	76.3	72.9	79.6	71.5	67.3	75.5	69.3	64.6	73.8
1992	75.8	72.3	79.1	76.5	73.2	79.8	71.8	67.7	75.7	69.6	65.0	73.9
1993	75.5	72.2	78.8	76.3	73.1	79.5	71.5	67.3	75.5	69.2	64.6	73.7
1994	75.7	72.3	79.0	76.4	73.2	79.6	71.7	67.5	75.8	69.6	64.9	74.1
1995	75.8	72.5	78.9	76.5	73.4	79.6	71.9	67.9	75.7	69.6	65.2	73.9
1996	76.1	73.0	79.0	76.8	73.8	79.6	72.6	68.9	76.1	70.3	66.1	74.2
1997	76.5	73.6	79.2	77.1	74.3	79.9	(NA)	(NA)	(NA)	71.2	67.3	74.7
Projections:[1] 1995	75.9	72.5	79.3	76.9	73.6	80.1	(NA)	(NA)	(NA)	69.7	64.8	74.5
2000	76.4	73.0	79.7	77.4	74.2	80.5	(NA)	(NA)	(NA)	69.7	64.6	74.7
2005	76.9	73.5	80.2	77.9	74.7	81.0	(NA)	(NA)	(NA)	69.9	64.5	75.0
2010	77.4	74.1	80.6	78.6	75.5	81.6	(NA)	(NA)	(NA)	70.4	65.1	75.5

NA Not available.   [1] Based on middle mortality assumptions; for details, see source. Source: U.S. Census Bureau, *Current Population Reports*, P25-1130.

Source: Except as noted, U.S. National Center for Health Statistics, *Vital Statistics of the United States*, annual, and *National Vital Statistics Reports (NVSR)* (formerly *Monthly Vital Statistics Reports*).

No. 128. Selected Life Table Values: 1979 to 1997

Age and sex	Total[1]			White			Black		
	1979-1981	1990	1997	1979-1981	1990	1997	1979-1981	1990	1997
AVERAGE EXPECTATION OF LIFE IN YEARS									
At birth: Male	70.1	71.8	73.6	70.8	72.7	74.3	64.1	64.5	67.3
Female	77.6	78.8	79.2	78.2	79.4	79.8	72.9	73.6	74.7
Age 20: Male	51.9	53.3	54.7	52.5	54.0	55.3	46.4	46.7	49.1
Female	59.0	59.8	60.1	59.4	60.3	60.5	54.9	55.3	56.1
Age 40: Male	33.6	35.1	36.2	34.0	35.6	36.6	29.5	30.1	31.7
Female	39.8	40.6	40.8	40.2	41.0	41.1	36.3	36.8	37.4
Age 50: Male	25.0	26.4	27.4	25.3	26.7	27.7	22.0	22.5	23.8
Female	30.7	31.3	31.6	31.0	31.6	31.8	27.8	28.2	28.8
Age 65: Male	14.2	15.1	15.8	14.3	15.2	15.9	13.3	13.2	14.2
Female	18.4	18.9	19.0	18.6	19.1	19.1	17.1	17.2	17.4
EXPECTED DEATHS PER 1,000 ALIVE AT SPECIFIED AGE[2]									
At birth: Male	13.9	10.3	(NA)	12.3	8.6	(NA)	23.0	19.7	(NA)
Female	11.2	8.2	(NA)	9.7	6.6	(NA)	19.3	16.3	(NA)
Age 20: Male	1.8	1.6	(NA)	1.8	1.4	(NA)	2.2	2.7	(NA)
Female	0.6	0.5	(NA)	0.6	0.5	(NA)	0.7	0.7	(NA)
Age 40: Male	3.0	3.1	(NA)	2.6	2.7	(NA)	6.9	7.1	(NA)
Female	1.6	1.4	(NA)	1.4	1.2	(NA)	3.2	3.1	(NA)
Age 50: Male	7.8	6.2	(NA)	7.1	5.6	(NA)	14.9	12.8	(NA)
Female	4.2	3.5	(NA)	3.8	3.2	(NA)	7.7	6.6	(NA)
Age 65: Male	28.2	22.9	(NA)	27.4	23.0	(NA)	38.5	36.8	(NA)
Female	14.3	13.5	(NA)	13.6	12.8	(NA)	21.6	21.4	(NA)
NUMBER SURVIVING TO SPECIFIED AGE PER 1,000 BORN ALIVE									
Age 20: Male	973	979	(NA)	975	981	(NA)	961	963	(NA)
Female	982	986	(NA)	984	988	(NA)	972	976	(NA)
Age 40: Male	933	938	(NA)	940	946	(NA)	885	880	(NA)
Female	965	971	(NA)	969	975	(NA)	941	944	(NA)
Age 50: Male	890	899	(NA)	901	912	(NA)	801	801	(NA)
Female	941	950	(NA)	947	957	(NA)	896	904	(NA)
Age 65: Male	706	741	(NA)	724	760	(NA)	551	571	(NA)
Female	835	851	(NA)	848	864	(NA)	733	751	(NA)

NA Not available.   [1] Includes other races not shown separately.   [2] See footnote 1, Table 129.

Source: U.S. National Center for Health Statistics, *U.S. Life Tables and Actuarial Tables, 1959-61, 1969-71, and 1979-81; Vital Statistics of the United States*, annual; and unpublished data.

No. 129. Expectation of Life and Expected Deaths, by Race, Sex, and Age: 1996

Age (years)	Expectation of life in years					Expected deaths per 1,000 alive at specified age [1]				
		White		Black			White		Black	
	Total	Male	Female	Male	Female	Total	Male	Female	Male	Female
At birth	76.1	73.9	79.7	66.1	74.2	7.32	6.67	5.44	16.02	13.25
1	75.7	73.4	79.1	66.2	74.2	0.54	0.54	0.39	0.99	0.82
2	74.7	72.4	78.1	65.2	73.2	0.40	0.39	0.30	0.73	0.67
3	73.7	71.4	77.1	64.3	72.3	0.31	0.30	0.24	0.56	0.54
4	72.8	70.5	76.2	63.3	71.3	0.26	0.25	0.20	0.47	0.43
5	71.8	69.5	75.2	62.4	70.3	0.23	0.23	0.18	0.42	0.35
6	70.8	68.5	74.2	61.4	69.4	0.21	0.22	0.16	0.39	0.29
7	69.8	67.5	73.2	60.4	68.4	0.20	0.21	0.15	0.36	0.24
8	68.8	66.5	72.2	59.4	67.4	0.18	0.19	0.14	0.31	0.21
9	67.8	65.5	71.2	58.4	66.4	0.16	0.16	0.13	0.25	0.20
10	66.9	64.5	70.2	57.5	65.4	0.14	0.14	0.12	0.19	0.20
11	65.9	63.5	69.2	56.5	64.4	0.15	0.14	0.13	0.19	0.22
12	64.9	62.6	68.3	55.5	63.4	0.19	0.20	0.15	0.30	0.25
13	63.9	61.6	67.3	54.5	62.5	0.29	0.33	0.20	0.53	0.29
14	62.9	60.6	66.3	53.5	61.5	0.42	0.50	0.26	0.86	0.34
15	61.9	59.6	65.3	52.6	60.5	0.57	0.70	0.34	1.23	0.41
16	61.0	58.7	64.3	51.6	59.5	0.71	0.88	0.41	1.58	0.48
17	60.0	57.7	63.3	50.7	58.6	0.82	1.02	0.46	1.90	0.54
18	59.1	56.8	62.4	49.8	57.6	0.89	1.12	0.47	2.17	0.59
19	58.1	55.8	61.4	48.9	56.6	0.93	1.18	0.45	2.38	0.64
20	57.2	54.9	60.4	48.0	55.7	0.96	1.24	0.43	2.60	0.69
21	56.2	54.0	59.5	47.2	54.7	1.00	1.29	0.42	2.83	0.75
22	55.3	53.0	58.5	46.3	53.7	1.03	1.33	0.41	2.98	0.81
23	54.3	52.1	57.5	45.4	52.8	1.04	1.34	0.42	3.04	0.88
24	53.4	51.2	56.5	44.6	51.8	1.04	1.32	0.45	3.04	0.96
25	52.4	50.2	55.6	43.7	50.9	1.04	1.30	0.48	3.01	1.04
26	51.5	49.3	54.6	42.8	49.9	1.04	1.28	0.50	3.00	1.13
27	50.6	48.4	53.6	42.0	49.0	1.07	1.30	0.53	3.05	1.22
28	49.6	47.4	52.6	41.1	48.0	1.11	1.35	0.56	3.19	1.33
29	48.7	46.5	51.7	40.2	47.1	1.18	1.44	0.59	3.40	1.44
30	47.7	45.6	50.7	39.4	46.2	1.26	1.55	0.63	3.64	1.56
31	46.8	44.6	49.7	38.5	45.2	1.34	1.65	0.67	3.87	1.68
32	45.8	43.7	48.8	37.6	44.3	1.42	1.74	0.71	4.09	1.82
33	44.9	42.8	47.8	36.8	43.4	1.50	1.83	0.76	4.30	1.97
34	44.0	41.9	46.8	36.0	42.5	1.59	1.92	0.81	4.50	2.14
35	43.0	40.9	45.9	35.1	41.6	1.68	2.01	0.87	4.71	2.31
36	42.1	40.0	44.9	34.3	40.7	1.78	2.12	0.94	4.96	2.50
37	41.2	39.1	43.9	33.4	39.8	1.89	2.23	1.00	5.25	2.68
38	40.3	38.2	43.0	32.6	38.9	2.00	2.36	1.07	5.61	2.87
39	39.3	37.3	42.0	31.8	38.0	2.13	2.49	1.15	6.02	3.07
40	38.4	36.4	41.1	31.0	37.1	2.26	2.65	1.24	6.47	3.28
41	37.5	35.5	40.1	30.2	36.2	2.41	2.82	1.34	6.93	3.50
42	36.6	34.6	39.2	29.4	35.3	2.57	3.00	1.45	7.42	3.73
43	35.7	33.7	38.2	28.6	34.5	2.74	3.18	1.56	7.93	3.96
44	34.8	32.8	37.3	27.8	33.6	2.91	3.37	1.69	8.47	4.21
45	33.9	31.9	36.4	27.1	32.8	3.11	3.58	1.83	9.04	4.47
46	33.0	31.0	35.4	26.3	31.9	3.33	3.83	2.00	9.65	4.75
47	32.1	30.1	34.5	25.6	31.0	3.59	4.13	2.20	10.28	5.08
48	31.2	29.2	33.6	24.8	30.2	3.89	4.47	2.44	10.94	5.47
49	30.3	28.4	32.7	24.1	29.4	4.23	4.88	2.72	11.63	5.90
50	29.5	27.5	31.7	23.4	28.5	4.62	5.33	3.04	12.37	6.38
51	28.6	26.6	30.8	22.7	27.7	5.05	5.84	3.39	13.16	6.90
52	27.7	25.8	29.9	21.9	26.9	5.50	6.37	3.74	14.01	7.42
53	26.9	25.0	29.1	21.3	26.1	5.97	6.94	4.09	14.92	7.93
54	26.0	24.1	28.2	20.6	25.3	6.48	7.55	4.46	15.91	8.46
55	25.2	23.3	27.3	19.9	24.5	7.02	8.20	4.86	16.89	9.00
56	24.4	22.5	26.4	19.2	23.7	7.62	8.94	5.30	17.95	9.62
57	23.6	21.7	25.6	18.6	23.0	8.35	9.83	5.84	19.27	10.37
58	22.8	20.9	24.7	17.9	22.2	9.24	10.91	6.50	20.94	11.32
59	22.0	20.1	23.9	17.3	21.4	10.25	12.16	7.25	22.89	12.42
60	21.2	19.4	23.0	16.7	20.7	11.37	13.53	8.08	25.13	13.67
61	20.4	18.6	22.2	16.1	20.0	12.54	14.97	8.96	27.39	14.95
62	19.7	17.9	21.4	15.6	19.3	13.70	16.44	9.84	29.26	16.12
63	19.0	17.2	20.6	15.0	18.6	14.81	17.92	10.69	30.49	17.11
64	18.2	16.5	19.8	14.5	17.9	15.91	19.44	11.56	31.25	18.00
65	17.5	15.8	19.1	13.9	17.2	17.05	21.02	12.47	31.69	18.80
70	14.1	12.6	15.4	11.2	13.9	26.00	32.40	19.51	46.35	29.43
75	11.1	9.8	12.0	9.0	11.2	38.94	48.59	30.62	64.58	41.18
80	8.4	7.3	8.9	7.0	8.5	59.67	74.31	49.47	89.27	59.20
85 and over	6.1	5.3	6.3	5.3	6.2	1,000.00	1,000.00	1,000.00	1,000.00	1,000.00

[1] Based on the proportion of the cohort who are alive at the beginning of an indicated age interval who will die before reaching the end of that interval. For example, out of every 1,000 people alive and exactly 50 years old at the beginning of the period, between 4 and 5 (4.62) will die before reaching their 51st birthdays.

Source: U.S. National Center for Health Statistics, Vital Statistics of the United States, annual; and unpublished data.

No. 130. Deaths and Death Rates, by Sex and Race: 1980 to 1997

[1,990 represents 1,990,000. **Rates are per 1,000 population for specified groups.** Excludes deaths of nonresidents of the United States and fetal deaths. For explanation of age-adjustment, see text, this section. The standard population for this table is the total population of the United States enumerated in 1940. See Appendix III]

Sex and race	1980	1985	1988	1989	1990	1991	1992	1993	1994	1995	1996	1997
Deaths [1] (1,000)	**1,990**	**2,086**	**2,168**	**2,150**	**2,148**	**2,170**	**2,176**	**2,269**	**2,279**	**2,312**	**2,315**	**2,315**
Male [1] (1,000)	1,075	1,098	1,126	1,114	1,113	1,122	1,122	1,162	1,163	1,173	1,164	1,154
Female [1] (1,000)	915	989	1,042	1,036	1,035	1,048	1,053	1,107	1,116	1,139	1,151	1,161
White (1,000)	1,739	1,819	1,877	1,854	1,853	1,869	1,874	1,951	1,960	1,987	1,993	2,001
Male (1,000)	934	950	965	951	951	956	957	988	989	997	992	989
Female (1,000)	805	869	911	903	902	912	917	963	971	990	1,001	1,012
Black (1,000)	233	244	264	268	266	270	269	282	282	286	282	273
Male (1,000)	130	134	144	146	145	147	147	154	153	154	149	142
Female (1,000)	103	111	120	121	120	122	123	129	129	132	133	131
Death rates [1]	**8.8**	**8.8**	**8.8**	**8.7**	**8.6**	**8.6**	**8.5**	**8.8**	**8.8**	**8.8**	**8.7**	**8.6**
Male [1]	9.8	9.5	9.5	9.3	9.2	9.1	9.0	9.2	9.2	9.1	9.0	8.8
Female [1]	7.9	8.1	8.3	8.2	8.1	8.1	8.1	8.4	8.4	8.5	8.5	8.5
White	8.9	9.0	9.1	8.9	8.9	8.9	8.8	9.1	9.1	9.1	9.1	9.0
Male	9.8	9.6	9.6	9.4	9.3	9.3	9.2	9.4	9.3	9.3	9.2	9.1
Female	8.1	8.4	8.7	8.5	8.5	8.5	8.4	8.8	8.8	8.9	9.0	9.0
Black	8.8	8.5	8.9	8.9	8.8	8.6	8.5	8.8	8.6	8.6	8.4	8.0
Male	10.3	9.9	10.3	10.3	10.1	10.0	9.8	10.1	9.9	9.8	9.4	8.8
Female	7.3	7.3	7.6	7.6	7.5	7.4	7.4	7.6	7.5	7.6	7.5	7.3
Age-adjusted death rates [1]	**5.9**	**5.5**	**5.4**	**5.3**	**5.2**	**5.1**	**5.0**	**5.1**	**5.1**	**5.0**	**4.9**	**4.8**
Male [1]	7.8	7.2	7.1	6.9	6.8	6.7	6.6	6.6	6.5	6.5	6.2	6.0
Female [1]	4.3	4.1	4.1	4.0	3.9	3.9	3.8	3.9	3.9	3.9	3.8	3.8
White	5.6	5.2	5.1	5.0	4.9	4.9	4.8	4.9	4.8	4.8	4.7	4.6
Male	7.5	6.9	6.7	6.5	6.4	6.3	6.2	6.3	6.2	6.1	5.9	5.7
Female	4.1	3.9	3.9	3.8	3.7	3.7	3.6	3.7	3.6	3.6	3.6	3.6
Black	8.4	7.9	8.1	8.1	7.9	7.8	7.7	7.9	7.7	7.7	7.4	7.0
Male	11.1	10.5	10.8	10.8	10.6	10.5	10.3	10.5	10.3	10.2	9.7	9.0
Female	6.3	5.9	6.0	5.9	5.8	5.8	5.7	5.8	5.7	5.7	5.6	5.4

[1] Includes other races, not shown separately.

Source: U.S. National Center for Health Statistics, *Vital Statistics of the United States*, annual; and *National Vital Statistics Reports (NVSR)* (formerly *Monthly Vital Statistics Report*).

No. 131. Death Rates, by Age, Sex, and Race: 1970 to 1997

[Number of deaths per 100,000 population in specified group. See headnote, Table 130]

Sex, year, and race	All ages [1]	Under 1 yr. old	1-4 yr. old	5-14 yr. old	15-24 yr. old	25-34 yr. old	35-44 yr. old	45-54 yr. old	55-64 yr. old	65-74 yr. old	75-84 yr. old	85 yr. old and over
MALE [2]												
1970	1,090	2,410	93	51	189	215	403	959	2,283	4,874	10,010	17,822
1980	977	1,429	73	37	172	196	299	767	1,815	4,105	8,817	18,801
1990	918	1,083	52	29	147	204	310	610	1,553	3,492	7,889	18,057
1995	914	844	45	27	141	205	333	599	1,417	3,285	7,377	17,979
1996	896	828	42	25	131	179	298	574	1,389	3,233	7,250	17,548
1997	881	807	39	24	122	158	264	546	1,332	3,195	7,141	17,559
White: 1970	1,087	2,113	84	48	171	177	344	883	2,203	4,810	10,099	18,552
1980	983	1,230	66	35	167	171	257	699	1,729	4,036	8,830	19,097
1990	931	896	46	26	131	176	268	549	1,467	3,398	7,845	18,268
1995	932	718	39	25	122	178	288	535	1,331	3,199	7,321	18,153
1996	918	683	37	23	114	155	260	516	1,305	3,158	7,206	17,871
1997	908	682	35	22	107	139	234	493	1,251	3,130	7,122	17,890
Black: 1970	1,187	4,299	151	67	321	560	957	1,778	3,257	5,803	9,455	12,222
1980	1,034	2,587	111	47	209	407	690	1,480	2,873	5,131	9,232	16,099
1990	1,008	2,112	86	41	252	431	700	1,261	2,618	4,946	9,130	16,955
1995	981	1,591	78	40	249	417	721	1,273	2,438	4,611	8,779	16,729
1996	940	1,748	71	38	233	361	629	1,191	2,395	4,432	8,615	16,006
1997	883	1,614	67	35	211	304	518	1,101	2,285	4,271	8,178	15,887
FEMALE [2]												
1970	808	1,864	75	32	68	102	231	517	1,099	2,580	6,678	15,518
1980	785	1,142	55	24	58	76	159	413	934	2,145	5,440	14,747
1990	812	856	41	19	49	74	138	343	879	1,991	4,883	14,274
1995	847	690	36	18	48	78	150	328	841	1,986	4,883	14,492
1996	850	680	34	18	46	75	145	323	827	1,979	4,868	14,445
1997	850	648	32	18	46	69	140	316	813	1,959	4,828	14,530
White: 1970	813	1,615	66	30	62	84	193	463	1,015	2,471	6,699	15,980
1980	806	963	49	23	56	65	138	373	876	2,067	5,402	14,980
1990	847	690	36	18	46	62	117	309	823	1,924	4,839	14,401
1995	891	572	31	17	44	64	126	294	788	1,925	4,831	14,639
1996	896	558	29	16	43	63	122	291	780	1,920	4,827	14,643
1997	900	536	28	16	43	60	120	286	766	1,904	4,803	14,739
Black: 1970	829	3,369	129	44	112	231	533	1,044	1,986	3,861	6,692	10,707
1980	733	2,124	84	31	71	150	324	768	1,561	3,057	6,212	12,367
1990	748	1,736	68	28	69	160	299	639	1,453	2,866	5,688	13,310
1995	759	1,342	63	27	70	167	328	619	1,350	2,824	5,840	13,472
1996	754	1,444	64	26	67	154	316	610	1,312	2,787	5,776	13,399
1997	733	1,350	51	27	60	132	283	583	1,295	2,710	5,592	13,502

[1] Includes unknown age. [2] Includes other races not shown separately.

Source: U.S. National Center for Health Statistics, *Vital Statistics of the United States*, annual; *National Vital Statistics Reports (NVSR)* (formerly *Monthly Vital Statistics Report*); and unpublished data.

Vital Statistics   95

No. 132. Deaths and Death Rates, by State: 1990 to 1997

[2,148 represents 2,148,000. By state of residence. Excludes deaths of nonresidents of the United States, except as noted. Caution should be used in comparing death rates by state; rates are affected by the population composition of the area. See also Appendix III]

State	Number of deaths (1,000)							Rate per 1,000 population [1]						
	1990	1992	1993	1994	1995	1996	1997	1990	1992	1993	1994	1995	1996	1997
United States..	2,148	2,176	2,269	2,279	2,312	2,315	2,315	8.6	8.5	8.8	8.8	8.8	8.7	8.6
Alabama.........	39	39	41	42	42	43	43	9.7	9.5	9.9	9.9	10.0	10.0	9.9
Alaska..........	2	2	2	2	3	3	2	4.0	3.9	3.8	4.0	4.2	4.3	4.1
Arizona..........	29	31	33	34	35	37	37	7.9	8.1	8.2	8.4	8.4	8.3	8.2
Arkansas	25	25	27	26	27	27	28	10.5	10.4	10.9	10.7	10.8	10.6	11.0
California	214	216	222	224	224	223	(NA)	7.2	7.0	7.0	7.1	7.1	7.0	(NA)
Colorado.........	22	22	24	24	25	26	26	6.6	6.5	6.7	6.6	6.7	6.7	6.6
Connecticut.......	28	28	29	29	29	30	29	8.4	8.6	8.9	8.9	9.0	9.0	8.9
Delaware	6	6	6	6	6	7	6	8.7	8.6	8.7	9.0	8.8	9.0	8.9
Dist. of Columbia ...	7	7	7	7	7	7	6	12.0	12.1	11.6	12.6	12.4	12.2	11.7
Florida	134	140	147	149	153	153	155	10.4	10.4	10.7	10.7	10.8	10.7	10.6
Georgia	52	53	56	57	58	59	59	8.0	7.8	8.1	8.0	8.1	8.0	7.9
Hawaii	7	7	7	7	8	8	8	6.1	6.0	6.2	6.2	6.4	6.7	6.7
Idaho...........	7	8	8	8	9	9	9	7.4	7.4	7.6	7.5	7.3	7.3	7.4
Illinois..........	103	102	107	107	108	106	103	9.0	8.8	9.2	9.1	9.2	9.0	8.7
Indiana..........	50	50	52	52	53	53	49	8.9	8.8	9.1	9.1	9.2	9.1	8.3
Iowa	27	27	28	28	28	28	28	9.7	9.5	9.9	9.8	9.9	9.8	9.7
Kansas..........	22	22	24	23	24	24	24	9.0	8.8	9.2	9.1	9.3	9.3	9.2
Kentucky	35	35	37	37	37	37	38	9.5	9.3	9.7	9.7	9.6	9.6	9.8
Louisiana	38	38	40	39	40	40	40	8.9	8.8	9.3	9.0	9.1	9.1	9.2
Maine...........	11	11	12	12	12	11	12	9.0	9.0	9.3	9.4	9.5	9.4	9.6
Maryland	38	39	40	41	42	42	42	8.0	7.9	8.7	8.2	8.3	8.3	8.2
Massachusetts.....	53	54	56	55	55	55	55	8.8	9.0	9.4	9.1	9.1	9.1	8.9
Michigan.........	79	79	83	83	84	84	84	8.5	8.4	8.7	8.7	8.8	8.7	8.6
Minnesota........	35	35	36	37	38	37	37	7.9	7.8	8.0	8.0	8.1	8.0	7.9
Mississippi	25	25	26	27	27	27	28	9.8	9.7	10.1	10.0	10.0	9.8	10.1
Missouri.........	50	51	54	54	54	54	55	9.8	9.8	10.8	10.2	10.2	10.1	10.1
Montana.........	7	7	7	7	8	8	8	8.6	8.6	8.9	8.6	8.8	8.8	8.9
Nebraska........	15	15	15	15	15	15	15	9.4	9.2	9.6	9.3	9.3	9.4	9.2
Nevada.........	9	10	11	12	13	13	13	7.8	7.7	7.8	8.2	8.2	8.2	8.0
New Hampshire....	8	9	9	9	9	9	10	7.7	7.7	7.9	7.8	8.0	8.1	8.1
New Jersey.......	70	71	73	72	74	73	72	9.1	9.1	9.2	9.1	9.3	9.2	8.9
New Mexico	11	11	12	12	13	12	13	7.0	7.1	7.3	7.3	7.4	7.3	7.4
New York	169	166	171	169	168	164	161	9.4	9.2	9.4	9.3	9.3	9.0	8.9
North Carolina.....	57	60	62	63	65	66	66	8.6	8.7	9.0	8.9	9.0	9.1	8.9
North Dakota......	6	6	6	6	6	6	6	8.9	9.0	9.3	9.2	9.3	9.3	9.5
Ohio	99	99	103	103	106	105	105	9.1	9.0	9.1	9.3	9.5	9.4	9.4
Oklahoma........	30	31	32	32	33	33	34	9.7	9.5	10.1	9.9	10.0	10.0	10.1
Oregon..........	25	26	28	27	28	29	29	8.8	8.7	9.0	8.9	9.0	9.0	8.9
Pennsylvania......	122	124	126	128	128	129	128	10.3	10.3	10.5	10.6	10.6	10.7	10.6
Rhode Island......	10	9	10	9	10	10	10	9.5	9.5	9.7	9.4	9.8	9.6	9.9
South Carolina.....	30	31	32	32	34	34	33	8.5	8.5	8.6	8.8	9.1	9.2	8.8
South Dakota	6	7	7	7	7	7	7	9.1	9.5	9.6	9.4	9.5	9.3	9.5
Tennessee	46	47	49	51	51	51	53	9.5	9.3	9.7	9.8	9.8	9.7	9.8
Texas...........	125	129	135	136	138	140	143	7.4	7.3	7.5	7.4	7.4	7.3	7.3
Utah	9	10	10	10	11	11	11	5.3	5.4	5.5	5.5	5.6	5.6	5.5
Vermont	5	5	5	5	5	5	5	8.2	8.4	8.5	8.2	8.5	8.3	8.9
Virginia..........	48	49	52	52	53	54	54	7.8	7.7	8.0	8.0	8.0	8.0	8.0
Washington.......	37	38	40	40	41	42	43	7.6	7.4	8.0	7.5	7.5	7.6	7.6
West Virginia......	19	20	20	20	20	20	21	10.8	10.9	11.0	11.1	11.1	11.2	11.6
Wisconsin........	43	42	45	44	45	45	45	8.7	8.5	8.7	8.7	8.8	8.7	8.7
Wyoming	3	3	3	3	4	4	4	7.1	7.5	7.3	7.3	7.7	7.5	7.8

NA Not available. [1] Rates based on enumerated resident population as of April 1 for 1990; estimated resident population as of July 1 for all other years.

Source: U.S. National Center for Health Statistics, Vital Statistics of the United States, annual; National Vital Statistics Reports (NVSR) (formerly Monthly Vital Statistics Report).

U.S. Census Bureau, Statistical Abstract of the United States: 1999

No. 133. Infant, Maternal, and Neonatal Mortality Rates and Fetal Mortality Ratios, by Race: 1980 to 1997

[Deaths per 1,000 live births, except as noted. Excludes deaths of nonresidents of United States. Race for live births tabulated according to race of mother, for infant and neonatal mortality rates. Beginning 1990, race for live births tabulated according to race of mother, for maternal mortality rates and mortality rates. See also Appendix III]

Item	1980	1990	1992	1993	1994	1995	1996	1997
Infant deaths [1]	12.6	9.2	8.5	8.4	8.0	7.6	7.2	7.1
White	10.9	7.6	6.9	6.8	6.6	6.3	6.0	6
Black and other	20.2	15.5	14.4	14.1	13.5	(NA)	(NA)	(NA)
Black	22.2	18.0	16.8	16.5	15.8	15.1	14.2	13.7
Maternal deaths [2]	9.2	8.2	7.8	7.5	8.3	7.1	7.6	(NA)
White	6.7	5.4	5.0	4.8	6.2	4.2	5.1	(NA)
Black and other	19.8	19.1	18.2	17.6	16.2	18.5	16.9	(NA)
Black	21.5	22.4	20.8	20.5	18.5	22.1	20.3	(NA)
Fetal deaths [3]	9.2	7.5	7.4	(NA)	(NA)	(NA)	(NA)	(NA)
White	8.2	6.4	6.3	(NA)	(NA)	(NA)	(NA)	(NA)
Black and other	13.4	11.9	11.7	(NA)	(NA)	(NA)	(NA)	(NA)
Neonatal deaths [4]	8.5	5.8	5.4	5.3	5.1	4.9	4.7	4.7
White	7.4	4.8	4.3	4.3	4.2	4.1	3.9	3.9
Black and other	13.2	9.9	9.2	9.0	8.6	(NA)	(NA)	(NA)
Black	14.6	11.6	10.8	10.7	10.2	9.8	9.2	9

NA Not available. [1] Represents deaths of infants under 1 year old, exclusive of fetal deaths. [2] Per 100,000 live births from deliveries and complications of pregnancy, childbirth, and the puerperium. Deaths are classified according to the ninth revision of the *International Classification of Diseases*; earlier years classified according to the revision in use at the time; see text, this section. [3] Includes only those deaths with stated or presumed period of gestation of 20 weeks or more. [4] Represents deaths of infants under 28 days old, exclusive of fetal deaths.

No. 134. Fetal and Infant Deaths—Number and Percent Distribution: 1970 to 1993

[State requirements for reporting of fetal deaths vary. Most states require reporting of fetal deaths of gestations of 20 weeks or more. There is substantial evidence that not all fetal deaths for which reporting is required are reported. For details of methodology, see Appendix III and source]

Year	Number					Percent distribution				
		Fetal deaths		Infant deaths			Fetal deaths		Infant deaths	
				Neonatal					Neonatal	
	Total	Early [1]	Late [2]	Early [3]	Late [4]	Post-neonatal [5]	Total	Early [1]	Late [2]	Early [3]	Late [4]	Post-neonatal [5]
1970	127,628	17,170	35,791	50,821	5,458	18,388	100.0	13.5	28.0	39.8	4.3	14.4
1980	78,879	10,754	22,599	25,492	5,126	14,908	100.0	13.6	28.7	32.3	6.5	18.9
1982	75,095	11,028	21,666	23,706	4,629	14,066	100.0	14.7	28.9	31.6	6.2	18.7
1983	71,379	10,933	19,819	22,315	4,192	14,120	100.0	15.3	27.8	31.3	5.9	19.8
1984	69,679	10,963	19,136	21,566	4,125	13,889	100.0	15.7	27.5	31.0	5.9	19.9
1985	69,691	10,958	18,703	21,865	4,314	13,851	100.0	15.7	26.8	31.4	6.2	19.9
1986	67,863	11,100	17,872	21,053	4,159	13,679	100.0	16.4	26.3	31.0	6.1	20.2
1987	67,757	11,656	17,693	20,471	4,156	13,781	100.0	17.2	26.1	30.2	6.1	20.3
1988	68,352	11,833	17,609	20,471	4,219	14,220	100.0	17.3	25.8	29.9	6.2	20.8
1989	70,124	12,397	18,072	20,796	4,372	14,487	100.0	17.7	25.8	29.7	6.2	20.7
1990	67,696	12,554	16,791	20,020	4,289	14,042	100.0	18.5	24.8	29.6	6.3	20.7
1991	65,000	12,310	15,924	18,916	4,062	13,788	100.0	18.9	24.5	29.1	6.2	21.2
1992	63,153	12,704	15,821	17,798	4,051	12,779	100.0	20.1	25.1	28.2	6.4	21.8
1993	55,387	12,588	14,243	(NA)	(NA)	(NA)	100.0	22.7	25.7	(NA)	(NA)	(NA)

NA Not available. [1] 20-27 weeks gestation. [2] 28 weeks or more gestation. [3] Less than 7 days. [4] 7-27 days. [5] 28 days-11 months.

No. 135. Infant Deaths and Infant Mortality Rates, by Cause of Death: 1990 to 1997

[Excludes deaths of nonresidents of the United States. Deaths classified according to ninth revision of *International Classification of Diseases*. See also Appendix III]

Cause of death	Number			Percent distribution			Infant mortality rate [1]		
	1990	1995	1997	1990	1995	1997	1990	1995	1997
Total	38,351	29,583	27,692	100	100	97	9.2	7.6	7.1
Congenital anomalies	8,239	6,554	6,063	21	22	21	2.0	1.7	1.6
Disorders relating to short gestation and unspecified low birth weight	4,013	3,933	3,727	10	13	13	1.0	1.0	1.0
Sudden infant death syndrome	5,417	3,397	2,705	14	11	9	1.3	0.9	0.7
Respiratory distress syndrome	2,850	1,454	1,262	7	5	4	0.7	0.4	0.3
Newborn affected by maternal complications of pregnancy	1,655	1,309	1,242	4	4	4	0.4	0.3	0.3
Newborn affected by complications of placenta, cord, and membranes	975	962	927	3	3	3	0.2	(NA)	0.2
Accidents and adverse effects	930	787	753	2	3	3	0.2	(NA)	0.2
Infections specific to the perinatal period	875	788	756	2	3	3	0.2	(NA)	0.2
Pneumonia and influenza	634	492	397	2	2	1	0.2	(NA)	0.1
Intrauterine hypoxia and birth asphyxia	762	475	456	2	2	1	0.2	(NA)	0.1
All other causes	12,001	9,432	9,404	31	32	33	2.9	(NA)	2.4

NA Not available. [1] Deaths of infants under 1 year old per 1,000 live births.

Source of Tables 133-135: U.S. National Center for Health Statistics, *Vital Statistics of the United States*, annual; *National Vital Statistics Reports (NVSR)* (formerly *Monthly Vital Statistics Report*); and unpublished data.

Vital Statistics 97

No. 136. Infant Mortality Rates, by Race—States: 1980 to 1996

[**Deaths per 1,000 live births, by place of residence.** Represents deaths of infants under 1 year old, exclusive of fetal deaths. Excludes deaths of nonresidents of the United States. See Appendix III]

State	Total [1]				White				Black			
	1980	1990	1995	1996	1980	1990	1995	1996	1980	1990	1995	1996
United States..	12.6	9.2	7.6	7.3	11.0	7.3	6.3	6.1	21.4	18.0	15.1	14.7
Alabama........	15.1	10.8	9.8	10.5	11.6	8.1	7.1	8.2	21.6	16.0	15.2	15.5
Alaska.........	12.3	10.5	7.7	7.2	9.4	7.6	6.1	5.8	19.5	(B)	(B)	(B)
Arizona........	12.4	8.8	7.5	7.6	11.8	7.8	7.2	7.1	18.4	20.6	17.0	20.5
Arkansas......	12.7	9.2	8.8	9.3	10.3	8.4	7.2	8.1	20.0	13.9	14.3	14.0
California	11.1	7.9	6.3	5.9	10.6	7.0	5.8	5.5	18.0	16.8	14.4	13.9
Colorado.......	10.1	8.8	6.5	6.6	9.8	7.8	6.0	6.4	19.1	19.4	16.8	14.7
Connecticut.....	11.2	7.9	7.2	6.4	10.2	6.3	6.5	5.3	19.1	17.6	12.6	14.9
Delaware	13.9	10.1	7.5	7.6	9.8	9.7	6.0	6.0	27.9	20.1	13.1	12.7
District of Columbia .	25.0	20.7	16.2	14.9	17.8	0.0	(B)	(NA)	26.7	24.6	19.6	17.6
Florida	14.6	9.6	7.5	7.5	11.8	6.7	6.0	5.8	22.8	16.8	13.0	13.3
Georgia........	14.5	12.4	9.4	9.2	10.8	7.4	6.5	6.3	21.0	18.3	15.1	14.9
Hawaii	10.3	6.7	5.8	5.8	11.6	6.1	(B)	4.4	(B)	(B)	(B)	(B)
Idaho.........	10.7	8.7	6.1	7.4	10.7	8.6	5.8	7.4	(NA)	(B)	(B)	(B)
Illinois	14.8	10.7	9.4	8.6	11.7	7.9	7.2	6.4	26.3	22.4	18.7	18.2
Indiana........	11.9	9.6	8.4	8.7	10.5	7.9	7.3	7.5	23.4	17.4	17.5	18.4
Iowa..........	11.8	8.1	8.2	7.0	11.5	7.9	7.8	6.5	27.2	21.9	21.2	22.9
Kansas........	10.4	8.4	7.0	8.3	9.5	8.0	6.2	7.2	20.6	17.7	17.6	23.1
Kentucky.......	12.9	8.5	7.6	7.5	12.0	8.2	7.4	6.9	22.0	14.3	10.7	13.6
Louisiana......	14.3	11.1	9.8	9.0	10.5	8.1	6.2	6.5	20.6	16.7	15.3	12.8
Maine..........	9.2	6.2	6.5	4.4	9.4	6.7	6.3	4.4	(B)	(B)	(B)	11.0
Maryland	14.0	9.5	8.9	8.5	11.6	6.8	6.0	5.7	20.4	17.1	15.3	14.5
Massachusetts.....	10.5	7.0	5.2	5.0	10.1	6.1	4.7	4.8	16.8	11.9	9.0	8.8
Michigan........	12.8	10.7	8.3	8.1	10.6	7.4	6.2	5.9	24.2	21.6	17.3	17.6
Minnesota........	10.0	7.3	6.7	5.9	9.6	6.7	6.0	5.1	20.0	23.7	17.6	14.5
Mississippi	17.0	12.1	10.5	11.0	11.1	7.4	7.0	8.0	23.7	16.2	14.7	14.6
Missouri	12.4	9.4	7.4	7.6	11.1	7.9	6.4	6.2	20.7	18.2	13.8	15.7
Montana........	12.4	9.0	7.0	7.0	11.8	6.0	7.0	6.8	(NA)	(B)	(B)	(B)
Nebraska.......	11.5	8.3	7.4	8.7	10.7	6.9	7.3	8.4	25.2	18.9	(B)	(B)
Nevada	10.7	8.4	5.7	6.2	10.0	8.2	5.5	5.4	20.6	14.2	(B)	13.7
New Hampshire....	9.9	7.1	5.5	5.0	9.9	6.0	5.5	5.0	22.5	(B)	(B)	(B)
New Jersey......	12.5	9.0	6.6	6.9	10.3	6.4	5.3	5.3	21.9	18.4	13.3	14.9
New Mexico......	11.5	9.0	6.2	6.2	11.3	7.6	6.1	6.1	23.1	(B)	(B)	(B)
New York	12.5	9.6	7.7	7.0	10.8	7.4	6.2	5.7	20.0	18.1	13.9	12.4
North Carolina.....	14.5	10.6	9.2	9.2	12.1	8.0	6.7	7.1	20.0	16.5	15.9	15.3
North Dakota.....	12.1	8.0	7.2	5.3	11.7	7.2	6.7	5.0	27.5	(B)	(B)	(B)
Ohio	12.8	9.8	8.7	7.7	11.2	7.8	7.3	6.3	23.0	19.5	17.5	16.2
Oklahoma........	12.7	9.2	8.3	8.5	12.1	9.1	8.0	7.7	21.8	14.3	15.1	17.6
Oregon.........	12.2	8.3	6.1	5.6	12.2	7.0	5.9	5.3	15.9	(B)	(B)	(B)
Pennsylvania......	13.2	9.6	7.8	7.8	11.9	7.4	6.2	6.4	23.1	20.5	17.6	16.9
Rhode Island.....	11.0	8.1	7.2	5.2	10.9	7.0	7.0	5.1	(B)	(B)	(B)	(B)
South Carolina.....	15.6	11.7	9.6	8.4	10.8	8.1	6.7	5.6	22.9	17.3	14.6	13.7
South Dakota	10.9	10.1	9.5	5.7	9.0	8.0	7.9	4.5	(NA)	(B)	(B)	(B)
Tennessee	13.5	10.3	9.3	8.5	11.9	7.3	6.8	6.7	19.3	17.9	17.9	15.4
Texas..........	12.2	8.1	6.5	6.3	11.2	6.7	5.9	5.7	18.8	14.7	11.7	11.7
Utah	10.4	7.5	5.4	6.0	10.5	6.0	5.3	5.9	27.3	(B)	(B)	(B)
Vermont	10.7	6.4	6.0	7.1	10.7	5.9	6.2	6.9	(B)	(B)	(B)	(B)
Virginia.	13.6	10.2	7.8	7.7	11.9	7.4	5.7	6.1	19.8	19.5	15.3	13.8
Washington.......	11.8	7.8	5.9	6.0	11.5	7.3	5.6	5.6	16.4	20.6	16.2	15.7
West Virginia......	11.8	9.9	7.9	7.4	11.4	8.1	7.6	6.9	21.5	(B)	(B)	(B)
Wisconsin........	10.3	8.2	7.3	7.3	9.7	7.7	6.3	6.1	18.5	19.0	18.6	18.8
Wyoming........	9.8	8.6	7.7	6.4	9.3	7.5	6.8	6.2	25.9	(S)	(B)	(B)

B Base figure too small to meet statistical standards for reliability. NA Not available. S Figure does not meet publication standards. [1] Includes other races, not shown separately.

Source: U.S. National Center for Health Statistics, *Vital Statistics of the United States,* annual; and unpublished data.

No. 137. Deaths and Death Rates, by Selected Causes: 1990 to 1997

[2,148.5 represents 2,148,500. Excludes deaths of nonresidents of the United States, except as noted. Beginning 1980, deaths classified according to ninth revision of *International Classification of Diseases*; for earlier years, classified according to revision in use at that time. See also Appendix III]

Cause of death	Deaths (1,000)				Crude death rate per 100,000 population [1]			
	1990	1995	1996	1997	1990	1995	1996	1997
All causes	**2,148.5**	**2,312.1**	**2,314.7**	**2,314.7**	**863.8**	**880.0**	**872.5**	**864.9**
Major cardiovascular diseases	916.0	951.4	950.2	942.7	368.3	362.1	358.2	352.2
Diseases of heart	720.1	737.6	733.4	725.8	289.5	280.7	276.4	271.2
Percent of total	33.5	31.9	31.7	31.4	33.5	31.9	31.7	31.4
Rheumatic fever and rheumatic heart disease	6.0	5.1	5.0	4.9	2.4	2.0	1.9	1.8
Hypertensive heart disease [2]	23.4	25.0	26.2	26.1	9.5	9.5	9.9	9.7
Ischemic heart disease	489.2	481.3	476.1	465.7	196.7	183.2	179.5	174.0
Other diseases of endocardium	13.0	16.2	17.2	17.7	5.2	6.2	6.5	6.6
All other forms of heart disease	188.4	207.4	206.4	209.0	75.8	78.9	77.8	78.1
Hypertension [2]	9.2	12.5	12.9	13.3	3.7	4.8	4.9	5.0
Cerebrovascular diseases	144.1	158.0	159.9	159.9	57.9	60.1	60.3	59.7
Atherosclerosis	18.0	16.7	16.7	15.8	7.3	6.4	6.3	5.9
Other	24.6	26.6	27.2	27.8	9.9	10.1	10.2	10.4
Malignancies [3]	505.3	538.5	539.5	537.4	203.2	204.9	203.4	200.8
Percent of total	23.5	23.3	23.3	23.2	23.5	23.3	23.3	23.2
Of respiratory and intrathoracic organs	146.4	156.4	157.3	158.2	58.9	59.5	59.3	59.1
Of digestive organs and peritoneum	120.8	126.6	126.5	126.1	48.6	48.2	47.7	47.1
Of genital organs	57.5	60.5	60.1	58.5	23.1	23.0	22.6	21.9
Of breast	43.7	44.2	43.4	42.2	17.6	16.8	16.4	15.8
Of urinary organs	20.7	22.6	23.0	23.3	8.3	8.6	8.7	8.7
Leukemia	18.6	20.1	20.3	20.2	7.5	7.7	7.7	7.5
Accidents and adverse effects	92.0	93.3	94.9	92.2	37.0	35.5	35.8	34.4
Motor vehicle	46.8	43.4	43.6	42.4	18.8	16.5	16.5	15.8
All other	45.2	50.0	51.3	49.8	18.2	19.0	19.3	18.6
Chronic obstructive pulmonary diseases and allied conditions	86.7	102.9	106.0	110.6	34.9	39.2	40.0	41.3
Bronchitis, chronic and unspecified	3.6	3.3	3.2	3.1	1.4	1.3	1.2	1.1
Emphysema	15.7	16.9	17.3	17.8	6.3	6.4	6.5	6.7
Asthma	4.8	5.6	5.7	5.3	1.9	2.1	2.1	2.0
Other	62.6	77.0	79.9	84.4	25.2	29.3	30.1	31.5
Pneumonia and influenza	79.5	82.9	83.7	88.4	32.0	31.6	31.6	33.0
Pneumonia	77.4	82.3	83.0	87.5	31.1	31.3	31.3	32.7
Influenza	2.1	0.6	0.7	0.9	0.8	0.2	0.3	0.3
Diabetes mellitus	47.7	59.3	61.8	62.3	19.2	22.6	23.3	23.3
Suicide	30.9	31.3	30.9	29.7	12.4	11.9	11.6	11.1
Chronic liver disease and cirrhosis	25.8	25.2	25.0	24.8	10.4	9.6	9.4	9.3
Other infectious and parasitic diseases	32.2	50.3	38.2	23.4	13.0	19.1	14.4	8.8
Homicide and legal intervention	24.9	22.9	21.0	18.8	10.0	8.7	7.9	7.0
Nephritis, nephrotic syndrome, and nephrosis	20.8	23.7	24.3	25.6	8.3	9.0	9.2	9.6
Septicemia	19.2	21.0	21.4	22.6	7.7	8.0	8.1	8.4
Certain conditions originating in the perinatal period	17.7	13.5	13.1	12.8	7.1	5.1	4.9	4.8
Congenital anomalies	13.1	11.9	11.8	11.7	5.3	4.5	4.5	4.4
Benign neoplasms [4]	6.8	7.8	7.6	7.8	2.7	3.0	2.9	2.9
Ulcer of stomach and duodenum	6.2	5.5	5.1	5.1	2.5	2.1	1.9	1.9
Hernia of abdominal cavity and intestinal obstruction [5]	5.8	6.2	6.5	6.5	2.3	2.4	2.4	2.4
Anemias	4.1	4.6	4.3	4.5	1.6	1.7	1.6	1.7
Cholelithiasis and other disorders of gall bladder	3.0	2.8	2.8	2.7	1.2	1.0	1.1	1.0
Nutritional deficiencies	3.0	3.6	3.7	3.9	1.2	1.4	1.4	1.5
Tuberculosis	1.8	1.3	1.2	1.2	0.7	0.5	0.5	0.4
Infections of kidney	1.3	0.9	0.9	0.8	0.5	0.3	0.3	0.3
Viral hepatitis	1.6	3.4	3.8	3.9	0.6	1.3	1.4	1.5
Meningitis	1.0	0.8	0.8	0.8	0.4	0.3	0.3	0.3
Acute bronchitis and bronchiolitis	0.6	0.5	0.5	0.5	0.3	0.2	0.2	0.2
Hyperplasia of prostate	0.5	0.4	0.5	0.4	0.2	0.2	0.2	0.2
Symptoms, signs, and ill-defined conditions	24.1	27.3	26.2	33.6	9.7	10.4	9.9	12.5
All other causes	172.9	214.1	223.5	234.7	69.5	81.5	84.3	87.7

[1] 1980 and 1990 based on resident population enumerated as of April 1. Other years based on resident population estimated as of July 1. [2] With or without renal disease. [3] Includes other types of malignancies not shown separately. [4] Includes neoplasms of unspecified nature; beginning 1980 also includes carcinoma in situ. [5] Without mention of hernia.

Source: U.S. National Center for Health Statistics, *Vital Statistics of the United States*, annual; and *National Vital Statistics Report (NVSR)* (formerly *Monthly Vital Statistics Report*); and unpublished data.

U.S. Census Bureau, Statistical Abstract of the United States: 1999

No. 138. Age-Adjusted Death Rates, by Selected Causes: 1990 to 1997

[Rates per 100,000 population. For explanation of age-adjustment, see text, this section. The standard population for this table is the total population of the United States enumerated in 1940. See also headnote, Table 137]

Cause of death	1990	1992	1993	1994	1995	1996	1997
All causes	520.2	504.5	513.3	507.4	503.9	491.6	478.2
Major cardiovascular diseases	189.8	180.4	181.8	176.8	174.9	170.7	165.4
Diseases of heart	152.0	144.3	145.3	140.4	138.3	134.5	129.9
Rheumatic fever and rheumatic heart disease	1.5	1.3	1.3	1.2	1.1	1.1	1.0
Hypertensive heart disease[1]	4.8	4.8	4.9	5.0	5.1	5.2	5.0
Hypertensive heart and renal disease	0.5	0.5	0.5	0.5	0.4	0.4	0.4
Ischemic heart disease	102.6	95.7	94.9	91.4	89.5	86.7	82.7
Other diseases of endocardium	2.5	2.6	2.6	2.6	2.6	2.7	2.7
Acute myocardial infarction	53.7	49.1	47.5	45.6	43.8	42.0	39.6
Old myocardial infarction and other	47.8	45.7	46.5	45.0	44.9	44.0	42.3
Hypertension[1]	1.9	2.0	2.2	2.2	2.3	2.3	2.3
Cerebrovascular diseases	27.7	26.2	26.5	26.5	26.7	26.4	25.9
Atherosclerosis	2.7	2.4	2.4	2.3	2.3	2.2	2.0
Intracerebral/intracranial hemorrage	5.2	5.1	5.1	5.0	5.1	5.2	5.5
Cerebral thrombosis	3.3	2.7	2.5	2.4	2.2	2.0	1.8
Cerebral embolism	0.1	0.1	0.1	0.1	0.1	0.1	0.1
Malignancies[2]	135.0	133.1	132.6	131.5	129.9	127.9	125.0
Of respiratory and intrathoracic organs	41.4	40.8	40.8	40.1	39.7	39.3	38.6
Of digestive organs and peritoneum	30.2	29.6	29.5	29.3	29.1	28.5	27.9
Of genital organs	13.6	13.5	13.2	13.2	12.8	12.5	11.9
Of breast	12.7	12.0	11.8	11.6	11.5	11.0	10.5
Of urinary organs	5.1	5.1	5.0	5.1	5.1	5.1	5.0
Leukemia	5.0	4.9	4.9	4.9	4.8	4.8	4.7
Of lip, oral cavity, and pharynx	2.4	2.3	2.3	2.1	2.1	2.1	2.0
Accidents and adverse effects	32.5	29.4	30.3	30.3	30.5	30.4	28.9
Motor vehicle	18.5	15.8	16.0	16.1	16.3	16.2	15.5
All other	14.0	13.7	14.4	14.2	14.2	14.2	13.4
Chronic obstructive pulmonary diseases and allied conditions	19.7	19.9	21.4	21.0	20.8	21.0	21.4
Bronchitis, chronic and unspecified	0.8	0.8	0.8	0.7	0.6	0.6	0.6
Emphysema	3.7	3.7	3.9	3.7	3.6	3.6	3.7
Asthma	1.4	1.4	1.4	1.5	1.5	1.5	1.4
Other	13.7	14.0	15.2	15.1	15.0	15.2	15.7
Pneumonia and influenza	14.0	12.7	13.5	13.0	12.9	12.8	13.2
Pneumonia	13.7	12.5	13.3	12.8	12.8	12.7	13.0
Influenza	0.3	0.2	0.2	0.2	0.1	0.1	0.1
Diabetes mellitus	11.7	11.9	12.4	12.9	13.3	13.6	13.4
Suicide	11.5	11.1	11.3	11.2	11.2	10.8	10.3
Chronic liver disease and cirrhosis	8.6	8.0	7.9	7.9	7.6	7.5	7.2
Homicide and legal intervention	10.2	10.5	10.7	10.3	9.4	8.5	7.5
Nephritis, nephrotic syndrome, and renal failure	3.9	4.0	4.1	3.9	4.0	3.9	4.1
Acute glomerulonephritis/nephrotic syndrome	0.1	0.1	(NA)	0.1	-	-	-
Septicemia	4.1	4.0	4.1	4.0	4.1	4.1	4.2
Other infectious and parasitic diseases	12.0	14.7	15.9	17.5	17.6	13.0	7.7
Benign neoplasms[3]	1.7	1.7	1.7	1.7	1.7	1.7	1.7
Ulcer of stomach and duodenum	1.3	1.2	1.2	1.2	1.0	0.9	0.9
Hernia of abdominal cavity and intestinal obstruction[4]	1.1	1.1	1.0	1.1	1.0	1.0	1.0
Anemias	0.9	0.9	0.9	0.9	0.9	0.8	0.8
Cholelithiasis and other disorders of gallbladder	0.6	0.5	0.5	0.5	0.5	0.5	0.5
Nutritional deficiencies	0.5	0.5	0.5	0.5	0.5	0.5	0.5
Tuberculosis	0.5	0.4	0.4	0.4	0.3	0.3	0.3
Tuberculosis of respiratory system	0.4	0.3	0.3	0.3	0.2	0.2	0.2
Other tuberculosis	0.1	0.1	0.1	0.1	0.1	0.1	0.1
Infections of kidney	0.2	0.2	0.2	0.2	0.2	0.2	0.1
Viral hepatitis	0.5	0.6	0.8	0.9	1.0	1.1	1.1
Meningitis	0.3	0.2	0.3	0.3	0.2	0.3	0.3
Acute bronchitis and bronchiolitis	0.1	0.1	0.1	0.1	0.1	0.1	0.1
Hyperplasia of prostate	0.1	0.1	0.1	0.1	0.1	0.1	0.2
Symptoms, signs, and ill-defined conditions	7.3	6.7	7.4	6.8	7.2	6.6	9.0
Meningococcal infection	0.1	0.1	0.1	0.1	0.1	0.1	0.1
Angina pectoris	0.2	0.2	0.2	0.2	0.1	0.1	0.1
Appendicitis	0.1	0.1	0.1	0.1	0.1	0.1	0.1
Complications of pregnancy, childbirth	0.1	0.1	0.1	0.1	0.1	0.1	0.1
Congenital anomalies	5.0	4.6	4.6	4.5	4.4	4.3	4.1
Perinatal period conditions	6.9	6.0	5.9	4.8	5.4	5.3	5.1
Birth trauma, intrauterine hypoxia, etc.	1.5	1.1	1.0	0.9	0.9	0.8	0.8

- Represents or rounds to zero. NA Not available. [1] With or without renal disease. [2] Includes other types of malignancies not shown separately. [3] Includes neoplasms of unspecified nature; also includes carcinoma in situ. [4] Without mention of hernia.

Source: U.S. National Center for Health Statistics, *Vital Statistics of the United States*, annual; and *National Vital Statistics Report (NVSR)* (formerly *Monthly Vital Statistics Report*); and unpublished data.

No. 139. Deaths, by Selected Causes and Selected Characteristics: 1996

[In thousands (2,314.7 represents 2,314,700). Excludes deaths of nonresidents of the U.S. Causes of deaths classified according to ninth revision of *International Classification of Diseases*. See also Appendix III]

Age, sex, and race	Total [1]	Heart disease	Cancer	Accidents and adverse effects	Cerebrovascular diseases	Chronic obstructive pulmonary diseases [2]	Pneumonia, flu	Suicide	Chronic liver disease, cirrhosis	Diabetes mellitus	Homicide and legal intervention
ALL RACES [3]											
Both sexes, total [4]	2,314.7	733.4	539.5	94.9	159.9	106.0	83.0	30.9	25.0	61.8	21.0
Under 1 years old	28.5	0.6	0.1	0.8	0.2	-	0.5	-	-	-	0.3
1 to 4 years old	5.9	0.2	0.4	2.1	-	0.1	0.2	-	-	-	0.4
5 to 9 years old	3.8	0.1	0.5	1.6	-	0.1	0.1	-	-	-	0.2
10 to 14 years old	4.6	0.2	0.5	1.8	-	0.1	0.1	0.3	-	-	0.3
15 to 19 years old	14.7	0.4	0.7	6.8	0.1	0.1	0.1	1.8	-	-	2.9
20 to 24 years old	17.8	0.6	0.9	7.1	0.1	0.1	0.1	2.5	-	0.1	3.6
25 to 29 years old	20.7	1.1	1.6	6.2	0.2	0.2	0.2	2.8	0.1	0.2	2.9
30 to 34 years old	30.4	2.3	3.2	6.6	0.5	0.2	0.4	3.0	0.4	0.4	2.5
35 to 39 years old	42.5	4.7	6.1	7.4	1.0	0.3	0.6	3.5	1.3	0.7	2.2
40 to 44 years old	53.5	8.5	10.9	6.9	1.7	0.5	0.9	3.3	2.3	1.2	1.6
45 to 49 years old	67.0	14.8	18.4	5.7	2.6	1.0	1.0	2.8	2.8	1.8	1.2
50 to 54 years old	77.3	20.3	26.2	4.1	3.1	1.8	1.1	2.1	2.6	2.5	0.7
55 to 59 years old	96.7	26.9	35.9	3.5	3.9	3.5	1.4	1.6	2.6	3.4	0.5
60 to 64 years old	137.0	40.5	51.0	3.4	5.7	6.6	2.1	1.3	2.8	5.0	0.4
65 to 69 years old	200.0	59.6	72.3	3.9	9.6	12.1	3.7	1.4	2.9	7.3	0.3
70 to 74 years old	273.8	85.3	88.5	4.9	15.7	18.1	6.8	1.4	2.8	9.3	0.2
75 to 79 years old	321.2	106.8	84.8	5.5	23.6	21.4	10.6	1.3	2.1	10.0	0.2
80 to 84 years old	342.1	123.0	69.7	6.2	30.9	19.5	15.6	1.0	1.4	9.0	0.1
85 years old and over	576.5	237.5	67.6	10.4	60.7	20.3	37.7	0.8	0.8	10.8	0.1
WHITE											
Both sexes, total [4]	1,993.0	645.5	469.4	79.4	138.3	97.9	73.5	27.9	21.4	49.5	10.3
Under 1 years old	18.8	0.4	0.1	0.5	0.2	-	0.3	-	-	-	0.2
1 to 4 years old	4.0	0.1	0.3	1.5	-	-	0.1	-	-	-	0.2
5 to 9 years old	2.7	0.1	0.4	1.1	-	-	0.1	-	-	-	0.2
10 to 14 years old	3.4	0.1	0.4	1.4	-	0.1	-	0.2	-	-	0.1
15 to 19 years old	10.6	0.3	0.5	5.7	-	0.1	0.1	1.5	-	-	1.2
20 to 24 years old	12.3	0.4	0.7	5.7	0.1	0.1	0.1	2.1	-	0.1	1.4
25 to 29 years old	14.4	0.7	1.3	5.0	0.2	0.1	0.1	2.4	0.1	0.1	1.2
30 to 34 years old	21.4	1.5	2.6	5.3	0.3	0.1	0.2	2.6	0.4	0.3	1.3
35 to 39 years old	30.3	3.4	4.8	6.0	0.7	0.2	0.4	3.1	1.0	0.5	1.2
40 to 44 years old	38.6	6.1	8.6	5.6	1.0	0.4	0.6	3.0	1.9	0.8	0.9
45 to 49 years old	50.2	11.2	14.7	4.6	1.7	0.7	0.7	2.6	2.3	1.3	0.7
50 to 54 years old	60.6	15.8	21.6	3.4	2.2	1.6	0.8	1.9	2.1	1.8	0.5
55 to 59 years old	77.5	21.4	29.8	2.8	2.8	3.0	1.1	1.5	2.1	2.5	0.3
60 to 64 years old	112.6	32.9	43.2	2.9	4.2	5.9	1.7	1.2	2.4	3.7	0.3
65 to 69 years old	170.4	50.6	62.7	3.3	7.5	11.1	3.0	1.3	2.6	5.7	0.2
70 to 74 years old	238.5	74.1	78.0	4.2	13.1	16.8	5.9	1.3	2.6	7.4	0.2
75 to 79 years old	286.3	95.2	75.8	4.9	20.6	20.1	9.5	1.2	2.0	8.3	0.1
80 to 84 years old	310.1	111.8	62.9	5.7	27.8	18.5	14.1	1.0	1.3	7.7	0.1
85 years old and over	529.7	219.3	61.1	9.7	55.8	19.2	34.6	0.7	0.7	9.4	0.1
BLACK											
Both sexes, total [4]	282.1	77.6	60.8	12.7	18.5	6.9	7.9	2.2	3.0	10.8	10.0
Under 1 years old	8.7	0.2	-	0.2	0.1	-	0.2	-	-	-	0.1
1 to 4 years old	1.6	0.1	0.1	0.5	0.1	-	0.2	-	-	-	0.1
5 to 9 years old	0.9	-	0.1	0.4	-	-	0.1	-	-	-	0.2
10 to 14 years old	0.9	-	0.1	0.4	-	-	0.1	-	-	-	0.1
15 to 19 years old	1.0	0.1	0.1	0.3	-	0.1	-	-	-	-	1.2
20 to 24 years old	3.5	0.1	0.1	0.8	-	0.1	-	0.2	-	-	1.4
25 to 29 years old	4.8	0.2	0.2	1.0	-	0.1	-	0.3	-	-	1.7
30 to 34 years old	5.6	0.3	0.3	0.9	0.1	0.1	0.1	0.3	-	0.1	1.6
35 to 39 years old	8.1	0.7	0.6	1.0	0.2	0.1	0.1	0.3	0.1	0.1	1.2
40 to 44 years old	11.1	1.2	1.1	1.1	0.3	0.1	0.2	0.3	0.2	0.2	1.0
45 to 49 years old	13.5	2.1	2.0	1.1	0.6	0.2	0.3	0.2	0.4	0.3	0.7
50 to 54 years old	15.0	3.3	3.2	1.0	0.8	0.2	0.3	0.1	0.5	0.5	0.4
55 to 59 years old	14.8	4.0	4.0	0.7	0.8	0.3	0.3	0.1	0.4	0.6	0.2
60 to 64 years old	17.0	4.9	5.3	0.5	1.0	0.4	0.3	0.1	0.4	0.8	0.2
65 to 69 years old	21.5	6.8	6.8	0.5	1.3	0.6	0.4	0.1	0.3	1.2	0.1
70 to 74 years old	26.0	8.0	8.5	0.5	1.8	0.8	0.6	0.1	0.3	1.4	0.1
75 to 79 years old	30.8	9.9	9.1	0.5	2.3	1.1	0.8	-	0.2	1.7	0.1
80 to 84 years old	30.2	10.1	7.8	0.5	2.5	1.1	0.9	-	0.1	1.5	-
85 years old and over	27.5	9.7	5.8	0.5	2.7	0.9	1.2	-	-	1.2	-

- Represents zero. [1] Includes other causes, not shown separately. [2] Includes allied conditions. [3] Includes other races, not shown separately. [4] Includes those deaths with age not stated.

Source: U.S. National Center for Health Statistics, *Vital Statistics of the United States*, annual.

U.S. Census Bureau, Statistical Abstract of the United States: 1999

No. 140. Deaths, by Age and Leading Cause: 1996

[Excludes deaths of nonresidents of the United States. Deaths classified according to ninth revision of *International Classification of Diseases*. See also Appendix III]

Age and leading cause of death	Number of deaths			Death rate per 100,000 population		
	Total	Male	Female	Total	Male	Female
All ages [1]	**2,314,690**	**1,163,569**	**1,151,121**	**872.5**	**896.4**	**849.7**
1 to 4 yrs. old, total	**5,948**	**3,349**	**2,599**	**38.3**	**42.2**	**34.3**
Leading causes of death:						
Accidents	2,147	1,290	857	13.8	16.2	11.3
Congenital anomalies	638	325	313	4.1	4.1	4.1
Malignant neoplasms (cancer).	424	246	178	2.7	3.1	2.3
Homicide and legal intervention	420	214	206	2.7	2.7	2.7
Heart disease.	217	111	106	1.4	1.4	1.4
HIV infection [2]	147	74	73	0.9	0.9	1.0
Pneumonia and influenza	168	91	77	1.1	1.1	1.0
Certain conditions originating in the perinatal period	60	44	(NA)	0.4	0.6	(NA)
Septicemia	83	47	36	0.5	0.6	0.5
Cerebrovascular diseases	(NA)	(NA)	25	(NA)	(NA)	0.3
5 to 14 yrs. old, total.	**8,330**	**5,003**	**3,327**	**21.7**	**25.4**	**17.8**
Leading causes of death:						
Accidents	3,433	2,183	1,250	8.9	11.1	6.7
Malignant neoplasms (cancer).	1,028	582	446	2.7	3.0	2.4
Homicide and legal intervention	514	311	203	1.3	1.6	1.1
Congenital anomalies	457	273	184	1.2	1.4	1.0
Suicide	302	225	77	0.8	1.1	0.4
Heart disease. . [2]	334	181	153	0.9	0.9	0.8
HIV infections [2]	177	96	81	0.5	0.5	0.4
Chronic obstructive pulmonary diseases .	165	97	68	0.4	0.5	0.4
Pneumonia and influenza	136	69	67	0.4	0.4	0.4
Benign neoplasms & carcinoma in situ . .	85	(NA)	46	0.2	(NA)	0.2
15 to 24 yrs. old, total.	**32,443**	**24,313**	**8,130**	**89.6**	**130.6**	**46.2**
Leading causes of death:						
Accidents	13,809	10,273	3,536	38.1	55.2	20.1
Homicide and legal intervention	6,548	5,655	893	18.1	30.4	5.1
Suicide	4,358	3,724	634	12.0	20.0	3.6
Malignant neoplasms (cancer).	1,632	955	677	4.5	5.1	3.8
Heart disease.	969	616	353	2.7	3.3	2.0
HIV infection [2]	413	243	170	1.1	1.3	1.0
Congenital anomalies	382	231	151	1.1	1.2	0.9
Chronic obstructive pulmonary disease . .	237	131	106	0.7	0.7	0.6
Pneumonia and influenza	203	106	97	0.6	0.6	0.6
Cerebrovascular diseases	167	96	71	0.5	0.5	0.4
25 to 44 yrs. old, total.	**147,180**	**100,374**	**46,806**	**175.7**	**240.4**	**111.4**
Leading causes of death:						
HIV infection [2]	21,685	17,505	4,180	25.9	41.9	10.0
Accidents	27,092	20,273	6,819	32.3	48.5	16.2
Malignant neoplasms (cancer).	21,894	9,996	11,898	26.1	23.9	28.3
Heart disease.	16,567	11,765	4,802	19.8	28.2	11.4
Suicide	12,602	10,148	2,454	15.0	24.3	5.8
Homicide and legal intervention	9,322	7,235	2,087	11.1	17.3	5.0
Chronic liver disease and cirrhosis	4,210	2,996	1,214	5.0	7.2	2.9
Cerebrovascular diseases	3,442	1,796	1,646	4.1	4.3	3.9
Diabetes mellitus	2,526	1,506	1,020	3.0	3.6	2.4
Pneumonia and influenza	2,029	1,233	796	2.4	3.0	1.9
45 to 64 yrs. old, total.	**378,054**	**232,041**	**146,013**	**703.6**	**892.4**	**526.6**
Leading causes of death:						
Malignant neoplasms (cancer).	131,455	69,965	61,490	244.7	269.1	221.8
Heart disease.	102,369	71,764	30,605	190.5	276.0	110.4
Accidents	16,717	11,826	4,891	31.1	45.5	17.6
Cerebrovascular diseases	15,468	8,495	6,973	28.8	32.7	25.1
Chronic obstructive pulmonary diseases .	12,847	6,715	6,132	23.9	25.8	22.1
Diabetes mellitus	12,687	6,802	5,885	23.6	26.2	21.2
Chronic liver disease and cirrhosis	10,743	7,708	3,035	20.0	29.6	10.9
HIV infection [2]	8,053	6,835	1,218	15.0	26.3	4.4
Suicide	7,762	5,990	1,772	14.4	23.0	6.4
Pneumonia and influenza	5,706	3,466	2,240	10.6	13.3	8.1
65 yrs. old and over, total	**1,713,725**	**782,151**	**931,574**	**5,061.1**	**5,634.7**	**4,662.5**
Leading causes of death:						
Heart disease.	612,199	275,249	336,950	1,808.0	1,982.9	1,686.4
Malignant neoplasms (cancer).	382,988	200,096	182,892	1,131.1	1,441.5	915.4
Cerebrovascular diseases	140,488	51,887	88,601	414.9	373.8	443.4
Chronic obstructive pulmonary diseases .	91,470	46,915	44,555	270.1	338.0	223.0
Pneumonia and influenza	74,979	32,721	42,258	221.4	235.7	211.5
Diabetes mellitus	46,376	19,244	27,132	137.0	138.6	135.8
Accidents	30,830	15,197	15,633	91.0	109.5	78.2
Alzheimer's disease.	21,077	6,835	14,242	62.2	49.2	71.3
Nephritis, nephrotic syndrome, and nephrosis.	20,869	9,673	11,196	61.6	69.7	56.0
Septicemia	17,337	6,914	10,423	51.2	49.8	52.2

NA Not available.   [1] Includes those deaths with age not stated.   [2] Human immunodeficiency virus.

Source: U.S. National Center for Health Statistics, *Vital Statistics of the United States*, annual; and unpublished data.

No. 141. Death Rates, by Leading Cause—States: 1996

[Deaths per 100,000 resident population enumerated as of April 1. By place of residence. Excludes deaths of nonresidents of the United States. Causes of death classified according to ninth revisions of International Classification of Diseases]

State	Total [1]	Heart disease	Cancer	Cerebro-vascular diseases [2]	Accidents and adverse effects	Motor vehicle accidents	Chronic obstructive pulmonary diseases [2]	Diabetes mellitus	HIV [3]	Suicide	Homicide
U.S. . . .	872.5	276.4	203.4	60.3	35.8	16.5	40.0	23.3	(NA)	11.6	7.9
AL	1,002.3	315.9	222.4	66.9	51.4	27.5	40.7	26.6	8.3	12.0	12.4
AK	425.4	85.0	106.4	23.4	52.2	16.1	18.6	10.7	(NA)	19.8	6.9
AZ	826.4	231.3	187.9	53.0	47.9	22.5	48.1	20.3	7.5	16.4	10.1
AR	1,057.2	331.6	237.5	91.4	50.3	25.3	44.5	23.0	(NA)	12.9	9.5
CA	700.9	214.0	160.2	51.9	29.8	13.3	35.8	17.0	13.2	10.7	9.6
CO	672.9	172.6	147.9	43.9	37.4	17.5	43.3	14.4	6.4	18.2	5.6
CT	902.8	303.2	218.2	59.7	31.9	10.0	37.0	21.7	12.0	8.9	5.3
DE	897.2	277.9	232.9	47.7	33.2	14.5	38.5	26.5	18.3	13.4	7.9
DC	1,219.4	298.0	254.0	67.6	33.0	10.9	29.8	37.2	99.6	(NA)	59.8
FL	1,065.6	345.4	261.8	68.6	37.5	19.5	53.5	26.4	21.5	15.0	8.3
GA	799.0	238.2	169.1	57.9	40.7	21.6	34.4	17.6	17.3	11.8	10.0
HI	671.4	206.6	157.2	52.1	31.1	11.7	20.2	18.1	6.1	10.7	3.5
ID	732.7	200.5	167.1	57.8	47.3	23.7	40.1	20.4	(NA)	14.9	4.2
IL	895.6	289.8	209.2	62.7	31.1	13.5	36.8	23.0	9.5	9.0	10.7
IN	906.9	287.9	213.8	67.6	35.8	16.6	44.6	25.5	(NA)	12.6	6.8
IA	976.2	322.0	227.7	79.7	38.3	17.2	47.2	21.2	(NA)	11.3	(NA)
KS	929.3	281.4	207.8	73.0	41.8	20.3	44.0	23.4	(NA)	13.0	5.6
KY	959.7	306.7	232.4	66.5	44.7	20.8	50.1	25.2	(NA)	12.6	6.0
LA	909.9	270.4	214.1	59.2	41.7	20.9	33.1	37.3	13.8	12.2	18.3
ME	944.3	284.8	237.4	58.8	31.8	14.2	53.0	24.4	(NA)	13.8	(NA)
MD	827.3	235.5	200.4	52.2	28.0	12.9	34.7	27.9	20.9	9.9	11.9
MA	908.2	276.5	229.0	55.1	21.0	7.5	40.1	22.2	10.0	8.0	(NA)
MI	871.6	292.0	204.1	60.0	32.1	16.5	38.4	24.5	(NA)	11.6	8.4
MN	798.3	215.4	189.9	65.0	35.3	13.6	36.1	23.8	(NA)	10.5	(NA)
MS	982.4	351.2	212.0	62.9	55.6	31.9	37.1	19.8	8.5	11.4	13.8
MO	1,006.0	340.1	223.2	70.5	44.6	21.0	46.7	23.8	6.0	14.2	8.7
MT	876.4	243.7	201.1	62.5	45.3	21.7	61.9	21.4	(NA)	19.8	4.2
NE	937.2	302.8	201.3	69.0	39.2	18.2	47.4	20.2	(NA)	11.4	4.2
NV	822.4	241.0	199.1	49.7	37.7	20.5	55.5	16.4	8.8	20.9	12.8
NH	808.2	251.0	205.3	59.0	24.5	11.5	42.4	24.6	(NA)	11.8	(NA)
NJ	916.4	298.8	229.3	53.8	28.7	10.4	35.2	29.6	22.0	7.3	(NA)
NM	728.4	186.5	159.9	46.2	55.9	25.9	38.1	25.2	(NA)	18.6	10.9
NY	904.0	345.0	209.8	45.4	26.1	9.7	33.6	19.4	31.3	7.3	7.5
NC	905.3	271.3	207.5	72.8	42.8	20.6	41.1	24.8	11.3	12.4	9.2
ND	934.1	291.7	216.3	78.9	37.8	16.8	43.4	25.5	(NA)	12.0	(NA)
OH	941.6	306.2	226.7	60.6	30.5	12.8	45.9	32.3	5.9	9.4	(NA)
OK	1,003.3	342.8	215.9	73.3	47.9	24.5	47.4	21.9	5.5	14.1	8.1
OR	902.5	239.4	209.5	81.8	42.2	16.6	51.2	22.3	6.4	16.2	4.7
PA	1,072.3	362.2	253.1	71.8	36.8	13.2	44.9	29.6	8.8	11.8	5.9
RI	964.0	329.7	254.1	59.1	21.0	7.9	41.4	26.9	6.8	8.4	(NA)
SC	920.7	273.0	206.0	77.1	46.4	24.4	39.4	25.3	14.4	13.4	10.2
SD	928.0	300.0	210.4	65.9	46.7	23.5	40.1	24.4	(NA)	16.9	(NA)
TN	966.6	305.3	218.4	75.4	49.6	24.6	43.2	23.5	7.3	13.0	10.1
TX	731.7	221.8	167.3	51.5	38.0	20.7	33.3	24.0	10.8	11.6	8.3
UT	555.5	144.3	105.2	42.2	32.2	17.1	23.0	20.9	(NA)	14.3	(NA)
VT	827.3	252.6	205.0	54.5	33.0	14.3	41.3	26.2	(NA)	11.2	(NA)
VA	801.5	240.8	190.4	57.8	33.5	13.3	33.9	18.9	8.8	12.4	8.0
WA	763.7	212.1	181.9	62.9	35.2	14.3	40.0	20.8	7.2	14.0	4.7
WV	1,118.4	386.4	255.9	66.8	41.8	18.5	60.2	36.6	(NA)	15.3	4.8
WI	874.9	275.2	203.2	71.4	35.8	15.5	38.8	22.7	(NA)	11.6	(NA)
WY	748.2	197.1	180.5	55.0	50.9	24.5	50.9	17.4	(NA)	18.3	(NA)

NA Not available. [1] Includes other causes not shown separately. [2] Includes allied conditions. [3] Human immunodeficiency virus.

Source: U.S. National Center for Health Statistics, *National Vital Statistics Report (NVSR)*.

U.S. Census Bureau, Statistical Abstract of the United States: 1999

No. 142. Estimated Deaths of Persons With Acquired Immunodeficiency Syndrome (AIDS) Deaths, by Selected Characteristics: 1992 to 1997

[Estimates adjusted for delays in reporting of deaths. Total estimates of less than 1,000, 1,000 to 2,499, 2,500 to 4,999, and 5,000 or more are rounded to the nearest 10, 25, 50, and 100 respectively. Annual estimates are through the most recent year for which reliable estimates are available. Because there is uncertainty in the estimates of deaths of persons with AIDS, changes over time in estimates of deaths of persons with AIDS should not be computed from these rounded estimates. See source, "Technical notes"]

Characteristic	1992	1993	1994	1995	1996	1997
Total	**39,790**	**43,306**	**47,533**	**48,250**	**35,863**	**20,539**
RACE/ETHNICITY						
White, not Hispanic	20,375	21,407	22,207	21,551	14,289	6,990
Black, not Hispanic	13,338	15,295	17,727	18,815	15,844	10,256
Hispanic	5,700	6,133	7,024	7,298	5,310	3,062
Asian/Pacific Islander	269	304	406	359	279	148
American Indian/Alaska Native	77	132	143	185	118	70
MALE ADULT/ADOLESCENT EXPOSURE CATEGORY						
Male total	34,570	37,080	39,940	40,084	28,950	16,017
Men who have sex with men	22,525	23,397	24,598	24,095	16,382	8,242
Injecting drug use	7,439	8,499	9,525	9,978	7,844	4,911
Men who have sex with men and inject drugs	2,677	2,949	3,260	3,205	2,366	1,275
Hemophilia/coagulation disorder	327	347	343	323	233	131
Heterosexual contact	1,044	1,383	1,759	2,106	1,844	1,288
Receipt of blood transfusion, blood components, or tissue	326	313	296	265	212	119
Risk not reported or identified	232	192	159	113	69	52
FEMALE ADULT/ADOLESCENT EXPOSURE CATEGORY						
Female total	4,817	5,721	7,043	7,645	6,507	4,313
Injecting drug use	2,608	2,983	3,525	3,630	3,109	2,048
Hemophilia/coagulation disorder	19	16	25	27	27	22
Heterosexual contact	1,835	2,408	3,202	3,706	3,164	2,124
Receipt of blood transfusion, blood components, or tissue	240	230	227	221	174	97
Risk not reported or identified	116	84	64	60	34	23
Pediatric[1] exposure category	403	505	549	521	406	209

[1] Less than 13 years old.

Source: Centers for Disease Control and Prevention, *HIV/AIDS Surveillance Report*, annual.

No. 143. Death Rates From Heart Disease, by Sex and Age: 1980 to 1996

[**Deaths per 100,000 population in specified age groups**. Beginning 1970, excludes deaths of nonresidents of the United States. Beginning 1980, deaths classified according to the ninth revision of the International Classification of Diseases. For earlier years, classified according to the revision in use at the time; see text, this section. See Appendix III]

Age at death and selected type of heart disease	Male					Female				
	1980	1990	1994	1995	1996	1980	1990	1994	1995	1996
Total U.S. rate [1]	369	298	284	283	277	305	282	279	279	276
25 to 34 years	11	10	11	11	11	5	5	6	6	6
35 to 44 years old	69	48	47	47	44	21	15	17	17	17
45 to 54 years old	283	183	171	169	162	85	61	57	56	57
55 to 64 years old	747	537	478	465	454	272	216	196	194	189
65 to 74 years old	1,728	1,250	1,133	1,102	1,065	829	617	566	558	544
75 to 84 years old	3,834	2,968	2,655	2,615	2,529	2,497	1,894	1,741	1,715	1,675
85 years old and over	8,753	7,418	7,123	7,040	6,834	7,351	6,478	6,253	6,268	6,108
Persons 45 to 54 years old:										
Ischemic heart	217.3	123.8	109.2	107.5	102.0	52.2	33.6	30.6	29.4	30.2
Rheumatic heart	3.1	1.1	1.0	0.7	0.8	4.3	1.9	1.4	1.3	1.3
Hypertensive heart [2]	8.3	7.6	8.7	8.8	8.9	5.5	4.3	4.1	3.9	4.2
Persons 55 to 64 years old:										
Ischemic heart	581.1	375.4	323.4	312.6	303.4	189.0	135.4	120.4	116.8	114.0
Rheumatic heart	6.2	3.4	2.4	2.2	1.8	9.2	4.7	3.7	3.4	3.3
Hypertensive heart [2]	21.8	18.1	17.3	18.2	19.0	13.3	10.9	9.5	9.3	9.9
Persons 65 to 74 years old:										
Ischemic heart	1,355.5	898.5	794.0	770.5	741.6	605.3	415.2	368.1	362.8	352.6
Rheumatic heart	11.8	7.1	5.9	4.5	4.6	18.6	10.5	9.1	8.3	7.9
Hypertensive heart [2]	44.3	33.2	29.4	30.9	31.0	36.2	25.9	21.4	22.1	21.2
Persons 75 to 84 years old:										
Ischemic heart	2,953.7	2,129.6	1,863.9	1,824.0	1,763.4	1,842.7	1,287.6	1,142.9	1,116.3	1,086.2
Rheumatic heart	16.7	12.3	11.1	10.7	10.4	25.4	22.5	18.5	17.9	16.8
Hypertensive heart [2]	90.7	67.9	59.3	59.7	60.3	101.1	69.7	61.7	62.4	64.1
Persons 85 years old and over:										
Ischemic heart	6,501.6	5,120.7	4,771.9	4,674.4	4,496.3	5,280.6	4,257.8	3,980.8	3,948.8	3,809.8
Rheumatic heart	19.5	18.7	19.2	21.5	17.4	25.8	33.3	28.1	28.8	28.4
Hypertensive heart [2]	180.3	154.3	143.0	154.9	162.8	250.8	212.1	216.3	223.2	232.7

[1] Includes persons under 25 years old, not shown separately.   [2] With or without renal disease.

Source: U.S. National Center for Health Statistics, *Vital Statistics of the United States*, annual; and unpublished data. <http://www.cdc.gov/nchswww/default.htm>

No. 144. Death Rates From Cancer, by Sex and Age: 1980 to 1996

[Deaths per 100,000 population in the specified age groups. See headnote, Table 143]

Age at death and selected type of cancer	Male 1980	Male 1990	Male 1994	Male 1995	Male 1996	Female 1980	Female 1990	Female 1994	Female 1995	Female 1996
Total [1]	205.3	221.3	220.7	219.5	(NA)	163.6	186.0	190.5	191.0	(NA)
25 to 34 years	13.4	12.6	(NA)	11.7	(NA)	14.0	12.6	(NA)	12.2	(NA)
35 to 44 years	44.0	38.5	(NA)	36.5	(NA)	53.1	48.1	(NA)	44.0	(NA)
45 to 54 years	188.7	162.5	(NA)	143.7	(NA)	171.8	155.5	(NA)	140.7	(NA)
55 to 64 years	520.8	532.9	(NA)	480.5	(NA)	361.7	375.2	(NA)	357.5	(NA)
65 to 74 years	1,093.2	1,122.2	(NA)	1,089.9	(NA)	607.1	677.4	(NA)	690.7	(NA)
75 to 84 years	1,790.5	1,914.4	(NA)	1,842.3	(NA)	903.1	1,010.3	(NA)	1,061.5	(NA)
85 years old and over	2,369.5	2,739.9	(NA)	2,837.3	(NA)	1,255.7	1,372.1	(NA)	1,429.1	(NA)
Persons, 35 to 44 years old:										
Respiratory, intrathoracic	12.6	9.1	8.0	7.8	6.5	6.8	5.4	4.9	5.1	5.3
Digestive organs, peritoneum	9.5	8.9	8.9	8.7	8.7	6.5	5.5	5.4	5.5	5.5
Breast	-	(B)	(B)	(B)	(NA)	17.9	17.8	15.2	15.0	14.2
Genital organs	0.7	0.6	0.6	0.7	0.6	8.3	7.3	6.6	6.7	6.5
Lymphatic and hematopoietic tissues, excl. leukemia	4.3	4.5	(NA)	36.5	(NA)	2.4	2.1	(NA)	44.0	(NA)
Urinary organs	1.4	1.5	1.3	1.5	1.4	0.6	0.6	0.7	0.7	0.6
Lip, oral cavity, and pharynx	1.8	1.3	1.1	1.1	1.1	0.5	0.3	0.4	0.4	0.4
Leukemia	3.2	2.5	2.2	2.4	2.1	2.6	2.2	1.8	1.7	1.7
Persons, 45 to 54 years old:										
Respiratory, intrathoracic	79.8	63.0	51.9	48.5	48.5	34.8	35.3	30.4	30.1	29.0
Digestive organs, peritoneum	44.3	40.4	38.7	36.6	36.6	27.8	23.3	21.3	21.0	20.2
Breast	0.2	0.3	0.2	0.3	(NA)	48.1	45.4	41.6	41.4	38.8
Genital organs	3.4	2.9	2.9	2.6	2.9	24.1	19.4	18.1	17.6	16.4
Lymphatic and hematopoietic tissues, excl. leukemia	10.2	10.9	(NA)	143.7	(NA)	6.6	6.0	(NA)	140.7	(NA)
Urinary organs	7.4	7.2	7.1	7.1	6.9	3.3	2.9	2.8	2.8	2.8
Lip, oral cavity, and pharynx	8.2	5.9	5.6	5.3	4.9	2.6	1.6	1.3	1.3	1.2
Leukemia	6.2	5.6	5.2	4.8	5.1	4.4	4.1	3.8	3.5	3.5
Persons, 55 to 64 years old:										
Respiratory, intrathoracic	223.8	232.6	206.8	190.7	190.7	74.5	107.6	105.3	104.8	102.2
Digestive organs, peritoneum	129.3	124.0	120.0	117.1	117.1	79.1	69.3	66.4	66.0	63.6
Breast	0.7	0.6	0.7	0.7	(NA)	80.5	78.6	69.8	69.8	67.4
Genital organs	23.5	27.9	24.0	23.6	22.2	46.8	40.1	39.0	37.2	37.1
Lymphatic and hematopoietic tissues, excl. leukemia	24.4	27.2	(NA)	480.5	(NA)	16.8	16.7	(NA)	357.5	(NA)
Urinary organs	22.9	23.5	22.5	21.9	22.1	8.9	8.8	8.8	9.1	8.7
Lip, oral cavity, and pharynx	17.9	16.2	13.5	12.7	12.8	6.0	4.7	4.0	4.3	4.1
Leukemia	14.7	14.7	14.8	14.5	14.0	9.3	8.8	8.5	8.7	8.5
Persons, 65 to 74 years old:										
Respiratory, intrathoracic	422.0	447.3	434.5	424.6	424.6	106.1	181.7	203.6	205.0	209.0
Digestive organs, peritoneum	284.1	267.4	260.8	255.0	255.0	173.6	153.0	149.7	149.9	147.1
Breast	1.1	1.1	1.4	1.1	(NA)	101.1	111.7	105.6	103.3	99.1
Genital organs	107.6	123.5	115.1	110.0	107.8	73.6	71.0	69.2	66.7	65.9
Lymphatic and hematopoietic tissues, excl. leukemia	48.1	56.8	(NA)	1,089.9	(NA)	34.4	39.5	(NA)	690.7	(NA)
Urinary organs	56.9	50.7	52.1	50.9	52.7	19.7	19.8	20.9	19.8	20.0
Lip, oral cavity, and pharynx	25.4	21.5	18.0	19.3	19.1	8.8	8.3	7.9	7.5	6.6
Leukemia	35.3	36.0	35.6	37.2	37.1	18.7	18.8	19.1	18.9	20.0
Persons, 75 to 84 years old:										
Respiratory, intrathoracic	511.5	594.4	576.7	566.9	566.9	98.0	194.5	236.4	245.1	251.1
Digestive organs, peritoneum	496.6	468.0	437.2	418.7	418.7	326.3	293.3	284.0	283.4	280.5
Breast	2.1	1.6	2.0	2.4	(NA)	126.4	146.3	145.9	142.0	139.8
Genital organs	315.4	358.5	350.7	333.9	321.7	95.7	95.3	96.7	96.3	95.0
Lymphatic and hematopoietic tissues, excl. leukemia	80.0	104.5	(NA)	1,842.3	(NA)	57.8	71.2	(NA)	1,061.5	(NA)
Urinary organs	112.4	107.5	105.3	105.4	101.0	37.4	38.5	39.9	39.3	39.9
Lip, oral cavity, and pharynx	31.4	26.1	23.5	23.2	21.1	10.9	11.6	10.6	10.3	10.5
Leukemia	71.5	71.9	71.5	75.1	71.4	38.5	38.8	38.3	39.9	40.8
Persons, 85 years old and over:										
Respiratory, intrathoracic	386.3	538.0	556.1	543.2	543.2	96.3	142.8	171.8	187.5	190.6
Digestive organs, peritoneum	705.8	699.5	661.4	644.0	644.0	504.3	497.6	477.2	478.8	478.3
Breast	2.6	2.4	3.9	4.2	(NA)	169.3	196.8	197.5	203.7	204.9
Genital organs	612.3	750.0	822.5	821.5	775.2	115.9	115.6	115.3	120.5	117.5
Lymphatic and hematopoietic tissues, excl. leukemia	93.2	140.5	(NA)	2,837.3	(NA)	63.0	90.0	(NA)	1,429.1	(NA)
Urinary organs	177.0	186.3	189.6	192.2	192.8	63.8	68.5	67.3	68.4	67.4
Lip, oral cavity, and pharynx	40.2	37.4	30.0	34.1	29.6	16.0	17.5	16.0	17.7	16.3
Leukemia	117.1	116.0	118.5	123.0	120.7	61.1	65.0	68.1	65.5	64.6

- Represents zero.   B Base figure too small to meet statistical standards for reliability.   NA Not available.   [1] Includes persons under 25 years of age and malignant neoplasms of other and unspecified sites, not shown separately.

Source: U.S. National Center for Health Statistics, *Vital Statistics of the United States,* annual; and unpublished data.

U.S. Census Bureau, Statistical Abstract of the United States: 1999

No. 145. Death Rates From Accidents and Violence, by Race and Sex: 1990 to 1996

[Rates are per 100,000 population. Excludes deaths of nonresidents of the United States. Deaths classified according to the ninth revision of the *International Classification of Diseases*. See text, this section. See Appendix III]

Cause of death	White						Black					
	Male			Female			Male			Female		
	1990	1995	1996	1990	1995	1996	1990	1995	1996	1990	1995	1996
Total [1]	81.2	(NA)	(NA)	32.1	(NA)	(NA)	142.0	(NA)	(NA)	38.6	(NA)	(NA)
Motor vehicle accidents	26.1	22.6	22.4	11.4	10.8	10.7	28.1	24.6	24.3	9.4	9.0	9.5
All other accidents	23.6	24.7	25.0	12.4	13.5	14.4	32.7	31.6	30.1	13.4	13.5	13.3
Suicide	22.0	21.4	19.3	5.3	(NA)	4.8	12.0	(NA)	11.4	2.3	(NA)	2.0
Homicide	9.0	(NA)	12.5	2.8	(NA)	2.5	69.2	56.3	51.5	13.5	(NA)	10.2

NA Not available. [1] Includes persons under 15 years old, not shown separately.

No. 146. Deaths and Death Rates From Accidents, by Type: 1980 to 1996

[See headnote, Table 145 and Appendix III]

Type of accident	Deaths (number)					Rate per 100,000 population				
	1980	1990	1994	1995	1996	1980	1990	1994	1995	1996
Total	105,718	91,983	(NA)	(NA)	(NA)	46.7	37.0	(NA)	(NA)	(NA)
Motor vehicle accidents	53,172	46,814	42,524	43,363	43,649	23.5	18.8	16.3	16.5	16.5
Traffic	51,930	45,827	41,507	42,331	42,522	22.9	18.4	15.9	16.1	16.0
Nontraffic	1,242	987	1,017	1,032	1,127	0.5	0.4	0.4	0.4	0.4
Water-transport accidents	1,429	923	723	762	675	0.6	0.4	0.3	0.3	0.3
Air and space transport accidents ..	1,494	941	1,075	851	1,061	0.7	0.4	0.4	0.3	0.4
Railway accidents	632	663	635	569	565	0.3	0.3	0.2	0.2	0.2
Accidental falls	13,294	12,313	13,450	13,986	14,986	5.9	5.0	5.2	5.3	5.6
Accidental drowning...........	6,043	3,979	3,404	3,790	3,488	2.7	1.6	1.3	1.4	1.3
Accidents caused by—										
Fires and flames	5,822	4,175	3,986	3,761	3,741	2.6	1.7	1.5	1.4	1.4
Firearms, unspecified and other ..	1,667	1,175	1,123	992	947	0.7	0.5	0.4	0.4	0.4
Handguns.	288	241	233	233	187	0.1	0.1	0.1	0.1	0.1
Electric current	1,095	670	561	559	482	0.5	0.3	0.2	0.2	0.2
Accidental poisoning by—										
Drugs and medicines	2,492	4,506	7,828	8,000	8,431	1.1	1.8	3.0	3.0	3.2
Other solid and liquid substances .	597	549	481	461	441	0.3	0.2	0.2	0.2	0.2
Gases and vapors	1,242	748	685	611	638	0.5	0.3	0.3	0.2	0.2
Complications due to medical procedures.	2,282	2,669	2,616	2,712	2,919	1.0	1.1	1.0	1.0	1.1
Inhalation and ingestion of objects ..	3,249	3,303	3,065	3,185	3,206	1.4	1.3	1.2	1.2	1.2

NA Not available.

Source of Tables 145-146: U.S. National Center for Health Statistics, *Vital Statistics of the United States*, annual; and unpublished data.

No. 147. Death Rates for Injury by Firearms, Sex, Race, and Age: 1996

[Death rate per 100,000 population. Deaths classified according to the ninth revision of the *International Classification of Diseases*]

Item	5-14 yrs old	15-24 yrs old	25-34 yrs old	35-44 yrs old	45-54 yrs old	55-64 yrs old	65-74 yrs old	75-84 yrs old	85 yrs and over
MALE									
Firearms: White	2.0	26.9	23.6	20.6	19.9	20.6	25.8	38.4	50.6
Black	4.5	131.6	88.6	44.7	30.2	21.7	19.6	18.6	(B)
Accidents: White............	0.5	1.7	0.8	0.6	0.5	0.6	0.6	0.6	(B)
Black............	1.0	4.0	1.1	0.9	(B)	(B)	(B)	(B)	(B)
Suicide: White	0.7	13.3	14.1	14.4	15.6	17.1	23.5	36.6	48.7
Black.............	(B)	12.8	10.9	8.4	6.9	8.2	11.1	10.9	(B)
Homicide: White	0.7	11.4	8.5	5.3	3.6	2.8	1.4	0.9	(B)
Black.............	2.9	112.6	75.6	35.0	22.5	12.4	7.8	7.7	(B)
FEMALE									
Firearms: White	0.6	3.8	4.3	4.8	4.5	3.2	2.8	2.7	1.7
Black	1.4	12.0	11.3	8.3	4.9	2.8	3.5	(B)	(B)
Accidents: White............	(B)	0.1	0.1	(B)	(B)	(B)	(B)	(B)	(B)
Black............	(B)	(B)	(B)	(B)	(B)	(B)	(B)	(B)	0.8
Suicide: White	0.2	1.8	2.3	2.9	3.0	2.4	2.1	1.8	(B)
Black.............	(B)	1.2	1.3	1.3	1.2	(B)	(B)	(B)	(B)
Homicide: White	0.4	1.8	1.8	1.8	1.3	0.7	0.6	0.8	(B)
Black.............	1.2	10.3	9.8	6.8	3.5	1.8	2.1	(B)	(B)

B Does not meet standard of reliability or precision.

Source: U.S. National Center for Health Statistics, *Advance Data From Vital and Health Statistics*, No. 231.

No. 148. Poisoning Deaths by Cause: 1980 to 1996

[Represents poisoning deaths of 50 or more. ICD-9 = International Classification of Diseases, Ninth Revision. N.e.c. = Not elsewhere classified]

Item	1980	1985	1990	1991	1992	1993	1994	1995	1996
Total poisoning deaths [1]	12,075	13,173	14,103	14,930	16,026	17,658	18,334	18,549	19,177
Drugs, total [1]	6,313	7,606	9,344	10,292	11,611	13,206	13,943	14,213	14,872
Unintentional poisoning by drugs, medicaments and biologicals	[1]2,492	3,612	4,506	5,215	5,951	7,382	7,828	8,000	8,431
Analgesics, antipyretics, and antirheumatics [1]	636	1,209	1,278	1,238	1,657	2,094	2,148	2,508	2,490
Opiates and related narcotics	322	867	931	872	1,279	1,728	1,732	2,118	2,075
Salicylates (incl. aspirin)	75	58	44	63	56	47	37	38	47
Aromatic analgesics, n.e.c. (incl. acetaminophen)	21	41	65	65	69	88	90	81	80
Other nonnarcotic analgesics	117	78	88	87	79	77	96	86	102
Barbiturates	155	42	22	26	21	17	15	10	19
Other sedatives and hypnotics	159	32	26	14	11	17	10	12	15
Tranquilizers [1]	110	102	67	76	65	64	63	72	82
Benzodiazepine-based	53	57	38	41	38	44	41	46	53
Other psychotropic agents [1]	161	165	217	193	269	315	355	373	344
Antidepressants	141	128	142	141	141	152	123	150	143
Psychostimulants (amphetamines, caffeine)	18	32	71	50	128	162	228	219	197
Drugs acting on central and autonomic nervous system	159	448	821	1,239	1,113	1,183	1,393	1,156	1,411
Local anaesthetics (cocaine, lidocaine, procaine, and tetracaine)	109	390	743	1,147	1,031	1,095	1,311	1,088	1,333
Antibiotics	50	50	51	57	55	43	44	26	47
Other drugs [1]	1,155	1,560	2,017	2,362	2,755	3,640	3,789	3,835	4,017
Primarily systemic agents	24	26	30	36	44	60	51	41	42
Agents primarily affecting cardiovascular system	190	225	257	282	218	213	244	226	227
Water, mineral, and uric acid metabolism drugs	13	68	112	85	75	74	72	43	44
Other	404	550	796	1,033	1,328	1,902	1,981	1,986	2,012
Unspecified	462	596	746	851	1,021	1,318	1,359	1,478	1,602
Suicide by drugs [1]	2,761	2,668	2,920	3,095	3,215	2,975	3,022	2,874	2,896
Analgesics, antipyretics, and antirheumatics	310	324	374	357	405	407	445	417	406
Barbiturates	498	220	137	158	154	115	133	102	98
Other sedatives and hypnotics	99	51	50	45	31	21	34	28	34
Tranquilizers and other psychotropic agents	754	856	939	988	1,000	913	888	757	740
Other specified drugs and medicaments	562	592	765	803	827	735	807	852	853
Unspecified drug or medicament	538	625	655	744	798	784	715	718	765
Undetermined intent-poisoning by drug [1]	826	778	955	1,049	1,401	1,742	1,834	1,878	1,864
Analgesics, antipyretics, and antirheumatics	202	229	247	271	491	689	687	750	737
Barbiturates	65	34	10	14	13	7	10	11	6
Tranquilizers and other psychotropic agents	140	102	161	147	159	168	180	161	166
Other specified drugs and medicaments	174	186	324	410	478	618	657	669	661
Unspecified drug or medicament	217	216	206	207	252	257	291	281	288
Nondependent abuse of drugs [1]	219	524	931	900	1,007	1,073	1,229	1,434	1,645
Tobacco	46	119	239	193	230	267	297	310	372
Morphine type	1	11	13	20	42	42	77	148	155
Cocaine type	1	18	85	153	146	176	238	300	304
Other, mixed or unspecified	167	370	587	531	574	573	589	646	781
Other solid and liquid substances [1]	1,833	1,557	1,612	1,560	1,589	1,575	1,570	1,505	1,529
Unintentional poisoning by other solid and liquid substances	[1]597	479	549	483	498	495	481	461	441
Alcohol, n.e.c. [1]	385	305	369	331	332	337	323	318	308
Other and unspecified ethyl alcohol and its products	182	171	168	151	168	146	152	143	140
Unspecified	163	98	144	110	117	140	125	124	131
Petroleum products, other solvents and their vapours, n.e.c	[1]78	75	80	75	63	49	54	57	50
Other solvents	51	54	66	55	48	39	43	44	43
Other and unspecified solid and liquid substances [1]	64	51	51	46	60	54	53	50	42
Suicide by other solid/liquid substances	[1]274	269	223	219	223	204	207	178	177
Agricultural & horticultural chemical & pharmaceutical preparations other than plant foods & fertilizers	[1]57	36	30	46	32	28	22	21	18
Corrosive and caustic substances	49	56	33	17	23	24	25	31	23
Other and unspecified solid and liquid substances	159	170	148	153	163	147	159	124	136
Undetermined intent-poisoning by other solids and liquids [1]	67	54	51	48	75	54	39	53	46
Other and unspecified solid and liquid substances	55	47	46	43	63	50	32	45	39
Nondependent abuse of alcohol	889	750	784	803	788	819	838	808	849
Gases and vapors, total [1]	3,929	4,010	3,147	3,078	2,826	2,877	2,821	2,831	2,776
Unintentional poisoning by gases and vapors [1]	1,242	1,079	748	736	633	660	685	611	638
Gas distributed by pipeline	61	49	33	20	21	14	24	27	23
Other utility gas and other carbon monoxide	[1]1,006	880	582	594	504	535	553	506	502
Liquified petroleum gas distributed in mobile containers	23	34	54	48	47	53	59	57	57
Motor vehicle exhaust gas	611	488	293	278	223	245	246	234	219
Carbon monoxide from incomplete combustion of other domestic fuels	106	126	85	104	69	77	59	44	52
Unspecified carbon monoxide	219	202	123	118	141	127	153	140	146
Other gases and vapours	175	150	133	122	108	111	108	78	113
Other specified gases and vapors	151	125	95	84	76	72	84	60	87
Suicide by gases in domestic use and other gases and vapors [1]	2,418	2,767	2,281	2,230	2,057	2,092	2,044	2,095	2,007
Motor vehicle exhaust gas	2,380	2,729	2,253	2,201	2,023	2,067	2,026	2,074	1,981
Other carbon monoxide	1,998	2,308	1,877	1,833	1,706	1,670	1,618	1,659	1,508
Undetermined intent-poisoning by other gases [1]	361	396	348	346	295	373	393	391	454
Motor vehicle exhaust gas	[1]246	151	110	97	112	103	79	107	116
Other carbon monoxide	177	93	70	54	69	62	49	67	61
	61	48	23	35	37	34	22	28	44

[1] Includes other causes not shown separately.

Source: U.S. Public Health Service; Compressed Mortality File, 1979-1996. National Center for Health Statistics, *Public Health*, Volume 113 Number 3, May/June 1998.

Sex, age, and method	1980	1985	1988	1989	1990	1991	1992	1993	1994	1995	1996
All races, both sexes	26,869	29,453	30,407	30,232	30,906	30,810	30,484	31,102	31,142	31,284	30,903
5 to 9 years old	3	3	6	4	6	1	10	6	4	7	4
10 to 14 years old	139	275	237	236	258	265	304	315	318	330	298
15 to 19 years old	1,797	1,849	2,059	2,009	1,979	1,899	1,847	1,884	1,948	1,890	1,817
20 to 24 years old	3,442	3,272	2,870	2,861	2,890	2,852	2,846	2,965	3,008	2,894	2,541
25 to 29 years old	3,228	3,364	3,355	3,299	3,192	3,086	2,864	2,979	3,026	2,880	2,816
30 to 34 years old	2,692	3,012	3,355	3,266	3,358	3,428	3,308	3,328	3,328	3,412	3,045
35 to 39 years old	2,150	2,528	2,909	2,937	3,098	3,089	3,177	3,248	3,397	3,332	3,476
40 to 44 years old	1,785	2,098	2,296	2,394	2,619	2,678	2,832	2,922	2,978	3,135	3,265
White, both sexes	24,829	27,087	27,790	27,424	28,086	27,996	27,611	28,035	27,976	28,187	27,856
5 to 9 years old	2	-	3	6	2	4	-	6	4	2	4
10 to 14 years old	130	243	195	196	219	228	265	258	269	284	244
15 to 19 years old	1,635	1,643	1,819	1,743	1,701	1,628	1,531	1,594	1,588	1,587	1,522
20 to 24 years old	3,057	2,866	2,489	2,399	2,481	2,450	2,404	2,443	2,490	2,416	2,117
25 to 29 years old	2,876	2,985	2,940	2,847	2,731	2,629	2,464	2,504	2,557	2,443	2,369
30 to 34 years old	2,391	2,674	2,904	2,850	2,952	3,045	2,895	2,940	2,933	2,977	2,640
35 to 39 years old	1,979	2,316	2,626	2,628	2,779	2,799	2,845	2,902	3,003	2,985	3,123
40 to 44 years old	1,639	1,948	2,124	2,189	2,404	2,470	2,582	2,665	2,719	2,857	2,979
Black, both sexes	1,607	1,795	2,022	2,153	2,111	2,097	2,143	2,259	2,271	2,231	(NA)
5 to 9 years old	1	-	-	2	2	1	1	2	-	1	-
10 to 14 years old	9	22	29	32	29	31	33	39	39	30	36
15 to 19 years old	108	135	167	175	183	183	223	213	263	229	195
20 to 24 years old	307	289	298	350	282	296	313	395	366	323	328
25 to 29 years old	278	294	325	340	357	344	303	353	325	321	301
30 to 34 years old	245	262	360	349	318	301	331	296	282	312	289
35 to 39 years old	133	175	226	244	252	237	257	265	296	266	267
40 to 44 years old	128	115	131	168	171	153	194	183	201	218	209
METHOD TOTAL, BOTH SEXES											
Drugs, medicaments, and biologicals	2,761	2,668	2,910	2,988	2,920	3,095	3,215	2,975	3,022	2,874	2,896
Other solid or liquid substances	274	269	223	227	223	219	223	204	207	178	177
Gases and vapors	2,418	2,767	2,692	2,228	2,281	2,230	2,057	2,092	2,044	2,095	2,007
Suicide by hanging[1]	3,691	4,264	4,375	4,484	4,444	4,561	4,678	4,627	4,745	5,217	5,330
Handgun	13,287	14,382	14,972	15,058	15,421	14,907	14,714	15,354	15,059	14,803	14,491
Other and unspecified firearms	2,109	2,981	3,197	3,120	3,464	3,619	3,455	3,586	3,706	3,700	3,675
All other	2,329	2,122	2,038	2,127	2,153	2,179	2,142	2,264	2,359	2,417	2,327
METHOD, WHITE											
Drugs, medicaments, and biologicals	2,620	2,503	2,694	2,774	2,703	2,894	2,979	2,742	2,756	2,643	2,690
Other solid or liquid substances	246	234	200	195	190	195	194	180	171	153	160
Gases and vapors	2,375	2,713	2,623	2,154	2,227	2,172	1,994	2,017	1,987	2,018	1,946
Suicide by hanging[1]	3,288	3,712	3,807	3,853	3,812	3,945	4,050	3,943	4,063	4,493	4,584
Handgun	12,346	13,318	13,763	13,767	14,126	13,626	13,412	13,967	13,603	13,468	13,130
Other and unspecified firearms	1,940	2,802	2,962	2,904	3,218	3,348	3,194	3,304	3,404	3,392	3,393
All other	2,014	1,805	1,741	1,777	1,810	1,816	1,788	1,882	1,992	2,020	1,953
METHOD, BLACK											
Drugs, medicaments, and biologicals	106	120	167	164	159	144	160	164	188	157	134
Other solid or liquid substances	17	26	15	23	22	14	12	14	24	13	10
Gases and vapors	29	39	52	53	30	44	46	49	33	57	39
Hanging[1]	263	334	376	408	374	375	379	418	394	406	409
Handgun	795	886	1,006	1,070	1,085	1,062	1,096	1,160	1,192	1,091	1,120
Other and unspecified firearms	151	146	176	171	178	191	185	205	201	213	205
All other	246	244	230	264	263	267	265	249	239	294	247

- Represents or rounds to zero.   NA Not available.   [1] Includes strangulation and suffocation.
Source: U.S. National Center for Health Statistics, *Vital Statistics of the United States*, annual, and unpublished data.

No. 150. Homicide Rates by Race, Sex, and Age: 1995 and 1996

[Rate per 100,000 population]

Age	White				Black			
	Male		Female		Male		Female	
	1995	1996	1995	1996	1995	1996	1995	1996
Total[1]	7.8	7.0	2.7	2.5	56.3	51.5	11.1	10.2
Under 1 year	7.1	6.5	5.0	6.8	19.4	23.1	19.2	21.1
1-4 yrs.	2.1	1.9	1.8	1.7	8.7	6.9	6.8	7.6
5-9 yrs.	0.7	0.8	0.6	0.7	2.1	2.0	1.5	1.8
10-14 yrs.	2.0	1.5	1.0	0.9	8.2	6.0	3.0	3.1
15-19 yrs.	14.7	12.2	3.9	2.9	110.5	100.9	16.4	12.9
20-24 yrs.	18.2	15.9	4.2	3.6	155.5	148.7	17.2	16.5
25-29 yrs.	14.3	12.0	4.4	3.5	113.9	109.2	19.6	17.8
30-34 yrs.	11.7	11.0	4.1	3.5	83.8	70.8	20.6	17.4
35-39 yrs.	9.4	9.2	3.5	3.5	61.1	56.1	17.0	16.2
40-44 yrs.	9.0	7.5	3.3	2.8	50.3	47.3	11.8	11.4
45-49 yrs.	6.7	6.0	2.6	2.6	44.5	37.3	6.9	9.4
50-54 yrs.	5.9	5.6	2.4	2.2	32.1	32.5	6.0	3.8
55-59 yrs.	5.4	5.2	2.0	1.6	29.4	24.3	5.5	4.4
60-64 yrs.	4.6	4.4	1.4	1.5	24.5	20.6	4.3	4.4
65-69 yrs.	3.8	3.9	1.5	1.6	21.4	15.3	5.7	3.8
70-74 yrs.	2.4	2.8	2.2	1.6	21.7	14.7	(B)	5.0
75-79 yrs.	2.5	2.7	2.0	2.0	19.5	14.8	9.2	(B)
80-84 yrs.	2.6	3.2	2.6	2.0	(B)	20.2	(B)	(B)
85 yrs. and over	3.5	2.8	2.1	2.4	(B)	(B)	14.4	(B)

B Base figure too small to meet statistical standards for reliability of a derived figure.   [1] Includes persons under 15 years old, not shown separately.
Source: U.S. National Center for Health Statistics, *Vital Statistics of the United States*, annual.

No. 151. Deaths and Death Rates for Injury by Firearms, by Race and Sex: 1980 to 1996

[Age-adjusted rates per 100,000 population]

Year	All races			White			All other Total			Black		
	Both sexes	Male	Female	Both sexes	Male	Female	Both sexes	Male	Female	Both sexes	Male	Female
NUMBER												
1980	33,780	28,322	5,458	24,849	20,714	4,135	8,931	7,608	1,323	8,505	7,265	1,240
1985	31,566	26,382	5,184	24,507	20,389	4,118	7,059	5,993	1,066	6,565	5,584	981
1990	37,155	31,736	5,419	26,299	22,249	4,050	10,856	9,487	1,369	10,175	8,922	1,253
1993	39,595	33,711	5,884	26,948	22,608	4,268	12,647	11,031	1,616	11,763	10,310	1,453
1994	38,505	33,021	5,484	26,403	22,408	3,995	12,102	10,613	1,489	11,223	9,880	1,343
1995	35,957	30,724	5,233	25,438	21,510	3,928	10,519	9,214	1,305	9,643	8,494	1,149
1996	34,040	29,183	4,857	24,114	20,511	3,603	9,926	8,672	1,254	9,175	8,050	1,125
RATE [1]												
1980	14.8	25.3	4.8	12.4	21.1	4.2	29.1	53.0	8.1	33.5	61.8	9.1
1985	12.7	21.8	4.2	11.4	19.4	3.9	19.7	35.4	5.7	23.2	42.2	6.5
1990	14.6	25.4	4.2	11.9	20.5	3.7	26.9	48.9	6.5	33.4	61.5	7.8
1993	15.6	26.9	4.6	12.2	20.7	3.9	30.1	54.4	7.3	37.6	68.8	8.8
1994	15.1	26.2	4.2	11.9	20.4	3.6	28.4	51.6	6.6	35.5	65.1	8.0
1995	13.9	24.1	4.0	11.3	19.3	3.5	24.4	44.4	5.7	30.3	55.6	6.8
1996	12.8	22.5	3.6	11.0	19.0	3.2	21.8	39.9	5.3	27.4	50.6	6.4

[1] Age-adjusted death rate. For method of computation see source.

No. 152. Deaths and Death Rates for Drug-Induced Causes, by Race and Sex: 1980 to 1996

[Age-adjusted rates per 100,000 population]

Year	All races			White			All other Total			Black		
	Both sexes	Male	Female	Both sexes	Male	Female	Both sexes	Male	Female	Both sexes	Male	Female
NUMBER												
1980	6,900	3,771	3,129	5,814	3,088	2,726	1,086	683	403	1,006	648	358
1985	8,663	5,342	3,321	6,946	4,172	2,774	1,717	1,170	547	1,600	1,107	493
1990	9,463	5,897	3,566	7,603	4,646	2,957	1,860	1,251	609	1,703	1,155	548
1993	13,275	9,052	4,223	10,394	7,005	3,389	2,881	2,047	834	2,688	1,924	764
1994	13,923	9,491	4,432	10,895	7,339	3,556	3,028	2,152	876	2,780	1,995	785
1995	14,218	9,909	4,309	11,173	7,730	3,443	3,045	2,179	866	2,800	2,011	789
1996	14,843	10,093	4,750	11,903	8,061	3,842	2,940	2,032	908	2,682	1,876	806
RATE [1]												
1980	3.0	3.4	2.6	2.9	3.2	2.6	3.7	4.9	2.5	4.1	5.8	2.7
1985	3.5	4.5	2.6	3.3	4.0	2.5	4.9	7.2	2.9	5.9	8.9	3.3
1990	3.6	4.6	2.6	3.3	4.2	2.5	4.6	6.7	2.8	5.7	8.4	3.4
1993	4.8	6.8	3.0	4.5	6.2	2.8	6.6	10.0	3.6	8.3	13.0	4.4
1994	5.0	7.0	3.0	4.7	6.5	2.9	6.8	10.5	3.7	8.6	13.4	4.4
1995	5.1	7.3	3.0	4.8	6.8	2.8	6.7	10.4	3.5	8.5	13.3	4.4
1996	5.2	7.3	3.2	5.0	6.9	3.1	6.3	9.5	3.6	8.0	12.2	4.4

[1] Age-adjusted death rate. For method of computation see source.

No. 153. Deaths and Death Rates for Alcohol-Induced Causes, by Race and Sex: 1980 to 1996

[Age-adjusted rates per 100,000 population]

Year	All races			White			All other Total			Black		
	Both sexes	Male	Female	Both sexes	Male	Female	Both sexes	Male	Female	Both sexes	Male	Female
NUMBER												
1980	19,765	14,447	5,318	14,815	10,936	3,879	4,950	3,511	1,439	4,451	3,170	1,281
1985	17,741	13,216	4,525	13,216	9,922	3,294	4,525	3,294	1,231	4,114	3,030	1,084
1990	19,757	14,842	4,915	14,904	11,334	3,570	4,853	3,508	1,345	4,337	3,172	1,165
1993	19,557	14,873	4,684	15,293	11,716	3,577	4,264	3,157	1,107	3,663	2,759	904
1994	20,163	15,293	4,870	15,853	12,154	3,699	4,310	3,139	1,171	3,648	2,700	948
1995	20,231	15,443	4,788	15,991	12,338	3,653	4,240	3,105	1,135	3,538	2,614	924
1996	19,770	14,926	4,844	15,868	12,057	3,811	3,902	2,869	1,033	3,224	2,400	824
RATE [1]												
1980	8.4	13.0	4.3	6.9	10.8	3.5	18.8	29.5	10.0	20.4	32.4	10.6
1985	7.0	11.0	3.4	5.8	9.2	2.8	14.6	23.5	7.2	16.8	27.7	8.0
1990	7.2	11.4	3.4	6.2	9.9	2.8	13.6	22.0	6.8	16.1	26.6	7.7
1993	6.7	10.8	3.0	6.1	9.7	2.7	10.8	17.8	5.0	12.5	21.3	5.5
1994	6.8	10.9	3.1	6.2	9.9	2.7	10.6	17.3	5.2	12.2	20.4	5.6
1995	6.7	10.8	3.0	6.2	9.9	2.7	10.1	16.7	4.8	11.5	19.4	5.3
1996	6.4	10.2	3.0	6.0	9.5	2.8	9.0	14.7	4.3	10.2	17.2	4.7

[1] Age-adjusted death rate. For method of computation see source.
Source of Tables 151-153: U.S. National Center for Health Statistics, *National Vital Statistics Report (NVSR)* (formerly *Monthly Vital Statistics Report*).

Vital Statistics 109

No. 154. Deaths—Life Years Lost and Mortality Costs, by Age, Sex, and Cause: 1996

[2,314 represents 2,314,000. **Life years lost:** Number of years person would have lived in absence of death. **Mortality cost:** value of lifetime earnings lost by persons who die prematurely, discounted at 6 percent]

Characteristic	Number of deaths (1,000)	Life years lost [1] Total (1,000)	Per death	Mortality cost [2] Total (mil.)	Per death
Total, 1996 .	2,314	37,907	16	437,338	188,996
Under 5 yrs. old..	34	2,602	77	19,099	561,729
5 to 14 yrs. old..	8	570	71	6,070	758,701
15 to 24 yrs. old.	32	1,874	59	32,357	1,011,142
25 to 44 yrs. old.	147	6,269	43	147,031	1,000,212
45 to 64 yrs. old.	378	9,657	26	169,816	449,249
65 yrs old and over.	1,714	16,935	10	62,966	36,736
Heart disease ...	733	9,121	12	134,813	183,919
Cancer.	540	8,808	16	96,569	178,831
Cerebrovascular diseases.....	144	1,724	12	13,515	93,853
Accidents and adverse effects .	95	3,204	34	56,553	595,294
Other.	802	15,051	19	135,888	169,437
Male.....	1,163	20,365	18	298,915	257,020
Under 5 yrs. old.	19	1,409	74	11,875	625,000
5 to 14 yrs. old.	5	330	66	4,007	801,441
15 to 24 yrs. old	24	1,368	57	25,780	1,074,146
25 to 44 yrs. old.	100	4,127	41	110,686	1,106,859
45 to 64 yrs. old.	232	5,587	24	116,731	503,153
65 yrs. old and over........	782	7,544	10	29,836	38,153
Heart disease ...	360	4,837	13	86,238	239,550
Cancer.	282	4,258	15	54,413	192,953
Cerebrovascular diseases.....	57	699	12	7,346	128,876
Accidents and adverse effects .	61	2,169	36	44,277	725,853
Other........	403	8,402	21	106,641	264,618
Female....	1,151	17,542	15	138,423	120,264
Under 5 yrs. old..	15	1,194	80	7,224	481,587
5 to 14 yrs. old ..	3	240	80	2,062	687,469
15 to 24 yrs. old	8	506	63	6,577	822,128
25 to 44 yrs. old	47	2,142	46	36,345	773,303
45 to 64 yrs. old	146	4,070	28	53,085	363,595
65 yrs. old and over.........	932	9,391	10	33,130	35,547
Heart disease ...	373	4,285	12	48,575	130,228
Cancer.	258	4,549	18	42,156	163,397
Cerebrovascular diseases.....	87	1,024	12	6,169	70,907
Accidents and adverse effects .	33	1,036	31	12,276	371,997
Other........	399	6,648	17	29,247	73,302

[1] Based on life expectancy at year of death. [2] Cost estimates based on the person's age, sex, life expectancy at the time of death, labor force participation rates, annual earnings, value of homemaking services, and a 4 percent discount rate by which to convert to present worth the potential aggregate earnings lost over the years.

Source: Institute for Health and Aging, University of California, San Francisco, CA, unpublished data.

No. 155. Marriages and Divorces: 1970 to 1997

Year	Marriages [1] Number (1,000)	Total	Men, 15 yrs. old and over [2]	Women, 15 yrs. old and over [2]	Unmarried women 15 yrs. old and over	15 to 44 yrs. old	Divorces and annulments Number (1,000)	Total [2]	Married women, 15 yrs. old and over
1970	2,159	10.6	31.1	28.4	76.5	140.2	708	3.5	14.9
1975	2,153	10.0	27.9	25.6	66.9	118.5	1,036	4.8	20.3
1980	2,390	10.6	28.5	26.1	61.4	102.6	1,189	5.2	22.6
1984	2,477	10.5	28.0	25.8	59.5	99.0	1,169	5.0	21.5
1985	2,413	10.1	27.0	24.9	57.0	94.9	1,190	5.0	21.7
1986	2,407	10.0	26.6	24.5	56.2	93.9	1,178	4.9	21.2
1987	2,403	9.9	26.3	24.3	55.7	92.4	1,166	4.8	20.8
1988	2,396	9.8	26.0	24.0	54.6	91.0	1,167	4.8	20.7
1989	2,403	9.7	25.8	23.9	54.2	91.2	1,157	4.7	20.4
1990	2,443	9.8	26.0	24.1	54.5	91.3	1,182	4.7	20.9
1991	2,371	9.4	(NA)	(NA)	54.2	86.8	1,189	4.7	20.9
1992	2,362	9.3	(NA)	(NA)	53.3	88.2	1,215	4.8	21.2
1993	2,334	9.0	(NA)	(NA)	52.3	86.8	1,187	4.6	20.5
1994	2,362	9.1	(NA)	(NA)	51.5	84.0	1,191	4.6	20.5
1995	2,336	8.9	(NA)	(NA)	50.8	83.0	1,169	4.4	19.8
1996	2,344	8.8	(NA)	(NA)	49.7	81.5	1,150	4.3	19.5
1997	2,384	8.9	(NA)	(NA)	(NA)	(NA)	1,163	4.3	(NA)

NA Not available. [1] Beginning 1980, includes nonlicensed marriages registered in California. [2] Rates for 1981-88 are revised and may differ from rates published previously.

No. 156. Percent Distribution of Marriages, by Marriage Order: 1970 to 1988

[Excludes marriages with marriage order not stated. See headnote, Table 158]

Marriage order	1970	1980	1981	1982	1983	1984	1985	1986	1987	1988
Total	100.0	100.0	100.0	100.0	100.0	100.0	100.0	100.0	100.0	100.0
First marriage of bride and groom	68.6	56.2	54.7	54.8	54.4	54.4	54.3	53.9	53.9	54.1
First marriage of bride, remarriage of groom . . .	7.6	11.3	11.8	11.6	11.6	11.5	11.5	11.3	11.3	11.1
Remarriage of bride, first marriage of groom . . .	7.3	9.8	10.1	10.3	10.3	10.5	10.7	11.2	11.3	11.4
Remarriage of bride and groom	16.5	22.7	23.4	23.3	23.5	23.4	23.4	23.6	23.5	23.4

Source of Tables 155 and 156: U.S. National Center for Health Statistics, *Vital Statistics of the United States*, annual; *National Vital Statistics Report (NVSR)* (formerly *Monthly Vital Statistics Report*); and unpublished data.

No. 157. Percent Distribution of Marriages, by Age, Sex, and Previous Marital Status: 1980 and 1990

[Data cover marriage registration area; see text, this section. Based on a sample and subject to sampling variability; for details, see source]

Sex and previous marital status	Total	Under 20 years old	20-24 years old	25-29 years old	30-34 years old	35-44 years old	45-64 years old	65 years old and over
WOMEN								
All marriages:[1]								
1980	100.0	21.1	37.1	18.7	9.3	7.8	5.0	1.0
1990	100.0	10.6	29.3	24.6	14.2	13.9	6.1	1.0
First marriages:[2]								
1980	100.0	30.4	47.3	16.0	4.0	1.6	0.6	0.1
1990	100.0	16.6	40.8	27.2	10.1	4.5	0.7	0.1
Remarriages:[2][3]								
1980	100.0	1.7	15.3	24.4	20.6	20.8	14.3	2.9
1990	100.0	0.6	8.0	19.9	21.7	31.3	16.0	2.7
Previously divorced:[4]								
1980	100.0	1.7	16.7	26.7	22.5	21.6	10.0	0.6
1990	100.0	0.6	8.6	20.9	23.0	32.5	13.6	0.6
MEN								
All marriages:[1]								
1980	100.0	8.5	35.7	23.8	12.3	10.5	7.4	1.8
1990	100.0	4.3	24.7	27.1	16.6	16.4	9.1	1.9
First marriages:[2]								
1980	100.0	12.7	50.0	25.7	7.5	2.9	1.1	0.1
1990	100.0	6.6	36.0	34.3	14.8	7.1	1.1	0.1
Remarriages:[2][3]								
1980	100.0	0.2	7.2	20.1	21.9	25.6	20.0	5.1
1990	100.0	0.1	3.6	13.8	19.9	33.8	23.8	5.1
Previously divorced:[4]								
1980	100.0	0.2	7.7	21.7	24.1	27.7	17.3	1.4
1990	100.0	0.1	3.8	14.8	21.2	35.8	22.6	1.7

[1] Includes marriage order not stated. [2] Excludes data for Iowa. [3] Includes remarriages of previously widowed. [4] Excludes remarriages in Michigan, Ohio, and South Carolina.

No. 158. Marriage Rates and Median Age of Bride and Groom, by Previous Marital Status: 1970 to 1990

[Data cover marriage registration area; see text, this section. Figures for previously divorced and previously widowed exclude data for Michigan and Ohio for all years, for South Carolina beginning 1975, and for the District of Columbia for 1970. Based on a sample and subject to sampling variability; for details, see source. For definition of median, see Guide to Tabular Presentation]

Year	Marriage rates [1]						Median age at marriage (years)					
	Women			Men			Women			Men		
	Single	Divorced	Widowed	Single	Divorced	Widowed	First marriage	Remarriage Divorced	Remarriage Widowed	First marriage	Remarriage Divorced	Remarriage Widowed
1970	93.4	123.3	10.2	80.4	204.5	40.6	20.6	30.1	51.2	22.5	34.5	58.7
1975	75.9	117.2	8.3	61.5	189.8	40.4	20.8	30.2	52.4	22.7	33.6	59.4
1980	66.0	91.3	6.7	54.7	142.1	32.2	21.8	31.0	53.6	23.6	34.0	61.2
1985	61.5	81.8	5.7	50.1	121.6	27.7	23.0	32.8	54.6	24.8	36.1	62.7
1986	59.7	79.5	5.5	49.1	117.8	26.8	23.3	33.1	54.3	25.1	36.6	62.9
1987	58.9	80.7	5.4	48.8	115.7	26.1	23.6	33.3	53.9	25.3	36.7	62.8
1988	58.4	78.6	5.3	48.3	109.7	25.1	23.7	33.6	53.9	25.5	37.0	63.0
1989	58.7	75.6	5.1	48.2	105.6	24.5	23.9	34.0	53.8	25.5	37.0	63.0
1990	57.7	76.2	5.2	47.0	105.9	23.8	24.0	34.2	54.0	25.9	37.4	63.1

[1] Rate per 1,000 population 15 years old and over in specified group.

No. 159. Divorces and Annulments—Duration of Marriage, Age at Divorce and Children Involved: 1970 to 1990

[Data cover divorce-registration area; see text, this section. Based on a sample and subject to sampling variability; for details, see source. Median age computed on data by single years of age]

Duration of marriage, age at divorce, and children involved	1970	1975	1980	1983	1984	1985	1986	1987	1988	1989	1990
Median duration of marriage (years)	6.7	6.5	6.8	7.0	6.9	6.8	6.9	7.0	7.1	7.2	7.2
Median age at divorce:											
Men (years)	32.9	32.2	32.7	34.0	34.3	34.4	34.6	34.9	35.1	35.4	35.6
Women (years)	29.8	29.5	30.3	31.5	31.7	31.9	32.1	32.5	32.6	32.9	33.2
Estimated number of children involved in divorce (1,000)	870	1,123	1,174	1,091	1,081	1,091	1,064	1,038	1,044	1,063	1,075
Avg. number of children per decree	1.22	1.08	0.98	0.94	0.92	0.92	0.90	0.89	0.89	0.91	0.90
Rate per 1,000 children under 18 years of age	12.5	16.7	17.3	17.4	17.2	17.3	16.8	16.3	16.4	16.8	16.8

Source of Tables 157-159: U.S. National Center for Health Statistics, *Vital Statistics of the United States*, annual; and *National Vital Statistics Report (NVSR)* (formerly *Monthly Vital Statistics Report*); and unpublished data.

No. 160. First Marriage Dissolution and Years Until Remarriage for Women, by Race and Hispanic Origin: 1988

[11,577 represents 11,577,000. For women 15 to 44 years old. Based on 1988 National Survey of Family Growth; see Appendix III. Marriage dissolution includes death of spouse, separation because of marital discord, and divorce]

Item	Number (1,000)	Years until remarriage (cumulative percent)					
		All	1	2	3	4	5
ALL RACES [1]							
Year of dissolution of first marriage:							
All years	11,577	56.8	20.6	32.8	40.7	46.2	49.7
1980-84	3,504	47.5	16.3	28.1	36.4	[2]41.1	[2]45.4
1975-79	3,235	65.3	21.9	36.0	44.7	52.7	55.4
1970-74	1,887	83.2	24.9	38.6	47.9	56.4	61.2
1965-69	1,013	89.9	32.6	48.7	60.2	65.0	72.8
WHITE							
Year of dissolution of first marriage:							
All years	10,103	59.9	21.9	35.2	43.5	49.4	53.0
1980-84	3,030	51.4	18.2	31.1	40.3	[2]45.2	[2]49.8
1975-79	2,839	69.5	23.2	38.5	46.9	55.6	58.4
1970-74	1,622	87.5	24.9	39.8	49.8	59.3	64.3
1965-69	893	91.0	34.7	52.3	64.9	69.3	76.9
BLACK							
Year of dissolution of first marriage:							
All years	1,166	34.0	10.9	16.5	19.6	22.7	25.0
1980-84	380	19.7	[3]4.7	[3]10.6	[3]12.9	[2]14.8	[2]14.8
1975-79	301	32.3	[3]11.4	[3]15.6	18.5	22.2	24.9
1970-74	227	59.0	22.3	29.4	35.3	38.7	42.3
1965-69	98	81.2	[3]20.9	[3]27.3	[3]31.3	40.8	52.1
Hispanic, [4] all years	942	44.7	12.5	16.6	22.7	27.8	29.9

[1] Includes other races. [2] The percent having remarried is biased downward because the women had not completed the indicated number of years since dissolution of first marriage at the time of the survey. [3] Figure does not meet standard of reliability or precision. [4] Hispanic persons may be of any race.

Source: National Center for Health Statistics, *Advance Data From Vital and Health Statistics*, No. 194.

No. 161. Marriage Experience for Women, by Age and Race: 1980 and 1990

[In percent. As of June. Based on Current Population Survey; see text, Section 1, Population]

Martial status and age	All races		White		Black		Hispanic [1]	
	1980	1990	1980	1990	1980	1990	1980	1990
Ever married:								
20 to 24 years old	49.5	38.5	52.2	41.3	33.3	23.5	55.4	45.8
25 to 29 years old	78.6	69.0	81.0	73.2	62.3	45.0	80.2	69.6
30 to 34 years old	89.9	82.2	91.6	85.6	77.9	61.1	88.3	83.0
35 to 39 years old	94.3	89.4	95.3	91.4	87.4	74.9	91.2	88.9
40 to 44 years old	95.1	92.0	95.8	93.4	89.7	82.1	94.2	92.8
45 to 49 years old	95.9	94.4	96.4	95.1	92.5	89.7	94.4	91.7
50 to 54 years old	95.3	95.5	95.8	96.1	92.1	91.9	95.0	91.8
Divorced after first marriage:								
20 to 24 years old	14.2	12.5	14.7	12.8	10.5	9.6	9.4	6.8
25 to 29 years old	20.7	19.2	21.0	19.8	20.2	17.8	13.9	13.5
30 to 34 years old	26.2	28.1	25.8	28.6	31.4	26.6	21.1	19.9
35 to 39 years old	27.2	34.1	26.7	34.6	32.9	35.8	21.9	29.7
40 to 44 years old	26.1	35.8	25.5	35.2	33.7	45.1	19.7	26.6
45 to 49 years old	23.1	35.2	22.7	35.5	29.0	39.8	23.9	24.6
50 to 54 years old	21.8	29.5	21.0	28.5	29.0	39.2	22.5	22.9
Remarried after divorce:								
20 to 24 years old	45.5	38.1	47.0	39.3	(B)	(B)	(B)	(B)
25 to 29 years old	53.4	51.8	56.4	52.8	27.9	44.4	(B)	49.5
30 to 34 years old	60.9	59.6	63.3	61.4	42.0	42.0	58.3	45.9
35 to 39 years old	64.9	65.0	66.9	66.5	50.6	54.0	45.2	51.2
40 to 44 years old	67.4	67.1	68.6	69.5	58.4	50.3	(B)	53.9
45 to 49 years old	69.2	65.9	70.4	67.2	62.7	55.0	(B)	51.0
50 to 54 years old	72.0	63.0	72.6	65.4	72.7	50.2	(B)	62.2
Redivorced after remarriage:								
20 to 24 years old	8.5	13.1	(NA)	(NA)	(NA)	(NA)	(NA)	(NA)
25 to 29 years old	15.6	17.8	(NA)	(NA)	(NA)	(NA)	(NA)	(NA)
30 to 34 years old	19.1	22.7	(NA)	(NA)	(NA)	(NA)	(NA)	(NA)
35 to 39 years old	24.7	28.5	(NA)	(NA)	(NA)	(NA)	(NA)	(NA)
40 to 44 years old	28.4	30.6	(NA)	(NA)	(NA)	(NA)	(NA)	(NA)
45 to 49 years old	25.1	36.4	(NA)	(NA)	(NA)	(NA)	(NA)	(NA)
50 to 54 years old	29.0	34.5	(NA)	(NA)	(NA)	(NA)	(NA)	(NA)

B Base is less than 75,000. NA Not available. [1] Persons of Hispanic origin may be of any race.

Source: U.S. Census Bureau, *Current Population Reports*, P23-180.

No. 162. Marriages and Divorces—Number and Rate, by State: 1990 to 1997

[2,443.00 represents 2,443,000. By place of occurrence]

State	Marriages [1] Number (1,000) 1990	1995	1997	Marriages [1] Rate per 1,000 population [2] 1990	1995	1997	Divorces [3] Number (1,000) 1990	1995	1997	Divorces [3] Rate per 1,000 population [2] 1990	1995	1997
U.S.	2,443.0	2,336.0	2,383.7	9.8	8.9	8.9	1,182.0	1,169.0	870.6	4.7	4.4	3.3
Alabama	43.3	42.0	44.7	10.6	9.9	10.3	25.3	26.0	22.4	6.1	6.1	5.2
Alaska	5.7	5.5	5.0	10.2	9.0	8.2	2.9	3.0	2.9	5.5	5.0	4.8
Arizona	37.0	38.9	40.2	10.0	9.2	8.8	25.1	27.6	26.4	6.9	6.6	5.8
Arkansas	35.7	36.6	35.2	15.3	14.7	14.0	16.8	16.0	14.8	6.9	6.5	5.9
California [4]	236.7	199.6	237.7	7.9	6.3	7.4	128.0	(NA)	(NA)	4.3	(NA)	-
Colorado	31.5	34.3	33.7	9.8	9.2	8.7	18.4	(NA)	(NA)	5.5	(NA)	-
Connecticut	27.8	22.6	22.6	7.9	6.7	6.9	10.3	10.6	11.2	3.2	2.9	3.4
Delaware	5.6	5.4	5.4	8.4	7.5	7.3	3.0	3.7	2.9	4.4	5.1	4.0
Dist. of Columbia .	4.7	3.5	3.8	8.2	6.4	7.1	2.7	1.9	1.2	4.5	3.4	2.2
Florida	142.3	144.3	161.0	10.9	10.2	11.0	81.7	79.5	83.0	6.3	5.6	5.7
Georgia	64.4	61.5	61.9	10.3	8.5	8.3	35.7	37.2	36.3	5.5	5.2	4.8
Hawaii	18.1	18.8	19.7	16.4	15.8	16.5	5.2	5.5	4.8	4.6	4.6	4.0
Idaho.	15.0	15.5	15.2	13.9	13.3	12.5	6.6	6.8	7.1	6.5	5.8	5.9
Illinois	97.1	83.2	94.8	8.8	7.0	7.9	44.3	38.8	40.0	3.8	3.3	3.3
Indiana	54.3	50.4	31.9	9.6	8.7	5.4	(NA)	(NA)	(NA)	(NA)	(NA)	-
Iowa	24.8	22.0	22.1	9.0	7.8	7.7	11.1	10.5	9.8	3.9	3.7	3.4
Kansas	23.4	22.1	20.4	9.2	8.6	7.8	12.6	10.7	11.5	5.0	4.2	4.4
Kentucky	51.3	47.6	44.7	13.5	12.3	11.4	21.8	22.9	22.1	5.8	5.9	5.6
Louisiana	41.2	40.8	35.9	9.6	9.4	8.2	(NA)	(NA)	(NA)	(NA)	(NA)	-
Maine	11.8	10.8	(NA)	9.7	8.7	-	5.3	5.5	4.5	4.3	4.4	3.7
Maryland	46.1	42.8	41.6	9.7	8.5	8.2	16.1	15.0	15.1	3.4	3.0	3.0
Massachusetts . .	47.8	43.6	42.4	7.9	7.2	6.9	16.8	13.5	16.2	2.8	2.2	2.6
Michigan	76.1	71.0	66.8	8.2	7.4	6.8	40.2	39.9	38.6	4.3	4.2	3.9
Minnesota	33.7	32.8	32.2	7.7	7.1	6.9	15.4	15.8	15.4	3.5	3.4	3.3
Mississippi	24.3	21.5	22.0	9.4	8.0	8.0	14.4	13.1	13.8	5.5	4.8	5.1
Missouri.	49.3	44.9	43.6	9.6	8.4	8.1	26.4	26.8	25.3	5.1	5.0	4.7
Montana	7.0	6.6	6.6	8.6	7.6	7.5	4.1	4.2	4.0	5.1	4.8	4.6
Nebraska	12.5	12.1	12.5	8.0	7.4	7.5	6.5	6.3	6.2	4.0	3.8	3.8
Nevada	123.4	134.8	134.9	99.0	88.1	80.3	13.3	12.4	17.5	11.4	8.1	10.4
New Hampshire. .	10.6	9.6	10.1	9.5	8.4	8.6	5.3	4.9	5.6	4.7	4.2	4.8
New Jersey	58.0	52.4	56.4	7.6	6.7	7.0	23.6	24.3	25.5	3.0	3.1	3.2
New Mexico	13.2	15.1	16.0	8.8	9.0	9.3	7.7	11.3	9.6	4.9	6.7	5.6
New York	169.3	147.4	172.8	8.6	8.1	9.5	57.9	56.0	65.5	3.2	3.1	3.6
North Carolina. . .	52.1	61.6	64.5	7.8	8.6	8.7	34.0	37.0	36.8	5.1	5.1	5.0
North Dakota . . .	4.8	4.6	4.4	7.5	7.2	6.8	2.3	2.2	2.0	3.6	3.4	3.2
Ohio	95.8	90.1	86.2	9.0	8.1	7.7	51.0	48.7	47.2	4.7	4.4	4.2
Oklahoma	33.2	28.5	27.7	10.6	8.7	8.3	24.9	21.8	19.1	7.7	6.7	5.8
Oregon	25.2	25.7	25.8	8.9	8.2	7.9	15.9	15.0	14.8	5.5	4.8	4.6
Pennsylvania . . .	86.8	75.8	77.3	7.1	6.3	6.4	40.1	39.4	38.7	3.3	3.3	3.2
Rhode Island . . .	8.1	7.4	8.1	8.1	7.5	8.2	3.8	3.7	3.2	3.7	3.7	3.2
South Carolina . .	55.8	44.6	42.1	15.9	12.1	11.1	16.1	14.8	15.2	4.5	4.0	4.0
South Dakota . . .	7.7	7.3	6.9	11.1	10.0	9.3	2.6	2.9	2.7	3.7	4.0	3.7
Tennessee	66.6	82.3	76.5	13.9	15.7	14.2	32.3	33.1	29.5	6.5	6.3	5.5
Texas	182.8	188.5	183.0	10.5	10.1	9.4	94.0	99.9	(NA)	5.5	5.3	-
Utah	19.0	21.6	20.5	11.2	11.1	9.9	8.8	8.9	9.2	5.1	4.6	4.4
Vermont.	6.1	6.1	6.1	10.9	10.3	10.4	2.6	2.8	2.8	4.5	4.8	4.7
Virginia	71.3	67.9	67.4	11.4	10.3	10.0	27.3	28.9	31.3	4.4	4.4	4.6
Washington	48.6	42.0	42.3	9.5	7.7	7.5	28.8	29.7	29.0	5.9	5.5	5.2
West Virginia . . .	13.2	11.2	10.6	7.2	6.1	5.8	9.7	9.4	9.6	5.3	5.1	5.3
Wisconsin.	41.2	36.3	35.7	7.9	7.1	6.9	17.8	17.5	17.1	3.6	3.4	3.3
Wyoming	4.8	5.2	4.9	10.7	10.7	10.2	3.1	3.2	3.0	6.6	6.7	6.2

- Represents zero.   NA Not available.   [1] Data are counts of marriages performed, except as noted.   [2] Based on total population residing in area; population enumerated as of April 1 for 1980; estimated as of July 1 for all other years.   [3] Includes annulments.   [4] Marriage data include nonlicensed marriages registered.

Source: U.S. National Center for Health Statistics, Vital Statistics of the United States, annual; National Vital Statistics Reports (NVSR) (formerly Monthly Vital Statistical Report).

U.S. Census Bureau, Statistical Abstract of the United States: 1999

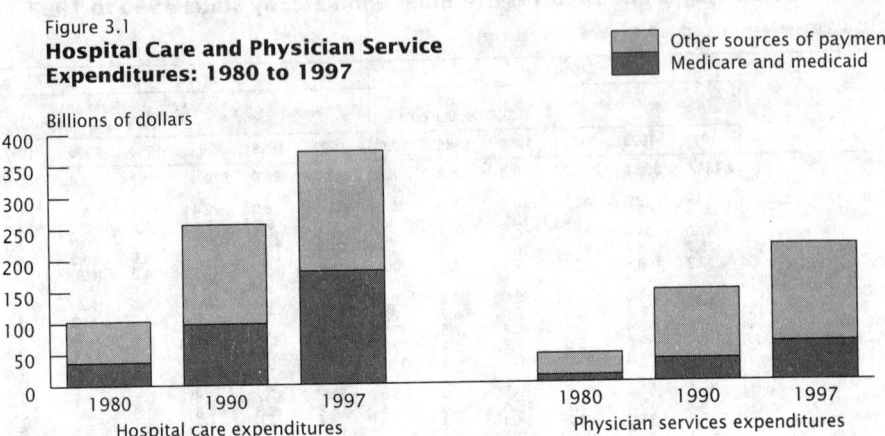

Figure 3.1
Hospital Care and Physician Service Expenditures: 1980 to 1997

Other sources of payment
Medicare and medicaid

Billions of dollars

Hospital care expenditures

1980   1990   1997

Physician services expenditures

1980   1990   1997

Source: Chart prepared by U.S. Census Bureau. For data, see Table 169.

Figure 3.2
Consumer Price Indexes—Medical Services and Commodities: 1990 to 1998

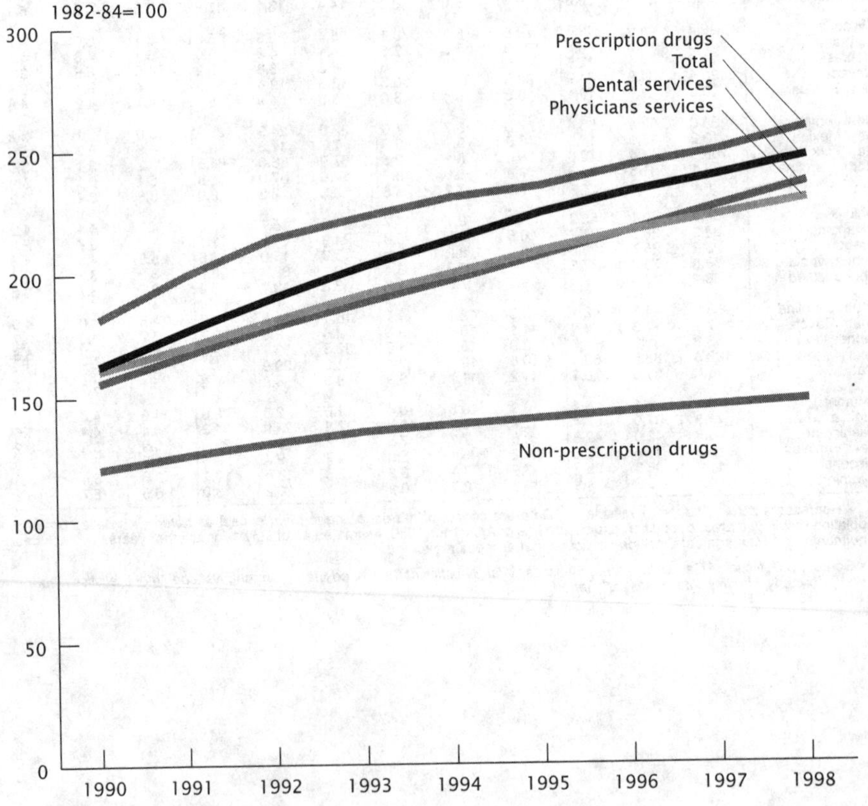

1982-84=100

Prescription drugs
Total
Dental services
Physicians services

Non-prescription drugs

1990   1991   1992   1993   1994   1995   1996   1997   1998

Source: Chart prepared by U.S. Census Bureau. For data, see Tables 183 and 778.

114 Health and Nutrition

Section 3

Health and Nutrition

This section presents statistics on health expenditures and insurance coverage, including medicare and medicaid, medical personnel, hospitals, nursing homes and other care facilities, incidence of acute and prevalence of chronic conditions, nutritional intake of the population, and food consumption. Summary statistics showing recent trends on health care and discussions of selected health issues are published annually by the U.S. National Center for Health Statistics (NCHS) in *Health, United States*. Data on national health expenditures, medical costs, and insurance coverage are compiled by the U.S. Health Care Financing Administration (HCFA) and appear in the quarterly *Health Care Financing Review* and in the annual *Medicare and Medicaid Statistical Supplement* to the *Health Care Financing Review*. Statistics on health insurance are also collected by NCHS and are published in Series 10 of *Vital and Health Statistics*. U.S. Census Bureau also publishes data on insurance coverage. Statistics on health facilities are collected by NCHS and are published in Series 14 of *Vital and Health Statistics*. Statistics on hospitals are published annually by the Health Forum, L.L.C., an American Hospital Association Company, in *Hospital Statistics*. Primary sources for data on nutrition are the quarterly *National Food Review* and the annual *Food Consumption, Prices, and Expenditures*, both issued by the U.S. Department of Agriculture. NCHS also conducts periodic surveys of nutrient levels in the population, including estimates of food and nutrient intake, overweight and obesity, hypercholesterolemia, hypertension, and clinical signs of malnutrition.

National health expenditures—HCFA compiles estimates of national health expenditures (NHE) to measure spending for health care in the United States. The NHE accounts are structured to show spending by type of expenditure (i.e., hospital care,

physician care, dental care, and other professional care; home health; drugs and other medical nondurables; vision products and other medical durables; nursing home care and other personal health expenditures; plus nonpersonal health expenditures for such items as public health, research, construction of medical facilities, administration, and the net cost of private health insurance) and by source of funding (e.g., private health insurance, out-of-pocket payments, and a range of public programs including medicare, medicaid, and those operated by the Department of Veterans Affairs (VA)).

Data used to estimate health expenditures come from existing sources which are tabulated for other purposes. The type of expenditure estimates rely upon statistics produced by such groups as the American Hospital Association, the Census Bureau, and the Department of Health and Human Services (HHS). Source of funding estimates are constructed using administrative and statistical records from the medicare and medicaid programs, the Department of Defense and VA medical programs, the Social Security Administration, Census Bureau's *Governmental Finances*, state and local governments, other HHS agencies, and other nongovernment sources. Detailed descriptions of sources and methods are published in an article titled "National health accounts: Lessons from the U.S. experience" in the summer 1992 edition of the *Health Care Financing Review*, Volume 13, Number 4. Revisions to the sources and methods, along with the most recent analysis of health care expenditure estimates, are published in the *Health Care Financing Review's* annual article on national health expenditures.

Medicare and medicaid—Since July 1966, the Federal medicare program has provided two coordinated plans for nearly all people age 65 and over: (1) A hospital

Health and Nutrition 115

insurance plan which covers hospital and related services and (2) a voluntary supplementary medical insurance plan, financed partially by monthly premiums paid by participants, which partly covers physicians' and related medical services. Such insurance also applies, since July 1973, to disabled beneficiaries of any age after 24 months of entitlement to cash benefits under the social security or railroad retirement programs and to persons with end stage renal disease.

Under medicaid, all states offer basic health services to certain very poor people: Individuals who are pregnant, aged, disabled or blind, and families with dependent children. Medicaid eligibility is automatic for almost all cash welfare recipients in these states. Thirty-nine states also extend medicaid to certain other persons who qualify, except for incomes above regular eligibility levels; those persons include those who have medical expenses which, when subtracted from their income, spend down to a state "medically needy" level or those who meet the higher "medically needy" income restrictions. Within Federal guidelines, each state determines its own medicaid eligibility criteria and the health services to be provided under medicaid. The cost of providing medicaid services is jointly shared by the Federal Government and the states.

Health resources—Hospital statistics based on data from the American Hospital Association's yearly survey are published annually in *Hospital Statistics* and cover all hospitals accepted for registration by the Association. To be accepted for registration, a hospital must meet certain requirements relating to number of beds, construction, equipment, medical and nursing staff, patient care, clinical records, surgical and obstetrical facilities, diagnostic and treatment facilities, laboratory services, etc. Data obtained from NCHS cover all U.S. hospitals which meet certain criteria for inclusion. The criteria are published in *Vital and Health Statistics* reports, Series 13. NCHS defines a hospital as a non-Federal short-term general or special facility with

six or more inpatient beds with an average stay of less than 60 days.

Statistics on the demographic characteristics of persons employed in the health occupations are compiled by the U.S. Bureau of Labor Statistics and reported in *Employment and Earnings* (monthly) (see Table 675, Section 13, Labor Force). Data based on surveys of health personnel and utilization of health facilities providing long-term care, ambulatory care, and hospital care are presented in NCHS Series 13 and Series 14, *Data on Health Resources Utilization* and *Data on Health Resources: Manpower and Facilities*. Statistics on patient visits to health care providers, as reported in health interviews, appear in NCHS Series 10, *National Health Interview Survey Data*.

The HCFA's *Health Care Financing Review* and its annual *Medicare and Medicaid Statistical Supplement* present data for hospitals and nursing homes as well as extended care facilities and home health agencies. These data are based on records of the medicare program and differ from those of other sources because they are limited to facilities meeting Federal eligibility standards for participation in medicare.

Data on patients in hospitals for the mentally ill and on mental health facilities are collected by the National Institute of Mental Health (NIMH) and appear in *Mental Health, U.S.*, the *Mental Health Statistics* reports, (series CN), and the Mental Health Statistical Note series.

Disability and illness—General health statistics, including morbidity, disability, injuries, preventive care, and findings from physiological testing are collected by NCHS in its National Health Interview Survey and its National Health and Nutrition Examination Surveys and appear in *Vital and Health Statistics*, Series 10 and 11, respectively. The Department of Labor compiles statistics on occupational injuries (see Section 13, Labor Force). Annual incidence data on notifiable diseases are compiled by the Public Health Service (PHS) at its Centers for Disease Control and Prevention in Atlanta, Georgia, and are published as a supplement to its *Morbidity and Mortality Weekly Report*. The list of diseases is revised annually and includes those which, by mutual agreement of the states and PHS, are communicable diseases of national importance.

Nutrition—Statistics on annual per capita consumption of food and its nutrient value are estimated by the U.S. Department of Agriculture and published quarterly in *National Food Review*. Historical data can be found in *Food Consumption, Prices, and Expenditures*, issued annually.

Statistics on food insufficiency and food and nutrient intake are collected by NCHS to estimate the diet of the Nation's population. NCHS also collects physical examination data to assess the population's nutritional status, including growth, overweight/obesity, nutritional deficiencies, and prevalence of nutrition-related conditions, such as hypertension, hypercholesterolemia, and diabetes.

Statistical reliability—For discussion of statistical collection, estimation, and sampling procedures and measures of reliability applicable to data from NCHS and HCFA, see Appendix III.

Figure 3.3
Per Capita Food Consumption, by Selected Products: 1980 to 1997

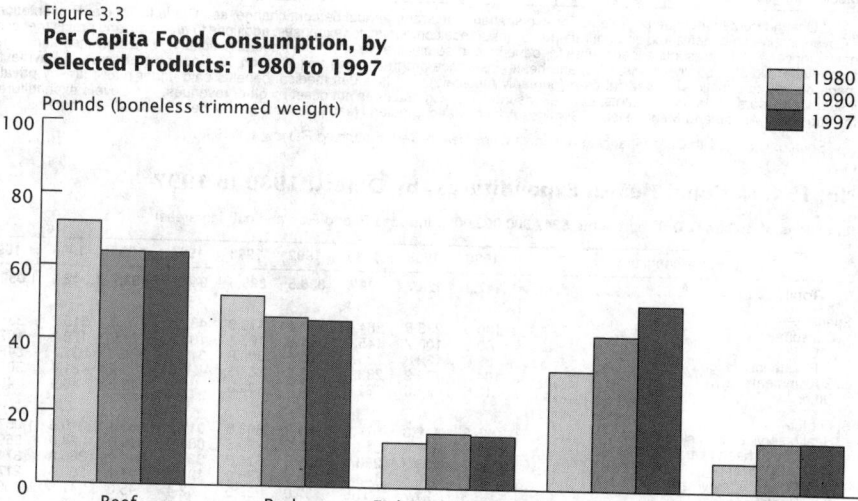

Source: Chart prepared by U.S. Census Bureau. For data, see Table 250.

No. 163. National Health Expenditures, by Type: 1980 to 1997

[In billions of dollars (247.3 represents $247,300,000,000), except percent. Includes Puerto Rico and outlying areas]

Type of expenditure	1980	1985	1990	1992	1993	1994	1995	1996	1997
Total	**247.3**	**428.7**	**699.4**	**836.5**	**898.5**	**947.7**	**993.7**	**1,042.5**	**1,092.4**
Annual percent change [1]	14.9	9.9	12.2	9.1	7.4	5.5	4.9	4.9	4.8
Private expenditures	**142.5**	**254.5**	**416.2**	**483.6**	**513.2**	**524.9**	**538.5**	**561.1**	**585.3**
Health services and supplies	138.0	248.0	405.9	472.5	501.3	513.1	527.6	549.5	571.9
Out-of-pocket payments	60.3	100.7	145.0	161.8	167.1	168.5	171.0	178.1	187.6
Insurance premiums [2]	69.8	132.8	239.6	285.5	306.8	315.1	324.3	337.1	348.0
Other	8.0	14.5	21.4	25.3	27.4	29.5	32.3	34.2	36.4
Medical research	0.3	0.5	1.0	1.2	1.2	1.3	1.3	1.4	1.5
Medical facilities construction	4.2	6.0	9.3	9.8	10.7	10.5	9.6	10.3	11.9
Public expenditures	**104.8**	**174.2**	**283.2**	**353.0**	**385.3**	**422.8**	**455.2**	**481.4**	**507.1**
Percent Federal of public	68.7	70.7	68.9	71.3	71.5	71.2	71.6	72.3	72.4
Health services and supplies	97.6	164.3	268.9	336.4	368.2	404.1	435.5	461.1	485.5
Medicare [3]	37.5	72.1	111.5	136.2	148.7	166.9	185.2	200.1	214.6
Public assistance medical payments [4]	28.0	44.4	80.4	111.9	126.8	140.0	151.6	159.7	165.2
Temporary disability insurance [5]	0.1	0.1	0.1	0.1	0.1	0.1	0.1	0.1	0.1
Workers' compensation (medical) [5]	5.1	8.0	16.1	19.0	18.5	18.6	17.1	15.2	14.1
Defense Dept. hospital, medical	4.4	7.5	11.6	13.0	13.3	13.2	13.4	13.3	13.4
Maternal, child health programs	0.9	1.3	1.9	2.1	2.2	2.3	2.4	2.4	2.5
Public health activities	6.7	11.6	19.6	23.4	25.3	28.2	30.4	34.0	38.5
Veterans' hospital, medical care	5.9	8.7	11.4	13.2	14.3	15.3	15.6	16.5	16.6
Medical vocational rehabilitation	0.3	0.4	0.6	0.6	0.6	0.7	0.7	0.7	0.8
State and local hospitals [6]	5.6	7.0	10.8	10.8	11.8	11.7	11.5	11.5	12.0
Other [7]	3.1	3.3	5.0	6.2	6.6	7.1	7.5	7.6	7.7
Medical research	5.2	7.3	11.3	13.0	13.3	14.6	15.4	15.7	16.5
Medical facilities construction	2.0	2.6	3.0	3.5	3.8	4.1	4.3	4.6	5.1

[1] Change from immediate prior year. For explanation of average annual percent change, see Guide to Tabular Presentation. [2] Covers insurance benefits and amount retained by insurance companies for expenses, additions to reserves, and profits (net cost of insurance). [3] Represents expenditures for benefits and administrative cost from Federal hospital and medical insurance trust funds under old-age, survivors, disability, and health insurance programs; see text, Section 12, Social Insurance. [4] Payments made directly to suppliers of medical care (primarily medicaid). [5] Includes medical benefits paid under public law by private insurance carriers, state governments, and self-insurers. [6] Expenditures not offset by other revenues. [7] Covers expenditures for Substance Abuse and Mental Health Services Administration, Indian Health Service; school health and other programs.

Source: U.S. Health Care Financing Administration, *Health Care Financing Review*, fall 1998.

No. 164. National Health Expenditures, by Object: 1980 to 1997

[In billions of dollars (247.3 represents $247,300,000,000). Includes Puerto Rico and outlying areas]

Object of expenditure	1980	1985	1990	1992	1993	1994	1995	1996	1997
Total	**247.3**	**428.7**	**699.4**	**836.5**	**898.5**	**947.7**	**993.7**	**1,042.5**	**1,092.4**
Spent by—									
Consumers	130.0	233.5	384.6	447.2	473.9	483.6	495.3	515.2	535.6
Out-of-pocket	60.3	100.7	145.0	161.8	167.1	168.5	171.0	178.1	187.6
Private insurance	69.8	132.8	239.6	285.5	306.8	315.1	324.3	337.1	348.0
Government	104.8	174.2	283.2	353.0	385.3	422.8	455.2	481.4	507.1
Other [1]	12.5	21.0	31.6	36.3	39.3	41.3	43.2	45.9	49.7
Spent for—									
Health services and supplies	235.6	412.3	674.8	809.0	869.5	917.2	963.1	1,010.6	1,057.5
Personal health care expenses	217.0	376.4	614.7	740.7	790.5	834.0	879.3	924.0	969.0
Hospital care	102.7	168.3	256.4	305.3	323.0	335.7	347.2	360.8	371.1
Physician services	45.2	83.6	146.3	175.9	185.9	193.0	201.9	208.5	217.6
Dental services	13.3	21.7	31.6	37.0	39.5	42.4	45.0	47.5	50.6
Other professional services [2]	6.4	16.6	34.7	42.1	46.1	49.6	53.6	57.5	61.9
Home health care	2.4	5.6	13.1	19.6	23.0	26.2	29.1	31.2	32.3
Drugs/other medical nondurables	21.6	37.1	59.9	71.2	76.2	81.6	88.9	98.3	108.9
Vision products/other med. durables [3]	3.8	6.7	10.5	11.9	12.3	12.5	13.1	13.4	13.9
Nursing home care	17.6	30.7	50.9	62.3	66.4	71.1	75.5	79.4	82.8
Other health services	4.0	6.1	11.2	15.4	18.0	21.9	25.1	27.4	29.9
Net cost of insurance and admin. [4]	11.9	24.3	40.5	44.9	53.7	55.1	53.3	52.5	50.0
Government public health activities	6.7	11.6	19.6	23.4	25.3	28.2	30.4	34.0	38.5
Medical research [5]	5.5	7.8	12.2	14.2	14.5	15.9	16.7	17.2	18.0
Medical facilities construction	6.2	8.5	12.3	13.4	14.5	14.6	13.9	14.8	16.9

[1] Includes nonpatient revenues, privately funded construction, and industrial inplant. [2] Includes services of registered and practical nurses in private duty, podiatrists, optometrists, physical therapists, clinical psychologists, chiropractors, naturopaths, and Christian Science practitioners. [3] Includes expenditures for eyeglasses, hearing aids, orthopedic appliances, artificial limbs, crutches, wheelchairs, etc. [4] Includes administrative expenses of federally financed health programs. [5] Research and development expenditures of drug companies and other manufacturers and providers of medical equipment and supplies are excluded from research expenditures, but are included in the expenditure class in which the product falls.

Source: U.S. Health Care Financing Administration, *Health Care Financing Review*, fall 1998

118   Health and Nutrition

No. 165. Health Services and Supplies—Per Capita Consumer Expenditures, by Object: 1980 to 1997

[In dollars, except percent. Based on Social Security Administration estimates of total U.S. population as of July 1, including Armed Forces and Federal employees abroad and civilian population of outlying areas. Excludes research and construction]

Object of expenditure	1980	1985	1990	1992	1993	1994	1995	1996	1997
Total, national	1,002	1,669	2,595	3,047	3,242	3,387	3,525	3,665	3,800
Annual percent change [1]	13.9	9.3	11.1	7.9	6.4	4.5	4.0	4.0	3.7
Hospital care	437	681	986	1,150	1,204	1,240	1,271	1,308	1,333
Physicians' services	192	338	563	663	693	713	739	756	782
Dentists' services	57	88	121	139	147	157	165	172	182
Other professional services [2]	27	67	133	159	172	183	196	208	223
Home health care	10	23	50	74	86	97	106	113	116
Drugs and other medical nondurables	92	150	230	268	284	301	325	357	391
Vision products and other medical durables [2]	16	27	40	45	46	46	48	49	50
Nursing home care	75	124	196	235	248	263	276	288	297
Other health services	17	25	43	58	67	81	92	100	108
Net cost of insurance and administration [2]	51	98	156	169	200	204	195	190	180
Government public health activities	29	47	75	88	94	104	111	124	138
Total, private consumer [3]	553	945	1,479	1,685	1,767	1,786	1,813	1,868	1,924
Hospital care	178	274	410	455	462	448	435	442	451
Physicians' services	135	234	381	454	474	481	492	501	515
Dentists' services	54	85	117	134	140	149	157	164	173
Other professional services [2]	19	50	99	113	122	128	136	145	157
Home health care	4	8	23	30	32	34	35	36	39
Drugs and other medical nondurables	85	137	205	237	249	263	283	308	334
Vision products and other medical durables [2]	14	21	29	30	30	29	28	27	26
Nursing home care	32	58	92	101	102	105	110	110	107
Net cost of insurance	33	76	122	131	155	150	138	135	124

[1] Change from immediate prior year. [2] See footnotes for corresponding objects in Table 164. [3] Represents out-of-pocket payments and private health insurance.

Source: U.S. Health Care Financing Administration, *Health Care Financing Review*, fall 1998.

No. 166. Government Expenditures for Health Services and Supplies: 1997

[In millions of dollars (485,546 represents $485,546,000,000). Includes Puerto Rico and outlying areas. Excludes medical research and construction]

Type of service	Total [1]	Federal	State and local	Medicare [2] (OASDHI)	Public assistance [3]	Other health services Veterans	Other health services Defense Dept. [4]	Other health services Workers' compensation [5]
Total [1]	485,546	351,791	133,755	214,569	165,250	16,636	13,432	14,116
Hospital care	228,420	185,634	42,785	123,714	60,479	13,608	9,973	6,434
Physician services	70,116	58,419	11,697	46,390	16,074	160	1,701	4,886
Home health care	17,652	15,387	2,266	12,767	4,886	-	-	-
Drugs and other medical nondurables	15,968	9,157	6,812	961	14,312	15	371	265
Nursing home care	51,449	34,522	16,927	10,150	39,568	1,731	-	-
Public health activities	38,490	4,131	34,359	-	-	-	-	-

- Represents zero. [1] Includes other items not shown separately. [2] Covers hospital and medical insurance payments and administrative costs under old-age, survivors, disability, and health insurance program. [3] Covers medicaid and other medical public assistance. Excludes funds paid into medicare trust fund by states to cover premiums for public assistance recipients and medically indigent persons. [4] Includes care for retirees and military dependents. [5] Medical benefits.

Source: U.S. Health Care Financing Administration, *Health Care Financing Review*, fall 1998.

No. 167. Personal Health Care—Third Party Payments and Private Consumer Expenditures: 1980 to 1997

[In billions of dollars (217.0 represents $217,000,000,000), except percent. See headnote, Table 168]

Item	1980	1985	1990	1992	1993	1994	1995	1996	1997
Personal health care expenditures	217.0	376.4	614.7	740.7	790.5	834.0	879.3	924.0	969.0
Third party payments, total	156.8	275.8	469.6	578.9	623.5	665.5	708.3	745.9	781.5
Percent of personal health care	72.2	73.3	76.4	78.2	78.9	79.8	80.6	80.7	80.6
Private insurance payments	62.0	114.1	207.7	250.6	265.2	274.5	286.6	299.8	313.5
Government expenditures	87.0	147.7	241.1	303.6	331.4	362.0	390.1	412.6	432.4
Other [1]	7.8	14.0	20.8	24.7	26.8	28.9	31.6	33.5	35.6
Private consumer expenditures [2]	122.3	214.7	352.8	412.4	432.3	443.0	457.6	477.9	501.0
Percent met by private insurance	50.7	53.1	58.9	60.8	61.4	62.0	62.6	62.7	62.6
Hospital care	41.8	67.8	106.6	120.9	124.0	121.2	118.8	121.9	125.4
Percent met by private insurance	87.2	87.0	89.6	88.7	88.6	89.6	90.3	90.3	90.1
Physicians' services	31.8	57.9	99.0	120.5	127.1	130.3	134.4	138.0	143.2
Percent met by private insurance	53.9	57.8	67.5	72.0	74.1	75.9	77.7	77.4	76.2

[1] Includes nonpatient revenues and industrial inplant health services. [2] Includes expenditures not shown separately. Represents out-of-pocket payments and private health insurance benefits. Excludes net cost of insurance.

Source: U.S. Health Care Financing Administration, *Health Care Financing Review*, fall 1998.

Health and Nutrition   119

No. 168. Personal Health Care Expenditures, by Object and Source of Payment: 1997

[In millions of dollars (969,005 represents $969,005,000,000), except as indicated. Includes Puerto Rico and outlying areas. Covers all expenditures for health services and supplies, except net cost of insurance and administration, government public health activities, and expenditures of philanthropic agencies for fund raising activities]

Object of expenditure	Private payments						Govern-ment	Third party pay-ments [2]
	Total	Consumer						
		Total	Total	Out of pocket pay-ments	Private health insur-ance	Other [1]		
Total	969,005	536,651	501,001	187,551	313,451	35,650	432,354	781,454
Hospital care..................	371,061	142,642	125,409	12,418	112,990	17,233	228,420	358,643
Physicians' services	217,628	147,512	143,220	34,072	109,148	4,292	70,116	183,556
Dentists' services .... [3]	50,648	48,371	48,130	23,862	24,268	241	2,277	26,786
Other professional services [3]	61,916	48,313	43,542	24,641	18,901	4,770	13,604	37,275
Home health care.............	32,318	14,665	10,721	7,024	3,698	3,944	17,652	25,294
Drugs/other medical nondurables ... [3]	108,872	92,904	92,904	53,000	39,905	-	15,968	55,873
Vision products/other med. durables [3] .	13,878	7,312	7,312	6,793	519	-	6,567	7,086
Nursing home care.............	82,774	31,325	29,763	25,741	4,022	1,562	51,449	57,033
Other health services	29,909	3,606	-	-	-	3,606	26,303	29,909

- Represents zero.   [1] Includes nonpatient revenues and industrial plant.   [2] Covers private health insurance, other private payments, and government.   [3] See footnotes for corresponding items on Table 164.

Source: U.S. Health Care Financing Administration, *Health Care Financing Review*, fall 1998.

No. 169. Hospital Care and Physician Service Expenditures, by Source of Payment: 1980 to 1997

[In billions of dollars (102.7 represents $102,700,000,000)]

Source of payment	Hospital care					Physician services				
	1980	1990	1995	1996	1997	1980	1990	1995	1996	1997
Total	102.7	256.4	347.2	360.8	371.1	45.2	146.3	201.9	208.5	217.6
Out-of-pocket payments	5.3	11.1	11.5	11.8	12.4	14.7	32.2	30.0	31.1	34.1
Third-party payments	97.4	245.4	335.7	348.9	358.6	30.6	114.2	171.8	177.4	183.6
Private health insurance	36.5	95.6	107.3	110.0	113.0	17.1	66.8	104.4	106.9	109.1
Other private funds	5.0	10.2	14.9	16.1	17.2	0.4	2.7	4.2	4.3	4.3
Government	55.9	139.6	213.5	222.8	228.4	13.1	44.7	63.2	66.2	70.1
Federal...............	42.1	105.4	170.6	179.6	185.6	10.0	35.6	50.9	54.4	58.4
State and local...........	13.7	34.2	42.9	43.2	42.8	3.1	9.1	12.4	11.8	11.7
Medicare [1]	26.4	68.7	108.9	116.3	123.7	8.0	29.2	39.9	42.8	46.4
Medicaid [2]	10.6	29.4	56.7	59.0	57.6	2.5	7.0	14.4	15.2	15.7

[1] Medicare expenditures come from Federal funds.   [2] Medicaid expenditures come from Federal and state and local funds.

Source: U.S. Health Care Financing Administration, Office of the Actuary, "National Health Expenditures Table 5;" published 29 October 1998; <http://www.hcfa.gov/stats/nhe-oact/tables/t13.htm> and "National Health Expenditures Table 6;" published 29 October 1998; <http://www.hcfa.gov/stats/nhe-oact/tables/t14.htm>.

No. 170. National Health Expenditures, by Source of Payment, 1980 to 1996, and Projections, 1998 to 2005

[In billions of dollars (247.3 represents $247,300,000,000). The health spending projections for 1998 to 2005 were based on the 1996 release of the national health expenditures (NHE). Subsequent releases of the NHE may not be consistent with these projections and should not be substituted for the 1996 historic estimates]

Source of payment	1980	1990	1996	Projections					
				1998	1999	2000	2001	2002	2005
Total	247.3	699.5	1,035.1	1,146.8	1,216.7	1,295.2	1,384.1	1,483.2	1,841.0
Private	142.5	415.1	552.0	606.4	649.6	696.5	746.6	802.3	992.3
Public......................	104.8	284.4	483.1	540.4	567.1	598.7	637.4	680.8	848.7
Medicare	37.5	112.1	203.1	231.1	241.2	252.9	267.8	285.0	356.1
Medicaid	26.1	75.4	147.7	165.5	175.6	188.0	203.2	220.0	283.6
Other	41.1	96.9	132.3	143.8	150.4	157.9	166.4	175.8	209.0
Federal	72.0	195.8	350.9	393.8	412.5	434.5	461.3	491.8	612.6
State and local	32.8	88.5	132.2	146.6	154.7	164.3	176.1	189.0	236.1

Source: U.S. Health Care Financing Administration, Office of the Actuary, "T01;" published 28 September 1998; <http://www.hcfa.gov/stats/NHE-Proj/tables/t01.htm>.

No. 171. National Health Expenditures by Object, 1980 to 1996, and Projections, 1998 to 2005

[In billions of dollars (247.3 represents $247,300,000,000). The health spending projections for 1998 to 2005 were based on the 1996 release of the national health expenditures (NHE). Subsequent releases of the NHE may not be consistent with these projections and should not be substituted for the 1996 historic estimates]

Object of expenditure	1980	1990	1996	Projections					
				1998	1999	2000	2001	2002	2005
Total	247.3	699.5	1,035.1	1,146.8	1,216.7	1,295.2	1,384.1	1,483.2	1,841.0
Health services and supplies.	235.6	675.0	1,003.6	1,113.2	1,182.1	1,259.3	1,346.7	1,444.4	1,797.1
Personal health care	217.0	614.7	907.2	998.2	1,056.1	1,124.2	1,203.2	1,290.0	1,603.2
Hospital care.	102.7	256.4	358.5	383.2	398.9	418.4	442.7	470.0	569.1
Physician services	45.2	146.3	202.1	221.4	235.8	253.1	272.0	292.7	366.4
Dental services	13.3	31.6	47.6	53.7	57.1	60.7	64.5	68.7	83.4
Other professional services	6.4	34.7	58.0	66.8	71.9	77.7	84.2	91.2	115.4
Home health care.	2.4	13.1	30.2	33.2	35.7	38.2	41.6	45.1	56.7
Drugs and other medical nondurables	21.6	59.9	91.4	106.1	114.9	124.5	135.0	146.6	188.8
Vision products and other medical durables	3.8	10.5	13.3	14.3	15.0	15.8	16.7	17.6	20.8
Nursing home care	17.6	50.9	78.5	87.3	91.3	96.4	102.3	108.6	130.9
Other personal health care.	4.0	11.2	27.6	32.4	35.5	39.3	44.2	49.7	71.6
Program administration and net cost of private health insurance . .	11.9	40.7	60.9	74.1	82.2	88.1	93.4	100.8	128.3
Government public health activities.	6.7	19.6	35.5	40.9	43.8	46.9	50.1	53.6	65.6
Research and construction	11.6	24.5	31.5	33.5	34.7	36.0	37.3	38.8	43.9
Research [1]	5.5	12.2	17.0	18.4	19.2	20.0	20.9	21.9	25.1
Construction.	6.2	12.3	14.5	15.1	15.5	15.9	16.4	16.9	18.9

[1] Research and development expenditures of drug companies and other manufacturers and providers of medical equipment and supplies are excluded from research expenditures, but are included in the expenditure class in which the product falls.
Source: U.S. Health Care Financing Administration, Office of the Actuary, "T02;" published 28 September 1998; <http://www.hcfa.gov/stats/NHE-Proj/tables/t02.htm>.

No. 172. Personal Health Care Expenditures, by Source of Payment, 1980 to 1996, and Projections, 1998 to 2005

[In billions of dollars (217.0 represents $217,000,000,000). The health spending projections for 1998 to 2005 were based on the 1996 release of the national health expenditures (NHE). Subsequent releases of the NHE may not be consistent with these projections and should not be substituted for the 1996 historic estimates]

Source of payment	1980	1990	1996	Projections					
				1998	1999	2000	2001	2002	2005
Total	217.0	614.7	907.2	998.2	1,056.1	1,124.2	1,203.2	1,290.0	1,603.2
Out-of-pocket payments	60.3	144.4	171.2	183.7	194.6	206.9	219.0	232.0	276.6
Third-party payments.	156.8	470.3	736.0	814.5	861.5	917.3	984.2	1,058.0	1,326.5
Private health insurance	62.0	206.7	292.3	321.6	345.3	372.8	404.0	437.7	550.8
Other private funds	7.8	21.3	31.7	35.5	38.1	40.8	43.6	46.6	56.4
Government	87.0	242.3	412.0	457.3	478.1	503.7	536.6	573.8	719.3
Federal	63.4	177.6	322.6	360.4	376.7	396.2	421.1	449.4	562.3
State and local	23.6	64.7	89.4	96.9	101.4	107.5	115.5	124.3	157.0
Medicare [1]	36.4	109.3	197.8	223.6	232.5	243.0	257.2	273.8	342.1
Medicaid [2]	24.8	71.4	139.7	154.9	164.2	175.9	190.5	206.3	266.5

[1] Medicare expenditures come from Federal funds. [2] Medicaid expenditures come from Federal and state and local funds.
Source: U.S. Health Care Financing Administration, Office of the Actuary, "T02a;" published 28 September 1998; <http://www.hcfa.gov/stats/NHE-Proj/tables/t02A.htm>.

No. 173. Medicare Enrollees and Expenditures: 1980 to 1997

[Enrollment as of July 1 (28.5 represents 28,500,000). Includes Puerto Rico and outlying areas and enrollees in foreign countries and unknown place of residence]

Item	1980	1985	1990	1993	1994	1995	1996	1997
ENROLLEES (mil.)								
Total.	28.5	31.1	34.2	36.3	36.9	37.5	38.1	38.4
Hospital insurance	28.1	30.6	33.7	35.9	36.5	37.1	37.7	38.1
Supplementary medical insurance	27.4	30.0	32.6	34.6	35.2	35.7	36.1	36.5
EXPENDITURES (mil. dol.)								
Total.	36,802	72,294	110,984	150,370	164,862	184,204	200,338	214,305
Hospital insurance [1]	25,557	48,414	66,997	94,391	104,545	117,604	129,929	140,180
Inpatient hospital	24,116	44,940	59,451	76,773	81,697	89,127	97,802	103,642
Skilled nursing facility	395	548	2,575	5,671	7,407	9,595	11,129	12,681
Home health agency	540	1,913	3,666	9,787	12,503	15,571	17,527	20,163
Hospice	-	43	358	1,059	1,486	1,883	1,999	2,120
Supplementary medical insurance [1] . . .	11,245	23,880	43,987	55,979	60,317	66,600	70,409	74,125
Physician	8,187	17,312	29,609	34,589	36,935	40,457	41,232	42,411
Outpatient hospital	1,897	4,319	8,482	12,632	14,042	15,625	16,447	17,416
Home health agency	234	38	74	120	154	200	227	228
Group practice prepayment.	203	720	2,827	4,632	6,439	6,808	8,847	10,980
Independent laboratory	114	558	1,476	2,006	2,048	2,065	1,846	1,722

- Represents zero. [1] Includes administrative expenses and, for hospital insurance, peer review activity, not shown separately.
Source: U.S. Health Care Financing Administration, Office of the Actuary, unpublished data.

U.S. Census Bureau, Statistical Abstract of the United States: 1999

No. 174. Medicare—Persons Served and Reimbursements: 1990 to 1997

[24,809 represents 24,809,000. Persons served are enrollees who use covered services, incurred expenses greater than the applicable deductible amounts and for whom medicare paid benefits. Reimbursements are amounts paid to providers for covered services. Excluded are retroactive adjustments resulting from end of fiscal year cost settlements and certain lump-sum interim payments. Also excluded are beneficiary (or third party payor) liabilities for applicable deductibles, coinsurance amounts, and charges for noncovered services. Includes data for enrollees living in outlying territories and foreign countries]

Type of coverage and service	Unit	Persons 65 years old and over			Disabled persons [1]		
		1990	1995	1997	1990	1995	1997
Persons served, total [2]	1,000 ...	24,809	27,379	26,587	2,390	3,333	3,547
Hospital insurance [2]	1,000 ...	6,367	7,147	7,360	680	933	986
Inpatient hospital	1,000 ...	5,906	6,148	6,220	644	844	887
Skilled-nursing services	1,000 ...	615	1,186	1,442	23	54	73
Home health services	1,000 ...	1,818	3,185	3,483	122	272	304
Supplementary medical insurance [2]	1,000 ...	24,687	27,234	26,237	2,365	3,299	3,499
Physicians' and other medical services	1,000 ...	24,193	26,621	25,707	2,249	3,184	3,363
Outpatient services	1,000 ...	14,055	17,597	18,093	1,496	2,281	2,510
Home health services	1,000 ...	38	42	47	-	-	-
Persons served per 1,000 enrollees, total [2]	Rate	802	826	791	734	759	737
Hospital insurance [2]	Rate	209	218	221	209	212	205
Inpatient hospital	Rate	194	188	187	198	192	184
Skilled-nursing services	Rate	20	36	43	7	12	15
Home health services	Rate	60	97	105	38	62	63
Supplementary medical insurance [2]	Rate	832	858	816	804	837	814
Physicians' and other medical services	Rate	815	839	799	764	808	783
Outpatient services	Rate	474	554	563	508	579	584
Home health services	Rate	1	1	2	-	-	-
Reimbursements, total	Mil. dol ..	88,778	138,948	152,772	11,239	21,024	23,796
Per person served	Dollars ..	3,578	5,075	5,746	4,703	6,308	6,710
Hospital insurance	Mil. dol ..	54,244	89,631	101,027	6,694	12,752	14,383
Inpatient hospital	Mil. dol ..	48,952	68,213	73,237	6,346	11,079	12,177
Skilled-nursing services	Mil. dol ..	1,886	7,504	10,831	85	374	564
Home health services	Mil. dol ..	3,406	13,914	16,960	264	1,300	1,641
Supplementary medical insurance	Mil. dol ..	34,533	49,317	51,744	4,545	8,272	9,414
Physicians' and other medical services	Mil. dol ..	27,379	37,069	38,206	2,831	4,888	5,474
Outpatient services	Mil. dol ..	7,077	12,045	13,319	1,714	3,384	3,940
Home health services	Mil. dol ..	78	203	219	-	-	-

- Represents or rounds to zero. [1] Age under 65; includes persons enrolled because of end-stage renal disease (ESRD) only.
[2] Persons are counted once for each type of covered service used, but are not double counted in totals.

Source: U.S. Health Care Financing Administration, *Medicare Program Statistics*, annual; and unpublished data.

No. 175. Medicare—Utilization and Charges: 1990 to 1997

[Fiscal year data, except as indicated (9,216 represents 9,216,000). Data reflect date expense was incurred based on bills submitted for payment and recorded in Health Care Financing Administration central records. Includes Puerto Rico, Virgin Islands, Guam, other outlying areas, and enrollees in foreign countries]

Item	Unit	Persons 65 years old and over				Disabled persons [1]			
		1990	1995	1996	1997	1990	1995	1996	1997
Hospital inpatient care:									
Admissions [2]	1,000...	9,216	10,574	10,521	10,698	1,257	1,442	1,572	1,599
Per 1,000 enrollees [3]	Rate ...	309	323	319	323	396	328	339	323
Covered days of care	Millions .	82	76	72	69	11	10	10	10
Per 1,000 enrollees [3]	Rate ...	2,702	2,313	2,153	2,097	3,464	2,351	2,289	2,097
Per admission	Days...	8.9	7.2	6.8	6.5	8.8	7.2	6.8	6.8
Hospital covered charges	Mil. dol. .	90,846	138,489	140,606	146,232	11,910	18,885	21,011	22,105
Per covered day	Dollars..	1,104	1,828	1,978	2,131	1,083	1,828	1,978	2,131
Percent of covered charges reimbursed [4]	Percent .	47.5	47.5	48.8	49.9	46.5	47.5	48.8	49.9
Physician allowed charges [5]	Mil. dol. .	30,447	41,409	36,212	(NA)	2,907	5,647	5,411	(NA)
Percent reimbursed	Percent .	77.0	76.2	76.0	(NA)	75.7	76.2	76.0	(NA)

NA Not available. [1] Disabled persons under age 65 and persons enrolled solely because of end-stage renal disease.
[2] Represents number of discharges and includes pass-through amounts, except for kidney acquisition. [3] Based on Hospital Insurance (HI) enrollment as of July 1. [4] Excludes retroactive adjustments resulting from end-of-fiscal year cost reports.
[5] Calendar year data.

Source: U.S. Health Care Financing Administration, unpublished data.

122   Health and Nutrition

No. 176. Medicare Trust Funds: 1980 to 1997

[In billions of dollars (23.9 represents $23,900,000,000)]

Type of trust fund	1980	1985	1990	1992	1993	1994	1995	1996	1997
Hospital insurance (HI):									
Net contribution income [1]	23.9	47.7	72.2	82.4	84.9	97.9	103.3	115.9	119.5
Interest received [2]	1.1	[3]3.4	8.5	10.5	12.5	10.7	10.8	10.2	9.6
Benefit payments	25.1	47.5	66.2	83.9	93.5	103.3	116.4	128.6	137.8
Assets, end of year	13.7	[4]20.5	98.9	124.0	127.8	132.8	130.3	124.9	115.6
Supplementary medical insurance (SMI):									
Net premium income	3.0	5.6	11.3	14.1	14.2	17.4	19.7	18.8	19.3
Transfers from general revenue	7.5	18.3	33.0	41.4	41.5	36.2	39.0	65.0	60.2
Interest received [2]	0.4	1.2	1.6	1.8	2.0	2.0	1.6	1.8	2.5
Benefit payments	10.6	22.9	42.5	49.3	55.8	58.6	65.0	68.6	72.8
Assets, end of year	4.5	10.9	15.5	24.2	24.1	19.4	13.1	28.3	36.1

[1] Includes income from taxation of benefits beginning in 1994. Includes premiums from aged ineligibles enrolled in HI. [2] Includes recoveries of amounts reimbursed from the trust fund. [3] Reflects interest on interfund borrowing. [4] Excludes $10.6 billion lent to the OASI Trust Fund (see Table 615).

Source: U.S. Health Care Financing Administration, *Annual Report of the Board of Trustees of the Federal Hospital Insurance Trust Fund* and *Annual Report of the Board of Trustees of the Federal Supplementary Medical Insurance Trust Fund.*

No. 177. Medicare—Summary, by State and Other Areas: 1995 and 1998

[For fiscal year ending in year shown. (37,496 represents 37,496,000)]

State and area	Enrollment [1] (1,000)		Payments [2] (mil. dol)		State and area	Enrollment [1] (1,000)		Payments [2] (mil. dol)	
	1995	1998	1995	1998		1995	1998	1995	1998
All areas	37,496	38,567	176,884	210,102	MO	832	845	3,821	4,695
U.S.	36,703	37,730	175,976	208,963	MT	130	134	489	534
					NE	249	251	840	1,080
AL	641	665	3,042	3,561	NV	192	219	894	1,105
AK	34	38	133	160	NH	156	163	597	648
AZ	597	641	2,717	2,986	NJ	1,169	1,182	5,603	6,908
AR	422	431	1,638	1,929	NM	211	224	710	829
CA	3,633	3,757	20,406	22,558	NY	2,639	2,659	13,904	17,065
CO	421	448	1,835	2,279	NC	1,025	1,086	4,276	5,296
CT	502	508	2,584	3,128	ND	103	103	412	480
DE	100	107	445	405	OH	1,666	1,681	7,262	8,835
DC	78	75	1,164	922	OK	487	497	2,178	2,373
FL	2,610	2,728	14,828	17,903	OR	467	478	1,685	1,832
GA	832	877	4,090	4,287	PA	2,069	2,079	10,796	13,183
HI	149	158	580	639	RI	168	169	772	1,022
ID	150	158	463	601	SC	508	541	1,926	2,563
IL	1,617	1,619	7,276	8,490	SD	117	118	563	504
IN	823	837	3,491	4,263	TN	770	800	4,083	4,728
IA	474	474	1,527	1,810	TX	2,076	2,177	11,504	14,666
KS	383	387	1,545	1,809	UT	187	197	708	888
KY	586	606	2,401	2,897	VT	83	86	284	289
LA	580	592	3,448	4,293	VA	817	857	2,979	3,657
ME	202	210	707	793	WA	687	713	2,603	2,883
MD	601	623	2,868	3,642	WV	329	333	1,208	1,528
MA	933	946	5,496	5,807	WI	761	771	2,673	3,267
MI	1,348	1,373	6,237	7,711	WY	60	63	180	218
MN	631	641	2,378	2,798	PR	477	512	875	1,086
MS	397	408	1,723	2,216	Other areas	317	325	33	54

[1] Hospital and/or medical insurance enrollment for 1995 as of September and for 1998 as of July 1. [2] Benefit payments for all areas represent 100 percent fee for service experience and actual HMO expenditures through the fiscal year and relate to the state of the provider.

Source: U.S. Health Care Financing Administration, unpublished data.

U.S. Census Bureau, Statistical Abstract of the United States: 1999

No. 178. Medicaid—Selected Characteristics of Persons Covered: 1990 to 1997

[In thousands, except percent (24,160 represents 24,160,000). Represents number of persons as of March of following year who were enrolled at any time in year shown. Person did not have to receive medical care paid for by medicaid in order to be counted. See headnote, Table 612]

Poverty status	1990	1995	1997							
			Total [1]	White	Black	His-panic [2]	Under 18 years old	18-44 years old	45-64 years old	65 years and over
Persons covered, total......	24,160	31,621	28,707	19,460	7,703	5,898	14,434	8,097	3,276	2,901
Below poverty level...........	15,175	16,900	15,386	9,521	4,940	3,744	8,550	4,356	1,520	958
Above poverty level	8,985	14,721	13,321	9,939	2,763	2,154	5,884	3,741	1,756	1,943
Percent of population										
covered.............	9.7	12.0	10.7	8.8	22.4	19.3	20.3	7.8	6.3	9.0
Below poverty level...........	45.2	46.4	43.2	39.0	54.2	45.1	60.6	32.4	32.8	28.4
Above poverty level	4.2	6.5	5.7	5.0	10.9	9.6	10.3	3.9	3.4	6.8

[1] Includes other races not shown separately.   [2] Persons of Hispanic origin may be of any race.

Source: U.S. Census Bureau, Current Population Reports, P60-201, earlier reports; and unpublished data.

No. 179. Medicaid—Recipients and Payments: 1980 to 1997

[For year ending September 30 (21,605 represents 21,605,000). Includes Puerto Rico (for 1980 through 1996) and outlying areas. Excludes Hawaii for 1997. Medical vendor payments are those made directly to suppliers of medical care]

Basis of eligibility and type of service	Recipients (1,000)					Payments (mil. dol.)				
	1980	1990	1995	1996	1997	1980	1990	1995	1996	1997
Total [1].............	21,605	25,255	36,282	36,118	33,579	23,311	64,859	120,141	121,685	123,551
Age 65 and over	3,440	3,202	4,119	4,285	3,954	8,739	21,508	36,527	36,947	37,721
Blindness..............	92	83	92	95	(NA)	124	434	848	869	(NA)
Disabled [2].............	2,819	3,635	5,767	6,126	6,129	7,497	23,969	48,570	51,196	54,129
AFDC [3] program	14,210	17,230	24,767	23,866	22,066	6,354	17,690	31,487	29,819	27,964
Other and unknown	1,499	1,105	1,537	1,746	1,429	596	1,257	2,708	2,853	3,737
Inpatient services in—										
General hospital........	3,680	4,593	5,561	5,362	4,746	6,412	16,674	26,331	25,176	23,143
Mental hospital.........	66	92	84	93	87	775	1,714	2,511	2,040	2,009
Intermediate care facilities, mentally retarded	121	147	151	140	136	1,989	7,354	10,383	9,555	9,798
Nursing facility services [4]....	1,398	1,461	1,667	1,594	1,603	7,887	17,693	29,052	29,630	30,504
Physicians	13,765	17,078	23,789	22,861	21,170	1,875	4,018	7,360	7,238	7,041
Dental	4,652	4,552	6,383	6,208	5,935	462	593	1,019	1,028	1,036
Other practitioner	3,234	3,873	5,528	5,342	5,142	198	372	986	1,094	979
Outpatient hospital	9,705	12,370	16,712	15,905	13,632	1,101	3,324	6,504	6,504	6,169
Clinic...............	1,531	2,804	5,322	5,070	4,713	320	1,688	4,280	4,222	4,252
Laboratory [5]............	3,212	8,959	13,064	12,607	11,074	121	721	1,180	1,208	1,033
Home health	392	719	1,639	1,727	1,861	332	3,404	9,406	10,868	12,237
Prescribed drugs	13,707	17,294	23,723	22,585	20,954	1,318	4,420	9,791	10,697	11,972
Family planning	1,129	1,752	2,501	2,366	2,091	81	265	514	474	418

NA Not available.   [1] Recipient data do not add due to small number of recipients that are reported in more than one category. Includes recipients of, and payments for, other care not shown separately.   [2] Permanently and totally. Beginning 1997, includes blind.   [3] Aid to families with dependent children.   [4] Nursing facility services includes skilled nursing facility services and intermediate care facility services for all other than the mentally retarded.   [5] Includes radiological services.

Source: U.S. Health Care Financing Administration, Office of Information Systems, Statistical Report on Medical Care: Eligibles, Recipients, Payments, and Services.

No. 180. Medicaid—Selected Utilization Measures: 1980 to 1997

[In thousands (2,255 represents 2,255,000). For year ending September 30. Includes Virgin Islands. See text, this section]

Measure	1980	1985	1990	1993	1994	1995	1996	1997
General hospitals:								
Recipients discharged	2,255	2,390	3,261	4,050	3,890	3,743	3,300	3,135
Total days of care	24,089	29,562	27,471	31,095	28,941	25,711	23,072	21,532
Nursing facilities: [1]								
Total recipients	1,395	1,375	1,461	1,610	1,639	1,667	1,594	1,497
Total days of care	273,497	277,996	360,044	422,965	400,785	400,123	409,663	388,985
Intermediate care facilities: [2]								
Total recipients	121	147	146	149	159	151	140	146
Total days of care	250,124	47,324	49,730	44,952	54,105	56,878	56,625	62,423

[1] Includes skilled nursing facilities and intermediate care facilities for all other than the mentally retarded.   [2] Mentally retarded.

Source: U.S. Health Care Financing Administration, Office of Information Systems, Statistical Report on Medical Care: Eligibles, Recipients, Payments, and Services.

No. 181. Medicaid—Summary, by State and Other Area: 1995 and 1997

[For year ending September 30. (36,282 represents 36,282,000)]

State and area	Recipients [1] (1,000) 1995	1997	Payments [2] (mil. dol.) 1995	1997	State and area	Recipients [1] (1,000) 1995	1997	Payments [2] (mil. dol.) 1995	1997
All areas ..	36,282	33,579	120,141	123,551	MO	695	540	2,039	2,097
U.S.....	35,210	33,562	119,885	123,544	MT.........	99	96	326	318
					NE.........	168	203	608	696
AL.........	539	546	1,455	1,571	NV.........	105	106	350	373
AK.........	68	73	252	321	NH.........	97	95	473	554
AZ.........	494	541	218	246	NJ.........	790	538	3,813	3,569
AR.........	353	370	1,376	1,302	NM.........	287	320	714	822
CA.........	5,017	4,855	10,521	11,433	NY.........	3,035	3,152	22,086	21,340
CO.........	294	251	1,063	1,124	NC.........	1,084	1,113	3,175	3,788
CT.........	380	202	2,125	2,003	ND.........	61	61	297	328
DE.........	79	84	324	275	OH.........	1,533	1,396	5,585	5,848
DC.........	138	128	532	696	OK.........	394	316	1,055	1,038
FL.........	1,735	1,597	4,802	4,885	OR.........	452	531	1,327	1,475
GA.........	1,147	1,208	3,076	3,090	PA.........	1,230	1,025	4,633	4,689
HI.........	52	(NA)	258	(NA)	RI.........	135	117	673	738
ID.........	115	115	360	432	SC.........	496	520	1,438	1,607
IL.........	1,552	1,400	5,600	5,783	SD.........	74	75	305	318
IN.........	559	515	1,878	2,382	TN.........	1,466	1,416	2,772	2,936
IA.........	304	294	1,036	1,083	TX.........	2,562	2,539	6,565	7,345
KS.........	256	233	831	919	UT.........	160	145	464	424
KY.........	641	664	1,945	2,269	VT.........	100	109	320	309
LA.........	785	746	2,708	2,336	VA.........	681	595	1,833	1,858
ME.........	153	167	760	780	WA.........	639	630	1,461	1,393
MD.........	414	402	2,019	2,201	WV.........	389	359	1,169	1,257
MA.........	728	723	3,972	3,855	WI.........	460	392	1,894	1,879
MI.........	1,168	1,133	3,409	3,591	WY.........	51	49	171	184
MN.........	473	371	2,550	2,359	PR	1,055	(NA)	244	(NA)
MS.........	520	504	1,266	1,424	VI	17	17	12	7

NA Not available. [1] Persons who had payments made on their behalf at any time during the fiscal year. [2] Payments are for fiscal year and reflect Federal and state contribution payments. Data exclude disproportionate hospital share payments.

Source: U.S. Health Care Financing Administration, Office of Information Systems, *Statistical Report on Medical Care: Eligibles, Recipients, Payments, and Services.*

No. 182. Medicaid Managed Care Enrollment, by State and Other Area: 1991 to 1997

[For year ending June 30. (28,280 represents 28,280,000)]

State and area	Total medicaid enrollment (1,000)	Managed care enrollment Number (1,000)	Percent of total	State and area	Total medicaid enrollment (1,000)	Managed care enrollment Number (1,000)	Percent of total
1991	28,280	2,696	9.5	MI.............	1,116	865	77.6
1992	30,926	3,635	11.8	MN.............	403	169	42.0
1993	33,430	4,809	14.4	MS.............	544	81	15.0
1994	33,634	7,794	23.2	MO.............	615	264	43.0
1995	33,373	9,800	29.4	MT.............	71	62	87.6
1996	33,241	13,330	40.1	NE.............	144	93	64.5
				NV.............	89	26	29.8
1997, total.	32,092	15,346	47.8	NH.............	71	9	12.8
				NJ.............	685	385	56.2
U.S	30,814	14,643	47.5	NM.............	242	139	57.5
AL	497	408	82.0	NY.............	2,296	661	28.8
AK	87	-	-	NC.............	825	351	42.5
AZ	432	349	80.9	ND.............	45	24	53.6
AR	268	159	59.6	OH.............	1,095	353	32.2
CA	4,791	1,854	38.7	OK.............	437	223	51.0
CO	229	184	80.5	OR.............	376	312	83.0
CT	360	232	64.4	PA.............	1,586	870	54.9
DE	81	65	80.8	RI.............	114	71	62.1
DC	125	81	64.6	SC.............	393	14	3.6
FL	1,411	897	63.6	SD.............	60	42	68.8
GA	882	561	63.6	TN.............	1,189	1,189	100.0
HI	167	135	81.1	TX.............	2,079	276	13.3
ID	81	32	40.3	UT.............	118	94	79.3
IL	1,370	187	13.7	VT.............	97	23	23.7
IN	405	220	54.3	VA.............	522	307	58.8
IA	218	88	40.6	WA.............	730	730	100.0
KS	185	94	51.0	WV.............	311	126	40.4
KY	527	268	50.9	WI.............	423	206	48.6
LA	636	40	6.4	WY.............	48	-	-
ME	156	13	8.0				
MD	465	348	74.7	PR	1,262	702	55.7
MA	716	462	64.5	VI	17	-	-

- Represents zero.

Source: U.S. Health Care Financing Administration, "Managed Care Trends;" published 27 February 1998; <http://www.hcfa.gov/medicaid/trends97.htm> and "Managed Care State Enrollment;" published 3 March 1998; <http://www.hcfa.gov/medicaid/mcsten97.htm>.

Health and Nutrition 125

No. 183. Consumer Price Indexes of Medical Care Prices: 1980 to 1998

[1982-1984=100. Indexes are annual averages of monthly data based on components of consumer price index for all urban consumers; for explanation, see text, Section 15, Prices]

Year	Medical care services					Medical care commodities	Annual percent change [2]				Medical care commodities
	Medical care	Total [1]	Professional services				Medical care	Medical care services			
			Total [1]	Physicians	Dental			Total [1]	Physicians	Dental	
1980	74.9	74.8	77.9	76.5	78.9	75.4	11.0	11.3	10.5	11.9	9.3
1985	113.5	113.2	113.5	113.3	114.2	115.2	6.3	6.1	5.9	6.2	7.2
1990	162.8	162.7	156.1	160.8	155.8	163.4	9.0	9.3	7.1	6.6	8.4
1991	177.0	177.1	165.7	170.5	167.4	176.8	8.7	8.9	6.0	7.4	8.2
1992	190.1	190.5	175.8	181.2	178.7	188.1	7.4	7.6	6.3	6.8	6.4
1993	201.4	202.9	184.7	191.3	188.1	195.0	5.9	6.5	5.6	5.3	3.7
1994	211.0	213.4	192.5	199.8	197.1	200.7	4.8	5.2	4.4	4.8	2.9
1995	220.5	224.2	201.0	208.8	206.8	204.5	4.5	5.1	4.5	4.9	1.9
1996	228.2	232.4	208.3	216.4	216.5	210.4	3.5	3.7	3.6	4.7	2.9
1997	234.6	239.1	215.4	222.9	226.6	215.3	2.8	2.9	3.0	4.7	2.3
1998	242.1	246.8	222.2	229.5	236.2	221.8	3.2	3.2	3.0	4.2	3.0

[1] Includes other services not shown separately. [2] Percent change from the immediate prior year.

Source: U.S. Bureau of Labor Statistics, *CPI Detailed Report*, January 1999.

No. 184. Average Annual Expenditures Per Consumer Unit for Health Care: 1985 to 1997

[In dollars, except percent. See text, Section 14, Income, and headnote, Table 738. For composition of regions, see map, inside front cover]

Item	Health care, total					Percent distribution		
	Amount	Percent of total expenditures	Health insurance	Medical services	Drugs and medical supplies [1]	Health insurance	Medical services	Drugs and medical supplies [1]
1985....................	1,108	4.7	375	496	238	33.8	44.8	21.5
1990....................	1,480	5.2	581	562	337	39.3	38.0	22.8
1991....................	1,554	5.2	656	555	344	42.2	35.7	22.1
1992....................	1,634	5.5	725	533	375	44.4	32.6	22.9
1993....................	1,776	5.8	800	574	402	45.0	32.3	22.6
1994....................	1,755	5.5	815	571	369	46.4	32.5	21.0
1995....................	1,732	5.4	860	512	360	49.7	29.6	20.8
1996....................	1,770	5.2	827	543	400	46.7	30.7	22.6
1997	**1,841**	**5.3**	**881**	**531**	**428**	**47.9**	**28.8**	**23.2**
Age of reference person:								
Under 25 years old..........	425	2.3	200	128	96	47.1	30.1	22.6
25 to 34 years old	1,236	3.5	577	422	236	46.7	34.1	19.1
35 to 44 years old	1,605	4.0	748	547	310	46.6	34.1	19.3
45 to 54 years old	1,945	4.3	845	658	442	43.4	33.8	22.7
55 to 64 years old	2,187	6.1	965	664	558	44.1	30.4	25.5
65 to 74 years old	2,900	10.4	1,547	636	717	53.3	21.9	24.7
75 years old and over........	2,799	13.8	1,494	475	829	53.4	17.0	29.6
Origin of reference person: Hispanic .	1,167	4.0	546	352	269	46.8	30.2	23.1
Non-Hispanic	1,903	5.4	912	548	443	47.9	28.8	23.3
Black	1,035	4.1	579	229	228	55.9	22.1	22.0
Other	1,950	5.4	922	572	456	47.3	29.3	23.4
Region of residence:								
Northeast.................	1,709	4.7	871	480	359	51.0	28.1	21.0
Midwest.................	1,903	5.6	912	521	470	47.9	27.4	24.7
South	1,902	5.9	931	502	469	48.9	26.4	24.7
West	1,793	4.6	775	638	379	43.2	35.6	21.1
Size of consumer unit:								
One person	1,249	6.0	575	369	305	46.0	29.5	24.4
Two or more persons	2,078	5.1	1,005	596	477	48.4	28.7	23.0
Two persons	2,301	6.3	1,160	548	594	50.4	23.8	25.8
Three persons	1,915	4.7	939	583	393	49.0	30.4	20.5
Four persons.............	1,938	4.3	884	666	388	45.6	34.4	20.0
Five persons or more	1,857	4.2	812	664	381	43.7	35.8	20.5
Income before taxes:								
Complete income reporters [2]	1,898	5.3	900	544	455	47.4	28.7	24.0
Quintiles of income:								
Lowest 20 percent........	1,169	7.3	570	246	354	48.8	21.0	30.3
Second 20 percent	1,808	7.7	877	446	485	48.5	24.7	26.8
Third 20 percent	1,853	5.9	874	499	479	47.2	26.9	25.8
Fourth 20 percent	2,067	4.8	997	631	440	48.2	30.5	21.3
Highest 20 percent	2,590	3.9	1,181	895	514	45.6	34.6	19.8
Incomplete reporters of income ..	1,617	5.5	805	479	333	49.8	29.6	20.6

[1] Includes prescription and nonprescription drugs. [2] A complete reporter is a consumer unit providing values for at least one of the major sources of income.

Source: Bureau of Labor Statistics, *Consumer Expenditure Survey*, annual.

126 Health and Nutrition

No. 185. Health Insurance Coverage Status, by Selected Characteristics: 1990 to 1997

[Persons as of following year for coverage in the year shown (**248.9 represents 248,900,000**). Government health insurance includes medicare, medicaid, and military plans. Based on Current Population Survey; see text, Section 1, Population, and Appendix III]

Characteristic	Number (mil.)							Percent			
	Total persons	Covered by private or government health insurance					Not covered by health insurance	Covered by private or government health insurance			Not covered by health insurance
		Total [1]	Private		Government			Total [1]	Private		
			Total	Group health [2]	Medicare	Medicaid				Medicaid	
1990	248.9	214.2	182.1	150.2	32.3	24.3	34.7	86.1	73.2	9.7	13.9
1992 [3]	256.8	218.2	181.5	148.8	33.2	29.4	38.6	85.0	70.7	11.5	15.0
1993 [3]	259.8	220.0	182.4	148.3	33.1	31.7	39.7	84.7	70.2	12.2	15.3
1994 [3]	262.1	222.4	184.3	159.6	33.9	31.6	39.7	84.8	70.2	12.1	15.2
1995 [3]	264.3	223.7	185.9	161.5	34.7	31.9	40.6	84.6	70.3	12.1	15.4
1996 [3]	266.8	225.1	187.4	163.2	35.2	31.5	41.7	84.4	70.2	11.8	15.6
1997, total [3][4]	**269.1**	**225.6**	**188.5**	**165.1**	**35.6**	**29.0**	**43.4**	**83.9**	**70.1**	**10.8**	**16.1**
Age:											
Under 18 years	71.7	60.9	48.0	44.9	0.4	14.7	10.7	85.0	66.9	20.5	15.0
Under 6 years	23.8	20.4	15.1	14.3	0.1	6.1	3.4	85.6	63.2	25.7	14.4
6 to 11 years	24.2	20.9	16.5	15.6	0.2	4.9	3.4	86.1	68.1	20.1	13.9
12 to 17 years	23.6	19.7	16.4	15.0	0.1	3.7	4.0	83.3	69.5	15.6	16.7
18 to 24 years	25.2	17.6	15.3	12.6	0.2	2.6	7.6	69.9	60.5	10.1	30.1
25 to 34 years	39.4	30.2	27.1	25.5	0.4	2.9	9.2	76.7	69.0	7.2	23.3
35 to 44 years	44.5	36.8	33.7	31.6	0.9	2.7	7.7	82.7	75.7	6.1	17.3
45 to 54 years	34.1	29.3	27.1	25.1	1.1	1.8	4.7	86.1	79.5	5.2	13.9
55 to 64 years	22.3	19.1	16.7	14.5	1.8	1.5	3.2	85.7	75.3	6.8	14.3
65 years and over	32.1	31.7	20.7	11.0	30.9	2.9	0.3	99.0	64.5	9.0	1.0
Sex: Male	131.7	108.6	92.8	82.6	15.3	12.1	23.1	82.4	70.4	9.2	17.6
Female	137.4	117.1	95.8	82.5	20.3	16.9	20.3	85.2	69.7	12.3	14.8
Race: White	221.7	188.4	161.7	140.6	31.1	19.7	33.2	85.0	72.9	8.9	15.0
Black	34.6	27.2	18.5	17.1	3.6	7.8	7.4	78.5	53.6	22.4	21.5
Hispanic origin [5]	30.8	20.2	13.8	12.8	2.0	6.0	10.5	65.8	44.7	19.4	34.2
Household income:											
Less than $25,000	72.2	53.9	28.6	19.2	18.7	20.3	18.4	74.6	39.6	28.1	25.4
$25,000-$49,999	80.4	65.8	58.3	51.2	10.2	5.8	14.5	81.9	72.5	7.3	18.1
$50,000-$74,999	56.2	50.5	48.0	44.9	3.4	1.6	5.7	89.9	85.5	2.9	10.1
$75,000 or more	60.3	55.5	53.6	49.8	3.3	1.2	4.9	91.9	88.9	2.0	8.1

[1] Includes other government insurance, not shown separately. Persons with coverage counted only once in total, even though they may have been covered by more that one type of policy. [2] Related to employment of self or other family members. [3] Beginning 1992, data based on 1990 census adjusted population controls. [4] Includes other races not shown separately. [5] Persons of Hispanic origin may be of any race.

Source: U.S. Census Bureau, *Current Population Reports*, P60-202; and unpublished data.

No. 186. Medical Care Benefit Coverage and Average Monthly Employee Contributions: 1980 to 1997

[Covers full-time employees in private nonfarm establishments. Based on a sample survey of establishments; for details, see source and headnotes, Tables 709 and 710]

Item	Medium and large establishments					Small establishments			
	1980	1991	1993	1995	1997	1990	1992	1994	1996
Percent of full-time employees participating	97	83	82	77	76	69	71	66	64
PERCENT DISTRIBUTION OF PARTICIPATING FULL-TIME EMPLOYEES									
Fee arrangement, total	100	100	100	100	100	100	100	100	100
Traditional fee-for-service [1]	(NA)	67	50	37	27	74	68	55	36
Preferred provider organization [2]	(NA)	16	26	34	40	13	18	24	35
Health maintenance organization [3]	(NA)	17	23	27	33	14	14	19	27
Other	(NA)	-	1	1	1	-	(Z)	1	2
Individual coverage:									
Employee contributions not required	(NA)	49	37	33	31	(NA)	(NA)	(NA)	48
Employee contributions required	26	51	61	67	69	42	47	52	52
Family coverage:									
Employee contributions not required	(NA)	31	21	22	20	(NA)	(NA)	(NA)	24
Employee contributions required	46	69	76	78	80	67	73	75	75
AVERAGE MONTHLY EMPLOYEE CONTRIBUTION (dol.)									
Individual coverage:									
Total	(NA)	27	32	34	39	25	37	41	43
Non-HMO [4]	(NA)	26	31	33	42	25	36	39	43
HMO	(NA)	29	32	36	34	25	39	49	41
Family coverage:									
Total	(NA)	97	107	118	130	109	151	160	182
Non-HMO [4]	(NA)	92	102	112	132	104	147	151	181
HMO	(NA)	118	122	133	126	135	168	190	182

- Represents zero. NA Not available. Z Less than 0.5 percent. [1] These plans pay for specific medical procedures as expenses are incurred. [2] Groups of hospitals and physicians that contract to provide comprehensive medical services at prearranged prices. To encourage use of organization members, the health plan limits reimbursement rates when participants use nonmember services. [3] Includes federally qualified and other HMOs that deliver comprehensive health care on a prepayment rather than fee-for-service basis. [4] Includes traditional fee-for-service plans, preferred provider plans, and exclusive provider organization plans.

Source: U.S. Bureau of Labor Statistics, *News*, USDL 98-240, June 15, 1998; *News*, USDL 99-02, January 7, 1999; and earlier releases.

No. 187. Private Establishments Offering Health Insurance, by Selected Characteristics: 1993

[As of December 31. (3,245 represents 3,245,000). Based on the National Employer Health Insurance Survey; for details on sample survey, see source]

Firm size [1] and industry group	Establishments offering—							Private employees, percent working in establishments offering health insurance
	One or more major health plans [2]		Two or more major plans [2] (percent)	Fee-for-service plan [3] (percent)	Any managed care plan [4] (percent)	Health maintenance organization [5] (percent)	Preferred provider organization [6] (percent)	
	Number (1,000)	Percent of all establishments						
Total [7]	3,245	51.6	18.6	52.0	55.5	25.9	35.0	83.1
Less than 10 employees.	1,311	33.2	10.1	56.0	47.5	20.5	28.7	39.2
10 to 24 employees.	583	67.1	11.7	47.9	56.9	25.3	34.7	68.8
25 to 99 employees.	493	83.0	17.3	43.4	63.6	29.6	39.6	84.2
100 to 499 employees	295	93.9	24.1	44.1	64.8	31.5	43.3	94.9
500 to 999 employees	90	96.8	29.3	53.0	59.1	27.0	42.6	98.6
1,000 or more employees	473	96.7	46.4	59.9	61.1	33.9	41.7	99.3
Agriculture, forestry, and fishing	66	30.2	8.7	55.4	47.1	16.3	32.8	54.7
Mining.	22	67.3	21.4	64.7	41.4	11.6	34.9	91.9
Construction.	214	40.4	20.6	57.1	51.6	23.5	30.8	63.1
Manufacturing.	311	60.8	19.1	50.2	58.8	29.6	34.3	93.3
Transportation, communication, and utilities.	168	65.8	23.2	49.9	60.7	27.0	40.1	91.2
Wholesale trade	330	64.9	17.1	52.0	56.1	23.3	37.0	86.9
Retail trade	637	43.6	19.3	54.6	52.7	25.2	33.2	72.1
Finance, insurance, and real estate .	352	64.8	26.6	50.6	59.2	30.8	38.2	91.3
Services	1,147	51.3	15.6	50.5	55.6	25.5	34.8	82.8

[1] Number of employees nationwide as reported by respondent. [2] Major health plans typically cover hospital care and doctor visits. [3] A plan in which the covered person seeks care from his or her own choice of providers on a fee-for-service basis. Either the patient or the provider submits the claims. Plans reported as fee-for-service with PPO riders were counted as PPO plans. [4] Covers both health maintenance organizations and preferred provider organizations (PPO). [5] Offers comprehensive health care from a specified set of providers for fixed periodic payments. HMO providers may be employees or under contract to the HMO. Care from providers outside the HMO is only covered in emergencies or when the patient is referred by an HMO provider. For this report, open-ended HMOs and Point of Service (POS) plans that include some HMO-like features but allow patients to use providers outside the HMO with higher patient costs, have been combined with HMOs. Exclusive Provider Organizations (EPO) are also combined with HMOs. [6] A plan in which the covered person may seek care from a provider associated with the plan (preferred provider) or a provider outside the plan (nonpreferred provider). Typically the patient pays more when he or she sees a nonpreferred provider. [7] Includes establishments with unknown characteristics.

No. 188. Percent of Private Employees Eligible and Enrolled in Employer's Health Plan: 1993

[As of December 31. (98,323 represents 98,323,000). Based on the National Employer Health Insurance Survey; for details on sample survey, see source]

Firm size [1] and industry group	All employees				Full-time employees		Part-time employees	
	Number (1,000)	Percent eligible for health benefits	Percent enrolled in employer's plan	Percent of eligible employees enrolled	Number (1,000)	Percent enrolled in employer's plan	Number (1,000)	Percent enrolled in employer's plan
Total [2]	98,323	67.9	57.6	84.8	76,861	70.8	21,462	10.2
Less than 25 employees.	26,453	41.7	33.3	79.9	19,494	43.9	6,959	3.5
25 to 99 employees.	16,250	66.6	53.8	80.8	12,634	68.2	3,616	3.5
100 to 999 employees	20,911	77.2	65.0	84.1	16,892	78.7	4,019	7.1
1,000 or more employees	34,710	82.9	73.4	88.5	27,842	86.0	6,868	22.3
Agriculture, forestry, and fishing .	1,590	38.1	30.8	81.0	1,140	42.2	450	[3]2.0
Mining.	771	87.3	82.1	94.0	723	86.8	48	[3]9.8
Construction.	4,545	51.9	42.4	81.7	4,053	46.6	492	7.8
Manufacturing.	19,211	86.5	78.3	90.5	18,080	82.4	1,131	13.1
Transportation, communication, and utilities.	6,231	80.2	72.5	90.3	5,251	81.5	979	24.0
Wholesale trade	6,590	77.2	67.2	87.0	5,788	75.2	802	9.3
Retail trade	17,843	45.2	34.3	75.9	10,481	54.2	7,362	5.9
Finance, insurance, and real estate	8,035	80.2	67.9	84.7	6,850	77.3	1,184	13.6
Services	33,509	65.5	53.7	82.0	24,495	69.0	9,014	12.0

[1] Number of employees nationwide as reported by respondent. [2] Includes establishments with unknown characteristics. [3] Figure does not meet standards of reliability or precision.

Source of Tables 187 and 188: U.S. National Center for Health Statistics, *Employer-Sponsored Health Insurance, State and National Estimates, 1997.*

No. 189. Private Establishments Offering Health Insurance and Employees Enrolled, by State: 1993

[As of December 31 (3,244.7 represents 3,244,700). Based on the National Employer Health Insurance Survey; for details on sample survey, see source]

State	One or more major health plans [1] — Number (1,000)	One or more major health plans [1] — Percent of all establishments	Any managed care plan [2] (percent)	Percent of employees enrolled in employer's plan	State	One or more major health plans [1] — Number (1,000)	One or more major health plans [1] — Percent of all establishments	Any managed care plan [2] (percent)	Percent of employees enrolled in employer's plan
U.S. ..	3,244.7	51.6	55.5	57.6	MO	71.2	52.2	64.8	56.7
AL	48.5	52.0	57.5	57.2	MT	11.7	40.0	40.7	41.2
AK	7.0	46.2	36.1	51.7	NE	22.2	46.2	36.6	47.8
AZ	46.8	49.7	75.5	53.7	NV	17.4	52.1	71.0	53.4
AR	25.9	40.3	37.2	51.8	NH	19.5	57.5	36.9	55.0
CA	379.8	47.0	84.2	54.4	NJ	94.0	52.0	41.5	62.5
CO	54.6	53.1	67.2	54.2	NM	21.3	49.4	54.9	46.7
CT	50.9	60.4	40.1	62.9	NY	227.1	54.6	50.9	61.3
DE	10.1	64.2	45.5	62.2	NC	86.6	51.9	37.5	62.6
DC	12.7	66.0	74.7	68.7	ND	10.1	49.1	29.0	46.1
FL	169.9	47.5	61.5	52.8	OH	135.6	54.7	48.1	60.8
GA	91.1	54.8	47.9	60.6	OK	36.7	43.9	57.1	47.4
HI	24.8	85.8	81.2	74.9	OR	47.0	51.6	69.3	57.2
ID	17.0	49.9	36.6	46.2	PA	158.7	61.0	37.1	64.1
IL	139.4	53.2	54.7	62.5	RI	16.2	64.5	65.9	63.9
IN	69.0	50.3	42.9	59.9	SC	40.1	48.8	34.9	59.7
IA	41.7	44.0	48.6	53.2	SD	10.5	44.7	24.6	44.7
KS	34.9	48.3	48.3	53.6	TN	53.5	48.2	57.1	61.5
KY	43.0	49.5	46.3	54.9	TX	186.5	44.7	48.6	53.3
LA	39.7	43.9	48.0	51.1	UT	21.3	47.3	61.6	48.4
ME	19.8	56.7	31.1	59.0	VT	11.1	55.0	47.3	50.6
MD	65.0	56.8	63.5	57.6	VA	85.1	55.7	51.6	57.6
MA	89.7	60.4	65.3	60.5	WA	81.9	56.4	75.0	58.4
MI	114.0	60.1	48.2	61.9	WV	19.3	51.9	26.9	54.0
MN	65.8	51.1	57.3	56.1	WI	66.2	52.6	50.3	54.8
MS	24.6	43.3	38.6	55.0	WY	8.0	47.3	20.6	44.4

[1] Major health plans typically cover hospital care and doctor visits. [2] Covers both health maintenance organizations and preferred provider organizations.

Source: U.S. National Center for Health Statistics, *Employer-Sponsored Health Insurance, State and National Estimates,* 1997.

No. 190. Persons With and Without Health Insurance Coverage, by State: 1997

[225,646 represents 225,646,000. Based on the Current Population Survey and subject to sampling error; see text, Section 1, Population, and Appendix III]

State	Total persons covered (1,000)	Total persons not covered — Number (1,000)	Total persons not covered — Percent of total	Children not covered — Number (1,000)	Children not covered — Percent of total	State	Total persons covered (1,000)	Total persons not covered — Number (1,000)	Total persons not covered — Percent of total	Children not covered — Number (1,000)	Children not covered — Percent of total
U.S.	225,646	43,448	16.1	10,743	15.0	MO	4,653	669	12.6	178	13.0
AL	3,588	659	15.5	151	14.4	MT	720	174	19.5	43	17.8
AK	525	116	18.1	31	15.0	NE	1,482	180	10.8	46	10.0
AZ	3,514	1,141	24.5	368	27.4	NV	1,423	301	17.5	90	19.9
AR	1,983	639	24.4	209	27.4	NH	1,059	141	11.8	33	9.6
CA	25,892	7,095	21.5	1,709	18.3	NJ	6,657	1,320	16.5	297	15.1
CO	3,337	592	15.1	137	13.4	NM	1,414	413	22.6	118	20.1
CT	2,904	395	12.0	93	11.0	NY	14,969	3,174	17.5	724	15.5
DE	652	98	13.1	28	14.1	NC	6,211	1,141	15.5	330	18.1
DC	434	84	16.2	17	14.7	ND	542	97	15.2	30	17.0
FL	11,582	2,817	19.6	639	20.3	OH	9,934	1,297	11.5	313	10.3
GA	6,303	1,344	17.6	363	16.8	OK	2,745	593	17.8	155	16.8
HI	1,094	89	7.5	15	5.3	OR	2,858	440	13.3	96	11.5
ID	1,034	223	17.7	72	18.7	PA	10,713	1,209	10.1	241	8.2
IL	10,592	1,506	12.4	382	11.0	RI	848	96	10.2	16	7.9
IN	5,196	669	11.4	195	12.3	SC	3,175	640	16.8	188	18.3
IA	2,490	340	12.0	84	11.1	SD	628	84	11.8	18	9.8
KS	2,286	304	11.7	69	9.7	TN	4,786	756	13.6	159	10.6
KY	3,335	587	15.0	142	14.5	TX	14,915	4,836	24.5	1,468	24.9
LA	3,423	827	19.5	232	21.3	UT	1,805	280	13.4	86	12.6
ME	1,043	182	14.9	41	15.0	VT	526	55	9.5	8	6.0
MD	4,380	677	13.4	126	10.1	VA	5,898	854	12.6	191	11.4
MA	5,249	755	12.6	115	8.4	WA	5,093	655	11.4	119	7.5
MI	8,661	1,133	11.6	211	8.1	WV	1,447	300	17.2	39	11.4
MN	4,329	438	9.2	105	7.5	WI	4,717	409	8.0	62	4.7
MS	2,187	550	20.1	144	18.4	WY	415	76	15.5	19	13.1

Source: U.S. Census Bureau; "Health Insurance Coverage: 1997 - Table 8;" published 3 February 1999; <http://www.census.gov/hhes/hlthins/hlthin97/hi97t8.html>; and unpublished data.

No. 191. Health Maintenance Organizations (HMOs): 1980 to 1998

[As of January 1, except as noted (9.1 represents 9,100,000). An HMO is a prepaid health plan delivering comprehensive care to members through designated providers, having a fixed periodic payment for health care services, and requiring members to be in a plan for a specified period of time (usually 1 year). A group HMO delivers health services through a physician group that is controlled by the HMO unit or contracts with one or more independent group practices to provide health services. An individual practice association (IPA) HMO contracts directly with physicians in independent practice, and/or contracts with one or more associations of physicians in independent practice, and/or contracts with one or more multispecialty group practices. Data are based on a census of HMOs. For composition of regions, see map, inside front cover]

Type of practice and size	1980 (June 30)	1985 (Dec. 31)	1990	1993	1994	1995	1996	1997	1998
NUMBER OF PLANS									
Total	235	478	572	551	540	550	628	651	651
Model type:									
I.P.A	97	244	360	332	319	323	366	284	317
Network.	138	234	212	150	117	107	122	109	122
Mixed	(NA)	(NA)	(NA)	69	104	120	140	258	212
Region:									
Northeast.	55	81	115	102	101	99	111	110	107
Midwest.	72	157	160	169	159	154	181	184	185
South	45	141	176	167	173	190	217	236	237
West	63	99	121	113	107	107	119	121	122
ENROLLMENT [1] (mil.)									
Total	9.1	21.0	33.0	38.4	42.2	46.2	52.5	58.8	64.8
Model type:									
I.P.A	1.7	6.4	13.7	15.3	16.1	17.4	21.7	21.0	24.8
Group	7.4	14.6	19.3	15.4	13.6	12.9	13.5	10.8	13.1
Mixed	(NA)	(NA)	(NA)	7.7	12.5	15.9	17.2	27.0	26.9
Federal program: [2]									
Medicaid [3]	0.3	0.6	1.2	1.7	2.6	3.5	4.7	5.5	7.8
Medicare	0.4	1.1	1.8	2.2	2.5	2.9	3.7	4.8	5.7

NA Not available.   [1] Excludes enrollees participating in open-ended plans.   [2] Refers to enrollment by medicaid or medicare beneficiaries, where the program contracts directly with the HMO to pay the appropriate annual premium.   [3] Enrollment for 1990 as of June 30.

Source: Interstudy Publications, Minneapolis, MN, *The InterStudy Competitive Edge*, annual (copyright).

No. 192. Annual Receipts/Revenue for the Health Service Industries: 1990 to 1997

[In millions of dollars (271,212 represents $271,212,000,000). Unless otherwise noted, receipts estimates are obtained from a sample of employer and nonemployer firms. Revenue estimates are obtained from a sample of employer firms only]

Industry	1987 SIC code [1]	1990	1993	1994	1995	1996	1997
TAXABLE FIRMS—RECEIPTS							
Health services [2]	80	271,212	335,108	351,419	376,279	398,353	421,317
Offices and clinics of MD's	801	128,871	154,242	159,616	167,969	172,926	179,718
Offices and clinics of dentists	802	31,502	38,946	41,663	44,909	47,411	50,979
Offices and clinics of doctors of osteopathy . .	803	3,254	4,159	4,354	4,698	4,749	4,952
Offices and clinics of other practitioners [2] . . .	804	20,139	25,367	25,891	27,357	28,409	29,850
Offices and clinics of chiropractors	8041	5,467	6,936	6,757	6,742	7,003	7,259
Offices and clinics of optometrists.	8042	4,799	5,715	6,021	6,113	6,330	6,491
Offices and clinics of podiatrists	8043	1,811	2,156	2,190	2,388	2,443	2,397
Nursing and personal care facilities	805	30,162	36,172	37,320	41,135	44,282	46,944
Hospitals [3] . . . . [3] .	806	26,487	33,331	35,143	38,417	44,669	50,154
General medical and surgical hospitals [3] . .	8062	20,442	26,683	27,993	30,704	36,496	40,920
Psychiatric hospitals [3]	8063	4,129	3,730	3,764	3,847	3,508	3,877
Specialty hospitals, except psychiatric [3]. . .	8069	1,916	2,918	3,386	3,866	4,665	5,357
Medical and dental laboratories	807	12,033	15,066	15,427	15,524	16,054	16,523
Medical laboratories.	8071	9,996	12,735	13,007	12,909	13,277	13,713
Dental laboratories.	8072	2,037	2,331	2,420	2,615	2,777	2,810
Home health care services	808	7,556	13,178	15,394	17,987	19,556	19,248
Miscellaneous allied services, n.e.c. [2][4]	809	11,208	14,647	16,611	18,283	20,297	22,949
Kidney dialysis centers	8092	1,451	2,468	2,898	3,259	3,391	3,723
Specialty outpatient facilities, n.e.c. [4]	8093	5,326	6,999	7,965	8,616	9,500	10,619
TAX EXEMPT FIRMS—REVENUE [3]							
Selected health services [2]	80 pt.	267,858	345,081	363,112	385,210	401,047	414,990
Offices and clinics of doctors of medicine . . .	801	12,888	19,647	21,882	24,873	26,153	28,447
Nursing and personal care facilities	805	12,132	15,972	16,564	17,570	18,510	19,712
Hospitals.	806	233,615	294,757	308,105	325,033	337,822	347,837
General medical and surgical hospitals . . .	8062	210,503	268,885	281,430	297,407	309,681	319,535
Psychiatric hospitals.	8063	11,008	10,243	9,848	9,211	9,291	9,742
Specialty hospitals, exc. psychiatric.	8069	12,104	15,629	16,827	18,415	18,850	18,560
Home health care services	808	3,874	6,608	7,428	7,943	8,043	8,083
Miscellaneous allied services, n.e.c. [2][4]	809	5,285	8,007	9,025	9,666	10,388	10,770
Kidney dialysis centers	8092	305	462	526	620	676	715
Specialty outpatient facilities, n.e.c. [4]	8093	3,519	4,737	5,320	5,661	5,957	5,896

[1] Based on the 1987 Standard Industrial Classification code; see text, Section 17, Business.   [2] Includes other industries not shown separately.   [3] Estimates are obtained from a sample of employer firms only.   [4] N.e.c. means not elsewhere classified.

Source: U.S. Census Bureau, *Current Business Reports, Service Annual Survey: 1997*, BS/97.

130   Health and Nutrition

No. 193. Employment in the Health Service Industries: 1980 to 1998

[In thousands (5,278 represents 5,278,000). See headnote Table 690]

Industry	1987 SIC code [1]	1980	1990	1995	1996	1997	1998
Health services [2]	80	5,278	7,814	9,230	9,478	9,720	9,904
Offices and clinics of MDs	801	802	1,338	1,609	1,678	1,743	1,817
Offices and clinics of dentists	802	(NA)	513	592	611	628	644
Offices and clinics of other practitioners	804	96	277	397	417	439	464
Nursing and personal care facilities	805	997	1,415	1,691	1,730	1,755	1,757
Skilled nursing care facilities	8051	(NA)	989	1,253	1,295	1,330	1,333
Intermediate care facilities	8052	(NA)	200	211	211	208	208
Other, n.e.c. [3]	8059	(NA)	227	227	225	216	216
Hospitals	806	2,750	3,549	3,772	3,812	3,869	3,953
General medical and surgical hospitals	8062	(NA)	3,268	3,474	3,514	3,567	3,642
Psychiatric hospitals	8063	(NA)	104	91	87	84	85
Specialty hospitals, exc. psychiatric	8069	(NA)	176	208	210	218	225
Medical and dental laboratories	807	(NA)	166	190	194	199	202
Home health care services	808	(NA)	291	629	675	713	680

NA Not available. [1] Based on the 1987 Standard Industrial Classification code; see text, Section 17, Business. [2] Includes other industries not shown separately. [3] N.e.c. means not elsewhere classified.

Source: U.S. Bureau of Labor Statistics, Bulletins 2445 and 2481, and *Employment and Earnings*, monthly, March and June issues.

No. 194. Physicians, by Selected Activity: 1980 to 1997

[In thousands (467.7 represents 467,700). 1980, 1985, and 1995-97, as of Dec. 31; other years as of Jan. 1, except as noted. Includes Puerto Rico and outlying areas]

Activity	1980	1985	1990	1994	1995	1996	1997
Doctors of medicine, total	467.7	552.7	615.4	684.4	720.3	737.8	756.7
Professionally active	435.5	511.1	560.0	619.8	646.0	663.9	684.6
Place of medical education:							
U.S. medical graduates	343.6	398.4	437.2	475.0	492.2	505.7	519.7
Foreign medical graduates [1]	91.8	112.7	122.8	144.8	153.8	158.3	164.9
Sex:							
Male	386.7	436.3	463.9	494.9	505.9	515.6	527.0
Female	48.7	74.8	96.1	124.9	140.1	148.3	157.7
Active non-Federal	417.7	489.5	539.5	597.3	624.9	643.5	665.2
Patient care	361.9	431.5	487.8	543.2	564.1	580.7	603.7
Office-based practice	271.3	329.0	359.9	407.0	427.3	445.8	458.2
General and family practice	47.8	53.9	57.6	58.2	59.9	61.8	62.0
Cardiovascular diseases	6.7	9.1	10.7	12.9	13.7	14.3	15.0
Dermatology	4.4	5.3	6.0	6.7	7.0	7.2	7.4
Gastroenterology	2.7	4.1	5.2	6.7	7.3	7.6	7.9
Internal medicine	40.5	52.7	57.8	67.9	72.6	77.9	81.4
Pediatrics	17.4	22.4	26.5	31.5	33.9	35.5	36.8
Pulmonary diseases	2.0	3.0	3.7	4.6	5.0	4.9	5.0
General surgery	22.4	24.7	24.5	24.2	24.1	25.4	27.9
Obstetrics and gynecology	19.5	23.5	25.5	28.2	29.1	29.9	30.1
Ophthalmology	10.6	12.2	13.1	14.3	14.6	14.9	15.1
Orthopedic surgery	10.7	13.0	14.2	16.6	17.1	17.6	18.5
Otolaryngology	5.3	5.8	6.4	6.9	7.1	7.2	7.4
Plastic surgery	2.4	3.3	3.8	4.3	4.6	5.0	5.3
Urological surgery	6.2	7.1	7.4	7.8	8.0	8.2	8.4
Anesthesiology	11.3	15.3	17.8	22.0	23.8	24.9	25.6
Diagnostic radiology	4.2	7.7	9.8	12.1	12.8	13.3	14.1
Emergency medicine	(NA)	(NA)	8.4	10.6	11.7	12.3	12.5
Neurology	3.2	4.7	5.6	7.1	7.6	7.9	8.2
Pathology, anatomical/clinical	6.0	6.9	7.3	8.7	9.0	9.7	10.2
Psychiatry	15.9	18.5	20.0	22.6	23.3	24.4	24.5
Other specialty	31.9	35.8	28.8	33.2	35.0	35.8	35.0
Hospital-based practice	90.6	102.5	127.9	136.1	136.8	134.9	145.3
Residents and interns [2]	59.6	72.2	89.9	91.5	93.7	90.6	95.8
Full-time hospital staff	31.0	30.3	38.0	44.6	43.1	44.3	49.5
Other professional activity [3]	35.2	44.0	39.0	39.9	40.3	42.8	41.5
Not classified	20.6	14.0	12.7	14.3	20.6	20.0	20.0
Federal	17.8	21.6	20.5	22.5	21.1	20.4	19.4
Patient care	14.6	17.3	16.1	19.3	18.1	18.2	16.9
Other professional activity [3]	3.2	4.3	4.4	3.2	3.0	2.2	2.4
Inactive/unknown address	32.1	41.6	55.4	64.7	74.3	73.8	72.1
Doctors of osteopathy [4]	18.8	24.0	30.9	35.0	35.7	37.3	38.9

NA Not available. [1] Foreign medical graduates received their medical education in schools outside the United States and Canada. [2] Includes clinical fellows. [3] Includes medical teaching, administration, research, and other. [4] As of July. Total DOs. Source: American Osteopathic Association, Chicago, IL.

Source: Except as noted, American Medical Association, Chicago, IL, *Physician Characteristics and Distribution in the U.S.*, annual (copyright).

U.S. Census Bureau, Statistical Abstract of the United States: 1999

No. 195. Dentists and Nurses: 1980 to 1996

[As of end of year (141 represents 141,000). Excludes Puerto Rico and outlying areas]

Item	Unit	1980	1985	1990	1992	1993	1994	1995	1996
Dentists, number [1]	1,000	141	156	[2]173	183	187	191	194	196
Active (exc. in Federal service) [3]	1,000	121	136	147	152	154	157	159	162
Rate per 100,000 population [4]	Rate	53	57	59	60	60	60	61	61
Nurses, number (active registered)	1,000	1,273	1,538	1,790	1,907	1,976	2,044	2,116	2,162
Rate per 100,000 population [4]	Rate	560	644	713	748	767	785	805	815

[1] Includes current year's graduates. [2] Revised since originally published. [3] Source: American Dental Association, Bureau of Economic and Behavioral Research, Master Membership file and periodic censuses. [4] Based on U.S. Census Bureau estimated resident population as of July 1. Estimates reflect revisions based on the 1990 Census of Population.

Source: Except as noted, U.S. Dept. of Health and Human Services, Health Resources and Services Administration, unpublished data.

No. 196. Health Professions Schools—Number, Enrollment, and Graduates: 1980 to 1997

[Data on the number of schools are reported as of the beginning of the academic year; all other data are reported as of the end of the academic year. Data are based on reporting by health professions schools]

Year	Medi-cine	Oste-opathy	Registered nursing Total	Bacca-laureate	Associ-ate degree	Diploma	Licensed practi-cal nursing	Den-tistry	Optom-etry	Phar-macy
NUMBER OF SCHOOLS [1]										
1980	126	14	1,385	377	697	311	1,299	60	16	72
1985	127	15	1,477	427	777	273	1,254	60	17	72
1988	127	15	1,465	467	789	209	1,068	58	17	74
1989	127	15	1,442	479	792	171	1,095	58	17	74
1990	127	15	1,457	488	812	157	1,171	58	17	74
1991	126	15	1,470	489	829	152	1,154	56	17	74
1992	126	15	1,484	501	838	145	1,125	55	17	74
1993	126	15	1,484	501	848	135	1,154	55	17	74
1994	126	16	1,493	507	857	129	1,159	54	17	74
1995	125	16	1,501	509	868	124	1,185	54	17	74
1996	125	16	1,516	521	876	119	1,210	54	17	74
1997	125	17	1,508	523	876	109	(NA)	54	17	78
FIRST-YEAR ENROLLMENT										
1980	16,930	1,426	105,952	35,414	53,633	16,905	56,316	6,132	1,202	8,035
1985	16,997	1,750	118,224	39,573	63,776	14,875	47,034	5,047	1,187	6,986
1988	16,713	1,692	94,269	28,505	57,375	8,389	43,774	4,370	1,268	7,751
1989	16,868	1,780	103,025	29,042	63,973	10,010	47,602	4,196	1,271	7,990
1990	16,756	1,844	108,580	29,858	68,634	10,088	52,969	3,979	1,258	8,033
1991	16,876	1,950	113,526	33,437	69,869	10,220	56,176	4,001	1,239	8,267
1992	17,071	1,974	122,656	37,886	74,079	10,691	58,245	4,047	1,355	8,343
1993	17,079	2,035	126,837	41,290	75,382	10,165	60,749	4,072	1,395	8,664
1994	17,121	2,162	129,897	42,953	77,343	9,601	60,632	4,100	1,351	8,970
1995	17,085	2,217	127,184	43,451	76,016	7,717	57,906	4,121	1,390	9,157
1996	17,058	2,274	119,205	40,048	72,930	6,227	(NA)	4,237	1,438	8,740
1997	16,935	2,535	(NA)	(NA)	(NA)	(NA)	(NA)	4,255	1,362	8,790
TOTAL ENROLLMENT										
1980	63,800	4,571	234,659	98,939	92,069	43,651	52,202	22,482	4,517	23,074
1985	67,016	6,547	237,232	95,008	104,968	37,256	48,840	20,588	4,569	18,646
1988	65,735	6,586	182,947	73,621	90,399	18,927	40,035	17,885	4,646	21,424
1989	65,300	6,614	184,924	70,078	95,986	18,860	42,808	17,094	4,708	22,447
1990	65,016	6,615	201,458	74,865	106,175	20,418	46,720	16,412	4,723	23,013
1991	65,163	6,792	221,170	81,788	117,413	21,969	52,749	15,951	4,760	23,238
1992	65,602	7,012	237,598	90,877	123,816	22,905	56,762	15,882	4,864	23,482
1993	66,142	7,375	257,983	102,128	132,603	23,252	59,095	15,980	5,078	26,287
1994	66,629	7,822	270,228	110,693	137,300	22,235	61,007	16,250	(NA)	27,143
1995	67,072	8,146	268,350	112,659	135,895	19,796	59,428	16,353	5,201	27,667
1996	66,970	8,475	261,219	109,505	135,235	16,479	56,028	16,552	5,312	28,060
1997	67,276	8,961	238,244	103,213	122,242	12,789	(NA)	16,570	5,210	28,027
GRADUATES										
1980	15,113	1,059	75,523	24,994	36,034	14,495	41,892	5,256	1,073	7,432
1985	16,318	1,474	82,075	24,975	45,208	11,892	36,955	5,353	1,114	5,735
1988	15,919	1,572	64,839	21,504	37,397	5,938	26,912	4,581	1,106	6,184
1989	15,630	1,609	61,660	18,997	37,837	4,826	30,368	4,312	1,143	6,560
1990	15,398	1,529	66,088	18,571	42,318	5,199	35,417	4,233	1,115	6,956
1991	15,427	1,534	72,230	19,264	46,794	6,172	38,100	3,995	1,224	7,122
1992	15,365	1,532	80,839	21,415	52,896	6,528	41,951	3,918	1,150	7,113
1993	15,466	1,606	88,149	24,442	56,770	6,937	44,822	3,778	1,167	7,380
1994	15,555	1,752	94,870	28,912	58,839	7,119	45,083	3,875	1,125	7,504
1995	15,888	1,843	97,052	31,254	58,749	7,049	44,234	3,908	1,219	7,837
1996	15,907	1,932	94,757	32,413	56,641	5,703	(NA)	3,810	1,210	8,003
1997	15,923	2,020	(NA)	(NA)	(NA)	(NA)	(NA)	(NA)	(NA)	(NA)
2000, proj.	16,112	1,934	79,660	26,490	47,790	5,380	(NA)	3,242	1,200	7,120

NA Not available. [1] Some nursing schools offer more than one type of program. Numbers shown for nursing are number of nursing programs.

Source: U.S. National Center for Health Statistics, Health United States, annual.

132 Health and Nutrition

No. 197. Active Non-Federal Physicians and Nurses, by State: 1997

[As of December. Excludes doctors of osteopathy, federally-employed persons, and physicians with addresses unknown. Includes all physicians not classified according to activity status]

State	Physicians Total	Rate [1]	Nurses Total	Rate [1]	State	Physicians Total	Rate [1]	Nurses Total	Rate [1]
United States..	656,197	245	2,203,000	823	Missouri	12,175	225	52,300	967
Alabama	8,399	194	33,200	768	Montana	1,655	188	7,300	831
Alaska	975	160	6,700	1,099	Nebraska	3,530	213	15,100	911
Arizona	9,094	200	34,600	760	Nevada	2,837	169	10,400	620
Arkansas	4,662	185	18,500	733	New Hampshire	2,694	230	11,100	947
California	78,502	244	178,500	555	New Jersey	23,101	287	66,500	825
Colorado	9,099	234	31,000	796	New Mexico	3,595	209	12,000	696
Connecticut	11,236	344	33,000	1,010	New York	68,017	375	169,500	934
Delaware	1,688	230	8,000	1,088	North Carolina	16,688	225	65,500	881
District of Columbia	3,722	702	8,600	1,623	North Dakota	1,401	219	7,200	1,123
Florida	34,100	232	123,700	843	Ohio	25,688	230	103,000	920
Georgia	15,292	204	54,700	730	Oklahoma	5,514	166	19,900	599
Hawaii	3,001	252	9,100	763	Oregon	7,152	221	27,500	848
Idaho	1,817	150	7,200	596	Pennsylvania	33,849	282	129,800	1,081
Illinois	30,373	253	107,200	894	Rhode Island	3,199	324	11,400	1,155
Indiana	11,238	192	47,600	812	South Carolina	7,609	201	29,200	771
Iowa	4,885	171	29,900	1,048	South Dakota	1,309	177	7,500	1,017
Kansas	5,246	202	22,300	857	Tennessee	12,983	242	47,300	881
Kentucky	8,018	205	31,500	806	Texas	37,987	196	127,100	656
Louisiana	10,384	239	33,600	772	Utah	4,060	197	13,300	644
Maine	2,663	214	13,300	1,071	Vermont	1,698	288	5,200	883
Maryland	18,469	362	43,400	852	Virginia	15,708	233	55,600	825
Massachusetts	24,597	402	72,900	1,192	Washington	12,859	229	44,000	784
Michigan	21,329	218	81,100	829	West Virginia	3,806	210	15,400	848
Minnesota	11,590	247	48,200	1,028	Wisconsin	11,630	224	46,400	892
Mississippi	4,273	156	20,600	754	Wyoming	801	167	4,400	917

[1] Per 100,000 resident population. Based on U.S. Census Bureau estimates as of July 1, 1997.

Source: Physicians: American Medical Association, Chicago, IL, *Physician Characteristics and Distribution in the U.S.*, annual (copyright); Nurses: U.S. Dept. of Health and Human Services, Health Resources and Services Administration, unpublished data.

No. 198. Physician Contacts, by Patient Characteristics: 1980 to 1996

[426 represents 426,000,000. See headnote, Table 222. Based on National Health Interview Survey; see Appendix III]

| Year | Total visits (mil.) | | | | Visits per person per year | | | | | | | | | |
| | Sex | | Race | | Sex | | Race | | Age (years) | | | | | |
	Male	Female	White	Black	Male	Female	White	Black	Under 5	5 to 17	18 to 24	25 to 44	45 to 64	65 and over
1980	426	610	903	115	4.0	5.4	4.8	4.5	[1]6.7	[2]3.2	[3]4.0	4.6	5.1	6.4
1985	498	733	1,074	132	4.4	6.1	5.4	4.7	[1]6.3	[2]3.1	[3]4.2	4.9	6.1	8.3
1988	530	774	1,139	136	4.5	6.2	5.6	4.6	7.0	3.4	3.8	5.1	6.1	8.7
1989	552	771	1,148	140	4.7	6.1	5.6	4.7	6.7	3.5	3.9	5.1	6.1	8.9
1990	558	806	1,178	148	4.7	6.4	5.7	4.9	6.9	3.2	4.3	5.1	6.4	9.2
1991	589	842	1,243	152	4.9	6.6	6.0	4.9	7.1	3.4	3.9	5.1	6.6	10.4
1992	624	889	1,286	181	5.1	6.9	6.1	5.8	6.9	3.5	4.1	5.4	7.2	10.6
1993	634	917	1,314	183	5.1	7.0	6.2	5.7	7.2	3.6	4.0	5.4	7.1	10.9
1994	652	930	1,350	179	5.2	7.0	6.3	5.4	6.8	3.5	3.9	5.5	7.3	11.3
1995	626	922	1,325	170	4.9	6.9	6.1	5.2	6.5	3.4	3.9	5.2	7.1	11.1
1996	633	933	1,339	180	4.9	6.9	6.1	5.4	6.5	3.3	4.1	4.9	7.2	11.7

[1] Under 6 years. [2] 6 to 16 years. [3] 17 to 24 years.

Source: U.S. National Center for Health Statistics, *Vital and Health Statistics*, Series 10, No. 200, and earlier reports; and unpublished data.

Health and Nutrition   133

No. 199. Visits to Office Based Physicians: 1997

[787,372 represents 787,372,000. Based on the 1997 National Ambulatory Medical Care Survey and subject to sampling error; see source for details]

Characteristic	Number of visits (1,000)	Percent distri- bution	Visits per person per year	Characteristic	Number of visits (1,000)	Percent distri- bution	Visits per person per year
All visits	787,372	100.0	3.0	American Indian/Eskimo/ Aleut	3,165	0.4	1.3
Age:							
Under 15 years old	137,361	17.4	2.3	Visit status:			
15 to 24 years old	62,488	7.9	1.7	Old patient	678,699	86.2	(X)
25 to 44 years old	203,701	25.9	2.4	New patient	99,321	12.6	(X)
45 to 64 years old	192,753	24.5	3.5	Unknown	9,352	1.2	(X)
65 to 74 years old	99,714	12.7	5.5				
75 years old and over . . .	91,355	11.6	6.5	Primary source of payment:			
				Private insurance	417,744	53.1	(X)
Sex:				Medicare	163,263	20.7	(X)
Male	315,891	40.1	2.4	Medicaid	64,047	8.1	(X)
Female	471,481	59.9	3.5	Worker's compensation . .	15,595	2.0	(X)
				Self pay	60,869	7.7	(X)
Race:				No charge	8,225	1.0	(X)
White	681,085	86.5	3.1	Other	41,000	5.2	(X)
Black	78,106	9.9	2.3	Unknown	16,629	2.1	(X)
Asian/Pacific Islander. . . .	25,015	3.2	2.5				

X Not applicable.

Source: U.S. National Center for Health Statistics, unpublished data.

No. 200. Medical Practice Characteristics, by Selected Specialty: 1985 to 1996

[Dollar figures in thousands (112.2 represents $112,200). Based on a sample telephone survey of 4,000 non-Federal office and hospital based patient care physicians, excluding residents. For details see source. For definition of mean, see Guide to Tabular Presentation]

Specialty	1985	1990	1992	1993	1994	1995	1996
Mean patient visits per week:							
All physicians [1]	117.1	120.9	114.8	112.4	109.6	107.6	109.4
General/Family practice	138.1	146.0	138.4	137.0	133.5	133.7	133.1
Internal medicine.	105.2	112.0	109.4	105.3	105.4	99.7	104.7
Surgery	108.2	107.6	101.6	98.3	98.8	97.1	95.1
Pediatrics.	130.8	134.0	126.9	130.9	125.5	125.9	121.1
Obstetrics/Gynecology	112.0	120.0	110.5	111.0	102.9	94.0	104.2
Mean hours in patient care per week:							
All physicians [1]	51.3	53.3	52.9	52.9	52.1	51.3	53.4
General/Family practice	53.6	55.0	53.1	54.0	51.9	52.9	53.5
Internal medicine.	52.4	55.7	55.5	56.0	56.6	53.9	57.2
Surgery	51.2	53.1	53.0	54.3	53.4	53.2	54.2
Pediatrics.	50.6	52.4	52.6	53.8	51.6	50.4	51.0
Obstetrics/Gynecology	56.9	60.4	58.8	58.9	58.1	54.6	60.5
Mean net income:							
All physicians [1]	112.2	164.3	181.7	189.3	182.4	195.5	199.0
General/Family practice	77.9	102.7	114.4	116.8	121.2	131.2	139.1
Internal medicine.	102.0	152.5	162.1	180.8	174.9	185.7	185.7
Surgery	155.0	236.4	250.5	262.7	255.2	269.4	275.2
Pediatrics.	76.2	106.5	123.9	135.4	126.2	140.5	140.6
Obstetrics/Gynecology	124.3	207.3	220.7	221.9	200.4	244.3	231.0
Mean professional expenses:							
All physicians [1]	102.7	150.0	183.4	182.2	183.1	201.6	217.6
General/Family practice	96.5	134.5	162.9	162.4	190.5	179.4	210.7
Internal medicine.	90.0	139.2	174.1	185.2	186.4	200.4	192.2
Surgery	135.7	201.0	245.1	245.9	249.9	265.1	307.2
Pediatrics.	87.3	138.0	173.7	167.4	157.8	208.5	212.4
Obstetrics/Gynecology	131.9	212.6	239.7	238.1	196.8	266.9	267.1
Mean liability premium:							
All physicians [1]	10.5	14.5	13.8	14.4	15.1	15.0	14.1
General/Family practice	6.8	7.8	8.2	7.9	10.2	9.0	8.4
Internal medicine.	5.8	9.2	8.6	9.0	8.6	9.4	8.9
Surgery	16.6	22.8	20.9	22.7	22.3	23.3	21.7
Pediatrics.	4.7	7.8	7.7	8.6	7.6	7.9	8.3
Obstetrics/Gynecology	23.5	34.3	34.4	33.7	37.4	38.6	35.2

[1] Includes other specialties not shown separately.

Source: American Medical Association, Chicago IL, *Socioeconomic Characteristics of Medical Practice*, annual (copyright).

No. 201. Percent of Women, 15 to 44 Years Old, Who Received Selected Medical Services From a Medical Care Provider: 1995

[In percent, except as indicated (60,201 represents 60,201,000)]

Characteristic	Number (1,000)	Pregnancy test	Pap smear	Pelvic exam	HIV test [1]	Other STD [2] test or treatment	Test or treatment for infection [3]
Total	60,201	16.0	61.9	61.3	17.3	7.6	21.0
AGE AT INTERVIEW							
15-19 years old	8,961	16.1	33.5	32.4	14.6	9.4	16.9
15-17 years old	5,452	11.4	23.0	23.4	12.1	7.1	12.2
18-19 years old	3,508	23.3	49.9	46.4	18.5	13.0	24.2
20-24 years old	9,041	27.4	68.7	66.5	23.7	14.0	28.1
25-29 years old	9,693	25.3	70.9	69.3	23.6	10.3	25.7
30-34 years old	11,065	17.4	69.5	70.3	18.5	6.5	21.8
35-39 years old	11,211	8.1	62.9	62.6	14.2	4.7	19.2
40-44 years old	10,230	4.3	62.7	63.2	10.0	2.2	15.1
RACE AND HISPANIC ORIGIN							
Hispanic	6,702	19.8	52.2	52.6	21.9	7.2	20.4
Non-Hispanic White	42,522	14.8	63.2	63.2	14.5	7.1	20.9
Non-Hispanic Black	8,210	19.8	67.6	63.0	28.7	11.4	24.8
Non-Hispanic other	2,767	14.3	47.7	47.7	14.7	(B)	13.6
MARITAL STATUS							
Never married	22,679	15.5	52.1	49.8	18.9	10.7	20.1
Currently married	29,673	17.3	68.5	69.0	14.5	4.7	20.9
Formerly married	7,849	12.4	64.8	65.3	23.1	9.7	24.2

B Figure does not meet standard of reliability. [1] Excludes HIV (human immunodeficiency virus) tests done as part of blood donation. [2] STD is sexually transmitted disease. [3] Refers to vaginal, urinary tract, and pelvic infections.

Source: U.S. National Center for Health Statistics, *Fertility, Family Planning, and Women's Health: New data from the 1995 National Survey of Family Growth, Vital and Health Statistics*, Series 23, No. 19, 1997.

No. 202. Use of Mammography for Women 40 Years Old and Over by Patient Characteristics: 1990 to 1994

[Percent of women having a mammogram within the past 2 years. Covers civilian noninstitutional population. Based on National Health Interview Survey; see Appendix III]

Characteristic	1990	1993	1994	Characteristic	1990	1993	1994
Total [1]	51.4	59.7	60.9	Years of school completed:			
40 to 49 years old	55.1	59.9	61.3	Less than 12 years	36.4	46.4	48.2
50 years old and over	49.7	59.7	60.6	12 years	52.7	59.0	61.0
50 to 64 years old	56.0	65.1	66.5	13 years or more	62.8	69.5	69.7
65 years old and over	43.4	54.2	55.0				
White, non-Hispanic	52.7	60.6	61.3	Poverty status: [3]			
Black, non-Hispanic	46.0	59.2	64.4	Below poverty	28.7	41.6	43.3
Hispanic origin [2]	45.2	50.9	51.9	At or above poverty	54.8	62.8	64.2

[1] Includes all other races not shown separately and unknown education level and poverty status. [2] Persons of Hispanic origin may be of any race. [3] For explanation of poverty level, see text, Section 14, Income.

Source: U.S. National Center for Health Statistics, *Health United States, 1996-97 and Injury Chartbook*, 1997.

No. 203. Average Cost to Community Hospitals Per Patient: 1980 to 1997

[In dollars, except percent. Covers non-Federal short-term general or special hospitals (excluding psychiatric or tuberculosis hospitals and hospital units of institutions). Total cost per patient based on total hospital expenses (payroll, employee benefits, professional fees, supplies, etc.). Data have been adjusted for outpatient visits]

Type of expense and hospital	1980	1985	1990	1991	1992	1993	1994	1995	1996	1997
Average cost per day, total	245	460	687	752	820	881	931	968	1,006	1,033
Annual percent change [1]	12.9	11.9	7.8	9.5	9.0	7.4	5.7	4.0	3.9	2.6
Nongovernmental nonprofit	246	463	692	758	828	898	950	994	1,042	1,074
For profit	257	500	752	820	889	914	924	947	945	962
State and local government	239	433	634	696	754	800	859	878	903	914
Average cost per stay, total	1,851	3,245	4,947	5,360	5,794	6,132	6,230	6,216	6,225	6,262
Nongovernmental nonprofit	1,902	3,307	5,001	5,393	5,809	6,178	6,257	6,279	6,344	6,393
For profit	1,676	3,033	4,727	5,134	5,548	5,643	5,529	5,425	5,207	5,219
State and local government	1,750	3,106	4,838	5,340	5,871	6,206	6,513	6,445	6,419	6,475

[1] Change from immediate prior year.

Source: Health Forum, An American Hospital Association Company, Chicago, IL, *Hospital Statistics 1999 Edition* (copyright).

U.S. Census Bureau, Statistical Abstract of the United States: 1999

No. 204. Hospitals—Summary Characteristics: 1980 to 1997

[For beds: **1,365 represents 1,365,000**. Covers hospitals accepted for registration by the American Hospital Association; see text, this section. Short-term hospitals have an average patient stay of less than 30 days; long-term, an average stay of longer duration. Special hospitals include obstetrics and gynecology; eye, ear, nose, and throat; rehabilitation; orthopedic; and chronic and other special hospitals except psychiatric, tuberculosis, alcoholism, and chemical dependency hospitals]

Item	1980	1985	1990	1992	1993	1994	1995	1996	1997
Number:									
All hospitals	6,965	6,872	6,649	6,539	6,467	6,374	6,291	6,201	6,097
With 100 beds or more	3,755	3,805	3,620	3,572	3,558	3,492	3,376	3,347	3,267
Non-Federal [1]	6,606	6,529	6,312	6,214	6,151	6,067	5,992	5,911	5,812
Community hospitals [2]	5,830	5,732	5,384	5,292	5,261	5,229	5,194	5,134	5,057
Nongovernmental nonprofit	3,322	3,349	3,191	3,173	3,154	3,139	3,092	3,045	3,000
For profit	730	805	749	723	717	719	752	759	797
State and local government	1,778	1,578	1,444	1,396	1,390	1,371	1,350	1,330	1,260
Long-term general and special	157	128	131	115	117	110	112	112	125
Psychiatric	534	610	757	774	741	696	657	636	601
Tuberculosis	11	7	4	4	4	5	3	3	4
Federal	359	343	337	325	316	307	299	290	285
Beds (1,000):									
All hospitals [3]	1,365	1,318	1,213	1,178	1,163	1,128	1,081	1,062	1,035
Rate per 1,000 population [4]	6.0	5.5	4.9	4.6	4.5	4.3	4.1	4.0	3.9
Beds per hospital	196	190	182	180	179	177	172	171	170
Non-Federal [1]	1,248	1,197	1,113	1,085	1,071	1,044	1,004	989	973
Community hospitals [2]	988	1,001	927	921	919	902	873	862	853
Rate per 1,000 population [4]	4.3	4.2	3.7	3.6	3.6	3.5	3.3	3.3	3.2
Nongovernmental nonprofit	692	707	657	656	649	637	610	598	591
For profit	87	104	102	99	99	101	106	109	115
State and local government	209	189	169	167	169	164	157	155	148
Long-term general and special	39	31	25	23	21	19	19	19	17
Psychiatric	215	169	158	139	131	121	110	106	100
Tuberculosis	2	1	(Z)	(Z)	(Z)	1	(Z)	(Z)	(Z)
Federal	117	112	98	89	87	84	78	73	62
Average daily census (1,000):									
All hospitals	1,060	910	844	807	783	745	710	685	673
Community hospitals [2]	747	649	619	604	592	568	548	531	528
Nongovernmental nonprofit	542	476	455	445	432	413	393	379	376
For profit	57	54	54	51	51	50	55	56	60
State and local government	149	119	111	108	109	104	100	96	92
Expenses (bil. dol.): [5]									
All hospitals	91.9	153.3	234.9	282.5	301.5	310.8	320.3	330.5	342.3
Non-Federal [1]	84.0	141.0	219.6	264.3	281.9	290.8	300.0	308.3	319.6
Community hospitals [2]	76.9	130.5	203.7	248.1	266.1	275.8	285.6	293.8	305.8
Nongovernmental nonprofit	55.8	96.1	150.7	183.8	197.2	204.2	209.6	216.0	225.3
For profit	5.8	11.5	18.8	22.5	23.1	23.4	26.7	28.4	31.2
State and local government	15.2	22.9	34.2	41.8	45.8	48.1	49.3	49.4	49.3
Long-term general and special	1.2	1.9	2.7	2.7	2.7	2.3	2.2	2.3	2.5
Psychiatric	5.8	8.3	12.9	13.2	12.7	12.3	11.7	12.0	11.0
Tuberculosis	0.1	0.1	0.1	(Z)	0.1	0.7	0.4	(Z)	0.1
Federal	7.9	12.3	15.2	18.2	19.6	20.0	20.2	22.3	22.7
Personnel (1,000): [6]									
All hospitals	3,492	3,625	4,063	4,236	4,289	4,270	4,273	4,276	4,333
Non-Federal [1]	3,213	3,326	3,760	3,930	3,970	3,969	3,971	3,981	4,036
Community hospitals [2]	2,873	2,997	3,420	3,620	3,677	3,692	3,714	3,725	3,790
Nongovernmental nonprofit	2,086	2,216	2,533	2,692	2,711	2,719	2,702	2,711	2,765
For profit	189	221	273	285	289	301	343	359	385
State and local government	598	561	614	643	676	672	670	654	640
Long-term general and special	56	58	55	49	45	38	38	40	37
Psychiatric	275	263	280	256	242	233	215	212	204
Tuberculosis	3	2	1	1	1	1	1	1	1
Federal	279	299	303	306	320	301	301	295	296
Outpatient visits (mil.)	263.0	282.1	368.2	417.9	435.7	453.6	483.2	505.5	520.6
Emergency	82.0	80.1	92.8	95.8	97.4	96.0	99.9	97.6	97.4

Z Less than 500 beds or $50 million. [1] Includes hospital units of institutions. [2] Short term (average length of stay less than 30 days) general and special (e.g., obstetrics and gynecology; eye, ear, nose and throat; rehabilitation etc. except psychiatric, tuberculosis, alcoholism and chemical dependency). Excludes hospital units of institutions. [3] Beginning 1990, number of beds at end of reporting period; prior years, average number in 12 month period. [4] Based on U.S. Census Bureau estimated resident population as of July 1. Estimates reflect revisions based on the 1990 Census of Population. [5] Excludes new construction. [6] Includes full-time equivalents of part-time personnel.

Source: Health Forum, An American Hospital Association Company, Chicago, IL, *Hospital Statistics 1999 Edition*, and prior years (copyright).

No. 205. Community Hospitals, by State: 1990 to 1997

[For beds: 928.1 represents 928,100. For definition of community hospitals see footnote 2, Table 204]

State	Number of hospitals			Beds (1,000)			Patients admitted (1,000)		Average daily census [1] (1,000)		Outpatient visits (mil.)	
	1990	1995	1997	1990	1995	1997	1995	1997	1995	1997	1995	1997
United States ...	5,384	5,194	5,057	928.1	872.7	853.3	30,945	31,577	547.6	527.5	414.3	450.1
Alabama	120	115	111	18.6	18.3	18.6	642	685	10.7	10.8	6.4	7.0
Alaska	16	17	17	1.2	1.3	1.4	40	40	0.7	1.1	0.8	0.9
Arizona	61	61	63	9.9	9.9	10.6	427	476	5.6	6.6	4.0	4.4
Arkansas	86	85	82	10.9	10.1	10.1	342	346	6.0	5.8	3.6	4.2
California	445	424	414	80.5	75.0	74.1	3,029	3,110	45.0	44.2	39.5	43.6
Colorado	69	69	67	10.4	9.3	9.1	340	366	5.4	5.0	5.5	6.2
Connecticut	35	34	34	9.6	7.5	7.2	338	338	5.5	5.0	5.7	7.2
Delaware	8	8	6	2.0	1.9	1.9	81	81	1.5	1.3	1.4	1.2
District of Columbia	11	12	12	4.5	3.8	3.6	154	129	2.7	2.6	1.2	1.2
Florida	224	212	206	50.7	49.7	49.8	1,772	1,883	29.4	29.2	16.9	18.7
Georgia	163	160	158	25.7	26.1	25.7	859	856	15.8	15.1	9.6	10.2
Hawaii	18	21	19	2.9	3.0	2.8	97	97	2.4	2.3	2.1	2.4
Idaho	43	41	42	3.2	3.4	3.5	104	108	1.8	1.9	1.7	2.1
Illinois	210	207	202	45.8	42.0	40.3	1,452	1,443	25.0	23.4	20.6	22.0
Indiana	113	115	112	21.8	19.4	19.4	699	695	11.3	11.2	11.8	12.4
Iowa	124	116	115	14.3	12.6	12.2	361	367	7.1	6.9	6.2	7.5
Kansas	138	132	130	11.8	10.8	10.8	291	298	5.8	5.7	4.0	4.7
Kentucky	107	104	105	15.9	15.1	15.4	534	543	9.0	8.7	6.1	6.8
Louisiana	140	130	127	19.1	19.1	18.6	622	650	10.6	10.1	8.0	8.6
Maine	39	39	38	4.5	4.0	3.7	142	143	2.6	2.3	2.5	2.7
Maryland	52	50	51	13.6	12.6	12.7	574	570	8.8	8.6	4.9	5.4
Massachusetts	101	96	84	21.7	18.9	17.4	751	764	13.0	11.7	13.5	13.6
Michigan	176	167	154	33.9	29.6	27.9	1,120	1,112	19.3	18.1	19.2	21.2
Minnesota	152	142	137	19.4	17.4	17.1	496	527	11.3	11.7	5.7	5.8
Mississippi	103	97	97	12.9	12.6	12.9	388	413	7.6	8.1	3.2	3.9
Missouri	135	126	123	24.3	21.9	20.9	714	730	12.6	11.8	9.9	9.6
Montana	55	55	54	4.6	4.2	4.5	96	99	2.7	2.8	1.3	1.5
Nebraska	90	91	87	8.5	7.9	7.8	183	191	4.5	4.6	2.5	2.5
Nevada	21	20	19	3.4	3.6	3.5	149	161	2.2	2.4	1.4	1.4
New Hampshire	27	29	28	3.5	3.4	3.0	110	110	2.1	1.9	1.8	2.1
New Jersey	95	92	85	28.9	29.9	28.1	1,068	1,096	21.4	19.1	12.8	14.1
New Mexico	37	36	36	4.2	3.7	3.6	156	163	2.1	2.1	2.5	2.9
New York	235	230	225	74.7	73.9	71.0	2,398	2,371	59.1	53.8	38.9	40.9
North Carolina	120	119	118	22.0	22.7	23.2	833	874	15.5	15.8	8.8	10.1
North Dakota	50	43	41	4.4	4.2	3.9	89	84	2.7	2.4	1.3	1.3
Ohio	190	180	170	43.1	37.8	36.1	1,375	1,376	22.2	21.0	22.0	24.0
Oklahoma	111	110	111	12.4	11.5	10.9	368	378	6.1	5.9	3.8	4.2
Oregon	70	64	61	8.1	7.2	7.0	296	309	3.8	3.7	5.8	5.6
Pennsylvania	238	225	217	52.6	48.5	45.7	1,810	1,756	33.8	30.6	26.9	27.7
Rhode Island	12	11	11	3.2	2.7	2.5	119	116	1.8	1.8	1.7	2.0
South Carolina	69	66	65	11.3	11.3	12.0	410	443	7.2	7.7	4.7	5.9
South Dakota	53	50	49	4.2	4.6	4.4	94	94	3.0	2.9	1.0	1.3
Tennessee	134	126	124	23.6	20.9	21.1	740	763	12.5	12.4	7.4	8.4
Texas	428	416	407	59.2	57.2	55.8	2,029	2,126	31.1	31.1	22.7	25.9
Utah	42	42	41	4.4	4.2	4.1	171	186	2.2	2.2	3.2	3.6
Vermont	15	14	14	1.7	1.8	1.6	55	52	1.3	1.1	1.0	0.9
Virginia	97	96	93	20.0	18.6	18.2	699	705	11.5	11.6	7.2	8.0
Washington	91	88	88	12.0	10.8	10.8	467	478	6.0	6.2	8.4	7.7
West Virginia	59	59	58	8.4	8.1	8.2	271	277	4.9	4.8	4.0	4.6
Wisconsin	129	127	124	18.6	17.0	16.7	550	551	10.2	9.5	8.2	9.3
Wyoming	27	25	25	2.2	2.0	2.0	43	44	1.1	1.0	0.7	0.8

[1] Inpatients receiving treatment each day; excludes newborn.

No. 206. Hospital Use Rates, by Type of Hospital: 1980 to 1997

Type of hospital	1980	1985	1990	1993	1994	1995	1996	1997
Community hospitals: [1]								
Admissions per 1,000 population [2]	159	141	125	119	118	118	117	118
Admissions per bed	37	33	34	33	34	35	36	37
Average length of stay [3] (days)	7.6	7.1	7.2	7.0	6.7	6.5	6.2	6.1
Outpatient visits per admission	5.6	6.5	9.7	11.9	12.5	13.4	14.1	14.3
Outpatient visits per 1,000 population [2]	890	919	1,208	1,423	1,471	1,577	1,659	1,682
Surgical operations (million [4])	18.8	20.1	21.9	22.8	23.0	23.2	23.6	24.2
Number per admission	0.5	0.6	0.7	0.7	0.7	0.7	0.8	0.8
Non-Federal psychiatric:								
Admissions per 1,000 population [2]	2.5	2.5	2.9	2.9	2.9	2.7	2.7	2.7
Days in hospital per 1,000 population [2]	295	224	190	149	136	124	117	109

[1] For definition of community hospitals, see footnote 2, Table 204. [2] Based on U.S. Census Bureau estimated resident population as of July 1. Estimates reflect revisions based on the 1990 Census of Population. [3] Number of inpatient days divided by number of admissions. [4] 18.8 represents 18,800,000.

Source of Tables 205 and 206: Health Forum, An American Hospital Association Company, Chicago, IL, Hospital Statistics 1999 Edition, and prior years (copyright).

U.S. Census Bureau, Statistical Abstract of the United States: 1999

No. 207. Hospital Utilization Rates: 1980 to 1996

[37,832 represents 37,832,000. Represents estimates of inpatients discharged from noninstitutional, short-stay hospitals, exclusive of federal hospitals. Excludes newborn infants. Based on sample data collected from the National Hospital Discharge Survey, a sample survey of hospital records of patients discharged in year shown; subject to sampling variability. For composition of regions, see map, inside front cover]

Selected characteristic	Patients discharged (1,000)	Patients discharged per 1,000 persons [1]			Days of care per 1,000 persons [1]			Average stay (days)		
		Total	Male	Female	Total	Male	Female	Total	Male	Female
1980.	37,832	168	139	194	1,217	1,068	1,356	7.3	7.7	7.0
1985 [2].	35,056	148	124	171	954	849	1,053	6.5	6.9	6.2
1990 [2].	30,788	124	102	144	792	704	875	6.4	6.9	6.1
1992 [2].	30,951	122	101	142	751	680	818	6.2	6.7	5.8
1993 [2].	30,825	120	98	141	720	644	792	6.0	6.5	5.6
1994 [2].	30,843	119	98	139	684	610	755	5.7	6.2	5.4
1995 [2].	30,722	118	96	138	630	561	695	5.4	5.8	5.0
1996, [2] total	30,545	116	94	136	606	543	665	5.2	5.8	4.9
Age:										
Under 1 year old	736	195	215	175	1,154	1,292	1,009	5.9	6.0	5.8
1 to 4 years old.	649	42	47	36	140	151	128	3.3	3.2	3.5
5 to 14 years old	822	21	23	20	92	103	81	4.3	4.5	4.1
15 to 24 years old	2,849	80	33	128	258	164	356	3.2	5.0	2.8
25 to 34 years old	4,077	102	44	160	360	241	477	3.5	5.5	3.0
35 to 44 years old	3,399	79	64	93	373	368	377	4.7	5.7	4.1
45 to 64 years old	6,294	117	121	114	624	659	592	5.3	5.5	5.2
65 to 74 years old	4,804	257	271	247	1,604	1,675	1,546	6.2	6.2	6.3
75 years old and over. . .	6,914	455	477	443	3,075	3,160	3,025	6.8	6.6	6.8
Region:										
Northeast	6,665	129	113	145	803	746	855	6.2	6.6	5.9
Midwest	7,107	115	95	133	574	519	626	5.0	5.4	4.7
South	11,085	120	96	143	621	554	684	5.2	5.8	4.8
West	5,688	98	74	122	440	378	502	4.5	5.1	4.1

[1] Based on U.S. Census Bureau estimated civilian population as of July 1. Estimates for 1980-90 do not reflect revisions based on the 1990 Census of Population. [2] Comparisons beginning 1990 with data for earlier years should be made with caution as estimates of change may reflect improvements in the design rather than true changes in hospital use.

Source: U.S. National Center for Health Statistics, *Vital and Health Statistics,* Series 13; and unpublished data.

No. 208. Hospital Discharges and Days of Care: 1996

[12,110 represents 12,110,000. See headnote, Table 207]

Age and first-listed diagnosis	Discharges		Days of care per 1,000 persons [1]	Average stay (days)	Age and first-listed diagnosis	Discharges		Days of care per 1,000 persons [1]	Average stay (days)
	Number (1,000)	Per 1,000 persons [1]				Number (1,000)	Per 1,000 persons [1]		
MALE					FEMALE				
All ages [2].	12,110	89.7	511.8	5.7	All ages [2].	18,435	115.3	531.6	4.6
					Under 15 years [3]	967	34.3	154.6	4.5
Under 15 years [3]	1,240	42.0	193.2	4.6	Pneumonia.	142	5.0	18.5	3.7
Pneumonia.	178	6.0	21.8	3.6	Injuries and poisoning.	81	2.9	12.4	4.3
Injuries and poisoning. . . .	142	4.8	17.1	3.6	Asthma	72	2.5	6.4	2.5
Asthma	123	4.2	11.6	2.8					
					15 to 44 years [3]	7,495	126.1	404.4	3.2
15 to 44 years [3]	2,831	47.7	263.2	5.5	Delivery	3,817	64.2	140.2	2.2
Injuries and poisoning. . . .	550	9.3	43.9	4.7	Injuries and poisoning.	315	5.3	20.1	3.8
Psychoses	277	4.7	44.6	9.5	Psychoses	299	5.0	48.2	9.6
Diseases of heart.	166	2.8	10.5	3.7					
Intervertebral disk disorders.	90	1.5	4.3	2.8	45 to 64 years [3]	3,156	113.8	592.0	5.2
					Diseases of heart.	455	16.4	75.8	4.6
45 to 64 years [3]	3,138	120.8	658.7	5.5	Malignant neoplasms	249	9.0	53.3	5.9
Diseases of heart.	793	30.5	139.3	4.6	Injuries and poisoning.	215	7.8	39.8	5.1
Injuries and poisoning. . . .	269	10.4	56.1	5.4	Pneumonia.	93	3.4	20.9	6.2
Malignant neoplasms	200	7.7	55.8	7.3	Diabetes	78	2.8	17.8	6.3
Cerebrovascular diseases . .	105	4.1	25.1	6.2					
					65 to 74 years [3]	2,551	246.6	1,546.6	6.3
65 to 74 years [3]	2,253	270.6	1,675.3	6.2	Diseases of heart.	553	53.4	298.5	5.6
Diseases of heart.	612	73.5	396.2	5.4	Injuries and poisoning.	209	20.2	135.3	6.7
Malignant neoplasms	196	23.5	171.0	7.3	Malignant neoplasms	205	19.8	133.9	6.8
Injuries and poisoning. . . .	132	15.8	103.3	6.5	Cerebrovascular diseases . .	125	12.0	76.9	6.4
Cerebrovascular diseases . .	127	15.3	92.0	6.0	Pneumonia.	111	10.8	79.5	7.4
Pneumonia.	108	13.0	89.2	6.9					
					75 years old and older [3] . .	4,266	442.8	3,025.3	6.8
75 years old and older [3] . .	2,648	476.6	3,160.4	6.6	Diseases of heart.	922	95.7	576.8	6.0
Diseases of heart.	635	114.3	616.5	5.4	Injuries and poisoning.	453	47.0	315.0	6.7
Pneumonia.	213	38.3	291.7	7.6	Cerebrovascular diseases . .	289	30.0	207.6	6.9
Malignant neoplasms	155	28.0	199.5	7.1	Pneumonia.	270	28.1	199.5	7.1
Injuries and poisoning. . . .	184	33.2	239.2	7.2	Malignant neoplasms	181	18.8	148.7	7.9
Cerebrovascular diseases . .	186	33.4	228.3	6.8					

[1] Based on U.S. Census Bureau estimated civilian population as of July 1. [2] Average length of stay and rates per 1,000 population are age-adjusted. [3] Includes other first-listed diagnoses not shown separately.

Source: U.S. National Center for Health Statistics, unpublished data.

No. 209. Hospital Discharges—Principal Source of Expected Payment: 1996

[30,545 represent 30,545,000. See headnote, Table 207]

Characteristic	Total discharges [1] (1,000)	Principal source of expected payment—percent distribution							
		Private insur- ance	Government				Self-pay	No charge	Other [2]
			Medicare	Medicaid	Workers' compen- sation	Other			
All ages	30,545	35.1	38.1	14.4	0.7	1.5	4.7	0.3	3.3
Under 15 years old	2,207	43.9	0.8	37.5	(X)	2.3	5.2	0.2	7.9
15 to 44 years old	10,325	49.6	5.3	25.6	1.2	2.2	8.3	0.6	4.6
45 to 64 years old	6,294	55.8	16.5	11.9	1.2	2.2	5.8	0.5	4.1
65 years old and over	11,718	9.6	85.7	1.7	0.2	0.3	0.7	(3)	1.0
SEX									
Male, all ages	12,110	33.8	41.2	10.8	1.3	1.7	5.5	0.4	3.4
Under 15 years old	1,240	44.1	0.8	37.4	(X)	2.5	5.2	0.2	7.9
15 to 44 years old	2,831	44.8	10.7	16.2	3.2	3.0	13.4	1.0	4.5
45 to 64 years old	3,138	54.9	18.2	10.2	1.6	2.4	5.9	0.4	4.2
65 years old and over	4,901	11.3	83.8	1.4	0.2	0.5	0.8	(3)	1.1
Female, all ages	18,435	36.0	36.1	16.8	0.4	1.3	4.1	0.3	3.3
Under 15 years old	967	43.6	0.8	37.6	(X)	2.2	5.2	0.2	8.0
15 to 44 years old	7,495	51.4	3.3	29.1	0.4	2.0	6.3	0.4	4.6
45 to 64 years old	3,156	56.7	14.8	13.5	0.8	2.1	5.8	0.4	3.9
65 years old and over	6,817	8.3	87.0	1.8	0.2	0.2	0.6	(3)	0.9
RACE									
White	19,738	36.1	42.4	10.5	0.8	1.2	4.1	0.3	2.8
All other	5,131	28.5	27.4	28.1	0.6	2.6	6.9	0.7	3.8
Not stated	5,676	37.7	32.9	15.6	0.5	1.5	4.6	(3)	4.9

X Not applicable.   [1] Includes discharges for whom expected source of payment was unknown.   [2] Includes all other nonprofit source of payment such as church, welfare, or United Way.   [3] Figure does not meet standards of reliability or precision.

Source: U.S. National Center for Health Statistics, unpublished data.

No. 210. Procedures for Inpatients Discharged From Short-Stay Hospitals: 1990 to 1996

[23,051 represents 23,051,000. Rates based on U.S. Census Bureau estimated civilian population as of July 1. Excludes newborn infants and discharges from federal hospitals. See headnote, Table 207]

Sex and type of procedure	Number of procedures (1,000)				Rate per 1,000 population			
	1990	1994	1995	1996	1990	1994	1995	1996
Surgical procedures, total [1]	23,051	22,629	22,530	22,980	92.4	87.4	86.2	87.0
Cardiac catheterization	995	1,048	1,068	1,161	4.0	4.0	4.1	4.4
Removal of coronary artery obstruction [2]	285	428	434	666	1.2	1.7	1.7	2.5
Reduction of fracture [3]	609	568	577	604	2.4	2.2	2.2	2.3
Coronary artery bypass graft	392	501	573	598	1.6	1.9	2.2	2.3
Male, total [1]	8,538	8,369	8,388	8,648	70.6	66.5	65.9	67.2
Cardiac catheterization	620	633	660	704	5.1	5.0	5.2	5.5
Prostatectomy	364	263	239	203	3.0	2.1	1.9	1.6
Removal of coronary artery obstruction [2]	200	280	285	452	1.7	2.2	2.2	3.5
Female, total [1]	14,513	14,260	14,142	14,333	113.0	107.1	105.3	105.9
Procedures to assist delivery	2,491	2,410	2,290	2,165	19.4	18.1	17.0	16.0
Repair of current obstetric laceration	795	910	964	1,061	6.2	6.8	7.2	7.8
Cesarean section	945	858	785	835	7.4	6.5	5.8	6.2
Hysterectomy	591	556	583	591	4.6	4.2	4.3	4.4
Diagnostic and other nonsurgical procedures [4]	17,455	18,081	17,278	17,417	70.0	69.8	66.1	66.0
Angiocardiography and arteriography [5]	1,735	1,804	1,834	1,964	7.0	7.0	7.0	7.4
Diagnostic ultrasound	1,608	1,310	1,181	1,177	6.4	5.1	4.5	4.5
Respiratory therapy	1,164	1,174	1,127	1,085	4.7	4.5	4.3	4.1
CAT scan [6]	1,506	1,028	967	995	6.0	4.0	3.7	3.8
Male, total [4]	7,378	7,501	7,261	7,350	61.0	59.6	57.1	57.1
Angiocardiography and arteriography [5]	1,051	1,058	1,076	1,165	8.7	8.4	8.5	9.1
Respiratory therapy	586	577	572	554	4.9	4.6	4.5	4.3
CAT scan [6]	736	500	473	493	6.1	4.0	3.7	3.8
Female, total [4]	10,077	10,580	10,016	10,067	78.5	79.5	74.6	74.4
Manual assisted delivery	750	974	866	1,030	5.9	7.3	6.5	7.6
Fetal EKG and fetal monitoring	1,377	1,099	935	896	10.8	8.3	7.0	6.6
Diagnostic ultrasound	941	771	682	676	7.3	5.8	5.1	5.0

[1] Includes other types of surgical procedures not shown separately.   [2] Beginning 1996 includes separately coded "insertion of stent".   [3] Excluding skull, nose, and jaw.   [4] Includes other nonsurgical procedures not shown separately.   [5] Using contrast material.   [6] Computerized axial tomography.

Source: U.S. National Center for Health Statistics, Vital and Health Statistics, Series 13; and unpublished data.

Health and Nutrition   139

No. 211. Organ Transplants and Grafts: 1985 to 1998

[As of end of year. Based on reports of procurement programs and transplant centers in the United States, except as noted]

Procedure	Number of procedures							Number of centers		Num- ber of people waiting, 1997	1-year patient survival rates, 1996 (percent)
	1985	1990	1993	1994	1995	1996	1997	1990	1998		
Transplant: [1]											
Heart........	719	2,108	2,297	2,341	2,361	2,343	2,292	148	153	3,897	86.2
Liver	602	2,690	3,439	3,652	3,925	4,065	4,167	85	124	9,637	84.7
Kidney........	7,695	9,877	11,020	11,393	11,901	12,152	12,307	232	250	38,236	98.0
Heart-lung	30	52	60	70	70	39	62	79	94	236	77.2
Lung	2	203	667	723	871	810	928	70	88	2,664	73.4
Pancreas/islet cell	130	528	774	842	1,025	1,024	1,061	84	124	361	94.2
Intestine.. [2]	(NA)	5	34	23	45	45	67	[3]107	32	94	68.8
Cornea grafts [2] ...	26,300	40,631	40,215	43,743	44,652	46,300	45,493	30	(NA)	2,603	(NA)
Bone grafts	(NA)	350,000	(NA)	(NA)	(NA)	450,000	(NA)	25	(NA)	(X)	(NA)
Skin grafts [4]	(NA)	5,500	(NA)	(NA)	5,500	9,000	(NA)		(NA)	(X)	(NA)

NA Not available.   X Not applicable.   [1] Simultaneous kidney-pancreas transplants are counted twice, both in kidney transplants and in pancreas transplants. Double kidney, double lung, and heart-lung transplants are counted as one transplant.   [2] 1985 and 1990, number of procedures and eye banks include Canada.   [3] Eye banks.   [4] Procedure data are shown in terms of square feet.

Source: Transplants: through 1990, U.S. Department of Health and Human Services, Public Health Service, Division of Organ Transplantation; beginning 1993, United Network for Organ Sharing, Richmond, VA; American Association of Tissue Banks, McLean, VA; and Eye Bank Association of America, Washington, DC; and unpublished data.

No. 212. Visits to Hospital Outpatient and Emergency Departments: 1995 and 1997

[In thousands (67,232 represents 67,232,000). An outpatient department is a hospital facility where nonurgent ambulatory care is provided under the supervision of a physician. Data for outpatient departments exclude clinics where only ancillary services, such as radiology, are provided. An emergency department is a hospital facility staffed by physicians for the provision of outpatient services to patients whose conditions require immediate attention and is staffed 24 hours a day. Data are for nonfederal short stay and general hospitals. Based on the National Hospital Ambulatory Care Surveys and subject to sampling error; see source for details]

Characteristic	Outpatient department		Emergency department		Characteristic	Outpatient department		Emergency department	
	1995	1997	1995	1997		1995	1997	1995	1997
All visits	67,232	[1]76,993	96,545	94,936	Visit status:				
Age:					Old patient	54,741	62,530	(NA)	(NA)
Under 15 years old ..	15,039	18,240	22,709	20,693	New patient	12,491	12,529	(NA)	(NA)
15 to 24 years old ..	8,307	8,753	15,681	14,412					
25 to 44 years old...	18,588	20,677	30,086	29,397	Primary expected source of payment: [3]				
45 to 64 years old ...	14,811	17,682	13,978	15,629	Private insurance ...	14,489	26,289	25,056	35,666
65 to 74 years old ...	6,004	6,677	6,057	6,201	Medicare	10,876	11,026	14,949	14,684
75 years old and over	4,482	4,963	8,033	8,604	Medicaid	19,333	21,439	22,041	17,010
Sex:					Worker's compensa- tion.............	834	945	3,776	3,293
Male	26,221	30,880	46,501	44,649	Self pay...........	7,113	7,245	16,113	15,336
Female	41,011	46,112	50,044	50,286	No charge	990	2,432	519	1,041
Race:					Other	2,930	4,329	2,471	2,833
White	50,110	56,138	74,593	72,165	Unknown source of payment.........	2,278	3,288	1,552	5,073
Black	15,022	18,432	19,284	20,570					
Asian/Pacific Islander.	1,926	2,277	1,963	1,679					
American Indian/ Eskimo/Aleut [2]	174	146	705	521					

NA Not available.   [1] Includes patients with unknown visit status.   [2] Figures do not meet standard of reliability or precision.   [3] For 1995 more than one source of payment may be reported.

Source: U.S. National Center for Health Statistics, Advance Data, No. 304, May 6, 1999 and prior issues; and unpublished data.

No. 213. Skilled Nursing Facilities: 1980 to 1997

[448 represents 448,000. Covers facilities and beds certified for participation under medicare as of midyear. Includes facilities which have transfer agreements with one or more participating hospitals, and are engaged primarily in providing skilled nursing care and related services for the rehabilitation of injured, disabled, or sick persons]

Item	Unit	1980	1990	1993	1994	1995	1996	1997
Skilled nursing facilities	Number .	5,155	9,008	11,472	12,584	13,281	14,177	14,860
Beds	1,000 .	448	512	623	649	657	672	685
Per 1,000 Medicare enrollees [1]	Rate ...	16.0	15.2	17.3	17.8	17.7	17.8	18.0

[1] Based on total number of beneficiaries enrolled in the medicare hospital insurance program as of July 1 of year stated.

Source: U.S. Health Care Financing Administration, Medicare Participating Providers and Suppliers of Health Services, 1980; and unpublished data.

No. 214. Ambulatory Surgery Visits and Procedures, by Type of Facility: 1995 and 1996

[19,638 represents 19,638,000. Excludes ambulatory surgery patients admitted to hospitals as inpatients. Hospital data cover only non-Federal short-stay and general hospitals. Freestanding facilities specializing in dentistry, podiatry, pain block, abortion, family planning, or birthing are excluded. Based on data collected from the National Survey of Ambulatory Surgery; for details, see source]

Utilization measure	All facilities		Hospitals		Freestanding centers	
	1995	1996	1995	1996	1995	1996
Number of visits (1,000)........	19,638	20,838	16,413	17,524	3,225	3,313
Rate per 1,000 population [1]	75.1	78.9	62.8	66.4	12.3	12.6
Number of procedures (1,000)	29,433	31,507	24,562	26,373	4,871	5,134
Rate per 1,000 population [1]	112.6	119.3	94.0	99.9	18.6	19.4

[1] Based on U.S. Census Bureau estimated civilian population, including institutionalized persons, as of July 1.

Source: U.S. National Center for Health Statistics, *Advance Data*, Nos. 296 and 300, December 24, 1997, and August 12, 1998.

No. 215. Ambulatory Surgery Procedures, by Sex and Age: 1996

[In thousands (31,507 represents 31,507,000). Covers procedures done on an ambulatory (outpatient) basis in hospitals and freestanding ambulatory surgery centers. Excludes procedures on ambulatory surgery patients admitted to hospitals as patients. Excluded specialties include dentistry, podiatry, abortion, family planning, birthing, pain block, and small procedures. Based on sample data collected from the National Survey of Ambulatory Surgery, a sample survey of medical records in hospitals and freestanding ambulatory surgery centers; subject to sampling variability]

Type of procedure	Sex			Age			
	Total	Male	Female	Under 15 years	15-44 years	45-64 years	65 years and over
Total [1]	**31,507**	**13,882**	**17,625**	**2,381**	**9,561**	**8,825**	**10,740**
Injection of agent into spinal canal........	534	224	310	(B)	166	199	169
Release of carpal tunnel	358	120	238	(B)	132	142	84
Extraction of lens	2,367	881	1,486	(B)	46	331	1,977
Insertion of prosthetic lens (pseudophakos)..	1,816	696	1,120	(B)	36	270	1,501
Myringotomy with insertion of tube........	524	313	211	490	16	(B)	(B)
Operations on nasal sinuses...........	463	229	234	33	223	163	43
Tonsillectomy with or without adenoidectomy.	383	164	219	263	109	(B)	(B)
Cardiac catheterization	472	298	175	(B)	47	206	213
Endoscopy of small intestine [2]	1,563	668	895	28	419	502	614
Endoscopy of large intestine [2]	1,913	855	1,058	15	380	696	822
Endoscopic polypectomy of large intestine ..	555	317	238	(B)	59	201	291
Repair of inguinal hernia	531	477	54	75	165	146	146
Laparoscopy	422	55	367	(B)	334	63	18
Cystoscopy with or without biopsy.......	703	422	281	26	137	205	336
Bilateral destruction or occlusion of fallopian tubes	320	(X)	320	-	314	(B)	(B)
Dilation and curettage of uterus.........	530	(X)	530	(B)	318	160	51
Arthroscopy of knee	629	357	272	9	325	212	83
Excision of semilunar cartilage of knee.....	455	275	180	(B)	198	178	76
Operations on muscle, tendon, fascia, and bursa	664	320	345	28	260	254	123
Local excision of lesion of breast (lumpectomy)..................	341	12	329	(B)	127	130	81
Excision or destruction of lesion or tissue of skin and subcutaneous tissue	877	412	465	71	330	258	217
Arteriography and angiocardiography using contrast material................	791	476	316	(B)	66	319	404
Injection or infusion of therapeutic or prophylactic substance............	464	203	260	(B)	135	165	155

- Represents zero.   B Figure too small to meet statistical standard for reliability.   X Not applicable.   [1] Includes other procedures not shown separately.   [2] With or without biopsy.

Source: U.S. National Center for Health Statistics, *Advance Data*, No. 296, December 24, 1997.

Health and Nutrition   141

No. 216. Home Health and Hospice Care Agencies, by Selected Characteristics: 1996

[In percent, except as indicated (13.5 represents 13,500). Based on the National Home and Hospice Care Survey. Home health care is provided to individuals and families in their place of residence. Hospice care is available in both the home and inpatient settings. See source for details. For composition of regions, see map, inside front cover]

Agency characteristic	Agencies, total	Current patients [1]			Discharges [2]		
		Total	Home health care	Hospice care	Total	Home health care	Hospice care
Total (1,000).................	13.5	2,486.8	2,427.5	59.4	8,168.9	7,775.7	393.2
PERCENT DISTRIBUTION							
Ownership:							
Proprietary...............	54.3	40.9	41.6	11.0	31.1	32.0	13.3
Voluntary nonprofit	34.3	49.9	49.0	84.6	61.5	60.3	85.2
Government and other..............	11.4	9.2	9.3	4.4	7.4	7.7	1.5
Certification:							
Medicare..................	88.2	92.5	92.4	96.8	95.3	95.3	95.3
Medicaid..................	86.0	93.6	93.6	93.8	95.7	95.8	94.3
Region:							
Northeast.................	15.0	26.2	26.5	15.0	29.7	30.2	18.2
Midwest..................	27.0	26.9	26.6	35.9	21.1	20.9	25.2
South...................	40.1	32.6	32.6	32.0	24.9	24.2	38.5
West....................	18.0	14.3	14.2	17.1	24.4	24.7	18.1

[1] Patients on the rolls of the agency as of midnight the day prior to the survey.   [2] Patients removed from the rolls of the agency during the 12 months prior to the day of the survey. A patient could be included more than once if the individual had more than one episode of care during the year.

Source: U.S. National Center for Health Statistics, *Advance Data*, No. 297, April 16, 1998, and prior issues.

No. 217. Home Health and Hospice Care Patients, by Selected Characteristics: 1996

[In percent, except as indicated (2,486.8 represents 2,486,800). See headnote, Table 216]

Item	Current patients [1]			Discharges [2]		
	Total	Home health care	Hospice care	Total	Home health care	Hospice care
Total (1,000)	2,486.8	2,427.5	59.4	8,168.9	7,775.7	393.2
PERCENT DISTRIBUTION						
Age at admission: [3]						
Under 45 years old............	14.1	14.3	7.3	19.0	19.5	8.1
45-54 years old..............	5.3	5.4	4.5	6.0	5.9	7.9
55-64 years old..............	7.8	7.7	10.3	8.7	8.4	14.8
65 years old and over............	72.4	72.2	77.7	66.1	66.1	67.5
65-69 years old	8.8	8.8	8.4	10.7	10.8	8.7
70-74 years old	13.0	12.9	16.2	13.3	13.2	15.6
75-79 years old	17.1	17.1	16.6	12.5	12.4	14.5
80-84 years old	16.6	16.7	15.2	14.1	14.2	12.3
85 years old and over	16.8	16.7	21.3	15.5	15.4	16.4
Sex:						
Male	33.2	32.9	44.9	37.2	36.5	50.3
Female	66.8	67.1	55.1	62.8	63.5	49.7
Race:						
White.....................	65.5	65.1	83.7	63.5	62.8	78.9
Black.....................	12.0	12.0	8.3	7.6	7.4	11.2
Other or unknown	22.5	22.9	8.0	28.9	29.8	9.9
Marital status: [4]						
Married...................	29.3	29.0	43.7	37.5	37.0	48.4
Widowed	35.3	35.3	32.2	24.8	24.6	29.4
Divorced or separated	4.2	4.1	9.3	5.0	5.0	6.5
Never married...............	18.5	18.7	8.5	18.0	18.4	9.3
Unknown	12.7	12.8	[5]6.3	14.6	15.0	6.4
Primary admission diagnosis:						
Neoplasms.................	6.5	5.2	59.6	11.6	8.6	70.6
Endocrine, nutritional and metabolic and immunity disorders	9.9	10.2	(5)	5.6	5.8	(5)
Diseases of the nervous system and sense organs	5.8	5.7	8.1	3.3	3.2	3.2
Diseases of the circulatory system ...	25.1	25.4	12.3	21.8	22.4	9.6
Diseases of the musculoskeletal system and connective tissue......	8.5	8.7	(5)	7.7	8.1	(5)
Injuries and poisoning............	6.7	6.9	(5)	11.9	12.5	(5)

[1] Patients on the rolls of the agency as of midnight the day prior to the survey.   [2] Patients removed from the rolls of the agency during the 12 months prior to the day of the survey. A patient could be included more than once if the individual had more than one episode of care during the year.   [3] Excludes unknown.   [4] For current patients, current marital status; for discharged patients, status at time of discharge.   [5] Figure does not meet standard of reliability or precision.

Source: U.S. National Center for Health Statistics, *Advance Data*, No. 297, April 16, 1998.

142   Health and Nutrition

No. 218. Elderly Home Health Patients: 1996

[**1,753 represents 1,753,000**. Covers the civilian population 65 years old and over who are home health care patients. Home health care is provided to individuals and families in their place of residence. Based on the 1996 National Home and Hospice Care Survey]

Item	Current patients [1]		Discharges [2]		Item	Current patients [1]		Discharges [2]	
	Number (1,000)	Per-cent	Number (1,000)	Per-cent		Number (1,000)	Per-cent	Number (1,000)	Per-cent
Total 65 yrs. old & over	**1,753**	**100.0**	**5,138**	**100.0**	Own income.	36	2.0	18	0.3
Received help with—					Medicare.	1,396	79.6	3,612	66.7
Bathing or showering. .	933	53.2	1,896	36.9	Medicaid	123	7.0	693	12.8
Dressing	804	45.8	1,707	33.2	Services rendered: [4]				
Eating.	162	9.2	347	6.7	Nursing services. . . .	1,476	84.2	4,505	87.7
Transferring in/out of					Social services	186	10.6	633	12.3
a bed or chair.	519	29.6	1,296	25.2	Counseling	40	2.3	830	1.6
Using the toilet room . .	396	22.6	963	18.7	Medications	171	9.8	368	7.2
Doing light housework .	682	38.9	1,216	23.7	Physical therapy	348	19.8	1,524	29.7
Managing money	49	2.8	29	0.6					
Shopping for groceries					Homemaker-				
or clothes	247	14.1	475	9.2	household services . .	493	28.1	967	18.8
Using the telephone . .	47	2.7	76	1.5	Nutrition services	58	3.3	99	1.9
Preparing meals	404	23.0	639	12.4	Physician services. . . .	64	3.7	110	2.1
Taking medications . . .	410	23.4	855	16.6	Occupational				
Primary source of					therapy	86	4.9	286	5.6
payment [3]:					Speech therapy/				
Private insurance	64	3.7	724	13.4	audiology.	27	1.6	86	1.7

[1] Patients on the rolls of the agency as of midnight the day prior to the survey.   [2] Patients removed from the rolls of the agency during the 12 months prior to the day of the survey. A patient could be included more than once if the individual had more than one episode of care during the year.   [3] For current patients, the expected source; for discharges the actual source for the entire episode.   [4] For current patients, services currently being provided; for discharges services provided during the 30 days prior to discharge.

Source: U.S. National Center for Health Statistics, *Advance Data*, No. 297, April 16, 1998.

No. 219. Nursing Homes—Selected Characteristics: 1985 and 1995

[Beds: **1,624 represents 1,624,000**. Covers nursing and related care homes in the conterminous United States that had three or more beds, were staffed for use by residents, and routinely provided nursing and personal care services. Excludes places providing only room and board and places serving specific health problems. Based on the 1995 National Nursing Home Survey, a two-stage survey sample of nursing homes and their residents. Subject to sampling variability. For composition of regions, see map, inside front cover]

Characteristic	Beds			Current residents		Full-time equivalent employment			
						Administrative, medical, and therapeutic		Nursing	
	Nursing homes	Number (1,000)	Per nursing home	Number (1,000)	Occu-pancy rate [1]	Number (1,000)	Rate per 100 beds	Number (1,000)	Rate per 100 beds
1985	19,100	1,624	85	1,491	91.8	(NA)	(NA)	(NA)	(NA)
1995, total	**16,700**	**1,771**	**106**	**1,549**	**87.4**	**20.1**	**1.1**	**914**	**51.6**
Ownership:									
Proprietary.	11,000	1,152	105	990	85.9	13.6	1.2	574	49.8
Voluntary nonprofit	4,300	468	109	421	89.9	4.9	1.0	254	54.3
Government and other. . . .	1,400	151	108	138	91.5	1.6	1.1	85	56.3
Certification:									
Medicare and medicaid									
certified	11,600	1,378	118	1,214	88.0	15.0	1.1	728	52.8
Medicare only.	[2]1,000	60	60	50	83.9	1.9	3.2	36	60.0
Medicaid only.	3,400	280	82	241	85.8	2.8	1.0	128	45.5
Not certified	[2]700	53	75	44	84.2	0.4	0.8	22	42.4
Bed size:									
Less than 50 beds	2,800	87	31	71	81.4	4.7	5.4	50	56.8
50-99 beds	5,900	430	73	378	87.9	5.2	1.2	221	51.4
100-199 beds.	6,700	903	135	794	88.0	8.4	0.9	469	51.9
200 beds or more	1,300	351	270	305	86.9	1.8	0.5	174	49.6
Region:									
Northeast	2,900	379	131	347	91.5	4.2	1.1	215	56.6
Midwest	5,600	564	101	495	87.7	4.8	0.9	264	46.8
South	5,500	573	104	495	86.4	6.3	1.1	300	52.3
West.	2,800	255	91	212	83.2	4.8	1.9	135	52.9
Affiliation [3]:									
Chain	9,100	978	108	857	87.7	(NA)	(NA)	(NA)	(NA)
Independent.	7,600	788	91	689	87.4	(NA)	(NA)	(NA)	(NA)

NA Not available.   [1] Number of residents divided by number of available beds multiplied by 100.   [2] Figure does not meet standards of reliability or precision.   [3] Excludes a small number of homes, beds, and residents with unknown affiliation.

Source: U.S. National Center for Health Statistics, *Advance Data*, No. 280, January 23, 1997.

Health and Nutrition   143

No. 220. Nursing Home Residents 65 Years Old and Over, by Selected Characteristics: 1995

[1,385 represents 1,385,000. Covers nursing and related care homes in the conterminous United States that had three or more beds, were staffed for use by residents, and routinely provided nursing and personal care services. Excludes places providing only room and board and places serving specific health problems. Based on the 1995 National Nursing Home Survey, a two-stage survey sample of nursing homes and their residents. Subject to sampling variability]

Characteristic [1]	Number (1,000)	Percent distri- bution	Item	Percent of elderly residents	Functional status	Percent of elderly residents receiving assistance
Total [2]	1,385	100.0	Type of aids used:		ADLs: [9]	
			Wheelchair	64.5	Bathing, showering. . . .	96.3
Male	343	24.7	Walker.	24.9	Dressing.	86.6
Female.	1,043	75.3	Hospital bed	78.4	Eating	45.1
					Transferring in or	
65 to 74 years	242	17.5	Vision impaired	26.4	out of beds or chair .	23.8
75 to 84 years	586	42.3	Hearing impaired.	22.4	Using toilet room	57.8
85 years and over	557	40.2				
			Type of nursing care:		IADLs: [10]	
White.	1,240	89.5	Skilled care [3] . . . . [3] .	46.1	Care of personal	
Black	118	8.5	Intermediate care [4]. . .	50.4	possessions	77.6
			Residential care [5] . . .	3.5	Managing money	69.2
Hispanic.	32	2.3			Securing personal . . .	
Non-Hispanic.	1,276	92.1	Primary source		items	76.8
			of payment: [6]		Using telephone	69.2
Living quarters:			Private sources [7]	28.9		
Private residence	510	36.8	Medicare	12.7		
Retirement home	31	2.2	Medicaid	55.7		
Board and care and/or			Other [8].	2.7		
residential facility. . . .	69	4.9				
Nursing home.	160	11.6				
Hospital.	562	40.6				
Mental health facility . .	15	1.1				

[1] At time of admission.   [2] Includes other and/or unknown, not shown separately.   [3] Skilled care indicates the greatest degree of medical care. Every patient is under the supervision of a physician and the facility has a transfer agreement with a nearby hospital. Twenty-four hour nursing care is provided with a physician on call to furnish medical care in case of emergency.   [4] Intermediate care is provided to individuals who do not require the degree of care or treatment normally given by a hospital or skilled nursing facility, but who do require health-related institutionalized care above the level of room and board.   [5] Residential care usually means providing residents with room, board, laundry services, some forms of personal care, and recreational activities and social services.   [6] In month before interview.   [7] Includes private insurance, own income, family support, social security benefits, and retirement funds.   [8] Includes supplemental security income, welfare, religious organizations, foundations, agencies, Veterans Administration contract, pensions, or other compensation, payment source not yet determined, and other and unknown sources.   [9] Activities of daily living.   [10] Instrumental activities of daily living.

Source: U.S. National Center for Health Statistics, *Advance Data*, No. 289, July 2, 1997.

No. 221. Mental Health Facilities—Summary, by Type of Facility: 1994

[Beds: 248.4 represents 248,400. Facilities, beds and inpatients as of year-end; other data are for calendar year or fiscal year ending in a month other than December since facilities are permitted to report on either a calendar or fiscal year basis. Excludes private psychiatric office practice and psychiatric service modes of all types in hospitals or outpatient clinics of Federal agencies other than U.S. Dept. of Veterans Affairs. Excludes data from Puerto Rico, Virgin Islands, Guam, and other territories]

Type of facility	Number of facilities	Inpatient beds		Inpatients		Average daily inpatients (1,000)	Inpatient care epi- sodes [2] (1,000)	Expenditure		Patient care staff [4] (1,000)
		Total (1,000)	Rate [1]	Total (1,000)	Rate [1]			Total (mil. dol.)	Per capita [3] (dol.)	
Total	5,392	248.4	97.0	190.8	73.5	190.5	2,388	33,135	128.0	370.9
Mental hospitals:										
State and county	256	79.3	30.6	70.0	26.9	69.5	308	7,824	30.2	100.2
Private [5]	889	69.0	27.8	50.1	19.4	48.8	568	8,829	34.1	72.4
General hospitals [6] . . .	1,612	53.0	20.5	35.8	13.8	37.1	1,102	5,344	20.6	74.3
Veterans Administration [7].	161	21.1	8.2	15.4	5.9	15.2	186	1,386	5.4	21.6
Other [8] [9]	2,474	26.0	9.9	19.5	7.5	19.9	224	9,752	37.7	102.4

[1] Rate per 100,000 population. Based on U.S. Census Bureau estimated civilian population as of July 1.   [2] "Inpatient care episodes" is defined as the number of residents in inpatient facilities at the beginning of the year plus the total additions to inpatient facilities during the year.   [3] Based on U.S. Census Bureau estimated civilian population as of July 1.   [4] Full-time equivalent.   [5] Includes residential treatment centers for emotionally disturbed children.   [6] Non-Federal hospitals with separate psychiatric services.   [7] Includes U.S. Department of Veterans Affairs (VA) neuropsychiatric hospitals, VA general hospitals with separate psychiatric settings and VA freestanding psychiatric outpatient clinics.   [8] Includes free-standing psychiatric outpatient facilities that provide only psychiatric outpatient services.   [9] Includes other multiservice mental health facilities with two or more settings, which are not elsewhere classified, as well as freestanding partial care facilities which only provide psychiatric partial care services. Number of facilities, expenditures, and staff data also include freestanding psychiatric partial care facilities.

Source: U.S. Substance Abuse and Mental Health Services Administration, Center for Mental Health Services, unpublished data.

No. 222. Days of Disability, by Type and Selected Characteristics: 1980 to 1996

[4,165 represents 4,165,000,000. Covers civilian noninstitutional population. Beginning 1985, the levels of estimates may not be comparable to estimates for 1980 because the later data are based on a revised questionnaire and field procedures; for further information, see source. Based on National Health Interview Survey; see Appendix III. For composition of regions, see map, inside front cover]

Item	Total days of disability (millions)						Days per person					
	1980	1985	1990	1994	1995	1996	1980	1985	1990	1994	1995	1996
Restricted-activity days [1]	4,165	3,453	3,669	4,143	4,097	3,825	19.1	14.8	14.9	16.0	15.6	14.5
Male	1,802	1,442	1,558	1,723	1,748	1,587	17.1	12.8	13.1	13.6	13.7	12.3
Female	2,363	2,011	2,111	2,420	2,349	2,237	21.0	16.6	16.7	18.2	17.5	16.5
White	3,518	2,899	3,057	3,375	3,392	3,154	18.7	14.5	14.8	15.7	15.6	14.3
Black	580	489	536	608	558	543	22.7	17.4	17.7	18.4	17.0	16.4
Under 65 years	3,228	2,557	2,734	3,070	3,091	2,857	16.6	12.4	12.6	13.4	13.4	12.3
65 years and over	937	895	936	1,073	1,006	968	39.2	33.1	31.4	34.6	32.0	30.5
Northeast	862	689	656	803	754	716	17.9	13.8	13.2	15.9	14.7	13.3
Midwest	989	744	836	879	865	819	17.2	12.7	14.0	13.9	13.9	12.9
South	1,415	1,308	1,404	1,443	1,561	1,432	19.8	16.3	16.7	16.4	16.9	15.8
West	899	712	773	1,017	917	857	22.0	15.7	14.8	17.6	16.4	15.2
Family income:												
Under $10,000	(NA)	893	662	681	649	554	(NA)	25.8	27.3	29.1	30.0	27.9
$10,000 to $19,999	(NA)	781	758	801	794	779	(NA)	16.7	19.1	21.5	21.0	21.1
$20,000 to $34,999	(NA)	791	715	825	824	702	(NA)	12.1	13.5	15.2	15.1	13.0
$35,000 or more	(NA)	568	912	1,051	1,133	1,083	(NA)	9.9	10.3	10.5	10.6	9.9
Bed-disability days [2]	1,520	1,436	1,521	1,603	1,593	1,566	7.0	6.1	6.2	6.2	6.1	5.9
Male	616	583	625	623	678	626	5.9	5.2	5.2	4.9	5.3	4.9
Female	904	852	896	980	915	940	8.0	7.1	7.1	7.4	6.8	6.9
Under 65 years	1,190	1,064	1,115	1,155	1,181	1,167	6.1	5.1	5.2	5.1	5.1	5.0
65 years and over	330	371	406	448	412	399	13.8	13.7	13.6	14.4	13.1	12.6
Work-loss days [3]	485	575	621	642	657	603	5.0	5.3	5.3	5.2	5.3	4.8
Male	271	287	303	311	307	282	4.9	4.8	4.7	4.6	4.5	4.1
Female	215	288	319	332	349	321	5.1	6.0	5.9	5.9	6.1	5.6
School-loss days [4]	204	217	212	225	229	206	5.3	4.8	4.6	4.5	4.5	4.0
Male	95	100	100	104	107	100	4.8	4.4	4.3	4.1	4.2	3.8
Female	109	117	112	121	122	105	5.7	5.3	5.0	5.0	4.9	4.2

NA Not available. [1] A day when a person cuts down on his activities for more than half a day because of illness or injury. Includes bed-disability, work-loss, and school-loss days. Total includes other races and unknown income, not shown separately. [2] A day when a person stayed in bed more than half a day because of illness or injury. Includes those work-loss and school-loss days actually spent in bed. [3] A day when a person lost more than half a workday because of illness or injury. Computed for persons 17 years of age and over (beginning 1985, 18 years of age and over) in the currently employed population, defined as those who were working or had a job or business from which they were not on layoff during the 2-week period preceding the week of interview. [4] Child's loss of more than half a school day because of illness or injury. Computed for children 6-16 years of age. Beginning 1985, children 5-17 years old.

Source: U.S. National Center for Health Statistics, *Vital and Health Statistics,* Series 10, No. 200; and earlier reports and unpublished data.

No. 223. Injuries, by Sex, Age and Type: 1980 to 1996

[68 represents 68,000,000. Covers civilian noninstitutional population and comprises incidents leading to restricted activity and/or medical attention. Beginning 1985, data not strictly comparable with other years. See headnote, Table 222. Based on National Health Interview Survey; see Appendix III]

Year	Injuries (mil.)			Rate per 100 population		
	Total	Male	Female	Total	Male	Female
1980	68	39	29	31.2	37.1	25.8
1985	63	35	28	26.8	30.6	23.1
1990	60	34	27	24.4	28.1	21.0
1994	62	33	29	23.8	25.8	22.0
1995	65	35	30	24.7	27.2	22.3
1996, total	57	32	26	21.7	24.6	18.9
Under 5 years	5	3	2	22.9	27.6	17.9
5 to 17 years	11	7	4	21.4	27.6	14.8
18 to 44 years	28	15	13	26.4	28.8	24.1
45 years and over	13	6	7	15.6	16.2	15.1
Fractures [1]	8	4	4	3.2	3.3	3.1
Sprains and strains	13	7	6	4.9	5.4	4.4
Open wounds and lacerations	9	6	3	3.4	4.9	2.0
Contusions [2]	10	6	4	3.8	4.6	2.9
Other	17	8	9	6.4	6.4	6.3

[1] Includes dislocations. [2] Includes superficial injuries.

Source: U.S. National Center for Health Statistics, *Vital and Health Statistics,* Series 10, No. 200, and earlier reports; and unpublished data.

U.S. Census Bureau, Statistical Abstract of the United States: 1999

No. 224. Injuries Associated With Consumer Products: 1996

[For products associated with more than 20,000 injuries in 1996. Estimates calculated from a representative sample of hospitals with emergency treatment departments in the United States. Data are estimates of the number of emergency room treated cases nationwide associated with various products. Product involvement does not necessarily mean the product caused the accident. Products were selected from the U.S. Consumer Product Safety Commission's National Electronic Injury Surveillance System]

Product	Number	Product	Number
Home workshop equipment:		Porches, balconies, open-side floors	122,343
Saws (hand or power)	89,786	Fences or fence posts	114,055
Hammers.	44,828	Glass doors	40,058
Household packaging and containers:		Handrails, railings, or banisters	39,299
Household containers and packaging	184,240	General household appliances:	
Bottles and jars.	84,785	Ranges	31,463
Bags.	25,366	Refrigerators.	26,376
Housewares:		Heating, cooling equipment: [3]	
Knives.	444,604	Pipes (excl. smoking pipes).	31,034
Drinking glasses	123,004	Home entertainment equipment:	
Tableware and flatware.	108,869	Televisions	35,023
Scissors	30,342	Sound recording equipment [4]	20,189
Waste containers, trash baskets, etc.	25,862	Personal use items:	
Home furnishing: [1]		Jewelry	53,854
Beds.	400,648	Razors and shavers.	40,242
Tables.	308,793	Coins	27,620
Chairs	279,815	Hair grooming equipment and accessories.	25,486
Bathtubs and showers	163,286	Yard and garden equipment:	
Ladders	151,327	Lawn mowers	71,912
Carpets, rugs	123,775	Pruning, trimming, and edging equipment .	36,204
Sofas, couches, davenports, etc.	109,954	Chain saws	35,132
Other furniture	58,812	Other unpowered garden tools.	22,002
Toilets	42,563	Sports and recreation equipment:	
Misc. decorating items	26,882	Bicycles.	566,085
Benches	25,623	Trampolines	83,399
Electric lighting equipment.	22,345	Swings or swing sets	82,882
Mirrors, mirror glass.	22,135	Playground climbing equipment	74,588
Home structures, construction: [2]		Swimming pools	72,933
Floors or flooring materials	987,385	All-terrain vehicles	63,600
Stairs or steps	984,300	Slides or sliding boards	45,792
Other doors (excl. garage)	318,185	Skateboards.	35,751
Ceilings and walls	228,431	Sleds	34,426
Household cabinets, racks, and shelves . .	221,458	Minibikes or trail bikes	27,891
Nails, screws, tacks, or bolts	191,037	BB's or pellets	21,807
Windows	138,875		

[1] Includes accessories. [2] Includes materials. [3] Includes ventilating equipment. [4] Includes reproducing equipment.

Source: National Safety Council, Itasca, IL, *Accident Facts, 1998 Edition* (copyright).

No. 225. Costs of Unintentional Injuries: 1997

[478.3 represents $478,300,000,000. Covers costs of deaths or disabling injuries together with vehicle accidents and fires]

Cost	Amount (bil. dol.)					Percent distribution				
	Total [1]	Motor vehicle	Work	Home	Other	Total [1]	Motor vehicle	Work	Home	Other
Total	478.3	200.3	127.7	99.9	66.1	100.0	100.0	100.0	100.0	100.0
Wage and productivity losses [2]	238.4	70.2	63.4	63.7	44.5	49.8	35.0	49.6	63.8	67.3
Medical expense	76.3	21.9	20.7	21.9	12.9	16.0	10.9	16.2	21.9	19.5
Administrative expenses [3]	82.4	56.2	26.5	4.5	3.9	17.2	28.1	20.8	4.5	5.9
Motor vehicle damage	49.8	49.8	2.0	(NA)	(NA)	10.4	24.9	1.6	(NA)	(NA)
Employer cost [4]	21.3	2.2	11.9	4.3	3.4	4.5	1.1	9.3	4.3	5.1
Fire loss	10.1	(NA)	3.2	5.5	1.4	2.1	(NA)	2.5	5.5	2.1

NA Not available. [1] Excludes duplication between work and motor vehicle ($15.7 billion in 1997). [2] Actual loss of wages and household production, and the present value of future earnings lost. [3] Includes the administrative cost of public and private insurance, and police and legal costs. [4] Estimate of the uninsured costs incurred by employers, representing the money value of time lost by noninjured workers.

Source: National Safety Council, Itasca, IL, *Accident Facts, 1998 Edition* (copyright).

No. 226. Specified Reportable Diseases—Cases Reported: 1980 to 1997

[190.9 represents 190,900. Figures should be interpreted with caution. Although reporting of some of these diseases is incomplete, the figures are of value in indicating trends of disease incidence. Includes cases imported from outside the United States]

Disease	1980	1985	1990	1992	1993	1994	1995	1996	1997
AIDS [1]	(NA)	8,249	41,595	45,472	103,533	78,279	71,547	66,885	58,492
Amebiasis	5,271	4,433	3,328	2,942	2,970	2,983	(2)	(2)	(2)
Aseptic meningitis	8,028	10,619	11,852	12,223	12,848	8,932	(2)	(2)	(2)
Botulism [3]	89	122	92	91	97	143	97	119	132
Brucellosis (undulant fever)	183	153	85	105	120	119	98	112	98
Chickenpox [4] (1,000)	190.9	178.2	173.1	158.4	134.7	151.2	120.6	83.5	93.6
Cholera	9	4	6	103	18	39	23	4	6
Cryptosporidiosis	(2)	(2)	(2)	(2)	(2)	(2)	(2)	(2)	2,566
Diphtheria	3	3	4	4	-	2	-	2	4
Encephalitis:									
Primary infectious	1,362	1,376	1,341	774	919	717	(2)	(2)	(2)
Post infectious	40	161	105	129	170	143	(2)	(2)	(2)
Escherichia coli 0157:H7	(2)	(2)	(2)	(2)	(2)	1,420	2,139	2,741	2,555
Haemophilus influenza	(2)	(2)	(2)	1,412	1,419	1,174	1,180	1,170	1,162
Hepatitis: B (serum) (1,000)	19.0	26.6	21.1	16.1	13.4	12.5	10.8	10.6	10.4
A (infectious) (1,000)	29.1	23.2	31.4	23.1	24.2	29.8	31.6	31.0	30.0
Unspecified (1,000)	11.9	5.5	1.7	0.9	0.6	0.4	(2)	(2)	(2)
C/Non-A, non-B (1,000) [5]	(2)	4.2	2.6	6.0	4.8	4.4	4.6	3.7	3.8
Legionellosis	(2)	830	1,370	1,339	1,280	1,615	1,241	1,198	1,163
Leprosy (Hansen disease)	223	361	198	172	187	136	144	112	122
Leptospirosis	85	57	77	54	51	38	(2)	(2)	(2)
Lyme disease	(2)	(2)	(2)	9,895	8,257	13,043	11,700	16,455	12,801
Malaria	2,062	1,049	1,292	1,087	1,411	1,229	1,419	1,800	2,001
Measles (1,000)	13.5	2.8	27.8	2.2	0.3	1.0	0.3	0.5	0.1
Meningococcal infections	2,840	2,479	2,451	2,134	2,637	2,886	3,243	3,437	3,308
Mumps (1,000)	8.6	3.0	5.3	2.6	1.7	1.5	0.9	0.8	0.7
Pertussis [6] (1,000)	1.7	3.6	4.6	4.1	6.6	4.6	5.1	7.8	6.6
Plague	18	17	2	13	10	17	9	5	4
Poliomyelitis, acute [7]	9	7	6	6	4	8	6	5	3
Psittacosis	124	119	113	92	60	38	64	42	33
Rabies, animal	6,421	5,565	4,826	8,589	9,377	8,147	7,811	6,982	8,105
Rabies, human	-	1	1	1	3	6	5	3	2
Rheumatic fever, acute [8]	432	90	108	75	112	112	(2)	(2)	(2)
Rubella [9]	3,904	630	1,125	160	192	227	128	238	181
Salmonellosis [10] (1,000)	33.7	65.3	48.6	40.9	41.6	43.3	46.0	45.5	41.9
Shigellosis [11] (1,000)	19.0	17.1	27.1	23.9	32.2	29.8	32.1	26.0	23.1
Tetanus	95	83	64	45	48	51	41	36	50
Toxic-shock syndrome	(2)	384	322	244	212	192	191	145	157
Trichinosis	131	61	129	41	16	32	29	11	13
Tuberculosis [12] (1,000)	27.7	22.2	25.7	26.7	25.3	24.4	22.9	21.3	19.9
Tularemia	234	177	152	159	132	96	(2)	(2)	(2)
Typhoid fever	510	402	552	414	440	441	369	396	365
Typhus fever:									
Flea-borne (endemic-murine)	81	37	50	28	25	(2)	(2)	(2)	(2)
Tick-borne (Rocky Mt. spotted fever)	1,163	714	651	502	456	465	590	831	409
Sexually transmitted diseases:									
Gonorrhea (1,000)	1,004	911	690	501	440	418	393	326	325
Syphilis (1,000)	69	68	134	113	101	82	69	53	47
Chlamydia (1,000)	(2)	(2)	(2)	(2)	(2)	(2)	478	499	527
Chancroid (1,000)	0.8	2.1	4.2	1.9	1.4	0.8	0.6	0.4	0.2

- Represents zero.   NA Not available.   [1] Acquired immunodeficiency syndrome was not a notifiable disease until 1984. Figures are shown for years in which cases were reported to the CDC. Beginning 1993, based on revised classification system and expanded surveillance case definition.   [2] Disease was not notifiable.   [3] Includes foodborne, infant, wound, and unspecified cases.   [4] Chickenpox was taken off the nationally notifiable list in 1991 but many states continue to report.   [5] Includes some persons positive for antibody to hepatitis C virus who do not have hepatitis.   [6] Whooping cough.   [7] Revised. Data subject to annual revisions.   [8] Based on reports from states; 37 in 1980, 31 in 1985, 30 in 1990, 26 in 1992 and 1993, and 27 in 1994.   [9] German measles.   [10] Excludes typhoid fever.   [11] Bacillary dysentery.   [12] Newly reported active cases.

Source: U.S. Centers for Disease Control and Prevention, Atlanta, GA, *Summary of Notifiable Diseases, United States, 1997*, *Morbidity and Mortality Weekly Report*, Vol. 46, No. 54, November 20, 1998.

No. 227. Selected Measures of Hospital Utilization for Patients Discharged With the Diagnosis of Human Immunodeficiency Virus (HIV): 1985 to 1997

[See headnote, Table 207]

Measure of utilization	Unit	1985	1990	1994	1995	1996	1997
Number of patients discharged [1]	1,000	23	146	234	249	227	178
Rate of patient discharges [2]	Rate	1.0	5.9	9.0	9.5	8.6	6.7
Number of days of care	1,000	387	2,188	2,317	2,326	2,123	1,448
Rate of days of care [2]	Rate	16.3	87.7	89.5	89.0	80.4	54.3
Average length of stay [3]	Days	17.1	14.9	9.9	9.3	9.4	8.1

[1] Comparisons beginning 1990 with data for earlier years should be made with caution as estimates of change may reflect improvements in the 1988 sample design rather than true changes in hospital use.   [2] Per 10,000 population. Based on U.S. Census Bureau estimated civilian population as of July 1. Population estimates for the 1980's do not reflect revised estimates based on the 1990 Census of Population.   [3] For similar data on all patients, see Table 207.

Source: National Center for Health Statistics, *Vital and Health Statistics*, Series 13; "Decreasing Hospital Use for HIV," *NCHS Health E-Stats*, No. 1, June 9, 1999; and unpublished data.

U.S. Census Bureau, Statistical Abstract of the United States: 1999

No. 228. AIDS Cases Reported, by Patient Characteristic: 1981 to 1998

[**Provisional.** For cases reported in the year shown. Data shown for 1990 and 1994-97 are as reported through December 1997; data for 1981-98 and 1998 are as reported through December 1998 and include Puerto Rico, Virgin Islands, Guam, and U.S. Pacific Islands. For data on AIDS deaths, see Table 142. Data are subject to retrospective changes and may differ from those data in Table 226]

Characteristic	1981-98, total	1990	1994	1995	1996	1997	1998
Total [1].............	688,200	41,529	77,103	70,864	66,497	58,443	48,269
Age:							
Under 5 years old.........	6,574	583	751	554	482	306	(NA)
5 to 12 years old..........	1,887	137	220	189	168	145	(NA)
13 to 19 years old.........	3,423	167	385	380	375	354	(NA)
20 to 29 years old.........	117,717	7,854	12,321	10,866	9,655	8,130	(NA)
30 to 39 years old.........	310,196	18,798	34,775	31,731	29,647	25,693	(NA)
40 to 49 years old.........	176,239	9,725	20,505	19,446	18,818	16,957	(NA)
50 to 59 years old.........	52,437	2,926	5,894	5,560	5,290	4,951	(NA)
60 years old and over	19,724	1,253	2,050	1,924	1,858	1,733	(NA)
Sex:							
Male..................	574,783	36,667	63,301	57,451	52,969	45,696	37,076
Female................	113,414	4,862	13,802	13,413	13,528	12,747	11,190
Race/ethnic group:							
Non-Hispanic White........	304,094	22,258	32,729	29,386	26,172	20,170	16,118
Non-Hispanic Black........	251,408	13,199	30,923	29,060	28,639	26,995	21,752
Hispanic..............	124,841	5,657	12,556	11,544	10,796	10,387	9,650
Other/unknown..........	7,857	415	895	874	890	891	749
Transmission category:							
Males, 13 years and over....	570,425	36,277	62,820	57,082	52,630	45,440	36,886
Men who have sex with men	326,051	23,797	35,255	30,953	27,460	20,894	16,642
Injecting drug use.........	126,889	6,957	15,124	13,329	11,801	9,737	7,869
Men who have sex with men and injecting drug use.........	43,640	2,809	4,529	3,805	3,153	2,262	1,984
Hemophilia/coagulation disorder ..	4,663	332	482	426	304	180	145
Heterosexual contact [2]	15,346	260	1,886	1,930	2,348	2,087	1,979
Heterosexual contact with injecting drug user	8,015	457	932	874	827	703	631
Transfusion [3]	4,784	449	369	341	270	217	156
Undetermined [4]	41,037	1,216	4,243	5,424	6,467	9,360	7,480
Females, 13 years and over ...	109,311	4,529	13,295	13,017	13,195	12,530	10,998
Injecting drug use.........	46,804	2,325	5,907	5,290	4,728	4,044	3,201
Hemophilia/coagulation disorder ..	248	16	28	26	22	16	17
Heterosexual contact [2]	24,897	506	3,431	3,518	3,781	3,293	2,913
Heterosexual contact with injecting drug user	18,231	1,035	2,029	1,873	1,870	1,349	1,212
Transfusion [3]	3,598	335	310	271	266	181	137
Undetermined [4]	15,533	312	1,590	2,039	2,528	3,647	3,518

NA Not available.   [1] Includes unknown, not shown separately.   [2] Includes persons who have had heterosexual contact with a person with human immunodeficiency virus (HIV) infection or at risk of HIV infection.   [3] Receipt of blood transfusion, blood components, or tissue.   [4] Includes persons for whom risk information is incomplete (because of death, refusal to be interviewed, or loss to followup), persons still under investigation, men reported only to have had heterosexual contact with prostitutes, and interviewed persons for whom no specific risk is identified.

Source: U.S. Centers for Disease Control and Prevention, Atlanta, GA, *HIV/AIDS Surveillance Reports*, semiannual.

No. 229. AIDS, Syphilis, Tuberculosis, and Measles Cases Reported, by State: 1997

[Diseases selected are those included in the Healthy People 2000 Indicators series]

State	AIDS	Syphilis	Tuber-culosis	Measles	State	AIDS	Syphilis	Tuber-culosis	Measles
U.S. ...	[1]58,492	46,540	19,851	138	MO	577	494	248	1
AL......	570	1,481	405	1	MT	41	5	18	-
AK......	52	12	78	-	NE	91	32	22	-
AZ......	448	600	296	5	NV	592	102	112	2
AR......	242	562	200	-	NH	55	23	17	1
CA......	7,029	3,823	4,056	24	NJ	3,226	1,129	718	3
CO......	380	154	94	-	NM	169	103	71	-
CT......	1,222	320	128	1	NY	13,189	5,639	2,265	16
DE......	231	113	39	-	NC	850	2,206	463	2
DC......	998	645	110	2	ND	13	-	12	-
FL......	6,098	2,746	1,400	8	OH	848	761	286	-
GA......	1,722	2,833	696	1	OK	283	405	212	1
HI	94	47	167	4	OR	305	48	161	-
ID	52	24	15	-	PA	1,912	1,182	528	8
IL......	1,842	1,953	974	7	RI	152	84	38	-
IN......	523	522	168	-	SC	779	1,135	328	1
IA......	101	72	74	-	SD	11	7	19	8
KS......	159	145	78	-	TN	784	2,366	467	-
KY......	361	403	198	-	TX	4,718	5,384	1,992	7
LA......	1,094	1,808	406	1	UT	152	56	36	1
ME......	51	13	21	-	VT	29	1	6	-
MD......	1,875	2,453	340	2	VA	1,175	1,103	350	1
MA......	863	731	268	16	WA	641	132	305	8
MI	882	785	374	2	WV	130	19	54	1
MN......	214	124	161	8	WI	255	315	130	1
MS.....	347	1,439	245	-	WY	16	1	2	-

- Represents zero.   [1] Includes 49 cases in persons with unknown state of residence.

Source: U.S. Centers for Disease Control and Prevention, Atlanta, GA, *Summary of Notifiable Diseases, United States, 1997, Morbidity and Mortality Weekly Report*, Vol. 46, No. 54, November 20, 1998.

No. 230. Children Immunized Against Specified Diseases: 1995 to 1997

[In percent. Covers civilian noninstitutionalized population ages 19 months to 35 months. Based on estimates from the National Immunization Survey. The health care providers of the children are contacted to verify and/or complete vaccination information. Results are based on race/ethnic status of the child]

Vaccination	1995, total	1996, total	1997					
			Total	White non-Hispanic	Hispanic	Black non-Hispanic	American Indian/ Alaskan Native	Asian/ Pacific Islander
Diphtheria-tetanus-pertussis (DPT)/ diphtheria-tetanus:								
3+ doses	95	95	95	97	93	95	92	95
4+ doses	79	81	81	84	77	78	80	80
Polio: 3+ doses.	88	91	91	92	90	90	91	88
Hib [1]: 3+ doses.	92	92	93	94	90	92	87	89
Measles containing (MCV)	90	91	91	92	88	90	92	89
Hepatitis B: 3+ doses.	68	82	84	85	81	83	83	88
4+ DPT/3+ polio/1+ MCV	76	78	78	80	74	74	78	75
4+ DPT/3+ polio/1+ MCV/3+ hiB	74	77	76	79	72	73	72	70

[1] Haemophilus B.

Source: U.S. Centers for Disease Control and Prevention, *Morbidity and Mortality Weekly Report*, Vol. 47, Nos. 26 and 44, July 10, 1998 and November 13, 1998.

No. 231. Acute Conditions, by Type: 1980 to 1996

[54 represents 54,000,000. Covers civilian noninstitutional population. Estimates include only acute conditions which were medically attended or caused at least 1 day of restricted activity. Based on National Health Interview Survey; see Appendix III. See headnote, Table 222. For composition of regions, see map, inside front cover]

Year and characteristic	Number of conditions (mil.)					Rate per 100 population				
	Infective and parasitic	Respiratory		Diges-tive system	Injuries	Infective and parasitic	Respiratory		Diges-tive system	Injuries
		Com-mon cold	Influ-enza				Com-mon cold	Influ-enza		
1980	54	(NA)	(NA)	25	73	24.6	(NA)	(NA)	11.4	33.4
1985	48	(NA)	(NA)	16	64	20.5	(NA)	(NA)	7.0	27.4
1990	52	61	107	13	60	21.0	25.0	43.4	5.3	24.4
1993	54	68	133	16	62	21.3	26.8	52.2	6.3	24.4
1994	54	66	90	16	62	20.9	25.4	34.8	6.1	23.8
1995	53	61	108	16	65	20.1	23.1	41.2	6.0	24.7
1996, total [1]	54	62	95	18	57	20.5	23.6	36.0	6.7	21.7
Under 5 years old.	11	10	11	2	5	57.0	48.6	53.7	9.6	22.9
5 to 17 years old	19	17	23	5	11	37.1	33.8	44.3	9.8	21.4
18 to 24 years old	6	6	10	2	8	23.2	23.8	40.5	6.4	31.5
25 to 44 years old	10	16	32	4	21	12.2	18.7	38.1	5.1	24.9
45 to 64 years old	6	9	14	3	8	11.0	16.4	26.1	5.3	14.6
65 years old and over . . .	2	5	6	2	5	6.5	15.7	18.6	6.6	17.2
Male	23	28	44	8	32	17.9	21.9	34.1	5.9	24.6
Female.	31	34	51	10	26	23.0	25.1	37.8	7.4	18.9
White.	46	51	82	15	49	21.0	23.3	37.3	6.8	22.1
Black	6	9	9	2	7	19.0	26.0	28.1	6.9	20.8
Northeast	11	12	15	3	12	21.3	21.7	28.3	4.8	21.9
Midwest	11	16	26	5	15	17.9	26.0	41.5	7.7	24.3
South.	23	17	26	7	18	25.5	19.2	28.8	7.4	20.4
West	8	17	27	3	12	14.7	29.6	48.7	6.1	20.5
Family income:										
Under $10,000	5	6	8	1	6	25.7	30.9	41.8	7.0	28.0
$10,000 to $19,999 . . .	6	7	12	3	10	16.5	18.9	33.7	8.0	25.8
$20,000 to $34,999 . . .	10	12	21	4	12	18.7	23.0	39.7	7.5	21.7
$35,000 or more	26	27	41	7	23	23.5	24.4	37.1	6.0	20.6

NA Not available.   [1] Includes other races and unknown income not shown separately.

Source: U.S. National Center for Health Statistics, *Vital and Health Statistics*, Series 10, No. 200, and earlier reports; and unpublished data.

Health and Nutrition   149

[33,638 represents 33,638,000. Covers civilian noninstitutional population. Conditions classified according to ninth revision of International Classification of Diseases. Based on National Health Interview Survey; see Appendix III. See headnote, Table 222]

Chronic condition	Conditions (1,000)	Rate [1]							
		Male				Female			
		Under 45 years old	45 to 64 years old	65 to 74 years old	75 years old and over	Under 45 years old	45 to 64 years old	65 to 74 years old	75 years old and over
Arthritis	33,638	26.1	193.0	394.6	437.9	35.8	284.0	500.3	576.4
Dermatitis, including eczema	8,249	24.1	28.6	[2]31.1	[2]34.9	36.4	47.0	[2]23.0	[2]16.0
Trouble with—									
Dry (itching) skin	6,627	15.0	23.1	[2]37.3	[2]73.0	24.4	34.3	[2]37.7	59.3
Ingrown nails	5,807	21.1	24.4	[2]40.1	[2]41.6	14.4	29.1	[2]29.0	[2]43.4
Corns and calluses	3,778	6.9	19.6	[2]25.4	[2]28.8	9.6	30.9	[2]28.5	[2]35.8
Visual impairments	8,280	21.7	61.0	90.6	125.1	12.2	36.4	52.6	91.4
Cataracts	7,022	[2]1.6	17.3	109.3	189.6	[2]2.1	29.0	186.4	203.9
Hearing impairments	22,044	34.0	183.4	342.6	457.9	26.4	82.9	184.5	315.5
Tinnitus	7,866	11.0	76.9	119.5	114.1	10.4	43.4	77.1	52.8
Deformities or orthopedic impairments	29,499	84.8	187.5	165.5	142.0	82.9	168.6	182.8	128.4
Hernia of abdominal cavity	4,470	7.8	35.0	49.3	[2]59.8	6.6	27.1	[2]29.6	64.0
Frequent indigestion	6,420	20.8	44.7	[2]28.1	[2]7.6	14.0	39.7	46.9	[2]38.1
Diabetes	7,627	6.1	56.9	117.4	129.0	9.0	59.4	83.1	85.8
Migraine	11,546	20.2	20.2	[2]1.5	[2]19.4	64.1	93.3	50.6	[2]33.9
Heart conditions	20,653	30.7	133.5	259.5	394.8	35.5	100.3	221.0	258.7
High blood pressure (Hypertension)	28,314	30.0	214.8	314.6	271.0	30.1	213.3	389.5	437.0
Varicose veins of lower extremities	7,399	[2]3.8	17.6	[2]38.2	[2]59.2	22.9	74.1	102.9	102.9
Hemorrhoids	8,531	16.7	47.8	[2]46.1	[2]31.2	25.0	59.1	94.3	54.2
Chronic bronchitis	14,150	48.4	41.0	57.9	[2]34.1	51.9	76.1	63.2	87.7
Asthma	14,596	49.8	30.4	[2]39.8	[2]33.7	68.1	65.5	46.8	56.8
Hay fever, allergic rhinitis without asthma	23,721	86.3	85.6	57.9	[2]26.1	92.1	122.8	65.1	106.3
Chronic sinusitis	33,161	93.5	140.5	119.4	93.7	131.7	205.5	133.1	109.6

[1] Conditions per 1,000 persons. [2] Figure does not meet standards of reliability or precision.

Source: U.S. National Center for Health Statistics, *Vital and Health Statistics,* Series 10, No. 200, and earlier reports; and unpublished data.

No. 233. Persons Using Assistive Technology Devices, by Age: 1994

[In thousands, except as indicated (4,565 represents 4,565,000). For the civilian noninstitutionalized population. Based on the National Health Interview Survey; see Appendix III]

Assistive device	Total	Under 45 years old	45 to 64 years old	65 years old and over
Any anatomical device [1]	4,565	2,491	1,325	748
Rate per 1,000 persons	17.6	14.0	26.3	24.1
Back brace	1,688	795	614	279
Neck brace	168	76	78	[2]13
Hand brace	332	171	119	42
Arm brace	320	209	86	[2]25
Leg brace	596	266	138	192
Foot brace	282	191	59	31
Knee brace	989	694	199	96
Other brace	399	239	104	56
Any artificial limb	199	69	59	70
Artificial leg or foot	173	58	50	65
Any mobility device [1]	7,394	1,151	1,699	4,544
Rate per 1,000 persons	28.5	6.5	33.7	146.5
Crutch	575	227	188	160
Cane	4,762	434	1,116	3,212
Walker	1,799	109	295	1,395
Medical shoes	677	248	226	203
Wheelchair	1,564	335	365	863
Scooter	140	12	53	75
Any hearing device [1]	4,484	439	969	3,076
Rate per 1,000 persons	17.3	2.5	19.2	99.2
Hearing aid	4,156	370	849	2,938
Amplified telephone	675	73	175	427
TDD/TTY [3]	104	58	[2]25	[2]21
Closed caption television	141	66	[2]32	43
Listening device	106	[2]26	[2]22	58
Signaling device	95	[2]37	[2]23	35
Any vision device [1]	527	123	135	268
Rate per 1,000 persons	2.0	0.7	2.7	8.6
Telescopic lenses	158	40	49	70
White cane	130	[2]35	48	47

[1] Numbers do not add to totals because a person could have used more than one device. [2] Figure does not meet standards of reliability or precision. [3] TDD/TTY is a typewriter-like device for the deaf that communicates over telephone lines using text.

Source: U.S. National Center for Health Statistics, *Advance Data,* No. 292, November 13, 1997.

No. 234. Disability Status of Children Under 15 Years Old: 1994-95

[For period October 1994 through January 1995 (11,942 represents 11,942,000). Covers civilian noninstitutional population and members of the Armed Forces living off post or with their families on post. The criteria for presence of disability varied by age. In general, a disability is considered a reduced ability to perform tasks one would normally do at a given stage in life. Based on the Survey of Income and Program Participation; for details, see source]

Age and disability status	Number (1,000)	Percent distribu-tion	Age and disability status	Number (1,000)	Percent distribu-tion
Children under 3 years old . . . . ₁ . .	11,942	100.0	Children 6 to 14 years old	35,011	100.0
With a developmental condition [1] . .	313	2.6	With any disability [3]	4,462	12.7
			With a severe disability.	659	1.9
Children 3 to 5 years old	12,427	100.0	Difficulty doing regular schoolwork .	2,170	6.2
With any disability [2]	652	5.2	With a learning disability.	1,559	4.5
With a developmental condition [1] . .	510	4.1	With a developmental disability [4] . .	451	1.3
Difficulty walking, running,			Difficulty with one or more ADLs [5] .	381	1.1
or using stairs.	235	1.9	Needs personal assistance	272	0.8

[1] A developmental condition for which the child has received therapy or diagnostic services. [2] Covers children with a developmental condition and/or difficulty walking, running, or using stairs. [3] Includes in addition to the disabilities listed below those children who have difficulty seeing, hearing, walking, running, or using stairs and those who use wheelchairs, canes, crutches, or walkers. [4] Includes the conditions of mental retardation, autism, and cerebral palsy. [5] See headnote, Table 236.

No. 235. Disability Status of Persons 15 Years Old and Over: 1994-95

[In thousands, except as noted (202,368 represents 202,368,000). See headnote, Table 234]

Disability status	Total	15 to 21 years	22 to 44 years	45 to 54 years	55 to 64 years	65 to 79 years	80 years and over
Total	202,368	25,146	95,002	30,316	20,647	24,471	6,785
With any disability.	48,481	3,047	14,105	7,412	7,497	11,568	4,853
Percent of total	24.0	12.1	14.9	24.5	36.3	47.3	71.5
With a severe disability	25,309	813	6,071	3,472	4,528	6,798	3,627
Difficulty with one or more ADLs [1]	8,194	154	1,425	952	1,235	2,565	1,864
Needs personal assistance	3,806	91	663	324	509	1,181	1,039
Difficulty with one or more IADLs [1]	12,260	385	2,364	1,360	1,662	3,747	2,743
Needs personal assistance with one or more ADLs or IADLs [1]	9,473	318	1,777	984	1,268	2,814	2,312

[1] See headnote, Table 236.

No. 236. Receipt of Personal Assistance by Persons With Disabilities: 1994-95

[9,342 represents 9,342,000. See headnote, Table 234. ADLs are activities of daily living and include getting around inside the home, getting in or out of a bed or chair, taking a bath or shower, dressing, eating, and using the toilet. IADLs are instrumental activities of daily living and include going outside the home, keeping track of money and bills, preparing meals, doing light housework, and using the telephone]

Relationship of first helper to person receiving assistance	Persons 15 years old and over				Persons 65 years old and over			
	Receiving assistance with an ADL or an IADL		Receiving assistance with an ADL		Receiving assistance with an ADL or an IADL		Receiving assistance with an ADL	
	Number (1,000)	Percent distribu-tion	Number (1,000)	Percent distribu-tion	Number (1,000)	Percent distribu-tion	Number (1,000)	Percent distribu-tion
Persons receiving assistance	9,342	100.0	3,777	100.0	5,046	100.0	2,202	100.0
Household member	4,478	47.9	2,154	57.0	2,360	46.8	1,208	54.9
Not a household member	4,864	52.1	1,623	43.0	2,686	53.2	994	45.1
Spouse	2,607	27.9	1,298	34.4	1,366	27.1	724	32.9
Daughter	1,710	18.3	688	18.2	1,120	22.2	465	21.1
Son	1,183	12.7	392	10.4	711	14.1	245	11.1
Parent.	800	8.6	280	7.4	(X)	(X)	(X)	(X)
Other relative	1,231	13.2	447	11.8	755	15.0	312	14.2
Nonrelative.	1,018	10.9	300	7.9	468	9.3	151	6.9
Paid help.	794	8.5	372	9.9	626	12.4	305	13.8

X Not applicable.

Source of Tables 234-236: U.S. Census Bureau, Current Population Reports, P70-61.

U.S. Census Bureau, Statistical Abstract of the United States: 1999

No. 237. Substance Abuse Treatment Facilities and Clients: 1997

[**As of October 1.** Based on the Uniform Facility Data Set (UFDS) survey, a census of all known facilities that provide substance abuse treatment in the United States and associated jurisdictions. Selected missing data for responding facilities were imputed]

Item	Number	Type of care and problem	Number of clients, 1997	Client characteristic	Number of clients, 1997
Facilities:		Total	929,166	Total	929,166
1995.	10,746	Outpatient rehab.	809,036	Under 18 yrs	81,456
1996.	10,641	24-hour rehab.	103,561	18 to 24 yrs	160,432
1997.	10,867	24-hour detoxification. . .	16,569	25 to 34 yrs	270,302
				35 to 44 yrs	264,553
				45 to 64 yrs	135,762
		Drug only.	305,431	65 yrs and over.	16,661
		Alcohol only	244,849	Male.	632,193
Clients:		Both alcohol & drug	378,886	Female	296,973
1995.	1,009,127				
1996.	940,141			White, non-Hispanic. . . .	524,996
1997.	929,166	Total with a drug problem [1]	684,317	Black, non-Hispanic. . . .	230,989
		Total with an alcohol problem [2]	623,735	Hispanic	132,470
				Asian/Pacific Islander. . .	7,697
				American Indian [3]	24,461
				Other	8,553

[1] The sum of clients with a drug problem and clients with both diagnoses.   [2] The sum of clients with an alcohol problem and clients with both diagnoses.   [3] Includes Alaskan native.

Source: U.S. Substance Abuse and Mental Health Services Administration, *Uniform Facility Data Set (UFDS): Annual surveys for 1995, 1996, and 1997.*

No. 238. Drug Use, by Type of Drug and Age Group: 1985 to 1997

[**In percent.** Current users are those who used drugs at least once within month prior to this study. Based on national samples of respondents residing in households. Subject to sampling variability; see source]

Age and type of drug	Ever used					Current user				
	1985	1990	1995	1996	1997	1985	1990	1995	1996	1997
12 YEARS OLD AND OVER										
Marijuana and hashish	29.4	30.5	31.0	32.0	32.9	9.7	5.4	4.7	4.7	5.1
Cocaine	11.2	11.2	10.3	10.3	10.5	3.0	0.9	0.7	0.8	0.7
Crack	(NA)	1.5	1.8	2.2	1.9	(NA)	0.3	0.2	0.3	0.3
Inhalants	7.9	5.7	5.7	5.6	5.7	0.6	0.4	0.4	0.4	0.4
Hallucinogens	6.9	7.9	9.5	9.7	9.6	1.2	0.4	0.7	0.6	0.8
PCP	2.0	2.0	3.2	3.2	3.0	(NA)	(NA)	-	0.1	0.1
LSD	4.6	5.8	7.5	7.7	7.8	(NA)	(NA)	0.3	0.2	0.2
Heroin	0.9	0.8	1.2	1.1	0.9	0.1	-	0.1	0.1	0.2
Stimulants [1]	7.3	5.5	4.9	4.7	4.5	1.8	0.6	0.4	0.4	0.3
Sedatives [1]	4.8	2.8	2.7	2.3	1.9	0.5	0.2	0.2	0.1	0.1
Tranquilizers [1]	7.6	4.0	3.9	3.6	3.2	2.2	0.6	0.4	0.4	0.4
Analgesics [1]	7.6	6.3	6.1	5.5	4.9	1.4	0.9	0.6	0.9	0.7
Alcohol.	84.9	82.2	82.3	82.6	81.9	60.2	52.6	52.2	51.0	51.4
Cigarettes.	78.0	75.4	71.8	71.6	70.5	38.7	32.6	28.8	28.9	29.6
Smokeless tobacco	(NA)	17.5	17.0	17.0	17.3	(NA)	3.9	3.3	3.2	3.2
12 to 17 YEARS OLD										
Marijuana and hashish	20.1	12.7	16.2	16.8	18.9	10.2	4.4	8.2	7.1	9.4
Cocaine	4.7	2.6	2.0	1.9	3.0	1.5	0.6	0.8	0.6	1.0
Alcohol.	56.1	48.8	40.6	38.8	39.7	41.2	32.5	21.1	18.8	20.5
Cigarettes.	50.7	45.1	38.1	36.3	38.7	29.4	22.4	20.2	18.3	19.9
18 TO 25 YEARS OLD										
Marijuana and hashish	57.6	50.4	41.4	44.0	41.5	21.7	12.7	12.0	13.2	12.8
Cocaine	24.3	19.3	9.8	10.2	8.9	8.1	2.3	1.3	2.0	1.2
Alcohol.	(NA)	87.6	84.4	83.8	83.5	70.1	62.8	61.3	60.0	58.4
Cigarettes.	75.3	70.7	67.7	68.5	67.7	47.4	40.9	35.3	38.3	40.6
26 TO 34 YEARS OLD										
Marijuana and hashish	54.1	56.5	51.8	50.5	47.9	19.0	9.5	6.7	6.3	6.0
Cocaine	23.6	25.4	21.6	20.9	18.4	6.3	1.9	1.2	1.5	0.9
Alcohol.	(NA)	(NA)	90.1	90.3	88.9	70.6	64.4	63.0	61.6	60.2
Cigarettes.	84.7	84.1	75.8	73.8	72.8	45.7	42.4	34.7	35.0	33.7
35 YEARS OLD AND OVER										
Marijuana and hashish	13.9	19.6	25.3	27.0	29.4	2.6	2.4	1.8	2.0	2.6
Cocaine	4.1	5.9	8.6	8.9	9.0	0.5	0.2	0.4	0.4	0.5
Alcohol.	(NA)	83.5	87.1	87.8	87.0	57.5	49.5	52.6	51.7	52.8
Cigarettes.	82.2	79.0	77.5	77.8	76.0	35.5	28.9	27.2	27.0	27.9

- Represents or rounds to zero.   NA Not available.   [1] Nonmedical use; does not include over-the-counter drugs.

Source: U.S. Substance Abuse and Mental Health Services Administration, *National Household Survey on Drug Abuse,* annual.

No. 239. Current Cigarette Smoking: 1985 to 1995

[In percent. Prior to 1994, a current smoker is a person who has smoked at least 100 cigarettes and who now smokes. Beginning 1994, definition includes persons who smoke only "some days". Excludes unknown smoking status. Based on the National Health Interview Survey; for details, see Appendix III]

Sex, age, and race	1985	1990	1994	1995	Sex, age, and race	1985	1990	1994	1995
Total smokers	30.1	25.5	25.5	24.7	Female, total	27.9	22.8	23.1	22.6
Male, total	32.6	28.4	28.2	27.0	18 to 24 years	30.4	22.5	25.2	21.8
18 to 24 years	28.0	26.6	29.8	27.8	25 to 34 years	32.0	28.2	28.8	(NA)
25 to 34 years	38.2	31.6	31.4	(NA)	35 to 44 years	31.5	24.8	26.8	(NA)
35 to 44 years	37.6	34.5	33.2	(NA)	45 to 64 years	29.9	24.8	22.8	24.0
45 to 64 years	33.4	29.3	28.3	27.1	65 years and over	13.5	11.5	11.1	11.5
65 years and over	19.6	14.6	13.2	14.3					
White, total	31.7	28.0	27.7	(NA)	White, total	27.7	23.4	23.7	(NA)
18 to 24 years	28.4	27.4	31.8	(NA)	18 to 24 years	31.8	25.4	28.5	(NA)
25 to 34 years	37.3	31.6	32.5	(NA)	25 to 34 years	32.0	28.5	30.2	(NA)
35 to 44 years	36.6	33.5	32.0	(NA)	35 to 44 years	31.0	25.0	27.1	(NA)
45 to 64 years	32.1	28.7	26.9	(NA)	45 to 64 years	29.7	25.4	23.2	(NA)
65 years and over	18.9	13.7	11.9	(NA)	65 years and over	13.3	11.5	11.1	(NA)
Black, total	39.9	32.5	33.7	(NA)	Black, total	31.0	21.2	21.7	(NA)
18 to 24 years	27.2	21.3	18.7	(NA)	18 to 24 years	23.7	10.0	11.8	(NA)
25 to 34 years	45.6	33.8	29.8	(NA)	25 to 34 years	36.2	29.1	24.8	(NA)
35 to 44 years	45.0	42.0	44.5	(NA)	35 to 44 years	40.2	25.5	28.2	(NA)
45 to 64 years	46.1	36.7	41.2	(NA)	45 to 64 years	33.4	22.6	23.5	(NA)
65 years and over	27.7	21.5	25.6	(NA)	65 years and over	14.5	11.1	13.6	(NA)

NA Not available.

Source: U.S. National Center for Health Statistics, *Health United States, 1996-97 and Injury Chartbook*, 1997, and U.S. Centers for Disease Control and Prevention, *Morbidity and Mortality Weekly Report*, Vol. 46, No. 51, December 26, 1997.

No. 240. Current Cigarette Smoking, by Sex and State: 1997

[In percent. Current cigarette smoking is defined as persons who reported having smoked 100 or more cigarettes during their lifetime and who currently smoke every day or some days. Based on the Behavioral Risk Factor Surveillance System, a telephone survey of health behaviors of the civilian, noninstitutionalized U.S. population, 18 years old and over; for details, see source]

State	Total	Male	Female	State	Total	Male	Female
U.S.	23.2	25.5	21.3	MO	28.7	31.7	26.0
				MT	20.5	20.8	20.2
AL	24.7	28.6	21.3	NE	22.2	24.4	20.2
AK	26.7	27.4	25.8	NV	27.7	25.7	29.8
AZ	21.1	22.1	20.2	NH	24.8	26.0	23.7
AR	28.5	32.1	25.2				
CA	18.4	22.4	14.5	NJ	21.5	23.3	19.8
				NM	22.1	21.6	22.6
CO	22.6	24.0	21.2	NY	23.1	25.0	21.5
CT	21.8	21.4	22.2	NC	25.8	29.7	22.3
DE	26.6	29.3	24.2	ND	22.2	24.3	20.3
DC	18.8	22.7	15.5				
FL	23.6	26.0	21.4	OH	25.1	26.3	24.0
				OK	24.6	25.2	24.1
GA	22.4	25.2	19.9	OR	20.7	22.1	19.4
HI	18.6	21.4	15.8	PA	24.3	26.2	22.5
ID	19.9	21.8	18.0	RI	24.2	25.6	23.0
IL	23.2	25.0	21.6				
IN	26.3	29.2	23.7	SC	23.4	29.5	17.8
				SD	24.3	28.1	20.8
IA	23.1	25.5	20.9	TN	26.9	27.9	26.0
KS	22.7	26.8	18.9	TX	22.6	28.0	17.5
KY	30.8	33.1	28.7	UT	13.7	16.1	11.5
LA	24.6	29.3	20.4				
ME	22.7	25.2	20.4	VT	23.2	25.1	21.5
				VA	24.6	26.2	23.1
MD	20.6	21.8	19.4	WA	23.9	25.1	22.7
MA	20.4	21.8	19.2	WV	27.4	27.1	27.7
MI	26.1	29.6	22.8	WI	23.2	25.6	21.0
MN	21.8	24.1	19.8	WY	24.0	24.0	24.1
MS	23.2	28.3	18.6				

Source: U.S. Centers for Disease Control and Prevention, *Morbidity and Mortality Weekly Report, Vol. 47, No. 43*, November 6, 1998.

No. 241. Cancer—Estimated New Cases, 1999, and Survival Rates, 1980-82 to 1989-95

[1,222 represents 1,222,000. The 5-year relative survival rate, which is derived by adjusting the observed survival rate for expected mortality, represents the likelihood that a person will not die from causes directly related to their cancer within 5 years. Survival data shown are based on those patients diagnosed while residents of an area listed below during the time periods shown. Data are based on information collected as part of the National Cancer Institute's Surveillance, Epidemiology and End Results (SEER) program, a collection of population-based registries in Connecticut, New Mexico, Utah, Iowa, Hawaii, Atlanta, Detroit, Seattle-Puget Sound, and San Francisco-Oakland]

Site	Estimated new cases,[1] 1999 (1,000) Total	Male	Female	White 1980-82	1983-85	1986-88	1989-95	Black 1980-82	1983-85	1986-88	1989-95
All sites [2]	1,222	624	598	52.0	53.8	56.6	60.9	39.7	39.8	42.5	47.7
Lung [3]	172	94	78	13.5	13.9	13.5	14.2	12.2	11.5	11.8	11.3
Breast [3]	176	1	175	77.1	79.2	83.8	86.0	65.9	63.5	69.2	71.0
Colon and rectum	130	62	67	54.8	57.6	60.7	61.8	46.5	47.9	52.1	51.7
Colon	95	43	52	55.6	58.4	61.5	62.4	49.2	49.2	52.5	51.8
Rectum	35	19	15	52.9	55.9	59.1	60.2	38.2	43.8	51.0	51.2
Prostate	179	179	(X)	74.5	76.2	82.6	93.1	64.7	64.1	69.0	83.6
Bladder	54	39	15	78.8	78.2	80.6	81.8	58.3	59.0	62.0	62.2
Corpus uteri	37	(X)	37	82.8	84.5	84.3	85.5	54.1	54.0	56.5	56.1
Non-Hodgkin's lymphoma [4]	57	33	24	51.7	54.3	52.8	51.9	50.0	44.8	49.8	41.3
Oral cavity and pharynx	30	20	10	55.4	55.1	55.1	55.5	30.8	35.1	34.8	33.8
Leukemia [4]	30	17	13	39.3	41.6	43.4	44.4	33.2	33.4	36.8	33.5
Melanoma of skin	44	26	18	83.0	84.6	87.6	87.9	60.9	74.4	65.9	67.6
Pancreas	29	14	15	2.9	2.9	3.0	4.1	4.7	5.4	6.2	3.6
Kidney	30	18	12	51.0	55.7	57.5	61.1	55.4	54.8	53.0	57.7
Stomach	22	14	8	16.5	16.3	19.1	19.3	19.4	18.6	18.9	21.6
Ovary [5]	25	(X)	25	38.6	40.2	41.9	49.9	38.6	41.7	38.6	47.2
Cervix uteri [5]	13	(X)	13	67.9	70.3	71.6	71.4	61.0	59.9	55.4	58.8

X Not applicable.   [1] Estimates provided by American Cancer Society are based on rates from the National Cancer Institute's SEER program.   [2] Includes other sites not shown separately.   [3] Survival rates for female only.   [4] All types combined.   [5] Invasive cancer only.

Source: U.S. National Institutes of Health, National Cancer Institute, *Cancer Statistics Review*, annual

No. 242. Cancer—Estimated New Cases and Deaths, by State: 1999

[In thousands (1,221.8 represents 1,221,800). Excludes basal and squamous cellskin cancers and in situ carcinomas except urinary bladder]

State	New cases[1] Total[2]	Lung	Female breast	Deaths Total[2]	Lung	Female breast	State	New cases[1] Total[2]	Lung	Female breast	Deaths Total[2]	Lung	Female breast
U.S...	1,221.8	171.6	175.0	563.1	158.9	43.3	MO	27.9	4.4	3.6	12.9	4.0	0.9
							MT	4.1	0.6	0.6	1.9	0.5	0.2
AL	21.1	2.9	2.5	9.7	2.7	0.6	NE	7.4	1.0	1.0	3.4	0.9	0.3
AK	1.4	0.2	0.2	0.6	0.2	0.1	NV	8.1	1.2	1.0	3.8	1.1	0.3
AZ	20.0	2.8	2.6	9.2	2.6	0.7	NH	5.4	0.8	0.7	2.5	0.7	0.2
AR	13.8	2.3	1.7	6.4	2.2	0.4							
CA	112.3	14.6	16.9	51.7	13.5	4.2	NJ.....	40.0	4.9	5.9	18.4	4.5	1.5
							NM	6.5	0.8	1.0	3.0	0.7	0.2
CO	13.3	1.6	2.0	6.2	1.5	0.5	NY	83.1	10.7	13.0	38.3	9.9	3.2
CT	15.1	2.0	2.1	7.0	1.8	0.5	NC	35.5	5.3	4.7	16.3	4.9	1.2
DE	3.8	0.6	0.5	1.8	0.6	0.1	ND	3.1	0.4	0.4	1.4	0.3	0.1
DC	3.0	0.4	0.5	1.4	0.3	0.1							
FL.....	88.0	13.0	11.9	40.6	12.1	2.9	OH	56.5	8.3	8.4	26.0	7.7	2.1
							OK	15.8	2.5	2.3	7.3	2.3	0.6
GA	29.1	4.4	4.0	13.4	4.1	1.0	OR	15.9	2.2	2.1	7.3	2.1	0.5
HI....	4.3	0.6	0.5	2.0	0.5	0.1	PA	66.6	9.0	10.0	30.7	8.4	2.5
ID....	4.6	0.6	0.7	2.1	0.5	0.2	RI.....	5.2	0.8	0.7	2.4	0.7	0.2
IL.....	56.8	7.8	8.5	26.2	7.3	2.1							
IN....	27.9	4.3	3.9	12.9	4.0	1.0	SC	17.9	2.5	2.6	8.2	2.3	0.6
							SD	3.4	0.4	0.5	1.6	0.4	0.1
IA....	14.3	2.0	2.1	6.6	1.8	0.5	TN	26.8	4.3	3.9	12.3	3.9	1.0
KS....	12.0	1.6	1.7	5.6	1.5	0.4	TX	77.4	11.5	11.3	35.7	10.6	2.8
KY....	20.5	3.5	2.7	9.5	3.3	0.7	UT	5.2	0.4	0.8	2.4	0.4	0.2
LA....	20.3	3.0	3.1	9.4	2.7	0.8							
ME	7.0	1.1	1.0	3.2	1.0	0.2	VT	2.6	0.4	0.3	1.2	0.3	0.1
							VA	29.0	4.1	4.2	13.3	3.8	1.0
MD	22.6	3.2	3.5	10.4	3.0	0.9	WA	23.8	3.4	3.3	11.0	3.1	0.8
MA	30.7	4.1	4.4	14.2	3.8	1.1	WV	10.6	1.7	1.2	4.9	1.6	0.3
MI....	44.2	6.4	6.5	20.4	5.9	1.6	WI.....	23.7	2.8	3.4	10.9	2.6	0.8
MN	19.4	2.4	2.8	9.0	2.2	0.7	WY	2.0	0.3	0.3	0.9	0.3	0.1
MS	13.0	1.8	1.7	6.0	1.7	0.4							

[1] Estimates are offered as a rough guide and should be interpreted with caution. They are calculated according to the distribution of estimated 1999 cancer deaths by state.   [2] Includes other types of cancer, not shown separately.

Source: American Cancer Society, Inc., Georgia, *Cancer Facts and Figures—1999* (copyright).

No. 243. Cumulative Percent Distribution of Population, by Height and Sex: 1988-94

[For persons 20 to 79 years old. Height was measured without shoes. Based on sample and subject to sampling variability; see source]

Height	Males 20-29 years	30-39 years	40-49 years	50-59 years	60-69 years	70-79 years	Females 20-29 years	30-39 years	40-49 years	50-59 years	60-69 years	70-79 years
Percent under—												
4'8"	-	-	-	-	-	-	0.6	0.1	-	-	0.2	1.7
4'9"	-	-	-	-	-	-	0.7	0.2	0.3	0.1	0.7	3.3
4'10"	-	-	-	-	0.1	-	1.2	0.7	0.7	1.9	1.7	4.9
4'11".	-	-	-	-	0.1	0.1	3.1	2.6	1.7	3.1	4.4	9.8
5'	0.1	-	0.2	-	0.4	0.1	6.0	5.5	5.3	6.6	9.9	15.4
5'1"	0.1	-	0.4	0.1	0.5	0.6	11.5	10.4	9.9	11.9	19.0	28.9
5'2"	0.5	0.8	0.7	0.2	0.7	1.9	21.8	18.5	18.8	24.4	34.3	45.6
5'3"	1.3	1.4	0.9	1.0	2.2	2.7	34.3	30.7	31.9	38.6	48.3	61.2
5'4"	3.4	2.2	1.7	2.5	5.8	7.8	48.9	42.9	49.2	52.6	65.5	74.5
5'5"	6.9	5.1	5.6	6.0	9.4	16.5	62.7	59.1	64.3	69.9	76.5	85.9
5'6"	11.7	10.1	12.1	11.7	15.8	27.3	74.0	71.8	77.0	81.6	87.8	93.9
5'7"	20.8	18.9	19.6	20.5	27.4	39.5	84.7	84.1	87.0	89.3	92.5	97.3
5'8"	32.0	28.3	28.0	32.6	38.6	53.4	92.4	91.6	94.5	95.6	96.7	99.2
5'9"	46.3	44.3	42.1	43.9	55.1	68.7	96.2	95.6	97.3	99.0	99.3	99.9
5'10"	58.7	58.0	58.1	60.6	68.8	79.5	98.6	98.1	98.9	99.6	99.8	100.0
5'11".	70.1	70.4	71.1	75.2	81.4	89.2	99.5	99.5	99.4	100.0	100.0	100.0
6'	81.2	79.7	81.5	85.4	90.0	94.1	100.0	100.0	100.0	100.0	100.0	100.0
6'1"	87.4	86.2	89.0	92.4	95.2	97.2	100.0	100.0	100.0	100.0	100.0	100.0
6'2"	94.7	92.4	94.4	96.4	98.2	99.3	100.0	100.0	100.0	100.0	100.0	100.0
6'3"	97.9	98.1	97.2	98.2	99.5	99.9	100.0	100.0	100.0	100.0	100.0	100.0

- Represents or rounds to zero.

Source: U.S. National Center for Health Statistics, unpublished data.

No. 244. Cumulative Percent Distribution of Population, by Weight and Sex: 1988-94

[For persons 20 to 79 years old. Weight measured includes clothes weight, estimated as ranging from .20 pounds to .62 pounds. Based on sample and subject to sampling variability; see source]

Weight	Males 20-29 years	30-39 years	40-49 years	50-59 years	60-69 years	70-79 years	Females 20-29 years	30-39 years	40-49 years	50-59 years	60-69 years	70-79 years
Percent under—												
90 pounds ...	-	-	-	-	-	-	0.5	0.5	-	0.3	0.2	1.8
100 pounds ..	-	-	-	-	0.2	0.2	3.8	2.0	1.6	1.3	1.7	4.7
110 pounds ..	0.5	0.1	0.2	0.1	0.8	0.4	13.3	7.7	5.5	3.7	5.6	9.2
120 pounds ..	1.8	1.0	0.7	0.6	1.5	1.7	27.0	17.8	12.6	9.5	13.8	19.0
130 pounds ..	6.7	3.4	3.3	2.2	3.1	5.8	46.1	31.4	25.1	19.7	24.3	31.6
140 pounds ..	15.8	7.8	6.7	5.4	7.5	13.2	58.7	44.3	37.4	30.0	36.2	46.6
150 pounds ..	29.0	17.0	14.1	9.9	15.5	23.3	70.4	55.5	49.4	42.0	48.8	57.3
160 pounds ..	42.1	27.6	23.0	16.2	24.5	35.2	76.5	65.3	59.3	52.7	61.3	67.9
170 pounds ..	54.9	42.0	32.4	28.9	36.1	48.4	82.6	72.6	70.0	61.5	71.3	77.6
180 pounds ..	66.7	54.9	48.6	41.5	48.2	59.5	87.6	78.3	78.6	70.9	79.0	84.6
190 pounds ..	76.2	66.4	61.0	55.2	60.5	73.1	90.1	82.2	82.6	77.0	84.3	90.2
200 pounds ..	82.1	74.8	70.1	68.5	72.5	82.6	92.5	86.2	87.4	83.8	89.1	92.8
210 pounds ..	86.8	81.2	78.0	77.4	81.0	87.8	94.5	89.3	90.5	89.0	92.6	94.6
220 pounds ..	90.4	86.3	83.8	84.4	87.1	93.2	96.0	92.1	93.2	92.1	94.7	95.7
230 pounds ..	92.9	91.6	88.8	89.3	92.6	95.7	97.7	94.2	94.9	93.7	96.4	96.3
240 pounds ..	95.4	94.3	92.6	92.6	95.7	96.7	98.7	96.0	97.3	95.1	97.3	97.5
250 pounds ..	96.2	95.5	94.1	94.5	97.2	97.4	99.0	96.7	97.6	96.7	97.6	98.8
260 pounds ..	97.2	96.6	95.7	96.3	98.0	98.5	99.4	97.5	98.1	97.9	98.8	99.3
270 pounds ..	97.9	97.4	96.5	97.3	98.6	99.4	99.7	98.7	98.4	98.1	99.2	99.5
280 pounds ..	98.7	97.6	97.5	98.1	98.9	99.8	99.8	98.7	98.7	98.7	99.4	99.8
290 pounds ..	99.0	98.0	97.8	98.6	99.5	100.0	99.9	99.1	99.0	98.8	99.6	99.9
300 pounds ..	99.3	98.2	98.7	99.0	99.5	100.0	100.0	99.4	99.2	99.0	99.8	99.9
310 pounds ..	99.3	98.5	98.9	99.2	100.0	100.0	100.0	99.7	99.4	99.9	99.8	100.0
320 pounds ..	99.5	98.6	99.2	99.5	100.0	100.0	100.0	99.9	99.9	99.9	99.8	100.0
330 pounds ..	99.5	98.8	99.3	99.5	100.0	100.0	100.0	99.9	99.5	100.0	99.8	100.0
340 pounds ..	99.5	99.3	99.3	99.9	100.0	100.0	100.0	99.9	99.6	100.0	99.9	100.0
350 pounds ..	99.6	99.7	99.3	100.0	100.0	100.0	100.0	99.9	100.0	100.0	99.9	100.0
360 pounds ..	99.6	99.8	99.3	100.0	100.0	100.0	100.0	99.9	100.0	100.0	100.0	100.0
370 pounds ..	99.6	98.8	99.3	100.0	100.0	100.0	100.0	99.9	100.0	100.0	100.0	100.0
380 pounds ..	99.6	99.8	99.4	100.0	100.0	100.0	100.0	99.9	100.0	100.0	100.0	100.0

- Represents or rounds to zero.

Source: U.S. National Center for Health Statistics, unpublished data.

Health and Nutrition 155

No. 245. Percent of Population Overweight, by Age, Sex, and Race: 1976 to 1994

[In percent. Overweight is defined for men as body mass index greater than or equal to 27.8 kilograms/meter squared, and for women as body mass index greater than or equal to 27.3 kilograms/meter squared. These points were used because they represent the sex-specific 85th percentiles for persons 20-29 years of age in the 1976-80 National Health and Nutrition Examination Survey (NHANES). Data are based on physical examinations of a sample of the civilian noninstitutional population in the NHANES]

Age, sex, and race	1976-80	1988-94	Age, sex, and race	1976-80	1988-94	Age, sex, and race	1976-80	1988-94
Persons 20 to 74 years old [1] . .	25.4	34.8	MALE			FEMALE [2]		
			20 to 34 years old . .	17.3	25.4	20 to 34 years old. .	16.8	25.6
Male . . [2]	24.0	33.7	35 to 44 years old. .	28.9	34.9	35 to 44 years old. .	27.0	36.8
Female [2]	26.5	35.9	45 to 54 years old. .	31.0	37.7	45 to 54 years old. .	32.5	45.4
			55 to 64 years old. .	28.1	43.7	55 to 64 years old. .	37.0	48.2
White male . [2]	24.2	34.3	65 to 74 years old. .	25.2	42.9	65 to 74 years old. .	38.4	42.3
White female [2]	24.4	33.9	75 years old and over	(NA)	27.7	75 years old and over	(NA)	35.1
Black male . [2]	25.7	34.0						
Black female [2]	44.3	53.0						

NA Not available.   [1] Age-adjusted. Includes other races not shown separately.   [2] Excludes pregnant women.

Source: U.S. National Center for Health Statistics, *Health, United States, 1996-97.*

No. 246. Self-Perception of Being Overweight: 1988-94

[In percent. See headnote, Table 245]

Age	Percent of overweight people who think they are overweight						Percent of population not overweight who think they are overweight					
	Total [1]		Non-Hispanic White		Non-Hispanic Black		Total [1]		Non-Hispanic White		Non-Hispanic Black	
	Male	Female	Male	Female	Male	Female	Male	Female	Male	Female	Male	Female
Total.	81.7	91.6	84.4	93.8	71.2	86.4	25.4	44.1	28.0	45.9	14.8	34.9
20 to 39 years old. . . .	82.4	93.7	86.6	95.7	73.4	90.0	24.4	45.0	27.3	46.1	12.7	37.6
40 to 59 years old. . . .	85.8	96.3	88.9	99.2	71.1	90.6	30.9	51.5	33.5	54.2	21.5	41.6
60 years old and over .	73.9	82.8	75.0	85.7	64.4	71.0	19.7	33.3	21.3	35.9	10.5	15.1

[1] Includes other races and persons of Hispanic origin not shown separately.

Source: U.S. National Center for Health Statistics, unpublished data.

No. 247. Healthy Eating Indexes, by Selected Food Groups and Dietary Guidelines: 1996

[Healthy Eating Index is comprised of the sum of 10 dietary component indices for a maximum possible score of 100. A score of 80 or above was judged to reflect a "good" diet. Each of the dietary components has a scoring range of zero to 10. Individuals with an intake at the recommended level received a maximum score of 10 points. A score of zero was assigned when no foods in a particular group were eaten. Intermediate scores were calculated proportionately. The indexes for grains, vegetables, fruits, milk, and meat groups measure the degree to which a person's diet conforms to the U.S. Department of Agriculture's (USDA) "Food Guide Pyramid" serving recommendations. The index was applied to USDA one-day food and nutrient intake data from the Continuing Survey of Food Intakes by Individuals. The data are based on a representative sample of individuals two years old and over excluding women who were pregnant or lactating at the time of the survey]

Food group and dietary guideline	Average score on one day	Percent receiving score of 10	Perfect score of 10 [1]	Score of zero
Healthy Eating Index.	63.8	[2]12.2	(X)	(X)
Grains [3]	6.7	22.2	6-11 servings	No servings
Vegetables [4]	6.3	31.8	3-5 servings	No servings
Fruits [4]	3.8	17.1	2-4 servings	No servings
Milk [5]	5.4	25.5	2-3 servings	No servings
Meat [6]	6.4	26.4	2-3 servings	No servings
Total fat [7]	6.9	37.5	30% or less energy from fat	45% or more energy from fat
Saturated fat [7].	6.4	40.1	Less than 10% energy from saturated fat	15% or more energy from saturated fat
Cholesterol	7.9	71.9	300 mg. or less	450 mg. or more
Sodium	6.3	34.7	2,400 mg. or less	4,800 mg or more
Variety [8]	7.6	53.0	8 different food items over 1 day	Fewer than 4 items over 1 day

X Not applicable.   [1] Depends on recommended energy intake. All amounts listed are based on a per day basis.   [2] Percent receiving a score of 80 or higher.   [3] One serving: a slice of bread, one-half cup of cooked pasta, or one-half cup of cooked cereal grains.   [4] One serving: one-half cup of cooked vegetables, 1 cup of raw leafy vegetables, or one-half cup of raw nonleafy chopped vegetables. Fruits are similar.   [5] One serving: one cup of milk or equivalent.   [6] Includes eggs, nuts, and some legumes. One serving: 2.5 ounces of lean meat or equivalent.   [7] Consumption of specified fat as a percentage of total food energy intake.   [8] Amount of variety in a person's diet over a 1-day period.

Source: U.S. Department of Agriculture, Center for Nutrition Policy and Promotion, unpublished data.

No. 248. Percentage of Adults Engaging in Leisure-Time Physical Activity: 1996

[In percent. Covers persons 18 years old and over. Based on response to question about physical activity in prior month. Based on a sample survey of approximately 122,000 persons in 50 states and the District of Columbia in 1996; for details, contact source]

Characteristic	No participation in physical activity	Participates in regular, sustained activity [1]	Participates in regular, vigorous activity [2]	Characteristic	No participation in physical activity	Participates in regular, sustained activity [1]	Participates in regular, vigorous activity [2]
Total............	29.5	19.6	12.9	30 to 44 years old...	28.3	19.0	14.9
				45 to 64 years old...	32.3	19.1	15.8
Male.............	27.3	20.3	11.6	65 to 74 years old...	36.2	19.3	15.4
Female...........	31.5	18.9	14.0	75 years old and over..........	47.3	14.1	11.1
White, non-Hispanic ...	27.6	20.3	14.0				
Black, non-Hispanic....	38.2	16.3	9.3	School years completed:			
Hispanic...........	36.6	17.1	8.6	Less than 12 years ..	50.3	13.8	6.2
Other.............	27.8	20.1	10.4	12 years	34.6	17.6	10.1
Males:				Some college (13-15 years)..........	24.4	20.8	13.4
18 to 29 years old...	19.7	24.3	6.7	College (16 or more years)..........	17.1	23.9	19.2
30 to 44 years old...	25.6	17.7	9.5				
45 to 64 years old...	32.5	17.9	14.4	Household income:			
65 to 74 years old...	32.1	25.5	18.2	Less than $10,000...	42.5	16.8	7.0
75 years old and over	36.9	22.3	19.5	$10,000 to $19,999 ..	40.0	17.2	8.5
				$20,000 to $34,999 ..	31.8	19.0	11.4
Females:				$35,000 to $49,999 ..	24.8	21.2	13.8
18 to 29 years old...	26.2	20.2	10.8	$50,000 and over ...	18.4	22.6	17.8

[1] Any type or intensity of activity that occurs 5 times or more per week and 30 minutes or more per occasion. [2] Rhythmic contraction of large muscle groups performed at 50 percent or more of estimated age- and sex-specific maximum cardiorespiratory capacity, 3 times per week or more for at least 20 minutes per occasion.

Source: U.S. National Center for Chronic Disease Prevention and Health Promotion, unpublished data.

No. 249. Nutrition—Nutrients in Foods Available for Civilian Consumption Per Capita Per Day: 1970 to 1994

[Computed by the Center for Nutrition Policy and Promotion (CNPP). Based on Economic Research Service (ERS) estimates of per capita quantities of food available for consumption from "Food Consumption, Prices, and Expenditures," on imputed consumption data for foods no longer reported by ERS, and on CNPP estimates of quantities of produce from home gardens. Food supply estimates do not reflect loss of food or nutrients from further marketing or home processing. Enrichment and fortification levels of iron, thiamin, riboflavin, niacin, vitamin A, vitamin B$_6$, vitamin B$_{12}$, and ascorbic acid are included]

Nutrient	Unit	1970-79	1980-89	1990	1993	1994
Food energy	Calories..........	3,300	3,400	3,600	3,700	3,800
Carbohydrate............	Grams...........	391	417	458	482	491
Protein	Grams...........	95	100	105	108	110
Total fat [1]	Grams...........	151	157	156	161	159
Saturated............	Grams...........	52	53	51	52	52
Monounsaturated	Grams...........	61	63	63	66	65
Polyunsaturated	Grams...........	28	31	32	32	31
Cholesterol	Milligrams.........	440	420	400	410	410
Vitamin A	Micrograms RE [2]....	1,530	1,510	1,530	1,530	1,520
Carotenes.............	Micrograms RE [2]....	580	620	670	670	660
Vitamin E	Milligrams α-TE [3]....	14.2	15.7	16.6	17.6	16.9
Vitamin C	Milligrams.........	109	114	111	122	124
Thiamin...............	Milligrams.........	2.1	2.4	2.6	2.7	2.7
Riboflavin.............	Milligrams.........	2.4	2.5	2.6	2.6	2.6
Niacin................	Milligrams.........	23.6	26.4	28.0	29.0	29.0
Vitamin B$_6$.............	Milligrams.........	2.0	2.1	2.2	2.3	2.3
Folacin	Micrograms.........	289	303	311	329	331
Vitamin B$_{12}$	Micrograms........	9.1	8.4	8.2	8.0	8.1
Calcium	Milligrams..........	880	900	940	950	960
Phosphorus	Milligrams..........	1,460	1,530	1,620	1,650	1,680
Magnesium	Milligrams..........	320	340	370	380	380
Iron	Milligrams..........	18.7	18.2	20.2	20.9	21.2
Zinc	Milligrams..........	12.1	12.3	12.7	13.0	13.2
Copper	Milligrams..........	1.6	1.7	1.8	1.9	1.9
Potassium	Milligrams........	3,470	3,530	3,650	3,750	3,780

[1] Includes other types of fat not shown separately. [2] Retinol equivalents. [3] Alpha-Tocopherol equivalents.

Source: U.S. Dept. of Agriculture, Center for Nutrition Policy and Promotion. Data published by Economic Research Service in *Food Consumption, Prices, and Expenditures*, annual.

No. 250. Per Capita Consumption of Major Food Commodities: 1980 to 1997

[In pounds, retail weight, except as indicated. Consumption represents the residual after exports, nonfood use and ending stocks are subtracted from the sum of beginning stocks, domestic production, and imports. Based on U.S. Census Bureau estimated population]

Commodity	Unit	1980	1985	1990	1994	1995	1996	1997
Red meat, total (boneless, trimmed weight) [1][2]	Pounds	126.4	124.9	112.3	114.7	115.1	112.8	111.0
Beef	Pounds	72.1	74.6	63.9	63.6	64.4	65.0	63.8
Veal	Pounds	1.3	1.5	0.9	0.8	0.8	1.0	0.9
Lamb and mutton	Pounds	1.0	1.1	1.0	0.9	0.9	0.8	0.8
Pork	Pounds	52.1	47.7	46.4	49.5	49.0	45.9	45.6
Poultry (boneless, trimmed weight) [2]	Pounds	40.8	45.5	56.3	63.3	62.9	64.4	64.8
Chicken	Pounds	32.7	36.4	42.4	49.3	48.8	49.8	50.9
Turkey	Pounds	8.1	9.1	13.8	14.1	14.1	14.6	13.9
Fish and shellfish (boneless, trimmed weight)	Pounds	12.4	15.0	15.0	15.1	14.9	14.7	14.5
Eggs	Number	271	255	234	238	235	237	239
Shell	Number	236	217	186	177	175	175	173
Processed	Number	35	38	48	61	61	62	66
Dairy products, total [3]	Pounds	543.2	593.7	568.4	586.0	584.4	575.5	579.8
Fluid milk products [4]	Gallons	27.9	27.1	26.2	25.3	24.9	24.9	24.6
Beverage milks	Gallons	27.6	26.7	25.7	24.8	24.3	24.4	24.0
Plain whole milk	Gallons	16.5	13.9	10.2	8.8	8.4	8.4	8.2
Plain reduced-fat milk (2%)	Gallons	6.3	7.9	9.1	8.7	8.2	8.0	7.7
Plain light and skim milks	Gallons	3.1	3.2	4.9	5.8	6.2	6.4	6.6
Flavored whole milk	Gallons	0.6	0.4	0.3	0.3	0.3	0.3	0.3
Flavored milks other than whole	Gallons	0.6	0.7	0.8	0.8	0.8	0.9	0.9
Buttermilk	Gallons	0.5	0.5	0.4	0.3	0.3	0.3	0.3
Yogurt (excl. frozen)	1/2 pints	4.6	7.3	7.4	8.6	9.4	8.9	9.5
Fluid cream products [5]	1/2 pints	10.5	13.5	14.3	15.2	15.9	16.4	17.0
Cream [6]	1/2 pints	6.3	8.2	8.7	9.2	9.5	10.2	10.7
Sour cream and dips	1/2 pints	3.4	4.3	4.7	5.2	5.5	5.4	5.6
Condensed and evaporated milks	Pounds	7.0	7.5	7.9	8.1	6.9	6.4	6.6
Whole milk	Pounds	3.8	3.6	3.2	2.6	2.3	2.3	2.6
Skim milk	Pounds	3.3	3.8	4.8	5.5	4.5	4.1	4.0
Cheese [7]	Pounds	17.5	22.5	24.6	26.8	27.3	27.7	28.0
American	Pounds	9.6	12.2	11.1	11.5	11.8	12.0	12.0
Cheddar	Pounds	6.9	9.8	9.0	9.1	9.1	9.2	9.6
Italian	Pounds	4.4	6.5	9.0	10.3	10.4	10.8	11.0
Mozzarella	Pounds	3.0	4.6	6.9	7.9	8.1	8.5	8.4
Other [8]	Pounds	3.4	3.9	4.5	5.0	5.0	5.0	5.1
Swiss	Pounds	1.3	1.3	1.4	1.2	1.1	1.1	1.0
Cream and Neufchatel	Pounds	1.0	1.2	1.7	2.2	2.1	2.2	2.3
Cottage cheese, total	Pounds	4.5	4.1	3.4	2.8	2.7	2.6	2.7
Lowfat	Pounds	0.8	1.0	1.2	1.2	1.2	1.2	1.3
Frozen dairy products	Pounds	26.4	27.9	28.4	29.9	29.4	28.6	28.7
Ice cream	Pounds	17.5	18.1	15.8	16.1	15.7	15.9	16.2
Lowfat ice cream	Pounds	7.1	6.9	7.7	7.6	7.5	7.6	7.9
Sherbet	Pounds	1.2	1.3	1.2	1.4	1.3	1.3	1.3
Frozen yogurt	Pounds	(NA)	(NA)	2.8	3.5	3.5	2.6	2.1
Fats and oils:								
Total, fat content only	Pounds	57.2	64.3	62.8	68.6	66.9	65.8	65.6
Butter (product weight)	Pounds	4.5	4.9	4.4	4.8	4.5	4.3	4.2
Margarine (product weight)	Pounds	11.3	10.8	10.9	9.9	9.2	9.2	8.6
Lard (direct use)	Pounds	2.6	1.8	1.9	2.3	2.2	2.3	2.3
Edible beef tallow (direct use)	Pounds	1.1	1.9	0.5	2.4	2.7	3.0	2.4
Shortening	Pounds	18.2	22.9	22.2	24.1	22.5	22.3	20.9
Salad and cooking oils	Pounds	21.2	23.6	24.8	26.3	26.9	26.1	28.7
Other edible fats and oils	Pounds	1.5	1.6	1.2	1.6	1.6	1.4	1.1
Flour and cereal products [9]	Pounds	144.7	156.6	182.0	194.1	192.5	198.4	200.1
Wheat flour	Pounds	116.9	124.6	136.0	144.5	141.8	148.8	149.7
Rice, milled	Pounds	9.4	9.1	16.2	19.2	20.1	18.9	19.5
Corn products	Pounds	12.9	17.2	21.9	22.5	22.7	22.9	23.1
Oat products	Pounds	3.9	4.0	6.5	6.5	6.5	6.6	6.5
Breakfast cereals [10]	Pounds	12.0	12.8	15.4	17.4	17.1	16.9	16.9
Ready-to-eat	Pounds	9.7	10.5	12.6	14.8	14.6	14.3	14.3
Ready-to-cook	Pounds	2.3	2.3	2.9	2.6	2.5	2.5	2.6
Caloric sweeteners, total [11]	Pounds	123.0	128.8	137.0	147.4	149.9	150.7	154.1
Sugar, refined cane and beet	Pounds	83.6	62.7	64.4	65.0	65.5	66.6	66.5
Corn sweeteners [12]	Pounds	38.2	64.8	71.1	81.0	83.0	82.8	86.2
High-fructose corn syrup	Pounds	19.0	45.2	49.6	56.8	58.4	59.4	62.4
Other:								
Cocoa beans	Pounds	3.4	4.6	5.4	4.8	4.6	5.3	5.1
Coffee (green beans)	Pounds	10.3	10.5	10.3	8.2	8.0	9.0	9.3
Peanuts (shelled)	Pounds	4.8	6.3	6.0	5.8	5.7	5.7	5.8
Tree nuts (shelled)	Pounds	1.8	2.5	2.4	2.3	1.9	2.0	2.2

NA Not available. [1] Excludes edible offals. [2] Excludes shipments to Puerto Rico and the other U.S. possessions. [3] Milk-equivalent, milkfat basis. Includes butter. [4] Fluid milk figures are aggregates of commercial sales and milk produced and consumed on farms. [5] Includes eggnog, not shown separately. [6] Heavy cream, light cream, and half and half. [7] Excludes full-skim American, cottage, pot, and baker's cheese. [8] Includes other cheeses not shown separately. [9] Includes rye flour and barley products not shown separately. Excludes quantities used in alcoholic beverages. [10] Partially overlaps flour and cereal products category. [11] Dry weight. Includes edible syrups (maple, molasses, etc.) and honey not shown separately. [12] Includes glucose and dextrose not shown separately.

Source: U.S. Department of Agriculture, Economic Research Service, *Food Consumption, Prices, and Expenditures, 1970-1997*; and *Agricultural Outlook*, monthly.

No. 251. Per Capita Utilization of Commercially Produced Fruits and Vegetables: 1980 to 1997

[In pounds, farm weight. Domestic food use of fresh fruits and vegetables reflects the fresh-market share of commodity production plus imports and minus exports]

Commodity	1980	1985	1990	1992	1993	1994	1995	1996	1997
Fruits and vegetables, total [1]	598.8	627.5	656.3	661.1	685.1	689.1	690.4	706.1	710.8
Fruits, total	262.4	269.4	273.5	268.0	285.4	284.3	285.4	289.8	294.7
Fresh fruits	104.8	110.6	116.3	123.5	124.9	126.5	124.6	129.0	133.2
Noncitrus	78.8	89.2	95.0	99.1	98.9	101.5	100.5	104.1	106.4
Apples	19.2	17.3	19.6	19.3	19.2	19.6	19.0	19.0	18.5
Bananas	20.8	23.5	24.4	27.3	26.8	28.1	27.4	28.0	27.7
Cantaloupes	5.8	8.5	9.2	8.5	8.7	8.6	9.2	10.6	11.7
Grapes	4.0	6.8	7.9	7.2	7.0	7.3	7.5	6.9	8.0
Peaches and nectarines	7.1	5.5	5.5	6.0	6.0	5.5	5.4	4.5	5.7
Pears	2.6	2.8	3.2	3.1	3.4	3.5	3.4	3.1	3.5
Pineapples	1.5	1.5	2.1	2.0	2.1	2.0	1.9	1.9	2.4
Plums and prunes	1.5	1.4	1.5	1.8	1.3	1.6	0.9	1.5	1.5
Strawberries	2.0	3.0	3.2	3.6	3.6	4.1	4.2	4.4	4.2
Watermelons	10.7	13.5	13.3	14.8	14.6	15.5	15.7	17.4	16.1
Other [2]	3.6	5.4	5.1	5.5	6.2	5.7	5.9	6.8	7.1
Fresh citrus	26.1	21.5	21.4	24.4	26.0	25.0	24.1	24.9	26.8
Oranges	14.3	11.6	12.4	12.9	14.2	13.1	12.0	12.8	14.1
Grapefruit	7.3	5.5	4.4	5.9	6.2	6.1	6.1	5.9	6.3
Other [3]	4.5	4.4	4.6	5.6	5.6	5.8	6.0	6.2	6.4
Processed fruits [4]	157.5	158.8	157.1	144.5	160.5	157.8	160.8	160.8	161.5
Frozen fruits [5]	3.0	3.1	3.7	3.7	3.6	3.6	4.0	3.8	3.5
Dried fruits [5]	11.2	12.7	12.1	10.8	12.6	12.9	12.8	11.4	10.8
Canned fruits [6]	23.8	20.9	21.0	22.9	20.7	21.0	17.5	18.8	20.5
Fruit juices [7]	118.9	121.8	120.1	106.4	123.3	119.9	126.2	126.6	126.1
Vegetables, total	336.4	358.1	382.8	393.2	399.8	404.8	405.0	416.2	416.0
Fresh vegetables	149.3	156.1	167.2	171.1	171.9	177.4	175.1	181.8	185.6
Asparagus (all uses)	0.3	0.5	0.6	0.6	0.6	0.6	0.6	0.6	0.7
Broccoli	1.4	2.6	3.4	3.4	2.9	3.9	4.4	4.5	5.2
Cabbage	8.1	8.8	8.8	8.9	9.7	9.7	8.7	9.2	10.2
Carrots	6.2	6.5	8.3	8.3	8.2	8.7	9.0	10.1	12.5
Cauliflower	1.1	1.8	2.2	1.8	1.7	1.6	1.4	1.5	1.6
Celery (all uses)	7.4	6.9	7.2	7.4	7.1	6.8	6.4	6.3	6.0
Corn	6.5	6.4	6.7	6.9	7.0	8.2	7.8	8.3	8.1
Cucumbers	3.9	4.4	4.7	5.0	5.3	5.5	5.7	6.0	6.3
Head lettuce	25.6	23.7	27.8	25.9	24.6	24.3	22.5	23.3	24.3
Mushrooms	1.2	1.8	2.0	2.0	2.0	2.0	2.1	2.1	2.2
Onions	11.4	13.6	15.1	16.2	16.5	16.5	17.6	17.9	17.9
Snap beans	1.3	1.3	1.1	1.5	1.5	1.6	1.7	1.4	1.4
Bell peppers (all uses)	2.9	3.8	4.5	5.7	6.2	6.5	6.3	7.3	7.2
Potatoes	51.1	46.3	46.8	48.6	49.3	50.3	49.2	50.0	47.9
Sweetpotatoes (all uses)	4.4	5.4	4.6	4.3	3.9	4.7	4.5	4.6	4.6
Tomatoes	12.8	14.9	15.5	15.5	16.0	16.5	17.2	18.0	18.9
Other fresh vegetables [8]	3.7	7.4	7.9	9.1	9.4	10.0	10.0	10.7	10.6
Processed vegetables	187.2	201.9	215.6	222.1	227.9	227.4	229.9	234.5	230.4
Selected vegetables for freezing	51.6	64.5	66.8	70.8	75.1	79.5	79.9	83.9	81.5
Selected vegetables for canning	102.7	99.4	110.7	111.6	112.1	107.8	110.2	108.5	105.9
Vegetables for dehydrating [9]	10.6	12.8	14.6	14.3	15.5	14.7	14.7	17.6	18.6
Potatoes for chips	16.5	17.6	16.4	17.2	17.5	17.0	16.6	16.4	15.9
Pulses [10]	5.8	7.6	7.1	8.2	7.7	8.5	8.5	8.5	8.5

[1] Excludes wine grapes. [2] Apricots, avocados, cherries, cranberries, kiwifruit, mangoes, papayas, and honeydew melons.
[3] Lemons, limes, tangerines, and tangelos. [4] Apples, apricots, blackberries, blueberries, boysenberries, cherries, loganberries, peaches, plums, prunes, raspberries, and strawberries. [5] Apples, apricots, dates, figs, peaches, pears, prunes, and raisins.
[6] Apples, apricots, cherries, olives, peaches, pears, pineapples, plums, and prunes. [7] Apple, cranberry, grape, grapefruit, lemon, lime, orange, pineapple, and prunes. [8] Artichokes, Brussels sprouts, eggplant, escarole, endive, garlic, romaine, leaf lettuce, radishes, and spinach. [9] Onions and potatoes. [10] Dry peas, lentils, and dry edible beans.

No. 252. Per Capita Consumption of Selected Beverages, by Type: 1980 to 1997

[In gallons. See headnote, Table 250]

Commodity	1980	1985	1990	1992	1993	1994	1995	1996	1997
Nonalcoholic	(NA)	(NA)	128.4	131.6	132.4	133.2	133.5	137.0	139.6
Milk (plain and flavored)	27.6	26.7	25.7	25.3	24.8	24.8	24.3	24.3	24.0
Whole	17.0	14.3	10.5	9.8	9.3	9.2	8.8	8.7	8.5
Reduced-fat, light, and skim	10.5	12.3	15.2	15.6	15.4	15.6	15.6	15.7	15.5
Tea	7.3	7.1	6.9	8.1	8.4	8.2	8.0	7.8	7.4
Coffee	26.7	27.4	26.9	25.9	23.5	21.1	20.5	22.5	23.5
Bottled water	2.4	4.5	8.0	8.2	9.4	10.7	11.6	12.5	13.1
Carbonated soft drinks	35.1	35.7	46.3	48.5	50.1	51.3	51.6	52.0	53.0
Diet	5.1	7.1	10.7	11.6	11.7	11.8	11.8	11.7	11.6
Regular	29.9	28.7	35.6	36.9	38.4	39.6	39.8	40.3	41.4
Fruit juices	7.4	7.8	7.9	8.6	8.5	8.8	8.7	8.9	9.2
Fruit drinks, cocktails, and ades	(NA)	(NA)	6.3	6.5	7.0	7.4	7.8	8.0	8.3
Canned iced tea	(NA)	(NA)	0.1	0.2	0.4	0.6	0.7	0.7	0.8
Vegetable juices	(NA)	(NA)	0.3	0.3	0.3	0.3	0.3	0.3	0.3
Alcoholic (adult population)	42.8	40.7	39.9	38.4	38.2	38.3	38.0	38.6	38.9
Beer	36.6	34.6	34.7	33.6	33.6	33.8	33.4	33.8	33.9
Wine [1]	3.2	3.5	3.0	2.7	2.6	2.6	2.7	2.9	3.0
Distilled spirits	3.0	2.6	2.2	2.0	2.0	1.9	1.9	1.9	1.9

NA Not available. [1] Beginning 1985, includes wine coolers.

Source of Tables 251 and 252: U.S. Dept. of Agriculture, Economic Research Service, *Food Consumption, Prices, and Expenditures,* annual; and *Agricultural Outlook,* monthly.

Health and Nutrition 159

Figure 4.1
**Educational Attainment, by Race and
Hispanic Origin: 1960 to 1998**

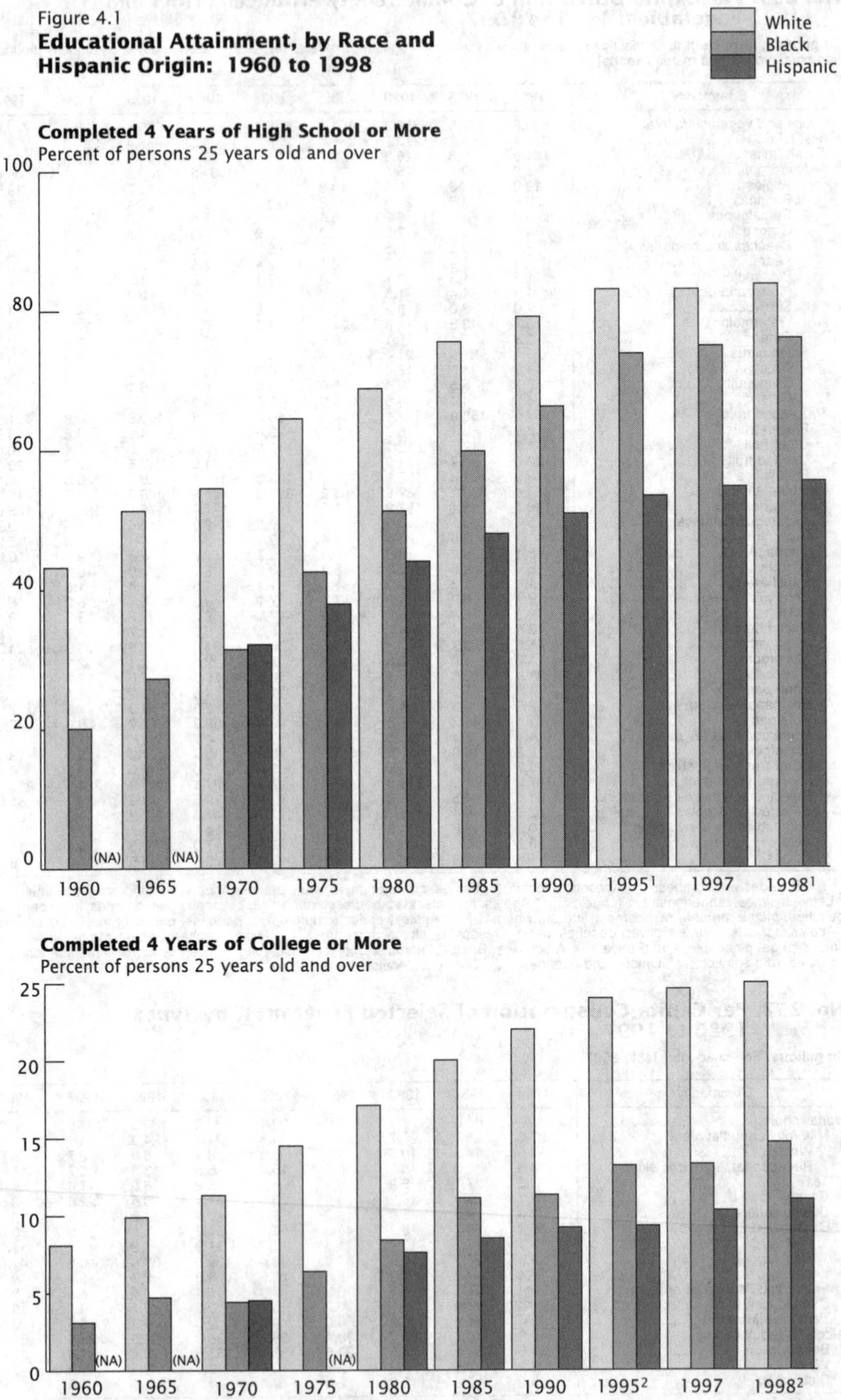

White
Black
Hispanic

Completed 4 Years of High School or More
Percent of persons 25 years old and over

Completed 4 Years of College or More
Percent of persons 25 years old and over

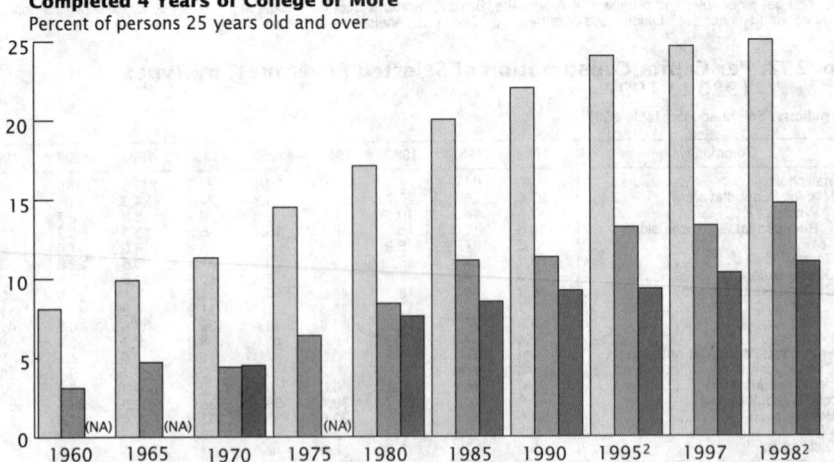

NA Not available. [1]High school graduate or more. [2]College graduate or more.
Note: Persons of Hispanic origin may be of any race.
Source: Chart prepared by U.S. Census Bureau. For data, see Table 263.

160 Education

Education

This section presents data primarily concerning formal education as a whole, at various levels, and for public and private schools. Data shown relate to the school-age population and school enrollment, educational attainment, education personnel, and financial aspects of education. In addition, data are shown for libraries, computer usage in schools, and adult education. The chief sources are the decennial census of population and the Current Population Survey (CPS), both conducted by the U.S. Census Bureau (see text, Section 1, Population); annual, biennial, and other periodic surveys conducted by the National Center for Education Statistics, a part of the U.S. Department of Education; and surveys conducted by the National Education Association.

The censuses of population have included data on school enrollment since 1840 and on educational attainment since 1940. The CPS has reported on school enrollment annually since 1945 and on educational attainment periodically since 1947.

The National Center for Education Statistics is continuing the pattern of statistical studies and surveys conducted by the U.S. Office of Education since 1870. The annual *Digest of Education Statistics* provides summary data on pupils, staff, finances, including government expenditures, and organization at the elementary, secondary, and higher education levels. It is also a primary source for detailed information on Federal funds for education, projections of enrollment, graduates, and teachers. *The Condition of Education*, issued annually, presents a summary of information on education of particular interest to policymakers.

Other sources of data include special studies by the National Center for Education Statistics and annual or biennial reports of education agencies in individual states.

The census of governments, conducted by the Census Bureau every 5 years (for the years ending in "2" and "7"), provides data on school district finances and state and local government expenditures for education. Reports published by the Bureau of Labor Statistics contain data relating civilian labor force experience to educational attainment (see also Tables 653, 677, and 684 in Section 13, Labor Force).

Types and sources of data—The statistics in this section are of two general types. One type, exemplified by data from the Census Bureau, is based on direct interviews with individuals to obtain information about their own and their family members' education. Data of this type relate to school enrollment and level of education attained, classified by age, sex, and other characteristics of the population. The school enrollment statistics reflect attendance or enrollment in any regular school within a given period; educational attainment statistics reflect the highest grade completed by an individual, or beginning 1992, the highest diploma or degree received.

For enrollment data starting in October 1994, the CPS used 1990 census population controls plus adjustment for undercount. Also the survey changed from paper to computer assisted technology. For years 1981 through 1993, 1980 census population controls were used; 1971 through 1980, 1970 census population controls had been used. These changes had little impact on summary measures (e.g., medians) and proportional measures (e.g., enrollment rates); however, use of the controls may have significant impact on absolute numbers.

Beginning with data for 1986, a new edit and tabulation package for school enrollment has been introduced. In 1988 a new

U.S. Census Bureau, Statistical Abstract of the United States: 1999

edit and tabulation package was introduced for educational attainment data.

The second type, generally exemplified by data from the National Center for Education Statistics and the National Education Association, is based on reports from administrators of educational institutions and of state and local agencies having jurisdiction over education. Data of this type relate to enrollment, attendance, staff, and finances for the Nation, individual states, and local areas.

Unlike the National Center for Education Statistics, the Census Bureau does not regularly include specialized vocational, trade, business, or correspondence schools in its surveys. The National Center for Education Statistics includes nursery schools and kindergartens that are part of regular grade schools in their enrollment figures. The Census Bureau includes all nursery schools and kindergartens. At the higher education level, the statistics of both agencies are concerned with institutions granting degrees or offering work acceptable for degree-credit, such as junior colleges.

School attendance—All states require that children attend school. While state laws vary as to the ages and circumstances of compulsory attendance, generally they require that formal schooling begin by age 6 and continue to age 16.

Schools—The National Center for Education Statistics defines a school as "a division of the school system consisting of students composing one or more grade groups or other identifiable groups, organized as one unit with one or more teachers to give instruction of a defined type, and housed in a school plant of one or more buildings. More than one school may be housed in one school plant, as is the case when the elementary and secondary programs are housed in the same school plant."

Regular schools are those which advance a person toward a diploma or degree. They include public and private nursery schools, kindergartens, graded schools, colleges, universities, and professional schools.

Public schools are schools controlled and supported by local, state, or Federal governmental agencies; private schools are those controlled and supported mainly by religious organizations or by private persons or organizations.

The Census Bureau defines *elementary* schools as including grades 1 through 8; *high* schools as including grades 9 through 12; and *colleges* as including junior or community colleges, regular 4-year colleges, and universities and graduate or professional schools. Statistics reported by the National Center for Education Statistics and the National Education Association by type of organization, such as elementary level and secondary level, may not be strictly comparable with those from the Census Bureau because the grades included at the two levels vary, depending on the level assigned to the middle or junior high school by the local school systems.

School year—Except as otherwise indicated in the tables, data refer to the school year which, for elementary and secondary schools, generally begins in September of the preceding year and ends in June of the year stated. For the most part, statistics concerning school finances are for a 12-month period, usually July 1 to June 30. Enrollment data generally refer to a specific point in time, such as fall, as indicated in the tables.

Statistical reliability—For a discussion of statistical collection, estimation, and sampling procedures and measures of statistical reliability applicable to the Census Bureau and the National Center for Education Statistics data, see Appendix III.

No. 253. School Enrollment: 1965 to 2008

[In thousands (54,394 represents 54,394,000). As of fall]

Year	All levels			K through grade 8		Grades 9 through 12		College	
	Total	Public	Private	Public	Private	Public	Private	Public	Private
1965	54,394	46,143	8,251	30,563	4,900	11,610	1,400	3,970	1,951
1970	59,838	52,322	7,516	32,558	4,052	13,336	1,311	6,428	2,153
1975	61,004	53,654	7,350	30,515	3,700	14,304	1,300	8,835	2,350
1980	58,305	50,335	7,971	27,647	3,992	13,231	1,339	9,457	2,640
1981	57,916	49,691	8,225	27,280	4,100	12,764	1,400	9,647	2,725
1982	57,591	49,262	8,330	27,161	4,200	12,405	1,400	9,696	2,730
1983	57,432	48,935	8,497	26,981	4,315	12,271	1,400	9,683	2,782
1984	57,150	48,686	8,465	26,905	4,300	12,304	1,400	9,477	2,765
1985	57,226	48,901	8,325	27,034	4,195	12,388	1,362	9,479	2,768
1986	57,709	49,467	8,242	27,420	4,116	12,333	1,336	9,714	2,790
1987	58,254	49,982	8,272	27,933	4,232	12,076	1,247	9,973	2,793
1988	58,485	50,349	8,136	28,501	4,036	11,687	1,206	10,161	2,894
1989	59,436	51,120	8,316	29,152	4,162	11,390	1,193	10,578	2,961
1990	60,267	52,061	8,206	29,878	4,095	11,338	1,137	10,845	2,974
1991	61,605	53,356	8,248	30,506	4,074	11,541	1,125	11,310	3,049
1992	62,686	54,208	8,478	31,088	4,212	11,735	1,163	11,385	3,103
1993	63,241	54,654	8,587	31,504	4,280	11,961	1,191	11,189	3,116
1994	63,986	55,245	8,741	31,898	4,360	12,213	1,236	11,189	3,116
1995	64,803	55,933	8,869	32,341	4,431	12,500	1,269	11,092	3,169
1996	65,674	56,682	8,993	32,759	4,486	12,834	1,297	11,090	3,210
1997, est.	66,170	57,161	9,010	32,951	4,545	13,003	1,322	11,208	3,143
1998, proj.	67,309	58,187	9,121	33,522	4,588	13,270	1,339	11,395	3,194
1999, proj.	67,871	58,668	9,203	33,722	4,616	13,420	1,354	11,525	3,233
2000, proj.	68,334	59,065	9,269	33,903	4,640	13,537	1,366	11,626	3,263
2001, proj.	68,728	59,402	9,324	34,055	4,661	13,643	1,376	11,705	3,287
2002, proj.	69,040	59,674	9,366	34,124	4,671	13,800	1,392	11,751	3,303
2003, proj.	69,338	59,923	9,413	34,124	4,671	13,951	1,407	11,849	3,335
2004, proj.	69,657	60,195	9,461	33,958	4,648	14,263	1,439	11,975	3,374
2005, proj.	69,942	60,436	9,506	33,756	4,620	14,579	1,471	12,101	3,415
2006, proj.	70,160	60,611	9,549	33,584	4,597	14,785	1,491	12,242	3,461
2007, proj.	70,305	60,721	9,584	33,489	4,584	14,854	1,498	12,378	3,502
2008, proj.	70,351	60,735	9,616	33,455	4,579	14,746	1,488	12,534	3,549

Source: U.S. National Center for Education Statistics, *Digest of Education Statistics*, annual, and *Projections of Education Statistics*, annual.

No. 254. School Expenditures, by Type of Control and Level of Instruction in Constant (1997-98) Dollars: 1960 to 1998

[In millions of dollars (131,342 represents $131,342,000,000). For school years ending in year shown. Total expenditures for public elementary and secondary schools include current expenditures, interest on school debt, and capital outlay. Data deflated by the Consumer Price Index, wage earners, and clerical workers through 1975; thereafter, all urban consumers, on a school year basis (supplied by the National Center for Education Statistics). See also Appendix III]

Year	Total	Elementary and secondary schools			Colleges and universities		
		Total	Public	Private [1]	Total	Public	Private [1]
1960	131,342	92,000	85,945	6,055	39,342	21,488	17,854
1970	293,123	184,899	174,195	10,704	108,223	69,510	38,713
1975	339,348	215,000	202,508	12,492	124,348	84,214	40,134
1980	345,070	214,929	199,928	15,001	130,141	86,324	43,817
1985	378,726	228,467	209,504	18,962	150,259	97,420	52,839
1986	400,554	240,494	220,874	19,620	160,059	104,148	55,911
1987	424,554	254,755	233,962	20,793	169,799	108,405	61,394
1988	437,542	262,490	241,127	21,362	175,052	111,501	63,551
1989	462,947	279,434	257,546	21,887	183,513	116,252	67,261
1990	485,990	294,211	271,028	23,183	191,779	122,779	69,001
1991	498,390	300,652	277,100	23,552	197,739	126,132	71,607
1992	506,716	305,741	282,101	23,640	200,974	127,171	73,804
1993	517,563	311,324	287,039	24,285	206,239	130,698	75,541
1994	527,909	318,033	293,476	24,557	209,875	132,269	77,606
1995	541,898	325,188	300,024	25,163	216,710	137,209	79,501
1996, prel.	554,382	333,127	307,374	25,753	221,256	138,975	82,281
1997, prel.	569,478	341,992	315,732	26,260	227,486	142,497	84,989
1998, est.	583,800	351,300	324,300	27,000	232,500	145,500	87,000

[1] Estimated.

Source: U.S. National Center for Education Statistics, *Digest Education Statistics*, annual.

No. 255. School Enrollment, Faculty, Graduates, and Finances, With Projections: 1990 to 2008

[As of fall, except as indicated (46,448 represents 46,448,000)]

Item	Unit	1990	1995	1997, est.	1998, proj.	2000, proj.	2005, proj.	2008, proj.
ELEMENTARY AND SECONDARY SCHOOLS								
School enrollment, total	1,000	46,448	50,540	51,821	52,718	53,445	54,426	54,268
Kindergarten through grade 8	1,000	33,973	36,772	37,495	38,110	38,543	38,376	38,034
Grades 9 through 12	1,000	12,475	13,769	14,324	14,608	14,902	16,050	16,234
Public	1,000	41,217	44,840	45,953	46,792	47,439	48,335	48,201
Kindergarten through grade 8	1,000	29,878	32,341	32,951	33,522	33,903	33,756	33,455
Grades 9 through 12	1,000	11,338	12,500	13,003	13,270	13,537	14,579	14,746
Private	1,000	5,232	5,700	5,867	5,927	6,006	6,091	6,067
Kindergarten through grade 8	1,000	4,095	4,431	4,545	4,588	4,640	4,620	4,579
Grades 9 through 12	1,000	1,137	1,269	1,322	1,339	1,366	1,471	1,488
Enrollment rate:								
5 and 6 year olds	Percent	96.5	96.0	96.5	(NA)	(NA)	(NA)	(NA)
7 to 13 year olds	Percent	99.6	98.9	99.1	(NA)	(NA)	(NA)	(NA)
14 to 17 year olds	Percent	95.8	96.3	96.6	(NA)	(NA)	(NA)	(NA)
Classroom teachers, total [1]	1,000	2,753	2,975	3,103	3,126	3,211	3,394	3,460
Public	1,000	2,398	2,595	2,710	2,728	2,802	2,963	3,022
Private	1,000	355	380	394	399	409	430	438
High school graduates, total [2]	1,000	2,503	2,548	2,708	2,751	2,875	2,985	(NA)
Public	1,000	2,235	2,281	2,433	2,465	2,576	2,675	(NA)
Public schools: [2]								
Average daily attendance (ADA)	1,000	38,427	41,502	42,924	43,372	43,973	44,803	(NA)
Constant (1997-98) dollars:								
Teachers' average salary	Dol.	39,958	39,484	39,385	(NA)	(NA)	(NA)	(NA)
Current school expenditure	Bil. dol.	244.0	267.0	281.7	(NA)	(NA)	(NA)	(NA)
Per pupil in ADA	Dol.	6,350	6,434	6,563	(NA)	(NA)	(NA)	(NA)
HIGHER EDUCATION								
Enrollment, total	1,000	13,819	14,262	14,350	14,590	14,889	15,516	16,083
Male	1,000	6,284	6,343	6,239	6,324	6,442	6,684	6,906
Full time	1,000	3,808	3,807	3,667	3,718	3,816	4,010	4,182
Part time	1,000	2,476	2,535	2,572	2,606	2,626	2,674	2,724
Female	1,000	7,535	7,919	8,111	8,266	8,447	8,833	9,177
Full time	1,000	4,013	4,321	4,424	4,562	4,727	5,075	5,380
Part time	1,000	3,521	3,598	3,687	3,704	3,720	3,758	3,797
Public	1,000	10,845	11,092	11,207	11,395	11,626	12,101	12,534
Four-year institutions	1,000	5,848	5,815	5,863	5,969	6,114	6,413	6,670
Two-year institutions	1,000	4,996	5,278	5,344	5,426	5,512	5,688	5,864
Private	1,000	2,974	3,169	3,143	3,195	3,263	3,415	3,549
Four-year institutions	1,000	2,730	2,955	2,914	2,961	3,024	3,165	3,288
Two-year institutions	1,000	244	215	229	234	239	250	260
Undergraduate	1,000	11,959	12,232	12,357	12,600	12,915	13,511	14,045
Graduate	1,000	1,586	1,732	1,716	1,716	1,706	1,728	1,752
First-time professional	1,000	273	298	277	273	269	278	286
Full-time equivalent	1,000	9,983	10,335	10,346	10,554	10,829	11,401	11,910
Public	1,000	7,558	7,752	7,799	7,959	8,168	8,593	8,974
Private	1,000	2,425	2,583	2,547	2,595	2,661	2,809	2,937
Faculty, total	1,000	817	932	936	952	947	(NA)	(NA)
Public	1,000	574	657	664	675	673	(NA)	(NA)
Private	1,000	244	275	273	277	274	(NA)	(NA)
Degrees conferred, total [2]	1,000	2,025	2,248	2,222	2,226	2,254	2,368	(NA)
Associate's	1,000	482	555	520	528	543	565	(NA)
Bachelor's	1,000	1,095	1,165	1,172	1,166	1,173	1,243	(NA)
Master's	1,000	337	406	406	410	418	438	(NA)
Doctorate's	1,000	39	45	45	46	47	49	(NA)
First-professional	1,000	72	77	78	76	73	73	(NA)

NA Not available.   [1] Full-time equivalents.   [2] For school year ending June the following year.

Source: U.S. National Center for Education Statistics, *Digest of Education Statistics*, annual, and *Projections of Educational Statistics*, annual.

U.S. Census Bureau, Statistical Abstract of the United States: 1999

No. 256. Federal Funds for Education and Related Programs: 1996 to 1998

[In millions of dollars (71,327.4 represents $71,327,400,000), except percent. For fiscal years ending in September. Figures represent on-budget funds]

Level, agency, and program	1996	1997	1998 [1]
Total, all programs	**71,327.4**	**73,136.8**	**75,077.5**
Percent of Federal budget outlays	4.6	4.6	4.5
Elementary/secondary education programs	**34,391.5**	**35,478.9**	**36,818.8**
Department of Education	14,323.8	14,511.2	14,787.3
Grants for the disadvantaged	7,020.5	7,201.6	6,235.9
School improvement programs	1,247.4	1,276.6	1,391.1
Indian education	77.4	56.0	55.0
Special education	3,222.2	3,305.5	3,812.4
Vocational and adult education	1,348.1	1,402.4	1,337.9
Education reform—Goals 2000	271.5	431.5	668.1
Department of Agriculture	8,408.1	8,830.2	9,320.2
Child nutrition programs	[3] 7,875.0	[3] 8,300.0	[3] 8,800.0
Agricultural Marketing Service—commodities [4]	400.0	400.0	400.0
Special milk program [3]	(3)	(3)	(3)
Department of Defense [2]	1,313.1	1,351.8	1,316.6
Overseas dependents schools	813.3	822.6	852.1
Section VI schools [5]	336.1	355.0	302.2
Department of Health and Human Services	5,185.9	5,110.2	5,195.4
Head Start	3,570.0	3,980.5	4,355.0
Social security student benefits	684.9	676.7	680.4
Department of the Interior [2]	486.5	558.4	535.6
Mineral Leasing Act and other funds	56.9	89.0	57.0
Indian Education	428.5	468.4	477.6
Department of Justice	175.9	191.4	222.2
Inmate programs	179.4	190.4	221.2
Department of Labor	4,084.0	4,432.0	4,990.0
Job Corps	1,114.0	1,185.0	1,203.0
Department of Veterans Affairs	344.3	402.2	347.8
Vocational rehab for disabled veterans	349.6	386.0	338.0
Other agencies and programs	70.0	91.4	103.7
Higher education programs [2]	**15,775.5**	**15,959.4**	**15,990.0**
Department of Education [2]	12,257.6	12,377.0	12,406.1
Student financial assistance	6,861.6	7,247.3	8,352.8
Federal Family Education Loans	3,664.0	3,313.8	1,967.8
Department of Agriculture	32.9	32.6	32.6
Department of Commerce	3.4	3.4	3.4
Department of Defense	864.9	913.6	923.5
Tuition assistance for military personnel	260.3	271.9	275.4
Service academies [6]	171.7	173.7	191.4
Senior ROTC	218.2	228.6	225.4

Level, agency, and program	1996	1997	1998 [1]
Professional development education	214.7	229.3	231.2
Department of Health and Human Services [2]	798.6	801.9	793.1
Health professions training programs	273.5	313.7	291.1
National Health Service Corps scholarships [7]	28.8	30.0	30.0
National Institutes of Health training grants [7]	457.0	417.0	429.8
Department of the Interior	132.5	165.6	167.8
Shared revenues, Mineral Leasing Act and other receipts—estimated education share	59.0	89.3	86.2
Indian programs	73.5	76.3	81.6
Department of Transportation	53.5	58.3	59.3
Department of Veterans Affairs [2]	1,074.7	992.7	1,024.8
Post-Vietnam veterans	44.4	16.3	11.7
All-volunteer-force educational assistance	922.8	863.9	898.8
Other agencies and programs [2]	557.5	614.3	579.4
National Endowment for the Humanities	30.9	25.8	20.5
National Science Foundation	262.0	355.0	358.0
United States Information Agency	239.4	204.8	172.0
Other education programs [2]	**4,828.0**	**5,021.2**	**5,171.4**
Department of Education [2]	3,085.6	2,882.3	2,961.8
Administration	502.9	412.6	437.1
Rehabilitative services and handicapped research	2,410.2	2,462.2	2,515.4
Department of Agriculture	412.9	413.6	408.7
Department of Health and Human Services	117.0	144.0	155.0
Department of Justice	35.1	46.1	39.8
Department of State	53.3	49.4	55.4
Department of the Treasury	59.0	51.0	73.0
Other agencies and programs [2]	1,065.2	1,434.8	1,477.6
Agency for International Development	307.0	355.6	347.7
Library of Congress	252.0	261.0	277.0
National Endowment for the Arts	0.5	2.8	2.3
National Endowment for the Humanities	62.4	68.7	72.4
Research programs at universities and related institutions [2]	**16,332.3**	**16,677.3**	**17,097.3**
Department of Agriculture	427.2	516.6	417.9
Department of Defense	1,663.7	1,452.8	1,364.8
Department of Energy	3,035.2	3,150.5	3,170.7
Department of Health and Human Services	6,784.9	7,210.2	7,422.1
National Aeronautics and Space Administration	1,754.6	1,652.2	1,699.0
National Science Foundation	2,041.5	2,040.0	2,115.3

[1] Estimated. [2] Includes other programs and agencies, not shown separately. [3] The Special Milk Program is included in the Child Nutrition Program. [4] Purchased under Section 32 of the Act of August 1935 for use in child nutrition programs. [5] Program provides for the education of dependents of Federal employees residing on Federal property where free public education is unavailable in the nearby community. [6] Instructional costs only including academics, audiovisual, academic computer center, faculty training, military training, physical education, and libraries. [7] Includes alcohol, drug abuse, and mental health training programs.

Source: U.S. National Center for Education Statistics, Digest of Education Statistics, 1998.

Education 165

No. 257. School Expenditures, by Source of Funds in Constant (1996-97) Dollars: 1980 to 1996

[For school years ending in year shown. (345.0 represents $345,000,000,000). Includes nursery, kindergarten, and special programs when provided by school system. Data are deflated by the Consumer Price Index for all urban consumers, on a school year basis (supplied by the U.S. National Center for Education Statistics). Distribution by source of funds is estimated]

Source of funds and control of school	Expenditures (bil. dol.)							Percent distribution		
	1980	1985	1990	1993	1994	1995	1996	1980	1990	1996
Total	345.0	378.8	486.0	518.8	527.9	541.9	554.4	100.0	100.0	100.0
Federal	39.4	32.6	40.2	45.5	46.5	47.0	47.1	11.4	8.3	8.5
State	134.0	147.0	181.1	181.4	181.6	191.3	197.4	38.8	37.3	35.6
Local	90.2	96.8	124.8	133.2	138.3	137.2	139.1	26.1	25.7	25.1
All other	81.5	102.3	139.9	158.6	161.5	166.4	170.7	23.6	28.8	30.8
Public	286.3	306.9	393.8	418.1	425.7	437.2	446.4	100.0	100.0	100.0
Federal	30.8	24.2	29.2	34.1	35.3	35.6	35.8	10.8	7.4	8.0
State	133.1	146.0	179.3	179.6	180.0	189.6	195.8	46.5	45.5	43.9
Local	89.8	96.5	124.3	132.7	137.7	136.8	138.5	31.4	31.6	31.0
All other	32.5	40.2	61.0	71.6	72.7	75.3	76.2	11.4	15.5	17.1
Private	58.8	71.9	92.2	100.7	102.3	104.6	108.0	100.0	100.0	100.0
Federal	8.5	8.4	11.0	11.4	11.3	11.4	11.3	14.5	11.9	10.5
State and local	1.3	1.4	2.3	2.2	2.2	2.2	2.2	2.1	2.5	2.0
All other	49.0	62.1	78.9	87.0	88.7	91.1	94.5	83.3	85.6	87.5
Elementary and secondary	215.0	228.5	294.2	311.4	318.0	325.2	333.1	100.0	100.0	100.0
Federal	19.6	13.9	16.6	20.0	20.7	20.4	20.4	9.1	5.6	6.1
State	93.1	102.2	128.2	131.5	132.5	140.3	146.0	43.3	43.6	43.8
Local	86.7	93.0	119.7	127.8	132.5	131.3	132.8	40.3	40.7	39.9
All other	15.6	19.6	29.7	32.2	32.4	33.2	33.9	7.3	10.1	10.2
Public	200.0	209.5	271.0	287.0	293.5	300.0	307.4	100.0	100.0	100.0
Federal	19.6	13.9	16.6	20.0	20.7	20.4	20.4	9.8	6.1	6.6
State	93.1	102.2	128.2	131.5	132.5	140.3	146.0	46.6	47.3	47.5
Local	86.7	93.0	119.7	127.8	132.5	131.3	132.8	43.3	44.2	43.2
All other [1]	0.6	0.6	6.6	7.8	7.8	8.1	8.2	0.3	2.4	2.7
Private	15.0	19.0	23.2	24.4	24.6	25.2	25.8	100.0	100.0	100.0
Higher education	130.2	150.3	191.8	207.3	209.9	216.7	221.2	100.0	100.0	100.0
Federal	19.8	18.7	23.7	25.5	25.9	26.7	26.7	15.2	12.3	12.1
State	40.8	45.0	52.9	50.0	49.1	51.0	51.4	31.4	27.6	23.2
Local	3.5	3.8	5.0	5.4	5.9	5.9	6.3	2.7	2.6	2.8
All other	65.8	82.7	110.2	126.5	129.1	133.1	136.8	50.6	57.4	61.9
Public	86.3	97.4	122.8	131.0	132.3	137.2	139.0	100.0	100.0	100.0
Federal	11.3	10.2	12.7	14.1	14.6	15.2	15.4	13.0	10.3	11.1
State	40.0	43.9	51.2	48.2	47.5	49.3	49.8	46.4	41.7	35.8
Local	3.1	3.5	4.5	4.9	5.3	5.5	5.8	3.6	3.7	4.1
All other	31.9	39.6	54.4	63.8	64.9	67.3	68.0	37.0	44.3	48.9
Private	43.8	52.9	69.0	76.3	77.6	79.5	82.3	100.0	100.0	100.0
Federal	8.5	8.4	11.0	11.4	11.3	11.4	11.3	19.5	15.9	13.7
State and local	1.3	1.4	2.3	2.2	2.2	2.2	2.2	2.9	3.3	2.7
All other	34.0	43.1	55.7	62.6	64.2	65.9	68.8	77.6	80.8	83.6

[1] Beginning in 1989-90, includes all fees for transportation, books, and food services.

Source: U.S. National Center for Education Statistics, Digest of Education Statistics, annual.

No. 258. School Enrollment, by Control and Level, With Projections: 1980 to 2008

[In thousands (58,305 represents 58,305,000). As of fall. Data are for regular day schools and exclude independent nursery schools and kindergartens, residential schools for exceptional children, subcollegiate departments of colleges, Federal schools for Indians, and federally operated schools on Federal installations. College data include degree-credit and nondegree-credit enrollment]

Control of school and level	1980	1985	1990	1995	1996, prel.	2000, proj.	2004, proj.	2005, proj.	2006, proj.	2007, proj.	2008, proj.
Total	58,305	57,226	60,267	64,803	65,674	68,334	69,657	69,942	70,160	70,305	70,351
Public	50,335	48,901	52,061	55,933	56,682	59,065	60,196	60,436	60,611	60,721	60,735
Private	7,971	8,325	8,206	8,869	8,993	9,269	9,461	9,506	9,549	9,584	9,616
Kindergarten through 8	31,639	31,229	33,973	36,772	37,245	38,543	38,606	38,376	38,181	38,073	38,034
Public	27,647	27,034	29,878	32,341	32,759	33,903	33,958	33,756	33,584	33,489	33,455
Private	3,992	4,195	4,095	4,431	4,486	4,640	4,648	4,620	4,597	4,584	4,579
Grades 9 through 12	14,570	13,750	12,475	13,769	14,131	14,902	15,702	16,050	16,276	16,352	16,234
Public	13,231	12,388	11,338	12,500	12,834	13,537	14,263	14,579	14,785	14,854	14,746
Private	1,339	1,362	1,137	1,269	1,297	1,366	1,439	1,471	1,491	1,498	1,488
College	12,097	12,247	13,819	14,262	14,300	14,889	15,349	15,516	15,703	15,880	16,083
Public	9,457	9,479	10,845	11,092	11,090	11,626	11,975	12,101	12,242	12,378	12,534
Private	2,640	2,768	2,974	3,169	3,210	3,263	3,374	3,415	3,461	3,502	3,549

Source: U.S. National Center for Education Statistics, Digest of Education Statistics, annual; Projections of Education Statistics, annual; and unpublished data.

No. 259. School Enrollment, by Age: 1970 to 1997

[As of October (60,357 represents 60,357,000). Covers civilian noninstitutional population enrolled in nursery school and above. Based on Current Population Survey, see text, Section 1, Population]

Age	1970	1980	1985	1990	1992	1993	1994	1995	1996	1997
ENROLLMENT (1,000)										
Total 3 to 34 years old	60,357	57,348	58,013	60,588	62,084	62,730	66,427	66,939	67,317	69,041
3 and 4 years old	1,461	2,280	2,801	3,292	3,063	3,275	3,917	4,042	3,959	4,194
5 and 6 years old	7,000	5,853	6,697	7,207	7,252	7,298	7,752	7,901	7,893	7,964
7 to 13 years old	28,943	23,751	22,849	25,016	25,768	26,110	26,768	27,003	26,936	27,616
14 and 15 years old	7,869	7,282	7,362	6,555	6,861	7,011	7,519	7,651	7,598	7,744
16 and 17 years old	6,927	7,129	6,654	6,098	6,272	6,339	6,895	6,997	7,220	7,538
18 and 19 years old	3,322	3,788	3,716	4,044	4,012	4,063	4,180	4,274	4,539	4,618
20 and 21 years old	1,949	2,515	2,708	2,852	3,027	2,810	3,133	3,025	3,017	3,231
22 to 24 years old	1,410	1,931	2,068	2,231	2,577	2,579	2,724	2,545	2,605	2,754
25 to 29 years old	1,011	1,714	1,942	2,013	1,907	1,942	2,070	2,216	2,265	2,223
30 to 34 years old	466	1,105	1,218	1,281	1,344	1,303	1,468	1,284	1,286	1,159
35 years old and over	(NA)	1,290	1,766	2,439	2,473	2,634	2,845	2,830	2,979	2,989
ENROLLMENT RATE										
Total 3 to 34 years old	56.4	49.7	48.3	50.2	51.4	51.8	53.3	53.7	54.1	55.6
3 and 4 years old	20.5	36.7	38.9	44.4	39.7	40.4	47.3	48.7	48.3	52.6
5 and 6 years old	89.5	95.7	96.1	96.5	95.5	95.4	96.7	96.0	94.0	96.6
7 to 13 years old	99.2	99.3	99.2	99.6	99.4	99.5	99.3	98.9	97.7	99.1
14 and 15 years old	98.1	98.2	98.1	99.0	99.1	98.9	98.8	98.9	98.0	98.9
16 and 17 years old	90.0	89.0	91.7	92.5	94.1	94.0	94.4	93.6	92.8	94.3
18 and 19 years old	47.7	46.4	51.6	57.3	61.4	61.6	60.2	59.4	61.5	61.5
20 and 21 years old	31.9	31.0	35.3	39.7	44.0	42.7	44.9	44.4	44.4	45.9
22 to 24 years old	14.9	16.3	16.9	21.0	23.7	23.6	24.1	23.2	24.8	26.4
25 to 29 years old	7.5	9.3	9.2	9.7	9.8	10.2	10.8	11.6	11.9	11.8
30 to 34 years old	4.2	6.4	6.1	5.8	6.1	5.9	6.7	6.0	6.1	5.7
35 years old and over	(NA)	1.4	1.6	2.1	2.1	2.2	2.3	2.2	2.3	2.3

NA Not available.

Source: U.S. Census Bureau, *Current Population Reports*, P20-516; and earlier reports.

No. 260. School Enrollment, by Race, Hispanic Origin, and Age: 1980 to 1997

[See headnote, Table 259. (47,673 represents 47,673,000)]

Age	White 1980	White 1990	White 1997	Black 1980	Black 1990	Black 1997	Hispanic origin [1] 1980	Hispanic origin [1] 1990	Hispanic origin [1] 1997
ENROLLMENT (1,000)									
Total 3 to 34 years old	47,673	48,899	54,142	8,251	8,854	10,876	4,263	6,073	9,032
3 and 4 years old	1,844	2,700	3,191	371	452	780	172	249	530
5 and 6 years old	4,781	5,750	6,266	904	1,129	1,269	491	835	1,360
7 to 13 years old	19,585	20,076	21,601	3,598	3,832	4,538	2,009	2,794	3,791
14 and 15 years old	6,038	5,265	6,099	1,088	1,023	1,220	568	739	1,018
16 and 17 years old	5,937	4,858	5,894	1,047	962	1,220	454	592	960
18 and 19 years old	3,199	3,271	3,688	494	596	659	226	329	537
20 and 21 years old	2,206	2,402	2,651	242	305	347	111	213	285
22 to 24 years old	1,669	1,781	2,143	196	274	393	93	121	252
25 to 29 years old	1,473	1,706	1,717	187	162	278	84	130	201
30 to 34 years old	942	1,090	892	124	119	171	54	72	98
35 years old and over	1,104	2,096	2,444	186	238	394	(NA)	145	188
ENROLLMENT RATE									
Total 3 to 34 years old	48.9	49.5	54.8	53.9	51.9	58.4	49.8	47.4	50.8
3 and 4 years old	36.3	44.9	50.9	38.2	41.6	60.0	28.5	29.8	36.6
5 and 6 years old	95.8	96.5	96.8	95.4	96.3	95.8	94.5	94.8	96.6
7 to 13 years old	99.2	99.6	99.1	99.4	99.8	99.3	99.2	99.4	99.1
14 and 15 years old	98.3	99.1	98.8	97.9	99.2	99.2	99.2	99.0	98.4
16 and 17 years old	88.6	92.5	94.5	90.6	91.7	93.4	81.8	85.4	91.1
18 and 19 years old	46.3	57.1	61.5	45.7	55.2	58.2	37.8	44.1	49.4
20 and 21 years old	31.9	41.0	46.4	23.4	28.4	35.9	19.5	27.2	28.9
22 to 24 years old	16.4	20.2	25.8	13.6	20.0	25.4	11.7	9.9	16.4
25 to 29 years old	9.2	9.9	11.3	8.8	6.1	10.7	6.9	6.3	7.3
30 to 34 years old	6.3	5.9	5.4	6.8	4.4	6.5	5.1	3.6	3.7
35 years old and over	1.3	2.1	2.2	1.8	2.1	2.8	(NA)	2.1	1.8

NA Not available. [1] Persons of Hispanic origin may be of any race.

Source: U.S. Census Bureau, *Current Population Reports*, P20-516; and earlier reports.

U.S. Census Bureau, Statistical Abstract of the United States: 1999

No. 261. Enrollment in Public and Private Schools: 1960 to 1997

[In millions (39.0 represents 39,000,000), except percent. As of October. For civilian noninstitutional population. For **1960**, 5 to 34 years old; for **1970 to 1985**, 3 to 34 years old; **beginning 1986**, for 3 years old and over]

Year	Public						Private					
	Total	Nursery	Kindergarten	Elementary	High School	College	Total	Nursery	Kindergarten	Elementary	High School	College
1960	39.0	(NA)	(¹)	27.5	9.2	2.3	7.2	(NA)	(¹)	4.9	1.0	1.3
1970	52.2	0.3	2.6	30.0	13.5	5.7	8.1	0.8	0.5	3.9	1.2	1.7
1975	52.8	0.6	2.9	27.2	14.5	7.7	8.2	1.2	0.5	3.3	1.2	2.0
1979	50.0	0.6	2.6	24.8	14.0	7.7	8.2	1.2	0.4	3.1	1.1	2.3
1980	(NA)	0.6	2.7	24.4	(NA)	(NA)	(NA)	1.4	0.5	3.1	(NA)	(NA)
1981	49.7	0.7	2.6	24.8	13.5	8.2	8.7	1.4	0.5	3.0	1.1	2.6
1982	49.2	0.7	2.7	24.4	13.0	8.4	8.2	1.4	0.6	3.0	1.1	2.6
1983	48.7	0.8	2.7	24.2	12.8	8.2	9.0	1.5	0.7	3.0	1.2	2.6
1984	49.0	0.8	3.0	24.1	12.7	8.5	8.3	1.6	0.5	2.7	1.1	2.4
1985	49.0	0.9	3.2	23.8	12.8	8.4	9.0	1.6	0.6	3.1	1.2	2.5
1986 ²	51.2	0.8	3.4	24.2	13.0	9.8	9.4	1.7	0.6	3.0	1.2	2.9
1987 ²	51.7	0.8	3.4	24.8	12.7	10.0	8.9	1.7	0.6	2.8	1.1	2.8
1988 ²	52.2	0.9	3.4	25.5	12.2	10.3	8.9	1.8	0.5	2.8	1.0	2.8
1989 ²	52.5	0.9	3.3	25.9	12.1	10.3	8.9	1.9	0.6	2.7	0.8	2.9
1990 ²	53.8	1.2	3.3	26.6	11.9	10.7	9.2	2.2	0.6	2.7	0.9	2.9
1991 ²	54.5	1.1	3.5	26.6	12.2	11.1	9.4	1.8	0.6	3.0	1.0	3.0
1992 ²	55.0	1.1	3.5	27.1	12.3	11.1	9.4	1.8	0.6	3.1	1.0	3.0
1993 ²	56.0	1.2	3.5	27.7	12.6	10.9	9.4	1.8	0.7	2.9	1.0	3.0
1994 ²	58.6	1.9	3.3	28.1	13.5	11.7	10.7	2.3	0.6	3.4	1.1	3.3
1995 ²	58.7	2.0	3.2	28.4	13.7	11.4	11.1	2.4	0.7	3.4	1.2	3.3
1996 ²	59.5	1.9	3.4	28.1	14.1	12.0	10.8	2.3	0.7	3.4	1.2	3.2
1997 ²	61.6	2.3	3.3	29.3	14.6	12.1	10.5	2.2	0.7	3.1	1.2	3.3
Percent White:												
1960	85.7	(NA)	(¹)	84.3	88.2	92.2	95.7	(NA)	(¹)	95.3	96.7	96.3
1970	84.5	84.4	84.6	83.1	85.6	90.7	93.4	91.1	88.2	94.1	96.1	92.8
1980	(NA)	68.2	80.7	80.9	(NA)	(NA)	(NA)	89.0	87.0	90.7	(NA)	(NA)
1990	79.8	71.7	78.3	78.9	79.2	84.1	87.4	89.6	83.2	88.2	89.4	85.0
1995	78.0	71.3	76.9	77.5	76.9	81.9	85.0	88.7	84.1	86.1	86.0	81.1
1997	77.6	69.7	77.4	77.4	77.1	80.3	84.0	85.4	82.4	85.3	86.5	81.6

NA Not available.   ¹ Included in elementary school.   ² See Table 311 for college enrollment 35 years old and over. Also data beginning 1986 based on a revised edit and tabulation package.

Source: U.S. Census Bureau, *Current Population Reports*, P20-516; and earlier reports.

No. 262. School Enrollment, by Sex and Level: 1960 to 1997

[In millions (46.3 represents 46,300,000). As of Oct. For the civilian noninstitutional population. For **1960**, persons 5 to 34 years old; **1970-1979**, 3 to 34 years old; **beginning 1980**, 3 years old and over. Elementary includes kindergarten and grades 1-8; high school, grades 9-12; and college, 2-year and 4-year colleges, universities, and graduate and professional schools. Data for college represent degree-credit enrollment]

Year	All levels ¹			Elementary			High school			College		
	Total	Male	Female	Total	Male	Female	Total	Male	Female	Total	Male	Female
1960	46.3	24.2	22.0	32.4	16.7	15.7	10.2	5.2	5.1	3.6	2.3	1.2
1970	60.4	31.4	28.9	37.1	19.0	18.1	14.7	7.4	7.3	7.4	4.4	3.0
1975	61.0	31.6	29.4	33.8	17.3	16.5	15.7	8.0	7.7	9.7	5.3	4.4
1978	58.6	30.1	28.6	31.5	16.1	15.3	15.5	7.8	7.6	9.8	5.1	4.7
1979	57.9	29.5	28.3	30.9	15.9	15.0	15.1	7.7	7.4	10.0	5.0	5.0
1980	58.6	29.6	29.1	30.6	15.8	14.9	14.6	7.3	7.3	11.4	5.4	6.0
1981 ²	58.4	29.5	28.9	30.1	15.5	14.7	14.4	7.3	7.1	11.8	5.6	6.2
1981 ³	59.9	30.3	29.6	31.0	15.9	15.0	14.7	7.5	7.3	12.1	5.8	6.3
1982	59.4	30.0	29.4	30.7	15.8	14.9	14.2	7.2	7.0	12.3	5.9	6.4
1983	59.3	30.1	29.2	30.6	15.7	14.8	14.1	7.1	7.0	12.4	6.0	6.3
1984	58.9	29.9	29.0	30.3	15.6	14.7	13.9	7.1	6.8	12.3	6.0	6.3
1985	59.8	30.0	29.7	30.7	15.7	15.0	14.1	7.2	6.9	12.5	5.9	6.6
1986	60.1	30.4	29.7	31.1	16.1	15.0	14.0	7.1	6.9	12.4	5.8	6.6
1986 ⁴	60.5	30.6	30.0	31.1	16.1	15.0	14.2	7.2	7.0	12.7	6.0	6.7
1987	60.6	30.7	29.9	31.6	16.3	15.3	13.8	7.0	6.8	12.7	6.0	6.7
1988	61.1	30.7	30.5	32.2	16.6	15.6	13.2	6.7	6.4	13.1	5.9	7.2
1989	61.5	30.8	30.7	32.5	16.7	15.8	12.9	6.6	6.3	13.2	6.0	7.2
1990	63.0	31.5	31.5	33.2	17.1	16.0	12.8	6.5	6.4	13.6	6.2	7.4
1991	63.9	32.1	31.8	33.8	17.3	16.4	13.1	6.8	6.4	14.1	6.4	7.6
1992	64.6	32.2	32.3	34.3	17.7	16.6	13.3	6.8	6.5	14.0	6.2	7.8
1993	65.4	32.9	32.5	34.8	17.9	16.9	13.6	7.0	6.6	13.9	6.3	7.6
1994	69.3	34.6	34.6	35.4	18.2	17.2	14.6	7.4	7.2	15.0	6.8	8.2
1995	69.8	35.0	34.8	35.7	18.3	17.4	15.0	7.7	7.3	14.7	6.7	8.0
1996	70.3	35.1	35.2	35.5	18.3	17.3	15.3	7.9	7.4	15.2	6.8	8.4
1997	72.0	35.9	36.2	36.3	18.7	17.6	15.8	8.0	7.7	15.4	6.8	8.6

¹ Beginning 1970, includes nursery schools, not shown separately.   ² Based on 1970 population controls.   ³ Based on 1980 population controls.   ⁴ Revised. Data beginning 1986, based on a revised edit and tabulation package.

Source: U.S. Census Bureau, *Current Population Reports*, P20-516; and earlier reports.

No. 263. Educational Attainment, by Race and Hispanic Origin: 1960 to 1998

[In percent. For persons 25 years old and over. 1960, 1970, and 1980 as of April 1 and based on sample data from the censuses of population. Other years as of March and based on the Current Population Survey; see text, Section 1, Population, and Appendix III. See Table 264 for data by sex]

Year	Total [1]	White	Black	Asian and Pacific Islander	Hispanic [2] Total [3]	Mexican	Puerto Rican	Cuban
COMPLETED 4 YEARS OF HIGH SCHOOL OR MORE								
1960	41.1	43.2	20.1	(NA)	(NA)	(NA)	(NA)	(NA)
1965	49.0	51.3	27.2	(NA)	(NA)	(NA)	(NA)	(NA)
1970	52.3	54.5	31.4	(NA)	32.1	24.2	23.4	43.9
1975	62.5	64.5	42.5	(NA)	37.9	31.0	28.7	51.7
1980	66.5	68.8	51.2	(NA)	44.0	37.6	40.1	55.3
1985	73.9	75.5	59.8	(NA)	47.9	41.9	46.3	51.1
1990	77.6	79.1	66.2	80.4	50.8	44.1	55.5	63.5
1995 [4]	81.7	83.0	73.8	(NA)	53.4	46.5	61.3	64.7
1996 [4]	81.7	82.8	74.3	83.2	53.1	46.9	60.4	63.8
1997 [4]	82.1	83.0	74.9	84.9	54.7	48.6	61.1	65.2
1998 [4]	82.8	83.7	76.0	(NA)	55.5	48.3	63.8	67.8
COMPLETED 4 YEARS OF COLLEGE OR MORE								
1960	7.7	8.1	3.1	(NA)	(NA)	(NA)	(NA)	(NA)
1965	9.4	9.9	4.7	(NA)	(NA)	(NA)	(NA)	(NA)
1970	10.7	11.3	4.4	(NA)	4.5	2.5	2.2	11.1
1975	13.9	14.5	6.4	(NA)	(NA)	(NA)	(NA)	(NA)
1980	16.2	17.1	8.4	(NA)	7.6	4.9	5.6	16.2
1985	19.4	20.0	11.1	(NA)	8.5	5.5	7.0	13.7
1990	21.3	22.0	11.3	39.9	9.2	5.4	9.7	20.2
1995 [4]	23.0	24.0	13.2	(NA)	9.3	6.5	10.7	19.4
1996 [4]	23.6	24.3	13.6	41.7	9.3	6.5	11.0	18.8
1997 [4]	23.9	24.6	13.3	42.2	10.3	7.5	10.7	19.7
1998 [4]	24.4	25.0	14.7	(NA)	11.0	7.5	11.9	22.2

NA Not available.   [1] Includes other races, not shown separately.   [2] Persons of Hispanic origin may be of any race.
[3] Includes persons of other Hispanic origin, not shown separately.   [4] Beginning 1995, persons who are high school graduates and those with a BA degree or higher.

Source: U.S. Census Bureau, *U.S. Census of Population, U.S. Summary,* PC80-1-C1, and *Current Population Reports* P20-455, P20-459, P20-462, P20-465RV, P20-475, P20-476, P20-489, P20-493, P20-505, P20-513; and unpublished data.

No. 264. Educational Attainment, by Race, Hispanic Origin, and Sex: 1960 to 1998

[In percent. See Table 263 for headnote and totals for both sexes]

Year	All races [1] Male	Female	White Male	Female	Black Male	Female	Asian and Pacific Islander Male	Female	Hispanic [2] Male	Female
COMPLETED 4 YEARS OF HIGH SCHOOL OR MORE										
1960	39.5	42.5	41.6	44.7	18.2	21.8	(NA)	(NA)	(NA)	(NA)
1965	48.0	49.9	50.2	52.2	25.8	28.4	(NA)	(NA)	(NA)	(NA)
1970	51.9	52.8	54.0	55.0	30.1	32.5	(NA)	(NA)	37.9	34.2
1975	63.1	62.1	65.0	64.1	41.6	43.3	(NA)	(NA)	39.5	36.7
1980	67.3	65.8	69.6	68.1	50.8	51.5	(NA)	(NA)	67.3	65.8
1985	74.4	73.5	76.0	75.1	58.4	60.8	(NA)	(NA)	48.5	47.4
1990	77.7	77.5	79.1	79.0	65.8	66.5	84.0	77.2	50.3	51.3
1995 [3]	81.7	81.6	83.0	83.0	73.4	74.1	(NA)	(NA)	52.9	53.8
1996 [3]	81.9	81.6	82.7	82.8	74.3	74.2	86.0	80.7	53.0	53.3
1997 [3]	82.0	82.2	82.9	83.2	73.5	76.0	(NA)	(NA)	54.9	54.6
1998 [3]	82.8	82.9	83.6	83.8	75.2	76.7	(NA)	(NA)	55.7	55.3
COMPLETED 4 YEARS OF COLLEGE OR MORE										
1960	9.7	5.8	10.3	6.0	2.8	3.3	(NA)	(NA)	(NA)	(NA)
1965	12.0	7.1	12.7	7.3	4.9	4.5	(NA)	(NA)	(NA)	(NA)
1970	13.5	8.1	14.4	8.4	4.2	4.6	(NA)	(NA)	7.8	4.3
1975	17.6	10.6	18.4	11.0	6.7	6.2	(NA)	(NA)	8.3	4.6
1980	20.1	12.8	21.3	13.3	8.4	8.3	(NA)	(NA)	9.4	6.0
1985	23.1	16.0	24.0	16.3	11.2	11.0	(NA)	(NA)	9.7	7.3
1990	24.4	18.4	25.3	19.0	11.9	10.8	44.9	35.4	9.8	8.7
1995 [3]	26.0	20.2	27.2	21.0	13.6	12.9	(NA)	(NA)	10.1	8.4
1996 [3]	26.0	21.4	26.9	21.8	12.4	14.6	46.4	37.3	10.3	8.3
1997 [3]	26.2	21.7	27.0	22.3	12.5	13.9	(NA)	(NA)	10.6	10.1
1998 [3]	26.5	22.4	27.3	22.8	13.9	15.4	(NA)	(NA)	11.1	10.9

NA Not available.   [1] Includes other races, not shown separately.   [2] Persons of Hispanic origin may be of any race.
[3] Beginning 1995, persons who are high school graduates and those with a BA degree or higher.

Source: U.S. Census Bureau, *U.S. Census of Population, 1960, 1970, and 1980, Vol.1;* and *Current Population Reports* P20-459, P20-489, P20-493, P20-505, P20-513; and unpublished data.

No. 265. Educational Attainment, by Selected Characteristic: 1998

[For persons 25 years old and over (172,211 represents 172,211,000). As of **March.** Based on the Current Population Survey; see text, Section 1, Population, and Appendix III. For composition of regions, see map inside front cover]

Characteristic	Population (1,000)	Percent of population—highest level					
		Not a high school graduate	High school graduate	Some college, but no degree	Asso- ciate's degree [1]	Bachelor's degree	Advanced degree
Total persons	172,211	17.2	33.8	17.2	7.5	16.4	7.9
Age:							
25 to 34 years old.	39,354	11.9	31.9	19.8	8.7	21.3	6.2
35 to 44 years old.	44,462	12.0	34.0	18.3	9.3	18.3	8.0
45 to 54 years old.	34,058	13.0	32.1	17.8	8.5	17.5	11.3
55 to 64 years old.	22,255	20.5	37.3	15.0	5.2	13.0	9.2
65 to 74 years old.	17,873	28.9	36.4	13.8	4.3	10.0	6.6
75 years old or over	14,209	38.0	33.2	13.0	3.2	8.1	4.4
Sex:							
Male.	82,376	17.2	32.3	17.1	6.9	17.1	9.4
Female	89,835	17.1	35.2	17.3	8.0	15.8	6.6
Race:							
White	145,078	16.3	33.9	17.2	7.7	16.8	8.1
Black	19,376	24.0	36.0	19.1	6.2	10.3	4.4
Other	7,756	16.5	25.5	13.5	7.1	24.7	12.8
Hispanic origin:							
Hispanic	16,044	44.5	26.8	12.6	5.1	7.8	3.2
Non-Hispanic	156,167	14.4	34.5	17.7	7.7	17.3	8.4
Region:							
Northeast	33,900	16.2	36.3	13.4	7.2	17.3	9.6
Midwest	39,600	14.2	37.3	17.4	8.0	15.7	7.4
South	60,909	19.9	33.9	16.8	6.8	15.3	7.3
West.	37,802	16.7	27.7	21.0	8.4	18.2	8.1
Marital status:							
Never married	25,752	16.0	30.2	18.6	7.1	19.9	8.3
Married spouse present	107,008	14.5	34.0	16.9	7.8	17.9	8.9
Married spouse absent	6,844	27.0	34.6	17.3	6.8	9.8	4.4
Separated	4,605	25.8	36.2	18.3	7.3	8.8	3.6
Widowed.	13,577	37.9	34.4	13.0	4.1	7.2	3.5
Divorced	19,030	15.6	36.8	20.0	8.8	12.3	6.4
Civilian labor force status:							
Employed	111,131	10.5	32.6	18.4	8.9	19.9	9.8
Unemployed	4,597	23.0	38.8	17.6	6.9	9.9	3.7
Not in the labor force.	55,822	30.2	35.9	14.7	4.7	10.0	4.5

[1] Includes vocational degrees.

Source: U.S. Census Bureau, *Current Population Reports*, P20-513; and unpublished data.

No. 266. Earnings, by Highest Degree Earned: 1998

[For persons 18 years old and over with earnings. Persons as of March. Earnings for prior year. Based on Current Population Survey; see text, Section 1, Population, and Appendix III. For definition of mean, see Guide to Tabular Presentation]

Characteristic	Total persons	Level of highest degree							
		Not a high school graduate	High school graduate only	Some college, no degree	Asso- ciate's	Bach- elor's	Master's	Profes- sional	Doctorate
MEAN EARNINGS (dol.)									
All persons [1]	29,514	16,124	22,895	24,804	29,872	40,478	51,183	95,148	77,445
Age:									
18 to 24 years old. . . .	11,264	7,737	12,001	9,813	15,931	19,444	23,007	14,045	4,158
25 to 34 years old. . . .	26,462	16,262	21,637	23,489	25,978	35,027	40,798	58,079	47,779
35 to 44 years old. . . .	34,081	18,532	26,235	30,353	32,429	45,298	56,922	115,697	77,982
45 to 54 years old. . . .	37,242	20,800	26,925	35,090	34,606	46,773	53,594	145,699	86,237
55 to 64 years old. . . .	35,924	21,096	26,202	26,392	32,063	45,129	53,547	145,699	79,931
65 years old and over .	21,588	13,482	13,734	21,880	33,313	29,958	26,154	54,246	65,543
Sex:									
Male.	36,556	19,575	28,307	31,268	36,392	50,056	63,220	109,206	87,426
Female	21,528	10,725	16,906	18,104	24,009	30,119	38,337	62,113	51,189
White	30,515	16,596	23,618	25,442	30,509	41,439	52,475	97,487	79,947
Male.	37,933	20,071	29,298	32,294	37,362	51,678	65,421	110,977	89,110
Female	21,799	10,700	17,166	18,083	24,059	30,041	38,428	63,450	54,587
Black	21,909	13,185	18,980	22,105	25,527	32,062	40,610	51,004	(B)
Male.	25,080	15,423	22,440	26,743	29,099	35,792	46,729	(B)	(B)
Female	19,161	10,607	15,789	18,346	23,416	29,091	37,425	(B)	(B)
Hispanic [2]	20,766	15,069	19,558	20,825	25,478	33,465	46,556	(B)	(B)
Male.	23,520	17,447	22,253	24,807	29,627	37,963	54,790	(B)	(B)
Female	16,781	10,503	15,747	16,258	21,705	29,173	35,425	(B)	(B)

B Base figure too small to meet statistical standards for reliability of a derived figure. [1] Includes other races, not shown separately. [2] Persons of Hispanic origin may be of any race.

Source: U.S. Census Bureau, *Current Population Reports*, P20-513.

No. 267. Educational Attainment, by State: 1990 and 1998

[In percent. As of March 1998 and April 1990. For persons 25 years old and over, except as indicated. Based on the 1990 Census of Population and the Current Population Survey; see text, Section 1, Population, and Appendix III]

State	1990						1998	
	Not a high school graduate	High school graduate or more	Bachelors degree or more			Drop- outs [1]	High school graduate or more	College graduate or more
			Total	Bachelor's degree	Advanced degree			
United States........	24.8	75.2	20.3	13.1	7.2	11.2	82.8	24.4
Alabama..............	33.1	66.9	15.7	10.1	5.5	12.6	78.8	20.6
Alaska...............	13.4	86.6	23.0	15.0	8.0	10.9	90.6	24.2
Arizona..............	21.3	78.7	20.3	13.3	7.0	14.4	81.9	21.9
Arkansas.............	33.7	66.3	13.3	8.9	4.5	11.4	76.8	16.2
California	23.8	76.2	23.4	15.3	8.1	14.2	80.1	26.4
Colorado.............	15.6	84.4	27.0	18.0	9.0	9.8	89.6	34.0
Connecticut..........	20.8	79.2	27.2	16.2	11.0	9.0	83.7	31.4
Delaware.............	22.5	77.5	21.4	13.7	7.7	10.4	85.2	25.1
District of Columbia	26.9	73.1	33.3	16.1	17.2	13.9	83.8	36.5
Florida	25.6	74.4	18.3	12.0	6.3	14.3	81.9	22.5
Georgia	29.1	70.9	19.3	12.9	6.4	14.1	80.0	20.7
Hawaii	19.9	80.1	22.9	15.8	7.1	7.5	84.6	24.0
Idaho	20.3	79.7	17.7	12.4	5.3	10.4	82.7	20.3
Illinois	23.8	76.2	21.0	13.6	7.5	10.6	84.2	25.8
Indiana..............	24.4	75.6	15.6	9.2	6.4	11.4	83.5	17.7
Iowa	19.9	80.1	16.9	11.7	5.2	6.6	87.7	20.3
Kansas..............	18.7	81.3	21.1	14.1	7.0	8.7	89.2	28.5
Kentucky	35.4	64.6	13.6	8.1	5.5	13.3	77.9	20.1
Louisiana............	31.7	68.3	16.1	10.5	5.6	12.5	78.6	19.5
Maine................	21.2	78.8	18.8	12.7	6.1	8.3	86.7	19.2
Maryland	21.6	78.4	26.5	15.6	10.9	10.9	84.7	31.8
Massachusetts........	20.0	80.0	27.2	16.6	10.6	8.5	85.6	31.0
Michigan.............	23.2	76.8	17.4	10.9	6.4	10.0	85.4	22.1
Minnesota............	17.6	82.4	21.8	15.6	6.3	6.4	89.4	31.0
Mississippi	35.7	64.3	14.7	9.7	5.1	11.8	77.3	19.5
Missouri	26.1	73.9	17.8	11.7	6.1	11.4	82.9	22.4
Montana.............	19.0	81.0	19.8	14.1	5.7	8.1	89.1	23.9
Nebraska............	18.2	81.8	18.9	13.1	5.9	7.0	87.7	20.9
Nevada	21.2	78.8	15.3	10.1	5.2	15.2	89.1	20.6
New Hampshire........	17.8	82.2	24.4	16.4	7.9	9.4	84.0	26.6
New Jersey...........	23.3	76.7	24.9	16.0	8.8	9.6	86.5	30.1
New Mexico	24.9	75.1	20.4	12.1	8.3	11.7	79.6	23.1
New York	25.2	74.8	23.1	13.2	9.9	9.9	81.5	26.8
North Carolina........	30.0	70.0	17.4	12.0	5.4	12.5	81.4	23.3
North Dakota.........	23.3	76.7	18.1	13.5	4.5	4.6	84.3	22.5
Ohio	24.3	75.7	17.0	11.1	5.9	8.9	86.2	21.5
Oklahoma............	25.4	74.6	17.8	11.8	6.0	10.4	84.6	20.5
Oregon..............	18.5	81.5	20.6	13.6	7.0	11.8	85.5	27.7
Pennsylvania.........	25.3	74.7	17.9	11.3	6.6	9.1	84.1	22.1
Rhode Island.........	28.0	72.0	21.3	13.5	7.8	11.1	80.7	27.8
South Carolina........	31.7	68.3	16.6	11.2	5.4	11.7	78.6	21.3
South Dakota	22.9	77.1	17.2	12.3	4.9	7.7	86.3	21.8
Tennessee	32.9	67.1	16.0	10.5	5.4	13.4	76.9	16.9
Texas	27.9	72.1	20.3	13.9	6.5	12.9	78.3	23.3
Utah	14.9	85.1	22.3	15.4	6.8	8.7	89.3	27.6
Vermont.............	19.2	80.8	24.3	15.4	8.9	8.0	86.7	27.1
Virginia..............	24.8	75.2	24.5	15.4	9.1	10.0	82.6	30.3
Washington...........	16.2	83.8	22.9	15.9	7.0	10.6	92.0	28.1
West Virginia.........	34.0	66.0	12.3	7.5	4.8	10.9	76.4	16.3
Wisconsin............	21.4	78.6	17.7	12.1	5.6	7.1	88.0	22.3
Wyoming	17.0	83.0	18.8	13.1	5.7	6.9	90.0	19.8

[1] For persons 16 to 19 years old. A dropout is a person who is not in regular school and who has not completed the 12th grade or received a general equivalency degree.

Source: U.S. Census Bureau, *1990 Census of Population*, CPH-L-96, and *Current Population Reports*, P20-513.

Education 171

No. 268. Nonfatal Crimes Against Students: 1995 and 1996

[For students aged 12 through 18 (3,667.0 represents 3,667,000). For crimes occurring at school or going to or from school. Based on the National Crime Victimization Survey; see Appendix III]

Student characteristic	1995				1996			
			Violent				Violent	
	Total	Theft	Total	Serious [1]	Total	Theft	Total	Serious [1]
Total (1,000)	3,667.0	2,213.9	1,453.2	273.5	3,347.7	2,075.6	1,272.1	255.0
RATE PER 1,000 STUDENTS								
Total [2]	143	86	57	11	128	79	49	10
Sex:								
Male	159	93	66	14	144	80	64	13
Female	125	78	47	7	111	79	32	6
Age:								
12 to 14 years old	188	105	83	15	161	94	67	10
15 to 18 years old	105	70	35	7	102	68	34	9
Race/ethnicity:								
White, non-Hispanic	154	95	59	8	137	85	51	7
Black, non-Hispanic	127	66	61	21	114	76	38	13
Hispanic	118	69	49	13	112	58	54	17
Other, non-Hispanic	108	80	28	[3]11	116	76	40	[3]11
Urbanicity: [4]								
Urban	136	79	58	18	131	77	55	16
Suburban	159	97	62	9	138	84	54	9
Rural	117	73	44	6	101	72	29	[3]4
Household income:								
Less than $7,500	91	30	61	25	86	55	31	[3]8
$7,500 to $14,999	113	60	53	16	95	54	41	11
$15,000 to $24,999	139	82	57	10	132	69	63	17
$25,000 to $34,999	164	94	70	15	138	80	57	11
$35,000 to $49,999	146	92	55	8	141	86	55	11
$50,000 to $74,999	157	104	54	10	147	99	48	9
$75,000 and over	180	121	60	[3]5	144	106	38	[3]5

[1] Includes rape, sexual assault, robbery, and aggravated assault. [2] Includes unknown household income. [3] Estimate based on fewer than 10 cases. [4] Urban—the largest city (or groupings of cities) of an MSA; suburban—those portions of metro areas outside central cities; rural—a place outside MSAs.

Source: U.S. National Center for Education Statistics and U.S. Bureau of Justice Statistics, *Indicators of School Crime and Safety, 1998.*

No. 269. Public Schools Reporting Criminal Incidents to the Police: 1996-97

[In percent. For crimes that took place in school buildings, on school buses or grounds, and places holding school-sponsored events. Based on the National Center for Education Statistics' Fast Response Survey System; see source for details]

School characteristic	Any incidents					Serious violent incidents [1]				
	Total	City [2]	Urban fringe [2]	Town [2]	Rural [2]	Total	City [2]	Urban fringe [2]	Town [2]	Rural [2]
Instructional level:										
Elementary school	45.1	46.9	47.0	52.6	34.2	4.2	6.1	3.3	2.0	5.1
Middle school	74.1	86.7	78.8	70.0	62.0	18.7	35.8	21.7	7.0	15.0
High school	76.9	88.8	84.0	84.2	64.1	20.6	48.0	33.0	12.7	9.4
School enrollment:										
Less than 300	37.8	(B)	(B)	44.9	38.0	3.9	(B)	(B)	8.8	2.5
300 to 999	59.6	54.2	59.2	67.3	56.8	9.3	12.5	9.0	3.2	13.9
1,000 or more	89.1	93.1	86.7	86.5	(B)	32.9	44.2	29.8	15.9	(B)
Minority enrollment:										
Less than 5 percent	46.7	(B)	47.2	53.9	40.8	5.8	(B)	5.9	3.3	7.3
5 to 19 percent	57.7	52.0	62.9	64.0	45.0	10.9	14.5	11.3	10.6	6.8
20 to 49 percent	58.1	54.7	58.5	66.7	53.3	11.1	19.1	10.1	5.0	8.0
50 percent or more	68.3	64.8	62.3	81.5	74.9	14.7	17.6	17.8	4.4	11.6
Free/reduced price lunch eligibility:										
Less than 20 percent	54.4	50.6	57.3	64.2	41.2	8.6	12.2	9.9	7.1	5.6
21 to 34 percent	53.2	56.0	65.5	57.2	39.5	11.7	18.4	13.3	7.1	11.6
35 to 49 percent	59.4	76.1	53.3	63.1	52.5	11.6	34.2	8.6	3.0	8.6
50 to 74 percent	58.8	60.8	54.7	66.6	52.0	8.9	22.9	10.3	2.0	2.3
75 percent or more	59.2	58.5	(B)	(B)	(B)	10.2	8.4	(B)	(B)	(B)

B Base figure too small to meet statistical standards for reliability of a derived figure. [1] Includes murder, rape or other sexual battery, suicide, physical attack or fight with a weapon, or robbery. [2] City—central city of an MSA; urban fringe—a place within an MSA but not its central city; town—a place outside an MSA, with a population greater than or equal to 2,500, and defined as urban by the U.S. Census Bureau; rural—a place with a population under 2,500 and defined as urban by the U.S. Census Bureau.

Source: U.S. National Center for Education Statistics and U.S. Bureau of Justice Statistics, *Indicators of School Crime and Safety, 1998.*

No. 270. Children Whose Parents Are Involved in School Activities: 1996

[In percent, except as indicated (22,920 represents 22,920,000). Based on the National Household Education Survey; see source for details]

Parental involvement	Students in grades K to 5					Students in grades 6 to 8				
		Two-parent families	One-parent families				Two-parent families	One-parent families		
	Total		Total	Mother	Father	Total		Total	Mother	Father
Total students (1,000)	22,920	16,363	6,557	5,886	671	11,098	7,800	3,298	2,867	431
Any adult attending a meeting	83.5	87.0	74.8	75.2	71.7	78.4	81.9	70.0	69.6	72.6
Only mother attended	38.2	26.5	67.5	75.2	(X)	37.0	27.1	60.5	69.6	(X)
Only father attended	4.4	3.2	7.3	(X)	71.7	6.2	4.9	9.5	(X)	72.6
Both attended	40.9	57.2	(X)	(X)	(X)	35.1	49.9	(X)	(X)	(X)
Any adult attending a conference	86.6	88.1	83.0	84.0	74.3	69.8	70.5	68.1	68.7	64.2
Only mother attended	51.6	42.1	75.4	84.0	(X)	42.3	34.9	59.7	68.7	(X)
Only father attended	5.4	4.5	7.6	(X)	74.3	6.3	5.4	8.4	(X)	64.2
Both attended	29.6	41.5	(X)	(X)	(X)	21.2	30.1	(X)	(X)	(X)
Any adult attending a class event	72.0	74.6	65.6	65.4	66.9	66.4	69.5	58.9	57.7	66.3
Only mother attended	33.2	23.0	58.7	65.4	(X)	25.5	15.1	50.2	57.7	(X)
Only father attended	4.2	3.1	6.9	(X)	66.9	4.7	3.0	8.7	(X)	66.3
Both attended	34.6	48.4	(X)	(X)	(X)	36.1	51.4	(X)	(X)	(X)
Any adult acted as a volunteer	49.6	54.9	36.4	37.4	28.1	30.8	34.7	21.5	21.9	18.7
Only mother attended	37.4	38.9	33.6	37.4	(X)	21.7	22.8	19.0	21.9	(X)
Only father attended	3.1	3.2	2.9	(X)	28.1	2.6	2.6	2.5	(X)	18.7
Both attended	9.1	12.8	(X)	(X)	(X)	6.5	9.2	(X)	(X)	(X)
Number of activities at least one parent participated in:										
None	3.6	2.4	6.6	6.1	11.1	8.0	5.5	14.0	14.4	10.9
One	7.3	6.1	10.2	10.3	9.9	12.6	12.1	13.9	13.2	18.5
Two	19.7	17.9	24.4	24.2	25.9	26.4	26.4	26.6	27.9	17.9
Three	32.6	31.8	34.5	34.6	33.2	31.9	32.4	30.8	28.9	43.5
Four	36.8	41.8	24.4	24.9	20.0	21.0	23.7	14.8	15.6	9.3
Number of activities mother participated in: [1]										
None	4.4	3.9	6.1	6.1	(X)	10.0	8.4	14.4	14.4	(X)
One	8.4	7.7	10.3	10.3	(X)	13.7	13.9	13.2	13.2	(X)
Two	20.9	19.7	24.2	24.2	(X)	27.0	26.6	27.9	27.9	(X)
Three	32.5	31.7	34.6	34.6	(X)	30.2	30.7	28.9	28.9	(X)
Four	33.8	37.0	24.9	24.9	(X)	19.1	20.3	15.6	15.6	(X)
Number of activities father participated in: [2]										
None	21.9	22.3	11.1	(X)	11.1	24.1	24.9	10.9	(X)	10.9
One	20.4	20.8	9.9	(X)	9.9	24.4	24.7	18.5	(X)	18.5
Two	26.7	26.8	25.9	(X)	25.9	25.3	25.7	17.9	(X)	17.9
Three	21.3	20.8	33.2	(X)	33.2	19.8	18.5	43.5	(X)	43.5
Four	9.7	9.3	20.0	(X)	20.0	6.4	6.2	9.3	(X)	9.3
Number of activities both parents participated in:										
None	25.3	25.3	(X)	(X)	(X)	29.0	29.0	(X)	(X)	(X)
One	22.3	22.3	(X)	(X)	(X)	25.9	25.9	(X)	(X)	(X)
Two	26.4	26.4	(X)	(X)	(X)	24.7	24.7	(X)	(X)	(X)
Three	19.2	19.2	(X)	(X)	(X)	16.3	16.3	(X)	(X)	(X)
Four	6.8	6.8	(X)	(X)	(X)	4.2	4.2	(X)	(X)	(X)

X Not applicable. [1] Regardless if father participated. [2] Regardless if mother participated.

Source: U.S. National Center for Education Statistics, *Fathers' Involvement in Their Children's School*, October 1997.

No. 271. Public Elementary Schools Holding Activities and Parental Attendance: 1996

[In percent. For grades K to 8 during school year ending in year shown. Based on survey and subject to sampling error; see source for details]

Type of activity	Schools holding activity	Estimate of typical parental attendance [1]				
		Most or all	More than half	About half	Less than half	Few
Open house or back-to-school night	97	49	31	13	6	1
Arts event [2]	96	36	30	16	13	5
Regularly scheduled school wide parent-teacher conferences	92	57	21	11	9	3
Sports event [3]	85	12	21	20	30	17
Science fairs or other academic demonstrations or events	84	19	24	20	23	14

[1] Estimated by person most knowledgeable about parental involvement programs. [2] Such as a play, dance, or musical performance. [3] Or other athletic demonstration.

Source: U.S. National Center for Education Statistics, Fast Response Survey System, NCES 98-032, *Parent Involvement in Children's Education: Efforts by Public Elementary Schools*, January 1998.

U.S. Census Bureau, Statistical Abstract of the United States: 1999

No. 272. Children With Difficulty Speaking English: 1979 to 1995

[In percent, except total. For children 5 to 17 years old (1,250 represents 1,250,000). For children reported to speak English less than "very well." Based on the Current Population Survey; see text Section 1, Population, and Appendix III]

Characteristic	1979	1989	1992	1995[1]
Total with difficulty speaking English (1,000)	1,250	1,850	2,178	2,431
Percent of children 5 to 17	2.8	4.4	4.9	5.1
Race and Hispanic origin:				
White, non-Hispanic	0.5	0.8	0.6	0.7
Black, non-Hispanic	0.3	0.5	1.3	0.9
Hispanic[2]	28.7	27.4	29.9	31.0
Other, non-Hispanic[3]	19.8	20.4	21.0	14.1
Region[4]:				
Northeast	2.9	4.8	5.3	5.0
Midwest	1.1	1.3	1.6	2.3
South	2.2	3.8	3.5	3.4
West	6.5	8.8	10.4	11.4
Percent speaking another language at home	32.7	34.9	34.2	36.5
White, non-Hispanic	17.3	22.6	17.2	19.0
Black, non-Hispanic	25.6	22.5	31.0	31.8
Hispanic[2]	38.2	38.5	39.0	41.9
Other, non-Hispanic[3]	44.9	38.1	36.1	31.1

[1] Reflects revised interviewing techniques and/or change in population controls to the 1990 Census-based estimates.
[2] Persons of Hispanic origin may be of any race. [3] Includes mostly Asian/Pacific Islanders, but also American Indian/Alaska Native children. [4] For composition of regions, see map, inside front cover.

Source: Federal Interagency Forum on Child and Family Statistics, *America's Children: National Indicators of Well-Being*, 1998.

No. 273. Preprimary School Enrollment—Summary: 1970 to 1997

[As of October. Civilian noninstitutional population (10,949 represents 10,949,000). Includes public and nonpublic nursery school and kindergarten programs. Excludes 5 year olds enrolled in elementary school. Based on Current Population Survey; see text, Section 1, Population and Appendix III]

Item	1970	1975	1980	1985	1990	1994	1995	1996	1997
NUMBER OF CHILDREN (1,000)									
Population, 3 to 5 years old	10,949	10,183	9,284	10,733	11,207	12,328	12,518	12,378	12,121
Total enrolled[1]	4,104	4,954	4,878	5,865	6,659	7,514	7,739	7,580	7,861
Nursery	1,094	1,745	1,981	2,477	3,378	4,162	4,331	4,147	4,438
Public	332	570	628	846	1,202	1,848	1,950	1,830	2,207
Private	762	1,174	1,353	1,631	2,177	2,314	2,381	2,317	2,231
Kindergarten	3,010	3,211	2,897	3,388	3,281	3,352	3,408	3,433	3,422
Public	2,498	2,682	2,438	2,847	2,767	2,819	2,799	2,853	2,847
Private	511	528	459	541	513	534	608	580	575
White	3,443	4,105	3,994	4,757	5,389	5,889	6,144	5,902	6,086
Black	586	731	725	919	964	1,289	1,236	1,245	1,356
Hispanic[2]	(NA)	(NA)	370	496	642	851	1,040	1,068	1,142
3 years old	454	683	857	1,035	1,205	1,385	1,489	1,506	1,529
4 years old	1,007	1,418	1,423	1,765	2,086	2,532	2,553	2,454	2,665
5 years old	2,643	2,852	2,598	3,065	3,367	3,597	3,697	3,621	3,667
ENROLLMENT RATE									
Total enrolled[1]	37.5	48.6	52.5	54.6	59.4	61.0	61.8	61.2	64.8
White	37.8	48.6	52.7	54.7	59.7	60.9	63.0	61.2	64.1
Black	34.9	48.1	51.8	55.8	57.8	64.2	58.9	60.8	68.6
Hispanic[2]	(NA)	(NA)	43.3	43.3	49.0	47.7	51.1	52.7	52.5
3 years old	12.9	21.5	27.3	28.8	32.6	33.9	35.9	37.2	38.7
4 years old	27.8	40.5	46.3	49.1	56.0	60.3	61.6	59.2	66.1
5 years old	69.3	81.3	84.7	86.5	88.8	88.9	87.5	86.5	88.6

NA Not available. [1] Includes races not shown separately. [2] Persons of Hispanic origin may be of any race. The method of identifying Hispanic children was changed in 1980 from allocation based on status of mother to status reported for each child. The number of Hispanic children using the new method is larger.

Source: U.S. Census Bureau, *Current Population Reports*, P20-516.

174 Education

No. 274. Public Elementary and Secondary Schools—Summary: 1980 to 1998

[For school year ending in year shown, except as indicated (48,041 represents 48,041,000). Data are estimates]

Item	Unit	1980	1985	1990	1995	1996	1997	1998
School districts, total	Number . . .	16,044	15,812	15,552	14,947	14,910	14,891	14,822
ENROLLMENT								
Population 5-17 years old [1]	1,000	48,041	44,787	44,949	48,196	49,014	49,807	50,491
Percent of resident population	Percent . . .	21.4	19.0	18.2	18.5	18.7	18.8	18.9
Fall enrollment [2]	1,000	41,778	39,354	40,527	43,898	44,649	45,344	45,924
Percent of population 5-17 years old	Percent . . .	87.0	87.9	90.2	91.1	91.1	91.0	91.0
Elementary [3]	1,000	24,397	23,830	26,253	28,148	28,581	28,925	29,241
Secondary [4]	1,000	17,381	15,524	14,274	15,750	16,068	16,419	16,682
Average daily attendance (ADA)	1,000	38,411	36,530	37,573	40,794	41,477	42,143	42,764
High school graduates	1,000	2,762	2,424	2,327	2,282	2,283	2,336	2,377
INSTRUCTIONAL STAFF								
Total [5]	1,000	2,521	2,473	2,685	2,929	2,970	3,042	3,087
Classroom teachers	1,000	2,211	2,175	2,362	2,567	2,606	2,668	2,705
Average salaries:								
Instructional staff	Dollar	16,715	24,666	32,638	38,331	39,465	40,562	41,598
Classroom teachers	Dollar	15,970	23,600	31,367	36,685	37,716	38,554	39,385
REVENUES								
Revenue receipts	Mil. dol . . .	97,635	141,013	208,656	273,364	286,927	301,404	314,187
Federal	Mil. dol . . .	9,020	9,533	13,184	18,766	19,323	20,387	21,338
State	Mil. dol . . .	47,929	69,107	100,787	130,139	138,045	147,396	155,321
Local	Mil. dol . . .	40,686	62,373	94,685	124,459	129,560	133,621	137,528
Percent of total:								
Federal	Percent . . .	9.2	6.8	6.3	6.9	6.7	6.8	6.8
State	Percent . . .	49.1	49.0	48.3	47.6	48.1	48.9	49.4
Local	Percent . . .	41.7	44.2	45.4	45.5	45.2	44.3	43.8
EXPENDITURES								
Total	Mil. dol . . .	96,105	139,382	209,698	276,502	292,323	308,077	323,879
Current expenditures (day schools)	Mil. dol . . .	85,661	127,230	186,583	242,729	254,254	268,026	280,023
Other current expenditures [6]	Mil. dol . . .	1,859	2,109	3,341	5,464	5,902	6,397	6,619
Capital outlay	Mil. dol . . .	6,504	7,529	16,012	21,904	25,189	25,849	29,132
Interest on school debt	Mil. dol . . .	2,081	2,514	3,762	6,406	6,978	7,806	8,104
Percent of total:								
Current expenditures (day schools)	Percent . . .	89.1	91.3	89.0	87.8	87.0	87.0	86.5
Other current expenditures [6]	Percent . . .	1.9	1.5	1.6	2.0	2.0	2.1	2.0
Capital outlay	Percent . . .	6.8	5.4	7.6	7.9	8.6	8.4	9.0
Interest on school debt	Percent . . .	2.2	1.8	1.8	2.3	2.4	2.5	2.5
In current dollars:								
Revenue receipts per pupil enrolled	Dollar	2,337	3,583	5,149	6,227	6,426	6,647	6,842
Current expenditures per pupil enrolled	Dollar	2,050	3,233	4,604	5,529	5,695	5,911	6,098
In constant (1998) dollars: [7]								
Revenue receipts per pupil enrolled	Dollar	4,870	5,476	6,555	6,695	6,726	6,764	6,842
Current expenditures per pupil enrolled	Dollar	4,273	4,941	5,862	5,945	5,960	6,015	6,098

[1] Estimated resident population as of July 1 of the previous year. Estimates reflect revisions based on the 1990 Census of Population.   [2] Fall enrollment of the previous year.   [3] Kindergarten through grade 6.   [4] Grades 7 through 12.   [5] Full-time equivalent.   [6] Current expenses for summer schools, adult education, post-high school vocational education, personnel retraining, etc., when operated by local school districts and not part of regular public elementary and secondary day-school program.   [7] Compiled by U.S. Census Bureau. Deflated by the Consumer Price Index, all urban consumers (for school year) supplied by U.S. National Center for Education Statistics.

Source: Except as noted, National Education Association, Washington, DC, Estimates of School Statistics Database (copyright).

U.S. Census Bureau, Statistical Abstract of the United States: 1999

No. 275. Elementary and Secondary Schools—Teachers and Pupil-Teacher Ratios With Projections: 1960 to 1998

[In thousands (1,600 represents 1,600,000), except ratios. As of **fall.** Data are for full-time equivalents. Schools are classified by type of organization, rather than by grade group; elementary includes kindergarten and secondary includes junior high]

Item	Total			Public			Private		
	Total	Elementary	Secondary	Total	Elementary	Secondary	Total	Elementary	Secondary
Number of teachers:									
1960	1,600	991	609	1,408	858	550	192	133	59
1970	2,292	1,283	1,009	2,059	1,130	929	233	153	80
1975	2,453	1,353	1,100	2,198	1,181	1,017	255	172	83
1980	2,485	1,401	1,084	2,184	1,189	995	301	212	89
1985	2,549	1,483	1,066	2,206	1,237	969	343	246	97
1988	2,668	1,604	1,064	2,323	1,353	970	345	251	94
1989	2,734	1,662	1,072	2,357	1,387	970	377	275	102
1990	2,753	1,680	1,073	2,398	1,426	972	355	254	101
1991	2,787	1,713	1,074	2,432	1,459	973	355	254	101
1992	2,822	1,752	1,070	2,459	1,492	967	363	260	103
1993	2,870	1,775	1,095	2,504	1,513	991	366	262	104
1994	2,926	1,794	1,132	2,552	1,528	1,024	373	266	108
1995	2,978	1,814	1,164	2,598	1,546	1,053	380	269	111
1996	3,053	1,856	1,197	2,666	1,582	1,084	387	274	113
1997, prel.	3,103	1,882	1,222	2,710	1,604	1,106	394	278	116
1998, proj.	3,126	1,894	1,233	2,728	1,612	1,116	399	281	117
Pupil-teacher ratio:									
1960	26.4	29.4	21.4	25.8	28.4	21.7	30.7	36.1	18.6
1970	22.4	24.6	19.5	22.3	24.3	19.8	23.0	26.5	16.4
1975	20.3	21.7	18.6	20.4	21.7	18.8	19.6	21.5	15.7
1980	18.6	20.1	16.6	18.7	20.4	16.8	17.7	18.8	15.0
1985	17.6	19.1	15.6	17.9	19.5	15.8	16.2	17.1	14.0
1988	17.0	18.6	14.7	17.3	19.0	14.9	15.2	16.1	12.8
1989	16.8	18.4	14.3	17.2	19.0	14.6	14.2	15.1	11.7
1990	16.9	18.5	14.3	17.2	19.0	14.6	14.7	16.1	11.3
1991	17.0	18.5	14.5	17.3	18.9	14.9	14.6	16.0	11.1
1992	17.1	18.4	14.8	17.4	18.8	15.2	14.8	16.2	11.3
1993	17.1	18.5	14.7	17.4	18.9	15.1	14.9	16.3	11.5
1994	17.1	18.6	14.7	17.3	18.9	15.1	15.0	16.4	11.4
1995	17.0	18.6	14.5	17.3	18.9	14.8	15.0	16.5	11.4
1996	16.8	18.4	14.3	17.1	18.8	14.6	14.9	16.4	11.5
1997, prel.	16.7	18.3	14.2	17.0	18.6	14.5	14.9	16.3	11.4
1998, proj.	16.9	18.5	14.4	17.2	18.9	14.7	14.9	16.3	11.4

Source: U.S. National Center for Education Statistics, *Digest of Education Statistics,* annual.

No. 276. Public Elementary and Secondary Schools, by Type and Size of School: 1996-97

[Enrollment in thousands (45,365 represents 45,365,000). Data reported by schools, rather than school districts]

Enrollment size of school	Number of schools					Enrollment [1]				
	Total	Elementary [2]	Secondary [3]	Combined [4]	Other [5]	Total	Elementary [2]	Secondary [3]	Combined [4]	Other [5]
Total	88,223	61,805	21,307	2,980	2,131	45,365	29,572	14,564	1,152	76
PERCENT										
Total	100.0	100.0	100.0	100.0	100.0	100.0	100.0	100.0	100.0	100.0
Under 100 students	9.2	6.0	14.3	31.5	60.0	0.8	0.6	1.0	3.6	19.4
100 to 199 students	9.4	8.7	10.5	15.2	18.7	2.7	2.8	2.2	5.7	19.3
200 to 299 students	11.3	12.2	8.6	10.3	10.8	5.4	6.5	3.0	6.4	19.3
300 to 399 students	13.2	15.4	7.7	7.8	6.0	8.8	11.2	3.8	7.0	15.1
400 to 499 students	13.2	15.8	6.9	6.5	2.0	11.3	14.8	4.4	7.5	6.3
500 to 599 students	11.8	13.8	6.7	6.5	0.5	12.2	15.8	5.2	9.2	2.1
600 to 699 students	8.8	9.9	6.2	5.6	-	10.8	13.3	5.8	9.3	-
700 to 799 students	6.2	6.6	5.2	3.5	0.4	8.7	10.4	5.6	6.7	2.0
800 to 999 students	7.4	7.1	8.8	5.2	0.5	12.5	13.2	11.2	12.1	3.4
1,000 to 1,499 students	6.2	4.0	13.3	4.9	0.7	14.1	9.6	23.1	15.2	6.5
1,500 to 1,999 students	2.0	0.4	6.8	1.9	0.2	6.5	1.4	16.7	8.4	2.1
2,000 to 2,999 students	1.1	0.1	4.3	0.8	-	5.0	0.4	14.3	5.1	-
3,000 or more students	0.2	-	0.8	0.3	0.2	1.4	-	3.8	3.8	4.5
Average enrollment	(X)	(X)	(X)	(X)	(X)	527	478	703	387	135

- Represents zero. X Not applicable. [1] Data for those schools reporting enrollment. [2] Includes schools beginning with grade 6 or below and with no grade higher than 8. [3] Includes schools with no grade lower than 7. [4] Includes schools with both elementary and secondary grades. [5] Includes special education, alternative, and other schools not classified by grade span.

Source: U.S. National Center for Education Statistics, *Digest of Education Statistics,* annual.

No. 277. Public Elementary and Secondary School Enrollment, by State: 1980 to 1996

[In thousands (27,647 represents 27,647,000), except rate. As of fall. Includes unclassified students]

State	K through grade 8 [1]				Grades 9 through 12				Enrollment rate [2]			
	1980	1985	1990	1996, prel.	1980	1985	1990	1996, prel.	1980	1985	1990	1996, prel.
United States ...	27,647	27,034	29,878	32,759	13,231	12,388	11,338	12,834	86.2	87.7	91.3	91.7
Alabama.........	528	517	527	540	231	213	195	208	87.6	89.6	93.3	95.8
Alaska..........	60	77	85	94	26	30	29	36	94.0	99.4	97.4	95.4
Arizona.........	357	386	479	588	157	162	161	211	88.9	90.8	93.3	95.4
Arkansas........	310	304	314	324	138	130	123	133	90.3	91.8	95.9	92.5
California	2,730	2,927	3,615	4,131	1,347	1,329	1,336	1,557	87.1	89.5	92.8	92.4
Colorado........	374	379	420	487	172	172	154	186	92.2	92.7	94.6	93.1
Connecticut......	364	321	347	389	168	141	122	138	83.3	83.4	90.2	92.6
Delaware........	62	63	73	78	37	30	27	33	79.5	80.1	87.4	87.1
District of Columbia .	71	62	61	61	29	25	19	18	91.8	96.8	100.9	105.7
Florida..........	1,042	1,086	1,370	1,653	468	476	492	589	84.4	86.7	92.6	91.3
Georgia.........	742	757	849	991	327	323	303	356	86.8	88.2	93.6	96.3
Hawaii	110	113	123	136	55	51	49	51	83.4	84.2	87.6	87.9
Idaho..........	144	149	160	169	59	59	61	76	95.4	93.6	96.9	95.4
Illinois.........	1,335	1,246	1,310	1,412	649	580	512	561	82.6	83.3	86.9	88.1
Indiana.........	708	654	676	690	347	312	279	294	88.0	88.4	90.4	90.7
Iowa	351	324	345	342	183	161	139	161	88.4	89.1	92.1	93.2
Kansas.........	283	286	320	328	133	125	117	138	88.7	91.0	92.6	92.2
Kentucky	464	449	459	466	206	195	177	190	83.7	85.8	90.5	92.8
Louisiana.......	544	573	586	575	234	215	199	218	80.2	83.9	88.2	89.3
Maine..........	153	142	155	156	70	64	60	58	91.6	93.3	96.5	93.8
Maryland	493	446	527	597	258	225	188	222	83.9	84.9	89.1	89.8
Massachusetts....	676	559	604	688	346	285	230	246	88.6	86.3	88.8	90.3
Michigan........	1,227	1,086	1,145	1,222	570	517	440	463	86.9	87.8	90.3	91.1
Minnesota.......	482	468	546	589	272	237	211	258	87.2	89.4	91.2	91.6
Mississippi	330	330	372	364	147	141	131	140	79.6	81.0	91.3	91.4
Missouri........	567	544	588	643	277	251	228	257	83.8	84.9	86.5	87.7
Montana........	106	108	111	115	50	46	42	50	92.9	93.8	93.8	93.8
Nebraska.......	189	184	198	203	91	82	76	89	86.6	87.7	88.7	89.0
Nevada	101	107	150	208	49	48	51	74	93.4	93.3	98.7	96.0
New Hampshire....	112	107	126	144	55	54	46	54	85.3	87.5	89.1	90.5
New Jersey.......	820	740	784	884	426	376	306	324	81.5	82.9	86.1	85.8
New Mexico	186	187	208	230	85	90	94	103	89.5	91.6	94.3	91.9
New York	1,838	1,703	1,828	2,000	1,033	918	770	843	80.8	82.3	86.6	88.5
North Carolina.....	786	749	783	886	343	337	304	324	90.1	91.2	94.8	91.9
North Dakota.....	77	84	85	82	40	35	33	38	85.9	89.2	92.8	95.6
Ohio	1,312	1,206	1,258	1,299	645	588	514	546	84.8	85.6	88.0	88.3
Oklahoma.......	399	414	425	445	179	178	154	175	92.9	94.3	95.1	95.9
Oregon.........	319	305	340	380	145	142	132	158	88.5	89.7	90.7	90.9
Pennsylvania.....	1,231	1,093	1,172	1,264	678	591	496	541	80.4	80.3	83.6	85.2
Rhode Island.....	98	90	102	110	51	44	37	41	80.1	81.2	87.3	88.6
South Carolina	426	424	452	468	193	183	170	185	88.1	89.6	94.0	94.3
South Dakota	86	88	95	99	42	37	34	44	87.4	90.7	89.7	95.4
Tennessee	602	575	598	658	252	239	226	248	87.8	88.3	93.5	94.9
Texas..........	2,049	2,261	2,511	2,800	851	871	872	1,029	92.4	93.2	98.4	98.7
Utah	250	299	325	328	93	105	122	154	98.2	96.3	97.7	98.2
Vermont........	66	63	71	76	29	27	25	30	87.9	89.3	93.9	96.5
Virginia........	703	665	728	796	307	303	270	300	90.7	94.0	94.2	93.5
Washington......	515	507	613	687	242	243	227	287	91.7	92.2	94.0	93.1
West Virginia.....	270	249	224	209	113	109	98	95	92.6	92.2	95.7	96.9
Wisconsin.......	528	501	566	605	303	267	232	274	82.1	83.8	86.0	87.5
Wyoming	70	74	71	67	28	29	27	32	97.3	97.0	97.3	97.4

[1] Data include a small number of prekindergarten students. [2] Percent of persons 5-17 years old. Based on enumerated resident population as of April 1, 1980, and 1990, and estimated resident population as of July 1 for other years. Data not adjusted for revisions based on the 1990 Census of Population.

Source: U.S. National Center for Education Statistics, *Digest of Education Statistics*, annual.

U.S. Census Bureau, Statistical Abstract of the United States: 1999

No. 278. Public Elementary and Secondary School Enrollment, by Grade: 1980 to 1996

[In thousands (40,877 represents 40,877,000). As of fall of year. Kindergarten includes nursery schools]

Grade	1980	1985	1988	1989	1990	1991	1992	1993	1994	1995	1996, prel.
Pupils enrolled	40,877	39,422	40,189	40,543	41,217	42,047	42,823	43,465	44,111	44,840	45,592
Kindergarten and grades 1 to 8 .	27,647	27,034	28,501	29,152	29,878	30,506	31,088	31,504	31,898	32,341	32,759
Kindergarten	2,689	3,192	3,433	3,486	3,610	3,686	3,817	3,922	4,047	4,173	4,208
First	2,894	3,239	3,460	3,485	3,499	3,556	3,542	3,529	3,593	3,671	3,769
Second................	2,800	2,941	3,223	3,289	3,327	3,360	3,431	3,429	3,440	3,507	3,596
Third	2,893	2,895	3,167	3,235	3,297	3,334	3,361	3,437	3,439	3,445	3,518
Fourth	3,107	2,771	3,051	3,182	3,248	3,315	3,342	3,361	3,426	3,431	3,447
Fifth	3,130	2,776	2,945	3,067	3,197	3,268	3,325	3,350	3,372	3,438	3,447
Sixth	3,038	2,789	2,937	2,987	3,110	3,239	3,303	3,356	3,381	3,395	3,486
Seventh	3,085	2,938	2,905	3,027	3,067	3,181	3,299	3,355	3,404	3,422	3,457
Eighth	3,086	2,982	2,853	2,853	2,979	3,020	3,129	3,249	3,302	3,356	3,398
Unclassified [1].........	924	511	527	540	543	545	539	515	494	502	434
Grades 9 to 12	13,231	12,388	11,687	11,390	11,338	11,541	11,735	11,961	12,213	12,500	12,834
Ninth	3,377	3,439	3,106	3,141	3,169	3,313	3,352	3,487	3,604	3,704	3,793
Tenth	3,368	3,230	2,895	2,868	2,896	2,915	3,027	3,050	3,131	3,237	3,316
Eleventh	3,195	2,866	2,749	2,629	2,612	2,645	2,656	2,751	2,748	2,826	2,925
Twelfth	2,925	2,550	2,650	2,473	2,381	2,392	2,431	2,424	2,488	2,487	2,582
Unclassified [1].........	366	303	288	279	282	275	269	248	242	245	218

[1] Includes ungraded and special education.

Source: U.S. National Center for Education Statistics, *Digest of Education Statistics,* annual.

No. 279. Public Elementary and Secondary School Teachers— Selected Characteristics: 1993-94

[For school year. (280 represents 280,000) Based on survey and subject to sampling error; for details, see source. Excludes prekindergarten teachers. See Table 295 for similar data on private school teachers]

Characteristic	Unit	Age				Sex		Race/ethnicity		
		Under 30 years old	30 to 39 years old	40 to 49 years old	Over 50 years old	Male	Female	White [1]	Black [1]	Hispanic
Total teachers [2]	1,000 ..	280	573	1,070	637	694	1,867	2,217	188	109
Highest degree held:										
Bachelor's	Percent .	83.9	59.4	46.3	40.9	46.2	54.1	51.8	48.4	62.8
Master's	Percent .	14.5	36.6	47.0	50.4	45.7	40.6	42.5	44.6	29.8
Education specialist......	Percent .	1.0	3.0	5.4	6.1	5.1	4.4	4.4	5.4	4.6
Doctorate	Percent .	0.1	0.3	0.7	1.4	1.3	0.5	0.7	0.9	1.4
Full-time teaching experience:										
Less than 3 years	Percent .	47.8	10.5	4.3	1.3	8.9	10.0	9.4	8.5	16.7
3 to 9 years	Percent .	52.2	48.7	16.9	7.3	21.6	26.9	25.5	20.8	32.1
10 to 20 years	Percent .	(X)	40.8	47.5	24.2	29.9	37.0	35.1	35.5	34.1
20 years or more	Percent .	(X)	(X)	31.3	67.1	39.6	26.1	30.0	35.2	17.1
Full-time teachers........	1,000 ..	259	518	974	590	643	1,698	2,012	182	103
Earned income.........	Dol. ...	27,151	31,596	38,106	42,243	41,031	34,781	36,576	36,200	35,197
Salary..............	Dol. ...	24,737	29,270	35,751	39,931	36,182	33,384	34,221	33,889	32,996
Supplemental contract during school year:										
Teachers receiving	1,000 ..	114	205	329	168	349	467	723	49	32
Salary..............	Dol. ...	1,777	2,163	2,107	2,109	2,923	1,442	2,067	2,325	1,930
Supplemental contract during summer:										
Teachers receiving	1,000 ..	52	102	161	86	147	254	328	41	24
Salary..............	Dol. ...	1,819	1,942	2,053	2,404	2,530	1,803	2,015	2,221	2,477
Teachers with nonschool employment:										
Teaching/tutoring	1,000 ..	12	25	50	32	37	81	100	11	6
Education related	1,000 ..	8	20	34	18	39	41	69	5	4
Not education related	1,000 ..	28	50	101	59	124	113	208	16	7

X Not applicable.   [1] Non-Hispanic.   [2] Includes teachers with no degrees and associates degrees, not shown separately.

Source: U.S. National Center for Education Statistics, *Digest of Education Statistics,* 1997; and unpublished data.

No. 280. Newly Hired Teachers, by Selected Characteristics: 1988 to 1994

[In percent. Based on sample and subject to sampling error; see source for details]

Characteristic	Public schools			Private schools		
	1988	1991	1994	1988	1991	1994
Total newly hired teachers	100.0	100.0	100.0	100.0	100.0	100.0
First-time teachers	30.6	41.7	45.8	25.2	34.0	42.4
Transfers.	36.6	34.3	31.4	38.1	36.1	34.3
Within state and sector.	20.8	21.6	20.2	19.0	18.1	14.6
Across state	8.3	7.1	7.1	8.3	7.0	11.5
Across sector	7.5	5.6	4.1	10.9	11.0	8.1
Reentrants	32.8	24.0	22.9	36.7	30.0	23.3
Main previous year activity:						
First-time teachers.	100.0	100.0	100.0	100.0	100.0	100.0
Work in education (nonteaching).	5.7	5.2	10.7	4.8	7.5	13.6
Work outside education.	11.0	10.0	11.6	24.5	20.6	19.9
College	66.5	58.4	56.7	51.8	48.7	43.1
Homemaking and childrearing	3.6	4.4	2.1	7.7	5.8	5.8
Other.	13.3	22.0	18.9	11.3	17.4	17.6
Substitute teaching	(NA)	18.0	17.2	(NA)	12.0	15.2
Reentrants.	100.0	100.0	100.0	100.0	100.0	100.0
Work in education (nonteaching).	10.3	19.1	15.0	8.9	11.7	19.9
Work outside education.	17.4	17.9	19.2	21.2	26.1	26.0
College	18.0	10.4	18.1	20.0	5.6	11.9
Homemaking and childrearing	27.8	19.3	14.6	28.6	23.1	21.4
Other.	26.5	33.3	33.1	21.3	33.6	20.9
Substitute teaching	(NA)	23.8	29.6	(NA)	18.7	18.1

NA Not available.

Source: U.S. Department of Education, National Center for Education Statistics, *Condition of Education, 1996*.

No. 281. Public Elementary and Secondary Schools—Number and Average Salary of Classroom Teachers, 1970 to 1998, and by State, 1998

[Estimates for school year ending in **June of year shown (2,008 represents 2,008,000)**. Schools classified by type of organization rather than by grade-group; elementary includes kindergarten]

Year and state	Teachers [1] (1,000)			Avg. salary ($1,000)			Year and state	Teachers [1] (1,000)			Avg. salary ($1,000)		
	Total	Elementary	Secondary	All teachers	Elementary	Secondary		Total	Elementary	Secondary	All teachers	Elementary	Secondary
1970	2,008	1,109	899	8.6	8.4	8.9	LA.	48.7	34.5	14.2	29.7	29.7	29.7
1975	2,171	1,169	1,001	11.7	11.3	12.0	ME	14.8	10.3	4.6	34.3	34.0	35.2
1980	2,211	1,206	1,005	16.0	15.6	16.5	MD	47.8	27.0	20.8	41.7	40.8	42.9
1985	2,175	1,212	963	23.6	23.2	24.2	MA	63.3	27.2	36.1	43.9	43.9	43.9
1988	2,282	1,308	974	28.0	27.5	28.8	MI	87.1	63.3	23.8	49.3	49.3	49.3
1989	2,324	1,354	970	29.6	29.0	30.2	MN	49.8	26.8	22.9	39.1	39.3	38.8
1990	2,362	1,390	972	31.4	30.8	32.0	MS	29.5	15.5	14.0	29.5	28.3	29.2
1991	2,409	1,435	974	33.1	32.5	33.9	MO	60.4	13.4	47.0	34.0	33.5	34.7
1992	2,429	1,466	963	34.1	33.5	34.8	MT	10.3	7.0	3.3	30.6	30.3	31.4
1993	2,466	1,496	970	35.0	34.4	35.9	NE	19.9	11.7	8.2	32.7	32.7	32.7
1994	2,512	1,517	995	35.7	35.2	36.6	NV.	15.7	9.3	6.4	37.1	36.8	37.5
1995	2,567	1,535	1,033	36.7	36.2	37.5	NH	12.6	8.8	3.9	36.6	36.6	36.6
1996	2,606	1,559	1,047	37.7	37.3	38.4	NJ	91.2	57.5	33.7	50.4	49.4	52.3
1997	2,668	1,607	1,061	38.6	38.2	39.1	NM	19.8	14.2	5.6	30.2	30.0	31.0
1998, U.S..	**2,705**	**1,608**	**1,097**	**39.4**	**39.1**	**39.9**	NY.	197.2	98.8	98.4	49.0	48.0	50.3
AL.	45.9	27.4	18.6	32.8	32.8	32.8	NC	76.8	47.8	29.0	33.3	33.2	33.6
AK.	8.2	5.2	3.0	51.7	51.7	51.7	ND	7.9	5.1	2.9	28.2	28.4	27.9
AZ.	41.8	32.2	9.6	34.4	33.9	33.9	OH	108.2	72.2	36.1	39.0	38.6	39.8
AR.	27.5	13.5	14.0	30.6	29.7	31.4	OK	40.5	21.1	19.3	30.6	30.5	30.8
CA.	239.6	176.2	63.4	43.7	43.2	45.2	OR	27.5	18.2	9.3	42.2	41.8	42.7
CO	36.8	18.6	18.2	37.1	36.9	37.2	PA.	106.5	54.7	51.8	47.7	47.1	48.2
CT.	38.2	27.3	10.9	50.7	50.5	52.3	RI	11.1	6.3	4.7	44.3	44.2	44.4
DE.	6.9	3.4	3.5	42.4	42.5	42.4	SC.	39.9	27.6	12.3	33.6	33.3	34.2
DC	5.7	3.4	2.3	46.4	46.8	47.7	SD.	9.5	6.7	2.8	27.3	27.4	27.1
FL.	126.4	64.5	61.9	34.5	34.5	34.5	TN.	52.0	37.8	14.2	35.3	35.0	36.4
GA	85.6	50.5	35.1	37.4	36.9	38.1	TX.	254.8	132.5	122.2	33.6	32.9	34.5
HI	10.9	6.1	4.9	38.4	38.4	38.4	UT.	21.1	11.0	10.0	33.0	33.1	33.1
ID	13.4	6.8	6.6	32.8	32.7	32.8	VT.	7.7	4.0	3.7	36.3	37.0	35.6
IL	119.6	84.1	35.5	43.9	42.0	48.1	VA.	77.6	47.8	29.9	36.7	35.5	38.2
IN	56.6	30.4	26.2	39.7	39.8	39.5	WA	48.9	28.0	21.0	38.8	38.8	38.8
IA	33.0	15.3	17.7	34.0	33.2	34.8	WV	20.8	12.5	8.3	33.4	33.1	33.8
KS.	31.5	16.5	15.0	36.8	36.8	36.8	WI	53.9	37.6	16.2	39.9	39.5	40.7
KY.	37.9	26.7	11.1	34.5	34.2	35.8	WY	6.7	3.3	3.4	32.0	32.2	31.9

[1] Full-time equivalent.

Source: National Education Association, Washington, DC, *Estimates of School Statistics Database* (copyright).

U.S. Census Bureau, *Statistical Abstract of the United States: 1999*

No. 282. Average Salary and Wages Paid in Public School Systems: 1980 to 1998

[**In dollars.** For school year ending in year shown. Data reported by a stratified sample of school systems enrolling 300 or more pupils. Data represent unweighted means of average salaries paid school personnel reported by each school system]

Position	1980	1985	1990	1993	1994	1995	1996	1997	1998
ANNUAL SALARY									
Central office administrators:									
Superintendent (contract salary) . . .	39,344	56,954	75,425	85,120	87,717	90,198	94,229	98,106	101,519
Deputy/assoc. superintendent	37,440	52,877	69,623	77,057	78,672	81,266	84,077	88,564	90,226
Assistant superintendent	33,452	48,003	62,698	70,525	72,701	75,236	77,007	80,176	82,339
Administrators for—									
Finance and business	27,147	40,344	52,354	57,864	59,997	61,323	63,840	65,797	67,724
Instructional services	29,790	43,452	56,359	62,508	64,676	66,767	68,463	70,788	73,058
Public relations/information	24,021	35,287	44,926	50,622	52,366	53,263	53,860	55,928	57,224
Staff personnel services	29,623	44,182	56,344	62,162	63,690	65,819	67,760	70,088	71,073
Subject area supervisors	23,974	34,422	45,929	51,407	52,837	54,534	56,145	58,776	60,359
School building administrators:									
Principals:									
Elementary.	25,165	36,452	48,431	54,905	56,906	58,589	60,922	62,903	64,653
Junior high/middle	27,625	39,650	52,163	58,620	60,651	62,311	64,452	66,859	68,740
Senior high.	29,207	42,094	55,722	63,054	64,993	66,596	69,277	72,410	74,380
Assistant principals:									
Elementary.	20,708	30,496	40,916	45,377	47,057	48,491	50,537	52,284	53,206
Junior high/middle	23,507	33,793	44,570	49,925	51,518	52,942	54,355	56,451	57,768
Senior high.	24,816	35,491	46,486	52,348	54,170	55,556	57,555	59,739	60,999
Classroom teachers.	15,913	23,587	31,278	35,291	36,531	37,264	38,706	39,580	40,133
Auxiliary professional personnel:									
Counselors	18,847	27,593	35,979	40,413	41,355	42,486	44,073	45,365	46,162
Librarians	16,764	24,981	33,469	37,945	39,319	40,418	41,761	43,315	44,310
School nurses	13,788	19,944	26,090	29,555	30,630	31,066	32,786	33,720	34,619
Secretarial/clerical personnel:									
Central office:									
Secretaries.	10,331	15,343	20,238	22,770	23,495	23,935	24,809	25,709	26,316
Accounting/payroll clerks.	10,479	15,421	20,088	22,605	23,275	24,042	25,009	25,881	26,249
Typists/data entry clerks	8,359	12,481	16,125	17,772	18,296	18,674	19,447	20,726	21,633
School building level:									
Secretaries.	8,348	12,504	16,184	18,104	18,692	19,170	20,076	20,709	21,215
Library clerks	6,778	9,911	12,152	13,311	13,809	14,381	14,791	15,349	15,742
HOURLY WAGE RATE									
Other support personnel:									
Teacher aides:									
Instructional	4.06	5.89	7.43	8.31	8.50	8.77	9.04	9.25	9.46
Noninstructional	3.89	5.60	7.08	7.82	8.14	8.29	8.52	8.88	8.82
Custodians	4.88	6.90	8.54	9.51	9.76	10.05	10.35	10.65	10.79
Cafeteria workers	3.78	5.42	6.77	7.56	7.72	7.89	8.15	8.30	8.56
Bus drivers	5.21	7.27	9.21	10.15	10.35	10.69	11.04	11.50	11.55

Source: Educational Research Service, Arlington, VA, *National Survey of Salaries and Wages in Public Schools*, annual, Vols. 2 and 3. (All rights reserved. Copyright.)

No. 283. Public School Employment: 1982 and 1996

[**In thousands (3,082 represents 3,082,000).** Covers full-time employment. Excludes Hawaii. 1982 also excludes District of Columbia and New Jersey. 1982 based on sample survey of school districts with 250 or more students. 1996 based on sample survey of school districts with 100 or more employees; see source for sampling variability]

Occupation	1982					1996				
	Total	Male	Female	White [1]	Black [1]	Total	Male	Female	White [1]	Black [1]
All occupations	**3,082**	**1,063**	**2,019**	**2,498**	**432**	**3,718**	**1,013**	**2,705**	**2,915**	**506**
Officials, administrators	41	31	10	36	3	47	27	19	39	5
Principals and assistant										
principals.	90	72	19	76	11	101	55	45	79	15
Classroom teachers [2]	1,680	534	1,146	1,435	186	2,051	522	1,529	1,735	198
Elementary schools	798	129	669	667	98	1,024	137	887	854	101
Secondary schools	706	363	343	619	67	755	324	431	651	69
Other professional staff	235	91	144	193	35	263	60	203	219	30
Teachers aides [3]	215	14	200	146	45	365	38	327	238	78
Clerical, secretarial staff.	210	4	206	177	19	258	6	252	200	29
Service workers [4]	611	316	295	434	132	633	304	330	407	151

[1] Excludes individuals of Hispanic origin. [2] Includes other classroom teachers, not shown separately. [3] Includes technicians. [4] Includes craftworkers and laborers.

Source: U.S. Equal Employment Opportunity Commission, *Elementary-Secondary Staff Information (EEO-5)*, biennial.

No. 284. Public Elementary and Secondary School Price Indexes: 1975 to 1997

[**1983=100**. For years ending **June 30**. Reflects prices paid by public elementary-secondary schools. For explanation of average annual percent change, see Guide to Tabular Presentation]

Year	Personnel compensation					Contracted services, supplies and equipment						
	Index, total	Total	Profes-sional salaries	Nonpro-fessional salaries	Fringe benefits	Total	Serv-ices	Sup-plies and materi-als	Equip-ment replace-ment	Library materi-als and text-books	Utilities	Fixed costs
1975 ..	52.7	53.4	56.0	55.6	40.9	50.4	55.7	58.0	53.7	53.8	34.5	45.2
1980 ..	76.6	75.9	76.7	77.8	71.0	79.2	77.4	85.9	79.6	82.1	71.1	77.9
1984 ..	105.0	106.0	105.7	104.5	108.3	101.7	105.6	99.6	103.4	107.8	94.3	105.4
1985 ..	112.0	113.7	113.4	111.3	117.1	105.5	112.4	103.2	107.2	111.0	96.1	110.8
1986 ..	118.5	121.1	121.4	117.6	123.3	108.3	117.4	103.0	109.3	120.8	93.7	116.2
1987 ..	123.3	127.4	128.4	121.9	128.8	107.5	123.7	101.5	112.9	126.5	75.3	122.7
1988 ..	129.8	134.5	135.5	127.5	137.0	111.8	126.1	105.9	113.4	140.0	78.1	128.4
1989 ..	136.3	141.6	142.2	133.3	147.0	116.2	131.8	112.0	116.0	149.4	75.1	134.6
1990 ..	144.3	150.0	150.1	139.4	159.3	122.6	137.7	119.2	121.2	171.7	82.1	140.3
1991 ..	152.3	158.3	158.1	146.5	169.8	129.7	142.5	122.7	125.7	189.4	92.6	144.9
1992 ..	158.5	165.4	165.8	152.4	175.8	132.0	148.0	122.5	128.5	199.0	90.8	148.9
1993 ..	162.2	169.6	169.2	155.1	184.5	133.9	151.5	121.9	131.8	205.6	90.4	153.8
1994 ..	167.1	175.1	175.1	159.3	190.2	136.5	154.0	122.7	135.4	218.4	90.6	158.7
1995 ..	170.9	179.2	178.9	163.7	194.9	139.3	157.2	124.4	138.7	230.7	89.7	163.9
1996 ..	177.3	185.6	185.7	169.2	200.3	145.9	161.8	138.7	143.2	227.9	91.0	169.1
1997 ..	181.7	190.2	190.2	174.5	204.2	149.4	165.2	137.7	145.2	238.0	100.1	172.9

Source: Research Associates of Washington, Arlington, VA, *Inflation Measures for Schools, Colleges, and Libraries*, annual (copyright).

No. 285. Finances of Public Elementary and Secondary School Systems, by Enrollment-Size Group: 1995-96

[**In millions of dollars (289,230 represents $289,230,000,000), except as indicated.** Data are estimates subject to sampling variability. For details, see source. See also Appendix III]

Item	All school systems	School systems with enrollment of—							
		50,000 or more	25,000 to 49,999	15,000 to 24,999	7,500 to 14,999	5,000 to 7,499	3,000 to 4,999	Under 3,000
Fall enrollment (1,000)	44,840	8,718	4,883	4,241	6,729	4,217	5,322	10,730
General revenue	289,230	56,236	29,657	24,878	42,096	27,428	34,861	74,074
From Federal sources	18,605	4,756	2,057	1,539	2,367	1,438	1,742	4,705
Through State	17,039	4,474	1,899	1,438	2,198	1,333	1,610	4,087
Compensatory programs	6,307	1,740	697	523	822	491	605	1,429
Handicapped programs	2,255	445	226	190	291	191	218	694
Child nutrition programs	5,229	1,408	646	480	712	425	513	1,045
Direct	1,566	283	159	101	169	106	131	618
From State sources [1]	139,168	26,468	15,039	13,377	20,970	12,651	15,572	35,090
General formula assistance	97,246	16,924	9,897	9,735	14,985	9,094	11,323	25,289
Handicapped programs	8,834	1,784	1,142	870	1,225	739	847	2,227
From local sources	131,457	25,012	12,560	9,961	18,759	13,338	17,547	34,278
Taxes	88,638	13,191	8,605	6,516	13,253	9,655	12,727	24,691
Contributions from parent	22,431	8,822	1,923	1,731	2,649	1,809	2,275	3,221
From other local governments	3,018	406	247	218	243	222	420	1,262
Current charges	7,876	1,223	799	708	1,152	757	956	2,281
School lunch	4,318	598	428	409	692	457	591	1,143
Other	9,494	1,370	986	789	1,461	896	1,168	2,823
General expenditure	292,807	57,451	30,150	25,236	42,574	27,782	35,154	74,460
Current spending	258,089	50,876	26,323	21,971	37,470	24,603	31,097	65,749
By function:								
Instruction	156,291	30,914	15,650	13,343	22,925	15,140	19,220	39,098
Support services	86,319	16,505	8,915	7,197	12,291	8,115	10,206	23,092
Other current spending	15,479	3,456	1,758	1,432	2,254	1,348	1,671	3,559
By object:								
Total salaries and wages	166,431	32,889	17,364	14,497	24,463	16,085	20,172	40,961
Total employee benefits	41,357	8,876	4,075	3,372	6,049	3,833	4,803	10,349
Other	50,301	9,111	4,884	4,102	6,958	4,685	6,122	14,439
Capital outlay	27,772	5,458	3,188	2,630	4,032	2,460	3,167	6,838
Interest on debt	5,793	1,084	592	557	885	555	767	1,354
Payments to other governments	1,154	33	46	78	188	165	124	520
Debt outstanding	109,924	21,773	11,139	10,073	16,142	10,273	14,818	25,706
Long-term	106,419	21,668	10,922	9,911	15,605	9,862	14,278	24,173
Short-term	3,505	105	217	161	538	412	540	1,533
Long-term debt issued	20,989	5,028	2,541	1,455	2,667	1,780	2,721	4,797
Long-term debt retired	9,207	1,684	895	847	1,381	896	1,226	2,277

[1] Includes other sources, not shown separately.

Source: U.S. Census Bureau, Internet site <http://www.census.gov/govs/www/school.html> (released June 1999).

U.S. Census Bureau, Statistical Abstract of the United States: 1999

No. 286. Public Elementary and Secondary Estimated Finances, 1980 to 1998, and by State, 1998

[In millions of dollars (101,724 represents $101,724,000,000), except as noted. For school years ending in June of year shown]

	Receipts						Expenditures				
	Revenue receipts								Current expenditures		
Year and state		Source				Non-revenue receipts[1]	Total[2]	Per capita[3] (dol.)	Ele-mentary and second-ary day schools	Average per pupil in ADA[4]	
	Total	Total	Federal	State	Local					Amount (dol.)	Rank
1980	101,724	97,635	9,020	47,929	40,686	4,089	96,105	428	85,661	2,230	(X)
1985	146,976	141,013	9,533	69,107	62,373	5,963	139,382	591	127,230	3,483	(X)
1990	218,126	208,656	13,184	100,787	94,685	9,469	209,698	850	186,583	4,966	(X)
1993	263,460	247,912	17,381	115,924	114,606	15,548	248,898	976	219,297	5,538	(X)
1994	275,121	259,587	18,434	119,443	121,710	15,534	262,485	1,018	230,773	5,749	(X)
1995	288,658	273,364	18,766	130,139	124,459	15,294	276,502	1,062	242,729	5,950	(X)
1996	306,148	286,927	19,323	138,045	129,560	19,221	292,323	1,112	254,254	6,134	(X)
1997	320,046	301,404	20,387	147,396	133,621	18,642	308,077	1,162	268,026	6,360	(X)
1998, total. .	333,149	314,187	21,338	155,321	137,528	18,961	323,879	1,210	280,023	6,548	(X)
Alabama.	4,125	4,030	380	2,601	1,049	94	4,369	1,011	3,669	5,110	45
Alaska.	1,325	1,183	148	752	283	142	1,303	2,138	1,202	10,650	1
Arizona.	4,858	4,389	344	2,109	1,936	469	4,843	1,064	3,792	4,937	48
Arkansas	2,462	2,322	193	1,536	594	139	2,544	1,008	2,230	5,222	42
California	35,479	35,055	3,108	19,921	12,026	425	34,786	1,081	30,159	5,345	41
Colorado.	4,625	4,184	235	1,860	2,089	441	4,423	1,136	3,636	5,704	36
Connecticut. . . .	5,117	5,113	236	2,065	2,812	4	5,117	1,566	4,719	9,218	4
Delaware	983	966	69	650	247	17	984	1,339	878	8,576	5
District of Columbia	496	452	67	-	385	44	598	1,129	566	8,069	7
Florida	16,079	14,583	1,058	7,068	6,457	1,496	15,763	1,074	12,646	6,137	30
Georgia	9,569	8,580	563	4,485	3,531	989	9,672	1,291	7,922	6,177	29
Hawaii	1,364	1,364	102	1,232	31	-	1,300	1,090	1,075	6,127	31
Idaho	1,436	1,345	88	870	387	91	1,356	1,122	1,164	4,973	47
Illinois	15,176	13,650	954	3,651	9,044	1,526	13,757	1,147	11,530	6,363	23
Indiana.	7,269	7,007	346	3,759	2,901	262	7,203	1,228	5,997	6,642	18
Iowa	3,388	3,189	117	1,727	1,345	199	3,074	1,077	2,716	5,713	35
Kansas	3,339	3,091	166	1,815	1,110	248	2,967	1,141	2,659	6,348	24
Kentucky	3,882	3,882	290	2,563	1,029	-	3,830	979	3,569	6,283	27
Louisiana	4,811	4,251	511	2,117	1,623	560	4,142	951	3,764	5,194	43
Maine.	1,562	1,520	95	698	727	42	1,562	1,258	1,463	7,107	15
Maryland	6,572	6,268	358	2,524	3,385	304	6,454	1,267	5,704	7,375	12
Massachusetts. .	7,533	7,533	385	2,720	4,428	-	7,312	1,196	6,931	7,861	9
Michigan.	14,691	13,579	896	11,102	1,581	1,111	13,400	1,370	11,866	7,673	11
Minnesota.	7,279	6,504	252	3,726	2,526	775	7,073	1,509	5,348	6,727	16
Mississippi	2,610	2,503	326	1,423	755	107	2,564	939	2,232	4,732	49
Missouri	6,168	5,841	345	2,337	3,159	327	5,545	1,025	4,669	5,597	38
Montana.	1,004	989	98	481	411	15	1,011	1,151	913	6,237	28
Nebraska	1,703	1,689	66	627	996	15	1,850	1,117	1,598	5,846	33
Nevada	2,037	1,755	74	551	1,130	282	2,015	1,200	1,500	5,601	37
New Hampshire .	1,466	1,365	43	84	1,239	100	1,338	1,142	1,194	6,556	20
New Jersey. . . .	12,651	12,556	390	4,738	7,428	95	12,663	1,571	12,042	10,427	2
New Mexico . . .	2,627	2,328	205	1,639	484	299	2,404	1,394	1,744	5,865	32
New York	29,881	27,691	1,807	11,165	14,719	2,190	28,610	1,577	25,198	9,812	3
North Carolina . .	7,518	7,128	506	4,690	1,932	390	7,530	1,013	6,669	5,830	34
North Dakota. . .	686	669	78	279	312	17	623	972	567	4,978	46
Ohio	13,793	12,694	858	5,495	6,341	1,099	13,504	1,206	11,084	6,539	21
Oklahoma.	3,373	3,119	302	1,951	866	254	3,132	943	2,705	4,634	50
Oregon.	3,930	3,525	250	2,175	1,100	405	3,844	1,185	3,296	6,719	17
Pennsylvania. . .	15,337	15,327	844	6,315	8,168	10	13,688	1,140	12,968	7,752	10
Rhode Island. . .	1,272	1,272	66	539	667	-	1,215	1,231	1,177	8,429	6
South Carolina. .	4,500	4,157	312	2,176	1,668	344	4,080	1,077	3,488	5,555	40
South Dakota . .	788	787	73	250	464	1	765	1,036	660	5,166	44
Tennessee	4,701	4,491	356	2,314	1,822	210	4,847	902	4,670	5,591	39
Texas.	26,362	23,920	1,833	10,282	11,805	2,442	26,102	1,346	22,554	6,291	26
Utah	2,250	2,249	141	1,409	699	1	2,197	1,064	1,771	3,900	51
Vermont	837	815	39	228	547	22	801	1,360	725	7,925	8
Virginia.	6,727	6,662	362	2,469	3,831	65	7,630	1,132	6,797	6,569	19
Washington. . . .	7,049	6,723	465	4,588	1,669	326	8,065	1,437	5,994	6,488	22
West Virginia. . .	2,226	2,176	187	1,368	622	49	2,220	1,223	1,991	7,110	14
Wisconsin.	7,551	7,054	304	3,881	2,869	497	7,159	1,376	6,041	7,272	13
Wyoming	681	661	45	318	299	20	647	1,347	570	6,312	25

- Represents or rounds to zero. X Not applicable. [1] Amount received by local education agencies from the sales of bonds and real property and equipment, loans, and proceeds from insurance adjustments. [2] Includes interest on school debt and other current expenditures not shown separately. [3] Based on U.S. Census Bureau estimated resident population, as of July 1, the previous year. Estimates reflect revisions based on the 1990 Census of Population. [4] Average daily attendance.

Source: National Education Association, Washington, DC, Estimates of School Statistics Database (copyright).

No. 287. Computers for Student Instruction in Elementary and Secondary Schools: 1998-99

[(52,289 represents 52,289,000) Market Data Retrieval collects student use computer information in elementary and secondary schools nationwide through a comprehensive annual technology survey that utilizes both mail and telephone methods]

Level	Total schools	Total enroll-ment (1,000)	Number of comput-ers [2] (1,000)	Students per com-puter	Schools, by location of computer [1] (percent) Class-rooms	Com-puter lab	Library/media center	Schools with Internet access (percent)	Students per computer with Internet access
U.S. total	**109,174**	**52,289**	**8,921**	**5.9**	**90.9**	**78.4**	**74.3**	**87.9**	**13.7**
Public schools, total	87,317	47,155	8,213	5.7	93.2	78.7	79.0	90.4	13.6
Elementary	51,459	23,681	3,742	6.3	94.4	72.7	78.4	88.4	17.3
Middle/Junior High	13,268	8,655	1,497	5.8	91.3	93.0	89.0	94.8	13.0
Senior High	15,632	12,479	2,437	5.1	91.5	88.5	82.1	95.0	11.0
K-12/other	6,958	2,341	536	4.4	90.6	75.1	56.9	88.0	6.5
Catholic schools, total	8,189	2,659	352	7.6	78.7	87.6	56.6	80.1	20.0
Elementary	6,793	1,972	256	7.7	80.8	86.3	51.1	77.0	27.6
Secondary	1,234	632	86	7.3	65.9	96.6	87.5	96.8	13.5
K-12/other	162	55	9	6.2	82.7	78.8	69.2	91.4	6.2
Other private schools, total	13,668	2,475	357	6.9	78.2	67.6	40.7	70.1	12.1
Elementary	6,773	1,069	148	7.2	82.9	61.4	35.2	67.5	13.1
Secondary	1,058	220	47	4.7	65.7	87.9	66.4	89.4	6.6
K-12/other	5,837	1,186	162	7.3	73.6	72.9	43.8	70.3	14.3

[1] Estimates based on responses of those indicating location of computers. Computers may also be in other locations.
[2] Includes estimates for schools not reporting number of computers.

Source: Market Data Retrieval, Shelton, CT, unpublished data (copyright).

No. 288. Public Schools With Access or Planned Access to the Internet: 1994 to 1998

[In percent. As of fall. Excludes special education, vocational education, and alternative schools. Based on sample and subject to sampling error; see source for details]

School characteristic	Percent of schools with Internet access 1994	1995	1996	1997	1998	Percent of instructional classrooms with internet access 1994	1995	1996	1997	1998	Percent of schools in 1996 having or expecting to have access to the Internet by the year 2000
Total [1]	35	50	65	78	89	3	8	14	27	51	95
Instructional level:											
Elementary	30	46	61	75	88	3	8	13	24	51	94
Secondary	49	65	77	89	94	4	8	16	32	52	98
Size of enrollment:											
Less than 300	30	39	57	75	87	3	9	15	27	54	93
300 to 999	35	52	66	78	89	3	8	13	28	53	96
1,000 or more	58	69	80	89	95	3	4	16	25	45	97
Percent minority enrollment:											
Less than 6 percent	38	52	65	84	91	6	9	18	37	57	95
6 to 20 percent	38	58	72	87	93	4	10	18	35	59	97
21 to 49 percent	38	54	65	73	91	4	9	12	22	52	98
50 percent or more	27	40	56	63	82	3	3	5	13	37	91
Percent of students eligible for free or reduced-price lunch:											
Less than 11 percent	40	62	78	88	87	4	9	18	36	62	97
11 to 30 percent	39	59	72	83	94	4	10	16	32	53	98
31 to 70 percent	33	47	58	78	91	3	7	14	27	52	93
71 percent or more	19	31	53	63	80	2	3	7	14	39	93

[1] Includes combined schools.

Source: U.S. National Center for Education Statistics, "Internet Access in Public Schools and Classrooms: 1994-98", Issue Brief, February 1999.

U.S. Census Bureau, Statistical Abstract of the United States: 1999

No. 289. Student Use of Computers at School: 1984 to 1997

[In percent. As of October. Based on the Current Population Survey and subject to sampling error; see Appendix III and source]

Characteristic	1984, total	1989, total	1993, total	1997 Total	1997 Prekinder-garten and kinder-garden	1997 Grades 1-8	1997 Grades 9-12	1997 1st to 4th year of college	1997 5th or later year of college
Total	27.3	42.7	59.0	68.8	36.5	79.3	70.5	64.7	55.5
Sex:									
Male.............	29.0	43.5	59.4	70.1	37.1	79.5	71.3	67.8	59.9
Female	25.5	41.9	58.7	67.6	35.7	79.0	69.6	62.2	52.1
Race/ethnicity:									
White [1]	30.0	45.7	61.6	71.1	38.7	84.0	71.9	64.3	53.8
Black [1]	16.8	32.6	51.5	66.3	33.5	71.6	72.9	69.2	55.8
Hispanic	18.6	34.9	52.3	61.5	31.0	68.3	63.1	63.3	54.7
Other	28.6	42.7	59.0	65.3	32.7	74.9	63.6	63.1	68.9
Household income:									
Less than $5,000	18.7	36.7	51.2	62.1	25.4	69.6	67.9	61.1	74.1
$5,000 to $9,999	21.0	36.1	53.3	63.5	35.1	70.1	61.6	69.8	74.8
$10,000 to $14,999...	22.4	38.4	56.4	66.2	33.3	74.1	68.2	64.1	70.5
$15,000 to $19,999...	25.9	41.5	58.1	65.9	33.0	74.9	66.7	62.1	69.4
$20,000 to $24,999...	26.7	42.4	56.4	66.9	34.2	74.9	69.2	64.0	65.8
$25,000 to $29,999...	30.5	46.1	60.0	68.5	38.9	77.7	72.0	63.1	53.7
$30,000 to $34,999...	30.5	44.2	59.1	67.6	34.6	79.9	70.4	55.2	47.7
$35,000 to $39,999...	32.3	45.2	60.7	69.0	34.6	79.9	70.1	61.5	55.2
$40,000 to $49,999...	32.8	44.7	59.3	70.5	34.7	81.6	74.1	63.3	52.0
$50,000 to $74,999 ..	35.5	47.0	62.6	71.7	39.3	84.0	72.8	67.2	48.5
$75,000 or more.....	36.0	51.2	64.6	72.1	43.2	85.7	71.6	68.1	50.1
Control of school:									
Public............	27.4	43.3	60.2	70.2	40.1	79.0	70.5	63.4	56.7
Private	26.5	38.9	52.1	60.7	29.6	82.1	69.6	70.4	53.0

[1] Non-Hispanic.

Source: U.S. National Center for Education Statistics, *Digest of Education Statistics*, 1998.

No. 290. Availability and Use of Selected Teaching Resources: 1996

[In percent. For resources available at the worksite or used for instructional purposes. Based in a sample survey conducted in the spring of 1996. For details, see source]

Resource	All teach-ers	Sex Male	Sex Female	Level [1] Ele-men-tary	Level [1] Sec-ondary	School system size Less than 3,000	School system size 3,000 to 24,999	School system size 25,000 or more	Race White	Race Minority
RESOURCE READILY AVAILABLE										
Personal computers..........	83.7	81.6	84.4	86.9	80.9	85.5	86.8	76.7	84.7	77.1
Computers with CD-ROM drive ...	58.2	62.8	56.6	58.9	57.6	60.5	60.9	51.1	59.7	44.4
Networked computers	45.0	50.5	43.1	41.2	48.4	48.6	46.0	39.1	45.5	41.6
Computers with modems	37.5	43.7	35.4	35.8	39.0	39.4	37.0	36.4	38.4	30.8
VCR....................	92.9	93.4	92.7	93.3	92.9	94.7	92.2	92.1	93.6	85.3
Television monitor	85.4	87.4	84.6	82.0	88.9	84.9	85.1	86.2	86.0	78.0
Hypermedia or multimedia software..............	39.9	43.6	38.6	41.3	38.8	40.0	40.4	38.9	40.7	33.7
Standard software	71.3	76.8	69.4	68.3	74.3	73.7	72.5	66.6	73.1	55.9
Specialized instructional software..	56.3	52.4	57.6	62.7	50.6	60.6	53.7	56.3	57.2	50.5
Online services/networks	35.3	42.8	32.6	29.3	40.7	40.4	35.0	30.1	36.7	24.5
Instructional laser/video disks	37.3	41.2	36.0	34.9	39.8	32.6	40.0	37.7	38.0	32.7
Instructional videotapes	79.7	77.6	80.4	78.5	80.7	81.3	81.2	75.4	80.8	70.8
Distance learning/video conferencing.............	11.2	13.9	10.2	7.9	14.2	14.2	9.7	10.4	10.9	14.2
RESOURCE REGULARY USED										
Personal computers..........	60.8	58.8	61.5	68.8	53.7	63.3	63.8	53.1	61.7	52.7
Computers with CD-ROM drive ...	29.4	34.0	27.8	32.0	26.8	33.2	30.8	22.9	30.5	17.0
Networked computers	23.9	28.4	22.3	23.6	24.1	27.1	24.1	20.1	24.5	19.6
Computers with modems	12.8	18.2	10.9	13.3	12.6	12.8	13.2	12.2	13.2	8.7
VCR....................	72.3	72.7	72.2	72.2	72.7	74.6	73.8	67.3	73.3	61.1
Television monitor	63.6	66.0	62.8	58.3	68.9	64.3	64.9	60.5	64.5	52.0
Hypermedia or multimedia software..............	20.0	20.3	19.9	23.5	16.8	18.8	21.9	17.8	20.5	15.0
Standard software	44.3	51.7	41.6	40.6	47.9	43.8	46.0	41.8	45.6	34.3
Specialized instructional software..	38.3	32.4	40.4	47.2	30.4	42.2	36.8	37.0	39.5	31.4
Online services/networks	8.9	13.4	7.3	7.9	9.8	9.4	9.3	7.7	9.6	3.8
Instructional laser/video disks	16.1	17.5	15.7	16.4	16.0	13.5	17.7	16.1	16.4	12.7
Instructional videotapes	62.7	59.7	63.7	63.7	62.2	65.9	64.0	56.6	63.6	54.3
Distance learning/video conferencing.............	2.7	3.7	2.4	1.9	3.6	3.2	2.5	2.8	2.4	4.7

[1] Level as determined by respondent.

Source: National Education Association, Washington, DC, *Status of the American Public School Teacher, 1995-1996* (copyright).

No. 291. Technology in Public Schools: 1992 to 1998

[For school year ending in year shown (5,781 represents 5,781,000). Based on surveys of school districts conducted in the spring and summer of the school year. For details, see source]

Technology	Number					Percent of total		
	1992	1995	1996	1997	1998	1992	1997	1998
Schools with interactive videodisk players [1]	6,502	27,059	29,759	30,417	46,804	8	36	54
Elementary [2]	2,921	14,594	16,200	16,614	25,907	6	32	49
Junior high [3]	1,258	5,460	6,009	6,124	9,202	10	43	64
Senior high [4]	2,106	6,661	7,195	7,322	10,687	14	42	61
Students represented (1,000)	5,781	18,552	20,258	20,706	(NA)	14	45	(NA)
Schools with modems [1]	13,597	35,696	40,147	40,876	61,930	16	48	71
Elementary [2]	5,831	18,858	21,733	22,234	35,066	11	43	66
Junior high [3]	2,608	6,546	7,286	7,417	10,996	20	53	76
Senior high [4]	5,001	9,930	10,682	10,781	14,540	30	63	83
Students represented (1,000)	10,717	22,372	24,688	25,136	(NA)	25	54	(NA)
Schools with networks [1]	4,184	27,805	31,986	32,299	49,178	5	38	56
Elementary [2]	1,583	13,582	16,189	16,441	26,422	3	32	50
Junior high [3]	776	5,194	5,971	6,035	9,003	6	43	62
Senior high [4]	1,736	8,839	9,562	9,565	12,853	10	55	73
Students represented (1,000)	3,754	17,540	19,997	20,193	(NA)	9	44	(NA)
Schools with CD-ROMs [1]	5,706	40,509	45,918	46,388	64,200	7	54	74
Elementary [2]	1,897	22,305	25,965	26,377	37,908	4	51	72
Junior high [3]	1,231	7,501	8,341	8,410	11,023	9	60	76
Senior high [4]	2,543	10,354	11,150	11,140	13,985	15	65	80
Students represented (1,000)	5,298	24,121	27,070	27,347	(NA)	12	59	(NA)
Schools with satellite dishes [1]	1,129	15,400	16,298	16,232	17,457	1	19	20
Elementary [2]	351	5,565	6,014	6,001	6,962	1	11	13
Junior high [3]	166	3,214	3,409	3,377	3,255	1	24	23
Senior high [4]	606	6,550	6,782	6,769	7,052	4	39	40
Students represented (1,000)	1,906	8,963	9,270	9,232	(NA)	4	20	(NA)
Schools with cable [1]	(NA)	63,639	64,310	64,171	66,409	(NA)	75	76
Elementary [2]	(NA)	38,336	38,714	38,678	39,431	(NA)	74	75
Junior high [3]	(NA)	11,518	11,575	11,554	11,862	(NA)	82	82
Senior high [4]	(NA)	13,114	13,282	13,208	13,778	(NA)	77	78
Students represented (1,000)	(NA)	36,284	36,950	36,870	(NA)	(NA)	80	(NA)

NA Not available. [1] Includes schools for special education and adult education, not shown separately. [2] Includes K-12, preschool, preschool through 3, K-6, and K-8. [3] Includes schools with grade spans of 4-8, 7-8, and 7-9. [4] Includes 7-12, 9-12, 10-12, vocational technical, and alternative high schools.

Source: Quality Education Data, Denver, CO, National Education Database.

No. 292. Student Participation in School Programs: 1993-94

[As of fall. (41,622 represents 41,622,000). Based on survey and subject to sampling error; for details see source]

Control and level	Total students		Percent of students participating in program or service							
	Number (1,000)	Percent distribu- tion	Bilin- gual educa- tion	English as a second lan- guage	Reme- dial reading	Reme- dial math- ematics	Pro- grams for the dis- abled	Pro- grams for the gifted and talented	Diag- nostic and pre- scrip- tive [1]	Ex- tended day
Public total	41,622	100.0	3.07	3.97	10.88	6.90	6.88	6.43	0.27	2.50
School level [2]:										
Elementary	26,886	64.6	3.98	4.75	13.46	7.77	6.76	6.25	0.31	3.58
Secondary	13,758	33.1	1.39	2.58	5.63	5.03	6.54	6.90	0.20	0.48
Combined	978	2.3	1.80	1.88	13.70	9.39	14.84	4.72	0.44	1.31
Private total	4,971	100.0	0.81	0.58	6.35	4.16	2.98	4.93	0.89	9.20
School level [2]:										
Elementary	2,803	56.4	0.77	0.45	7.22	4.33	0.93	3.34	0.94	12.48
Secondary	811	16.3	0.19	0.62	4.24	3.06	3.43	8.56	0.47	0.23
Combined	1,356	27.3	1.25	0.83	5.82	4.46	6.95	6.05	1.03	7.76

[1] Includes testing for reading and cognitive disabilities, for example. [2] Elementary schools have grade 6 or lower and no grade higher than 8. Secondary schools have no grade lower than 7. Combined schools have grades lower than 7 and higher than 8.

Source: U.S. National Center for Education Statistics, *Digest of Education Statistics*, 1998.

U.S. Census Bureau, Statistical Abstract of the United States: 1999

No. 293. Children and Youth With Disabilities Served by Selected Programs: 1990 to 1998

[For school year ending in year shown (4,210.8 represents 4,210,800). Excludes outlying areas. Through 1994, for persons age 6 to 21 years old served under IDEA (Individuals with Disabilities Act) Part B and Chapter 1 of ESEA (Elementary and Secondary Education Act), SOP (State Operated Programs); beginning 1995, IDEA, Part B only]

Item	1990	1993	1994	1995	1996	1997	1998
All conditions (1,000)................	4,210.8	4,586.2	4,730.4	4,859.1	5,028.7	5,177.6	5,339.4
PERCENT DISTRIBUTION							
Specific learning disabilities	48.6	51.3	50.9	51.2	51.3	51.2	51.0
Speech or language impairments	23.1	21.7	21.4	20.9	20.3	20.1	19.8
Mental retardation....................	13.0	11.3	11.3	11.4	11.3	11.2	11.0
Serious emotional disturbance	9.0	8.7	8.7	8.8	8.7	8.6	8.5
Hearing impairments..................	1.3	1.3	1.3	1.3	1.3	1.3	1.3
Orthopedic impairments................	1.1	1.1	1.2	1.2	1.2	1.3	1.3
Other health impairments..............	1.2	1.4	1.7	2.2	2.6	3.1	3.6
Visually impaired	0.5	0.5	0.5	0.5	0.5	0.5	0.5
Multiple disabilities	2.0	2.2	2.3	1.8	1.8	1.9	2.0
Deaf-blind..........................	(Z)	(Z)	(Z)	(Z)	(Z)	(Z)	(Z)
Autism	(NA)	0.3	0.4	0.5	0.6	0.7	0.8
Traumatic brain injury	(NA)	0.1	0.1	0.1	0.2	0.2	0.2

NA Not available.   Z less than .05 percent.

Source: U.S. Department of Education, Office of Special Education Programs, Data Analysis System (DANS).

No. 294. Catholic Elementary and Secondary Schools: 1967 to 1998

[As of October 1 (3,860 represents 3,860,000). Regular sessions only]

Item	Unit	1967	1970	1975	1980	1985	1990	1995	1996	1997	1998
Elementary schools...	Number .	10,133	9,362	8,340	8,043	7,811	7,291	7,022	7,005	7,004	6,990
Pupils enrolled , ...	1,000...	3,860	3,355	2,252	2,269	2,061	1,884	2,011	2,014	2,015	2,013
Teachers, total [1] ...	1,000...	110	112	99	97	97	91	119	108	106	106
Religious	1,000...	61	52	35	25	18	11	10	8	7	8
Lay	1,000...	49	60	64	72	78	80	109	99	98	98
Secondary schools ...	Number .	2,192	1,981	1,653	1,516	1,434	1,296	1,228	1,226	1,219	1,227
Pupils enrolled , ...	1,000...	1,081	1,008	890	837	760	592	624	631	634	636
Teachers, total [1] ...	1,000...	51	55	50	49	50	40	48	46	47	47
Religious	1,000...	30	29	20	14	11	7	6	5	5	4
Lay	1,000...	21	26	30	35	39	34	42	41	42	43

[1] Beginning 1995, includes part-time teachers.

Source: National Catholic Educational Association, (NCEA) Washington, DC, *United States Catholic Elementary and Secondary Schools school year: Annual Statistical Report on Schools, Enrollment & Staffing* (copyright.)

No. 295. Private Elementary and Secondary School Teachers— Selected Characteristics: 1993-94

[For school year (65 represents 65,000). Based on survey and subject to sampling error; for details, see source. See Table 279 for similar data on public school teachers]

Characteristic	Unit	Age				Sex		Race/ethnicity		
		Under 30 years old	30 to 39 years old	40 to 49 years old	Over 50 years old	Male	Female	White [1]	Black [1]	Hispanic
Total teachers [2] ...	1,000...	65	94	131	88	93	285	348	12	12
Highest degree held:										
Bachelor's	Percent .	78.8	63.1	54.0	47.2	47.3	62.8	59.4	55.8	57.4
Master's.........	Percent .	10.8	25.7	35.1	40.5	40.6	26.3	30.2	26.4	19.9
Education specialist .	Percent .	1.0	2.6	3.4	3.8	2.6	3.0	2.6	4.8	4.4
Doctorate	Percent .	0.2	1.4	2.0	2.6	4.3	0.8	1.6	1.0	2.3
Full-time teaching experience:										
Less than 3 years ..	Percent .	54.9	21.7	12.6	7.2	21.7	20.6	20.4	26.9	25.5
3 to 9 years	Percent .	44.9	51.2	29.8	13.4	28.2	35.8	33.6	34.9	41.8
10 to 20 years.....	Percent .	0.1	27.1	45.5	30.2	28.7	29.9	30.0	27.9	21.6
20 years or more ...	Percent .	(Z)	(Z)	12.1	49.2	21.4	13.7	16.0	10.3	11.1
Full-time teachers ...	1,000...	53	82	103	62	70	231	277	9	9
Earned income	Dol.....	18,384	21,344	22,190	24,113	27,196	20,007	21,578	23,094	22,912
Salary	Dol.....	16,062	19,108	20,631	22,500	23,003	18,815	19,717	20,333	20,740

Z Less than .05 percent.   [1] Non-Hispanic.   [2] Includes teachers with no degrees and associates degrees, not shown separately.

Source: U.S. National Center for Education Statistics, *Digest of Education Statistics*, 1997.

No. 296. Scholastic Assessment Test (SAT) Scores and Characteristics of College-Bound Seniors: 1967 to 1998

[For school year ending in year shown. Data are for the SAT I: Reasoning Tests. SAT I: Reasoning Test replaced the SAT in March 1994. Scores between the two tests have been equated to the same 200-800 scale and are thus comparable. Scores for 1995 and prior years have been recentered and revised]

Type of test and characteristic	Unit	1967	1970	1975	1980	1985	1990	1995	1996	1997	1998
AVERAGE TEST SCORES [1]											
Verbal, total [2]	Point ...	543	537	512	502	509	500	504	505	505	505
Male	Point ...	540	536	515	506	514	505	505	507	507	509
Female	Point ...	545	538	509	498	503	496	502	503	503	502
Math, total [2]	Point ...	516	512	498	492	500	501	506	508	511	512
Male	Point ...	535	531	518	515	522	521	525	527	530	531
Female	Point ...	495	493	479	473	480	483	490	492	494	496
PARTICIPANTS											
Total [3]	1,000 ...	(NA)	(NA)	996	922	977	1,026	1,068	1,085	1,127	1,173
Male	Percent .	(NA)	(NA)	49.9	48.2	48.3	47.8	46.4	46.5	46.1	46.2
White	Percent .	(NA)	(NA)	86.0	82.1	81.0	73.0	69.2	68.7	68.0	67.0
Black	Percent .	(NA)	(NA)	7.9	9.1	7.5	10.0	10.7	10.8	10.8	11.0
Obtaining scores [1] of—											
600 or above:											
Verbal	Percent .	(NA)	(NA)	(NA)	(NA)	(NA)	20.3	21.9	21.1	20.9	21.0
Math	Percent .	(NA)	(NA)	(NA)	(NA)	(NA)	20.4	23.4	22.7	23.4	23.7
Below 400:											
Verbal	Percent .	(NA)	(NA)	(NA)	(NA)	(NA)	17.3	16.4	15.9	16.1	16.1
Math	Percent .	(NA)	(NA)	(NA)	(NA)	(NA)	15.8	16.0	16.0	15.2	15.3
Selected intended area of study:											
Business and commerce	Percent .	(NA)	(NA)	11.5	18.6	21.0	20.9	13.3	12.8	12.8	13.6
Engineering	Percent .	(NA)	(NA)	6.7	11.1	11.7	10.2	8.8	8.5	8.4	8.6
Social science	Percent .	(NA)	(NA)	7.7	7.8	7.5	12.6	11.6	11.3	11.0	10.5
Education	Percent .	(NA)	(NA)	9.1	6.1	4.7	7.5	8.1	8.2	8.6	8.9

NA Not available. [1] Minimum score, 200; maximum score, 800. [2] 1967 and 1970 are estimates based on total number of persons taking SAT. [3] 996 represents 996,000.

Source: College Entrance Examination Board, New York, NY, *National College-Bound Senior*, annual (copyright).

No. 297. American College Testing (ACT) Program Scores and Characteristics of College-Bound Students: 1970 to 1998

[For academic year ending in year shown. Except as indicated, test scores and characteristics of college-bound students. Through 1980, data based on 10 percent sample; thereafter, based on all ACT tested seniors]

Type of test and characteristic	Unit	1970	1975	1980	1985	1990 [1]	1994 [1]	1995 [1]	1996 [1]	1997 [1]	1998 [1]
TEST SCORES [2]											
Composite	Point ...	19.9	18.6	18.5	18.6	20.6	20.8	20.8	20.9	21.0	21.0
Male	Point ...	20.3	19.5	19.3	19.4	21.0	20.9	21.0	21.0	21.1	21.2
Female	Point ...	19.4	17.8	17.9	17.9	20.3	20.7	20.7	20.8	20.8	20.9
English	Point ...	18.5	17.7	17.9	18.1	20.5	20.3	20.2	20.3	20.3	20.4
Male	Point ...	17.6	17.1	17.3	17.6	20.1	19.8	19.8	19.8	19.9	19.9
Female	Point ...	19.4	18.3	18.3	18.6	20.9	20.7	20.6	20.7	20.7	20.8
Math	Point ...	20.0	17.6	17.4	17.2	19.9	20.2	20.2	20.2	20.6	20.8
Male	Point ...	21.1	19.3	18.9	18.6	20.7	20.8	20.9	20.9	21.3	21.5
Female	Point ...	18.8	16.2	16.2	16.0	19.3	19.6	19.7	19.7	20.1	20.2
Reading [3]	Point ...	19.7	17.4	17.2	17.4	(NA)	21.2	21.3	21.3	21.3	21.4
Male	Point ...	20.3	18.7	18.2	18.3	(NA)	21.1	21.1	21.0	21.2	21.1
Female	Point ...	19.0	16.4	16.4	16.6	(NA)	21.4	21.4	21.6	21.5	21.6
Science reasoning [4]	Point ...	20.8	21.1	21.1	21.2	(NA)	20.9	21.0	21.1	21.1	21.1
Male	Point ...	21.6	22.4	22.4	22.6	(NA)	21.6	21.6	21.7	21.7	21.8
Female	Point ...	20.0	20.0	20.0	20.0	(NA)	20.4	20.5	20.5	20.6	20.6
PARTICIPANTS [5]											
Total [6]	1,000 ...	788	714	822	739	817	892	945	925	959	995
Male	Percent .	52	46	45	46	46	45	44	44	44	43
White	Percent .	(NA)	77	83	82	79	76	75	77	74	73
Black	Percent .	4	7	8	8	9	10	10	10	10	11
Obtaining composite scores [7] of—											
27 or above	Percent .	14	14	13	14	12	13	13	13	14	14
18 or below	Percent .	21	33	33	32	35	34	34	34	33	33
Planned educational major:											
Business [8]	Percent .	18	21	20	21	20	14	14	13	11	12
Engineering [9]	Percent .	8	6	8	9	9	9	9	9	8	7
Social science [9]	Percent .	10	9	6	7	10	9	9	9	8	9
Education	Percent .	16	12	9	6	8	10	9	9	9	10

NA Not available. [1] Beginning 1990, not comparable with previous years because a new version of the ACT was introduced. Estimated average composite scores for prior years: 1989, 20.6; 1988, 1987, and 1986, 20.8. [2] Minimum score, 1; maximum score, 36. [3] Prior to 1990, social studies; data not comparable with previous years. [4] Prior to 1990, natural sciences; data not comparable with previous years. [5] Beginning 1985, data are for seniors who graduated in year shown and had taken the ACT in their junior or senior years. Data by race are for those responding to the race question. [6] 788 represents 788,000. [7] Prior to 1990, 26 or above and 15 or below. [8] Includes political and persuasive (e.g. sales) fields through 1975; thereafter, business and commerce. [9] Includes religion through 1975.

Source: The ACT, Inc., Iowa City, IA, *High School Profile Report*, annual.

U.S. Census Bureau, Statistical Abstract of the United States: 1999

No. 298. Proficiency Test Scores for Selected Subjects, by Characteristic: 1977 to 1996

[Based on The National Assessment of Educational Progress Tests which are administered to a representative sample of students in public and private schools. Test scores can range from 0 to 500. For details, see source]

Test and year	Total	Sex		Race			Parental education				
		Male	Female	White [1]	Black [1]	His-panic origin	Less than high school	High school	More than high school		
									Total	Some college	College gradu-ate
READING											
9 year olds:											
1979-80	215	210	220	221	189	190	194	213	226	(NA)	(NA)
1987-88	212	208	216	218	189	194	193	211	220	(NA)	(NA)
1993-94	211	207	215	218	185	186	189	207	221	(NA)	(NA)
1995-96	212	207	218	220	190	194	197	207	220	(NA)	(NA)
13 year olds:											
1979-80	259	254	263	264	233	237	239	254	271	(NA)	(NA)
1987-88	258	252	263	261	243	240	247	253	265	(NA)	(NA)
1993-94	258	251	266	265	234	235	237	251	269	(NA)	(NA)
1995-96	259	253	265	267	236	240	241	252	270	(NA)	(NA)
17 year olds:											
1979-80	286	282	289	293	243	261	262	278	299	(NA)	(NA)
1987-88	290	286	294	295	274	271	267	282	300	(NA)	(NA)
1993-94	288	282	295	296	266	263	268	276	299	(NA)	(NA)
1995-96	287	280	294	294	265	265	267	273	297	(NA)	(NA)
WRITING [2]											
4th graders:											
1983-84	204	201	208	211	182	189	179	192	217	208	218
1987-88	206	199	213	215	173	190	194	199	212	211	212
1993-94	205	196	214	214	173	189	188	202	(NA)	212	212
1995-96	207	200	214	216	182	191	190	203	(NA)	205	214
8th graders:											
1983-84	267	258	276	272	247	247	258	261	276	271	278
1987-88	264	254	274	269	246	250	254	258	271	275	271
1993-94	265	254	278	272	245	252	250	259	(NA)	270	275
1995-96	264	251	276	271	242	246	245	258	(NA)	270	274
11th graders:											
1983-84	290	281	299	297	270	259	274	284	299	298	300
1987-88	291	282	299	296	275	274	276	285	299	296	299
1993-94	285	276	293	291	267	271	269	279	(NA)	286	293
1995-96	283	275	292	289	267	269	260	275	(NA)	287	291
MATHEMATICS											
9 year olds:											
1977-78	219	217	220	224	192	203	200	219	231	230	231
1985-86	222	222	222	227	202	205	201	218	231	229	231
1993-94	231	232	230	237	212	210	210	225	(NA)	239	238
1995-96	231	233	229	237	212	215	220	221	(NA)	238	240
13 year olds:											
1977-78	264	264	265	272	230	238	245	263	280	273	284
1985-86	269	270	268	274	249	254	252	263	278	274	280
1993-94	274	276	273	281	252	256	255	266	(NA)	277	285
1995-96	274	276	272	281	252	256	254	267	(NA)	278	283
17 year olds:											
1977-78	300	304	297	306	268	276	280	294	313	305	317
1985-86	302	305	299	308	279	283	279	293	310	305	314
1993-94	306	309	304	312	286	291	284	295	(NA)	305	318
1995-96	307	310	305	313	286	292	281	297	(NA)	307	317
SCIENCE											
9 year olds:											
1976-77	220	222	218	230	175	192	199	223	233	237	232
1985-86	224	227	221	232	196	199	204	220	235	236	235
1993-94	231	232	230	240	201	201	211	225	(NA)	239	239
1995-96	230	232	228	239	201	207	215	222	(NA)	242	240
13 year olds:											
1976-77	247	251	244	256	208	213	224	245	264	260	266
1985-86	251	256	247	259	222	226	229	245	262	258	264
1993-94	257	259	254	267	224	232	234	247	(NA)	260	269
1995-96	256	261	252	266	226	232	232	248	(NA)	260	266
17 year olds:											
1976-77	290	297	282	298	240	262	265	284	304	296	309
1985-86	289	295	282	298	253	259	258	277	300	295	304
1993-94	294	300	289	306	257	261	256	279	(NA)	295	311
1995-96	296	300	292	307	260	269	261	282	(NA)	297	308
HISTORY, 1993-94											
4th graders	205	203	206	215	177	180	177	197	(NA)	214	216
8th graders:	259	259	259	267	239	243	241	251	(NA)	264	270
12th graders	286	288	285	292	265	267	263	276	(NA)	287	296
GEOGRAPHY, 1993-94											
4th graders	206	208	203	218	168	183	186	197	(NA)	216	216
8th graders	260	262	258	270	229	239	238	250	(NA)	265	272
12th graders	285	288	281	291	258	268	263	274	(NA)	286	294

NA Not available. [1] Non-Hispanic. [2] Writing scores revised from previous years; previous writing scores were recorded on a 0 to 400 rather than 0 to 500 scale.

Source: U.S. National Center for Education Statistics, *Digest of Education Statistics*, annual.

No. 299. Advanced Placement Program—Summary: 1997 and 1998

[Includes exams taken by candidates abroad. In 1998 this represents 24,705 examinations taken by 16,911 students in 638 schools abroad. Minus sign (-) indicates decrease]

Item	Schools repre- sented, 1998	Program total 1997	Program total 1998	Percent change, 1997-98	1998 Grade level of test taker 10th grade	1998 Grade level of test taker 11th grade	1998 Grade level of test taker 12th grade	1998 Sex of test taker Male	1998 Sex of test taker Female
Exams taken, total [1]	(X)	921,601	1,016,657	10	52,174	342,280	598,823	471,415	545,242
By subject area:									
Art History	671	6,756	7,332	9	755	1,735	4,691	2,668	4,664
Art, Drawing	1,045	3,180	3,686	16	37	696	2,861	1,679	2,007
Art, General	1,703	7,122	8,094	14	106	1,367	6,371	3,046	5,048
Biology	5,646	70,812	75,461	7	5,662	27,234	40,810	32,466	42,995
Calculus AB	9,037	111,834	117,671	5	1,063	14,399	100,059	62,515	55,156
Calculus BC	2,583	22,668	27,088	19	408	4,449	21,726	16,687	10,401
Chemistry	4,397	41,874	44,937	7	1,721	22,566	19,788	25,662	19,275
Computer Science—A	1,208	7,311	6,478	-11	704	2,431	3,194	5,301	1,177
Computer Science—AB	859	4,526	4,057	-10	380	1,501	2,103	3,562	495
Economics-Micro	1,184	11,901	13,243	11	219	2,035	10,665	7,697	5,546
Economics-Macro	1,324	15,725	17,668	12	257	2,265	14,773	10,148	7,520
English Language/ Composition	4,396	67,322	80,016	19	683	54,964	23,195	30,473	49,543
English Literature/ Composition	9,471	158,416	167,194	6	125	9,325	155,033	60,839	106,355
Environmental Science	456	-	5,163	(X)	133	1,436	3,431	2,360	2,803
European History	2,945	43,170	48,298	12	21,775	7,549	18,095	23,587	24,711
French Language	2,687	13,605	13,721	1	614	3,444	9,244	4,216	9,505
French Literature	350	1,523	1,618	6	64	288	1,221	453	1,165
German Language	1,086	3,297	3,493	6	188	732	2,424	1,676	1,817
Government and Politics—U.S.	3,236	45,328	49,934	10	1,341	4,889	42,827	24,265	25,669
Government and Politics—Comparative	753	6,563	6,835	4	320	815	5,571	3,712	3,123
International English Language	67	2,510	3,752	49	4	88	68	1,574	2,178
Latin—Vergil	533	2,956	3,311	12	287	1,604	1,374	1,709	1,602
Latin—Literature	373	1,744	2,055	18	112	884	1,008	1,008	1,047
Music Theory	1,062	3,369	4,084	21	318	1,190	2,481	2,079	2,005
Physics—B	2,510	21,542	24,276	13	399	8,056	15,365	15,950	8,326
Physics—Mechanics	1,672	11,944	12,939	8	91	1,350	11,283	9,510	3,429
Physics—Electricity and Magnetism	1,004	5,848	6,415	10	46	511	5,753	4,982	1,433
Psychology	1,483	18,628	21,974	18	507	5,734	15,345	7,650	14,324
Spanish Language	4,419	45,966	51,424	12	4,349	17,157	28,005	18,545	32,879
Spanish Literature	850	6,134	6,975	14	375	1,954	4,419	2,323	4,652
Statistics	1,299	7,667	15,486	102	513	2,876	11,776	8,109	7,377
U.S. History	7,415	150,340	161,979	8	8,618	136,756	13,864	74,964	87,015
Candidates taking exams [1]	(X)	581,554	635,168	9	47,847	239,859	330,117	282,997	352,171

- Represents zero.   X Not applicable.   [1] Includes students and exams taken in other grades not shown separately.

Source: The College Board, New York, NY, Advanced Placement Program, *National Summary Report*, 1998 (copyright).

No. 300. Foreign Language Enrollment in Public High Schools: 1970 to 1994

[In thousands (13,301.9 represents 13,301,900), except percent. As of fall, for grades 9 through 12]

Language	1970	1974	1976	1978	1982	1985	1990	1994
Total enrollment	13,301.9	13,648.9	13,952.1	13,941.4	12,879.3	12,466.5	11,099.6	11,847.5
Enrolled in all foreign languages	3,779.3	3,294.5	3,174.0	3,200.1	2,909.8	4,028.9	4,256.9	5,001.9
Percent of all students	28.4	24.1	22.7	23.0	22.6	32.3	38.4	42.2
Enrolled in modern foreign languages [1]	3,514.1	3,127.3	3,023.5	3,048.3	2,740.2	3,852.0	4,093.0	4,813.0
Spanish	1,810.8	1,678.1	1,717.0	1,631.4	1,562.8	2,334.4	2,611.4	3,219.8
French	1,230.7	977.9	888.4	856.0	858.0	1,133.7	1,089.4	1,105.9
German	410.5	393.0	352.7	330.6	266.9	312.2	295.4	326.0
Italian	27.3	40.2	45.6	45.5	44.1	47.3	40.4	43.8
Japanese	(NA)	(NA)	(NA)	(NA)	6.2	8.6	25.1	42.3
Russian	20.2	15.1	11.3	8.8	5.7	6.4	16.5	16.4
Percent of all students [1]	26.4	22.9	21.7	21.9	21.3	30.9	36.9	40.6
Spanish	13.6	12.3	12.3	11.7	12.1	18.7	23.5	27.2
French	9.3	7.2	6.4	6.1	6.7	9.1	9.8	9.3
German	3.1	2.9	2.5	2.4	2.1	2.5	2.7	2.8
Italian	0.2	0.3	0.3	0.3	0.3	0.4	0.4	0.4
Japanese	(NA)	(NA)	(NA)	(NA)	0.1	0.1	0.2	0.4
Russian	0.2	0.1	0.1	0.1	(Z)	0.1	0.2	0.1

NA Not available.   Z Less than .05 percent.   [1] Includes other foreign languages, not shown separately.

Source: The American Council on the Teaching of Foreign Languages, Yonkers, NY, *Foreign Language Enrollments in Public Secondary Schools, Fall 1994.*

U.S. Census Bureau, Statistical Abstract of the United States: 1999

No. 301. Public High School Graduates, by State: 1980 to 1998

[In thousands (2,747.7 represents 2,747,000). For school year ending in year shown]

State	1980	1990	1995	1998, est.	State	1980	1990	1995	1998, est.
United States	2,747.7	2,320.3	2,273.5	2,433.4	Missouri	62.3	49.0	48.9	51.9
Alabama	45.2	40.5	36.3	35.3	Montana	12.1	9.4	10.1	10.6
Alaska	5.2	5.4	5.8	6.1	Nebraska	22.4	17.7	18.0	20.3
Arizona	28.6	32.1	31.0	36.1	Nevada	8.5	9.5	10.0	11.6
Arkansas	29.1	26.5	24.6	25.9	New Hampshire	11.7	10.8	10.1	9.3
California	249.2	236.3	255.2	282.7	New Jersey	94.6	69.8	67.4	72.2
Colorado	36.8	33.0	32.4	34.7	New Mexico	18.4	14.9	14.9	15.4
Connecticut	37.7	27.9	26.4	28.8	New York	204.1	143.3	132.4	140.5
Delaware	7.6	5.6	5.2	5.9	North Carolina	70.9	64.8	59.5	59.4
District of Columbia	5.0	3.6	3.0	2.7	North Dakota	9.9	7.7	7.8	8.1
Florida	87.3	88.9	89.8	95.4	Ohio	144.2	114.5	109.4	109.0
Georgia	61.6	56.6	56.7	63.0	Oklahoma	39.3	35.6	33.3	33.6
Hawaii	11.5	10.3	9.4	9.8	Oregon	29.9	25.5	26.7	27.7
Idaho	13.2	12.0	14.2	15.1	Pennsylvania	146.5	110.5	104.1	111.4
Illinois	135.6	108.1	105.2	113.9	Rhode Island	10.9	7.8	7.8	7.0
Indiana	73.1	60.0	56.1	58.2	South Carolina	38.7	32.5	30.7	34.0
Iowa	43.4	31.8	31.3	33.8	South Dakota	10.7	7.7	8.4	12.0
Kansas	30.9	25.4	26.1	27.8	Tennessee	49.8	46.1	43.6	46.0
Kentucky	41.2	38.0	37.6	37.0	Texas	171.4	172.5	170.3	185.1
Louisiana	46.3	36.1	36.5	36.9	Utah	20.0	21.2	27.7	32.0
Maine	15.4	13.8	11.5	12.6	Vermont	6.7	6.1	5.9	6.2
Maryland	54.3	41.6	41.4	43.9	Virginia	66.6	60.6	58.3	64.4
Massachusetts	73.8	55.9	47.7	49.9	Washington	50.4	45.9	49.3	55.0
Michigan	124.3	93.8	84.6	93.7	West Virginia	23.4	21.9	20.1	20.1
Minnesota	64.9	49.1	49.4	54.9	Wisconsin	69.3	52.0	51.7	56.3
Mississippi	27.6	25.2	23.8	24.2	Wyoming	6.1	5.8	5.9	6.1

Source: U.S. National Center for Education Statistics, *Digest of Education Statistics*, annual.

No. 302. High School Dropouts, by Race and Hispanic Origin: 1975 to 1997

[In percent. As of October]

Item	1975	1980	1985	1989 [1]	1990	1991	1992	1993	1994	1995	1996	1997
EVENT DROPOUTS [2]												
Total [3]	5.8	6.0	5.2	4.5	4.0	4.0	4.3	4.2	5.0	5.4	4.7	4.3
White	5.4	5.6	4.8	3.9	3.8	3.7	4.1	4.1	4.7	5.1	4.5	4.2
Male	5.0	6.4	4.9	4.1	4.1	3.6	3.8	4.1	4.6	5.4	4.8	4.9
Female	5.8	4.9	4.7	3.8	3.5	3.8	4.4	4.1	4.9	4.8	4.1	3.5
Black	8.7	8.3	7.7	7.7	5.1	6.2	4.9	5.4	6.2	6.1	6.3	4.8
Male	8.3	8.0	8.3	6.9	4.1	5.5	3.3	5.7	6.5	7.9	4.6	4.1
Female	9.0	8.5	7.2	8.6	6.0	7.0	6.7	5.0	5.7	4.4	7.8	5.7
Hispanic [4]	10.9	11.5	9.7	7.7	8.0	7.3	7.9	5.4	9.2	11.6	8.4	8.6
Male	10.1	16.9	9.3	7.6	8.7	10.4	5.8	5.7	8.4	10.9	9.2	10.4
Female	11.6	6.9	9.8	7.7	7.2	4.8	8.6	5.0	10.1	12.5	7.6	6.7
STATUS DROPOUTS [5]												
Total [3]	15.6	15.6	13.9	14.4	13.6	14.2	12.7	12.7	13.3	13.9	12.8	13.0
White	13.9	14.4	13.5	14.1	13.5	14.2	12.2	12.2	12.7	13.6	12.5	12.4
Male	13.5	15.7	14.7	15.4	14.2	15.4	13.3	13.0	13.6	14.3	12.9	13.8
Female	14.2	13.2	12.3	12.8	12.8	13.1	11.1	11.5	11.7	13.0	12.1	10.9
Black	27.3	23.5	17.6	16.4	15.1	15.6	16.3	16.4	15.5	14.4	16.0	16.7
Male	27.8	26.0	18.8	18.6	13.6	15.4	15.5	15.6	17.5	14.2	17.4	17.5
Female	26.9	21.5	16.6	14.5	16.2	15.8	17.1	17.2	13.7	14.6	14.7	16.1
Hispanic [4]	34.9	40.3	31.5	37.7	37.3	39.6	33.9	32.7	34.7	34.7	34.5	30.6
Male	32.6	42.6	35.8	40.3	39.8	44.4	38.4	34.7	36.1	34.2	36.2	33.2
Female	36.8	38.1	27.0	35.0	34.5	34.5	29.6	31.0	33.1	35.4	32.7	27.6

[1] Beginning 1989 reflects new editing procedures for cases with missing data on school enrollment. [2] Percent of students who drop out in a single year without completing high school. For grades 10 to 12. [3] Includes other races, not shown separately. [4] Persons of Hispanic origin may be of any race. [5] Percent of the population who have not completed high school and are not enrolled, regardless of when they dropped out. For persons 18 to 24 years old.

Source: U.S. Census Bureau, *Current Population Reports*, P20-516.

U.S. Census Bureau, Statistical Abstract of the United States: 1999

No. 303. High School Dropouts by Age, Race, and Hispanic Origin: 1970 to 1997

[As of October (4,670 represents 4,670,000). For persons 14 to 24 years old. See Table 305 for definition of dropouts]

Age and race	Number of dropouts (1,000)					Percent of population				
	1970	1980	1990	1995	1997	1970	1980	1990	1995	1997
Total dropouts [1][2]	4,670	5,212	3,854	3,963	3,708	12.2	12.0	10.1	9.9	9.1
16 to 17 years	617	709	418	406	387	8.0	8.8	6.3	5.4	4.9
18 to 21 years	2,138	2,578	1,921	1,980	1,929	16.4	15.8	13.4	14.2	13.3
22 to 24 years	1,770	1,798	1,458	1,491	1,307	18.7	15.2	13.8	13.6	12.5
White [2]	3,577	4,169	3,127	3,098	2,842	10.8	11.3	10.1	9.7	8.8
16 to 17 years	485	619	334	314	294	7.3	9.2	6.4	5.4	4.7
18 to 21 years	1,618	2,032	1,516	1,530	1,489	14.3	14.7	13.1	13.8	12.7
22 to 24 years	1,356	1,416	1,235	1,181	987	16.3	14.0	14.0	13.4	11.9
Black [2]	1,047	934	611	605	693	22.2	16.0	10.9	10.0	11.2
16 to 17 years	125	80	73	70	73	12.8	6.9	6.9	5.8	5.6
18 to 21 years	500	486	345	328	354	30.5	23.0	16.0	15.8	16.9
22 to 24 years	397	346	185	194	257	37.8	24.0	13.5	12.5	16.6
Hispanic [2][3]	(NA)	919	1,122	1,355	1,196	(NA)	29.5	26.8	24.7	21.0
16 to 17 years	(NA)	92	89	94	77	(NA)	16.6	12.9	10.7	7.3
18 to 21 years	(NA)	470	502	652	561	(NA)	40.3	32.9	29.9	27.1
22 to 24 years	(NA)	323	523	598	542	(NA)	40.6	42.8	37.4	35.3

NA Not available.   [1] Includes other groups not shown separately.   [2] Includes persons 14 to 15 years, not shown separately.   [3] Persons of Hispanic origin may be of any race.

Source: U.S. Census Bureau, *Current Population Reports*, P20-516; and earlier reports.

No. 304. Enrollment Status, by Race, Hispanic Origin, and Sex: 1975 and 1997

[As of October (15,693 represents 15,693,000). For persons 18 to 21 years old. For the civilian noninstitutional population. Based on the Current Population Survey; see text, Section 1, Population, and Appendix III]

Characteristic	Total persons 18 to 21 years old (1,000)		Percent distribution							
			Enrolled in high school		High school graduates				Not high school graduates	
					Total		In college			
	1975	1997	1975	1997	1975	1997	1975	1997	1975	1997
Total [1]	15,693	14,550	5.7	9.2	78.0	77.5	33.5	44.7	16.3	13.3
White	13,448	11,706	4.7	8.0	80.6	79.2	34.6	46.1	14.7	12.7
Black	1,997	2,100	12.5	14.6	60.4	68.7	24.9	33.4	27.0	16.9
Hispanic [2]	899	2,072	12.0	11.8	57.2	60.7	24.4	27.5	30.8	27.1
Male [1]	7,584	7,338	7.4	10.7	76.6	74.6	35.4	42.0	15.9	14.7
White	6,545	5,982	6.2	9.1	79.7	76.5	36.9	43.5	14.1	14.3
Black	911	992	15.9	18.8	55.0	63.0	23.9	28.1	29.0	18.4
Hispanic [2]	416	1,108	17.3	12.8	54.6	57.1	25.2	23.9	27.9	30.0
Female [1]	8,109	7,212	4.2	7.6	79.2	80.5	31.8	47.5	16.6	11.8
White	6,903	5,724	3.2	6.9	81.4	82.0	32.4	48.8	15.3	11.1
Black	1,085	1,107	9.7	10.7	65.0	73.9	25.8	38.1	25.4	15.4
Hispanic [2]	484	964	7.6	10.8	59.3	65.0	23.6	31.7	33.1	23.8

[1] Includes other races not shown separately.   [2] Persons of Hispanic origin may be of any race.

Source: U.S. Census Bureau, *Current Population Reports*, P20-516; and earlier reports.

No. 305. Employment Status of High School Graduates and School Dropouts: 1980 to 1998

[In thousands (11,622 represents 11,622,000), except percent. As of October. For civilian noninstitutional population 16 to 24 years old. Based on Current Population Survey; see text, Section 1, Population, and Appendix III]

Employment status, sex, and race	Graduates [1]				Dropouts [2]			
	1980	1990	1995 [3]	1998 [3]	1980	1990	1995 [3]	1998 [3]
Civilian population	11,622	8,370	6,627	6,659	5,254	3,800	3,876	3,942
In labor force	9,795	7,107	5,530	5,668	3,549	2,506	2,443	2,579
Percent of population	84.3	84.9	83.4	85.1	67.5	66.0	63.0	65.4
Employed.	8,567	6,279	4,863	5,147	2,651	1,993	1,894	2,174
Percent of labor force	87.5	88.3	87.9	90.8	74.7	79.5	77.5	84.3
Unemployed	1,228	828	667	520	898	513	549	405
Unemployment rate, total [4]	12.5	11.7	12.1	9.2	25.3	20.5	22.5	15.7
Male	13.5	11.1	11.7	8.6	23.5	18.8	19.2	13.9
Female	11.5	12.3	12.5	9.9	28.7	23.5	28.8	19.3
White	10.8	9.0	10.5	7.2	21.6	17.0	19.1	14.1
Black	26.1	26.0	20.3	18.8	43.9	43.3	48.0	24.5
Not in labor force	1,827	1,262	1,097	992	1,705	1,294	1,433	1,363
Percent of population	15.7	15.1	16.6	14.9	32.5	34.1	37.0	34.6

[1] For persons not enrolled in college who have completed 4 years of high school only.   [2] For persons not in regular school and who have not completed the 12th grade nor received a general equivalency degree.   [3] See footnote 2, Table 649.   [4] Includes other races not shown separately.

Source: U.S. Bureau of Labor Statistics, Bulletin 2307; *News*, USDL 99-175, June 25, 1999; and unpublished data.

Education   191

No. 306. General Educational Development (GED) Credentials Issued: 1974 to 1996

[GEDs issued in thousands (295 represents 295,000). Includes outlying areas]

Year	GEDs issued	Percent distribution by age of test taker				
		Under 19 years old	20 to 24 years old	25 to 29 years old	30 to 34 years old	35 years old and over
1974	295	35	27	13	9	17
1975	342	33	26	14	9	18
1980	488	37	27	13	8	15
1985	427	33	26	15	10	16
1990	419	35	25	14	10	17
1992	465	32	28	13	11	16
1993	476	33	27	14	11	16
1994	499	34	26	13	10	16
1995	513	37	25	13	10	15
1996	514	40	25	13	9	15

Source: U.S. National Center for Education Statistics, *Digest of Education Statistics,* 1998.

No. 307. College Enrollment of Recent High School Graduates: 1960 to 1997

[High school graduates in thousands (1,679 represents 1,679,000). For persons 16 to 24 who graduated from high school in the preceeding 12 months. Includes persons receiving GEDs. Based on surveys and subject to sampling error]

Year	Number of high school graduates					Percent enrolled in college [2]				
	Total [1]	Male	Female	White	Black	Total [1]	Male	Female	White	Black
1960	1,679	756	923	1,565	(NA)	45.1	54.0	37.9	45.8	(NA)
1965	2,659	1,254	1,405	2,417	(NA)	50.9	57.3	45.3	51.7	(NA)
1970	2,757	1,343	1,414	2,461	(NA)	51.8	55.2	48.5	52.0	(NA)
1975	3,186	1,513	1,673	2,825	(NA)	50.7	52.6	49.0	51.2	(NA)
1980	3,089	1,500	1,589	2,682	361	49.3	46.7	51.8	49.9	41.8
1982	3,100	1,508	1,592	2,644	384	50.6	49.0	52.1	52.0	36.5
1983	2,964	1,390	1,574	2,496	392	52.7	51.9	53.4	55.0	38.5
1984	3,012	1,429	1,583	2,514	438	55.2	56.0	54.5	57.9	40.2
1985	2,666	1,286	1,380	2,241	333	57.7	58.6	56.9	59.4	42.3
1986	2,786	1,331	1,455	2,307	386	53.8	55.9	51.9	56.0	36.5
1987	2,647	1,278	1,369	2,207	337	56.8	58.4	55.3	56.6	51.9
1988	2,673	1,334	1,339	2,187	382	58.9	57.0	60.8	60.7	45.0
1989	2,454	1,208	1,245	2,051	337	59.6	57.6	61.6	60.4	52.8
1990	2,355	1,169	1,185	1,921	341	59.9	57.8	62.0	61.5	46.3
1991	2,276	1,139	1,137	1,867	320	62.4	57.6	67.1	64.6	45.6
1992	2,398	1,216	1,182	1,900	353	61.7	59.6	63.8	63.4	47.9
1993	2,338	1,118	1,219	1,910	302	62.6	59.7	65.4	62.8	55.6
1994	2,517	1,244	1,273	2,065	318	61.9	60.6	63.2	63.6	50.9
1995	2,599	1,238	1,361	2,088	356	61.9	62.6	61.4	62.6	51.4
1996	2,660	1,297	1,363	2,092	416	65.0	60.1	69.7	65.8	55.3
1997	2,769	1,354	1,415	2,228	394	67.0	63.5	70.3	67.5	59.6

NA Not available.   [1] Includes other races, not shown separately.   [2] As of October.

Source: U.S. National Center for Education Statistics, *Digest of Education Statistics,* annual.

No. 308. College Enrollment, by Sex and Attendance Status: 1983 to 1997

[As of fall. In thousands (12,465 represents 12,465,000)]

Sex and age	1983		1989		1993		1996, prel.		1997, est.	
	Total	Part time	Total	Part time	Total	Part time	Total	Part time	Total	Part time
Total	12,465	5,204	13,539	5,878	14,305	6,177	14,300	6,087	14,350	6,259
Male	6,024	2,264	6,190	2,450	6,427	2,537	6,344	2,528	6,239	2,572
14 to 17 years old	102	16	71	12	83	10	92	21	88	12
18 to 19 years old	1,256	158	1,342	113	1,224	138	1,342	231	1,374	207
20 to 21 years old	1,241	205	1,189	198	1,294	209	1,224	263	1,215	260
22 to 24 years old	1,158	382	1,090	367	1,260	392	1,175	323	1,038	359
25 to 29 years old	1,115	624	1,038	639	950	564	993	553	954	540
30 to 34 years old	570	384	603	439	661	484	480	337	561	390
35 years old and over	583	494	857	682	955	739	1,039	801	1,009	805
Female	6,441	2,940	7,349	3,428	7,877	3,640	7,956	3,558	8,111	3,687
14 to 17 years old	142	16	101	12	93	6	137	45	99	15
18 to 19 years old	1,496	179	1,515	184	1,416	172	1,662	257	1,715	233
20 to 21 years old	1,125	204	1,253	213	1,414	279	1,419	282	1,429	273
22 to 24 years old	884	378	1,104	470	1,263	493	1,141	407	1,101	436
25 to 29 years old	947	658	1,052	732	1,058	689	1,131	669	1,075	661
30 to 34 years old	721	553	750	563	811	575	714	478	688	455
35 years old and over	1,126	953	1,574	1,253	1,824	1,427	1,752	1,421	2,004	1,614

Source: U.S. National Center for Education Statistics, *Digest of Education Statistics,* annual.

No. 309. College Enrollment, by Selected Characteristics: 1980 to 1996

[In thousands (12,086.8 represents 12,086,800). As of fall. Totals may differ from other tables because of adjustments to underreported and nonreported racial/ethnic data. Nonresident alien students are not distributed among racial/ethnic groups]

Characteristic	1980	1988	1990	1992	1993	1994	1995, prel.	1996, est.
Total	12,086.8	13,819.5	14,359.0	14,487.4	14,304.8	14,278.8	14,261.8	14,300.3
Male	5,868.1	6,284.4	6,501.8	6,524.0	6,427.5	6,371.9	6,342.5	6,344.0
Female	6,218.7	7,535.1	7,857.1	7,963.4	7,877.4	7,906.9	7,919.2	7,956.3
Public	9,456.4	10,844.7	11,309.6	11,384.6	11,189.1	11,133.7	11,092.4	11,090.2
Private	2,630.4	2,974.8	3,049.4	3,101.7	3,115.7	3,145.1	3,169.4	3,210.1
2-year	4,521.4	5,240.1	5,651.9	5,722.4	5,565.9	5,529.7	5,492.5	5,497.4
4-year	7,565.4	8,579.4	8,707.1	8,765.0	8,738.9	8,749.1	8,769.3	8,802.8
Undergraduate	10,469.1	11,959.2	12,439.3	12,537.7	12,324.0	12,262.6	12,232.0	12,259.4
Graduate	1,340.9	1,586.2	1,639.1	1,668.7	1,688.4	1,721.5	1,732.0	1,743.1
First professional . . .	276.8	274.1	280.5	280.9	292.4	294.7	297.6	297.7
White [1]	9,833.0	10,723.0	10,989.8	10,875.4	10,600.0	10,427.0	10,311.2	10,226.0
Male	4,772.9	4,861.3	4,962.2	4,884.6	4,755.0	4,650.7	4,594.1	4,553.0
Female	5,060.1	5,861.7	6,027.6	5,990.8	5,845.1	5,776.3	5,717.2	5,673.1
Public	7,656.1	8,385.4	8,622.2	8,492.8	8,226.6	8,056.3	7,945.4	7,848.3
Private	2,176.9	2,337.6	2,367.5	2,382.6	2,373.4	2,370.6	2,365.9	2,377.7
2-year	3,558.5	3,954.3	4,198.8	4,131.2	3,960.6	3,861.7	3,794.0	3,742.8
4-year	6,274.5	6,768.7	6,791.0	6,744.3	6,639.5	6,565.3	6,517.2	6,483.2
Undergraduate	8,480.7	9,272.6	9,507.7	9,387.6	9,100.4	8,916.0	8,805.6	8,730.9
Graduate	1,104.7	1,228.4	1,258.0	1,267.2	1,273.8	1,286.8	1,282.3	1,273.9
First professional . . .	247.7	222.0	224.0	220.6	225.9	224.2	223.3	221.2
Black [1]	1,106.8	1,247.1	1,335.4	1,392.9	1,412.8	1,448.6	1,473.7	1,499.4
Male	463.7	484.7	517.0	536.9	543.7	549.7	555.9	563.6
Female	643.0	762.4	818.4	856.0	869.1	898.9	917.8	935.8
Public	876.1	976.5	1,053.4	1,100.5	1,114.3	1,144.6	1,160.7	1,177.3
Private	230.7	270.6	281.9	292.3	298.5	304.1	313.0	322.2
2-year	472.5	524.3	577.6	601.6	599.0	615.0	621.5	629.3
4-year	634.3	722.8	757.7	791.2	813.7	833.6	852.2	870.2
Undergraduate	1,018.8	1,147.2	1,229.3	1,280.6	1,290.4	1,317.3	1,333.6	1,352.6
Graduate	75.1	83.9	88.9	94.1	102.2	110.6	118.6	125.5
First professional . . .	12.8	16.0	17.2	18.2	20.2	20.7	21.4	21.4
Hispanic	471.7	782.6	866.6	955.0	988.8	1,045.6	1,093.8	1,152.2
Male	231.6	354.0	390.5	427.7	441.2	464.0	480.2	501.3
Female	240.1	428.6	476.0	527.3	547.6	581.6	613.7	650.9
Public	406.2	671.4	742.1	822.3	851.3	898.7	937.1	987.6
Private	65.5	111.1	124.5	132.7	137.5	146.8	156.8	164.7
2-year	255.1	424.2	483.7	545.0	556.8	582.9	608.4	644.2
4-year	216.6	358.3	382.9	409.9	432.0	462.7	485.5	508.1
Undergraduate	433.1	724.6	804.2	887.8	918.1	968.3	1,012.0	1,065.6
Graduate	32.1	47.2	50.9	55.3	57.9	63.9	68.0	72.7
First professional . . .	6.5	10.9	11.4	12.0	12.8	13.4	13.8	14.0
American Indian [1] .	83.9	102.8	113.7	119.3	121.7	127.4	131.3	134.0
Male	37.8	43.1	47.6	50.2	51.2	53.0	54.8	55.7
Female	46.1	59.7	66.1	69.1	70.5	74.4	76.5	78.2
Public	74.2	90.4	100.2	103.3	106.4	110.7	113.8	116.3
Private	9.7	12.4	13.6	15.9	15.3	16.6	17.5	17.7
2-year	47.0	54.9	62.6	64.4	63.2	66.2	65.6	66.7
4-year	36.9	47.9	51.2	54.9	58.5	61.2	65.7	67.2
Undergraduate	77.9	95.5	105.8	110.9	112.7	117.4	120.7	122.9
Graduate	5.2	6.2	6.6	7.0	7.3	8.1	8.5	8.9
First professional . . .	0.8	1.1	1.3	1.5	1.7	1.8	2.1	2.2
Asian [1]	286.4	572.5	637.2	697.0	724.4	774.3	797.4	823.6
Male	151.3	294.9	325.1	351.5	363.1	385.0	393.3	403.6
Female	135.2	277.6	312.0	345.6	361.3	389.3	404.1	420.0
Public	239.7	461.0	516.3	565.9	586.3	622.1	638.0	657.1
Private	46.7	111.6	120.9	131.1	138.2	152.2	159.4	166.5
2-year	124.3	215.2	255.7	289.5	295.0	312.5	314.9	322.9
4-year	162.1	357.3	381.5	407.5	429.4	461.8	482.4	500.7
Undergraduate	248.7	500.5	558.7	613.0	634.2	674.1	692.0	713.2
Graduate	31.6	53.2	57.6	61.5	65.2	72.6	75.6	79.0
First professional . . .	6.1	18.8	20.8	22.5	25.0	27.6	29.6	31.4
Nonresident alien .	305.0	391.5	416.4	447.7	457.1	455.9	454.4	464.9
Male	210.8	246.3	259.4	273.1	273.4	269.5	264.3	266.7
Female	94.2	145.2	157.0	174.6	183.7	186.4	190.1	198.2
Public	204.1	260.0	275.3	299.5	304.3	301.2	297.5	303.7
Private	100.8	131.5	141.0	148.1	152.7	154.7	156.9	161.3
2-year	64.1	67.1	73.5	90.6	91.2	91.4	88.1	91.5
4-year	240.9	324.4	342.8	357.0	365.9	364.5	366.2	373.5
Undergraduate	209.9	218.7	233.6	257.9	268.2	269.4	267.6	274.1
Graduate	92.2	167.3	177.0	183.6	182.0	179.5	179.5	183.2
First professional . . .	2.9	5.4	5.8	6.2	6.9	7.0	7.3	7.7

[1] Non-Hispanic.

Source: U.S. National Center for Education Statistics, *Digest of Education Statistics*, annual.

Education   193

No. 310. Foreign (Nonimmigrant) Student Enrollment in College: 1976 to 1998

[For fall of the previous year. (179 represents 179,000)]

Region of origin	Enrollment (1,000)									Percent enrolled in—					
										Engineering		Science[1]		Business	
	1976	1980	1985	1990	1994	1995	1996	1997	1998	1980	1996	1980	1996	1980	1996
All regions ...	179	286	342	387	449	453	454	458	481	25	16	8	8	16	21
Africa..........	25	36	40	25	21	21	21	22	23	20	14	9	8	19	20
Nigeria	11	16	18	4	2	2	2	2	2	19	11	9	10	22	18
Asia[2]..........	97	165	200	245	294	292	290	291	308	32	19	8	9	16	22
China: Taiwan ...	11	18	23	31	37	36	33	30	31	17	18	15	6	17	25
Hong Kong	12	10	10	11	14	13	12	11	10	22	15	9	4	26	37
India..........	10	9	15	26	35	34	32	31	34	31	36	16	9	21	15
Indonesia	1	2	7	9	11	12	13	12	13	27	21	7	2	21	45
Iran	20	51	17	7	4	3	3	2	2	45	31	7	17	11	7
Japan	7	12	13	30	44	45	46	46	47	7	3	5	4	19	18
Malaysia	2	4	22	14	14	14	14	15	15	13	31	14	3	22	36
Saudi Arabia	3	10	8	4	4	4	4	4	5	30	29	4	4	14	14
South Korea	3	5	16	22	31	34	36	37	43	17	12	11	8	15	16
Thailand	7	7	7	7	9	11	12	13	15	17	17	6	3	26	40
Europe.........	14	23	33	46	62	65	67	68	72	15	9	9	9	14	22
Latin America[3] ...	30	42	49	48	45	47	47	50	51	20	13	8	7	14	23
Mexico........	5	6	6	7	8	9	9	9	10	16	16	7	6	11	22
Venezuela......	5	10	10	3	4	4	4	5	5	30	16	8	5	11	25
North America	10	16	16	19	23	23	24	24	23	8	5	6	7	13	11
Canada........	10	15	15	18	22	23	23	23	22	8	5	6	7	12	11
Oceania........	3	4	4	4	4	4	4	4	4	5	5	7	7	16	16

[1] Physical and life sciences.   [2] Includes countries not shown separately.   [3] Includes Central America, Caribbean, and South America.

Source: Institute of International Education, New York, NY, Open Doors, annual (copyright).

No. 311. College Enrollment, by Sex, Age, Race, and Hispanic Origin: 1980 to 1997

[In thousands (11,387 represents 11,387,000). As of October for the civilian noninstitutional population, 14 years old and over. Based on the Current Population Survey; see text, Section 1, Population, and Appendix III]

Characteristic	1980	1985	1989[1]	1990	1991	1992	1993	1994	1995	1996	1997
Total[2]	11,387	12,524	13,180	13,621	14,057	14,035	13,898	15,022	14,715	15,226	15,436
Male[3]	5,430	5,906	5,950	6,192	6,439	6,192	6,324	6,764	6,703	6,820	6,843
18 to 24 years	3,604	3,749	3,717	3,922	3,954	3,912	3,994	4,152	4,089	4,187	4,374
25 to 34 years	1,325	1,464	1,443	1,412	1,605	1,392	1,406	1,589	1,561	1,523	1,509
35 years old and over ..	405	561	716	772	832	789	873	958	985	1,013	899
Female[3]	5,957	6,618	7,231	7,429	7,618	7,844	7,574	8,258	8,013	8,406	8,593
18 to 24 years	3,625	3,788	4,085	4,042	4,218	4,429	4,199	4,576	4,452	4,582	4,829
25 to 34 years	1,378	1,599	1,639	1,749	1,680	1,732	1,688	1,830	1,788	1,920	1,760
35 years old and over ..	802	1,100	1,396	1,546	1,636	1,575	1,616	1,766	1,684	1,765	1,892
White[3]	9,925	10,781	11,243	11,488	11,686	11,710	11,434	12,222	12,021	12,189	12,442
18 to 24 years	6,334	6,500	6,631	6,635	6,813	6,916	6,763	7,118	7,011	7,123	7,495
25 to 34 years	2,328	2,604	2,597	2,698	2,661	2,582	2,505	2,735	2,686	2,644	2,522
35 years old and over ..	1,051	1,448	1,868	2,023	2,107	2,053	2,068	2,267	2,208	2,254	2,297
Male	4,804	5,103	5,136	5,235	5,304	5,210	5,222	5,524	5,535	5,453	5,552
Female	5,121	5,679	6,107	6,253	6,382	6,499	6,212	6,698	6,486	6,735	6,890
Black[3]	1,163	1,263	1,287	1,393	1,477	1,424	1,545	1,800	1,772	1,901	1,903
18 to 24 years	688	734	835	894	828	886	861	1,001	988	983	1,085
25 to 34 years	289	295	275	258	373	302	386	440	426	519	423
35 years old and over ..	156	213	146	207	257	208	284	323	334	354	372
Male	476	552	480	587	629	527	636	745	710	764	723
Female	686	712	807	807	848	897	909	1,054	1,062	1,136	1,180
Hispanic origin[3][4]	443	580	754	748	830	918	995	1,187	1,207	1,223	1,260
18 to 24 years	315	375	453	435	516	586	602	662	745	706	806
25 to 34 years	118	189	170	168	196	214	249	312	250	310	254
35 years old and over ..	(NA)	(NA)	114	130	109	102	129	205	193	184	151
Male	222	279	353	364	347	388	442	529	568	529	555
Female	221	299	401	384	483	530	553	658	639	693	704

NA Not available.   [1] Beginning 1989, based on a revised edit and tabulation package.   [2] Includes other races not shown separately.   [3] Includes persons 14 to 17 years old, not shown separately.   [4] Persons of Hispanic origin may be of any race.

Source: U.S. Census Bureau, Current Population Reports, P20-516; and earlier reports.

U.S. Census Bureau, Statistical Abstract of the United States: 1999

No. 312. Higher Education—Summary: 1970 to 1996

[Institutions, staff, and enrollment as of fall (474 represents 474,000). Finances for fiscal year ending in the following year. Covers universities, colleges, professional schools, junior and teachers colleges, both publicly and privately controlled, regular session. Includes estimates for institutions not reporting. See also Appendix III]

Item	Unit	1970	1980	1985	1990	1992	1993	1994	1995	1996, est.
ALL INSTITUTIONS										
Number of institutions [1]	Number...	2,556	3,231	3,340	3,559	3,638	3,632	3,688	3,706	(NA)
4-year	Number...	1,665	1,957	2,029	2,141	2,169	2,190	2,215	2,244	(NA)
2-year	Number...	891	1,274	1,311	1,418	1,469	1,442	1,473	1,462	(NA)
Instructional staff—										
(Lecturer or above) [2]	1,000	474	686	715	817	877	915	915	932	890
Percent full-time	Percent...	78	66	64	61	(NA)	60	(NA)	59	(NA)
Total enrollment [3]	1,000	8,581	12,097	12,247	13,819	14,486	14,305	14,279	14,262	14,300
Male	1,000	5,044	5,874	5,818	6,284	6,524	6,427	6,372	6,343	6,344
Female	1,000	3,537	6,223	6,429	7,535	7,963	7,877	7,907	7,919	7,956
4-year institutions	1,000	6,262	7,571	7,716	8,579	8,765	8,739	8,749	8,769	8,803
2-year institutions	1,000	2,319	4,526	4,531	5,240	5,722	5,566	5,530	5,493	5,497
Full-time	1,000	5,816	7,098	7,075	7,821	8,162	8,128	8,138	8,129	8,213
Part-time	1,000	2,765	4,999	5,172	5,998	6,325	6,177	6,141	6,133	6,087
Public	1,000	6,428	9,457	9,479	10,845	11,385	11,189	11,134	11,092	11,090
Private	1,000	2,153	2,640	2,768	2,974	3,102	3,116	3,145	3,169	3,210
Undergraduate [4]	1,000	7,376	10,475	10,597	11,959	12,538	12,324	12,263	12,232	12,259
Men	1,000	4,254	5,000	4,962	5,380	5,583	5,484	5,422	5,401	5,411
Women	1,000	3,122	5,475	5,635	6,579	6,955	6,840	6,840	6,831	6,848
First-time freshmen	1,000	2,063	2,588	2,292	2,257	2,184	2,161	2,133	2,169	2,193
First professional	1,000	173	278	274	273	281	292	295	298	298
Men	1,000	159	199	180	167	169	173	174	174	172
Women	1,000	15	78	94	107	112	120	121	124	125
Graduate [4]	1,000	1,031	1,343	1,376	1,586	1,669	1,688	1,721	1,732	1,743
Men	1,000	630	675	677	737	772	771	776	768	760
Women	1,000	400	670	700	849	896	917	946	965	983
Current funds revenues [5]	Mil. dol ...	23,879	65,585	100,438	149,766	170,881	179,227	189,121	197,973	(NA)
Tuition and fees	Mil. dol ...	5,021	13,773	23,117	37,434	45,346	48,647	51,507	55,260	(NA)
Federal government	Mil. dol ...	4,190	9,748	12,705	18,236	21,015	22,076	23,243	23,939	(NA)
State government	Mil. dol ...	6,503	20,106	29,912	39,481	41,248	41,910	44,343	45,693	(NA)
Auxiliary enterprises	Mil. dol ...	3,125	7,287	10,674	14,903	16,663	17,538	18,336	18,868	(NA)
Current funds expenditures [5]	Mil. dol ...	23,375	64,053	97,536	146,088	165,241	173,351	182,969	190,476	(NA)
Educational and general [6]	Mil. dol ...	17,616	50,074	76,128	114,140	128,978	136,024	144,158	151,446	(NA)
Auxiliary enterprises	Mil. dol ...	2,988	7,288	10,528	14,272	15,562	16,429	17,205	17,599	(NA)
Endowment (market value)	Mil. dol ...	13,714	23,465	50,281	72,049	92,239	96,013	109,707	128,837	(NA)
2-YEAR INSTITUTIONS										
Number of institutions [1][7]	Number...	891	1,274	1,311	1,418	1,469	1,442	1,473	1,462	(NA)
Public	Number...	654	945	932	972	1,024	1,021	1,036	1,047	(NA)
Private	Number...	237	329	379	446	445	421	437	415	(NA)
Instructional staff—										
(Lecturer or above) [2]	1,000	92	192	211	(NA)	(NA)	290	(NA)	285	(NA)
Enrollment [3][4]	1,000	2,319	4,526	4,531	5,240	5,722	5,566	5,530	5,493	5,497
Public	1,000	2,195	4,329	4,270	4,996	5,485	5,337	5,308	5,278	5,283
Private	1,000	124	198	261	244	238	229	221	215	214
Male	1,000	1,375	2,047	2,002	2,233	2,413	2,345	2,323	2,329	2,348
Female	1,000	945	2,479	2,529	3,007	3,309	3,220	3,207	3,164	3,149
Current funds revenue [5]	Mil. dol ...	2,504	8,505	12,293	18,021	20,805	21,961	22,977	24,614	(NA)
Tuition and fees	Mil. dol ...	413	1,618	2,618	4,029	5,218	5,594	5,643	6,323	(NA)
State government	Mil. dol ...	926	3,961	5,659	8,001	8,647	8,730	9,252	9,848	(NA)
Local government	Mil. dol ...	701	1,623	2,027	3,044	3,524	3,936	4,139	4,324	(NA)
Current funds expenditures	Mil. dol ...	2,327	8,212	11,976	17,494	19,941	21,187	22,078	23,522	(NA)
Education and general [6]	Mil. dol ...	2,073	7,608	11,118	16,270	18,578	19,763	20,616	22,053	(NA)
Instruction	Mil. dol ...	1,205	3,764	5,398	7,903	9,018	9,476	9,829	10,312	(NA)

NA Not available. [1] Beginning 1980, number of institutions includes count of branch campuses. Due to revised survey procedures, data beginning 1990 are not comparable with previous years. [2] Due to revised survey methods, data beginning 1990 not comparable with previous years. [3] Beginning 1980, branch campuses counted according to actual status, e.g., 2-year branch in 2-year category; previously a 2-year branch included in university category. [4] Includes unclassified students. (Students taking courses for credit, but are not candidates for degrees.) [5] Includes items not shown separately. [6] Data for 1970 are not strictly comparable with later years. [7] Beginning 1980, includes schools accredited by the National Association of Trade and Technical Schools.

Source: U.S. National Center for Education Statistics, *Digest of Education Statistics*, annual; *Projections of Education Statistics*, annual; and unpublished data.

Education **195**

No. 313. Colleges—Number, 1995 and Enrollment, 1996, by State

[Number of institutions beginning in academic year. Opening fall enrollment of resident and extension students attending full time or part time (**14,300 represents 14,300,000**). Excludes students taking courses for credit by mail, radio, or TV, and students in branches of U.S. institutions operated in foreign countries. See Appendix III]

State	Number of institutions, 1995 [1]	1996 Enrollment, prel. (1,000)							Minority enrollment			Nonresident alien
		Total	Male	Female	Public	Private	Full time	White [2]	Total [3]	Black [2]	Hispanic	
United States	3,706	14,300	6,344	7,956	11,090	3,210	8,213	10,226	3,609	1,499	1,152	465
Alabama	82	219	96	124	197	23	150	157	58	52	2	4
Alaska	9	29	12	17	28	1	12	22	5	1	1	1
Arizona	45	277	125	152	253	23	131	200	69	9	40	8
Arkansas	38	101	43	58	89	11	68	80	18	15	1	2
California	348	1,883	841	1,041	1,625	258	887	923	878	144	383	82
Colorado	59	243	111	132	209	34	131	194	43	8	23	6
Connecticut	42	155	68	88	98	58	83	123	26	12	8	6
Delaware	9	45	19	26	37	8	26	35	8	6	1	1
District of Columbia	19	74	33	41	7	67	49	36	30	22	3	8
Florida	114	641	277	364	531	110	309	418	203	88	92	20
Georgia	120	318	135	183	249	69	214	215	95	81	5	8
Hawaii	17	61	27	34	47	14	35	16	39	1	1	6
Idaho	12	60	27	33	49	11	41	55	4	(Z)	2	1
Illinois	169	721	316	405	532	189	371	504	199	92	64	18
Indiana	78	286	131	155	221	65	191	246	31	18	7	9
Iowa	59	177	81	96	126	51	122	157	13	5	3	7
Kansas	54	172	77	95	155	17	96	146	21	8	6	6
Kentucky	61	178	74	104	147	30	118	158	17	12	1	3
Louisiana	36	204	86	118	175	29	145	133	64	54	5	6
Maine	33	56	22	33	38	18	32	53	2	(Z)	(Z)	1
Maryland	57	261	108	152	217	43	128	170	81	59	6	10
Massachusetts	118	410	179	231	173	237	261	317	68	23	18	25
Michigan	109	547	239	308	459	88	278	437	93	60	12	18
Minnesota	107	275	122	154	209	67	164	244	24	8	4	7
Mississippi	46	126	54	72	115	11	93	84	41	38	1	2
Missouri	101	291	127	164	189	101	170	244	39	26	5	8
Montana	26	43	20	23	38	5	33	37	5	(Z)	1	1
Nebraska	35	119	54	66	100	20	68	107	9	3	2	3
Nevada	10	73	33	41	72	2	24	55	16	4	6	2
New Hampshire	30	64	27	37	36	28	39	60	3	1	1	1
New Jersey	61	328	143	186	265	64	177	223	94	39	32	11
New Mexico	35	104	43	60	98	6	51	57	45	3	33	2
New York	311	1,028	437	591	572	455	665	672	312	137	103	44
North Carolina	121	373	160	213	303	70	241	276	91	75	5	6
North Dakota	20	41	20	20	37	4	32	36	3	(Z)	(Z)	1
Ohio	156	538	240	297	405	132	337	448	73	51	8	16
Oklahoma	45	177	81	96	154	23	107	134	35	13	4	8
Oregon	45	165	76	89	141	24	92	138	21	3	6	6
Pennsylvania	217	622	293	329	335	287	391	519	86	52	12	17
Rhode Island	12	72	32	40	37	35	46	61	9	3	3	3
South Carolina	59	174	72	102	148	26	111	127	45	40	2	3
South Dakota	21	35	16	20	29	7	26	31	3	(Z)	(Z)	1
Tennessee	76	247	108	139	194	53	162	198	44	37	3	5
Texas	179	955	437	519	838	117	521	582	347	95	202	27
Utah	17	152	76	76	114	37	96	137	10	1	4	5
Vermont	22	35	15	20	20	15	24	33	2	(Z)	(Z)	1
Virginia	89	354	154	200	292	61	202	260	86	58	8	8
Washington	64	292	129	164	252	40	180	232	51	11	11	9
West Virginia	28	86	38	48	75	11	60	79	5	4	1	2
Wisconsin	66	299	132	167	245	54	182	264	28	13	6	7
Wyoming	9	31	13	18	30	1	18	28	2	(Z)	1	(Z)
U.S. military [4]	10	82	69	13	82	-	20	65	16	11	3	1

- Represents zero.   Z Fewer than 500.   [1] Branch campuses counted as separate institutions.   [2] Non-Hispanic.   [3] Includes other races not shown separately.   [4] Service schools.

Source: U.S. National Center for Education Statistics, *Digest of Education Statistics,* annual.

No. 314. Higher Education Price Indexes: 1970 to 1997

[1983=100. For years ending June 30. Reflects prices paid by colleges and universities]

Year	Index, total	Personnel compensation				Contracted services, supplies, and equipment					
		Total	Professional salaries	Nonprofessional salaries	Fringe benefits	Total	Services	Supplies and materials	Equipment	Library acquisitions	Utilities
1970 ..	39.5	42.1	47.7	38.8	24.7	31.9	42.8	37.6	41.9	25.7	16.3
1972 ..	44.3	47.1	52.0	44.9	31.1	36.0	47.8	39.8	45.1	34.9	19.2
1973 ..	46.7	49.8	54.3	47.6	34.7	37.6	49.9	41.1	46.5	37.7	20.2
1974 ..	49.9	52.8	57.2	50.6	38.6	41.4	52.2	46.5	49.4	41.6	24.8
1975 ..	54.3	56.3	60.3	54.6	42.9	48.5	56.8	58.0	58.3	46.7	31.8
1976 ..	57.8	60.0	63.5	59.0	47.8	51.3	59.1	60.7	61.7	52.1	34.4
1977 ..	61.5	63.5	66.4	63.1	52.8	55.7	62.6	63.8	64.8	56.8	40.5
1978 ..	65.7	67.6	69.9	68.1	58.4	60.2	66.6	66.6	69.3	63.2	45.9
1979 ..	70.5	72.4	74.1	73.4	64.5	65.1	71.2	71.7	74.7	70.0	50.3
1980 ..	77.5	78.4	79.4	80.2	72.6	75.0	77.0	84.6	81.6	77.8	64.1
1981 ..	85.8	85.8	86.3	87.7	81.8	85.9	85.2	95.6	89.6	85.9	79.7
1982 ..	93.9	93.5	93.7	94.6	91.5	94.9	94.2	100.4	96.4	93.5	92.4
1983 ..	100.0	100.0	100.0	100.0	100.0	100.0	100.0	100.0	100.0	100.0	100.0
1984 ..	104.8	105.4	104.7	105.1	108.3	103.0	104.9	99.7	102.3	105.3	102.5
1985 ..	110.8	112.0	111.4	109.2	117.7	107.1	110.8	103.0	104.8	111.3	105.3
1986 ..	116.3	118.8	118.2	112.8	127.7	109.0	115.1	102.6	107.2	121.2	103.1
1987 ..	120.9	125.4	125.0	116.3	137.4	107.4	119.7	99.0	108.9	132.9	91.0
1988 ..	126.1	131.7	130.9	120.6	147.1	109.8	123.0	101.1	120.5	140.5	87.7
1989 ..	132.8	139.5	138.8	125.3	158.7	112.8	128.8	108.3	115.1	153.5	85.3
1990 ..	140.8	148.3	147.6	130.3	171.3	118.7	134.0	114.3	119.6	167.0	90.1
1991 ..	148.2	156.5	155.6	135.4	184.4	123.2	139.8	116.4	123.3	179.8	92.2
1992 ..	153.4	162.4	160.8	140.2	193.8	126.9	145.7	115.2	126.3	193.9	93.3
1993 ..	157.9	167.6	165.0	144.2	204.2	129.4	149.5	113.2	128.6	204.3	94.7
1994 ..	163.3	173.4	170.3	148.2	214.1	133.9	154.8	114.3	130.8	216.2	98.7
1995 ..	168.3	179.1	176.1	152.5	221.4	136.1	158.0	115.7	133.5	228.8	96.8
1996 ..	173.3	184.1	181.7	157.3	224.5	141.3	163.8	130.1	137.0	245.0	93.3
1997 ..	178.6	189.0	187.2	162.1	226.7	148.0	167.3	128.6	139.3	260.9	106.1

Source: Research Associates of Washington, Arlington, VA, *Inflation Measures for Schools, Colleges, and Libraries,* annual (copyright).

No. 315. Institutions of Higher Education—Finances: 1980 to 1996

[In millions of dollars (58,520 represents $58,520,000,000). For fiscal years ending in year shown. For coverage, see headnote, Table 312. See also Appendix III]

Item	1980	1985	1990	1993	1994	1995	1996 Total	1996 Public	1996 Private
Current funds revenues.......	58,520	92,473	139,635	170,881	179,227	189,121	197,973	123,501	74,472
Tuition and fees	11,930	21,283	33,926	45,346	48,647	51,507	55,260	23,257	32,003
Federal government	8,902	11,509	17,255	21,015	22,076	23,243	23,939	13,672	10,267
State government	18,378	27,583	38,349	41,248	41,910	44,343	45,693	44,243	1,450
Local government	1,588	2,387	3,640	4,445	4,998	5,166	5,608	5,075	533
Private gifts, grants, and contracts [1]	2,808	4,896	7,781	9,660	10,203	10,867	11,903	5,089	6,814
Endowment earnings	1,177	2,096	3,144	3,628	3,670	3,988	4,562	721	3,841
Educational activities [2].....	1,239	2,127	3,632	5,038	5,294	5,603	5,531	3,529	2,002
Auxiliary enterprises	6,481	10,100	13,938	16,663	17,538	18,336	18,868	11,595	7,272
Hospitals.................	(3)	7,475	13,217	18,124	18,960	19,100	18,612	12,276	6,336
Other funds revenues [4]	6,015	3,015	4,753	5,715	5,931	6,967	7,998	4,044	3,954
Current funds expenditures [5]...	56,914	89,951	134,656	165,241	173,351	182,969	190,476	119,525	70,952
Educational and general.....	44,543	70,061	105,585	128,978	136,023	144,158	151,446	96,086	55,360
Instruction	18,497	28,777	42,146	50,341	52,776	55,720	57,810	38,653	19,157
Institutional support	5,054	8,587	12,674	15,250	15,926	16,845	18,256	10,710	7,545
Research..............	5,099	7,552	12,506	15,291	16,118	17,110	17,518	12,076	5,442
Plant operation [6]	4,700	7,345	9,458	10,784	11,368	11,746	12,331	8,005	4,326
Academic support	3,876	6,074	9,438	11,073	11,678	12,279	13,297	9,004	4,293
Libraries..............	1,624	2,362	3,254	3,685	3,908	4,166	4,293	2,691	1,603
Student services	2,567	4,178	6,388	8,165	8,563	9,060	9,631	5,810	3,820
Scholarships and fellowships .	2,200	3,670	6,656	10,148	11,238	12,285	13,195	5,085	8,110
Unrestricted funds	905	1,962	3,854	5,949	6,645	7,329	8,213	2,457	5,756
Restricted funds	1,296	1,709	2,802	4,199	4,593	4,956	4,982	2,628	2,355
Public service	1,817	2,861	4,690	5,935	6,242	6,691	7,007	5,321	1,686
Mandatory transfers	732	1,016	1,630	1,991	2,115	2,423	2,401	1,420	980
Auxiliary enterprises [5]	6,486	10,012	13,204	15,562	16,429	17,205	17,599	11,309	6,290
Hospitals [5].............	4,757	8,010	12,679	17,050	17,510	18,071	17,941	11,879	6,062
Independent operations [5]	1,128	1,868	3,187	3,652	3,387	3,534	3,491	251	3,240

[1] Private grants represent nongovernmental revenue for sponsored research and other sponsored programs; includes private contracts. [2] Sales and service of educational departments only. [3] Included in other. [4] Includes sales and services of federally funded research and development centers, and others sources. [5] Includes mandatory transfers which are primarily current expenditures for plant. [6] Includes maintenance.

Source: U.S. National Center for Education Statistics, *Digest of Education Statistics,* annual.

No. 316. Federal Student Financial Assistance: 1990 to 1999

[For award years July 1 of year shown to the following June 30 (19,677 represents ($19,677,000,000). Funds utilized exclude operating costs, etc., and represent funds given to students]

Award year impact data	1990	1991	1992	1993	1994	1995	1996	1997	1998, est.	1999, est.
FUNDS UTILIZED (mil. dol.)										
Total	19,677	20,342	21,926	29,274	32,683	35,477	38,865	38,107	40,451	41,903
Federal Pell Grants	4,906	5,793	6,176	5,655	5,520	5,472	5,780	6,326	7,211	7,373
Federal Supplemental Educational Opportunity Grant	503	586	651	753	755	764	762	811	777	774
Federal Work-Study	728	760	780	771	757	764	776	906	1,002	1,044
Federal Perkins Loan	870	868	892	919	971	1,029	1,022	1,062	1,058	1,058
Federal Direct Student Loan (FDSL)	(X)	(X)	(X)	(X)	1,790	8,296	9,796	9,838	10,400	11,363
Federal Family Education Loans (FFEL)	12,669	12,336	13,427	21,177	22,891	19,152	20,729	19,163	20,003	20,291
NUMBER OF AWARDS (1,000)										
Total	10,258	10,312	11,039	12,614	13,082	13,667	14,516	14,355	14,933	15,306
Federal Pell Grants	3,562	3,786	4,002	3,756	3,675	3,612	3,666	3,725	3,838	3,811
Federal Supplemental Educational Opportunity Grant	761	771	976	1,068	1,057	1,083	1,191	1,116	1,109	1,118
Federal Work-Study	687	697	714	712	701	702	691	746	892	930
Federal Perkins Loan	660	654	669	685	663	688	674	679	698	698
Federal Direct Student Loan (FDSL)	(X)	(X)	(X)	(X)	474	2,339	2,762	2,864	3,018	3,122
Federal Family Education Loans (FFEL)	4,587	4,403	4,677	6,394	6,512	5,243	5,531	5,225	5,378	5,627
AVERAGE AWARD (dol.)										
Total	1,918	1,973	1,986	2,321	2,498	2,596	2,677	2,655	2,709	2,738
Federal Pell Grants	1,377	1,530	1,543	1,506	1,502	1,515	1,577	1,698	1,879	1,935
Federal Supplemental Educational Opportunity Grant	661	665	667	705	715	706	640	727	701	701
Federal Work-Study	1,059	1,090	1,092	1,084	1,081	1,087	1,123	1,215	1,123	1,123
Federal Perkins Loan	1,318	1,326	1,333	1,342	1,464	1,497	1,516	1,564	1,516	1,516
Federal Direct Student Loan (FDSL)	(X)	(X)	(X)	(X)	3,779	3,548	3,547	3,435	3,445	3,639
Federal Family Education Loans (FFEL)	2,762	2,802	2,871	3,312	3,515	3,653	3,748	3,667	3,719	3,606
COHORT DEFAULT RATE [1]										
Federal Perkins Loan	(NA)	(NA)	12.24	11.42	10.76	12.57	12.95	12.47	(X)	(X)
FFEL/FDSL Combined Rates [2]	22.40	17.80	15.00	11.60	10.70	10.40	9.60	(NA)	(X)	(X)

NA Not available.   X Not applicable.   [1] As of June 30. Represents the percent of borrowers entering repayment status in year shown who defaulted in the following year. For the Perkins Loans, prior to 1992-93 the default rate was based on the dollar amount of loans outstanding.   [2] Prior to 1995, this rate was FFEL-only.
Source: U.S. Dept. of Education, Office of Postsecondary Education, unpublished data.

No. 317. Finances of Public Colleges, 1990 to 1996, and by State, 1997

[For academic years ending in year shown (7,959.7 represents 7,959,700). Data provided by the state higher education finance officers, except as noted]

State	FTE [1] enrollment (1,000)	Appropriations for current operations [2] (mil. dol.)	Net tuition revenues (mil. dol.)[3]	State	FTE [1] enrollment (1,000)	Appropriations for current operations [2] (mil. dol.)	Net tuition revenues (mil. dol.)[3]
Total, 1990	7,959.7	33,853.9	11,264.7	Michigan	313.8	1,372.5	1,779.5
Total, 1992	8,325.4	34,928.8	14,180.6	Minnesota	157.3	404.4	872.6
Total, 1993	8,397.7	35,172.0	15,746.3	Mississippi	117.8	216.0	463.9
Total, 1994	8,334.0	36,497.0	16,623.4	Missouri	130.2	491.0	729.3
Total, 1995	8,262.7	38,655.2	17,406.8	Montana	33.1	84.3	117.2
Total, 1996	8,267.1	40,077.5	18,465.2	Nebraska	66.8	124.5	323.6
Total, 1997	**8,315.2**	**19,235.2**	**42,057.0**	Nevada	37.3	46.7	212.9
Alabama	170.9	424.7	697.4	New Hampshire	27.9	169.0	84.7
Alaska	17.2	38.7	156.9	New Jersey [4]	181.6	576.4	1,155.3
Arizona	165.7	330.4	827.2	New Mexico	62.8	98.6	392.8
Arkansas	75.4	164.8	352.2	New York	422.1	1,111.2	2,218.8
California	1,309.2	1,330.9	6,674.5	North Carolina	237.8	385.9	1,519.9
Colorado	136.3	444.9	513.7	North Dakota	30.9	64.0	120.5
Connecticut	56.7	208.9	430.9	Ohio	336.1	1,120.4	1,490.4
Delaware	27.2	176.2	173.7	Oklahoma	111.5	221.4	562.8
District of Columbia	4.8	13.5	37.8	Oregon	99.0	264.7	449.1
Florida	402.4	518.1	1,849.5	Pennsylvania	279.7	1,273.4	1,414.8
Georgia	217.2	417.1	1,314.0	Rhode Island	24.8	108.6	134.9
Hawaii	30.6	51.1	210.6	South Carolina	125.4	355.0	524.5
Idaho	40.6	55.4	232.3	South Dakota	21.4	63.8	87.7
Illinois	357.0	509.7	1,977.2	Tennessee	155.5	317.8	727.8
Indiana	173.5	571.5	846.8	Texas	628.2	1,174.1	2,976.3
Iowa	106.1	300.0	589.8	Utah	83.4	148.1	411.8
Kansas	100.3	224.7	502.1	Vermont	15.2	135.1	37.3
Kentucky	115.0	260.3	456.7	Virginia	217.7	670.8	918.6
Louisiana	136.1	330.6	495.5	Washington	194.8	330.8	954.2
Maine	27.2	100.6	165.2	West Virginia	60.8	153.5	194.4
Maryland	155.2	479.2	732.8	Wisconsin	179.6	441.0	1,030.9
Massachusetts	114.3	317.3	766.4	Wyoming	23.9	43.6	147.0

[1] Full-time equivalent (FTE). Credit and noncredit program enrollment including summer session. Excludes medical enrollments.   [2] State and local appropriations. Includes aid to students attending in-state public institutions. Excludes sums for research, agriculture stations and cooperative extension, and hospitals and medical schools.   [3] Excludes appropriated aid to students attending in-state public institutions.   [4] Estimated by source.
Source: Research Associates of Washington, Arlington, VA, State Profiles: Financing Public Higher Education, annual (copyright).

No. 318. Institutions of Higher Education—Charges: 1985 to 1998

[In dollars. Estimated. **For the entire academic year ending in year shown.** Figures are average charges per full-time equivalent student. Room and board are based on full-time students]

Academic control and year	Tuition and required fees [1]				Board rates [2]				Dormitory charges			
	All institutions	2-yr. colleges	4-yr. colleges	Other 4-yr. schools	All institutions	2-yr. colleges	4-yr. colleges	Other 4-yr. schools	All institutions	2-yr. colleges	4-yr. colleges	Other 4-yr. schools
Public:												
1985.....	971	584	1,386	1,117	1,241	1,302	1,276	1,201	1,196	921	1,237	1,200
1990.....	1,356	756	2,035	1,608	1,635	1,581	1,728	1,561	1,513	962	1,561	1,554
1991.....	1,454	824	2,159	1,707	1,691	1,594	1,767	1,641	1,612	1,050	1,658	1,655
1992.....	1,624	937	2,410	1,933	1,780	1,612	1,852	1,745	1,731	1,074	1,789	1,782
1993.....	1,782	1,025	2,604	2,192	1,841	1,668	1,982	1,761	1,756	1,106	1,856	1,787
1994.....	1,942	1,125	2,820	2,360	1,880	1,681	1,993	1,828	1,873	1,190	1,897	1,958
1995.....	2,057	1,192	2,977	2,499	1,949	1,712	2,108	1,866	1,959	1,232	1,992	2,044
1996.....	2,179	1,239	3,151	2,660	2,020	1,681	2,192	1,937	2,057	1,297	2,104	2,133
1997.....	2,271	1,276	3,323	2,778	2,111	1,789	2,282	2,025	2,148	1,339	2,187	2,232
1998 est...	2,365	1,318	3,489	2,876	2,180	1,864	2,380	2,076	2,243	1,419	2,280	2,338
Private:												
1985.....	5,315	3,485	6,843	5,135	1,462	1,294	1,647	1,405	1,426	1,424	1,753	1,309
1990.....	8,174	5,196	10,348	7,778	1,948	1,811	2,339	1,823	1,923	1,663	2,411	1,774
1991.....	8,772	5,570	11,379	8,389	2,074	1,989	2,470	1,943	2,063	1,744	2,654	1,889
1992.....	9,434	5,752	12,192	9,053	2,252	2,090	2,727	2,098	2,221	1,789	2,860	2,038
1993.....	9,942	6,059	13,055	9,533	2,344	1,875	2,825	2,197	2,348	1,970	3,018	2,151
1994.....	10,572	6,370	13,874	10,100	2,434	1,970	2,946	2,278	2,490	2,067	3,277	2,261
1995.....	11,111	6,914	14,537	10,653	2,509	2,023	3,035	2,362	2,587	2,233	3,469	2,347
1996.....	11,864	7,094	15,605	11,297	2,606	2,098	3,218	2,429	2,738	2,371	3,680	2,473
1997.....	12,498	7,236	16,552	11,871	2,663	2,181	3,142	2,520	2,878	2,537	3,826	2,602
1998 est...	13,013	7,536	17,197	12,388	2,742	2,321	3,224	2,608	2,990	2,624	4,001	2,717

[1] For in-state students.   [2] Beginning 1990, rates reflect 20 meals per week, rather than meals served 7 days a week.

Source: U.S. National Center for Education Statistics, *Digest of Education Statistics*, annual.

No. 319. Voluntary Financial Support of Higher Education: 1970 to 1997

[For school years ending in years shown (1,780 represents $1,780,000,000); enrollment as of fall of preceding year. Voluntary support, as defined in Gift Reporting Standards, excludes income from endowment and other invested funds as well as all support received from Federal, state, and local governments and their agencies and contract research]

Item	Unit	1970	1980	1985	1990	1994	1995	1996	1997
Estimated support, total [1]	Mil. dol.	1,780	3,800	6,320	9,800	12,350	12,750	14,250	16,000
Individuals................	Mil. dol.	822	1,757	2,876	4,770	6,210	6,540	7,440	8,500
Alumni..............	Mil. dol.	381	910	1,460	2,540	3,410	3,600	4,040	4,650
Business corporations	Mil. dol.	269	696	1,574	2,170	2,510	2,560	2,800	3,050
Foundations.............	Mil. dol.	434	903	1,175	1,920	2,540	2,460	2,815	3,200
Religious organizations	Mil. dol.	102	155	208	240	240	250	255	250
Current operations	Mil. dol.	960	2,250	3,800	5,440	6,710	7,230	7,850	8,500
Capital purposes..........	Mil. dol.	820	1,550	2,520	4,360	5,640	5,520	6,400	7,500
Enrollment, higher education...	1,000 ..	8,094	11,570	12,242	13,539	14,306	14,279	14,210	13,917
Support per student.........	Dollars .	220	328	516	724	863	893	1,003	1,150
In **1996-97** dollars	Dollars .	925	672	776	906	939	944	1,031	1,150
Expenditures, higher education .	Bil. dol .	24.7	62.47	98.26	150.56	189.73	201.53	212.40	224.50
Expenditures per student	Dollars .	3,052	5,399	8,026	11,120	13,262	14,114	14,947	16,131
In **1996-97** dollars	Dollars .	12,833	11,050	12,065	13,913	14,571	14,920	15,288	16,131
Institutions reporting support	Number.	1,045	1,019	1,114	1,056	992	1,086	1,104	1,061
Total support reported	Mil. dol.	1,472	3,055	5,295	8,214	10,326	10,992	12,251	13,801
Private 4-year institutions	Mil. dol .	1,154	2,178	3,522	5,072	6,103	6,500	7,163	8,023
Public 4-year institutions......	Mil. dol .	292	856	1,728	3,056	4,138	4,382	4,943	5,654
2-year colleges............	Mil. dol .	26	20	45	85	84	110	145	124

[1] Includes other contributions, not shown separately.

Source: Council for Aid to Education, New York, NY, *Voluntary Support of Education*, annual.

No. 320. Average Salaries for College Faculty Members: 1996 to 1998

[In thousands of dollars (50.4 represents $50,400). **For academic year ending in year shown.** Figures are for 9 months teaching for full-time faculty members in 4-year institutions. Fringe benefits averaged in 1996, $12,600 in public institutions and $14,600 in private institutions, in 1997, $12,600 in public institutions and $14,700 in private institutions, and in 1998, $13,200 in public institutions and $15,800 in private institutions]

Type of control and academic rank	1996	1997	1998	Type of control and academic rank	1996	1997	1998
Public: All ranks.............	50.4	52.0	53.6	Private: [1] All ranks...........	57.5	59.3	61.5
Professor.................	63.9	65.8	68.0	Professor	75.6	78.2	81.8
Associate professor.........	48.2	49.7	51.2	Associate professor	51.5	52.7	54.5
Assistant professor.........	40.2	41.3	42.4	Assistant professor.........	42.4	43.4	44.9
Instructor	30.8	31.8	32.4	Instructor	32.9	33.1	34.5

[1] Excludes church-related colleges and universities.

Source: American Association of University Professors, Washington, DC, *AAUP Annual Report on the Economic Status of the Profession.*

U.S. Census Bureau, Statistical Abstract of the United States: 1999

No. 321. Employees in Higher Education Institutions, by Sex and Occupation: 1976 to 1995

[In thousands (1,863.8 represents 1,863,800). As of fall. Based on survey and subject to sampling error; see source]

Year and status	Total	Professional staff										Nonpro-fessional staff, total
		Total	Executive, administrative, and managerial		Faculty [1]		Research/instruction assistants		Other			
		Total	Male	Female	Male	Female	Male	Female	Male	Female		
1976, total	1,863.8	1,073.1	74.6	26.6	460.6	172.7	106.5	53.6	87.5	91.0		790.7
Full time	1,339.9	709.4	72.0	25.0	326.8	107.2	18.6	9.4	76.2	74.1		630.5
Part time.	523.9	363.7	2.6	1.7	133.7	65.4	87.9	44.2	11.3	16.9		160.2
1991, total	2,545.2	1,595.5	85.4	59.3	525.6	300.7	119.1	78.6	165.4	261.3		949.8
Full time	1,812.9	1,031.8	82.9	56.2	366.2	169.4	(NA)	(NA)	142.2	214.8		781.1
Part time.	732.3	563.7	2.5	3.1	159.4	131.2	119.1	78.6	23.2	46.4		168.7
1993, total	2,602.6	1,687.3	82.7	60.9	561.1	354.4	120.4	82.4	166.7	258.6		915.3
Full time	1,783.5	1,039.1	80.1	57.7	363.4	182.3	(NA)	(NA)	142.7	212.9		744.4
Part time.	819.1	648.2	2.7	3.2	197.7	172.1	120.4	82.4	24.0	45.8		170.9
1995, total	2,662.1	1,744.9	82.1	65.3	562.9	368.8	124.0	91.9	177.2	272.7		917.2
Full time	1,801.4	1,066.5	79.2	61.8	360.2	190.7	(NA)	(NA)	151.5	223.2		734.9
Part time.	860.7	678.4	2.9	3.6	202.7	178.1	124.0	91.9	25.6	49.5		182.3

NA Not available.   [1] Instruction and research.

Source: U.S. Center for Education Statistics, *Fall Staff in Postsecondary Institutions, 1995*, March 1998.

No. 322. Faculty in Institutions of Higher Education: 1970 to 1995

[In thousands (474 represents 474,000), except percent. As of fall. Based on survey and subject to sampling error; see source]

Year	Total	Employment status		Control		Level		Percent		
		Full time	Part time	Public	Private	4-Year	2-Year	Part time	Public	2-Year
1970	474	369	104	314	160	382	92	22	66	19
1975	628	440	188	443	185	467	161	30	71	26
1976	633	434	199	449	184	467	166	31	71	26
1977	678	448	230	492	186	485	193	34	73	28
1979	675	445	230	488	187	494	182	34	72	27
1980	686	450	236	495	191	494	192	34	72	28
1981	705	461	244	509	196	493	212	35	72	30
1982	710	462	248	506	204	493	217	35	71	31
1983	724	471	254	512	212	504	220	35	71	30
1984	717	462	255	505	212	504	213	36	70	30
1985	715	459	256	503	212	504	211	36	70	30
1986	722	459	263	510	212	506	216	36	71	30
1987	793	523	270	553	240	548	246	34	70	31
1989	824	524	300	577	247	584	241	36	70	29
1991	826	536	291	581	245	591	235	35	70	28
1993	915	546	370	650	265	626	289	40	71	32
1995	932	551	381	657	275	647	285	41	70	31

Source: U.S. Center for Education Statistics, *Fall Staff in Postsecondary Institutions, 1995*, March 1998.

No. 323. Higher Education Registrations in Foreign Languages: 1970 to 1995

[As of fall (1,111.5 represents 1,111,500)]

Item	1970	1972	1974	1977	1980	1983	1986	1990	1995
Registrations [1] (1,000)	1,111.5	1,008.9	946.6	933.5	924.8	966.0	1,003.2	1,184.1	1,138.8
Index (1960=100).	171.8	155.9	146.3	144.3	142.9	149.3	155.0	183.0	176.0
By selected language (1,000):									
Spanish	389.2	364.5	362.2	376.7	379.4	386.2	411.3	533.9	606.3
French	359.3	293.1	253.1	246.1	248.4	270.1	275.3	272.5	205.4
German	202.6	177.1	152.1	135.4	126.9	128.2	121.0	133.3	96.3
Italian	34.2	33.3	33.0	33.3	34.8	38.7	40.9	49.7	43.8
Japanese	6.6	8.3	9.6	10.7	11.5	16.1	23.5	45.7	44.7
Russian	36.1	36.4	32.5	27.8	24.0	30.4	34.0	44.6	24.7
Latin.	27.6	24.4	25.2	24.4	25.0	24.2	25.0	28.2	25.9
Chinese	6.2	10.0	10.6	9.8	11.4	13.2	16.9	19.5	26.5
Ancient Greek	16.7	20.6	24.4	25.8	22.1	19.4	17.6	16.4	16.3
Hebrew.	16.6	21.1	22.4	19.4	19.4	18.2	15.6	13.0	13.1
Portuguese	5.1	4.8	5.1	5.0	4.9	4.4	5.1	6.2	6.5
Arabic.	1.3	1.7	2.0	3.1	3.5	3.4	3.4	3.5	4.4
12 languages as percent of total .	99.1	98.7	98.5	98.3	98.5	98.6	98.6	98.5	97.8

[1] Includes other foreign languages, not shown separately.

Source: Association of Departments of Foreign Languages, New York, NY, *ADFL Bulletin*, Vol. 28, No. 2, and earlier issues (copyright).

No. 324. College Freshmen—Summary Characteristics: 1970 to 1998

[In percent, except as indicated. As of fall for first-time full-time freshmen. Based on sample survey and subject to sampling error; see source]

Characteristic	1970	1980	1985	1990	1994	1995	1996	1997	1998
Sex:									
Male	55	49	48	46	46	46	46	46	46
Female	45	51	52	54	54	54	54	54	54
Applied to three or more colleges	[1]15	26	29	36	36	36	37	36	37
Average grade in high school:									
A- to A+	16	21	21	23	28	28	32	32	33
B- to B+	58	60	59	58	56	56	54	54	54
C to C+	27	19	20	19	15	15	14	14	13
D	1	1	1	-	-	-	-	-	-
Political orientation:									
Liberal	34	20	21	23	23	21	22	22	21
Middle of the road	45	60	57	55	53	54	53	55	57
Conservative	17	17	19	20	21	20	21	19	19
Probable field of study:									
Arts and humanities	16	9	8	9	8	10	10	9	10
Biological sciences	4	4	4	4	7	7	7	6	6
Business	16	24	27	21	16	16	16	16	17
Education	11	7	7	10	10	10	11	10	11
Engineering	9	12	11	8	8	7	8	9	8
Physical science	2	3	2	2	2	2	2	2	2
Social science	14	7	8	10	10	9	9	8	8
Professional	(NA)	15	13	15	19	18	16	15	15
Technical	4	6	5	4	3	4	2	4	4
Data processing/computer programming	(NA)	2	2	1	1	1	1	2	2
Other [2]	(NA)	(NA)	16	16	17	17	19	19	18
Communications	(NA)	2	2	2	2	2	2	2	2
Computer science	(NA)	1	2	2	2	2	3	3	4
Recipient of financial aid:									
Pell grant	(NA)	33	19	23	23	23	20	22	21
Supplemental educational opportunity grant	(NA)	8	5	7	6	6	6	6	6
State scholarship or grant	(NA)	16	14	16	16	16	17	17	17
College grant	(NA)	13	19	22	26	26	29	27	29
Federal guaranteed student loan	(NA)	21	23	23	29	29	26	25	25
Perkins loan [3]	(NA)	9	6	8	9	9	9	9	9
College loan	(NA)	4	4	6	8	10	9	11	10
College work-study grant	(NA)	15	10	10	13	13	12	12	12
Attitudes—agree or strongly agree:									
Activities of married women are best confined to home and family	48	27	22	25	25	24	24	25	(X)
Capital punishment should be abolished	56	34	27	22	20	21	22	24	23
Legalize marijuana	38	39	22	19	32	34	33	35	32
There is too much concern for the rights of criminals	52	66	(NA)	(NA)	73	73	72	70	73
Abortion should be legalized	(NA)	54	55	65	60	58	56	54	51
Aspires to an advanced degree	49	49	51	61	64	64	67	67	65
Male	57	50	52	60	62	61	65	63	61
Female	41	47	50	62	66	66	68	69	67
Median family income ($1,000)	12	23	34	43	48	49	53	53	53

- Represents or rounds to zero. NA Not available. X Not applicable. [1] 1969 data. [2] Includes other fields, not shown separately. [3] National Direct Student Loan prior to 1990.

Source: The Higher Education Research Institute, University of California, Los Angeles, CA, The American Freshman: National Norms, annual.

No. 325. Freshman Enrollment in Remedial Courses, by Institutional Characteristic: 1995

[In percent, except number of freshmen (2,128 represents 2,128,000). As of fall. Remedial courses are those developed for students lacking skills necessary to perform college-level work as required by the institution. Based on survey and subject to sampling error; for details, see source]

Institutional characteristic	Number of freshmen (1,000)	Institutions offering courses				Freshmen taking courses			
		Total	Reading	Writing	Math	Total	Reading	Writing	Math
All institutions	2,128	78	57	71	72	29	13	17	24
Control:									
Public, 2 year	943	100	99	99	99	41	20	25	34
Private, 2 year	56	63	29	61	62	26	11	18	23
Public, 4 year	726	81	52	71	78	22	8	12	18
Private, 4 year	403	63	34	52	51	13	7	8	9
Minority enrollment:									
High [1]	338	94	87	85	93	43	25	29	35
Low [2]	1,790	76	53	70	70	26	11	15	21

[1] Total enrollment, excluding nonresident aliens, is less than 50% White, non-Hispanic. [2] Total enrollment, excluding nonresident aliens, is more than 50% White, Non-Hispanic.

Source: U.S. National Center for Education Statistics, "Remedial Education at Higher Education Institutions in Fall of 1995," NCES 97-584.

No. 326. College Population, by Selected Characteristics: 1987 and 1997

[In thousands (190,058 represents 190,058,000), except percent. As of **October**. Based on the Current Population Survey. See text, Section 1, Population, and Appendix III]

Characteristic	Total population	Enrolled in college							
		Total	Type of school			Percent enrolled full time	Percent employed		
			2-year	4-year	Graduate school		Total	Full time	Part time
Total, 1987 [1]	**190,058**	**12,719**	**3,648**	**6,656**	**2,415**	**62.6**	**60.4**	**31.7**	**28.7**
Male	90,610	6,030	1,522	3,356	1,152	67.2	60.6	31.7	28.9
Female.	99,449	6,689	2,127	3,299	1,264	58.4	60.1	31.6	28.5
White.	162,757	10,731	3,039	5,617	2,075	61.6	62.2	32.6	29.6
Black	21,520	1,351	422	748	181	66.3	50.5	28.6	21.9
Hispanic origin [2]	13,687	739	307	342	90	57.3	65.5	37.0	28.6
14 to 19 years old	21,410	3,284	1,111	2,172	1	88.1	44.0	7.6	36.4
20 and 21 years old	7,078	2,642	624	1,961	58	84.4	53.3	14.5	38.8
22 to 24 years old	11,712	2,006	457	1,055	494	67.2	62.5	29.8	32.7
25 to 34 years old	42,374	2,985	851	996	1,137	36.4	74.0	55.8	18.2
35 years and older	107,484	1,802	605	471	725	22.3	83.1	62.8	20.3
Total, 1997 [1]	**207,727**	**15,436**	**4,078**	**8,331**	**3,027**	**66.3**	**62.2**	**33.0**	**29.2**
Male	100,067	6,843	1,663	3,876	1,304	70.4	59.5	33.9	25.6
Female.	107,660	8,593	2,415	4,455	1,723	63.1	64.2	32.2	32.0
White.	173,542	12,442	3,290	6,745	2,407	65.3	64.3	33.6	30.7
Black	24,749	1,903	541	1,031	331	67.2	55.0	34.3	20.7
Hispanic origin [2]	21,039	1,260	475	679	105	63.3	61.0	32.0	29.0
15 to 19 years old	19,463	3,533	1,178	2,327	30	89.7	43.1	8.8	34.3
20 and 21 years old	7,040	3,143	760	2,320	63	87.8	55.5	13.9	41.6
22 to 24 years old	10,423	2,699	528	1,609	562	73.3	65.0	28.9	36.1
25 to 34 years old	39,276	3,270	806	1,164	1,299	47.9	74.0	54.1	19.9
35 years and older	131,526	2,791	807	911	1,073	27.3	77.4	64.4	13.0

[1] Includes other races, not shown separately. [2] Persons of Hispanic origin may be of any race.

Source: U.S. Census Bureau, *Current Population Reports*, P20-443 and P20-516.

No. 327. Salary Offers to Candidates for Degrees: 1996 to 1998

[In dollars. Data are average beginning salaries based on offers made by business, industrial, government, and nonprofit and educational employers to graduating students. Data from representative colleges throughout the United States]

Field of study	Bachelor's			Master's [1]			Doctor's		
	1996	1997	1998	1996	1997	1998	1996	1997	1998
Accounting . . . . . . [2] . . .	29,375	30,154	32,825	32,965	33,636	36,492	(NA)	(NA)	(NA)
Business, general [2]	27,274	29,346	31,454	42,193	42,618	51,231	(NA)	(NA)	(NA)
Marketing	26,777	28,031	29,231	[3]42,046	[3]47,422	[3]53,563	(NA)	(NA)	(NA)
Engineering:									
Civil	31,308	33,031	35,335	35,702	37,947	41,584	[3]51,198	[3]49,746	[3]54,167
Chemical.	41,443	42,802	45,104	43,733	45,469	[3]48,593	[3]59,536	62,343	
Computer	37,529	40,093	43,865	43,488	50,485	51,610	[3]55,332	[3]63,367	[3]64,417
Electrical.	38,025	39,546	43,282	45,655	50,166	53,534	62,447	[3]64,158	66,716
Mechanical	37,036	38,287	41,260	43,181	45,974	48,695	[3]54,676	[3]61,037	[3]58,922
Nuclear [4]	[3]37,453	[3]37,050	[3]41,517	[3]40,840	[3]43,001	[3]45,090	(NA)	(NA)	(NA)
Petroleum	39,770	43,444	49,926	[3]42,630	[3]48,350	[3]50,760	(NA)	(NA)	(NA)
Engineering technology . . .	33,826	35,498	39,390	(NA)	(NA)	(NA)	(NA)	(NA)	(NA)
Chemistry	29,743	34,135	33,892	[3]37,360	[3]37,050	[3]37,145	[3]55,160	[3]54,671	54,219
Mathematics	29,745	32,151	36,203	[3]36,996	[3]38,360	[3]41,186	[3]52,000	[3]53,969	[3]52,368
Physics	[3]30,484	[3]35,554	[3]36,139	[3]40,305	[3]42,500	[3]42,964	[3]56,787	[3]62,403	45,601
Humanities . . . . [2]	24,285	25,078	28,447	(NA)	(NA)	(NA)	(NA)	(NA)	(NA)
Social sciences [5]	24,635	25,103	27,149	(NA)	(NA)	(NA)	(NA)	(NA)	(NA)
Computer science	35,222	37,215	41,949	44,204	44,331	52,648	[3]61,352	[3]63,058	[3]62,500

NA Not available. [1] Candidates with 1 year or less of full-time nonmilitary employment. [2] For master's degree, offers are after nontechnical undergraduate degree. [3] Fewer than 50 offers reported. [4] Includes engineering physics. [5] Excludes economics.

Source: National Association of Colleges and Employers, Bethlehem, PA, *Salary Survey, A Study of Beginning Offers*, annual (copyright).

No. 328. Time Spent Earning Bachelor's Degree, by Selected Characteristic: 1993

[As of spring (36,787 represents 36,787,000). Based on Survey of Income and Program Participation; for details, see source]

Characteristic	Total with bachelor's degrees (1,000)	Years to B.A. degree from end of high school						Mean duration [1]
		Number (1,000)			Percent			
		4 years or less	5 years or less	6 years or less	4 years or less	5 years or less	6 years or less	
All persons..............	36,787	15,624	23,810	27,334	42.5	64.7	74.3	6.29
Male...................	19,351	7,321	11,695	13,827	37.8	60.4	71.5	6.28
Female.................	17,436	8,302	12,115	13,508	47.6	69.5	77.5	6.30
White......	32,279	14,161	21,201	24,235	43.9	65.7	75.1	6.24
Male...................	17,258	6,717	10,537	12,411	38.9	61.1	71.9	6.22
Female.................	15,021	7,444	10,664	11,824	49.6	71.0	78.7	6.26
Black..........	2,314	713	1,258	1,473	30.8	54.4	63.7	7.19
Male...................	926	264	493	570	28.5	53.2	61.6	6.98
Female.................	1,388	448	764	904	32.3	55.0	65.1	7.33
Hispanic origin [2].............	1,367	363	689	852	26.6	50.4	62.3	6.79
Male...................	693	187	308	407	27.0	44.4	58.7	7.06
Female.................	674	176	381	445	26.1	56.5	66.0	6.50
Field of bachelor's degree: [3]								
Agriculture/Forestry.........	395	103	209	293	26.1	52.9	74.2	5.78
Biology................	624	241	416	471	38.6	66.7	75.5	6.34
Business/Management	5,282	1,952	3,117	3,628	37.0	59.0	68.7	6.72
Economics	660	321	433	479	48.6	65.6	72.6	6.35
Education.............	3,613	1,522	2,338	2,658	42.1	64.7	73.6	7.03
Engineering...........	2,577	729	1,392	1,733	28.3	54.0	67.2	6.66
English/Journalism...........	1,137	553	743	854	48.6	65.3	75.1	6.28
Home Economics...........	337	177	262	284	52.5	77.7	84.3	4.71
Law........	145	73	98	104	(B)	(B)	(B)	6.33
Liberal Arts/Humanities	2,188	894	1,413	1,592	40.9	64.6	72.8	6.44
Mathematics/Statistics	567	283	412	457	49.9	72.7	80.6	5.28
Medicine/Dentistry	142	39	74	104	(B)	(B)	(B)	6.32
Nursing/Pharmacy/Technical Health	1,626	498	914	1,092	30.6	56.2	67.2	7.10
Physical/Earth Sciences	614	194	362	470	31.6	59.0	76.5	6.25
Police Science/Law Enforcement .	326	95	182	240	29.1	55.8	73.6	6.11
Psychology..............	815	328	555	619	40.2	68.1	76.0	6.02
Religion/Theology	138	52	66	71	(B)	(B)	(B)	7.64
Social Sciences...........	1,760	683	1,113	1,333	38.8	63.2	75.7	6.44
Vo-tech Studies.............	181	64	121	135	(B)	(B)	(B)	7.39
Other...........	1,816	735	1,082	1,302	40.5	59.6	71.7	6.63
Advanced degree	11,843	6,089	8,507	9,417	51.4	71.8	79.5	5.67

B Base is less than 200,000 persons.   [1] For definition of mean, see Guide to Tabular Presentation.   [2] Persons of Hispanic origin may be of any race.   [3] For persons whose highest degree is the B.A.

Source: U.S. Census Bureau, unpublished data.

No. 329. Earned Degrees Conferred, by Level and Sex: 1960 to 1996

[In thousands (477 represents 477,000), except percent. Includes Alaska and Hawaii]

Year ending	All degrees		Associate's		Bachelor's		Master's		First professional		Doctor's	
	Total	Percent male	Male	Female	Male	Female	Male	Female	Male	Female	Male	Female
1960 [1]	477	65.8	(NA)	(NA)	254	138	51	24	(NA)	(NA)	9	1
1965	660	61.5	(NA)	(NA)	282	212	81	40	27	1	15	2
1970	1,271	59.2	117	89	451	341	126	83	33	2	26	4
1975	1,666	56.0	191	169	505	418	162	131	49	7	27	7
1980	1,731	51.1	184	217	474	456	151	147	53	17	23	10
1981	1,752	50.3	189	228	470	465	147	149	53	19	23	10
1982	1,788	49.8	197	238	473	480	146	150	52	20	22	10
1983	1,815	49.6	204	246	479	490	145	145	51	22	22	11
1984	1,819	49.6	203	250	482	492	144	141	51	23	22	11
1985	1,828	49.3	203	252	483	497	143	143	50	25	22	11
1986	1,830	49.0	196	250	486	502	144	145	49	25	22	12
1987	1,823	48.4	191	245	481	510	141	148	47	25	22	12
1988	1,835	48.0	190	245	477	518	145	154	45	25	23	12
1989	1,873	47.3	186	250	483	535	149	161	45	26	23	13
1990	1,940	46.6	191	264	492	560	154	171	44	27	24	14
1991	2,025	45.8	199	283	504	590	156	181	44	28	25	15
1992	2,108	45.6	207	297	521	616	162	191	45	29	25	15
1993	2,167	45.5	212	303	533	632	169	200	45	30	26	16
1994	2,206	45.1	215	315	532	637	176	211	45	31	27	17
1995	2,218	44.9	218	321	526	634	179	219	45	31	27	18
1996	2,248	44.2	220	336	522	642	179	227	45	32	27	18

NA Not available.   [1] First-professional degrees are included with bachelor's degrees.

Source: U.S. National Center for Education Statistics, Digest of Education Statistics, annual.

Education   203

No. 330. Degrees and Awards Earned Below Bachelor's, by Field: 1996

[Covers associate degrees and other awards based on postsecondary curriculums of less than 4 years in institutions of higher education]

Field of study	Less than 1-year awards		1- to less than 4-year awards		Associate degrees	
	Total	Women	Total	Women	Total	Women
Total	100,888	53,530	139,688	83,810	555,216	335,702
Agriculture and natural resources	1,749	422	1,874	549	6,182	1,964
Architecture and related programs	2	2	10	9	256	216
Area, ethnic, and cultural studies	180	137	133	114	111	83
Biological/life sciences	79	24	529	205	2,037	1,220
Business management and administrative services [1]	17,799	12,644	28,133	23,600	99,447	72,091
Communications and communications technologies.	505	243	557	240	3,944	1,698
Computer and information sciences	4,349	2,040	3,570	1,868	9,658	4,704
Construction trades	4,212	229	4,021	200	2,141	106
Consumer and personal services.	1,615	1,240	6,460	4,764	7,721	2,754
Education	569	423	677	627	9,750	6,641
Engineering and engineering technologies.	2,581	421	8,325	1,026	35,199	4,414
English language and literature/letters	128	86	37	26	1,310	839
Foreign languages and literatures	419	264	29	22	607	444
Health professions and related sciences	33,993	25,893	45,185	38,637	101,872	84,577
Home economics and vocational home economics	4,144	2,877	4,295	3,879	8,192	7,435
Law and legal studies	850	707	2,006	1,719	9,106	7,987
Liberal/general studies and humanities	152	86	481	340	174,970	106,976
Library science.	117	107	57	49	94	81
Mathematics	1	-	1	-	758	295
Mechanics and repairers	4,614	322	15,624	754	12,524	801
Multi/interdisciplinary studies	439	370	134	60	8,611	4,399
Parks, recreation, leisure, and fitness	95	61	130	78	936	391
Physical sciences	86	47	81	30	2,612	1,154
Precision production trades	4,009	724	8,104	1,393	10,217	2,098
Protective services	10,156	2,202	2,821	813	19,196	5,769
Psychology	24	18	52	39	1,583	1,177
Public administration and services	544	361	548	419	4,218	3,453
R.O.T.C. and military technologies	-	-	-	-	556	42
Social sciences and history	22	12	29	20	4,021	2,533
Theological studies, religion and philosophy	149	89	561	255	691	332
Transportation and material moving	6,180	826	749	120	1,571	246
Visual and performing arts	831	432	3,861	1,576	13,534	7,728
Undistributed and unclassified.	295	221	614	379	1,591	1,054

- Represents zero. [1] Includes marketing.

Source: U.S. National Center for Education Statistics, *Digest of Education Statistics, 1998.*

No. 331. Bachelor's Degrees Earned, by Field: 1971 to 1996

Field of study	1971	1980	1990	1995	1996	Percent female	
						1971	1996
Total	839,730	929,417	1,051,344	1,160,134	1,164,792	43.4	55.1
Agriculture and natural resources	12,672	22,802	12,900	19,841	21,431	4.2	36.8
Architecture and environmental design .	5,570	9,132	9,364	8,756	8,352	11.9	36.1
Area, ethnic and cultural studies	2,582	2,840	4,613	5,706	5,786	52.4	65.7
Biological sciences/life sciences	35,743	46,370	37,204	55,984	60,994	29.1	52.7
Business and management	114,729	184,867	248,698	234,323	227,102	9.1	48.6
Communications [1]	10,802	28,616	51,308	48,803	48,003	35.3	58.8
Computer and information sciences . . .	2,388	11,154	27,257	24,404	24,098	13.6	27.5
Education	176,307	118,038	105,112	106,079	105,509	74.5	75.1
Engineering [1]	50,046	68,893	81,322	78,154	77,437	0.8	16.1
English language and literature/letters .	64,342	32,541	47,519	51,901	50,698	65.6	66.0
Foreign languages and literatures	20,536	12,089	12,386	13,775	13,952	74.0	69.8
Health sciences	25,226	63,920	58,302	79,855	84,036	77.1	81.6
Home economics	11,167	18,411	14,491	15,345	15,803	97.3	88.1
Law and legal studies	545	683	1,592	2,032	2,052	5.0	72.9
Liberal/general studies	7,481	23,196	27,985	33,356	33,997	33.6	60.6
Library and archival sciences	1,013	398	77	50	58	92.0	86.2
Mathematics	24,937	11,872	15,176	13,723	13,143	37.9	45.7
Military technologies	357	38	196	27	7	0.3	65.0
Multi/interdisciplinary studies	6,286	11,277	16,267	26,033	26,515	22.8	49.3
Parks and recreation.	1,621	5,753	4,582	12,889	13,983	34.7	30.2
Philosophy, religion, and theology	11,890	13,276	12,068	12,854	12,746	25.5	36.0
Physical sciences [1]	21,412	23,410	16,066	19,177	19,647	13.8	38.4
Protective services	2,045	15,015	15,354	24,157	24,810	9.2	73.0
Psychology	38,187	42,093	53,952	72,083	73,291	44.4	78.8
Public affairs	5,466	16,644	13,908	18,586	19,849	68.4	47.9
Social sciences [2]	155,324	103,662	118,083	128,154	126,479	36.8	59.2
Visual and performing arts	30,394	40,892	39,934	48,690	49,296	59.7	21.9
Unclassified.	662	1,535	5,628	5,397	5,718	0.9	21.9

- Represents zero. [1] Includes technologies. [2] Includes history.

Source: U.S. National Center for Education Statistics, *Digest of Education Statistics*, annual.

No. 332. Master's and Doctorate's Degrees Earned, by Field: 1971 to 1996

Level and field of study	1971	1980	1990	1995	1996	Percent female 1971	Percent female 1996
MASTER'S DEGREES							
Total	230,509	298,081	324,301	397,629	406,301	40.1	55.9
Agriculture and natural resources	2,457	3,976	3,382	4,252	4,569	5.9	42.0
Architecture and related programs	1,705	3,139	3,499	3,923	3,993	13.8	40.9
Area, ethnic and cultural studies	1,032	852	1,212	1,639	1,713	38.3	53.4
Biological sciences/life sciences	5,728	6,510	4,869	5,393	6,157	33.6	52.9
Business management and administrative services	25,977	54,484	76,676	93,809	93,982	3.9	37.6
Communications and technologies	1,856	3,082	4,362	5,609	5,604	34.6	61.3
Computer and information sciences	1,588	3,647	9,677	10,326	10,151	10.3	26.7
Education	87,666	101,819	84,881	101,242	106,253	56.2	76.3
Engineering and engineering technologies	16,443	16,243	24,772	29,670	28,566	1.1	17.2
English language and literature/letters	10,686	6,189	6,567	7,845	7,893	60.6	64.3
Foreign languages	5,217	2,854	2,760	3,136	3,124	64.2	67.4
Health sciences	5,749	15,704	20,321	31,243	33,398	55.3	79.0
Home economics	1,452	2,690	2,100	2,864	2,917	93.9	83.0
Law and legal studies	955	1,817	1,888	2,511	2,751	4.8	36.4
Liberal arts and sciences, general studies and humanities	885	2,646	1,999	2,565	2,778	44.6	65.4
Library science	7,001	5,374	4,341	5,057	5,099	81.3	79.0
Mathematics	5,695	3,382	4,146	4,181	4,031	27.1	38.8
Military technologies	2	46	-	124	136	-	2.9
Multi/interdisciplinary studies	821	2,306	2,834	2,457	2,347	25.0	53.9
Parks and recreation	218	647	529	1,755	1,751	29.8	48.0
Philosophy, religion, and theology	4,036	5,126	6,265	6,620	6,409	27.1	39.1
Physical sciences and science technologies	6,367	5,219	5,449	5,753	5,847	13.3	32.2
Protective services	194	1,805	1,151	1,706	1,812	10.3	36.5
Psychology	5,717	9,938	10,730	13,921	13,792	40.6	72.4
Public administration and services	7,785	17,560	17,399	23,501	24,229	50.0	71.4
Social sciences [1]	16,539	12,176	11,634	14,845	15,012	28.5	46.1
Visual and performing arts	6,675	8,708	8,481	10,277	10,280	47.4	57.6
Unclassified	63	142	2,377	1,405	1,707	-	24.9
DOCTORATE'S DEGREES							
Total	32,107	32,615	38,371	44,446	44,652	14.3	39.9
Agriculture and natural resources	1,086	991	1,295	1,264	1,271	2.9	26.4
Architecture and related programs	36	79	103	141	141	8.3	31.9
Area, ethnic and cultural studies	144	151	131	186	184	16.7	48.9
Biological sciences/life sciences	3,645	3,636	3,844	4,645	4,780	16.3	42.0
Business management and administrative services	757	753	1,093	1,394	1,368	2.8	28.8
Communications and technologies	145	193	273	321	345	13.1	44.9
Computer and information sciences	128	240	627	884	867	2.3	14.5
Education	6,041	7,314	6,502	6,905	6,676	21.0	62.2
Engineering and engineering technology	3,638	2,507	4,981	6,128	6,380	0.6	12.5
English language and literature/letters	1,650	1,294	1,078	1,561	1,535	28.8	61.6
Foreign languages	988	755	724	905	876	34.6	55.8
Health sciences	466	786	1,536	2,069	2,119	16.5	56.6
Home economics	123	192	301	388	414	61.0	71.7
Law and legal studies	20	40	111	88	91	-	35.2
Liberal arts and sciences, general studies and humanities	32	192	63	90	75	31.3	56.0
Library science	39	73	42	55	53	28.2	81.1
Mathematics	1,249	763	966	1,226	1,209	7.6	20.4
Multi/interdisciplinary studies	59	209	272	238	441	6.8	50.6
Parks and recreation	2	21	35	149	104	50.0	37.5
Philosophy, religion, and theology	866	1,693	1,756	2,098	2,070	5.8	18.4
Physical sciences and science technologies	4,390	3,089	4,164	4,483	4,571	5.6	23.1
Protective services	1	18	38	26	38	-	42.1
Psychology	2,144	3,395	3,811	3,822	3,711	24.0	66.1
Public administration and services	174	342	508	556	499	24.1	55.9
Social sciences [1]	3,660	3,230	3,010	3,725	3,760	13.9	37.8
Visual and performing arts	621	655	849	1,080	1,067	22.2	50.9
Unclassified	3	4	258	19	7	-	28.6

- Represents zero.   [1] Includes history.

Source: U.S. National Center for Education Statistics, *Digest of Education Statistics*, annual.

Education 205

No. 333. First Professional Degrees Earned in Selected Professions: 1970 to 1996

[First professional degrees include degrees which require at least 6 years of college work for completion (including at least 2 years of preprofessional training). See Appendix III]

Type of degree and sex of recipient	1970	1975	1980	1985	1990	1992	1993	1994	1995	1996
Medicine (M.D.):										
Institutions conferring degrees.....	86	104	112	120	124	120	122	121	119	119
Degrees conferred, total.........	8,314	12,447	14,902	16,041	15,075	15,243	15,531	15,368	15,537	15,341
Percent to women...........	8.4	13.1	23.4	30.4	34.2	35.7	37.7	37.9	38.8	40.9
Dentistry (D.D.S. or D.M.D.):										
Institutions conferring degrees.....	48	52	58	59	57	52	55	53	53	53
Degrees conferred, total.........	3,718	4,773	5,258	5,339	4,100	3,593	3,605	3,787	3,897	3,697
Percent to women...........	0.9	3.1	13.3	20.7	30.9	32.3	33.9	38.5	36.4	35.8
Law (LL.B. or J.D.):										
Institutions conferring degrees.....	145	154	179	181	182	177	184	185	183	183
Degrees conferred, total.........	14,916	29,296	35,647	37,491	36,485	38,848	40,302	40,044	39,349	39,828
Percent to women...........	5.4	15.1	30.2	38.5	42.2	42.7	42.5	43.0	42.6	43.5
Theological (B.D., M.Div., M.H.L.):										
Institutions conferring degrees.....	(NA)	(NA)	(NA)	(NA)	(NA)	(NA)	(NA)	186	192	184
Degrees conferred, total.........	5,298	5,095	7,115	7,221	5,851	5,251	5,447	5,967	5,978	5,879
Percent to women...........	2.3	6.8	13.8	18.5	24.8	23.3	24.8	24.8	25.7	25.2

NA Not available.

Source: U.S. National Center for Education Statistics, *Digest of Education Statistics*, annual.

No. 334. Degrees Earned, by Level and Race/Ethnicity: 1981 to 1996

[For **school year ending in year shown.** Data exclude some institutions not reporting field of study and are slight undercounts of degrees awarded]

Level of degree and race/ethnicity	Total						Percent distribution	
	1981	1985	1990	1994	1995	1996	1981	1996
Associate's degrees, total	410,174	429,815	450,263	529,106	538,545	553,625	100.0	100
White, non-Hispanic.............	339,167	355,343	369,580	418,301	419,323	425,028	82.7	76.8
Black, non-Hispanic.............	35,330	35,791	35,327	45,461	47,142	51,672	8.6	9.3
Hispanic	17,800	19,407	22,195	32,074	36,013	38,163	4.3	6.9
Asian or Pacific Islander..........	8,650	9,914	13,482	18,433	20,717	23,091	2.1	4.2
American Indian/Alaskan Native......	2,584	2,953	3,530	4,871	5,492	5,556	0.6	1.0
Nonresident alien	6,643	6,407	6,149	9,966	9,858	10,115	1.6	1.8
Bachelor's degrees, total	934,800	968,311	1,048,631	1,165,973	1,158,788	1,163,036	100.0	100.0
White, non-Hispanic.............	807,319	826,106	884,376	936,227	913,377	904,709	86.4	77.8
Black, non-Hispanic.............	60,673	57,473	61,063	83,576	87,203	91,166	6.5	7.8
Hispanic	21,832	25,874	32,844	50,241	54,201	58,288	2.3	5.0
Asian or Pacific Islander..........	18,794	25,395	39,248	55,660	60,478	64,359	2.0	5.5
American Indian/Alaskan Native......	3,593	4,246	4,392	6,189	6,606	6,970	0.4	0.6
Nonresident alien	22,589	29,217	26,708	34,080	36,923	37,544	2.4	3.2
Master's degrees, total	294,183	280,421	322,465	385,419	397,052	405,521	100.0	100.0
White, non-Hispanic.............	241,216	223,628	251,690	288,288	292,784	297,558	82.0	73.4
Black, non-Hispanic.............	17,133	13,939	15,446	21,937	24,171	25,801	5.8	6.4
Hispanic	6,461	6,864	7,950	11,913	12,907	14,412	2.2	3.6
Asian or Pacific Islander..........	6,282	7,782	10,577	15,267	16,842	18,161	2.1	4.5
American Indian/Alaskan Native......	1,034	1,256	1,101	1,697	1,621	1,778	0.4	0.4
Nonresident alien	22,057	26,952	35,701	46,317	48,727	47,811	7.5	11.8
Doctor's degrees, total	32,839	32,307	38,113	43,149	44,427	44,645	100.0	100.0
White, non-Hispanic.............	25,908	23,934	25,880	27,156	27,826	27,756	78.9	62.2
Black, non-Hispanic.............	1,265	1,154	1,153	1,393	1,667	1,636	3.9	3.7
Hispanic	456	677	788	903	984	999	1.4	2.2
Asian or Pacific Islander..........	877	1,106	1,235	2,025	2,690	2,646	2.7	5.9
American Indian/Alaskan Native......	130	119	99	134	130	158	0.4	0.4
Nonresident alien	4,203	5,317	8,958	11,538	11,130	11,450	12.8	25.6
First-professional degrees, total ..	71,340	71,057	70,744	75,418	75,800	76,641	100.0	100.0
White, non-Hispanic.............	64,551	63,219	60,240	60,140	59,402	59,456	90.5	77.6
Black, non-Hispanic.............	2,931	3,029	3,410	4,444	4,747	5,016	4.1	6.5
Hispanic	1,541	1,884	2,427	3,134	3,231	3,476	2.2	4.5
Asian or Pacific Islander..........	1,456	1,816	3,362	5,892	6,397	6,617	2.0	8.6
American Indian/Alaskan Native......	192	248	257	371	412	463	0.3	0.6
Nonresident alien	669	861	1,048	1,437	1,611	1,613	0.9	2.1

Source: U.S. National Center for Education Statistics, *Digest of Education Statistics*, annual.

No. 335. College and University Libraries—Summary: 1975 to 1995

[For school year ending in year shown, except enrollment as of fall of the prior year (10,322 represents 10,322,000). Prior to 1982, includes outlying areas]

Item	1975	1982	1985	1988	1990	1992	1995
Number of libraries	2,972	3,104	3,322	3,438	3,274	3,274	3,639
Total enrollment (1,000)	10,322	12,372	12,242	12,767	13,539	14,359	14,279
COLLECTIONS (1,000)							
Number of volumes	447,059	567,826	631,727	706,504	717,042	749,429	792,707
Volumes added during year.	23,242	19,507	20,658	21,907	19,003	20,982	22,460
Number of serial subscriptions.	4,434	4,890	6,317	6,416	5,748	6,966	6,780
STAFF							
Total	56,836	58,476	58,476	67,251	69,359	67,166	68,920
Librarians and professional	23,530	23,816	21,822	25,115	26,101	26,341	27,376
OPERATING EXPENDITURES ($1,000)							
Total [1]	1,091,784	1,943,769	2,404,524	2,770,075	3,257,813	3,648,654	4,317,847
Salaries.	592,568	1,081,894	1,156,138	1,451,551	1,693,813	1,889,368	2,058,375
Collection.	327,904	561,199	750,282	891,281	1,040,928	1,197,293	1,374,407

[1] Includes other expenditures, not shown separately.

Source: U.S. National Center for Education Statistics, *Digest of Education Statistics,* 1997; and Academic Library Survey.

No. 336. Libraries—Number, by Type: 1980 to 1997

Type	1980	1985	1990	1997	Type	1980	1985	1990	1997
Total [1]	31,564	32,323	34,613	37,591	Junior college	1,191	1,188	1,233	1,270
United States.	28,638	29,843	30,761	33,108	Colleges,				
Public	8,717	8,849	9,060	9,815	universities	3,400	3,846	3,360	3,430
Public branches.	5,936	6,330	5,833	6,435	Departmental . . .	1,489	1,824	1,454	1,452
Special [2]	7,649	7,530	9,051	9,898	Law, medicine,				
Medicine.	1,674	1,667	1,861	1,900	religious	269	531	501	491
Religious.	913	839	946	1,010	Government	1,260	1,574	1,735	1,897
Law [3]	417	435	647	1,153	Armed Forces	485	526	489	363
Academic.	4,591	5,034	4,593	4,700	Outlying areas	113	114	110	(NA)

NA Not available. [1] Includes Canadian libraries and libraries in regions administered by the United States, not shown separately. Data are exclusive of elementary and secondary school libraries. Law libraries with fewer than 10,000 volumes are included only if they specialize in a particular field. [2] Includes other types of special libraries, not shown separately. Increase between 1980 and 1990 is due mainly to revised criteria for identifying special libraries and improved methods of counting. [3] Increase in 1997 due to increased effort in identifying special libraries.

Source: R.R. Bowker Co., New York, NY, *The Bowker Annual: Library and Book Trade Almanac* and *American Library Directory,* annual. (Copyright by Reed Elsevier Inc.)

No. 337. Public Libraries, by Selected Characteristics: 1996

[Based on survey of public libraries (5,905 represents $5,905,000,000). Data are for public libraries in the 50 states and the District of Columbia. The response rates for these items are between 97 and 100 percent]

Population of service area	Number of—		Operating income—			Paid staff [3]		Books and serial volumes (per capita)
	Public libraries	Stationary outlets [1]	Total (mil, dol.) [2]	Source (percent)		Total	Librarians with ALA-MLS [4]	
				State govern-ment	Local govern-ment			
Total	8,946	16,047	5,905	12.2	78.1	117,812	27,353	2.8
1,000,000 or more. . . .	20	864	771	10.9	75.2	13,954	4,104.2	2.5
500,000 to 999,000 . . .	52	1,132	999	17.2	74.6	17,531	4,674.7	2.6
250,000 to 499,999 . . .	90	1,039	688	10.7	82.6	12,526	3,241.4	2.4
100,000 to 249,999 . . .	313	1,960	959	10.1	81.9	19,341	4,516.1	2.2
50,000 to 99,999.	510	1,573	729	13.5	78.5	15,096	3,420.1	2.5
25,000 to 49,999.	863	1,662	718	12.3	78.8	15,046	3,436.1	2.9
10,000 to 24,999.	1,679	2,162	643	10.2	78.7	13,945	2,843.2	3.5
5,000 to 9,999	1,498	1,677	239	11.8	74.4	5,792	804.6	4.2
2,500 to 4,999	1,327	1,365	92	7.1	74.2	2,518	220.6	5.3
1,000 to 2,499	1,636	1,653	52	5.7	69.9	1,590	76.9	7.7
Fewer than 1,000	958	960	14	7.3	66.4	473	15.4	13.8

[1] The sum of central and branches libraries. The total number of central libraries was 8,923; the total of branch libraries was 7,124. [2] Includes income from the Federal Government (1.0%) and other sources (8.7%), not shown separately. [3] Full-time equivalents. [4] Librarians with master's degrees from a graduate library education program accredited by the American Library Association (ALA). Total librarians, including those without ALA-MLS, was 39,096.

Source: U.S. National Center for Education Statistics, *Public Libraries in the United States: 1996.*

No. 338. Household Use of Public Library Services: 1996

[For the 50 states and DC **(99,088 represents 99,088,000)**. Based on a survey conducted between January and April 1996; see source for details]

Item	All households	Households with children under 18 years old	Households with no children under 18 years old
Number of households (1,000)	99,088	36,225	62,863
PERCENT USING PUBLIC LIBRARIES			
Used in the past year.	65	82	54
Used on the past month	44	61	35
Way of using—			
Borrow or drop off books or tapes	36	53	26
Go for other purpose [1]	18	26	14
Called library to renew book or to get information [2] . . .	14	18	12
Linked to library from home computer	4	5	3
Purpose for using—			
Enjoyment or hobbies [3]	32	45	24
To get information for personal use.	20	22	18
School or class assignment.	19	38	7
Work assignment or to keep up to date at work	8	10	7
To get information to help find a job	5	5	5
For program or activity for children 6 to 12 years old	4	7	2
For activity for children under 6	4	8	1

[1] Including a lecture, story hour, or using equipment.   [2] Information other than library hours or directions.   [3] Including borrowing books or tapes or to attend activities.
Source: U.S. Department of Education, National Center for Education Statistics, *Use of Public Library Services by Households in the United States: 1996*, February 1997.

No. 339. Children Who Participated in Various Literacy Programs With a Parent or Family Member: 1991 to 1996

[In percent. For children 3 to 5 years old. Based on the National Household Education Survey; see source for details]

Characteristic	Read to 3 or more times in the prior week			Told a story at least once in the prior week			Visited a library in the past month		
	1991	1995	1996	1991	1995	1996	1991	1995	1996
Total participating [1]	**71.4**	**83.1**	**82.9**	**72.0**	**81.4**	**82.0**	**36.6**	**41.2**	**38.2**
School enrollment status:									
Not enrolled	68.8	81.5	80.0	72.3	80.3	80.0	30.5	32.0	31.5
Center-based programs [2]	75.2	85.8	85.2	74.1	82.7	84.0	41.0	46.3	42.6
Kindergarten [2]	71.1	81.3	83.8	68.8	81.0	81.9	41.7	47.3	42.1
Race/ethnicity:									
White [3]	77.7	89.0	88.9	73.8	83.9	83.9	40.7	45.1	42.5
Black [3]	59.0	73.7	75.9	66.0	74.4	76.6	27.8	34.1	34.1
Hispanic	53.0	61.5	65.3	68.4	75.1	79.3	24.5	28.0	25.9
Parents highest education level:									
Less than high school diploma	53.8	64.4	58.8	67.4	71.9	72.8	18.3	18.3	19.4
High school diploma or GED	63.5	77.9	77.4	68.2	77.6	79.9	26.0	31.5	30.1
Some college/vocational/technical. .	74.0	85.3	86.5	74.2	82.9	84.6	38.5	40.9	37.1
Bachelor's degree	82.1	89.7	90.9	74.7	85.0	83.2	52.0	53.5	51.9
Graduate/professional school. . . .	88.3	94.0	96.1	78.4	88.2	85.8	59.1	62.8	59.5

[1] Includes other race/ethnic groups, not shown separately.   [2] Center-based includes Head Start, nursery school, and prekindergarten; kindergarten includes transitional kindergarten, kindergarten and pre-first grade.   [3] Non-Hispanic.
Source: U.S. Department of Education, National Center for Education Statistics, *Condition of Education, 1998*.

No. 340. Public Library Use of the Internet: 1998

[In percent, except number of outlets. As of spring. Based on sample survey; see source for details]

Item		Metropolitan status [1]			Poverty status [2]		
	Total	Urban	Sub-urban	Rural	Less than 20 percent	20 to 40 percent	More than 40 percent
All libraries outlets [3]	**15,718**	**2,691**	**4,933**	**8,094**	**12,757**	**2,644**	**317**
Percent of total	100.0	17.1	31.4	51.5	81.2	16.8	2.0
Connected to the Internet	83.6	91.0	88.1	78.4	84.1	80.9	83.3
Connected with public access.	73.3	84.0	76.7	67.6	73.2	72.8	79.5
Public access services provided—							
Only text-based terminals	5.8	13.4	5.3	3.2	5.7	5.0	16.1
Some graphical workstations	94.2	86.6	94.7	96.8	94.3	95.0	83.9
Speed of access—							
Less than 28.8kpbs	4.2	3.6	3.7	4.7	4.8	0.9	3.8
28.8kpbs to 56kpbs	28.7	7.7	21.3	42.2	30.6	21.6	11.1
56kpbs	32.7	33.5	35.1	30.7	32.0	34.8	42.6
Greater than 56kpbs	33.7	53.5	39.1	22.2	31.8	42.4	40.9
Special software/hardware for persons with disabilities on: all workstations	2.9	2.3	1.2	4.2	2.4	5.3	0.8
Some workstations	13.6	24.1	15.1	8.3	12.7	16.9	23.0
No workstations	83.6	73.8	83.7	87.5	84.9	77.9	76.1
Filtering software not used on workstations . . .	85.3	82.9	83.3	87.9	85.8	83.1	85.4
With acceptable use policies	84.8	87.3	85.9	83.1	84.5	86.6	86.3

[1] Urban = inside central city; Suburban = in metro area, outside of a central city; Rural = outside a metro area.   [2] Determined by the 1990 poverty status of the service area of the outlet.   [3] Central libraries and branches; excludes bookmobiles.
Source: The American Library Association, Washington, D.C., *The 1998 National Survey of U.S. Public Library Outlet Internet Connectivity: Final Report*, September 1998, by John Carlo Bartot and Charles R. McClure.

No. 341. Participation in Adult Education: 1994-95

[In thousands (189,543 represents 189,543,000), except percent. For the civilian noninstitutional population 17 years old and over not enrolled full-time in elementary or secondary school at the time of the survey. Adult education is considered any enrollment in any educational activity at any time in the prior 12 months. Based on survey and subject to sampling error; source for details]

Characteristic	Adult population (1,000)	Number taking adult ed. courses (1,000)	Participants in adult education				
			Percent of total	Reason for taking course (percent)[1]			
				Personal/social	Advance on the job	Train for a new job	Complete degree or diploma
Total....................	189,543	76,261	40	44	54	11	10
Age: 17 to 24 years old............	22,407	10,539	47	39	33	21	19
25 to 34 years old............	40,326	19,508	48	41	56	14	8
35 to 44 years old............	42,304	20,814	49	40	64	10	9
45 to 54 years old............	31,807	14,592	46	39	65	7	10
55 to 64 years old............	21,824	6,117	28	52	54	4	6
65 years old and over	30,876	4,691	15	86	14	1	3
Sex: Male..................	90,256	34,450	38	34	60	10	10
Female..................	99,287	41,811	42	51	49	12	9
Race/ethnicity:							
White [2]..................	144,587	59,982	41	44	57	10	9
Black [2]..................	20,806	7,704	37	45	48	13	12
Hispanic	15,689	5,281	34	40	37	13	11
Other races [2].............	8,461	3,294	39	40	45	16	13
Marital status:							
Never married	38,627	17,094	44	37	44	20	15
Currently married	114,678	48,200	42	45	58	8	8
Other	36,238	10,967	30	48	52	9	8
Children under 18 in household:							
Yes	77,787	36,103	46	43	56	11	9
No	111,756	40,158	36	44	52	11	10
Educational attainment:							
Up to 8th grade	12,808	1,283	10	52	20	8	9
9th to 12th grade	16,511	3,332	20	45	27	10	18
High school diploma or GED.....	62,956	19,341	31	44	49	10	6
Vocational school after high school	6,327	2,648	42	44	57	8	8
Some college..............	34,433	16,978	49	45	47	16	13
Associate's degree	9,975	5,601	56	39	64	9	9
Bachelor's or higher	46,535	27,078	58	43	65	9	9
Labor force status:							
Employed	117,826	59,734	51	37	64	10	10
Unemployed	8,155	2,983	37	39	27	25	13
Not in the labor force.........	63,562	13,544	21	72	15	11	8
Occupation: [3]							
Professional................	16,814	12,219	73	37	74	8	10
Executive, administrative and managerial..............	12,500	7,070	57	37	76	8	10
Technical and related support	4,812	3,300	69	32	73	9	11
Sales workers	15,666	7,131	46	41	53	12	11
Administrative support [4]..........	20,460	10,727	52	43	62	11	6
Service	17,355	8,238	47	37	51	14	12
Agriculture, forestry, and fishing....	1,908	500	26	40	49	6	12
Precision production, craft and repair	11,441	4,977	43	30	62	8	11
Machine operators, assemblers [5]...	8,309	2,515	30	28	58	10	9
Transportation and materials moving	4,488	1,295	29	35	60	13	12
Handlers, equipment cleaners, helpers and laborers	1,989	519	26	33	43	24	5
Nonclassifiable, undetermined.....	2,022	1,194	59	35	71	6	4
Household income:							
Under $10,000..............	30,198	6,883	23	48	25	20	12
$10,001 to $15,000...........	13,523	3,610	27	51	32	17	10
$15,001 to $20,000...........	13,116	4,176	32	45	38	15	12
$20,001 to $25,000...........	13,812	4,339	31	47	44	13	11
$25,001 to $30,000...........	16,386	6,208	38	45	46	13	11
$30,001 to $40,000...........	28,628	12,220	43	45	46	13	11
$40,001 to $50,000...........	20,446	9,567	47	41	55	11	9
$50,001 to $75,000...........	29,161	15,169	52	39	61	10	8
More than $75,000	24,274	14,089	58	43	67	7	8

[1] Reason for taking at least one course. Includes duplication. Excludes "to improve basic skills," cited by no more than 6 percent of participants. [2] Non-Hispanic. [3] For those employed in the 12 months prior to the interview. Excludes those participating exclusively in full-time credential programs. [4] Includes clerical. [5] Includes inspectors.

Source: U.S. National Center for Education Statistics, 1995 National Household Education Survey.

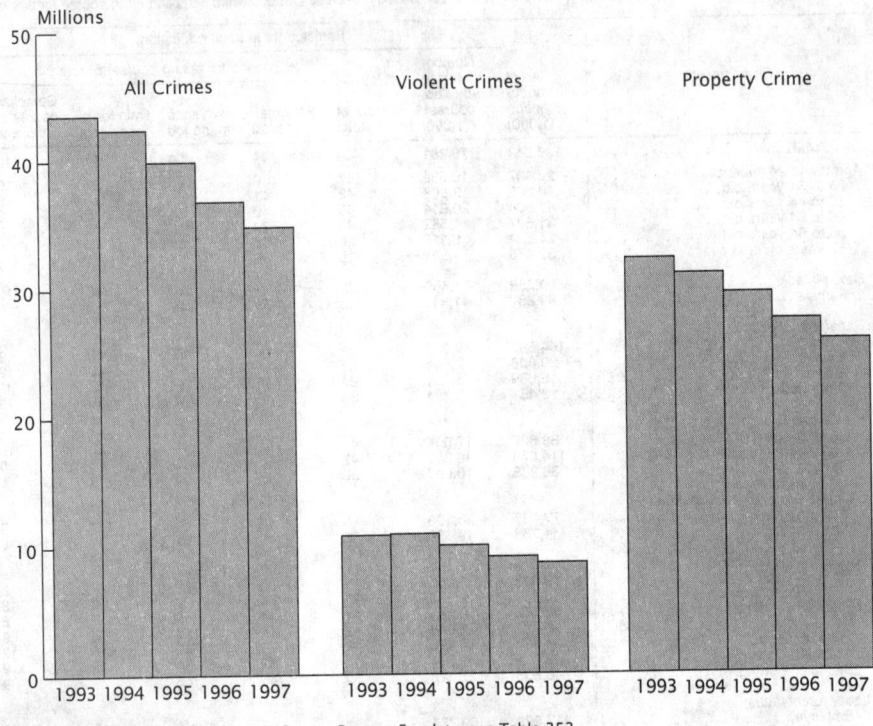

Figure 5.1
Criminal Victimization: 1993 to 1997

Millions

All Crimes

Violent Crimes

Property Crime

1993 1994 1995 1996 1997   1993 1994 1995 1996 1997   1993 1994 1995 1996 1997

Source: Chart prepared by U.S. Census Bureau. For data, see Table 353.

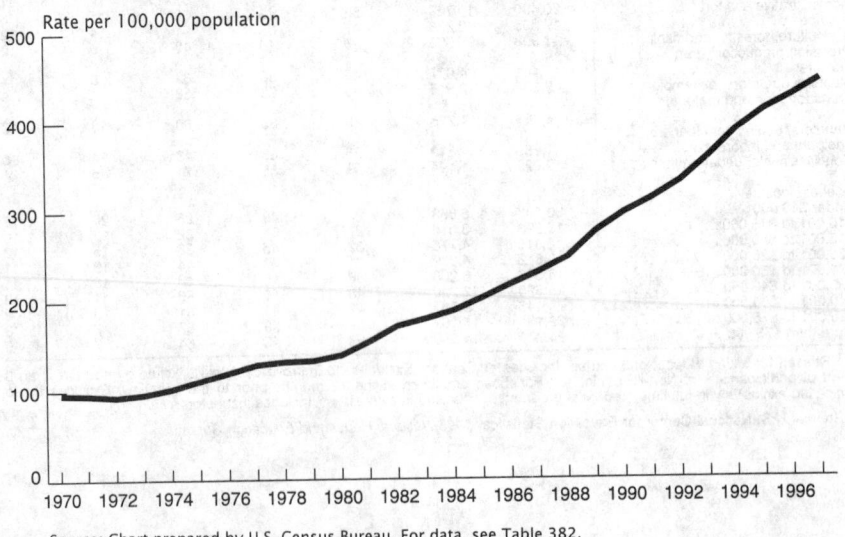

Figure 5.2
**Federal and State Prisoners per 100,000
Estimated Population: 1970 to 1997**

Rate per 100,000 population

1970 1972 1974 1976 1978 1980 1982 1984 1986 1988 1990 1992 1994 1996

Source: Chart prepared by U.S. Census Bureau. For data, see Table 382.

210 Law Enforcement, Courts, and Prisons

Section 5

Law Enforcement, Courts, and Prisons

This section presents data on crimes committed, victims of crimes, arrests, and data related to criminal violations and the criminal justice system. The major sources of these data are the Bureau of Justice Statistics (BJS), the Federal Bureau of Investigation (FBI), and the Administrative Office of the U.S. Courts. BJS issues several reports, including *Sourcebook of Criminal Justice Statistics, Criminal Victimization in the United States, Prisoners in State and Federal Institutions, Children in Custody, National Survey of Courts, Census of State Correctional Facilities and Survey of Prison Inmates, Census of Jails and Survey of Jail Inmates, Parole in the United States, Capital Punishment,* and the annual *Expenditure and Employment Data for the Criminal Justice System.* The Federal Bureau of Investigation's major annual report is *Crime in the United States,* which presents data on reported crimes as gathered from state and local law enforcement agencies.

Legal jurisdiction and law enforcement—Law enforcement is, for the most part, a function of state and local officers and agencies. The U.S. Constitution reserves general police powers to the states. By act of Congress, Federal offenses include only offenses against the U.S. Government and against or by its employees while engaged in their official duties and offenses which involve the crossing of state lines or an interference with interstate commerce. Excluding the military, there are 52 separate criminal law jurisdictions in the United States: 1 in each of the 50 states, 1 in the District of Columbia, and the Federal jurisdiction. Each of these has its own criminal law and procedure and its own law enforcement agencies. While the systems of law enforcement are quite similar among the states, there are often substantial differences in the penalties for like offenses.

Law enforcement can be divided into three parts: Investigation of crimes and arrests of persons suspected of committing them; prosecution of those charged with crime; and the punishment or treatment of persons convicted of crime.

Crime—There are two major approaches taken in determining the extent of crime. One perspective is provided by the FBI through its Uniform Crime Reporting Program (UCR). The FBI receives monthly and annual reports from law enforcement agencies throughout the country, currently representing 95 percent of the national population. Each month, city police, sheriffs, and state police file reports on the number of index offenses that become known to them. The FBI Crime Index offenses are as follows: *Murder and nonnegligent manslaughter* is based on police investigations, as opposed to the determination of a medical examiner or judicial body, includes willful felonious homicides and excludes attempts and assaults to kill, suicides, accidental deaths, justifiable homicides, and deaths caused by negligence; *forcible rape* includes forcible rapes and attempts; *robbery* includes stealing or taking anything of value by force or violence or threat of force or violence and includes attempted robbery; *aggravated assault* includes assault with intent to kill; *burglary* includes any unlawful entry to commit a felony or a theft and includes attempted burglary and burglary followed by larceny; *larceny* includes theft of property or articles of value without use of force and violence or fraud and excludes embezzlement, "con games," forgery, etc.; *motor vehicle theft* includes all cases where vehicles are driven away and abandoned but excludes vehicles taken for temporary use and returned by the taker. Arson was added as the eighth Index offense in April 1979 following a Congressional mandate. *Arson* includes

Law Enforcement, Courts, and Prisons 211

any willful or malicious burning or attempt to burn, with or without intent to defraud, a dwelling house, public building, motor vehicle or aircraft, personal property of another, etc. The monthly Uniform Crime Reports also contain data on crimes cleared by arrest and on characteristics of persons arrested for all criminal offenses. In summarizing and publishing crime data, the FBI depends primarily on the adherence to the established standards of reporting for statistical accuracy, presenting the data as information useful to persons concerned with the problem of crime and criminal-law enforcement.

National Crime Victimization Survey (NCVS)—A second perspective on crime is provided by this survey (formerly known as the National Crime Survey until August 1991) of the Bureau of Justice Statistics. Details about the crimes come directly from the victims. No attempt is made to validate the information against police records or any other source.

The NCVS measures rape, robbery, assault, household and personal larceny, burglary, and motor vehicle theft. The NCVS includes offenses reported to the police, as well as those not reported.

Police reporting rates (percent of victimizations) varied by type of crime. In 1994, for instance, 32 percent of the rapes/sexual assaults were reported; 55 percent of the robberies; 40 percent of assaults; 33 percent of personal thefts; 51 percent of the household burglaries; and 78 percent of motor vehicle thefts.

Murder and kidnaping are not covered. Commercial burglary and robbery were dropped from the program during 1977. The so-called victimless crimes, such as drunkenness, drug abuse, and prostitution, also are excluded, as are crimes for which it is difficult to identify knowledgeable respondents or to locate data records.

Crimes of which the victim may not be aware also cannot be measured effectively. Buying stolen property may fall into this category, as may some instances of embezzlement. Attempted crimes of many

types probably are under recorded for this reason. Events in which the victim has shown a willingness to participate in illegal activity also are excluded.

In any encounter involving a personal crime, more than one criminal act can be committed against an individual. For example, a rape may be associated with a robbery or a household offense, such as a burglary, can escalate into something more serious in the event of a personal confrontation. In classifying the survey-measured crimes, each criminal incident has been counted only once—by the most serious act that took place during the incident and ranked in accordance with the seriousness classification system used by the Federal Bureau of Investigation. The order of seriousness for crimes against persons is as follows: Rape, robbery, assault, and larceny.

Consequently, if a person were both robbed and assaulted, the event would be classified as robbery; if the victim suffered physical harm, the crime would be categorized as robbery with injury. Personal crimes take precedence over household offenses.

A victimization, basic measure of the occurrence of crime, is a specific criminal act as it affects a single victim. The number of victimizations is determined by the number of victims of such acts. Victimization counts serve as key elements in computing rates of victimization. For crimes against persons, the rates are based on the total number of individuals age 12 and over or on a portion of that population sharing a particular characteristic or set of traits. As general indicators of the danger of having been victimized during the reference period, the rates are not sufficiently refined to represent true measures of risk for specific individuals or households.

An incident is a specific criminal act involving one or more victims; therefore the number of incidents of personal crimes is lower than that of victimizations.

Courts—Statistics on criminal offenses and the outcome of prosecutions are

U.S. Census Bureau, Statistical Abstract of the United States: 1999

incomplete for the country as a whole, although data are available for many states individually. The only national compilations of such statistics were made by the Census Bureau for 1932 to 1945 covering a maximum of 32 states and by the Bureau of Justice Statistics for 1986, 1988, 1990, and 1992 based on a nationally representative sample survey.

The bulk of civil and criminal litigation in the country is commenced and determined in the various state courts. Only when the U.S. Constitution and acts of Congress specifically confer jurisdiction upon the Federal courts may civil or criminal litigation be heard and decided by them. Generally, the Federal courts have jurisdiction over the following types of cases: Suits or proceedings by or against the United States; civil actions between private parties arising under the Constitution, laws, or treaties of the United States; civil actions between private litigants who are citizens of different states; civil cases involving admiralty, maritime, or prize jurisdiction; and all matters in bankruptcy. The Administrative Office of the United States Courts has compiled statistics on the caseload of the Federal courts annually since 1940.

There are several types of courts with varying degrees of legal jurisdiction. These jurisdictions include original, appellate, general, and limited or special. A court of original jurisdiction is one having the authority initially to try a case and pass judgment on the law and the facts; a court of appellate jurisdiction is one with the legal authority to review cases and hear appeals; a court of general jurisdiction is a trial court of unlimited original jurisdiction in civil and/or criminal cases, also called a "major trial court"; a court of limited or special jurisdiction is a trial court with legal authority over only a particular class of cases, such as probate, juvenile, or traffic cases.

The 94 Federal courts of original jurisdiction are known as the U.S. district courts. One or more of these courts is established in every state and one each in the District of Columbia, Puerto Rico, the Virgin Islands, the Northern Mariana Islands, and Guam. Appeals from the district courts are taken to intermediate appellate courts of which there are 13, known as U.S. courts of appeals and the United States Court of Appeals for the Federal Circuit. The Supreme Court of the United States is the final and highest appellate court in the Federal system of courts.

Juvenile offenders—For statistical purposes, the FBI and most states classify as juvenile offenders persons under the age of 18 years who have committed a crime or crimes.

Delinquency cases are all cases of youths referred to a juvenile court for violation of a law or ordinance or for seriously "antisocial" conduct. Several types of facilities are available for those adjudicated delinquent, ranging from the short-term physically unrestricted environment to the long-term very restrictive atmosphere.

Prisoners—Data on prisoners in Federal and state prisons and reformatories were collected annually by the Census Bureau until 1950, by the Federal Bureau of Prisons until 1971, transferred then to the Law Enforcement Assistance Administration, and, in 1979, to the Bureau of Justice Statistics. Adults convicted of criminal activity may be given a prison or jail sentence. A prison is a confinement facility having custodial authority over adults sentenced to confinement of more than 1 year. A jail is a facility, usually operated by a local law enforcement agency, holding persons detained pending adjudication and/or persons committed after adjudication to 1 year or less. Nearly every state publishes annual data either for its whole prison system or for each separate state institution.

Statistical reliability—For discussion of statistical collection, estimation and sampling procedures, and measures of statistical reliability pertaining to the National Crime Victimization Survey and Uniform Crime Reporting Program, see Appendix III.

No. 342. Crimes and Crime Rates, by Type of Offense: 1987 to 1997

[Data refer to offenses known to the police. Rates are based on the U.S. Census Bureau estimated resident population as of July 1, 1990, enumerated as of April 1. See source for details. Minus sign (-) indicates decrease. For definitions of crimes, see text, this section]

Item and year		Violent crime					Property crime			
	Total	Total	Mur-der [1]	Forcible rape	Rob-bery	Aggra-vated assault	Total	Burglary	Lar-ceny—theft	Motor vehicle theft
Number of offenses (1,000):										
1987	13,509	1,484	20.1	91.1	518	855	12,025	3,236	7,500	1,289
1988	13,923	1,566	20.7	92.5	543	910	12,357	3,218	7,706	1,433
1989	14,251	1,646	21.5	94.5	578	952	12,605	3,168	7,872	1,565
1990	14,476	1,820	23.4	102.6	639	1,055	12,656	3,074	7,946	1,636
1991	14,873	1,912	24.7	106.6	688	1,093	12,961	3,157	8,142	1,662
1992	14,438	1,932	23.8	109.1	672	1,127	12,506	2,980	7,915	1,611
1993	14,145	1,926	24.5	106.0	660	1,136	12,219	2,835	7,821	1,563
1994	13,990	1,858	23.3	102.2	619	1,113	12,132	2,713	7,880	1,539
1995	13,863	1,799	21.6	97.5	581	1,099	12,064	2,594	7,998	1,472
1996	13,494	1,689	19.7	96.3	536	1,037	11,805	2,506	7,905	1,394
1997	13,175	1,635	18.2	96.1	498	1,022	11,540	2,461	7,726	1,354
Percent change, number of offenses:										
1987 to 1997	-2.5	10.2	-9.4	5.5	-3.8	19.6	-4.0	-24.0	3.0	5.0
1994 to 1995	-0.9	-3.2	-7.3	-4.6	-6.1	-1.3	-0.6	-4.4	1.5	-4.4
1995 to 1996	-2.7	-6.1	-8.8	-1.3	-7.8	-5.6	-2.1	-3.4	-1.2	-5.3
1996 to 1997	-2.4	-3.2	-7.6	-0.1	-7.0	-1.4	-2.2	-1.8	-2.3	-2.9
Rate per 100,000 population:										
1987	5,550.0	609.7	8.3	37.4	212.7	351.3	4,940.3	1,329.6	3,081.3	529.4
1988	5,664.2	637.2	8.4	37.6	220.9	370.2	5,027.1	1,309.2	3,134.9	582.9
1989	5,741.0	663.1	8.7	38.1	233.0	383.4	5,077.9	1,276.3	3,171.3	630.4
1990	5,820.3	731.8	9.4	41.2	257.0	424.1	5,088.5	1,235.9	3,194.8	657.8
1991	5,897.8	758.1	9.8	42.3	272.7	433.3	5,139.7	1,252.0	3,228.8	659.0
1992	5,660.2	757.5	9.3	42.8	263.6	441.8	4,902.7	1,168.2	3,103.0	631.5
1993	5,484.4	746.8	9.5	41.1	255.9	440.3	4,737.6	1,099.2	3,032.4	606.1
1994	5,373.5	713.6	9.0	39.3	237.7	427.6	4,660.0	1,042.0	3,026.7	591.3
1995	5,275.9	684.6	8.2	37.1	220.9	418.3	4,591.3	987.1	3,043.8	560.4
1996	5,086.6	636.5	7.4	36.3	201.9	390.9	4,450.1	944.8	2,979.7	525.6
1997	4,922.7	610.8	6.8	35.9	186.1	382.0	4,311.9	919.6	2,886.5	505.8
Percent change, rate per 100,000 population:										
1987 to 1997	-7.2	3.0	-14.0	-4.2	-10.3	12.9	-8.5	-29.7	-1.0	3.5
1994 to 1995	-1.8	-4.1	-8.9	-5.6	-7.1	-2.2	-1.5	-5.3	0.6	-5.2
1995 to 1996	-3.6	-7.0	-9.8	-2.2	-8.6	-6.6	-3.1	-4.3	-2.1	-6.2
1996 to 1997	-3.2	-4.0	-8.1	-1.1	-7.8	-2.3	-3.1	-2.7	-3.1	-3.8

[1] Includes nonnegligent manslaughter.

Source: U.S. Federal Bureau of Investigation, *Crime in the United States*, annual.

No. 343. Crimes and Crime Rates, by Type and Area: 1997

[In thousands (13,175 represents 13,175,000), except rate. Rate per 100,000 population; see headnote, Table 342. Estimated totals based on reports from city and rural law enforcement agencies representing 96 percent of the national population. For definitions of crimes, see text, this section]

Type of crime	United States		Metropolitan areas [1]		Other cities		Rural areas	
	Total	Rate	Total	Rate	Total	Rate	Total	Rate
Total	**13,175**	**4,923**	**11,358**	**5,325**	**1,152**	**5,207**	**665**	**2,064**
Violent crime	1,635	611	1,460	684	101	455	74	231
Murder and nonnegligent manslaughter	18	7	16	7	1	4	1	5
Forcible rape	96	36	80	38	8	36	8	25
Robbery	498	186	476	223	16	72	6	18
Aggravated assault	1,022	382	888	416	76	343	59	183
Property crime	11,540	4,312	9,899	4,641	1,051	4,752	591	1,833
Burglary	2,461	920	2,055	963	206	932	200	622
Larceny-theft	7,725	2,887	6,584	3,087	793	3,586	349	1,082
Motor vehicle theft	1,354	506	1,260	591	52	234	42	129

[1] For definition, see Appendix II.

Source: U.S. Federal Bureau of Investigation, *Crime in the United States*, annual.

No. 344. Crime Rates, by State, 1995 to 1997, and by Type, 1997

[**Offenses known to the police per 100,000 population.** Based on the U.S. Census Bureau estimated resident population as of July 1. For definitions of crimes, see text, this section]

State			1997									
				Violent crime					Property crime			
	1995, total	1996, total	Total	Total	Murder [1]	Forcible rape	Robbery	Aggravated assault	Total	Burglary	Larceny—theft	Motor vehicle theft
United States .	**5,276**	**5,087**	**4,923**	**611**	**6.8**	**35.9**	**186**	**382**	**4,312**	**920**	**2,887**	**506**
Alabama	4,848	4,820	4,890	565	9.9	32.3	161	362	4,325	1,014	2,955	357
Alaska.	5,754	5,450	5,273	701	8.9	66.2	106	520	4,571	702	3,412	457
Arizona	8,214	7,067	7,195	624	8.2	32.8	166	417	6,571	1,319	4,282	970
Arkansas.	4,691	4,699	4,719	527	9.9	43.5	112	362	4,192	1,013	2,864	315
California.	5,831	5,208	4,865	798	8.0	31.6	253	506	4,067	927	2,431	709
Colorado	5,396	5,119	4,650	363	4.0	43.1	83	233	4,287	796	3,077	414
Connecticut	4,503	4,228	3,984	391	3.8	22.6	153	212	3,593	738	2,410	445
Delaware	5,159	4,895	5,138	678	2.5	65.0	180	431	4,460	768	3,185	508
District of Columbia [2] . .	12,174	11,897	9,839	2,024	56.9	41.2	851	1,075	7,815	1,316	5,068	1,431
Florida.	7,702	7,497	7,272	1,024	6.9	51.9	276	689	6,248	1,460	4,057	732
Georgia	6,004	6,310	5,792	607	7.5	31.1	207	361	5,185	1,086	3,503	595
Hawaii.	7,199	6,585	6,023	278	4.0	31.3	118	125	5,745	1,073	4,127	545
Idaho [3]	4,402	4,013	3,925	257	3.2	28.9	20	205	3,668	758	2,709	201
Illinois [3]	5,456	5,320	5,141	861	9.2	37.1	278	537	4,280	871	2,943	466
Indiana	4,632	4,498	4,466	515	7.3	32.9	132	342	3,952	822	2,702	428
Iowa	4,102	3,649	3,816	310	1.8	20.3	56	232	3,506	772	2,500	234
Kansas [3]	4,887	4,682	4,564	409	6.0	42.4	93	268	4,154	971	2,934	250
Kentucky [3]	3,352	3,166	3,127	317	5.8	33.4	91	187	2,810	682	1,880	248
Louisiana.	6,676	6,839	6,449	856	15.7	41.3	239	560	5,593	1,239	3,748	606
Maine	3,285	3,394	3,132	121	2.0	20.5	21	78	3,011	664	2,215	132
Maryland	6,295	6,062	5,653	847	9.9	35.6	337	464	4,807	941	3,264	602
Massachusetts	4,342	3,837	3,675	644	1.9	26.9	109	506	3,031	662	1,888	481
Michigan	5,183	5,118	4,917	590	7.8	51.9	153	378	4,327	826	2,833	668
Minnesota	4,497	4,463	4,414	338	2.8	52.2	115	168	4,076	753	2,942	381
Mississippi	4,515	4,523	4,630	469	13.1	39.0	137	280	4,161	1,187	2,632	342
Missouri.	5,121	5,084	4,815	577	7.9	28.2	156	385	4,237	868	2,878	491
Montana [3]	4,797	4,494	4,409	132	4.8	19.5	20	88	4,277	569	3,460	248
Nebraska.	4,545	4,437	4,284	438	3.0	24.5	66	345	3,845	592	2,919	334
Nevada	6,579	5,992	6,065	799	11.2	59.9	302	425	5,266	1,310	3,167	788
New Hampshire [3]	2,655	2,824	2,640	113	1.4	33.7	23	55	2,526	393	1,997	136
New Jersey	4,704	4,333	4,057	493	4.2	21.5	211	256	3,564	756	2,297	511
New Mexico	6,428	6,602	6,907	853	7.7	50.4	171	624	6,053	1,452	3,884	717
New York	4,560	4,132	3,911	689	6.0	22.5	309	351	3,222	652	2,131	439
North Carolina	5,640	5,526	5,492	607	8.3	31.6	173	395	4,885	1,347	3,209	329
North Dakota	2,866	2,669	2,711	87	0.9	24.8	6	55	2,624	359	2,085	180
Ohio	4,405	4,456	4,515	435	4.7	40.8	159	231	4,079	849	2,824	406
Oklahoma	5,597	5,653	5,495	560	6.9	45.7	104	403	4,935	1,206	3,287	442
Oregon	6,564	5,997	6,270	444	2.9	40.3	118	284	5,825	1,033	4,198	595
Pennsylvania	3,365	3,556	3,432	442	5.9	27.4	156	253	2,989	568	2,054	368
Rhode Island	4,245	3,994	3,654	334	2.5	36.8	72	223	3,321	718	2,178	425
South Carolina	6,064	6,214	6,134	990	8.4	48.9	176	757	5,144	1,232	3,493	419
South Dakota	3,061	2,970	3,245	197	1.4	48.4	23	124	3,048	554	2,377	116
Tennessee	5,363	5,449	5,512	790	9.5	56.9	214	509	4,722	1,172	2,922	629
Texas	5,684	5,709	5,481	603	6.8	41.2	157	398	4,878	1,034	3,320	523
Utah	6,091	5,986	5,996	334	2.4	47.5	68	216	5,661	891	4,327	444
Vermont	3,434	3,003	2,828	120	1.5	26.5	13	78	2,709	613	1,960	136
Virginia	3,989	3,968	3,876	345	7.2	27.0	125	187	3,531	571	2,679	281
Washington	6,270	5,909	5,926	441	4.3	51.4	120	265	5,486	1,106	3,812	568
West Virginia	2,458	2,483	2,469	219	4.1	19.5	43	152	2,250	586	1,483	181
Wisconsin	3,886	3,821	3,678	271	4.0	20.3	101	146	3,407	571	2,534	303
Wyoming	4,320	4,254	4,181	255	3.5	28.5	18	205	3,926	625	3,166	135

[1] Includes nonnegligent manslaughter. [2] Includes offenses reported by the police at the National Zoo. [3] Complete data were not available; therefore, it was necessary for the crime counts to be estimated for 1995 and 1996.

Source: U.S. Federal Bureau of Investigation, *Crime in the United States*, annual.

Law Enforcement, Courts, and Prisons 215

No. 345. Crime Rates, by Type—Selected Large Cities: 1997

[**Offenses known to the police per 100,000 population.** Based on the U.S. Census Bureau estimated resident population as of July 1. For definitions of crimes, see text, this section]

City ranked by population size, 1997[1]	Crime index, total	Violent crime					Property crime			
		Total	Murder	Forcible rape	Robbery	Aggravated assault	Total	Burglary	Larceny—theft	Motor vehicle theft
New York, NY	4,861.6	1,268.5	10.5	29.5	610.7	617.8	3,593.1	739.0	2,145.2	708.9
Los Angeles, CA	5,776.3	1,596.5	16.3	39.9	579.1	961.3	4,179.8	852.7	2,332.6	994.5
Chicago, IL	(2)	(2)	27.4	(2)	914.3	1,320.4	7,008.6	1,469.1	4,324.5	1,215.1
Houston, TX	7,263.6	1,174.5	14.1	43.9	452.2	664.3	6,089.1	1,330.5	3,604.2	1,154.4
San Diego, CA	4,985.6	827.7	5.7	32.5	220.2	569.4	4,157.9	689.9	2,553.9	914.0
Phoenix, AZ	9,608.0	884.9	14.9	36.5	317.7	515.8	8,723.0	1,793.3	5,256.5	1,673.2
Dallas, TX	9,335.8	1,383.8	19.4	69.0	522.0	773.4	7,952.0	1,647.3	4,693.3	1,611.4
San Antonio, TX	8,050.5	401.7	9.2	59.5	196.1	136.9	7,648.8	1,274.5	5,544.3	830.0
Detroit, MI	11,669.1	2,151.5	45.9	94.8	803.6	1,207.3	9,517.6	1,891.9	4,351.9	3,273.8
Honolulu, HI	6,067.4	299.5	3.9	29.2	137.9	128.5	5,768.0	994.6	4,138.5	634.9
San Jose, CA	3,870.2	736.6	5.1	44.6	108.0	578.8	3,133.6	521.2	2,144.2	468.2
Indianapolis, IN	6,743.4	1,132.3	18.7	71.0	427.9	614.8	5,611.1	1,474.2	3,146.9	990.0
San Francisco, CA	6,893.8	1,133.5	7.8	30.9	610.7	484.1	5,760.4	948.4	3,830.5	981.5
Baltimore, MD	10,783.3	2,420.3	43.4	66.7	1,199.2	1,111.1	8,363.0	1,772.5	5,363.2	1,227.2
Jacksonville, FL	8,252.6	1,343.3	10.7	86.3	337.2	909.1	6,909.3	1,756.9	4,382.6	769.8
Columbus, OH	9,735.9	933.5	13.1	108.5	484.0	327.9	8,802.4	2,097.6	5,594.9	1,109.9
Memphis, TN	10,041.7	1,856.7	21.6	147.1	822.0	865.9	8,185.0	2,426.9	3,961.0	1,797.2
Milwaukee, WI	7,587.0	1,053.0	19.4	48.8	565.3	419.4	6,534.1	1,084.8	4,129.5	1,319.8
El Paso, TX	6,960.2	791.3	3.9	36.7	174.0	576.7	6,168.9	530.6	5,055.5	582.8
Charlotte-Mecklenburg, NC	9,409.9	1,630.8	10.5	61.4	483.3	1,075.6	7,779.1	1,852.8	5,146.2	780.1
Boston, MA	6,817.4	1,420.8	7.7	63.1	491.5	858.5	5,396.5	774.9	3,228.7	1,392.9
Seattle, WA	10,350.7	914.1	9.0	39.8	380.3	485.0	9,436.6	1,487.4	6,655.0	1,294.2
Austin, TX	7,870.0	645.7	7.3	51.8	235.1	351.5	7,224.3	1,375.1	5,031.8	817.4
Nashville, TN	11,091.4	1,746.7	21.1	103.4	485.6	1,136.7	9,344.7	1,660.8	6,147.3	1,536.5
Washington, DC	9,827.2	2,023.8	56.9	41.2	850.5	1,075.2	7,803.4	1,316.3	5,056.3	1,430.8
Denver, CO	5,803.4	672.3	13.1	67.7	238.3	353.2	5,131.1	1,227.9	2,806.2	1,097.0
Cleveland, OH	7,455.5	1,458.6	15.5	128.5	772.6	542.1	5,996.9	1,640.3	2,880.4	1,476.2
New Orleans, LA	9,355.8	1,720.3	54.7	78.8	813.1	773.8	7,635.5	1,659.5	4,055.8	1,920.1
Tucson, AZ	9,965.8	1,052.8	10.3	59.9	297.6	685.1	8,913.0	1,424.3	6,085.4	1,403.3
Fort Worth, TX	7,317.8	902.5	15.5	55.5	293.4	538.2	6,415.4	1,375.4	4,187.1	852.9
Portland, OR	11,199.6	1,604.4	9.7	75.2	411.2	1,108.3	9,595.2	1,561.8	6,492.3	1,541.1
Oklahoma City, OK	11,655.6	1,073.0	12.5	86.6	295.9	677.9	10,582.7	2,071.4	7,547.6	963.7
Kansas City, KS	10,952.1	1,895.5	22.1	92.2	599.7	1,181.5	9,056.6	1,911.4	5,502.2	1,642.9
Long Beach, CA	4,898.2	944.5	12.6	28.1	415.1	488.8	3,953.7	964.3	2,039.5	949.9
Virginia Beach, VA	4,482.0	239.7	4.3	23.0	116.0	96.4	4,242.3	673.7	3,358.4	210.2
Albuquerque, NM	11,118.3	1,317.1	11.4	62.6	401.1	841.9	9,801.2	1,982.0	6,021.4	1,797.8
Atlanta, GA	13,921.6	3,048.5	35.6	87.0	1,128.9	1,797.0	10,873.1	2,181.9	6,821.4	1,869.7
Fresno, CA	9,480.6	1,205.0	15.1	48.4	452.1	689.4	8,275.6	1,673.2	4,796.6	1,805.8
Miami, FL	12,828.8	2,813.7	26.3	48.2	1,153.0	1,586.2	10,015.2	2,283.5	5,771.0	1,960.6
Sacramento, CA	8,890.4	968.2	10.7	41.9	482.1	433.4	7,922.2	1,790.2	4,501.4	1,630.5
Tulsa, OK	7,472.2	1,204.3	10.5	72.8	240.3	880.7	6,268.0	1,666.5	3,629.1	972.4
St. Louis, MO	13,576.7	2,542.5	40.6	59.6	946.9	1,495.4	11,034.1	2,676.7	6,204.6	2,152.8
Oakland, CA	10,100.5	2,184.5	26.3	81.2	924.4	1,152.7	7,915.9	1,572.4	5,019.7	1,323.9
Minneapolis, MN	11,439.5	1,850.1	15.9	147.3	909.0	777.9	9,589.4	2,263.3	5,730.7	1,595.4
Pittsburgh, PA	5,817.7	786.4	14.2	49.5	436.8	285.9	5,031.3	950.9	3,283.2	797.2
Omaha, NE	7,236.2	1,385.4	8.8	50.0	232.6	1,094.0	5,850.8	899.8	3,964.8	986.2
Mesa, AZ	7,730.1	728.5	3.7	35.9	128.4	560.5	7,001.6	1,218.5	4,799.6	983.5
Toledo, OH	8,526.5	823.1	7.7	72.0	337.6	405.9	7,703.4	1,789.9	4,973.8	939.7
Wichita, KS	8,037.9	833.4	10.1	72.2	281.9	469.1	7,204.5	1,510.7	4,976.4	717.5
Buffalo, NY	8,095.4	1,284.5	14.7	73.6	702.6	493.6	6,810.9	1,915.4	3,656.7	1,238.8
Arlington, TX	6,621.7	797.4	4.0	41.8	173.6	577.9	5,824.3	1,007.0	4,141.5	675.8
Tampa, FL	12,260.1	2,663.8	11.7	88.4	846.7	1,717.1	9,596.3	2,202.6	5,983.7	1,410.0
Santa Ana, CA	4,035.9	675.2	9.0	30.5	327.6	308.1	3,360.7	537.6	1,925.2	897.9
Corpus Christi, TX	10,219.0	984.1	6.2	52.9	146.9	778.2	9,234.8	1,500.4	7,173.9	560.6
Anaheim, CA	4,187.9	678.1	5.2	34.5	280.3	358.0	3,509.8	783.7	2,045.3	680.8
Louisville, KY	6,906.7	1,112.2	22.4	46.3	559.0	484.5	5,794.5	1,620.9	3,150.0	1,023.6
Birmingham, AL	9,590.0	1,375.2	39.2	80.7	485.8	769.5	8,214.8	1,884.2	5,110.9	1,219.7
St. Paul, MN	7,909.7	886.6	8.9	85.2	308.3	484.2	7,023.1	1,487.2	4,558.6	977.3
Aurora, CO	6,188.4	621.1	6.4	83.5	187.7	343.5	5,567.4	867.1	3,890.7	809.5
Newark, NJ	10,728.0	2,734.7	21.6	64.3	1,302.5	1,346.4	7,993.3	1,728.2	4,091.3	2,173.9
Anchorage, AK	5,971.4	738.9	9.0	68.1	196.0	465.9	5,232.5	755.4	3,944.3	532.8
St. Petersburg, FL	8,939.1	2,098.4	8.4	80.2	500.9	1,508.9	6,840.7	1,612.7	4,520.1	708.0
Raleigh, NC	7,747.3	907.5	9.3	41.0	292.4	564.8	6,839.7	1,468.3	4,805.9	565.6
Norfolk, VA	7,598.8	974.1	22.2	55.6	476.8	419.5	6,624.8	1,018.8	5,086.0	519.9
Riverside, CA	5,881.2	1,008.2	9.3	39.1	305.1	654.6	4,873.1	1,117.4	2,856.8	898.9

[1] Resident population estimated by the FBI. [2] The rates for forcible rape, violent crime, and crime index are not shown because the forcible rape figures were not in accordance with national Uniform Crime Reporting guidelines.

Source: U.S. Federal Bureau of Investigation, *Crime in the United States,* annual.

No. 346. Murder—Circumstances and Weapons Used or Cause of Death: 1990 to 1997

[Based solely on police investigation. For definition of murder, see text, this section]

Characteristic	1990	1995	1996	1997	Characteristic	1990	1995	1996	1997
Murders, total . . .	20,273	20,232	16,967	15,839	Other motives	19.4	21.6	19.8	17.2
Percent distribution . . .	100.0	100.0	100.0	100.0	Unknown	24.8	28.9	30.1	31.8
CIRCUMSTANCES					TYPE OF WEAPON OR CAUSE OF DEATH				
Felonies, total	20.8	17.7	18.8	18.8					
Robbery	9.2	9.3	9.5	9.5	Guns	64.3	68.2	67.5	67.8
Narcotics	6.7	5.1	5.0	5.1	Handguns	49.8	55.8	54.6	53.3
Sex offenses	1.1	0.2	0.6	0.6	Cutting or stabbing . .	17.4	12.6	13.7	13.0
Other felonies	3.7	3.2	4.1	3.5	Blunt objects [1]	5.4	4.5	4.7	4.6
Suspected felonies . . .	0.7	0.6	0.4	1.0	Personal weapons [2] . . .	5.5	5.9	6.1	6.3
Argument, total	34.4	31.2	31.0	31.2	Strangulations,				
Property or money . .	2.5	1.7	1.9	1.8	asphyxiations	2.0	1.8	2.0	2.0
Romantic triangle . .	2.0	1.4	1.1	1.1	Fire	1.4	0.8	1.0	1.0
Other arguments . . .	29.8	28.2	27.8	28.3	All other [3]	4.0	6.1	5.0	5.4

[1] Refers to club, hammer, etc.   [2] Hands, fists, feet, etc.   [3] Includes poison, drowning, explosives, narcotics, and unknown.
Source: U.S. Federal Bureau of Investigation, *Crime in the United States*, annual.

No. 347. Murder Victims, by Age, Sex, and Race: 1997

Age	Total	Sex			Race			
		Male	Female	Unknown	White	Black	Other	Unknown
Total	**15,839**	**12,227**	**3,587**	**25**	**7,496**	**7,692**	**456**	**195**
Percent distribution	100.0	77.2	22.6	0.2	47.3	48.6	2.9	1.2
Under 18 yrs. old	1,790	1,253	536	1	843	836	93	18
18 yrs. old and over	13,746	10,772	2,974	-	6,524	6,751	352	119
Infant (under 1 yr. old)	242	143	99	-	142	82	10	8
1 to 4 yrs. old	319	158	160	1	163	140	12	4
5 to 8 yrs. old	114	62	52	-	61	45	7	1
9 to 12 yrs. old	99	58	41	-	62	30	6	1
13 to 16 yrs. old	583	455	128	-	245	299	37	2
17 to 19 yrs. old	1,624	1,413	211	-	619	943	52	10
20 to 24 yrs. old	2,916	2,508	408	-	1,109	1,732	58	17
25 to 29 yrs. old	2,175	1,811	364	-	914	1,180	58	23
30 to 34 yrs. old	1,842	1,398	444	-	865	925	38	14
35 to 39 yrs. old	1,581	1,149	432	-	765	756	44	16
40 to 44 yrs. old	1,213	895	318	-	631	536	31	15
45 to 49 yrs. old	888	648	240	-	504	338	38	8
50 to 54 yrs. old	540	401	139	-	345	174	16	5
55 to 59 yrs. old	372	268	104	-	240	112	13	7
60 to 64 yrs. old	275	201	74	-	161	101	10	3
65 to 69 yrs. old	211	149	62	-	136	68	4	3
70 to 74 yrs. old	198	131	67	-	142	51	5	-
75 yrs. old and over	344	177	167	-	263	75	6	-
Age unknown	303	202	77	24	129	105	11	58

- Represents zero.
Source: U.S. Federal Bureau of Investigation, *Crime in the United States*, annual.

No. 348. Homicide Victims, by Race and Sex: 1980 to 1997

[Rates per 100,000 resident population in specified group. Excludes deaths to nonresidents of United States. Deaths classified according to the ninth revision of the *International Classification of Diseases*]

Year	Homicide victims					Homicide rate [2]				
	Total [1]	White		Black		Total [1]	White		Black	
		Male	Female	Male	Female		Male	Female	Male	Female
1980	24,278	10,381	3,177	8,385	1,898	10.7	10.9	3.2	66.6	13.5
1981	23,646	9,941	3,125	8,312	1,825	10.3	10.4	3.1	64.8	12.7
1982	22,358	9,260	3,179	7,730	1,743	9.6	9.6	3.1	59.1	12.0
1983	20,191	8,355	2,880	6,822	1,672	8.6	8.6	2.8	51.4	11.3
1984	19,796	8,171	2,956	6,563	1,677	8.4	8.3	2.9	48.7	11.2
1985	19,893	8,122	3,041	6,616	1,666	8.3	8.2	2.9	48.4	11.0
1986	21,731	8,567	3,123	7,634	1,861	9.0	8.6	3.0	55.0	12.1
1987	21,103	7,979	3,149	7,518	1,969	8.7	7.9	3.0	53.3	12.6
1988	22,032	7,994	3,072	8,314	2,089	9.0	7.9	2.9	58.0	13.2
1989	22,909	8,337	2,971	8,888	2,074	9.2	8.2	2.8	61.1	12.9
1990	24,932	9,147	3,006	9,981	2,163	10.0	9.0	2.8	69.2	13.5
1991	26,513	9,581	3,201	10,628	2,330	10.5	9.3	3.0	72.0	14.2
1992	25,488	9,456	3,012	10,131	2,187	10.0	9.1	2.8	67.5	13.1
1993	26,009	9,054	3,232	10,640	2,297	10.1	8.6	3.0	69.7	13.6
1994	24,926	9,055	2,921	10,083	2,124	9.6	8.5	2.6	65.1	12.4
1995	22,895	8,336	3,028	8,847	1,936	8.7	7.8	2.7	56.3	11.1
1996	20,971	7,570	2,747	8,183	1,800	7.9	7.0	2.5	51.5	10.2
1997	18,774	(NA)	(NA)	(NA)	(NA)	7.0	(NA)	(NA)	(NA)	(NA)

NA Not available.   [1] Includes races not shown separately.   [2] Rate based on enumerated population figures as of April 1 for 1980 and 1990; July 1 estimates for other years.
Source: U.S. National Center for Health Statistics, *Vital Statistics of the United States*, annual, and unpublished data.

Law Enforcement, Courts, and Prisons   217

No. 349. Forcible Rape—Number and Rate: 1980 to 1997

[For definition of rape, see text, this section]

Item	1980	1985	1990	1991	1992	1993	1994	1995	1996	1997
NUMBER										
Total..................	82,990	88,670	102,560	106,590	109,060	106,010	102,220	97,460	96,250	96,122
By force	63,599	71,060	86,541	91,522	93,825	92,360	89,297	85,249	84,053	84,790
Attempt..................	19,391	17,610	16,019	15,068	15,235	13,650	12,923	12,211	12,197	11,332
RATE										
Per 100,000 population	36.8	37.1	41.2	42.3	42.8	41.1	39.3	37.1	36.3	35.9
Per 100,000 females	71.6	72.3	80.5	82.5	83.5	80.3	76.7	72.5	71.0	70.4
Per 100,000 females 12 years old and over.............	86.3	86.6	96.6	100.9	100.5	96.4	92.0	87.1	85.3	84.4
AVERAGE ANNUAL PERCENT CHANGE IN RATE [1]										
Per 100,000 population	6.1	3.9	8.1	2.7	1.2	-4.0	-4.4	-5.6	-2.2	-1.1
Per 100,000 females 12 years old and over..............	6.0	4.3	8.2	4.5	-0.4	-4.1	-4.6	-5.3	-2.1	-1.1

[1] Represents annual average from prior year shown except for 1980, from 1979; for 1985, from 1984; and for 1990, from 1989.

Source: U.S. Federal Bureau of Investigation, *Population-at-Risk Rates and Selected Crime Indicators*, annual.

No. 350. Robbery and Property Crimes, by Type and Selected Characteristic: 1990 to 1997

[For definition of crime, see text, this section]

Item	Number of offenses (1,000)				Rate per 100,000 inhabitants				Average value lost (dol.)	
	1990	1995	1996	1997	1990	1995	1996	1997	1996	1997
Robbery, total [1]	639	581	536	498	257.0	220.9	201.9	186.1	929	995
Type of crime:										
Street or highway	359	315	274	249	144.2	120.0	103.4	93.1	667	720
Commercial house	73	71	72	69	29.5	27.2	27.2	25.6	1,477	1,474
Gas station	18	13	13	12	7.1	5.1	4.9	4.4	487	715
Convenience store	39	30	32	28	15.6	11.4	11.9	10.5	567	576
Residence...............	62	63	57	58	25.1	24.0	21.5	21.6	1,133	1,133
Bank	9	9	11	10	3.8	3.5	4.0	3.6	4,207	4,802
Weapon used:										
Firearm................	234	238	218	198	94.1	90.6	82.2	73.9	(NA)	(NA)
Knife or cutting instrument	76	53	48	42	30.7	20.1	18.1	15.9	(NA)	(NA)
Other dangerous weapon	61	53	62	67	24.5	20.2	28.0	24.9	(NA)	(NA)
Strongarm..............	268	236	207	191	107.7	90.0	78.2	71.5	(NA)	(NA)
Burglary, total	3,074	2,595	2,506	2,461	1,235.9	987.6	944.8	919.6	1,332	1,334
Forcible entry	2,150	1,737	1,651	1,615	864.5	661.2	622.2	603.4	(NA)	(NA)
Unlawful entry	678	657	650	669	272.8	250.1	245.0	249.9	(NA)	(NA)
Attempted forcible entry........	245	201	206	177	98.7	76.4	77.6	66.3	(NA)	(NA)
Residence	2,033	1,736	1,666	1,640	817.4	660.6	628.2	612.8	1,350	1,305
Nonresidence	1,041	859	840	821	418.5	327.0	316.6	306.8	1,296	1,391
Occurred during the night	1,135	905	868	827	456.4	344.4	327.1	309.1	(NA)	(NA)
Occurred during the day	1,151	1,000	902	886	462.8	380.5	340.0	330.9	(NA)	(NA)
Larceny-theft, total.......	7,946	8,001	7,905	7,726	3,194.8	3,044.9	2,979.7	2,886.5	532	585
Pocket picking..............	81	51	35	46	32.4	19.4	13.3	17.1	320	466
Purse snatching.............	82	51	47	47	32.8	19.5	17.6	17.4	296	403
Shoplifting................	1,291	1,205	1,214	1,179	519.1	458.4	457.8	440.5	120	130
From motor vehicles.........	1,744	1,940	1,999	1,975	701.3	738.5	753.6	737.8	518	584
Motor vehicle accessories	1,185	964	844	770	476.3	367.0	318.3	287.6	387	390
Bicycles	443	501	439	430	178.2	190.5	165.5	160.7	263	293
From buildings.............	1,118	1,004	1,007	1,051	449.4	382.1	379.6	392.5	894	963
From coin-operated machines....	63	50	48	45	25.4	18.9	17.9	16.7	296	453
Other..................	1,940	2,235	2,271	2,184	780.0	850.5	856.2	816.2	723	785
Motor vehicles, total [2]	1,636	1,473	1,394	1,354	657.8	560.5	525.5	505.8	5,372	5,416
Automobiles	1,304	1,154	1,092	1,042	524.3	439.2	411.8	389.3	(NA)	(NA)
Trucks and buses...........	238	240	230	240	95.5	91.2	86.6	89.7	(NA)	(NA)

NA Not available. [1] Includes other crimes not shown separately. [2] Includes other types of motor vehicles not shown separately.

Source: U.S. Federal Bureau of Investigation, *Population-at-Risk Rates and Selected Crime Indicators*, annual.

U.S. Census Bureau, Statistical Abstract of the United States: 1999

No. 351. Hate Crimes—Number of Incidents, Offenses, Victims, and Offenders, by Bias Motivation: 1997

[The FBI collected statistics on hate crimes from 11,211 law enforcement agencies representing over 223 million inhabitants in 1997. Hate crime offenses cover incidents motivated by race, religion, sexual orientation, ethnicity/national origin, and disability]

Bias motivation	Incidents	Offenses	Victims [1]	Known offenders [2]
Total bias motivations	8,049	9,861	10,255	8,474
Race, total	4,710	5,898	6,084	5,444
Anti-White	993	1,267	1,293	1,520
Anti-Black.	3,120	3,838	3,951	3,301
Anti-American Indian/Alaskan native	36	44	46	45
Anti-Asian/Pacific Islander	347	437	466	351
Anti-multiracial group	214	312	328	227
Ethnicity/national origin, total	836	1,083	1,132	906
Anti-Hispanic.	491	636	649	614
Anti-other ethnicity/national origin	345	447	483	292
Religion, total.	1,385	1,483	1,586	792
Anti-Jewish.	1,087	1,159	1,247	598
Anti-Catholic.	31	32	32	16
Anti-Protestant	53	59	61	19
Anti-Islamic.	28	31	32	22
Anti-other religious group	159	173	184	120
Anti-multireligious group	24	26	27	11
Anti-atheism/agnosticism/etc	3	3	3	6
Sexual orientation, total.	1,102	1,375	1,401	1,315
Anti-male homosexual	760	912	927	1,032
Anti-female homosexual	188	229	236	158
Anti-homosexual	133	210	214	103
Anti-heterosexual	12	14	14	14
Anti-bisexual	9	10	10	8
Disability, total	12	12	12	14
Anti-physical	9	9	9	11
Anti-mental	3	3	3	3
Multiple bias	4	10	40	3

[1] The term "victim" may refer to a person, business, institution, or a society as a whole. [2] The term "known offender" does not imply that the identity of the suspect is known, but only that an attribute of the suspect is identified which distinguishes him/her from an unknown offender.

Source: U.S. Federal Bureau of Investigation, *Hate Crime Statistics*, annual; and <http://www.fbi.gov/ucr/hc97all.pdf> (accessed 30 March 1999).

No. 352. Hate Crimes Reported, by State: 1997

[See headnote, Table 351]

State	Number of participating agencies	Population	Agencies submitting incidents	Incidents reported	State	Number of participating agencies	Population	Agencies submitting incidents	Incidents reported
U.S.	11,211	222,856,059	1,732	8,049	Missouri	194	3,958,650	33	157
Alabama	282	4,076,423	-	-	Montana	95	791,645	7	15
Alaska	1	255,634	1	10	Nebraska	10	208,189	1	3
Arizona	85	4,308,394	28	330	Nevada	34	1,677,000	7	45
Arkansas	194	2,524,624	-	-	New Hampshire. .	(1)	(1)	(1)	(1)
California	720	32,252,340	242	1,831	New Jersey	567	8,060,900	257	694
Colorado	232	3,893,977	35	113	New Mexico	58	1,085,811	1	24
Connecticut . . .	59	1,932,906	48	113					
Delaware	54	730,117	12	58	New York	502	17,619,783	32	853
Dist. of Columbia .	1	529,000	1	6	North Carolina. . .	445	7,348,121	22	42
Florida	580	14,954,150	39	93	North Dakota . . .	84	502,699	2	2
					Ohio	304	7,167,639	42	265
Georgia	5	427,963	2	45	Oklahoma	300	3,317,000	25	41
Hawaii	(1)	(1)	(1)	(1)	Oregon	171	3,239,829	18	105
Idaho	119	1,205,564	23	46	Pennsylvania . . .	1,108	11,779,853	27	168
Illinois	96	5,205,187	83	339	Rhode Island . . .	45	987,000	13	43
Indiana	139	3,103,389	23	62	South Carolina . .	316	3,758,844	35	71
Iowa	230	2,707,822	25	55					
Kansas	1	315,690	1	55	South Dakota . . .	42	402,991	5	34
Kentucky	213	2,481,612	20	48	Tennessee	167	2,332,713	15	46
Louisiana	147	3,165,841	3	4	Texas	924	19,417,481	85	333
Maine	131	1,240,324	17	57	Utah	124	2,044,259	22	49
Maryland	148	5,097,287	34	321	Vermont	20	310,916	3	3
					Virginia	409	6,737,051	40	105
Massachusetts . .	359	6,042,890	116	441	Washington	229	5,491,897	51	190
Michigan	465	6,463,486	148	461	West Virginia . . .	32	367,499	3	3
Minnesota	312	4,685,499	58	214	Wisconsin.	345	5,172,844	24	50
Mississippi	75	1,144,219	-	-	Wyoming	38	331,107	3	6

- Represents or rounds to zero. [1] Did not report.

Source: U.S. Federal Bureau of Investigation, *Hate Crime Statistics*, annual; and <http://www.fbi.gov/ucr/hc97all.pdf> (accessed 30 March 1999).

Law Enforcement, Courts, and Prisons   219

No. 353. Criminal Victimizations and Victimization Rates: 1994 to 1997

[Based on National Crime Victimization Survey; see text, this section and Appendix III]

Type of crime	Number of victimizations (1,000)				Victimization rates [1]			
	1994	1995	1996	1997	1994	1995	1996	1997
All crimes, total	42,359	39,926	36,796	34,788	(X)	(X)	(X)	(X)
Personal crimes [2]	11,349	10,436	9,443	8,971	53.1	46.2	43.5	40.8
Crimes of violence	10,860	10,022	9,125	8,614	50.8	44.5	42.0	39.2
Completed violence	3,205	2,960	2,700	2,679	15.0	12.9	12.4	12.2
Attempted/threatened violence	7,654	7,061	6,425	5,935	35.8	31.6	29.6	27.0
Rape/sexual assault	433	363	307	311	2.0	1.6	1.4	1.4
Rape/attempted rape	316	252	197	194	1.5	1.1	0.9	0.9
Rape	168	153	98	115	0.8	0.7	0.4	0.5
Attempted rape	149	99	99	79	0.7	0.4	0.5	0.4
Sexual assault	117	112	110	117	0.5	0.5	0.5	0.5
Robbery	1,299	1,171	1,134	944	6.1	5.3	5.2	4.3
Completed/property taken	795	753	757	607	3.7	3.5	3.5	2.8
With injury	288	224	250	243	1.3	1.0	1.1	1.1
Without injury	507	529	508	363	2.4	2.4	2.3	1.7
Attempted to take property	504	418	377	337	2.4	1.8	1.7	1.5
With injury	122	84	79	73	0.6	0.4	0.4	0.3
Without injury	382	335	298	265	1.8	1.4	1.4	1.2
Assault	9,128	8,487	7,683	7,359	42.7	37.6	35.4	33.5
Aggravated	2,478	2,050	1,910	1,883	11.6	8.8	8.8	8.6
With injury	679	533	513	595	3.2	2.4	2.4	2.7
Threatened with weapon	1,799	1,517	1,397	1,288	8.4	6.4	6.4	5.9
Simple	6,650	6,437	5,773	5,476	31.1	28.9	26.6	24.9
With minor injury	1,466	1,426	1,240	1,258	6.9	6.0	5.7	5.7
Without injury	5,184	5,012	4,533	4,218	24.3	22.9	20.9	19.2
Personal theft [3]	489	414	318	357	2.3	1.7	1.5	1.6
Property crimes	31,011	29,490	27,353	25,817	307.6	279.5	266.3	248.3
Household burglary	5,482	5,004	4,845	4,635	54.4	47.4	47.2	44.6
Completed	4,573	4,232	4,056	3,893	45.4	40.0	39.5	37.4
Attempted forcible entry	910	773	789	742	9.0	7.4	7.7	7.1
Motor vehicle theft	1,764	1,717	1,387	1,433	17.5	16.2	13.5	13.8
Completed	1,172	1,163	938	1,007	11.6	10.8	9.1	9.7
Attempted	591	554	449	426	5.9	5.5	4.4	4.1
Theft	23,765	22,769	21,120	19,749	235.7	215.9	205.7	189.9
Completed [4]	22,743	21,857	20,303	18,960	225.6	207.6	197.7	182.3
Attempted	1,022	911	818	789	10.1	8.4	8.0	7.6

X Not applicable.   [1] Per 1,000 persons age 12 or older or per 1,000 households.   [2] The victimization survey cannot measure murder because of the inability to question the victim.   [3] Includes pocket picking, purse snatching, and attempted purse snatching.   [4] Includes thefts in which the amount taken was not ascertained.

Source: U.S. Bureau of Justice Statistics, *Criminal Victimization*, annual.

No. 354. Victimization Rates, by Type of Violent Crime and Characteristic of the Victim: 1997

[Rate per 1,000 persons age 12 years or older. Based on National Crime Victimization Survey; see text, this section and Appendix III]

Characteristic	Crimes of violence						Personal theft
	All crimes of violence	Rape/ sexual assault	Robbery	Assault			
				Total	Aggra- vated	Simple	
Total	39.2	1.4	4.3	33.5	8.6	24.9	1.6
Male	45.8	0.3	6.1	39.4	10.9	28.4	1.6
Female	33.0	2.5	2.6	27.9	6.4	21.6	1.7
12 to 15 yrs. old	87.9	2.5	8.2	77.1	15.1	62.0	2.8
16 to 19 yrs. old	96.2	5.6	10.2	80.4	24.6	55.8	3.5
20 to 24 yrs. old	67.8	2.4	7.4	57.9	17.0	40.9	1.8
25 to 34 yrs. old	46.9	2.3	4.7	39.9	9.5	30.4	1.1
35 to 49 yrs. old	32.2	0.6	3.7	27.9	7.4	20.4	1.6
50 to 64 yrs. old	14.6	0.2	2.2	12.2	2.8	9.4	1.1
65 yrs. old and over	4.4	0.2	0.9	3.4	0.6	2.8	1.2
White	38.3	1.4	3.8	33.1	8.2	24.9	1.4
Black	49.0	1.6	7.4	39.9	12.2	27.7	3.3
Other	28.0	1.1	5.0	21.9	6.1	15.8	0.8
Hispanic	43.1	1.5	7.3	34.3	10.4	24.0	2.4
Non-Hispanic	38.3	1.4	3.9	33.0	8.3	24.7	1.5
Household income:							
Less than $7,500	71.0	5.2	10.1	55.6	13.6	42.0	2.7
$7,500-$14,999	51.2	2.2	7.0	42.0	11.8	30.3	2.0
$15,000-$24,999	40.1	1.5	4.6	34.0	10.4	23.6	1.7
$25,000-$34,999	40.2	1.5	4.2	34.6	8.2	26.4	1.5
$35,000-$49,999	38.7	0.6	2.9	35.2	8.6	26.6	1.4
$50,000-$74,999	33.7	0.7	3.1	30.1	7.2	22.8	1.6
$75,000 or more	30.7	1.1	3.7	26.0	4.7	21.4	1.4

Source: U.S. Bureau of Justice Statistics, *Criminal Victimization*, annual.

No. 355. Victim-Offender Relationship in Crimes of Violence, by Characteristic of the Criminal Incident: 1997

[In percent. Covers only crimes of violence. Based on National Crime Victimization Survey; see text, this section and Appendix III]

Characteristic of incident	Total	Rape/ sexual assault	Robbery	Assault Total	Aggra- vated[1]	Simple
Total	**100**	**100**	**100**	**100**	**100**	**100**
Victim/offender relationship: [2]						
Relatives	9	10	6	9	7	10
Well-known	27	39	13	28	24	29
Casual acquaintance	16	20	9	17	12	18
Stranger	48	31	72	46	56	43
Time of day:						
6 a.m. to 6 p.m.	53	35	42	55	46	58
6 p.m. to midnight	35	33	43	34	41	31
Midnight to 6 a.m.	11	30	13	10	13	9
Location of crime:						
At or near victim's home or lodging	29	39	24	29	31	28
Friend's/relative's/neighbor's home	9	28	5	8	10	8
Commercial places	13	8	6	14	11	15
Parking lots/garages	7	5	12	6	7	6
School	13	3	6	14	6	17
Streets other than near victim's home	18	5	35	17	24	14
Other [3]	12	12	12	12	12	11
Victim's activity:						
At work or traveling to or from work	21	11	15	22	20	23
School	12	4	8	13	7	14
Activities at home	23	38	14	24	27	23
Shopping/errands	4	-	7	4	3	4
Leisure activities away from home	22	31	22	22	26	21
Traveling	9	6	19	7	11	6
Other	9	11	14	8	6	9
Distance from victim's home:						
Inside home or lodging	15	34	15	15	15	14
Near victim's home	16	8	11	17	20	16
1 mile or less	20	19	30	19	18	19
5 miles or less	24	15	27	24	21	25
50 miles or less	21	16	13	23	23	23
More than 50 miles	4	7	4	3	4	3
Weapons:						
No weapons present	72	92	45	75	5	100
Weapons present	28	9	55	25	95	-
Firearm	9	3	26	8	29	-
Other type of weapon [4]	18	5	28	18	67	-

- Represents zero. [1] An aggravated assault is any assault in which an offender possesses or uses a weapon or inflicts serious injury. [2] Excludes "don't know" relationships. [3] Includes areas on public transportation or inside station, in apartment yard, park, field, playground, or other areas. [4] Includes knives, other sharp objects, blunt objects, and other types of weapons.
Source: U.S. Bureau of Justice Statistics, *Criminal Victimization*, annual.

No. 356. Property Victimization Rates, by Selected Household Characteristic: 1997

[Victimizations per 1,000 households. Based on National Crime Victimization Survey; see text, this section and Appendix III]

Characteristic	Total	Burglary	Motor vehicle theft	Theft
Total	**248.3**	**44.6**	**13.8**	**189.9**
Race:				
White	242.3	42.3	11.9	188.1
Black	292.0	62.5	24.1	205.3
Other	237.4	36.2	23.3	177.9
Ethnicity:				
Hispanic	329.4	60.9	29.6	238.9
Non-Hispanic	240.8	43.2	12.5	185.2
Household income:				
Less than $7,500	258.8	79.5	10.0	169.3
$7,500-$14,999	236.3	53.9	9.1	173.3
$15,000-$24,999	242.4	47.2	14.1	181.2
$25,000-$34,999	260.3	42.4	15.8	202.0
$35,000-$49,999	271.7	39.8	17.2	214.6
$50,000-$74,999	270.9	35.0	11.7	224.2
$75,000 or more	292.8	42.4	16.3	234.1
Residence:				
Urban	309.9	56.5	20.1	233.3
Suburban	235.4	38.9	12.7	183.8
Rural	187.7	40.1	7.1	140.5
Form of tenure:				
Home owned	211.7	35.8	11.1	164.8
Home rented	316.0	60.9	18.7	236.5

Source: U.S. Bureau of Justice Statistics, *Criminal Victimization*, annual.

Law Enforcement, Courts, and Prisons   221

No. 357. Juvenile Arrests for Selected Offenses: 1980 to 1997

[169,439 represents 169,439,000. Juveniles are persons between the ages 10-17]

Offense	1980	1985	1990	1991	1992	1993	1994	1995	1996	1997
Number of contributing agencies . .	8,178	11,263	10,765	10,148	11,058	10,277	10,693	10,037	10,026	9,471
Population covered (1,000)	169,439	206,269	204,543	189,962	217,754	213,705	208,035	206,762	195,805	194,925
NUMBER										
Violent crime, total.	77,220	75,077	97,103	95,677	118,358	122,434	125,141	123,131	104,455	99,342
Murder.	1,475	1,384	2,661	2,626	3,025	3,473	3,114	2,812	2,184	1,873
Forcible rape.	3,668	5,073	4,971	4,766	5,451	5,490	4,873	4,556	4,228	4,102
Robbery.	38,529	31,833	34,944	35,632	42,639	44,598	47,046	47,240	39,788	36,059
Aggravated assault	33,548	36,787	54,527	52,653	67,243	68,873	70,108	68,523	58,255	57,308
Weapon law violations	21,203	27,035	33,123	37,575	49,903	54,414	52,278	46,506	40,145	39,001
Drug abuse, total	86,685	78,660	66,300	58,603	73,232	90,618	124,931	149,236	148,783	154,540
Sale and manufacturing	13,004	14,846	24,575	22,929	25,331	27,635	32,746	34,077	32,558	30,642
Heroin/cocaine.	1,318	2,851	17,511	16,915	17,881	18,716	20,327	19,187	17,465	15,778
Marijuana	8,876	8,646	4,372	3,579	4,853	6,144	8,812	10,682	11,489	11,168
Synthetic narcotics	465	414	346	570	663	455	465	701	614	671
Dangerous nonnarcotic drugs .	2,345	2,935	2,346	1,865	1,934	2,320	3,142	3,507	2,990	3,025
Possession.	73,681	63,814	41,725	35,674	47,901	62,983	92,185	115,159	116,225	123,898
Heroin/cocaine.	2,614	7,809	15,194	13,747	16,855	17,726	21,004	21,253	17,560	18,104
Marijuana	64,465	50,582	20,940	16,490	25,004	37,915	61,003	82,015	87,712	93,579
Synthetic narcotics	1,524	1,085	1,155	885	897	1,008	1,227	2,047	1,713	1,987
Dangerous nonnarcotic drugs .	5,078	4,338	4,436	4,552	5,145	6,334	8,951	9,844	9,240	10,228

Source: U.S. Federal Bureau of Investigation, *Crime in the United States*, annual.

No. 358. Persons Arrested, by Charge, Race, Sex, and Age: 1997

[11,521.1 represents 11,521,100. Represents arrests (not charges) reported by approximately 10,000 agencies with a total 1997 population of approximately 200 million as estimated by FBI]

Offense charged	Total arrests (1,000)						Percent—		
	Total	White	Black	American Indian or Alaskan Native	Asian or Pacific Islander	Total (1,000)	Male	Under 18 yrs. old	18 to 24 yrs. old
Total	**11,521.1**	**7,608.8**	**3,644.7**	**136.8**	**130.8**	**11,553.4**	**78.9**	**17.3**	**27.3**
Serious crimes [1]	2,051.6	1,264.7	731.8	22.6	32.5	2,054.8	74.8	29.6	25.9
Murder and nonnegligent manslaughter	14.2	5.9	8.0	0.1	0.2	14.2	90.0	13.8	43.6
Forcible rape.	24.1	13.7	9.9	0.2	0.3	24.1	98.8	16.9	26.2
Robbery	118.8	46.9	69.8	0.6	1.6	118.9	90.2	30.5	35.1
Aggravated assault	403.4	241.6	152.7	3.9	5.2	404.1	81.0	13.9	25.4
Burglary	259.5	174.6	78.9	2.7	3.3	259.8	88.2	36.7	28.1
Larceny/theft	1,091.8	700.1	358.7	13.5	19.4	1,093.6	65.6	33.4	23.1
Motor vehicle theft	126.2	72.0	50.5	1.4	2.3	126.3	85.5	38.4	31.1
Arson	13.7	10.1	3.4	0.1	0.1	13.7	85.3	54.3	16.8
All other nonserious crimes. . . .	9,469.5	6,344.1	2,912.8	114.2	98.3	9,498.6	79.8	6.5	27.6
Other assaults.	1,012.8	628.6	360.1	12.8	11.4	1,014.5	78.8	15.5	22.7
Forgery and counterfeiting. . .	90.8	58.7	30.2	0.5	1.4	90.9	63.4	6.6	31.7
Fraud	323.1	207.8	110.8	1.6	2.8	323.5	58.3	7.0	26.7
Embezzlement	12.7	8.0	4.4	0.1	0.2	12.7	53.2	7.9	33.6
Stolen property—buying, receiving, possessing	113.5	64.4	46.8	0.9	1.4	113.7	84.6	25.8	34.1
Vandalism.	234.1	169.9	58.7	2.9	2.6	234.4	85.3	44.0	25.1
Weapons; carrying, possessing etc.	164.4	94.5	66.9	1.1	1.8	164.5	91.6	23.5	34.4
Prostitution and commercialized vice	81.7	47.1	32.9	0.4	1.3	81.8	40.0	1.5	18.3
Sex offenses (except forcible rape and prostitution)	76.2	55.4	18.9	0.9	1.0	76.3	91.3	18.4	18.4
Drug abuse violations	1,242.0	750.4	477.0	6.2	8.5	1,243.4	82.9	14.1	33.8
Gambling	18.9	8.4	9.8	0.1	0.6	18.9	87.4	12.4	29.6
Offenses against family and children	107.9	71.7	33.2	1.0	2.0	108.3	75.8	5.4	18.7
Driving under the influence . .	966.1	841.8	100.1	14.6	9.6	980.9	84.6	1.3	21.7
Liquor laws.	561.7	433.7	110.3	13.5	4.1	562.7	81.0	17.9	44.2
Drunkenness.	512.6	411.9	86.8	11.8	2.1	514.1	87.6	3.1	20.9
Disorderly conduct	626.0	387.0	226.6	8.2	4.3	626.7	78.1	24.8	29.5
Vagrancy	23.6	12.0	11.2	0.4	0.1	23.6	77.7	13.3	27.4
Suspicion	4.5	2.9	1.5	0.1	0.0	4.5	79.3	24.7	29.4
Curfew and loitering law violations.	154.4	107.3	43.1	1.9	2.2	154.6	70.0	100.0	(X)
Runaways	143.4	111.4	25.5	1.6	5.0	144.0	41.9	100.0	(X)
All other offenses (except traffic	2,999.1	1,871.4	1,058.2	33.7	35.9	3,004.7	81.0	10.9	28.3

X Not applicable.   [1] Includes arson.

Source: U.S. Federal Bureau of Investigation, *Crime in the United States*, annual.

U.S. Census Bureau, Statistical Abstract of the United States: 1999

No. 359. Drug Use by Arrestees in Major U.S. Cities, by Type of Drug and Sex: 1998

[**Percent testing positive.** Based on data from the Arrestee Drug Abuse Monitoring Program]

City	Male				Female			
	Any drug [1]	Marijuana	Cocaine	Heroin	Any drug [1]	Marijuana	Cocaine	Heroin
Albuquerque, NM	64.8	35.9	38.7	8.2	73.1	24.0	59.1	15.4
Atlanta, GA	65.7	26.0	51.3	1.3	(NA)	(NA)	(NA)	(NA)
Chicago, IL	74.2	41.5	44.9	18.3	71.5	19.7	55.5	27.0
Cleveland, OH	65.2	36.8	36.8	6.0	58.1	27.0	40.5	1.4
Dallas, TX	63.4	43.1	29.0	2.3	48.9	24.2	29.5	4.8
Denver, CO	68.8	41.3	39.6	4.2	68.7	29.9	49.9	3.4
Detroit, MI.	68.2	46.5	28.2	6.8	60.2	21.5	46.2	21.5
Houston, TX	59.9	35.8	35.8	7.5	51.7	20.1	37.3	7.0
Indianapolis, IN	66.8	45.1	34.2	1.8	67.1	31.2	43.2	4.5
Las Vegas, NV	56.8	25.8	24.2	2.6	70.3	21.6	35.1	13.5
Los Angeles, CA	64.4	27.3	42.7	5.6	71.0	21.8	44.7	8.8
Miami, FL	61.5	29.2	47.3	2.4	(NA)	(NA)	(NA)	(NA)
New Orleans, LA	67.3	38.3	46.0	12.9	50.5	22.1	38.7	3.4
New York, NY	76.9	38.7	47.1	16.2	82.1	23.4	67.0	21.8
Oklahoma City, OK.	69.0	53.1	27.3	1.9	(NA)	(NA)	(NA)	(NA)
Philadelphia, PA.	78.7	44.9	44.5	18.4	77.4	23.7	60.9	14.9
Phoenix, AZ	62.7	32.2	31.1	5.7	70.6	24.9	39.6	7.3
Portland, OR	71.5	36.9	29.2	15.5	74.3	23.2	36.7	25.1
Sacramento, CA.	70.8	44.1	18.2	3.2	72.8	28.2	30.7	8.4
San Antonio, TX.	56.0	41.1	27.0	9.6	37.8	17.5	20.0	8.6
San Diego, CA.	68.6	36.4	19.1	9.3	63.9	26.7	20.4	6.7
San Jose, CA	48.2	24.8	8.0	4.4	41.5	13.6	9.5	4.8
Seattle, WA.	65.4	35.4	35.9	17.4	81.0	37.9	56.9	17.2
Tucson, AZ	63.1	39.2	39.4	6.8	57.0	21.5	41.3	7.4
Washington, DC.	65.3	38.0	33.3	9.7	65.3	28.5	40.4	9.8

NA Not available. [1] Includes other drugs not shown separately.

Source: U.S. National Institute of Justice, *Drug Use Forecasting*, annual.

No. 360. Drug Arrest Rates for Drug Abuse Violations, 1990 to 1997, and by Region, 1997

[**Rate per 100,000 inhabitants.** Based on the U.S. Census Bureau estimated resident population as of **July 1**, except **1990**, enumerated as of **April 1**. For composition of regions, see map, inside front cover]

Offense	1990	1995	1996	1997				
				Total	Region			
					North-east	Midwest	South	West
Drug arrest rate, total	**435.3**	**564.7**	**558.4**	**602.5**	**723.8**	**398.6**	**545.4**	**725.9**
Sale and/or manufacture	139.0	140.7	137.0	135.8	225.7	97.7	104.2	131.5
Heroin or cocaine [1]	93.7	83.7	78.2	75.0	167.0	24.9	61.1	56.7
Marijuana.	26.4	32.7	35.0	34.5	46.3	32.7	28.2	34.0
Synthetic or manufactured drugs	2.7	3.9	3.4	4.3	3.2	2.1	7.0	3.6
Other dangerous nonnarcotic drugs . .	16.2	20.3	20.5	22.0	9.1	37.9	7.9	37.3
Possession . . . . [1]	296.3	423.9	421.4	466.7	498.1	301.0	441.2	594.3
Heroin or cocaine [1]	144.4	157.4	142.7	155.4	216.1	57.8	130.7	209.4
Marijuana.	104.9	192.7	205.3	225.9	257.7	191.5	268.2	175.2
Synthetic or manufactured drugs	6.6	8.5	7.9	9.6	5.9	6.3	11.6	12.4
Other dangerous nonnarcotic drugs . .	40.4	65.4	65.5	75.8	18.3	45.4	30.7	197.3

[1] Includes other derivatives such as morphine, heroin, and codeine.

Source: U.S. Federal Bureau of Investigation, *Crime in the United States,* annual.

No. 361. Federal Drug Seizures, by Type of Drug: 1990 to 1998

[**In pounds. For fiscal years ending in year shown.** Reflects the combined drug seizure effort of the Drug Enforcement Administration, the Federal Bureau of Investigation, the U.S. Customs Services, and beginning October 1993 the U.S. Border Patrol within the jurisdiction of the United States as well as maritime seizures by the U.S. Coast Guard. Based on reports to the Federal-wide Drug Seizure System, which eliminates duplicate reporting of a seizure involving more than one Federal agency]

Drug	1990	1991	1992	1993	1994	1995	1996	1997	1998
Total	1,238,425	1,591,277	1,881,693	1,845,998	2,397,037	2,913,227	3,181,573	3,338,636	3,794,034
Heroin.	1,704	3,067	2,552	3,516	2,883	2,971	3,373	3,115	3,384
Cocaine.	235,891	246,318	304,086	244,315	309,928	233,447	254,437	253,536	263,988
Cannabis	500,415	670,946	787,527	799,083	1,042,113	1,338,405	1,461,881	1,540,992	1,763,331
Marijuana	483,353	499,097	783,479	773,004	1,040,999	1,306,528	1,429,786	1,487,942	1,762,734
Hashish	17,062	171,849	4,048	26,080	1,114	31,876	32,096	53,051	597

Source: U.S. Drug Enforcement Administration, unpublished data from Federal-wide Drug Seizure System.

U.S. Census Bureau, Statistical Abstract of the United States: 1999

No. 362. Immigration Border Patrol and Investigation Activities: 1980 to 1995

[For fiscal years ending in year shown. See text, Section 9, State and Local Government]

Item	Unit	1980	1985	1989	1990	1991	1992	1993	1994	1995
BORDER PATROL										
Border patrol agents:										
Authorized number [1]	Number...	2,484	3,228	4,804	4,852	4,968	4,948	4,143	4,559	5,259
On duty	Number...	2,329	3,023	3,857	4,360	4,312	4,759	3,991	4,226	4,881
Border patrol obligations	Mil. dol...	82.5	141.9	246.4	261.1	295.5	325.8	354.5	376.8	457.2
Persons apprehended [1]	1,000....	766.6	1,272.4	906.5	1,123.2	1,152.7	1,221.9	1,281.7	1,046.6	1,336.5
Deportable aliens located [2]	1,000....	759.4	1,262.4	893.0	1,103.4	1,132.9	1,199.6	1,263.5	1,031.7	1,324.2
Mexican	1,000....	734.2	1,218.7	832.2	1,054.8	1,095.1	1,168.9	1,230.1	999.9	1,293.5
Canadian	1,000....	5.3	5.9	5.3	5.7	6.7	6.2	5.2	3.4	3.5
Other	1,000....	19.9	37.8	55.5	42.8	31.1	24.4	28.1	28.4	27.2
Number of seizures	Number...	1,920	7,827	10,789	17,275	14,261	14,241	10,995	9,134	9,327
Value of seizures	Mil. dol...	116.1	122.0	1,212.7	843.6	950.2	1,247.9	1,383	1,598	733.0
Narcotics	Mil. dol...	110.3	119.8	1,191.5	797.8	910.1	1,216.8	1,338	1,556	686.6
INVESTIGATIONS										
Deportable aliens located	1,000....	150.9	83.9	61.1	64.1	63.6	57.4	60.4	61.6	68.9
Mexican	1,000....	83.3	48.3	33.1	35.8	35.5	36.2	38.8	40.1	46.3
Canadian	1,000....	1.5	1.1	0.5	0.4	0.5	0.4	0.4	0.5	0.5
Other	1,000....	66.1	34.5	28.5	30.0	29.7	20.8	21.1	21.1	22.0

[1] Covers deportable aliens located and U.S. citizens engaged in smuggling or other immigration violations. [2] Beginning 1989, includes apprehension by the anti smuggling unit.

Source: U.S. Immigration and Naturalization Service, Statistical Yearbook, annual; and unpublished data.

No. 363. Authorized Intercepts of Communication—Summary: 1980 to 1996

[Data for jurisdictions with statutes authorizing or approving interception of wire or oral communication]

Item	1980	1985	1987	1988	1989	1990	1991	1992	1993	1994	1995	1996
Jurisdictions: [1]												
With wiretap statutes	28	32	33	34	37	40	41	41	41	41	41	46
Reporting interceptions	22	22	22	23	25	25	23	23	23	18	19	24
Intercept applications authorized	564	784	673	738	763	872	856	919	976	1,154	1,058	1,149
Intercept installations	524	722	634	678	720	812	802	846	938	1,100	1,024	1,035
Federal	79	235	233	286	305	321	349	332	444	549	527	574
State	445	487	401	392	415	491	453	514	494	551	497	461
Intercepted communications, average [2]	1,058	1,320	1,299	1,251	1,656	1,487	1,584	1,861	1,801	2,139	2,028	1,969
Incriminating	315	275	230	316	337	321	290	347	364	373	459	422
Persons arrested [3]	1,871	2,469	2,226	2,486	2,804	2,057	2,364	2,685	2,428	2,852	2,577	2,464
Convictions [3]	259	660	506	543	706	420	605	607	413	772	494	502
Major offense specified:												
Gambling	199	206	135	126	111	116	98	66	96	86	95	114
Drugs	282	434	379	435	471	520	536	634	679	876	732	821
Homicide and assault	13	25	18	14	20	21	21	35	28	19	30	41
Other	70	119	141	163	161	204	201	184	173	173	201	173

[1] Jurisdictions include Federal government, states, and District of Columbia. [2] Average per authorized installation. [3] Based on information received from intercepts installed in year shown; additional arrests/convictions will occur in subsequent years but are not shown here.

Source: Administrative Office of the U.S. Courts, Report on Applications for Orders Authorizing or Approving the Interception of Wire, Oral or Electronic Communications (Wiretap Report), annual.

No. 364. Presale Handgun Checks—Inquiries and Rejections: 1996 and 1997

[In thousands (2,593 represents 2,593,000), except rates. Estimates]

Inquiries and rejections	1996			1997		
	All states	Original Brady states [1]	Brady states during 1996	All states	Original Brady states [1]	Brady states during 1997
Inquiries and rejections:						
Inquiries/applications	2,593	1,213	816	2,671	1,197	803
Rejected	70	44	25	69	42	24
Rate	2.7	3.6	3.1	2.6	3.5	3.0
Reasons for rejection:						
Felony indictment/conviction	47	35	15	43	30	12
Other	23	9	10	26	12	12

[1] Original Brady states are the 32 states required to follow presale review procedures set out in the Brady Act when it became effective on February 28, 1994. At the end of 1997, 23 of the 32 were still Brady states.

Source: U.S. Bureau of Justice Statistics, Presale Handgun Checks, 1996 and 1997.

No. 365. U.S. Population Who Had Face-to-Face Contact With Police, by Race and Ethnicity, and Reason for Contact: 1996

[215,529 represents 215,529.000. Persons having multiple contacts or more than one reason for any single contact appear in table more than once; therefore, may not add to total. Covers persons 12 years old and over. Based on the Police-Public Contact Survey of 6,421 persons; data subject to sampling variability]

Reason for contact	Number having contact (1,000)				Percent having contact			
	Total	White	Black	Hispanic [1]	Total	White	Black	Hispanic [1]
Population total	215,529	163,883	25,394	17,159	(X)	(X)	(X)	(X)
For any reason.............	44,556	36,262	3,964	2,593	20.7	22.1	15.6	15.1
I reported a crime	12,722	10,640	1,049	634	5.9	6.5	4.1	3.7
I asked police for help	10,087	8,393	744	500	4.7	5.1	2.9	2.9
I reported a problem	7,892	6,449	508	557	3.7	3.9	2.0	3.2
Police ticketed me.............	10,947	8,988	815	865	5.1	5.5	3.2	5.0
I was in a traffic accident	5,454	4,501	501	241	2.5	2.7	2.0	1.4
I witnessed an accident	2,326	2,007	151	102	1.1	1.2	0.6	0.6
I was the victim of a crime	6,755	5,753	343	360	3.1	3.5	1.4	2.1
I witnessed a crime	3,467	2,776	419	179	1.6	1.7	1.6	1.0
Police suspected me of a crime....	2,611	1,945	197	326	1.2	1.2	0.8	1.9
Police asked why I was there	2,690	2,070	361	84	1.2	1.3	1.4	0.5
Police had a warrant for my arrest ..	492	378	84	30	0.2	0.2	0.3	0.2
I had a casual encounter	8,042	6,901	640	327	3.7	4.2	2.5	1.9
I attended a community meeting ...	2,437	1,986	285	32	1.1	1.2	1.1	0.2
Some other reason	14,066	11,760	1,075	724	6.5	3.9	2.0	3.2

X Not applicable.   [1] Persons of Hispanic origin may be of any race.

Source: U.S. Bureau of Justice Statistics, *Police Use of Force, National Collection of Data*, November 1997.

No. 366. Full-Time Sworn Police Officers in State and Local Government— Number and Rate: 1996

[As of June. Rate based on the U.S. Census Bureau estimated resident population as of July 1]

State	Num- ber [1]	Rate per 10,000 [2]	Type of agency			State	Num- ber [1]	Rate per 10,000 [2]	Type of agency		
			Local	State	Sheriff				Local	State	Sheriff
U.S...	663,535	25	410,956	54,587	152,922	MO	12,998	24	8,836	996	2,421
AL	9,767	23	6,484	581	1,963	MT	1,682	19	690	212	616
AK	1,254	21	740	290	-	NE	3,297	20	1,929	464	794
AZ	10,088	23	6,967	952	1,563	NV	4,363	27	2,565	375	935
AR	5,819	23	3,244	522	1,410	NH	2,305	20	1,862	245	129
CA	69,134	22	35,939	6,219	22,869	NJ	28,058	35	19,891	2,702	3,145
CO	9,896	26	5,451	581	3,324	NM	4,134	24	2,462	435	889
CT	8,525	26	6,411	1,022	886	NY	71,221	39	54,657	3,972	5,852
DE	1,660	23	923	540	24	NC	16,953	23	9,505	1,380	5,264
DC	3,909	72	3,587	-	-	ND	1,141	18	561	120	364
FL	37,395	26	19,652	1,740	14,124	OH	23,811	21	15,932	1,391	5,179
GA	19,115	26	10,241	878	6,752	OK	7,232	22	4,951	756	1,014
HI	2,989	25	2,746	-	-	OR	6,064	19	3,245	824	1,921
ID	2,524	21	1,142	192	1,053	PA	24,873	21	17,655	4,114	1,239
IL	38,192	32	26,151	1,988	8,426	RI	2,422	24	1,958	193	153
IN	10,931	19	6,426	1,207	2,618	SC	8,675	23	4,004	892	3,037
IA	5,043	18	3,037	433	1,343	SD	1,464	20	847	155	344
KS	6,183	24	3,616	552	1,683	TN ...	12,152	23	7,076	768	3,520
KY	6,466	17	4,089	984	1,113	TX [3] ..	47,767	25	28,269	2,873	11,326
LA	16,125	37	5,733	873	8,720	UT	3,699	18	1,882	355	1,198
ME	2,318	19	1,426	337	321	VT	981	17	548	290	87
MD	13,828	27	8,923	1,625	1,438	VA	18,448	28	8,911	1,662	6,605
MA	17,935	29	13,068	2,565	1,540	WA	9,292	17	5,430	906	2,553
MI	20,568	21	13,288	2,164	4,435	WV	2,977	16	1,416	595	726
MN	7,994	17	5,006	484	2,139	WI	12,678	25	7,640	497	3,886
MS	5,813	21	3,326	535	1,474	WY	1,377	29	618	151	507

- Represents zero.   [1] Includes special police not shown separately.   [2] Based on resident population as of July 1.   [3] Texas includes sworn personnel of constable offices, not shown separately.

Source: U.S. Bureau of Justice Statistics, *Census of State and Local Law Enforcement Agencies, 1996*, Series NCJ 164618, June 1998.

U.S. Census Bureau, Statistical Abstract of the United States: 1999

No. 367. General Purpose Law Enforcement Agencies—Number and Employment: 1996

Type of agency	Number of agencies [1]	Number of employees					
		Full time			Part time		
		Total	Sworn	Civilian	Total	Sworn	Civilian
Total	18,769	921,978	663,535	258,443	97,770	47,712	50,058
Local police	13,578	521,985	410,956	111,029	61,453	30,976	30,477
Sheriff	3,088	257,712	152,922	104,790	22,412	10,845	11,567
State police	49	83,742	54,587	29,155	1,303	132	1,171
Special police	1,316	56,229	43,082	13,147	12,003	5,202	6,801
Texas constable	738	2,310	1,988	322	599	557	42

[1] The number of agencies reported here is the result of a weighted sample and not an exact enumeration.

Source: U.S. Bureau of Justice Statistics, *Census of State and Local Law Enforcement Agencies, 1996*, Series NCJ 164618, June 1998.

No. 368. Federal Agencies Employing 500 or More Full-Time Officers With Authority to Carry Firearms and Make Arrests—Number of Officers: 1993 and 1996

[As of December]

Selected agency	1993	1996
All agencies [1]	68,825	74,493
U.S. Customs Service	10,120	9,749
Federal Bureau of Investigation	10,075	10,389
Federal Bureau of Prisons	9,984	11,329
Immigration and Naturalization Service.	9,466	12,403
Administrative Office of the U.S. Courts	3,763	2,777
Internal Revenue Service	3,621	3,784
U.S. Postal Inspection Service	3,587	3,576
Drug Enforcement Administration	2,813	2,946
U.S. Secret Service	2,186	3,185
National Park Service	2,160	2,148
U.S. Marshals Service.	2,153	2,650
Bureau of Alcohol, Tobacco and Firearms	1,959	1,869
U.S. Capitol Police	1,080	1,031
U.S. Forest Service	732	619
GSA - Federal Protective Services.	732	643
U.S. Fish and Wildlife Service.	620	869

[1] Includes agencies not shown separately.

Source: U.S. Bureau of Justice Statistics, *Federal Law Enforcement Officers, 1993* and *1996, Series* NCJ-164617, December 1997.

No. 369. Law Enforcement Officers Killed and Assaulted: 1989 to 1997

[Covers officers killed feloniously and accidentally in line of duty; includes Federal officers. For composition of regions, see map inside front cover]

Item	1989	1990	1991	1992	1993	1994	1995	1996	1997
OFFICERS KILLED									
Total killed	145	133	124	130	129	141	133	112	132
Northeast	23	13	16	16	12	17	16	17	14
Midwest	22	20	26	15	27	30	19	21	25
South	67	69	55	68	57	50	63	46	55
West	23	23	18	23	22	30	32	18	31
Puerto Rico	8	8	8	8	11	9	2	10	7
Outlying areas, foreign countries	2	-	1	-	-	5	1	-	-
ASSAULTS									
Population (1,000) [1]	189,641	199,834	191,397	217,997	210,658	221,572	194,781	166,038	199,816
Number of—									
Agencies represented	9,213	9,512	9,263	10,862	9,809	10,626	8,938	7,808	8,692
Police officers	380,232	414,037	405,069	460,430	454,105	480,343	421,414	373,575	451,980
Total assaulted	62,172	72,276	62,852	81,252	66,975	64,912	56,686	46,695	49,151
Firearm	3,154	3,665	3,532	4,455	4,002	3,168	2,238	1,887	1,844
Knife or cutting instrument . . .	1,379	1,650	1,493	2,095	1,574	1,513	1,301	871	895
Other dangerous weapon . . .	5,778	7,436	7,014	8,604	7,551	7,210	6,299	5,084	5,389
Hands, fists, feet, etc	51,861	59,519	50,813	66,098	53,848	53,021	46,848	38,853	41,023

- Represents zero. [1] Represents the number of persons covered by agencies shown.

Source: U.S. Federal Bureau of Investigation, *Law Enforcement Officers Killed and Assaulted*, annual.

No. 370. U.S. Supreme Court—Cases Filed and Disposition: 1980 to 1997

[Statutory term of court begins first Monday in **October**]

Action	1980	1990	1991	1992	1993	1994	1995	1996	1997
Total cases on docket	**5,144**	**6,316**	**6,770**	**7,245**	**7,786**	**8,100**	**7,565**	**7,602**	**7,692**
Appellate cases on docket...........	2,749	2,351	2,451	2,441	2,442	2,515	2,456	2,430	2,432
From prior term	527	365	365	379	342	377	361	375	347
Docketed during present term	2,222	1,986	2,086	2,062	2,100	2,138	2,095	2,055	2,085
Cases acted upon [1]	2,324	2,042	2,125	2,140	2,099	2,185	2,130	2,124	2,142
Granted review	167	114	103	83	78	83	92	74	75
Denied, dismissed, or withdrawn	1,999	1,802	1,914	1,920	1,947	2,016	1,945	1,955	1,990
Summarily decided	90	81	52	84	34	52	62	66	36
Cases not acted upon	425	309	326	301	343	330	326	306	290
Pauper cases on docket	2,371	3,951	4,307	4,792	5,332	5,574	5,098	5,165	5,253
Cases acted upon	2,027	3,436	3,768	4,261	4,621	4,983	4,514	4,613	4,616
Granted review	17	27	17	14	21	10	13	13	14
Denied, dismissed, or withdrawn ...	1,968	3,369	3,716	4,209	4,566	4,955	4,439	4,582	4,581
Summarily decided	32	28	22	25	30	14	55	15	14
Cases not acted upon	344	515	539	531	711	591	584	552	637
Original cases on docket	24	14	12	12	12	11	11	7	7
Cases disposed of during term	7	3	1	1	1	2	5	2	1
Total cases available for argument .	**264**	**201**	**196**	**166**	**145**	**136**	**145**	**140**	**138**
Cases disposed of	162	131	130	120	105	97	93	92	97
Cases argued	154	125	127	116	99	94	90	90	96
Cases dismissed or remanded without argument	8	6	3	4	6	3	3	2	1
Cases remaining	102	70	66	46	40	39	52	48	41
Cases decided by signed opinion	144	121	120	111	93	91	87	87	93
Cases decided by per curiam opinion.....	8	4	3	4	6	3	3	3	1
Number of signed opinions...........	123	112	107	107	84	82	75	80	91

[1] Includes cases granted review and carried over to next term, not shown separately.

Source: Office of the Clerk, Supreme Court of the United States, unpublished data.

No. 371. U.S. Courts of Appeals—Cases Commenced and Disposition: 1980 to 1997

[For years ending **June 30**]

Item	1980	1990	1991	1992	1993	1994	1995	1996	1997
Cases commenced [1]	23,200	40,898	42,033	46,032	49,770	48,815	49,671	51,524	52,571
Criminal..........	4,405	9,493	9,949	10,956	11,885	11,052	10,171	10,653	10,740
U.S. civil..........	4,654	6,626	6,663	7,113	7,758	7,518	7,761	8,681	8,710
Private civil........	10,200	20,490	20,798	22,862	24,030	24,781	25,992	27,188	26,716
Administrative appeals ..	2,950	2,578	2,764	3,052	3,824	3,560	3,345	2,858	4,131
Cases terminated [1]	20,887	38,520	41,414	42,933	47,466	48,546	50,085	49,359	51,295
Criminal..........	3,993	7,509	9,198	9,830	11,043	11,519	11,320	9,995	10,522
U.S. civil..........	4,346	6,379	6,579	6,797	7,462	7,637	7,710	7,831	8,751
Private civil........	8,942	20,369	20,698	21,628	23,437	23,943	25,574	25,999	26,365
Administrative appeals ..	2,643	2,582	3,148	2,801	3,464	3,480	3,254	3,131	3,615
Cases disposed of [2]	10,607	21,006	22,707	23,162	25,567	26,475	28,187	26,988	26,287
Affirmed or granted	8,017	16,629	17,988	18,463	20,604	21,371	22,825	21,696	21,170
Reversed or denied	1,845	2,565	2,503	2,681	2,514	2,636	2,679	2,533	2,353
Other...........	745	1,812	2,216	2,018	2,449	2,468	2,683	2,759	2,764
Median months [3].......	8.9	10.1	10.2	10.5	10.4	10.5	10.5	10.3	11.1

[1] Includes original proceedings and bankruptcy appeals not shown separately. [2] Terminated on the merits after hearing or submission. [3] Prior to 1985, the figure is from filing of complete record to final disposition; beginning 1985, figure is from filing notice of appeal to final disposition. For definition of median, see Guide to Tabular Presentation.

No. 372. U.S. District Courts—Civil and Criminal Cases: 1980 to 1997

[In thousands (168.8 represents 168,800), except percent. For years ending **June 30**]

Case and defendant status	1980	1990	1991	1992	1993	1994	1995	1996	1997
Civil cases: Commenced	168.8	217.9	207.7	226.9	228.6	236.0	239.0	272.7	265.2
Cases terminated [1]	155.0	213.4	211.7	239.6	225.2	228.9	226.1	246.4	249.0
No court action	68.7	51.6	44.6	51.4	44.0	40.5	37.0	36.8	37.4
Court action, total	86.2	161.8	166.5	187.6	181.2	188.4	189.1	209.6	211.7
Before pretrial	53.8	127.0	136.9	153.4	152.3	159.6	161.6	183.3	183.8
Pretrial	22.4	25.5	21.1	26.2	21.1	21.0	19.7	18.8	20.5
Trials	10.1	9.2	8.4	8.0	7.9	7.8	7.7	7.5	7.4
Percent reaching trial...	6.5	4.3	4.0	3.4	3.5	3.4	3.4	3.1	3.0
Criminal cases: Commenced [2] ...	28.0	46.5	45.1	47.5	45.7	44.9	44.2	47.1	48.7
Defendants disposed of [3]	36.6	56.5	56.7	58.4	59.5	61.2	55.3	59.5	62.1
Not convicted	8.0	9.8	10.0	10.0	9.2	10.0	9.0	8.5	7.5
Convicted............	28.6	46.7	46.8	48.4	50.4	51.1	46.3	51.0	54.5
Imprisonment	13.2	27.8	29.2	31.1	34.2	34.5	31.7	36.5	39.9
Probation	11.1	14.2	13.8	13.1	12.6	12.8	11.5	11.6	11.9
Fine and other........	4.4	4.7	3.8	4.3	3.7	3.9	3.2	2.9	2.9

[1] Excludes land condemnation cases. [2] Excludes transfers. [3] Includes Guam, Virgin Islands, and Northern Mariana Islands; 1980 includes Canal Zone.

Source of Tables 371 and 372: Administrative Office of the U.S. Courts, *Statistical Tables for the Federal Judiciary*, annual.

Law Enforcement, Courts, and Prisons   227

No. 373. U.S. District Courts—Civil Cases Commenced and Pending: 1994 to 1997

[For years ending June 30]

Type of case	Cases commenced				Cases pending			
	1994	1995	1996	1997	1994	1995	1996	1997
Cases total [1]	235,996	239,013	272,661	265,151	217,963	224,378	243,703	268,620
Contract actions [1]	31,988	31,619	33,413	38,858	29,697	27,337	26,999	27,539
Recovery of overpayments [2]	2,591	2,099	3,583	8,070	1,227	1,041	2,301	3,838
Real property actions	7,468	7,282	6,276	5,761	5,855	5,073	4,486	3,901
Tort actions	48,067	44,511	67,029	52,710	47,186	52,334	65,823	82,570
Personal injury	44,734	41,102	63,222	48,266	43,638	48,789	62,087	78,483
Personal injury product liability [1]	23,977	17,631	38,170	23,294	20,694	24,166	34,096	47,001
Asbestos	7,111	6,821	6,760	8,184	3,704	3,524	2,037	2,446
Other personal injury	20,757	23,471	25,052	24,972	22,944	24,623	27,991	31,482
Personal property damage	3,333	3,409	3,807	4,444	3,548	3,545	3,736	4,087
Actions under statutes	148,344	155,495	165,922	167,807	135,020	139,487	144,094	150,772
Civil rights [1]	31,521	35,566	40,476	43,166	33,271	37,512	42,545	45,995
Employment	15,256	18,225	22,150	23,707	17,359	20,375	24,212	26,600
Bankruptcy suits	5,675	5,138	4,737	4,217	4,705	4,541	3,938	3,570
Commerce (ICC rates, etc.)	1,228	613	1,622	483	693	446	760	498
Environmental matters	1,059	1,136	1,158	973	1,864	1,823	1,869	1,623
Prisoner petitions	56,283	62,597	69,352	64,262	45,417	47,382	50,353	49,973
Forfeiture and penalty	3,548	2,670	2,255	2,301	3,359	2,399	1,989	1,880
Labor laws	15,800	15,030	15,068	15,320	12,346	11,829	11,742	12,089
Protected property rights [3]	7,051	6,990	6,800	7,511	5,963	5,998	6,273	6,711
Securities commodities and exchanges	1,742	1,870	1,741	1,737	3,130	2,969	2,872	2,562
Social Security laws	11,142	10,168	8,517	13,047	12,302	11,310	9,153	12,952
Tax suits	2,275	2,144	2,078	2,294	1,884	1,692	1,646	1,638
Freedom of information	566	481	465	400	502	500	496	393

[1] Includes other types not shown separately. [2] Includes enforcement of judgments in student loan cases, and overpayments of veterans benefits. [3] Includes copyright, patent, and trademark rights.

Source: Administrative Office of the U.S. Courts, *Statistical Tables for the Federal Judiciary*, annual.

No. 374. U.S. District Courts—Offenders Convicted and Sentenced to Prison, and Length of Sentence: 1997

Most serious offense of conviction	Offenders convicted	Convicted offenders sentenced to prison	Length of sentence (mo.)	Most serious offense of conviction	Offenders convicted	Convicted offenders sentenced to prison	Length of sentence (mo.)
Total [1]	56,570	39,431	58.9	Drug offenses [2]	20,093	17,964	79.5
				Possession	1,937	1,180	62.6
Violent offenses	3,097	2,696	83.4	Trafficking and manufacturing	18,121	16,764	80.8
Property offenses	15,054	7,709	22.8	Public-order offenses	18,180	11,057	45.2
Fraudulent offenses [2]	11,616	6,282	20.8	Regulatory offenses	1,950	782	26.6
Embezzlement	1,092	513	14.3	Other offenses	16,230	10,275	46.6
Fraud [3]	9,302	5,086	21.1	Weapons	2,916	2,668	101.6
Forgery	265	116	13.1	Immigration	6,523	5,502	22.3
Other offenses [2]	3,438	1,427	31.8	Tax law violations [4]	876	346	20.0
Larceny	2,547	850	21.5				

[1] Total may include offenders for whom offense category could not be determined. [2] Includes offenses not shown separately. [3] Excludes tax fraud. [4] Includes tax fraud.

Source: U.S. Bureau of Justice Statistics, *Compendium of Federal Justice Statistics*, annual.

No. 375. Federal Prosecutions of Public Corruption: 1980 to 1996

[As of Dec. 31. Prosecution of persons who have corrupted public office in violation of Federal Criminal Statutes]

Prosecution status	1980	1985	1987	1988	1989	1990	1991	1992	1993	1994	1995	1996
Total: [1] Indicted	727	1,157	1,276	1,274	1,348	1,176	1,452	1,189	1,371	1,165	1,051	984
Convicted	602	997	1,081	1,067	1,149	1,084	1,194	1,081	1,362	969	878	902
Awaiting trial	213	256	368	288	375	300	346	380	403	332	323	244
Federal officials: Indicted	123	563	651	629	695	615	803	624	627	571	527	456
Convicted	131	470	545	529	610	583	665	532	595	488	438	459
Awaiting trial	16	90	118	86	126	103	149	139	133	124	120	64
State officials: Indicted	72	79	102	66	71	96	115	84	113	99	61	109
Convicted	51	66	76	69	54	79	77	92	133	97	61	83
Awaiting trial	28	20	26	14	18	28	42	24	39	17	23	40
Local officials: Indicted	247	248	246	276	269	257	242	232	309	248	236	219
Convicted	168	221	204	229	201	225	180	211	272	202	191	190
Awaiting trial	82	49	89	79	122	98	88	91	132	96	89	60

[1] Includes individuals who are neither public officials nor employees but who were involved with public officials or employees in violating the law, not shown separately.

Source: U.S. Department of Justice, *Federal Prosecutions of Corrupt Public Officials, 1970-1980* and *Report to Congress on the Activities and Operations of the Public Integrity Section*, annual.

No. 376. Delinquency Cases Disposed by Juvenile Courts, by Reason for Referral: 1986 to 1996

[In thousands (1,180 represents 1,180,000, except rate). A delinquency offense is an act committed by a juvenile for which an adult could be prosecuted in a criminal disposition of a case involves taking a definite action such as waiving the case to criminal court, dismissing the case, placing the youth on probation, placing the youth in a facility for delinquents, or such actions as fines, restitution, and community service]

Reason for referral	1986	1987	1988	1989	1990	1991	1992	1993	1994	1995	1996
All delinquency offenses .	1,180	1,181	1,190	1,236	1,320	1,413	1,484	1,515	1,605	1,703	1,758
Case rate [1]	45.5	46.2	47.0	49.1	51.7	54.4	55.8	55.8	58.2	60.7	61.8
Violent offenses	71	66	70	80	97	109	121	124	135	141	137
Criminal homicide	2	1	2	2	2	2	2	3	3	3	2
Forcible rape	5	4	4	5	5	6	6	7	6	7	7
Robbery	26	22	22	23	28	31	33	35	37	39	37
Aggravated assault	39	38	43	51	62	70	79	80	88	93	90
Property offenses	518	519	518	545	564	613	617	593	594	619	623
Burglary	142	134	132	136	146	154	158	149	142	139	141
Larceny	327	331	325	334	341	381	381	374	381	416	422
Motor vehicle theft	43	48	55	68	71	72	71	63	61	53	52
Arson	6	6	7	7	7	7	8	8	9	11	9
Delinquency offenses	590	595	601	611	658	690	746	798	877	943	998
Simple assault	101	105	109	114	128	139	155	171	184	204	217
Vandalism	87	86	84	85	100	112	118	119	124	120	120
Drug law violations	72	72	81	78	71	65	73	91	125	159	176
Obstruction of justice	72	74	75	77	80	76	80	90	102	109	126
Other [2]	258	258	253	256	278	298	320	328	343	351	359

[1] Number of cases disposed per 1,000 youth (ages 10 to 17) at risk.   [2] Includes such offenses as stolen property offenses, trespassing, weapons offenses, other sex offenses, liquor law violations, disorderly conduct, and miscellaneous offenses.

Source: National Center for Juvenile Justice, Pittsburgh, PA, *Juvenile Court Statistics*, annual.

No. 377. Delinquency Cases and Case Rates, by Sex and Race: 1987 to 1996

[A delinquency offense is an act committed by a juvenile for which an adult could be prosecuted in a criminal court. Disposition of a case involves taking a definite action such as waiving the case to criminal court, dismissing the case, placing the youth on probation, placing the youth in a facility for delinquents, or such actions as fines, restitution, and community service. Offenses may not add to total sex and race categories due to rounding]

Sex, race, and offense	Number of cases			Case rate [1]		
	1987	1992	1996	1987	1992	1996
Male, total	954,100	1,197,100	1,359,000	72.7	87.7	92.9
Person	152,900	243,500	285,800	11.7	17.8	19.5
Property	578,400	693,500	671,100	44.1	50.8	45.9
Drugs	60,800	63,900	151,100	4.6	4.7	10.3
Public order	162,000	196,200	251,000	12.3	14.4	17.2
Female, total	226,700	286,700	398,600	18.2	22.2	28.8
Person	38,000	64,700	95,700	3.0	5.0	6.9
Property	134,000	167,100	203,300	10.7	12.9	14.7
Drugs	11,300	8,700	25,200	0.9	0.7	1.8
Public order	43,400	46,100	74,400	3.5	3.6	5.4
White, total	831,800	975,800	1,158,600	40.2	45.8	51.0
Person	110,200	177,000	224,600	5.3	8.3	9.9
Property	522,100	604,500	611,500	25.2	28.4	26.9
Drugs	48,200	37,500	114,100	2.3	1.8	5.0
Public order	151,300	156,700	208,400	7.3	7.4	9.2
Black, total	315,000	453,800	530,100	82.4	113.7	124.1
Person	76,000	121,300	143,100	19.9	30.4	33.5
Property	168,000	221,300	223,700	43.9	55.4	52.3
Drugs	22,300	33,500	57,800	5.8	8.4	13.5
Public order	48,700	77,700	105,500	12.7	19.5	24.7
Other races, total	34,000	54,300	69,000	32.5	42.6	46.7
Person	4,700	9,900	13,800	4.5	7.8	9.3
Property	22,400	34,900	39,200	21.4	27.3	26.6
Drugs	1,600	1,600	4,400	1.5	1.3	3.0
Public order	5,400	7,900	11,500	5.1	6.2	7.8

[1] Cases per 1,000 youth at risk.

Source: National Center for Juvenile Justice, Pittsburgh, PA, *Juvenile Court Statistics*, annual.

U.S. Census Bureau, Statistical Abstract of the United States: 1999

No. 378. Child Abuse and Neglect Cases Substantiated and Indicated— Victim Characteristics: 1990 to 1997

[Based on reports alleging child abuse and neglect that were referred for investigation by the respective child protective services agency in each state. The reporting period may be either calendar or fiscal year. The majority of states provided duplicated counts. Also, varying number of states reported the various characteristics presented below. A substantiated case represents a type of investigation disposition that determines that there is sufficient evidence under state law to conclude that maltreatment occurred or that the child is at risk of maltreatment. An indicated case represents a type of disposition that concludes that there was a reason to suspect maltreatment had occurred]

Item	1990		1995		1996		1997	
	Number	Percent	Number	Percent	Number	Percent	Number	Percent
TYPES OF SUBSTANTIATED MALTREATMENT								
Victims, total [1][2]	690,658	(X)	970,285	(X)	969,018	(X)	798,358	(X)
Neglect	338,770	49.1	507,015	52.3	500,032	51.6	436,630	54.7
Physical abuse	186,801	27.0	237,840	24.5	229,332	23.7	195,517	24.5
Sexual abuse	119,506	17.3	122,964	12.7	119,397	12.3	97,425	12.2
Emotional maltreatment	45,621	6.6	42,051	4.3	55,473	5.7	49,146	6.2
Medical neglect	(NA)	(NA)	28,541	2.9	25,758	2.7	18,866	2.4
SEX OF VICTIM								
Victims, total [2]	794,101	100.0	809,634	100.0	808,370	100.0	669,057	100.0
Male	357,367	45.0	381,075	47.1	384,280	47.5	316,842	47.4
Female	405,409	51.1	425,193	52.5	419,656	51.9	349,606	52.3
AGE OF VICTIM								
Victims, total [2]	807,965	100.0	808,575	100.0	807,854	100.0	668,059	100.0
1 year and younger	106,507	13.2	103,335	12.8	101,055	12.5	83,921	12.6
2 to 5 years old	192,018	23.8	215,303	26.6	208,754	25.8	167,658	25.1
6 to 9 years old	175,609	21.7	195,400	24.2	200,888	24.9	166,718	25.0
10 to 13 years old	150,507	18.6	154,682	19.1	158,247	19.6	130,840	19.6
14 to 17 years old	116,015	14.4	121,548	15.0	123,872	15.3	97,348	14.6
18 and over	5,464	0.7	7,506	0.9	6,466	0.8	3,063	0.5

NA Not available.   X Not applicable.   [1] More than one type of maltreatment may be substantiated per child. Therefore, totals for this category will add up to more than 100 percent. Victim totals and maltreatment types are based on subset of states which reported both the number of child victims and maltreatment incidences by type for that year. [2] Includes other and unknown not shown separately.

No. 379. Child Abuse and Neglect Cases Reported and Investigated, by State: 1997

[Based on reports alleging child abuse and neglect that were referred for investigation by the respective child protective services agency in each state. The reporting period may be either calendar or fiscal year. The majority of states were unable to provide unduplicated counts. Only nine jurisdictions (Alaska, Hawaii, Michigan, Montana, Ohio, Oregon, South Carolina, Vermont, and Washington) provided unduplicated counts of children subject of report. Excludes the Armed Forces]

State	Population under 18 years old	Reports, Number of reports [1]	Reports, Number of children subject of a report	Investigation disposition, number of children substantiated [2]	State	Population under 18 years old	Reports, Number of reports [1]	Reports, Number of children subject of a report	Investigation disposition, number of children substantiated [2]
U.S. . .	69,527,944	1,941,253	2,700,369	889,665	MO	1,406,425	51,151	80,185	15,845
					MT	229,530	10,885	21,568	3,611
AL	1,071,708	[3]25,626	37,873	19,489	NE	444,681	8,140	16,654	4,054
AK	188,329	11,616	11,616	9,017	NV	442,856	14,685	(NA)	(NA)
AZ	1,278,063	38,229	80,622	24,005	NH	296,090	6,429	9,015	1,092
AR	662,692	21,671	36,340	5,109	NJ	1,987,124	[3]70,024	70,024	10,982
CA	8,951,653	380,528	480,443	174,170					
CO	1,015,529	30,647	18,893	5,532	NM	499,322	18,224	23,454	8,213
CT	792,161	29,676	34,152	18,178	NY	4,560,031	141,482	234,205	72,000
DE	177,411	6,659	9,657	4,416	NC	1,873,403	[3]104,950	104,950	33,347
DC	107,204	4,656	11,518	5,341	ND	165,208	4,219	6,870	(NA)
FL	3,471,316	124,810	186,726	79,785	OH	2,838,641	(NA)	(NA)	(NA)
GA	1,987,811	48,770	79,848	45,504	OK	878,305	33,375	51,001	13,800
					OR	810,699	17,187	27,499	9,742
HI	302,592	[3]4,218	4,221	2,559	PA	2,864,082	[3]22,688	22,688	5,691
ID	351,352	12,144	32,522	8,283	RI	233,654	8,486	10,182	3,481
IL	3,174,223	66,613	115,344	38,936	SC	955,641	20,573	39,333	8,684
IN	1,497,455	31,483	47,170	15,624					
IA	725,325	(NA)	(NA)	(NA)	SD	197,338	[4]5,441	4,874	2,491
KS	687,931	31,451	45,459	18,592	TN	1,324,789	[3]32,383	32,383	10,803
KY	961,202	[3]45,001	45,001	20,783	TX	5,577,135	109,598	162,974	39,638
LA	1,190,878	27,908	46,287	14,825	UT	688,077	17,044	27,219	9,356
ME	297,266	4,591	10,041	3,746	VT	145,519	2,223	2,309	1,041
MD	1,268,552	30,330	48,528	14,198	VA	1,644,386	33,273	51,227	10,025
MA	1,451,374	37,722	64,008	29,815	WA	1,454,654	35,838	38,200	21,806
MI	2,504,757	59,829	147,628	20,654	WV	411,746	17,579	(NA)	(NA)
MN	1,250,685	17,358	26,252	10,777	WI	1,346,376	[3]43,406	43,406	14,625
MS	752,998	17,869	(NA)	(NA)	WY	131,765	2,565	(NA)	(NA)

NA Not available.   [1] Except as noted, reports are on incident/family based basis or based on number of reported incidents regardless of the number of children involved in the incidents.   [2] Type of investigation disposition that determines that there is sufficient evidence under state law to conclude that maltreatment occurred or that the child is at risk of maltreatment.   [3] Child-based report that enumerates each child who is a subject of a report.   [4] South Dakota has both child and incident based reports.

Source of Tables 378 and 379: U.S. Department of Health and Human Services, National Center on Child Abuse and Neglect, National Child Abuse and Neglect Data System, *Child Maltreatment 1997: Reports From the States to the National Child Abuse and Neglect System,* April 1999.

No. 380. Jail Inmates, by Sex and Race: 1987 to 1997

[Data are for midyear. Excludes Federal and state prisons or other correctional institutions; institutions exclusively for juveniles; state-operated jails in Alaska, Connecticut, Delaware, Hawaii, Rhode Island, and Vermont; and other facilities which retain persons for less than 48 hours. As of **June 30**. Data for 1993 based on National Jail Census; for other years, based on sample survey and subject to sampling variability]

Characteristic	1987	1990	1992	1993	1994	1995	1996	1997
Total inmates [1]	295,873	405,320	444,584	459,804	486,474	507,044	518,492	567,079
Male	270,172	368,002	403,768	415,576	437,600	455,400	462,400	507,195
Female.	23,920	37,318	40,816	44,228	48,800	51,600	56,100	59,884
White [2]	168,647	186,989	191,362	180,914	253,500	266,200	285,000	306,500
Black [2]	124,267	174,335	195,156	203,463	224,900	232,000	220,600	246,200
Other races [2]	2,959	5,321	5,831	6,178	8,100	8,800	12,800	14,400
Hispanic [3]	41,422	57,449	62,961	69,200	74,900	74,400	80,900	88,800
Non-Hispanic.	254,451	347,871	381,623	390,600	411,600	432,600	437,600	478,200

[1] 1990 to 1993, includes 31,356, 43,138, and 52,235, persons, respectively, of unknown race not shown separately. [2] Beginning 1993, data represent White, non-Hispanic and Black, non-Hispanic and rounded to nearest 100. [3] Hispanic persons may be of any race. Data for 1993 to 1996 are estimated and rounded to nearest 100.

Source: U.S. Bureau of Justice Statistics, through 1994, Jail Inmates, annual; beginning 1995, *Prison and Jail Inmates at Midyear*, annual.

No. 381. State and Federal Correctional Facilities—Inmates and Staff: 1990 and 1995

[Covers all state and Federal correctional institutions or places of confinement such as prisons, prison farms, boot camps, and community based halfway houses and work release centers. Excludes jails and other regional detention centers, private facilities, facilities for the military, Immigration and Naturalization Service, Bureau of Indian Affairs, U.S. Marshall Service, and correctional hospital wards not operated by correctional authorities]

Characteristic	1990	1995	Characteristic	1990	1995
FACILITIES			INMATES		
Total	1,287	1,500	Total	715,649	1,023,572
Type of facility:			Male.	675,624	961,210
Confinement.	1,037	1,196	Female	40,025	62,362
Community.	250	304	Type of facility:		
Federal	80	125	Confinement.	698,570	992,333
State.	1,207	1,375	Community.	17,079	31,239
Size of facility:			Federal	56,821	81,930
Fewer than 500.	816	854	State.	658,828	941,642
500-999.	260	286	Custody level:		
1,000-2,499.	185	306	Maximum/close/high.	150,205	202,174
2,500 or more	26	54	Medium	292,372	415,688
Age of facility:			Minimum/low	219,907	366,227
Less than 10 years	314	497	Not classified	53,165	39,483
10-19 years old.	163	273			
20-49 years old.	373	366	STAFF		
50-99 years old.	379	310	Total	264,201	347,320
100 years old or more . . .	58	45	Federal.	18,451	25,379
Not reported	-	9	State	245,750	321,941

- Represents or rounds to zero.

Source: U.S. Bureau of Justice Statistics, *Census of State and Federal Correctional Facilities, 1995*.

No. 382. Federal and State Prisoners, by Sex: 1980 to 1997

[Based on the U.S. Census Bureau estimated resident population, as of **December 31**. Includes all persons under jurisdiction of Federal and state authorities rather than those in the custody of such authorities. Represents inmates sentenced to maximum term of more than a year]

Year	Total	Rate [1]	Male	Female	Year	Total	Rate [1]	Male	Female
1980	315,974	139	303,643	12,331	1989	680,907	276	643,643	37,264
1981	353,167	154	338,940	14,227	1990	739,980	297	699,416	40,564
1982	394,374	171	378,045	16,329	1991	789,610	313	745,808	43,802
1983	419,820	179	402,391	17,429	1992	846,277	332	799,776	46,501
1984	443,398	188	424,193	19,205	1993	932,074	359	878,037	54,037
1985	480,568	202	458,972	21,296	1994	1,016,691	389	956,566	60,125
1986	522,084	217	497,540	24,544	1995	1,085,363	411	1,021,463	63,900
1987	560,812	231	533,990	26,822	1996	1,138,984	427	1,069,257	69,727
1988	603,732	247	573,587	30,145	1997	1,197,590	445	1,123,478	74,112

[1] Rate per 100,000 estimated population.

Source: U.S. Bureau of Justice Statistics, *Prisoners in State and Federal Institutions on December 31*, annual,

U.S. Census Bureau, Statistical Abstract of the United States: 1999

No. 383. Alcohol or Drug Use at Time of Offense of State and Federal Prisoners, by Type of Offense: 1997

Type of offense	Number of prisoners [1] (est.)		Prisoners who reported being under the influence at time of offense (percent)					
			Alcohol		Drugs		Alcohol or drugs	
	State	Federal	State	Federal	State	Federal	State	Federal
Total	1,046,705	88,018	37.2	20.4	32.6	22.4	52.5	34.0
Violent offenses......	494,349	13,021	41.7	24.5	29.0	24.5	51.9	39.8
Murder	122,435	1,288	44.6	38.7	26.8	29.4	52.4	52.4
Negligent manslaughter . . .	16,592	53	52.0	(B)	17.4	(B)	56.0	(B)
Sexual assault [2]	89,328	713	40.0	32.3	21.5	7.9	45.2	32.3
Robbery	148,001	8,770	37.4	18.0	39.9	27.8	55.6	37.6
Assault	97,897	1,151	45.1	46.0	24.2	13.8	51.8	50.5
Other violent.	20,096	1,046	39.6	32.2	29.0	15.9	48.2	37.2
Property offenses.....	230,177	5,964	34.5	15.6	36.6	10.8	53.2	22.6
Burglary.	111,884	294	37.2	(B)	38.4	(B)	55.7	(B)
Larceny/theft	43,936	414	33.7	(B)	38.4	(B)	54.2	(B)
Motor vehicle theft.	19,279	216	32.2	(B)	39.0	(B)	51.2	(B)
Fraud	28,102	4,283	25.2	10.4	30.5	6.5	42.8	14.5
other property..........	26,976	757	36.0	22.8	30.6	16.4	53.2	34.6
Drug offenses	216,254	55,069	27.4	19.8	41.9	25.0	52.4	34.6
Possession	92,373	10,094	29.6	21.3	42.6	25.1	53.9	36.0
Trafficking	117,926	40,053	25.5	19.4	41.0	25.9	50.9	35.0
Other drug	5,955	4,922	29.9	19.7	47.1	17.1	59.2	29.0
Public-order offenses ..	103,344	13,026	43.2	20.6	23.1	15.6	56.2	30.2
Weapons.............	25,642	6,025	28.3	23.0	22.4	24.4	41.8	37.1
Other public-order	77,702	7,001	48.1	18.5	23.3	8.1	60.9	24.1

B Too few cases in the sample to permit calculation.   [1] Based on cases with valid offense data. See Methodology for differences from other BJS prisoner counts.   [2] Includes rape and other sexual assault.

Source: U.S. Bureau of Justice Statistics, *Substance Abuse and Treatment, State and Federal Prisoners, 1997*, released December 1998, Series NCJ 172871, revised March 11, 1999.

No. 384. Prisoners Under Jurisdiction of State and Federal Correctional Authorities—Summary, by State: 1980 to 1997

[For years ending December 31]

State	1980	1990	1996	1997, advance Total	Percent change, 1996-1997	State	1980	1990	1996	1997, advance Total	Percent change, 1996-1997
U.S. [1].	329,821	773,919	1,183,368	1,244,554	5.2	MO	5,726	14,943	22,003	23,998	9.1
AL	6,543	15,665	21,760	22,290	2.4	MT	739	1,425	2,293	2,242	-2.2
AK [2] ..	822	2,622	3,716	4,220	13.6	NE	1,446	2,403	3,287	3,402	3.5
AZ [3] ..	4,372	14,261	22,493	23,484	4.4	NV	1,839	5,322	8,439	9,024	6.9
AR	2,911	7,322	9,407	10,021	6.5	NH	326	1,342	2,062	2,164	4.9
CA	24,569	97,309	146,049	157,547	7.9	NJ	5,884	21,128	27,490	28,361	3.2
CO	2,629	7,671	12,438	13,461	8.2	NM	1,279	3,187	4,724	4,688	-0.8
CT [2] ..	4,308	10,500	17,851	18,521	3.8	NY	21,815	54,895	69,709	70,026	0.5
DE [2] ..	1,474	3,471	5,110	5,435	6.4	NC	15,513	18,411	30,647	31,638	3.2
DC [2] ..	3,145	9,947	9,376	9,353	-0.2	ND	253	483	722	797	10.4
FL [3] ..	20,735	44,387	63,763	64,565	1.3	OH	13,489	31,822	46,174	48,002	4.0
GA [3] ..	12,178	22,411	35,139	36,450	3.7	OK [4] ..	4,796	12,285	19,593	20,542	4.8
HI [2] ..	985	2,533	4,011	4,949	23.4	OR	3,177	6,492	8,661	7,999	-7.6
ID [3] ..	817	1,961	3,832	3,946	3.0	PA	8,171	22,290	34,537	34,964	1.2
IL [3] ..	11,899	27,516	38,852	40,788	5.0	RI [2] ..	813	2,392	3,271	3,371	3.1
IN [3] ..	6,683	12,736	16,960	17,903	5.6	SC	7,862	17,319	20,446	21,173	3.6
IA [3] ..	2,481	3,967	6,342	6,938	9.4	SD	635	1,341	2,063	2,239	8.5
KS	2,494	5,775	7,756	7,911	2.0	TN	7,022	10,388	15,626	16,659	6.6
KY	3,588	9,023	12,910	14,600	13.1	TX	29,892	50,042	132,383	140,729	6.3
LA	8,889	18,599	26,779	29,265	9.3	UT [2] ..	932	2,496	3,972	4,284	7.9
ME	814	1,523	1,426	1,620	13.6	VT [2] ..	480	1,049	1,119	1,270	13.5
MD [3][4]	7,731	17,848	22,050	22,232	0.8	VA	8,920	17,593	27,655	28,385	2.6
MA [3][4]	3,185	8,345	11,796	11,947	1.3	WA	4,399	7,995	12,527	13,214	5.5
MI [3][4]	15,124	34,267	42,349	44,771	5.7	WV	1,257	1,565	2,749	3,172	15.4
MN	2,001	3,176	5,158	5,326	3.3	WI	3,980	7,465	12,991	14,682	13.0
MS	3,902	8,375	13,859	15,447	11.5	WY	534	1,110	1,499	1,566	4.5

[1] State-level data excludes Federal inmates.   [2] Includes both jail and prison inmates (state has combined jail and prison system).   [3] Numbers are for custody rather than jurisdiction counts.   [4] Data are for custody counts until 1995 when jurisdiction counts are reported.

Source: U.S. Bureau of Justice Statistics, *Prisoners in 1997*, and earlier reports.

No. 385. Adults on Probation, in Jail or Prison, or on Parole: 1980 to 1997

[As of December 31, except jail counts as June 30]

Year	Total [1]	Probation	Jail	Prison	Parole	Male	Female
1980	1,840,400	1,118,097	[2]182,288	319,598	220,438	(NA)	(NA)
1981	2,006,600	1,225,934	[2]195,085	360,029	225,539	(NA)	(NA)
1982	2,192,600	1,357,264	207,853	402,914	224,604	(NA)	(NA)
1983	2,475,100	1,582,947	221,815	423,898	246,440	(NA)	(NA)
1984	2,689,200	1,740,948	233,018	448,264	266,992	(NA)	(NA)
1985	3,011,400	1,968,712	254,986	487,593	300,203	2,606,000	405,500
1986	3,239,400	2,114,621	272,735	526,436	325,638	2,829,100	410,300
1987	3,459,600	2,247,158	294,092	562,814	355,505	3,021,000	438,600
1988	3,714,100	2,356,483	341,893	607,766	407,977	3,223,000	491,100
1989	4,055,600	2,522,125	393,303	683,367	456,803	3,501,600	554,000
1990	4,348,000	2,670,234	403,019	743,382	531,407	3,746,300	601,700
1991	4,535,600	2,728,472	424,129	792,535	590,442	3,913,000	622,600
1992	4,762,600	2,811,611	441,781	850,566	658,601	4,050,300	712,300
1993	4,944,000	2,903,061	455,500	909,381	676,100	4,215,800	728,200
1994	5,141,300	2,981,022	479,800	990,147	690,371	4,377,400	763,900
1995	5,335,100	3,077,861	499,300	1,078,542	679,421	4,546,400	828,100
1996	5,475,000	3,161,030	510,400	1,127,528	676,045	(NA)	(NA)
1997, total [3]	5,690,700	3,261,888	557,974	1,185,800	685,033	(NA)	(NA)

NA Not available. [1] Totals may not add due to individuals having multiple correctional statuses. [2] Estimated. [3] Totals may not add due to rounding.

Source: U.S. Bureau of Justice Statistics, *Correctional Populations in the United States*, annual.

No. 386. Prisoners Under Sentence of Death, by Characteristic: 1980 to 1997

[As of December 31. Excludes prisoners under sentence of death who remained within local correctional systems pending exhaustion of appellate process or who had not been committed to prison]

Characteristic	1980	1987	1988	1989	1990	1991	1992	1993	1994	1995	1996	1997
Total [1]	688	1,967	2,117	2,243	2,346	2,466	2,575	2,727	2,905	3,064	3,242	3,335
White	418	1,128	1,235	1,308	1,368	1,450	1,508	1,575	1,653	1,732	1,833	1,876
Black and other	270	839	882	935	978	1,016	1,067	1,152	1,252	1,332	1,409	1,459
Under 20 years	11	10	11	6	8	14	12	13	19	20	17	14
20 to 24 years	173	222	195	191	168	179	188	211	231	264	288	275
25 to 34 years	334	969	1,048	1,080	1,110	1,087	1,078	1,066	1,088	1,088	1,088	1,075
35 to 54 years	186	744	823	917	1,006	1,129	1,212	1,330	1,449	1,583	1,711	1,818
55 years and over	10	39	47	56	64	73	85	96	103	119	138	153
Years of school completed:												
7 years or less	68	181	180	183	178	173	181	185	186	191	196	199
8 years	74	183	184	178	186	181	180	183	198	195	201	204
9 to 11 years	204	650	692	739	775	810	836	885	930	979	1,040	1,065
12 years	162	591	657	695	729	783	831	887	939	995	1,037	1,077
More than 12 years	43	168	180	192	209	222	232	244	255	272	282	286
Unknown	163	211	231	263	279	313	315	332	382	422	486	504
Marital status:												
Never married	268	856	898	956	998	1,071	1,132	1,222	1,320	1,412	1,507	1,561
Married	229	571	594	610	632	663	663	671	707	718	739	744
Divorced [2]	217	557	632	684	726	746	780	823	863	924	996	1,030
Time elapsed since sentencing:												
Less than 12 months	185	295	293	231	231	252	265	262	280	287	306	242
12 to 47 months	389	804	812	809	753	718	720	716	755	784	816	849
48 to 71 months	102	412	409	408	438	441	444	422	379	423	447	462
72 months and over	38	473	610	802	934	1,071	1,146	1,316	1,476	1,560	1,673	1,782
Legal status at arrest:												
Not under sentence	384	1,123	1,207	1,301	1,345	1,415	1,476	1,562	1,662	1,764	1,881	1,946
Parole or probation [3]	115	480	545	585	578	615	702	754	800	866	894	909
Prison or escaped	45	91	93	94	128	102	101	102	103	110	112	114
Unknown	170	290	272	270	305	321	296	298	325	314	355	366

[1] Revisions to the total number of prisoners were not carried to the characteristics except for race. [2] Includes persons married but separated, widows, widowers, and unknown. [3] Includes prisoners on mandatory conditional release, work release, leave, AWOL, or bail. Covers 28 prisoners in 1990, and 29 in 1991 and 1992, 33 in 1993 and 1995, 31 in 1994 and 1996, and 30 in 1997.

Source: U.S. Bureau of Justice Statistics, *Capital Punishment*, annual.

U.S. Census Bureau, Statistical Abstract of the United States: 1999

No. 387. Movement of Prisoners Under Sentence of Death: 1980 to 1997

[Prisoners reported under sentence of death by civil authorities. The term "under sentence of death" begins when the court pronounces the first sentence of death for a capital offense]

Status	1980	1987	1988	1989	1990	1991	1992	1993	1994	1995	1996	1997
Under sentence of death, Jan. 1 [1] [2]	595	1,800	1,967	2,117	2,243	2,346	2,465	2,580	2,727	2,905	3,064	3,242
Received death sentence [1] [2]	203	299	296	251	244	266	265	282	306	310	299	256
White	125	190	196	133	147	163	147	146	162	168	174	146
Black	77	106	91	114	94	101	114	130	136	138	119	106
Dispositions other than executions	101	90	128	102	108	116	124	108	112	105	99	89
Executions	-	25	11	16	23	14	31	38	31	56	45	74
Under sentence of death, Dec. 31 [1] [2]	688	1,967	2,117	2,243	2,346	2,466	2,575	2,727	2,890	3,054	3,242	3,335
White	425	1,128	1,238	1,308	1,368	1,450	1,508	1,575	1,645	1,730	1,833	1,876
Black	268	813	853	898	940	1,016	1,029	1,111	1,197	1,275	1,358	1,406

- Represents zero. [1] Includes races other than White or Black. [2] Revisions to total number of prisoners under death sentence not carried to this category.

Source: U.S. Bureau of Justice Statistics, *Capital Punishment*, annual.

No. 388. Prisoners Executed Under Civil Authority, by Race: 1930 to 1998

[Excludes executions by military authorities. The Army (including the Air Force) carried out 160 (148 between 1942 and 1950; 3 each in 1954, 1955, and 1957; and 1 each in 1958, 1959, and 1961). Of the total, 106 were executed for murder (including 21 involving rape), 53 for rape, and 1 for desertion. The Navy carried out no executions during the period]

Year or period	Total [1]	White	Black	Executed for murder Total [1]	White	Black	Executed for rape Total [1]	White	Black	Executed, other offenses [2] Total [1]	White	Black
All years, 1930-97	4,291	1,971	2,201	3,692	1,884	1,770	455	48	405	70	39	31
1930 to 1939	1,667	827	816	1,514	803	687	125	10	115	28	14	14
1940 to 1949	1,284	490	781	1,064	458	595	200	19	179	20	13	7
1950 to 1959	717	336	376	601	316	280	102	13	89	14	7	7
1960 to 1967	191	98	93	155	87	68	28	6	22	8	5	3
1968 to 1976	-	-	-	-	-	-	-	-	-	-	-	-
1977 to 1997	432	265	162	432	265	167	-	-	-	-	-	-
1985	18	11	7	18	11	7	-	-	-	-	-	-
1986	18	11	7	18	11	7	-	-	-	-	-	-
1987	25	13	12	25	13	12	-	-	-	-	-	-
1988	11	6	5	11	6	5	-	-	-	-	-	-
1989	16	8	8	16	8	8	-	-	-	-	-	-
1990	23	16	7	23	16	7	-	-	-	-	-	-
1991	14	7	7	14	7	7	-	-	-	-	-	-
1992	31	19	11	31	19	11	-	-	-	-	-	-
1993	38	23	14	38	23	14	-	-	-	-	-	-
1994	31	20	11	31	20	11	-	-	-	-	-	-
1995	56	33	22	56	33	22	-	-	-	-	-	-
1996	45	31	14	45	31	14	-	-	-	-	-	-
1997	74	45	27	74	45	27	-	-	-	-	-	-
1998, prel.	68	48	18	(NA)	(NA)	(NA)	(NA)	(NA)	(NA)	(NA)	(NA)	(NA)

- Represents zero. NA Not available. [1] Includes races other than White or Black. [2] Includes 25 armed robbery, 20 kidnapping, 11 burglary, 8 espionage (6 in 1942 and 2 in 1953), and 6 aggravated assault.

Source: Through 1978, U.S. Law Enforcement Assistance Administration; thereafter, U.S. Bureau of Justice Statistics, *Correctional Populations in the United States,* annual; and *Capital Punishment,* annual.

No. 389. Prisoners Under Sentence of Death and Executed Under Civil Authority, by States: 1977 to 1998

[Alaska, District of Columbia, Hawaii, Iowa, Maine, Massachusetts, Michigan, Minnesota, New York, North Dakota, Rhode Island, Vermont, West Virginia, and Wisconsin are jurisdictions without a death penalty]

State	1977 to 1998	1995	1996	1997	1998	State	1977 to 1998	1995	1996	1997	1998	State	1977 to 1998	1995	1996	1997	1998
U.S.	432	56	45	74	68	ID	1	-	-	-	-	NC	8	2	-	-	3
AL	16	2	1	3	1	IL	10	5	1	2	1	OK	9	3	2	1	4
AZ	8	1	2	2	4	IN	5	-	1	1	1	SC	13	1	6	2	7
AR	16	2	1	4	1	LA	24	1	1	1	-	TX	144	19	3	37	20
CA	4	-	2	-	1	MD	2	-	-	1	1	UT	5	-	1	-	-
DE	8	1	3	-	-	MS	4	-	-	-	-	VA	46	5	8	9	13
FL	39	3	2	1	4	MO	29	6	6	6	3	WA	2	-	-	-	1
GA	22	2	2	-	1	NE	3	-	1	1	-	WY	1	-	-	-	-
						NV	6	-	1	-	1						

- Represents zero.

Source: Through 1978, U.S. Law Enforcement Assistance Administration; thereafter, U.S. Bureau of Justice Statistics, *Capital Punishment,* annual.

No. 390. Fire Losses—Total and Percent Change: 1980 to 1997

[5,579 represents 5,579,000,000. Includes allowance for uninsured and unreported losses but excludes losses to government property and forests. Represents incurred losses]

Year	Total (mil. dol.)	Per capita[1]	Year	Total (mil. dol.)	Per capita[1]	Year	Total (mil. dol.)	Per capita[1]
1980	5,579	24.56	1986	8,488	35.21	1992	13,588	53.29
1981	5,625	24.53	1987	8,504	34.96	1993	11,331	43.96
1982	5,894	25.61	1988	9,626	39.11	1994	12,778	49.09
1983	6,320	27.20	1989	9,514	38.33	1995	11,887	45.24
1984	7,602	32.35	1990	9,495	38.07	1996	12,544	47.30
1985	7,753	32.70	1991	11,302	44.83	1997	11,372	42.49

[1] Based on U.S. Census Bureau estimated resident population as of July 1.

Source: Insurance Information Institute, New York, NY, *Insurance Facts*, annual (copyright).

No. 391. Fires—Number and Loss, by Type and Property Use: 1994 to 1997

[2,054 represents 2,054,000. Based on annual sample survey of fire departments. No adjustments were made for unreported fires and losses. Property loss includes direct property loss only]

Type and property use	Number (1,000)				Property loss (mil. dol.)			
	1994	1995	1996	1997	1994	1995	1996	1997
Fires, total	2,054	1,966	1,975	1,795	8,151	8,918	9,406	8,525
Structure	614	574	578	552	6,867	7,620	7,933	7,087
Outside of structure[1]	66	61	63	57	120	77	91	99
Brush and rubbish	795	778	766	662	-	-	-	-
Vehicle	422	406	414	397	1,111	1,152	1,333	1,269
Other	157	147	154	127	53	69	49	70
Structure by property use:								
Public assembly	17	15	16	15	334	336	330	327
Educational	9	9	9	8	91	84	65	58
Institutional	11	9	8	8	20	31	24	25
Stores and offices	30	29	27	27	598	[2]681	665	612
Residential[3]	451	426	428	407	4,317	4,363	4,962	4,585
1-2 family units[3]	341	320	324	303	3,537	3,615	4,121	3,735
Apartments	97	94	93	93	678	649	748	718
Other residential[4]	13	12	11	11	102	99	93	132
Storage[5]	43	39	41	36	568	710	949	577
Industry, utility, defense[6]	19	18	18	17	758	[6]1,248	[7]733	723
Special structures	34	29	31	34	181	167	205	180

- Represents zero. [1] Includes outside storage, crops, timber, etc. [2] Includes an estimated $135 million in property loss that occurred in the explosion and fire in the Federal office building in Oklahoma City on April 19, 1995. [3] Includes mobile homes. [4] Includes hotels and motels, college dormitories, boarding houses, etc. [5] Data underreported as some incidents were handled by private fire brigades or fixed suppression systems which do not report. [6] Includes estimated losses of $500 million in an industrial complex fire in Massachusetts and $200 million in a manufacturing plant in Georgia in 1995. [7] Includes $280 million in property in a storage property fire in New Orleans, Louisiana in 1996.

Source: National Fire Protection Association, Quincy, MA, "1997 U.S. Fire Loss," *NFPA Journal*, September 1998, and prior issues (copyright 1998).

No. 392. Fires and Property Loss for Incendiary and Suspicious Fires and Civilian Fire Deaths and Injuries, by Selected Property Type: 1994 to 1997

[614 represents 614,000. Based on sample survey of fire departments]

Characteristic	1994	1995	1996	1997	Characteristic	1994	1995	1996	1997
NUMBER (1,000)					**CIVILIAN FIRE DEATHS**				
Structure fires, total	614	574	578	552	Deaths, total[3]	4,275	4,585	4,990	4,050
Structure fires of incendiary or suspicious origin	86	91	85	78	Residential property	3,465	3,695	4,080	3,390
Fires of incendiary origin	53	58	52	52	One- and two-family dwellings	2,785	3,035	3,470	2,700
Fires of suspicious origin	33	33	33	26	Apartments	640	605	565	660
					Vehicles	630	535	710	480
PROPERTY LOSS[1] (mil. dol.)					**CIVILIAN FIRE INJURIES**				
Structure fires, total	6,867	7,620	7,933	7,087	Injuries, total[3]	27,250	25,775	25,550	23,750
Structure fires of incendiary or suspicious origin	1,447	1,647	1,405	1,309	Residential property	20,025	19,125	19,300	17,775
Fires of incendiary origin	964	[2]1,116	897	802	One- and two-family dwellings	14,000	13,450	13,700	12,300
Fires of suspicious origin	483	531	508	507	Apartments	5,475	5,200	5,175	5,000
					Vehicles	2,625	2,525	2,225	2,125

[1] Direct property loss only. [2] Includes $135 million in property loss that occurred in the explosion and fire in the Federal office building in Oklahoma City on April 19, 1995. [3] Includes other not shown separately.

Source: National Fire Protection Association, Quincy, MA, "1997 U.S. Fire Loss," *NFPA Journal*, September 1998, and prior issues (copyright 1998).

Figure 6.1
Number and Volume of Oil Spills in U.S. Water: 1990 to 1997

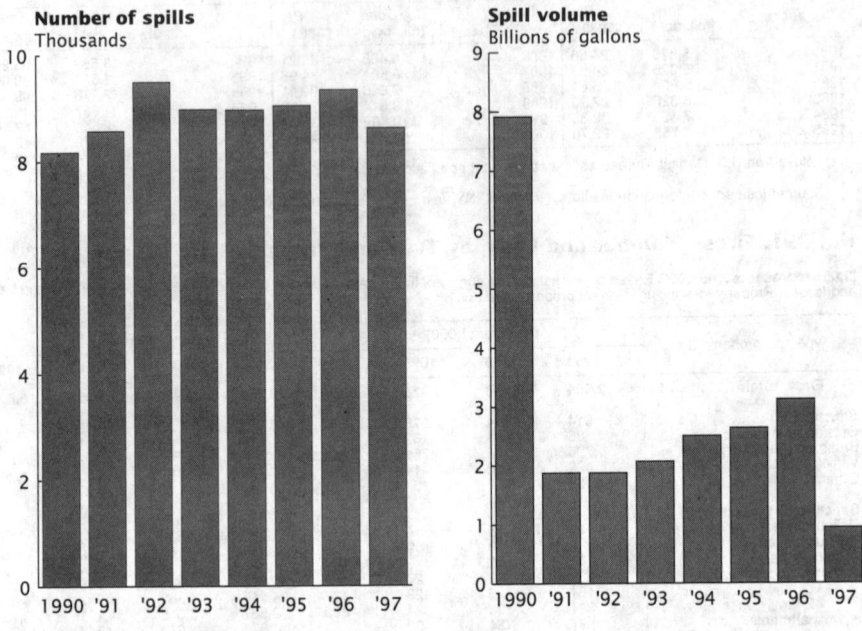

Number of spills
Thousands

Spill volume
Billions of gallons

Source: Chart prepared by U.S. Census Bureau. For data, see Table 402.

Figure 6.2
Toxic Chemical Releases, by Industry: 1988 to 1996

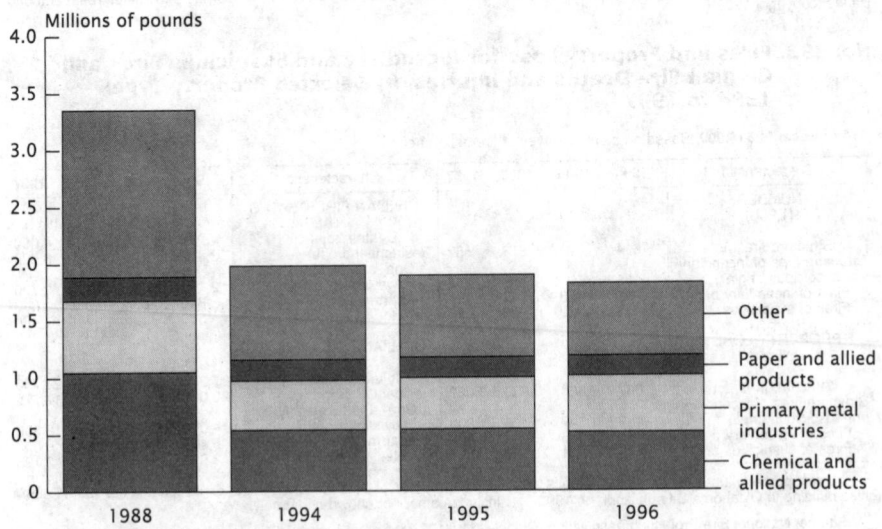

Millions of pounds

Other

Paper and allied products

Primary metal industries

Chemical and allied products

Source: Chart prepared by U.S. Census Bureau. For data, see Table 412.

U.S. Census Bureau, Statistical Abstract of the United States: 1999

Section 6

Geography and Environment

This section presents a variety of information on the physical environment of the United States, starting with basic area measurement data and ending with climatic data for selected weather stations around the country. The subjects covered between those points are mostly concerned with environmental trends but include such related subjects as land use, water consumption, air pollutant emissions, toxic releases, oil spills, hazardous waste sites, municipal waste and recycling, threatened and endangered wildlife, and the environmental industry.

The information in this section is selected from a wide range of Federal agencies that compile the data for various administrative or regulatory purposes, such as the Environmental Protection Agency, U.S. Geological Survey, National Oceanic and Atmospheric Administration, Soil Conservation Service, and General Services Administration. Other agencies include the U.S. Census Bureau, which presents nationwide area measurement information and the Bureau of Economic Analysis, which compiles data on pollution abatement and control expenditures.

Area—For the 1990 census, area measurements were calculated by computer based on the information contained in a single, consistent geographic database, the TIGER ™ file (described below), rather than relying on historical, local, and manually calculated information. This especially affects water area figures reported in 1990; these had only included those bodies of water of least 40 acres and those streams with a width of at least one-eighth of a statute mile from 1940 to 1980. Water area figures for 1990 increased because the data reflected all water recorded in the Census Bureau's

geographic database including coastal, Great Lakes, and territorial waters.

Geography—The U.S. Geological Survey conducts investigations, surveys, and research in the fields of geography, geology, topography, geographic information systems, mineralogy, hydrology, and geothermal energy resources as well as natural hazards. In cooperation with state and local agencies, the U.S. Geological Survey prepares and publishes topographic, land use/land cover, geologic, and hydrologic maps and digital data compilations. The U.S. Geological Survey provides United States cartographic data through the Earth Sciences Information Center, water resources data through the National Water Data Exchange (NAWDEX), and a variety of research and Open-File reports which are announced monthly in *New Publications of the U.S. Geological Survey.*

In a joint project with the Census Bureau, the U.S. Geological Survey provided the basic information on geographic features for input into a national geographic and cartographic database prepared by the Census Bureau, called the TIGER ™ (Topologically Integrated Geographic Encoding and Referencing) System. Maps prepared by the Census Bureau show the names and boundaries of various types of legal and statistical entities, such as places, county subdivisions, and larger areas and are available as of the specific decennial census. An inventory is available for the 1990 census, both on computer tape and CD-ROM as the *1990 TIGER/GICS (Geographic Identification Code Scheme)* and for the 1992 economic censuses in the *Geographic Reference Manual* (EC97-R-1). The Census Bureau maintains a current inventory of governmental units and their legal boundaries through its Boundary and Annexation

Geography and Environment 237

U.S. Census Bureau, Statistical Abstract of the United States: 1999

Survey. The TIGER ™ System contains information on the legal and statistical entities used by the Census Bureau, as well as on both manmade and natural features, such as streets, roads, railroads, rivers, and lakes; information is available to the public in the form of machine-readable TIGER extract files.

An inventory of the Nation's land resources by type of use/cover was conducted by the Soil Conservation Service in 1982, 1987, and 1992. The results, published in the *1992 National Inventory of Land Resources*, cover all non-Federal land in Puerto Rico, the Virgin Islands, and the United States except Alaska. An update to cover 1997 is expected to be released in late 1999 and early 2000.

Environment—The principal Federal agency responsible for pollution abatement and control activities is the Environmental Protection Agency (EPA). It is responsible for establishing and monitoring national air quality standards, water quality activities, solid and hazardous waste disposal, and control of toxic substances. Many of these series now appear on the EPA web site at the Center for Environmental Information and Statistics and can be accessed at http://www.epa.gov/ceis/.

National Ambient Air Quality Standards (NAAQS) for suspended particulate matter, sulfur dioxide, photochemical oxidants, carbon onoxide, and nitrogen dioxide were originally set by the EPA in April 1971. Every 5 years, each of the NAAQS is reviewed and revised if new health or welfare data indicates that a change is necessary. The standard for photochemical oxidants, now called ozone, was revised in February 1979. Also, a new NAAQS for lead was promulgated in October 1978 and for suspended particulate matter in 1987.

Table 404 gives some of the health-related standards for the six air pollutants having NAAQS. Responsibility for demonstrating compliance with or progress toward achieving these standards lies with the state agencies. In 1997, there were 1,734 non-Federal sampling stations for particulates, 658 for sulfur dioxide, 538 for carbon monoxide, 1,019 for ozone, 409 for nitrogen dioxide, and 381 for lead. Data from these state networks are periodically submitted to EPA's National Aerometric Information Retrieval System (AIRS) for summarization in annual reports on the nationwide status and trends in air quality; for details, see *National Air Quality and Emissions Trends Report, 1997*.

Climate—NOAA, through the National Weather Service and the National Environmental Satellite, Data, and Information Service, is responsible for data on climate. NOAA maintains about 11,600 weather stations, of which over 3,000 produce autographic precipitation records, about 600 take hourly readings of a series of weather elements, and the remainder record data once a day. These data are reported monthly in the *Climatological Data* and *Storm Data*, published monthly, and annually in the *Local Climatological Data* (published by location for major cities).

The normal climatological temperatures, precipitation, and degree days listed in this publication are derived for comparative purposes and are averages for the 30-year period, 1961-90. For stations that did not have continuous records for the entire 30 years from the same instrument site, the normals have been adjusted to provide representative values for the current location. The information in all other tables is based on data from the beginning of the record at that location through 1997, except as noted.

No. 393. Land and Water Area of States and Other Entities: 1990

[One square mile=2.59 square kilometers. Excludes territorial water, which was included in the 1993 edition of the *Statistical Abstract*]

State and other area	Total area Sq. mi.	Total area Sq. km.	Land area Sq. mi.	Land area Sq. km.	Water area Total Sq. mi.	Water area Total Sq. km.	Water area Inland sq. mi.	Water area Coastal sq. mi.	Water area Great Lakes sq. mi.
United States . . .	3,717,796	9,629,091	3,536,278	9,158,960	181,518	470,131	78,937	42,528	60,052
Alabama	52,237	135,293	50,750	131,443	1,486	3,850	968	519	-
Alaska.	615,230	1,593,444	570,374	1,477,268	44,856	116,177	17,501	27,355	-
Arizona	114,006	295,276	113,642	294,333	364	943	364	-	-
Arkansas	53,182	137,742	52,075	134,875	1,107	2,867	1,107	-	-
California	158,869	411,470	155,973	403,971	2,895	7,499	2,674	222	-
Colorado	104,100	269,618	103,729	268,658	371	960	371	-	-
Connecticut	5,544	14,358	4,845	12,550	698	1,808	161	538	-
Delaware	2,396	6,206	1,955	5,062	442	1,144	71	371	-
District of Columbia . . .	68	177	61	159	7	18	7	-	-
Florida.	59,928	155,214	53,937	139,697	5,991	15,517	4,683	1,308	-
Georgia.	58,977	152,750	57,919	150,010	1,058	2,740	1,011	47	-
Hawaii.	6,459	16,729	6,423	16,636	36	93	36	-	-
Idaho	83,574	216,456	82,751	214,325	823	2,131	823	-	-
Illinois	57,918	150,007	55,593	143,987	2,325	6,021	750	-	1,575
Indiana	36,420	94,328	35,870	92,904	550	1,424	315	-	235
Iowa	56,276	145,754	55,875	144,716	401	1,038	401	-	-
Kansas	82,282	213,110	81,823	211,922	459	1,189	459	-	-
Kentucky	40,411	104,665	39,732	102,907	679	1,759	679	-	-
Louisiana	49,651	128,595	43,566	112,836	6,085	15,759	4,153	1,931	-
Maine	33,741	87,388	30,865	79,939	2,876	7,449	2,263	613	-
Maryland	12,297	31,849	9,775	25,316	2,522	6,533	680	1,842	-
Massachusetts	9,241	23,934	7,838	20,300	1,403	3,634	424	979	-
Michigan	96,705	250,465	56,809	147,136	39,895	103,329	1,704	-	38,192
Minnesota	86,943	225,182	79,617	206,207	7,326	18,975	4,780	-	2,546
Mississippi	48,286	125,060	46,914	121,506	1,372	3,553	781	591	-
Missouri.	69,709	180,546	68,898	178,446	811	2,100	811	-	-
Montana	147,046	380,849	145,556	376,991	1,490	3,859	1,490	-	-
Nebraska	77,358	200,358	76,878	199,113	481	1,245	481	-	-
Nevada	110,567	286,367	109,806	284,396	761	1,971	761	-	-
New Hampshire	9,283	24,044	8,969	23,231	314	813	314	-	-
New Jersey	8,215	21,277	7,419	19,215	796	2,062	371	425	-
New Mexico	121,598	314,939	121,364	314,334	234	605	234	-	-
New York.	53,989	139,833	47,224	122,310	6,766	17,523	1,888	976	3,901
North Carolina	52,672	136,421	48,718	126,180	3,954	10,241	3,954	-	-
North Dakota	70,704	183,123	68,994	178,695	1,710	4,428	1,710	-	-
Ohio	44,828	116,103	40,953	106,067	3,875	10,036	376	-	3,499
Oklahoma	69,903	181,048	68,679	177,877	1,224	3,171	1,224	-	-
Oregon	97,132	251,571	96,002	248,646	1,129	2,925	1,050	80	-
Pennsylvania	46,058	119,291	44,820	116,083	1,239	3,208	490	-	749
Rhode Island	1,231	3,189	1,045	2,707	186	482	168	18	-
South Carolina	31,189	80,779	30,111	77,988	1,078	2,791	1,006	72	-
South Dakota	77,121	199,744	75,896	196,571	1,225	3,174	1,225	-	-
Tennessee	42,146	109,158	41,219	106,758	926	2,400	926	-	-
Texas	267,277	692,248	261,914	678,358	5,363	13,890	4,959	404	-
Utah	84,904	219,902	82,168	212,815	2,736	7,086	2,736	-	-
Vermont	9,615	24,903	9,249	23,956	366	947	366	-	-
Virginia	42,326	109,625	39,598	102,558	2,729	7,067	1,000	1,728	-
Washington	70,637	182,949	66,581	172,445	4,055	10,503	1,545	2,511	-
West Virginia	24,231	62,759	24,087	62,384	145	375	145	-	-
Wisconsin	65,499	169,643	54,314	140,672	11,186	28,971	1,831	-	9,355
Wyoming	97,818	253,349	97,105	251,501	714	1,848	714	-	-
Other areas:									
Puerto Rico.	3,508	9,085	3,427	8,875	81	210	65	16	-
American Samoa . . .	90	233	77	200	13	33	7	6	-
Guam	217	561	210	543	7	18	7	-	-
No. Mariana Islands .	189	490	179	464	10	26	2	8	-
Palau.	241	624	177	458	64	165	40	24	-
Virgin Islands of the U.S	171	443	134	346	37	96	17	20	-

- Represents or rounds to zero.

Source: U.S. Census Bureau, *1990 Census of Population and Housing*, Series CPH-2; and unpublished data from the TIGER/Geographic Information Control System (TIGER/GICS) computer file. Corrections have been made subsequent to the 1990 Census reports.

Geography and Environment 239

[As of end of fiscal year; see text, Section 9, State and Local Government. Total land area figures are not comparable with those in Table 393]

State	Total (1,000 acres)	Not owned by Federal Government (1,000 acres)	Owned by Federal Government [1] Acres (1,000)	Percent	State	Total (1,000 acres)	Not owned by Federal Government (1,000 acres)	Owned by Federal Government [1] Acres (1,000)	Percent
United States.	2,271,343	1,708,262	563,081	24.8	Missouri	44,248	42,590	1,658	3.7
Alabama	32,678	31,598	1,080	3.3	Montana	93,271	67,786	25,485	27.3
Alaska	365,482	193,694	171,788	47.0	Nebraska	49,032	48,517	515	1.1
Arizona	72,688	41,351	31,337	43.1	Nevada	70,264	14,183	56,082	79.8
Arkansas	33,599	30,860	2,740	8.2	New Hampshire	5,769	5,035	734	12.7
California	100,207	55,449	44,757	44.7	New Jersey	4,813	4,712	102	2.1
Colorado	66,486	42,357	24,129	36.3	New Mexico	77,766	51,548	26,218	33.7
Connecticut	3,135	3,128	7	0.2	New York	30,681	30,484	197	0.6
Delaware	1,266	1,264	2	0.2	North Carolina	31,403	29,374	2,028	6.5
District of Columbia.	39	30	9	23.5	North Dakota	44,452	43,040	1,413	3.2
Florida	34,721	32,077	2,645	7.6	Ohio	26,222	25,942	280	1.1
Georgia	37,295	35,837	1,458	3.9	Oklahoma	44,088	43,410	678	1.5
Hawaii	4,106	3,755	350	8.5	Oregon	61,599	29,789	31,809	51.6
Idaho	52,933	19,941	32,992	62.3	Pennsylvania	28,804	28,182	623	2.2
Illinois	35,795	35,390	405	1.1	Rhode Island	677	674	3	0.5
Indiana	23,158	22,764	394	1.7	South Carolina	19,374	18,440	935	4.8
Iowa	35,860	35,831	30	0.1	South Dakota	48,882	46,304	2,577	5.3
Kansas	52,511	52,161	350	0.7	Tennessee	26,728	25,152	1,576	5.9
Kentucky	25,512	24,430	1,083	4.2	Texas	168,218	166,209	2,008	1.2
Louisiana	28,868	28,123	745	2.6	Utah	52,697	18,799	33,898	64.3
Maine	19,848	19,702	145	0.7	Vermont	5,937	5,560	377	6.3
Maryland	6,319	6,162	157	2.5	Virginia	25,496	23,217	2,279	8.9
Massachusetts	5,035	4,983	52	1.0	Washington	42,694	30,755	11,939	28.0
Michigan	36,492	32,513	3,980	10.9	West Virginia	15,411	14,333	1,077	7.0
Minnesota	51,206	47,137	4,069	7.9	Wisconsin	35,011	33,278	1,733	5.0
Mississippi	30,223	28,946	1,276	4.2	Wyoming	62,343	31,465	30,878	49.5

[1] Excludes trust properties.

Source: U.S. General Services Administration, *Inventory Report on Real Property Owned by the United States Throughout the World,* annual.

No. 395. Land Cover/Use, by State: 1992

[In millions of acres (1,940.0 represents 1,940,000,000). Excludes Alaska and District of Columbia]

State	Total surface area [1]	Non-Federal Total	Developed [2]	Rural land Total	Rural land Crop land	State	Total surface area [1]	Non-Federal Total	Developed [2]	Rural land Total	Rural land Crop land
Total......	1,940.0	1,483.1	92.4	1,390.8	382.3	Montana	94.1	65.7	1.1	64.6	15.0
						Nebraska	49.5	48.1	1.3	46.9	19.2
United States..	1,937.7	1,480.9	91.9	1,389.0	382.0	Nevada	70.8	10.0	0.4	9.6	0.8
						New Hampshire..	5.9	5.0	0.6	4.4	0.1
Alabama	33.1	31.2	2.0	29.1	3.1						
Arizona	73.0	42.4	1.4	41.0	1.2	New Jersey	5.0	4.5	1.6	3.0	0.6
Arkansas	34.0	29.8	1.3	28.5	7.7	New Mexico	77.8	50.2	0.9	49.3	1.9
California	101.6	52.9	5.0	47.9	10.1	New York	31.4	29.8	3.0	26.8	5.6
						North Carolina.	33.7	28.5	3.5	24.9	6.0
Colorado	66.6	42.2	1.7	40.5	8.9	North Dakota	45.2	42.2	1.3	40.8	24.7
Connecticut	3.2	3.1	0.8	2.2	0.2						
Delaware	1.3	1.2	0.2	1.0	0.5	Ohio	26.5	25.7	3.6	22.1	11.9
Florida	37.5	30.4	4.6	25.8	3.0	Oklahoma	44.8	42.4	1.9	40.5	10.1
Georgia	37.7	34.6	3.1	31.5	5.2	Oregon	62.1	29.2	1.1	28.0	3.8
Hawaii	4.1	3.6	0.2	3.5	0.3	Pennsylvania	29.0	27.8	3.4	24.4	5.6
Idaho	53.5	19.5	0.6	18.9	5.6	Rhode Island	0.8	0.7	0.2	0.5	0.0
Illinois	36.1	34.8	3.1	31.7	24.1						
Indiana	23.2	22.3	2.1	20.2	13.5	South Carolina	19.9	18.0	1.9	16.1	3.0
						South Dakota	49.4	45.5	1.1	44.3	16.4
Iowa	36.0	35.4	1.8	33.6	25.0	Tennessee	27.0	24.7	2.2	22.6	4.9
Kansas	52.7	51.5	2.0	49.5	26.6	Texas	170.8	163.7	8.2	155.5	28.3
Kentucky	25.9	24.0	1.7	22.3	5.1	Utah	54.3	16.9	0.6	16.3	1.8
Louisiana	30.6	26.4	1.8	24.6	6.0						
Maine	21.3	19.5	0.7	18.8	0.4	Vermont	6.2	5.5	0.3	5.2	0.6
						Virginia	26.1	22.8	2.2	20.6	2.9
Maryland	6.7	6.0	1.1	4.9	1.7	Washington	43.6	29.9	1.9	28.1	6.7
Massachusetts	5.3	4.8	1.3	3.5	0.3	West Virginia	15.5	14.1	0.7	13.4	0.9
Michigan	37.5	33.0	3.7	29.4	9.0	Wisconsin	35.9	32.7	2.4	30.4	10.8
Minnesota	54.0	47.1	2.4	44.7	21.4	Wyoming	62.6	32.0	0.5	31.5	2.3
Mississippi	30.5	28.0	1.3	26.7	5.7						
Missouri	44.6	41.7	2.3	39.4	13.3	Caribbean	2.3	2.2	0.4	1.8	0.4

[1] Includes water area not shown separately.   [2] Includes urban and built-up areas in units of 10 acres or greater, and rural transportation.

Source: U.S. Dept. of Agriculture, Soil Conservation Service, and Iowa State University, Statistical Laboratory; *Summary Report, 1992 National Resources Inventory.*

No. 396. Extreme and Mean Elevations, by State and Other Area

[One foot=.305 meter]

State and other area	Highest point Name	Elevation Feet	Meters	Lowest point Name	Elevation Feet	Meters	Approximate mean elevation Feet	Meters
U.S.....	**Mt. McKinley (AK)**	**20,320**	**6,198**	**Death Valley (CA)**.....	**-282**	**-86**	**2,500**	**763**
AL........	Cheaha Mountain	2,405	733	Gulf of Mexico	(¹)	(¹)	500	153
AK........	Mount McKinley.......	20,320	6,198	Pacific Ocean.........	(¹)	(¹)	1,900	580
AZ........	Humphreys Peak.......	12,633	3,853	Colorado River........	70	21	4,100	1,251
AR........	Magazine Mountain	2,753	840	Ouachita River........	55	17	650	198
CA........	Mount Whitney	14,494	4,419	Death Valley.........	-282	-86	2,900	885
CO........	Mt. Elbert..........	14,433	4,402	Arkansas River.......	3,350	1,022	6,800	2,074
CT........	Mt. Frissell on South slope	2,380	726	Long Island Sound	(¹)	(¹)	500	153
DE........	Ebright Road, [2] New Castle County.....	448	137	Atlantic Ocean	(¹)	(¹)	60	18
DC........	Tenleytown at Reno Reservoir	410	125	Potomac River........	1	(Z)	150	46
FL........	Sec. 30, T6N, R20W, Walton County...........	345	105	Atlantic Ocean	(¹)	(¹)	100	31
GA........	Brasstown Bald	4,784	1,459	Atlantic Ocean	(¹)	(¹)	600	183
HI........	Puu Wekiu	13,796	4,208	Pacific Ocean.........	(¹)	(¹)	3,030	924
ID........	Borah Peak	12,662	3,862	Snake River..........	710	217	5,000	1,525
IL........	Charles Mound	1,235	377	Mississippi River......	279	85	600	183
IN........	Franklin Twp., Wayne Co .	1,257	383	Ohio River...........	320	98	700	214
IA........	Sec. 29, T100N, R41W, Osceola County [3]	1,670	509	Mississippi River......	480	146	1,100	336
KS........	Mount Sunflower	4,039	1,232	Verdigris River.......	679	207	2,000	610
KY........	Black Mountain	4,139	2,162	Mississippi River......	257	78	750	229
LA........	Driskill Mountain	535	163	New Orleans	-8	-2	100	31
ME........	Mount Katahdin	5,267	1,606	Atlantic Ocean	(¹)	(¹)	600	183
MD........	Backbone Mountain	3,360	1,025	Atlantic Ocean	(¹)	(¹)	350	107
MA........	Mount Greylock.......	3,487	1,064	Atlantic Ocean	(¹)	(¹)	500	153
MI........	Mount Arvon.........	1,979	604	Lake Erie...........	571	174	900	275
MN........	Eagle Mountain, Cook Co .	2,301	702	Lake Superior........	600	183	1,200	366
MS........	Woodall Mountain	806	246	Gulf of Mexico	(¹)	(¹)	300	92
MO........	Taum Sauk Mountain	1,772	540	St. Francis River......	230	70	800	244
MT........	Granite Peak	12,799	3,904	Kootenai River.......	1,800	549	3,400	1,037
NE........	Johnson Twp., Kimball Co .	5,424	1,654	Missouri River.......	840	256	2,600	793
NV........	Boundary Peak	13,140	4,007	Colorado River........	479	146	5,500	1,678
NH........	Mount Washington	6,288	1,918	Atlantic Ocean	(¹)	(¹)	1,000	305
NJ........	High Point	1,803	550	Atlantic Ocean	(¹)	(¹)	250	76
NM........	Wheeler Peak........	13,161	4,014	Red Bluff Reservoir ...	2,842	867	5,700	1,739
NY........	Mount Marcy.........	5,344	1,630	Atlantic Ocean	(¹)	(¹)	1,000	305
NC........	Mount Mitchell.......	6,684	2,039	Atlantic Ocean	(¹)	(¹)	700	214
ND........	White Butte, Slope Co .	3,506	1,069	Red River...........	750	229	1,900	580
OH........	Campbell Hill	1,549	472	Ohio River..........	455	139	850	259
OK........	Black Mesa	4,973	1,517	Little River.........	289	88	1,300	397
OR........	Mount Hood	11,239	3,428	Pacific Ocean.........	(¹)	(¹)	3,300	1,007
PA........	Mount Davis	3,213	980	Delaware River.......	(¹)	(¹)	1,100	336
RI........	Jerimoth Hill	812	248	Atlantic Ocean	(¹)	(¹)	200	61
SC........	Sassafras Mountain	3,560	1,086	Atlantic Ocean	(¹)	(¹)	350	107
SD........	Harney Peak.........	7,242	2,209	Big Stone Lake.......	966	295	2,200	671
TN........	Clingmans Dome	6,643	2,026	Mississippi River......	178	54	900	275
TX........	Guadalupe Peak	8,749	2,668	Gulf of Mexico	(¹)	(¹)	1,700	519
UT........	Kings Peak..........	13,528	4,126	Beaverdam Wash	2,000	610	6,100	1,861
VT........	Mount Mansfield	4,393	1,340	Lake Champlain	95	29	1,000	305
VA........	Mount Rogers........	5,729	1,747	Atlantic Ocean	(¹)	(¹)	950	290
WA........	Mount Rainier.......	14,410	4,395	Pacific Ocean.........	(¹)	(¹)	1,700	519
WV........	Spruce Knob.........	4,861	1,483	Potomac River.......	240	73	1,500	458
WI........	Timms Hill	1,951	595	Lake Michigan	579	177	1,050	320
WY........	Gannett Peak........	13,804	4,210	Belle Fourche River....	3,099	945	6,700	2,044
Other areas:								
Puerto Rico	Cerro de Punta	4,390	1,339	Atlantic Ocean	(¹)	(¹)	1,800	549
American Samoa...	Lata Mountain........	3,160	964	Pacific Ocean.........	(¹)	(¹)	1,300	397
Guam ...	Mount Lamlam	1,332	406	Pacific Ocean.........	(¹)	(¹)	330	101
Virgin Is. ...	Crown Mountain	1,556	475	Atlantic Ocean	(¹)	(¹)	750	229

Z Less than 0.5 meter. [1] Sea level. [2] At DE-PA state line. [3] "Sec." denotes section; "T," township; "R," range; "N," north; and "W," west.

Source: U.S. Geological Survey, for highest and lowest points, *Elevations and Distances in the United States, 1990*; for mean elevations, 1983 edition.

No. 397. Water Areas for Selected Major Bodies of Water: 1990

[Includes only that portion of body of water under the jurisdiction of the United States, excluding Hawaii. One square mile=2.59 square kilometers]

Body of water and state	Area Sq. mi.	Area Sq. km.	Body of water and state	Area Sq. mi.	Area Sq. km.
Atlantic Coast water bodies:			Leech Lake (MN)	162	419
Chesapeake Bay (MD-VA)	2,747	7,115	Lake St. Clair (MI) [1]	161	416
Pamlico Sound (NC)	1,622	4,200	Eufaula Lake (OK)	157	407
Long Island Sound (CT-NY)	914	2,368			
Delaware Bay (DE-NJ)	614	1,591	Sam Rayburn Reservoir (TX)	150	389
Cape Cod Bay (MA)	598	1,548	Goose Lake (CA-OR)	147	381
Albemarle Sound (NC)	492	1,274	Utah Lake (UT)	139	361
Biscayne Bay (FL)	218	565	Lake Marion (SC)	139	360
Buzzards Bay (MA)	215	558	Lake Francis Case (SD)	134	346
Tangier Sound (MD-VA)	172	445	Lake Pend Oreille (ID)	133	343
Currituck Sound (NC)	116	301	Lake Texoma (OK-TX)	132	342
Pocomoke Sound (MD-VA)	111	286	Yellowstone Lake (WY)	131	339
Chincoteague Bay (MD-VA)	105	272	Livingston Reservoir (TX)	127	330
Great South Bay (NY)	94	243	Franklin D. Roosevelt Lake (WA)	124	322
Core Sound (NC)	88	229	Moosehead Lake (ME)	116	301
			Clark Hill Lake (GA-SC)	105	272
Gulf Coast water bodies:			Lake Maurepas (LA)	91	235
Mississippi Sound (AL-LA-MS)	813	2,105	Lake Moultrie (SC)	89	230
Laguna Madre (TX)	733	1,897	Lake Winnibigoshish (MN)	87	225
Lake Pontchartrain (LA)	631	1,635	Hartwell Lake (GA-SC)	86	224
Florida Bay (FL)	616	1,596	Upper Klamath Lake (OR)	85	221
Breton Sound (LA)	511	1,323	Harry S. Truman Reservoir (MO)	84	217
Mobile Bay (AL)	310	802	Oneida Lake (NY)	80	207
Lake Borgne (LA-MS)	271	702	Malheur Lake (OR)	75	195
Matagorda Bay (TX)	253	656			
Atchafalaya Bay (LA)	245	635	Alaska water bodies:		
Galveston Bay (TX)	236	611	Chatham Strait	1,559	4,039
			Prince William Sound	1,382	3,579
Tampa Bay (FL)	212	549	Clarence Strait	1,199	3,107
Vermilion Bay (LA)	189	489	Iliamna Lake	1,022	2,646
Corpus Christi Bay (TX)	151	392	Frederick Sound	792	2,051
West Cote Blanche Bay (LA)	146	378	Sumner Strait	791	2,048
Trinity Bay (TX)	129	335	Stephens Passage	702	1,819
Choctawhatchee Bay (FL)	122	315	Kvichak Bay	640	1,659
San Antonio Bay (TX)	118	306	Montague Strait	463	1,198
Timbalier Bay (LA)	112	291	Becharof Lake	447	1,158
Charlotte Harbor (FL)	112	291	Icy Strait	436	1,130
Aransas Bay (TX)	104	268	Hotham Inlet	433	1,120
Apalachicola Bay (FL)	101	262	Selawik Lake	403	1,044
Terrebonne Bay (LA)	99	256	Nushagak Bay	393	1,018
East Cote Blanche Bay (LA)	94	243	Baird Inlet	348	902
St. George Sound (FL)	93	240			
Sabine Lake (LA-TX)	89	229	Yakutat Bay	345	894
White Lake (LA)	85	221	Teshekpuk Lake	324	839
Old Tampa Bay (FL)	83	214	Behm Canal	324	839
Bon Secour Bay (AL)	79	204	Turnagain Arm	322	834
Pine Island Sound (FL)	75	194	Kachemak Bay	310	803
			Glacier Bay	310	803
Pacific Coast water bodies:			Stefansson Sound	301	780
Puget Sound (WA)	808	2,092	Revillagigedo Channel	295	764
San Francisco Bay (CA)	264	684	Kasegaluk Lagoon	293	759
Willapa Bay (WA)	125	325	Cordova Bay	241	623
Hood Canal (WA)	117	303	Sitka Sound	229	593
			Naknek Lake	225	582
Interior water bodies:			Eschscholtz Bay	210	543
Lake Michigan (IL-IN-MI-WI)	22,342	57,866	Stepovak Bay	206	534
Lake Superior (MI-MN-WI) [1]	20,557	53,243	Keku Strait	206	534
Lake Huron (MI) [1]	8,800	22,792			
Lake Erie (MI-NY-OH-PA) [1]	5,033	13,036	Port Clarence	187	486
Lake Ontario (NY) [1]	3,446	8,926	Orca Bay	184	476
Great Salt Lake (UT)	1,836	4,756	Knik Arm	169	437
Green Bay (MI-WI)	1,396	3,617	Dall Lake	167	433
Lake Okeechobee (FL)	663	1,717	Knight Island Passage	167	432
Lake Sakakawea (ND)	563	1,459	Scammon Bay	163	423
Lake Oahe (ND-SD)	538	1,394	Port Moller	159	412
Lake of the Woods (MN) [1]	462	1,196	Ernest Sound	158	410
Lake Champlain (NY-VT) [1]	414	1,072	Spafarief Bay	157	405
Fort Peck Lake (MT)	379	981	Pavlov Bay	153	396
Salton Sea (CA)	364	944	Shishmaref Inlet	153	395
Toledo Bend Reservoir (LA-TX)	268	694	Smith Bay	140	363
Lower Red Lake (MN)	257	666	Seymour Canal	140	361
Lake Powell (AZ-UT)	250	649	Sitkalidak Strait	135	349
Kentucky Lake (KY-TN)	234	605	Tlevak Strait	135	349
Lake Mead (AZ-NV)	233	603			
Lake Winnebago (WI)	206	535	Lake Clark	130	336
Mille Lacs Lake (MN)	200	518	Lynn Canal	130	336
Flathead Lake (MT)	191	495	Chignik Bay	119	309
Lake Tahoe (CA-NV)	187	486	Elson Lagoon	119	309
Upper Red Lake (MN)	186	483	Bucareli Bay	119	307
Pyramid Lake (NV)	170	440	Hinchinbrook Entrance	118	306

[1] Area measurements for Lake Champlain, Lake Erie, Lake Huron, Lake Ontario, Lake St. Clair, Lake Superior, and Lake of the Woods include only those portions under the jurisdiction of the United States.

Source: U.S. Census Bureau, unpublished data from the Census TIGER ™ database.

U.S. Census Bureau, Statistical Abstract of the United States: 1999

No. 398. Flows of Largest U.S. Rivers—Length, Discharge, and Drainage Area

River	Location of mouth	Source stream (name and location)	Length (miles) [1]	Average discharge at mouth (1,000 cubic ft. per second)	Drainage area (1,000 sq. mi.)
Missouri	Missouri.	Red Rock Creek, MT	2,540	76.2	[5]529
Mississippi	Louisiana.	Mississippi River, MN.	[2]2,340	[3]593	[4] [5]1,150
Yukon	Alaska.	McNeil River, Canada	1,980	225	[5]328
St. Lawrence	Canada.	North River, MN	1,900	348	[5]396
Rio Grande	Mexico-Texas	Rio Grande, CO	1,900	-	336
Arkansas	Arkansas	East Fork Arkansas River, CO . . .	1,460	41	161
Colorado.	Mexico	Colorado River, CO	1,450	-	246
Atchafalaya [6]	Louisiana.	Tierra Blanca Creek, NM	1,420	58	95.1
Ohio	Illinois-Kentucky . .	Allegheny River, PA	1,310	281	203
Red.	Louisiana.	Tierra Blanca Creek, NM	1,290	56	93.2
Brazos	Texas	Blackwater Draw, NM.	1,280	-	45.6
Columbia	Oregon-Washington.	Columbia River, Canada.	1,240	265	[5]258
Snake	Washington	Snake River, WY.	1,040	56.9	108
Platte	Nebraska.	Grizzly Creek, CO	990	-	84.9
Pecos	Texas	Pecos River, NM.	926	-	44.3
Canadian	Oklahoma	Canadian River, CO.	906	-	46.9
Tennessee	Kentucky	Courthouse Creek, NC	886	68	40.9
Colorado (of Texas) .	Texas	Colorado River, TX	862	-	42.3
North Canadian . . .	Oklahoma	Corrumpa Creek, NM.	800	-	17.6
Mobile	Alabama	Tickanetley Creek, GA	774	67.2	44.6
Kansas.	Kansas	Arikaree River, CO	743	-	59.5
Kuskokwim	Alaska.	South Fork Kuskokwim River, AK .	724	67	48
Yellowstone.	North Dakota	North Folk Yellowstone River, WY	692	-	70
Tanana.	Alaska.	Nabesna River, AK	659	41	44.5
Gila	Arizona	Middle Fork Gila River, NM	649	-	58.2

- Represents zero.   [1] From source to mouth.   [2] The length from the source of the Missouri River to the Mississippi River and thence to the Gulf of Mexico is about 3,710 miles.   [3] Includes about 167,000 cubic ft. per second diverted from the Mississippi into the Atchafalaya River but excludes the flow of the Red River.   [4] Excludes the drainage areas of the Red and Atchafalaya Rivers.   [5] Drainage area includes both the United States and Canada.   [6] In east-central Louisiana, the Red River flows into the Atchafalaya River, a distributary of the Mississippi River. Data on average discharge, length, and drainage area include the Red River, but exclude all water diverted into the Atchafalaya from the Mississippi River.

Source: U.S. Geological Survey, *Largest Rivers in the United States,* Open File Report 87-242, May 1990.

No. 399. U.S. Water Withdrawals and Consumptive Use Per Day, by End Use: 1940 to 1995

[Includes Puerto Rico. Withdrawal signifies water physically withdrawn from a source. Includes fresh and saline water; excludes water used for hydroelectric power]

Year	Total (bil. gal.)	Per capita [1] (gal.)	Irrigation (bil. gal.)	Public supply [2] Total (bil. gal.)	Public supply [2] Per capita[3] (gal.)	Rural [4] (bil. gal.)	Industrial and misc. [5] (bil. gal.)	Steam electric utilities (bil. gal.)
WITHDRAWALS								
1940.	140	1,027	71	10	75	3.1	29	23
1950.	180	1,185	89	14	145	3.6	37	40
1955.	240	1,454	110	17	148	3.6	39	72
1960.	270	1,500	110	21	151	3.6	38	100
1965.	310	1,602	120	24	155	4.0	46	130
1970.	370	1,815	130	27	166	4.5	47	170
1975.	420	1,972	140	29	168	4.9	45	200
1980.	440	1,953	150	34	183	5.6	45	210
1985.	399	1,650	137	38	189	7.8	31	187
1990.	408	1,620	137	41	195	7.9	30	195
1995.	402	1,500	134	43	192	8.9	26	190
CONSUMPTIVE USE								
1960.	61	339	52	3.5	25	2.8	3.0	0.2
1965.	77	403	66	5.2	34	3.2	3.4	0.4
1970.	87	427	73	5.9	36	3.4	4.1	0.8
1975.	96	451	80	6.7	38	3.4	4.2	1.9
1980.	100	440	83	7.1	38	3.9	5.0	3.2
1985.	92	380	74	([6])	([6])	9.2	6.1	6.2
1990.	94	370	76	([6])	([6])	8.9	6.7	4.0
1995.	100	374	81	([6])	([6])	9.9	4.8	3.7

[1] Based on U.S. Census Bureau resident population as of July 1.   [2] Includes commercial water withdrawals.   [3] Based on population served.   [4] Rural farm and nonfarm household and garden use, and water for farm stock and dairies.   [5] For 1940 to 1960, includes manufacturing and mineral industries, rural commercial industries, air-conditioning, resorts, hotels, motels, military and other state and Federal agencies, and miscellaneous; thereafter, includes manufacturing, mining and mineral processing, ordnance, construction, and miscellaneous.   [6] Public supply consumptive use included in end-use categories.

Source: 1940-1960, U.S. Bureau of Domestic Business Development, based principally on committee prints, *Water Resources Activities in the United States,* for the Senate Committee on National Water Resources, U.S. Senate, thereafter, U.S. Geological Survey, *Estimated Use of Water in the United States in 1995,* circular 1200, and previous quinquennial issues.

U.S. Census Bureau, Statistical Abstract of the United States: 1999

No. 400. Water Withdrawals and Consumptive Use— States and Other Area: 1995

[In millions of gallons per day, (401,500 represents 401,500,000,000) except as noted. Figures may not add due to rounding. Withdrawal signifies water physically withdrawn from a source. Includes fresh and saline water]

State or other area	Total	Per capita (gal. per day) fresh	Source Ground water	Source Surface water	Selected major uses Irrigation	Selected major uses Public supply [2]	Selected major uses Industrial	Selected major uses Thermo-electric	Consumptive use [1] fresh water
U.S. [2]	401,500	1,280	77,500	324,000	134,000	43,600	26,200	190,000	100,000
Alabama......	7,100	1,670	445	6,650	139	875	753	5,200	532
Alaska.......	329	350	132	196	0.6	90	197	30	25
Arizona.......	6,830	1,620	2,840	3,990	5,670	846	197	62	3,830
Arkansas.....	8,800	3,540	5,460	3,340	5,940	419	187	1,780	4,140
California	45,900	1,130	14,700	31,300	28,900	5,740	802	9,630	25,500
Colorado.....	13,800	3,690	2,270	11,600	12,700	732	191	115	5,230
Connecticut..	4,450	389	166	4,290	28	448	11	3,940	97
Delaware	1,500	1,050	110	1,390	48	101	64	1,270	71
District of Columbia	10	18	0.5	9.7	-	-	0.5	9.7	15
Florida........	18,200	509	4,340	13,800	3,470	2,360	649	11,600	2,780
Georgia......	5,820	799	1,190	4,630	722	1,250	676	3,070	1,170
Hawaii........	1,930	853	531	1,400	652	218	20	970	542
Idaho.........	15,100	13,000	2,830	12,300	13,000	254	76	-	4,360
Illinois	19,900	1,680	953	19,000	180	1,950	527	17,100	857
Indiana.......	9,140	1,570	709	8,430	116	784	2,410	5,690	505
Iowa.........	3,030	1,070	528	2,510	39	418	301	2,130	290
Kansas.......	5,240	2,040	3,510	1,720	3,380	384	77	1,260	3,620
Kentucky	4,420	1,150	226	4,190	12	521	375	3,450	318
Louisiana	9,850	2,270	1,350	8,500	769	677	2,580	5,480	1,930
Maine.........	326	178	80	246	27	135	16	136	48
Maryland.....	7,730	289	246	7,480	57	907	331	6,360	150
Massachusetts..	5,510	189	351	5,160	82	759	88	4,570	180
Michigan.....	12,100	1,260	862	11,200	227	1,490	1,910	8,370	667
Minnesota....	3,390	736	714	2,680	157	573	438	2,090	417
Mississippi	3,200	1,140	2,590	614	1,740	377	294	375	1,570
Missouri......	7,030	1,320	891	6,140	567	757	63	5,550	692
Montana......	8,860	10,200	217	8,640	8,550	161	80	22	1,960
Nebraska	10,500	6,440	6,200	4,350	7,550	328	175	2,350	7,020
Nevada	2,300	1,480	896	1,400	1,640	479	95	27	1,340
New Hampshire .	1,320	388	81	1,240	6.3	130	50	1,110	35
New Jersey....	6,110	269	580	5,530	125	1,120	486	4,360	210
New Mexico...	3,510	2,080	1,700	1,800	2,990	337	69	55	1,980
New York	16,800	567	1,010	15,800	30	3,140	321	13,100	469
North Carolina..	9,290	1,070	535	8,750	239	939	385	7,420	713
North Dakota...	1,120	1,750	122	1,000	117	85	17	819	181
Ohio	10,500	944	905	9,620	27	1,560	650	8,190	791
Oklahoma.....	2,040	543	1,220	822	864	597	285	124	716
Oregon.......	7,910	2,520	1,050	6,860	6,170	572	379	9.0	3,210
Pennsylvania...	9,680	802	860	8,820	16	1,730	1,930	5,930	565
Rhode Island...	411	138	27	383	2.3	121	7.3	275	19
South Carolina..	6,200	1,690	322	5,880	53	614	703	4,810	321
South Dakota..	460	631	187	273	269	97	32	5.3	249
Tennessee	10,100	1,920	435	9,640	24	831	868	8,300	233
Texas........	29,600	1,300	8,780	20,800	9,450	3,420	2,920	13,500	10,500
Utah.........	4,460	2,200	790	3,670	3,530	506	253	48	2,200
Vermont......	565	967	50	515	3.9	66	12	452	24
Virginia......	8,260	826	358	7,900	30	911	622	6,620	218
Washington....	8,860	1,620	1,760	7,100	6,470	1,300	652	376	3,080
West Virginia...	4,620	2,530	146	4,470	-	217	1,330	3,010	352
Wisconsin.....	7,250	1,420	759	6,490	169	692	453	5,820	443
Wyoming	7,060	14,700	335	6,720	6,590	100	118	220	2,800
Puerto Rico....	2,840	154	135	2,680	107	443	15	2,260	187
Virgin Islands...	202	113	0.7	201	-	7.8	20	173	1.9

- Represents zero. [1] Water that has been evaporated, transpired, or incorporated into products, plant, or animal tissue and therefore is not available for immediate reuse. [2] Includes Puerto Rico and Virgin Islands.

Source: U.S. Geological Survey, *Estimated Use of Water in the United States in 1995*, circular 1200.

No. 401. National Ambient Water Quality in Rivers and Streams— Violation Rate: 1980 to 1995

[In percent. Violation level based on U.S. Environmental Protection Agency water quality criteria. Violation rate represents the proportion of all measurements of a specific water quality pollutant which exceeds the "violation level" for that pollutant. "Violation" does not necessarily imply a legal violation. Data based on U.S. Geological Survey's National Stream Quality Accounting Network (NASQAN) data system; for details, see source. Years refer to water years. A water year begins in Oct. and ends in Sept. μg=micrograms; mg=milligrams. For metric conversion, see page ix]

Pollutant	Violation level	1980	1985	1989	1990	1991	1992	1993	1994	1995
Fecal coliform bacteria....	Above 200 cells per 100 ml..	31	28	30	26	15	28	31	28	35
Dissolved oxygen	Below 5 mg per liter.	5	3	3	2	2	2	(Z)	2	1
Phosphorus, total, as phosporous	Above 1.0 mg per liter	4	3	2	3	2	2	2	2	4
Lead, dissolved	Above 50 μg per liter	(Z)	(Z)	(Z)	(Z)	(Z)	(Z)	(NA)	(NA)	(NA)
Cadmium, dissolved	Above 10 μg per liter	1	(Z)	(Z)	(Z)	(Z)	(Z)	(NA)	(NA)	(NA)

NA Not available.   Z Less than one.

Source: U.S. Geological Survey, national-level data, unpublished; state-level data, *Water-Data Report,* annual series prepared in cooperation with the state governments.

No. 402. Oil Spills in U.S. Water—Number and Volume: 1994 to 1997

[Based on reported discharges into U.S. navigable waters, including territorial waters (extending 3 to 12 miles from the coastline), tributaries, the contiguous zone, onto shoreline, or into other waters that threaten the marine environment. Data found in Marine Safety Management System]

Spill characteristic	Number of spills				Spill volume (1,000 gal.)			
	1994	1995	1996	1997	1994	1995	1996	1997
Total	8,960	9,038	9,335	8,624	2,499,273	2,638,229	3,117,831	942,574
Size of spill (gallons):								
1-100	8,440	8,614	8,904	8,299	77,961	48,936	43,434	39,082
101-1,000	371	324	322	243	130,979	115,140	114,831	81,895
1,001-3,000	79	52	57	40	151,756	91,426	102,008	78,117
3,001-5,000	22	19	20	14	88,479	73,598	86,389	58,016
5,001-10,000	23	9	12	15	165,824	63,853	92,163	109,288
10,001-50,000	18	15	15	11	437,238	354,824	351,106	282,176
50,001-100,000	3	2	-	1	290,342	155,950	-	84,000
100,000-1,000,000	4	3	5	1	1,146,694	1,734,502	2,327,900	210,000
1,000,000 and over.	-	-	-	-	-	-	-	-
Body of water:								
Atlantic ocean	206	267	119	87	799,549	48,313	27,980	40,875
Pacific ocean	666	648	491	505	128,752	69,053	29,209	32,841
Gulf of Mexico	1,350	1,485	2,403	2,341	205,151	253,040	45,145	105,462
Great Lakes.	240	282	228	156	15,984	3,103	3,507	4,311
Lakes.	16	26	19	29	318	92	52	210,270
Rivers and canals	1,814	1,849	1,984	1,821	383,171	1,156,002	475,550	182,676
Bays and sounds	1,062	1,109	793	811	72,022	41,004	1,092,207	46,450
Harbors.	1,016	1,176	992	858	346,649	148,229	288,252	45,932
Other	2,590	2,196	2,306	2,016	537,677	919,393	1,155,929	273,775
Source:								
Tankship	172	148	122	124	69,694	125,491	219,311	22,429
Tankbarge	393	353	313	252	955,582	1,101,938	1,163,258	165,649
All other vessels	4,681	4,977	5,151	4,971	308,343	396,724	298,451	192,801
Facilities	2,258	586	509	838	677,016	868,900	406,384	204,935
Pipelines	55	30	17	32	62,340	11,894	978,392	224,122
All other nonvessels	796	500	552	486	348,577	77,428	23,527	72,208
Unknown.	605	2,444	2,671	1,921	77,721	55,854	28,508	60,430

- Represents or rounds to zero.

Source: U.S. Coast Guard, <http://www.uscg.mil/hq/g-m/nmc/response/stats/Summary.htm>; (accessed 15 June 1999).

No. 403. Wastewater Treatment Facilities: 1988 to 1996

[Covers treatment facilities, which are structures designed to treat wastewater, storm water, or combined sewer overflows prior to discharging to the environment. Treatment is accomplished by subjecting the wastewater to a combination of physical, chemical, and/or biological processes that reduce the concentration of contaminants]

Level of treatment	Number of facilities			1996		
				Present design capacity (mgd [2])	Number of persons served	
	1988	1992	1996		Total	Percent of U.S.
Total	15,591	15,613	16,024	42,225	189,710,899	71.8
Nondischarge [1]	1,854	1,981	2,032	1,421	7,660,876	2.9
Less than secondary.	1,789	868	176	3,054	17,177,492	6.5
Secondary	8,536	9,086	9,388	17,734	81,944,349	31.0
Greater than secondary.	3,412	3,678	4,428	20,016	82,928,182	31.4

[1] Facilities that do not discharge effluent to surface waters.   [2] Millions of gallons per day.

Source: U.S. Environmental Protection Agency, Office of Wastewater Management, *1996 Clean Water Needs Survey Report to Congress.*

Geography and Environment   245

No. 404. National Ambient Air Pollutant Concentrations: 1987 to 1997

[Data represent annual composite averages of pollutant based on daily 24-hour averages of monitoring stations, except carbon monoxide is based on the second-highest, nonoverlapping, 8-hour average; ozone, average of the second-highest daily maximum 1-hour value; and lead, quarterly average of ambient lead levels. Based on data from the Aerometric Information Retrieval System. $\mu g/m^3$=micrograms of pollutant per cubic meter of air; ppm=parts per million]

Pollutant	Unit	Monitor- ing stations, number	Air quality stand- ard [1]	1987	1990	1993	1994	1995	1996	1997
Carbon monoxide	ppm	368	[2]9	6.71	5.8	4.9	5.0	4.5	4.2	3.9
Ozone	ppm	660	[3].12	0.124	0.112	0.108	0.107	0.112	0.105	0.105
Sulfur dioxide	ppm	486	.03	0.009	0.008	0.007	0.007	0.006	0.006	0.005
Particulates (PM-10) [4]	$\mu g/m^3$	845	50	(NA)	29.5	26.2	26.2	25.1	24.2	24.0
Nitrogen dioxide	ppm	224	.053	0.021	0.020	0.019	0.020	0.019	0.018	0.018
Lead	$\mu g/m^3$	195	[5]1.5	0.16	0.09	0.05	0.05	0.04	0.04	0.04

NA Not available.   [1] Refers to the primary National Ambient Air Quality Standard that protects the public health.   [2] Based on 8-hour standard of 9 ppm.   [3] Based on 1-hour standard of .12 ppm.   [4] The particulates (PM-10) standard replaced the previous standard for total suspended particulates in 1987.   [5] Based on 3-month standard of 1.5 $\mu g/m^3$.
Source: U.S. Environmental Protection Agency, *National Air Quality and Emissions Trends Report*, annual.

No. 405. National Air Pollutant Emissions: 1970 to 1997

[In thousands of tons, except as indicated. PM-10=Particulate matter of less than 10 microns. Methodologies to estimate data for 1970 to 1984 period and 1985 to present emissions differ. Beginning with 1985, the estimates are based on a modified National Acid Precipitation Assessment Program inventory]

Year	PM-10	PM-10, fugitive dust[1]	Sulfur dioxide	Nitrogen dioxides	Volatile organic compounds	Carbon monoxide	Lead
1970	13,190	(NA)	31,161	21,639	30,817	128,761	220,869
1975	7,803	(NA)	28,011	23,151	25,895	115,968	159,659
1980	7,287	(NA)	25,905	24,875	26,167	116,702	74,153
1984	6,220	(NA)	23,470	23,172	25,572	114,262	42,217
1985	4,695	40,889	23,230	23,488	24,227	115,644	22,890
1986	4,553	46,582	22,544	23,329	23,480	110,437	14,763
1987	4,492	38,041	22,308	22,806	23,193	108,879	7,681
1988	5,424	55,851	22,767	24,526	24,167	117,169	7,053
1989	4,590	48,650	22,907	24,057	22,383	104,447	5,468
1990	5,425	24,419	23,678	23,436	20,935	95,794	4,975
1991	5,329	24,122	23,056	23,520	21,063	97,790	4,168
1992	5,515	23,865	22,818	23,789	20,642	94,400	3,808
1993	3,680	24,196	22,476	24,046	20,830	94,526	3,911
1994	5,294	25,461	21,878	24,345	21,465	98,854	4,043
1995	4,306	22,454	19,189	23,768	20,558	89,151	3,924
1996	8,481	24,716	19,812	23,465	19,293	90,929	3,910
1997	8,428	25,153	20,369	23,582	19,214	87,451	3,915

NA Not available.   [1] Sources such as agricultural tilling, construction, mining and quarrying, paved roads, unpaved roads, and wind erosion.

No. 406. Air Pollutant Emissions, by Pollutant and Source: 1997

[In thousands of tons, except as indicated. See headnote, Table 405]

Source	Particu- lates[1]	Sulfur dioxide	Nitrogen oxides	Volatile organic compounds	Carbon monoxide	Lead
Total	33,581	20,369	23,582	19,214	87,451	3,915
Fuel combustion, stationary sources	1,101	17,259	10,724	860	4,817	496
Electric utilities	290	13,082	6,178	51	406	64
Industrial	314	3,365	3,270	217	1,110	17
Other fuel combustion	497	813	1,276	593	3,301	415
Residential	388	179	858	568	3,042	7
Industrial processes	861	1,664	804	1,527	4,779	2,251
Chemical and allied product manufacture	70	301	167	458	1,287	159
Metals processing	220	552	102	73	2,465	2,038
Petroleum and related industries	41	385	115	538	364	(NA)
Other	530	427	421	458	663	54
Solvent utilization	6	1	3	6,483	6	(NA)
Storage and transport	114	2	6	1,377	26	(NA)
Waste disposal and recycling	296	50	103	449	1,242	646
Highway vehicles	268	320	7,035	5,230	50,257	19
Light-duty gas vehicles and motorcycle	56	129	2,875	2,755	27,036	12
Light-duty trucks	40	96	1,901	1,968	18,364	7
Heavy-duty gas vehicles	9	11	326	268	3,349	-
Diesels	163	84	1,932	239	1,508	(NA)
Off highway [2]	466	1,060	4,560	2,430	16,755	503
Miscellaneous [3]	30,469	13	346	858	9,568	(NA)

- Represents or rounds to zero.   NA Not available.   [1] Represents both PM-10 and PM-10 fugitive dust; see Table 405.   [2] Includes emissions from farm tractors and other farm machinery, construction equipment, industrial machinery, recreational marine vessels, and small general utility engines such as lawn mowers.   [3] Includes emissions such as from forest fires and other kinds of burning, various agricultural activities, fugitive dust from paved and unpaved roads, and other construction and mining activities, and natural sources.
Source of Tables 405 and 406: U.S. Environmental Protection Agency, *National Air Pollutant Emission Trends, 1900-1997.*

No. 407. Emissions of Greenhouse Gases, by Type and Source: 1990 to 1997

[Emission estimates were mandated by Congress through Section 1605(a) of the Energy Policy Act of 1992 (title XVI). Gases that contain carbon can be measured either in terms of the full molecular weight of the gas or just in terms of their carbon content]

Type and source	Unit	1990	1992	1993	1994	1995	1996	1997
Carbon dioxide:								
Carbon content, total [1]	Mil. metric tons ..	1,355.9	1,360.6	1,393.6	1,413.8	1,428.1	1,478.8	1,500.8
Energy sources	Mil. metric tons ..	1,346.1	1,352.1	1,379.8	1,398.4	1,411.7	1,460.6	1,479.6
Methane:								
Gas, total [1]	Mil. metric tons ..	30.20	30.41	29.68	29.91	30.02	29.15	29.11
Energy sources	Mil. metric tons ..	10.79	10.83	10.11	10.13	10.36	9.89	9.99
Landfills	Mil. metric tons ..	11.11	10.89	10.82	10.75	10.66	10.54	10.38
Agricultural sources	Mil. metric tons ..	8.18	8.56	8.62	8.90	8.86	8.59	8.60
Nitrous oxide, total	1,000 metric tons .	964	1,008	1,022	1,080	1,037	1,021	1,011
Agriculture	1,000 metric tons .	646	670	670	706	650	635	642
Energy sources	1,000 metric tons .	208	228	237	252	265	260	264
Industrial sources	1,000 metric tons .	94	93	98	103	104	107	87
Nitrogen oxide, total [1]	Mil. metric tons ..	21.55	21.87	22.18	22.55	21.68	21.26	(NA)
Energy related	Mil. metric tons ..	20.41	20.86	21.20	21.41	20.68	20.24	(NA)
Stationary source fuel combustion .	Mil. metric tons ..	9.85	9.89	10.05	9.97	9.79	9.49	(NA)
Transportation	Mil. metric tons ..	10.55	10.98	11.14	11.45	10.88	10.75	(NA)
Nonmethane volatile organic compounds:								
(VOCs), total [1]	Mil. metric tons ..	18.92	18.68	18.85	19.46	18.59	17.23	(NA)
Energy related	Mil. metric tons ..	8.90	8.83	8.77	9.07	8.35	8.16	(NA)
Transportation	Mil. metric tons ..	8.00	7.82	7.88	8.18	7.38	7.19	(NA)
Industrial processes	Mil. metric tons ..	8.18	8.50	8.65	8.79	8.81	8.21	(NA)
Solid waste disposal	Mil. metric tons ..	0.89	0.92	0.95	0.95	0.97	0.39	(NA)
Carbon monoxide, total	Mil. metric tons ..	87.44	86.16	86.32	90.29	81.26	80.43	(NA)
Energy related	Mil. metric tons ..	71.96	74.61	74.61	76.27	69.61	68.71	(NA)
Transportation	Mil. metric tons ..	67.10	69.16	69.67	71.40	64.36	63.45	(NA)
Stationary source fuel combustion	Mil. metric tons ..	4.86	5.45	4.94	4.87	5.25	5.26	(NA)
Industrial processes	Mil. metric tons ..	4.33	4.12	4.22	4.18	4.18	4.19	(NA)
Chlorofluorocarbons (CFCs) gases [2]	1,000 metric tons .	193	143	141	104	97	63	46
Hydrofluorocarbons	1,000 metric tons .	7	4	7	9	13	18	22
Hydrochlorofluorocarbons (HCFCs) gases [3]	1,000 metric tons .	80	84	82	93	107	119	133
Other chemicals:								
Carbon tetrachloride	1,000 metric tons .	32	22	19	16	5	(NA)	(NA)
Methyl cloroform	1,000 metric tons .	158	108	93	77	46	4	(NA)
Sulfur hexafluoride	1,000 metric tons .	1	1	1	1	1	1	1

NA Not available.   [1] Includes minor sources not shown separately.   [2] Covers principally CFC-11, CFC-12, and CFC-113.
[3] Covers principally HCFC-22.

Source: U.S. Energy Information Administration, *Emissions of Greenhouse Gases in the United States*, annual.

No. 408. Municipal Solid Waste Generation, Recovery, and Disposal: 1980 to 1997

[In millions of tons (151.5 represents 151,500,000), except as indicated. Covers post-consumer residential and commercial solid wastes which comprise the major portion of typical municipal collections. Excludes mining, agricultural and industrial processing, demolition and construction wastes, sewage sludge, and junked autos and obsolete equipment wastes. Based on material-flows estimating procedure and wet weight as generated]

Item and material	1980	1990	1991	1992	1993	1994	1995	1996	1997
Waste generated	151.5	205.2	204.6	208.9	211.8	214.2	211.4	209.2	217.0
Per person per day (lb.)	3.7	4.5	4.4	4.5	4.5	4.4	4.4	4.3	4.4
Materials recovered	14.5	33.6	37.0	40.6	43.8	50.8	55.0	57.4	60.8
Per person per day (lb.)	0.35	0.7	0.8	0.9	0.9	1.1	1.1	1.2	1.2
Combustion for energy recovery	2.7	29.7	30.1	30.5	30.9	31.2	34.5	36.1	36.7
Per person per day (lb.)	0.06	0.7	0.7	0.7	0.7	0.7	0.7	0.7	0.8
Combustion without energy recovery .	11.0	2.2	2.2	2.2	1.6	1.3	1.0	(NA)	(NA)
Per person per day (lb.)	0.27	0.05	0.05	0.05	0.03	0.03	0.02	(NA)	(NA)
Landfill, other disposal	123.3	139.7	135.3	135.7	135.5	130.9	120.8	115.7	119.5
Per person per day (lb.)	2.97	3.1	2.9	2.9	2.9	2.8	2.5	2.4	2.4
Percent distribution of generation:									
Paper and paperboard	36.1	35.4	34.7	35.5	36.6	37.7	38.6	38.1	38.6
Glass	9.9	6.4	6.2	6.3	6.4	6.2	6.1	5.9	5.5
Metals	9.6	8.1	8.1	7.7	7.5	7.6	7.5	7.7	7.7
Plastics	5.2	8.3	8.7	8.8	9.0	9.0	8.9	9.4	9.9
Rubber and leather	2.8	2.8	2.9	2.8	2.7	2.9	2.9	3.0	3.0
Textiles	1.7	2.8	3.0	3.2	3.2	3.4	3.5	3.7	3.8
Wood	4.4	6.0	6.2	5.9	5.8	5.3	4.9	5.2	5.3
Food wastes	8.7	10.1	10.2	10.1	10.0	10.0	10.3	10.4	10.1
Yard wastes	18.2	17.1	17.1	16.8	15.7	14.7	14.0	13.3	12.8
Other wastes	3.4	3.0	3.1	2.9	3.0	3.2	3.3	3.3	3.3

NA Not available.

Source: Franklin Associates, Ltd., Prairie Village, KS, *Characterization of Municipal Solid Waste in the United States: 1998*. Prepared for the U.S. Environmental Protection Agency.

U.S. Census Bureau, Statistical Abstract of the United States: 1999

No. 409. Generation and Recovery of Selected Materials in Municipal Solid Waste: 1980 to 1997

[In millions of tons (151.5 represents 151,500,000), except as indicated. Covers post-consumer residential and commercial solid wastes which comprise the major portion of typical municipal collections. Excludes mining, agricultural and industrial processing, demolition and construction wastes, sewage sludge, and junked autos and obsolete equipment wastes. Based on material-flows estimating procedure and wet weight as generated]

Item and material	1980	1990	1991	1992	1993	1994	1995	1996	1997
Waste generated, total	**151.5**	**205.2**	**204.6**	**208.9**	**211.8**	**214.2**	**211.4**	**209.2**	**217.0**
Paper and paperboard.	54.7	72.7	71.0	74.3	77.4	80.8	81.7	79.7	83.8
Ferrous metals.	11.6	12.6	12.7	12.1	11.9	11.8	11.6	11.8	12.3
Aluminum	1.8	2.8	2.8	2.9	2.9	3.0	3.0	3.0	3.0
Other nonferrous metals.	1.1	1.1	1.1	1.1	1.1	1.4	1.3	1.3	1.3
Glass	15.0	13.1	12.6	13.1	13.6	13.4	12.8	12.3	12.0
Plastics.	7.9	17.1	17.7	18.4	19.0	19.3	18.9	19.8	21.5
Yard waste	27.5	35.0	35.0	35.0	33.3	31.5	29.7	27.9	27.7
Other wastes	31.9	50.7	51.7	52.1	52.5	53.1	52.4	53.5	55.3
Materials recovered, total	**14.5**	**33.6**	**37.0**	**40.6**	**43.8**	**50.8**	**55.0**	**57.4**	**60.8**
Paper and paperboard.	11.9	20.2	22.5	24.5	25.5	29.5	32.7	33.2	34.9
Ferrous metals.	0.4	2.6	3.1	3.4	3.9	4.0	4.1	4.4	4.7
Aluminum	0.3	1.0	1.0	1.1	1.0	1.2	1.0	1.0	1.1
Other nonferrous metals.	0.5	0.7	0.7	0.7	0.7	1.0	0.8	0.8	0.8
Glass	0.8	2.6	2.6	2.9	3.0	3.1	3.1	3.2	2.9
Plastics.	-	0.4	0.5	0.6	0.7	0.9	1.0	1.1	1.1
Yard waste	-	4.2	4.8	5.4	6.9	8.0	9.0	10.4	11.5
Other wastes	0.6	1.8	1.9	2.0	2.1	3.1	3.2	3.3	3.8
Percent of generation recovered, total	**9.6**	**16.4**	**18.1**	**19.4**	**20.7**	**23.7**	**26.0**	**27.4**	**28.0**
Paper and paperboard.	21.8	27.8	31.7	33.0	32.9	36.5	40.0	41.6	41.7
Ferrous metals.	3.4	20.4	24.1	27.7	32.8	33.9	35.5	37.2	38.4
Aluminum	16.7	35.9	35.5	38.7	35.7	37.8	34.6	34.3	35.1
Other nonferrous metals.	45.5	66.4	65.5	63.4	63.1	73.3	64.3	66.7	65.4
Glass	5.3	20.0	20.3	22.0	22.1	23.3	24.5	25.8	24.3
Plastics.	-	2.2	2.5	3.3	3.5	4.9	5.2	5.4	5.2
Yard waste	-	12.0	13.7	15.4	20.8	25.4	30.3	37.2	41.4
Other wastes	1.9	3.6	3.7	3.9	4.0	5.9	6.1	6.2	6.8

- Represents zero.

Source: Franklin Associates, Ltd., Prairie Village, KS, *Characterization of Municipal Solid Waste in the United States: 1998.* Prepared for the U.S. Environmental Protection Agency.

No. 410. Curbside Recycling Programs—Number and Population Served, by Region: 1995 and 1996

[For composition of regions, see map, inside front cover]

Region	Number of programs		Population served [1]			
			Total (1,000)		Percent	
	1995	1996	1995	1996	1995	1996
Total	**7,375**	**8,817**	**121,335**	**134,630**	**46**	**51**
Northeast	2,210	3,427	37,256	43,052	72	83
South.	1,281	1,318	31,521	32,798	34	35
Midwest	2,985	3,198	25,487	27,454	41	44
West	899	874	27,071	31,326	49	55

[1] Calculated using population of states reporting data.

Source: Franklin Associates, Ltd., Prairie Village, KS, *Characterization of Municipal Solid Waste in the United States: 1998.* Prepared for the U.S. Environmental Protection Agency. Also in *Biocycle Magazine.*

No. 411. Toxic Chemical Releases and Transfers, by Media: 1988 to 1996

[In thousands of pounds (3,352,959 represents 3,352,959,000), except as indicated. Based on reports filed as required by section 313 of the Emergency Planning and Community Right-to-Know Act (EPCRA, or Title III of the Superfund Amendments and Reauthorization Act of 1986), Public Law 99-499. Owners and operators of facilities that are classified within Standard Classification Code groups 20 through 39, have 10 or more full-time employees, and that manufacture, process, or otherwise uses any listed toxic chemical in quantities greater than the established threshold in the course of a calendar year are covered and required to report]

Media	Core chemicals [1]				Expanded chemical list [2]	
	1988	1994	1995	1996	1995	1996
Total facilities reporting	20,436	20,946	20,356	19,726	22,378	21,626
Total releases	3,352,959	1,982,786	1,895,290	1,823,765	2,530,786	2,433,507
On-site releases	2,966,497	1,723,558	1,639,512	1,558,759	2,250,353	2,138,770
Total air emissions	2,180,862	1,280,286	1,191,260	1,095,413	1,567,430	1,452,090
Fugitive air	680,929	351,433	304,738	276,183	388,750	355,272
Point source air	1,499,933	928,853	886,522	819,230	1,178,680	1,096,818
Surface water	164,551	39,795	35,919	45,144	159,768	173,288
Underground injection	161,969	114,136	139,908	118,222	240,175	204,329
Releases to land	459,114	289,341	272,425	299,980	282,979	309,063
Off-site releases	386,462	259,228	255,778	265,006	280,433	294,736
Total transfers off-site for further waste management	(NA)	3,046,596	3,056,371	2,933,850	3,289,504	3,156,867
Tranfers to recycling	(NA)	2,200,760	2,173,559	2,094,268	2,237,557	2,150,594
Transfers to energy recovery. . .	(NA)	459,576	488,955	446,488	517,242	477,057
Transfers to treatment	369,204	221,230	236,497	248,020	286,937	290,097
Transfers to POTWs [3]	254,808	159,935	155,174	141,995	245,374	235,814
Other off-site transfers	43,279	5,094	2,187	3,079	2,394	3,306
Other on-site waste management .	(NA)	14,222,807	13,682,935	14,041,722	21,483,644	17,744,197
Recycled on-site	(NA)	6,518,368	6,139,070	6,209,510	11,530,186	7,842,595
Energy recovery on-site	(NA)	3,138,177	2,688,189	2,585,786	2,837,074	2,761,739
Treated on-site	(NA)	4,566,261	4,855,676	5,246,426	7,116,384	7,139,862

NA Not available.   [1] Excludes chemicals removed from the list, those added in 1990, 1991, 1994, and 1995, and aluminum oxide, ammonia, hydrochloric acid, and sulfuric acid. Chemicals covered for all reporting years.   [2] The Environmental Protection Agency added 286 chemicals and chemical categories to the EPCRA section list of 313 list of toxic chemicals.   [3] POTW (Publicly Owned Treatment Work) is a wastewater treatment facility that is owned by a state or municipality.

Source: U.S. Environmental Protection Agency, *1996 Toxics Release Inventory.*

No. 412. Toxic Chemical Releases, by Industry: 1988 to 1996

[In thousands of pounds (3,352,959 represents 3,352,959,000). Based on reports filed as required by section 313 of the Emergency Planning and Community Right-to-Know Act (EPCRA, or Title III of the Superfund Amendments and Reauthorization Act of 1986), Public Law 99-499. Owners and operators of facilities that are classified within Standard Classification Code groups 20 through 39, have 10 or more full-time employees, and that manufacture, process, or otherwise uses any listed toxic chemical in quantities greater than the established threshold in the course of a calendar year are covered and required to report]

Industry	1987 SIC[1] code	Core chemicals [2]				Expanded chemical list [3]	
		1988	1994	1995	1996	1995	1996
Total	(X)	3,352,959	1,982,786	1,895,290	1,823,765	2,530,786	2,433,507
Food and kindred products	20	8,378	6,014	5,120	5,121	86,467	83,303
Tobacco products	21	342	135	95	73	2,034	4,153
Textile mill products	22	35,798	16,346	15,656	15,280	18,501	17,328
Apparel and other textile products . .	23	1,026	1,381	1,260	1,742	1,287	1,865
Lumber and wood products.	24	32,982	32,986	30,435	27,117	34,835	36,243
Furniture and fixtures.	25	62,363	52,135	41,530	35,652	41,780	35,877
Paper and allied products	26	207,603	185,334	178,775	172,799	238,317	227,563
Printing and publishing.	27	61,188	34,387	30,896	28,270	31,156	28,466
Chemical and allied products.	28	1,047,782	537,483	539,600	513,043	844,232	785,178
Petroleum and coal products	29	72,781	46,877	42,593	43,077	64,141	68,887
Rubber and misc. plastic products . .	30	158,314	125,462	114,765	105,358	127,168	116,409
Leather and leather products.	31	13,024	5,104	4,026	3,814	4,476	4,242
Stone, clay, glass products	32	40,539	17,359	19,053	23,264	32,324	38,740
Primary metal industries	33	629,354	433,886	455,029	496,663	524,041	564,535
Fabricated metals products	34	160,370	99,572	90,441	77,611	97,039	90,254
Industrial machinery and equipment . .	35	69,747	27,120	22,852	19,162	26,203	22,061
Electronic, electric equipment	36	132,719	36,672	31,457	33,753	40,456	41,765
Transportation equipment	37	208,392	128,139	114,746	105,232	121,155	111,353
Instruments and related products . . .	38	58,085	14,328	12,955	10,359	17,859	15,350
Miscellaneous.	39	32,593	15,350	13,286	9,843	13,869	10,270
Multiple codes	20-39	308,351	149,011	122,437	91,158	152,531	120,779
No codes.	20-39	11,229	17,704	8,281	5,377	10,918	8,885

X Not applicable.   [1] Standard Industrial Classification, see text, Section 13, Labor Force.   [2] Chemicals covered for all reporting years.   [3] The Environmental Protection Agency added 286 chemicals and chemical categories to the EPCRA section list of 313 list of toxic chemicals.

Source: U.S. Environmental Protection Agency, *1996 Toxics Release Inventory.*

Geography and Environment   249

No. 413. Toxic Releases, by State: 1988 to 1996

[In thousands of pounds (3,352,959 represents 3,352,959,000). Excludes delisted chemicals, chemicals added in 1990, 1991, 1994, and 1995, and aluminum oxice, ammonia, hydorchloric acid, and sulfuric acid. See headnote, Table 412]

State and outlying area	Core chemicals				State and outlying area	Core chemicals			
	1988	1994	1995	1996		1988	1994	1995	1996
Total...	3,352,959	1,982,786	1,895,290	1,823,765	MT	35,630	46,460	42,644	47,204
U.S. total .	3,337,537	1,971,577	1,885,211	1,815,062	NE	16,936	13,735	11,171	8,881
AL	109,690	96,649	100,495	89,469	NV	2,352	3,209	3,369	3,294
AK	3,715	1,095	2,164	1,684	NH	13,866	2,395	1,940	1,750
AZ	66,236	30,775	33,875	46,258	NJ	45,018	14,025	12,399	10,645
AR	41,078	29,329	24,495	22,915	NM	30,386	17,230	17,946	18,339
CA	109,318	42,362	36,146	30,989	NY	99,656	37,902	30,361	26,028
CO	15,736	4,081	3,489	3,690	NC	132,027	80,753	72,493	67,973
CT	37,800	11,219	8,644	6,388	ND	1,195	988	1,207	773
DE	8,635	4,096	2,902	1,986	OH	202,152	116,096	122,236	115,228
DC	1	56	57	9	OK	32,895	15,344	15,995	15,216
FL	61,527	71,434	52,111	46,914	OR	21,562	18,011	18,449	24,647
GA	86,767	43,827	39,792	38,468	PA	134,852	95,110	95,914	90,529
HI	848	531	562	448	RI	7,713	6,789	3,017	2,452
ID	7,349	9,149	10,081	10,753	SC	66,070	47,640	48,112	47,374
IL	134,594	89,071	82,882	76,549	SD	2,393	2,108	1,872	1,364
IN	184,554	82,653	88,801	91,419	TN	126,484	104,915	94,684	88,191
IA	43,028	22,728	21,124	17,500	TX	318,632	199,765	205,724	187,485
KS	30,301	17,408	17,612	17,570	UT	123,836	67,175	69,144	73,876
KY	66,444	32,512	30,570	30,941	VT	1,734	632	544	294
LA	250,845	114,824	122,286	129,789	VA	112,329	43,829	40,613	40,555
ME	15,356	6,879	6,594	5,273	WA	28,273	20,770	22,336	21,890
MD	20,037	11,451	11,858	9,381	WV	39,416	20,852	19,679	17,445
MA	31,879	9,950	8,351	8,951	WI	60,707	39,397	32,875	31,566
MI	132,693	103,055	85,889	78,426	WY	16,741	880	1,144	1,356
MN	55,948	20,826	18,338	15,846	Guam	-	-	3	3
MS	59,600	42,834	39,671	39,321	Puerto Rico .	12,829	9,693	8,840	7,468
MO	90,704	56,772	50,552	49,770	Virgin Island .	2,593	1,516	1,236	1,232

- Represents zero.

Source: U.S. Environmental Protection Agency, *1996 Toxics Release Inventory.*

No. 414. Hazardous Waste Sites on the National Priority List, by State: 1998

[Includes both proposed and final sites listed on the National Priorities List for the Superfund program as authorized by the Comprehensive Environmental Response, Compensation, and Liability Act of 1980 and the Superfund Amendments and Reauthorization Act of 1986]

State and outlying area	Total sites	Rank	Percent distri- bution	Fed- eral	Non- Fed- eral	State and outlying area	Total sites	Rank	Percent distri- bution	Fed- eral	Non- Fed- eral
Total	1,258	(X)	(X)	161	1,097	Montana	9	42	0.7	-	9
						Nebraska	10	38	0.8	1	9
United States . . .	1,245	(X)	100.0	160	1,085	Nevada	1	49	0.1	-	1
Alabama	12	32	1.0	3	9	New Hampshire	18	20	1.4	1	17
Alaska	7	43	0.6	6	1	New Jersey	111	1	8.9	6	105
Arizona	10	39	0.8	3	7	New Mexico	11	34	0.9	1	10
Arkansas	11	36	0.9	-	11	New York	84	4	6.7	4	80
California	96	3	7.7	23	73	North Carolina	24	17	1.9	2	22
Colorado	17	22	1.4	3	14	North Dakota	-	50	0.0	-	-
Connecticut	14	29	1.1	1	13	Ohio	36	10	2.9	5	31
Delaware	17	23	1.4	1	16	Oklahoma	12	30	1.0	1	11
District of Columbia .	1	(X)	0.1	1	-	Oregon	11	35	0.9	2	9
Florida	53	6	4.3	6	47	Pennsylvania	100	2	8.0	6	94
Georgia	16	25	1.3	2	14	Rhode Island	12	31	1.0	2	10
Hawaii	4	45	0.3	3	1	South Carolina	25	16	2.0	2	23
Idaho	9	41	0.7	2	7	South Dakota	2	48	0.2	1	1
Illinois	43	8	3.5	4	39	Tennessee	15	28	1.2	4	11
Indiana	30	13	2.4	-	30	Texas	32	11	2.6	4	28
Iowa	17	21	1.4	1	16	Utah	16	24	1.3	4	12
Kansas	11	37	0.9	2	9	Vermont	9	40	0.7	-	9
Kentucky	16	26	1.3	1	15	Virginia	27	15	2.2	9	18
Louisiana	15	27	1.2	1	14	Washington	47	7	3.8	14	33
Maine	12	33	1.0	3	9	West Virginia	7	44	0.6	2	5
Maryland	18	19	1.4	8	10	Wisconsin	40	9	3.2	-	40
Massachusetts	31	12	2.5	8	23	Wyoming	3	46	0.2	1	2
Michigan	71	5	5.7	1	70						
Minnesota	27	14	2.2	2	25	Guam	2	(X)	(X)	1	1
Mississippi	3	47	0.2	-	3	Puerto Rico	9	(X)	(X)	-	9
Missouri	22	18	1.8	3	19	Virgin Islands	2	(X)	(X)	-	2

- Represents zero. X Not applicable.

Source: U.S. Environmental Protection Agency, *Supplementary Materials: National Priorities List, Proposed Rule,* December 1998.

250 Geography and Environment

No. 415. Environmental Industry—Revenues and Employment, by Industry Segment: 1980 to 1998

[59.0 represents $59,000,000,000. Covers approximately 59,000 private and public companies engaged in environmental activities]

Industry segment	Revenue (bil. dol.)					Employment (1,000)				
	1980	1990	1995	1997	1998	1980	1990	1995	1997	1998
Industry total	59.0	150.3	179.5	186.1	191.5	462.5	1,174.3	1,327.0	1,348.0	(NA)
Analytical services [1]	0.4	1.5	1.2	1.1	1.1	6.0	20.2	14.1	12.7	(NA)
Wastewater treatment works [2]	10.9	20.4	23.4	24.4	25.3	53.9	95.0	101.5	104.8	(NA)
Solid waste management [3]	11.2	26.1	32.5	34.9	35.9	83.2	209.5	243.4	249.9	(NA)
Hazardous waste management [4] . .	0.6	6.3	6.2	5.8	5.7	6.8	56.9	52.5	49.4	(NA)
Remediation/industrial services . . .	2.4	11.1	11.1	11.2	11.4	6.9	107.2	98.1	96.0	(NA)
Consulting & engineering	1.7	12.5	15.5	15.3	15.2	20.5	144.2	180.2	174.4	(NA)
Water equipment & chemicals	6.9	13.5	16.5	18.2	19.1	62.4	97.9	110.2	117.0	(NA)
Instrument manufacturing	0.2	2.0	3.0	3.3	3.4	2.5	18.8	26.2	28.7	(NA)
Air pollution control equipment [5] . .	3.3	13.1	14.8	15.7	16.2	28.3	82.7	107.2	111.2	(NA)
Waste management equipment [6] . .	3.5	8.7	9.9	9.8	10.0	41.9	88.8	93.8	94.2	(NA)
Process & prevention technology . .	0.1	0.4	0.8	0.9	1.0	2.1	8.9	19.5	21.2	(NA)
Water utilities [7]	11.9	19.8	25.3	27.6	28.5	76.9	104.7	118.2	121.3	(NA)
Resource recovery [8]	4.4	13.1	16.9	15.3	15.9	48.7	118.4	136.0	141.2	(NA)
Environmental energy sources [9] . .	1.5	1.8	2.4	2.7	2.9	22.4	21.1	26.1	26.4	(NA)

NA Not available. [1] Covers environmental laboratory testing and services. [2] Mostly revenues collected by municipal entities. [3] Covers such activities as collection, transportation, transfer stations, disposal, landfill ownership, and management for solid waste. [4] Transportation and disposal of hazardous, medical, and nuclear waste. [5] Includes stationery and mobile sources. [6] Includes vehicles, containers, liners, processing, and remediation equipment. [7] Revenues generated from the sale of water. [8] Revenues generated from the sale of recovered metals, paper, plastic, etc. [9] Includes solar, wind, geothermal, and conservation devices.

Source: Environmental Business International, Inc., San Diego, CA, *Environmental Business Journal*, monthly (copyright).

No. 416. Threatened and Endangered Wildlife and Plant Species— Number: 1999

[As of **April.** Endangered species: One in danger of becoming extinct throughout all or a significant part of its natural range. Threatened species: One likely to become endangered in the foreseeable future]

Item	Mam- mals	Birds	Rep- tiles	Amphib- ians	Fishes	Snails	Clams	Crusta- ceans	Insects	Arach- nids	Plants
Total listings	336	274	114	26	121	29	71	20	41	5	706
Endangered species, total.	312	253	79	17	80	19	63	17	32	5	569
United States	61	75	14	9	69	18	61	17	28	5	568
Foreign	251	178	65	8	11	1	2	-	4	-	1
Threatened species, total.	24	21	35	9	41	10	8	3	9	-	137
United States	8	15	21	8	41	10	8	3	9	-	135
Foreign	16	6	14	1	-	-	-	-	-	-	2

- Represents zero. [1] Species outside United States and outlying areas as determined by Fish and Wildlife Service.

Source: U.S. Fish and Wildlife Service, *Endangered Species Technical Bulletin*, quarterly.

No. 417. Tornadoes, Floods, Tropical Storms, and Lightning: 1987 to 1997

Item	1987	1988	1989	1990	1991	1992	1993	1994	1995	1996	1997
Tornadoes, number [1]	656	702	856	1,133	1,132	1,298	1,176	1,082	1,235	1,170	1,148
Tornado days	151	156	160	181	179	195	186	199	178	196	196
Lives lost, total	59	32	50	53	39	39	33	69	30	25	67
Most in a single tornado	30	5	21	29	17	12	7	22	6	5	27
Floods and flash floods: Lives lost.	70	31	85	142	61	62	103	91	80	131	117
North Atlantic tropical storms and hurricanes [2]	7	12	11	14	8	7	8	7	19	13	7
Number of hurricanes reaching U.S. mainland.	1	1	3	-	1	1	1	-	2	2	1
Total direct deaths from tropical storms and hurricanes	3	550	84	123	17	28	273	1,175	121	138	4
Direct deaths on U.S. mainland .	-	6	56	10	17	26	9	38	29	33	4
Property loss in U.S.	8	59	7,670	57	1,500	26,500	57	973	3,729	3,600	100
Lightning: Deaths	86	69	67	74	73	41	43	74	85	52	42
Injuries	364	311	322	252	432	292	295	577	510	309	306

- Represents zero. [1] A violent, rotating column of air descending from a cumulonimbus cloud in the form of a tubular- or funnel-shaped cloud, usually characterized by movements along a narrow path and wind speeds from 100 to over 300 miles per hour. Also known as a "twister" or "waterspout." [2] Source: National Hurricane Center, Coral Gables, FL, unpublished data. Tropical storms have maximum winds of 39 to 73 miles per hour; hurricanes have maximum winds of 74 miles per hour or higher.

Source: Except as noted, U.S. National Oceanic and Atmospheric Administration, *Storm Data*, monthly.

U.S. Census Bureau, Statistical Abstract of the United States: 1999

No. 418. Major U.S. Weather Disasters: 1980 to Early 1999

[1.3 represents $1,300,000,000. Covers only weather related disasters costing $1 billion or more]

Event	Description	Time period	Estimated cost (bil. dol.)	Deaths
Arkansas-Tennessee tornados	Two outbreaks of tornadoes in 6-day period	January 1999	1.3	31
Texas flooding	Severe flooding in southeast Texas from two heavy rain events with 10-20 in. totals	Oct.-Nov. 1998	1.0	31
Hurricane Georges	Category 2 hurricane in Puerto Rico, Florida Keys, and Gulf coasts of LA, MS, AL, and FL	Sept. 1998	3-4	16
Hurricane Bonnie	Category 3 hurricane in eastern NC and VA	August 1998	1.0	2
Southern drought/heat wave	Severe drought and heat wave from TX/OK eastward to the Carolinas	Summer 1998	6.0	200
Southeast severe weather	Tornadoes and flooding related to strong El Nino in the southeast	Winter/ spring 1998	1.0	Over 130
Northeast ice storm	Intense ice storm hits ME, NH, VT, and NY	January 1998	1.4	16
Northern plains flooding	Severe flooding in Dakotas and Minnesota due to heavy spring snowmelt	April-May 1997	2.0	11
MS and OH valleys flooding and tornadoes	Tornadoes and severe flooding hit the states of AR, MO, MS, TN, IL, IN, KY, OH, and WV	March 1997	1.0	67
West Coast flooding	Flooding from rains and snowmelt in CA, WA, OR, ID, NV, & MT	Dec. 1996-Jan. 1997	2-3	36
Hurricane Fran	Category 3 hurricane in NC and VA	Sept. 1996	5.0	37
Southern Plains severe drought	Drought in agricultural areas of TX & OK	Fall 1995-summer 1996	Over $4	(NA)
Pacific Northwest severe flooding	Flooding from heavy rain & snowmelt in OR, WA, ID, and MT	Feb. 1996	1.0	9
Blizzard of '96 followed by flooding	Heavy snowstorm followed by severe flooding in Appalachians, Mid-Atlantic, and Northeast	Jan. 1996	3.0	187
Hurricane Opal	Category 3 hurricane in FL, AL, parts of GA, TN, & Carolinas	Oct. 1995	Over 3	27
Hurricane Marilyn	Category 2 hurricane in Virgin Islands	Sept. 1995	2.1	13
TX/OK/LA/MS severe weather and flooding	Flooding, hail, & tornadoes across TX, OK, parts of LA, MS, Dallas & New Orleans hardest hit	May 1995	5-6	32
California flooding	Flooding from frequent winter storms across much of CA	Jan.-Mar. 1995	3.0	27
Western fire season	Severe fire season in western states due to dry weather	Summer-fall 1994	1.0	(NA)
Texas flooding	Flooding from torrential rain & thunderstorms across southeast TX	Oct. 1994	1.0	19
Tropical Storm Alberto	Flooding due to 10 to 25 inch rain across GA, AL, part of FL	July 1994	1.0	32
Southeast ice storm	Intense ice storm in pts of TX, OK, AR, LA, MS, AL, TN, GA, SC, NC, & VA	Feb. 1994	3.0	9
California wildfires	Out-of-control wildfires over southern CA	Fall 1993	1.0	4
Midwest flooding	Extreme flooding across central U.S.	Summer 1993	15-20	48
Drought/heat wave	Extreme drought/heatwave across southeastern U.S.	Summer 1993	1.0	(NA)
Storm/blizzard	"Storm of the Century" hits entire eastern seaboard	Mar. 1993	3-6	270
Nor'easter of 1992	Slow-moving storm batters northeast U.S. coast, New England hardest hit	Dec. 1992	1-2	19
Hurricane Iniki	Category 4 hurricane hit Hawaiian island of Kauai	Sept. 1992	1.8	7
Hurricane Andrew	Category 4 hurricane hit FL & LA	Aug. 1992	27.0	58
Oakland firestorm	Oakland, CA firestorm due to low humidity & high winds	Oct. 1991	1.5	25
Hurricane Bob	Category 2 hurricane—mainly coastal NC, Long Island, & New England	Aug. 1991	1.5	18
TX/OK/LA/AR flooding	Torrential rains cause flooding along Trinity, Red, and Arkansas rivers	May 1990	1.0	
Hurricane Hugo	Category 4 hurricane hit Puerto Rico & Virgin Islands, devastated NC & SC	Sept. 1989	Over 9	86
Drought/heat wave	Drought/heatwave over central & eastern U.S.	Summer 1988	40.0	5,000-10,000
Hurricane Juan	Category 1 hurricane, flooding most severe problem, hit LA and southeast U.S.	Oct.-Nov. 1985	1.5	63
Hurricane Elena	Category 3 hurricane across FL to LA	Aug.-Sept. 1985	1.3	4
Florida freeze	Severe freeze central/northern FL, damage to citrus industry	Jan. 1985	1.2	-
Florida freeze	Severe freeze central/northern FL, damage to citrus industry	Dec. 1983	2.0	-
Hurricane Alicia	Category 3 hurricane across TX	Aug. 1983	3.0	21
Drought/heat wave	Drought/heatwave over central & eastern U.S.	June-Sept. 1980	20.0	10,000

- Represents zero.   NA Not available or not reported.

Source: U.S. National Oceanic and Atmospheric Administration, National Climatic Data Center. *"Billion Dollar U.S. Weather Disaster, 1980-1999,"* and release date: April 7, 1999; <http://www.ncdc.noaa.gov/ol/reports/billionz.html>.

252   Geography and Environment

No. 419. Highest and Lowest Temperatures, by State Through 1997

State	Highest temperatures Station	Temperature (F)	Date	Lowest temperatures Station	Temperature (F)	Date
U.S.	Greenland Ranch, CA . .	134	Jul. 10, 1913	Prospect Creek, AK . . .	-80	Jan. 23, 1971
AL.	Centerville	112	Sep. 5, 1925	New Market	-27	Jan. 30, 1966
AK.	Fort Yukon.	100	Jun. 27, 1915	Prospect Creek.	-80	Jan. 23, 1971
AZ.	Lake Havasu City	128	Jun. 29, 1994	Hawley Lake	-40	Jan. 7, 1971
AR.	Ozark	120	Aug. 10, 1936	Pond.	-29	Feb. 13, 1905
CA.	Greenland Ranch	134	Jul. 10, 1913	Boca.	-45	Jan. 20, 1937
CO.	Bennett.	118	Jul. 11, 1888	Maybell	-61	Feb. 1, 1985
CT.	Danbury	106	Jul. 15, 1995	Falls Village	-32	Feb. 16, 1943
DE.	Millsboro	110	Jul. 21, 1930	Millsboro	-17	Jan. 17, 1893
FL.	Monticello	109	Jun. 29, 1931	Tallahassee	-2	Feb. 13, 1899
GA.	Louisville	112	Jul. 24, 1952	CCC Camp F-16.	-17	Jan. 27, 1940
HI	Pahala	100	Apr. 27, 1931	Mauna Kea Obs. 111.2. .	12	May 17, 1979
ID	Orofino	118	Jul. 28, 1934	Island Park Dam	-60	Jan. 18, 1943
IL	East St. Louis	117	Jul. 14, 1954	Elizabeth	-35	[1]Feb. 3, 1996
IN	Collegeville	116	Jul. 14, 1936	New Whiteland	-36	Jan. 19, 1994
IA	Keokuk	118	Jul. 20, 1934	Elkader	-47	[1]Feb. 3, 1996
KS.	Alton (near)	121	[1]Jul. 24, 1936	Lebanon	-40	Feb. 13, 1905
KY.	Greensburg	114	Jul. 28, 1930	Shelbyville	-37	Jan. 19, 1994
LA.	Plain Dealing	114	Aug. 10, 1936	Minden	-16	Feb. 13, 1899
ME.	North Bridgton	105	[1]Jul. 10, 1911	Van Buren	-48	Jan. 19, 1925
MD	Cumberland & Frederick .	109	[1]Jul. 10, 1936	Oakland	-40	Jan. 13, 1912
MA.	New Bedford & Chester. .	107	Aug. 2, 1975	Chester	-35	Jan. 12, 1981
MI	Mio	112	Jul. 13, 1936	Vanderbilt	-51	Feb. 9, 1934
MN	Moorhead	114	[1]Jul. 6, 1936	Tower	-60	Feb. 2, 1996
MS.	Holly Springs	115	Jul. 29, 1930	Corinth	-19	Jan. 30, 1966
MO	Warsaw & Union.	118	[1]Jul. 14, 1954	Warsaw.	-40	Feb. 13, 1905
MT	Medicine Lake	117	Jul. 5, 1937	Rogers Pass	-70	Jan. 20, 1954
NE.	Minden	118	[1]Jul. 24, 1936	Camp Clarke	-47	Feb. 12, 1899
NV.	Laughlin	125	Jun. 29, 1994	San Jacinto	-50	Jan. 8, 1937
NH	Nashua.	106	Jul. 4, 1911	Pittsburg	-46	Jan. 28, 1925
NJ.	Runyon	110	Jul. 10, 1936	River Vale	-34	Jan. 5, 1904
NM	Waste Isolat Pilot Plt . . .	122	Jun. 27, 1994	Gavilan	-50	Feb. 1, 1951
NY.	Troy	108	Jul. 22, 1926	Old Forge	-52	[1]Feb. 18, 1979
NC	Fayetteville	110	Aug. 21, 1983	Mt. Mitchell	-34	Jan. 21, 1985
ND	Steele.	121	Jul. 6, 1936	Parshall.	-60	Feb. 15, 1936
OH	Gallipolis (near)	113	[1]Jul. 21, 1934	Milligan	-39	Feb. 10, 1899
OK	Tipton.	120	[1]Jun. 27, 1994	Watts	-27	Jan. 18, 1930
OR	Pendleton	119	Aug. 10, 1898	Seneca	-54	[1]Feb. 10, 1933
PA.	Phoenixville	111	[1]Jul. 10, 1936	Smethport	-42	Jan. 5, 1904
RI	Providence	104	Aug. 2, 1975	Kingston	-23	Jan. 11, 1942
SC.	Camden	111	[1]Jun. 28, 1954	Caesars Head	-19	Jan. 21, 1985
SD.	Gannvalley	120	Jul. 5, 1936	McIntosh	-58	Feb. 17, 1936
TN.	Perryville.	113	[1]Aug. 9, 1930	Mountain City	-32	Dec. 30, 1917
TX.	Seymour	120	Aug. 12, 1936	Seminole	-23	[1]Feb. 8, 1933
UT.	Saint George	117	Jul. 5, 1985	Peter's Sink	-69	Feb. 1, 1985
VT.	Vernon	105	Jul. 4, 1911	Bloomfield	-50	Dec. 30, 1933
VA.	Balcony Falls	110	Jul. 15, 1954	Mtn. Lake Bio. Stn. . . .	-30	Jan. 22, 1985
WA	Ice Harbor Dam	118	[1]Aug. 5, 1961	Mazama & Winthrop . . .	-48	Dec. 30, 1968
WV	Martinsburg	112	[1]Jul. 10, 1936	Lewisburg	-37	Dec. 30, 1917
WI.	Wisconsin Dells	114	Jul. 13, 1936	Danbury	-54	Jan. 24, 1922
WY	Basin	114	Jul. 12, 1900	Riverside R.S.	-66	Feb. 9, 1933

[1] Also on earlier dates at the same or other places.

Source: U.S. National Oceanic and Atmospheric Administration, <http://www.ncdc.noaa.gov/ol/climate/> (accessed May 11, 1999).

No. 420. Normal Daily Mean, Maximum, and Minimum Temperatures—Selected Cities

[In Fahrenheit degrees. Airport data except as noted. Based on standard 30-year period, 1961 through 1990]

State	Station	Daily mean temperature			Daily maximum temperature			Daily minimum temperature		
		Jan.	July	Annual average	Jan.	July	Annual average	Jan.	July	Annual average
AL	Mobile	49.9	82.3	67.5	59.7	91.3	77.4	40.0	73.2	57.4
AK	Juneau	24.2	56.0	40.6	29.4	63.9	46.9	19.0	48.1	34.1
AZ	Phoenix	53.6	93.5	72.6	65.9	105.9	85.9	41.2	81.0	59.3
AR	Little Rock.	39.1	81.9	61.8	49.0	92.4	72.5	29.1	71.5	51.0
CA	Los Angeles	56.8	69.1	63.0	65.7	75.3	70.4	47.8	62.8	55.5
	Sacramento	45.2	75.7	60.8	52.7	93.2	73.5	37.7	58.1	48.1
	San Diego.	57.4	71.0	64.2	65.9	76.2	70.8	48.9	65.7	57.6
	San Francisco	48.7	62.7	57.1	55.6	71.6	65.2	41.8	53.9	49.0
CO	Denver.	29.7	73.5	50.3	43.2	88.2	64.2	16.1	58.6	36.2
CT	Hartford	24.6	73.7	49.9	33.2	85.0	60.2	15.8	62.2	39.5
DE	Wilmington	30.6	76.4	54.2	38.7	85.6	63.6	22.4	67.1	44.8
DC	Washington	34.6	80.0	58.0	42.3	88.5	66.9	26.8	71.4	49.2
FL	Jacksonville.	52.4	81.6	68.0	64.2	91.4	78.9	40.5	71.9	57.1
	Miami.	67.2	82.6	75.9	75.2	89.0	82.8	59.2	76.2	69.0
GA	Atlanta	41.0	78.8	61.3	50.4	88.0	71.2	31.5	69.5	51.3
HI	Honolulu.	72.9	80.5	77.2	80.1	87.5	84.4	65.6	73.5	70.0
ID	Boise.	29.0	74.0	50.9	36.4	90.2	62.8	21.6	57.7	39.1
IL	Chicago.	21.0	73.2	49.0	29.0	83.7	58.6	12.9	62.6	39.5
	Peoria	21.6	75.5	50.7	29.9	85.7	60.4	13.2	65.4	41.0
IN	Indianapolis.	25.5	75.4	52.3	33.7	85.5	62.1	17.2	65.2	42.4
IA	Des Moines.	19.4	76.6	49.9	28.1	86.7	59.8	10.7	66.5	40.0
KS	Wichita.	29.5	81.4	56.2	39.8	92.8	67.4	19.2	69.9	45.0
KY	Louisville	31.7	77.2	56.1	40.3	87.0	66.0	23.2	67.3	46.0
LA	New Orleans	51.3	81.9	68.1	60.8	90.6	77.6	41.8	73.1	58.5
ME	Portland	20.8	68.6	45.4	30.3	78.8	54.9	11.4	58.3	35.8
MD	Baltimore	31.8	77.0	55.1	40.2	87.2	65.0	23.4	66.8	45.2
MA	Boston	28.6	73.5	51.3	35.7	81.8	59.0	21.6	65.1	43.6
MI	Detroit	22.9	72.3	48.6	30.3	83.3	58.1	15.6	61.3	39.0
	Sault Ste. Marie.	12.9	63.8	39.7	21.1	76.3	49.6	4.6	51.3	29.8
MN	Duluth	7.0	66.1	38.5	16.2	77.1	47.9	-2.2	55.1	29.0
	Minneapolis-St. Paul . .	11.8	73.6	44.9	20.7	84.0	54.3	2.8	63.1	35.3
MS	Jackson	44.1	81.5	64.2	55.6	92.4	76.4	32.7	70.5	52.0
MO	Kansas City.	25.7	78.5	53.6	34.7	88.7	63.6	16.7	68.2	43.7
	St. Louis.	29.3	79.8	56.1	37.7	89.3	65.4	20.8	70.4	46.7
MT	Great Falls	21.2	68.2	44.8	30.6	83.3	56.4	11.6	53.2	33.1
NE	Omaha.	21.1	76.9	50.6	31.3	87.9	61.5	10.9	65.9	39.5
NV	Reno	32.9	71.6	50.8	45.1	91.9	66.8	20.7	51.3	34.7
NH	Concord	18.6	69.5	45.1	29.8	82.4	57.0	7.4	56.5	33.1
NJ	Atlantic City.	30.9	74.7	53.0	40.4	84.5	63.2	21.4	64.8	42.8
NM	Albuquerque	34.2	78.5	56.2	46.8	92.5	70.1	21.7	64.4	42.2
NY	Albany	20.6	71.8	47.4	30.2	84.0	58.1	11.0	59.6	36.6
	Buffalo	23.6	71.1	47.7	30.2	80.2	55.8	17.0	61.9	39.5
	New York [1]	31.5	76.8	54.7	37.6	85.2	62.3	25.3	68.4	47.1
NC	Charlotte.	39.3	79.3	60.1	49.0	88.9	70.4	29.6	69.6	49.7
	Raleigh.	38.9	78.1	59.3	48.9	88.0	70.1	28.8	68.1	48.4
ND	Bismarck	9.2	70.4	41.6	20.2	84.4	53.8	-1.7	56.4	29.4
OH	Cincinnati	28.1	75.1	53.2	36.6	85.5	63.2	19.5	64.8	43.2
	Cleveland.	24.8	71.9	49.6	31.9	82.4	58.7	17.6	61.4	40.5
	Columbus	26.4	73.2	51.4	34.1	83.7	61.2	18.5	62.7	41.6
OK	Oklahoma City.	35.9	82.0	60.0	46.7	93.4	71.1	25.2	70.6	48.8
OR	Portland	39.6	68.2	53.6	45.4	79.9	62.6	33.7	56.5	44.5
PA	Philadelphia	30.4	76.7	54.3	37.9	86.1	63.4	22.8	67.2	45.1
	Pittsburgh	26.1	72.1	50.3	33.7	82.6	59.9	18.5	61.6	40.7
RI	Providence	27.9	72.7	50.4	36.6	82.1	59.8	19.1	63.2	41.0
SC	Columbia	43.8	80.8	63.1	55.3	91.6	75.1	32.1	70.0	50.9
SD	Sioux Falls	13.8	74.3	45.5	24.3	86.3	56.8	3.3	62.3	34.2
TN	Memphis.	39.7	82.6	62.3	48.5	92.3	72.1	30.9	72.9	52.4
	Nashville.	36.2	79.3	59.1	45.9	89.5	69.8	26.5	68.9	48.4
TX	Dallas-Fort Worth	43.4	85.3	65.4	54.1	96.5	76.3	32.7	74.1	54.6
	El Paso	42.8	82.3	63.2	56.1	96.1	77.5	29.4	68.4	49.0
	Houston	50.4	82.6	67.9	61.0	92.7	78.6	39.7	72.4	57.3
UT	Salt Lake City	27.9	77.9	52.0	36.4	92.2	63.6	19.3	63.7	40.3
VT	Burlington	16.3	70.5	44.6	25.1	81.2	54.0	7.5	59.7	35.2
VA	Norfolk	39.1	78.2	59.2	47.3	86.4	67.8	30.9	70.0	50.6
	Richmond	35.7	78.0	57.7	45.7	88.4	68.8	25.7	67.5	46.6
WA	Seattle-Tacoma	40.1	65.2	52.0	45.0	75.2	59.4	35.2	55.2	44.6
	Spokane.	27.1	68.8	47.3	33.2	83.1	57.5	20.8	54.4	36.9
WV	Charleston	32.1	75.1	55.0	41.2	85.7	65.8	23.0	64.4	44.2
WI	Milwaukee.	18.9	70.9	46.1	26.1	79.9	54.3	11.6	62.0	37.9
WY	Cheyenne	26.5	68.4	45.6	37.7	82.2	58.0	15.2	54.6	33.2
PR	San Juan	77.0	82.6	80.2	83.2	88.5	86.4	70.8	76.8	74.0

[1] City office data.

Source: U.S. National Oceanic and Atmospheric Administration, *Climatography of the United States*, No. 81.

254 Geography and Environment

No. 421. Highest Temperature of Record—Selected Cities

[In **Fahrenheit degrees.** Airport data, except as noted. For period of record through 1997]

State	Station	Length of record (yr.)	Jan.	Feb.	Mar.	Apr.	May	June	July	Aug.	Sept.	Oct.	Nov.	Dec.	Annual
AL	Mobile.........	56	84	82	90	94	100	102	104	102	99	93	87	81	104
AK	Juneau	53	57	57	59	72	82	86	90	83	73	61	56	54	90
AZ	Phoenix........	60	88	92	100	105	113	122	121	116	118	107	93	88	122
AR	Little Rock	56	83	85	91	95	98	105	112	108	106	97	86	80	112
CA	Los Angeles	62	88	92	95	102	97	104	97	98	110	106	101	94	110
	Sacramento	47	70	76	88	95	105	115	114	110	108	101	87	72	115
	San Diego	57	88	90	93	98	96	101	95	98	111	107	97	88	111
	San Francisco	70	72	78	85	92	97	106	105	100	103	99	85	75	106
CO	Denver........	61	73	76	84	90	96	104	104	101	97	89	79	75	104
CT	Hartford........	43	65	73	87	96	99	100	102	101	99	91	81	74	102
DE	Wilmington.......	50	75	78	86	94	96	100	102	101	100	91	85	74	102
DC	Washington......	56	79	82	89	95	99	101	104	105	101	94	86	75	105
FL	Jacksonville	56	85	88	91	95	100	103	105	102	100	96	88	84	105
	Miami	55	88	89	92	96	96	98	98	98	97	95	89	87	98
GA	Atlanta	49	79	80	89	93	95	101	105	102	98	95	84	79	105
HI	Honolulu	28	88	88	88	91	93	92	94	93	95	94	93	89	95
ID	Boise	58	63	71	81	92	98	109	111	110	102	94	74	65	111
IL	Chicago........	39	65	71	88	91	93	104	104	101	99	91	78	71	104
	Peoria........	58	70	72	86	92	93	105	103	103	100	90	81	71	105
IN	Indianapolis	58	71	74	85	89	93	102	104	102	100	90	81	74	104
IA	Des Moines	58	65	73	91	93	98	103	105	108	101	95	76	69	108
KS	Wichita	45	75	87	89	96	100	110	113	110	107	95	85	83	113
KY	Louisville	50	77	77	86	91	95	102	105	101	104	92	84	76	105
LA	New Orleans	51	83	85	89	92	96	100	101	102	101	92	87	84	102
ME	Portland	57	64	64	85	86	94	98	99	103	95	88	74	69	103
MD	Baltimore........	47	75	79	87	94	98	101	104	105	100	92	83	77	105
MA	Boston	46	66	70	81	94	95	100	102	102	100	90	79	73	102
MI	Detroit.........	39	62	65	81	89	93	104	102	100	98	91	77	68	104
	Sault Ste. Marie ...	57	45	47	75	85	89	93	97	98	95	80	67	60	98
MN	Duluth.........	56	52	55	78	88	90	94	97	97	95	86	70	55	97
	Minneapolis-St. Paul	59	58	60	83	95	96	102	105	102	98	90	75	63	105
MS	Jackson........	34	82	85	89	94	99	105	106	102	104	95	88	84	106
MO	Kansas City	25	69	77	86	93	92	105	107	109	102	92	82	70	109
	St. Louis.......	40	76	85	89	93	94	102	107	107	104	94	85	76	107
MT	Great Falls.......	60	67	70	78	89	93	101	105	106	98	91	76	69	106
NE	Omaha	61	69	78	89	97	99	105	114	110	104	96	80	72	114
NV	Reno	56	70	75	83	89	96	103	104	105	101	91	77	70	105
NH	Concord	56	68	67	85	95	97	98	102	101	98	90	80	68	102
NJ	Atlantic City	54	78	75	87	94	99	106	104	102	99	90	84	75	106
NM	Albuquerque......	58	69	76	85	89	98	107	105	101	100	91	77	72	107
NY	Albany	51	65	68	86	92	94	99	100	99	100	89	82	71	100
	Buffalo	54	72	70	81	94	90	96	97	99	98	87	80	74	99
	New York [1]......	129	72	75	86	96	99	101	106	104	102	94	84	72	106
NC	Charlotte	58	78	81	90	93	100	103	103	103	104	98	85	77	104
	Raleigh	53	79	84	92	95	97	104	105	105	104	98	88	79	105
ND	Bismarck	58	62	69	81	93	98	107	109	109	105	95	75	65	109
OH	Cincinnati.......	36	69	73	84	89	93	102	103	102	98	88	81	75	103
	Cleveland	56	73	70	83	88	92	104	103	102	101	90	82	77	104
	Columbus	58	74	73	85	89	94	102	100	101	100	90	80	76	102
OK	Oklahoma City	44	80	92	93	100	104	105	110	110	102	96	87	86	110
OR	Portland	57	63	71	80	87	100	100	107	107	105	92	73	65	107
PA	Philadelphia	56	74	74	87	94	97	100	104	101	100	96	81	72	104
	Pittsburgh	45	69	73	82	89	91	98	103	100	97	87	82	74	103
RI	Providence.......	44	69	72	80	98	95	97	102	104	100	86	78	70	104
SC	Columbia	50	84	84	91	94	101	107	107	107	101	101	90	83	107
SD	Sioux Falls.......	52	66	70	87	94	100	110	108	108	104	94	76	61	110
TN	Memphis	56	78	81	85	94	99	104	108	105	103	95	85	81	108
	Nashville	58	78	84	86	91	97	106	107	104	105	94	84	79	107
TX	Dallas-Fort Worth ..	44	88	95	96	95	103	113	110	108	106	102	89	88	113
	El Paso........	58	80	83	89	98	104	114	112	108	104	96	87	80	114
	Houston........	28	84	91	91	95	99	103	104	107	102	96	89	85	107
UT	Salt Lake City	69	62	69	78	86	95	104	107	106	100	89	75	69	107
VT	Burlington	54	66	62	84	91	93	100	100	101	94	85	75	65	101
VA	Norfolk	49	78	82	88	97	100	101	103	104	99	95	86	80	104
	Richmond.......	68	80	83	93	96	100	104	105	102	103	99	86	80	105
WA	Seattle-Tacoma....	53	64	70	75	85	93	96	100	99	98	89	74	64	100
	Spokane	50	59	63	71	90	96	101	103	108	98	86	67	56	108
WV	Charleston	50	79	78	89	94	93	98	104	101	102	92	85	80	104
WI	Milwaukee	57	62	65	82	91	93	101	103	103	98	89	77	63	103
WY	Cheyenne	62	66	71	74	83	90	100	100	96	95	83	73	69	100
PR	San Juan	43	92	96	96	97	96	97	95	97	97	98	96	94	98

[1] City office data.

Source: U.S. National Oceanic and Atmospheric Administration, *Comparative Climatic Data,* annual.

U.S. Census Bureau, Statistical Abstract of the United States: 1999

No. 422. Lowest Temperature of Record—Selected Cities

[In **Fahrenheit degrees.** Airport data, except as noted. For period of record through 1997]

State	Station	Length of record (yr.)	Jan.	Feb.	Mar.	Apr.	May	June	July	Aug.	Sept.	Oct.	Nov.	Dec.	Annual
AL	Mobile.........	56	3	11	21	32	43	49	60	59	42	30	22	8	3
AK	Juneau........	53	-22	-22	-15	6	25	31	36	27	23	11	-5	-21	-22
AZ	Phoenix.......	60	17	22	25	32	40	50	61	60	47	34	25	22	17
AR	Little Rock......	56	-4	-5	11	28	40	46	54	52	37	29	17	-1	-5
CA	Los Angeles.....	62	23	32	34	39	43	48	49	51	47	41	34	32	23
	Sacramento.....	47	23	23	26	32	36	41	48	49	43	36	26	18	18
	San Diego.....	57	29	36	39	41	48	51	55	57	51	43	38	34	29
	San Francisco....	70	24	25	30	31	36	41	43	42	38	34	25	20	20
CO	Denver........	61	-25	-30	-11	-2	22	30	43	41	17	3	-8	-25	-30
CT	Hartford.......	43	-26	-21	-6	9	28	37	44	36	30	17	1	-14	-26
DE	Wilmington......	50	-14	-6	2	18	30	41	48	43	36	24	14	-7	-14
DC	Washington.....	56	-5	4	11	24	34	47	54	49	39	29	16	1	-5
FL	Jacksonville......	56	7	19	23	34	45	47	61	63	48	36	21	11	7
	Miami.........	55	30	32	32	46	53	60	69	68	68	51	39	30	30
GA	Atlanta.......	49	-8	5	10	26	37	46	53	55	36	28	3	-	-8
HI	Honolulu.......	28	53	53	55	57	60	65	66	67	66	61	57	54	53
ID	Boise........	58	-17	-15	6	19	22	31	35	34	23	11	-3	-25	-25
IL	Chicago........	39	-27	-19	-8	7	24	36	40	41	28	17	1	-25	-27
	Peoria........	58	-25	-19	-10	14	25	39	47	41	26	19	-2	-23	-25
IN	Indianapolis.....	58	-27	-21	-7	16	28	37	44	41	28	17	-2	-23	-27
IA	Des Moines......	58	-24	-26	-22	9	30	38	47	40	26	14	-4	-22	-26
KS	Wichita.......	45	-12	-21	-2	15	31	43	51	48	31	18	1	-16	-21
KY	Louisville.......	50	-22	-19	-1	22	31	42	50	46	33	23	-1	-15	-22
LA	New Orleans....	51	14	16	25	32	41	50	60	60	42	35	24	11	11
ME	Portland.......	57	-26	-39	-21	8	23	33	40	33	23	15	3	-21	-39
MD	Baltimore......	47	-7	-3	6	20	32	40	50	45	35	25	13	-	-7
MA	Boston........	46	-12	-4	6	16	34	45	50	47	38	28	15	-7	-12
MI	Detroit........	39	-21	-15	-4	10	25	36	41	38	29	17	9	-10	-21
	Sault Ste. Marie ...	57	-36	-35	-24	-2	18	26	36	29	25	16	-10	-31	-36
MN	Duluth........	56	-39	-39	-29	-5	17	27	35	32	22	8	-23	-34	-39
	Minneapolis-St. Paul	59	-34	-32	-32	2	18	34	43	39	26	13	-17	-29	-34
MS	Jackson.......	34	2	10	15	27	38	47	51	55	35	26	17	4	2
MO	Kansas City.....	25	-17	-19	-10	12	30	42	51	43	31	17	1	-23	-23
	St. Louis.......	52	-13	-17	-3	18	30	42	44	44	31	18	4	-16	-17
MT	Great Falls......	60	-37	-35	-29	-6	15	31	40	30	20	-11	-25	-43	-43
NE	Omaha........	61	-23	-21	-16	5	27	38	44	43	25	13	-9	-23	-23
NV	Reno	56	-16	-16	-2	13	18	25	33	24	20	8	1	-16	-16
NH	Concord.......	56	-33	-37	-16	8	21	30	35	29	21	10	-5	-22	-37
NJ	Atlantic City.....	54	-10	-11	5	12	25	37	42	40	32	20	10	-7	-11
NM	Albuquerque.....	58	-17	-5	8	19	28	40	52	50	37	21	-7	-7	-17
NY	Albany........	51	-28	-21	-21	10	26	36	40	34	24	16	5	-22	-28
	Buffalo.......	54	-16	-20	-7	12	26	35	43	38	32	20	9	-10	-20
	New York [1].......	129	-6	-15	3	12	32	44	52	50	39	28	5	-13	-15
NC	Charlotte.......	58	-5	5	4	24	32	45	53	53	39	24	11	2	-5
	Raleigh	53	-9	-	11	23	31	38	48	46	37	19	11	4	-9
ND	Bismarck.......	58	-44	-43	-31	-12	15	30	35	33	11	-10	-30	-43	-44
OH	Cincinnati.......	36	-25	-11	-11	15	27	39	47	43	31	16	1	-20	-25
	Cleveland......	56	-20	-15	-5	10	25	31	41	38	32	19	3	-15	-20
	Columbus	58	-22	-13	-6	14	25	35	43	39	31	20	5	-17	-22
OK	Oklahoma City	44	-4	-3	3	20	37	47	53	51	36	16	11	-8	-8
OR	Portland.......	57	-2	-3	19	29	29	39	43	44	34	26	13	6	-3
PA	Philadelphia......	56	-7	-4	7	19	28	44	51	44	35	25	15	1	-7
	Pittsburgh	45	-22	-12	-1	14	26	34	42	39	31	16	-1	-12	-22
RI	Providence......	44	-13	-7	1	14	29	41	48	40	33	20	6	-10	-13
SC	Columbia.......	50	-1	5	4	26	34	44	54	53	40	23	12	4	-1
SD	Sioux Falls.......	52	-36	-31	-23	5	17	33	38	34	22	9	-17	-28	-36
TN	Memphis.......	56	-4	-11	12	29	38	48	52	48	36	25	9	-13	-13
	Nashville	58	-17	-13	2	23	34	42	51	47	36	26	-1	-10	-17
TX	Dallas-Fort Worth ..	44	4	7	15	29	41	51	59	56	43	29	20	-1	-1
	El Paso........	58	-8	8	14	23	31	46	57	56	41	25	1	5	-8
	Houston	28	12	20	22	31	44	52	62	60	48	29	19	7	7
UT	Salt Lake City.....	69	-22	-30	2	14	25	35	40	37	27	16	-14	-21	-30
VT	Burlington	54	-30	-30	-20	2	24	33	39	35	25	15	-2	-26	-30
VA	Norfolk	49	-3	8	18	28	36	45	54	49	45	27	20	7	-3
	Richmond	68	-12	-10	11	23	31	40	51	46	35	21	10	-1	-12
WA	Seattle-Tacoma....	53	-	1	11	29	28	38	43	44	35	28	6	6	-
	Spokane	50	-22	-24	-7	17	24	33	37	35	24	10	-21	-25	-25
WV	Charleston.......	50	-16	-12	-	19	26	33	46	41	34	17	6	-12	-16
WI	Milwaukee	57	-26	-26	-10	12	21	33	40	44	28	18	-5	-20	-26
WY	Cheyenne	62	-29	-34	-21	-8	16	25	38	36	8	-1	-16	-28	-34
PR	San Juan........	43	61	62	60	64	66	69	69	70	69	67	66	63	60

- Represents zero.   [1] City office data.

Source: U.S. National Oceanic and Atmospheric Administration, *Comparative Climatic Data,* annual.

No. 423. Normal Monthly and Annual Precipitation—Selected Cities

[In Inches. Airport data, except as noted. Based on standard 30-year period, 1961 through 1990]

State	Station	Jan.	Feb.	Mar.	Apr.	May	June	July	Aug.	Sept.	Oct.	Nov.	Dec.	Annual
AL	Mobile	4.76	5.46	6.41	4.48	5.74	5.04	6.85	6.96	5.91	2.94	4.10	5.31	63.96
AK	Juneau	4.54	3.75	3.28	2.77	3.42	3.15	4.16	5.32	6.73	7.84	4.91	4.44	54.31
AZ	Phoenix	0.67	0.68	0.88	0.22	0.12	0.13	0.83	0.96	0.86	0.65	0.66	1.00	7.66
AR	Little Rock	3.42	3.61	4.91	5.49	5.17	3.57	3.60	3.26	4.05	3.75	5.20	4.83	50.86
CA	Los Angeles	2.40	2.51	1.98	0.72	0.14	0.03	0.01	0.15	0.31	0.34	1.76	1.66	12.01
	Sacramento	3.73	2.87	2.57	1.16	0.27	0.12	0.05	0.07	0.37	1.08	2.72	2.51	17.52
	San Diego	1.80	1.53	1.77	0.79	0.19	0.07	0.02	0.10	0.24	0.37	1.45	1.57	9.90
	San Francisco	4.35	3.17	3.06	1.37	0.19	0.11	0.03	0.05	0.20	1.22	2.86	3.09	19.70
CO	Denver	0.50	0.57	1.28	1.71	2.40	1.79	1.91	1.51	1.24	0.98	0.87	0.64	15.40
CT	Hartford	3.41	3.23	3.63	3.85	4.12	3.75	3.19	3.65	3.79	3.57	4.04	3.91	44.14
DE	Wilmington	3.03	2.91	3.43	3.39	3.84	3.55	4.23	3.40	3.43	2.88	3.27	3.48	40.84
DC	Washington	2.72	2.71	3.17	2.71	3.66	3.38	3.80	3.91	3.31	3.02	3.12	3.12	38.63
FL	Jacksonville	3.31	3.93	3.68	2.77	3.55	5.69	5.60	7.93	7.05	2.90	2.19	2.72	51.32
	Miami	2.01	2.08	2.39	2.85	6.21	9.33	5.70	7.58	7.63	5.64	2.66	1.83	55.91
GA	Atlanta	4.75	4.81	5.77	4.26	4.29	3.56	5.01	3.66	3.42	3.05	3.86	4.33	50.77
HI	Honolulu	3.55	2.21	2.20	1.54	1.13	0.50	0.59	0.44	0.78	2.28	3.00	3.80	22.02
ID	Boise	1.45	1.07	1.29	1.24	1.08	0.81	0.35	0.43	0.80	0.75	1.48	1.36	12.11
IL	Chicago	1.53	1.36	2.69	3.64	3.32	3.78	3.66	4.22	3.82	2.41	2.92	2.47	35.82
	Peoria	1.51	1.42	2.91	3.77	3.70	3.99	4.20	3.10	3.87	2.65	2.69	2.44	36.25
IN	Indianapolis	2.32	2.46	3.79	3.70	4.00	3.49	4.47	3.64	2.87	2.63	3.23	3.34	39.94
IA	Des Moines	0.96	1.11	2.33	3.36	3.66	4.46	3.78	4.20	3.53	2.62	1.79	1.32	33.12
KS	Wichita	0.79	0.96	2.43	2.38	3.81	4.31	3.13	3.02	3.49	2.22	1.59	1.20	29.33
KY	Louisville	2.86	3.30	4.66	4.23	4.62	3.46	4.51	3.54	3.16	2.71	3.70	3.64	44.39
LA	New Orleans	5.05	6.01	4.90	4.50	4.56	5.84	6.12	6.17	5.51	3.05	4.42	5.75	61.88
ME	Portland	3.53	3.33	3.67	4.08	3.62	3.44	3.09	2.87	3.09	3.90	5.17	4.55	44.34
MD	Baltimore	3.05	3.12	3.38	3.09	3.72	3.67	3.69	3.92	3.41	2.98	3.32	3.41	40.76
MA	Boston	3.59	3.62	3.69	3.60	3.25	3.09	2.84	3.24	3.06	3.30	4.22	4.01	41.51
MI	Detroit	1.76	1.74	2.55	2.95	2.92	3.61	3.18	3.43	2.89	2.10	2.67	2.82	32.62
	Sault Ste. Marie	2.42	1.74	2.30	2.35	2.71	3.14	2.71	3.61	3.69	3.23	3.45	2.88	34.23
MN	Duluth	1.22	0.80	1.91	2.25	3.03	3.82	3.61	3.99	3.84	2.49	1.80	1.24	30.00
	Minneapolis-St. Paul	0.95	0.88	1.94	2.42	3.39	4.05	3.53	3.62	2.72	2.19	1.55	1.08	28.32
MS	Jackson	5.24	4.70	5.82	5.57	5.05	3.18	4.51	3.77	3.55	3.26	4.81	5.91	55.37
MO	Kansas City	1.09	1.10	2.51	3.12	5.04	4.72	4.38	4.01	4.86	3.29	1.92	1.58	37.62
	St. Louis	1.81	2.12	3.58	3.50	3.97	3.72	3.85	2.85	3.12	2.68	3.28	3.03	37.51
MT	Great Falls	0.91	0.57	1.10	1.41	2.52	2.39	1.24	1.54	1.24	0.78	0.66	0.85	15.21
NE	Omaha	0.74	0.77	2.04	2.66	4.52	3.87	3.51	3.24	3.72	2.28	1.49	1.02	29.86
NV	Reno	1.07	0.99	0.71	0.38	0.69	0.46	0.28	0.32	0.39	0.38	0.87	0.99	7.53
NH	Concord	2.51	2.53	2.72	2.91	3.14	3.15	3.23	3.32	2.81	3.23	3.66	3.16	36.37
NJ	Atlantic City	3.46	3.06	3.62	3.56	3.33	2.64	3.83	4.14	2.93	2.82	3.58	3.32	40.29
NM	Albuquerque	0.44	0.46	0.54	0.52	0.50	0.59	1.37	1.64	1.00	0.89	0.43	0.50	8.88
NY	Albany	2.36	2.27	2.93	2.99	3.41	3.62	3.18	3.47	2.95	2.83	3.23	2.93	36.17
	Buffalo	2.70	2.31	2.68	2.87	3.14	3.55	3.08	4.17	3.49	3.09	3.83	3.67	38.58
	New York [1]	3.42	3.27	4.08	4.20	4.42	3.67	4.35	4.01	3.89	3.56	4.47	3.91	47.25
NC	Charlotte	3.71	3.84	4.43	2.68	3.82	3.39	3.92	3.73	3.50	3.36	3.23	3.48	43.09
	Raleigh	3.48	3.69	3.77	2.59	3.92	3.68	4.01	4.02	3.19	2.86	2.98	3.24	41.43
ND	Bismarck	0.45	0.43	0.77	1.67	2.18	2.72	2.14	1.72	1.49	0.90	0.49	0.51	15.47
OH	Cincinnati	2.59	2.69	4.24	3.75	4.28	3.84	4.24	3.35	2.88	2.86	3.46	3.15	41.33
	Cleveland	2.04	2.19	2.91	3.14	3.49	3.70	3.52	3.40	3.44	2.54	3.17	3.09	36.63
	Columbus	2.18	2.24	3.27	3.21	3.93	4.04	4.31	3.72	2.96	2.15	3.22	2.86	38.09
OK	Oklahoma City	1.13	1.56	2.71	2.77	5.22	4.31	2.61	2.60	3.84	3.23	1.98	1.40	33.36
OR	Portland	5.35	3.85	3.56	2.39	2.06	1.48	0.63	1.09	1.75	2.67	5.34	6.13	36.30
PA	Philadelphia	3.21	2.79	3.46	3.62	3.75	3.74	4.28	3.80	3.42	2.62	3.34	3.38	41.41
	Pittsburgh	2.54	2.39	3.41	3.15	3.59	3.71	3.75	3.21	2.97	2.36	2.85	2.92	36.85
RI	Providence	3.88	3.61	4.05	4.11	3.76	3.33	3.18	3.63	3.48	3.69	4.43	4.38	45.53
SC	Columbia	4.42	4.12	4.82	3.28	3.68	4.80	5.50	6.09	3.67	3.04	2.90	3.59	49.91
SD	Sioux Falls	0.51	0.64	1.64	2.52	3.03	3.40	2.68	2.85	3.02	1.78	1.09	0.70	23.86
TN	Memphis	3.73	4.35	5.41	5.46	4.98	3.57	3.79	3.43	3.53	3.01	5.10	5.74	52.10
	Nashville	3.58	3.81	4.85	4.37	4.88	3.57	3.97	3.46	3.46	2.62	4.12	4.61	47.30
TX	Dallas-Fort Worth	1.83	2.18	2.77	3.50	4.88	2.98	2.31	2.21	3.39	3.52	2.29	1.84	33.70
	El Paso	0.40	0.41	0.29	0.20	0.25	0.67	1.54	1.58	1.70	0.76	0.44	0.57	8.81
	Houston	3.29	2.96	2.92	3.21	5.24	4.96	3.60	3.49	4.89	4.27	3.79	3.45	46.07
UT	Salt Lake City	1.11	1.23	1.91	2.12	1.80	0.93	0.81	0.86	1.28	1.44	1.29	1.40	16.18
VT	Burlington	1.82	1.63	2.23	2.76	3.12	3.47	3.65	4.06	3.30	2.88	3.13	2.42	34.47
VA	Norfolk	3.78	3.47	3.70	3.06	3.81	3.82	5.06	4.81	3.90	3.15	2.85	3.23	44.64
	Richmond	3.24	3.16	3.61	2.96	3.84	3.62	5.03	4.40	3.34	3.53	3.17	3.26	43.16
WA	Seattle-Tacoma	5.38	3.99	3.54	2.33	1.70	1.50	0.76	1.14	1.88	3.23	5.83	5.91	37.19
	Spokane	1.98	1.49	1.49	1.18	1.41	1.26	0.67	0.72	0.73	0.99	2.15	2.42	16.49
WV	Charleston	2.91	3.04	3.63	3.31	3.94	3.59	4.99	4.01	3.24	2.89	3.59	3.39	42.53
WI	Milwaukee	1.60	1.45	2.67	3.50	2.84	3.24	3.47	3.53	3.38	2.41	2.51	2.33	32.93
WY	Cheyenne	0.40	0.39	1.03	1.37	2.39	2.08	2.09	1.69	1.27	0.74	0.53	0.42	14.40
PR	San Juan	2.81	2.15	2.35	3.76	5.93	4.00	4.37	5.32	5.28	5.71	5.94	4.72	52.34

[1] City office data.

Source: U.S. National Oceanic and Atmospheric Administration, *Climatography of the United States*, No. 81.

U.S. Census Bureau, Statistical Abstract of the United States: 1999

No. 424. Average Number of Days With Precipitation of .01 Inch or More—Selected Cities

[Airport data, except as noted. For period of record through 1997]

State	Station	Length of record (yr.)	Jan.	Feb.	Mar.	Apr.	May	June	July	Aug.	Sept.	Oct.	Nov.	Dec.	Annual
AL	Mobile	56	11	10	10	8	9	11	16	14	10	6	8	10	122
AK	Juneau	53	18	17	18	17	17	16	17	18	20	24	20	21	222
AZ	Phoenix	58	4	4	4	2	1	1	4	5	3	3	3	4	36
AR	Little Rock	55	10	9	10	10	10	8	8	7	7	7	8	9	105
CA	Los Angeles	62	6	6	6	3	1	-	1	*	*	1	2	3	5	35
	Sacramento	58	10	9	9	5	3	1	*	*	1	3	7	9	57
	San Diego	57	7	6	7	4	2	1	*	-	1	2	4	6	42
	San Francisco	70	11	10	10	6	3	1	*	*	1	4	7	10	62
CO	Denver	61	6	6	9	9	11	9	9	9	6	5	6	5	89
CT	Hartford	43	11	10	12	11	12	11	10	10	9	9	11	12	128
DE	Wilmington	50	11	9	11	11	11	10	9	9	8	8	10	10	117
DC	Washington	56	10	9	11	10	11	9	10	9	8	7	9	9	113
FL	Jacksonville	56	8	8	8	6	8	13	15	15	13	9	7	8	117
	Miami	55	7	6	6	6	10	15	16	17	17	14	8	7	131
GA	Atlanta	63	12	10	11	9	9	10	12	10	8	7	9	10	115
HI	Honolulu	48	10	9	9	9	7	6	7	6	7	9	9	10	98
ID	Boise	58	12	10	10	8	8	6	2	3	4	6	10	11	90
IL	Chicago	39	11	9	12	13	11	10	9	9	9	9	11	11	126
	Peoria	58	9	8	11	12	11	10	9	8	9	8	9	10	114
IN	Indianapolis	58	12	10	13	12	12	10	10	9	8	8	10	12	126
IA	Des Moines	58	8	7	10	11	11	11	9	9	9	8	7	8	108
KS	Wichita	44	5	5	8	8	11	9	8	8	8	6	5	6	86
KY	Louisville	50	11	10	13	12	12	10	10	8	8	8	10	11	124
LA	New Orleans	49	10	9	9	7	8	11	14	13	10	6	7	10	115
ME	Portland	57	11	10	12	12	13	11	10	9	9	9	12	12	129
MD	Baltimore	47	11	9	11	11	11	9	9	9	8	8	9	10	114
MA	Boston	46	12	10	12	11	12	11	9	10	9	9	11	12	127
MI	Detroit	39	13	11	13	13	11	10	10	9	10	10	12	13	136
	Sault Ste. Marie	56	19	15	13	11	11	11	10	11	13	14	17	19	166
MN	Duluth	56	12	9	11	11	12	13	12	11	12	10	11	12	134
	Minneapolis-St. Paul	59	9	7	10	10	11	12	10	10	10	8	9	9	115
MS	Jackson	34	11	9	10	8	9	8	10	10	8	7	8	10	109
MO	Kansas City	25	7	7	10	11	12	10	9	9	8	7	8	7	105
	St. Louis	40	9	8	11	11	11	9	9	8	8	8	10	9	111
MT	Great Falls	60	9	8	9	9	12	12	8	8	7	6	7	8	101
NE	Omaha	61	6	7	9	10	12	10	9	9	8	6	6	7	99
NV	Reno	55	6	6	6	4	4	3	2	2	2	3	5	6	51
NH	Concord	56	11	10	11	12	12	11	10	10	9	9	11	11	126
NJ	Atlantic City	54	11	10	11	11	10	9	9	9	8	7	9	10	113
NM	Albuquerque	58	4	4	5	3	5	4	9	10	6	5	4	4	61
NY	Albany	51	12	11	12	12	13	11	10	10	10	9	12	12	135
	Buffalo	54	20	17	16	14	13	11	10	10	11	12	16	19	169
	New York [1]	128	11	10	11	11	11	10	11	10	8	8	9	10	121
NC	Charlotte	58	10	10	11	9	10	10	11	10	7	7	8	10	112
	Raleigh	53	10	10	10	9	10	9	11	10	8	7	8	9	113
ND	Bismarck	58	8	7	8	8	10	11	9	8	7	6	7	8	96
OH	Cincinnati	50	12	11	13	13	12	11	10	9	8	8	11	12	130
	Cleveland	56	16	14	15	14	13	11	10	10	10	11	15	16	156
	Columbus	58	13	11	14	13	13	11	11	9	8	9	12	13	137
OK	Oklahoma City	58	5	6	7	8	10	9	6	7	7	6	5	6	83
OR	Portland	57	18	16	17	15	12	9	4	5	8	12	18	19	152
PA	Philadelphia	57	11	9	11	11	11	10	9	9	8	10	10	10	117
	Pittsburgh	45	16	14	16	14	13	12	11	10	10	10	13	16	153
RI	Providence	44	11	10	12	11	11	11	9	9	9	9	11	12	125
SC	Columbia	50	10	10	10	8	9	10	12	11	8	6	7	9	110
SD	Sioux Falls	52	6	7	9	9	11	11	10	9	8	6	7	6	98
TN	Memphis	47	10	9	11	10	9	9	9	7	7	6	9	10	107
	Nashville	56	11	10	12	11	11	10	10	9	8	7	10	11	119
TX	Dallas-Fort Worth	44	7	7	7	8	9	7	5	5	7	6	6	6	79
	El Paso	58	4	3	2	2	2	3	8	8	6	4	3	4	49
	Houston	28	11	9	9	7	9	9	9	9	9	8	8	9	106
UT	Salt Lake City	69	10	9	10	10	8	5	5	6	5	6	8	9	91
VT	Burlington	54	14	12	13	13	14	12	12	12	12	12	14	15	155
VA	Norfolk	49	11	10	11	10	10	9	11	10	8	8	8	9	116
	Richmond	60	10	9	11	9	11	9	11	9	8	7	8	9	113
WA	Seattle-Tacoma	53	18	15	17	14	11	9	5	6	9	13	18	19	155
	Spokane	50	14	11	11	9	9	8	5	5	6	8	13	15	113
WV	Charleston	50	15	14	15	14	13	12	13	11	9	9	12	14	152
WI	Milwaukee	57	11	9	12	12	12	11	10	9	9	9	11	11	125
WY	Cheyenne	62	6	6	9	10	12	11	11	10	8	6	6	6	101
PR	San Juan	42	17	13	13	13	16	15	19	18	17	17	19	19	196

[1] City office data.

Source: U.S. National Oceanic and Atmospheric Administration, *Comparative Climatic Data*, annual.

258 Geography and Environment

No. 425. Snow and Ice Pellets—Selected Cities

[**In inches.** Airport data, except as noted. For period of record through 1997. T denotes trace]

State	Station	Length of record (yr.)	Jan.	Feb.	Mar.	Apr.	May	June	July	Aug.	Sept.	Oct.	Nov.	Dec.	Annual
AL	Mobile	55	0.1	0.1	0.1	T	T	-	T	-	-	-	T	0.1	0.4
AK	Juneau	53	25.9	19.4	15.2	3.3	-	T	-	-	T	1	12.5	22.3	99.6
AZ	Phoenix	60	T	-	T	T	T	-	-	-	-	T	-	-	T
AR	Little Rock	55	2.4	1.5	0.5	T	T	-	-	-	-	T	0.2	0.6	5.2
CA	Los Angeles	62	T	T	T	-	-	-	-	-	-	-	T	T	T
	Sacramento	49	T	T	T	-	T	-	-	-	-	-	-	T	T
	San Diego	57	T	-	T	-	-	-	-	-	-	-	T	T	T
	San Francisco	69	-	T	T	-	-	-	-	-	-	-	T	T	T
CO	Denver	61	8.1	7.5	12.5	8.9	1.6	-	T	T	1.6	3.7	9.1	7.3	60.3
CT	Hartford	42	13	12	10	1.5	-	T	-	-	-	0.1	2.1	10.3	49.0
DE	Wilmington	49	6.8	6.1	3.3	0.2	T	T	T	-	-	0.1	0.9	3.3	20.7
DC	Washington	54	5.5	5.4	2.2	T	T	-	T	T	-	-	0.8	2.8	16.7
FL	Jacksonville	56	T	-	-	T	-	T	T	-	-	-	-	-	T
	Miami	55	-	-	-	-	-	-	-	-	-	-	-	-	-
GA	Atlanta	62	0.9	0.5	0.4	T	-	-	-	-	-	T	-	0.2	2.0
HI	Honolulu	51	-	-	-	-	-	-	-	-	-	-	-	-	-
ID	Boise	58	6.5	3.7	1.6	0.6	0.1	T	T	T	-	0.1	2.3	5.8	20.7
IL	Chicago	38	10.7	8.2	6.6	1.6	0.1	T	T	T	T	0.4	1.9	8.3	37.8
	Peoria	54	6.6	5.4	3.9	0.8	-	-	T	-	T	0.1	2	5.9	24.7
IN	Indianapolis	66	6.7	5.7	3.4	0.5	-	T	T	-	T	0.2	1.9	5.1	23.5
IA	Des Moines	57	8.3	7.2	6	1.8	-	T	T	-	T	0.3	3.1	6.7	33.4
KS	Wichita	44	4.4	4.1	2.5	0.2	T	T	T	T	T	-	1.3	3.2	15.7
KY	Louisville	50	5.4	4.3	3.3	0.1	T	T	T	-	-	0.1	1	2.1	16.3
LA	New Orleans	50	-	0.1	T	T	T	-	-	-	-	-	T	0.1	0.2
ME	Portland	57	19.6	17.2	13	3.1	0.2	-	-	-	T	0.2	3.3	14.7	71.3
MD	Baltimore	47	6.3	6.8	3.8	0.1	T	-	-	-	-	-	1	3.2	21.2
MA	Boston	61	12.8	11.8	8	0.9	-	-	-	-	T	-	1.3	7.6	42.4
MI	Detroit	39	10.4	9.2	6.9	1.7	T	-	-	-	T	0.2	2.9	9.9	41.2
	Sault Ste. Marie	55	29	18.4	14.7	5.8	0.5	T	-	T	0.1	2.4	15.8	31.1	117.8
MN	Duluth	54	17.7	11.5	13.6	6.7	0.7	T	-	T	0.1	1.5	12.9	15.7	80.4
	Minneapolis-St. Paul	59	10	8.3	10.6	2.8	0.1	T	T	T	-	0.5	8	9.5	49.8
MS	Jackson	34	0.5	0.2	0.2	-	-	-	-	-	-	-	-	0.1	1.0
MO	Kansas City	63	5.8	4.5	3.4	0.8	T	T	T	-	T	0.1	1.2	4.4	20.2
	St. Louis	61	5.4	4.5	4	0.5	-	T	T	-	-	T	1.4	3.8	19.6
MT	Great Falls	60	9.6	8.4	10.5	7.3	1.7	0.3	T	0.1	1.5	3.4	7.4	8.3	58.5
NE	Omaha	62	7.3	6.6	6.3	1	0.1	T	-	-	T	0.3	2.6	5.6	29.8
NV	Reno	54	5.8	5.2	4.3	1.2	0.8	-	-	-	-	0.3	2.4	4.3	24.3
NH	Concord	56	18	14.6	11.2	2.5	0.1	T	-	-	T	0.1	4.1	13.8	64.4
NJ	Atlantic City	51	5	5.3	2.5	0.3	T	T	T	-	-	T	0.4	2.2	15.7
NM	Albuquerque	58	2.5	2.1	1.8	0.6	-	T	T	T	T	0.1	1.2	2.6	10.9
NY	Albany	51	16.5	14.3	11.5	2.6	0.1	T	-	-	T	0.2	4.3	14.8	64.3
	Buffalo	54	23.9	18.3	11.7	3.2	0.2	T	T	T	T	0.3	11.4	23	92.0
	New York [1]	129	7.6	8.7	5.1	0.9	T	-	-	-	-	-	0.9	5.4	28.6
NC	Charlotte	58	2	1.6	1.2	-	T	-	-	-	-	T	0.1	0.5	5.4
	Raleigh	53	2.3	2.5	1.3	-	T	T	T	-	-	-	0.1	0.8	7.0
ND	Bismarck	58	7.7	6.9	8.7	4	0.9	T	T	T	0.2	1.8	6.8	7	44.0
OH	Cincinnati	50	7.3	5.4	4.4	0.5	-	T	-	-	-	0.3	2	3.7	23.6
	Cleveland	56	13.2	12.2	10.5	2.4	0.1	T	T	-	T	0.6	5.4	11.9	56.3
	Columbus	50	8.8	6.2	4.6	0.9	-	T	T	-	T	0.1	2.2	5.4	28.2
OK	Oklahoma City	58	3.1	2.4	1.5	T	T	T	T	-	T	-	0.5	1.8	9.3
OR	Portland	55	3.2	1.1	0.4	T	-	T	-	T	T	-	0.4	1.4	6.5
PA	Philadelphia	55	6.1	6.6	3.7	0.3	T	T	T	-	-	-	0.7	3.2	20.6
	Pittsburgh	45	11.9	9.3	8.8	1.7	0.1	T	T	T	T	0.4	3.5	8.3	44.0
RI	Providence	44	10.1	10	7.5	0.7	0.2	-	-	-	T	-	1.1	6.8	36.5
SC	Columbia	50	0.4	0.8	0.2	T	-	-	-	T	-	-	T	0.3	1.7
SD	Sioux Falls	52	6.7	8.2	9.2	2.8	T	T	T	-	-	0.8	5.6	7.2	40.5
TN	Memphis	47	2.2	1.4	0.8	T	T	T	T	-	-	-	0.1	0.6	5.1
	Nashville	56	3.7	3	1.5	-	-	T	-	T	-	-	0.4	1.4	10.0
TX	Dallas-Fort Worth	43	1.1	0.9	0.2	T	T	-	-	-	-	T	0.1	0.2	2.5
	El Paso	57	1.3	0.8	0.4	0.3	T	T	T	-	T	-	0.9	1.6	5.3
	Houston	63	0.2	0.2	-	T	T	-	-	-	-	-	T	T	0.4
UT	Salt Lake City	69	13.9	9.7	9.3	4.9	0.6	T	T	T	0.1	1.3	6.9	11.8	58.5
VT	Burlington	54	19.1	16.7	13	4.2	0.2	-	T	-	-	0.2	6.9	18.3	78.6
VA	Norfolk	48	2.8	3	1	-	T	-	-	-	-	-	0.2	2	7.7
	Richmond	60	4.8	4	2.4	0.1	T	-	T	-	-	-	0.4	2	13.7
WA	Seattle-Tacoma	52	4.9	1.6	1.3	0.1	T	-	T	-	T	-	1.1	2.4	11.4
	Spokane	50	15.7	7.6	3.9	0.6	0.1	T	-	-	T	0.4	6.4	14.7	49.4
WV	Charleston	49	11.1	8.7	5.4	0.9	-	T	T	T	T	0.2	2.4	5.3	34.0
WI	Milwaukee	57	13.5	9.8	8.4	1.8	0.1	T	T	T	T	0.2	3.2	10.3	47.3
WY	Cheyenne	62	6.7	6.3	12	9.2	3.2	0.2	T	T	0.9	3.8	7.2	6.2	55.7
PR	San Juan	42	-	-	-	-	-	-	-	-	-	T	-	-	T

- Represents zero or rounds to zero.   [1] City office data.

Source: U.S. National Oceanic and Atmospheric Administration, *Comparative Climatic Data*, annual.

U.S. Census Bureau, *Statistical Abstract of the United States: 1999*

No. 426. Sunshine, Average Wind Speed, Heating and Cooling Degree Days, and Average Relative Humidity—Selected Cities

[Airport data, except as noted. For period of record through 1997, except as noted. M=morning. A=afternoon]

State	Station	Average percentage of possible sunshine [1] — Length of record (yr.)	Annual	Average wind speed (m.p.h.) — Length of record (yr.)	Annual	Jan.	July	Heating degree days	Cooling degree days	Average relative humidity (percent) — Length of record (yr.)	Annual M	Annual A	Jan. M	Jan. A	July M	July A
AL	Mobile	47	60	49	8.9	10.2	6.9	1,702	2,627	35	87	59	82	62	90	62
AK	Juneau	47	23	52	8.3	8.0	7.5	8,897	-	31	80	69	79	76	78	66
AZ	Phoenix	57	81	52	6.2	5.3	7.1	1,350	4,162	37	50	23	65	32	43	20
AR	Little Rock	35	60	55	7.8	8.4	6.7	3,155	2,005	36	83	57	80	62	86	55
CA	Los Angeles	60	72	49	7.5	6.7	7.9	1,458	727	38	78	65	71	60	86	68
	Sacramento	49	73	47	7.9	7.2	8.9	2,749	1,237	35	81	45	90	70	75	28
	San Diego	55	72	57	7.0	6.0	7.5	1,256	984	37	77	63	71	57	82	66
	San Francisco	68	71	70	10.6	7.2	13.6	3,016	145	38	84	62	86	67	86	59
CO	Denver	61	67	47	8.6	8.6	8.3	6,020	679	35	67	40	63	49	68	34
CT	Hartford	41	52	43	8.4	9.0	7.3	6,151	677	38	77	52	72	56	79	51
DE	Wilmington	47	55	49	9.0	9.8	7.8	4,937	1,046	50	78	55	75	60	80	54
DC	Washington	48	55	49	9.4	10.0	8.3	4,047	1,549	37	75	53	70	56	77	53
FL	Jacksonville	47	61	48	7.9	8.1	7.0	1,434	2,551	61	88	56	87	58	89	58
	Miami	46	68	48	9.2	9.5	7.9	200	4,198	33	84	61	84	59	84	63
GA	Atlanta	61	59	59	9.1	10.4	7.7	2,991	1,667	37	82	56	78	59	88	59
HI	Honolulu	47	74	48	11.3	9.5	13.1	-	4,474	28	72	56	81	61	68	51
ID	Boise	56	58	58	8.7	8.0	8.4	5,861	754	38	69	43	80	71	54	22
IL	Chicago	37	52	39	10.4	11.7	8.4	6,536	752	39	80	61	77	69	82	58
	Peoria	52	53	54	9.9	11.1	7.8	6,148	982	38	83	63	80	70	87	61
IN	Indianapolis	64	51	49	9.6	10.9	7.5	5,615	1,014	38	84	62	81	71	87	60
IA	Des Moines	46	55	48	10.7	11.5	8.9	6,497	1,036	36	80	61	77	68	83	58
KS	Wichita	39	62	44	12.2	12.0	11.3	4,791	1,628	44	80	56	79	63	79	50
KY	Louisville	47	53	50	8.3	9.5	6.8	4,514	1,288	37	81	58	77	65	85	58
LA	New Orleans	47	60	49	8.1	9.3	6.1	1,513	2,655	49	88	64	85	67	91	66
ME	Portland	54	55	57	8.7	9.1	7.6	7,378	268	57	79	59	76	61	80	59
MD	Baltimore	45	58	47	9.0	9.7	7.8	4,707	1,137	44	77	54	72	57	80	53
MA	Boston	60	55	60	12.5	13.8	11.0	5,641	678	33	72	58	68	58	74	56
MI	Detroit	37	49	39	10.3	12.0	8.5	6,569	626	39	81	60	80	70	82	54
	Sault Ste. Marie	54	43	56	9.2	9.6	7.8	9,316	131	36	85	67	81	74	89	62
MN	Duluth	47	49	48	11.0	11.6	9.4	9,818	180	36	81	64	77	70	85	60
	Minneapolis-St. Paul	57	54	59	10.5	10.5	9.4	7,981	682	38	79	61	75	67	81	56
MS	Jackson	30	59	34	7.2	8.4	5.6	2,467	2,215	34	91	59	86	65	94	61
MO	Kansas City	23	59	25	10.7	11.3	9.3	5,393	1,288	25	81	61	77	65	85	59
	St. Louis	47	55	48	9.7	10.6	8.0	4,758	1,534	37	82	60	81	67	84	57
MT	Great Falls	57	51	56	12.6	15.0	10.0	7,741	388	36	67	45	66	61	67	31
NE	Omaha	49	59	61	10.5	10.9	8.8	6,300	1,072	33	81	60	78	66	85	60
NV	Reno	53	69	55	6.6	5.6	7.2	5,674	328	34	69	31	79	51	61	18
NH	Concord	54	55	55	6.7	7.3	5.7	7,554	328	32	81	54	76	59	84	51
NJ	Atlantic City	37	56	39	9.9	10.9	8.3	5,169	826	33	82	56	78	59	83	58
NM	Albuquerque	56	76	58	8.9	8.0	8.9	4,425	1,244	37	59	29	68	40	59	27
NY	Albany	57	49	59	8.9	9.7	7.5	6,894	507	32	80	57	78	63	81	55
	Buffalo	52	43	58	11.9	14.1	10.3	6,747	477	37	80	62	79	72	78	55
	New York [2]	42	64	60	9.3	10.7	7.6	4,805	1,096	63	72	56	68	60	75	55
NC	Charlotte	49	58	48	7.4	7.8	6.6	3,341	1,582	37	82	53	78	56	86	56
	Raleigh	47	59	48	7.7	8.5	6.7	3,457	1,417	33	85	54	79	55	89	58
ND	Bismarck	56	55	58	10.2	10.0	9.2	8,968	488	38	81	58	75	69	84	49
OH	Cincinnati	44	49	50	9.0	10.6	7.2	5,248	996	35	82	60	79	68	85	57
	Cleveland	54	45	56	10.5	12.2	8.6	6,201	621	37	80	62	78	70	81	57
	Columbus	46	48	48	8.3	9.8	6.5	5,708	797	38	80	59	77	68	84	56
OK	Oklahoma City	44	64	49	12.3	12.6	10.9	3,659	1,859	32	80	56	78	60	80	51
OR	Portland	47	39	49	7.9	10.0	7.6	4,522	371	57	85	59	85	75	82	45
PA	Philadelphia	55	56	45	9.1	10.6	7.3	4,954	1,101	38	76	55	73	59	79	54
	Pittsburgh	43	44	42	8.3	8.9	7.3	5,968	654	37	79	57	76	66	83	54
RI	Providence	19	58	48	8.6	9.1	7.8	5,884	606	34	75	55	71	56	77	56
SC	Columbia	48	60	49	6.8	7.2	6.3	2,649	1,966	31	87	51	82	54	89	54
SD	Sioux Falls	50	57	49	11.1	11.0	9.8	7,809	744	34	82	62	78	69	84	56
TN	Memphis	43	59	48	9.8	10.0	7.5	3,082	2,118	58	81	58	78	64	84	58
	Nashville	54	57	56	8.0	9.1	6.5	3,729	1,616	32	84	58	79	64	89	58
TX	Dallas-Fort Worth	42	64	44	10.7	11.0	9.8	2,407	2,603	34	82	57	80	61	81	50
	El Paso	53	80	55	8.8	8.3	8.3	2,708	2,094	37	56	27	65	35	61	29
	Houston	26	56	28	7.8	8.2	6.9	1,599	2,700	28	90	61	85	65	93	59
UT	Salt Lake City	69	62	68	8.8	7.5	9.5	5,765	1,047	38	67	43	79	69	52	22
VT	Burlington	52	44	54	9.0	9.8	8.0	7,771	388	32	77	59	73	64	78	53
VA	Norfolk	47	58	49	10.6	11.5	8.9	3,495	1,422	49	78	57	75	59	82	59
	Richmond	50	56	49	7.7	8.1	6.9	3,963	1,348	63	83	53	80	57	85	56
WA	Seattle-Tacoma [3]	51	38	49	9.0	9.6	8.3	4,908	190	38	83	62	81	74	81	49
	Spokane	48	48	50	8.9	8.8	8.6	6,842	398	38	78	52	85	79	64	28
WV	Charleston	47	48	50	6.0	7.2	4.8	4,646	1,031	50	83	56	78	63	90	59
WI	Milwaukee	55	52	57	11.5	12.6	9.7	7,324	479	37	80	65	76	69	82	62
WY	Cheyenne	60	64	40	12.9	15.3	10.4	7,326	285	38	65	45	57	50	70	38
PR	San Juan	40	76	42	8.4	8.4	9.7	-	5,558	42	79	65	82	64	79	67

- Represents zero. [1] Percent of days that are either clear or partly cloudy. [2] Airport data for sunshine. [3] Does not represent airport data.

Source: U.S. National Oceanic and Atmospheric Administration, *Comparative Climatic Data,* annual.

260 Geography and Environment

Parks, Recreation, and Travel

This section presents data on national parks and forests, state parks, recreational activities, the arts and humanities, and domestic and foreign travel.

Parks and recreation—The Department of the Interior has responsibility for administering the national parks. As part of this function, issues reports relating to the usage of public parks for recreation purposes. The National Park Service publishes information on visits to national park areas in its annual report, *National Park Statistical Abstract. The National Parks: Index (year)* is a biannual report which has appeared under a variety of Index titles prior to 1985. Beginning with the 1985 edition, the report has appeared under the current title. The Index contains brief descriptions, with acreages, of each area administered by the Service, plus certain "related" areas. A statistical summary of Service-administered areas is also presented. The annual *Federal Recreation Fee Report* summarizes the prior year's recreation fee receipts and recreation visitation statistics for seven Federal land managing agencies.

Statistics for state parks are compiled by the National Association of State Park Directors which issues its *Annual Information Exchange*. The Department of Agriculture's Forest Service, in its *Report of the Forest Service*, issues data on recreational uses of the national forests.

Visitation—Statistics presented on visitation to reporting areas are collected by several different agencies and groups. The methodology used to collect these results may vary accordingly, from visual counts and estimates to the use of electromagnetic traffic counters. In using and comparing these data, one should also be aware of several different definitions that follow: Recreation visit, which is the entry of any person into an area for recreation purposes; nonrecreation visits, which include visits going to and from inholdings, through traffic, tradespeople and personnel with business in the area; and visitor hour, which constitutes the presence of a person in a recreation area or site for recreational purposes for periods of time aggregating 60 minutes.

Recreation and leisure activities—Data on the participation in various recreation and leisure time activities are based on several sample surveys. Data on participation in fishing, hunting, and other forms of wildlife-associated recreation are published periodically by the U.S. Department of Interior, Fish and Wildlife Service. The most recent data are from the 1991 survey. Data on participation in various sports recreation activities are published by the National Sporting Goods Association.

Travel—Information on foreign travel and personal expenditures abroad, as well as expenditures by foreign citizens traveling in the United States, is compiled annually by the U.S. Bureau of Economic Analysis and published in selected issues of the monthly *Survey of Current Business*. Statistics on arrivals to the United States are reported by the International Trade Administration (ITA). Sources of statistics on departures from the United States include the Department of Transportation's *International Air Travel Statistics* and other sources. Data on domestic travel, business receipts and employment of the travel industry, and travel expenditures are published by the U.S. Travel Data Center, which is the research department of the Travel Industry Association and the national non-profit center for travel and tourism research which is located in Washington, DC. Other data on household transportation characteristics may be found in Section 21, Land Transportation.

[For fiscal years ending in year shown, except as noted; see text, Section 10, Federal Government. (986.1 represents $986,100,000). Includes data for five areas in Puerto Rico and Virgin Islands, one area in American Samoa, and one area in Guam]

Item	1990	1991	1992	1993	1994	1995	1996	1997
Finances (mil. dol.): [1]								
Expenditures reported	986.1	1,104.4	1,268.7	1,429.4	1,404.0	1,445.0	1,391.0	1,473.0
Salaries and wages	459.1	495.3	518.1	596.1	627.2	633.0	650.0	683.0
Improvements, maintenance	160.0	179.6	212.1	224.8	222.9	234.0	234.0	246.0
Construction	108.5	134.1	193.3	226.8	205.6	192.0	168.0	188.0
Other	258.5	295.4	345.2	379.7	348.3	386.0	339.0	356.0
Funds available	1,505.5	1,988.4	2,274.8	2,346.5	2,307.7	2,225.0	2,116.0	2,301.0
Appropriations	1,052.5	1,284.7	1,392.8	1,334.0	1,388.8	1,325.0	1,346.0	1,625.0
Other [2]	453.0	703.7	882.0	1,012.5	918.9	900.0	770.0	676.0
Revenue from operations	78.6	78.1	88.3	89.5	97.0	106.3	133.2	174.8
Recreation visits (millions): [3]								
All areas	258.7	267.8	274.7	273.1	268.6	269.6	265.8	275.3
National parks [4]	57.7	57.4	58.7	59.8	63.0	64.8	63.1	65.3
National monuments	23.9	25.8	26.6	26.5	23.6	23.5	23.6	24.1
National historical, commemorative, archaeological [5]	57.5	61.0	63.3	61.9	59.5	56.9	59.0	63.0
National parkways	29.1	28.8	30.7	30.4	29.3	31.3	30.9	31.6
National recreation areas [4]	47.2	49.8	50.3	50.8	52.3	53.7	52.6	51.6
National seashores and lakeshores	23.3	24.4	23.9	24.1	24.0	22.5	20.3	22.4
National Capital Parks	7.5	7.5	8.1	9.1	5.4	5.5	6.1	5.1
Miscellaneous other areas	12.5	13.1	13.1	10.5	11.8	11.4	11.3	12.1
Recreation overnight stays (millions) [3]	17.6	17.7	18.3	17.7	18.3	16.8	16.6	15.8
In commercial lodgings	3.9	4.0	4.1	4.0	3.9	3.8	3.7	3.6
In Park Service campgrounds	7.9	7.8	8.1	7.5	7.6	7.1	6.5	6.3
In tents	4.1	4.2	4.4	4.1	4.2	3.9	3.7	3.6
In recreation vehicles	3.8	3.6	3.7	3.4	3.4	3.2	2.8	2.7
In backcountry	1.7	2.0	2.2	2.4	2.4	2.2	2.1	2.2
Other	4.2	3.9	3.9	3.8	4.4	3.7	3.7	3.8
Land (1,000 acres): [6]								
Total	76,362	76,607	76,492	75,515	74,905	77,355	77,458	77,457
Parks	46,089	46,135	46,208	45,521	48,111	49,307	49,315	49,384
Recreation areas	3,344	3,346	3,347	3,349	3,351	3,353	3,353	3,329
Other	26,929	27,126	26,937	26,645	23,443	24,695	24,790	24,744
Acquisition, gross	21	66	23	39	32	27	98	142
By purchase	18	15	21	29	29	25	10	36
By gift	2	43	1	10	1	1	3	2
By transfer or exchange	3	8	1	1	(Z)	(Z)	85	104
Exclusion	1	(Z)	(Z)	(Z)	(Z)	(Z)	(Z)	(Z)
Acquisition, net	21	66	23	39	32	27	98	142

Z Less than 500 acres. [1] Financial data are those associated with the National Park System. Certain other functions of the National Park Service (principally the activities absorbed from the former Heritage Conservation and Recreation Service in 1981) are excluded. [2] Includes funds carried over from prior years. [3] For calendar year. [4] For 1990, combined data for North Cascades National Park and two adjacent National Recreation Areas are included in National Parks total. [5] Includes military areas. [6] Federal land only, as of Dec. 31. Federal land acreages, in addition to National Park Service administered lands, also include lands within national park system area boundaries but under the administration of other agencies. Year-to-year changes in the Federal lands figures include changes in the acreages of these other lands and hence often differ from "net acquisition."
Source: U.S. National Park Service, Visits, National Park Statistical Abstract, annual; and unpublished data. Other data are unpublished.

No. 428. National Forest Recreation Use, Summary: 1980 to 1996

[Estimated for year ending September 30 (233,549 represents 233,549,000). Represents recreational use of National Forest land and water in states which have a Forest Service recreation program]

Year and activity	Recreation visitor-days [1] (1,000)	Percent	State	Recreation visitor-days [1] 1996 (1,000)	State or other area	Recreation visitor-days [1] 1996 (1,000)
1980	233,549	100.0	U.S.	341,200	NV	3,857
1984	227,554	100.0			NH	3,354
1985	225,407	100.0	AL	689	NM	9,326
1986	226,533	100.0	AK	6,962	NY	39
1987	238,458	100.0	AZ	35,000	NC	6,979
1988	242,316	100.0	AR	2,210	ND	133
1989	252,495	100.0	CA	71,165	OH	524
1990	263,051	100.0	CO	30,971	OK	393
1991	278,849	100.0	FL	2,960	OR	37,030
1992	287,691	100.0	GA	2,925	PA	3,268
1993	295,473	100.0	ID	15,365	SC	1,011
1994	330,348	100.0	IL	1,188	SD	3,571
1995	345,083	100.0	IN	684	TN	3,309
1996, total	341,200	100.0	KS	86	TX	2,302
Mechanized travel and viewing scenery	122,141	35.8	KY	2,326	UT	19,378
Camping, picnicking, and swimming	87,082	25.5	LA	599	VT	1,395
Hiking, horseback riding, and water travel	33,099	9.7	MA	158	VA	4,927
Winter sports	19,708	5.8	MI	4,866	WA	24,797
Hunting	19,384	5.7	MN	5,982	WV	1,499
Resorts, cabins, and organization camps	17,702	5.2	MS	1,828	WI	2,527
Fishing	18,160	5.3	MO	2,518	WY	9,114
Nature studies	3,299	1.0	MT	13,495		
Other [2]	20,627	6.0	NE	320	PR	171

[1] One recreation visitor-day is the recreation use of National Forest land or water that aggregates 12 visitor-hours. This may entail 1 person for 12 hours, 12 persons for 1 hour, or any equivalent combination of individual or group use, either continuous or intermittent. [2] Includes team sports, gathering forest products, attending talks and programs, and other uses.
Source: U.S. Forest Service, Annual Report.

[For year ending June 30 (12,484 represents 12,484,000). Data are shown as reported by state park directors. In some states, park agency has under its control forests, fish and wildlife areas, and/or other areas. In other states, agency is responsible for state parks only]

State	Acreage (1,000)	Visitors (1,000) [1]	Revenue Total ($1,000)	Percent of operating expenditures	State	Acreage (1,000)	Visitors (1,000) [1]	Revenue Total ($1,000)	Percent of operating expenditures
United States ...	12,484	783,400	590,054	44.6	Missouri	135	16,706	5,909	23.8
Alabama	50	5,826	23,321	83.5	Montana	51	1,371	1,117	22.9
Alaska	3,289	4,055	1,930	38.2	Nebraska	133	9,491	12,196	72.7
Arizona	46	2,245	4,287	41.6	Nevada	132	3,131	1,532	23.1
Arkansas	51	7,773	12,998	53.8	New Hampshire	154	910	5,575	104.3
California	1,356	115,741	63,183	34.4	New Jersey	334	14,570	7,142	27.0
Colorado	348	11,767	10,264	57.4	New Mexico	91	3,202	3,345	25.2
Connecticut	176	8,140	3,611	40.1	New York	308	67,006	54,106	45.1
Delaware	17	2,724	5,594	44.2	North Carolina	144	10,701	2,541	16.5
Florida	511	13,741	23,459	50.6	North Dakota	20	1,095	719	36.5
Georgia	71	13,691	16,927	33.4	Ohio	204	58,122	23,061	41.4
Hawaii	25	15,071	266	4.8	Oklahoma	71	15,997	20,585	98.5
Idaho	42	2,288	3,341	46.0	Oregon	92	39,678	12,854	41.7
Illinois	401	40,391	5,369	13.6	Pennsylvania	283	34,387	12,077	19.9
Indiana	178	17,548	23,361	107.1	Rhode Island	9	3,046	3,039	50.6
Iowa	63	12,404	2,900	31.9	South Carolina	82	9,518	14,630	69.5
Kansas	29	6,690	3,200	52.5	South Dakota	94	6,442	6,235	76.7
Kentucky	43	8,636	41,964	64.9	Tennessee	135	28,938	23,921	53.0
Louisiana	39	1,339	2,478	22.9	Texas	629	21,818	12,897	39.6
Maine	587	1,963	1,654	25.4	Utah	114	7,301	6,565	35.3
Maryland	292	10,559	9,614	32.8	Vermont	65	897	4,950	93.3
Massachusetts	277	13,169	3,523	11.2	Virginia	66	4,903	5,457	41.8
Michigan	266	23,416	32,511	88.5	Washington	263	48,539	10,905	35.7
Minnesota	247	8,331	10,250	47.7	West Virginia	196	7,971	15,559	58.6
Mississippi	24	4,745	5,994	43.5	Wisconsin	127	13,235	10,454	69.7
					Wyoming	127	2,171	683	14.8

[1] Includes overnight visitors.

Source: National Association of State Park Directors, Tuscon, AZ, *1998 Annual Information Exchange.*

No. 430. Personal Consumption Expenditures for Recreation: 1990 to 1996

[In billions of dollars (281.6 represents $281,600,000,000), except percent. Represents market value of purchases of goods and services by individuals and nonprofit institutions]

Type of product or service	1990	1991	1992	1993	1994	1995	1996
Total recreation expenditures	281.6	292.0	310.8	340.2	370.2	402.5	431.1
Percent of total personal consumption [1]	7.3	7.3	7.4	7.6	7.8	8.1	8.3
Books and maps	16.5	16.9	17.7	19.0	20.6	22.1	23.2
Magazines, newspapers, and sheet music	21.5	21.9	21.6	22.7	24.5	25.5	26.5
Nondurable toys and sport supplies	31.6	32.8	34.2	36.6	39.7	42.2	45.4
Wheel goods, sports and photographic equipment [2]	29.8	29.5	29.9	32.6	35.6	39.1	42.0
Video and audio products, computer equipment, and musical instruments	53.8	57.3	61.2	68.1	78.5	85.2	89.7
Radio and television repair	4.2	4.0	4.2	4.5	4.5	4.9	5.1
Flowers, seeds, and potted plants	11.1	11.3	12.3	12.7	13.4	13.9	14.9
Admissions to specified spectator amusements	15.1	15.7	16.6	18.1	19.0	20.2	22.1
Motion picture theaters	5.2	5.3	5.0	5.2	5.6	6.0	6.3
Legitimate theaters and opera, and entertainments of nonprofit institutions [3]	5.6	6.0	6.8	7.8	8.2	8.7	9.3
Spectator sports [4]	4.4	4.5	4.8	5.1	5.2	5.5	6.4
Clubs and fraternal organizations except insurance [5]	8.9	9.6	10.3	11.2	11.8	12.7	13.0
Commercial participant amusements [6]	23.0	23.8	27.2	31.5	36.2	41.5	46.2
Pari-mutuel net receipts	3.4	3.3	3.3	3.3	3.3	3.3	3.5
Other [7]	62.7	65.9	72.4	80.0	83.1	91.9	99.6

[1] See Table 729. [2] Includes boats and pleasure aircraft. [3] Except athletic. [4] Consists of admissions to professional and amateur athletic events and to racetracks, including horse, dog, and auto. [5] Consists of dues and fees excluding insurance premiums. [6] Consists of billiard parlors; bowling alleys; dancing, riding, shooting, skating, and swimming places; amusement devices and parks; golf courses; sightseeing buses and guides; private flying operations; casino gambling; and other commercial participant amusements. [7] Consists of net receipts of lotteries and expenditures for purchases of pets and pet care services, cable TV, film processing, photographic studios, sporting and recreation camps, video cassette rentals, and recreational services, not elsewhere classified.

Source: U.S. Bureau of Economic Analysis, *The National Income and Product Accounts of the United States, 1929-94,* Vol.1, and *Survey of Current Business,* August, 1997.

No. 431. Expenditures Per Consumer Unit for Entertainment and Reading: 1985 to 1997

[Data are **annual averages. In dollars, except as indicated.** Based on Consumer Expenditure Survey; see text, Section 14, Income, for description of survey. See also headnote, Table 738. For composition of regions, see map, inside front cover]

Year and characteristic	Entertainment and reading		Entertainment				Reading
	Total	Percent of total expenditures	Total	Fees and admissions	Television, radios, and sound equipment	Other equipment and services [1]	Reading
1985.	1,311	5.6	1,170	320	371	479	141
1988.	1,479	5.7	1,329	353	416	560	150
1989.	1,581	5.7	1,424	377	429	618	157
1990.	1,575	5.6	1,422	371	454	597	153
1991.	1,635	5.5	1,472	378	468	627	163
1992.	1,662	5.6	1,500	379	492	629	162
1993.	1,792	5.8	1,626	414	590	621	166
1994.	1,732	5.5	1,567	439	533	595	165
1995.	1,775	5.5	1,612	433	542	637	163
1996.	1,993	5.9	1,834	459	561	814	159
1997, total	**1,977**	**5.7**	**1,813**	**471**	**577**	**766**	**164**
Age of reference person:							
Under 25 years old.	1,115	6.0	1,051	263	437	350	64
25 to 34 years old	1,997	5.7	1,865	424	618	822	132
35 to 44 years old	2,289	5.7	2,129	574	671	884	160
45 to 54 years old	2,621	5.8	2,416	679	683	1054	205
55 to 64 years old	2,098	5.8	1,900	451	561	888	198
65 to 74 years old	1,495	5.4	1,300	390	470	440	195
75 years old and over	1,009	5.0	861	180	314	367	148
Origin of reference person:							
Hispanic.	1,203	4.1	1,137	237	474	426	66
Non-Hispanic	2,048	5.8	1,875	492	587	796	173
Race of reference person:							
White and other.	2,115	5.9	1,940	509	587	845	175
Black.	949	3.7	872	191	507	174	77
Region of residence:							
Northeast.	1,961	5.4	1,769	528	581	660	192
Midwest.	2,085	6.2	1,915	468	560	886	170
South	1,691	5.2	1,561	358	570	633	130
West	2,339	6.0	2,153	604	605	943	186
Size of consumer unit:							
One person	1,136	5.4	1,011	296	394	321	125
Two or more persons	2,312	5.7	2,133	541	651	941	179
Two persons	2,166	5.9	1,969	468	563	937	197
Three persons	2,289	5.6	2,118	517	669	932	171
Four persons	2,643	5.8	2,462	698	770	995	181
Five persons or more	2,327	5.3	2,191	575	718	899	136

[1] Other equipment and services includes pets, toys, and playground equipment; sports, exercise, and photographic equipment; and recreational vehicles.

Source: U.S. Bureau of Labor Statistics, *Consumer Expenditure Survey, annual.*

No. 432. Motion Pictures and Amusement and Recreation Services— Annual Receipts: 1990 to 1997

[**In millions of dollars (39,982 represents $39,982,000,000).** For taxable employer and nonemployer firms. Based on the Service Annual Survey; see Appendix III]

Kind of business	1987 SIC code [1]	1990	1993	1994	1995	1996	1997
Motion pictures.	78	39,982	49,799	53,504	57,184	60,279	63,010
Production, distribution, and allied services	781, 782	28,888	37,653	40,256	43,264	46,274	48,216
Theaters	783	6,088	5,977	6,233	6,530	7,044	7,589
Video tape rental.	784	5,006	6,169	7,015	7,390	6,961	7,204
Amusement and recreation services.	79	50,126	63,651	68,453	77,452	85,733	93,794
Dance studios, schools, and halls.	791	626	880	906	947	1,046	1,075
Theatrical producers (except motion picture), bands, orchestras, and entertainers	792	10,735	15,408	16,050	17,479	19,597	21,655
Bowling centers.	793	2,800	2,724	2,709	2,681	2,751	2,765
Commercial sports.	794	8,636	9,870	11,090	13,056	14,589	16,669
Professional sports clubs and promoters	7941	3,702	5,056	6,138	7,695	8,841	10,034
Racing, including track operation	7948	4,934	4,814	4,952	5,360	5,748	6,635
Miscellaneous amusement and recreation services [2] . .	799	27,329	34,769	37,698	43,290	47,748	51,631
Physical fitness facilities	7991	3,623	3,961	4,033	4,412	4,975	5,713
Public golf courses	7992	2,254	2,828	3,059	3,584	3,979	4,290
Coin-operated amusement devices.	7993	2,146	2,763	2,965	3,254	3,491	3,651
Amusement parks	7996	4,922	5,641	5,858	6,298	6,777	7,312
Membership sports and recreation clubs	7997	4,825	5,965	6,379	6,765	7,427	7,657

[1] 1987 Standard Industrial Classification code; see text, Section 17, Business.   [2] Includes kinds of businesses, not shown separately.

Source: U.S. Census Bureau, *Current Business Reports, Service Annual Survey: 1997,* BS/97.

No. 433. Quantity of Books Sold and Value of U.S. Domestic Consumer Expenditures: 1982 to 1997

[Includes all titles released by publishers in the United States and imports which appear under the imprints of American publishers. (1,732 represents 1,732,000,000). Multivolume sets, such as encyclopedias, are counted as one unit]

Type of publication and market area	Units sold (mil.)					Consumer expenditures (mil. dol.)				
	1982	1985	1990	1995	1997	1982	1985	1990	1995	1997
Total [1]	1,723	1,788	2,005	2,186	2,144	9,889	12,611	19,043	25,154	26,450
Hardbound, total	646	694	824	827	758	6,190	7,969	11,789	15,011	15,343
Softbound, total	1,077	1,094	1,181	1,359	1,386	3,699	4,642	7,254	10,143	11,107
Trade	459	553	705	813	759	2,484	3,660	6,498	9,340	9,173
Adult	315	360	403	465	424	2,028	2,871	4,777	7,060	6,832
Juvenile	144	193	301	348	335	456	789	1,721	2,280	2,341
Religious	144	134	130	148	157	706	926	1,362	1,792	1,958
Professional	106	110	131	146	146	1,630	2,043	2,957	4,153	4,465
Bookclubs	133	130	108	123	134	510	582	705	949	1,113
Elhi text	233	234	209	237	275	1,067	1,415	1,948	2,384	2,866
College text	115	110	137	142	154	1,388	1,575	2,319	2,708	3,110
Mail order publications	134	121	138	92	83	581	650	752	578	539
Mass market paperbacks— rack sized	382	382	433	470	419	1,102	1,244	1,775	2,322	2,220
General retailers	756	829	1,010	1,145	1,078	3,743	5,103	8,465	11,888	11,958
College stores	224	225	255	274	274	1,910	2,309	3,403	4,311	4,698
Libraries and institutions [2]	80	80	88	97	96	888	1,090	1,592	2,111	2,210
Schools [2]	262	260	244	273	309	1,313	1,685	2,365	2,896	3,388
Direct to consumers	319	300	304	289	291	1,889	2,214	2,901	3,544	3,820
Other	82	94	104	108	96	146	210	316	404	378

[1] Types of publications include university press publications and subscription reference works, not shown separately.   [2] Elhi libraries included in schools.

Source: Book Industry Study Group, Inc., New York, NY, *Book Industry Trends, 1998*, annual (copyright).

No. 434. Book Purchasing by Adults: 1991 and 1997

[In percent. Excludes books purchased for or by children under age 13. Based on a survey of 16,000 households conducted over 12 months ending in December of year shown. For details, see source]

Characteristic	Total		Mass market [1]		Trade [2]		Hardcover	
	1991	1997	1991	1997	1991	1997	1991	1997
Total	100.0	100.0	100.0	100.0	100.0	100.0	100.0	100.0
Age of purchaser:								
Under 25 years old	4.3	5.6	3.7	4.4	5.2	7.2	4.4	5.3
25 to 34 years old	18.8	15.4	13.9	13.2	25.4	17.9	19.6	14.6
35 to 44 years old	23.7	26.0	22.8	21.4	25.2	29.8	23.7	25.8
45 to 54 years old	22.4	25.0	26.0	25.0	18.5	25.7	20.5	24.8
55 to 64 years old	15.6	13.3	15.8	15.9	13.9	9.5	17.2	15.5
65 years old and over	15.2	14.7	17.8	20.1	11.8	9.9	14.6	14.0
Household income:								
Under $30,000	37.1	32.8	41.7	37.9	32.6	29.8	34.1	29.9
$30,000 to 49,999	27.2	25.4	27.3	26.4	27.7	25.4	26.5	24.3
$50,000 to 59,999	11.0	8.9	9.8	8.7	12.3	9.6	11.5	8.3
$60,000 to 69,999	6.9	9.3	7.0	7.8	7.2	9.8	6.3	10.6
$70,000 and over	17.8	23.6	14.2	19.2	20.2	25.4	21.6	26.9
Household size:								
Singles	20.8	19.6	17.7	18.9	24.1	20.2	22.8	19.8
Families with no children	40.4	42.6	42.3	43.2	38.0	41.9	39.7	42.7
Families with children	38.8	37.8	40.0	37.9	37.9	37.9	37.5	37.5
Age of reader:								
Under 25 years old	7.3	8.0	5.2	5.8	10.1	11.5	7.7	7.0
25 to 34 years old	18.7	15.9	14.1	13.9	24.7	19.2	20.2	16.0
35 to 44 years old	22.9	23.8	22.3	20.4	24.0	26.9	22.7	24.9
45 to 54 years old	20.8	22.6	24.9	23.8	16.5	22.5	18.4	24.1
55 to 64 years old	14.9	13.3	15.9	16.2	12.7	9.3	15.6	12.3
65 years old and over	15.4	16.4	17.6	19.9	12.0	10.6	15.6	15.7
Category of book:								
Popular fiction	54.9	50.4	93.0	93.6	14.9	16.9	31.8	36.0
General nonfiction	10.3	8.9	3.6	2.5	15.6	10.1	16.5	15.1
Cooking/crafts	10.2	10.2	0.4	0.3	20.6	15.8	18.2	15.6
Other	24.6	30.5	3.0	3.6	48.9	57.2	33.5	33.3
Sales outlet:								
Independent	32.5	17.2	26.5	10.0	44.9	26.1	29.0	15.9
Chain book store	22.0	25.2	17.2	21.9	27.4	27.3	25.2	26.8
Book clubs	16.6	20.3	17.8	22.5	9.5	14.4	22.6	24.2
Other [3]	28.9	37.3	38.5	45.6	18.2	32.2	23.2	33.1

[1] "Pocket size" books sold primarily through magazine and news outlets, supermarkets, variety stores, etc.   [2] All paperback books, except mass market.   [3] Includes mail order, price clubs, discount stores, food/drug stores, used book stores, and other outlets.

Source: Book Industry Study Group, Inc., New York, NY, *Consumer Research Study on Book Purchasing*, annual (copyright).

U.S. Census Bureau, Statistical Abstract of the United States: 1999

No. 435. Profile of Consumer Expenditures for Sound Recordings: 1990 to 1998

[In percent, except total value (7,541.1 represents $7,541,100,000). Based on monthly telephone surveys of the population 10 years old and over]

Item	1990	1995	1998	Item	1990	1995	1998
Total value (mil. dol.)	7,541.1	12,320.3	13,723.5	Music club	8.9	14.3	9.0
PERCENT DISTRIBUTION [1]				Mail order.............	2.5	4.0	2.9
				Internet ..	(NA)	(NA)	1.1
Age: 10 to 14 years........	7.6	8.0	9.1	Music type: [2]			
15 to 19 years...........	18.3	17.1	15.8	Rock	36.1	33.5	25.7
20 to 24 years...........	16.5	15.3	12.2	Country	9.6	16.7	14.1
25 to 29 years...........	14.6	12.3	11.4	R&B	11.6	11.3	12.8
30 to 34 years...........	13.2	12.1	11.4	Pop	13.7	10.1	10.0
35 to 39 years...........	10.2	10.8	12.6	Rap...................	8.5	6.7	9.7
40 to 44 years...........	7.8	7.5	8.3	Classical	3.1	2.9	3.3
45 years and over	11.1	16.1	18.1	Jazz	4.8	3.0	1.9
Sex: Male	54.4	53.0	48.7	Oldies	0.8	1.0	0.7
Female	45.6	47.0	51.3	Gospel................	2.5	3.1	6.3
Sales outlet:				Soundtracks	0.8	0.9	1.7
Record store...........	69.8	52.0	50.8	New age	1.1	0.7	0.6
Other store...........	18.5	28.2	34.4	Children's............	0.5	0.5	0.4

NA Not available.   [1] Percent distributions exclude nonresponses and responses of don't know.   [2] As classified by respondent.

Source: Recording Industry Association of America, Inc., Washington, DC, *1998 Consumer Profile*.

No. 436. Household Pet Ownership: 1996

[(31.2 represents 31,200,000). Based on a sample survey of 80,000 households in 1996; for details, see source]

Item	Unit	Dog	Cat	Pet bird	Horse
Households owning companion pets [1]	Million . . .	31.2	27.0	4.6	1.5
Percent of all households.................	Percent . . .	31.6	27.3	4.6	1.5
Average number owned................	Number . . .	1.7	2.2	2.7	2.7
Total companion pet population [1]	Million . . .	52.9	59.1	12.6	4.0
Households obtaining veterinary care [2].............	Percent . . .	85.3	67.7	10.8	59.1
Average visits per household per year	Number . . .	2.6	1.9	0.2	2.3
PERCENT DISTRIBUTION OF HOUSEHOLDS OWNING PETS					
Annual household income:					
Under $12,500	Percent . . .	12.7	13.9	17.3	9.5
$12,500 to $24,999	Percent . . .	19.1	19.7	20.9	20.3
$25,000 to $39,999	Percent . . .	21.6	21.5	22.0	21.8
$40,000 to $59,999	Percent . . .	21.5	21.2	17.5	23.1
$60,000 and over	Percent . . .	25.2	23.7	22.3	25.4
Family size: [1]					
One person	Percent . . .	13.2	16.8	12.7	12.1
Two persons	Percent . . .	31.0	32.6	27.9	29.1
Three persons	Percent . . .	21.4	20.6	20.4	22.0
Four or more persons	Percent . . .	34.5	29.9	38.9	36.7

[1] As of December.   [2] During 1996.

Source: American Veterinary Medical Association, Schaumburg, IL, *U.S. Pet Ownership and Demographics Sourcebook, 1997* (copyright).

No. 437. Household Participation in Lawn and Garden Activities: 1993 to 1997

[For calendar year (22,410 represents $22,410,000,000). Based on national household sample survey conducted by the Gallup Organization. Subject to sampling variability; see source]

Activity	Percent households engaged in—					Retail sales (mil. dol.)				
	1993	1994	1995	1996	1997	1993	1994	1995	1996	1997
Total	71	74	72	64	67	22,410	25,897	22,242	22,519	26,639
Lawn care.............	54	56	53	47	45	6,446	8,417	7,621	6,925	6,366
Indoor houseplants........	31	37	30	31	29	689	999	864	791	1,107
Flower gardening	39	44	38	37	38	2,396	3,147	2,107	2,987	3,404
Insect control...........	24	28	24	24	21	1,080	1,127	1,049	1,734	1,342
Shrub care	28	30	25	25	24	1,274	1,133	774	1,059	1,441
Vegetable gardening.......	26	31	28	26	23	1,063	1,476	1,359	1,341	1,914
Tree care	21	22	17	20	18	2,011	1,408	1,002	1,362	1,892
Landscaping	24	26	20	22	23	5,006	5,797	5,524	3,964	6,153
Flower bulbs	22	28	21	21	21	453	635	377	521	573
Fruit trees...........	13	14	11	12	11	759	389	241	349	455
Container gardening	11	12	12	10	11	441	359	377	387	558
Raising transplants	10	11	8	8	7	201	182	187	238	383
Herb gardening	8	10	8	9	8	175	112	140	144	168
Growing berries	6	6	5	5	5	126	85	55	90	60
Ornamental gardening......	6	5	5	5	6	290	264	144	158	251
Water gardening	(NA)	5	5	4	5	(NA)	367	421	469	572

NA Not available.   [1] Starting plants in advance of planting in ground.

Source: The National Gardening Association, Burlington, VT, *National Gardening Survey*, annual (copyright).

No. 438. Participants in Wildlife Related Recreation Activities: 1996

[In thousands (39,694 represents 39,694,000). For persons 16 years old and over engaging in activity at least once in 1996. Based on survey and subject to sampling error; see source for details]

Participant	Number	Days of participation	Trips	Participant	Number	Days of participation
Total sportsmen [1]	39,694	882,569	729,495	Wildlife watchers [1]	62,868	(X)
Total anglers	35,246	625,893	506,557	Nonresidential [2]	23,652	313,790
Freshwater	29,734	515,115	420,010	Observe wildlife	22,878	278,683
Excluding Great Lakes ..	28,921	485,474	402,814	Photograph wildlife ..	12,038	79,342
Great Lakes	2,039	20,095	17,195	Feed wildlife........	9,976	89,606
Saltwater.............	9,438	103,034	86,547	Residential [3]	60,751	(X)
Total hunters	13,975	256,676	222,938	Observe wildlife	44,063	(X)
Big game	11,288	153,784	113,971	Photograph wildlife ..	16,021	(X)
Small game	6,945	75,117	63,744	Feed wild birds [4]	54,122	(X)
Migratory birds	3,073	26,501	22,509	Visit public parks....	11,011	(X)
Other animals.........	1,521	24,522	22,714	Maintain plantings or natural areas	13,401	(X)

X Not applicable. [1] Detail does not add to total due to multiple responses and nonresponse. [2] Persons taking a trip of at least 1 mile for activity. [3] Activity wihin 1 mile of home. [4] Or other wildlife.

No. 439. Expenditures for Wildlife Related Recreation Activities: 1996

[See headnote, Table 438. (37,797 represents $37,797,000,000)]

Type of expenditure	Fishing			Hunting			Wildlife watching		
	Expenditures (mil. dol.)	Spenders Number (1,000)	Percent of anglers	Expenditures (mil. dol.)	Spenders Number (1,000)	Percent of hunters	Expenditures (mil. dol.)	Spenders Number (1,000)	Percent of watchers
Total [1]	37,797	34,002	96	20,613	13,769	99	29,228	52,729	84
Food and lodging	5,990	28,452	81	2,512	11,073	79	5,352	17,922	76
Food	4,256	28,267	80	2,078	11,060	79	3,447	17,761	75
Lodging	1,734	8,020	23	434	1,909	14	1,905	6,783	29
Transportation	3,730	28,741	82	1,780	12,022	86	2,943	20,260	86
Public	559	1,780	5	145	479	3	811	2,229	9
Private	3,171	28,382	81	1,634	11,926	85	2,132	19,863	84
Other trip-related costs ...	5,661	28,398	81	864	4,378	31	1,150	9,340	39
Sport specific equipment [2] ...	5,309	24,726	70	5,519	11,278	81	8,230	47,355	75
Auxiliary equipment [3]	1,037	6,006	17	1,233	5,730	41	858	4,763	8
Special equipment [4]	12,828	3,599	10	4,521	805	6	7,564	1,094	2
Other expenditures [5]	3,242	24,944	71	4,185	12,471	89	3,132	23,827	40

[1] Total not adjusted for multiple responses or nonresponse. [2] Items owned primarily for each specific activity, such as rods and reels for fishing and guns and rifles for hunting. [3] Equipment such as camping gear owned for wildlife-associated recreation. [4] "Big ticket" equipment such as campers and boats owned for wildlife-associated recreation. [5] Books, magazines, membership dues and contributions, land leasing and ownership, licenses and plantings.

Source of Tables 438 and 439: U.S. Fish and Wildlife Service, 1996 National Survey of Fishing, Hunting, and Wildlife Associated Recreation.

No. 440. Participation in NCAA Sports: 1996-97

[Excludes sports sponsored by fewer than 10 institutions]

Sport	Males			Females		
	Teams	Athletes	Average squad	Teams	Athletes	Average squad
Total	7,705	200,627	(X)	7,684	128,209	(X)
Baseball	829	24,442	29.5	(X)	(X)	(X)
Basketball........	950	15,141	15.9	966	13,392	13.9
Crew [1]	49	1,820	37.2	(X)	(X)	(X)
Cross country	792	10,271	13.0	838	10,141	12.1
Fencing	36	657	18.3	42	558	13.3
Field hockey	(X)	(X)	(X)	228	4,857	21.3
Football	601	53,984	89.8	(X)	(X)	(X)
Golf	678	7,197	10.6	282	2,323	8.2
Gymnastics [2]	28	413	14.8	91	1,311	14.4
Ice hockey	125	3,608	28.9	22	436	19.8
Lacrosse	182	5,705	31.4	182	4,068	22.4
Rifle...........	42	408	9.7	(X)	(X)	(X)
Rowing..........	(X)	(X)	(X)	97	3,951	40.7
Skiing...........	40	575	14.4	40	455	11.4
Soccer..........	681	17,053	25.0	691	14,829	21.5
Softball..........	(X)	(X)	(X)	770	13,167	17.1
Squash [1]	25	418	16.7	26	381	14.6
Swimming........	368	7,508	20.4	432	8,745	20.2
Tennis..........	776	7,999	10.3	859	8,223	9.6
Track, indoor	512	15,957	31.2	528	13,061	24.7
Track, outdoor	625	19,305	30.9	644	15,578	24.2
Volleyball	74	1,052	14.2	923	12,284	13.3
Water polo [2]	42	893	21.3	23	452	19.6
Wrestling	250	6,219	24.9	(X)	(X)	(X)

X Not applicable. [1] Sport recognized by the NCAA but does not have an NCAA championship. [2] Sport recognized by the NCAA but does not have an NCAA championship for women.

Source: The National Collegiate Athletic Association (NCAA), Overland Park, KS, 1996-97 Participation Study.

U.S. Census Bureau, Statistical Abstract of the United States: 1999

No. 441. Selected Spectator Sports: 1985 to 1997

[47,742 represents 47,742,000]

Sport	Unit	1985	1987	1990	1993	1994	1995	1996	1997
Baseball, major leagues: [1]									
Attendance	1,000	47,742	53,182	55,512	71,237	50,010	51,288	61,665	64,921
Regular season	1,000	46,824	52,011	54,824	70,257	50,010	50,469	60,097	63,168
National League	1,000	22,292	24,734	24,492	36,924	25,808	25,110	30,379	31,885
American League	1,000	24,532	27,277	30,332	33,333	24,202	25,359	29,718	31,283
Playoffs [2]	1,000	591	784	479	636	(X)	533	1,300	1,349
World Series	1,000	327	387	209	344	(X)	286	268	404
Players' salaries: [3]									
Average	$1,000	371	412	598	1,076	1,168	1,111	1,120	1,337
Basketball: [4][5]									
NCAA—Men's college:									
Teams	Number	753	760	767	831	858	868	866	865
Attendance	1,000	26,584	26,798	28,741	28,527	28,390	28,548	28,225	27,738
NCAA—Women's college:									
Teams	Number	746	756	782	826	859	864	874	879
Attendance	1,000	2,072	2,156	2,777	4,193	4,557	4,962	5,234	6,734
Pro: [6]									
Teams	Number	23	23	27	27	27	27	29	29
Attendance, total [7]	1,000	11,534	13,190	18,586	19,120	19,350	19,883	21,833	21,677
Regular season	1,000	10,506	12,065	17,369	17,778	17,984	18,516	20,513	20,305
Average per game	Number	11,141	12,795	15,690	16,060	16,246	16,727	17,252	17,077
Players' salaries:									
Average	$1,000	325	440	750	1,300	1,700	1,900	2,000	2,200
Football:									
NCAA college: [5]									
Teams	Number	509	507	533	560	568	565	566	581
Attendance	1,000	34,952	35,008	35,330	34,871	36,460	35,638	36,083	36,858
National Football League: [8]									
Teams	Number	28	28	28	28	(NA)	(NA)	(NA)	(NA)
Attendance, total [9]	1,000	14,058	[10]15,180	17,666	14,772	(NA)	(NA)	(NA)	(NA)
Regular season	1,000	13,345	[10]11,406	13,960	13,967	(NA)	(NA)	(NA)	(NA)
Average per game	Number	59,567	[10]54,315	62,321	62,352	(NA)	(NA)	(NA)	(NA)
Postseason games [11]	1,000	711	656	848	805	(NA)	(NA)	(NA)	(NA)
Players' salaries: [12]									
Average	$1,000	194	203	352	683	637	714	791	725
Median base salary	$1,000	140	175	236	330	325	335	350	340
National Hockey League: [13]									
Regular season attendance	1,000	11,621	12,118	12,344	15,714	10,646	15,658	16,237	15,701
Playoffs attendance	1,000	1,153	1,337	1,442	1,440	1,329	1,447	1,423	1,384
Horse racing: [14][15]									
Racing days	Number	13,745	14,208	13,841	13,237	13,082	13,243	12,457	11,958
Attendance	1,000	73,346	70,105	63,803	45,688	42,065	38,934	43,367	41,846
Pari-mutuel turnover	Mil. dol	12,222	13,122	7,162	13,718	14,143	14,592	14,902	15,220
Revenue to government	Mil. dol	625	608	624	472	452	456	444	422
Greyhound: [14]									
Total performances	Number	9,590	11,156	14,915	17,976	17,035	16,110	15,151	14,557
Attendance	1,000	23,853	26,215	28,660	(NA)	(NA)	(NA)	(NA)	14,306
Pari-mutuel turnover	Mil. dol	2,702	3,193	3,422	3,255	2,948	2,730	2,433	2,291
Revenue to government	Mil. dol	201	221	235	195	183	157	139	114
Jai alai: [14]									
Total performances	Number	2,736	2,906	3,620	3,200	3,146	2,748	2,542	2,648
Games played	Number	32,260	38,476	(NA)	43,056	42,607	37,052	34,346	(NA)
Attendance	1,000	4,722	6,816	5,329	4,194	3,684	3,208	(NA)	2,125
Total handle	Mil. dol	664.0	707.5	545.5	384.2	330.7	296.4	273.4	251
Revenue to government	Mil. dol	50	51	39	27	22	13	12	10
Professional rodeo: [16]									
Rodeos	Number	617	637	754	791	782	739	742	742
Performances	Number	1,887	1,832	2,159	2,269	2,245	2,217	2,229	2,229
Members	Number	5,239	5,342	5,693	5,760	6,415	6,894	7,084	7,084
Permit-holders (rookies)	Number	2,534	2,746	3,290	2,888	3,346	3,835	4,141	4,141

NA Not available. X Not applicable. [1] Source: The National League of Professional Baseball Clubs, New York, NY, *National League Green Book;* and The American League of Professional Baseball Clubs, New York, NY, *American League Red Book.* [2] Beginning 1996, two rounds of playoffs were played. Prior years had one round. [3] Source: Major League Baseball Players Association, New York, NY. [4] Season ending in year shown. [5] Source: National Collegiate Athletic Assn., Overland Park, KS. For women's attendance total, excludes double-headers with men's teams. [6] Source: National Basketball Assn., New York, NY. For season ending in year shown. [7] Includes All-Star game, not shown separately. [8] Source: National Football League, New York, NY. [9] 1987 and 1990 includes preseason attendance, not shown separately. [10] Season was interrupted by a strike. [11] Includes Pro Bowl, a nonchampionship game and Super Bowl. [12] Source: National Football League Players Association, Washington, DC. [13] For season beginning in year shown. Source: National Hockey League, Montreal, Quebec. [14] Source: Association of Racing Commissioners International, Inc., Lexington, KY. [15] Includes thoroughbred, harness, quarter horse, and fairs. [16] Source: Professional Rodeo Cowboys Association, Colorado Springs, CO., *Official Professional Rodeo Media Guide,* annual (copyright).

Source: Compiled from sources listed in footnotes.

268 Parks, Recreation, and Travel

U.S. Census Bureau, Statistical Abstract of the United States: 1999

No. 442. Selected Recreational Activities: 1975 to 1997

[26 represents 26,000,000]

Activity	Unit	1975	1980	1985	1990	1994	1995	1996	1997
Softball, amateur: [1]									
Total participants [2]	Million	26	30	41	41	42	42	42	42
Youth participants	1,000	450	650	712	1,100	1,209	1,350	1,416	1,438
Adult teams [3]	1,000	66	110	152	188	196	187	183	178
Youth teams [3]	1,000	9	18	31	46	68	74	79	80
Golfers (one round or more) [4][5]	1,000	13,036	15,112	17,520	27,800	24,300	25,000	24,737	26,474
Golf rounds played [5]	1,000	308,562	357,701	414,777	502,000	464,800	490,200	477,400	547,200
Golf facilities	Number	11,370	12,005	12,346	12,846	13,683	14,074	14,341	14,602
Classification:									
Private	Number	4,770	4,839	4,861	4,810	4,367	4,324	4,306	4,257
Daily fee	Number	5,014	5,372	5,573	6,024	7,126	7,491	7,729	7,984
Municipal	Number	1,586	1,794	1,912	2,012	2,190	2,259	2,306	2,361
Tennis: [6]									
Players	1,000	[7]34,000	(NA)	13,000	21,000	16,500	17,820	19,499	19,500
Courts	1,000	130	(NA)	220	220	240	240	245	245
Indoor	1,000	8	(NA)	14	14	15	15	15	15
Tenpin bowling: [8]									
Participants, total	Million	62.5	72.0	67.0	71.0	79.0	79.0	91.0	91.0
Male	Million	29.9	34.0	32.0	35.4	36.3	36.3	41.8	41.8
Female	Million	32.6	38.0	35.0	35.6	42.6	42.6	49.2	49.2
Establishments	Number	8,577	8,591	8,275	7,611	7,183	7,049	6,880	6,688
Lanes	1,000	141	154	155	148	142	139	136	133
Membership, total [9]	1,000	8,751	9,664	8,064	6,588	5,201	4,925	4,662	4,405
American Bowling Congress	1,000	4,300	4,688	3,657	3,036	2,455	2,370	2,261	2,135
Women's Bowling Congress	1,000	3,692	4,187	3,714	2,859	2,191	2,036	1,917	1,798
Young American Bowling Alliance [10]	1,000	759	789	693	693	555	519	484	472
Motion picture theaters [11]	1,000	15	18	21	24	26	28	30	32
Four-wall	1,000	11	14	18	23	26	27	29	31
Drive-in	1,000	4	4	3	1	(Z)	1	1	1
Receipts, box office	Mil. dol.	2,115	2,749	3,749	5,022	5,396	5,494	5,912	6,366
Admission, average price	Dollars	2.05	2.69	3.55	4.23	4.18	4.35	4.42	4.59
Attendance	Million	1,033	1,022	1,056	1,189	1,292	1,263	1,339	1,388
Boating: [12]									
Recreational boats owned	1,000	(NA)	11,832	13,778	15,987	16,239	15,375	15,830	16,284
Retail expenditures on boating [13]	Mil. dol.	4,800	7,370	13,284	13,731	14,071	17,226	17,753	19,344
Retail units purchased:									
Total all boats [14]	1,000	(NA)	570	637	504	563	649	619	596
Outboard boats	1,000	(NA)	290	305	227	220	231	215	200
Inboard boats	1,000	(NA)	8	17	15	11	12	11	12
Sterndrive boats	1,000	(NA)	56	115	97	90	94	95	92
Jet boats [15]	1,000	(NA)	69	34	19	(NA)	15	14	12
Canoes	1,000	(NA)	105	79	75	100	98	93	104
Personal watercraft [16]	1,000	(NA)	21	50	42	142	200	191	176
Boat trailers	1,000	(NA)	176	192	165	176	207	194	181
Outboard motors	1,000	(NA)	315	392	352	308	317	308	302
Sterndrive and inboard engines	1,000	(NA)	88	155	134	114	120	120	116

NA Not available.   Z Fewer than 500.   [1] Source: Amateur Softball Association, Oklahoma City, OK.   [2] Amateur Softball Association teams and other amateur softball teams.   [3] Amateur Softball Association teams only.   [4] Source: National Golf Foundation, Jupiter, FL.   [5] Prior to 1990, for persons 5 years of age and over; thereafter for persons 12 years of age and over.   [6] Source: Tennis Industry Association, North Palm Beach, FL. Players for persons 12 years old and over who played at least once.   [7] 1974 data.   [8] For season ending in year shown. Persons 5 years old and over. Source: Bowling Headquarters, Greendale, WI.   [9] Membership totals are for U.S., Canada and for U.S. military personnel worldwide.   [10] Prior to 1985, represents American Jr. Bowling Congress and ABC/WIBC Collegiate Division.   [11] Source: Motion Picture Association of America, Inc., Encino, CA. For 1975, figures represent theaters; thereafter, screens.   [12] Source: National Marine Manufacturers Association, Chicago, IL.   [13] Represents estimated expenditures for new and used boats, motors and engines, accessories, safety equipment, fuel, insurance, docking, maintenance, launching, storage, repairs, and other expenses.   [14] 1980 through 1990 includes auxiliary sailboats; 1980 through 1992 includes inflatable boats, not shown separately.   [15] 1980 through 1990, count of nonpowered sailboats.   [16] 1980 through 1990, count of sailboats.

Source: Compiled from sources listed in footnotes.

U.S. Census Bureau, Statistical Abstract of the United States: 1999

No. 443. Participation in Selected Sports Activities: 1997

[In thousands (240,328 represents 240,328,000), except rank. For persons 7 years of age or older. Except as indicated, a participant plays a sport more than once in the year]

Activity	All persons Number	Rank	Sex Male	Female	Age 7-11 years	12-17 years	18-24 years	25-34 years	35-44 years	45-54 years	55-64 years	65 years and over	Household income (dol.) Under 15,000	15,000-24,999	25,000-34,999	35,000-49,999	50,000-74,999	75,000 and over
SERIES I SPORTS [1]																		
Total	240,328	(X)	116,731	123,594	19,527	23,053	24,689	39,624	43,930	33,592	21,815	34,095	39,603	33,976	34,657	44,837	48,304	38,948
Number participated in—																		
Aerobic exercising [2]	26,259	11	6,231	20,028	816	2,113	4,490	6,920	5,454	3,237	1,585	1,644	3,009	3,117	3,494	5,161	5,348	6,130
Backpacking [3]	12,005	20	7,287	4,718	1,101	1,781	2,067	3,264	2,472	939	291	91	1,730	1,708	1,642	1,904	2,865	2,156
Badminton	5,611	28	2,608	3,004	1,326	1,215	626	793	1,238	257	105	52	1,760	597	838	1,408	1,157	852
Baseball	14,146	17	10,960	3,186	4,733	3,672	1,532	1,596	1,679	692	169	73	1,714	1,716	2,042	2,996	3,069	2,709
Basketball	30,660	9	21,260	9,400	6,836	7,883	4,900	5,177	4,013	1,233	324	293	3,613	3,260	4,492	5,703	7,405	6,187
Bicycle riding [2]	45,119	5	24,889	20,230	11,199	8,500	4,489	6,559	7,321	3,612	1,849	1,590	5,782	5,022	5,939	8,095	10,792	9,490
Billiards	36,969	8	23,139	13,830	1,870	3,720	8,608	10,332	7,681	3,157	907	694	5,427	4,915	5,799	6,671	7,515	6,642
Bowling	44,770	6	23,577	21,193	5,718	7,123	7,323	8,903	8,460	3,898	1,518	1,827	5,337	6,045	5,863	8,265	11,035	8,226
Calisthenics [2]	10,955	24	5,266	5,690	1,541	1,899	1,535	1,928	1,676	1,136	568	673	1,678	1,268	1,495	1,663	2,340	2,512
Camping [4]	46,611	4	25,136	21,475	5,844	6,452	5,338	9,463	9,949	5,272	2,375	1,917	5,714	5,692	7,214	9,194	10,845	7,951
Exercise walking [2]	76,276	1	28,182	48,095	3,275	3,864	7,258	13,357	15,777	13,521	8,478	10,746	11,560	10,038	10,577	13,285	16,100	14,717
Exercising with equipment [2]	47,868	3	22,175	25,693	768	3,507	7,125	10,910	10,792	7,105	3,595	4,066	5,144	5,062	6,112	8,314	11,089	12,147
Fishing—fresh water	38,956	7	26,760	12,196	4,839	5,025	3,923	7,263	8,093	4,852	2,814	2,150	5,537	5,687	6,422	7,830	7,757	5,723
Fishing—salt water	11,562	22	8,256	3,306	862	1,197	1,000	2,277	2,725	1,762	857	882	1,322	1,462	1,472	2,223	2,807	2,276
Football—tackle	8,219	27	7,436	783	1,845	2,982	1,673	1,058	336	222	57	47	1,383	1,302	1,014	1,782	1,692	1,046
Football—touch	11,877	21	9,406	2,471	2,617	3,694	2,326	1,836	921	339	109	34	1,895	1,572	1,603	2,226	2,511	2,070
Golf	26,216	12	20,583	5,633	1,059	2,250	2,923	5,864	6,077	3,708	1,958	2,378	1,661	2,285	2,724	4,370	6,783	8,392
Hiking	28,356	10	15,404	12,952	2,990	3,269	3,545	6,302	6,058	3,578	1,620	995	3,768	3,345	3,279	4,877	6,607	6,479
Hunting with firearms	17,015	15	15,167	1,848	500	2,084	2,213	3,872	3,922	2,333	1,306	785	3,211	2,315	2,531	3,578	4,378	2,003
Martial arts	4,896	29	3,115	1,780	1,125	908	769	917	578	377	100	122	1,146	636	413	663	921	1,116
Racquetball [2]	4,511	30	3,249	1,262	209	386	1,372	1,232	834	337	94	46	534	511	606	882	961	1,016
Running/jogging [2]	21,688	13	12,662	9,026	1,913	4,241	4,008	4,664	3,884	1,951	696	330	2,496	2,239	2,437	3,577	4,956	5,983
Skiing—alpine/downhill	8,866	25	5,177	3,689	910	1,325	1,577	2,112	1,726	878	246	93	350	321	753	1,490	2,321	3,631
Skiing—cross country	2,517	31	1,259	1,258	156	367	225	362	648	500	151	108	147	122	250	558	321	1,025
Soccer	13,651	18	8,303	5,348	5,630	4,106	1,319	1,167	1,012	187	138	91	1,441	1,066	1,591	2,372	3,613	3,568
Softball [2]	16,339	16	8,966	7,373	2,392	3,432	2,783	3,703	2,699	1,025	174	129	1,894	1,808	2,297	3,657	3,855	2,827
Swimming [2]	59,547	2	28,087	31,460	10,986	10,430	6,952	9,198	10,753	5,443	2,945	2,842	6,654	6,092	7,049	11,662	13,959	14,131
Table tennis	8,834	26	5,334	3,500	1,294	1,877	1,358	1,456	1,784	701	194	170	993	920	1,023	1,176	2,116	2,604
Target shooting	13,487	19	10,949	2,538	963	1,809	2,000	3,047	3,165	1,531	654	318	1,683	1,914	1,824	2,730	3,119	2,217
Tennis	11,106	23	6,264	4,842	1,022	1,765	1,736	2,590	2,160	1,092	449	291	1,002	656	1,205	1,780	2,403	4,060
Volleyball	17,836	14	8,719	9,117	1,801	4,864	2,904	3,758	3,047	1,102	236	125	2,246	2,027	2,337	3,223	4,269	3,734

U.S. Census Bureau, Statistical Abstract of the United States: 1999

Activity	All persons		Sex		Age								Household income (dol.)					
	Number	Rank	Male	Female	7-11 years	12-17 years	18-24 years	25-34 years	35-44 years	45-54 years	55-64 years	65 years and over	Under 15,000	15,000-24,999	25,000-34,999	35,000-49,999	50,000-74,999	75,000 and over
SERIES II SPORTS [5]																		
Total	240,325	(X)	116,731	123,594	19,527	23,053	24,689	39,624	43,930	33,592	21,815	34,095	40,558	33,935	35,468	42,893	48,070	39,401
Number participating in—																		
Archery (target)	4,658	15	3,407	1,252	584	992	1,001	768	717	500	53	43	732	1,295	580	830	830	391
Boating, motor/power	27,174	1	15,668	11,506	2,541	3,013	2,802	5,522	6,075	3,602	2,002	1,617	2,250	2,192	3,999	5,227	7,135	6,372
Canoeing	7,089	10	4,371	2,718	678	1,083	810	1,531	1,481	918	278	312	766	601	914	1,354	2,101	1,354
Dart throwing	21,444	3	13,042	8,402	1,817	2,033	3,627	6,668	4,741	1,767	615	176	3,368	2,640	3,637	3,822	4,783	3,195
Hunting with bow arrow	5,338	14	4,947	391	171	466	872	1,505	1,335	558	313	119	692	662	1,013	1,223	1,037	710
Ice hockey	1,925	20	1,660	265	304	407	481	396	245	51	20	21	162	131	267	397	573	395
Ice/figure skating	7,867	9	3,137	4,730	2,055	1,934	838	1,301	1,084	411	162	81	553	672	911	1,445	2,143	2,143
Mountain biking-off road	8,109	8	5,553	2,556	996	1,192	1,179	2,663	1,352	515	151	61	969	909	1,241	1,551	1,650	1,790
Mountain biking-on road	15,953	5	9,270	6,683	2,143	2,114	2,028	4,737	2,981	1,242	459	248	2,092	1,854	1,971	2,887	3,517	3,633
Roller hockey	3,034	17	2,598	435	978	1,038	470	383	129	16	20	-	258	222	312	481	971	791
Roller skating/in-line wheels	26,550	2	13,114	13,436	9,152	7,163	3,195	4,119	2,070	539	156	156	2,504	2,443	3,638	5,095	7,303	5,566
Roller skating/traditional 2x2 wheel	10,902	6	4,029	6,873	3,871	2,470	1,025	1,695	1,197	461	139	43	1,247	1,614	2,052	2,299	2,369	1,320
Sailing	3,449	16	2,019	1,429	297	384	218	746	631	554	265	354	233	228	470	341	899	1,279
Scuba (open water)	2,293	19	1,577	717	-	172	325	527	699	456	108	6	111	105	258	278	541	1,001
Skate boarding	6,334	12	4,996	1,337	2,651	2,399	774	334	121	18	26	10	1,006	603	980	1,174	1,488	1,083
Snorkeling	6,268	13	3,382	2,885	324	509	741	1,543	1,632	1,021	331	167	357	231	529	962	1,792	2,397
Snowboarding	2,516	18	1,921	595	426	976	471	493	103	20	27	-	175	251	534	442	602	512
Step aerobics	9,555	7	1,035	8,520	51	448	1,898	3,148	2,013	1,145	404	446	1,289	1,288	1,411	1,620	1,982	1,965
Water skiing	6,464	11	4,000	2,465	440	1,196	1,130	1,881	1,195	446	91	85	459	549	742	1,094	1,690	1,930
Wind surfing	525	21	388	137	-	81	137	103	127	47	28	-	80	8	46	63	99	228
Work out at club	21,128	4	10,034	11,094	273	1,234	4,203	6,059	4,286	2,778	1,181	1,114	2,111	2,037	2,758	3,428	4,536	6,259

- Represents or rounds to zero. X Not applicable. [1] Based on a sampling of 15,000 households. [2] Participant engaged in activity at least six times in the year. [3] Includes wilderness camping. [4] Vacation/overnight. [5] Based on a sampling of 20,000 households.

Source: National Sporting Goods Association, Mt. Prospect, IL, Sports Participation in 1997: Series I and Series II (copyright).

No. 444. High School Students Engaged in Organized Physical Activity: 1997

[In percent. For students in grades 9 to 12. Based on the Youth Risk Behavior Survey, a school-based survey and subject to sampling error; for details see source]

Characteristic	Participation on sports team		Enrollment in physical education class		
	Run by school	Run by other organization	Total	Exercised 20 minutes or more per class	Attended daily
All students.	**49.5**	**38.3**	**48.8**	**73.9**	**27.4**
Male	55.5	45.4	52.0	78.5	29.8
Grade 9	57.2	51.3	69.6	78.5	43.0
Grade 10	58.0	47.3	56.0	77.5	32.8
Grade 11	54.0	41.6	43.5	78.3	22.5
Grade 12	53.4	42.6	42.3	80.1	23.2
Female	42.3	29.8	44.9	67.5	24.6
Grade 9	48.5	36.8	68.7	68.7	42.1
Grade 10	45.0	34.7	50.1	65.8	28.1
Grade 11	40.7	26.4	34.2	62.5	15.5
Grade 12	35.7	21.9	28.4	73.3	13.9
White, non-Hispanic	54.6	41.4	49.5	74.1	23.8
Male	58.7	46.6	51.8	79.4	25.8
Female	49.4	34.7	46.7	66.7	21.3
Black, non-Hispanic	44.3	38.0	46.3	71.0	32.5
Male	56.4	51.8	53.7	73.9	37.1
Female	32.9	25.1	39.4	67.3	28.2
Hispanic	40.2	32.9	51.6	73.8	38.4
Male	46.9	40.5	52.6	78.6	39.3
Female	32.3	24.0	50.3	67.7	37.3

Source: U.S. Centers for Disease Control and Prevention, Atlanta, GA, *Youth Risk Behavior Surveillance—United States, 1997, Morbidity and Mortality Weekly Report,* Vol. 47, No. 5, August 14, 1998.

No. 445. Participation in High School Athletic Programs: 1971 to 1998

[Data based on number of state associations reporting and may underrepresent the number of schools with and participants in athletic programs]

Year	Participants [1]		Sex and sport	Most popular sports, 1997-98 [2]	
	Males	Females		Schools	Participants
1971	3,666,917	294,105	MALES		
1972-73	3,770,621	817,073			
1973-74	4,070,125	1,300,169	Football	13,243	971,335
1975-76	4,109,021	1,645,039	Basketball	16,617	544,463
1977-78	4,367,442	2,083,040	Track & field (outdoor)	14,612	471,175
1978-79	3,709,512	1,854,400	Baseball	14,407	449,897
1979-80	3,517,829	1,750,264	Soccer	8,859	309,484
1980-81	3,503,124	1,853,789	Wrestling	8,900	229,176
1981-82	3,409,081	1,810,671	Cross country	11,693	178,672
1982-83	3,355,558	1,779,972	Golf	11,935	159,501
1983-84	3,303,599	1,747,346	Tennis	9,364	137,827
1984-85	3,354,284	1,757,884	Swimming & diving	5,098	83,781
1985-86	3,344,275	1,807,121	FEMALE		
1986-87	3,364,082	1,836,356			
1987-88	3,425,777	1,849,684	Basketball	16,428	454,000
1988-89	3,416,844	1,839,352	Track & field (outdoor)	14,284	395,955
1989-90	3,398,192	1,858,659	Volleyball	13,019	373,219
1990-91	3,406,355	1,892,316	Softball (fast pitch)	12,326	333,374
1991-92	3,429,853	1,940,801	Soccer	7,468	246,687
1992-93	3,416,389	1,997,489	Tennis	9,297	151,539
1993-94	3,472,967	2,130,315	Cross country	11,097	150,846
1994-95	3,536,359	2,240,461	Swimming & diving	5,360	126,062
1995-96	3,634,052	2,367,936	Competitive spirit squads	3,154	58,737
1996-97	3,740,262	2,470,826	Field hockey	1,491	56,589
1997-98	3,763,120	2,570,333			

[1] A participant is counted in the number of sports participated in. [2] Ten most popular sports for each sex in terms of number of participants.

Source: National Federation of State High School Associations, Kansas City, MO, *The 1997 High School Athletics Participation Survey* (copyright).

272   Parks, Recreation, and Travel

No. 446. Sporting Goods Sales, by Product Category: 1990 to 1998

[In millions of dollars (48,250 represents $48,250,000,000), except percent. Based on a sample survey of consumer purchases of 80,000 households, (100,000 beginning 1995), except recreational transport, which was provided by industry associations. Excludes Alaska and Hawaii]

Selected product category	1990	1991	1992	1993	1994	1995	1996	1997	1998, proj.
Sales, all products	48,250	47,104	47,110	49,129	53,453	58,428	61,574	64,109	66,495
Annual percent change [1]	-0.7	-2.4	(Z)	4.3	8.8	9.3	5.4	4.1	3.7
Percent of retail sales	2.6	2.5	2.4	2.4	2.4	2.5	2.5	2.5	2.5
Athletic and sport clothing [2]	10,130	10,731	8,990	9,096	9,521	10,311	11,127	11,935	12,412
Athletic and sport footwear [2]	11,654	11,787	11,733	11,084	11,120	11,415	12,815	13,319	13,687
Walking shoes	2,950	2,689	2,688	2,673	2,543	2,841	3,079	3,236	3,397
Gym shoes, sneakers	2,536	2,545	2,397	2,016	1,869	1,741	1,996	1,980	2,059
Jogging and running shoes	1,110	1,192	1,232	1,231	1,069	1,043	1,132	1,482	1,586
Tennis shoes	740	759	748	599	556	480	541	545	556
Aerobic shoes	611	600	590	500	356	372	401	380	342
Basketball shoes	918	974	984	874	867	999	1,192	1,134	1,066
Cross training shoes	679	879	799	877	1,101	1,191	1,417	1,450	1,377
Golf shoes	226	249	260	275	238	225	231	239	265
Athletic and sport equipment [2]	11,964	12,062	12,846	13,880	15,257	17,442	17,743	17,697	18,225
Firearms and hunting	2,202	2,091	2,533	2,722	3,490	3,003	2,521	2,562	2,639
Exercise equipment	1,824	2,106	2,050	2,602	2,449	2,960	3,232	2,948	2,889
Golf	1,219	1,149	1,338	1,248	1,342	3,194	3,560	3,734	4,033
Camping	1,072	1,006	903	906	1,017	1,205	1,127	1,151	1,198
Fishing tackle	776	711	678	716	717	737	725	694	687
Snow skiing	606	577	627	611	652	646	707	723	752
In-line skating and wheel sports	(NA)	(NA)	(NA)	510	545	608	590	553	530
Tennis	287	295	296	267	257	241	296	319	335
Archery	265	270	334	285	306	287	276	281	292
Baseball and softball	217	214	245	323	295	251	277	284	301
Water skis	88	63	55	51	51	54	55	56	55
Bowling accessories	155	155	164	159	157	156	154	154	157
Recreational transport	14,502	12,524	13,541	15,069	17,555	19,259	19,888	21,158	22,171
Pleasure boats	7,644	5,862	5,765	6,246	7,679	9,064	9,399	10,139	10,636
Recreational vehicles	4,113	3,615	4,412	4,775	5,690	5,895	6,327	6,904	7,389
Bicycles and supplies	2,423	2,686	2,973	3,534	3,470	3,390	3,187	3,156	3,187
Snowmobiles	322	362	391	515	715	910	974	959	960

NA Not available. Z Less than .05 percent. [1] Represents change from immediate prior year. [2] Includes other products not shown separately.

Source: National Sporting Goods Association, Mt. Prospect, IL, *The Sporting Goods Market in 1998*; and prior issues (copyright).

No. 447. Consumer Purchases of Sporting Goods, by Consumer Characteristics: 1997

[In percent. Based on sample survey of consumer purchases of 100,000 households. Excludes Alaska and Hawaii]

Characteristic	Total households	Footwear				Equipment					
		Aerobic shoes	Gym shoes/ sneakers	Jogging/ running shoes	Walking shoes	Fishing tackle	Camping equipment	Exercise equipment	Hunting equipment	Team sports equipment	Golf equipment
Total	100	100	100	100	100	100	100	100	100	100	100
Age of user:											
Under 14 years old	20.2	9.5	47.0	12.6	6.4	6.0	13.0	-	4.0	45.0	4.0
14 to 17 years old	5.8	6.7	13.1	14.5	3.4	6.0	9.0	3.0	3.0	26.0	5.0
18 to 24 years old	9.3	8.9	6.3	8.5	4.2	6.0	9.0	5.0	10.0	8.0	5.0
25 to 34 years old	14.5	29.5	10.0	19.2	11.3	22.0	28.0	23.0	23.0	10.0	22.0
35 to 44 years old	16.5	22.5	9.5	17.8	17.2	24.0	21.0	23.0	26.0	7.0	17.0
45 to 64 years old	21.0	19.3	11.1	23.3	36.7	27.0	15.0	35.0	28.0	3.0	35.0
65 years old and over	12.7	3.6	3.0	4.1	20.8	6.0	2.0	10.0	6.0	-	12.0
Multiple ages	-	-	-	-	-	3.0	3.0	1.0	-	1.0	-
Sex of user:											
Male	49.0	16.4	53.0	54.6	37.6	82.0	62.0	40.0	92.0	80.0	84.0
Female	51.0	83.6	47.0	45.4	62.4	14.0	32.0	56.0	7.0	19.0	16.0
Both sexes	-	-	-	-	-	4.0	6.0	4.0	1.0	1.0	-
Education of household head:											
Less than high school	9.2	5.2	7.6	3.9	6.9	7.0	5.0	7.0	7.0	5.0	2.0
High school	24.6	20.3	23.6	15.6	23.1	26.0	18.0	20.0	27.0	18.0	11.0
Some college	35.9	36.5	38.7	32.7	36.0	42.0	38.0	31.0	41.0	36.0	37.0
College graduate	30.3	38.0	30.1	47.8	34.0	25.0	39.0	42.0	25.0	41.0	50.0
Annual household income:											
Under $15,000	20.3	6.9	12.7	8.0	13.0	8.0	9.0	7.0	10.0	7.0	2.0
$15,000 to $24,999	16.7	13.7	14.2	9.4	15.8	15.0	14.0	10.0	17.0	10.0	9.0
$25,000 to $34,999	13.6	10.8	14.3	12.3	12.8	15.0	13.0	11.0	14.0	12.0	7.0
$35,000 to $49,999	16.6	16.7	19.6	20.6	16.2	21.0	20.0	18.0	19.0	19.0	14.0
$50,000 to $74,999	23.0	35.5	27.4	33.1	27.5	27.0	28.0	32.0	28.0	36.0	37.0
$75,000 and over	9.8	16.4	11.8	16.6	14.7	14.0	16.0	22.0	12.0	16.0	31.0

- Represents or rounds to zero.

Source: National Sporting Goods Association, Mt. Prospect, IL, *The Sporting Goods Market in 1998* (copyright).

Parks, Recreation, and Travel 273

No. 448. Participation in Various Leisure Activities: 1997

[In percent, except as indicated (195.6 represents 195,600,000). Covers activities engaged in at least once in the prior 12 months. See headnote, Table 450. See also Table 451]

Item	Adult population (mil.)	Attendance at— Movies	Sports events	Amusement park	Participation in— Exercise program	Playing sports	Charity work	Home improvement/repair	Computer hobbies
Total	195.6	66	41	57	76	45	43	66	40
Sex: Male	94.2	66	49	58	75	56	40	71	44
Female	101.4	65	34	57	77	35	46	61	37
Race: Hispanic	19.1	59	35	66	69	35	31	61	25
White	146.1	68	44	56	78	48	45	70	43
African-American	22.1	60	35	55	74	34	44	51	37
American Indian	3.0	65	34	59	83	49	34	58	37
Asian	5.3	76	29	58	70	48	41	58	62
Age: 18 to 24 years old	23.7	88	51	76	85	67	35	57	68
25 to 34 years old	40.1	79	51	70	82	63	41	63	51
35 to 44 years old	45.3	73	46	68	79	52	50	76	47
45 to 54 years old	33.7	65	42	53	77	40	46	75	40
55 to 64 years old	20.9	46	33	40	69	19	44	71	23
65 to 74 years old	19.6	38	21	29	65	23	40	55	11
75 years old and over	12.3	28	16	18	56	13	40	44	7
Education: Grade school	13.7	14	13	34	46	13	20	40	1
Some high school	26.9	52	25	54	66	30	31	59	19
High school graduate	62.0	62	38	58	74	41	36	65	35
Some college	50.3	78	48	64	81	54	50	71	52
College graduate	25.2	82	59	61	87	61	55	76	63
Graduate school	17.4	81	55	53	88	57	67	73	59
Income: $10,000 or less	15.0	37	15	39	55	19	32	42	19
$10,001 to $20,000	26.5	46	26	51	69	27	34	53	22
$20,001 to $30,000	29.4	56	28	55	72	40	37	61	30
$30,001 to $40,000	32.1	71	42	64	77	46	47	68	40
$40,001 to $50,000	25.9	73	51	67	80	51	42	75	47
$50,001 to $75,000	35.0	82	54	65	86	60	50	80	54
$75,001 to $100,000	16.2	81	66	64	86	61	51	79	64
Over $100,000	15.5	87	65	56	90	66	59	81	69

Source: U.S. National Endowment for the Arts, *1997 Survey of Public Participation in the Arts,* Research Division Report #39, December 1998.

No. 449. Arts and Humanities—Selected Federal Aid Programs: 1980 to 1997

[In millions of dollars (188.1 represents 188,100,000), except as indicated. For fiscal years ending in year shown, see text, Section 9, State and Local Government]

Type of fund and program	1980	1985	1990	1992	1993	1994	1995	1996	1997
National Endowment for the Arts:									
Funds available [1]	188.1	171.7	170.8	163.0	159.7	158.1	152.1	86.9	98.4
Program appropriation	97.0	118.7	124.3	123.0	120.0	116.3	109.0	63.5	65.8
Matching funds [2]	42.9	29.5	32.4	30.3	27.4	29.4	28.5	17.2	16.8
Grants awarded (number)	5,505	4,801	4,475	4,229	4,096	3,843	3,685	1,751	1,098
Funds obligated [3]	166.4	149.4	157.6	154.6	148.4	145.2	147.9	75.3	94.4
Partnership agreements	22.1	24.4	26.1	37.0	42.0	40.7	39.2	25.9	30.0
Music	13.6	15.3	16.5	14.9	12.4	10.9	10.9	5.4	(X)
Museums	11.2	11.9	12.1	11.1	9.9	9.4	9.0	3.8	(X)
Theater	8.4	10.6	10.6	9.4	8.3	8.8	7.3	5.2	(X)
Dance	8.0	9.0	9.6	8.2	7.9	7.6	7.1	4.2	(X)
Media arts	8.4	9.9	13.9	12.0	10.2	10.9	8.9	3.0	(X)
Challenge [4]	50.8	20.7	19.7	13.8	11.7	9.6	21.1	4.0	(X)
Visual arts	7.3	6.2	5.9	5.6	5.1	4.8	4.4	1.2	(X)
Other	36.6	41.3	43.1	42.7	40.9	42.5	40.0	22.6	(X)
National Endowment for the Humanities:									
Funds available [1]	186.2	125.6	140.6	156.5	158.5	157.9	151.4	93.1	93.9
Program appropriation	100.3	95.2	114.2	131.2	131.9	131.4	125.7	77.2	80.0
Matching funds [2]	38.4	30.4	26.3	25.2	26.5	26.5	25.7	15.9	13.9
Grants awarded (number)	2,917	2,241	2,195	2,199	2,197	1,881	1,871	815	900
Funds obligated [3]	185.5	125.7	141.0	159.1	160.3	159.0	151.8	93.4	94.8
Education programs	18.3	17.9	16.3	20.0	20.8	19.6	19.2	13.5	10.5
State programs	26.0	24.4	29.6	31.8	32.4	32.2	32.0	29.0	29.5
Research grants	32.0	24.4	22.5	25.3	23.7	23.4	22.2	5.1	8.5
Fellowship program	18.0	15.3	15.3	17.4	18.9	17.7	16.5	5.1	5.6
Challenge [4]	53.5	19.6	14.6	12.4	14.2	14.4	13.8	9.9	9.9
Public programs	25.1	24.1	25.4	27.0	26.7	27.5	25.8	12.5	12.6
Preservation and access	(X)	(X)	17.5	25.1	23.5	24.1	22.2	18.3	18.2
National Capital Arts and Cultural Affairs Program	(X)	(X)	(X)	(X)	(X)	(X)	(X)	(X)	(X)
Other	12.6	(X)	(X)	(X)	(X)	(X)	(X)	(X)	(X)

X Not applicable. [1] Includes other funds, shown separately. Excludes administrative funds. Gifts are included in 1980; excluded thereafter. [2] Represents Federal funds obligated only upon receipt or certification by Endowment of matching non-Federal gifts. [3] Includes obligations for new grants, supplemental awards on previous years' grants, and program contracts. Beginning with 1997 data, the grantmaking structure changed from discipline-based categories to thematic ones. [4] Program designed to stimulate new sources and higher levels of giving to institutions for the purpose of guaranteeing long-term stability and financial independence. Program requires a match of at least 3 private dollars to each Federal dollar. Funds for challenge grants are not allocated by program area because they are awarded on a grant-by-grant basis.

Source: U.S. National Endowment for the Arts, *Annual Report;* and U.S. National Endowment for the Humanities, *Annual Report.*

No. 450. Attendance Rates for Various Arts Activities: 1997

[In percent. For persons 18 years old and over. Excludes elementary and high school performances. Based on the 1997 household survey Public Participation in the Arts. Data are subject to sampling error; see source. See also Tables 448 and 451]

Item	Attendance at least once in the prior 12 months at—								
	Jazz performance	Classical music performance	Opera	Musical play	Non-musical play	Ballet	Art museum	Historic park	Reading literature[1]
Total	12	16	5	25	16	6	35	47	63
Sex: Male	13	14	4	22	15	4	34	48	55
Female	11	17	5	27	17	8	36	46	71
Race: Hispanic	7	8	3	16	10	5	29	33	50
White	12	18	5	27	17	7	36	51	65
African American	16	10	2	22	16	4	31	37	60
American Indian	11	9	5	15	5	1	22	42	56
Asian	10	16	7	20	18	4	42	44	69
Age: 18 to 24 years old	15	16	5	26	20	7	38	46	70
25 to 34 years old	13	11	4	23	13	5	37	49	61
35 to 44 years old	14	14	4	26	15	7	37	52	64
45 to 54 years old	13	20	6	29	20	7	40	54	66
55 to 64 years old	9	16	5	23	14	5	30	45	58
65 to 74 years old	8	18	4	24	15	5	28	37	59
75 years old and over	4	14	3	15	13	4	20	25	61
Education: Grade school	2	2	-	6	3	2	6	13	29
Some high school	3	4	2	13	7	2	14	27	46
High school graduate	7	8	2	16	9	4	25	41	58
Some college	15	18	5	28	19	7	43	56	72
College graduate	21	28	10	44	28	11	58	67	80
Graduate school	28	45	14	50	37	14	70	73	86
Income: $10,000 or less	5	4	2	12	10	2	16	23	45
$10,001 to $20,000	6	8	2	12	7	3	20	29	53
$20,001 to $30,000	8	10	2	17	10	4	26	39	62
$30,001 to $40,000	11	13	3	21	16	5	32	50	62
$40,001 to $50,000	11	15	5	23	15	6	37	52	64
$50,001 to $75,000	16	22	8	32	20	8	46	62	72
$75,001 to $100,000	23	26	6	41	27	10	55	65	75
Over $100,000	27	35	13	51	32	13	60	69	76

[1] Includes novels, short stories, poetry, or and plays.

Source: U.S. National Endowment for the Arts, *1997 Survey of Public Participation in the Arts*, Research Division Report No. #39, December 1998.

No. 451. Participation in Various Arts Activities: 1997

[In percent. Covers activities engaged in at least once in the prior 12 months. See Table 448 and headnote, Table 450]

Item	Playing classical music	Modern dancing[1]	Drawing	Pottery work[2]	Weaving	Photography[3]	Creative writing	Buying art work	Singing in groups
Total	1	13	16	15	28	17	12	35	10
Sex: Male	9	13	15	16	5	16	10	36	9
Female	13	12	17	14	49	18	14	34	12
Race: Hispanic	7	14	17	11	17	12	8	33	7
White	12	12	15	16	30	17	12	36	8
African American	8	11	16	11	25	18	14	43	26
American Indian	9	21	18	25	28	28	10	35	7
Asian	12	17	27	13	28	22	21	19	9
Age: 18 to 24 years old	13	20	39	21	22	28	32	42	14
25 to 34 years old	10	13	18	17	25	18	13	43	9
35 to 44 years old	11	13	15	18	29	18	12	40	9
45 to 54 years old	15	11	13	18	29	18	10	37	13
55 to 64 years old	9	8	9	10	29	10	5	31	11
65 to 74 years old	6	14	7	10	32	10	5	23	10
75 years old and over	6	9	4	3	28	5	6	8	7
Education: Grade school	2	4	4	7	14	8	2	24	11
Some high school	4	11	13	15	22	12	8	35	9
High school graduate	8	12	15	16	28	13	9	31	9
Some college	14	16	20	18	32	22	17	35	13
College graduate	18	10	18	13	32	23	14	41	9
Graduate school	20	15	18	13	26	22	19	41	12
Income: $10,000 or less	5	9	15	8	28	11	8	29	13
$10,001 to $20,000	7	10	13	12	27	14	8	27	9
$20,001 to $30,000	8	12	17	16	26	14	12	26	11
$30,001 to $40,000	10	14	15	20	29	18	11	44	13
$40,001 to $50,000	11	12	16	17	29	18	13	35	8
$50,001 to $75,000	15	13	17	18	28	18	17	32	10
$70,001 to $100,000	15	18	18	17	24	23	13	41	11
Over $100,000	18	12	12	14	23	23	11	46	9

[1] Dancing other than ballet (e.g. folk and tap). [2] Includes ceramics, jewelry, leatherwork, and metalwork. [3] Includes making movies or video as an artistic activity.

Source: U.S. National Endowment for the Arts, *1997 Survey of Public Participation in the Arts*, Research Division Report No. #39, December 1998.

Parks, Recreation and Travel   275

No. 452. Performing Arts—Selected Data: 1985 to 1997

[Sales, receipts, and expenditures in millions of dollars (209 represents $209,000,000). For season ending in year shown, except as indicated]

Item	1985	1989	1990	1991	1992	1993	1994	1995	1996	1997
Legitimate theater: [1]										
Broadway shows:										
New productions	33	33	39	28	39	35	38	33	39	36
Attendance (mil.) [2] [3]	7.3	8.1	8.0	7.3	7.4	7.9	8.1	9.0	9.5	10.6
Playing weeks [2] [3]	1,078	1,093	1,062	971	905	1,019	1,061	1,118	1,144	1,349
Gross ticket sales	209	262	282	267	293	328	356	406	436	499
Broadway road tours:										
Attendance (mil.)	8.2	8.3	11.1	13.0	13.0	15.0	16.0	16.0	18.1	18.0
Playing weeks	993	869	944	1,152	1,171	1,296	1,249	1,242	1,345	1,334
Gross ticket sales	226	256	367	450	503	626	705	701	796	782
Nonprofit professional theatres: [4]										
Companies reporting	217	192	185	184	182	177	231	215	228	197
Gross income	234.7	349.0	307.6	333.9	359.1	342.5	455.1	444.4	450.7	565.0
Earned income	146.1	224.6	188.4	202.6	222.5	209.7	277.4	281.2	274.0	349.9
Contributed income	88.6	124.4	119.2	131.3	136.6	132.8	177.7	163.1	176.7	215.1
Gross expenses	239.3	349.2	306.3	336.7	365.6	349.3	460.2	444.9	439.5	526.6
Productions	2,710	2,469	2,265	2,277	2,310	2,319	2,929	2,646	3,074	2,295
Performances	52,341	53,263	46,131	48,695	46,184	44,933	59,542	56,608	56,954	51,453
Total attendance (mil.)	14.2	18.7	15.2	16.9	16.0	16.5	20.7	18.6	17.1	17.2
OPERA America professional member companies: [5]										
Number of companies reporting [6]	97	101	98	98	100	85	86	88	83	91
Expenses [6] [7]	216.4	311.7	321.2	346.7	371.8	389.5	404.9	435.0	466.7	534.1
Performances [7]	1,909	2,429	2,336	2,283	2,424	1,945	1,982	2,251	2,019	2,137
Total attendance (mil.) [7] [8]	6.7	7.4	7.5	7.6	7.3	5.5	6.0	6.5	6.5	6.9
Main season attendance (mil.) [7] [9]	3.3	4.0	4.1	4.3	4.3	3.6	3.7	3.9	3.9	4.0
Symphony orchestras: [10]										
Concerts	19,573	20,630	18,931	18,074	19,778	18,389	17,795	29,328	28,887	26,906
Attendance (mil.)	24.0	25.8	24.7	26.7	26.3	24.0	24.4	30.9	31.1	31.9
Gross revenue	252.4	353.2	377.5	394.5	414.0	430.5	442.5	536.2	558.9	575.5
Concert income	168.6	231.0	253.3	273.8	284.1	294.1	303.6	368.6	383.7	390.5
Endowment income	(NA)	46.8	52.1	52.5	55.3	59.7	60.4	76.2	79.9	91.4
Other earned income	83.8	75.4	72.1	68.2	74.6	76.8	78.5	91.4	95.3	93.5
Operating expenses	426.1	583.5	621.7	662.2	683.0	689.9	710.0	858.8	892.4	937.1
Artistic personnel	231.9	310.2	327.3	355.8	398.9	378.8	389.9	464.7	473.9	487.1
Concert production	69.2	89.0	104.3	110.3	117.2	114.3	129.3	160.6	166.0	175.1
Advertising and promotion	32.5	47.5	51.3	57.3	58.3	63.1	67.3	75.2	82.9	90.8
General and administrative	51.3	68.4	73.3	75.6	76.2	73.6	74.4	87.2	88.2	91.6
Other	41.3	68.4	65.6	63.2	32.4	60.1	49.1	71.1	81.5	92.5
Support	188.1	249.0	257.8	281.2	279.6	293.0	293.1	351.0	382.8	401.1
Tax supported grants	42.2	54.5	55.6	58.3	49.1	48.0	46.4	55.5	57.6	54.5
Private sector support	145.9	194.5	202.1	222.9	230.5	245.0	246.7	295.5	325.3	346.6
Development expenses	20.8	30.9	31.4	36.7	36.0	38.0	37.9	38.8	42.8	44.9
Net support	167.3	218.2	226.4	244.6	243.6	255.0	255.2	312.2	340.0	356.2

NA Not available. [1] Source: The League of American Theaters and Producers, Inc., New York, NY. [2] All shows (new productions and holdovers from previous seasons). [3] Eight performances constitute one playing week. [4] Source: Theatre Communications Group, New York, NY. For years ending on or prior to Aug. 31. [5] Source: OPERA America, Washington, DC. For years ending on or prior to Aug 31. [6] United States companies. [7] Prior to 1993, United States and Canadian companies; beginning 1993, US companies only. [8] Includes educational performances, outreach, etc. [9] For paid performances. [10] Source: American Symphony Orchestra League, Inc., Washington, DC. For years ending Aug. 31. Prior to 1995 represents 254 U.S. orchestras; beginning 1995, represents all U.S. orchestras, excluding college/university and youth orchestras. Also, beginning 1995, data based on 1,200 orchestras; prior data based on 254.

Source: Compiled from sources listed in footnotes.

No. 453. Boy Scouts and Girl Scouts—Membership and Units: 1970 to 1998

[In thousands (6,287 represents 6,287,000). Boy Scouts as of Dec. 31; Girl Scouts as of Sept. 30. Includes Puerto Rico and outlying areas]

Item	1970	1975	1980	1985	1990	1993	1994	1995	1996	1997	1998
BOY SCOUTS OF AMERICA											
Membership	6,287	5,318	4,318	4,845	5,448	5,354	5,378	5,457	5,629	5,835	6,043
Boys	4,683	3,933	3,207	3,755	4,293	4,165	4,188	4,256	4,399	4,574	4,756
Adults	1,604	1,385	1,110	1,090	1,155	1,189	1,190	1,201	1,230	1,262	1,287
Total units (packs, troops, posts, groups)	157	150	129	134	130	128	129	132	135	139	143
GIRL SCOUTS OF THE U.S.A.											
Membership	3,922	3,234	2,784	2,802	3,269	3,438	3,363	3,318	3,390	3,525	3,567
Girls	3,248	2,723	2,250	2,172	2,480	2,612	2,561	2,534	2,584	2,671	2,708
Adults	674	511	534	630	788	826	802	784	807	855	858
Total units (troops, groups)	164	159	154	166	202	221	218	215	219	223	226

Source: Boy Scouts of America, National Council, Irving, TX, Annual Report; and Girl Scouts of the United States of America, New York, NY, Annual Report.

No. 454. Travel by U.S. Residents—Summary: 1985 to 1997

[In millions (497.8 represents 497,800,000), except party size. See headnote, Table 455]

Type of trip	1985	1990	1991	1992	1993	1994	1995	1996	1997
All travel: Total trips [1]	497.8	589.4	592.4	650.7	648.2	665.3	669.7	682.8	715.9
Person trips	808.3	956.0	980.1	1,063.0	1,057.5	1,139.1	1,172.6	1,161.2	1,256.1
Party size	1.6	1.6	1.7	1.6	1.6	1.7	1.8	1.7	1.8
Business travel: Total trips	156.6	182.8	176.9	210.8	210.4	193.2	207.8	192.8	207.4
Person trips	196.1	221.8	224.0	278.0	275.4	246.7	275.2	251.2	275.5
Party size	1.3	1.2	1.3	1.3	1.3	1.3	1.3	1.3	1.3
Pleasure travel: Total trips	301.2	361.1	364.3	411.7	413.4	434.3	413.0	432.5	443.2
Person trips	539.5	649.4	666.6	736.4	740.0	781.2	809.5	807.8	862.4
Party size	1.8	1.8	1.8	1.8	1.8	1.8	1.9	1.9	1.9
Vacation travel: Total trips	264.5	328.7	327.7	352.8	352.2	343.4	349.7	375.5	388.6
Person trips	487.8	591.6	605.3	637.1	633.2	664.6	680.4	706.1	751.8
Party size	1.8	1.8	1.9	1.8	1.8	1.9	1.9	1.9	1.9

[1] Includes other trips, not shown separately.

Source: Travel Industry Association of America, Washington, DC, *National Travel Survey*, annual (copyright).

No. 455. Characteristics of Business Trips and Pleasure Trips: 1985 to 1997

[Represents trips to places 100 miles or more from home by one or more household members traveling together (156.6 represents 156,600,000). Based on a monthly telephone survey of 1,500 U.S. adults. For details, see source]

Characteristic	Unit	Business trips				Pleasure trips			
		1985	1990	1995	1997	1985	1990	1995	1997
Total trips	Millions...	156.6	182.8	207.8	207.4	301.2	361.1	413.0	443.2
Average household members on trip	Number...	1.3	1.2	1.3	1.3	1.8	1.8	1.9	1.9
Average nights per trip [1]	Nights...	3.6	3.7	3.1	3.2	5.6	4.4	3.8	3.8
Average miles per trip [2]	Miles.....	1,180	1,020	1,022	1,128	1,010	867	781	901
Traveled primarily by auto/truck/RV [3] rental car	Percent...	51	58	63	60	73	77	84	80
Traveled primarily by air	Percent...	44	37	35	38	21	18	13	16
Used a rental car while on trip	Percent...	20	14	22	25	6	7	8	9
Stayed in a hotel while on trip	Percent...	62	71	66	65	39	37	39	39
Used a travel agent	Percent...	28	21	24	27	13	12	9	11
Also a vacation trip	Percent...	13	17	14	18	80	82	74	74
Male travelers	Percent...	67	71	74	70	48	49	53	53
Female travelers	Percent...	33	29	26	30	52	51	47	47
Household income:									
Less than $40,000	Percent...	58	42	25	25	73	63	47	42
$40,000 or more	Percent...	42	56	75	75	27	38	53	58

[1] Includes no overnight stays.   [2] United States only.   [3] Recreational vehicle.

Source: Travel Industry Association of America, Washington, DC, *National Travel Survey*, annual (copyright).

No. 456. Arrangement of Passenger Transportation—Receipts and Expenses, by Source: 1990 to 1997

[In millions of dollars (10,921 represents $10,921,000,000). For taxable employer firms in SIC 472. Based on the 1987 Standard Industrial Classification code; see text, Section 17, Business]

Item	1990	1992	1993	1994	1995	1996	1997
RECEIPTS							
Total	10,921	10,573	11,032	11,710	12,754	13,725	14,812
Air carriers	5,837	5,881	6,211	6,544	7,174	7,689	8,332
Water carriers	474	523	529	584	679	653	649
Hotels and motels	771	744	773	846	951	1,045	1,151
Motor coaches	403	379	363	348	342	421	466
Railroads	127	110	122	116	122	147	156
Rental cars	175	187	216	264	335	363	402
Packaged tours	2,250	1,989	2,143	2,397	2,539	2,706	2,875
Other	884	760	671	609	612	701	781
EXPENSES							
Total	9,912	9,705	10,051	10,706	11,258	12,238	13,166
Annual payroll	3,891	3,924	4,013	4,489	4,745	5,114	5,460
Employer contributions to Social Security and other supplemental benefits	519	526	573	664	718	791	802
Lease and rental payments	919	873	838	767	786	850	898
Advertising and promotion	722	653	670	652	607	697	691
Taxes and licenses	158	135	140	153	160	152	181
Utilities	352	371	417	448	505	544	553
Depreciation	409	326	339	365	393	412	506
Purchased office supplies	321	300	288	313	324	337	370
Purchased repair services	156	124	129	142	151	161	195
Other	2,465	2,473	2,644	2,713	2,869	3,180	3,510

Source: U.S. Census Bureau, *Current Business Reports, Service Annual Survey: 1997*, BS/97.

Parks, Recreation, and Travel   277

No. 457. Domestic Travel Expenditures, by State: 1996

[386,125 represents $386,125,000,000. Represents U.S. spending on domestic overnight trips and day trips of 100 miles or more away from home. Excludes spending by foreign visitors and by U.S. residents in U.S. territories and abroad]

State	Total (mil. dol.)	Share of total (percent)	Rank	State	Total (mil. dol.)	Share of total (percent)	Rank	State	Total (mil. dol.)	Share of total (percent)	Rank
U.S., total	386,125	100.0	(X)	KY	4,313	1.1	29	OH	10,528	2.7	11
AL	4,328	1.1	28	LA	6,503	1.7	20	OK	3,220	0.8	35
AK	1,191	0.3	46	ME	1,668	0.4	42	OR	4,543	1.2	27
AZ	6,811	1.8	18	MD	6,091	1.6	22	PA	11,937	3.1	8
AR	3,212	0.8	36	MA	8,596	2.2	14	RI	848	0.2	51
CA	50,215	13.0	1	MI	8,958	2.3	13	SC	5,715	1.5	23
CO	7,434	1.9	17	MN	5,312	1.4	24	SD	975	0.3	49
CT	4,047	1.0	30	MS	3,452	0.9	32	TN	8,172	2.1	15
DE	915	0.2	50	MO	7,701	2.0	16	TX	24,669	6.4	3
DC	3,420	0.9	33	MT	1,609	0.4	43	UT	3,287	0.9	34
FL	33,360	8.6	2	NE	2,204	0.6	39	VT	1,167	0.3	47
GA	11,199	2.9	9	NV	15,492	4.0	6	VA	10,545	2.7	10
HI	6,684	1.7	19	NH	1,725	0.4	41	WA	6,434	1.7	21
ID	1,777	0.5	40	NJ	12,494	3.2	7	WV	1,523	0.4	44
IL	16,945	4.4	5	NM	3,131	0.8	37	WI	5,129	1.3	25
IN	4,971	1.3	26	NY	23,158	6.0	4	WY	1,365	0.4	45
IA	3,474	0.9	31	NC	9,724	2.5	12				
KS	2,971	0.8	38	ND	984	0.3	48				

X Not applicable.

Source: Travel Industry Association of America, Washington, DC, *Impact of Travel on State Economies, 1996* (copyright).

No. 458. International Travelers and Expenditures: 1988 to 1997

[For coverage, see Table 459. Minus sign (-) indicates deficit (39,843 represents $39,843,000,000)]

Year	Travel and passenger fare (mil. dol.)				U.S. net travel and passenger payments (mil. dol.)	U.S. travelers to foreign countries (1,000)	Foreign visitors to the U.S. (1,000)
	Payments by U.S. travelers		Receipts from foreign visitors				
	Total [1]	Expenditures abroad	Total [1]	Travel receipts			
1988	39,843	32,114	38,409	29,434	-1,434	40,669	33,942
1989	41,665	33,416	46,863	36,205	5,198	41,138	36,365
1990	47,880	37,349	58,305	43,007	10,425	44,623	39,363
1991	45,334	35,322	64,237	48,384	18,903	41,566	42,674
1992	49,155	38,552	71,360	54,742	22,205	43,898	47,261
1993	52,123	40,713	74,403	57,875	22,280	44,411	45,779
1994	56,844	43,782	75,414	58,417	18,570	46,450	44,753
1995	59,579	44,916	82,304	63,395	22,725	50,763	43,318
1996	63,866	48,048	90,164	69,751	26,298	52,311	46,489
1997	69,455	51,220	94,163	73,268	24,708	52,735	47,754

[1] Includes passenger fares not shown separately.

Source: U.S. Dept. of Commerce, International Trade Administration, Tourism Industries, Internet site <http://www.tinet.ita.doc.gov>.

No. 459. Foreign Travel: 1990 to 1997

[In thousands (44,623 represents 44,623,000). U.S. travelers cover residents of the United States, its territories and possessions. Foreign travelers to the United States include travelers for business and pleasure, international travelers in transit through the United States, and students; excludes travel by international personnel and international businessmen employed in the United States]

Item and area	1990	1991	1992	1993	1994	1995	1996	1997
U.S. travelers to foreign countries....	44,623	41,566	43,898	44,411	46,450	50,763	52,311	52,735
Canada	12,252	12,003	11,819	12,024	12,542	12,933	12,909	13,401
Mexico	16,381	15,042	16,114	15,285	15,759	18,771	19,616	17,700
Total overseas	15,990	14,521	15,965	17,102	18,149	19,059	19,786	21,634
Europe	8,043	6,316	7,136	7,491	8,167	8,596	8,706	9,800
Foreign travelers to the U.S.	39,363	42,674	47,262	45,779	44,753	43,318	46,489	47,754
Canada	17,263	19,113	18,598	17,293	14,974	14,663	15,301	15,127
Mexico	7,041	7,406	10,872	9,824	11,321	8,016	8,530	8,433
Total overseas	15,059	16,155	17,791	18,662	18,458	20,639	22,658	24,194
Europe	6,659	7,360	8,262	8,630	8,119	8,793	9,727	10,390
South America	1,328	1,575	1,770	2,026	2,112	2,449	2,461	2,831
Central America	412	444	481	545	513	509	524	564
Caribbean	1,137	1,061	1,004	1,098	1,031	1,044	1,133	1,189
Far East	4,360	4,579	5,097	5,165	5,551	6,616	7,500	7,756
Middle East	365	357	373	419	403	454	480	552
Oceania	662	641	654	609	556	588	629	680
Africa	137	139	150	169	173	186	205	234

Source: U.S. Dept. of Commerce, International Trade Administration, Tourism Industries, Internet site <http://www.tinet.ita.doc.gov>.

U.S. Census Bureau, Statistical Abstract of the United States: 1999

No. 460. Top States and Cities Visited by Overseas Travelers: 1996 and 1997

[22,658 represents 22,658,000]. Includes travelers for business and pleasure, international travelers in transit through the United States, and students; excludes travel by international personnel and international businessmen employed in the United States]

State	Overseas visitors (1,000) 1996	1997	Market share (percent) 1996	1997	City	Overseas visitors (1,000) 1996	1997	Market share (percent) 1996	1997
Total overseas travelers [1].	22,658	24,194	100.0	100.0					
California	6,004	6,436	26.5	26.6	New York City	4,532	5,008	20.0	20.7
Florida	5,710	6,073	25.2	25.1	Los Angeles	3,603	3,920	15.9	16.2
New York	4,804	5,274	21.2	21.8	Miami.	3,127	3,315	13.8	13.7
Hawaii	3,059	3,073	13.5	12.7	San Francisco	2,923	2,855	12.9	11.8
Nevada	2,062	2,202	9.1	9.1	Orlando	2,583	2,782	11.4	11.5
Guam	1,292	1,355	5.7	5.6	Oahu/Honolulu.	2,402	2,468	10.6	10.2
Massachusetts.	1,156	1,210	5.1	5.0	Las Vegas	1,971	2,105	8.7	8.7
Illinois	1,178	1,137	5.2	4.7	Washington, DC.	1,382	1,427	6.1	5.9
Texas.	974	1,040	4.3	4.3	Boston	1,065	1,137	4.7	4.7
Arizona.	997	968	4.4	4.0	Chicago	1,110	1,089	4.9	4.5
New Jersey.	634	726	2.8	3.0	San Diego.	702	823	3.1	3.4
Georgia	657	653	2.9	2.7	Anaheim.	589	605	2.6	2.5
Pennsylvania.	702	629	3.1	2.6	Tampa/St. Petersburg	589	556	2.6	2.3
Washington.	612	581	2.7	2.4	Atlanta	566	532	2.5	2.2
Colorado.	566	532	2.5	2.2	Seattle	544	532	2.4	2.2
North Carolina	363	484	1.6	2.0	Maui	544	508	2.4	2.1
Ohio	385	436	1.7	1.8	Houston	408	460	1.8	1.9
Utah	498	411	2.2	1.7	Dallas/Ft. Worth.	385	436	1.7	1.8
Louisiana	408	363	1.8	1.5	San Jose	408	411	1.8	1.7
Virginia.	340	363	1.5	1.5	Ft. Lauderdale	317	387	1.4	1.6
Michigan.	363	339	1.6	1.4	Philadelphia	431	387	1.9	1.6
Oregon.	249	315	1.1	1.3	Phoenix	408	387	1.8	1.6
Connecticut.	227	290	1.0	1.2	New Orleans	363	339	1.6	1.4
Maryland	272	266	1.2	1.1	Denver.	363	315	1.6	1.3
Minnesota.	272	266	1.2	1.1	Monterey	227	266	1.0	1.1
Tennessee	227	266	1.0	1.1	Riverside/San Bernardino .	227	266	1.0	1.1
South Carolina.	181	242	0.8	1.0	Monterey	227	266	1.0	1.1
Wisconsin.	159	242	0.7	1.0	Portland	159	242	0.7	1.0
Missouri	159	194	0.7	0.8	Sacramento	204	242	0.9	1.0

[1] Includes other states and cities, not shown separately.

Source: U.S. Dept. of Commerce, International Trade Administration, Internet site <http://www.tinet.ita.doc.gov>.

No. 461. Foreign Visitors for Pleasure Admitted, by Country of Last Residence: 1985 to 1996

[In thousands (6,609 represents 6,609,000). For years ending September 30. See headnote, Table 7, Section 1, Population]

Country	1985	1990	1995	1996	Country	1985	1990	1995	1996
Total [1]	6,609	13,418	17,612	19,110	Africa [2]	101	105	137	157
					Egypt.	16	16	16	19
Europe [2]	2,048	5,383	7,012	7,478	Nigeria.	25	11	10	12
Austria	34	87	146	158	Oceania [2]	282	562	478	512
Belgium	39	95	153	170	Australia	195	380	327	342
Denmark	36	75	78	89	New Zealand.	74	153	115	127
Finland	24	83	47	53					
France.	226	566	738	767	North America.	1,664	2,463	2,240	2,314
Greece	34	43	44	43	Canada	79	119	127	121
Ireland	55	81	126	151	Mexico.	773	1,061	893	908
Italy.	155	308	427	437	Caribbean [2]	584	963	831	907
Netherlands	82	214	308	325	Bahamas, The	211	332	234	292
Norway	41	80	71	80	Barbados	17	34	36	37
Poland.	40	55	36	45	Cayman Islands	18	31	31	34
Soviet Union.	2	53	54	71	Dominican Republic . .	57	137	138	140
Spain.	64	183	248	262	Haiti.	56	57	43	39
Sweden	71	230	142	165	Jamaica	74	132	130	144
Switzerland	110	236	321	337	Netherlands Antilles . .	27	31	32	27
United Kingdom.	598	1,899	2,342	2,495	Trinidad and Tobago . .	71	81	64	70
Germany [3]	373	969	1,550	1,624	Central America [2].	228	320	387	376
					Costa Rica	41	62	91	87
Asia [2]	1,866	3,830	5,666	5,445	El Salvador	38	46	63	62
China (Mainland China					Guatemala	53	91	99	97
and Taiwan)	83	187	378	363	Panama	38	43	54	54
Hong Kong	64	111	162	174	South America [2]	606	1,016	1,978	2,000
India	52	75	75	84	Argentina	66	136	320	339
Israel.	80	128	160	186	Brazil.	148	300	710	723
Japan	1,277	2,846	3,986	3,621	Chile	28	54	117	121
Korea	26	120	427	513	Colombia	123	122	174	187
Philippines	59	76	85	86	Ecuador.	42	57	77	78
Saudi Arabia	31	33	45	42	Peru	44	97	98	101
Singapore	23	32	61	72	Venezuela	122	199	400	362

[1] Includes countries unknown or not reported.   [2] Includes countries not shown separately.   [3] Data prior to 1995 for former West Germany.

Source: U.S. Immigration and Naturalization Service, *Statistical Yearbook*, annual.

Parks, Recreation, and Travel 279

Figure 8.1
**Participation in Elections for President and Representatives—
Percent of Voting-Age Population: 1972 to 1998**

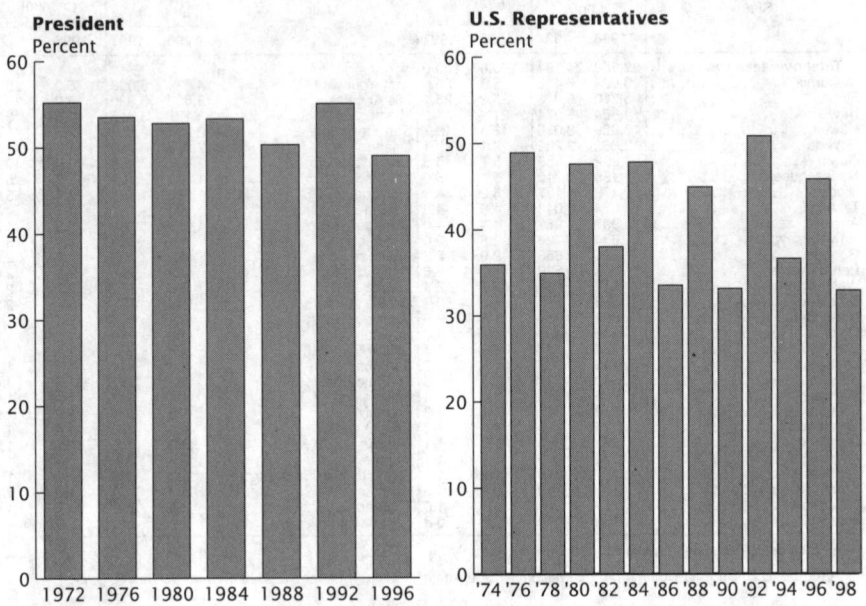

Source: Chart prepared by U.S. Census Bureau. For data, see Table 489.

Figure 8.2
Political Campaign Receipts: 1979 to 1998

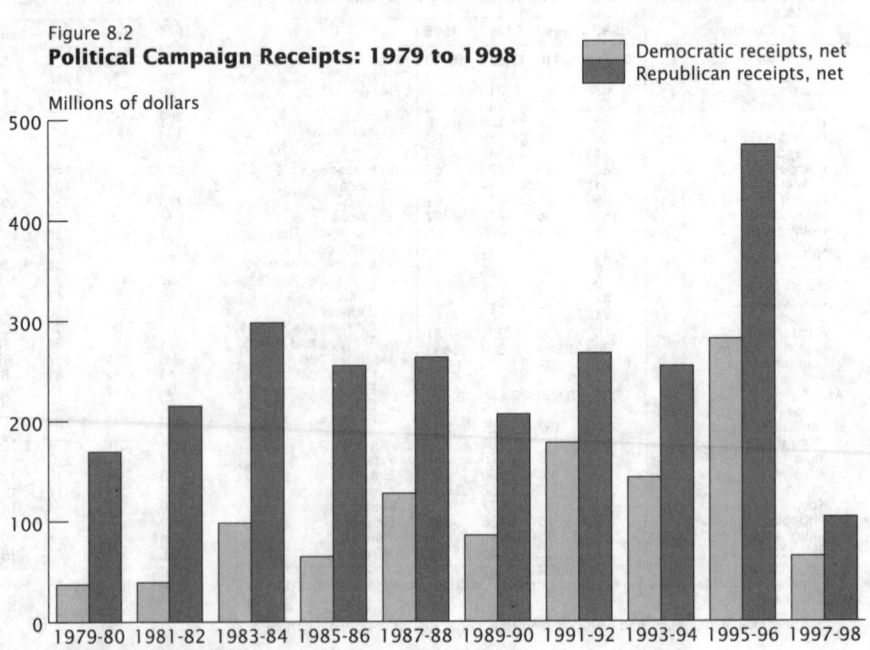

Source: Chart prepared by U.S. Census Bureau. For data, see Table 492.

280 Elections

Section 8
Elections

This section relates primarily to Presidential, congressional, and gubernatorial elections. Also presented are summary tables on congressional legislation; state legislatures; Black, Hispanic, and female officeholders; population of voting age; voter participation; and campaign finances.

Official statistics on Federal elections, collected by the Clerk of the House, are published biennially in *Statistics of the Presidential and Congressional Election* and *Statistics of the Congressional Election*. Federal and state elections data appear also in *America Votes*, a biennial volume published by Congressional Quarterly, Inc., Washington, DC. Federal elections data also appear in the U.S. Congress, *Congressional Directory*, and in official state documents. Data on reported registration and voting for social and economic groups are obtained by the U.S. Census Bureau as part of the Current Population Survey (CPS) and are published in *Current Population Reports*, Series P20 (see text, Section 1).

Almost all Federal, state, and local governmental units in the United States conduct elections for political offices and other purposes. The conduct of elections is regulated by state laws or, in some cities and counties, by local charter. An exception is that the U.S. Constitution prescribes the basis of representation in Congress and the manner of electing the President and grants to Congress the right to regulate the times, places, and manner of electing Federal officers. Amendments to the Constitution have prescribed national criteria for voting eligibility. The 15th Amendment, adopted in 1870, gave all citizens the right to vote regardless of race, color, or previous condition of servitude. The 19th Amendment, adopted in 1919, further extended the right to vote to all citizens regardless of sex. The payment of poll taxes

as a prerequisite to voting in Federal elections was banned by the 24th Amendment in 1964. In 1971, as a result of the 26th Amendment, eligibility to vote in national elections was extended to all citizens, 18 years old and over.

Presidential election—The Constitution specifies how the President and Vice President are selected. Each state elects, by popular vote, a group of electors equal in number to its total of members of Congress. The 23d Amendment, adopted in 1961, grants the District of Columbia three presidential electors, a number equal to that of the least populous state. Subsequent to the election, the electors meet in their respective states to vote for President and Vice President. Usually, each elector votes for the candidate receiving the most popular votes in his or her state. A majority vote of all electors is necessary to elect the President and Vice President. If no candidate receives a majority, the House of Representatives, with each state having one vote, is empowered to elect the President and Vice President, again, with a majority of votes required.

The 22d Amendment to the Constitution, adopted in 1951, limits presidential tenure to two elective terms of 4 years each or to one elective term for any person who, upon succession to the Presidency, has held the office or acted as President for more than 2 years.

Congressional election—The Constitution provides that Representatives be apportioned among the states according to their population, that a census of population be taken every 10 years as a basis for apportionment, and that each state have at least one Representative. At the time of each apportionment, Congress decides what the total number of Representatives will be. Since 1912, the total has been 435,

U.S. Census Bureau, Statistical Abstract of the United States: 1999

except during 1960 to 1962 when it increased to 437, adding one Representative each for Alaska and Hawaii. The total reverted to 435 after reapportionment following the 1960 census. Members are elected for 2-year terms, all terms covering the same period. The District of Columbia, American Samoa, Guam, and the Virgin Islands each elect one nonvoting Delegate, and Puerto Rico elects a nonvoting Resident Commissioner.

The Senate is composed of 100 members, two from each state, who are elected to serve for a term of 6 years. One-third of the Senate is elected every 2 years. Senators were originally chosen by the state legislatures. The 17th Amendment to the Constitution, adopted in 1913, prescribed that Senators be elected by popular vote.

Voter eligibility and participation— The Census Bureau publishes estimates of the population of voting age and the percent casting votes in each state for Presidential and congressional election years. These voting-age estimates include a number of persons who meet the age requirement but are not eligible to vote, (e.g. aliens and some institutionalized persons). In addition, since 1964, voter participation and voter characteristics data have been collected during November of election years as part of the CPS. These survey data include noncitizens in the voting age population estimates but exclude members of the Armed Forces and the institutional population.

Statistical reliability—For a discussion of statistical collection and estimation, sampling procedures, and measures of statistical reliability applicable to Census Bureau data, see Appendix III.

Figure 8.3
Popular Vote Cast for President, by Major Political Party: 1972 to 1996

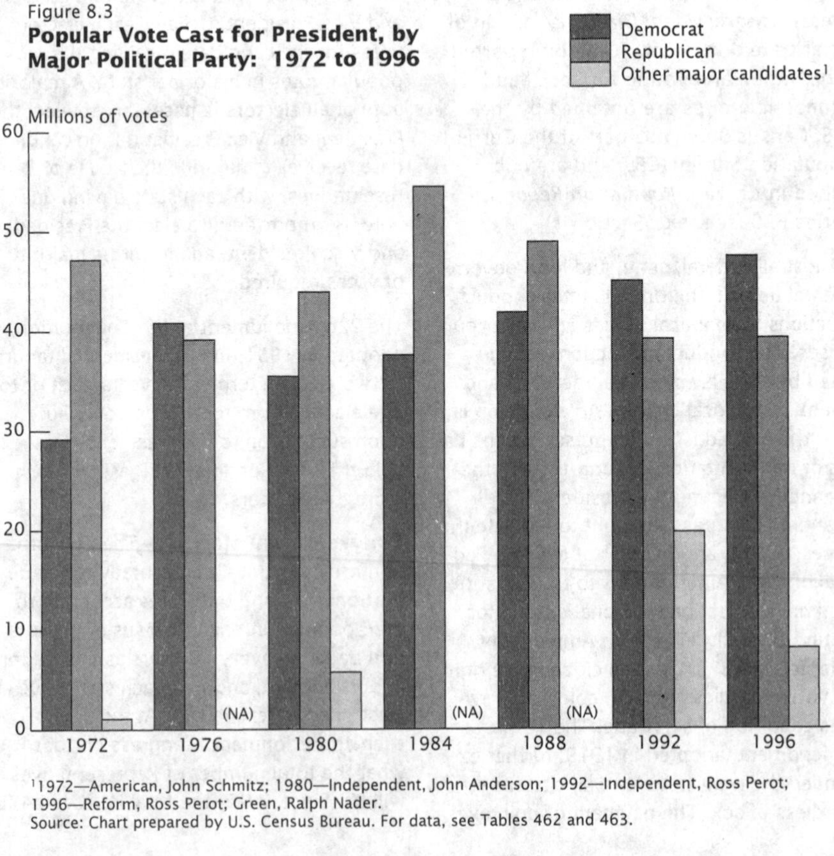

Democrat
Republican
Other major candidates[1]

[1]1972—American, John Schmitz; 1980—Independent, John Anderson; 1992—Independent, Ross Perot; 1996—Reform, Ross Perot; Green, Ralph Nader.
Source: Chart prepared by U.S. Census Bureau. For data, see Tables 462 and 463.

No. 462. Vote Cast for President, by Major Political Party: 1936 to 1996

[Prior to 1960, excludes Alaska and Hawaii; prior to 1964, excludes DC. Vote cast for major party candidates include the votes of minor parties cast for those candidates]

Year	Candidates for President		Vote cast for President							
				Democratic			Republican			
	Democratic	Republican	Total popular vote [1] (1,000)	Popular vote		Electoral vote	Popular vote		Electoral vote
				Number (1,000)	Percent		Number (1,000)	Percent	
1936	F. D. Roosevelt	Landon	45,655	27,757	60.8	523	16,684	36.5	8
1940	F. D. Roosevelt	Willkie	49,900	27,313	54.7	449	22,348	44.8	82
1944	F. D. Roosevelt	Dewey	47,977	25,613	53.4	432	22,018	45.9	99
1948	Truman	Dewey	48,794	24,179	49.6	303	21,991	45.1	189
1952	Stevenson	Eisenhower	61,551	27,315	44.4	89	33,936	55.1	442
1956	Stevenson	Eisenhower	62,027	26,023	42.0	73	35,590	57.4	457
1960	Kennedy	Nixon	68,838	34,227	49.7	303	34,108	49.5	219
1964	Johnson	Goldwater	70,645	43,130	61.1	486	27,178	38.5	52
1968	Humphrey	Nixon	73,212	31,275	42.7	191	31,785	43.4	301
1972	McGovern	Nixon	77,719	29,170	37.5	17	47,170	60.7	520
1976	Carter	Ford	81,556	40,831	50.1	297	39,148	48.0	240
1980	Carter	Reagan	86,515	35,484	41.0	49	43,904	50.7	489
1984	Mondale	Reagan	92,653	37,577	40.6	13	54,455	58.8	525
1988	Dukakis	Bush	91,595	41,809	45.6	111	48,886	53.4	426
1992	Clinton	Bush	104,425	44,909	43.0	370	39,104	37.4	168
1996	Clinton	Dole	96,278	47,402	49.2	379	39,199	40.7	159

[1] Include votes for minor party candidates, independents, unpledged electors, and scattered write-in votes.

Source: Congressional Quarterly, Inc., Washington, DC, *America at the Polls 2*, 1965, and *America Votes*, biennial (copyright).

No. 463. Vote Cast for Leading Minority Party Candidates for President: 1936 to 1996

[See headnote, table 462]

Year	Candidate	Party	Popular vote (1,000)	Candidate	Party	Popular vote (1,000)
1936	William Lemke	Union	892	Norman Thomas	Socialist	188
1940	Norman Thomas	Socialist	116	Roger Babson	Prohibition	59
1944	Norman Thomas	Socialist	79	Claude Watson	Prohibition	75
1948	Strom Thurmond	States' Rights	1,176	Henry Wallace	Progressive	1,157
1952	Vincent Hallinan	Progressive	140	Stuart Hamblen	Prohibition	73
1956	T. Coleman Andrews	States' Rights	111	Eric Hass	Socialist Labor	44
1960	Eric Hass	Socialist Labor	48	Rutherford Decker	Prohibition	46
1964	Eric Hass	Socialist Labor	45	Clifton DeBerry	Socialist Workers	33
1968	George Wallace	American Independent	9,906	Henning Blomen	Socialist Labor	53
1972	John Schmitz	American	1,099	Benjamin Spock	People's	79
1976	Eugene McCarthy	Independent	757	Roger McBride	Libertarian	173
1980	John Anderson	Independent	5,720	Ed Clark	Libertarian	921
1984	David Bergland	Libertarian	228	Lyndon H. LaRouche	Independent	79
1988	Ron Paul	Libertarian	432	Lenora B. Fulani	New Alliance	217
1992	H. Ross Perot	Independent	19,742	Andre Marrou	Libertarian	292
1996	H. Ross Perot	Reform Party	8,085	Ralph Nader	Green	685

Source: Congressional Quarterly, Inc. Washington, DC, *America at the Polls 1920-1996*, 1997; and *America Votes*, biennial (copyright).

No. 464. Democratic and Republican Percentages of Two-Party Presidential Vote, by Selected Characteristics of Voters: 1992 and 1996

[In percent. Covers citizens of voting age living in private housing units in the contiguous United States. Percentages for Democratic Presidential vote are computed by subtracting the percentage Republican vote from 100 percent; third-party or independent votes are not included as valid data. Data are from the National Election Studies and are based on a sample and subject to sampling variability; for details, see source]

Characteristic	1992		1996		Characteristic	1992		1996	
	Democratic	Republican	Democratic	Republican		Democratic	Republican	Democratic	Republican
Year of birth:					Race:				
1959 or later	58	42	58	42	White	53	47	54	46
1943 to 1958	58	42	58	42	Black	94	6	99	1
1927 to 1942	56	44	56	44	Education:				
1911 to 1926	62	38	64	36	Grade school	68	32	82	18
1895 to 1910	58	42	57	43	High school	62	38	60	40
Sex:					College	52	48	49	51
Male	55	45	51	50	Union household	68	32	75	25
Female	61	39	65	35	Non-union household	57	43	54	46

Source: Center for Political Studies, University of Michigan, Ann Arbor, MI, unpublished data (copyright).

U.S. Census Bureau, Statistical Abstract of the United States: 1999

No. 465. Electoral Vote Cast for President, by Major Political Party—States: 1956 to 1996

[D=Democratic, R=Republican. For composition of regions, see inside front cover]

State	1956[1]	1960[2]	1964	1968[3]	1972[4]	1976[5]	1980	1984	1988[6]	1992	1996
Democratic	73	303	486	191	17	297	49	13	111	370	379
Republican	457	219	52	301	520	240	489	525	426	168	159
Northeast: Democratic .	-	121	126	102	14	86	4	-	53	106	106
Republican .	133	12	-	24	108	36	118	113	60	-	-
Midwest: Democratic ..	13	71	149	31	-	58	10	10	29	100	100
Republican ..	140	82	-	118	145	87	135	127	108	29	29
South: Democratic	60	101	121	45	3	149	31	3	8	68	80
Republican	105	50	47	77	165	20	138	174	168	116	104
West: Democratic	-	10	90	13	-	4	4	-	21	96	93
Republican	79	75	5	82	102	97	98	111	90	23	26
AL	[1]D-10	[2]D-5	R-10	([3])	R-9	D-9	R-9	R-9	R-9	R-9	R-9
AK	(X)	R-3	D-3	R-3	R-3	R-3	R-3	R-3	R-3	R-3	R-3
AZ	R-4	R-4	R-5	R-5	R-6	R-6	R-6	R-7	R-7	R-8	D-8
AR	D-8	D-8	D-6	([3])	R-6	D-6	R-6	R-6	R-6	D-6	D-6
CA	R-32	R-32	D-40	R-40	R-45	R-45	R-45	R-47	R-47	D-54	D-54
CO	R-6	R-6	D-6	R-6	R-7	R-7	R-7	R-8	R-8	D-8	R-8
CT	R-8	D-8	D-8	D-8	R-8	R-8	R-8	R-8	R-8	D-8	D-8
DE	R-3	D-3	D-3	R-3	R-3	D-3	R-3	R-3	R-3	D-3	D-3
DC	(X)	(X)	D-3	D-3	D-3	D-3	D-3	D-3	D-3	D-3	D-3
FL	R-10	R-10	D-14	R-14	R-17	D-17	R-17	R-21	R-21	R-25	D-25
GA	D-12	D-12	R-12	([3])	R-12	D-12	D-12	R-12	R-12	D-13	R-13
HI	(X)	D-3	D-4	D-4	R-4	D-4	D-4	D-4	D-4	D-4	D-4
ID	R-4	R-4	R-4	R-4	R-4	R-4	R-4	R-4	R-4	R-4	R-4
IL	R-27	R-27	D-26	R-26	R-26	R-26	R-26	R-24	R-24	D-22	D-22
IN	R-13	R-13	D-13	R-13	R-13	R-13	R-13	R-12	R-12	R-12	R-12
IA	R-10	R-10	D-9	R-9	R-8	R-8	R-8	R-8	D-8	D-7	D-7
KS	R-8	R-8	D-7	R-7	R-7	R-7	R-7	R-7	R-7	R-6	R-6
KY	R-10	R-10	D-9	R-9	R-9	D-9	R-9	R-9	R-9	D-8	D-8
LA	R-10	D-10	R-10	([3])	R-10	D-10	R-10	R-10	R-10	D-9	D-9
ME	R-5	R-5	D-4	D-4	R-4	R-4	R-4	R-4	R-4	D-4	D-4
MD	R-9	D-9	D-10	D-10	R-10	D-10	D-10	R-10	R-10	D-10	D-10
MA	R-16	D-16	D-14	D-14	D-14	D-14	D-14	R-13	D-13	D-12	D-12
MI	R-20	D-20	D-21	D-21	R-21	R-21	R-21	R-20	R-20	D-10	D-10
MN	R-11	D-11	D-10	D-10	D-10	D-10	D-10	D-10	D-10	D-10	D-10
MS	D-8	([2])	R-7	([3])	R-7	D-7	R-7	R-7	R-7	R-7	R-7
MO	D-13	D-13	D-12	R-12	R-12	D-12	R-12	R-11	R-11	D-11	D-11
MT	R-4	R-4	D-4	R-4	R-4	R-4	R-4	R-4	R-4	D-3	R-3
NE	R-6	R-6	D-5	R-5	R-5	R-5	R-5	R-5	R-5	R-5	R-5
NV	R-3	D-3	D-3	R-3	R-3	R-3	R-3	R-4	R-4	D-4	D-4
NH	R-4	R-4	D-4	R-4	R-4	R-4	R-4	R-4	R-4	D-4	D-4
NJ	R-16	D-16	D-17	R-17	R-17	R-17	R-17	R-16	R-16	D-15	D-15
NM	R-4	D-4	D-4	R-4	R-4	R-4	R-4	R-5	R-5	D-5	D-5
NY	R-45	D-45	D-43	D-43	R-41	D-41	R-41	R-36	D-36	D-33	D-33
NC	D-14	D-14	D-13	[3]R-12	R-13	D-13	R-13	R-13	R-13	R-14	R-14
ND	R-4	R-4	D-4	R-4	R-3	R-3	R-3	R-3	R-3	R-3	R-3
OH	R-25	R-25	D-26	R-26	R-25	D-25	R-25	R-23	R-23	D-21	D-21
OK	R-8	[2]R-7	D-8	R-8	R-8	R-8	R-8	R-8	D-7	D-7	D-7
OR	R-6	R-6	D-6	R-6	R-6	R-6	R-6	R-7	D-7	D-7	D-7
PA	R-32	R-32	D-29	R-29	R-27	D-27	R-27	R-25	R-25	D-23	D-23
RI	R-4	D-4	D-4	D-4	R-4	D-4	D-4	D-4	D-4	D-4	D-4
SC	D-8	D-8	R-8	R-8	R-8	D-8	R-8	R-8	R-8	R-8	R-8
SD	R-4	R-4	D-4	R-4	R-4	R-4	R-4	R-3	R-3	R-3	R-3
TN	R-11	R-11	D-11	R-11	R-10	D-10	R-10	R-11	R-11	D-11	D-11
TX	R-24	R-24	D-25	D-25	R-26	D-26	R-26	R-29	R-29	R-32	R-32
UT	R-4	R-4	D-4	R-4	R-4	R-4	R-4	R-5	R-5	R-5	R-5
VT	R-3	R-3	D-3	R-3	R-3	R-3	R-3	R-3	R-3	R-3	R-3
VA	R-12	R-12	D-12	R-12	[4]R-11	R-12	R-12	R-12	R-12	R-13	R-13
WA	R-9	R-9	D-9	D-9	R-9	[5]R-8	R-9	R-10	D-10	D-11	D-11
WV	R-8	D-8	D-7	D-7	R-6	D-6	D-6	R-6	[6]D-5	D-5	D-5
WI	R-12	R-12	D-12	R-12	R-11	D-11	R-11	R-11	D-11	D-11	D-11
WY	R-3	R-3	D-3	R-3	R-3	R-3	R-3	R-3	R-3	R-3	R-3

- Represents zero. X Not applicable. [1] Excludes one electoral vote cast for Walter B. Jones in Alabama. [2] Excludes 15 electoral votes cast for Harry F. Byrd as follows: AL 6, MS 8, and OK 1. [3] Excludes 46 electoral votes cast for American Independent George C. Wallace as follows: AL 10, AR 6, GA 12, LA 10, MS 7, and NC 1. [4] Excludes one electoral vote cast for Libertarian John Hospers in Virginia. [5] Excludes one electoral vote cast for Ronald Reagan in Washington. [6] Excludes one electoral vote cast for Lloyd Bentsen for President in West Virginia.

Source: 1956-72, U.S. Congress, Clerk of the House, *Statistics of the Presidential and Congressional Election*, quadrennial; 1976-96, Congressional Quarterly, Inc., Washington DC, *America Votes*, biennial (copyright).

No. 466. Popular Vote Cast for President, by Political Party—States: 1992 and 1996

[In thousands (104,425 represents 104,425,000), except percent]

State	1992 Total [1]	1992 Democratic Party	1992 Republican Party	1992 Perot (Reform Party) [2]	1996 Total [1]	1996 Democratic Party	1996 Republican Party	1996 Perot (Reform Party) [2]	Percent of total vote Democratic Party	Percent of total vote Republican Party	Percent of total vote Perot (Reform Party) [2]
United States..	104,425	44,909	39,104	19,742	96,278	47,402	39,199	8,085	49.2	40.7	8.4
Alabama.........	1,688	690	804	183	1,534	662	769	92	43.2	50.1	6.0
Alaska.........	259	78	102	73	242	80	123	26	33.3	50.8	10.9
Arizona.........	1,487	543	572	354	1,404	653	622	112	46.5	44.3	8.0
Arkansas........	951	506	337	99	884	475	325	70	53.7	36.8	7.9
California	11,132	5,121	3,631	2,296	10,019	5,120	3,828	698	51.1	38.2	7.0
Colorado.........	1,569	630	563	366	1,511	671	692	100	44.4	45.8	6.6
Connecticut.......	1,616	682	578	349	1,393	736	483	140	52.8	34.7	10.0
Delaware	290	126	102	59	271	140	99	29	51.8	36.6	10.6
District of Columbia .	228	193	21	10	186	158	17	4	85.2	9.3	1.9
Florida	5,314	2,073	2,173	1,053	5,304	2,547	2,245	484	48.0	42.3	9.1
Georgia	2,321	1,009	995	310	2,299	1,054	1,081	146	45.8	47.0	6.4
Hawaii	373	179	137	53	360	205	114	27	56.9	31.6	7.6
Idaho..........	482	137	203	130	492	165	257	63	33.6	52.2	12.7
Illinois.........	5,050	2,453	1,734	841	4,311	2,342	1,587	346	54.3	36.8	8.0
Indiana.........	2,306	848	989	456	2,136	887	1,007	224	41.5	47.1	10.5
Iowa	1,355	586	505	253	1,234	620	493	105	50.3	39.9	8.5
Kansas.........	1,157	390	450	312	1,074	388	583	93	36.1	54.3	8.6
Kentucky	1,493	665	617	204	1,389	637	623	120	45.8	44.9	8.7
Louisiana	1,790	816	733	211	1,784	928	713	123	52.0	39.9	6.9
Maine..........	679	263	207	207	606	313	186	86	51.6	30.8	14.2
Maryland	1,985	989	707	281	1,781	966	682	116	54.3	38.3	6.5
Massachusetts.....	2,774	1,319	805	631	2,557	1,572	718	227	61.5	28.1	8.9
Michigan.........	4,275	1,871	1,555	825	3,849	1,990	1,481	337	51.7	38.5	8.7
Minnesota........	2,348	1,021	748	563	2,193	1,120	766	258	51.1	35.0	11.8
Mississippi	982	400	488	86	894	394	440	52	44.1	49.2	5.8
Missouri	2,392	1,054	811	519	2,158	1,026	890	217	47.5	41.2	10.1
Montana.........	411	155	144	107	407	168	180	55	41.3	44.1	13.6
Nebraska	738	217	344	174	677	237	363	71	35.0	53.7	10.5
Nevada	506	189	176	133	464	204	199	44	43.9	42.9	9.5
New Hampshire	538	209	202	121	499	246	196	48	49.3	39.4	9.7
New Jersey.......	3,344	1,436	1,357	522	3,076	1,652	1,103	262	53.7	35.9	8.5
New Mexico	570	262	213	92	556	273	233	32	49.2	41.9	5.8
New York	6,927	3,444	2,347	1,091	6,316	3,756	1,933	503	59.5	30.6	8.0
North Carolina....	2,612	1,114	1,135	358	2,516	1,108	1,226	168	44.0	48.7	6.7
North Dakota......	308	99	136	71	266	107	125	33	40.1	46.9	12.2
Ohio	4,940	1,985	1,894	1,036	4,534	2,148	1,860	483	47.4	41.0	10.7
Oklahoma........	1,390	473	593	320	1,207	488	582	131	40.4	48.3	10.8
Oregon..........	1,463	621	476	354	1,378	650	538	121	47.2	39.1	8.8
Pennsylvania	4,960	2,239	1,792	903	4,506	2,216	1,801	431	49.2	40.0	9.6
Rhode Island......	453	213	132	105	390	233	105	44	59.7	26.8	11.2
South Carolina.....	1,203	480	578	139	1,152	506	573	64	44.0	49.8	5.6
South Dakota	336	125	137	73	324	139	151	31	43.0	46.5	9.7
Tennessee	1,983	934	841	200	1,894	909	864	106	48.0	45.6	5.6
Texas..........	6,154	2,282	2,496	1,355	5,612	2,460	2,736	379	43.8	48.8	6.7
Utah	744	183	323	203	666	222	362	66	33.3	54.4	10.0
Vermont	290	134	88	66	258	138	80	31	53.4	31.1	12.0
Virginia.........	2,559	1,039	1,151	349	2,417	1,091	1,138	160	45.1	47.1	6.6
Washington.......	2,288	993	731	542	2,254	1,123	841	201	49.8	37.3	8.9
West Virginia......	684	331	242	109	636	328	234	72	51.5	36.8	11.3
Wisconsin........	2,531	1,041	931	544	2,196	1,072	845	227	48.8	38.5	10.4
Wyoming	201	68	79	51	212	78	105	26	36.8	49.8	12.3

[1] Includes other parties.   [2] D=Democratic, R=Republican. Leading party vote refers to the party vote representing either a majority or a plurality for the victorious party in the area shown.

Source: Congressional Quarterly, Inc., Washington, DC, America Votes, biennial (copyright).

Elections   285

No. 467. Vote Cast for United States Senators, 1996 and 1998, and Incumbent Senators, 1998—States

[D=Democrat; R=Republican]

State	1996 Total (1,000)[1]	1996 Percent for leading party	1998 Total (1,000)[1]	1998 Percent for leading party	Incumbent Senators Name, party, and year	Incumbent Senators Name, party, and year
Alabama......	1,499	R-52.5	1,293	R-63.2	Jeff Sessions (R) 2003	Richard C. Shelby (R) 2005
Alaska.......	232	R-76.7	222	R-74.5	Frank H. Murkowski (R) 2005	Ted Stevens (R) 2003
Arizona......	(X)	(X)	1,013	R-68.7	John McCain (R) 2005	Jon Kyl (R) 2001
Arkansas.....	846	R-52.7	701	D-55.1	Blanche Lincoln (D) 2005	Tim Hutchinson (R) 2003
California....	(X)	(X)	8,315	D-53.1	Barbara Boxer (D) 2005	Dianne Feinstein (D) 2001
Colorado.....	1,470	R-51.1	1,327	R-62.5	Ben N. Campbell (R) 2005	Wayne Allard (R) 2003
Connecticut....	(X)	(X)	964	D-65.1	Christopher J. Dodd (D) 2005	Joseph I. Lieberman (D) 2001
Delaware	276	D-60.0	(X)	(X)	Joseph R. Biden Jr. (D) 2003	William V. Roth, Jr. (R) 2001
Florida.......	(X)	(X)	3,900	D-62.5	Bob Graham (D) 2005	Connie Mack (R) 2001
Georgia	2,259	D-48.9	1,754	R-52.4	Paul Coverdell (R) 2005	Max Cleland (D) 2003
Hawaii	(X)	(X)	398	D-79.2	Daniel K. Akaka (D) 2001	Daniel K. Inouye (D) 2005
Idaho........	497	R-57.0	378	R-69.5	Larry E. Craig (R) 2003	Michael D. Crapo (R) 2005
Illinois.......	4,251	D-56.1	3,395	R-50.3	Peter Fitzgerald (R) 2005	Richard J. Durbin (D) 2003
Indiana.......	(X)	(X)	1,589	D-63.7	Evan Bayh (D) 2005	Richard G. Lugar (R) 2001
Iowa.........	1,224	D-51.8	948	R-68.4	Tom Harkin (D) 2003	Charles E. Grassley (R) 2005
Kansas.......	[2]1,065	R-53.9	727	R-65.3	Sam Brownback (R) 2005	Pat Roberts (R) 2003
Kentucky	1,307	R-55.5	1,145	R-49.7	Jim Bunning (R) 2005	Mitch McConnell (R) 2003
Louisiana [3]....	1,700	D-50.2	969	D-64.0	John B. Breaux (D) 2005	Mary Landrieu (D) 2003
Maine........	607	R-49.2	(X)	(X)	Susan Collins (R) 2003	Olympia Snowe (R) 2001
Maryland	(X)	(X)	1,507	D-70.5	Barbara A. Mikulski (D) 2005	Paul S. Sarbanes (D) 2001
Massachusetts..	2,556	D-52.2	(X)	(X)	Edward M. Kennedy (D) 2001	John F. Kerry (D) 2003
Michigan......	3,763	D-58.4	(X)	(X)	Carl Levin (D) 2003	Spencer Abraham (R) 2001
Minnesota.....	2,183	D-50.3	(X)	(X)	Paul David Wellstone (D) 2003	Rod Grams (R) 2001
Mississippi....	879	R-71.0	(X)	(X)	Thad Cochran (R) 2003	Trent Lott (R) 2001
Missouri	(X)	(X)	1,577	R-52.7	Christopher S. Bond (R) 2005	John Ashcroft (R) 2001
Montana......	407	D-49.6	(X)	(X)	Max Baucus (D) 2003	Conrad Burns (R) 2001
Nebraska	677	R-56.1	(X)	(X)	Chuck Hagel (R) 2003	J. Robert Kerrey (D) 2001
Nevada	(X)	(X)	436	D-47.9	Harry Reid (D) 2005	Richard H. Bryan (D) 2001
New Hampshire.	493	R-49.2	315	R-67.8	Judd Gregg (R) 2005	Robert C. Smith (R) 2003
New Jersey....	2,884	D-52.7	(X)	(X)	Robert G. Torricelli (D) 2003	Frank R. Lautenberg (D) 2001
New Mexico ...	552	R-64.7	(X)	(X)	Jeff Bingaman (D) 2001	Pete V. Domenici (R) 2003
New York	(X)	(X)	4,671	D-54.6	Daniel P. Moynihan (D) 2001	Charles E. Schumer (D) 2005
North Carolina..	2,556	R-52.6	2,012	D-51.2	John Edwards (D) 2005	Jesse Helms (R) 2003
North Dakota...	(X)	(X)	213	D-63.2	Byron L. Dorgan (D) 2005	Kent Conrad (D) 2001
Ohio	(X)	(X)	3,404	R-56.5	George V. Voinovich (R) 2005	Mike DeWine (R) 2001
Oklahoma.....	1,183	R-56.7	860	R-66.4	James Inhofe (R) 2003	Don Nickles (R) 2005
Oregon.......	1,360	R-49.8	1,118	D-61.1	Gordon Smith (R) 2003	Ron Wyden (D) 2005
Pennsylvania...	(X)	(X)	2,958	R-61.3	Rick Santorum (R) 2001	Arlen Specter (R) 2005
Rhode Island...	363	D-63.5	(X)	(X)	Jack Reed (D) 2003	John H. Chafee (R) 2001
South Carolina..	1,161	R-53.4	1,068	D-52.7	Ernest F. Hollings (D) 2005	Strom Thurmond (R) 2003
South Dakota ..	324	D-51.3	262	D-62.1	Thomas A. Daschle (D) 2005	Tim Johnson (D) 2003
Tennessee	1,779	R-61.4	(X)	(X)	Fred Thompson (R) 2003	Bill Frist (R) 2001
Texas........	5,527	R-54.8	(X)	(X)	Kay Bailey Hutchison (R) 2001	Phil Gramm (R) 2003
Utah	(X)	(X)	495	R-64.0	Robert F. Bennett (R) 2005	Orrin G. Hatch (R) 2001
Vermont	(X)	(X)	214	D-72.2	Patrick J. Leahy (D) 2005	James M. Jeffords (R) 2001
Virginia......	2,355	R-52.5	(X)	(X)	Charles S. Robb (D) 2001	John W. Warner (R) 2003
Washington....	(X)	(X)	1,889	D-58.4	Patty Murray (D) 2005	Slade Gorton (R) 2001
West Virginia...	596	D-76.6	(X)	(X)	Robert C. Byrd (D) 2001	John D. Rockefeller IV (D) 2003
Wisconsin.....	(X)	(X)	1,761	D-50.5	Herb Kohl (D) 2001	Russell Feingold (D) 2005
Wyoming	211	R-54.1	(X)	(X)	Mike Enzi (R) 2003	Craig Thomas (R) 2001

X Not applicable. [1] Includes vote cast for minor parties. [2] Kansas had elections to fill two Senate seats in 1996. Pat Roberts was elected to fill the full-term seat vacated by the retiring Nancy Kassenbaum. Sam Brownback was elected to fill the short-term seat vacated by Robert Dole, who resigned in 1996 to run for President. [3] Louisiana holds an open-primary election with candidates from all parties running on the same ballot. Any candidate who receives a majority is elected.

Source: Congressional Quarterly, Inc., Washington, DC, *America Votes*, biennial (copyright).

No. 468. Vote Cast for United States Representatives, by Major Political Party—States: 1990 to 1998

[In thousands (61,513 represents 61,513,000), except percent. In each state, totals represent the sum of votes cast in each Congressional District or votes cast for Representative at Large in states where only one member is elected. In all years there are numerous districts within the state where either the Republican or Democratic party had no candidate. In some states the Republican and Democratic vote includes votes cast for the party candidate by endorsing parties]

State	1990 Total [1]	1990 Democratic	1990 Republican	1990 Percent for leading party	1996 Total [1]	1996 Democratic	1996 Republican	1996 Percent for leading party	1998 Total [1]	1998 Democratic	1998 Republican	1998 Percent for leading party
U.S. [2]...	61,513	32,565	27,648	D-52.9	89,863	43,626	43,902	R-48.9	65,897	31,482	32,255	R-48.9
AL........	1,017	690	315	D-67.9	1,469	656	786	R-53.5	1,215	545	666	R-54.8
AK........	192	92	99	R-51.7	234	85	139	R-59.4	223	77	140	R-62.6
AZ [3]......	966	345	621	R-64.3	1,356	521	801	R-59.0	1,004	407	574	R-57.1
AR........	665	369	296	D-55.5	863	396	456	R-52.8	525	169	320	R-60.9
CA........	7,287	3,568	3,347	D-49.0	9,482	4,707	4,292	D-49.6	7,990	4,040	3,510	D-50.6
CO........	1,001	504	487	D-50.3	1,461	597	833	R-57.0	1,274	533	716	R-56.2
CT........	1,037	489	546	R-52.6	1,294	724	547	D-55.9	954	496	442	D-51.9
DE........	177	116	58	D-65.5	267	73	186	R-69.5	181	57	120	R-66.4
DC [3 4]....	160	98	42	D-61.7	(NA)	(NA)	(NA)	(NA)	(NA)	(NA)	(NA)	(NA)
FL [3 4]....	2,378	1,213	1,163	D-51.0	4,692	2,037	2,640	R-56.3	1,213	581	558	D-47.9
GA........	1,394	855	539	D-61.3	2,163	1,011	1,152	R-53.3	1,632	592	1,040	R-63.7
HI........	341	216	118	D-63.3	353	196	136	D-55.5	397	261	119	D-65.7
ID........	315	183	131	D-58.2	494	194	290	R-58.7	379	169	205	R-54.0
IL........	3,077	1,646	1,349	D-53.5	4,128	2,267	1,813	D-54.9	3,215	1,566	1,625	R-50.5
IN........	1,514	831	683	D-54.9	2,105	944	1,119	R-53.1	1,576	673	862	R-54.7
IA........	792	401	385	D-50.6	1,201	533	650	R-54.1	901	338	552	R-61.3
KS........	781	394	387	D-50.4	1,049	425	591	R-56.4	727	272	450	R-61.9
KY........	764	353	397	R-52.0	1,238	507	731	R-59.0	1,099	456	637	R-58.0
LA........	106	106	-	D-100.0	660	262	398	R-60.3	310	213	97	D-68.7
ME........	517	284	233	D-55.0	600	379	211	D-63.2	415	281	125	D-67.7
MD........	1,091	566	517	D-51.9	1,639	877	762	D-53.5	1,482	792	690	D-53.5
MA........	2,051	1,420	567	D-69.2	2,409	1,585	781	D-65.8	1,742	1,306	413	D-75.0
MI........	2,434	1,321	1,089	D-54.3	3,700	1,945	1,679	D-52.6	2,985	1,469	1,438	D-49.2
MN........	1,781	1,042	736	D-58.5	2,141	1,180	895	D-55.1	2,040	1,090	863	D-53.5
MS........	369	299	69	D-81.2	904	397	488	R-54.0	551	263	232	D-47.7
MO........	1,353	728	625	D-53.8	2,116	1,116	833	D-52.8	1,572	788	748	D-50.1
MT........	317	157	160	R-50.5	404	175	212	R-52.4	332	147	176	R-53.0
NE........	587	277	309	R-52.7	662	204	450	R-68.0	526	105	393	R-74.7
NV........	313	144	151	R-48.2	450	173	249	R-55.3	410	79	275	R-67.1
NH........	291	141	149	R-51.2	491	221	247	R-50.3	318	124	190	R-59.8
NJ........	1,827	837	911	R-49.9	2,823	1,352	1,399	R-49.6	1,815	902	858	D-49.7
NM........	359	146	214	R-59.5	548	271	261	D-49.4	498	228	246	R-49.5
NY........	3,662	1,830	1,662	D-50.0	5,551	3,041	2,358	D-54.8	4,267	2,278	1,858	D-53.4
NC........	2,011	1,076	935	D-53.5	2,514	1,136	1,340	R-53.3	1,904	827	1,014	R-53.3
ND........	234	153	81	D-65.2	263	145	114	D-55.1	213	120	88	D-56.2
OH........	3,418	1,807	1,590	D-52.9	4,388	2,031	2,192	R-49.9	3,375	1,594	1,752	R-51.9
OK........	857	519	338	D-60.6	1,180	430	723	R-61.3	859	314	538	R-62.7
OR........	1,053	667	342	D-63.4	1,335	724	558	D-54.3	1,090	631	402	D-57.9
PA........	2,851	1,293	1,552	R-54.5	4,316	2,223	2,038	D-51.5	2,896	1,381	1,472	R-50.8
RI........	347	182	165	D-52.5	360	241	108	D-66.9	293	204	77	D-69.5
SC........	670	383	275	D-57.2	1,057	345	683	R-64.6	974	370	580	R-59.6
SD........	257	174	83	D-67.6	323	120	186	R-57.7	259	64	194	R-75.1
TN........	717	369	289	D-51.5	1,784	856	889	R-49.8	914	412	470	R-51.4
TX........	3,278	1,763	1,498	D-53.8	5,219	2,323	2,785	R-53.4	3,462	1,531	1,787	R-51.6
UT........	442	234	191	D-52.9	664	264	386	R-58.2	471	127	304	R-64.6
VT........	210	6	83	I-56.0	255	24	83	I-58.1	215	(X)	71	R-32.9
VA........	1,153	663	411	D-57.5	2,199	1,027	1,117	R-50.8	1,149	514	542	R-47.2
WA........	1,313	696	596	D-53.0	2,174	1,130	1,021	D-52.0	1,858	980	819	D-52.8
WV........	375	251	123	D-67.1	522	458	64	D-87.8	351	283	29	D-80.6
WI........	1,256	597	652	R-51.9	2,150	1,012	1,121	R-52.1	1,673	762	880	R-52.6
WY........	158	71	87	R-55.1	210	86	116	R-55.2	174	67	101	R-57.8

- Represents zero.   NA Not available.   X Not applicable.   [1] Includes vote cast for minor parties. Total for 1996 includes results from 431 districts, including 14 where members were elected without major party opposition (7 won by the Republicans and 7 by the Democrats). In four districts (three in Louisiana and one in Florida) candidates ran unopposed and no vote was recorded.   [2] Includes vote cast for nonvoting Delegate at Large in District of Columbia, except for 1994 and 1996.   [3] State law does not require tabulation of votes for unopposed candidates.   [4] In 1990 Districts 8, 10, 12, 13, and 16 were unopposed; in 1994 Districts 4, 10, 13, 14, 18, and 23 were unopposed; in 1996 District 4 was unopposed.

Source: Congressional Quarterly, Inc., Washington, DC, *America Votes*, biennial (copyright).

U.S. Census Bureau, Statistical Abstract of the United States: 1999

No. 469. Vote Cast for United States Representatives, by Major Political Party—Congressional Districts: 1998

[In some states the Democratic and Republican vote includes votes cast for the party candidate by endorsing parties]

State and district	Democratic candidate Name	Percent of total	Republican candidate Name	Percent of total	State and district	Democratic candidate Name	Percent of total	Republican candidate Name	Percent of total
AL....	(X)	(X)	(X)	(X)	44th .	Waite	35.7	Bono	60.1
1st..	[1]	[1]	Callahan	99.4	45th .	Neal	37.3	Rohrabacher	58.7
2d..	Fondren	30.7	Everett	69.3	46th .	Sanchez	56.4	Dornan	39.3
3d..	Turnham	41.9	Riley	58.1	47th .	Avalos	29.5	Cox	67.6
4th..	Bevill	43.5	Aderholt	56.4	48th .	[1]	[1]	Packard	76.9
5th..	Cramer	69.7	Aust	30.3	49th .	Kehoe	46.6	Bilbray	48.8
6th..	Smalley	28.1	Bachus	71.8	50th .	Filner	99.2	[1]	[1]
7th..	Hilliard	98.0	[1]	[1]	51st .	Kripke	34.7	Cunningham	61.0
AK....	Duncan	34.6	Young	62.6	52d .	[1]	[1]	Hunter	75.7
AZ....	(X)	(X)	(X)	(X)	CO....	(X)	(X)	(X)	(X)
1st..	Mendoza	35.4	Salmon	64.6	1st .	DeGette	66.9	McClanahan	30.1
2d..	Pastor	67.8	Barron	28.0	2d .	Udall	49.9	Greenlee	47.4
3d..	Starky	32.7	Stump	67.3	3d .	Kelley	31.5	McInnis	66.1
4th..	Ehst	31.2	Shadegg	64.7	4th .	Kirkpatrick	40.7	Schaffer	59.3
5th..	Volgy	45.2	Kolbe	51.6	5th .	Alford	26.0	Hefley	72.7
6th..	Owens	43.7	Hayworth	53.0	6th .	Strauss	41.5	Tancredo	55.9
AR....	(X)	(X)	(X)	(X)	CT....	(X)	(X)	(X)	(X)
1st..	Berry	[1]	[1]	[1]	1st .	Larson	58.1	O'Connor	41.4
2d..	Snyder	58.0	Wyrick	42.0	2d .	Gejdenson	61.0	Koval	35.5
3d..	[1]	[1]	Hutchinson	80.7	3d .	DeLauro	71.3	Reust	27.4
4th..	Smith	42.5	Dickey	57.5	4th .	Kantrowitz	29.9	Shays	69.1
CA....	(X)	(X)	(X)	(X)	5th .	Maloney	49.9	Nielsen	48.4
1st..	Thompson	61.9	Luce	32.8	6th .	Koskoff	39.6	Johnson	58.1
2d..	Braden	34.5	Herger	62.5	DE....	Williams	31.8	Castle	66.4
3d..	Dunn	45.0	Ose	52.4	FL....	(X)	(X)	(X)	(X)
4th..	Shapiro	34.4	Doolittle	62.2	1st .	[1]	[1]	Scarborough	99.5
5th..	Matsui	71.9	Dinsmore	26.0	2d .	Boyd	95.2	[1]	[1]
6th..	Woolsey	68.0	McAuliffe	29.7	3d .	Brown	55.4	Randall	44.6
7th..	Miller	76.7	Reece	23.3	4th .	[1]	[1]	Fowler	[1]
8th..	Pelosi	85.8	Martz	12.0	5th .	Thurman	66.3	[1]	[1]
9th..	Lee	82.8	Sanders	13.2	6th .	[1]	[1]	Stearns	[1]
10th..	Tauscher	53.5	Ball	43.4	7th .	[1]	[1]	Mica	[1]
11th..	Figueroa	36.2	Pombo	61.4	8th .	Krulick	34.2	McCollum	65.8
12th..	Lantos	74.0	Evans Jr	21.1	9th .	[1]	[1]	Bilirakis	[1]
13th..	Stark	71.2	Goetz	26.6	10th .	[1]	[1]	Young	[1]
14th..	Eshoo	68.6	Haugen	28.4	11th .	Davis	64.9	Chillura	35.1
15th..	Lane	37.9	Campbell	60.5	12th .	[1]	[1]	Canady	[1]
16th..	Lofgren	72.8	Thayn	23.4	13th .	[1]	[1]	Miller	[1]
17th..	Farr	64.5	McCampbell	32.7	14th .	[1]	[1]	Goss	[1]
18th..	Condit	86.8	[1]	[1]	15th .	Golding	36.9	Weldon	63.1
19th..	[1]	[1]	Radanovich	79.4	16th .	[1]	[1]	Foley	[1]
20th..	Dooley	60.7	Unruh	39.3	17th .	Meek	[1]	[1]	[1]
21st..	[1]	[1]	Thomas	78.9	18th .	(1)	[1]	Ros([1]) Lehtin	[1]
22d..	Capps	55.1	Bordonaro	43.0	19th .	Wexler	[1]	[1]	[1]
23d..	Gonzalez	39.9	Gallegly	60.1	20th .	Deutsch	[1]	[1]	[1]
24th..	Sherman	57.3	Hoffman	38.5	21st .	Cusack	25.2	Diaz([1]) Balar	74.8
25th..	[1]	[1]	McKeon	74.7	22d .	[1]	[1]	Shaw	[1]
26th..	Berman	82.5	[1]	[1]	23d .	Hastings	[1]	[1]	[1]
27th..	Gordon	46.4	Rogan	50.7	GA....	(X)	(X)	(X)	(X)
28th..	Nelson	39.3	Dreier	57.6	1st .	[1]	[1]	Kingston	100.0
29th..	Waxman	73.9	Gottlieb	22.6	2d .	Bishop	56.8	McCormick	43.2
30th..	Becerra	81.2	Parker	18.8	3d .	[1]	[1]	Collins	100.0
31st..	Martinez	70.0	Moreno	22.6	4th .	McKinney	61.1	Warren	38.9
32d..	Dixon	86.7	Ardito	11.3	5th .	Lewis	78.5	Lewis Sr	21.5
33d..	Roybal([1]) Allard	87.2	Miller	12.8	6th .	Pelphrey	29.3	Gingrich	70.7
34th..	Napolitano	67.6	Perez	28.6	7th .	Williams	44.6	Barr	55.4
35th..	Waters	89.3	[1]	[1]	8th .	Cain	37.6	Chambliss	62.4
36th..	Hahn	46.6	Kuykendall	48.9	9th .	[1]	[1]	Deal	100.0
37th..	Millender([1]) McDonald	85.1	Lankster	14.9	10th .	Freeman	40.4	Norwood	59.6
38th..	Mathews	44.3	Horn	52.9	11th .	Littman	30.7	Linder	69.3
39th..	Groom	34.0	Royce	62.6	HI....	(X)	(X)	(X)	(X)
40th..	Conaway	31.9	Lewis	64.9	1st .	Abercrombie	61.6	Ward	36.3
41st..	Ansari	40.7	Miller	53.2	2d .	Mink	69.4	Douglass	24.3
42d..	Brown	55.3	Pirozzi	40.3	ID....	(X)	(X)	(X)	(X)
43d..	Rayburn	37.8	Calvert	55.7	1st .	Williams	44.7	Chenoweth	55.3
					2d .	Stallings	44.7	Simpson	52.5

See footnotes at end of table.

U.S. Census Bureau, Statistical Abstract of the United States: 1999

[See headnote, p. 288]

State and district	Democratic candidate Name	Percent of total	Republican candidate Name	Percent of total	State and district	Democratic candidate Name	Percent of total	Republican candidate Name	Percent of total
IL.	(X)	(X)	(X)	(X)	4th . .	Frank.	98.4	(¹)	(¹)
1st . .	Rush	87.1	Ahimaz	10.6	5th . .	Meehan	70.7	Coleman . . .	29.3
2d . .	Jackson Jr. . . .	89.4	Gordon III . .	9.6	6th . .	Tierney	54.6	Torkildsen . . .	42.4
3d . .	Lipinski	72.5	Marshall . . .	27.5	7th . .	Markey	70.6	Long	29.3
4th . .	Gutierrez	81.7	Birch.	15.9	8th . .	Capuano	81.7	Hyde.	11.6
5th . .	Blagojevich. . .	74.0	Spitz.	26.0	9th . .	Moakley	99.4	(¹)	(¹)
6th . .	Cramer	30.1	Hyde.	67.3	10th .	Delahunt	70.0	Bleicken	29.9
7th . .	Davis.	92.9	(¹)	(¹)	**MI**	(X)	(X)	(X)	(X)
8th . .	Rothman	31.4	Crane	68.6	1st . .	Stupak.	58.7	McManus. . . .	39.5
9th . .	Schakowsky . .	74.6	Sohn.	23.1	2d . .	Shrauger . . .	29.8	Hoekstra . . .	68.7
10th .	(¹)	(¹)	Porter	100.0	3d . .	Ferguson Jr. . .	24.7	Ehlers	73.1
11th .	Mueller	41.2	Weller	58.8	4th . .	(¹)	(¹)	Camp	91.3
12th .	Costello	60.4	Price.	39.6	5th . .	Barcia	71.2	Brewster . . .	27.1
13th .	Hynes	39.0	Biggert	61.0	6th . .	Annen	28.1	Upton	70.1
14th .	Cozzi Jr.	30.2	Hastert	69.8	7th . .	Berryman . . .	40.1	Smith	57.5
15th .	Prussing.	38.4	Ewing	61.6	8th . .	Stabenow. . . .	57.4	Munsell	38.6
16th .	(¹)	(¹)	Manzullo	100.0	9th . .	Kildee	55.9	McMillin. . . .	41.9
17th .	Evans	51.6	Baker	48.4	10th .	Bonior	52.4	Palmer	45.3
18th .	(¹)	(¹)	LaHood	100.0	11th .	Reeds	33.7	Knollenberg . .	63.9
19th .	Phelps	58.3	Winters	41.7	12th .	Levin	55.9	Tourna	42.0
20th .	Verticchio	38.7	Shimkus . . .	61.3	13th .	Rivers	58.1	Hickey.	39.8
IN	(X)	(X)	(X)	(X)	14th .	Conyers Jr. . .	86.9	Collins.	11.1
1st . .	Visclosky	72.5	Petyo	26.2	15th .	Kilpatrick . . .	87.0	Boyd(¹)Fields .	10.3
2d . .	Boles.	38.0	McIntosh . . .	60.6	16th .	Dingell Jr. . . .	66.6	Morse	31.0
3d . .	Roemer	58.1	Holtz.	41.9	**MN.**	(X)	(X)	(X)	(X)
4th . .	Wehrle.	36.7	Souder	63.3	1st . .	Beckman	45.2	Gutknecht . . .	54.7
5th . .	Steele	36.0	Buyer	62.5	2d . .	Minge	57.0	Duehring . . .	36.1
6th . .	Kern	16.8	Burton	72.0	3d . .	Leino.	23.5	Ramstad . . .	71.9
7th . .	Hillenberg. . . .	28.1	Pease	68.9	4th . .	Vento	53.7	Newinski	39.8
8th . .	Riecken	46.0	Hostettler . . .	52.1	5th . .	Sabo	66.9	Taylor	27.6
9th . .	Hill	50.8	Leising	47.9	6th . .	Luther	50.0	Kline	46.0
10th .	Carson.	58.3	Hofmeister . . .	39.4	7th . .	Peterson	71.7	Edin	28.1
IA	(X)	(X)	(X)	(X)	8th . .	Oberstar	66.0	Shuster	26.5
1st . .	Rush	42.3	Leach	56.5	**MS.**	(X)	(X)	(X)	(X)
2d . .	Tully	44.0	Nussle.	55.2	1st . .	Weathers	30.6	Wicker.	67.2
3d . .	Boswell	56.9	McKibben . . .	41.1	2d . .	Thompson . . .	71.2	(¹)	(¹)
4th . .	Dvorak.	33.9	Ganske	65.2	3d . .	(¹)	(¹)	Pickering . . .	84.6
5th . .	(¹)	(¹)	Latham	99.2	4th . .	Shows	53.4	Hosemann . . .	44.9
KS.	(X)	(X)	(X)	(X)	5th . .	Taylor*	77.8	McConnell . . .	19.1
1st . .	Phillips.	19.3	Moran	80.7	**MO**	(X)	(X)	(X)	(X)
2d . .	Clark	39.0	Ryun.	61.0	1st . .	Clay*	72.6	Soluade.	24.5
3d . .	Moore	52.4	Snowbarger . .	47.6	2d . .	Ross	28.3	Talent*	70.0
4th . .	Lawing	38.6	Tiahrt	58.3	3d . .	Gephardt* . . .	55.8	Federer	42.0
KY	(X)	(X)	(X)	(X)	4th . .	Skelton*	71.0	Noland	27.2
1st . .	Barlow	44.8	Whitfield . . .	55.2	5th . .	McCarthy* . . .	65.9	Bennett	31.0
2d . .	Evans	35.3	Lewis	63.7	6th . .	Danner	70.9	Bailey	26.8
3d . .	Gorman	47.5	Northup.	51.5	7th . .	Perkel	24.3	Blunt.	72.6
4th . .	Lucas	53.4	Williams.	46.6	8th . .	Heckemeyer . .	35.7	Emerson ⁵ . .	62.6
5th . .	Bailey(¹)Barner	21.8	Rogers	78.2	9th . .	Vogt	35.5	Hulshof	62.2
6th . .	Scorsone	46.0	Fletcher.	53.1	**MT.**	Deschamps . .	44.4	Hill	53.0
LA ²	(X)	(X)	(X)	(X)	**NE.**	(X)	(X)	(X)	(X)
1st . .	(¹)	(¹)	Livingston ³ . .	(¹)	1st . .	Eret.	26.4	Bereuter . . .	73.5
2d . .	Jefferson ³ . . .	86.0	(¹)	(¹)	2d . .	Scott	34.2	Terry	65.5
3d . .	(¹)	(¹)	Tauzin ³	(¹)	3d . .	(¹)	(¹)	Barrett.	84.3
4th . .	(¹)	(¹)	McCrery ³ . . .	(¹)	**NV.**	(X)	(X)	(X)	(X)
5th . .	(¹)	(¹)	Cooksey	(¹)	1st . .	Berkley	49.2	Chairez	45.7
6th . .	McKeithen . . .	49.3	Baker ⁵	50.7	2d . .	(¹)	(¹)	Gibbons	81.1
7th . .	John ⁴	(¹)	(¹)	(¹)	**NH.**	(X)	(X)	(X)	(X)
ME.	(X)	(X)	(X)	(X)	1st . .	Flood.	33.1	Sununu	66.8
1st . .	Allen	60.3	Connelly	35.5	2d . .	Rauh	44.8	Bass	53.1
2d . .	Baldacci	76.2	Reisman	23.8	**NJ**	(X)	(X)	(X)	(X)
MD.	(X)	(X)	(X)	(X)	1st . .	Andrews.	73.2	Richards	22.6
1st . .	Pinder	30.8	Gilchrest	69.2	2d . .	Hunsberger . .	30.8	LoBiondo . . .	65.9
2d . .	Bosley	30.7	Ehrlich.	69.3	3d . .	Polansky	35.1	Saxton	62.0
3d . .	Cardin	77.6	Harby	22.4	4th . .	Schneider. . . .	35.0	Smith	62.2
4th . .	Wynn.	85.7	Kimble.	14.3	5th . .	Schneider. . . .	33.3	Roukema	63.7
5th . .	Hoyer	65.4	Ostrom	34.6	6th . .	Pallone	57.0	Ferguson	40.3
6th . .	McCown.	36.6	Bartlett	63.4	7th . .	Connelly.	44.4	Franks.	52.5
7th . .	Cummings . . .	85.7	Kondner	14.3	8th . .	Pascrell Jr. . . .	62.1	Kirnan	35.4
8th . .	Neas	39.6	Morella	60.3	9th . .	Rothman	64.6	Lonegan	33.8
MA.	(X)	(X)	(X)	(X)	10th .	Payne	83.5	Wnuck.	10.8
1st . .	Olver	71.7	Morgan	28.3	11th .	Scollo	29.6	Frelinghuysen.	67.7
2d . .	Neal	99.0	(¹)	(¹)	12th .	Holt.	50.1	Pappas	47.2
3d . .	McGovern . . .	56.9	Amorello	41.5	13th .	Menendez . . .	80.1	de Leon.	16.6

See footnotes at end of table.

U.S. Census Bureau, Statistical Abstract of the United States: 1999

No. 469. Vote Cast for United States Representatives, by Major Political Party—Congressional Districts: 1998—Continued

[See headnote, p. 288]

State and district	Democratic candidate Name	Percent of total	Republican candidate Name	Percent of total	State and district	Democratic candidate Name	Percent of total	Republican candidate Name	Percent of total
NM....	(X)	(X)	(X)	(X)	13th .	Brown	61.5	Drake	38.5
1st ..	Maloof	41.9	Wilson	48.4	14th .	Sawyer	62.7	Watkins	37.3
2d ..	Baca	42.1	Skeen	57.9	15th .	Miller	28.5	Pryce	65.7
3d ..	Udall	53.2	Redmond	43.3	16th .	Ferguson	36.0	Regula	64.0
NY....	(X)	(X)	(X)	(X)	17th .	Traficant	68.2	Alberty	31.8
1st ..	Holst	35.9	Forbes	64.1	18th .	Burch	39.7	Ney	60.3
2d ..	Bace	29.5	Lazio	66.2	19th .	Kelley	33.6	LaTourette	66.4
3d ..	Langberg	34.9	King	64.3	OK....	(X)	(X)	(X)	(X)
4th ..	McCarthy	52.6	Becker	46.6	1st ..	Plowman	38.2	Largent	61.8
5th ..	Ackerman	65.0	Pinzon	33.1	2d ..	Pharaoh	39.8	Coburn	57.7
6th ..	Meeks	100.0	(¹)	(¹)	3d ..	Roberts	38.0	Watkins	62.0
7th ..	Crowley	69.0	Dillon	25.6	4th ..	Odom	38.5	Watts	61.5
8th ..	Nadler	86.0	Howard	14.0	5th ..	Smothermon	31.8	Istook	68.2
9th ..	Weiner	66.4	Telano	23.4	6th ..	Barby	33.2	Lucas	65.0
10th ..	Towns	92.3	Brown	6.2	OR....	(X)	(X)	(X)	(X)
11th ..	Owens	90.0	Greene	8.7	1st ..	Wu	50.1	Bordonaro	47.1
12th ..	Velazquez	83.6	Markgraf	11.6	2d ..	Campbell	34.8	Walden	61.5
13th ..	Prisco	34.2	Fossella	64.8	3d ..	Blumenauer	83.9	(¹)	(¹)
14th ..	Maloney	77.4	Kupferman	22.6	4th ..	DeFazio	70.1	Webb	28.6
15th ..	Rangel	93.1	Cunningham	5.8	5th ..	Hooley	54.9	Shannon	40.5
16th ..	Serrano	95.4	Bayley Jr.	3.5	PA....	(X)	(X)	(X)	(X)
17th ..	Engel	88.0	Flumefreddo	12.0	1st ..	Brady	81.2	Harrison	16.6
18th ..	Lowey	82.8	(¹)	(¹)	2d ..	Fattah	86.5	Mulligan	13.5
19th ..	Collins	33.6	Kelly	62.2	3d ..	Borski	59.3	Dougherty	40.7
20th ..	Feiner	38.8	Gilman	58.3	4th ..	Klink	63.8	Turzai	36.2
21st ..	McNulty	74.2	Ayers	25.8	5th ..	(¹)	(¹)	Peterson	84.8
22d ..	Bordewich	42.1	Sweeney	55.3	6th ..	Holden	61.0	Meckley	39.0
23d ..	(¹)	(¹)	Boehlert	80.8	7th ..	D'Urso	28.2	Weldon	71.8
24th ..	Tallon	21.0	McHugh	79.0	8th ..	Tuthill	32.6	Greenwood	63.2
25th ..	Rothenberg	30.6	Walsh	69.4	9th ..	(¹)	(¹)	Shuster	99.5
26th ..	Hinchey	61.8	Walker	31.3	10th ..	Casey	48.4	Sherwood	48.7
27th ..	Cook	42.7	Reynolds	57.3	11th ..	Kanjorski	66.8	Urban	33.2
28th ..	Slaughter	64.8	Kaplan	30.8	12th ..	Murtha	68.5	Holloway	31.5
29th ..	LaFalce	57.0	Collins	40.7	13th ..	Hoeffel	51.6	Fox	46.6
30th ..	Peoples	32.2	Quinn	67.8	14th ..	Coyne	60.5	Ravotti	38.3
31st ..	Rossiter	25.3	Houghton	68.0	15th ..	Afflerbach	45.0	Toomey	55.0
NC....	(X)	(X)	(X)	(X)	16th ..	Yorczyk	29.5	Pitts	70.5
1st ..	Clayton	62.2	Tyler	37.0	17th ..	(¹)	(¹)	Gekas	99.8
2d ..	Etheridge	57.4	Page	41.7	18th ..	Doyle	67.7	Walker	32.3
3d ..	Williams	37.1	Jones Jr.	81.9	19th ..	Ropp	28.5	Goodling	67.6
4th ..	Price	57.4	Roberg	41.6	20th ..	Mascara	99.8	(¹)	(¹)
5th ..	Robinson	31.7	Burr	67.6	21st ..	Klemens	36.6	English	63.4
6th ..	(¹)	(¹)	Coble	88.6	RI	(X)	(X)	(X)	(X)
7th ..	McIntyre	91.3	(¹)	(¹)	1st ..	Kennedy	66.8	Santa	27.7
8th ..	Taylor	48.2	Hayes	50.7	2d ..	Weygand	72.0	Matson	24.8
9th ..	Blake	29.5	Myrick	69.3	SC....	(X)	(X)	(X)	(X)
10th ..	(¹)	(¹)	Ballenger	85.6	1st ..	(¹)	(¹)	Sanford	91.0
11th ..	Young	42.2	Taylor	56.6	2d ..	Frederick	41.0	Spence	57.8
12th ..	Watt	56.0	Keadle	42.2	3d ..	(¹)	(¹)	Graham	99.7
ND....	Pomeroy	56.2	Cramer	41.1	4th ..	Reese	40.2	DeMint	57.7
OH....	(X)	(X)	(X)	(X)	5th ..	Spratt	57.9	Burkhold	40.4
1st ..	Qualls	47.0	Chabot	53.0	6th ..	Clyburn	72.6	McLeod	25.8
2d ..	Sanders	24.2	Portman	75.8	SD....	Moser	24.9	Thune	75.1
3d ..	Hall	69.3	Shondel	30.7	TN....	(X)	(X)	(X)	(X)
4th ..	McClain	36.2	Oxley	63.8	1st ..	White	30.8	Jenkins	69.1
5th ..	Darrow	33.3	Gillmor	66.7	2d ..	(¹)	(¹)	Duncan Jr.	88.6
6th ..	Strickland	57.0	Hollister	43.0	3d ..	Lewis Jr.	32.6	Wamp	66.0
7th ..	Minor	27.7	Hobson	67.2	4th ..	Cooper	40.4	Hilleary	59.6
8th ..	Griffin	29.3	Boehner	70.7	5th ..	Clement	82.8	(¹)	(¹)
9th ..	Kaptur	81.2	Emery	18.8	6th ..	Gordon	54.6	Massey	45.3
10th ..	Kucinich	66.8	Slovenic	33.2	7th ..	(¹)	(¹)	Bryant	99.5
11th ..	Tubbs Jones	80.4	Hereford	13.0	8th ..	Tanner	100.0	(¹)	(¹)
12th ..	Brown	32.8	Kasich	67.2	9th ..	Ford Jr.	78.7	Burdikoff	18.9

See footnotes at end of table.

U.S. Census Bureau, Statistical Abstract of the United States: 1999

No. 469. Vote Cast for United States Representatives, by Major Political Party—Congressional Districts: 1998—Continued

[See headnote, p. 288]

State and district	Democratic candidate — Name	Percent of total	Republican candidate — Name	Percent of total
TX	(X)	(X)	(X)	(X)
1st . .	Sandlin	59.4	Boemer	40.6
2d . .	Turner	58.4	Babin	40.8
3d . .	(1)	(1)	Johnson	91.2
4th . .	Hall	57.6	Lohmeyer	40.9
5th . .	Morales	43.4	Sessions	55.8
6th . .	Boothe	25.9	Barton	72.9
7th . .	(1)	(1)	Archer	93.3
8th . .	(1)	(1)	Brady[6]	92.8
9th . .	Lampson[7] . .	63.7	Cottar	36.3
10th .	Doggett	85.2	(1)	(1)
11th .	Edwards	82.4	(1)	(1)
12th .	Hall	36.3	Granger	61.9
13th .	Harmon	31.0	Thornberry . . .	67.9
14th .	Sneary	44.5	Paul	55.3
15th .	Hinojosa	58.4	Haughey	41.6
16th .	Reyes	87.9	(1)	(1)
17th .	Stenholm . . .	53.6	Izzard	45.3
18th .	Jackson[1]Lee	89.9	(1)	(1)
19th .	Blakenship . . .	16.4	Combest	83.6
20th .	Gonzalez . . .	63.2	Walker	35.6
21st .	(1)	(1)	Smith	91.4
22d . .	Kemp	33.7	DeLay	65.2
23d . .	Jones	35.1	Bonilla	63.8
24th .	Frost	57.5	Terry	40.9
25th .	Bentsen[8] . . .	57.9	Sanchez	41.3
26th .	(1)	(1)	Armey	88.1
27th .	Ortiz	63.3	Stone	35.2
28th .	Rodriguez . . .	90.5	(1)	(1)
29th .	Green	92.8	(1)	(1)
30th .	Johnson[9] . . .	72.2	Kelleher	26.8
UT	(X)	(X)	(X)	(X)
1st . .	Beierlein	30.4	Hansen	67.7
2d . .	Eskelsen	43.5	Cook	52.8
3d . .	(1)	(1)	Cannon	76.9
VT[10]	(1)	(1)	Candon	32.9
VA	(X)	(X)	(X)	(X)
1st . .	(1)	(1)	Bateman	76.4
2d . .	Pickett	94.3	(1)	(1)
3d . .	Scott	76.0	(1)	(1)
4th . .	Sisisky	97.0	(1)	(1)
5th . .	Goode Jr. . . .	98.9	(1)	(1)
6th . .	Bowers	30.7	Goodlatte	69.3
7th . .	(1)	(1)	Bliley	78.7
8th . .	Moran	66.7	Miller	33.1
9th . .	Boucher	60.9	Barta	39.1
10th .	Brooks	25.2	Wolf	71.6
11th .	(1)	(1)	Davis III	81.7
WA	(X)	(X)	(X)	(X)
1st . .	Inslee	49.8	Smith	44.1
2d . .	Cammermeyer .	44.8	Metcalf	55.2
3d . .	Baird	54.7	Benton	45.3
4th . .	Pross	24.4	Hastings	69.1
5th . .	Lyons	38.1	Nethercutt . . .	56.9
6th . .	Dicks	68.4	Lawrence	31.6
7th . .	McDermott . . .	88.2	(1) / Behrens[1]	(1)
8th . .	Benedict	40.3	Dunn	59.7
9th . .	Smith	64.7	Taber	35.3
WV . . .	(X)	(X)	(X)	(X)
1st . .	Mollohan	84.7	(1)	(1)
2d . .	Wise	73.0	Kay	21.4
3d . .	Rahall II	86.6	(1)	(1)
WI	(X)	(X)	(X)	(X)
1st . .	Spottswood . . .	42.7	Ryan	57.1
2d . .	Baldwin	52.5	Musser	46.7
3d . .	Kind	71.5	Brechler	28.4
4th . .	Kleczka	57.9	Reynolds	42.0
5th . .	Barrett	78.2	Melvin	21.6
6th . .	(1)	(1)	Petri	92.6
7th . .	Obey	60.6	West	39.3
8th . .	Johnson	45.4	Green	54.6
9th . .	(1)	(1)	Sensenbren-ner .	91.3
WY . . .	Farris	38.7	Cubin	57.8

X Not applicable.   [1] No candidate.   [2] Louisiana holds an open-primary election with candidates from all parties running on the same ballot. Any candidate who receives a majority is elected; if no candidate receives 50 percent, there is a run-off election in November between the top two finishers.   [3] Candidate listed won seat in open-primary.   [4] There were two Democratic candidates; Hunter Lundy received 46.9 percent of Democratic votes.   [5] Jo Ann Emerson ran as an independent but caucused in the 105th Congress with the Democrats.   [6] There were two Republican candidates; Gene Fontenot received 38.9 percent of Republican votes.   [7] There were two Democratic candidates; Geraldine Sam received 9.4 percent of Democratic votes.   [8] There were two Democratic candidates; Beverly Clark received 16.9 percent of Democratic votes.   [9] There were two additional Democratic candidates who received a total of 15.7 percent of Democratic candidates.   [10] The winning candidate was Bernard Sanders, an Independent, who received 49.9 percent of the vote.

Source: Congressional Quarterly Inc., *Congressional Quarterly Weekly Report* (copyright).

No. 470. Composition of Congress, by Political Party: 1971 to 1997

[D=Democratic, R=Republican. Data for beginning of first session of each Congress (as of January 3), except as noted. Excludes vacancies at beginning of session]

Year	Party and President	Congress	House — Majority party	House — Minority party	House — Other	Senate — Majority party	Senate — Minority party	Senate — Other
1971 [1]	R (Nixon)	92d	D-254	R-180	-	D-54	R-44	2
1973 [1][2]	R (Nixon)	93d	D-239	R-192	1	D-56	R-42	2
1975 [3]	R (Ford)	94th	D-291	R-144	-	D-60	R-37	2
1977 [4]	D (Carter)	95th	D-292	R-143	-	D-61	R-38	1
1979 [4]	D (Carter)	96th	D-276	R-157	-	D-58	R-41	1
1981 [4]	R (Reagan)	97th	D-243	R-192	-	R-53	D-46	1
1983	R (Reagan)	98th	D-269	R-165	-	R-54	D-46	-
1985	R (Reagan)	99th	D-252	R-182	-	R-53	D-47	-
1987	R (Reagan)	100th	D-258	R-177	-	D-55	R-45	-
1989	R (Bush)	101st	D-259	R-174	-	D-55	R-45	-
1991 [5]	R (Bush)	102d	D-267	R-167	1	D-56	R-44	-
1993 [5]	D (Clinton)	103d	D-258	R-176	1	D-57	R-43	-
1995 [5][6]	D (Clinton)	104th	R-230	D-204	1	R-52	D-48	-
1996 [5][6]	D (Clinton)	104th	R-236	D-197	1	R-53	D-46	-
1997 [5][6]	D (Clinton)	105th	R-226	D-207	2	R-55	D-45	-

- Represents zero.   [1] Senate had one Independent and one Conservative-Republican.   [2] House had one Independent-Democrat.   [3] Senate had one Independent, one Conservative-Republican, and one undecided (New Hampshire).   [4] Senate had one Independent.   [5] House had one Independent-Socialist.   [6] As of beginning of second session.

Source: U.S. Congress, Joint Committee on Printing, *Congressional Directory*, annual; beginning 1977, biennial.

No. 471. Composition of Congress, by Political Party Affiliation—States: 1989 to 1997

[Figures are for the beginning of the first session (as of January 3), except as noted. Dem.=Democratic; Rep.=Republican]

State	Representatives								Senators							
	101st Cong.,[1] 1989		102d Cong.,[2] 1991		103rd Cong.,[2] 1993		104th Cong.,[2][3][4] 1997		101st Cong., 1989		102d Cong., 1991		103rd Cong., 1993		104th Cong.,[3][5] 1997	
	Dem.	Rep.	Dem.	Rep.	Dem.	Rep.	Dem.	Rep.	Dem.	Rep.	Dem.	Rep.	Dem.	Rep.	Dem.	Rep.
U.S.	259	174	267	167	258	176	197	236	55	45	56	44	57	43	46	53
AL	4	2	5	2	4	3	2	5	2	-	2	-	2	-	-	2
AK	-	1	-	1	-	1	-	1	-	2	-	2	-	2	-	2
AZ	1	4	1	4	3	3	1	5	1	1	1	1	1	1	-	2
AR	3	1	3	1	2	2	2	2	2	-	2	-	2	-	1	1
CA	27	18	26	19	30	22	29	23	1	1	1	1	1	1	-	2
CO	3	3	3	3	2	4	2	4	1	1	2	-	2	-	2	-
CT	3	3	3	3	3	3	4	2	2	-	2	-	2	-	1	1
DE	1	-	1	-	-	1	-	1	1	1	1	1	1	1	1	1
FL	10	9	9	10	10	13	8	15	1	1	1	1	1	1	1	1
GA	9	1	9	1	7	4	3	8	2	-	2	-	1	1	1	1
HI	1	1	2	-	2	-	2	-	2	-	2	-	2	-	2	-
ID	1	1	-	2	-	2	-	2	-	2	-	2	-	2	-	2
IL	14	8	15	7	12	8	10	10	2	-	2	-	2	-	2	-
IN	6	3	8	2	7	3	4	6	-	2	1	1	1	1	-	2
IA	2	4	2	4	1	4	1	4	1	1	-	2	-	2	-	2
KS	2	3	2	3	2	2	-	4	1	1	-	2	-	2	-	2
KY	4	3	4	3	4	2	1	5	1	1	1	1	1	1	1	1
LA	4	4	4	4	4	3	2	5	2	-	2	-	2	-	2	-
ME	1	1	1	1	1	1	2	-	1	1	1	1	1	1	-	2
MD	6	2	5	3	4	4	4	4	2	-	2	-	2	-	2	-
MA	10	1	10	1	8	2	10	-	2	-	2	-	2	-	2	-
MI	11	7	11	7	10	6	10	6	2	-	1	1	1	1	1	1
MN	5	3	6	2	6	2	6	2	-	2	-	2	-	2	1	1
MS	4	1	5	-	5	-	2	3	-	2	-	2	-	2	1	1
MO	5	4	6	3	6	3	5	4	-	2	-	2	-	2	1	1
MT	1	1	1	1	1	-	-	1	1	1	1	1	1	1	1	1
NE	1	2	1	2	1	2	-	3	2	-	2	-	2	-	2	-
NV	1	1	1	1	1	1	-	2	-	2	-	2	-	2	-	2
NH	-	2	1	1	1	1	-	2	2	-	2	-	2	-	2	-
NJ	8	6	8	6	7	6	6	7	2	-	2	-	2	-	2	-
NM	1	2	1	2	1	2	-	3	1	1	1	1	1	1	1	1
NY	21	13	21	13	18	13	18	13	1	1	1	1	1	1	1	1
NC	8	3	7	4	8	4	6	6	1	1	1	1	-	2	-	2
ND	1	-	1	-	-	1	1	-	2	-	2	-	2	-	1	1
OH	11	10	11	10	10	9	8	11	1	1	1	1	1	1	1	1
OK	4	2	4	2	4	1	4	1	-	2	-	2	-	2	-	2
OR	3	2	4	1	4	1	4	1	-	2	-	2	1	1	1	1
PA	12	11	11	12	11	10	11	10	1	1	1	1	1	1	1	1
RI	-	2	1	1	1	1	2	-	1	1	1	1	1	1	1	1
SC	4	2	4	2	3	3	2	4	1	1	1	1	1	1	1	1
SD	1	-	1	-	1	-	-	1	2	-	1	1	1	1	2	-
TN	6	3	6	3	6	3	4	5	2	-	2	-	2	-	-	2
TX	19	8	19	8	21	9	17	13	1	1	1	1	1	1	-	2
UT	1	2	2	1	2	1	-	3	1	1	-	2	-	2	-	2
VT	-	1	-	1	-	1	-	1	1	1	1	1	1	1	1	1
VA	5	5	6	4	7	4	6	5	1	1	1	1	1	1	1	1
WA	5	3	5	3	8	1	3	6	2	-	2	-	2	-	2	-
WV	4	-	4	-	3	-	3	-	2	-	2	-	2	-	2	-
WI	5	4	4	5	4	5	5	4	1	1	1	1	2	-	2	-
WY	-	1	-	1	-	1	-	1	-	2	-	2	-	2	-	2

- Represents zero. [1] Alabama and Indiana had one vacancy each. [2] Vermont had one Independent-Socialist Representative. [3] As of beginning of second session. [4] California had one vacancy. [5] Oregon had one vacancy.

Source: U.S. Congress, Joint Committee on Printing, *Congressional Directory*, biennial; and unpublished data.

U.S. Census Bureau, Statistical Abstract of the United States: 1999

No. 472. Members of Congress—Incumbents Reelected: 1964 to 1998

	Representatives						Senators					
		Incumbent candidates						Incumbent candidates				
			Reelected		Defeated in—				Reelected		Defeated in—	
Year	Retire-ments [1]	Total	Num-ber	Per-cent of candi-dates	Pri-mary	General election	Retire-ments [1]	Total	Num-ber	Per-cent of candi-dates	Pri-mary	General election
PRESIDENTIAL-YEAR ELECTIONS												
1964	33	397	344	86.6	8	45	2	33	28	84.8	1	4
1968	23	409	396	96.8	4	9	6	28	20	71.4	4	4
1972	40	390	365	93.6	12	13	6	27	20	74.1	2	5
1976	47	384	368	95.8	3	13	8	25	16	64.0	-	9
1980	34	398	361	90.7	6	31	5	29	16	55.2	4	9
1984	22	411	392	95.4	3	16	4	29	26	89.7	-	3
1988	23	409	402	98.3	1	6	6	27	23	85.2	-	4
1992	65	368	325	88.3	[2]19	[3]24	7	28	23	82.1	1	4
1996	50	384	361	94.0	2	21	13	21	19	90.5	1	1
MIDTERM ELECTIONS												
1966	22	411	362	88.1	8	41	3	32	28	87.5	3	1
1970	29	401	379	94.5	10	12	4	31	24	77.4	1	6
1974	43	391	343	87.7	8	40	7	27	23	85.2	2	2
1978	49	382	358	93.7	5	19	10	25	15	60.0	3	7
1982	40	393	354	90.1	[2]10	29	3	30	28	93.3	-	2
1986	40	394	385	97.7	3	6	6	28	21	75.0	-	7
1990	27	406	390	96.1	1	15	3	32	31	96.9	-	1
1994	48	387	349	90.2	4	34	9	26	24	92.3	-	2
1998	23	404	395	97.8	1	6	5	29	26	89.7	-	3

- Represents zero.   [1] Does not include persons who died or resigned before the election.   [2] Number of incumbents defeated in primaries by other incumbents due to redistricting: six in 1982 and four in 1992.   [3] Five incumbents defeated in general election by other incumbents due to redistricting.

Source: Ornstein, Norman J., Thomas E. Mann, and Michael J. Malbin, *Vital Statistics on Congress, 1993-1994*, beginning 1995, Beginning 1995, Congressional Quarterly, Inc., Washington, DC, *America Votes, biennial (copyright)*.

No. 473. Members of Congress—Selected Characteristics: 1981 to 1995

[As of beginning of first session of each Congress (January 3). Figures for Representatives exclude vacancies]

Members of congress and year	Male	Fe-male	Black [1]	API [2]	His-panic [3]	Age [4] (in years)					Seniority [5]				
						Under 40	40 to 49	50 to 59	60 to 69	70 and over	Less than 2 yrs.	2 to 9 yrs.	10 to 19 yrs.	20 to 29 yrs.	30 yrs. or more
REPRESENTATIVES															
97th Cong., 1981 . . .	416	19	[6]17	3	6	94	142	132	54	13	77	231	96	23	8
98th Cong., 1983 . . .	413	21	[7]21	3	8	86	145	132	57	14	83	224	88	28	11
99th Cong., 1985 . . .	412	22	[7]20	3	10	71	154	131	59	19	49	237	104	34	10
100th Cong., 1987 . .	412	23	[7]23	4	11	63	153	137	56	26	51	221	114	37	12
101st Cong., 1989 . .	408	25	[7]24	5	10	41	163	133	74	22	39	207	139	35	13
102d Cong., 1991 . .	407	28	[7]26	3	11	39	152	134	86	24	55	178	147	44	11
103d Cong., 1993 [6] .	388	47	[7]38	4	17	47	151	128	89	15	118	141	132	32	12
104th Cong., 1995 . .	388	47	[9]40	4	17	53	155	135	79	13	92	188	110	36	9
SENATORS															
97th Cong., 1981 . . .	98	2	-	3	-	9	35	36	14	6	19	51	17	11	2
98th Cong., 1983 . . .	98	2	-	2	-	7	28	39	20	6	5	61	21	10	3
99th Cong., 1985 . . .	98	2	-	2	-	4	27	38	25	6	8	56	27	7	2
100th Cong., 1987 . .	98	2	-	2	-	5	30	36	22	7	14	41	36	7	2
101st Cong., 1989 . .	98	2	-	2	-	-	30	40	22	8	23	22	43	10	2
102d Cong., 1991 . .	98	2	-	2	-	-	23	46	24	7	5	34	47	10	4
103d Cong., 1993 [6] .	93	7	1	2	-	1	16	48	22	12	15	30	39	11	5
104th Cong., 1995 . .	92	8	1	2	-	1	14	41	27	17	12	38	30	15	5

- Represents zero.   [1] Source: Joint Center for Political and Economic Studies, Washington, DC.   [2] Asian and Pacific Islanders. Source: Library of Congress, Congressional Research Service, "Asian Pacific Americans in the United States Congress", Report 94-767 GOV.   [3] Source: National Association of Latino Elected and Appointed Officials, Washington, DC, *National Roster of Hispanic Elected Officials*, annual.   [4] Some members do not provide date of birth.   [5] Represents consecutive years of service.   [6] Does not include District of Columbia or Virgin Islands delegate.   [7] Includes District of Columbia delegate but not Virgin Islands delegate.   [8] Includes members elected to fill vacant seats through June 14, 1993.   [9] Includes District of Columbia and Virgin Islands delegate.

Source: Except as noted, compiled by U.S. Census Bureau from data published in *Congressional Directory*, biennial.

U.S. Census Bureau, Statistical Abstract of the United States: 1999

No. 474. U.S. Congress—Measures Introduced and Enacted and Time in Session: 1979 to 1996

[Excludes simple and concurrent resolutions]

Item	96th Cong., 1979-80	97th Cong., 1981-82	98th Cong., 1983-84	99th Cong., 1985-86	100th Cong., 1987-88	101st Cong., 1989-90	102d Cong., 1991-92	103d Cong., 1993-94	104th Cong., 1995-96
Measures introduced	12,583	11,490	11,156	9,885	9,588	6,664	6,775	8,544	6,808
Bills	11,722	10,582	10,134	8,697	8,515	5,977	6,212	7,883	6,545
Joint resolutions	861	908	1,022	1,188	1,073	687	563	661	263
Measures enacted	736	529	677	483	761	666	609	473	337
Public	613	473	623	466	713	650	589	465	333
Private.	123	56	54	17	48	16	20	8	4
HOUSE OF REPRESENTATIVES									
Number of days	326	303	266	281	298	281	280	265	290
Number of hours.	1,876	1,420	1,705	1,794	1,659	1,688	1,796	1,887	2,445
Number of hours per day	5.8	4.7	6.4	6.4	5.6	6.0	6.4	7.1	8.4
SENATE									
Number of days	333	312	281	313	307	274	287	291	343
Number of hours.	2,324	2,158	1,951	2,531	2,341	2,254	2,292	2,514	2,876
Number of hours per day	7.0	6.9	6.9	8.1	7.6	8.2	8.0	8.6	8.4

Source: U.S. Congress, *Congressional Record* and *Daily Calendar*, selected issues.

No. 475. Congressional Bills Vetoed: 1961 to 1997

Period	President	Total vetoes	Regular vetoes	Pocket vetoes	Vetoes sustained	Bills passed over veto
1961-63	Kennedy	21	12	9	21	-
1963-69	Johnson	30	16	14	30	-
1969-74	Nixon	43	26	17	36	7
1974-77	Ford	66	48	18	54	12
1977-81	Carter	31	13	18	29	2
1981-89	Reagan	78	39	39	69	9
1989-93	Bush.	44	29	15	43	1
1993-97	Clinton	20	20	-	19	1

- Represents zero.

Source: U.S. Congress, Senate Library, *Presidential Vetoes ... 1789-1968*; U.S. Congress, *Calendars of the U.S. House of Representatives and History of Legislation*, annual.

No. 476. Congressional Staff, by Location of Employment: 1972 to 1995

[Excludes those persons employed in Congressional support agencies such as the U.S. General Accounting Office, the Library of Congress, and the Congressional Budget Office]

Year	Personal staff House	Personal staff Senate	Year	Standing committee staff House	Standing committee staff Senate	Location of employment	1985	1990	1991	1993	1995
1972 . .	5,280	2,426	1970. .	702	635	Total	18,136	17,625	17,851	(NA)	16,184
1980 . .	7,371	3,746	1980. .	1,917	1,191						
1981 . .	7,487	3,945	1981. .	1,843	1,022	House of Representatives. . .	11,636	11,064	11,041	10,791	9,913
1982 . .	7,511	4,041	1982. .	1,839	1,047	Committee staff [2]	2,146	2,173	2,321	2,070	1,266
1983 . .	7,606	4,059	1983. .	1,970	1,075	Personal staff	7,528	7,496	7,278	7,390	7,186
1984 . .	7,385	3,949	1984. .	1,944	1,095	Leadership staff.	144	156	149	137	134
1985 . .	7,528	4,097	1985. .	2,009	1,080	Officers of House, staff . . .	1,818	1,239	1,293	1,194	1,327
1986 . .	[1]7,920	[1]3,774	1986. .	1,954	1,075						
1987 . .	7,584	4,075	1987. .	2,024	1,074	Senate	6,369	6,425	6,665	6,529	6,163
			1988. .	1,976	970	Committee staff [2]	1,178	1,207	1,154	1,032	796
1989 . .	7,569	3,837	1989. .	1,986	1,013	Personal staff	4,097	4,162	4,294	4,200	4,247
1990 . .	7,496	4,162	1990. .	1,993	1,090	Leadership staff.	118	94	125	132	126
1991 . .	7,278	4,294	1991. .	2,201	1,030	Officers of Senate, staf . . .	976	962	1,092	1,165	994
1992 . .	7,597	4,249	1992. .	2,178	1,008						
1993 . .	7,400	4,138	1993. .	2,118	897	Joint committee staff	131	136	145	(NA)	108
1994 . .	7,390	4,200	1994. .	2,046	958						
1995 . .	7,186	4,247	1995. .	1,246	732						

NA Not available. [1] House figure is average for year, and Senate figure only covers period following implementation of Gramm-Rudman budget reductions. [2] Covers standing, select, and special committees.

Source: Ornstein, Norman J., Thomas E. Mann, and Michael J. Malbin, *Vital Statistics on Congress, 1993-1994*, Congressional Quarterly, Inc., Washington, DC, 1994, and unpublished data (copyright).

No. 477. Number of Governors, by Political Party Affiliation: 1970 to 1999

[Reflects figures after inaugurations for each year]

Year	Demo-cratic	Repub-lican	Indepen-dent/other	Year	Demo-cratic	Repub-lican	Indepen-dent/other	Year	Demo-cratic	Repub-lican	Indepen-dent/other
1970	18	32	-	1989	28	22	-	1995	19	30	1
1975	36	13	1	1990	29	21	-	1996	18	31	1
1980	31	19	-	1991 [1]	29	19	2	1997	17	32	1
1985	34	16	-	1992	28	20	2	1998	17	32	1
1987	26	24	-	1993	30	18	2	1999	17	31	1
1988	27	23	-	1994	29	19	2				

- Represents zero.   [1] Reflects result of runoff election in Arizona in February 1991.

Source: National Governors' Association, Washington, DC, 1970-87 and 1991-99, *Directory of Governors of the American States, Commonwealths & Territories,* annual; and 1988-90, *Directory of Governors,* annual (copyright).

No. 478. Vote Cast for and Governor Elected, by State: 1990 to 1998

[In thousands (1,216 represents 1,216,000), except percent. D=Democratic, R=Republican, I=Independent]

State	1990 Total vote [1]	1990 Percent leading party	1994 Total vote [1]	1994 Percent leading party	1996 Total vote [1]	1996 Percent leading party	1998 Total vote [1]	1998 Percent leading party	Candidate elected at most recent election
AL......	1,216	R-52.1	1,202	605	594	R-50.3	1,318	D-57.7	Donald Siegelman
AK......	195	I-38.9	213	87	88	D-41.1	220	D-51.3	Tony Knowles
AZ......	941	R-52.4	1,129	593	501	R-52.5	1,018	R-60.9	Jane Dee Hull
AR......	696	D-57.5	717	288	429	D-59.8	706	R-59.8	Mike Huckabee
CA......	7,699	R-49.2	8,659	4,778	3,518	R-55.2	8,385	D-58.0	Gray Davis
CO	1,011	D-61.9	1,116	432	619	D-55.5	1,321	R-49.1	Bill Owens
CT......	1,141	I-40.4	1,147	415	375	R-36.2	1,000	R-62.9	John G. Rowland
DE......	(X)	(X)	(X)	(X)	(X)	(X)	(X)	(X)	Thomas R. Carper
FL......	3,531	D-56.5	4,206	2,071	2,135	D-50.8	3,964	R-55.3	Jeb Bush
GA......	1,450	D-52.9	1,545	756	789	D-51.1	1,793	D-52.5	Roy Barnes
HI......	340	D-59.8	369	108	135	D-36.6	408	D-50.1	Benjamin J. Cayetano
ID......	321	D-68.2	413	216	181	R-52.3	381	R-67.7	Dirk Kempthorne
IL......	3,257	R-50.7	3,107	1,984	1,070	R-63.9	3,359	R-51.0	George Ryan
IN......	(X)	(X)	(X)	(X)	(X)	(X)	(X)	(X)	Frank L. O'Bannon
IA......	976	R-60.6	997	566	414	R-56.8	956	D-52.3	Tom Vilsack
KS......	783	D-48.6	821	526	295	R-64.1	743	R-73.4	Bill Graves
KY [2]...	(X)	(X)	(X)	(X)	(X)	(X)	(X)	(X)	Paul E. Patton
LA......	(X)	(X)	(X)	(X)	(X)	(X)	(X)	(X)	Mike Foster
ME......	522	R-46.7	511	118	173	I-35.4	421	R-18.9	Angus King
MD......	1,111	D-59.8	1,410	702	708	D-50.2	1,536	D-55.1	Parris N. Glendening
MA	2,343	R-50.2	2,164	1,533	612	R-70.9	1,903	R-50.8	Argeo Paul Cellucci
MI......	2,565	R-49.8	3,088	1,899	1,188	R-61.5	3,027	R-62.2	John Engler
MN [2]...	1,807	R-49.6	1,766	1,094	589	R-62.0	2,091	R-34.3	Jesse Ventura
MS [2]...	(X)	(X)	(X)	(X)	(X)	(X)	(X)	(X)	Kirk Fordice
MO	(X)	(X)	(X)	(X)	(X)	(X)	(X)	(X)	Mel Carnahan
MT	(X)	(X)	(X)	(X)	(X)	(X)	(X)	(X)	Marc Racicot
NE......	587	D-49.9	580	148	423	D-73.0	545	R-53.9	Mike Johanns
NV......	321	D-64.8	371	157	200	D-53.9	434	R-51.6	Kenny Guinn
NH......	295	R-60.3	312	218	80	R-69.9	319	D-66.1	Jeanne Shaheen
NJ......	2,254	D-61.2	2,506	(X)	(X)	R-49.3	2,418	R-46.9	Christine Todd Whitman
NM......	411	D-54.6	468	233	187	R-49.8	499	R-54.5	Gary E. Johnson
NY......	4,057	D-53.2	5,204	2,539	2,365	R-48.8	4,735	R-54.3	George E. Pataki
NC......	(X)	(X)	(X)	(X)	(X)	(X)	(X)	(X)	James B. Hunt
ND......	(X)	(X)	(X)	(X)	(X)	(X)	(X)	(X)	Edward T. Schafer
OH......	3,478	R-55.7	3,346	2,402	836	R-71.8	3,354	R-50.0	Bob Taft
OK......	911	D-57.4	995	467	295	R-46.9	874	R-57.9	Frank Keating
OR......	1,113	D-45.7	1,221	518	622	D-50.9	1,113	D-64.4	John Kitzhaber
PA......	3,053	D-67.7	3,585	1,628	1,430	R-45.4	3,025	R-57.4	Tom Ridge
RI......	357	D-74.1	361	171	157	R-47.4	306	R-51.0	Lincoln C. Almond
SC......	761	R-69.5	934	471	447	R-50.4	1,071	D-53.2	Jim Hodges
SD......	257	R-58.9	312	173	126	R-55.4	260	R-64.0	William J. Janklow
TN......	790	D-60.8	1,487	807	664	R-54.3	976	R-68.6	Don Sundquist
TX......	3,893	D-49.5	4,396	2,351	2,017	R-53.5	3,738	R-68.2	George W. Bush
UT......	(X)	(X)	(X)	(X)	(X)	(X)	(X)	(X)	Michael O. Leavitt
VT......	211	R-51.8	212	40	146	D-68.7	218	D-55.7	Howard Dean
VA......	1,789	D-50.1	1,794	(X)	(X)	R-58.3	1,736	R-55.8	James S. Gilmore
WA......	(X)	(X)	(X)	(X)	(X)	(X)	(X)	(X)	Gary Locke
WV......	(X)	(X)	(X)	(X)	(X)	(X)	(X)	(X)	Cecil H. Underwood
WI......	1,380	R-58.2	1,563	1,051	483	R-67.3	1,756	R-59.7	Tommy G. Thompson
WY......	160	D-65.4	201	118	81	R-58.7	175	R-55.6	Jim Geringer

X Not applicable.   [1] Includes minor party and scattered votes.   [2] Voting years 1987, 1991, and 1995.

Source: Congressional Quarterly, Inc., Washington, DC, *America Votes,* biennial; and unpublished data (copyright).

U.S. Census Bureau, Statistical Abstract of the United States: 1999

No. 479. Composition of State Legislatures, by Political Party Affiliation: 1990 to 1996

[Data reflect election results in year shown for most states; and except as noted, results in previous year for other states. Figures reflect immediate results of elections, including holdover members in state houses which do not have all of their members running for re-election. Dem.=Democrat, Rep.=Republican. In general, Lower House refers to body consisting of State Representatives; Upper House, of State Senators]

State	Lower house								Upper house							
	1990 [1][2]		1992 [3][4]		1994 [5][6]		1996 [5][6]		1990 [1][7]		1992 [3][8]		1994 [5][7]		1996 [9]	
	Dem.	Rep.	Dem.	Rep.	Dem.	Rep.	Dem.	Rep.	Dem.	Rep.	Dem.	Rep.	Dem.	Rep.	Dem.	Rep.
U.S. . .	3,242	2,202	3,186	2,223	2,817	2,603	2,886	2,539	1,186	757	1,132	799	1,021	905	998	931
AL [10] . .	82	23	82	23	74	31	72	33	28	7	27	8	23	12	22	12
AK [11] . .	23	17	20	18	17	22	16	24	10	10	10	10	8	12	7	13
AZ [12] . .	27	33	25	35	22	38	22	38	17	13	12	18	11	19	12	18
AR [11] . .	90	9	88	11	88	12	86	13	31	4	30	5	28	7	28	6
CA [11] . .	47	33	47	33	39	40	43	37	25	13	21	16	21	17	25	15
CO [11] . .	27	38	31	34	24	41	24	41	12	23	16	19	16	19	15	20
CT [12] . .	87	64	85	64	90	61	97	54	20	16	19	17	17	19	19	17
DE [11] . .	17	24	18	23	14	27	14	27	15	6	15	6	12	9	13	8
FL [11] . .	74	46	71	49	63	57	59	61	22	18	20	20	19	21	17	23
GA [12] . .	145	35	128	51	114	65	106	74	45	11	41	15	35	20	34	22
HI [11] . .	45	6	47	4	44	7	39	12	22	3	22	3	23	2	23	2
ID [12] . .	28	56	20	50	13	57	11	59	21	21	12	23	8	27	5	30
IL [11] . .	72	46	67	51	54	64	60	58	31	28	27	32	26	33	28	31
IN [11] . .	52	48	55	45	44	56	50	50	24	26	22	28	20	30	19	31
IA [11] . .	55	45	49	51	36	64	46	54	29	21	27	23	27	23	21	29
KS [11] . .	63	62	59	66	45	80	48	77	18	22	13	27	13	27	13	27
KY [11] . .	68	32	71	29	64	36	64	36	27	11	25	13	21	17	20	18
LA [10] . .	89	16	88	16	86	17	76	28	34	5	33	6	33	6	25	14
ME [12] . .	97	54	93	58	77	74	81	69	21	14	20	15	16	18	19	15
MD [10] . .	116	25	116	25	100	41	100	41	38	9	38	9	32	15	32	15
MA [12] . .	118	37	123	34	125	34	134	25	25	15	31	9	30	10	34	6
MI [11] . .	61	49	55	55	53	56	58	52	18	20	16	22	16	22	16	22
MN [11] . .	78	56	85	49	71	63	70	64	46	21	45	22	43	21	42	24
MS [10] . .	98	23	91	29	89	31	86	33	43	9	37	15	36	14	34	18
MO [11] . .	99	64	98	65	87	76	88	75	23	11	20	14	19	15	19	15
MT [11] . .	61	39	47	53	33	67	35	65	29	21	30	20	19	31	16	34
NE [11] . .	(13)	(13)	(13)	(13)	(13)	(13)	(13)	(13)	(13)	(13)	(13)	(13)	(13)	(13)	(13)	(13)
NV [11] . .	22	19	27	12	21	21	25	17	10	10	10	11	8	13	9	12
NH [12] . .	125	268	136	258	112	286	143	255	11	13	11	13	6	18	9	15
NJ [11] . .	22	58	27	53	28	52	30	50	13	27	16	24	16	24	16	24
NM [11] . .	49	21	53	17	46	24	42	28	26	16	27	15	27	15	25	17
NY [12] . .	95	55	100	50	94	56	96	54	26	35	26	35	26	36	26	35
NC [12] . .	81	39	78	42	52	68	59	61	36	14	39	11	26	24	30	20
ND [11] . .	48	58	33	65	23	75	26	72	27	26	25	24	20	29	19	30
OH [11] . .	61	38	53	46	43	56	39	60	12	21	13	20	13	20	12	21
OK [11] . .	68	33	70	31	65	36	65	36	37	11	37	11	35	13	33	15
OR [11] . .	28	32	28	32	26	34	29	31	20	10	16	14	11	19	10	20
PA [11] . .	107	94	105	98	101	102	99	104	24	26	24	25	21	29	20	30
RI [12] . .	89	11	85	15	84	16	84	16	45	5	39	11	40	10	41	9
SC [11] . .	79	43	71	52	58	62	53	70	33	13	30	16	29	17	26	20
SD [12] . .	25	45	28	42	24	46	23	47	17	18	20	15	16	19	13	22
TN [11] . .	57	42	63	36	59	40	61	38	20	13	19	14	18	15	18	15
TX [11] . .	93	57	91	58	89	61	82	68	22	9	18	13	17	14	14	16
UT [11] . .	31	44	26	49	20	55	20	55	10	19	11	18	10	19	9	20
VT [12] . .	73	75	87	57	86	61	89	57	15	15	14	16	12	18	17	13
VA [11] . .	58	41	52	47	52	47	53	46	22	18	22	18	22	18	20	20
WA [11] . .	58	40	65	33	38	60	45	53	24	25	28	21	25	24	23	26
WV [11] . .	74	26	79	21	69	30	74	25	33	1	32	2	26	8	25	9
WI [11] . .	58	41	51	47	48	51	47	52	19	14	16	17	16	17	17	16
WY [11] . .	22	42	19	41	13	47	17	43	10	20	10	20	10	20	9	21

[1] Status as of May 1992; reflects results of elections held in LA, KY, MS, and NJ in 1991.   [2] Excludes one Independent each for MA, MS, NH, SC, and VA; one Independent Democrat for NH; two Independents for VT; one vacancy each for AR, NV, and SC; two vacancies for PA; four vacancies for MA; and five vacancies for NH.   [3] Status as of November 11, 1993.   [4] Excludes one Independent each for AR, LA, NH, SC, and VA; two Independents each for AK and MS; four Independents for VT; members of political parties other than Democratic, Republican, or Independent (one in MA, two in VT, and four in NH); one vacancy each for GA, NH, TX, and WI; two vacancies each for CT and MA; and three vacancies for NV.   [5] Status as of December 7, 1994.   [6] Excludes one Independent each for AK, CA, LA, and VA; two Independents each for MS and VT; four Independents for SC; members of political parties other than Democratic, Republican, or Independent (one each in MA and VT and two in NH); one undecided in GA; and one vacancy each in LA, MI, and WV.   [7] Excludes two Independents for CA; and one vacancy for NV.   [8] Excludes two Independents for CA; and one vacancy each for CA and PA.   [9] Excludes one Independent in ME, two independents in CA, one vacancy in GA, two vacancies in MS, and three vacancies in MN.   [10] Members of both houses serve 4-year terms.   [11] Upper House members serve 4-year terms and Lower House members serve 2-year terms.   [12] Members of both houses serve 2-year terms.   [13] Single chamber (unicameral body) of 49 members, elected without party designation.

Source: The Council of State Governments, Lexington, KY, *State Elective Officials and the Legislatures*, biennial (copyright); thereafter, National Conference of State Legislatures, Denver, CO, unpublished data.

No. 480. Political Party Control of State Legislatures, by Party: 1975 to 1997

[As of beginning of year. Until 1972 there were two nonpartisan legislatures in Minnesota and Nebraska. Since then only Nebraska has had a nonpartisan legislature]

Year	Legislatures under— Democratic control	Split control or tie	Republican control	Year	Legislatures under— Democratic control	Split control or tie	Republican control	Year	Legislatures under— Democratic control	Split control or tie	Republican control
1975...	37	7	5	1985...	27	11	11	1993...	25	16	8
1977...	36	8	5	1987...	28	12	9	1994...	24	17	8
1979...	30	7	12	1989 [2]	28	13	8	1995...	18	12	19
1981...	28	6	15	1990...	29	11	9	1996...	16	15	18
1983 [1]	34	4	11	1992...	29	14	6	1997...	20	11	18

[1] Two 1984 midterm recall elections resulted in a change in control of the Michigan State Senate. At the time of the 1984 election, therefore, Democrats controlled 33 legislatures.   [2] A party change during the year by a Democratic representative broke the tie in the Indiana House of Representatives, giving the Republicans control of both chambers.

Source: National Conference of State Legislatures, Denver, CO, *State Legislatures*, periodic.

No. 481. Local Elected Officials, by Sex, Race, Hispanic Origin, and Type of Government: 1992

Sex, race, and Hispanic origin		General purpose			Special purpose	
	Total	County	Municipal	Town, township	School district	Special district
Total	**493,830**	**58,818**	**135,531**	**126,958**	**88,434**	**84,089**
Male	324,255	43,563	94,808	76,213	54,443	55,228
Female	100,531	12,525	26,825	27,702	24,730	8,749
Sex not reported	69,044	2,730	13,898	23,043	9,261	20,112
White	405,905	52,705	114,880	102,676	73,894	61,750
Black	11,542	1,715	4,566	369	4,222	670
American Indian, Eskimo, Aleut	1,800	147	776	86	564	227
Asian, Pacific Islander	514	80	97	16	184	137
Hispanic	5,859	906	1,701	216	2,466	570
Non-Hispanic	413,902	53,741	118,618	102,931	76,398	62,214
Race, Hispanic origin not reported	74,069	4,171	15,212	23,811	9,570	21,305

Source: U.S. Census Bureau, *1992 Census of Governments, Popularly Elected Officials*, (GC92(1)-2).

No. 482. Women Holding State Public Offices, by Office and State: 1998

[As of **January**. For data on women in U.S. Congress, see Table 473]

State	State-wide elective executive office [1]	State legislature	State	State-wide elective executive office [1]	State legislature	State	State-wide elective executive office [1]	State legislature
United States .	**82**	**1,617**	Kentucky	-	13	North Dakota	4	25
Alabama	3	6	Louisiana	1	17	Ohio	2	29
Alaska	1	8	Maine	-	48	Oklahoma	4	15
Arizona	4	33	Maryland	1	56	Oregon	1	24
Arkansas	2	23	Massachusetts	-	47	Pennsylvania	1	31
California	2	26	Michigan	2	34	Rhode Island	1	39
Colorado	3	37	Minnesota	3	63	South Carolina	1	20
Connecticut	2	54	Mississippi	-	22	South Dakota	4	18
Delaware	4	16	Missouri	2	42	Tennessee	1	18
Florida	1	38	Montana	2	35	Texas	1	33
Georgia	2	40	Nebraska	2	13	Utah	2	18
Hawaii	1	13	Nevada	1	21	Vermont	-	60
Idaho	2	25	New Hampshire	1	131	Virginia	-	22
Illinois	2	45	New Jersey	1	20	Washington	4	58
Indiana	3	29	New Mexico	1	30	West Virginia	-	20
Iowa	1	32	New York	1	43	Wisconsin	-	31
Kansas	2	49	North Carolina	1	30	Wyoming	2	17

- Represents zero.   [1] Excludes women elected to the judiciary, women appointed to State cabinet-level positions, women elected to executive posts by the legislature, and elected members of university Board of Trustees or board of education.

Source: Center for the American Woman and Politics, Eagleton Institute of Politics, Rutgers University, New Brunswick, NJ, information releases, (copyright).

U.S. Census Bureau, Statistical Abstract of the United States: 1999

No. 483. Black Elected Officials, by Office, 1970 to 1996, and State, 1997

[As of January 1997, no Black elected officials had been identified in Hawaii, Idaho, Montana, North Dakota, or Utah]

State	Total	U.S. and state legislatures[1]	City and county offices[2]	Law enforcement[3]	Education[4]	State	Total	U.S. and state legislatures[1]	City and county offices[2]	Law enforcement[3]	Education[4]
1970 (Feb.)	1,469	179	715	213	362	MD	195	38	115	32	10
1980 (July)	4,890	326	2,832	526	1,206	MA	33	7	21	3	2
1985 (Jan.)	6,016	407	3,517	661	1,431	MI	333	19	134	51	129
1990 (Jan.)	7,335	436	4,485	769	1,645	MN	14	1	3	7	3
1995 (Jan.)	8,385	604	4,954	987	1,840	MS	803	46	519	98	140
1996 (Jan.)	8,545	606	5,023	994	1,922	MO	188	16	136	14	22
1997 (Jan.)	8,617	617	5,052	996	1,952	NE	4	1	2	-	1
						NV	16	5	5	4	2
AL	726	36	551	52	87	NH	2	2	-	-	-
AK	1	-	1	-	-	NJ	222	14	124	-	84
AZ	17	4	3	5	5	NM	5	2	-	2	1
AR	484	13	262	60	149	NY	311	32	75	78	126
CA	255	14	72	79	90	NC	506	27	354	29	96
CO	20	4	4	10	2	OH	231	20	129	30	52
CT	63	14	38	4	7	OK	102	6	76	1	19
DE	25	4	16	2	3	OR	7	4	1	2	-
DC	147	3	139	-	5	PA	162	19	55	58	30
FL	216	23	146	32	15	RI	10	9	1	-	-
GA	579	48	389	37	105	SC	542	35	323	12	172
ID	1	-	-	1	-	TN	174	17	108	26	23
IL	545	26	310	55	154	TX	448	18	293	45	92
IN	80	13	51	10	6	UT	1	-	-	1	-
IA	11	1	7	1	2	VT	1	1	-	-	-
KS	21	7	6	4	4	VA	333	15	137	17	164
KY	58	5	42	5	6	WA	23	2	9	10	2
LA	645	35	362	112	136	WV	19	2	14	3	-
ME	3	1	2	-	-	WI	35	8	17	4	6

- Represents zero.   [1] Includes elected state administrators.   [2] County commissioners and councilmen, mayors, vice mayors, aldermen, regional officials, and others.   [3] Judges, magistrates, constables, marshals, sheriffs, justices of the peace, and others.   [4] Members of state education agencies, college boards, school boards, and others.

Source: Joint Center for Political and Economic Studies, Washington, DC, *Black Elected Officials: A Statistical Summary*, 1993-1997, annual (copyright).

No. 484. Hispanic Public Officials, by Office, 1985 to 1994, and by State, 1994

[As of September. For states not shown, no Hispanic public officials had been identified]

State	Total	State executives and legislators[1]	County and municipal officials	Judicial and law enforcement	Education and school boards	State	Total	State executives and legislators[1]	County and municipal officials	Judicial and law enforcement	Education and school boards
1985 (Sept.)	3,147	129	1,316	517	1,185	IN	8	1	5	1	1
1986 (Sept.)	3,202	132	1,352	530	1,188	KS	7	5	1	-	1
1987 (Sept.)	3,317	138	1,412	568	1,199	LA	12	3	1	8	-
1988 (Sept.)	3,360	135	1,425	574	1,226	MD	2	-	1	-	1
1989 (Sept.)	3,783	143	1,724	575	1,341	MA	1	-	-	-	1
1990 (Sept.)	4,004	144	1,819	583	1,458	MI	8	-	5	1	2
1991 (Sept.)	4,202	151	1,867	596	1,588	MN	3	2	1	-	-
1992 (Sept.)	4,994	150	1,908	628	2,308	MO	1	-	1	-	-
1993 (Sept.)	5,170	182	2,023	633	2,332	MT	2	-	-	1	1
1994 (Sept.)	5,459	199	2,197	651	2,412	NE	3	-	2	-	1
1994	5,459	199	2,197	651	2,412	NV	4	1	-	1	2
						NJ	37	2	17	1	17
AK	1	1	-	-	-	NM	716	50	410	105	151
AZ	341	11	144	50	136	NY	83	12	13	11	47
AR	2	1	-	-	1	OH	4	-	1	2	1
CA	796	16	349	50	381	OK	1	-	1	-	-
CO	201	9	140	10	42	OR	5	-	3	1	1
CT	26	12	9	-	5	PA	8	1	3	1	3
DE	1	-	1	-	-	RI	1	1	-	-	-
DC	1	-	-	1	-	TX	2,215	41	1,022	389	763
FL	64	16	33	12	3	UT	1	1	-	-	-
HI	2	2	-	-	-	WA	14	2	4	2	6
ID	2	1	1	-	-	WI	2	-	2	-	-
IL	881	7	26	3	[2]845	WY	3	1	2	-	-

- Represents zero.   [1] Includes U.S. Representatives.   [2] Includes local school council members in the Chicago area.

Source: National Association of Latino Elected and Appointed Officials, Washington, DC, *National Roster of Hispanic Elected Officials*, annual.

U.S. Census Bureau, Statistical Abstract of the United States: 1999

No. 485. Public Confidence Levels in Selected Public and Private Institutions: 1996

[Based on a sample survey of 2,719 persons 18 years old and over conducted during the spring and subject to sampling variability; see source]

Institution	Level of confidence				
	A great deal	Quite a lot	Some	Very little	Can't say/no answer
Religious organizations	23.6	31.1	31.3	12.3	1.7
Higher education (colleges or univ.)	18.3	38.7	28.3	7.5	7.1
Private elementary or secondary education	15.1	35.3	33.4	9.7	6.5
Youth development and recreation organizations	14.8	35.2	32.7	11.6	5.7
Federated charitable appeals	12.6	26.3	34.9	21.6	4.5
Health organizations	10.8	28.2	42.0	15.9	3.1
Environmental organizations	9.4	23.1	41.0	20.3	6.2
Human service organizations	9.1	28.1	42.6	15.1	5.0
Recreational organizations (adult)	7.8	27.5	41.9	13.4	9.4
Arts, culture, & humanities organizations	9.3	26.7	39.8	14.3	9.9
Private and community foundations	7.6	24.0	42.3	13.5	12.6
Public /society benefit organizations [1]	7.5	22.7	43.4	20.8	5.6
International/foreign organizations [2]	6.3	19.1	37.5	24.2	12.8
Small businesses	15.3	40.8	32.6	7.6	3.6
Military	16.9	37.0	31.0	12.1	3.1
Public higher educ. (colleges or univ.)	15.0	36.4	34.2	11.6	2.8
Public elementary or secondary education	13.3	31.7	37.2	15.3	2.4
Organized labor	6.6	17.7	40.9	29.3	5.6
Media (e.g. newspapers, TV, radio)	6.3	22.7	39.5	29.7	1.8
Work-related organizations	6.1	21.5	47.2	17.4	7.9
Major corporations	4.9	18.7	44.2	27.4	4.8
State government	4.1	22.2	44.9	26.4	2.5
Organizations that lobby for a particular cause	4.0	15.7	42.7	29.5	8.1
Political organizations, parties	3.8	10.8	39.2	42.6	3.7
Local government	5.4	25.9	43.3	23.1	2.3
Federal government	5.2	17.5	43.9	31.1	2.2
Congress	3.4	12.4	41.7	39.0	3.5

[1] Civil rights, social justice, or community improvement organizations.   [2] Culture exchange or relief organizations.

Source: Hodgkinson, Virginia, Murray Weitzman, and the Gallup Organization, Inc., *Giving & Volunteering in the United States: 1996 Edition*. (Copyright and published by INDEPENDENT SECTOR, Washington, DC, 1996.)

No. 486. Political Party Identification of the Adult Population, by Degree of Attachment, 1972 to 1994, and by Selected Characteristics, 1994

[In percent. Covers citizens of voting-age living in private housing units in the contiguous United States. Data are from the National Election Studies and are based on a sample and subject to sampling variability; for details, see source]

Year and selected characteristic	Total	Strong Democrat	Weak Democrat	Independent Democrat	Independent	Independent Republican	Weak Republican	Strong Republican	Apolitical
1972	100	15	26	11	13	11	13	10	1
1980	100	18	23	11	13	10	14	9	2
1984	100	17	20	11	11	12	15	12	2
1986	100	18	22	10	12	11	15	11	2
1988	100	18	18	12	11	13	14	14	2
1990	100	20	19	12	11	12	15	10	2
1992	100	18	18	14	12	12	14	11	1
1994	100	15	19	13	10	12	15	16	1
1994									
Age:									
17 to 24 year	100	9	20	22	10	8	19	10	1
25 to 34 years old . .	100	11	19	14	12	11	16	16	1
35 to 44 years old . .	100	13	18	14	12	11	14	18	-
45 to 54 years old . .	100	15	16	15	7	16	12	17	1
55 to 64 years old . .	100	18	22	8	8	16	12	15	-
65 to 74 years old . .	100	28	17	6	8	13	14	15	-
75 to 99 years old . .	100	19	26	9	9	5	17	13	2
Sex:									
Male	100	13	17	12	11	14	14	18	1
Female	100	18	21	13	10	9	15	13	1
Race:									
White.	100	12	19	12	10	13	16	17	1
Black.	100	38	23	20	8	4	2	3	1
Education:									
Grade school	100	26	26	7	13	7	11	6	4
High school.	100	15	22	14	13	10	13	11	1
College	100	14	16	13	7	13	16	21	-

- Represents zero.   [1] Includes other characteristics, not shown separately.

Source: Center for Political Studies, University of Michigan, Ann Arbor, MI, unpublished data. Data prior to 1988 published in Warren E. Miller and Santa A. Traugott, *American National Election Studies Data Sourcebook, 1952-1986*, Harvard University Press, Cambridge, MA, 1989 (copyright).

U.S. Census Bureau, Statistical Abstract of the United States: 1999

No. 487. Voting-Age Population, Percent Reporting Registered, and Voted: 1980 to 1998

[As of November. Covers civilian noninstitutional population 18 years old and over. Includes aliens. Figures are based on Current Population Survey (see text, Section 1, Population, and Appendix III) and differ from those in Table 489 based on population estimates and official vote counts]

| Characteristic | Voting-age population (mil.) | | | | | | | Percent reporting they registered | | | | | | | | Percent reporting they voted | | | | | | | |
| | | | | | | | | Presidential election years | | | | Congressional election years | | | | Presidential election years | | | | Congressional election years | | | |
	1980	1988	1990	1992	1994	1996	1998	1980	1988	1992	1996	1986	1990	1994	1998	1980	1988	1992	1996	1986	1990	1994	1998
Total[1]	**157.1**	**178.1**	**182.1**	**185.7**	**190.3**	**193.7**	**198.2**	**66.9**	**66.6**	**68.2**	**65.9**	**64.3**	**62.2**	**62.0**	**62.1**	**59.2**	**57.4**	**61.3**	**54.2**	**46.0**	**45.0**	**44.6**	**41.9**
18 to 20 years old	12.3	10.7	10.8	9.7	10.3	10.8	11.4	44.7	44.9	48.3	51.2	35.4	35.4	45.5	37.2	35.7	33.2	38.5	31.2	18.6	18.4	16.5	13.5
21 to 24 years old	15.9	14.8	14.0	14.6	14.9	13.9	14.1	52.7	50.6	55.3	51.2	46.6	43.3	45.5	43.1	43.1	38.3	45.7	33.4	22.0	22.3	19.2	28.0
25 to 34 years old	35.7	42.7	42.7	41.6	41.6	40.1	38.6	62.4	58.0	58.0	56.9	55.8	55.5	51.5	52.4	54.6	48.0	53.2	43.1	35.1	33.8	32.2	40.7
35 to 44 years old	25.6	35.2	37.9	39.7	41.9	43.3	44.4	70.6	69.3	69.2	66.5	67.9	65.5	63.3	62.4	64.4	61.3	63.6	54.9	49.3	48.4	46.0	53.6
45 to 64 years old	43.6	45.9	46.9	49.1	50.9	53.7	57.4	75.8	75.5	78.0	73.5	74.8	76.5	71.0	71.1	69.3	67.9	70.0	(NA)	58.7	55.8	60.7	59.5
65 years old and over	24.1	28.8	29.9	30.8	31.1	31.9	32.3	74.6	78.4	78.0	77.0	76.9	76.5	75.6	75.4	65.1	68.8	70.1	(NA)	60.9	60.3	60.7	59.5
Male	74.1	84.5	86.6	88.6	91.0	92.6	95.2	66.6	65.2	66.9	64.4	63.4	61.2	60.8	60.6	59.1	56.4	60.2	52.8	45.8	44.6	44.4	41.4
Female	83.0	93.6	95.5	97.1	99.3	101.0	103.0	67.1	67.8	69.3	67.3	65.0	63.1	63.2	63.5	59.4	58.3	62.3	55.5	46.1	45.4	44.9	42.4
White	137.7	152.9	155.6	157.8	160.3	162.8	165.8	68.4	67.9	70.1	67.7	65.3	63.8	64.2	63.9	60.9	59.1	63.6	56.0	47.0	46.7	46.9	43.3
Black	16.4	19.7	20.4	21.0	21.8	22.5	23.3	60.0	64.5	63.9	63.5	64.0	58.8	58.3	60.2	50.5	51.5	54.0	50.6	43.2	39.2	37.0	39.6
Hispanic[2]	8.2	12.9	13.8	14.7	17.5	18.4	20.3	36.3	35.5	35.0	35.7	35.9	32.3	30.0	33.7	29.9	28.8	28.9	26.7	24.2	21.0	19.1	20.0
Region:[3]																							
Northeast	35.5	37.9	38.1	38.3	38.4	38.3	38.5	64.8	64.8	67.0	64.7	62.0	61.0	60.9	60.8	58.5	57.4	61.2	54.5	44.4	45.2	45.2	41.2
Midwest	41.5	43.3	43.9	44.4	44.5	45.2	45.9	73.8	72.5	74.6	71.6	70.7	68.2	68.7	68.2	65.8	62.9	67.2	59.3	49.5	48.6	48.8	47.3
South	50.6	60.7	62.4	63.7	66.4	68.1	70.1	64.5	65.6	67.2	65.9	63.0	61.3	60.7	62.7	55.6	54.5	59.0	52.2	43.0	42.4	40.5	38.6
West	29.5	36.2	37.7	39.3	41.0	42.1	43.7	63.3	63.0	63.6	60.8	60.8	57.7	58.1	56.0	57.2	55.6	58.5	51.8	48.4	45.0	46.4	42.3
School years completed:																							
8 years or less	22.7	19.1	17.7	15.4	14.7	14.1	13.3	53.0	47.5	43.9	40.7	50.5	44.0	40.1	40.2	42.6	36.7	35.1	28.1	32.7	27.7	23.2	24.6
High school:																							
1 to 3 years	22.5	21.1	21.0	[4]21.0	[4]20.7	21.0	21.0	54.6	52.8	[4]50.4	47.9	52.4	47.9	[4]44.7	43.4	45.6	41.3	[4]41.2	33.8	33.8	30.9	[4]27.0	25.0
4 years	61.2	70.0	71.5	[5]65.3	[5]64.9	65.2	65.6	66.4	64.6	[5]64.9	62.2	62.9	60.0	[5]58.9	58.6	58.9	54.7	[5]57.5	49.1	44.1	42.2	[5]40.5	37.1
College:																							
1 to 3 years	26.7	34.3	36.3	[6]46.7	[6]50.4	50.9	52.9	74.4	73.5	[6]75.4	72.9	70.0	68.7	[6]68.4	68.3	67.2	64.5	[6]68.7	60.5	49.9	50.0	[6]49.1	46.2
4 years or more	24.0	33.6	35.6	[7]37.4	[7]39.4	42.5	45.4	84.3	83.1	[7]84.8	80.4	77.8	77.3	[7]76.3	75.1	79.9	77.6	[7]81.0	73.0	62.5	62.5	[7]63.1	57.2
Employed	95.0	113.8	115.5	116.3	122.6	125.6	135.7	68.7	67.1	69.9	67.0	64.4	62.6	62.9	62.6	61.8	58.4	63.8	55.2	45.7	45.1	45.2	41.2
Unemployed	6.9	5.8	6.7	8.3	6.7	6.4	6.7	50.3	50.4	53.7	52.5	50.6	44.6	46.4	48.5	41.2	38.6	46.2	37.2	31.2	27.9	28.3	28.4
Not in labor force	55.2	58.5	59.9	61.1	61.2	61.6	62.5	65.8	67.2	66.8	65.1	65.4	63.4	61.9	62.1	57.0	57.3	58.7	54.1	48.2	46.7	45.3	44.5

NA Not available. [1] Includes other races not shown separately. [2] Hispanic persons may be of any race. [3] For composition of regions, see map, inside front cover. [4] Represents those who completed 9th to 12th grade, but have no high school diploma. [5] High school graduate. [6] Some college or associate degree. [7] Bachelor's or advanced degree.

Source: U.S. Census Bureau, Current Population Reports, P20-453 and P20-466; and unpublished data.

No. 488. Persons Reported Registered and Voted, by State: 1996

[See headnote, Table 487]

State	Voting-age population (1,000)	Percent of voting-age population		State	Voting-age population (1,000)	Percent of voting-age population	
		Registered	Voted			Registered	Voted
U.S.	**193,651**	**65.9**	**54.2**	MS	1,942	71.6	55.1
AL	3,139	73.8	55.6	MO	3,925	75.5	61.1
AK	404	75.5	59.5	MT	649	75.1	67.3
AZ	3,149	58.5	47.3	NE	1,181	74.1	61.0
AR	1,843	64.4	51.5	NV	1,176	59.0	47.8
CA	22,871	56.1	48.4	NH	862	71.7	60.1
CO	2,859	70.0	58.8	NJ	5,944	63.3	54.7
CT	2,409	69.9	58.5	NM	1,213	61.7	51.7
DE	536	64.0	54.7	NY	13,408	61.0	50.9
DC	402	73.0	59.6	NC	5,364	68.5	54.0
FL	10,886	61.8	50.7	ND	456	90.5	65.8
GA	5,303	66.1	49.6	OH	8,192	68.4	58.7
HI	839	55.1	43.1	OK	2,356	70.1	58.5
ID	835	68.4	60.1	OR	2,395	72.9	61.1
IL	8,598	67.7	55.6	PA	8,996	65.6	55.0
IN	4,238	68.5	55.8	RI	725	71.7	60.6
IA	2,113	73.0	61.1	SC	2,716	68.2	54.5
KS	1,823	68.9	62.0	SD	523	74.8	64.3
KY	2,906	69.4	52.8	TN	4,014	65.9	53.1
LA	3,098	73.4	61.8	TX	13,434	61.9	46.2
ME	926	81.5	67.7	UT	1,334	64.5	53.0
MD	3,766	65.9	54.4	VT	434	72.0	59.5
MA	4,560	66.7	56.3	VA	4,955	66.5	56.4
MI	7,018	72.0	58.1	WA	4,059	70.0	60.0
MN	3,375	78.3	66.9	WV	1,423	64.7	50.2
				WI	3,736	77.6	62.4

Source: U.S. Census Bureau, unpublished data.

No. 489. Participation in Elections for President and U.S. Representatives: 1932 to 1998

[As of **November**. Estimated resident population 21 years old and over, 1932-70, except as noted, and 18 years old and over thereafter; includes Armed Forces. Prior to 1960, excludes Alaska and Hawaii. District of Columbia is included in votes cast for President beginning 1964 and in votes cast for Representative from 1972 to 1992]

Year	Resident population (incl. aliens) of voting age [1] (1,000)	Votes cast				Year	Resident population (incl. aliens) of voting age [1] (1,000)	Votes cast			
		For President [2] (1,000)	Percent of voting-age population	For U.S. Representatives (1,000)	Percent of voting-age population			For President [2] (1,000)	Percent of voting-age population	For U.S. Representatives (1,000)	Percent of voting-age population
1932	75,768	39,758	52.5	37,657	49.7	1966	116,638	(X)	(X)	52,908	45.4
1934	77,997	(X)	(X)	32,256	41.4	1968	120,285	73,212	60.9	66,288	55.1
1936	80,174	45,654	56.9	42,886	53.5	1970	124,498	(X)	(X)	54,173	43.5
1938	82,354	(X)	(X)	36,236	44.0	1972	140,777	77,719	55.2	71,430	50.7
1940	84,728	49,900	58.9	46,951	55.4	1974	146,338	(X)	(X)	52,495	35.9
1942	86,465	(X)	(X)	28,074	32.5	1976	152,308	81,556	53.5	74,422	48.9
1944	85,654	47,977	56.0	45,103	52.7	1978	158,369	(X)	(X)	55,332	34.9
1946	92,659	(X)	(X)	34,398	37.1	1980	163,945	86,515	52.8	77,995	47.6
1948	95,573	48,794	51.1	45,933	48.1	1982	169,643	(X)	(X)	64,514	38.0
1950	98,134	(X)	(X)	40,342	41.1	1984	173,995	92,653	53.3	83,231	47.8
1952	99,929	61,551	61.6	57,571	57.6	1986	177,922	(X)	(X)	59,619	33.5
1954	102,075	(X)	(X)	42,580	41.7	1988	181,956	91,595	50.3	81,786	44.9
1956	104,515	62,027	59.3	58,426	55.9	1990	185,812	(X)	(X)	61,513	33.1
1958	106,447	(X)	(X)	45,818	43.0	1992	189,524	104,425	55.1	96,239	50.8
1960	109,672	68,838	62.8	64,133	58.5	1994	193,650	(X)	(X)	70,781	36.6
1962	112,952	(X)	(X)	51,267	45.4	1996	196,507	96,278	49.0	89,863	45.8
1964	114,090	70,645	61.9	65,895	57.8	1998	200,929	(X)	(X)	66,033	32.9

X Not applicable.   [1] Population 18 and over in Georgia, 1944-70, and in Kentucky, 1956-70; 19 and over in Alaska and 20 and over in Hawaii, 1960-70.   [2] Source: 1932-58, U.S. Congress, Clerk of the House, *Statistics of the Presidential and Congressional Election,* biennial.

Source: Except as noted, U.S. Census Bureau, *Current Population Reports,* P25-1085; Congressional Quarterly, Inc., Washington, DC *America Votes,* biennial (copyright).

U.S. Census Bureau, Statistical Abstract of the United States: 1999

No. 490. Resident Population of Voting Age and Percent Casting Votes—States: 1990 to 1998

[As of **November**. **Estimated population, 18 years old and over**. Includes Armed Forces stationed in each state, aliens, and institutional population]

State	Voting-age population							Percent casting votes for—				
	1990 (1,000)	1992 (1,000)	1994 (1,000)	1996 (1,000)	1998, proj., (1,000) Total	Black	His-panic [1]	Presidential electors 1992	1996	U.S. Representatives 1992	1994	1998
U.S. ...	185,812	189,524	193,650	196,928	200,927	23,715	19,947	55.1	49.0	50.8	36.0	32.9
AL......	2,995	3,080	3,138	3,221	3,293	787	28	54.8	47.7	49.9	37.1	36.9
AK......	382	405	429	423	437	16	16	63.8	56.9	58.6	44.0	51.1
AZ......	2,696	2,812	2,923	3,321	3,547	121	675	52.9	45.4	71.8	54.0	28.3
AR......	1,737	1,774	1,817	1,854	1,882	270	35	53.6	47.5	61.0	36.7	27.9
CA......	22,124	22,521	23,225	23,095	23,665	1,690	6,653	49.4	43.3	65.6	49.3	33.8
CO	2,447	2,579	2,713	2,841	2,961	120	370	60.8	53.1	56.6	43.3	43.0
CT......	2,534	2,508	2,486	2,471	2,464	206	172	64.4	56.4	51.9	44.8	38.7
DE......	507	521	534	551	568	102	17	55.6	49.6	57.2	43.0	31.8
DC......	481	467	452	428	414	238	29	48.7	42.7	46.9	34.6	32.9
FL......	10,180	10,422	10,856	11,055	11,383	1,530	1,638	51.0	48.0	43.2	33.8	10.7
GA	4,791	5,006	5,159	5,432	5,678	1,507	153	46.4	42.6	50.2	33.6	28.7
HI	841	866	900	875	878	27	62	43.1	40.8	50.1	36.6	45.3
ID	707	750	803	847	888	5	54	64.3	58.2	58.5	41.2	42.7
IL	8,495	8,598	8,712	8,703	8,755	1,215	775	58.7	49.2	56.6	38.5	36.7
IN	4,105	4,209	4,298	4,346	4,410	334	94	54.8	48.9	55.8	39.7	35.7
IA	2,061	2,073	2,112	2,135	2,157	38	36	65.3	57.7	52.7	36.0	41.8
KS.....	1,819	1,840	1,889	1,896	1,925	105	86	62.9	56.6	56.2	34.9	37.8
KY.....	2,740	2,798	2,857	2,926	2,990	202	22	53.4	47.5	55.9	43.0	36.8
LA.....	2,988	3,045	3,100	3,117	3,149	932	81	58.8	56.9	65.0	38.6	9.9
ME	924	932	931	943	957	5	7	72.9	64.5	63.3	47.7	43.3
MD	3,640	3,705	3,750	3,786	3,824	1,018	127	53.6	46.7	69.5	52.0	38.8
MA	4,646	4,616	4,564	4,677	4,731	258	234	60.1	55.3	59.9	46.3	36.8
MI	6,851	6,947	6,983	7,177	7,266	958	168	61.5	54.5	61.0	45.2	41.1
MN	3,222	3,272	3,362	3,417	3,483	87	52	71.8	64.3	64.5	50.4	58.6
MS	1,832	1,873	1,905	1,966	2,014	670	16	52.4	45.6	65.9	58.6	27.4
MO	3,813	3,851	3,902	3,981	4,042	410	55	62.1	54.2	61.1	47.9	38.9
MT	579	600	623	647	658	2	9	68.4	62.9	61.1	43.3	50.4
NE.....	1,152	1,164	1,192	1,211	1,231	45	46	63.4	56.1	45.9	30.2	42.7
NV.....	929	1,011	1,088	1,204	1,314	92	177	50.1	39.3	46.7	30.3	31.2
NH	835	838	843	869	890	7	12	64.2	58.0	53.0	36.5	35.7
NJ.......	5,927	5,964	5,974	6,023	6,075	828	680	56.1	51.2	48.8	35.9	29.9
NM.....	1,075	1,121	1,167	1,216	1,250	33	465	50.8	46.0	42.1	(NA)	39.8
NY.....	13,683	13,705	13,646	13,610	13,590	2,278	1,760	50.5	46.5	48.8	38.4	31.4
NC	5,061	5,190	5,364	5,512	5,685	1,165	106	50.3	45.8	40.9	29.3	33.5
ND	462	462	467	475	476	3	5	66.7	56.3	48.7	29.6	44.7
OH	8,066	8,207	8,313	8,334	8,401	879	116	60.2	54.3	41.8	31.7	40.2
OK.....	2,310	2,352	2,394	2,423	2,463	173	76	59.1	49.9	44.2	29.0	34.9
OR.....	2,140	2,220	2,311	2,404	2,484	42	123	65.9	57.5	[2]47.2	[2]26.3	43.9
PA.....	9,091	9,161	9,212	9,150	9,118	804	201	54.1	49.0	49.0	33.3	31.8
RI......	776	768	764	754	751	33	40	59.0	52.0	48.6	27.5	39.0
SC......	2,587	2,669	2,740	2,792	2,886	802	31	45.1	41.5	45.5	36.2	33.7
SD......	498	505	522	533	538	4	5	66.6	61.1	52.0	35.5	48.1
TN......	3,685	3,796	3,913	4,009	4,120	617	41	52.2	47.1	51.5	32.6	22.2
TX......	12,222	12,681	13,166	13,748	14,299	1,685	3,799	48.5	41.2	42.7	28.3	24.2
UT......	1,104	1,169	1,246	1,347	1,432	13	87	63.6	50.3	50.1	39.0	32.9
VT......	422	429	429	442	448	3	5	67.5	58.6	[3]22.4	[3](X)	48.0
VA	4,716	4,855	4,967	5,058	5,165	979	175	52.7	47.5	54.2	40.5	22.2
WA	3,650	3,812	4,000	4,112	4,257	143	223	60.0	54.7	44.3	31.3	43.6
WV	1,349	1,376	1,389	1,401	1,406	43	7	49.7	45.0	51.0	38.8	25.0
WI	3,616	3,675	3,777	3,819	3,877	186	82	68.9	57.4	55.3	40.7	43.2
WY	319	329	343	348	354	3	17	61.0	60.1	67.3	56.5	49.2

NA Not available.   X Not applicable.   [1] Persons of Hispanic origin may be of any race.   [2] State law does not require tabulation of votes for unopposed candidates.   [3] See footnote 6, Table 468.

Source: Compiled by U.S. Census Bureau. Population data from U.S. Census Bureau, *Current Population Reports*, P25-1117 and Statistical Brief (SB/96-2); votes cast from Elections Research Center, Chevy Chase, MD, *America Votes*, biennial, (copyright); and 1994, Congressional Quarterly Inc., *Congressional Quarterly Weekly Report*, Vol. 53, No. 15, April 15, 1995 (copyright).

No. 491. Sources of Voter Registration Applications: 1995-96

[Based on a report to the United States Congress on the impact of the National Voter Registration Act of 1993 on the administration of elections for Federal office during the preceding 2-year period, 1995 through 1996. Based on survey results from 43 states and the District of Columbia. Six states are exempt from the provisions of the Act. Vermont is excluded because of state constitutional impediments]

State	Total	Motor vehicle offices			Public assis-tance offices	Disability services	Armed Forces offices	State desig-nated sites	All other services
		Total	Percent of total	By mail					
United States ...	41,452,428	13,722,233	33.1	12,330,015	2,602,748	178,015	76,008	1,732,475	10,810,934
Alabama.........	560,500	90,356	16.1	106,199	80,096	3,202	4,730	17,512	258,405
Alaska..........	170,669	55,215	32.4	21,264	3,673	133	8	40,668	49,708
Arizona.........	524,042	81,317	15.5	272,550	17,845	2,662	7,278	57,108	85,282
Arkansas.......	282,023	114,325	40.5	28,324	28,324	1,570	956	6,670	77,873
California	5,761,575	818,927	14.2	2,372,689	129,273	4,132	2,094	25,219	2,409,241
Colorado........	554,343	303,422	54.7	52,644	12,255	1,460	2,292	3,264	179,006
Connecticut......	338,203	35,323	10.4	97,829	21,061	221	919	9,843	173,007
Delaware	159,302	128,626	80.7	5,956	7,889	2,135	917	632	13,147
District of Columbia .	320,968	276,653	86.2	13,743	14,268	129	387	15,788	
Florida	2,723,303	1,202,599	44.2	706,163	158,836	9,396	4,787	56,231	585,291
Georgia	1,469,269	772,419	52.6	295,283	103,942	2,046	231	140,762	154,586
Hawaii..........	139,399	27,370	19.6	103,709	1,040	-	-	2,606	4,674
Idaho [1]	(X)	(X)	(X)	(X)	(X)	(X)	(X)	(X)	(X)
Illinois.........	887,874	295,255	33.3	94,681	33,837	26,676	1,706	5,068	430,651
Indiana.........	1,059,666	287,198	27.1	478,351	83,853	8,388	2,697	55,208	143,971
Iowa	731,514	240,316	32.9	142,058	26,345	950	507	-	321,338
Kansas.........	377,279	186,604	49.5	56,228	8,419	1,028	630	11,122	113,248
Kentucky	1,495,553	731,840	48.9	50,505	63,477	4,624	1,061	23,402	620,644
Louisiana	1,345,799	291,805	21.7	226,014	74,636	5,709	4,826	35,605	707,204
Maine..........	269,673	106,434	39.5	46,254	16,849	118	54	7,538	92,426
Maryland	473,449	165,267	34.9	222,233	982	671	188	25,802	58,306
Massachusetts....	619,966	96,097	15.5	301,088	10,895	2,258	1,043	92,910	115,675
Michigan........	1,493,541	1,211,238	81.1	64,717	79,538	8,371	4,237	-	125,440
Minnesota [1]......	(X)	(X)	(X)	(X)	(X)	(X)	(X)	(X)	(X)
Mississippi	268,459	-	-	77,938	33,203	4,255	1,097	-	151,966
Missouri	937,209	409,323	43.7	135,076	143,135	4,507	1,361	15,851	227,956
Montana........	90,017	51,690	57.4	21,553	473	211	232	-	15,858
Nebraska	294,282	125,477	42.6	25,784	9,564	1,929	780	204	130,544
Nevada	289,345	150,695	52.1	94,025	13,200	340	512	-	30,573
New Hampshire [1]...	(X)	(X)	(X)	(X)	(X)	(X)	(X)	(X)	(X)
New Jersey......	1,425,826	172,607	12.1	39,358	54,579	6,790	-	374,686	777,806
New Mexico	203,052	35,650	17.6	78,109	16,668	543	170	6,671	65,241
New York	3,275,102	699,644	21.4	2,020,088	358,105	32,216	892	90,292	73,865
North Carolina	1,449,659	539,287	37.2	229,122	74,882	8,097	3,496	139,477	455,298
North Dakota [1].....	(X)	(X)	(X)	(X)	(X)	(X)	(X)	(X)	(X)
Ohio	1,866,048	528,762	28.3	360,675	100,129	4,041	2,155	240,236	630,050
Oklahoma.......	554,679	228,138	41.1	124,795	58,811	1,213	178	1,760	139,784
Oregon.........	802,724	199,065	24.8	401,234	38,446	5,174	-	3,432	155,373
Pennsylvania......	1,846,786	597,625	32.4	959,041	59,462	950	4,953	6,342	218,413
Rhode Island.....	41,131		75.9	5,569	3,822	523	-	-	-
South Carolina	117,197	93,881	80.1		20,615	2,051	650	-	-
South Dakota	94,117	5,030	5.3	14,993	13,906	648	2,022	3,582	53,936
Tennessee	776,156	186,563	24.0	222,871	147,830	-	4,568	28,126	186,198
Texas..........	3,340,587	1,494,846	44.8	1,050,413	353,550	7,690	5,991	129,066	299,031
Utah	330,169	84,743	25.7	93,404	24,913	754	2,165	47,229	76,961
Vermont[2]	(X)	(X)	(X)	(X)	(X)	(X)	(X)	(X)	(X)
Virginia.........	664,754	181,128	27.3	228,418	54,051	2,428	906	775	197,048
Washington......	883,722	350,304	39.6	330,403	22,859	5,360	2,292	7,313	165,191
West Virginia.....	143,497	37,952	26.5	34,683	23,212	2,416	40	4,475	40,719
Wisconsin [1].......	(X)	(X)	(X)	(X)	(X)	(X)	(X)	(X)	(X)
Wyoming [1]	(X)	(X)	(X)	(X)	(X)	(X)	(X)	(X)	(X)

- Represents zero.   X Not applicable.   [1] Exempt from the National Voter Registration Act of 1993.   [2] Has not yet implemented to National Voter Registration Act of 1993.

Source: Federal Election Commission, Executive Summary—Report to the Congress, June 1997.

Elections   303

No. 492. Political Party Financial Activity, by Major Political Party: 1981 to 1998

[In millions of dollars ($39.3 represents $39,300,000). Covers financial activity during 2-year calendar period indicated. Some political party financial activities, such as building funds and state and local election spending, are not reported to the source. Also excludes contributions earmarked to Federal candidates through the party organizations, since some of those funds never passed through the committees' accounts]

Year and type of committee	Democratic				Republican			
	Receipts, net [1]	Disburse-ments, net [1]	Contribu-tions to candi-dates	Monies spent on behalf of party's nomi-nees [2]	Receipts, net [1]	Disburse-ments, net [1]	Contribu-tions to candi-dates	Monies spent on behalf of party's nomi-nees [2]
1981-82	39.3	40.1	1.7	3.3	215.0	214.0	5.6	14.3
1983-84	98.5	97.4	2.6	9.0	297.9	300.8	4.9	20.1
1985-86	64.8	65.9	1.7	9.0	255.2	258.9	3.4	14.3
1987-88	127.9	121.9	1.8	17.9	263.3	257.0	3.4	22.7
1989-90	85.8	90.9	1.5	8.7	206.3	213.5	2.9	10.7
1991-92	177.7	171.9	1.9	28.1	267.3	256.1	3.0	33.9
1993-94, total	143.3	141.8	2.2	21.2	254.4	243.7	3.0	20.6
1995-96, total	281.5	274.8	2.1	22.6	474.0	465.3	3.8	31.0
1997-98, total [3]	189.0	184.3	1.2	27.1	319.6	310.5	2.6	15.7
National committee	64.8	65.3	-	6.0	104.0	105.1	0.4	3.9
Senatorial committee	35.6	35.8	0.3	8.4	53.4	53.7	0.3	-
Congressional committee. . . .	25.2	24.7	0.4	3.0	72.7	71.7	0.8	5.1
State and local	63.4	58.5	0.5	9.6	89.4	80.0	1.1	6.7

- Represents zero.   [1] Excludes monies transferred between affiliated committees.   [2] Monies spent in the general election. Minus sign (-) indicates refunds for expenditures.   [3] Excludes "Other national" activity.

Source: U.S. Federal Election Commission, *FEC Reports on Financial Activity, Final Report, Party and Non-Party Political Committees,* biennial.

No. 493. Independent Expenditures for Presidential and Congressional Campaigns: 1985 to 1996

[In thousands of dollars ($10,205 represents $10,205,000). Covers campaign finance activity during 2-year calendar period indicated. An "independent expenditure" is money spent to support or defeat a clearly identified candidate. According to Federal election law, such an expenditure must be made without cooperation or consultation with the candidate or his/her campaign. Independent expenditures are not limited, as are contributions]

Type of office and year	All parties			Democrats		Republicans		Others	
	Total	For	Against	For	Against	For	Against	For	Against
TOTAL									
1985-86	10,205	8,832	1,373	3,450	888	5,376	485	6	-
1987-88	21,341	16,654	4,687	2,865	4,248	13,784	439	6	-
1989-90	5,774	4,177	1,597	1,530	735	2,645	862	2	-
1991-92	11,052	8,710	2,342	3,044	1,483	5,548	847	118	12
1993-94	4,980	3,256	1,724	672	1,119	2,571	590	13	15
1995-96	21,744	11,016	10,728	1,186	6,491	9,714	4,228	116	9
PRESIDENTIAL									
1985-86	841	795	45	76	28	719	17	-	-
1987-88	14,127	10,628	3,499	568	3,352	10,054	146	6	-
1989-90	497	322	174	5	169	318	5	-	-
1991-92	4,431	3,695	736	583	561	3,052	163	60	12
1993-94	112	27	85	12	84	15	(Z)	-	1
1995-96	1,436	601	835	111	761	459	74	31	-
SENATE									
1985-86	5,312	4,331	980	988	632	3,343	348	(Z)	-
1987-88	4,401	3,641	761	831	617	2,810	143	2	-
1989-90	3,506	2,362	1,144	756	428	1,604	716	1	-
1991-92	2,604	1,912	692	1,025	462	886	230	(Z)	-
1993-94	2,627	1,612	1,015	261	476	1,351	539	26	1
1995-96	14,821	7,041	7,780	347	5,499	6,668	2,280		
HOUSE OF REPRESENTATIVES									
1985-86	4,053	3,706	347	2,386	227	1,314	120	6	-
1987-88	2,813	2,385	427	1,466	279	920	149	(Z)	-
1989-90	1,772	1,493	279	770	138	723	141	-	-
1991-92	4,017	3,103	914	1,436	460	1,610	454	57	-
1993-94	2,241	1,617	624	399	559	1,205	51	13	14
1995-96	5,487	3,374	2,113	728	231	2,587	1,874	59	8

- Represents zero.   Z Less than $500.

Source: U.S. Federal Election Commission, *FEC Index of Independent Expenditures, 1987-88,* May 1989; press release of May 19, 1989; and unpublished data.

No. 494. Political Action Committees—Number, by Committee Type: 1980 to 1998

[As of December 31]

Committee type	1980	1985	1990	1993	1994	1995	1996	1997	1998
Total	2,551	3,992	4,172	4,210	3,954	4,016	4,079	3,844	3,798
Corporate	1,206	1,710	1,795	1,789	1,660	1,674	1,642	1,597	1,567
Labor	297	388	346	337	333	334	332	332	321
Trade/membership/health	576	695	774	761	792	815	838	825	821
Nonconnected	374	1,003	1,062	1,121	980	1,020	1,103	931	935
Cooperative	42	54	59	56	53	44	41	42	39
Corporation without stock	56	142	136	146	136	129	123	117	115

Source: U.S. Federal Election Commission, press release of January 1999.

No. 495. Political Action Committees—Financial Activity Summary, by Committee Type: 1993 to 1998

[In millions of dollars ($391.8 represents $391,800,000). Covers financial activity during 2-year calendar period indicated. Data have not been adjusted for transfers between affiliated committees]

Committee type	Receipts			Disbursements [1]			Contributions to candidates		
	1993-94	1995-96	1997-98	1993-94	1995-96	1997-98	1993-94	1995-96	1997-98
Total	391.8	437.5	502.6	388.1	430.0	470.8	189.6	217.9	219.9
Corporate	115.0	133.8	144.1	116.8	130.6	137.6	69.6	78.2	78.0
Labor	90.3	104.1	111.3	88.4	99.8	98.2	41.9	48.0	44.6
Trade/membership/health	96.4	106.0	119.6	94.1	105.4	114.4	52.9	60.2	62.3
Nonconnected	76.9	81.2	114.3	75.1	81.3	107.8	18.2	24.0	28.2
Cooperative	4.4	3.9	4.5	4.5	4.2	4.3	3.0	3.0	2.4
Corporation without stock	8.9	8.5	8.8	9.2	8.7	8.5	4.1	4.5	4.4

[1] Comprises contributions to candidates, independent expenditures, and other disbursements.

Source: U.S. Federal Election Commission, FEC Reports on Financial Activity, Final Report, Party and Non-Party Political Committees, biennial.

No. 496. Presidential Campaign Finances—Federal Funds for General Election: 1980 to 1996

[In millions of dollars ($62.7 represents $62,700,000). Based on FEC certifications, audit reports, and Dept. of Treasury reports]

1980		1988		1992		1996	
Candidate	Amount	Candidate	Amount	Candidate	Amount	Candidate	Amount
Total [1]	62.7	Total	92.2	Total	110.4	Total	152.6
Anderson [1]	4.2	Bush	46.1	Bush	55.2	Clinton	61.8
Carter	29.4	Dukakis	46.1	Clinton	55.2	Dole	61.8
Reagan	29.2			Perot	-	Perot	29.0

- Represents zero.   [1] John Anderson, as the candidate of a new party, was permitted to raise funds privately. Total receipts for the Anderson campaign, including Federal funds, were $17.6 million, and total expenditures were $15.6 million.

Source: U.S. Federal Election Commission, periodic press releases.

No. 497. Presidential Campaign Finances—Primary Campaign Receipts and Disbursements: 1987 to 1996

[In millions of dollars ($213.8 represents $213,800,000). Covers campaign finance activity during 2-year calendar period indicated. Covers candidates who received Federal matching funds or who had significant financial activity]

Item	Total			Democratic			Republican		
	1987-88 [1]	1991-92 [2]	1995-96	1987-88	1991-92	1995-96	1987-88	1991-92	1995-96
Receipts, total [3]	213.8	125.2	243.9	91.9	70.0	46.2	116.0	49.7	187.0
Individual contributions	141.1	82.4	126.4	59.4	44.7	31.3	76.8	34.4	93.1
Federal matching funds	65.7	41.5	56.0	30.1	24.4	14.0	34.7	15.0	41.6
Disbursements	210.7	118.7	(NA)	90.2	64.4	(NA)	114.6	48.8	(NA)

NA Not available.   [1] Includes a minor party candidate who sought several party nominations and a Democratic candidate who did not receive Federal matching funds, but who had significant financial activity.   [2] Includes other parties, not shown separately.   [3] Includes other types of receipts, not shown separately.

Source: U.S. Federal Election Commission, FEC Reports on Financial Activity, Final Report, Presidential Pre-Nomination Campaigns, quadrennial.

U.S. Census Bureau, Statistical Abstract of the United States: 1999

No. 498. Congressional Campaign Finances—Receipts and Disbursements: 1993 to 1998

[Covers all campaign finance activity during 2-year calendar period indicated for primary, general, run-off, and special elections. for 1993-94 relates to 2,045 House of Representatives candidates and 331 Senate candidates; Data have been adjusted to eliminate transfers between all committees within a campaign. For further information on legal limits of contributions, see Federal Election Campaign Act of 1971, as amended]

Item	House of Representatives						Senate					
	Amount (mil. dol.)			Percent distribution			Amount (mil. dol.)			Percent distribution		
	1993-94	1995-96	1997-98	1993-94	1995-96	1997-98	1993-94	1995-96	1997-98	1993-94	1995-96	1997-98
Total receipts [1]	421.3	505.4	493.8	100	100	100	319.1	285.1	287.6	100	100	100
Individual contributions.	216.1	276.5	256.0	51	55	52	186.4	167.5	166.8	58	59	58
Other committees	132.4	155.8	158.7	31	31	32	47.2	45.6	48.1	15	16	17
Candidate loans	43.9	42.6	48.2	10	8	10	43.5	40.3	52.3	14	14	18
Candidate contributions	10.3	7.3	5.4	2	1	1	24.9	16.4	1.4	8	6	(Z)
Democrats.	216.7	233.1	233.4	51	46	47	133.6	126.5	134.1	42	44	47
Republicans.	201.8	266.9	255.8	48	53	52	183.6	157.7	153.0	58	55	53
Others	2.8	5.4	4.5	1	1	1	2.0	0.9	0.4	1	(Z)	(Z)
Incumbents	224.1	281.7	294.4	53	56	60	113.3	81.8	135.5	36	29	47
Challengers	100.6	121.6	96.2	24	24	19	119.2	79.2	113.9	37	28	40
Open seats [2]	96.6	72.2	103.2	23	14	21	86.6	124.1	37.7	27	44	13
Total disbursements . . .	407.2	477.8	452.5	100	95	100	318.8	287.5	287.9	100	100	100
Democrats.	213.4	221.1	211.1	46	44	47	136.3	127.4	134.6	43	44	47
Republicans.	191.0	251.4	237.2	53	50	52	180.6	159.1	152.9	57	55	53
Others	2.8	5.3	4.2	1	1	1	2.0	0.9	0.4	1	(Z)	(Z)
Incumbents	213.5	258.1	257.2	54	51	57	115.1	85.4	137.3	36	30	48
Challengers	99.1	119.6	94.7	25	24	21	118.3	78.9	112.5	37	27	39
Open seats [2]	94.6	100.2	100.6	21	20	22	85.5	123.1	38.1	27	43	13

Z Less than $50,000 or 0.5 percent.   [1] Includes other types of receipts, not shown separately.   [2] Elections in which an incumbent did not seek re-election.

Source: U.S. Federal Election Commission, *FEC Reports on Financial Activity, Final Report, U.S. Senate and House Campaigns*, biennial.

No. 499. Contributions to Congressional Campaigns by Political Action Committees (PAC), by Type of Committee: 1981 to 1998

[In millions of dollars (61.1 represents $61,100,000). Covers amounts given to candidates in primary, general, run-off, and special elections during the 2-year calendar period indicated. For number of political action committees, see Table 494]

Type of committee	Total [1]	Democrats	Republicans	Incumbents	Challengers	Open seats [2]
HOUSE OF REPRESENTATIVES						
1981-82	61.1	34.2	26.8	40.8	10.9	9.4
1983-84	75.7	46.3	29.3	57.2	11.3	7.2
1985-86	87.4	54.7	32.6	65.9	9.1	12.4
1987-88	102.2	67.4	34.7	82.2	10.0	10.0
1989-90	108.5	72.2	36.2	87.5	7.3	13.6
1991-92	127.4	85.4	41.7	94.4	12.2	20.8
1993-94	132.4	88.2	43.9	101.4	12.7	18.3
1995-96, total . [3]	159.8	79.4	79.7	117.2	21.4	20.1
1997-98, total [3]	162.1	79.1	82.8	127.0	15.2	19.8
Corporate	51.7	16.7	35.0	45.4	2.1	4.2
Trade association [4]	47.5	18.0	29.4	39.0	3.1	5.3
Labor.	37.9	34.5	3.3	26.6	5.4	5.7
Nonconnected [5]	20.2	7.7	12.4	11.7	4.2	4.3
SENATE						
1981-82	22.6	11.2	11.4	14.3	5.2	3.0
1983-84	29.7	14.0	15.6	17.9	6.3	5.4
1985-86	45.3	20.2	25.1	23.7	10.2	11.4
1987-88	45.7	24.2	21.5	28.7	8.0	9.0
1989-90	41.2	20.2	21.0	29.5	8.2	3.5
1991-92	51.2	29.0	22.2	31.9	9.4	10.0
1997-98, total [3]	57.8	24.1	33.6	43.8	6.8	7.2
Corporate	26.3	8.4	17.9	20.6	2.7	3.0
Trade association [4]	14.9	5.5	9.4	11.3	1.6	1.9
Labor.	6.7	6.0	0.7	4.6	1.0	1.1
Nonconnected [5]	7.9	3.3	4.6	5.6	1.3	1.0

[1] Includes other parties, not shown separately.   [2] Elections in which an incumbent did not seek re-election.   [3] Includes other types of political action committees not shown separately.   [4] Includes membership organizations and health organizations.   [5] Represents "ideological" groups as well as other issue groups not necessarily ideological in nature.

Source: U.S. Federal Election Commission, *FEC Reports on Financial Activity, Party and Non-Party Political Committees, Final Report*, biennial.

Section 9

State and Local Government Finances and Employment

This section presents data on revenues, expenditures, debt, and employment of state and local governments. Nationwide statistics relating to state and local governments, their numbers, finances, and employment, are compiled primarily by the U.S. Census Bureau through a program of censuses and surveys. Every fifth year (for years ending in "2" and "7") the Census Bureau conducts a census of governments involving collection of data for all governmental units in the United States. In addition, the Census Bureau conducts annual surveys which cover all the state governments and a sample of local governments.

Annually, the Census Bureau releases information on the Internet which presents financial data for the Federal Government, nationwide totals for state and local governments, and state-local data by states. Also released annually is a series on state, city, county, and school finances and on state and local public employment. There is also a series of quarterly data releases covering tax revenue and finances of major public employee retirement systems.

Basic information for Census Bureau statistics on governments is obtained by mail canvass from state and local officials; however, financial data for each of the state governments and for many of the large local governments are compiled from their official records and reports by Census Bureau personnel. In over two thirds of the states, all or part of local government financial data are obtained through central collection arrangements with state governments. Financial data on the Federal Government is primarily based on the *Budget* published by the Office of Management and Budget (see text, Section 10, Federal).

Governmental units—The governmental structure of the United States includes, in addition to the Federal Government and the states, thousands of local governments—counties, municipalities, townships, school districts, and numerous kinds of "special districts." In 1997, 87,453 local governments were identified by the census of governments. As defined by the census, governmental units include all agencies or bodies having an organized existence, governmental character, and substantial autonomy. While most of these governments can impose taxes, many of the special districts-such as independent public housing authorities, and numerous local irrigation, power, and other types of districts are financed from rentals, charges for services, benefit assessments, grants from other governments, and other nontax sources. The count of governments excludes semi-autonomous agencies through which states, cities, and counties sometimes provide for certain functions—for example, "dependent" school systems, state institutions of higher education, and certain other "authorities" and special agencies which are under the administrative or fiscal control of an established governmental unit.

Finances—The financial statistics relate to government fiscal years ending June 30 or at some date within the 12 previous months. The following governments are exceptions and are included as though they were part of the June 30 group; ending September 30, the state governments of Alabama and Michigan, the District of Columbia, and Alabama school districts; and ending August 31, the state government of Texas and Texas school districts. New York State ends its

U.S. Census Bureau, Statistical Abstract of the United States: 1999

fiscal year on March 31. The Federal Government ended the fiscal year June 30 until 1976 when its fiscal year, by an act of Congress, was revised to extend from Oct. 1 to Sept. 30. A 3-month quarter (July 1 to Sept. 30, 1976) bridged the transition.

Nationwide government finance statistics have been classified and presented in terms of uniform concepts and categories, rather than according to the highly diverse terminology, organization, and fund structure utilized by individual governments. Accordingly, financial statistics which appear here for the Federal Government and for individual states or local governments have been standardized and may not agree directly with figures appearing in the original sources.

Statistics on governmental finances distinguish among general government, utilities, liquor stores, and insurance trusts. General government comprises all activities except utilities, liquor stores, and insurance trusts. Utilities include government water supply, electric light and power, gas supply, and transit systems. Liquor stores are operated by 17 states and by local governments in 6 states. Insurance trusts relate to employee retirement, unemployment compensation, and other social insurance systems administered by the Federal, state, and local governments.

Data for cities or counties relate only to municipal or county and their dependent agencies and do not include amounts for other local governments in the same geographic location. Therefore, expenditure figures for "education" do not include spending by the separate school districts which administer public schools within most municipal or county areas. Variations in the assignment of governmental responsibility for public assistance, health, hospitals, public housing, and other functions to a lesser degree also have an important effect upon reported amounts of city or county expenditure, revenue, and debt. Therefore, any comparisons based upon these figures should be made with caution and with due recognition of variations that exist among areas in the relative role of the municipal corporation.

Employment and payrolls—These data are based mainly on mail canvassing of state and local governments. Payroll includes all salaries, wages, and individual fee payments for the month specified, and employment relates to all persons on governmental payrolls during a pay period of the month covered—including paid officials, temporary help, and (unless otherwise specified) part-time as well as full-time personnel. Beginning 1986, statistics for full-time equivalent employment have been computed with a formula using hours worked by part-time employees. A payroll based formula was used prior to 1985. Full-time equivalent employment statistics were not computed for 1985. Figures shown for individual governments cover major dependent agencies such as institutions of higher education, as well as the basic central departments and agencies of the government.

Statistical reliability—For a discussion of statistical collection and estimation, sampling procedures, and measures of statistical reliability applicable to Census Bureau data, see Appendix III.

No. 500. Number of Governmental Units, by Type: 1942 to 1997

Type of government	1942	1952 [1]	1962	1967	1972	1977	1982	1987	1992	1997
Total	155,116	116,807	91,237	81,299	78,269	79,913	81,831	83,237	85,006	87,504
U.S. Government	1	1	1	1	1	1	1	1	1	1
State government	48	50	50	50	50	50	50	50	50	50
Local governments	155,067	116,756	91,186	81,248	78,218	79,862	81,780	83,186	84,955	87,453
County	3,050	3,052	3,043	3,049	3,044	3,042	3,041	3,042	3,043	3,043
Municipal	16,220	16,807	18,000	18,048	18,517	18,862	19,076	19,200	19,279	19,372
Township and town	18,919	17,202	17,142	17,105	16,991	16,822	16,734	16,691	16,656	16,629
School district	108,579	67,355	34,678	21,782	15,781	15,174	14,851	14,721	14,422	13,726
Special district	8,299	12,340	18,323	21,264	23,885	25,962	28,078	29,532	31,555	34,683

[1] Adjusted to include units in Alaska and Hawaii which adopted statehood in 1959.

No. 501. Number of Local Governments, by Type—States: 1997

State	All governmental units [1]	County	Municipal	Township [1]	School district	Special district [2] Total [3]	Natural resources	Fire protection	Housing & community development
United States	87,453	3,043	19,372	16,629	13,726	34,683	6,983	5,601	3,469
Alabama	1,131	67	446	-	127	491	71	5	154
Alaska	175	12	149	-	-	14	-	-	13
Arizona	637	15	87	-	231	304	79	152	-
Arkansas	1,516	75	491	-	311	639	232	74	126
California	4,607	57	471	-	1,069	3,010	472	369	79
Colorado	1,869	62	269	-	180	1,358	168	249	96
Connecticut	583	-	30	149	17	387	1	65	94
Delaware	336	3	57	-	19	257	236	-	3
District of Columbia	2	-	1	-	-	1	-	-	-
Florida	1,081	66	394	-	95	526	132	56	105
Georgia	1,344	156	535	-	180	473	36	2	206
Hawaii	19	3	1	-	-	15	14	-	-
Idaho	1,147	44	200	-	114	789	182	144	10
Illinois	6,835	102	1,288	1,433	944	3,068	935	827	113
Indiana	3,198	91	569	1,008	294	1,236	134	2	63
Iowa	1,876	99	950	-	394	433	249	68	26
Kansas	3,950	105	627	1,370	324	1,524	260	-	204
Kentucky	1,366	119	434	-	176	637	131	144	17
Louisiana	467	60	302	-	66	39	3	-	-
Maine	832	16	22	467	98	229	16	-	30
Maryland	420	23	156	-	-	241	156	-	20
Massachusetts	861	12	44	307	85	413	18	16	252
Michigan	2,775	83	534	1,242	584	332	82	2	-
Minnesota	3,501	87	854	1,794	360	406	114	-	176
Mississippi	936	82	295	-	164	395	251	-	62
Missouri	3,416	114	944	324	537	1,497	181	273	143
Montana	1,144	54	128	-	362	600	125	159	12
Nebraska	2,894	93	535	455	681	1,130	84	419	126
Nevada	205	16	19	-	17	153	35	16	5
New Hampshire	575	10	13	221	166	165	10	14	21
New Jersey	1,421	21	324	243	552	281	16	200	2
New Mexico	881	33	99	-	96	653	609	-	6
New York	3,413	57	615	929	686	1,126	2	912	-
North Carolina	952	100	527	-	-	325	155	-	94
North Dakota	2,758	53	363	1,341	237	764	80	289	38
Ohio	3,597	88	941	1,310	666	592	97	60	73
Oklahoma	1,799	77	592	-	578	552	98	20	105
Oregon	1,493	36	240	-	258	959	195	263	22
Pennsylvania	5,070	66	1,023	1,546	516	1,919	7	-	91
Rhode Island	119	-	8	31	4	76	3	34	26
South Carolina	716	46	269	-	91	310	48	97	45
South Dakota	1,810	66	309	956	177	302	107	60	34
Tennessee	940	93	343	-	14	490	112	-	100
Texas	4,700	254	1,177	-	1,087	2,182	428	103	395
Utah	683	29	230	-	40	384	77	24	17
Vermont	691	14	49	237	279	112	14	20	10
Virginia	483	95	231	-	1	156	47	-	-
Washington	1,812	39	275	-	296	1,202	163	402	45
West Virginia	704	55	232	-	55	362	15	-	39
Wisconsin	3,059	72	583	1,266	442	696	184	-	171
Wyoming	654	23	97	-	56	478	119	61	-

- Represents zero. [1] Includes "town" governments in the six New England States and in Minnesota, New York, and Wisconsin. [2] Single function districts. [3] Includes other special districts not shown separately.

Source of Tables 500 and 501: U.S. Census Bureau, *1997 Census of Governments, Government Organization*, Series GC97(1).

U.S. Census Bureau, Statistical Abstract of the United States: 1999

No. 502. County, Municipal, and Township Governments: 1997

[Number of governments as of **January 1997.** Population enumerated as of **July 1, 1994.** Consolidated city-county governments are classified as municipal rather than county governments. Township governments include "towns" in the six New England States, Minnesota, New York, and Wisconsin]

Population-size group	County governments			Municipal governments			Township governments		
		Population, 1994			Population, 1994			Population, 1994	
	Number, 1997	Number (1,000)	Percent	Number, 1997	Number (1,000)	Percent	Number, 1997	Number (1,000)	Percent
Total	3,043	236,107	100	19,372	161,605	100	16,629	54,662	100
250,000 or more	183	128,741	55	66	46,417	29	4	1,758	3
100,000 to 299,999	264	40,234	17	142	20,687	13	31	4,259	8
50,000 to 99,999	378	26,583	11	346	23,595	15	84	5,626	10
25,000 to 49,999	604	21,543	9	590	20,623	13	257	8,750	16
10,000 to 24,999	908	15,047	6	1,378	21,606	13	744	11,509	21
5,000 to 9,999	413	3,105	1	1,618	11,504	7	1,064	7,403	14
2,500 to 4,999	178	668	-	2,096	7,426	5	1,836	6,422	12
1,000 to 2,499	86	165	-	3,723	5,965	4	3,606	5,766	11
Less than 1,000	29	21	-	9,413	3,782	2	9,003	3,169	6

- Represents or rounds to zero.

Source: U.S. Census Bureau, *1997 Census of Governments, Government Organization*, Series GC97(1).

Figure 9.1
Lottery Ticket Sales—Type of Game and Use of Proceeds: 1997

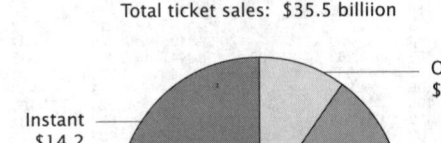

Type of Game
Total ticket sales: $35.5 billiion

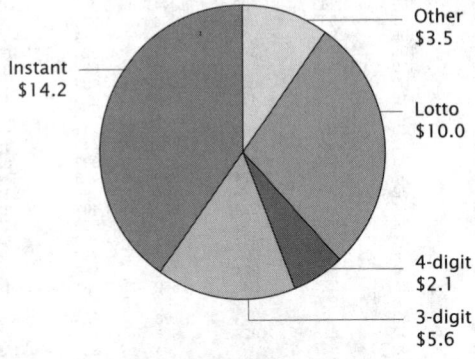

Instant
$14.2

Other
$3.5

Lotto
$10.0

4-digit
$2.1

3-digit
$5.6

Proceeds
Total ticket sales: $12.0 billiion

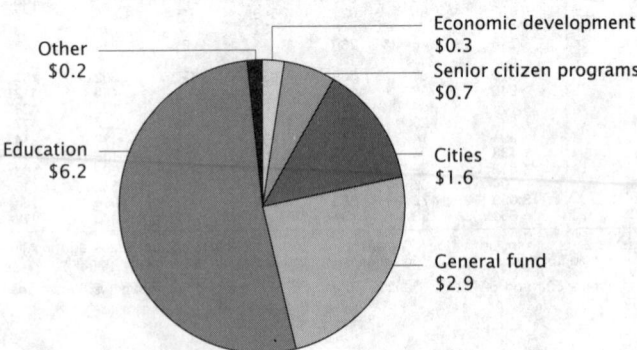

Other
$0.2

Education
$6.2

Economic development
$0.3

Senior citizen programs
$0.7

Cities
$1.6

General fund
$2.9

Source: Chart prepared by U.S. Census Bureau. For data, see Table 529.

U.S. Census Bureau, Statistical Abstract of the United States: 1999

No. 503. All Governments—Revenue, Expenditure, and Debt: 1990 to 1996

[(2,047 represents $2,047,000,000,000) except where indicated. For fiscal year ending in year shown; see text, this section. Local government amounts are estimates subject so sampling variation; see Appendix III and source]

Item	All govern-ments (bil. dol.)	Federal[1] Total (bil. dol.)	Federal[1] Percent of total	State and local (bil. dol.) Total	State and local (bil. dol.) State	State and local (bil. dol.) Local	Per capita[2] (dollars) Total	Per capita[2] (dollars) Federal	Per capita[2] (dollars) State and local
Revenue: [3]									
1990................	2,047	1,155	56.4	[4]1,032	632	580	[4]8,229	4,641	4,149
1995................	2,759	1,573	57.0	[4]1,418	906	757	[4]10,500	5,986	5,396
1996................	(NA)	(NA)	(NA)	[4]1,514	967	804	(X)	(X)	5,709
Intergovernmental:									
1990.............	(X)	3	(X)	[4]137	126	191	(X)	12	550
1995.............	(X)	3	(X)	[4]229	216	259	(X)	12	872
1996.............	(X)	(NA)	(X)	[4]235	221	270	(X)	(X)	886
General, own sources:									
1990.............	1,493	780	52.2	713	391	322	6,002	3,137	2,865
1995.............	1,956	1,015	51.9	941	523	417	7,444	3,863	3,581
1996.............	(NA)	(NA)	(NA)	988	549	439	3,725	(X)	3,725
Taxes: [3]									
1990.............	1,134	632	55.7	502	301	201	4,558	2,542	2,016
1995.............	1,505	844	56.1	661	399	261	5,728	3,212	2,516
1996.............	(NA)	(NA)	(NA)	689	418	271	2,598	(X)	2,598
Property:									
1990...........	156	(X)	(X)	156	6	150	626	(X)	626
1995...........	203	(X)	(X)	203	10	194	773	(X)	773
1996...........	(NA)	(X)	(X)	209	10	199	788	(X)	788
Individual income:									
1990...........	573	467	81.6	106	96	10	2,301	1,877	425
1995...........	728	590	81.0	138	126	12	2,771	2,245	525
1996...........	(NA)	(NA)	(NA)	147	134	13	554	(X)	554
Corporate income:									
1990...........	117	94	80.3	24	22	2	471	376	95
1995...........	188	157	83.5	31	29	2	715	598	118
1996...........	(NA)	(NA)	(NA)	32	29	3	121	(X)	121
Sales or gross receipts:									
1990...........	232	[5]54	23.3	178	147	31	932	[5]217	715
1995...........	312	[5]75	24.0	237	197	40	1,187	[5]285	902
1996...........	(NA)	(NA)	(NA)	249	206	43	939	(X)	939
Current charges and miscellaneous:									
1990.............	359	148	41.3	211	91	120	1,444	596	849
1995.............	451	171	37.9	280	124	156	1,716	651	1,066
1996.............	(NA)	(NA)	(NA)	299	131	168	1,127	(X)	1,127
Expenditures: [3]									
1990................	2,219	1,393	62.8	[4]976	572	581	[4]8,921	5,601	3,924
1995................	2,820	1,705	60.5	[4]1,351	837	759	[4]11,630	6,491	5,143
1996................	(NA)	(NA)	(NA)	[4]1,398	860	794	[4]5,272	(X)	5,272
Intergovernmental:									
1990.............	(X)	147	(X)	[4]3	175	6	(X)	591	13
1995.............	(X)	233	(X)	[4]4	241	8	(X)	887	15
1996.............	(X)	(X)	(X)	[4]4	252	8	(X)	(X)	15
Direct: [3]									
1990.............	2,219	1,246	56.2	973	397	575	8,919	5,009	3,911
1995.............	2,820	1,472	52.2	1,348	596	751	10,732	5,602	5,130
1996.............	(NA)	(NA)	(NA)	1,394	608	786	5,257	(X)	5,257
Current operation:									
1990.............	1,190	490	41.2	700	258	442	4,785	1,970	2,814
1995.............	1,471	486	33.0	986	396	590	5,598	1,850	3,752
1996.............	(NA)	(NA)	(NA)	1,021	406	616	3,850	(X)	3,850
Capital outlay:									
1990...........	221	98	44.3	123	46	78	888	394	495
1995...........	226	75	33.2	151	58	94	860	285	575
1996...........	(NA)	(NA)	(NA)	159	59	100	600	(X)	600
Debt outstanding: [6]									
1990................	4,127	3,266	79.2	861	318	542	16,589	13,129	3,459
1995................	6,116	5,001	81.8	1,115	427	688	23,276	19,033	4,243
1996................	(NA)	(NA)	(NA)	1,170	452	717	4,412	(X)	4,412

NA Not available. X Not applicable. [1] Data adjusted to system for reporting state and local data; therefore, differ from figures in Section 10 tables. [2] 1990 based on enumerated resident population as of April 1, all other years based on estimated resident population as of July 1. [3] Includes amounts not shown separately. [4] Excludes duplicate transactions between levels of government; see source. [5] Includes customs. [6] End of fiscal year.

Source: U.S. Census Bureau, 1990, *Government Finances*, GF, No. 5, annual; thereafter, <http://www.census.gov/govs/www/index.html> (accessed 5 May 1999).

State and Local Government Finances and Employment 311

No. 504. All Governments—Detailed Finances: 1996

[In millions of dollars (1,572,588 represents $1,572,588,000,000), except as indicated. For fiscal year ending in year shown; see text, this section. Local government amounts are estimates subject to sampling variation; see Appendix III and source]

Item	Federal [1]	State and local Total	State	Local	Per capita [2] (dol.) Fed- eral [1]	State and local
Revenue	**1,572,588**	**1,513,633**	**966,808**	**803,737**	**5,985**	**5,708**
Intergovernmental revenue	3,060	234,891	221,369	270,480	12	886
Revenue from own sources	1,569,528	1,278,743	745,439	533,257	5,973	4,822
General revenue from own sources	1,015,042	987,930	549,147	438,736	3,863	3,725
Taxes [3]	844,415	689,038	418,390	270,602	3,214	2,598
Property	(X)	209,440	9,974	199,467	(X)	790
Individual income	590,243	146,844	133,547	13,296	2,246	554
Corporation income	157,004	32,009	29,316	2,693	598	121
Sales and gross receipts	75,185	248,993	206,115	42,832	286	939
Customs duties	19,438	(X)	(X)	(X)	74	(X)
General	(X)	169,071	139,363	29,709	(X)	638
Selective [3]	55,747	79,922	66,752	13,123	212	301
Motor fuel	28,669	26,833	25,988	844	109	101
Alcoholic beverages	7,523	3,988	3,667	275	29	15
Tobacco products	5,878	7,520	7,338	183	22	28
Public utilities	9,365	15,920	8,615	7,306	36	60
Motor vehicle and operators' licenses	(X)	14,939	13,848	1,090	(X)	56
Death and gift	14,763	5,352	5,320	32	56	20
Charges and miscellaneous [3]	170,627	298,892	130,757	168,135	649	1,127
Current charges [3]	95,860	182,201	67,259	114,942	365	687
National defense and international relations	9,612	(X)	(X)	(X)	37	(X)
Postal service	53,311	(X)	(X)	(X)	203	(X)
Education [3]	(X)	49,741	37,592	12,150	(X)	188
School lunch sales	(X)	4,307	16	4,290	(X)	16
Higher education	(X)	41,546	37,100	4,445	(X)	157
Natural resources	13,042	2,076	1,573	503	50	8
Hospitals	223	50,544	15,533	35,011	1	191
Sewerage	(X)	21,067	27	21,041	(X)	79
Solid waste management	2	9,019	347	8,672	-	34
Parks and recreation	113	4,916	1,000	3,916	-	19
Housing and community development	2,459	3,605	374	3,231	9	14
Airports	27	8,170	705	7,465	-	31
Sea and inland port facilities	1,491	2,131	600	1,531	6	8
Highways	(X)	5,610	3,517	2,093	(X)	21
Interest earnings	12,973	57,592	28,621	28,971	49	217
Special assessments	(X)	3,123	102	3,021	(X)	12
Sale of property	4,666	856	209	647	18	3
Utility and liquor store revenue	(X)	75,326	7,079	68,247	(X)	284
Insurance trust revenue	554,486	215,487	189,213	26,273	2,110	813
Expenditure	**1,705,486**	**1,397,634**	**859,599**	**794,318**	**6,491**	**5,270**
Intergovernmental expenditure	233,389	3,920	252,005	8,198	888	15
Direct expenditure	1,472,097	1,393,714	607,594	786,120	5,602	5,256
General expenditure [3]	913,806	1,189,356	503,306	686,050	3,478	4,485
Education [3]	26,660	398,859	106,565	292,294	101	1,504
Elementary and secondary education	(X)	279,353	2,447	276,906	(X)	1,053
Higher education	(X)	100,736	85,348	15,388	(X)	380
Public welfare	57,246	40,588	23,118	17,470	218	153
Hospitals	11,990	70,648	29,063	41,585	46	266
Health	14,531	40,166	22,180	17,986	55	151
Highways	731	79,092	47,548	31,545	3	298
Police protection	6,862	44,683	6,499	38,184	26	168
Fire protection	(X)	17,709	(X)	17,709	(X)	67
Corrections	3,065	37,510	25,294	12,216	12	141
Natural resources	39,742	15,819	12,306	3,512	151	60
Sewerage	(X)	24,665	1,527	23,138	(X)	93
Solid waste management	2,711	14,700	1,620	13,080	10	55
Housing and community development	16,278	22,666	2,369	20,297	62	85
Governmental administration	(X)	54,991	23,360	31,631	(X)	207
Parks and recreation	2,250	19,137	3,063	16,073	9	72
Interest on general debt	233,225	58,912	25,410	33,502	888	222
Utility	(X)	92,509	8,043	84,465	(X)	349
Liquor store expenditure	(X)	3,099	2,593	506	(X)	12
Insurance trust expenditure	558,291	108,751	93,652	15,099	2,125	410
By character and object:						
Current operation	486,041	1,021,155	405,527	615,629	1,850	3,851
Capital outlay	74,648	158,911	58,927	99,984	284	599
Construction	9,929	116,076	46,934	69,142	38	438
Equip., land, and existing structures	64,719	42,835	11,994	30,842	246	162
Assistance and subsidies	119,892	36,154	23,313	12,841	456	136
Interest on debt (general and utility)	233,225	68,743	26,175	42,568	888	259
Insurance benefits and repayments	558,291	108,751	93,652	15,099	2,125	410
Expenditure for salaries and wages [4]	*162,392*	*447,638*	*129,577*	*318,061*	*618*	*1,688*

- Represents or rounds to zero.   X Not applicable.   [1] 1995 data.   [2] Based on estimated resident population as of July 1.
See Table 2.   [3] Includes amounts not shown separately.   [4] Included in items shown above.

Source: U.S. Census Bureau <http://www.census.gov/pub/ govs/www/index.html> (accessed 20 May 1999), and unpublished data.

No. 505. All Governments—Capital Outlays: 1980 to 1996

[In millions of dollars (99,386 represents $99,386,000,000), except percent. For fiscal year ending in year shown; see text, this section. Local government amounts are subject to sampling variation; see Appendix III and source]

Level and function	1980	1985	1990	1992	1993	1994	1995	1996
Total	99,386	156,912	220,960	227,798	221,227	217,328	226,088	(NA)
Federal Government:								
Total	36,492	77,014	97,891	93,095	85,328	79,827	74,648	(NA)
Annual percent change [1]. . . .	10.9	6.3	-1.9	-2.6	-8.3	-6.5	-6.5	(NA)
Direct expenditure	526,330	924,889	1,246,131	889,494	1,364,873	1,412,364	1,472,097	(NA)
Percent of direct expenditure .	6.9	8.3	7.9	10.5	6.3	5.7	5.1	(NA)
By function:								
National defense [2]	28,161	64,154	75,624	69,061	61,754	59,160	53,826	(NA)
Education.	97	39	41	90	86	145	221	(NA)
Highways	132	121	181	310	210	203	185	(NA)
Health and hospitals	673	916	1,096	1,594	1,703	1,508	1,740	(NA)
Natural resources	4,046	4,092	4,698	5,466	6,122	2,990	3,261	(NA)
Housing [3].	317	1,935	4,343	4,017	3,942	3,557	3,918	(NA)
Air transportation.	151	785	664	879	916	909	791	(NA)
Water transportation [4].	1,003	583	385	506	739	495	369	(NA)
Other	1,912	4,389	10,859	11,172	9,856	10,837	10,337	(NA)
State and local governments:								
Total	62,894	79,898	123,069	134,703	135,899	137,501	151,440	158,911
Annual percent change [1]. . . .	7.0	13.1	9.9	2.3	0.9	1.2	10.1	4.9
Direct expenditure	432,328	656,188	972,662	1,146,853	1,213,723	1,115,997	1,347,763	1,393,714
Percent of direct expenditure .	14.5	12.2	12.7	11.7	11.2	12.3	11.2	11.4
By function:								
Education [5]	10,737	13,477	25,997	30,845	31,359	29,012	35,708	40,302
Higher education	2,972	4,629	7,441	9,180	8,949	8,959	10,461	11,006
Elementary and secondary.	7,362	8,358	18,057	21,319	22,102	19,693	24,808	28,868
Highways	19,133	23,900	33,867	37,031	36,980	39,503	42,561	43,453
Health and hospitals	2,443	2,709	3,848	4,331	5,291	4,464	4,883	5,160
Natural resources	1,052	1,736	2,545	2,266	2,137	2,349	2,891	3,042
Housing [3].	2,248	3,217	3,997	4,182	4,890	4,066	4,527	4,704
Air transportation.	1,391	1,875	3,434	4,605	5,413	5,170	3,802	3,814
Water transportation [4].	623	717	924	778	996	1,483	1,101	1,246
Sewerage	6,272	5,926	8,356	8,926	10,261	7,989	8,894	9,326
Parks and recreation	2,023	2,196	3,877	3,934	3,849	3,919	4,085	4,869
Utilities	9,933	13,435	16,601	17,785	15931	18,180	19,028	18,755
Water.	3,335	4,160	6,873	7,567	6,490	6,893	7,466	7,381
Electric.	4,572	5,247	3,976	3,950	3,760	4,030	3,715	3,522
Transit	1,921	3,830	5,443	5,836	5,253	6,966	7,507	7,533
Gas	105	198	310	432	428	290	340	318
Other	7,039	10,711	19,623	20,020	18,793	21,366	23,961	24,239

NA Not available. [1] Change from prior year shown. [2] Includes international relations and U.S. service schools. [3] Includes community development. [4] Includes terminals. [5] Includes other education.
Source: U.S. Census Bureau, 1980-92; *Historical Statistics on Governmental Finances and Employment*; and *Government Finances*, Series GF, No. 5, annual; thereafter, <http://www.census.gov/govs/www/index.html> (accessed 20 May 1999).

No. 506. All Governments—Expenditure for Public Works: 1980 to 1996

[In millions of dollars (72,177 represents $72,177,000,000). Public works include expenditures on highways, airports, water transport and terminals, sewerage, solid waste management, water supply, and mass transit systems. Represents direct expenditures excluding intergovernmental grants]

Item	Total	High-ways	Airport transpor-tation	Water transport and ter-minals	Sewer-age	Solid waste manage-ment	Water supply	Mass transit
1980: Total.	72,177	33,745	5,071	3,278	9,892	3,322	9,228	7,641
Federal	5,114	434	2,570	2,110	-	-	-	-
State	22,832	20,661	360	360	334	-	91	1,026
Local	44,231	12,650	2,141	808	9,558	3,322	9,137	6,615
Capital expenditures (percent) . . .	48	57	30	50	63	11	36	25
1990: Total.	146,762	61,913	10,983	4,524	18,309	10,144	22,101	18,788
Federal	7,911	856	4,499	2,556	-	-	-	-
State	43,787	36,464	635	504	636	891	136	4,521
Local	95,064	24,593	5,848	1,464	17,673	9,253	21,966	14,267
Capital expenditures (percent) . . .	42	55	37	29	46	18	31	29
1994: Total.	180,634	72,758	15,896	5,476	21,624	14,041	26,617	24,221
Federal	10,021	691	6,482	2,848	-	-	-	-
State	52,534	43,812	788	635	1,318	1,370	176	4,434
Local	118,079	28,255	8,626	1,993	20,305	12,671	26,441	19,788
Capital expenditures (percent) . . .	40	55	38	36	37	13	26	29
1995: Total.	192,985	77,840	15,085	5,016	23,583	17,701	28,041	25,719
Federal	12,837	731	6,688	2,707	-	2,711	-	-
State	56,392	46,893	783	604	1,462	1,658	178	4,814
Local	123,756	30,216	7,614	1,706	22,121	13,331	27,863	20,904
Capital expenditures (percent) . . .	39	55	30	29	38	11	27	29
1996: Total.	(NA)	(NA)	(NA)	(NA)	(NA)	(NA)	(NA)	(NA)
Federal	(NA)	(NA)	(NA)	(NA)	(NA)	(NA)	(NA)	(NA)
State	89,392	79,092	796	784	1,527	1,620	184	5,388
Local	142,895	47,548	7,997	1,794	23,138	13,080	28,766	20,573
Capital expenditures (percent) . . .	(NA)	(NA)	(NA)	(NA)	(NA)	(NA)	(NA)	(NA)
Capital expenditures	(NA)	(NA)	(NA)	(NA)	(NA)	(NA)	(NA)	(NA)

- Represents or rounds to zero. NA Not available.
Source: U.S. Census Bureau, 1980-90, *Government Finances*, Series GF, No. 5, annual; thereafter, <http://www.census.gov/govs/www/index.html> (accessed 20 May 1999), *State and Local Government Finance Estimates by State*, annual, and unpublished data.

State and Local Government Finances and Employment 313

No. 507. Federal Grants-in-Aid Summary: 1970 to 1999

[(24,065 represents $24,065,000,000), except as indicated. For fiscal year ending in year shown; see text, this section. Minus sign (-) indicates decrease]

Year	Total grants (mil. dol.)	Annual percent change [1]	Grants to individuals — Total (mil. dol.)	Grants to individuals — Percent of total grants	Grants as percent of— State/local govt. expenditures from own sources [2]	Grants as percent of— Federal outlays	Grants as percent of— Gross domestic product	Constant (1992) dollars — Total grants (bil. dol.)	Constant (1992) dollars — Annual percent change [1]
1970	24,065	19.3	8,717	36.3	30.9	12.3	2.4	86.9	11.8
1975	49,791	14.8	16,752	33.7	36.6	15.0	3.2	126.6	3.3
1980	91,385	9.6	32,619	35.7	42.9	15.5	3.4	155.7	-1.1
1985	105,852	8.5	49,321	46.6	32.0	11.2	2.6	135.6	4.7
1990	135,325	11.0	75,685	57.0	26.9	10.8	2.4	144.7	6.2
1991	154,519	14.2	90,744	59.9	28.3	11.7	2.6	158.6	9.6
1992	178,065	15.2	110,016	63.0	30.7	12.9	2.9	178.1	12.3
1993	193,612	8.7	121,519	64.2	31.5	13.7	3.0	188.6	6.0
1994	210,596	8.8	131,123	64.2	32.7	14.4	3.1	200.5	6.3
1995	224,991	6.8	141,183	64.8	33.5	14.8	3.1	208.5	3.8
1996	227,811	1.3	142,802	64.8	32.8	14.6	3.0	206.7	-1.3
1997	234,160	2.8	144,189	63.6	32.2	14.6	2.9	208.1	0.1
1998	246,093	7.2	155,852	64.2	32.4	14.9	2.9	215.2	4.9
1999, est	262,164	8.1	164,194	62.7	(NA)	15.2	3.0	225.2	5.7

NA Not available. [1] Average annual percent change from prior year shown. For explanation, see Guide to Tabular Presentation. 1970, change from 1969. [2] Outlays as defined in the national income and product accounts.

Source: U. S. Office of Management and Budget, based on *Historical Tables* and *Analytical Prospectives, Budget of the United States Government,* annual.

No. 508. Federal Aid to State and Local Governments: 1970 to 1999

[In millions of dollars (24,065 represents $24,065,000,000). For fiscal year ending in year shown; See text, this section. Includes trust funds]

Program	1970	1980	1990	1995	1996	1997	1998	1999, est.
Grant-in-aid shared revenue [1]	[2]24,065	91,385	135,325	224,991	227,811	234,160	246,093	262,164
National defense	37	93	241	68	38	-	12	3
Energy	25	499	461	492	481	440	424	456
Natural resources and environment	411	5,363	3,745	4,148	3,900	4,121	3,829	4,276
Environmental Protection Agency	194	4,603	2,874	2,912	2,779	2,907	2,746	2,972
Agriculture	604	569	1,285	780	641	634	668	746
Commerce and Housing Credit	4	3	-	5	8	9	9	8
Transportation [1]	4,599	13,022	19,174	25,787	25,957	26,846	26,144	29,137
Airports [3]	83	590	1,220	1,826	1,655	1,489	1,511	1,670
Highways [3]	4,395	9,208	14,711	19,475	19,366	20,304	19,791	22,748
Urban mass transit [3]	104	3,129	3,730	4,353	4,291	4,499	4,221	3,946
Community and regional development [1]	1,780	6,486	4,965	7,230	7,850	8,161	7,653	8,697
Appalachian regional development	184	335	124	182	230	236	180	145
Community development block grants	(X)	3,902	2,818	4,333	4,545	4,517	4,621	4,965
Education, employment, training, social services [1]	6,417	21,862	23,359	34,125	34,034	34,735	36,467	38,911
Compensatory education for the disadvantaged	1,470	3,370	4,437	6,785	7,006	7,187	7,800	6,666
School improvement programs	86	523	1,080	1,288	1,140	1,187	1,260	1,373
Bilingual and immigrant education	-	166	152	189	160	171	204	351
Federally affected areas impact aid	622	622	799	803	945	651	689	968
Vocational and adult education	285	854	1,287	1,449	1,323	1,382	1,425	1,292
Payments to states for Family Support Activities	81	383	265	953	931	445	48	39
Social services-block grants to states	574	2,763	2,749	2,797	2,484	2,571	2,441	2,050
Children and family services programs	390	1,548	2,618	4,463	4,494	4,876	5,052	5,553
Training and employment assistance	954	6,191	3,042	3,620	3,231	3,324	3,399	3,728
Office of libraries	105	154	127	109	156	132	121	166
Health [1]	3,849	15,758	43,890	93,587	97,650	98,974	105,833	114,834
Alcohol, drug abuse, and mental health [4]	146	679	1,241	2,444	2,083	1,622	2,236	2,331
Grants to states for medicaid [4]	2,727	13,957	41,103	89,070	91,990	95,552	101,234	108,534
Income security [1]	5,795	18,495	35,189	55,122	53,375	54,965	58,870	58,991
Family support payments to states [4]	4,142	6,888	12,246	17,133	16,670	5,345	2,171	2,738
Food stamps-administration [4]	559	412	2,130	2,740	3,030	3,122	3,673	3,642
Child nutrition and special milk programs [4]	380	3,388	4,871	7,387	7,757	8,141	8,436	8,936
Housing assistance [4]	436	3,435	9,516	18,416	16,762	17,717	19,668	18,431
Veterans benefits and services [4]	18	90	134	253	266	277	288	330
Administration of justice	42	529	574	1,222	1,547	2,845	3,658	3,816
General government [5]	479	8,616	2,309	2,172	2,064	2,153	2,238	1,959

- Represents zero or rounds to zero. X Not applicable. [1] Includes items not shown separately. [2] Includes $5 million for international affairs subsequently provided to a private institution. [3] Trust funds. [4] Includes grants for payments to individuals. [5] Includes general purpose fiscal assistance.

Source: U.S. Office of Management and Budget, *Historical Tables, Budget of the United States Government,* annual.

No. 509. Federal Aid to State and Local Governments—Selected Programs, by State: 1998

[In millions of dollars (253,274 represents $253,274,000,000), except per capita. For fiscal year ending September 30]

State and outlying area	Federal aid [1]		USDA food and nutrition service	OESE [3] compensatory education [4]	Education for the disadvantaged	HHS [5] Administration for children and families [6]	Medicaid	HUD [7] Lower income housing assistance [8]	Community development	ETA [9] employment/training	DOT [10] highway trust fund
	Total	Per capita [2] (dol.)									
United States [11]	253,274	937	8,346	10,622	8,450	32,427	101,001	3,216	4,621	6,728	19,191
Alabama	3,814	876	168	180	158	283	1,654	79	79	93	284
Alaska	1,413	2,301	24	110	30	132	251	14	15	45	213
Arizona	3,821	818	166	303	146	484	1,308	33	54	106	268
Arkansas	2,414	951	96	106	97	217	1,075	19	16	54	292
California	29,826	913	1,072	1,307	1,110	5,747	10,128	118	506	1,085	1,678
Colorado	2,632	663	84	117	92	318	877	14	46	75	254
Connecticut	3,313	1,012	64	98	86	472	1,461	54	47	93	334
Delaware	3,070	4,129	22	43	29	252	587	42	103	47	98
District of Columbia	680	1,299	24	30	24	72	224	9	7	20	101
Florida	9,754	654	448	500	429	1,272	3,707	88	189	259	703
Georgia	5,696	745	311	277	242	659	2,260	97	98	125	423
Hawaii	1,178	987	38	90	26	195	303	9	34	44	143
Idaho	934	760	32	44	33	104	325	1	15	37	127
Illinois	9,838	817	320	474	408	1,397	3,585	299	255	290	661
Indiana	4,052	687	126	163	143	454	1,686	33	91	111	444
Iowa	2,182	762	73	69	64	269	898	1	39	59	246
Kansas	1,861	708	88	107	73	240	691	10	32	44	198
Kentucky	4,010	1,019	143	175	160	406	1,861	38	64	87	296
Louisiana	4,794	1,097	226	265	230	457	2,273	53	84	111	276
Maine	1,582	1,272	33	45	38	170	756	9	20	40	120
Maryland	4,030	785	20	152	116	483	1,410	73	56	124	355
Massachusetts	7,218	1,174	140	193	173	795	3,043	92	131	141	912
Michigan	8,334	849	219	442	393	1,359	3,329	56	159	189	606
Minnesota	4,086	865	138	131	105	569	1,633	35	105	85	291
Mississippi	2,993	1,087	151	167	149	291	1,393	21	45	61	187
Missouri	4,704	865	151	178	145	518	2,074	31	74	100	385
Montana	1,104	1,254	27	77	31	108	283	8	14	29	192
Nebraska	1,395	839	56	73	42	150	540	6	24	33	127
Nevada	1,026	587	35	31	26	111	276	16	15	49	116
New Hampshire	916	773	17	25	21	88	379	6	17	25	95
New Jersey	7,041	868	161	238	193	798	2,903	140	127	225	495
New Mexico	2,178	1,254	98	158	75	266	726	8	29	52	170
New York	28,293	1,557	621	393	261	4,240	14,235	788	401	487	1,186
North Carolina	6,514	863	251	211	169	738	2,912	78	90	140	662
North Dakota	989	1,550	23	41	7	84	244	6	84	25	150
Ohio	9,494	847	238	410	360	1,362	3,997	135	192	237	716
Oklahoma	2,800	837	128	152	104	323	1,019	23	62	77	259
Oregon	3,218	981	90	114	98	332	1,127	11	39	97	333
Pennsylvania	11,104	925	251	471	419	1,248	4,840	221	284	313	855
Rhode Island	1,262	1,276	21	36	31	154	529	15	23	34	90
South Carolina	3,355	875	147	135	117	294	1,660	26	43	78	247
South Dakota	999	1,353	28	71	26	72	260	11	22	20	160
Tennessee	5,364	988	174	182	160	456	2,635	80	63	100	446
Texas	15,154	767	791	997	824	1,386	6,645	84	307	415	1,079
Utah	1,551	739	71	57	43	174	519	3	22	41	143
Vermont	748	1,266	15	27	23	96	267	2	9	21	100
Virginia	3,708	546	129	99	47	405	1,289	53	60	125	460
Washington	5,001	879	135	211	146	678	1,903	30	82	177	422
West Virginia	2,185	1,206	65	43	31	222	1,017	13	35	58	221
Wisconsin	4,220	808	110	191	155	689	1,713	14	79	103	367
Wyoming	775	1,612	14	21	8	46	128	2	6	16	126
Outlying areas	4,281	1,000	11,719	391	601	277	167	109	126	193	113
Puerto Rico	3,677	953	150	354	328	247	152	82	124	159	82

[1] Includes programs not shown separately. [2] Based on estimated resident population as of July 1, 1998. [3] Department of Education, Office of Elementary and Secondary Education. [4] For the disadvantaged. [5] Department of Health and Human Services. [6] Includes family support payments (Aid to Families With Dependent Children), social services block grants, children and family services, foster care and adoption assistance, low-income home energy assistance, community services block grants, refugee assistance, and assistance for legalized aliens. [7] Department of Housing and Urban Development. [8] Includes public housing, housing payments (section 8) to public agencies, and college housing. [9] Department of Labor, Employment and Training Administration, Insurance and Employment Service Operations, and Community Service. [10] Department of Transportation, Highway Trust Fund. [11] Includes undistributed amounts not shown separately.

Source: U.S. Census Bureau, *Federal Aid to States for Fiscal Year, 1998*, series FAS/98.

U.S. Census Bureau, Statistical Abstract of the United States: 1999

No. 510. State and Local Government Receipts and Current Expenditures in the National Income and Product Accounts: 1980 to 1997

[In billions of dollars (361.4 represents $361,400,000,000). For explanation of national income, see text, Section 14, Income, Expenditures, and Wealth]

Item	1980	1985	1990	1991	1992	1993	1994	1995	1996	1997
Receipts	361.4	528.7	728.9	784.2	844.3	894.4	949.2	999.0	1,043.4	1,090.4
Personal tax and nontax receipts	56.2	94.0	139.1	147.8	159.7	167.4	176.8	189.4	200.2	214.3
Income taxes	42.6	72.1	106.3	110.4	118.1	124.2	131.2	140.3	149.1	159.8
Nontaxes	5.0	9.9	15.6	19.2	22.5	23.4	24.8	26.7	28.8	31.0
Other	8.6	11.9	17.3	18.2	19.1	19.8	20.8	22.4	22.3	23.5
Corporate profits tax accruals	14.5	20.2	22.5	23.6	24.4	26.9	29.9	31.1	34.5	37.6
Indirect business tax and nontax accruals [1]	172.3	271.4	377.6	398.4	423.7	445.6	469.8	489.3	508.9	528.1
Sales taxes	82.9	131.1	183.2	190.0	202.2	214.8	228.2	239.4	249.8	257.4
Property taxes	68.8	107.0	155.5	167.6	177.5	185.0	191.4	197.4	202.3	208.8
Contributions for social insurance	29.7	42.8	57.4	60.9	64.3	68.7	73.4	77.3	81.4	86.2
Federal grants-in-aid	88.7	100.3	132.4	153.4	172.2	185.8	199.2	211.9	218.3	224.2
Current expenditures	307.0	437.8	648.8	708.4	758.0	807.0	852.3	895.9	938.0	982.6
Consumption expenditures	261.3	382.6	550.1	579.4	603.6	631.6	663.8	698.6	730.9	762.9
Transfer payments to persons	65.7	101.9	166.5	199.0	227.2	247.2	264.3	280.6	294.8	311.8
Net interest paid	-19.3	-38.9	-51.7	-53.3	-54.7	-52.4	-55.1	-59.6	-61.7	-65.2
Interest received by government	38.7	81.0	112.1	116.8	119.4	116.9	118.8	123.7	126.3	129.8
Less: Dividends received	1.9	4.5	9.0	9.5	10.1	10.5	11.4	12.5	13.6	14.6
Subsidies	0.4	0.3	0.4	0.4	0.4	0.4	0.4	0.3	0.3	0.3
Less: Current surplus of government enterprises	-0.9	3.7	7.5	7.6	8.4	9.3	9.7	11.5	12.7	12.6
Current surplus or deficit	54.4	91.0	80.1	75.8	86.3	87.4	96.8	103.1	105.3	107.8
Social insurance funds	26.9	47.0	59.9	64.3	68.0	67.8	68.9	70.5	71.3	71.4
Other	27.5	44.0	20.2	11.5	18.3	19.7	27.9	32.5	34.1	36.3

[1] Includes other items not shown separately.

Source: U.S. Bureau of Economic Analysis, *National Income and Product Accounts of the United States, 1929-94*, Vol.1 and *Survey of Current Business*, August 1997.

No. 511. State and Local Government Consumption Expenditures and Transfers in the National Income and Product Accounts: 1980 to 1997

[In billions of dollars (324.4 represents $324,400,000,000). For explanation of national income, see text, Section 14, Income, Expenditures, and Wealth]

Expenditure	1980	1985	1990	1991	1992	1993	1994	1995	1996	1997
Consumption expenditures and gross investment [1]	324.4	464.9	672.6	703.4	735.8	765.0	802.8	846.0	886.7	928.9
Consumption expenditures	261.3	382.6	550.1	579.4	603.6	631.6	663.8	698.6	730.9	762.9
Durable goods [2]	4.7	7.4	10.9	11.7	12.4	13.2	13.9	14.7	15.3	15.8
Nondurable goods	28.8	38.7	56.5	58.4	60.9	64.3	67.8	73.0	78.2	80.6
Services	227.8	336.5	482.8	509.4	530.3	554.2	582.1	610.9	637.5	666.5
Gross investment	63.1	82.3	122.5	123.9	132.2	133.4	138.9	147.4	155.7	166.0
Structures	55.1	67.6	98.5	100.5	108.1	108.7	113.4	121.0	128.5	138.4
Equipment	8.1	14.8	23.9	23.4	24.0	24.7	25.6	26.4	27.3	27.6
Transfers	65.7	101.9	166.5	199.0	227.2	247.2	264.3	280.6	294.8	(NA)
Benefits from social insurance funds	17.8	30.4	49.6	55.1	61.0	66.0	71.1	76.8	83.5	(NA)
State and local employee retirement	15.1	25.5	40.6	44.7	49.6	54.8	60.3	66.3	72.9	(NA)
Temporary disability insurance	0.8	1.4	2.2	2.8	3.0	2.3	2.2	2.1	2.1	(NA)
Workers' compensation	2.0	3.5	6.9	7.6	8.4	8.9	8.6	8.4	8.6	(NA)
Public assistance	42.8	65.7	108.1	134.4	156.0	170.0	180.9	190.3	197.0	(NA)
Medical care [3]	24.6	41.8	76.7	100.2	119.7	132.5	141.7	151.3	159.9	(NA)
Family Assistance [3]	12.4	15.4	19.8	22.0	23.3	24.0	24.3	23.3	21.7	(NA)
Supplemental Security Income	2.0	2.3	3.8	3.8	4.1	3.9	3.8	3.8	3.6	(NA)
General assistance	1.4	2.4	3.0	2.9	3.3	3.3	3.4	3.4	3.5	(NA)
Energy assistance	1.3	2.1	1.6	1.6	1.6	1.5	2.0	1.5	1.4	(NA)
Other [4]	1.0	1.6	3.2	3.8	4.0	4.8	5.7	7.0	6.8	(NA)
Education	2.4	3.5	5.3	5.7	6.0	6.6	7.6	8.5	9.1	(NA)
Employment and training	1.7	0.9	0.9	0.9	1.1	1.1	1.1	1.2	1.1	(NA)
Other [5]	0.8	1.3	2.5	2.9	3.1	3.4	3.7	3.9	4.1	(NA)

NA Not available. [1] Gross government investment consists of general government and government enterprise expenditures for fixed assets; inventory investment is included in government consumption expenditures. [2] Consumption expenditures for durable goods excludes expenditures classified as investment, except for goods transferred to foreign countries by the Federal Government. [3] Consists of aid to families with dependent children. Beginning with 1996, assistance programs operating under the personal responsibility and work opportunity act of 1996. [4] Consists of emergency assistance and medical insurance premium payments paid on behalf of indigents. [5] Consists largely of foster care, veterans benefits, Alaska dividends, and crime victim payments.

Source: U.S. Bureau of Economic Analysis, *National Income and Product Accounts of the United States, 1929-94*, Vol. 1, and *Survey of Current Business*, August 1997.

No. 512. State and Local Governments—Summary of Finances: 1980 to 1996

[In millions of dollars (451,537 represents $451,537,000,000), except as indicated. For fiscal year ending in year shown; see text, this section. Local government amounts are estimates subject to sampling variation; see Appendix III and source]

Item	Total (mil. dol.)				Per capita [1] (dol.)			
	1980	1990	1995	1996	1980	1990	1995	1996
Revenue [2]	451,537	1,032,115	1,417,925	1,513,633	1,993	4,150	5,396	5,708
From Federal Government	83,029	136,802	228,771	234,891	367	550	871	886
Public welfare	24,921	59,961	115,799	119,201	110	241	441	449
Highways	8,980	14,368	19,879	19,279	40	58	76	73
Education	14,435	23,233	34,045	36,224	-	93	130	137
Health and hospitals	2,513	5,904	11,113	11,915	11	24	42	45
Housing and community development	3,905	9,655	15,255	15,585	17	39	58	59
Other and unallocable	28,275	23,683	32,681	32,687	125	95	124	123
From state and local sources	368,509	895,313	1,189,153	1,278,742	1,627	3,600	4,526	4,822
General, net intergovernmental	299,293	712,700	940,733	987,930	1,321	2,865	3,580	3,725
Taxes	223,463	501,619	660,577	689,038	986	2,017	2,514	2,598
Property	68,499	155,613	203,451	209,440	302	626	774	790
Sales and gross receipts	79,927	177,885	237,268	248,993	353	715	903	939
Individual income	42,080	105,640	137,931	146,844	186	425	525	554
Corporation income	13,321	23,566	31,406	32,000	59	95	120	121
Other	19,636	38,915	50,521	51,752	87	156	192	195
Charges and miscellaneous	75,830	211,081	280,156	298,892	335	849	1,066	1,127
Utility and liquor stores	25,560	58,642	72,271	75,325	113	236	275	284
Water supply system	6,766	17,674	23,879	25,433	30	71	91	96
Electric power system	11,387	29,268	34,627	35,476	50	118	132	134
Transit system	2,397	5,216	6,540	6,889	11	21	25	26
Gas supply system	1,809	3,043	3,588	3,795	8	12	14	14
Liquor stores	3,201	3,441	3,637	3,732	14	14	14	14
Insurance trust revenue [3]	43,656	123,970	176,149	215,487	193	498	670	813
Employee retirement	25,441	94,268	122,595	165,411	112	379	467	624
Unemployment compensation	13,529	18,441	37,225	33,864	60	74	142	128
Direct expenditure	432,328	972,662	1,347,763	1,393,714	1,908	3,911	5,129	5,256
By function:								
Direct general expenditure [3]	367,340	834,786	1,146,188	1,189,356	1,622	3,356	4,362	4,485
Education [3]	133,211	288,148	378,273	398,859	588	1,159	1,440	1,504
Elementary and secondary	92,930	202,009	264,240	279,353	410	812	1,006	1,053
Higher education	33,919	73,418	97,048	100,736	150	295	369	380
Highways	33,311	61,057	77,109	79,092	147	245	293	298
Public welfare	45,552	110,518	193,110	193,480	201	444	735	730
Health	8,387	24,223	38,020	40,166	37	97	145	151
Hospitals	23,787	50,412	67,926	70,648	105	203	259	266
Police protection	13,494	30,577	41,055	44,683	60	123	156	168
Fire protection	5,718	13,186	17,009	17,709	25	53	65	67
Natural resources	5,509	12,330	15,251	15,819	24	50	58	60
Sanitation and sewerage	13,214	28,453	38,573	39,365	58	114	147	148
Housing and community development	6,062	15,479	21,509	22,666	27	62	82	85
Parks and recreation	6,520	14,326	17,888	19,137	29	58	68	72
Financial administration	6,719	16,217	22,380	22,633	30	65	85	85
Interest on general debt [4]	14,747	49,739	56,970	58,912	65	200	217	222
Utility and liquor stores [4]	36,191	77,801	94,235	95,608	160	313	359	361
Water supply system	9,228	22,101	28,041	28,950	41	89	107	109
Electric power system	15,016	30,997	34,021	34,084	66	125	129	129
Gas supply system	1,715	2,989	25,719	3,514	8	12	98	13
Transit system	7,641	18,788	3,434	25,961	34	76	13	98
Liquor stores	2,591	2,926	3,020	3,099	11	12	11	12
Insurance trust expenditure [3]	28,797	63,321	107,340	108,751	127	255	409	410
Employee retirement	14,008	38,355	61,427	68,010	56	154	234	256
Unemployment compensation	12,070	16,499	35,204	29,509	53	66	134	111
By character and object:								
Current operation	307,811	700,131	985,693	1,021,155	1,359	2,815	3,751	3,851
Capital outlay	62,894	123,069	151,440	158,911	278	495	576	599
Construction	51,492	89,114	110,012	116,076	227	358	419	438
Equipment, land, and existing structures	11,402	33,955	41,429	42,835	50	137	158	162
Assistance and subsidies	15,222	27,227	36,867	36,154	67	109	140	136
Interest on debt (general and utility)	17,604	58,914	66,423	68,743	78	237	253	259
Insurance benefits and repayments	28,797	63,321	107,340	108,751	127	255	409	410
Expenditure for salaries and wages	163,896	341,158	430,950	447,638	723	1,372	1,640	1,688
Debt outstanding, year end	335,603	860,584	1,115,370	1,169,714	1,481	3,460	4,245	4,411
Long-term	322,456	841,278	1,088,331	1,145,666	1,423	3,382	4,142	4,320
Short-term	13,147	19,306	27,039	24,048	58	78	103	91
Long-term debt:								
Issued	42,364	108,468	129,337	141,087	187	436	492	532
Retired	17,404	64,831	95,070	106,501	77	261	362	402

- Represents zero. [1] 1980 and 1990 based on enumerated resident population as of April 1. Other years based on estimated resident population as of July 1; see Table 2. [2] Aggregates exclude duplicative transactions between state and local governments; see source. [3] Includes amounts not shown separately. [4] Interest on utility debt included in "utility expenditure." For total interest on debt, see "Interest on debt (general and utility)."

Source: U.S. Census Bureau, 1980-90, *Government Finances*, GF, No. 5, annual; thereafter, <http://www.census.gov/govs/www/estimate.html> (accessed 21 May 1999).

State and Local Government Finances and Employment **317**

No. 513. State and Local Governments—Revenue, by State: 1996

[In millions of dollars ($1,513,633 represents $1,513,633,000,000). For fiscal year ending in year shown; see text, this section]

State	Total revenue [1]	General revenue Total	Intergovernmental from Federal Government	Taxes Total	Property	Sales and gross receipts	Charges and miscellaneous	Utility and liquor stores	Insurance trust revenue
United States ...	1,513,633	1,222,821	234,891	689,038	209,440	248,993	298,892	75,326	215,487
Alabama	19,617	16,214	3,615	7,632	999	3,905	4,967	1,599	1,804
Alaska...........	10,002	8,332	1,121	2,301	680	239	4,910	223	1,446
Arizona..........	20,787	16,873	3,163	10,163	3,114	4,541	3,547	2,042	1,873
Arkansas.........	11,396	9,319	2,271	4,851	754	2,320	2,197	427	1,651
California........	200,998	155,497	31,217	86,215	22,779	30,856	38,066	12,506	32,994
Colorado.........	20,785	16,979	3,102	9,244	2,841	3,460	4,633	1,136	2,670
Connecticut	20,766	18,164	3,015	12,543	4,657	3,932	2,607	388	2,214
Delaware.........	4,432	3,962	677	2,046	299	246	1,239	136	333
District of Columbia ...	5,675	4,910	1,871	2,481	702	794	558	377	388
Florida...........	74,196	60,703	9,360	33,557	11,813	17,578	17,786	4,174	9,319
Georgia..........	38,006	31,283	5,805	17,309	4,793	6,822	8,169	2,282	4,441
Hawaii...........	7,821	6,641	1,342	3,842	613	1,992	1,458	175	1,004
Idaho	5,932	4,740	910	2,542	652	861	1,287	160	1,033
Illinois..........	63,909	52,928	9,332	32,660	12,510	10,969	10,937	2,239	8,741
Indiana..........	25,793	23,125	3,937	12,980	4,029	3,804	6,209	1,125	1,543
Iowa	14,320	12,715	2,303	6,983	2,384	2,243	3,429	565	1,041
Kansas	12,874	11,025	1,760	6,373	1,987	2,325	2,893	805	1,043
Kentucky.........	18,515	15,562	3,378	8,413	1,411	3,211	3,771	713	2,240
Louisiana.........	21,458	18,227	4,446	8,466	1,359	4,644	5,315	661	2,570
Maine	6,145	5,627	1,330	3,231	1,352	937	1,065	157	361
Maryland	25,843	22,571	3,666	14,132	3,795	3,765	4,774	570	2,702
Massachusetts	37,025	32,077	6,243	19,123	6,475	3,954	6,711	1,754	3,194
Michigan	52,580	43,872	8,184	24,828	7,098	8,380	10,860	1,637	7,071
Minnesota	30,794	24,922	3,846	14,569	4,116	4,611	6,508	1,216	4,656
Mississippi	12,516	10,674	2,790	5,143	1,208	2,658	2,740	571	1,271
Missouri..........	25,647	20,221	4,013	11,687	2,616	4,870	4,521	1,019	4,407
Montana	4,505	3,802	1,044	1,782	776	269	976	96	606
Nebraska.........	9,898	7,440	1,291	4,181	1,579	1,401	1,967	1,821	638
Nevada	9,124	7,009	914	4,266	879	2,778	1,829	310	1,806
New Hampshire	5,589	4,673	915	2,619	1,766	429	1,140	283	633
New Jersey	53,661	43,694	6,713	27,449	12,815	7,394	9,532	1,164	8,803
New Mexico.......	10,147	8,086	1,925	3,877	474	2,083	2,283	250	1,811
New York.........	154,432	122,097	24,889	72,495	23,262	19,402	24,712	5,538	26,798
North Carolina	35,885	29,864	5,800	16,486	3,458	6,115	7,578	2,658	3,363
North Dakota	3,439	2,941	703	1,441	412	598	797	64	434
Ohio	64,538	48,318	9,567	27,961	7,967	8,621	10,789	2,072	14,149
Oklahoma	14,996	11,971	2,266	6,558	1,014	2,762	3,146	778	2,247
Oregon	22,126	16,018	3,926	7,238	2,332	740	4,855	816	5,291
Pennsylvania	64,439	52,534	10,574	30,280	8,689	9,037	11,680	2,466	9,439
Rhode Island	5,769	4,714	1,154	2,711	1,151	784	850	96	958
South Carolina	18,369	15,096	3,276	7,328	1,953	2,709	4,492	1,573	1,700
South Dakota	3,446	2,903	754	1,439	558	696	711	135	408
Tennessee........	27,197	20,027	4,964	9,992	2,266	6,075	5,071	4,629	2,540
Texas...........	89,318	74,847	13,787	40,705	15,248	20,642	20,355	5,029	9,442
Utah	10,459	8,434	1,910	4,294	1,008	1,787	2,231	1,171	854
Vermont	3,189	2,869	765	1,518	680	406	586	144	176
Virginia	31,667	26,477	3,813	15,627	4,847	4,860	7,037	1,306	3,884
Washington	37,557	26,810	4,400	15,467	4,673	9,347	6,943	3,281	7,466
West Virginia	8,746	7,590	2,164	3,643	727	1,490	1,784	151	1,004
Wisconsin	33,829	24,384	3,896	15,205	5,438	4,205	5,283	729	8,717
Wyoming	3,478	3,058	784	1,165	435	443	1,110	106	314

[1] Includes items not shown separately.

Source: U.S Census Bureau; <http://www.census.gov/govs/www/esti96.html> (accessed 21 May 1999).

No. 514. State and Local Governments—Expenditures and Debt, by State: 1996

[In millions of dollars (1,397,634 represents $1,397,634,000,000), except as indicated. For fiscal year ending in year shown; see text, this section]

State	General expenditure										
	Total			Selected functions (direct expenditures)							
	Total expenditure[1]	Amount	Per capita[2] (dol.)	Direct expenditures	Education	Public welfare	Health and hospitals	Highways	Police protection	Utility expenditures	Debt outstanding
United States.....	**1,397,634**	**1,393,714**	**5,256**	**1,189,356**	**398,859**	**193,480**	**110,813**	**79,092**	**44,683**	**92,509**	**1,169,714**
Alabama......	19,303	19,303	4,498	16,585	5,796	2,366	2,980	1,147	502	1,529	11,615
Alaska......	7,215	7,108	11,745	6,291	1,550	623	244	698	146	305	6,799
Arizona......	20,028	20,028	4,519	16,950	6,148	2,625	835	1,241	777	1,956	19,211
Arkansas.....	9,661	9,659	3,856	8,679	3,164	1,587	876	823	254	399	5,812
California	187,314	185,237	5,832	151,433	43,799	24,103	15,318	6,402	7,209	16,218	143,791
Colorado......	19,204	19,197	5,033	16,193	6,072	2,144	1,072	1,177	600	1,456	19,254
Connecticut....	19,797	19,797	6,065	17,478	5,332	2,817	1,339	1,017	560	556	25,571
Delaware	4,218	4,217	5,800	3,783	1,362	463	207	339	128	151	5,508
District of Columbia	5,817	5,817	10,780	4,184	669	1,172	432	89	248	1,138	4,137
Florida	68,581	68,580	4,754	60,773	18,027	7,383	6,011	4,580	3,034	4,712	65,164
Georgia	35,129	35,129	4,790	30,647	11,150	4,691	3,799	2,052	1,005	2,875	23,701
Hawaii	7,570	7,557	6,365	6,555	1,549	915	492	343	181	285	7,206
Idaho........	5,073	5,073	4,277	4,545	1,810	560	402	439	154	108	2,323
Illinois	59,756	59,756	5,007	50,951	17,013	8,831	3,644	3,602	2,278	3,394	52,419
Indiana.......	24,272	24,252	4,162	22,044	9,214	3,241	2,048	1,466	621	1,176	15,391
Iowa	13,467	13,431	4,715	12,218	4,633	1,789	1,339	1,380	333	534	6,355
Kansas.......	12,214	12,214	4,725	10,826	4,247	1,133	997	1,338	364	762	8,051
Kentucky	16,653	16,653	4,289	14,634	5,328	2,789	961	1,187	372	769	19,401
Louisiana	20,679	20,679	4,765	18,391	5,652	2,975	2,665	1,286	682	760	16,323
Maine........	6,006	5,999	4,846	5,402	1,788	1,275	292	488	129	93	4,681
Maryland	24,711	24,711	4,886	21,728	7,724	2,963	1,031	1,306	895	811	22,249
Massachusetts..	36,639	36,452	5,992	30,730	8,055	5,779	2,814	2,282	1,116	2,785	40,635
Michigan......	49,070	49,002	5,034	43,425	17,242	6,768	4,131	2,363	1,461	1,415	31,611
Minnesota.....	27,891	27,891	6,000	24,715	8,252	4,670	2,253	1,949	652	1,245	22,067
Mississippi	11,712	11,712	4,322	10,487	3,649	1,607	1,593	995	287	444	6,149
Missouri	21,614	21,614	4,026	19,176	7,132	2,949	1,739	1,566	720	1,160	13,873
Montana......	4,199	4,199	4,790	3,723	1,469	525	221	416	102	69	2,928
Nebraska.....	8,986	8,977	5,447	6,941	2,827	1,018	621	719	177	1,801	6,222
Nevada	7,951	7,946	4,965	6,867	2,035	698	586	682	342	355	8,166
New Hampshire .	5,192	5,192	4,478	4,724	1,625	1,030	128	333	146	69	6,937
New Jersey....	49,032	48,973	6,116	42,022	14,576	7,095	2,021	2,576	1,797	2,079	41,630
New Mexico ...	8,598	8,598	5,034	7,818	2,614	1,170	794	839	282	261	5,427
New York	145,293	144,338	7,956	120,189	32,959	25,048	12,322	5,944	4,620	10,554	149,701
North Carolina..	33,978	33,978	4,649	28,992	10,231	4,584	4,166	1,920	998	2,921	21,501
North Dakota...	2,958	2,958	4,602	2,662	1,020	395	80	282	54	88	1,742
Ohio	55,041	55,038	4,927	45,854	16,628	7,904	3,781	2,821	1,723	2,089	28,954
Oklahoma.....	13,568	13,527	4,104	11,630	4,525	1,627	1,225	944	402	755	8,967
Oregon.......	18,459	18,459	5,777	15,090	5,296	2,127	1,256	1,072	532	1,102	12,450
Pennsylvania...	60,353	60,227	5,005	51,091	18,025	9,861	3,209	2,968	1,735	2,975	58,490
Rhode Island...	5,582	5,562	5,629	4,780	1,496	867	335	265	164	116	6,518
South Carolina..	17,864	17,864	4,780	15,036	5,289	2,560	2,669	724	448	1,763	12,102
South Dakota ..	3,082	3,082	4,181	2,833	951	409	143	385	80	111	2,406
Tennessee	25,759	25,759	4,854	19,975	6,378	3,770	2,569	1,490	660	4,621	22,490
Texas........	83,495	83,495	4,387	72,366	27,859	10,243	7,866	5,125	2,582	6,209	75,988
Utah	9,883	9,882	4,887	8,259	3,428	961	557	544	265	1,115	11,479
Vermont	2,905	2,893	4,934	2,627	1,043	505	65	268	67	122	2,257
Virginia.......	29,030	29,030	4,354	26,135	10,023	3,288	1,912	2,264	910	1,261	24,233
Washington....	34,611	34,581	6,266	27,018	9,428	3,800	2,520	1,995	806	3,967	31,770
West Virginia...	8,437	8,437	4,635	7,342	2,653	1,589	438	745	133	130	6,499
Wisconsin.....	26,742	26,610	5,143	23,862	9,154	3,928	1,437	1,915	873	850	19,692
Wyoming	3,043	3,042	6,336	2,695	969	256	378	303	78	89	1,870

[1] Includes items not shown separately.   [2] Based on estimated resident population as of July 1.

Source: U.S. Census Bureau, <http://www.census.gov/govs/www/esti96.html> (accessed 17 June 1999).

U.S. Census Bureau, Statistical Abstract of the United States: 1999

No. 515. State and Local Governments—Per Capita Summary of Finances, by State: 1996

[In millions of dollars (1,513,633 represents $1,513,633,000,000), except as indicated. For fiscal year ending in year shown; see text, this section]

State	Revenue [1]						Expenditures [1]		Debt outstanding	
					Inter-governmental					
					From state/local sources	Per capita [2] (dol.)	Direct general expenditures	Per capita [2] (dol.)	Total	Per capita [2] (dol.)
	All revenue	Per capita [2] (dol.)	General revenue	Per capita [2] (dol.)						
United States..	1,513,633	5,708	1,222,821	4,611	987,930	3,725	1,189,356	4,485	1,169,714	4,411
Alabama.........	19,617	4,572	16,214	3,779	12,599	2,936	16,585	3,865	11,615	2,707
Alaska..........	10,002	16,526	8,332	13,767	7,211	11,915	6,291	10,395	6,799	11,234
Arizona.........	20,787	4,690	16,873	3,807	13,709	3,093	16,950	3,824	19,211	4,334
Arkansas	11,396	4,549	9,319	3,720	7,047	2,813	8,679	3,465	5,812	2,320
California	200,998	6,328	155,497	4,896	124,281	3,913	151,433	4,768	143,791	4,527
Colorado........	20,785	5,450	16,979	4,452	13,877	3,639	16,193	4,246	19,254	5,048
Connecticut.....	20,766	6,362	18,164	5,565	15,150	4,642	17,478	5,355	25,571	7,834
Delaware	4,432	6,095	3,962	5,450	3,285	4,518	3,783	5,203	5,508	7,575
District of Columbia .	5,675	10,516	4,910	9,099	3,039	5,631	4,184	7,752	4,137	7,665
Florida..........	74,196	5,144	60,703	4,208	51,343	3,559	60,773	4,213	65,164	4,517
Georgia	38,006	5,182	31,283	4,265	25,477	3,474	30,647	4,179	23,701	3,232
Hawaii	7,821	6,587	6,641	5,594	5,300	4,464	6,555	5,521	7,206	6,069
Idaho..........	5,932	5,001	4,740	3,996	3,829	3,228	4,545	3,832	2,323	1,958
Illinois.........	63,909	5,355	52,928	4,435	43,596	3,653	50,951	4,270	52,419	4,393
Indiana.........	25,793	4,426	23,125	3,968	19,188	3,293	22,044	3,783	15,391	2,641
Iowa	14,320	5,027	12,715	4,463	10,412	3,655	12,218	4,289	6,355	2,231
Kansas.........	12,874	4,981	11,025	4,266	9,266	3,585	10,826	4,188	8,051	3,115
Kentucky	18,515	4,769	15,562	4,008	12,184	3,138	14,634	3,769	19,401	4,997
Louisiana	21,458	4,944	18,227	4,200	13,781	3,175	18,391	4,238	16,323	3,761
Maine..........	6,145	4,963	5,627	4,545	4,296	3,470	5,402	4,363	4,681	3,781
Maryland	25,843	5,110	22,571	4,463	18,906	3,738	21,728	4,296	22,249	4,399
Massachusetts.....	37,035	6,087	32,077	5,273	25,834	4,247	30,730	5,052	40,635	6,680
Michigan........	52,580	5,402	43,872	4,507	35,688	3,666	43,425	4,461	31,611	3,248
Minnesota........	30,794	6,625	24,922	5,362	21,077	4,535	24,715	5,317	22,067	4,747
Mississippi	12,516	4,618	10,674	3,939	7,884	2,909	10,487	3,870	6,149	2,269
Missouri	25,647	4,777	20,221	3,766	16,208	3,019	19,176	3,572	13,873	2,584
Montana.........	4,505	5,138	3,802	4,337	2,758	3,146	3,723	4,247	2,928	3,339
Nebraska........	9,898	6,006	7,440	4,514	6,149	3,731	6,941	4,211	6,222	3,775
Nevada	9,124	5,701	7,009	4,379	6,095	3,808	6,867	4,291	8,166	5,103
New Hampshire....	5,589	4,820	4,673	4,030	3,758	3,241	4,724	4,074	6,937	5,983
New Jersey.......	53,661	6,701	43,694	5,456	36,981	4,618	42,022	5,248	41,630	5,199
New Mexico.....	10,147	5,941	8,086	4,734	6,160	3,607	7,818	4,578	5,427	3,178
New York	154,432	8,512	122,097	6,730	97,207	5,358	120,189	6,625	149,701	8,252
North Carolina ...	35,885	4,910	29,864	4,086	24,064	3,293	28,992	3,967	21,501	2,942
North Dakota.....	3,439	5,350	2,941	4,575	2,238	3,482	2,662	4,141	1,742	2,709
Ohio	64,538	5,778	48,318	4,326	38,751	3,469	45,854	4,105	28,954	2,592
Oklahoma........	14,996	4,550	11,971	3,632	9,705	2,944	11,630	3,529	8,967	2,721
Oregon.........	22,126	6,924	16,018	5,013	12,093	3,784	15,090	4,723	12,450	3,896
Pennsylvania.....	64,439	5,355	52,534	4,366	41,960	3,487	51,091	4,246	58,490	4,860
Rhode Island.....	5,769	5,838	4,714	4,771	3,561	3,603	4,780	4,837	6,518	6,596
South Carolina.....	18,369	4,915	15,096	4,040	11,820	3,163	15,036	4,024	12,102	3,238
South Dakota	3,446	4,674	2,903	3,938	2,149	2,915	2,833	3,843	2,406	3,263
Tennessee	27,197	5,124	20,027	3,774	15,064	2,838	19,975	3,764	22,490	4,238
Texas	89,318	4,693	74,847	3,932	61,059	3,208	72,366	3,802	75,988	3,992
Utah	10,459	5,172	8,434	4,171	6,524	3,226	8,259	4,084	11,479	5,676
Vermont.........	3,189	5,439	2,869	4,894	2,104	3,588	2,627	4,481	2,257	3,849
Virginia.........	31,667	4,749	26,477	3,971	22,663	3,399	26,135	3,920	24,233	3,635
Washington.......	37,557	6,805	26,810	4,858	22,410	4,061	27,018	4,896	31,770	5,757
West Virginia.....	8,746	4,805	7,590	4,170	5,427	2,981	7,342	4,034	6,499	3,571
Wisconsin........	33,829	6,538	24,384	4,712	20,488	3,960	23,862	4,612	19,692	3,806
Wyoming	3,478	7,246	3,058	6,371	2,275	4,738	2,695	5,613	1,870	3,896

[1] Includes items not shown separately. [2] Based on estimated resident population as of July 1.

Source: U.S. Census Bureau, <http://www.census.gov/govs/www/esti96.html> (accessed 17 June 1999); and unpublished data.

No. 516. Long-Term Municipal New Issues for State and Local Governments: 1980 to 1998

[In billions of dollars (45.6 represents $45,600,000,000)]

Item	1980	1985	1990	1992	1993	1994	1995	1996	1997	1998
Long-term municipal new issues	45.6	202.4	125.9	231.7	289.9	162.2	156.2	181.4	214.3	279.7
General obligation	13.7	39.6	40.2	80.3	91.4	55.6	60.2	64.2	72.2	92.6
Revenue	31.9	162.8	85.7	151.3	198.5	106.7	96.0	117.3	142.1	187.1
Competitive	19.3	27.8	30.2	44.3	55.6	49.5	41.0	47.0	47.8	65.2
Negotiated	26.4	174.6	95.9	187.3	234.3	112.8	115.4	134.4	166.5	214.5
States with largest issuance: [2]										
California	3.6	25.3	15.7	25.9	38.3	25.4	20.2	24.9	27.7	33.9
New York	2.9	12.7	16.9	22.0	30.7	18.8	18.8	20.8	27.4	36.3
Texas	3.8	21.2	6.5	17.1	16.3	10.3	10.4	11.6	15.3	18.1
Florida	2.2	13.2	5.9	13.3	17.7	7.7	9.1	10.0	10.5	14.7
Illinois	2.3	9.2	6.3	10.9	11.7	7.9	6.6	8.8	9.6	10.1
All Others	30.8	120.8	74.6	142.5	175.2	92.1	91.1	105.3	123.8	166.6
Type of issuer: [3]										
City, town, or village	8.5	36.5	22.7	44.5	51.3	26.6	27.9	30.3	34.8	44.3
College or university	0.2	2.9	1.5	3.7	4.7	2.4	2.5	4.5	3.3	4.6
County/parish	4.6	15.8	10.0	20.1	24.4	17.2	13.3	16.8	15.5	21.2
Direct issuer	-	0.4	0.2	0.7	0.8	0.6	0.4	1.0	0.8	2.1
District	3.9	15.6	15.2	31.8	38.2	21.7	22.4	27.5	33.7	43.6
Local authority	9.2	51.1	20.7	41.0	56.5	26.3	27.9	33.7	41.5	53.9
State authority	14.1	68.1	40.6	64.6	85.7	47.6	47.2	53.2	66.0	85.2
State	5.1	12.1	15.0	25.2	28.2	19.8	14.6	14.3	18.7	24.7
Refunding	1.6	70.5	25.3	122.2	194.6	49.8	47.5	605.2	81.2	120.8
New Capital	45.6	202.4	125.9	231.6	289.9	162.3	156.2	181.4	214.3	279.7
General use of proceeds:										
Airports	0.4	3.0	5.2	7.2	5.7	4.3	4.7	5.2	6.4	10.2
Combined utilities	0.3	2.4	1.0	2.8	1.9	1.2	0.7	1.2	1.5	1.8
Economic development	0.2	2.5	2.1	4.6	6.0	4.2	2.5	1.8	2.9	3.5
Education	4.0	20.4	20.5	35.0	43.4	26.9	28.5	35.0	42.7	56.5
Health care	3.1	30.0	12.6	20.8	29.2	13.8	11.5	16.6	22.1	33.4
Industrial development	1.0	2.9	1.9	2.4	2.4	2.1	3.2	2.8	3.5	3.6
Multi-family housing	2.5	20.2	3.1	5.7	6.2	4.9	6.1	6.7	5.4	6.4
Nursing homes/life care retirement	0.3	1.2	1.6	2.4	2.5	2.4	1.9	3.0	3.6	4.8
Other miscellaneous	11.1	37.3	36.2	67.1	82.7	48.8	44.2	55.2	57.0	71.5
Pollution control	2.3	10.0	2.5	6.2	8.1	7.0	5.0	5.5	5.6	9.7
Electric & public power	4.4	23.2	5.2	15.7	27.8	6.3	4.8	5.7	6.5	15.6
Single family housing	10.6	16.4	12.5	8.9	8.2	10.5	10.0	10.4	13.6	12.9
Solid waste/resource recovery	0.4	3.8	3.0	3.4	5.1	3.8	3.3	2.2	3.6	2.4
Student loans	0.2	4.0	0.4	5.1	4.8	3.3	4.4	4.2	3.9	4.9
Transportation	1.3	11.0	7.6	17.9	21.0	9.4	11.3	10.3	16.6	20.5
Water, sewer, and gas facilities	3.1	13.4	9.3	25.0	33.2	12.5	13.2	14.3	18.2	20.9
Waterfront/seaports	0.5	1.5	0.5	1.5	1.6	0.8	0.8	1.3	1.2	0.9

- Represents or rounds to zero. [1] Excludes issues with a final maturity of less than 13 months, private placements, and not-for-profit cooperative utilities. [2] Ranked by 1998 Long-Term Municipal New Issue Volume. [3] Includes outlying areas.

Source: Tromson Financial Securities Data Company, Newark, NJ, Municipal New Issues Database (copyright).

No. 517. State and Local Governments—Indebtedness: 1980 to 1996

[In billions of dollars (335.6 represents $335,600,000,000), except per capita. For fiscal year ending in year shown; see text, this section. Local government amounts are estimates subject to sampling variation; see Appendix III and source]

Item	Debt outstanding						Long term		
		Per capita [1] (dol.)	Long-term			Short-term	Net long term	Debt issued	Debt retired
	Total		Local schools [2]	Utilities	All other				
1980: Total	335.6	1,481	32.3	55.2	235.0	13.1	262.9	42.4	17.4
State	122.0	540	3.8	4.6	111.4	2.1	79.8	16.4	5.7
Local	213.6	943	28.5	50.6	123.5	11.0	183.1	25.9	11.7
1985: Total	568.6	2,390	43.8	90.8	414.5	19.6	430.5	101.2	43.5
State	211.9	893	6.7	8.6	193.8	2.8	110.4	41.7	16.4
Local	356.7	1,499	37.1	82.2	220.6	16.8	320.1	59.5	27.2
1990: Total	860.6	3,459	60.4	134.8	646.1	19.3	477.0	108.5	64.8
State	318.3	1,282	4.4	12.3	298.8	2.8	125.5	43.5	22.9
Local	542.3	2,180	56.0	122.4	347.4	16.5	351.5	65.0	42.0
1993: Total	1,016.2	3,943	89.2	157.6	746.8	22.6	617.1	195.0	146.3
State	389.7	1,515	9.4	14.8	361.7	3.9	176.9	77.1	60.7
Local	628.0	2,437	79.8	142.7	385.2	18.9	440.2	118.4	86.3
1994: Total	1,074.7	4,129	143.5	164.9	438.0	26.7	672.8	207.8	166.6
State	411.0	1,582	10.4	16.7	162.0	4.9	200.8	78.5	61.3
Local	663.7	2,550	86.2	148.2	276.0	21.8	472.0	129.3	105.3
1995: Total	1,115.3	4,244	118.2	163.9	756.0	27.0	835.3	129.3	95.1
State	427.2	1,629	11.3	17.0	345.0	6.1	205.3	52.6	37.5
Local	688.1	2,619	107.0	146.9	411.0	20.9	629.9	76.8	57.6
1996: Total	1,169.7	4,411	130.7	170.3	868.8	24.0	890.2	141.1	106.5
State	452.4	1,709	11.2	16.3	424.9	5.8	224.4	60.2	42.4
Local	717.3	2,705	119.5	154.0	443.8	18.2	665.7	80.9	64.1

[1] 1980 and 1990 based on enumerated resident population as of April 1; other years based on estimated resident population as of July 1; see Table 2. [2] Includes debt for education activities other than higher education.

Source: U.S. Census Bureau, 1980-90, State and Local Government Finance Estimates, annual; thereafter, <http://www.census.gov/govs/www/estimate.html> (accessed 21 May 1999).

State and Local Government Finances and Employment 321

No. 518. Bond Ratings for State Governments, by State: 1998

[As of fourth quarter. Key to investment grade ratings are in declining order of quality. The ratings from AA to CCC may be modified by the addition of a plus or minus sign to show relative standing within the major rating categories. **S&P:** AAA, AA, A, BBB, BB, B, CCC, CC, C; **Moody's:** Aaa, Aa, A, Baa, Ba, B, Caa, Ca, C; Numerical modifiers 1, 2, and 3 are added to letter-rating. **Fitch:** AAA, AA, A, BBB, BB, B, CCC, CC, C]

State	Standard & Poor's	Moody's	Fitch	State	Standard & Poor's	Moody's	Fitch
Alabama	AA	Aa3	AA	Montana	AA-	Aa3	(1)
Alaska	AA	Aa2	AA	Nebraska	(1)	(1)	(1)
Arizona	(1)	(1)	(1)	Nevada	AA	Aa2	(1)
Arkansas	AA	Aa3	AA	New Hampshire	AA+	Aa2	AA+
California	A+	Aa3	AAA	New Jersey	AA+	Aa1	AA+
Colorado	(1)	(1)	(1)	New Mexico	AA+	Aa1	(1)
Connecticut	AA	Aa3	AA	New York	A	A2	A+
Delaware	AA+	Aa1	(1)	North Carolina	AAA	Aaa	AAA
Florida	AA+	Aa2	AA	North Dakota	(1)	Aa3	(1)
Georgia	AAA	Aaa	AAA	Ohio	AA+	Aa1	AA+
Hawaii	A+	A1	AA-	Oklahoma	AA	Aa3	AA
Idaho	(1)	(1)	(1)	Oregon	AA	Aa2	AA
Illinois	AA	Aa2	AA	Pennsylvania	AA	Aa3	AA
Indiana	AA+	(1)	(1)	Rhode Island	AA-	A1	AA-
Iowa	(1)	(1)	(1)	South Carolina	AAA	Aaa	AAA
Kansas	AA+	(1)	(1)	South Dakota	(1)	(1)	(1)
Kentucky	AA	(1)	(1)	Tennessee	AAA	Aaa	AAA
Louisiana	A-	A2	A	Texas	AA	Aa2	AA+
Maine	AA+	Aa2	AA	Utah	AAA	Aaa	AAA
Maryland	AAA	Aaa	AAA	Vermont	AA	Aa2	AA
Massachusetts	AA-	Aa3	AA-	Virginia	AAA	Aaa	AAA
Michigan	AA+	Aa1	AA+	Washington	AA+	Aa1	AA+
Minnesota	AAA	Aaa	AAA	West Virginia	AA-	A1	AA-
Mississippi	AA	Aa3	AA	Wisconsin	A+	Aa2	AA+
Missouri	AAA	Aaa	AAA	Wyoming	AA	(1)	(1)

¹ Not reviewed.

Sources: Standard & Poors, New York, NY; Moody's Investors Service, New York, NY (copyright); and Fitch IBCA, New York, NY (copyright).

No. 519 Bond Ratings for City Governments, by Largest Cities: 1998

[As of fourth quarter. For key to ratings, see headnote in table above]

Cities ranked by 1994 population	Standard & Poors	Moody's	Fitch IBCA	Cities ranked by 1994 population	Standard & Poors	Moody's	Fitch IBCA
New York, NY	A-	A3	A-	Honolulu, HI	AA	Aa2	(1)
Los Angeles, CA	AA	Aa2	(1)	Tulsa, OK	AA	Aa2	(1)
Chicago, IL	A+	A1	AA-	Sacramento, CA	AA	Aa2	(1)
Houston, TX	AA-	Aa3	AA	Miami, FL	BB	Ba1	(1)
Philadelphia, PA	BBB	Baa2	BBB	St. Louis, MO	A-	Baa1	BBB
San Diego, CA	AA	Aa1	AA+	Oakland, CA	AA-	A1	A+
Phoenix, AZ	AA+	Aa1	(1)	Pittsburgh, PA	BBB	Baa1	BBB+
Dallas, TX	AAA	Aaa	AA	Cincinnati, OH	AA+	Aa1	(1)
San Antonio, TX	AA+	Aa2	AA	Minneapolis, MN	AAA	Aaa	(1)
Detroit, MI	BBB+	Baa1	BBB+	Omaha, NE	AAA	Aaa	(1)
San Jose, CA	A+	(1)	(1)	Toledo, OH	A	A3	(1)
Indianapolis, IN	AAA	Aaa	AAA	Colorado Springs, CO	AA-	Aa3	(1)
San Francisco, CA	AA-	Aa3	AA	Mesa, AZ	AA-	A1	(1)
Baltimore, MD	A	A1	AAA	Buffalo, NY	BBB	Baa3	(1)
Jacksonville, FL	(1)	Aa2	AA	Wichita, KS	AA	Aa2	(1)
Columbus, OH	AAA	AAA	(1)	Santa Ana, CA	(1)	(1)	(1)
Milwaukee, WI	AA+	Aa1	AA+	Arlington, TX	AA	Aa3	(1)
Memphis, TN	AA	Aa2	AA	Tampa, FL	(1)	(1)	(1)
El Paso, TX	AA	Aa3	AA-	Anaheim, CA	AA	Aa2	(1)
Washington, DC	BB	Ba1	BB+	Corpus Christi, TX	A+	A3	(1)
Boston, MA	A+	Aa3	A+	Louisville, KY	AA-	Aa3	(1)
Seattle, WA	AA+	Aaa	(1)	Birmingham, AL	AA	Aa3	AA
Austin, TX	AA	Aa2	AA	St. Paul, MN	AA+	Aa2	(1)
Nashville-Davidson, TN	AA	Aa2	AA	Newark, NJ	BAB+	Baa1	(1)
Denver, CO	AA	Aa2	AA	Anchorage, AK	A	A1	(1)
Cleveland, OH	A	A2	A	Aurora, CO	AA-	A1	(1)
New Orleans, LA	BBB+	Baa2	(1)	Riverside, CA	(1)	(1)	(1)
Oklahoma City, OK	AA	Aa2	(1)	Norfolk, VA	AA	A1	(1)
Fort Worth, TX	AA	Aa2	AA	St Petersburg, FL	A+	A1	(1)
Portland, OR	(1)	Aaa	(1)	Lexington-Fayette, KY	AA+	(1)	(1)
Kansas City, MO	AA	Aa3	(1)	Raleigh, NC	AAA	Aaa	(1)
Charlotte, NC	AAA	Aaa	(1)	Rochester, NY	AA	A1	(1)
Tucson, AZ	AA	Aa3	(1)	Baton Rouge, LA	(1)	(1)	(1)
Long Beach, CA	AA-	(1)	(1)	Jersey City, NJ	BBB	Baa3	(1)
Virginia Beach, VA	AA	Aa2	(1)	Stockton CA	(1)	(1)	(1)
Albuquerque, NM	AA	Aa3	AA	Akron, OH	AA-	A2	(1)
Atlanta, GA	AA	Aa3	(1)	Mobile, AL	AAA	A2	(1)
Fresno, CA	A+	(1)	(1)	Richmond, VA	AA	A1	(1)

¹ Not reviewed.

Sources: Standard & Poors, New York, NY; Moody's Investors Service, New York, NY, (copyright); and Fitch IBCA, New York, NY (copyright).

No. 520. State Resources, Expenditures, and Balances: 1998 and 1999

[In millions of dollars (845,136 represents $845,136,000,000). For fiscal year ending in year shown; see text; this section. General funds exclude special funds earmarked for particular purposes, such as highway trust funds and Federal funds; they support most on-going broad-based state services and are available for appropriation to support any governmental activity. Minus sign (-) indicates deficit]

State	Expenditures by fund source					State general fund					
	Total, 1998	1999 [1]				Resources [3][4]		Expenditures [4]		Balance [5]	
		Total [2]	General fund	Federal funds	Other state funds	1998	1999 [1]	1998	1999 [1]	1998	1999 [1]
Total . . . . United States . . .	845,136 826,714	903,613 884,044	427,476 420,850	232,739 229,191	222,279 213,359	445,990 439,845	461,371 454,658	416,373 410,320	440,837 434,124	25,744 25,744	18,827 18,827
Alabama.	12,910	14,074	4,908	4,233	4,918	4,739	4,940	4,688	4,906	51	34
Alaska.	4,381	5,152	2,296	1,418	1,238	1,852	1,291	2,359	2,324	-	-
Arizona.	13,026	14,140	5,720	3,785	4,607	5,745	5,960	5,219	5,900	526	61
Arkansas	8,900	9,259	2,990	2,218	3,965	2,903	3,046	2,844	3,009	59	37
California	104,477	110,998	57,262	34,715	15,618	55,949	59,368	52,874	58,271	[6]3,075	[6]1,097
Colorado.	9,855	11,031	5,270	2,255	3,506	5,761	6,523	4,721	5,293	[6]901	667
Connecticut.	14,873	15,351	10,079	2,359	1,845	10,142	10,513	9,829	10,484	313	29
Delaware	4,237	4,400	2,196	585	1,499	2,439	2,673	1,900	2,196	[6]539	[6]477
Florida	43,294	45,390	18,003	9,206	16,633	17,479	18,185	17,078	18,185	401	-
Georgia	22,060	22,183	11,647	5,269	4,782	13,606	13,649	12,403	13,064	1,203	[6]585
Hawaii	6,433	7,407	3,194	1,223	2,354	3,368	3,424	3,214	3,244	154	180
Idaho.	3,079	3,375	1,611	997	762	1,482	1,629	1,446	1,612	36	17
Illinois	29,557	38,117	16,975	7,508	11,422	20,790	22,516	19,588	21,416	1,202	1,100
Indiana.	14,771	14,967	6,669	4,295	3,809	9,618	10,255	7,894	8,395	1,320	1,366
Iowa	10,087	10,159	4,544	2,272	3,343	4,769	4,849	4,359	4,526	415	331
Kansas.	8,101	8,557	4,193	2,003	2,280	4,556	4,835	3,799	4,223	757	612
Kentucky	13,628	16,443	6,428	4,364	5,651	6,689	6,594	5,958	6,181	356	33
Louisiana	15,255	15,712	5,823	4,432	5,094	5,942	5,926	5,771	5,819	94	107
Maine.	4,170	4,552	2,143	1,491	846	2,145	2,387	1,898	2,202	98	186
Maryland	16,233	17,221	8,484	3,674	4,475	8,236	8,779	7,816	8,530	420	[6]249
Massachusetts.	21,743	22,926	15,193	5,383	1,350	18,223	18,922	17,285	18,507	254	96
Michigan.	29,953	30,812	8,801	8,144	13,864	8,818	8,986	8,647	8,811	55	27
Minnesota.	16,723	18,258	11,598	3,801	2,549	12,739	12,536	10,212	11,042	2,527	1,494
Mississippi	7,840	9,373	3,024	2,702	2,858	3,136	3,319	2,933	3,127	101	96
Missouri	13,864	15,956	7,056	4,330	4,570	6,927	7,212	6,657	7,056	270	156
Montana.	2,513	2,658	1,033	921	704	1,067	1,091	1,023	1,048	44	43
Nebraska	4,784	4,753	2,232	1,226	1,295	2,363	2,529	1,932	2,231	431	166
Nevada	(NA)	(NA)	(NA)	(NA)	(NA)	1,519	1,554	1,451	1,534	86	79
New Hampshire	2,401	2,503	953	862	629	959	990	918	970	41	20
New Jersey.	25,386	27,646	17,739	6,420	3,234	18,149	18,834	16,753	17,784	[6]1,257	[6]1,050
New Mexico	7,014	7,523	3,127	2,690	1,706	3,287	3,437	3,061	3,227	[6]227	[6]193
New York	71,695	77,555	33,817	23,162	18,340	34,985	37,413	34,347	36,614	[6]638	[6]799
North Carolina	21,912	22,523	13,112	5,497	3,464	12,305	13,350	11,436	13,037	[6]115	313
North Dakota.	2,034	2,329	786	856	684	825	830	728	761	[6]97	[6]69
Ohio	34,454	35,965	18,332	5,961	10,544	18,287	19,009	17,087	18,158	139	216
Oklahoma.	9,280	10,298	4,351	2,834	3,029	4,373	4,700	4,200	4,460	174	240
Oregon.	13,044	14,132	4,543	3,288	6,301	4,806	4,790	4,333	4,430	473	361
Pennsylvania.	34,080	37,354	18,098	10,987	7,683	17,718	18,409	17,289	18,098	265	307
Rhode Island.	3,710	4,208	1,966	1,198	930	2,009	2,138	1,876	2,062	132	76
South Carolina	12,934	13,201	4,589	3,923	4,516	5,420	5,221	4,904	4,782	[6]517	[6]439
South Dakota	1,950	1,958	731	708	519	723	751	702	734	-	2
Tennessee	14,740	15,672	6,571	5,623	3,125	6,259	6,573	5,816	6,421	349	152
Texas.	43,057	44,859	27,531	13,253	3,803	29,758	25,460	26,733	22,124	3,025	3,337
Utah	6,092	6,396	3,237	1,349	1,465	3,128	3,286	3,042	3,245	86	41
Vermont	1,797	1,951	758	676	474	824	831	876	831	-	-
Virginia.	19,065	19,927	8,983	3,415	6,978	9,306	10,585	8,335	10,195	971	391
Washington	18,968	18,416	9,745	4,718	3,337	10,162	10,723	9,330	9,827	[6]832	[6]896
West Virginia.	5,409	5,592	2,048	2,120	1,252	2,678	2,728	2,543	2,723	125	1
Wisconsin	18,983	18,943	9,943	4,357	4,643	10,300	10,540	9,695	9,989	[6]554	[6]551
Wyoming	1,962	1,869	518	485	866	584	570	518	518	[6]40	[6]52
Puerto Rico	18,422	19,569	6,626	3,548	8,920	6,145	6,713	6,053	6,713	(NA)	-

- Represents zero. NA Not available. [1] Estimated. [2] Includes bonds not shown separately. [3] Includes funds budgeted, adjustments, and balances from previous year. [4] May or may not include budget stabilization fund transfers, depending on state accounting practices. [5] Resources less expenditures. Total excludes Puerto Rico. [6] Ending balance is held in a budget stabilization fund.

Source: Expenditures by fund from National Association of State Budget Officers, Washington, DC, 1998 State Expenditure Report, and State General Fund from National Governors' Association and NASBO, Fiscal Survey of the States, semi-annual (copyright).

State and Local Government Finances and Employment 323

No. 521. State Governments—Summary of Finances: 1980 to 1997

[In millions of dollars (293,358 represents $293,358,000,000), except where indicated. For fiscal year ending in year shown; see text, this section]

Item	Total (mil. dol.)				Per capita [1] (dollars)			
	1980	1990	1996	1997	1980	1990	1996	1997
Borrowing and revenue	293,356	672,994	1,026,450	1,093,486	1,299	2,712	3,879	4,092
Borrowing	16,394	40,532	60,152	54,064	73	163	227	202
Revenue	276,962	632,462	966,298	1,039,422	1,226	2,549	3,651	3,890
General revenue	233,592	517,720	770,006	814,382	1,034	2,087	2,910	3,048
Taxes	137,075	300,779	418,264	443,335	607	1,212	1,580	1,659
Sales and gross receipts	67,855	147,404	205,687	215,737	300	594	777	807
General	43,168	99,929	139,279	147,069	191	403	526	550
Motor fuels	9,722	19,379	25,981	27,132	43	78	98	102
Alcoholic beverages	2,478	3,191	3,667	3,698	11	13	14	14
Tobacco products	3,738	5,541	7,338	7,451	17	22	28	28
Other	8,750	19,365	29,423	30,387	39	78	111	114
Licenses	8,690	18,849	27,036	28,217	38	76	102	106
Motor vehicles	4,936	9,850	12,740	12,965	22	40	48	49
Corporations in general	1,388	3,096	5,158	5,882	6	12	19	22
Other	2,366	5,903	9,138	9,370	10	24	35	35
Individual income	37,089	96,076	133,976	144,668	164	387	506	541
Corporation net income	13,321	21,751	29,316	30,662	59	88	111	115
Property	2,892	5,775	9,974	10,297	13	23	38	39
Other	7,227	10,922	12,275	13,754	32	44	46	51
Charges and miscellaneous	32,190	90,612	130,273	140,454	142	365	492	526
Intergovernmental revenue	64,326	126,329	221,469	230,592	285	509	837	863
From Federal Government	61,892	118,353	208,100	215,421	274	477	786	806
Public welfare	24,680	59,397	118,154	123,087	109	239	446	461
Education	12,765	21,271	34,055	33,663	57	86	129	126
Highways	8,860	13,931	18,809	19,346	39	56	71	72
Health and hospitals	2,309	5,475	11,067	11,676	10	22	42	44
Other	13,278	17,279	26,015	27,649	69	96	98	103
From local governments	2,434	7,976	13,370	15,171	11	32	51	57
Utility revenue	1,304	3,305	3,919	4,046	6	13	15	15
Liquor store revenue	2,765	2,907	3,160	3,292	12	12	12	12
Insurance trust revenue [2]	39,301	108,530	189,213	217,703	174	437	715	815
Employee retirement	21,146	78,898	139,316	168,184	94	318	526	629
Unemployment compensation	13,468	18,370	33,685	34,882	60	74	127	131
Expenditure and debt redemption	263,494	592,213	902,353	935,208	1,166	2,386	3,410	3,500
Expenditure	257,812	572,318	859,959	893,827	1,141	2,306	3,249	3,345
General expenditure	228,223	508,284	755,277	788,176	1,010	2,048	2,854	2,950
Education	87,939	184,935	263,519	275,821	389	745	996	1,032
Public welfare	44,219	104,971	195,731	203,204	196	423	740	760
Health	6,485	20,029	32,612	33,880	29	81	123	127
Hospitals	11,370	22,637	29,421	29,313	50	91	111	110
Highways	25,044	44,249	58,255	60,204	111	178	220	225
Police protection	2,263	5,166	7,173	7,501	10	21	27	28
Correction	4,449	17,266	27,324	29,043	20	70	103	109
Natural resources	4,346	9,909	12,862	12,909	19	40	49	48
Housing and community development	601	2,856	3,836	3,839	3	12	14	14
Other and unallocable	41,507	96,266	99,877	132,462	184	388	377	496
Utility expenditure	2,401	7,131	8,043	7,783	11	29	30	29
Liquor store expenditure	2,206	2,452	2,593	2,697	10	10	10	10
Insurance trust expenditure [2]	24,981	54,452	94,045	95,172	111	219	355	356
Employee retirement	10,256	29,562	53,083	56,570	45	119	201	212
Unemployment compensation	12,006	16,423	29,337	27,475	53	66	111	103
By character and object:								
Intergovernmental expenditure	84,504	175,028	252,102	264,207	374	705	953	989
Direct expenditure	173,307	397,291	607,856	629,620	767	1,601	2,297	2,356
Current operation	108,131	258,046	405,416	425,898	479	1,040	1,532	1,594
Capital outlay	23,325	45,524	58,915	59,658	103	183	223	223
Construction	19,736	34,803	46,924	46,991	87	140	177	176
Other capital outlay	(X)	(X)	11,991	12,667	(X)	(X)	45	47
Land and existing structure	1,345	3,471	2,968	(NA)	6	14	11	(NA)
Equipment	2,243	7,250	9,022	(NA)	10	29	34	(NA)
Assistance and subsidies	9,818	16,902	23,313	21,867	43	68	88	82
Interest on debt	7,052	22,387	26,167	27,025	31	90	99	101
Insurance benefits [4]	24,981	54,452	94,045	95,171	111	219	355	356
Debt redemption	5,682	19,895	42,395	41,381	25	80	160	155
Debt outstanding, year end	121,958	318,254	447,339	455,698	540	1,282	1,690	1,705
Long-term	119,821	315,490	441,489	453,556	530	1,271	1,668	1,697
Full-faith and credit	49,364	74,972	118,549	119,514	219	302	448	447
Nonguaranteed	70,457	240,518	322,940	334,042	312	969	1,220	1,250
Short-term	2,137	2,764	5,849	2,142	9	11	22	8
Net long-term	79,810	125,524	219,392	222,393	353	506	829	832
Full-faith and credit only	39,357	63,481	108,955	109,513	174	256	412	410

NA Not available.   X Not applicable.   [1] 1980 and 1990 based on enumerated resident population as of April 1; other years based on estimated resident population as of July 1.   [2] Includes other items not shown separately.   [3] Includes repayments.   [4] Less cash and investment assets specifically held for redemption of long-term debt.

Source: U.S. Census Bureau, *State Government Finances*, Series GF, No. 3, annual; <http://www.census.gov/ftp/pub/govs/www/state.html>; (accessed 17 June 1999).

No. 522. State Governments—Summary of Revenue, by State: 1997

[In millions of dollars (1,039,423 represents $1,039,423,000,000), except as noted. For fiscal year ending in year shown; see text, this section. Includes local shares of state imposed taxes. N.E.C. = Not elsewhere classified]

State	Total revenue [1]	General revenue Total	Per capita [2] Total (dol.)	Rank	Intergovernmental revenue Total	From Federal Government	Charges and miscellaneous Total	Current charges	Miscellaneous general/ revenue	Insurance trust revenue
United States..	1,039,423	814,382	3,048	(X)	230,592	215,421	140,454	72,303	68,151	217,703
Alabama	14,008	11,487	2,658	39	3,554	3,503	2,449	1,780	670	2,382
Alaska.	9,439	7,425	12,179	1	1,042	1,037	4,764	300	4,463	1,993
Arizona	13,692	11,499	2,525	46	3,237	2,936	1,428	714	714	2,168
Arkansas	8,844	7,290	2,889	29	2,264	2,253	1,249	792	457	1,554
California	131,349	103,929	3,229	20	30,345	27,719	11,917	7,207	4,710	27,269
Colorado	12,780	9,945	2,555	44	2,596	2,578	2,059	1,187	872	2,835
Connecticut	14,520	13,015	3,983	7	2,944	2,938	1,925	905	1,020	1,483
Delaware	4,211	3,469	4,719	2	672	650	1,054	492	562	733
Florida.	41,432	34,281	2,336	50	8,297	7,947	4,904	1,884	3,019	7,146
Georgia.	24,028	19,714	2,632	40	6,007	5,949	2,809	1,501	1,309	4,315
Hawaii.	6,701	5,527	4,636	3	1,303	1,300	1,136	776	360	1,174
Idaho	4,289	3,402	2,814	33	849	839	592	291	301	839
Illinois	39,038	32,068	2,675	38	8,714	7,912	4,810	1,987	2,823	6,970
Indiana	17,537	15,992	2,727	36	3,859	3,700	3,032	1,783	1,248	1,545
Iowa	9,509	8,360	2,929	25	2,008	1,920	1,666	1,056	610	1,059
Kansas	7,950	7,264	2,792	34	1,840	1,808	1,195	755	440	685
Kentucky	15,033	12,431	3,179	22	3,464	3,454	2,148	1,217	932	2,601
Louisiana	15,929	13,529	3,108	23	4,329	4,287	3,554	1,828	1,726	2,396
Maine	5,215	4,059	3,268	18	1,299	1,293	741	305	435	1,086
Maryland	20,128	14,800	2,905	27	3,411	3,304	2,784	1,443	1,341	5,236
Massachusetts . . .	26,538	23,811	3,894	8	5,809	5,312	4,697	1,907	2,790	2,658
Michigan	45,509	33,857	3,462	14	8,267	7,780	5,734	3,438	2,296	11,169
Minnesota	22,882	17,207	3,671	10	3,626	3,449	2,358	1,262	1,096	5,674
Mississippi	9,400	7,895	2,890	28	2,904	2,788	974	743	232	1,363
Missouri.	16,601	13,774	2,547	45	3,720	3,697	2,238	1,154	1,084	2,827
Montana	3,524	2,879	3,276	17	959	942	611	275	335	612
Nebraska.	5,537	4,740	2,861	30	1,164	1,141	1,028	665	363	797
Nevada	6,494	4,386	2,613	42	830	780	523	295	228	2,082
New Hampshire . .	3,561	2,796	2,385	48	988	840	893	387	505	525
New Jersey	36,087	26,963	3,346	15	6,363	5,989	6,185	2,952	3,233	8,655
New Mexico	8,188	6,963	4,039	6	1,973	1,926	1,668	622	1,045	1,225
New York.	95,442	75,383	4,154	5	30,470	24,278	10,048	4,175	5,873	17,884
North Carolina . . .	25,527	21,696	2,920	26	6,318	5,869	2,699	1,664	1,036	3,831
North Dakota	2,818	2,427	3,786	9	812	776	551	396	155	391
Ohio	45,250	30,792	2,751	35	8,993	8,708	5,382	3,015	2,367	14,069
Oklahoma	11,328	8,704	2,620	41	2,170	2,095	1,474	1,011	463	2,356
Oregon	15,004	11,286	3,480	13	3,518	3,420	2,822	1,235	1,587	3,528
Pennsylvania	49,318	35,212	2,932	24	9,420	9,344	6,415	3,687	2,728	13,372
Rhode Island	4,229	3,501	3,546	11	1,109	1,051	748	290	459	719
South Carolina . . .	13,805	10,750	2,838	32	3,162	3,041	2,207	1,600	608	2,355
South Dakota	2,316	1,920	2,603	43	673	665	479	192	287	395
Tennessee	15,696	13,366	2,488	47	5,065	5,003	1,684	1,189	495	2,330
Texas	63,864	45,546	2,349	49	13,800	13,281	8,721	3,815	4,906	18,318
Utah	7,724	5,903	2,859	31	1,592	1,577	1,300	892	408	1,725
Vermont	2,370	2,053	3,487	12	667	664	486	297	190	290
Virginia	24,322	18,089	2,685	37	3,545	3,393	4,917	2,805	2,112	5,975
Washington	26,841	18,213	3,244	19	4,112	4,052	2,898	1,810	1,088	8,358
West Virginia	7,467	6,038	3,326	16	2,040	2,033	1,092	595	497	1,381
Wisconsin	23,592	16,649	3,201	21	3,637	3,367	2,826	1,631	1,194	6,943
Wyoming	2,559	2,095	4,365	4	851	833	582	103	479	427

See footnotes at end of table.

U.S. Census Bureau, Statistical Abstract of the United States: 1999

[See headnote, page 325]

State	All taxes			Sales and gross receipts taxes							
	Per capita						Selective sales taxes				
	Total [1]	Total (dol.)	Rank	Total property taxes	Total [1]	Total general sales taxes	Total [1]	Alcoholic beverages and tobacco sales	Insurance premiums	Motor fuels sales	Public utilities
United States	443,335	1,659	(X)	10,297	215,737	147,069	68,668	11,149	9,219	27,132	8,605
Alabama........	5,484	1,269	1	131	2,866	1,506	1,361	187	156	473	414
Alaska	1,619	2,656	46	54	96	(X)	96	27	28	36	3
Arizona.........	6,834	1,501	33	257	3,803	2,855	948	214	138	505	88
Arkansas	3,777	1,497	32	8	2,018	1,429	588	121	66	352	(X)
California	61,667	1,916	11	3,612	25,222	19,974	5,248	942	1,284	2,822	43
Colorado........	5,290	1,359	44	(X)	2,179	1,413	766	92	114	491	7
Connecticut......	8,146	2,493	3	-	4,165	2,598	1,567	165	186	544	179
Delaware	1,743	2,371	5	(X)	253	(X)	253	33	43	102	23
Florida	21,080	1,436	39	788	16,081	12,068	4,013	996	487	1,481	576
Georgia	10,898	1,455	37	38	4,905	3,916	990	215	222	553	(X)
Hawaii	3,088	2,590	2	(X)	1,926	1,457	469	75	77	75	114
Idaho..........	1,961	1,622	20	(X)	924	622	302	36	47	212	3
Illinois	18,545	1,547	23	204	8,796	5,296	3,500	485	127	1,221	889
Indiana.........	9,101	1,552	26	4	4,132	3,043	1,089	123	138	617	5
Iowa	4,686	1,642	27	(X)	2,228	1,500	728	112	106	386	(X)
Kansas.........	4,230	1,626	21	44	2,007	1,476	531	119	90	303	1
Kentucky	6,819	1,744	15	415	3,194	1,883	1,311	81	276	407	(X)
Louisiana	5,646	1,297	45	25	2,759	1,828	931	138	250	495	13
Maine..........	2,019	1,626	6	42	965	683	282	78	43	156	-
Maryland	8,604	1,689	17	236	3,695	2,095	1,600	127	166	614	156
Massachusetts.....	13,305	2,176	22	-	4,217	2,876	1,341	343	298	603	(X)
Michigan........	19,856	2,030	7	1,688	8,872	7,132	1,740	674	186	841	(X)
Minnesota.......	11,223	2,394	4	10	4,776	3,115	1,661	245	181	539	-
Mississippi	4,017	1,470	38	23	2,665	1,916	749	96	103	356	(X)
Missouri	7,816	1,445	34	16	3,702	2,592	1,110	138	186	649	-
Montana........	1,309	1,489	40	235	274	(X)	274	31	37	175	19
Nebraska	2,548	1,538	16	5	1,281	866	416	64	40	277	3
Nevada	3,034	1,807	19	61	2,601	1,699	903	72	97	217	6
New Hampshire....	915	780	28	1	459	(X)	459	62	53	111	57
New Jersey.......	14,415	1,789	50	3	7,192	4,415	2,777	326	294	465	1,162
New Mexico	3,322	1,927	14	34	1,807	1,346	461	60	61	237	7
New York	34,865	1,921	13	(X)	12,140	7,353	4,787	851	681	474	1,683
North Carolina.....	12,678	1,706	12	(X)	5,316	3,057	2,259	218	247	997	312
North Dakota.....	1,064	1,660	10	2	606	311	295	29	21	104	27
Ohio	16,418	1,467	35	18	8,055	5,234	2,821	378	346	1,368	713
Oklahoma........	5,061	1,524	30	(X)	1,941	1,273	668	134	143	347	15
Oregon..........	4,946	1,525	31	-	674	(X)	674	166	76	421	9
Pennsylvania......	19,377	1,613	24	203	9,221	6,055	3,166	491	377	790	718
Rhode Island.....	1,644	1,665	18	4	813	490	324	63	33	124	69
South Carolina.....	5,381	1,421	41	14	2,735	2,032	703	148	78	328	38
South Dakota	768	1,042	49	(X)	609	411	198	31	34	95	2
Tennessee	6,616	1,232	47	(X)	5,087	3,840	1,247	153	244	723	7
Texas..........	23,025	1,188	48	(X)	18,404	11,362	7,042	1,086	673	2,383	368
Utah	3,011	1,458	36	(X)	1,580	1,265	315	52	45	217	(X)
Vermont	899	1,528	42	10	490	184	225	27	19	58	8
Virginia.........	9,628	1,429	29	22	3,767	2,119	1,648	125	219	735	124
Washington.......	11,202	1,995	8	1,927	8,289	6,572	1,717	417	212	685	241
West Virginia	2,906	1,601	9	3	1,515	831	683	42	77	228	193
Wisconsin	10,187	1,959	25	76	4,231	2,865	1,366	254	102	694	312
Wyoming	662	1,380	43	86	282	215	67	6	13	47	(X)

See footnotes at end of table.

U.S. Census Bureau, Statistical Abstract of the United States: 1999

No. 522. State Governments—Revenue, by State: 1997—Continued

[See headnote, page 325]

State	License taxes					Income			Other taxes	
	Total[1]	Corpora-tion license	Hunting and fishing license	Motor vehicle and opera-tors license	Occu-pancy and business license, n.e.c.	Total[1]	Indi-vidual income	Corpora-tion net income	Total[1]	Death and gift
United States	28,217	5,882	1,015	12,965	5,823	175,330	144,668	30,662	13,755	5,913
Alabama.........	424	110	17	171	100	1,914	1,688	227	148	45
Alaska.........	78	1	16	29	31	331	(X)	331	1,060	2
Arizona.	437	6	15	323	50	2,269	1,668	601	67	67
Arkansas	222	8	20	97	66	1,477	1,247	230	52	19
California	2,963	41	74	1,511	1,122	29,077	23,273	5,804	794	757
Colorado.	261	4	54	139	41	2,785	2,560	224	65	35
Connecticut.	341	11	3	211	78	3,338	2,807	530	302	227
Delaware	579	391	1	28	149	836	663	173	76	32
Florida	1,370	122	15	809	251	1,233	(X)	1,233	1,608	537
Georgia	405	31	21	202	70	5,468	4,741	726	81	60
Hawaii.........	90	2	-	61	17	1,044	977	68	28	22
Idaho..........	148	1	23	46	39	850	712	138	39	4
Illinois.........	1,215	124	24	769	237	8,091	6,287	1,804	238	199
Indiana.........	194	5	15	116	45	4,655	3,751	904	116	115
Iowa	421	35	18	262	70	1,941	1,720	221	96	88
Kansas.........	212	21	12	129	32	1,804	1,513	291	163	76
Kentucky	427	148	17	153	90	2,498	2,205	293	285	95
Louisiana	436	248	22	96	55	1,940	1,560	380	486	78
Maine..........	117	3	12	56	33	869	772	97	26	15
Maryland	350	13	11	190	117	4,112	3,769	343	211	106
Massachusetts.....	431	20	6	245	56	8,395	7,182	1,213	262	203
Michigan........	1,016	11	45	653	216	8,159	5,930	2,229	121	79
Minnesota........	821	3	37	510	228	5,478	4,779	699	138	48
Mississippi	266	75	11	117	40	1,017	791	226	45	12
Missouri	562	89	27	237	155	3,449	3,038	411	87	81
Montana........	151	1	29	49	27	488	406	82	160	15
Nebraska	165	6	10	74	51	1,075	937	137	22	15
Nevada	303	15	-	98	95	(X)	(X)	(X)	69	28
New Hampshire....	121	4	6	56	36	261	53	208	74	41
New Jersey.......	742	130	12	400	111	6,089	4,825	1,264	388	313
New Mexico	134	2	11	87	25	921	748	173	427	18
New York	945	67	31	613	72	20,596	17,554	3,042	1,183	889
North Carolina.....	775	230	15	346	98	6,440	5,459	981	147	145
North Dakota......	77	-	7	38	27	239	163	75	140	5
Ohio	1,355	481	30	557	220	6,879	6,141	737	111	102
Oklahoma........	701	40	12	546	88	1,919	1,698	221	501	81
Oregon.........	512	5	26	334	115	3,657	3,273	384	103	34
Pennsylvania......	1,920	971	45	506	280	7,151	5,575	1,576	883	615
Rhode Island......	80	10	1	47	20	729	640	89	18	13
South Carolina.....	411	40	14	96	97	2,172	1,933	239	49	28
South Dakota	94	1	12	30	41	37	(X)	37	29	21
Tennessee	738	401	19	201	72	608	128	480	184	61
Texas..........	3,265	1,831	65	786	429	(X)	(X)	(X)	1,355	207
Utah	90	4	14	48	13	1,305	1,128	177	35	10
Vermont.........	68	1	5	39	17	368	323	45	44	18
Virginia.........	431	26	19	264	87	5,153	4,728	425	256	92
Washington.......	510	11	29	244	150	(X)	(X)	(X)	477	88
West Virginia......	151	6	15	75	25	1,037	786	251	200	17
Wisconsin........	614	71	49	226	236	5,177	4,538	639	88	51
Wyoming	78	5	19	45	3	(X)	(X)	(X)	217	4

- Represents or rounds to zero.   X Not applicable.   [1] Includes amounts not shown separately.   [2] Based on estimated resident population as of July 1.   [3] Special tax rate on specific items.

Source: U.S. Census Bureau; <http://www.census.gov/govs/www/index.html> (accessed 18 June 1999).

U.S. Census Bureau, Statistical Abstract of the United States: 1999

[In millions of dollars (893,827 represents $893,827,000,000), except as indicated. For fiscal year ending in year shown; see text, this section]

State	Total expenditure [1]	General expenditure Total Amount	Per capita [2] (dol.)	Inter-govern-mental	Direct expend-itures	Educa-tion	Public welfare	Health and hospitals	High-ways	Police protection
United States..	893,827	788,176	2,950	264,207	629,620	275,821	203,204	63,193	60,204	7,501
Alabama.......	12,945	11,669	2,700	3,292	9,652	5,175	2,538	1,449	837	93
Alaska........	5,722	5,160	8,463	1,015	4,707	1,199	742	188	590	57
Arizona........	12,419	11,266	2,474	4,528	7,890	4,033	2,688	614	1,167	132
Arkansas......	7,685	7,103	2,815	1,967	5,717	2,819	1,667	624	763	60
California......	117,643	102,853	3,196	49,636	68,008	35,546	30,205	9,001	4,581	1,039
Colorado	10,861	9,381	2,410	3,017	7,844	4,192	2,221	393	810	55
Connecticut ...	13,826	11,952	3,658	2,481	11,345	2,894	2,915	1,380	756	110
Delaware......	3,404	3,098	4,215	576	2,828	1,070	501	227	262	52
Florida........	37,464	34,658	2,361	11,900	25,564	11,599	7,693	2,402	3,159	320
Georgia.......	21,975	20,448	2,730	6,141	15,834	8,938	5,335	1,344	1,084	172
Hawaii........	6,093	5,421	4,548	156	5,937	1,557	983	515	322	7
Idaho	3,674	3,251	2,689	1,067	2,607	1,346	599	130	397	32
Illinois........	35,302	31,266	2,608	9,148	26,154	9,160	9,164	2,549	2,597	303
Indiana	16,370	15,400	2,626	5,508	10,863	6,411	3,221	634	1,648	153
Iowa	9,348	8,622	3,021	2,869	6,479	3,595	1,738	679	1,095	59
Kansas	7,496	6,875	2,643	2,326	5,171	3,037	1,124	605	1,013	41
Kentucky......	12,949	11,634	2,975	2,918	10,031	4,398	3,207	751	1,091	121
Louisiana......	14,286	12,790	2,938	3,171	11,115	4,558	2,960	1,459	850	192
Maine	4,441	3,961	3,190	773	3,669	1,122	1,337	262	362	39
Maryland	16,200	14,002	2,748	3,536	12,663	4,401	3,023	1,099	1,245	251
Massachusetts ...	25,791	23,589	3,858	5,637	20,154	4,956	5,881	2,212	2,144	267
Michigan	36,092	32,546	3,328	14,145	21,947	14,309	6,723	3,467	2,059	253
Minnesota	18,443	16,796	3,583	6,942	11,501	6,176	4,459	930	776	89
Mississippi.....	9,006	8,014	2,934	2,686	6,320	2,752	1,891	670	1,265	56
Missouri.......	14,230	13,082	2,419	3,944	10,286	5,051	3,066	1,010	1,265	156
Montana	3,204	2,826	3,216	715	2,489	1,020	501	192	344	33
Nebraska......	4,802	4,548	2,744	1,210	3,592	1,588	1,030	544	596	46
Nevada.......	5,130	4,328	2,578	1,772	3,358	1,677	654	156	370	39
New Hampshire ..	3,324	2,891	2,467	414	2,910	624	905	180	306	29
New Jersey	29,430	23,053	2,861	6,383	23,047	7,282	4,826	1,729	1,593	236
New Mexico.....	7,059	6,486	3,762	2,075	4,984	2,516	1,253	591	644	58
New York......	83,243	70,017	3,858	25,638	57,605	16,243	27,594	5,459	2,764	344
North Carolina ...	22,864	20,955	2,820	7,315	15,550	8,561	4,733	1,682	1,888	219
North Dakota	2,426	2,222	3,467	540	1,886	773	452	102	230	9
Ohio	37,407	30,705	2,743	10,442	26,965	11,233	7,961	2,228	2,468	204
Oklahoma	9,593	8,286	2,495	2,625	6,968	3,691	1,723	616	806	53
Oregon	12,388	10,367	3,197	3,208	9,180	3,603	2,390	805	1,024	146
Pennsylvania ...	39,296	33,709	2,806	9,844	29,452	10,513	10,019	3,076	2,493	647
Rhode Island ..	4,002	3,373	3,416	506	3,495	914	869	328	192	33
South Carolina ...	12,847	11,127	2,937	2,929	9,918	3,903	2,622	1,314	665	160
South Dakota	2,070	1,947	2,639	435	1,635	581	389	99	282	16
Tennessee......	14,284	13,304	2,477	3,645	10,639	4,670	3,987	1,118	1,299	96
Texas	48,887	44,124	2,276	12,806	36,081	18,303	11,525	3,293	3,291	294
Utah	6,818	6,285	3,044	1,673	5,145	3,025	990	492	584	58
Vermont	2,123	1,971	3,348	312	1,811	645	523	59	191	30
Virginia	19,287	17,807	2,643	5,337	13,949	7,048	3,234	1,704	2,140	326
Washington	22,207	18,803	3,349	5,682	16,525	7,803	4,059	1,574	1,558	202
West Virginia	7,145	6,099	3,360	1,626	5,520	2,386	1,603	217	783	41
Wisconsin	18,200	16,229	3,120	6,993	11,206	6,286	3,223	943	1,277	59
Wyoming.......	2,127	1,877	3,911	702	1,424	637	259	102	289	14

See footnotes at end of table.

U.S. Census Bureau, Statistical Abstract of the United States: 1999

No. 523. State Governments—Expenditures and Debt, by State: 1997—Continued

[See headnote, page 328]

State	General expenditure								Debt outstanding		
	Selected functions										
	Corrections	Natural resources	Parks and recreation	Governmental administration	Interest on general debt	Utility expenditures	Liquor stores expenditures	Insurance trust expenditures	Cash and security holdings	Total	Per capita [2] (dol.)
United States..	29,043	12,909	3,900	28,656	26,310	7,783	2,697	95,172	1,784,947	455,697	1,705
Alabama	234	176	16	301	224	-	142	1,134	21,639	3,780	875
Alaska.	152	289	15	334	227	24	-	539	34,320	3,291	5,397
Arizona	564	167	44	331	159	28	-	1,124	25,615	2,742	602
Arkansas.	206	138	49	246	122	-	-	582	11,899	2,248	891
California.	3,968	2,011	249	3,164	2,482	74	-	14,716	226,142	45,337	1,409
Colorado	456	152	47	334	236	5	-	1,475	23,591	3,402	874
Connecticut	494	76	38	584	948	217	-	1,657	22,887	17,051	5,219
Delaware.	123	55	27	245	209	39	-	266	7,510	3,434	4,671
Florida.	1,849	1,104	148	1,536	905	80	-	2,726	65,401	16,022	1,092
Georgia.	882	373	169	487	385	-	-	1,527	36,320	6,186	826
Hawaii.	128	71	144	248	328	-	-	672	10,843	5,253	4,406
Idaho	103	116	20	119	102	-	39	385	7,294	1,598	1,322
Illinois	951	268	195	1,055	1,526	-	-	4,036	59,776	23,801	1,985
Indiana	419	162	58	372	288	-	-	970	23,269	6,140	1,047
Iowa	200	212	18	312	114	-	62	664	18,889	2,014	706
Kansas	206	165	6	254	71	-	-	621	8,826	1,211	466
Kentucky	260	215	105	468	384	9	-	1,306	24,059	7,120	1,821
Louisiana.	417	313	190	483	544	3	-	1,493	26,722	7,030	1,615
Maine	66	116	9	159	173	-	47	433	6,400	3,203	2,579
Maryland	741	317	158	668	602	358	-	1,840	40,443	9,873	1,938
Massachusetts . . .	811	202	143	982	1,771	95	-	2,106	35,435	29,386	4,806
Michigan	1,291	325	55	718	787	-	374	3,172	60,166	14,431	1,476
Minnesota	325	360	99	493	309	-	-	1,647	36,925	4,862	1,037
Mississippi	212	163	116	265	152	-	114	877	14,574	2,455	899
Missouri.	368	263	38	637	443	-	-	1,148	32,267	7,579	1,401
Montana	73	146	6	143	131	-	29	349	6,727	2,056	2,339
Nebraska.	106	131	23	128	90	-	-	254	6,895	1,494	902
Nevada.	180	66	15	201	156	46	-	755	12,360	2,769	1,650
New Hampshire . .	60	30	12	151	380	-	209	223	9,090	5,848	4,990
New Jersey	1,002	245	372	965	1,377	1,562	-	4,815	63,138	26,591	3,300
New Mexico	186	85	43	257	124	-	-	572	18,665	2,458	1,426
New York.	2,287	299	328	3,467	3,767	4,299	-	8,927	153,766	74,078	4,082
North Carolina . . .	935	408	91	592	297	-	-	1,910	42,723	5,677	764
North Dakota	21	103	10	81	57	-	-	204	4,562	900	1,404
Ohio	1,263	316	93	1,121	865	-	263	6,439	113,511	13,437	1,201
Oklahoma	352	154	53	354	165	252	-	1,055	16,869	3,795	1,143
Oregon	429	257	38	661	361	1	115	1,905	24,103	5,841	1,801
Pennsylvania	1,078	436	108	1,086	1,181	-	677	4,911	77,929	15,368	1,279
Rhode Island	120	25	31	215	300	37	-	593	9,587	5,302	5,370
South Carolina . . .	429	174	50	316	209	640	-	1,080	20,140	5,350	1,412
South Dakota	60	84	18	82	117	-	-	123	5,697	1,841	2,495
Tennessee	469	169	98	331	203	4	-	976	22,632	3,315	617
Texas	2,253	572	67	1,239	843	-	-	4,763	121,587	12,462	643
Utah	175	167	31	296	130	-	72	461	12,538	2,451	1,187
Vermont	44	62	12	116	112	1	26	125	3,672	2,037	3,461
Virginia	824	141	51	776	599	3	227	1,249	42,855	9,941	1,475
Washington	562	464	73	451	536	-	230	3,174	47,230	9,493	1,691
West Virginia	95	145	47	267	179	4	40	1,003	7,478	3,040	1,674
Wisconsin	574	298	57	478	584	-	-	1,971	53,026	9,832	1,890
Wyoming	37	123	18	88	57	-	31	219	6,955	872	1,816

- Represents or rounds to zero.   [1] Includes items not shown separately.   [2] Based on estimated resident population as of July 1.

Source: U.S. Census Bureau, <http://www.census.gov/govs/www/st97.html> (accessed 21 June 1999).

State and Local Government Finances and Employment   329

No. 524. Local Governments—Revenue, by State: 1996

[In millions of dollars (803,737 represents $803,737,000,000), except as noted. For fiscal year ending in year shown; see text, this section]

State	Total revenue [1]	General revenue Total	Per capita [2] (dol.)	Intergovernmental revenue From Federal Government	Intergovernmental revenue From state governments	Taxes Total	Taxes Property	General sales	Current charges and miscellaneous	Utility revenue
United States..	803,737	709,216	2,674	26,906	243,574	270,602	199,467	29,709	168,135	67,674
Alabama	9,902	8,345	1,945	314	2,980	2,374	864	961	2,677	1,463
Alaska.	2,549	2,314	3,824	109	796	782	624	109	627	207
Arizona	12,698	10,511	2,372	396	4,167	3,753	2,751	731	2,195	2,020
Arkansas	4,278	3,830	1,529	116	1,521	1,148	746	301	1,045	427
California.	123,892	103,549	3,260	4,485	43,881	28,468	19,404	4,315	26,715	12,363
Colorado	11,862	10,462	2,743	376	2,924	4,423	2,841	1,289	2,739	1,136
Connecticut	8,687	8,078	2,475	286	2,265	4,713	4,657	-	814	367
Delaware	1,479	1,326	1,823	44	633	362	299	-	286	129
District of Columbia.	5,675	4,910	9,099	1,871	-	2,481	702	468	558	377
Florida.	43,455	38,648	2,679	1,189	10,646	13,829	11,058	356	12,985	4,169
Georgia	21,195	18,536	2,527	486	5,497	7,016	4,757	1,525	5,536	2,282
Hawaii.	1,619	1,444	1,216	122	174	762	613	-	386	175
Idaho	2,592	2,479	2,090	67	1,035	687	653	-	690	113
Illinois	36,051	31,755	2,661	1,460	8,889	15,105	12,297	1,135	6,301	2,239
Indiana	13,762	12,579	2,159	313	4,393	4,543	4,026	-	3,331	1,125
Iowa	7,488	6,994	2,455	246	2,330	2,542	2,384	60	1,876	477
Kansas	7,170	6,294	2,435	102	2,124	2,394	1,946	289	1,674	805
Kentucky	7,342	6,607	1,702	237	2,605	1,924	999	-	1,841	713
Louisiana.	10,171	9,403	2,167	362	2,982	3,559	1,338	1,928	2,499	661
Maine	2,614	2,527	2,042	88	733	1,335	1,309	-	371	87
Maryland	13,153	11,911	2,355	540	3,237	5,965	3,569	-	2,169	369
Massachusetts . . .	17,905	15,309	2,517	889	5,603	6,668	6,475	-	2,148	1,686
Michigan	28,031	25,240	2,593	871	12,621	6,128	5,458	-	5,620	1,162
Minnesota	16,751	15,213	3,273	384	6,324	4,327	4,107	25	4,178	1,063
Mississippi	6,182	5,744	2,119	182	2,443	1,283	1,184	1	1,836	437
Missouri.	12,049	10,652	1,984	322	3,432	4,477	2,601	1,015	2,420	1,019
Montana	1,716	1,659	1,892	68	627	571	546	-	393	57
Nebraska	5,885	3,890	2,360	127	960	1,812	1,574	143	990	1,821
Nevada	4,852	4,588	2,867	150	1,691	1,371	823	83	1,377	264
New Hampshire . .	2,479	2,417	2,085	53	302	1,782	1,765	-	281	60
New Jersey	25,625	24,900	3,109	289	7,582	13,064	12,813	-	3,965	718
New Mexico.	3,962	3,712	2,173	176	1,915	816	437	302	806	250
New York.	91,383	82,105	4,526	2,517	25,932	38,345	23,262	6,171	15,311	3,382
North Carolina . . .	19,416	16,736	2,290	500	6,461	4,604	3,446	884	5,171	2,370
North Dakota	1,327	1,253	1,949	71	427	456	410	30	298	64
Ohio	30,204	28,340	2,537	1,198	9,133	12,312	7,950	932	5,698	1,698
Oklahoma	6,764	6,192	1,879	147	2,299	1,941	1,014	813	1,805	532
Oregon	9,649	9,016	2,821	659	3,179	2,887	2,332	-	2,291	632
Pennsylvania	31,499	28,878	2,400	1,511	9,768	11,985	8,468	100	5,614	1,773
Rhode Island	2,103	1,974	1,998	101	552	1,157	1,141	-	164	88
South Carolina . . .	8,328	7,395	1,979	213	2,436	2,215	1,941	54	2,531	929
South Dakota	1,480	1,335	1,811	67	311	708	558	121	249	116
Tennessee.	15,715	10,785	2,032	275	3,225	3,813	2,266	1,110	3,472	4,629
Texas	51,020	45,051	2,367	1,175	12,696	19,093	15,248	2,340	12,087	5,029
Utah	5,200	4,116	2,036	198	1,459	1,388	1,008	247	1,071	1,083
Vermont	1,303	1,179	2,011	118	256	677	670	-	127	116
Virginia	15,933	14,199	2,130	436	4,316	6,726	4,828	594	2,721	1,057
Washington	18,651	15,498	2,808	566	5,827	4,880	2,872	1,058	4,225	3,028
West Virginia	3,226	3,101	1,704	85	1,325	878	724	-	813	106
Wisconsin	15,814	14,663	2,834	317	6,068	5,620	5,354	144	2,657	728
Wyoming	1,650	1,574	3,279	31	589	454	352	75	500	72

- Represents or rounds to zero. [1] Includes items not shown separately. [2] Based on estimated resident population as of July.

Source: U.S. Census Bureau, <http://www.census.gov/govs/www/esti96.html> (accessed 26 April 1999; and unpublished data).

U.S. Census Bureau, Statistical Abstract of the United States: 1999

No. 525. Local Governments—Expenditures and Debt, by State: 1996

[In millions of dollars (794,318 represents $794,318,000,000), except as indicated. For fiscal year ending in year shown; see text, this section]

State	Total expenditure [1]	Total Amount	Per capita [2] (dol.)	Direct expenditures	Education	Public welfare	Health and hospitals	Highways	Police protection	Utility expenditures	Debt outstanding
United States.....	794,318	693,946	2,617	686,050	292,953	37,776	60,322	31,600	38,187	84,465	717,322
Alabama	10,262	8,680	2,023	8,670	3,556	41	1,669	448	426	1,529	7,970
Alaska............	2,536	2,244	3,708	2,244	957	17	112	110	99	284	3,622
Arizona	12,673	10,650	2,403	10,387	4,574	770	362	516	662	1,931	16,275
Arkansas	4,245	3,835	1,531	3,834	1,999	4	288	250	203	399	3,670
California	121,559	102,738	3,235	101,408	32,996	11,765	10,032	3,317	6,298	16,118	97,932
Colorado	11,877	10,279	2,695	10,235	3,977	586	728	603	548	1,452	15,677
Connecticut	8,694	8,169	2,503	8,167	4,206	174	75	325	455	370	4,102
Delaware	1,483	1,372	1,887	1,369	803	1	9	93	82	97	1,229
District of Columbia ...	5,817	4,184	7,752	4,184	669	1,172	432	89	248	1,138	4,137
Florida...........	43,383	38,407	2,663	38,293	14,943	281	3,627	1,553	2,742	4,648	49,649
Georgia..........	20,439	17,378	2,369	17,343	7,858	83	2,919	834	858	2,875	17,501
Hawaii............	1,755	1,470	1,238	1,470	-	12	19	73	176	285	2,089
Idaho.............	2,580	2,471	2,083	2,462	1,237	32	311	177	126	108	869
Illinois............	34,221	29,437	2,467	29,408	13,246	395	1,414	1,678	2,016	3,394	29,742
Indiana...........	14,043	12,818	2,200	12,713	5,967	489	1,493	512	478	1,176	9,275
Iowa	7,331	6,785	2,382	6,708	3,216	127	797	670	272	534	4,291
Kansas	7,245	6,410	2,480	6,409	3,198	40	498	474	324	762	6,890
Kentucky.........	7,638	6,858	1,766	6,856	3,441	37	455	227	269	761	12,371
Louisiana.........	9,686	8,835	2,036	8,827	3,738	77	1,185	472	548	760	8,871
Maine	2,503	2,409	1,946	2,409	1,295	32	59	146	95	93	1,522
Maryland	12,481	11,688	2,311	11,610	5,804	68	282	471	688	418	12,558
Massachusetts	17,201	13,633	2,241	13,100	6,074	168	634	634	865	2,697	11,340
Michigan..........	27,323	25,184	2,587	25,081	12,352	440	2,137	1,485	1,245	1,415	17,943
Minnesota.........	16,719	15,127	3,254	15,035	6,049	1,064	1,314	1,232	566	1,245	17,208
Mississippi.........	6,002	5,557	2,050	5,556	2,629	26	1,009	388	236	444	3,917
Missouri..........	12,106	10,758	2,004	10,756	5,495	77	721	651	616	1,160	6,744
Montana	1,766	1,699	1,938	1,693	988	28	75	92	80	69	683
Nebraska..........	5,669	3,803	2,307	3,796	2,045	56	252	286	141	1,801	4,820
Nevada...........	4,741	4,469	2,793	4,467	1,510	70	450	330	303	272	5,908
New Hampshire	2,405	2,330	2,010	2,275	1,213	180	18	129	120	69	1,104
New Jersey	24,761	24,124	3,013	23,758	11,629	1,298	792	843	1,558	657	16,028
New Mexico	3,928	3,667	2,147	3,645	1,633	53	237	203	226	261	3,281
New York..........	91,534	80,684	4,447	76,740	27,332	11,859	6,629	3,176	4,280	5,897	76,579
North Carolina	19,708	16,501	2,258	16,234	7,039	980	3,038	310	803	2,921	16,988
North Dakota	1,318	1,224	1,905	1,213	605	41	13	118	47	88	923
Ohio	29,700	27,548	2,466	27,415	12,221	1,436	2,177	1,404	1,541	2,089	16,327
Oklahoma	6,800	6,257	1,899	6,255	3,088	18	701	326	350	524	5,078
Oregon	9,714	8,571	2,682	8,567	4,070	53	634	532	430	1,101	6,364
Pennsylvania	31,216	27,641	2,297	27,631	12,982	1,408	1,254	942	1,117	2,975	43,444
Rhode Island	2,006	1,885	1,908	1,885	1,049	7	3	55	135	78	1,012
South Carolina	8,203	7,096	1,899	7,073	3,331	23	1,434	130	315	1,109	6,777
South Dakota	1,480	1,345	1,824	1,341	673	17	37	140	60	111	702
Tennessee	15,483	10,648	2,006	10,608	4,254	112	1,547	540	578	4,617	19,420
Texas	50,226	43,259	2,273	43,212	21,815	296	5,214	1,603	2,291	6,209	61,413
Utah.............	5,243	4,128	2,041	4,123	2,096	22	158	187	221	1,115	9,015
Vermont	1,147	1,023	1,744	1,023	663	-	4	109	34	120	539
Virginia	15,710	14,226	2,134	14,175	6,684	691	504	459	751	1,257	15,440
Washington	18,962	14,894	2,699	14,861	6,261	29	1,189	954	687	3,967	22,779
West Virginia	3,189	3,048	1,674	3,045	1,813	1	242	40	94	125	3,669
Wisconsin	15,936	14,924	2,884	14,901	6,936	1,115	847	1,209	814	850	10,566
Wyoming..........	1,668	1,576	3,283	1,575	746	7	290	58	68	89	1,071

- Represents or rounds to zero. [1] Includes items not shown separately. [2] Based on estimated resident population as of July 1.

Source: U.S. Census Bureau, <http://www.census.gov/govs/www/esti96.html>; (accessed 26 April 1999); and unpublished data.

U.S. Census Bureau, Statistical Abstract of the United States: 1999

No. 526. Estimated State and Local Taxes Paid by a Family of Four in Selected Cities: 1997

[Data based on average family of four (two wage earners and two school age children) owning their own home and living in a city where taxes apply. Comprises state and local sales, income, auto, and real estate taxes. For definition of median, see Guide to Tabular Presentation]

City	Total taxes paid, by gross family income level (dollars)					Total taxes paid as percent of income				
	$25,000	$50,000	$75,000	$100,000	$150,000	$25,000	$50,000	$75,000	$100,000	$150,000
Albuquerque, NM . . .	1,684	3,794	6,529	9,171	14,634	6.7	7.6	8.7	9.2	9.8
Atlanta, GA	1,951	4,444	7,466	10,253	15,682	7.8	8.9	10.0	10.3	10.5
Baltimore, MD	2,037	5,490	8,597	11,381	16,908	8.1	11.0	11.5	11.4	11.3
Boston, MA	2,181	5,004	8,075	10,816	16,250	8.7	10.0	10.8	10.8	10.8
Charlotte, NC	1,869	4,180	6,930	9,704	14,808	7.5	8.4	9.2	9.7	9.9
Chicago, IL	2,124	4,177	6,565	8,625	12,724	8.5	8.4	8.8	8.6	8.5
Columbus, OH	2,154	4,571	7,472	10,333	16,141	8.6	9.1	10.0	10.3	10.8
Denver, CO	1,647	3,591	5,698	7,675	11,449	6.6	7.2	7.6	7.7	7.6
Detroit, MI	2,551	5,278	8,215	10,907	16,276	10.2	10.6	11.0	10.9	10.9
Honolulu, HI	2,168	4,778	7,905	10,805	16,551	8.7	9.6	10.5	10.8	11.0
Houston, TX	1,325	2,433	3,808	4,869	6,986	5.3	4.9	5.1	4.9	4.7
Indianapolis, IN	1,945	3,716	5,717	7,528	11,144	7.8	7.4	7.6	7.5	7.4
Jacksonville, FL	982	1,769	2,841	3,664	5,303	3.9	3.5	3.8	3.7	3.5
Kansas City, MO . . .	2,175	4,231	6,704	9,160	14,124	8.7	8.5	8.9	9.2	9.4
Las Vegas, NV	1,450	2,296	3,520	4,461	6,272	5.8	4.6	4.7	4.5	4.2
Los Angeles, CA . . .	1,970	4,222	7,526	11,004	17,795	7.9	8.4	10.0	11.0	11.9
Memphis, TN.	1,519	2,467	3,999	5,208	7,726	6.1	4.9	5.3	5.2	5.2
Milwaukee, WI	2,371	5,421	8,574	11,420	17,077	9.5	10.8	11.4	11.4	11.4
Minneapolis, MN . . .	1,679	4,584	8,167	11,349	17,678	6.7	9.2	10.9	11.3	11.8
New Orleans, LA . . .	1,449	3,335	5,747	7,798	11,859	5.8	6.7	7.7	7.8	7.9
New York City, NY . .	2,123	5,707	9,872	13,878	22,006	8.5	11.4	13.2	13.9	14.7
Oklahoma City, OK. .	2,095	4,167	6,855	9,318	14,236	8.4	8.3	9.1	9.3	9.5
Omaha, NE.	2,081	4,321	7,284	10,050	15,926	8.3	8.6	9.7	10.0	10.6
Philadelphia, PA. . . .	3,241	6,098	9,136	11,882	17,314	13.0	12.2	12.2	11.9	11.5
Phoenix, AZ	2,051	3,889	6,123	8,292	12,466	8.2	7.8	8.2	8.3	8.3
Portland, ME.	2,705	6,094	10,139	13,752	20,964	10.8	12.2	13.5	13.8	14.0
Seattle, WA	1,871	3,188	4,823	6,135	8,754	7.5	6.4	6.4	6.1	5.8
Virginia Beach, VA . .	2,214	4,297	6,892	9,296	13,859	8.9	8.6	9.2	9.3	9.2
Washington, DC. . . .	2,203	4,660	7,933	10,984	17,033	8.8	9.3	10.6	11.0	11.4
Wichita, KS.	1,894	3,661	6,251	8,697	13,455	7.6	7.3	8.3	8.7	9.0
Average [1]	2,027	4,221	6,885	9,318	14,148	8.1	8.4	9.2	9.3	9.4
Median [1]	1,970	4,180	6,870	9,318	14,549	7.9	8.4	9.2	9.3	9.7

[1] Based on selected cities and District of Columbia. For complete list of cities, see Table 527.

Source: Government of the District of Columbia, Department of Finance and Revenue, *Tax Rates and Tax Burdens in the District of Columbia: A Nationwide Comparison,* annual.

No. 527. Residential Property Tax Rates in Selected Cities: 1997

[Effective tax rate is amount each jurisdiction considers based upon assessment level used. Assessment level is ratio of assessed value to assumed market value. Nominal rate is announced rates it levied at taxable value of house]

City	Effective tax rate per $100		Assessment level (percent)	Nominal rate per $100	City	Effective tax rate per $100		Assessment level (percent)	Nominal rate per $100
	Rank	Rate				Rank	Rate		
Newark, NJ.	1	3.91	16.4	23.85	Billings, MT.	28	1.24	74.0	1.68
Bridgeport, CT.	2	3.73	56.9	6.55	Columbia, SC	29	1.42	4.0	35.47
Manchester, NH. . . .	3	3.40	109.0	3.12	Louisville, KY	30	1.12	90.0	1.25
Milwaukee, WI.	4	2.97	96.4	3.08	Wichita, KS.	31	1.23	11.5	10.73
Providence, RI	5	3.20	100.0	3.20	Albuquerque, NM. . . .	32	1.38	33.3	4.13
Des Moines, IA	6	2.36	54.9	4.30	Boston, MA	33	1.35	100.0	1.35
Detroit, MI	7	2.58	43.9	5.88	Minneapolis, MN	34	1.25	87.5	1.43
Philadelphia, PA	8	2.64	32.0	8.26	Little Rock, AR	35	1.19	18.6	6.39
Houston, TX	9	2.70	100.0	2.70	Kansas City, MO	36	1.20	19.0	6.30
Portland, ME.	10	2.46	100.0	2.46	Seattle, WA	37	1.18	91.2	1.29
Omaha, NE	11	2.23	93.0	2.40	Wilmington, DE	38	1.10	50.4	2.19
Baltimore, MD.	12	2.42	40.0	6.06	Virginia Beach, VA. . .	39	1.12	91.9	1.22
Sioux Falls, SD	13	1.75	85.0	2.06	Charlotte, NC	40	1.08	86.3	1.26
Atlanta, GA.	14	2.05	40.0	5.11	Jacksonville, FL.	41	1.11	100.0	1.11
Burlington, VT.	15	2.02	100.0	2.02	Oklahoma City, OK . .	42	1.13	11.0	10.30
Fargo, ND	16	1.93	4.1	46.96	Las Vegas, NV	43	1.03	35.0	2.94
Indianapolis, IN	17	1.53	15.0	10.21	Jackson, MS.	44	1.28	10.0	12.75
Charleston, WV	18	0.92	60.0	1.53	Washington, DC	45	0.96	99.5	0.96
Boise City, ID	19	1.78	98.4	1.81	New York City, NY . . .	46	0.75	7.0	10.79
Phoenix, AZ	20	1.69	10.0	16.90	Denver, CO	47	0.73	9.7	7.54
Columbus, OH	21	1.82	35.0	5.20	Cheyenne, WY	48	0.77	9.5	8.10
Chicago, IL.	22	1.92	20.4	9.44	Los Angeles, CA	49	0.79	75.0	1.05
New Orleans, LA. . . .	23	1.65	10.0	16.50	Birmingham, AL.	50	0.79	10.0	7.86
Portland, OR.	24	1.65	100.0	1.65	Honolulu, HI	51	0.39	100.0	0.39
Salt Lake City, UT . . .	25	1.21	97.0	1.25	Unweighted average .	(X)	1.67	56.1	6.65
Anchorage, AK	26	1.79	96.0	1.87	Median	(X)	1.42	(X)	(X)
Memphis, TN.	27	1.42	22.4	6.34					

X Not applicable.

Source: Government of the District of Columbia, Department of Finance and Revenue, *Tax Rates and Tax Burdens in the District of Columbia: A Nationwide Comparison,* annual.

U.S. Census Bureau, Statistical Abstract of the United States: 1999

[In millions of dollars ($35,844 represents $35,844,000,000). For fiscal years; see text, this section]

State	Gross revenue (mil. dol.)	Amusement taxes [1]	Parimutuel taxes	Lottery revenue			
				Total [2] (mil. dol.)	Apportionment of funds (percent)		
					Prizes	Administration	Proceeds available from ticket sales
United States.....	35,844	1,899	424	33,521	19,300	1,877	12,344
Alabama............	4	-	4	(X)	(X)	(X)	(X)
Alaska.............	2	2	(X)	(X)	(X)	(X)	(X)
Arizona............	238	1	3	235	132	25	78
Arkansas...........	8	1	7	(X)	(X)	(X)	78
California.........	2,020	(X)	90	1,930	1,032	176	722
Colorado...........	347	-	7	340	215	30	95
Connecticut........	992	210	11	772	451	68	253
Delaware...........	224	(X)	-	224	54	4	166
Florida............	2,030	(X)	65	1,965	1,028	118	819
Georgia............	1,536	(X)	(X)	1,536	857	116	563
Hawaii.............	(X)	(X)	(X)	(X)	(X)	(X)	(X)
Idaho..............	87	(X)	-	87	53	15	18
Illinois...........	1,779	277	40	1,462	827	63	572
Indiana............	533	(X)	3	529	323	30	176
Iowa...............	280	121	3	156	97	23	36
Kansas.............	174	1	4	169	98	20	51
Kentucky...........	554	-	19	536	348	32	155
Louisiana..........	264	1	5	258	140	18	100
Maine..............	150	(X)	4	146	82	15	50
Maryland...........	1,056	9	3	1,044	552	98	394
Massachusetts......	3,020	7	10	3,002	2,237	69	696
Michigan...........	1,499	(X)	12	1,487	852	49	586
Minnesota..........	413	62	1	349	224	61	64
Mississippi........	193	193	(X)	(X)	(X)	(X)	(X)
Missouri...........	533	121	(X)	412	242	36	134
Montana............	27	(X)	-	27	14	6	6
Nebraska...........	85	8	1	77	40	17	20
Nevada.............	493	493	(X)	(X)	(X)	(X)	(X)
New Hampshire......	173	2	5	166	106	7	53
New Jersey.........	1,812	309	1	1,502	796	43	663
New Mexico.........	87	4	1	82	41	17	23
New York...........	3,686	1	42	3,644	2,026	87	1,531
North Carolina.....	(X)	(X)	(X)	(X)	(X)	(X)	(X)
North Dakota.......	11	11	(X)	(X)	(X)	(X)	(X)
Ohio...............	2,460	(X)	15	2,445	1,312	86	1,046
Oklahoma...........	17	13	4	(X)	(X)	(X)	(X)
Oregon.............	1,374	-	1	1,373	613	217	543
Pennsylvania.......	1,636	-	24	1,611	869	59	683
Rhode Island.......	482	(X)	6	476	373	5	98
South Carolina.....	27	27	(X)	(X)	(X)	(X)	(X)
South Dakota.......	119	-	1	119	15	8	95
Tennessee..........	(X)	(X)	(X)	(X)	(X)	(X)	(X)
Texas..............	3,422	24	14	3,385	2,152	59	1,174
Utah...............	(X)	(X)	(X)	(X)	(X)	(X)	(X)
Vermont............	77	(X)	-	77	46	5	26
Virginia...........	898	-	(X)	898	457	87	354
Washington.........	412	-	4	408	258	55	95
West Virginia......	194	(X)	10	184	93	20	71
Wisconsin..........	413	1	4	409	244	32	133
Wyoming............	(X)	(X)	(X)	(X)	(X)	(X)	(X)

- Represents or rounds to zero. X Not applicable. [1] Represents nonlicense taxes. [2] Excludes commissions.
Source: U.S. Census Bureau, unpublished data.

No. 529. Lottery Sales—Type of Game, 1980 to 1998 and Use of Proceeds, 1964-95

[In millions of dollars (2,393 represents $2,393,000,000). For fiscal years]

Game	1980	1990	1995	1997	1998	Use of proceeds	Cumulative [1] 1965-95	Government proceeds 1997
Total ticket sales	2,393	20,017	31,931	35,486	35,588	Total [2]...........	92,922	11,959
Passive [3]................	206	(NA)	(NA)	(NA)	(NA)	Education	52,061	6,204
Instant [4]................	527	5,204	11,511	14,217	13,882	General fund	21,133	2,946
Three-digit [5]............	1,554	4,572	5,737	5,639	5,643	Cities	9,013	1,580
Four-digit [5].............	55	1,302	1,941	2,111	2,232	Senior citizen programs .	8,708	701
Lotto [6]..................	52	8,563	10,594	9,996	9,854	Taxes	(NA)	32
Other [7]..................	(NA)	409	2,148	3,523	3,978	Economic development .	1,385	349
						Infrastructure	(NA)	81
State proceeds (net income) [8]..	978	7,703	11,100	11,959	12,102	Environment...........	485	31

NA Not available. [1] Cumulative profits track lottery revenue to government from March 12, 1964 - June 30, 1995. [2] Includes other not shown separately. [3] Also known as draw game or ticket. Player must match his ticket to winning numbers drawn by lottery. Players cannot choose their numbers. [4] Player scratches a latex section on ticket which reveals instantly whether ticket is a winner. [5] Players choose and bet on three or four digits, depending on game, with various payoffs for different straight order or mixed combination bets. [6] Players typically select six digits out of a large field of numbers. Varying prizes are offered for matching three through six numbers drawn by lottery. [7] Includes breakopen tickets, spiel, keno, video lottery, etc. [8] Sales minus prizes and expenses equal net government income.
Source: TLF Publications, Inc., Boyds, MD, 1999 World Lottery Almanac annual; LaFleur's Fiscal 1998 Lottery Special Report; and LaFleur's Lottery World Government Profits Report (copyright).

State and Local Government Finances and Employment   333

No. 530. City Governments—Revenue for Largest Cities: 1996

[In millions of dollars (49,292 represents $49,292,000,000). For fiscal years ending in year shown; see text, this section. Cities ranked by size of population estimated as of July 1, 1996 except Honolulu ranked by county population. Data reflect inclusion of fiscal activity of dependent school systems where applicable]

Cities ranked by 1996 population	Total revenue	General revenue Total	Intergov. Total	Intergov. From Federal Govt	Intergov. From state/local govt	Intergov. From local govt	Own sources Total	Taxes Total	Taxes Property	Sales & gross receipts Total	Sales General sales	Sales Public utilities	Current charges Total	Current charges Parks and recreation	Current charges Sewerage[1]	Misc. Total	Misc. Interest earnings	Utility revenue[2]	Employee retirement revenue
New York City, NY [3]	49,292	41,024	16,419	1,895	14,414	110	24,605	18,182	7,179	3,863	2,742	366	4,769	29	828	1,655	630	2,374	5,893
Los Angeles, CA	8,483	4,437	960	501	374	84	3,477	1,822	607	803	277	450	1,220	44	427	435	294	2,342	1,704
Chicago, IL	5,036	4,057	1,146	349	797	-	2,911	1,723	653	883	154	385	724	17	119	464	286	268	711
Houston, TX	2,327	1,644	121	88	30	3	1,523	864	447	388	248	109	485	15	262	174	97	255	428
Philadelphia, PA [3]	4,513	3,495	1,249	366	717	166	2,246	1,686	351	132	82	-	419	36	194	141	105	694	323
San Diego, CA	1,716	1,353	330	170	99	60	1,023	417	130	234	135	30	264	21	194	341	164	179	184
Phoenix, AZ	1,528	1,282	411	98	279	33	871	440	122	288	194	56	287	30	104	144	73	151	95
Dallas, TX	1,628	1,300	88	63	22	3	1,212	555	285	258	151	83	476	22	178	181	71	143	185
San Antonio, TX	1,748	724	115	35	69	11	609	295	144	140	96	13	221	15	141	94	64	962	62
Detroit, MI	2,868	1,805	807	214	561	32	998	632	228	53	-	53	251	17	185	115	47	181	882
Honolulu, HI [3]	1,120	988	142	74	67	1	846	528	417	65	-	19	217	17	180	101	54	132	-
San Jose, CA	1,115	876	121	22	59	40	755	401	121	179	100	67	251	14	146	102	47	12	227
Indianapolis, IN [3]	1,106	1,067	279	72	206	2	788	447	353	25	-	-	266	17	63	75	61	7	32
San Francisco, CA [3]	4,542	3,302	1,285	213	1,070	1	2,017	981	459	271	103	61	682	32	132	354	196	273	967
Jacksonville, FL [3]	1,752	872	141	69	72	-	731	356	219	125	49	68	181	4	100	194	180	770	111
Baltimore, MD [3]	2,395	1,946	1,045	70	919	55	901	674	463	46	-	26	99	7	59	129	67	66	382
Columbus, OH	888	770	124	42	76	6	646	383	26	8	-	-	191	7	121	71	34	118	-
Milwaukee, WI	1,042	690	367	71	296	-	323	163	153	10	-	-	103	3	40	57	38	56	296
Memphis, TN	2,157	1,108	724	20	388	316	385	221	176	45	34	12	114	38	57	50	30	947	102
El Paso, TX	441	343	48	31	13	4	295	167	87	58	34	13	84	4	50	44	29	50	48
Washington, DC [3]	5,101	4,661	1,662	1,609	50	3	2,998	2,481	702	794	468	190	265	25	69	252	57	53	388
Boston, MA [3]	2,296	2,022	906	50	855	1	1,115	771	719	30	-	-	244	30	96	100	36	86	188
Seattle, WA	1,358	895	134	30	95	9	762	434	143	187	93	72	256	14	191	72	26	401	61
Austin, TX	1,444	728	68	30	37	1	661	240	119	106	80	12	347	3	110	74	54	637	78
Nashville-Davidson, TN [3]	1,987	1,236	259	2	256	1	977	628	351	199	164	9	209	32	92	140	119	695	56
Denver, CO [3]	1,612	1,446	343	29	314	-	1,103	489	131	306	270	13	484	6	64	130	97	97	69
Cleveland, OH	898	656	169	84	85	1	486	319	136	60	-	-	101	7	17	66	45	242	-
New Orleans, LA.	822	719	147	83	63	1	573	322	73	249	185	28	156	11	63	95	20	56	47
Oklahoma City, OK	547	490	47	23	23	1	443	278	51	227	208	19	131	7	63	34	20	50	8
Fort Worth, TX	604	465	76	23	53	-	389	222	131	88	88	-	95	9	76	71	56	81	58
Portland, OR	656	598	102	38	35	29	496	284	127	22	-	-	111	12	75	102	58	57	1
Kansas City, MO	840	689	80	33	39	8	609	393	30	135	88	31	116	-	35	100	56	60	90
Charlotte, NC	639	588	180	49	121	10	408	178	116	54	31	10	142	10	65	88	58	34	17
Tucson, AZ	576	446	181	61	120	-	265	174	30	135	116	19	54	3	11	38	20	95	35
Long Beach, CA	1,017	850	131	17	114	-	718	190	124	66	41	12	450	9	99	78	27	164	3
Virginia Beach, VA [3]	857	816	299	28	271	-	517	418	284	134	31	33	62	9	37	37	37	41	-
Albuquerque, NM	639	584	201	59	142	-	383	172	56	106	88	11	138	9	72	73	53	55	-
Atlanta, GA	968	751	114	35	73	6	637	241	124	117	81	27	289	19	94	106	66	86	131

- Represents or rounds to zero. [1] Includes solid waste management. [2] Includes water, electric, and transit. [3] Represents, in effect, city-county consolidated government.

Source: U.S. Census Bureau, unpublished data.

U.S. Census Bureau, Statistical Abstract of the United States: 1999

No. 531. City Governments—Expenditures and Debt for Largest Cities: 1996

[In millions of dollars (48,018 represents $48,018,000,000). For fiscal year ending in year shown; see text, this section. Regarding intercity comparisons, see text, this section]

Cities ranked by 1996 population	Total expenditure	Total direct expenditure	General expenditure Total	Education	Housing and community development	Public welfare	Health and hospitals	Police protection	Fire protection	Correction	Highways	Parks and recreation	Sewerage	Solid waste management	Governmental administration	General public buildings	Interest on general debt	Utility expenditure	Employee retirement expenditure	Debt outstanding
New York City, NY [1]	48,018	45,184	38,753	8,813	2,487	7,510	4,301	2,519	838	1,071	1,223	373	1,222	712	895	289	1,853	4,569	4,697	44,149
Los Angeles, CA	7,572	7,511	4,655	15	362	-	30	806	297	3	170	210	379	144	268	106	344	2,120	797	9,181
Chicago, IL	4,768	4,693	3,890	1	170	132	129	821	270	14	405	43	101	163	114	40	452	285	594	7,448
Houston, TX [1]	2,261	2,238	1,777	-	45	-	79	356	171	-	154	97	297	53	84	-	181	387	96	4,407
Philadelphia, PA [1]	4,310	4,221	3,244	16	140	294	418	358	130	221	105	90	169	71	271	134	76	709	357	3,515
San Diego, CA	1,791	1,787	1,460	-	131	-	2	186	77	5	80	149	408	71	65	17	160	266	65	1,985
Phoenix, AZ	1,479	1,472	1,221	11	73	-	-	193	120	-	74	113	100	51	87	21	141	224	34	2,854
Dallas, TX	1,447	1,416	1,197	-	18	-	18	177	103	5	72	85	100	29	86	28	203	135	116	3,776
San Antonio, TX	1,648	1,645	796	15	15	32	34	136	81	1	67	70	83	42	36	5	53	827	24	3,928
Detroit, MI	2,329	2,239	1,653	5	81	-	98	287	96	-	130	103	198	107	137	10	94	332	345	2,195
Honolulu, HI [1]	1,253	1,253	1,022	-	101	-	11	118	50	-	31	77	121	99	82	20	120	232	-	1,588
San Jose, CA [1]	873	855	790	-	88	-	3	132	67	-	47	64	121	58	38	5	78	21	63	1,504
Indianapolis, IN [1]	1,417	1,406	1,346	1	115	90	241	101	46	32	57	71	64	36	99	4	78	28	43	2,255
San Francisco, CA [1]	3,813	3,710	2,959	71	77	354	685	235	139	66	43	173	189	36	186	78	118	563	290	4,270
Jacksonville, FL [1]	1,859	1,831	1,075	-	61	10	47	104	68	39	37	180	47	64	57	13	210	726	58	4,821
Baltimore, MD [1]	1,999	1,991	1,802	673	102	1	75	202	90	-	84	82	100	42	100	19	202	132	127	1,296
Columbus, OH	851	840	720	-	23	-	29	136	96	7	55	53	89	43	44	16	81	132	-	1,361
Milwaukee, WI	834	798	705	-	78	-	18	147	67	-	44	7	64	52	44	17	63	-	98	532
Memphis, TN	2,097	2,079	1,110	575	22	2	7	109	73	-	36	75	40	37	17	7	30	895	93	818
El Paso, TX [1]	461	458	344	-	9	-	24	69	29	-	22	25	49	17	24	2	23	91	26	568
Washington, DC [1]	4,955	4,771	4,368	669	101	1,172	432	248	89	292	89	60	110	29	256	53	29	91	496	3,824
Boston, MA [1]	2,129	1,890	1,890	-	64	100	266	192	96	70	66	22	99	32	56	14	313	32	207	1,151
Seattle, WA	1,511	1,402	975	-	52	-	20	115	75	12	111	192	96	75	71	4	47	471	65	1,701
Austin, TX	1,434	1,423	691	-	9	7	74	74	48	-	41	52	47	21	32	4	19	716	26	3,302
Nashville-Davidson, TN [1]	1,977	1,977	1,144	423	31	12	119	89	62	31	34	27	68	24	81	-	94	754	79	2,835
Denver, CO [1]	1,867	1,804	1,716	-	61	176	211	107	59	42	44	88	55	22	87	19	106	119	33	5,054
Cleveland, OH	947	944	644	-	88	3	26	149	72	-	52	45	9	30	43	2	60	303	-	1,322
Oklahoma City, OK	763	763	652	-	13	-	25	63	33	5	21	18	54	20	67	16	38	75	36	968
Fort Worth, TX	511	511	438	-	82	-	-	82	71	41	36	50	42	20	21	-	55	66	7	702
Portland, OR	495	494	374	-	13	-	8	69	37	-	32	25	50	17	43	3	59	83	38	806
Kansas City, MO	719	715	624	-	36	-	-	82	63	-	66	49	136	13	61	23	58	53	42	1,155
Charlotte, NC	831	806	720	-	49	-	50	104	50	4	30	56	40	18	13	7	38	66	45	1,005
Tucson, AZ	587	579	423	-	12	1	3	104	35	-	42	10	24	22	1	1	30	156	8	1,353
Long Beach, CA [1]	1,086	1,086	412	-	31	5	1	62	51	-	63	47	-	69	44	6	81	133	13	730
Virginia Beach, VA [1]	856	855	910	407	86	-	42	154	51	18	74	44	4	51	51	21	44	174	2	1,849
Albuquerque, NM	737	737	658	-	25	16	21	63	21	24	24	42	19	60	26	4	56	85	-	812
Atlanta, GA	1,114	1,094	866	-	12	1	8	99	54	19	56	64	72	32	55	39	80	144	103	1,379

- Represents or rounds to zero.   [1] Represents, in effect, city-county consolidated government.

Source: U.S. Census Bureau, unpublished data.

State and Local Government Finances and Employment   335

No. 532. County Governments—Revenue for Largest Counties: 1996

[In millions of dollars (13,988 represents $13,988,000,000). For fiscal years ending in year shown; see text, this section. Counties ranked by size of population estimated as of July 1, 1998. Data relate only to county governments and their dependent agencies and do not include amounts for other local governments in the same geographic location such as separate school districts; excluded are areas having certain type of county characteristics but included as part of another government. See tables 530-531, for details see text, this section and source]

Counties ranked by 1996 population	Total revenue	General revenue — Total	Intergov. — Total	Federal — Total	Federal — Housing and urban	State — Total	State — Public welfare	State — Health and hospitals	From local gov't	Own sources — Total	Taxes — Total	Taxes — Property	Sales & gross receipts — Total	Sales & gross receipts — General sales	Current charges — Total	Current charges — Parks and recreation	Current charges — Sewerage [1]	Current charges — Hospitals	Misc. general revenue — Total	Misc. general revenue — Interest on debt
Los Angeles, CA	13,988	11,391	8,100	235	193	7,602	4,392	1,114	263	3,291	1,696	1,532	98	43	903	78	39	448	691	233
Cook, IL	2,267	1,938	376	22	20	352	126	55	2	1,563	1,130	735	382	231	349	33	-	187	84	57
Harris, TX	1,505	1,505	327	22	-	241	-	201	63	1,179	712	655	16	12	195	2	64	65	272	238
San Diego, CA	2,831	2,388	1,701	70	54	1,544	894	12	87	688	405	358	-	-	155	2	6	-	128	33
Maricopa, AZ	1,408	1,408	770	43	14	707	345	173	20	638	300	288	10	8	237	13	79	154	101	72
Orange, CA	2,459	2,132	1,167	24	18	1,079	444	284	64	966	245	216	10	8	261	18	54	-	460	214
Wayne, MI	1,392	1,315	677	112	7	503	83	-	62	638	235	230	-	-	256	-	-	-	146	34
Dade, FL	4,068	3,858	745	352	136	389	31	59	5	3,113	1,127	775	288	73	1,545	-	402	570	441	258
Dallas, TX	911	886	170	2	-	146	-	109	22	716	360	324	3	-	294	15	-	228	62	48
King, WA	1,474	1,416	312	44	2	201	59	69	68	1,104	704	344	264	230	315	15	229	78	85	70
Santa Clara, CA	1,640	1,640	1,078	38	12	996	588	110	44	562	336	311	4	3	135	7	10	38	91	47
San Bernardino, CA	1,848	1,713	1,236	72	15	1,105	723	6	59	477	170	146	16	12	155	10	47	-	152	71
Broward, FL	1,173	1,138	145	25	5	119	-	-	3	993	493	407	61	-	342	-	131	13	159	120
Middlesex, MA	143	61	29	-	-	27	-	-	2	32	11	-	-	-	19	-	-	-	2	-
Riverside, CA	1,496	1,496	964	19	10	878	489	100	68	532	236	199	20	16	137	11	42	197	159	87
Cuyahoga, OH	1,144	1,144	457	9	7	444	221	125	5	686	372	206	135	127	219	-	4	36	95	79
Alameda, CA	1,505	1,418	921	18	6	869	564	150	33	497	281	175	95	88	119	12	-	-	97	34
Suffolk, NY	1,793	1,703	496	8	5	451	221	43	37	1,207	1,011	402	595	593	115	3	10	128	82	50
Bexar, TX	609	609	123	4	15	108	64	26	11	486	227	207	6	-	145	4	-	130	114	106
Nassau, NY	1,645	1,645	381	21	10	360	181	63	1	1,264	949	476	470	463	236	6	-	53	79	34
Tarrant, TX	554	554	166	10	25	145	52	51	11	389	241	219	7	5	78	-	10	19	70	62
Allegheny, PA	1,103	1,033	515	31	6	483	137	103	1	518	286	275	9	-	185	11	145	-	47	30
Oakland, MI	725	665	396	7	14	261	17	-	128	269	168	163	9	-	55	-	46	-	46	32
Sacramento, CA	1,793	1,634	864	17	3	824	502	56	23	770	331	180	118	95	282	14	56	186	158	88
Hennepin, MN	1,122	1,122	431	27	11	391	242	-	14	691	351	348	9	-	264	23	-	247	76	48
Clark, NV	1,696	1,532	316	28	4	236	-	94	52	1,216	545	192	231	222	521	5	143	-	150	108
Franklin, OH	614	612	284	4	-	255	82	-	24	329	245	167	67	60	32	3	4	-	52	42
St Louis, MO	492	463	56	12	12	41	-	3	3	407	336	70	260	222	27	1	-	189	44	31
Palm Beach, FL	1,003	977	114	6	-	88	3	27	10	863	418	300	102	-	277	23	-	202	168	86
Erie, NY	1,255	1,216	322	26	11	306	219	114	7	894	537	220	308	303	284	3	184	-	73	40
Milwaukee, WI	1,113	952	429	44	29	377	132	14	8	523	193	148	44	-	300	19	-	220	30	10
Fairfax, VA	2,570	2,128	371	55	14	308	27	-	18	1,757	1,389	1,112	176	102	271	-	43	-	97	83
Hillsborough, FL	1,264	1,189	223	43	-	179	62	62	8	966	380	288	81	54	438	3	16	-	147	81
Westchester, NY	1,645	1,640	416	13	-	385	239	60	1	1,223	666	436	228	221	502	-	17	351	55	40
Contra Costa, CA	1,053	1,000	428	19	5	401	204	73	5	572	197	168	15	10	305	1	86	154	70	40
Pinellas, FL	641	599	73	12	5	60	60	-	5	526	298	219	72	46	144	-	-	-	84	58

- Represents or rounds to zero.   [1] Includes solid waste management.

Source: U.S. Census Bureau, unpublished data.

U.S. Census Bureau, Statistical Abstract of the United States: 1999

No. 533. County Governments—Expenditures and Debt for Largest Counties: 1996

[In millions of dollars (12,421 represents $12,421,000,000). For fiscal year ending in year shown; see text, this section. See headnote, Table 532]

Counties ranked by 1996 population	Total expenditure	Total direct expenditure	General expenditure: Total	Education	Housing and community development	Public welfare	Health	Hospitals	Police protection	Correction	Highways	Parks and recreation	Natural resouces	Sewerage and solid waste management	Governmental administration	General public buildings	Interest on general debt	Utility expenditure	Employee retirement expenditure	Debt outstanding
Los Angeles, CA	12,421	11,862	11,545	370	220	4,087	780	1,568	1,072	612	185	202	171	43	1,099	91	343	38	837	5,452
Cook, IL	2,061	2,040	1,926	2	20	11	58	639	62	254	86	90	-	-	403	55	97	-	135	1,611
Harris, TX	1,569	1,569	1,569	-	13	19	97	378	116	215	128	26	45	-	198	23	268	-	-	4,915
San Diego, CA	2,331	2,316	2,223	83	50	879	269	-	99	155	31	12	7	79	376	4	64	10	99	650
Maricopa, AZ	1,434	1,231	1,434	18	14	518	49	191	54	58	81	85	36	15	179	-	72	-	-	1,152
Orange, CA	2,079	2,035	1,982	68	21	551	173	-	104	127	66	57	52	43	328	24	259	-	97	3,599
Wayne, MI	1,310	1,250	1,239	-	-	94	263	697	21	103	92	6	110	100	131	8	63	-	71	1,007
Dade, FL	4,390	4,387	3,961	-	209	51	24	396	311	202	77	100	19	469	228	2	320	429	-	5,713
Dallas, TX	912	908	907	-	5	13	94	40	23	170	12	-	-	-	108	19	44	-	5	763
King, WA	1,558	1,534	1,253	1	13	-	194	222	65	61	89	74	30	256	184	20	128	5	-	1,984
Santa Clara, CA	1,760	1,696	1,760	93	5	507	158	323	37	182	55	21	2	16	247	41	52	-	-	816
San Bernardino, CA	1,917	1,860	1,839	74	1	673	103	-	107	82	4	14	38	77	148	5	57	305	72	1,419
Broward, FL	1,127	1,090	1,021	-	15	21	74	-	125	89	42	39	11	126	104	18	138	-	-	2,103
Middlesex, MA	1,482	1,397	1,481	80	25	454	99	99	99	103	56	7	87	18	156	16	98	6	-	1,307
Riverside, CA	109	109	64	-	-	-	-	14	-	37	-	-	-	-	5	3	-	106	45	5
Cuyahoga, OH	1,096	1,084	1,096	18	10	216	191	319	15	61	28	214	78	11	128	2	80	-	-	1,344
Alameda, CA	1,770	1,687	1,694	216	9	486	183	194	31	66	37	22	3	-	177	28	65	-	76	697
Suffolk, NY	1,777	1,550	1,645	-	5	360	117	-	314	58	25	1	5	45	92	5	69	-	-	1,437
Bexar, TX	613	571	612	200	1	44	34	256	16	103	12	32	2	-	58	101	106	132	1	1,200
Nassau, NY	1,967	1,768	1,965	-	8	303	89	210	318	67	49	4	-	105	71	3	96	-	-	2,696
Tarrant, TX	512	512	512	27	31	12	67	172	13	56	15	24	-	-	68	25	55	2	2	927
Allegheny, PA	1,034	984	997	-	6	131	180	95	23	52	35	9	56	85	93	-	96	-	-	1,467
Oakland, MI	643	631	616	44	95	2	132	7	28	92	84	21	19	189	81	1	20	-	-	336
Sacramento, CA	1,748	1,720	1,672	-	5	580	106	-	60	67	95	112	4	53	169	22	113	16	37	2,208
Hennepin, MN	1,059	1,055	1,059	-	11	165	184	273	39	70	45	13	38	27	97	43	23	8	11	685
Clark, NV	1,600	1,587	1,438	-	5	44	21	264	159	36	194	43	-	-	108	11	142	-	69	2,761
Franklin, OH	620	602	619	-	12	145	200	-	16	50	51	11	-	3	71	13	45	162	-	566
St Louis, MO	496	337	487	-	-	-	32	-	44	61	66	43	-	93	39	19	24	1	-	324
Palm Beach, FL	928	900	879	-	3	22	25	-	107	80	37	97	26	25	154	13	58	-	10	685
Erie, NY	1,243	1,060	1,217	67	5	476	46	179	26	43	20	35	-	182	35	2	56	49	-	1,672
Milwaukee, WI	1,060	996	898	-	47	210	30	256	15	28	31	40	10	36	78	23	29	26	-	717
Fairfax, VA	2,351	2,320	2,102	1,039	17	113	29	-	94	55	64	33	35	113	55	-	123	101	61	572
Hillsborough, FL	1,317	1,307	1,227	-	-	57	29	286	108	99	44	1	1	19	98	30	107	135	114	2,406
Westchester, NY	1,754	1,554	1,725	60	5	443	76	353	16	65	40	20	17	113	59	1	82	90	-	2,231
Contra Costa, CA	1,135	1,135	1,068	38	7	243	119	193	40	39	40	-	13	19	110	-	39	28	67	735
Pinellas, FL	624	594	587	-	-	10	50	-	61	-	63	-	-	58	105	-	44	37	-	802

- Represents or rounds to zero.

Source: U.S. Census Bureau, unpublished data.

U.S. Census Bureau, Statistical Abstract of the United States: 1999

[Employees in thousands (16,213 represents 16,213,000), payroll in millions of dollars (19,935 represents $19,935,000,000). For 1980 to 1995 as of October; 1997 as of March, 1996 data are not available. Covers full-time and part-time employees. Local government data are estimates subject to sampling variation; see Appendix III and source]

Type of government	1980	1985	1989	1990	1991	1992	1993	1994	1995	1997
EMPLOYEES (1,000)										
Total	16,213	16,690	17,879	18,369	18,554	18,745	18,823	19,420	19,521	19,540
Federal (civilian)[1]	2,898	3,021	3,114	3,105	3,103	3,047	2,999	2,952	2,895	2,807
State and local	13,315	13,669	14,765	15,263	15,452	15,698	15,824	16,468	16,626	16,733
Percent of total	82	82	83	83	83	84	84	85	85	86
State	3,753	3,984	4,365	4,503	4,521	4,595	4,673	4,694	4,719	4,733
Local	9,562	9,685	10,400	10,760	10,930	11,103	11,151	11,775	11,906	12,000
Counties	1,853	1,891	2,085	2,167	2,196	2,253	2,270	(NA)	(NA)	(NA)
Municipalities	2,561	2,467	2,569	2,642	2,662	2,665	2,644	(NA)	(NA)	(NA)
School districts	4,270	4,416	4,774	4,950	5,045	5,134	(NA)	(NA)	(NA)	(NA)
Townships	394	392	405	418	415	424	(NA)	(NA)	(NA)	(NA)
Special districts	484	519	568	585	612	627	(NA)	(NA)	(NA)	(NA)
OCTOBER PAYROLLS (mil. dol.)										
Total	19,935	28,945	36,763	39,228	41,237	43,120	(NA)	(NA)	(NA)	49,156
Federal (civilian)[1]	5,205	7,580	8,636	8,999	9,687	9,937	(NA)	(NA)	(NA)	9,744
State and local	14,730	21,365	28,127	30,229	31,551	33,183	34,540	36,545	37,714	39,412
Percent of total	74	74	77	77	77	77	(NA)	(NA)	(NA)	80
State	4,285	6,329	8,443	9,083	9,437	9,828	10,288	10,666	10,927	11,413
Local	10,445	15,036	19,684	21,146	22,113	23,355	24,252	25,878	26,787	27,999
Counties	1,936	2,819	3,855	4,192	4,404	4,698	4,839	(NA)	(NA)	(NA)
Municipalities	2,951	4,191	5,274	5,564	5,784	6,207	6,328	(NA)	(NA)	(NA)
School districts	4,683	6,746	8,852	9,551	9,975	10,394	(NA)	(NA)	(NA)	(NA)
Townships	330	446	599	642	664	685	(NA)	(NA)	(NA)	(NA)
Special districts	546	834	1,104	1,197	1,287	1,370	(NA)	(NA)	(NA)	(NA)

NA Not available.   [1] Includes employees outside the United States.

Source: U.S. Census Bureau, *Historical Statistics on Governmental Finances and Employment,* and *Public Employment,* series GE, No. 1, annual; <http://www.census.gov/govs/www/apes.html> (accessed 12 July 1999).

No. 535. All Governments—Employment and Payroll, by Function: 1997

[Employees in thousands (19,540 represents 19,540,000), payroll in millions of dollars ($49,406 represent $49,406,000,000). As of March. Covers full-time and part-time employees. Local government data are estimates subject to sampling variation; see Appendix III and source]

Function	Employees (1,000)					October payrolls (mil. dol.)				
	Total	Federal (civilian)[1]	State and local Total	State	Local	Total	Federal (civilian)[1]	State and local Total	State	Local
Total	19,540	2,807	16,733	4,733	12,000	49,406	9,994	39,412	11,413	27,999
National defense[2]	777	777	(X)	(X)	(X)	2,689	2,689	(X)	(X)	(X)
Postal Service	854	854	(X)	(X)	(X)	2,768	2,768	(X)	(X)	(X)
Space research and technology	20	20	(X)	(X)	(X)	105	105	(X)	(X)	(X)
Elem. and secondary educ.	6,408	(X)	6,408	50	6,358	14,713	(X)	14,713	119	14,594
Higher education	2,451	(X)	2,451	1,965	486	4,800	(X)	4,800	3,994	806
Other education	111	11	350	99	251	662	45	617	259	358
Health	548	136	412	170	243	1,508	493	1,015	461	554
Hospitals	1,223	163	1,060	495	565	3,085	481	2,603	1,239	1,364
Public welfare	507	9	498	225	273	1,212	40	1,172	561	612
Social insurance administration	165	69	96	96	(X)	522	263	259	259	(X)
Police protection	951	95	856	94	762	3,064	419	2,645	307	2,338
Fire protection	356	(X)	356	(X)	356	990	(X)	990	(X)	990
Correction	708	30	679	458	220	1,776	(NA)	1,776	1,183	592
Streets & highways	552	4	548	252	297	1,396	(NA)	1,396	677	719
Air transportation	86	48	38	3	35	385	273	111	9	103
Water transport/Terminals	28	15	13	5	8	81	41	40	14	26
Solid waste management	115	(X)	115	1	113	272	(X)	272	6	266
Sewerage	129	(X)	129	1	128	353	(X)	353	4	349
Parks & recreation	354	24	330	40	291	572	78	495	75	420
Natural resources	397	191	206	165	40	1,227	732	496	409	86
Housing & community dev.	141	18	123	-	123	368	76	292	-	292
Water supply	164	-	164	1	163	436	-	436	3	433
Electric power	80	-	80	6	74	302	-	302	28	274
Gas supply	10	-	10	-	10	26	-	26	-	26
Transit	197	(X)	197	19	178	676	(X)	676	79	597
Libraries	160	4	156	1	155	252	19	234	1	232
State liquor stores	9	(X)	9	9	(X)	16	(X)	16	16	(X)
Financial administration	533	139	394	172	221	1,446	479	968	464	504
Other government administration	406	22	384	60	323	779	85	694	157	537
Judicial and legal	419	53	366	139	228	1,305	235	1,071	467	604
Other & unallocable	680	124	555	206	349	1,853	550	1,303	622	681

- Represents or rounds to zero.   NA Not available.   X Not applicable.   [1] Includes employees outside the United States. [2] Includes international relations.

Source: U.S. Census Bureau; <http://www.census.gov/pub/govs/www/apes.html> (accessed 12 July 1999).

No. 536. State and Local Government—Employer Costs Per Hour Worked: 1998

[In dollars. As of March. Based on a sample; see source for details. For additional data, see Table 707]

Item	Total compensation	Wages and salaries	Benefits Total	Paid leave	Supplemental pay	Insurance	Retirement and savings	Legally required benefits	Other [1]
Total workers	**27.28**	**19.19**	**8.10**	**2.11**	**0.23**	**2.15**	**1.94**	**1.63**	**0.04**
Occupational group:									
White-collar occupations	30.34	21.89	8.45	2.19	0.14	2.27	2.07	1.74	0.04
Professional specialty and technical	35.76	26.54	9.22	2.15	0.16	2.41	2.45	2.00	0.06
Teachers	39.88	30.13	9.75	2.01	0.07	2.62	2.84	2.14	0.08
Executive, admin., & managerial	34.50	24.01	10.49	3.47	0.17	2.33	2.47	2.03	(Z)
Admin. support including clerical	17.48	11.60	5.88	1.59	0.09	1.98	1.10	1.10	0.02
Blue-collar occupations	22.08	14.38	7.70	2.09	0.39	2.06	1.58	1.56	0.03
Service occupations	20.10	12.97	7.13	1.85	0.45	1.79	1.73	1.27	0.03
Industry group:									
Services	28.62	20.80	7.82	1.91	0.15	2.17	1.90	1.64	0.05
Health services	22.20	14.95	7.25	2.26	0.57	1.72	1.10	1.57	0.03
Hospitals	22.81	15.43	7.38	2.35	0.55	1.70	1.14	1.61	0.03
Educational services	29.97	22.03	7.93	1.84	0.09	2.23	2.06	1.67	0.05
Elementary and secondary education	29.57	21.88	7.68	1.67	0.06	2.34	1.94	1.61	0.06
Higher education	31.53	22.86	8.66	2.31	0.17	1.94	2.39	1.85	(Z)
Public administration	24.73	16.24	8.49	2.46	0.34	2.05	2.10	1.52	0.03

Z Cost per hour worked is less than 1 cent.   [1] Includes severance pay and supplemental unemployment benefits.

Source: U.S. Bureau of Labor Statistics, *News, Employer Costs for Employee Compensation-March 1998*, USDL 98-285.

No. 537. State and Local Government—Full-Time Employment and Salary, by Sex and Race/Ethnic Group: 1973 to 1997

[As of June 30. (3,809 represents 3,809,000). Excludes school systems and educational institutions. Based on reports from state governments (44 in 1973; 48 in 1975, 1976, and 1979; 47 in 1977 and 1983; 45 in 1978; 42 in 1980; 49 in 1981 and 1984 through 1987; and 50 in 1989 through 1991) and a sample of county, municipal, township, and special district jurisdictions employing 15 or more nonelected, nonappointed full-time employees. Data for 1993 only for state and local governments with 100 or more employees. Data for 1974, 1982, 1988, 1992, and 1994 not available. For definition of median, see Guide to Tabular Presentation]

Year and occupation	Employment (1,000)				Minority			Median annual salary ($1,000)			Minority		
	Total	Male	Female	White [1]	Total [2]	Black [1]	Hispanic [3]	Male	Female	White [1]	Total [2]	Black [1]	Hispanic [3]
1973	3,809	2,486	1,322	3,115	693	523	125	9.6	7.0	8.8	7.5	7.4	7.4
1975	3,899	2,436	1,464	3,102	797	602	147	11.3	8.2	10.2	8.8	8.6	8.9
1976	4,369	2,724	1,645	3,490	880	664	165	11.8	8.6	10.7	9.2	9.1	9.4
1977	4,415	2,737	1,678	3,480	935	705	175	12.4	9.1	11.3	9.7	9.5	9.9
1978	4,447	2,711	1,736	3,481	966	723	181	13.3	9.7	12.0	10.4	10.1	10.7
1979	4,576	2,761	1,816	3,568	1,008	751	192	14.1	10.4	12.8	10.9	10.6	11.4
1980	3,987	2,350	1,637	3,146	842	619	163	15.2	11.4	13.8	11.8	11.5	12.3
1981	4,665	2,740	1,925	3,591	1,074	780	205	17.7	13.1	16.1	13.5	13.3	14.7
1983	4,492	2,674	1,818	3,423	1,069	768	219	20.1	15.3	18.5	15.9	15.6	17.3
1984	4,580	2,700	1,880	3,458	1,121	799	233	21.4	16.2	19.6	17.4	16.5	18.4
1985	4,742	2,789	1,952	3,563	1,179	835	248	22.3	17.3	20.6	18.4	17.5	19.2
1986	4,779	2,797	1,982	3,549	1,230	865	259	23.4	18.1	21.5	19.6	18.7	20.2
1987	4,849	2,818	2,031	3,600	1,249	872	268	24.2	18.9	22.4	20.9	19.3	21.1
1989	5,257	3,030	2,227	3,863	1,394	961	308	26.1	20.6	24.1	22.1	20.7	22.7
1990	5,374	3,071	2,302	3,918	1,456	994	327	27.3	21.8	25.2	23.3	22.0	23.8
1991	5,459	3,110	2,349	3,965	1,494	1,011	340	28.4	22.7	26.4	23.8	22.7	24.5
1993	5,024	2,820	2,204	3,588	1,436	948	341	30.6	24.3	28.5	25.9	24.2	26.8
1995, total	5,315	2,960	2,355	3,781	1,534	993	379	33.5	27.0	31.4	26.3	26.8	28.6
Officials/administrators	299	201	98	250	48	31	12	52.7	45.2	50.6	44.9	47.7	49.0
Professionals	1,313	624	689	999	314	183	68	41.4	36.1	38.9	35.8	35.0	36.3
Technicians	481	280	202	359	122	71	34	33.3	27.4	31.1	29.6	27.8	29.2
Protective service	931	788	142	687	244	160	69	34.1	28.9	33.7	32.3	30.5	35.5
Paraprofessionals	380	105	275	231	149	114	26	23.8	21.9	23.1	22.3	21.0	22.2
Admin. support	926	123	803	627	299	187	82	24.6	22.9	23.0	23.1	23.0	23.0
Skilled craft	408	389	19	306	102	62	30	31.1	25.6	30.8	30.7	30.3	31.1
Service/maintenance	578	450	128	321	258	186	59	25.0	19.9	24.1	25.6	22.9	24.5
1997, total	5,205	2,898	2,307	3,676	1,529	973	392	34.6	27.9	32.2	30.2	27.4	29.5
Officials/administrators	296	197	99	247	49	31	12	54.8	47.2	52.5	50.7	49.7	50.7
Professionals	1,291	605	686	974	317	183	71	42.3	36.6	39.1	37.3	35.5	37.0
Technicians	456	265	191	338	118	68	33	34.4	27.8	31.7	29.7	28.4	28.7
Protective service	969	813	156	704	265	171	77	35.0	29.2	34.6	32.2	30.5	36.5
Paraprofessionals	369	100	269	221	148	111	27	25.1	22.6	24.1	22.8	21.1	23.0
Admin. support	882	117	765	590	292	179	83	25.3	23.5	23.7	23.6	23.4	23.5
Skilled craft	406	385	21	302	104	62	31	31.9	26.4	31.5	31.2	31.0	32.2
Service/maintenance	536	416	120	299	237	168	56	25.7	19.9	24.9	23.9	22.8	24.4

[1] Non-Hispanic.   [2] Includes other minority groups not shown separately.   [3] Persons of Hispanic origin may be of any race.

Source: U.S. Equal Employment Opportunity Commission, *State and Local Government Information Report*, biennially.

State and Local Government Finances and Employment   339

No. 538. State and Local Government Full-Time Equivalent Employment, by Selected Function and State: 1997

[In thousands (1,484.1 represents 1,484,100) for March. Local government amounts are estimates subject to sampling variation; see Appendix III and source]

State	Education Total		Elem. & secondary		Higher education		Public welfare		Health		Hospitals	
	Total	Local	State	Local	State	Local	State	Local	State	Local	State	Local
United States.....	**1,484.1**	**5,766.4**	**40.7**	**5,480.2**	**1,352.2**	**286.2**	**220.9**	**254.1**	**162.6**	**214.8**	**468.7**	**515.7**
Alabama	34.8	92.0	-	92.0	31.4	-	4.0	1.2	7.0	4.4	11.7	22.9
Alaska.	7.7	13.3	2.9	13.3	4.2	-	1.9	0.2	0.6	0.4	0.3	0.4
Arizona	26.1	96.4	-	86.7	23.4	9.7	5.9	1.6	2.1	2.5	0.7	3.4
Arkansas	18.2	58.1	-	58.1	15.5	-	3.7	0.3	4.6	0.2	4.9	4.3
California	119.2	616.8	-	546.9	114.5	69.9	3.7	49.0	11.2	34.2	31.9	63.6
Colorado	34.6	80.0	-	78.7	33.2	1.3	1.5	4.9	1.1	2.3	4.0	8.1
Connecticut	16.4	69.3	-	69.3	13.5	-	4.8	1.8	2.0	1.5	10.7	-
Delaware	7.1	13.5	-	13.5	6.8	-	1.4	-	1.7	0.2	2.3	-
District of Columbia . . .	(X)	11.5	(X)	10.7	(X)	0.7	(X)	1.2	(X)	1.4	(X)	4.0
Florida.	45.8	287.0	-	265.8	43.8	21.2	9.1	5.3	14.3	5.6	17.0	31.6
Georgia	41.4	177.2	-	176.4	35.9	0.8	7.6	0.6	4.8	11.9	12.9	39.5
Hawaii.	29.8	-	22.9	-	6.8	-	1.1	0.1	2.8	0.2	3.3	-
Idaho	9.1	28.1	-	27.2	8.6	0.9	1.9	0.2	1.3	0.7	0.9	4.7
Illinois	55.8	251.7	-	231.0	52.8	20.6	13.3	6.3	3.1	7.1	15.2	15.0
Indiana	48.8	126.4	-	126.4	47.7	-	5.1	1.5	1.7	2.9	5.8	22.8
Iowa	27.5	71.2	-	65.4	26.3	5.7	3.2	1.4	0.3	2.1	7.8	8.3
Kansas	18.5	73.0	-	67.1	17.8	5.9	1.7	0.8	0.9	3.1	5.6	6.2
Kentucky	29.5	92.4	-	92.4	25.4	-	4.7	0.7	1.9	3.9	5.2	4.4
Louisiana	31.7	101.1	-	100.7	27.9	0.3	6.0	0.5	5.8	1.1	21.1	12.6
Maine	6.4	31.9	0.1	31.9	5.4	-	2.3	0.5	1.2	0.2	0.5	0.7
Maryland	19.8	104.6	-	96.0	17.8	8.5	7.3	2.4	5.9	3.6	6.1	-
Massachusetts	22.5	125.7	-	125.6	21.8	0.2	7.4	2.0	5.4	2.5	17.8	5.5
Michigan	63.9	208.5	-	196.2	63.3	12.3	13.5	2.2	2.1	9.2	14.4	7.7
Minnesota	39.1	106.5	-	106.5	37.5	-	2.3	10.5	2.1	3.6	4.7	10.5
Mississippi	17.0	69.3	-	62.8	15.3	6.6	3.2	0.5	3.3	0.2	9.4	17.7
Missouri.	29.6	122.1	-	117.1	27.5	5.0	7.5	2.5	4.3	4.1	13.6	8.1
Montana	7.4	20.8	-	20.7	6.6	0.1	1.5	0.5	0.4	0.7	1.3	0.8
Nebraska.	10.7	42.4	-	39.7	10.1	2.7	2.8	0.8	0.8	0.4	4.6	4.2
Nevada	7.3	28.4	-	28.4	7.2	-	1.1	0.4	0.7	0.4	1.8	4.4
New Hampshire	5.5	24.7	-	24.7	5.2	-	1.3	2.1	0.9	0.2	0.9	0.3
New Jersey	44.9	173.3	14.4	162.1	26.9	11.2	5.4	11.1	2.7	3.7	16.5	5.2
New Mexico	16.1	44.0	-	41.4	15.2	2.6	1.4	0.4	2.7	0.3	5.4	2.9
New York	50.0	412.8	-	390.3	45.2	22.5	7.2	51.9	8.8	17.2	50.0	52.0
North Carolina	45.5	172.6	-	159.0	42.6	13.6	1.4	13.2	2.3	14.8	15.8	17.7
North Dakota	7.0	13.3	-	13.3	6.6	-	0.3	0.8	1.2	0.3	1.2	-
Ohio	66.8	215.4	-	210.1	64.5	5.3	2.2	24.5	3.8	16.4	16.0	12.7
Oklahoma	27.0	80.9	-	80.9	24.8	-	5.8	0.4	4.1	1.1	5.8	9.3
Oregon	16.3	69.3	-	60.8	15.2	8.5	4.8	0.8	1.6	3.7	7.0	2.7
Pennsylvania	52.1	208.2	-	201.1	49.2	7.1	12.1	20.1	1.6	5.1	15.6	-
Rhode Island	7.2	19.1	0.4	19.1	6.2	-	1.9	0.1	1.3	0.1	1.3	-
South Carolina	27.2	82.6	-	82.6	24.3	-	5.0	0.3	8.0	1.9	9.6	19.9
South Dakota	5.3	17.3	-	17.0	4.9	0.2	0.9	0.3	0.5	0.2	1.0	0.5
Tennessee.	36.2	102.3	-	102.3	34.3	-	4.5	3.5	2.9	3.3	10.5	13.2
Texas	85.7	539.5	-	509.0	80.9	30.5	21.9	3.6	10.4	18.1	40.7	44.1
Utah	23.6	40.2	-	40.2	22.6	-	3.1	0.4	1.5	1.2	4.9	0.8
Vermont	4.7	13.6	-	13.6	4.4	-	1.1	-	0.5	-	0.2	-
Virginia	42.4	155.4	-	154.1	39.6	1.3	2.0	7.0	5.1	5.3	13.1	2.8
Washington	49.6	88.4	-	88.4	48.9	-	7.6	1.0	6.5	3.9	7.5	10.0
West Virginia	13.3	40.7	-	40.7	11.9	-	0.1	-	0.7	1.4	1.9	3.5
Wisconsin	28.8	117.0	-	107.9	27.6	9.0	1.1	12.8	1.9	5.8	7.6	3.0
Wyoming	3.3	16.4	-	14.7	3.2	1.7	0.6	-	0.5	0.2	0.9	4.1

See footnote at end of table.

U.S. Census Bureau, Statistical Abstract of the United States: 1999

[In thousands, for March. Local government amounts are estimates subject to sampling variation; see Appendix III and source]

State	Highways		Police protection		Fire protection		Corrections		Parks and recreation		Government administration	
	State	Local	State	Local	State	Local	State	Local	State	Local	State	Local
United States ...	247.7	282.9	92.2	706.2	(X)	277.2	435.7	212.9	34.3	195.5	356.5	598.1
Alabama	4.0	7.0	1.2	10.6	(X)	4.8	4.2	2.6	0.8	3.3	5.8	7.2
Alaska	2.7	0.7	0.4	1.2	(X)	0.6	1.3	-	0.1	0.5	2.7	1.7
Arizona	3.0	4.1	1.7	13.0	(X)	4.6	8.2	3.9	0.4	3.6	5.6	13.8
Arkansas	3.6	3.5	0.9	5.7	(X)	2.2	3.6	1.4	0.8	0.8	2.9	5.6
California	16.4	20.9	12.3	80.3	(X)	29.8	44.2	28.5	2.9	30.5	23.7	80.3
Colorado	3.1	4.9	1.1	10.3	(X)	4.2	4.6	3.0	0.2	5.7	5.5	9.5
Connecticut	3.9	3.6	1.7	8.1	(X)	4.4	8.1	-	0.4	2.1	7.1	4.5
Delaware	1.5	0.4	0.8	1.3	(X)	0.3	2.0	-	0.2	0.3	2.3	0.9
District of Columbia ...	(X)	0.5	(X)	4.3	(X)	1.6	(X)	3.7	(X)	0.6	(X)	3.1
Florida	11.6	13.5	4.0	46.4	(X)	18.6	37.7	13.6	1.1	15.1	24.4	35.5
Georgia	5.9	7.8	2.2	19.6	(X)	8.7	17.2	6.2	2.7	4.4	5.3	16.5
Hawaii	0.8	1.0	-	3.4	(X)	1.7	2.2	-	0.2	1.9	4.0	2.2
Idaho	1.7	1.5	0.4	2.5	(X)	1.0	1.6	0.8	0.2	0.6	1.8	2.8
Illinois	8.0	11.3	4.1	39.3	(X)	15.2	14.4	8.9	0.7	14.9	11.6	29.9
Indiana	4.3	6.3	2.0	12.5	(X)	6.3	6.2	4.0	0.1	3.1	5.1	14.8
Iowa	3.0	5.3	1.0	5.6	(X)	1.7	2.4	0.9	0.1	1.6	4.5	5.2
Kansas	3.8	5.1	1.0	6.9	(X)	2.5	3.5	1.8	0.5	1.9	4.8	6.7
Kentucky	5.6	2.9	1.8	6.5	(X)	3.0	5.1	2.1	1.5	1.2	8.3	5.2
Louisiana	5.8	4.8	1.1	11.8	(X)	4.3	6.8	4.3	1.2	3.2	5.9	10.1
Maine	2.8	1.7	0.4	2.4	(X)	1.4	1.2	0.6	0.1	0.6	2.1	2.3
Maryland	4.7	4.9	2.3	14.0	(X)	5.9	10.8	2.5	0.6	6.1	9.1	7.9
Massachusetts	4.4	6.1	2.0	16.8	(X)	12.4	6.1	5.3	1.1	2.0	12.9	8.8
Michigan	3.4	9.0	3.0	21.2	(X)	7.9	16.7	4.9	0.4	5.1	7.1	23.4
Minnesota	5.0	6.9	0.9	9.4	(X)	2.2	3.5	3.9	0.5	4.1	5.9	12.1
Mississippi	3.3	5.6	1.0	7.1	(X)	3.2	4.1	1.3	0.4	0.9	2.1	7.1
Missouri	6.5	7.0	2.3	14.4	(X)	5.7	9.0	2.5	0.6	3.5	7.2	10.5
Montana	1.8	1.3	0.4	1.8	(X)	0.6	0.8	0.5	0.1	0.4	1.5	2.2
Nebraska	2.3	2.9	0.7	3.5	(X)	1.2	2.0	1.0	0.3	1.3	1.8	4.1
Nevada	1.5	1.4	0.6	4.5	(X)	1.9	3.0	1.4	0.2	2.2	2.4	5.3
New Hampshire	1.9	1.5	0.4	2.8	(X)	1.4	1.1	0.5	0.3	0.3	1.7	1.7
New Jersey	7.7	10.3	3.6	27.8	(X)	6.8	8.4	6.2	2.0	5.0	19.2	18.9
New Mexico	2.4	1.7	0.6	4.6	(X)	1.7	4.0	1.4	0.7	1.6	3.9	4.3
New York	14.1	26.7	5.4	74.7	(X)	23.7	34.2	25.9	2.5	10.2	40.0	40.3
North Carolina	12.3	3.5	3.3	17.4	(X)	5.8	19.2	4.1	0.8	4.0	10.3	10.4
North Dakota	0.9	1.0	0.2	1.2	(X)	0.3	0.4	0.2	0.1	0.7	1.3	1.4
Ohio	7.9	12.9	2.4	27.4	(X)	14.2	16.3	7.7	0.7	7.6	11.9	31.4
Oklahoma	4.2	5.2	1.7	8.2	(X)	4.0	10.6	1.0	1.8	2.1	5.2	6.0
Oregon	3.4	4.3	1.4	6.3	(X)	3.7	3.5	3.0	0.3	2.4	8.0	6.3
Pennsylvania	13.8	10.5	6.5	24.5	(X)	6.0	13.8	11.3	1.3	3.8	13.7	30.2
Rhode Island	0.9	0.9	0.3	2.6	(X)	2.3	1.6	0.0	0.1	0.3	2.5	1.9
South Carolina	5.0	2.4	2.2	8.7	(X)	3.2	8.4	2.1	0.6	2.1	4.3	7.4
South Dakota	1.3	1.5	0.3	1.4	(X)	0.4	0.8	0.4	0.1	0.4	1.2	1.7
Tennessee	4.8	6.8	1.8	13.5	(X)	6.0	7.3	4.6	1.1	3.9	5.1	10.1
Texas	14.0	17.9	3.5	52.7	(X)	18.7	43.0	20.6	1.0	13.1	17.0	38.4
Utah	1.8	1.5	0.7	4.1	(X)	1.5	2.6	0.8	0.3	1.8	3.2	3.8
Vermont	1.1	0.9	0.5	0.8	(X)	0.3	0.9	-	0.1	0.2	1.3	0.9
Virginia	9.8	4.1	2.4	15.0	(X)	7.1	13.2	6.5	0.7	6.1	7.8	14.3
Washington	6.4	6.7	1.9	10.7	(X)	6.7	7.1	3.8	0.5	4.2	5.7	14.6
West Virginia	5.9	0.9	0.9	2.6	(X)	0.9	1.0	0.4	0.6	0.8	2.8	3.3
Wisconsin	1.9	9.0	0.9	13.6	(X)	4.3	7.2	2.8	0.2	2.8	6.0	10.9
Wyoming	1.9	0.7	0.2	1.4	(X)	0.3	0.7	0.3	0.1	0.5	0.9	1.4

- Represents or rounds to zero.   X Not applicable.

Source: U.S. Census Bureau, <http://www.cenus.gov/ftp/pub/govs/www/apes/97html>; (accessed July 99).

State and Local Government Finances and Employment 341

No. 539. State and Local Government Employment and Average Earnings, by State: 1990 and 1997

[In thousands (3,840 represents 3,840,000), except as noted. For March]

State	Full-time equivalent employment (1,000)				Full-time equivalent employment per 10,000 population [2]				Average March earnings [3] (dol.)			
	State		Local [1]		State		Local [1]		State		Local [1]	
	1990	1997	1990	1997	1990	1997	1990	1997	1990	1997	1990	1997
United States..	3,840	3,987	9,239	10,227	154	149	371	382	2,472	3,292	2,364	3,058
Alabama.........	79	81	148	175	196	188	367	406	2,196	2,740	1,749	2,214
Alaska	22	22	21	23	401	367	385	379	3,543	3,938	3,491	4,012
Arizona..........	50	61	136	165	137	134	370	363	2,334	2,926	2,540	2,952
Arkansas	43	49	78	91	182	192	330	360	1,922	2,593	1,545	2,055
California	325	335	1,091	1,194	109	104	367	371	3,209	4,336	3,073	3,988
Colorado........	54	59	130	153	165	153	395	393	2,765	4,752	2,292	2,968
Connecticut......	58	60	98	104	178	183	299	319	3,018	3,733	2,854	3,815
Delaware	21	22	17	19	314	298	250	257	2,245	3,073	2,458	2,963
District of Columbia .	(X)	(X)	57	46	(X)	(X)	939	873	(X)	(X)	3,024	3,956
Florida..........	160	187	497	544	123	128	384	370	2,095	2,920	2,247	2,658
Georgia	112	111	270	324	173	149	418	433	2,037	2,801	1,872	2,397
Hawaii	49	52	13	14	445	434	120	120	2,317	2,890	2,536	3,270
Idaho...........	19	23	37	46	186	186	372	381	2,100	2,676	1,772	2,510
Illinois	145	141	416	460	127	118	364	384	2,520	3,476	2,463	3,305
Indiana..........	89	87	196	221	161	148	354	376	2,496	3,105	2,036	2,697
Iowa	57	56	107	113	207	196	387	395	2,936	4,092	2,024	2,736
Kansas..........	50	44	104	118	200	171	421	455	2,077	3,025	1,979	2,533
Kentucky	75	72	114	135	204	183	310	345	2,141	2,987	1,823	2,273
Louisiana	85	94	155	170	200	217	368	390	2,047	2,796	1,713	2,086
Maine...........	22	20	42	46	179	162	345	372	2,352	2,927	1,978	2,628
Maryland	89	80	159	172	186	157	333	337	2,609	3,421	2,776	3,457
Massachusetts.....	93	90	196	214	155	147	325	350	2,541	3,468	2,554	3,286
Michigan........	144	138	316	333	155	141	340	340	2,858	4,161	2,646	3,632
Minnesota........	70	71	163	189	160	152	374	403	2,936	4,173	2,552	3,397
Mississippi	47	51	105	122	183	188	407	448	1,824	2,503	1,543	1,952
Missouri.........	74	89	171	202	145	164	334	373	1,965	2,532	2,052	2,505
Montana.........	17	18	35	33	211	208	434	372	2,072	2,942	1,959	2,598
Nebraska	29	30	68	75	186	179	430	455	2,075	2,551	2,089	2,691
Nevada	19	23	42	57	160	137	348	337	2,502	3,433	2,574	3,496
New Hampshire	16	17	33	39	145	145	301	331	2,352	2,919	2,215	2,986
New Jersey.......	112	123	304	298	145	153	393	370	2,859	3,835	2,698	3,936
New Mexico	40	41	57	70	262	238	379	406	2,100	2,632	1,783	2,256
New York	285	250	866	860	158	138	482	474	2,997	3,748	2,795	3,710
North Carolina	107	122	244	294	161	165	368	395	2,372	2,969	2,065	2,563
North Dakota......	15	15	20	21	234	240	314	331	2,057	2,860	2,138	2,914
Ohio	139	140	385	421	128	125	355	376	2,510	3,452	2,236	2,998
Oklahoma........	65	72	116	129	208	217	369	390	1,975	2,238	1,761	2,207
Oregon..........	52	54	100	118	184	166	353	364	2,302	3,460	2,322	3,345
Pennsylvania......	127	150	361	366	107	125	304	304	2,437	3,412	2,403	3,183
Rhode Island......	21	20	27	29	205	204	266	295	2,586	3,531	2,656	3,364
South Carolina.....	79	78	116	144	227	205	333	380	1,956	2,535	1,848	2,422
South Dakota	13	13	24	27	192	180	349	360	1,979	2,703	1,733	2,384
Tennessee	79	82	175	194	163	152	358	362	2,055	2,772	1,883	2,327
Texas...........	223	262	706	850	131	135	415	439	2,192	2,787	1,952	2,450
Utah	37	45	51	64	216	219	294	309	2,000	2,828	2,092	2,889
Vermont.........	13	12	18	18	233	211	312	303	2,302	2,724	2,090	2,742
Virginia..........	117	106	221	253	188	157	356	376	2,267	3,023	2,248	2,813
Washington.......	91	108	164	185	187	193	336	330	2,459	3,611	2,515	3,941
West Virginia......	34	32	59	60	188	178	326	330	1,919	2,559	1,862	2,392
Wisconsin........	67	65	183	202	136	124	375	388	2,503	3,908	2,372	3,311
Wyoming	11	11	24	27	239	230	539	571	2,045	2,403	2,110	2,729

X Not applicable. [1] Estimates subject to sampling variation; see Appendix III and source. [2] Based on estimated resident population as of July 1. [3] For full-time employees.

Source: U.S. Census Bureau, 1990, *Public Employment,* Series GE, No. 1, annual; thereafter, <http://www.census.gov/pub/govs/www/apes.html>; (accessed 12 July 1999).

No. 540. City Government Employment and Payroll—Largest Cities: 1990 and 1997

[1997 for March; prior years for October. In thousands (456.2 represents 456,200). See footnote 1, Table 530, for those areas representing city-county consolidated governments]

Cities ranked by 1996 population	Total employment (1,000)		Full-time equivalent employment [1]				Payroll (mil. dol.)		Average earnings for full-time employees (dol.)	
			Total (1,000)		Per 10,000 population [1]					
	1990	1997	1990	1997	1990	1997	1990	1997	1990	1997
New York, NY [2][3]	456.2	413.5	394.6	391.5	539	530	1,091.7	1,295.0	2,783	3,433
Los Angeles, CA	51.3	48.8	50.8	47.8	146	134	176.5	201.3	3,488	4,280
Chicago, IL	41.6	41.7	41.6	41.7	149	153	124.9	175.1	3,002	4,198
Houston, TX	19.6	23.1	19.6	22.9	120	131	40.4	57.7	2,061	2,504
Philadelphia, PA	32.4	29.9	31.9	29.0	201	196	89.1	95.3	2,843	3,305
San Diego, CA	10.4	11.4	9.8	10.6	88	91	28.8	39.5	3,019	3,819
Phoenix, AZ	11.9	12.3	11.4	12.0	116	103	31.7	42.2	2,876	3,585
San Antonio, TX	13.4	15.2	12.8	15.2	134	143	28.4	44.4	2,227	2,991
Dallas, TX	14.9	15.8	14.5	14.9	144	141	28.2	39.4	1,945	2,726
Detroit, MI	22.1	17.8	21.2	17.5	206	174	49.8	54.0	2,390	3,114
Honolulu, HI	9.9	10.0	9.2	9.3	110	107	23.7	30.4	2,600	3,305
San Jose, CA	5.9	6.8	4.9	6.2	62	74	16.0	28.8	3,453	4,882
Indianapolis, IN	12.8	11.5	12.5	11.2	171	151	23.1	29.5	1,910	2,688
San Francisco, CA	25.8	27.4	25.7	27.3	356	372	93.8	105.3	3,648	3,852
Jacksonville, FL	10.8	10.7	9.8	9.8	154	144	23.8	31.2	2,582	3,280
Baltimore, MD [2]	29.7	29.2	29.1	28.0	395	415	73.2	82.6	2,540	3,027
Columbus, OH	7.7	8.5	7.5	8.2	118	125	17.8	25.2	2,416	3,128
El Paso, TX	4.9	5.7	4.8	5.6	94	94	9.5	13.6	1,973	2,440
Memphis, TN [2]	21.7	23.1	21.1	21.8	341	366	47.6	57.6	2,287	2,664
Milwaukee, WI	9.0	8.5	8.6	8.1	137	138	20.6	28.4	2,431	3,527
Boston, MA [2]	20.9	23.2	20.9	22.2	363	397	49.8	72.1	2,391	3,311
Washington, DC [2][3]	49.6	39.4	47.9	38.5	789	708	138.7	133.2	2,930	3,493
Austin, TX	10.0	10.5	9.6	9.8	203	181	20.9	27.3	2,186	2,846
Seattle, WA	11.2	9.7	10.2	9.5	198	181	32.3	38.7	3,274	4,156
Nashville-Davidson, TN [2]	17.9	21.4	16.9	18.6	347	364	41.8	39.3	2,510	2,154
Cleveland, OH	8.9	9.5	8.2	9.0	163	180	20.6	27.3	2,521	3,075
Denver, CO	13.0	14.4	11.9	13.8	254	277	31.1	43.7	2,649	3,255
Portland, OR	4.8	5.9	4.5	5.2	97	107	14.6	20.1	3,305	3,982
Fort Worth, TX	5.5	6.1	5.2	5.5	117	114	11.1	13.7	2,171	2,615
New Orleans, LA	9.8	10.6	9.6	10.3	194	215	15.5	23.7	1,623	2,358
Oklahoma City, OK	4.8	5.1	4.5	4.8	101	101	10.5	14.8	2,430	3,269
Tucson, AZ	5.0	5.9	4.7	5.1	114	113	11.5	14.7	2,528	2,974
Charlotte, NC	5.0	4.8	4.8	4.7	115	106	11.5	13.5	2,399	2,922
Kansas City, MO	6.4	6.6	6.3	6.5	145	147	14.9	18.3	2,390	2,830
Virginia Beach, VA [2]	14.4	17.6	13.1	15.5	334	360	28.4	37.8	2,232	2,660
Long Beach, CA	5.7	5.8	5.4	5.1	126	121	17.7	17.4	3,413	3,578
Albuquerque, NM	6.9	8.4	6.2	6.5	161	154	12.2	16.1	2,040	2,521
Atlanta, GA	8.3	8.1	8.1	8.0	205	198	18.4	21.2	2,286	2,669
Fresno, CA	2.9	2.8	2.7	2.8	77	70	7.9	11.3	2,944	4,070
Tulsa, OK	4.4	4.5	4.2	4.3	115	114	10.5	12.2	2,555	2,850
Las Vegas, NV	1.9	2.4	2.0	2.3	77	62	4.9	9.1	2,563	3,933
Sacramento, CA	4.2	4.2	3.9	4.2	105	112	11.3	17.8	3,021	4,211
Baton Rouge, LA	6.0	6.8	5.0	6.1	132	164	11.0	14.9	2,255	2,533
Oakland, CA	4.6	5.1	4.1	4.0	111	110	15.3	19.0	3,948	4,807
Omaha, NE	2.9	3.5	2.7	3.2	79	88	7.9	10.3	3,051	3,576
Minneapolis, MN	6.4	9.0	5.7	5.7	154	158	15.2	18.8	2,815	3,405
Miami, FL	4.3	3.2	4.0	3.2	113	90	14.6	12.2	3,771	3,855
St. Louis, MO	7.8	8.3	7.4	7.9	186	225	17.0	22.0	2,363	2,805
Pittsburgh, PA	5.9	4.3	5.6	4.2	152	119	12.3	13.5	2,240	3,362
Cincinnati, OH	7.0	6.5	6.3	6.4	173	184	16.1	18.0	2,634	2,926
Colorado Springs, CO	5.9	6.8	5.3	6.4	188	184	13.3	19.9	2,618	3,202
Mesa, AZ	2.3	3.1	2.3	3.1	81	89	6.8	10.2	2,898	3,365
Wichita, KS	2.7	3.5	2.6	3.1	87	96	5.4	8.6	2,083	2,841
Toledo, OH	3.0	3.1	3.0	3.1	91	97	8.6	10.0	2,847	3,241
Buffalo, NY [2]	13.1	12.4	12.4	11.2	379	362	31.3	39.3	2,596	3,702
Santa Ana, CA	2.0	2.3	1.7	1.9	58	64	6.8	8.8	4,144	5,324
Arlington, TX	1.8	5.7	1.8	5.3	68	181	4.5	14.9	2,538	2,845
Anaheim, CA	3.7	3.1	2.6	2.5	99	86	8.6	10.4	3,728	4,807
Tampa, FL	4.3	4.2	4.2	4.1	151	145	10.5	12.1	2,505	2,969
Corpus Christi, TX	3.2	3.4	3.0	3.2	116	114	5.9	7.8	2,009	2,485
Newark, NJ	5.1	5.7	4.9	5.4	177	202	8.3	19.9	1,698	3,846
Louisville, KY	4.5	4.7	4.3	4.5	159	172	9.1	10.5	2,180	2,397
St. Paul, MN	3.6	3.6	3.4	3.3	124	127	10.5	11.9	3,265	3,741
Birmingham, AL	3.9	4.2	3.8	4.1	142	157	8.4	10.5	2,243	2,619
Riverside, CA	2.0	2.4	2.0	2.2	88	85	7.0	7.9	3,459	3,938
Aurora, CO	1.9	2.2	1.9	2.2	84	85	4.8	7.3	2,586	3,387
Anchorage, AK	8.8	9.2	7.9	7.8	351	312	28.4	30.8	3,706	4,082
Raleigh, NC	3.0	3.0	3.0	2.7	141	113	5.0	7.6	2,297	2,861
Lexington-Fayette, KY	3.0	3.4	3.0	3.4	133	141	6.0	7.0	1,929	2,084
St Petersburg, FL	3.0	2.9	3.0	2.8	125	119	7.0	8.3	2,412	2,966
Norfolk, VA [2]	10.5	13.2	9.8	11.5	376	494	21.9	29.8	2,268	2,634
Stockton, CA	2.0	2.1	1.0	1.8	47	78	5.0	5.9	3,554	3,429
Jersey City, NJ	4.0	3.8	3.0	3.6	131	157	10.0	13.6	3,172	3,971
Rochester, NY	9.0	10.5	8.0	9.8	347	441	27.0	34.0	3,315	3,576
Akron, OH	6.0	3.2	5.0	3.1	224	142	11.0	9.0	2,255	2,934
Lincoln, NE	4.0	3.8	3.0	3.5	156	168	7.0	9.5	2,367	2,761

[1] 1990 based on enumerated resident population as of April 1, 1990. 1997 based on estimated resident population as of March 1, 1997.   [2] Includes city-operated elementary and secondary schools.   [3] Includes city-operated university or college.

Source: U.S. Census Bureau, City Employment, GE-90-2; and unpublished data.

State and Local Government Finances and Employment 343

No. 541. County Government Employment and Payroll—Largest Counties: 1997

[For March. See text, this section. See headnote, Table 532]

Counties ranked by 1996 population	Total employment (1,000)	Full-time equivalent employment (1,000)	Per 10,000 population [1]	Payroll (mil. dol.)	Avg. earnings, full-time employees (dol.)	Counties ranked by 1996 population	Total employment (1,000)	Full-time equivalent employment (1,000)	Per 10,000 population [1]	Payroll (mil. dol.)	Avg. earnings, full-time employees (dol.)
Los Angeles, CA	88.8	84.4	93	319.1	3,801	Hudson, NJ	3.4	3.2	57	9.2	2,993
Cook, IL	28.1	28.1	54	90.1	3,210	Delaware, PA	3.1	3.1	56	5.9	1,912
Harris, TX	19.2	18.9	61	50.5	2,680	Snohomish, WA	2.1	2.1	38	7.2	3,491
San Diego, CA	19.1	18.0	67	55.5	3,112	Cobb, GA	4.5	4.1	76	12.0	3,008
Maricopa, AZ	14.4	12.3	47	26.6	2,223	Kent, MI	2.1	2.0	37	5.2	2,679
Orange, CA	16.6	16.0	62	53.9	3,381	Summit, OH	3.5	3.4	64	8.0	2,350
Wayne, MI	6.6	6.5	30	20.6	3,199	Wake, NC	16.1	13.9	261	34.0	2,414
Dade, FL	36.5	35.6	169	118.6	3,414	San Joaquin, CA	7.8	6.5	122	17.5	2,839
Dallas, TX	12.4	12.2	61	31.2	2,553	Tulsa, OK	1.6	1.5	27	2.9	2,028
King, WA	14.2	12.5	77	43.0	3,470	Bernalillo, NM	1.4	1.4	26	4.3	3,260
Santa Clara, CA	15.6	13.6	85	54.4	4,063	Bristol, MA	0.7	0.7	14	1.9	2,714
San Bernardino, CA	15.7	14.9	93	48.1	3,271	Camden, NJ	4.0	3.6	71	12.6	3,567
Broward, FL	10.2	10.1	70	29.8	2,996	Union, NJ	5.1	3.7	74	13.5	3,789
Middlesex, MA	0.9	0.9	6	2.7	3,055	Jefferson, CO	2.5	2.4	48	6.4	2,742
Riverside, CA	13.5	12.9	92	44.7	3,522	Hidalgo, TX	1.5	1.5	30	2.7	1,850
Cuyahoga, OH	14.7	14.7	105	40.1	2,737	Ramsey, MN	3.8	3.4	71	11.7	3,494
Alameda, CA	11.2	10.2	75	39.7	3,858	Passaic, NJ	3.9	3.6	75	13.0	3,743
Suffolk, NY	13.7	12.5	93	50.1	4,076	Lake, IN	1.9	1.8	38	3.8	2,091
Bexar, TX	8.2	7.9	61	18.7	2,368	Gwinnett, GA	3.5	3.3	69	8.7	2,667
Nassau, NY	18.4	17.5	135	73.0	4,395	Ocean, NJ	3.3	3.0	64	9.4	3,128
Tarrant, TX	6.9	6.7	51	15.7	2,403	New Castle, DE	2.0	1.6	33	4.8	3,281
Allegheny, PA	7.4	7.2	56	16.7	2,344	El Paso, CO	2.0	1.9	40	4.9	2,613
Oakland, MI	5.9	4.8	42	15.5	3,478	Anne Arundel, MD	13.8	12.5	268	43.8	3,698
Sacramento, CA	12.1	12.0	107	42.2	3,521	Onondaga, NY	6.2	5.5	119	14.6	2,750
Hennepin, MN	12.3	10.3	97	35.2	3,421	Plymouth, MA	0.7	0.7	15	2.1	3,161
Clark, NV	13.5	12.3	117	44.8	3,724	Arapahoe, CO	1.8	1.8	39	5.1	2,917
Franklin, OH	6.6	6.3	62	20.7	3,378	Jefferson, LA	9.8	9.1	200	22.7	2,538
St Louis, MO	4.0	3.8	38	11.1	2,897	Brevard, FL	3.5	3.3	72	7.4	2,302
Palm Beach, FL	8.0	7.9	80	22.8	2,887	Lucas, OH	3.8	3.8	83	9.4	2,549
Erie, NY	13.4	11.2	117	33.3	3,107	Lancaster, PA	2.3	2.1	46	4.5	2,243
Milwaukee, WI	7.8	7.4	80	22.9	3,106	Morris, NJ	4.4	3.5	78	9.7	2,967
Fairfax, VA	32.7	31.1	346	96.5	3,200	Hampden, MA	1.0	1.0	22	2.7	2,786
Hillsborough, FL	13.5	12.7	142	31.5	2,526	Polk, FL	3.8	3.6	83	8.8	2,447
Westchester, NY	10.6	10.3	115	38.7	3,842	Douglas, NE	2.1	1.9	44	4.8	2,698
Contra Costa, CA	9.3	8.4	95	38.4	4,821	Genesee, MI	1.8	1.8	41	6.3	3,693
Pinellas, FL	5.5	5.4	62	14.3	2,673	Sedgwick, KS	2.2	2.1	49	6.6	3,114
Shelby, TN	11.3	11.2	129	28.2	2,530	Will, IL	1.8	1.7	39	4.8	2,890
Du Page, IL	3.2	3.0	35	9.1	3,120	Sonoma, CA	5.3	4.8	113	18.5	4,101
Hamilton, OH	5.8	5.6	66	14.8	2,637	Burlington, NJ	3.7	3.4	82	9.0	2,813
Bergen, NJ	7.1	6.1	72	21.0	3,521	Dane, WI	2.3	2.0	48	6.3	3,254
Salt Lake, UT	5.1	4.0	48	11.4	3,149	Stanislaus, CA	4.8	4.5	109	14.9	3,475
Montgomery, MD	37.5	30.1	367	108.0	3,898	Volusia, FL	2.7	2.5	61	5.8	2,362
Macomb, MI	2.9	2.7	35	7.9	3,022	Chester, PA	2.2	2.0	50	5.0	2,508
Pima, AZ	7.2	6.5	85	16.5	2,582	Johnson, KS	3.1	2.9	70	6.8	2,456
Prince Georges, MD	25.8	23.8	311	71.4	3,174	Spokane, WA	1.8	1.8	44	5.0	2,834
Orange, FL	9.0	7.9	104	20.9	2,653	Mobile, AL	2.0	2.0	51	4.2	2,064
Essex, NJ	7.0	5.9	79	18.8	3,211	Santa Barbara, CA	5.0	4.6	120	15.8	3,571
Fresno, CA	6.8	6.6	89	19.1	3,021	Washington, OR	1.3	1.3	33	4.1	3,303
Monroe, NY	6.8	5.9	82	17.0	2,950	Lee, FL	2.9	2.8	75	6.8	2,427
Worcester, MA	0.7	0.7	10	1.8	2,707	Guilford, NC	12.0	10.9	288	26.6	2,493
Baltimore, MD	22.4	19.9	277	57.3	3,044	Westmoreland, PA	2.2	2.1	56	4.5	2,141
Fulton, GA	6.3	6.2	87	14.8	2,359	Stark, OH	2.8	2.8	76	5.7	2,033
Ventura, CA	8.1	7.9	111	28.0	3,597	Collin, TX	1.0	1.0	27	2.4	2,413
Montgomery, PA	3.3	3.2	45	6.8	2,156	Kane, IL	1.2	1.2	33	2.9	2,368
Middlesex, NJ	5.2	4.7	68	16.3	3,634	York, PA	1.9	1.8	49	3.7	2,040
Essex, MA	0.9	0.7	11	2.2	2,878	Solano, CA	2.9	2.7	72	8.7	3,343
San Mateo, CA	5.7	5.5	81	20.3	3,898	Knox, TN	9.1	8.7	240	17.8	2,039
Travis, TX	3.6	3.4	50	8.4	2,492	Polk, IA	1.9	1.9	52	5.8	3,188
El Paso, TX	3.4	3.3	48	7.6	2,402	Hillsborough, NH	0.7	0.7	19	1.6	2,391
Jefferson, KY	3.3	3.2	48	8.2	2,552	Berks, PA	5.9	2.2	63	5.0	2,276
Jefferson, AL	4.9	4.8	72	12.9	2,705	Pulaski, AR	1.3	1.2	36	2.8	2,235
Pierce, WA	3.2	3.0	46	10.9	3,619	Denton, TX	1.1	1.1	30	2.4	2,334
Jackson, MO	2.2	2.2	34	4.6	2,080	Monterey, CA	4.1	3.9	113	13.0	3,384
Norfolk, MA	0.9	0.9	14	2.4	2,751	Tulare, CA	3.7	3.5	102	10.8	3,167
Oklahoma, OK	2.0	1.9	31	3.4	1,773	Greenville, SC	1.5	1.4	40	3.2	2,299
Multnomah, OR	4.4	3.8	61	8.6	2,418	Waukesha, WI	1.4	1.3	39	3.5	2,714
Kern, CA	8.6	8.3	134	26.2	3,186	Seminole, FL	2.2	2.1	64	5.3	2,528
Mecklenburg, NC	20.8	18.2	305	44.6	2,507	Mercer, NJ	3.8	3.0	92	10.2	3,540
Monmouth, NJ	5.8	5.1	86	15.9	3,240	Dakota, MN	1.5	1.4	43	4.4	3,226
Dekalb, GA	5.8	5.6	96	15.3	2,745	Orange, NY	3.4	2.9	91	8.5	2,904
Lake, IL	2.1	1.9	33	6.0	3,119	Clackamas, OR	2.0	1.8	54	5.9	3,504
Bucks, PA	2.4	2.4	41	6.2	2,642	Butler, OH	1.9	1.8	55	4.2	2,359
Montgomery, OH	4.9	4.6	82	12.8	2,757	Utah, UT	0.7	0.6	20	1.7	2,750

[1] 1997 based on estimated resident population as of July 1, 1998.

Source: U.S. Census Bureau, unpublished data.

344 State and Local Government Finances and Employment

Section 10
Federal Government Finances and Employment

This section presents statistics relating to the financial structure and the civilian employment of the Federal Government. The fiscal data cover taxes, other receipts, outlays, and debt. The principal sources of fiscal data are *The Budget of the United States Government* and related documents, published annually by the Office of Management and Budget (OMB), and the Department of the Treasury's *United States Government Annual Report* and its *Appendix.* Detailed data on tax returns and collections are published annually by the Internal Revenue Service. The personnel data relate to staffing and payrolls. They are published by the Office of Personnel Management and the Bureau of Labor Statistics. The primary source for data on public lands is *Public Land Statistics*, published annually by the Bureau of Land Management, Department of the Interior. Data on federally owned land and real property are collected by the General Services Administration and presented in its annual *Inventory Report on Real Property Owned by the United States Throughout the World.*

Budget concept—Under the unified budget concept, all Federal monies are included in one comprehensive budget. These monies comprise both Federal funds and trust funds. Federal funds are derived mainly from taxes and borrowing and are not restricted by law to any specific government purpose. Trust funds, such as the Unemployment Trust Fund, collect certain taxes and other receipts for use in carrying out specific purposes or programs in accordance with the terms of the trust agreement or statute. Fund balances include both cash balances with Treasury and investments in U.S. securities. Part of the balance is obligated, part unobligated. Prior to 1985, the budget totals, under provisions of law, excluded some Federal

activities—including the Federal Financing Bank, the Postal Service, the Synthetic Fuels Corporation, and the lending activities of the Rural Electrification Administration. The Balanced Budget and Emergency Deficit Control Act of 1985 (P.L.99-177) repealed the off-budget status of these entities and placed social security (Federal old-age and survivors insurance and the Federal disability insurance trust funds) off-budget. Though social security is now off-budget and, by law, excluded from coverage of the congressional budget resolutions, it continues to be a Federal program.

Receipts arising from the Government's sovereign powers are reported as governmental receipts; all other receipts, i.e., from business-type or market-oriented activities, are offset against outlays. Outlays are reported on a checks-issued (net) basis (i.e., outlays are recorded at the time the checks to pay bills are issued).

Debt concept—For most of U.S. history, the total debt consisted of debt borrowed by the Treasury (i.e., public debt). The present debt series, includes both public debt and agency debt. The *gross Federal debt* includes money borrowed by the Treasury and by various Federal agencies; it is the broadest generally used measure of the Federal debt. *Total public debt* is covered by a statutory debt limitation and includes only borrowing by the Treasury.

Treasury receipts and outlays—All receipts of the Government, with a few exceptions, are deposited to the credit of the U.S. Treasury regardless of ultimate disposition. Under the Constitution, no money may be withdrawn from the Treasury unless appropriated by the Congress.

The day-to-day cash operations of the Federal Government clearing through the accounts of the U.S. Treasury are reported in the *Daily Treasury Statement*. Extensive detail on the public debt is published in the *Monthly Statement of the Public Debt of the United States*.

Budget receipts such as taxes, customs duties, and miscellaneous receipts, which are collected by Government agencies, and outlays represented by checks issued and cash payments made by disbursing officers as well as government agencies are reported in the *Daily Treasury Statement of Receipts and Outlays of the United States Government* and in the Treasury's *United States Government Annual Report* and its *Appendix*. These deposits in and payments from accounts maintained by Government agencies are on the same basis as the unified budget.

The quarterly *Treasury Bulletin* contains data on fiscal operations and related Treasury activities, including financial statements of Government corporations and other business-type activities.

Income tax returns and tax collections—Tax data are compiled by the Internal Revenue Service of the Treasury Department. The *Annual Report of the Commissioner and Chief Counsel of the Internal Revenue Service* gives a detailed account of tax collections by kind of tax and by regions, districts, and states. The agency's annual *Statistics of Income* reports present detailed data from individual income tax returns and corporation income tax returns. The quarterly *Statistics of Income Bulletin* has, in general, replaced the supplemental *Statistics of Income* publications which presented data on such diverse subjects as tax-exempt organizations, unincorporated businesses, fiduciary income tax and estate tax returns, sales of capital assets by individuals, international income and taxes reported by corporations and individuals, and estate tax wealth.

Employment and payrolls—The Office of Personnel Management collects employment and payroll data from all departments and agencies of the Federal Government,

except the Central Intelligence Agency, the National Security Agency, and the Defense Intelligence Agency. Employment figures represent the number of persons who occupied civilian positions at the end of the report month shown and who are paid for personal services rendered for the Federal Government, regardless of the nature of appointment or method of payment. Federal payrolls include all payments for personal services rendered during the report month and payments for accumulated annual leave of employees who separate from the service. Since most Federal employees are paid on a biweekly basis, the calendar month earnings are partially estimated on the basis of the number of work days in each month where payroll periods overlap.

Federal employment and payroll figures are published by the Office of Personnel Management in its *Federal Civilian Workforce Statistics—Employment and Trends*. It also publishes biennial employment data for minority groups, data on occupations of white- and blue-collar workers, and data on employment by geographic area; reports on salary and wage distribution of Federal employees are published annually. General schedule is primarily white-collar; wage system primarily blue-collar. Data on Federal employment are also issued by the Bureau of Labor Statistics in its *Monthly Labor Review* and in Employment and Earnings and by the U.S. Census Bureau in its annual *Public Employment*.

Public lands—The data on applications, entries, selections, patents, and certifications refer to transactions which involve the disposal, under the public land laws (including the homestead laws), of Federal public lands to non-Federal owners. In general, original entries and selections are applications to secure title to public lands which have been accepted as properly filed (i.e., allowed). Some types of applications, however, are not reported until issuance of the final certificate, which passes equitable title to the land to the applicant.

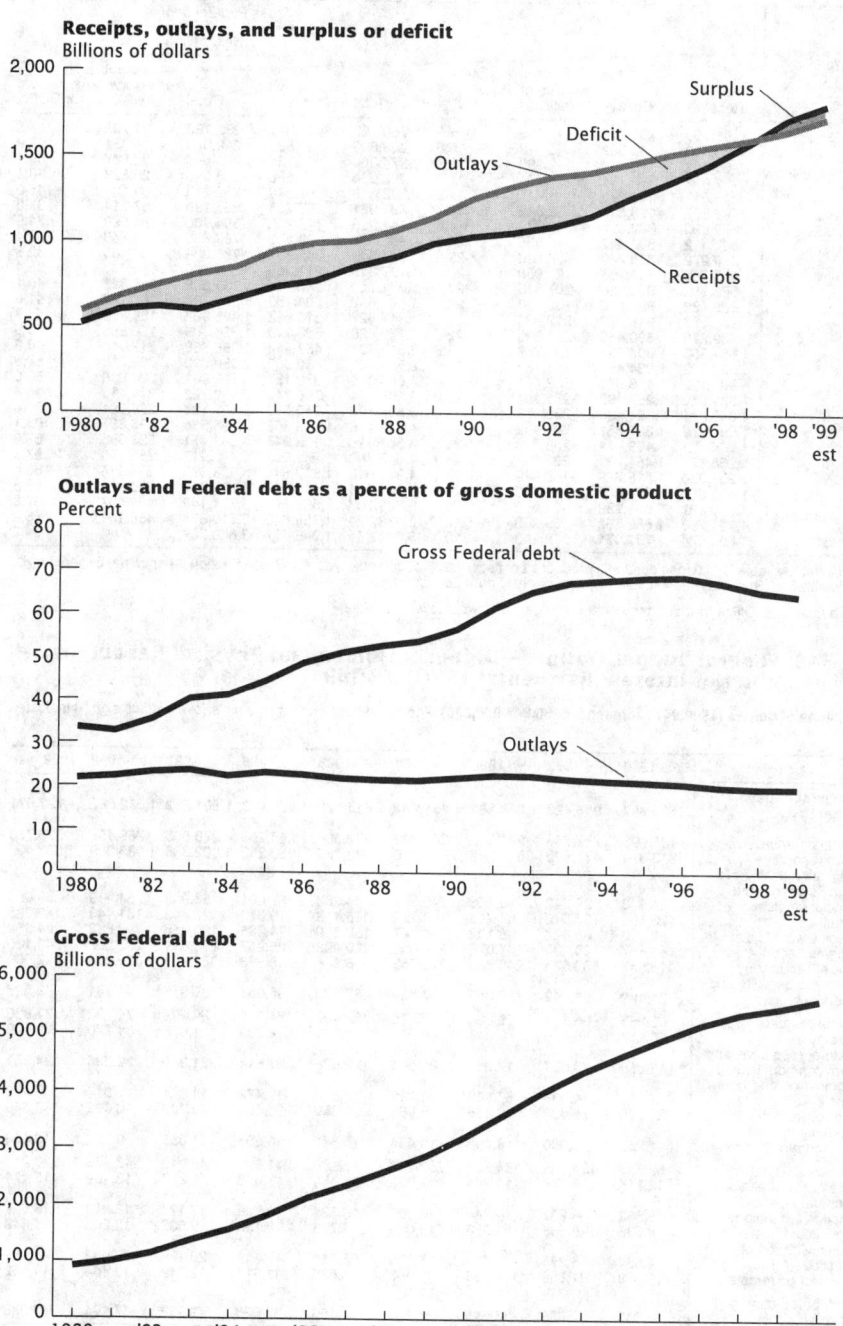

Figure 10.1
Federal Budget Summary: 1980 to 1999

Receipts, outlays, and surplus or deficit
Billions of dollars

Surplus
Deficit
Outlays
Receipts

Outlays and Federal debt as a percent of gross domestic product
Percent

Gross Federal debt

Outlays

Gross Federal debt
Billions of dollars

Source: Chart prepared by U.S. Census Bureau. For data, see Table 542.

Federal Government Finances and Employment 347

No. 542. Federal Budget—Summary: 1945 to 1999

[In millions of dollars ($45,159 represents $45,159,000,000), except percent. For fiscal years ending in year shown; see text, Section 9, State and Local Government. The Balanced Budget and Emergency Deficit Control Act of 1985 put all the previously off-budget Federal entities into the budget and moved social security off-budget. Minus sign (-) indicates deficit or decrease]

Year	Receipts	Outlays	Surplus or deficit(-)	Outlays as percent of GDP [1]	Gross Federal debt [2] Total	Federal gov't account	Held by the public Total	Federal Reserve System	As percent of GDP [1]
1945	45,159	92,712	-47,553	41.9	260,123	24,941	235,182	21,792	117.5
1950	39,443	42,562	-3,119	15.6	256,853	37,830	219,023	18,331	93.9
1955	65,451	68,444	-2,993	17.3	274,366	47,751	226,616	23,607	69.4
1960	92,492	92,191	301	17.8	290,525	53,686	236,840	26,523	56.1
1965	116,817	118,228	-1,411	17.2	322,318	61,540	260,778	39,100	46.9
1970	192,807	195,649	-2,842	19.4	380,921	97,723	283,198	57,714	37.8
1975	279,090	332,332	-53,242	21.4	541,925	147,225	394,700	84,993	34.9
1980	517,112	590,947	-73,835	21.7	909,050	199,212	709,838	120,846	33.4
1981	599,272	678,249	-78,976	22.2	994,845	209,507	785,338	124,466	32.6
1982	617,766	745,755	-127,989	23.2	1,137,345	217,560	919,785	134,497	35.4
1983	600,562	808,380	-207,818	23.6	1,371,710	240,114	1,131,596	155,527	40.1
1984	666,486	851,874	-185,388	22.3	1,564,657	264,159	1,300,498	155,122	41.0
1985	734,088	946,423	-212,334	23.1	1,817,521	317,612	1,499,908	169,806	44.3
1986	769,215	990,460	-221,245	22.6	2,120,629	383,919	1,736,709	190,855	48.5
1987	854,353	1,004,122	-149,769	21.8	2,346,125	457,444	1,888,680	212,040	50.9
1988	909,303	1,064,489	-155,187	21.5	2,601,307	550,507	2,050,799	229,218	52.5
1989	991,190	1,143,671	-152,481	21.4	2,868,039	678,157	2,189,882	220,088	53.6
1990	1,031,969	1,253,163	-221,194	22.0	3,206,564	795,841	2,410,722	234,410	56.4
1991	1,055,041	1,324,400	-269,359	22.6	3,598,498	910,362	2,688,137	258,591	61.4
1992	1,091,279	1,381,681	-290,402	22.5	4,002,136	1,003,302	2,998,834	296,397	65.1
1993	1,154,401	1,409,414	-255,013	21.8	4,351,416	1,103,945	3,247,471	325,653	67.2
1994	1,258,627	1,461,731	-203,104	21.4	4,643,705	1,211,588	3,432,117	355,150	67.8
1995	1,351,830	1,515,729	-163,899	21.1	4,921,018	1,317,645	3,603,373	374,114	68.4
1996	1,453,062	1,560,512	-107,450	20.7	5,181,934	1,448,967	3,732,968	390,924	68.6
1997	1,579,292	1,601,232	-21,940	20.0	5,369,707	1,598,559	3,771,148	424,507	67.2
1998	1,721,798	1,652,552	69,246	19.7	5,478,724	1,758,846	3,719,878	458,131	65.2
1999, est	1,806,334	1,727,071	79,263	19.7	5,614,934	1,945,197	3,669,737	(NA)	64.2

NA Not available.   [1] Gross domestic product as of fiscal year; for calendar year GDP, see Section 14, Income, Expenditures, and Wealth.   [2] See text, this section, for discussion of debt concept.

Source: U.S. Office of Management and Budget, *Historical Tables*, annual.

No. 543. Federal Budget Outlays—Defense, Human and Physical Resources, and Net Interest Payments: 1980 to 1999

[In millions of dollars ($590,947 represents $590,947,000,000). For fiscal year ending in year shown. Minus sign (-) indicates offsets]

Outlays	1980	1985	1990	1994	1995	1996	1997	1998	1999, est.
Federal outlays, total	**590,947**	**946,423**	**1,253,163**	**1,461,731**	**1,515,729**	**1,560,512**	**1,601,232**	**1,652,552**	**1,727,071**
National defense	133,995	252,748	299,331	281,642	272,066	265,753	270,505	268,456	276,730
Human resources.	313,374	471,822	619,329	869,410	923,765	958,232	1,002,336	1,033,389	1,087,406
Education, training, employment, and social services	31,843	29,342	38,755	46,307	54,263	52,001	53,008	54,919	60,065
Health.	23,169	33,542	57,716	107,122	115,418	119,378	123,843	131,440	143,095
Medicare.	32,090	65,822	98,102	144,747	159,855	174,225	190,016	192,822	204,982
Income security	86,557	128,230	147,076	214,085	220,493	225,967	230,899	233,202	243,130
Social security	118,547	188,623	248,623	319,565	335,846	349,676	365,257	379,225	392,608
Veterans benefits and services.	21,169	26,262	29,058	37,584	37,890	36,985	39,313	41,781	43,526
Physical resources	65,985	56,821	126,004	70,575	59,197	64,231	59,992	74,732	77,830
Energy	10,156	5,609	3,341	5,219	4,936	2,839	1,475	1,270	49
Natural resources and environment	13,858	13,357	17,080	21,064	22,078	21,614	21,369	22,396	24,261
Commerce and housing credit	9,390	4,337	67,600	-4,228	-17,808	-10,472	-14,624	1,014	452
Transportation	21,329	25,838	29,485	38,066	39,350	39,565	40,767	40,332	42,640
Community and regional development.	11,252	7,680	8,498	10,454	10,641	10,685	11,005	9,720	10,428
Net interest	52,538	129,504	184,221	202,957	232,169	241,090	244,016	243,359	227,244
International affairs . . .	12,714	16,176	13,764	17,083	16,434	13,496	15,228	13,109	15,474
General science, space/technology . . .	5,832	8,627	14,444	16,227	16,724	16,709	17,174	18,219	18,529
Agriculture	8,839	25,565	11,958	15,046	9,778	9,159	9,032	12,206	21,449
Administration of justice	4,584	6,270	9,993	15,256	16,216	17,548	20,173	22,832	24,467
General government . .	13,028	11,588	10,734	11,307	13,835	11,914	12,749	13,444	14,852
Undistributed offsetting receipts	-19,942	-32,698	-36,615	-37,772	-44,455	-37,620	-49,973	-47,194	-40,028

Source: U. S. Office of Management and Budget, *Historical Tables*, annual.

No. 544. Federal Receipts, by Source: 1980 to 1999

[In millions of dollars ($517,112 represents $517,112,000,000). For fiscal years ending in year shown; see text, Section 9, State and Local Government. Receipts reflect collections. Covers both Federal funds and trust funds; see text, this section. Excludes government-sponsored but privately-owned corporations, Federal Reserve System, District of Columbia government, and money held in suspense as deposit funds]

Source	1980	1985	1990	1995	1997	1998	1999, est.
Total receipts [1]	**517,112**	**734,088**	**1,031,969**	**1,351,830**	**1,579,292**	**1,721,798**	**1,806,334**
Individual income taxes	244,069	334,531	466,884	590,244	737,466	828,586	868,945
Corporation income taxes	64,600	61,331	93,507	157,004	182,293	188,677	182,210
Social insurance and retirement receipts	157,803	265,163	380,047	484,473	539,371	571,831	608,824
Excise taxes	24,329	35,992	35,345	57,484	56,924	57,673	68,075
Social insurance and retirement receipts [1]	157,803	265,163	380,048	484,473	539,371	571,831	608,824
Employment and general retirement	138,748	234,646	353,891	451,045	506,751	540,014	575,740
Old-age and survivors insurance:							
Trust funds (off-budget)	96,581	169,822	255,031	284,091	336,729	358,784	383,176
Disability insurance (off-budget)	16,628	16,348	26,625	66,988	55,261	57,015	60,860
Hospital insurance	23,217	44,871	68,556	96,024	110,710	119,863	127,363
Railroad retirement/pension fund:							
Trust funds	2,323	2,213	2,292	2,424	2,440	2,583	2,656
Railroad social security equivalent account	(NA)	1,391	1,387	1,518	1,611	1,769	1,685
Unemployment insurance	15,336	25,758	21,635	28,878	28,202	27,484	28,765
Trust funds	15,336	25,758	21,635	28,878	28,202	27,484	28,765
Total excise taxes [1]	**24,329**	**35,992**	**35,345**	**57,484**	**56,924**	**57,673**	**68,075**
Federal funds	15,563	19,097	15,591	26,941	27,831	21,665	17,592
Alcohol	5,601	5,562	5,695	7,216	7,257	7,215	7,240
Tobacco	2,443	4,779	4,081	5,878	5,873	5,657	5,213
Crude oil windfall profit	6,934	6,348	(NA)	(NA)	(NA)	(NA)	(NA)
Telephone	(NA)	2,147	2,995	3,794	4,543	4,910	5,213
Ozone depleting chemicals/products	(NA)	(NA)	360	616	130	98	52
Transportation fuels	(NA)	(NA)	(NA)	8,491	7,107	589	811
Trust funds	8,766	16,894	19,754	30,543	29,093	36,008	50,483
Highway	6,620	13,015	13,867	22,611	23,867	26,628	38,464
Airport and airway	1,874	2,851	3,700	5,534	4,007	8,111	10,397
Black lung disability	272	581	665	608	614	636	638
Inland waterway	(NA)	40	63	103	96	91	102
Hazardous substance superfund	(NA)	273	818	867	71	(NA)	147
Post-closure liability (hazardous waste)	(NA)	7	-1	(NA)	(NA)	(NA)	(NA)
Oil spill liability	(NA)	(NA)	143	211	1	(NA)	35
Aquatic resources	(NA)	126	218	306	316	290	376
Leaking underground storage tank	(NA)	(NA)	122	165	-2	136	212
Vaccine injury compensation	(NA)	(NA)	159	138	123	116	112

NA Not available.   [1] Totals reflect interfund and intragovernmental transactions and/or other functions, not shown separately.

Source: U.S. Office of Management and Budget, *Historical Tables*, annual.

No. 545. Federal Trust Fund Receipts, Outlays, and Balances: 1996 to 1998

[In billions of dollars ($835 represents $835,000,000,000). For fiscal years ending in year shown. Receipts deposited. Outlays on a checks-issued basis less refunds collected. Balances: That which have not been spent. See text, this section, for discussion of the budget concept and trust funds]

Description	Income			Outlays			Balances [1]		
	1996	1997	1998	1996	1997	1998	1996	1997	1998
Total [2]	**835**	**878**	**932**	**720**	**752**	**771**	**1,391**	**1,515**	**1,669**
Airport and airway trust fund	3	5	9	7	6	6	8	6	9
Federal employees health benefits fund	16	16	17	16	17	17	7	7	6
Federal civilian employees retirement fund	68	71	73	40	42	44	402	431	461
Federal old-age, survivors and disability insurance trust funds	418	449	481	352	367	382	550	631	730
Foreign military sales trust fund	15	15	14	14	15	14	6	-	-
Highway trust fund	(NA)	25	29	(NA)	25	25	(NA)	22	18
Health insurance trust funds:									
Medicare: Federal hospital insurance	124	129	138	128	138	137	125	116	117
Federal supplemental medical insurance	82	81	83	69	73	77	27	35	41
Military retirement fund	33	38	38	29	30	31	131	139	146
Railroad retirement trust funds	9	9	10	8	8	8	14	15	17
Unemployment trust funds	32	33	32	26	24	24	54	62	71
Veterans life insurance trust funds	2	2	2	2	2	2	14	14	14
Other trust funds [3]	10	10	10	9	9	9	31	31	33

- Represents or rounds to zero.   NA Not available.   [1] Balances available on a cash basis (rather than an authorization basis) at the end of the year. Balances are primarily invested in Federal debt securities.   [2] Includes funds not shown separately.   [3] Effective August 9, 1989, the permanent insurance fund of the FDIC was classified under law as a Federal fund.

Source: U.S. Office of Management and Budget, *Analytical Perspectives*, annual.

Federal Government Finances and Employment **349**

No. 546. Federal Budget Outlays in Constant (1992) Dollars: 1980 to 1999

[Dollar amounts in billions of dollars ($1,015.9 represents $1,015,900,000,000). For fiscal years ending in year shown; see text, Section 9, State and Local Government. Given the inherent imprecision in deflating outlays, the data shown in constant dollars present a reasonable perspective—not precision. The deflators and the categories that are deflated are as comparable over time as feasible. Minus sign (-) indicates offset]

Outlay	1980	1985	1990	1992	1993	1994	1995	1996	1997	1998	1999, est.
Constant (1992) dollar outlays, total	1,015.9	1,208.6	1,353.6	1,381.7	1,374.8	1,392.8	1,410.2	1,419.7	1,429.0	1,450.4	1,489.9
National defense [1]	229.4	306.1	324.6	298.4	286.6	271.9	256.8	242.3	241.1	236.6	240.6
Nondefense, total	786.5	902.5	1,029.1	1,083.3	1,088.2	1,120.9	1,153.5	1,177.4	1,187.8	1,213.7	1,249.2
Payments for individuals. . .	484.5	564.4	632.3	727.6	761.1	780.9	810.6	826.7	846.5	855.6	880.0
Direct payments [2] . . .	427.7	499.1	548.9	615.5	640.3	652.5	675.5	692.5	713.9	715.9	736.0
Grants to state and local governments . .	56.8	65.2	83.4	112.2	120.9	128.5	135.1	134.2	132.6	139.7	144.0
All other grants	98.8	70.2	61.1	65.6	67.5	71.8	73.3	72.5	75.6	75.5	81.2
Net interest [2]	88.6	165.2	197.8	199.4	193.7	193.1	215.7	219.7	218.2	215.0	198.2
All other [2]	149.7	145.3	177.9	130.0	101.4	109.6	93.2	90.1	88.7	106.0	122.0
Undistributed offsetting receipts [2] . .	-35.1	-42.6	-40.0	-39.3	-35.6	-34.5	-39.2	-31.6	-41.1	-38.4	-32.1
Total outlays as percent of GDP	21.7	23.1	22.0	22.5	21.8	21.4	21.1	20.7	20.0	19.7	19.7
National defense [1]	4.9	6.2	5.3	4.9	4.5	4.1	3.8	3.5	3.4	3.2	3.2
Nondefense, total	16.8	16.9	16.8	17.6	17.3	17.2	17.3	17.2	16.6	16.5	16.6
Payments for individuals. . .	10.2	10.4	10.3	11.8	12.1	12.0	12.2	12.0	11.9	11.6	11.7
Direct payments [2] . . .	9.0	9.2	8.9	10.0	10.2	10.0	10.1	10.1	10.0	9.7	9.8
Grants to state and local governments . .	1.2	1.2	1.4	1.8	1.9	2.0	2.0	2.0	1.9	1.9	1.9
All other grants	2.2	1.4	1.0	1.1	1.1	1.1	1.1	1.1	1.1	1.0	1.1
Net interest [2]	1.9	3.2	3.2	3.2	3.1	3.0	3.2	3.2	3.1	2.9	2.6
All other [2]	3.2	2.8	2.9	2.1	1.6	1.7	1.4	1.3	1.3	1.5	1.7
Undistributed offsetting receipts [2] . .	-0.7	-0.8	-0.6	-0.6	-0.6	-0.6	-0.6	-0.5	-0.6	-0.6	-0.5
Percent of outlays, total . .	100.0	100.0	100.0	100.0	100.0	100.0	100.0	100.0	100.0	100.0	100.0
National defense [1]	22.7	26.7	23.9	21.6	20.7	19.3	17.9	17.0	16.9	16.2	16.0
Nondefense, total	77.3	73.3	76.1	78.4	79.3	80.7	82.1	83.0	83.1	83.8	84.0
Payments for individuals. . .	47.1	45.1	46.6	52.7	55.5	56.2	57.7	58.3	59.3	59.1	59.3
Direct payments [2] . . .	41.6	39.9	40.5	44.5	46.7	47.0	48.1	48.8	50.0	49.4	49.6
Grants to state and local governments . .	5.5	5.2	6.2	8.1	8.8	9.3	9.6	9.5	9.3	9.7	9.7
All other grants	9.9	6.0	4.6	4.7	4.9	5.1	5.2	5.1	5.3	5.2	5.5
Net interest [2]	8.9	13.7	14.7	14.4	14.1	13.9	15.3	15.4	15.2	14.7	13.2
All other [2]	14.8	12.0	13.1	9.4	7.5	8.0	6.7	6.5	6.3	7.5	8.4
Undistributed offsetting receipts [2] . .	-3.4	-3.5	-2.9	-2.8	-2.7	-2.6	-2.9	-2.4	-3.1	-2.9	-2.3

[1] Includes a small amount of grants to state and local governments and direct payments for individuals. [2] Includes some off-budget amounts; most of the off-budget amounts are direct payments for individuals (social security benefits).

Source: U.S. Office of Management and Budget, *Historical Tables*, annual.

No. 547. Federal Outlays, by Agency: 1990 to 1999

[In millions of dollars ($1,253,163 represents $1,253,163,000,000)]

Department or other unit	1990	1995	1996	1997	1998	1999, est.
Total outlays.	1,253,163	1,515,729	1,560,512	1,601,232	1,652,552	1,727,071
Legislative Branch	2,241	2,625	2,273	2,363	2,600	2,850
The Judiciary Branch.	1,646	2,903	3,059	3,259	3,467	3,913
Agriculture.	46,012	56,665	54,352	52,547	53,947	63,412
Commerce	3,734	3,401	3,702	3,783	4,046	4,767
Defense-Military	289,755	259,556	253,253	258,322	256,122	263,556
Education	22,972	31,205	29,727	30,009	31,463	34,360
Energy	12,084	17,617	16,203	14,467	14,438	15,544
Health and Human Services	175,531	303,081	319,803	339,535	350,568	375,532
Housing and Urban Development	20,167	29,044	25,236	27,527	30,227	32,324
Interior	5,790	7,378	6,725	6,720	7,218	8,426
Justice	6,507	10,788	11,954	14,310	16,168	16,458
Labor	25,215	32,092	32,492	30,458	30,007	34,923
State	4,802	6,267	5,739	6,033	5,382	6,791
Transportation	28,650	38,777	38,780	39,832	39,463	41,873
Treasury	255,172	348,579	364,629	379,342	390,140	385,976
Veterans Affairs	28,998	37,771	36,920	39,280	41,773	43,474
Corps of Engineers	3,324	3,745	3,627	3,598	3,845	4,209
Other Defense-Civil Programs.	21,692	27,977	28,952	30,282	31,216	32,311
Environmental Protection Agency.	5,108	6,351	6,046	6,164	6,284	6,667
Executive Office of the President.	158	215	202	221	237	374
Federal Emergency Management Administration . .	2,183	3,136	3,102	3,326	2,096	2,668
General Services Administration	-93	831	732	1,084	1,091	328
International Assistance Programs	10,086	11,129	9,665	10,126	8,974	10,130
National Aeronautics and Space Administration . .	12,429	13,378	13,881	14,360	14,206	14,043
National Science Foundation	1,838	2,845	3,012	3,130	3,188	3,259
Office of Personnel Management.	31,949	41,276	42,870	45,404	46,305	48,266
Small Business Administration.	692	677	873	333	-77	-866
Social Security Administration (On-budget)	18,147	31,753	31,365	34,939	38,134	41,122
Social Security Administration (Off-budget)	244,998	330,370	343,869	358,372	370,069	381,316
Other Independent Agencies (On-budget)	68,679	-6,102	2,646	-2,876	10,773	5,377
Other Independent Agencies (Off-budget)	1,626	-1,969	-180	-49	217	964
Undistributed offsetting receipts	-98,930	-137,632	-134,997	-154,969	-161,035	-160,394

Source: U.S. Office of Management and Budget, *Historical Tables*, annual.

350   Federal Government Finances and Employment

No. 548. Federal Outlays, by Detailed Function: 1990 to 1999

[In millions of dollars ($1,253,163 represents $1,253,163,000,000)]

Superfunction and function	1990	1995	1996	1997	1998	1999, est.
Total outlays.	1,253,163	1,515,729	1,560,512	1,601,232	1,652,552	1,727,071
National defense, total.	299,331	272,066	265,753	270,505	268,456	276,730
Department of Defense—Military [1]	289,755	259,442	253,187	258,311	256,122	263,556
Military personnel.	75,622	70,809	66,669	69,724	68,976	71,957
Operation and maintenance.	88,340	91,078	88,759	92,461	93,473	96,839
Procurement.	80,972	54,982	48,913	47,690	48,206	48,422
Research, develop., test, and evaluation . . .	37,458	34,594	36,494	37,015	37,420	36,758
Military construction	5,080	6,823	6,683	6,187	6,044	5,287
Family housing	3,501	3,571	3,828	4,003	3,871	3,894
Atomic energy defense activities	8,988	11,777	11,644	11,275	11,268	12,012
Defense-related activities	587	847	922	919	1,066	1,162
International affairs, total	13,764	16,434	13,496	15,228	13,109	15,474
International develop. & humanitarian assist. . . .	5,498	7,599	6,160	6,054	5,446	5,714
International security assistance.	8,652	5,252	4,565	4,632	5,135	5,737
Conduct of foreign affairs	3,050	4,192	3,761	3,919	3,262	4,617
Foreign info. and exchange activities . . .	1,103	1,417	1,187	1,173	1,159	1,216
International financial programs	-4,539	-2,026	-2,177	-550	-1,893	-1,810
General science, space & technology, total	14,444	16,724	16,709	17,174	18,219	18,529
General science and basic research	2,835	4,131	4,016	4,118	5,353	5,738
Space flight, research, and supporting activities	11,609	12,593	12,693	13,056	12,866	12,791
Energy, total	3,341	4,936	2,839	1,475	1,270	49
Energy supply.	1,976	3,584	1,649	626	181	-894
Energy conservation	365	671	624	572	621	560
Emergency energy preparedness.	442	223	141	23	233	182
Energy information, policy, & regulation . . .	559	458	425	254	235	201
Natural resources & environment, total [1]	17,080	22,078	21,614	21,369	22,396	24,261
Water resources	4,401	4,791	4,617	4,536	4,721	5,454
Conservation and land management.	3,553	5,318	5,396	5,067	5,475	5,074
Recreational resources.	1,876	2,801	2,673	2,785	2,984	3,952
Pollution control and abatement	5,170	6,513	6,182	6,292	6,422	6,855
Agriculture, total	11,958	9,778	9,159	9,032	12,206	21,449
Farm income stabilization	9,761	7,020	6,477	6,272	9,297	18,405
Agricultural research and services	2,197	2,758	2,682	2,760	2,909	3,044
Commerce and housing credit, total [1]	67,600	-17,808	-10,472	-14,624	1,014	452
Mortgage credit.	3,845	-1,038	-5,025	-4,006	-2,934	-1,112
Postal Service	2,116	-1,839	-58	77	303	964
Deposit insurance	57,891	-17,827	-8,394	-14,384	-4,371	-5,047
Transportation, total [1]	29,485	39,350	39,565	40,767	40,332	42,640
Ground transportation	18,954	25,297	25,650	26,795	26,004	28,333
Air transportation.	7,234	10,020	10,135	10,138	10,622	10,559
Water transportation.	3,151	3,732	3,460	3,554	3,507	3,502
Community & regional development, total	8,498	10,641	10,685	11,005	9,720	10,428
Community development	3,530	4,744	4,860	4,962	5,118	5,437
Area and regional development	2,868	2,615	2,667	2,691	2,456	2,570
Disaster relief and insurance	2,100	3,282	3,158	3,352	2,146	2,421
Education, training, employ., & social serv.	38,755	54,263	52,001	53,008	54,919	60,065
Elementary, secondary, & vocational education .	9,918	14,694	14,871	15,073	16,571	16,989
Higher education.	11,107	14,172	12,191	12,298	12,070	14,047
Research and general education aids	1,577	2,120	2,215	2,136	2,271	2,448
Training and employment	5,619	7,430	7,030	6,681	6,636	7,941
Social services	9,723	14,882	14,769	15,811	16,335	17,532
Health, total.	57,716	115,418	119,378	123,843	131,440	143,095
Health care services	47,642	101,931	106,622	109,973	116,336	126,190
Health research and training	8,611	11,569	10,827	11,847	13,073	14,681
Consumer & occupational health & safety	1,462	1,918	1,929	2,023	2,031	2,224
Medicare.	98,102	159,855	174,225	190,016	192,822	204,982
Income security, total [1]	147,076	220,493	225,967	230,899	233,202	243,130
General retirement & disability insurance [2] . . .	5,148	5,106	5,234	4,721	4,632	2,312
Federal employee retirement & disability	52,037	65,882	68,071	71,539	73,485	76,262
Unemployment compensation	18,889	23,638	24,898	22,888	22,070	25,178
Housing assistance	15,891	27,520	26,754	27,798	28,741	28,376
Food and nutrition assistance	23,964	37,594	37,933	36,061	33,585	35,271
Social security	248,623	335,846	349,676	365,257	379,225	392,608
Veterans benefits and services, total [1]	29,058	37,890	36,985	39,313	41,781	43,526
Income security for veterans	15,241	18,966	18,201	20,407	21,322	22,640
Veterans educ., training & rehab	278	1,124	1,114	1,156	1,102	1,337
Hospital & medical care for veterans.	12,134	16,428	16,586	17,093	17,545	17,933
Veterans housing	517	329	66	-342	837	468
Administration of justice, total	9,993	16,216	17,548	20,173	22,832	24,467
General government, total	10,734	13,835	11,914	12,749	13,444	14,852
Net interest, total	184,221	232,169	241,090	244,016	243,359	227,244
Interest on the public debt.	264,724	332,414	343,955	355,796	363,793	353,429
Interest received by on-budget trust funds . . .	-46,321	-59,871	-60,869	-63,776	-67,208	-67,233
Interest received by off-budget trust funds	-15,991	-33,305	-36,507	-41,214	-46,630	-51,869
Allowances, total	(X)	(X)	(X)	(X)	(X)	3,118
Undistributed offsetting receipts, total	-36,615	-44,455	-37,620	-49,973	-47,194	-40,028

X Not applicable.   [1] Includes functions not shown separately.   [2] Includes social security.

Source: U.S. Office of Management and Budget, *Historical Tables*, annual.

No. 549. Tax Expenditures Estimates, by Function: 1998 to 2001

[In millions of dollars ($2,095 represents $2,095,000,000). For years ending **Sept. 30.** Tax expenditures are defined as *revenue losses* attributable to provisions of the Federal tax laws which allow a special exclusion, exemption, or deduction from gross income or which provide a special credit, a preferential rate of tax, or a deferral of liability. Represents tax expenditures of **$1.5 billion or more in 2001**]

Function and provision	1998	1999	2000	2001, est.
National defense:				
Current law tax expenditures	2,095	2,120	2,140	2,160
Exclusion of benefits and allowances to armed forces personnel	2,095	2,120	2,140	2,160
International affairs:				
Current law tax expenditures	11,040	12,410	12,265	13,100
Exclusion of income earned abroad by U.S. citizens	1,990	2,235	2,500	2,800
Exclusion of income of foreign sales corporations	2,150	2,250	2,400	2,550
Deferral of income from controlled foreign corporations [1]	5,500	5,800	6,200	6,600
Energy: Total, current law tax expenditures.	1,535	1,575	1,625	1,630
Natural resources and environment:				
Total, current law tax expenditures.	1,460	1,515	1,555	1,620
Commerce and housing:				
Current law tax expenditures	219,320	227,555	236,210	245,090
Financial institutions and insurance:				
Exclusion of interest on life insurance savings	13,465	14,200	14,990	15,810
Housing: Deductibility of mortgage interest on owner-occupied homes	51,700	52,990	55,100	57,590
Deductibility of state and local property tax on owner-occupied homes	17,770	18,595	19,495	20,535
Capital gains exclusion on home sales	17,475	18,000	18,540	19,095
Exception from passive loss rules for $25,000 of rental loss	4,735	4,455	4,215	4,000
Credit for low-income housing investment.	3,120	3,225	3,335	3,485
Accelerated depreciation on rental housing [1]	2,405	2,740	3,095	4,170
Commerce: Capital gains (except agriculture, timber, iron ore, and coal) [1]	38,275	39,415	40,585	41,795
Step-up basis of capital gains at death	24,570	25,800	27,090	28,240
Accelerated depreciation of buildings other than rental housing [1]	6,270	4,895	3,430	2,385
Accelerated depreciation of machinery and equipment [1]	28,885	32,505	35,465	36,830
Graduated corporation income tax rate [1]	5,400	5,360	5,360	5,620
Transportation:				
Current law tax expenditures	1,645	1,690	1,740	1,810
Exclusion of reimbursed employee parking expenses	1,560	1,595	1,630	1,690
Education, training, employment, and social services:				
Current law tax expenditures	29,885	37,580	40,035	42,025
Education: HOPE tax credit	200	4,015	4,855	5,325
Lifetime Learning tax credit	110	2,510	2,655	2,970
Deductibility of charitable contributions (education).	2,880	2,940	3,065	3,195
Training, employment, and social services:				
Exclusion of employer-provided child care	1,325	1,385	1,445	1,510
Credit for child and dependent care expenses.	2,485	2,455	2,425	2,395
Deductibility of charitable contributions, other than education and health	18,580	19,150	20,055	21,005
Proposals affecting tax expenditures	-	165	1,577	3,656
Health: Current law tax expenditures.	80,545	85,810	91,795	97,885
Exclusion of employer contrib. for medical ins. premiums and medical care . . .	67,920	72,535	77,670	83,095
Workers' compensation insurance premiums	4,260	4,420	4,585	4,755
Deductibility of medical expenses.	3,615	3,775	3,985	4,215
Deductibility of charitable contributions (health).	2,560	2,630	2,730	2,860
Income security: Current law tax expenditures.	117,906	132,388	135,291	138,642
Exclusion of workmens compensation benefits	5,140	5,330	5,475	5,940
Net exclusion of pension contributions and earnings:				
Employer plans	82,215	82,195	84,350	86,670
Individual Retirement Accounts.	10,565	10,770	11,170	11,440
Keogh plans	3,930	4,025	4,255	4,495
Exclusion of other employee benefits:				
Premiums on group term life insurance	2,030	2,075	2,120	2,170
Additional deduction for the elderly.	1,690	1,720	1,740	1,795
Earned income tax credit	6,351	5,118	4,971	5,142
Child credit	3,525	18,740	18,725	18,430
Social Security: Current law tax expenditures	22,770	23,415	24,650	25,930
Exclusion of social security benefits:				
Social security benefits for retired workers	16,780	17,210	18,125	19,045
Social security benefits for disabled	2,265	2,420	2,615	2,820
Social security benefits for dependents and survivors.	3,725	3,785	3,910	4,065
Veterans' benefits and services:				
Current law tax expenditures	2,990	3,120	3,265	3,415
Exclusion of veterans' death benefits and disability compensation	2,820	2,940	3,070	3,210
General purpose fiscal assistance:				
Current law tax expenditures	56,805	59,175	61,570	64,140
Exclusion of interest on public purpose bonds	20,050	20,250	20,450	20,660
Deductibility of nonbusiness state and local taxes other than on owner-occupied homes.	32,795	34,925	37,000	39,235
Tax credit for corps. receiving income from doing business in U.S. possessions .	3,960	4,000	4,120	4,245

- Represents zero.   [1] Normal tax method.

Source: U.S. Office of Management and Budget, *Budget of the United States Government*, annual.

U.S. Census Bureau, Statistical Abstract of the United States: 1999

No. 550. United States Government—Balance Sheet: 1990 to 1998

[In millions of dollars ($70,415 represents $70,415,000,000). For fiscal year ending in year shown]

Item	1990	1995	1996	1997	1998
Assets, total	70,415	89,349	103,432	121,273	139,401
Cash and monetary assets, total................	60,839	84,080	86,056	81,242	87,586
U.S. Treasury operating cash:					
Federal Reserve account.................	7,638	8,620	7,700	7,692	4,952
Tax and loan note accounts..............	32,517	29,329	36,525	35,930	33,926
Special drawing rights (SDR):					
Total holdings	10,666	11,035	10,177	9,997	10,106
SDR's certificates issued to Federal Reserve banks....	-8,518	-10,168	-9,718	-9,200	-9,200
Monetary assets with IMF [1]	8,883	14,682	15,428	14,045	21,155
Other cash and monetary assets:					
U.S. Treasury monetary assets	1,572	356	87	87	87
Cash and other assets held outside the Treasury Account .	8,079	29,697	21,133	18,670	21,523
U.S. Treasury time deposits	(NA)	528	4,724	4,021	4,543
Loan financing accounts:					
Guaranteed loans.......................	(NA)	-12,714	-13,750	-13,905	-13,391
Direct loans...........................	(NA)	19,732	32,780	53,816	65,289
Miscellaneous asset accounts	9,576	-1,748	-1,654	120	-83
Total assets and excess of liabilities over assets........	2,479,165	3,674,266	3,795,179	3,834,651	3,781,994
Excess of liabilities over assets at beginning of fiscal year...	2,188,926	3,421,723	3,584,917	3,691,894	3,713,378
Add: Total deficit for fiscal year...............	220,388	163,916	107,445	-21,957	70,215
Subtotal	(NA)	3,585,639	3,692,362	3,713,850	3,643,163
Deduct: Other transactions not applied to surplus or deficit ..	564	722	615	472	569
Excess of liabilities over assets at close of fiscal year......	2,408,750	3,584,917	3,691,747	3,713,378	3,642,594
Liabilities, total.........................	2,479,165	3,674,266	3,795,179	3,834,651	3,781,994
Borrowing from the public, total................	2,470,166	3,603,299	3,732,957	3,771,141	3,719,864
Public debt securities outstanding	3,233,313	4,973,985	5,224,812	5,413,147	5,526,194
Premium and discount on public debt securities	59,811	-79,996	-77,932	-76,633	-76,849
Total public debt securities	(NA)	4,893,989	5,146,880	5,336,514	5,449,345
Agency securities outstanding................	32,758	26,955	35,043	33,187	29,372
Federal securities, total..................	3,266,073	4,920,944	5,181,923	5,369,700	5,478,717
Deduct: Net Federal securities held as investments by					
government accounts......................	795,907	1,317,645	1,448,967	1,598,559	1,758,853
Accrued interest payable	43,799	50,611	45,605	46,083	45,448
Special drawing rights allocated by IMF [1]	6,823	7,380	7,052	6,689	6,719
Deposit fund liabilities	8,306	8,186	7,213	6,800	6,041
Miscellaneous liability accounts (checks outstanding, etc.) .	9,882	4,790	2,352	3,938	3,923

NA Not available.   [1] IMF = International Monetary Funds.

Source: U.S. Dept. of Treasury, *United States Government Annual Report.*

No. 551. Federal Participation in the Credit Market: 1970 to 2000

[In millions of dollars, except percents]

Item	1970	1980	1990	1995	1996	1997	1998	1999 est.	2000 est.
Total, Federal and federally assisted borowing	16.2	122.5	376.9	323.2	361.1	208.7	300.3	317.4	221.7
Federal borrowing from the public .	35.0	69.5	220.8	171.3	129.6	38.2	-51.3	-50.1	-97.9
Guaranteed borrowing..........	7.8	31.6	40.7	26.2	89.9	57.8	58.5	102.1	97.9
Government-sponsored enterprise borrowing	4.9	21.4	115.4	125.7	141.5	112.8	293.1	265.3	221.7
Total, Federal and federally assisted lending	15.9	79.9	133.5	90.4	255.1	178.4	341.5	423.7	332.1
Direct loans.................	3.0	24.2	2.8	1.6	4.0	12.8	6.8	14.7	11.1
Guaranteed loans.............	7.8	31.6	40.7	26.2	89.9	57.8	58.5	102.1	97.9
Government-sponsored enterprise loans	5.2	24.1	90.0	68.2	161.2	107.9	276.2	306.9	223.1
Total net borrowing in credit market	88.2	336.9	704.1	705.6	713.7	687.1	933.8	(NA)	(NA)
Federal borrowing participation rate (percent)..............	18.4	36.4	53.5	45.8	50.6	30.4	32.2	(NA)	(NA)
Total net lending in credit market..	88.2	336.9	704.1	705.6	713.7	687.1	933.7	(NA)	(NA)
Federal lending participation rate (percent)................	18.0	23.7	19.0	12.8	35.7	26.0	36.6	(NA)	(NA)

NA Not available.

Source: U.S. Office of Management and Budget, *Analytical Perspectives,* annual.

U.S. Census Bureau, Statistical Abstract of the United States: 1999

No. 552. Summary of Federal Debt: 1990 to 1998

[In millions of dollars ($3,266,073 represents $3,266,073,000,000). Based on end of fiscal year]

Item	1990	1995	1996	1997	1998
Debt outstanding, total	3,266,073	5,000,945	5,259,854	5,446,333	5,555,565
Public debt securities	3,233,313	4,973,983	5,224,811	5,413,146	5,526,193
Agency securities.	32,758	26,962	35,043	33,187	29,372
Securities held by—					
Government accounts, total	795,907	1,320,800	1,454,608	1,605,557	1,769,497
Public debt securities	795,762	1,320,784	1,447,001	1,598,459	1,765,580
Agency securities	145	16	7,606	7,098	3,917
The public, total	2,470,166	3,680,145	3,805,246	3,840,776	3,786,068
Public debt securities	2,437,551	3,653,199	3,777,810	3,814,687	3,760,613
Agency securities	32,613	26,946	27,437	26,089	25,455
Interest-bearing public debt, total.	**3,210,943**	**4,950,644**	**5,220,790**	**5,407,528**	**5,518,681**
Marketable, total	2,092,759	3,260,447	3,418,371	3,439,616	3,331,030
Treasury bills	482,454	742,462	761,232	701,909	637,648
Treasury notes	1,218,081	1,980,343	2,098,670	2,122,172	2,009,115
Treasury bonds	377,224	522,643	543,469	576,151	610,444
Treasury inflation-indexed notes	(Z)	(Z)	(Z)	24,384	58,823
Federal Financing Bank	15,000	15,000	15,000	15,000	15,000
Nonmarketable, total.	1,118,184	1,690,197	1,802,419	1,967,912	2,187,651
U.S. savings bonds	122,152	181,181	184,147	182,665	180,816
Foreign series:					
Government	36,041	40,950	37,488	34,909	35,079
Government account series, total.	779,412	1,324,270	1,454,690	1,608,478	1,777,329
Airport and airway trust fund	14,312	11,145	7,682	6,360	8,550
Bank insurance fund	8,438	20,117	22,186	26,329	27,445
Employees life insurance fund	9,561	15,839	16,962	18,038	19,377
Exchange stabilization fund	1,863	2,399	11,853	15,460	15,981
Federal disability insurance trust fund	11,254	35,150	50,051	63,513	76,947
Federal employees retirement funds	223,229	357,539	377,677	407,202	440,145
Federal hospital insurance trust fund.	96,249	129,864	125,805	116,621	118,250
Federal Housing Administration	6,678	6,277	7,894	13,643	14,518
Fed. old-age & survivors insurance trust fund	203,717	447,947	499,403	567,445	653,282
Fed. S&L Corp., resolution fund	929	528	694	1,806	2,087
Fed. supplementary medical insur. trust fund	14,286	13,513	27,175	34,464	39,502
Government life insurance fund	184	106	99	(Z)	(Z)
Highway trust fund	9,530	8,954	11,660	22,341	17,926
National service life insurance fund.	10,917	11,954	12,007	12,023	12,008
Postal Service fund	3,063	1,249	860	860	1,000
Railroad retirement account.	8,356	12,129	14,763	17,486	19,764
Treasury deposit funds	304	130	77	74	71
Unemployment trust fund	50,186	47,098	53,849	61,880	70,598
Other	106,376	202,332	213,993	222,933	239,878
State and local government series.	161,248	113,368	95,674	111,863	164,431
Domestic series	18,886	29,995	29,995	29,995	29,995
Other	447	432	424	1	1
MATURITY DISTRIBUTION					
Amount outstanding, privately held	**1,841,903**	**2,870,781**	**3,011,185**	**2,998,846**	**2,856,637**
Maturity class:					
Within 1 year	626,297	1,002,875	1,058,558	1,017,913	940,572
1-5 years.	630,144	1,157,492	1,212,258	1,206,993	1,105,175
5-10 years	267,573	290,111	306,643	321,622	319,331
10-20 years	82,713	87,297	111,360	154,205	157,347
20 years and over	235,176	333,006	322,366	298,113	334,212

Z Less than $500,000.

Source: U.S. Department of the Treasury, *Treasury Bulletin*, quarterly.

No. 553. U.S. Savings Bonds: 1980 to 1998

[In billions of dollars ($73 represents $73,000,000), except percent. As of end of fiscal year, see text, Section 9, State and Local Government]

Item	1980	1985	1990	1991	1992	1993	1994	1995	1996	1997	1998
Amounts outstanding, total [1]	73	77	123	134	149	167	177	182	184	183	181
Funds from sales	5	5	8	9	14	17	9	7	6	5	3
Accrued discounts	4	5	8	10	9	9	9	9	10	9	7
Redemptions [2]	17	6	8	8	7	8	9	12	2	2	11
Percent of total outstanding. . .	23.0	7.4	6.1	5.6	5.0	4.7	5.3	6.5	1.4	1.1	6.1

[1] Interest-bearing debt only for amounts end of year. [2] Matured and unmatured bonds.

Source: U.S. Dept. of the Treasury, *Treasury Bulletin*, quarterly.

No. 554. Federal Funds—Summary Distribution, by State: 1998

[In millions of dollars ($1,484,177 represents $1,484,177,000,000). For year ending Sept. 30. Data for grants, salaries and wages, and direct payments to individuals are on an expenditures basis; procurement is on obligation basis]

State	Federal funds		Defense	Non-defense	Direct pay-ments to individuals	Procure-ment	Grants to state and local govern-ments	Salaries and wages
	Total [1]	Per capita [2] (dol.)						
United States [3]..	**1,484,177**	**5,491**	**226,444**	**1,257,733**	**835,619**	**209,260**	**269,128**	**170,171**
Alabama	25,297	5,813	4,501	20,796	15,089	3,104	4,161	2,944
Alaska	4,767	7,763	1,467	3,300	1,194	863	1,427	1,282
Arizona	24,067	5,155	4,753	19,315	13,595	3,793	4,147	2,533
Arkansas	13,016	5,128	938	12,078	9,048	475	2,440	1,054
California	161,571	4,946	29,072	132,498	86,771	25,365	32,090	17,344
Colorado	21,009	5,291	4,632	16,377	10,164	4,300	3,048	3,496
Connecticut	19,424	5,933	3,920	15,504	10,600	3,814	3,653	1,357
Delaware	3,553	4,776	382	3,172	2,293	215	678	367
District of Columbia	24,034	45,955	2,274	21,761	3,298	5,200	4,101	11,436
Florida	83,558	5,602	12,201	71,357	58,414	7,128	10,320	7,696
Georgia	37,144	4,861	8,118	29,026	20,324	4,603	6,233	5,984
Hawaii	8,442	7,076	3,394	5,048	3,641	1,053	1,190	2,557
Idaho	5,961	4,850	535	5,426	3,235	1,019	1,055	652
Illinois	55,467	4,605	3,313	52,154	35,246	4,576	10,156	5,490
Indiana	26,098	4,424	2,510	23,588	17,796	2,233	4,152	1,917
Iowa	14,535	5,079	719	13,815	10,241	930	2,424	941
Kansas	13,426	5,107	2,061	11,365	8,497	1,316	1,934	1,680
Kentucky	23,161	5,884	3,269	19,892	12,588	3,850	4,236	2,488
Louisiana	22,900	5,242	2,441	20,459	13,839	2,351	4,708	2,002
Maine	7,463	5,999	1,442	6,021	4,088	1,025	1,602	748
Maryland	41,565	8,094	8,738	32,827	18,083	10,417	5,022	8,042
Massachusetts	37,173	6,047	5,103	32,070	20,864	5,451	8,019	2,840
Michigan	41,917	4,270	1,852	40,065	28,613	1,871	8,618	2,814
Minnesota	20,399	4,317	1,591	18,808	12,701	1,795	4,199	1,704
Mississippi	15,314	5,565	2,429	12,885	9,176	1,613	3,025	1,500
Missouri	32,682	6,009	5,678	27,004	18,221	6,341	5,065	3,055
Montana	5,465	6,210	367	5,098	3,337	376	1,139	614
Nebraska	8,253	4,963	868	7,385	5,292	487	1,511	963
Nevada	7,566	4,331	955	6,611	4,846	805	1,081	835
New Hampshire	5,272	4,449	702	4,569	3,258	524	1,042	448
New Jersey	40,373	4,975	4,068	36,304	25,715	4,091	7,108	3,458
New Mexico	12,933	7,446	1,605	11,329	5,036	3,769	2,547	1,581
New York	99,766	5,489	4,746	95,020	58,464	5,995	28,066	7,240
North Carolina	35,677	4,728	5,123	30,554	21,645	2,064	7,133	4,833
North Dakota	4,131	6,475	477	3,654	2,253	258	1,067	554
Ohio	52,006	4,640	4,434	47,571	33,663	4,368	9,733	4,242
Oklahoma	18,205	5,439	2,970	15,234	11,128	1,381	3,059	2,637
Oregon	15,119	4,607	820	14,299	9,646	728	3,275	1,471
Pennsylvania	67,350	5,612	5,417	61,933	44,501	5,163	12,381	5,306
Rhode Island	6,039	6,112	722	5,317	3,644	313	1,368	715
South Carolina	19,870	5,180	3,235	16,635	11,611	2,489	3,525	2,246
South Dakota	4,319	5,852	310	4,009	2,487	317	1,007	508
Tennessee	30,497	5,615	2,272	28,225	17,238	5,116	5,510	2,633
Texas	92,019	4,657	15,994	76,024	51,152	13,893	15,809	11,164
Utah	8,728	4,156	1,305	7,423	4,430	1,180	1,727	1,392
Vermont	2,895	4,898	188	2,706	1,659	154	803	278
Virginia	55,830	8,221	23,079	32,752	21,525	18,523	4,423	11,360
Washington	31,186	5,482	6,416	24,770	16,232	4,920	5,422	4,612
West Virginia	10,697	5,906	364	10,332	6,870	488	2,480	859
Wisconsin	21,883	4,189	986	20,896	14,426	1,295	4,697	1,464
Wyoming	2,743	5,702	283	2,460	1,343	175	850	376

[1] Includes other programs not shown separately.   [2] Based on U.S. Census Bureau resident population as of July 1.
[3] Includes outlying areas, not shown separately.

Source: U.S. Census Bureau, Federal Expenditures by State for Fiscal Year, annual.

Federal Government Finances and Employment 355

No. 555. Per Capita Federal Balance of Payments, by State: 1990 to 1997

[For year ending Sept. 30. Represents Federal spending within the borders of the 50 states, including defense and excluding interest payments on the Federal debt. Each state runs a balance of payments surplus or deficit with the Federal Government. Put another way, each state indirectly subsidizes or is being subsidized by the other states]

State	1990	1994	1995	1996	1997					
					Amount	Rank	Spending	Rank	Taxes	Rank
Alabama.	1,857	1,723	1,593	1,453	1,603	10	5,821	9	4,218	35
Alaska	1,003	1,957	1,057	1,365	2,019	6	6,589	5	4,570	30
Arizona.	1,118	870	803	655	372	23	4,630	35	4,258	34
Arkansas	1,028	1,009	934	1,073	1,251	16	5,185	20	3,934	42
California	-463	-128	-208	-283	-366	35	4,632	34	4,997	16
Colorado.	860	131	-133	-144	-444	38	4,774	29	5,218	12
Connecticut.	1,693	-2,307	-2,209	-1,917	-2,272	50	4,571	36	6,844	1
Delaware	-1,913	-1,722	-1,483	-992	-1,030	43	4,210	41	5,240	11
District of Columbia	26,381	32,111	32,441	33,554	35,520	(X)	41,912	(X)	6,392	(X)
Florida	45	316	375	285	338	24	5,607	13	5,269	9
Georgia	-180	349	131	67	-59	30	4,932	25	4,991	17
Hawaii	769	1,101	1,020	1,414	1,788	8	5,391	17	3,603	50
Idaho	1,401	501	611	633	637	20	4,691	32	4,054	40
Illinois	-1,553	-1,680	-1,680	-1,673	-1,688	48	4,040	46	5,728	3
Indiana.	-449	-645	-747	-679	-511	39	4,158	42	4,670	29
Iowa	252	169	-156	172	131	26	4,661	33	4,530	31
Kansas.	278	115	-62	-96	-174	34	4,746	30	4,919	18
Kentucky	1,096	999	1,450	1,155	1,541	11	5,653	12	4,112	39
Louisiana	1,045	1,628	1,423	1,277	1,521	13	5,482	14	3,961	41
Maine.	737	1,199	1,057	1,147	1,454	15	5,228	19	3,774	46
Maryland	1,291	1,773	1,600	1,387	1,767	9	7,476	2	5,709	4
Massachusetts.	22	-199	-244	-365	-518	40	5,067	23	5,585	5
Michigan.	-1,017	-1,174	-1,439	-1,416	-1,383	45	4,067	44	5,450	8
Minnesota.	-590	-1,194	-1,466	-1,343	-1,325	44	4,220	40	5,545	6
Mississippi	2,185	2,548	2,332	2,451	2,234	5	5,871	8	3,637	49
Missouri	1,502	1,585	1,289	1,904	1,108	17	5,938	7	4,829	22
Montana.	1,564	1,529	1,668	1,721	1,925	7	5,818	10	3,893	43
Nebraska	548	-118	-44	-32	-138	33	4,729	31	4,867	20
Nevada	-871	-1,012	-1,165	-909	-1,413	46	4,044	45	5,457	7
New Hampshire	-1,561	-1,303	-1,354	-1,375	-1,419	47	3,680	50	5,099	15
New Jersey.	-2,243	-1,981	-1,983	-1,958	-1,946	49	3,956	47	5,902	2
New Mexico	3,731	3,519	3,473	3,335	3,464	1	7,156	3	3,691	48
New York	-961	-1,126	-1,030	-789	-785	41	4,339	37	5,124	13
North Carolina	-196	30	75	33	134	25	4,837	26	4,703	28
North Dakota.	1,951	2,230	1,748	1,577	2,788	2	6,993	4	4,206	36
Ohio	-204	-542	-552	-442	-429	37	4,321	38	4,750	25
Oklahoma.	919	1,058	1,176	1,289	1,539	12	5,389	18	3,850	44
Oregon.	-5	-366	-360	-373	-387	36	4,317	39	4,704	27
Pennsylvania.	-194	-147	11	3	44	28	4,808	27	4,764	24
Rhode Island.	136	202	411	356	633	21	5,102	22	4,469	32
South Carolina.	1,526	1,219	1,207	1,052	983	18	5,184	21	4,201	38
South Dakota.	1,582	1,233	1,154	1,223	1,507	14	5,814	11	4,307	33
Tennessee	617	764	748	749	741	19	5,475	15	4,734	26
Texas.	-52	-111	65	-1	-42	29	4,800	28	4,843	21
Utah	1,480	576	787	273	94	27	3,936	49	3,842	45
Vermont	-630	-449	-12	62	-87	31	4,117	43	4,204	37
Virginia.	2,408	2,273	2,836	2,353	2,648	3	7,896	1	5,248	10
Washington.	353	-261	48	-111	-99	32	5,008	24	5,107	14
West Virginia.	1,424	1,910	2,005	1,981	2,235	4	5,946	6	3,711	47
Wisconsin.	-712	-1,077	-1,147	-1,061	-965	42	3,936	48	4,901	19
Wyoming	880	203	327	244	622	22	5,406	16	4,784	23

X Not applicable.

Source: Jay H. Walder and Herman B. Leonard, *The Federal Budget and the States*, annual.

U.S. Census Bureau, Statistical Abstract of the United States: 1999

No. 556. Tax Returns Filed—Examination Coverage: 1988 to 1997

[In thousands ($103,251 represents $103,251,000, except as indicated. Return classification as Schedule C or C-EZ (nonfarm sole proprietorships) or Schedule F (farm proprietorships) for audit examination purposes was based on the largest source of income on the return and certain other characteristics. Therefore, some returns with business activity are reflected in the nonbusiness individual income tax return statistics in the table below (and vise versa), so that the statistics for the number of returns with Schedule C is not comparable to the number of nonfarm sole proprietorship returns in Table 864. Series completely revised starting with fiscal year 1988]

Year and item	Returns filed [1]	Returns examined					Average tax and penalty per return (dollars)		
		Total	Percent coverage	By—			Revenue agents [3]	Tax auditors	Service centers
				Revenue agents	Tax auditors	Service centers [2]			
INDIVIDUAL RETURNS									
1988	103,251	1,621	1.57	353	532	736	997,696	2,188	1,950
1989	107,029	1,385	1.29	243	543	599	246,371	1,827	1,649
1990	109,868	1,145	1.04	202	517	426	309,566	1,962	2,432
1991	112,305	1,313	1.17	200	500	613	664,440	2,398	2,738
1992	113,829	1,206	1.06	210	537	459	1,365,896	2,280	2,539
1993	114,719	1,059	0.92	251	506	303	103,250	2,625	2,974
1994	113,754	1,226	1.08	364	456	406	246,785	3,113	1,963
1995	114,683	1,919	1.67	339	459	1,122	204,616	3,497	1,404
1996	116,060	1,942	1.67	252	509	1,180	818,753	3,051	1,714
1997 [4]									
Individual, total	118,363	1,519	1.28	210	506	804	802,549	3,460	2,963
1040A, TPI under $25,000 [5]	45,699	659	1.44	22	136	501	16,794	3,250	3,179
Non 1040, TPI under $25,000 [5]	13,091	158	1.21	14	57	86	47,318	2,117	2,674
TPI $25,000 under $50,000 [5]	27,932	196	0.7	21	103	72	15,861	2,148	1,696
TPI $50,000 under $100,000 [5]	18,274	140	0.77	22	77	42	23,418	2,586	1,524
TPI $100,000 and over [5]	5,261	120	2.27	45	35	40	359,105	6,319	5,400
Sch C—TGR under $25,000 [6]	2,465	79	3.19	13	38	27	26,221	3,829	2,764
Sch C—TGR $25,000 under $100,000 [6]	3,140	81	2.57	22	42	17	10,750	5,580	1,991
Sch C—TGR $100,000 and over [6]	1,771	73	4.13	46	15	12	4,983,432	11,162	2,952
Sch F—TGR under $100,000 [6]	450	6	1.28	1	2	2	6,183	1,631	853
Sch F—TGR $100,000 and over [6]	271	7	2.75	4	1	3	82,186	7,350	1,920
Corporation (except S Corporation)	2,609	70	2.67	68	(NA)	2	4,532,951	(NA)	145,623
Fiduciary	3,261	6	0.18	3	(NA)	3	28,034	(NA)	1,831
Estate	91	12	12.9	11	(NA)	0.3	122,775	(NA)	7,733
Gift	232	2	0.9	2	(NA)	0.0001	10,728,731	2,728	(NA)
Employment	28,723	61	0.18	47	13	0.9	145,833	5,856	942
Excise	786	25	3.14	22	2	(NA)	260,906	494	(NA)
Windfall profit	(NA)	(NA)	(NA)	(NA)	(NA)	(NA)	(NA)	(NA)	(NA)
Miscellaneous taxable	(NA)	0.5	(NA)	0.05	(NA)	0.0012	368,017	(NA)	(NA)
Partnerships	1,653	10	0.59	8	(NA)	2	(NA)	(NA)	(NA)
S Corporations (nontaxable)	2,291	24	1.04	23	(NA)	1	(NA)	(NA)	(NA)
Miscellaneous nontaxable [7]	(NA)	0.2	(NA)	0.02	(NA)	(NA)	(NA)	(NA)	(NA)

NA Not available. [1] Returns filed in previous calendar year. [2] Includes taxpayer contacts by correspondence. [3] Mostly reflects coordinated examination of large corporations and related returns. [4] Includes activities to protect release of funds in Treasury in response to taxpayer efforts to recoup tax previously assessed and paid with penalty. [5] Total positive income, i.e., excludes losses. [6] Total gross receipts. [7] Includes Domestic International Sales Corporations, Interest-Charge Domestic International Sales Corporations, Real Estate Investment Mortgage Conduits, and other.

Source: U.S. Internal Revenue Service, *IRS Data Book, 1997* Publication 55B.

No. 557. Internal Revenue Gross Collections, by Source: 1980 to 1997

[For fiscal year ending in year shown; see text, Section 9, State and Local Government]

Source of revenue	Collections (bil. dol.)					Percent of total				
	1980	1990	1995	1996	1997	1980	1990	1995	1996	1997
All taxes	519	1,078	1,389	1,500	1,623	100.0	100.0	100.0	100.0	100.0
Individual income taxes	288	540	676	745	825	54.9	50.1	48.7	50.1	50.7
Withheld by employers	224	388	534	533	580	43.1	36.0	38.4	35.9	35.7
Employment taxes [1]	128	367	465	492	529	24.7	34.0	33.5	33.1	32.6
Old-age and disability insurance	123	358	455	482	518	23.6	33.2	32.8	32.4	31.9
Unemployment insurance	3	6	6	6	6	0.6	0.4	0.4	0.4	0.4
Corporation income taxes	72	110	174	189	204	13.9	10.2	12.5	12.6	12.6
Estate and gift taxes	7	12	15	18	20	1.3	1.1	1.1	1.2	1.2
Excise taxes	25	49	59	56	59	4.7	4.5	4.2	3.7	3.6

[1] Includes railroad retirement, not shown separately.

Source: U.S. Internal Revenue Service, *Annual Report*, and Bureau of Alcohol, Tobacco, and Firearms, *Alcohol and Tobacco Tax Collections*.

No. 558. Federal Individual Income Tax Returns With Adjusted Gross Income (AGI)—Summary: 1990 and 1996

[Includes Puerto Rico and Virgin Islands. Includes returns of resident aliens, based on a sample of unaudited returns as filed. Data are not comparable for all years because of tax changes and other changes, as indicated. See *Statistics of Income, Individual Income Tax Returns* publications for a detailed explanation. See Appendix III]

Item	Number of returns (1,000)		Amount (mil. dol.)		Average amount (dollars)	
	1990	1996	1990	1996	1990	1996
Total returns	113,717	120,351	3,405,427	4,535,974	29,947	37,690
Adjusted gross income (AGI)	3,405,427	4,535,974	3,405,427	4,535,974	1,000	1,000
Salaries and wages.	96,730	102,749	2,599,401	3,376,872	26,873	32,865
Taxable interest received	70,370	67,159	227,084	165,673	3,227	2,467
Tax-exempt interest.	3,917	5,001	40,228	48,217	10,270	9,641
Dividends in AGI.	22,904	27,710	80,169	104,255	3,500	3,762
Business or profession net income.	11,222	12,535	161,657	20,030	14,405	1,598
Business or profession net loss.	3,416	4,201	20,227	23,126	5,921	5,505
Net capital gain in AGI	9,217	17,442	123,783	260,696	13,430	14,946
Net capital loss in AGI	5,071	4,622	9,552	8,879	1,884	1,921
Sales of property other than capital assets, net gain . .	866	818	6,300	6,532	7,275	7,985
Sales of property other than capital assets, net loss . .	825	1,004	4,829	8,816	5,853	8,781
Pensions and annuities in AGI.	17,014	19,272	159,294	238,787	9,363	12,390
Unemployment compensation in AGI	8,014	7,995	15,453	19,327	1,928	2,417
Social security benefits in AGI.	5,083	7,366	19,687	53,203	3,873	7,223
Rent net income	3,934	4,426	25,886	37,528	6,580	8,479
Rent net loss	5,163	4,763	33,450	27,639	6,479	5,803
Royalty net income	1,171	1,080	4,534	5,967	3,872	5,525
Royalty net loss	49,133	29,775	126	71	3	2
Partnerships and S [1] Corporations net income	3,210	3,791	112,030	190,739	34,900	50,314
Partnerships and S [1] Corporations net loss	2,767	2,201	45,007	43,960	16,266	19,973
Estate or trust net income	445	489	4,633	8,465	10,411	17,311
Estate or trust net loss.	74	44	468	749	6,324	17,023
Farm net income.	996	728	11,395	8,915	11,441	12,246
Farm net loss.	1,325	1,461	11,829	16,027	8,928	10,970
Statutory adjustments, total	16,648	18,425	33,974	42,647	2,041	2,315
Individual retirement arrangements.	5,224	4,374	9,858	8,628	1,887	1,973
Self-employed retirement plans	824	1,079	6,778	8,979	8,226	8,322
Deduction for self-employment tax	11,006	13,204	9,921	14,044	901	1,064
Self-employment health insurance	2,754	3,147	1,627	2,785	591	885
Exemptions, total [2]	227,549	238,626	227,549	238,626	1,000	1,000
Age 65 or older	18,717	20,354	18,717	20,354	1,000	1,000
Deductions, total	112,796	119,412	789,942	998,644	7,003	8,363
Standard deductions	80,621	83,997	331,457	426,103	4,111	5,073
Returns with additional standard deductions for age 65 or older or for blindness	10,954	11,043	10,616	13,294	969	1,204
Itemized deductions, total [3]	32,175	35,415	458,485	572,541	14,250	16,167
Medical and dental expenses.	5,091	5,397	21,457	27,002	4,215	5,003
Taxes paid.	31,594	34,855	140,011	203,776	4,432	5,846
Interest paid	29,395	29,803	208,354	233,151	7,088	7,823
Home mortgage interest paid	26,679	29,436	189,233	220,203	7,093	7,481
Charitable contributions	29,230	31,592	57,243	86,159	1,958	2,727
Taxable income	93,148	96,577	2,263,661	3,089,667	24,302	31,992
Income tax before credits	93,089	96,522	453,128	666,724	4,868	6,907
Tax credits, total [2]	12,484	15,851	6,831	11,304	547	713
Child care credit	6,144	5,974	2,549	2,531	415	424
Elderly and disabled credit	340	168	62	32	182	190
Foreign tax	772	2,106	1,682	3,539	2,179	1,680
General business credit	263	298	616	743	2,342	2,493
Income tax after credits	89,844	90,907	446,296	655,420	4,967	7,210
Income tax, total [4]	89,862	90,929	447,127	658,245	4,976	7,239
Minimum tax	(NA)	(NA)	(NA)	(NA)	(NA)	(NA)
Alternative minimum tax.	132	478	830	2,813	6,288	5,885
Earned income credit	12,542	19,464	7,542	28,825	601	1,481
Used to offset income tax before credits	5,702	8,195	1,617	3,563	284	435
Used to offset other taxes.	1,355	3,028	659	2,105	486	695
Excess earned income credit (refundable)	8,698	15,380	5,266	23,157	605	1,506
Tax payments, total	104,816	112,926	495,922	737,610	4,731	6,532
Excess social security tax withheld.	931	1,179	905	1,313	972	1,114
Estimated tax payments.	12,806	12,334	91,607	141,571	7,153	11,478
Payments with requests for extension of filing time . . .	1,305	1,423	16,704	32,447	12,800	22,802
Taxes due at time of filing	26,987	30,602	56,561	85,337	2,096	2,789
Tax overpayments, total.	83,508	86,492	88,479	128,964	1,060	1,491
Overpayment refunds	80,514	83,669	78,103	111,681	970	1,335

NA Not available. [1] S Corporations are certain small corporations with up to 35 shareholders. [2] Includes items not shown separately. Beginning 1996, total exemptions amount is after limitation. Beginning 1996, total itemized deductions are after limitation. [4] Includes minimum tax or alternative minimum tax.

Source: U.S. Internal Revenue Service, *Statistics of Income Bulletin*, and *Statistics of Income, Individual Income Tax Returns*, annual.

No. 559. Individual Income Tax Returns—Number, Income Tax, and Average Tax, by Size of Adjusted Gross Income: 1995 and 1996

[Number in thousands; money amounts in billions of dollars, except as indicated]

Size of adjusted gross income	Number of returns 1995	Number of returns 1996, prel.	Adjusted gross income (AGI) 1995	Adjusted gross income (AGI) 1996, prel.	Taxable income 1995	Taxable income 1996, prel.	Income tax total [1] 1995	Income tax total [1] 1996, prel.	Tax as percent of AGI [2] 1995	Tax as percent of AGI [2] 1996, prel.	Average tax ($1,000) [2] 1995	Average tax ($1,000) [2] 1996, prel.
Total........	118,218	120,351	4,189.4	4,536.0	2,813.8	4,536.0	588.4	658.2	14.1	14.5	6.8	7.2
Less than $1,000 [3] .	3,204	3,260	-53.9	-53.1	0.1	-53.1	0.1	0.1	-0.2	-0.2	0.2	0.3
$1,000-$2,999	6,526	6,472	13.0	12.8	0.9	12.8	0.2	0.2	1.2	1.2	0.1	0.1
$3,000-$4,999	5,860	6,050	23.2	24.1	1.3	24.1	0.2	0.3	1.0	1.1	0.1	0.1
$5,000-$6,999	5,680	5,398	34.0	32.4	2.9	32.4	0.4	0.4	1.3	1.3	0.2	0.3
$7,000-$8,999 ...	5,593	5,470	44.9	43.7	6.7	43.7	1.0	0.9	2.2	2.0	0.3	0.3
$9,000-$10,999 ...	5,372	5,438	53.7	54.4	10.7	54.4	1.6	1.7	3.0	3.1	0.5	0.5
$11,000-$12,999. .	5,555	5,202	66.6	62.3	17.2	62.3	2.6	2.2	3.9	3.5	0.8	0.7
$13,000-$14,999 . .	5,344	5,316	74.8	74.5	23.9	74.5	3.2	3.1	4.3	4.1	0.9	0.9
$15,000-$16,999 . .	4,837	4,919	77.3	78.7	29.2	78.7	3.8	3.8	4.9	4.8	1.1	1.1
$17,000-$18,999 . .	4,402	4,597	79.3	82.7	34.0	82.7	4.3	4.5	5.5	5.5	1.3	1.4
$19,000-$21,999 . .	6,507	6,210	133.4	127.2	64.9	127.2	8.6	7.9	6.5	6.2	1.5	1.6
$22,000-$24,999 . .	5,610	5,609	131.8	131.5	71.1	131.5	10.1	9.5	7.6	7.2	1.9	1.9
$25,000-$29,999 . .	7,848	8,062	215.2	221.1	125.1	221.1	18.5	18.8	8.6	8.5	2.4	2.4
$30,000-$39,999 . .	12,380	12,549	430.5	436.4	270.6	436.4	42.4	42.4	9.9	9.7	3.5	3.4
$40,000-$49,999 . .	9,099	9,539	406.6	426.8	269.4	426.8	43.6	46.3	10.7	10.8	4.8	4.9
$50,000-$74,999 . .	13,679	14,323	828.3	871.8	579.8	871.8	100.3	104.9	12.1	12.0	8.2	7.3
$75,000-$99,999 . .	5,374	5,801	458.5	498.4	335.0	498.4	67.7	73.3	14.8	14.7	16.0	12.6
$100,000-$199,999 .	4,075	4,613	532.0	603.7	411.6	603.7	97.2	109.8	18.3	18.2	31.3	23.8
$200,000-$499,999 .	1,007	1,199	292.1	347.4	249.4	347.4	74.6	87.7	25.6	25.2	95.0	73.2
$500,000-$999,999 .	178	214	120.3	144.8	106.6	144.8	36.3	43.5	30.2	30.1	258.2	203.7
$1,000,000 or more .	87	111	227.6	314.4	203.5	314.4	71.5	97.0	31.4	30.8	1,077.0	875.0

[1] Consists of income after credits, and alternative minimum tax.   [2] Computed using taxable returns only.   [3] In addition to low income taxpayers, this size class (and others) includes taxpayers with "tax preferences," not reflected in adjusted gross income or taxable income which are subject to the "alternative minimum tax" (included in total income tax).

Source: U.S. Internal Revenue Service, *Statistics of Income Bulletin*, quarterly and *Statistics of Income, Individual Income Tax Returns*, annual.

No. 560. Individual Income Tax Returns—Itemized Deductions and Statutory Adjustments, by Size of Adjusted Gross Income: 1996

[Preliminary]

Item	Unit	Total	Under $10,000	$10,000 to $19,999	$20,000 to $29,999	$30,000 to $39,999	$40,000 to $49,999	$50,000 to $99,999	$100,000 and over
Returns with itemized deductions:									
Number [1]	1,000 ..	35,415	700	2,134	3,388	4,275	4,566	14,696	5,654
Amount	Mil. dol.	572,541	6,892	21,844	34,259	45,010	53,059	215,606	195,871
Medical and dental expenses:									
Returns	1,000 ..	5,397	444	1,148	1,047	855	700	1,071	131
Amount	Mil. dol.	27,002	2,617	6,254	4,057	3,434	2,518	6,122	2,001
Taxes paid:									
Returns, total	1,000 ..	34,855	608	1,959	3,303	4,203	4,528	14,627	5,628
State, local income taxes ..	1,000 ..	29,717	303	1,345	2,674	3,646	3,891	12,898	4,960
Real estate taxes........	1,000 ..	31,348	498	1,645	2,793	3,682	3,993	13,456	5,282
Amount, total	Mil. dol.	203,776	1,057	4,059	7,427	11,606	15,005	73,072	91,550
State, local income taxes ..	Mil. dol.	124,376	133	827	2,693	5,303	7,574	41,185	66,660
Real estate taxes........	Mil. dol.	71,233	842	2,936	4,246	5,642	6,612	28,416	22,541
Interest paid:									
Returns..............	1,000 ..	29,803	432	1,433	2,685	3,560	3,922	12,977	4,794
Amount...............	Mil. dol.	233,151	2,791	8,472	13,482	20,295	23,947	94,070	70,093
Home mortgages interest:									
Returns..............	1,000 ..	29,436	421	1,407	2,658	3,544	3,891	12,878	4,638
Amount...............	Mil. dol.	220,203	2,731	8,266	13,184	19,961	23,710	92,233	60,118
Contributions:									
Returns..............	1,000 ..	31,592	458	1,625	2,807	3,668	4,019	13,607	5,408
Amount...............	Mil. dol.	86,159	647	2,362	3,651	5,302	6,614	27,642	39,942
Employee business expense:									
Returns..............	1,000 ..	11,184	68	410	903	1,448	1,605	5,280	1,469
Amount...............	Mil. dol.	36,582	189	1,276	2,536	3,898	4,626	16,118	7,940
Returns with statutory adjus'mts: [2]									
Returns	1,000 ..	18,425	3,048	2,963	2,650	2,209	1,787	3,606	2,161
Amount of adjustments	Mil. dol	42,647	2,498	3,573	3,768	3,818	3,355	9,707	15,927
Payments to IRAs: [3]									
Returns..............	1,000 ..	4,374	282	655	945	820	590	707	376
Amount...............	Mil. dol.	8,628	534	1,179	1,533	1,485	985	1,788	1,124
Payments to Keogh plans:									
Returns..............	1,000 ..	1,079	8	38	43	66	86	356	483
Amount...............	Mil. dol.	8,979	31	102	110	224	306	1,790	6,418
Alimony paid:									
Returns	1,000 ..	597	40	56	58	68	68	178	130
Amount	Mil. dol.	5,668	370	233	264	404	369	1,211	2,818

[1] After limitations.   [2] Includes disability income exclusion, employee business expenses, moving expenses, forfeited interest penalty, alimony paid, deduction for expense of living abroad, and other data not shown separately.   [3] Individual Retirement Account.

Source: U.S. Internal Revenue Service, *Statistics of Income, Individual Income Tax Returns*, annual.

No. 561. Federal Individual Income Tax Returns—Adjusted Gross Income (AGI), by Source of Income and Income Class for Taxable Returns: 1996

[In millions of dollars ($90,929 represents $90,929,000,000), except as indicated. Minus sign (-) indicates net loss was greater than net income. See headnote, Table 558]

Item	Total [1]	Under $10,000	$10,000 to $19,999	$20,000 to $29,999	$30,000 to $39,999	$40,000 to $49,999	$50,000 to $99,999	$100,000 and over
Number of returns (1,000)........	90,929	10,048	16,277	16,417	12,464	9,497	20,094	6,132
Source of income:								
Adjusted gross income (AGI)......	4,341,871	52,468	245,462	408,100	433,449	424,920	1,368,290	1,409,182
Salaries and wages	3,177,472	46,530	176,090	331,451	360,748	352,709	1,109,486	800,458
Percent of AGI for taxable returns	73.2	88.7	71.7	81.2	83.2	83.0	81.1	56.8
Interest received	153,365	4,452	15,980	13,341	12,648	11,125	36,372	59,447
Dividends in AGI	99,344	2,171	5,336	5,462	5,147	5,666	21,709	53,853
Business; profession, net profit less loss.................	160,287	1,671	8,310	11,523	12,014	12,135	41,209	73,425
Pensions and annuities in AGI ...	224,712	3,818	30,154	32,732	26,743	23,876	74,357	33,031
Sales of property, [2] net gain less loss	246,560	3,210	3,170	4,033	3,715	5,076	28,789	198,566
Rents and royalties, net income less loss.... [3]	21,535	148	732	619	70	322	1,915	17,727
Other sources, [3] net	297,678	-8,985	7,986	12,579	16,092	17,320	64,095	188,596
Percent of all returns: [4]								
Number of returns	75.6	8.4	13.5	13.6	10.4	7.9	16.7	5.1
Adjusted gross income	95.7	1.2	5.4	9.0	9.6	9.4	30.2	31.1
Salaries and wages	94.1	1.4	5.2	9.8	10.7	10.4	32.9	23.7
Interest received	92.6	2.7	9.7	8.1	7.6	6.7	22.0	35.9
Dividends in AGI	95.3	2.1	5.1	5.2	4.9	5.4	20.8	51.7
Business; profession, net profit less loss.................	90.6	0.9	4.7	6.5	6.8	6.9	23.3	41.5
Pensions and annuities in AGI.....	94.1	1.6	12.6	13.7	11.2	10.0	31.1	13.8
Sales of property, [2] net gain less loss..................	98.8	1.3	1.3	1.6	1.5	2.0	11.5	79.6

[1] Includes a small number of taxable returns with no adjusted gross income. [2] Includes sales of capital assets and other property; net gain less loss. [3] Excludes rental passive losses disallowed in the computation of adjusted gross income; net income less loss. [4] Without regard to taxability.

Source: U.S. Internal Revenue Service, *Statistics of Income,* annual.

No. 562. Federal Individual Income Tax Returns, by State: 1996

State	Number of returns (1,000)	Adjusted gross income (AGI) [2]	Income tax Total [3] (mil. dol.)	Income tax Per capita [4] (dol.)	State	Number of returns (1,000)	Adjusted gross income (AGI) [2]	Income tax Total [3] (mil. dol.)	Income tax Per capita [4] (dol.)
U.S....	120,787	4,520,289	693,529	2,614	MO.......	2,416	82,981	12,032	2,245
					MT.......	400	11,169	1,469	1,671
AL......	1,844	58,948	8,149	1,907	NE......	775	25,569	3,619	2,191
AK......	349	11,152	1,749	2,881	NV......	800	32,413	5,438	3,392
AZ......	1,910	68,178	9,964	2,250	NH......	573	22,686	3,535	3,042
AR......	1,066	31,216	4,109	1,637	NJ......	3,818	178,847	29,709	3,719
CA......	13,488	540,864	84,951	2,665	NM......	748	22,026	2,902	1,694
CO......	1,839	71,805	11,050	2,890	NY......	8,031	345,391	57,574	3,166
CT......	1,581	81,344	14,789	4,517	NC......	3,395	115,538	15,975	2,181
DE......	350	13,759	2,036	2,808	ND......	293	8,646	1,198	1,860
DC......	270	11,230	1,936	3,565	OH......	5,358	182,384	26,376	2,361
FL......	6,749	245,122	40,152	2,788	OK......	1,392	42,029	5,694	1,725
GA......	3,305	120,331	17,652	2,401	OR......	1,472	52,529	7,424	2,317
HI.......	550	19,538	2,592	2,189	PA......	5,515	201,766	30,535	2,533
ID.......	508	16,378	2,207	1,856	RI.......	456	16,461	2,336	2,360
IL.......	5,489	226,033	36,941	3,118	SC......	1,682	53,031	7,035	1,902
IN.......	2,691	94,528	13,585	2,326	SD......	333	9,765	1,419	1,939
IA.......	1,300	42,583	5,804	2,035	TN......	2,416	81,348	12,340	2,320
KS......	1,151	41,095	5,969	2,321	TX......	8,243	289,049	46,031	2,406
KY......	1,637	51,611	6,981	1,797	UT......	847	29,962	3,960	1,980
LA......	1,795	56,475	8,177	1,879	VT......	278	9,098	1,257	2,134
ME......	567	17,719	2,338	1,881	VA......	3,057	121,332	17,953	2,690
MD......	2,418	102,323	15,051	2,967	WA.......	2,544	101,042	16,005	2,893
MA......	2,899	127,380	21,070	3,459	WV......	722	21,281	2,757	1,510
MI	4,368	168,850	25,756	2,685	WI	2,427	87,899	12,457	2,414
MN......	2,188	86,639	13,007	2,792	WY....	223	7,758	1,314	2,732
MS......	1,122	31,356	4,039	1,487	Other [5]....	1,139	31,829	5,127	(NA)

NA Not available. [1] Includes returns constructed by Internal Revenue Service for certain self-employment tax returns. [2] Less deficit. [3] Includes additional tax for tax preferences, self-employment tax, tax from investment credit recapture, and other income-related taxes. Total is before earned income credit. [4] Based on resident population as of July 1. [5] Includes returns filed from Army Post Office and Fleet Post Office addresses by members of the armed forces stationed overseas; returns by other U.S. citizens abroad; and returns filed by residents of Puerto Rico with income from sources outside of Puerto Rico or with income earned as U.S. government employees.

Source: U.S. Internal Revenue Service, *Statistics of Income Bulletin,* quarterly.

No. 563. Federal Individual Income Tax—Tax Liability, Effective and Marginal Tax Rates, for Selected Income Groups: 1990 to 1998

[Refers to income after exclusions. Effective rate represents tax liability divided by stated income. The marginal tax rate is the percentage of the first additional dollar of income which would be paid in income tax. Computations assume the low income allowance, standard deduction, zero bracket amount, or itemized deductions equal to 10 percent of adjusted gross income, whichever is greatest. Excludes self-employment tax]

Adjusted gross income	1990	1993	1994	1995	1996	1997	1998
TAX LIABILITY							
Single person, no dependents:							
$5,000	-	-	-306	-314	-323	-332	-341
$10,000	705	593	563	540	518	480	455
$20,000	2,205	2,093	2,063	2,040	2,018	1,980	1,958
$25,000	2,988	2,843	2,813	2,790	2,768	2,730	2,708
$35,000	5,718	5,233	5,093	4,973	4,846	4,692	4,559
$50,000	9,498	9,069	8,957	8,865	8,766	8,654	8,549
$75,000	16,718	15,719	15,555	15,418	15,270	15,107	14,951
Married couple, two dependents: [1]							
$5,000	-700	-975	-1,500	-1,800	-2,000	-2,000	-2,000
$10,000	-953	-1,511	-2,528	-3,110	-3,556	-3,556	-3,756
$20,000	926	235	-359	-832	-1,324	-1,414	-1,811
$25,000	1,703	1,410	1,275	929	479	389	-8
$35,000	3,203	2,910	2,828	2,768	2,715	2,625	2,565
$50,000	5,960	5,160	5,078	5,018	4,965	4,875	4,815
$75,000	12,386	11,471	11,216	11,030	10,831	10,576	10,371
EFFECTIVE RATE							
Single person, no dependents:							
$5,000 [2]	-	-	-6.1	-6.3	-6.5	-6.6	-6.8
$10,000	7.1	5.9	5.6	5.4	5.2	4.8	4.6
$20,000	11.0	10.5	10.3	10.2	10.1	9.9	9.8
$25,000	12.0	11.4	11.3	11.2	11.1	10.9	10.8
$35,000	16.3	15.0	14.6	14.2	13.8	13.4	13
$50,000	19.0	18.1	17.9	17.7	17.5	17.3	17.1
$75,000	22.3	21.0	20.7	20.6	20.4	20.1	19.9
Married couple, two dependents: [2]							
$5,000 [3]	-14.0	-19.5	-30.0	-36.0	-40	-40	-40
$10,000 [4]	-9.5	-15.1	-25.3	-31.1	-35.6	-35.6	-37.6
$20,000 [4]	4.6	1.2	-1.8	-4.2	-6.6	-7.1	-9.1
$25,000	6.8	5.6	5.1	3.7	1.9	1.6	-
$35,000	9.2	8.3	8.1	7.9	7.8	7.5	7.3
$50,000	11.9	10.3	10.2	10.0	9.9	9.8	9.6
$75,000	16.5	15.3	15.0	14.7	14.4	14.1	13.8
MARGINAL TAX RATE							
Single person, no dependents:							
$5,000	-	7.7	-	-	-	-	-
$10,000	15	15	15	15	15	15	22.7
$20,000	15	15	15	15	15	15	15
$25,000	28	15	15	15	15	15	15
$35,000	28	28	28	28	28	28	28
$50,000	28	28	28	28	28	28	28
$75,000	33	31	31	31	31	31	31
Married couple, two dependents: [1]							
$5,000 [3]	-14	-19.5	-30	-36	-40	-40	-40
$10,000 [4]	-	-	-	-			
$20,000 [4]	25	28.9	32.7	35.2	36.1	36.1	36.1
$25,000	15	15	32.7	35.2	36.1	36.1	36.1
$35,000	15	15	15	15	15	15	15
$50,000	28	15	15	15	15	15	15
$75,000	28	28	28	28	28	28	28

- Represents zero. [1] Only one spouse is assumed to work. [2] Beginning 1994, refundable earned income credit. [3] Refundable earned income credit. [4] Beginning 1990, refundable earned income credit.

Source: U.S. Dept. of the Treasury, Office of Tax Analysis, unpublished data.

No. 564. Federal Individual Income Tax—Current Income Equivalent to 1995 Constant Income for Selected Income Groups: 1990 to 1998

[Constant 1995 dollar incomes calculated by using the NIPA Personal Consumption Expenditure (PCE) Implicit Price Deflator (1992=100): 1990, 92.9; 1992, 100.0; 1993, 102.6; 1994, 105.2; 1995, 107.6; 1996, 109.8; 1997, 111.8; and 1998, 112.7]

Adjusted gross income	1990	1993	1994	1995	1996	1997	1998
REAL INCOME EQUIVALENT							
Single person, no dependents:							
$5,000	4,320	4,770	4,890	5,000	5,100	5,200	5,240
$10,000	8,640	9,540	9,780	10,000	10,200	10,400	10,480
$20,000	17,280	19,090	19,550	20,000	20,410	20,790	20,960
$25,000	21,590	23,860	24,440	25,000	25,510	25,990	26,190
$35,000	30,230	33,410	34,220	35,000	35,710	36,380	36,670
$50,000	43,190	47,720	48,880	50,000	51,020	51,980	52,390
$75,000	64,780	71,580	73,320	75,000	76,530	77,960	78,580
Married couple, two dependents:[1]							
$5,000	4,320	4,770	4,890	5,000	5,100	5,200	5,240
$10,000	8,640	9,540	9,780	10,000	10,200	10,400	10,480
$20,000	17,280	19,090	19,550	20,000	20,410	20,790	20,960
$25,000	21,590	23,860	24,440	25,000	25,510	25,990	26,190
$35,000	30,230	33,410	34,220	35,000	35,710	36,380	36,670
$50,000	43,190	47,720	48,880	50,000	51,020	51,980	52,390
$75,000	64,780	71,580	73,320	75,000	76,530	77,960	78,580
EFFECTIVE RATE (percent)							
Single person, no dependents:							
$5,000 [2]	-	-	-6.3	-6.3	-6.3	-6.4	-6.5
$10,000	5.8	5.5	5.4	5.4	5.4	5.2	5.1
$20,000	10.4	10.2	10.2	10.2	10.2	10.1	10
$25,000	11.3	11.2	11.2	11.2	11.1	11.1	11
$35,000	14.7	14.3	14.2	14.2	14.1	14.0	13.7
$50,000	18.0	17.8	17.7	17.7	17.7	17.6	17.5
$75,000	21.1	20.6	20.6	20.6	20.5	20.4	20.3
Married couple, two dependents:[1]							
$5,000 [3]	-14.0	-19.5	-30.0	-36.0	-40.0	-40.0	-40.0
$10,000 [4]	-11.0	-15.8	-25.8	-31.1	-34.9	-34.2	-35.8
$20,000 [4]	1.4	-0.0	-2.6	-4.2	-5.8	-5.4	-7.0
$25,000	5.5	5.2	4.5	3.7	2.6	2.9	1.6
$35,000	8.2	8.0	7.9	7.9	7.9	7.8	7.7
$50,000	10.3	10.1	10.0	10.0	10.0	9.9	9.9
$75,000	15.1	14.8	14.7	14.7	14.7	14.5	14.3
MARGINAL TAX RATE (percent)							
Single person, no dependents:							
$5,000	-	-	-	-	-	-	-
$10,000	15	15	15	15	15	15	15
$20,000	15	15	15	15	15	15	15
$25,000	15	15	15	15	15	15	15
$35,000	28	28	28	28	28	28	28
$50,000	28	28	28	28	28	28	28
$75,000	33	31	31	31	31	31	31
Married couple, two dependents:[1]							
$5,000 [3]	-14	-19.5	-30	-36	-40	-40	-40
$10,000 [4]	-	-	-	-	-	-	-
$20,000 [4]	25	28.9	32.7	35.2	36.1	36.1	36.1
$25,000	15	15	32.7	35.2	36.1	36.1	36.1
$35,000	15	15	15	15	15	15	15
$50,000	15	15	15	15	15	15	15
$75,000	28	28	28	28	28	28	28

- Represents zero. [1] Only one spouse is assumed to work. [2] Beginning 1994, refundable earned income credit. [3] Refundable earned income credit. [4] Refundable earned income credit.

Source: U.S. Dept. of the Treasury, Office of Tax Analysis, unpublished data.

No. 565. Paid Full-Time Federal Civilian Employment, All Areas: 1990 to 1998

[As of March 31. Excludes employees of Congress and Federal courts, maritime seamen of Dept. of Commerce, and small number for whom rates were not reported. See text, this section, for explanation of general schedule and wage system]

Compensation authority	Employees (1,000)				Average pay			
	1990	1995	1997	1998	1990	1995	1997	1998
Total	2,697	2,620	2,506	2,490	31,174	(NA)	43,873	(NA)
General Schedule	1,506	1,417	1,290	1,258	31,239	40,568	43,239	44,824
Wage System	369	269	237	222	26,565	32,084	33,834	34,763
Postal pay system [1]	661	753	765	792	29,264	33,665	35,069	35,670
Other	161	181	214	218	41,149	53,639	58,782	60,678

NA Not available. [1] Source: Employees—U.S. Postal Service, Annual Report of the Postmaster General. Average pay—U.S. Postal Service, Comprehensive Statement of Postal Operations, annual.

Source: Except as noted, U.S. Office of Personnel Management, Pay Structure of the Federal Civil Service, annual.

No. 566. Federal Civilian Employment, by Branch and Agency: 1990 and 1998

[For fiscal year ending in year shown; excludes Central Intelligence Agency, National Security Agency; and, as of November 1984, the Defense Intelligence Agency; and, as of October 1996, the National Imagery and Mapping Agency]

Agency	1990	1998	Percent change 1990-95	Percent change 1997-98
Total, all agencies	**3,128,267**	**2,789,495**	**-6.6**	**0.1**
Legislative Branch, total	37,495	30,474	-11.0	-2.8
Judicial Branch	23,605	31,742	22.8	3.6
Executive Branch, total	3,067,167	2,727,279	-6.8	0.1
Office of Management and Budget	574	505	-7.0	-1.4
Executive Departments	2,065,542	1,646,245	-13.7	-0.8
State	25,288	24,713	-1.7	2.5
Treasury	158,655	140,873	-1.7	0.4
Defense	1,034,152	717,901	-19.5	-4.2
Justice	83,932	122,759	23.0	4.7
Interior	77,679	72,434	-1.6	1.6
Agriculture	122,594	105,664	-7.6	-11.6
Commerce	69,920	50,041	-47.4	43.8
Labor	17,727	15,894	-8.6	0.7
Health & Human Services	123,959	59,813	-51.8	0.5
Housing & Urban Development	13,596	10,063	-13.0	-7.7
Transportation	67,364	64,859	-5.7	1.1
Energy	17,731	16,156	10.5	-5.4
Education	4,771	4,677	4.5	0.8
Veterans Affairs [1]	248,174	240,398	6.3	-1.2
Independent agencies:				
American Battle Monuments Commission	396	357	-5.3	-0.6
Armed Forces Retirement Home	966	848	(X)	-6.8
Arms Control & Disarmament Agency	216	222	23.1	-7.5
Board of Government Federal Reserve System	1,525	1,669	11.7	-2.7
Commodity Futures Trading Commission	542	583	0.4	2.1
Consumer Product Safety Commission	520	468	-6.5	-1.5
Corp Natl & Community Service	(X)	538	(X)	-0.2
Defense Nuclear Facilities Safety Board	25	100	324.0	-2.0
Environmental Protection Agency	17,123	18,787	4.6	4.1
Equal Employment Opportunity Commission	2,880	2,571	-2.9	-2.3
Export-Import Bank of U.S.	343	413	29.2	-1.4
Farm Credit Administration	515	299	-26.2	-1.3
Federal Communications Commission	1,778	1,988	19.0	-4.4
Federal Deposit Insurance Corporation	17,641	7,778	-16.3	-5.9
Federal Election Commission	250	320	30.8	6.7
Federal Emergency Management Agency	3,137	5,812	67.5	18.9
Federal Housing Finance Board [2]	65	120	73.8	6.2
Federal Labor Relations Auth	251	215	-12.0	-0.5
Federal Maritime Commission	230	142	-26.5	2.9
Federal Med & Council Svc	316	282	-6.0	1.1
Federal Ret Thrift Invest Board	93	111	18.3	-0.9
Federal Trade Commission	988	1,004	0.8	4.0
General Services Administration	20,277	14,207	-18.6	-0.7
Holocaust Memorial Council	26	228	696.2	8.6
Int Boun & Wat Comm (U.S. & Mexico)	260	258	-9.2	4.0
International Trade Commission	491	417	-10.0	7.8
National Archives & Records Administration	3,120	2,610	-9.2	-7.8
National Aeronautics & Space Administration	24,872	18,899	-13.0	-4.8
Natl Credit Union Admin	900	882	1.3	-5.3
Natl Fnd Arts & Humanities	547	350	-9.9	4.2
Natl Labor Relations Board	2,263	1,866	-9.4	-6.3
Natl Science Foundation	1,318	1,194	-2.0	-1.3
Natl Trans Safety Board	366	443	0.5	14.2
Nuclear Regulatory Commission	3,353	2,995	-4.2	-2.8
Office of Personnel Management	6,636	3,576	-34.4	-0.7
Panama Canal Commission	8,240	9,966	10.0	1.9
Peace Corps	1,178	1,059	0.1	-3.2
Pension Benefit Guar Corp	574	750	24.7	0.9
Railroad Retirement Board	1,772	1,289	-12.9	-2.9
Securities & Exchange Commission	2,302	2,826	23.9	-1.2
Selective Service System	288	188	-24.3	-7.4
Small Business Administration	5,128	4,574	-0.8	4.4
Smithsonian Institution, summary	5,092	5,166	6.9	-0.4
Social Security Administration	(X)	65,257	(X)	-2.6
Tennessee Valley Authority	28,392	13,818	-41.7	-4.8
U.S. Information Agency	8,555	6,378	-12.6	-2.4
U.S. International Development Cooperation Agency	4,698	2,800	-20.1	-5.7
U.S. Postal Service	816,886	871,467	3.5	2.1

X Not applicable.   [1] Formerly Veterans Administration.   [2] Formerly Federal Home Loan Bank Board.

Source: U.S. Office of Personnel Management, *Federal Civilian Workforce Statistics— Employment and Trends*, bimonthly.

Federal Government Finances and Employment   363

No. 567. Federal Civilian Employment and Annual Payroll, by Branch: 1970 to 1998

[Employment in thousands (2,997 represents 2,997,000); payroll in millions of dollars ($27,322 represents $27,322,000,000). Average annual employment. For fiscal year ending in year shown; see text, Section 9, State and Local Government. Includes employees in U.S. territories and foreign countries. Data represent employees in active-duty status, including intermittent employees. Annual employment figures are averages of monthly figures. Excludes Central Intelligence Agency, National Security Agency, and, as of November 1984, the Defense Intelligence Agency, and as of October 1996, the National Imagery and Mapping Agency]

Year	Employment						Payroll				
	Total	Percent of U.S. employed [1]	Executive		Legislative	Judicial	Total	Executive		Legislative	Judicial
			Total	Defense				Total	Defense		
1970	[2]2,997	3.8	2,961	1,263	29	7	27,322	26,894	11,264	338	89
1971	2,899	3.7	2,861	1,162	31	7	29,475	29,007	11,579	369	98
1972	2,882	3.5	2,842	1,128	32	8	31,626	31,102	12,181	411	112
1973	2,822	3.3	2,780	1,076	33	9	33,240	32,671	12,414	447	121
1974	2,825	3.3	2,781	1,041	35	9	35,661	35,035	12,789	494	132
1975	2,877	3.4	2,830	1,044	37	10	39,126	38,423	13,418	549	154
1976	2,879	3.2	2,831	1,025	38	11	42,259	41,450	14,699	631	179
1977	2,855	3.1	2,803	997	39	12	45,895	44,975	15,696	700	219
1978	2,875	3.0	2,822	987	40	13	49,921	48,899	16,995	771	251
1979	2,897	2.9	2,844	974	40	13	53,590	52,513	18,065	817	260
1980	[3]2,987	3.0	2,933	971	40	14	58,012	56,841	18,795	883	288
1981	2,909	2.9	2,855	986	40	15	63,793	62,510	21,227	922	360
1982	2,871	2.9	2,816	1,019	39	16	65,503	64,125	22,226	980	398
1983	2,878	2.9	2,823	1,033	39	16	69,878	68,420	23,406	1,013	445
1984	2,935	2.8	2,879	1,052	40	17	74,616	73,084	25,253	1,081	451
1985	3,001	2.8	2,944	1,080	39	18	80,599	78,992	28,330	1,098	509
1986	3,047	2.8	2,991	1,089	38	19	82,598	80,941	29,272	1,112	545
1987	3,075	2.7	3,018	1,084	38	19	85,543	83,797	29,786	1,153	593
1988	3,113	2.7	3,054	1,073	38	21	88,841	86,960	29,609	1,226	656
1989	3,133	2.7	3,074	1,067	38	22	92,847	90,870	30,301	1,266	711
1990	[4]3,233	2.7	3,173	1,060	38	23	99,138	97,022	31,990	1,329	787
1991	3,101	2.7	3,038	1,015	38	25	104,273	101,965	32,956	1,434	874
1992	3,106	2.6	3,040	1,004	39	27	108,054	105,402	31,486	1,569	1,083
1993	3,043	2.5	2,976	952	39	28	114,323	111,523	32,755	1,609	1,191
1994	2,993	2.4	2,928	900	37	28	116,138	113,264	32,144	1,613	1,260
1995	2,943	2.4	2,880	852	34	28	118,304	115,328	31,753	1,598	1,379
1996	2,881	2.3	2,819	811	32	29	119,321	116,385	31,569	1,519	1,417
1997	2,816	2.2	2,755	768	31	30	119,603	116,693	31,431	1,515	1,396
1998	2,783	2.1	2,721	730	31	31	121,964	118,800	30,315	1,517	1,647

[1] Civilian only. See Table 646. [2] Includes 33,000 temporary census workers. [3] Includes 81,116 temporary census workers.
[4] Includes 111,020 temporary census workers.
Source: U.S. Office of Personnel Management, *Federal Civilian Workforce Statistics—Employment and Trends*, bimonthly; and unpublished data.

No. 568. Federal Executive Branch (Non-Postal) Employment, by Race and National Origin: 1990 to 1998

[As of **Sept. 30.** Covers total employment for only Executive branch agencies participating in OPMs Central Personnel Data File (CPDF)]

Pay system	1990	1995	1996	1997	1998
All personnel	2,150,359	1,960,577	1,890,406	1,830,300	1,804,591
White, non-Hispanic..............	1,562,846	1,394,690	1,341,157	1,293,244	1,269,790
General schedule and related......	1,218,188	1,101,108	1,060,863	1,027,440	1,010,793
Grades 1-4 ($12,960 - $23,203)	132,028	79,195	67,988	63,775	61,909
Grades 5-8 ($19,969 - $35,610)....	337,453	288,755	275,093	264,288	255,344
Grades 9-12 ($30,257 - $57,043)...	510,261	465,908	451,651	434,228	425,617
Grades 13-15 ($52,176 - $94,287)...	238,446	267,250	266,131	265,149	267,923
Total executives/senior pay levels [1]	9,337	13,307	13,319	13,465	13,634
Wage pay system.................	244,220	186,184	174,364	164,755	157,639
Other pay systems	91,101	94,091	92,611	87,584	87,724
Black...........................	356,867	327,302	313,810	303,415	300,661
General schedule and related....	272,657	258,586	249,959	243,932	242,587
Grades 1-4 ($12,960 - $23,203)...	65,077	41,381	34,993	32,439	30,668
Grades 5-8 ($19,969 - $35,610)...	114,993	112,962	109,571	106,037	103,985
Grades 9-12 ($30,257 - $57,043)..	74,985	79,795	80,065	79,124	79,999
Grades 13-15 ($52,176 - $94,287)..	17,602	24,448	25,330	26,332	27,935
Total executives/senior pay levels [1]	479	942	967	1,002	1,044
Wage pay system.................	72,755	55,637	51,189	47,261	45,492
Other pay systems	10,976	12,137	11,695	11,220	11,538
Hispanic	115,170	115,964	115,644	114,740	115,545
General schedule and related....	83,218	86,762	86,598	87,427	89,155
Grades 1-4 ($12,960 - $23,203)...	15,738	11,081	9,798	9,320	9,213
Grades 5-8 ($19,969 - $35,610)...	28,727	31,152	31,437	31,843	31,877
Grades 9-12 ($30,257 - $57,043)..	31,615	34,056	34,431	34,742	35,864
Grades 13-15 ($52,176 - $94,287)..	7,138	10,473	10,932	11,522	12,201
Total executives/senior pay levels [1]	154	382	376	409	454
Wage pay system.................	26,947	22,128	21,416	20,565	19,341
Other pay systems	4,851	6,692	7,254	6,339	6,595
American Indian, Alaska Natives, and Asian and Pacific Islander	115,476	122,621	119,795	118,901	118,595

[1] General schedule pay rates and senior pay levels effective as of January 1998.
Source: Office of Personnel Management, Central Personnel Data File.

No. 569. Paid Civilian Employment in the Federal Government: 1996

[As of **December 31**. Excludes Central Intelligence Agency, Defense Intelligence Agency, seasonal and on-call employees, and National Security Agency]

State	Total (1,000)	Percent Defense	Percent change, 1994-96	State	Total (1,000)	Percent Defense	Percent change, 1994-96
United States	**2,735**	**26.2**	**-5.8**	Missouri	58	21.9	-9.9
Alabama	52	42.0	-5.3	Montana	11	10.5	-13.4
Alaska	14	32.4	-6.9	Nebraska	15	23.9	-6.4
Arizona	40	21.6	-1.0	Nevada	12	18.1	-2.7
Arkansas	20	19.3	-0.8	New Hampshire	8	15.1	-7.7
California	269	31.1	-8.7	New Jersey	68	28.1	-5.8
Colorado	52	23.6	-8.5	New Mexico	26	31.2	-4.4
Connecticut	22	13.4	-10.2	New York	139	9.3	-4.3
Delaware	5	28.9	-13.2	North Carolina	55	31.6	1.5
District of Columbia	185	7.3	-9.4	North Dakota	8	23.3	-0.4
Florida	112	25.6	-1.8	Ohio	86	32.1	-6.8
Georgia	87	37.5	-5.2	Oklahoma	42	46.7	-0.3
Hawaii	24	72.9	-2.4	Oregon	28	10.1	-6.7
Idaho	11	13.1	-0.4	Pennsylvania	112	26.7	-11.6
Illinois	97	15.6	-8.4	Rhode Island	11	41.6	1.1
Indiana	40	30.2	-4.1	South Carolina	26	38.8	-14.5
Iowa	20	7.2	-4.5	South Dakota	10	13.3	-0.6
Kansas	25	22.2	-5.5	Tennessee	52	10.1	-1.5
Kentucky	34	28.9	-5.8	Texas	172	29.9	-2.0
Louisiana	34	24.5	-2.3	Utah	29	44.3	-7.0
Maine	13	42.5	-4.5	Vermont	6	9.9	5.2
Maryland	126	26.2	-4.9	Virginia	151	58.4	-5.8
Massachusetts	54	15.2	-9.4	Washington	62	38.8	-6.5
Michigan	55	14.9	-8.9	West Virginia	18	10.0	1.7
Minnesota	33	7.5	-3.8	Wisconsin	29	11.1	-4.0
Mississippi	24	39.9	-4.4	Wyoming	6	16.2	-10.7

Source: U.S. Office of Personnel Management, *Biennial Report of Employment by Geographic Area*.

No. 570. Federal General Schedule Employee Pay Increases: 1965 to 1998

[Percent change from prior year shown, except 1965, change from 1964. Represents legislated pay increases. For some years data based on range, for details see source]

Date	Pay increase	Date	Pay increase	Date	Pay increase
1965	3.6	1976	5.2	1989	4.1
1966	2.9	1977	7.0	1990	3.6
1967	4.5	1978	5.5	1991	4.1
1968	4.9	1979	7.0	1992	4.2
1969	9.1	1980	9.1	1993	3.7
1970	6.0	1981	4.8	1994	-
1971	6.0	1982	4.0	1995	2.0
1972	5.5	1984	4.0	1996	2.0
1972	5.1	1985	3.5	1997	2.3
1973	4.8	1986	-	1998	2.3
1974	5.5	1987	3.0		
1975	5.0	1988	2.0		

- Represents zero.

Source: U.S. Office of Personnel Management, *Pay Structure of the Federal Civil Service*, annual.

No. 571. Turnover Data for the Executive Branch—All Areas: 1983 to 1997

[Turnover data exclude Legislative and Judicial branches, U.S. Postal Service, Postal Rate Commission]

Year	Accessions Total	New hires	Separations Total	Quits	Total employment Average	Change from prior year	Percent change
1983	540,267	423,123	472,628	177,430	2,158,755	8,216	0.4
1984	533,865	427,349	496,426	193,195	2,178,273	19,498	0.9
1985	541,787	451,516	484,742	185,453	2,210,487	32,214	1.5
1986	466,191	379,267	478,595	182,124	2,207,807	-2,680	-0.1
1987	515,958	431,687	440,797	176,813	2,207,828	21	(Z)
1988	463,413	375,561	448,025	175,374	2,226,642	18,814	0.9
1989	515,759	435,911	483,850	172,376	2,233,981	7,339	0.3
1990	819,554	716,066	799,237	165,099	2,348,458	114,477	5.1
1991	495,123	351,112	515,673	134,175	2,224,389	-124,069	-5.3
1992	430,021	290,883	446,126	129,167	2,238,635	14,246	0.6
1993	382,399	253,374	423,830	127,140	2,189,416	-49,219	-2.2
1994	317,509	219,026	398,134	111,096	2,114,387	-75,029	-3.4
1995	345,166	222,025	457,246	91,909	2,037,890	-76,542	-3.6
1996	266,473	199,463	356,566	80,922	1,960,892	-76,953	-3.8
1997	283,517	208,725	333,431	81,574	1,895,295	65,597	-3.3

Z Less than .05 percent.

Source: U.S. Office of Personnel Management, *Monthly Report of Federal Civilian Employment*.

No. 572. Accessions to and Separations From Employment in the Federal Government: 1995 and 1998

[As of September 30]

Agency	Accessions Number 1995	1998	Rate 1995	1998	Separations Number 1995	1998	Rate 1995	1998
Total, all agencies	556,695	574,392	19.2	21.0	638,733	538,645	22.1	19.7
Legislative Branch, total [1]	1,074	1,079	6.6	7.9	1,985	1,655	12.2	12.1
General Accounting Office	39	205	0.9	6.2	392	316	8.9	9.6
Government Printing Office	77	138	1.8	4.0	318	297	7.6	8.6
Library of Congress	540	382	11.6	8.7	642	561	13.8	12.8
Judicial Branch	-	-	-	0.0	-	-	-	0.0
Executive Branch, total	555,621	573,313	19.3	21.1	636,748	536,990	22.1	19.7
Executive Office of the President	384	369	24.3	23.0	373	343	23.6	21.4
Executive Departments	257,125	301,025	14.0	18.3	422,606	299,153	23.0	18.2
State	3,338	3,823	13.3	15.7	3,919	3,259	15.6	13.3
Treasury	24,532	59,161	15.0	39.9	52,634	50,264	32.2	33.9
Defense	104,088	90,686	12.2	12.4	155,722	125,177	18.3	17.2
Justice	14,958	14,537	14.9	12.1	7,496	7,097	7.5	5.9
Interior	12,936	16,202	17.1	23.3	16,147	13,237	21.4	19.0
Agriculture [3]	25,365	27,142	23.3	26.9	41,384	27,531	37.9	27.3
Commerce [3]	5,900	32,458	15.8	82.1	6,460	10,934	17.3	27.7
Labor	1,438	1,809	8.7	11.4	2,003	1,713	12.2	10.8
Health & Human Services [2]	8,774	9,562	9.3	16.1	78,780	8,751	83.7	14.7
Housing & Urban Development	489	746	4.0	7.5	1,952	1,220	15.8	12.2
Transportation	2,673	4,308	4.2	6.7	4,740	4,179	7.4	6.5
Energy	2,087	691	10.5	4.2	2,671	1,626	13.4	9.9
Education	683	453	13.8	9.7	354	261	7.2	5.6
Veterans Affairs [4]	49,864	39,447	19.0	16.3	48,344	43,904	18.5	18.1
Independent agencies [1]	298,112	271,919	28.6	25.3	213,769	237,494	20.5	22.1
Board of Governors, Fed RSRV System	231	207	13.7	12.3	199	274	11.8	16.3
Environmental Protection Agency	2,232	2,678	12.3	14.6	2,078	1,752	11.5	9.6
Equal Employment Opportunity Comm	129	73	4.5	2.8	156	88	5.4	3.4
Federal Deposit Insurance Corporation	360	659	2.2	8.4	4,404	1,106	26.8	14.0
Fed Emergency Management Agency	3,165	1,834	60.2	35.9	3,059	2,234	58.2	43.8
General Services Administration	292	601	1.7	4.2	2,552	664	14.8	4.7
National Aeronautics & Space Admin	2,004	1,222	8.9	6.3	3,673	2,102	16.2	10.9
National Archives & Records Admin	583	369	20.0	13.5	307	332	10.5	12.2
Nuclear Regulatory Commission	98	130	3.0	4.3	263	197	8.0	6.5
Office of Personnel Management	506	491	10.3	13.6	1,407	551	28.6	15.3
Panama Canal Comm	1,744	1,451	19.6	14.9	1,246	1,263	14.0	13.0
Railroad Retirement Board	46	40	2.9	3.1	185	79	11.6	6.1
Securities and Exchange Commission	584	509	21.1	18.0	356	440	12.8	15.6
Small Business Administration	1,065	1,212	18.1	27.2	2,799	1,046	47.6	23.5
Smithsonian Institution	707	548	13.1	12.7	980	620	18.2	14.4
Tennessee Valley Authority	674	372	4.1	2.6	2,873	1,015	17.3	7.2
U.S. Information Agency	356	308	4.7	4.8	836	725	11.0	11.3
U.S. International Dev Coop Agency	333	276	8.6	9.6	665	408	17.2	16.6
U.S. Postal Service	210,447	252,474	25.0	29.2	179,494	215,693	21.3	24.9

- Represents zero.   [1] Includes other branches, or other agencies, not shown separately.   [2] Sizable changes due to the Social Security Administration which was separated from the Department of Health and Human Services to become an independent agency effective April 1995.   [3] Includes Census Enumerators for the 2000 Decennial Census.   [4] Formerly Veterans Administration.

Source: U.S. Office of Personnel Management, *Federal Civilian Workforce Statistics— Employment and Trends*, bimonthly.

No. 573. Federal Land and Buildings Owned and Leased and Predominant Land Usage: 1990 to 1997

[For fiscal years ending in years shown; see text, Section 9, State and Local Government. Covers Federal real property throughout the world, except as noted. Cost of land figures represent total cost of property owned in year shown. For further details see source. For data on Federal land by state, see Table 394]

Item	Unit	1990	1993	1994	1995	1996	1997
Federally owned:							
Land, worldwide	1,000 acres	650,014	650,513	677,802	549,670	563,278	563,231
United States	1,000 acres	649,802	650,322	676,615	549,474	563,129	563,081
Buildings	1,000	(NA)	(NA)	(NA)	(NA)	(NA)	(NA)
United States	1,000	446	440	448	424	430	430
Buildings floor area (sq. ft.)	Mil. sq/ft.	(NA)	(NA)	(NA)	(NA)	(NA)	(NA)
United States	Mil. sq/ft.	2,859	2,783	2,944	2,793	2,930	2,935
Costs	Mil. dol.	187,865	194,181	209,318	199,387	217,857	222,391
Land	Mil. dol.	(NA)	20,134	20,947	18,972	22,952	22,914
Buildings	Mil. dol.	(NA)	96,223	115,633	113,018	123,897	128,530
Structures and facilities	Mil. dol.	(NA)	77,824	72,738	67,398	71,008	70,946
Federally leased:							
Land, worldwide	1,000 acres	994	941	1,119	1,385	1,373	1,374
United States	1,000 acres	938	898	1,055	1,351	1,339	1,340
Buildings	1,000	(NA)	(NA)	(NA)	(NA)	(NA)	(NA)
United States	Number	47,291	43,130	53,128	77,896	77,232	76,761
Buildings floor area (sq. ft.)	Mil. sq/ft.	(NA)	(NA)	(NA)	(NA)	(NA)	(NA)
United States	Mil. sq/ft.	234	252	276	275	277	276
Annual rental	Mil. dol.	2,590	3,706	3,766	3,633	3,739	3,613
United States	Mil. dol.	2,125	2,727	3,105	3,174	3,214	3,212

NA Not available.   [1] Excludes data for Dept. of Defense military functions outside United States.   [2] Includes other uses not shown separately.

Source: U.S. General Services Administration, *Inventory Report on Real Property Owned by the United States Throughout the World,* annual.

Section 11

National Defense and Veterans Affairs

This section presents data on national defense and its human and financial costs; active and reserve military personnel; ships, equipment and aircraft; and federally sponsored programs and benefits for veterans. The principal sources of these data are the annual *Selected Manpower Statistics* and the *Atlas/Data Abstract for the United States and Selected Areas* issued by the Office of the Secretary of Defense; *Annual Report of Secretary of Veterans Affairs, Department of Veterans Affairs*, and *The Budget of the United States Government*, Office of Management and Budget. For more data on expenditures, personnel, and ships, see Section 30.

Department of Defense (DOD)—The Department of Defense is responsible for providing the military forces of the United States. It includes the Office of the Secretary of Defense, the Joint Chiefs of Staff, the Army, the Navy, the Air Force, and the defense agencies. The President serves as Commander in Chief of the Armed Forces; from him, the authority flows to the Secretary of Defense and through the Joint Chiefs of Staff to the commanders of unified and specified commands (e.g., Strategic Air Command).

Reserve components—Reserve personnel of the Armed Forces consist of the Army National Guard, Army Reserve, Naval Reserve, Marine Corps Reserve, Air National Guard, Air Force Reserve, and Coast Guard Reserve. They provide trained personnel available for active duty in the Armed Forces in time of war or national emergency and at such other times as authorized by law.

The National Guard has dual Federal-state responsibilities and uses jointly provided equipment, facilities, and budget support. The President is empowered to mobilize the National Guard and to use such of the Armed Forces as he considers necessary to enforce Federal authority in any state.

The ready reserve includes selected reservists who are intended to assist active forces in a war and the individual ready reserve who, in a major war, would be used to fill out active and reserve units and later would be a source of combat replacements; a portion of the ready reserve serves in an active status. The standby reserve cannot be called to active duty unless the Congress gives explicit approval. The retired reserve represents a low potential for mobilization.

Department of Veterans Affairs—The Department of Veterans Affairs administers laws authorizing benefits for eligible former and present members of the Armed Forces and for the beneficiaries of deceased members. Veterans benefits available under various acts of Congress include compensation for service-connected disability or death; pensions for non-service-connected disability or death; vocational rehabilitation, education, and training; home loan insurance; life insurance; health care; special housing and automobiles or other conveyances for certain disabled veterans; burial and plot allowances; and educational assistance to families of deceased or totally disabled veterans, servicemen missing in action, or prisoners of war. Since these benefits are legislated by Congress, the dates they were enacted and the dates they apply to veterans may be different from the actual dates the conflicts occurred.

VA estimates of veterans cover all persons with active duty service during periods of war or armed conflict and until 1982 include those living outside the United States.

U.S. Census Bureau, Statistical Abstract of the United States: 1999

No. 574. National Defense Outlays and Veterans Benefits: 1960 to 1999

[For fiscal year ending in year shown; see text, Section 9, State and Local Government. Includes outlays of Department of Defense, Department of Veterans Affairs, and other agencies for activities primarily related to national defense and veterans programs. For explanation of average annual percent change, see Guide to Tabular Presentation. Minus sign (-) indicates decline]

Year	National defense and veterans outlays				Annual percent change [1]			Defense outlays, percent of—	
	Defense outlays								
	Total outlays (bil. dol.)	Current dollars (bil. dol.)	Constant (1992) dollars (bil. dol.)	Veterans outlays (bil. dol.)	Total outlays	Defense outlays	Veterans outlays	Federal outlays	Gross domestic product [2]
1960	53.5	48.1	260.3	5.4	2.5	2.4	3.1	52.2	9.3
1965	56.3	50.6	248.9	5.7	-6.8	-7.6	0.7	42.8	7.4
1966	64.1	58.1	274.0	6.0	13.7	14.8	3.5	43.2	7.7
1967	78.1	71.4	323.4	6.7	22.1	22.9	13.8	45.4	8.8
1968	88.9	81.9	352.2	7.0	13.8	14.7	4.4	46.0	9.4
1969	90.2	82.5	337.4	7.7	1.3	0.7	8.5	44.9	8.7
1970	90.4	81.7	315.4	8.7	0.3	-1.0	13.6	41.8	8.1
1971	88.7	78.9	287.1	9.8	-1.9	-3.5	12.7	37.5	7.3
1972	89.9	79.2	263.7	10.7	1.4	0.4	9.8	34.3	6.7
1973	88.7	76.7	239.6	12.0	1.3	-3.1	12.0	31.2	5.9
1974	92.6	79.3	228.3	13.3	4.6	3.5	11.4	29.5	5.5
1975	103.1	86.5	224.1	16.6	11.2	9.0	24.0	26.0	5.6
1976	108.0	89.6	216.8	18.4	4.8	3.6	11.0	24.1	5.2
1976, TQ [3]	26.3	22.3	52.1	4.0	(X)	(X)	(X)	23.2	4.9
1977	115.2	97.2	216.4	18.0	6.7	8.5	-2.1	23.8	4.9
1978	123.5	104.5	217.4	19.0	7.1	7.5	5.2	22.8	4.7
1979	136.2	116.3	221.9	19.9	10.4	11.3	5.0	23.1	4.7
1980	155.1	134.0	229.4	21.1	13.9	15.2	6.3	22.7	4.9
1981	180.4	157.5	241.8	22.9	16.3	17.6	8.5	23.2	5.2
1982	209.2	185.3	263.6	23.9	15.9	17.6	4.2	24.8	5.8
1983	234.7	209.9	284.0	24.8	12.1	13.3	3.3	26.0	6.1
1984	253.0	227.4	287.4	25.6	7.8	8.3	3.2	26.7	6.0
1985	279.0	252.7	306.1	26.3	10.3	11.1	2.7	26.7	6.2
1986	299.9	273.4	324.7	26.5	7.4	8.2	0.4	27.6	6.2
1987	309.0	282.0	330.0	27.0	3.0	3.1	1.5	28.1	6.1
1988	319.7	290.4	333.9	29.3	3.6	3.0	9.7	27.3	5.9
1989	333.6	303.6	338.3	30.0	4.3	4.5	2.4	26.5	5.7
1990	328.3	299.3	324.6	29.0	-1.6	-1.4	-3.3	23.9	5.3
1991	304.5	273.3	283.3	31.2	-7.2	-8.7	7.6	20.6	4.7
1992	332.3	298.4	298.4	33.9	12.0	12.4	8.0	21.6	4.9
1993	326.6	291.1	286.6	35.5	-1.9	-2.4	4.6	20.7	4.5
1994	319.0	281.6	271.9	37.4	-2.3	-3.3	5.4	19.3	4.1
1995	309.9	272.1	256.8	37.8	-2.9	-3.4	1.1	17.9	3.8
1996	302.7	265.8	242.3	36.9	-2.3	-2.3	-2.4	17.0	3.5
1997	309.8	270.5	241.1	39.3	2.3	1.8	6.5	16.9	3.4
1998	310.3	268.5	236.6	41.8	0.2	-0.7	6.3	16.2	3.2
1999, est	320.2	276.7	240.6	43.5	3.2	3.1	4.1	16.0	3.2

X Not applicable. [1] Change from prior year shown; for 1960, change from 1955. [2] Represents fiscal year GDP; for definition, see text, Section 14, Income, Expenditures, and Wealth. [3] Transition quarter, July-Sept.

Source: U.S. Office of Management and Budget, *Historical Tables,* annual.

No. 575. Federal Budget Outlays for National Defense Functions: 1980 to 1999

[In billions of dollars ($134.0 represents $134,000,000,000), except percent. For fiscal year ending in year shown; see text, Section 9, State and Local Government. Minus sign (-) indicates decline]

Defense function	1980	1985	1990	1991	1992	1993	1994	1995	1996	1997	1998	1999, est.
Total................	134.0	252.7	299.3	273.3	298.4	291.1	281.6	272.1	265.8	270.5	268.5	276.7
Percent change [1]......	15.2	11.1	-1.4	-8.7	9.2	-2.4	-3.3	-3.4	-2.3	1.8	-0.7	3.1
Defense Dept., military	130.9	245.2	289.8	262.4	286.9	278.6	268.6	259.4	253.2	258.3	256.1	263.6
Military personnel	40.9	67.8	75.6	83.4	81.2	75.9	73.1	70.8	66.7	69.7	69.0	72.0
Percent of military	31.2	27.7	26.1	31.8	28.3	27.2	27.2	27.3	26.3	27.0	26.9	27.3
Operation, maintenance.....	44.8	72.4	88.3	101.8	92.0	94.1	87.9	91.1	88.8	92.5	93.5	96.8
Procurement	29.0	70.4	81.0	82.0	74.9	69.9	61.8	55.0	48.9	47.7	48.2	48.4
Research and development ..	13.1	27.1	37.5	34.6	34.6	37.0	34.8	34.6	36.5	37.0	37.4	36.8
Military construction	2.5	4.3	5.1	3.5	4.3	4.8	5.0	6.8	6.7	6.2	6.0	5.3
Family housing...........	1.7	2.6	3.5	3.3	3.3	3.3	3.3	3.6	3.8	4.0	3.9	3.9
Other [2]................	-1.1	0.6	-1.2	-46.2	-3.3	-6.4	2.7	-2.4	1.8	1.2	-1.9	0.4
Atomic energy activities [3]	2.9	7.1	9.0	10.0	10.6	11.0	11.9	11.8	11.6	11.3	11.3	12.0
Defense-related activities [4]	0.2	0.5	0.6	0.9	0.8	1.5	1.1	0.8	0.9	0.9	1.1	1.2

[1] Change from immediate prior year. [2] Revolving and management funds, trust funds, special foreign currency program, allowances, and offsetting receipts. [3] Defense activities only. [4] Includes civil defense activities.

Source: U.S. Office of Management and Budget, *Historical Tables,* annual.

No. 576. National Defense—Budget Authority and Outlays: 1980 to 1999

[In billions of dollars ($143.9 represents $143,900,000,000), except percent. For fiscal year ending in year shown, except as noted; see text, Section 9, State and Local Government]

Item	1980	1985	1990	1992	1993	1994	1995	1996	1997	1998	1999, est.
Budget authority [1]	143.9	294.7	303.3	295.1	281.1	263.3	266.3	266.0	270.3	271.3	276.2
Department of Defense-Military [2]	140.7	286.8	293.0	282.1	267.2	251.4	255.7	254.4	258.0	258.5	262.6
Atomic energy defense activities[1]	3.0	7.3	9.7	12.0	12.1	10.9	10.1	10.7	11.4	11.7	12.5
Defense-related activities	0.2	0.5	0.6	1.0	1.8	1.1	0.6	0.9	1.0	1.0	1.1
Outlays (Defense) [1]	134.0	252.7	299.3	298.4	291.1	281.6	272.1	265.8	270.5	268.5	276.7
Department of Defense-Military	130.9	245.2	289.8	286.9	278.6	268.6	259.4	253.2	258.3	256.1	263.6
Atomic energy defense activities[1]	2.9	7.1	9.0	10.6	11.0	11.9	11.8	11.6	11.3	11.3	12.0
Defense-related activities	0.2	0.5	0.6	0.8	1.5	1.1	0.8	0.9	0.9	1.1	1.2

[1] Includes defense budget authority, balances, and outlays by other departments. [2] Excluding accruals.

Source: U.S. Office of Management and Budget, *Historical Tables,* annual.

No. 577. Defense-Related Employment and Spending: 1977 to 1996, and Projections to 2006

[Dollar amounts in billions of chain-weighted 1992 dollars ($4,279.3 represents $4,279,300,000,000]

Item	1977	1987	1996	2002	2006	Change				
						1977-87	1987-96	1996-2002	1996-2006	1987-2006
Spending (bil. dol.):										
Gross domestic product (GDP)	4,279.3	5,648.4	6,911.0	7,739.9	8,539.1	1,369.1	1,262.6	828.9	1,628.1	2,890.7
Defense purchases	266.4	409.2	314.9	265.4	257.3	142.8	-94.3	-49.5	-57.6	-151.9
As percent of GDP:										
Defense purchases	6.2	7.2	4.6	3.4	3.0	1.0	-2.7	-1.1	-1.5	-4.2
Employment, total [1] (1,000)	95,588	116,523	133,884	144,646	152,370	20,935	17,361	10,762	18,485	35,847
Defense-related	4,767	6,942	4,492	3,744	3,595	2,175	-2,450	-748	-897	-3,347
As percent of total employment:										
Defense related	4.99	5.96	3.36	2.59	2.36	0.97	-2.60	-0.77	-1.00	-3.60
Civilian, Defense Dept.	1.07	0.96	0.61	0.51	0.49	-0.10	-0.36	-0.10	-0.12	-0.48
Civilian, other gov't	0.02	0.04	0.02	0.01	0.01	0.01	-0.02	-0.01	-0.01	-0.03
Armed Forces	2.17	1.92	1.14	1.00	0.95	-0.25	-0.77	-0.15	-0.20	-0.97
Private	1.73	3.04	1.59	1.07	0.92	1.31	-1.46	-0.52	-0.67	-2.13

[1] Total employed, including resident Armed Forces, plus Department of Defense estimates of Armed Forces abroad.

Source: U.S. Bureau of Labor Statistics, *Monthly Labor Review,* July 1998.

No. 578. Military and Civilian Personnel and Expenditures: 1990 to 1997

Item	1990	1993	1994	1995	1996	1997
Personnel, total [1] (1,000)	**3,693**	**3,762**	**3,623**	**3,391**	**3,252**	**3,081**
Active duty military	1,185	1,171	1,131	1,085	1,056	1,045
Expenditures, total (mil. dol.) [2]	**209,904**	**214,655**	**210,138**	**209,695**	**211,740**	**205,764**
Prime contract awards [3] (mil. dol.)	121,254	114,145	110,316	109,005	109,408	106,561
Major area of work (mil. dol.):						
Aircraft, fixed wing	6,329	6,926	6,277	7,543	8,950	12,904
Guided missiles	928	793	494	495	625	2,831

[1] Includes those based ashore and excludes those temporarily shore-based, in a transient status, or afloat. [2] Includes expenditures not shown separately. [3] Represents contract awards over $25,000.

Source: U.S. Dept. of Defense, *Atlas/Data Abstract for the United States and Selected Areas,* annual.

National Defense and Veterans Affairs **369**

No. 579. Military Prime Contract Awards to All Businesses, by Program: 1980 to 1997

[In billions of dollars ($83.7 represents $83,700,000,000). Net values for **fiscal year ending in year shown;** see text, Section 9, State and Local Government. Includes all new prime contracts; debit or credit changes in contracts are also included. Actions cover official awards, amendments, or other changes in prime contracts to obtain military supplies, services, or construction. Excludes term contracts and contracts which do not obligate a firm total dollar amount or fixed quantity, but includes job orders, task orders, and delivery orders against such contracts]

DOD procurement program	1980	1990	1991	1992	1993	1994	1995	1996	1997
Total	83.7	144.7	150.9	136.3	138.3	132.2	131.4	132.2	128.4
Intragovernmental [1]	10.2	10.0	11.9	9.6	12.9	11.1	12.3	13.0	11.5
For work outside the U.S.	5.4	7.1	9.2	5.9	5.8	5.6	5.6	6.4	6.4
Educ. and nonprofit institutions	1.5	3.5	3.6	3.4	3.4	3.3	3.3	3.3	3.6
With business firms for work in the U.S. [2] . .	66.7	123.8	125.9	117.2	116.0	112.0	110.0	109.5	106.9
Major hard goods	41.0	79.1	74.1	67.1	64.5	59.2	56.0	55.1	52.5
Aircraft	12.5	24.0	23.6	24.1	23.0	23.5	18.8	20.3	18.4
Electronics and communication equip. .	9.6	18.5	15.2	14.2	14.2	12.4	12.3	11.5	12.1
Missiles and space systems	7.9	17.1	16.4	13.1	12.1	11.6	10.6	10.2	9.5
Ships	6.0	10.3	9.3	8.3	9.0	6.8	9.1	7.1	6.8
Tanks, ammo. and weapons	5.1	9.2	9.6	7.4	6.2	4.9	5.3	5.9	5.7
Services	5.9	14.6	16.9	17.3	17.5	17.7	18.6	19.2	20.2

[1] Covers only purchases from other Federal agencies and reimbursable purchases on behalf of foreign governments.
[2] Includes Department of Defense. Includes other business not shown separately. Contracts awarded for work in U.S. possessions, and other areas subject to complete sovereignty of United States; contracts in a classified location; and any intragovernmental contracts entered into overseas.

Source: U.S. Dept. of Defense, *Prime Contract Awards*, semiannual.

No. 580. Department of Defense Contract Awards, Payroll, and Civilian and Military Personnel—States: 1997

[For years ending **Sept. 30. Contracts** refer to awards made in year specified; expenditures relating to awards may extend over several years. **Civilian employees** include United States citizen and foreign national direct hire civilians subject to Office of Management and Budget (OMB) ceiling controls and civilian personnel involved in civil functions in the United States. Excludes indirect hire civilians and those direct hire civilian not subject to OMB ceiling controls. **Military personnel** include active duty personnel based ashore. Excludes personnel temporarily shore-based in a transient status, or afloat. **Payroll outlays** include the gross earnings of civilian and active duty military personnel for services rendered to the government and for cash allowances for benefits. Excludes employer's share of employee benefits, accrued military retirement benefits, and most permanent change of station costs]

State	Contract awards [1] (mil. dol.)	Payroll (mil. dol.)	Personnel (1,000) Civilian	Personnel (1,000) Military	State	Contract awards [1] (mil. dol.)	Payroll (mil. dol.)	Personnel (1,000) Civilian	Personnel (1,000) Military
U.S. . . .	106,561	97,296	689.2	1,045.3	MO	4,766	1,407	10.5	15.1
AL	2,107	2,150	22.1	15.6	MT	81	255	1.2	3.6
AK	628	840	4.7	16.1	NE	261	691	3.6	9.0
AZ	1,977	1,919	8.4	22.3	NV	257	726	2.1	7.8
AR	191	764	3.7	5.2	NH	388	272	1.3	0.4
CA	18,477	12,396	79.0	122.0	NJ	3,016	1,589	18.1	7.5
CO	1,900	2,267	11.5	29.4	NM	512	1,129	8.1	13.2
CT	2,536	602	2.8	5.7	NY	3,178	1,675	12.3	18.9
DE	104	301	1.5	3.9	NC	1,110	4,062	17.3	91.9
DC	1,526	1,192	12.8	14.5	ND	127	370	1.7	8.7
FL	6,394	6,910	28.3	57.4	OH	2,676	2,256	26.1	8.2
GA	3,950	4,090	31.8	62.9	OK	751	2,085	19.4	27.1
HI	957	2,226	17.2	34.8	OR	168	517	2.8	0.9
ID	147	345	1.4	4.5	PA	3,039	2,213	29.9	3.6
IL	1,248	2,073	14.7	30.4	RI	275	481	4.5	3.3
IN	1,721	867	9.9	1.3	SC	919	2,127	10.2	33.7
IA	438	250	1.5	0.5	SD	89	230	1.3	3.1
KS	688	936	5.7	16.7	TN	1,211	924	5.0	1.9
KY	1,201	1,433	7.8	33.9	TX	7,411	8,070	49.7	111.0
LA	1,759	1,283	8.0	17.5	UT	442	892	12.4	4.9
ME	946	544	5.2	2.0	VT	97	88	0.5	0.1
MD	3,889	3,346	33.9	30.5	VA	11,188	10,544	82.0	84.5
MA	4,910	866	7.4	3.3	WA	2,517	3,713	23.8	37.9
MI	1,101	805	7.9	1.2	WV	150	275	1.8	0.5
MN	1,091	407	2.5	0.9	WI	565	403	3.2	0.7
MS	1,431	1,277	9.7	12.4	WY	48	214	1.0	3.5

[1] Military awards for supplies, services, and construction. Net value of contracts of over $25,000 for work in each state and DC. Figures reflect impact of prime contracting on state distribution of defense work. Often the state in which a prime contractor is located in is not the state where the subcontracted work is done. See also headnote, Table 579. Undistributed civilians and military personnel, their payrolls, and prime contract awards for performance in classified locations are excluded.

Source: U.S. Dept. of Defense, *Atlas/Data Abstract for the United States and Selected Areas*, annual.

No. 581. Worldwide Military Expenditures: 1987 to 1995

[In billions of dollars ($1,051 represents $1,051,000,000,000). For military expenditures and Armed Forces by country, see Section 30, Comparative International Statistics. GNP=Gross national product]

Country group	1987	1988	1989	1990	1991	1992	1993	1994	1995
Current dollars, total [1]	1,051	1,080	1,089	1,106	1,049	974	912	879	865
United States	288	293	304	306	280	305	298	288	278
Percent of total.	27.4	27.1	27.9	27.7	26.7	31.3	32.6	32.8	32.1
Developed countries [2]	881	911	922	912	848	771	732	695	668
Developing countries [2]	170	169	167	193	200	203	180	184	197
NATO countries [3]	464	472	492	504	483	504	496	485	471
Constant (1995) dollars, total [1] . .	1,360	1,349	1,305	1,271	1,159	1,048	957	901	865
United States	373	366	364	352	310	328	312	295	278
Percent of total.	27.4	27.1	27.9	27.7	26.7	31.3	32.6	32.8	32.1
Developed countries [2]	1,140	1,138	1,105	1,048	937	829	768	712	668
Developing countries [2]	220	211	200	222	221	219	189	189	197
NATO countries [3]	601	590	590	579	533	542	519	497	471
Percent of GNP	5.0	4.8	4.5	4.3	3.9	3.6	3.3	3.0	2.8
United States	6.1	5.8	5.6	5.3	4.7	4.9	4.5	4.2	3.8
Developed countries [2]	5.1	4.8	4.6	4.3	3.8	3.6	3.3	3.0	2.8
Developing countries [2]	4.9	4.4	4.1	4.4	4.3	3.6	3.0	2.8	2.8
NATO countries [3]	4.6	4.3	4.2	4.0	3.7	3.7	3.5	3.3	3.0

[1] Includes countries not shown separately. [2] Twenty-eight developed countries; see Table 582 for selected countries; for complete list, see source. [3] North Atlantic Treaty Organization.

No. 582. Arms Trade in Constant (1995) Dollars—Selected Countries: 1994 to 1996

[In millions of dollars ($38,520 represents $38,520,000,000), except percent. Because some countries exclude arms imports or exports from their trade statistics and their "total" imports and exports are therefore understated, and because arms transfers may be estimated independently of trade data, the ratio of arms to total imports or exports may be overstated and may even exceed 100 percent]

Country	1994	1995	1996 Total	1996 Arms imports as percent of total imports	Country	1994	1995	1996 Total	1996 Arms imports as percent of total imports
World total [1] . .	38,520	40,640	42,630	0.8	India	188	407	400	1.1
EXPORTERS [1]					Iran	406	306	350	2.2
					Iraq	-	-	-	-
Canada	703	377	460	0.1	Israel	1,250	789	925	2.9
China: Mainland .	755	662	600	1.1	Italy	438	397	575	0.3
Czech Republic. .	323	102	100	0.2	Japan	2,084	1,630	2,400	0.7
France.	1,459	2,139	3,200	0.1					
Poland.	73	41	50	0.2	Jordan.	52	81	110	2.5
United Kingdom. .	5,419	5,195	6,100	0.5	Kuwait.	406	1,324	1,700	22.5
United States . . .	22,510	22,620	23,500	0.1	Libya.	10	-	10	0.2
Germany	1,667	1,732	825	0.2	Morocco.	135	61	50	0.5
					Nicaragua.	-	-	10	0.9
IMPORTERS [1]					North Korea	135	122	-	(NA)
					Oman	302	438	380	8.3
Afghanistan	21	20	60	40.0	Pakistan.	344	535	170	1.4
Algeria.	167	244	110	1.2	Peru	63	275	160	1.7
Angola.	755	122	90	(NA)	Poland.	21	71	60	0.2
Argentina	42	51	80	0.3					
Australia.	1,042	1,324	1,300	2.0	Romania	-	10	20	0.2
					Saudi Arabia	8,128	9,168	9,800	35.3
Canada	302	224	260	0.1	South Korea	2,188	1,732	1,100	0.7
Cuba.	-	-	-	-	Spain	755	336	675	0.6
Czech Republic. .	104	20	60	0.2	Syria	52	112	90	1.7
Egypt	1,771	2,343	1,800	13.8					
El Salvador.	31	31	30	1.1	Turkey.	1,980	1,732	1,400	3.3
					United Kingdom. .	1,146	968	1,500	0.5
Ethiopia	-	5	10	(NA)	*United States* . . .	*1,146*	*1,121*	*1,100*	*0.1*
Germany	1,016	840	900	0.2	Venezuela	198	122	190	1.9
Greece	677	469	625	(NA)	Vietnam	83	377	10	0.1
Hungary.	10	31	50	0.3	Yemen (Sanaa) . .	261	143	80	(NA)

- Represents or rounds to zero. NA Not available. [1] Includes countries not shown separately.

Source of Tables 581 and 582: U.S. Arms Control and Disarmament Agency, *World Military Expenditures and Arms Transfers*, annual.

National Defense and Veterans Affairs **371**

No. 583. Arms Transfers—Cumulative Value for Period 1994-96, by Major Supplier and Recipient Country

[In millions of dollars ($119,565 represents $119,565,000,000)]

Recipient	Total [1]	Supplier United States	United Kingdom	Russia	West Germany	France	China: Mainland
World, total	**119,565**	**67,210**	**16,405**	**8,490**	**4,045**	**6,675**	**1,970**
Africa [1]							
North Africa	990	280	5	305	-	60	15
Algeria	525	20	-	300	-	-	-
Libya	25	-	-	-	-	-	-
Morocco	250	170	-	-	-	-	-
Subsahara Africa	1,880	75	55	625	-	130	70
Angola	920	20	-	550	-	-	-
Nigeria	45	10	-	-	-	-	-
Rwanda	20	5	-	-	-	-	-
Zimbabwe	100	-	-	-	-	50	-
Americas:							
Central America & Caribbean	380	355	-	-	-	10	-
Cuba	-	-	-	-	-	-	-
El Salvador	80	80	-	-	-	-	-
North America (NAFTA)	4,510	875	960	60	320	360	40
Canada	765	525	-	-	-	200	-
Mexico	415	350	-	-	-	-	-
United States	3,330	-	950	40	320	160	40
South America	3,370	1,350	210	120	100	265	40
Brazil	770	440	170	-	60	50	-
Chile	710	90	-	-	-	60	-
Colombia	200	160	-	-	-	-	-
Venezuela	510	370	-	-	-	-	-
Asia:							
Central Asia & Caucasus	910	80	-	665	30	-	5
Middle East	44,475	22,505	12,900	1,655	220	3,180	690
Egypt	5,675	5,000	-	210	-	130	-
Iran	1,025	-	-	320	-	-	500
Israel	2,865	2,600	-	-	150	-	-
Kuwait	3,405	1,900	675	750	-	60	-
Saudi Arabia	26,585	11,700	11,200	-	60	2,000	-
Syria	230	-	-	-	-	-	-
United Arab Emirates	2,270	800	260	200	-	750	-
Yemen	480	5	-	-	-	-	-
East Asia	25,580	15,820	1,830	3,270	1,335	920	510
Burma	315	-	-	-	-	-	-
China:							
Mainland	2,565	120	-	2,000	-	-	(X)
Taiwan	4,090	3,300	-	-	-	775	-
Indonesia	1,260	300	725	-	90	-	-
Japan	6,020	6,000	-	-	-	-	-
Korea, South	4,780	3,200	70	80	1,200	-	-
Malaysia	1,990	360	950	550	-	-	-
Singapore	1,290	950	-	-	-	-	-
Thailand	1,715	1,100	-	-	-	-	110
South Asia	2,605	280	100	740	-	440	480
India	985	110	-	650	-	-	-
Pakistan	1,040	140	70	-	-	440	230
Europe							
Eastern Europe	2,045	220	20	750	75	20	-
Hungary	90	20	-	-	-	-	-
Western Europe	24,910	20,255	270	265	1,460	1,215	-
Belgium	890	600	-	-	-	280	-
Denmark	445	410	-	-	-	-	-
Finland	1,360	1,200	-	70	-	-	-
France	695	550	-	-	-	(X)	-
Germany	2,710	2,600	-	-	(X)	-	-
Greece	1,770	1,100	-	-	410	50	-
Italy	1,410	1,300	90	-	-	-	-
Netherlands	1,565	1,500	-	-	-	-	-
Norway	755	575	-	-	-	130	-
Portugal	555	500	-	-	-	-	-
Spain	1,690	1,400	-	-	-	90	-
Sweden	1,125	850	-	-	270	-	-
Switzerland	570	500	-	-	-	-	-
Turkey	4,985	3,200	-	190	700	350	-
United Kingdom	3,570	3,500	(X)	-	-	-	-
Oceania	4,285	2,020	40	-	500	-	-
Australia	3,500	1,800	-	-	500	-	-
New Zealand	760	220	-	-	-	-	-

- Represents $2.5 million or less.　X Not applicable.　[1] Includes countries not shown separately.

Source: U.S. Arms Control and Disarmament Agency, *World Military Expenditures and Arms Transfers*, annual.

No. 584. U.S. Military Sales and Assistance to Foreign Governments: 1989 to 1997

[In millions of dollars, ($16,614 represents $16,614,000,000). For fiscal year ending in year shown; see text, Section 9, State and Local Government. Department of Defense (DOD) sales deliveries cover deliveries against DOD sales orders sales orders authorized under Arms Export Control Act, as well as earlier and applicable legislation. For details regarding individual programs, see source]

Item	1989	1990	1991	1992	1993	1994	1995	1996	1997
Military sales agreements	8,783	16,614	17,325	13,888	31,109	13,292	8,950	10,300	8,778
Military constr. sales agrmts	75	636	799	148	660	58	25	83	30
Military sales deliveries [1]	7,585	8,065	9,191	10,389	11,666	9,736	12,158	11,716	19,331
Military sales financing . . . .[2]. .	4,273	4,758	4,693	4,274	4,124	3,917	3,712	3,836	3,530
Military assistance programs [2] . .	535	137	177	116	540	321	119	340	70
Military assist. program delivery [3] .	53	27	150	82	60	1	8	25	112
IMET program/deliveries [3]	46	43	46	42	43	22	26	39	43

[1] Includes military construction sales deliveries. [2] Also includes Military Assistance Service Funded (MASF) program data, section 506(a) drawdown authority, and MAP Merger Funds. [3] Includes Military Assistance Service Funded (MASF) program data and section 506(a) drawdown authority.

No. 585. U.S. Military Sales Deliveries, by Country: 1989 to 1997

[In millions of dollars ($7,585 represents $7,585,000,000). For fiscal years ending in year shown; see text, Section 9, State and Local Government. Represents Department of Defense military sales]

Country	1989	1990	1991	1992	1993	1994	1995	1996	1997
Total [1]	7,585	8,065	9,191	10,389	11,666	9,736	12,158	11,716	19,331
Australia	583	384	205	156	259	354	308	229	197
Canada	144	119	164	123	230	169	128	164	84
China: Taiwan	393	455	549	711	818	845	1,353	853	5,696
Egypt	321	440	574	1,094	1,363	1,029	1,619	1,169	1,226
Germany	632	366	476	511	356	152	240	405	212
Greece	137	114	124	163	226	236	221	210	717
Israel	230	146	238	720	782	412	328	386	504
Italy	64	61	61	52	72	181	54	77	51
Japan	206	272	518	571	380	785	753	786	512
Kuwait	46	52	110	858	893	221	485	628	1,391
Netherlands	384	397	387	236	114	140	157	397	174
Portugal	32	72	40	89	82	228	90	19	71
Saudi Arabia	963	1,137	3,016	2,603	3,574	2,083	3,676	2,903	4,697
South Korea	316	328	230	309	306	381	442	342	483
Spain	656	406	155	138	203	403	193	419	220
Thailand	210	175	178	100	106	151	356	340	200
Turkey	621	761	627	703	756	937	374	483	1,167
United Kingdom	131	205	243	154	227	202	108	153	235

[1] Includes countries not shown.

Source of Tables 584 and 585: U.S. Defense Security Assistance Agency, *Foreign Military Sales, Foreign Military Construction Sales,* and *Military Assistance Facts,* annual.

No. 586. Summary of Active and Reserve Military Personnel and Forces

Item	Cold War (1990)	2000	Quadrennial defense review (QDR) target	Item	Cold War (1990)	2000	Quadrennial defense review (QDR) target
Military personnel (1,000):				Reserve	2	1	1
Active	2,069	1,385	1,363				
Selected reserve	1,128	865	835	Battle force ships [3]	546	314	306
Army:				Marine Corps:			
Divisions:				Divisions:			
Active	18	[1]10	[1]10	Active	3	3	3
National Guard	10	[2]8	[2]8	Reserve	1	1	1
				Air wings:			
Air Force:				Active	3	3	3
Fighter wing:				Reserve	1	1	1
Active	24	13	12	Strategic nuclear forces:			
Reserve	12	7	8	Intercontinental ballistic missiles .	1,000	550	500
				Warheads	2,450	2,000	[4]500
Navy:				Ballistic missile submarines . . .	31	18	[4]14
Aircraft carriers:				Sea-launched ballistic missiles . .	568	432	336
Active	15	11	11	Warheads	4,864	3,456	[5]
Training	1	1	1				
Air wings:							
Active	13	10	10	Heavy bombers	324	[6]90	[6]92

[1] Plus two armored cavalry regiments. [2] Plus 18 separate brigades. [3] Includes active and reserve ships. [4] Upon entry-into-force of START II. [5] Not over 1,750. [6] Does not include 95 B-1 bombers dedicated to conventional missions.

Source: U.S. Office of Management and Budget, *Budget of the United States Government,* annual.

National Defense and Veterans Affairs   373

U.S. Census Bureau, *Statistical Abstract of the United States: 1999*

No. 587. Department of Defense Manpower: 1950 to 1997

[In thousands ($1,459 represents $1,459,000). As of **end of fiscal year**; see text, Section 9, State and Local Government. Includes National Guard, Reserve, and retired regular personnel on extended or continuous active duty. Excludes Coast Guard. Other officer candidates are included under enlisted personnel]

Year	Total [1][2]	Army					Navy [3]					Marine corps					Air Force				
		Total [2]	White	Black	Officers	Enlisted	Total [2]	White	Black	Officers	Enlisted	Total [2]	White	Black	Officers	Enlisted	Total [2]	White	Black	Officers	Enlisted
1950	1,459	593	(NA)	(NA)	73	519	381	(NA)	(NA)	45	333	74	(NA)	(NA)	7	67	411	(NA)	(NA)	57	354
1955	2,935	1,109	(NA)	(NA)	122	986	661	(NA)	(NA)	75	583	205	(NA)	(NA)	18	187	960	(NA)	(NA)	137	823
1960	2,475	873	(NA)	(NA)	101	770	617	(NA)	(NA)	70	545	171	(NA)	(NA)	16	154	815	(NA)	(NA)	130	683
1965	2,654	969	(NA)	(NA)	112	855	670	(NA)	(NA)	78	588	190	(NA)	(NA)	17	173	825	(NA)	(NA)	132	690
1966	3,092	1,200	(NA)	(NA)	118	1,080	743	(NA)	(NA)	80	659	262	(NA)	(NA)	21	241	887	(NA)	(NA)	131	753
1967	3,375	1,442	(NA)	(NA)	144	1,297	750	(NA)	(NA)	82	664	285	(NA)	(NA)	24	262	897	(NA)	(NA)	135	759
1968	3,546	1,570	(NA)	(NA)	166	1,402	764	(NA)	(NA)	85	674	307	(NA)	(NA)	25	283	905	(NA)	(NA)	140	762
1969	3,458	1,512	(NA)	(NA)	173	1,337	774	(NA)	(NA)	85	684	310	(NA)	(NA)	26	284	862	(NA)	(NA)	135	723
1970	3,065	1,323	(NA)	(NA)	167	1,153	691	(NA)	(NA)	81	606	260	(NA)	(NA)	25	235	791	(NA)	(NA)	130	657
1971	2,713	1,124	(NA)	(NA)	149	972	622	(NA)	(NA)	75	542	212	(NA)	(NA)	22	191	755	(NA)	(NA)	126	625
1972	2,322	811	(NA)	(NA)	121	687	587	(NA)	(NA)	73	511	198	(NA)	(NA)	20	178	726	(NA)	(NA)	122	600
1973	2,252	801	(NA)	(NA)	116	682	564	(NA)	(NA)	71	490	196	(NA)	(NA)	19	177	691	(NA)	(NA)	115	572
1974	2,162	783	(NA)	(NA)	106	674	546	(NA)	(NA)	67	475	189	(NA)	(NA)	19	170	644	(NA)	(NA)	110	529
1975	2,128	784	503	229	103	678	535	436	55	66	466	196	142	39	19	177	613	460	80	105	503
1976	2,082	779	502	232	99	678	525	443	58	64	458	192	145	39	19	174	585	468	83	100	481
1977	2,075	782	504	230	98	680	530	450	62	63	462	192	149	38	19	173	571	476	87	96	470
1978	2,062	772	512	220	98	670	530	462	66	63	463	191	152	37	18	172	570	483	88	95	470
1979	2,027	759	520	215	97	657	523	455	67	62	457	185	153	36	18	167	559	486	89	96	459
1980	2,051	777	503	229	99	674	527	436	55	63	460	188	142	39	18	170	558	460	80	98	456
1981	2,083	781	502	232	102	675	540	443	58	65	470	191	145	39	18	172	570	468	83	99	467
1982	2,109	780	504	230	103	673	553	450	62	67	481	192	149	38	19	173	583	476	87	102	476
1983	2,123	780	512	220	106	669	558	462	66	68	485	194	152	37	20	174	592	483	88	105	483
1984	2,138	780	520	215	108	668	565	455	67	69	491	196	153	36	20	176	597	486	89	106	486
1985	2,151	781	523	211	110	667	571	459	70	71	495	198	152	37	20	178	602	488	90	108	489
1986	2,169	781	524	210	110	667	581	464	75	72	504	199	151	38	20	179	608	491	92	109	495
1987	2,174	781	519	212	108	668	587	467	81	72	510	200	150	38	20	179	607	489	92	107	495
1988	2,138	772	507	213	107	660	593	466	85	72	516	197	147	38	20	177	576	462	88	105	467
1989	2,130	770	497	218	107	658	593	461	91	72	516	197	146	38	20	177	571	458	87	104	463
1990	2,044	732	466	213	104	624	579	446	93	72	503	197	145	38	20	177	535	428	82	100	431
1991	1,986	711	452	204	104	603	570	439	92	71	495	194	144	36	20	174	510	409	77	97	409
1992	1,807	610	388	173	95	511	542	415	88	69	468	185	138	32	19	165	470	377	70	90	376
1993	1,705	572	365	158	88	480	510	390	84	66	439	178	134	30	18	160	444	357	65	84	356
1994	1,610	541	344	147	85	452	469	355	78	62	403	174	131	28	18	156	426	341	62	81	341
1995	1,518	509	322	137	83	422	435	326	75	59	372	175	130	28	18	157	400	318	58	78	318
1996	1,472	491	(NA)	(NA)	81	407	417	(NA)	(NA)	57	355	175	(NA)	(NA)	18	157	389	(NA)	(NA)	76	309
1997	1,439	492	(NA)	(NA)	79	408	396	(NA)	(NA)	56	335	174	(NA)	(NA)	18	156	377	(NA)	(NA)	74	299

NA Not available. [1] Beginning 1980, excludes Navy Reserve personnel on active duty for Training and Administration of Reserves (TARS). From 1969, the full-time Guard and Reserve. [2] Includes Cadets and other not shown separately. [3] Prior to 1980, includes Navy Reserve personnel on active duty for Training and Administration of Reserves (TARS).

Source: U.S. Dept. of Defense, *Selected Manpower Statistics*, annual.

No. 588. United States Military and Civilian Personnel in Installations: 1997

[As of September 30]

State	Military personnel				Civilian personnel			
	Total	Army	Navy/MC	Air Force	Total [1]	Army	Navy/MC	Air Force
U.S.	1,056,173	398,528	342,647	314,998	689,187	224,770	193,959	164,489
AL.	15,570	9,581	916	5,073	22,104	17,436	28	2,688
AK.	16,069	6,561	259	9,249	4,689	2,699	23	1,729
AZ.	22,297	5,952	4,290	12,055	8,350	3,534	425	3,384
AR.	5,161	497	116	4,548	3,703	2,702	24	859
CA.	121,971	7,985	89,148	24,838	78,963	7,877	41,906	17,463
CO	29,433	14,796	967	13,670	11,501	3,277	35	4,854
CT.	5,713	26	5,573	114	2,778	474	1,188	245
DE.	3,889	9	20	3,860	1,462	179	-	1,202
DC	14,501	4,560	6,140	3,801	12,782	4,756	6,636	1,078
FL.	57,426	2,488	28,472	26,466	28,294	2,399	14,146	8,380
GA	62,947	47,892	5,444	9,611	31,827	12,155	4,870	11,419
HI	34,826	15,249	15,963	3,614	17,216	4,779	9,361	1,951
ID	4,524	20	80	4,424	1,431	650	60	671
IL	30,399	713	23,663	6,023	14,732	7,888	1,884	3,264
IN	1,251	652	428	171	9,910	1,622	3,235	1,170
IA	462	225	132	105	1,453	873	4	509
KS.	16,659	13,361	219	3,079	5,684	4,121	3	1,058
KY.	33,875	33,301	265	309	7,839	5,726	296	221
LA	17,511	8,495	3,261	5,755	7,952	4,156	1,612	1,683
ME	2,036	241	1,618	177	5,229	284	4,273	287
MD	30,453	8,874	15,176	6,403	33,900	12,985	15,584	2,374
MA	3,256	458	588	2,210	7,392	1,885	410	3,568
MI	1,239	589	391	259	7,946	4,900	21	1,565
MN	884	365	371	148	2,512	1,358	27	786
MS	12,362	500	3,063	8,799	9,677	3,799	2,604	2,939
MO	15,078	10,022	1,688	3,368	10,525	6,707	234	1,260
MT	3,574	21	18	3,535	1,151	418	2	666
NE.	8,953	74	501	8,378	3,583	1,583	18	1,544
NV.	7,813	28	1,158	6,627	2,138	246	406	1,258
NH	404	10	258	136	1,264	528	268	294
NJ.	7,472	1,015	1,024	5,433	18,112	10,777	4,350	1,652
NM	13,154	471	394	12,289	8,092	3,443	94	3,917
NY.	18,853	15,701	2,301	851	12,287	7,598	182	2,530
NC	91,855	41,320	41,240	9,295	17,255	6,126	7,695	1,235
ND	8,698	23	5	8,670	1,674	412	1	1,138
OH	8,174	582	647	6,945	26,122	1,468	107	13,290
OK	27,060	16,150	758	10,152	19,421	4,082	86	13,639
OR	889	239	399	251	2,815	2,045	11	723
PA	3,566	1,661	1,555	350	29,933	9,246	9,426	1,624
RI	3,271	83	3,028	160	4,525	270	3,921	248
SC.	33,653	11,455	12,696	9,502	10,155	2,819	4,139	1,759
SD.	3,102	92	12	2,998	1,260	484	-	705
TN	1,864	323	1,245	296	5,049	2,709	502	952
TX.	110,956	63,578	6,995	40,383	49,680	18,366	1,966	24,008
UT.	4,896	298	154	4,444	12,421	2,168	24	8,259
VT.	125	22	19	84	545	267	1	231
VA.	84,463	26,921	43,200	14,342	81,998	21,230	36,922	4,354
WA	37,896	20,809	9,315	7,772	23,824	5,624	14,854	1,885
WV	547	227	285	35	1,820	1,320	83	388
WI	689	357	101	231	3,247	2,209	11	884
WY	3,534	4	11	3,519	965	201	1	699

- Represents zero. [1] Includes other DOD organizations not shown separately.

Source: U.S. Dept. of Defense, *Selected Manpower Statistics*, annual.

No. 589. Military Personnel on Active Duty, by Location: 1980 to 1997

[In thousands (2,051 represents 2,051,000). As of **end of fiscal year**; see text, Section 9, State and Local Government]

Item	1980	1985	1989	1990	1991	1992	1993	1994	1995	1996	1997
Total.	2,051	2,151	2,130	2,044	1,986	1,807	1,705	1,611	1,518	1,472	1,439
Shore-based [1].	1,840	1,920	1,884	1,794	1,743	1,589	1,505	1,431	1,351	1,317	1,294
Afloat [2].	211	231	246	252	243	218	200	180	167	155	145
United States [3].	1,562	1,636	1,620	1,437	1,539	1,463	1,397	1,324	1,280	1,231	1,211
Foreign countries.	488	516	510	609	448	344	308	287	238	240	227

[1] Includes Navy personnel temporarily on shore. [2] Includes Marine Corps. [3] Includes outlying areas.
Source: U.S. Dept. of Defense, *Selected Manpower Statistics*, annual.

No. 590. U.S. Military Personnel on Active Duty in Selected Foreign Countries: 1997

[As of **end of fiscal year**]

Country	1997	Country	1997	Country	1997
In foreign countries [1] .	227,258	Egypt	5,846	Norway	107
Ashore	207,978	El Salvador	28	Oman	28
Afloat	19,280	Finland	18	Pakistan	29
		France	74	Panama	5,400
Antarctica	22	Germany	60,053	Paraguay	11
Argentina	27	Greece	498	Peru	29
Australia	333	Greenland	131	Philippines	35
Austria	34	Guatemala	18	Poland	19
Bahamas, The	24	Haiti	239	Portugal	1,066
Bahrain	748	Honduras	427	Qatar	26
Barbados	10	Hungary	4,220	Rep. of Korea	35,663
Belgium	1,679	Iceland	1,960	Romania	12
Bolivia	26	India	25	Russia	68
Bosnia and Herzegovina . . .	8,170	Indonesia	48	Saudi Arabia	1,722
Brazil	45	Israel	40	Senegal	16
Bulgaria	19	Italy	11,677	Serbia	13
Burma	10	Jamaica	11	Singapore	168
Canada	179	Japan	41,257	South Africa	25
Chile	25	Jordan	30	Spain	3,575
China	58	Kenya	31	Sweden	12
Colombia	32	Korea, Republic of	35,663	Switzerland	22
Cote D'Ivoire	19	Kuwait	1,640	Syria	10
Croatia	866	Macedonia	518	Thailand	126
Cuba (Guantanamo)	1,527	Malaysia	19	Tunisia	193
Cyprus	25	Mexico	27	Turkey	2,864
Czech Republic	18	Morocco	16	Ukraine	10
Denmark	39	Netherlands	703	United Arab Emirates	22
Diego Garcia	705	New Zealand	25	United Kingdom	11,379
Dominican Republic	12	Nicaragua	15	Venezuela	35
Ecuador	164	Nigeria	16	Zambabwe	11

[1] Includes areas not shown separately.
Source: U.S. Department of Defense, *Selected Manpower Statistics*, annual.

No. 591. Coast Guard Personnel on Active Duty: 1970 to 1997

[As of **end of fiscal year**; see text, Section 9, State and Local Government]

Year	Total	Officers	Cadets	Enlisted	Year	Total	Officers	Cadets	Enlisted
1970	37,689	5,512	653	31,524	1992	39,388	7,507	919	30,962
1975	36,788	5,630	1,177	29,981	1993	39,234	7,628	907	30,699
1980	39,381	6,463	877	32,041	1994	37,802	7,656	881	29,265
1985	38,595	6,775	733	31,087	1995	36,731	7,462	841	28,401
1990	36,939	6,876	927	29,136	1996	35,229	7,270	830	27,129
1991	38,377	7,192	900	30,285	1997	34,890	7,100	845	26,945

Source: U.S. Dept. of Transportation, *Annual Report of the Secretary of Transportation*.

No. 592. U.S. Active Duty Military Deaths, by Manner of Death: 1980 to 1998

Manner of death	1980-98	1980	1985	1990	1991	1992	1993	1994	1995	1996	1997	1998
Deaths, total	32,151	2,391	2,016	1,526	1,787	1,332	1,245	1,109	1,055	1,008	864	815
Accident	19,077	1,577	1,215	864	931	712	672	548	572	518	463	420
Illness	5,848	401	400	275	323	253	215	217	167	180	177	156
Homicide	1,769	161	97	71	108	112	89	86	59	65	43	28
Self-inflicted	4,429	236	273	250	233	222	246	231	242	210	159	155
Pending/undetermined . . .	465	15	26	42	44	32	13	8	9	14	22	53
Hostile deaths	563	1	5	24	148	1	10	19	6	21	-	3
Deaths per 100,000	(X)	116.6	93.7	74.7	90.0	73.7	73.0	68.9	69.5	68.5	60.1	57.9
Nonhostile deaths per 100,000	(X)	116.5	93.5	73.5	82.5	73.7	72.4	67.7	69.1	67.1	60.1	57.7
Accidents per 100,000 . . .	(X)	76.9	56.5	42.3	46.9	39.4	39.4	34.0	37.7	35.2	32.2	29.9
Illnesses per 100,000 . . .	(X)	19.6	18.6	13.5	16.3	14.0	12.6	13.5	11.0	12.2	12.3	11.1
Homicides per 100,000 . . .	(X)	7.9	4.5	3.5	5.4	6.2	5.2	5.3	3.9	4.4	3.0	2.0
Self-inflicted per 100,000 . .	(X)	11.5	12.7	12.2	11.7	12.3	14.4	14.3	15.9	14.3	11.1	11.0

- Represents zero.   X Not applicable.
Source: U.S. Dept. of Defense, *DoD Worldwide U.S. Active Duty Military Personnel*.

376   National Defense and Veterans Affairs

No. 593. Armed Forces Personnel—Summary of Major Conflicts

[For Revolutionary War, number of personnel serving not known, but estimates range from 184,000 to 250,000; for War of 1812, 286,730 served; for Mexican War, 78,718 served. Dates of the major conflicts may differ from those specified in various laws providing benefits for veterans]

Item	Unit	Civil War [1]	Spanish-American War	World War I	World War II	Korean conflict	Vietnam conflict
Personnel serving [2]	1,000 ...	2,213	307	4,735	[3]16,113	[4]5,720	[5]8,744
Average duration of service	Months ..	20	8	12	33	19	23
Service abroad: Personnel serving.	Percent..	(NA)	[6]29	53	73	[7]56	(NA)
Average duration [8]	Months ..	(NA)	1.5	6	16	13	(NA)
Casualties: [9] Battle deaths [2]	1,000 ...	140	(Z)	53	292	34	[10]47
Wounds not mortal [2]	1,000 ...	282	2	204	671	103	[10]153
Draftees: Classified.	1,000 ...	777	(X)	24,234	36,677	9,123	[5]75,717
Examined	1,000 ...	522	(X)	3,764	17,955	3,685	[5]8,611
Rejected	1,000 ...	160	(X)	803	6,420	1,189	[5]3,880
Inducted	1,000 ...	46	(X)	2,820	10,022	1,560	[5]1,759

NA Not available. X Not applicable. Z Fewer than 500. [1] Union forces only. Estimates of the number serving in Confederate forces range from 600,000 to 1.5 million. [2] Source: U.S. Department of Defense, *Selected Manpower Statistics*, annual. [3] Covers Dec. 1, 1941, to Dec. 31, 1946. [4] Covers June 25, 1950, to July 27, 1953. [5] Covers Aug. 4, 1964, to Jan. 27, 1973. [6] Army and Marines only. [7] Excludes Navy. Covers July 1950 through Jan. 1955. Far East area only. [8] During hostilities only. [9] For periods covered, see footnotes 3, 4, and 5. [10] Covers Jan. 1, 1961, to Jan. 27, 1973. Includes known military service personnel who have died from combat related wounds.

Source: Except as noted, the President's Commission on Veterans' Pensions, *Veterans' Benefits in the United States*, Vol. I, 1956; and U.S. Dept. of Defense, unpublished data.

No. 594. Enlisted Military Personnel Accessions: 1990 to 1997

[In thousands (461.1 represents 461,100). For years ending Sept. 30]

Branch of service	1990	1995	1996	1997	Branch of service	1990	1995	1996	1997
Total	461.1	357.3	367.6	380.1	First enlistments	62.1	36.4	39.2	43.7
First enlistments	216.4	160.0	174.6	184.6	Reenlistments	58.6	41.4	40.6	41.6
Reenlistments	237.0	180.8	181.0	187.4	Marine Corps	47.7	46.7	48.7	50.0
Reserves to active duty	15.6	16.6	12.0	8.1	First enlistments	32.9	34.4	34.5	35.1
Army	181.7	135.9	146.0	162.3	Reenlistments	14.4	11.9	0.4	14.7
First enlistments	84.8	57.7	69.7	75.3	Air Force	104.4	81.3	81.6	74.5
Reenlistments	96.5	77.7	76.2	87.0	First enlistments	36.6	31.4	31.2	30.5
Navy	135.3	93.4	91.3	93.3	Reenlistments	67.5	49.7	50.3	44.0

Source: U.S. Dept. of Defense, *Selected Manpower Statistics*, annual.

No. 595. Military Personnel on Active Duty: 1990 to 1997

[In thousands ($2,043.7 represents $2,043,700). As of Sept. 30]

Rank/grade	1990	1992	1993	1994	1995	1996	1997
Total [1]	2,043.7	1,807.2	1,705.1	1,610.5	1,518.2	1,471.7	1,438.6
Recruit—E-1	97.6	83.2	75.4	73.3	63.4	69.3	74.1
Private—E-2	140.3	110.9	114.1	108.2	99.7	99.0	100.8
Pvt. 1st class—E-3	280.1	233.5	214.6	208.4	197.1	200.4	196.0
Corporal—E-4	427.8	383.5	352.2	322.2	317.2	283.8	264.8
Sergeant—E-5	361.5	305.1	295.6	281.0	261.4	254.8	250.6
Staff Sgt.—E-6	239.1	227.4	214.6	198.1	180.5	172.6	169.6
Sgt. 1st class—E-7	134.1	130.5	124.7	119.7	109.3	107.7	104.7
Master Sgt.—E-8	38.0	33.2	31.6	29.9	28.8	28.8	27.6
Sgt. Major—E-9	15.3	13.5	12.8	12.1	11.1	10.7	10.8
Warrant Officer—W-1	3.2	2.2	2.4	2.4	2.0	2.1	2.0
Chief Warrant—W-4	3.0	2.7	2.4	2.4	2.2	2.0	1.9
2d Lt.—O-1	31.9	25.8	25.0	24.8	25.6	25.2	24.8
1st Lt.—O-2	37.9	33.5	29.7	27.3	26.1	25.8	25.5
Captain—O-3	106.6	100.2	93.0	89.2	84.3	81.0	78.3
Major—O-4	53.2	50.4	48.0	44.8	43.9	43.9	43.1
Lt. Colonel—O-5	32.3	30.9	29.5	29.0	28.7	28.2	28.0
Colonel—O-6	14.0	13.2	12.5	12.2	11.7	11.6	11.4
Brig. General—O-7	0.5	0.5	0.4	0.5	0.4	0.4	0.4
Major General—O-8	0.4	0.3	0.3	0.3	0.3	0.3	0.3
Lt. General—O-9	0.1	0.1	0.1	0.1	0.1	0.1	0.1
General—O-10	(Z)	(Z)	(Z)	(Z)	(Z)	(Z)	(Z)

Z Fewer than 50. [1] Includes cadets and midshipmen and warrant officers, W-2 and W-3.

Source: U.S. Dept. of Defense, *Selected Manpower Statistics*, annual, and Office of the Comptroller, unpublished data.

National Defense and Veterans Affairs 377

No. 596. Military Reserve Personnel: 1980 to 1998

[In thousands (1,349 represents 1,349,000). As of end of fiscal year; see text, Section 9, State and Local Government. Excludes U.S. Coast Guard Reserve. The ready reserve includes selected reservists who are intended to assist active forces in a war and the individual ready reserve who, in a major war, would be used to fill out active and reserve units and later would be a source of combat replacements; a portion of the ready reserve serves in an active status. The standby reserve cannot be called to active duty unless the Congress gives its explicit approval. The retired reserve represents a low potential for mobilization]

Reserve status and branch of service	1980	1985	1988	1989	1990	1991	1992	1993	1994	1995	1996	1997	1998
Total reserves [1]	1,349	1,610	1,677	1,661	1,671	1,786	1,883	1,867	1,805	1,659	1,550	1,461	1,369
Ready reserve	1,263	1,566	1,642	1,631	1,641	1,758	1,858	1,841	1,779	1,633	1,523	1,438	1,341
Standby reserve	86	44	34	29	29	28	25	26	26	26	28	23	29
Retired reserve	338	372	469	477	462	474	442	461	482	506	530	550	562
Army [1 2]	804	1,045	1,070	1,062	1,050	1,124	1,156	1,132	1,077	1,001	921	862	799
Navy [1 2]	207	214	244	248	252	271	297	302	317	280	262	238	218
Marine Corps [1]	94	92	87	82	83	96	107	112	109	104	102	100	99
Air Force [1 2]	243	259	275	270	286	295	323	321	302	274	265	261	253

[1] Less retired reserves.   [2] Includes Army national guard.   [3] Includes Air national guard.

Source: U.S. Dept. of Defense, *Official Guard and Reserve Manpower Strengths and Statistics,* quarterly.

No. 597. Ready Reserve Personnel Profile—Race and Sex: 1990 to 1998

Item	Race					Percent distribution			
	Total	White	Black	Asian	American Indian	White	Black	Asian	American Indian
1990	1,641,475	1,289,367	271,470	14,616	7,695	78.5	16.5	0.9	0.5
1993	1,840,650	1,425,255	309,699	21,089	9,068	77.4	16.8	1.1	0.5
1994	1,779,436	1,366,387	297,519	22,190	8,870	76.8	16.7	1.2	0.5
1995	1,633,497	1,254,592	273,847	21,792	8,591	76.8	16.8	1.3	0.5
1996	1,522,451	1,166,628	249,114	21,240	8,226	76.6	16.4	1.4	0.5
1998, total [1]	1,340,557	1,022,851	209,814	21,411	7,531	76.3	15.7	1.6	0.6
Male	1,128,421	885,231	154,183	18,142	6,052	78.4	13.7	1.6	0.5
Officers	174,620	148,390	12,041	2,285	464	85.0	6.9	1.3	0.3
Enlisted	953,801	736,841	142,142	15,857	5,588	77.3	14.9	1.7	0.6
Female	211,874	137,607	55,624	3,269	1,479	64.9	26.3	1.5	0.7
Officers	40,141	29,939	6,313	542	114	74.6	15.7	1.4	0.3
Enlisted	171,733	107,668	49,311	2,727	1,365	62.7	28.7	1.6	0.8

[1] Includes unknown sex.

Source: U.S. Dept. of Defense, *Official Guard and Reserve Manpower Strengths and Statistics,* annual.

No. 598. Military Reserve Costs: 1980 to 1996

[In millions of dollars ($7,969 represents $7,969,000,000). As of end of fiscal year; see text, Section 9, State and Local Government. Army and Air Force data include National Guard]

Type of cost	1980	1985	1990	1991	1992	1993	1994	1995	1996
Total	7,969	19,414	21,526	21,811	21,867	22,825	20,269	20,424	21,539
Operations and maintenance	3,526	5,734	6,687	7,398	7,714	8,095	8,173	8,832	8,782
Personnel	2,456	7,703	8,621	8,543	9,272	9,062	9,564	9,258	9,322
Procurement	1,459	5,009	4,914	4,480	3,533	4,398	1,168	1,102	2,292
Active-duty support	408	566	638	700	731	682	632	658	715
Construction	120	402	666	690	617	588	732	574	428

Source: U.S. Dept. of Defense, unpublished data.

No. 599. National Guard—Summary: 1980 to 1997

[As of end of fiscal year; see text, Section, 9 State and Local Government. Includes Puerto Rico]

Item	Unit	1980	1985	1990	1992	1993	1994	1995	1996	1997
Army National Guard:										
Units	Number	3,379	4,353	4,055	6,727	6,339	6,000	5,872	5,643	5,500
Personnel [1]	1,000	368	438	444	427	410	397	375	373	370
Funds obligated [2]	Bil. dol.	1.8	4.4	5.2	6.3	6.3	6.0	6.0	5.9	5.7
Value of equipment	Bil. dol.	7.6	18.8	29.0	29.0	31.0	31.0	33.0	33.0	33.0
Air National Guard:										
Units	Number	1,054	1,184	1,339	1,425	1,330	1,665	1,604	1,588	(NA)
Personnel [1]	1,000	96	109	118	119	117	114	110	110	108
Funds obligated [2]	Bil. dol.	1.7	2.8	3.2	1.9	2.6	3.1	4.2	4.6	4.5
Value of equipment (est.) [3]	Bil. dol.	5.2	21.4	26.4	38.3	41.7	40.2	38.3	40.1	42.0

NA Not available.   [1] Officers and enlisted personnel.   [2] Federal funds; includes personnel, operations, maintenance, and military construction.   [3] Beginning 1985, increase due to repricing of aircraft to current year dollars to reflect true replacement value. Beginning 1993 includes value of aircraft and support equipment.

Source: National Guard Bureau, *Annual Review of the Chief, National Guard Bureau;* and unpublished data.

No. 600. Veterans—States: 1998

[In thousands (25,062 represents 25,062,000). As of end of fiscal year; see text, Section 9, State and Local Government. Data were estimated starting with veteran's place of residence as of April 1, 1980; 1990 based on 1990 census population data, extended to later years on the basis of estimates of veteran interstate migration, separations from the Armed Forces, and mortality; not directly comparable with earlier estimates previously published by the VA. Excludes 541,000 veterans whose only active-duty military service of less than 2 years occurred since Sept. 30, 1980, and who failed to satisfy the minimum service requirement. Also excludes a small indeterminate number of National Guard personnel or reservists who incurred service-connected disabilities while on an initial tour of active duty for training only]

State	Total veterans [1]	War veterans [1]	World War II	Korean conflict	Vietnam era [2]	Persian Gulf War
United States.	**25,062**	**19,207**	**6,300**	**4,148**	**8,132**	**2,037**
Alabama.	413	321	101	74	134	46
Alaska	63	44	7	7	30	4
Arizona.	447	342	120	80	146	30
Arkansas	249	195	66	43	79	27
California	2,707	2,026	646	457	931	172
Colorado.	369	281	76	61	142	29
Connecticut.	320	244	87	53	97	20
Delaware	76	57	19	12	24	7
District of Columbia	47	37	13	9	14	5
Florida.	1,671	1,298	531	306	490	117
Georgia	667	492	128	101	245	62
Hawaii	113	83	23	19	42	9
Idaho.	108	83	27	17	36	11
Illinois	1,019	795	266	165	313	83
Indiana.	572	437	136	90	179	51
Iowa	278	223	73	48	85	26
Kansas.	250	196	64	42	84	19
Kentucky	355	278	88	58	116	34
Louisiana	355	281	92	58	114	39
Maine.	150	113	34	23	50	14
Maryland	513	375	113	80	171	39
Massachusetts.	561	430	161	95	163	33
Michigan.	913	701	219	136	287	84
Minnesota.	444	340	101	71	148	33
Mississippi	224	176	58	40	67	28
Missouri	565	438	141	97	181	48
Montana.	91	72	22	15	30	9
Nebraska	160	126	40	29	50	15
Nevada	185	137	42	35	65	9
New Hampshire	132	98	29	21	46	10
New Jersey.	698	541	203	122	198	43
New Mexico	167	127	39	27	59	15
New York	1,454	1,121	396	236	408	124
North Carolina	691	522	160	113	231	61
North Dakota.	56	44	13	10	18	5
Ohio	1,143	886	293	178	350	104
Oklahoma.	330	262	87	60	115	25
Oregon.	360	279	91	55	124	28
Pennsylvania.	1,306	1,022	379	213	375	105
Rhode Island.	104	81	31	18	31	7
South Carolina.	370	279	83	60	129	38
South Dakota	71	56	17	14	21	8
Tennessee	501	385	117	81	170	46
Texas.	1,578	1,206	362	258	572	135
Utah	131	104	35	23	43	11
Vermont	61	45	13	9	20	5
Virginia.	684	505	143	113	256	56
Washington.	614	460	132	97	230	46
West Virginia.	191	154	53	34	59	18
Wisconsin.	489	374	119	77	150	41
Wyoming	44	35	10	7	16	4

[1] Veterans who served in more than one wartime period are counted only once. "All veterans" includes Vietnam era (no prior wartime service), Korean conflict (no prior wartime service), World War II, post Vietnam era, Persian Gulf War era, and other.
[2] Excludes reservists.

Source: U.S. Dept. of Veterans Affairs, Management Sciences Service (008B2), *Annual Report of the Secretary of Veterans Affairs*.

National Defense and Veterans Affairs   379

No. 601. Veterans Living in the United States and Puerto Rico, by Age and by Service: 1998

[In thousands, except as indicated. As of July, 1. Estimated. Excludes 500,000 veterans whose active military service of less than 2 years occurred since Sept. 30, 1980. See headnote, Table 600]

Age	Total veterans	Wartime veterans						Peace-time veterans
		Total [1]	Persian Gulf	Vietnam era	Korean conflict	World War II	World War I	
All ages.......	25,188	19,300	2,048	8,166	4,179	6,319	5	5,888
Under 30 years old ...	914	831	831	-	-	-	-	83
30-34 years old	1,150	493	493	-	-	-	-	657
35-39 years old	1,427	257	230	27	-	-	-	1,170
40-44 years old	1,740	896	205	767	-	-	-	844
45-49 years old	2,537	2,357	179	2,323	-	-	-	181
50-54 years old	3,369	3,155	79	3,137	-	-	-	214
55-59 years old	2,373	1,187	24	1,164	17	-	-	1,186
60-64 years old	2,396	1,154	7	328	927	-	-	1,242
65 years old and over .	9,281	8,971	2	421	3,235	6,319	5	310

- Represents zero. [1] Veterans who served in more than one wartime period are counted only once.

Source: U.S. Dept. of Veterans Affairs, Office of Policy *Veteran Population*, annual.

No. 602. Disabled Veterans Receiving Compensation: 1980 to 1998

[In thousands ($2,274 represents $2,274,000), except as indicated. As of end of fiscal year; see text, Section 9, State and Local Government). Represents veterans receiving compensation for service-connected disabilities. Totally disabled refers to veterans with any disability, mental or physical, deemed to be total and permanent which prevents the individual from maintaining a livelihood and are rated for disability at 100 percent]

Military service	1980	1985	1990	1992	1993	1994	1995	1996	1997	1998
Disabled, all periods [1]	2,274	2,240	2,184	2,181	2,198	2,218	2,236	2,253	2,263	2,277
Peace-time	262	352	444	500	471	492	514	529	539	550
World War I [1]	30	12	3	2	1	1	1	(Z)	(Z)	(Z)
World War II...............	1,193	1,049	876	805	769	731	692	655	616	578
Korea	236	223	209	202	198	195	191	187	182	179
Vietnam..................	553	604	652	671	682	694	705	714	724	729
Persian Gulf...............	(X)	(X)	(X)	(X)	76	106	134	168	202	241
Totally disabled, all periods [1] .	121	136	131	132	135	138	143	150	156	161
Peace-time	20	26	27	28	28	29	30	32	33	34
World War I [1]	3	1	(Z)	(Z)	(Z)	(Z)	(Z)	(Z)	(Z)	(Z)
World War II...............	51	54	43	39	37	36	34	33	31	30
Korea	16	17	16	15	15	15	15	15	15	14
Vietnam..................	31	38	44	49	52	56	61	67	73	78
Persian Gulf...............	(X)	(X)	(X)	(X)	2	2	3	3	4	5
Compensation (mil. dol.).....	6,104	8,270	9,284	10,031	10,545	11,056	11,644	11,072	13,004	(NA)

X Not applicable. Z Less than 500. [1] Includes Spanish-American War and Mexican Border service, not shown separately.

Source: U.S. Dept. of Veterans Affairs, *Annual Report of the Secretary of Veterans Affairs;* and unpublished data.

No. 603. Veterans Benefits—Expenditures, by Program: 1980 to 1998

[In millions of dollars ($23,187 represents $23,187,000,000). For fiscal years ending in year shown; see text, Section 9, State and Local Government. Beginning with fiscal year 1990, data are for outlays]

Program	1980	1985	1990	1993	1994	1995	1996	1997	1998
Total	23,187	29,359	28,998	35,460	37,401	37,775	36,915	39,277	41,776
Medical programs	6,042	9,227	11,582	14,603	15,430	16,255	16,337	16,900	17,575
Construction.............	300	557	661	622	695	641	698	597	515
General operating expenses ...	605	765	811	904	906	954	961	1,063	877
Compensation and pension....	11,044	14,037	14,674	16,882	17,188	17,765	17,056	19,284	20,289
Vocational rehabilitation and education..............	2,350	1,164	452	863	1,119	1,127	1,212	1,287	1,310
All other [1]	2,846	3,609	818	1,586	2,062	1,034	652	145	1,209

[1] Includes insurance and indemnities, and miscellaneous funds and expenditures. (Excludes expenditures from personal funds of patients.)

Source: U.S. Dept. of Veterans Affairs, *Trend Data,* annual.

No. 604. Veterans Compensation and Pension Benefits—Number on Rolls and Average Payment, by Period of Service and Status: 1980 to 1998

[As of **Sept. 30.** Living refers to veterans receiving compensation for disability incurred or aggravated while on active duty and war veterans receiving pension and benefits for nonservice connected disabilities. Deceased refers to deceased veterans whose dependents were receiving pensions and compensation benefits]

Period of service and veteran status	Veterans on rolls (1,000)							Average payment (annual basis) [1] (dol.)			
	1980	1990	1994	1995	1996	1997	1998	1980	1990	1991	1992
Total.	4,646	3,584	3,342	3,330	3,308	3,281	3,263	2,370	4,335	4,552	4,712
Living veterans	3,195	2,746	2,659	2,669	2,671	2,667	2,668	2,600	4,320	4,491	4,611
Service connected	2,273	2,184	2,218	2,236	2,253	2,263	2,277	2,669	4,250	4,406	4,593
Nonservice connected. .	922	562	441	433	418	404	391	2,428	4,591	4,837	4,689
Deceased veterans	1,451	838	683	662	637	614	595	1,863	4,382	4,761	5,071
Service connected	358	320	308	307	306	305	303	3,801	7,349	7,815	8,244
Nonservice connected. .	1,093	518	376	355	332	309	291	1,228	2,548	2,748	2,810
Prior to World War I	14	4	2	2	2	2	1	1,432	2,616	2,921	3,073
Living	(Z)	(Z)	(Z)	(Z)	(Z)	(Z)	(Z)	2,634	10,502	10,441	8,176
World War I	692	198	105	89	74	61	51	1,683	3,435	3,674	3,754
Living	198	18	4	3	2	1	1	2,669	6,922	7,239	6,476
World War II	2,520	1,723	1,375	1,307	1,237	1,165	1,097	2,307	4,052	4,238	4,334
Living	1,849	1,294	1,018	961	902	842	785	2,462	4,123	4,278	4,333
Korean conflict [2]	446	390	371	368	360	351	342	2,691	5,105	5,330	5,462
Living	317	305	292	290	285	278	271	2,977	5,103	5,288	5,390
Peacetime	312	495	539	559	574	582	592	3,080	4,132	4,216	4,292
Living. . . . . . [3] . . .	262	444	492	514	529	539	550	2,828	3,709	3,789	3,866
Vietnam era [3]	662	774	842	868	889	913	932	2,795	4,945	5,242	5,551
Living	569	685	746	766	784	804	819	2,709	4,671	4,936	5,234
Persian Gulf War [4]	(X)	(X)	108	138	173	207	247	(X)	(X)	(X)	1,673
Living	(X)	(X)	106	134	169	203	242	(X)	(X)	(X)	1,386

X Not applicable.   Z Fewer than 500.   [1] Annual basis.   Averages calculated by multiplying average monthly payment by 12.   [2] Service during period June 27, 1950, to Jan. 31, 1955.   [3] Service from Aug. 5, 1964, to May 7, 1975.   [4] Service from Aug. 2, 1990, to the present.

Source: U.S. Dept. of Veterans Affairs, *Annual Report of the Secretary of Veterans Affairs;* and unpublished data.

No. 605. Veterans Administration Health Care Summary: 1990 to 1997

[For years ending **Sept. 30**]

Item	Unit	1990	1995	1997	Item	Unit	1990	1995	1997
Facilities operating:					Obligations [2]	Mil. dol . .	11,827	16,548	17,546
Hospitals	Number .	172	173	172	Prescriptions dispensed .	Millions. .	58.6	66.1	65.2
Domiciliaries	Number .	32	39	40	Laboratory . . . . . . [3] . .	Millions. .	188	(NA)	(NA)
Outpatient clinics. . . .	Number .	339	391	438	Inpatients treated [3]	1,000 . .	1,113	1,035	827
Nursing home units . .	Number .	126	131	131	Average daily	1,000 . . .	88	81	67
Employment [1]	1,000 . . .	199	205	190	Outpatient visits	Millions. .	22.6	27.6	31.9

NA Not available.   [1] Net full-time equivalent.   [2] 1980, cost basis; thereafter, obligation basis.   [3] Based on the number of discharges and deaths during the fiscal year, plus the number on the rolls (bed occupants and patients on authorized leave of absence) at the end of the fiscal year. Excludes interhospital transfers.

Source: U.S. Dept. of Veterans Affairs, *Annual Report of the Secretary of Veterans Affairs; Directory of VA Facilities,* biennial; and unpublished data.

No. 606. Veterans Assistance—Education and Training: 1980 to 1998

[In thousands ($1,107 represents $1,107,000), except where indicated. For fiscal years ending in year shown; see text, Section 9, State and Local Governments. Represents persons in training during year]

Program	1980	1990	1993	1994	1995	1996	1997	1998
Veteran Education Assistance [1]	1,107	102	246	284	292	296	297	297
Institutions of higher education	842	94	223	258	264	270	267	265
Resident schools other than college	149	6	18	19	19	18	18	18
Correspondence schools	42	1	3	4	(NA)	3	4	4
On-the-job training	74	1	2	3	4	5	8	9
Children's Educational Assistance	82.6	37.5	36.4	35.7	34.8	35.7	36.2	37.2
Institutions of higher education	75.5	35.3	34.3	33.7	33.1	34	34.4	35.3
Schools other than college	6.5	2.1	2.0	1.9	1.7	1.6	1.7	1.8
Special restorative training	0.1	(Z)	(Z)	(Z)	(Z)	(Z)	(Z)	(Z)
On-the-job training	0.5	0.1	(Z)	(Z)	(Z)	(Z)	0.1	0.1
Spouses, Widows/Widowers Educational Assistance Program	13.0	4.5	4.4	4.6	4.6	5.0	5.2	5.5
Institutions of higher education	10.8	4.1	4.0	4.1	4.2	4.5	4.7	5.0
Schools other than college	2.2	0.4	0.4	0.4	0.4	0.4	0.4	0.5
Disabled Veterans Vocational Rehab.	25.5	27.8	40.7	44.2	47.9	51.8	53.8	(NA)
Guaranteed and insured loans	297.4	196.6	383.3	602.2	263.1	320.8	258.8	(NA)
Guaranteed and insured loans, (mil. dol.) . .	14,815	15,779	34,635	55,141	25,341	32,609	27,042	(NA)
Guaranty and insurance (mil. dol.)	6,370	5,561	11,601	18,332	8,383	10,525	8,632	(NA)

NA Not available.   Z Fewer than 50.   [1] Data for 1980 are for Post-Korean Conflict GI Bill (Title 38 USC Chapter 34). Data for 1990-94 or 1990-98 are for Active Duty Montgomery GI Bill (Title 38 USC Chapter 30).

Source: U.S. Dept. of Veterans Affairs, *Annual Report of the Secretary of Veterans Affairs;* and unpublished data.

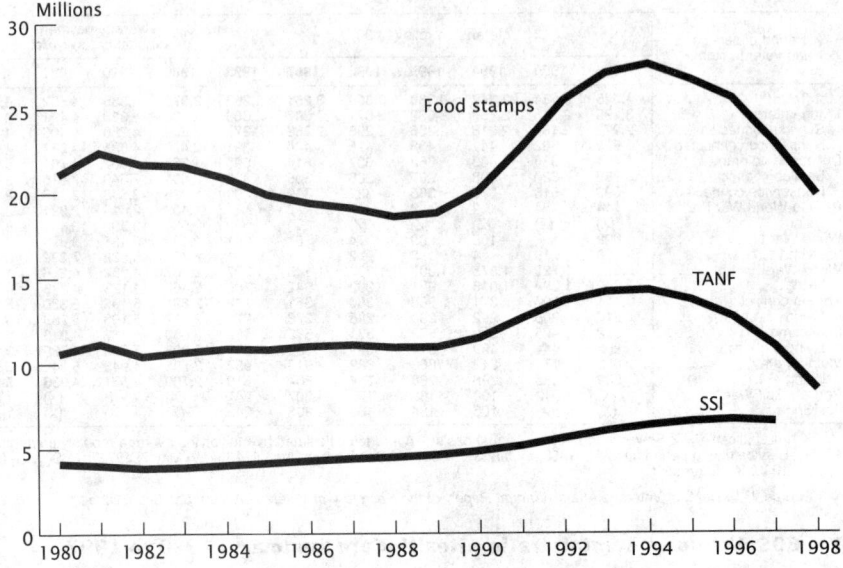

Figure 12.1
SSI, TANF[1], and Food Stamp Recipients: 1980 to 1998

Millions

Food stamps

TANF

SSI

[1]Supplemental security income (SSI), temporary assistance for needy families (TANF).
Source: Chart prepared by U.S. Census Bureau. For data, see Tables 631, 633, and 635.

Figure 12.2
**Percent of Households Contributing to Charity
by Annual Amount: 1995**

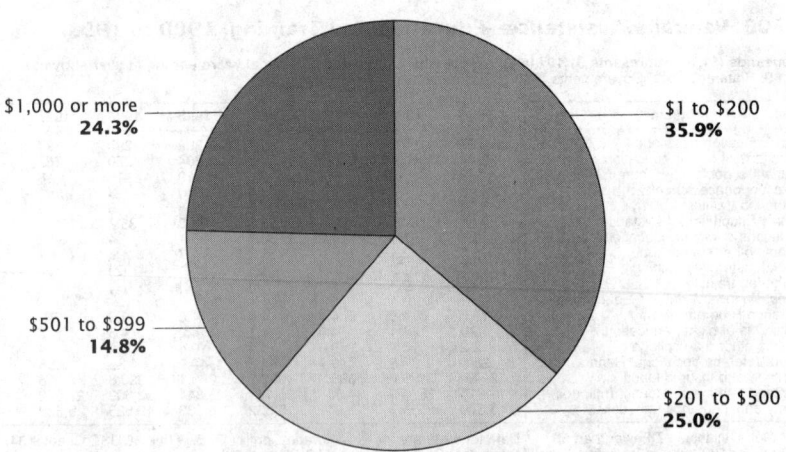

$1,000 or more
24.3%

$1 to $200
35.9%

$501 to $999
14.8%

$201 to $500
25.0%

Source: Chart prepared by U.S. Census Bureau. For data, see Table 645.

382 Social Insurance and Human Services

Section 12

Social Insurance and Human Services

This section presents data related to governmental expenditures for social welfare; governmental programs for old-age, survivors, disability, and health insurance (OASDHI); governmental employee retirement; private pension plans; government unemployment and temporary disability insurance; Federal supplemental security income payments and aid to the needy; child and other welfare services; and Federal food programs. Also included here are selected data on workers' compensation and vocational rehabilitation, child support, child care, charity contributions, and philanthropic trusts and foundations.

The principal sources for these data are the Social Security Administration's quarterly *Social Security Bulletin* and the *Annual Statistical Supplement to the Social Security Bulletin* which present current data on many of the programs. Current data on employment security are published annually in the Department of Labor's *Unemployment Insurance, Financial Data.*

Social insurance under the Social Security Act— Programs established by the Social Security Act provide protection against wage loss resulting from retirement, prolonged disability, death, or unemployment, and protection against the cost of medical care during old age and disability. The Federal OASDI program provides monthly benefits to retired or disabled insured workers and their dependents and to survivors of insured workers. To be eligible, a worker must have had a specified period of employment in which OASDI taxes were paid. A worker becomes eligible for full benefits at age 65, although reduced benefits may be obtained up to 3 years earlier; the worker's spouse is under the same limitations. Survivor benefits are payable to dependents of deceased insured workers. Disability benefits are payable to an insured worker under age 65

with a prolonged disability and to the disabled worker's dependents on the same basis as dependents of retired workers. Disability benefits are provided at age 50 to the disabled widow or widower of a deceased worker who was fully insured at the time of death. Disabled children, aged 18 or older, of retired, disabled, or deceased workers are also eligible for benefits. A lump sum benefit is generally payable on the death of an insured worker to a spouse or minor children. For information on the medicare program, see Section 3, Health.

Retirement, survivors, disability, and hospital insurance benefits are funded by a payroll tax on annual earnings (up to a maximum of earnings set by law) of workers, employers, and the self-employed. The maximum taxable earnings are adjusted annually to reflect increasing wage levels (see Table 614). Effective January 1994, there is no dollar limit on wages and self-employment income subject to the hospital insurance tax. Tax receipts and benefit payments are administered through Federal trust funds. Special benefits for uninsured persons; hospital benefits for persons aged 65 and over with specified amounts of social security coverage less than that required for cash benefit eligibility; and that part of the cost of supplementary medical insurance not financed by contributions from participants are financed from federal general revenues.

Unemployment insurance is presently administered by the U.S. Employment and Training Administration and each state's employment security agency. By agreement with the U.S. Secretary of Labor, state agencies also administer unemployment compensation for eligible ex-service members and Federal employees, unemployment assistance under the Disaster Relief Act of 1970, and workers assistance and relocation allowances under the Trade Act. Under

U.S. Census Bureau, Statistical Abstract of the United States: 1999

state unemployment insurance laws, benefits related to the individual's past earnings are paid to unemployed eligible workers. State laws vary concerning the length of time benefits are paid and their amount. In most states, benefits are payable for 26 weeks and, during periods of high unemployment, extended benefits are payable under a Federal-state program to those who have exhausted their regular state benefits. The basic benefit can vary among states by over 100 percent. Some states also supplement the basic benefit with allowances for dependents.

Unemployment insurance is funded by a Federal unemployment tax levied on the taxable payrolls of most employers. Taxable payroll under the Federal act and 12 state laws is the first $7,000 in wages paid each worker during a year. Forty-one states have taxable payrolls above $7,000. Employers are allowed a percentage credit of taxable payroll for contributions paid to states under state unemployment insurance laws. The remaining percent of the Federal tax finances administrative costs, the Federal share of extended benefits, and advances to states. About 97 percent of wage and salary workers are covered by unemployment insurance.

Retirement programs for government employees—The Civil Service Retirement System (CSRS) and the Federal Employees' Retirement System (FERS) are the two major programs providing age and service, disability, and survivor annuities for Federal civilian employees. In general, employees hired after December 31, 1983, are covered under FERS and the social security program (OASDHI), and employees on staff prior to that date are members of CSRS and are covered under medicare. CSRS employees were offered the option of transferring to FERS during 1987 and 1998. There are separate retirement systems for the uniformed services (supplementing OASDHI) and for certain special groups of Federal employees. State and local government employees are covered for the most part by state and local retirement systems similar to the Federal Civil Service Retirement

System. In many jurisdictions these benefits supplement OASDHI coverage.

Workers' compensation—All states provide protection against work-connected injuries and deaths, although some states exclude certain workers (e.g., domestic help). Federal laws cover Federal employees, private employees in the District of Columbia, and longshoremen and harbor workers. In addition, the Social Security Administration and the Department of Labor administer "black lung" benefits programs for coal miners disabled by pneumoconiosis and for specified dependents and survivors. Specified occupational diseases are compensable to some extent. In most states, benefits are related to the worker's salary. The benefits may or may not be augmented by dependents' allowances or automatically adjusted to prevailing wage levels.

Income support—Income support programs are designed to provide benefits for persons with limited income and resources. The Supplemental Security Income (SSI) program and Temporary Assistance for Needy Families (TANF) program are the major programs providing monthly payments. In addition, a number of programs provide money payments or in-kind benefits for special needs or purposes. Several programs offer food and nutritional services. Also, various Federal-state programs provide energy assistance, public housing, and subsidized housing to individuals and families with low incomes. General assistance may also be available at the state or local level.

The SSI program, administered by the Social Security Administration, provides income support to persons aged 65 or older and blind or disabled adults and children. Eligibility requirements and Federal payment standards are nationally uniform. Most states supplement the basic SSI payment for all or selected categories of persons.

The Personal Responsibility and Work Opportunity Reconciliation Act of 1996

U.S. Census Bureau, Statistical Abstract of the United States: 1999

contained provisions that replaced the Aid to Families With Dependent Children (AFDC), Job Opportunities and Basic Skills (JOBS), and Emergency Assistance programs with the Temporary Assistance for Needy Families block grant program. This law contains strong work requirements, comprehensive child support enforcement, support for families moving from welfare to work, and other features. The TANF became effective as soon as each state submitted a complete plan implementing TANF, but no later than July 1, 1997. The AFDC program provided cash assistance based on need, income, resources, and family size.

Federal Food Stamp program—Under the food stamp program, single persons and those living in households meeting nationwide standards for income and assets may receive coupons redeemable for food at most retail food stores. The monthly amount of coupons a unit receives is determined by household size and income. Households without income receive the determined monthly cost of a nutritionally adequate diet for their household size. This amount is updated to account for food price increases. Households with income receive the difference between the amount of a nutritionally adequate diet and 30 percent of their income, after certain allowable deductions.

To qualify for the program, a household must have less than $2,000 in disposable assets ($3,000 if one member is aged 60 or older), gross income below 130 percent of the official poverty guidelines, and net income below 100 percent of the poverty guidelines. Households with a person aged 60 or older or a disabled person receiving SSI, social security, or veterans' disability benefits may have gross income exceeding 130 percent of the poverty guidelines. All households must meet these requirements, even those receiving other Federal assistance payments. Households are certified for varying lengths of time, depending on their income sources and individual circumstances.

Health and welfare services—Programs providing health and welfare services are aided through federal grants to states for child welfare services, vocational rehabilitation, activities for the aged, maternal and child health services, maternity and infant care projects, comprehensive health services, and a variety of public health activities. For information about the medicaid program, see Section 3, Health.

Noncash benefits—The U.S. Census Bureau annually collects data on the characteristics of recipients of noncash (in-kind) benefits to supplement the collection of annual money income data in the Current Population Survey (see text, Section 1, Population, and Section 15, Prices). Noncash benefits are those benefits received in a form other than money which serve to enhance or improve the economic well-being of the recipient. As for money income, the data for noncash benefits are for the calendar year prior to the date of the interview. The major categories of noncash benefits covered are public transfers (e.g., food stamps, school lunch, public housing, and medicaid) and employer or union-provided benefits to employees.

Statistical reliability— For discussion of statistical collection, estimation, and sampling procedures and measures of statistical reliability applicable to HHS and Census Bureau data, see Appendix III.

U.S. Census Bureau, Statistical Abstract of the United States: 1999

No. 607. Social Welfare Expenditures Under Public Programs: 1980 to 1995

[In billions of dollars (493 represents $493,000,000,000), except percent. See headnote, Table 609]

Year	Total	Social insurance	Public aid	Health and medical programs [1]	Veterans programs	Education	Housing	Other social welfare	All health and medical care [2]
Total:									
1980	493	230	73	27	21	121	7	14	100
1985	732	370	98	39	27	172	13	14	171
1990	1,049	514	147	61	31	258	19	18	274
1992	1,267	619	208	70	36	292	21	22	353
1993	1,367	659	221	75	36	332	21	23	382
1994	1,436	684	238	80	38	344	27	25	409
1995	1,505	705	254	86	39	366	29	27	435
Federal:									
1980	303	191	49	13	21	13	6	9	69
1985	451	310	63	18	27	14	11	8	122
1990	617	422	93	27	30	18	17	9	190
1992	750	496	139	32	35	20	17	11	250
1993	805	534	152	33	36	20	19	11	276
1994	853	557	163	35	37	24	25	12	295
1995	888	580	170	37	38	23	27	12	308
State and local:									
1980	190	39	23	14	(Z)	108	1	5	31
1985	281	59	35	21	(Z)	158	2	6	49
1990	432	92	54	34	(Z)	240	3	9	84
1992	517	123	69	38	1	272	3	11	103
1993	561	125	69	42	1	312	2	12	106
1994	583	126	75	45	1	320	2	13	114
1995	617	126	83	49	1	342	2	14	127
Percent Federal:									
1980	62	83	68	47	99	11	91	65	69
1985	62	84	64	46	99	8	88	56	71
1990	59	82	63	44	98	7	85	50	69
1993	59	81	69	44	98	6	91	48	72
1994	59	82	68	43	98	7	92	48	72
1995	59	82	67	43	98	6	93	47	71
Per capita (current dollars): [3]									
1980	2,126	990	314	118	92	523	30	59	434
1985	3,009	1,516	405	161	111	708	52	56	705
1990	4,123	2,017	579	243	120	1,018	77	71	1,081
1993	5,238	2,523	849	287	137	1,275	80	87	1,466
1994	5,446	2,591	905	305	141	1,308	103	94	1,554
1995	5,622	2,632	949	320	144	1,368	109	99	1,628
Per capita (constant (1995) dollars): [3] [4]									
1980	3,788	1,764	560	210	164	932	53	105	764
1985	4,131	2,081	556	223	152	972	71	77	969
1990	4,741	2,319	665	279	138	1,170	89	81	1,243
1993	5,487	2,644	889	301	144	1,335	84	91	1,536
1994	5,570	2,650	925	312	144	1,338	105	96	1,589
1995	5,622	2,632	949	320	144	1,368	109	99	1,628

Z Less than $500 million.   [1] Excludes program parts of social insurance, public aid, veterans, and other social welfare. [2] Combines "Health and medical programs" with medical services included in social insurance, public aid, veterans, vocational rehabilitation, and antipoverty programs.   [3] Excludes payments within foreign countries for education, veterans, OASDHI, and civil service retirement.   [4] Constant dollar figures are based on implicit price deflators for personal consumption expenditures published by U.S. Bureau of Economic Analysis in *Survey of Current Business.*

No. 608. Social Welfare Expenditures Under Public Programs as Percent of GDP and Total Government Outlays: 1980 to 1995

[493 represents $493,000,000,000. See headnote, Table 609]

Year	Total expenditures				Federal				State and local government			
	Total (bil. dol.)	Percent change [1]	Percent of—		Total (bil. dol.)	Percent change [1]	Percent of—		Total (bil. dol.)	Percent change [1]	Percent of—	
			Total GDP [2]	Total govt. outlays			Total GDP [2]	Total Federal outlays			Total GDP [2]	Total state and local outlays
1980	493	14.7	18.6	57.2	303	15.2	11.4	54.4	190	13.8	7.2	62.9
1985	732	8.0	18.4	54.4	451	7.1	11.3	48.7	281	9.3	7.1	68.8
1990	1,049	9.6	18.5	58.2	617	9.1	10.9	51.4	432	10.3	7.6	74.0
1992	1,267	9.2	20.6	63.7	750	10.8	12.2	57.4	517	7.0	8.4	77.6
1993	1,367	7.8	21.1	66.6	805	7.2	12.4	60.0	561	8.5	8.7	80.7
1994	1,436	5.1	21.0	64.5	853	6.1	12.5	57.4	583	3.7	8.5	80.4
1995	1,505	4.8	20.9	67.5	888	4.1	12.4	60.2	617	5.8	8.6	83.6

[1] Percent change from immediate prior year.   [2] Gross domestic product.

Source of Tables 607 and 608: U.S. Social Security Administration, *Social Security Bulletin,* Vol. 60, No. 3, 1997; and unpublished data.

Social Welfare Expenditures, by Source of Funds and Public Program: 1990 to 1995

[In millions of dollars (616,639 represents $616,639,000,000). For fiscal years ending in year shown; see text, Section 9, State and Local Government. Represents outlays from trust funds (mostly social insurance funds built up by earmarked contributions from insured persons, their employers, or both) and budgetary outlays from general revenues. Includes administrative expenditures, capital outlay, and some expenditures and payments outside the United States]

Program	Federal				State and local			
	1990	1993	1994	1995	1990	1993	1994	1995
Total	616,639	805,336	852,876	888,358	432,167	561,418	582,944	616,779
Social insurance	422,257	534,212	557,321	579,804	91,565	124,998	126,458	125,680
Old-age, survivors, disability, health ...	355,264	449,277	477,340	496,356	(X)	(X)	(X)	(X)
Health insurance (medicare)........	109,709	148,094	161,393	164,713	(X)	(X)	(X)	(X)
Public employee retirement [1]	53,541	61,632	63,733	67,022	36,851	50,928	55,520	60,980
Railroad employee retirement	7,230	7,921	8,025	8,106	(X)	(X)	(X)	(X)
Unemployment insurance and employment services [2]	3,096	12,124	4,972	5,156	16,878	28,597	26,279	21,146
Other railroad employee insurance [3] ..	105	86	83	78	(X)	(X)	(X)	(X)
State temporary disability insurance [4] ..	(X)	(X)	(X)	(X)	3,224	3,316	3,201	3,189
Workers' compensation [5]	3,021	3,173	3,168	3,085	34,613	42,157	41,458	40,365
Hospital and medical benefits......	457	597	688	668	13,849	17,116	15,512	16,032
Public aid.	92,858	151,850	162,675	170,260	53,953	69,149	75,351	83,270
Public assistance [6]	54,747	95,340	100,209	107,599	50,347	65,285	71,546	79,620
Medical assistance payments [7].....	40,690	77,367	81,192	89,113	35,485	47,771	53,012	61,756
Social services	2,065	2,785	2,734	2,797	688	928	911	932
Supplemental security income	13,625	22,642	26,281	26,488	3,605	3,864	3,805	3,650
Food stamps	16,254	24,497	25,274	25,319	(X)	(X)	(X)	(X)
Other [8]	8,232	9,372	10,911	10,854	(X)	(X)	(X)	(X)
Health and medical programs.	27,204	33,189	34,770	36,767	34,282	41,528	45,465	48,740
Hospital and medical care.........	14,816	18,575	18,601	19,373	11,155	12,042	12,962	12,531
Civilian programs	3,654	5,166	5,466	5,951	11,155	12,042	12,962	12,531
Defense Department [9]	11,162	13,409	13,134	13,422	(X)	(X)	(X)	(X)
Maternal and child health programs ...	492	595	615	612	1,374	1,590	1,657	1,736
Medical research............	9,172	10,690	11,739	12,544	1,676	2,090	2,249	2,438
Medical facilities construction......	413	166	102	429	1,922	2,878	3,137	3,369
School health	(X)	(X)	(X)	(X)	1,113	1,320	1,489	1,667
Other	2,311	3,164	3,714	3,809	17,043	21,608	23,971	26,999
Veterans programs	30,428	35,806	37,262	38,385	488	572	633	687
Pensions and compensation	15,793	17,205	17,481	18,070	(X)	(X)	(X)	(X)
Health and medical programs	12,004	15,410	16,231	16,654	(X)	(X)	(X)	(X)
Education	523	938	1,098	1,118	(X)	(X)	(X)	(X)
Life insurance [10]	1,038	905	972	946	(X)	(X)	(X)	(X)
Welfare and other	1,070	1,348	1,479	1,596	488	572	633	687
Education [11]	18,374	20,455	24,084	23,472	240,011	311,542	320,007	342,153
Elementary and secondary [12]	9,944	13,238	15,514	15,301	189,333	239,268	245,492	262,574
Construction [13]	23	5	9	2	10,613	22,283	19,684	24,808
Higher.	6,747	5,285	6,577	6,164	50,678	72,273	74,514	79,580
Construction [13]	-	35	23	29	3,953	8,955	8,959	10,461
Vocational and adult [13]	1,293	1,495	1,504	1,508	([12])	([12])	([12])	([12])
Housing.	16,612	18,985	24,987	27,276	2,856	1,798	2,045	2,085
Other social welfare	8,905	10,838	11,777	12,394	9,012	11,832	12,985	14,164
Vocational rehabilitation	1,661	1,830	1,963	2,031	466	549	597	599
Medical services and research	415	458	491	508	116	137	149	150
Institutional care [14]	143	143	150	152	486	579	633	722
Child nutrition [15]	5,470	7,139	7,626	7,992	1,696	2,253	2,473	2,661
Child welfare [16]	253	295	295	292	(NA)	(NA)	(NA)	(NA)
Special CSA and ACTION programs [17] ...	169	208	204	222	(X)	(X)	(X)	(X)
Welfare, not elsewhere classified [18] ...	1,209	1,223	1,540	1,704	6,365	8,451	9,282	10,182

- Represents zero. NA Not available. X Not applicable. [1] Excludes refunds to those leaving service. Federal data include military retirement. [2] Includes compensation for Federal employees and ex-servicemen, trade adjustment and cash training allowance, and payments under extended, emergency, disaster, and special unemployment insurance programs. [3] Unemployment and temporary disability insurance. [4] Cash and medical benefits in five areas. Includes private plans where applicable. [5] Benefits paid by private insurance carriers, state funds, and self-insurers. Federal includes black lung benefit programs. [6] Includes payments under state general assistance programs and work incentive activities, not shown separately. [7] Medicaid payments and state and local general assistance medical payments. [8] Refugee assistance, surplus food for the needy, and work-experience training programs under the Comprehensive Employment and Training Act. Includes low-income energy assistance program. [9] Includes medical care for military dependent families. [10] Excludes servicemen's group life insurance. [11] Federal expenditures include administrative costs (Department of Education) and research, not shown separately. [12] All state and local vocational education costs included with elementary-secondary. [13] Construction costs of vocational and adult education programs included under elementary-secondary expenditures. [14] Federal expenditures represent primarily surplus foods for nonprofit institutions. [15] Surplus food for schools and programs under National School Lunch and Child Nutrition Acts. [16] Represents primarily child welfare services under Title V of the Social Security Act. [17] Represents domestic volunteer programs under ACTION. [18] Federal expenditures include administrative expenses of the Secretary of Health and Human Services, Indian welfare and guidance, and aging and juvenile delinquency activities. State and local include antipoverty and manpower programs, child care and adoption services, legal assistance, and other unspecified welfare services.

Source: U.S. Social Security Administration, *Social Security Bulletin*, Vol. 60, No. 3, 1997; and unpublished data.

No. 610. Public Income-Maintenance Programs—Cash Benefit Payments: 1980 to 1995

[In billions of dollars (228.1 represents $228,100,000,000). Includes payments outside the United States and benefits to dependents, where applicable]

Program	1980	1985	1988	1989	1990	1991	1992	1993	1994	1995
Total [1]	228.1	335.2	393.8	421.9	457.5	504.2	544.9	557.7	584.4	608.3
Percent of personal income [2]	10.1	9.9	9.7	9.6	9.5	10.2	10.4	10.2	10.1	10.0
OASDI [3]	120.3	186.1	216.4	229.6	245.6	265.6	284.3	302.4	316.8	332.6
Public employee retirement [4]	40.6	63.0	78.0	83.8	90.4	97.3	103.7	112.6	119.3	128.0
Railroad retirement	4.9	6.3	6.7	6.9	7.2	7.5	7.7	7.9	8.0	8.1
Veterans' pensions, compensation	11.4	14.1	14.7	15.3	15.8	16.3	16.5	17.2	17.5	18.1
Unemployment benefits [5]	18.9	14.4	13.2	16.4	20.0	31.3	37.3	21.5	21.6	22.0
Temporary disability benefits	1.4	1.8	2.8	2.9	3.2	3.9	4.0	3.3	3.2	3.2
Workers' compensation [6]	9.7	22.3	30.3	33.8	37.6	41.7	45.7	45.3	44.6	43.4
Public assistance	12.1	15.3	17.0	17.4	19.3	20.1	22.4	21.0	23.3	22.8
Supplemental security income	7.9	11.1	14.7	14.9	17.2	19.6	23.4	26.5	30.1	30.1

[1] Includes lump sum death benefits, not shown separately. Lump sum death benefits for state and local government employee retirement systems are not available beginning 1988. [2] For base data, see Table 730. [3] Old-age, survivors, and disability insurance under Federal Social Security Act; see text for this section. [4] Excludes refunds of contributions to employees who leave service. [5] Beginning 1985, covers state unemployment insurance, Ex-Servicemen's Compensation Act and railroad unemployment insurance only. [6] Includes black lung benefits.

Source: U.S. Social Security Administration, *Social Security Bulletin*, quarterly; and unpublished data.

No. 611. Number of Families Receiving Specified Sources of Income, by Characteristic of Householder and Family Income: 1997

[In thousands (70,884 represents 70,884,000). Families as of March 1998. Based on Current Population Survey; see text, Sections 1, Population and 14, Income, and Appendix III]

Source of income	Total families [1]	Under 65 years old	65 years old and over	White	Black	Hispanic origin [2]	Under $15,000	$15,000 to $24,999	$25,000 to $34,999
Total [1]	70,884	59,614	11,270	59,515	8,408	6,961	8,870	9,250	9,079
Earnings	60,607	56,071	4,536	50,858	7,087	6,071	5,225	6,539	7,512
Wages and salary	58,587	54,515	4,072	49,034	6,989	5,927	4,836	6,163	7,241
Social security, railroad retirement	16,371	5,912	10,459	14,252	1,717	973	2,322	3,699	2,965
Supplemental security income (SSI)	2,460	1,938	523	1,699	621	379	974	603	317
Public assistance	2,682	2,624	58	1,632	928	621	1,956	427	133
Veterans payments	1,541	889	652	1,359	143	72	134	206	212
Unemployment compensation	4,230	4,020	210	3,465	574	483	409	591	593
Workers compensation	1,523	1,404	119	1,325	151	165	124	169	260
Retirement income	9,920	4,174	5,746	8,971	699	344	367	1,470	1,847
Private pensions	6,296	2,380	3,916	5,745	416	215	266	1,124	1,310
Military retirement	959	595	364	827	95	28	17	61	79
Federal employee pensions	1,137	403	734	1,031	77	43	26	114	186
State or local employee pensions	1,880	726	1,154	1,689	139	63	53	177	299
Alimony	235	222	13	219	6	15	20	22	62
Child support	4,305	4,286	19	3,527	694	371	892	673	691
Education assistance	4,836	4,707	129	3,891	690	360	445	525	517

[1] Includes other items not shown separately. [2] Persons of Hispanic origin may be of any race.

Source: U.S. Census Bureau, "09 Table of Contents"; published 17 December 1998; <http://ferret.bls.census.gov/macro/031998/faminc/09000.htm>.

No. 612. Households Receiving Means-Tested Noncash Benefits: 1980 to 1997

[In thousands (82,368 represents 82,368,000), except percent. Households as of March of following year. Covers civilian noninstitutional population, including persons in the Armed Forces living off post or with their families on post. A means-tested benefit program requires that the household's income and/or assets fall below specified guidelines in order to qualify for benefits. There are general trends toward underestimation of noncash beneficiaries. Households are classified according to poverty status of family or nonfamily householder; for explanation of poverty level, see text, Section 14, Income. Data for 1980 and 1990 based on 1980 census population controls; beginning 1995, based on 1990 census population controls. Based on Current Population Survey; see text, Section 1, Population, and Appendix III]

Type of benefit received	1980	1990	1995	1996	1997 Below poverty level Total	1997 Below poverty level Number	1997 Below poverty level Percent distribution	1997 Above poverty level
Total households	82,368	94,312	99,627	101,018	102,528	12,960	100	89,568
Food stamps	6,769	7,163	8,388	8,263	7,256	4,924	38	2,332
School lunch	5,532	6,252	8,607	8,922	7,585	3,342	26	4,243
Public housing	2,777	4,339	4,846	4,981	4,778	2,728	21	2,050
Medicaid	8,287	10,321	14,111	14,486	13,589	6,063	47	7,526

Source: U.S. Census Bureau, "Current Population Survey, Annual Demographic Survey, March Supplement;" published 24 September 1998; <http://ferret.bls.census.gov/macro/031998/noncash/1001.htm> and *Current Population Reports*, P-60 reports.

Cash and Noncash Benefits for Persons With Limited Income: 1995 and 1996

[For years ending September 30, except as noted (366,594 represents $366,594,000,000). Programs covered provide cash, goods, or services to persons who make no payment and render no service in return. In case of job and training programs and some educational benefits, recipients must work or study for wages, training allowances, stipends, grants, or loans. Most of the programs base eligibility on individual, household, or family income, but some use group or area income tests; and a few offer help on the basis of presumed need]

Program	Average monthly recipients (1,000)		Expenditures (mil. dol.)					
			Total		Federal		State and local	
	1995	1996	1995	1996	1995	1996	1995	1996
Total	(X)	(X)	366,594	367,712	258,382	261,311	108,212	106,401
Medical care [1]	(X)	(X)	174,556	177,575	101,338	103,568	73,218	74,007
Medicaid [2][3]	41,388	41,284	156,395	159,357	89,070	91,205	67,325	68,152
Veterans [4][5][6]	1,561	1,587	8,642	8,697	8,642	8,697	-	-
General assistance [6]	(NA)	(NA)	5,464	5,429	-	-	5,464	5,429
Indian health services [2][3]	1,257	1,285	1,960	1,984	1,960	1,984	-	-
Maternal and child health services	12,200	13,000	1,113	1,105	684	679	429	426
Cash aid [1]	(X)	(X)	91,598	91,673	67,923	69,637	23,675	22,036
Supplemental security income [3][7]	6,715	6,894	30,567	30,367	26,839	26,934	3,728	3,433
A.F.D.C. [3][8]	13,619	12,649	25,553	23,677	13,788	12,698	11,765	10,979
Earned income tax credit (refunded portion) [9]	52,128	53,706	19,040	21,566	19,040	21,566	-	-
Foster care	261	267	5,747	5,853	3,066	3,114	2,681	2,739
General assistance [9]	989	767	3,559	2,880	-	-	3,559	2,880
Pensions for needy veterans [10][11]	798	705	3,018	3,086	3,018	3,086	-	-
Food benefits [1]	(X)	(X)	38,627	39,036	36,797	37,116	1,830	1,921
Food stamps [3][12]	28,000	26,800	27,438	27,344	25,678	25,494	1,760	1,850
School lunch program [13][14]	14,400	14,600	4,581	4,784	4,581	4,784	(NA)	(NA)
Women, infants and children [3][15]	6,900	7,200	3,451	3,688	3,451	3,688	-	-
School breakfast [13]	5,500	6,200	1,021	1,088	1,021	1,088	-	-
Child and adult care food program [16]	1,300	1,300	905	945	905	945	-	-
Nutrition program for elderly [17] . .	3,401	(NA)	690	691	620	620	70	71
Housing benefits [1]	(X)	(X)	27,272	27,208	24,948	25,096	2,325	2,113
Low-income housing asst. (Sec. 8) [18]	3,012	3,095	15,824	15,015	15,824	15,015	-	-
Low-rent public housing [18][19] . . .	1,411	1,414	4,449	4,710	4,449	4,710	(NA)	(NA)
Rural housing loans [20][21] . . .	32	41	1,983	2,716	1,983	2,716	-	-
Interest reduction payments [18] . .	501	493	661	651	661	651	-	-
Home investment partnerships [3][21][22]	67	71	3,269	3,136	963	1,039	2,306	2,097
Education aid [1]	(X)	(X)	16,092	16,275	15,137	15,320	955	955
Pell grants [23][24]	3,952	3,600	6,634	6,144	6,634	6,144	-	-
Head Start [23]	751	752	4,417	4,461	3,534	3,569	883	892
Stafford loans [23]	3,516	3,716	2,702	3,339	2,702	3,339	-	-
Services [1]	(NA)	(NA)	11,329	10,136	6,012	5,452	5,317	4,684
Social services (Title 20) [25]	(NA)	(NA)	7,168	6,095	2,800	2,381	4,368	3,714
Child care for AFDC recipients and ex-recipients [26]	583	(NA)	1,675	1,737	950	980	725	757
Child care and development block grant	663	(NA)	935	935	935	935	-	-
Jobs and training [1]	(X)	(X)	5,437	4,567	4,626	3,955	811	612
Training for disadvantaged adults and youth [27]	507	426	1,124	977	1,124	977	-	-
JOBS (for AFDC recipients) [28] . .	632	650	1,767	1,281	1,051	765	716	516
Job Corps	100	100	1,089	1,094	1,089	1,094	-	-
Summer youth employment program [29]	489	409	867	625	867	625	-	-
Energy assistance [1]	(X)	(X)	1,682	1,239	1,601	1,167	81	73
Low-income energy assistance [3][30][31]	5,500	4,300	1,402	1,064	1,386	1,055	16	9

- Represents zero.   NA Not available.   X Not applicable.   [1] Includes other programs not shown separately.   [2] Recipient data represent unduplicated annual number.   [3] Expenditures include administrative expenses.   [4] Medical care for veterans with a nonservice-connected disability.   [5] Recipients are estimated number of inpatients.   [6] Estimated expenditures.   [7] Includes State-administered SSI supplements.   [8] Aid to families with dependent children program. Excludes data for foster care program and child support operations (cost and collections).   [9] Estimated recipients.   [10] Estimated recipients as of September.   [11] Includes dependents and survivors.   [12] Includes Puerto Rico's nutritional assistance program.   [13] Free and reduced-price segments.   [14] Includes estimate of commodity assistance.   [15] Special supplemental food program for women, infants, and children.   [16] Recipient data are numbers of children receiving free or reduced price meals and snacks in child care centers and estimates of children in family day care homes with incomes below 185 percent of poverty.   [17] No income test required but preference given to those with greatest need.   [18] Recipient data represent units eligible for payment at end of year.   [19] Includes operating subsidies and HUD-administered Indian housing.   [20] Recipient data represent total families or dwelling units during year.   [21] Expenditure data represent amounts obligated.   [22] Recipient data are housing units provided or rehabilitated.   [23] Recipient data are total numbers for the school year ending in year shown.   [24] Expenditure data are appropriations available for school year ending the fiscal year named.   [25] Nonfederal expenditure data are rough estimates.   [26] Recipient data are estimated number of children served.   [27] Recipient data are total number of participants.   [28] Job opportunities and basic skills training program (JOBS).   [29] Total participants (June-August).   [30] Households served during the year with heating and winter crisis aid.   [31] Federal funds include amounts transferred to other programs serving the needy.

Source: Library of Congress, Congressional Research Service, "Cash and Noncash Benefits for Persons With Limited Income: Eligibility Rules, Recipient and Expenditure Data, FYs 1994-96," CRS Report, 98-226.

Social Insurance and Human Services   389

No. 614. Social Security—Covered Employment, Earnings, and Contribution Rates: 1980 to 1998

[140.4 represents 140,400,000. Includes Puerto Rico, Virgin Islands, American Samoa, and Guam Represents all reported employment. Data are estimated. OASDHI=Old-age, survivors, disability, and health insurance; SMI=Supplementary medical insurance]

Item	Unit	1980	1985	1990	1992	1993	1994	1995	1996	1997	1998
Workers with insured status [1]	Million . .	140.4	150.9	164.0	167.5	169.1	170.7	172.9	174.8	177.0	179.1
Male.	Million . .	76.6	80.7	86.5	87.9	88.5	89.1	90.0	90.9	91.8	92.7
Female	Million . .	63.8	70.1	77.5	79.6	80.6	81.6	82.9	84.0	85.3	86.4
Under 25 years old	Million . .	25.7	22.0	21.3	20.1	19.5	19.0	18.8	18.5	18.5	18.7
25 to 34 years old	Million . .	36.5	40.1	41.6	40.8	40.3	39.8	39.4	38.8	38.1	37.2
35 to 44 years old	Million . .	23.0	29.9	36.4	38.1	38.9	39.7	40.5	41.3	41.9	42.3
45 to 54 years old	Million . .	18.6	19.2	22.8	25.6	26.8	28.2	29.5	30.7	31.9	33.1
55 to 59 years old	Million . .	9.3	9.0	8.7	9.0	9.3	9.5	9.7	10.1	10.7	11.2
60 to 64 years old	Million . .	8.2	8.8	8.8	8.5	8.5	8.4	8.4	8.5	8.7	8.9
65 to 69 years old	Million . .	7.0	7.5	8.2	8.2	8.2	8.1	8.1	8.1	8.0	7.9
70 years old and over	Million . .	12.1	14.3	16.3	17.3	17.7	18.1	18.5	18.8	19.3	19.6
Workers reported with—											
Taxable earnings [2]	Million . .	113	120	134	134	136	138	141	144	147	(NA)
Maximum earnings [2]	Million . .	10	8	8	8	8	8	8	9	9	(NA)
Earnings in covered employ-											
ment [2]	Bil. dol . .	1,329	1,942	2,704	2,916	3,023	3,169	3,359	3,568	3,853	(NA)
Reported taxable [2]	Bil. dol . .	1,178	1,725	2,359	2,533	2,636	2,785	2,920	3,076	3,292	(NA)
Percent of total	Percent . .	88.6	88.8	87.2	86.8	87.2	87.9	86.9	86.2	85.5	(NA)
Average per worker:											
Total earnings [2]	Dollars . .	11,761	16,125	20,227	21,776	22,205	22,929	23,814	24,863	26,258	(NA)
Taxable earnings [2]	Dollars . .	10,430	14,326	17,642	18,911	19,364	20,152	20,700	21,431	22,440	(NA)
Annual maximum taxable earnings [3]	Dollars . .	25,900	39,600	51,300	55,500	57,600	60,600	61,200	62,700	65,400	68,400
Contribution rates for OASDHI: [4]											
Each employer and employee . .	Percent .	6.13	7.05	7.65	7.65	7.65	7.65	7.65	7.65	7.65	7.65
Self-employed [5]	Percent .	8.10	14.10	15.30	15.30	15.30	15.30	15.30	15.30	15.30	15.30
SMI, monthly premium [6]	Dollars . .	9.60	15.50	28.60	31.80	36.60	41.10	46.10	42.50	43.80	43.80

NA Not available. [1] Estimated number fully insured for retirement and/or survivor benefits as of end of year. [2] Includes self-employment. [3] The maximum taxable earnings for HI was $130,200 in 1992 and 135,000 in 1993. Beginning 1994 upper limit on earnings subject to HI taxes was repealed. [4] As of January 1, 1999, each employee and employer pays 7.65 percent and the self-employed pay 15.3 percent. [5] Self-employed pays 11.8 percent in 1985. The additional amount is supplied from general revenues. Beginning 1990, self-employed pays 15.3 percent, and half of the tax is deductible for income tax purposes and for computing self-employment income subject to social security tax. [6] 1980, as of July 1; beginning 1985, as of January 1. As of January 1, 1999, the monthly premium is $45.50.

Source: U.S. Social Security Administration, Annual Statistical Supplement to the Social Security Bulletin; and unpublished data.

No. 615. Social Security Trust Funds: 1980 to 1997

[In billions of dollars (103.5 represents $103,500,000,000)]

Type of trust fund	1980	1985	1990	1992	1993	1994	1995	1996	1997
Old-age and survivors insurance (OASI):									
Net contribution income [1]	103.5	180.2	272.4	286.8	296.2	298.3	310.1	328.0	357.4
Interest received [2]	1.8	1.9	16.4	24.3	27.0	29.9	32.8	35.7	39.8
Benefit payments [3]	105.1	[4]67.2	223.0	[4]254.9	[4]267.8	279.1	291.6	302.9	316.3
Assets, end of year	22.8	[5]35.8	214.2	319.2	369.3	413.5	458.5	514.0	589.1
Disability insurance (DI):									
Net contribution income [1]	13.3	17.4	28.7	30.4	31.5	51.7	54.7	57.7	56.5
Interest received [2]	0.5	0.9	0.9	1.1	0.8	1.2	2.2	3.0	4.0
Benefit payments [3]	15.5	18.8	24.8	[4]31.1	[4]34.6	37.7	40.9	44.2	45.7
Assets, end of year	3.6	[6]6.3	11.1	12.3	9.0	22.9	37.6	52.9	66.4

[1] Includes deposits by states and deductions for refund of estimated employee-tax overpayment. Beginning in 1985, includes government contributions on deemed wage credits for military service in 1957 and later. Includes tax credits on net earnings from self-employment in 1985-89. Includes taxation of benefits beginning in 1985. [2] In 1985-90, includes interest on advance tax transfers. Beginning 1985, includes interest on reimbursement for unnegotiated checks. Data for 1985 reflect interest on interfund borrowing. [3] Includes payments for vocational rehabilitation services furnished to disabled persons receiving benefits because of their disabilities. Beginning in 1985, amounts reflect deductions for unnegotiated benefit checks. [4] Data adjusted to reflect 12 months of benefit payments. [5] Includes $13.2 billion borrowed from the DI and HI Trust Funds (see Table 176). [6] Excludes $2.5 billion lent to the OASI Trust Fund.

Source: U.S. Social Security Administration, Annual Report of Board of Trustees, OASI, DI, HI, and SMI Trust Funds. Also published in Social Security Bulletin, quarterly.

No. 616. Social Security (OASDI)—Benefits, by Type of Beneficiary: 1980 to 1998

[35,526 represents 35,526,000. A person eligible to receive more than one type of benefit is generally classified or counted only once as a retired-worker beneficiary. OASDI=Old-age, survivors, and disability insurance. See also headnote, Table 614 and Appendix III]

Type of beneficiary	1980	1985	1990	1992	1993	1994	1995	1996	1997	1998
Number of benefits [1] (1,000) .	35,526	37,027	39,825	41,504	42,243	42,882	43,386	43,736	43,971	44,246
Retired workers [2] (1,000)	19,583	22,432	24,838	25,758	26,104	26,408	26,673	26,898	27,275	27,511
Disabled workers [3] (1,000)	2,861	2,657	3,011	3,468	3,726	3,963	4,185	4,386	4,508	4,698
Wives and husbands [2] [4] (1,000) . .	3,480	3,375	3,367	3,382	3,367	3,337	3,290	3,194	3,129	3,054
Children (1,000)	4,610	3,319	3,187	3,391	3,527	3,654	3,734	3,803	3,772	3,769
Under age 18	3,426	2,699	2,497	2,664	2,777	2,887	2,956	3,010	2,970	2,963
Disabled children [5]	451	526	600	637	656	673	686	697	705	713
Students [6]	734	94	89	90	94	94	92	96	97	93
Of retired workers	642	457	422	432	436	440	442	443	441	439
Of deceased workers	2,609	1,917	1,776	1,808	1,836	1,864	1,884	1,898	1,893	1,884
Of disabled workers	1,359	945	989	1,151	1,255	1,350	1,409	1,463	1,438	1,446
Widowed mothers [7] (1,000)	563	372	304	294	289	283	275	242	230	221
Widows and widowers [2] [8] (1,000) . .	4,415	4,863	5,111	5,205	5,224	5,232	5,226	5,210	5,053	4,990
Parents [2] (1,000)	15	10	6	5	5	4	4	4	3	3
Special benefits [9] (1,000)	93	32	7	4	2	2	1	1	(Z)	(NA)
AVERAGE MONTHLY BENEFIT CURRENT DOLLARS										
Retired workers [2]	341	479	603	653	674	697	720	745	765	780
Retired worker and wife [2]	567	814	1,027	1,111	1,145	1,184	1,221	1,262	1,295	(NA)
Disabled workers [3] [4]	371	484	587	626	642	661	682	704	722	733
Wives and husbands [2] [4]	164	236	298	322	332	343	354	369	379	386
Children of retired workers	140	198	259	285	297	309	322	337	349	358
Children of deceased workers	240	330	406	432	443	456	469	487	500	510
Children of disabled workers	110	142	164	170	173	178	183	194	201	208
Widowed mothers [7]	246	332	409	438	448	464	478	515	532	545
Widows and widowers, nondisabled [2]	311	433	556	608	630	655	680	707	731	749
Parents [2]	276	378	482	526	547	570	591	614	636	651
Special benefits [9]	105	138	167	178	183	187	192	197	201	(NA)
Number of benefits awarded (1,000)	4,215	3,796	3,717	4,051	4,001	3,940	3,882	3,793	3,866	(NA)
Retired workers [2]	1,620	1,690	1,665	1,708	1,661	1,625	1,609	1,581	1,719	(NA)
Disabled workers [3]	389	377	468	637	635	632	646	624	587	(NA)
Wives and husbands [2] [4]	469	440	379	383	365	345	322	302	319	(NA)
Children	1,174	714	695	795	816	824	809	798	757	(NA)
Widowed mothers [7]	108	72	58	56	56	55	52	49	44	(NA)
Widows and widowers [2] [8]	452	502	452	472	466	459	445	438	440	(NA)
Parents [2]	1	(Z)	(Z)	(Z)	(Z)	(Z)	(Z)	(Z)	(Z)	(NA)
Special benefits [9]	1	1	(Z)	(Z)	(Z)	(Z)	(Z)	(Z)	(Z)	(NA)
BENEFIT PAYMENTS DURING YEAR (bil. dol.)										
Total [10]	120.5	186.2	247.8	286.0	302.4	316.8	332.6	347.1	362.0	375.0
Monthly benefits [11]	120.1	186.0	247.6	285.8	302.2	316.6	332.4	346.9	361.8	374.8
Retired workers [2]	70.4	116.8	156.8	179.4	188.4	196.4	205.3	213.4	223.6	232.3
Disabled workers [3]	12.8	16.5	22.1	27.9	30.9	33.7	36.6	39.6	41.1	43.5
Wives and husbands [2] [4]	6.4	10.5	14.0	15.8	16.4	16.9	17.3	17.7	18.2	18.4
Children	10.5	10.7	12.0	13.6	14.6	15.3	16.1	17.1	17.6	18.1
Under age 18	7.4	8.5	9.0	10.1	10.8	11.4	11.9	12.6	13.0	(NA)
Disabled children [5]	1.0	1.8	2.5	3.0	3.3	3.4	3.6	3.8	4.0	(NA)
Students [6]	2.1	0.4	0.5	0.5	0.5	0.6	0.6	0.6	0.6	(NA)
Of retired workers	1.1	1.1	1.3	1.5	1.6	1.6	1.7	1.8	1.9	1.9
Of deceased workers	7.4	7.8	8.6	9.4	9.9	10.3	10.7	11.2	11.7	11.9
Of disabled workers	2.0	1.8	2.2	2.7	3.1	3.4	3.7	4.0	4.1	4.2
Widowed mothers [7]	1.6	1.5	1.4	1.5	1.5	1.6	1.6	1.5	1.5	1.4
Widows and widowers [2] [8]	17.6	29.3	40.7	47.1	49.7	52.1	54.8	57.0	59.3	60.5
Parents [2]	0.1	0.1	(Z)	(Z)	(Z)	(Z)	(Z)	(Z)	(Z)	(Z)
Special benefits [9]	0.1	0.1	(Z)	(Z)	(Z)	(Z)	(Z)	(Z)	(Z)	(Z)
Lump sum	0.4	0.2	0.2	0.2	0.2	0.2	0.2	0.2	0.2	0.2

NA Not available.   Z Fewer than 500 or less than $50 million.   [1] Number of benefit payments in current-payment status, i.e., actually being made at a specified time with no deductions or with deductions amounting to less than a month's benefits. Total excludes special benefits (see footnote 9) since the cost of paying benefits to these beneficiaries is reimbursed from the general fund of the Treasury.   [2] 62 years and over.   [3] Disabled workers under age 65.   [4] Includes wife beneficiaries with entitled children in their care and entitled divorced wives.   [5] 18 years old and over. Disability began before age 18 and, beginning 1973, before age 22.   [6] Full-time students aged 18-21 through 1984 and aged 18 and 19 beginning 1985.   [7] Includes surviving divorced mothers with entitled children in their care and widowed fathers with entitled children in their care.   [8] Includes widows aged 60-61, surviving divorced wives aged 60 and over, disabled widows and widowers aged 50 and over; and widowers aged 60-61.   [9] Benefits for persons aged 72 and over not insured under regular or transitional provisions of Social Security Act.   [10] Represents total disbursements of benefit checks by the U.S. Dept. of the Treasury during the years specified.   [11] Distribution by type estimated.

Source: U.S. Social Security Administration, *Annual Statistical Supplement* to the *Social Security Bulletin;* and unpublished data.

U.S. Census Bureau, Statistical Abstract of the United States: 1999

No. 617. Social Security—Beneficiaries, Annual Payments, and Average Monthly Benefit, 1980 to 1997 and by State and Other Area, 1997

[Number of beneficiaries in current-payment status (**35,585 represents 35,585,000**) and average monthly benefit as of **December**. Data for number of beneficiaries and average monthly benefit based on 10-percent sample of administrative records. See also headnote, Table 616, and Appendix III]

Year, state, and other area	Number of beneficiaries (1,000)				Annual payments (mil. dol.)				Average monthly benefit (dol.)		
	Total	Retired workers and dependents[1]	Survivors	Disabled workers and dependents	Total	Retired workers and dependents[1]	Survivors[2]	Disabled workers and dependents	Retired workers[3]	Disabled workers	Widows and widowers[4]
1980	35,585	23,309	7,598	4,678	120,472	78,025	27,010	15,437	341	371	311
1985	37,058	25,989	7,162	3,907	186,195	128,536	38,824	18,836	479	484	433
1990	39,832	28,369	7,197	4,266	247,796	172,042	50,951	24,803	603	587	557
1994	42,878	29,913	7,371	5,592	316,835	214,895	64,223	37,717	697	661	655
1995	43,380	30,139	7,379	5,862	332,581	224,381	67,302	40,898	720	682	680
1996	43,737	30,314	7,347	6,077	347,088	232,938	69,976	44,174	745	705	707
1997, total[5] .	43,976	30,649	7,171	6,156	361,970	243,590	72,721	45,659	765	722	731
United States..	42,940	30,015	6,952	5,967	356,363	240,546	71,246	44,573	717	693	656
Alabama	795	493	153	149	6,076	3,646	1,405	1,025	(NA)	(NA)	(NA)
Alaska.	48	30	9	8	370	233	78	59	752	708	680
Arizona	735	535	102	98	6,096	4,296	1,047	753	775	747	757
Arkansas	510	322	90	98	3,815	2,331	807	677	698	687	643
California	4,037	2,915	609	512	33,749	23,433	6,342	3,974	777	733	763
Colorado	511	353	78	80	4,100	2,719	789	592	745	716	733
Connecticut	568	429	76	63	5,164	3,813	863	488	840	738	814
Delaware	127	91	19	17	1,095	758	207	130	795	755	781
Dist. of Columbia. .	76	52	14	9	545	359	110	70	644	661	600
Florida.	3,082	2,306	420	355	25,462	18,391	4,389	2,682	763	729	755
Georgia	1,044	663	187	194	8,122	5,024	1,710	1,388	727	697	667
Hawaii.	172	135	22	15	1,385	1,059	213	113	754	738	698
Idaho	184	132	28	24	1,463	1,014	277	171	742	711	744
Illinois	1,816	1,295	304	217	15,961	10,938	3,325	1,697	806	749	788
Indiana	971	679	158	133	8,397	5,681	1,719	997	799	731	778
Iowa	538	394	86	58	4,474	3,123	922	430	765	707	747
Kansas	434	314	69	51	3,680	2,564	747	369	785	701	772
Kentucky	719	425	134	161	5,490	3,103	1,244	1,143	713	721	654
Louisiana.	702	417	158	127	5,323	2,995	1,451	877	711	726	668
Maine	243	166	34	42	1,847	1,224	340	283	705	658	692
Maryland	693	493	120	81	5,811	3,955	1,220	637	767	746	741
Massachusetts . . .	1,051	749	147	155	8,818	6,081	1,587	1,151	769	712	765
Michigan	1,605	1,108	271	225	14,225	9,455	2,979	1,791	820	778	784
Minnesota	716	526	112	78	5,886	4,130	1,174	582	754	706	732
Mississippi	500	294	95	111	3,578	2,066	789	723	680	670	607
Missouri.	977	672	158	147	7,929	5,272	1,591	1,066	751	705	724
Montana	153	107	24	22	1,232	819	246	167	745	727	726
Nebraska.	283	206	45	32	2,305	1,613	475	217	754	683	753
Nevada	252	185	32	34	2,104	1,491	336	277	773	762	762
New Hampshire . .	190	138	25	27	1,600	1,126	274	200	772	726	770
New Jersey	1,317	974	194	148	12,067	8,678	2,182	1,207	842	767	809
New Mexico	264	177	46	42	1,988	1,288	412	288	717	704	690
New York.	2,964	2,110	440	414	26,072	18,043	4,734	3,295	814	764	781
North Carolina . . .	1,276	853	198	225	9,989	6,526	1,835	1,628	729	693	659
North Dakota	115	82	22	12	892	595	215	82	718	679	699
Ohio	1,905	1,312	343	250	16,198	10,594	3,700	1,903	782	735	762
Oklahoma	582	398	104	80	4,599	3,005	1,010	584	729	709	704
Oregon	551	409	78	65	4,637	3,308	833	496	777	718	768
Pennsylvania	2,328	1,693	387	248	20,111	13,952	4,248	1,911	787	741	770
Rhode Island . . .	189	139	24	26	1,580	1,134	255	192	764	694	762
South Carolina . . .	650	421	107	122	5,052	3,218	951	883	729	703	650
South Dakota	135	95	24	15	1,025	694	231	100	706	651	686
Tennessee.	946	606	168	172	7,373	4,577	1,570	1,226	727	691	673
Texas	2,526	1,704	486	336	20,011	12,901	4,714	2,395	742	715	711
Utah	230	165	35	30	1,878	1,311	359	208	770	705	777
Vermont	101	70	15	16	812	550	151	112	751	690	733
Virginia	979	662	164	153	7,780	5,066	1,592	1,122	736	716	687
Washington	807	590	115	102	6,923	4,886	1,253	785	796	723	781
West Virginia	385	231	79	75	3,139	1,772	789	578	754	767	700
Wisconsin	884	648	133	103	7,531	5,317	1,441	773	783	723	768
Wyoming	74	52	11	10	604	419	109	76	769	741	742
Puerto Rico. . . .	636	344	122	169	3,378	1,669	756	954	497	607	451
Guam	8	5	2	1	46	27	14	5	542	632	505
Amer. Samoa . .	5	2	2	2	22	7	9	7	432	516	388
Virgin Islands . .	12	8	2	1	79	53	16	10	631	686	550
Abroad.	375	269	90	16	2,057	1,275	677	105	488	626	518

NA Not available. [1] Includes special benefits for persons aged 72 and over not insured under regular or transitional provisions of Social Security Act. [2] Includes lump-sum payments to survivors of deceased workers. [3] Excludes persons with special benefits. [4] Nondisabled only. [5] Includes those with state or area unknown.

Source: U.S. Social Security Administration, *Social Security Bulletin*, quarterly.

No. 618. Public Employee Retirement Systems—Participants and Finances: 1980 to 1996

[For fiscal year of retirement system, except data for the Thrift Savings Plan are for calendar year (4,629 represents 4,629,000)]

Retirement plan	Unit	1980	1985	1990	1991	1992	1993	1994	1995	1996
TOTAL PARTICIPANTS [1]										
Federal retirement systems:										
Defined benefit:										
Civil Service Retirement System	1,000..	4,629	4,919	4,167	4,086	4,014	3,808	3,808	3,731	3,663
Federal Employees Retirement System [2]	1,000..	(X)	(X)	1,180	1,325	1,367	1,764	1,764	1,512	1,615
Military Service Retirement System [3]	1,000..	3,380	3,672	3,763	3,732	3,579	3,511	3,451	3,387	3,372
Thrift Savings Plan [4]	1,000..	(X)	(X)	1,625	1,776	1,900	2,036	2,119	2,195	2,300
State and local retirement systems [5][6]	1,000..	(NA)	15,234	16,858	17,502	18,310	13,466	13,290	14,734	15,153
ACTIVE PARTICIPANTS										
Federal retirement systems:										
Defined benefit:										
Civil Service Retirement System	1,000..	2,700	2,800	1,826	1,726	1,654	1,525	1,443	1,525	1,343
Federal Employees Retirement System [2]	1,000..	(X)	(X)	1,136	1,260	1,276	1,318	1,375	1,318	1,447
Military Service Retirement System [3]	1,000..	2,050	2,192	2,130	2,064	1,868	1,763	1,666	1,572	1,525
Thrift Savings Plan [4]	1,000..	(X)	(X)	1,419	1,593	1,300	1,812	1,876	1,930	1,800
State and local retirement systems [5][6]	1,000..	(NA)	10,364	11,345	11,696	11,998	11,940	11,849	12,524	13,051
ASSETS										
Total	Bil. dol..	258	529	1,047	1,150	1,276	1,384	1,519	1,655	1,854
Federal retirement systems	Bil. dol..	73	154	326	367	411	455	494	537	581
Defined benefit	Bil. dol..	73	154	318	355	394	434	468	502	534
Civil Service Retirement System [2]	Bil. dol..	73	142	220	237	256	277	294	311	328
Federal Employees Retirement System [2]	Bil. dol..	(X)	(X)	18	24	32	41	50	60	71
Military Service Retirement System [3]	Bil. dol..	([7])	12	80	94	106	116	124	131	135
Thrift Savings Plan [4]	Bil. dol..	(X)	(X)	8	12	16	21	26	35	47
State and local retirement systems [5]	Bil. dol..	185	374	721	783	866	929	1,025	1,118	1,273
CONTRIBUTIONS										
Total	Bil. dol..	83	106	103	111	107	120	121	127	129
Federal retirement systems	Bil. dol..	19	54	61	65	68	68	67	67	66
Defined benefit	Bil. dol..	19	54	59	62	64	63	62	61	60
Civil Service Retirement System [2]	Bil. dol..	19	27	28	29	30	31	31	31	32
Federal Employees Retirement System [2]	Bil. dol..	(X)	(X)	4	5	6	6	6	6	6
Military Service Retirement System [3]	Bil. dol..	([7])	27	27	28	28	26	25	24	22
Thrift Savings Plan [4]	Bil. dol..	(X)	(X)	2	3	4	5	5	6	6
State and local retirement systems [5]	Bil. dol..	64	52	42	46	39	52	54	60	63
BENEFITS										
Total	Bil. dol..	39	62	89	96	101	117	124	125	131
Federal retirement systems	Bil. dol..	27	40	53	56	58	63	65	66	66
Defined benefit	Bil. dol..	27	40	53	56	58	62	64	65	69
Civil Service Retirement System [2]	Bil. dol..	15	23	31	33	33	35	36	37	39
Federal Employees Retirement System [2]	Bil. dol..	(X)	(X)	(Z)	(Z)	(Z)	(Z)	(Z)	1	1
Military Service Retirement System [3]	Bil. dol..	12	17	22	23	25	27	28	28	29
Thrift Savings Plan [4]	Bil. dol..	(X)	(X)	(Z)	(Z)	(Z)	1	1	1	1
State and local retirement systems [5]	Bil. dol..	12	22	36	39	44	54	59	59	65

NA Not available.   X Not applicable.   Z Less than $500 million.   [1] Includes active, separated vested, retired employees, and survivors.   [2] The Federal Employees Retirement System was established June 6, 1986.   [3] Includes nondisability and disability retirees, surviving families, and all active personnel with the exception of active reserves.   [4] The Thrift Savings Plan (a defined contribution plan) was established April 1, 1987.   [5] Excludes state and local plans that are fully supported by employee contributions.   [6] Not adjusted for double counting of individuals participating in more than one plan.   [7] The Military Retirement System was unfunded until October 1, 1984.

Source: Employee Benefit Research Institute, Washington, DC, *EBRI Databook on Employee Benefits, Sixth Edition* (copyright).

No. 619. Federal Civil Service Retirement: 1980 to 1998

[As of **Sept. 30** or for **year ending Sept. 30 (2,720 represents 2,720,000)**. Covers both Civil Service Retirement System and Federal Employees Retirement System]

Item	Unit	1980	1985	1990	1993	1994	1995	1996	1997	1998
Employees covered [1]	1,000..	2,720	2,750	2,945	2,843	2,778	2,668	2,629	2,681	2,658
Annuitants, total	1,000..	1,675	1,955	2,143	2,242	2,263	2,311	2,333	2,352	2,369
Age and service	1,000..	905	1,122	1,288	1,378	1,398	1,441	1,459	1,474	1,488
Disability	1,000..	343	332	297	274	268	263	260	257	253
Survivors	1,000..	427	501	558	589	597	607	614	621	628
Receipts, total [2]	Mil. dol.	24,389	40,790	52,689	62,878	63,390	65,684	67,339	70,227	72,156
Employee contributions	Mil. dol	3,686	4,679	4,501	4,703	4,610	4,498	4,398	4,358	4,274
Federal government contributions..	Mil. dol	15,562	22,301	27,368	32,668	32,434	33,130	33,991	35,386	36,188
Disbursements, total [3]	Mil. dol	14,977	23,203	31,416	35,123	36,532	38,435	39,711	41,722	43,058
Age and service annuitants [4]	Mil. dol	12,639	19,414	26,495	29,288	30,440	32,070	32,970	34,697	35,806
Survivors	Mil. dol	1,912	3,158	4,366	5,377	5,607	5,864	6,221	6,518	6,763
Average monthly benefit:										
Age and service	Dollars .	992	1,189	1,369	1,537	1,587	1,643	1,698	1,749	1,847
Disability	Dollars .	723	881	1,008	1,120	1,141	1,164	1,184	1,204	1,216
Survivors	Dollars .	392	528	653	760	789	819	849	881	905
Cash and security holdings	Bil. dol.	73.7	142.3	238.0	317.4	344.3	366.2	394.1	422.2	451.3

[1] Excludes employees in leave without pay status.   [2] Includes interest on investments.   [3] Includes refunds, death claims, and administration.   [4] Includes disability annuitants.

Source: U.S. Office of Personnel Management, *Civil Service Retirement and Disability Trust Fund Annual Report.*

State and Local Government Retirement Systems—Beneficiaries and Finances: 1980 to 1997

[In billions of dollars, except as indicated (37.3 represents $37,300,000,000). For fiscal years closed during the 12 months ending June 30]

Year and level of government	Number of beneficiaries (1,000)	Receipts					Benefits and withdrawals			Cash and security holdings
		Total	Employee contributions	Government contributions		Earnings on investments	Total	Benefits	Withdrawals	
				State	Local					
1980: All systems	(NA)	37.3	6.5	7.6	10.0	13.3	14.0	12.2	1.8	185
State-administered	(NA)	28.6	5.3	7.4	5.6	10.3	10.3	8.8	1.4	145
Locally administered	(NA)	8.7	1.2	0.2	4.3	3.0	3.8	3.4	0.4	41
1990: All systems	4,026	111.3	13.9	14.0	18.6	64.9	38.4	36.0	2.4	721
State-administered	3,232	89.2	11.6	14.0	11.5	52.0	29.6	27.6	2.0	575
Locally administered	794	22.2	2.2	(Z)	7.0	12.9	8.8	8.4	0.4	145
1995: All systems	4,979	148.8	18.6	16.6	24.4	89.2	61.4	58.8	2.7	1,118
State-administered	4,025	123.3	15.7	16.2	15.4	76.0	48.0	45.8	2.2	914
Locally administered	954	25.5	2.9	0.4	9.0	13.3	13.5	13.0	0.5	204
1997: All systems	5,348	224.7	20.8	20.6	24.4	159.0	75.7	68.9	3.4	1,476
State-administered	4,273	188.4	17.4	20.2	16.9	133.9	58.9	53.7	2.8	1,222
Locally administered	1,074	36.3	3.4	0.4	7.5	25.1	16.8	15.2	0.6	254

NA Not available.   Z Less than $50 million.

Source: U.S. Census Bureau, *Finances of Employee-Retirement Systems of State and Local Governments*, Series GF, No. 2, annual.

No. 621. Private Pension Plans—Summary, by Type of Plan: 1980 to 1995

[488.9 represents 488,900. "Pension plan" is defined by the Employee Retirement Income Security Act (ERISA) as "any plan, fund, or program which was heretofore or is hereafter established or maintained by an employer or an employee organization, or by both, to the extent that such plan (a) provides retirement income to employees, or (b) results in a deferral of income by employees for periods extending to the termination of covered employment or beyond, regardless of the method of calculating the contributions made to the plan, the method of calculating the benefits under the plan, or the method of distributing benefits from the plan." A defined benefit plan provides a definite benefit formula for calculating benefit amounts - such as a flat amount per year of service or a percentage of salary times years of service. A defined contribution plan is a pension plan in which the contributions are made to an individual account for each employee. The retirement benefit is dependent upon the account balance at retirement. The balance depends upon amounts contributed, investment experience, and, in the case of profit sharing plans, amounts which may be allocated to the account due to forfeitures by terminating employees. Employee Stock Ownership Plans (ESOP) and 401(k) plans (see Table 624) are included among defined contribution plans. Data are based on Form 5500 series reports filed with the Internal Revenue Service]

Item	Unit	Total				Defined contribution plan				Defined benefit plan			
		1980	1985	1990	1995	1980	1985	1990	1995	1980	1985	1990	1995
Number of plans [1]	1,000	488.9	632.1	712.3	693.4	340.8	462.0	599.2	623.9	148.1	170.2	113.1	69.5
Total participants [2][3]	Million	57.9	74.7	76.9	87.5	19.9	35.0	38.1	47.7	38.0	39.7	38.8	39.7
Active participants [2][4]	Million	49.0	62.3	61.8	66.2	18.9	33.2	35.5	42.7	30.1	29.0	26.3	23.5
Contributions [5]	Bil. dol	66.2	95.1	98.8	158.8	23.5	53.1	75.8	117.4	42.6	42.0	23.0	41.4
Benefits [6]	Bil. dol	35.3	101.9	129.4	183.0	13.1	47.4	63.0	97.9	22.1	54.5	66.4	85.1

[1] Excludes all plans covering only one participant.   [2] Includes double counting of workers in more than one plan.   [3] Total participants include active participants, vested separated workers, and retirees.   [4] Any workers currently in employment covered by a plan and who are earning or retaining credited service under a plan. Includes any nonvested former employees who have not yet incurred breaks in service.   [5] Includes both employer and employee contributions.   [6] Benefits paid directly from trust and premium payments made from plan to insurance carriers. Excludes benefits paid directly by insurance carriers.

Source: U.S. Dept. of Labor, Pension and Welfare Benefits Administration, *Private Pension Plan Bulletin*, winter 1996 and unpublished data.

No. 622. Percent of Full-Time Employees Participating in Retirement Plans: 1991 to 1997

[In percent. Covers full-time employees in private nonfarm establishments. Based on a sample survey of establishments; for details, see source]

Type of retirement plan	1991	1993	1995	1997
Total [1]	78	78	80	79
Defined benefit	59	56	52	50
Defined contribution	48	49	55	57
401(k) plans [2]	44	43	54	55

[1] Some employees participate in both defined benefit and defined contribution plans, but are counted just once in total.   [2] A 401(k) plan is a qualified retirement plan that allows participants to have a portion of their compensation (otherwise payable in cash) contributed pretax to a retirement account on their behalf.

Source: U.S. Bureau of Labor Statistics, *News*, USDL 99-02, January 7, 1999.

[60,711 represents 60,711,000. Covers workers as of **March 1998** who had earnings in 1997. Based on Current Population Survey; see text, Section 1, Population and Appendix III]

Sex and age	Number with coverage (1,000)				Percent of total workers			
	Total[1]	White	Black	Hispanic[2]	Total[1]	White	Black	Hispanic[2]
Total	**60,711**	**51,559**	**6,622**	**3,747**	**42.0**	**42.4**	**40.7**	**26.2**
Male	33,689	29,193	3,130	2,173	43.9	44.5	41.4	25.7
Under 65 years old . . .	33,028	28,607	3,080	2,143	44.6	45.3	41.7	25.7
15 to 24 years old . .	1,571	1,320	186	148	12.6	12.5	13.8	8.2
25 to 44 years old . .	18,591	15,898	1,855	1,350	48.0	48.9	44.7	28.0
45 to 64 years old . .	12,866	11,390	1,038	645	56.3	56.9	54.9	37.6
65 years old and over .	661	586	50	30	24.2	23.6	29.2	21.8
Female	27,022	22,365	3,492	1,575	39.8	39.9	40.1	26.9
Under 65 years old . . .	26,532	21,928	3,462	1,562	40.4	40.5	40.7	27.0
15 to 24 years old . .	1,319	1,086	181	114	11.3	11.3	11.9	9.3
25 to 44 years old . .	14,869	12,101	2,062	947	44.1	44.4	43.4	29.5
45 to 64 years old . .	10,344	8,741	1,219	500	50.9	50.8	54.4	37.5
65 years old and over .	490	437	29	13	22.3	22.4	15.5	15.8

[1] Includes other races, not shown separately. [2] Hispanic persons may be of any race.

Source: U.S. Census Bureau, "Current Population Survey, Annual Demographic Survey, March Supplement;" published 13 October 1998; <http://ferret.bls.census.gov/macro/031998/noncash/8000.htm>.

No. 624. 401(k) Plans—Summary: 1985 to 1994

[10,339 represents 10,339,000. A 401(k) plan is a qualified retirement plan that allows participants to have a portion of their compensation (otherwise payable in cash) contributed pretax to a retirement account on their behalf]

Item	1985	1989	1990	1991	1992	1993	1994
Number of plans[1]	29,869	83,301	97,614	111,314	139,704	154,527	174,945
Active participants[2] (1,000)	10,339	17,337	19,548	19,126	22,404	23,138	26,206
Assets (mil. dol.)	143,939	357,015	384,854	440,259	552,959	616,316	674,681
Contributions (mil. dol.)	24,322	46,081	48,998	51,533	64,345	69,322	75,878
Benefits (mil. dol.)	16,399	30,875	32,028	32,734	43,166	44,206	50,659
Percentage of all private defined contribution plans:							
Assets	34	52	54	53	58	58	62
Contributions	46	63	65	64	69	68	72
Benefits	35	47	51	51	58	57	62

[1] Excludes single-participant plans. [2] May include some employees who are eligible to participate in the plan, but have not elected to join. 401(k) participants may participate in one or more additional plans.

Source: Employee Benefit Research Institute, Washington, DC, *EBRI Databook on Employee Benefits*, Sixth Edition (copyright).

No. 625. State Unemployment Insurance, by State and Other Area: 1997

[7,325 represents 7,325,000. See headnote, Table 626. For state data on insured unemployment, see Table 686]

State and other area	Beneficiaries, first payments (1,000)	Benefits paid (mil. dol.)	Avg. weekly unemployment benefits (dol.)
Total .	7,325	19,735	193
AL	135	194	145
AK	44	121	176
AZ	69	144	147
AR	93	182	198
CA	1,073	2,628	152
CO	64	162	213
CT	114	367	211
DE	21	68	194
DC	21	79	233
FL	246	646	192
GA	180	279	162
HI	38	164	269
ID	45	94	187
IL	320	1,165	217
IN	121	257	186
IA	79	179	205
KS	49	128	204
KY	114	222	176
LA	69	141	133
ME	42	98	152
MD	107	332	196
MA	178	725	263
MI	348	912	222
MN	110	355	242
MS	61	114	142
MO	140	275	154
MT	27	56	166
NE	27	51	163
NV	64	175	204
NH	18	34	165
NJ	283	1,144	259
NM	30	75	158
NY	490	1,754	204
NC	201	357	198
ND	19	38	176
OH	254	691	208
OK	41	86	177
OR	137	362	198
PA	430	1,430	228
RI	49	151	224
SC	92	169	169
SD	9	16	156
TN	165	305	163
TX	345	943	196
UT	34	75	193
VT	21	49	174
VA	101	187	179
WA	198	698	240
WV	56	133	180
WI	211	463	188
WY	11	27	182
PR . . .	132	229	94
VI . . .	2	6	166

Source: U.S. Employment and Training Administration, *Unemployment Insurance Financial Handbook*, annual.

No. 626. State Unemployment Insurance—Summary: 1980 to 1997

[3,356 represents 3,356,000. Includes unemployment compensation for state and local government employees where covered by state law]

Item	Unit	1980	1985	1990	1991	1992	1993	1994	1995	1996	1997
Insured unemployment, avg. weekly..	1,000...	3,356	2,617	2,522	3,342	3,245	2,751	2,670	2,572	2,596	2,323
Percent of covered employment [1]..	Percent .	3.9	2.9	2.4	3.1	3.1	2.6	2.5	2.3	2.3	2.0
Percent of civilian unemployed....	Percent .	43.9	31.5	35.8	38.7	33.8	30.8	33.4	34.7	35.9	34.5
Unemployment benefits, avg. weekly .	Dollars..	100	128	162	170	174	180	182	187	189	193
Percent of weekly wage........	Percent .	36.6	35.3	36.0	36.4	35.4	36.0	35.7	35.5	34.5	33.5
Weeks compensated............	Million ..	149.0	119.3	116.0	155.1	150.2	125.6	123.4	118.3	119.0	106.6
Beneficiaries, first payments [2].......	1,000...	9,992	8,372	8,629	10,075	9,243	7,884	7,959	8,035	7,995	7,325
Average duration of benefits [2].......	Weeks ..	14.9	14.2	13.4	15.4	16.2	15.9	15.5	14.7	14.9	14.6
Claimants exhausting benefits......	1,000...	3,072	2,572	2,323	3,472	3,838	3,204	2,977	2,662	2,739	2,485
Percent of first payment [3]........	Percent .	33.2	31.2	29.4	34.8	39.9	39.2	36.3	34.3	33.4	32.8
Contributions collected [4]........	Bil. dol..	11.4	19.3	15.2	14.5	17.0	19.8	21.8	21.2	21.8	19.7
Benefits paid...............	Bil. dol..	14.2	14.7	18.0	25.5	25.1	21.8	21.5	21.2	21.8	19.7
Funds available for benefits [5]....	Bil. dol..	6.6	10.1	37.9	30.5	25.8	28.0	31.3	35.4	38.6	43.8
Average employer contribution rate [6]	Percent .	2.4	3.1	2.0	1.9	2.2	2.5	2.6	2.4	2.3	2.1

[1] Insured unemployment as percent of average covered employment in preceding year.   [2] Weeks compensated divided by first payment.   [3] Based on first payments for 12-month period ending June 30.   [4] Contributions from employers; also employees in states which tax workers.   [5] End of year. Sum of balances in state clearing accounts, benefit-payment accounts, and state accounts in Federal unemployment trust funds.   [6] As percent of taxable wages.
Source: U.S. Employment and Training Administration, *Unemployment Insurance Financial Handbook*, annual.

No. 627. Persons With Work Disability, by Selected Characteristics: 1998

[In thousands, except percent (17,157 represents 17,157,000). As of **March**. Covers civilian noninstitutional population and members of Armed Forces living off post or with their families on post. Persons are classified as having a work disability if they (1) have a health problem or disability which prevents them from working or which limits the kind or amount of work they can do; (2) have a service-connected disability or ever retired or left a job for health reasons; (3) did not work in survey reference week or previous year because of long-term illness or disability; or (4) are under age 65, and are covered by medicare or receive supplemental security income. Based on Current Population Survey; see text, Section 1, Population, and Appendix III]

Age and participation status in assistance programs	Total [1]	Male	Female	White	Black	Hispanic [2]
Persons with work disability	**17,157**	**8,291**	**8,867**	**13,289**	**3,163**	**1,740**
16 to 24 years old..............	1,368	675	693	984	313	183
25 to 34 years old..............	2,131	987	1,144	1,628	424	251
35 to 44 years old..............	4,035	2,029	2,006	3,002	890	419
45 to 54 years old..............	4,488	2,123	2,365	3,543	746	396
55 to 64 years old..............	5,136	2,477	2,659	4,131	790	491
Percent work disabled of total population ...	10.0	9.8	10.1	9.3	14.7	9.0
16 to 24 years old..............	4.1	4.1	4.2	3.7	6.3	3.8
25 to 34 years old..............	5.5	5.1	5.8	5.2	8.1	4.6
35 to 44 years old..............	9.1	9.3	9.0	8.2	16.3	9.1
45 to 54 years old..............	13.2	12.8	13.6	12.3	20.4	14.7
55 to 64 years old..............	23.1	23.2	23.0	21.6	35.5	30.1
Percent of work disabled—						
Receiving social security income...........	31.5	34.3	29.0	32.1	31.1	26.7
Receiving food stamps	20.2	16.2	24.0	16.8	34.0	27.7
Covered by medicaid................	33.9	29.3	38.1	30.4	48.1	42.9
Residing in public housing	6.6	5.0	8.1	4.8	14.3	10.1
Residing in subsidized housing	3.5	3.0	4.0	3.0	5.2	5.5

[1] Includes other races not shown separately.   [2] Hispanic persons may be of any race.
Source: U.S. Census Bureau, unpublished data.

No. 628. Vocational Rehabilitation—Summary: 1980 to 1997

[For year ending September 30. Includes Puerto Rico, Guam, Virgin Islands, American Samoa, Northern Mariana Islands, and the Republic of Palau. State agencies, using matching state and Federal funds, provide vocational rehabilitation services to eligible individuals with disabilities to enable them to prepare for and engage in gainful employment. Services may include counseling, guidance and work related placement services, physical and mental restoration, training and rehabilitation technology]

Item	Unit	1980	1985	1990	1992	1993	1994	1995	1996	1997
Federal and state expenditures [1]........	Mil. dol..	1,076	1,452	1,910	2,240	2,241	2,517	2,714	2,844	3,046
Federal expenditures..............	Mil. dol..	817	1,100	1,525	1,731	1,691	1,891	2,054	2,104	2,164
Applicants processed for program eligibility.	1,000...	717	594	625	713	713	675	625	578	617
Percent accepted into program	Percent .	58	60	57	57	61	72	76	76	79
Total persons rehabilitated [2]..........	1,000...	277	228	216	192	194	203	210	213	212
Rehabilitation rate [3].............	Percent .	64	64	62	58	56	49	46	61	61
Severely disabled persons rehabilitated [2][4].	1,000...	143	135	146	134	139	149	159	166	168
Rehabilitation rate [3].............	Percent .	61	62	62	57	55	49	46	60	60
Percent of total persons rehabilitated ...	Percent .	51	59	68	70	72	74	76	78	79
Persons served, total [5]............	1,000...	1,095	932	938	949	1,049	1,194	1,250	1,226	1,267
Persons served, severely disabled [4][5]	1,000...	606	581	640	668	762	882	940	951	1,005
Percent of total persons served	Percent .	55	62	68	70	73	74	75	78	79

[1] Includes expenditures only under the basic support provisions of the Rehabilitation Act.   [2] Persons successfully placed into gainful employment.   [3] Persons rehabilitated as a percent of all active case closures (whether rehabilitated or not); beginning 1996, as a percent of persons who required services.   [4] An individual with a severe disability is an individual whose severe physical or mental impairment seriously limits one or more functional capacities in terms of an employment outcome, and whose vocational rehabilitation can be expected to require multiple vocational rehabilitation services over an extended period of time.   [5] Includes active cases accepted for rehabilitation services during year plus active cases on hand at beginning of year.
Source: U.S. Dept. of Education, Rehabilitation Services Administration, *Caseload Statistics of State Vocational Rehabilitation Agencies in Fiscal Years*, and *State Vocational Rehabilitation Agency Program Data in Fiscal Years*, both annual.

No. 629. Workers' Compensation Payments: 1980 to 1996

[In billions of dollars, except as indicated (79 represents 79,000,000). See headnote, Table 630]

Item	1980	1985	1989	1990	1991	1992	1993	1994	1995	1996
Workers covered [1] (mil.)	79	84	104	106	104	104	106	109	113	(NA)
Premium amounts paid [2]	22.3	29.2	48.0	53.1	55.2	57.4	60.8	60.5	57.0	55.2
Private carriers [2]	15.7	19.5	31.9	35.1	35.7	34.5	35.6	34.0	31.6	(NA)
State funds	3.0	3.5	7.2	8.0	8.7	9.6	10.9	11.2	10.5	(NA)
Federal programs [3]	1.1	1.7	2.0	2.2	2.1	2.5	2.5	2.5	2.6	(NA)
Self-insurers	2.4	4.5	6.9	7.9	8.7	10.8	11.8	12.8	12.4	(NA)
Annual benefits paid [2]	13.6	22.2	34.3	38.2	42.2	45.7	45.3	44.7	43.5	42.4
By private carriers [2]	7.0	12.3	19.9	22.2	24.5	25.3	24.1	22.6	21.4	20.5
From state funds [4]	4.3	5.7	8.0	8.7	9.7	10.7	10.6	10.6	10.9	10.9
Employers' self-insurance [5]	2.3	4.1	6.4	7.2	7.9	9.7	10.6	11.5	11.2	10.9
Type of benefit:										
Medical/hospitalization	3.9	7.5	13.4	15.2	16.8	17.6	17.5	17.2	16.7	16.6
Compensation payments	9.7	14.7	20.9	23.1	25.3	28.1	27.8	27.5	26.7	25.8
Disability	8.4	13.1	19.2	21.2	23.3	26.0	25.4	25.5	24.8	(NA)
Survivor	1.3	1.7	1.7	1.8	2.0	2.1	2.4	2.0	2.0	(NA)
Percent of covered payroll: [1]										
Workers' compensation costs [6][7]	1.96	1.82	2.04	2.13	2.16	2.13	2.17	2.05	1.83	1.67
Benefits [7]	1.07	1.30	1.43	1.49	1.64	1.66	1.58	1.52	1.39	1.28

NA Not available. [1] Data for years 1980 and 1985 not comparable with later years. [2] Premium and benefit amounts include estimated benefit payments under insurance policy deductible provisions. Deductible benefits are allocated to private carriers and state funds. [3] Includes Federal employer compensation program and that portion of Federal black lung benefits program financed from employer contributions. [4] Net cash and medical benefits paid by competitive and exclusive state funds and by Federal workers' compensation programs, including black lung benefit program. [5] Cash and medical benefits paid by self-insurers, plus value of medical benefits paid by employers carrying workers' compensation policies that exclude standard medical coverage. [6] Premiums written by private carriers and state funds, and benefits paid by self-insurers increased by 5-10 percent prior to 1992 and by 11 percent for 1992-95 for administrative costs. Also includes benefits paid and administrative costs of Federal system for government employees. [7] Excludes programs financed from general revenue—black lung benefits and supplemental pensions in some states.

Source: 1980-1993, U.S. Social Security Administration, *Annual Statistical Supplement* to the *Social Security Bulletin*. Beginning 1994, National Academy of Social Insurance, Washington, DC, *Workers' Compensation: Benefits, Coverage, and Costs, 1994-95*, and *1996, New Estimates*.

No. 630. Workers' Compensation Payments, by State: 1990 to 1996

[In millions of dollars (38,238 represents $38,238,000,000). Calendar-year data, except fiscal-year data for Federal civilian and other programs and for some states with state funds. Payments represent compensation and medical benefits and include insurance losses paid by private insurance carriers (compiled from state workers' compensation agencies and A.M. Best Co); disbursements of state funds (compiled from the A.M. Best Co., state workers' compensation agencies and U.S. Census Bureau); and self-insurance payments, estimated from available state data. Includes benefit payments under Longshore and Harbor Workers' Compensation Act for states in which such payments are made]

State	1990	1993	1994	1995	1996	State	1990	1993	1994	1995	1996
Total [1]	38,238	45,330	44,697	43,512	42,362	Nebraska	137	160	156	141	199
						Nevada	339	553	432	365	383
Alabama	444	[2]479	[2]480	516	525	New Hampshire	169	194	178	169	188
Alaska	113	122	112	106	122	New Jersey	844	968	[2]957	[2]972	931
Arizona	371	402	406	386	459	New Mexico	228	182	162	145	151
Arkansas	229	224	209	159	160	New York	1,752	2,370	[2]2,725	[2]2,780	2,559
California	6,065	7,625	7,390	[2]7,177	6,830	North Carolina	480	671	565	495	501
Colorado	595	683	612	584	679	North Dakota	60	60	75	71	67
Connecticut	694	[2]848	[2]773	[2]733	672	Ohio	1,960	2,353	2,149	2,303	2,432
Delaware	75	[2]88	[2]103	[2]103	115	Oklahoma	369	493	550	580	645
District of Columbia	86	122	115	113	90	Oregon	573	468	468	463	506
Florida	1,976	2,296	2,720	2,518	2,707	Pennsylvania	2,019	[2]2,774	[2]2,582	[2]2,663	2,534
Georgia	735	911	812	699	822	Rhode Island	219	185	160	138	122
Hawaii	216	324	343	326	288	South Carolina	277	[2]344	[2]339	[2]353	372
Idaho	105	125	147	148	128	South Dakota	56	72	78	63	82
Illinois	1,607	1,668	1,582	1,438	1,643	Tennessee	463	487	449	400	432
Indiana	350	364	378	361	410	Texas	2,896	[2]2,694	[2]2,232	[2]2,006	1,820
Iowa	231	240	233	233	261	Utah	187	165	152	140	155
Kansas	266	307	[2]302	[2]280	270	Vermont	61	73	67	65	74
Kentucky	383	595	585	498	507	Virginia	507	539	591	557	560
						Washington	883	1,068	1,087	1,129	1,193
Louisiana	575	531	531	516	557	West Virginia	389	476	510	529	524
Maine	380	341	282	286	314	Wisconsin	561	608	609	608	648
Maryland	505	548	558	522	597	Wyoming	49	76	77	75	74
Massachusetts	1,235	[2]1,017	[2]917	[2]773	700						
Michigan	1,205	[2]1,594	[2]1,589	[2]1,585	1,559	Federal programs:					
Minnesota	582	809	[2]783	[2]733	740	Civilian employees	1,448	1,822	1,859	1,880	1,912
Mississippi	198	214	[2]213	[2]218	224	Black lung benefits [3]	1,435	1,356	1,306	1,222	1,154
Missouri	496	656	785	733	619	Other [4]	11	11	(NA)	(NA)	(NA)
Montana	150	167	154	151	150						

NA Not available. [1] Totals for 1993-95 include an amount for benefits under deductible provisions not distributed by state. [2] Includes benefits under deductible provisions. [3] Includes payments by Social Security Administration and by Department of Labor. [4] Primarily payments made to dependents of reservists who died while on active duty in the Armed Forces.

Source: U.S. Social Security Administration, *Social Security Bulletin*, summer 1995, and selected prior issues. Beginning 1994, National Academy of Social Insurance, Washington, DC, *Workers' Compensation: Benefits, Coverage, and Costs, 1994-95*, and *1996, New Estimates*.

U.S. Census Bureau, Statistical Abstract of the United States: 1999

No. 631. Supplemental Security Income—Recipients and Payments: 1980 to 1997

[As of **December (4,142 represents 4,142,000)**. See also Appendix III]

Program	Unit	1980	1985	1990	1992	1993	1994	1995	1996	1997
Recipients, total [1]	1,000...	4,142	4,138	4,817	5,566	5,984	6,296	6,514	6,614	6,495
Aged	1,000...	1,808	1,504	1,454	1,471	1,475	1,466	1,446	1,413	1,363
Blind	1,000...	78	82	84	85	85	85	84	82	81
Disabled	1,000...	2,256	2,551	3,279	4,010	4,424	4,745	4,984	5,119	5,052
Payments, total [2]	Mil. dol .	7,941	11,060	16,599	22,233	24,557	25,877	27,628	28,792	29,052
Aged	Mil. dol .	2,734	3,035	3,736	4,140	4,248	4,367	4,467	4,507	4,532
Blind	Mil. dol .	190	264	334	371	375	375	375	372	375
Disabled	Mil. dol .	5,014	7,755	12,521	17,711	19,928	21,131	22,782	23,906	24,006
Average monthly payment, total [1]	Dollars..	168	226	299	358	345	351	358	363	351
Aged	Dollars..	128	164	213	227	237	243	251	261	268
Blind	Dollars..	213	274	342	362	359	364	370	379	382
Disabled	Dollars..	198	261	337	407	381	384	389	391	373

[1] Federally administered payments only.   [2] Includes data not available by reason for eligibility.

Source: U.S. Social Security Administration, *Social Security Bulletin*, quarterly, and *Annual Statistical Supplement to the Social Security Bulletin*.

No. 632. Supplemental Security Income (SSI)—Recipients and Payments, by State and Other Area: 1995 to 1997

[Recipients as of **December (6,514 represents 6,514,000)**. Data cover Federal SSI payments and/or federally-administered state supplementation. For explanation of methodology, see Appendix III]

State and other area	Recipients (1,000)			Payments for year (mil. dol.)			State and other area	Recipients (1,000)			Payments for year (mil. dol.)		
	1995	1996	1997	1995	1996	1997		1995	1996	1997	1995	1996	1997
Total .	6,514	6,614	6,495	27,037	28,252	28,371	MT......	14	14	14	53	55	54
U.S....	6,513	6,613	6,494	27,035	28,250	28,368	NE......	21	22	21	76	81	81
AL......	165	167	163	600	631	633	NV......	21	22	22	79	86	88
AK......	7	7	7	27	29	30	NH......	11	11	11	39	42	44
AZ......	73	76	76	288	308	316	NJ......	144	146	144	594	616	628
AR......	94	94	91	326	335	335	NM.....	45	46	45	166	174	177
CA......	1,032	1,045	1,023	5,391	5,594	5,513	NY......	589	606	598	2,724	2,895	2,932
CO......	57	58	56	217	229	230	NC......	191	195	193	639	687	699
CT......	45	46	46	181	194	195	ND......	9	9	9	29	30	30
DE......	11	11	11	40	43	46	OH......	248	254	247	1,044	1,106	1,111
DC......	20	20	20	83	85	85	OK......	74	75	74	266	279	283
FL......	338	353	353	1,300	1,408	1,449	OR......	47	48	48	183	196	198
GA......	199	201	199	692	728	744	PA......	265	270	269	1,159	1,214	1,235
HI......	19	20	19	82	88	89	RI......	24	25	25	100	107	109
ID......	17	17	17	63	67	69	SC......	111	112	110	384	402	410
IL......	267	268	253	1,160	1,199	1,145	SD......	14	14	13	47	50	49
IN......	89	91	89	348	367	370	TN......	180	179	172	648	667	658
IA......	42	42	41	148	153	153	TX......	404	412	407	1,391	1,460	1,491
KS......	38	38	36	141	150	146	UT......	20	21	20	80	85	86
KY......	165	170	168	635	672	676	VT......	13	13	13	50	50	50
LA......	182	182	175	717	731	728	VA......	130	133	131	471	497	507
ME......	31	28	28	96	99	100	WA	92	95	94	398	424	432
MD......	82	85	85	332	353	364	WV	68	70	69	276	294	297
MA......	164	166	168	700	728	740	WI	112	95	91	487	377	370
MI	210	214	209	896	943	945	WY	6	6	6	21	23	23
MN.....	62	64	63	235	250	253	N. Mari-						
MS.....	141	141	136	504	517	518	ana	1	1	1	2	2	3
MO	114	116	113	431	455	453							

Source: U.S. Social Security Administration, *Social Security Bulletin*, quarterly, and *Annual Statistical Supplement* to the *Social Security Bulletin*.

No. 633. Temporary Assistance for Needy Families (TANF)—Families and Recipients: 1980 to 1999

[In thousands (3,642 represents 3,642,000). **Average monthly families and recipients, except as noted**. Prior to TANF, the cash assistance program to families was called Aid to Families With Dependent Children (1980-96). Under the new welfare law (Personal Responsibility and Work Opportunity Reconciliation Act of 1996), the program became TANF. See text, this section. Includes Puerto Rico, Guam, and Virgin Islands]

Year	Families	Recipients	Year	Families	Recipients
1980	3,642	10,597	1990	3,974	11,460
1981	3,871	11,160	1991	4,374	12,592
1982	3,569	10,431	1992	4,768	13,625
1983	3,651	10,659	1993	4,981	14,143
1984	3,725	10,866	1994	5,046	14,226
1985	3,692	10,813	1995	4,876	13,652
1986	3,748	10,997	1996	4,553	12,649
1987	3,784	11,065	1997	3,946	10,936
1988	3,748	10,920	1998	3,179	8,770
1989	3,771	10,934	1999 (March)	2,668	7,335

Source: U.S. Administration for Children and Families, "Temporary Assistance for Needy Families (TANF): 1936-1999;" <http://www.acf.dhhs.gov/news/stats/3697.htm>; (accessed: 20 September 1999).

No. 634. Temporary Assistance for Needy Families (TANF)—Recipients by State and Other Area: 1995 and 1998

[In thousands (4,963 represents 4,963,000). 1995, as of **January**; 1998, as of **September**. See headnote, Table 633]

State and other area	Families 1995	Families 1998	Recipients 1995	Recipients 1998	State and other area	Families 1995	Families 1998	Recipients 1995	Recipients 1998
Total	4,963	2,896	13,931	7,955	MT	12	7	34	20
U.S.	4,904	2,854	13,747	7,826	NE	15	12	42	36
AL	47	22	122	52	NV	16	9	42	23
AK	13	9	37	28	NH	11	6	29	14
AZ	71	37	195	100	NJ	120	69	321	182
AR	25	13	65	31	NM	35	25	105	78
CA	926	657	2,692	1,909	NY	461	316	1,266	862
CO	39	17	111	46	NC	127	70	318	162
CT	61	41	171	118	ND	5	3	15	8
DE	11	7	26	14	OH	233	124	630	320
DC	27	20	72	54	OK	46	22	127	58
FL	241	96	657	246	OR	40	18	108	44
GA	141	69	389	172	PA	209	125	611	346
HI	22	17	65	46	RI	23	19	62	54
ID	9	2	24	3	SC	50	21	134	52
IL	240	152	710	449	SD	6	3	18	9
IN	68	38	197	117	TN	106	57	282	149
IA	37	23	103	63	TX	280	127	765	346
KS	29	13	82	33	UT	17	10	47	28
KY	76	47	194	113	VT	10	7	28	19
LA	82	47	258	122	VA	74	39	189	94
ME	22	14	61	38	WA	103	67	291	185
MD	81	42	228	109	WV	39	12	108	35
MA	105	62	286	166	WI	74	10	214	34
MI	207	108	612	309	WY	5	1	15	2
MN	61	47	180	141	PR	56	39	172	118
MS	53	19	146	45	GU	2	2	8	7
MO	91	55	260	139	VI	1	1	4	4

Source: U.S. Administration for Children and Families, "Change in Welfare Caseloads;" published: 27 January 1999; <http://www.acf.dhhs.gov/news/stats/case-fam.htm>; and "Change in Welfare Caseloads;" published: 27 January 1999; <http://www.acf.dhhs.gov/news/stats/caseload.htm>.

U.S. Census Bureau, Statistical Abstract of the United States: 1999

No. 635. Federal Food Programs: 1980 to 1998

[For fiscal years ending in year shown; see text, Section 9, State and Local Government. Program data include Puerto Rico, Virgin Islands, Guam, American Samoa, Northern Marianas, and the former Trust Territory when a Federal food program was operated in these areas. Participation data are average monthly figures except as noted (21.1 represents 21,100,000). Participants are not reported for the commodity distribution programs. Cost data are direct Federal benefits to recipients; they exclude Federal administrative payments and applicable state and local contributions. Federal costs for commodities and cash-in-lieu of commodities are shown separately from direct cash benefits for those programs receiving both]

Program	Unit	1980	1985	1990	1994	1995	1996	1997	1998
Food Stamp:									
Participants	Million	21.1	19.9	20.1	27.5	26.6	25.5	22.9	19.8
Federal cost	Mil. dol.	8,721	10,744	14,187	22,749	22,765	22,440	19,548	16,879
Monthly average coupon value per recipient	Dollars	34.47	44.99	58.92	69.01	71.27	73.21	71.27	71.08
Nutrition assistance program for Puerto Rico: [1]									
Federal cost	Mil. dol.	(X)	825	937	1,079	1,131	1,143	1,174	1,204
National school lunch program (NSLP):									
Free lunches served	Million	1,671	1,657	1,662	2,049	2,090	2,128	2,194	2,190
Reduced-price lunches served	Million	308	255	273	298	309	326	347	361
Children participating [2]	Million	26.6	23.6	24.1	25.3	25.7	25.9	26.3	26.6
Federal cost	Mil. dol.	2,279	2,578	3,214	4,291	4,467	4,662	4,934	5,084
School breakfast (SB):									
Children participating [2]	Million	3.6	3.4	4.1	5.8	6.3	6.6	6.9	7.1
Federal cost	Mil. dol.	288	379	596	959	1,048	1,119	1,214	1,264
Special supplemental food program (WIC): [3]									
Participants	Million	1.9	3.1	4.5	6.5	6.9	7.2	7.4	7.4
Federal cost	Mil. dol.	584	1,193	1,637	2,325	2,516	2,690	2,815	2,811
Child and adult care (CC): [4]									
Participants [5]	Million	0.7	1.0	1.5	2.2	2.4	2.4	2.5	2.6
Federal cost	Mil. dol.	207	390	720	1,196	1,296	1,360	1,392	1,373
Federal cost of commodities donated to— [6]									
Child nutrition (NSLP, CC, SF, and SB)	Mil. dol.	930	840	646	764	733	734	661	767

X Not applicable. [1] Puerto Rico was included in the food stamp program until June 30, 1982. [2] Average monthly participation (excluding summer months of June through August). Includes children in public and private elementary and secondary schools and in residential child care institutes. [3] WIC serves pregnant and postpartum women, infants, and children up to age 5. [4] Program provides year-round subsidies to feed preschool children in child care centers and family day care homes. Certain care centers serving disabled or elderly adults also receive meal subsidies. [5] Average quarterly daily attendance at participating institutions. [6] Includes the Federal cost of commodity entitlements, cash-in-lieu of commodities, and bonus foods. SF=summer feeding program.

Source: U.S. Dept. of Agriculture, Food and Nutrition Service. In "Annual Historical Review of FNS Programs" and unpublished data.

No. 636. Federal Food Stamp Program, by State: 1995 to 1998

[Participation data are average monthly number (26,619 represents 26,619,000). For years ending Sept. 30. Food stamp costs are for benefits only and exclude administrative expenditures]

State	Persons (1,000)			Benefits (mil. dol.)			State	Persons (1,000)			Benefits (mil. dol.)		
	1995	1997	1998	1995	1997	1998		1995	1997	1998	1995	1997	1998
Total [1]	26,619	22,854	19,787	22,765	19,548	16,879	MS	480	399	329	383	313	254
U.S.	26,579	22,816	19,744	22,714	19,496	16,822	MO	576	478	411	488	401	345
							MT	71	67	62	57	55	52
AL	525	469	427	441	393	357	NE	105	97	95	77	72	68
AK	45	45	42	50	52	50	NV	99	82	72	91	74	63
AZ	480	364	296	414	316	251	NH	58	46	40	44	35	30
AR	272	266	256	212	214	206	NJ	551	491	425	506	449	384
CA	3,175	2,815	2,259	2,473	2,372	2,018	NM	239	205	175	196	168	145
CO	252	217	191	217	182	157	NY	2,183	1,914	1,627	2,065	1,775	1,487
CT	226	210	196	169	170	162	NC	614	586	528	495	478	422
DE	57	54	46	47	41	34	ND	41	38	34	32	29	25
DC	94	90	85	93	91	85	OH	1,155	874	734	1,017	744	607
FL	1,395	1,192	991	1,307	1,061	849	OK	375	322	288	315	256	231
GA	816	698	632	700	597	535	OR	289	259	238	254	216	198
HI	125	127	122	177	189	178	PA	1,173	1,009	907	1,006	865	765
ID	80	70	62	59	53	47	RI	93	85	73	82	70	58
IL	1,151	1,020	923	1,056	933	848	SC	364	349	333	297	281	264
IN	470	348	313	382	293	263	SD	50	47	45	40	39	37
IA	184	161	141	141	125	110	TN	662	586	538	554	475	438
KS	184	149	119	144	112	83	TX	2,558	2,034	1,636	2,246	1,765	1,427
KY	520	444	412	413	372	346	UT	119	98	92	90	78	75
LA	711	575	537	629	512	468	VT	59	53	46	46	40	34
ME	132	124	115	112	103	100	VA	546	476	397	450	379	307
MD	399	354	323	365	320	282	WA	476	445	362	417	387	320
MA	410	340	293	315	262	222	WV	309	287	269	253	239	224
MI	971	839	772	806	678	588	WI	320	232	193	220	158	130
MN	308	260	220	240	192	173	WY	34	29	25	28	23	21

[1] Includes Guam and the Virgin Islands. Several outlying areas receive nutrition assistance grants in lieu of food stamp assistance (e.g., Puerto Rico, American Samoa, and the Northern Marianas).

Source: U.S. Dept. of Agriculture, Food and Nutrition Service. In "Annual Historical Review of FNS Programs" and unpublished data.

400   Social Insurance and Human Services

No. 637. Child Support—Award and Recipiency Status of Custodial Parent: 1995

[In thousands except as noted (13,739 represents 13,739,000). Custodial parents 15 years and older with own children under 21 years of age present from absent parents as of spring 1996. Covers civilian noninstitutional population. Based on Current Population Survey; see text, section 1, Population and Appendix III. For definition of mean, see Guide to Tabular Presentation]

Award and recipiency status	All custodial parents				Custodial parents below poverty level			
	Total				Total			
	Number	Percent distribution	Mothers	Fathers	Number	Percent distribution	Mothers	Fathers
Total.	13,739	(X)	11,634	2,105	4,172	(X)	3,871	301
With child support agreement or award . . .	7,967	(X)	7,123	844	2,103	(X)	1,979	124
Supposed to receive payments in 1995.	6,966	100.0	6,233	733	1,761	100.0	1,654	108
Actually received payments in 1995 . .	4,769	68.5	4,353	416	1,067	60.6	1,024	44
Received full amount	2,718	39.0	2,482	236	432	24.5	415	17
Received partial payments.	2,051	29.4	1,871	180	635	36.1	609	26
Did not receive payments in 1995. . .	2,198	31.6	1,880	318	694	39.4	630	64
Child support not awarded	5,772	(X)	4,511	1,261	2,069	(X)	1,892	177
MEAN INCOME AND CHILD SUPPORT								
Received child support payments in 1995:								
Mean total money income (dol.).	22,543	(X)	21,829	30,030	6,855	(X)	6,855	(B)
Mean child support received (dol.)	3,732	(X)	3,767	3,370	2,531	(X)	2,519	(B)
Received the full amount due:								
Mean total money income (dol.)	25,092	(X)	24,355	32,839	6,734	(X)	6,695	(B)
Mean child support received (dol.). .	5,044	(X)	5,086	4,606	4,082	(X)	4,135	(B)
Received partial payments:								
Mean total money income (dol.). . . .	19,166	(X)	18,477	26,338	6,937	(X)	6,964	(B)
Mean child support received (dol.). .	1,993	(X)	2,016	1,746	1,477	(X)	1,420	(B)
Received no payments in 1995:								
Mean total money income (dol.).	17,398	(X)	16,093	25,122	6,043	(X)	6,160	(B)
Without child support agreement or award:								
Mean total money income (dol.).	18,927	(X)	14,068	36,312	5,660	(X)	5,614	6,152

B Base too small to meet statistical standards for reliability.   X Not applicable.

Source: U.S. Census Bureau, *Current Population Reports*, P60-196.

No. 638. Child Support Enforcement Program—Caseload and Collections: 1980 to 1997

[For years ending Sept. 30 (5,432 represents 5,432,000). Includes Puerto Rico, Guam, and the Virgin Islands. The child support enforcement program locates absent parents, establishes paternity of children born out-of-wedlock, and establishes and enforces support orders. By law, these services are available to all families that need them. The program is operated at the state and local government level but 68 percent of administrative costs are paid by the Federal government. Child support collected for families not receiving Aid to Families with Dependent Children (AFDC) goes to the family to help it remain self-sufficient. Most of the child support collected on behalf of AFDC families goes to Federal and state governments to offset AFDC payments. Based on data reported by state agencies. Minus sign (-) indicates net outlay]

Item	Unit	1980	1985	1990	1993	1994	1995	1996	1997
Total cases	1,000 . . .	5,432	8,401	12,796	17,125	18,610	19,162	19,319	19,057
AFDC and AFDC arrears only caseload . . .	1,000 . . .	(NA)	(NA)	7,953	9,638	10,420	10,379	9,971	9,109
AFDC cases	1,000 . . .	4,583	6,242	5,872	7,472	7,986	7,880	7,380	6,462
AFDC arrears only cases [1]	1,000 . . .	(NA)	(NA)	2,082	2,166	2,434	2,499	2,591	2,647
Non-AFDC cases	1,000 . . .	849	2,159	4,843	7,487	8,190	8,783	9,348	9,948
Cases for which a collection was made:									
AFDC cases	1,000 . . .	503	684	701	879	926	976	940	865
AFDC arrears only cases [1]	1,000 . . .	(NA)	(NA)	224	289	308	343	402	495
Non-AFDC cases	1,000 . . .	243	654	1,363	1,958	2,169	2,408	2,612	2,851
Percentage of cases with collections:									
AFDC cases	Percent .	11.0	11.0	11.9	11.8	11.6	12.4	12.7	13.4
AFDC arrears only cases [1]	Percent .	(NA)	(NA)	10.8	13.4	12.7	13.7	15.5	18.7
Non-AFDC cases	Percent .	28.7	30.3	28.1	26.1	26.5	27.4	27.9	28.7
Absent parents located, total	1,000 . . .	643	878	2,062	3,777	4,204	4,950	5,779	6,420
Paternities established, total	1,000 . . .	144	232	393	554	592	659	718	804
Support orders established, total [2]	1,000 . . .	374	669	1,022	1,026	1,025	1,051	1,082	1,250
FINANCES									
Collections, total . . . . [3]	Mil. dol .	1,478	2,694	6,010	8,907	9,850	10,828	12,020	13,364
AFDC collections [3]	Mil. dol . .	603	1,090	1,750	2,416	2,550	2,690	2,855	2,843
State share	Mil. dol . .	274	415	620	847	891	939	1,014	1,159
Incentive payments to states.	Mil. dol . .	72	145	264	339	407	400	409	412
Federal share.	Mil. dol . .	246	341	533	777	762	822	888	1,044
Payments to AFDC families [4]	Mil. dol . .	10	189	334	446	457	474	480	157
Non-AFDC collections.	Mil. dol . .	874	1,604	4,260	6,491	7,300	8,138	9,165	10,521
Administrative expenditures, total	Mil. dol . .	466	814	1,606	2,241	2,556	3,012	3,049	3,429
State share	Mil. dol . .	117	243	545	724	816	917	1,015	(NA)
Federal share.	Mil. dol . .	349	571	1,061	1,517	1,741	2,095	2,040	(NA)
Program savings, total.	Mil. dol . .	127	86	-190	-278	-496	-852	-738	-801
State share	Mil. dol . .	230	317	338	462	482	422	408	(NA)
Federal share.	Mil. dol . .	-103	-231	-528	-740	-978	-1,273	-1,151	(NA)
Total fees and costs recovered for non-AFDC cases	Mil. dol . .	5	3	22	31	33	33	37	41
Percentage of AFDC payments recovered .	Percent .	5.2	7.3	10.3	12.0	12.5	13.6	15.5	(NA)

NA Not available.   [1] Reflects cases that are no longer receiving AFDC but still have outstanding child support due.
[2] Through 1990 includes modifications to orders.   [3] Beginning 1993 includes medical support payments not shown separately.
[4] Beginning 1985, states were required to pass along to the family the first $50 of any current child support collected each month.

Source: U.S. Department of Health and Human Services, Office of Child Support Enforcement, *Annual Report to Congress*.

Social Insurance and Human Services   401

No. 639. Regular Child Care Arrangements for Children Under 6 Years Old, by Type of Arrangement: 1995

[In percent, except as indicated (21,421 represents 21,421,000). Estimates are based on children under 6 years old who have yet to enter kindergarten. Based on 14,064 interviews from a sample survey of the civilian, noninstitutional population in households with telephones; see source for details]

Characteristic	Children		Type of nonparental arrangement				No non-parental arrange-ment
	Number (1,000)	Percent distribution	Total [1]	In relative care	In non-relative care	In center-based program [2]	
Total................	21,421	100	60	21	18	31	40
Race-ethnicity:							
White, non-Hispanic........	13,996	65	62	18	21	33	38
Black, non-Hispanic.........	3,344	16	66	31	12	33	34
Hispanic................	2,838	13	46	23	12	17	54
Other................	1,243	6	58	25	13	28	42
Mother's employment status: [3]							
35 or more hours per week....	7,101	34	88	33	32	39	12
Less than 35 hours per week ..	4,034	19	75	30	26	35	25
Looking for work...........	1,635	8	42	16	4	25	58
Not in labor force	8,354	40	32	7	6	22	68
Household income:							
Less than $10,001	4,502	21	50	22	10	25	50
$10,001 to $20,000.........	2,909	14	54	27	12	24	46
$20,001 to $30,000.........	3,385	16	53	22	14	25	47
$30,001 to $40,000.........	3,047	14	60	23	20	27	40
$40,001 to $50,000.........	2,304	11	63	19	22	32	37
$50,001 to $75,000.........	3,063	14	74	20	26	40	26
$75,001 or more...........	2,211	10	77	14	30	49	23

[1] Columns do not add to total because some children participated in more than one type of nonparental arrangement. [2] Center-based programs include day care centers, head start programs, preschool, prekindergartens, and other early childhood programs. [3] Children without mothers are not included.

Source: U.S. National Center for Education Statistics, *Statistics in Brief*, October 1995 (NCES 95-824).

No. 640. Licensed Child Care Centers and Family Child Care Providers, by State: 1998

[Centers as of February; family child care providers as of August]

State	Licensed child care centers	Licensed family child care providers	State	Licensed child care centers	Licensed family child care providers
United States......	98,374	290,817	Missouri	1,515	2,570
			Montana	251	1,580
Alabama	1,335	3,195	Nebraska	743	3,844
Alaska	226	1,484	Nevada............	405	636
Arizona............	1,483	1,557	New Hampshire	790	451
Arkansas...........	1,935	1,562			
California...........	12,885	36,422	New Jersey	3,200	4,400
			New Mexico	600	241
Colorado...........	2,396	6,040	New York	3,374	19,169
Connecticut	1,555	5,287	North Carolina	3,670	4,824
Delaware...........	262	1,980	North Dakota	98	2,887
District of Columbia....	360	234			
Florida	5,971	8,477	Ohio..............	3,760	8,826
			Oklahoma	1,818	4,113
Georgia	1,148	6,309	Oregon............	930	10,660
Hawaii	494	500	Pennsylvania	3,416	4,663
Idaho	511	1,360	Rhode Island	340	758
Illinois.............	2,725	9,594			
Indiana............	659	3,285	South Carolina.......	1,689	2,038
			South Dakota........	153	1,150
Iowa..............	1,555	4,796	Tennessee..........	2,693	2,856
Kansas............	1,377	8,315	Texas	7,575	13,760
Kentucky...........	1,861	825	Utah..............	320	2,690
Louisiana	1,907	10,000			
Maine.............	904	2,400	Vermont	500	1,440
			Virginia	2,340	4,953
Maryland...........	2,125	12,202	Washington	1,837	8,725
Massachusetts.......	2,221	11,005	West Virginia	307	5,000
Michigan...........	4,619	17,035	Wisconsin	2,269	7,516
Minnesota..........	1,514	15,559	Wyoming...........	210	736
Mississippi.........	1,543	908			

Source: Children's Foundation, Washington, DC, *1998 Child Care Licensing Study* and *1998 Family Child Care Licensing Study* (copyright).

No. 641. Foster Care—Homes and Children in Out-of-Home Care, by State: 1995 and 1996

[Number of foster homes covers only licensed, certified and approved foster homes. Out-of-home care includes children placed into family foster care, kinship (relative) foster care, group homes, and residential group care]

State	Number of foster homes, 1995	Children in out-of-home care Number, 1995	1996 Number	1996 Rate per 1,000 children
United States...	142,374	483,629	530,496	7.7
Alabama	1,528	3,593	3,941	3.7
Alaska	931	1,881	1,770	9.6
Arizona	1,669	5,979	6,158	5.4
Arkansas	612	2,507	2,449	3.7
California	(NA)	74,364	104,406	11.8
Colorado	3,347	7,186	7,415	7.4
Connecticut	1,427	7,839	7,042	8.8
Delaware	300	851	821	4.7
Florida	4,929	10,789	24,129	7.0
Georgia	3,614	14,582	15,426	7.9
Hawaii	1,086	1,652	1,921	6.3
Idaho	759	913	827	2.4
Illinois	13,667	53,342	54,540	17.3
Indiana	4,991	9,649	9,849	6.6
Iowa	2,365	4,195	4,197	5.8
Kansas	(NA)	6,345	6,264	9.1
Kentucky	1,636	3,800	3,510	3.6
Louisiana	2,628	6,034	6,203	5.0
Maine	1,169	2,312	2,488	8.3
Maryland	3,341	11,818	11,768	9.1
Massachusetts	7,033	13,241	13,046	9.2
Michigan	6,850	14,987	15,663	6.2
Minnesota	5,000	8,452	8,654	6.9
Mississippi	978	2,945	3,089	4.1
Missouri	4,135	9,423	10,272	7.4
Montana	(NA)	1,606	2,422	10.4
Nebraska	629	3,326	3,446	7.8
Nevada	711	2,486	2,218	5.3
New Hampshire	880	1,527	1,644	5.6
New Jersey	3,598	8,014	8,651	4.4
New Mexico	633	2,064	1,872	3.7
New York	20,410	53,562	53,285	11.7
North Carolina	4,098	12,692	10,880	5.9
North Dakota	560	1,102	912	5.4
Ohio	9,145	17,134	18,811	6.6
Oklahoma	1,516	5,063	5,937	6.7
Oregon	3,134	5,937	6,300	7.8
Pennsylvania	(NA)	23,653	21,377	7.4
Rhode Island	611	3,284	2,721	11.6
South Carolina	1,620	5,181	5,036	5.4
South Dakota	481	922	795	3.9
Tennessee	2,724	9,511	9,114	6.9
Texas	3,452	15,734	15,008	2.8
Utah	1,029	2,118	2,333	3.4
Vermont	990	1,483	1,356	9.2
Virginia	4,500	6,973	6,788	4.2
Washington	6,867	9,715	8,841	6.2
West Virginia	791	2,954	3,113	7.4
Wisconsin	(NA)	7,875	8,424	6.3
Wyoming	(NA)	1,034	1,192	8.9

NA Not available.

Source: Petit, M.R. & Curtis, P.A., *Child Abuse and Neglect: A Look at the States, 1998 CWLA Stat Book*, and previous editions, Child Welfare League of America, Washington, DC, 1998 (copyright).

No. 642. Head Start—Enrollment and Congressional Appropriations: 1970 to 1997

[For fiscal years ending in year shown; see text, Section 9, State and Local Government (477 represents 477,000)]

Year	Enrollment (1,000)	Appropriation (mil. dol.)	Year	Enrollment (1,000)	Appropriation (mil. dol.)	Age and race	Enrollment, 1997 (percent)
1970	477	326	1984	442	996	Under 3 years old	4
1971	398	360	1985	452	1,075	3 years old	30
1972	379	376	1986	452	1,040	4 years old	60
1973	379	401	1987	447	1,131	5 years old and over	6
1974	353	404	1988	448	1,206		
1975	349	404	1989	451	1,235	White	31
1976	349	441	1990	541	1,552	Black	36
1977	333	475	1991	583	1,952	Hispanic	26
1978	391	625	1992	621	2,202	American Indian	4
1979	388	680	1993	714	2,776	Asian	3
1980	376	735	1994	740	3,326		
1981	387	819	1995	751	3,534		
1982	396	912	1996	752	3,569		
1983	415	912	1997	794	3,981		

Source: U.S. Administration for Children and Families, "Head Start 1998 Fact Sheet;" <http://www.acf.dhhs.gov/programs/hsb/facts98.htm>; (accessed: 22 July 1998).

Social Insurance and Human Services   403

No. 643. Percent of Adult Population Doing Volunteer Work: 1995

[Volunteers are persons who worked in some way to help others for no monetary pay during the previous year. Based on a sample survey of 2,719 persons 18 years old and over conducted during the spring of the following year and subject to sampling variability; see source]

Age, sex, race, and Hispanic origin	Percent of population volunteering	Average hours volunteered per week	Educational attainment and household income	Percent of population volunteering	Average hours volunteered per week	Type of activity	Percent of population involved in activity
Total........	48.8	4.2	Elementary school ...	18.7	(B)	Arts, culture, humanities..	6.2
			Some high school....	26.1	3.3	Education	17.5
18-24 years old.....	38.4	2.8	High school graduate .	43.1	4.0	Environment	7.1
25-34 years old.....	50.8	4.3	Technical, trade, or			Health............	13.2
35-44 years old.....	55.0	4.3	business school....	51.2	4.4	Human services	12.7
45-54 years old.....	55.3	4.5	Some college	56.3	3.9		
55-64 years old.....	47.9	4.8	College graduate	70.7	4.8	Informal	20.3
65-74 years old.....	44.7	4.1				International, foreign	1.6
75 years old and over.	33.7	4.4	Under $10,000......	34.7	3.6	Political organizations ...	3.8
			$10,000-$19,999	34.3	3.2	Private, community	
Male	45.1	4.2	$20,000-$29,999	45.2	3.7	foundations	2.7
Female	52.2	4.2	$30,000-$39,999	46.0	3.7		
			$40,000-$49,999	52.7	5.8	Public and societal benefit	6.7
White	51.9	4.2	$50,000-$59,999	64.1	5.1	Recreation - adults	7.3
Black...........	35.3	4.5	$60,000-$74,999	56.4	4.4	Religion	25.8
			$75,000-$99,999	64.8	4.0	Work-related organizations	7.9
Hispanic [1]	40.4	4.3	$100,000 or more....	69.4	4.4	Youth development	15.4

B Base figure too small to meet statistical standards for reliability.   [1] Hispanic persons may be of any race.

No. 644. Charity Contributions—Average Dollar Amount and Percent of Household Income, 1991 to 1995, and by Age of Respondent and Household Income, 1995

[Estimates cover households' contribution activity for the year and are based on respondents' replies as to contribution and volunteer activity of household. See headnote, Table 643]

Year and age	All contributing households		Contributors and volunteers		Household income	All contributing households		Contributors and volunteers	
	Average amount (dol.)	Percent of household income	Average amount (dol.)	Percent of household income		Average amount (dol.)	Percent of household income	Average amount (dol.)	Percent of household income
1991	899	2.2	1,155	2.6	**1995—**				
1993	880	2.1	1,193	2.6	Under $10,000 ...	295	4.3	(B)	(B)
1995, total.....	1,017	2.2	1,279	2.6	$10,000-$19,999 ..	425	2.8	444	2.9
18-24 years.....	287	0.7	344	0.7	$20,000-$29,999 ..	578	2.3	658	2.6
25-34 years.....	743	1.6	922	2.0	$30,000-$39,999 ..	722	2.1	928	2.7
35-44 years.....	1,342	2.6	1,653	3.0	$40,000-$49,999 ..	576	1.3	677	1.5
45-54 years.....	955	1.8	1,142	2.1	$50,000-$59,999 ..	1,001	1.8	1,142	2.1
55-64 years.....	1,791	3.6	2,473	4.5	$60,000-$74,999 ..	1,301	1.9	1,443	2.1
65-74 years.....	980	2.8	1,125	3.0	$75,000-$99,999 ..	1,582	1.8	1,682	2.0
75 years and over..	839	3.7	1,078	5.0	$100,000 and over.	3,379	3.4	4,195	4.2

B Base too small to meet statistical standards for reliability.

No. 645. Charity Contributions—Percent of Households Contributing, by Dollar Amount, 1991 to 1995, and Type of Charity, 1995

[In percent, except as noted. See headnote, Tables 643 and 644]

Annual amount of household contributions	All households			Givers			Type of charity	1995 Percentage of households	1995 Average contribution [1] (dol.)
	1991	1993	1995	1991	1993	1995			
None	27.8	26.6	31.5	(X)	(X)	(X)	Arts, culture, humanities.	9.4	216
Givers	72.2	73.4	68.5	100.0	100.0	100.0	Education	20.3	318
$1 to $100....	14.9	20.9	15.2	24.9	32.3	24.3	Environment........	11.5	106
$101 to $200 ..	8.1	9.8	7.2	13.5	15.2	11.6	Health............	27.3	214
$201 to $300 ..	7.3	5.6	5.7	12.2	8.6	9.2	Human services	25.1	271
$301 to $400 ..	3.3	3.7	4.7	5.6	5.8	7.5	International.........	6.1	283
$401 to $500 ..	3.2	4.0	5.2	5.4	6.2	8.3	Private, community		
$501 to $600 ..	2.6	3.0	3.0	4.4	4.6	4.7	foundations	6.1	181
$601 to $700 ..	2.5	2.0	2.6	4.2	3.1	4.1	Public, societal benefit ..	10.3	122
$701 to $999 ..	3.4	2.9	3.7	5.7	4.6	6.0	Recreation - adults	7.0	161
$1,000 or more.	14.5	12.8	15.2	24.2	19.7	24.3	Religion...........	48.0	868
Not reported ..	12.4	8.6	5.9	(X)	(X)	(X)	Youth development	20.9	137

X Not applicable.   [1] Average contribution per contributing household.

Source of Tables 643-645: Hodgkinson, Virginia, Murray Weitzman, and the Gallup Organization, Inc., *Giving and Volunteering in the United States: 1996 Edition.* (Copyright and published by INDEPENDENT SECTOR, Washington, DC, fall 1996.)

No. 646. Private Philanthropy Funds, by Source and Allocation: 1980 to 1997

[In billions of dollars (48.6 represents $48,600,000,000). Estimates for sources of funds based on U.S. Internal Revenue Service reports of individual charitable deductions, household surveys of giving by Independent Sector, and, for 1980 and 1985, an econometric model. For corporate giving, data are those prepared by the Council for Aid to Education. Data about foundation donations are based upon surveys of foundations and data provided by the Foundation Center. Estimates of the allocation of funds were derived from surveys of nonprofits conducted by source and other groups]

Source and allocation	1980	1985	1988	1989	1990	1991	1992	1993	1994	1995	1996	1997
Total funds	48.6	71.7	88.0	98.4	101.4	105.0	110.4	116.5	119.2	124.3	133.5	143.5
Individuals	40.7	57.4	70.0	79.5	81.0	84.3	87.7	92.0	92.5	95.7	102.4	109.3
Foundations	2.8	4.9	6.2	6.6	7.2	7.7	8.6	9.5	9.7	10.6	12.0	13.4
Corporations	2.3	4.6	5.3	5.5	5.5	5.3	5.9	6.5	7.0	7.3	7.6	8.2
Charitable bequests	2.9	4.8	6.6	7.0	7.6	7.8	8.2	8.5	10.0	10.7	11.5	12.6
Allocation:												
Religion	22.2	38.2	45.2	47.8	49.8	50.0	54.9	56.3	60.2	66.3	70.7	75.0
Health	5.3	7.7	9.6	9.9	9.9	9.7	10.2	10.8	11.5	12.6	13.9	14.0
Education	5.0	8.2	10.2	11.0	12.4	13.5	14.3	15.4	16.6	17.6	19.2	21.5
Human service	4.9	8.5	10.5	11.4	11.8	11.1	11.6	12.5	11.7	11.7	12.2	12.7
Arts, culture and humanities . .	3.2	5.1	6.8	7.5	7.9	8.8	9.3	9.6	9.7	10.0	10.9	10.6
Public/societal benefit	1.5	2.2	3.2	3.8	4.9	4.9	5.1	5.4	6.1	7.1	7.6	8.4
Environment/wildlife	(¹)	(¹)	2.2	1.9	2.5	2.8	2.9	3.0	3.3	3.8	3.8	4.1
International	(¹)	(¹)	0.9	1.0	1.3	1.5	1.5	1.6	1.9	1.8	1.7	2.0
Unclassified ²	4.6	-2.9	-4.4	-0.3	-3.0	-1.7	-4.4	-4.4	-8.2	-13.9	-15.7	-16.0
Gifts to foundations	2.0	4.7	3.9	4.4	3.8	4.5	5.0	6.3	6.3	7.5	9.3	11.2

¹ Included in "Unclassified."   ² Money received by charities but not allocated to sources.

Source: AAFRC Trust for Philanthropy, New York, NY, *Giving USA* annual (copyright).

No. 647. Foundations—Number and Finances, by Asset Size: 1997

[Figures are for latest year reported by foundations (329,910 represents $329,910,000,000). Covers nongovernmental nonprofit organizations with funds and programs managed by their own trustees or directors, whose goals were to maintain or aid social, educational, religious, or other activities deemed to serve the common good. Excludes organizations that make general appeals to the public for funds, act as trade associations for industrial or other special groups, or do not currently award grants]

Asset size	Number	Assets (mil. dol.)	Gifts received (mil. dol.)	Expenditures (mil. dol.)	Grants (mil. dol.)	Percent distribution				
						Number	Assets	Gifts received	Expenditures	Grants
Total	44,146	329,910	15,833	20,049	15,985	100.0	100.0	100.0	100.0	100.0
Under $50,000	7,739	134	345	444	413	17.5	(Z)	2.2	2.2	2.6
$50,000-$99,999	3,414	249	102	131	112	7.7	0.1	0.6	0.7	0.7
$100,000-$249,999	6,553	1,087	265	290	227	14.8	0.3	1.7	1.4	1.4
$250,000-$499,999	5,701	2,066	335	328	276	12.9	0.6	2.1	1.6	1.7
$500,000-$999,999	5,644	4,033	504	470	392	12.8	1.2	3.2	2.3	2.5
$1,000,000-$4,999,999	9,643	21,738	2,126	2,025	1,686	21.8	6.6	13.4	10.1	10.5
$5,000,000-$9,999,999 . . .	2,236	15,742	1,281	1,266	1,007	5.1	4.8	8.1	6.3	6.3
$10,000,000-$49,999,999 . . .	2,439	51,459	3,706	3,815	3,131	5.5	15.6	23.4	19.0	19.6
$50,000,000-$99,999,999 . . .	385	27,067	1,758	1,678	1,356	0.9	8.2	11.1	8.4	8.5
$100,000,000-$249,999,999 . .	227	35,608	1,687	2,084	1,644	0.5	10.8	10.7	10.4	10.3
$250,000,000 or more	165	170,728	3,724	7,518	5,743	0.4	51.7	23.5	37.5	35.9

Z Less than 0.05 percent.

Source: The Foundation Center, New York, NY, *Guide to U.S. Foundations, Their Trustees, Officers, and Donors*, annual.

No. 648. Foundations—Grants Reported, by Subject Field and Recipient Organization: 1997

[Covers grants of $10,000 or more in size. Based on reports of 1,016 foundations. Grant sample totaling $7.9 billion represented over half of all grant dollars awarded by private, corporate, and community foundations. For definition of foundations, see headnote, Table 647]

Subject field	Number of grants		Dollar value		Recipient organization [1]	Number of grants		Dollar value	
	Number	Percent distribution	Amount (mil. dol.)	Percent distribution		Number	Percent distribution	Amount (mil. dol.)	Percent distribution
Total	86,203	100.0	7,945	100.0	Arts/humanities org.	3,093	3.6	240	3.0
Arts and culture	12,424	14.4	1,013	12.7	Community improvement				
Education	18,285	21.2	1,902	23.9	organizations	4,218	4.9	360	4.5
Environment & animals . .	4,992	5.8	414	5.2	Educational institutions	24,258	28.1	2,968	37.4
Health	11,366	13.2	1,324	16.7	Colleges & universities . . .	12,079	14.0	1,672	21.0
Human services	19,630	22.8	1,227	15.4	Educational support				
International affairs,					agencies	5,271	6.1	610	7.7
development & peace . .	2,720	3.2	300	3.8	Schools	4,725	5.5	340	4.3
Public/societal benefit . .	10,176	11.8	970	12.2	Hospitals/medical care				
Science and technology .	2,352	2.7	428	5.4	facilities	3,743	4.3	391	4.9
Social sciences	1,691	2.0	199	2.5	Human service agencies	15,665	18.2	861	10.8
Religion	2,454	2.8	158	2.0	Museums/historical societies .	3,525	4.1	364	4.6
Other	113	0.1	9	0.1	Recreation organizations . . .	967	1.1	81	1.0

[1] Grants may be awarded to multiple types of recipient organizations and would thereby be double-counted.

Source: The Foundation Center, New York, NY, *The Foundation Grants Index*, 1998.

U.S. Census Bureau, Statistical Abstract of the United States: 1999

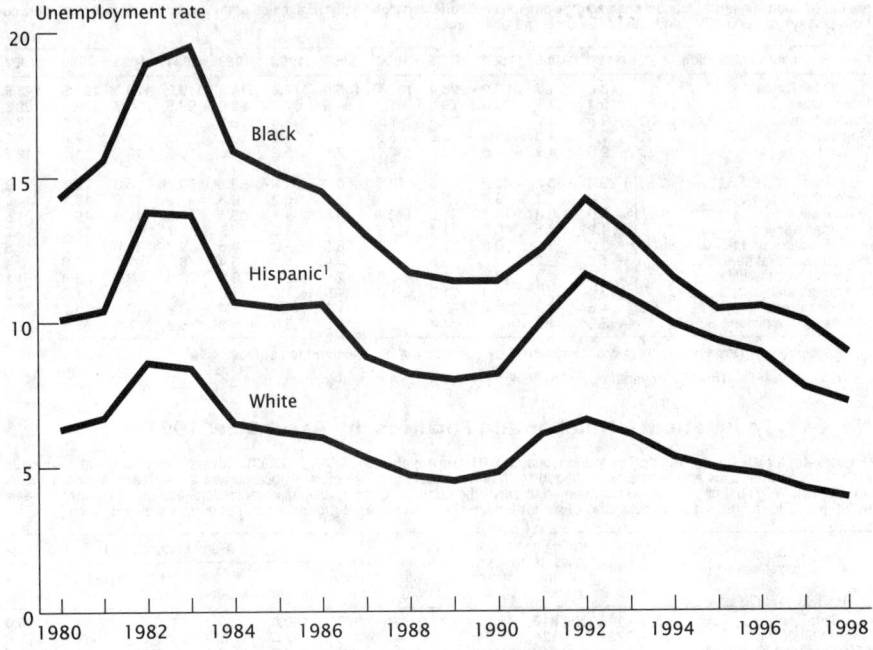

Figure 13.1
Unemployment Rate, by Race and Hispanic Origin: 1980 to 1998

Unemployment rate

Black

Hispanic[1]

White

[1] Persons of Hispanic origin may be of any race.
Source: Chart prepared by U.S. Census Bureau. For data, see Table 651.

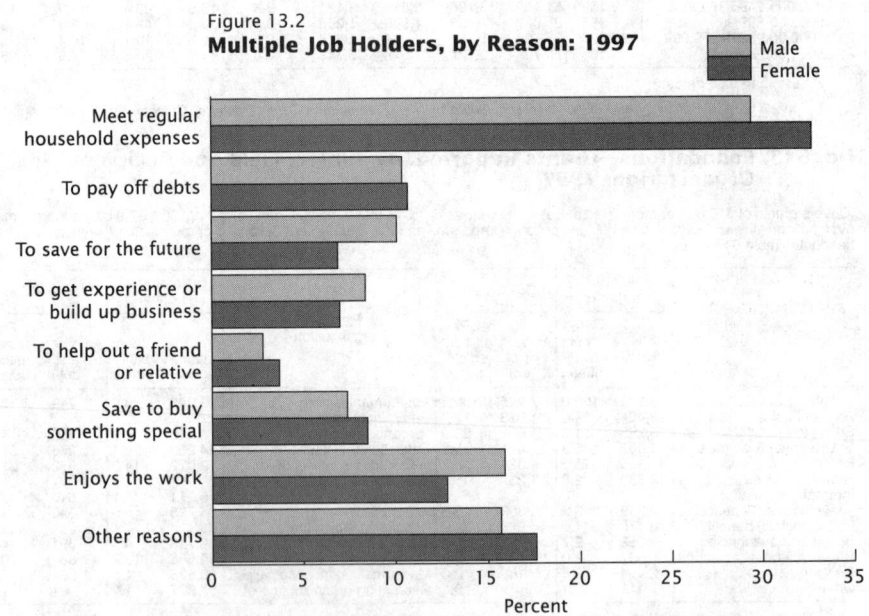

Figure 13.2
Multiple Job Holders, by Reason: 1997

Male
Female

Meet regular household expenses

To pay off debts

To save for the future

To get experience or build up business

To help out a friend or relative

Save to buy something special

Enjoys the work

Other reasons

Percent

Source: Chart prepared by U.S. Census Bureau. For data, see Table 669.

406 Labor Force, Employment, and Earnings

Section 13
Labor Force, Employment, and Earnings

This section presents statistics on the labor force; its distribution by occupation and industry affiliation; and the supply of, demand for, and conditions of labor. The chief source of these data is the Current Population Survey (CPS) conducted by the U.S. Census Bureau for the Bureau of Labor Statistics (BLS). Comprehensive historical and current data are available from the BLS Internet site <http://stats.bls.gov/cpshome.htm>. These data are published on a current basis by the BLS monthly publication *Employment and Earnings*. Detailed data on the labor force are also available from the Census Bureau's decennial census of population.

Types of data—Most statistics in this section are obtained by two methods: household interviews or questionnaires and reports of establishment payroll records. Each method provides data which the other cannot suitably supply. Population characteristics, for example, are readily obtainable only from the household survey, while detailed industrial classifications can be readily derived only from establishment records.

Household data are obtained from a monthly sample survey of the population. The CPS is used to gather data for the calendar week including the 12th of the month and provides current comprehensive data on the labor force (see text, Section 1, Population). The CPS provides information on the work status of the population without duplication since each person is classified as employed, unemployed, or not in the labor force. Employed persons holding more than one job are counted only once, according to the job at which they worked the most hours during the survey week.

Monthly, quarterly, and annual data from the CPS are published by the Bureau of Labor Statistics in *Employment and Earnings*.

Data presented include national totals of the number of persons in the civilian labor force by sex, race, Hispanic origin, and age; the number employed; hours of work; industry and occupational groups; and the number unemployed, reasons for, and duration of unemployment. Annual data shown in this section are averages of monthly figures for each calendar year, unless otherwise specified.

The CPS also produces annual estimates of employment and unemployment for each state, 50 large metropolitan statistical areas, and selected cities. These estimates are published by BLS in its annual *Geographic Profile of Employment and Unemployment*. More detailed geographic data (e.g., for counties and cities) are provided by the decennial population censuses.

Data based on establishment records are compiled by BLS and cooperating state agencies as part of an ongoing Current Employment Statistics program. Survey data, gathered monthly from a sample of employers through mail questionnaires or electronic interviewing, are supplemented by data from other government agencies and adjusted at intervals to data from government social insurance program reports. The estimates exclude self-employed persons, private household workers, unpaid family workers, agricultural workers, and the Armed Forces. In March 1998, reporting establishments employed 8 million manufacturing workers (44 percent of the total manufacturing employment at the time), 19 million workers in private nonmanufacturing industries (22 percent of the total in private nonmanufacturing), and 15 million Federal, state, and local government employees (76 percent of total government).

The establishment survey counts workers each time they appear on a payroll during the reference period (as with the CPS, the

Labor Force, Employment, and Earnings   407

week including the 12th of the month). Thus, unlike the CPS, a person with two jobs is counted twice. The establishment survey is designed to provide detailed industry information for the Nation, states, and metropolitan areas on nonfarm wage and salary employment, average weekly hours, and average hourly and weekly earnings. Establishment survey data also are published in *Employment and Earnings*. Historical national data are available on the site <http://stats.bls.gov/ceshome.htm>.

Labor force—According to the CPS definitions, the civilian labor force comprises all civilians in the noninstitutional population 16 years and over classified as "employed" or "unemployed" according to the following criteria: Employed civilians comprise (a) all civilians, who, during the reference week, did any work for pay or profit (minimum of an hour's work) or worked 15 hours or more as unpaid workers in a family enterprise and (b) all civilians who were not working but who had jobs or businesses from which they were temporarily absent for noneconomic reasons (illness, weather conditions, vacation, labor-management dispute, etc.) whether they were paid for the time off or were seeking other jobs. Unemployed persons comprise all civilians who had no employment during the reference week, who made specific efforts to find a job within the previous 4 weeks (such as applying directly to an employer, or to a public employment service, or checking with friends) and who were available for work during that week, except for temporary illness. Persons on layoff from a job and expecting recall also are classified as unemployed. All other civilian persons, 16 years old and over, are "not in the labor force."

Beginning in 1982, changes in the estimation procedures and the introduction of 1980 census data caused substantial increases in the population and estimates of persons in all labor force categories. Rates on labor force characteristics, however, were essentially unchanged. In order to avoid major breaks in series, some 30,000 labor force series were adjusted back to 1970. The effect of the 1982 revisions on various data series and an explanation of the adjustment procedure used are described in "Revisions in the Current Population Survey in January 1982," in the February 1982 issue of *Employment and Earnings*. The revisions did not, however, smooth out the breaks in series occurring between 1972 and 1979, and data users should make allowances for them in making certain data comparisons.

Beginning in January 1985, and again in January 1986, the CPS estimation procedures were revised due to the implementation of a new sample design (for the 1985 revision) and to reflect an explicit estimate of the number of undocumented immigrants (for the 1986 revision). The greatest impact of these revisions was on estimates of persons of Hispanic origin. Where possible these estimates were revised back to January 1980. A description of the changes and an indication of their effect on the national estimates of labor force characteristics appear in the February 1985 and February 1986 issues of *Employment and Earnings*, respectively.

Beginning in January 1994, several changes were introduced into the CPS that effect all data comparisons with prior years. These changes include the results of a major redesign of the survey questionnaire and collection methodology, revisions to some of the labor force concepts and definitions, and the introduction of 1990 census population controls, adjusted for the estimated undercount. An explanation of the changes and their effects on the labor force data appears in "Revisions in the Current Population Survey Effective January 1994" in the February 1994 issue of *Employment and Earnings*.

Beginning 1996, 1990 census population controls, adjusted for the estimated undercount, were extended back to January 1990. A discussion of the changes and their effects on the labor force data appears in "Revisions In Household Survey Data Effective February 1996" in the March 1996 issue of *Employment and Earnings*.

Beginning in January 1997, the CPS reflects updated 1990 census-based population controls. The greatest impact of the new population controls was on estimates for persons of Hispanic origin. An explanation of the changes and their effects on labor force estimates appear in "Revisions in the Current Population Survey Effective January 1997" in the February 1997 issue of *Employment and Earnings*.

Beginning in January 1998, the CPS reflects the introduction of new composite estimation procedures and revised 1990 census-based controls. An explanation of the changes and their effects on labor force estimates appear in "Revisions in the Current Population Survey Effective January 1998" in the February 1998 issue of *Employment and Earnings*.

Hours and earnings—Average hourly earnings, based on establishment data, are gross earnings (i.e., earnings before payroll deductions) and include overtime premiums; they exclude irregular bonuses and value of payments in kind. Hours are those for which pay was received. Wages and salaries from the CPS consist of total monies received for work performed by an employee during the income year. It includes wages, salaries, commissions, tips, piece-rate payments, and cash bonuses earned before deductions were made for taxes, bonds, union dues, etc. Persons who worked 35 hours or more are classified as working full time.

Industry and Occupational groups—Industry data derived from the CPS for 1983-91 utilize the 1980 census industrial classification developed from the 1972 SIC. CPS data from 1971 to 1982 were based on the 1970 census classification system which was developed from the 1967 SIC. Most of the industry categories were not affected by the change in classification.

Establishments responding to the establishment survey are classified according to the *Standard Industrial Classification (SIC) Manual*. See text, Section 17, Business, for information about the SIC manual.

The occupational classification system used in the 1980 census and in the CPS for 1983-91, evolved from the 1980 Standard Occupational Classification (SOC) system, first introduced in 1977. Occupational categories used in the 1980 census classification system are so radically different from the 1970 census system used in the CPS through 1982, that their implementation represented a break in historical data series. In cases where data have not yet been converted to the 1980 classifications and still reflect the 1970 classifications (e.g., Table 704), comparisons between the two systems should not be made. To help users bridge the data gap, a limited set of estimates was developed for the 1972-82 period based on the new classifications. The estimates were developed by means of applying conversion factors created by double coding a 20-percent sample of CPS occupational records for 6 months during 1981-82. For further details, contact BLS.

Beginning in January 1992, the occupational and industrial classification system used in the 1990 census were introduced into the CPS. (These systems were largely based on the 1980 Standard Occupational Classification and the 1987 Standard Industrial Classification.) There were a few breaks in comparability between the 1980 and 1990 census-based systems, particularly within the "technical, sales, and administrative support" categories. The most notable changes in industry classification were the shift of several industries from "business services" to "professional services" and the splitting of some industries into smaller, more detailed categories. A number of industry titles were changed as well, with no change in content.

Productivity—BLS publishes data on productivity as measured by output per hour (labor productivity), output per combined unit of labor and capital input (multifactor productivity), and, for manufacturing industries, output per combined unit of capital, labor, energy, materials, and purchased service inputs. Labor productivity and related indexes are published for the business sector as a whole and its major subsectors: nonfarm business, manufacturing, nonfinancial corporations, 178 specific industries, and various functional areas of the Federal Government. Multifactor

Labor Force, Employment, and Earnings 409

productivity and related measures are published for the private business sector and its major subsectors. Productivity indexes which take into account capital, labor, energy, materials, and service inputs are published for the 21 major industry groups which comprise the manufacturing sector, the utility services industry group, and for the following industries: cotton and synthetic broadwoven fabrics, household furniture, tire and inner tubes, footwear, steel, metal stampings, farm and garden machinery, refrigeration and heating equipment, motor vehicles, and railroad transportation industries. The major sector data are published in the BLS quarterly news release, *Productivity and Costs* and in the annual *Multifactor Productivity Measures* release. The specific industry productivity measures are published annually in the BLS Bulletin, *Productivity Measures for Selected Industries and Government Services*. Detailed information on methods, limitations, and data sources appears in the BLS *Handbook of Methods*, BLS Bulletin 2490 (1997), Chapters 10 and 11.

Unions—As defined here, unions include traditional labor unions and employee associations similar to labor unions. Data on union membership status provided by BLS are for employed wage and salary workers and relate to their principal job. Earnings by union membership status are usual weekly earnings of full-time wage and salary workers. The information is collected through the Current Population Survey. Collective bargaining settlements data are available for bargaining situations involving 1,000 or more workers in private industry and state and local government.

Work stoppages—Work stoppages include all strikes and lockouts known to BLS which last for at least 1 full day or shift and involve 1,000 or more workers. All stoppages, whether or not authorized by a union, legal or illegal, are counted. Excluded are work slowdowns and instances where employees report to work late or leave early to attend mass meetings or mass rallies.

Seasonal adjustment—Many economic statistics reflect a regularly recurring seasonal movement which can be estimated on the basis of past experience. By eliminating that part of the change which can be ascribed to usual seasonal variation (e.g., climate or school openings and closings), it is possible to observe the cyclical and other nonseasonal movements in the series. However, in evaluating deviations from the seasonal pattern—that is, changes in a seasonally adjusted series—it is important to note that seasonal adjustment is merely an approximation based on past experience. Seasonally adjusted estimates have a broader margin of possible error than the original data on which they are based, since they are subject not only to sampling and other errors, but also are affected by the uncertainties of the adjustment process itself.

Statistical reliability—For discussion of statistical collection, estimation, sampling procedures, and measures of statistical reliability applicable to Census Bureau and BLS data, see Appendix III.

No. 649. Employment Status of the Civilian Population: 1950 to 1998

[In thousands (104,995 represents 104,995,000), except as indicated. Annual averages of monthly figures. For the civilian noninstitutional population 16 years old and over. Based on Current Population Survey; see text, Section 1, Population, and Appendix III]

Year	Civilian noninstitutional population	Civilian labor force				Unemployed		Not in labor force	
		Total	Percent of population	Employed	Employ-ment/population ratio [1]	Number	Percent of labor force	Number	Percent of population
1950	104,995	62,208	59.2	58,918	56.1	3,288	5.3	42,787	40.8
1960	117,245	69,628	59.4	65,778	56.1	3,852	5.5	47,617	40.6
1970	137,085	82,771	60.4	78,678	57.4	4,093	4.9	54,315	39.6
1980	167,745	106,940	63.8	99,303	59.2	7,637	7.1	60,806	36.2
1981	170,130	108,670	63.9	100,397	59.0	8,273	7.6	61,460	36.1
1982	172,271	110,204	64.0	99,526	57.8	10,678	9.7	62,067	36.0
1983	174,215	111,550	64.0	100,834	57.9	10,717	9.6	62,665	36.0
1984	176,383	113,544	64.4	105,005	59.5	8,539	7.5	62,839	35.6
1985	178,206	115,461	64.8	107,150	60.1	8,312	7.2	62,744	35.2
1986	180,587	117,834	65.3	109,597	60.7	8,237	7.0	62,752	34.7
1987	182,753	119,865	65.6	112,440	61.5	7,425	6.2	62,888	34.4
1988	184,613	121,669	65.9	114,968	62.3	6,701	5.5	62,944	34.1
1989 [2]	186,393	123,869	66.5	117,342	63.0	6,528	5.3	62,523	33.5
1990 [2]	189,164	125,840	66.5	118,793	62.8	7,047	5.6	63,324	33.5
1991	190,925	126,346	66.2	117,718	61.7	8,628	6.8	64,578	33.8
1992	192,805	128,105	66.4	118,492	61.5	9,613	7.5	64,700	33.6
1993	194,838	129,200	66.3	120,259	61.7	8,940	6.9	65,638	33.7
1994 [2]	196,814	131,056	66.6	123,060	62.5	7,996	6.1	65,758	33.4
1995	198,584	132,304	66.6	124,900	62.9	7,404	5.6	66,280	33.4
1996	200,591	133,943	66.8	126,708	63.2	7,236	5.4	66,647	33.2
1997 [2]	203,133	136,297	67.1	129,558	63.8	6,739	4.9	66,837	32.9
1998 [2]	205,220	137,673	67.1	131,463	64.1	6,210	4.5	67,547	32.9

[1] Civilian employed as a percent of the civilian noninstitutional population.   [2] Data not strictly comparable with data for earlier years. See text, this section, and February 1994, March 1996, February 1997, and February 1998 issues of *Employment and Earnings*.

Source: U.S. Bureau of Labor Statistics, Bulletin 2307; and *Employment and Earnings*, monthly.

No. 650. Civilian Labor Force and Participation Rates, With Projections: 1970 to 2006

[For civilian noninstitutional population 16 years old and over (82.8 represents 82,800,000). Annual averages of monthly figures. Rates are based on annual average civilian noninstitutional population of each specified group and represent proportion of each specified group in the civilian labor force. Based on Current Population Survey; see text, Section 1, Population, and Appendix III]

Race, sex, and age	Civilian labor force (millions)						Participation rate (percent)					
	1970	1980	1990 [1]	1995	1998 [1]	2006, proj.	1970	1980	1990 [1]	1995	1998 [1]	2006, proj.
Total [2]	82.8	106.9	125.8	132.3	137.7	148.8	60.4	63.8	66.5	66.6	67.1	67.1
White	73.6	93.6	107.4	112.0	115.4	123.6	60.2	64.1	66.9	67.1	67.3	67.8
Male	46.0	54.5	59.6	61.1	63.0	66.0	80.0	78.2	77.1	75.7	75.6	74.3
Female	27.5	39.1	47.8	50.8	52.4	57.6	42.6	51.2	57.4	59.0	59.4	61.7
Black	[3]9.2	10.9	13.7	14.8	16.0	17.2	61.8	61.0	64.0	63.7	65.6	63.1
Male	5.2	5.6	6.8	7.2	7.5	8.0	76.5	70.3	71.0	69.0	69.0	65.4
Female	4.0	5.3	6.9	7.6	8.4	9.2	49.5	53.1	58.3	59.5	62.8	61.3
Hispanic [4]	(NA)	6.1	10.7	12.3	14.3	17.4	(NA)	64.0	67.4	65.8	67.9	65.8
Male	(NA)	3.8	6.5	7.4	8.6	10.2	(NA)	81.4	81.4	79.1	79.8	77.1
Female	(NA)	2.3	4.2	4.9	5.7	7.2	(NA)	47.4	53.1	52.6	55.6	54.3
Male	51.2	61.5	69.0	71.4	74.0	78.2	79.7	77.4	76.4	75.0	74.9	73.1
16 to 19 years	4.0	5.0	4.1	4.0	4.2	4.6	56.1	60.5	55.7	54.8	53.3	51.5
20 to 24 years	5.7	8.6	7.9	7.3	7.2	8.3	83.3	85.9	84.4	83.1	82.0	81.1
25 to 34 years	11.3	17.0	19.9	18.7	17.8	16.5	96.4	95.2	94.1	93.0	93.2	92.5
35 to 44 years	10.5	11.8	17.5	19.2	20.2	18.5	96.9	95.5	94.3	92.3	92.6	90.7
45 to 54 years	10.4	9.9	11.1	13.4	15.0	18.0	94.3	91.2	90.7	88.8	89.2	87.7
55 to 64 years	7.1	7.2	6.6	6.5	7.3	9.9	83.0	72.1	67.8	66.0	68.1	68.3
65 years and over	2.2	1.9	2.0	2.2	2.2	2.6	26.8	19.0	16.3	16.8	16.5	17.3
Female	31.5	45.5	56.8	60.9	63.7	70.6	43.3	51.5	57.5	58.9	59.8	61.4
16 to 19 years	3.2	4.4	3.7	3.7	4.0	4.4	44.0	52.9	51.6	52.2	52.3	51.0
20 to 24 years	4.9	7.3	6.8	6.3	6.4	7.2	57.7	68.9	71.3	70.3	73.0	71.8
25 to 34 years	5.7	12.3	16.1	15.5	15.0	14.4	45.0	65.5	73.5	74.9	76.3	77.6
35 to 44 years	6.0	8.6	14.7	16.6	17.3	17.0	51.1	65.5	76.4	77.2	77.1	80.2
45 to 54 years	6.5	7.0	9.1	11.8	13.4	17.2	54.4	59.9	71.2	74.4	76.2	79.9
55 to 64 years	4.2	4.7	4.9	5.4	6.0	8.8	43.0	41.3	45.2	49.2	51.2	55.8
65 years and over	1.1	1.2	1.5	1.6	1.6	1.7	9.7	8.1	8.6	8.8	8.6	8.7

NA Not available.   [1] See footnote 2, Table 649.   [2] Beginning 1980, includes other races, not shown separately.   [3] For 1970, Black and other.   [4] Persons of Hispanic origin may be of any race.

Source: U.S. Bureau of Labor Statistics, *Employment and Earnings*, monthly, January issues; *Monthly Labor Review*, November 1997; and unpublished data.

Labor Force, Employment, and Earnings   411

No. 651. Employment Status of the Civilian Population: 1970 to 1998

[In thousands (137,085 represents 137,085,000), except as indicated. Annual averages of monthly figures. For the civilian noninstitutional population 16 years old and over. Based on Current Population Survey; see text, Section 1, Population, and Appendix III]

Year, sex, race, and Hispanic origin	Civilian noninstitutional population	Civilian labor force			Employment/population ratio [1]	Unemployed		Not in labor force	
		Total	Percent of population	Employed		Number	Percent of labor force	Number	Percent of population
Total: [2]									
1970.........	137,085	82,771	60.4	78,678	57.4	4,093	4.9	54,315	39.6
1980.........	167,745	106,940	63.8	99,303	59.2	7,637	7.1	60,806	36.2
1985.........	178,206	115,461	64.8	107,150	60.1	8,312	7.2	62,744	35.2
1990 [3]......	189,164	125,840	66.5	118,793	62.8	7,047	5.6	63,324	33.5
1995.........	198,584	132,304	66.6	124,900	62.9	7,404	5.6	66,280	33.4
1996.........	200,591	133,943	66.8	126,708	63.2	7,236	5.4	66,647	33.2
1997 [3]......	203,133	136,297	67.1	129,558	63.8	6,739	4.9	66,837	32.9
1998 [3]......	205,220	137,673	67.1	131,463	64.1	6,210	4.5	67,547	32.9
Male:									
1970.........	64,304	51,228	79.7	48,990	76.2	2,238	4.4	13,076	20.3
1980.........	79,398	61,453	77.4	57,186	72.0	4,267	6.9	17,945	22.6
1985.........	84,469	64,411	76.3	59,891	70.9	4,521	7.0	20,058	23.7
1990 [3]......	90,377	69,011	76.4	65,104	72.0	3,906	5.7	21,367	23.6
1995.........	95,178	71,360	75.0	67,377	70.8	3,983	5.6	23,818	25.0
1996.........	96,206	72,087	74.9	68,207	70.9	3,880	5.4	24,119	25.1
1997 [3]......	97,715	73,261	75.0	69,685	71.3	3,577	4.9	24,454	25.0
1998 [3]......	98,758	73,959	74.9	70,693	71.6	3,266	4.4	24,799	25.1
Female:									
1970.........	72,782	31,543	43.3	29,688	40.8	1,855	5.9	41,239	56.7
1980.........	88,348	45,487	51.5	42,117	47.7	3,370	7.4	42,861	48.5
1985.........	93,736	51,050	54.5	47,259	50.4	3,791	7.4	42,686	45.5
1990 [3]......	98,787	56,829	57.5	53,689	54.3	3,140	5.5	41,957	42.5
1995.........	103,406	60,944	58.9	57,523	55.6	3,421	5.6	42,462	41.1
1996.........	104,385	61,857	59.3	58,501	56.0	3,356	5.4	42,528	40.7
1997 [3]......	105,418	63,036	59.8	59,873	56.8	3,162	5.0	42,382	40.2
1998 [3]......	106,462	63,714	59.8	60,771	57.1	2,944	4.6	42,748	40.1
White:									
1970.........	122,174	73,556	60.2	70,217	57.5	3,339	4.5	48,618	39.8
1980.........	146,122	93,600	64.1	87,715	60.0	5,884	6.3	52,523	35.9
1985.........	153,679	99,926	65.0	93,736	61.0	6,191	6.2	53,753	35.0
1990 [3]......	160,625	107,447	66.9	102,261	63.7	5,186	4.8	53,178	33.1
1995.........	166,914	111,950	67.1	106,490	63.8	5,459	4.9	54,965	32.9
1996.........	168,317	113,108	67.2	107,808	64.1	5,300	4.7	55,209	32.8
1997 [3]......	169,993	114,693	67.5	109,856	64.6	4,836	4.2	55,301	32.5
1998 [3]......	171,478	115,415	67.3	110,931	64.7	4,484	3.9	56,064	32.7
Black:									
1973.........	14,917	8,976	60.2	8,128	54.5	846	9.4	5,941	39.8
1980.........	17,824	10,865	61.0	9,313	52.2	1,553	14.3	6,959	39.0
1985.........	19,664	12,364	62.9	10,501	53.4	1,864	15.1	7,299	37.1
1990 [3]......	21,477	13,740	64.0	12,175	56.7	1,565	11.4	7,737	36.0
1995.........	23,246	14,817	63.7	13,279	57.1	1,538	10.4	8,429	36.3
1996.........	23,604	15,134	64.1	13,542	57.4	1,592	10.5	8,470	35.9
1997 [3]......	24,003	15,529	64.7	13,969	58.2	1,560	10.0	8,474	35.3
1998 [3] [4]...	24,373	15,982	65.6	14,556	59.7	1,426	8.9	8,391	34.4
Hispanic: [4]									
1980.........	9,598	6,146	64.0	5,527	57.6	620	10.1	3,451	36.0
1985.........	11,915	7,698	64.6	6,888	57.8	811	10.5	4,217	35.4
1990 [3]......	15,904	10,720	67.4	9,845	61.9	876	8.2	5,184	32.6
1995.........	18,629	12,267	65.8	11,127	59.7	1,140	9.3	6,362	34.2
1996.........	19,213	12,774	66.5	11,642	60.6	1,132	8.9	6,439	33.5
1997 [3]......	20,321	13,796	67.9	12,726	62.6	1,069	7.7	6,526	32.1
1998 [3]......	21,070	14,317	67.9	13,291	63.1	1,026	7.2	6,753	32.1
Mexican:									
1986.........	7,377	4,941	67.0	4,387	59.5	555	11.2	2,436	33.0
1990 [3]......	9,752	6,707	68.8	6,146	63.0	561	8.4	3,045	31.2
1995.........	11,609	7,765	66.9	7,016	60.4	750	9.7	3,844	33.1
1996.........	11,762	7,943	67.5	7,209	61.3	734	9.2	3,819	32.5
1997 [3]......	12,443	8,546	68.7	7,884	63.4	662	7.7	3,897	31.3
1998 [3]......	13,216	9,096	68.8	8,431	63.8	664	7.3	4,121	31.2
Puerto Rican:									
1986.........	1,494	804	53.8	691	46.3	113	14.0	690	46.2
1990 [3]......	1,718	960	55.9	870	50.6	91	9.5	758	44.1
1995.........	1,896	1,098	57.9	974	51.4	123	11.2	798	42.1
1996.........	2,017	1,170	58.0	1,057	52.4	112	9.6	848	42.0
1997 [3]......	2,139	1,293	60.4	1,166	54.5	127	9.8	846	39.6
1998 [3]......	2,080	1,249	60.0	1,145	55.0	104	8.3	832	40.0
Cuban:									
1986.........	842	570	67.7	533	63.3	36	6.4	272	32.3
1990 [3]......	918	603	65.7	559	60.9	44	7.2	315	34.3
1995.........	1,019	613	60.2	568	55.7	45	7.4	406	39.8
1996.........	991	637	64.3	591	59.7	46	7.2	354	35.7
1997 [3]......	1,025	646	63.0	603	58.8	43	6.6	379	37.0
1998 [3]......	1,062	651	61.3	612	57.6	39	6.0	411	38.7

[1] Civilian employed as a percent of the civilian noninstitutional population. [2] Includes other races, not shown separately. [3] See footnote 2, Table 649. [4] Persons of Hispanic origin may be of any race. Includes persons of other Hispanic origin, not shown separately.

Source: U.S. Bureau of Labor Statistics, Bulletin 2307; and Employment and Earnings, monthly, January issues.

No. 652. Civilian Labor Force—Percent Distribution, by Sex and Age: 1960 to 1998

[For civilian noninstitutional population 16 years old and over (**69,628 represents 69,628,000**). Annual averages of monthly figures. Based on Current Population Survey; see text, Section 1, Population, and Appendix III]

Year and sex	Civilian labor force (1,000)	Percent distribution						
		16 to 19 years	20 to 24 years	25 to 34 years	35 to 44 years	45 to 54 years	55 to 64 years	65 yrs. and over
Total: 1960	69,628	7.0	9.6	20.7	23.4	21.3	13.5	4.6
1970	82,771	8.8	12.8	20.6	19.9	20.5	13.6	3.9
1980 ¹	106,940	8.8	14.9	27.3	19.1	15.8	11.2	2.9
1990 ¹	125,840	6.2	11.7	28.6	25.5	16.1	9.2	2.7
1995	132,304	5.9	10.3	25.8	27.0	19.1	9.0	2.9
1998 ¹	137,673	6.0	9.9	23.8	27.3	20.6	9.6	2.8
Male: 1960	46,388	6.0	8.9	22.1	23.6	20.6	13.8	4.9
1970	51,228	7.8	11.2	22.1	20.4	20.3	13.9	4.2
1980 ¹	61,453	8.1	14.0	27.6	19.3	16.1	11.8	3.1
1990 ¹	69,011	5.9	11.4	28.8	25.3	16.1	9.6	2.9
1995	71,360	5.7	10.3	26.2	26.9	18.8	9.1	3.1
1998 ¹	73,959	5.7	9.8	24.1	27.4	20.2	9.8	3.0
Female: 1960	23,240	8.8	11.1	17.8	22.8	22.7	12.8	3.9
1970	31,543	10.3	15.5	18.1	18.9	20.7	13.2	3.3
1980 ¹	45,487	9.6	16.1	26.9	19.0	15.4	10.4	2.6
1990 ¹	56,829	6.5	12.0	28.3	25.8	16.1	8.7	2.6
1995	60,944	6.1	10.4	25.5	27.2	19.4	8.8	2.7
1998 ¹	63,714	6.3	10.1	23.6	27.1	21.0	9.4	2.5

¹ See footnote 2, Table 649.
Source: U.S. Bureau of Labor Statistics, Bulletin 2307, and *Employment Earnings*, monthly, January issues.

No. 653. Civilian Labor Force and Participation Rates, by Educational Attainment, Sex, Race, and Hispanic Origin: 1992 to 1998

[**As of March.** For the civilian noninstitutional population 25 to 64 years of age (**102,387 represents 102,387,000**). See Table 684 for unemployment data. Based on Current Population Survey; see text, Section 1, Population, and Appendix III]

Year, sex, and race	Civilian labor force					Participation rate ¹				
	Total (1,000)	Percent distribution				Total	Less than high school diploma	High school graduates, no degree	Less than a bachelor's degree	College graduate
		Less than high school diploma	High school graduate, no degree	Less than a bachelor's degree	College graduate					
Total: ²										
1992	102,387	12.2	36.2	25.2	26.4	79.0	60.3	78.3	83.5	88.4
1994 ³	104,868	11.0	34.0	27.6	27.3	78.9	58.3	77.8	83.2	88.2
1995	106,519	10.8	33.1	27.8	28.3	79.3	59.8	77.3	83.2	88.7
1996	108,037	10.9	32.9	27.7	28.5	79.4	60.2	77.9	83.7	87.8
1997 ³	110,514	10.9	33.0	27.4	28.6	80.1	61.7	82.5	83.7	88.5
1998 ³	111,857	10.7	32.8	27.4	29.1	80.2	63.0	78.4	83.5	88.0
Male:										
1992	55,917	13.9	34.7	23.8	27.5	88.6	75.1	89.0	91.8	93.7
1994 ³	56,633	12.7	32.9	25.8	28.6	87.0	71.5	86.8	90.3	93.2
1995	57,454	12.2	32.3	25.7	29.7	87.4	72.0	86.9	90.1	93.8
1996	58,121	12.7	32.2	26.0	29.1	87.5	74.3	86.9	90.0	92.9
1997 ³	59,268	12.8	32.2	25.8	29.2	87.7	75.2	86.4	90.6	93.5
1998 ³	59,905	12.3	32.3	25.8	29.6	87.8	75.3	86.7	90.0	93.4
Female:										
1992	46,469	10.2	37.9	26.9	25.0	70.0	45.6	69.1	76.2	82.2
1994 ³	48,235	9.1	35.3	29.8	25.8	71.1	44.7	70.0	77.0	82.5
1995	49,065	9.1	34.1	30.2	26.6	71.5	47.2	68.9	77.3	82.8
1996	49,916	8.8	33.7	29.7	27.8	71.8	45.7	69.8	78.1	82.3
1997 ³	51,246	8.7	34.0	29.3	28.0	72.8	47.1	71.4	77.6	83.2
1998 ³	51,953	8.8	33.3	29.3	28.6	73.0	49.8	70.9	77.8	82.3
White:										
1992	87,656	11.3	36.1	25.5	27.1	79.8	61.5	78.7	83.8	88.7
1994 ³	89,009	10.5	33.7	27.7	28.1	79.8	60.3	78.3	83.5	88.5
1995	90,192	10.0	32.8	27.8	29.3	80.1	61.6	77.9	83.4	88.8
1996	91,506	10.4	32.8	27.5	29.3	80.4	62.5	78.6	83.9	88.2
1997 ³	93,119	10.4	32.8	27.3	29.5	81.0	63.8	79.2	83.9	89.0
1998 ³	93,527	10.2	32.7	27.4	29.8	80.6	63.8	78.6	83.5	88.3
Black:										
1992	10,936	19.2	40.3	24.9	15.6	74.4	55.4	76.9	83.4	89.1
1994 ³	11,368	14.5	39.3	29.2	17.0	73.5	49.4	75.2	82.5	89.5
1995	11,695	14.1	38.6	29.6	17.7	74.2	51.0	74.5	82.8	90.9
1996	11,891	14.2	37.2	31.2	17.4	73.7	50.1	74.3	83.0	87.9
1997 ³	12,253	14.3	37.8	31.3	16.6	74.9	52.9	75.0	83.8	89.0
1998 ³	12,893	14.3	37.3	30.1	18.2	77.7	59.3	77.0	85.0	88.8
Hispanic: ⁴										
1992	7,702	39.1	30.2	19.3	11.4	73.8	64.6	77.5	84.2	87.1
1994 ³	8,984	38.6	28.7	21.5	11.1	73.2	63.9	77.5	81.9	86.3
1995	9,298	38.9	28.2	21.3	11.6	73.2	64.7	75.9	81.9	87.9
1996	9,683	38.9	28.5	21.2	11.3	74.2	65.0	78.2	83.7	87.2
1997 ³	10,556	37.4	28.1	22.1	12.4	75.9	66.4	79.4	85.3	87.7
1998 ³	10,922	37.3	29.1	20.3	13.3	75.8	67.9	78.8	82.3	86.9

¹ See headnote, Table 650. ² Includes other races, not shown separately. ³ See footnote 2, Table 649. ⁴ Persons of Hispanic origin may be of any race.
Source: U.S. Bureau of Labor Statistics, unpublished data.

Labor Force, Employment, and Earnings 413

No. 654. Characteristics of the Civilian Labor Force, by State: 1997

[In thousands (136,297 represents 136,297,000), except ratio and rate. Preliminary. For civilian noninstitutional population, 16 years old and over. Annual averages of monthly figures. Because of separate processing and weighting procedures, the totals for the United States may differ from results obtained by aggregating totals for states]

State	Total Number	Total Female	Employed Total	Employed Female	Employed/population ratio [1]	Unemployed Total Number	Unemployed Total Female	Unemployed Rate [2] Total	Unemployed Rate [2] Male	Unemployed Rate [2] Female	Participation rate [3] Male	Participation rate [3] Female
United States .	136,297	63,036	129,558	59,873	63.8	6,739	3,162	4.9	4.9	5.0	75.0	59.8
Alabama	2,168	1,005	2,058	945	61.8	110	59	5.1	4.4	5.9	72.7	58.1
Alaska	315	143	290	134	68.3	25	9	7.9	9.2	6.3	80.4	67.9
Arizona	2,185	972	2,083	923	60.8	102	50	4.6	4.3	5.1	72.6	55.3
Arkansas	1,214	573	1,150	545	59.8	64	28	5.3	5.7	4.8	69.9	56.9
California	15,941	7,048	14,937	6,598	62.1	1,004	449	6.3	6.2	6.4	75.2	57.6
Colorado	2,152	988	2,081	956	70.4	70	32	3.3	3.2	3.3	78.8	66.8
Connecticut	1,723	836	1,635	800	64.8	88	36	5.1	5.9	4.3	73.9	63.2
Delaware	382	186	366	179	64.6	15	7	4.0	4.4	3.6	72.2	62.8
Dist. of Columbia .	258	132	238	121	56.9	20	11	7.9	7.2	8.6	66.5	57.8
Florida	7,119	3,302	6,781	3,142	59.3	339	160	4.8	4.7	4.8	69.8	55.4
Georgia	3,907	1,833	3,730	1,740	66.2	177	93	4.5	4.1	5.1	77.9	61.6
Hawaii	597	294	559	278	63.5	38	16	6.4	7.2	5.6	72.8	63.4
Idaho	633	285	599	269	66.8	34	16	5.3	5.2	5.5	77.8	63.3
Illinois	6,196	2,850	5,904	2,721	65.3	291	129	4.7	4.8	4.5	77.0	60.7
Indiana	3,086	1,417	2,978	1,368	66.8	108	49	3.5	3.5	3.5	78.0	61.2
Iowa	1,579	754	1,528	732	70.3	51	23	3.3	3.5	3.0	78.6	67.2
Kansas	1,368	641	1,317	614	67.8	52	27	3.8	3.4	4.2	77.6	63.9
Kentucky	1,917	912	1,814	855	60.4	103	57	5.4	4.6	6.2	70.7	57.7
Louisiana	2,014	952	1,891	887	58.3	123	65	6.1	5.4	6.9	69.5	55.5
Maine	659	310	624	295	64.1	36	16	5.4	5.7	5.0	73.5	62.3
Maryland	2,784	1,342	2,642	1,275	67.7	141	67	5.1	5.1	5.0	77.0	66.0
Massachusetts . .	3,260	1,548	3,129	1,493	66.2	131	56	4.0	4.4	3.6	75.5	62.9
Michigan	4,962	2,309	4,753	2,210	64.0	209	98	4.2	4.2	4.3	74.6	59.6
Minnesota	2,625	1,203	2,539	1,171	72.1	86	33	3.3	3.7	2.7	81.1	67.9
Mississippi	1,262	600	1,190	559	58.4	72	41	5.7	4.7	6.9	68.7	55.9
Missouri	2,893	1,395	2,770	1,341	67.9	123	54	4.2	4.6	3.9	77.4	65.0
Montana	455	212	431	203	63.6	24	10	5.4	6.0	4.6	72.8	61.9
Nebraska	906	421	883	410	71.4	24	11	2.6	2.6	2.6	80.8	66.3
Nevada	883	392	847	376	66.6	36	16	4.1	4.1	4.2	77.1	61.9
New Hampshire . .	646	297	625	287	69.6	20	10	3.1	3.0	3.3	79.0	64.9
New Jersey	4,198	1,950	3,982	1,851	64.3	216	99	5.1	5.2	5.1	76.7	59.7
New Mexico	815	370	764	347	59.6	51	23	6.2	6.2	6.3	70.9	56.5
New York	8,835	4,108	8,269	3,839	59.1	566	269	6.4	6.3	6.6	71.8	55.5
North Carolina . . .	3,844	1,799	3,705	1,729	66.1	139	69	3.6	3.4	3.9	75.8	61.9
North Dakota . . .	348	164	339	160	70.7	9	4	2.5	2.6	2.5	78.4	67.0
Ohio	5,707	2,672	5,445	2,542	63.6	262	130	4.6	4.4	4.8	74.0	60.2
Oklahoma	1,601	739	1,535	704	61.6	66	35	4.1	3.6	4.7	73.2	56.2
Oregon	1,728	771	1,627	727	64.6	101	44	5.8	5.9	5.7	76.4	60.9
Pennsylvania . . .	5,979	2,805	5,668	2,664	61.1	311	141	5.2	5.3	5.0	73.1	56.9
Rhode Island . . .	502	243	476	230	63.4	27	13	5.3	5.2	5.4	74.3	60.6
South Carolina . .	1,931	920	1,843	868	63.6	87	53	4.5	3.4	5.7	74.7	59.6
South Dakota . . .	390	186	378	180	69.2	12	6	3.1	2.9	3.3	77.9	65.4
Tennessee	2,708	1,286	2,562	1,223	61.6	146	63	5.4	5.8	4.9	71.7	59.1
Texas	9,850	4,419	9,320	4,172	65.2	530	247	5.4	5.2	5.6	78.3	60.1
Utah	1,040	466	1,008	451	69.5	32	15	3.1	3.1	3.2	81.5	62.5
Vermont	327	159	314	153	68.7	13	6	4.0	4.1	3.8	77.0	66.6
Virginia	3,413	1,618	3,278	1,545	64.2	135	72	4.0	3.5	4.5	73.5	60.7
Washington	2,989	1,337	2,847	1,272	66.8	142	65	4.8	4.7	4.8	78.4	62.1
West Virginia . . .	803	368	748	346	51.6	55	22	6.9	7.6	6.1	64.1	47.8
Wisconsin	2,949	1,389	2,841	1,338	72.0	108	51	3.7	3.7	3.7	79.8	69.7
Wyoming	251	114	239	108	65.5	13	6	5.1	4.7	5.5	76.2	62.0

[1] Civilian employment as a percent of civilian noninstitutional population.   [2] Percent unemployed of the civilian labor force.
[3] Percent of civilian noninstitutional population of each specified group in the civilian labor force.

Source: U.S. Bureau of Labor Statistics, "Local Area Unemployment Statistics, Geographic Profile" Internet site <http://146.142.4.24/cgi-bin/surveymost?gp> (accessed 2 August 1999).

No. 655. Civilian Labor Force, by Selected Metropolitan Area: 1998

[For the civilian noninstitutional population 16 years old and over (137,673 represents 137,673,000). Annual averages of monthly figures. Data are derived from the Local Area Unemployment Statistics Program. For composition of metropolitan areas, see Appendix II]

Metropolitan areas ranked by labor force size, 1998	Civilian labor force (1,000)	Unemployment rate [1]	Metropolitan areas ranked by labor force size, 1998	Civilian labor force (1,000)	Unemployment rate [1]
U.S. total	137,673	4.5	Indianapolis, IN MSA	835	2.5
Los Angeles-Long Beach, CA PMSA	4,641	6.5	Columbus, OH MSA	812	2.7
Chicago, IL PMSA	4,164	4.3	Milwaukee-Waukesha, WI PMSA	809	3.3
New York, NY PMSA	4,092	7.3	San Antonio, TX MSA	759	3.7
Washington, DC-MD-VA-WV PMSA	2,559	3.2	Sacramento, CA PMSA	758	4.9
Philadelphia, PA-NJ PMSA	2,493	4.3	Fort Lauderdale, FL PMSA	757	4.5
Detroit, MI PMSA	2,255	3.5	Charlotte-Gastonia-Rock Hill, NC-SC MSA	746	2.7
Houston, TX PMSA	2,129	4.1	Norfolk-Virginia Beach-Newport News, VA-NC MSA	735	3.5
Atlanta, GA MSA	2,123	3.3	Las Vegas, NV-AZ MSA	698	4.2
Dallas, TX PMSA	1,870	3.2	Austin-San Marcos, TX MSA	682	2.6
Boston, MA-NH PMSA	1,817	2.8	Salt Lake City-Ogden, UT MSA	681	3.6
Minneapolis-St. Paul, MN-WI MSA	1,678	2.0	Bergen-Passaic, NJ PMSA	673	4.4
Phoenix-Mesa, AZ MSA	1,507	2.7	Nashville, TN MSA	642	2.7
Orange County, CA PMSA	1,435	2.9	Middlesex-Somerset-Hunterdon, NJ PMSA	633	3.3
Nassau-Suffolk, NY PMSA	1,399	3.2	Greensboro-Winston-Salem-High Point, NC MSA	632	2.7
Riverside-San Bernardino, CA PMSA	1,382	6.1	Raleigh-Durham-Chapel Hill, NC MSA	622	1.7
Seattle-Bellevue-Everett, WA PMSA	1,382	3.1	New Orleans, LA MSA	621	4.9
St. Louis, MO-IL MSA	1,321	4.3	Grand Rapids-Muskegon-Holland, MI MSA	595	3.0
San Diego, CA MSA	1,319	3.5	Hartford, CT MSA	581	3.5
Baltimore, MD PMSA	1,299	5.1	Rochester, NY MSA	575	4.0
Oakland, CA PMSA	1,191	3.9	Buffalo-Niagara Falls, NY MSA	575	5.3
Tampa-St. Petersburg-Clearwater, FL MSA	1,173	3.0	Providence-Fall River-Warwick, RI-MA MSA	573	4.9
Pittsburgh, PA MSA	1,151	4.6	Memphis, TN-AR-MS MSA	552	3.7
Denver, CO PMSA	1,128	3.2	Louisville, KY-IN MSA	549	3.3
Cleveland-Lorain-Elyria, OH PMSA	1,106	4.4	Oklahoma City, OK MSA	534	3.8
Portland-Vancouver, OR-WA PMSA	1,048	4.2	Jacksonville, FL MSA	534	3.1
Miami, FL PMSA	1,037	6.5	Monmouth-Ocean, NJ PMSA	515	4.3
Newark, NJ PMSA	1,010	4.5	West Palm Beach-Boca Raton, FL MSA	508	5.5
Kansas City, MO-KS MSA	967	3.8	Richmond-Petersburg, VA MSA	507	2.6
San Jose, CA PMSA	963	3.2			
San Francisco, CA PMSA	949	3.0			
Fort Worth-Arlington, TX PMSA	879	3.3			
Orlando, FL MSA	842	3.0			
Cincinnatti, OH-KY-IN PMSA	839	3.4			

[1] Percent unemployed of the civilian labor force.

Source: U.S. Bureau of Labor Statistics, Local Area Unemployment Statistics program.

No. 656. School Enrollment and Labor Force Status: 1980 and 1998

[In thousands (37,103 represents 37,103,000), except percent. As of October. For the civilian noninstitutional population 16 to 24 years old. Based on Current Population Survey; see text, Section 1, Population, and Appendix III]

Characteristic	Population		Civilian labor force		Employed		Unemployed		
	1980	1998 [1]	1980	1998 [1]	1980	1998 [1]	1980, total	1998 [1] Total	1998 [1] Rate [2]
Total, 16 to 24 years [3]	37,103	33,445	24,918	21,691	21,454	19,575	3,464	2,116	9.8
Enrolled in school [3]	15,713	18,174	7,454	9,207	6,433	8,241	1,021	967	10.5
16 to 19 years	11,126	12,370	4,836	5,533	4,029	4,778	807	756	13.7
20 to 24 years	4,587	5,804	2,618	3,674	2,404	3,463	214	211	5.7
Sex:									
Male	7,997	9,058	3,825	4,448	3,259	3,927	566	520	11.7
Female	7,716	9,116	3,629	4,760	3,174	4,313	455	446	9.4
College level	7,664	9,445	3,996	5,646	3,632	5,250	364	396	7.0
Full-time	6,396	7,939	2,854	4,306	2,554	3,982	300	324	7.5
Race:									
White	13,242	14,392	6,687	7,721	5,889	7,020	798	701	9.1
Below college	6,566	6,759	3,095	3,000	2,579	2,600	516	400	13.3
College level	6,678	7,633	3,592	4,720	3,310	4,419	282	301	6.4
Black	2,028	2,653	595	1,098	406	884	189	214	19.5
Below college	1,282	1,516	294	454	174	315	120	139	30.5
College level	747	1,137	300	644	230	569	70	75	11.7
Not enrolled [3]	21,390	15,271	17,464	12,484	15,021	11,334	2,443	1,149	9.2
White	18,103	12,340	15,121	10,332	13,318	9,528	1,803	804	7.8
Black	2,864	2,364	2,055	1,733	1,451	1,433	604	300	17.3

[1] See footnote 2, Table 649.   [2] Percent of civilian labor force in each category.   [3] Includes other races, not shown separately.

Source: U.S. Bureau of Labor Statistics, Bulletin 2307; News, USDL 99-75, June 25, 1999; and unpublished data.

No. 657. Labor Force Participation Rates, by Marital Status, Sex, and Age: 1960 to 1998

[Annual averages of monthly figures. See Table 654 for definition of participation rate. Based on Current Population Survey; see text, Section 1, Population, and Appendix III]

Marital status and year	Male participation rate							Female participation rate						
	Total	16-19 years	20-24 years	25-34 years	35-44 years	45-64 years	65 and over	Total	16-19 years	20-24 years	25-34 years	35-44 years	45-64 years	65 and over
Single:														
1960 ..	69.8	42.6	80.3	91.5	88.6	80.1	31.2	58.6	30.2	77.2	83.4	82.9	79.8	24.3
1970 ..	65.5	54.6	73.8	87.9	86.2	75.7	25.2	56.8	44.7	73.0	81.4	78.6	73.0	19.7
1975 ..	68.7	57.9	77.9	86.7	83.2	69.9	21.0	59.8	49.6	72.5	80.8	78.6	68.3	15.8
1980 ..	72.6	59.9	81.3	89.2	82.2	66.9	16.8	64.4	53.6	75.2	83.3	76.9	65.6	13.9
1985 ..	73.8	56.3	81.5	89.4	84.6	65.5	15.6	66.6	52.3	76.3	82.4	80.8	67.9	9.8
1990 [1]	74.8	55.1	81.6	89.9	84.5	67.3	15.7	66.7	51.7	74.5	80.9	80.8	66.2	12.1
1994 [1]	73.9	53.6	80.5	88.4	83.1	67.8	17.8	66.7	51.4	73.6	78.9	78.7	68.8	12.7
1995 ..	73.7	54.4	80.3	88.7	81.4	67.0	17.9	66.8	52.2	72.9	80.2	79.5	67.3	11.6
1996 .	73.3	52.8	79.8	89.1	82.1	67.4	18.2	67.1	51.5	73.3	80.9	79.4	68.5	12.2
1997 [1]	73.1	51.9	80.1	89.0	82.1	68.5	14.8	67.9	51.0	75.1	82.3	80.1	70.8	11.5
1998 [1]	73.3	52.9	79.7	89.1	82.5	70.2	15.2	68.5	52.4	75.3	83.0	80.9	69.9	9.7
Married: [2]														
1960 ..	89.2	91.5	97.1	98.8	98.6	93.7	36.6	31.9	27.2	31.7	28.8	37.2	36.0	6.7
1970 ..	86.1	92.3	94.7	98.0	98.1	91.2	29.9	40.5	37.8	47.9	38.8	46.8	44.0	7.3
1975 ..	83.0	92.9	95.3	97.4	97.1	86.8	23.3	44.3	46.2	57.0	48.4	52.0	43.8	7.0
1980 ..	80.9	91.3	96.9	97.5	97.2	84.3	20.5	49.8	49.3	61.4	58.8	61.8	46.9	7.3
1985 ..	78.7	91.0	95.6	97.4	96.8	81.7	16.8	53.8	49.6	65.7	65.8	68.1	49.4	6.6
1990 [1]	78.6	92.1	95.6	96.9	96.7	82.6	17.5	58.4	49.5	66.1	69.6	74.0	56.5	8.5
1994 [1]	77.4	88.7	94.2	95.9	95.6	81.9	18.1	60.7	48.9	65.8	71.6	75.8	61.9	9.4
1995 ..	77.5	89.2	94.9	96.3	95.4	82.4	18.0	61.0	51.6	64.7	72.0	75.7	62.7	9.1
1996 .	77.6	84.4	94.5	96.4	95.4	83.2	18.3	61.2	48.6	66.0	71.7	75.8	63.7	9.0
1997 [1]	77.7	84.6	94.9	96.1	95.7	83.6	18.3	61.6	50.1	66.1	71.9	76.0	64.6	8.9
1998 [1]	77.6	83.8	95.0	96.4	95.8	83.7	17.5	61.2	49.8	66.1	71.6	74.5	64.9	8.9
Other: [3]														
1960 ..	63.1	(B)	96.9	95.2	94.4	83.2	22.7	41.6	43.5	58.0	63.1	70.0	60.0	11.4
1970 ..	60.7	(B)	90.4	93.7	91.1	78.5	19.3	40.3	48.6	60.3	64.6	68.8	61.9	10.0
1975 ..	63.4	(B)	88.8	92.4	89.4	73.4	15.4	40.1	47.6	65.3	68.6	69.2	59.0	8.3
1980 ..	67.5	(B)	92.6	94.1	91.9	73.3	13.7	43.6	50.0	68.4	76.5	77.1	60.2	8.2
1985 ..	68.7	(B)	95.1	93.7	91.8	72.8	11.4	45.1	51.9	66.2	76.9	81.6	61.0	7.5
1990 [1]	68.9	(B)	93.1	93.0	90.7	74.9	12.0	47.2	53.9	65.4	77.0	82.1	65.0	8.4
1994 [1]	66.8	(B)	91.0	90.3	88.6	72.6	11.9	47.5	46.2	66.6	74.3	80.4	67.6	8.7
1995 ..	66.2	(B)	92.7	90.9	88.2	72.4	12.1	47.4	55.8	67.2	77.1	80.7	67.2	8.4
1996 .	66.4	(B)	90.9	90.8	88.8	73.1	11.5	48.1	42.6	70.7	78.5	82.1	67.7	8.0
1997 [1]	67.4	60.8	89.9	92.1	89.6	74.7	13.2	48.6	49.7	70.4	80.2	81.9	68.6	8.1
1998 [1]	66.9	66.2	89.1	93.0	89.1	73.7	13.1	48.8	50.4	73.7	81.0	82.8	68.6	8.4

B For 1960, percentage not shown where base is less than 50,000; beginning 1970, 35,000.   [1] See footnote 2, Table 649.   [2] Spouse present.   [3] Widowed, divorced, and married (spouse absent).

Source: U.S. Bureau of Labor Statistics, Bulletins 2217 and 2340; and unpublished data.

No. 658. Marital Status of Women in the Civilian Labor Force: 1960 to 1998

[Annual averages of monthly figures (23,240 represent 23,240,000). For civilian noninstitutional population 16 years old and over. Based on the Current Population Survey; see text, Section 1, Population, and Appendix III]

Year	Female labor force (1,000)				Female participation rate [3]			
	Total	Single	Married [1]	Other [2]	Total	Single	Married [1]	Other [2]
1960	23,240	5,410	12,893	4,937	37.7	58.6	31.9	41.6
1965	26,200	5,976	14,829	5,396	39.3	54.5	34.9	40.7
1970	31,543	7,265	18,475	5,804	43.3	56.8	40.5	40.3
1975	37,475	9,125	21,484	6,866	46.3	59.8	44.3	40.1
1980	45,487	11,865	24,980	8,643	51.5	64.4	49.9	43.6
1982	47,755	12,460	25,971	9,324	52.6	65.1	51.1	44.8
1983	48,503	12,659	26,468	9,376	52.9	65.0	51.8	44.4
1984	49,709	12,867	27,199	9,644	53.6	65.6	52.8	44.7
1985	51,050	13,163	27,894	9,993	54.5	66.6	53.8	45.1
1986	52,413	13,512	28,623	10,277	55.3	67.2	54.9	45.6
1987	53,658	13,885	29,381	10,393	56.0	67.4	55.9	45.7
1988	54,742	14,194	29,921	10,627	56.6	67.7	56.7	46.2
1989	56,030	14,377	30,548	11,104	57.4	68.0	57.8	47.0
1990 [4]	56,829	14,612	30,901	11,315	57.5	66.7	58.4	47.2
1991	57,178	14,681	31,112	11,385	57.4	66.2	58.5	46.8
1992	58,141	14,872	31,700	11,570	57.8	66.2	59.3	47.1
1993	58,795	15,031	31,980	11,784	57.9	66.2	59.4	47.2
1994 [4]	60,239	15,333	32,888	12,018	58.8	66.7	60.7	47.5
1995	60,944	15,467	33,359	12,118	58.9	66.8	61.0	47.4
1996 [4]	61,857	15,842	33,618	12,397	59.3	67.1	61.2	48.1
1997 [4]	63,036	16,492	33,802	12,742	59.8	67.9	61.6	48.6
1998 [4]	63,714	17,087	33,857	12,771	59.8	68.5	61.2	48.8

[1] Husband present.   [2] Widowed, divorced, or separated.   [3] See Table 654 for definition of participation rate.   [4] See footnote 2, Table 649.

Source: U.S. Bureau of Labor Statistics, Bulletin 2307; and unpublished data.

416 Labor Force, Employment, and Earnings

No. 659. Employment Status of Women, by Marital Status and Presence and Age of Children: 1960 to 1998

[As of **March (5.4 represents 5,400,000).** For 1960, civilian noninstitutional persons 14 years and over, thereafter 16 years old and over. Based on Current Population Survey; see text, Section 1, Population, and Appendix III]

Item	Total			With any children								
				Total			Children 6 to 17 only			Children under 6		
	Single	Mar-ried [1]	Other [2]	Single	Mar-ried [1]	Other [2]	Single	Mar-ried [1]	Other [2]	Single	Mar-ried [1]	Other [2]
IN LABOR FORCE (mil.)												
1960	5.4	12.3	4.9	(NA)	6.6	1.5	(NA)	4.1	1.0	(NA)	2.5	0.4
1970	7.0	18.4	5.9	(NA)	10.2	1.9	(NA)	6.3	1.3	(NA)	3.9	0.6
1980	11.2	24.9	8.8	0.6	13.7	3.6	0.2	8.4	2.6	0.3	5.2	1.0
1985	12.9	27.7	10.3	1.1	14.9	4.0	0.4	8.5	2.9	0.7	6.4	1.1
1990	14.0	31.0	11.2	1.5	16.5	4.2	0.6	9.3	3.0	0.9	7.2	1.2
1995	15.0	33.6	12.0	2.1	18.0	4.6	0.8	10.2	3.3	1.3	7.8	1.3
1996 [3]	15.4	33.4	12.4	2.2	17.8	4.7	0.9	10.2	3.4	1.4	7.6	1.3
1997 [3]	16.2	33.9	12.8	2.8	18.2	4.7	1.0	10.6	3.4	1.8	7.6	1.3
1998 [3]	16.9	34.1	12.9	3.0	18.1	4.5	1.2	10.5	3.3	1.8	7.7	1.2
PARTICIPATION RATE [4]												
1960	44.1	30.5	40.0	(NA)	27.6	56.0	(NA)	39.0	65.9	(NA)	18.6	40.5
1970	53.0	40.8	39.1	(NA)	39.7	60.7	(NA)	49.2	66.9	(NA)	30.3	52.2
1980	61.5	50.1	44.0	52.0	54.1	69.4	67.6	61.7	74.6	44.1	45.1	60.3
1985	65.2	54.2	45.6	51.6	60.8	71.9	64.1	67.8	77.8	46.5	53.4	59.7
1990	66.4	58.2	46.8	55.2	66.3	74.2	69.7	73.6	79.7	48.7	58.9	63.6
1995	65.5	61.1	47.3	57.5	70.2	75.3	67.0	76.2	79.5	53.0	63.5	66.3
1996 [3]	65.2	61.1	48.2	60.5	70.0	77.0	71.8	76.7	80.6	55.1	62.7	69.2
1997 [3]	66.8	62.1	48.7	68.1	71.1	79.1	74.0	77.6	81.1	65.1	63.6	74.2
1998 [3]	68.1	61.8	49.4	72.5	70.6	79.7	81.2	76.8	82.7	67.3	63.7	72.5
EMPLOYMENT (mil.)												
1960	5.1	11.6	4.6	(NA)	6.2	1.3	(NA)	3.9	0.9	(NA)	2.3	0.4
1970	6.5	17.5	5.6	(NA)	9.6	1.8	(NA)	6.0	1.2	(NA)	3.6	0.6
1980	10.1	23.6	8.2	0.4	12.8	3.3	0.2	8.1	2.4	0.2	4.8	0.9
1985	11.6	26.1	9.4	0.9	13.9	3.5	0.3	8.1	2.6	0.5	5.9	0.9
1990	12.9	29.9	10.5	1.2	15.8	3.8	0.5	8.9	2.7	0.7	6.9	1.1
1995	13.7	32.3	11.3	1.8	17.2	4.2	0.7	9.8	3.1	1.1	7.3	1.2
1996 [3]	14.1	32.3	11.7	1.8	17.1	4.4	0.7	9.8	3.2	1.1	7.3	1.2
1997 [3]	14.7	32.8	12.1	2.3	17.5	4.3	0.9	10.3	3.1	1.4	7.3	1.1
1998 [3]	15.6	33.0	12.2	2.5	17.4	4.2	1.1	10.1	3.1	1.4	7.3	1.1
UNEMPLOY-MENT RATE [5]												
1960	6.0	5.4	6.2	(NA)	6.0	8.4	(NA)	4.9	6.8	(NA)	7.8	12.5
1970	7.1	4.8	4.8	(NA)	6.0	7.2	(NA)	4.8	5.9	(NA)	7.9	9.8
1980	10.3	5.3	6.4	23.2	5.9	9.2	15.6	4.4	7.9	29.2	8.3	12.8
1985	10.2	5.7	8.5	23.8	6.6	12.1	15.4	5.5	10.6	28.5	8.0	16.1
1990	8.2	3.5	5.7	18.4	4.2	8.5	14.5	3.8	7.7	20.8	4.8	10.2
1995	8.7	3.9	5.8	16.6	4.3	8.1	11.8	3.6	7.1	19.5	5.3	10.8
1996 [3]	8.6	3.4	5.5	18.5	3.5	6.4	15.7	3.2	5.1	20.3	3.9	9.7
1997 [3]	8.8	3.2	5.8	16.9	3.5	9.0	13.5	2.9	7.9	18.8	4.4	11.7
1998 [3]	7.5	3.2	5.0	15.1	3.8	6.7	11.8	3.2	5.3	17.5	4.5	10.6

NA Not available.   [1] Husband present.   [2] Widowed, divorced, or separated.   [3] See footnote 2, Table 649.   [4] Percent of women in each specific category in the labor force.   [5] Unemployed as a percent of civilian labor force in specified group.

Source: U.S. Bureau of Labor Statistics, Bulletin 2307; and unpublished data.

No. 660. Labor Force Participation Rates for Wives, Husband Present, by Age of Own Youngest Child: 1975 to 1998

[As of **March.** For civilian noninstitutional population, 16 years old and over. For definition of participation rate, see Table 659. Based on Current Population Survey; see text, Section 1, Population, and Appendix III]

Presence and age of child	Total			White			Black		
	1975	1985	1998 [1]	1975	1985	1998 [1]	1975	1985	1998 [1]
Wives, total	44.4	54.2	61.8	43.6	53.3	61.0	54.1	63.8	69.6
No children under 18	43.8	48.2	54.1	43.6	47.5	53.5	47.6	55.2	59.0
With children under 18	44.9	60.8	70.6	43.6	59.9	70.0	58.4	71.7	79.4
Under 6, total	36.7	53.4	63.7	34.7	52.1	62.6	54.9	69.6	76.2
Under 3	32.7	50.5	61.4	30.7	49.4	60.5	50.1	66.2	74.6
1 year or under	30.8	49.4	61.8	29.2	48.6	60.7	50.0	63.7	76.9
2 years	37.1	54.0	61.8	35.1	52.7	61.5	56.4	69.9	73.2
3 to 5 years	42.2	58.4	67.1	40.1	56.6	65.9	61.2	73.8	78.3
3 years	41.2	55.1	63.8	39.0	52.7	63.8	62.7	72.3	70.9
4 years	41.2	59.7	67.8	38.7	58.4	66.0	64.9	70.6	80.9
5 years	44.4	62.1	70.9	43.8	59.9	69.5	56.3	79.1	82.6
6 to 13 years	51.8	68.2	76.1	50.7	67.7	75.8	65.7	73.3	82.0
14 to 17 years	53.5	67.0	78.4	53.4	66.6	78.3	52.3	74.4	81.0

[1] See footnote 2, Table 649.

Source: U.S. Bureau of Labor Statistics, Bulletin 2340; and unpublished data.

Labor Force, Employment, and Earnings   **417**

No. 661. Families With Own Children—Employment Status of Parents: 1995 and 1998

[Annual average of monthly figures (33,544 represents 33,544,000). For families with own children. Based on the Current Population Survey, see text, Section 1, Population, and Appendix III]

Characteristic	Number (1,000) 1995	Number (1,000) 1998	Percent distribution 1995	Percent distribution 1998	Characteristic	Number (1,000) 1995	Number (1,000) 1998	Percent distribution 1995	Percent distribution 1998
WITH OWN CHILDREN UNDER 18					Father employed, not mother	2,921	3,074	22.5	22.8
Total families	33,544	34,232	100.0	100.0	Neither parent employed	517	431	4.0	3.2
Parent(s) employed	29,659	31,100	88.4	90.9	Families maintained by women [1]	4,360	4,638	100.0	100.0
No parent employed	3,886	3,130	11.6	9.1	Mother employed	3,142	3,573	72.1	77.0
					Mother not employed	1,219	1,065	27.9	23.0
Married-couple families	24,604	24,820	100.0	100.0					
Parent(s) employed	23,643	24,088	96.1	97.1	Families maintained by men [1]	908	1,075	100.0	100.0
Mother employed	16,629	16,911	67.6	68.1	Father employed	766	913	84.3	84.9
Both parents employed	15,491	15,906	63.0	64.1	Father not employed	143	162	15.7	15.1
Mother employed, not father	1,137	1,005	4.6	4.0	WITH OWN CHILDREN UNDER 6				
Father employed, not mother	7,014	7,178	28.5	28.9					
Neither parent employed	962	731	3.9	2.9	Total families	15,275	15,023	100.0	100.0
					Parent(s) employed	13,267	13,550	86.9	90.2
Families maintained by women [1]	7,433	7,573	100.0	100.0	No parent employed	2,007	1,473	13.1	9.8
Mother employed	4,755	5,440	64.0	71.8	Married-couple families	11,604	11,324	100.0	100.0
Mother not employed	2,678	2,133	36.0	28.2	Parent(s) employed	11,159	11,023	96.2	97.3
					Mother employed	7,066	6,920	60.9	61.1
Families maintained by men [1]	1,507	1,839	100.0	100.0	Both parents employed	6,646	6,567	57.3	58.0
Father employed	1,261	1,572	83.7	85.5	Mother employed, not father	421	352	3.6	3.1
Father not employed	245	266	16.3	14.5	Father employed, not mother	4,092	4,103	35.3	36.2
WITH OWN CHILDREN 6 to 17					Neither parent employed	445	301	3.8	2.7
Total families	18,270	19,209	100.0	100.0	Families maintained by women [1]	3,073	2,936	100.0	100.0
Parent(s) employed	16,391	17,551	89.7	91.4	Mother employed	1,613	1,867	52.5	63.6
No parent employed	1,878	1,658	10.3	8.6	Mother not employed	1,460	1,068	47.5	36.4
Married-couple families	13,001	13,496	100.0	100.0	Families maintained by men [1]	598	763	100.0	100.0
Parent(s) employed	12,484	13,065	96.0	96.8	Father employed	496	660	82.8	86.5
Mother employed	9,562	9,991	73.6	74.0	Father not employed	102	104	17.1	13.6
Both parents employed	8,846	9,338	68.0	69.2					
Mother employed, not father	717	653	5.5	4.8					

[1] No spouse present.

Source: U.S. Bureau of Labor Statistics, News, USDL97-195, June 16, 1997; and unpublished data.

No. 662. Employed Civilians and Weekly Hours: 1970 to 1998

[In thousands (78,678 represents 78,678,000, except as indicated. For civilian noninstitutional population 16 years old and over. Annual averages of monthly figures. Based on Current Population Survey; see text, Section 1, Population, and Appendix III]

Item	1970	1980	1990 [1]	1994 [1]	1995	1996	1997 [1]	1998 [1]
Total employed	78,678	99,303	118,793	123,060	124,900	126,708	129,558	131,463
Age:								
16 to 19 years old	6,144	7,710	6,581	6,161	6,419	6,500	6,661	7,051
20 to 24 years old	9,731	14,087	13,401	12,758	12,443	12,138	12,380	12,557
25 to 34 years old	16,318	27,204	33,935	32,286	32,356	32,077	31,809	31,394
35 to 44 years old	15,922	19,523	30,817	33,599	34,202	35,051	35,908	36,278
45 to 54 years old	16,473	16,234	19,525	23,348	24,378	25,514	26,744	27,587
55 to 64 years old	10,974	11,586	11,189	11,228	11,435	11,739	12,296	12,872
65 years old and over	3,118	2,960	3,346	3,681	3,666	3,690	3,761	3,725
Class of worker:								
Nonagriculture	75,215	95,938	115,570	119,651	121,460	123,264	126,159	128,085
Wage and salary worker	69,491	88,525	106,598	110,517	112,448	114,171	116,983	119,019
Self-employed	5,221	7,000	8,719	9,003	8,902	8,971	9,056	8,962
Unpaid family workers	502	413	253	131	110	122	120	103
Agriculture	3,463	3,364	3,223	3,409	3,440	3,443	3,399	3,378
Wage and salary worker	1,154	1,425	1,740	1,715	1,814	1,869	1,890	2,000
Self-employed	1,810	1,642	1,378	1,645	1,580	1,518	1,457	1,341
Unpaid family workers	499	297	105	49	45	56	51	38
Weekly hours:								
Nonagriculture:								
Wage and salary workers	38.3	38.1	39.2	39.1	39.2	39.2	39.4	39.2
Self-employed	45.0	41.2	40.8	39.5	39.4	39.6	39.7	39.6
Unpaid family workers	37.9	34.7	34.0	33.7	33.5	34.1	32.6	34.0
Agriculture:								
Wage and salary workers	40.0	41.6	41.2	41.0	41.1	41.5	41.6	40.6
Self-employed	51.0	49.3	46.8	43.0	43.5	43.1	42.7	43.3
Unpaid family workers	40.0	38.6	38.5	39.0	42.0	38.0	44.3	36.2

[1] See footnote 2, Table 649.

Source: U.S. Bureau of Labor Statistics, Employment and Earnings, monthly, January issues; and unpublished data.

418 Labor Force, Employment, and Earnings

No. 663. Employed Workers Actively Seeking a New Job: 1997

[As of February. In thousands (112,819 represents 112,819,000), except rate. For employed wage and salary workers 16 old and over (except as indicated) responding to the question on actively seeking work in the prior 3 months Based on the Current Population Survey; see text, Section 1, Population, and Appendix III]

| Characteristic | Total employed | Persons responding to search question | | | Characteristic | Total employed | Persons responding to search question | | |
		Total	Actively seeking work	Percent			Total	Actively seeking work	Percent
Total	**112,819**	**110,546**	**5,528**	**5.0**	Professional specialty . . .	17,477	17,186	921	5.4
Age:					Technical and related				
16 to 19 years old	5,951	5,828	400	6.9	support.	4,042	3,998	206	5.2
20 to 24 years old	11,645	11,326	949	8.4	Sales.	12,493	12,247	774	6.3
25 to 34 years old	29,278	28,590	1,825	6.4	Administrative support,				
35 to 44 years old	31,126	30,579	1,396	4.6	including clerical.	17,843	17,585	816	4.6
45 to 54 years old	22,474	22,078	732	3.3	Private household	731	644	20	3.1
55 to 64 years old	9,843	9,698	203	2.1	Protective service.	2,138	2,097	80	3.8
65 years old and over. . .	2,502	2,447	23	0.9	Service, except private				
Sex: Male	58,797	57,655	3,071	5.3	households and protec-				
Female	54,022	52,891	2,457	4.6	tive	12,808	12,425	658	5.3
Educational attainment: [1]					Precision production,				
Less than high school					craft, and repair	11,803	11,586	458	4.0
diploma	9,669	9,389	310	3.3	Machine operators,				
High school diploma, no					assemblers, and inspec-				
college	31,326	30,672	969	3.2	tors	7,691	7,534	330	4.4
Some college or associ-					Transportation and mate-				
ate degree	26,676	26,265	1,296	4.9	rial moving occupations .	4,787	4,653	178	3.8
Bachelor's degree or					Handlers, equipment				
more	27,552	27,065	1,604	5.9	cleaners, helpers and				
Occupation:					laborers	4,517	4,396	314	7.1
Executive, administrative,					Farming, forestry and				
and managerial	14,887	14,639	694	4.7	fishing	1,604	1,558	78	5.0

[1] Persons 25 years old and over.

Source: U.S. Bureau of Labor Statistics, Current Population Survey, February 1997, unpublished data.

No. 664. Persons At Work, by Hours Worked: 1998

[For civilian noninstitutional population 16 years old and over (125,877 represents 125,877,000). Annual averages of monthly figures. Based on Current Population Survey; see text, Section 1, Population, and Appendix III]

| Hours of work | Persons at work (1,000) | | | Percent distribution | | |
	Total	Agriculture industries	Non-agriculture industries	Total	Agriculture industries	Non-agriculture industries
Total	**125,877**	**3,217**	**122,660**	**100.0**	**100.0**	**100.0**
1 to 34 hours.	33,132	987	32,146	26.3	30.7	26.2
1 to 4 hours.	1,336	71	1,265	1.1	2.2	1.0
5 to 14 hours	4,914	218	4,696	3.9	6.8	3.8
15 to 29 hours	15,545	465	15,081	12.3	14.4	12.3
30 to 34 hours	11,337	232	11,105	9.0	7.2	9.1
35 hours and over	92,745	2,231	90,514	73.7	69.3	73.8
35 to 39 hours	8,731	174	8,556	6.9	5.4	7.0
40 hours	44,224	760	43,464	35.1	23.6	35.4
41 hours and over.	39,790	1,297	38,494	31.6	40.3	31.4
41 to 48 hours	14,608	268	14,340	11.6	8.3	11.7
49 to 58 hours	14,520	387	14,133	11.5	12.0	11.5
60 hours and over	10,663	642	10,020	8.5	20.0	8.2
Average weekly hours:						
Total at work	39.3	41.6	39.2	(X)	(X)	(X)
Persons usually working full time . . .	43.2	47.9	43.1	(X)	(X)	(X)

X Not applicable.

Source: U.S. Bureau of Labor Statistics, Employment and Earnings, monthly, January, 1999 issue.

No. 665. Persons With a Job But Not at Work: 1970 to 1998

[In thousands (4,645 represents 4,645,000), except percent. For civilian noninstitutional population 16 years old and over. Annual averages of monthly figures. Based on Current Population Survey; see text, Section 1, Population, and Appendix III]

Reason for not working	1970	1975	1980	1985	1990 [1]	1993	1994 [1]	1995	1996	1997 [1]	1998 [1]
All industries, number	**4,645**	**5,221**	**5,881**	**5,789**	**6,160**	**6,041**	**5,619**	**5,582**	**5,768**	**5,555**	**5,586**
Percent of employed	5.9	6.1	5.9	5.4	5.2	5.0	4.6	4.5	4.6	4.3	4.2
Reason for not working:											
Vacation	2,341	2,815	3,320	3,338	3,529	3,328	2,877	2,982	3,085	2,942	3,033
Illness	1,324	1,343	1,426	1,308	1,341	1,295	1,184	1,084	1,090	1,114	1,095
Bad weather	128	139	155	141	90	153	165	122	256	146	130
Industrial dispute	156	95	105	42	24	24	15	21	11	20	10
All other	696	829	876	960	1,177	1,241	1,378	1,373	1,325	1,334	1,318

[1] See footnote 2, Table 649.

Source: U.S. Bureau of Labor Statistics, Employment and Earnings, monthly, January issues; and unpublished data.

Labor Force, Employment, and Earnings   419

No. 666. Self-Employed Workers, by Industry and Occupation: 1970 to 1998

[In thousands (7,031 represents 7,031,000). For civilian noninstitutional population 16 years old and over. Annual averages of monthly figures. Data from 1994 forward are not fully comparable with data for prior years because of the introduction of the occupational and industrial classification used in the 1990 census. Based on the Current Population Survey; see text, Section 1, Population, and Appendix III]

Item	1970	1980	1990 [1]	1994 [1]	1995	1996	1997 [1]	1998 [1]
Total self-employed..............	7,031	8,642	10,097	10,648	10,482	10,490	10,513	10,303
Industry: Agriculture	1,810	1,642	1,378	1,645	1,580	1,518	1,457	1,341
Nonagriculture	5,221	7,000	8,719	9,003	8,902	8,971	9,056	8,962
Mining.....................	14	28	24	13	16	15	14	21
Construction...................	687	1,173	1,457	1,506	1,460	1,496	1,492	1,519
Manufacturing..................	264	358	427	426	433	406	422	428
Transportation and public utilities	196	282	301	385	396	432	438	430
Trade	1,667	1,899	1,851	1,906	1,772	1,760	1,761	1,640
Finance, insurance, and real estate	254	458	630	625	660	674	629	609
Services	2,140	2,804	4,030	4,142	4,166	4,189	4,300	4,317
Occupation:								
Managerial and professional specialty......	(NA)	(NA)	3,050	3,106	3,147	3,288	3,432	3,400
Technical, sales, and administrative support..	(NA)	(NA)	2,240	2,380	2,341	2,304	2,219	2,117
Service occupations	(NA)	(NA)	1,207	1,178	1,190	1,198	1,179	1,198
Precision production, craft, and repair......	(NA)	(NA)	1,675	1,740	1,618	1,595	1,651	1,697
Operators, fabricators, and laborers	(NA)	(NA)	567	639	631	634	629	584
Farming, forestry, and fishing	(NA)	(NA)	1,358	1,605	1,556	1,471	1,403	1,307

NA Not available.   [1] See footnote 2, Table 649.

Source: U.S. Bureau of Labor Statistics, Bulletin 2307; *Employment and Earnings*, monthly, January issues; and unpublished data.

No. 667. Self-Employed Persons With Home-Based Businesses: 1997

[As of May (4,125 represents 4,125,000). For persons at work 16 years and over in nonagricultural industries who worked in home-based businesses as part of their primary job. Based on the Current Population Survey; see text, Section 1, Population, and Appendix III]

Characteristic	Total [1] (1,000)	Percent distribution by hours worked at home				Mean hours	
		Less than 8 hours	8 hours or more			Worked at home	Total at work on primary job
			Total	35 hours or more			
Total	4,125	30.4	69.6	29.3		23.0	37.3
SEX							
Male........................	2,157	36.2	63.8	25.5		20.4	42.1
Female......................	1,968	24.2	75.8	33.5		25.9	31.9
RACE AND HISPANIC ORIGIN							
White.......................	3,868	30.5	69.5	29.0		22.9	36.9
Black.......................	135	29.2	70.8	47.0		29.1	42.7
Hispanic origin [2]	156	27.8	72.2	31.3		23.8	35.9
OCCUPATION							
Managerial and professional.............	1,714	28.3	71.7	28.2		23.1	37.0
Exec., admin., and managerial............	1,014	28.3	71.7	29.0		23.8	39.6
Professional......................	700	28.3	71.7	27.1		22.1	33.2
Technical, sales and administrative [3]	1,016	33.4	66.6	22.5		19.5	32.0
Sales	722	34.4	65.6	24.1		20.2	35.8
Administrative support	259	33.1	66.9	15.5		16.7	20.1
Service........................	616	12.0	88.0	58.3		36.9	42.1
Precision production, craft, and repair.........	564	50.1	49.9	15.1		14.8	41.9
Operators, fabricators, and laborers	215	36.1	63.9	22.4		20.0	38.0
INDUSTRY							
Construction	726	49.5	50.5	14.3		14.3	44.3
Manufacturing	193	13.6	86.4	38.5		29.1	36.5
Transportation and public utilities............	132	52.8	47.2	18.0		14.9	35.7
Wholesale trade...................	185	28.9	71.1	30.2		22.3	39.4
Retail trade	532	38.9	61.1	19.2		19.1	30.5
Finance, insurance, and real estate	291	22.5	77.5	23.6		20.9	34.5
Services	2,054	23.0	77.0	37.8		27.4	36.8

[1] Includes persons who worked at home but did not report the number of hours worked. These persons are excluded from the distribution.   [2] Persons of Hispanic origin may be of any race.   [3] Includes other occupations, not shown separately.

Source: U.S. Bureau of Labor Statistics, *News*, USDL 98-93, March 11, 1998.

420   Labor Force, Employment, and Earnings

No. 668. Multiple Jobholders: 1998

[Annual average of monthly figures (7,926 represents 7,926,000). For the civilian noninstitutional population 16 years old and over. Multiple jobholders are employed persons who, either 1) had jobs as wage or salary workers with two employers or more; 2) were self-employed and also held a wage and salary job; or 3) were unpaid family workers on their primary jobs but also held wage and salary job. Based on the Current Population Survey; see text, Section 1, Population, and Appendix III]

Characteristic	Total		Male		Female	
	Number (1,000)	Percent of employed	Number (1,000)	Percent of employed	Number (1,000)	Percent of employed
Total [1]	7,926	6.0	4,178	5.9	3,748	6.2
Age:						
16 to 19 years old	335	4.8	138	3.9	198	5.7
20 to 24 years old	788	6.3	363	5.5	425	7.2
25 to 54 years old	6,011	6.3	3,228	6.3	2,783	6.3
55 to 64 years old	682	5.3	378	5.4	303	5.2
65 years old and over.............	109	2.9	71	3.3	39	2.5
Race and Hispanic origin:						
White........................	6,832	6.2	3,622	6.0	3,210	6.4
Black........................	802	5.5	406	5.9	396	5.2
Hispanic origin [2]	503	3.8	299	3.7	204	3.9
Marital status:						
Married, spouse present	4,414	5.8	2,664	6.2	1,750	5.3
Widowed, divorced, or separated	1,385	6.7	498	5.8	887	7.3
Single, never married	2,127	6.1	1,016	5.3	1,110	7.0
Full- or part-time status:						
Primary job full time, secondary job......	4,478	(X)	2,608	(X)	1,870	(X)
Both jobs part time...............	1,635	(X)	512	(X)	1,124	(X)
Both jobs full time	266	(X)	188	(X)	78	(X)
Hours vary on primary or secondary job. . .	1,504	(X)	848	(X)	656	(X)

X Not applicable. [1] Includes a small number of persons who work part time on their primary job and full time on their secondary job(s), not shown separately. Includes other races, not shown separately. [2] Persons of Hispanic origin may be of any race.

Source: U.S. Bureau of Labor Statistics, *Employment and Earnings*, monthly, January 1999 issue.

No. 669. Reasons for Multiple Jobholding: 1997

[As of May (8,751 represents 8,751,000). See headnote, Table 668]

Characteristic		Percent distribution by reason							
	Total (1,000)	Meet regular houshold expenses	To pay off debts	To save for the future	To get experi- ence or build up a busi- ness	To help out a friend or relative	To get extra money to buy some- thing special	Enjoys the work on the second job	Other reasons
Total [1]	8,751	30.9	10.5	8.7	7.7	3.2	7.9	14.5	16.6
Age:									
16 to 24 years old	1,274	24.7	18.2	11.4	5.2	2.3	13.0	6.5	18.5
25 to 54 years old	6,648	33.0	9.8	8.4	8.5	3.3	6.7	14.4	15.7
55 years old and over. . .	829	23.6	4.6	6.2	5.0	3.7	9.4	26.9	20.7
Race and Hispanic origin:									
White..............	7,566	29.7	9.8	8.8	8.0	3.5	8.0	15.2	17.1
Black...............	874	38.9	14.1	7.9	5.6	1.4	7.0	11.4	13.8
Hispanic origin [2]	557	39.5	9.5	9.7	5.4	3.1	11.1	4.7	17.1
Males	4,720	29.4	10.4	10.1	8.4	2.8	7.4	15.9	15.7
Single	1,238	24.5	15.6	11.1	8.0	2.3	10.2	10.3	18.0
Married, spouse present .	2,910	31.2	8.1	10.1	8.2	3.0	6.3	19.2	13.9
Widowed, divorced, or separated	573	30.6	10.5	7.9	9.8	2.8	7.2	11.0	20.3
Females	4,031	32.7	10.7	6.9	7.0	3.7	8.5	12.8	17.6
Single	1,145	28.7	15.5	9.4	3.6	2.5	12.9	9.0	18.3
Married, spouse present .	1,941	28.8	7.2	6.5	9.9	4.1	7.4	16.5	19.5
Widowed, divorced, or separated	946	45.4	12.2	4.9	5.1	4.3	5.4	9.9	12.8
Women who maintain families.	577	52.5	12.0	5.0	1.6	2.1	6.1	8.3	12.5

[1] Due to estimation procedures, the number of multiple jobholders differs from the regularly published monthly data. Includes other races, not shown separately. [2] Persons of Hispanic origin may be of any race.

Source: U.S. Bureau of Labor Statistics, unpublished data.

No. 670. Distribution of Workers, by Tenure With Current Employer, by Selected Characteristic: 1998

[As of February (115,892 represents 115,892,000). For employed wage and salary workers 16 years old and over. Based on the Current Population Survey and subject to sampling error; see source and Appendix III]

Characteristic	Number employed (1,000)	Percent distribution by tenure with current employer								Median years [1]
		12 months or less	13 to 23 months	2 years	3 to 4 years	5 to 9 years	10 to 14 years	15 to 19 years	20 years or more	
Total [2]	115,892	27.8	7.9	4.9	15.8	17.9	10.7	6.1	9.0	3.6
AGE AND SEX										
16 to 19 years old	6,461	77.9	10.2	6.1	5.5	0.3	-	-	-	0.7
20 years old and over	109,431	24.8	7.7	4.8	16.4	18.9	11.3	6.5	9.5	4.0
20 to 24 years old	11,967	53.5	13.1	9.1	18.4	5.9	(Z)	-	-	1.1
25 to 34 years old	29,291	31.3	10.4	6.0	21.9	21.5	8.0	0.9	-	2.7
35 to 44 years old	31,684	20.5	6.7	4.0	15.6	22.0	15.9	9.7	5.6	5.0
45 to 54 years old	23,482	14.7	5.2	3.4	12.5	18.7	13.6	10.2	21.7	8.1
55 to 64 years old	10,377	11.6	4.0	2.6	11.0	17.3	14.2	10.4	28.9	10.1
65 years old and over	2,631	16.1	3.5	3.6	13.1	18.6	13.9	9.5	21.7	7.8
Male	60,113	26.9	7.5	4.7	15.9	17.4	10.5	6.2	10.9	3.8
16 to 19 years old	3,143	78.3	10.4	5.0	5.9	0.4	-	-	-	0.7
20 years old and over	56,970	24.1	7.3	4.7	16.4	18.3	11.1	6.6	11.5	4.2
20 to 24 years old	6,270	52.1	12.1	10.3	19.4	6.0	(Z)	-	-	1.2
25 to 34 years old	15,637	30.6	9.6	5.7	22.6	22.2	8.4	1.0	-	2.8
35 to 44 years old	16,568	19.2	6.5	3.5	14.7	21.8	16.7	10.8	6.8	5.5
45 to 54 years old	11,866	14.3	4.6	3.1	12.2	16.2	11.5	10.7	27.5	9.4
55 to 64 years old	5,333	11.3	3.9	2.6	10.1	15.9	12.2	8.3	35.8	11.2
65 years old and over	1,297	16.5	4.9	4.3	14.2	17.7	15.1	6.3	20.9	7.1
Female	55,779	28.7	8.3	5.1	15.8	18.3	10.9	6.0	6.9	3.4
16 to 19 years old	3,318	77.4	10.0	7.2	5.2	0.2	-	-	-	0.7
20 years old and over	52,461	25.6	8.2	5.0	16.4	19.5	11.6	6.3	7.4	3.8
20 to 24 years old	5,697	55.0	14.2	7.7	17.3	5.7	(Z)	-	-	1.1
25 to 34 years old	13,654	32.2	11.3	6.4	21.2	20.8	7.4	0.7	-	2.5
35 to 44 years old	15,116	21.9	6.8	4.5	16.6	22.3	15.0	8.6	4.2	4.5
45 to 54 years old	11,616	15.2	5.8	3.8	12.8	21.3	15.7	9.7	15.8	7.2
55 to 64 years old	5,044	11.9	4.2	2.6	11.9	18.9	16.3	12.6	21.6	9.6
65 years old and over	1,334	15.7	2.1	3.0	12.0	19.6	12.6	12.6	22.4	8.7
RACE AND HISPANIC ORIGIN										
White	97,341	27.5	8.0	4.8	15.7	18.0	10.8	6.2	9.2	3.6
Male	51,234	26.6	7.5	4.6	15.7	17.3	10.7	6.4	11.2	3.9
Female	46,108	28.4	8.6	5.0	15.6	18.7	11.0	5.9	6.9	3.4
Black	13,298	29.1	6.3	5.4	16.6	16.8	10.0	6.4	9.4	3.5
Male	6,123	28.7	6.1	5.2	16.5	17.3	9.2	6.0	11.1	3.6
Female	7,175	29.5	6.5	5.6	16.6	16.3	10.7	6.7	8.0	3.4
Hispanic origin [3]	12,695	31.4	8.4	6.5	19.6	17.4	8.6	3.6	4.4	2.8
Male	7,468	30.7	7.9	6.1	19.9	18.1	8.1	4.0	5.2	3.0
Female	5,227	32.5	9.1	7.0	19.0	16.5	9.3	3.2	3.3	2.6

- Represents zero.   Z Less than 0.05 percent.   [1] For definition of median, see Guide to Tabular Presentation.   [2] Includes other races, not shown separately.   [3] Persons of Hispanic origin may be of any race.
Source: U. S. Bureau of Labor Statistics, *News*, USDL 98-387, September 23, 1998, and unpublished data.

No. 671. Part-Time Workers, by Reason: 1998

[In thousands (33,132 represents 33,132,000), except hours. For persons working 1 to 34 hours per per week. For civilian noninstitutional population 16 years old and over. Annual average of monthly figures. Based on the Current Population Survey and subject to sampling error; see text, Section 1, Population, and Appendix III]

Reason	All industries			Nonagricultural industries		
	Total	Usually work—		Total	Usually work—	
		Full time	Part time		Full time	Part time
Total working fewer than 35 hours	33,132	12,260	20,872	32,146	11,929	20,217
Economic reasons	3,665	1,322	2,343	3,501	1,238	2,263
Slack work or business conditions	2,095	1,056	1,038	1,997	998	999
Could find only part-time work	1,258	-	1,258	1,228	-	1,228
Seasonal work	135	89	47	102	66	37
Job started or ended during the week	177	177	-	174	174	-
Noneconomic reasons	29,467	10,938	18,530	28,645	10,691	17,954
Child-care problems	856	89	767	843	87	755
Other family or personal obligations	5,551	688	4,863	5,390	673	4,716
Health or medical limitations	717	-	717	683	-	683
In school or training	6,394	97	6,297	6,245	94	6,151
Retired or Social Security limit on earnings	1,889	-	1,889	1,775	-	1,775
Vacation or personal day	3,487	3,487	-	3,420	3,420	-
Holiday, legal, or religious	3,399	3,399	-	3,357	3,357	-
Weather related curtailment	489	489	-	426	426	-
Other	6,685	2,689	3,997	6,508	2,634	3,874
Average hours per week:						
Economic reasons	22.9	23.9	22.4	23.0	24.0	22.4
Noneconomic reasons	22.1	26.6	19.5	22.2	26.7	19.6

- Represents or rounds to zero.
Source: U.S. Bureau of Labor Statistics, *Employment and Earnings*, monthly, January 1999 issue.

No. 672. Displaced Workers, by Selected Characteristics: 1998

[In percent, except total (3,578 represents 3,578,000). As of February. For persons 20 years old and over with tenure of 3 years or more who lost or left a job between January 1995 and December 1997 because of plant closings or moves, slack work, or the abolishment of their positions. Data revised since originally published. Based on Current Population Survey and subject to sampling error; see source and Appendix III]

Characteristic	Total (1,000)	Employment status			Reason for job loss		
		Employed	Unem-ployed	Not in the labor force	Plant or company closed down or moved	Slack work	Position or shift abolished
Total [1]	**3,578**	**75.9**	**10.0**	**14.1**	**47.2**	**21.2**	**31.6**
20 to 24 years old	108	61.2	11.8	27.0	43.1	38.7	18.2
25 to 54 years old	2,835	81.5	9.9	8.5	47.1	20.9	32.0
55 to 64 years old	471	59.6	9.9	30.4	46.0	17.7	36.4
65 years old and over ...	163	34.7	10.6	54.8	54.0	25.7	20.3
Males	1,898	78.8	12.0	9.3	44.0	26.0	30.0
20 to 24 years old	49	(2)	(2)	(2)	(2)	(2)	(2)
25 to 54 years old	1,488	84.3	11.3	4.4	45.3	25.5	29.2
55 to 64 years old	280	61.9	12.6	25.4	42.8	16.4	40.8
65 years old and over	81	42.0	16.8	41.3	40.3	40.6	19.1
Females	1,680	72.6	7.8	19.5	50.7	15.8	33.5
20 to 24 years old	59	(2)	(2)	(2)	(2)	(2)	(2)
25 to 54 years old	1,347	78.4	8.5	13.1	49.2	15.7	35.1
55 to 64 years old	191	56.2	6.0	37.8	50.7	19.5	29.8
65 years old and over	82	27.4	4.3	68.2	67.7	10.9	21.5
White	3,063	76.0	9.4	14.6	46.0	21.3	32.7
Black	366	73.1	16.3	10.6	53.1	17.7	29.2
Hispanic origin [3]	354	71.6	15.4	13.0	57.8	26.0	16.2

[1] Includes other races, not shown separately. [2] Data not shown where base is less than 75,000. [3] Persons of Hispanic origin may be of any race.
Source: U.S. Bureau of Labor Statistics, *News*, USDL 98-347, August 19, 1998.

No. 673. Percent Distribution of Employed Persons by Disability Status: 1991 to 1994

[(119,432 represents 119,432,000). Data from the Survey of Income and Program Participation]

Disability status	1991	1993	1994	Disability status	1991	1993	1994
All employed persons (1,000) ..	119,432	122,614	125,591	Lifting and carrying........	2.3	2.6	2.5
Total of employed persons..	100.0	100.0	100.0	Climbing stairs...........	2.3	2.6	2.6
				Walking 3 city blocks	2.4	2.6	2.7
With no disability..........	86.6	86.2	86.2				
With a disability...........	13.4	13.8	13.8	With an ADL [1] limitation	0.8	1.0	0.9
Severe	2.8	3.2	3.4	With an IADL [2] limitation......	1.1	1.3	1.4
Not severe	10.6	10.6	10.4	Needs personal assistance and			
				an ADL or IADL..........	0.7	0.9	0.9
With a functional limitation	8.4	8.9	7.9	Uses a wheelchair.........	0.1	0.1	0.1
Severe	1.7	2.0	2.1	Does not use a wheelchair,			
With difficulty:				but uses a cane, crutches,			
Seeing words and letters....	2.0	2.2	1.6	or a walker	0.4	0.5	0.4
Hearing normal conversation .	3.2	3.5	2.7				

[1] ADLs are activities of daily living and include getting around inside the home, getting in or out of a bed or chair, taking a bath or shower, dressing, eating, and using the toilet. [2] IADLs are instrumental activities of daily living and include going outside the home, keeping track of money and bills, preparing meals, doing light housework, and using the telephone.
Source: U.S. Census Bureau, Internet site <http://www.census.gov/hhes/www/disable/dissipp.html> (Accessed 18 June 1997)

No. 674. Persons Not in the Labor Force: 1998

[In thousands (67,547 represents 67,547,000). Annual average of monthly figures. For the civilian noninstitutional population 16 years old and over. Based on the Current Population Survey; see text, Section 1, Population, and Appendix III]

Status and reason	Total	Age			Sex	
		16 to 24 yrs. old	25 to 54 yrs. old	55 yrs. old and over	Male	Female
Total not in the labor force	**67,547**	**11,343**	**18,732**	**37,472**	**24,799**	**42,748**
Do not want a job now [1]	62,735	9,491	16,580	36,664	22,790	39,945
Want a job now	4,812	1,852	2,152	807	2,008	2,803
In the previous year—						
Did not search for a job............	2,859	1,011	1,240	608	1,134	1,725
Did search for a job [2]	1,953	841	912	200	875	1,078
Not available for work now	643	332	275	36	250	392
Available for work now, not looking for work. . .	1,310	509	637	164	624	686
Reason for not currently looking:						
Discouraged over job prospects [3]	331	108	170	53	198	133
Family responsibilities.............	143	37	93	13	23	120
In school or training	206	173	32	1	105	102
Ill health or disability.............	104	14	69	21	52	52
Other [4]	525	177	273	75	247	278

[1] Includes some persons who are not asked if they want a job. [2] Persons who had a job in the prior 12 months must have searched since the end of that job. [3] Includes such things as believes no work available, could not find work, lacks necessary schooling or training, employer thinks too young or old, and other types of discrimination. [4] Includes such things as child care and transportation problems.
Source: U.S. Bureau of Labor Statistics, *Employment and Earnings*, monthly, January 1999 issue.

Labor Force, Employment, and Earnings 423

No. 675. Employed Civilians, by Occupation, Sex, Race, and Hispanic Origin: 1983 and 1998

[For civilian noninstitutional population 16 years old and over (**100,834 represents 100,834,000**). Annual average of monthly figures. Based on Current Population Survey; see text, Section 1, Population, and Appendix III. Persons of Hispanic origin may be of any race. See headnote, Table 666]

Occupation	1983 Total employed (1,000)	Percent of total Female	Black	Hispanic	1998 [1] Total employed (1,000)	Percent of total Female	Black	Hispanic
Total	**100,834**	**43.7**	**9.3**	**5.3**	**131,463**	**46.2**	**11.1**	**10.1**
Managerial and professional specialty	**23,592**	**40.9**	**5.6**	**2.6**	**38,937**	**49.0**	**7.6**	**5.0**
Executive, administrative, and managerial [2]	10,772	32.4	4.7	2.8	19,054	44.4	7.2	5.4
Officials and administrators, public	417	38.5	8.3	3.8	630	48.5	12.1	4.5
Financial managers	357	38.6	3.5	3.1	705	53.3	6.8	4.4
Personnel and labor relations managers	106	43.9	4.9	2.6	162	65.9	7.7	4.3
Purchasing managers	82	23.6	5.1	1.4	136	39.4	5.0	5.5
Managers, marketing, advertising and public relations	396	21.8	2.7	1.7	772	38.5	3.8	3.4
Administrators, education and related fields	415	41.4	11.3	2.4	752	62.2	10.6	4.2
Managers, medicine and health	91	57.0	5.0	2.0	725	79.2	6.8	5.3
Managers, properties and real estate	305	42.8	5.5	5.2	517	52.2	7.1	9.4
Management-related occupations [2]	2,966	40.3	5.8	3.5	4,700	57.1	9.7	5.4
Accountants and auditors	1,105	38.7	5.5	3.3	1,616	58.2	9.4	4.9
Professional specialty [2]	12,820	48.1	6.4	2.5	19,883	53.3	7.9	4.6
Architects	103	12.7	1.6	1.5	158	17.5	2.0	5.2
Engineers [2]	1,572	5.8	2.7	2.2	2,052	11.1	4.1	3.8
Aerospace engineers	80	6.9	1.5	2.1	86	8.4	3.3	2.6
Chemical engineers	67	6.1	3.0	1.4	69	16.5	4.6	1.0
Civil engineers	211	4.0	1.9	3.2	296	12.1	2.0	4.6
Electrical and electronic	450	6.1	3.4	3.1	629	9.0	5.3	3.7
Industrial engineers	210	11.0	3.3	2.4	262	18.3	5.3	5.6
Mechanical	259	2.8	3.2	1.1	335	7.0	3.3	2.0
Mathematical and computer scientists [2]	463	29.6	5.4	2.6	1,747	28.9	7.2	4.2
Computer systems analysts, scientists	276	27.8	6.2	2.7	1,471	26.9	7.2	3.6
Operations and systems researchers and analysts	142	31.3	4.9	2.2	212	41.9	8.8	8.5
Natural scientists [2]	357	20.5	2.6	2.1	519	30.9	3.9	3.0
Chemists, except biochemists	98	23.3	4.3	1.2	133	32.9	6.1	3.1
Biological and life scientists	55	40.8	2.4	1.8	104	38.8	3.3	1.5
Medical scientists	(3)	(3)	(3)	(3)	83	45.2	5.6	5.2
Health diagnosing occupations [2]	735	13.3	2.7	3.3	1,083	26.3	4.2	4.0
Physicians	519	15.8	3.2	4.5	740	26.6	4.9	4.8
Dentists	126	6.7	2.4	1.0	155	19.8	2.8	2.0
Health assessment and treating occupations [2]	1,900	85.8	7.1	2.2	2,898	85.2	8.9	3.4
Registered nurses	1,372	95.8	6.7	1.8	2,032	92.5	9.3	3.2
Pharmacists	158	26.7	3.8	2.6	180	44.0	4.1	5.1
Dietitians	71	90.8	21.0	3.7	90	86.0	18.2	4.3
Therapists [2]	247	76.3	7.6	2.7	528	75.4	7.3	3.8
Respiratory therapists	69	69.4	6.5	3.7	103	60.8	11.7	2.0
Physical therapists	55	77.0	9.7	1.5	134	72.9	4.2	5.4
Speech therapists	51	90.5	1.5	-	105	92.6	1.9	6.3
Physicians' assistants	51	36.3	7.7	4.4	68	52.6	10.6	2.8
Teachers, college and university	606	36.3	4.4	1.8	919	42.3	5.8	3.6
Teachers, except college and university [2]	3,365	70.9	9.1	2.7	4,962	75.3	10.0	5.4
Prekindergarten and kindergarten	299	98.2	11.8	3.4	586	97.8	14.4	8.0
Elementary school	1,350	83.3	11.1	3.1	1,951	84.0	10.5	5.6
Secondary school	1,209	51.8	7.2	2.3	1,225	56.9	8.9	4.2
Special education	81	82.2	10.2	2.3	381	82.0	11.0	4.7
Counselors, educational and vocational	184	53.1	13.9	3.2	230	68.8	13.2	5.5
Librarians, archivists, and curators	213	84.4	7.8	1.6	236	80.8	5.9	5.4
Librarians	193	87.3	7.9	1.8	208	83.4	5.2	5.9
Social scientists and urban planners [2]	261	46.8	7.1	2.1	430	54.7	6.7	5.2
Economists	98	37.9	6.3	2.7	137	46.3	3.6	6.5
Psychologists	135	57.1	8.6	1.1	232	62.1	10.2	4.0
Social, recreation, and religious workers [2]	831	43.1	12.1	3.8	1,329	55.1	17.5	5.9
Social workers	407	64.3	18.2	6.3	749	68.4	23.4	6.4
Recreation workers	65	71.9	15.7	2.0	132	75.1	15.9	4.8
Clergy	293	5.6	4.9	1.4	325	12.0	8.7	6.1
Lawyers and judges	651	15.8	2.7	1.0	951	28.6	4.3	3.0
Lawyers	612	15.3	2.6	0.9	912	28.5	4.0	3.0
Writers, artists, entertainers, and athletes [2]	1,544	42.7	4.8	2.9	2,353	51.4	6.2	5.6
Authors	62	46.7	2.1	0.9	130	55.0	2.2	1.3
Technical writers	(3)	(3)	(3)	(3)	73	57.4	3.5	1.2
Designers	393	52.7	3.1	2.7	692	58.0	3.0	6.6
Musicians and composers	155	28.0	7.9	4.4	183	39.7	10.8	7.2
Actors and directors	60	30.8	6.6	3.4	130	38.7	8.2	4.5
Painters, sculptors, craft-artists, and artist printmakers	186	47.4	2.1	2.3	241	53.9	4.7	5.0
Photographers	113	20.7	4.0	3.4	154	38.1	5.5	7.1
Editors and reporters	204	48.4	2.9	2.1	274	51.0	8.9	3.1
Public relations specialists	157	50.1	6.2	1.9	170	66.3	8.8	4.0
Announcers	(3)	(3)	(3)	(3)	60	17.1	10.7	5.0
Athletes	58	17.6	9.4	1.7	91	23.7	12.7	3.7

See footnotes at end of table.

U.S. Census Bureau, Statistical Abstract of the United States: 1999

No. 675. Employed Civilians, by Occupation, Sex, Race, and Hispanic Origin: 1983 and 1998—Continued

[See headnote, page 424]

Occupation	1983 Total employed (1,000)	1983 Female	1983 Black	1983 Hispanic	1998[1] Total employed (1,000)	1998 Female	1998 Black	1998 Hispanic
Technical, sales, and administrative support	**31,265**	**64.6**	**7.6**	**4.3**	**38,521**	**64.2**	**11.1**	**8.3**
Technicians and related support	3,053	48.2	8.2	3.1	4,261	53.6	10.4	6.6
Health technologists and technicians[2]	1,111	84.3	12.7	3.1	1,733	81.6	13.9	7.0
Clinical laboratory technologists and technicians	255	76.2	10.5	2.9	359	78.5	15.0	6.4
Dental hygienists	66	98.6	1.6	-	112	99.1	3.9	3.9
Radiologic technicians	101	71.7	8.6	4.5	170	69.5	8.2	2.0
Licensed practical nurses	443	97.0	17.7	3.1	381	96.0	17.4	5.8
Engineering and related technologists and technicians[2]	822	18.4	6.1	3.5	970	20.8	8.6	7.6
Electrical and electronic technicians	260	12.5	8.2	4.6	431	16.9	9.3	8.8
Drafting occupations	273	17.5	5.5	2.3	228	19.3	3.5	6.2
Surveying and mapping technicians	(3)	(3)	(3)	(3)	71	12.8	3.5	8.2
Science technicians[2]	202	29.1	6.6	2.8	285	43.3	8.8	5.8
Biological technicians	52	37.7	2.9	2.0	108	68.2	4.0	4.9
Chemical technicians	82	26.9	9.5	3.5	75	21.2	12.9	5.3
Technicians, except health, engineering, and science[2]	917	35.3	5.0	2.7	1,273	42.8	7.2	5.6
Airplane pilots and navigators	69	2.1	-	1.6	113	3.4	1.9	2.5
Computer programmers	443	32.5	4.4	2.1	613	28.5	6.4	4.9
Legal assistants	128	74.0	4.3	3.6	370	82.0	8.1	7.2
Sales occupations	11,818	47.5	4.7	3.7	15,850	50.3	8.9	7.9
Supervisors and proprietors	2,958	28.4	3.6	3.4	4,719	40.1	6.5	6.3
Sales representatives, finance and business services[2]	1,853	37.2	2.7	2.2	2,668	43.6	7.6	4.8
Insurance sales	551	25.1	3.8	2.5	592	41.5	9.1	4.2
Real estate sales	570	48.9	1.3	1.5	749	53.0	3.9	4.1
Securities and financial services sales	212	23.6	3.1	1.1	477	29.1	6.4	3.7
Advertising and related sales	124	47.9	4.5	3.3	186	58.3	8.9	3.1
Sales representatives, commodities, except retail	1,442	15.1	2.1	2.2	1,584	26.0	2.9	5.4
Sales workers, retail and personal services	5,511	69.7	6.7	4.8	6,784	65.4	12.5	10.7
Cashiers	2,009	84.4	10.1	5.4	3,025	78.2	16.8	12.7
Sales-related occupations	54	58.7	2.8	1.3	94	72.7	6.6	3.7
Administrative support, including clerical	16,395	79.9	9.6	5.0	18,410	78.6	13.1	9.0
Supervisors	676	53.4	9.3	5.0	698	60.1	15.1	5.9
Computer equipment operators	605	63.9	12.5	6.0	375	54.7	14.1	7.1
Computer operators	597	63.7	12.1	6.0	371	54.8	14.2	6.8
Secretaries, stenographers, and typists[2]	4,861	98.2	7.3	4.5	3,599	97.6	9.6	7.0
Secretaries	3,891	99.0	5.8	4.0	2,914	98.4	8.5	7.0
Typists	906	95.6	13.8	6.4	580	94.3	16.5	7.1
Information clerks	1,174	88.9	8.5	5.5	1,965	89.0	11.5	10.7
Receptionists	602	96.8	7.5	6.6	1,006	95.5	10.5	12.5
Records processing occupations, except financial[2]	866	82.4	13.9	4.8	1,063	79.2	14.5	10.6
Order clerks	188	78.1	10.6	4.4	246	75.2	20.2	11.4
Personnel clerks, except payroll and time keeping	64	91.1	14.9	4.6	74	87.1	14.0	15.9
Library clerks	147	81.9	15.4	2.5	173	75.5	10.3	6.1
File clerks	287	83.5	16.7	6.1	348	80.3	14.5	10.8
Records clerks	157	82.8	11.6	5.6	205	82.5	10.7	11.9
Financial records processing[2]	2,457	89.4	4.6	3.7	2,214	92.1	7.7	6.5
Bookkeepers, accounting, and auditing clerks	1,970	91.0	4.3	3.3	1,726	93.0	6.8	6.0
Payroll and time keeping clerks	192	82.2	5.9	5.0	146	89.7	10.6	8.8
Billing clerks	146	88.4	6.2	3.9	185	87.2	9.3	7.9
Cost and rate clerks	96	75.6	5.9	5.3	52	83.7	8.9	9.2
Billing, posting, and calculating machine operators	(3)	(3)	(3)	(3)	105	94.1	15.7	6.1
Duplicating, mail and other office machine operators	68	62.6	16.0	6.1	81	55.7	18.9	16.6
Communications equipment operators	256	89.1	17.0	4.4	175	81.7	25.9	14.3
Telephone operators	244	90.4	17.0	4.3	159	85.8	26.8	13.1
Mail and message distributing occupations	799	31.6	18.1	4.5	984	38.0	21.1	10.3
Postal clerks, except mail carriers	248	36.7	26.2	5.2	319	47.2	28.2	8.5
Mail carrier, postal service	259	17.1	12.5	2.7	333	29.7	17.1	9.9
Mail clerks, except postal service	170	50.0	15.8	5.9	178	49.7	24.5	12.4
Messengers	122	26.2	16.7	5.2	155	23.1	11.4	12.3
Material recording, scheduling, and distributing[2][4]	1,562	37.5	10.9	6.6	1,945	45.1	14.1	12.7
Dispatchers	157	45.7	11.4	4.3	235	49.4	11.0	8.7
Production coordinators	182	44.0	6.1	2.2	255	56.7	5.3	7.0
Traffic, shipping, and receiving clerks	421	22.6	9.1	11.1	628	31.6	17.3	17.0
Stock and inventory clerks	532	38.7	13.3	5.5	452	42.9	15.5	14.8
Weighers, measurers, and checkers	79	47.2	16.9	5.8	51	52.4	22.8	9.4
Expediters	112	57.5	8.4	4.3	272	67.9	12.7	10.4
Adjusters and investigators	675	69.9	11.1	5.1	1,813	74.7	16.3	8.0
Insurance adjusters, examiners, and investigators	199	65.0	11.5	3.3	476	72.1	12.2	6.6
Investigators and adjusters, except insurance	301	70.1	11.3	4.8	1,049	75.6	17.1	7.7
Eligibility clerks, social welfare	69	88.7	12.9	9.4	94	85.8	17.5	14.7
Bill and account collectors	106	66.4	8.5	6.5	195	70.5	21.5	9.3
Miscellaneous administrative support[2]	2,397	85.2	12.5	5.9	3,496	83.1	14.7	9.7
General office clerks	648	80.6	12.7	5.2	735	81.1	15.3	10.8
Bank tellers	480	91.0	7.5	4.3	416	89.5	11.0	9.0
Data entry keyers	311	93.6	18.6	5.6	711	81.8	17.4	8.4
Statistical clerks	96	75.7	7.5	3.4	100	80.5	19.4	7.1
Teachers' aides	348	93.7	17.8	12.6	633	93.0	15.1	13.5

See footnotes at end of table.

U.S. Census Bureau, Statistical Abstract of the United States: 1999

No. 675. Employed Civilians, by Occupation, Sex, Race, and Hispanic Origin: 1983 and 1998—Continued

[See headnote, page 424]

Occupation	1983				1998 [1]			
	Total employed (1,000)	Fe-male	Black	His-panic	Total employed (1,000)	Fe-male	Black	His-panic
Service occupations	13,857	60.1	16.6	6.8	17,836	59.5	17.6	15.0
Private household [2]	980	96.1	27.8	8.5	847	94.6	13.7	30.9
Child care workers	408	96.9	7.9	3.6	278	96.5	9.4	19.5
Cleaners and servants	512	95.8	42.4	11.8	549	94.3	15.4	37.0
Protective service	1,672	12.8	13.6	4.6	2,417	17.8	19.1	8.5
Supervisors, protective service	127	4.7	7.7	3.1	214	9.3	14.2	7.5
Supervisors, police and detectives	58	4.2	9.3	1.2	118	11.3	10.5	6.0
Firefighting and fire prevention	189	1.0	6.7	4.1	250	2.5	10.9	5.3
Firefighting occupations	170	1.0	7.3	3.8	228	2.3	11.8	3.9
Police and detectives	645	9.4	13.1	4.0	1,062	16.3	19.4	8.8
Police and detectives, public service	412	5.7	9.5	4.4	602	11.5	15.2	10.0
Sheriffs, bailiffs, and other law enforcement officers . .	87	13.2	11.5	4.0	161	17.0	16.8	8.0
Correctional institution officers	146	17.8	24.0	2.8	299	25.4	29.2	6.8
Guards	711	20.6	17.0	5.6	891	26.0	22.4	9.2
Guards and police, except public service	602	13.0	18.9	6.2	753	19.0	25.1	9.9
Service except private household and protective	11,205	64.0	16.0	6.9	14,572	64.4	17.6	15.1
Food preparation and service occupations [2]	4,860	63.3	10.5	6.8	6,071	56.5	11.8	17.0
Bartenders	338	48.4	2.7	4.4	324	54.6	4.3	6.7
Waiters and waitresses	1,357	87.8	4.1	3.6	1,379	78.3	5.4	11.3
Cooks	1,452	50.0	15.8	6.5	2,135	40.9	16.6	21.9
Food counter, fountain, and related occupations	326	76.0	9.1	6.7	339	69.1	10.3	10.8
Kitchen workers, food preparation	138	77.0	13.7	8.1	269	69.0	12.1	11.1
Waiters' and waitresses' assistants	364	38.8	12.6	14.2	559	53.4	10.7	18.8
Health service occupations	1,739	89.2	23.5	4.8	2,480	88.5	30.1	10.0
Dental assistants	154	98.1	6.1	5.7	230	98.1	6.1	12.1
Health aides, except nursing	316	86.8	16.5	4.8	337	78.9	24.4	9.3
Nursing aides, orderlies, and attendants [2]	1,269	88.7	27.3	4.7	1,913	89.0	34.0	9.8
Cleaning and building service occupations [2]	2,736	38.8	24.4	9.2	3,112	44.5	22.8	20.5
Maids and housemen	531	81.2	32.3	10.1	653	82.8	26.7	25.0
Janitors and cleaners	2,031	28.6	22.6	8.9	2,233	34.8	21.7	19.6
Personal service occupations [2]	1,870	79.2	11.1	6.0	2,909	81.5	13.5	9.8
Barbers	92	12.9	8.4	12.1	66	18.5	39.4	11.8
Hairdressers and cosmetologists	622	88.7	7.0	5.7	763	90.8	11.3	8.2
Attendants, amusement and recreation facilities	131	40.2	7.1	4.3	215	43.2	9.3	5.6
Public transportation attendants	63	74.3	11.3	5.9	124	86.3	12.9	4.1
Welfare service aides	77	92.5	24.2	10.5	92	86.8	25.1	15.9
Family child care providers	(NA)	(NA)	(NA)	(NA)	486	97.1	11.2	10.7
Early childhood teachers' assistants	(NA)	(NA)	(NA)	(NA)	453	95.9	16.0	11.8
Precision production, craft, and repair	12,328	8.1	6.8	6.2	14,411	8.3	8.0	12.4
Mechanics and repairers [2]	4,158	3.0	6.8	5.3	4,786	4.0	7.9	10.4
Mechanics and repairers, except supervisors [2]	3,906	2.8	7.0	5.5	4,527	4.0	8.0	10.5
Vehicle and mobile equipment mechanics/repairers [2] . . .	1,683	0.8	6.9	6.0	1,845	1.0	7.6	12.6
Automobile mechanics	800	0.5	7.8	6.0	877	0.8	8.3	13.7
Aircraft engine mechanics	95	2.5	4.0	7.6	153	3.7	8.6	11.7
Electrical and electronic equipment repairers [2] . . .	674	7.4	7.3	4.5	866	11.1	10.8	9.0
Data processing equipment repairers	98	9.3	6.1	4.5	274	16.9	7.5	8.0
Telephone installers and repairers	247	9.9	7.8	3.7	232	12.0	11.9	9.2
Construction trades	4,289	1.8	6.6	6.0	5,594	2.0	7.1	14.0
Construction trades, except supervisors	3,784	1.9	7.1	6.1	4,839	2.0	7.5	14.9
Carpenters	1,160	1.4	5.0	5.0	1,346	1.2	5.3	13.7
Extractive occupations	196	2.3	3.3	6.0	125	1.4	7.0	11.8
Precision production occupations	3,685	21.5	7.3	7.4	3,907	23.0	9.5	12.7
Operators, fabricators, and laborers	16,091	26.6	14.0	8.3	18,256	24.6	15.7	16.0
Machine operators, assemblers, and inspectors [2]	7,744	42.1	14.0	9.4	7,791	37.3	15.4	17.2
Textile, apparel, and furnishings machine operators [2] . . .	1,414	82.1	18.7	12.5	954	72.1	19.4	25.1
Textile sewing machine operators	806	94.0	15.5	14.5	511	82.1	16.4	30.2
Pressing machine operators	141	66.4	27.1	14.2	91	81.0	27.8	35.2
Fabricators, assemblers, and hand working occupations .	1,715	33.7	11.3	8.7	2,090	33.1	14.3	14.5
Production inspectors, testers, samplers, and weighers .	794	53.8	13.0	7.7	770	48.0	14.8	16.3
Transportation and material moving occupations	4,201	7.8	13.0	5.9	5,363	10.2	16.3	11.9
Motor vehicle operators	2,978	9.2	13.5	6.0	4,069	11.5	16.2	12.0
Trucks drivers	2,195	3.1	12.3	5.7	3,012	5.3	14.9	12.0
Transportation occupations, except motor vehicles	212	2.4	6.7	3.0	167	4.1	17.3	3.8
Material moving equipment operators	1,011	4.8	12.9	6.3	1,127	6.2	16.2	12.8
Industrial truck and tractor operators	369	5.6	19.6	8.2	534	8.9	22.7	18.3
Handlers, equipment cleaners, helpers, and laborers [2] . . .	4,147	16.8	15.1	8.6	5,102	20.3	15.6	18.4
Freight, stock, and material handlers	1,488	15.3	15.3	7.1	1,988	23.7	17.4	14.3
Laborers, except construction	1,024	19.4	16.0	8.6	1,298	21.8	16.6	16.6
Farm operators and managers	1,450	12.1	1.3	0.7	1,187	23.1	1.3	2.4
Other agricultural and related occupations	2,072	19.9	11.7	14.0	2,171	17.7	6.8	34.8
Farm workers	1,149	24.8	11.6	15.9	835	17.2	4.2	44.9
Forestry and logging occupations	126	1.4	12.8	2.1	91	6.7	8.1	6.9

- Represents or rounds to zero.   NA Not available.   [1] See footnote 2, Table 649.   [2] Includes other occupations, not shown separately.   [3] Level of total employment below 50,000.   [4] Includes clerks.

Source: U.S. Bureau of Labor Statistics, *Employment and Earnings*, monthly, January issues; and unpublished data.

No. 676. Employment Projections, by Occupation: 1996 and 2006

[In thousands (3,146 represents 3,146,000), except percent. Estimates based on the Current Employment Statistics estimates and the Occupational Employment Statistics estimates. See source for methodological assumptions]

Occupation	Employment 1996	Employment 2006	Change Number	Change Percent	Education and training category
LARGEST JOB GROWTH					
Cashiers.	3,146	3,677	530	17	Short-term on-the-job training
Systems analysts	506	1,025	520	103	Bachelor's degree
General managers and top executives	3,210	3,677	467	15	Work experience plus bachelor's or higher degree
Registered nurses	1,971	2,382	411	21	Associate's degree
Salespersons, retail	4,072	4,481	408	10	Short-term on-the-job training
Truck drivers light and heavy	2,719	3,123	404	15	Short-term on-the-job training
Home health aides	495	873	378	76	Short-term on-the-job training
Teacher aides and educational assistants	981	1,352	370	38	Short-term on-the-job training
Nursing aides, orderlies, and attendants	1,312	1,645	333	25	Short-term on-the-job training
Receptionists and information clerks	1,074	1,392	318	30	Short-term on-the-job training
Teachers, secondary school	1,406	1,718	312	22	Bachelor's degree
Child care workers	830	1,129	299	36	Short-term on-the-job training
Clerical supervisors and managers	1,369	1,630	262	19	Work experience in a related occupation
Database administrators, computer support specialists [1]	212	461	249	118	Bachelor's degree
Marketing and sales worker supervisors	2,316	2,562	246	11	Work experience in a related occupation
Maintenance repairers, general utility	1,362	1,608	246	18	Long-term on-the-job training
Food counter, fountain, and related workers . . .	1,720	1,963	243	14	Short-term on-the-job training
Teachers, special education	407	648	241	59	Bachelor's degree
Computer engineers	216	451	235	109	Bachelor's degree
Food preparation workers	1,253	1,487	234	19	Short-term on-the-job training
Hand packers and packagers	986	1,208	222	23	Short-term on-the-job training
Guards	955	1,175	221	23	Short-term on-the-job training
General office clerks	3,111	3,326	215	7	Short-term on-the-job training
Waiters and waitresses	1,957	2,163	206	11	Short-term on-the-job training
Social workers	585	772	188	32	Bachelor's degree
Adjustment clerks	401	584	183	46	Short-term on-the-job training
Cooks, short order and fast food	804	978	174	22	Short-term on-the-job training
Personal and home care aides	202	374	171	85	Short-term on-the-job training
Food service and lodging managers	589	757	168	28	Work experience in a related occupation
Medical assistants	225	391	166	74	Moderate-term on-the-job training
FASTEST GROWING					
Database administrators, computer support specialists [1]	212	461	249	118	Bachelor's degree
Computer engineers	216	451	235	109	Bachelor's degree
Systems analysts	506	1,025	520	103	Bachelor's degree
Personal and home care aides	202	374	171	85	Short-term on-the-job training
Physical and corrective therapy assistants and aides . . .	84	151	66	79	Moderate-term on-the-job training
Home health aides	495	873	378	76	Short-term on-the-job training
Medical assistants	225	391	166	74	Moderate-term on-the-job training
Desktop publishing specialists	30	53	22	74	Long-term on-the-job training
Physical therapists	115	196	81	71	Bachelor's degree
Occupational therapy assistants and aides	16	26	11	69	Moderate-term on-the-job training
Paralegals	113	189	76	68	Associate's degree
Occupational therapists	57	95	38	66	Bachelor's degree
Teachers, special education	407	648	241	59	Bachelor's degree
Human services workers	178	276	98	55	Moderate-term on-the-job training
Data processing equipment repairers	80	121	42	52	Postsecondary vocational training
Medical records technicians	87	132	44	51	Associate's degree
Speech-language pathologists and audiologists .	87	131	44	51	Master's degree
Dental hygienists	133	197	64	48	Associate's degree
Amusement and recreation attendants	288	426	138	48	Short-term on-the-job training
Physician assistants	64	93	30	47	Bachelor's degree
Respiratory therapists	82	119	37	46	Associate's degree
Adjustment clerks	401	584	183	46	Short-term on-the-job training
Engineering, science, and computer systems managers . . .	343	498	155	45	Work experience plus bachelor's or higher degree
Emergency medical technicians	150	217	67	45	Postsecondary vocational training
Manicurists	43	62	19	45	Postsecondary vocational training
Bill and account collectors	269	381	112	42	Short-term on-the-job training
Residential counselors	180	254	74	41	Bachelor's degree
Instructors and coaches, sports and physical training . . .	303	427	123	41	Moderate-term on-the-job training
Dental assistants	202	278	77	38	Moderate-term on-the-job training
Securities and financial services sales workers .	263	363	100	38	Bachelor's degree

[1] All other computer specialists.

Source: U.S. Bureau of Labor Statistics, *Monthly Labor Review*, November 1997.

U.S. Census Bureau, Statistical Abstract of the United States: 1999

No. 677. Occupations of the Employed, by Selected Characteristics: 1998

[In thousands (58,326 represents 58,326,000). Annual averages of monthly figures. For civilian noninstitutional population 25 to 64 years old. Based on Current Population Survey; see text, Section 1, Population, and Appendix III]

Sex, race, and educational attainment	Total employed	Managerial/ professional	Tech./ sales/ administrative	Service[1]	Precision production[2]	Operators/ fabricators[3]	Farming, forestry, fishing
Male, total [4]	58,326	18,176	10,984	4,980	11,510	10,658	2,018
Less than a high school diploma	6,776	369	477	889	1,872	2,509	659
High school graduates, no college	18,581	2,212	3,041	1,895	5,358	5,326	748
Less than a bachelor's degree	15,007	3,595	3,753	1,558	3,438	2,273	390
College graduates	17,961	11,999	3,712	636	842	549	221
White	49,886	16,130	9,400	3,726	10,224	8,572	1,834
Less than a high school diploma	5,734	328	409	678	1,662	2,071	586
High school graduates, no college	15,757	2,000	2,595	1,352	4,830	4,311	670
Less than a bachelor's degree	12,756	3,226	3,169	1,188	3,030	1,773	370
College graduates	15,639	10,576	3,226	508	701	418	209
Black	5,702	1,078	991	920	908	1,681	123
Less than a high school diploma	752	24	40	138	147	348	55
High school graduates, no college	2,206	144	320	423	409	857	54
Less than a bachelor's degree	1,655	268	406	283	285	401	12
College graduates	1,088	642	225	76	68	74	3
Female, total [4]	49,805	17,424	19,364	7,694	1,071	3,738	513
Less than a high school diploma	4,129	247	855	1,665	185	1,053	124
High school graduates, no college	16,177	2,399	7,678	3,494	504	1,900	203
Less than a bachelor's degree	14,704	4,283	7,378	2,019	277	633	115
College graduates	14,795	10,496	3,454	517	105	153	71
White	41,096	14,999	16,236	5,744	837	2,802	479
Less than a high school diploma	3,132	199	694	1,183	144	800	112
High school graduates, no college	13,383	2,125	6,644	2,602	397	1,424	191
Less than a bachelor's degree	12,072	3,683	6,051	1,552	219	460	109
College graduates	12,509	8,991	2,847	408	76	119	67
Black	6,360	1,637	2,310	1,568	142	686	16
Less than a high school diploma	724	32	118	389	25	151	8
High school graduates, no college	2,219	213	807	746	67	382	6
Less than a bachelor's degree	2,093	481	1,056	377	38	139	2
College graduates	1,324	912	329	57	11	14	1

[1] Includes private household workers. [2] Includes craft and repair. [3] Includes laborers. [4] Includes other races, not shown separately.

Source: U.S. Bureau of Labor Statistics, unpublished data.

No. 678. Employment, by Industry: 1970 to 1998

[In thousands (78,678 represents 78,678,000), except percent. See headnote, Table 652. Data for 1990, and also beginning 1995, not strictly comparable with other years due to changes in industrial classification]

Industry	1970	1980	1990[1]	1995[1]	1998 Total	1998 Percent Female	1998 Percent Black	1998 Percent Hispanic[2]
Total employed	78,678	99,303	118,793	124,900	131,463	46.2	11.1	10.1
Agriculture	3,463	3,364	3,223	3,440	3,378	24.4	4.1	22.0
Mining	516	979	724	627	620	13.7	4.6	9.0
Construction	4,818	6,215	7,764	7,668	8,518	9.4	6.4	12.7
Manufacturing	20,746	21,942	21,346	20,493	20,733	31.8	10.5	11.2
Transportation, communication, and other public utilities	5,320	6,525	8,168	8,709	9,307	29.1	15.1	9.5
Wholesale and retail trade	15,008	20,191	24,622	26,071	27,203	47.2	9.6	11.4
Wholesale trade	2,672	3,920	4,669	4,986	5,090	30.0	7.4	10.8
Retail trade	12,336	16,270	19,953	21,086	22,113	51.1	10.1	11.6
Finance, insurance, real estate	3,945	5,993	8,051	7,983	8,605	58.7	10.5	7.1
Services[3]	20,385	28,752	39,267	43,953	47,212	62.1	12.2	8.7
Business and repair services[3]	1,403	3,848	7,485	7,526	8,708	36.6	11.6	10.8
Advertising	147	191	277	267	308	51.2	6.1	6.8
Services to dwellings and buildings	(NA)	370	827	829	791	48.8	16.5	21.2
Personnel supply services	(NA)	235	710	853	1,027	60.2	20.8	12.1
Computer and data processing	(NA)	221	805	1,136	1,780	29.7	6.8	4.1
Detective/protective services	(NA)	213	378	506	573	21.0	26.0	11.1
Automobile services	600	952	1,457	1,459	1,536	13.5	9.8	14.9
Personal services[3]	4,276	3,839	4,733	4,375	4,451	70.3	13.5	17.3
Private households	1,782	1,257	1,036	971	967	90.7	15.1	29.3
Hotels and lodging places	979	1,149	1,818	1,495	1,371	57.7	15.4	18.4
Entertainment and recreation[3]	717	1,047	1,526	2,238	2,530	45.0	9.0	8.4
Professional and related services[3]	12,904	19,853	25,351	29,661	31,392	69.5	12.5	6.9
Hospitals	2,843	4,036	4,700	4,961	5,116	76.3	16.0	6.6
Health services, except hospitals	1,628	3,345	4,673	5,967	6,388	79.0	14.7	7.9
Elementary, secondary schools	6,126	5,550	5,994	6,653	7,131	75.3	12.4	7.4
Colleges and universities	(4)	2,108	2,637	2,768	2,792	52.5	10.1	5.8
Social services	828	1,590	2,239	2,979	3,240	81.8	17.5	8.8
Legal services	429	776	1,215	1,335	1,356	56.0	6.0	6.2
Public administration[5]	4,476	5,342	5,627	5,957	5,887	43.6	16.5	6.6

NA Not available. [1] See footnote 2, Table 649. [2] Persons of Hispanic origin may be of any race. [3] Includes industries not shown separately. [4] Included with elementary/secondary schools. [5] Includes workers involved in uniquely governmental activities, e.g., judicial and legislative.

Source: U.S. Bureau of Labor Statistics, Employment and Earnings, monthly, January issues; and unpublished data.

No. 679. Employment by Selected Industry, With Projections: 1986 to 2006

[(111,374 represents 111,374,000). Figures may differ from those in other tables since these data exclude establishments not elsewhere classified (SIC 99); in addition, agriculture services (SIC 074, 5, 8) are included in agriculture, not services. See source for details. Minus sign (-) indicates decrease]

Industry	1987 SIC [1] code	Employment (1,000)			Annual growth rate	
		1986	1996	2006, proj.	1986-1996	1996-2006, proj.
Total	(X)	111,374	132,352	150,927	1.7	1.3
Nonfarm wage and salary	(X)	98,727	118,732	136,318	1.9	1.4
Goods-producing (excluding agriculture)	(X)	24,538	24,431	24,451	-0.0	0.0
Mining	10-14	778	574	443	-3.0	-2.5
Construction	15,16,17	4,810	5,400	5,900	1.2	0.9
Manufacturing	20-39	18,951	18,457	18,108	-0.3	-0.2
Durable manufacturing	24,25,32	11,200	10,766	10,514	-0.4	-0.2
Lumber and wood products	24	724	780	797	0.7	0.2
Furniture and fixtures.	25	498	504	509	0.1	0.1
Stone, clay and glass products	32	558	541	497	-0.3	-0.8
Primary metal industries.	33	752	711	633	-0.6	-1.2
Blast furnaces/basic steel products	331	273	240	197	-1.3	-2.0
Fabricated metal products	34	1,422	1,448	1,378	0.2	-0.5
Industrial machinery and equipment	35	2,074	2,112	2,087	0.2	-0.1
Computer equipment	357	469	363	314	-2.5	-1.4
Electronic and other electric equipment [2] . .	36	1,774	1,651	1,627	-0.7	-0.1
Communications equipment.	366	296	269	255	-0.9	-0.5
Electronic components	367	610	610	700	-0.0	1.4
Transportation equipment.	37	2,003	1,781	1,792	-1.2	0.1
Motor vehicles and equipment	371	872	963	929	1.0	-0.4
Instruments and related products [2]	38	1,036	854	787	-1.9	-0.8
Measuring/controlling devices	382	312	297	265	-0.5	-1.1
Medical instruments and supplies	384	213	268	310	2.3	1.5
Miscellaneous manufacturing industries . .	39	361	387	408	0.7	0.5
Nondurable manufacturing	20-23,26	7,751	7,691	7,593	-0.1	-0.1
Food and kindred products	20	1,605	1,693	1,713	0.5	0.1
Tobacco manufactures	21	59	41	30	-3.4	-3.1
Textile mill products	22	703	624	588	-1.2	-0.6
Apparel and other textile products	23	1,100	864	714	-2.4	-1.9
Paper and allied products	26	667	681	702	0.2	0.3
Printing and publishing.	27	1,456	1,538	1,501	0.5	-0.2
Chemicals and allied products	28	1,021	1,032	1,070	0.1	0.4
Petroleum and coal products	29	169	142	118	-1.7	-1.8
Rubber/misc. plastics products	30	822	981	1,091	1.8	1.1
Leather and leather products	31	149	96	65	-4.3	-3.8
Service producing	(X)	74,189	94,300	111,867	2.4	1.7
Transportation, communications, utilities . .	40-42,44	5,247	6,260	7,111	1.8	1.3
Transportation	40-42,44	3,051	4,038	4,774	2.8	1.7
Communications	48	1,275	1,337	1,360	0.5	0.2
Electric, gas, and sanitary services	49	921	885	976	-0.4	1.0
Wholesale trade	50,51	5,751	6,483	7,228	1.2	1.1
Retail trade	52-59	17,878	21,625	23,875	1.9	1.0
Eating and drinking places	58	5,902	7,499	8,884	2.4	1.7
Finance, insurance, and real estate	60-67	6,275	6,899	7,651	1.0	1.0
Services	70-87,89	22,346	33,586	44,852	4.2	2.9
Hotels and other lodging places	70	1,378	1,716	1,978	2.2	1.4
Personal services.	72	1,008	1,184	1,294	1.6	0.9
Business services [2]	73	3,931	7,254	10,835	6.3	4.1
Advertising	731	204	242	270	1.7	1.1
Services to buildings	734	685	897	1,097	2.7	2.0
Personnel supply services	736	990	2,646	4,039	10.3	4.3
Computer and data processing services . .	737	588	1,208	2,509	7.5	7.6
Auto repair, services, and garages	75	762	1,084	1,482	3.6	3.2
Miscellaneous repair shops	76	322	375	425	1.5	1.3
Motion pictures	78	320	522	628	5.0	1.9
Video tape rental	784	94	155	173	5.1	1.1
Amusement and recreation services	79	895	1,466	1,998	5.1	3.1
Health services	80	6,528	9,469	12,620	3.8	2.9
Offices of health practitioners	801,2,3,4	1,752	2,751	4,046	4.6	3.9
Nursing and personal care facilities	805	1,245	1,732	2,377	3.4	3.2
Hospitals, private	806	3,037	3,814	4,229	2.3	1.0
Health services, n.e.c. [3]	807,8,9	494	1,172	1,968	9.0	5.3
Legal services	81	747	930	1,187	2.2	2.5
Educational services	82	1,421	2,020	2,478	3.6	2.1
Social services	83	1,406	2,403	3,461	5.5	3.7
Museums, botanical, zoological gardens	84	52	85	109	5.0	2.5
Membership organizations	86	1,536	2,185	2,428	3.6	1.1
Engineering, management, and services	87,89	2,042	2,893	3,930	3.5	3.1
Government	(X)	16,693	19,447	21,150	1.5	0.8
Federal government	(X)	2,899	2,757	2,670	-0.5	-0.3
State and local government	(X)	13,794	16,690	18,480	1.9	1.0
Agriculture	01,02,07	3,327	3,642	3,618	0.9	-0.1
Private households	88	1,235	928	775	-2.8	-1.8
Nonagriculture self-employed and unpaid family . .	(X)	8,085	9,051	10,216	1.1	1.2

X Not applicable. [1] 1987 Standard Industrial Classification; see text, Section 17, Business. [2] Includes other industries, not shown separately. [3] N.e.c. means not elsewhere classified.

Source: U.S. Bureau of Labor Statistics, *Monthly Labor Review*, November 1997.

No. 680. Unemployed Workers—Summary: 1980 to 1998

[In thousands (7,637 represents 7,637,000), except as indicated. For civilian noninstitutional population 16 years old and over. Annual averages of monthly figures. For data on unemployment insurance, see Table 626]

Age, sex, race, Hispanic origin	1980	1985	1990 [1]	1994 [1]	1995	1996	1997 [1]	1998 [1]
UNEMPLOYED								
Total [2]	7,637	8,312	7,047	7,996	7,404	7,236	6,739	6,210
16 to 19 years old	1,669	1,468	1,212	1,320	1,346	1,306	1,271	1,205
20 to 24 years old	1,835	1,738	1,299	1,373	1,244	1,239	1,152	1,081
25 to 44 years old	2,964	3,681	3,323	3,694	3,390	3,262	2,989	2,677
45 to 64 years old	1,075	1,331	1,109	1,456	1,269	1,289	1,199	1,125
65 years and over	94	93	105	153	153	139	127	122
Male	4,267	4,521	3,906	4,367	3,983	3,880	3,577	3,266
16 to 19 years old	913	806	667	740	744	733	694	686
20 to 24 years old	1,076	944	715	768	673	675	636	583
25 to 44 years old	1,619	1,950	1,803	1,968	1,776	1,689	1,504	1,308
45 to 64 years old	600	766	662	803	697	707	674	621
65 years and over	58	55	59	88	94	76	69	69
Female	3,370	3,791	3,140	3,629	3,421	3,356	3,162	2,944
16 to 19 years old	755	661	544	580	602	573	577	519
20 to 24 years old	760	794	584	605	571	564	516	498
25 to 44 years old	1,345	1,732	1,519	1,726	1,615	1,574	1,486	1,370
45 to 64 years old	473	566	447	653	574	582	525	503
65 years and over	36	39	46	66	60	63	58	53
White [3]	5,884	6,191	5,186	5,892	5,459	5,300	4,836	4,484
16 to 19 years old	1,291	1,074	903	960	952	939	912	876
20 to 24 years old	1,364	1,235	899	952	866	854	765	731
Black [3]	1,553	1,864	1,565	1,666	1,538	1,592	1,560	1,426
16 to 19 years old	343	357	268	300	325	310	302	281
20 to 24 years old	426	455	349	351	311	327	327	301
Hispanic [3][4]	620	811	876	1,187	1,140	1,132	1,069	1,026
16 to 19 years old	145	141	161	198	205	199	197	214
20 to 24 years old	138	171	167	220	209	217	206	194
Full-time workers	6,269	6,793	5,677	6,513	5,909	5,803	5,395	4,916
Part-time workers	1,369	1,519	1,369	1,483	1,495	1,433	1,344	1,293
UNEMPLOYMENT RATE (percent) [5]								
Total [2]	7.1	7.2	5.6	6.1	5.6	5.4	4.9	4.5
16 to 19 years old	17.8	18.6	15.5	17.6	17.3	16.7	16.0	14.6
20 to 24 years old	11.5	11.1	8.8	9.7	9.1	9.3	8.5	7.9
25 to 44 years old	6.0	6.2	4.9	5.3	4.8	4.6	4.2	3.8
45 to 64 years old	3.7	4.5	3.5	4.0	3.4	3.3	3.0	2.7
65 years and over	3.1	3.2	3.0	4.0	4.0	3.6	3.3	3.2
Male	6.9	7.0	5.7	6.2	5.6	5.4	4.9	4.4
16 to 19 years old	18.3	19.5	16.3	19.0	18.4	18.1	16.9	16.2
20 to 24 years old	12.5	11.4	9.1	10.2	9.2	9.5	8.9	8.1
25 to 44 years old	5.6	5.9	4.8	5.2	4.7	4.4	3.9	3.4
45 to 64 years old	3.5	4.5	3.7	4.1	3.5	3.4	3.1	2.8
65 years and over	3.1	3.1	3.0	4.0	4.3	3.4	3.0	3.1
Female	7.4	7.4	5.5	6.0	5.6	5.4	5.0	4.6
16 to 19 years old	17.2	17.6	14.7	16.2	16.1	15.2	15.0	12.9
20 to 24 years old	10.4	10.7	8.5	9.2	9.0	9.0	8.1	7.8
25 to 44 years old	6.4	6.6	4.9	5.4	5.0	4.9	4.6	4.2
45 to 64 years old	4.0	4.6	3.2	3.9	3.3	3.3	2.8	2.6
65 years and over	3.1	3.3	3.1	4.0	3.7	4.0	3.6	3.3
White [3]	6.3	6.2	4.7	5.3	4.9	4.7	4.2	3.9
16 to 19 years old	15.5	15.7	13.5	15.1	14.5	14.2	13.6	12.6
20 to 24 years old	9.9	9.2	7.3	8.1	7.7	7.8	6.9	6.5
Black [3]	14.3	15.1	11.4	11.5	10.4	10.5	10.0	8.9
16 to 19 years old	38.5	40.2	30.9	35.2	35.7	33.6	32.4	27.6
20 to 24 years old	23.6	24.5	19.9	19.5	17.7	18.8	18.3	16.8
Hispanic [3][4]	10.1	10.5	8.2	9.9	9.3	8.9	7.7	7.2
16 to 19 years old	22.5	24.3	19.5	24.5	24.1	23.6	21.6	21.3
20 to 24 years old	12.1	12.6	9.1	11.8	11.5	11.8	10.3	9.4
Experienced workers [6]	6.9	6.8	5.3	5.9	5.4	5.2	4.7	4.3
Women maintaining families	9.2	10.4	8.3	8.9	8.0	8.2	8.1	7.2
Married men, wife present [2]	4.2	4.3	3.4	3.7	3.3	3.0	2.7	2.4
White	3.9	4.0	3.1	3.4	3.0	2.8	2.5	2.2
Black	7.4	8.0	6.2	6.0	5.0	4.9	4.3	3.9
Percent without work for—								
Fewer than 5 weeks	43.2	42.1	46.3	34.1	36.5	36.4	37.7	42.2
5 to 10 weeks	23.4	22.2	23.5	20.6	22.0	21.8	21.9	22.1
11 to 14 weeks	9.0	8.0	8.5	9.5	9.6	9.8	9.9	9.3
15 to 26 weeks	13.8	12.3	11.7	15.5	14.6	14.6	14.8	12.3
27 weeks and over	10.7	15.4	10.0	20.3	17.3	17.4	15.8	14.1
Unemployment duration, average (weeks)	11.9	15.6	12.0	18.8	16.6	16.7	15.8	14.5

[1] See footnote 2, Table 649. [2] Includes other races, not shown separately. [3] Includes other ages, not shown separately. [4] Persons of Hispanic origin may be of any race. [5] Unemployed as percent of civilian labor force in specified group. [6] Wage and salary workers.

Source: U.S. Bureau of Labor Statistics, *Employment and Earnings*, monthly, January issues; and unpublished data.

No. 681. Unemployed Persons, by Sex and Reason: 1970 to 1998

[In thousands (2,238 represents 2,238,000). For civilian noninstitutional population 16 years old and over. Annual averages of monthly figures. Based on Current Population Survey; see text, Section 1, Population, and Appendix III]

Sex and reason	1970	1980	1985	1990 [1]	1991	1992	1993	1994 [1]	1995	1996	1997 [1]	1998 [1]
Male, total......	**2,238**	**4,267**	**4,521**	**3,906**	**4,946**	**5,523**	**5,055**	**4,367**	**3,983**	**3,880**	**3,577**	**3,266**
Job losers [2]......	1,199	2,649	2,749	2,257	3,172	3,593	3,150	2,416	2,190	2,158	1,902	1,703
Job leavers.......	282	438	409	528	507	495	507	408	407	372	414	368
Reentrants.......	533	776	876	806	891	978	939	1,265	1,113	1,076	1,004	931
New entrants.....	224	405	487	315	375	457	459	278	273	273	257	264
Female, total....	**1,855**	**3,370**	**3,791**	**3,140**	**3,683**	**4,090**	**3,885**	**3,629**	**3,421**	**3,356**	**3,162**	**2,944**
Job losers [2]......	614	1,297	1,390	1,130	1,522	1,796	1,699	1,399	1,286	1,212	1,135	1,119
Job leavers.......	267	453	468	513	497	507	469	383	417	402	381	366
Reentrants.......	696	1,152	1,380	1,124	1,247	1,307	1,259	1,521	1,412	1,435	1,334	1,201
New entrants.....	279	468	552	373	416	480	459	326	306	307	312	257

[1] See footnote 2, Table 649.   [2] Beginning 1994, persons who completed temporary jobs are identified separately and are included as job losers.

Source: U.S. Bureau of Labor Statistics, *Employment and Earnings*, monthly, January issues; and Bulletin 2307; and unpublished data.

No. 682. Unemployment Rates, by Industry, 1975 to 1998, and by Sex, 1980 and 1998

[In percent. For civilian noninstitutional population 16 years old and over. Annual averages of monthly figures. Rate represents unemployment as a percent of labor force in each specified group. Data for 1985-90 not strictly comparable with other years due to changes in industrial classification]

Industry	1975	1980	1985	1990 [1]	1995 [1]	1998 [1]	Male 1980	Male 1998 [1]	Female 1980	Female 1998 [1]
All unemployed [2].............	**8.5**	**7.1**	**7.2**	**5.6**	**5.6**	**4.5**	**6.9**	**4.4**	**7.4**	**4.6**
Industry: [3]										
Agriculture.....................	10.4	11.0	13.2	9.8	11.1	8.3	9.7	7.9	15.1	9.3
Mining........................	4.1	6.4	9.5	4.8	5.2	3.2	6.7	3.4	4.5	1.8
Construction	18.0	14.1	13.1	11.1	11.5	7.5	14.6	7.7	8.9	5.9
Manufacturing.................	10.9	8.5	7.7	5.8	4.9	3.9	7.4	3.3	10.8	5.2
Transportation and public utilities.....	5.6	4.9	5.1	3.9	4.5	3.4	5.1	3.3	4.4	3.5
Wholesale and retail trade......	8.7	7.4	7.6	6.4	6.5	5.5	6.6	5.1	8.3	6.0
Finance, insurance, and real estate	4.9	3.4	3.5	3.0	3.3	2.5	3.2	2.3	3.5	2.6
Services	7.1	5.9	6.2	5.0	5.4	4.5	6.3	4.7	5.8	4.4
Government....................	4.1	4.1	3.9	2.7	2.9	2.2	3.9	2.0	4.3	2.3

[1] See footnote 2, Table 649.   [2] Includes the self-employed, unpaid family workers, and persons with no previous work experience, not shown separately.   [3] Covers unemployed wage and salary workers.

Source: U.S. Bureau of Labor Statistics, *Employment and Earnings*, monthly, January issues.

No. 683. Unemployment by Occupation, 1990 to 1998, and by Sex, 1998

[For civilian noninstitutional population 16 years old and over (7,047 represents 7,047,000). Annual averages of monthly data. Rate represents unemployment as a percent of the labor force for each specified group. Based on Current Population Survey; see text, Section 1, Population, and Appendix III. See also headnote, Table 666]

Occupation	Number (1,000) 1990 [1]	Number (1,000) 1995 [1]	Number (1,000) 1998 [1]	Unemployment rate 1990 [1]	Unemployment rate 1995 [1]	Unemployment rate 1998 [1] Total	Unemployment rate 1998 [1] Male	Unemployment rate 1998 [1] Female
Total [2]	**7,047**	**7,404**	**6,210**	**5.6**	**5.6**	**4.5**	**4.4**	**4.6**
Managerial and professional specialty	666	880	722	2.1	2.4	1.8	1.7	2.0
Executive, administrative, and managerial	350	420	343	2.3	2.4	1.8	1.6	2.0
Professional specialty	316	460	380	2.0	2.5	1.9	1.8	2.0
Technical sales, and administrative support.......	1,641	1,744	1,550	4.3	4.5	3.9	3.3	4.2
Technicians and related support..........	116	113	96	2.9	2.8	2.2	2.3	2.1
Sales occupations...................	720	795	745	4.8	5.0	4.5	3.3	5.6
Administrative support, including clerical	804	836	710	4.1	4.3	3.7	4.0	3.6
Service occupations	1,139	1,378	1,216	6.6	7.5	6.4	6.3	6.4
Private household	47	99	74	5.6	10.7	8.0	8.7	8.0
Protective service	74	86	85	3.6	3.7	3.4	3.1	5.0
Service except private household and protective..	1,018	1,193	1,057	7.1	7.9	6.8	7.5	6.3
Precision production, craft, and repair	861	860	630	5.9	6.0	4.2	4.1	4.8
Mechanics and repairers	175	182	149	3.8	4.0	3.0	3.1	2.3
Construction trades	483	501	338	8.5	9.0	5.7	5.6	10.4
Other precision production, craft, and repair.....	202	177	143	4.7	4.2	3.4	3.1	4.6
Operators, fabricators, and laborers............	1,714	1,618	1,304	8.7	8.2	6.7	6.3	7.7
Machine operators, assemblers, inspectors	727	629	494	8.1	7.4	6.0	5.0	7.6
Transportation and material moving occupations..	329	329	279	6.3	6.0	4.9	4.8	6.3
Handlers, equipment cleaners, helpers, laborers..	657	660	531	11.6	11.7	9.4	9.6	8.8
Construction laborers	177	179	136	18.1	18.7	14.2	14.2	16.0
Farming, forestry, and fishing	237	311	244	6.4	7.9	6.5	6.1	8.0

[1] See footnote 2, Table 649.   [2] Includes persons with no previous work experience and those whose last job was in the Armed Forces.

Source: U.S. Bureau of Labor Statistics, *Employment and Earnings*, monthly, January issues.

Labor Force, Employment, and Earnings **431**

No. 684. Unemployed and Unemployment Rates, by Educational Attainment, Sex, Race, and Hispanic Origin: 1992 to 1998

[As of March (6,846 represents 6,846,000). For the civilian noninstitutional population 25 to 64 years old. See Table 653 for civilian labor force and participation rate data. Based on Current Population Survey; see text, Section 1, Population, and Appendix III]

Year, sex, and race	Unemployed (1,000)					Unemployment rate [1]				
	Total	Less than high school diploma	High school graduates, no degree	Less than a bachelor's degree	College graduate	Total	Less than high school diploma	High school graduate, no degree	Less than a bachelor's degree	College graduate
Total: [2]										
1992 ...	6,846	1,693	2,851	1,521	782	6.7	13.5	7.7	5.9	2.9
1995 ...	5,065	1,150	1,833	1,329	753	4.8	10.0	5.2	4.5	2.5
1997 [3] ..	4,902	1,253	1,853	1,157	640	4.4	10.4	5.1	3.8	2.0
1998 [3] ..	4,463	1,018	1,751	1,111	582	4.0	8.5	4.8	3.6	1.8
Male:										
1992	4,207	1,151	1,709	854	493	7.5	14.8	8.8	6.4	3.2
1995	2,925	765	1,064	656	440	5.1	10.9	5.7	4.4	2.6
1997 [3] ...	2,797	752	1,069	616	359	4.7	9.9	5.6	4.0	2.1
1998 [3] ...	2,461	592	989	575	306	4.1	8.0	5.1	3.7	1.7
Female:										
1992	2,639	542	1,142	666	289	5.7	11.4	6.5	5.3	2.5
1995	2,140	385	770	673	313	4.4	8.6	4.6	4.5	2.4
1997 [3] ...	2,105	500	783	541	281	4.1	11.3	4.5	3.6	2.0
1998 [3] ...	2,002	426	762	537	276	3.9	9.3	4.4	3.5	1.9
White:										
1992	5,247	1,285	2,146	1,176	641	6.0	12.9	6.8	5.3	2.7
1995	3,858	831	1,362	1,054	612	4.3	9.2	4.6	4.2	2.3
1997 [3] ...	3,674	910	1,395	867	502	3.9	9.4	4.6	3.4	1.8
1998 [3] ...	3,282	711	1,283	814	474	3.5	7.5	4.2	3.2	1.7
Black:										
1992	1,353	361	619	291	81	12.4	17.2	14.1	10.7	4.8
1995	905	225	377	218	86	7.7	13.7	8.4	6.3	4.1
1997 [3] ...	997	291	381	235	89	8.1	16.6	8.2	6.1	4.4
1998 [3] ...	948	248	402	248	50	7.3	13.4	8.4	6.4	2.1
Hispanic: [4]										
1992	757	408	224	88	36	9.8	13.6	9.6	5.9	4.2
1995	746	393	211	102	40	8.0	10.9	8.1	5.2	3.7
1997 [3] ...	768	379	221	128	39	7.3	9.6	7.5	5.5	3.0
1998 [3] ...	647	337	176	94	41	5.9	8.3	5.5	4.2	2.8

[1] Percent unemployed of the civilian labor force. [2] Includes other races, not shown separately. [3] See footnote 2, Table 649. [4] Persons of Hispanic origin may be of any race.

Source: U.S. Bureau of Labor Statistics, unpublished data.

No. 685. Unemployed Persons, by Reason of Unemployment: 1998

[Annual averages of monthly data (6,210 represents 6,210,000). Based on Current Population Survey; see text, Section 1, Population, and Appendix III]

Age, sex, and reason	Total unemployed (1,000)	Less than 5 weeks	5 to 14 weeks	Percent distribution by duration		
				15 weeks and over		
				Total	15 to 26 weeks	27 weeks or longer
Total 16 years old and over	6,210	42.2	31.4	26.4	12.3	14.1
16 to 19 years old................	1,205	51.2	33.2	15.7	8.3	7.3
Total 20 years old and over	**5,005**	**40.1**	**31.0**	**28.9**	**13.2**	**15.7**
Males	2,580	38.8	30.8	30.5	13.2	17.3
Job losers and persons who completed temporary	1,588	39.9	32.1	28.1	13.6	14.5
On temporary layoff..............	483	55.3	30.2	14.5	9.8	4.8
Not on temporary layoff	1,105	33.1	32.9	34.0	15.3	18.7
Permanent job losers	763	31.6	32.1	36.3	16.6	19.7
Persons who completed temporary jobs....................	343	36.6	34.5	28.9	12.5	16.4
Job leavers	318	44.7	31.5	23.8	10.9	12.9
Reentrants	611	34.7	26.9	38.5	13.4	25.0
New entrants.................	63	20.5	32.3	47.3	10.9	36.4
Females	2,424	41.5	31.2	27.3	13.3	14.0
Job losers and persons who completed temporary	1,053	42.5	32.2	25.3	14.2	11.1
On temporary layoff..............	322	58.6	28.4	13.0	8.2	4.8
Not on temporary layoff	731	35.3	33.9	30.8	16.9	13.9
Permanent job losers	527	32.1	34.9	33.0	18.4	14.7
Persons who completed temporary jobs....................	204	43.7	31.3	24.9	13.0	11.9
Job leavers	330	49.6	30.9	19.5	10.2	9.3
Reentrants	944	38.6	30.3	31.1	13.3	17.8
New entrants.................	97	31.1	30.6	38.2	13.6	24.6

Source: U.S. Bureau of Labor Statistics, Employment and Earnings, monthly, January 1999 issue.

No. 686. Total Unemployed and Insured Unemployed—States: 1980 to 1998

[For civilian noninstitutional population 16 years old and over (**7,637 represents 7,637,000**). Annual averages of monthly figures. Total unemployment estimates based on the Current Population Survey; see text, Section 1, Population, and Appendix III. U.S. totals derived by independent population controls; therefore state data may not add to U.S. totals]

State	Total unemployed Number (1,000) 1980	1985	1990[2]	1998[2]	Total unemployed Percent[1] 1980	1985	1990[2]	1998[2]	Insured unemployed[3] Number (1,000) 1996	1997	Insured unemployed Percent[4] 1996	1997
United States..	7,637	8,312	7,047	6,210	7.1	7.2	5.6	4.5	[5]2,595.6	[5]2,322.6	[5]2.3	[5]2.0
Alabama	147	160	130	91	8.8	8.9	6.9	4.2	33.7	30.1	2.0	1.7
Alaska	18	24	19	18	9.7	9.7	7.0	5.8	13.1	12.1	5.5	5.0
Arizona	83	96	99	94	6.7	6.5	5.5	4.1	25.4	21.0	1.4	1.1
Arkansas	76	91	78	67	7.6	8.7	7.0	5.5	29.6	28.2	2.9	2.7
California	790	934	874	969	6.8	7.2	5.8	5.9	443.1	386.5	3.6	3.0
Colorado	88	101	89	86	5.9	5.9	5.0	3.8	22.5	18.9	1.3	1.0
Connecticut	94	83	95	57	5.9	4.9	5.2	3.4	41.2	33.9	2.7	2.2
Delaware	22	17	19	15	7.7	5.3	5.2	3.8	8.0	6.1	2.3	1.7
Dist. of Columbia. .	24	27	22	24	7.3	8.4	6.6	8.8	8.0	8.2	1.9	2.0
Florida.	251	320	390	310	5.9	6.0	6.0	4.3	87.3	79.5	1.5	1.3
Georgia.	163	188	182	169	6.4	6.5	5.5	4.2	39.2	37.0	1.2	1.1
Hawaii.	21	27	16	37	4.9	5.6	2.9	6.2	15.1	13.4	3.0	2.7
Idaho	34	37	29	33	7.9	7.9	5.9	5.0	14.1	12.7	3.0	2.6
Illinois	459	513	369	277	8.3	9.0	6.2	4.5	129.7	115.4	2.4	2.1
Indiana	252	215	149	96	9.6	7.9	5.3	3.1	34.1	31.4	1.3	1.2
Iowa	82	112	62	43	5.8	8.0	4.3	2.8	21.3	19.0	1.6	1.4
Kansas	53	62	57	54	4.5	5.0	4.5	3.8	15.9	14.1	1.4	1.2
Kentucky	133	161	104	89	8.0	9.5	5.9	4.6	30.1	27.0	1.9	1.7
Louisiana	121	229	117	118	6.7	11.5	6.3	5.7	26.7	23.7	1.6	1.4
Maine	39	30	33	29	7.8	5.4	5.2	4.4	14.8	12.8	2.9	2.5
Maryland	140	104	122	125	6.5	4.6	4.7	4.6	43.7	37.8	2.2	1.8
Massachusetts . . .	162	120	195	109	5.6	3.9	6.0	3.3	70.2	63.5	2.5	2.2
Michigan	534	433	350	194	12.4	9.9	7.6	3.9	99.1	89.4	2.4	2.1
Minnesota	125	133	117	68	5.9	6.0	4.9	2.5	36.1	34.0	1.6	1.4
Mississippi	79	116	90	68	7.5	10.3	7.6	5.4	23.6	19.9	2.3	1.9
Missouri.	167	158	151	119	7.2	6.4	5.8	4.2	44.7	40.8	1.9	1.7
Montana	23	31	24	26	6.1	7.7	6.0	5.6	9.8	8.7	3.0	2.6
Nebraska	31	44	18	25	4.1	5.5	2.2	2.7	7.7	7.2	1.0	0.9
Nevada	27	41	33	40	6.2	8.0	4.9	4.3	16.4	17.4	2.1	2.1
New Hampshire . .	22	21	36	19	4.7	3.9	5.7	2.9	5.7	4.8	1.1	0.9
New Jersey	260	217	206	192	7.2	5.7	5.1	4.6	110.6	96.1	3.2	2.8
New Mexico	42	57	46	51	7.5	8.8	6.5	6.2	11.8	11.9	1.9	1.9
New York	597	544	467	498	7.5	6.5	5.3	5.6	210.1	188.7	2.8	2.5
North Carolina . . .	187	168	144	131	6.6	5.4	4.2	3.5	54.0	47.8	1.6	1.4
North Dakota	15	20	13	11	5.0	5.9	4.0	3.2	3.9	4.2	1.4	1.5
Ohio	426	455	310	242	8.4	8.9	5.7	4.3	84.4	75.7	1.7	1.5
Oklahoma	66	112	86	74	4.8	7.1	5.7	4.5	14.4	12.4	1.2	1.0
Oregon	107	116	83	98	8.3	8.8	5.6	5.6	45.9	41.2	3.3	2.9
Pennsylvania	425	443	315	275	7.8	8.0	5.4	4.6	167.5	146.5	3.4	2.9
Rhode Island	34	25	35	24	7.2	4.9	6.8	4.9	18.4	15.8	4.4	3.7
South Carolina . . .	96	107	83	75	6.9	6.8	4.8	3.8	29.6	25.1	1.9	1.5
South Dakota	16	18	13	11	4.9	5.1	3.9	2.9	2.6	2.4	0.8	0.7
Tennessee	152	180	126	116	7.3	8.0	5.3	4.2	47.3	43.0	2.0	1.8
Texas	352	565	544	487	5.2	7.0	6.3	4.8	121.7	114.8	1.6	1.4
Utah	40	43	35	40	6.3	5.9	4.3	3.8	8.4	8.5	1.0	1.0
Vermont	16	13	15	11	6.4	4.8	5.0	3.4	7.2	6.6	2.8	2.5
Virginia	128	160	141	102	5.0	5.6	4.3	2.9	28.0	24.6	1.0	0.8
Washington	156	170	125	145	7.9	8.1	4.9	4.8	84.6	72.8	3.7	3.1
West Virginia	74	100	64	53	9.4	13.0	8.4	6.6	19.2	16.8	3.0	2.6
Wisconsin	167	171	114	99	7.2	7.2	4.4	3.4	56.9	52.7	2.3	2.1
Wyoming	9	18	13	12	4.0	7.1	5.5	4.8	4.2	3.4	2.0	1.7

[1] Total unemployment as percent of civilian labor force.   [2] See footnote 2, Table 649.   [3] Source: U.S. Employment and Training Administration, *Unemployment Insurance, Financial Handbook,* annual updates.   [4] Insured unemployment as percent of average covered employment in the previous year.   [5] Includes 55,000 in Puerto Rico and the Virgin Islands in 1996 and 56,900 in 1997.

Source: Except as noted, U.S. Bureau of Labor Statistics, *Geographic Profile of Employment and Unemployment,* annual.

No. 687. Job Openings and Placements and Help-Wanted Advertising: 1970 to 1997

[(**6,130 represents 6,130,000**). Openings 1970 and 1980, for years ending Sept. 30; beginning 1985, for years ending June 30]

Item	1970	1980	1985	1990	1993	1994	1995	1996	1997
Job openings: [1]									
Received (1,000)	6,130	8,122	7,529	5,651	6,343	6,619	5,917	6,039	6,568
Average per month	511	677	627	471	529	552	493	503	547
Nonagricultural placements [1] (1,000) . .	4,604	5,610	3,270	3,714	3,375	3,360	2,859	2,687	2,456
Index of help-wanted advertising in newspapers [2] (1987=100)	60	84	91	84	69	83	85	83	87

[1] As reported by state employment agencies. Beginning 1985, all placements. Placements include duplication for individuals placed more than once.   [2] Source: The Conference Board, New York, NY (copyright). Index based on the number of advertisements in classified sections of 51 newspapers, each in a major employment area.

Source: Except as noted, U.S. Employment and Training Administration, unpublished data.

Labor Force, Employment, and Earnings   433

No. 688. Nonfarm Establishments—Employees, Hours, and Earnings, by Industry: 1970 to 1998

[Based on data from establishment reports. Includes all full- and part-time employees who worked during, or received pay for, any part of the pay period reported. Excludes proprietors, the self-employed, farm workers, unpaid family workers, private household workers, and Armed Forces. Establishment data shown here conform to industry definitions in the 1987 Standard Industrial Classification and are adjusted to March 1997 employment benchmarks, and reflect historical corrections to previously published data. Based on the Current Employment Statistics Program; see Appendix III]

Item and year		Goods-producing				Service-producing						
	Total	Total	Mining	Construction	Manufacturing	Total	Transportation and public utilities	Wholesale trade	Retail trade	Finance, insurance, and real estate	Services	Government
EMPLOYEES (1,000)												
1970	70,880	23,578	623	3,588	19,367	47,302	4,515	4,006	11,034	3,645	11,548	12,554
1980	90,406	25,658	1,027	4,346	20,285	64,748	5,146	5,292	15,018	5,160	17,890	16,241
1985	97,387	24,842	927	4,668	19,248	72,544	5,233	5,727	17,315	5,948	21,927	16,394
1990	109,403	24,905	709	5,120	19,076	84,497	5,777	6,173	19,601	6,709	27,934	18,304
1992	108,601	23,231	635	4,492	18,104	85,370	5,718	5,997	19,356	6,602	29,052	18,645
1993	110,713	23,352	610	4,668	18,075	87,361	5,811	5,981	19,773	6,757	30,197	18,841
1994	114,163	23,908	601	4,986	18,321	90,256	5,984	6,162	20,507	6,896	31,579	19,128
1995	117,191	24,265	581	5,160	18,524	92,925	6,132	6,378	21,187	6,806	33,117	19,305
1996	119,608	24,493	580	5,418	18,495	95,115	6,253	6,482	21,597	6,911	34,454	19,419
1997	122,690	24,934	592	5,686	18,657	97,756	6,395	6,648	22,011	7,091	36,040	19,570
1998	125,832	25,256	575	5,965	18,716	100,576	6,549	6,825	22,475	7,341	37,525	19,862
PERCENT DISTRIBUTION												
1970	100.0	33.3	0.9	5.1	27.3	66.7	6.4	5.7	15.6	5.1	16.3	17.7
1980	100.0	28.4	1.1	4.8	22.4	71.6	5.7	5.9	16.6	5.7	19.8	18.0
1985	100.0	25.5	1.0	4.8	19.8	74.5	5.4	5.9	17.8	6.1	22.5	16.8
1990	100.0	22.8	0.6	4.7	17.4	77.2	5.3	5.6	17.9	6.1	25.5	16.7
1992	100.0	21.4	0.6	4.1	16.7	78.6	5.3	5.5	17.8	6.1	26.8	17.2
1993	100.0	21.1	0.6	4.2	16.3	78.9	5.2	5.4	17.9	6.1	27.3	17.0
1994	100.0	20.9	0.5	4.4	16.0	79.1	5.2	5.4	18.0	6.0	27.7	16.8
1995	100.0	20.7	0.5	4.4	15.8	79.3	5.3	5.5	18.1	5.8	28.2	16.5
1996	100.0	20.5	0.5	4.5	15.5	79.5	5.2	5.4	18.1	5.8	28.8	16.2
1997	100.0	20.3	0.5	4.6	15.2	79.7	5.2	5.4	17.9	5.8	29.4	16.0
1998	100.0	20.1	0.5	4.7	14.9	79.9	5.2	5.4	17.9	5.8	29.8	15.8
WEEKLY HOURS [1]												
1970	37.1	(NA)	42.7	37.3	39.8	(NA)	40.5	39.9	33.8	36.7	34.4	(NA)
1980	35.3	(NA)	43.3	37.0	39.7	(NA)	39.6	38.4	30.2	36.2	32.6	(NA)
1985	34.9	(NA)	43.4	37.7	40.5	(NA)	39.5	38.4	29.4	36.4	32.5	(NA)
1990	34.5	(NA)	44.1	38.2	40.8	(NA)	38.4	38.1	28.8	35.8	32.5	(NA)
1992	34.4	(NA)	43.9	38.0	41.0	(NA)	38.3	38.2	28.8	35.8	32.5	(NA)
1993	34.5	(NA)	44.3	38.5	41.4	(NA)	39.3	38.2	28.8	35.8	32.5	(NA)
1994	34.7	(NA)	44.8	38.9	42.0	(NA)	39.7	38.4	28.9	35.8	32.5	(NA)
1995	34.5	(NA)	44.7	38.9	41.6	(NA)	39.4	38.3	28.8	35.9	32.4	(NA)
1996	34.4	(NA)	45.3	39.0	41.6	(NA)	39.6	38.3	28.8	35.9	32.4	(NA)
1997	34.6	(NA)	45.4	38.9	42.0	(NA)	39.7	38.4	28.9	36.1	32.6	(NA)
1998	34.6	(NA)	43.9	38.8	41.7	(NA)	39.5	38.4	29.1	36.4	32.7	(NA)
HOURLY EARNINGS [1]												
1970	3.23	(NA)	3.85	5.24	3.35	(NA)	3.85	3.43	2.44	3.07	2.81	(NA)
1980	6.66	(NA)	9.17	9.94	7.27	(NA)	8.87	6.95	4.88	5.79	5.85	(NA)
1985	8.57	(NA)	11.98	12.32	9.54	(NA)	11.40	9.15	5.94	7.94	7.90	(NA)
1990	10.01	(NA)	13.68	13.77	10.83	(NA)	12.92	10.79	6.75	9.97	9.83	(NA)
1992	10.57	(NA)	14.54	14.15	11.46	(NA)	13.43	11.39	7.12	10.82	10.54	(NA)
1993	10.83	(NA)	14.60	14.38	11.74	(NA)	13.55	11.74	7.29	11.35	10.78	(NA)
1994	11.12	(NA)	14.88	14.73	12.07	(NA)	13.78	12.06	7.49	11.83	11.04	(NA)
1995	11.43	(NA)	15.30	15.09	12.37	(NA)	14.13	12.43	7.69	12.32	11.39	(NA)
1996	11.82	(NA)	15.62	15.47	12.77	(NA)	14.45	12.87	7.99	12.80	11.79	(NA)
1997	12.28	(NA)	16.17	16.03	13.17	(NA)	14.93	13.44	8.34	13.33	12.28	(NA)
1998	12.77	(NA)	16.95	16.56	13.49	(NA)	15.34	14.01	8.75	14.06	12.84	(NA)
WEEKLY EARNINGS [1]												
1970	120	(NA)	164	195	133	(NA)	156	137	82	113	97	(NA)
1980	235	(NA)	397	368	289	(NA)	351	267	147	210	191	(NA)
1985	299	(NA)	520	464	386	(NA)	450	351	175	289	257	(NA)
1990	345	(NA)	603	526	442	(NA)	496	411	194	357	319	(NA)
1992	364	(NA)	638	538	470	(NA)	514	435	205	387	343	(NA)
1993	374	(NA)	647	554	486	(NA)	533	448	210	406	350	(NA)
1994	386	(NA)	667	573	507	(NA)	547	463	216	424	359	(NA)
1995	394	(NA)	684	587	515	(NA)	557	476	221	442	369	(NA)
1996	407	(NA)	708	603	531	(NA)	572	493	230	460	382	(NA)
1997	425	(NA)	734	624	553	(NA)	593	516	241	481	400	(NA)
1998	442	(NA)	744	643	563	(NA)	606	538	255	512	420	(NA)

NA Not available. [1] Average hours and earnings. Private production and related workers in mining, manufacturing, and construction; nonsupervisory employees in other industries.

Source: U.S. Bureau of Labor Statistics, *Employment and Earnings*, monthly, June issues and Internet site <http://stats.bls.gov/ceshome.htm>.

No. 689. Employees in Nonfarm Establishments—States: 1980 to 1998

[In thousands (90,406 represents 90,406,000). For coverage, see headnote, Table 688. National totals differ from the sum of the State figures because of differing benchmarks among States and differing industrial and geographic stratification. Based on 1987 *Standard Industrial Classification Manual*, see text, Section 17, Business]

State			1998							
	1980	1995	Total [1]	Construction	Manufacturing	Transportation and public utilities	Wholesale and retail trade	Finance, insurance, and real estate	Services	Government
United States ...	90,406	117,191	125,832	5,965	18,716	6,549	29,300	7,341	37,525	19,862
Alabama.........	1,356	1,804	1,906	102	379	92	439	87	449	347
Alaska..........	169	262	275	13	15	26	57	13	69	74
Arizona.........	1,014	1,796	2,078	144	217	101	499	139	626	339
Arkansas	742	1,069	1,123	48	254	68	256	45	263	186
California........	9,849	12,422	13,584	602	1,960	694	3,122	798	4,220	2,164
Colorado........	1,251	1,834	2,051	132	207	129	493	135	618	322
Connecticut......	1,427	1,562	1,645	59	279	76	356	136	513	227
Delaware	259	366	400	22	60	16	87	49	112	54
District of Columbia .	616	643	615	9	13	16	48	29	274	227
Florida..........	3,576	5,996	6,677	351	496	336	1,684	430	2,415	957
Georgia	2,159	3,402	3,740	182	593	242	930	200	999	586
Hawaii	404	533	530	[2]21	16	41	132	36	172	112
Idaho	330	477	522	32	76	25	132	23	127	103
Illinois	4,850	5,593	5,894	238	977	347	1,334	405	1,767	815
Indiana.........	2,130	2,787	2,918	145	684	144	688	141	709	400
Iowa	1,110	1,358	1,446	62	262	69	354	83	379	236
Kansas.........	945	1,198	1,312	62	213	75	318	62	334	241
Kentucky	1,210	1,643	1,753	84	321	102	416	70	443	294
Louisiana	1,579	1,772	1,897	128	192	114	442	87	510	367
Maine..........	418	538	570	25	87	24	143	30	168	94
Maryland	1,712	2,183	2,324	142	178	109	539	134	787	435
Massachusetts.....	2,654	2,977	3,177	108	448	136	721	217	1,135	412
Michigan........	3,443	4,274	4,514	186	966	178	1,067	210	1,242	659
Minnesota.......	1,770	2,379	2,560	102	444	128	614	156	727	382
Mississippi	829	1,075	1,132	55	245	54	244	42	262	223
Missouri	1,970	2,521	2,687	127	421	166	633	162	758	416
Montana........	280	351	373	19	25	22	100	17	107	78
Nebraska	628	816	875	41	119	56	212	57	238	151
Nevada	400	786	925	85	42	48	189	43	392	112
New Hampshire	385	540	588	23	108	20	152	31	173	79
New Jersey	3,060	3,601	3,801	135	478	260	886	248	1,221	570
New Mexico	465	682	721	44	45	33	171	32	203	178
New York	7,207	7,872	8,229	283	917	412	1,662	736	2,799	1,415
North Carolina	2,380	3,460	3,773	214	825	172	852	178	933	594
North Dakota......	245	302	318	15	24	18	81	16	90	71
Ohio	4,367	5,221	5,475	227	1,095	241	1,325	299	1,512	763
Oklahoma.......	1,138	1,316	1,441	54	186	82	332	73	404	278
Oregon.........	1,045	1,418	1,557	83	245	76	384	95	417	255
Pennsylvania......	4,753	5,253	5,496	219	945	286	1,231	318	1,773	704
Rhode Island......	398	440	458	15	79	16	99	29	157	63
South Carolina.....	1,189	1,646	1,787	106	364	77	430	80	420	309
South Dakota	238	344	361	16	50	17	90	22	95	71
Tennessee	1,747	2,499	2,637	123	515	158	624	125	704	384
Texas..........	5,851	8,023	8,939	496	1,107	542	2,107	495	2,515	1,510
Utah	551	908	1,024	68	134	59	243	55	280	177
Vermont........	200	270	286	14	48	13	66	12	87	46
Virginia.........	2,157	3,070	3,310	189	405	173	733	175	1,023	602
Washington......	1,608	2,347	2,596	143	380	136	625	135	710	466
West Virginia.....	646	688	719	35	82	39	163	29	207	141
Wisconsin.......	1,938	2,559	2,712	113	617	127	610	144	707	393
Wyoming	210	219	228	16	11	14	53	9	51	58

[1] Includes mining, not shown separately.   [2] Hawaii includes mining with construction.

Source: U.S. Bureau of Labor Statistics, *Employment and Earnings*, monthly, May issues. Compiled from data supplied by cooperating state agencies.

Labor Force, Employment, and Earnings   435

[Annual averages of monthly figures (90,406 represents 90,406,000). Covers all full- and part-time employees who worked during, or received pay for, any part of the pay period including the 12th of the month. For mining and manufacturing, data refer to production and related workers; for construction, to employees engaged in actual construction work; and for other industries, to nonsupervisory employees and working supervisors. See also headnote, Table 688]

Industry	1987 SIC [1] code	All employees (1,000)			Production workers					
					Total (1,000)			Average hourly earnings (dollars)		
		1980	1990	1998	1980	1990	1998	1980	1990	1998
Total.	(X)	90,406	109,403	125,832	(NA)	(NA)	(NA)	(NA)	(NA)	(NA)
Private sector [2]	(X)	74,166	91,098	105,970	60,331	73,774	86,716	6.66	10.01	12.77
Mining	(B)	1,027	709	575	762	509	436	9.17	13.68	16.95
Metal mining	10	98	58	51	74	46	39	10.26	14.05	18.25
Coal mining	12	246	147	91	204	119	75	10.86	16.71	19.16
Oil and gas extraction.	13	560	395	326	389	261	242	8.59	12.94	16.83
Nonmetallic minerals, except fuels	14	123	110	108	96	83	82	7.52	11.58	14.72
Construction.	(C)	4,346	5,120	5,965	3,421	3,974	4,617	9.94	13.77	16.56
General building contractors	15	1,173	1,298	1,399	900	938	980	9.22	13.01	15.87
Heavy construction, except building . . .	16	895	770	824	720	643	690	9.20	13.34	16.15
Special trade contractors.	17	2,278	3,051	3,743	1,802	2,393	2,947	10.63	14.20	16.90
Manufacturing.	(D)	20,285	19,076	18,716	14,214	12,947	12,896	7.27	10.83	13.49
Durable goods.	(X)	12,159	11,109	11,097	8,416	7,363	7,597	7.75	11.35	13.99
Lumber and wood products [3]	24	704	733	804	587	603	661	6.57	9.08	11.11
Logging	241	88	85	79	71	70	62	8.64	11.22	12.55
Sawmills and planing mills	242	215	198	181	190	172	158	6.70	9.22	11.10
Millwork, plywood, and structural members.	243	206	262	306	170	210	246	6.44	9.04	11.26
Wood containers	244	43	45	53	37	38	45	4.95	6.64	8.85
Mobile homes	2451	46	41	73	36	33	62	6.08	8.67	11.50
Furniture and fixtures [3]	25	466	506	524	376	400	417	5.49	8.52	10.89
Household furniture	251	301	289	282	253	241	239	5.12	7.87	10.28
Office furniture	252	51	68	66	40	51	48	5.91	9.64	11.80
Partitions and fixtures	254	63	78	90	47	57	67	6.68	9.77	11.65
Stone, clay, and glass products [3] . . .	32	629	556	563	486	432	440	7.50	11.12	13.60
Flat glass	321	18	17	17	14	13	13	9.65	15.15	18.60
Glass and glassware, pressed and blown	322	124	83	72	105	72	59	7.97	12.40	15.52
Products of purchased glass	323	45	60	63	32	46	49	6.50	9.75	12.11
Cement, hydraulic.	324	31	18	18	25	14	13	10.55	13.90	18.54
Structural clay products	325	46	36	33	34	28	26	6.14	9.55	11.88
Pottery and related products.	326	47	39	38	39	31	30	6.25	9.62	11.94
Concrete, gypsum, and plaster	327	204	206	223	157	157	173	7.45	10.76	13.10
Primary metal industries [3]	33	1,142	756	711	878	574	557	9.77	12.92	15.48
Blast furnaces and basic steel products	331	512	276	233	396	212	180	11.39	14.82	18.43
Iron and steel foundries	332	209	132	132	167	105	108	8.20	11.55	13.96
Primary nonferrous metals	333	71	46	39	53	34	30	10.63	14.36	17.04
Nonferrous rolling and drawing	335	211	172	168	151	124	129	8.81	12.29	14.60
Nonferrous foundries (castings). . . .	336	90	84	92	72	66	75	7.30	10.21	12.35
Fabricated metal products [3]	34	1,609	1,419	1,489	1,194	1,045	1,122	7.45	10.83	13.07
Metal cans and shipping containers . .	341	75	50	37	63	43	31	9.84	14.27	16.69
Cutlery, handtools, and hardware . . .	342	164	131	126	125	96	97	7.02	10.78	12.29
Plumbing and heating, exc. electric . .	343	71	60	59	52	43	42	6.59	9.75	11.88
Fabricated structural metal products	344	506	427	457	351	303	334	7.27	10.16	12.50
Screw machine products	345	109	96	108	84	73	84	6.96	10.70	13.30
Metal forgings and stampings	346	260	225	257	205	178	203	8.56	12.70	15.25
Industrial machinery and equipment [3] . .	35	2,517	2,095	2,189	1,614	1,260	1,382	8.00	11.77	14.45
Engines and turbines	351	135	89	83	87	58	53	9.73	14.55	17.22
Farm and garden machinery.	352	169	106	102	116	78	74	8.78	10.99	13.80
Construction and related machinery . .	353	389	229	253	255	141	165	8.60	11.92	13.69
Metalworking machinery	354	398	330	349	290	236	249	8.13	12.27	15.33
Special industry machinery.	355	194	159	182	125	94	99	7.53	11.90	15.08
General industrial machinery	356	300	247	266	196	158	169	7.95	11.32	14.05
Computer and office equipment. . . .	357	420	438	375	181	137	145	6.75	11.51	15.32
Refrigeration and service machinery	358	175	177	202	120	125	146	7.23	10.93	13.00
Electronic and other elec. equip. [3] . .	36	1,771	1,673	1,700	(⁴)	1,055	1,066	(⁴)	10.30	13.11
Electric distribution equipment. . . .	361	117	97	83	82	67	56	6.96	10.15	13.09
Electrical industrial apparatus	362	232	169	153	163	119	106	(⁴)	10.00	12.48
Household appliances	363	162	124	115	128	99	91	6.95	10.26	12.43
Electric lighting and wiring equip . . .	364	211	189	182	157	136	130	6.43	10.12	12.72
Household audio and video equip . . .	365	109	85	78	79	59	50	6.42	9.68	11.94
Communications equipment	366	(⁴)	264	277	(⁴)	133	128	(⁴)	11.03	14.02
Electronic components and accessories.	367	539	582	667	325	329	401	6.05	10.00	13.25
Transportation equipment [3]	37	1,881	1,989	1,874	1,220	1,224	1,252	9.35	14.08	17.56
Motor vehicles and equipment	371	789	812	988	575	617	759	9.85	14.56	17.94
Aircraft and parts	372	633	712	523	344	345	264	9.28	14.79	19.11
Ship and boat building and repairing	373	221	188	162	176	141	123	8.22	10.94	13.36
Railroad equipment.	374	71	33	34	53	25	26	9.93	13.41	16.91
Guided missiles, space vehicles, and parts	376	111	185	89	35	57	24	9.22	14.39	19.98

See footnotes at end of table.

U.S. Census Bureau, Statistical Abstract of the United States: 1999

[See headnote, p. 436]

Industry	1987 SIC [1] code	All employees (1,000)			Production workers					
					Total (1,000)			Average hourly earnings (dollars)		
		1980	1990	1998	1980	1990	1998	1980	1990	1998
Durable goods—Continued	(X)									
Instruments and related products	38	1,022	1,006	859	[4]	499	430	[4]	11.29	13.77
Search and navigation equipment . . .	381	[4]	284	160	[4]	94	44	[4]	14.62	17.32
Measuring and controlling devices. . .	382	[4]	323	300	[4]	180	154	[4]	10.68	13.87
Medical instruments and supplies . . .	384	[4]	246	279	[4]	144	165	[4]	9.85	12.79
Ophthalmic goods	385	44	43	37	31	30	25	5.30	8.18	10.23
Photographic equipment and supplies	386	135	100	77	67	43	36	8.83	14.08	16.29
Watches, clocks, watchcases, and parts	387	22	11	7	17	8	6	5.24	7.70	10.42
Misc. manufacturing industries [3]	39	418	375	386	313	272	269	5.46	8.61	10.87
Jewelry, silverware, and plated ware .	391	56	52	49	40	37	34	5.76	9.23	11.36
Toys and sporting goods	394	117	104	102	88	76	69	5.01	7.94	10.42
Pens, pencils, office and art supplies .	395	37	34	30	27	24	21	5.58	8.89	11.28
Costume jewelry and notions	396	[4]	33	23	[4]	25	17	[4]	7.40	9.72
Nondurable goods	(X)	8,127	7,968	7,619	5,798	5,584	5,299	6.56	10.12	12.75
Food and kindred products [3]	20	1,708	1,661	1,705	1,175	1,194	1,266	6.85	9.62	11.80
Meat products	201	358	422	501	298	359	426	6.99	7.94	9.66
Dairy products	202	175	155	142	96	95	97	6.86	10.56	13.57
Preserved fruits and vegetables	203	246	247	230	202	206	193	5.94	8.95	11.34
Grain mill products	204	144	128	125	99	89	88	7.67	11.52	14.89
Bakery products	205	230	213	209	139	133	141	7.14	10.85	12.75
Sugar and confectionery products . . .	206	108	99	99	81	78	78	6.56	10.26	13.05
Fats and oils	207	44	31	35	32	22	24	7.03	10.10	12.84
Beverages	208	234	184	184	105	78	90	8.12	13.51	16.11
Tobacco products	21	69	49	40	54	36	31	7.74	16.23	18.67
Cigarettes	211	46	35	27	35	26	20	9.23	19.57	24.34
Textile mill products [3]	22	848	691	596	737	593	505	5.07	8.02	10.39
Broadwoven fabric mills, cotton. . . .	221	150	91	69	135	82	62	5.25	8.31	10.91
Broadwoven fabric mills, synthetics . .	222	116	77	64	104	68	55	5.30	8.63	11.25
Broadwoven fabric mills, wool.	223	19	17	13	16	14	11	5.21	8.61	10.82
Narrow fabric mills	224	23	24	21	20	20	17	4.63	7.39	9.52
Knitting mills	225	224	205	161	194	179	137	4.77	7.37	9.47
Textile finishing, except wool.	226	74	62	63	62	50	52	5.39	8.45	10.64
Carpets and rugs	227	54	61	66	44	50	55	5.20	8.25	10.36
Yarn and thread mills	228	125	103	84	113	92	75	4.76	7.68	10.05
Apparel and other textile products [3]	23	1,264	1,036	771	1,079	869	620	4.56	6.57	8.52
Men's and boys' suits and coats . . .	231	77	50	28	67	42	23	5.34	7.34	8.69
Men's and boys' furnishings	232	362	274	186	310	235	157	4.23	6.06	7.98
Women's and misses outerwear	233	417	328	232	360	274	183	4.61	6.26	8.18
Women's and children's undergarments	234	90	62	32	76	51	25	4.15	6.18	8.14
Girls' and children's outerwear	236	64	56	26	55	47	21	4.20	5.95	8.07
Paper and allied products [3]	26	685	697	682	519	522	519	7.84	12.31	15.50
Papermills	262	178	180	155	133	136	121	9.05	15.10	19.80
Paperboard mills	263	65	52	50	51	40	39	9.28	15.26	19.57
Paperboard containers and boxes . . .	265	205	209	218	157	162	169	6.94	10.39	13.12
Misc. converted paper products . . .	267	220	241	247	163	174	181	6.89	10.79	13.49
Printing and publishing [3]	27	1,252	1,569	1,566	699	871	845	7.53	11.24	13.44
Newspapers	271	420	474	444	164	166	148	7.72	11.17	13.20
Periodicals	272	90	129	139	16	47	45	7.16	11.95	14.82
Books	273	101	121	128	52	66	63	6.76	10.10	12.69
Commercial printing	275	410	552	577	304	401	411	7.85	11.52	13.70
Blankbooks and bookbinding	278	62	72	66	51	56	50	5.78	8.83	10.52
Chemicals and allied products [3]	28	1,107	1,086	1,036	626	600	582	8.30	13.54	17.13
Industrial inorganic chemicals	281	161	138	115	88	70	62	9.07	14.66	19.12
Plastics materials and synthetics. . . .	282	205	180	154	137	116	102	8.21	13.97	17.91
Drugs.	283	196	237	274	97	105	125	7.69	12.90	17.03
Soap, cleaners, and toilet goods	284	141	159	157	86	98	98	7.67	11.71	13.94
Paints and allied products	285	65	61	52	33	31	28	7.39	11.99	14.42
Industrial organic chemicals	286	174	155	137	88	86	80	9.67	15.97	20.51
Agricultural chemicals	287	72	56	51	45	34	31	8.12	13.73	17.11
Petroleum and coal products [3]	29	198	157	136	125	103	89	10.10	16.24	20.90
Petroleum refining	291	155	118	93	93	75	60	10.94	17.58	23.52
Asphalt paving and roofing materials .	295	31	27	28	24	21	21	7.69	12.87	15.51
Rubber and misc. plastics products [3] . . .	30	764	888	1,006	588	687	780	6.58	9.76	11.87
Tires and inner tubes	301	115	84	79	81	62	59	9.74	15.42	18.65
Rubber and plastics footwear	302	22	11	6	20	9	5	4.43	6.66	10.07
Leather and leather products [3]	31	233	133	82	197	109	62	4.58	6.91	9.34
Leather tanning and finishing	311	19	15	12	16	12	10	6.10	9.04	12.05
Footwear, except rubber	314	144	74	35	123	63	28	4.42	6.61	8.91
Luggage	316	16	11	10	12	8	7	4.90	6.91	9.16
Handbags and personal leather goods.	317	30	15	9	25	12	5	4.33	6.08	8.22

See footnotes at end of table.

U.S. Census Bureau, Statistical Abstract of the United States: 1999

[See headnote, p. 436]

Industry	1987 SIC [1] code	All employees (1,000)			Production workers					
					Total (1,000)			Average hourly earnings (dollars)		
		1980	1990	1998	1980	1990	1998	1980	1990	1998
Transp. and public utilities [3]	(E)	5,146	5,777	6,549	4,293	4,781	5,426	8.87	12.92	15.34
Railroad transportation	40	532	279	232	(4)	(4)	(4)	(4)	(4)	(4)
Class I railroads, plus Amtrak [5]	4011	482	241	205	(4)	(4)	(4)	[6]9.92	16.08	17.95
Local and interurban passenger transit	41	265	338	462	244	308	422	6.34	9.23	11.17
Trucking and warehousing	42	(4)	1,395	1,707	(NA)	1,215	1,495	(4)	11.68	13.62
Water transportation	44	211	177	186	(4)	(4)	(4)	(4)	(4)	(4)
Transportation by air	45	(4)	968	1,157	(4)	(4)	(4)	(4)	(4)	(4)
Pipelines, except natural gas	46	21	19	14	15	14	12	10.50	17.04	20.64
Transportation services	47	(4)	336	449	159	270	367	6.94	10.38	13.64
Communication [3]	48	1,357	1,309	1,487	1,014	978	1,083	8.50	13.51	17.30
Telephone communication	481	1,072	913	1,023	779	658	716	8.72	14.13	17.79
Radio and television broadcasting ...	483	192	234	246	154	193	202	7.44	12.71	17.79
Cable and other pay television services	484	(4)	126	185	(4)	105	151	(4)	10.50	14.14
Electric, gas, and sanitary services [3]	49	829	957	855	678	759	685	8.90	15.23	19.97
Electric services	491	391	454	363	316	351	294	9.12	15.80	21.01
Gas production and distribution	492	168	165	140	138	129	109	8.27	14.25	18.56
Combination utility services	493	197	193	157	162	156	122	9.64	17.58	24.30
Sanitary services	495	50	115	163	44	99	134	7.16	11.55	15.70
Wholesale trade	(F)	5,292	6,173	6,825	4,328	4,959	5,471	6.95	10.79	14.01
Retail trade [3]	(G)	15,018	19,601	22,475	13,484	17,358	19,741	4.88	6.75	8.75
General merchandise stores	53	2,245	2,540	2,790	2,090	2,380	2,590	4.77	6.83	8.59
Food stores	54	2,384	3,215	3,545	2,202	2,953	3,213	6.24	7.31	9.07
Automotive dealers and service stations	55	1,689	2,063	2,351	1,430	1,718	1,951	5.66	8.92	12.09
Apparel and accessory stores	56	957	1,183	1,105	820	991	924	4.30	6.25	8.45
Furniture and home furnishings stores	57	606	820	1,062	502	670	874	5.53	8.53	11.87
Eating and drinking places	58	4,626	6,509	7,746	4,256	5,905	6,958	3.69	4.97	6.35
Finance, insurance, real estate	(H)	5,160	6,709	7,341	3,907	4,860	5,390	5.79	9.97	14.06
Depository institutions	60	(4)	2,251	2,041	(4)	1,632	1,468	(4)	8.43	10.83
Nondepository institutions	61	(4)	373	620	(4)	270	426	(4)	10.40	14.55
Security and commodity brokers	62	227	424	649	(4)	(4)	(4)	(4)	(4)	(4)
Insurance carriers	63	1,224	1,462	243	854	982	(4)	6.29	11.18	(4)
Insurance, agents, brokers, service	64	464	663	1,586	(4)	(4)	1,199	(4)	(4)	16.65
Real estate	65	989	1,315	743	(4)	(4)	(4)	(4)	(4)	(4)
Holding and other investment offices	67	115	221	1,460	(4)	(4)	(4)	(4)	(4)	(4)
Services [3]	(I)	17,890	27,934	37,525	15,921	24,387	32,740	5.85	9.83	12.84
Hotels and other lodging places	70	1,076	1,631	1,771	(4)	(4)	(4)	(4)	(4)	(4)
Hotels and motels	701	1,038	1,578	1,718	954	1,398	1,509	4.45	6.98	8.92
Personal services [3]	72	818	1,104	1,181	(4)	(4)	(4)	(4)	(4)	(4)
Laundry, cleaning, garment services	721	356	426	441	318	379	388	4.47	6.82	8.40
Beauty shops	723	284	372	402	264	333	355	4.26	7.10	9.40
Business services [3]	73	2,564	5,139	8,546	(4)	4,522	7,571	(4)	4.92	12.55
Advertising	731	153	235	268	116	169	193	8.07	13.51	17.57
Personnel supply services	736	543	1,535	3,161	(4)	(4)	(4)	(4)	(4)	(4)
Employment agencies	7361	(4)	246	338	(4)	(4)	(4)	(4)	(4)	(4)
Help supply services	7363	(4)	1,288	2,824	(4)	1,245	2,738	(4)	8.09	10.18
Computer and data processing services	737	304	772	1,603	254	603	1,283	7.16	15.11	21.16
Prepackaged software	7372	(4)	113	269	(4)	(4)	(4)	(4)	(4)	(4)
Data processing and preparation	7374	(4)	197	272	(4)	(4)	(4)	(4)	(4)	(4)
Auto repair, services, and parking	75	571	914	1,159	488	756	941	6.10	8.77	11.06
Automotive repair shops	753	350	524	635	297	429	499	6.52	9.67	12.43
Motion pictures	78	(4)	408	565	(4)	344	470	(4)	10.95	14.62
Motion picture theaters	783	124	112	134	(4)	(4)	(4)	(4)	(4)	(4)
Amusement and recreation services	79	(4)	1,076	1,688	(4)	944	1,476	(4)	8.11	9.67
Health services [3]	80	5,278	7,814	9,904	4,712	6,948	8,773	5.68	10.41	13.72
Offices and clinics of medical doctors	801	802	1,338	1,817	(4)	1,105	1,497	(4)	10.58	14.28
Nursing and personal care facilities	805	997	1,415	1,757	898	1,279	1,580	4.17	7.24	9.76
Hospitals	806	2,750	3,549	3,953	2,522	3,248	3,622	6.06	11.79	15.46
Home health care services	808	(4)	291	680	(4)	269	627	(4)	8.72	11.50
Legal services	81	498	908	982	427	748	784	7.35	14.16	18.05
Educational services	82	1,138	1,661	2,207	(4)	(4)	(4)	(4)	(4)	(4)
Social services	83	1,134	1,734	2,628	990	1,494	2,275	4.26	7.11	9.20
Membership organizations	86	1,539	1,946	2,271	(4)	(4)	(4)	(4)	(4)	(4)
Engineering and management services	87	(4)	2,478	3,236	(4)	1,886	2,472	(4)	13.56	17.86
Government	(J)	16,241	18,304	19,862	(NA)	(NA)	(NA)	(NA)	(NA)	(NA)
Federal government	(X)	2,866	3,085	2,686	(NA)	(NA)	(NA)	(NA)	(NA)	(NA)
State government	(X)	3,610	4,305	4,648	(NA)	(NA)	(NA)	(NA)	(NA)	(NA)
Local government	(X)	9,765	10,914	12,527	(NA)	(NA)	(NA)	(NA)	(NA)	(NA)

NA Not available.   X Not applicable.   [1] 1987 Standard Industrial Classification, see text, Section 17, Business   [2] Excludes government.   [3] Includes industries not shown separately.   [4] Included in totals; not available separately.   [5] For changes in "Class I" classification, see text, Section 21, Land Transportation.   [6] Includes all employees except executives, officials, and staff assistants who received pay during the month.

Source: U.S. Bureau of Labor Statistics, *Employment and Earnings*, monthly, June issues and Internet site <http://stats.bls.gov/ceshome.htm>.

No. 691. Establishments Providing Training to Employees: 1995

[In percent, except hours. For May through October. For private establishments with 50 or more employees. Formal training is structured, planned in advances and with a defined curriculum. Based on the 1995 Survey of Employer-Provided Training; see source for details]

Establishment characteristic	Establish-ments providing formal training [1]	Employees receiving formal training [1]	Hours of training per employee		
			Formal training		Informal training [2]
			Employer survey	Employee survey	
Total..........................	92.5	69.8	10.7	13.4	31.1
Size: 50 to 99 employees	90.8	61.6	5.7	8.2	31.9
100 to 499 employees.................	94.4	73.0	12.1	13.5	34.5
500 or more employees.................	98.1	71.0	12.0	16.6	26.0
Industry:					
Mining...........................	96.7	94.7	14.4	17.2	18.9
Construction	94.7	71.2	5.0	11.4	36.1
Manufacturing:					
Durable goods	88.1	78.3	11.7	20.8	30.3
Nondurable goods..................	95.2	85.4	11.9	21.7	18.5
Transportation, communications and public utilities ..	96.5	81.4	18.3	17.6	19.7
Retail trade	88.7	48.8	3.7	4.2	32.6
Finance, insurance and real estate.............	95.6	87.4	16.6	15.9	34.7
Services	93.5	70.7	11.0	13.2	37.0

[1] In the prior 12 months. Measured by the employer survey. [2] Measured by the employee survey.

Source: U.S. Bureau of Labor Statistics, *Monthly Labor Review*, June 1998.

No. 692. Employees Receiving Employer-Provided Training: 1995

[In percent, except hours. See headnote, Table 691]

Employee characteristic	Employees receiving formal training [1]	Hours of training per employee		Employee characteristic	Employees receiving formal training [1]	Hours of training per employee	
		Formal training [2]	Informal training [2]			Formal training [2]	Informal training [2]
Total	69.8	13.4	31.1	Occupation: managerial and professional........	80.2	4.3	22.4
Age: 24 years old and under.	63.4	2.7	21.4	Professional, para-			
25 to 34 years old	78.5	14.0	32.5	professional and tech. ...	84.8	22.3	38.7
35 to 44 years old	74.7	15.4	30.3	Sales, clerical, and			
45 to 54 years old	64.7	17.2	39.0	admin. support	72.5	10.2	23.2
55 years old and over ...	50.7	5.7	17.1	Service	49.8	5.6	22.1
				Production [3]	66.3	15.2	38.5
Sex: Male	66.5	12.2	35.4				
Female	73.1	14.6	26.9				
				Tenure in current job:			
Education: High school				2 years or less	67.5	8.9	56.5
graduate or less	60.1	10.9	24.8	2 to 5 years	56.8	4.5	19.5
Some college	67.8	14.3	37.0	5 to 10 years	79.7	19.5	27.0
BA degree or more	89.7	16.1	31.8	More than 10 years	75.3	21.1	20.5

[1] In the prior 12 months. [2] Measured by the employee survey. [3] Includes construction, operating, maintenance, and material handling.

Source: U.S. Bureau of Labor Statistics, *Monthly Labor Review*, June 1998.

No. 693. Adults Taking Work-Related Adult Education Classes: 1995

[In thousands (178,618 represents 178,618,000), except percent. For the civilian noninstitutionalized population 16 years old noninstitutional population 16 years old and over not enrolled in elementary or secondary school. Excludes retired persons over 70 years old who did not work for pay in the prior year. Excludes classes such as basic skills, personal development, etc. See also, Table 341]

Occupation	Total popu-lation	Participants		Occupation	Total popu-lation	Participants	
		Number	Per-cent			Number	Per-cent
Total...............	178,618	39,655	22	Service.................	20,080	4,192	21
				Precision production, craft			
Health assessment, treatment ..	2,337	1,667	71	and repair..............	12,667	2,811	22
Health diagnosing	859	576	67	Transportation and materials			
Teacher, below college	5,414	2,837	52	moving.................	5,311	825	16
Other professional [1]	7,903	3,739	47	Machine operators, assemblers			
Executive, admin., managerial ..	13,098	5,509	42	and inspectors	9,484	1,392	15
College teacher	1,254	511	41	Agriculture, forestry and fishing..	2,336	270	12
Technical and related support...	5,240	2,268	43	Handlers, equipment cleaning,			
Miscellaneous	2,311	819	35	helpers and laborers	2,456	273	11
Admin. support, incl. clerical....	22,968	6,646	29				
Sales workers	18,179	4,214	23	No job in the past year	46,720	1,107	2

[1] For example, includes engineers, scientists, and social scientists.

Source: U.S. Center for Education Statistics, *Adult Participation in Work-Related Courses, 1994-95*, October 1998, NCES 98-309.

No. 694. Annual Indexes of Output Per Hour for Selected Three-Digit SIC Industries: 1988 to 1997

[See text, Section 13, Labor Force. Minus sign (-) indicates decrease]

Industry	1987 SIC code [1]	Indexes (1987=100)						Average annual percent change [2]
		1988	1990	1994	1995	1996	1997	
Mining:								
Bituminous coal and lignite mining	122	111.7	118.7	148.1	155.9	168.0	176.8	5.9
Crude petroleum and natural gas	131	101.0	97.0	112.4	119.4	123.7	126.1	2.3
Manufacturing:								
Meat products	201	100.1	97.1	101.2	102.4	97.7	(NA)	-0.3
Dairy products	202	108.4	107.3	111.9	116.6	115.9	(NA)	1.7
Preserved fruits and vegetables	203	97.0	95.6	107.6	109.1	109.4	(NA)	1.0
Grain mill products	204	101.3	105.3	108.4	115.3	107.7	(NA)	0.8
Bakery products	205	96.8	92.7	96.4	97.3	95.4	(NA)	-0.5
Sugar and confectionery products	206	99.4	102.8	105.4	107.5	112.7	(NA)	1.3
Beverages	208	106.0	117.7	130.9	134.3	135.7	(NA)	3.4
Miscellaneous food and kindred products . . .	209	107.0	99.3	101.0	103.1	107.6	(NA)	0.8
Broadwoven fabric mills, cotton	221	99.6	103.1	122.1	134.0	137.8	(NA)	3.6
Knitting mills	225	96.3	107.5	134.3	138.6	150.8	(NA)	4.7
Yarn and thread mills	228	102.1	110.2	130.7	137.4	146.6	(NA)	4.3
Men's and boys' furnishings	232	100.1	102.1	111.7	123.4	134.0	(NA)	3.3
Women's and misses' outerwear	233	101.4	104.1	127.4	135.5	144.2	(NA)	4.2
Miscellaneous fabricated textile products	239	96.6	99.9	107.8	109.2	106.3	(NA)	0.7
Logging	241	93.7	86.3	87.8	86.0	86.0	(NA)	-1.7
Sawmills and planing mills	242	100.7	99.8	103.3	110.2	114.9	(NA)	1.6
Millwork, plywood, and structural members . .	243	98.9	98.0	94.5	92.7	92.2	(NA)	-0.9
Wood buildings and mobile homes	245	97.8	103.1	98.3	97.0	97.0	(NA)	-0.3
Miscellaneous wood products	249	95.9	107.7	111.8	115.4	114.2	(NA)	1.5
Household furniture	251	99.4	104.5	112.5	116.9	122.2	(NA)	2.3
Partitions and fixtures	254	95.7	95.6	98.9	101.2	97.3	(NA)	-0.3
Paper mills	262	103.9	102.3	110.2	119.0	111.9	(NA)	1.3
Paperboard containers and boxes	265	99.7	101.3	108.4	105.1	106.5	(NA)	0.7
Miscellaneous converted paper products	267	101.1	101.4	110.8	113.4	114.6	(NA)	1.5
Newspapers	271	96.9	90.6	79.9	79.0	77.1	(NA)	-2.8
Periodicals	272	97.9	93.9	82.4	88.5	90.9	(NA)	-1.1
Books	273	99.1	96.6	103.0	101.5	100.5	(NA)	0.1
Miscellaneous publishing	274	96.7	92.2	97.5	94.8	93.4	(NA)	-0.8
Blankbooks and bookbinding	278	95.6	99.4	105.4	108.7	115.0	(NA)	1.6
Industrial inorganic chemicals	281	105.7	106.7	102.0	109.2	110.4	(NA)	1.1
Plastics materials and synthetics	282	98.8	100.9	125.0	128.7	125.1	(NA)	2.5
Drugs	283	101.1	103.9	105.5	108.9	112.9	(NA)	1.4
Soaps, cleaners, and toilet goods	284	102.0	103.8	111.2	118.6	121.4	(NA)	2.2
Industrial organic chemicals	286	109.8	101.4	100.0	98.8	98.4	(NA)	-0.2
Miscellaneous chemical products	289	95.4	97.3	105.7	107.8	110.2	(NA)	1.1
Petroleum refining	291	105.3	109.2	123.8	132.3	142.0	(NA)	4.0
Tires and inner tubes	301	102.9	103.0	124.1	131.1	138.8	(NA)	3.7
Fabricated rubber products, n.e.c. [3] . . .	306	104.3	109.2	119.2	121.6	120.3	(NA)	2.1
Miscellaneous plastics products, n.e.c. [3]	308	100.5	105.6	120.4	120.7	124.9	(NA)	2.5
Glass and glassware, pressed or blown	322	100.6	104.8	112.9	115.7	121.9	(NA)	2.2
Concrete, gypsum, and plaster products . . .	327	100.8	102.3	101.5	104.5	107.5	(NA)	0.8
Miscellaneous nonmetallic mineral products . .	329	103.0	95.4	106.3	107.8	111.3	(NA)	1.2
Blast furnace and basic steel products	331	112.6	109.6	142.4	142.7	153.6	(NA)	4.9
Iron and steel foundries	332	104.0	106.1	113.0	112.7	115.7	(NA)	1.6
Nonferrous rolling and drawing	335	95.5	92.7	101.1	99.1	103.9	(NA)	0.4
Nonferrous foundries (castings)	336	102.6	104.0	112.1	117.8	122.6	(NA)	2.3
Cutlery, handtools, and hardware	342	97.8	97.3	109.2	111.3	117.9	(NA)	1.8
Fabricated structural metal products	344	100.4	98.8	107.7	105.8	106.7	(NA)	0.7
Screw machine products, bolts, etc.	345	98.5	96.1	107.2	109.7	110.4	(NA)	1.1
Metal forgings and stampings	346	101.5	95.6	108.5	109.3	113.7	(NA)	1.4
Metal services, n.e.c. [3]	347	108.3	104.7	123.0	127.7	127.5	(NA)	2.7
Miscellaneous fabricated metal products	349	101.4	97.5	103.0	106.4	108.6	(NA)	0.9
Engines and turbines	351	106.8	106.5	122.3	122.7	136.9	(NA)	3.6
Farm and garden machinery	352	106.3	116.5	125.0	134.7	136.6	(NA)	3.5
Construction and related machinery	353	106.5	107.0	117.7	122.1	123.8	(NA)	2.4
Metalworking machinery	354	101.0	101.1	109.9	114.8	114.7	(NA)	1.5
Special industry machinery	355	104.6	107.5	121.2	132.3	134.7	(NA)	3.4
General industrial machinery	356	106.0	101.5	106.7	109.0	110.0	(NA)	1.1
Refrigeration and service machinery	358	102.1	103.6	110.7	112.7	114.4	(NA)	1.5
Industrial machinery, n.e.c. [3]	359	106.5	107.3	127.3	138.8	142.1	(NA)	4.0
Electric distribution equipment	361	105.4	106.3	131.8	143.0	145.1	(NA)	4.2
Electrical industrial apparatus	362	104.5	107.5	134.5	150.4	154.1	(NA)	4.9
Household appliances	363	103.0	105.8	131.4	127.3	126.7	(NA)	2.7

See footnotes at end of table.

U.S. Census Bureau, Statistical Abstract of the United States: 1999

[See headnote, page 440]

Industry	1987 SIC code [1]	Indexes (1987=100)						Average annual percent change [2]
		1988	1990	1994	1995	1996	1997	
Manufacturing—Continued:								
Electric lighting and wiring equipment. . .	364	101.9	99.9	113.4	113.7	117.4	(NA)	1.8
Communications equipment	366	110.4	120.9	164.8	169.6	189.6	(NA)	7.4
Miscellaneous electrical equipment and supplies.	369	102.8	90.6	110.5	114.1	123.0	(NA)	2.3
Motor vehicles and equipment.	371	103.2	102.4	107.1	104.1	104.1	(NA)	0.4
Aircraft and parts	372	100.5	98.8	109.5	107.8	112.6	(NA)	1.3
Ship and boat building and repairing . . .	373	99.4	103.7	103.8	97.9	100.5	(NA)	0.1
Guided missiles, space vehicles, parts . .	376	104.8	115.7	117.5	118.7	127.3	(NA)	2.7
Search and navigation equipment	381	104.8	112.7	132.1	149.5	141.8	(NA)	4.0
Measuring and controlling devices	382	103.1	106.1	133.8	146.4	150.4	(NA)	4.6
Medical instruments and supplies.	384	104.4	116.3	126.1	130.9	140.4	(NA)	3.8
Photographic equipment and supplies. . .	386	105.6	107.8	132.7	129.5	129.0	(NA)	2.9
Toys and sporting goods	394	104.8	108.1	109.7	113.6	120.0	(NA)	2.0
Miscellaneous manufactures	399	104.5	107.9	106.2	108.2	113.5	(NA)	1.4
Transportation:								
US postal service [4]	431	99.9	104.0	106.6	106.5	104.7	108.3	0.8
Air transportation [5]	4512,13, 22 (pts.)	99.5	92.9	105.7	108.6	111.1	112.1	1.1
Utilities:								
Telephone communications.	481	106.2	113.3	142.2	148.1	159.4	160.2	4.8
Radio and television broadcasting	483	103.1	104.9	110.1	109.6	105.9	101.3	0.1
Cable and other pay TV services.	484	102.0	92.5	83.3	84.3	81.6	84.1	-1.7
Electric utilities	491,3(pt.)	104.9	110.1	126.8	135.0	146.5	150.5	4.2
Gas utilities	492,3(pt.)	105.5	94.8	102.2	107.5	116.0	119.9	1.8
Trade:								
Lumber and other building materials dealers	521	101.0	103.6	117.9	117.0	121.5	124.0	2.2
Paint, glass, and wallpaper stores	523	102.8	106.0	124.6	126.8	132.1	132.3	2.8
Hardware stores	525	108.6	110.5	114.2	110.7	115.2	115.8	1.5
Retail nurseries, lawn and garden supply stores	526	106.7	83.9	116.6	117.1	136.6	119.3	1.8
Department stores	531	99.2	94.2	111.2	113.4	121.0	125.7	2.3
Variety stores.	533	101.9	151.2	191.8	205.8	232.6	246.1	9.4
Miscellaneous general merchandise stores	539	100.8	116.4	160.9	164.0	165.1	165.7	5.2
Grocery stores	541	98.9	94.6	92.9	91.9	90.2	89.1	-1.2
Retail bakeries	546	89.8	89.7	90.1	91.2	87.3	97.6	-0.2
New and used car dealers	551	103.4	106.1	108.7	107.1	108.2	107.3	0.7
Auto and home supply stores	553	103.2	102.7	107.0	112.6	113.9	109.7	0.9
Gasoline service stations	554	103.0	102.6	116.5	120.4	117.2	116.5	1.5
Men's and boys' wear stores.	561	106.0	113.7	118.1	117.9	126.3	139.1	3.4
Women's clothing stores	562	97.8	101.5	115.8	122.8	133.6	134.1	3.0
Family clothing stores	565	102.0	104.5	121.2	135.2	140.5	143.2	3.7
Shoe stores	566	102.7	106.1	124.4	131.5	142.6	143.5	3.7
Miscellaneous apparel and accessory stores	569	96.3	88.6	105.4	131.2	139.9	128.0	2.5
Furniture and homefurnishings stores . .	571	98.6	101.8	110.5	114.7	122.5	125.7	2.3
Household appliance stores	572	98.5	102.8	116.8	131.6	132.0	149.4	4.1
Radio, television, computer, and music stores	573	118.6	119.6	178.8	200.0	209.3	220.4	8.2
Eating and drinking places	581	102.8	104.0	98.9	97.6	95.2	93.7	-0.6
Drug and proprietary stores	591	101.9	103.6	104.5	105.2	107.5	113.8	1.3
Liquor stores	592	98.2	105.2	98.1	102.0	110.3	107.8	0.8
Used merchandise stores.	593	105.3	100.3	111.6	111.6	121.6	122.1	2.0
Miscellaneous shopping goods stores. . .	594	100.7	104.2	111.5	117.2	119.5	124.5	2.2
Nonstore retailers	596	105.6	108.8	130.6	125.7	138.3	148.0	4.0
Fuel dealers.	598	95.6	84.4	99.7	112.3	113.3	106.5	0.6
Retail stores, n.e.c. [3]	599	105.9	113.7	121.3	120.5	130.6	137.8	3.3
Finance and services:								
Commercial banks	602	102.8	107.7	122.3	127.6	130.9	134.1	3.0
Hotels and motels	701	97.6	96.1	109.6	110.1	109.7	107.9	0.8
Laundry, cleaning, and garment services.	721	97.2	101.8	104.0	105.5	108.7	108.1	0.8
Photographic studios, portrait	722	100.1	96.6	117.4	129.3	126.4	135.4	3.1
Beauty shops.	723	95.1	96.8	99.8	103.5	106.3	108.9	0.9
Funeral services and crematories.	726	102.5	90.9	103.8	99.7	97.1	101.3	0.1
Automotive repair shops.	753	105.7	106.9	112.3	119.5	114.1	115.8	1.5
Motion picture theaters	783	107.1	115.8	106.5	101.4	100.4	100.8	0.1

NA Not available. [1] 1987 Standard Industrial Classification; see text, Section 17, Business. [2] Average annual percent change, 1987 to current year, based on compound rate formula. [3] N.e.c. means not elsewhere classified. [4] Refers to output per full-time equivalent employee years on fiscal basis. [5] Refers to output per employee.

Source: U.S. Bureau of Labor Statistics, Internet site <http://stats.bls.gov/iprhome.htm>.

Labor Force, Employment, and Earnings   441

No. 695. Productivity and Related Measures: 1970 to 1998

[See text, this section, Labor Force. Minus sign (-) indicates decrease]

Item	1970	1980	1985	1990	1994	1995	1996	1997	1998
INDEXES (1992=100)									
Output per hour, business sector	70.6	84.2	91.7	96.1	100.7	101.0	103.7	105.2	107.8
Nonfarm business	72.7	86.0	92.3	96.3	100.6	101.2	103.7	104.9	107.3
Manufacturing	54.4	70.4	82.8	93.0	105.3	109.4	113.8	119.4	124.4
Output,[1] business sector	52.0	73.0	85.7	98.6	107.0	109.9	114.5	119.8	125.3
Nonfarm business	52.1	73.4	85.8	98.8	107.0	110.2	114.8	119.9	125.5
Manufacturing	56.8	75.7	86.6	97.5	109.1	113.8	118.0	125.7	130.9
Hours,[2] business sector	73.6	86.6	93.5	102.6	106.2	108.8	110.4	113.8	116.3
Nonfarm business	71.8	85.4	92.9	102.6	106.3	108.9	110.7	114.3	117.0
Manufacturing	104.4	107.5	104.6	104.8	103.6	104.0	103.7	105.3	105.2
Compensation per hour,[3] business sector	23.6	54.5	73.1	90.8	104.4	106.8	110.7	114.7	119.7
Nonfarm business	23.8	54.8	73.4	90.7	104.2	106.7	110.4	114.3	119.1
Manufacturing	23.8	55.8	75.3	91.0	105.8	108.3	110.7	115.3	120.4
Real hourly compensation,[3] business sector	85.4	92.8	95.3	97.4	98.8	98.4	99.0	100.3	103.0
Nonfarm business	86.1	93.4	95.7	97.3	98.7	98.2	98.7	99.9	102.5
Manufacturing	86.2	95.0	98.2	97.7	100.1	99.7	99.0	100.8	103.7
Unit labor costs,[4] business sector	33.5	64.7	79.7	94.4	103.7	105.8	106.8	109.0	111.1
Nonfarm business	32.8	63.8	79.5	94.2	103.6	105.4	106.5	108.9	111.0
Manufacturing	43.8	79.3	91.0	97.9	100.5	99.0	97.2	96.6	96.8
ANNUAL PERCENT CHANGE [5]									
Output per hour, business sector	2.0	-0.3	1.6	0.7	0.6	0.3	2.7	1.5	2.4
Nonfarm business	1.4	-0.4	1.0	0.5	0.5	0.6	2.4	1.2	2.2
Manufacturing	1.1	0.3	3.8	2.5	3.0	3.9	4.1	4.9	4.2
Output,[1] business sector	-0.1	-1.2	3.9	0.8	4.1	2.7	4.0	4.5	4.6
Nonfarm business	-0.2	-1.2	3.6	0.7	3.9	3.0	4.1	4.5	4.6
Manufacturing	-4.8	-4.3	3.0	0.4	5.3	4.3	3.7	6.5	4.1
Hours,[2] business sector	-2.0	-0.9	2.2	0.2	3.5	2.4	1.5	3.1	2.2
Nonfarm business	-1.6	-0.8	2.5	0.3	3.3	2.4	1.6	3.2	2.4
Manufacturing	-5.9	-4.6	-0.7	-2.1	2.2	0.4	-0.4	1.6	-0.1
Compensation per hour,[3] business sector	7.8	10.8	4.9	5.7	1.8	2.3	3.6	3.6	4.3
Nonfarm business	7.2	10.8	4.6	5.5	1.9	2.4	3.5	3.5	4.2
Manufacturing	7.1	11.9	5.4	4.7	2.8	2.4	2.2	4.2	4.5
Real hourly compensation,[3] business sector	1.9	-2.4	1.3	0.3	-0.7	-0.5	0.7	1.2	2.7
Nonfarm business	1.4	-2.4	1.0	0.1	-0.6	-0.5	0.6	1.2	2.6
Manufacturing	1.3	-1.4	1.8	-0.6	0.2	-0.4	-0.8	1.8	2.9
Unit labor costs,[4] business sector	5.7	11.1	3.2	5.0	1.2	2.0	0.9	2.1	1.9
Nonfarm business	5.7	11.2	3.6	5.0	1.4	1.8	1.1	2.3	1.9
Manufacturing	5.9	11.6	1.6	2.2	-0.3	-1.4	-1.8	-0.7	0.2

[1] Refers to gross sectoral product, annual weighted. [2] Hours at work of all persons engaged in the business and nonfarm business sectors (employees, proprietors, and unpaid family workers); employees' and proprietors' hours in manufacturing. [3] Wages and salaries of employees plus employers' contributions for social insurance and private benefit plans. Also includes an estimate of same for self-employed. Real compensation deflated by the consumer price index for all urban consumers, see text, Section 15, Prices. [4] Hourly compensation divided by output per hour. [5] All changes are from the immediate prior year.

Source: U.S. Bureau of Labor Statistics, News USDL 99-53, Productivity and Costs; and Internet site <http://stats.bls.gov/lprhome.htm>.

No. 696. Workers Using Computers on the Job: 1993 and 1997

[In percent, except as indicated (51,106 represents 51,106,000). For workers 18 years old and over. Based on the Current Population Survey and subject to sampling error; see Appendix III and source]

Characteristic	Number using computers[1] (1,000)	Percent of total	Type of application						
			Analysis/ spread-sheets	Book-keeping/ inventory	Com-munica-tions [2]	Data-bases	Desktop publish-ing	Sales and telemar-keting	Word process-ing
Total, 1993	51,106	45.8	36.1	45.0	38.7	34.5	22.3	16.2	44.4
Total, 1997	63,885	49.8	40.9	66.4	47.0	34.1	26.1	22.1	57.0
Age:									
18 to 24 years old	6,007	37.1	28.2	70.3	35.3	23.4	18.4	23.5	43.1
25 to 29 years old	7,984	52.5	41.7	69.8	46.6	35.0	25.8	23.4	58.3
30 to 39 years old	18,864	53.3	44.0	67.0	49.1	35.4	28.3	24.0	58.5
40 to 49 years old	18,182	54.9	43.6	65.8	48.6	36.9	27.1	20.6	58.9
50 to 59 years old	10,092	50.7	39.1	62.8	49.0	33.5	26.1	19.6	58.8
60 years old and over	2,755	32.6	33.5	62.1	42.2	28.8	21.6	21.3	54.1
Sex: Male	30,336	44.1	46.5	64.3	51.4	36.8	29.4	24.6	53.9
Female	33,549	56.5	35.8	68.3	43.1	31.6	23.1	19.9	59.8
Occupation:									
Executive, admin., managerial	14,528	77.5	60.1	76.3	61.4	47.2	32.6	30.9	74.5
Professional specialty	13,900	71.7	44.4	45.1	55.8	37.8	40.3	9.8	68.7
Teachers, below college	2,961	60.3	33.1	31.9	39.7	27.5	42.3	4.6	73.6
Teachers, college and univ.	759	79.9	51.5	27.1	74.6	40.2	41.3	5.4	83.5
Technical/related support	3,226	75.1	42.9	51.8	49.4	36.9	26.1	7.7	49.6
Sales workers	8,277	54.8	38.4	83.0	43.0	31.3	21.0	57.2	46.1
Admin. support, inc. clerical	14,235	77.6	31.4	75.0	39.4	28.3	17.0	15.9	56.2
Service workers	2,752	16.4	15.7	52.3	27.6	17.4	9.6	11.0	34.4
Precision prod., craft/repair	3,501	25.0	29.6	62.8	31.6	22.5	18.2	11.1	29.0
Operators, laborers[3]	3,154	17.3	19.1	63.1	21.3	14.6	12.6	9.2	17.4
Farming, forestry and fishing	311	9.3	40.2	79.3	22.8	33.0	11.2	19.1	33.7

[1] Includes other applications, not shown separately. A person may be counted in more than one application. [2] Includes bulletin boards and electronic mail. [3] Includes fabricators.

Source: U.S. National Center for Education Statistics, Digest of Education Statistics, 1994 and 1998.

No. 697. Annual Total Compensation and Wages and Salary Accruals Per Full-Time Equivalent Employee, by Industry: 1990 to 1997

[In dollars. Wage and salary accruals include executives' compensation, bonuses, tips, and payments-in-kind; total compensation includes in addition to wages and salaries, employer contributions for social insurance, employer contributions to private and welfare funds, director's fees, jury and witness fees, etc. Based on the 1987 Standard Industrial Classification Code (SIC); See text, Section 17, Business]

Industry	Annual total compensation				Annual wages and salary			
	1990	1995	1996	1997	1990	1995	1996	1997
Domestic industries	32,093	37,783	38,792	40,249	26,396	30,902	32,034	33,438
Agriculture, forestry, and fisheries	18,638	21,076	21,819	22,892	16,014	18,200	19,017	19,951
Mining	46,053	57,143	58,809	61,303	38,081	46,624	48,353	50,910
Construction	33,701	37,358	38,377	39,650	27,832	30,444	31,641	32,944
Manufacturing	37,048	44,750	45,672	47,856	30,148	35,803	37,256	39,291
Transportation	36,636	40,756	41,634	42,934	29,019	32,264	33,285	34,507
Communication	46,481	59,678	60,913	63,107	38,930	49,525	50,756	52,872
Electric, gas, and sanitary services	48,057	61,006	62,616	65,228	39,538	48,831	50,438	52,663
Wholesale trade	37,394	44,526	46,076	48,154	31,810	37,812	39,319	41,272
Retail trade	18,678	21,238	21,731	22,484	16,065	18,296	18,823	19,562
Finance, insurance, and real estate	37,905	49,554	53,314	56,689	32,071	41,674	45,237	48,283
Services	29,141	34,051	34,822	35,955	24,996	29,003	29,973	31,184
Government	37,142	44,877	46,282	47,683	28,195	33,930	34,958	36,091

Source: U.S. Bureau of Economic Analysis, *National Income and Product Accounts of the United States, 1929-94*, vol.2; and *Survey of Current Business*, August 1998.

No. 698. Average Hourly and Weekly Earnings, by Private Industry Group: 1980 to 1998

[Average earnings include overtime. Data are for production and related workers in mining, manufacturing, and construction, and nonsupervisory employees in other industries. Excludes agriculture. See headnote, Table 688]

Private industry group	Current dollars					Constant (1982) dollars [1]				
	1980	1985	1990	1995	1998	1980	1985	1990	1995	1998
AVERAGE HOURLY EARNINGS										
Total	6.66	8.57	10.01	11.43	12.77	7.78	7.77	7.52	7.39	7.75
Mining	9.17	11.98	13.68	15.30	16.95	10.71	10.86	10.28	9.90	10.29
Construction	9.94	12.32	13.77	15.09	16.56	11.61	11.17	10.35	9.76	10.05
Manufacturing	7.27	9.54	10.83	12.37	13.49	8.49	8.65	8.14	8.00	8.19
Transportation, public utilities	8.87	11.40	12.92	14.13	15.34	10.36	10.34	9.71	9.14	9.31
Wholesale trade	6.95	9.15	10.79	12.43	14.01	8.12	8.30	8.11	8.04	8.50
Retail trade	4.88	5.94	6.75	7.69	8.75	5.70	5.39	5.07	4.97	5.31
Finance, insurance, real estate	5.79	7.94	9.97	12.32	14.06	6.76	7.20	7.49	7.97	8.53
Services	5.85	7.90	9.83	11.39	12.84	6.83	7.16	7.39	7.37	7.79
AVERAGE WEEKLY EARNINGS										
Total	235	299	345	394	442	275	271	259	255	268
Mining	397	520	603	684	744	464	471	453	442	452
Construction	368	464	526	587	643	430	421	395	380	390
Manufacturing	289	386	442	515	563	337	350	332	333	341
Transportation, public utilities	351	450	496	557	606	410	408	373	360	368
Wholesale trade	267	351	411	476	538	312	319	309	308	326
Retail trade	147	175	194	221	255	172	158	146	143	155
Finance, insurance, real estate	210	289	357	442	512	245	262	268	286	311
Services	191	257	319	369	420	223	233	240	239	255

[1] Earnings in current dollars divided by the Consumer Price Index (CPI-W) on a 1982 base; see text, Section 15, Prices.

Source: U.S. Bureau of Labor Statistics, *Employment and Earnings*, monthly, March and June issues; and Internet site <http://stats.bls.gov/ceshome.htm>

No. 699. Annual Percent Changes in Earnings and Compensation: 1980 to 1998

[Annual percent change from immediate prior year. Minus sign (-) indicates decrease]

Item	1980	1985	1990	1993	1994	1995	1996	1997	1998
Current dollars:									
Hourly earnings, total [1]	8.1	3.0	3.6	2.5	2.7	2.8	3.4	3.9	4.0
Hourly earnings, manufacturing [2]	8.5	3.8	3.3	2.4	2.8	2.5	3.2	3.1	2.4
Compensation per employee-hour [3]	10.7	4.5	5.4	2.2	1.9	2.3	3.5	3.5	4.2
Constant (1982) dollars:									
Hourly earnings, total [1]	-4.8	-0.4	-1.6	-0.3	0.1	-0.1	0.5	1.6	2.6
Hourly earnings, manufacturing [2]	-4.5	0.3	-1.7	-0.4	0.2	-0.4	0.4	0.9	1.1
Compensation per employee-hour [3]	-2.5	0.9	0.0	-0.7	-0.7	-0.5	0.6	1.2	2.6
Consumer Price Index (CPI-U) [4]	13.5	3.6	5.4	3.0	2.6	2.8	3.0	2.3	1.6

[1] Production or nonsupervisory workers on private nonfarm payrolls.   [2] Production and related workers.   [3] Nonfarm business sector.   [4] See text, Section 15, Prices.

Source: U.S. Bureau of Labor Statistics, News USDL 99-53, *Productivity and Costs*.

Labor Force, Employment, and Earnings   443

No. 700. Average Annual Pay, by State: 1996 and 1997

[In dollars, except percent change. For workers covered by state unemployment insurance laws and for Federal civilian workers covered by unemployment compensation for Federal employees, approximately 97 percent of wage and salary civilian employment in 1997. Excludes most agricultural workers on small farms, all Armed Forces, elected officials in most states, railroad employees, most domestic workers, most student workers at school, employees of certain nonprofit organizations, and most self-employed individuals. Pay includes bonuses, cash value of meals and lodging, and tips and other gratuities]

State	Average annual pay 1996 [1]	Average annual pay 1997, prel.	Percent change, 1996-97	State	Average annual pay 1996 [1]	Average annual pay 1997, prel.	Percent change, 1996-97
United States......	28,946	30,336	4.8	Missouri...........	26,601	27,782	4.4
Alabama...........	25,180	26,138	3.8	Montana...........	21,146	21,947	3.8
Alaska............	32,461	33,157	2.1	Nebraska..........	23,294	24,566	5.5
Arizona............	26,387	27,654	4.8	Nevada............	27,788	28,677	3.2
Arkansas..........	22,294	23,268	4.4	New Hampshire......	27,691	29,296	5.8
California..........	31,776	33,485	5.4	New Jersey........	35,928	37,513	4.4
Colorado..........	28,520	30,067	5.4	New Mexico........	23,716	24,684	4.1
Connecticut........	36,592	38,895	6.3	New York..........	36,816	38,497	4.6
Delaware..........	30,711	32,185	4.8	North Carolina......	25,410	26,672	5.0
District of Columbia....	44,458	46,775	5.2	North Dakota.......	21,242	22,047	3.8
Florida............	25,641	26,569	3.6	Ohio..............	27,776	29,088	4.7
Georgia...........	27,492	29,020	5.6	Oklahoma..........	23,329	24,243	3.9
Hawaii............	27,363	28,358	3.6	Oregon............	27,028	28,420	5.2
Idaho.............	23,353	24,053	3.0	Pennsylvania.......	28,973	30,161	4.1
Illinois............	31,296	33,018	5.5	Rhode Island.......	27,194	28,664	5.4
Indiana...........	26,477	27,633	4.4	South Carolina......	24,049	25,004	4.0
Iowa..............	23,679	24,811	4.8	South Dakota.......	20,724	21,645	4.4
Kansas...........	24,609	25,693	4.4	Tennessee.........	25,963	27,235	4.9
Kentucky..........	24,463	25,574	4.5	Texas.............	28,129	29,690	5.6
Louisiana	24,541	25,754	4.9	Utah..............	24,572	25,689	4.5
Maine............	23,850	24,899	4.4	Vermont...........	24,480	25,496	4.1
Maryland..........	30,295	31,765	4.9	Virginia...........	28,003	29,548	5.5
Massachusetts......	33,937	35,710	5.2	Washington........	28,881	30,768	6.5
Michigan..........	31,522	32,761	3.9	West Virginia.......	24,075	24,716	2.7
Minnesota.........	28,866	30,254	4.8	Wisconsin.........	26,021	27,327	5.0
Mississippi........	21,822	22,772	4.4	Wyoming..........	22,870	23,864	4.3

[1] Revised since originally published.

Source: U.S. Bureau of Labor Statistics, *News* USDL 99-171, June 23, 1999, *Average Annual Pay by State and Industry.*

No. 701. Average Annual Pay, by Selected Metropolitan Areas: 1996 and 1997

[In dollars. Metropolitan areas ranked by average pay 1997. Includes data for Metropolitan Statistical Areas and Primary Metropolitan Statistical Areas defined as of June 30, 1996. In the New England areas, the New England County Metropolitan Area (NECMA) definitions were used. See source for details. See also headnote, Table 700]

Metropolitan area	1996	1997, prel.	Metropolitan area	1996	1997, prel.
Metropolitan areas.........	30,238	31,717	Saginaw-Bay City-Midland, MI......	31,117	32,117
San Jose, CA.................	44,824	48,702	Portland-Vancouver, OR-WA.......	29,935	31,606
New York, NY	45,007	47,281	Rochester, MN................	30,662	31,517
San Francisco, CA	40,017	42,583	Monmouth-Ocean, NJ...........	29,919	31,506
New Haven-Bridgeport-Stamford-			Rochester, NY................	30,235	31,353
Waterbury-Danbury, CT ...	39,495	42,485	Baltimore, MD	29,957	31,326
Middlesex-Somerset-Hunterdon, NJ..	39,630	41,796	Springfield, IL...............	29,700	31,171
Newark, NJ	38,894	40,411	Dutchess County, NY	30,546	31,104
Trenton, NJ	37,598	39,835	Cleveland-Lorain-Elyria, OH	29,705	31,089
Bergen-Passaic, NJ............	36,845	38,509	Austin-San Marcos, TX	28,702	31,059
Washington, DC-MD-VA-WV	36,385	38,487	Sacramento, CA..............	29,560	31,028
Jersey City, NJ..............	36,833	38,455	St. Louis, MO-IL..............	29,474	30,995
Detroit, MI..................	35,747	37,126	Raleigh-Durham-Chapel Hill, NC ...	29,091	30,908
Hartford, CT.................	34,844	36,643	Charlotte-Gastonia-Rock Hill, NC-SC .	29,287	30,826
Oakland, CA	34,427	36,377	Yolo, CA	29,067	30,739
Seattle-Bellevue-Everett, WA	33,586	36,311	Lansing-East Lansing, MI.........	29,101	30,688
Boston-Worcester-Lawrence-Lowell-			Milwaukee-Waukesha, WI	29,076	30,673
Brockton, MA-NH	34,357	36,210	Bloomington-Normal, IL	29,970	30,587
Chicago, IL.................	33,910	35,894	Indianapolis, IN..............	29,133	30,517
Kokomo, IN.................	34,787	35,815	Cincinnati, OH-KY-IN...........	29,022	30,492
Dallas, TX..................	32,983	35,012	Ventura, CA.................	28,289	30,454
Houston, TX.................	32,895	34,930	San Diego, CA	28,845	30,364
Los Angeles-Long Beach, CA	33,476	34,846	Pittsburgh, PA	29,060	30,363
Wilmington-Newark, DE-MD	33,220	34,841	Racine, WI..................	27,973	30,341
Anchorage, AK...............	33,501	34,788	Dayton-Springfield, OH	28,486	30,312
Philadelphia, PA-NJ...........	33,076	34,375	Fort Worth-Arlington, TX	28,515	30,040
Nassau-Suffolk, NY............	32,879	34,341	Richmond-Petersburg, VA	28,704	30,025
Orange County, CA............	32,179	33,767	Nashville, TN................	28,143	29,880
Flint, MI...................	33,294	33,640	West Palm Beach-Boca Raton, FL...	29,057	29,821
Minneapolis-St. Paul, MN-WI	31,935	33,577	Kansas City, MO-KS	28,772	29,819
Denver, CO	31,614	33,374	Albany-Schenectady-Troy, NY	28,712	29,725
Atlanta, GA	31,337	33,259	Allentown-Bethlehem-Easton, PA....	28,759	29,699
Boulder-Longmont, CO	30,968	33,198	Birmingham, AL	28,511	29,637
New London-Norwich, CT	32,003	33,043	Grand Rapids-Muskegon-Holland, MI .	28,486	29,632
Ann Arbor, MI................	31,041	32,643	Decatur, IL	28,425	29,525
Huntsville, AL................	31,472	32,543	Honolulu, HI.................	28,336	29,511
Brazoria, TX.................	30,781	32,205	Janesville-Beloit, WI	27,832	29,457

Source: U.S. Bureau of Labor Statistics, *News* USDL 99-232, August 25, 1999 *Average Annual Pay Levels in Metropolitan Areas.*

444   Labor Force, Employment, and Earnings

No. 702. Full-Time Wage and Salary Workers—Number and Earnings: 1985 to 1998

[In current dollars of usual weekly earnings. Data represent annual averages (77,002 represents 77,002,000). See text, this section, and headnote Table 666, for a discussion of occupational data. Based on Current Population Survey; see text, Section 1, Population, and Appendix III. For definition of median, see Guide to Tabular Presentation]

Characteristic	Number of workers (1,000)				Median weekly earnings (dol.)			
	1985	1990 [1]	1995 [1]	1998 [1]	1985	1990 [1]	1995 [1]	1998 [1]
All workers [2]	77,002	85,804	89,282	95,595	343	412	479	523
Male	45,589	49,564	51,222	54,313	406	481	538	598
16 to 24 years old.	6,956	6,824	6,118	6,325	240	282	303	334
25 years old and over	38,632	42,740	45,104	47,988	442	512	588	639
Female.	31,414	36,239	38,060	41,282	277	346	406	456
16 to 24 years old.	5,621	5,227	4,366	4,721	210	254	275	305
25 years old and over	25,793	31,012	33,695	36,561	296	369	428	485
White.	66,481	72,811	74,874	79,403	355	424	494	545
Male.	40,030	42,797	43,747	46,087	417	494	566	615
Female	26,452	30,014	31,127	33,316	281	353	415	468
Black	8,393	9,820	10,596	11,776	277	329	383	426
Male.	4,367	4,983	5,279	5,751	304	361	411	468
Female	4,026	4,837	5,317	6,025	252	308	355	400
Hispanic origin [3].	(NA)	7,812	8,719	10,532	(NA)	304	329	370
Male.	(NA)	5,000	5,597	6,716	(NA)	318	350	390
Female	(NA)	2,812	3,122	3,816	(NA)	278	305	337
Occupation, male:								
Managerial and professional	11,078	12,255	13,684	14,941	583	729	829	905
Exec., admin., managerial.	5,835	6,389	7,172	7,746	593	740	833	915
Professional specialty.	5,243	5,866	6,512	7,195	571	719	827	895
Technical, sales, and administrative support	8,803	9,677	9,894	10,439	420	493	556	606
Tech. and related support	1,563	1,762	1,688	1,773	472	567	641	701
Sales	4,227	4,692	5,000	5,299	431	502	579	622
Admin. support, incl. clerical	3,013	3,224	3,206	3,368	391	436	489	518
Service	3,947	4,602	4,779	5,291	272	317	357	389
Private household	13	12	15	19	(B)	(B)	(B)	(B)
Protective.	1,327	1,531	1,691	1,817	391	477	552	613
Other service	2,607	3,059	3,073	3,455	230	271	300	325
Precision production [4]	10,026	10,259	10,046	10,741	408	486	534	587
Mechanics and repairers.	3,752	3,687	3,658	3,926	400	475	538	599
Construction trades	3,308	3,650	3,541	3,989	394	478	507	545
Other	2,966	2,922	2,847	2,826	433	508	574	611
Operators, fabricators and laborers	10,585	11,464	11,529	11,564	325	375	413	456
Machine operators, assemblers, and inspectors.	4,403	4,594	4,576	4,482	341	387	421	472
Transportation and material moving . .	3,459	3,752	3,870	3,977	369	416	482	519
Handlers, equipment cleaners, helpers, and laborers	2,724	3,118	3,083	3,105	261	306	328	362
Farming, forestry, and fishing	1,150	1,306	1,290	1,337	216	261	294	307
Occupation, female:								
Managerial and professional	8,302	10,575	12,609	14,363	399	510	605	655
Exec., admin., managerial.	3,492	4,758	5,803	6,705	383	484	570	626
Professional specialty.	4,810	5,816	6,806	7,658	408	534	632	682
Technical, sales, and administrative support	14,622	16,290	16,004	16,933	269	331	383	419
Tech. and related support	1,200	1,476	1,506	1,734	331	417	480	511
Sales	2,929	3,554	3,862	4,338	226	290	330	372
Admin. support, incl. clerical	10,494	11,260	10,636	10,862	270	332	384	418
Service	3,963	4,577	4,838	5,301	185	230	264	296
Private household	330	305	324	362	130	171	193	220
Protective.	156	217	266	323	278	405	438	481
Other service	3,477	4,055	4,249	4,616	188	230	264	295
Precision production [4]	906	900	957	949	268	316	371	408
Mechanics and repairers.	144	139	150	155	392	458	550	519
Construction trades	53	50	66	64	265	393	400	408
Other	709	711	741	730	253	299	346	392
Operators, fabricators, and laborers	3,482	3,722	3,462	3,518	216	261	297	327
Machine operators, assemblers, and inspectors.	2,778	2,878	2,559	2,505	216	259	296	328
Transportation and material moving . .	189	227	261	345	252	314	354	373
Handlers, equipment cleaners, helpers and laborers	514	616	642	669	209	249	284	311
Farming, forestry, and fishing	138	175	190	218	185	216	249	272

B Data not shown where base is less than 50,000.   NA Not available.   [1] See footnote 2, Table 649.   [2] Includes other races, not shown separately.   [3] Persons of Hispanic origin may be of any race.   [4] Includes craft and repair.

Source: U.S. Bureau of Labor Statistics, Bulletin 2307, and *Employment and Earnings*, monthly, January issues; and unpublished data.

Labor Force, Employment, and Earnings   445

No. 703. Workers With Earnings, by Occupation of Longest Held Job and Sex: 1997

[Covers persons 15 years old and over as of **March 1997 (67,736 represents 67,736,000).** Based on Current Population Survey; see text, Section 1, Population, and Appendix III. For definition of median, see Guide to Tabular Presentation]

Major occupation of longest job held	All workers				Year round, full time			
	Women		Men		Women		Men	
	Number (1,000)	Median earnings	Number (1,000)	Median earnings	Number (1,000)	Median earnings	Number (1,000)	Median earnings
Total [1]	67,736	16,716	76,694	26,843	37,683	24,973	54,909	33,674
Executive, administrators, and managerial	8,852	29,301	10,448	45,970	6,611	33,037	9,046	50,149
Professional specialty	11,176	29,257	9,639	44,401	6,679	35,417	7,516	50,402
Technical and related support	2,580	23,733	2,074	34,751	1,735	27,576	1,591	37,705
Sales	9,244	10,535	8,566	27,550	4,077	21,392	6,108	35,655
Admin. support, incl. clerical	16,188	17,825	4,312	23,126	9,790	22,474	3,035	29,442
Precision production, craft and repair	1,364	16,466	14,176	27,429	865	21,649	10,629	31,496
Machine operators, assemblers, and inspectors	3,347	14,411	5,249	23,991	2,090	17,683	4,026	26,969
Transportation and material moving	591	12,345	5,216	23,739	247	21,024	3,641	28,227
Handlers, equipment cleaners, helpers, and laborers	1,159	9,056	4,806	12,469	465	15,774	2,304	21,475
Service workers	12,376	8,603	8,481	13,145	4,807	15,964	4,703	22,335
Private household	982	4,852	37	(B)	225	12,648	7	(B)
Service, except private household	11,395	9,072	8,444	13,207	4,583	16,120	4,696	22,359
Farming, forestry, and fishing	742	6,235	3,013	11,645	223	17,301	1,651	17,394

B Base less than 75,000.   [1] Includes persons whose longest job was in the Armed Forces.

Source: U.S. Census Bureau, *Current Population Reports* P60-200.

No. 704. Employment Cost Index (ECI), Compensation by Industry and Occupation: 1982 to 1998

[As of **December.** The ECI is a measure of the rate of change in employee compensation (wages, salaries, and employer costs for employee benefits). Data are not seasonally adjusted: 1982-1985 based on fixed employment counts from 1970 Census of Population; 1986-94 based on fixed employment counts from the 1980 Census of Population; Beginning 1995 based primarily on 1990 Occupational Employment Survey]

Item	Indexes (June 1989=100)						Percent change for 12 months ending Dec.—				
	1982	1985	1990	1995	1997	1998	1985	1990	1995	1997	1998
Civilian workers [1]	74.8	86.8	107.6	127.2	135.2	139.8	4.3	4.9	2.7	3.3	3.4
Workers, by occupational group:											
White-collar occupations	72.9	85.8	108.3	128.0	136.5	141.4	4.9	5.2	2.9	3.5	3.6
Blue-collar occupations	78.2	88.4	106.5	125.8	132.4	136.1	3.3	4.4	2.5	2.6	2.8
Service occupations	74.3	87.2	108.0	127.4	135.6	140.0	3.9	5.1	2.5	3.5	3.2
Workers, by industry division:											
Manufacturing	76.9	87.8	107.2	128.3	135.3	138.9	3.3	5.1	2.6	2.4	2.7
Nonmanufacturing	73.9	86.4	107.8	126.8	135.1	139.9	4.7	4.9	2.8	3.5	3.6
Service industries	70.5	84.1	110.2	129.4	137.6	141.7	4.7	6.3	2.4	3.3	3.0
Public administration [2]	71.9	85.4	108.7	128.3	135.1	139.9	4.9	5.3	3.3	2.5	3.6
Private industry workers [3]	75.8	87.3	107.0	126.7	135.1	139.8	3.9	4.6	2.6	3.4	3.5
Workers, by occupational group:											
White-collar occupations	73.7	86.4	107.4	127.6	136.7	142.0	4.9	4.9	2.8	3.8	3.9
Blue-collar occupations	78.4	88.5	106.4	125.6	132.3	135.9	3.1	4.4	2.4	2.6	2.7
Service occupations	76.3	88.4	107.3	125.2	134.1	138.0	3.0	4.7	1.9	4.0	2.9
Workers, by industry division:											
Manufacturing	76.9	87.8	107.2	128.3	135.3	138.9	3.3	5.1	2.6	2.4	2.7
Nonmanufacturing	75.1	87.0	106.9	125.9	134.7	139.7	4.3	4.5	2.7	3.8	3.7
Service industries	(NA)	84.1	109.3	129.4	138.5	142.7	(NA)	6.2	2.2	3.8	3.0
Business services	(NA)	(NA)	107.4	126.3	138.6	145.9	(NA)	6.0	2.7	5.2	5.3
Health services	(NA)	83.7	110.8	132.2	138.1	139.0	(NA)	6.8	2.7	2.7	0.7
Hospitals	(NA)	(NA)	110.7	131.3	136.5	139.9	(NA)	7.0	2.1	2.1	2.5
Workers by bargaining status:											
Union	79.6	90.1	106.2	127.7	133.5	137.5	2.6	4.3	2.8	2.1	3.0
Nonunion	74.3	86.3	107.3	126.5	135.3	140.1	4.6	4.8	2.7	3.8	3.5
State and local government	70.8	84.6	110.4	129.3	135.7	139.8	5.6	5.8	2.9	2.3	3.0
Workers, by occupational group:											
White-collar occupations	70.4	84.2	110.9	129.1	135.5	139.3	5.8	6.0	2.9	2.3	2.8
Blue-collar workers	73.9	86.7	108.7	128.0	134.2	137.8	5.3	4.8	2.6	2.3	2.7
Workers, by industry division:											
Service industries	70.0	84.0	111.3	129.6	136.0	139.7	5.9	6.3	2.8	2.2	2.7
Schools	69.0	83.6	111.6	129.8	136.2	139.9	6.2	6.0	2.8	2.1	2.7
Elementary and secondary	68.6	83.6	112.1	130.1	135.8	139.3	6.4	6.3	2.8	2.0	2.6
Colleges and universities	(NA)	(NA)	110.2	128.7	137.2	141.5	(NA)	5.3	2.5	2.4	3.1
Services, excluding schools [4]	73.1	85.2	110.2	129.4	135.3	138.8	4.7	6.8	3.0	2.5	2.6
Public administration [2]	71.9	85.4	108.7	128.3	135.1	139.9	4.9	5.3	3.3	2.5	3.6

NA Not available.   [1] Includes private industry and state and local government workers and excludes farm, household, and federal government workers.   [2] Consists of legislative, judicial, administrative, and regulatory activities.   [3] Excludes farm and household workers.   [4] Includes library, social, and health services. Formerly called hospitals and other services.

Source: U.S. Bureau of Labor Statistics, News, *Employment Cost Index,* quarterly; and Internet site <http://stats.bls.gov/ecthome.htm>.

446   Labor Force, Employment, and Earnings

No. 705. Federal Minimum Wage Rates: 1954 to 1996

Year	Value of the minimum wage [1]		Year	Value of the minimum wage [1]	
	Current dollars	Constant (1996) dollars [2]		Current dollars	Constant (1996) dollars [2]
1954	0.75	4.37	1976	2.30	6.34
1955	0.75	4.39	1977	2.30	5.95
1956	1.00	5.77	1978	2.65	6.38
1957	1.00	5.58	1979	2.90	6.27
1958	1.00	5.43	1980	3.10	5.90
1959	1.00	5.39	1981	3.35	5.78
1960	1.00	5.30	1982	3.35	5.45
1961	1.15	6.03	1983	3.35	5.28
1962	1.15	5.97	1984	3.35	5.06
1963	1.25	6.41	1985	3.35	4.88
1964	1.25	6.33	1986	3.35	4.80
1965	1.25	6.23	1987	3.35	4.63
1966	1.25	6.05	1988	3.35	4.44
1967	1.40	6.58	1989	3.35	4.24
1968	1.60	7.21	1990	3.80	4.56
1969	1.60	6.84	1991	4.25	4.90
1970	1.60	6.47	1992	4.25	4.75
1971	1.60	6.20	1993	4.25	4.61
1972	1.60	6.01	1994	4.25	4.50
1973	1.60	5.65	1995	4.25	4.38
1974	2.00	6.37	1996	4.75	4.75
1975	2.10	6.12			

[1] Effective September 1, 1997, the Federal minimum wage rose to $5.15; $5.03 in constant 1996 dollars. [2] Adjusted for inflation using the CPI-U; see text, Section 15, Prices.

Source: U.S. Employment Standards Administration, Internet site <http://www.dol.gov/esa/public/minwage/main.htm> (accessed 25 May 1999).

No. 706. Workers Paid Hourly Rates, by Selected Characteristics: 1998

[Data are annual averages (71,440 represents 71,440,000). For employed wage and salary workers. Based on Current Population Survey; see text, Section 1, Population, and Appendix III]

Characteristic	Number of workers [1] (1,000)				Percent of all workers paid hourly rates			Median hourly earnings of workers paid hourly rates [2]
	Total paid hourly rates	At or below $5.15			At or below $5.15			
		Total	At $5.15	Below $5.15	Total	At $5.15	Below $5.15	
Total, 16 years and over [3] ..	71,440	4,427	1,593	2,834	6.2	2.2	4.0	$9.10
16 to 24 years	16,361	2,260	883	1,377	13.8	5.4	8.4	6.58
16 to 19 years.	6,482	1,348	558	790	20.8	8.6	12.2	5.88
25 years and over	55,080	2,166	710	1,456	3.9	1.3	2.6	10.13
Male, 16 years and over ..	35,761	1,667	628	1,039	4.7	1.8	2.9	10.06
16 to 24 years	8,411	936	400	536	11.1	4.8	6.4	6.91
16 to 19 years.	3,219	585	257	328	18.2	8.0	10.2	5.98
25 years and over	27,349	731	228	503	2.7	0.8	1.8	11.72
Women, 16 years and over.	35,680	2,759	965	1,794	7.7	2.7	5.0	8.23
16 to 24 years	7,949	1,324	483	841	16.7	6.1	10.6	6.24
16 to 19 years.	3,263	763	301	462	23.4	9.2	14.2	5.78
25 years and over	27,730	1,435	482	953	5.2	1.7	3.4	9.13
White	58,512	3,559	1,269	2,290	6.1	2.2	3.9	9.22
Black	9,773	705	274	431	7.2	2.8	4.4	8.39
Hispanic origin [4]	9,065	669	276	393	7.4	3.0	4.3	7.92
Full-time workers	54,093	1,793	596	1,197	3.3	1.1	2.2	10.01
Part-time workers [5]	17,198	2,621	993	1,628	15.2	5.8	9.5	6.53
Private sector industries . . .	62,796	4,142	1,471	2,671	6.6	2.3	4.3	8.90
Goods-producing [6]	19,179	497	177	320	2.6	0.9	1.7	10.36
Service-producing [7]	43,617	3,645	1,294	2,351	8.4	3.0	5.4	8.12
Public sector	8,644	285	122	163	3.3	1.4	1.9	11.16

[1] Excludes the incorporated self-employed. [2] For definition of median, see Guide to Tabular Presentation. [3] Includes races not shown separately. Also includes a small number of multiple jobholders whose full- part- time status can not be determined for their principal job. [4] Persons of Hispanic origin may be of any race. [5] Working fewer than 35 hours per week. [6] Includes agriculture, mining, construction, and manufacturing. [7] Includes transportation and public utilities; wholesale trade; finance, insurance, and real estate; private households; and other service industries.

Source: U.S. Bureau of Labor Statistics, unpublished data.

U.S. Census Bureau, Statistical Abstract of the United States: 1999

No. 707. Employer Costs for Employee Compensation Per Hour Worked: 1998

[In dollars. As of March, for private industry workers. Based on a sample of establishments; see source for details]

Compensation component	Total	Goods producing[1]	Service producing[2]	Manu-facturing	Non-manu-facturing	Union members	Non-union members	Full-time workers	Part-time workers
Total compensation ...	18.50	22.26	17.31	22.29	17.66	23.59	17.80	20.95	10.01
Wages and salaries	13.47	15.35	12.88	15.22	13.09	15.38	13.21	15.03	8.10
Total benefits	5.02	6.91	4.42	7.07	4.57	8.22	4.58	5.93	1.90
Paid leave	1.16	1.47	1.07	1.68	1.05	1.57	1.11	1.42	0.27
Vacation	0.58	0.76	0.52	0.86	0.51	0.85	0.54	(NA)	(NA)
Holiday	0.40	0.53	0.36	0.62	0.35	0.51	0.39	(NA)	(NA)
Sick	0.14	0.11	0.14	0.13	0.14	0.14	0.14	(NA)	(NA)
Other	0.05	0.06	0.05	0.07	0.05	0.07	0.05	(NA)	(NA)
Supplemental pay	0.56	0.85	0.47	0.91	0.48	0.95	0.51	0.68	0.15
Premium pay	0.22	0.47	0.14	0.48	0.16	0.60	0.17	(NA)	(NA)
Nonproduction bonuses	0.29	0.30	0.29	0.34	0.28	0.21	0.30	(NA)	(NA)
Shift pay	0.05	0.07	0.04	0.09	0.04	0.14	0.04	(NA)	(NA)
Insurance	1.10	1.62	0.94	1.70	0.97	2.15	0.96	1.34	0.27
Health insurance	1.00	1.48	0.85	1.54	0.88	1.97	0.86	(NA)	0.14
Retirement and savings	0.55	0.82	0.46	0.76	0.50	1.29	0.45	0.67	0.14
Defined benefit	0.24	0.45	0.18	0.40	0.21	1.00	0.14	(NA)	(NA)
Defined contributions	0.30	0.37	0.28	0.36	0.29	0.29	0.31	(NA)	(NA)
Legally required	1.63	2.09	1.48	1.93	1.56	2.18	1.55	1.78	1.08
Social Security	1.12	1.30	1.07	1.30	1.08	1.33	1.09	(NA)	(NA)
Federal unemployment	0.03	0.03	0.03	0.03	0.03	0.03	0.03	(NA)	(NA)
State unemployment	0.11	0.14	0.10	0.12	0.11	0.14	0.11	(NA)	(NA)
Workers compensation	0.36	0.63	0.28	0.48	0.33	0.69	0.31	(NA)	(NA)
Other benefits[3]	0.03	0.07	-	0.08	-	0.08	0.02	0.03	-

- Represents or rounds to zero.   NA Not available.   [1] Mining, construction, and manufacturing.   [2] Transportation, communications, and public utilities, wholesale and retail trade, finance, insurance, and real estate, and services.   [3] Includes severance pay, and supplemental unemployment benefits.

Source: U.S. Bureau of Labor Statistics, News, Employer Costs for Employee Compensation, USDL, 98-285.

No. 708. Employees With Employer- or Union-Provided Pension Plans or Group Health Plans: 1997

[Total in thousands (144,582 represents 144,582,000). For wage and salary workers 15 years old and over as of March 1998. Based on Current Population Survey; see text, Section 1, Population, and Appendix III. Data based on 1990 population controls]

Occupation	Total (1,000)	Percent Included in pension plan	Percent With group health plan	Characteristic	Total (1,000)	Percent Included in pension plan	Percent With group health plan
Total	144,582	42.0	52.8	AGE			
Executive, admin., managerial ...	19,313	55.3	67.2	Total	144,582	42.0	52.8
Professional specialty	20,819	59.6	66.8	15 to 24 years old	24,049	12.0	21.6
				25 to 44 years old	72,442	46.2	57.8
Technical/related support	4,656	55.2	65.4	45 to 64 years old	43,155	53.8	63.1
Sales workers	17,824	30.2	42.8	65 years old and over	4,937	23.3	40.8
Admin. support, inc. clerical	20,565	47.1	56.3	WORK EXPERIENCE			
				Worked	144,582	42.0	52.8
Precision prod., craft/repair	15,544	41.8	56.0	Full time	113,977	49.8	62.1
				50 weeks or more	92,648	55.1	67.5
Mach. operators, assemblers[1] ...	8,601	44.3	61.4	27 to 49 weeks	12,513	33.6	47.9
Transportation/material moving[2] ...	5,809	40.8	55.2	26 weeks or fewer	8,816	16.2	25.1
Handlers, equipment cleaners[2] ...	5,968	25.6	36.5	Part time	30,605	13.0	18.4
				50 weeks or more	13,880	17.9	24.2
Service workers	20,879	23.1	32.5	27 to 49 weeks	6,624	14.7	18.3
Private households	1,019	1.2	8.7	26 weeks or fewer	10,101	5.2	10.3
Other	19,860	24.2	33.7	EMPLOYER SIZE			
				Under 25 persons	42,394	14.2	28.2
Farming, forestry and fishing	3,776	9.2	20.9	25 to 99 persons	18,374	35.8	52.3
				100 to 499 persons	19,051	49.0	61.7
Armed Forces	828	70.0	32.7	500 to 999 persons	8,091	57.8	66.5
				Over 1,000 persons	56,671	60.2	66.4

[1] Includes inspectors.   [2] Includes helpers and laborers.

Source: U.S. Census Bureau, unpublished data.

448   Labor Force, Employment, and Earnings

No. 709. Employee Benefits in Medium and Large Firms: 1997

[In percent. Covers full-time employees in private industry. Medium and large establishments exclude establishments with fewer than 100 workers. Covers only benefits for which the employer pays part or all of the premium or expenses involved, except unpaid family leave. Based on a sample survey of establishments; for details, see source. For data on employee benefits in small establishments, see Table 710]

Employee benefit program	All employees	Professional, technical and related	Clerical and sales	Blue collar and service	Employee benefit program	All employees	Professional, technical and related	Clerical and sales	Blue collar and service
Paid time off:					Tax-deferred savings:				
Holidays	89	89	91	88	With employer contribution	46	56	51	38
Vacations	95	96	97	94	With no employer contribution	9	11	8	8
Personal leave	20	23	33	13	Income continuation plans:				
Funeral leave	81	84	85	76	Severance pay	36	48	43	26
Jury duty leave	87	92	89	83	Supplemental unemployment benefits	5	2	2	7
Military leave	47	60	50	38	Family benefits:				
Sick leave	56	73	73	38	Child care	10	14	10	7
Family leave	2	3	3	1	Adoption assistance	10	16	12	6
Unpaid family leave	93	95	96	91	Long-term care insurance	7	10	11	4
Disability benefits:					Flexible workplace	2	5	3	(Z)
Short-term disability	55	54	52	58	Health promotion programs:				
Long-term disability	43	62	52	28	Wellness programs	36	44	36	32
Insurance:					Employee assistance programs	61	75	63	52
Medical care	76	79	78	74	Fitness center	21	31	19	16
Dental care	59	64	59	56	Miscellaneous benefits:				
Vision care	26	28	25	24	Job-related travel accident insurance	42	56	46	32
Life insurance	87	94	91	81	Nonproduction bonuses	42	43	43	40
Retirement	79	89	81	72	Subsidized commuting	6	10	7	3
Defined benefit	50	52	49	50	Educational assistance:				
Defined contribution	57	70	63	46	Job-related	67	81	68	58
Savings and thrift	39	49	45	30	Non-job related	20	25	18	18
Deferred profit sharing	13	15	15	12					
Employee stock ownership	4	6	6	3					
Money purchase pension	8	12	6	6					

Z Less than 0.5 percent.

Source: U.S. Bureau of Labor Statistics, *News,* USDL 99-02, January 7, 1999.

No. 710. Employee Benefits in Small Firms: 1996

[In percent. Covers full-time employees in private industry. Small establishments are establishments with fewer than 100 workers. Covers only benefits for which the employer pays part or all of the premium or expenses involved, except certain tax deferred earnings arrangements. Based on a sample survey of establishments; for details, see sources. For data on employee benefits in medium and large establishments, see Table 709]

Employee benefit program	All employees	Professional, technical and related	Clerical and sales	Blue collar and service	Employee benefit program	All employees	Professional, technical and related	Clerical and sales	Blue collar and service
Paid time off:					Income contribution plans:				
Holidays	80	86	91	71	Severance pay	15	23	19	9
Vacations	86	90	95	79	Supplemental unemployment benefits	(Z)	(NA)	(Z)	(Z)
Personal leave	14	21	18	8	Family benefits:				
Funeral leave	51	60	60	42	Employer assistance for child care	2	4	2	(Z)
Jury duty leave	59	74	68	47	Employer provided funds	1	2	2	(Z)
Military leave	18	25	23	12	On-site child care	1	2	(Z)	(Z)
Sick leave	50	66	64	35	Off-site child care	1	2	(Z)	(Z)
Family leave	2	3	3	1	Health promotion programs:				
Insurance:					Wellness programs	8	11	9	5
Short-term disability	29	32	33	25	Employee assistance programs	14	18	19	10
Long-term disability	22	39	30	10	Fitness center	4	6	5	3
Medical care	64	76	69	56	Miscellaneous benefits:				
Fee-for-service[1]	36	31	34	41	Job-related travel accident insurance	12	17	16	7
HMO[1]	27	27	28	25	Nonproduction bonuses	44	44	46	43
PPO[1]	35	41	36	32	Subsidized commuting	1	3	2	1
Dental care	31	40	35	24	Educational assistance:				
Life insurance	62	72	68	54	Job-related	38	56	45	27
Retirement	46	56	53	37	Non-job related	5	6	6	4
Defined benefit	15	12	16	15					
Defined contribution	38	51	46	28					
Tax deferred earnings arrangements:									
With employer contribution	24	30	31	17					
With no employer contribution	4	8	4	3					

NA Not available.   Z Less than 0.5 percent.   [1] Percent of participants receiving medical care insurance.

Source: U.S. Bureau of Labor Statistics, *News,* USDL 98-240, June 15, 1998.

Labor Force, Employment, and Earnings   449

[Data for 1997 are preliminary estimates (**13.8 represents 13,800**). Excludes homicides and suicides. Estimates based on data from the U.S. National Center for Health Statistics, state vital statistics departments, state industrial commissions and beginning 1992, Bureau of Labor Statistics, Census of Occupational Fatalities. Numbers of workers based on data from the U.S. Bureau of Labor Statistics]

Year	Deaths Total Number (1,000)	Rate [1]	Deaths Manufacturing Number (1,000)	Rate [1]	Deaths Nonmanufacturing Number (1,000)	Rate [1]	Disabling injuries [2] (mil.)	Year and industry group	Deaths Number (1,000)	Rate [1]	Disabling injuries [2] (1,000)
1960 ..	13.8	21	1.7	10	12.1	25	2.0	**Total, 1997** [3]	5,100	4	3,800
1965 ..	14.1	20	1.8	10	12.3	24	2.1	Agriculture [4]	720	20	140
1970 ..	13.8	18	1.7	9	12.1	21	2.2	Mining and quarrying [5] .	150	24	20
1975 ..	13.0	15	1.6	9	11.4	17	2.2	Construction	1,060	14	390
1980 ..	13.2	13	1.7	8	11.5	15	2.2	Manufacturing	670	3	640
1990 ..	10.1	9	1.0	5	9.1	9	3.9	Transportation and			
1994 ..	5.3	4	0.7	4	4.3	4	3.5	utilities	900	12	380
1995 ..	5.0	4	0.6	4	4.3	4	3.6	Trade [6]	470	2	720
1996 ..	5.0	4	0.7	3	4.3	4	3.9	Services [7]	640	1	960
1997 ..	5.1	4	0.7	3	4.3	4	3.8	Government	490	3	550

[1] Per 100,000 workers. [2] Disabling injury defined as one which results in death, some degree of physical impairment, or renders the person unable to perform regular activities for a full day beyond the day of the injury. [3] Includes deaths where industry is not known. [4] Includes forestry and fishing. [5] Includes oil and gas extraction. [6] Includes wholesale and retail trade. [7] Includes finance, insurance, and real estate.

Source: National Safety Council, Itasca, IL, *Accident Facts*, annual (copyright).

No. 712. Worker Deaths, Injuries, and Production Time Lost: 1995 to 1997

[**45.7 represents 45,700**. Data may not agree with Table 711 because data here are not revised]

Item	Deaths (1,000) 1995	1996	1997	Disabling injuries [1] (mil.) 1995	1996	1997	Production time lost (mil. days) In the current year 1995	1996	1997	In future years [2] 1995	1996	1997
All accidents	45.7	43.9	43.3	9.9	10.2	9.6	225	230	220	455	430	420
On the job	5.3	4.8	5.1	3.6	3.9	3.8	75	80	80	65	60	60
Off the job	40.4	39.1	38.2	6.3	6.3	5.8	150	150	140	390	370	360
Motor vehicle	22.9	22.2	22.0	1.2	1.3	1.2	(NA)	(NA)	(NA)	(NA)	(NA)	(NA)
Public nonmotor vehicle ...	7.5	7.4	6.8	2.3	2.4	2.3	(NA)	(NA)	(NA)	(NA)	(NA)	(NA)
Home	10.0	9.5	9.4	2.8	2.6	2.3	(NA)	(NA)	(NA)	(NA)	(NA)	(NA)

NA Not available. [1] See footnote 2, Table 711, for a definition of disabling injuries. [2] Based on an average of 5,850 days lost in future years per fatality and 565 days lost in future years per permanent injury.

Source: National Safety Council, Itasca, IL, *Accident Facts*, annual (copyright).

No. 713. Incidence Rates for Nonfatal Injuries and Illnesses— Selected Industries: 1995 and 1996

[**Rates per 100 full-time employees.** Industries shown are those with highest rates in 1997. For nonfarm employment data, see Table 690. Rates refer to any occupational injury or illness resulting in (1) lost workday cases, or (2) nonfatal cases without lost workdays. Incidence rates were calculated as: Number of injuries and illnesses divided by total hours worked by all employees during year multiplied by 200,000 as base for 100 full-time equivalent workers (working 40 hours per week, 50 weeks a year)]

Industry	1987 SIC [1] code	1995	1996	Industry	1987 SIC [1] code	1995	1996
Private Industry	(X)	7.4	7.1	Secondary nonferrous metals	334	21.0	18.9
Meat packing plants	2011	30.3	32.1	Primary aluminum	3334	13.6	18.8
Malleable iron foundries	3322	16.7	27.6	Transportation equipment, n.e.c. ...	3799	15.2	18.6
Gray and ductile iron foundries	3321	25.8	26.6	Structural wood members, n.e.c. [2] ...	2439	20.5	18.1
Motor vehicles and car bodies......	3711	26.1	25.5	Canned and cured fish and seafoods .	2091	15.3	17.9
Metal sanitary ware............	3431	29.4	24.4	Air transportation, scheduled [3] ...	451	19.3	17.7
Vitreous plumbing fixtures	3261	16.3	23.9	Boat building and repairing........	3732	16.2	17.6
Mobile homes	2451	26.2	22.6	Aluminum die-castings...........	3363	19.9	17.4
Ship building and repairing........	3731	27.4	21.4	Burial caskets	3995	8.9	17.3
Truck trailers	3715	19.4	21.3	Iron and steel forgings...........	3462	19.4	17.3
Automotive stampings	3465	23.2	20.0	Construction machinery	3531	16.3	17.0
Leather tanning and finishing	311	19.1	19.9	Travel trailers and campers	3792	19.7	16.9
Aluminum foundries............	3365	17.1	19.8	Fabricated structural metal	3441	16.7	16.8
Steel foundries, n.e.c.	3325	26.4	19.1	Fresh and frozen prepared fish	2092	14.4	16.8

X Not applicable. [1] 1987 Standard Industrial Classification; see text, Section 17, Business. [2] N.e.c. means not elsewhere classified.

Source: U.S. Bureau of Labor Statistics, *Occupational Injuries and Illnesses in the United States by Industry*, annual.

No. 714. Nonfatal Occupational Injury and Illness Incidence Rates: 1996 and 1997

[Rates per 100 full-time employees. See headnote, Table 713]

Industry	1987 SIC [1] code	1996	1997	Industry	1987 SIC [1] code	1996	1997
Private sector [2]	(X)	7.4	7.1	Local passenger transit	41	10.3	8.0
Agriculture, forestry, fishing [2]	A	8.7	8.4	Trucking and warehousing	42	10.4	10.0
Mining [3]	B	5.4	5.9	Water transportation	44	9.8	8.6
Metal mining [3]	10	5.0	4.9	Transportation by air	45	17.9	16.4
Coal mining [3]	12	8.0	7.8	Pipelines, except natural gas	46	2.0	3.7
Oil and gas extraction	13	5.0	5.9	Transportation services	47	3.5	3.9
Nonmetallic minerals, exc. fuels	14	4.8	4.7	Communications	48	3.5	3.4
Construction	C	9.9	9.5	Electric, gas, sanitary services	49	6.9	6.9
General building contractors	15	9.0	8.5	**Wholesale and retail trade**	F, G	6.8	6.7
Heavy construction, except building	16	9.0	8.7	Wholesale trade	F	6.6	6.5
Special trade contractors	17	10.4	10.0	Retail trade	G	6.9	6.8
Manufacturing	D	10.6	10.3	**Finance, insurance, real estate**	H	2.4	2.2
Durable goods	(X)	11.6	11.3	Depository institutions	60	1.8	1.8
Lumber and wood products	24	14.2	13.5	Nondepository institutions	61	1.1	1.2
Furniture and fixtures	25	12.2	12.0	Security and commodity brokers	62	0.6	0.7
Stone, clay, and glass products	32	12.4	11.8	Insurance carriers	63	2.1	2.2
Primary metal industries	33	15.0	15.0	Insurance agents, brokers, and service	64	1.4	1.3
Fabricated metal products	34	14.4	14.2	Real estate	65	5.4	4.7
Industrial machinery and equip.	35	9.9	10.0	Holding and other investment offices	67	2.8	2.0
Electronic/other electric equip.	36	6.8	6.6	**Services [4]**	I	6.0	5.6
Transportation equipment	37	16.3	15.4	Hotels and other lodging places	70	9.0	8.4
Instruments/related products	38	5.1	4.8	Personal services	72	3.8	3.8
Miscellaneous manufacturing industries	39	9.5	8.9	Business services	73	3.9	3.6
Nondurable goods	(X)	9.2	8.8	Auto repair, services, and parking	75	5.9	6.3
Food and kindred products	20	15.0	14.5	Miscellaneous repair services	76	6.3	7.4
Tobacco products	21	6.7	5.9	Motion pictures	78	(NA)	3.1
Textile mill products	22	7.8	6.7	Amusement and recreation services	79	9.5	8.1
Apparel and other textile products	23	7.4	7.0	Health services	80	9.1	8.4
Paper and allied products	26	7.9	7.3	Legal services	81	1.1	0.8
Printing and publishing	27	6.0	5.7	Educational services	82	3.4	2.9
Chemicals and allied products	28	4.8	4.8	Social services	83	7.2	6.4
Petroleum and coal products	29	4.6	4.3	Museums, botanical, zoological gardens	84	(NA)	7.4
Rubber and misc. plastics products	30	12.3	11.9	Engineering and management services	87	2.0	1.9
Leather and leather products [3]	31	10.7	10.6	Services, n.e.c. [5]	89	(NA)	1.3
Transportation/public utilities [3]	E	8.7	8.2				
Railroad transportation [3]	40	3.5	3.4				

NA Not available.   X Not applicable.   [1] 1987 Standard Industrial Classification; see text, Section 17, Business.   [2] Excludes farms with fewer than 11 employees.   [3] Data conforming to OSHA definitions for employers in the railroad industry and for mining operators in coal, metal, and nonmetal mining. Independent mining contractors are excluded from the coal, metal, and nonmetal mining industries.   [4] Includes categories not shown separately.   [5] N.e.c. means not elsewhere classified.

Source: U.S. Bureau of Labor Statistics, *Occupational Injuries and Illnesses in the United States by Industry,* annual.

No. 715. Workplace Violence: 1992-96

[Based on the National Crime Victimization Surveys; see text, Section 5, Law Enforcement, and Appendix III. (2,009.4 represents 2,009,400)]

Characteristic of violence victims	Percent	Occupation	Average annual number (1,000)	Rate [1]	Occupation	Average annual number (1,000)	Rate [1]
Total [2]	100.0	**Total [4]**	2,009.4	14.8	Teachers:		
Sex: Male	66.8	Medical:			Elementary	35.4	16.0
Female	33.2	Physicians	10.0	15.7	Junior High	47.3	57.4
Race: White	88.6	Nurses	69.5	24.8	High school	33.3	28.9
Black	8.9	Medical technicians	24.5	21.4	Higher ed.	6.6	2.5
Other	2.5	Other	56.8	10.7	Special ed.	9.0	40.7
Ethnicity: [3]		Mental health:			Other	14.4	10.1
Hispanic	6.6	Professional	50.3	79.5	Retail sales:		
Non-Hispanic	92.1	Custodial	8.7	63.3	Convenience/liquor		
Age: 12 to 17 years	2.4	Other	43.5	64.0	store	61.5	68.4
18 to 24 years	17.9				Gas station	15.5	79.1
25 to 34 years	32.9	Law enforcement:			Bar	26.4	91.3
35 to 49 years	37.0	Police	234.2	306.0	Other	228.2	17.5
50 to 59 years	7.2	Private security	71.1	117.3	Transportation:		
60 to 64 years	1.5	Corrections officer	58.3	217.8	Taxi driver	16.1	183.8
65 years and over	1.1	Other	67.6	61.5	Bus driver	17.2	45.0
					Other	43.2	10.0

[1] Rate per 1,000 workers.   [2] Includes 1,023 average annual homicide victims.   [3] Ethnicity was unknown for 1.3% of victims.   [4] Includes other occupations, not shown separately.

Source: U.S. Bureau of Justice Statistics, *Workplace Violence, 1992-96.*

U.S. Census Bureau, Statistical Abstract of the United States: 1999

No. 716. Fatal Occupational Injuries, by Industry and Event: 1997

[For the 50 states and DC. Based on the 1997 Census of Fatal Occupational Injuries. Due to methodological differences, data differ from those in Table 711. For details, see source]

Industry	1987 SIC[1] code	Fatalities[2]	Event or exposure—Percent distribution					Rate[5]
			Transportation incidents	Assaults/ violent acts	Contact with objects[3]	Falls	Exposure[4]	
Total	(X)	6,218	42	18	17	12	9	5
Private industry	(X)	5,594	40	18	18	12	9	5
Agriculture, forestry, fishing	A	830	49	7	25	8	9	23
Mining[6]	B	158	30	-	39	9	9	25
Coal mining	12	32	19	-	63	-	13	
Oil and gas extraction	13	85	27	-	28	14	8	23
Construction	C	1,107	26	3	18	34	17	14
General building contractors	15	194	24	5	14	40	15	-
Heavy construction, except building	16	252	44	-	27	10	15	-
Special trade contractors	17	648	19	2	16	42	18	-
Manufacturing[6]	D	743	30	9	40	7	8	4
Food and kindred products	20	78	41	10	26	10	12	5
Lumber and wood products	24	199	25	-	67	4	3	24
Transportation and public utilities[6]	E	1,002	69	13	7	4	6	13
Local passenger transit	41	106	26	74	-	-	-	19
Trucking and warehousing	42	569	81	5	7	4	2	22
Transportation by air	45	83	88	-	-	-	-	10
Electric, gas, sanitary services	49	89	34	6	15	5	30	8
Wholesale trade	F	241	51	12	18	7	7	5
Retail trade[6]	G	665	19	64	5	5	5	3
Food stores	54	189	9	82	-	4	2	5
Automotive dealer and service stations	55	115	27	49	9	-	7	5
Eating and drinking places	58	150	10	78	-	5	5	2
Finance, insurance, real estate	H	97	38	36	4	17	4	1
Services[6]	I	722	41	27	12	9	8	2
Business services	73	181	42	24	11	10	11	3
Auto repair, services, and parking	75	109	33	25	26	-	7	7
Government	J	624	57	19	6	5	9	3

- No data reported or data do not meet publication standards.   X Not applicable.   [1] 1987 Standard Industrial Classification code, see text Section 17, Business.   [2] Includes 29 fatalities for which there was insufficient information to determine industry classification. Includes fatalities caused by other events and exposures, not shown separately.   [3] Includes equipment.   [4] Exposure to harmful substances or environments.   [5] Rate per 100,000 employed civilians 16 years old and over.   [6] Includes other industries, not shown separately.

Source: U.S. Bureau of Labor Statistics, *USDL News,* 98-336, August 12, 1998; and unpublished data.

No. 717. Work Stoppages: 1960 to 1998

[Excludes work stoppages involving fewer than 1,000 workers and lasting less than 1 day. Information is based on reports of labor disputes appearing in daily newspapers, trade journals, and other public sources. The parties to the disputes are contacted by telephone, when necessary, to clarify details of the stoppages]

Year	Number of work stoppages[1]	Workers involved[2] (1,000)	Days idle		Year	Number of work stoppages[1]	Workers involved[2] (1,000)	Days idle	
			Number[3] (1,000)	Percent estimated working time[4]				Number[3] (1,000)	Percent estimated working time[4]
1960	222	896	13,260	0.09	1983	81	909	17,461	0.08
1965	268	999	15,140	0.10	1984	62	376	8,499	0.04
1969	412	1,576	29,397	0.16	1985	54	324	7,079	0.03
1970	381	2,468	52,761	0.29	1986	69	533	11,861	0.05
1971	298	2,516	35,538	0.19	1987	46	174	[5]4,481	0.02
1972	250	975	16,764	0.09	1988	40	118	[5]4,381	0.02
1973	317	1,400	16,260	0.08	1989	51	452	16,996	0.07
1974	424	1,796	31,809	0.16	1990	44	185	5,926	0.02
1975	235	965	17,563	0.09	1991	40	392	4,584	0.02
1976	231	1,519	23,962	0.12	1992	35	364	3,989	0.01
1977	298	1,212	21,258	0.10	1993	35	182	3,981	0.01
1978	219	1,006	23,774	0.11	1994	45	322	5,020	0.02
1979	235	1,021	20,409	0.09	1995	31	192	5,771	0.02
1980	187	795	20,844	0.09	1996	37	273	4,887	0.02
1981	145	729	16,908	0.07	1997	29	339	4,497	0.01
1982	96	656	9,061	0.04	1998	34	387	5,116	0.02

[1] Beginning in year indicated.   [2] Workers counted more than once if involved in more than one stoppage during the year.   [3] Resulting from all stoppages in effect in a year, including those that began in an earlier year.   [4] Agricultural and government employees are included in the total working time; private household and forestry and fishery employees are excluded.   [5] Revised since originally published.

Source: U.S. Bureau of Labor Statistics, *Compensation and Working Conditions,* monthly through 1995, thereafter quarterly.

U.S. Census Bureau,   Statistical Abstract of the United States: 1999

No. 718. Labor Union Membership, by Sector: 1983 to 1998

[See headnote, Table 720. **17,717.4** represents 17,717,400]

Sector	1983	1985	1990	1993	1994	1995	1996	1997	1998
TOTAL (1,000)									
Wage and salary workers:									
Union members	17,717.4	16,996.1	16,739.8	16,598.1	16,740.3	16,359.6	16,269.4	16,109.9	16,211.4
Covered by unions	20,532.1	19,358.1	19,057.8	18,646.4	18,842.5	18,346.3	18,158.1	17,923.0	17,918.3
Public sector workers:									
Union members.	5,737.2	5,743.1	6,485.0	7,017.8	7,091.0	6,927.4	6,854.4	6,746.7	6,905.3
Covered by unions.	7,112.2	6,920.6	7,691.4	8,162.4	8,191.8	7,986.6	7,829.7	7,668.0	7,814.7
Private sector workers:									
Union members.	11,980.2	11,253.0	10,254.8	9,580.3	9,649.4	9,432.1	9,415.0	9,363.3	9,306.1
Covered by unions.	13,419.9	12,437.5	11,366.4	10,484.0	10,650.6	10,359.8	10,328.4	10,255.0	10,103.6
PERCENT									
Wage and salary workers:									
Union members	20.1	18.0	16.1	15.8	15.5	14.9	14.5	14.1	13.9
Covered by unions	23.3	20.5	18.3	17.7	17.4	16.7	16.2	15.6	15.4
Public sector workers:									
Union members.	36.7	35.7	36.5	37.7	38.7	37.7	37.6	37.2	37.5
Covered by unions.	45.5	43.1	43.3	43.8	44.7	43.5	43.0	42.3	42.5
Private sector workers:									
Union members.	16.5	14.3	11.9	11.1	10.8	10.3	10.0	9.7	9.5
Covered by unions.	18.5	15.9	13.2	12.1	11.9	11.3	11.0	10.6	10.3

Source: The Bureau of National Affairs, Inc., Washington, DC, *Union Membership and Earnings Data Book: Compilations from the Current Population Survey (1999 edition)*, (copyright by BNA PLUS); authored by Barry Hirsch and David Macpherson of Florida State University. Internet site <http://www.bna.com/bnaplus/databook.html>.

No. 719. Union Members, by Selected Characteristics: 1998

[**Annual averages of monthly data (116,730 represents 116,730,000).** Covers employed wage and salary workers 16 years old and over. Excludes self-employed workers whose businesses are incorporated although they technically qualify as wage and salary workers. Based on Current Population Survey, see text, Section 1, Population, and Appendix III]

Characteristic	Employed wage and salary workers			Median usual weekly earnings [3] (dol.)			
	Total (1,000)	Percent					
		Union members [1]	Represented by unions [2]	Total	Union members [1]	Represented by unions [2]	Not represented by unions
Total [4].	**116,730**	**13.9**	**15.4**	**523**	**659**	**653**	**499**
16 to 24 years old	19,164	5.3	6.0	319	415	410	315
25 to 34 years old	29,121	11.4	12.7	502	595	591	489
35 to 44 years old	31,865	15.7	17.3	597	683	678	576
45 to 54 years old	23,579	20.1	22.1	620	716	712	592
55 to 64 years old	10,427	18.4	20.2	592	697	692	560
65 years and over	2,574	7.5	8.3	405	610	597	383
Men.	60,973	16.2	17.4	598	699	696	573
Women	55,757	11.4	13.1	456	596	593	430
White.	**97,531**	**13.5**	**14.8**	**545**	**683**	**678**	**513**
Men.	51,700	15.8	17.0	615	719	716	591
Women	45,831	10.8	12.4	468	610	607	443
Black.	**13,894**	**17.7**	**19.7**	**426**	**578**	**572**	**398**
Men.	6,452	20.7	22.6	468	597	592	424
Women	7,443	15.1	17.2	400	537	533	376
Hispanic [5].	**12,374**	**11.9**	**13.2**	**370**	**540**	**541**	**350**
Men.	7,360	12.7	13.8	390	585	584	367
Women	5,015	10.6	12.3	337	478	481	322
Full-time workers	95,595	15.5	17.1	523	659	653	499
Part-time workers	20,862	6.5	7.5	(X)	(X)	(X)	(X)
Managerial and professional specialty	33,102	12.8	15.2	759	789	774	756
Technical sales, and admin. support	35,379	9.2	10.4	477	575	569	463
Service occupations	16,594	13.3	14.5	327	557	542	305
Precision, production, craft, and repair	12,274	22.1	23.1	572	753	747	514
Operators, fabricators, and laborers	17,443	21.3	22.3	415	585	580	381
Farming, forestry, and fishing	1,938	4.6	5.2	302	471	462	299
Agricultural wage and salary workers	1,739	1.5	1.8	315	(B)	(B)	314
Private nonagri. wage and salary workers . .	96,590	9.6	10.4	509	626	620	496
Mining.	589	12.2	13.4	684	733	723	673
Construction	5,946	17.8	18.4	534	790	783	496
Manufacturing	19,763	15.8	16.8	551	606	603	532
Transportation and public utilities	7,147	25.8	27.0	624	731	724	586
Wholesale and retail trade, total.	24,230	5.3	5.7	410	480	476	405
Finance, insurance, and real estate	7,420	2.0	2.6	577	545	554	578
Services	31,493	5.6	6.6	498	540	548	494
Government	18,401	37.5	42.5	620	694	688	558

B Data not shown where base is less than 50,000.   X Not applicable.   [1] Members of a labor union or an employee association similar to a labor union.   [2] Members of a labor union or an employee association similar to a union as well as workers who report no union affiliation but whose jobs are covered by a union or an employee association contract.   [3] For full-time employed wage and salary workers.   [4] Includes races not shown separately. Also includes a small number of multiple jobholders whose full- part- time status can not be determined for their principal job.   [5] Persons of Hispanic origin may be of any race.
Source: U.S. Bureau of Labor Statistics, *Employment and Earnings*, monthly, January 1999 issue.

Labor Force, Employment, and Earnings   453

No. 720. Labor Union Membership, by State: 1983 and 1998

[Annual averages of monthly figures (**17,717.4 represents 17,717,400**). For wage and salary workers in agriculture and non-agriculture. Data represent union members by place of residence. Based on the Current Population Survey and subject to sampling error. For methodological details, see source]

State	Union members (1,000) 1983	Union members (1,000) 1998	Workers covered by unions (1,000) 1983	Workers covered by unions (1,000) 1998	Percent of workers— Union members 1983	Union members 1998	Covered by unions 1983	Covered by unions 1998	Private manufacturing sector union members 1983	Private manufacturing sector union members 1998
United States..	17,717.4	16,211.4	20,532.1	17,918.3	20.1	13.9	23.3	15.4	27.8	15.8
Alabama [1]	228.2	180.2	268.2	218.4	16.9	9.7	19.8	11.8	25.9	13.8
Alaska	41.7	51.5	49.2	57.8	24.9	20.4	29.3	22.9	23.3	2.7
Arizona [1]	125.0	123.2	156.4	146.2	11.4	6.5	14.3	7.7	7.8	4.2
Arkansas [1]	82.2	61.1	103.2	72.1	11.0	6.2	13.8	7.3	18.7	9.3
California	2,118.9	2,154.0	2,505.2	2,407.6	21.9	16.1	25.9	18.1	21.0	9.2
Colorado.	177.9	171.4	209.6	189.4	13.6	9.1	16.0	10.0	13.1	8.6
Connecticut.	314.0	262.6	345.1	271.9	22.7	17.5	25.0	18.1	28.1	16.5
Delaware	49.2	46.3	54.1	50.2	20.1	13.6	22.1	14.7	27.3	20.0
District of Columbia	52.4	30.1	69.4	34.0	19.5	13.5	25.9	15.3	17.6	18.9
Florida [1]	393.7	407.8	532.9	538.4	10.2	6.7	13.8	8.9	11.3	5.4
Georgia [1]	267.0	256.8	345.1	289.0	11.9	7.4	15.3	8.4	16.9	7.2
Hawaii	112.6	130.2	124.9	136.4	29.2	26.5	32.4	27.7	35.6	26.2
Idaho [1]	41.3	42.1	53.7	55.6	12.5	7.8	16.2	10.3	19.0	10.2
Illinois	1,063.8	1,004.4	1,205.1	1,064.2	24.2	18.9	27.4	20.0	32.4	21.8
Indiana.	503.3	431.3	544.5	471.6	24.9	16.2	27.0	17.7	48.7	25.7
Iowa [1]	185.9	166.4	231.3	197.0	17.2	12.5	21.5	14.8	40.3	20.4
Kansas [1]	125.2	92.7	170.4	114.0	13.7	7.9	18.7	9.7	25.5	17.1
Kentucky	223.7	218.9	259.8	248.1	17.9	13.1	20.8	14.8	37.4	20.4
Louisiana [1]	204.2	134.5	267.8	172.1	13.8	7.8	18.1	10.0	24.9	22.8
Maine.	88.0	66.1	100.4	75.1	21.0	12.6	24.0	14.3	24.8	24.2
Maryland	346.5	331.3	423.1	378.9	18.5	14.1	22.6	16.1	29.2	17.3
Massachusetts.	603.2	453.1	661.4	493.7	23.7	15.9	26.0	17.4	26.7	14.0
Michigan.	1,005.4	953.8	1,084.6	995.8	30.4	21.6	32.8	22.6	46.2	32.2
Minnesota.	393.9	421.6	439.4	443.3	23.2	18.8	25.9	19.8	22.3	14.2
Mississippi [1]	79.4	61.2	99.7	105.6	9.9	5.6	12.5	9.7	18.9	8.5
Missouri	374.4	336.0	416.7	369.5	20.8	13.7	23.2	15.1	36.6	18.4
Montana.	49.5	48.8	55.5	53.5	18.3	13.9	20.5	15.3	33.0	16.4
Nebraska [1]	80.6	77.2	94.8	104.0	13.6	10.3	16.0	13.8	19.1	15.3
Nevada [1]	90.0	133.8	106.7	148.8	22.4	17.0	26.6	18.9	10.8	2.8
New Hampshire.	48.5	61.7	60.8	70.5	11.5	11.0	14.4	12.6	10.6	7.5
New Jersey	822.1	792.9	918.2	851.0	26.9	22.0	30.0	23.7	31.4	21.1
New Mexico	52.6	63.2	70.6	78.5	11.8	9.4	15.8	11.7	11.9	6.0
New York	2,155.6	1,899.8	2,385.9	1,994.8	32.5	25.4	36.0	26.7	31.0	19.5
North Carolina [1]	178.7	139.8	238.1	173.1	7.6	4.2	10.2	5.2	6.9	2.9
North Dakota [1]	28.4	25.5	35.1	26.9	13.2	9.1	16.3	9.6	27.4	12.9
Ohio	1,011.0	932.0	1,125.0	991.8	25.1	19.0	27.9	20.2	40.9	26.9
Oklahoma	131.5	116.6	168.2	132.8	11.5	8.6	14.7	9.8	25.2	16.3
Oregon.	222.9	231.9	261.9	248.0	22.3	16.1	26.2	17.3	28.7	12.2
Pennsylvania.	1,195.7	827.3	1,350.0	896.0	27.5	16.3	31.1	17.7	42.3	20.0
Rhode Island.	85.8	81.1	93.7	83.6	21.5	19.0	23.5	19.6	16.9	10.8
South Carolina [1]	69.6	78.1	100.6	87.7	5.9	4.5	8.6	5.1	5.5	6.2
South Dakota [1]	26.8	20.8	34.8	26.0	11.5	6.4	14.9	8.0	19.0	7.5
Tennessee [1]	252.4	183.3	300.9	220.2	15.1	7.9	18.0	9.5	21.4	11.5
Texas [1]	583.7	503.1	712.8	603.4	9.7	5.9	11.9	7.0	16.1	7.5
Utah [1]	81.6	61.6	100.9	78.3	15.2	6.8	18.9	8.6	14.9	5.5
Vermont.	25.9	25.3	31.5	29.4	12.6	9.4	15.3	11.0	13.5	5.8
Virginia [1]	268.3	208.7	346.1	232.9	11.7	6.8	15.1	7.6	21.2	9.9
Washington.	419.9	537.3	499.7	584.8	27.1	21.2	32.3	23.0	35.5	25.6
West Virginia.	142.7	83.3	160.6	91.6	25.3	12.6	28.5	13.8	41.3	25.8
Wisconsin.	465.5	470.0	526.7	491.7	23.8	18.7	26.9	19.6	36.0	22.5
Wyoming [1]	27.1	19.7	31.8	23.1	13.9	9.6	16.2	11.3	14.6	14.5

[1] Right to work state.

Source: The Bureau of National Affairs, Inc., Washington, DC, *Union Membership and Earnings Data Book: Compilations from the Current Population Survey,* (1999 edition) (copyright by BNA PLUS); authored by Barry Hirsch and David Macpherson of Florida State University. Internet site <http://www.bna.com/bnaplus/databook.html>

Section 14

Income, Expenditures, and Wealth

This section presents data on gross domestic product (GDP), gross national product (GNP), national and personal income, saving and investment, money income, poverty, and national and personal wealth. The data on income and expenditures measure two aspects of the U.S. economy. One aspect relates to the national income and product accounts (NIPAs), a summation reflecting the entire complex of the Nation's economic income and output and the interaction of its major components; the other relates to the distribution of money income to families and individuals or consumer income.

The primary source for data on GDP, GNP, national and personal income, gross saving and investment, and fixed reproducible tangible wealth is the *Survey of Current Business*, published monthly by the Bureau of Economic Analysis (BEA). A comprehensive revision to the NIPAs was completed in January 1996. Discussions of the revision appeared in the July, September, and October 1995 the January/February 1996, and the May 1997 issues of the *Survey of Current Business*. Summary historical estimates appeared in the August 1997 issue of the *Survey of Current Business*. Detailed historical data appear in the *National Income and Product Accounts of the United States, 1929-94*.

Sources of income distribution data are the decennial censuses of population and the Current Population Survey (CPS), both products of the U.S. Census Bureau (see text, Section 1). Annual data on income of families, individuals, and households are presented in *Current Population Reports, Consumer Income*, P60 series.

Data on individuals' saving and assets are published by the Board of Governors of the Federal Reserve System in the quarterly *Flow of Funds Accounts*; and detailed information on personal wealth is published periodically by the Internal Revenue Service (IRS) in *SOI Bulletin*.

National income and product—Gross domestic product is the total output of goods and services produced by labor and property located in the United States, valued at market prices. GDP can be viewed in terms of the expenditure categories that comprise its major components—purchases of goods and services by consumers and government, gross private domestic investment, and net exports of goods and services. The goods and services included are largely those bought for final use (excluding illegal transactions) in the market economy. A number of inclusions, however, represent imputed values, the most important of which is rental value of owner-occupied housing. GDP, in this broad context, measures the output attributable to the factors of production located in the United States. Gross state product (GSP) is the gross market value of the goods and services attributable to labor and property located in a state. It is the state counterpart of the Nation's gross domestic product.

As part of the comprehensive revision released in January 1996, BEA replaced its fixed-weighted (1987 dollars) index as the featured measure of real GDP with an index based on chain-type annual weights. Changes in the new featured measures of real output and prices are calculated as the average of changes based on weights for the current and preceding years. (Components of real output are weighted by price, and components of prices are weighted by output.) These annual changes are "chained" (multiplied) together to form a time series that allows for the effects of changes in relative prices and

U.S. Census Bureau, Statistical Abstract of the United States: 1999

changes in the composition of output over time. Quarterly and monthly changes are also based on annual weights. The new output indexes are expressed as 1992=100, and for recent years, in 1992 dollars; the new price indexes are based to 1992=100.

Chained (1992) dollar estimates of most components of GDP are not published for periods prior to 1982, because during periods far from the base period, the levels of the components may provide misleading information about their contributions to an aggregate. Values are published in index form (1992=100) for 1929 to the present to allow users to calculate the percent changes for all components, changes which are accurate for all periods. In addition, the Bureau of Economic Analysis publishes estimates of the contribution of major components to the percent change in GDP for all periods.

Gross national product measures the output attributable to all labor and property supplied by United States residents. GNP differs from "national income" mainly in that GNP includes allowances for depreciation and for indirect business taxes (sales and property taxes); see Table 727.

In December 1991, the Bureau of Economic Analysis began featuring gross domestic product rather than gross national product as the primary measure of U.S. production. GDP is now the standard measure of growth because it is the appropriate measure for much of the short-term monitoring and analysis of the economy. In addition, the use of GDP facilitates comparisons of economic activity in the United States with that in other countries.

National income is the aggregate of labor and property earnings which arises in the current production of goods and services. It is the sum of employee compensation, proprietors' income, rental income of persons, corporate profits, and net interest. It measures the total factor costs of the goods and services produced by the economy. Income is measured before deduction of taxes.

Capital consumption adjustment for corporations and for nonfarm sole proprietorships and partnerships is the difference between capital consumption based on income tax returns and capital consumption measured using empirical evidence on prices of used equipment and structures in resale markets, which have shown that depreciation for most types of assets approximates a geometric pattern. The tax return data are valued at historical costs and reflect changes over time in service lives and depreciation patterns as permitted by tax regulations. *Inventory valuation adjustment* represents the difference between the book value of inventories used up in production and the cost of replacing them.

Personal income is the current income received by persons from all sources minus their personal contributions for social insurance. Classified as "persons" are individuals (including owners of unincorporated firms), nonprofit institutions that primarily serve individuals, private trust funds, and private noninsured welfare funds. Personal income includes transfers (payments not resulting from current production) from government and business such as social security benefits, public assistance, etc., but excludes transfers among persons. Also included are certain nonmonetary types of income—chiefly estimated net rental value to owner-occupants of their homes and the value of services furnished without payment by financial intermediaries. Capital gains (net losses) are excluded.

Disposable personal income is personal income less personal tax and nontax payments. It is the income available to persons for spending or saving. Personal tax and nontax payments are tax payments (net of refunds) by persons (except personal contributions for social insurance) that are not chargeable to business expense and certain personal payments to general government that are treated like taxes. Personal taxes include income, estate and gift, and personal property taxes and motor vehicle licenses. Nontax payments include passport fees, fines and forfeitures, and donations.

U.S. Census Bureau, Statistical Abstract of the United States: 1999

Consumer Expenditure Survey—The Consumer Expenditure Survey program was begun in late 1979. The principal objective of the survey is to collect current consumer expenditure data which provide a continuous flow of data on the buying habits of American consumers. The data are necessary for future revisions of the Consumer Price Index.

The survey conducted by the Census Bureau for the Bureau of Labor Statistics consists of two components: (1) An interview panel survey in which the expenditures of consumer units are obtained in five interviews conducted every 3 months, and (2) a diary or recordkeeping survey completed by participating households for two consecutive 1-week periods.

Each component of the survey queries an independent sample of consumer units representative of the U.S. total population.

Over 52 weeks of the year, 5,000 consumer units are sampled for the diary survey. Each consumer unit keeps a diary for two 1-week periods yielding approximately 10,000 diaries a year. The interview sample is selected on a rotating panel basis, targeted at 5,000 consumer units per quarter. Data are collected in 88 urban and 16 rural areas of the country that are representative of the U.S. total population. The survey includes students in student housing. Data from the two surveys are combined; integration is necessary to permit analysis of total family expenditures because neither the diary nor quarterly interview survey was designed to collect a complete account of consumer spending.

Distribution of money income to families and individuals—Money income statistics are based on data collected in various field surveys of income conducted since 1936. Since 1947, the Census Bureau has collected the data on an annual basis and published them in *Current Population Reports*, P60 series. In each of the surveys, field representatives interview samples of the population with respect to income received during the previous year. Money income as defined by the Bureau of the Census differs from the BEA concept of "personal income."

Data on consumer income collected in the CPS by the Census Bureau cover money income received (exclusive of certain money receipts such as capital gains) before payments for personal income taxes, social security, union dues, medicare deductions, etc. Therefore, money income does not reflect the fact that some families receive part of their income in the form of noncash benefits (see Section 12) such as food stamps, health benefits, and subsidized housing; that some farm families receive noncash benefits in the form of rent-free housing and goods produced and consumed on the farm; or that noncash benefits are also received by some nonfarm residents which often take the form of the use of business transportation and facilities, full or partial payments by business for retirement programs, medical and educational expenses, etc. These elements should be considered when comparing income levels. For data on noncash benefits, see Section 12. None of the aggregate income concepts (GDP, national income, or personal income) is exactly comparable with money income, although personal income is the closest.

In October 1983, the Census Bureau began to collect data under the new Survey of Income and Program Participation (SIPP). The information supplied by this survey is expected to provide better measures of the status and changes in income distribution and poverty of households and persons in the United States. The data collected in SIPP will be used to study Federal and state aid programs (such as food stamps, welfare, medicaid, and subsidized housing), to estimate program costs and coverage, and to assess the effects of proposed changes in program eligibility rules or benefit levels. The core questions are repeated at each interview and cover labor force activity, the types and amounts of income received, and participation status in various programs. The core also contains questions covering attendance in post-secondary schools and private health insurance

U.S. Census Bureau, Statistical Abstract of the United States: 1999

coverage. Various supplements or topical modules covering areas such as educational attainment, assets and liabilities, and pension plan coverage are periodically included.

Poverty—Families and unrelated individuals are classified as being above or below the poverty level using the poverty index originated at the Social Security Administration in 1964 and revised by Federal Interagency Committees in 1969 and 1980.

The poverty index is based solely on money income and does not reflect the fact that many low-income persons receive noncash benefits such as food stamps, medicaid, and public housing. The index is based on the Department of Agriculture's 1961 Economy Food Plan and reflects the different consumption requirements of families based on their size and composition. The poverty thresholds are updated every year to reflect changes in the Consumer Price Index. The following technical changes to the thresholds were made in 1981: (1) distinctions based on sex of householder have been eliminated; (2) separate thresholds for farm families have been dropped; and (3) the matrix has been expanded to families of nine or more persons from the old cutoff of seven or more persons. These changes have been incorporated in the calculation of poverty data beginning with 1981. In the recent past, the Census Bureau has published a number of technical papers that presented experimental poverty estimates (see Table 770) based on income definitions that counted the value of selected government noncash benefits. The Census Bureau has also published annual reports on after-tax income (see Tables 745 and 746). The *Current Population Reports*, Series P60-186RD brings together the benefit and tax data that previously appeared in the separate reports. This report shows the distribution of income among households and the prevalence of poverty under the official definition of money income and under definitions that add or subtract income components.

The poverty statistics presented by the Census Bureau and Congressional Budget Office reflect alternative adjustments for inflation. The study used a variation of the Consumer Price Index to adjust poverty thresholds for the effects of changing prices since 1967. The alternative measure of inflation uses estimates of the cost of renting equivalent housing to assess homeownership costs; this methodology has been used in the official Consumer Price Index since 1983. See text, Section 15, and source for more details.

Statistical reliability—For a discussion of statistical collection and estimation, sampling procedures, and measures of statistical reliability pertaining to Census Bureau data, see Appendix III.

U.S. Census Bureau, Statistical Abstract of the United States: 1999

No. 721. GDP in Current and Real (1992) Dollars: 1960 to 1998

[In billions of dollars (526.6 represents $526,600,000,000). For explanation of gross domestic product and chained dollars, see text, this section]

Item	1960	1970	1980	1984	1985	1986	1987	1988	1989
CURRENT DOLLARS									
Gross domestic product (GDP)...	526.6	1,035.6	2,784.2	3,902.4	4,180.7	4,422.2	4,692.3	5,049.6	5,438.7
Personal consumption expenditures	332.2	648.1	1,760.4	2,492.3	2,704.8	2,892.7	3,094.5	3,349.7	3,594.8
Durable goods................	43.3	85.0	213.5	325.1	361.1	398.7	416.7	451.0	472.8
Nondurable goods	152.9	272.0	695.5	883.6	927.6	957.2	1,014.0	1,081.1	1,163.8
Services.....................	136.0	291.1	851.4	1,283.6	1,416.1	1,536.8	1,663.8	1,817.6	1,958.1
Gross private domestic investment.....	78.8	150.2	465.9	715.6	715.1	722.5	747.2	773.9	829.2
Fixed investment	75.5	148.1	473.5	648.1	688.9	712.9	722.9	763.1	797.5
Change in business inventories	3.2	2.2	-7.6	67.5	26.2	9.6	24.2	10.9	31.7
Net exports of goods and services	2.4	1.2	-14.9	-102.0	-114.2	-131.5	-142.1	-106.1	-80.4
Exports	25.3	57.0	278.9	303.1	303.0	320.7	365.7	447.2	509.3
Imports	22.8	55.8	293.8	405.1	417.2	452.2	507.9	553.2	589.7
Government consumption expenditures and gross investment.............	113.2	236.1	572.8	796.6	875.0	938.5	992.8	1,032.0	1,095.1
Federal	65.6	115.9	248.4	372.6	410.1	435.2	455.7	457.3	477.2
National defense	54.9	90.6	174.2	282.7	312.4	332.4	350.4	354.0	360.6
State and local	47.6	120.2	324.4	424.0	464.9	503.3	537.2	574.7	617.9
CHAINED (1992) DOLLARS									
Gross domestic product (GDP)...	2,262.9	3,397.6	4,615.0	5,140.1	5,323.5	5,487.7	5,649.5	5,865.2	6,062.0
Personal consumption expenditures	1,432.6	2,197.8	3,009.7	3,407.6	3,566.5	3,708.7	3,822.3	3,972.7	4,064.6
Durable goods................	(NA)	(NA)	(NA)	374.9	411.4	448.4	454.9	483.5	496.2
Nondurable goods	(NA)	(NA)	(NA)	1,151.8	1,178.3	1,215.9	1,239.3	1,274.4	1,303.5
Services.....................	(NA)	(NA)	(NA)	1,883.0	1,977.3	2,041.4	2,126.9	2,212.4	2,262.3
Gross private domestic investment.....	270.5	426.1	628.3	833.4	823.8	811.8	821.5	828.2	863.5
Fixed investment	(NA)	(NA)	(NA)	762.4	799.3	805.0	799.4	818.3	832.0
Change in business inventories	(NA)	(NA)	(NA)	75.3	30.2	11.1	26.4	11.7	33.3
Net exports of goods and services	(NA)	(NA)	(NA)	-127.3	-147.9	-163.9	-156.2	-114.4	-82.7
Exports	86.8	158.1	331.4	328.4	337.3	362.2	402.0	465.8	520.2
Imports	108.1	223.1	321.3	455.7	485.2	526.1	558.2	580.2	603.0
Government consumption expenditures and gross investment.............	617.2	866.8	941.4	1,018.4	1,080.1	1,135.0	1,165.9	1,180.9	1,213.9
Federal	(NA)	(NA)	(NA)	463.7	495.6	518.4	534.4	524.6	531.5
National defense	(NA)	(NA)	(NA)	348.1	374.1	393.4	409.2	405.5	401.6
State and local	(NA)	(NA)	(NA)	555.0	584.7	616.9	631.8	656.6	682.6

Item	1990	1991	1992	1993	1994	1995	1996	1997	1998
CURRENT DOLLARS									
Gross domestic product (GDP)...	5,743.8	5,916.7	6,244.4	6,558.1	6,947.0	7,269.6	7,661.6	8,110.9	8,511.0
Personal consumption expenditures	3,839.3	3,975.1	4,219.8	4,459.2	4,717.0	4,953.9	5,215.7	5,493.7	5,807.9
Durable goods................	476.5	455.2	488.5	530.2	579.5	611.0	643.3	673.0	724.7
Nondurable goods	1,245.3	1,277.6	1,321.8	1,370.7	1,428.4	1,473.6	1,539.2	1,600.6	1,662.4
Services.....................	2,117.5	2,242.3	2,409.4	2,558.4	2,709.1	2,869.2	3,033.2	3,220.1	3,420.8
Gross private domestic investment.....	799.7	736.2	790.4	876.2	1,007.9	1,043.2	1,131.9	1,256.0	1,367.1
Fixed investment	791.6	738.5	783.4	855.7	946.6	1,012.5	1,099.8	1,188.6	1,307.8
Change in business inventories	8.0	-2.3	7.0	20.5	61.2	30.7	32.1	67.4	59.3
Net exports of goods and services	-71.3	-20.5	-29.5	-60.7	-90.9	-83.9	-91.2	-93.4	-151.2
Exports	557.3	601.8	639.4	658.6	721.2	819.4	873.8	965.4	959.0
Imports	628.6	622.3	669.0	719.3	812.1	903.3	965.0	1,058.8	1,110.2
Government consumption expenditures and gross investment.............	1,176.1	1,225.9	1,263.8	1,283.4	1,313.0	1,356.4	1,405.2	1,454.6	1,487.1
Federal	503.6	522.6	528.0	518.3	510.2	509.1	518.4	520.2	520.6
National defense	373.1	383.5	375.8	360.7	349.2	344.4	351.0	346.0	340.4
State and local	672.6	703.4	735.8	765.0	802.8	847.3	886.8	934.4	966.5
CHAINED (1992) DOLLARS									
Gross domestic product (GDP)...	6,136.3	6,079.4	6,244.4	6,389.6	6,610.7	6,761.7	6,994.8	7,269.8	7,551.9
Personal consumption expenditures	4,132.2	4,105.8	4,219.8	4,343.6	4,486.0	4,605.6	4,752.4	4,913.5	5,153.3
Durable goods................	493.3	462.0	488.5	523.8	561.2	589.1	626.1	668.6	737.1
Nondurable goods	1,316.1	1,302.9	1,321.8	1,351.0	1,389.9	1,417.6	1,450.9	1,486.3	1,544.1
Services.....................	2,321.3	2,341.0	2,409.4	2,468.9	2,535.5	2,599.6	2,676.7	2,761.5	2,879.5
Gross private domestic investment.....	815.0	738.1	790.4	863.6	975.7	996.1	1,084.1	1,206.4	1,330.1
Fixed investment	805.8	741.3	783.4	842.8	915.5	966.0	1,050.6	1,138.0	1,267.8
Change in business inventories	10.4	-3.0	7.0	22.1	60.6	27.7	30.0	63.2	57.4
Net exports of goods and services	-61.9	-22.3	-29.5	-70.2	-104.6	-96.5	-111.2	-136.1	-238.2
Exports	564.4	599.9	639.4	658.2	712.4	792.6	860.0	970.0	984.7
Imports	626.3	622.2	669.0	728.4	817.0	889.0	971.2	1,106.1	1,222.9
Government consumption expenditures and gross investment.............	1,250.4	1,258.0	1,263.8	1,252.1	1,252.3	1,254.5	1,268.2	1,285.0	1,296.9
Federal	541.9	539.4	528.0	505.7	486.6	470.6	465.6	458.0	453.3
National defense	401.5	397.5	375.8	354.4	336.9	323.5	319.1	308.9	300.4
State and local	708.6	718.7	735.8	746.4	765.7	783.9	802.7	827.1	843.8

NA Not available.

Source: U.S. Bureau of Economic Analysis, *National Income and Product Accounts of the United States, 1929-94*, Vol. 1; and *Survey of Current Business*, May 1999.

Income, Expenditures, and Wealth 459

[In billions of dollars (5,743.8 represents $5,743,800,000,000). Data are based on the 1987 SIC. Data include nonfactor charges (capital consumption allowances, indirect business taxes, etc.) as well as factor charges against gross product; corporate profits and capital consumption allowances have been shifted from a company to an establishment basis]

Industry	Current dollars				Chained (1992) dollars			
	1990	1995	1996	1997	1990	1995	1996	1997
Gross domestic product	5,743.8	7,269.6	7,661.6	8,110.9	6,136.3	6,761.7	6,994.8	7,269.8
Private industries	4,951.4	6,306.9	6,667.9	7,083.3	5,246.0	5,896.5	6,119.9	6,395.3
Agriculture, forestry, and fishing	108.7	109.5	130.4	131.7	99.3	106.2	114.2	127.6
Farms	79.5	72.3	91.6	90.2	70.7	72.0	78.6	90.3
Agricultural services	29.1	37.2	38.8	41.5	28.6	34.7	36.2	38.0
Mining [1]	112.3	98.7	113.8	120.5	96.9	107.4	103.0	109.9
Construction	245.2	286.4	311.9	328.8	247.5	254.2	268.5	274.4
Manufacturing	1,031.4	1,282.2	1,309.1	1,378.9	1,090.0	1,271.6	1,293.8	1,369.9
Durable goods	572.8	716.8	737.3	784.0	600.4	727.0	769.0	838.6
Lumber and wood products	31.8	40.9	39.1	42.8	37.0	31.7	31.4	33.1
Furniture and fixtures	15.4	19.4	20.5	22.1	15.8	18.7	18.6	19.7
Stone, clay, and glass products	24.8	30.2	31.3	33.7	25.5	27.2	27.6	29.3
Primary metal industries	42.6	51.7	51.5	53.2	39.0	44.1	46.9	48.0
Fabricated metal products	69.4	87.6	93.1	99.3	72.6	87.8	88.6	93.0
Industrial machinery	114.8	141.5	148.8	158.9	113.2	162.9	183.2	215.2
Electronic & other electric equipment	94.9	136.7	141.6	157.3	92.5	178.7	213.2	261.2
Motor vehicles and equipment	46.1	85.2	82.4	85.4	56.8	77.7	73.2	77.8
Other transportation equipment	60.5	46.1	49.0	50.7	69.1	43.3	43.9	44.1
Instruments and related products	52.2	49.1	55.5	55.9	58.7	42.0	40.2	36.3
Misc. manufacturing industries	20.2	23.3	24.6	24.8	22.2	22.8	23.3	23.1
Nondurable goods	458.6	570.5	571.8	594.9	489.4	545.1	527.8	537.6
Food and kindred products	94.2	123.2	116.0	118.5	103.2	125.8	105.7	106.7
Tobacco manufactures	16.4	17.3	17.0	18.4	24.9	23.8	22.5	21.3
Textile mill products	21.7	24.5	24.7	25.5	22.6	26.4	25.6	25.7
Apparel and other textile products	25.2	27.4	26.7	28.4	26.5	28.6	27.0	28.2
Paper and allied products	45.3	58.9	56.6	55.0	44.1	44.4	46.4	48.9
Printing and publishing	73.9	84.7	92.4	98.4	84.5	77.1	76.1	76.7
Chemicals and allied products	110.3	156.1	155.8	158.8	117.3	139.6	140.3	141.2
Petroleum and coal products	33.0	28.3	29.6	35.2	28.4	30.4	32.3	32.4
Rubber and misc. plastic products	34.0	44.9	48.6	52.0	34.4	47.1	49.5	53.7
Leather and leather products	4.6	5.2	4.4	4.8	4.8	4.7	4.1	4.3
Transportation and public utilities	482.1	616.4	649.3	676.3	491.7	592.2	626.4	644.3
Transportation	176.4	226.1	237.0	255.5	176.7	216.1	229.7	241.5
Railroad transportation	19.6	22.9	23.4	24.1	18.7	26.1	28.2	28.2
Local & interurban passenger transit	9.0	12.2	13.0	13.8	10.3	11.4	11.3	11.3
Trucking and warehousing	75.8	98.0	92.9	97.9	73.7	89.1	86.5	87.3
Water transportation	9.7	10.9	11.7	12.8	10.7	11.0	10.7	11.0
Transportation by air	39.4	53.9	65.2	74.4	39.5	50.6	63.5	72.6
Pipelines, except natural gas	5.0	4.9	5.2	5.6	4.8	4.9	6.3	6.8
Transportation services	17.8	23.2	25.5	26.8	19.2	23.2	24.0	25.1
Communications	146.6	193.3	207.5	211.6	149.2	180.7	191.5	196.4
Telephone and telegraph	119.1	145.2	157.0	158.6	120.6	138.6	152.4	160.6
Radio and television broadcasting	27.6	48.1	50.4	53.1	28.6	41.8	39.5	37.3
Electric, gas, and sanitary services	159.1	197.0	204.9	209.2	168.4	195.5	205.3	206.3
Wholesale trade	367.2	491.4	519.8	562.8	360.5	455.8	486.6	532.0
Retail trade	503.5	641.0	673.0	712.9	546.4	626.4	665.9	713.5
Finance, insurance, and real estate [2]	1,024.1	1,362.3	1,448.6	1,570.3	1,109.0	1,206.2	1,246.0	1,286.0
Depository institutions	169.2	229.1	240.6	266.4	214.9	193.4	192.0	191.9
Nondepository institutions	21.5	39.7	44.3	56.3	25.6	32.6	35.4	39.3
Security and commodity brokers	39.7	73.4	96.5	106.6	41.2	78.4	104.1	120.5
Insurance carriers	69.3	118.5	122.0	146.0	70.2	91.2	87.6	93.5
Insurance agents, brokers & services	37.1	46.7	48.0	50.7	40.8	42.1	41.7	43.1
Real estate	671.9	843.8	892.2	935.0	706.8	776.6	799.5	814.8
Services	1,059.4	1,445.4	1,544.2	1,656.8	1,181.7	1,305.3	1,349.1	1,398.6
Hotels and other lodging places	46.1	61.3	65.6	69.0	49.2	56.2	57.5	56.8
Personal services	38.2	47.4	47.8	51.5	41.7	43.2	42.4	44.1
Business services	199.0	284.9	322.1	364.7	216.5	271.3	295.7	323.1
Auto repair, services, and garages	48.9	63.6	68.3	73.3	54.0	56.5	60.2	64.4
Motion pictures	20.4	26.3	28.4	30.5	22.1	24.4	25.2	26.6
Amusement and recreation services	39.1	56.6	61.3	66.7	42.8	50.5	52.7	56.2
Health services	307.9	0.0	445.5	460.1	356.9	373.3	377.3	379.0
Legal services	80.7	96.6	100.7	106.6	91.5	85.7	86.0	87.0
Educational services	39.8	55.3	58.1	61.5	44.3	49.0	49.4	50.4
Social services & membership organizations	29.6	46.4	49.0	52.2	32.5	43.4	44.6	46.3
Other services	147.8	198.8	214.6	234.6	160.4	183.7	192.8	201.3
Government	792.5	962.7	993.7	1,027.6	867.0	876.5	877.8	884.0
Federal	293.5	327.7	334.8	338.1	327.7	296.8	290.2	286.9
State and local	499.0	635.0	658.9	689.6	539.4	579.7	587.6	597.4

[1] For additional natural resource industries, see Table 1147.   [2] For additional finance, insurance, and real estate data, see Table 794.

Source: U.S. Bureau of Economic Analysis, *Survey of Current Business*, November 1998.

No. 723. Gross Domestic Product in Current and Real (1992) Dollars, by Type of Product and Sector: 1990 to 1998

[In billions of dollars (5,743.8 represents $5,743,800,000,000). For explanation of chained dollars, see text, this section]

Item	1990	1992	1993	1994	1995	1996	1997	1998
CURRENT DOLLARS								
Gross domestic product......	5,743.8	6,244.4	6,558.1	6,947.0	7,269.6	7,661.6	8,110.9	8,511.0
PRODUCT								
Goods	2,203.8	2,321.0	2,422.1	2,581.4	2,675.6	2,812.4	2,978.5	3,104.0
Durable goods	938.2	955.0	1,028.8	1,106.1	1,175.7	1,249.5	1,343.8	1,416.2
Nondurable goods.	1,265.7	1,366.0	1,393.3	1,475.3	1,499.9	1,562.9	1,634.8	1,687.8
Services	3,016.9	3,411.1	3,589.5	3,772.3	3,974.9	4,179.5	4,414.1	4,641.0
Structures.	523.1	512.3	546.5	593.2	619.1	669.7	718.3	765.9
SECTOR								
Business	4,796.9	5,184.4	5,453.1	5,801.6	6,080.6	6,432.9	6,836.5	7,189.7
Nonfarm	4,717.3	5,103.8	5,380.1	5,718.1	6,008.3	6,341.3	6,746.3	7,105.4
Farm	79.6	80.6	73.0	83.5	72.3	91.6	90.2	84.3
Households and institutions	237.9	279.1	296.5	312.7	331.4	345.0	361.4	380.6
General government	709.0	781.0	808.5	832.7	857.6	883.6	912.9	940.7
Federal	252.7	274.4	276.9	275.2	275.4	279.2	281.3	281.9
State and local	456.3	506.6	531.6	557.5	582.2	604.4	631.7	658.8
CHAINED (1992) DOLLARS								
Gross domestic product......	6,136.3	6,244.4	6,389.6	6,610.7	6,761.7	6,994.8	7,269.8	7,551.9
PRODUCT								
Goods	2,304.8	2,321.0	2,391.5	2,514.2	2,591.0	2,708.8	2,867.9	3,011.6
Durable goods	966.5	955.0	1,023.1	1,089.7	1,167.0	1,247.7	1,364.8	1,476.1
Nondurable goods.	1,337.9	1,366.0	1,368.5	1,424.9	1,425.8	1,464.2	1,509.6	1,546.9
Services	3,295.4	3,411.1	3,469.5	3,542.9	3,615.7	3,701.7	3,798.7	3,916.5
Structures.	533.3	512.3	528.7	554.9	557.3	588.5	612.5	637.1
SECTOR								
Business	5,097.0	5,184.4	5,317.2	5,530.6	5,677.4	5,903.5	6,164.9	6,433.8
Nonfarm	5,026.5	5,103.8	5,246.2	5,446.0	5,604.9	5,824.3	6,074.3	6,340.6
Farm	70.8	80.6	71.0	85.0	72.0	78.6	90.3	92.4
Households and institutions	264.1	279.1	290.1	297.9	304.8	311.8	321.5	328.8
General government	774.7	781.0	782.3	782.6	780.2	781.2	786.2	793.6
Federal	280.3	274.4	267.7	258.4	248.2	240.7	235.4	231.9
State and local	494.5	506.6	514.5	524.2	532.1	540.8	551.3	562.5

Source: U.S. Bureau of Economic Analysis, *National Income and Product Accounts of the United States, 1929-94*, Vol. 1; and *Survey of Current Business*, May 1999.

No. 724. GDP Components in Current Dollars—Annual Percent Change: 1989 to 1998

[Change from previous year; for 1989, change from 1988. For explanation of chained dollars, see text, this section. Minus sign (-) indicates decrease]

Item	1989	1990	1991	1992	1993	1994	1995	1996	1997	1998
Gross domestic product (GDP) .	7.7	5.6	3.0	5.5	5.0	5.9	4.6	5.4	5.9	4.9
Personal consumption expenditures. . .	7.3	6.8	3.5	6.2	5.7	5.8	5.0	5.3	5.3	5.7
Durable goods	4.8	0.8	-4.5	7.3	8.5	9.3	5.4	5.3	4.6	7.7
Nondurable goods.	7.7	7.0	2.6	3.5	3.7	4.2	3.2	4.4	4.0	3.9
Services	7.7	8.1	5.9	7.5	6.2	5.9	5.9	5.7	6.2	6.2
Gross private domestic investment . . .	7.1	-3.6	-7.9	7.4	10.8	15.0	3.5	8.5	11.0	8.8
Fixed investment	4.5	-0.7	-6.7	6.1	9.2	10.6	7.0	8.6	8.1	10.0
Nonresidential.	6.7	1.7	-5.0	1.9	8.3	9.1	10.1	8.3	9.2	9.0
Structures.	6.1	4.4	-9.5	-6.9	4.2	4.6	9.1	7.8	10.7	2.8
Producers' durable equipment .	7.0	0.3	-2.5	6.3	10.0	11.3	10.6	8.5	8.7	11.4
Residential.	-0.5	-6.7	-11.4	18.0	11.5	13.7	-0.4	9.5	5.2	12.7
Exports of goods and services	13.9	9.4	8.0	6.3	3.0	9.5	13.6	6.6	10.5	-0.7
Exports of goods	14.1	7.2	7.0	5.2	2.5	10.8	14.6	5.9	11.3	-1.1
Exports of services	13.4	15.3	10.5	8.7	4.3	6.4	11.3	8.4	8.4	0.4
Imports of goods and services	6.6	6.6	-1.0	7.5	7.5	12.9	11.2	6.8	9.7	4.9
Imports of goods.	7.2	4.9	-1.4	8.8	8.8	14.2	11.9	6.8	9.8	5.0
Imports of services	4.1	14.6	0.8	2.1	1.9	6.9	7.7	7.1	9.3	4.3
Govt. consumption expenditures and gross investment	6.1	7.4	4.2	3.1	1.6	2.3	3.3	3.6	3.5	2.2
Federal	4.4	5.5	3.8	1.0	-1.8	-1.6	-0.2	1.8	0.3	0.1
National defense	1.9	3.5	2.8	-2.0	-4.0	-3.2	-1.4	1.9	-1.4	-1.6
Nondefense	12.9	11.8	6.6	9.5	3.6	2.1	2.3	1.7	4.1	3.4
State and local	7.5	8.9	4.6	4.6	4.0	4.9	5.6	4.7	5.4	3.4

Source: U.S. Bureau of Economic Analysis, *National Income and Product Accounts of the United States, 1929-94*, Vol. 1; and *Survey of Current Business*, August 1997 and May 1998.

Income, Expenditures, and Wealth   461

No. 725. Gross State Product in Current and Real (1992) Dollars: 1990 to 1996

[In billions of dollars (5,659.8 represents $5,659,800,000,000). For definition of gross state product or chained dollars, see text, this section]

State	Current dollars					Chained (1992) dollars [1]				
	1990	1993	1994	1995	1996	1990	1993	1994	1995	1996
United States [1] ...	5,659.8	6,440.0	6,868.0	7,228.3	7,631.0	6,046.5	6,274.5	6,535.6	6,707.6	6,923.8
Alabama............	71.1	83.0	89.3	95.0	99.2	75.5	80.9	85.5	88.4	90.7
Alaska.............	25.4	22.5	21.9	23.7	24.2	25.2	22.1	21.5	22.7	21.4
Arizona............	68.5	85.0	95.4	104.0	111.5	72.9	82.8	91.2	97.3	102.6
Arkansas	37.9	46.5	50.4	53.4	56.4	40.0	45.3	48.2	49.9	51.5
California	792.7	843.1	876.0	913.5	962.7	845.2	819.1	835.5	855.1	880.1
Colorado...........	74.4	92.9	100.7	107.9	116.2	79.0	90.8	96.8	101.6	106.8
Connecticut........	98.5	107.5	112.6	118.6	124.0	105.2	103.9	107.0	110.2	113.0
Delaware..........	21.0	23.7	24.1	26.9	28.3	23.2	26.0	26.2	27.1	28.9
District of Columbia	40.7	47.0	48.1	49.7	51.2	45.3	46.8	46.6	46.7	47.8
Florida	255.2	300.7	321.7	339.0	360.5	273.0	291.6	305.7	314.3	326.1
Georgia	140.5	170.9	186.0	200.8	216.0	150.0	166.4	178.2	187.4	197.1
Hawaii	32.4	35.2	35.2	36.0	36.3	34.9	36.3	35.6	34.9	34.9
Idaho.............	17.5	22.4	24.5	26.9	27.9	18.5	21.8	23.5	25.5	25.9
Illinois............	273.4	312.3	336.9	352.9	370.8	290.8	306.8	325.6	333.8	345.5
Indiana............	109.6	129.7	141.4	148.8	155.8	116.3	126.5	135.1	139.6	144.1
Iowa	55.0	62.0	68.7	71.4	76.3	58.0	60.4	66.0	67.5	70.3
Kansas............	51.3	58.2	61.9	64.1	68.0	54.3	56.7	59.4	60.3	62.0
Kentucky	67.7	79.9	86.1	90.6	95.4	72.3	78.2	83.4	86.4	89.3
Louisiana..........	91.1	94.7	103.9	112.9	121.1	93.7	92.3	100.7	107.5	109.6
Maine.............	23.2	25.1	26.2	27.7	28.9	24.8	24.4	24.9	25.4	26.0
Maryland	113.7	124.6	132.9	137.4	143.2	122.3	121.4	126.5	127.6	130.2
Massachusetts.......	158.9	174.0	186.0	195.9	208.6	169.9	168.9	177.3	183.0	191.0
Michigan...........	188.0	217.3	240.6	251.8	263.3	202.1	211.2	228.9	234.9	241.0
Minnesota..........	99.5	114.6	124.6	131.4	141.6	105.1	110.9	118.4	122.0	128.7
Mississippi	38.7	46.6	50.8	53.6	56.4	40.8	45.2	48.4	50.2	51.7
Missouri	104.1	118.3	129.1	137.5	145.1	111.3	115.5	123.4	128.5	132.8
Montana...........	13.3	16.1	16.9	17.7	18.5	13.9	15.7	16.2	16.6	16.9
Nebraska..........	33.2	38.4	42.1	43.7	47.2	34.9	37.4	40.4	41.3	43.2
Nevada............	31.3	39.5	44.5	48.7	53.7	33.1	38.6	42.3	44.8	48.3
New Hampshire......	23.7	27.2	29.3	31.8	34.1	25.2	26.4	28.0	30.0	31.7
New Jersey.........	214.1	243.9	255.8	266.1	276.4	227.7	236.4	242.8	246.9	251.1
New Mexico	26.7	36.3	40.9	40.8	42.7	27.9	35.6	39.8	39.6	40.4
New York	498.3	541.1	565.2	587.7	613.3	535.6	527.6	543.7	549.6	563.3
North Carolina......	142.5	168.6	182.3	192.2	204.2	154.5	165.2	177.9	183.9	190.9
North Dakota.......	11.4	12.7	13.7	14.5	15.7	11.9	12.4	13.2	13.7	14.3
Ohio	227.1	256.6	276.7	292.1	304.4	241.6	250.2	264.7	273.6	280.7
Oklahoma..........	56.9	64.0	66.0	68.6	72.8	59.5	62.3	63.6	65.0	66.7
Oregon............	57.0	68.9	74.7	80.8	87.0	60.8	66.5	70.6	75.0	79.4
Pennsylvania........	245.8	283.1	296.8	313.3	328.5	261.9	273.6	281.6	290.6	298.7
Rhode Island.......	21.5	23.3	23.9	25.0	25.6	23.1	22.6	22.8	23.3	23.3
South Carolina......	65.4	75.2	80.7	85.3	89.5	69.5	73.6	77.7	80.1	82.7
South Dakota	12.9	16.3	17.5	18.7	20.3	13.7	15.9	16.8	17.5	18.4
Tennessee	94.2	116.7	127.9	134.9	140.8	100.5	113.4	121.9	125.8	128.7
Texas.............	388.9	453.0	484.1	514.2	551.8	404.1	438.9	465.5	486.1	502.9
Utah	31.1	38.1	42.0	45.6	50.4	32.9	37.1	40.2	42.4	45.9
Vermont	11.6	13.0	13.6	13.9	14.6	12.3	12.6	13.0	13.0	13.5
Virginia............	148.1	170.0	178.8	187.0	197.8	160.6	167.1	173.4	177.0	183.2
Washington.........	114.1	136.4	144.7	150.0	159.6	122.2	132.1	137.2	138.7	143.8
West Virginia	28.0	31.9	34.5	36.0	37.2	29.3	31.5	33.5	34.3	35.0
Wisconsin..........	99.2	117.7	125.8	132.7	139.2	105.0	115.1	120.8	124.6	128.7
Wyoming	13.5	14.6	14.9	15.8	16.8	13.4	14.6	15.1	15.7	15.8

[1] For chained (1992) dollar estimates, states will not add to U.S. total.

Source: U.S. Bureau of Economic Analysis, Survey of Current Business, June 1998.

No. 726. Gross State Product in Chained (1992) Dollars, by Industry: 1996

[In billions of dollars (6,923.8 represents $6,923,800,000,000). For definition of gross state product or chained dollars, see text, this section. Industries based on 1987 Standard Industrial Classification]

State	Total [1]	Farms, forestry, fisheries [2]	Construction	Manufacturing	Transportation, public utilities	Wholesale trade	Retail trade	Finance, insurance, real estate	Services	Government [3]
United States [4] ..	6,923.8	111.7	264.3	1,323.7	611.7	493.3	648.5	1,255.9	1,342.9	839.6
Alabama	90.7	1.8	3.6	21.0	8.8	6.0	9.5	10.6	13.9	14.0
Alaska.	21.4	0.3	0.8	1.1	3.5	0.7	1.5	2.3	2.5	4.3
Arizona	102.6	1.7	5.6	16.8	8.2	6.7	11.4	18.3	19.6	13.0
Arkansas	51.5	2.5	1.9	13.2	5.9	3.3	5.6	5.5	7.2	6.0
California	880.1	18.1	27.3	138.7	62.8	62.9	83.0	189.7	194.8	99.6
Colorado	106.8	1.8	5.4	14.4	12.1	7.0	10.9	17.7	22.1	13.8
Connecticut	113.0	0.8	3.5	20.8	7.2	7.9	8.9	30.3	23.6	9.9
Delaware	28.9	0.3	0.8	5.6	1.4	1.1	1.6	13.0	3.5	2.4
District of Columbia . . .	47.8	0.0	0.4	1.1	2.6	0.6	1.3	8.7	14.6	18.6
Florida.	326.1	5.8	14.7	28.8	30.4	25.2	39.2	67.8	73.4	40.1
Georgia.	197.1	3.3	7.2	37.9	22.7	18.1	18.8	29.9	34.0	24.4
Hawaii.	34.9	0.4	1.5	1.0	3.5	1.4	4.1	9.3	7.0	7.0
Idaho	25.9	1.5	1.4	5.8	2.4	1.6	2.7	3.0	4.0	3.3
Illinois	345.5	4.4	13.4	71.9	32.3	27.2	29.0	65.3	67.2	33.4
Indiana	144.1	2.4	6.2	48.3	11.9	9.0	13.8	17.4	20.7	13.7
Iowa	70.3	4.9	2.7	18.4	5.8	5.0	6.1	9.3	10.1	7.8
Kansas	62.0	2.6	2.5	11.8	7.1	5.1	6.4	7.4	9.9	8.6
Kentucky	89.3	2.1	3.2	26.6	7.6	5.3	8.2	9.1	12.4	11.7
Louisiana	109.6	1.3	4.4	21.9	10.2	6.2	9.2	13.4	16.5	11.8
Maine	26.0	0.5	1.1	4.9	2.0	1.6	3.1	4.6	4.7	3.5
Maryland	130.2	1.2	6.2	12.0	10.6	8.6	12.2	26.5	29.1	23.6
Massachusetts	191.0	1.1	5.7	33.5	12.4	14.2	15.9	43.9	47.2	17.3
Michigan	241.0	2.2	8.7	68.6	16.5	18.0	22.7	36.0	42.5	24.6
Minnesota	128.7	3.6	5.3	26.7	10.3	11.2	11.9	21.2	24.0	13.8
Mississippi	51.7	1.5	1.9	12.8	5.7	3.0	5.5	5.4	7.8	7.6
Missouri.	132.8	2.3	5.8	29.6	14.1	10.2	12.8	18.8	24.1	14.7
Montana	16.9	0.8	0.8	1.3	2.3	1.1	1.8	2.2	3.1	2.7
Nebraska	43.2	3.7	1.8	6.6	4.9	3.3	3.8	5.9	7.0	6.0
Nevada	48.3	0.4	3.9	2.5	3.9	2.4	4.9	8.6	15.1	4.8
New Hampshire	31.7	0.2	1.0	8.1	2.5	2.0	3.0	6.5	5.8	2.8
New Jersey	251.1	1.4	8.4	36.8	25.6	24.0	19.6	55.8	52.8	26.6
New Mexico	40.4	0.7	1.7	8.2	3.2	1.7	3.7	5.1	6.6	6.8
New York.	563.3	2.5	15.2	71.7	46.3	36.0	40.8	167.2	122.6	60.9
North Carolina	190.9	4.1	7.4	56.8	15.2	12.5	17.7	25.2	27.4	24.1
North Dakota	14.3	1.4	0.7	1.2	1.7	1.3	1.4	1.7	2.4	2.1
Ohio	280.7	2.9	10.1	80.7	22.3	20.6	27.2	40.3	46.9	28.6
Oklahoma	66.7	1.3	2.0	12.7	6.9	4.2	7.1	7.7	11.0	10.6
Oregon	79.4	2.3	4.1	17.4	6.3	6.6	7.4	12.1	13.9	9.3
Pennsylvania	298.7	2.9	10.8	66.7	27.5	18.4	27.5	51.8	60.5	31.0
Rhode Island	23.3	0.2	0.8	4.3	1.7	1.4	2.2	5.0	5.1	2.8
South Carolina	82.7	1.1	3.6	23.4	6.7	4.9	8.9	10.3	11.7	11.9
South Dakota	18.4	1.7	0.6	3.1	1.5	1.2	1.7	3.4	2.7	2.2
Tennessee	128.7	1.4	4.8	31.1	10.3	9.9	14.9	16.4	24.0	15.4
Texas	502.9	6.4	20.8	90.8	55.4	38.4	46.6	66.6	86.7	57.9
Utah	45.9	0.5	2.5	6.8	4.2	3.0	5.0	7.1	8.6	6.7
Vermont	13.5	0.3	0.5	2.7	1.2	0.9	1.4	2.3	2.6	1.6
Virginia	183.2	1.7	7.5	30.3	16.1	10.6	15.7	31.2	34.7	34.3
Washington	143.8	4.0	6.6	19.4	12.0	11.3	15.0	25.0	28.8	21.5
West Virginia	35.0	0.2	1.5	6.2	4.8	1.9	3.2	3.6	5.3	4.6
Wisconsin	128.7	2.6	5.2	38.3	9.2	8.4	11.7	19.7	20.0	13.5
Wyoming	15.8	0.3	0.5	0.9	2.5	0.5	1.1	1.6	1.4	2.0

[1] Includes mining not shown separately.   [2] Includes agricultural services.   [3] Includes Federal civilian and military and state and local government.   [4] States will not add to U.S. total as chained-dollar estimates are usually not additive.

Source: U.S. Bureau of Economic Analysis, *Survey of Current Business*, June 1998.

Income, Expenditures, and Wealth   463

No. 727. Relation of GDP, GNP, Net National Product, National Income, Personal Income, Disposable Personal Income, and Personal Saving: 1990 to 1998

[In billions of dollars (5,743.8 represents $5,743,800,000,000). For definitions, see text, this section]

Item	1990	1992	1993	1994	1995	1996	1997	1998
Gross domestic product..........	5,743.8	6,244.4	6,558.1	6,947.0	7,269.6	7,661.6	8,110.9	8,511.0
Plus: Receipts of factor income from the rest of the world [1]............	177.5	137.9	150.8	176.5	225.2	235.5	265.5	269.2
Less: Payments of factor income to the rest of the world [2]............	156.4	126.8	132.1	168.3	207.6	223.1	273.5	289.6
Equals: Gross national product......	5,764.9	6,255.5	6,576.8	6,955.2	7,287.1	7,674.0	8,102.9	8,490.5
Less: Consumption of fixed capital.....	651.5	713.5	727.9	777.5	800.8	832.0	871.8	908.0
Equals: Net national product [3]	5,113.4	5,542.0	5,848.9	6,177.7	6,486.3	6,842.0	7,231.1	7,582.5
Less: Indirect business tax and nontax liability........................	442.6	505.6	532.5	568.5	581.2	606.4	627.2	655.3
Plus: Subsidies [4]...................	25.3	27.1	31.1	26.6	25.1	22.0	21.9	27.1
Equals: National income [3]........	4,652.1	4,990.4	5,266.8	5,590.7	5,923.7	6,256.0	6,646.5	6,994.7
Less: Corporate profits [5]............	397.1	428.0	492.8	570.5	672.4	750.4	817.9	824.6
Net interest...................	467.3	414.3	402.5	412.3	420.6	418.6	432.0	449.3
Contributions for social insurance	518.5	571.4	596.0	630.5	658.9	688.0	727.0	767.5
Wage accruals less disbursements ...	0.1	-15.8	4.4	13.3	13.4	9.3	3.7	4.0
Plus: Personal interest income........	704.4	667.2	651.0	668.1	704.9	719.4	747.3	764.8
Personal dividend income	142.9	159.4	185.3	171.0	192.8	248.2	260.3	263.1
Government transfer payments to persons	666.5	835.7	889.8	930.9	990.1	1,041.5	1,083.3	1,120.8
Business transfer payments to persons	21.3	22.5	22.1	23.7	25.8	26.4	27.2	28.2
Equals: Personal income	4,804.2	5,277.2	5,519.2	5,757.9	6,072.1	6,425.2	6,784.0	7,126.1
Less: Personal tax and nontax payments..	624.8	650.5	690.0	739.1	795.0	890.5	989.0	1,098.3
Equals: Disposable personal income..	4,179.4	4,626.7	4,829.2	5,018.9	5,277.0	5,534.7	5,795.1	6,027.9
Less: Personal outlays.............	3,958.1	4,341.0	4,580.7	4,842.1	5,097.2	5,376.2	5,674.1	6,000.2
Equals: Personal saving...........	221.3	285.6	248.5	176.8	179.8	158.5	121.0	27.7

[1] Consists largely of receipts by U.S. residents of interest and dividends and reinvested earnings of foreign affiliates of U.S. corporations. [2] Consists largely of payments to foreign residents of interest and dividends and reinvested earnings of U.S. affiliates of foreign corporations. [3] Includes items not shown separately. [4] Less current surplus of government enterprises. [5] With inventory valuation and capital consumption adjustments.

Source: U.S. Bureau of Economic Analysis, *National Income and Product Accounts of the United States, 1929-94*, Vol. 1; and *Survey of Current Business*, May 1999.

No. 728. Selected Per Capita Income and Product Items in Current and Real (1992) Dollars: 1960 to 1998

[In dollars. Based on U.S. Census Bureau estimated population including Armed Forces abroad; based on quarterly averages. For explanation of chained dollars, see text, this section]

Year	Current dollars					Chained (1992) dollars			
	Gross domestic product	Gross national product	Personal income	Disposable personal income	Personal consumption expenditures	Gross domestic product	Gross national product	Disposable personal income	Personal consumption expenditures
1960	2,913	2,931	2,277	2,008	1,838	12,512	12,585	8,660	7,926
1970	5,050	5,081	4,077	3,545	3,160	16,520	16,616	12,022	10,717
1971	5,419	5,456	4,328	3,805	3,383	16,853	16,959	12,345	10,975
1972	5,894	5,935	4,703	4,074	3,671	17,579	17,694	12,770	11,508
1973	6,524	6,584	5,217	4,553	4,018	18,412	18,572	13,539	11,950
1974	6,998	7,071	5,672	4,928	4,353	18,178	18,360	13,310	11,756
1975	7,550	7,611	6,091	5,367	4,765	17,896	18,032	13,404	11,899
1976	8,341	8,419	6,673	5,837	5,268	18,713	18,878	13,793	12,446
1977	9,201	9,295	7,315	6,362	5,797	19,426	19,611	14,095	12,846
1978	10,292	10,392	8,176	7,097	6,418	20,185	20,367	14,662	13,258
1979	11,361	11,507	9,105	7,861	7,079	20,541	20,794	14,899	13,417
1980	12,226	12,381	10,037	8,665	7,730	20,252	20,497	14,813	13,216
1981	13,547	13,698	11,132	9,566	8,440	20,542	20,756	15,009	13,245
1982	13,961	14,095	11,744	10,145	8,943	19,896	20,076	15,053	13,270
1983	14,998	15,135	12,379	10,803	9,744	20,499	20,675	15,332	13,829
1984	16,508	16,640	13,602	11,929	10,543	21,744	21,904	16,309	14,415
1985	17,529	17,614	14,464	12,629	11,341	22,320	22,418	16,654	14,954
1986	18,374	18,427	15,200	13,289	12,019	22,801	22,857	17,039	15,409
1987	19,323	19,359	16,013	13,896	12,743	23,264	23,300	17,164	15,740
1988	20,605	20,659	17,076	14,905	13,669	23,934	23,988	17,678	16,211
1989	21,984	22,042	18,194	15,790	14,531	24,504	24,559	17,854	16,430
1990	22,979	23,064	19,220	16,721	15,360	24,549	24,632	17,996	16,532
1991	23,416	23,478	19,715	17,242	15,732	24,060	24,121	17,809	16,249
1992	24,447	24,490	20,660	18,113	16,520	24,447	24,490	18,113	16,520
1993	25,403	25,476	21,379	18,706	17,273	24,750	24,822	18,221	16,825
1994	26,647	26,678	22,086	19,251	18,093	25,357	25,389	18,308	17,207
1995	27,621	27,687	23,071	20,050	18,822	25,691	25,758	18,640	17,499
1996	28,849	28,895	24,193	20,840	19,639	26,338	26,389	18,989	17,894
1997	30,278	30,248	25,325	21,633	20,508	27,138	27,125	19,349	18,342
1998	31,492	31,416	26,368	22,304	21,490	27,943	27,891	19,790	19,068

Source: U.S. Bureau of Economic Analysis, *National Income and Product Accounts of the United States, 1929-94*, Vol. 2; and *Survey of Current Business*, May 1999.

464 Income, Expenditures, and Wealth

No. 729. Personal Consumption Expenditures in Current and Real (1992) Dollars, by Type: 1990 to 1997

[In billions of dollars (3,839.3 represents $3,893,300,000,000). For definition of "chained" dollars, see text, this section]

Expenditure	Current dollars				Chained (1992) dollars			
	1990	1995	1996	1997	1990	1995	1996	1997
Total expenditures [1]	3,839.3	4,953.9	5,215.7	5,493.7	4,132.2	4,605.6	4,752.4	4,913.5
Food and tobacco [1]	672.5	780.4	805.2	832.3	713.5	736.8	740.0	745.7
Food purchased for off-premise consumption	404.8	461.9	477.0	494.2	423.3	434.9	436.6	442.3
Purchased meals and beverages [2]	218.0	261.0	268.8	277.2	231.6	246.1	247.4	248.4
Tobacco products	42.0	48.6	50.2	51.4	50.9	47.4	47.5	46.4
Clothing, accessories, and jewelry [1]	262.7	321.8	338.0	353.3	279.4	324.2	345.7	361.8
Shoes	31.9	36.9	38.5	39.8	34.0	37.2	39.0	40.4
Clothing	173.8	216.8	226.9	237.9	183.7	222.7	236.9	247.7
Jewelry and watches	31.2	39.4	41.4	43.1	34.0	37.7	41.2	44.5
Personal care	57.3	71.8	75.0	79.4	60.6	68.1	70.1	73.0
Housing [1]	586.3	750.4	787.4	829.8	627.2	688.6	700.9	717.4
Owner-occupied nonfarm dwellings-space rent	410.7	532.4	559.1	590.3	437.6	487.4	496.0	508.9
Tenant-occupied nonfarm dwellings-space rent	150.1	184.8	193.2	203.2	160.0	171.4	174.7	178.7
Household operation [1]	436.2	559.4	592.8	620.7	457.0	533.0	555.6	578.4
Furniture [3]	39.0	47.7	50.6	54.8	40.6	44.3	46.4	50.4
Semidurable house furnishings [4]	21.2	28.7	30.7	32.8	22.0	26.8	28.7	30.6
Cleaning and polishing preparations	41.9	52.3	54.6	56.5	43.7	50.3	51.2	52.5
Household utilities	138.3	168.0	176.6	178.5	146.7	159.0	161.9	160.1
Electricity	71.9	87.9	90.3	90.2	76.1	84.3	85.1	84.6
Gas	26.8	31.3	35.2	36.0	27.7	30.5	32.9	31.5
Water and other sanitary services	27.5	37.9	38.9	41.1	31.9	33.1	32.8	33.8
Fuel oil and coal	12.0	10.9	12.2	11.2	11.2	11.2	11.2	10.3
Telephone and telegraph	60.4	87.7	97.1	104.2	61.3	85.5	94.7	105.0
Medical care [1]	615.6	875.0	912.4	957.3	691.1	766.9	782.6	803.6
Drug preparations and sundries [5]	65.1	85.5	91.1	98.1	74.5	79.6	83.0	88.2
Physicians	140.8	191.5	198.2	205.2	158.5	166.2	170.8	174.5
Dentists	32.9	47.6	49.5	52.6	37.7	41.1	40.8	41.5
Hospitals and nursing homes [6]	265.7	374.3	389.8	408.1	299.0	336.9	341.1	350.2
Health insurance [7]	37.4	57.9	57.4	58.0	41.3	37.1	36.2	35.8
Medical care [7]	31.3	45.6	45.0	46.1	35.3	34.8	34.0	33.6
Personal business [1]	290.1	388.8	416.2	459.1	331.3	354.3	364.6	377.2
Expense of handling life insurance [8]	56.4	75.7	77.4	80.2	61.2	68.8	66.2	65.2
Legal services	41.8	49.4	53.0	55.9	46.4	44.4	46.1	46.7
Funeral and burial expenses	9.0	12.2	13.3	13.8	10.1	10.5	10.9	10.7
Transportation	463.3	574.1	611.6	636.4	491.3	531.5	551.7	569.7
User-operated transportation [1]	426.9	531.9	567.3	588.3	454.2	491.1	509.0	525.3
New autos	92.4	86.6	85.8	86.2	98.1	80.2	78.2	78.5
Net purchases of used autos	31.6	53.0	55.8	57.3	35.0	41.4	42.4	44.1
Tires, tubes, accessories, etc.	29.4	36.2	38.5	38.8	30.0	36.7	39.1	39.7
Repair, greasing, washing, parking, storage, rental, and leasing	84.1	128.7	143.6	154.9	94.7	117.5	128.6	137.0
Gasoline and oil	96.6	115.6	124.5	126.5	108.1	114.3	116.0	117.9
Purchased local transportation	7.8	9.1	10.0	10.4	8.6	8.5	8.4	8.6
Mass transit systems	5.2	6.0	6.5	6.8	5.7	5.5	5.5	5.7
Taxicab	2.6	3.2	3.5	3.6	2.9	3.0	3.0	3.0
Purchased intercity transportation [1]	28.5	33.0	34.3	37.7	28.6	31.9	34.4	35.9
Railway (commutation)	0.8	0.8	0.8	0.8	0.8	0.7	0.7	0.7
Bus	1.0	1.1	1.1	1.2	1.1	1.2	1.2	1.2
Airline	23.9	27.9	28.5	31.5	23.7	27.2	29.2	30.4
Recreation [1][9]	281.6	404.2	432.3	462.9	291.8	399.1	429.9	466.9
Magazines, newspapers, and sheet music	21.5	25.7	27.6	29.1	23.8	23.1	23.9	25.0
Nondurable toys and sport supplies	31.6	42.3	45.1	47.8	32.6	41.9	44.5	47.6
Video and audio products, computing equipment, musical instruments	53.8	86.4	92.0	96.5	47.9	103.6	123.8	146.8
Education and research	80.7	112.0	119.7	129.4	89.3	98.7	102.0	106.8
Higher education	44.0	62.4	65.7	69.6	50.2	53.7	54.0	54.8
Religious and welfare activities	100.4	138.6	151.1	157.6	106.6	127.8	137.0	140.4
Foreign travel and other, net	-7.4	-22.7	-26.1	-24.4	-24.4	-20.1	-21.4	-17.1
Foreign travel by U.S. residents	41.2	51.2	54.7	59.9	46.1	48.3	50.5	54.5
Less: Expenditures in the United States by nonresidents	51.6	75.2	82.0	86.0	57.7	69.6	73.0	74.1

[1] Includes other expenditures not shown separately.   [2] Consists of purchases (including tips) of meals and beverages from retail, service, and amusement establishments; hotels; dining and buffet cars; schools; school fraternities; institutions; clubs; and industrial lunch rooms. Includes meals and beverages consumed both on and off-premise.   [3] Includes mattresses and bedsprings.   [4] Consists largely of textile house furnishings including piece goods allocated to house furnishing use. Also includes lamp shades, brooms, and brushes.   [5] Excludes drug preparations and related products dispensed by physicians, hospitals, and other medical services.   [6] Consists of (1) current expenditures (including consumption of fixed capital) of nonprofit hospitals and nursing homes and (2)payments by patients to proprietary and government hospitals and nursing homes.   [7] Consists of (1) premiums, less benefits and dividends, for health hospitalization and accidental death and dismemberment insurance provided by commercial insurance carriers and (2)administrative expenses (including consumption of fixed capital) of Blue Cross and Blue Shield plans and of other independent prepaid and self-insured health plans.   [8] Consists of (1) operating expenses of life insurance carriers and private noninsured pension plans and (2) premiums less benefits and dividends of fraternal benefit societies. Excludes expenses allocated by commercial carriers to accident and health insurance.   [9] For additional details, see Table 430.

Source: U.S. Bureau of Economic Analysis, *National Income and Product Accounts of the United States, 1929-94, Vol. 1;* and *Survey of Current Business,* August 1998.

Income, Expenditures, and Wealth   465

No. 730. Personal Income and Its Disposition: 1990 to 1998

[**In billions of dollars (4,804.2 represents $4,804,200,000,000), except as indicated.** For definition of personal income and chained dollars, see text, this section]

Item	1990	1992	1993	1994	1995	1996	1997	1998
Personal income	**4,804.2**	**5,277.2**	**5,519.2**	**5,757.9**	**6,072.1**	**6,425.2**	**6,784.0**	**7,126.1**
Wage and salary disbursements	2,757.5	2,986.4	3,089.6	3,240.7	3,428.5	3,631.1	3,889.8	4,149.9
Commodity-producing industries [1] . .	754.2	765.7	781.2	824.4	863.9	909.0	975.0	1,026.9
Manufacturing. . . . [2]	561.2	583.5	592.9	620.8	647.9	674.6	719.5	751.5
Distributive industries [2]	634.1	680.3	699.4	741.4	782.9	823.3	879.8	939.6
Service industries [3]	852.1	972.6	1,024.7	1,072.7	1,158.9	1,257.9	1,370.8	1,494.0
Government	517.2	567.8	584.3	602.2	622.7	640.9	664.2	689.3
Other labor income.	300.6	351.3	385.1	405.0	401.6	387.0	392.9	406.9
Proprietors' income [4]	374.0	423.8	450.8	471.6	488.1	527.7	551.2	577.2
Rental income of persons [5]	61.0	79.4	105.7	124.4	133.7	150.2	158.2	162.6
Personal dividend income	142.9	159.4	185.3	171.0	192.8	248.2	260.3	263.1
Personal interest income.	704.4	667.2	651.0	668.1	704.9	719.4	747.3	764.8
Transfer payments to persons	687.8	858.2	912.0	954.7	1,015.9	1,068.0	1,110.4	1,149.0
Less: Personal contributions for social insurance	*223.9*	*248.4*	*260.3*	*277.5*	*293.6*	*306.3*	*326.2*	*347.4*
Less: Personal tax and nontax payments.	*624.8*	*650.6*	*690.0*	*739.1*	*795.0*	*890.5*	*989.0*	*1,098.3*
Equals: Disposable person.	**4,179.4**	**4,626.7**	**4,829.2**	**5,018.9**	**5,277.0**	**5,534.7**	**5,795.1**	**6,027.9**
Less: Personal outlays	*3,958.1*	*4,341.0*	*4,580.7*	*4,842.1*	*5,097.2*	*5,376.2*	*5,674.1*	*6,000.2*
Personal consumption expenditures . .	3,839.3	4,219.8	4,459.2	4,717.0	4,953.9	5,215.7	5,493.7	5,807.9
Interest paid by persons	108.9	111.7	108.2	110.9	127.6	143.6	161.5	172.4
Personal transfer payments to the rest of the world (net).	9.9	9.6	13.3	14.2	15.7	16.9	18.9	19.9
Equals: Personal saving.	**221.3**	**285.7**	**248.5**	**176.8**	**179.8**	**158.5**	**121.0**	**27.7**
Addenda:								
Disposable personal income:								
Total, billions of chained (1992) dollars.	4,498.2	4,626.7	4,703.9	4,772.9	4,906.0	5,043.0	5,183.1	5,348.5
Per capita (dollars):								
Current dollars	16,721.0	18,113.0	18,706.0	19,251	20,050	20,840	21,633	22,304
Chained (1992) dollars	17,996.0	18,113.0	18,221.0	18,308	18,640	18,989	19,349	19,790
Personal saving as percentage of disposable personal income	5.3	6.2	5.1	3.5	3.4	2.9	2.1	0.5

[1] Comprises agriculture, forestry, fishing, mining, construction, and manufacturing.   [2] Comprises transportation, communication, public utilities, and trade.   [3] Comprises finance, insurance, real estate, services, and rest of world.   [4] With capital consumption and inventory valuation adjustments.   [5] With capital consumption adjustment.

Source: U.S. Bureau of Economic Analysis, *National Income and Product Accounts of the United States, 1929-94*, Vol. 1; and *Survey of Current Business*, May 1999.

No. 731. Gross Saving and Investment: 1990 to 1998

[**In billions of dollars (903.1 represents $903,100,000,000)**]

Item	1990	1992	1993	1994	1995	1996	1997	1998
Gross saving	**903.1**	**904.3**	**949.5**	**1,079.2**	**1,187.4**	**1,274.5**	**1,406.3**	**1,468.0**
Gross private saving	860.3	970.7	979.3	1,030.2	1,106.2	1,114.5	1,141.6	1,090.4
Personal saving	221.3	285.6	248.5	176.8	179.8	158.5	121.0	27.7
Undistributed corporate profits [1]	104.7	115.5	131.9	201.4	256.1	262.4	296.7	305.4
Undistributed profits	79.4	93.9	104.5	166.1	219.3	192.3	213.2	198.5
Inventory valuation adjustment.	-13.5	-7.5	-8.5	-16.1	-22.6	-1.2	6.9	14.5
Capital consumption adjustment	38.9	29.1	36.0	51.4	59.4	71.4	76.6	92.3
Corporate consumption of fixed capital . .	350.3	376.4	388.4	412.3	431.1	452.0	477.3	500.6
Noncorporate consumption of fixed capital.	184.0	209.0	206.1	226.3	225.9	232.3	242.8	252.7
Wage accruals less disbursements.	-	-15.8	4.4	13.3	13.4	9.3	3.7	4.0
Gross government saving	42.7	-66.5	-29.8	49.0	81.2	160.0	264.7	377.6
Federal	-94.0	-215.0	-182.7	-117.2	-103.7	-39.6	49.5	142.5
State and local	136.7	148.6	152.9	166.2	184.8	199.6	215.2	235.1
Capital grants received by the U.S. (net) . .								
Gross investment.	**920.5**	**949.1**	**1,002.1**	**1,093.8**	**1,160.9**	**1,242.3**	**1,350.5**	**1,391.5**
Gross private domestic investment	799.7	790.4	876.2	1,007.9	1,043.2	1,131.9	1,256.0	1,367.1
Gross government investment	199.4	209.1	204.5	205.9	218.3	229.7	235.4	237.0
Net foreign investment	-78.6	-50.5	-78.6	-120.0	-100.6	-119.2	-140.9	-212.6
Statistical discrepancy	**17.4**	**44.8**	**52.6**	**14.6**	**-26.5**	**-32.2**	**-55.8**	**-76.5**

- Represents or rounds to zero.   [1] With inventory valuation and capital consumption adjustments.

Source: U.S. Bureau of Economic Analysis, *National Income and Product Accounts of the United States, 1929-94*, Vol. 1; and *Survey of Current Business*, May 1999.

No. 732. Personal Income, by State: 1990 to 1998

[In billions of dollars (4,778.3 represents $4,778,300,000,000), except percent. 1998 preliminary. Represents a measure of income received from all sources during the calendar year by residents of each state. Data exclude federal employees overseas and U.S. residents employed by private U.S. firms on temporary foreign assignment. Totals may differ from those in Tables 727, 728, and 730. For definition of average annual percent change, see Guide to Tabular Presentation]

State	Current dollars				Constant (1992) dollars [1]				Average annual percent change		Percent distribution	
	1990	1995	1997	1998	1990	1995	1997	1998	1990-97	1997-98	1990	1998
United States..	4,778.3	6,059.1	6,770.7	7,139.1	5,142.9	5,633.2	6,055.5	6,334.6	2.8	4.6	100.0	100.0
Alabama........	61.6	81.3	89.3	93.3	66.3	75.6	79.9	82.8	3.2	3.6	1.3	1.3
Alaska.........	11.7	14.4	15.2	15.8	12.5	13.4	13.6	14.0	1.4	2.9	0.2	0.2
Arizona.........	61.1	86.5	100.2	107.7	65.8	80.4	89.6	95.5	5.3	6.6	1.3	1.5
Arkansas	33.0	44.5	49.4	51.6	35.5	41.4	44.2	45.8	3.7	3.6	0.7	0.7
California	639.3	754.8	846.8	898.4	688.1	701.7	757.4	797.2	1.6	5.3	13.4	12.6
Colorado........	63.7	90.9	105.1	113.8	68.6	84.5	94.0	101.0	5.4	7.4	1.3	1.6
Connecticut......	87.0	104.6	117.2	123.1	93.6	97.3	104.8	109.2	1.9	4.2	1.8	1.7
Delaware	14.4	18.4	20.9	22.2	15.5	17.1	18.7	19.7	3.2	5.3	0.3	0.3
District of Columbia ..	15.5	17.9	18.9	19.5	16.7	16.6	16.9	17.3	0.2	2.4	0.3	0.3
Florida	249.0	321.5	364.0	385.6	268.0	298.9	325.5	342.1	3.3	5.1	5.2	5.4
Georgia	113.1	156.0	178.9	191.2	121.7	145.0	160.0	169.7	4.7	6.1	2.4	2.7
Hawaii	24.0	29.4	30.5	31.2	25.8	27.3	27.3	27.7	0.9	1.5	0.5	0.4
Idaho..........	15.5	22.1	24.7	25.9	16.7	20.5	22.0	23.0	4.7	4.5	0.3	0.4
Illinois	234.6	298.2	332.0	347.8	252.5	277.3	296.9	308.6	2.7	3.9	4.9	4.9
Indiana.........	95.4	124.0	136.1	142.9	102.6	115.3	121.7	126.8	2.9	4.2	2.0	2.0
Iowa	46.9	58.0	66.0	68.5	50.5	53.9	59.0	60.8	2.6	3.1	1.0	1.0
Kansas.........	44.5	55.3	62.4	65.7	47.9	51.4	55.8	58.3	2.6	4.5	0.9	0.9
Kentucky	55.7	71.7	80.4	84.7	60.0	66.7	71.9	75.1	3.1	4.5	1.2	1.2
Louisiana	62.3	81.5	89.1	93.3	67.1	75.8	79.7	82.8	2.9	3.9	1.3	1.3
Maine..........	21.1	24.7	27.2	28.6	22.7	22.9	24.4	25.3	1.2	3.7	0.4	0.4
Maryland	107.9	131.3	146.1	153.8	116.1	122.1	130.7	136.4	2.0	4.4	2.3	2.2
Massachusetts.....	139.7	170.2	191.0	201.6	150.3	158.2	170.8	178.9	2.2	4.7	2.9	2.8
Michigan........	174.1	226.2	244.1	253.8	187.4	210.3	218.3	225.2	2.6	3.2	3.6	3.6
Minnesota........	84.9	109.3	123.0	130.0	91.4	101.6	110.0	115.3	3.1	4.8	1.8	1.8
Mississippi	32.7	44.6	49.4	52.2	35.2	41.5	44.2	46.3	3.9	4.8	0.7	0.7
Missouri	90.4	115.0	127.8	132.8	97.3	106.9	114.3	117.9	2.7	3.1	1.9	1.9
Montana........	12.0	15.9	17.3	17.8	12.9	14.8	15.5	15.8	3.1	1.9	0.3	0.2
Nebraska........	27.7	34.4	39.1	41.2	29.8	32.0	35.0	36.5	2.7	4.3	0.6	0.6
Nevada	24.6	37.5	44.5	47.5	26.5	34.9	39.8	42.2	7.0	6.0	0.5	0.7
New Hampshire....	23.0	29.0	32.5	34.4	24.8	27.0	29.1	30.5	2.7	4.8	0.5	0.5
New Jersey.......	193.0	235.4	260.7	275.4	207.8	218.9	233.2	244.4	1.9	4.8	4.0	3.9
New Mexico......	22.0	30.4	33.3	34.6	23.7	28.2	29.8	30.7	3.9	3.0	0.5	0.5
New York	416.0	500.6	548.9	576.8	447.7	465.4	490.9	511.8	1.5	4.3	8.7	8.1
North Carolina	110.8	150.9	172.2	181.4	119.3	140.3	154.0	160.9	4.3	4.5	2.3	2.5
North Dakota......	9.7	11.6	12.9	13.8	10.5	10.8	11.5	12.3	1.5	7.0	0.2	0.2
Ohio	196.8	247.4	270.5	281.7	211.8	230.1	241.9	250.0	2.2	3.3	4.1	3.9
Oklahoma........	49.1	60.7	67.4	70.5	52.9	56.4	60.3	62.6	2.2	3.8	1.0	1.0
Oregon.........	49.8	67.9	77.6	81.3	53.6	63.1	69.4	72.1	4.4	3.9	1.0	1.1
Pennsylvania.....	230.4	280.1	308.3	321.5	248.0	260.5	275.8	285.3	1.8	3.4	4.8	4.5
Rhode Island.....	19.8	23.3	25.3	26.5	21.3	21.6	22.7	23.5	1.1	3.5	0.4	0.4
South Carolina.....	54.0	69.5	77.7	81.7	58.1	64.6	69.5	72.5	3.0	4.3	1.1	1.1
South Dakota	10.8	13.8	15.5	16.3	11.6	12.8	13.9	14.5	3.1	4.3	0.2	0.2
Tennessee	79.8	110.5	121.9	127.9	85.8	102.7	109.1	113.5	4.1	4.0	1.7	1.8
Texas..........	294.7	398.6	459.6	493.1	317.2	370.5	411.0	437.6	4.4	6.5	6.2	6.9
Utah	24.6	36.0	41.7	44.1	26.5	33.4	37.3	39.2	5.9	5.1	0.5	0.6
Vermont	10.0	12.4	13.5	14.3	10.7	11.5	12.1	12.7	2.1	5.0	0.2	0.2
Virginia.........	124.4	158.1	175.9	186.0	133.9	147.0	157.3	165.0	2.7	4.9	2.6	2.6
Washington.......	96.1	128.6	148.5	159.1	103.4	119.6	132.8	141.2	4.3	6.3	2.0	2.2
West Virginia......	25.4	31.8	34.0	35.1	27.3	29.5	30.4	31.1	1.8	2.3	0.5	0.5
Wisconsin........	86.7	112.8	125.1	131.0	93.3	104.9	111.9	116.2	3.1	3.8	1.8	1.8
Wyoming	7.8	9.9	10.8	11.1	8.4	9.2	9.7	9.9	2.4	2.1	0.2	0.2

[1] Implicit price deflator for personal consumption expenditures is used as a deflator.

Source: U.S. Bureau of Economic Analysis, *Survey of Current Business*, May 1999, and unpublished data.

Income, Expenditures, and Wealth   467

No. 733. Personal Income Per Capita in Current and Constant (1992) Dollars, by State: 1990 to 1998

[1998 preliminary. See headnote, Table 732]

State	Current dollars				Constant (1992) dollars [1]				Income rank	
	1990	1995	1997	1998	1990	1995	1997	1998	1990	1998
United States.	19,156	23,059	25,288	26,412	20,618	21,438	22,617	23,436	(X)	(X)
Alabama.	15,213	19,041	20,672	21,442	16,374	17,703	18,489	19,026	42	40
Alaska	21,073	23,971	24,969	25,675	22,681	22,286	22,332	22,782	9	20
Arizona.	16,608	20,078	21,998	23,060	17,875	18,667	19,674	20,461	35	35
Arkansas	14,025	17,934	19,595	20,346	15,095	16,673	17,525	18,053	49	46
California	21,363	23,983	26,314	27,503	22,993	22,297	23,535	24,404	8	12
Colorado.	19,290	24,304	27,015	28,657	20,762	22,596	24,162	25,428	18	9
Connecticut.	26,453	32,073	35,863	37,598	28,472	29,819	32,075	33,361	1	1
Delaware	21,590	25,603	28,493	29,814	23,238	23,803	25,483	26,454	6	6
District of Columbia	25,646	32,398	35,704	37,278	27,603	30,121	31,933	33,077	(X)	(X)
Florida	19,127	22,676	24,799	25,852	20,587	21,082	22,180	22,939	19	19
Georgia	17,385	21,696	23,882	25,020	18,712	20,171	21,359	22,201	28	23
Hawaii	21,529	24,848	25,598	26,137	23,172	23,102	22,894	23,192	7	17
Idaho	15,346	18,961	20,392	21,081	16,517	17,628	18,238	18,705	41	43
Illinois	20,494	25,135	27,688	28,873	22,058	23,368	24,763	25,619	11	8
Indiana.	17,167	21,427	23,202	24,219	18,477	19,921	20,751	21,490	30	29
Iowa	16,885	20,412	23,120	23,925	18,174	18,977	20,678	21,229	33	32
Kansas.	17,940	21,481	23,972	24,981	19,309	19,971	21,440	22,166	22	24
Kentucky	15,085	18,601	20,570	21,506	16,236	17,294	18,397	19,083	43	39
Louisiana	14,773	18,826	20,458	21,346	15,900	17,503	18,297	18,941	45	41
Maine.	17,159	19,995	21,937	22,952	18,468	18,590	19,620	20,366	31	36
Maryland	22,482	26,141	28,674	29,943	24,198	24,304	25,645	26,569	5	5
Massachusetts.	23,210	28,097	31,239	32,797	24,981	26,122	27,939	29,101	3	3
Michigan.	18,699	23,407	24,956	25,857	20,126	21,762	22,320	22,943	20	18
Minnesota.	19,348	23,736	26,243	27,510	20,824	22,068	23,471	24,410	16	11
Mississippi	12,706	16,574	18,098	18,958	13,676	15,409	16,186	16,822	50	50
Missouri	17,639	21,540	23,629	24,427	18,985	20,026	21,133	21,674	25	28
Montana	15,038	18,286	19,660	20,172	16,186	17,001	17,583	17,899	44	47
Nebraska	17,536	21,029	23,618	24,754	18,874	19,551	21,123	21,965	26	27
Nevada	20,209	24,541	26,514	27,200	21,751	22,816	23,713	24,135	12	14
New Hampshire	20,728	25,313	27,766	29,022	22,310	23,534	24,833	25,752	10	7
New Jersey	24,883	29,568	32,356	33,937	26,782	27,490	28,938	30,113	2	2
New Mexico	14,480	18,029	19,298	19,936	15,585	16,762	17,260	17,689	46	48
New York	23,106	27,587	30,250	31,734	24,869	25,648	27,055	28,158	4	4
North Carolina	16,649	20,996	23,168	24,036	17,919	19,520	20,721	21,327	34	31
North Dakota.	15,264	18,149	20,103	21,675	16,429	16,873	17,980	19,232	40	38
Ohio	18,116	22,217	24,163	25,134	19,498	20,655	21,611	22,302	21	21
Oklahoma.	15,613	18,544	20,305	21,072	16,804	17,241	18,160	18,697	37	44
Oregon.	17,423	21,618	23,920	24,766	18,753	20,099	21,393	21,975	27	26
Pennsylvania.	19,371	23,268	25,670	26,792	20,849	21,633	22,959	23,773	17	16
Rhode Island	19,698	23,520	25,667	26,797	21,201	21,867	22,956	23,777	14	15
South Carolina.	15,427	18,789	20,508	21,309	16,604	17,468	18,342	18,908	39	42
South Dakota	15,488	18,724	21,076	22,114	16,670	17,408	18,850	19,622	38	37
Tennessee	16,309	21,109	22,699	23,559	17,554	19,625	20,301	20,904	36	33
Texas.	17,290	21,320	23,707	24,957	18,609	19,821	21,203	22,145	29	25
Utah	14,214	18,054	20,185	21,019	15,299	16,785	18,053	18,650	47	45
Vermont	17,677	21,246	23,017	24,175	19,026	19,753	20,586	21,451	24	30
Virginia.	20,021	23,943	26,109	27,385	21,549	22,260	23,351	24,299	13	13
Washington.	19,605	23,677	26,451	27,961	21,101	22,013	23,657	24,810	15	10
West Virginia.	14,176	17,441	18,724	19,362	15,258	16,215	16,746	17,180	48	49
Wisconsin	17,692	21,960	24,048	25,079	19,042	20,417	21,508	22,253	23	22
Wyoming	17,174	20,685	22,596	23,167	18,485	19,231	20,209	20,556	32	34

X Not applicable.   [1] Implicit price deflator for personal consumption expenditures is used as a deflator.

Source: U.S. Bureau of Economic Analysis, Survey of Current Business, May 1999, and unpublished data.

No. 734. Disposable Personal Income Per Capita in Current and Constant (1992) Dollars, by State: 1990 and 1998

[In dollars. 1998 preliminary]

State	Current dollars 1990	1998	Constant[1] (1992) dollars 1990	1998	State	Current dollars 1990	1998	Constant[1] (1992) dollars 1990	1998
United States.	16,657	22,353	17,928	19,834	Missouri	15,444	20,932	16,623	18,573
Alabama	13,554	18,818	14,588	16,697	Montana	13,136	17,455	14,138	15,488
Alaska	18,124	21,645	19,507	19,206	Nebraska	15,401	21,286	16,576	18,887
Arizona.	14,632	19,686	15,749	17,468	Nevada.	17,527	22,799	18,864	20,230
Arkansas.	12,542	17,837	13,499	15,827	New Hampshire . .	18,455	24,991	19,863	22,175
California.	18,391	23,044	19,794	20,447	New Jersey	21,500	28,313	23,141	25,122
Colorado.	16,758	23,963	18,037	21,263	New Mexico.	12,938	17,502	13,925	15,530
Connecticut	22,792	30,215	24,531	26,810	New York	19,568	26,061	21,061	23,124
Delaware.	18,485	24,959	19,896	22,146	North Carolina . . .	14,553	20,491	15,664	18,182
District of Columbia.	21,752	30,729	23,412	27,266	North Dakota	13,580	19,130	14,616	16,974
Florida.	16,901	22,064	18,191	19,578	Ohio.	15,786	21,224	16,991	18,832
Georgia	15,214	21,273	16,375	18,876	Oklahoma	13,601	18,308	14,639	16,245
Hawaii	18,340	22,428	19,740	19,901	Oregon.	15,099	20,670	16,251	18,341
Idaho	13,470	18,130	14,498	16,087	Pennsylvania	16,886	22,786	18,175	20,218
Illinois.	17,688	24,173	19,038	21,449	Rhode Island	17,285	23,017	18,604	20,423
Indiana.	14,962	20,577	16,104	18,258	South Carolina. . . .	13,650	18,520	14,692	16,433
Iowa.	14,682	20,607	15,802	18,285	South Dakota.	13,930	19,779	14,993	17,550
Kansas.	15,652	21,254	16,846	18,859	Tennessee.	14,693	20,689	15,814	18,358
Kentucky.	13,226	18,542	14,235	16,453	Texas	15,379	21,928	16,553	19,457
Louisiana	13,272	18,771	14,285	16,656	Utah.	12,405	17,842	13,352	15,831
Maine.	15,059	19,762	16,208	17,535	Vermont	15,434	20,773	16,612	18,432
Maryland.	19,149	24,903	20,610	22,097	Virginia	17,330	23,002	18,652	20,410
Massachusetts	19,813	26,719	21,325	23,708	Washington	17,201	24,015	18,514	21,309
Michigan.	16,266	21,710	17,507	19,264	West Virginia	12,652	17,120	13,617	15,191
Minnesota	16,542	22,563	17,804	20,020	Wisconsin	15,275	20,925	16,441	18,567
Mississippi.	11,575	17,067	12,458	15,144	Wyoming.	15,168	19,619	16,325	17,408

[1] Constant dollars based on the implicit price deflator for personal consumption expenditures.

Source: U.S. Bureau of Economic Analysis, *Survey of Current Business*, May 1999, unpublished data.

No. 735. Personal Income, by Selected Large Metropolitan Area: 1995 to 1997

[As defined June 30, 1994. CMSA=Consolidated Metropolitan Statistical Area; MSA=Metropolitan Statistical Area. See Appendix II]

Metropolitan area ranked by 1997 population	Personal income 1995 (mil. dol.)	1996 (mil. dol.)	1997 (mil. dol.)	Annual percent change, 1996-97	Per capita personal income 1995 (dol.)	1996 (dol.)	1997 (dol.)	Percent of national average, 1997
United States	6,059,091	6,408,103	6,770,650	5.7	23,059	24,164	25,288	100.0
New York-No. New Jersey-Long Island, NY-NJ-CT-PA CMSA	619,350	654,862	688,267	5.1	31,352	33,031	34,560	136.7
Los Angeles-Riverside-Orange County, CA CMSA	355,870	373,755	393,604	5.3	23,321	24,318	25,313	100.1
Chicago-Gary-Kenosha, IL-IN-WI CMSA .	235,526	248,253	262,357	5.7	27,296	28,555	29,981	118.6
Washington-Baltimore, DC-MD-VA-WV CMSA	202,626	213,221	225,524	5.8	28,601	29,838	31,265	123.6
San Francisco-Oakland-San Jose, CA CMSA	200,245	215,695	232,660	7.9	30,562	32,571	34,634	137.0
Philadelphia-Wilmington-Atlantic City, PA-NJ-DE-MD CMSA	158,253	166,947	175,008	4.8	26,493	27,936	29,292	115.8
Boston-Worcester-Lawrence-Lowell-Brockton, MA-NH (NECMA).	164,632	174,335	185,340	6.3	28,612	30,124	31,808	125.8
Detroit-Ann Arbor-Flint, MI CMSA.	139,276	143,074	149,232	4.3	25,889	26,374	27,419	108.4
Dallas-Fort Worth, TX CMSA.	113,904	123,121	134,293	9.1	25,612	27,023	28,709	113.5
Houston-Galveston-Brazoria, TX CMSA. .	105,523	112,366	121,775	8.4	25,408	26,566	28,225	111.6
Atlanta, GA	87,823	95,356	102,678	7.7	25,603	26,993	28,253	111.7
Miami-Fort Lauderdale, FL CMSA . . .	78,661	83,186	86,917	4.5	22,619	23,459	24,131	95.4
Seattle-Tacoma-Bremerton, WA CMSA . .	86,045	92,306	100,810	9.2	26,363	27,855	29,839	118.0
Cleveland-Akron, OH CMSA	71,327	74,337	77,920	4.8	24,499	25,495	26,733	105.7
Phoenix-Mesa, AZ CMSA	58,249	63,395	68,597	8.2	21,887	23,025	24,137	95.4
Minneapolis-St. Paul, MN-WI CMSA. . . .	74,448	79,350	84,193	6.1	27,315	28,739	30,123	119.1
San Diego, CA	60,432	63,908	67,998	6.4	22,882	23,903	24,965	98.7
St. Louis, MO-IL	63,014	65,847	69,547	5.6	24,785	25,824	27,177	107.5
Pittsburgh, PA.	56,561	59,485	61,928	4.1	23,703	25,054	26,243	103.8
Denver-Boulder-Greeley, CO CMSA	60,179	64,674	69,800	7.9	27,024	28,483	30,099	119.0
Tampa-St. Petersburg-Clearwater, FL . . .	48,799	51,926	55,356	6.6	22,440	23,654	24,879	98.4
Portland-Salem, OR-WA CMSA	47,988	52,031	55,815	7.3	23,697	25,100	26,396	104.4
Cincinnati-Hamilton, OH-KY-IN CMSA. . .	44,660	47,149	50,006	6.1	23,427	24,574	25,855	102.2
Kansas City, MO-KS	40,847	43,133	45,714	6.0	24,233	25,450	26,627	105.3
Sacramento-Yolo, CA.	37,445	39,292	41,621	5.9	23,326	24,099	25,138	99.4
Milwaukee-Racine, WI CMSA	41,484	43,512	45,898	5.5	25,230	26,433	27,899	110.3

U.S. Bureau of Economic Analysis, *Survey of Current Business*, May 1999.

Income, Expenditures, and Wealth   469

No. 736. Flow of Funds Accounts—Composition of Individuals' Savings: 1980 to 1996

[In billions of dollars (323.2 represents $323,200,000,000). Combined statement for households, farm business, and nonfarm non- corporate business. Minus sign (-) indicates decrease]

Composition of savings	1980	1985	1990	1991	1992	1993	1994	1995	1996
Increase in financial assets	323.2	622.5	590.8	418.1	529.8	512.4	542.8	492.7	541.5
Checkable deposits and currency	9.2	41.8	-19.0	43.2	98.9	54.5	-8.9	-38.2	-47.7
Time and savings deposits	125.5	119.7	48.7	-54.2	-76.5	-106.9	-5.8	152.6	144.4
Money market fund shares	23.9	2.3	26.9	9.1	-41.3	5.9	13.7	95.5	90.8
Securities	3.1	81.6	198.1	127.4	252.3	194.3	205.7	-56.5	-35.7
Open market paper	-5.0	-7.0	6.2	-29.9	-3.3	15.6	-10.5	0.3	11.4
U.S. savings bonds	-7.3	5.3	8.5	11.9	19.1	14.7	8.0	5.1	2.0
Other Treasury securities	19.6	3.7	61.3	-22.0	59.6	11.8	153.2	5.0	-62.1
Agency securities	4.8	12.2	41.5	12.3	36.8	-31.4	149.4	-31.9	54.8
Municipal securities	8.3	94.9	27.7	40.2	-27.2	-27.2	-51.9	-50.7	-21.4
Corporate and foreign bonds	-14.6	2.6	45.1	29.6	-8.5	37.3	2.1	51.4	27.7
Corporate equities	-4.3	-111.2	-28.8	-23.6	33.1	-57.7	-138.1	-176.1	-245.5
Mutual fund shares	1.8	81.2	36.6	109.0	142.8	231.3	93.7	140.4	197.4
Private life insurance reserves	9.7	10.4	25.3	25.6	27.7	35.7	34.3	44.8	35.2
Private insured pension reserves	22.3	55.6	95.9	46.4	76.7	86.3	71.2	66.7	69.2
Private noninsured pension reserves	60.2	126.6	64.1	72.5	81.8	82.7	87.1	98.3	85.2
Govt. insurance and pension reserves	35.8	69.0	85.7	83.0	83.7	81.8	93.7	75.4	97.4
Investment in tangible assets	4.1	11.2	32.9	17.5	-7.1	0.9	17.8	-49.7	-25.0
Miscellaneous assets	29.2	103.5	30.8	46.4	32.4	76.9	30.8	101.9	123.5
Gross investment in tangible assets.	407.5	661.1	815.8	758.3	823.0	897.9	1,021.5	1,050.9	1,107.4
Consumption of fixed capital	296.0	409.8	577.9	612.4	633.9	674.2	716.3	724.5	756.2
Net investment in tangible assets.	111.4	251.3	237.9	145.8	189.1	223.7	305.2	326.4	351.2
Residential structures	58.8	105.2	113.3	92.0	114.5	142.3	164.7	164.0	178.9
Other fixed assets [1]	31.5	35.4	23.3	4.1	-10.1	4.8	22.2	53.8	60.5
Consumer durables.	27.3	103.9	98.4	50.9	79.6	81.5	104.3	109.1	112.8
Inventories [1]	-6.2	6.8	2.9	-1.1	5.1	-4.8	13.9	-0.5	-1.0
Net increase in liabilities	196.6	435.5	267.3	217.4	204.0	297.1	401.6	441.9	478.0
Mortgage debt on nonfarm homes	94.1	174.7	226.2	177.7	188.9	186.6	203.4	195.7	277.4
Other mortgage debt [1]	50.9	98.1	16.9	5.3	-28.8	-17.8	3.7	21.5	45.7
Consumer credit	2.3	73.9	16.1	-13.7	5.0	61.5	126.3	141.6	94.4
Policy loans	6.7	-0.1	4.1	4.8	5.7	5.6	7.8	10.5	7.1
Security credit	7.3	18.9	-3.7	16.3	-1.6	22.6	-1.1	3.5	14.5
Other liabilities [1]	35.3	70.1	7.7	27.1	34.8	38.5	61.5	69.1	38.8
Personal saving (Flow of Funds measure) [2] . . .	238.0	438.3	561.4	346.5	514.9	439.0	446.4	377.2	414.7
Personal saving as a percentage of disposable personal income	12.1	14.6	13.5	8.0	11.2	9.2	8.9	7.1	7.4

[1] Includes corporate farms. [2] Net acquisition of financial assets plus net investment in tangible assets minus net increase in liabilities.

Source: Board of Governors of the Federal Reserve System, *Flow of Funds Accounts*, quarterly.

No. 737. Annual Expenditure Per Child by Husband-Wife Families, by Family Income and Expenditure Type: 1998

[In dollars. Expenditures based on data from the 1990-92 Consumer Expenditure Survey updated to 1998 dollars using the Consumer Price Index. For more on the methodology, see report cited below]

Age of child	Expenditure type							
	Total	Housing	Food	Trans- por- tation	Clothing	Health care	Child care and educa- tion	Miscel- lan- eous [1]
INCOME: LESS THAN $36,000								
Less than 2 yrs. old	5,950	2,270	850	720	390	410	720	590
3 to 5 yrs. old	6,060	2,240	940	690	380	390	820	600
6 to 8 yrs. old	6,180	2,170	1,210	810	420	450	480	640
9 to 11 yrs. old	6,210	1,960	1,450	880	470	490	290	670
12 to 14 yrs. old	7,020	2,180	1,520	990	780	500	210	840
15 to 17 yrs. old	6,920	1,760	1,650	1,330	690	530	340	620
INCOME: $36,000-$60,600								
Less than 2 yrs. old	8,240	3,070	1,010	1,070	450	540	1,190	910
3 to 5 yrs. old	8,460	3,040	1,170	1,040	440	520	1,320	930
6 to 8 yrs. old	8,520	2,970	1,490	1,160	490	590	850	970
9 to 11 yrs. old	8,470	2,760	1,750	1,230	540	640	550	1,000
12 to 14 yrs. old	9,200	2,980	1,770	1,330	910	640	400	1,170
15 to 17 yrs. old	9,340	2,560	1,960	1,690	810	680	700	940
INCOME: MORE THAN $60,600								
Less than 2 yrs. old	12,260	4,880	1,340	1,490	600	620	1,800	1,530
3 to 5 yrs. old	12,530	4,850	1,520	1,470	580	600	1,960	1,550
6 to 8 yrs. old	12,440	4,780	1,830	1,580	640	680	1,350	1,580
9 to 11 yrs. old	12,320	4,570	2,120	1,650	700	730	940	1,610
12 to 14 yrs. old	13,170	4,790	2,230	1,760	1,150	740	720	1,780
15 to 17 yrs. old	13,510	4,370	2,350	2,130	1,050	780	1,270	1,560

[1] Expenses include personal care items, entertainment, and reading materials.

Source: Dept. of Agriculture, Center for Nutrition Policy and Promotion, *Expenditures on Children by Families, 1998 Annual Report*.

No. 738. Average Annual Expenditures of All Consumer Units, by Race, Hispanic Origin, and Age of Householder: 1997

[In dollars. Based on Consumer Expenditure Survey. Data are averages for the noninstitutional population. Expenditures reported here are out-of-pocket]

Item	All consumer units	Black	Hispanic	Under 25 yrs.	25 to 34 yrs.	35 to 44 yrs.	45 to 54 yrs.	55 to 64 yrs.	65 yrs. and over
Expenditures, total	**$34,819**	**$25,509**	**$29,333**	**$18,450**	**$34,902**	**$40,413**	**$45,239**	**$35,954**	**$24,413**
Food	4,801	3,571	4,869	2,838	4,650	5,666	6,028	5,085	3,486
Food at home	2,880	2,515	3,363	1,566	2,758	3,382	3,440	3,139	2,293
Cereals and bakery products	453	376	468	249	432	540	548	470	360
Cereals and cereal products	161	148	190	97	168	197	189	160	118
Bakery products	292	228	279	151	264	344	359	310	242
Meats, poultry, fish, and eggs	743	861	1,057	385	702	865	915	830	580
Beef	224	244	326	125	219	264	284	231	162
Pork	157	194	225	75	144	174	193	187	133
Other meats	96	97	114	51	84	120	111	110	77
Poultry	145	185	189	78	146	174	172	150	111
Fish and seafood	89	106	144	37	80	97	117	114	67
Eggs	33	35	58	20	28	35	38	37	30
Dairy products	314	210	346	169	303	387	359	325	252
Fresh milk and cream	128	87	169	79	125	164	138	122	106
Other dairy products	186	123	178	90	177	224	221	203	146
Fruits and vegetables	476	402	607	242	434	525	558	549	433
Fresh fruits	150	113	199	77	137	161	174	169	147
Fresh vegetables	143	107	208	64	124	151	174	185	128
Processed fruits	102	99	114	55	97	117	117	108	92
Processed vegetables	80	84	87	46	76	95	93	87	65
Other food at home	895	666	884	520	887	1,066	1,060	965	668
Nonalcoholic beverages	245	194	263	160	232	294	292	267	178
Food away from home	1,921	1,056	1,506	1,272	1,893	2,283	2,588	1,946	1,193
Alcoholic beverages	309	137	206	253	380	348	358	283	197
Housing	11,272	9,044	9,907	5,860	11,774	13,415	13,892	11,090	8,082
Shelter	6,344	5,098	5,797	3,656	6,964	7,864	7,829	5,783	4,003
Owned dwellings	3,935	2,235	2,672	381	3,435	5,244	5,586	4,059	2,612
Mortgage interest and charges	2,225	1,369	1,750	224	2,368	3,448	3,396	1,927	547
Property taxes	971	469	527	101	639	1,054	1,303	1,195	1,060
Maintenance, repair, insurance, other	738	397	395	57	429	743	887	936	1,006
Rented dwellings	1,983	2,721	2,972	3,002	3,291	2,234	1,515	1,145	1,051
Other lodging	426	143	153	273	238	386	729	579	340
Utilities, fuels, and public services	2,412	2,461	2,169	1,092	2,229	2,694	2,890	2,654	2,157
Natural gas	301	324	265	88	264	327	321	342	338
Electricity	909	909	761	390	785	1,015	1,114	1,013	839
Fuel oil and other fuels	108	41	55	11	69	108	147	126	131
Telephone	809	945	833	550	893	921	952	842	551
Water and other public services	286	241	256	55	218	323	357	331	297
Household operations	548	379	322	191	659	724	554	402	452
Personal services	263	245	202	132	493	450	146	59	108
Other household expenses	285	134	120	58	167	274	409	343	343
Housekeeping supplies	455	289	398	163	403	524	552	523	412
Household furnishings and equipment	1,512	818	1,220	759	1,518	1,609	2,066	1,728	1,059
Household textiles	79	53	63	45	70	80	116	100	54
Furniture	387	277	368	257	475	430	515	390	190
Floor coverings	78	37	26	18	69	57	70	101	124
Major appliances	169	105	144	76	149	181	193	246	141
Small appliances, misc. housewares	92	30	73	46	76	97	131	123	65
Miscellaneous household equipment	707	316	547	317	678	764	1,041	768	484
Apparel and services	1,729	1,631	1,958	1,247	1,957	2,062	2,107	1,656	1,045
Men and boys	407	332	490	269	453	496	550	357	219
Women and girls	680	550	668	466	700	793	834	684	480
Children under 2 years old	77	78	140	111	163	90	51	34	22
Footwear	315	357	417	250	342	390	347	337	189
Other apparel products and services	250	314	243	151	300	293	325	243	135
Transportation	6,457	4,754	5,585	3,734	7,051	7,254	8,734	6,708	3,812
Vehicle purchases (net outlay)	2,736	2,036	2,367	1,737	3,238	3,038	3,704	2,641	1,482
Cars and trucks, new	1,229	712	772	513	1,159	1,378	1,808	1,374	777
Cars and trucks, used	1,464	1,307	1,594	1,196	2,007	1,594	1,849	1,267	686
Gasoline and motor oil	1,098	798	1,095	693	1,123	1,294	1,430	1,188	648
Other vehicle expenses	2,230	1,640	1,785	1,087	2,295	2,556	3,079	2,369	1,376
Vehicle finance charges	293	307	254	162	418	349	388	260	95
Maintenance and repair	682	454	548	324	598	788	942	760	491
Vehicle insurance	755	596	675	341	746	837	994	851	549
Rent, lease, licenses, other	501	282	308	260	533	582	755	499	241
Public transportation	393	280	339	217	395	365	522	509	305
Health care [1]	1,841	1,035	1,167	425	1,236	1,605	1,945	2,187	2,855
Entertainment [2]	1,813	872	1,137	1,051	1,865	2,129	2,416	1,900	1,103
Personal care products and services	528	631	479	292	530	586	637	541	441
Reading	164	77	66	64	132	160	205	198	174
Education	571	269	456	1,114	483	604	1,068	281	153
Tobacco products and smoking supplies	264	170	111	200	261	329	312	292	156
Miscellaneous	847	563	694	275	757	989	1,106	1,061	619
Cash contributions	1,001	669	398	157	484	945	1,431	1,208	1,326
Personal insurance and pensions	3,223	2,086	2,299	940	3,341	4,322	4,998	3,466	964
Life and other personal insurance	379	321	205	47	239	383	604	523	334
Pensions and Social Security	2,844	1,765	2,095	893	3,102	3,939	4,394	2,943	630
Personal taxes	**3,241**	**1,548**	**1,929**	**660**	**3,376**	**4,278**	**4,863**	**3,500**	**1,325**

[1] For additional health care expenditures, see Table 184.   [2] For additional recreation expenditures, see Table 431.

Source: U.S. Bureau of Labor Statistics, *Consumer Expenditures in 1997;* and unpublished data.

Income, Expenditures, and Wealth   471

No. 739. Average Annual Expenditures of All Consumer Units, by Region and Size of Unit: 1997

[See headnote, Table 738. For composition of regions, see map, inside front cover]

Item	Region				Size of consumer unit				
	North-east	Mid-west	South	West	One person	Two per-sons	Three per-sons	Four per-sons	Five or more
Expenditures, total	**$36,070**	**$33,791**	**$32,226**	**$39,037**	**$20,923**	**$36,617**	**$40,926**	**$45,225**	**$43,929**
Food	5,358	4,631	4,426	5,077	2,579	4,886	5,513	6,463	7,177
Food at home	2,970	2,739	2,771	3,125	1,354	2,787	3,370	4,101	4,860
Cereals and bakery products	504	446	415	474	218	423	522	666	781
Cereals and cereal products	177	154	149	175	72	142	186	243	311
Bakery products	326	292	266	299	146	281	336	423	470
Meats, poultry, fish, and eggs	789	663	753	774	309	717	877	1,056	1,361
Beef	214	207	235	233	88	211	264	326	428
Pork	141	153	173	150	65	156	182	218	289
Other meats	112	101	88	90	42	88	117	138	179
Poultry	177	119	141	151	61	137	175	213	257
Fish and seafood	108	58	85	110	37	94	103	120	146
Eggs	36	25	31	41	15	33	37	41	61
Dairy products	327	308	290	345	152	294	361	461	537
Fresh milk and cream	130	129	119	140	60	115	144	190	243
Other dairy products	198	179	171	205	92	178	217	270	294
Fruits and vegetables	525	430	438	541	245	486	542	629	753
Fresh fruits	169	146	131	170	83	159	158	194	235
Fresh vegetables	162	122	125	176	72	151	177	172	218
Processed fruits	115	92	93	116	56	98	115	145	162
Processed vegetables	79	70	89	79	34	79	92	118	137
Other food at home	825	892	876	991	430	867	1,066	1,289	1,428
Nonalcoholic beverages	228	240	253	251	120	243	280	348	389
Food away from home	2,388	1,892	1,655	1,952	1,225	2,099	2,144	2,362	2,318
Alcoholic beverages	379	306	229	377	246	405	289	285	255
Housing	12,480	10,532	9,877	13,255	7,586	11,541	12,896	14,346	13,890
Shelter	7,539	5,653	5,070	8,089	4,742	6,249	7,183	7,885	7,645
Owned dwellings	4,704	3,785	3,059	4,818	2,003	4,044	4,637	5,789	5,311
Mortgage interest and charges	2,351	1,955	1,779	3,143	941	2,031	2,806	3,634	3,518
Property taxes	1,569	1,088	630	838	550	1,113	1,105	1,260	1,110
Maintenance, repair, insurance, other	784	742	650	836	512	900	727	895	684
Rented dwellings	2,298	1,477	1,694	2,731	2,512	1,650	2,025	1,586	2,005
Other lodging	536	391	317	541	227	555	521	510	329
Utilities, fuels, and public services	2,480	2,452	2,463	2,220	1,563	2,458	2,808	3,035	3,168
Natural gas	396	446	185	238	197	311	338	373	402
Electricity	830	834	1,094	762	555	942	1,066	1,155	1,210
Fuel oil and other fuels	255	115	55	48	66	119	127	137	120
Telephone	785	778	839	817	583	789	954	995	1,016
Water and other public services	215	279	290	355	161	296	323	375	420
Household operations	473	458	534	745	265	447	735	986	738
Personal services	219	248	249	346	57	86	460	648	524
Other household expenses	254	210	286	399	208	361	275	337	215
Housekeeping supplies	418	485	427	501	222	496	529	664	552
Household furnishings and equipment	1,570	1,484	1,383	1,699	794	1,892	1,641	1,776	1,788
Household textiles	86	78	64	99	44	100	83	96	85
Furniture	424	354	386	392	220	478	385	496	435
Floor coverings	102	85	63	72	29	141	76	59	49
Major appliances	145	160	187	173	84	217	184	200	199
Small appliances, misc. housewares	91	95	75	117	56	99	106	135	85
Miscellaneous household equipment	723	711	608	847	361	857	807	791	935
Apparel and services	1,916	1,707	1,620	1,755	866	1,703	2,053	2,420	2,695
Men and boys	432	446	350	432	197	352	533	607	671
Women and girls	722	713	648	657	382	705	793	905	926
Children under 2 years old	80	63	69	103	11	44	139	149	161
Footwear	339	298	323	298	162	294	344	483	511
Other apparel products and services	343	186	231	266	113	308	243	276	426
Transportation	5,830	6,367	6,473	7,120	3,239	6,860	8,223	8,856	8,147
Vehicle purchases (net outlay)	2,040	2,784	3,055	2,811	1,244	2,958	3,588	3,788	3,449
Cars and trucks, new	973	1,216	1,486	1,062	650	1,493	1,489	1,619	1,107
Cars and trucks, used	1,052	1,544	1,541	1,633	578	1,400	2,061	2,121	2,290
Gasoline and motor oil	979	1,107	1,112	1,174	567	1,116	1,364	1,512	1,532
Other vehicle expenses	2,223	2,131	2,062	2,624	1,148	2,319	2,814	3,146	2,799
Vehicle finance charges	214	307	335	281	100	305	416	411	440
Maintenance and repair	584	659	657	838	391	691	798	965	883
Vehicle insurance	808	684	727	831	417	790	961	1,019	906
Rent, lease, licenses, other	617	480	343	674	239	533	640	751	571
Public transportation	587	345	243	511	280	467	457	410	367
Health care [1]	1,709	1,903	1,902	1,793	1,249	2,301	1,915	1,938	1,857
Entertainment [2]	1,769	1,915	1,561	2,153	1,011	1,969	2,118	2,462	2,191
Personal care products and services	521	506	544	530	305	573	631	654	668
Reading	192	170	130	186	125	197	171	181	136
Education	772	512	449	647	447	421	743	830	736
Tobacco products and smoking supplies	260	302	268	217	169	266	339	303	350
Miscellaneous	821	824	806	965	694	871	1,085	841	845
Cash contributions	765	989	1,057	1,145	811	1,242	927	980	951
Personal insurance and pensions	3,298	3,128	2,883	3,819	1,597	3,381	4,024	4,665	4,031
Life and other personal insurance	386	361	421	322	170	431	474	543	426
Pensions and Social Security	2,912	2,767	2,461	3,497	1,427	2,950	3,550	4,122	3,605
Personal taxes	**3,170**	**3,318**	**2,399**	**4,529**	**2,011**	**3,857**	**3,780**	**3,912**	**3,104**

[1] For additional health care expenditures, see Table 184. [2] For additional recreation expenditures, see Table 431.

Source: U.S. Bureau of Labor Statistics, *Consumer Expenditures in 1997;* and unpublished data.

No. 740. Average Annual Expenditures of All Consumer Units, by Type of Expenditure: 1990 to 1997

[In dollars, except units (96,968 represent 96,968,000). See headnote, Table 738]

Type	1990	1991	1992	1993	1994	1995	1996	1997
Number of consumer units (1,000)	96,968	97,918	100,019	100,049	102,210	103,024	104,212	105,576
Total expenditures.	28,381	29,614	29,846	30,692	31,751	32,277	33,797	34,819
Food	4,296	4,271	4,273	4,399	4,411	4,505	4,698	4,801
Food at home	2,485	2,651	2,643	2,735	2,712	2,803	2,876	2,880
Meats, poultry, fish, and eggs . . .	668	709	687	734	732	752	737	743
Dairy products	295	294	302	295	289	297	312	314
Fruits and vegetables.	408	429	428	444	437	457	490	476
Other food at home	746	815	814	827	825	856	889	895
Food away from home.	1,811	1,620	1,631	1,664	1,698	1,702	1,823	1,921
Alcoholic beverages	293	297	301	268	278	277	309	309
Housing.	8,703	9,252	9,477	9,636	10,106	10,465	10,747	11,272
Shelter	4,836	5,191	5,411	5,415	5,686	5,932	6,064	6,344
Fuels, utilities, public services.	1,890	1,990	1,984	2,112	2,189	2,193	2,347	2,412
Apparel and services	1,618	1,735	1,710	1,676	1,644	1,704	1,752	1,729
Transportation.	5,120	5,151	5,228	5,453	6,044	6,016	6,382	6,457
Vehicle purchase	2,129	2,111	2,189	2,319	2,725	2,639	2,815	2,736
Gasoline and motor oil.	1,047	995	973	977	986	1,006	1,082	1,098
Other transportation	1,944	1,741	1,776	1,843	1,953	2,016	2,058	2,230
Health care.	1,480	1,554	1,634	1,776	1,755	1,732	1,770	1,841
Entertainment	1,422	1,472	1,500	1,626	1,567	1,612	1,834	1,813
Reading	153	163	162	166	165	163	159	164
Tobacco products, smoking supplies . .	274	276	275	268	259	269	255	264
Personal insurance and pensions	2,593	2,787	2,750	2,908	2,957	2,967	3,060	3,223
Life and other personal insurance	345	356	353	399	398	374	353	379
Pensions and Social Security	2,248	2,431	2,397	2,509	2,559	2,593	2,707	2,844

Source: U.S. Bureau of Labor Statistics, Consumer Expenditures in 1997; and earlier reports.

No. 741. Average Annual Expenditures of All Consumer Units, by Metropolitan Area: 1996-97

[In dollars. Metropolitan areas defined June 30, 1983, CMSA=Consolidated Metropolitan Statistical Area; MSA=Metropolitan Statistical Area; PMSA=Primary Metropolitan Statistical Area. See text, Section 1, Population, and Appendix II. See headnote, Table 738]

Metropolitan area	Total expendi- tures [1]	Food	Housing Total [1]	Shel- ter	Apparel and serv- ices	Transportation Total [1]	Vehicle pur- chases	Gaso- line and motor oil	Health care
Anchorage, AK MSA.	51,276	6,782	16,273	9,709	1,623	10,459	5,136	1,206	1,738
Atlanta, GA MSA	39,373	4,031	13,663	7,746	2,039	7,603	3,235	1,173	2,087
Baltimore, MD MSA.	34,716	5,186	11,258	6,725	1,831	5,522	2,401	947	1,614
Boston-Lawrence-Salem, MA-NH CMSA	37,069	4,297	13,616	8,377	1,956	6,698	2,656	1,056	1,753
Buffalo-Niagara Falls, NY CMSA.	(NA)	(NA)	(NA)	(NA)	(NA)	(NA)	(NA)	(NA)	(NA)
Chicago-Gary-Lake County, IL-IN-WI CMSA	37,787	5,141	12,887	7,685	2,415	6,169	2,454	1,045	1,929
Cincinnati-Hamilton, OH-KY-IN CMSA . .	36,179	4,904	11,572	6,456	1,623	6,970	3,339	1,036	1,810
Cleveland-Akron-Lorain, OH CMSA	36,110	4,548	11,478	5,827	1,671	6,641	2,828	997	1,975
Dallas-Fort Worth, TX CMSA	42,355	5,572	12,457	6,656	2,060	10,188	5,814	1,385	1,922
Denver-Boulder-Greeley, CO CMSA . .	41,718	4,918	13,218	8,089	2,310	8,138	3,286	1,137	1,743
Detroit-Ann Arbor, MI CMSA.	35,376	5,452	11,141	6,189	2,532	6,687	2,240	1,132	1,494
Honolulu, HI MSA.	41,992	5,672	13,638	9,371	2,215	7,955	3,521	1,046	1,618
Houston-Galveston-Brazoria, TX CMSA	38,208	4,830	11,810	6,365	1,867	8,590	4,225	1,334	1,901
Kansas City, MO-Kansas City, KS CMSA	35,373	5,365	10,636	5,545	1,868	6,116	2,399	1,139	1,862
Los Angeles-Long Beach, CA PMSA . .	39,400	4,952	14,950	9,676	1,804	6,926	2,270	1,238	1,528
Miami-Fort Lauderdale, FL CMSA	31,876	5,053	11,322	6,857	1,590	5,045	1,815	924	1,325
Milwaukee, WI PMSA	35,684	4,539	11,770	7,354	1,744	5,251	1,926	996	1,453
Minneapolis-St. Paul, MN-WI MSA	44,025	5,571	12,935	7,752	1,943	8,562	3,241	1,374	2,015
New York-Northern New Jersey- Long Island, NY-NJ-CT CMSA	38,470	5,927	14,234	9,267	2,211	5,202	1,225	847	1,736
Philadelphia-Wilmington-Trenton, PA-NJ-DE-MD CMSA	34,489	3,879	12,694	8,067	1,964	5,732	1,755	1,016	1,466
Phoenix-Mesa, AZ MSA.	36,537	3,954	12,715	7,024	1,790	7,044	2,833	1,110	1,833
Pittsburgh-Beaver Valley, PA CMSA. . .	34,873	4,906	10,967	5,479	1,775	6,769	3,108	1,061	1,804
Portland-Vancouver, OR-WA CMSA. . . .	40,050	5,035	12,937	7,948	2,138	7,409	3,598	1,037	1,926
San Diego, CA MSA	37,974	4,666	15,065	9,927	1,682	5,893	1,967	1,052	1,747
San Francisco-Oakland-San Jose, CA CMSA	44,668	6,174	15,074	9,910	2,021	7,301	2,684	1,164	1,808
Seattle-Tacoma, WA CMSA	40,440	5,241	14,226	8,820	1,952	7,712	3,521	1,169	1,557
St. Louis-East St. Louis-Alton, MO-IL CMSA.	34,717	4,861	10,734	5,293	1,906	6,203	2,640	1,070	1,580
Tampa-St. Petersburg-Clearwater, FL MSA.	34,084	4,526	11,059	5,597	1,315	6,958	2,931	1,016	1,953
Washington, DC-MD-VA MSA.	47,935	5,701	17,405	10,927	2,284	7,979	3,184	1,179	2,165

NA Not available.   [1] Includes expenditures not shown separately.

Source: U.S. Bureau of Labor Statistics, Consumer Expenditures, annual; and Internet <http://stats.bls.gov:80/csxmsa.html> (accessed 8 June 1999).

Income, Expenditures, and Wealth   473

No. 742. Money Income of Households—Percent Distribution, by Income Level, Race, and Hispanic Origin, in Constant (1997) Dollars: 1970 to 1997

[Constant dollars based on CPI-U-X1 deflator. Households as of **March** of **following** year. Based on Current Population Survey; see text, Section 1, Population, and text, this section, and Appendix III. For definition of median, see Guide to Tabular Presentation]

Year	Number of house-holds (1,000)	Percent distribution							Median income (dollars)
		Under $10,000	$10,000-$14,999	$15,000-$24,999	$25,000-$34,999	$35,000-$49,999	$50,000-$74,999	$75,000 and over	
ALL HOUSEHOLDS [1]									
1970	64,778	13.4	7.5	15.1	16.1	21.1	17.7	9.0	33,942
1975	72,867	12.6	8.7	15.9	15.3	19.4	18.3	9.9	33,699
1980	82,368	12.4	8.2	15.8	14.0	19.2	18.4	12.0	34,538
1985	88,458	12.3	8.2	15.1	14.1	17.9	17.9	14.4	35,229
1990	94,312	11.6	7.9	14.8	13.8	17.7	18.2	16.0	36,770
1995	99,627	11.4	8.4	15.3	14.0	16.7	17.7	16.5	35,887
1996	101,018	11.5	8.4	15.1	13.6	16.1	18.2	17.1	36,306
1997	102,528	11.0	8.1	14.9	13.3	16.3	18.1	18.4	37,005
WHITE									
1970	57,575	12.2	7.0	14.5	16.1	21.8	18.6	9.7	35,353
1975	64,392	11.2	8.2	15.6	15.2	20.0	19.3	10.6	35,241
1980	71,872	10.8	7.7	15.4	14.1	19.7	19.4	12.8	36,437
1985	76,576	10.7	7.8	14.8	14.1	18.4	18.8	15.5	37,154
1990	80,968	9.8	7.5	14.6	14.0	18.1	19.1	17.0	38,352
1995	84,511	9.8	8.0	15.1	14.0	17.0	18.5	17.7	37,667
1996	85,059	9.8	8.0	14.9	13.7	16.4	19.0	18.1	38,014
1997	86,106	9.5	7.8	14.6	13.2	16.5	18.8	19.7	38,972
BLACK									
1970	6,180	24.3	12.2	20.9	15.8	14.5	9.2	3.0	21,518
1975	7,489	24.6	13.5	18.8	15.9	14.3	9.8	3.2	21,156
1980	8,847	25.3	12.8	19.2	13.3	14.7	10.5	4.2	20,992
1985	9,797	25.2	11.9	18.3	13.6	14.1	11.1	5.6	22,105
1990	10,671	25.8	11.3	16.5	13.0	15.0	11.5	6.9	22,934
1995	11,577	22.8	11.3	18.0	14.3	14.6	11.9	7.2	23,583
1996	12,109	22.6	11.5	17.6	13.9	14.1	12.6	7.8	24,021
1997	12,474	21.4	10.5	17.9	14.2	14.9	13.1	7.9	25,050
HISPANIC [2]									
1975	2,948	16.5	11.2	21.8	17.2	18.7	10.8	3.8	25,317
1980	3,906	16.1	10.5	20.2	16.5	17.1	13.6	6.0	26,622
1985	5,213	17.3	12.1	18.6	15.3	16.9	12.7	7.1	26,051
1990	6,220	16.2	11.5	18.5	15.7	17.1	12.9	8.1	27,421
1995	7,939	18.8	11.8	21.0	15.2	14.1	12.1	6.9	24,075
1996	8,225	16.7	12.0	20.8	14.9	15.0	12.5	8.1	25,477
1997	8,590	16.8	10.7	19.7	15.0	16.6	12.2	9.1	26,628

[1] Includes other races not shown separately.   [2] Persons of Hispanic origin may be of any race. Income data for Hispanic origin households are not available prior to 1972.

No. 743. Money Income of Households—Median Income, by Race and Hispanic Origin, in Current and Constant (1997) Dollars: 1970 to 1997

[In dollars. See headnote, Table 742]

Year	Median income in current dollars					Median income in constant (1997) dollars				
	All house-holds [1]	White	Black	Asian, Pacific Islander	His-panic [2]	All house-holds [1]	White	Black	Asian, Pacific Islander	His-panic [2]
1970	8,734	9,097	5,537	(NA)	(NA)	33,942	35,353	21,518	(NA)	(NA)
1980	17,710	18,684	10,764	(NA)	13,651	34,538	36,437	20,992	(NA)	26,622
1985	23,618	24,908	14,819	(NA)	17,465	35,229	37,154	22,105	(NA)	26,051
1986	24,897	26,175	15,080	(NA)	18,352	36,460	38,331	22,083	(NA)	26,875
1987 [3]	26,061	27,458	15,672	(NA)	19,336	36,820	38,794	22,142	(NA)	27,319
1988	27,225	28,781	16,407	32,267	20,359	36,937	39,048	22,260	43,777	27,621
1989	28,906	30,406	18,083	36,102	21,921	37,415	39,356	23,406	46,729	28,374
1990	29,943	31,231	18,676	38,450	22,330	36,770	38,352	22,934	47,217	27,421
1991	30,126	31,569	18,807	36,449	22,691	35,501	37,201	22,162	42,952	26,739
1992 [4]	30,636	32,209	18,755	37,801	22,597	35,047	36,846	21,455	43,243	25,850
1993	31,241	32,960	19,533	38,347	22,886	34,700	36,610	21,696	42,593	25,420
1994	32,264	34,028	21,027	40,482	23,421	34,942	36,852	22,772	43,842	25,365
1995	34,076	35,766	22,393	40,614	22,860	35,887	37,667	23,583	42,773	24,075
1996	35,492	37,161	23,482	43,276	24,906	36,306	38,014	24,021	44,269	25,477
1997	37,005	38,972	25,050	45,249	26,628	37,005	38,972	25,050	45,249	26,628

NA Not available.   [1] Includes other races not shown separately.   [2] Persons of Hispanic origin may be of any race.
[3] Beginning 1987, data based on revised processing procedures and not directly comparable with prior years.   [4] Based on 1990 census population controls.

Source of Tables 742 and 743: U.S. Census Bureau, *Current Population Reports*, P60-200; and Internet site <http://www.census.gov/hhes/income/histinc/inchhdet.html> (accessed 8 May 1999).

No. 744. Money Income of Households—Distribution, by Income Level and Selected Characteristics: 1997

Characteristic	Number of households (1,000)	Under $10,000	$10,000- $14,999	$15,000- $24,999	$25,000- $34,999	$35,000- $49,999	$50,000- $74,999	$75,000 and over	Median income (dollars)
Total [1]	**102,528**	**11,296**	**8,326**	**15,244**	**13,586**	**16,698**	**18,531**	**18,847**	**37,005**
Age of householder:									
15 to 24 years	5,435	1,141	595	1,223	952	810	460	254	22,583
25 to 34 years	19,033	1,635	1,302	2,683	2,947	3,820	4,062	2,584	38,174
35 to 44 years	23,943	1,686	1,181	2,702	3,000	4,319	5,580	5,475	46,359
45 to 54 years	19,547	1,318	876	1,947	2,097	3,084	4,406	5,818	51,875
55 to 64 years	13,072	1,440	871	1,710	1,540	2,168	2,300	3,044	41,356
65 years and over	21,497	4,075	3,500	4,979	3,052	2,496	1,723	1,671	20,761
White	86,106	8,188	6,716	12,549	11,350	14,170	16,190	16,945	38,972
Black	12,474	2,672	1,316	2,238	1,766	1,859	1,637	985	25,050
Hispanic [2]	8,590	1,441	916	1,691	1,290	1,429	1,047	778	26,628
Northeast	19,810	2,393	1,546	2,648	2,374	3,033	3,532	4,283	38,929
Midwest	24,236	2,418	1,836	3,560	3,278	4,138	4,723	4,283	38,316
South	36,578	4,445	3,143	5,840	5,143	5,981	6,279	5,748	34,345
West	21,905	2,039	1,800	3,196	2,792	3,546	3,997	4,533	39,162
Size of household:									
One person	26,327	6,692	4,171	5,453	3,688	3,058	2,024	1,241	18,762
Two persons	32,965	2,027	2,177	5,255	5,099	5,894	6,214	6,299	39,343
Three persons	17,331	1,177	891	2,084	1,963	3,052	4,028	4,136	47,115
Four persons	15,358	738	586	1,350	1,623	2,756	3,873	4,432	53,165
Five persons	7,048	436	290	692	756	1,310	1,658	1,906	50,407
Six persons	2,232	139	114	239	296	411	503	530	46,465
Seven or more persons	1,267	88	96	170	160	216	231	305	42,343
Type of household:									
Family households	70,880	4,346	3,911	9,068	9,157	12,500	15,380	16,516	45,347
Married-couple	54,317	1,471	2,085	5,886	6,473	9,981	13,205	15,216	51,681
Male householder, wife absent	3,911	271	262	605	711	709	805	548	36,634
Female householder, husband absent	12,652	2,604	1,564	2,578	1,974	1,810	1,370	754	23,040
Nonfamily households	31,648	6,949	4,415	6,176	4,429	4,197	3,151	2,331	21,705
Male householder	14,133	2,167	1,508	2,715	2,193	2,303	1,844	1,402	27,592
Female householder	17,516	4,782	2,907	3,461	2,236	1,895	1,306	928	17,613
Educational attainment of householder: [3]									
Total	**97,093**	**10,155**	**7,731**	**14,021**	**12,635**	**15,888**	**18,070**	**18,594**	**38,190**
Less than 9th grade	7,369	2,223	1,344	1,664	843	690	375	231	15,541
9th to 12th grade (no diploma)	9,686	2,321	1,402	2,079	1,303	1,240	898	443	19,851
High school graduate	30,739	3,254	2,657	5,245	4,729	5,691	5,755	3,409	33,779
Some college, no degree	17,225	1,227	1,287	2,429	2,591	3,121	3,533	3,038	40,015
Associate degree	7,263	417	389	900	940	1,357	1,742	1,518	45,258
Bachelor's degree or more	24,811	712	652	1,704	2,229	3,789	5,768	9,956	63,292
Bachelor's degree	16,098	529	456	1,276	1,604	2,581	4,020	5,633	59,048
Master's degree	5,735	136	140	323	462	873	1,257	2,544	68,115
Professional degree	1,693	29	27	58	88	213	261	1,017	92,228
Doctorate degree	1,285	19	29	47	76	122	231	762	87,232
Tenure:									
Owner occupied	67,873	4,376	4,198	8,567	8,240	11,474	14,517	16,501	45,821
Renter occupied	32,954	6,505	3,882	6,347	5,135	4,975	3,829	2,281	24,514
Occupier paid no cash rent	1,701	414	246	331	212	249	185	66	20,376
Work experience of householder:									
Total	**102,528**	**11,296**	**8,326**	**15,244**	**13,586**	**16,698**	**18,531**	**18,847**	**37,005**
Worked	73,415	3,551	3,779	9,103	9,963	13,673	16,342	17,003	45,877
Worked at full-time jobs	63,318	1,917	2,697	7,263	8,681	12,100	15,053	15,608	48,488
50 weeks or more	53,665	755	1,649	5,566	7,299	10,470	13,564	14,363	51,336
27 to 49 weeks	6,311	454	618	1,062	914	1,189	1,122	951	36,263
26 weeks or less	3,341	707	430	635	467	441	367	293	23,254
Worked at part-time jobs	10,098	1,633	1,082	1,841	1,283	1,574	1,289	1,396	28,437
50 weeks or more	5,090	554	537	953	693	828	682	843	31,640
27 to 49 weeks	2,224	326	206	417	282	378	327	287	30,652
26 weeks or less	2,784	754	339	471	308	367	280	266	21,023
Did not work	29,113	7,745	4,546	6,141	3,623	3,024	2,188	1,844	18,143

[1] Includes other races not shown separately. [2] Persons of Hispanic origin may be of any race. [3] Persons 25 years old and over.

Source: U.S. Census Bureau, *Current Population Reports*, P60-200, Money Income in the United States: 1997.

Income, Expenditures, and Wealth 475

No. 745. Household Income Before and After Taxes in Current and Constant (1997) Dollars: 1980 to 1997

[In dollars, except as indicated. Households as of **March of the following year**. Income in current and 1997 CPI-U-X1 adjusted dollars]

Year	Number of house-holds (1,000)	Current dollars				Constant (1997) dollars			
		Mean		Median		Mean		Median	
		Before taxes	After taxes	Before taxes	After taxes	Before taxes	After taxes	Before taxes	After taxes
1980	82,368	21,063	16,272	17,710	14,551	41,077	31,733	34,538	28,377
1985 [1]	88,458	29,066	22,646	23,618	19,401	43,356	33,780	35,229	28,939
1990	94,312	37,403	29,188	29,943	24,546	45,931	35,843	36,770	30,143
1991	95,669	37,922	29,640	30,126	24,955	44,688	34,928	35,501	29,407
1992 [2]	96,426	38,840	30,425	30,636	25,474	44,432	34,806	35,047	29,142
1993 [3]	97,107	41,428	32,092	31,241	26,112	46,015	35,645	34,700	29,003
1994 [4]	98,990	43,133	33,315	32,264	26,973	46,713	36,080	34,942	29,212
1995 [5]	99,627	44,938	34,592	34,076	28,249	47,326	36,431	35,887	29,750
1996	101,018	47,123	36,008	35,492	29,312	48,204	36,834	36,306	29,985
1997	102,528	49,692	37,656	37,005	30,648	49,692	37,656	37,005	30,648

[1] Recording of amounts for earnings from longest job increased to $299,999. Full implementation of 1980 census-based sample design.   [2] Implementation of 1990 census population controls.   [3] Data collection method changed from paper and pencil to computer assisted interviewing. In addition, the March 1994 income supplement was revised to allow for the coding of different income amounts on selected questionnaire items. Limits either increased or decreased in the following categories: earnings increased to $999,999; social security increased to $49,999; supplemental security income and public assistance increased to $24,999; veterans' benefits increased to $99,999; child support and alimony decreased to $49,999.   [4] Introduction of 1990 census sample design.   [5] Full implementation of the 1990 census-based sample design and metropolitan definitions, 7,000 household sample reduction, and revised race edits.

Source: U.S. Census Bureau, Internet site <http://www.census.gov/hhes/income/histinc/incexper.html> (accessed 8 June 1999).

No. 746. Mean-Taxes Paid and Taxes Paid as a Percentage of Total Mean Before-Tax Income by Type of Tax in Current and Constant (1997) Dollars: 1980 to 1997

[Households as of **March of the following year**. Mean taxes paid in current and 1997 CPI-U-X1 adjusted dollars]

Type of tax and year	Mean taxes paid				Type of tax and year	Mean taxes paid			
	Number (1,000)	Current dollars (dollars)	Constant 1997 dollars (dollars)	As a percent of mean before-tax income		Number (1,000)	Current dollars (dollars)	Constant 1997 dollars (dollars)	As a percent of mean before-tax income
One or more taxes paid:					1993 [3]	62,459	2,045	2,271	4.4
1980	76,171	5,180	10,102	23.1	1994 [4]	63,626	2,194	2,376	4.1
1985	81,943	6,947	10,362	22.5	1995 [5]	64,827	2,296	2,418	4.2
1990	87,597	8,896	10,924	22.4	1996	65,856	2,467	2,524	4.3
1991	88,636	9,007	10,614	22.3	1997	67,164	2,674	2,674	4.5
1992	89,232	9,178	10,499	22.2	FICA payroll taxes:				
1993	89,561	10,217	11,348	23.1	1980	62,061	1,114	2,173	4.6
1994	91,540	10,768	11,662	23.4	1985 [1]	66,090	1,894	2,825	5.6
1995	92,754	11,292	11,892	23.7	1990	70,942	2,692	3,306	6.2
1996	94,236	12,118	12,396	24.3	1991	71,466	2,807	3,308	6.3
1997	95,850	13,077	13,077	24.9	1992 [2]	72,516	2,889	3,305	6.3
Federal income taxes:					1993 [3]	72,264	2,961	3,289	6.1
1980	61,316	4,011	7,822	15.3	1994 [4]	74,050	3,107	3,365	6.1
1985 [1]	68,019	4,675	6,973	13.2	1995 [5]	75,096	3,193	3,363	6.1
1990	70,255	5,806	7,130	12.4	1996	76,724	3,330	3,406	6.0
1991	69,842	5,901	6,954	12.3	1997	77,999	3,508	3,508	6.1
1992 [2]	68,957	6,029	6,897	12.1	Property taxes on own home:				
1993 [3]	68,786	7,098	7,884	13.3	1980	52,328	575	1,121	2.3
1994 [4]	69,501	7,591	8,221	13.5	1985 [1]	53,298	811	1,210	2.3
1995 [5]	70,926	7,935	8,357	13.7	1990	58,472	1,125	1,382	2.5
1996	72,009	8,637	8,835	14.3	1991	59,403	1,119	1,319	2.5
1997	73,941	9,445	9,445	14.9	1992 [2]	59,838	1,213	1,388	2.6
State income taxes:					1993 [3]	60,554	1,230	1,366	2.5
1980	52,591	859	1,675	3.3	1994 [4]	62,121	1,257	1,361	2.4
1985 [1]	57,033	1,330	1,984	3.8	1995 [5]	63,377	1,361	1,433	2.5
1990	61,875	1,710	2,100	3.8	1996	64,559	1,433	1,466	2.6
1991	62,314	1,761	2,075	3.8	1997	65,998	1,390	1,390	2.3
1992 [2]	62,247	1,837	2,101	3.9					

[1] See footnote 1, Table 745.   [2] See footnote 2, Table 745.   [3] See footnote 3, Table 745.   [4] See footnote 4, Table 745.   [5] See footnote 5, Table 745.

Source: U.S. Census Bureau, Internet site <http://www.census.gov/hhes/income/histinc/rdi02.html> (accessed 8 June 1999).

No. 747. Money Income of Households—Median Income and Income Level, by Household Type: 1997

[See headnote, Table 742]

Item	Family households					Nonfamily households		
	All house-holds	Total	Married couple	Male house-holder, wife absent	Female house-holder, husband absent	Total [1]	Single-person household	
							Male house-holder	Female house-holder
MEDIAN INCOME (dollars)								
All households.	37,005	45,347	51,681	36,634	23,040	21,705	23,871	15,530
White	38,972	47,454	52,199	38,511	25,670	22,380	25,415	15,818
Black	25,050	29,915	45,372	28,593	17,962	17,073	17,139	13,738
Hispanic [2]	26,628	29,253	34,317	28,249	16,393	16,807	16,524	9,666
NUMBER (1,000)								
All households.	102,528	70,880	54,317	3,911	12,652	31,648	11,010	15,317
Under $5,000	3531	1698	593	120	985	1835	672	1055
$5,000 to $9,999.	7765	2650	878	374	1619	5116	1367	3598
$10,000 to $14,999	8326	3910	2085	262	1564	4415	1366	2805
$15,000 to $19,999	7837	4465	2783	307	1375	3372	1218	1802
$20,000 to $24,999	7406	4603	3102	299	1202	2804	1091	1342
$25,000 to $34,999	6913	4655	3156	405	1094	2258	861	1023
$35,000 to $49,999	6111	4364	3377	272	715	1747	718	637
$50,000 to $74,999	4864	3898	3295	210	393	966	335	307
$75,000 to $99,999	2399	2046	1816	88	141	353	143	60
$100,000 and over	9,661	8,516	7,976	220	321	1,145	380	241

[1] Includes other nonfamily households not shown separately.   [2] Persons of Hispanic origin may be of any race.

Source: U.S. Census Bureau, *Current Population Reports*, P60-200.

No. 748. Money Income of Households—Median Income, by State, in Constant (1997) Dollars: 1987 to 1997

[Constant dollars based on the CPI-U-X1 deflator. Data based on the Current Population Survey; see text, Section 1, Population, and text, this section, and Appendix III. The CPS is designed to collect reliable data on income primarily at the national level and secondarily at the regional level. When the income data are tabulated by state, the estimates are considered less reliable and, therefore, particular caution should be used when trying to interpret the results]

State	1987	1990	1995 [1]	1996	1997	State	1987	1990	1995 [1]	1996	1997
U.S.	**$36,714**	**$36,770**	**$35,887**	**$36,306**	**$37,005**						
						MO	33,513	33,564	36,676	35,051	36,553
AL	27,881	28,682	27,372	30,997	31,939	MT	28,927	28,705	29,232	29,342	29,212
AK	46,953	48,258	50,503	53,990	47,994	NE	32,874	33,748	34,679	34,794	34,692
AZ	37,792	35,887	32,503	32,363	32,740	NV	37,975	39,324	38,000	39,424	38,854
AR	26,600	27,981	27,186	27,745	26,162	NH	45,689	50,109	41,253	40,311	40,998
CA	42,592	40,880	38,976	39,703	39,694						
						NJ	48,377	47,565	46,259	48,557	48,021
CO	37,407	37,740	42,870	41,890	43,233	NM	29,328	30,748	27,372	25,662	30,086
CT	46,429	47,732	42,382	43,085	43,985	NY	37,277	38,794	34,783	36,222	35,798
DE	41,317	37,827	36,784	40,211	43,033	NC	32,157	32,332	33,679	36,418	35,840
DC	38,790	33,637	32,382	32,699	31,860	ND	31,897	31,024	30,635	32,192	31,661
FL	34,599	32,769	31,326	31,344	32,455						
						OH	36,413	36,856	36,798	34,852	36,134
GA	37,743	33,845	35,911	33,242	36,663	OK	30,646	29,944	27,709	28,067	31,351
HA	49,481	47,795	45,129	42,730	40,934	OR	35,375	35,957	38,307	36,306	37,247
ID	29,324	31,075	34,413	35,505	33,404	PA	35,920	35,618	36,359	35,700	37,517
IL	38,266	39,962	40,094	40,462	41,283	RI	39,972	39,257	37,238	37,835	34,797
IN	31,816	33,068	35,159	35,953	38,889						
						SC	35,391	35,287	30,616	35,460	34,262
IA	31,351	33,510	37,407	33,971	33,783	SD	29,883	30,173	31,150	30,203	29,694
KS	36,145	36,738	31,954	33,333	36,471	TN	29,923	27,743	30,557	31,496	30,636
KY	29,208	30,430	31,394	33,157	33,452	TX	34,927	34,664	33,742	33,831	35,075
LA	30,163	27,513	29,434	30,956	33,260	UT	37,482	37,014	38,419	37,888	42,775
MA	33,343	33,726	35,658	35,492	32,772						
						VT	35,908	38,188	35,622	33,100	35,053
MD	49,407	47,717	43,222	45,002	46,685	VA	42,380	43,070	38,147	40,111	42,957
MA	45,552	44,511	40,624	40,400	42,023	WA	38,598	39,434	37,458	37,518	44,562
MI	39,139	36,763	38,362	40,125	38,742	WV	24,311	27,184	26,202	25,826	27,488
MN	39,676	38,639	39,949	41,932	42,564	WI	37,255	37,713	43,132	40,919	39,595
MS	26,156	24,779	27,948	27,289	28,499	WY	38,981	36,177	33,205	31,663	33,423

[1] Full implementation of the 1990 census-based sample design and metropolitan definitions, 7,000 household sample reduction, and revised race edits.

Source: U.S. Census Bureau, *Current Population Reports*, P60-200; and <http://www.census.gov/hhes/income/histinc/inchhdet.html> (accessed 23 March 1999).

No. 749. Money Income of Families—Percent Distribution, by Income Level, Race, and Hispanic Origin, in Constant (1997) Dollars: 1970 to 1997

[Constant dollars based on CPI-U-X1 deflator. Families as of **March** of following year. Beginning with 1980, based on householder concept and restricted to primary families. Based on Current Population Survey; see text, Section 1, Population, and text, this section, and Appendix III. For definition of median, see Guide to Tabular Presentation]

Year	Number of families (1,000)	Percent distribution							Median income (dollars)
		Under $10,000	$10,000-$14,999	$15,000-$24,999	$25,000-$34,999	$35,000-$49,999	$50,000-$74,999	$75,000 and over	
ALL FAMILIES [1]									
1970	52,227	7.0	6.2	14.5	17.0	24.1	20.6	10.5	38,345
1980	60,309	6.6	6.2	14.3	14.2	21.4	22.4	14.9	40,999
1985	63,558	7.5	6.2	13.7	14.0	19.3	21.3	17.9	41,371
1990	66,322	7.1	5.8	12.9	13.5	19.1	21.5	20.3	43,414
1995	69,597	6.9	6.2	13.6	13.8	18.0	20.9	20.7	42,769
1996	70,241	7.3	5.9	13.2	13.4	17.5	21.5	21.2	43,271
1997	70,884	6.8	5.7	13.0	12.8	17.4	21.3	22.8	44,568
WHITE									
1970	46,535	5.9	5.5	13.7	17.0	24.9	21.7	11.3	39,779
1980	52,710	5.3	5.4	13.6	14.2	22.0	23.6	16.0	42,717
1985	54,991	6.0	5.5	13.1	14.0	19.9	22.3	19.2	43,484
1990	56,803	5.3	5.0	12.5	13.6	19.5	22.6	21.5	45,332
1995	58,872	5.2	5.5	13.0	13.8	18.4	21.9	22.1	44,913
1996	58,934	5.6	5.3	12.6	13.4	17.9	22.6	22.7	45,783
1997	59,515	5.3	5.1	12.5	12.7	17.7	22.1	24.5	46,754
BLACK									
1970	4,928	17.3	12.1	22.1	17.5	16.6	10.9	3.5	24,401
1980	6,317	17.7	13.1	19.8	14.3	16.7	13.1	5.4	24,717
1985	6,921	19.9	11.5	18.7	14.2	15.6	13.2	6.9	25,039
1990	7,471	20.2	11.7	16.2	13.3	16.3	13.7	8.7	26,308
1995	8,055	18.2	10.5	17.8	14.6	16.0	13.7	9.2	27,350
1996	8,455	18.5	10.5	17.6	14.1	15.4	14.6	9.4	27,131
1997	8,408	17.0	9.8	17.7	14.2	15.5	16.0	9.9	28,602
HISPANIC ORIGIN [2]									
1980	3,235	12.2	10.5	20.2	17.3	18.4	15.0	6.4	28,699
1985	4,206	13.9	12.1	18.9	15.6	17.5	14.2	7.9	28,381
1990	4,981	13.5	11.3	19.2	15.4	17.6	14.0	9.0	28,773
1995	6,287	15.2	11.5	22.2	15.9	14.6	13.0	7.7	25,876
1996	6,631	14.2	11.6	21.3	15.5	15.3	13.2	8.9	26,780
1997	6,961	13.8	10.9	20.1	15.3	17.2	12.7	10.0	28,142

[1] Includes other races not shown separately.   [2] Persons of Hispanic origin may be of any race.

No. 750. Money Income of Families—Median Income, by Race and Hispanic Origin, in Current and Constant (1997) Dollars: 1970 to 1997

[See headnote, Table 742]

Year	Median income in current dollars					Median income in constant (1997) dollars				
	All families [1]	White	Black	Asian, Pacific Islander	His-panic [2]	All families [1]	White	Black	Asian, Pacific Islander	His-panic [2]
1970	9,867	10,236	6,279	(NA)	(NA)	38,345	39,779	24,401	(NA)	(NA)
1980	21,023	21,904	12,674	(NA)	14,716	40,999	42,717	24,717	(NA)	28,699
1985 [3]	27,735	29,152	16,786	(NA)	19,027	41,371	43,484	25,039	(NA)	28,381
1986	29,458	30,809	17,604	(NA)	19,995	43,139	45,117	25,780	(NA)	29,281
1987 [4]	30,970	32,385	18,406	(NA)	20,300	43,756	45,755	26,005	(NA)	28,681
1988	32,191	33,915	19,329	36,560	21,769	43,674	46,013	26,224	49,602	29,534
1989	34,213	35,975	20,209	40,351	23,446	44,284	46,564	26,158	52,229	30,347
1990	35,353	36,915	21,423	42,246	23,431	43,414	45,332	26,308	51,878	28,773
1991	35,939	37,783	21,548	40,974	23,895	42,351	44,524	25,392	48,284	28,158
1992 [5]	36,573	38,670	21,103	42,255	23,555	41,839	44,238	24,141	48,339	26,946
1993 [6]	36,959	39,300	21,542	44,456	23,654	41,051	43,652	23,927	49,378	26,273
1994 [7]	38,782	40,884	24,698	46,122	24,318	42,001	44,277	26,748	49,950	26,336
1995 [8]	40,611	42,646	25,970	46,356	24,570	42,769	44,913	27,350	48,820	25,876
1996	42,300	44,756	26,522	49,105	26,179	43,271	45,783	27,131	50,232	26,780
1997	44,568	46,754	28,602	51,850	28,142	44,568	46,754	28,602	51,850	28,142

NA Not available.   [1] Includes other races not shown separately.   [2] Persons of Hispanic origin may be of any race. [3] Recording of amounts for earnings from longest job increased to $299,999.   [4] Implementation of a new March CPS processing system.   [5] Implementation of 1990 census population controls.   [6] See text, Section 14, for information on data collection change.   [7] Introduction of 1990 census sample design.   [8] Full implementation of the 1990 census-based sample design and metropolitan definitions, 7,000 household sample reduction, and revised race edits.

Source of Tables 749 and 750: U.S. Census Bureau, Current Population Reports, P60-200.

478   Income, Expenditures, and Wealth

No. 751. Share of Aggregate Income Received by Each Fifth and Top 5 Percent of Families: 1970 to 1997

[Families as of March of the following year. Income in constant 1997 CPI-U-X1 adjusted dollars]

Year	Num- ber (1,000)	Income at selected positions (dollars)					Percent distribution of aggregate income					
		Upper limit of each fifth				Top 5 percent	Low- est 5th	Sec- ond 5th	Third 5th	Fourth 5th	Highest 5th	Top 5 percent
		Lowest	Second	Third	Fourth							
1970	52,227	19,820	32,333	43,910	60,357	94,240	5.4	12.2	17.6	23.8	40.9	15.6
1975	56,245	19,954	32,857	45,694	63,266	99,099	5.6	11.9	17.7	24.2	40.7	14.9
1980	60,309	20,282	34,148	48,365	67,866	107,260	5.3	11.6	17.6	24.4	41.1	14.6
1985	63,558	19,816	34,138	49,451	71,940	117,787	4.8	11.0	16.9	24.3	43.1	16.1
1990	66,322	20,687	35,666	51,625	75,510	125,696	4.6	10.8	16.6	23.8	44.3	17.4
1991	67,173	20,033	34,305	50,672	74,229	121,169	4.5	10.7	16.6	24.1	44.2	17.1
1992 [1]	68,216	19,119	33,946	50,335	73,272	121,275	4.3	10.5	16.5	24.0	44.7	17.6
1993 [2]	68,506	18,849	33,322	50,016	74,190	125,714	4.1	9.9	15.7	23.3	47.0	20.3
1994 [3]	69,313	19,429	33,898	50,901	75,808	130,006	4.2	10.0	15.7	23.3	46.9	20.1
1995	69,597	20,084	34,738	51,589	76,101	130,228	4.4	10.1	15.8	23.2	46.5	20.0
1996	70,241	20,132	35,102	52,258	77,044	130,937	4.2	10.0	15.8	23.1	46.8	20.3
1997	70,884	20,586	36,000	53,616	80,000	137,080	4.2	9.9	15.7	23.0	47.2	20.7
White	59,515	22,576	38,258	55,783	82,442	142,400	4.6	10.2	15.7	22.8	46.8	20.7
Black	8,408	11,396	21,875	36,052	57,000	95,684	3.4	9.1	15.6	25.1	46.8	17.6
Hispanic origin [4]	6,961	12,642	22,200	34,963	53,548	96,460	3.9	9.2	14.9	22.8	49.3	21.6

[1] Based on 1990 census population controls. [2] See text, this section, for explanation of changes in data collection method. [3] Introduction of new 1990 census sample design. [4] Persons of Hispanic origin may be of any race.

Source: U.S. Census Bureau, *Current Population Reports*, P60-200; and <http://www.census.gov/hhes/income/histinc/index.html> (accessed 23 March 1999).

No. 752. Money Income of Families—Distribution, by Family Characteristics and Income Level: 1997

[See headnote, Table 749. For composition of regions, see map inside front cover]

Characteristic	Number of fami- lies (1,000)	Income level (1,000)							Median income (dollars)
		Under $10,000	$10,000 to $14,999	$15,000 to $24,999	$25,000 to $34,999	$35,000 to $49,999	$50,000 to $74,999	$75,000 and over	
All families	**70,884**	**4,816**	**4,054**	**9,250**	**9,079**	**12,357**	**15,112**	**16,217**	**44,568**
Age of householder:									
15 to 24 years old	3,018	720	361	659	456	443	264	114	20,820
25 to 34 years old	13,639	1,363	922	1,814	1,846	2,637	3,080	1,977	39,979
35 to 44 years old	18,872	1,151	826	1,934	2,120	3,285	4,734	4,820	50,424
45 to 54 years old	14,695	530	500	1,112	1,420	2,303	3,640	5,189	59,959
55 to 64 years old	9,391	484	407	991	1,081	1,700	1,997	2,731	50,241
65 years old and over	11,270	567	1,037	2,739	2,156	1,989	1,398	1,385	30,660
White	59,515	3,185	3,047	7,454	7,552	10,527	13,172	14,578	46,754
Black	8,408	1,428	824	1,486	1,193	1,302	1,344	832	28,602
Hispanic origin [1]	6,961	956	759	1,397	1,066	1,199	887	697	28,142
Northeast	13,338	904	608	1,570	1,596	2,158	2,853	3,648	48,328
Midwest	16,594	898	797	1,993	2,122	3,093	3,862	3,829	46,734
South	25,682	2,008	1,689	3,718	3,492	4,565	5,230	4,981	41,001
West	15,270	1,006	959	1,968	1,869	2,542	3,167	3,760	45,590
Type of family:									
Married-couple families	54,321	1,488	2,100	5,899	6,497	9,978	13,200	15,159	51,591
Male householder, wife absent	3,911	358	292	703	707	694	716	440	32,960
Female householder, husband absent	12,652	2,971	1,661	2,647	1,875	1,685	1,195	618	21,023
Unrelated subfamilies	575	219	86	133	69	51	14	3	13,692
Education attainment of householder: [2]									
Total	67,866	4,096	3,693	8,590	8,622	11,913	14,848	16,103	45,874
Less than 9th grade	4,667	690	799	1,267	728	624	341	219	21,208
9th to 12th grade (no diploma)	6,604	1,027	753	1,465	1,085	1,101	778	395	25,465
High school graduate (includes equivalency)	21,991	1,439	1,152	3,261	3,517	4,610	4,991	3,021	40,040
Some college, no degree	12,107	559	562	1,358	1,666	2,338	2,964	2,661	46,936
Associate degree	5,226	162	174	506	556	1,005	1,468	1,355	52,393
Bachelor's degree or more	17,272	221	253	733	1,071	2,235	4,306	8,454	73,578
Bachelor's degree	11,201	156	185	581	797	1,616	3,079	4,788	67,230
Master's degree	3,903	46	46	109	194	451	868	2,188	81,734
Professional degree	1,249	10	12	25	50	111	203	839	106,942
Doctorate degree	919	8	10	18	30	58	156	638	103,203

[1] Persons of Hispanic origin may be of any race. [2] Persons 25 years old and over.

Source: U.S. Census Bureau, *Current Population Reports*, P60-200.

U.S. Census Bureau, Statistical Abstract of the United States: 1999

No. 753. Money Income of Families—Work Experience, by Income Level: 1997

[See headnote, Table 749]

Characteristic	Number of families (1,000)	Income level (1,000)							Median income (dollars)
		Under $10,000	$10,000 to $14,999	$15,000 to $24,999	$25,000 to $34,999	$35,000 to $49,999	$50,000 to $74,999	$75,000 and over	
All families	70,884	4,816	4,054	9,250	9,079	12,357	15,112	16,217	44,568
Number of earners:									
No earners	9,835	2,168	1,378	2,624	1,508	1,095	609	454	19,731
One earner	20,494	2,287	1,960	4,055	3,483	3,455	2,876	2,379	30,204
Two earners or more	40,555	361	716	2,570	4,088	7,807	11,628	13,383	58,972
Two earners	31,752	340	674	2,348	3,645	6,486	9,067	9,192	55,443
Three earners	6,638	20	41	201	390	1,128	2,018	2,840	68,028
Four earners or more	2,165	2	2	21	53	193	543	1,352	85,978
Work experience of householder:									
Worked	53,783	2,188	2,180	5,401	6,287	9,860	13,230	14,637	51,268
Worked at full-time jobs	46,789	1,258	1,592	4,376	5,405	8,631	12,111	13,416	53,302
50 weeks or more	40,012	488	955	3,298	4,526	7,424	10,937	12,384	56,309
27 to 49 weeks	4,370	272	365	656	565	858	871	784	40,651
26 weeks or less	2,407	498	271	422	314	350	303	249	25,347
Worked at part-time jobs	6,994	930	588	1,025	882	1,228	1,120	1,221	35,725
50 weeks or more	3,537	312	273	517	464	633	599	738	39,213
27 to 49 weeks	1,560	187	120	218	178	325	285	247	38,010
26 weeks or less	1,897	432	194	290	240	270	236	235	26,362

No. 754. Median Income of Families, by Type of Family in Current and Constant (1997) Dollars: 1970 to 1997

[See headnote, Table 749]

Year	Current dollars						Constant (1997) dollars					
	Total	Married-couple families			Male householder, no wife present	Female householder, no husband present	Total	Married-couple families			Male householder, no wife present	Female householder, no husband present
		Total	Wife in paid labor force	Wife not in paid labor force				Total	Wife in paid labor force	Wife not in paid labor force		
1970	9,867	10,516	12,276	9,304	9,012	5,093	38,345	40,867	47,707	36,157	35,022	19,792
1980	21,023	23,141	26,879	18,972	17,519	10,408	40,999	45,129	52,419	36,999	34,165	20,297
1985	27,735	31,100	36,431	24,556	22,622	13,660	41,371	46,390	54,342	36,629	33,744	20,376
1990	35,353	39,895	46,777	30,265	29,046	16,932	43,414	48,991	57,442	37,166	35,669	20,793
1991	35,939	40,995	48,169	30,075	28,351	16,692	42,351	48,309	56,763	35,441	33,409	19,670
1992 [1]	36,573	41,890	49,775	30,174	27,576	17,025	41,839	47,921	56,941	34,518	31,546	19,476
1993	36,959	43,005	51,204	30,218	26,467	17,443	41,051	47,767	56,874	33,564	29,398	19,374
1994 [2]	38,782	44,959	53,309	31,176	27,751	18,236	42,001	48,690	57,733	33,763	30,054	19,750
1995 [3]	40,611	47,062	55,823	32,375	30,358	19,691	42,769	49,563	58,790	34,096	31,972	20,738
1996	42,300	49,707	58,381	33,748	31,600	19,911	43,271	50,848	59,721	34,522	32,325	20,368
1997	44,568	51,591	60,669	36,027	32,960	21,023	44,568	51,591	60,669	36,027	32,960	21,023

[1] Based on 1990 census population controls.   [2] See text, this section, for information on data collection change.   [3] Introduction of 1990 census sample design.

No. 755. Married-Couple Families—Number and Median Income, by Work Experience of Husbands and Wives and Presence of Children: 1997

[As of **March 1998.** Based on Current Population Survey; see text, Section 1, Population, and text, this section, and Appendix III]

Work experience of husband or wife	Number (1,000)					Median income (dollars)				
	All married-couple families	No related children	One or more related children under 18 years old			All married-couple families	No related children	One or more related children under 18 years old		
			Total	One child	Two children or more			Total	One child	Two children or more
All married-couple families	54,321	27,892	26,430	10,057	16,372	51,591	48,588	54,395	56,324	52,857
Husband worked	43,384	18,404	24,980	9,365	15,615	57,794	61,190	55,905	58,075	54,588
Wife worked	32,834	14,020	18,814	7,482	11,331	61,837	65,624	59,733	61,486	57,974
Wife year-round, full-time worker	18,962	8,907	10,055	4,455	5,600	67,053	70,445	64,859	66,726	62,848
Wife did not work	10,550	4,384	6,166	1,882	4,284	43,482	45,421	42,095	42,887	41,783
Husband year-round, full-time worker	35,618	14,009	21,609	8,052	13,557	61,495	66,268	58,688	60,667	57,220
Wife worked	27,493	11,103	16,390	6,499	9,891	64,902	69,982	61,713	63,369	60,761
Wife year-round, full-time worker	16,244	7,392	8,852	3,921	4,931	69,507	73,280	66,477	68,173	65,354
Wife did not work	8,125	2,906	5,219	1,553	3,666	48,510	51,866	46,454	46,864	46,109
Husband did not work	10,937	9,488	1,449	693	757	27,639	28,253	22,880	28,329	19,602
Wife worked	2,861	2,084	778	382	396	37,239	39,784	30,014	32,530	25,990
Wife year-round, full-time worker	1,600	1,124	476	247	229	44,548	47,962	38,347	39,041	37,405
Wife did not work	8,076	7,404	672	311	361	24,986	25,656	17,542	21,406	15,256

Source of Tables 753-755: U.S. Census Bureau, *Current Population Reports*, P60-200; and <http://www.census.gov/hhes/income/histinc/index.htm> (accessed 23 March 1999).

No. 756. Money Income of Persons—Selected Characteristics, by Income Level: 1997

[Persons as of **March of following year.** Covers persons 15 years old and over. For definition of median, see Guide to Tabular Presentation. For composition of regions, see map, inside front cover]

Characteristic	All persons (1,000)	Persons with income Number (1,000)									Median income (dollars)
		Total (1,000)	Under [1] $5,000	$5,000 to $9,999	$10,000 to $14,999	$15,000 to $24,999	$25,000 to $34,999	$35,000 to $49,999	$50,000 to $74,999	$75,000 and over	
MALE											
Total	101,123	94,168	8,578	9,598	10,695	17,800	14,740	14,367	10,938	7,451	25,212
15 to 24 years old	18,747	13,905	5,201	2,969	1,983	2,329	950	307	91	77	7,468
25 to 34 years old	19,526	18,936	880	1,291	2,138	4,561	4,138	3,281	1,860	787	25,996
35 to 44 years old	22,054	21,456	887	1,374	1,554	3,446	3,978	4,434	3,555	2,228	32,851
45 to 54 years old	16,598	16,203	599	924	1,044	2,290	2,438	3,366	3,261	2,281	37,624
55 to 64 years old	10,673	10,361	516	917	1,061	1,671	1,558	1,827	1,391	1,419	31,151
65 yr. old and over . . .	13,524	13,308	495	2,124	2,916	3,504	1,678	1,153	780	659	17,768
Northeast.	19,341	17,953	1,663	1,788	1,917	3,163	2,515	2,883	2,340	1,683	26,378
Midwest.	23,265	22,086	2,041	2,024	2,301	4,059	3,842	3,646	2,612	1,561	26,285
South.	35,610	32,950	2,898	3,547	3,880	6,752	5,434	4,748	3,402	2,289	23,896
West.	22,907	21,179	1,977	2,239	2,597	3,826	2,949	3,089	2,584	1,918	24,832
White	85,219	80,400	6,903	7,527	8,979	14,962	12,678	12,602	9,829	6,921	26,115
Black . . [2]	11,283	9,671	1,254	1,605	1,264	2,062	1,459	1,176	635	216	18,096
Hispanic [2]	10,944	9,585	1,069	1,490	1,824	2,338	1,237	890	487	250	16,216
Education attainment of householder: [3]											
Total	82,376	80,263	3,377	6,629	8,712	15,471	13,790	14,060	10,848	7,375	28,919
Less than 9th grade. . .	6,159	5,839	495	1,633	1,439	1,356	492	271	83	69	12,157
9th to 12th grade [4] . . .	8,018	7,601	623	1,229	1,479	2,020	1,137	697	289	126	16,818
High school graduate [5] .	26,575	25,777	1,147	1,994	3,139	6,277	5,273	4,729	2,443	774	25,453
Some college, no degree	14,122	13,892	482	832	1,366	2,684	2,776	2,840	1,994	917	30,536
Associate degree	5,670	5,591	191	295	424	978	1,081	1,310	945	367	32,930
Bachelor's degree or more	21,832	21,563	438	646	865	2,155	3,031	4,214	5,093	5,122	47,126
Bachelor's degree . .	14,090	13,900	338	467	650	1,647	2,288	2,830	3,244	2,436	41,949
Master's degree. . . .	4,640	4,583	62	115	138	359	491	936	1,241	1,242	52,530
Professional degree	1,749	1,741	18	50	45	80	156	245	292	855	72,274
Doctorate degree . . .	1,353	1,338	20	13	33	69	96	202	316	588	68,643
FEMALE											
Total	108,168	97,447	18,456	19,077	14,123	19,472	11,813	8,207	4,351	1,947	13,703
15 to 24 years old	18,333	13,626	5,705	3,331	1,918	1,856	530	179	90	17	6,342
25 to 34 years old	19,828	18,081	3,005	2,345	2,407	4,573	3,054	1,708	717	273	17,647
35 to 44 years old	22,407	20,809	3,364	2,657	2,606	4,426	3,246	2,653	1,276	583	18,706
45 to 54 years old	17,459	16,231	2,248	1,909	1,924	3,554	2,537	2,176	1,312	570	20,534
55 to 64 years old	11,582	10,607	1,930	2,048	1,476	2,072	1,341	870	593	277	14,376
65 yr. old and over . . .	18,558	18,093	2,205	6,786	3,792	2,992	1,106	621	363	228	10,062
Northeast.	21,285	19,283	3,412	3,808	2,717	3,469	2,526	1,838	1,033	480	14,333
Midwest.	25,167	23,417	4,435	4,491	3,389	4,954	2,800	1,970	1,019	359	13,899
South.	38,347	34,154	6,602	7,101	4,931	7,158	3,972	2,547	1,257	585	13,036
West.	23,368	20,592	4,008	3,677	3,085	3,891	2,514	1,852	1,041	523	14,002
White	89,489	81,352	15,500	15,597	11,890	16,060	9,898	6,950	3,727	1,730	13,792
Black	13,715	11,961	2,046	2,779	1,661	2,697	1,407	858	414	99	13,048
Hispanic [2]	10,485	8,055	1,959	1,976	1,384	1,415	668	441	152	61	10,260
Education attainment of householder: [3]											
Total	89,835	83,821	12,752	15,746	12,205	17,616	11,283	8,028	4,260	1,930	15,573
Less than 9th grade. . .	6,623	5,647	1,241	2,549	1,089	555	134	42	26	12	7,505
9th to 12th grade [4] . . .	8,758	7,661	1,623	2,738	1,539	1,204	372	112	38	36	8,861
High school graduate [5] .	31,599	29,332	4,797	6,145	5,076	7,328	3,521	1,656	557	253	13,407
Some college, no degree.	15,516	14,667	2,190	2,103	2,215	3,629	2,324	1,405	602	209	17,153
Associate degree	7,198	6,914	804	755	834	1,715	1,339	959	397	110	21,073
Bachelor's degree or more	20,142	19,590	2,097	1,457	1,452	3,186	3,593	3,855	2,641	1,310	29,781
Bachelor's degree . .	14,215	13,787	1,701	1,172	1,089	2,534	2,643	2,511	1,464	673	26,401
Master's degree. . . .	4,592	4,488	293	229	303	526	816	1,064	918	339	35,882
Professional degree	820	807	70	28	47	95	85	154	120	209	45,199
Doctorate degree . . .	515	508	34	27	14	31	49	127	138	90	46,545

[1] Includes persons with income deficit. [2] Persons of Hispanic origin may be of any race. [3] Persons 25 years old and over.
[4] No diploma attained. [5] Includes high school equivalency.

Source: U.S. Census Bureau, *Current Population Reports*, P60-200.

No. 757. Median Income of Persons With Income in Constant (1997) Dollars, by Sex, Race, and Hispanic Origin: 1980 to 1997

[Persons as of **March of following year**. Persons 15 years old and over. Constant dollars based on CPI-U-X1 deflator]

Item	Male					Female				
	1980	1990	1995	1996	1997	1980	1990	1995	1996	1997
NUMBER WITH INCOME (1,000)										
All races	78,661	88,220	92,066	93,439	94,168	80,826	92,245	96,007	96,558	97,447
White	69,420	76,480	79,022	80,041	80,400	70,573	78,566	80,608	80,741	81,352
Black	7,387	8,820	9,339	9,410	9,671	8,596	10,687	11,607	11,817	11,961
Asian and Pacific Islander	(NA)	2,235	3,095	3,277	3,330	(NA)	2,333	3,025	3,226	3,415
Hispanic [1]	3,996	6,767	8,577	9,305	9,585	3,617	5,903	7,478	7,744	8,055
White, not Hispanic origin	65,564	69,987	70,754	71,084	71,150	67,084	72,939	73,506	73,445	73,709
MEDIAN INCOME IN CONSTANT (1997) DOLLARS										
All races	24,436	24,920	23,761	24,381	25,212	9,595	12,366	12,775	13,109	13,703
White	25,992	25,997	25,165	25,521	26,115	9,648	12,669	12,971	13,258	13,792
Black	15,619	15,802	16,857	16,869	18,096	8,932	10,227	11,544	12,042	13,048
Asian and Pacific Islander	(NA)	23,816	23,340	23,190	25,046	(NA)	13,614	13,546	14,970	14,312
Hispanic [1]	18,837	16,541	15,629	15,791	16,216	8,591	9,249	9,403	9,702	10,260
White, not Hispanic origin	26,680	26,964	26,835	26,893	27,559	9,712	12,993	13,488	13,824	14,389

NA Not available.   [1] Persons of Hispanic origin may be of any race.

No. 758. Average Earnings of Year-Round, Full-Time Workers, by Educational Attainment: 1997

[In dollars. For persons 18 years old and over as of March 1998]

Age and sex	All workers	Less than 9th grade	High school		College		
			9th to 12th grade (no diploma)	High school graduate (includes equivalency)	Some college, no degree	Associate degree	Bachelor's degree or more
Male, total	43,709	22,746	27,638	32,611	39,367	40,465	66,393
18 to 24 years old	20,294	13,377	15,576	19,470	21,945	23,297	28,498
25 to 34 years old	34,807	17,714	24,517	28,772	32,354	34,670	48,688
35 to 44 years old	45,780	24,304	26,285	34,790	40,919	42,968	67,652
45 to 54 years old	52,429	23,261	35,163	38,340	45,568	44,431	74,985
55 to 64 years old	55,702	28,510	36,561	38,179	55,987	44,129	86,816
65 years old and over	51,148	33,425	32,911	30,549	54,905	(B)	68,470
Female, total	29,261	14,957	18,594	22,656	26,562	29,776	41,626
18 to 24 years old	17,510	(B)	13,915	15,727	15,506	19,894	26,297
25 to 34 years old	27,805	13,526	18,814	21,289	24,127	25,431	37,321
35 to 44 years old	31,273	13,820	19,409	23,011	28,561	31,090	46,154
45 to 54 years old	32,524	15,419	18,430	24,624	31,350	35,932	45,105
55 to 64 years old	28,876	16,826	19,317	25,243	29,535	30,773	40,203
65 years old and over	27,567	(B)	(B)	22,523	27,596	(B)	36,825

B Base figure too small to meet statistical standards for reliability of derived figure.

No. 759. Per Capita Money Income in Current and Constant (1997) Dollars, by Race and Hispanic Origin: 1970 to 1997

[In dollars. Constant dollars based on CPI-U-X1 deflator. As of March of following year]

Year	Current dollars					Constant (1997) dollars				
	All races [1]	White	Black	Asian, Pacific Islander	His-panic [2]	All races [1]	White	Black	Asian, Pacific Islander	His-panic [2]
1970	3,177	3,354	1,869	(NA)	(NA)	12,346	13,034	7,263	(NA)	(NA)
1980	7,787	8,233	4,804	(NA)	4,865	15,186	16,056	9,369	(NA)	9,488
1985 [3]	11,013	11,671	6,840	(NA)	6,613	16,427	17,409	10,203	(NA)	9,864
1990	14,387	15,265	9,017	(NA)	8,424	17,667	18,745	11,073	(NA)	10,345
1991	14,617	15,510	9,170	(NA)	8,662	17,225	18,277	10,806	(NA)	10,207
1992 [4]	14,847	15,785	9,239	15,691	8,591	16,985	18,058	10,569	(NA)	9,828
1993	15,777	16,800	9,863	15,691	8,830	17,524	18,660	10,955	17,428	9,808
1994	16,555	17,611	10,650	16,902	9,435	17,929	19,073	11,534	18,305	10,218
1995	17,227	18,304	10,982	16,567	9,300	18,143	19,277	11,566	17,448	9,794
1996	18,136	19,181	11,899	17,921	10,048	18,552	19,621	12,172	18,332	10,279
1997	19,241	20,425	12,351	18,226	10,773	19,241	20,425	12,351	18,226	10,773

NA Not available.   [1] Includes other races not shown separately.   [2] Persons of Hispanic origin may be of any race.   [3] Beginning 1985, data based on revised Hispanic population controls.   [4] Based on 1990 population controls.

Source of Tables 757-759: U.S. Census Bureau, *Current Population Reports*, P60-200; and Internet site, <http://www.census.gov/hhes/income/histinc/index.html> (accessed 15 March 1999).

No. 760. Persons Below Poverty Level and Below 125 Percent of Poverty Level: 1960 to 1997

[Persons as of **March of the following year**. Based on Current Population Survey; see text, Section 1, Population, and text, this section, and Appendix III]

Year	Number below poverty level (1,000)					Percent below poverty level					Below 125 percent of poverty level	
	All races [1]	White	Black	Asian and Pacific Islander	His-panic [2]	All races [1]	White	Black	Asian and Pacific Islander	His-panic [2]	Number (1,000)	Percent of total popula-tion
1960	39,851	28,309	(NA)	(NA)	(NA)	22.2	17.8	(NA)	(NA)	(NA)	54,560	30.4
1970	25,420	17,484	7,548	(NA)	(NA)	12.6	9.9	33.5	(NA)	(NA)	35,624	17.6
1975	25,877	17,770	7,545	(NA)	2,991	12.3	9.7	31.3	(NA)	23.0	37,182	17.6
1976	24,975	16,713	7,595	(NA)	2,783	11.8	9.1	31.1	(NA)	26.9	35,509	16.7
1977	24,720	16,416	7,726	(NA)	2,700	11.6	8.9	31.3	(NA)	24.7	35,659	16.7
1978	24,497	16,259	7,625	(NA)	2,607	11.4	8.7	30.6	(NA)	22.4	34,155	15.8
1979 [3] . . .	26,072	17,214	8,050	(NA)	2,921	11.7	9.0	31.0	(NA)	21.6	36,616	16.4
1980	29,272	19,699	8,579	(NA)	3,491	13.0	10.2	32.5	(NA)	21.8	40,658	18.1
1981	31,822	21,553	9,173	(NA)	3,713	14.0	11.1	34.2	(NA)	25.7	43,748	19.3
1982 [4] . . .	34,398	23,517	9,697	(NA)	4,301	15.0	12.0	35.6	(NA)	26.5	46,520	20.3
1983	35,303	23,984	9,882	(NA)	4,633	15.2	12.1	35.7	(NA)	29.9	47,150	20.3
1984	33,700	22,955	9,490	(NA)	4,806	14.4	11.5	33.8	(NA)	28.0	45,288	19.4
1985	33,064	22,860	8,926	(NA)	5,236	14.0	11.4	31.3	(NA)	28.4	44,166	18.7
1986 [5] . . .	32,370	22,183	8,983	(NA)	5,117	13.6	11.0	31.1	(NA)	29.0	43,486	18.2
1987	32,221	21,195	9,520	1,021	5,422	13.4	10.4	32.4	16.1	27.3	43,032	17.9
1988	31,745	20,715	9,356	1,117	5,357	13.0	10.1	31.3	17.3	28.0	42,551	17.5
1989	31,528	20,785	9,302	939	5,430	12.8	10.0	30.7	14.1	26.7	42,653	17.3
1990	33,585	22,326	9,837	858	6,006	13.5	10.7	31.9	12.2	26.2	44,837	18.0
1991 [6] . . .	35,708	23,747	10,242	996	6,339	14.2	11.3	32.7	13.8	28.1	47,527	18.9
1992	38,014	25,259	10,827	985	7,592	14.8	11.9	33.4	12.7	29.6	50,592	19.7
1993	39,265	26,226	10,877	1,134	8,126	15.1	12.2	33.1	15.3	30.6	51,801	20.0
1994	38,059	25,379	10,196	974	8,416	14.5	11.7	30.6	14.6	30.7	50,401	19.3
1995	36,425	24,423	9,872	1,411	8,574	13.8	11.2	29.3	14.6	30.3	48,761	18.5
1996	36,529	24,650	9,694	1,454	8,697	13.7	11.2	28.4	14.5	29.4	49,310	18.5
1997	35,574	24,396	9,116	1,468	8,308	13.3	11.0	26.5	14.0	27.1	47,853	17.8

NA Not available.   [1] Includes other races not shown separately.   [2] Persons of Hispanic origin may be of any race.
[3] Population controls based on 1980 census; see text, this section, and text, Section 1, Population.   [4] Beginning 1983, data based on revised Hispanic population controls and not directly comparable with prior years.   [5] Beginning 1987, data based on revised processing procedures and not directly comparable with prior years.   [6] Beginning 1992, based on 1990 population controls.
Source: U.S. Census Bureau, *Current Population Reports*, P60-201.

No. 761. Children Below Poverty Level, by Race and Hispanic Origin: 1960 to 1997

[Persons as of **March of the following year**. Covers only related children in families under 18 years old. Based on Current Population Survey; see text, Section 1, Population, and text, this section, and Appendix III]

Year	Number below poverty level (1,000)				Percent below poverty level			
	All races [1]	White	Black	Hispanic [2]	All races [1]	White	Black	Hispanic [2]
1960	17,288	11,229	(NA)	(NA)	26.5	20.0	(NA)	(NA)
1970	10,235	6,138	3,922	(NA)	14.9	10.5	41.5	(NA)
1980	11,114	6,817	3,906	1,718	17.9	13.4	42.1	33.0
1981	12,068	7,429	4,170	1,874	19.5	14.7	44.9	35.4
1982	13,139	8,282	4,388	2,117	21.3	16.5	47.3	38.9
1983 [3]	13,427	8,534	4,273	2,251	21.8	17.0	46.2	37.7
1984	12,929	8,086	4,320	2,317	21.0	16.1	46.2	38.7
1985	12,483	7,838	4,057	2,512	20.1	15.6	43.1	39.6
1986	12,257	7,714	4,037	2,413	19.8	15.3	42.7	37.1
1987 [4]	12,275	7,398	4,234	2,606	19.7	14.7	44.4	38.9
1988	11,935	7,095	4,148	2,576	19.0	14.0	42.8	37.3
1989	12,001	7,164	4,257	2,496	19.0	14.1	43.2	35.5
1990	12,715	7,696	4,412	2,750	19.9	15.1	44.2	37.7
1991	13,658	8,316	4,637	2,977	21.1	16.1	45.6	39.8
1992 [5]	14,521	8,752	5,015	3,440	21.6	16.5	46.3	39.0
1993	14,961	9,123	5,030	3,666	22.0	17.0	45.9	39.9
1994	14,610	8,826	4,787	3,956	21.2	16.3	43.3	41.1
1995	13,999	8,474	4,644	3,938	20.2	15.5	41.5	39.3
1996	13,764	8,488	4,411	4,090	19.8	15.5	39.5	39.9
1997	13,422	8,441	4,116	3,865	19.2	15.4	36.8	36.4

NA Not available.   [1] Includes other races not shown separately.   [2] Persons of Hispanic origin may be of any race.
[3] Beginning 1983, data based on revised Hispanic population controls and not directly comparable with prior years.   [4] Beginning 1987, data based on revised processing procedures and not directly comparable with prior years.   [5] Beginning 1992, based on 1990 population controls.
Source: U.S. Census Bureau, *Current Population Reports*, P60-201.

Income, Expenditures, and Wealth   483

No. 762. Weighted Average Poverty Thresholds: 1980 to 1997

[Official poverty thresholds; see text, this section]

Size of unit	1980[1]	1990	1991	1992	1993	1994	1995	1996	1997
One person (unrelated individual	$4,190	$6,652	$6,932	$7,143	$7,363	$7,547	$7,763	7,995	8,183
Under 65 years..............	4,290	6,800	7,086	7,299	$7,518	7,710	7,929	8,163	8,350
65 years and over...........	3,949	6,268	6,532	6,729	6,930	7,108	7,309	7,525	7,698
Two persons	5,363	8,509	8,865	9,137	9,414	9,661	9,933	10,233	10,473
Householder under 65 years	5,537	8,794	9,165	9,443	9,728	9,976	10,259	10,564	10,805
Householder 65 years and over ...	4,983	7,905	8,241	8,487	8,740	8,967	9,219	9,491	9,712
Three persons	6,565	10,419	10,860	11,186	11,522	11,821	12,158	12,516	12,802
Four persons	8,414	13,359	13,924	14,335	14,763	15,141	15,569	16,036	16,400
Five persons	9,966	15,792	16,456	16,952	17,449	17,900	18,408	18,952	19,380
Six persons	11,269	17,839	18,587	19,137	19,718	20,235	20,804	21,389	21,886
Seven persons................	12,761	20,241	21,058	21,594	22,383	22,923	23,552	24,268	24,802
Eight persons................	14,199	22,582	23,582	24,053	24,838	25,427	26,237	27,091	27,593
Nine or more persons	16,896	26,848	27,942	28,745	29,529	30,300	31,280	31,971	32,566

[1] Poverty levels for nonfarm families.

Source: U.S. Census Bureau, *Current Population Reports*, P60-201; and <http://www.census.gov/hhes/poverty/histpov/hstpov1.html> (accessed 15 March 1999).

No. 763. Persons Below Poverty Level, by Selected Characteristics: 1997

[Persons as of **March 1998.** Based on Current Population Survey; see text, Section 1, Population, and text, this section, and Appendix III. For composition of regions, see map, inside front cover]

Age and region	Number below poverty level (1,000)				Percent below poverty level			
	All races [1]	White	Black	Hispanic [2]	All races [1]	White	Black	Hispanic [2]
Total	35,574	24,396	9,116	8,308	13.3	11.0	26.5	27.1
Under 18 years old.....	14,113	8,990	4,225	3,972	19.9	16.1	37.2	36.8
18 to 24 years old	4,416	3,131	1,041	979	17.5	15.5	28.0	25.8
25 to 34 years old	4,759	3,327	1,106	1,201	12.1	10.5	20.9	21.9
35 to 44 years old	4,251	2,928	1,063	992	9.6	8.0	19.3	21.5
45 to 54 years old	2,439	1,817	489	427	7.2	6.3	13.3	15.8
55 to 59 years old	1,092	778	270	191	9.0	7.4	22.2	20.5
60 to 64 years old	1,127	857	222	161	11.2	9.9	22.1	22.9
65 years old and over...	3,376	2,569	700	384	10.5	9.0	26.0	23.8
65 to 74 years old....	1,641	1,198	383	214	9.2	7.6	23.8	21.1
75 years old and over .	1,735	1,370	316	170	12.2	10.7	29.3	28.2
Northeast	6,474	4,373	1,788	1,533	12.6	10.2	28.5	31.8
Midwest	6,493	4,546	1,696	532	10.4	8.3	27.4	23.4
South..............	13,748	8,473	4,895	2,500	14.6	11.7	25.7	25.3
West	8,858	7,004	738	3,744	14.6	13.8	24.9	27.4

[1] Includes other races not shown separately. [2] Persons of Hispanic origin may be of any race.

Source: U.S. Census Bureau, *Current Population Reports*, P60-201; and unpublished data.

No. 764. Persons 65 Years Old and Over Below Poverty Level: 1980 to 1997

[Persons as of **March of following year.** Based on the Current Population Survey, see text, Section 1, Population, and text, this section, and Appendix III]

Characteristic	Number below poverty level (1,000)					Percent below poverty level				
	1980	1990	1995	1996	1997	1980	1990	1995	1996	1997
Total	3,871	3,658	3,318	3,428	3,376	15.7	12.2	10.5	10.8	10.5
White	3,042	2,707	2,572	2,667	2,569	13.6	10.1	9.0	9.4	9.0
Black	783	860	629	661	700	38.1	33.8	25.4	25.3	26.0
Asian and Pacific Islander.	(NA)	62	89	63	87	(NA)	12.1	14.3	9.7	12.3
Hispanic [1]	179	245	342	370	384	30.8	22.5	23.5	24.4	23.8
In families	(NA)	1,172	1,058	1,190	1,143	(NA)	5.8	5.0	5.6	5.3
Unrelated individuals	(NA)	2,479	2,260	2,237	2,233	(NA)	24.7	21.4	20.9	21.0

NA Not available.   [1] Persons of Hispanic origin may be of any race.

Source: U.S. Census Bureau, *Current Population Reports*, P60-201; and earlier reports.

No. 765. Persons Below Poverty Level, by State: 1980 to 1997

[Based on the Current Population Survey; see text, Section 1, Population, and text, this section, and Appendix III. The CPS is designed to collect reliable data on income primarily at the national level and secondarily at the regional level. When the income data are tabulated by state, the estimates are considered less reliable and, therefore, particular caution should be used when trying to interpret the results; for additional detail, see source]

State	Number below poverty level (1,000)					Percent below poverty level				
	1980	1990 [1]	1995	1996	1997	1980	1990 [1]	1995	1996	1997
United States	29,272	33,585	36,425	36,529	35,574	13.0	13.5	13.8	13.7	13.3
Alabama.	810	779	882	595	665	21.2	19.2	20.1	14.0	15.7
Alaska.	36	57	45	54	56	9.6	11.4	7.1	8.2	8.8
Arizona.	354	484	700	980	797	12.8	13.7	16.1	20.5	17.2
Arkansas	484	472	376	449	515	21.5	19.6	14.9	17.2	19.7
California	2,619	4,128	5,342	5,472	5,459	11.0	13.9	16.7	16.9	16.6
Colorado.	247	461	335	412	320	8.6	13.7	8.8	10.6	8.2
Connecticut.	255	196	318	392	282	8.3	6.0	9.7	11.7	8.6
Delaware	68	48	74	63	72	11.8	6.9	10.3	8.6	9.6
District of Columbia	131	120	122	130	113	20.9	21.1	22.2	24.1	21.8
Florida	1,692	1,896	2,321	2,037	2,056	16.7	14.4	16.2	14.2	14.3
Georgia	727	1,001	878	1,097	1,109	13.9	15.8	12.1	14.8	14.5
Hawaii	81	121	122	142	164	8.5	11.0	10.3	12.1	13.9
Idaho	138	157	167	140	183	14.7	14.9	14.5	11.9	14.7
Illinois	1,386	1,606	1,459	1,429	1,349	12.3	13.7	12.4	12.1	11.2
Indiana.	645	714	545	428	515	11.8	13.0	9.6	7.5	8.8
Iowa	311	289	352	279	270	10.8	10.4	12.2	9.6	9.6
Kansas.	215	259	273	287	250	9.4	10.3	10.8	11.2	9.7
Kentucky	701	628	572	658	623	19.3	17.3	14.7	17.0	15.9
Louisiana	868	952	849	873	691	20.3	23.6	19.7	20.5	16.3
Maine.	158	162	138	135	124	14.6	13.1	11.2	11.2	10.1
Maryland	389	468	520	522	422	9.5	9.9	10.1	10.3	8.4
Massachusetts.	542	626	665	622	732	9.5	10.7	11.0	10.1	12.2
Michigan.	1,194	1,315	1,174	1,068	1,006	12.9	14.3	12.2	11.2	10.3
Minnesota.	342	524	427	458	457	8.7	12.0	9.2	9.8	9.6
Mississippi	591	684	630	575	455	24.3	25.7	23.5	20.6	16.7
Missouri	625	700	484	500	627	13.0	13.4	9.4	9.5	11.8
Montana	102	134	133	155	139	13.2	16.3	15.3	17.0	15.6
Nebraska	199	167	159	169	163	13.0	10.3	9.6	10.2	9.8
Nevada	70	119	173	133	190	8.3	9.8	11.1	8.1	11.0
New Hampshire	63	68	60	73	109	7.0	6.3	5.3	6.4	9.1
New Jersey.	659	711	617	726	737	9.0	9.2	7.8	9.2	9.3
New Mexico	268	319	457	472	387	20.6	20.9	25.3	25.5	21.2
New York	2,391	2,571	3,020	3,058	2,979	13.8	14.3	16.5	16.7	16.5
North Carolina	877	829	877	885	839	15.0	13.0	12.6	12.2	11.4
North Dakota.	99	87	76	69	87	15.5	13.7	12.0	11.0	13.6
Ohio	1,046	1,256	1,285	1,424	1,231	9.8	11.5	11.5	12.7	11.0
Oklahoma.	406	481	548	556	456	13.9	15.6	17.1	16.6	13.7
Oregon.	309	267	360	382	382	11.5	9.2	11.2	11.8	11.6
Pennsylvania.	1,142	1,328	1,464	1,374	1,337	9.8	11.0	12.2	11.6	11.2
Rhode Island.	97	71	102	104	120	10.7	7.5	10.6	11.0	12.7
South Carolina.	534	548	744	482	500	16.8	16.2	19.9	13.0	13.1
South Dakota	127	93	103	82	117	18.8	13.3	14.5	11.8	16.5
Tennessee	884	833	846	878	791	19.6	16.9	15.5	15.9	14.3
Texas.	2,247	2,684	3,270	3,180	3,297	15.7	15.9	17.4	16.6	16.7
Utah	148	143	168	153	185	10.0	8.2	8.4	7.7	8.9
Vermont	62	61	61	74	54	12.0	10.9	10.3	12.6	9.3
Virginia.	647	705	648	795	858	12.4	11.1	10.2	12.3	12.7
Washington.	538	434	677	666	529	12.7	8.9	12.5	11.9	9.2
West Virginia.	297	328	300	323	286	15.2	18.1	16.7	18.5	16.4
Wisconsin	403	448	449	460	422	8.5	9.3	8.5	8.8	8.2
Wyoming	49	51	59	58	66	10.4	11.0	12.2	11.9	13.5

[1] Beginning 1990, data based on revised processing procedures and not directly comparable with prior years.

Source: U.S. Census Bureau, *Current Population Reports*, P60-201, and <http://www.census.gov/hhes/poverty/histpov/hstpov21.html> (accessed 15 March 1999).

U.S. Census Bureau, Statistical Abstract of the United States: 1999

No. 766. Persons Below Poverty Level, by Race and Family Status: 1990 to 1997

Race and family status	Number below poverty level (mil.)					Percent below poverty level				
	1990	1994	1995	1996	1997	1990	1994	1995	1996	1997
All persons [1]	**33.6**	**38.1**	**36.4**	**36.5**	**35.6**	**13.5**	**14.5**	**13.8**	**13.7**	**13.3**
In families	25.2	29.0	27.5	27.4	26.2	12.0	13.1	12.3	12.2	11.6
Householder	7.1	8.1	7.5	7.7	7.3	10.7	11.6	10.8	11.0	10.3
Related children under 18 years .	12.7	14.6	14.0	13.8	13.4	19.9	21.2	20.2	19.8	19.2
Unrelated individuals	7.4	8.3	8.2	8.5	8.7	20.7	21.5	20.9	20.8	20.8
Male	2.9	3.3	3.4	3.3	3.4	16.9	17.8	18.0	17.0	17.4
Female	4.6	5.0	4.9	5.1	5.2	24.0	24.9	23.5	24.2	24.0
In families with female householder, no spouse present. .	12.6	14.4	14.2	13.8	13.5	37.2	38.6	36.5	35.8	35.1
Householder	3.8	4.2	4.1	4.2	4.0	33.4	34.6	32.4	32.6	31.6
Related children under 18 years.	7.4	8.4	8.4	8.0	7.9	53.4	52.9	50.3	49.3	49.0
White [1]	**22.3**	**25.4**	**24.4**	**24.7**	**24.4**	**10.7**	**11.7**	**11.2**	**11.2**	**11.0**
In families	15.9	18.5	17.6	17.6	17.3	9.0	10.1	9.6	9.6	9.3
Householder	4.6	5.3	5.0	5.1	5.0	8.1	9.1	8.5	8.6	8.4
Related children under 18 years.	7.7	8.8	8.5	8.5	8.4	15.1	16.3	15.5	15.5	15.4
Unrelated individuals	5.7	6.3	6.3	6.5	6.6	18.6	19.3	19.0	18.9	18.9
Black [1]	**9.8**	**10.2**	**9.9**	**9.7**	**9.1**	**31.9**	**30.6**	**29.3**	**28.4**	**26.5**
In families	8.2	8.4	8.2	8.0	7.4	31.0	29.6	28.5	27.6	25.5
Householder	2.2	2.2	2.1	2.2	2.0	29.3	27.3	26.4	26.1	23.6
Related children under 18 years.	4.4	4.8	4.6	4.4	4.1	44.2	43.3	41.5	39.5	36.8
Unrelated individuals	1.5	1.6	1.6	1.6	1.6	35.1	34.8	32.6	32.2	31.0

[1] Includes other races and members of unrelated subfamilies not shown separately.

Source: U.S. Census Bureau, *Current Population Reports*, P60-201; and earlier reports.

No. 767. Monthly Measures of Poverty Status, by Selected Characteristics: 1993-94 Period

[Covers 2-year calendar period. Based on Survey of Income and Program Participation, see text, this section]

Characteristic	Persons poor in an average month of 1994		Persons poor 2 or more months of 1994		Persons poor all 24 months of 1993-94		Median duration of poverty spells (months)
	Number (1,000)	Percent	Number (1,000)	Percent	Number (1,000)	Percent	
Total [1]	**40,009**	**15.4**	**54,800**	**21.4**	**13,105**	**5.3**	**4.5**
Under 18 years old	17,169	24.5	22,529	32.4	6,489	9.4	5.3
18 to 64 years old	19,652	12.3	28,317	18.1	5,156	3.4	4.0
65 years old and over	3,188	10.2	3,954	13.5	1,459	5.4	6.7
White	27,543	12.7	38,861	18.3	7,793	3.8	4.2
Black	10,304	31.2	13,059	40.2	4,461	14.1	6.8
Hispanic origin [2]	8,555	31.4	10,940	41.8	3,262	13.5	5.0
Region: [3]							
Northeast	7,303	14.1	9,892	19.3	2,822	5.5	4.4
Midwest	8,740	13.2	12,069	18.4	2,571	4.0	3.9
South	14,701	16.8	20,044	23.3	5,085	6.1	5.6
West	9,265	16.8	12,795	24.3	2,628	5.2	4.4
Educational attainment: [4]							
Less than 4 years of high school . . .	9,507	24.8	12,221	33.0	3,736	10.5	6.4
High school graduate, no college . . .	8,263	11.6	11,973	17.3	2,120	3.1	4.0
One or more years of college	5,071	6.3	8,077	10.1	759	1.0	3.7
Disability status: [5]							
With a work disability	7,059	21.6	8,991	29.8	2,519	8.6	5.8
With no work disability	15,539	10.5	23,445	15.9	3,444	2.4	4.0

[1] Includes other characteristics not shown separately. [2] Persons of Hispanic origin may be of any race. [3] For composition of regions, see map, inside front cover. [4] Persons 18 years old and over. [5] Persons 15 to 69 years old.

Source: U.S. Census Bureau, unpublished data from the Survey of Income and Program Participation.

No. 768. Families Below Poverty Level and Below 125 Percent of Poverty Level: 1960 to 1997

[Families as of **March of the following year.** Based on Current Population Survey, see text, Section 1, Population, and text, this section, and Appendix III]

Year	Number below poverty level (1,000)				Percent below poverty level				Below 125 percent of poverty level	
	All races [1]	White	Black	His-panic [2]	All races [1]	White	Black	His-panic [2]	Number (1,000)	Percent
1960	8,243	6,115	(NA)	(NA)	18.1	14.9	(NA)	(NA)	11,525	25.4
1970	5,260	3,708	1,481	(NA)	10.1	8.0	29.5	(NA)	7,516	14.4
1975	5,450	3,838	1,513	627	9.7	7.7	27.1	25.1	7,974	14.2
1976	5,311	3,560	1,617	598	9.4	7.1	27.9	23.1	7,647	13.5
1977	5,311	3,540	1,637	591	9.3	7.0	28.2	21.4	7,713	13.5
1978 [3]	5,280	3,523	1,622	559	9.1	6.9	27.5	20.4	7,417	12.8
1979 [3]	5,461	3,581	1,722	614	9.2	6.9	27.8	20.3	7,784	13.1
1980	6,217	4,195	1,826	751	10.3	8.0	28.9	23.2	8,764	14.5
1981	6,851	4,670	1,972	792	11.2	8.8	30.8	24.0	9,568	15.7
1982	7,512	5,118	2,158	916	12.2	9.6	33.0	27.2	10,279	16.7
1983 [4]	7,647	5,220	2,161	981	12.3	9.7	32.3	25.9	10,358	16.7
1984	7,277	4,925	2,094	991	11.6	9.1	30.9	25.2	9,901	15.8
1985	7,223	4,983	1,983	1,074	11.4	9.1	28.7	25.5	9,753	15.3
1986	7,023	4,811	1,987	1,085	10.9	8.6	28.0	24.7	9,476	14.7
1987 [5]	7,005	4,567	2,117	1,168	10.7	8.1	29.4	25.5	9,338	14.3
1988	6,874	4,471	2,089	1,141	10.4	7.9	28.2	23.7	9,284	14.1
1989	6,784	4,409	2,077	1,133	10.3	7.8	27.8	23.4	9,267	14.0
1990	7,098	4,622	2,193	1,244	10.7	8.1	29.3	25.0	9,564	14.4
1991	7,712	5,022	2,343	1,372	11.5	8.8	30.4	26.5	10,244	15.3
1992 [6]	8,144	5,255	2,484	1,529	11.9	9.1	31.1	26.7	10,959	16.1
1993	8,393	5,452	2,499	1,625	12.3	9.4	31.3	27.3	11,203	16.4
1994	8,053	5,312	2,212	1,724	11.6	9.1	27.3	27.8	10,771	15.5
1995	7,532	4,994	2,127	1,695	10.8	8.5	26.4	27.0	10,223	14.7
1996	7,708	5,059	2,206	1,748	11.0	8.6	26.1	26.4	10,476	14.9
1997	7,324	4,990	1,985	1,721	10.3	8.4	23.6	24.7	10,032	14.2

NA Not available. [1] Includes other races not shown separately. [2] Persons of Hispanic origin may be of any race. [3] Population controls based on 1980 census; see text, this section. [4] Beginning 1983, data based on revised Hispanic population controls and not directly comparable with prior years. [5] Beginning 1987, data based on revised processing procedures and not directly comparable with prior years. [6] Beginning 1992, based on 1990 population controls.

Source: U.S. Census Bureau, *Current Population Reports,* P60-201.

No. 769. Families Below Poverty Level, by Selected Characteristics: 1997

Characteristic	Number below poverty level (1,000)				Percent below poverty level			
	All races [1]	White	Black	His-panic [2]	All races [1]	White	Black	His-panic [2]
Total	7,324	4,990	1,985	1,721	10.3	8.4	23.6	24.7
Age of householder:								
15 to 24 years old.	897	580	299	213	31.0	26.5	49.6	35.8
25 to 34 years old.	2,204	1,496	603	540	16.2	13.6	29.4	27.8
35 to 44 years old.	1,982	1,323	557	522	10.5	8.5	23.7	26.1
45 to 54 years old.	849	620	176	208	5.8	5.0	11.1	17.8
55 to 64 years old.	658	485	138	121	7.0	6.0	16.0	17.9
65 years old and over	678	457	193	99	6.0	4.5	21.1	18.1
Education of householder: [3]								
No high school diploma	2,713	1,903	674	993	24.1	21.0	37.9	35.1
High school diploma, no college	2,179	1,454	636	285	9.9	7.8	22.8	17.7
Some college, less than Bachelor's degree . .	1,136	785	301	160	6.6	5.4	14.1	13.1
Bachelor's degree or more	344	240	55	53	2.0	1.6	5.2	7.8
Work experience of householder:								
Total [4].	6,640	4,532	1,787	1,621	11.1	9.2	23.9	25.3
Worked during year.	3,864	2,677	1,011	940	7.5	6.2	16.4	17.9
Year-round, full-time.	1,279	944	273	422	3.3	2.9	6.3	11.2
Not year-round, full-time	2,584	1,734	738	518	21.1	17.5	35.4	35.4
Did not work	2,776	1,855	776	681	34.3	29.0	58.8	58.4

[1] Includes other races not shown separately. [2] Hispanic persons may be of any race. [3] Householder 25 years old and over. [4] Persons 16 years old and over.

Source: U.S. Census Bureau, *Current Population Reports,* P60-201.

Income, Expenditures, and Wealth 487

[Persons as of **March 1998**. For explanation of income definitions, see text, this section]

Definition number	Definition	Number below poverty level (1,000)				Percent below poverty level			
		All races[1]	White	Black	His-panic[2]	All races[1]	White	Black	His-panic[2]
	All persons	268,480	221,200	34,458	30,637	(X)	(X)	(X)	(X)
	INCOME BEFORE TAXES								
1	Money income excluding capital gains[3]	35,574	24,396	9,116	8,308	13.3	11.0	26.5	27.1
2	Definition 1 less government money transfers	56,390	41,794	12,027	9,894	21.0	18.9	34.9	32.3
3	Definition 2 plus capital gains	56,161	41,620	11,977	9,855	20.9	18.8	34.8	32.2
4	Definition 3 plus health insurance supplements to wage or salary income[4]	54,573	40,500	11,600	9,472	20.3	18.3	33.7	30.9
	INCOME AFTER TAXES								
5	Definition 4 less Social Security payroll taxes	57,138	42,315	12,194	10,103	21.3	17.7	35.4	33.0
6	Definition 5 less Federal income taxes (excluding EITC)[5]	57,520	42,582	12,276	10,202	21.4	17.8	35.6	33.3
7	Definition 6 plus EITC[5]	53,601	39,800	11,337	9,038	20.0	16.7	32.9	29.5
8	Definition 7 less state income taxes	54,036	40,132	11,398	9,076	20.1	16.8	33.1	29.6
9	Definition 8 plus nonmeans-tested government cash transfers[6]	35,849	24,266	9,418	7,950	13.4	10.3	27.3	25.9
10	Definition 9 plus value of Medicare	34,748	23,503	9,120	7,801	12.9	10.6	26.5	25.5
11	Definition 10 plus value of regular-price school lunches	34,748	23,503	9,120	7,801	12.9	10.6	26.5	25.5
12	Definition 11 plus means-tested government cash transfers[7]	32,113	21,901	8,267	7,336	12.0	9.9	24.0	23.9
13	Definition 12 plus value of Medicaid	30,119	20,624	7,719	6,803	11.2	9.3	22.4	22.2
14	Definition 13 plus means-tested government noncash transfers[8]	26,940	18,680	6,648	6,018	10.0	8.4	19.3	19.6
15	Definition 14 plus net imputed return on equity in own home[9]	24,659	16,902	6,200	5,676	9.2	7.6	18.0	18.5

X Not applicable.   [1] Includes other races not shown separately.   [2] Persons of Hispanic origin may be of any race.   [3] Official definition based on income before taxes and includes government cash transfers.   [4] Employer contributions to the health insurance plans of employees.   [5] Earned Income Tax Credit.   [6] Includes social security and railroad retirement, veterans payments, unemployment and workers' compensation, Black Lung payments, Pell Grants, and other government educational assistance.   [7] Includes AFDC and other public assistance or welfare payments, Supplemental Security Income, and veterans payments. Households must meet certain eligibility requirements in order to qualify for these benefits.   [8] Includes medicaid, food stamps, subsidies from free or reduced-price school lunches, and rent subsidies.   [9] Estimated amount of income a household would receive if it chose to shift amount held as home equity into an interest bearing account.

Source: U.S. Census Bureau, *Current Population Reports*, P60-201; and unpublished data.

No. 771. Family Net Worth—Mean and Median Net Worth in Constant (1995) Dollars, by Selected Family Characteristics: 1989 to 1995

[**Net worth in thousands of constant (1995) dollars (225.9 represents $225,900)**. Constant dollar figures are based on consumer price index for all urban consumers published by U.S. Bureau of Labor Statistics. Families include one-person units and as used in this table are comparable to the U.S. Census Bureau household concept. Based on Survey of Consumer Finance; see Appendix III. For definition of median, see Guide to Tabular Presentation]

Family characteristic	1989			1992			1995		
	Percent of families	Net worth		Percent of families	Net worth		Percent of families	Net worth	
		Mean	Median		Mean	Median		Mean	Median
All families	100.0	225.9	57.0	100.0	201.1	52.9	100.0	208.1	55.6
Age of family head:									
Under 35 years old	28.1	58.0	9.5	25.8	50.4	10.1	24.8	42.0	10.7
35 to 44 years old	21.5	180.2	67.6	22.8	144.8	46.3	23.0	141.5	51.0
45 to 54 years old	15.1	330.8	114.7	16.2	287.9	84.2	17.9	290.0	90.6
55 to 64 years old	13.9	373.1	118.7	13.2	362.0	122.9	12.5	372.4	111.3
65 to 74 years old	12.5	341.0	93.6	12.6	308.9	105.8	12.0	344.9	106.9
75 years old and over	8.9	296.2	89.2	9.4	231.3	93.2	9.8	257.2	92.3
Family income in constant (1995) dollars:[1]									
Less than $10,000	15.5	29.0	1.6	15.5	30.8	3.3	16.1	43.6	4.7
$10,000 to $24,999	24.5	70.0	24.0	27.7	69.8	27.6	26.9	77.2	30.0
$25,000 to $49,999	29.8	127.3	56.0	29.6	125.0	55.1	30.6	117.7	53.4
$50,000 to $99,999	22.0	247.2	129.5	20.1	241.3	122.9	19.8	256.0	121.1
$100,000 and more	8.3	1,350.4	547.1	7.1	1,284.2	498.7	6.5	1,435.3	482.0
Education of householder:									
No high school diploma	24.3	99.1	28.5	20.4	76.2	21.3	18.5	83.2	22.7
High school diploma	32.2	135.8	45.0	29.9	120.9	41.4	31.7	128.9	50.7
Some college	15.6	226.9	56.5	17.8	186.0	63.2	19.1	184.9	45.2
College degree	27.8	440.6	136.0	31.9	364.3	103.1	30.7	379.4	102.6
Tenure:									
Owner occupied	63.9	326.8	122.0	63.9	290.3	106.5	64.7	297.9	101.4
Renter occupied or other	36.1	47.5	2.3	63.1	43.0	3.6	35.3	43.5	4.5

[1] Income for year preceding the survey.

Source: Board of Governors of the Federal Reserve System, *Federal Reserve Bulletin*, January 1997, and unpublished revisions. Results from the 1998 survey are expected to be released around the end of 1999.

No. 772. Nonfinancial Assets Held by Families, by Type of Asset: 1995

[Median value in thousands of dollars (82.8 represents $82,800). Constant dollar figures are based on consumer price index for all urban consumers published by U.S. Bureau of Labor Statistics. Families include one-person units and, as used in this table, are comparable to the U.S. Census Bureau household concept. For definition of family, see text, Section 1, Population. Based on Survey of Consumer Finance; see Appendix III. For data on financial assets, see Table 801. For definition of median, see Guide to Tabular Presentation]

Age of family head, and family income	Total	Vehicles	Primary residence	Investment real estate	Business	Other non-financial
PERCENT OF FAMILIES OWNING ASSET						
All families, total	**91.1**	**84.2**	**64.7**	**18.0**	**11.1**	**9.0**
Age of family head:						
Under 35 years old	87.4	84.1	37.9	7.0	8.4	7.3
35 to 44 years old	91.0	85.0	64.7	14.7	14.4	10.1
45 to 54 years old	93.8	88.3	75.4	25.0	15.4	11.3
55 to 64 years old	94.1	88.4	82.3	27.3	12.6	10.2
65 to 74 years old	92.7	82.4	79.4	27.9	8.7	9.0
75 years old and over	89.9	72.2	72.5	16.3	3.8	5.6
Family income:						
Less than $10,000	68.6	56.6	37.5	7.2	4.8	3.7
$10,000 to $24,999	90.2	83.3	56.2	11.3	7.0	6.3
$25,000 to $49,999	96.8	92.3	68.0	16.6	9.8	9.7
$50,000 to $99,999	99.0	93.4	84.7	26.9	16.8	11.3
$100,000 and more	99.4	90.8	90.9	51.6	32.6	23.9
Current work status of householder:						
Professional, managerial	96.6	91.1	70.5	24.8	9.7	14.5
Technical, sales, clerical	93.0	88.0	63.4	11.4	6.4	10.9
Precision production	97.1	93.2	67.0	16.1	7.4	8.8
Machine operators and laborers	93.8	92.1	61.0	14.1	5.6	6.8
Service occupations	86.9	83.7	50.4	9.0	3.7	2.1
Self-employed	96.1	86.1	74.2	33.1	58.2	15.5
Retired	88.2	76.3	70.5	18.9	3.3	5.8
Other not working	67.3	59.7	35.3	8.5	4.1	6.0
Tenure:						
Owner occupied	100.0	90.8	100.0	22.8	13.7	10.5
Renter occupied or other	74.8	72.2	-	9.0	6.5	6.5
MEDIAN VALUE [1]						
All families, total	**82.8**	**9.9**	**89.0**	**50.0**	**45.0**	**8.8**
Age of family head:						
Under 35 years old	21.7	8.9	76.0	30.0	22.0	5.0
35 to 44 years old	95.9	10.7	95.0	47.0	35.0	10.0
45 to 54 years old	113.0	12.6	100.0	59.0	70.0	10.0
55 to 64 years old	108.0	11.3	85.0	75.0	65.0	10.0
65 to 74 years old	94.6	8.2	82.5	57.0	100.5	14.0
75 years old and over	79.0	5.3	80.0	22.4	37.5	8.0
Family income:						
Less than $10,000	14.0	3.6	38.5	16.2	50.0	5.2
$10,000 to $24,999	44.7	6.1	65.0	26.4	30.0	7.5
$25,000 to $49,999	81.9	11.0	80.0	45.0	25.0	5.8
$50,000 to $99,999	145.7	16.2	120.0	60.0	33.0	15.0
$100,000 and more	304.5	23.8	200.0	130.0	320.0	18.0
Current work status of householder:						
Professional, managerial	129.1	12.5	130.0	55.5	18.0	10.6
Technical, sales, clerical	82.5	10.3	90.0	44.5	24.0	9.0
Precision production	72.7	12.1	80.0	37.5	20.0	5.0
Machine operators and laborers	56.3	10.8	65.0	30.0	20.0	8.0
Service occupations	36.3	7.0	70.0	30.0	80.2	10.0
Self-employed	180.1	12.7	120.0	100.0	75.0	8.0
Retired	78.0	7.4	75.0	45.0	100.0	10.0
Other not working	22.0	6.4	60.0	50.0	21.0	7.0
Tenure:						
Owner occupied	115.8	11.9	89.0	50.0	55.0	10.0
Renter occupied or other	7.5	6.4	(B)	35.0	22.0	5.0

- Represents or rounds to zero.   B Base too small to meet statistical standards for reliability of derived figure.   [1] Median value of financial asset for families holding such assets.

Source: Board of Governors of the Federal Reserve System, *Federal Reserve Bulletin*, January 1997, and unpublished revisions. Results from the 1998 survey are expected to be released around the end of 1999.

Income, Expenditures, and Wealth   489

No. 773. Household and Nonprofit Organization Sector Balance Sheet: 1980 to 1998

[In billions of dollars (10,950 represents $10,950,000,000,000). As of **December 31**. For details of financial assets and liabilities, see Table 800]

Item	1980	1985	1990	1992	1993	1994	1995	1996	1997	1998
Assets [1]	10,950	16,684	24,308	27,214	28,574	29,529	32,540	35,224	39,111	43,037
Tangible assets [1]	4,366	6,535	9,324	9,731	9,980	10,316	10,789	11,316	12,091	12,916
Real estate	3,422	5,235	7,405	7,664	7,805	8,018	8,398	8,833	9,517	10,202
Consumer durable goods	918	1,265	1,866	2,005	2,108	2,226	2,317	2,406	2,492	2,630
Financial assets [1]	6,584	10,149	14,985	17,483	18,594	19,212	21,751	23,908	27,020	30,121
Deposits	1,517	2,484	3,265	3,250	3,183	3,157	3,365	3,538	3,790	4,089
Checkable deposits and currency	251	342	409	547	593	564	505	438	423	424
Time and savings deposits	1,203	1,941	2,477	2,349	2,236	2,224	2,388	2,556	2,725	2,882
Money market fund shares	62	193	365	339	338	351	449	508	600	746
Credit market instruments [1]	425	849	1,513	1,679	1,672	1,979	1,938	1,969	1,795	1,738
U.S. government securities	165	270	530	630	613	940	859	911	749	650
Treasury	160	242	405	486	505	689	594	567	382	310
Savings bonds	73	80	126	157	172	180	185	187	187	187
Corporate equities	894	1,107	1,778	2,896	3,191	2,990	3,995	4,528	5,333	6,280
Mutual fund shares	46	198	468	728	991	1,052	1,265	1,582	2,048	2,486
Pension fund reserves	971	2,087	3,497	4,367	4,828	5,057	5,821	6,568	7,681	8,770
Equity in noncorporate business	2,156	2,608	3,233	3,128	3,187	3,370	3,578	3,776	4,097	4,164
Liabilities	1,427	2,330	3,706	4,077	4,321	4,640	5,004	5,357	5,739	6,250
Credit market instruments	1,376	2,239	3,582	3,926	4,139	4,454	4,804	5,135	5,472	5,958
Home mortgages	906	1,411	2,489	2,797	2,923	3,097	3,275	3,498	3,737	4,106
Consumer credit	355	604	805	798	859	984	1,123	1,212	1,264	1,334
Net worth	9,523	14,355	20,602	23,137	24,253	24,889	27,536	29,867	33,372	36,787

[1] Includes types of assets and/or liabilities not shown separately.

Source: Board of Governors of the Federal Reserve System, *Balance Sheets for the U.S. Economy*.

No. 774. Net Stock of Fixed Reproducible Tangible Wealth: 1980 to 1997

[In billions of dollars (10,323 represents $10,323,000,000,000). As of **December 31**]

Item	1980	1985	1990	1991	1992	1993	1994	1995	1996	1997
CURRENT DOLLARS										
Net stock	10,323	13,737	18,284	18,718	19,480	20,508	21,717	22,706	23,766	24,883
Private	7,154	9,583	12,707	12,955	13,484	14,199	15,065	15,736	16,497	17,316
Nonresidential equipment	1,375	1,850	2,452	2,520	2,590	2,687	2,823	2,980	3,117	3,258
Information processing and related equipment	225	413	586	603	629	650	674	692	724	768
Industrial equipment	525	646	877	898	917	946	991	1,053	1,090	1,127
Transportation equipment	306	395	473	491	510	539	581	627	662	692
Other equipment	319	396	516	527	534	552	577	609	641	670
Nonresidential structures	2,266	3,155	4,107	4,177	4,303	4,529	4,776	4,977	5,195	5,468
Nonresidential buildings, excluding farm	1,169	1,787	2,518	2,594	2,686	2,835	3,011	3,146	3,306	3,513
Utilities	695	853	1,017	1,032	1,062	1,120	1,160	1,204	1,236	1,269
Residential	3,513	4,578	6,098	6,208	6,539	6,928	7,407	7,718	8,122	8,526
Housing units	2,898	3,730	4,984	5,057	5,327	5,667	6,078	6,320	6,641	6,965
Government	2,251	2,889	3,711	3,827	3,991	4,201	4,426	4,653	4,864	5,075
Equipment	300	425	552	577	600	618	635	649	650	641
Structures	1,952	2,464	3,159	3,250	3,391	3,583	3,791	4,004	4,214	4,434
Federal	698	889	1,090	1,127	1,169	1,227	1,263	1,295	1,327	1,335
Defense	483	613	744	768	798	839	858	868	878	866
State and local	1,554	2,000	2,621	2,701	2,822	2,974	3,163	3,358	3,537	3,740
Consumer durable goods	918	1,265	1,866	1,935	2,005	2,108	2,226	2,317	2,406	2,492
Motor vehicles	257	392	591	593	608	629	659	688	713	723
Furniture and household equipment	459	605	846	885	926	986	1,046	1,092	1,141	1,194
Other	203	268	429	457	471	493	521	537	552	575
CHAINED (1992) DOLLARS										
Net stock	14,269	16,178	18,586	18,883	19,212	19,603	20,037	20,538	21,097	21,689
Private	9,950	11,346	12,890	13,078	13,278	13,536	13,830	14,162	14,540	14,944
Nonresidential equipment	1,855	2,178	2,507	2,538	2,579	2,649	2,749	2,880	3,031	3,206
Nonresidential structures	3,177	3,697	4,142	4,205	4,251	4,300	4,345	4,406	4,476	4,552
Residential	4,921	5,471	6,240	6,335	6,448	6,587	6,738	6,884	7,047	7,212
Government	3,127	3,382	3,778	3,856	3,936	4,004	4,064	4,137	4,215	4,287
Federal	969	1,022	1,126	1,139	1,149	1,150	1,147	1,144	1,147	1,138
State and local	2,156	2,357	2,652	2,717	2,787	2,854	2,918	2,995	3,070	3,150
Consumer durable goods	1,198	1,455	1,919	1,950	1,998	2,064	2,144	2,243	2,351	2,475

Source: U.S. Bureau of Economic Analysis, *Fixed Reproducible Tangible Wealth, 1925-95*; and *Survey of Current Business*, September 1998.

Section 15

Prices

This section presents indexes of producer and consumer prices, actual prices for selected commodities, and energy prices. The primary sources of these data are monthly publications of the Department of Labor, Bureau of Labor Statistics (BLS), which include *Monthly Labor Review, Consumer Price Index, Detailed Report, Producer Price Indexes,* and *U.S. Import and Export Price Indexes.* The Department of Commerce, Bureau of Economic Analysis is the source for gross domestic product measures.

Producer price index (PPI)—This index, dating from 1890, is the oldest continuous statistical series published by BLS. It is designed to measure average changes in prices received by producers of all commodities, at all stages of processing, produced in the United States.

The index has undergone several revisions (see *Monthly Labor Review,* February 1962, April 1978, and August 1988). It is now based on approximately 10,000 individual products and groups of products along with about 100,000 quotations per month. Indexes for the net output of manufacturing and mining industries have been added in recent years. Prices used in constructing the index are collected from sellers and generally apply to the first significant large-volume commercial transaction for each commodity—i.e., the manufacturer's or other producer's selling price or the selling price on an organized exchange or at a central market.

The weights used in the index represent the total net selling value of commodities produced or processed in this country. Values are f.o.b. (free-on-board) production point and are exclusive of excise taxes. Effective with the release of data for January 1988, many important producer price indexes were changed to a new reference base year, 1982=100, from 1967=100. The

reference year of the PPI shipment weights has been taken primarily from the 1987 Census of Manufactures. For further detail regarding the PPI, see the BLS *Handbook of Methods,* Bulletin 2490 (April 1997), Chapter 16. The PPI web page is <http://stats.bls.gov/ppihome.htm>.

Consumer price indexes (CPI)—The CPI is a measure of the average change in prices over time in a "market basket" of goods and services purchased either by urban wage earners and clerical workers or by all urban consumers. In 1919, BLS began to publish complete indexes at semi-annual intervals, using a weighting structure based on data collected in the expenditure survey of wage-earner and clerical-worker families in 1917-19 (BLS Bulletin 357, 1924). The first major revision of the CPI occurred in 1940, with subsequent revisions in 1953, 1964, 1978, 1987, and 1998.

Beginning with the release of data for January 1988 in February 1988, most Consumer Price Indexes shifted to a new reference base year. All indexes previously expressed on a base of 1967=100, or any other base through December 1981, have been rebased to 1982-84=100. The expenditure weights are based upon data tabulated from the Consumer Expenditure Surveys for 1993, 1994, and 1995.

BLS publishes CPIs for two population groups: (1) a CPI for all urban consumers (CPI-U) which covers approximately 80 percent of the total population; and (2) a CPI for urban wage earners and clerical workers (CPI-W) which covers 32 percent of the total population. The CPI-U includes, in addition to wage earners and clerical workers, groups which historically have been excluded from CPI coverage, such as professional, managerial, and technical workers; the self-employed; short-term workers;

the unemployed; and retirees and others not in the labor force.

The current CPI is based on prices of food, clothing, shelter, fuels, transportation fares, charges for doctors' and dentists' services, drugs, etc. purchased for day-to-day living. Prices are collected in 87 areas across the country from over 50,000 housing units and 23,000 establishments. Area selection was based on the 1990 census. All taxes directly associated with the purchase and use of items are included in the index. Prices of food, fuels, and a few other items are obtained every month in all 87 locations. Prices of most other commodities and services are collected monthly in the three largest geographic areas and every other month in other areas.

In calculating the index, each item is assigned a weight to account for its relative importance in consumers' budgets. Price changes for the various items in each location are then averaged. Local data are then combined to obtain a U.S. city average. Separate indexes are also published for regions, area size-classes, cross-classifications of regions and size-classes, and for 26 local areas, usually consisting of the Metropolitan Statistical Area (MSA); see Appendix II. Area definitions are those established by the Office of Management and Budget in 1983. Definitions do not include revisions made since 1992. Area indexes do not measure differences in the level of prices among cities; they only measure the average change in prices for each area since the base period. For further detail regarding the CPI, see the BLS *Handbook of Methods*, Bulletin 2490, Chapter 17; the *Consumer Price Index*, and the CPI home page: <http://stats.bls.gov/cpihome.htm>. In January 1983, the method of measuring home-ownership costs in the CPI-U was changed to a rental equivalence approach. This treatment calculates homeowner costs of shelter based on the implicit rent owners would pay to rent the homes they own. The rental equivalence approach was introduced into the CPI-W in 1985. The CPI-U was used to prepare the consumer price tables in this section.

Other price indexes—Chain-weighted price indexes are weighted averages of the detailed price indexes used in the deflation of goods and services that make up the gross domestic product (GDP). The weights used for the most recent year reflect the composition of goods and services in the preceding year; for all other years, the weights reflect the composition of goods and services in the preceding year and the current year. Chain-weighted price indexes provide the most reliable comparisons; another index, the gross domestic purchases chained price index, measures the average price of goods and services purchased in the United States. The difference between these two measures is due to net exports. Both price indexes are expressed in terms of the base year value 1992=100.

Measures of inflation—Inflation is defined as a time of generally rising prices for goods and factors of production. The Bureau of Labor Statistics samples prices of items in a representative market basket and publishes the result as the CPI. The media invariably announce the inflation rate as the percent change in the CPI from month to month. A much more meaningful indicator of inflation is the percent change from the same month of the prior year. The Producer Price Index measures prices at the producer level only. The PPI shows the same general pattern of inflation as does the CPI but is more volatile. The PPI can be roughly viewed as a leading indicator. It often tends to foreshadow trends that later occur in the CPI.

Other measures of inflation include the gross domestic purchases chain-weighted price index, the index of industrial materials prices; the Dow Jones Commodity Spot Price Index; Futures Price Index; the Employment Cost Index, the Hourly Compensation Index, or the Unit Labor Cost Index as a measure of the change in cost of the labor factor-of production; and changes in long-term interest rates that are often used to measure changes in the cost of the capital factor of production.

U.S. Census Bureau, Statistical Abstract of the United States: 1999

International price indexes—The BLS International Price Program produces export and import price indexes for nonmilitary goods traded between the United States and the rest of the world.

The export price index provides a measure of price change for all products sold by U.S. residents to foreign buyers. The import price index provides a measure of price change for goods purchased from other countries by U.S. residents. The reference period for the indexes is 1990=100, unless otherwise indicated. The product universe for both the import and export indexes includes raw materials, agricultural products, semifinished manufactures, and finished manufactures, including both capital and consumer goods. Price data for these items are collected primarily by mail questionnaire. In nearly all cases, the data are collected directly from the exporter or importer, although in a few cases, prices are obtained from other sources.

To the extent possible, the data gathered refer to prices at the U.S. border for exports and at either the foreign border or the U.S. border for imports. For nearly all products, the prices refer to transactions completed during the first week of the month. Survey respondents are asked to indicate all discounts, allowances, and rebates applicable to the reported prices, so that the price used in the calculation of the indexes is the actual price for which the product was bought or sold.

In addition to general indexes for U.S. exports and imports, indexes are also published for detailed product categories of exports and imports. These categories are defined according to the five-digit level of detail for the Bureau of Economic Analysis End-use Classification, the three-digit level of detail for the Standard International Trade Classification (SITC), and the four-digit level of detail for the Harmonized System. Aggregate import indexes by country or region of origin are also available.

No. 775. Purchasing Power of the Dollar: 1950 to 1998

[Indexes: PPI, 1982=$1.00; CPI, 1982-84=$1.00. Producer prices prior to 1961 and consumer prices prior to 1964, exclude Alaska and Hawaii. Producer prices based on finished goods index. Obtained by dividing the average price index for the 1982=100, PPI; 1982-84=100, CPI base periods (100.0) by the price index for a given period and expressing the result in dollars and cents. Annual figures are based on average of monthly data]

Year	Annual average as measured—by		Year	Annual average as measured—by		Year	Annual average as measured—by	
	Producer prices	Consumer prices		Producer prices	Consumer prices		Producer prices	Consumer prices
1950	$3,546	$4,151	1966	2.841	3.080	1982	1.000	1.035
1951	3.247	3.846	1967	2.809	2.993	1983	0.984	1.003
1952	3.268	3.765	1968	2.732	2.873	1984	0.964	0.961
1953	3.300	3.735	1969	2.632	2.726	1985	0.955	0.928
1954	3.289	3.717	1970	2.545	2.574	1986	0.969	0.913
1955	3.279	3.732	1971	2.469	2.466	1987	0.949	0.880
1956	3.195	3.678	1972	2.392	2.391	1988	0.926	0.846
1957	3.077	3.549	1973	2.193	2.251	1989	0.880	0.807
1958	3.012	3.457	1974	1.901	2.029	1990	0.839	0.766
1959	3.021	3.427	1975	1.718	1.859	1991	0.822	0.734
1960	2.994	3.373	1976	1.645	1.757	1992	0.812	0.713
						1993	0.802	0.692
1961	2.994	3.340	1977	1.546	1.649	1994	0.797	0.675
1962	2.985	3.304	1978	1.433	1.532	1995	0.782	0.656
1963	2.994	3.265	1979	1.289	1.380	1996	0.762	0.638
1964	2.985	3.220	1980	1.136	1.215	1997	0.759	0.623
1965	2.933	3.166	1981	1.041	1.098	1998	0.766	0.600

Source: U.S. Bureau of Labor Statistics. Monthly data in U.S. Bureau of Economic Analysis, *Survey of Current Business.*

U.S. Census Bureau, Statistical Abstract of the United States: 1999

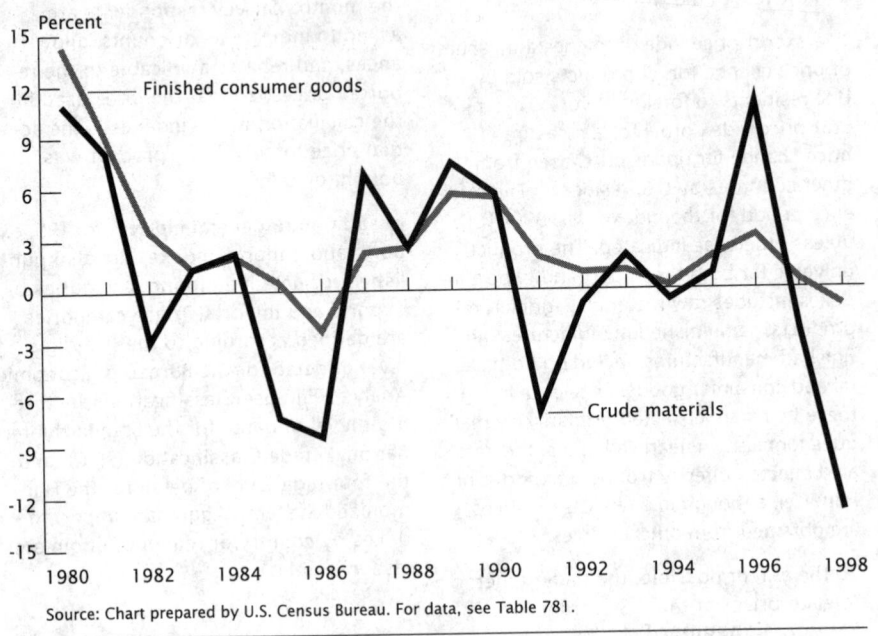

Figure 15.1
Annual Percent Change in Producer Price Indexes by Stage of Processing: 1980 to 1998

Percent

Finished consumer goods

Crude materials

Source: Chart prepared by U.S. Census Bureau. For data, see Table 781.

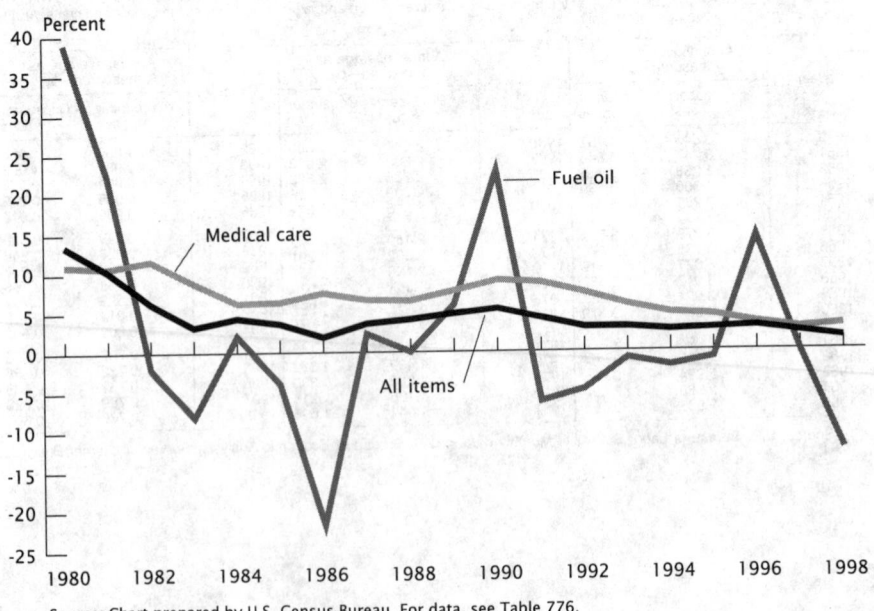

Figure 15.2
Annual Percent Change in Consumer Price Indexes: 1980 to 1998

Percent

Fuel oil

Medical care

All items

Source: Chart prepared by U.S. Census Bureau. For data, see Table 776.

494 Prices

No. 776. Consumer Price Indexes (CPI-U), by Major Groups: 1980 to 1998

[1982-84=100. Represents annual averages of monthly figures. Reflects buying patterns of all urban consumers. Minus sign (-) indicates decrease. See text, this section]

Year	All items	Commodities	Energy	Food	Shelter	Apparel and upkeep	Transportation	Medical care	Fuel oil	Electricity	Utility (piped) gas	Telephone services
1980	82.4	86.0	86.0	86.8	81.0	90.9	83.1	74.9	87.7	75.8	65.7	77.7
1985	107.6	105.4	101.6	105.6	109.8	105.0	106.4	113.5	94.6	108.9	104.8	111.7
1986	109.6	104.4	88.2	109.0	115.8	105.9	102.3	122.0	74.1	110.4	99.7	117.2
1987	113.6	107.7	88.6	113.5	121.3	110.6	105.4	130.1	75.8	110.0	95.1	116.5
1988	118.3	111.5	89.3	118.2	127.1	115.4	108.7	138.6	75.8	111.5	94.5	116.0
1989	124.0	116.7	94.3	125.1	132.8	118.6	114.1	149.3	80.3	114.7	97.1	117.2
1990	130.7	122.8	102.1	132.4	140.0	124.1	120.5	162.8	98.6	117.4	97.3	117.7
1991	136.2	126.6	102.5	136.3	146.3	128.7	123.8	177.0	92.4	121.8	98.5	119.7
1992	140.3	129.1	103.0	137.9	151.2	131.9	126.5	190.1	88.0	124.2	100.3	120.4
1993	144.5	131.5	104.2	140.9	155.7	133.7	130.4	201.4	87.2	126.7	106.5	121.2
1994	148.2	133.8	104.6	144.3	160.5	133.4	134.3	211.0	85.6	126.7	108.5	123.1
1995	152.4	136.4	105.2	148.4	165.7	132.0	139.1	220.5	84.8	129.6	102.9	124.0
1996	156.9	139.9	110.1	153.3	171.0	131.7	143.0	228.2	97.0	131.8	107.2	125.9
1997	160.5	141.8	111.5	157.3	176.3	132.9	144.3	234.6	96.9	132.5	114.6	127.7
1998	163.0	141.9	102.9	160.7	182.1	133.0	141.6	242.1	84.8	127.4	112.4	100.7
PERCENT CHANGE												
1980	13.5	12.3	30.9	8.6	17.6	7.1	17.9	11.0	39.0	15.5	19.2	2.5
1985	3.6	2.1	0.7	2.3	5.6	2.8	2.6	6.3	-4.0	3.4	-0.7	3.9
1986	1.9	-0.9	-13.2	3.2	5.5	0.9	-3.9	7.5	-21.7	1.4	-4.9	4.9
1987	3.6	3.2	0.5	4.1	4.7	4.4	3.0	6.6	2.3	-0.4	-4.6	-0.6
1988	4.1	3.5	0.8	4.1	4.8	4.3	3.1	6.5	-	1.4	-0.6	-0.4
1989	4.8	4.7	5.6	5.8	4.5	2.8	5.0	7.7	5.9	2.9	2.8	1.0
1990	5.4	5.2	8.3	5.8	5.4	4.6	5.6	9.0	22.8	2.4	0.2	0.4
1991	4.2	3.1	0.4	2.9	4.5	3.7	2.7	8.7	-6.3	3.7	1.2	1.7
1992	3.0	2.0	0.5	1.2	3.3	2.5	2.2	7.4	-4.8	2.0	1.8	0.6
1993	3.0	1.9	1.2	2.2	3.0	1.4	3.1	5.9	-0.9	2.0	6.2	0.7
1994	2.6	1.7	0.4	2.4	3.1	-0.2	3.0	4.8	-1.9	0.0	1.9	1.6
1995	2.8	1.9	0.6	2.8	3.2	-1.0	3.6	4.5	-0.9	2.3	-5.2	0.7
1996	3.0	2.6	4.7	3.3	3.2	-0.2	2.8	3.5	14.4	1.7	4.2	1.5
1997	2.3	1.4	1.3	2.6	3.1	0.9	0.9	2.8	-0.1	0.5	6.9	1.4
1998	1.6	0.1	-7.7	2.7	3.3	0.1	-1.9	3.2	-12.5	-3.8	-1.9	-

- Represents zero.

Source: Bureau of Labor Statistics, Monthly Labor Review and Handbook of Labor Statistics, periodic.

No. 777. Consumer Price Indexes (CPI-U)—Selected Areas: 1998

[1982-84=100, except as indicated. Represents annual averages of monthly figures. Local area CPI indexes are byproducts of the national CPI program. Each local index has a smaller sample size than the national index and is therefore, subject to substantially more sampling and other measurement error. As a result, local area indexes show greater volatility than the national index, although their long- term trends are similar. Area definitions are those established by the Office of Management and Budget in 1983. For further detail see the U.S. Bureau of Labor Statistics Handbook of Methods, Bulletin 2285, Chapter 19, the Consumer Price Index, and Report 736, the CPI: 1987 Revision. See also text, this section]

Area	All items	Food and beverages	Food	Housing	Apparel and upkeep	Transportation	Medical care	Fuel and other utilities
U.S. city average	**163.0**	**161.1**	**160.7**	**160.4**	**133.0**	**141.6**	**242.1**	**128.5**
Anchorage, AK MSA	146.9	147.3	147.5	131.0	125.6	144.9	255.7	148.4
Atlanta, GA MSA	161.2	164.7	169.1	161.1	137.6	127.8	245.0	142.1
Boston-Lawrence-Salem, MA-NH CMSA	171.7	165.8	166.3	165.8	147.0	139.5	313.9	119.1
Chicago-Gary-Lake County, IL-IN-WI CMSA	165.0	164.8	164.3	164.2	121.6	138.0	244.3	120.1
Cincinnati-Hamilton, OH-KY-IN CMSA	155.1	148.4	146.8	149.9	129.0	136.6	224.5	126.6
Cleveland-Akron-Lorain, OH CMSA	159.8	163.3	165.0	158.4	129.9	141.8	214.7	130.1
Dallas-Fort Worth, TX CMSA	153.6	160.1	157.8	143.2	136.6	138.5	229.0	128.4
Denver-Boulder, CO CMSA	161.9	151.6	153.6	154.4	100.6	166.5	275.0	128.6
Detroit-Ann Arbor, MI CMSA	159.8	154.6	153.7	153.6	133.7	148.9	230.6	124.3
Honolulu, HI MSA	171.5	159.1	159.1	176.0	112.2	162.5	226.1	131.0
Houston-Galveston-Brazoria, TX CMSA	146.8	150.9	150.3	129.6	140.9	135.7	235.4	107.8
Kansas City, MO-KS CMSA	157.8	159.7	160.8	151.8	129.1	137.2	217.7	134.5
Los Angeles-Anaheim-Riverside, CA CMSA	162.3	167.3	165.5	160.1	123.1	142.6	236.7	146.1
Miami-Fort Lauderdale, FL CMSA	160.5	169.0	169.4	153.5	152.1	144.2	227.3	118.0
Milwaukee, WI PMSA	160.3	157.5	158.6	159.9	118.7	140.8	239.8	112.6
Minneapolis-St. Paul, MN-WI MSA	158.3	166.6	163.6	145.0	144.2	141.9	229.6	119.2
New York-Northern New Jersey-Long Island, NY-NJ-CT CMSA	173.6	166.1	165.3	175.9	127.9	151.1	255.0	116.5
Philadelphia-Wilmington-Trenton, PA-NJ-DE-MD CMSA	168.2	155.1	154.1	170.1	106.2	149.3	254.8	132.2
Pittsburgh-Beaver Valley, PA CMSA	159.2	153.6	152.4	160.1	142.5	130.3	235.0	143.6
Portland-Vancouver, OR-WA CMSA	167.1	153.7	154.1	168.4	132.4	146.9	223.1	138.0
San Diego, CA MSA	166.9	165.0	163.0	170.1	125.1	149.4	240.9	117.7
San Francisco-Oakland-San Jose, CA CMSA	165.5	166.3	167.1	174.4	115.9	132.0	228.0	140.7
Seattle-Tacoma, WA CMSA	167.7	165.2	165.7	170.9	126.5	145.4	232.7	121.4
St. Louis-East St. Louis, MO-IL CMSA	154.5	158.4	156.8	147.0	126.2	138.4	233.9	123.5
Tampa-St. Petersburg-Clearwater, FL MSA[1]	137.5	132.7	132.6	132.2	144.1	124.2	192.1	119.8
Washington-Baltimore, DC-MD-VA-WV CMSA[2]	102.1	101.6	101.5	103.1	[2]99.3	[2]98.4	104.4	105.6

[1] 1987=100. [2] 1997=100; except "Apparel and upkeep" and "Transportation," 1996=100.

Source: U.S. Bureau of Labor Statistics, Monthly Labor Review and CPI Detailed Report, January issues.

No. 778. Consumer Price Indexes for All Urban Consumers (CPI-U) for Selected Items and Groups: 1980 to 1998

[1982-84=100. Annual averages of monthly figures. See headnote, Table 776]

Item	1980	1990	1992	1993	1994	1995	1996	1997	1998
All items	82.4	130.7	140.3	144.5	148.2	152.4	156.9	160.5	163.0
Food and beverages	86.7	132.1	138.7	141.6	144.9	148.9	153.7	157.7	161.1
Food	86.8	132.4	137.9	140.9	144.3	148.4	153.3	157.3	160.7
Food at home	88.4	132.3	136.8	140.1	144.1	148.8	154.3	158.1	161.1
Cereals and bakery products	83.9	140.0	151.5	156.6	163.0	167.5	174.0	177.6	181.1
Cereals and cereal products	84.2	141.1	153.3	157.9	164.8	167.1	168.9	169.5	171.5
Cereals	76.3	158.6	175.4	183.3	190.6	192.5	190.0	187.5	189.9
Rice, pasta, and cornmeal	90.9	122.0	128.3	129.7	139.7	140.2	144.2	148.8	150.5
Bakery products	83.8	139.2	150.4	155.7	161.9	167.4	176.1	181.1	185.4
White bread	85.9	136.4	146.2	152.2	159.0	165.5	177.5	183.8	187.3
Cookies, cakes, and cupcakes	81.5	142.7	155.6	159.3	165.1	169.1	174.1	179.2	181.2
Meats, poultry, fish and eggs	92.0	130.0	130.9	135.5	137.2	138.8	144.8	148.5	147.3
Meats	92.7	128.5	130.7	134.6	135.4	135.5	140.2	144.4	141.6
Beef and veal	98.4	128.8	132.3	137.1	136.0	134.9	134.5	136.8	136.5
Ground beef excl. canned	104.6	118.1	118.9	121.7	119.7	116.1	114.3	116.4	116.1
Chuck roast	99.8	130.3	137.1	141.9	140.3	138.7	140.0	142.3	(NA)
Round steak	98.9	125.1	129.9	134.4	133.0	130.4	129.3	130.1	(NA)
Sirloin steak	96.2	130.6	132.4	138.5	137.5	138.7	137.6	139.0	(NA)
Pork	81.9	129.8	127.8	131.7	133.9	134.8	148.2	155.9	148.5
Bacon	73.5	113.4	104.6	110.8	118.1	120.0	148.9	164.0	152.0
Chops	82.9	140.2	138.9	144.6	144.2	144.2	153.0	155.2	146.8
Ham	85.5	132.4	135.6	137.9	139.3	139.6	149.2	156.3	150.0
Poultry	93.7	132.5	131.4	136.9	141.5	143.5	152.4	156.6	157.1
Fresh whole chicken	94.4	134.9	131.9	138.0	140.1	142.2	152.6	158.5	159.6
Fresh, frozen chicken parts	91.7	135.9	134.4	140.1	145.6	146.0	155.0	157.4	157.2
Fish and seafood	87.5	146.7	151.7	156.6	163.7	171.6	173.1	177.1	181.7
Canned fish and seafood	93.7	119.5	118.7	121.5	123.8	125.5	125.9	128.4	132.6
Fresh, frozen fish, seafood	84.1	161.4	168.7	174.5	183.6	194.1	196.0	200.7	(NA)
Eggs	88.6	124.1	108.3	117.1	114.3	120.5	142.1	140.0	135.4
Dairy products	90.9	126.5	128.5	129.4	131.7	132.8	142.1	145.5	150.8
Fruits and vegetables	82.1	149.0	155.4	159.0	165.0	177.7	183.9	187.5	198.2
Fresh fruits and vegetables	81.8	(NA)	(NA)	(NA)	186.7	206.0	211.8	215.4	231.2
Fresh fruits	84.8	170.9	184.2	188.8	201.2	219.0	234.4	236.3	246.5
Apples	92.1	147.5	179.5	169.0	174.0	183.5	202.3	199.6	202.3
Bananas	91.5	138.2	139.9	135.5	143.6	153.8	159.0	159.6	160.9
Oranges, tangerines	72.6	160.6	176.2	190.1	189.9	224.5	239.3	226.1	251.5
Fresh vegetables	79.0	151.1	157.9	168.7	172.3	193.1	189.2	194.6	215.8
Potatoes	81.0	162.6	141.5	154.6	174.3	174.7	180.6	174.2	185.2
Lettuce	77.8	150.3	155.7	178.2	170.3	221.2	185.7	200.1	229.1
Tomatoes	81.9	160.8	171.8	168.0	173.5	188.3	198.2	213.6	239.2
Processed fruits and vegetables	82.6	(NA)	(NA)	(NA)	134.5	137.5	144.4	147.9	(NA)
Processed fruits	82.1	136.9	137.7	132.3	133.1	137.2	145.2	148.8	(NA)
Processed vegetables	83.1	127.5	128.8	130.8	136.6	138.3	143.9	147.2	(NA)
Coffee	111.6	117.5	110.7	109.8	140.4	163.1	149.2	168.0	163.4
Food away from home	83.4	(NA)	(NA)	(NA)	145.7	149.0	152.7	157.0	161.1
Lunch	83.8	133.9	141.3	144.0	146.4	149.6	153.3	157.7	(NA)
Dinner	84.2	132.3	138.9	141.3	143.8	147.1	150.7	154.7	(NA)
Alcoholic beverages	86.4	129.3	147.3	149.6	151.5	153.9	158.5	162.8	165.7
Alcoholic beverages at home	87.3	123.0	141.6	142.2	142.5	143.1	146.8	149.5	150.6
Beer and ale	84.8	123.6	143.5	143.2	143.4	143.9	147.4	148.2	148.5
Distilled spirits	89.8	125.7	141.5	143.2	144.3	145.7	147.5	150.8	152.7
Wine	89.5	114.4	132.6	134.0	133.3	133.6	139.3	145.5	147.3
Alcoholic beverages away from home	82.9	144.4	162.5	167.4	171.6	176.5	182.7	189.4	195.0
Housing	81.1	128.5	137.5	141.2	144.8	148.5	152.8	156.8	160.4
Shelter	81.0	140.0	151.2	155.7	160.5	165.7	171.0	176.3	182.1
Renters' cost	(NA)	146.7	160.9	165.0	169.4	174.3	180.2	186.4	(NA)
Rent, residential	80.9	138.4	146.9	150.3	154.0	157.8	162.0	166.7	(NA)
Tenants' insurance	78.9	130.6	136.5	140.8	145.8	150.9	154.7	159.2	(NA)
Homeowners' costs	(NA)	144.8	155.3	160.2	165.5	171.0	176.5	181.5	(NA)
Owners' equivalent rent	(NA)	144.8	155.5	160.5	165.8	171.3	176.8	181.9	187.8
Household insurance	(NA)	135.3	142.2	146.9	152.3	157.4	161.0	165.3	(NA)
Maintenance and repair	82.4	122.2	128.6	130.6	130.8	135.0	139.0	143.7	(NA)
Fuels and other utilities	75.4	111.6	117.8	121.3	122.8	123.7	127.5	130.8	128.5
Fuels	74.8	104.5	108.1	111.2	111.7	111.5	115.2	117.9	113.7
Fuel oil and other	86.1	99.3	90.7	90.3	88.8	88.1	99.2	99.8	90.0
Fuel oil	87.7	98.6	88.0	87.2	85.6	84.8	97.0	96.9	84.8
Gas (piped) and electricity	71.4	109.3	114.8	118.5	119.2	119.2	122.1	125.1	121.2
Electricity	75.8	117.4	124.2	126.7	126.7	129.6	131.8	132.5	127.4
Utility (piped) gas	65.7	97.3	100.3	106.5	108.5	102.9	107.2	114.6	112.4
Telephone services	77.7	117.7	120.4	121.2	123.1	124.0	125.9	127.7	(NA)
Local charges	72.8	149.3	155.7	156.4	156.9	160.4	160.8	163.1	165.7
Interstate toll charges	83.3	68.2	68.0	69.6	75.2	74.9	77.9	77.3	75.5
Intrastate toll charges	85.2	95.1	91.4	90.7	90.2	86.0	89.4	93.9	95.7
Water and sewerage maintenance	74.0	150.2	172.1	181.4	190.6	196.5	204.5	210.0	217.3
Cable television	(NA)	158.4	186.2	198.9	197.4	200.7	212.6	228.7	245.2
Refuse collection	(NA)	171.2	207.3	220.5	231.4	241.2	246.0	250.5	256.7

See footnotes at end of table.

496 Prices

No. 778. Consumer Price Indexes for All Urban Consumers (CPI-U) for Selected Items and Groups: 1980 to 1998—Continued

[1982-84=100. Annual averages of monthly figures. See headnote, Table 776]

Item	1980	1990	1992	1993	1994	1995	1996	1997	1998
Household furnishings and operations......	86.3	113.3	118.0	119.3	121.0	123.0	124.7	125.4	126.6
Housefurnishings..................	88.5	106.7	109.0	109.5	111.0	111.2	111.3	110.6	(NA)
Furniture and bedding............	88.0	115.7	120.6	123.5	128.2	130.9	134.1	134.5	135.0
Bedroom furniture..............	83.5	118.5	126.8	132.5	135.1	136.4	139.3	141.5	141.3
Sofas	(NA)	118.4	119.4	120.1	125.2	132.8	141.5	142.0	(NA)
Living room chairs and tables	(NA)	116.7	121.9	125.0	132.7	136.6	136.9	136.7	(NA)
Appliances and electronic equip.......	93.5	87.8	84.6	83.4	82.3	80.0	77.8	75.3	(NA)
Video and audio equipment.........	100.7	80.8	78.4	77.1	76.0	73.9	71.3	99.4	101.1
Television...................	104.6	74.6	72.4	70.7	69.9	68.1	64.5	61.7	59.2
Video products other than TV......	(NA)	91.5	81.0	78.5	73.8	70.3	66.3	63.4	(NA)
Audio products	97.7	93.2	94.4	93.9	93.8	92.1	90.7	88.9	85.2
Housekeeping supplies.............	83.2	125.2	129.6	130.7	132.3	137.1	141.1	143.1	145.7
Housekeeping services.............	84.3	120.1	132.1	135.8	138.5	143.7	148.0	151.9	(NA)
Postage	76.2	125.1	145.3	145.3	145.3	160.3	160.3	160.3	160.3
Apparel and upkeep	90.9	124.1	131.9	133.7	133.4	132.0	131.7	132.9	133.0
Apparel commodities	92.9	122.0	129.4	131.0	130.4	128.7	128.2	129.1	(NA)
Apparel commodities less footwear	93.0	122.8	130.2	131.9	131.2	129.3	128.5	129.4	129.3
Men's and boy's apparel	89.4	120.4	126.5	127.5	126.4	126.2	127.7	130.1	131.8
Women's and girl's apparel	96.0	122.6	130.4	132.6	130.9	126.9	124.7	126.1	126.0
Infants' and toddlers'............	85.5	125.8	129.3	127.1	128.1	127.2	129.7	129.0	126.1
Footwear.......................	91.8	117.4	125.0	125.9	126.0	125.4	126.6	127.6	128.0
Transportation	83.1	120.5	126.5	130.4	134.3	139.1	143.0	144.3	141.6
Private transportation	84.2	118.8	124.6	127.5	131.4	136.3	140.0	141.0	137.9
New vehicles..................	88.5	121.4	129.2	132.7	137.6	141.0	143.7	144.3	143.4
New cars	88.4	121.0	128.4	131.5	136.0	139.0	141.4	141.7	140.7
New trucks	(NA)	121.6	130.9	135.7	141.7	145.9	149.5	151.4	151.1
Used cars....................	62.3	117.6	123.2	133.9	141.7	156.5	157.0	151.1	150.6
Motor fuel...................	97.4	101.2	99.0	98.0	98.5	100.0	106.3	106.2	92.2
Automobile maintenance and repair.......	81.5	130.1	141.3	145.9	150.2	154.0	158.4	162.7	167.1
Automobile insurance..............	82.0	177.9	205.5	216.7	224.8	234.3	243.9	251.6	254.3
Automobile finance charges..........	86.4	99.6	86.1	78.6	83.8	99.0	94.4	93.6	(NA)
Vehicle rental, registration, other........	78.3	148.1	162.3	169.8	174.2	177.9	181.1	185.4	102.5
Public transportation	69.0	142.6	151.4	167.0	172.0	175.9	181.9	186.7	190.3
Airline fares...................	68.0	148.4	155.2	178.7	185.5	189.7	192.5	199.2	205.3
Other intercity transportation	73.1	143.3	152.5	150.9	152.8	153.3	156.0	155.1	160.4
Intracity transportation..............	69.7	133.5	146.9	150.7	152.7	157.5	173.2	175.8	174.2
Medical care	74.9	162.8	190.1	201.4	211.0	220.5	228.2	234.6	242.1
Medical care commodities...........	75.4	163.4	188.1	195.0	200.7	204.5	210.4	215.3	221.8
Prescription drugs	72.5	181.7	214.7	223.0	230.6	235.0	242.9	249.3	258.6
Nonprescription drugs, medical sup.....	(NA)	120.6	131.2	135.5	138.1	140.5	143.1	145.4	147.7
Medical care services..............	74.8	162.7	190.5	202.9	213.4	224.2	232.4	239.1	246.8
Professional medical services........	77.9	156.1	175.8	184.7	192.5	201.0	208.3	215.4	222.2
Physicians' services	76.5	160.8	181.2	191.3	199.8	208.8	216.4	222.9	229.5
Dental services	78.9	155.8	178.7	188.1	197.1	206.8	216.5	226.6	236.2
Eye care....................	(NA)	117.3	127.0	130.4	133.0	137.0	139.3	141.5	144.1
Hospital and related services........	69.2	178.0	214.0	231.9	245.6	257.8	269.5	278.4	287.5
Hospital rooms..............	68.0	175.4	208.7	226.4	239.2	251.2	261.0	(NA)	(NA)
Entertainment	83.6	132.4	142.3	145.8	150.1	153.9	159.1	162.5	(NA)
Entertainment commodities	84.5	124.0	131.3	133.4	136.1	138.7	143.0	144.2	(NA)
Reading materials	77.7	136.2	150.9	156.2	161.3	168.1	176.4	179.0	184.1
Newspapers	79.4	134.6	154.8	161.1	168.2	178.7	188.9	191.3	(NA)
Magazines, periodicals, and books....	75.9	137.9	147.4	151.8	155.1	158.4	165.0	167.8	(NA)
Sporting goods, equipment	88.5	114.9	120.2	120.1	122.2	123.5	123.4	122.6	121.9
Sport vehicles, including bicycles....	87.9	115.3	119.7	120.6	122.3	125.3	125.7	124.5	125.3
Toys, hobbies; other entertainment	86.5	121.5	124.7	126.0	127.4	127.8	131.9	133.3	(NA)
Pet supplies and expenses............	83.3	124.6	128.1	128.8	130.9	132.3	139.0	142.7	143.5
Entertainment services	82.3	143.2	155.9	160.8	166.8	172.0	178.1	183.8	(NA)
Club membership..............	(NA)	117.0	125.2	128.4	130.7	132.8	133.3	132.1	(NA)
Admissions	83.8	151.2	164.5	167.3	175.2	182.3	192.1	198.9	205.5
Tobacco and smoking products	72.0	181.5	219.8	228.4	220.0	225.7	232.8	243.7	274.8
Personal care.......................	81.9	130.4	138.3	141.5	144.6	147.1	150.1	152.7	156.7
Personal care services.............	83.7	132.8	140.0	144.0	147.4	151.5	156.6	162.4	166.0
Beauty parlor services for women	83.4	133.0	139.8	143.6	147.7	150.9	155.9	161.4	(NA)
Haircuts, etc. for men	84.4	131.5	140.3	144.6	147.9	153.4	158.5	165.5	(NA)
Personal and educational expenses	70.9	170.2	197.4	210.7	223.2	235.5	247.5	259.7	(NA)
School books and supplies	71.4	171.3	190.3	197.6	205.5	214.4	226.9	238.4	250.8
Personal and educational services	70.8	170.4	198.1	211.9	224.8	237.3	249.3	261.6	(NA)
Tuition and other school fees...........	71.2	175.7	208.5	225.3	239.8	253.8	267.1	280.4	294.2
College tuition...............	70.8	175.0	213.5	233.5	249.8	264.8	279.8	294.1	306.5
Elementary and high school tuition	72.3	182.8	213.7	228.9	242.6	259.2	272.8	288.1	307.9
Day care and nursery school	(NA)	(NA)	108.3	113.6	119.6	124.5	129.4	134.3	140.9
All commodities	86.0	122.8	129.1	131.5	133.8	136.4	139.9	141.8	141.9
All commodities less food..................	85.7	117.4	124.2	126.3	127.9	129.8	132.6	133.4	132.0
Energy	86.0	102.1	103.0	104.2	104.6	105.2	110.1	111.5	102.9

NA Not available.

Source: U.S. Bureau of Labor Statistics, *Monthly Labor Review* and *CPI Detailed Report*, January issues.

No. 779. Cost of Living Index—Selected Metropolitan Areas: Fourth Quarter 1998

[Measures relative price levels for consumer goods and services in participating areas for a mid-management standard of living. The nationwide average equals 100, and each index is read as a percent of the national average. The index does not measure inflation, but compares prices at a single point in time. Excludes taxes. Metropolitan areas as defined by the Office of Management and Budget. For definitions and components of MSAs, see source for details]

Metropolitan areas	Composite index (100%)	Grocery items (16%)	Housing (28%)	Utilities (8%)	Transportation (10%)	Health care (5%)	Misc. goods and services (33%)
Anniston, AL MSA	94.1	100.9	87.1	99.7	92.1	86.9	97.0
Birmingham, AL MSA	96.5	96.6	93.4	101.3	93.9	96.4	98.6
Decatur, AL MSA	95.8	96.5	90.3	92.0	100.0	94.7	99.9
Florence, AL MSA	94.3	100.0	88.7	93.5	87.7	93.1	98.8
Gadsden, AL MSA	93.1	99.8	76.2	103.6	86.3	93.6	103.7
Huntsville, AL MSA	93.0	95.1	83.4	86.2	97.6	98.7	99.6
Mobile, AL MSA	93.0	97.7	82.9	106.5	97.4	83.5	96.1
Montgomery, AL MSA	97.2	98.0	93.3	100.4	100.9	97.7	98.1
Flagstaff, AZ-UT MSA	109.1	105.7	121.0	107.1	108.7	118.6	99.7
Las Vegas, NV-AZ MSA	98.7	100.3	86.8	113.7	100.9	108.6	102.3
Phoenix-Mesa, AZ MSA	101.6	103.7	96.9	106.5	113.1	111.6	98.4
Tucson, AZ MSA	99.3	106.4	96.0	120.8	95.2	98.1	94.9
Yuma, AZ	104.0	106.8	98.8	146.0	110.1	109.7	94.2
Fayetteville-Springdale-Rogers, AR MSA	92.4	91.0	89.2	87.1	96.4	89.3	96.3
Fort Smith, AR-OK MSA	87.3	85.2	76.0	84.9	88.2	86.4	98.4
Jonesboro, AR MSA	89.7	92.2	85.7	91.4	85.8	85.7	93.3
Little Rock-North Little Rock, AR MSA	94.7	103.3	80.7	115.6	100.2	94.5	95.7
Bakersfield, CA MSA	102.8	110.0	86.7	120.2	110.2	105.9	106.0
Frenso, CA MSA	103.4	105.3	94.5	116.3	114.4	108.1	103.0
Los Angeles-Long Beach, CA PMSA	128.5	116.1	164.3	121.2	117.2	117.2	111.1
Oakland, CA PMSA	163.0	118.3	266.1	107.4	132.1	154.4	121.2
Riverside-San Bernardino, CA PSMA	112.0	106.0	104.4	151.4	111.6	143.1	107.1
Salinas, CA MSA	133.2	113.7	198.2	99.8	124.5	140.3	97.2
Santa Barbara-Santa Maria-Lompac, CA MSA	113.0	112.0	128.3	113.2	114.0	121.8	98.8
Visalia-Tulare-Porterville, CA MSA	106.6	108.6	97.5	116.7	109.6	120.9	107.7
Colorodo Springs, CO MSA	99.7	100.5	112.0	68.6	101.8	122.0	92.5
Denver, CO PMS	109.1	112.6	121.6	85.3	112.6	125.2	99.0
Fort Collins-Loveland, CO MSA	104.1	112.5	109.5	78.9	103.4	114.3	100.1
Grand Junction, CO MSA	104.0	108.5	112.2	85.0	110.0	102.5	97.8
Greeley, CO PMSA	107.6	107.7	124.3	84.9	96.9	105.1	102.5
Pueblo, CO MSA	92.5	111.5	78.0	80.1	91.7	105.6	96.8
New Haven,-Meriden, CT PMSA	122.3	107.5	145.7	168.7	101.7	122.3	104.7
Dover, DE MSA	101.9	108.9	94.1	122.2	97.6	94.4	102.7
Wilmington-Newark, DE-MD PMSA	111.5	116.4	118.3	134.2	96.0	105.0	103.5
Washington DC-MD-VA-WV PMSA	123.0	112.3	148.2	95.1	125.2	119.5	113.4
Daytona Beach, FL MSA	93.2	99.0	83.0	108.6	91.5	98.5	95.0
Ft Lauderdale, FL MSA	107.7	104.2	112.0	109.0	99.8	111.8	107.3
Fort Walton Beach FL, MSA	97.2	101.2	93.5	92.6	98.7	99.7	98.6
Jacksonville, FL MSA	97.0	103.4	85.4	99.9	104.8	95.0	101.0
Miami, FL PMSA	107.7	102.9	113.0	103.0	106.8	101.6	108.0
Orlando, FL MSA	100.5	98.9	95.1	104.8	98.1	106.6	104.6
Panama City, FL MSA	98.4	103.1	97.8	97.9	102.2	99.7	95.3
Pensacola, FL MSA	97.6	102.8	87.3	93.0	105.1	109.8	100.9
Sarasota-Bradenton, FL MSA	100.9	96.9	102.9	98.7	97.7	104.3	102.2
Tallahassee, FL MSA	103.7	101.7	105.1	120.0	103.0	104.1	99.6
Tampa-St Petersburg-Clearwater, FL MSA	105.1	104.4	111.4	98.6	102.8	112.3	101.4
West Palm Beach-Boca Raton, FL MSA	108.2	104.2	111.4	112.6	108.3	110.2	106.1
Albany, GA MSA	90.3	97.1	73.9	107.6	92.2	84.4	96.9
Atlanta, GA MSA	103.3	106.0	101.8	97.5	100.7	109.2	104.6
Augusta-Aiken, GA-SC MSA	92.1	93.5	83.7	98.7	97.6	96.6	94.5
Macon, GA MSA	96.9	101.5	87.1	111.8	89.4	86.1	103.4
Savannah, GA MSA	101.2	97.9	106.7	100.8	90.9	97.1	102.1
Boise City, ID MSA	102.9	101.7	110.8	74.9	105.2	112.6	101.5
Pocatello, ID	96.8	99.7	97.5	80.5	99.2	97.6	97.8
Chanpaign-Urbana, IL MSA	105.2	100.3	113.9	102.3	105.2	96.6	102.3
Davenport-Moline-Rock Island, IA-IL MSA	97.8	99.7	93.0	97.3	105.6	100.8	98.2
Decatur, IL MSA	92.6	102.3	78.7	99.5	101.1	85.6	96.4
Peoria-Perkin, IL MSA	105.7	102.2	106.9	98.3	107.4	97.5	108.8
Rockford, IL MSA	96.0	97.6	93.7	103.2	98.2	100.1	94.2
Springfield, IL MSA	97.4	101.9	96.8	84.5	93.8	106.7	98.5
Elkhart-Goshen, IN MSA	97.4	99.4	95.3	102.4	93.7	94.4	98.5
Evansville-Henderson, IN-KY MSA	96.3	90.6	104.3	90.6	90.4	91.9	96.1
Fort Wayne, IN MSA	93.1	97.3	89.1	98.0	92.6	88.2	94.1
Indianapolis, IN MSA	95.4	91.1	100.6	98.2	96.2	96.4	92.1
Lafayette, IN MSA	98.5	93.8	101.0	108.9	95.2	99.8	96.8

498 Prices

No. 779. Cost of Living Index—Selected Metropolitan Areas: Fourth Quarter 1998—Continued

[See headnote, page 498]

Metropolitan areas	Composite index (100%)	Grocery items (16%)	Housing (28%)	Utilities (8%)	Transportation (10%)	Health care (5%)	Misc. goods and services (33%)
Muncie, IN MSA	96.9	94.4	97.4	105.0	101.0	92.0	95.2
South Bend, IN MSA	92.9	96.6	89.5	102.6	90.4	102.0	91.0
Cedar Rapids, IA MSA	97.8	93.0	93.4	111.7	102.3	92.4	99.8
Des Moines, IA MSA	97.2	93.8	91.5	98.8	100.7	97.0	102.4
Waterloo-Cedar Falls, IA MSA	95.0	89.8	93.9	99.1	98.9	87.6	97.3
Lawerence, KS MSA	102.6	98.9	107.2	101.8	92.6	93.8	105.0
Wichita, KS MSA	94.8	88.5	88.3	104.9	99.0	106.2	98.0
Cincinnati, OH-KY-IN PMSA	91.6	95.1	86.4	92.1	93.6	96.9	92.9
Clarksville-Hopkinsville, TN-KY MSA	93.9	97.5	83.7	94.1	88.1	93.4	102.6
Lexington, KY MSA	97.1	101.5	93.3	87.9	94.5	97.7	101.1
Louisville, KY-IN MSA	94.6	92.9	90.6	98.2	102.0	89.4	96.4
Baton Rouge, LA MSA	101.0	104.0	96.4	121.1	106.5	101.8	96.8
Lafayette, LA MSA	97.4	96.5	103.4	86.3	97.8	87.3	96.8
Lake Charles, LA MSA	97.0	92.7	93.2	115.0	94.6	87.5	100.2
Monroe, LA MSA	94.5	88.1	83.9	105.1	104.4	91.1	101.6
Shreveport-Bossier City, LA MSA	93.1	86.6	97.6	94.4	92.9	91.1	92.4
Baltimore, MD PMSA	97.1	96.8	94.4	110.8	102.1	93.7	95.1
Cumberland, MD-WV MSA	104.8	106.9	108.3	125.0	89.6	95.8	101.8
Boston, MA-NH PMSA	144.4	113.0	213.8	124.2	117.5	133.3	115.5
Fitchburg-Leominster, MA PMSA	101.4	107.0	93.5	108.8	102.9	117.6	100.7
Springfield, MA MSA	118.3	119.9	132.2	126.5	104.0	131.0	106.3
Grand Rapids-Muskegon-Holland, MI MSA	107.6	111.8	115.0	102.9	102.6	102.5	102.6
Lansing-East Lansing, MI MSA	107.1	105.3	131.1	80.8	97.4	100.2	98.1
Minneapolis-St Paul, MW-WI MSA	102.3	98.3	95.6	103.3	111.6	117.6	104.5
Rochester, MN MSA	103.0	101.0	99.4	94.1	105.6	122.8	105.3
St Cloud, MD MSA	98.6	100.1	93.3	91.3	104.6	98.7	102.3
Biloxi-Gulfport-Pascagoula, MS MSA	99.6	104.4	90.4	107.3	101.9	93.1	103.5
Hattiesburg, MS MSA	96.2	101.6	90.4	102.2	91.5	82.7	100.4
Jackson, MS MSA	89.8	86.4	87.5	101.5	90.8	79.9	91.8
Columbia, MO MSA	94.9	99.4	85.7	88.4	100.3	98.2	100.1
Joplin, MO MSA	86.7	88.6	76.7	86.2	81.0	96.3	94.6
St Joseph, MO MSA	96.6	86.2	106.1	84.9	90.4	99.2	97.9
St Louis, MO MSA	97.7	101.7	97.0	98.5	96.6	108.7	94.8
Springfield, MO MSA	94.7	99.3	90.4	75.3	103.9	98.1	97.5
Billings, MT MSA	102.5	104.4	99.0	85.4	114.0	107.2	104.6
Great Falls, MT MSA	99.9	100.8	102.7	86.2	101.6	103.0	99.5
Missoula, MT MSA	103.5	106.4	106.4	82.4	109.2	103.1	103.2
Lincoln, NE MSA	99.1	95.0	110.9	83.1	97.1	87.2	97.4
Omaha, NE-IA MSA	94.0	96.3	93.0	86.8	100.0	91.8	94.1
Las Vegas, NV-AZ MSA	104.3	115.0	104.1	87.7	111.3	117.8	99.1
Reno, NV MSA	110.5	110.1	120.4	94.4	110.0	118.8	105.0
Manchester, NH PMSA	110.4	100.3	112.2	146.1	98.6	115.9	107.8
Albuquerque, NM MSA	101.0	102.7	102.9	94.9	94.4	102.3	101.9
Las Cruces, NM MSA	99.0	100.1	102.1	100.8	96.2	97.5	96.4
Santa Fe, NM MSA	121.2	103.9	167.2	87.7	115.4	109.2	102.4
Binghamton, NY MSA	96.6	100.8	83.9	131.4	101.5	91.7	96.1
Buffalo-Niagara Falls, NY MSA	97.3	112.4	85.6	133.3	95.4	86.4	93.5
Elmira, NY MSA	100.9	107.0	84.0	155.6	108.9	90.4	98.3
Glens Falls, NY MSA	104.1	106.1	89.5	154.2	112.2	95.9	102.1
Nassau-Suffolk, NY PMSA	141.8	125.5	174.0	166.8	116.7	159.5	121.1
New York, NY PMSA	225.3	142.8	442.6	178.2	120.1	183.6	130.4
Syracuse,NY MSA	101.6	111.4	87.6	136.0	104.7	105.1	98.9
Asheville, NC MSA	102.3	100.2	114.8	96.2	103.5	91.0	95.5
Charlotte-Gastonia-Rock Hill, NC-SC MSA	100.1	101.4	101.3	96.9	99.6	94.2	100.3
Greensboro-Winston-Salem-High Point, NC MSA	95.9	97.8	92.9	97.9	88.3	98.1	99.0
Greenville, NC MSA	97.8	98.9	89.3	125.3	86.2	94.0	101.9
Hickory-Morganton-Lenior, NC MSA	96.9	100.1	94.0	97.0	88.9	83.4	102.4
Raleigh-Durham-Chapel Hill, NC MSA	100.8	98.8	110.3	102.6	93.2	97.3	96.2
Wilmington, NC MSA	104.5	101.1	111.5	108.2	101.4	97.1	101.4
Bismarck, ND MSA	98.9	102.9	98.8	87.7	93.5	95.7	101.8
Fargo-Moorhead, ND-MN MSA	96.0	94.8	88.6	104.6	93.7	102.6	100.5
Grand Forks, ND-MN MSA	100.3	96.6	100.6	91.1	98.8	92.6	105.8
Cincinnati, OH-KY-IN PMSA	97.8	93.7	99.9	100.5	99.7	95.7	97.2
Cleveland-Lorain-Elyria, OH PMSA	111.9	106.3	120.3	129.1	112.9	124.9	101.0
Columbus, OH MSA	99.6	104.6	95.3	123.2	102.5	89.8	95.7
Dayton-Springfield, OH MSA	99.8	92.4	104.0	107.4	104.1	99.1	96.7
Lima, OH MSA	97.9	108.0	90.6	103.4	103.4	88.1	97.6
Mansfield, OH MSA	96.6	98.7	91.7	130.5	97.3	84.9	93.0
Toledo, OH MSA	102.2	102.9	94.1	130.2	102.7	99.7	102.2
Youngstown-Warren, OH MSA	91.0	97.1	84.9	117.8	85.6	86.7	89.1

U.S. Census Bureau, Statistical Abstract of the United States: 1999

No. 779. Cost of Living Index—Selected Metropolitan Areas: Fourth Quarter 1998—Continued

[See headnote, page 498]

Metropolitan areas	Composite index (100%)	Grocery items (16%)	Housing (28%)	Utilities (8%)	Transportation (10%)	Health care (5%)	Misc. goods and services (33%)
Enid, OK MSA	92.8	95.9	82.4	88.5	87.9	94.2	102.5
Lawton, OK MSA	92.4	96.2	79.2	89.8	100.8	97.5	99.1
Oklahoma City, OK MSA	91.0	92.5	76.5	95.6	98.4	89.9	99.4
Tulsa, OK MSA	92.1	94.1	87.8	87.8	83.1	94.8	98.1
Eugene-Springfield, OR MSA	105.3	101.2	120.1	71.8	109.3	124.3	98.7
Portland-Vancouver, OR-WA PMSA	110.3	105.2	125.4	80.5	113.6	121.9	104.5
Salem, OR PMSA	104.0	98.4	113.4	83.0	102.3	117.8	102.3
Altoona, PA MSA	100.7	102.3	101.6	120.2	92.4	87.2	98.9
Lancaster, PA MSA	110.3	99.2	121.7	119.9	103.2	90.1	108.8
Philadelphia, PA-NJ PMSA	121.9	106.9	145.2	155.5	115.0	98.0	107.1
Scranton-Wilkes Barre-Hazelton, PA MSA	96.1	98.7	90.3	95.9	91.5	94.0	101.5
Williamsport, PA MSA	98.0	93.1	96.8	109.6	94.4	91.3	100.6
York, PA MSA	100.8	93.6	106.2	118.9	98.0	81.6	99.1
Charleston-North Charlston, SC MSA	101.8	98.6	101.6	114.1	93.3	102.2	103.0
Columbia, SC MSA	97.1	94.5	93.3	121.2	86.7	89.4	100.1
Greenville-Spatanburg-Anderson, SC MSA	99.3	101.9	95.6	101.9	94.5	96.2	102.4
Myrtle Beach, SC MSA	100.6	102.8	94.5	122.5	97.1	91.0	101.8
Sumter, SC MSA	92.4	97.9	72.0	106.6	94.8	91.4	102.9
Rapid City, SD MSA	99.9	105.4	97.6	104.0	101.0	92.4	99.0
Sioux Falls, SD MSA	95.7	97.2	89.5	97.7	101.8	99.9	97.2
Chattanooga, TN-GA MSA	96.0	97.6	93.7	91.1	88.1	91.9	101.3
Clarksville-Hopkinsville, TN-KY MSA	91.3	93.8	82.3	84.9	95.5	92.2	97.9
Jackson, TN MSA	92.1	92.3	83.8	93.6	103.8	84.4	96.2
Johnson City-Kingsport-Bristol, TN-VA MSA	90.5	91.8	91.1	90.0	85.0	82.5	92.4
Knoxville, TN MSA	96.0	98.2	86.8	95.0	91.7	95.9	104.2
Memphis, TN-AR-MS MSA	92.4	95.7	92.0	78.6	93.6	93.8	94.0
Nashville, TN MSA	95.0	93.8	92.7	88.0	97.7	92.5	98.7
Abilene, TX MSA	92.6	85.4	84.1	100.4	101.3	98.9	97.9
Amarillo, TX MSA	91.2	92.9	88.0	77.3	96.0	85.5	96.0
Austin-San Marcos, TX MSA	96.5	87.5	93.3	89.3	106.2	99.2	102.0
Beaumont-Port Arthur, TX MSA	93.4	86.5	89.0	102.0	97.9	91.6	97.2
Brownsville-Harlingen-San Benito, TX MSA	92.5	94.8	81.1	102.7	101.3	94.9	95.7
Bryan-College Station, TX MSA	91.7	99.0	79.1	100.2	95.0	99.2	94.6
Dallas, TX PMSA	100.6	97.9	99.2	97.9	104.1	107.3	101.6
Fort Worth-Arlington, TX PMSA	91.5	86.5	85.8	88.1	98.0	94.1	97.1
Houston, TX PMSA	93.7	93.7	83.3	90.1	106.0	107.3	97.7
Killeen-Temple, TX MSA	98.2	91.1	86.9	117.5	99.0	106.7	104.9
Lubbock, TX MSA	91.0	91.0	86.3	71.3	95.5	99.1	97.1
McAllen-Edinburg-Mission, TX MSA	92.4	83.2	81.8	109.2	99.4	91.7	99.7
Odessa-Midland, TX MSA	89.8	91.2	74.5	85.4	98.6	94.7	99.8
San Angelo, TX MSA	91.0	89.3	77.3	85.2	100.6	99.3	100.8
San Antonio, TX MSA	90.7	88.1	83.0	81.2	93.4	90.5	100.0
Sherman-Denison, TX MSA	92.2	88.3	83.7	99.7	95.1	100.3	97.5
Texarkana, TX-AR MSA	89.9	88.5	75.7	91.9	98.0	105.2	97.5
Tyler, TX MSA	94.9	88.0	89.9	105.9	98.0	91.3	99.5
Victoria, TX MSA	90.3	82.7	89.9	99.7	89.1	96.2	91.5
Waco, TX MSA	89.4	89.0	75.3	117.2	96.4	78.9	94.4
Wichita Falls, TX MSA	91.2	95.1	75.9	95.1	103.0	92.6	97.5
Provo-Orem, UT MSA	100.0	99.4	99.6	85.4	111.8	118.3	97.7
Salt Lake City-Ogden, UT MSA	106.6	106.9	118.5	79.8	108.9	103.6	102.7
Burlington, VT MSA	114.2	105.5	126.3	133.0	100.5	114.5	107.8
Johnson City-Kingsport-Bristol, TN-VA MSA	85.1	98.6	80.1	76.6	88.3	75.8	85.3
Norfolk-Virginia Beach-Newport News VA-NC MSA	97.3	97.6	90.0	119.2	104.7	95.8	95.9
Richmond-Petersburg, VA MSA	105.9	93.4	110.2	128.2	103.0	102.6	104.2
Roanoke, VA MSA	95.5	96.0	96.5	88.4	89.8	94.6	98.0
Washington DC-MD-VA-WV PMSA	108.5	105.9	102.1	120.3	135.0	113.3	103.6
Bellingham, WA MSA	105.8	103.1	123.9	67.8	98.6	119.5	101.2
Bremerton, WA MSA	105.1	104.1	111.6	95.9	101.7	136.4	98.6
Richland-Kennewick-Pasco, WA MSA	99.0	100.4	92.6	73.0	100.3	126.1	105.7
Spokane, WA MSA	101.6	99.6	114.8	64.7	96.0	122.1	98.8
Tacoma, WA MSA	103.3	106.3	106.4	72.1	107.9	131.6	101.2
Yakima, WA MSA	103.9	102.2	111.7	77.5	100.5	133.5	101.2
Appletone-Oshkosh-Neenah, WI MSA	97.1	91.4	101.1	88.3	106.8	96.9	95.6
Eau Claire, WI MSA	98.7	99.6	99.7	99.8	101.7	107.4	95.0
Green Bay, WI MSA	97.2	93.6	100.8	75.3	102.6	101.8	99.0
Sheboygan, WI MSA	97.5	100.9	106.0	74.0	103.0	95.4	92.9
Wausau, WI MSA	102.5	98.3	115.7	82.8	98.1	104.2	99.1
Cheyenne, WY MSA	97.8	108.8	93.7	78.7	95.4	103.7	100.3
Saskatoon, SK CMA	90.8	97.6	94.1	68.1	102.8	48.2	92.9

Source: ACCRA, 4232 King St., Alexandria, VA 22302-1507, *ACCRA Cost of Living Index*, Fourth Quarter 1998 (copyright).

No. 780. Annual Percent Changes From Prior Year in Consumer Prices—United States and OECD Countries: 1990 to 1998

[Covers member countries of Organization for Economic Cooperation (OECD). For consumer price indexes for OECD countries, see Section 30, Comparative International Statistics]

Country	1990	1993	1994	1995	1996	1997	1998
United States	5.4	3.0	2.6	2.8	2.9	2.3	(NA)
OECD	5.8	4.2	4.4	5.5	5.1	4.2	(NA)
Australia.	7.3	1.8	1.9	4.6	2.6	0.2	0.8
Canada	4.8	1.9	0.2	2.2	1.6	1.6	1.0
Japan	3.1	1.2	0.7	-0.1	0.1	1.7	(NA)
New Zealand.	6.1	1.3	1.8	3.8	2.3	1.2	1.3
Austria	3.3	3.6	3.0	2.2	1.5	1.3	0.9
Belgium	3.4	2.8	2.4	1.5	2.1	1.6	1.0
Denmark.	2.7	1.3	2.0	2.1	2.1	2.2	1.9
Finland.	6.1	2.2	1.1	0.8	0.6	1.2	1.4
France	3.4	2.1	1.7	1.8	2.0	1.2	0.7
Greece.	20.4	14.4	10.7	8.9	8.2	5.5	4.8
Ireland	3.3	1.4	2.3	2.5	1.7	1.4	2.4
Italy [1]	6.1	4.2	3.9	5.4	3.8	1.8	1.7
Luxembourg	3.7	3.6	2.2	1.9	1.3	1.4	1.0
Netherlands	2.5	2.6	2.8	1.9	2.0	2.2	2.0
Norway.	4.1	2.3	1.4	2.5	1.3	2.6	2.3
Portugal [2]	13.4	6.7	5.4	4.2	3.1	2.3	2.8
Spain.	6.7	4.6	4.7	4.7	3.6	2.0	1.8
Sweden	10.5	4.7	2.4	2.9	0.8	0.9	(NA)
Switzerland	5.4	3.3	0.9	1.8	0.8	0.5	0.0
Turkey [2]	60.3	66.1	105.2	89.1	80.3	85.7	84.6
United Kingdom	9.5	1.6	2.5	3.4	2.5	3.1	3.4
Germany	2.7	4.5	2.7	1.8	1.5	1.7	1.0

NA Not available.   [1] Households of wage and salary earners.   [2] Excludes rent.

Source: Organization for Economic Cooperation and Development, Paris, France, *Main Economic Indicators,* monthly (copyright).

No. 781. Producer Price Indexes, by Stage of Processing: 1980 to 1998

[1982=100. Minus sign (-) indicates decline. See text this section]

Year	Crude materials				Interme-diate materi-als, sup-plies, and com-ponents	Finished goods		Consumer foods		Finished consumer goods excl. food
	Total	Food-stuffs and feed-stuffs	Fuel	Crude nonfood materials except fuel		Con-sumer goods	Capital equip-ment	Crude	Pro-cessed	
1980	95.3	104.6	69.4	91.8	90.3	88.6	85.8	93.9	92.3	87.1
1981	103.0	103.9	84.8	109.8	98.6	96.6	94.6	104.4	97.2	96.1
1982	100.0	100.0	100.0	100.0	100.0	100.0	100.0	100.0	100.0	100.0
1983	101.3	101.8	105.1	98.8	100.6	101.3	102.8	102.4	100.9	101.2
1984	103.5	104.7	105.1	101.0	103.1	103.3	105.2	111.4	104.9	102.2
1985	95.8	94.8	102.7	94.3	102.7	103.8	107.5	102.9	104.8	103.3
1986	87.7	93.2	92.2	76.0	99.1	101.4	109.7	105.6	107.4	98.5
1987	93.7	96.2	84.1	88.5	101.5	103.6	111.7	107.1	109.6	100.7
1988	96.0	106.1	82.1	85.9	107.1	106.2	114.3	109.8	112.7	103.1
1989	103.1	111.2	85.3	95.8	112.0	112.1	118.8	119.6	118.6	108.9
1990	108.9	113.1	84.8	107.3	114.5	118.2	122.9	123.0	124.4	115.3
1991	101.2	105.5	82.9	97.5	114.4	120.5	126.7	119.3	124.4	118.7
1992	100.4	105.1	84.0	94.2	114.7	121.7	129.1	107.6	124.4	120.8
1993	102.4	108.4	87.1	94.1	116.2	123.0	131.4	114.4	126.5	121.7
1994	101.8	106.5	82.4	97.0	118.5	123.3	134.1	111.3	127.9	121.6
1995	102.7	105.8	72.1	105.8	124.9	125.6	136.7	118.8	129.8	124.0
1996	113.8	121.5	92.6	105.7	125.7	129.5	138.3	129.2	133.8	127.6
1997	111.1	112.2	101.3	103.5	125.6	130.2	138.2	126.6	135.1	128.2
1998	96.7	103.8	86.4	84.5	123.0	128.9	137.5	127.0	134.8	126.4
PERCENT CHANGE										
1980	10.9	4.6	21.1	22.0	15.2	14.3	10.7	1.7	6.3	18.5
1981	8.1	-0.7	22.2	21.6	9.2	9.0	10.3	11.2	5.3	10.3
1982	-2.9	-3.8	17.9	19.6	1.4	3.5	5.7	-4.2	2.9	4.1
1983	1.3	1.8	5.1	-8.9	0.6	1.3	2.8	2.4	0.9	1.2
1984	2.2	2.8	-	-1.2	2.5	2.0	2.3	8.8	4.0	1.0
1985	-7.4	-9.5	-2.3	2.2	-0.4	0.5	2.2	-7.6	-0.1	1.1
1986	-8.5	-1.7	-10.2	-6.6	-3.5	-2.3	2.0	2.6	2.5	-4.6
1987	6.8	3.2	-8.8	-19.4	2.4	2.2	1.8	1.4	2.0	2.2
1988	2.5	10.3	-2.4	16.4	5.5	2.5	2.3	2.5	2.8	2.4
1989	7.4	4.8	3.9	-2.9	4.6	5.6	3.9	8.9	5.2	5.6
1990	5.6	1.7	-0.6	11.5	2.2	5.4	3.5	2.8	4.9	5.9
1991	-7.1	-6.7	-2.2	12.0	-0.1	1.9	3.1	-3.0	-	2.9
1992	-0.8	-0.4	1.3	-9.1	0.3	1.0	1.9	-9.8	-	1.8
1993	2.0	3.1	3.7	-3.4	1.3	1.1	1.8	6.3	1.7	0.7
1994	-0.6	-1.8	-5.4	-0.1	2.0	0.2	2.1	-2.7	1.1	-0.1
1995	0.9	-0.7	-12.5	3.1	5.4	1.9	1.9	6.7	1.5	2.0
1996	10.8	14.8	28.4	-0.1	0.6	3.1	1.2	8.8	3.1	2.9
1997	-2.4	-7.7	9.4	-2.1	-0.1	0.5	-0.1	-2.0	1.0	0.5
1998	-13.0	-7.5	-14.7	-18.4	-2.1	-1.0	-0.5	0.3	-0.2	-1.4

- Represents or rounds to zero.

Source: U.S. Bureau of Labor Statistics, *Producer Price Indexes,* monthly and annual.

No. 782. Producer Price Indexes, by Stage of Processing: 1990 to 1998

[1982=100, except as indicated]

Stage of processing	1990	1992	1993	1994	1995	1996	1997	1998
Finished goods	**119.2**	**123.2**	**124.7**	**125.5**	**127.9**	**131.3**	**131.8**	**130.6**
Finished consumer goods	**118.2**	**121.7**	**123.0**	**123.3**	**125.6**	**129.5**	**130.2**	**128.9**
Finished consumer foods.	**124.4**	**123.3**	**125.7**	**126.8**	**129.0**	**133.6**	**134.5**	**134.3**
Fresh fruits and melons...................	118.1	84.0	84.5	82.7	85.8	100.8	99.4	90.0
Fresh and dry vegetables.................	118.1	115.0	135.2	129.0	144.4	135.0	123.1	139.5
Eggs for fresh use (Dec. 1991=100)	(NA)	78.6	86.6	80.9	86.3	105.1	97.1	90.1
Bakery products......................	141.0	152.5	156.6	160.0	164.3	169.8	173.9	175.8
Milled rice..........................	102.5	108.8	101.3	118.3	113.1	129.4	127.3	124.8
Pasta products (June 1985=100).............	114.1	118.2	121.5	127.1	125.0	127.4	125.1	122.6
Beef and veal	116.0	109.5	112.9	103.6	100.9	100.2	102.8	99.5
Pork.............................	119.8	98.9	105.7	101.4	101.5	120.9	123.1	96.6
Processed young chickens.................	111.0	104.9	109.5	113.3	113.5	121.5	118.6	125.2
Processed turkeys.....................	107.6	102.3	101.0	108.5	104.9	105.5	101.0	94.9
Finfish and shellfish	147.2	156.1	156.5	161.4	170.8	165.9	178.1	183.0
Dairy products.......................	117.2	117.9	118.1	119.4	119.7	130.4	128.1	138.1
Processed fruits and vegetables	124.7	120.8	118.2	121.1	122.4	127.6	126.4	125.8
Confectionery end products	140.0	151.4	154.1	156.9	160.7	166.9	168.3	168.9
Soft drinks	122.3	125.6	126.2	127.0	133.1	134.0	133.2	134.8
Roasted coffee	113.0	100.5	100.5	128.2	146.5	129.2	152.9	144.4
Shortening and cooking oils	123.2	115.1	122.9	138.6	142.5	138.5	137.8	143.4
Finished consumer goods excluding foods ...	**115.3**	**120.8**	**121.7**	**121.6**	**124.0**	**127.6**	**128.2**	**126.4**
Alcoholic beverages	117.2	126.1	126.0	124.8	128.5	132.8	135.1	135.2
Women's apparel	116.1	119.9	120.2	119.7	119.6	119.9	120.5	121.9
Men's and boy's apparel	120.2	126.0	127.7	128.5	130.3	132.1	132.7	133.2
Girls', children's, and infants' apparel	115.3	119.0	120.1	119.9	121.6	122.4	122.9	122.0
Textile house furnishings	109.5	113.7	115.8	117.3	119.5	122.3	122.6	123.1
Footwear	125.6	132.0	134.4	135.5	139.2	141.6	143.7	144.7
Residential electric power (Dec. 1990=100).......	(NA)	107.5	109.8	109.8	111.8	112.8	112.8	110.8
Residential gas (Dec. 1990=100)	(NA)	100.9	107.3	108.8	104.4	110.4	116.5	114.0
Gasoline...........................	78.7	68.1	63.9	61.7	63.7	72.8	71.9	53.3
Fuel oil No. 2........................	73.3	61.7	59.1	56.0	56.6	69.5	64.8	48.1
Pharmaceutical preps, ethical (Prescription)	200.8	231.7	242.2	250.0	257.0	265.4	273.5	322.3
Pharmaceutical preps, proprietary (Over-counter)...	156.8	173.6	180.0	183.2	186.5	185.1	184.8	184.5
Soaps and synthetic detergents	117.7	120.6	122.2	121.4	122.9	125.2	126.4	126.1
Cosmetics and other toilet preparations	121.6	126.7	129.1	128.7	129.0	130.2	130.6	133.0
Tires, tubes, and tread	96.8	98.9	98.9	98.6	100.2	97.0	95.2	94.0
Sanitary papers and health products	135.3	136.9	134.6	133.2	144.4	149.9	147.1	145.1
Newspaper circulation...................	144.1	166.6	169.5	174.9	185.6	198.8	201.9	202.7
Periodical circulation....................	150.3	160.0	164.8	171.1	176.6	180.6	188.1	193.5
Book publishing	153.4	165.9	169.1	175.8	185.0	193.9	200.1	205.2
Household furniture	125.1	130.0	133.4	138.0	141.8	144.5	146.2	148.3
Floor coverings	119.0	120.3	120.2	121.5	123.7	126.6	128.0	128.2
Household appliances...................	110.8	111.4	112.9	112.8	112.4	112.7	110.1	108.9
Home electronic equipment	82.7	82.0	80.2	80.3	78.9	79.0	77.1	76.1
Household glassware	132.5	141.6	142.9	147.4	153.2	157.3	161.3	162.8
Household flatware.....................	122.1	125.2	130.7	133.9	138.3	138.4	138.5	139.2
Lawn and garden equipment, except tractors	123.0	125.3	126.2	128.4	130.4	132.3	132.2	131.7
Passenger cars	118.3	126.9	129.8	133.9	134.1	135.4	133.6	131.9
Toys, games, and children's vehicles	118.1	121.4	121.5	122.4	124.3	125.3	125.2	124.3
Sporting and athletic goods	112.6	118.2	118.6	120.1	122.0	123.3	124.7	126.2
Tobacco products.....................	221.4	275.3	260.3	224.7	231.3	237.4	248.9	283.4
Mobile homes	117.5	121.7	127.8	137.0	145.6	149.8	152.2	154.2
Jewelry, platinum, and karat gold	122.8	123.5	125.6	127.3	127.8	129.4	129.2	128.1
Costume jewelry and novelties	125.3	132.1	133.2	134.1	135.1	136.9	139.9	139.5
Capital equipment	**122.9**	**129.1**	**131.4**	**134.1**	**136.7**	**138.3**	**138.2**	**137.5**
Agricultural machinery and equipment	121.7	129.5	133.6	137.0	142.9	146.8	149.0	149.9
Construction machinery and equipment	121.6	128.7	132.0	133.7	136.7	139.8	142.2	145.1
Metal cutting machine tools	129.8	138.9	141.1	143.1	148.0	152.6	156.0	159.9
Metal forming machine tools................	128.7	135.9	138.4	141.9	145.7	149.6	153.9	157.7
Tools, dies, jigs, fixtures, and industrial molds	117.2	125.1	128.4	131.4	133.8	136.2	138.1	138.8
Pumps, compressors, and equipment	119.2	129.1	132.8	135.2	139.4	143.5	146.5	149.0
Industrial material handling equipment	115.0	118.4	120.2	122.4	125.3	127.4	129.7	131.3

See footnote at end of table.

U.S. Census Bureau, Statistical Abstract of the United States: 1999

No. 782. Producer Price Indexes, by Stage of Processing: 1990 to 1998—Continued

[1982=100, except as indicated]

Stage of processing	1990	1992	1993	1994	1995	1996	1997	1998
Capital equipment—Continued								
Electronic computers (Dec. 1990=100)	(NA)	73.2	62.9	58.0	51.8	42.4	33.2	24.7
Textile machinery	128.8	138.9	143.7	144.9	146.7	148.4	152.1	152.7
Paper industries machinery (June 1982=100)	134.8	142.7	144.9	147.5	151.0	153.8	157.4	160.3
Printing trades machinery	124.9	126.8	129.5	130.9	133.6	136.8	138.8	141.5
Transformers and power regulators	120.9	123.5	123.0	125.3	128.9	129.7	129.5	131.0
Communication/related equip. (Dec. 1985=100)	106.1	107.9	109.1	110.8	112.1	113.0	114.0	114.0
X-ray and electromedical equipment	109.8	113.8	114.0	112.4	111.8	109.9	107.4	106.7
Oil field and gas field machinery	102.4	107.6	108.2	110.8	114.1	117.8	122.8	125.8
Mining machinery and equipment	121.0	127.4	129.5	131.1	135.6	139.0	140.3	142.2
Office and store machines and equipment	109.5	111.0	111.0	111.3	111.5	112.0	112.4	112.3
Commercial furniture.	133.4	138.1	140.5	144.7	148.2	151.7	154.3	155.2
Light motor trucks.	130.0	142.4	150.3	157.1	159.0	160.3	158.9	155.1
Heavy motor trucks.	120.3	128.6	133.9	138.7	144.1	144.5	140.4	142.1
Truck trailers	110.8	115.1	118.2	122.2	131.7	130.7	130.3	135.0
Civilian aircraft (Dec. 1985=100)	115.3	128.8	131.5	135.4	141.8	147.3	150.0	150.1
Ships (Dec. 1985=100)	110.1	122.1	129.1	131.1	132.8	138.7	143.7	145.7
Railroad equipment.	118.6	123.7	125.2	129.2	134.8	137.2	134.7	134.9
Intermediate materials, supplies, and components	**114.5**	**114.7**	**116.2**	**118.5**	**124.9**	**125.7**	**125.6**	**123.0**
Intermediate foods and feeds	**113.3**	**110.7**	**112.7**	**114.8**	**114.8**	**128.1**	**125.4**	**116.1**
Flour	103.6	109.5	108.9	110.4	123.0	136.8	118.7	109.2
Refined sugar	122.7	119.8	118.2	118.2	119.3	123.7	123.6	119.8
Confectionery materials	101.2	102.2	98.9	112.4	109.1	107.9	105.4	93.8
Crude vegetable oils	115.8	97.1	110.5	135.0	130.0	118.1	116.6	131.1
Prepared animal feeds	107.4	108.3	111.0	111.3	109.1	135.3	132.9	107.9
Intermediate materials less foods and feeds . .	**120.9**	**122.0**	**123.8**	**127.1**	**135.2**	**134.0**	**134.2**	**133.5**
Synthetic fibers	106.7	103.4	103.6	104.1	109.4	111.3	111.1	109.8
Processed yarns and threads	112.6	110.8	107.8	108.4	112.8	114.7	114.0	112.7
Gray fabrics	117.2	120.6	118.6	116.8	121.2	121.4	121.9	121.6
Leather	177.5	163.7	168.6	179.6	191.4	177.9	182.7	178.5
Liquefied petroleum gas	77.4	65.8	63.6	58.2	65.1	84.7	84.5	60.1
Commercial electric power	115.3	124.4	127.2	128.8	131.7	131.6	131.7	130.5
Industrial electric power.	119.6	129.6	130.6	129.2	130.8	131.6	130.8	130.0
Commercial natural gas (Dec. 1990=100)	(NA)	96.7	102.7	103.7	96.5	103.2	109.8	106.6
Industrial natural gas (Dec. 1990=100).	(NA)	94.2	101.6	99.5	90.9	98.9	109.3	104.2
Natural gas to electric utilities (Dec. 1990=100)	(NA)	98.8	93.5	90.2	87.7	90.4	96.9	80.5
Jet fuels	76.0	61.9	59.0	53.9	55.0	66.7	62.9	46.0
No. 2 Diesel fuel	74.1	61.9	60.5	56.0	57.0	70.0	64.5	47.3
Residual fuel	57.7	45.9	49.6	48.2	52.6	59.8	59.5	43.8
Industrial chemicals	113.2	109.3	110.4	114.3	128.4	126.7	126.4	121.6
Prepared paint	124.8	131.6	133.3	135.3	142.1	147.2	152.1	155.0
Paint materials	136.3	131.1	131.5	132.1	139.4	141.3	141.5	143.8
Medicinal and botanical chemicals	102.2	111.3	120.7	125.4	128.3	128.6	133.4	135.0
Fats and oils, inedible	88.1	93.0	95.6	110.6	126.9	133.3	132.3	116.9
Mixed fertilizers	103.3	102.6	99.0	105.7	111.1	114.7	113.6	115.3
Nitrogenates	92.3	95.4	99.3	112.3	129.4	130.5	132.3	108.2
Phosphates	96.5	92.5	82.8	95.5	109.1	116.3	110.4	112.5
Other agricultural chemicals	119.9	129.2	134.7	140.8	144.3	146.1	147.8	149.7
Plastic resins and materials	124.1	116.4	117.1	122.4	143.5	133.1	137.3	125.6
Synthetic rubber.	111.9	103.8	105.7	108.9	126.3	122.2	119.3	117.2
Plastic construction products	117.2	112.7	116.6	122.9	133.8	130.9	128.2	126.2
Unsupported plastic film, sheet, and shapes	119.0	120.3	121.4	122.8	135.6	132.7	131.7	128.1
Plastic parts and components for manufacturing . . .	112.9	113.3	113.9	113.5	115.9	117.5	117.2	117.1
Softwood lumber	123.8	148.6	193.0	198.1	178.5	189.5	206.5	182.4
Hardwood lumber.	131.0	140.7	163.3	168.3	167.0	163.9	174.1	178.7
Millwork	130.4	143.3	156.6	162.4	163.8	166.6	170.9	171.1
Plywood	114.2	133.3	152.8	158.6	153.3	156.4	159.3	157.6
Woodpile	151.3	118.9	104.2	115.9	183.2	133.1	128.6	122.0
Paper.	128.8	123.2	123.8	126.0	159.0	149.4	143.9	146.0
Paperboard.	135.7	134.3	130.0	140.5	183.1	155.1	144.4	151.7
Paper boxes and containers	129.9	130.6	129.9	136.1	163.8	153.9	144.7	154.7
Building paper and board.	112.2	119.6	132.7	144.1	144.9	137.2	129.6	132.8

See footnote at end of table.

U.S. Census Bureau, Statistical Abstract of the United States: 1999

[1982=100, except as indicated]

Stage of processing	1990	1992	1993	1994	1995	1996	1997	1998
Intermediate materials less foods and feeds—Continued								
Commercial printing (June 1982=100)	128.0	131.1	134.8	136.5	144.5	148.3	148.7	152.1
Foundry and forge shop products	117.2	120.1	121.3	123.9	129.3	132.6	134.1	135.0
Steel mill products	112.1	106.4	108.2	113.4	120.1	115.6	116.4	113.9
Primary nonferrous metals....................	133.4	108.1	98.1	115.7	146.8	126.2	126.2	106.7
Aluminum mill shapes........................	127.9	121.9	120.4	127.7	160.4	144.8	147.5	142.1
Copper and brass mill shapes	174.6	166.0	150.7	167.3	195.2	179.0	177.3	153.4
Nonferrous wire and cable..................	142.6	136.7	133.1	139.8	151.5	147.5	148.1	140.9
Metal containers...........................	114.0	113.9	109.7	108.1	117.2	110.0	108.1	108.7
Hardware	125.9	132.7	135.2	137.5	141.1	143.8	145.6	147.0
Plumbing fixtures and brass fittings	144.3	153.1	155.9	159.6	166.0	171.1	174.5	175.1
Heating equipment..........................	131.6	137.3	140.4	142.5	147.5	151.2	152.4	153.2
Fabricated structural metal products	121.8	122.1	123.2	127.3	135.1	137.8	140.3	142.5
Fabricated ferrous wire products (June 1982=100)..	114.6	117.5	119.3	122.6	125.7	126.8	128.0	130.1
Other miscellaneous metal products	120.7	121.1	121.4	122.7	124.9	125.7	126.2	126.2
Mechanical power transmission equipment	125.3	132.1	136.2	140.5	146.9	151.5	154.8	157.7
Air conditioning and refrigeration equipment	122.1	125.4	126.0	127.0	130.2	132.7	132.6	134.6
Metal valves, excluding fluid power (Dec. 1982=100)................................	125.3	133.7	137.2	140.3	145.3	149.8	153.3	156.6
Ball and roller bearings	130.6	139.0	141.9	145.7	152.0	157.8	162.9	165.2
Wiring devices	132.2	134.8	138.6	141.5	147.2	151.2	154.0	154.2
Motors, generators, motor generator sets	132.9	136.6	138.6	140.2	143.9	145.6	144.7	145.8
Switchgear and switchboard equipment	124.4	131.5	134.6	136.8	140.3	142.6	145.6	148.3
Electronic components and accessories	118.4	117.5	117.7	116.6	113.6	108.9	104.0	100.1
Internal combustion engines.................	120.2	128.4	130.2	132.9	135.6	138.8	140.1	140.7
Machine shop products	124.3	126.8	128.0	129.7	131.3	133.6	135.2	136.3
Flat glass	107.5	106.5	107.3	110.5	113.2	110.0	108.4	107.2
Cement	103.7	106.3	111.7	119.5	128.1	134.0	139.4	145.7
Concrete products	113.5	117.2	120.2	124.6	129.4	133.2	136.0	140.1
Asphalt felts and coatings	97.1	96.2	96.8	95.3	100.0	100.0	99.9	99.6
Gypsum products..........................	105.2	99.9	108.3	136.1	154.5	154.0	170.8	177.2
Glass containers	120.4	125.1	125.8	127.5	130.5	129.1	125.7	125.9
Motor vehicle parts.........................	111.2	113.1	113.8	114.3	116.0	116.2	115.4	114.6
Aircraft engines and engine parts (Dec. 1985=100) .	113.5	125.0	127.7	130.7	132.8	134.7	135.7	136.9
Aircraft parts and auxiliary equipment, n.e.c. (June 1985=100)................................	117.7	128.0	131.2	134.0	135.7	139.3	141.3	142.6
Photographic supplies.......................	127.6	125.6	124.3	124.7	126.8	128.9	130.0	128.9
Medical/surgical/personal aid devices.	127.3	133.9	137.8	140.4	141.3	143.1	143.1	143.3
Crude materials for further processing	108.9	100.4	102.4	101.8	102.7	113.8	111.1	96.7
Crude foodstuffs and feedstuffs.	113.1	105.1	108.4	106.5	105.8	121.5	112.2	103.8
Wheat	87.6	98.5	98.4	104.8	118.6	136.6	108.2	87.8
Corn	100.9	96.0	92.9	100.1	109.0	158.5	110.1	91.7
Slaughter cattle	122.5	115.4	116.7	105.8	99.5	95.8	97.9	92.5
Slaughter hogs	94.1	70.7	76.1	65.9	70.2	88.6	87.0	52.2
Slaughter broilers/fryers......................	119.5	115.2	125.9	127.7	129.1	148.0	137.2	151.8
Slaughter turkeys	116.9	106.6	113.1	119.6	120.3	121.5	112.9	110.4
Fluid milk	100.8	96.1	94.1	95.7	93.6	107.9	97.5	112.6
Soybeans	100.8	97.3	104.8	106.0	102.2	127.9	131.0	103.4
Cane sugar, raw...........................	119.2	112.1	113.2	115.2	119.7	118.6	116.8	117.2
Crude nonfood materials	101.5	93.5	94.7	94.8	96.8	104.5	106.4	88.3
Raw cotton	118.2	89.8	91.9	121.3	156.2	130.0	116.5	111.0
Leaf tobacco	95.8	101.0	100.3	100.2	102.5	105.1	(NA)	104.6
Cattle hides...............................	217.8	171.4	180.2	200.9	209.9	186.5	196.1	153.3
Coal......................................	97.5	95.0	96.1	96.7	95.0	94.5	96.3	93.1
Natural gas...............................	80.4	80.6	84.7	78.8	66.6	91.2	101.7	83.7
Crude petroleum	71.0	58.0	51.4	47.1	51.1	62.2	57.5	35.7
Logs and timber...........................	142.8	164.8	212.3	219.1	204.4	206.8	214.4	208.2
Wastepaper...............................	138.9	117.5	117.4	209.5	371.1	141.6	163.3	146.0
Iron ore	83.3	83.7	82.7	82.7	91.8	96.7	96.3	95.5
Iron and steel scrap	166.0	139.2	172.5	192.9	202.7	191.1	188.9	164.9
Nonferrous metal ores (Dec. 1983=100)	98.3	75.4	67.2	81.4	101.6	90.2	82.2	66.9
Copper base scrap	181.3	162.9	136.1	155.5	193.5	166.3	157.7	116.3
Aluminum base scrap	172.6	137.6	129.2	172.9	209.4	173.4	195.1	162.8
Construction sand, gravel, and crushed stone	125.4	130.6	134.0	137.9	142.3	145.6	148.2	152.7

NA Not available.

Source: U.S. Bureau of Labor Statistics, *Producer Price Indexes, Producer Price Indexes*, monthly and annual.

No. 783. Producer Price Indexes for the Net Output of Selected Industries: 1990 to 1998

[Indexes are based on selling prices reported by establishments of all sizes by probability sampling. Manufacturing industries selected by shipment value. N.e.c.= not elsewhere classified. See text, Section 27, Domestic Trade]

Industry	SIC code [1]	Index base	1990	1995	1996	1997	1998
Iron ores	1011	12/84	82.2	91.0	95.7	95.3	94.5
Copper ores	1021	06/88	112.8	157.1	117.0	110.4	78.0
Lead and zinc ores	1031	12/85	(X)	103.1	109.4	138.6	107.2
Gold ores	1041	06/85	113.8	115.9	117.0	100.9	90.0
Metal mining services	1081	12/85	108.6	111.4	112.5	116.8	122.2
Metal ores, n.e.c.	1099	12/85	137.9	119.3	110.5	100.8	90.3
Bituminous coal and lignite	1211	12/81	100.5	95.3	95.0	95.9	92.7
Anthracite mining	1231	12/79	157.8	158.9	158.6	159.0	160.1
Coal Mining Services	1241	06/85	107.0	105.7	109.2	108.1	108.1
Crude petroleum and natural gas liquids	1331	06/96	(X)	(X)	(X)	115.6	86.0
Drilling oil and gas wells	1381	12/85	91.3	104.2	115.1	143.7	154.9
Oil and gas exploration services	1382	12/85	73.1	103.4	103.7	105.6	114.5
Oil and gas field services, n.e.c.	1389	12/85	103.8	111.0	108.2	112.7	113.8
Dimension stone	1411	06/85	113.4	126.4	132.2	138.2	142.2
Crushed and broken limestone	1422	12/83	119.0	130.9	132.4	134.5	137.4
Crushed and broken granite, n.e.c.	1423	12/83	124.1	153.6	156.5	159.7	166.3
Crushed and broken stone, n.e.c.	1429	12/83	122.8	137.1	143.0	145.4	147.9
Construction sand and gravel	1442	06/82	126.9	146.6	151.1	155.3	162.9
Industrial sand	1446	06/82	119.3	134.2	136.6	138.9	142.2
Kaolin and ball clay	1455	06/84	111.9	115.2	116.5	117.1	115.6
Clay and related minerals, n.e.c.	1459	06/84	118.7	128.8	130.2	131.7	133.4
Potash, soda, and borate minerals	1474	12/84	116.4	113.7	121.2	117.4	119.0
Phosphate rock	1475	12/82	93.8	98.0	101.8	(NA)	(NA)
Chemicals and fertilizer mineral mining, n.e.c.	1479	12/89	102.8	95.1	91.8	92.7	93.4
Non-metallic minerals (except fuels) services	1481	06/85	102.7	100.0	103.4	104.7	104.7
Miscellaneous nonmetallic minerals	1499	06/85	110.3	126.8	130.3	133.5	136.7
Meat packing plants	2011	12/80	119.8	105.9	110.9	113.5	101.4
Sausage and other prepared meats	2013	12/82	112.7	108.5	115.5	118.8	113.3
Poultry slaughtering and processing	2015	12/81	118.9	120.5	127.1	124.7	127.0
Natural and processed cheese	2022	06/81	110.3	110.8	119.6	115.7	126.2
Dry, condensed, and evaporated milk products	2023	12/83	118.8	131.1	139.5	138.7	146.5
Ice cream and frozen desserts	2024	06/83	122.2	125.8	130.5	135.1	142.0
Fluid milk	2026	12/82	121.4	123.3	134.3	133.6	140.3
Canned specialties	2032	12/82	132.8	154.3	157.7	163.0	165.4
Canned fruits, vegetables, preserves, jams, and jellies	2033	06/81	129.9	131.8	138.4	137.7	137.0
Pickled fruits/veg./veg. sauces/seasonings/ salad dressings	2035	06/81	142.9	157.0	160.9	161.2	162.4
Frozen fruits and vegetables	2037	06/81	138.3	134.8	141.5	139.2	138.6
Frozen specialties	2038	12/82	127.3	133.2	135.7	136.8	137.0
Flour and other grain mill products	2041	06/83	102.2	116.0	133.3	114.3	103.3
Cereal breakfast foods	2043	12/83	145.2	169.4	174.5	168.2	161.4
Wet corn milling	2046	06/85	114.7	124.5	133.6	123.6	107.1
Dog and cat food	2047	12/85	115.5	124.6	130.7	132.1	132.4
Prepared animal feeds, n.e.c.	2048	12/80	91.5	98.3	119.8	112.2	95.2
Bread and other bakery products, except cookies and crackers	2051	06/80	159.4	189.4	195.7	199.7	201.3
Cookies and crackers	2052	06/83	141.9	156.5	161.4	167.0	170.3
Candy and other confectionery products, and chewing gum	2064	06/83	122.9	137.8	143.8	146.2	146.7
Soybean oil mill products	2075	12/79	84.4	87.7	98.6	103.2	86.7
Malt beverages	2082	06/82	115.2	124.0	127.7	128.0	128.1
Bottled and canned soft drinks	2086	06/81	127.2	140.2	141.2	140.5	142.4
Flavoring extracts and syrups, n.e.c.	2087	12/85	115.5	125.5	127.7	130.7	131.3
Fresh or frozen packaged fish	2092	12/82	129.4	149.4	140.0	145.2	151.7
Coffee	2095	06/81	120.0	152.6	138.7	161.8	153.8
Potato and corn chips, and similar snacks	2096	06/91	(X)	104.3	106.5	109.4	111.1
Food preparations, n.e.c.	2099	12/85	114.3	121.4	124.1	127.5	128.4
Cigarettes	2111	12/82	197.6	204.3	210.5	223.3	260.4
Cotton broadwoven fabric	2211	12/80	109.3	118.6	119.1	118.5	117.4
Manmade fiber and silk broadwoven fabric	2221	06/81	115.6	112.4	113.0	115.0	114.8
Knit outerwear	2253	12/84	111.1	116.7	117.9	118.6	118.9
Carpet and rugs	2273	06/90	(X)	102.2	104.4	105.9	106.6
Spun yarn	2281	12/82	106.2	105.8	106.1	104.7	102.4
Men's and boys' separate trousers and slacks	2325	12/81	120.7	130.7	133.1	133.4	136.5
Women's, misses', and juniors' dresses	2335	12/80	125.6	124.9	125.4	126.0	126.7
Women's, misses', and juniors' outerwear, n.e.c.	2339	06/83	104.2	106.6	108.4	110.9	110.9
House furnishings, n.e.c.	2392	06/83	108.0	116.8	120.4	120.5	119.5
Automotive trimmings, apparel findings, and related products	2396	12/83	107.6	110.2	117.2	120.1	124.2
Logging camps and logging contractors	2411	12/81	135.6	194.3	185.8	191.2	188.2
Sawmills and planing mills	2421	12/80	109.9	150.8	152.0	163.1	151.5
Millwork	2431	06/83	120.4	152.1	153.6	156.4	157.2
Wood kitchen cabinets	2434	06/84	120.4	144.3	147.3	150.4	153.1
Softwood plywood	2436	12/80	102.5	158.0	139.5	142.4	142.9
Mobile homes	2451	06/81	122.5	151.0	155.3	157.8	159.8
Wood household furniture, except upholstered	2511	12/79	158.9	186.3	189.7	192.3	195.8
Upholstered wood household furniture	2512	06/82	121.5	132.9	136.3	138.1	140.1
Nonwood office furniture	2522	12/79	169.5	188.1	192.4	193.5	191.5
Public building and related furniture	2531	12/84	118.4	130.0	133.7	135.9	136.0
Paper mills	2621	06/81	134.0	164.8	152.2	143.2	145.3
Paperboard mills	2631	12/82	146.0	203.2	169.8	158.2	165.4

See footnotes at end of table.

U.S. Census Bureau, Statistical Abstract of the United States: 1999

[See headnote, page 505]

Industry	SIC code [1]	Index base	1990	1995	1996	1997	1998
Corrugated and solid fiber boxes	2653	03/80	139.6	186.5	168.7	154.9	168.8
Folding paperboard boxes	2657	12/83	129.1	141.4	143.4	142.2	143.6
Paper coated and laminated, n.e.c.	2672	06/93	(X)	108.2	110.5	110.1	109.6
Plastics, foil and coated paper bags	2673	12/83	150.2	161.4	158.6	160.9	156.5
Sanitary Paper Products	2676	06/83	130.0	149.5	150.3	147.8	146.0
Newspaper publishing	2711	12/79	220.4	286.7	306.9	317.7	328.5
Periodical publishing	2721	12/79	205.7	246.3	253.2	263.2	276.8
Book Publishing	2731	12/80	175.2	214.3	224.7	232.1	238.0
Miscellaneous publishing	2741	06/84	133.8	167.1	174.5	181.1	187.8
Commercial printing, lithographic	2752	06/82	127.9	145.0	149.0	149.8	153.3
Commercial printing, n.e.c.	2759	06/82	136.1	154.4	158.2	159.4	160.9
Manifold business forms	2761	12/83	124.6	163.9	168.4	165.8	167.1
Industrial inorganic chemicals, n.e.c.	2819	12/82	117.9	125.2	136.0	135.5	132.3
Plastic materials and resins	2821	12/80	139.5	159.0	149.6	153.9	139.5
Noncellulosic manmade fibers	2824	06/81	102.7	107.9	109.3	107.7	106.6
Medicinal chemicals and botanical products (in bulk)	2833	06/82	104.9	129.2	129.8	134.2	136.3
Pharmaceutical preparations	2834	06/81	203.5	249.9	253.9	259.1	289.9
In vivo and In vitro diagnostics	2835	03/80	152.3	165.3	166.6	167.4	177.8
Biological products, except diagnostics	2836	06/91	(X)	109.9	111.2	112.3	115.8
Soap and other detergents	2841	06/83	115.2	121.7	123.8	124.6	124.8
Specialty cleaning, polishing and sanitation preparations	2842	06/83	118.6	129.2	129.6	130.8	132.6
Toilet preparations	2844	03/80	153.2	167.1	168.5	168.9	171.7
Paints and Allied Products	2851	06/83	125.0	143.1	147.4	152.1	154.9
Cyclic (coal tar) crudes and intermediates, organic dyes and pigments	2865	12/82	114.1	125.0	118.3	115.2	109.3
Industrial organic chemicals, n.e.c.	2869	12/82	125.6	163.0	171.2	171.5	168.0
Agricultural chemicals, n.e.c.	2879	06/82	114.7	135.2	136.5	137.6	139.4
Adhesives and sealants	2891	12/83	123.4	145.1	146.1	148.8	151.4
Chemicals and chemical preparations, n.e.c.	2899	06/85	112.5	128.9	130.3	133.2	134.3
Petroleum Refining	2911	06/85	90.1	74.5	85.3	83.1	62.3
Tires and inner tubes	3011	06/81	103.0	108.5	105.2	103.4	102.2
Fabricated rubber products, n.e.c.	3069	06/83	114.4	128.6	130.6	132.1	132.4
Unsupported plastic film and sheet	3081	06/93	(X)	112.4	108.9	108.3	103.8
Plastic bottles	3085	06/93	(X)	110.3	107.0	107.1	105.5
Plastic foam products	3086	06/93	(X)	110.6	110.7	109.7	108.6
Custom compounding of purchased plastic resins	3087	06/93	(X)	108.2	108.1	106.7	107.4
Plastic products n.e.c.	3089	06/93	(X)	105.8	106.4	106.3	106.3
Products of purchased glass	3231	06/83	117.6	126.8	126.3	127.1	127.5
Concrete products	3272	12/79	127.8	144.4	148.1	151.6	156.7
Ready-mixed concrete	3273	06/81	114.3	131.3	135.2	138.0	142.3
Blast furnaces and steel mills	3312	06/82	110.8	118.5	114.0	114.2	111.4
Cold finishing of steel shapes - mfpm	3316	06/82	111.5	122.0	116.4	116.7	114.7
Steel pipe and tubes - mfpm	3317	06/82	111.8	127.0	126.7	131.8	132.7
Gray iron foundries	3321	12/80	123.4	137.7	141.5	143.0	143.3
Primary copper	3331	06/80	152.4	194.4	144.8	137.3	106.2
Secondary nonferrous metals	3341	06/80	97.0	102.1	94.0	94.5	85.9
Rolling, drawing and extruding of copper	3351	12/80	149.4	161.6	151.1	149.9	131.9
Aluminum sheet, plate, foil and welded tube products	3353	06/81	129.6	165.6	148.4	152.9	145.5
Nonferrous wire drawing and insulating	3357	12/82	148.7	157.4	153.7	154.5	148.1
Metal cans	3411	06/81	116.6	118.7	112.0	110.4	110.2
Hardware, n.e.c.	3429	06/85	110.6	121.7	123.7	125.0	126.0
Fabricated structural metal	3441	06/82	118.6	126.2	130.7	132.8	136.8
Metal doors, sash and trim	3442	06/83	126.3	148.5	151.1	152.5	152.9
Fabricated plate work (boiler shops)	3443	03/80	142.3	155.6	159.1	161.9	164.7
Sheet metal work	3444	12/82	129.4	137.6	137.7	138.6	139.9
Bolts, nuts, screws, rivets, and washers	3452	06/82	115.8	122.2	124.2	125.6	127.0
Automotive stampings	3465	12/82	112.6	111.7	112.5	112.8	112.1
Metal stampings, n.e.c.	3469	06/84	121.1	126.6	127.3	128.5	128.9
Metal coating and allied services	3479	12/84	114.5	116.6	118.0	119.4	119.1
Industrial Valves	3491	06/91	(X)	111.7	114.8	117.3	119.7
Fabricated metal products, n.e.c.	3499	06/85	117.6	127.4	128.5	129.9	131.8
Turbines and turbine generator sets	3511	06/82	134.3	148.1	145.7	146.9	146.9
Internal combustion engines, n.e.c.	3519	12/82	115.7	131.2	134.3	135.7	136.2
Farm machinery and equipment	3523	12/82	116.8	133.2	136.7	138.8	140.4
Lawn and garden equipment	3524	12/82	116.6	124.1	125.9	126.0	124.9
Construction machinery	3531	12/80	137.6	157.2	161.6	164.4	167.8
Special tools, dies, jigs, fixtures and industrial molds	3544	06/81	124.5	140.1	142.5	144.1	144.9
Special industry machinery, n.e.c.	3559	12/81	137.5	156.5	160.5	163.3	166.0
Pumps and pumping equipment	3561	12/83	119.9	141.3	146.1	150.4	153.3
General industrial machinery, n.e.c.	3569	12/84	123.4	143.4	147.0	149.5	151.3
Electronic computers	3571	12/90	(X)	53.8	45.2	36.5	29.1
Computer storage devices	3572	12/92	(X)	67.2	57.6	51.1	45.3
Computer peripheral equipment, n.e.c.	3577	12/93	(X)	95.7	93.1	90.5	84.5
Refrigeration and heating equipment	3585	12/82	119.0	126.0	128.2	129.2	131.3
Service industry machinery, n.e.c.	3589	06/82	130.5	150.6	154.6	159.3	161.7
Machinery, except electrical, n.e.c.	3599	06/84	113.9	121.4	123.4	125.4	126.9
Switchgear and switchboard apparatus	3613	06/85	118.5	132.4	133.6	135.0	138.2
Electric motors and generators	3621	06/83	127.5	137.5	139.1	138.6	139.8
Relays and industrial controls	3625	06/85	115.4	130.7	133.6	137.8	140.4

See footnotes at end of table.

U.S. Census Bureau, Statistical Abstract of the United States: 1999

No. 783. Producer Price Indexes for the Net Output of Selected Industries: 1990 to 1998—Continued

[See headnote, page 505]

Industry	SIC code [1]	Index base	1990	1995	1996	1997	1998
Household audio & video equipment.............	3651	03/80	86.5	82.6	82.4	80.5	79.7
Telephone & telegraph apparatus.............	3661	12/85	112.0	118.2	119.7	119.4	117.9
Radio and television broadcast and communication equipment.............................	3663	12/91	(X)	103.5	104.2	105.7	105.5
Printed circuit boards......................	3672	06/91	(X)	95.1	95.9	95.0	93.9
Semiconductors and related devices...........	3674	06/81	105.0	91.3	84.8	76.7	70.6
Electrical equipment for internal combustion engines ..	3694	12/82	118.2	126.7	128.2	128.8	127.9
Motor vehicles and passenger car bodies	3711	06/82	119.9	139.1	140.4	138.7	136.8
Truck and bus bodies......................	3713	12/82	125.4	145.5	149.9	153.5	155.3
Motor vehicle parts and accessories............	3714	12/82	108.9	113.5	114.0	113.1	112.6
Aircraft...............................	3721	12/85	116.0	137.3	140.5	142.3	142.6
Aircraft engines and engine parts..............	3724	12/85	112.6	130.9	133.4	134.8	135.7
Ship building and repairing	3731	12/85	114.0	127.6	130.1	133.3	134.8
Railroad equipment.......................	3743	06/84	114.2	127.6	129.6	127.4	127.5
Search/detection/navigation/&guidance sys&aero/ nautical nav syst	3812	12/91	(X)	104.8	105.5	107.0	109.0
Industrial process control instruments	3823	06/83	126.4	138.2	142.2	147.7	149.9
Electrical measuring and integrating instruments.....	3825	12/83	117.7	133.8	134.2	135.0	135.1
Laboratory analytical instruments	3826	12/85	107.6	114.6	115.9	117.5	118.4
Surgical and medical instruments and apparatus.....	3841	06/82	120.0	129.7	130.9	129.0	127.9
Surgical, orthopedic and prosthetic appliances and supplies..............................	3842	06/83	133.5	154.8	156.1	158.1	160.5
Electromedical equipment...................	3845	06/85	103.0	109.7	107.9	104.7	103.8
Photographic equipment and supplies...........	3861	12/83	112.2	113.8	114.9	113.5	110.0
Sporting and athletic goods, n.e.c.	3949	12/85	114.1	123.6	125.3	127.5	129.1
Signs and advertising displays................	3993	12/85	112.5	129.6	132.1	134.3	136.2

SERVICES

Industry	SIC code [1]	Index base	1990	1995	1996	1997	1998
Railroads, line haul operations................	4011	12/84	107.5	111.7	111.5	112.1	113.4
Local trucking without storage................	4212	06/93	(X)	102.9	102.9	104.6	104.8
Trucking, except local	4213	06/92	(X)	105.1	107.6	110.7	114.1
Local trucking with storage	4214	06/93	(X)	110.7	11.9	112.2	113.0
Courier services, except by air................	4215	12/92	(X)	109.5	113.0	116.4	122.2
Farm product warehousing and storage..........	4221	12/92	(X)	104.0	102.4	102.9	104.1
Refrigerated warehousing and storage	4222	12/91	(X)	104.2	104.6	105.1	105.5
General warehousing and storage	4225	06/93	(X)	103.1	104.3	105.5	107.2
United States Postal Service.................	4311	06/89	100.0	132.2	132.3	132.3	132.3
Deep sea foreign transportation of freight	4412	06/88	113.1	113.3	114.1	113.1	116.4
Domestic deep sea transportation of freight	4424	06/88	106.7	121.5	122.0	124.5	120.9
Marine cargo handling	4491	12/91	(X)	102.1	101.6	103.7	105.0
Tugging and towing services.................	4492	12/92	(X)	107.2	110.9	113.3	115.7
Air transportation, scheduled................	4512	12/89	110.6	137.8	148.1	153.9	152.6
Air courier services	4513	12/89	105.0	109.5	113.9	115.1	113.2
Air transportation, nonscheduled..............	4522	06/92	(X)	103.6	105.0	104.5	106.0
Airports, flying fields, and airport services	4581	06/92	(X)	102.8	106.6	109.7	112.5
Crude petroleum pipelines	4612	06/86	94.2	113.4	104.7	96.0	96.8
Refined petroleum pipelines	4613	06/86	100.8	104.6	104.3	105.3	104.8
Travel agencies	4724	12/89	107.3	111.3	109.9	114.5	112.5
Freight transportation arrangement.............	4731	12/94	(X)	99.8	101.5	101.4	99.8
Telephone communications, except radiotelephone	4813	06/95	(X)	(X)	99.9	99.6	98.5
Radio broadcasting.......................	4832	06/88	109.2	128.8	140.6	148.5	151.2
Cable and other pay television services...........	4841	06/93	(X)	98.5	103.3	108.3	112.4
Electric power and natural gas utilities...........	4981	12/90	(X)	109.4	111.1	112.0	110.4
Scrap and waste materials	5093	12/86	140.7	181.8	147.6	152.7	131.7
Operators and lessors of nonresidential buildings	6512	12/95	(X)	(X)	99.6	101.0	103.1
Real estate agents and managers..............	6531	12/95	(X)	(X)	99.6	100.8	102.5
Hotels and motels	7011	06/93	(X)	106.1	110.1	115.6	119.8
Advertising agencies	7311	06/95	(X)	(X)	101.7	103.8	105.3
Building cleaning and maintenance services, n.e.c.	7349	12/94	(X)	101.0	102.4	104.5	105.6
Employment agencies	7361	06/94	(X)	102.0	103.0	104.5	106.4
Help supply services	7363	06/94	(X)	103.1	105.1	106.9	109.1
Prepackaged software	7372	12/97	(X)	(X)	(X)	(X)	100.6
Truck rental and leasing, without drivers	7513	06/91	(X)	103.7	106.5	104.5	104.7
Passenger car rental, without drivers	7514	12/91	(X)	123.8	119.3	130.5	132.5
Offices and clinics of doctors of medicine	8011	12/93	(X)	106.8	107.6	109.0	11.2
Skilled and intermediate care facilities...........	8053	12/94	(X)	103.7	110.0	114.7	119.4
General medical and surgical hospitals	8062	12/92	(X)	109.9	112.5	113.6	114.5
Psychiatric hospitals	8063	12/92	(X)	110.4	113.7	112.0	108.2
Specialty hospitals, except psychiatric...........	8069	12/92	(X)	110.9	113.6	114.7	117.1
Medical laboratories......................	8071	06/94	(X)	104.0	105.3	106.1	106.4
Home health care services	8082	12/96	(X)	(X)	(X)	103.3	106.1
Legal services	8111	12/96	(X)	(X)	(X)	102.5	106.2
Engineering design, analysis, and consulting services .	8711	12/96	(X)	(X)	(X)	102.3	105.0
Architectural design, analysis, and consulting services .	8712	12/96	(X)	(X)	(X)	102.0	105.5
Accounting, auditing, and bookkeeping services	8721	06/95	(X)	(X)	102.9	105.7	108.2

NA Not available.   X Not applicable.   [1] Standard Industrial Classification code.

Source: U.S. Bureau of Labor Statistics, *Producer Price Indexes*, monthly.

Prices   507

No. 784. Chain-Type Price Indexes for Personal Consumption Expenditures: 1980 to 1998

[1992=100. For explanation of "chain-type", see text, Section 14, Income]

Item	1980	1985	1990	1993	1994	1995	1996	1997	1998
Personal consumption expenditures..	**58.5**	**75.8**	**92.9**	**102.7**	**105.2**	**107.6**	**109.8**	**111.8**	**112.7**
Durable goods	75.6	87.8	96.6	101.2	103.3	103.7	102.8	100.7	98.3
Motor vehicles and parts	68.3	83.2	93.8	103.3	107.2	110.8	112.7	112.7	111.9
Furniture and household equipment	92.0	100.9	101.5	98.6	98.6	96.0	92.3	88.2	84.2
Nondurable goods.	65.3	78.7	94.6	101.5	102.8	104.0	106.1	107.7	107.7
Food	63.6	77.5	95.1	101.7	103.9	106.1	109.0	111.7	113.5
Clothing and shoes	72.5	81.6	94.5	101.0	100.3	97.7	96.2	96.4	94.7
Gasoline and oil.	97.8	99.4	101.8	99.1	99.6	101.1	107.3	107.3	93.5
Fuel oil and coal	93.7	104.6	107.8	99.6	98.0	97.2	108.6	109.6	99.6
Services	51.0	71.6	91.2	103.6	106.9	110.4	113.3	116.6	118.8
Housing	52.4	73.9	93.5	102.8	105.7	109.0	112.3	115.7	119.4
Household operation	60.3	87.7	94.2	102.8	104.9	105.8	107.9	108.7	106.9
Electricity and gas	62.1	92.4	95.2	103.1	103.7	103.9	106.3	108.8	105.1
Other household operation	59.1	83.8	93.5	102.6	105.7	107.2	109.0	108.7	108.0
Transportation.	56.0	71.1	89.9	104.3	106.3	109.0	110.9	113.2	114.7
Medical care	43.6	65.6	89.2	106.2	110.5	115.0	117.5	120.2	122.8
Other.	51.8	69.3	90.2	102.2	105.4	109.5	113.0	117.9	120.1

Source: U.S. Bureau of Economic Analysis, *The National Income and Product Accounts of the United States*, 1929-94, Vol. 2; and *Survey of Current Business*, August 1997 and May 1999.

No. 785. Chain-Type Price Indexes for Gross Domestic Product: 1990 to 1998

[1992=100. For explanation of "chain-type", see text, Section 14, Income]

Item	1990	1993	1994	1995	1996	1997	1998
Gross domestic product	**93.6**	**102.6**	**105.1**	**107.5**	**109.5**	**111.6**	**112.7**
Personal consumption expenditures.	92.9	102.7	105.2	107.6	109.8	111.8	112.7
Durable goods	96.6	101.2	103.3	103.7	102.8	100.7	98.3
Nondurable goods.	94.6	101.5	102.8	104.0	106.1	107.7	107.7
Services	91.2	103.6	106.9	110.4	113.3	116.6	118.8
Gross private domestic investment	98.4	101.5	103.3	104.7	104.5	104.1	102.8
Fixed investment	98.2	101.5	103.4	104.8	104.7	104.5	103.2
Nonresidential	98.4	100.7	101.9	102.4	101.5	100.2	97.7
Structures	98.8	103.3	107.0	111.4	114.3	118.2	121.6
Producers' durable equipment	98.2	99.6	99.9	99.0	96.8	93.9	89.8
Residential.	97.8	103.7	107.1	110.9	113.0	116.0	118.4
Exports of goods and services	98.7	100.1	101.2	103.4	101.6	99.5	97.4
Exports of goods	101.8	99.1	100.0	101.8	98.2	94.8	91.7
Exports of services	91.7	102.3	104.3	107.3	110.2	112.2	112.9
Imports of goods and services	100.4	98.8	99.4	101.6	99.4	95.7	90.7
Imports of goods.	102.2	98.5	98.9	101.1	98.1	93.9	88.3
Imports of services	93.2	100.0	101.6	104.3	105.9	105.3	103.8
Government consumption expend [1]	94.1	102.5	104.9	108.1	110.8	113.2	114.7
Federal	92.9	102.5	104.8	108.2	111.4	113.6	114.8
National defense	92.9	101.8	103.6	106.5	110.0	112.0	113.3
Nondefense	92.8	104.3	107.7	112.1	114.6	117.3	118.5
State and local	94.9	102.5	104.9	108.1	110.5	113.0	114.6

[1] And gross investment.

Source: U.S. Bureau of Economic Analysis, *The National Income and Product Accounts of the United States*, 1929-94, ; and *Survey of Current Business*, August 1997 and May 1999.

No. 786. Commodity Research Bureau Futures Price Index: 1980 to 1998

[1967=100. Index computed daily. Represents unweighted geometric average of commodity futures prices (through 6 months forward) of 17 major commodity futures markets. Represents end-of-year index]

Item	1980	1985	1988	1989	1990	1991	1992	1993	1994	1995	1996	1997	1998
All commodities	**308.5**	**229.2**	**251.8**	**229.9**	**222.6**	**208.0**	**205.9**	**212.4**	**229.7**	**237.1**	**247.9**	**229.1**	**191.2**
Softs [1]	426.0	398.2	365.2	271.7	276.0	264.4	232.4	246.9	352.3	354.4	322.2	408.7	344.8
Industrials	324.6	211.7	248.2	249.6	245.5	217.2	224.7	235.0	263.6	272.5	266.3	210.9	185.3
Grains and oilseeds [2]	312.1	198.5	261.9	205.7	171.2	196.1	196.9	193.8	191.2	218.6	284.7	210.7	172.8
Energy	(NA)	96.5	156.5	210.0	246.0	182.2	192.6	151.8	173.8	180.0	224.0	180.4	135.0
Oilseeds [3]	314.6	245.4	309.6	254.2	223.6	195.4	218.8	239.8	259.9	277.5	307.9	(3)	(3)
Livestock and meats	217.4	206.9	199.1	206.5	226.2	174.0	179.8	201.4	192.3	192.4	241.7	238.1	186.7
Metals (precious) [4]	531.4	256.6	318.7	296.9	257.8	226.0	228.5	242.2	273.9	276.0	271.3	249.3	234.3

NA Not available. [1] Prior to 1997, reported as imported. [2] Prior to 1997, reported as grains. [3] Incorporated into grains and oilseeds beginning 1997. [4] Prior to 1979, index for metals only.

Source: Bridge Commodity Research Bureau (CRB), Chicago, IL, *CRB Commodity Index Report*, weekly (copyright.)

508 Prices

No. 787. Indexes of Spot Primary Market Prices: 1980 to 1998

[1967=100. Computed weekly for 1980; daily thereafter. Represents unweighted geometric average of price quotations of 23 commodities; much more sensitive to changes in market conditions than is a monthly producer price index]

Items and number of commodities	1980	1985	1989	1990	1991	1992	1993	1994	1995	1996	1997	1998
All commodities (23)	**265.1**	**251.4**	**281.3**	**279.2**	**235.3**	**242.3**	**237.7**	**261.5**	**290.6**	**297.7**	**271.8**	**235.2**
Foodstuffs (10).	260.9	248.1	222.5	231.5	197.7	201.3	208.3	215.5	229.1	251.3	227.3	197.5
Raw industrials (13)	268.0	253.6	329.0	317.0	265.2	275.5	260.4	299.2	348.2	334.9	307.5	265.3
Livestock and products (5)	250.5	284.5	285.2	306.9	286.6	276.4	291.3	296.9	314.6	338.4	306.1	232.3
Metals (5)	257.9	220.2	347.1	313.9	348.8	262.7	236.2	262.1	306.7	296.7	269.8	218.5
Textiles and fibers (4)	234.7	220.8	253.5	259.4	201.8	218.6	205.3	252.6	286.0	274.6	261.5	237.5
Fats and oils (4).	229.5	273.1	208.1	193.3	185.0	180.7	190.1	209.6	228.3	245.7	257.1	236.0

Source: Bridge Commodity Research Bureau, Chicago, IL, *CRB Commodity Index Report*, weekly (copyright).

No. 788. Average Prices of Selected Fuels and Electricity: 1980 to 1998

[In dollars per unit, except electricity, in cents per kWh. Represents price to end-users, except as noted]

Type	Unit [1]	1980	1990	1991	1992	1993	1994	1995	1996	1997	1998
Crude oil, composite [2]. . .	Barrel	28.07	22.22	19.06	18.43	16.41	15.59	17.23	20.71	19.04	12.57
Motor gasoline: [3]											
Unleaded regular	Gallon.	1.25	1.16	1.14	1.13	1.11	1.11	1.15	1.23	1.23	1.12
Unleaded premium . . .	Gallon.	(NA)	1.35	1.32	1.32	1.30	1.31	1.34	1.41	1.42	1.25
No. 2 heating oil.	Gallon.	0.79	0.73	0.67	0.63	0.60	0.57	0.56	0.67	0.59	0.42
No. 2 diesel fuel.	Gallon.	0.82	0.73	0.65	0.62	0.60	0.55	0.56	0.68	0.61	0.44
Residual fuel oil	Gallon.	0.61	0.44	0.34	0.34	0.34	0.35	0.39	0.46	0.42	0.30
Natural gas, residential . .	1,000 cu/ft. .	3.68	5.80	5.82	5.89	6.16	6.41	6.06	6.34	6.94	6.91
Electricity, residential. . . .	kWh	5.36	7.83	8.04	8.21	8.32	8.38	8.40	8.36	8.43	8.26

NA Not available. [1] See headnote. [2] Refiner acquisition cost. [3] Average, all service.

Source: U.S. Energy Information Administration, *Monthly Energy Review.*

No. 789. Weekly Food Cost, by Type of Family: 1990 and 1998

[In dollars. Assumes that food for all meals and snacks is purchased at the store and prepared at home. See source for details on estimation procedures]

Family type	December 1990				October 1998			
	Thrifty plan	Low-cost plan	Moderate-cost plan	Liberal plan	Thrifty plan	Low-cost plan	Moderate-cost plan	Liberal plan
FAMILIES								
Family of two:								
20-50 years.	48.10	60.60	74.70	92.70	58.40	74.00	91.20	113.50
51 years and over	45.60	58.30	71.80	85.80	54.80	71.20	88.00	105.40
Family of four:								
Couple, 20-50 years and children—								
1-2 and 3-5 years	70.10	87.30	106.60	131.00	84.80	106.60	130.30	160.40
6-8 and 9-11 years	80.10	102.60	128.30	154.40	97.90	125.70	156.50	188.60
INDIVIDUALS [1]								
Child:								
1-2 years	12.70	15.40	18.00	21.80	15.20	18.70	22.00	26.70
3-5 years	13.70	16.80	20.70	24.90	16.50	20.60	25.40	30.50
6-8 years	16.60	22.20	27.90	32.50	20.50	27.40	34.00	39.60
9-11 years	19.80	25.30	32.50	37.60	24.30	31.00	39.60	45.80
Male:								
12-14 years.	20.60	28.60	35.70	42.00	25.20	35.00	43.40	51.00
15-19 years.	21.40	29.60	36.80	42.60	25.90	36.00	44.90	51.80
20-50 years.	22.90	29.30	36.60	44.30	27.90	35.90	44.70	54.20
51 years and over	20.90	27.90	34.30	41.10	25.10	34.20	42.10	50.50
Female:								
12-19 years.	20.80	24.80	30.10	36.30	25.00	30.10	36.60	44.20
20-50 years.	20.80	25.80	31.30	40.00	25.20	31.40	38.20	49.00
51 years and over	20.60	25.10	30.10	36.90	24.70	30.50	37.90	45.30

[1] The costs given are for individuals in four-person families. For individuals in other size families, the following adjustments are suggested: one-person, add 20 percent; two-person, add 10 percent; three-person, add 5 percent; five- or six-person, subtract 5 percent; seven- (or more) person, subtract 10 percent.

Source: U.S. Dept. of Agriculture, *Agricultural Research Service*, monthly.

Prices 509

No. 790. Food—Retail Prices of Selected Items: 1990 to 1998

[In dollars per pound, except as indicated. As of December]

Food	1990	1991	1992	1993	1994	1995	1996	1997	1998
Cereals and bakery products:									
Flour, white, all purpose	0.24	0.22	0.23	0.22	0.23	0.24	0.30	0.28	0.28
Rice, white, lg. grain, raw	0.49	0.51	0.53	0.50	0.53	0.55	0.55	0.58	0.54
Spaghetti and macaroni	0.85	0.86	0.86	0.84	0.87	0.88	0.84	0.88	0.88
Bread, whole wheat	(NA)	1.05	1.09	1.12	1.12	1.15	1.30	1.30	1.32
Meats, poultry, fish and eggs:									
Ground beef, 100% beef	1.63	1.58	1.50	1.57	1.38	1.40	1.42	1.39	1.39
T-bone steak	5.45	5.21	5.39	5.77	5.86	5.92	5.87	6.07	6.40
Pork:									
Bacon, sliced	2.28	1.99	1.86	2.02	1.89	2.17	2.64	2.61	2.58
Chops, center cut, bone-in	3.32	3.12	3.15	3.24	3.03	3.29	3.44	3.39	3.03
Sausage	2.42	2.24	2.14	1.99	1.85	1.92	2.15	2.08	2.43
Poultry:									
Chicken, fresh, whole	0.86	0.86	0.88	0.91	0.90	0.94	1.00	1.00	1.06
Turkey, frozen, whole	0.96	0.91	0.93	0.95	0.98	0.99	1.02	0.98	0.95
Eggs, Grade A, large, (dozen)	1.00	1.01	0.93	0.87	0.87	1.16	1.31	1.17	1.09
Dairy products:									
Milk, fresh, whole, fortified (1/2 gal.)	1.39	1.40	1.39	1.43	1.44	1.48	1.65	1.61	(NA)
Butter, salted, grade AA, stick	1.92	1.94	1.64	1.61	1.54	1.73	2.17	2.46	3.18
Fresh fruits and vegetables:									
Apples, red Delicious	0.77	0.86	0.76	0.78	0.72	0.83	0.89	0.90	0.85
Bananas	0.43	0.42	0.40	0.41	0.46	0.45	0.48	0.46	0.51
Oranges, navel	0.56	0.65	0.52	0.56	0.55	0.64	0.59	0.58	0.61
Pears, Anjou	0.79	0.88	0.80	0.89	(NA)	(NA)	1.06	0.85	0.98
Potatoes, white	0.32	0.28	0.31	0.36	0.34	0.38	0.33	0.37	0.38
Tomatoes, field grown	0.86	0.79	1.23	1.31	1.43	1.51	1.21	1.62	1.80
Cabbage	0.39	0.46	0.38	0.37	0.45	0.41	0.40	0.46	0.42

NA Not available.

Source: U.S. Bureau of Labor Statistics, *Monthly Labor Review* and *CPI Detailed Report*, January issues.

No. 791. Import Price Indexes—Selected Commodities: 1990 to 1998

[1995=100. Indexes are weighted by the 1990 Tariff Schedule of the United States Annotated, a scheme for describing and reporting product composition and value of U.S. imports. Import prices are based on U.S. dollar prices paid by importer. F.o.b. = Free on board; c.i.f. = Cost, insurance, and freight; n.e.s. = Not elsewhere specified]

Commodity	1990 [1]	1992	1993	1994	1995	1996	1997	1998
All commodities	90.3	94.3	94.4	95.8	100.8	100.1	98.2	92.6
Food and live animals	84.9	84.3	87.0	93.9	100.1	94.7	103.7	98.0
Meat	116.3	110.4	115.6	105.9	99.1	90.4	101.9	98.3
Fish	77.9	86.9	86.9	97.6	101.6	97.5	103.6	109.4
Crustaceans; fresh, chilled, frozen, salted or dried . .	73.3	79.3	80.1	97.7	103.4	95.0	103.5	106.4
Beverages and tobacco	86.1	98.4	97.7	98.2	99.7	103.6	107.5	109.6
Crude materials	82.4	77.5	77.1	86.3	99.8	94.3	97.4	87.7
Mineral fuels and related products	92.9	110.1	101.6	96.9	105.1	110.6	104.6	77.6
Crude petroleum and petroleum products	91.7	110.4	100.8	96.4	105.4	111.0	104.0	73.4
Natural gas	112.7	105.5	113.8	105.4	101.2	108.2	113.3	111.9
Chemicals and related products	88.3	91.2	92.1	92.0	100.7	98.8	96.4	93.6
Intermediate manufactured products	88.8	88.8	88.6	90.2	99.8	99.2	96.8	94.0
Machinery and transport equipment	90.2	94.5	95.9	97.6	100.6	98.6	95.7	91.8
Computer equipment and office machines	119.2	114.2	109.7	104.0	100.4	91.7	81.2	70.4
Computer equipment	143.0	131.7	121.9	109.1	99.7	93.0	80.8	66.5
Telecommunications [2]	102.0	99.0	99.9	99.2	100.5	97.3	93.4	89.4
Electrical machinery and equipment	92.0	95.2	96.9	98.9	101.6	95.5	90.2	84.5
Road vehicles	84.3	90.4	92.8	96.6	100.0	100.4	100.8	101.1
Miscellaneous manufactured articles	92.1	96.6	97.9	98.2	100.4	100.7	100.2	98.6
Plumbing, heating & lighting fixtures	95.3	98.2	98.8	96.4	100.4	99.5	96.2	96.0
Furniture and parts	93.7	97.7	98.4	98.2	100.7	100.8	102.9	100.2
Articles of apparel and clothing	97.6	98.8	99.2	99.2	100.1	101.5	102.6	102.7
Footwear	97.2	100.7	99.4	98.4	100.0	101.3	101.1	100.7

[1] June 1990 may not equal 100 because indexes were reweighted to an "average" trade value in 1990. [2] Includes sound recording and reproducing equipment.

Source: U.S. Bureau of Labor Statistics, *News, U.S. Import and Export Price Indexes*, monthly.

No. 792. Export Price Indexes—Selected Commodities: 1990 to 1998

[1990=100. Indexes are weighted by 1980 export values according to the Schedule B classification system of the U.S. Census Bureau. Prices used in these indexes were collected from a sample of U.S. manufacturers of exports and are factory transaction prices, except as noted. F.a.s. = free alongside ship. N.e.s. = not elsewhere specified. F.o.b. = free on board]

Commodity	1990 [1]	1992	1993	1994	1995	1996	1997	1998
All commodities.....................	**91.5**	**92.8**	**93.2**	**94.8**	**100.5**	**101.4**	**99.3**	**96.1**
Food and live animals.......................	89.0	87.8	83.5	88.7	97.4	122.0	98.5	90.9
Meat........................	84.9	91.5	96.2	92.5	99.9	101.6	95.3	97.8
Fish.........................	83.6	83.3	82.0	83.3	103.2	89.4	85.3	80.7
Cereals and cereal preparations	90.6	87.4	75.7	84.9	95.4	145.6	92.3	82.6
Wheat...................	80.4	77.7	67.4	65.4	91.1	129.3	87.1	75.4
Maize...................	97.6	91.8	78.8	94.9	98.0	165.3	90.4	80.9
Fruits and vegetables	83.6	82.0	84.4	89.8	96.2	105.7	101.6	98.4
Feeding stuff for animals	93.2	97.6	96.2	101.4	98.3	122.5	127.2	95.0
Miscellaneous food products.............	100.4	100.6	100.8	98.3	101.3	103.2	103.5	105.0
Beverages and tobacco......................	86.4	95.5	98.4	98.7	99.9	100.6	100.8	99.9
Tobacco and tobacco manufactures	86.6	95.5	98.3	98.6	100.0	100.6	100.9	99.7
Crude materials........................	80.4	74.7	79.6	86.4	104.1	90.3	93.4	82.0
Raw hides and skins	105.1	80.8	79.1	94.3	103.4	95.7	100.8	84.8
Oil seeds and oleaginous fruits	97.0	98.3	97.8	112.7	96.6	127.0	134.6	102.6
Cork and wood...................	66.4	71.7	105.1	97.3	102.1	94.7	93.2	82.0
Pulp and waste paper	64.7	53.4	45.4	61.1	111.6	56.8	65.9	64.0
Textile fibers........................	81.8	68.6	66.6	83.7	106.9	91.1	83.4	79.3
Cotton textile fibers	83.4	64.1	62.2	81.4	107.9	90.2	80.6	78.7
Crude fertilizers and minerals	101.9	101.5	96.7	97.3	99.4	96.8	97.8	97.0
Metalliferous ores and metal scrap..............	83.4	71.1	70.1	76.2	104.2	89.3	91.7	76.6
Ferrous waste and scrap	85.2	70.2	84.5	81.6	99.6	93.3	93.5	74.2
Nonferrous base metal waste and scrap	85.3	73.8	62.0	79.6	100.2	86.8	89.2	70.1
Mineral fuels and related materials	100.1	95.0	96.6	96.0	102.0	109.1	110.9	103.2
Coal, coke and briquettes..................	103.2	99.8	96.8	96.8	100.3	103.1	102.0	100.1
Crude petroleum and petroleum products	99.9	92.0	96.0	95.7	103.6	113.7	119.4	106.8
Animal and vegetable oils, fats and waxes	86.6	79.7	82.7	92.5	96.5	95.4	94.7	107.9
Chemicals and related products	85.6	85.5	84.4	86.9	102.6	97.1	96.5	92.6
Organic chemicals......................	81.7	78.8	77.9	79.8	106.8	87.8	84.9	77.1
Hydrocarbons, n.e.s. and derivatives, f.a.s.	82.9	69.1	71.2	82.0	115.7	90.8	95.0	75.0
Alcohols, phenols, phenol-alcohols, & deriv., f.a.s...	77.4	74.9	75.0	71.8	105.9	88.0	81.5	80.2
Chemical materials and products, n.e.s.	85.9	89.5	91.9	94.6	100.0	102.0	103.9	100.6
Intermediate manufactured products	86.9	87.6	87.7	90.9	100.8	97.9	98.2	97.9
Rubber manufactures	84.9	90.6	93.1	93.7	99.8	102.8	103.2	101.9
Paper and paperboard products	81.1	80.2	76.5	78.4	103.3	87.3	83.5	83.8
Textiles	89.7	95.1	96.2	96.1	101.1	103.8	103.3	103.2
Nonmetallic mineral manufactures	91.1	94.6	96.4	98.1	100.1	101.2	104.3	106.7
Nonferrous metals........................	88.4	77.5	71.7	81.6	99.7	93.4	93.4	88.1
Manufactures of metals, n.e.s................	88.0	91.4	92.7	94.7	100.1	101.5	104.4	107.0
Machinery and transport equipment [2]............	95.3	99.7	99.8	99.4	100.0	100.9	100.6	98.7
Power generating machinery [3]...........	86.5	94.9	95.9	97.7	99.4	100.4	106.0	107.1
Rotating electric plant and parts thereof, n.e.s.	89.2	93.7	95.0	96.2	100.4	102.4	103.1	103.1
Machinery specialized for particular industries	88.0	93.5	95.8	97.3	99.9	102.7	104.2	105.2
Agricultural machinery and parts [4]	90.3	94.6	96.8	98.7	100.3	102.0	102.8	103.1
Civil engineering and contractors, plant and equip. .	87.6	90.4	93.5	97.1	100.2	101.5	103.1	105.8
Metalworking machinery....................	89.0	97.4	99.1	98.8	100.0	102.3	104.3	108.4
General industrial machines, parts, n.e.s.	89.2	94.9	96.8	98.4	99.4	102.5	105.2	106.1
Computer equipment and office machines	132.0	124.5	115.3	106.5	100.8	93.7	84.7	76.5
Computer equipment	148.1	138.7	123.2	111.0	101.5	90.1	79.1	73.8
Telecommunications [5]	94.1	101.8	102.9	100.9	100.3	101.1	99.6	98.7
Electrical machinery and equipment	96.8	100.3	100.2	99.9	100.7	99.1	96.5	92.1
Electronic valves, diodes, transistors & integr. cir. ..	101.6	104.7	103.3	101.0	101.7	97.9	91.8	84.4
Road vehicles	92.1	96.2	97.3	98.4	99.8	101.0	101.8	101.9
Miscellaneous manufactured articles	91.7	98.3	99.0	99.1	99.9	100.8	101.7	100.8

[1] June 1990 may not equal 100 because indexes were reweighted to an "average" trade value in 1990.   [2] Excludes military and commercial aircraft.   [3] Includes equipment.   [4] Excludes tractors.   [5] Includes sound recording and reproducing equipment.

Source: U.S. Bureau of Labor Statistics, *U.S. Import and Export Price Indexes*, monthly.

Prices   511

No. 793. Refiner/Reseller Sales Price of Gasoline, by State: 1995 to 1997

[In cents per gallon. As of **March**. Represents all refinery and gas plant operators' sales through company-operated retail outlets. Gasoline prices exclude excise taxes]

State	Gasoline excise taxes, 1997	Average, all grades			Midgrade			Premium		
		1995	1996	1997	1995	1996	1997	1995	1996	1997
United States	(NA)	**63.0**	**71.5**	**70.3**	**67.3**	**76.0**	**75.1**	**72.4**	**80.4**	**79.4**
Alabama	18	61.3	69.5	67.5	64.2	72.7	70.3	69.1	77.3	75.7
Alaska	8	81.8	90.0	90.9	93.9	103.7	101.8	92.3	102.5	101.9
Arizona	18	70.2	80.3	78.4	73.2	85.6	85.2	81.0	91.1	90.0
Arkansas	19	58.7	67.7	66.2	61.9	70.7	68.8	66.0	75.4	73.5
California	19	68.1	78.0	79.0	71.4	81.1	84.2	79.2	87.7	90.3
Colorado	22	63.6	73.3	72.6	68.4	78.1	76.5	70.9	80.5	79.9
Connecticut	39	72.3	74.7	73.2	72.3	78.2	77.9	78.2	83.6	81.9
Delaware	23	67.4	73.5	71.6	69.6	76.1	74.7	76.0	81.7	80.5
District of Columbia . .	20	77.8	85.4	82.0	75.9	83.8	80.6	83.3	91.2	86.6
Florida	13	63.2	71.2	70.0	65.3	73.6	72.9	72.7	80.4	79.3
Georgia	8	60.5	68.2	66.2	62.9	70.8	69.0	68.3	76.0	74.0
Hawaii	16	96.7	103.7	101.9	98.8	106.7	106.1	104.9	112.7	111.6
Idaho	26	67.3	77.8	79.6	69.8	80.0	82.8	75.0	84.7	88.1
Illinois	20	63.0	73.8	70.9	71.6	82.8	78.4	74.2	84.0	81.6
Indiana	16	61.0	70.2	67.8	65.7	75.2	71.6	69.4	78.6	76.5
Iowa	20	59.5	70.2	68.8	66.8	75.9	72.5	66.3	76.8	75.2
Kansas	18	57.5	67.6	66.4	62.9	73.5	71.9	64.2	74.6	73.1
Kentucky	16	61.9	70.8	69.2	65.5	74.6	73.2	69.3	77.9	77.2
Louisiana	20	58.5	66.2	65.7	63.2	70.2	70.3	66.0	74.2	72.1
Maine	19	64.8	71.4	71.1	70.0	77.0	75.8	72.6	78.7	79.1
Maryland	24	69.2	77.0	73.7	71.2	79.1	76.2	77.2	85.0	81.0
Massachusetts	21	69.5	75.2	74.6	73.5	80.3	80.5	78.3	82.9	83.1
Michigan	16	61.2	71.8	68.4	65.2	76.0	72.5	69.3	79.9	76.8
Minnesota	20	62.6	72.6	71.6	68.0	78.7	74.3	69.5	79.7	78.2
Mississippi	18	58.1	66.4	65.5	61.8	70.1	69.8	66.1	74.2	73.6
Missouri	17	59.4	69.8	68.9	64.5	75.9	74.8	66.6	77.1	77.0
Montana	28	69.0	79.9	77.3	72.0	81.9	79.9	76.4	88.4	86.6
Nebraska	26	59.8	69.9	68.7	63.7	74.0	73.0	66.9	77.1	75.9
Nevada	24	66.9	78.6	78.1	70.3	82.6	81.8	77.1	88.0	87.3
New Hampshire	20	71.5	77.8	76.6	74.9	80.8	81.2	80.2	86.8	86.7
New Jersey	11	66.3	71.6	70.7	73.8	79.9	79.1	75.3	80.9	80.6
New Mexico	19	64.1	74.7	73.3	69.3	78.7	76.0	72.0	82.4	81.6
New York	22	67.8	74.3	74.4	72.3	79.5	79.4	78.4	84.5	83.7
North Carolina	23	60.2	68.5	67.3	62.6	70.9	70.1	68.0	76.2	75.2
North Dakota	20	62.2	72.5	70.4	68.3	77.7	75.8	71.6	81.6	79.1
Ohio	22	61.3	70.6	68.4	65.8	74.5	72.2	70.5	79.3	77.6
Oklahoma	17	56.0	65.5	64.4	63.2	72.8	70.7	63.7	72.9	71.4
Oregon	24	67.7	77.2	76.2	72.6	82.9	82.8	80.4	88.0	86.8
Pennsylvania	22	64.2	70.7	69.1	67.4	73.7	72.3	72.9	78.7	77.4
Rhode Island	29	66.0	73.3	72.6	70.0	76.7	77.4	75.4	81.7	81.6
South Carolina	17	60.5	68.5	66.7	62.6	71.3	69.4	68.7	76.8	74.8
South Dakota	20	62.2	72.6	70.9	67.5	77.0	73.3	70.3	80.4	79.0
Tennessee	21	60.3	68.9	67.4	62.7	71.3	70.5	67.8	76.5	75.2
Texas	20	57.8	65.3	63.8	63.9	71.4	69.9	66.2	73.7	72.3
Utah	19	67.6	77.3	79.3	70.2	79.9	82.0	73.9	83.3	85.8
Vermont	16	72.0	78.8	77.6	74.3	81.6	81.9	80.9	87.7	86.0
Virginia	18	63.8	71.6	69.4	66.1	73.9	72.0	72.2	80.0	77.3
Washington	23	69.9	79.8	77.2	75.0	84.6	82.4	82.0	90.7	88.4
West Virginia	21	65.3	73.6	71.3	68.1	76.4	74.3	73.8	81.9	79.8
Wisconsin	27	61.6	71.8	68.6	65.4	75.9	73.1	69.5	79.2	76.5
Wyoming	9	65.1	76.0	75.4	70.1	80.7	81.8	72.8	83.5	83.8

NA Not available.

Source: U.S. Energy Information Administration, *Petroleum Marketing Monthly.*

Section 16
Banking, Finance, and Insurance

This section presents data on the Nation's finances, various types of financial institutions, money and credit, securities, and insurance. The primary sources of these data are publications of several departments of the Federal Government, especially the Treasury Department, and independent agencies such as the Federal Deposit Insurance Corporation, the Federal Reserve System, and the Securities and Exchange Commission. National data on insurance are available primarily from private organizations, such as the American Council of Life Insurance.

Flow of funds—The flow of funds accounts of the Federal Reserve System (see Tables 797 to 800) bring together statistics on all of the major forms of financial instruments to present an economy-wide view of asset and liability relationships. In flow form, the accounts relate borrowing and lending to one another and to the nonfinancial activities that generate income and production. Each claim outstanding is included simultaneously as an asset of the lender and as a liability of the debtor. The accounts also indicate the balance between asset totals and liability totals over the economy as a whole. Several publications of the Board of Governors of the Federal Reserve System contain information on the flow of funds accounts: Summary data on flows and outstandings, in the *Federal Reserve Bulletin, Flow of Funds Accounts of the United States* (quarterly), and *Annual Statistical Digest*; and concepts and organization of the accounts, in *Guide to the Flow of Funds Accounts* (1993). Data are also available at the Board's web site <http://www.federalreserve.gov/releases>.

Banking system—Banks in this country are organized under the laws of both the states and the Federal Government and are regulated by several bank supervisory agencies. National banks are supervised by the Comptroller of the Currency. *Reports of*

Condition have been collected from national banks since 1863. Summaries of these reports are published in the Comptroller's *Annual Report*, which also presents data on the structure of the national banking system.

The Federal Reserve System was established in 1913 to exercise central banking functions, some of which are shared with the U.S. Treasury. It includes national banks and such state banks that voluntarily join the system. Statements of state bank members are consolidated by the Board of Governors of the Federal Reserve System with data for national banks collected by the Comptroller of the Currency into totals for all member banks of the system. Balance sheet data for member banks and other commercial banks are published quarterly in the *Federal Reserve Bulletin*. The Federal Deposit Insurance Corporation (FDIC), established in 1933, insures each depositor up to $100,000. Major item balance sheet and income data for all commercial banks are published in the *FDIC Quarterly Banking Profile*. This publication is also available on the Internet at the following address: <http://www.fdic.gov>. Balance sheet and income data for individual institutions are also available at this site in the Institution Directory (ID) system.

The FDIC is the primary Federal regulator of state-chartered banks that are not members of the Federal Reserve System and of most savings banks insured by the Bank Insurance Fund (BIF). The agency also has certain backup supervisory authority, for safety and soundness purposes, over state-chartered banks that are members of the Federal Reserve System, national banks, and savings associations.

Savings institutions—Savings institutions are primarily involved in credit extension in the form of mortgage loans. Statistics on savings institutions are collected by

Banking, Finance, and Insurance   513

the U.S. Office of Thrift Supervision and the FDIC. The Financial Institutions Reform, Recovery, and Enforcement Act of 1989 (FIRREA) authorized the establishment of the Resolution Trust Corporation (RTC) which was responsible for the disposal of assets from failed savings institutions. FIRREA gave the FDIC the job of managing the Federal deposit insurance fund for savings institutions (SAIF=Savings Association Insurance Fund). Major balance sheet and income data for all insured savings institutions are published in the *FDIC Quarterly Banking Profile.*

Credit unions—Federally chartered credit unions are under the supervision of the National Credit Union Administration. State-chartered credit unions are supervised by the respective state supervisory authorities. The Administration publishes comprehensive program and statistical information on all Federal and federally insured state credit unions in the *Annual Report of the National Credit Union Administration.* Deposit insurance (up to $100,000 per account) is provided to members of all Federal and those state credit unions that are federally-insured by the National Credit Union Share Insurance Fund which was established in 1970. Deposit insurance for state chartered credit unions is also available in some states under private or state-administered insurance programs.

Other credit agencies—Insurance companies, finance companies dealing primarily in installment sales financing, and personal loan companies represent important sources of funds for the credit market. Statistics on loans, investments, cash, etc., of life insurance companies are published principally by the American Council of Life Insurance in its *Life Insurance Fact Book* and in the *Federal Reserve Bulletin.* Consumer credit data are published currently in the *Federal Reserve Bulletin.*

Government corporations and credit agencies make available credit of specified types or to specified groups of private borrowers, either by lending directly or by insuring or guaranteeing loans made by private lending institutions.

Data on operations of government credit agencies, along with other government corporations, are available in reports of individual agencies; data on their debt outstanding are published in the *Federal Reserve Bulletin.*

Currency—Currency, including coin and paper money, represents about 42 percent of all media of exchange in the United States, with most payments made by check. All currency is now issued by the Federal Reserve Banks.

Securities—The Securities and Exchange Commission (SEC) was established in 1934 to protect the interests of the public and investors against malpractices in the securities and financial markets and to provide the fullest possible disclosure of information regarding securities to the investing public. Statistical data are published in the *SEC Annual Report.*

Insurance—Insuring companies, which are regulated by the various states or the District of Columbia, are classified as either life or property. Companies that underwrite accident and health insurance only and those that underwrite accident and health insurance in addition to one or more property lines are included with property insurance. Insuring companies, other than those classified as life, are permitted to underwrite one or more property lines provided they are so licensed and have the necessary capital or surplus.

There are a number of published sources for statistics on the various classes of insurance—life, health, fire, marine, and casualty. Organizations representing certain classes of insurers publish reports for these classes. Among them are the annual commercial publishers, such as The National Underwriter Company whose *Argus Chart* (annual) contains financial and operating data for individual health and accident insurance companies, including Blue Cross and Blue Shield Plans. The American Council of Life Insurance publishes statistics on life insurance purchases, ownership, benefit payments, and assets in its *Life Insurance Fact Book.*

No. 794. Gross Domestic Product in Finance, Insurance, and Real Estate, in Current and Real (1992) Dollars: 1990 to 1996

[In billions of dollars, except percent (1,024.1 represents $1,024,100,000,000). For definition of gross domestic product, see text, Section 14, Income. Based on 1987 Standard Industrial Classification; see text, Section 17, Business]

Industry	Current dollars				Chained (1992) dollars [1]			
	1990	1994	1995	1996	1990	1994	1995	1996
Finance, insurance, real estate, total	1,024.1	1,267.6	1,361.3	1,448.5	1,109.0	1,196.9	1,231.1	1,258.5
Percent of gross domestic product	17.8	18.2	18.7	19.0	18.1	18.1	18.3	18.2
Depository institutions	169.2	207.4	229.6	247.4	214.9	197.0	193.4	192.0
Nondepository institutions	21.5	36.1	39.0	49.9	25.6	33.9	32.6	35.4
Security and commodity brokers	39.7	78.5	79.5	90.0	41.2	83.0	81.9	92.2
Insurance carriers	69.3	108.8	126.5	136.6	70.2	91.3	105.1	110.1
Insurance agents, brokers, and service	37.1	45.0	47.1	50.4	40.8	41.6	42.1	43.6
Real estate	671.9	802.9	842.7	886.2	706.8	758.3	775.6	793.3
Nonfarm housing services	492.2	607.3	642.8	673.3	525.6	573.3	587.9	596.8
Other real estate	179.6	195.6	199.9	212.9	179.8	185.0	187.7	196.6
Holding and other investment offices	15.5	-11.1	-3.2	-12.0	12.3	12.9	12.6	12.6

[1] See text, Section 14, Income.

Source: U.S. Bureau of Economic Analysis, *Survey of Current Business*, May 1998.

No. 795. Finance, Insurance, and Real Estate Establishments—Number, Revenues, Payroll, and Employees: 1992 and 1997

[Preliminary (586 represents 586,000). Covers only establishments with payroll]

Kind of business	1987 SIC code [1]	Establishments (1,000)		Revenue (bil. dol.)		Annual payroll (bil. dol.)		Paid employees (1,000)	
		1992	1997	1992	1997	1992	1997	1992	1997
Finance, insurance, real estate	(H)	586	(S)	1,832	(S)	212	(S)	6,510	(S)
Depository institutions	60	105	110	532	699	57	77	2,100	2,130
Nondepository institutions	61	39	52	135	212	15	24	446	589
Security and commodity brokers	62	31	48	109	250	34	67	406	643
Insurance carriers	63	39	41	796	988	51	66	1,517	1,587
Insurance agents, brokers, and service	64	122	131	52	74	19	26	636	720
Real estate	65	229	254	142	191	26	35	1,231	1,394
Holding and other investment offices	67	20	(S)	66	(S)	9	(S)	174	(S)

S Figure does not meet publication standards. [1] Standard Industrial Classification; see text, Section 17, Business.

Source: U.S. Census Bureau, *1997 Economic Census, Core Business Statistics Series, Advance*, EC97X-CS1.

No. 796. Finance, Insurance, and Real Estate—Establishments, Employees, and Payroll: 1990 and 1996

[544.7 represents 544,700. Covers establishments with payroll. Employees are for the week including March 12. Most Government employees are excluded. For statement on methodology, see Appendix III]

Kind of business	1987 SIC code [1]	Establishments (1,000)		Employees (1,000)		Payroll (bil. dol.)	
		1990	1996	1990	1996	1990	1996
Finance, insurance, real estate	(H)	544.7	650.1	6,957	7,194	197.4	285.0
Depository institutions [2][3]	60	81.2	105.1	2,033	2,061	48.4	65.8
Commercial banks	602	52.3	67.4	1,472	1,507	35.6	47.5
Savings institutions	603	21.7	16.1	417	263	8.8	8.0
Nondepository institutions [2][3]	61	42.0	48.2	506	540	14.0	21.7
Personal credit institutions	614	25.0	19.0	236	183	5.5	6.4
Mortgage bankers and brokers	616	10.9	21.9	153	226	4.6	9.0
Security and commodity brokers [2]	62	25.2	45.6	411	568	26.6	57.7
Security brokers and dealers	621	15.9	25.5	308	411	20.8	44.4
Insurance carriers [2]	63	43.3	41.8	1,407	1,537	41.5	59.3
Life insurance	631	14.1	11.8	572	548	16.3	19.7
Medical service and health insurance [2]	632	2.1	3.3	188	306	5.1	11.2
Hospital and medical service plans	6324	1.0	2.2	139	248	3.8	9.3
Fire, marine, and casualty insurance	633	18.3	20.4	533	595	17.0	25.1
Insurance agents, brokers, and service	64	110.8	127.3	712	695	20.3	24.7
Real estate [2]	65	217.0	252.6	1,374	1,422	28.5	35.4
Real estate operators and lessors	651	95.7	100.6	509	499	8.7	10.2
Real estate agents and managers	653	72.2	124.5	585	757	13.3	20.6
Holding and other investment offices	67	22.6	28.3	263	303	10.0	16.6
Administrative and auxiliary	(X)	2.6	1.3	251	68	8.2	3.8

X Not applicable. [1] Standard Industrial Classification; see text, Section 17, Business. [2] Includes industries not shown separately. [3] Includes Government employees.

Source: U.S. Census Bureau, *County Business Patterns*, annual.

Banking, Finance, and Insurance 515

No. 797. Flow of Funds Accounts—Financial Assets of Financial and Nonfinancial Institutions, by Holder Sector: 1980 to 1998

[In billions of dollars (14,080 represents $14,080,000,000,000). As of Dec. 31]

Sector	1980	1985	1990	1992	1993	1994	1995	1996	1997	1998
All sectors	14,080	24,081	36,707	42,287	45,800	47,986	54,058	59,907	67,888	76,078
Households [1]	6,584	10,149	14,985	17,483	18,594	19,212	21,751	23,908	27,020	30,121
Nonfinancial business	1,624	2,964	4,168	4,478	4,860	5,179	5,724	6,265	6,818	7,221
Farm business	24	33	47	53	57	59	61	61	62	63
Nonfarm noncorporate	145	435	486	492	514	553	604	644	681	724
Nonfinancial corporations	1,455	2,496	3,634	3,932	4,289	4,567	5,059	5,560	6,075	6,434
State and local government	301	645	963	1,034	1,083	1,026	994	1,008	1,043	1,130
U.S. Government	229	372	440	474	489	436	438	437	432	438
U.S. Govt.-sponsored enterprises	195	324	478	552	631	782	897	989	1,099	1,405
Federally-related mortgage pools	114	369	1,020	1,272	1,357	1,472	1,570	1,711	1,826	2,018
Monetary authorities	174	243	342	382	424	452	472	495	534	567
Commercial banking [2]	1,482	2,376	3,337	3,655	3,892	4,160	4,494	4,710	5,175	5,635
U.S.-chartered commercial banks	1,266	1,990	2,644	2,775	2,932	3,123	3,322	3,445	3,742	4,094
Foreign banking offices in U.S.	98	144	367	509	542	590	666	715	811	802
Nonbank finance	2,884	5,688	9,034	10,710	11,865	12,414	14,295	16,251	19,096	22,133
Funding corporations	16	135	247	336	327	366	372	489	606	747
Savings institutions	792	1,275	1,323	1,060	1,020	1,009	1,013	1,032	1,029	1,088
Credit unions	68	135	217	265	282	294	311	330	354	394
Life insurance	464	796	1,351	1,587	1,755	1,863	2,064	2,246	2,515	2,819
Other insurance	182	299	533	598	642	678	740	778	852	884
Private pension funds	513	1,228	1,608	2,009	2,252	2,352	2,755	3,155	3,706	4,331
State and local govt. retirement funds	197	399	920	1,168	1,256	1,294	1,518	1,715	2,094	2,344
Finance companies	197	338	547	556	557	600	672	715	757	827
Mortgage companies	16	25	49	60	60	36	33	41	32	35
Real estate investment trusts	3	8	13	14	17	22	26	30	52	60
Mutual funds	62	246	608	993	1,375	1,477	1,853	2,342	2,989	3,626
Closed-end investment funds	8	8	53	93	116	118	134	145	148	148
Money market funds	76	242	493	539	560	603	745	891	1,049	1,334
Security brokers, dealers	45	156	262	382	479	455	568	636	779	841
Asset-backed securities issuers	-	39	285	421	504	577	717	865	1,078	1,392
Bank personal trusts, estates	245	358	522	630	661	670	775	842	1,055	1,263
Rest of the world	493	951	1,940	2,247	2,605	2,853	3,423	4,133	4,846	5,410

- Represents zero.   [1] Includes nonprofit organizations.   [2] Includes other sectors not shown separately.

No. 798. Flow of Funds Accounts—Credit Market Debt Outstanding: 1980 to 1998

[In billions of dollars (4,734 represents $4,734,000,000,000). As of Dec. 31. N.e.c.= Not elsewhere classified]

Item	1980	1985	1990	1992	1993	1994	1995	1996	1997	1998
Credit market debt	4,734	8,628	13,745	15,195	16,167	17,212	18,445	19,794	21,200	23,291
U.S. government	735	1,590	2,498	3,080	3,336	3,492	3,637	3,782	3,805	3,752
Non-Federal domestic nonfinancial	3,223	5,543	8,345	8,753	9,099	9,526	10,085	10,661	11,373	12,378
Households [1]	1,376	2,239	3,582	3,926	4,139	4,454	4,804	5,135	5,472	5,958
Corporations	910	1,609	2,488	2,475	2,536	2,687	2,913	3,113	3,366	3,709
Nonfarm noncorporate business	431	843	1,148	1,115	1,119	1,122	1,152	1,199	1,259	1,348
Farm business	161	173	135	135	138	142	145	150	156	163
State and local government	344	678	992	1,102	1,168	1,122	1,070	1,063	1,119	1,200
Rest of the world	197	237	286	316	386	371	442	519	570	592
Financial sectors	579	1,258	2,616	3,046	3,346	3,822	4,281	4,833	5,453	6,569
Commercial banking	91	188	198	195	208	228	251	264	309	382
Thrift institutions [2]	55	111	140	88	100	113	115	141	161	214
Life insurance companies	-	-	-	-	-	1	1	2	2	2
Government-sponsored enterprises [3]	163	264	399	448	528	701	807	897	995	1,300
Federally-related mortgage pools	114	369	1,020	1,272	1,357	1,472	1,570	1,711	1,826	2,018
Asset-backed securities issuers	-	39	287	422	506	579	720	874	1,089	1,406
Finance companies	127	224	374	386	385	434	484	530	554	616
Mortgage companies	12	17	25	30	30	19	19	32	27	28
Real estate investment trusts	5	5	12	14	17	31	37	44	80	146
Security brokers, dealers	-	1	15	22	34	34	29	27	35	43
Funding corporations	13	39	147	169	180	211	249	313	374	414
CORPORATE CREDIT MARKET DEBT OUTSTANDING, BY TYPE OF INSTRUMENT										
Total	910	1,609	2,488	2,475	2,536	2,687	2,913	3,113	3,366	3,709
Commercial paper	28	72	117	107	118	139	157	156	169	193
Municipal securities [4]	46	127	115	118	125	132	135	138	142	148
Corporate bonds	366	578	1,008	1,155	1,230	1,253	1,326	1,399	1,490	1,622
Bank loans, n.e.c.	230	424	545	488	478	521	588	634	706	790
Other loans and advances	110	248	473	413	388	421	454	475	521	569
Savings institutions	1	15	17	6	5	5	6	8	9	12
Finance companies	78	135	241	238	224	247	271	279	287	320
U.S. government	8	14	9	8	8	8	10	9	8	8
Acceptance liabilities to banks	17	28	29	20	17	15	14	13	11	7
Rest of the world	5	56	172	130	114	122	122	129	143	141
Asset-backed securities issuers	-	-	4	10	19	24	30	38	62	81
Mortgages	131	159	229	194	197	220	253	311	339	389

- Represents or rounds to zero.   [1] Includes nonprofit organizations.   [2] Covers savings institutions and credit unions.   [3] U.S. Government.   [4] Industrial revenue bonds. Issued by state and local governments to finance private investment and secured in interest and principal by the industrial user of the funds.

Source of Tables 797 and 798: Board of Governors of the Federal Reserve System, *Flow of Funds Accounts*, March 1999 quarterly diskettes. Data are also published in the quarterly Z.1 release.

No. 799. Flow of Funds Accounts—Financial Assets and Liabilities of Financial and Nonfinancial Institutions, by Sector and Type of Instrument: 1998

[In billions of dollars (76,078 represents $76,078,000,000,000). As of Dec. 31. Preliminary. A=Assets; L=Liabilities and equity, SDR=Special drawing rights, IMF=International Monetary Fund. RPs=Repurchase agreements. N.e.c. = Not elsewhere classified]

Type of instrument	All sectors, total A	All sectors, total L	Domestic nonfinancial — Total A	Domestic nonfinancial — Total L	Households [1] A	Households [1] L	Business A	Business L	State and local governments A	State and local governments L	Federal government A	Federal government L	Financial sectors A	Financial sectors L	Rest of the world A	Rest of the world L
Total	76,078	74,247	38,909	35,130	30,121	6,250	7,221	23,100	1,130	1,236	438	4,544	31,759	35,254	5,410	3,863
Gold stock and SDRs	22	–	–	–												
IMF position	24	24	11	–							11		11			24
Official foreign exchange	36	36	24	–							24		–0			36
Treasury currency, SDR certificates	35	27	16	27							16	27	20			
Foreign deposits	88	661	58	–	38		20						35			661
Interbank claims	211	184											70	184	141	
Checkable deposits, currency	1,316	1,335	958		424		478		33		23		101	1,335	257	
Time and savings deposits	3,434	3,434	3,149		2,882		173		90		5		199	3,434	86	
Money market fund shares	1,334	1,334	903		746		158						431	1,334		
Fed. funds and security RPs	719	878	162				3		159				485	878	72	
Credit market instruments	23,291	23,291	2,985	16,130	1,738	5,958	355	5,220	679	1,200	214	3,752	17,797	6,569	2,508	592
Open-market paper	1,173	1,173	173	193	63		29	193	80				887	907	113	73
U.S. Treasury securities [2]	3,724	3,724	600	3,724	310		53		237			3,724	1,834		1,290	
Federal agency securities [3]	3,347	3,347	556	29	340		33		182			29	2,489	3,318	302	
Municipal securities	1,464	1,464	500	1,464	447		48	148	4	1,190			965			
Corporate and foreign bonds	3,894	3,894	524	1,622	475			1,622	50				2,708	1,864	662	408
Bank loans, n.e.c	1,316	1,316		1,144		67		1,077					1,316	113		52
Other loans	1,258	1,258	169	917		205	116	702	125	10	169		948	290	141	59
Mortgages	5,782	5,782	389	5,705	102	4,226	75	1,479			45		5,393	77		
Consumer credit	1,334	1,334	75	1,334		1,334							1,259			
Other corporate equities [4]	15,438	15,438	6,356	10,040	6,280			10,040	76				7,972	4,202	1,110	1,196
Mutual fund shares [5]	3,626	3,626	2,609		2,486				48				1,017	3,626		
Trade credit [6]	1,801	1,481	1,518	1,412		121	1,495	1,173		36	23	81	227	19	56	51
Security credit	570	570	274	152	274	152							295	417		
Life insurance reserves	707	707		34	707							34		673		
Pension fund reserves	8,770	8,770		643	8,770							643		8,127		
Taxes payable	49	147	49	100				100	28		21			47		
Investment in bank personal trusts	1,291	1,291	1,291		1,291									1,291		
Proprietors' equity	4,164	4,164	4,164	4,157	4,164			4,157								
Miscellaneous claims	9,152	6,848	4,904	2,435	322	18	4,463	2,410	19		101	7	3,068	3,110	1,180	1,303

– Represents or rounds to zero. [1] Includes nonprofit organizations. [2] Includes savings bonds and other nonmarketable debt held by public. [3] Issues by agencies in the budget and by government-sponsored enterprises in financial sectors, issues backed by federally-related mortgage pools, and loan participation certificates. [4] Assets shown at market value. [5] Nonbank finance liability is redemption value of shares of open-end investment companies. [6] Asset is corporate only; noncorporate credit deducted in liability total to conform to quarterly flow tables.

Source: Board of Governors of the Federal Reserve System, Flow of Funds Accounts, quarterly.

No. 800. Flow of Funds Accounts—Assets of Households: 1980 to 1998

[As of **December 31** (6,584 represents $6,584,000,000,000). Includes nonprofit organizations]

Type of instrument	Total (bil. dol.)							Percent distribution		
	1980	1985	1990	1995	1996	1997	1998	1980	1990	1998
Total financial assets	6,584	10,149	14,985	21,751	23,908	27,020	30,121	100.0	100.0	100.0
Deposits	1,517	2,484	3,265	3,365	3,538	3,790	4,089	23.0	21.8	13.6
Foreign deposits	-	8	13	23	35	42	38	-	0.1	0.1
Checkable deposits and currency	251	342	409	505	438	423	424	3.8	2.7	1.4
Time and savings deposits	1,203	1,941	2,477	2,388	2,556	2,725	2,882	18.3	16.5	9.6
Money market fund shares	62	193	365	449	508	600	746	0.9	2.4	2.5
Credit market instruments	425	849	1,513	1,938	1,969	1,795	1,738	6.5	10.1	5.8
Open-market paper	38	35	63	48	52	59	63	0.6	0.4	0.2
U.S. Government securities	165	270	530	859	911	749	650	2.5	3.5	2.2
Treasury issues	160	242	405	594	567	382	310	2.4	2.7	1.0
Savings bonds	73	80	126	185	187	187	187	1.1	0.8	0.6
Other Treasury	88	162	279	409	380	195	123	1.3	1.9	0.4
Agency issues	5	29	125	265	344	367	340	0.1	0.8	1.1
Municipal securities	104	346	575	459	435	421	447	1.6	3.8	1.5
Corporate and foreign bonds	31	77	201	461	463	461	475	0.5	1.3	1.6
Mortgages	86	120	144	111	108	105	102	1.3	1.0	0.3
Corporate equities [1]	894	1,107	1,778	3,995	4,528	5,333	6,280	13.6	11.9	20.8
Mutual fund shares	46	198	468	1,265	1,582	2,048	2,486	0.7	3.1	8.3
Security credit	16	35	62	128	163	215	274	0.2	0.4	0.9
Life insurance reserves [2]	221	264	392	566	611	665	707	3.3	2.6	2.3
Pension fund reserves [2]	971	2,087	3,497	5,821	6,568	7,681	8,770	14.7	23.3	29.1
Investment in bank personal trusts	265	384	552	803	872	1,083	1,291	4.0	3.7	4.3
Equity in noncorporate business	2,156	2,608	3,233	3,578	3,776	4,097	4,164	32.7	21.6	13.8
Miscellaneous assets	74	133	224	292	301	312	322	1.1	1.5	1.1

- Represents zero. [1] Only those directly held and those in closed-end funds. Other equities are included in mutual funds, life insurance and pension reserves, and bank personal trusts. [2] See also Table 853.

Source: Board of Governors of the Federal Reserve System, *Flow of Funds Accounts*, March 1999 diskettes. Data are also published in the quarterly Z.1 release.

No. 801. Financial Assets Held by Families, by Type of Asset: 1992 and 1995

[**Median value in thousands of constant 1995 dollars** (12.2 represents $12,200). Constant dollar figures are based on consumer price index data published by U.S. Bureau of Labor Statistics. Families include one-person units; for definition of family, see text, Section 1, Population. Based on Survey of Consumer Finance; see Appendix III. For definition of median, see Guide to Tabular Presentation]

Age of family head and family income	Any financial asset [1]	Transaction accounts [2]	Certificates of deposit	Savings bonds	Stocks [3]	Mutual funds [4]	Retirement accounts [5]	Life insurance (cash value)	Other managed [6]
PERCENT OF FAMILIES OWNING ASSET									
1992, total	90.3	87.0	16.7	22.3	17.0	10.4	38.0	34.8	4.0
1995, total	90.7	87.1	14.3	22.8	15.2	12.3	43.0	31.9	3.9
Under 35 years old	86.6	80.8	7.2	20.4	10.8	8.0	38.0	22.7	1.6
35 to 44 years old	91.8	87.3	8.1	31.0	14.6	11.2	52.1	29.2	3.5
45 to 54 years old	92.3	89.0	12.3	25.3	17.6	16.3	55.0	38.4	3.0
55 to 64 years old	90.5	88.2	17.1	20.2	15.0	16.1	47.7	37.4	7.6
65 to 74 years old	92.2	91.3	23.9	16.8	18.6	14.9	35.5	37.4	5.9
75 years old and over	93.9	92.9	34.7	15.3	19.8	10.2	15.5	35.6	5.2
Less than $10,000	67.6	60.6	8.0	5.5	2.6	1.8	6.5	15.9	0.5
$10,000 to $24,999	87.9	82.6	15.8	12.8	8.8	4.8	24.1	25.3	3.6
$25,000 to $49,999	97.7	94.9	13.9	26.9	14.0	12.7	52.2	33.5	4.2
$50,000 to $99,999	99.5	98.6	16.1	39.3	26.7	21.9	70.5	44.4	5.5
$100,000 and more	100.0	99.9	19.6	36.3	43.9	38.1	83.6	52.6	7.7
MEDIAN VALUE [7]									
1992, total	12.2	2.5	11.2	0.7	8.7	17.4	15.5	3.3	21.7
1995, total	14.0	2.1	10.0	1.0	8.8	20.0	16.0	5.0	30.0
Under 35 years old	5.0	1.2	5.3	0.5	3.0	5.5	5.0	3.5	4.5
35 to 44 years old	12.3	2.0	6.0	1.0	4.5	10.0	12.5	5.3	10.8
45 to 54 years old	26.0	3.0	12.0	1.0	10.0	21.0	27.5	7.8	56.7
55 to 64 years old	30.0	3.1	14.0	1.5	19.4	56.0	30.0	5.5	50.0
65 to 74 years old	21.1	3.2	20.0	1.5	20.0	55.0	29.2	5.0	35.0
75 years old and over	22.6	5.0	11.0	4.8	18.0	50.0	23.5	5.0	65.0
Less than $10,000	1.3	0.7	8.0	0.2	2.0	25.0	5.0	1.6	51.0
$10,000 to $24,999	5.5	1.4	10.0	0.8	6.0	8.5	6.0	3.0	24.0
$25,000 to $49,999	12.3	1.9	10.0	0.7	6.0	13.0	10.0	5.0	20.0
$50,000 to $99,999	42.0	4.5	15.0	1.3	7.5	20.0	24.0	8.0	38.0
$100,000 and more	213.3	16.9	17.0	1.2	29.0	58.5	84.0	15.0	70.0

[1] Includes other types of financial assets, not shown separately. [2] Checking, savings, and money market accounts. [3] Covers only those stocks that are directly held by families outside mutual funds, IRAs, Keogh or pension accounts. [4] Excludes money market mutual funds, individual retirement accounts (IRAs), Keogh accounts, and any type of pension plan invested in mutual funds. [5] Covers IRAs, Keogh accounts, and employer-provided pension plans from which withdrawals can be made, such as 401(k) plans. [6] Includes trusts, annuities, managed investment accounts, and other such assets. [7] Median value of financial asset for families holding such assets.

Source: Board of Governors of the Federal Reserve System, *Federal Reserve Bulletin*, January 1997, and unpublished revisions.

518   Banking, Finance, and Insurance

No. 802. Flow of Funds Accounts—Liabilities of Households: 1980 to 1998

[As of **December 31 (1,427 represents $1,427,000,000,000)**. Includes nonprofit organizations]

Type of instrument	Total (bil. dol.)							Percent distribution		
	1980	1985	1990	1995	1996	1997	1998	1980	1990	1998
Total liabilities	**1,427**	**2,330**	**3,706**	**5,004**	**5,357**	**5,739**	**6,250**	**100.0**	**100.0**	**100.0**
Credit market instruments	1,376	2,239	3,582	4,804	5,135	5,472	5,958	96.4	96.6	95.3
Home mortgages	906	1,411	2,489	3,275	3,498	3,737	4,106	63.5	67.2	65.7
Consumer credit	355	604	805	1,123	1,212	1,264	1,334	24.9	21.7	21.3
Municipal securities	17	81	87	98	105	115	127	1.2	2.3	2.0
Bank loans, n.e.c. [1]	28	31	18	55	48	57	67	2.0	0.5	1.1
Other loans	55	79	101	160	173	191	205	3.8	2.7	3.3
Commercial mortgages	15	33	83	93	100	108	120	1.0	2.2	1.9
Security credit	25	51	39	79	94	131	152	1.7	1.0	2.4
Trade payables	14	24	69	103	109	117	121	1.0	1.9	1.9
Unpaid life insurance premiums [2]	13	15	16	18	18	19	18	0.9	0.4	0.3

[1] Not elsewhere classified. [2] Includes deferred premiums.

Source: Board of Governors of the Federal Reserve System, *Flow of Funds Accounts*, March 1999 diskettes.

No. 803. Financial Debt Held by Families, by Type of Debt: 1992 and 1995

[**Median debt in thousands of constant 1995 dollars (19.5 represents $19,500)**. See headnote, Table 801]

Age of family head and family income	Any debt	Mortgage, home equity	Installment	Other lines of credit	Credit card	Investment real estate	Other debt [1]
PERCENT OF FAMILIES HOLDING DEBTS							
1992, total	73.6	39.1	46.2	2.4	43.8	7.8	8.8
1995, total	**74.9**	**41.0**	**46.2**	**1.9**	**47.4**	**6.4**	**8.5**
Under 35 years old	83.7	32.9	62.6	2.7	54.8	2.8	7.6
35 to 44 years old	87.2	54.2	60.2	2.1	56.1	6.8	10.5
45 to 54 years old	86.6	61.9	53.7	2.2	56.6	10.8	12.9
55 to 64 years old	74.1	45.3	34.8	1.6	43.4	11.6	7.7
65 to 74 years old	54.3	25.1	16.7	1.3	30.8	5.3	5.3
75 years old and over	28.7	6.8	9.0	-	17.7	1.7	2.9
Less than $10,000	48.1	9.2	25.8	(B)	24.7	2.0	6.1
$10,000 to $24,999	67.7	25.2	40.7	1.3	42.0	2.3	8.5
$25,000 to $49,999	83.6	47.3	54.2	2.0	55.8	5.9	8.3
$50,000 to $99,999	89.2	68.0	60.2	3.2	63.1	10.1	8.9
$100,000 and more	85.8	73.1	38.7	4.3	38.9	25.9	14.1
MEDIAN DEBT [2]							
1992, total	19.5	47.5	5.0	2.2	1.1	26.0	2.7
1995, total	**22.4**	**51.7**	**6.1**	**3.6**	**1.5**	**30.0**	**2.0**
Under 35 years old	15.0	62.0	7.1	1.4	1.3	22.8	1.5
35 to 44 years old	37.6	61.0	5.6	2.0	1.9	30.0	2.0
45 to 54 years old	40.7	50.0	7.2	5.5	2.0	30.0	3.0
55 to 64 years old	21.5	37.0	5.0	3.4	1.3	40.0	4.0
65 to 74 years old	7.6	19.0	4.9	3.8	0.8	40.0	2.0
75 years old and over	1.9	18.1	3.4	(B)	0.4	8.0	4.0
Less than $10,000	2.5	18.0	2.6	(B)	0.6	11.4	2.7
$10,000 to $24,999	8.8	27.6	3.8	1.5	1.2	10.7	1.2
$25,000 to $49,999	23.9	45.0	6.7	3.9	1.5	26.0	1.7
$50,000 to $99,999	64.3	67.0	9.0	2.2	2.0	35.0	3.5
$100,000 and more	118.0	100.0	8.5	7.0	2.5	48.0	7.0

- Represents or rounds to zero. B Base figure too small. [1] Includes loans on insurance policies, loans against pension accounts, and other unclassified loans. [2] Median amount of financial debt for families holding such debts.

No. 804. Percent Distribution of Amount of Debt Held by Families: 1992 and 1995

[See headnote, Table 805]

Type of debt	1992	1995	Purpose of debt	1992	1995	Type of lending institution	1992	1995
Total	**100.0**	**100.0**	**Total**	**100.0**	**100.0**	**Total**	**100.0**	**100.0**
Home mortgage and home equity lines of credit	64.1	67.3	Home purchase	59.8	67.0	Commercial bank	33.1	34.7
			Home improvement . .	2.3	1.9	Savings and loan	16.5	10.7
			Investment, excluding real estate	1.6	0.4	Credit union	4.0	4.4
Installment loans	10.3	11.0	Vehicles	6.2	7.0	Finance or loan company .	13.6	20.8
Credit card balances . .	2.8	3.6	Goods and services . .	5.0	4.8	Brokerage	3.3	2.1
Other lines of credit . .	0.7	0.5	Investment real estate .	20.7	16.1	Real estate lender	14.3	13.0
Investment real estate mortgages	19.9	15.0	Education	2.5	2.6	Individual lender	4.4	5.3
Other debt	2.1	2.6	Other loans	2.1	0.3	Other nonfinancial	1.5	0.8
						Government	2.0	1.3
						Credit and store cards . .	3.0	3.6
						Other loans	4.4	3.3

Source of Tables 803 and 804: Board of Governors of the Federal Reserve System, *Federal Reserve Bulletin*, January 1997 and unpublished revisions.

Banking, Finance, and Insurance 519

No. 805. Ratios of Debt Payments to Family Income: 1989 to 1995

[In percent. Constant dollar figures are based on consumer price index data published by U.S. Bureau of Labor Statistics. Families include one-person units; for definition of family, see text, Section 1, Population. Based on Survey of Consumer Finance; see Appendix III. For definition of median, see Guide to Tabular Presentation]

Age of family head and family income (constant (1995) dollars)	Ratio of debt payments to family income						Percent of debtors with—					
	Aggregate			Median			Ratios above 40 percent			Any payment 60 days or more past due		
	1989	1992	1995	1989	1992	1995	1989	1992	1995	1989	1992	1995
All families	15.6	15.7	14.8	16.1	16.3	16.3	11.0	11.5	11.0	7.2	6.0	7.0
Under 35 years old	18.1	16.9	17.5	17.2	16.5	16.7	13.0	10.5	11.1	11.1	8.2	8.7
35 to 44 years old.........	19.3	18.4	17.2	18.4	19.2	18.1	8.9	12.2	10.0	6.4	7.0	7.7
45 to 54 years old.........	15.3	17.4	15.8	16.6	16.8	16.7	12.5	11.4	10.8	4.5	5.3	7.3
55 to 64 years old.........	16.9	14.4	14.1	13.6	15.4	14.1	10.4	15.5	15.5	7.3	4.6	3.1
65 to 74 years old.........	6.5	10.3	9.6	11.3	10.9	13.3	8.3	8.5	8.4	3.3	1.1	5.3
75 years old and over	2.7	4.6	3.5	10.0	5.5	3.8	12.4	9.4	8.7	1.1	2.0	5.3
Less than $10,000	17.9	16.8	22.7	22.0	19.4	16.0	27.9	28.8	27.2	21.2	11.1	8.5
$10,000 to $24,999	12.7	16.3	16.3	17.2	15.5	17.4	14.4	15.7	15.9	11.8	9.2	11.1
$25,000 to $49,999	16.5	17.0	16.9	16.4	16.7	16.9	9.9	9.7	8.3	4.5	6.2	7.8
$50,000 to $99,999	16.8	16.0	16.6	16.1	16.9	16.7	5.5	4.7	4.9	4.6	2.1	2.8
$100,000 and more	14.6	14.1	10.6	13.2	14.6	11.0	7.1	4.3	3.6	1.2	0.5	1.4

Source: Board of Governors of the Federal Reserve System, *Federal Reserve Bulletin*, January 1997, and unpublished revisions.

No. 806. Selected Financial Institutions—Number and Assets, by Asset Size: 1998

[As of December (5,440.9 represents $5,440,900,000,000). FDIC=Federal Deposit Insurance Corporation]

Asset size	Number of institutions			Assets (bil. dol.)		
	FDIC-insured			FDIC-insured		
	Commercial banks	Savings institutions	Credit unions [1]	Commercial banks [2]	Savings institutions	Credit unions [1]
Total................	8,774	1,687	10,995	5,440.9	1,087.7	388.7
Less than $5.0 million.........	42	7	4,916	0.1	(Z)	9.1
$5.0 million to $9.9 million	158	24	1,721	1.2	0.2	12.3
$10.0 million to $24.9 million	1,043	115	1,860	18.8	2.1	30.0
$25.0 million to $49.9 million	1,915	198	1,042	70.8	7.5	36.8
$50.0 million to $99.9 million	2,250	356	681	161.4	26.3	48.0
$100.0 million to $499.9 million...	2,696	727	665	537.5	165.1	137.1
$500.0 million to $999.9 million...	278	115	80	189.5	79.6	52.9
$1.0 billion to $2.9 billion	212	91	26	336.9	145.8	40.0
$3.0 billion or more..........	180	54	4	4,124.7	661.0	22.5
	Percent distribution					
Total................	100.0	100.0	100.0	100.0	100.0	100.0
Less than $5.0 million.........	0.5	0.4	44.7	(Z)	(Z)	2.3
$5.0 million to $9.9 million	1.8	1.4	15.7	(Z)	(Z)	3.2
$10.0 million to $24.9 million	11.9	6.8	16.9	0.3	0.2	7.7
$25.0 million to $49.9 million	21.8	11.7	9.5	1.3	0.7	9.5
$50.0 million to $99.9 million	25.6	21.1	6.2	3.0	2.4	12.3
$100.0 million to $499.9 million...	30.7	43.1	6.0	9.9	15.2	35.3
$500.0 million to $999.9 million...	3.2	6.8	0.7	3.5	7.3	13.6
$1.0 billion to $2.9 billion	2.4	5.4	0.2	6.2	13.4	10.3
$3.0 billion or more..........	2.1	3.2	(Z)	75.8	60.8	5.8

Z Less than $50 million or 0.05 percent. [1] Source: National Credit Union Administration, *National Credit Union Administration Yearend Statistics 1998*. Excludes nonfederally insured state chartered credit unions and federally insured corporate credit unions. [2] Includes foreign branches of U.S. banks.
Source: Except as noted, U.S. Federal Deposit Insurance Corporation, *Statistics on Banking, 1998*.

No. 807. Banking Offices, by Type of Bank: 1980 to 1998

[As of December 31. Includes Puerto Rico and outlying areas. Covers all FDIC-insured commercial banks and savings institutions. Commercial banks include insured branches of foreign banks. Data for 1980 include automatic teller machines which were reported by many banks as branches]

Item	1980	1985	1990	1993	1994	1995	1996	1997	1998
All banking offices	(NA)	82,366	84,329	80,541	81,127	81,305	82,461	83,159	84,123
Number of banks	(NA)	18,033	15,192	13,261	12,641	12,002	11,478	10,945	10,481
Number of branches	(NA)	64,333	69,137	67,280	68,486	69,303	70,983	72,214	73,642
Commercial banks	53,172	57,657	62,705	63,610	65,049	65,830	66,703	68,428	69,985
Number of banks.............	14,434	14,407	12,377	10,999	10,489	9,972	9,553	9,165	8,794
Number of branches	38,738	43,250	50,328	52,611	54,560	55,858	57,150	59,263	61,191
Savings institutions	(NA)	24,709	21,624	16,931	16,078	15,475	15,758	14,731	14,138
Number of banks.............	(NA)	3,626	2,815	2,262	2,152	2,030	1,925	1,780	1,687
Number of branches	(NA)	21,083	18,809	14,669	13,926	13,445	13,833	12,951	12,451

NA Not available.
Source: U.S. Federal Deposit Insurance Corporation, *Statistics on Banking*, annual and *The FDIC Quarterly Banking Profile Graph Book*.

No. 808. Retail Fees and Services of Banks: 1996 and 1997

[In dollars, except as noted. Data for 1996 as of November or December; 1997 data as of June. For most services, fees are reported in terms of (1) the proportion of those banks offering a service that charge for the service and (2) the average fee charged by the institutions that charge for the service. Based on a random sample of depository institutions belonging to the Bank Insurance Fund, whose members are predominantly commercial banks]

Type of account or service	1996	1997	Type of account or service	1996	1997
NONINTEREST CHECKING ACCOUNT			AUTOMATED TELLER MACHINES (ATMs)		
Percent offering.	97.8	98.7	Percent offering.	72.9	79.4
Single-balance, single-fee account: [1]			Annual fee:		
Percent offering	32.9	39.3	Percent charging	13.4	16.7
Monthly fee (low balance)	6.34	6.09	Average	7.94	11.51
Minimum balance to avoid fee	480	479	Fees for customer transactions on us: [4]		
Minimum balance to open	123	124	Withdrawals:		
Fee-only account: [2]			Percent charging.	6.8	7.4
Percent offering	34.2	33.3	Average	0.59	0.65
Monthly fee (low balance)	5.02	4.49	Balance inquiries:		
Check charge:			Percent charging.	4.4	6.7
Percent charging.	45.8	32.4	Average	0.70	0.65
Average	0.34	0.38	Fees for customer transactions on others: [4]		
Minimum balance to open	82	61	Withdrawals:		
			Percent charging.	79.8	67.0
NOW ACCOUNTS [3]			Average	1.10	1.06
Percent offering.	97.3	97.6	Balance inquiries:		
Single-fee account: [1]			Percent charging.	64.7	55.2
Percent offering	44.0	56.7	Average	1.03	0.99
Monthly fee (low balance)	8.11	7.81	Surcharge: [5]		
Minimum balance to avoid fee	1,079	1,052	Percent charging	44.8	60.1
Minimum balance to open	654	663	Average	1.19	1.14

[1] A monthly fee for balances below the minimum, no monthly fee for balances above the minimum, and no other charges. [2] A monthly fee, no minimum balance to eliminate the fee, and a charge per check in some cases. [3] NOW (negotiable order of withdrawal) accounts are checking accounts that pay interest and often have fee structures that differ from those of noninterest checking accounts. [4] An institution's "customer" is one who has an account at the institution. A customer's ATM transactions in which the machine used is that of the customer's institution are called "on us"; a customer's transactions in which the machine used is that of another institution are called "on others". [5] An ATM surcharge is a fee imposed by the ATMs institution, typically on every transaction by the machine's noncustomer users.

Source: Board of Governors of the Federal Reserve Systems, *Annual Report to the Congress on Retail Fees and Services of Depository Institutions*, June 1998.

No. 809. Insured Commercial Banks—Assets and Liabilities: 1980 to 1998

[In billions of dollars, except as indicated (1,856 represents $1,856,000,000,000). As of Dec. 31. Includes outlying areas. Except as noted, includes foreign branches of U.S. banks]

Item	1980	1985	1990	1993	1994	1995	1996	1997	1998 [1]
Number of banks reporting	14,435	14,417	12,343	10,958	10,450	9,940	9,528	9,142	8,774
Assets, total.	**1,856**	**2,731**	**3,389**	**3,706**	**4,011**	**4,313**	**4,578**	**5,015**	**5,441**
Net loans and leases.	1,006	1,608	2,055	2,097	2,306	2,550	2,758	2,916	3,181
Real estate loans	269	438	830	923	998	1,080	1,139	1,244	1,345
Home equity loans [2]	(NA)	(NA)	61	73	76	79	85	98	97
Commercial and industrial loans. . .	391	578	615	539	589	661	710	796	899
Loans to individuals	187	309	404	419	487	535	562	561	571
Credit cards and related plans . .	(NA)	(NA)	134	153	187	216	232	231	229
Farm loans.	32	36	33	37	39	40	41	45	46
Other loans and leases.	158	288	242	239	251	292	364	329	381
Less: Reserve for losses.	10	23	56	53	52	53	53	55	57
Less: Unearned income	21	18	14	7	6	6	5	4	4
Loans to non-U.S. borrowers [3]	196	235	190	180	201	232	279	302	334
Percent of total loans and leases	19	14	9	8	9	9	10	10	10
Investment securities	325	439	605	837	823	811	801	872	980
Other	524	684	730	772	881	952	1,020	1,227	1,280
Domestic office assets.	1,533	2,326	2,999	3,258	3,483	3,728	3,906	4,267	4,733
Foreign office assets	323	406	390	448	527	585	672	748	708
Liabilities and capital, total	**1,856**	**2,731**	**3,389**	**3,706**	**4,011**	**4,313**	**4,578**	**5,015**	**5,441**
Noninterest-bearing deposits [4]	432	471	489	572	572	612	664	676	719
Interest-bearing deposits [5]	1,049	1,646	2,162	2,182	2,302	2,416	2,533	2,745	2,963
Subordinated debt.	7	15	24	37	41	44	51	62	73
Other liabilities	260	429	496	618	783	892	954	1,113	1,224
Equity capital	108	169	219	296	312	350	375	418	462
Domestic office deposits.	1,187	1,796	2,357	2,424	2,443	2,573	2,724	2,896	3,110
Foreign office deposits.	294	322	293	330	432	454	474	526	572

NA Not available. [1] Preliminary. [2] For one- to four-family residential properties. [3] Includes leases and commercial and industrial loans to non-U.S. addressees, loans to foreign governments, real estate loans in foreign offices, and loans to banks in foreign countries. [4] Prior to 1984, demand deposits. [5] Prior to 1984, time and savings deposits.

Source: U.S. Federal Deposit Insurance Corporation, *The FDIC Quarterly Banking Profile, Annual Report*, and *Statistics on Banking*, annual.

Banking, Finance, and Insurance **521**

No. 810. Insured Commercial Banks—Income and Selected Measures of Financial Condition: 1980 to 1998

[In billions of dollars, except as indicated (177.4 represents $177,400,000,000). Includes outlying areas. Includes foreign branches of U.S. banks]

Item	1980	1985	1990	1993	1994	1995	1996	1997	1998 [1]
Interest income	177.4	248.2	320.5	245.1	257.8	302.4	312.7	339.5	362.1
Interest expense	120.1	157.3	204.9	105.7	111.3	148.2	150.0	165.0	179.3
Net interest income	57.3	90.9	115.5	139.3	146.6	154.2	162.8	174.5	182.8
Provisions for loan losses	4.5	17.8	32.1	16.8	11.0	12.6	16.3	19.8	22.2
Noninterest income	13.3	31.1	54.9	75.0	76.3	82.4	93.6	104.5	123.7
Percent of net operating revenue [2]	18.8	25.5	32.2	35.0	34.2	34.8	36.5	37.5	40.4
Noninterest expense	46.7	82.4	115.7	139.7	144.2	149.7	160.7	170.0	194.0
Income taxes	5.0	5.6	7.7	19.9	22.4	26.1	28.2	31.9	32.0
Securities gain/loss, net	-0.5	1.6	0.5	3.1	-0.6	0.5	1.1	1.8	3.1
Extraordinary gains, net	-	0.2	0.6	2.1	-	-	0.1	-	0.5
Net income	14.0	18.0	16.0	43.0	44.6	48.7	52.4	59.2	61.9
From domestic operations	11.9	16.3	14.2	36.0	39.3	43.1	46.0	53.1	56.7
From foreign operations	2.0	1.7	1.8	7.0	5.3	5.7	6.3	6.1	5.2
PERFORMANCE RATIOS									
Return on assets [3] (percent)	0.80	0.70	0.48	1.20	1.15	1.17	1.19	1.23	1.19
Return on equity [4] (percent)	13.66	11.31	7.45	15.34	14.61	14.66	14.46	14.70	13.95
Net interest margin [5] (percent)	3.66	4.09	3.94	4.40	4.36	4.29	4.27	4.21	4.07
Net charge-offs [6]	3.6	13.6	29.7	17.5	11.2	12.2	15.5	18.3	20.7
Net charge-offs to loans and leases, total (percent) .	0.36	0.84	1.43	0.85	0.50	0.49	0.58	0.63	0.67
Net charge-off rate, credit card loans (percent) . . .	(NA)	2.95	3.86	3.42	3.00	3.98	4.66	5.34	5.26
CONDITION RATIOS									
Equity capital to assets (percent)	5.80	6.20	6.45	8.00	7.78	8.11	8.20	8.33	8.50
Noncurrent assets plus other real estate owned to assets [7] (percent)	(NA)	1.87	2.94	1.61	1.01	0.85	0.75	0.66	0.65
Percentage of banks losing money	3.7	17.1	13.4	4.9	4.0	3.6	4.2	4.5	5.8

- Represents or rounds to zero. NA Not available. [1] Preliminary. [2] Net operating revenue equals net interest income plus noninterest income. [3] Net income (including securities transactions and nonrecurring items) as a percentage of average total assets. [4] Net income as a percentage of average total equity capital. [5] Interest income less interest expense as a percentage of average earning assets (i.e. the profit margin a bank earns on its loans and investments). [6] Total loans and leases charged off (removed from balance sheet because of uncollectibility), less amounts recovered on loans and leases previously charged off. [7] The sum of loans, leases, debt securities and other assets that are 90 days or more past due, or in nonaccrual status plus foreclosed property.

No. 811. Insured Commercial Banks—Selected Measures of Financial Condition, by Asset Size and Region: 1998

[In percent, except as indicated. Preliminary. See headnote, Table 810]

Asset size and region	Number of banks	Return on assets	Return on equity	Equity capital to assets	Noncurrent assets plus other real estate owned to total assets	Net charge-offs to loans and leases	Percentage of banks losing money
Total	8,774	1.19	13.95	8.50	0.65	0.67	5.8
Less than $100 million . . .	5,408	1.14	10.15	10.95	0.71	0.30	8.2
$100 million to $1 billion .	2,974	1.31	13.57	9.52	0.62	0.39	2.0
$1 billion to $10 billion. . .	321	1.52	15.96	9.46	0.71	1.02	1.9
$10 billion or more	71	1.08	13.82	7.86	0.64	0.65	1.4
Northeast [1]	693	1.07	14.10	7.81	0.78	0.91	7.6
Southeast [2]	1,444	1.31	14.47	9.10	0.55	0.43	8.9
Central [3]	1,904	1.25	14.71	8.27	0.56	0.44	4.0
Midwest [4]	2,265	1.50	16.66	8.72	0.57	0.74	2.6
Southwest [5]	1,518	1.14	12.41	8.83	0.59	0.42	5.7
West [6]	950	1.11	11.39	9.29	0.67	0.86	11.4

[1] CT, DE, DC, ME, MD, MA, NH, NJ, NY, PA, PR, RI, and VT. [2] AL, FL, GA, MS, NC, SC, TN, VA, and WV. [3] IL, IN, KY, MI, OH, and WI. [4] IA, KS, MN, MO, NE, ND, and SD. [5] AR, LA, NM, OK, and TX. [6] AK, AZ, CA, CO, HI, ID, MT, NV, OR, Pacific Islands, UT, WA, and WY.

Source of Tables 810 and 811: U.S. Federal Deposit Insurance Corporation, *Annual Report; Statistics on Banking*, annual; and *FDIC Quarterly Banking Profile*.

No. 812. Insured Commercial Banks—Delinquency Rates on Loans: 1990 to 1998

[In percent. Seasonally adjusted. Delinquent loans are those past due 30 days or more and still accruing interest as well as those in nonaccrual status]

Type of loan	1990	1991	1992	1993	1994	1995	1996	1997	1998
Total loans.	5.98	5.81	4.82	3.36	2.50	2.46	2.39	2.25	2.21
Real estate	7.34	7.30	6.04	4.35	3.09	2.82	2.64	2.34	2.16
Residential [1]	(NA)	3.39	2.91	2.47	2.10	2.26	2.37	2.30	2.11
Commercial [2]	(NA)	11.80	10.02	6.95	4.51	3.58	2.99	2.33	2.09
Consumer	4.09	4.15	3.55	2.96	2.71	3.29	3.70	3.77	3.77
Credit cards	(NA)	5.32	4.68	3.90	3.27	3.93	4.61	4.80	4.76
Other	(NA)	3.56	2.97	2.45	2.39	2.88	3.08	3.10	3.17
Commercial and industrial	5.89	5.63	4.45	2.86	2.06	1.94	1.83	1.61	1.78
Agricultural	4.78	4.81	4.20	3.17	2.71	2.76	3.22	2.65	2.82

NA Not available. [1] Residential real estate loans include loans secured by one- to four-family properties, including home equity lines of credit. [2] Commercial real estate loans include construction and land development loans, loans secured by multifamily residences, and loans secured by nonfarm, nonresidential real estate.

Source: Board of Governors of the Federal Reserve System; "Delinquency Rates, All Banks, SA;" <http://www.bog.frb.fed.us/releases/ChargeOff/delallsa.txt>; (accessed: 30 March 1999).

No. 813. U.S. Banking Offices of Foreign Banks—Summary: 1980 to 1997

[In billions of dollars, except as indicated (201 represents $201,000,000,000). As of December. Covers agencies, branches, subsidiary commercial banks, and New York State investment companies]

Item	1980	1985	1990	1993	1994	1995	1996	1997	Share [1] 1980	1990	1995	1997
Assets	201	441	791	856	944	984	989	1,120	11.9	21.4	21.7	21.2
Loans, total	121	247	398	380	419	461	460	493	13.4	18.0	17.3	16.1
Business	60	109	193	196	216	249	264	281	18.2	30.8	35.1	33.2
Deposits	80	237	384	466	523	523	527	592	6.6	14.5	17.6	17.6

[1] Percent of "domestically owned" commercial banks plus U.S. offices of foreign banks.

Source: Board of Governors of the Federal Reserve System, unpublished data.

No. 814. Foreign Lending by U.S. Banks, by Type of Borrower and Country: 1998

[In millions of dollars (367,397 represents $367,397,000,000). As of December. Covers 108 U.S. banking organizations which do nearly all of the foreign lending in the country. Data represent claims on foreign residents and institutions held at all domestic and foreign offices of covered banks. Data cover only cross-border and nonlocal currency lending. These result from a U.S. bank's office in one country lending to residents of another country or lending in a currency other than that of the borrower's country. Excludes local currency loans and other claims and local currency liabilities held by banks' foreign offices on residents of the country in which the office was located (e.g. Deutsche mark loans to German residents booked at the German branch of the reporting U.S. bank). Criteria for country selection is $4.5 billion or more]

Country	Total	Bank	Public	Private non-bank	Country	Total	Bank	Public	Private non-bank
Total [1]	367,397	111,651	109,827	145,920	Italy.	17,835	3,859	12,016	1,960
					Japan	34,012	4,924	25,514	3,574
Argentina	11,602	2,170	2,846	6,586	Korea, South	6,859	3,703	1,446	1,710
Australia.	5,246	1,294	1,143	2,809	Mexico.	19,457	1,429	7,836	10,192
Belgium	5,738	2,358	1,451	1,929	Netherlands	13,176	4,930	2,414	5,832
Brazil.	13,295	3,978	2,879	6,438	Netherlands Antilles . .	5,178	164	45	4,969
Canada	12,180	3,218	2,389	6,573	Spain	5,353	1,732	1,507	2,114
Cayman Islands.	15,497	6,123	184	9,190	Sweden	4,931	1,190	2,124	1,617
France.	21,125	9,650	6,274	5,201	Switzerland.	7,507	3,023	1,335	3,149
Germany	31,358	9,976	16,684	4,698	Turkey	4,541	1,939	942	1,660
Hong Kong	4,825	2,215	18	2,592	United Kingdom.	38,123	19,018	1,015	18,090

[1] Includes other countries, not shown separately.

Source: Board of Governors of the Federal Reserve System, Federal Financial Institutions Examination Council, statistical release.

No. 815. Insured Commercial Banks, by State and Other Area: 1998

[In billions of dollars, except number of banks (5,440.9 represents $5,440,900,000,000). As of December 31. Includes foreign branches of U.S. banks]

State	Number	Assets	Deposits	State	Number	Assets	Deposits
Total	8,774	5,440.9	3,681.5	Nebraska	315	28.0	23.0
United States.	8,756	5,398.4	3,655.1	Nevada.	26	27.5	8.8
Alabama	160	140.9	101.8	New Hampshire	19	16.1	11.1
Alaska	6	5.1	3.8	New Jersey	72	96.9	74.2
Arizona.	43	42.3	25.1	New Mexico.	58	15.0	11.4
Arkansas.	202	25.1	21.5	New York	153	1,143.7	677.5
California.	336	516.0	398.9	North Carolina	67	665.7	414.5
Colorado.	195	36.1	31.3	North Dakota	114	10.8	8.1
Connecticut	28	6.5	5.1	Ohio.	220	267.4	170.4
Delaware.	34	131.3	54.2	Oklahoma	309	35.6	28.7
District of Columbia.	7	1.3	1.0	Oregon	42	6.3	5.3
Florida	250	81.2	62.5	Pennsylvania	197	198.4	137.0
Georgia	349	76.6	47.3	Rhode Island	7	90.5	56.6
Hawaii	12	24.2	16.6	South Carolina	77	19.0	15.6
Idaho	17	1.8	1.6	South Dakota	104	29.7	11.7
Illinois.	745	297.3	207.6	Tennessee.	204	102.5	76.4
Indiana	169	73.4	54.5	Texas	799	179.9	149.2
Iowa.	443	46.6	38.0	Utah.	50	45.2	22.9
Kansas	393	34.0	28.9	Vermont	21	7.6	6.4
Kentucky.	261	52.3	39.9	Virginia	152	75.0	52.0
Louisiana	150	49.0	39.5	Washington	78	12.7	10.6
Maine	17	5.0	4.0	West Virginia	89	23.6	18.8
Maryland.	80	44.6	33.5	Wisconsin	344	81.7	62.2
Massachusetts	44	137.5	94.5	Wyoming	52	10.1	9.1
Michigan	165	117.2	87.0	American Samoa.	1	0.1	(Z)
Minnesota	514	147.8	103.7	Puerto Rico	12	41.5	25.6
Mississippi.	96	26.9	21.6	Guam	2	0.8	0.7
Missouri	382	79.6	62.0	Pacific Islands.	1	(Z)	(Z)
Montana	89	9.9	8.2	Virgin Islands	2	0.1	0.1

Z Less than $50 million.

Source: U.S. Federal Deposit Insurance Corporation, Statistics on Banking, annual.

Banking, Finance, and Insurance   523

No. 816. Federal and State-Chartered Credit Unions—Summary: 1980 to 1998

[Except as noted, as of **December 31 (24,519 represents 24,519,000).** Federal data include District of Columbia, Puerto Rico, Canal Zone, Guam, and Virgin Islands. Excludes state-insured, privately-insured, and noninsured state-chartered credit unions and corporate central credit unions which have mainly other credit unions as members]

Year	Operating credit unions		Number of failed institutions [1]	Members (1,000)		Assets (mil. dol.)		Loans outstanding (mil. dol.)		Savings (mil. dol.)	
	Federal	State		Federal	State	Federal	State	Federal	State	Federal	State
1980	12,440	4,910	239	24,519	12,338	40,092	20,870	26,350	14,582	36,263	18,469
1985	10,125	4,920	94	29,579	15,689	78,188	41,525	48,241	26,168	71,616	37,917
1990	8,511	4,349	164	36,241	19,454	130,073	68,133	83,029	44,102	117,892	62,082
1993	7,696	4,621	37	39,756	23,997	172,854	104,316	94,640	57,695	153,506	93,482
1994	7,498	4,493	33	40,837	24,295	182,529	106,937	110,090	65,769	160,226	94,797
1995	7,329	4,358	26	42,163	24,927	193,781	112,860	120,514	71,606	170,300	99,838
1996	7,152	4,240	19	43,546	25,652	206,695	120,193	134,127	79,661	180,969	105,743
1997	6,981	4,257	16	43,491	27,921	215,104	136,074	140,104	92,117	187,822	119,359
1998	6,814	4,181	14	43,865	29,674	231,904	156,787	144,849	100,890	202,651	137,347

[1] Through 1994 for year ending September 30; 1995 reflects 15-month period from October 1994 through December 1995; beginning 1996 reflects calendar year. A failed institution is defined as a credit union which has ceased operation because it was involuntarily liquidated or merged with assistance from the National Credit Union Share Insurance Fund. Assisted mergers were not identified until 1981.

Source: National Credit Union Administration, *Annual Report of the National Credit Union Administration*, and unpublished data.

No. 817. Insured Savings Institutions—Financial Summary: 1985 to 1998

[In billions of dollars, except number of institutions (1,263 represents $1,263,000,000,000). As of **December 31**. Includes Puerto Rico, Guam, and Virgin Islands. Covers SAIF (Savings Association Insurance Fund)- and BIF (Bank Insurance Fund)-insured savings institutions. Excludes institutions in Resolution Trust Corporation conservatorship and, beginning 1992, excludes one self-liquidating institution. Minus sign (-) indicates loss]

Item	1985	1990	1991	1992	1993	1994	1995	1996	1997	1998
Number of institutions	3,626	2,815	2,561	2,390	2,262	2,152	2,030	1,924	1,780	1,687
Assets, total	1,263	1,259	1,113	1,030	1,001	1,009	1,026	1,028	1,026	1,088
Loans and leases, net	821	812	724	648	626	635	648	681	692	714
Liabilities, total...........	1,218	1,192	1,044	956	922	929	940	942	937	993
Deposits	1,023	987	907	828	774	737	742	728	704	705
Equity capital............	45	68	69	74	78	80	86	86	89	94
Interest and fee income.....	119	117	98	78	66	63	71	72	69	71
Interest expense	101	91	70	46	35	33	43	42	41	42
Net interest income.......	17	26	28	32	32	30	28	30	29	29
Net income.............	6	-5	1	7	7	6	8	7	9	10

Source: U.S. Federal Deposit Insurance Corporation, *Statistics on Banking*, annual and *FDIC Quarterly Banking Profile*.

No. 818. Volume of Long-Term Mortgage Loans Originated, by Type of Property, 1980 to 1997, and by Lender, 1997

[In billions of dollars (197.2 represents $197,200,000,000). Covers credit extended in primary mortgage markets for financing real estate acquisitions]

Type of property	1980	1985	1990	1993	1994	1995	1996	Total [1]	1997, by lender			
									Commercial banks	Mortgage companies	Savings and loan	Life insurance companies
Loans, total....	197.2	430.0	710.5	1,241.7	1,019.2	930.0	1,126.2	1,118.4	395.0	505.3	141.2	24.4
1-4 unit family home..	133.8	289.8	458.4	1,019.9	768.7	639.4	785.3	859.1	206.6	494.5	130.9	0.4
New units	49.1	59.0	110.7	117.3	114.6	110.7	178.2	111.2	43.2	50.4	14.5	0.1
Existing units	84.6	230.8	347.7	902.5	654.2	528.7	607.2	747.9	163.4	444.1	116.4	0.3
Multifamily residential .	12.5	31.9	32.6	31.7	32.7	39.2	47.1	47.9	25.4	10.7	4.8	1.4
New units	8.6	10.6	6.5	4.4	4.5	5.4	8.5	7.9	4.3	1.7	0.2	0.7
Existing units	3.9	21.3	26.0	27.3	28.2	33.8	38.7	40.0	21.1	9.0	4.6	0.7
Nonresidential	35.9	99.4	209.5	172.5	190.0	220.8	268.2	193.2	153.5	-	5.5	21.7
Farm properties	15.0	9.0	10.0	17.6	27.8	30.6	25.6	18.1	9.5	-	0.0	0.8

- Represents zero. [1] Includes other lenders not shown separately.

Source: U.S. Dept. of Housing and Urban Development, monthly and quarterly press releases based on the Survey of Mortgage Lending Activity.

No. 819. Characteristics of Conventional First Mortgage Loans for Purchase of Single-Family Homes: 1990 to 1998

[In percent, except as indicated (154.1 represents $154,100). Annual averages. Covers fully amortized conventional mortgage loans used to purchase nonfarm homes. Excludes refinancing loans, nonamortized and balloon loans, loans insured by the Federal Housing Administration, and loans guaranteed by the Veterans Administration. Based on a sample of mortgage lenders, including savings and loans associations, savings banks, commercial banks, and mortgage companies]

Loan characteristics	New homes						Previously occupied homes					
	1990	1994	1995	1996	1997	1998	1990	1994	1995	1996	1997	1998
Contract interest rate,[1]												
all loans	9.7	7.3	7.7	7.6	7.6	6.9	9.8	7.3	7.7	7.6	7.5	7.0
Fixed-rate loans	10.1	7.9	8.0	7.8	7.7	7.1	10.1	8.0	8.0	7.8	7.7	7.1
Adjustable-rate loans [2]. . . .	8.9	6.5	7.2	7.0	6.9	6.4	8.9	6.2	7.0	6.9	6.7	6.3
Initial fees, charges [3]	1.98	1.29	1.20	1.21	1.01	0.88	1.74	1.07	0.93	0.93	0.97	0.84
Effective interest rate, [4]												
all loans	10.1	7.5	7.9	7.8	7.7	7.1	10.1	7.5	7.8	7.7	7.7	7.1
Fixed-rate loans	10.4	8.1	8.2	8.0	7.9	7.2	10.4	8.2	8.2	8.0	7.9	7.2
Adjustable-rate loans [2]. . . .	9.2	6.6	7.2	7.2	7.0	6.5	9.2	6.4	7.1	7.1	6.9	6.5
Term to maturity (years).	27.3	27.5	27.7	27.1	28.2	28.4	27.0	27.1	27.4	26.8	27.3	27.7
Purchase price ($1,000)	154.1	170.7	175.4	182.6	181.4	195.0	140.3	136.4	137.3	150.2	161.0	169.5
Loan to price ratio	74.9	78.7	78.6	78.1	80.4	80.1	74.9	80.1	80.1	79.1	79.2	78.7
Percent of number of loans with adjustable rates	31	41	37	26	21	17	27	39	31	27	22	12

[1] Initial interest rate paid by the borrower as specified in the loan contract.   [2] Loans with a contractual provision for periodic adjustments in the contract interest rate.   [3] Includes all fees, commissions, discounts and "points" paid by the borrower, or seller, in order to obtain the loan. Excludes those charges for mortgage, credit, life or property insurance; for property transfer; and for title search and insurance.   [4] Contract interest rate plus fees and charges amortized over a 10-year period.

Source: U.S. Federal Housing Finance Board, *Rates & Terms on Conventional Home Mortgages, Annual Summary.*

No. 820. Mortgage Debt Outstanding, by Type of Property and Holder: 1980 to 1998

[In billions of dollars (1,465 represents $1,465,000,000,000). As of **Dec. 31**. Includes Puerto Rico and Guam]

Type of property and holder	1980	1985	1990	1991	1992	1993	1994	1995	1996	1997	1998
Mortgage debt, total.	**1,465**	**2,374**	**3,794**	**3,948**	**4,063**	**4,206**	**4,392**	**4,610**	**4,928**	**5,257**	**5,782**
Residential nonfarm	1,111	1,742	2,961	3,134	3,293	3,448	3,632	3,820	4,065	4,328	4,738
One- to four-family homes.	970	1,537	2,674	2,851	3,019	3,178	3,357	3,533	3,756	3,999	4,376
Savings institutions	487	554	600	538	490	470	478	482	514	521	534
Mortgage pools or trusts [1]	125	407	1,046	1,230	1,400	1,519	1,658	1,771	1,941	2,106	2,381
Government National Mortgage Association	92	207	392	416	411	405	441	461	494	523	522
Federal Home Loan Mortgage Corp . .	13	100	308	352	402	443	488	512	552	577	643
Federal National Mortgage Assoc . .	(X)	54	291	363	436	487	521	570	633	688	804
Private mortgage conduits [2]	(NA)	(NA)	(NA)	(NA)	(NA)	(NA)	209	228	262	318	411
Commercial banks	162	215	458	486	511	561	616	669	699	763	811
Individuals and others [3].	117	239	403	422	414	390	370	372	376	389	426
Federal and related agencies	61	110	153	163	194	230	228	229	220	213	217
Federal National Mortgage Assoc . .	52	92	94	101	124	151	159	164	155	150	148
Life insurance companies	18	12	13	11	11	9	7	8	7	7	7
Five or more units	141	205	287	283	273	269	275	287	309	330	362
Commercial.	256	526	754	735	690	677	677	706	776	839	949
Farm	97	106	79	79	80	81	83	85	87	90	95
TYPE OF HOLDER											
Savings institutions	603	760	802	705	628	598	596	597	628	632	643
Commercial banks	264	431	849	881	901	948	1,013	1,090	1,145	1,245	1,338
Life insurance companies.	131	172	268	260	242	224	211	213	208	207	212
Individuals and others [3].	206	404	555	569	561	533	524	538	586	614	665
Mortgage pools or trusts [1]	146	439	1,081	1,267	1,445	1,576	1,732	1,863	2,065	2,273	2,632
Government National Mortgage Assoc. . . .	94	212	404	425	420	414	451	472	506	537	537
Federal Home Loan Mortgage Corp	17	100	316	359	408	447	491	515	554	579	646
Federal National Mortgage Association . . .	(X)	55	300	372	445	496	530	583	651	710	835
Farmers Home Administration [4]	32	48	(Z)	(Z)	(Z)	(Z)	(Z)	(Z)	(Z)	(Z)	(Z)
Private mortgage conduits.	(NA)	(NA)	(NA)	(NA)	(NA)	(NA)	260	293	353	447	613
Federal and related agencies	115	167	239	266	286	326	316	309	295	286	292
Federal National Mortgage Association . . .	57	98	105	112	137	166	174	179	169	161	158
Farmers Home Administration [4]	3	1	41	42	42	41	42	42	42	41	41
Federal Land Banks.	38	47	29	29	29	28	29	28	30	31	33
Federal Home Loan Mortgage Corp	5	14	22	27	34	47	42	44	47	48	57
Federal Housing and Veterans Admin	4	4	7	9	11	11	10	10	6	4	3
Government National Mortgage Assoc. . . .	5	1	(Z)	(Z)	(Z)	(Z)	(Z)	(Z)	(Z)	(Z)	(Z)
Federal Deposit Insurance Corp	(X)	(X)	(X)	(X)	(X)	14	8	4	2	1	(Z)
Resolution Trust Corporation	(X)	(X)	33	46	32	17	10	2	(X)	(X)	(X)

NA Not available.   X Not applicable.   Z Less than $500 million.   [1] Outstanding principal balances of mortgage pools backing securities insured or guaranteed by the agency indicated. Includes other pools not shown separately.   [2] Includes securitized home equity loans.   [3] Includes mortgage companies, real estate investment trusts, state and local retirement funds, noninsured pension funds, state and local credit agencies, credit unions, and finance companies.   [4] FmHA-guaranteed securities sold to the Federal Financing Bank were reallocated from FmHA mortgage pools to FmHA mortgage holdings in 1986 because of accounting changes by the Farmers Home Administration.

Source: Board of Governors of the Federal Reserve System, *Federal Reserve Bulletin*, monthly.

Banking, Finance, and Insurance   525

No. 821. Estimated Home Equity Debt Outstanding, by Type and Source of Credit: 1990 to 1998

[In billions of dollars (258 represents $258,000,000,000). A "traditional home equity loan" is a closed-end loan extended for a specific period that generally requires repayment of interest and principal in equal monthly installments. Such a loan typically has a fixed interest rate. A "home equity line of credit" is a revolving account that permits borrowing from time to time, at the home-owner's discretion, up to the amount of the credit line. It usually has a more flexible repayment schedule and a variable interest rate. Based on reports from lending institutions and data from the Survey of Consumers, a sample survey of households]

Year	Home equity lines of credit				Traditional home equity loans			
	Total	All lenders	Commercial banks	Other sources	All lenders	Commercial banks	Other sources	
1990	258	105	61	44	153	54	99	
1992	258	114	73	41	144	50	94	
1993	261	110	73	37	151	49	102	
1994	274	116	76	40	158	54	104	
1995	299	123	79	44	176	61	115	
1996	347	132	85	47	215	69	146	
1997	420	152	98	54	268	76	192	
1998	470	153	96	57	317	80	237	

Source: Board of Governors of the Federal Reserve System, *Federal Reserve Bulletin*, July 1994 and April 1998; and unpublished data.

No. 822. Home Equity Lending—Percentage of Homeowners With Credit, Sources of Credit, and Uses for Funds Borrowed: 1993-94 and 1997

[In percent. See headnote, Table 821]

Item	Home equity lines of credit		Traditional home equity loans		Uses for funds borrowed	1997[1]	
	1993-94	1997	1993-94	1997		Home equity lines of credit	Traditional home equity loans
Percentage of homeowners with home equity credit	8	8	5	5	Home improvement	69	45
					Repayment of other debts	49	61
					Education	19	2
SOURCE OF HOME EQUITY CREDIT					Real estate	9	10
Total	100	100	100	100	Auto or truck	37	6
Commercial banks [2]	60	61	29	44	Medical expenses	10	2
Savings institutions [2]	21	16	30	20	Business expenses	18	4
Credit unions [3]	13	16	11	13	Vacation	13	1
Other creditors [3]	7	7	29	24	Other [4]	1	1

[1] Percentages sum to more than 100 because respondents were allowed to cite multiple uses for a single loan or drawdown and more than one draw for one line of credit. [2] Includes savings banks and savings and loan associations. [3] Includes finance and loan companies, brokerage firms, mortgage companies, and individuals. [4] Includes purchase of furniture or appliance, purchase of boat or other recreational vehicle, payment of taxes, and personal financial investments.

Source: Board of Governors of the Federal Reserve System, *Federal Reserve Bulletin*, April 1998.

No. 823. Mortgage Delinquency and Foreclosure Rates: 1980 to 1998

[In percent, except as indicated (30,033 represents 30,033,000). Covers one- to four-family residential nonfarm mortgage loans]

Item	1980	1985	1990	1993	1994	1995	1996	1997	1998
Number of mortgage loans outstanding (1,000)	30,033	34,004	40,638	44,562	47,462	49,111	50,064	51,279	52,508
Delinquency rates: [1]									
Total	5.0	5.8	4.7	4.2	4.1	4.3	4.3	4.3	4.4
Conventional loans	3.1	4.0	3.0	2.7	2.6	2.8	2.8	2.8	2.9
VA loans	5.3	6.6	6.4	6.3	6.3	6.4	6.7	6.9	7.1
FHA loans	6.6	7.5	6.7	7.1	7.3	7.6	8.1	8.1	8.5
Foreclosure rates: [2]									
Total	0.5	1.0	0.9	1.0	0.9	0.9	1.0	1.1	1.1
Conventional loans	0.2	0.7	0.7	0.8	0.7	0.7	0.7	0.7	0.7
VA loans	0.6	1.1	1.2	1.3	1.3	1.3	1.6	1.8	1.8
FHA loans	0.7	1.3	1.3	1.5	1.5	1.4	1.6	2.0	2.2

[1] Number of loans delinquent 30 days or more as percentage of mortgage loans serviced in survey. Annual average of quarterly figures. [2] Percentage of loans in the foreclosure process at yearend, not seasonally adjusted.

Source: Mortgage Bankers Association of America, Washington, DC, *National Delinquency Survey*, quarterly.

No. 824. Consumer Credit Outstanding and Finance Rates: 1980 to 1998

[In billions of dollars, except percent (350.1 represents $350,100,000,000). Estimated amounts of seasonally adjusted credit outstanding as of end of year; finance rates, annual averages]

Type of credit	1980	1985	1990	1992	1993	1994	1995	1996	1997	1998
Total	350.1	584.7	796.4	779.9	839.1	960.7	1,095.7	1,181.9	1,233.1	1,308.4
Automobile	112.0	210.9	282.4	262.7	288.1	327.9	364.2	392.3	413.4	447.2
Revolving [1]	55.1	122.1	223.3	278.2	310.0	365.6	443.2	499.5	531.1	558.6
Other [2]	183.0	251.7	290.7	239.1	241.1	267.2	288.3	290.1	288.6	302.6
FINANCE RATES (percent)										
Commercial banks:										
New automobiles (48 months) [3]	14.32	12.91	11.78	9.29	8.09	8.12	9.57	9.05	9.02	8.72
Other consumer goods (24 months)	15.48	15.94	15.46	14.04	13.47	13.19	13.94	13.54	13.90	13.74
Credit-card plans	17.31	18.69	18.17	17.78	16.83	16.04	15.90	15.63	15.77	15.71
Finance companies:										
New automobiles	14.82	11.98	12.54	9.93	9.48	9.79	11.19	9.83	7.12	6.30
Used automobiles	19.10	17.58	15.99	13.80	12.79	13.49	14.48	13.53	13.27	12.64

[1] Consists mainly of outstanding balances on credit card accounts, but also includes borrowing under check credit and overdraft plans, and unsecured personal lines of credit. [2] Includes noninstallment credit. [3] For 1980, maturities were 36 months for new car loans.

Source: Board of Governors of the Federal Reserve System, *Federal Reserve Bulletin*, monthly; and *Annual Statistical Digest*.

No. 825. Credit Cards—Holders, Numbers, Spending, and Debt, 1990 and 1997, and Projections, 2000

[122 represents 122,000,000]

Type of credit card	Cardholders (mil.)			Number of cards (mil.)			Credit card spending (bil. dol.)			Credit card debt (bil. dol.)		
	1990	1997	2000, proj.	1990	1997	2000, proj.	1990	1997	2000, proj.	1990	1997	2000, proj.
Total [1]	122	149	157	1,013	1,387	1,499	467	1,080	1,419	243	560	677
Bank [2]	79	100	105	213	403	458	243	678	891	154	397	486
Oil company	85	79	79	123	109	105	28	38	46	3	4	5
Phone	97	116	126	141	173	183	14	19	22	2	2	3
Retail store	96	108	114	459	614	652	75	121	147	51	88	99
Travel and entertainment [3]	16	23	24	28	31	38	85	160	232	20	33	40
Other [4]	10	7	7	49	57	63	22	64	81	13	36	44

[1] Cardholders may hold more than one type of card. [2] Visa and MasterCard credit cards. Excludes debit cards. [3] Includes American Express and Diners Club. [4] Includes Air Travel Card, automobile rental, Discover (except for cardholders), and miscellaneous cards.

Source: HSN Consultants Inc., Oxnard, CA, *The Nilson Report*, twice-monthly. (Copyright used by permission.)

No. 826. Usage of General Purpose Credit Cards by Families: 1989 to 1995

[General purpose credit cards include Mastercard, Visa, Optima, and Discover cards. All dollar figures are given in constant 1995 dollars based on consumer price index data as published by U.S. Bureau of Labor Statistics. Families include one-person units; for definition of family, see text, Section 1, Population. Based on Survey of Consumer Finance; see Appendix III. For definition of median, see Guide to Tabular Presentation]

Age of family head and family income	Percent having a general purpose credit card	Median number of cards	Median new charges on last month's bills	Percent having a balance after last month's bills	Median balance [1]	Percent of cardholding families who—		
						Almost always pay off the balance	Some-times pay off the balance	Hardly ever pay off the balance
1989, total	55.8	2	$100	52.0	$1,200	53.1	21.5	25.4
1992, total	62.2	2	100	52.8	1,100	52.8	19.6	27.6
1995, total	66.4	2	200	56.3	1,500	51.9	20.4	27.7
Under 35 years old	59.0	2	100	69.2	1,500	40.2	23.5	36.3
35 to 44 years old	68.5	2	200	68.1	1,900	40.7	26.9	32.4
45 to 54 years old	75.4	2	200	64.8	1,800	47.1	22.5	30.4
55 to 64 years old	71.9	2	200	48.0	1,800	59.3	18.4	22.3
65 to 74 years old	68.3	2	200	30.8	800	72.0	12.9	15.1
75 years old and over	54.6	1	100	18.2	700	85.8	2.5	11.7
Less than $10,000	26.3	1	100	55.8	1,000	56.4	12.4	31.2
$10,000 to $24,999	53.3	2	100	57.0	1,500	50.9	17.2	31.9
$25,000 to $49,999	75.0	2	100	59.2	1,500	47.6	20.9	31.5
$50,000 to $99,999	93.1	2	200	59.4	2,000	49.7	25.3	25.1
$100,000 and more	97.1	3	800	35.4	2,100	73.7	17.2	9.1

[1] Among families having a balance.

Source: Board of Governors of the Federal Reserve System, unpublished data.

Banking, Finance, and Insurance **527**

No. 827. Consumer Payment Systems by Method of Payment: 1990 to 2000

[91.8 represents 91,800,000,000]

	Transactions				Volume				
Method of payment	Number (bil.)		Percent distribution		Amount (bil. dol.)			Percent distribution		
	1997	2000, proj.	1997	2000, proj.	1990	1997	2000, proj.	1990	1997	2000, proj.
Total	91.8	103.4	100.0	100.0	2,972	4,289	5,005	100.0	100.0	100.0
Paper	69.3	71.3	75.5	69.0	2,511	3,147	3,331	84.5	73.4	66.6
Personal checks [1]	29.7	29.2	32.3	28.2	(NA)	2,246	2,417	(NA)	52.4	48.3
Cash	37.4	40.3	40.8	39.0	(NA)	748	759	(NA)	17.4	15.2
Money orders	1.1	1.2	1.2	1.2	(NA)	99	110	(NA)	2.3	2.2
Travelers cheques	0.3	0.3	0.4	0.3	(NA)	20	17	(NA)	0.5	0.4
Official checks [2]	0.1	0.1	0.1	0.1	(NA)	19	22	(NA)	0.4	0.4
Food stamps.	0.6	0.2	0.7	0.2	(NA)	15	6	(NA)	0.3	0.1
Cards . . . . . . [3]	21.5	30.2	23.4	29.2	441	1,035	1,482	14.8	24.1	29.6
Credit cards [4]	16.5	19.1	18.0	18.4	(NA)	906	1,163	(NA)	21.1	23.2
Debit cards [4]	3.4	8.4	3.7	8.1	(NA)	119	292	(NA)	2.8	5.8
Stored value cards [5]	1.4	2.2	1.5	2.2	(NA)	6	14	(NA)	0.1	0.3
EBT cards [6]	0.2	0.6	0.2	0.5	(NA)	4	13	(NA)	0.1	0.3
Electronic . . . . [7] . .	1.0	1.8	1.1	1.8	20	107	192	0.7	2.5	3.8
Preauthorized payments [7]	0.8	1.3	0.9	1.3	(NA)	87	144	(NA)	2.0	2.9
Remote payments [8]	0.2	0.5	0.2	0.5	(NA)	21	47	(NA)	0.5	1.0

NA Not available. [1] Excludes repayments and prepayments involving other payment systems. [2] Official checks include cashier's checks, teller checks, and certified checks purchased from financial institutions. Excludes those purchased by businesses. [3] Credit cards include general purpose cards usable at all kinds of merchants and proprietary cards usable only at selected outlets. Includes purchases on commercial cards and business-related spending on personal cards. Cash advances are excluded. [4] Debit cards include general purpose cards carrying the Visa or MasterCard brand, electronic funds transfer (EFT) brands of regional EFT systems, proprietary commercial cards issued by private firms to drivers in the long-haul trucking industry, and proprietary merchant cards issued by supermarkets and gasoline marketers. Cash withdrawals at ATM's and cash back over the counter are excluded. [5] Stored value cards are used primarily for telephone calls, although most major gasoline marketers and department stores also had products on the market. Many phone cards were acquired by collectors and never used. [6] Electronic benefits transfer (EBT) cards were issued to replace paper scrip food stamps at participating merchants. [7] Preauthorized payments are handled electronically through an automated clearing house. Mortgages are excluded. [8] Remote payments are made using a telephone, on-line computer service, or the Internet. Also included are utility-bill payments made by clerk-assisted electronic banking machines at supermarkets, ATM's, and self-service kiosks.

Source: HSN Consultants Inc., Oxnard, CA, The Nilson Report, Number 680, November 1998. (Copyright used by permission.)

No. 828. Debit Cards—Numbers, Transactions, and Volume, 1990 to 1997, and Projections, 2000

[173 represents 173,000,000]

Type of debit card	Number of cards (mil.)				Number of transactions (mil.)				Volume (bil. dol.)			
	1990	1995	1997	2000, proj.	1990	1995	1997	2000, proj.	1990	1995	1997	2000, proj.
Total [1]	173	240	291	353	273	1,558	3,912	9,408	12	62	163	368
Bank [2]	9	40	80	122	127	829	2,465	6,008	8	36	110	244
EFT systems [3]	160	190	200	219	129	672	1,388	3,335	3	23	49	120
Other [4]	4	10	11	12	17	57	59	65	1	3	4	4

[1] Increasingly, bank cards and EFT cards are the same pieces of plastic that carry multiple brands. The total card figure shown does not include any duplication. [2] Visa Check Card and MasterCard MasterMoney. [3] Cards issued by financial institution members of regional and national switches. EFT=Electronic fund transfer. [4] Commercial fuel cards issued by private-label firms plus retail cards such as those issued by supermarkets and oil companies.

Source: HSN Consultants Inc., Oxnard, CA, The Nilson Report, bimonthly. (Copyright used by permission.)

No. 829. Electronic Funds Transfer Volume: 1980 to 1998

[Electronic funds transfer cover automated teller machine (ATM) transactions and transactions at point-of-sale (POS) terminals. Point-of-sale terminals are electronic terminals in retail stores that allow a customer to pay for goods through a direct debit to a customer's account at the bank]

Item	Unit	1980	1985	1990	1993	1994	1995	1996	1997	1998
Total number of transactions	Million. .	(NA)	3,579	5,942	8,135	8,958	10,464	11,830	12,362	12,960
ATM transactions	Million . .	(NA)	3,565	5,751	7,705	8,334	9,689	10,684	10,920	11,160
POS transactions	Million . .	(NA)	14	191	430	624	775	1,146	1,442	1,800
ATM terminals, total [1]	1,000. . .	18.5	60.0	80.2	94.8	109.1	122.7	139.1	165.0	187.0
Monthly transactions per terminal . .	Number . .	5,405	4,951	5,980	6,772	6,459	6,580	6,399	5,515	4,977
Shared terminals	1,000. . .	(NA)	35.5	75.3	92.6	108.1	122.6	139.0	165.0	187.0
Proprietary terminals	1,000. . .	(NA)	24.5	4.9	2.3	1.0	0.1	0.1	(NA)	(NA)
POS terminals, total [2]	1,000. . .	(NA)	(NA)	53	155	341	529	875	1,300	1,700

NA Not available. [1] As of September. [2] As of June.

Source: Faulkner & Gray, Chicago, IL, Faulkner & Gray/EFT Network Data Book-1998, September 26, 1997 and unpublished data (copyright).

No. 830. Money Stock: 1980 to 1998

[In billions of dollars (408 represents $408,000,000,000). As of December. Seasonally adjusted averages of daily figures]

Item	1980	1981	1982	1983	1984	1985	1986	1987	1988	1989	1990	1991	1992	1993	1994	1995	1996	1997	1998
M1, total	408	436	474	521	551	619	724	750	786	793	825	897	1,024	1,129	1,150	1,127	1,081	1,075	1,093
Currency [1]	115	123	133	146	156	168	181	197	212	223	247	267	293	322	354	372	394	424	459
Travelers checks [2]	.3	4	4	4	4	5	5	6	6	6	7	7	7	7	8	8	8	8	8
Demand deposits [3]	261	231	234	238	243	267	303	288	287	279	277	290	340	385	384	389	403	396	377
Other checkable deposits [4]	28	79	104	132	147	180	236	260	281	285	294	332	384	415	404	357	276	246	249
M2, total	1,600	1,756	1,911	2,128	2,312	2,497	2,734	2,833	2,996	3,160	3,279	3,380	3,434	3,487	3,502	3,649	3,824	4,047	4,413
M1	408	436	474	521	551	619	724	750	786	793	825	897	1,024	1,129	1,150	1,127	1,081	1,075	1,093
Non-M1 components in M2	1,192	1,320	1,437	1,607	1,760	1,878	2,010	2,083	2,210	2,367	2,455	2,483	2,410	2,358	2,352	2,522	2,743	2,972	3,320
Money market funds, retail	64	153	186	138	167	177	210	225	246	322	358	373	355	357	386	456	523	602	763
Savings deposits (including MMDAs) [5]	400	344	400	685	705	815	941	937	926	894	923	1,044	1,187	1,219	1,150	1,135	1,272	1,400	1,605
Commercial banks	186	159	190	363	389	457	534	535	542	541	582	665	754	785	753	775	905	1,023	1,190
Thrift institutions	215	185	210	322	315	359	407	403	384	353	342	380	433	434	397	360	367	377	415
Small time deposits [6]	729	823	851	784	889	886	858	921	1,037	1,151	1,173	1,066	868	782	816	932	948	969	952
Commercial banks	286	348	380	351	388	386	369	392	451	534	611	602	508	468	503	575	594	626	626
Thrift institutions	442	475	471	433	501	499	489	529	586	618	563	463	360	314	314	357	354	343	326
M3, total	1,996	2,255	2,461	2,699	2,993	3,210	3,501	3,692	3,935	4,091	4,156	4,209	4,220	4,280	4,354	4,619	4,956	5,405	6,016
M2	1,600	1,756	1,911	2,128	2,312	2,497	2,734	2,833	2,996	3,160	3,279	3,380	3,434	3,487	3,502	3,649	3,824	4,047	4,413
Non-M2 components in M3 [7]	396	499	550	571	681	712	767	859	939	931	876	829	786	792	852	969	1,132	1,358	1,604
Large time deposits [8]	260	304	325	316	403	422	420	467	518	541	482	418	354	334	364	421	493	576	638
Commercial banks	215	250	261	220	256	271	270	304	344	380	361	334	287	273	300	347	415	490	549
Thrift institutions	45	54	64	97	147	152	150	163	175	161	121	83	67	62	65	74	78	86	89
Repurchase agreements [9]	58	68	72	97	107	121	146	178	197	169	151	131	142	173	196	199	211	253	298
Eurodollars [9]	61	89	104	117	109	104	116	121	132	109	103	92	80	73	86	94	114	149	152
Money market funds, institution only	16	38	49	41	62	65	86	93	93	111	140	188	210	212	205	256	313	380	516

[1] Currency outside U.S. Treasury, Federal Reserve Banks and the vaults of depository institutions. [2] Outstanding amount of nonbank issuers. [3] At commercial banks and foreign-related institutions. [4] Consists of negotiable order of withdrawal (NOW) and automatic transfer service (ATS) accounts at all depository institutions, credit union share draft balances, and demand deposits at thrift institutions. [5] Money market deposit accounts (MMDA). [6] Issued in amounts of less than $100,000. Includes retail repurchase agreements. Excludes individual retirement accounts (IRAs) and Keogh accounts. [7] Issued in amounts of $100,000 or more. [8] Excludes those booked at international banking facilities. [9] Excludes those held by money market mutual funds, depository institutions, U.S. Government, foreign banks, and official institutions. [9] Excludes those held by depository institutions and money market mutual funds.

Source: Board of Governors of the Federal Reserve System, Federal Reserve Bulletin, monthly, and Money Stock, Liquid Assets, and Debt Measures, Federal Reserve Statistical Release H.6, weekly.

Banking, Finance, and Insurance   529

No. 831. Money Market Interest Rates and Mortgage Rates: 1980 to 1998

[Percent per year. Annual averages of monthly data, except as indicated]

Type	1980	1985	1987	1988	1989	1990	1991	1992	1993	1994	1995	1996	1997	1998
Federal funds, effective rate	13.35	8.10	6.66	7.57	9.21	8.10	5.69	3.52	3.02	4.21	5.83	5.30	5.46	5.35
Prime rate charged by banks	15.26	9.93	8.21	9.32	10.87	10.01	8.46	6.25	6.00	7.15	8.83	8.27	8.44	8.35
Eurodollar deposits, 3-month	14.00	8.27	7.07	7.85	9.16	8.16	5.86	3.70	3.18	4.63	5.93	5.38	5.61	5.45
Bankers acceptances, 3-month [1]	12.67	7.91	6.75	7.56	8.87	7.93	5.70	3.62	3.13	4.56	5.81	5.31	5.54	5.39
Bankers acceptances, 6-month [1]	12.20	7.95	6.78	7.60	8.67	7.80	5.67	3.67	3.21	4.83	5.80	5.31	5.57	5.30
Large negotiable CDs:														
3-month, secondary market	13.07	8.05	6.86	7.73	9.09	8.15	5.83	3.68	3.17	4.63	5.92	5.39	5.62	5.47
6-month, secondary market	12.94	8.24	7.01	7.91	9.08	8.17	5.91	3.76	3.28	4.96	5.98	5.47	5.73	5.44
Taxable money market funds [2]	12.68	7.71	6.12	7.11	8.87	7.82	5.71	3.36	2.70	3.75	5.48	4.95	5.10	5.04
Tax-exempt money market funds [2]	(NA)	4.90	4.14	4.79	5.90	5.45	4.13	2.58	1.97	2.38	3.39	2.99	3.14	2.94
Certificates of deposit (CDs): [3]														
6-month	(NA)	7.83	6.47	7.18	8.34	7.35	5.67	3.46	2.84	3.37	4.92	4.68	4.86	4.50
1-year	(NA)	8.29	6.77	7.47	8.41	7.42	5.88	3.72	3.12	3.94	5.39	4.95	5.16	4.72
2½-year	(NA)	9.00	7.16	7.77	8.33	7.52	6.29	4.47	3.73	4.49	5.69	5.14	5.40	4.83
5-year	(NA)	9.66	7.66	8.11	8.30	7.71	6.83	5.62	4.88	5.30	6.00	5.46	5.67	4.98
U.S. Government securities:														
Secondary market: [4]														
3-month Treasury bill	11.39	7.47	5.78	6.67	8.11	7.50	5.38	3.43	3.00	4.25	5.49	5.01	5.06	4.78
6-month Treasury bill	11.32	7.65	6.03	6.91	8.03	7.46	5.44	3.54	3.12	4.64	5.56	5.08	5.18	4.83
1-year Treasury bill	10.85	7.81	6.33	7.13	7.92	7.35	5.52	3.71	3.29	5.02	5.60	5.22	5.36	4.80
Auction average: [5]														
3-month Treasury bill	11.51	7.47	5.82	6.68	8.12	7.51	5.42	3.45	3.02	4.29	5.51	5.02	5.07	4.81
6-month Treasury bill	11.37	7.64	6.05	6.92	8.04	7.47	5.49	3.57	3.14	4.66	5.59	5.09	5.18	4.85
1-year Treasury bill	10.75	7.76	6.33	7.17	7.91	7.36	5.54	3.75	3.33	4.98	5.69	5.23	5.36	4.85
Home mortgages:														
HUD series: [6]														
FHA insured, secondary market [7]	13.44	12.24	10.16	10.49	10.24	10.17	9.25	8.46	7.46	8.68	8.18	8.19	7.89	7.04
Conventional, new-home [8]	13.95	12.28	10.17	10.30	10.21	10.08	9.20	8.43	7.37	8.58	8.05	8.03	7.76	7.00
Conventional, existing-home [8]	13.95	12.29	10.17	10.31	10.22	10.08	9.20	8.43	7.37	8.59	8.05	8.03	7.76	7.01
Conventional, 15 yr. fixed [3]	(NA)	11.53	10.04	10.14	10.05	9.67	8.76	7.80	6.65	7.77	7.39	7.28	7.16	6.58
Conventional, 30 yr. fixed [3]	(NA)	11.90	10.40	10.38	10.26	10.01	9.09	8.27	7.17	8.28	7.86	7.76	7.57	6.92

NA Not available.   [1] Yields are quoted on a bank-discount basis, rather than an investment yield basis (which would give a higher figure). Based on representative closing yields. From Jan. 1, 1981, rates of top-rated banks only.   [2] 12 month return for period ending December 31. Source: IBC Financial Data, Inc., Ashland, MA, *IBC's Money Market Insight*, monthly (copyright).   [3] Annual averages. Source: Financial Rates, Inc., North Palm Beach, FL, *Bank Rate Monitor*, weekly (copyright).   [4] Averages based on daily closing bid yields in secondary market, bank discount basis.   [5] Averages computed on an issue-date basis; bank discount basis.   [6] HUD=Housing and Urban Development.   Averages based on quotations for 1 day each month as compiled by FHA.   [8] Primary market.   [9] Average contract rates on new commitments.

Source: Except as noted, Board of Governors of the Federal Reserve System, *Federal Reserve Bulletin*, monthly, and *Annual Statistical Digest*.

No. 832. Bond Yields: 1980 to 1998

[Percent per year. Annual averages of daily figures, except as indicated]

Type	1980	1985	1990	1991	1992	1993	1994	1995	1996	1997	1998
U.S. Treasury, constant maturities: [1][2]											
1-year	12.00	8.42	7.89	5.86	3.89	3.43	5.32	5.94	5.52	5.63	5.05
2-year	11.73	9.27	8.16	6.49	4.77	4.05	5.94	6.15	5.84	5.99	5.13
3-year	11.51	9.64	8.26	6.82	5.30	4.44	6.27	6.25	5.99	6.10	5.14
5-year	11.45	10.12	8.37	7.37	6.19	5.14	6.69	6.38	6.18	6.22	5.15
7-year	11.40	10.50	8.52	7.68	6.63	5.54	6.91	6.50	6.34	6.33	5.28
10-year	11.43	10.62	8.55	7.86	7.01	5.87	7.69	6.57	6.44	6.35	5.26
20-year	(NA)	(NA)	(NA)	(NA)	(NA)	6.29	7.47	6.95	6.83	6.69	5.72
30-year	11.27	10.79	8.61	8.14	7.67	6.59	7.37	6.88	6.71	6.61	5.58
U.S. Govt., long-term bonds [2][3]	10.81	10.75	8.74	8.16	7.52	6.45	7.41	6.93	6.80	6.67	5.69
State and local govt. bonds, Aaa	7.86	8.60	6.97	6.56	6.09	5.38	5.77	5.80	5.52	5.32	4.93
State and local govt. bonds, Baa	9.02	9.58	7.30	6.99	6.48	5.83	6.17	6.10	5.79	5.50	5.14
Municipal (Bond Buyer, 20 bonds)	8.59	9.10	7.27	6.92	6.44	5.60	6.18	5.95	5.76	5.52	5.09
Corporate Aaa seasoned [4]	11.94	11.37	9.32	8.77	8.14	7.22	7.97	7.59	7.37	7.27	6.53
Corporate Baa seasoned [4]	13.67	12.72	10.36	9.80	8.98	7.93	8.63	8.20	8.05	7.87	7.22
Corporate (Moody's) [4][5]	12.75	12.05	9.77	9.23	8.55	7.54	8.26	7.83	7.66	7.54	6.87
Industrials (49 bonds) [6]	12.35	11.80	9.77	9.25	8.52	7.51	8.21	7.76	7.58	7.47	6.79
Public utilities (51 bonds) [7]	13.15	12.29	9.76	9.21	8.57	7.56	8.30	7.90	7.74	7.63	7.00

NA Not available. [1] Yields on the more actively traded issues adjusted to constant maturities by the U.S. Treasury. [2] Yields are based on closing bid prices quoted by at least five dealers. [3] Averages (to maturity or call) for all outstanding bonds neither due nor callable in less than 10 years, including several very low yielding "flower" bonds. [4] Source: Moody's Investors Service, New York, NY. [5] For 1980 and 1985 includes railroad bonds which were discontinued as part of composite in 1989. [6] Covers 40 bonds for 1980 and 38 bonds for 1985. [7] Covers 40 bonds for 1980 and 1985.
Source: Except as noted, Board of Governors of the Federal Reserve System, Federal Reserve Bulletin, monthly.

No. 833. Volume of Debt Markets by Type of Security: 1990 to 1998

[In billions of dollars (2,780 represents $2,780,000,000,000). Covers debt markets as represented by the source]

Type of security	1990	1993	1994	1995	1996	1997	1998
NEW ISSUE VOLUME							
Total	2,780	4,829	5,268	6,745	8,159	9,406	10,494
U.S. Treasury securities [1]	1,531	2,066	2,112	2,331	2,485	2,169	1,969
Federal agency debt	637	1,380	2,228	3,506	4,500	5,730	6,403
Municipal	163	340	205	198	226	267	321
Mortgage-backed securities [2]	235	568	359	269	371	368	727
Asset-backed securities [3]	42	59	75	107	151	185	198
Corporate debt [4]	173	416	289	333	428	687	877
DAILY TRADING VOLUME							
Total	111.2	204.6	237.7	246.3	274.0	300.5	352.8
U.S. Treasury securities [1][5]	111.2	173.6	191.3	193.2	203.7	212.1	226.6
Federal agency debt [5]	(NA)	8.9	16.0	23.7	31.1	40.2	47.6
Municipal [6]	(NA)	(NA)	(NA)	(NA)	1.1	1.1	7.7
Mortgage-backed securities [2][5]	(NA)	22.1	30.4	29.4	38.1	47.1	70.9
VOLUME OF SECURITIES OUTSTANDING							
Total	7,431	9,100	9,633	10,404	11,233	12,098	12,905
U.S. Treasury securities [1]	2,196	2,990	3,126	3,307	3,460	3,457	3,356
Federal agency debt [7]	435	571	739	845	926	1,023	1,070
Municipal	1,184	1,378	1,342	1,294	1,296	1,368	1,464
Mortgage-backed securities [2]	1,024	1,350	1,442	1,570	1,711	1,826	2,019
Asset-backed securities [3]	102	179	205	298	391	518	629
Money market instruments [8]	1,157	972	1,035	1,177	1,394	1,693	1,978
Corporate debt [4][7]	1,334	1,662	1,747	1,913	2,055	2,214	2,390

NA Not available. [1] Marketable public debt. [2] Includes only Government National Mortgage Association (GNMA), Federal National Mortgage Association (FNMA), and Federal Home Loan Mortgage Corporation (FHLMC) mortgage-backed securities. [3] Excludes mortgage-backed assets. [4] Includes non-convertible corporate debt, Yankee bonds, and MTNs (Medium-Term Notes), but excludes Federal and agency debt. [5] Primary dealer transactions. [6] Beginning September 1998 includes customer-to-dealer and dealer-to-dealer transactions. [7] The Bond Market Association estimates. [8] Commercial paper, bankers acceptances, and large time deposits.
Source: The Bond Market Association, New York, NY. Copyright. Based on data supplied by Board of Governors of the Federal Reserve System, U.S. Dept. of Treasury, Securities Data Company, FHLMC, FNMA, GNMA, Federal Home Loan Banks, Student Loan Marketing Association, Federal Farm Credit Banks, Tennessee Valley Authority, and Municipal Securities Rulemaking Board.

No. 834. Commercial Paper Outstanding, by Type of Company: 1980 to 1998

[In billions of dollars (124 represents $124,000,000,000). As of December 31. Seasonally adjusted. Commercial paper is an unsecured promissory note having a fixed maturity of no more than 270 days]

Type of company	1980	1985	1990	1991	1992	1993	1994	1995	1996	1997	1998
All issuers	124	299	563	529	546	555	595	675	775	967	1,163
Financial companies [1]	88	214	415	396	398	399	431	487	591	766	936
Dealer-placed paper [2]	20	78	215	213	227	219	223	276	361	513	628
Directly-placed paper [3]	68	135	200	183	172	180	208	211	230	253	308
Nonfinancial companies [4]	37	85	148	133	148	156	165	188	185	201	227

[1] Institutions engaged primarily in commercial, savings, and mortgage banking; sales, personal, and mortgage financing; factoring, finance leasing, and other business lending; insurance underwriting; and other investment activities. [2] Includes all financial company paper sold by dealers in the open market. [3] As reported by financial companies that place their paper directly with investors. [4] Includes public utilities and firms engaged primarily in such activities as communications, construction, manufacturing, mining, wholesale and retail trade, transportation, and services.
Source: Board of Governors of the Federal Reserve System, Federal Reserve Bulletin, monthly.

No. 835. Total Returns of Stocks, Bonds, and Treasury Bills: 1950 to 1998

[In percent. Average annual percent change. Stock return data are based on the Standard & Poor's 500 index]

| Period | Stocks | | | | Treasury bills, total return | Bonds (10-year), total return |
	Total return	Capital gains	Dividends and reinvestment	Total return after inflation		
1950 to 1959	19.28	13.58	5.02	16.69	2.02	0.73
1960 to 1969	7.78	4.39	3.62	5.13	4.06	2.42
1970 to 1979	5.82	1.60	4.15	-0.14	6.42	5.84
1980 to 1989	17.54	12.59	4.42	11.87	9.21	13.06
1990 to 1998	17.17	14.86	2.01	13.77	4.99	9.68

Source: Global Financial Data, Alhambra, CA, "Global Financial Data, US Sector Total Returns;" <http://www.globalfindata.com/april.htm>; (accessed: 27 April 1998); and unpublished data (copyright).

No. 836. Equities, Corporate Bonds, and Municipal Securities—Holdings and Net Purchases, by Type of Investor: 1990 to 1998

[In billions of dollars (3,537 represents $3,537,000,000,000). Holdings as of Dec. 31. Minus sign (-) indicates net sales]

| Type of investor | Holdings | | | | | Net purchases | | | | |
	1990	1995	1996	1997	1998	1990	1995	1996	1997	1998
EQUITIES [1]										
Total [2]	3,537	8,331	10,062	12,776	15,438	-37.7	-3.1	-3.4	-78.8	-178.4
Household sector [3]	1,778	3,995	4,528	5,333	6,280	-26.3	-192.0	-281.5	-513.9	-500.0
State and local governments	5	26	47	63	76	1.5	12.1	14.5	1.3	2.6
Rest of the world [4]	244	528	657	916	1,110	-16.0	16.6	11.0	64.2	42.5
Bank personal trusts and estates	190	225	249	401	538	0.5	1.6	-17.3	72.3	45.9
Life insurance companies	82	315	410	561	746	-5.7	18.6	42.1	93.2	92.1
Other insurance companies	80	134	149	186	204	-7.0	-0.6	-6.8	3.0	-5.1
Private pension funds	595	1,238	1,491	1,864	2,232	-4.1	5.9	-9.6	-16.1	-52.7
State and local retirement funds	293	753	956	1,306	1,593	13.2	41.3	52.2	53.5	65.7
Mutual funds	233	1,025	1,470	2,019	2,523	14.4	87.4	193.0	166.8	143.5
CORPORATE & FOREIGN BONDS										
Total [2]	1,706	2,824	3,127	3,440	3,894	125.2	319.6	303.8	345.7	453.9
Household sector [3]	201	461	463	461	475	45.1	88.5	2.7	32.2	14.1
Rest of the world [4]	217	369	453	540	662	5.3	58.1	83.7	86.8	122.3
Commercial banking	89	111	112	143	181	4.6	8.4	1.4	27.8	38.0
Savings institutions	76	79	69	59	89	-19.3	-8.2	-9.9	-9.9	29.9
Life insurance companies	567	870	949	1,026	1,086	56.5	90.7	79.2	77.0	59.9
Other insurance companies	89	123	142	157	158	10.4	12.7	18.3	16.4	1.4
Private pension funds	146	207	228	256	301	15.2	5.6	21.2	27.7	45.3
State and local retirement funds	172	163	180	199	245	5.2	-4.2	16.7	19.3	45.3
Money market mutual funds	2	22	24	36	81	-1.7	6.4	2.4	12.5	44.8
Mutual funds	59	196	229	274	339	4.7	23.3	33.8	44.4	65.1
Brokers and dealers	29	76	91	100	81	-4.0	12.0	14.5	9.2	-18.6
MUNICIPAL SECURITIES [5]										
Total [2]	1,184	1,293	1,296	1,367	1,464	49.3	-48.2	2.6	71.4	96.8
Household sector [3]	575	459	435	421	447	27.7	-42.9	-24.3	24.3	25.9
Commercial banking	117	93	94	97	105	-16.4	-4.2	0.9	2.4	8.2
Bank personal trusts and estates	81	108	104	105	106	7.7	-5.9	-4.3	0.8	1.0
Other insurance companies	137	161	175	194	196	1.8	7.0	14.4	5.1	1.7
Money market mutual funds	84	128	144	167	193	13.9	14.3	16.8	22.5	26.0
Mutual funds	113	210	213	220	243	13.9	3.2	3.1	6.5	23.6
Closed-end funds	14	60	62	62	63	2.0	6.2	2.1	-	1.2

- Represents or rounds to zero. [1] Excludes mutual fund shares. [2] Includes other types not shown separately. [3] Includes nonprofit organizations. [4] Holdings of U.S. issues by foreign residents. [5] Includes loans.

Source: Board of Governors of the Federal Reserve System, *Flow of Funds Accounts*, March 1999 quarterly diskettes. Data are also published in the quarterly Z.1 release.

U.S. Census Bureau, Statistical Abstract of the United States: 1999

No. 837. Purchases and Sales by U.S. Investors of Foreign Bonds and Stocks, 1980 to 1998, and by Selected Country, 1998

[In billions of dollars (3.1 represents $3,100,000,000). See headnote, Table 838. Minus sign (-) indicates net sales by U.S. investors or a net inflow of capital into the United States]

Year and country	Net purchases			Total transactions [1]			Bonds		Stocks	
	Total	Bonds	Stocks	Total	Bonds	Stocks	Pur-chases	Sales	Pur-chases	Sales
1980...................	3.1	1.0	2.1	53	35	18	18	17	10	8
1985...................	7.9	4.0	3.9	212	166	46	85	81	25	21
1990...................	31.2	21.9	9.2	907	652	255	337	315	132	123
1991...................	46.8	14.8	32.0	949	675	273	345	330	153	121
1992...................	47.9	15.6	32.3	1,375	1,043	332	529	514	182	150
1993...................	143.1	80.4	62.7	2,126	1,572	554	826	746	308	245
1994...................	57.3	9.2	48.1	2,526	1,706	820	858	848	434	386
1995...................	98.7	48.4	50.3	2,569	1,827	741	938	890	396	346
1996...................	110.6	51.4	59.3	3,239	2,279	960	1,165	1,114	510	450
1997...................	89.1	48.2	40.9	4,505	2,952	1,553	1,500	1,452	797	756
1998, total [2]..............	10.7	18.7	-8.0	4,562	2,689	1,873	1,354	1,335	932	941
United Kingdom	-1.0	14.6	-15.6	2,066	1,278	787	646	632	386	401
Canada..................	1.2	4.7	-3.5	433	326	107	165	161	52	55
Bermuda	1.4	-0.7	2.1	247	212	34	106	107	18	16
Japan...................	1.7	-2.0	3.6	227	70	157	34	36	81	77
British West Indies	4.9	1.1	3.7	164	99	65	50	49	34	31
Brazil	-0.4	-0.7	0.3	152	104	48	52	52	24	24
Netherlands Antilles..........	4.8	-0.5	5.3	130	36	95	18	18	50	45
Germany................	10.2	12.3	-2.2	105	21	84	17	4	41	43
France	-1.3	-0.3	-0.9	95	48	47	24	24	23	24
Argentina................	1.2	1.7	-0.5	89	77	11	40	38	5	6

[1] Total purchases plus total sales.   [2] Includes other countries, not shown separately.

Source: U.S. Dept. of Treasury, *Treasury Bulletin*, quarterly.

No. 838. Foreign Purchases and Sales of U.S. Securities, by Type of Security, 1980 to 1998, and by Selected Country, 1998

[In billions of dollars (15.8 represents $15,800,000,000). Covers transactions in all types of long-term domestic securities by foreigners as reported by banks, brokers, and other entities in the United States (except nonmarketable U.S. Treasury notes, foreign series; and nonmarketable U.S. Treasury bonds and notes, foreign currency series). Data cover new issues of securities, transactions in outstanding issues, and redemptions of securities. Includes transactions executed in the United States for the account of foreigners and transactions executed abroad for the account of reporting institutions and their domestic customers. Data by country show the country of domicile of the foreign buyers and sellers of the securities; in the case of outstanding issues, this may differ from the country of the original issuer. The term "foreigner" covers all institutions and individuals domiciled outside the United States, including U.S. citizens domiciled abroad and the foreign branches, subsidiaries, and other affiliates abroad of U.S. banks and businesses; the central governments, central banks, and other official institutions of foreign countries; and international and regional organizations. "Foreigner" also includes persons in the United States to the extent that they are known by reporting institutions to be acting on behalf of foreigners. Minus sign (-) indicates net sales by foreigners or a net outflow of capital from the United States]

Year and country	Net purchases					Total transactions [4]				
	Total	Trea-sury bonds and notes [1]	U.S. Govt. corpora-tions [2] bonds	Corpo-rate bonds [3]	Corpo-rate stocks	Total	Trea-sury bonds and notes [1]	U.S. Govt. corpora-tions [2] bonds	Corpo-rate bonds [3]	Corpo-rate stocks
1980	15.8	4.9	2.6	2.9	5.4	198	97	17	9	75
1985	78.3	29.2	4.3	39.8	4.9	1,256	968	46	84	159
1990	34.7	17.9	6.3	9.7	-15.1	4,204	3,620	104	117	362
1991	58.1	19.9	10.2	16.9	11.1	4,706	4,016	124	155	411
1992	73.2	39.3	18.3	20.8	-5.1	5,282	4,444	204	187	448
1993	111.1	23.6	35.4	30.6	21.6	6,314	5,195	263	239	618
1994	140.4	78.8	21.7	38.0	1.9	6,562	5,343	297	222	699
1995	231.9	134.1	28.7	57.9	11.2	7,243	5,828	222	278	915
1996	370.2	232.2	41.7	83.7	12.5	8,965	7,134	241	422	1,169
1997	387.9	184.2	49.9	84.3	69.6	12,759	9,546	469	617	2,126
1998, total [5]	278.2	46.7	54.8	122.7	54.1	15,039	10,268	990	643	3,138
United Kingdom	134.2	12.1	29.8	67.9	24.3	6,634	5,526	143	337	629
British West Indies	14.6	0.9	-0.4	9.5	4.6	1,146	436	277	60	373
Japan	20.0	13.0	6.6	1.7	-1.4	1,112	901	71	12	129
Bermuda	9.1	5.1	-5.7	11.5	-1.8	936	254	205	45	432
Canada	1.9	0.6	0.5	5.6	-4.8	860	673	341	14	95
France	14.9	5.4	0.2	3.2	6.1	668	264	1	10	393
Netherlands Antilles	-15.5	-13.2	(Z)	0.8	-3.1	481	239	3	5	235
Germany	15.1	0.1	0.4	4.0	10.6	277	155	5	14	102
Singapore..........	1.4	7.8	2.3	-0.2	-8.5	233	165	1	5	56
Hong Kong	7.1	9.7	-0.5	(Z)	-2.1	197	162	13	2	21

Z Less than $50 million.   [1] Marketable bonds and notes.   [2] Includes federally-sponsored agencies.   [3] Includes transactions in directly placed issues abroad by U.S. corporations and issues of states and municipalities.   [4] Total purchases plus total sales.   [5] Includes other countries, not shown separately.

Source: U.S. Dept. of Treasury, *Treasury Bulletin*, quarterly.

Banking, Finance, and Insurance 533

No. 839. New Security Issues of Corporations, by Type of Offering: 1985 to 1997

[In billions of dollars (239.2 represents $239,200,000,000). Represents gross proceeds of issues maturing in more than 1 year. Figures are the principal amount or the number of units multiplied by the offering price. Excludes secondary offerings, employee stock plans, investment companies other than closed-end, intracorporate transactions, equities sold abroad, and Yankee bonds. Stock data include ownership securities issued by limited partnerships]

Type of offering	1985	1989	1990	1991	1992	1993	1994	1995	1996	1997
Total	239.2	377.8	339.1	465.2	559.8	769.1	583.2	673.6	767.4	923.6
Bonds, total	203.7	320.0	298.9	389.8	471.5	646.6	498.0	573.0	651.1	811.4
Public, domestic	119.7	179.7	188.8	286.9	378.1	487.0	365.2	408.7	524.0	653.2
Private placement, domestic ...	46.2	117.4	87.0	74.9	65.9	121.2	76.1	87.5	43.7	55.0
Sold abroad	37.8	22.9	23.1	28.0	27.6	38.4	56.8	76.8	83.4	103.2
Stocks, total	35.5	57.9	40.2	75.4	88.3	122.5	85.2	100.6	116.3	112.2
Preferred	6.5	6.2	4.0	17.1	21.3	18.9	12.5	10.9	33.2	29.8
Common	29.0	26.0	19.4	48.2	57.1	82.7	47.8	57.6	83.1	82.4
Private placement	(NA)	25.6	16.7	10.1	9.9	20.9	24.8	32.1	(NA)	(NA)

NA Not available.

Source: Board of Governors of the Federal Reserve System, *Federal Reserve Bulletin*, monthly, and *Annual Statistical Digest*.

No. 840. Stock Prices and Yields: 1990 to 1998

[Closing values as of end of December, except as noted]

Index	1990	1993	1994	1995	1996	1997	1998
STOCK PRICES							
Standard & Poor's indices: [1]							
S&P 500 composite (1941-43=10)	330.2	466.5	459.3	615.9	740.7	970.4	1,229.2
Industrials	387.1	543.9	548.9	719.7	870.0	1,121.4	1,479.2
Utilities	144.8	176.4	151.9	201.7	198.8	235.8	259.6
S&P 400 Midcap Index (1982=100)	100.0	179.4	169.4	217.8	255.6	333.4	392.3
Russell indices: [2]							
Russell 1000 (Dec. 31, 1986=130)...........	171.22	250.71	244.65	328.89	393.75	513.79	642.87
Russell 2000 (Dec. 31, 1986=135)..........	132.16	258.59	250.36	315.97	362.61	437.02	421.96
Russell 3000 (Dec. 31, 1986=140)..........	180.85	270.13	263.44	351.91	419.44	543.05	664.27
N.Y. Stock Exchange common stock index							
Composite (Dec. 31, 1965=50)	180.49	259.08	250.94	329.51	392.30	511.19	596.05
Yearly high	201.55	261.16	267.78	331.73	401.08	515.24	601.76
Yearly low	161.76	235.15	241.79	249.86	320.90	386.36	462.69
Industrial (Dec. 31, 1965=50).............	223.60	315.26	318.10	413.29	494.38	630.38	743.65
Transportation (Dec. 31, 1965=50)	141.49	270.48	222.46	301.96	352.30	466.25	482.38
Utility (Dec. 31, 1965=100)	182.60	229.92	198.41	252.90	259.91	335.19	445.94
Finance (Dec. 31, 1965=50)	122.07	216.82	195.80	274.25	351.17	495.96	521.42
American Stock Exchange Composite Index							
(Dec. 29, 1996=550).....................	(NA)	(NA)	(NA)	550.00	572.34	684.61	688.99
NASDAQ composite index (Feb. 5, 1971=100)	373.8	776.8	752.0	1,052.1	1,291.0	1,570.4	2,192.7
Industrial	406.1	805.8	753.8	964.7	1,109.6	1,221.0	1,304.3
Insurance	451.8	920.6	925.9	1,292.6	1,465.4	1,798.0	1,796.8
Bank	254.9	689.4	697.1	1,009.4	1,273.5	2,083.2	1,838.0
Dow-Jones and Co., Inc.:							
Composite (65 stocks).................	920.6	1,381.0	1,274.4	1,693.2	2,025.8	2,607.4	2,870.8
Industrial (30 stocks).................	2,633.7	3,754.1	3,834.4	5,117.1	6,448.3	7,908.3	9,181.4
Transportation (20 stocks)..............	910.2	1,762.3	1,455.0	1,981.0	2,255.7	3,256.5	3,149.3
Utility (15 stocks)...................	209.7	229.3	181.5	225.4	232.5	273.1	312.3
Wilshire 5000 equity index							
(Dec. 31, 1980=1404.596)	3,101.4	4,657.8	4,540.6	6,057.2	7,274.2	9,298.2	11,317.5
COMMON STOCK YIELDS (percent)							
Standard & Poor's composite index (500 stocks): [3]							
Dividend-price ratio [4]...................	3.61	2.78	2.82	2.56	2.19	1.77	1.34
Earnings-price ratio [5]...................	6.47	4.46	5.83	6.09	5.24	4.57	3.10

NA Not available. [1] The S&P 500 composite index includes 400 industrial stocks, 20 transportation, 40 public utility, and 40 financial stocks. The S&P Midcap Index shows the 400 largest capitalization stocks in the United States after the S&P 500. [2] The Russell 1000 and 3000 indices show respectively the 1,000 and 3,000 largest capitalization stocks in the United States. The Russell 2000 index shows the 2,000 largest capitalization stocks in the United States after the first 1,000. [3] Source: U.S. Council of Economic Advisors, *Economic Report of the President*, annual. [4] Aggregate cash dividends (based on latest known annual rate) divided by aggregate market value based on Wednesday closing prices. Averages of monthly figures. [5] Averages of quarterly ratios which are ratio of earnings (after taxes) for 4 quarters ending with particular quarter to price index for last day of that quarter.

Source: Except as noted, Global Financial Data, Alhambra, CA, "GFD Standard and Poor's Sectors;" <http://www.globalfindata. com/tbspsect.htm>; "US Stock Market Capitalization Indices;" <http://www.globalfindata.com/tbcap.htm>; and "Global Financial Data Dow Jones Industrial Average;" <http://www.globalfindata.com/tbdjia.htm>; (all accessed 19 April 1999) and unpublished data (copyright).

No. 841. Dow-Jones U.S. Equity Market Index, by Industry: 1990 to 1998

[As of end of year]

Industry	1990	1993	1994	1995	1996	1997	1998
U.S. Equity Market Index, total	305.59	442.19	433.07	581.43	700.56	922.34	1,169.34
Basic materials	299.67	443.38	456.55	540.47	614.63	680.77	630.44
Consumer, cyclical	325.98	596.43	532.55	635.01	711.02	961.83	1,340.80
Consumer, noncyclical.	543.87	684.89	740.25	1,052.90	1,287.32	1,738.25	2,192.39
Conglomerates.	354.20	655.57	638.07	891.54	1,228.43	1,794.92	2,463.15
Energy	262.85	290.55	286.70	358.74	442.09	533.72	522.82
Financial services.	233.04	436.98	408.25	611.76	809.78	1,203.36	1,303.63
Industrial.	288.12	432.52	399.79	499.93	581.94	700.74	737.60
Technology	242.10	361.45	406.48	570.55	730.45	891.62	1,446.78
Utilities	248.91	316.02	272.82	362.66	359.67	473.01	631.38

Source: Dow Jones & Company, Inc., New York, NY, Wall Street Journal, selected issues (copyright).

No. 842. Sales of Stocks and Options on Registered Exchanges: 1980 to 1997

[522 represents $522,000,000,000. Excludes over-the-counter trading]

Exchange	Unit	1980	1985	1990	1991	1992	1993	1994	1995	1996	1997
Market value of all sales, all exchanges [1] [2]	Bil. dol . . .	522	1,260	1,752	1,903	2,149	2,734	2,966	3,690	4,735	6,879
New York	Bil. dol. . . .	398	1,024	1,394	1,534	1,759	2,278	2,483	3,078	4,013	5,848
American	Bil. dol. . . .	47	38	65	67	69	83	83	105	131	204
Chicago	Bil. dol. . . .	21	79	74	77	87	107	98	114	136	213
CBOE [3]	Bil. dol. . . .	28	38	81	74	63	65	87	107	130	179
Pacific	Bil. dol. . . .	13	40	53	63	65	70	70	94	108	151
Philadelphia	Bil. dol. . . .	11	23	41	39	49	55	51	59	68	89
STOCKS [4]											
Shares sold, all exchanges [2] . .	Billion	15.5	37.0	53.3	58.0	65.5	82.8	90.5	106.4	125.7	159.7
New York	Billion	12.4	30.2	43.8	47.7	53.3	68.7	76.7	90.1	108.2	138.8
American	Billion	1.7	2.1	3.1	3.1	3.6	4.5	4.3	4.8	5.3	6.2
Chicago	Billion	0.6	2.3	2.5	2.7	3.0	3.8	3.5	3.9	4.2	6.0
Pacific	Billion	0.4	1.4	1.7	2.1	2.1	2.3	2.1	2.7	3.0	3.2
Market value, all exchanges [2] .	Bil. dol. . . .	476	1,200	1,612	1,776	2,032	2,610	2,817	3,507	4,511	6,559
New York	Bil. dol. . . .	398	1,023	1,390	1,532	1,758	2,276	2,482	3,076	4,011	5,847
American	Bil. dol. . . .	35	26	36	40	42	54	56	73	86	139
Chicago	Bil. dol. . . .	21	79	74	77	87	107	98	114	136	213
Pacific	Bil. dol. . . .	11	37	45	63	58	62	59	79	92	123

[1] Includes market value of stocks, rights, warrants, and options trading beginning 1990. [2] Includes other registered exchanges, not shown separately. [3] Chicago Board Options Exchange, Inc. [4] Includes voting trust certificates, American Depository Receipts, and certificate of deposit for stocks.
Source: U.S. Securities and Exchange Commission, SEC Monthly Statistical Review (discontinued Feb. 1989); and unpublished data.

No. 843. NASDAQ—Securities Listed and Volume of Trading: 1980 to 1998

Item	Unit	1980	1985	1990	1992	1993	1994	1995	1996	1997	1998
Member firms	Number. . .	2,932	6,307	5,827	5,254	5,296	5,426	5,451	5,553	5,597	5,592
Branch offices	Number. . .	7,555	15,375	24,457	33,484	44,181	57,105	58,119	60,151	62,966	70,752
Companies listed	Number. . .	2,894	4,136	4,132	4,113	4,611	4,902	5,112	5,556	5,487	5,126
Issues	Number. . .	3,050	4,784	4,706	4,768	5,393	5,761	5,955	6,384	6,208	5,666
Shares traded	Billion	6.7	20.7	33.4	48.5	66.5	74.4	101.2	138.1	163.9	202.0
Average daily volume . .	Million . . .	26.5	82.1	131.9	190.8	263.0	295.1	401.4	543.7	647.8	801.7
Value of shares traded . . .	Bil. dol. . . .	69	234	452	891	1,350	1,449	2,398	2,302	4,482	5,759

Source: National Association of Securities Dealers, Washington, DC, Fact Book, annual.

No. 844. Volume of Trading on New York Stock Exchange: 1980 to 1998

[11,562 represents 11,562,000,000. Round lot: A unit of trading or a multiple thereof. On the NYSE the unit of trading is generally 100 shares in stocks. For some inactive stocks, the unit of trading is 10 shares. Odd lot: An amount of stock less than the established 100-share unit or 10-share unit of trading]

Item	Unit	1980	1985	1990	1992	1993	1994	1995	1996	1997	1998
Shares traded. . .	Million .	11,562	27,774	39,946	51,826	67,461	74,003	87,873	105,477	134,404	171,188
Round lots	Million . .	11,352	27,511	39,665	51,376	66,923	73,420	87,218	104,636	133,312	169,745
Average daily shares	Million . .	45	109	157	202	265	291	346	412	527	674
High day	Million . .	84	181	292	389	379	483	653	681	1,201	1,216
Low day	Million . .	16	62	57	95	90	114	118	130	155	247
Odd lots	Million . .	209	263	282	450	538	583	656	841	1,091	1,443
Value of shares traded	Bil. dol .	382	981	1,336	1,765	2,305	2,477	3,110	4,102	5,833	7,395
Round lots	Bil. dol. .	375	970	1,325	1,745	2,283	2,454	3,083	4,064	5,778	7,318
Odd lots	Bil. dol. .	8	10	11	19	22	22	27	38	56	77
Bond volume [1] . .	Mil. dol .	5,190	9,047	10,893	11,629	9,743	7,197	6,979	5,529	5,046	3,836
Daily average . .	Mil. dol .	20.5	35.9	43.1	45.8	38.5	28.6	27.7	21.8	19.9	15.2

[1] Par value.
Source: New York Stock Exchange, Inc., New York, NY, Fact Book, annual (copyright).

Banking, Finance, and Insurance 535

No. 845. Securities Listed on New York Stock Exchange: 1980 to 1998

[As of **December 31**, except **cash dividends** are for **calendar year** (602 represent $602,000,000,000)]

Item	Unit	1980	1985	1990	1991	1992	1993	1994	1995	1996	1997	1998
BONDS												
Number of issuers	Number .	1,045	1,010	743	705	636	574	583	564	563	533	474
Number of issues.	Number .	3,057	3,856	2,912	2,727	2,354	2,103	2,141	2,097	2,064	1,965	1,858
Face value	Bil. dol . .	602	1,327	1,689	2,219	2,009	2,342	2,526	2,773	2,845	2,625	2,554
STOCKS												
Companies	Number .	1,570	1,541	1,774	1,885	2,088	2,361	2,570	2,675	2,907	3,047	3,114
Number of issues.	Number .	2,228	2,298	2,284	2,426	2,658	2,904	3,060	3,126	3,285	3,358	3,382
Shares listed	Billion .	33.7	52.4	90.7	99.6	115.8	131.1	142.3	154.7	176.9	207.1	239.3
Market value	Bil. dol . .	1,243	1,950	2,820	3,713	4,035	4,541	4,448	6,013	7,300	9,413	10,864
Average price	Dollars . .	36.87	37.20	31.08	37.27	34.83	34.65	31.26	38.86	41.26	45.45	45.40
Cash dividends on common stock [1]	Bil. dol . .	53.1	74.2	103.2	123.4	109.7	120.2	130.0	147.0	150.6	159.4	179.0

[1] Beginning 1990 estimate based on average annual yield of the NYSE composite index.

Source: New York Stock Exchange, Inc., New York, NY, *Fact Book*, annual (copyright).

No. 846. Stock Ownership, by Age of Head of Family and Family Income: 1989 to 1995

[**Median value in thousands of constant 1995 dollars (10.4 represents $10,400).** Constant dollar figures are based on consumer price index data published by U.S. Bureau of Labor Statistics. Families include one-person units; for definition of family, see text, Section 1, Population. Based on Survey of Consumer Finance; see Appendix III. For definition of median, see Guide to Tabular Presentation]

Age of family head and family income (constant (1995) dollars)	Families having direct or indirect stock holdings (percent)			Median value among families with holdings			Stock holdings' share of group's financial assets (percent)		
	1989	1992	1995	1989	1992	1995	1989	1992	1995
All families	31.6	36.6	40.3	10.4	11.4	14.5	28.6	34.1	41.5
Under 35 years old	22.3	28.4	36.7	3.7	3.8	5.1	20.4	25.2	31.6
35 to 44 years old	38.9	42.5	46.4	6.3	8.1	10.0	30.1	31.4	41.5
45 to 54 years old	41.8	46.2	48.9	16.1	16.3	25.6	36.2	41.1	44.5
55 to 64 years old	36.1	45.3	40.0	22.6	27.1	30.0	28.5	38.3	47.0
65 to 74 years old	26.7	30.0	34.2	24.9	17.9	34.0	26.4	31.6	36.2
75 years old and over	25.9	25.6	27.8	30.7	27.1	20.0	25.0	25.5	39.8
Less than $10,000	3.3	6.8	6.2	35.0	5.9	2.9	12.1	15.3	13.6
$10,000 to $24,999	13.0	18.7	23.2	7.4	4.3	6.0	12.0	15.3	28.1
$25,000 to $49,999	32.3	40.8	47.3	5.5	7.6	9.0	18.3	24.4	32.1
$50,000 to $99,999	52.4	63.4	67.3	10.4	15.2	23.4	23.5	34.5	43.2
$100,000 and more	81.8	78.5	81.1	55.2	75.4	97.7	36.6	40.7	47.3

Source: Board of Governors of the Federal Reserve System, *Federal Reserve Bulletin*, January 1997, and unpublished revisions.

No. 847. Household Ownership of Mutual Funds, by Age and Income: 1998

[**In percent.** Includes money market, stock, bond and hybrid, variable annuity, IRA, Keogh, and employer-sponsored retirement plan fund owners. An estimated 44,400,000 households own mutual funds. Based on a sample survey of 3,000 households; for details, see source]

Age of household head and household income	All house-holds, percent distri-bution	Households owning mutual funds		Age of household head and household income	All house-holds, percent distri-bution	Households owning mutual funds	
		Percent distri-bution	Percent of all house-holds			Percent distri-bution	Percent of all house-holds
Total	100	100	44				
Less than 25 years old	5	3	24	Less than $25,000	27	9	13
25 to 34 years old.	20	18	42	$25,000 to $34,999.	17	11	28
35 to 44 years old.	22	26	52	$35,000 to $49,999.	17	19	47
45 to 54 years old.	18	22	53	$50,000 to $74,999.	22	31	62
55 to 64 years old.	13	15	51	$75,000 to $99,999.	8	14	72
65 years old and over	22	16	31	$100,000 and over	9	16	77

Source: Investment Company Institute, Washington, DC, *Fundamentals, Investment Company Institute Research in Brief,* Vol. 8, No. 1, March 1999 (copyright).

No. 848. Mutual Fund Shares—Holdings and Net Purchases, by Type of Investor: 1990 to 1998

[In billions of dollars (608.4 represents $608,400,000,000). Holdings as of **Dec. 31.** Minus sign (-) indicates net sales]

Type of investor	Holdings					Net purchases				
	1990	1995	1996	1997	1998	1990	1995	1996	1997	1998
Total	608.4	1,852.8	2,342.4	2,989.4	3,626.1	53.7	147.4	237.6	265.1	275.6
Households, nonprofit organizations	467.8	1,265.0	1,582.1	2,048.5	2,485.6	27.5	94.7	176.2	254.9	255.2
Nonfinancial corporate business. . .	9.7	45.7	59.9	69.1	75.4	-1.0	4.6	3.3	-8.2	-8.0
State and local governments	4.8	35.0	41.0	44.6	48.3	3.3	5.9	6.0	3.6	3.6
Commercial banking	1.9	2.3	2.6	8.1	11.3	-0.3	0.3	0.3	0.8	1.7
Credit unions	1.4	2.8	2.6	2.4	3.6	0.2	0.2	-0.3	-0.2	1.2
Bank personal trusts and estates . .	62.7	253.5	293.6	342.2	406.5	9.7	9.5	3.9	-7.8	2.6
Life insurance companies	30.7	27.7	39.1	36.5	31.3	12.6	13.5	7.0	-14.1	-12.0
Private pension funds	29.2	220.7	321.4	438.0	564.1	1.6	18.6	41.1	36.2	31.2

Source: Board of Governors of the Federal Reserve System, *Flow of Funds Accounts*, March 1999 quarterly diskettes. Data are also published in the quarterly Z.1 release.

No. 849. Mutual Funds—Summary: 1980 to 1998

[Number of funds, accounts, and assets as of **December 31 (12.1 represents 12,100,000).** A mutual fund is an open-end investment company that continuously issues and redeems shares that represent an interest in a pool of financial assets]

Type of fund	Unit	1980	1985	1990	1993	1994	1995	1996	1997	1998
Number of funds, total	Number. .	564	1,528	3,105	4,558	5,357	5,761	6,293	6,684	7,314
Equity funds . . . . , ...	Number . .	267	579	1,127	1,615	1,944	2,211	2,626	2,951	3,513
Income and bond funds [1] . . . . . . , .	Number . .	191	492	1,235	2,023	2,450	2,553	2,679	2,720	2,775
Money market funds, tax-exempt [2] . .	Number . .	10	111	235	292	319	325	323	331	341
Money market funds, taxable [3]	Number . .	96	346	508	628	644	672	665	682	685
Shareholder accounts, total. . . .	Millions. .	12.1	34.7	62.6	93.6	114.8	131.8	150.8	171.3	206.0
Equity funds	Millions . .	5.8	11.5	23.0	42.5	59.0	70.7	87.1	103.6	125.4
Income and bond funds [1]	Millions . .	1.5	8.3	16.6	27.5	30.5	30.9	31.5	32.0	41.8
Money market funds, tax-exempt [2] . .	Millions . .	(NA)	0.5	1.4	2.0	2.0	2.3	2.3	2.7	2.4
Money market funds, taxable [3]	Millions . .	4.8	14.4	21.6	21.6	23.3	27.9	29.9	33.0	36.4
Assets, total	Bil. dol . .	135	496	1,067	2,075	2,161	2,820	3,539	4,468	5,525
Equity funds	Bil. dol . .	44	117	246	749	866	1,269	1,751	2,368	2,978
Income and bond funds [1]	Bil. dol . .	14	135	323	761	684	798	887	1,041	1,195
Money market funds, tax-exempt [2] . .	Bil. dol . .	2	36	84	103	111	123	140	161	189
Money market funds, taxable [3]	Bil. dol . .	74	208	415	462	500	630	762	898	1,163
Sales, total	Bil. dol . .	248	954	1,565	3,189	3,077	3,602	4,675	5,800	7,230
Equity funds	Bil. dol . .	6	30	71	229	271	307	471	602	722
Income and bond funds [1]	Bil. dol . .	4	84	79	282	203	170	213	267	336
Money market funds, tax-exempt [2] . .	Bil. dol . .	5	109	197	342	369	397	468	536	639
Money market funds, taxable [3]	Bil. dol . .	232	730	1,219	2,336	2,234	2,728	3,522	4,393	5,534
Redemptions, total	Bil. dol . .	217	865	1,471	2,905	2,929	3,315	4,267	5,324	6,649
Equity funds	Bil. dol . .	6	18	45	93	142	172	243	362	534
Income and bond funds [1]	Bil. dol . .	3	15	53	139	188	141	156	179	213
Money market funds, tax-exempt [2] . .	Bil. dol . .	4	99	190	337	370	386	455	518	612
Money market funds, taxable [3]	Bil. dol . .	204	732	1,183	2,337	2,229	2,616	3,414	4,265	5,289

NA Not available.   [1] Includes municipal bond funds and, beginning 1996, hybrid funds which invest in both equity and bond.   [2] Funds invest in municipal securities with relatively short maturities.   [3] Funds invest in short-term, high-grade securities sold in the money market.

Source: Investment Company Institute, Washington, DC, *Mutual Fund Fact Book*, annual (copyright).

Banking, Finance, and Insurance   537

No. 850. Mutual Fund Retirement Assets: 1990 to 1997

[In billions of dollars, except percent (230 represents $230,000,000,000). Based on data from the Institute's Annual Questionnaire for Retirement Statistics. The 1997 survey gathered data from 7,088 mutual fund share classes representing 82 percent of mutual fund industry assets. Assets were estimated for all non-respondent funds to produce total industry retirement plan assets. Reporting funds were grouped by investment objective and ratios were calculated of the reported retirement assets to the total net assets for each type of retirement plan. These ratios were used to estimate data for non-respondents. A similar survey was conducted of brokers to ascertain the amount of retirement assets held in street name and omnibus accounts. The results of the broker survey and the mutual fund survey were combined to produce total mutual fund retirement assets]

Type of account	1990	1991	1992	1993	1994	1995	1996	1997
Mutual fund retirement assets . .	230	358	485	649	738	1,000	1,250	1,596
Percent of total retirement								
assets	6	8	9	11	12	14	16	17
Individual retirement accounts (IRAs) . . .	147	198	250	342	372	509	642	822
Employer-sponsored retirement plans . . .	84	160	234	308	366	491	608	774
Defined contribution plans [1]	77	149	219	285	340	464	574	734
401(k) plans [2]	35	46	82	140	176	258	329	444
Percent of total 401(k) assets . . .	9	10	15	23	26	33	37	42
403(b) plans [3]	15	68	74	86	90	119	146	185
457 plans [4]	2	2	3	3	6	8	11	14
Other defined contribution plans . . .	25	34	60	56	69	79	89	92
Defined benefit plans	7	11	16	22	26	27	34	39
Percent of all mutual funds:								
Mutual fund retirement assets	22	26	29	31	34	35	35	36
Individual retirement accounts (IRAs) . . .	14	14	15	17	17	18	18	18
Employer-sponsored retirement plans . . .	8	12	14	15	17	17	17	17

[1] Defined-contribution plans other than 401(k) plans include profit-sharing, stock bonus, and money-purchase plans without 401(k) features as well as 403(b), 457, and Keogh plans. The source no longer collects separate assets data for Keogh plan holdings of mutual funds, and these assets are now included in other defined-contribution plan assets. [2] See headnote, Table 624. [3] Section 403(b) of the Internal Revenue Code permits employees of certain charitable organizations, nonprofit hospitals, universities, and public schools to establish tax-sheltered retirement programs. These plans may invest in either annuity contracts or mutual fund shares. [4] These plans are deferred compensation arrangements for government employees and employees of certain tax-exempt organizations.

Source: Investment Company Institute, Washington, DC, *Fundamentals, Investment Company Institute Research in Brief,* Vol. 7, No. 2, July 1998, and "Retirement Assets Held in Mutual Funds by Type of Plan, 1980-1997;" <http://www.ici.org/retirement/retirementstatshist.html>; (accessed: 30 March 1999) (copyright).

No. 851. Individual Retirement Accounts (IRA) Plans—Value, by Type of Holder: 1985 to 1996

[As of **December 31** (200 represents $200,000,000,000). Estimated]

Type of holder	Amount (bil. dol.)									Percent distribution		
	1985	1989	1990	1991	1992	1993	1994	1995	1996	1985	1990	1996
Total	200	455	529	657	746	868	941	1,170	1,347	100	100	100
Savings institutions	56	98	95	91	85	76	72	73	72	28	18	5
Commercial banks	52	99	119	134	137	134	136	143	144	26	22	11
Mutual funds	32	112	127	169	211	284	305	411	511	16	24	38
Self directed	29	82	117	181	225	271	318	415	483	15	22	36
Life insurance companies	17	38	42	50	56	70	79	94	106	9	8	8
Credit unions	14	26	29	32	32	32	32	34	33	7	6	2

Source: Investment Company Institute, Washington, DC, *Mutual Fund Fact Book,* annual (copyright).

No. 852. 401(k) Plan Assets—Summary, 1985 to 1997, and Projections, 2000

Year	Total assets (bil. dol.)	Type of asset	Percent of companies offering investment option, 1997	Assets, 1997		Financial institution managing assets	Assets, 1997	
				Amount (bil. dol.)	Percent distribution		Amount (bil. dol.)	Percent distribution
1985	105	Total	(X)	985	100	All defined contribution		
1989	270	Guaranteed investment				plans [2]	1,730	100
1990	300	account [1]	52	177	18	Insurance companies. . .	450	26
1991	350	Equity	96	325	33	Banks	433	25
1992	410	Money market.	55	30	3	Mutual fund groups	588	34
1993	475	Balanced account . . .	64	108	11	Other	260	15
1994	525							
1995	675	Bond fund	69	69	7	401(k) plans	985	100
1996	810	Company stock	22	207	21	Insurance companies. . .	217	22
1997	985	Other.	(NA)	(NA)	(NA)	Banks	207	21
						Mutual fund groups	414	42
2000, proj. .	1,475					Other	148	15

NA Not available.   X Not applicable.   [1] Covers bank certificate of deposits, guaranteed investment contracts (GICs), GIC alternatives, and insurance company participating contracts.   [2] Includes 401(k) plans.

Source: Spectrum Group, San Francisco, CA, *1997 Marketplace Update,* 1997 (copyright).

U.S. Census Bureau, Statistical Abstract of the United States: 1999

No. 853. Assets of Private and Public Pension Funds, by Type of Fund: 1980 to 1998

[In billions of dollars. As of end of year. Except for corporate equities, represents book value. Excludes social security trust funds and U.S. government pension funds; see Tables 615 and 619]

Type of pension fund	1980	1985	1990	1993	1994	1995	1996	1997	1998
Total, all types	882	1,887	3,125	4,344	4,531	5,275	5,964	7,033	8,076
Private funds	685	1,488	2,205	3,088	3,237	3,757	4,249	4,939	5,732
Insured . . . . [1] [2]	172	260	596	836	885	1,002	1,095	1,234	1,401
Noninsured [1] [2]	513	1,228	1,608	2,252	2,352	2,755	3,155	3,706	4,331
Credit market instruments [2] . . [2] . .	151	331	491	615	661	717	769	835	953
U.S. Government securities [2] . .	51	196	289	351	402	444	470	503	562
Treasury	32	138	198	240	272	299	315	334	362
Corporate and foreign bonds . .	78	97	146	209	201	207	228	256	301
Corporate equities	232	516	595	992	996	1,238	1,491	1,864	2,232
Mutual fund shares	7	11	29	116	150	221	321	438	564
Unallocated insurance contracts [3] .	-	132	189	207	210	211	220	235	262
State and local pension funds [2]	197	399	920	1,256	1,294	1,518	1,715	2,094	2,344
Credit market instruments [2] . [2] . . .	147	252	424	433	456	483	529	566	633
U.S. government securities [2] . . .	40	124	224	231	246	271	299	317	336
Treasury	21	83	140	163	171	176	191	205	195
Corporate and foreign bonds	92	107	172	167	168	163	180	199	245
Corporate equities	44	120	293	531	543	753	956	1,306	1,593

- Represents zero.   [1] Covers all pension funds of corporations, nonprofit organizations, unions, and multi-employer groups. Also includes deferred profit-sharing plans and Federal Employees Retirement System (FERS) Thrift Savings Fund. Excludes health, welfare, and bonus plans.   [2] Includes other types of assets not shown separately.   [3] Assets held at life insurance companies (e.g., guaranteed investment contracts (GICs), variable annuities).

Source: Board of Governors of the Federal Reserve System, *Flow of Funds Accounts*, March 1999 quarterly diskettes. Data are also published in the quarterly Z.1 release.

No. 854. Securities Industry—Revenues and Expenses: 1980 to 1997

[In millions of dollars (19,829 represents $19,829,000,000)]

Type	1980	1985	1990	1991	1992	1993	1994	1995	1996	1997
Revenues, total.	19,829	49,844	71,356	84,890	90,584	108,844	112,758	143,414	172,411	207,245
Commissions	6,777	10,955	12,032	14,210	16,249	19,905	19,847	23,215	27,866	32,662
Trading/investment gains	5,091	14,549	15,746	22,641	21,838	25,427	20,219	28,963	30,768	35,958
Underwriting profits	1,571	4,987	3,728	6,593	8,300	11,249	6,844	8,865	12,613	14,611
Margin interest	2,151	2,746	3,179	2,771	2,690	3,235	4,668	6,470	7,386	10,630
Mutual fund sales	278	2,754	3,242	4,176	5,950	8,115	6,887	7,434	10,081	12,422
Other	3,960	13,854	33,428	34,498	35,557	40,913	54,293	68,468	83,697	100,961
Expenses, total.	16,668	43,342	70,566	76,234	81,467	95,805	109,266	132,089	155,433	187,281
Interest expense	3,876	11,470	28,093	27,512	24,576	26,616	40,250	56,877	64,698	80,659
Compensation	7,619	18,112	22,931	26,916	32,071	39,125	37,595	41,541	51,033	58,558
Commissions/clearance paid	1,055	2,314	2,959	3,200	3,722	5,338	5,360	5,700	7,364	8,864
Other	4,119	11,446	16,583	18,605	21,098	24,726	26,060	27,970	32,338	39,200
Net income, pretax	3,160	6,502	790	8,656	9,117	13,039	3,492	11,325	16,978	19,964

Source: U.S. Securities and Exchange Commission, *Annual Report*.

No. 855. Health Insurance—Premium Income and Benefit Payments of Insurance Companies: 1980 to 1996

[In billions of dollars (43.7 represents $43,700,000,000). Includes Puerto Rico and other U.S. outlying areas. Represents premium income of and benefits paid by insurance companies only. Excludes Blue Cross-Blue Shield plans, medical-society sponsored plans, and all other independent plans]

Item	1980	1985	1988	1989	1990	1991	1992	1993	1994	1995	1996
Premiums [1]	43.7	75.2	98.2	108.0	112.9	116.4	125.0	124.7	129.3	133.9	137.1
Group policies [2]	36.8	64.4	87.6	96.1	100.2	103.0	110.4	110.2	114.1	116.4	116.3
Individual and family policies . . .	6.9	10.8	10.6	11.8	12.7	13.3	14.6	14.5	15.2	17.5	20.8
Benefit payments	37.0	60.0	83.0	89.4	92.5	97.6	104.8	103.6	106.3	110.1	113.8
Group policies [2]	33.0	53.7	76.4	82.2	84.4	88.8	95.2	94.1	95.9	98.1	99.0
Individual and family policies . . .	4.0	6.3	6.6	7.2	8.2	8.8	9.6	9.3	10.4	12.0	14.8
Type of coverage:											
Loss of income	5.3	5.6	6.4	7.2	7.4	7.5	8.3	8.1	7.8	8.2	9.2
Medical expense	27.9	47.2	66.4	72.0	73.8	77.9	82.9	81.4	84.0	85.8	(NA)
Dental	2.8	5.3	6.3	6.5	6.4	6.4	7.1	7.0	7.0	7.7	(NA)
Medicare supplement	1.0	1.9	3.8	3.7	5.0	5.8	6.4	6.9	7.5	8.4	(NA)

NA Not available.   [1] Earned premiums.   [2] Insurance company group premiums and benefit payments include administrative service agreements and minimum premium plans.

Source: Health Insurance Association of America, Washington, DC, *Source Book of Health Insurance Data*, annual.

U.S. Census Bureau, Statistical Abstract of the United States: 1999

No. 856. Property and Casualty Insurance—Summary: 1990 to 1997

[In billions of dollars (217.8 represents $217,800,000,000). Minus sign (-) indicates loss]

Item	1990	1991	1992	1993	1994	1995	1996	1997
Premiums, net written	217.8	223.0	227.8	241.7	250.7	259.8	268.6	276.1
Automobile, private [1]	78.4	82.8	88.4	93.4	96.8	102.0	107.7	113.6
Automobile, commercial [1]	17.0	16.6	16.1	16.3	16.7	17.2	17.6	18.0
Liability other than auto	22.1	20.9	21.1	22.1	23.6	23.4	24.5	25.0
Fire and allied lines	7.1	7.2	7.1	7.9	8.7	9.4	9.9	9.1
Homeowners' multiple peril	18.6	19.3	20.5	21.5	22.6	24.0	25.4	26.9
Commercial multiple peril	17.7	17.0	16.4	17.3	17.8	18.8	18.9	19.0
Workers' compensation	31.0	31.3	29.7	30.3	28.9	26.2	25.1	24.0
Marine, inland and ocean	5.7	5.5	5.5	6.1	6.7	7.1	7.5	7.6
Accident and health	5.0	5.1	5.4	6.8	7.2	7.8	7.8	8.2
Other lines	15.2	17.4	17.6	20.0	21.7	23.9	24.2	24.7
Losses and expenses	234.7	239.3	259.6	250.7	263.3	268.4	277.1	272.6
Underwriting gain/loss	-20.9	-19.4	-33.3	-15.1	-19.0	-14.2	-13.8	-1.1
Net investment income	32.9	34.2	33.7	32.6	33.7	36.8	38.0	41.5
Operating earnings after taxes	9.0	10.4	5.8	19.3	10.9	20.6	24.4	36.8
Assets	556.3	601.4	637.3	671.5	704.6	765.2	806.1	870.1
Policyholders' surplus	138.4	158.7	163.1	182.3	193.3	230.0	255.5	308.5

[1] Includes premiums for automobile liability and physical damage.

Source: Insurance Information Institute, New York, NY, *The Fact Book, Property/Casualty Insurance Facts*, annual (copyright).

No. 857. Automobile Insurance—Average Expenditures Per Insured Vehicle, by State: 1995 to 1997

[In dollars. The average expenditures for automobile insurance in a state are affected by a number of factors, including the underlying rate structure, the coverages purchased, the deductibles and limits selected, the types of vehicles insured, and the distribution of driver characteristics]

State	1995	1996	1997	State	1995	1996	1997	State	1995	1996	1997
U.S.	667	691	706	KS	474	495	516	ND	381	402	436
				KY	555	581	597	OH	531	553	572
AL	549	578	616	LA	788	803	841	OK	526	545	566
AK	730	751	776	ME	472	470	478	OR	565	585	621
AZ	727	785	819	MD	732	759	772	PA	667	687	718
AR	500	558	566	MA	898	833	803	RI	870	870	866
CA	794	798	776	MI	645	697	736	SC	582	602	629
CO	722	751	774	MN	628	654	671	SD	428	448	470
CT	881	899	909	MS	579	604	648	TN	519	557	586
DE	784	806	828	MO	573	599	614	TX	711	726	740
DC	959	993	1,039	MT	468	479	501	UT	547	581	610
FL	739	783	759	NE	452	475	505	VT	512	514	519
GA	597	628	653	NV	759	803	848	VA	553	550	566
HI	963	959	912	NH	609	612	616	WA	650	666	693
ID	447	465	479	NJ	1,013	1,099	1,126	WV	646	671	707
IL	612	638	666	NM	639	660	690	WI	506	533	548
IN	542	548	571	NY	906	960	953	WY	433	452	477
IA	429	445	456	NC	501	518	556				

Source: National Association of Insurance Commissioners, Kansas City, MO, *State Average Expenditures and Premiums for Personal Automobile Insurance*, annual (copyright).

No. 858. Life Insurance in Force in the United States—Summary: 1980 to 1997

[As of **December 31** or **calendar year**, as applicable (**402 represents 402,000,000**). Covers life insurance with life insurance companies only. Represents all life insurance in force on lives of U.S. residents whether issued by U.S. or foreign companies. For definition of household, see text, Section 1, Population]

Year	Number of policies, total (mil.)	Life insurance in force — Value (bil. dol.)					Average size policy in force (dollars)				Average amount ($1,000)		Disposable personal income per household ($1,000)
		Total	Ordinary	Group	Industrial	Credit [1]	Ordinary	Group	Industrial	Credit [1]	Per household	Per insured household	
1980	402	3,541	1,761	1,579	36	165	11,920	13,410	620	2,110	41.9	51.1	24.4
1985	386	6,053	3,247	2,562	28	216	22,780	19,720	640	3,100	66.6	82.2	34.6
1990	389	9,393	5,367	3,754	24	248	37,910	26,630	670	3,500	98.4	124.5	44.6
1992	366	10,406	5,942	4,241	21	202	42,960	29,930	700	3,610	106.6	136.6	48.2
1993	363	11,105	6,428	4,456	20	200	45,770	31,430	700	3,850	111.6	143.1	49.7
1994	390	11,057	6,407	4,442	19	189	45,870	26,338	659	3,609	113.9	146.3	51.7
1995	393	11,638	6,816	4,603	18	201	49,090	27,051	664	3,554	119.1	148.9	54.3
1996	372	12,590	7,294	5,067	18	211	52,285	32,577	686	4,189	127.5	157.3	56.6
1997	373	13,196	7,689	5,277	18	212	56,044	32,221	714	4,482	132.4	165.8	58.1

[1] Insures borrower to cover consumer loan in case of death.

Source: American Council of Life Insurance, Washington, DC, *Life Insurance Fact Book*, annual (copyright).

U.S. Census Bureau, Statistical Abstract of the United States: 1999

No. 859. Life Insurance Purchases in the United States— Number and Amount: 1980 to 1997

[29,007 represents 29,007,000. Excludes revivals, increases, dividend additions, and reinsurance acquired. Includes long-term credit insurance (life insurance on loans of more than 10 years' duration). See also headnote, Table 858]

Year	Number of policies purchased (1,000)				Amount purchased (bil. dol.)			
	Total	Ordinary	Group	Industrial	Total	Ordinary	Group	Industrial
1980	29,007	14,750	11,379	2,878	573	386	183	4
1985	33,880	17,104	16,243	533	[1]1,231	911	[1]320	1
1990	28,791	14,066	14,592	133	1,529	1,070	459	(Z)
1992	28,382	13,350	14,930	102	1,489	1,048	441	(Z)
1993	31,238	13,574	17,574	90	1,678	1,101	577	(Z)
1994	32,225	13,675	18,390	160	1,611	1,051	560	(Z)
1995	31,999	12,466	19,404	129	1,543	1,005	538	(Z)
1996	30,782	11,926	18,761	95	1,650	1,035	615	(Z)
1997	31,708	11,667	19,973	68	1,831	1,142	689	(Z)

Z Less than $500 million.   [1] Includes Federal Employees' Group Life Insurance: $11 billion in 1985.

Source: American Council of Life Insurance, Washington, DC, *Life Insurance Fact Book*, annual (copyright).

No. 860. U.S. Life Insurance Companies—Summary: 1980 to 1997

[As of **December 31** or **calendar year**, as applicable **(130.9 represents $130,900,000,000)**. Covers domestic and foreign business of U.S. companies. Beginning 1994 includes annual statement data for companies that primarily are health insurance companies]

Item	Unit	1980	1985	1990	1991	1992	1993	1994	1995	1996	1997
U.S. companies [1]	Number	1,958	2,261	2,195	2,064	1,944	1,844	2,136	2,079	1,679	1,620
Income	**Bil. dol.**	**130.9**	**234.0**	**402.2**	**411.0**	**426.9**	**466.4**	**492.6**	**528.1**	**561.1**	**610.6**
Life insurance premiums	Bil. dol	40.8	60.1	76.7	79.3	83.9	94.4	98.9	102.8	107.6	115.0
Annuity considerations	Bil. dol	22.4	53.9	129.1	123.6	132.6	156.4	153.0	158.4	178.4	197.5
Health insurance premiums	Bil. dol	29.4	41.8	58.3	60.9	65.5	68.7	86.2	90.0	92.2	92.7
Investment and other	Bil. dol	38.3	78.2	138.2	147.2	144.9	146.8	154.5	176.9	182.9	205.3
Payments to life insurance beneficiaries	Bil. dol	12.9	18.2	24.6	25.4	27.2	28.8	32.6	34.5	43.6	43.9
Payments under life insurance and annuity contracts	Bil. dol	25.2	48.3	63.8	66.2	67.8	71.2	168.2	193.1	210.7	239.2
Surrender values under life insurance [2]	Bil. dol	6.7	15.6	18.0	16.3	16.8	16.9	18.0	19.5	24.5	24.2
Surrender values under annuity policies [2]	Bil. dol	(NA)	(NA)	(NA)	(NA)	(NA)	(NA)	92.8	105.4	115.7	140.8
Policy dividends	Bil. dol	6.8	10.1	12.0	12.1	12.2	12.7	15.9	17.8	18.1	18.0
Annuity payments	Bil. dol	10.2	21.3	32.6	36.6	37.6	40.3	40.4	48.5	51.1	55.1
Matured endowments	Bil. dol	0.9	0.8	0.7	0.7	0.6	0.6	0.6	1.0	0.7	0.6
Other payments	Bil. dol	0.6	0.5	0.6	0.5	0.6	0.6	0.5	0.9	0.6	0.6
Health insurance benefit payments	Bil. dol	23.0	27.3	40.0	42.6	45.0	46.0	60.1	64.7	66.7	67.4
BALANCE SHEET											
Assets	**Bil. dol.**	**479**	**826**	**1,408**	**1,551**	**1,665**	**1,839**	**1,942**	**2,144**	**2,328**	**2,579**
Government securities	Bil. dol	33	125	211	269	320	384	396	409	411	391
Corporate securities	Bil. dol	227	374	711	788	863	982	1,072	1,241	1,416	1,658
Percent of total assets	Percent	47.4	45.3	50.5	50.8	51.8	53.4	55.2	57.9	60.8	64.3
Bonds	Bil. dol	180	297	583	624	670	730	791	869	962	1,060
Stocks	Bil. dol	47	77	128	165	192	252	282	372	454	598
Mortgages	Bil. dol	131	172	270	265	247	229	215	212	212	210
Real estate	Bil. dol	15	29	43	47	51	54	54	52	50	46
Policy loans	Bil. dol	41	54	63	66	72	78	85	96	102	105
Other	Bil. dol	32	72	110	115	112	112	120	133	137	169
Interest earned on assets [3]	Percent	8.02	9.63	8.89	8.63	8.08	7.52	7.14	7.34	7.20	7.17
Obligations and surplus funds [4]	Bil. dol	479	826	1,408	1,551	1,665	1,839	1,942	2,144	2,340	2,583
Policy reserves [5]	**Bil. dol.**	**390**	**665**	**1,197**	**1,305**	**1,407**	**1,550**	**1,644**	**1,812**	**1,966**	**2,165**
Annuities [6]	Bil. dol	181	411	815	894	960	1,062	1,118	1,238	1,340	1,483
Group	Bil. dol	140	303	516	548	560	602	612	619	690	762
Individual [7]	Bil. dol	41	108	299	346	400	460	505	619	650	721
Life insurance	Bil. dol	198	236	349	372	402	436	468	511	556	606
Health insurance	Bil. dol	11	19	33	38	45	51	58	63	70	75
Asset valuation reserve	Bil. dol	6	11	15	19	21	25	25	30	33	36
Capital and surplus	Bil. dol	34	57	91	106	115	128	137	151	147	160

NA Not available.   [1] Beginning 1994 includes life insurance companies that sell accident and health insurance.
[2] Beginning with 1994, "surrender values" include annuity withdrawals of funds, which were not included in prior years.   [3] Net rate.   [4] Includes other obligations not shown separately.   [5] Includes the business of health insurance departments of life companies.   [6] Beginning 1996 data are not comparable with prior years' data due to a change in the treatment of separate account annuities.   [7] Includes reserves for supplementary contracts with and without life contingencies.

Source: American Council of Life Insurance, Washington, DC, *Life Insurance Fact Book*, annual (copyright).

U.S. Census Bureau, Statistical Abstract of the United States: 1999

Figure 17.1
Patents Issued: 1990 to 1997

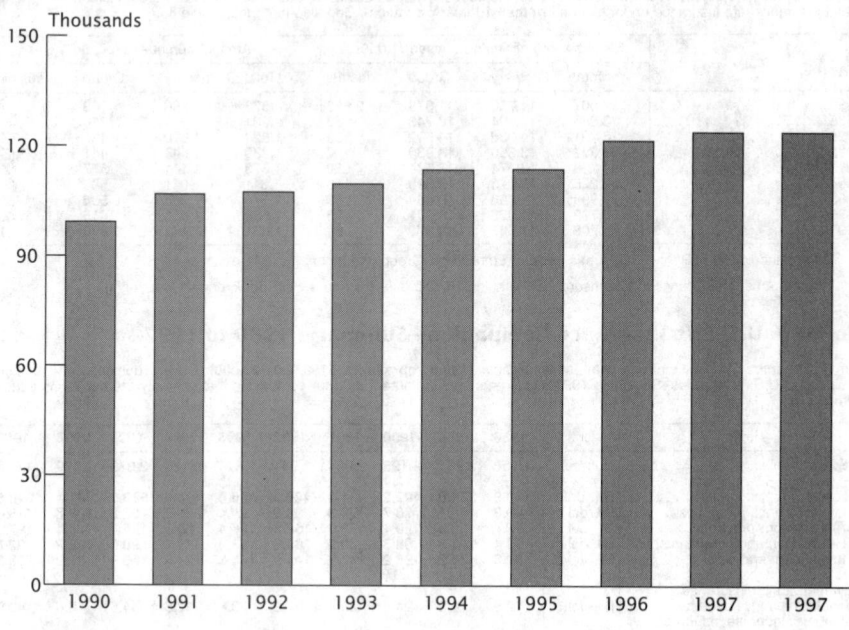

Source: Chart prepared by U.S. Census Bureau. For data, see Table 893.

Figure 17.2
Bankruptcy Cases Filed: 1990 to 1998

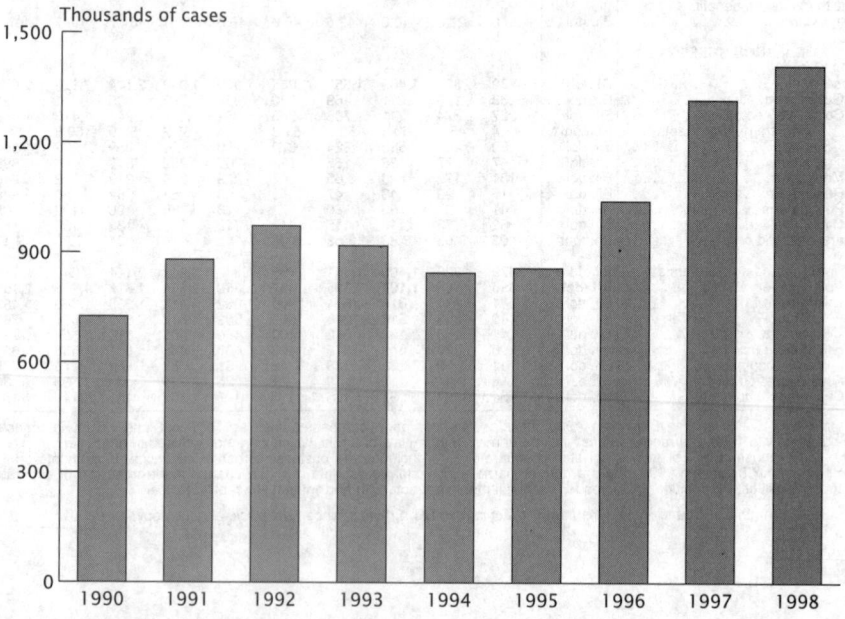

Source: Chart prepared by U.S. Census Bureau. For data, see Table 887.

542 Business Enterprise

Section 17

Business Enterprise

This section relates to the place and behavior of the business firm and to business initiative in the American economy. It includes data on the number, type, and size of businesses; financial data of domestic and multinational U.S. corporations; business investments, expenditures, and profits; sales and inventories; and business failures.

The principal sources of these data are the *Survey of Current Business*, published by the Bureau of Economic Analysis (BEA), the *Federal Reserve Bulletin*, issued by the Board of Governors of the Federal Reserve System, the annual *Statistics of Income* (SOI) reports of the Internal Revenue Service (IRS), *The Business Failure Record* issued by the Dun & Bradstreet Corporation, Murray Hill, NJ. ; and the *Quarterly Financial Report for Manufacturing, Mining, and Trade Corporations (QFR)*.

Business firms—A firm is generally defined as a business organization under a single management and may include one or more establishments. The terms firm, business, company, and enterprise are used interchangeably throughout this section. A firm doing business in more than one industry is classified by industry according to the major activity of the firm as a whole. The industrial classification is based on the Standard Industrial Classification (SIC) Manual.

The IRS concept of a business firm relates primarily to the legal entity used for tax reporting purposes. A **sole proprietorship** is an unincorporated business owned by one person including large enterprises with many employees and hired managers and part-time operations in which the owner is the only person involved. A **partnership** is an unincorporated business owned by two or more persons, each of whom has a financial interest in the business. A **corporation** is a business that is legally incorporated under state laws. While many corporations file consolidated tax returns, most corporate tax returns represent individual corporations, some of which are affiliated through common ownership or control with other corporations filing separate returns.

Economic censuses—The economic censuses constitute comprehensive and periodic canvasses of the Nation's industrial and business activities. The first economic census of the United States was conducted as part of the 1810 decennial census, when inquiries on manufacturing were included with the census of population. Minerals data were collected in 1840. The first censuses of construction and business were taken for 1929. An integrated economic census program was begun for 1954. In that year, the censuses covered the retail and wholesale trades, selected service industries, manufactures, and mineral industries. In 1992, coverage was expanded to 95 percent of the private U.S. economy. The economic censuses are taken at 5-year intervals covering years ending in "2" and "7." Special surveys are conducted every 5 years as part of the economic censuses to determine the extent of business ownership by specific minority groups and women.

Industrial groups—Establishments are classified into industries on the basis of their principal product or activity in accordance with the 1987 *Standard Industrial Classification (SIC) Manual*, Office of Management and Budget. The SIC is a classification structure for the entire national economy. The structure provides data on a division and industry code basis, according to the level of industrial detail. For example, manufacturing is a major industrial division; food and kindred products (Code 20) is one of its major groups. One of the

U.S. Census Bureau, Statistical Abstract of the United States: 1999

ways this group is further divided is into meat products (Code 201) and meat packing plants (Code 2011).

Changes in industry presentation—The country detail in this presentation is identical to that in the 1989 benchmark survey and in the intervening annual surveys. However, three changes have affected the industry detail. First, beginning with the publication of the preliminary 1994 benchmark survey results, the data for nonbank U.S. parents and foreign affiliates exclude savings institutions and credit unions. The change in coverage reflects the reclassification of savings institutions and credit unions from the "finance, except banking" industry (which is covered by the nonbank data) to the industry "depository institutions" (which will replace the industry "banking" in the publication of the final 1994 benchmark results). This change will not materially affect the comparisons of the data for 1993 with the data for 1994, because in 1993, only one U.S. parent and no foreign affiliates were classified as a savings institution or credit union.

Second, beginning with the preliminary 1994 benchmark survey results, the "communication and public utilities" group was disaggregated and the "metal mining" and "nonmetallic minerals mining" groups were aggregated in the industry table stub. Third, beginning with the revised 1993 annual estimates, the names of two industry groups were changed; the group "machinery, except electrical" is now called "industrial machinery and equipment," and the group "electric and electronic equipment" is now called "electronic and other electric equipment."

North American Industry Classification System (NAICS)—The United States has a new industry classification system! On April 9, 1997, the Office of Management and Budget (OMB) announced its decision to adopt the North American Industry Classification System (NAICS pronounced Nakes) as the industry classification system used by the statistical agencies of the United States. NAICS replaces the

1987 Standard Industrial Classification (SIC).

NAICS is based on a consistent, economic concept. Establishments that use the same or similar processes to produce goods or services are grouped together. The SIC, developed in the 1930s and revised periodically over the past 50 years, was not based on a consistent economic concept. Some industries are demand based while others are production based.

NAICS recognizes the changing and growing services-based economy of the United States and its North American neighbors. NAICS includes 1,170 industries of which 565 are service-based industries. The SIC had 1,004 industries of which 416 were service-related industries. Three hundred and fifty eight new industries are recognized in NAICS, 250 of which are services producing industries. There are 20 sectors in NAICS of which 16 are services related. The SIC had 10 divisions of which 5 were service related.

NAICS provides for comparable statistics among the North American countries. In addition, it provides for more comparable information with the Internal Standard Industrial Classification of All Economic Activities (ISIC). The SIC did not.

NAICS is a six-digit system that provides for comparability among the three countries at the five-digit level, albeit with a few exceptions. The SIC was a four-digit system that was not linked in any way to the systems of Canada and Mexico. A six-digit system was adopted for NAICS to provide for increased flexibility in the system. NAICS allows each country to recognize activities that are important in the respective countries, but may not be large enough or important enough to recognize in all three countries. The sixth digit is reserved for this purpose.

The nomenclature of the groupings within the system is different in NAICS. NAICS calls the highest level of aggregation in the system a sector; the SIC referred to this grouping as a division.

U.S. Census Bureau, Statistical Abstract of the United States: 1999

No. 861. Number of Returns and Business Receipts, by Type of Business Size of Receipts: 1980 to 1996

[**2,711 represents 2,711,000.** Covers active enterprises only. Figures are estimates based on sample of unaudited tax returns; see Appendix III. The industrial distribution is based on data collected from companies; see text, this section]

Size-class of receipts	Returns (1,000)					Business receipts [1] (bil. dol.)				
	1980	1990	1994	1995	1996	1980	1990	1994	1995	1996
Corporations.	2,711	3,717	4,342	4,474	4,631	6,172	10,914	12,858	13,969	14,890
Under $25,000 [2]	557	879	1,029	1,030	1,060	4	5	3	4	5
$25,000 to $49,999	208	252	275	288	286	8	9	10	11	11
$50,000 to $99,999	323	359	427	447	480	22	26	32	33	35
$100,000 to $499,999.	926	1,162	1,356	1,393	1,444	224	291	342	350	364
$500,000 to $999,999.	280	416	489	513	521	197	294	346	361	368
$1,000,000 or more	418	649	766	803	841	5,717	10,289	12,126	13,210	14,107
Partnerships.	1,380	1,554	1,494	1,581	1,654	286	541	732	854	1,042
Under $25,000 [2]	638	963	899	931	956	5	4	4	4	4
$25,000 to $49,999	182	126	121	133	141	7	5	4	5	5
$50,000 to $99,999	184	133	131	142	146	13	10	9	10	10
$100,000 to $499,999.	290	222	228	245	268	64	51	52	56	61
$500,000 to $999,999.	48	52	54	59	64	33	36	37	42	45
$1,000,000 or more	37	57	62	69	80	164	435	625	738	917
Nonfarm proprietorships [3]	9,730	14,783	16,154	16,424	16,956	411	731	791	807	844
Under $25,000 [2]	6,916	10,196	11,163	11,317	11,577	44	69	75	76	78
$25,000 to $49,999	1,079	1,660	1,868	1,983	2,091	39	58	67	71	74
$50,000 to $99,999	836	1,282	1,409	1,393	1,473	59	91	101	99	105
$100,000 to $499,999.	796	1,444	1,503	1,514	1,579	159	296	308	310	319
$500,000 to $999,999.	74	143	141	147	165	50	97	95	100	110
$1,000,000 or more	29	57	71	70	71	60	119	145	151	158

[1] Excludes investment income except for partnerships and corporations in finance, insurance, and real estate. Starting 1990, investment income no longer included for S corporations. S corporations are certain small companies with 35 shareholders (15 in 1980), mostly individuals, electing to be taxed through shareholders.   [2] Includes firms with no receipts.   [3] Number of businesses for 1980. Number of nonfarm sole proprietorship returns is not available by size prior to 1981. However, the number of returns and the number of businesses are very closely related. The ratio of number of returns to the number of businesses is approximately 1 to 1.3.

Source: U.S. Internal Revenue Service, *Statistics of Income; Statistics of Income Bulletin;* and unpublished data.

No. 862. Number of Returns, Receipts, and Net Income, by Type of Business and Industry: 1980 to 1996

[**8,932 represents 8,932,000.** See headnote, Table 861. Minus sign (-) indicates net loss]

Item	Number of returns (1,000)			Business receipts [2] (bil. dol.)			Net income (less loss) [3] (bil. dol.)		
	Nonfarm proprietorships [1]	Partnerships	Corporations	Nonfarm proprietorships [1]	Partnerships	Corporations	Nonfarm proprietorships [1]	Partnerships	Corporations
1980.	8,932	1,380	2,711	411	286	6,172	55	8	239
1985.	11,929	1,714	3,277	540	349	8,050	79	-9	240
1988.	13,679	1,654	3,563	672	516	9,804	126	15	413
1989.	14,298	1,635	3,628	693	524	10,440	133	14	389
1990.	14,783	1,554	3,717	731	541	10,914	141	17	371
1991 [4].	15,181	1,515	3,803	713	539	10,963	142	21	345
1992.	15,495	1,485	3,869	737	571	11,272	154	43	402
1993.	15,848	1,468	3,965	757	627	11,814	156	67	498
1994.	16,154	1,493	4,342	791	731	12,858	167	83	577
1995 [4].	16,424	1,581	4,474	807	854	13,969	169.0	107	714
1996 [4].	16,955	1,654	4,631	843	1,042	14,890	177	145	806
Agriculture, forestry, fishing [5]. . .	552	131	159	20	15	112	3	1	3
Mining.	108	25	36	6	24	128	(Z)	5	8
Construction.	2,097	74	471	127	45	700	22	3	18
Manufacturing.	507	34	326	32	150	4,567	4	10	286
Transportation, public utilities. . .	825	30	206	42	101	1,184	6	7	75
Wholesale and retail trade [6] . . .	3,151	168	1,142	261	212	4,383	17	5	73
Wholesale	351	23	364	41	84	2,074	5	3	33
Retail.	2,800	145	775	220	128	2,303	11	3	40
Finance, insurance, real estate .	1,271	892	723	65	247	2,407	22	70	299
Services	8,234	297	1,557	287	249	1,409	102	44	44

Z Less than $500 million.   [1] In 1980, represents individually owned businesses, including farms; thereafter, represents only nonfarm proprietors, i.e., business owners.   [2] Excludes investment income except for partnerships and corporations in finance, insurance, and real estate. Starting 1985, investment income no longer included for S corporations.   [3] Net income (less loss) is defined differently by form of organization, basically as follows: (a) Proprietorships: Total taxable receipts less total business deductions, including cost of sales and operations, depletion, and certain capital expensing, excluding charitable contributions and owners' salaries; (b) Partnerships: Total taxable receipts (including investment income except capital gains) less deductions, including cost of sales and operations and certain payments to partners, excluding charitable contributions, oil and gas depletion, and certain capital expensing; (c) Corporations: Total taxable receipts (including investment income, capital gains, and income from foreign subsidiaries deemed received for tax purposes, except for S corporations beginning 1985) less business deductions, including cost of sales and operations, depletion, certain capital expensing, and officers' compensation excluding S corporation charitable contributions and investment expenses starting 1985; net income is before income tax.   [4] Includes businesses not allocable to individual industries.   [5] Represents agricultural services only.   [6] Includes trade business not identified as wholesale or retail.

Source: U.S. Internal Revenue Service, *Statistics of Income,* various publications.

No. 863. Number of Returns and Business Receipts, by Industry, Type of Business, and Size of Business Receipts: 1996

[Number of returns in thousands (16,955 represents 16,955,000); receipts and net income in billions of dollars (843 represents $843,000,000,000). Covers active enterprises only. Figures are estimates based on a sample of unaudited tax returns; see Appendix III. The industrial distribution is based on data collected from establishments; see text, this section]

Industry	Nonfarm proprietorships	Partnerships	Corporations				
			Under $1 mil.[1]	$1 mil.-$4.9 mil.	$5 mil.-$9.9 mil.	$10 mil.-$49.9 mil.	$50 mil. or more
Total:[2] Number	16,955	1,654	3,791	626	101	91	22
Business receipts[3]	843	1,042	783	1,326	705	1,856	10,220
Net income (less loss)	177	145	4	31	20	75	676
Agriculture, forestry, fishing: Number	552	131	143	13	2	1	(Z)
Business receipts[3]	20	15	24	27	12	20	29
Mining: Number	108	25	31	3	1	1	(Z)
Business receipts[3]	6	24	5	7	5	14	97
Construction: Number	2,097	74	359	90	12	9	1
Business receipts[3]	127	45	97	191	84	173	155
Manufacturing: Number	507	34	206	77	18	19	6
Business receipts[3]	32	150	50	174	126	387	3,830
Transportation, public utilities: Number	825	30	162	33	6	3	1
Business receipts[3]	42	101	31	71	40	66	977
Wholesale and retail trade: Number	3,151	168	826	229	39	41	8
Business receipts[3]	261	212	225	489	269	849	2,551
Finance, insurance, real estate: Number	1,271	892	668	38	7	8	3
Business receipts[3]	65	247	74	84	52	159	2,038
Services: Number	8,234	297	1,386	143	17	10	2
Business receipts[3]	287	249	276	284	118	187	544

Z Less than 500 returns. [1] Includes businesses without receipts. [2] Includes businesses not allocable to individual industries. [3] Excludes investment income except for partnerships and corporations (other than S corporations) in finance, insurance, and real estate.

Source: U.S. Internal Revenue Service, *Statistics of Income,* various publications; and unpublished data.

No. 864. Sole Proprietorships—Selected Income and Deduction Items: 1980 to 1996

[In millions of dollars (21,996 represents $21,996,000,000) except as indicated. Covers nonfarm sole proprietorships. All figures are estimates based on sample. Tax law changes have affected the comparability of the data over time; see *Statistics of Income* reports for a description]

Item	1980	1985	1990	1991	1992	1993	1994	1995	1996
Number of returns (1,000)	8,932	11,929	14,783	15,181	15,495	15,848	16,154	16,424	16,955
Businesses with net income (1,000)	(NA)	8,641	11,222	11,551	11,720	11,872	12,187	12,213	12,524
Inventory, end of year	21,996	24,970	30,422	29,783	29,898	31,795	33,602	33,356	33,785
Business receipts	411,206	540,045	730,606	712,568	737,082	757,215	790,630	807,364	843,234
Income from sales and operations	407,169	528,675	719,008	700,681	725,666	746,306	778,494	796,597	831,546
Business deductions[1]	356,258	461,273	589,250	571,154	583,147	600,765	623,833	638,127	666,461
Cost of goods sold/operations[1]	209,890	232,294	291,010	272,627	274,220	289,578	301,004	306,959	316,421
Purchases	168,302	(NA)	210,225	200,861	204,317	210,260	216,365	219,305	220,029
Labor costs	10,922	14,504	22,680	21,918	18,838	20,685	23,497	24,383	26,002
Materials and supplies	12,909	(NA)	30,195	28,072	28,825	32,701	34,304	34,427	40,473
Commissions	3,333	(NA)	8,816	7,628	10,457	8,707	9,029	9,592	10,792
Salaries and wages (net)	26,561	38,266	46,998	48,890	52,316	52,046	53,649	54,471	56,322
Car and truck expenses	13,378	17,044	21,766	22,594	23,920	26,714	30,845	32,785	36,700
Rent paid	9,636	15,259	23,392	23,643	25,148	25,008	26,769	27,503	28,516
Repairs	5,032	(NA)	8,941	9,159	9,706	9,847	10,385	10,172	10,715
Taxes paid	7,672	(NA)	10,342	10,629	12,618	13,062	13,600	13,471	13,736
Utilities	4,790	(NA)	13,539	13,260	14,547	16,069	16,918	17,206	18,162
Insurance	6,003	(NA)	13,358	13,065	13,260	13,173	13,289	12,978	13,195
Interest paid	7,190	11,914	13,312	12,077	10,406	9,431	9,170	10,057	10,567
Depreciation	13,953	26,291	23,735	23,076	23,274	24,964	26,158	26,738	27,883
Pension and profit sharing plans	141	311	586	519	528	636	605	649	707
Net income (less loss)	54,947	78,773	141,430	141,516	153,960	156,459	166,799	169,262	176,756
Businesses with net income	68,010	98,776	161,657	162,427	173,473	176,983	187,845	191,729	200,124

NA Not available. [1] Includes other amounts not shown separately.

Source: U.S. Internal Revenue Service, *Statistics of Income Bulletin.*

No. 865. Partnerships—Selected Items, by Industry: 1980 to 1996

[In millions of dollars, (597,504 represents $597,504,000,000) except number of partners and partnerships in thousands. Covers active partnerships only. Includes partnerships not allocable by industry. Figures are estimates based on samples. See Appendix III]

Year	Number of partnerships (1,000)			Number of partners	Total assets [1]	Business receipts [2,3]	Total deductions [3]	Net income less loss [3]	Net income [3]	Net loss [3]
	Total	With net income	With net loss							
All industries:										
1980	1,380	774	605	8,420	597,504	285,967	283,749	8,249	45,062	36,813
1985	1,714	876	838	13,245	1,269,434	349,169	376,001	-8,884	77,045	85,928
1990	1,554	854	700	17,095	1,735,285	540,647	549,603	16,610	116,318	99,708
1993	1,468	870	598	15,627	2,118,268	626,515	589,358	66,652	137,441	70,788
1994	1,494	890	604	14,990	2,295,212	731,834	680,052	82,183	150,928	68,745
1995	1,581	955	626	15,606	2,718,648	853,831	783,603	106,829	178,651	71,822
1996	1,654	1,010	644	15,662	3,368,166	1,042,136	943,352	145,218	228,158	82,939
Agriculture, forestry, fishing:										
1980	126	72	54	381	24,595	21,611	22,859	472	2,539	2,067
1985	136	76	60	585	27,027	6,529	10,495	-1,049	2,797	3,846
1990	125	77	48	503	27,580	9,497	11,805	1,667	3,905	2,238
1993	120	76	44	588	38,947	10,343	12,517	2,019	3,989	1,970
1994	123	72	51	575	41,517	11,324	13,682	1,608	3,985	2,377
1995	129	75	54	603	43,481	13,270	16,207	1,330	4,183	2,853
1996	131	80	51	594	46,605	14,716	17,835	1,357	4,394	3,036
Mining:										
1980	35	15	20	722	24,742	13,201	18,248	-4,208	3,920	8,128
1985	62	33	30	2,207	66,930	19,922	21,920	1,482	7,884	6,402
1990	41	29	14	2,149	58,246	19,967	20,869	2,183	7,009	4,825
1993	32	21	11	1,431	51,367	17,364	18,073	2,148	6,070	3,922
1994	27	17	10	1,010	45,532	15,902	17,323	984	5,076	4,092
1995	26	15	11	828	55,503	17,813	19,004	1,111	5,272	4,161
1996	25	16	9	746	68,122	23,545	21,846	4,865	8,737	3,872
Construction:										
1980	67	51	16	160	9,811	18,407	17,202	1,560	2,119	559
1985	57	41	16	134	15,008	21,476	20,080	2,207	2,743	536
1990	59	45	15	162	17,989	30,716	29,672	1,908	3,020	1,112
1993	62	45	17	154	13,917	26,863	25,279	2,176	2,884	708
1994	66	48	18	159	15,171	31,140	29,065	2,654	3,127	474
1995	71	48	22	167	16,653	35,881	33,936	2,527	3,338	810
1996	74	51	23	179	20,592	45,117	43,055	3,114	4,036	922
Transportation, public utilities:										
1980	20	11	10	73	9,291	5,868	5,821	248	1,092	844
1985	25	15	10	186	26,468	11,253	14,814	-3,066	1,360	4,426
1990	25	14	11	503	63,334	32,800	35,989	-117	5,887	6,004
1993	21	11	10	652	115,596	58,852	58,198	4,119	9,319	5,200
1994	23	12	11	635	126,351	66,407	64,863	5,627	11,118	5,491
1995	26	14	12	656	158,869	76,796	75,538	6,750	13,209	6,459
1996	30	16	13	647	200,208	101,127	101,891	7,051	18,121	11,070
Manufacturing:										
1980	30	20	10	92	11,252	15,327	16,142	-472	1,199	1,671
1985	30	12	18	105	24,838	22,588	24,225	-1,085	1,228	2,314
1990	28	15	13	246	59,789	65,354	65,833	1,166	4,791	3,626
1993	25	16	9	231	84,184	89,861	88,889	3,940	7,482	3,542
1994	30	18	12	224	93,494	107,569	104,551	6,584	9,853	3,268
1995	30	19	12	223	108,926	124,007	120,741	9,221	13,034	3,812
1996	34	19	15	233	127,699	149,775	146,680	9,696	14,088	4,392
Wholesale and retail trade:										
1980	200	123	77	487	17,727	65,793	63,988	2,475	3,374	900
1985	201	113	88	493	20,568	69,079	68,119	1,977	3,467	1,490
1990	176	100	77	481	28,423	98,120	97,131	2,610	4,717	2,107
1993	157	88	69	471	35,278	110,890	109,854	3,076	5,304	2,229
1994	153	87	66	443	44,367	142,116	140,295	4,301	6,344	2,043
1995	164	93	71	501	59,436	171,905	170,756	3,996	7,171	3,175
1996	168	91	72	534	80,882	212,077	210,482	5,464	9,330	3,866
Finance, insurance, and real estate:										
1980	637	313	325	5,566	454,531	87,133	91,382	-4,249	15,169	19,418
1985	844	369	475	7,755	979,787	92,309	118,237	-25,929	30,383	56,311
1990	822	401	422	10,846	1,329,452	64,313	87,011	-19,213	47,577	66,790
1993	793	443	350	9,944	1,612,142	127,908	113,480	15,260	59,062	43,802
1994	810	465	345	9,881	1,750,671	161,365	137,240	24,125	65,369	41,245
1995	849	505	344	10,317	2,074,641	196,234	151,712	44,522	82,871	38,349
1996	892	548	344	10,262	2,587,697	246,681	176,958	69,724	112,749	43,025
Services:										
1980	263	169	94	938	45,510	58,627	48,106	12,424	15,649	3,224
1985	341	207	134	1,713	106,597	104,197	96,202	16,541	26,942	10,400
1990	267	173	96	2,153	150,063	161,702	145,789	26,453	39,383	12,930
1993	256	169	87	2,146	166,806	184,434	162,846	33,887	43,300	9,413
1994	261	170	91	2,060	177,992	195,933	172,926	36,318	46,048	9,730
1995	282	186	96	2,297	200,562	217,684	195,402	37,394	49,561	12,168
1996	297	187	110	2,455	235,679	248,883	224,417	43,883	56,614	12,731

[1] Total assets are understated because not all partnerships file complete balance sheets. [2] Includes investment income for partnerships in finance, insurance, and real estate. [3] Beginning 1985, only net (not gross) income from farming, rents, and royalties are included.

Source: U.S. Internal Revenue Service, *Statistics of Income Bulletin,* and *Partnership Returns—1978-1996. Partnership Returns—1978-1994,* and *Statistics of Income Bulletin.*

No. 866. Partnerships—Selected Income and Balance Sheet Items: 1980 to 1996

[In billions of dollars (598 represents $598,000,000,000), except as indicated. Covers active partnerships only. All figures are estimates based on samples. See Appendix III]

Item	1980	1985	1990	1991	1992	1993	1994	1995	1996
Number of returns (1,000)	1,380	1,714	1,554	1,515	1,485	1,468	1,494	1,581	1,654
Number with net income (1,000)	774	876	854	856	856	870	890	955	1,010
Number of partners (1,000)	8,420	13,245	17,095	15,801	15,735	15,627	14,990	15,606	15,662
Assets [1][2]	598	1,269	1,735	1,817	1,907	2,118	2,295	2,719	3,368
Depreciable assets (net)	239	696	681	696	701	698	712	767	848
Inventories, end of year	33	27	57	57	62	71	76	88	137
Land	70	152	215	213	213	207	208	221	232
Liabilities [1][2]	489	1,069	1,415	1,460	1,508	1,620	1,662	1,886	2,235
Accounts payable	34	41	67	63	79	80	81	91	121
Short-term debt [3]	48	103	88	117	115	131	126	124	126
Long-term debt [4]	178	382	498	491	486	489	508	544	607
Nonrecourse loans	119	328	470	474	476	478	463	466	474
Partners' capital accounts [2]	109	200	320	357	399	499	633	832	1,133
Receipts [1]	292	367	566	563	597	656	762	890	1,089
Business receipts	271	303	483	483	515	561	732	854	1,042
Interest received	11	21	21	20	16	16	19	31	33
Deductions [1]	284	376	550	541	554	589	680	784	943
Cost of goods sold/operations	114	146	243	237	249	273	335	395	486
Salaries and wages	22	34	56	58	62	65	70	80	94
Taxes paid	10	8	9	10	10	11	12	13	15
Interest paid	28	29	30	28	25	27	36	43	49
Depreciation	22	54	60	58	60	60	22	23	29
Net income (less loss)	8	-9	17	21	43	67	82	107	145
Net income	45	77	116	113	122	137	151	179	228

[1] Includes items not shown separately. [2] Assets, liabilities, and partners' capital accounts are understated because not all partnerships file complete balance sheets. [3] Mortgages, notes, and bonds payable in less than 1 year. [4] Mortgages, notes, and bonds payable in 1 year or more.

Source: U.S. Internal Revenue Service, *Statistics of Income*, various issues.

No. 867. Corporate Funds—Sources and Uses: 1980 to 1998

[In billions of dollars (421.8 represents $421,800,000,000), except percent. Covers nonfarm nonfinancial corporate business. See text this section]

Item	1980	1985	1990	1992	1993	1994	1995	1996	1997	1998
Sources	421.8	737.9	592.6	600.0	698.1	758.9	882.0	953.8	987.2	1,079.6
Internal	199.9	358.2	409.1	438.6	480.2	524.3	524.4	588.4	624.8	692.2
U.S. undistributed profits	69.4	26.0	23.6	33.7	48.2	81.4	86.9	92.7	(NA)	78.8
IVA and CCA [1]	-74.5	46.8	-8.9	-9.1	-7.5	-8.7	-19.0	7.4	(NA)	110.5
Capital consumption allowances	186.3	264.0	349.5	372.6	386.1	418.3	430.7	461.3	489.5	432.4
Foreign earnings [2]	18.7	21.4	44.8	41.5	53.4	41.6	59.3	62.0	60.6	70.5
External [3]	221.9	379.7	183.5	161.3	217.9	241.6	403.3	385.5	362.4	387.4
Credit market funds	78.7	83.9	47.0	60.9	68.9	(NA)	(NA)	(NA)	(NA)	64.6
Securities and mortgages	35.9	11.5	-26.6	66.8	85.3	(NA)	(NA)	(NA)	(NA)	-90.5
Equity issues	10.4	-84.5	-63.0	27.0	21.3	(NA)	(NA)	(NA)	(NA)	-267.0
Bonds and mortgages [4]	25.5	96.0	36.4	39.8	64.0	(NA)	(NA)	(NA)	(NA)	176.5
Loans and short-term paper	42.8	72.4	73.6	-5.9	-16.4	(NA)	(NA)	(NA)	(NA)	155.1
Profit taxes payable	2.9	-3.2	-5.0	7.2	2.0	(NA)	(NA)	(NA)	(NA)	5.2
Trade debt	29.1	43.0	28.4	33.4	36.4	(NA)	(NA)	(NA)	(NA)	-18.0
Foreign direct invest'mt in U.S	13.2	256.0	55.9	59.8	42.9	42.9	50.7	59.7	81.8	164.7
Miscellaneous liabilities	111.1	256.0	113.1	59.8	110.6	75.4	171.1	243.3	135.3	170.9
Uses	419.7	643.7	509.7	554.4	787.9	(NA)	(NA)	(NA)	(NA)	1,075.3
Capital expenditures	250.7	369.6	394.5	386.9	430.6	511.1	567.7	592.5	675.7	707.4
Increase in financial assets	168.9	274.1	115.3	167.5	357.3	(NA)	(NA)	(NA)	(NA)	367.9
Discrepancy (sources less uses)	2.1	94.2	82.9	45.6	-899.8	(NA)	(NA)	(NA)	(NA)	4.3

NA Not available   [1] Inventory valuation and capital consumption adjustment.   [2] Foreign earnings of subsidiaries retained abroad.   [3] Net increases in liability.   [4] Includes industrial pollution control revenue bonds issued by state and local governments.

Source: Board of Governors of the Federal Reserve System. Data derived from *Flow of Funds Accounts*, annual.

No. 868. Nonfinancial Corporate Business-Sector Balance Sheet: 1987 to 1996

[In billions of dollars (8,343 represents $8,343,000,000,000). Represents year-end outstandings]

Item	1987	1988	1989	1990	1991	1992	1993	1994	1995	1996
Assets	8,343	9,074	9,621	9,817	9,800	9,788	10,120	10,753	11,488	12,281
Tangible assets (current cost)	5,440	5,788	6,102	6,183	6,036	5,856	5,831	6,185	6,513	6,876
Real estate[1]	3,083	3,289	3,472	3,429	3,247	3,007	2,874	3,051	3,187	3,383
Equipment[2]	1,568	1,653	1,736	1,828	1,876	1,925	1,994	2,092	2,223	2,361
Inventories[2]	789	847	894	925	913	924	963	1,042	1,103	1,132
Financial assets[3]	2,903	3,286	3,520	3,634	3,764	3,932	4,289	4,567	4,976	5,405
Checkable deposits and currency	105	135	151	167	183	189	203	222	239	286
Time and savings deposits	117	99	90	73	67	52	74	68	66	69
Trade receivables	805	896	938	967	961	989	1,035	1,107	1,206	1,269
Liabilities	3,774	4,192	4,533	4,729	4,830	5,110	5,389	5,627	6,022	6,379
Credit market instruments[3]	1,984	2,188	2,381	2,492	2,432	2,470	2,528	2,667	2,876	3,053
Municipal securities[4]	116	116	116	115	114	114	114	109	96	79
Corporate bonds[5]	784	887	961	1,008	1,087	1,155	1,230	1,253	1,326	1,399
Mortgages	202	208	235	233	215	193	201	223	259	313
Net worth (market value)	4,569	4,882	5,088	5,088	4,970	4,678	4,732	5,125	5,466	5,902

[1] At market value. [2] At replacement (current) cost. [3] Includes items not shown separately. [4] Industrial revenue bonds. Issued by state and local governments to finance private investment and secured in interest and principal by the industrial user of the funds. [5] Through 1992, corporate bonds include net issues by Netherlands Antillean financial subsidiaries, and U.S. direct investment abroad excludes net inflows from those bond issues.

Source: Board of Governors of the Federal Reserve System, *Balance Sheets for the U.S. Economy.*

No. 869. Corporations—Selected Financial Items: 1980 to 1996

[In billions of dollars (7,617 represents $7,617,000,000,000), except as noted. Covers active corporations only. All corporations are required to file returns except those specifically exempt. See source for changes in law affecting comparability of historical data. Based on samples; see Appendix III]

Item	1980	1985	1990	1991	1992	1993	1994	1995	1996
Number of returns (1,000)	2,711	3,277	3,717	3,803	3,869	3,965	4,342	4,474	4,631
Number with net income (1,000)	1,597	1,820	1,911	1,942	2,064	2,145	2,392	2,455	2,588
S Corporation returns[1] (1,000)	545	725	1,575	1,698	1,785	1,902	2,024	2,153	2,304
Assets[2]	7,617	12,773	18,190	19,030	20,002	21,816	23,446	26,014	28,642
Cash	529	683	771	787	806	812	853	962	1,097
Notes and accounts receivable	1,985	3,318	4,198	4,191	4,169	4,532	4,768	5,307	5,783
Inventories	535	715	894	884	915	947	1,126	1,045	1,079
Investments in Govt. obligations	266	917	921	1,069	1,248	1,290	1,309	1,363	1,339
Mortgage and real estate	894	1,259	1,538	1,529	1,567	1,627	1,661	1,713	1,825
Other investments	1,214	2,414	4,137	4,750	4,971	5,701	6,265	7,429	8,657
Depreciable assets	2,107	3,174	4,318	4,549	4,755	4,969	5,284	5,571	5,923
Depletable assets	72	112	129	142	131	137	148	154	169
Land	93	141	210	215	221	230	239	242	254
Liabilities[2]	7,617	12,773	18,190	19,030	20,002	21,816	23,446	26,014	28,642
Accounts payable	542	892	1,094	1,681	1,605	1,466	1,606	1,750	1,905
Short-term debt[3]	505	1,001	1,803	1,500	1,560	1,569	1,831	2,034	2,328
Long-term debt[4]	987	1,699	2,665	2,698	2,742	2,871	3,100	3,335	3,651
Capital stock	417	920	1,585	1,741	1,881	2,042	2,132	2,194	2,278
Paid-in or capital surplus	532	1,421	2,814	3,257	3,656	4,223	4,790	5,446	6,427
Retained earnings[5]	1,070	1,366	1,410	1,441	1,431	1,662	1,698	2,191	2,519
Net worth	1,944	3,304	4,739	5,277	5,700	(NA)	7,031	8,132	9,495
Receipts[3][6]	6,361	8,398	11,410	11,436	11,742	12,270	13,360	14,539	15,526
Business receipts[6][7]	5,732	7,370	9,860	9,966	10,360	10,866	11,884	12,786	13,659
Interest[8]	367	635	977	920	829	808	882	1,039	1,082
Rents and royalties	54	105	133	137	140	130	132	145	156
Deductions[3][6]	6,125	8,158	11,033	11,087	11,330	11,765	12,775	13,821	14,728
Cost of sales and operations[7]	4,205	4,894	6,611	6,654	6,772	7,052	7,625	8,206	8,707
Compensation of officers	109	171	205	201	221	226	282	304	319
Rent paid on business property	72	135	185	193	196	201	223	232	248
Taxes paid	163	201	251	258	274	290	322	326	341
Interest paid	345	569	825	733	597	546	611	744	771
Depreciation	157	304	333	334	346	364	403	437	474
Advertising	52	92	126	129	134	140	157	163	177
Net income (less loss)[6][9]	239	240	371	345	402	498	577	714	806
Net income	297	364	553	536	570	659	740	881	987
Deficit	58	124	182	191	168	161	162	166	180
Income subject to tax	247	266	366	350	378	437	494	565	640
Income tax before credits[10]	104	109	119	116	126	149	168	194	224
Tax credits[3]	42	48	32	29	30	35	37	42	53
Foreign tax credit	25	24	25	21	22	23	25	30	40
Income tax after credits[11]	62	61	96	93	102	(NA)	136	156	171

NA Not available. [1] Represents certain small corporations with up to 35 shareholders (15 in 1980), mostly individuals, electing to be taxed at the shareholder level. [2] Includes items not shown separately. [3] Payable in less than 1 year. [4] Payable in 1 year or more. [5] Appropriated and unappropriated. [6] Except for 1980, receipts, deductions and net income of S corporations are limited to those from trade or business. Those from investments are excluded. [7] Beginning 1988, includes gross sales and cost of sales of securities, commodities, and real estate by exchanges, brokers, or dealers selling on their own accounts. Previously, net gain included in total receipts only. Excludes investment income. [8] Includes tax-exempt interest in state and local government obligations. [9] Excludes regulated investment companies. [10] Consists of regular (and alternative tax) only. [11] Includes minimum tax, alternative minimum tax, adjustments for prior year credits, and other income-related taxes.

Source: U.S. Internal Revenue Service, *Statistics of Income, Corporation Income Tax Returns,* annual.

U.S. Census Bureau, Statistical Abstract of the United States: 1999

No. 870. Corporations—Selected Financial Items, by Industry: 1980 to 1996

[In billions of dollars ($40.7 represents $40,700,000,000), except as indicated. Covers active corporations only. Industrial distribution based on data collected from companies; see text, this section. Excludes corporations not allocable by industry]

Industry	1980	1985	1990	1992	1993	1994	1995	1996
Agriculture, forestry, and fishing:								
Returns (1,000)	81	103	126	138	141	147	148	159
Assets	40.7	52.7	68.3	71.8	74.6	79.9	86.3	94.1
Liabilities [1]	29.3	37.2	45.0	46.7	46.9	50.6	56.2	61.4
Receipts [2]	52.1	70.5	88.1	95.6	98.3	100.9	107.6	119.7
Deductions [2]	51.4	70.6	86.9	94.0	96.7	99.6	106.0	117.2
Net income (less loss) [2]	0.7	-0.1	1.2	1.6	1.6	1.3	1.6	2.6
Mining:								
Returns (1,000)	26	41	40	37	35	35	35	36
Assets	126.9	240.8	219.2	218.2	224.0	239.7	268.7	299.1
Liabilities [1]	72.9	136.0	108.9	112.1	112.6	121.1	136.6	147.4
Receipts [2]	176.7	142.0	111.4	112.8	112.1	115.7	126.8	141.3
Deductions [2]	169.1	145.4	106.5	110.3	109.6	112.3	121.4	133.4
Net income (less loss) [2]	7.8	-2.5	5.3	2.7	2.6	3.6	5.5	8.2
Construction:								
Returns (1,000)	272	318	407	408	417	433	450	471
Assets	132.9	215.3	243.8	231.1	240.4	249.1	265.8	284.6
Liabilities [1]	100.1	160.6	180.0	159.5	164.6	170.9	179.3	192.2
Receipts [2]	267.2	387.2	534.7	499.4	538.3	592.8	637.1	710.5
Deductions [2]	262.1	382.8	527.8	493.9	530.7	581.2	622.6	692.6
Net income (less loss) [2]	5.3	4.4	6.8	5.5	7.5	11.6	14.5	17.9
Manufacturing:								
Returns (1,000)	243	277	302	300	307	312	320	326
Assets	1,709.5	2,644.4	3,921.3	4,113.1	4,225.1	4,525.5	4,941.1	5,425.2
Liabilities [1]	960.3	1,544.7	2,529.1	2,701.2	2,784.4	2,936.6	3,201.5	3,458.3
Receipts [2]	2,404.3	2,831.1	3,688.7	3,760.3	3,890.7	4,218.8	4,585.5	4,902.7
Deductions [2]	2,290.6	2,733.1	3,545.1	3,633.8	3,741.6	4,024.3	4,354.6	4,653.0
Net income (less loss) [2]	125.7	113.8	171.4	143.6	173.2	219.1	260.9	286.1
Transportation and public utilities:								
Returns (1,000)	111	138	160	178	176	187	194	206
Assets	758.4	1,246.4	1,522.0	1,642.0	1,770.7	1,826.3	1,903.2	2,069.5
Liabilities [1]	467.7	755.9	1,013.4	1,106.3	1,190.9	1,207.2	1,270.1	1,355.3
Receipts [2]	523.8	772.4	936.3	997.6	1,037.2	1,103.2	1,156.7	1,257.0
Deductions [2]	504.0	747.8	901.0	956.5	984.9	1,036.1	1,084.7	1,182.4
Net income (less loss) [2]	20.0	25.1	35.4	41.8	52.9	68.3	72.9	75.4
Wholesale and retail trade:								
Returns (1,000)	800	917	1,023	1,053	1,073	1,106	1,132	1,142
Assets	646.9	1,010.0	1,447.3	1,581.9	1,702.8	1,795.2	1,919.7	2,016.2
Liabilities [1]	424.6	723.7	1,092.5	1,177.7	1,254.2	1,303.1	1,385.8	1,447.6
Receipts [2]	1,955.5	2,473.9	3,309.0	3,503.9	3,709.5	4,052.2	4,310.3	4,490.1
Deductions [2]	1,919.5	2,440.4	3,279.1	3,463.4	3,659.8	3,984.0	4,247.6	4,418.3
Net income (less loss) [2]	38.3	33.1	30.1	41.3	49.7	68.5	63.6	73.4
Finance, insurance, and real estate:								
Returns (1,000)	493	518	609	635	641	682	683	724
Assets	4,022.2	7,029.5	10,193.3	11,480.5	12,831.7	13,895.3	15,677.3	17,360.1
Liabilities [1]	3,491.7	5,867.5	8,051.3	8,531.3	9,288.5	10,053.1	11,008.7	11,754.8
Receipts [2 3]	697.5	1,182.0	1,954.7	1,900.4	1,940.3	1,976.5	2,278.1	2,406.9
Deductions [2]	652.6	1,104.6	1,809.9	1,724.3	1,723.3	1,773.1	1,985.8	2,076.6
Net income (less loss) [2]	33.1	60.7	109.9	147.0	185.2	169.3	256.8	299.1
Services:								
Returns (1,000)	671	939	1,029	1,100	1,158	1,424	1,504	1,557
Assets	178.2	331.0	572.8	661.6	744.8	833.9	950.7	1,092.3
Liabilities [1]	125.3	241.1	429.7	465.0	508.6	570.3	643.1	729.2
Receipts [2]	279.9	534.6	779.3	869.5	941.6	1,198.0	1,335.7	1,496.2
Deductions [2]	271.8	528.7	769.0	851.1	916.5	1,162.5	1,297.5	1,453.2
Net income (less loss) [2]	8.2	5.9	10.6	18.5	25.4	35.6	38.4	44.0
ANNUAL PERCENT CHANGE RECEIPTS [4]								
Agriculture, forestry, and fishing	-2.4	5.9	1.7	11.3	2.8	2.6	6.6	11.2
Mining	33.3	15.0	8.8	9.2	-0.6	3.1	9.6	11.4
Construction	5.7	14.4	3.3	-3.0	7.8	10.1	7.5	11.5
Manufacturing	11.7	2.3	4.5	2.8	3.5	8.4	8.7	6.9
Transportation and public utilities	17.5	6.4	3.3	4.5	4.0	6.3	4.8	8.6
Wholesale and retail trade	11.6	7.2	3.9	3.6	5.9	9.2	6.4	4.1
Finance, insurance, and real estate	24.3	14.4	4.6	-1.2	2.1	1.8	15.3	5.6
Services	14.2	9.0	6.0	7.4	8.3	27.2	11.5	12.0

[1] Liabilities does not include net worth.   [2] Beginning 1989, receipts, deductions, and net income of S corporations are limited to those from trade or business; those from investments are generally excluded. S corporations are certain small corporations with up to 35 shareholders (15 in 1980), mostly individuals, electing to be taxed at the shareholder level.   [3] Beginning 1989, includes gross sales (previously net sales) of securities, commodities, and real estate by exchanges, brokers, or dealers selling on their own account.   [4] Change from preceding year.

Source: U.S. Internal Revenue Service, *Statistics of Income, Corporation Income Tax Returns*, annual.

No. 871. Corporations, by Asset-Size Class and Industry: 1996

[In millions of dollars (94,140 represents $94,140,000,000), except number of returns and percent distribution. Covers active corporations only. Excludes corporations not allocable by industry. The industrial distribution is based on data collected from companies; see text, this section. Detail may not add to total because of rounding]

Industry	Total	Asset-size class					
		Under $10 mil. [1]	$10-$24.9 mil.	$25-$49.9 mil.	$50-$99.9 mil.	$100-$249.9 mil.	$250 mil. and over
Agriculture, forestry, and fishing:							
Returns	158,963	157,365	1,333	141	59	43	21
Assets	94,140	53,138	12,386	4,865	4,111	6,128	13,512
Receipts	119,737	74,699	17,380	5,701	5,116	8,052	8,788
Deductions	117,166	73,556	16,960	5,596	5,057	7,833	8,164
Net income (less loss)	2,614	1,120	414	98	60	217	704
Mining:							
Returns	35,799	33,993	1,231	210	119	106	138
Assets	299,106	11,573	12,912	7,310	8,315	17,168	241,827
Receipts	141,278	18,756	10,795	5,089	4,863	10,042	91,732
Deductions	133,386	17,957	10,091	4,976	4,630	9,491	86,240
Net income (less loss)	8,153	792	693	107	231	555	5,774
Construction:							
Returns	471,230	463,719	6,770	427	191	80	43
Assets	284,595	136,378	63,054	14,729	13,430	13,543	43,462
Receipts	710,467	431,501	140,576	32,711	25,619	26,317	53,744
Deductions	692,582	421,443	136,480	32,019	25,111	25,739	51,789
Net income (less loss)	17,878	10,023	4,042	675	495	575	2,068
Manufacturing:							
Returns	325,689	301,051	17,299	2,974	1,689	1,258	1,417
Assets	5,425,185	154,603	180,640	104,675	118,933	196,387	4,669,946
Receipts	4,902,669	442,629	345,813	168,076	174,466	248,815	3,522,870
Deductions	4,652,961	432,367	333,298	162,014	167,017	236,817	3,321,448
Net income (less loss)	286,060	10,311	12,467	6,064	7,508	12,162	237,547
Transportation and public utilities:							
Returns	205,777	200,753	3,469	520	317	264	453
Assets	2,069,453	55,539	36,100	18,000	22,729	41,286	1,895,800
Receipts	1,257,011	180,290	51,554	18,285	23,243	32,911	950,728
Deductions	1,182,369	178,922	50,597	18,104	22,778	31,359	880,610
Net income (less loss)	75,400	1,348	940	178	474	1,539	70,921
Wholesale and retail trade:							
Returns	1,142,491	1,114,130	23,769	2,275	1,006	725	586
Assets	2,016,232	375,511	233,321	78,803	70,766	112,163	1,145,669
Receipts	4,490,074	1,415,291	787,785	224,792	180,361	260,126	1,621,719
Deductions	4,418,321	1,400,311	777,215	221,108	177,230	255,809	1,586,648
Net income (less loss)	73,353	14,928	10,503	3,675	3,148	4,338	36,762
Finance, insurance, and real estate:							
Returns	723,754	688,951	15,675	4,896	4,412	4,669	5,151
Assets	17,360,053	233,118	174,022	175,949	316,366	738,486	15,722,111
Receipts [2]	2,406,855	231,274	50,027	31,948	41,039	88,582	1,963,985
Deductions	2,076,614	223,264	48,566	30,362	34,791	71,635	1,667,996
Net income (less loss)	299,149	7,520	1,127	1,020	4,847	13,316	271,319
Services:							
Returns	1,557,401	1,545,608	9,109	1,151	680	450	403
Assets	1,092,310	225,760	91,965	41,071	47,717	73,296	612,500
Receipts	1,496,216	793,464	137,643	47,748	50,683	66,167	400,511
Deductions	1,453,204	773,655	136,284	47,342	50,040	64,756	381,128
Net income (less loss)	43,952	19,734	1,336	368	627	1,414	20,473
PERCENT DISTRIBUTION RECEIPTS							
Agriculture, forestry, and fishing	100.0	62.4	14.5	4.8	4.3	6.7	7.3
Mining	100.0	13.3	7.6	3.6	3.4	7.1	64.9
Construction	100.0	60.7	19.8	4.6	3.6	3.7	7.6
Manufacturing	100.0	9.0	7.1	3.4	3.6	5.1	71.9
Transportation and public utilities	100.0	14.3	4.1	1.5	1.8	2.6	75.6
Wholesale and retail trade	100.0	31.5	17.5	5.0	4.0	5.8	36.1
Finance, insurance, and real estate [2]	100.0	9.6	2.1	1.3	1.7	3.9	81.6
Services	100.0	53.0	9.2	3.2	3.4	4.4	26.8

[1] Includes returns with zero assets. [2] Includes investment income.

Source: U.S. Internal Revenue Service, *Statistics of Income, Corporation Income Tax Returns,* annual.

No. 872. Advance Comparative Statistics for the United States (1987 Basis): 1992 and 1997

[162.1 represents 162,100,000,000. These data are preliminary and are subject to change; they will be superceded by data released in later reports. Includes only establishments with payroll. For meaning of abbreviations and symbols, see text this section]

Industry	1987 SIC code	Establishments (number)		Sales/receipts/revenues/shipments (bil. dol.)		Annual payroll (bil. dol.)		Paid employees (thousands)	
		1992	1997	1992	1997	1992	1997	1992	1997
MINERAL INDUSTRIES									
Total.		30,787	26,100	162.1	158.5	24.2	22.1	638.2	550.1
Metal mining	10	1,023	839	9.9	11.6	2.1	2.2	52.9	50.2
Coal mining.	12	3,069	1,929	27.1	23.3	5.5	4.3	134.5	95.6
Oil & gas extraction	13	20,891	17,781	111.5	106.8	13.4	12.0	344.9	304.7
Nonmetallic minerals, except fuels.	14	5,804	5,551	13.6	16.8	3.2	3.6	105.9	99.6
CONSTRUCTION INDUSTRIES									
Total		572,851	631,595	539.1	832.5	117.7	170.3	4,668.3	5,616.8
Building construction—general contractors & operative builders	15	168,407	182,315	220.2	362.4	27.1	39.2	1,096.9	1,266.2
Heavy construction other than buildings construction.	16	37,180	38,983	98.5	128.4	23.7	29.3	799.4	858.2
Construction—special trade contractors . . .	17	367,263	410,297	220.3	341.7	66.9	101.9	2,772.0	3,492.3
MANUFACTURES									
Total		370,912	377,673	3,004.7	3,964.8	494.1	596.2	16,948.9	17,634.0
Food & kindred products	20	20,798	20,913	407.0	480.3	36.8	43.1	1,502.7	1,567.2
Tobacco products	21	114	141	35.2	36.3	1.5	1.6	38.0	34.5
Textile mill products	22	5,886	6,134	70.8	82.8	12.4	13.6	616.4	557.8
Apparel & other textile products	23	23,093	23,345	71.7	81.0	15.3	15.5	985.3	840.5
Lumber & wood products	24	35,807	36,712	81.6	111.4	13.9	18.7	655.8	756.9
Furniture & fixtures	25	11,658	12,059	43.8	62.4	10.2	13.3	471.1	522.9
Paper & allied products	26	6,416	6,509	133.2	160.0	20.5	23.8	626.3	623.8
Printing & publishing	27	65,392	62,073	166.2	206.4	41.1	49.1	1,492.1	1,519.8
Chemicals & allied products	28	12,004	12,401	305.4	404.4	32.5	38.4	848.6	843.5
Petroleum & coal products	29	2,124	2,136	150.2	173.4	5.0	5.4	114.4	106.9
Rubber & miscellaneous plastics products .	30	15,842	16,648	113.6	159.1	23.2	30.0	906.7	1,031.2
Leather & leather products	31	2,040	1,846	9.7	9.9	1.8	1.8	101.1	84.0
Stone, clay, & glass products	32	16,254	16,413	62.5	88.3	13.1	16.5	468.8	509.7
Primary metal industries	33	6,501	6,559	138.3	192.9	22.2	26.9	662.1	692.9
Fabricated metal products	34	36,429	38,194	166.5	233.7	39.0	51.1	1,362.3	1,555.7
Industrial machinery & equipment	35	53,956	56,315	258.7	407.7	57.2	75.0	1,738.9	2,001.7
Electronic & other electric equipment	36	16,922	17,129	216.8	345.5	44.2	57.9	1,438.8	1,573.9
Transportation equipment	37	11,287	12,323	399.3	520.5	62.7	68.5	1,646.9	1,587.1
Instruments & related products	38	11,354	11,811	134.9	157.9	33.1	35.6	907.1	832.4
Miscellaneous mfg industries	39	17,035	18,012	39.5	50.8	8.4	10.5	365.5	391.7
TRANSPORTATION, COMMUNICATIONS, & UTILITIES									
Total		252,953	293,882	791.2	1,146.2	152.5	204.7	4,934.2	5,822.7
Passenger transportation	41	17,805	19,616	12.6	18.8	5.2	7.7	354.9	455.2
Motor freight transportation & warehousing .	42	110,908	133,360	143.8	197.6	39.9	55.8	1,580.1	1,963.5
Water transportation	44	8,147	9,245	29.2	36.3	5.2	6.3	171.3	180.3
Transportation by air.	45	9,363	11,364	33.0	48.6	7.4	10.4	272.6	360.0
Pipelines, except natural gas	46	844	984	7.1	8.3	-	0.1	16.8	14.9
Transportation services	47	46,593	52,117	23.9	41.6	7.9	12.7	329.2	433.8
Communications	48	39,244	44,890	230.7	370.3	47.1	68.7	1,294.2	1,570.2
Electric, gas, & sanitary services	49	20,049	22,306	311.0	424.7	39.2	42.2	915.0	844.8
WHOLESALE TRADE									
Total		495,457	518,215	3,238.5	4,212.3	173.3	234.4	5,791.3	6,507.0
Durable goods	50	313,464	335,300	1,593.9	2,293.8	105.2	147.5	3,349.1	3,879.5
Nondurable goods	51	181,993	182,915	1,644.6	1,918.5	68.1	86.9	2,442.2	2,627.5
Merchant wholesalers:									
Total		414,836	440,211	1,847.3	2,498.4	128.0	177.9	4,587.9	5,295.4
Durable goods	50	264,611	285,686	902.8	1,322.5	78.3	114.0	2,714.0	3,235.5
Nondurable goods	51	150,225	154,525	944.5	1,175.9	49.7	63.9	1,873.9	2,059.9
RETAIL TRADE									
Total		1,526,215	1,566,049	1,894.9	2,562.1	222.9	293.6	18,407.5	21,349.1
Building materials, hardware, garden supply, & mobile home dlr	52	69,483	69,028	98.8	153.8	11.8	17.5	665.7	854.5
General merchandise stores	53	34,606	35,444	245.3	328.6	24.5	30.6	2,078.5	2,494.9
Food stores	54	180,568	174,284	369.2	419.8	37.2	43.4	2,969.3	3,147.0
Automotive dealers & gasoline service stations.	55	201,707	200,807	529.9	785.3	39.4	55.7	1,942.6	2,290.8
Apparel & accessory stores	56	145,490	126,099	101.7	118.6	12.0	13.7	1,144.6	1,121.5
Home furniture, furnishings, & equipment stores.	57	110,073	115,207	93.2	138.0	11.9	16.4	702.2	868.3
FINANCIAL, INSURANCE, AND REAL ESTATE INDUSTRIES									
Total		585,580	(S)	1,831.5	-	211.6	-	6,509.6	-
Depository institutions	60	104,505	109,700	532.1	698.7	57.3	76.9	2,100.1	2,130.1
Nondepository credit institutions	61	39,439	52,116	135.4	212.4	15.5	24.3	445.6	588.9
Security & commodity brokers, dealers, exchanges, & services.	62	31,177	48,070	108.9	249.8	33.8	67.1	406.4	642.9
Insurance carriers.	63	38,977	40,728	796.0	988.3	50.5	65.7	1,516.6	1,586.6
Insurance agents, brokers, & services	64	121,662	131,330	51.7	74.3	18.9	25.8	635.5	720.4
Real estate	65	229,493	254,023	141.7	190.5	26.2	35.3	1,231.5	1,393.6

See footnotes at end of table.

U.S. Census Bureau, Statistical Abstract of the United States: 1999

No. 872. Advance Comparative Statistics for the United States (1987 Basis): 1992 and 1997—Continued

[These data are preliminary and are subject to change; they will be superceded by data released in later reports. Includes only establishments with payroll. For meaning of abbreviations and symbols, see text this section]

Industry	1987 SIC code	Establishments (number)		Sales/receipts/ revenues/ship- ments (mil. dol.)		Annual payroll (mil. dol.)		Paid employees (number)	
		1992	1997	1992	1997	1992	1997	1992	1997
SERVICE INDUSTRIES									
Total.		2,034,346	2,306,942	1,648.9	2,453.3	639.4	921.9	27,399.3	34,223.9
Hotels, rooming houses, camps, & other lodging places	70	51,817	(S)	70.0	-	19.8	-	1,506.7	(S)
Personal services.	72	197,101	204,636	43.3	53.3	14.4	17.9	1,217.6	1,311.4
Business services.	73	306,551	398,192	274.9	550.5	109.3	215.5	5,542.4	8,749.9
Automotive repair, services, & parking	75	171,970	192,252	70.0	101.0	15.5	22.9	863.9	1,109.6
Miscellaneous repair services.	76	71,576	67,053	30.7	38.5	9.7	11.6	428.1	426.8
Motion pictures	78	41,857	45,961	44.0	63.7	9.8	13.7	478.1	568.9
Amusement & recreation services	79	83,871	97,485	57.8	95.0	18.9	29.5	1,119.6	1,529.5
Health services	80	465,356	498,881	623.5	814.8	274.6	346.7	10,017.2	11,369.7
Legal services	81	153,462	168,206	102.3	123.7	40.0	48.2	945.0	977.9
Educational services.	82	21,018	27,244	10.2	17.0	3.4	5.5	196.3	256.4
Social services.	83	140,849	162,365	67.0	94.3	24.8	34.4	1,912.3	2,273.1
Museums, art galleries, & botanical & zoological gardens	84	3,553	5,425	3.4	6.4	1.2	1.8	69.6	88.5
Membership organizations	86	72,386	66,458	36.3	46.5	10.2	12.6	602.5	597.2
Eng, acctg, research, mgt, & rel serv (exc noncomm research org)	87	238,392	297,402	207.6	330.5	84.6	129.3	2,418.9	3,139.2
Services, n.e.c.	89	14,587	(S)	8.0	-	3.1	-	81.1	(S)

- Represents zero. S Figure does not meet publication standards.

Source: U.S. Census Bureau. 1997 Economic Census: Advance Summary Statistics for the United States 1997 NAICS Basis.

No. 873. Advance Summary Statistics for the United States (1997 NAICS Basis): 1997

[158.1 represents 158,100,000,000. Data are preliminary and are subject to change; they will be superceded by data released in later reports. Includes only establishments with payroll. Definition of paid employees varies among sectors. See text in sector specific reports for exact definitions]

Description	NAICS code	Establish- ments (number)	Revenue/ shipments/ sales/ receipts (bil. dol.)	Annual payroll (bil. dol.)	Paid employees (thousands)
Mining, total		**25,868**	**158.1**	**22.1**	**547.6**
Oil & gas extraction	211	8,300	87.3	5.7	116.9
Mining (except oil & gas).	212	7,539	50.2	9.7	233.4
Support activities for mining	213	10,029	20.6	6.6	197.3
Utilities, total		**15,558**	**391.2**	**36.9**	**711.1**
Utilities.	221	15,558	391.2	36.9	711.1
Construction, total.		**649,601**	**865.3**	**174.7**	**5,732.7**
Building, developing, & general contracting	233	198,124	391.1	42.6	1,357.8
Heavy construction.	234	42,010	133.9	30.7	900.0
Special trade contractors	235	409,467	340.3	101.4	3,474.9
Manufacturing, total.		**364,377**	**3,855.5**	**574.1**	**16,999.6**
Food mfg	311	26,970	425.3	38.9	1,489.6
Beverage & tobacco product mfg	312	2,774	96.6	6.8	177.3
Textile mills	313	4,714	60.1	10.3	400.7
Textile product mills	314	7,226	31.9	4.8	220.9
Apparel mfg	315	17,831	67.7	13.1	744.1
Leather & allied product mfg.	316	1,824	10.7	1.9	89.7
Wood product mfg	321	17,101	88.7	14.4	572.1
Paper mfg.	322	5,925	150.7	22.3	573.5
Printing & related support activities	323	43,054	98.7	26.4	846.7
Petroleum & coal products mfg.	324	2,143	178.9	5.6	110.0
Chemical mfg	325	13,482	417.7	40.8	903.3
Plastics & rubber products mfg	326	16,686	159.0	29.8	1,024.4
Nonmetallic mineral product mfg	327	16,404	88.1	16.5	508.9
Primary metal mfg	331	5,298	173.9	24.1	609.3
Fabricated metal product mfg	332	62,684	245.9	57.3	1,780.0
Machinery mfg	333	30,580	271.5	53.4	1,435.0
Computer & electronic product mfg	334	17,240	431.4	71.4	1,689.8
Electrical equipment, appliance, & component mfg . .	335	7,108	112.4	19.0	595.2
Transportation equipment mfg	336	13,206	577.9	80.2	1,886.6
Furniture & related product mfg.	337	20,694	65.4	15.1	606.7
Miscellaneous mfg	339	31,433	102.9	22.1	735.8
Wholesale trade, total		**453,184**	**4,055.0**	**215.7**	**582.4**
Wholesale trade, durable goods	421	290,260	2,189.6	133.7	340.8
Wholesale trade, nondurable goods.	422	162,924	1,865.4	82.0	2,410.6
Merchant wholesalers, total.		375,155	2,337.2	159.1	4,607.9
Wholesale trade, durable goods	421	240,621	1,214.4	100.2	2,764.8
Wholesale trade, nondurable goods	422	134,534	1,122.8	59.0	1,843.0

See footnotes at end of table.

U.S. Census Bureau, Statistical Abstract of the United States: 1999

[2,456.6 represents 2,456,600,000,000. Data are preliminary and are subject to change; they will be superceded by data released in later reports. Includes only establishments with payroll. Definition of paid employees varies among sectors. See text in sector specific reports for exact definitions]

Description	NAICS code	Establish-ments (number)	Revenue/ shipments/ sale/ receipts (bil. dol.)	Annual payroll (bil. dol.)	Paid employees (thousands)
Retail trade, total		1,120,249	2,456.6	238.8	14,115.6
Motor vehicle & parts dealers.	441	122,970	647.5	50.6	1,743.0
Furniture & home furnishings stores	442	64,498	71.8	9.9	483.3
Electronics & appliance stores	443	43,480	70.3	7.3	350.3
Building material & garden equipment & supplies dealers .	444	93,115	230.3	25.8	1,124.4
Food & beverage stores	445	149,919	401.0	40.8	2,909.5
Health & personal care stores	446	83,194	117.7	15.3	904.5
Gasoline stations.	447	126,059	197.8	11.5	917.9
Clothing & clothing accessories stores.	448	156,752	138.7	16.8	1,335.7
Sporting goods, hobby, book, & music stores	451	68,963	62.8	7.3	566.7
General merchandise stores	452	36,636	330.2	30.8	2,505.9
Miscellaneous store retailers	453	130,081	79.5	10.2	757.9
Nonstore retailers	454	44,582	109.1	12.5	516.4
Transportation & warehousing, total		177,770	318.5	82.4	2,927.1
Air transportation.	[1]481	3,611	21.4	2.8	91.5
Water transportation.	483	1,923	24.9	2.8	72.8
Truck transportation.	484	103,836	141.9	38.6	1,302.4
Transit & ground passenger transportation	485	16,006	13.9	5.6	342.1
Pipeline transportation	486	2,354	24.4	2.6	49.1
Scenic & sightseeing transportation.	487	2,288	1.7	0.5	22.1
Support activities for transportation	488	30,358	40.3	12.5	408.7
Couriers & messengers.	492	10,923	39.7	14.0	531.2
Warehousing & storage.	493	6,471	10.3	2.8	107.1
Information, total		115,386	641.7	135.2	3,222.0
Publishing industries.	511	33,375	172.2	41.3	969.9
Motion picture & sound recording industries	512	22,100	49.2	9.6	289.4
Broadcasting & telecommunications	513	44,007	367.8	68.1	1,555.3
Information services & data processing services	514	15,904	52.4	16.2	407.4
Finance & insurance, total.		398,169	2,254.5	263.3	5,767.8
Monetary authorities central bank	521	42	24.6	0.9	21.7
Credit intermediation & related activities.	522	166,835	886.8	100.3	2,715.7
Securities intermediation & related activities	523	58,020	269.3	70.0	704.8
Insurance carriers & related activities	524	172,010	1,062.4	91.4	2,306.1
Funds, trusts, & other financial vehicles (part)	525	1,262	11.4	0.7	19.6
Real estate & rental & leasing, total		289,871	249.5	43.6	1,761.2
Real estate.	531	222,540	162.8	29.7	1,170.9
Rental & leasing services	532	65,099	79.2	12.9	569.4
Professional, scientific, & technical services, total. .	541	621,605	608.6	233.3	5,416.1
Professional, scientific, & technical services	541	621,605	608.6	233.3	5,416.1
Administrative & support & waste management & remediation services, total		276,588	302.8	137.7	7,439.2
Administrative & support services	561	260,252	262.5	128.8	7,159.4
Waste management & remediation services	562	16,336	40.3	8.9	279.8
Educational services, total.		40,996	20.9	6.6	332.5
Educational services.	611	40,996	20.9	6.6	332.5
Health care & social assistance, total		645,841	889.6	379.3	13,616.9
Ambulatory health care services.	621	454,853	347.8	155.2	4,405.8
Hospitals	622	6,892	391.8	157.3	4,979.4
Nursing & residential care facilities	623	57,359	92.8	42.2	2,477.4
Social assistance.	624	126,737	57.2	24.7	1,754.3
Arts, entertainment, & recreation, total		99,690	103.1	32.3	1,571.9
Performing arts, spectator sports, & related industries . .	711	31,201	37.7	14.4	325.7
Museums, historical sites, & similar institutions	712	5,564	6.5	1.8	91.1
Amusement, gambling, & recreation industries	713	62,925	58.8	16.1	1,155.1

[1] Excludes large passenger carriers, etc. Railroad transportation and U.S. Postal Service industries are out of scope for the 1977 Economic Census.

Source: U.S. Census Bureau. 1997 Economic Census: Advance Summary Statistics for the United States 1997 NAICS Basis.

No. 874. Employees and Payroll, by Employment-Size Class: 1980 to 1996

[1,035 represents $1,035,000,000,000. Excludes government employees, railroad employees, self-employed persons, etc. See "General Explanation" in source for definitions and statement on reliability of data. An **establishment** is a single physical location where business is conducted or where services or industrial operations are performed]

Employment-size class	Unit	1980	1985	1990	1991	1992	1993	1994	1995	1996
Employees, total [1]	1,000 .	74,844	81,111	93,476	92,302	92,801	94,789	96,733	100,335	102,199
Under 20 employees	1,000 .	19,423	21,810	24,373	24,482	25,000	25,233	25,373	25,785	26,115
20 to 99 employees	1,000 .	21,168	23,539	27,414	26,906	27,030	27,443	28,138	29,202	29,697
100 to 499 employees	1,000 .	17,840	19,410	22,926	22,369	22,227	23,195	24,048	25,364	26,086
500 to 999 employees	1,000 .	5,689	5,716	6,551	6,325	6,270	6,449	6,663	7,021	7,274
1,000 or more employees	1,000 .	10,716	10,645	12,212	12,220	12,275	12,470	12,513	12,962	13,026
Annual payroll, total [1]	Bil. dol	1,035	1,514	2,104	2,145	2,272	2,363	2,488	2,666	2,849
Under 20 employees	Bil. dol.	231	352	485	502	536	554	579	608	647
20 to 99 employees	Bil. dol.	261	388	547	555	586	611	650	696	747
100 to 499 employees	Bil. dol.	249	362	518	523	550	582	621	675	730
500 to 999 employees	Bil. dol.	91	126	174	175	186	191	202	219	240
1,000 or more employees	Bil. dol.	208	286	381	390	413	424	436	467	485

[1] Prior to 1987, totals for employees and annual payroll have been revised. Detail may not add to totals because revisions for size class are not available.

Source: U.S. Census Bureau, *County Business Patterns*, annual.

No. 875. Establishments, Employees, and Payroll, by Industry: 1980 to 1996

[4,543 represents 4,543,000. Beginning 1990, data are based on the 1987 Standard Industrial Classification (SIC). Prior to 1990, data are based on the 1972 SIC]

Industry	Establishments (1,000)				Employees (1,000)				Payroll (bil. dol.)			
	1980	1990	1995	1996	1980	1990	1995	1996	1980	1990	1995	1996
All industries [1]	4,543	6,176	6,613	6,739	74,844	93,476	100,335	102,199	1,035	2,104	2,666	2,849
Agricultural services [2]	46	85	108	113	290	531	630	664	3	9	12	13
Mining	30	30	27	27	994	723	627	574	22	27	26	26
Construction	418	578	634	658	4,473	5,239	5,039	5,207	75	132	147	161
Manufacturing	319	378	390	393	21,165	19,173	18,613	18,558	355	544	631	660
Transportation [3]	168	235	285	295	4,623	5,592	5,924	6,057	88	166	201	212
Wholesale trade	385	476	518	531	5,211	6,328	6,606	6,665	89	181	227	240
Retail trade	1,223	1,530	1,568	1,579	15,047	19,815	21,085	21,487	124	242	300	318
Finance and insurance [4]	421	545	628	650	5,295	6,956	6,998	7,194	77	197	256	285
Services	1,278	2,059	2,386	2,461	17,186	28,800	34,707	35,750	197	599	864	933

[1] Includes nonclassifiable establishments not shown separately.   [2] Includes forestry and fisheries.   [3] Includes public utilities.   [4] Includes real estate.

Source: U.S. Census Bureau, *County Business Patterns*, annual.

No. 876. Establishments, Employees, and Payroll, by Employment-Size Class and Industry: 1996

[6,739 represents 6,739,000. See headnote, Table 874. Data are based on the 1987 Standard Industrial Classification]

Employment-size class	Unit	All industries [1]	Agricultural services [2]	Mining	Construction	Manufacturing	Transportation [3]	Wholesale trade	Retail trade	Finance and insurance [4]	Services
Establishments, total	1,000 ..	6,739	113	27	658	393	295	531	1,579	650	2,461
Under 20 employees	1,000 ..	5,843	107	22	605	264	245	456	1,326	593	2,194
20 to 99 employees	1,000 ..	741	5	4	47	91	41	67	224	48	214
100 to 499 employees	1,000 ..	138	420	1	5	33	9	8	29	8	47
500 to 999 employees	1,000 ..	11	18	1	(Z)	(Z)	4	1	(Z)	1	1	4
1,000 or more employees	1,000 ..	6	8	(Z)	(Z)	2	(Z)	(Z)	(Z)	(Z)	3
Employees, total	1,000 ..	102,199	664	574	5,207	18,558	6,057	6,665	21,487	7,194	35,750
Under 20 employees	1,000 ..	26,155	383	102	2,297	1,531	1,072	2,277	7,000	2,343	9,074
20 to 99 employees	1,000 ..	29,697	(D)	164	1,770	4,026	1,687	2,542	8,847	1,886	8,585
100 to 499 employees	1,000 ..	26,086	(D)	189	847	6,685	1,630	1,380	4,939	1,499	8,844
500 to 999 employees	1,000 ..	7,274	12	57	130	2,498	509	245	453	550	2,819
1,000 or more employees	1,000 ..	13,026	10	62	163	3,818	1,158	221	249	918	6,428
Annual payroll, total	Bil. dol.	2,849	13	26	161	660	212	240	318	285	933
Under 20 employees	Bil. dol	647	8	4	61	43	30	76	100	77	249
20 to 99 employees	Bil. dol	747	(D)	7	58	123	54	89	121	74	216
100 to 499 employees	Bil. dol	730	(D)	10	31	220	60	54	78	64	210
500 to 999 employees	Bil. dol	240	295	3	5	91	21	11	11	25	73
1,000 or more employees	Bil. dol	485	253	3	6	182	47	11	8	45	184

D Withheld to avoid disclosing data for individual companies; data are included in higher-level totals.   Z Less than 500 establishments.   [1] Includes nonclassifiable establishments not shown separately.   [2] Includes forestry and fisheries.   [3] Includes public utilities.   [4] Includes real estate.

Source: U.S. Census Bureau, *County Business Patterns*, annual.

U.S. Census Bureau, Statistical Abstract of the United States: 1999

No. 877. Major Industries—Private Firms, Establishments, Annual Payroll, and Estimated Receipts by Firm Size, 1996

[5,478.0 represents 5,478,000. Firms are an aggregation of all establishments owned by a parent company within an industry. Employment is measured in March and payroll is annual leading to some firms with zero employment]

Industry and data type	Unit	All industries employment size of firm								
		Total	0	1 to 4	5 to 9	10 to 19	20 to 99	100 to 499	Less than 500	More than 500
Total:										
Firms.	1,000 . .	5,478.0	718.0	2,609.8	996.4	585.8	476.3	76.1	5,462.4	15.6
Establishments.	1,000 . .	6,738.5	720.2	2,617.8	1,013.4	624.6	636.3	280.6	5,892.9	845.5
Employment	1,000 . .	102,187.3	-	5,485.7	6,541.3	7,854.5	18,643.2	14,649.8	53,174.5	49,012.8
Annual payroll	Bil. dol .	2,848.6	27.6	123.2	144.7	185.5	465.2	384.0	1,330.3	1,518.4
Receipts estimated . . .	Bil. dol .	16,654.6	138.0	841.3	819.0	1,006.9	2,817.2	2,168.5	7,790.9	8,863.8
Agric. services, forestry, and fishing:										
Firms.	1,000 . .	111.5	24.9	51.1	19.7	10.6	4.7	0.4	111.4	0.1
Establishments.	1,000 . .	113.1	24.9	51.1	19.8	10.6	4.8	0.6	111.8	1.3
Employment	1,000 . .	664.4	-	106.4	129.7	138.7	158.6	53.5	586.9	77.4
Annual payroll	Bil. dol .	13.3	0.5	1.9	2.2	2.6	3.2	1.0	11.5	1.8
Receipts estimated . . .	Bil. dol .	40.7	1.6	6.0	6.2	6.7	8.5	3.6	32.8	7.9
Mining:										
Firms.	1,000 . .	21.1	2.4	9.8	3.2	2.4	2.3	0.5	20.7	0.4
Establishments.	1,000 . .	26.9	2.4	9.9	3.3	2.5	2.8	1.5	22.4	4.5
Employment	1,000 . .	574.3	-	19.8	21.2	32.0	86.3	78.0	237.4	336.9
Annual payroll	Bil. dol .	26.5	0.2	0.5	0.6	1.0	3.0	3.3	8.6	17.9
Receipts estimated . . .	Bil. dol .	163.9	0.9	5.2	5.2	6.0	18.4	18.9	54.4	109.4
Construction:										
Firms.	1,000 . .	651.9	106.7	317.0	113.6	64.3	44.9	4.6	651.3	0.7
Establishments.	1,000 . .	658.4	106.7	317.1	113.7	64.4	45.6	6.1	653.7	4.7
Employment	1,000 . .	5,207.5	-	663.8	742.6	858.6	1,643.8	750.7	4,659.5	548.0
Annual payroll	Bil. dol .	160.9	3.2	14.9	17.5	23.5	52.5	27.3	138.9	22.0
Receipts estimated . . .	Bil. dol .	726.9	14.7	86.1	80.3	99.9	224.0	121.0	625.9	101.0
Manufacturing:										
Firms.	1,000 . .	332.6	29.0	101.0	61.2	52.9	67.1	16.5	327.6	4.9
Establishments.	1,000 . .	393.4	29.0	101.1	61.3	53.2	71.4	28.2	344.2	49.2
Employment	1,000 . .	18,558.5	-	229.2	410.8	722.4	2,775.7	3,005.0	7,143.1	11,415.4
Annual payroll	Bil. dol .	659.7	2.1	5.1	9.6	18.7	78.9	90.3	204.7	455.0
Receipts estimated . . .	Bil. dol .	3,546.3	12.6	25.8	42.8	79.1	361.2	480.8	1,002.3	2,544.0
Transportation, communications & public utilities:										
Firms.	1,000 . .	217.7	31.2	101.7	35.6	22.8	20.8	3.9	216.1	1.7
Establishments.	1,000 . .	295.5	31.3	102.0	36.0	24.1	26.6	12.6	232.6	62.8
Employment	1,000 . .	6,057.3	-	208.9	232.8	307.2	797.3	635.9	2,182.0	3,875.3
Annual payroll	Bil. dol .	211.9	1.1	4.2	5.0	7.1	20.4	18.7	56.6	155.3
Receipts estimated . . .	Bil. dol .	1,078.8	4.9	25.4	22.5	29.9	86.1	81.2	250.1	828.7
Wholesale trade:										
Firms.	1,000 . .	417.0	43.4	181.6	78.7	54.5	47.2	8.2	413.6	3.4
Establishments.	1,000 . .	531.5	43.5	182.2	80.2	59.0	68.9	29.0	462.8	68.7
Employment	1,000 . .	6,664.9	-	388.7	520.0	728.2	1,713.3	1,044.5	4,394.6	2,270.2
Annual payroll	Bil. dol .	240.3	1.8	11.6	15.4	22.5	55.4	36.0	142.7	97.6
Receipts, estimated . .	Bil. dol .	4,045.2	32.2	265.0	273.4	353.5	1,004.2	602.3	2,530.6	1,514.6
Retail trade:										
Firms.	1,000 . .	1,103.5	138.4	465.2	225.4	141.9	116.3	13.3	1,100.5	3.0
Establishments.	1,000 . .	1,579.3	139.5	467.9	231.2	154.4	165.0	77.0	1,234.9	344.4
Employment	1,000 . .	21,487.3	-	1,039.2	1,488.8	1,894.1	4,367.1	2,221.3	11,010.5	10,476.9
Annual payroll	Bil. dol .	317.7	3.6	13.3	18.8	24.3	65.7	36.3	161.8	155.8
Receipts estimated . . .	Bil. dol .	2,424.8	23.7	133.5	152.2	182.4	546.2	302.8	1,340.8	1,084.0
Finance, insurance & real estate:										
Firms.	1,000 . .	453.3	58.1	271.5	60.6	29.6	24.7	5.8	450.2	3.1
Establishments.	1,000 . .	650.1	58.3	272.5	62.4	34.2	44.9	29.6	501.8	148.3
Employment	1,000 . .	7,185.3	-	523.4	389.2	391.2	942.7	821.0	3,067.5	4,117.8
Annual payroll	Bil. dol .	284.8	2.4	12.5	11.1	12.6	31.6	29.8	100.1	184.7
Receipts estimated . . .	Bil. dol .	2,260.6	12.0	82.7	54.3	59.4	177.9	210.4	596.7	1,663.8
Services:										
Firms.	1,000 . .	2,175.6	267.3	1,101.3	398.0	209.0	158.7	32.6	2,167.0	8.6
Establishments.	1,000 . .	2,461.3	268.0	1,104.0	403.9	221.7	205.8	96.1	2,299.7	161.6
Employment	1,000 . .	35,747.9	-	2,289.3	2,596.2	2,775.2	6,152.4	6,039.9	19,853.0	15,894.9
Annual payroll	Bil. dol .	933.0	12.3	59.1	64.4	73.2	154.5	141.3	504.7	428.2
Receipts estimated . . .	Bil. dol .	2,363.3	33.4	210.4	181.6	189.7	390.3	347.5	1,353.0	1,010.3
Unclassified:										
Firms.	1,000 . .	29.0	16.5	10.2	1.5	0.5	0.2	-	29.0	-
Establishments.	1,000 . .	29.0	16.5	10.2	1.5	0.5	0.2	-	29.0	-
Employment	1,000 . .	40.0	-	17.0	10.0	7.0	6.0	-	40.0	-
Annual payroll	Bil. dol .	0.7	0.4	0.2	0.1	0.1	0.1	-	0.7	-
Receipts estimated . . .	Bil. dol .	4.2	2.0	1.0	0.5	0.4	0.3	-	4.2	-

- Represents or rounds to zero.

Source: Office of Advocacy, U.S. Small Business Administration, based on data provided by the U.S. Department of Commerce, U.S. Census Bureau, *Statistics of U.S. Businesses.*

556 Business Enterprise

No. 878. Private Employer Firms, Establishments, Employment, Annual Payroll, and Estimated Receipts by Firm Size: 1990 to 1996

[Firms are an aggregation of all establishments owned by a parent company. Employment is measured in March and payroll is annual leading to some firms with zero employment. This table illustrates the changing importance of firm sizes over time, not job growth as firms can grow or decline and change firm size cells over time]

Item	All industries—employment size of firm							
	Total	0-4	5-9	10-19	20-99	100-499	Less than 500	More than 500
Employer firms:								
1990	5,073,795	3,020,935	952,030	562,610	453,732	70,465	5,059,772	14,023
1994	5,276,964	3,208,235	964,985	563,097	452,383	73,267	5,261,967	14,997
1995	5,369,068	3,249,573	981,094	576,866	469,869	76,222	5,353,624	15,444
1996	5,478,047	3,327,783	996,356	585,844	476,312	76,136	5,462,431	15,616
Establishments:								
1990	6,175,559	3,032,253	970,580	599,529	590,496	254,747	5,447,605	727,954
1994	6,509,065	3,218,076	982,695	608,804	631,324	283,782	5,724,681	784,384
1995	6,612,721	3,259,795	998,264	618,268	638,616	283,993	5,798,936	813,785
1996	6,738,476	3,338,051	1,013,353	624,610	636,285	280,635	5,892,934	845,542
Employment:								
1990	93,469,275	5,116,914	6,251,632	7,543,360	17,710,042	13,544,849	50,166,797	43,302,478
1994	96,721,594	5,318,961	6,332,580	7,543,777	17,693,995	14,118,375	51,007,688	45,713,906
1995	100,314,946	5,395,432	6,440,349	7,734,080	18,422,228	14,660,421	52,652,510	47,662,436
1996	102,187,297	5,485,712	6,541,288	7,854,502	18,643,192	14,649,808	53,174,502	49,012,795
Annual payroll ($mil.):								
1990	2,103,971	116,857	114,006	144,451	352,391	279,452	1,007,156	1,096,815
1994	2,487,960	134,649	131,667	166,476	408,053	335,574	1,176,419	1,311,541
1995	2,665,922	141,538	137,083	175,388	437,065	361,061	1,252,135	1,413,787
1996	2,848,623	150,825	144,692	185,491	465,230	384,020	1,330,258	1,518,365
Receipts (est.) ($mil.):								
1990	9,450,656	626,679	569,640	681,192	1,715,443	1,316,747	4,909,700	4,540,956
1994	14,840,452	880,764	752,675	928,380	2,531,403	1,930,758	7,023,980	7,816,472
1995	15,751,365	919,735	778,864	965,259	2,678,293	2,062,235	7,404,386	8,346,979
1996	16,654,636	979,261	818,958	1,006,930	2,817,214	2,168,503	7,790,866	8,863,770

Source: Office of Advocacy, U.S. Small Business Administration based on data provided by the Department of Commerce, U.S. Census Bureau, unpublished data.

No. 879. Employer Firm Births and Deaths by Employment Size of Firms: 1989-95

[Longitudinal data for establishments active (payroll) in first quarter of the year (establishments with 0 employment in the first quarter were excluded). New firm births are classified by their employment size at the first quarter. Represents private establishments excluding railroad, domestic and farms. The number of continuing firms was calculated from static and longitudinal data. Existing firms with ownership changes are considered continuing firms]

Item	New firms (original locations)				Deaths (original locations)			
	Total	Less than 20	Less than 500	More than 500	Total	Less than 20	Less than 500	More than 500
Firms:								
1989-1990	584,892	558,478	584,660	232	531,400	502,685	530,991	409
1990-1991	541,141	515,870	540,889	252	546,518	516,964	546,149	369
1991-1992	544,596	519,014	544,278	318	521,606	492,746	521,176	430
1992-1993	564,504	539,601	564,093	411	492,651	466,550	492,266	385
1993-1994	570,587	546,437	570,337	250	503,563	476,667	503,125	438
1994-1995	594,369	568,896	594,119	250	497,246	472,441	496,874	372
Employment:								
1989-1990	3,211,064	1,886,311	3,090,643	120,421	3,198,829	1,683,174	2,988,436	210,393
1990-1991	3,105,363	1,712,856	2,907,351	198,012	3,208,099	1,723,159	3,044,470	163,629
1991-1992	3,200,969	1,703,491	2,863,799	337,170	3,126,463	1,602,579	2,894,127	232,336
1992-1993	3,438,106	1,750,662	3,053,765	384,341	2,906,260	1,515,896	2,697,656	208,604
1993-1994	3,105,753	1,760,322	2,889,507	216,246	3,077,307	1,549,072	2,800,933	276,374
1994-1995	3,322,001	1,836,153	3,049,456	272,545	2,822,627	1,516,552	2,633,587	189,040

Source: Office of Advocacy, U.S. Small Business Administration from data provided by Department of Commerce, U.S. Census Bureau, unpublished data.

No. 880. Private Employer Firms, Employment, and Estimated Receipts by Firm Size and State: 1996

[5,478.0 represents 5,478,000. Firms are an aggregation of all establishments owned by a parent company within a state. Establishments are locations with active payroll in any quarter. Employment is measured in March and payroll is annual leading to some firms with zero employment]

State	Employer firms (1,000) Employment size of firm			Employment (1,000) Employment size of firm			Estimated receipts (bil. dol.) Employment size of firm		
	Total	Less than 20	More than 500	Total	Less than 20	More than 500	Total	Less than 20	More than 500
United States ...	5,478.0	4,910.0	15.6	102,187.3	19,881.5	49,012.8	16,655	2,805	8,864
Alabama	80.4	69.4	2.1	1,568.8	293.2	794.2	222	36	120
Alaska	15.3	13.6	0.5	183.5	51.4	65.4	37	8	16
Arizona	86.7	74.5	2.3	1,599.3	304.0	777.3	225	38	124
Arkansas	52.1	45.5	1.4	911.9	184.2	452.3	120	21	63
California	625.8	552.6	5.0	11,131.1	2,225.7	5,096.3	1,950	345	993
Colorado	105.5	92.5	2.5	1,601.1	355.0	720.7	252	48	130
Connecticut	79.2	68.7	1.9	1,433.7	276.7	692.3	297	48	167
Delaware	18.4	15.2	1.2	333.0	58.7	178.4	64	8	43
District of Columbia	16.3	12.7	1.0	387.0	54.3	198.0	62	9	35
Florida	341.6	308.1	3.7	5,357.9	1,151.2	2,612.8	714	154	352
Georgia	150.1	129.8	3.5	3,036.6	523.8	1,649.1	484	76	283
Hawaii	24.3	20.9	0.7	424.1	89.6	187.1	61	13	31
Idaho	30.1	26.3	0.8	393.7	105.3	152.0	58	12	25
Illinois	249.0	215.5	4.1	4,978.0	886.0	2,459.3	893	141	485
Indiana	116.4	99.3	2.7	2,433.1	432.5	1,190.0	380	53	209
Iowa	65.7	56.8	1.5	1,163.1	236.5	523.3	189	29	95
Kansas	60.4	51.8	1.7	1,011.7	212.7	442.3	167	27	88
Kentucky	71.6	61.1	2.0	1,370.7	260.5	654.2	211	31	119
Louisiana	81.0	69.4	1.9	1,498.1	298.3	664.1	241	36	138
Maine	32.3	28.6	0.8	437.5	108.4	172.4	63	12	29
Maryland	103.3	89.0	2.3	1,831.4	370.3	843.2	282	50	144
Massachusetts	137.9	119.3	2.7	2,778.5	484.8	1,371.2	472	78	249
Michigan	192.2	167.2	2.9	3,758.0	714.7	1,799.3	647	100	361
Minnesota	108.9	93.6	2.2	2,134.8	385.8	995.6	353	56	181
Mississippi	48.3	41.9	1.4	883.3	172.6	441.5	116	19	62
Missouri	118.2	102.3	2.6	2,210.5	415.3	1,078.7	347	54	189
Montana	26.8	24.0	0.6	265.6	89.9	72.4	37	10	14
Nebraska	40.4	34.9	1.2	693.5	145.5	324.0	112	17	57
Nevada	34.0	28.4	1.4	718.7	115.0	395.6	93	16	48
New Hampshire	30.8	26.5	0.9	482.1	106.4	206.6	72	15	32
New Jersey	196.5	174.5	2.9	3,208.8	654.9	1,521.7	666	119	352
New Mexico	35.4	30.3	1.3	519.8	124.2	205.3	71	14	34
New York	411.1	369.2	4.0	6,789.5	1,359.7	3,219.3	1,323	242	683
North Carolina	153.6	134.3	3.0	3,058.7	549.4	1,611.3	448	71	255
North Dakota	17.7	15.2	0.5	235.1	62.1	75.1	37	9	14
Ohio	213.7	183.8	3.5	4,640.0	801.0	2,316.3	717	103	398
Oklahoma	69.7	60.7	1.7	1,084.7	243.4	458.3	156	30	76
Oregon	82.4	72.1	1.8	1,237.1	290.1	503.9	191	37	86
Pennsylvania	234.9	204.2	3.6	4,729.1	862.8	2,313.7	737	114	400
Rhode Island	25.2	21.8	0.8	381.5	82.2	164.4	53	11	24
South Carolina	74.0	64.3	2.0	1,433.1	266.8	759.9	194	31	112
South Dakota	20.3	17.6	0.6	272.2	70.3	98.9	39	9	16
Tennessee	103.3	88.6	2.7	2,193.2	369.2	1,171.0	327	49	185
Texas	359.4	315.7	4.5	6,952.6	1,292.8	3,529.9	1,163	191	657
Utah	41.1	34.8	1.4	781.9	146.6	384.0	111	17	59
Vermont	18.8	16.6	0.5	225.2	63.9	74.2	32	7	12
Virginia	133.7	116.2	2.8	2,523.7	479.4	1,270.6	379	59	213
Washington	132.9	117.3	2.3	2,003.3	459.1	855.8	337	62	167
West Virginia	34.3	29.8	1.1	529.3	122.4	230.3	78	13	43
Wisconsin	114.0	97.7	2.1	2,220.7	421.2	991.4	348	51	182
Wyoming	15.5	13.7	0.5	157.7	51.9	47.7	27	6	13

Source: U.S. Small Business Administration, Office of Advocacy, based on data provided by the U.S. Department of Commerce, U.S. Census Bureau, unpublished data.

No. 881. Small Establishments, Employees, and Payroll, by Employment-Size Class and Industry: 1996

Employment size-class	Unit	All indust-ries [1]	Agricul-tural serv-ices [2]	Manu-facturing	Transpor-tation [3]	Whole-sale trade	Retail trade	Finance and insur-ance [4]	Services
Establishments, total	Number. . .	6,738,541	113,000	393,060	295,205	531,220	1,579,264	650,161	2,461,235
1 to 4 employees.	Number. . .	3,698,120	76,367	136,245	160,078	268,251	716,010	410,078	1,464,163
5 to 9 employees.	Number. . .	1,316,760	20,129	66,776	48,942	109,463	368,278	116,285	466,138
10 to 19 employees	Number. . .	827,726	10,913	60,894	35,699	78,635	241,646	66,513	263,517
20 + employees.	Number. . .	895,935	5,591	129,145	50,486	74,871	253,330	57,285	267,417
Employees, total	1,000	102,199	664	18,558	6,057	6,665	21,487	7,194	35,750
1 to 4 employees.	1,000	6,287	107	243	262	486	1,299	692	2,491
5 to 9 employees.	1,000	8,701	132	450	323	728	2,455	765	3,056
10 to 19 employees	1,000	11,127	144	838	487	1,063	3,245	886	3,527
20 + employees.	1,000	76,084	(D)	17,027	4,985	4,388	14,487	4,851	26,676
Annual payroll.	Mil. dol . . .	2,848,955	13,289	659,644	211,880	240,314	317,660	285,032	933,003
1 to 4 employees.	Mil. dol . . .	185,512	2,443	8,429	8,180	17,898	24,561	23,628	80,586
5 to 9 employees.	Mil. dol . . .	196,430	2,323	11,224	8,318	22,805	32,616	23,520	76,600
10 to 19 employees	Mil. dol . . .	264,870	2,796	23,196	13,680	34,907	42,354	29,699	91,978
20 + employees.	Mil. dol . . .	2,202,144	(D)	616,795	181,702	164,704	218,129	208,185	683,839

D Withheld to avoid disclosing data for individual companies; data are included in higher-level totals. [1] Includes establishments not shown separately. [2] Includes forestry and fisheries. [3] Includes public utilities. [4] Includes real estate.

Source: U.S. Census Bureau, *County Business Patterns,* annual.

No. 882. Women-Owned Firms by Major Industry Group: 1992

[Based on the 1987 SIC system. Includes individual proprietorships, partnerships and subchapter S corporations. Detail may not add to total due to rounding]

Major industry group	All firms		Firms with paid employees			
	Firms (number)	Sales and receipts ($1,000)	Firms (number)	Sales and receipts ($1,000)	Employees (number)	Annual payroll ($1,000)
All industries.	**5,888,883**	**642,484,352**	**817,773**	**550,425,116**	**6,252,029**	**104,786,488**
Agric. services, forestry, & fishing	82,526	4,987,572	15,254	3,787,251	69,542	1,002,688
Mining	37,205	6,905,374	2,731	5,940,020	30,563	841,127
Construction	183,695	45,978,168	64,746	41,579,094	371,788	8,827,641
Manufacturing	152,346	90,634,753	41,038	88,751,252	803,428	18,574,330
Transportation & public utilities	141,623	25,822,193	31,049	23,026,912	290,081	5,841,177
Wholesale trade.	154,542	12,487,093	45,591	120,625,000	385,814	9,846,339
Retail trade.	1,093,342	155,852,751	244,488	139,694,945	1,850,074	19,926,963
Finance, insurance, and real estate . . .	602,802	51,748,279	56,040	33,084,796	295,871	6,347,967
Services	3,158,444	130,745,314	307,443	92,823,096	2,145,482	33,415,073
Industries not classified	282,358	4,962,855	9,394	1,112,750	9,386	163,185

Source: U.S. Census Bureau, *Women-Owned Businesses Enterprises,* Series WB92-1.

No. 883. Minority-Owned Firms—Comparison of Business Ownership by Minority Group and Gender: 1987 and 1992

[Based on the 1987 Standard Industrial Classification (SIC). Data includes individual proprietorships, partnerships, and subchapter S corporations. Detail may not add to total due to rounding]

Sex and race	Firms		Percent change, 1987-1992	Percent of total		Sales/receipts		Percent change, 1987-1992	Percent of total	
	1987	1992		1987	1992	1987 (mil. dol.)	1992 (mil. dol.)		1987	1992
All minorities . . .	**1,213,750**	**1,965,565**	**61.9**	**(X)**	**(X)**	**77,840**	**202,011**	**160.0**	**(X)**	**(X)**
Men	825,441	1,248,130	51.2	68.0	63.5	59,847	152,245	154.9	76.9	75.4
Women	388,309	717,435	84.8	32.0	36.5	17,993	49,767	176.6	23.1	24.6
Black	424,165	620,912	46.4	34.9	31.6	19,763	32,197	62.9	25.4	15.9
Men	265,887	343,666	29.3	21.9	17.5	13,232	23,688	77.1	17.0	11.7
Women	158,278	277,246	75.2	13.0	14.1	6,531	8,510	30.3	8.4	4.2
Hispanic	422,373	771,708	82.7	34.8	39.3	24,732	72,824	194.5	31.8	36.0
Men	307,348	525,330	70.9	25.3	26.7	20,403	55,645	172.2	26.2	27.5
Women	115,025	246,378	114.2	9.5	12.5	4,328	17,180	297.0	5.6	8.5
API/AIAN [1]:										
Men	258,514	397,779	53.9	21.3	20.2	26,700	74,856	180.4	34.3	37.1
Women	118,197	208,647	76.5	9.7	10.6	7,336	24,853	238.8	9.4	12.3

X Not Applicable. [1] API/AIAN = Asian, Pacific Islander, American Indian, and Alaska Native.

Source: U.S. Census Bureau, *Survey of Minority-Owned Businesses, Summary 1992,* Series MB92-4.

U.S. Census Bureau, Statistical Abstract of the United States: 1999

No. 884. Business Starts and Employment: 1990 to 1998

[647 represents 647,000]

Item	1990	1991	1992	1993	1994	1995	1996	1997	1998
New incorporations (1,000)	647	629	667	707	742	767	786	799	(NA)
Failures [1], total	60,747	88,140	97,069	86,133	71,558	71,128	71,931	84,342	71,857
Rate per 10,000 concerns	74	107	110	109	86	82	80	89	76
Current liabilities [2] (mil. dol.) . . .	56,130	96,825	94,318	47,756	28,978	37,284	29,569	24,802	23,868
Business starts, total	158,930	155,672	164,086	166,154	188,387	168,158	170,475	166,740	155,141
Agriculture, forestry & fishing	2,295	2,306	2,160	2,195	2,644	2,199	2,295	2,275	2,451
Mining	1,054	944	805	772	680	564	589	655	588
Construction	20,801	19,165	18,259	17,533	18,213	16,980	18,624	18,513	17,016
Manufacturing	15,315	14,927	14,043	13,789	12,927	12,172	12,908	13,144	11,876
Transportation & public utilities . . .	6,281	6,409	6,578	6,846	7,683	7,161	7,993	8,741	8,559
Wholesale trade.	18,170	18,284	18,419	17,958	16,409	14,956	16,019	15,780	13,983
Retail trade	43,109	40,653	40,318	38,707	38,949	36,381	38,407	36,377	33,151
Finance, insurance & real estate. .	9,550	9,139	9,581	10,314	11,746	10,362	11,222	12,198	12,317
Services	38,471	39,011	40,555	41,349	49,328	44,586	50,077	50,253	48,500
Unclassifiable establishments	3,884	4,834	13,368	16,691	29,808	22,797	12,341	8,804	6,700
Employment, total	827,012	731,621	800,827	780,804	758,134	738,606	846,973	939,310	906,105
Agriculture, forestry & fishing	8,518	7,344	7,422	5,198	7,099	6,146	7,794	10,001	10,105
Mining	8,431	6,444	6,164	4,312	3,184	4,697	4,248	6,790
Construction	80,096	63,495	59,361	53,432	54,210	53,118	64,478	82,336	78,920
Manufacturing	139,506	121,238	122,483	119,487	105,255	104,660	108,644	125,007	111,507
Transportation & public utilities . . .	45,373	38,093	45,227	44,885	41,617	43,583	50,072	59,144	59,972
Wholesale trade.	75,914	69,235	79,247	78,924	66,186	59,933	69,001	73,281	70,297
Retail trade	207,752	184,698	203,698	191,484	174,270	176,159	200,354	211,007	195,802
Finance, insurance & real estate. .	54,872	46,831	56,665	57,199	55,857	54,610	61,185	70,982	75,113
Services	205,481	192,938	219,120	222,054	243,296	233,482	278,292	299,137	294,331
Unclassifiable establishments	1,069	1,305	1,085	1,977	6,032	3,731	2,456	4,167	3,268

NA Not available. [1] Includes concerns discontinued following assignment, voluntary or involuntary petition in bankruptcy, attachment, execution, foreclosure, etc. [2] Liabilities exclude long-term publicly held obligations; offsetting assets are not taken into account.

Source: Dun & Bradstreet Corporation, Murray Hill, NJ,07974-0027 *A Decade of Business Starts*; and *Monthly Failure Report* (copyright).

No. 885. Business Starts and Business Failures, by State: 1997 and 1998

State	Business starts		Number of failures		State	Business starts		Number of failures	
	1997	1998	1997	1998		1997	1998	1997	1998
United States . . .	166,740	155,141	84,342	71,857	Missouri.	2,435	2,163	1,555	1,321
Alabama	2,480	2,645	632	546	Montana	419	397	191	201
Alaska.	267	271	179	177	Nebraska	648	565	491	383
Arizona	3,110	2,868	1,219	1,225	Nevada	1,672	1,465	628	677
Arkansas	1,183	1,091	1,131	748	New Hampshire.	718	708	432	322
California	22,497	21,582	20,277	17,679					
					New Jersey	7,481	6,412	2,649	2,024
Colorado	3,276	3,041	3,117	2,483	New Mexico	961	887	647	585
Connecticut	2,123	2,069	640	530	New York	14,450	13,403	5,093	4,233
Delaware	602	508	33	28	North Carolina.	4,578	4,371	1,051	846
District of Columbia . .	696	537	91	75	North Dakota	255	229	138	144
Florida.	13,032	13,029	2,597	2,047					
					Ohio	5,122	4,829	2,862	2,524
Georgia	5,383	5,471	1,186	800	Oklahoma	1,499	1,367	1,559	990
Hawaii.	696	593	647	781	Oregon	1,837	1,823	1,201	1,109
Idaho.	784	639	685	441	Pennsylvania	6,450	5,525	3,154	2,641
Illinois	6,525	5,542	3,527	3,291	Rhode Island	511	544	188	150
Indiana	2,928	2,611	856	473					
					South Carolina	2,014	2,023	418	410
Iowa	1,199	1,020	528	244	South Dakota	286	281	284	275
Kansas	1,109	967	1,272	1,140	Tennessee	3,239	2,835	1,746	1,369
Kentucky	1,859	1,824	568	270	Texas	11,859	10,936	7,329	6,785
Louisiana	2,028	1,849	303	377	Utah	1,527	1,417	586	388
Maine	570	577	398	259					
					Vermont	291	261	150	80
Maryland	3,668	3,139	1,502	1,283	Virginia	3,779	3,502	903	860
Massachusetts	3,766	3,425	1,687	1,200	Washington	3,223	2,956	3,015	2,528
Michigan	4,881	4,293	1,949	1,551	West Virginia	555	623	320	305
Minnesota	2,336	2,111	1,220	1,711	Wisconsin.	2,515	2,357	1,221	1,005
Mississippi	1,171	1,347	147	177	Wyoming	247	213	140	166

Source: The Dun & Bradstreet Corporation, Murray Hill, NJ, 07974-0027 A Decade of Business Starts, monthly; (copyright), and *Business Failure Record*, annual, (copyright).

U.S. Census Bureau, Statistical Abstract of the United States: 1999

No. 886. Business Failures, by Industry: 1990 to 1998

Industry	Number					Rate per 10,000 firms				
	1990	1995	1996	1997	1998	1990	1995	1996	1997	1998
Total	60,747	71,128	71,931	84,342	71,857	74	82	80	89	76
Agriculture, forestry, fishing	1,733	2,231	2,723	2,977	2,547	50	85	102	103	47
Mining	388	200	189	163	173	88	57	60	52	58
Construction	8,162	9,158	9,801	11,057	9,568	91	106	112	118	102
Manufacturing	4,740	4,383	4,093	4,224	3,314	92	88	83	81	64
Food and kindred products	232	216	230	221	176	91	91	93	86	70
Textile mill products	102	117	126	126	90	97	122	139	131	93
Apparel, other textile products	318	394	359	358	274	114	151	141	134	103
Lumber and wood products	420	318	375	397	127	97	89	107	107	33
Furniture and fixtures	258	229	184	161	43	151	144	120	100	27
Paper and allied products	68	51	57	46	605	105	76	84	63	830
Printing and publishing	734	815	696	772	605	74	81	69	74	60
Chemicals and allied products	139	126	123	112	82	86	81	78	66	47
Petroleum refining and coal products	21	14	14	13	9	83	67	64	56	38
Rubber and misc. products	158	128	156	121	94	101	80	98	74	58
Leather and leather products	40	28	32	32	27	113	92	110	105	88
Stone, clay, and glass products	161	125	106	122	84	80	74	64	70	47
Primary metal products	115	59	59	67	57	123	69	71	79	67
Fabricated metal products	397	354	311	311	242	90	83	73	71	55
Machinery, exc. electric	656	565	486	511	456	84	75	65	66	58
Electric and electronic	287	255	217	228	189	114	104	88	87	72
Transportation equipment	242	160	154	140	104	147	114	109	93	69
Instruments and related equipment	120	121	92	116	70	68	68	52	60	36
Miscellaneous	272	308	316	368	310	74	76	74	78	64
Transportation, public utilities	2,630	2,733	3,362	4,402	3,824	94	90	107	132	115
Wholesale trade	4,423	4,149	3,957	3,912	3,138	77	71	69	67	56
Retail trade	12,972	12,952	13,476	15,132	12,640	65	73	72	79	70
Finance, insurance, real estate	3,819	4,293	4,138	4,634	3,261	60	60	57	62	43
Services	16,119	21,850	22,928	29,752	28,547	49	54	59	73	72
Public administration	10	24	23	27	25	(NA)	(NA)	(NA)	(NA)	(NA)
Nonclassifiable establishments	5,751	9,221	7,241	8,062	4,820	(NA)	(NA)	(NA)	(NA)	(NA)

NA Not available.

Source: The Dun and Bradstreet Corporation, Murray Hill, NJ 07974-0027; *Business Failure Record*, annual (copyright).

No. 887. Bankruptcy Cases, by State: 1995 to 1998

[In thousands (858.1 represents 858,100). For years ending June 30. Includes outlying areas, not shown separately. Covers only bankruptcy cases filed under the Bankruptcy Reform Act of 1978. Bankruptcy: legal recognition that a company or individual is insolvent and must restructure or liquidate. Petitions "filed" means the commencement of a proceeding through the presentation of a petition to the clerk of the court]

State	1995	1996	1997	1998	State	1995	1996	1997	1998
United States	858.1	1,042.1	1,317.0	1,411.4	Missouri	15.1	19.8	24.2	27.4
Alabama	24.3	29.3	33.3	33.8	Montana	2.1	2.5	3.2	3.7
Alaska	0.9	1.0	1.3	1.4	Nebraska	3.4	4.6	5.7	6.1
Arizona	14.8	18.0	23.2	24.7	Nevada	7.3	8.9	12.3	14.4
Arkansas	7.9	11.2	14.7	16.5	New Hampshire	3.1	3.4	4.3	5.1
California	140.4	164.3	200.1	211.3	New Jersey	25.5	30.6	38.8	44.5
Colorado	13.1	14.9	17.9	18.9	New Mexico	3.7	5.2	6.8	7.9
Connecticut	8.5	10.2	12.7	13.5	New York	48.8	56.1	69.8	76.9
Delaware	1.4	1.9	2.4	2.7	North Carolina	14.0	18.9	24.9	26.5
District of Columbia	1.4	1.6	2.2	2.8	North Dakota	1.2	1.5	1.9	2.1
Florida	43.4	51.9	67.4	76.4	Ohio	32.4	38.8	50.1	55.5
Georgia	42.1	50.9	59.9	62.6	Oklahoma	13.2	16.1	20.8	22.5
Hawaii	1.8	2.4	3.8	5.1	Oregon	13.2	15.1	17.9	17.9
Idaho	3.7	4.8	6.2	7.5	Pennsylvania	22.0	28.2	38.3	45.2
Illinois	39.2	48.5	60.3	64.6	Rhode Island	3.0	3.8	5.1	5.4
Indiana	22.3	26.0	33.7	38.5	South Carolina	6.9	8.5	10.7	11.3
Iowa	5.9	7.6	9.6	9.7	South Dakota	1.3	1.7	2.1	2.3
Kansas	8.5	10.1	12.5	13.2	Tennessee	35.5	43.7	52.1	52.6
Kentucky	13.0	16.6	20.6	22.1	Texas	43.8	54.2	69.5	72.0
Louisiana	13.4	17.1	22.6	23.2	Utah	6.9	8.0	10.6	13.5
Maine	1.9	2.6	3.6	4.4	Vermont	0.9	1.2	1.7	1.9
Maryland	16.3	20.4	28.8	34.5	Virginia	25.5	31.7	40.7	43.4
Massachusetts	14.3	15.9	22.5	22.1	Washington	18.6	25.0	31.7	33.6
Michigan	22.7	28.0	36.1	41.2	West Virginia	3.8	4.9	7.6	8.8
Minnesota	14.1	16.3	19.9	19.5	Wisconsin	11.8	14.4	17.9	19.6
Mississippi	10.6	13.3	18.2	19.1	Wyoming	1.2	1.5	2.0	2.1

Source: Administrative Office of the U.S. Courts, unpublished data.

U.S. Census Bureau, Statistical Abstract of the United States: 1999

No. 888. Bankruptcy Petitions Filed and Pending, by Type and Chapter: 1985 to 1998

[For years ending June 30. Covers only bankruptcy cases filed under the Bankruptcy Reform Act of 1978. **Bankruptcy:** legal recognition that a company or individual is insolvent and must restructure or liquidate. Petitions "filed" means the commencement of a proceeding through the presentation of a petition to the clerk of the court; "pending" is a proceeding in which the administration has not been completed]

Item	1985	1990	1992	1993	1994	1995	1996	1997	1998
Total filed	364,536	725,484	972,490	918,734	845,257	858,104	1,042,110	1,316,999	1,429,451
Business [1]	66,651	64,688	72,650	66,428	56,748	51,288	52,938	53,993	50,202
Nonbusiness [2]	297,885	660,796	899,840	852,306	788,509	806,816	989,172	1,263,006	1,379,249
Voluntary	362,939	723,886	971,047	917,350	844,087	856,991	1,040,915	1,315,782	1,428,550
Involuntary	1,597	1,598	1,443	1,384	1,170	1,113	1,195	1,217	901
Chapter 7 [3]	244,650	505,337	679,662	638,916	578,903	581,390	712,129	917,274	1,015,453
Chapter 9 [4]	3	7	15	9	17	12	10	9	5
Chapter 11 [5]	21,425	19,591	24,029	20,579	17,098	13,221	12,859	11,159	9,613
Chapter 12 [6]	(X)	1,351	1,634	1,434	976	904	1,063	1,006	845
Chapter 13 [7]	98,452	199,186	267,121	257,777	248,246	262,551	316,024	387,521	403,501
Section 304 [8]	6	12	29	19	17	26	24	29	34
Total pending	608,945	961,919	1,237,357	1,183,009	1,134,036	1,090,446	1,169,112	1,331,290	1,389,585

X Not applicable. [1] Business bankruptcies include those filed under chapters 7, 9, 11, or 12. [2] Bankruptcies include those filed under chapters 7, 11, or 13. [3] Chapter 7, liquidation of nonexempt assets of businesses or individuals. [4] Chapter 9, adjustment of debts of a municipality. [5] Chapter 11, individual or business reorganization. [6] Chapter 12, adjustment of debts of a family farmer with regular income, effective November 26, 1986. [7] Chapter 13, adjustment of debts of an individual with regular income. [8] Chapter 11 U.S.C., Section 304, cases ancillary to foreign proceedings.

Source: Administrative Office of the U.S. Courts, *Statistical Tables for the Federal Judiciary*.

No. 889. Small Business Administration Loans to Small Businesses: 1980 to 1996

[For fiscal year ending in year shown; see text, Section 9, State and Local Government. A small business must be independently owned and operated, must not be dominant in its particular industry, and must meet standards set by the Small Business Administration as to its annual receipts or number of employees. Loans include both direct and guaranteed loans to small business establishments. Does not include Disaster Assistance Loans]

Loans approved	Unit	1980	1985	1989	1990	1991	1992	1993	1994	1995	1996
Loans, all businesses	1,000...	31.7	19.3	17.0	18.8	20.6	26.4	29.4	40.4	60.1	52.7
Loans, minority-owned businesses ..	1,000...	6.0	2.8	2.4	2.4	3.1	3.9	4.5	6.8	10.4	9.1
Percent of all business loans....	Percent	19	15	14	13	15	15	15	18	19	19
Value of total loans [1]	Mil. dol.	3,858	3,217	3,490	4,354	4,861	6,596	7,591	9,527	9,854	10,177
Minority business loans [2]	Mil. dol.	470	324	385	473	764	1,033	1,178	1,754	1,885	2,124

[1] Includes both SBA and bank portions of loans. [2] SBA direct loans and guaranteed portion of bank loans only.

Source: U.S. Small Business Administration, Management Information Summary, unpublished data.

No. 890. Venture Capital Commitments, by Source: 1980 to 1997

[Investment in venture capital partnerships]

Source	1980	1985	1990	1991	1992	1993	1994	1995	1996	1997
Capital commitments (mil. dol.)..	661	2,327	1,847	1,271	2,548	2,545	3,764	4,227	7,501	9,060
PERCENT DISTRIBUTION										
Individuals/families	16	13	11	12	11	7	12	17	7	13
Endowments/foundations	14	8	13	24	18	11	21	23	11	9
Insurance companies/banks	13	11	9	5	15	11	9	19	3	1
Foreign investors	8	23	7	12	11	4	2	1	2	-
Corporations	19	12	7	5	3	8	9	2	19	29
Pension funds	30	33	53	42	42	59	46	38	55	41

- Represents zero.

Source: Venture Economics Investor Services, Boston, MA, *Venture Capital Journal*, monthly.

No. 891. Mergers and Acquisitions—Summary: 1985 to 1998

[Covers transactions valued at $5 million or more. Values based on transactions for which price data revealed. **All activity** includes mergers, acquisitions, acquisitions of partial interest that involve a 40% stake in the target or an investment of at least $100 million, divestitures, and leveraged transactions that result in a change in ownership. **Divestiture:** sale of a business, division, or subsidiary by corporate owner to another party. **Leveraged buyout:** acquisition of a business in which buyers use mostly borrowed money to finance purchase price and incorporate debt into capital structure of business after change in ownership]

Item	Unit	1985	1990	1992	1993	1994	1995	1996	1997	1998
All activity:										
Number	Number	1,719	4,239	3,502	3,722	4,383	4,981	5,639	8,770	9,634
Value	Bil. dol.	149.6	205.6	125.3	420.4	524.9	895.8	1,059.3	1,610.3	2,480.2
Divestitures:										
Number	Number	780	1,907	1,598	1,993	2,005	2,227	2,423	3,189	3,304
Value	Bil. dol.	51	90.8	57.2	213.4	236.9	365.3	319.0	616.2	554.8
Leveraged buyouts:										
Number	Number	154	177	199	621	173	206	169	198	238
Value	Bil. dol.	16.3	17.6	7.2	1.64	10.6	23.6	17.4	24.1	27.2
Foreign acquisitions of U.S. companies:										
Number	Number	259	773	361	(NA)	(NA)	80	73	441	483
Value	Bil. dol.	27.9	56.4	17.6	(NA)	(NA)	3.5	2.9	64.8	232.5
U.S. acquisitions overseas:										
Number	Number	91	392	455	197	207	317	364	539	746
Value	Bil. dol.	3.7	20.5	13.7	19.5	21.1	62.6	59.3	87.8	127.8

NA Not available.

No. 892. Mergers and Acquisitions, by Industry: 1998

[See headnote Table 891]

Industry	U.S. company acquiring U.S. company		Foreign company acquiring U.S. company		U.S. company acquiring foreign company	
	Number	Value (mil. dol.)	Number	Value (mil. dol.)	Number	Value (mil. dol.)
Total activity [1]	3,882	1,378,564.6	483	232,505.1	746	127,760.9
Construction firms	76	3,494.9	6	1,314.3	8	344.0
Food and kindred products	56	11,089.3	10	359.1	23	5,380.5
Tobacco products	(NA)	(NA)	1	729.3	1	12.0
Textile and apparel products	32	3,648.9	8	479.1	2	584.8
Wood products, furniture, and fixtures	20	2,914.5	5	631.1	4	61.1
Paper and allied products	19	16,637.0	9	911.6	10	3,460.9
Chemicals and allied products	37	14,275.9	13	2,327.2	15	2,824.1
Drugs	52	9,071.8	16	2,734.0	13	1,428.2
Stone, clay, glass and concrete products	23	3,843.7	3	792.5	9	3,846.1
Metal and metal products	84	12,155.2	10	2,008.5	24	1,408.0
Machinery	90	24,549.5	7	228.4	19	1,369.7
Computer and office equipment	39	12,139.8	11	9,746.3	13	1,490.9
Prepackaged software	160	19,782.5	36	3,059.4	38	2,793.9
Electronic and electrical equipment	101	26,438.6	25	2,938.6	29	11,996.4
Communications equipment	47	5,006.3	15	6,005.5	20	1,615.4
Transportation equipment	34	21,649.7	9	43,520.0	19	2,497.2
Aerospace and aircraft	16	1,296.7	2	85.0	4	354.9
Measuring, medical, photo equip; clocks	104	28,158.3	24	3,676.3	25	3,336.0
Transportation and shipping (except air)	8	1,788.9	2	222.0	6	5,666.9
Air transportation and shipping	60	2,613.3	10	4,065.5	21	1,681.9
Telecommunications	101	206,600.2	15	13,086.6	29	4,904.3
Radio & television broadcasting stations	137	108,477.3	5	341.7	11	4,872.3
Printing, publishing, and allied services	39	8,007.2	11	9,751.8	7	411.6
Electric, gas, water distribution	57	29,988.7	6	16,767.4	30	19,649.0
Sanitary services	26	23,760.0	1	14.5	2	486.4
Hotels and casinos	122	18,939.7	8	489.4	21	1,840.8
Amusement and recreation services	46	5,411.5	3	140.6	7	245.4
Motion picture production and distribution	27	3,474.4	1	420.0	4	146.4
Personal services	7	1,977.4	1	11.0	1	68.6
Business services	433	75,834.2	37	6,305.8	81	5,506.2
Advertising services	31	3,194.3	4	54.4	10	2,163.6
Repair services	18	2,657.0	1	14.8	3	1,411.5
Wholesale trade—durable goods	93	6,612.4	7	296.8	16	1,250.9
Retail trade—general merchandise and apparel.	23	20,812.6	1	6.0	2	220.0
Commercial banks, bank holding companies	253	241,677.7	1	9,082.1	13	1,878.2
Real estate, mortgage bankers and brokers	482	46,668.9	46	4,577.5	24	5,275.9
Investment & commodity firms, dealers, exchanges	120	37,363.9	18	3,407.2	34	4,797.7
Insurance	96	61,680.2	16	7,068.5	23	4,289.8
Other financial	5	1,671.9	1	45.4		
Agriculture, forestry, and fishing	17	4,087.3	3	415.0	10	1,477.4
Mining	28	6,415.8	7	2,108.6	16	1,034.7
Oil and gas; petroleum refining	147	118,128.6	19	56,178.8	38	7,594.3
Holding companies, except banks	2	640.8	1	27.6	2	164.0
Public administration	4	109.8	1	1,100.0	2	169.7

NA Not available.   [1] Includes other items not shown separately.

Source of Tables 891 and 892: Thompson Financial Securities Data, Newark, NJ, Merger & Corporate Transactions Database (copyright).

Business Enterprise   563

No. 893. Patents and Trademarks: 1980 to 1997

[In thousands (113.0 represents 113,000). Calendar year data. Covers patents issued to citizens of the United States and residents of foreign countries. For data on foreign countries, see Table 1380]

Item	1980	1990	1991	1992	1993	1994	1995	1996	1997
Patent applications filed...........	113.0	176.7	178.4	187.2	189.4	206.9	226.6	211.6	233.0
Inventions	104.3	164.6	164.3	173.1	174.7	189.9	212.4	195.2	215.3
Designs	7.8	11.3	13.1	13.1	13.6	15.8	15.4	15.2	16.5
Botanical plants	0.2	0.4	0.4	0.4	0.4	0.5	0.5	0.7	0.6
Reissues..................	0.6	0.5	0.6	0.6	0.6	0.7	0.6	0.6	0.5
Patents issued.................	66.2	99.2	106.8	107.4	109.7	113.6	113.8	121.7	124.1
Inventions	61.8	90.4	96.5	97.4	98.3	101.7	101.4	109.6	112.0
Individuals	13.8	17.3	18.1	17.3	16.5	17.3	17.4	18.2	17.6
Corporations: United States.....	27.7	36.1	39.2	40.3	41.8	44.0	44.0	48.7	50.2
Foreign [1]	19.1	36.0	38.1	38.7	38.8	38.8	39.1	41.5	42.9
U.S. Government...........	1.2	1.0	1.2	1.2	1.2	1.3	1.0	0.9	0.9
Designs	3.9	8.0	9.6	9.3	10.6	11.1	11.7	11.4	11.4
Botanical plants	0.1	0.3	0.4	0.3	0.4	0.5	0.4	0.4	0.4
Reissues.................	0.3	0.4	0.3	0.4	0.3	0.3	0.3	0.3	0.3
U.S. residents [2]	40.8	52.8	57.7	58.7	61.1	64.2	64.4	69.3	69.9
Foreign country resident[2]	25.4	46.2	49.0	48.7	48.7	49.3	49.4	52.4	54.2
Percent of total	38.4	46.7	46.0	45.3	44.3	43.4	43.4	43.0	43.7
Other published documents [3]	(Z)	0.1	0.1	0.1	0.1	0.1	0.1	0.1	0.1
Trademarks:									
Applications filed..............	46.8	127.3	123.3	127.8	150.4	161.1	188.9	200.6	224.4
Issued	24.7	60.8	52.4	85.8	86.9	70.1	92.5	98.6	119.9
Trademarks	18.9	53.6	46.6	80.2	80.6	63.9	85.6	93.7	112.5
Trademark renewals..........	5.9	7.2	5.8	5.6	6.3	6.2	6.9	7.7	7.4

Z Less than 50. [1] Includes patents to foreign governments. [2] Includes patents for inventions, designs, botanical plants, and reissues. [3] Includes Defensive Publications, a practice which began in November 1968 and ended in July 1986; and Statutory Invention Registrations, the current practice, which began May 1985. These documents are patent applications, which are published to provide the defensive properties of a patent, but do not have the enforceable rights of a patent.

Source: U.S. Patent and Trademark Office. Fiscal-year figures are published in the *Commissioner of Patents and Trademarks Annual Report.*

No. 894. Patents, by State: 1997

[Includes only U.S. patents granted to residents of the United States and territories]

State	Total	Inventions	Designs	Botanical plants	Reissues	State	Total	Inventions	Designs	Botanical plants	Reissues
U.S. [1]	69,857	61,707	7,747	230	173	Mississippi	182	156	26	-	-
						Missouri......	870	731	130	7	2
Alabama......	345	300	45	-	-	Montana......	105	88	15	-	2
Alaska	60	46	14	-	-	Nebraska	185	164	20	1	-
Arizona.......	1,162	1,048	114	-	-	Nevada	226	181	45	-	-
Arkansas	152	125	25	2	-	New Hampshire .	503	458	41	1	3
California	12,904	11,290	1,475	114	25						
						New Jersey....	3,458	3,186	261	2	9
Colorado......	1,344	1,220	123	-	1	New Mexico ...	281	261	15	1	4
Connecticut....	1,644	1,403	237	2	2	New York	5,421	4,814	585	7	15
Delaware	368	357	11	-	-	North Carolina .	1,500	1,262	236	2	-
District of						North Dakota...	50	42	6	-	2
Columbia	59	52	7	-	-						
Florida	2,550	2,159	358	30	3	Ohio	3,280	2,715	542	17	6
						Oklahoma.....	453	416	37	-	-
Georgia.......	1,112	966	141	3	2	Oregon.......	1,103	793	305	5	-
Hawaii.......	93	77	14	2	-	Pennsylvania...	2,931	2,697	219	6	9
Idaho	597	565	30	-	2	Rhode Island...	303	249	53	-	1
Illinois	3,537	3,007	516	4	10						
Indiana.......	1,331	1,215	113	1	2	South Carolina .	499	430	67	-	2
						South Dakota ..	53	46	7	-	-
Iowa	450	398	50	-	2	Tennessee	744	644	95	3	2
Kansas.......	322	260	62	-	-	Texas........	4,439	4,140	276	6	17
Kentucky	350	291	54	1	4	Utah	666	613	51	-	2
Louisiana	408	376	31	-	1						
Maine........	109	93	16	-	-	Vermont......	290	276	14	-	-
						Virginia.......	914	818	93	-	3
Maryland	1,257	1,170	85	-	2	Washington....	1,510	1,350	154	5	1
Massachusetts..	2,830	2,575	243	4	8	West Virginia...	165	147	18	-	-
Michigan......	3,074	2,838	221	4	11	Wisconsin.....	1,526	1,301	218	-	7
Minnesota.....	2,058	1,829	218	-	11	Wyoming	60	51	9	-	-

- Represents zero. [1] Includes U.S. territories not shown separately.

Source: U.S. Patent and Trademark Office, Technology Assessment and Forecast Data Base.

U.S. Census Bureau, Statistical Abstract of the United States: 1999

No. 895. Patents, by Industry: 1980 to 1997

[Based on the 1972 Standard Industrial Classification (SIC). Includes all patents for inventions granted to residents of the United States, its territories, and foreign citizens. Individual industries may not add to total since a patent may be recorded in more than one industry category. Except for total, data for all years have been revised to reflect the U.S. Patent Classification System as of 1993]

Industry	SIC code	1980	1985	1990	1995	1996	1997
Total	(X)	61,819	71,661	90,364	101,419	109,645	111,983
Durable goods:							
Stone, clay, and glass products	32	1,243	1,320	1,618	1,534	1,711	1830
Primary metals	33, 3462-3	705	779	913	903	843	753
Fabricated metal products [1]	34	5,013	5,568	6,792	5,924	6,218	5952
Machinery, except electrical	35	14,378	16,832	19,140	21,201	23,299	23547
Electronic and other electric equipment	36, 3825	10,774	13,946	19,203	25,523	27,754	27640
Transportation equipment	37, 348	3,091	3,737	4,723	4,459	4,825	4498
Instruments and related products [2]	38	7,414	8,917	12,252	14,378	15,678	15726
Nondurable goods:							
Food and kindred products	20	483	546	728	600	650	543
Textile mill products	22	428	513	514	629	630	634
Chemicals and allied products	28	9,879	10,278	12,522	13,604	14,685	17210
Oil and gas extraction, petroleum products . .	13, 29	595	802	662	641	532	462
Rubber and miscellaneous plastics products . .	30	2,581	3,020	3,763	3,890	4,026	4074
Other industries	(X)	5,235	5,404	7,534	8,133	8,794	9114

X Not applicable. [1] Excludes SIC groups 3462, 3463, and 348. [2] Excludes SIC group 3825.

Source: U.S. Patent and Trademark Office, *Patenting Trends in the United States, State Country Report, 1963-1996.*

No. 896. New Product Introductions of Consumer Packaged Goods: 1980 to 1997

[Consumer packaged goods: consumable products packaged by the manufacturer for retail sale primarily through grocery and drug stores. New product: a product not previously offered for sale by a particular manufacturer including new varieties, formats, sizes, and packaging for existing products]

Item	Food	Beverages	Health and beauty	Household products	Pet products	Miscella-neous products
Domestic and imports:						
1980	1,192	256	834	331	86	197
1985	2,327	585	1,222	463	139	294
1990	3,453	630	1,531	432	164	154
1991	3,130	589	1,614	422	175	113
1992	2,987	587	1,869	417	213	127
1993	3,107	767	2,068	376	173	161
1994	3,883	807	2,655	378	161	97
1995	3,891	809	2,419	314	123	134
1996	3,889	977	3,051	369	160	148
1997, total	3,793	1,205	3,492	366	216	122
Percent:						
New brands [1]	19.8	30.8	20.1	22.7	31.9	34.4
Brand extensions [2]	1.6	1.3	1.1	2.5	-	-
Line extensions [3]	78.6	67.9	78.8	74.8	68.1	65.6
Types of new product innovation (percent): [4]						
Formulation [5]	56.5	61.6	48.4	50.0	47.1	46.9
New market [6]	1.0	-	0.7	3.1	-	3.1
Packaging [7]	14.0	20.2	9.7	17.2	11.8	9.4
Positioning [8]	24.6	18.2	39.8	29.7	41.2	25.0
Technology [9]	-	-	1.4	-	-	12.5
Merchandising	3.9	-	-	-	-	3.1
CUMULATIVE						
Domestic, except imports, 1980-97	47,796	10,093	29,520	6,447	2,575	2,965
Imports, 1980-97 [10]	4,075	1,314	1,389	261	75	178
International, 1985-97 [11]	18,206	5,712	15,534	3,043	2,914	985

- Represents or rounds to zero. [1] Product introduced under completely or partly new brand name. [2] Product introduced in a category with an existing brand name which has not been used in the category before. [3] Introduction of a new variety, format, size, or package of an existing product/brand name. [4] Product which offers consumers something significantly different from existing products. [5] Added or new ingredient which offers a benefit not previously provided by existing products in its category. [6] Special category for new products which do not compete with any existing category of products. [7] New product packaged in a way that makes it easier to store, handle, prepare, or dispense than others in its category. [8] New product presented for new users or uses compared to existing products in its category. [9] New product with added consumer benefits resulting from use of a new technology. [10] New products introduced in the United States by foreign companies. [11] New products introduced by U.S. and foreign companies outside the United States.

Source: Marketing Intelligence Service Ltd., Naples, NY, *Product Alert Weekly.* Publication contains extract from data base, Product scan.

U.S. Census Bureau, Statistical Abstract of the United States: 1999

No. 897. Net Stock of Fixed Private Capital, by Industry: 1990 to 1997

[In billions of dollars. (12,707 represents $12,707,000,000,000) except quantity indexes, 1992=100. Estimates as of Dec. 31. Based on the 1987 Standard Industrial Classification]

Industry	Current dollars				Quantity indexes (1992=100)			
	1990	1995	1996	1997	1990	1995	1996	1997
Fixed private capital	12,707	15,736	16,497	17,316	97.1	106.7	109.5	112.5
Nonresidential	6,559	7,957	8,311	8,725	97.4	106.6	109.7	113.2
Agriculture, forestry, and fishing	317	360	370	383	102.1	101.5	102.6	103.9
Farms	283	311	318	329	103.6	99.6	100.1	101.0
Agricultural services, forestry, and fishing . .	34	49	52	54	91.0	115.9	120.8	125.7
Mining	441	441	457	481	103.8	97.4	96.4	97.3
Metal mining	29	34	35	37	100.2	103.6	104.0	107.1
Coal mining	32	35	36	38	105.0	103.8	103.2	104.6
Oil and gas extraction	361	351	365	385	104.0	96.1	94.8	95.4
Nonmetallic minerals, except fuels	19	21	21	22	104.5	100.5	100.3	102.8
Construction	77	85	88	93	107.8	103.1	105.7	110.1
Manufacturing	1,203	1,427	1,481	1,533	97.8	104.6	107.3	109.6
Durable goods	630	732	761	793	99.4	104.6	107.6	111.0
Lumber and wood products	25	28	30	31	104.0	103.9	106.2	108.3
Furniture and fixtures	11	13	13	14	100.9	105.1	107.3	108.8
Stone, clay, and glass products	40	43	44	45	102.8	98.1	99.3	101.6
Primary metal industries	118	127	128	129	101.9	97.8	97.6	97.0
Fabricated metal products	68	79	82	85	101.0	104.5	107.0	109.9
Industrial machinery and equipment	110	125	128	133	98.8	103.2	105.6	109.1
Electronic and other electric equipment . .	91	118	129	139	97.7	116.5	127.1	136.3
Motor vehicles and equipment	63	81	86	92	97.3	111.3	116.0	122.5
Other transportation equipment	49	53	53	55	98.3	97.4	96.8	97.8
Instruments and related products	43	52	53	56	94.4	104.7	107.2	111.3
Miscellaneous manufacturing industries . .	11	14	14	14	98.3	104.2	107.1	108.4
Nondurable goods	573	695	720	740	96.2	104.7	106.9	108.1
Food and kindred products	117	141	146	150	96.8	104.3	106.4	107.1
Tobacco products	9	9	9	10	102.1	96.9	97.1	97.4
Textile mill products	33	37	38	38	102.1	101.3	100.7	99.7
Apparel and other textile products	11	13	13	14	99.4	105.0	105.8	106.7
Paper and allied products	83	96	98	100	97.1	100.8	101.5	102.2
Printing and publishing	51	59	60	61	97.2	102.9	104.4	105.3
Chemicals and allied products	154	196	206	214	93.8	107.4	111.1	113.8
Petroleum and coal products	74	91	92	93	95.0	103.3	103.2	102.4
Rubber and miscellaneous plastics products	38	51	55	58	95.4	113.9	121.7	126.3
Leather and leather products	3	3	3	3	104.2	96.3	94.7	94.4
Transportation and public utilities.	1,849	2,204	2,278	2,360	98.3	104.9	107.1	109.2
Transportation	588	689	717	738	101.6	102.9	104.5	106.2
Railroad transportation	315	350	362	365	102.7	97.7	97.2	97.1
Local and interurban passenger transit . .	18	18	18	19	108.7	96.1	95.8	97.2
Trucking and warehousing.	73	99	108	113	105.0	122.8	133.3	139.2
Water transportation	35	36	37	37	105.3	97.5	96.3	95.2
Transportation by air	82	102	105	110	95.5	101.8	103.0	107.3
Pipelines, except natural gas	38	46	47	50	99.4	103.9	105.5	106.8
Transportation services	27	39	42	44	95.2	123.5	132.1	140.1
Communications	430	521	555	591	95.5	110.5	116.8	123.7
Telephone and telegraph.	374	438	462	487	96.4	107.9	113.0	118.3
Radio and television.	56	83	92	105	89.9	126.4	139.9	156.9
Electric, gas, and sanitary services.	831	994	1,006	1,031	97.5	103.5	104.2	104.3
Electric services.	605	704	710	722	98.9	102.2	102.7	102.4
Gas services.	163	199	202	210	95.5	103.5	104.3	104.8
Sanitary services	64	91	95	99	89.6	115.0	117.4	119.5
Wholesale trade.	281	369	398	429	95.6	117.0	126.4	136.6
Retail trade	380	502	539	578	94.1	111.6	117.6	123.4
Finance, insurance, and real estate	1,489	1,872	1,959	2,074	95.1	107.3	110.4	114.4
Depository institutions	269	354	370	388	91.5	110.6	114.5	118.5
Nondepository institutions	73	105	115	127	97.4	132.4	146.8	164.2
Security and commodity brokers	10	11	11	12	102.8	104.9	107.1	110.9
Insurance carriers	104	164	175	185	84.2	123.8	131.0	137.8
Insurance agents, brokers, and service	6	6	6	7	101.3	101.3	101.6	103.2
Real estate	998	1,200	1,247	1,318	97.0	102.9	104.6	107.2
Holding and other investment offices . . .	29	31	34	37	102.6	101.6	107.2	115.9
Services	523	698	742	794	94.1	115.4	122.0	129.8
Hotels and other lodging places.	101	114	120	127	100.9	101.2	103.9	107.1
Personal services	21	25	26	27	96.9	106.8	109.7	110.5
Business services	87	115	122	130	95.7	127.1	139.7	155.8
Auto repair, services, and parking	68	106	114	122	86.5	121.0	128.9	139.0
Miscellaneous repair services	9	12	12	13	97.0	111.8	115.3	124.2
Motion pictures	16	26	29	32	89.1	130.7	144.9	159.6
Amusement and recreation services	33	45	49	53	97.1	117.1	124.2	131.2
Other services	187	256	271	290	92.6	114.6	120.1	126.4
Health services	100	146	155	165	89.3	118.1	122.9	129.1
Legal services.	18	19	19	19	99.5	99.6	100.3	102.1
Educational services	11	17	20	23	93.7	127.8	146.4	162.9
Other [1]	59	74	78	83	96.5	110.0	115.5	121.3
Residential.	6,147	7,779	8,186	8,591	96.8	106.8	109.3	111.9
Farms	158	183	188	193	100.1	100.8	100.9	101.0
Real estate	5,989	7,596	7,997	8,398	96.7	106.9	109.5	112.1

[1] Consists of social services, membership organizations, and miscellaneous professional services.

Source: U.S. Bureau of Economic Analysis, *Survey of Current Business*, September 1998.

No. 898. Fixed Nonresidential Private Capital: 1980 to 1997

[In billions of dollars (3,641 represents $3,641,000,000,000) except as indicated. End-of-year stocks; depreciation over entire calendar year. Data refer to privately owned assets and are based on the fixed capital formation components of the gross domestic product. Excludes residential capital and government enterprises; includes nonprofit institutions. Net stock and depreciation estimates are usually based on geometric depreciation rates]

Item	1980	1990	1992	1993	1994	1995	1996	1997
CURRENT DOLLARS								
Net stocks	3,641	6,559	6,893	7,216	7,599	7,957	8,311	8,725
Equipment	1,375	2,452	2,590	2,687	2,823	2,980	3,116	3,258
Structures	2,266	4,107	4,303	4,529	4,776	4,977	5,195	5,467
Depreciation	225	440	472	486	513	535	559	588
Equipment	164	325	352	362	379	398	417	438
Structures	61	114	120	124	133	137	142	149
QUANTITY INDEXES (1992=100)								
Net stocks	73.68	97.36	100.00	101.74	103.82	106.57	109.71	113.23
Equipment	71.95	97.22	100.00	102.72	106.61	111.67	117.55	124.32
Structures	74.73	97.44	100.00	101.16	102.20	103.64	105.29	107.09
Depreciation	65.04	95.53	100.00	101.48	105.46	108.46	112.94	118.72
Equipment	62.97	95.45	100.00	102.15	106.00	110.64	116.51	123.95
Structures	71.19	95.75	100.00	99.56	103.90	102.38	103.16	104.68

Source: U.S. Bureau of Economic Analysis, *Survey of Current Business,* and unpublished data.

No. 899. Gross Private Domestic Investment in Current and Real (1992) Dollars: 1989 to 1997

[In billions of dollars (773.9 represents $773,900,000,000)]

Item	1989	1990	1991	1992	1993	1994	1995	1996	1997
CURRENT DOLLARS									
Gross private domestic investment	829.2	799.7	736.2	790.4	876.2	1,007.9	1,043.2	1,131.9	1,256.0
Net private domestic investment	314.1	265.4	179.8	205.1	281.7	369.2	386.2	447.6	535.9
Fixed investment	797.5	791.6	738.5	783.4	855.7	946.6	1,012.5	1,099.8	1,188.6
Consumption of fixed capital	515.1	534.3	556.4	585.4	594.5	638.6	657.0	684.3	720.2
Net fixed investment	282.4	257.4	182.1	198.1	261.2	308.0	355.5	415.5	468.4
Nonresidential	566.2	575.9	547.3	557.9	604.1	660.6	727.7	787.9	860.7
Structures	192.3	200.8	181.7	169.2	176.4	184.5	201.3	216.9	240.2
Producers' durable equiment	373.9	375.1	365.6	388.7	427.7	476.1	526.4	571.0	620.5
Residential	231.3	215.7	191.2	225.6	251.6	286.0	284.8	311.8	327.9
Change in business inventories	31.7	8.0	-2.3	7.0	20.5	61.2	30.7	32.1	67.4
Gross government investment	182.7	199.4	200.5	209.1	204.5	205.9	218.3	229.7	235.4
Net government investment	72.4	82.2	77.0	81.0	71.1	67.1	74.5	82.0	83.8
Federal	15.1	16.3	12.7	11.1	3.1	-2.5	-4.4	-3.1	-10.8
State and local	57.3	65.8	64.3	69.9	67.9	69.6	78.9	85.0	94.5
Structures	102.0	112.6	114.3	123.6	125.0	129.6	140.3	148.5	158.2
Equipment	80.7	86.8	86.2	85.5	79.5	76.4	78.0	81.2	77.2
CHAINED (1992) DOLLARS									
Gross private domestic investment	863.5	815.0	738.1	790.4	863.6	975.7	996.1	1,084.1	1,206.4
Net private domestic investment	322.6	267.3	177.3	205.1	280.4	360.5	375.7	441.6	534.2
Fixed investment	832.0	805.8	741.3	783.4	842.8	915.5	966.0	1,050.6	1,138.0
Consumption of fixed capital	540.9	547.7	560.8	585.4	583.1	615.2	620.4	642.4	672.2
Net fixed investment	291.1	258.2	180.4	198.1	259.6	300.4	345.6	408.1	465.7
Nonresidential	588.8	585.2	547.7	557.9	600.2	648.4	710.6	776.6	859.4
Structures	201.2	203.3	181.6	169.2	170.8	172.5	180.7	189.7	203.2
Producers' durable equiment	387.6	381.9	366.2	388.7	429.6	476.8	531.7	589.8	660.9
Residential	243.2	220.6	193.4	225.6	242.6	267.0	256.8	275.9	282.8
Change in business inventories	33.3	10.4	-3.0	7.0	22.1	60.6	27.7	30.0	63.2
Gross government investment [1]	192.5	204.6	202.2	209.1	200.4	196.0	201.6	208.6	211.3
Net government investment	74.7	83.0	77.0	81.0	69.9	63.9	67.8	73.0	73.9
Federal	14.2	15.6	12.2	11.1	3.5	-2.1	-3.3	-1.8	-7.7
State and local	60.5	67.4	64.8	69.9	66.4	66.0	71.1	74.6	81.1
Structures	107.7	115.3	115.3	123.6	121.7	122.0	126.8	130.1	134.0
Equipment	84.7	89.3	86.9	85.5	78.6	73.9	74.7	78.4	76.9

[1] See text, Section 14, Income.

Source: U.S. Bureau of Economic Analysis, *National Income and Product Accounts, Volume 1, 1929-94,* and *Survey of Current Business,* August 1997.

U.S. Census Bureau, Statistical Abstract of the United States: 1999

No. 900. Capital Expenditures: 1996 and 1997

[In millions of dollars (870,221 represents 870,221,000,000). Based on 1987 Standard Industrial Classification code (SIC)]

Item	SIC code	Capital expenditures					
		Companies				Nonemployer businesses	
		Total, 1996	Total, 1997	One or more employee, 1996	One or more employee, 1997	1996	1997
STRUCTURES AND EQUIPMENT							
Total	(X)	807,070	870,221	707,110	770,799	99,960	99,422
Structures	(X)	243,427	272,669	204,345	235,537	39,082	37,132
New	(X)	223,588	253,822	191,867	224,478	31,721	29,344
Used	(X)	19,839	18,849	12,478	11,060	7,361	7,789
Equipment	(X)	563,641	597,550	502,762	535,261	60,878	62,289
New	(X)	526,016	561,103	481,785	515,049	44,231	46,054
Used	(X)	37,625	36,447	20,977	20,212	16,648	16,235
CAPITAL LEASE AND CAPITALIZED INTEREST EXPENSES							
Capital leases	(X)	15,675	16,066	13,023	14,549	2,652	1,517
Capitalized interest	(X)	(NA)	(NA)	6,827	7,241	(NA)	(NA)
INDUSTRY							
Total expenditures	(X)	(NA)	(NA)	707,110	770,799	(NA)	(NA)
Mining	(X)	(NA)	(NA)	30,155	37,412	(NA)	(NA)
Construction	15-17	(NA)	(NA)	13,806	15,531	(NA)	(NA)
Manufacturing industries	20-39	(NA)	(NA)	191,762	192,271	(NA)	(NA)
Durable goods	24, 25, 32-39	(NA)	(NA)	109,898	108,331	(NA)	(NA)
Nondurable goods	20-23, 26-31	(NA)	(NA)	81,864	83,940	(NA)	(NA)
Transportation	40-42, 44-47	(NA)	(NA)	36,698	45,045	(NA)	(NA)
Communications	48	(NA)	(NA)	57,133	68,403	(NA)	(NA)
Utilities	49	(NA)	(NA)	36,744	38,719	(NA)	(NA)
Electric and gas services	491, 493	(NA)	(NA)	25,531	26,503	(NA)	(NA)
Gas, water, and other utilities	492, 494-497	(NA)	(NA)	11,212	12,216	(NA)	(NA)
Wholesale trade	50, 51	(NA)	(NA)	26,026	28,847	(NA)	(NA)
Retail trade	52-59	(NA)	(NA)	55,831	55,868	(NA)	(NA)
Finance	60-62, 67	(NA)	(NA)	87,144	91,328	(NA)	(NA)
Insurance and real estate	63-65	(NA)	(NA)	23,410	29,270	(NA)	(NA)
Services	07-09, 70-89	(NA)	(NA)	145,896	165,113	(NA)	(NA)

NA Not available.   X Not applicable.

Source: U.S. Census Bureau, Annual Capital Expenditures.

No. 901. Composite Indexes of Economic Cyclical Indicators: 1980 to 1997

Item	Unit	1980	1990	1994	1995	1996	1997
Leading index, composite	1992=100	89.3	99.2	101.3	100.8	102.0	103.8
Average weekly hours, manufacturing	Hours	39.7	40.8	41.9	41.6	41.6	42.0
Average weekly initial claims for unemployment insurance	1,000	488.9	385.9	342.0	358.3	351.6	319.4
Manufacturers' new orders, consumer goods and materials (1992 dol.)	Mil. dol.	96,153	118,017	136,312	139,592	142,199	151,576
Vendor performance, slower deliveries diffusion index	Percent	40.6	47.9	60.1	52.8	50.5	53.9
Manufacturers' new orders, nondefense capital goods (1992 dol.)	Mil. dol.	27,142	34,598	34,629	38,783	42,066	45,195
Building permits, new private housing units	1,000	1,246.4	1,155.1	1,366.9	1,335.8	1,419.1	1,444.6
Stock prices, 500 common stocks	1941-43=100	118.8	334.6	460.3	541.6	670.8	872.7
Money supply, M2 (1992 dol.)	Bil. dol.	2,636	3,476	3,328	3,321	3,414	3,517
Interest rate spread, 10-year treasury bonds less Federal funds	Percent	-1.9	0.5	2.9	0.7	1.1	0.9
Index of consumer expectations	Percent	56.8	70.2	83.8	83.2	85.7	97.7
Coincident index, composite	1992=100	80.1	100.2	106.1	109.6	112.6	116.4
Employees on nonagricultural payrolls	Millions	90,418	109,404	114,131	117,187	119,590	122,677
Personal income less transfer payments (1992 dol.)	Bil. dol.	3,371	4,422	4,581	4,713	4,890	5,078
Industrial production	1992=100	79.7	98.9	109.2	114.5	118.5	124.4
Manufacturing and trade sales (1992 dol.)	Bil. dol.	434,290	562,978	627,972	652,755	675,345	714,249
Lagging index, composite	1992=100	103.7	106.8	100.2	103.5	104.4	104.7
Average duration of unemployment	Weeks	11.9	12.0	18.8	16.6	16.7	15.8
Inventories to sales ratio, manufacturing and trade	Ratio	1.5	1.5	1.4	1.4	1.4	1.4
Labor cost per unit of output, manufacturing	Percent	10.0	4.2	-2.5	-1.3	-1.2	0.9
Average prime rate	Percent	15.3	10.0	7.1	8.8	8.3	8.4
Commercial and industrial loans (1992 dol.)	Bil. dol.	345,348	566,029	463,454	517,670	535,297	556,275
Consumer installment credit to personal income ratio	Ratio	15.2	16.4	15.6	17.0	17.9	17.9
Consumer price index for services	Percent	14.6	5.8	3.0	3.5	3.3	2.8

Source: The Conference Board, New York, NY 10022-6601, Business Cycle Indicators, monthly (copyright).

568 Business Enterprise

No. 902. Business Cycle Expansions and Contractions—Months of Duration: 1919 to 1997

[A trough is the low point of a business cycle; a peak is the high point. Contraction or recession is the period from peak to subsequent trough; expansion is the period from trough to subsequent peak. Business cycle reference dates are determined by the National Bureau of Economic Research, Inc.]

Business cycle reference date				Contraction (trough from previous peak)	Expansion (trough to peak)	Length of cycle	
Trough		Peak				Trough from previous trough	Peak from previous peak
Month	Year	Month	Year				
March	1919	January	1920	[1]7	10	[2]51	[1]17
July	1921	May	1923	18	22	28	40
July	1924	October	1926	14	27	36	41
November	1927	August	1929	13	21	40	34
March	1933	May	1937	43	50	64	93
June	1938	February	1945	13	80	63	93
October	1945	November	1948	8	37	88	45
October	1949	July	1953	11	45	48	56
May	1954	August	1957	10	39	55	49
April	1958	April	1960	8	24	47	32
February	1961	December	1969	10	106	34	116
November	1970	November	1973	11	36	117	47
March	1975	January	1980	16	58	52	74
July	1980	July	1981	6	12	64	18
November	1982	July	1990	16	92	28	108
March	1991	(X)	(X)	8	(X)	100	(X)
Average, all cycles:							
1854 to 1991 (31 cycles)				18	35	53	[3]53
1854 to 1919 (16 cycles)				22	27	48	[4]49
1919 to 1945 (six cycles)				18	35	53	53
1945 to 1991 (nine cycles)				11	50	61	61
Average, peacetime cycles:							
1854 to 1991 (26 cycles)				19	29	48	[5]48
1854 to 1919 (14 cycles)				22	24	46	[6]47
1919 to 1945 (5 cycles)				20	26	46	45
1945 to 1991 (7 cycles)				11	43	53	53

X Not applicable.   [1] Previous peak: August 1918.   [2] Previous trough: December 1914.   [3] 30 cycles.   [4] 15 cycles.   [5] 25 cycles.   [6] 13 cycles.

Source: National Bureau of Economic Research, Inc., Cambridge, MA, unpublished data.

No. 903. Manufacturing and Trade—Sales and Inventories: 1980 to 1997

[In billions of dollars, (393 represents $393,000,000,000), except ratios]

Item	1980	1985	1990	1992	1993	1994	1995	1996	1997
Sales, average monthly	**393**	**507**	**546**	**567**	**595**	**638**	**683**	**715**	**750**
Manufacturing	185	233	243	250	261	279	300	310	327
Retail trade	96	138	150	154	162	173	189	200	208
Merchant wholesalers	112	136	154	163	173	186	194	205	214
Inventories [1]	**(NA)**	**664**	**841**	**843**	**869**	**932**	**992**	**1,010**	**1,053**
Manufacturing	(NA)	335	405	383	384	405	431	437	456
Retail trade	(NA)	182	196	208	217	235	254	256	273
Merchant wholesalers	(NA)	147	240	252	268	292	307	316	324
Inventory-sales ratios [2]	**(NA)**	**1.31**	**1.52**	**1.48**	**1.44**	**1.41**	**1.43**	**1.40**	**1.38**
Manufacturing	(NA)	1.44	1.65	1.54	1.47	1.41	1.41	1.40	1.37
Retail trade	(NA)	1.32	1.29	1.32	1.32	1.30	1.31	1.29	1.27
Merchant wholesalers	(NA)	1.08	1.56	1.52	1.51	1.51	1.56	1.52	1.50

NA Not available.   [1] Seasonally adjusted end-of-year data. See text, this section.   [2] End-of-year seasonally adjusted inventories to seasonally adjusted sales.

Source: U.S. Council of Economic Advisors, *Economic Report of the President,* annual.

U.S. Census Bureau, Statistical Abstract of the United States: 1999

No. 904. Manufacturing Corporations—Number, Assets, and Profits, by Asset Size: 1980 to 1998

[Corporations and assets as of **end of 4th quarter**; profits for **entire year.** Based on complete canvass. The asset value for complete canvass was $25 million in 1980 and raised in 1988 to $50 million. Asset sizes less than these values are sampled, except as noted. For details regarding methodology, see source for first quarter, 1988]

Year	Unit	Total	Asset-size Under [1] $10 mil.	$10-$25 mil.	$25-$50 mil.	$50-$100 mil.	$100-$250 mil.	$250 mil.-$1 bil.	$1 bil. and over
Corporations:									
1980	Number	(NA)	(NA)	1,777	941	590	491	369	244
1985	Number	(NA)	(NA)	(NA)	896	744	608	428	281
1989	Number	(NA)	(NA)	(NA)	(NA)	781	750	579	347
1990	Number	(NA)	(NA)	(NA)	(NA)	834	774	597	367
1991	Number	(NA)	(NA)	(NA)	(NA)	868	799	608	373
1992	Number	(NA)	(NA)	(NA)	(NA)	881	829	621	387
1993	Number	(NA)	(NA)	(NA)	(NA)	956	843	648	407
1994	Number	(NA)	(NA)	(NA)	(NA)	983	903	712	417
1995	Number	(NA)	(NA)	(NA)	(NA)	574	639	727	447
1996	Number	(NA)	(NA)	(NA)	(NA)	532	620	745	484
1997	Number	(NA)	(NA)	(NA)	(NA)	470	615	748	529
1998	Number	(NA)	(NA)	(NA)	(NA)	416	531	753	549
Assets:									
1980	Mil. dol	1,384,474	126,639	43,569	34,930	41,963	75,284	179,959	882,129
1985	Mil. dol	1,932,766	153,883	64,324	52,669	58,019	96,748	208,403	1,298,720
1989	Mil. dol	2,503,761	144,774	73,493	56,554	68,146	117,228	282,595	1,760,971
1990	Mil. dol	2,629,458	142,498	74,477	55,914	72,554	123,967	287,512	1,872,536
1991	Mil. dol	2,688,422	140,056	70,567	58,549	72,694	127,748	295,743	1,923,066
1992	Mil. dol	2,798,625	143,766	70,446	65,718	75,967	132,742	302,287	2,007,698
1993	Mil. dol	2,904,869	149,763	72,854	61,243	81,389	134,388	317,774	2,087,457
1994	Mil. dol	3,080,231	148,751	81,505	66,405	82,116	138,950	358,100	2,204,404
1995	Mil. dol	3,345,229	155,618	87,011	68,538	87,262	159,133	370,263	2,417,403
1996	Mil. dol	3,574,407	163,928	87,096	69,722	93,205	156,702	398,651	2,605,102
1997	Mil. dol	3,746,797	167,921	87,398	76,034	85,186	157,130	397,559	2,775,570
1998	Mil. dol	3,998,804	170,618	88,430	69,450	86,850	148,164	417,209	3,018,082
Net profit: [2]									
1980	Mil. dol	92,443	7,770	2,235	1,904	2,479	4,532	11,485	62,041
1985	Mil. dol	87,647	8,601	2,551	2,305	2,819	3,628	7,312	60,431
1989	Mil. dol	135,141	10,378	5,171	2,920	3,092	4,415	11,665	97,501
1990	Mil. dol	110,128	8,527	5,160	2,769	2,661	3,525	7,110	80,377
1991	Mil. dol	66,407	6,820	4,271	2,564	1,704	1,707	5,027	44,316
1992	Mil. dol	22,085	9,567	4,748	3,245	3,034	4,553	5,919	-8,979
1993	Mil. dol	83,156	11,195	5,415	3,439	3,218	3,584	4,555	51,750
1994	Mil. dol	174,874	14,131	7,057	4,072	4,996	6,745	14,626	123,250
1995	Mil. dol	198,151	13,224	5,668	3,767	5,771	7,000	16,549	146,172
1996	Mil. dol	224,869	15,802	6,872	4,266	5,664	7,935	16,059	168,271
1997	Mil. dol	244,505	17,948	8,383	4,153	4,675	7,074	18,433	183,836
1998	Mil. dol	237,661	18,302	6,409	3,754	4,734	5,607	14,147	184,707

NA Not available.   [1] Beginning 1986, excludes estimates for corporations with less than $250,000 in assets at time of sample selection. Prior periods include estimates for corporations in this size category.   [2] After taxes.

Source: U.S. Census Bureau, *Quarterly Financial Report for Manufacturing, Mining and Trade Corporations.*

No. 905. U.S. Largest Public Companies—Profitability and Growth: 1997

[In percent. For fiscal years ending in the 12 month period ending September 30. See source for details. Minus sign (-) indicates decrease]

Industry	Profitability— return on capital [1] 5-year average	Latest 12 months	Growth Sales [2] 5-year average	Latest 12 months	Earnings per share 5-year average	Latest 12 months	Debt/ capital, latest 12 months (percent)
All industries, median	10.5	10.3	8.9	7.9	6.7	14.9	32.8
Aerospace and defense	13.4	12.6	4.0	8.9	7.2	10.7	32.1
Business services and supplies	12.4	10.9	14.9	13.3	9.2	19.8	28.7
Capital goods	13.1	14.7	10.4	7.6	14.0	15.7	30.7
Chemicals	13.2	11.6	6.5	2.0	11.2	12.2	32.0
Computers and software	15.1	14.4	26.0	10.6	16.5	19.6	15.4
Construction	10.1	12.4	11.7	9.9	22.7	25.6	39.9
Consumer durables	10.0	11.1	10.4	6.4	8.0	13.1	33.6
Energy distributors	6.6	6.5	4.6	6.6	3.3	-0.3	36.8
Energy extractors	8.7	11.4	4.7	9.8	-20.7	33.3	30.3
Entertainment and information	10.5	8.7	7.8	9.5	9.0	40.0	40.9
Financial services	12.2	11.7	10.2	11.4	14.4	20.8	41.8
Food distributors	10.1	9.1	7.3	4.7	-17.3	10.4	46.5
Food, drink and tobacco	10.1	10.4	6.2	4.0	-7.3	18.6	40.9
Forest products and packaging	7.6	4.8	7.2	-0.9	(NS)	-44.8	39.6
Health care products	14.6	12.7	11.1	8.8	8.6	15.5	19.4
Health care services	10.4	7.4	24.9	22.3	6.0	23.5	35.4
Household and personal products	9.4	11.7	7.8	7.0	-11.3	28.8	36.0
Insurance	11.7	12.3	6.2	8.4	7.6	14.9	15.8
Metals	9.7	7.8	7.6	3.8	(NS)	-13.7	30.1
Retailing	9.5	9.0	11.2	9.5	-13.0	16.8	27.9
Telecommunications	10.2	11.3	15.1	11.5	9.3	12.8	28.9
Travel and transport	8.9	9.6	10.4	8.9	-3.0	16.4	38.9

NS Not significant.   [1] After-tax profits, the amount remaining if the interest paid on long-term debt was taxed, and minority interest divided by a firm's total capitalization. Total capitalization is long-term debt, common and preferred equity, deferred taxes, investment tax credits, and minority interest in consolidated subsidiaries.   [2] Net sales plus other operating revenue.

Source: Forbes, Inc., New York, NY, *Forbes Annual Report on American Industry,* (Copyright).

No. 906. 500 Largest Industrial Corporations—Selected Financial Items: 1980 to 1996

[78.1 represents $78,100]

Item	Unit	1980	1990	1991	1992	1993	1994	1995	1996
Sales per employee	$1,000 ...	78.1	153.9	159.2	169.3	174.5	(NA)	(NA)	(NA)
Changes in profits	Percent ...	3.6	-11.6	[1]-41.0	[1]-100.4	[1]1.8	13.8	15.0	12.2
Sales per dollar of stockholder's equity	Dollar	3.00	2.97	2.81	2.91	3.02	(NA)	(NA)	(NA)
Return on stockholder's equity	Percent ...	14.4	12.7	[2]10.2	[2]9.0	[2]10.3	13.7	14.0	13.9
Return on sales	Percent ...	4.8	4.1	3.1	2.4	2.9	(NA)	(NA)	(NA)
Total return to investors [3]	Percent ...	21.1	-10.2	29.5	9.1	11.1	-1.0	32.8	30.5

NA Not available. [1] Changes in profits of -41% in 1991 and -100.4% in 1992 include charge-offs for accounting rule change on retiree health benefits. Changes before charge-offs were -35.8%, 18.3%, and 15.1% in 1991, 1992 and 1993 respectively. [2] For 1991-92 data, the return is on common stockholders' equity. For prior years and again with 1993 data, the return is on total equity. [3] Includes both price appreciation and dividend yield, i.e., to an investor in the company's stock.

No. 907. 1000 Largest Industrial Corporations—Selected Financial Items, by Industry: 1987 and 1997

[Data are medians. For explanation of terms, see source. Minus sign (-) indicates decrease. For definition of median, see Guide to Tabular Presentation]

Industry	Revenue, percent change from 1996	Profits					Total return to investors (percent)	
		Percent change from 1996	As per-cent of revenue	As per-cent of assets	As per-cent of stock-holders' equity	Earnings per share, 1987-97 ann. rate	1987-97 ann. rate	1997
Aerospace	13	18	5	6	21	7	21	20
Apparel	7	24	7	9	19	6	12	-1
Beverages	4	17	6	8	17	9	21	32
Building materials, glass	9	66	7	8	23	-2	14	3
Chemicals	2	3	6	6	17	7	14	19
Computer and data services	11	15	5	7	14	14	17	35
Computer peripherals	13	70	7	12	22	13	22	33
Computers, office equipment	12	21	5	5	16	10	12	24
Diversified outsourcing services	15	21	2	6	21	14	19	64
Electronics, electrical equip	10	11	5	7	15	9	17	20
Electronics, network communications	33	25	14	17	22	27	21	-15
Electronics, semiconductors	4	6	12	10	16	23	15	7
Food	4	18	3	7	17	10	18	43
Food services	7	12	2	4	12	15	18	19
Forest and paper products	1	-59	2	2	4	-4	10	6
Industrial and farm equipment	10	17	5	6	16	9	15	31
Insurance: Life, health (stock)	9	36	8	1	11	12	23	42
Insurance: property and casualty (stock)	7	28	9	3	12	9	20	41
Metal products	8	20	8	7	17	12	17	36
Metals	3	19	4	5	13	8	14	-5
Motor vehicles and parts	6	36	4	4	17	6	14	37
Petroleum refining	-	6	5	6	14	7	14	22
Pharmaceuticals	8	12	14	13	27	14	23	34
Pipelines	37	-19	3	2	8	6	20	16
Publishing, printing	8	-	7	7	15	8	14	38
Savings institutions	10	20	10	1	11	5	22	61
Scientific, photo, and control equip	8	-	7	7	14	10	14	13
Securities	22	25	10	1	19	15	29	81
Soaps, cosmetics	6	17	7	10	27	13	23	32
Utilities, gas and electric	6	-	8	3	11	1	14	27
Wholesalers	11	14	1	3	11	9	15	18

- Represents or rounds to zero.

Source of Tables 906-907: Time Warner, New York, NY, *The Fortune Directories* (copyright).

U.S. Census Bureau, Statistical Abstract of the United States: 1999

No. 908. Corporate Profits, Taxes, and Dividends: 1990 to 1998

[In billions of dollars (372 represents $372,000,000,000). Covers corporations organized for profit and other entities treated as corporations. Represents profits to U.S. residents, without deduction of depletion charges and exclusive of capital gains and losses; intercorporate dividends from profits of domestic corporations are eliminated; net receipts of dividends, reinvested earnings of incorporated foreign affiliates, and earnings of unincorporated foreign affiliates are added]

Item	1990	1993	1994	1995	1996	1997	1998
Profits before tax	372	464	535	636	680	734	718
Profits tax liability	141	164	187	211	226	246	240
Profits after tax	231	301	349	425	454	488	478
Dividends	152	197	182	205	262	275	279
Undistributed profits	79	103	166	219	192	213	199
Inventory valuation adjustment (IVA)	-14	-7	-16	-23	-1	7	15
Capital consumption adjustment	39	34	51	59	71	77	92
Net interest	467	399	412	421	419	432	449
Addenda:							
Corporate profits after tax with IVA/CCA [1]	257	328	384	461	524	572	585
Net cash flow with inventory IVA/CCA [1]	455	520	614	687	714	774	806
Undistributed profits with IVA/CCA [1]	105	131	201	256	262	297	305
Consumption of fixed capital	350	389	412	431	452	477	501
Less: Inventory valuation adjustment (IVA)	-14	-7	-16	-23	-1	7	15
Equals: Net cash flow	469	527	630	710	716	767	791

[1] Inventory valuation adjustment/capital consumption adjustment.

Source: U.S. Bureau of Economic Analysis, *National Income and Product Accounts of the Unites States* and *Survey of Current Business,* August 1997.

No. 909. Corporate Profits, by Industry: 1990 to 1997

[In millions of dollars, (371,685 represents $371,685,000,000). Profits are without inventory valuation and capital consumption adjustments. Minus sign (-) indicates loss. See headnote, Table 908]

Industry	Before taxes				After taxes			
	1990	1995	1996	1997	1990	1995	1996	1997
Corporate profits	371,685	635,621	680,194	734,376	231,221	424,646	454,106	488,290
Domestic industries [1]	305,945	546,079	583,804	635,352	165,481	335,104	357,716	389,266
Agriculture, forestry, and fishing	1,619	1,802	2,826	2,992	993	1,134	2,076	2,178
Mining	2,459	4,549	6,183	6,578	876	3,235	4,659	4,561
Construction	10,999	17,408	21,368	17,993	8,781	14,708	18,208	15,334
Manufacturing	115,543	194,472	193,454	212,158	67,503	128,856	123,152	131,357
Transportation	934	11,511	15,364	17,038	-1,993	7,269	10,445	11,278
Communications	20,014	33,713	35,701	30,975	11,831	21,419	22,078	16,401
Wholesale trade	19,839	32,141	37,108	47,415	13,695	22,725	26,196	33,393
Retail trade	24,382	46,583	53,888	60,133	15,426	34,080	39,717	43,976
Finance, insurance, and real estate	65,354	110,117	117,497	138,119	17,873	32,507	37,637	57,509
Services	20,241	52,946	58,041	62,445	14,901	42,399	45,515	48,002
Rest of the world	65,740	89,542	96,390	99,024	65,740	89,542	96,390	99,024

[1] Consists of receipts by all U.S. residents, including both corporations and persons, of earnings of unincorporated foreign affiliates, dividends from their incorporated foreign affiliates, and their share of their incorporated foreign affiliates, net of corresponding outflows.

No. 910. Corporate Profits With Inventory Valuation and Capital Consumption Adjustments—Financial and Nonfinancial Industries: 1980 to 1998

[In billions of dollars (167.1 represents $167,100,000,000). See headnote, Table 908]

Item	1980	1985	1990	1992	1993	1994	1995	1996	1997	1998
Corporate profits with IVA/CCA [1]	167.1	304.0	397.1	428.0	492.1	570.5	672.4	750.4	817.9	824.6
Domestic industries	131.6	270.6	331.3	363.1	422.5	497.1	582.8	654.0	718.9	729.0
Rest of the world	35.5	33.4	65.7	64.9	69.6	73.4	89.5	96.4	99.0	95.7
Corporate profits with IVA [1]	198.3	230.5	358.2	398.9	457.7	519.1	613.0	679.0	741.2	732.3
Domestic industries	162.9	197.1	292.5	334.0	388.1	445.7	523.4	582.6	642.2	636.6
Financial	24.3	29.0	68.6	83.7	91.0	69.4	104.6	110.7	130.0	134.2
Nonfinancial	138.5	168.1	223.8	250.3	297.2	376.3	418.8	471.8	512.3	502.4
Manufacturing	75.8	81.6	112.3	96.3	109.7	151.6	183.9	195.6	214.4	192.8
Transportation and public utilities	18.3	34.3	43.2	57.8	70.6	83.1	86.0	92.7	88.4	90.4
Wholesale trade	16.7	20.6	17.2	23.0	25.5	29.4	26.2	37.9	49.8	51.3
Retail trade	6.1	22.5	20.6	32.2	39.2	46.0	43.3	51.8	61.2	67.2
Other	21.6	9.1	30.6	41.0	52.1	66.2	79.5	93.8	98.5	100.7

[1] Inventory valuation adjustment and capital consumption adjustment.

Source of Tables 909-910: U.S. Bureau of Economic Analysis, *National Income and Product Accounts of the Unites States, 1929-94,* forthcoming, and *Survey of Current Business,* September 1998.

No. 911. Manufacturing, Mining, and Trade Corporations—Profits and Stockholders' Equity Ratios: 1990 to 1998

[Averages of quarterly figures at annual rates. manufacturing data exclude estimates for corporations with less than $250,000 in assets at time of sample selection. Data are not necessarily comparable from year to year due to changes in accounting procedures, industry classifications, sampling procedures, etc.; for detail, see source. Based on sample; see source for discussion of methodology. Minus sign (-) indicates loss]

Industry	Ratio of profits to stockholders' equity (percent)				Profits per dollar of sales (cents)				Ratio of stockholders' equity to debt			
	1990	1995	1997	1998	1990	1995	1997	1998	1990	1995	1997	1998
Manufacturing corporations.....	10.6	16.0	16.7	15.7	3.9	5.6	6.2	6.1	1.3	1.4	1.5	1.4
Durable goods..................	7.9	15.4	16.3	16.4	3.0	5.2	5.8	5.9	1.6	1.8	1.9	1.7
Lumber and wood products........	(NA)	12.6	20.1	15.0	(NA)	3.5	5.1	3.8	(NA)	1.8	1.6	1.3
Furniture and fixtures............	(NA)	7.9	16.4	19.5	(NA)	2.2	4.4	4.8	(NA)	1.7	1.8	1.5
Stone, clay, and glass products	5.2	12.2	11.9	18.5	1.7	4.4	3.8	6.3	0.8	1.1	1.1	1.1
Primary metal industries	9.2	19.0	12.7	10.1	2.5	5.4	4.2	3.5	1.1	1.3	1.5	1.3
Iron and steel	6.1	14.8	12.1	7.7	0.9	3.9	3.6	2.4	0.6	1.3	1.4	1.2
Nonferrous metals	10.2	22.1	13.2	12.2	3.9	6.7	4.9	4.6	1.7	1.3	1.6	1.4
Fabricated metal products	11.7	13.0	19.2	18.1	3.3	3.5	5.7	5.5	1.3	1.2	1.3	1.2
Machinery, exc. electrical.........	8.1	12.1	15.4	13.7	4.3	4.3	5.5	5.1	2.2	1.8	2.0	1.7
Electrical and electronic equipment ...	7.5	18.8	16.4	12.0	3.0	8.3	7.9	6.0	1.6	2.4	2.7	2.4
Transportation equipment	3.8	17.4	20.9	33.4	1.2	4.5	5.4	7.8	1.9	2.1	2.0	1.6
Motor vehicles and equipment ...	-1.0	21.0	23.4	45.2	-0.5	4.7	5.5	9.3	2.2	2.6	2.6	1.9
Aircraft, guided missiles and parts ..	11.5	10.6	17.3	17.9	3.4	3.6	5.2	5.0	1.6	1.7	1.3	1.3
Instruments and related products ...	12.8	13.7	11.3	9.0	6.5	7.6	6.7	5.2	1.6	2.3	1.9	1.6
Miscellaneous manufacturing	(NA)	11.1	16.5	15.7	(NA)	3.2	4.6	4.2	(NA)	1.7	1.6	1.4
Nondurable goods...............	13.1	16.6	17.1	15.1	4.8	6.0	6.7	6.2	1.2	1.2	1.3	1.2
Food and kindred products [1]	16.1	18.4	19.9	20.7	4.0	5.4	5.5	5.8	0.8	1.0	0.9	0.9
Tobacco products.............	(1)	(1)	(1)	(1)	(1)	(1)	(1)	(1)	(1)	(1)	(1)	(1)
Textile mill products	2.7	4.9	9.7	10.7	0.6	1.3	2.8	3.2	0.7	0.9	1.1	1.1
Apparel (includes leather)	(NA)	12.5	24.5	17.3	(NA)	2.7	4.6	3.4	(NA)	1.1	0.9	1.0
Paper and allied products	10.6	20.9	5.7	7.8	4.2	6.9	2.2	2.9	1.1	0.9	0.9	0.9
Printing and publishing	8.2	14.8	11.7	15.3	3.6	6.1	5.9	8.3	1.2	1.3	1.4	1.6
Chemicals and allied products	16.8	21.0	20.5	20.2	7.9	9.1	9.9	9.9	1.4	1.2	1.3	1.2
Industrial..................	13.1	16.2	13.1	12.2	6.6	6.6	5.5	5.3	1.4	1.0	1.0	1.0
Drugs....................	27.1	26.7	23.4	29.1	15.7	14.4	14.1	15.9	2.2	1.4	1.6	1.5
Residual of chemicals	(NA)	20.3	25.3	17.6	(NA)	7.6	11.0	8.5	(NA)	1.3	1.4	1.3
Petroleum and coal products	12.7	10.6	18.9	6.5	5.6	4.9	9.2	3.9	1.7	1.7	2.5	2.1
Rubber and misc. plastics products ...	6.9	15.3	15.5	15.0	1.8	4.1	4.4	4.4	1.0	1.3	1.2	1.1
Mining corporations [2]	8.2	2.1	8.4	-5.7	5.8	1.9	8.4	-5.5	1.3	1.4	1.6	1.3
Retail trade corporations [2]......	8.4	10.0	11.8	13.4	1.0	1.6	2.0	2.3	0.6	1.0	1.1	1.1
Wholesale trade corporations [2] ..	5.0	9.1	10.7	9.2	0.6	1.2	1.5	1.4	1.0	0.8	1.0	1.0

NA Not available. [1] Tobacco included in food and kindred products. [2] Asset cut-off raised to $50 million from $25 million in 1985.

No. 912. Manufacturing Corporations—Selected Finances: 1980 to 1998

[In billions of dollars (1,328 represents $1,328,000,000,000). Data are not necessarily comparable from year to year due to changes in accounting procedures, industry classifications, sampling procedures, etc.; for detail, see source]

Year	All manufacturing corps.					Durable goods industries					Nondurable goods industries				
	Profits			Stockholders' equity[1]	Debt[2]	Profits			Stockholders' equity[1]	Debt[2]	Profits			Stockholders' equity[1]	Debt[2]
	Sales	Before taxes	After taxes			Sales	Before taxes	After taxes			Sales	Before taxes	After taxes		
1980 ..	1,328	115	70	497	292	657	58	35	240	143	671	57	36	257	149
1982 ..	1,742	154	99	601	371	866	72	45	293	177	876	82	54	308	193
1983 ..	1,913	146	93	668	368	889	57	36	318	168	1,024	88	57	350	200
1984 ..	2,145	159	101	743	405	980	67	42	350	166	1,165	91	60	393	239
1985 ..	2,039	108	71	770	454	913	35	22	356	187	1,126	74	49	415	267
1986 ..	2,114	133	86	813	501	974	49	30	372	203	1,141	84	56	440	298
1987 ..	2,335	166	108	864	553	1,108	76	49	396	229	1,228	90	59	469	324
1988 ..	2,331	137	88	866	622	1,143	62	39	421	265	1,189	76	49	445	357
1989 ..	2,221	129	83	875	733	1,126	52	33	436	308	1,095	77	51	438	425
1990 ..	2,378	173	116	901	782	1,178	78	53	444	328	1,200	95	63	457	453
1988 [3]	2,596	215	154	958	(X)	1,285	92	67	469	(X)	1,312	124	87	489	(X)
1989 ..	2,745	188	135	999	(X)	1,357	75	56	501	(X)	1,389	113	80	498	(X)
1990 ..	2,811	158	110	1,044	(X)	1,357	57	41	515	(X)	1,454	101	69	529	(X)
1991 ..	2,761	99	66	1,064	814	1,304	14	7	507	338	1,457	85	59	557	476
1992 [4]	2,890	31	22	1,035	819	1,390	-34	-24	474	335	1,500	65	46	561	485
1993 ..	3,015	118	83	1,040	819	1,490	39	27	483	327	1,525	79	56	557	492
1994 ..	3,256	244	175	1,110	815	1,658	121	87	533	316	1,598	123	88	577	500
1995 ..	3,528	275	198	1,241	862	1,808	131	94	614	333	1,721	144	104	627	529
1996 ..	3,758	307	225	1,348	920	1,942	147	106	674	366	1,816	160	119	674	554
1997 ..	3,922	331	244	1,464	953	2,076	167	121	744	386	1,847	164	123	721	566
1998 ..	3,934	318	238	1,513	1,062	2,145	173	126	772	455	1,789	145	112	741	606

X Not applicable. [1] In the old series, "income taxes" refers to Federal income taxes only, as state and local income taxes had already been deducted. In the new series, no income taxes have been deducted. [2] Annual data are average equity for the year (using four end-of-quarter figures). [3] Beginning 1988, profits before and after income taxes reflect inclusion of minority stockholders' interest in net income before and after income taxes. [4] Data for 1992 (most significantly 1992:I) reflect the early adoption of Financial Accounting Standards Board Statement 106 (Employer's Accounting for Post-Retirement Benefits Other Than Pensions) by a large number of companies during the fourth quarter of 1992. Data for 1993: I also reflect adoption of Statement 106. Corporations must show the cumulative effect of a change in accounting principle in the first quarter of the year in which the change is adopted.

Source of Tables 911 and 912: Through 1981, U.S. Federal Trade Commission; thereafter, U.S. Census Bureau, *Quarterly Financial Report for Manufacturing, Mining, and Trade Corporations.* In U.S. Council of Economic Advisers, *Economic Report of the President,* annual.

Business Enterprise 573

No. 913. U.S. Multinational Companies—Gross Product: 1995 and 1996

[In millions of dollars (1,831,046 represents $1,831,046,000,000). Gross product measures valued added by a firm. Consists of nonbank U.S. parent companies and their nonbank foreign affiliates. A U.S. parent comprises the domestic operations of a multinational and is a U.S. person that owns or controls 10 percent or more of the voting securities, or the equivalent, of a foreign business enterprise. A U.S. person can be an incorporated business enterprise. A majority-owned foreign affiliate is a foreign business enterprise in which a U.S. parent company owns or controls 50 percent or more of the voting securities]

Industry	U.S. multinationals		U.S. parents		Majority-owned foreign affiliates	
	1995	1996	1995	1996	1995	1996
All industries...................	1,831,046	1,965,438	1,365,470	1,466,999	462,959	498,439
Petroleum........................	205,044	229,265	110,014	124,818	95,030	104,447
Manufacturing....................	1,023,697	1,060,715	723,182	752,784	300,515	307,931
Food and kindred products............	119,282	111,905	78,223	75,322	41,059	36,583
Chemical and allied products............	182,827	(NA)	116,949	127,746	65,878	69,938
Primary and fabricated metals............	59,387	59,376	39,937	39,716	19,450	19,660
Industrial machinery and equipment [1].....	139,767	145,119	88,818	93,670	50,949	51,449
Electronic and other electric equipment [1].....	103,693	122,232	77,286	87,913	26,407	34,319
Transportation equipment..............	202,108	209,154	152,834	162,188	49,274	46,966
Other........................	216,632	215,245	169,135	166,229	47,497	49,016
Wholesale trade...................	39,127	57,229	30,853	42,425	8,274	14,804
Finance (exc. dep. inst.), insurance & real estate .	72,489	92,933	52,813	69,768	19,676	23,165
Finance, except depository institutions	22,370	(NA)	18,205	28,568	4,165	6,941
Insurance......................	41,677	(NA)	32,815	38,478	8,862	9,215
Real estate	(D)	(NA)	1,667	1,795	31	(D)
Holding companies	5,286	(NA)	127	928	5,159	5,131
Services........................	118,328	140,597	97,623	113,882	20,705	26,715
Hotels and other lodging places...........	9,178	(NA)	7,557	8,981	1,621	1,639
Business services...................	51,915	(NA)	38,667	49,188	13,248	17,750
Advertising.....................	5,181	(NA)	2,820	3,109	2,361	2,568
Equipment rental (exc. auto, computers) ...	1,288	(NA)	1,100	1,064	188	135
Computer and data processing..........	24,094	(NA)	18,481	28,035	5,613	9,859
Business services, n.e.c...............	21,352	(NA)	16,266	16,980	5,086	5,188
Automotive rental and leasing	3,717	(NA)	3,346	3,326	371	(D)
Motion pictures, television tape and film	11,613	(NA)	10,126	11,286	1,487	(D)
Health services...................	17,569	(NA)	17,218	18,360	351	211
Engineering and architectural services [1]	6,077	(NA)	5,301	5,251	776	1,000
Management and public relations..........	5,210	(NA)	3,621	4,289	1,589	1,843
Other	13,051	(NA)	11,788	13,201	1,263	2,001
Other industries.....................	372,360	140,597	350,984	363,323	21,376	21,377

D Figure withheld to avoid disclosure pertaining to a specific organization or individual.   NA Not available.   [1] For changes in industry definition, see text.

Source: U.S. Bureau of Economic Analysis, Survey of Current Business, September 1998.

No. 914. U.S. Multinational Companies—Selected Characteristics: 1996

[Preliminary. In billions of dollars ($7,805.1 represents $7,805,100,000,000), except as indicated. Consists of nonbank U.S. parent companies and their nonbank foreign affiliates. U.S. parent is a U.S. person that owns or controls directly or indirectly, 10 percent or more of the voting securities of an incorporated foreign business enterprise, or an equivalent interest in an unincorporated foreign business enterprise. A U.S. person can be an incorporated business enterprise. A foreign affiliate is a foreign business enterprise owned or controlled by a U.S. parent company]

Industry [1]	U.S. parents				Foreign affiliates				U.S. exports shipped to foreign affiliates	U.S. imports shipped from foreign affiliates
	Total assets	Sales	Employment (1,000)	Employee compensation	Total assets	Sales	Employment (1,000)	Employee compensation		
All industries.......	7,805.1	4,497.6	18,755.1	843.8	3,075.5	2,227.0	7,616.5	254.0	194.1	162.3
Petroleum.............	554.6	435.9	484.3	31.4	295.6	380.4	236.0	12.1	3.6	12.7
Manufacturing.........	2,636.4	2,123.4	8,949.3	463.4	846.6	1,041.4	4,477.9	142.7	124.8	134.1
Food and kindred products	214.1	212.3	958.2	32.0	111.2	121.2	557.1	14.1	3.1	2.9
Chemical and allied products	471.7	327.1	1,038.0	66.6	204.6	199.3	611.1	25.6	14.9	7.7
Primary and fabricated metals.............	118.4	119.3	574.6	26.2	42.2	43.0	244.7	7.8	2.9	3.5
Industrial machinery and equipment	289.8	271.6	1,151.9	61.9	110.2	167.3	527.2	21.3	19.0	28.2
Electronic and electric equipment	402.2	284.9	1,192.8	59.1	77.2	99.9	838.5	15.8	20.1	20.5
Transportation equipment.	650.2	499.6	1,683.5	111.3	133.2	233.8	707.5	26.5	49.9	58.3
Other manufacturing	490.0	408.6	2,350.3	106.3	168.0	176.9	991.9	31.5	15.0	13.0
Wholesale trade.......	178.4	350.5	685.4	26.4	210.5	393.1	563.3	27.5	59.9	13.2
Finance (deposit institutions), insurance, real estate...............	3,047.5	522.3	1,069.6	72.9	1,333.5	117.4	196.2	10.8	-	-
Services..............	293.2	217.3	2,381.3	79.0	131.7	115.6	829.1	32.0	2.2	0.4
Other................	1,095.0	848.1	5,205.1	170.8	257.7	179.2	1,314.0	28.8	3.7	2.0

- Represents zero.   [1] Represents industry of U.S. parent or industry of foreign affiliate.

Source: U.S. Bureau of Economic Analysis, Survey of Current Business, September 1998.

Gross Product, Employment, and Capital Expenditures of Nonbank U.S. MNCs, U.S. Parents, and Foreign Affiliates: 1990 to 1996

[Gross product and capital expenditures in millions of dollars; employees in thousands]

Item	1990	1992	1993	1994	1995	1996 [1]	Percent change at annual rates		
							1989-94	1994-95	1995-96
GROSS PRODUCT									
MNCs worldwide:									
Parents and all affiliates .	(NA)	(NA)	(NA)	(NA)	(NA)	(NA)	(NA)	(NA)	(NA)
Parents and MOFAs [2] ...	(NA)	(NA)	(NA)	1,717,488	1,831,046	1,965,438	4.7	6.6	7.3
Parents.............	(NA)	(NA)	(NA)	1,313,792	1,365,470	1,466,999	4.7	3.9	7.4
Affiliates, total.........	(NA)	(NA)	(NA)	(NA)	(NA)	(NA)	(NA)	(NA)	(NA)
MOFAs...........	356,033	361,524	359,179	403,696	465,576	498,439	4.8	15.3	7.1
Other............	(NA)	(NA)	(NA)	(NA)	(NA)	(NA)	(NA)	(NA)	(NA)
EMPLOYEES									
MNCs worldwide:									
Parents and all affiliates .	25,264	24,190	24,222	25,670	25,921	26,392	0.2	1.0	1.8
Parents and MOFAs....	23,786	22,812	22,760	24,273	24,500	24,933	0.3	0.9	1.8
Parents.............	18,430	17,530	17,537	18,565	18,576	18,775	-0.2	0.1	1.1
Affiliates, total.........	6,834	6,660	6,685	7,105	7,345	7,617	1.4	3.4	3.7
MOFAs...........	5,356	5,282	5,223	5,707	5,924	6,158	2.2	3.8	4.0
Other............	1,478	1,378	1,461	1,398	1,421	1,459	-1.5	1.7	2.6
CAPITAL EXPENDITURES									
MNCs worldwide:									
Parents and all affiliates .	(NA)	(NA)	(NA)	328,240	(NA)	(NA)	3.7	(NA)	(NA)
Parents and MOFAs....	274,614	272,049	271,661	303,364	323,616	340,101	3.5	6.7	5.1
Parents.............	213,079	208,834	207,437	231,917	248,017	258,997	3.1	6.9	4.4
Affiliates, total.........	(NA)	(NA)	(NA)	96,323	(NA)	(NA)	5.1	(NA)	(NA)
MOFAs...........	61,535	63,215	64,224	71,447	75,599	81,104	4.6	5.8	7.3
Other............	(NA)	(NA)	(NA)	24,876	(NA)	(NA)	6.7	(NA)	(NA)

NA Not available. [1] Break-in-series. See source, appendix for details. [2] Majority-Owned Foreign Affiliate.

Source: U.S. Bureau of Economic Analysis, *Survey of Current Business,* December, October 1997.

No. 916. Nonbank U.S. MNCs, U.S. Parents, and MOFAs by Industry of U.S. Parent: 1989 and 1996

[In billions of dollars ($1,364.9 represents $1,364,900,000,000)]

Item	MNCs			Parents			MOFAs		
	Gross product	Profit-type return	Capital expenditures	Gross product	Profit-type return	Capital expenditures	Gross product	Profit-type return	Capital expenditures
1989									
All industries	1,364.9	251.4	258.8	1,044.9	164.9	201.8	320.0	86.5	57.0
Petroleum	165.7	31.3	41.5	93.1	15.8	26.8	72.6	15.5	14.7
Manufacturing	793.8	147.0	132.0	586.6	86.2	98.7	207.2	60.8	33.3
Food and kindred products	79.5	19.5	12.0	60.3	14.6	9.4	19.2	5.0	2.7
Chemicals and allied products	141.0	38.4	27.8	97.1	23.4	20.3	43.9	15.0	7.5
Primary and fabricated metals	45.8	9.6	7.3	37.6	6.3	5.4	8.2	3.3	1.9
Industrial machinery and equip....	116.1	16.2	18.5	70.9	1.8	11.5	45.3	14.4	6.9
Electronic/other electric equip	68.5	12.4	13.6	56.1	9.2	11.0	12.4	3.2	2.6
Transportation equipment	160.3	22.0	24.4	121.1	11.6	18.6	39.2	10.4	5.7
Other manufacturing	182.6	28.8	28.4	143.4	19.3	22.4	39.2	9.5	6.0
Wholesale trade	28.8	5.6	6.1	22.6	3.2	5.0	6.2	2.5	1.1
Finance (except banking), insurance and real estate	62.7	20.2	9.4	50.5	16.4	7.6	12.2	3.8	1.9
Services	67.0	7.8	16.7	57.1	5.9	13.6	9.9	1.8	3.1
Other industries	246.9	39.5	53.1	235.0	37.4	50.2	12.0	2.1	3.0
1996									
All industries	1,965.4	450.9	340.1	1,467.0	325.3	259.0	498.4	125.6	81.1
Petroleum	229.3	50.4	40.8	124.8	25.9	23.4	104.4	24.5	17.4
Manufacturing	1,060.7	239.1	161.8	752.8	158.1	114.2	307.9	81.0	47.6
Food and kindred products	111.9	32.6	12.4	75.3	23.6	9.1	36.6	9.1	3.3
Chemicals and allied products	197.7	60.7	30.9	127.7	34.7	20.6	69.9	26.0	10.3
Primary and fabricated metals	59.4	8.8	7.8	39.7	6.0	6.0	19.7	2.8	1.8
Industrial machinery and equip....	145.1	31.4	19.1	93.7	18.0	12.9	51.4	13.4	6.2
Electronic/other electric equip	122.2	33.5	28.8	87.9	22.2	20.9	34.3	11.4	7.8
Transportation equipment	209.2	33.5	32.5	162.2	26.1	20.7	47.0	7.5	11.8
Other manufacturing	215.2	38.4	30.3	166.2	27.6	23.9	49.0	10.8	6.4
Wholesale trade	57.2	10.2	10.2	42.4	6.1	8.4	14.8	4.1	1.8
Finance (except banking), insurance and real estate	92.9	47.2	14.0	69.4	37.7	11.5	23.2	9.4	2.5
Services	140.6	22.8	21.6	113.9	18.2	18.3	26.7	4.6	3.3
Other industries	384.7	81.2	91.6	363.3	79.2	83.2	21.4	2.0	8.4

Source: U.S. Bureau of Economic Analysis, *Survey of Current Business,* September 1998.

Business Enterprise 575

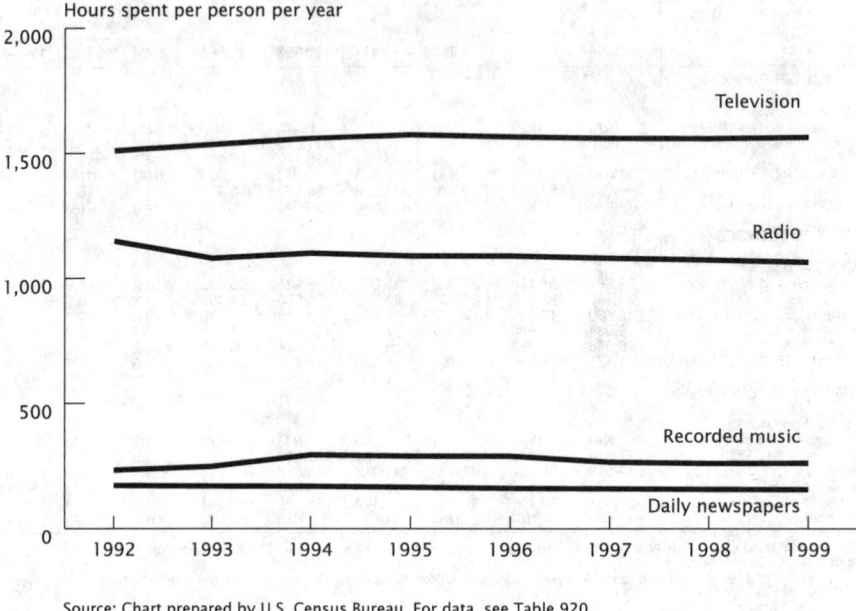

Figure 18.1
Media Usage by Consumers: 1992 to 1999

Hours spent per person per year

Television

Radio

Recorded music

Daily newspapers

Source: Chart prepared by U.S. Census Bureau. For data, see Table 920.

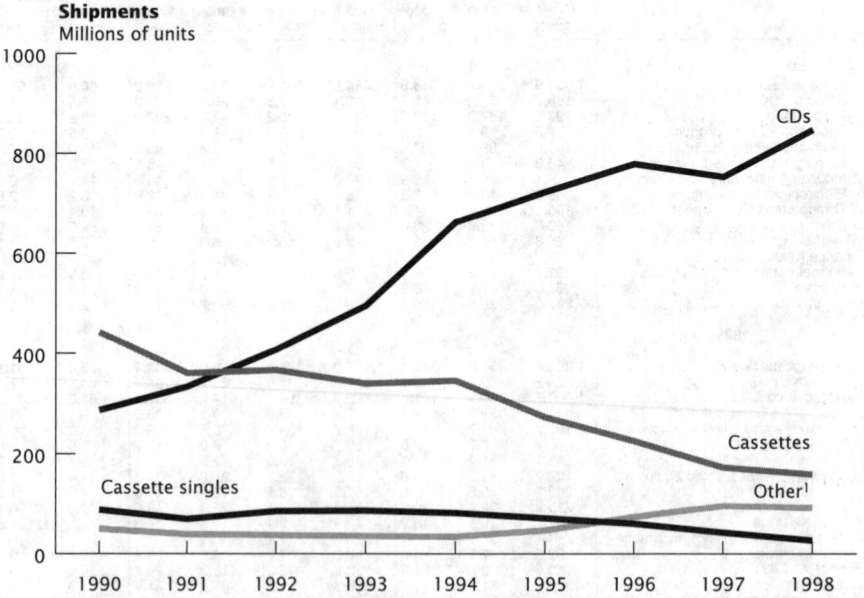

Figure 18.2
Shipments of Recording Media: 1990 to 1998

Shipments
Millions of units

CDs

Cassettes

Cassette singles

Other[1]

[1] Includes CD singles, vinyl albums and singles, and music video.
Source: Chart prepared by U.S. Census Bureau. For data, see Table 936.

576 Communications and Information Technology

Section 18
Communications and Information Technology

This section presents statistics on the various communications media: telephone, telegraph, radio, television, newspapers, and periodicals and the usage, finances, and operations of the Postal Service. Expenditure data for advertising in the media are also included.

Communication media—The U.S. Census Bureau's *Annual Survey of Communication Services* (ASCS) covers all employer firms with one or more establishments that are primarily engaged in providing point-to-point communication services, whether by wire or radio, and whether intended to be received aurally or visually. This includes telephone communications, including cellular and other radiotelephone services; telegraph and other message communications, such as electronic mail services, facsimile transmission services, telex services, etc.; radio and television broadcasting stations and networks; cable and other pay television services; and other communication services, such as radar station operations, satellite earth stations, satellite or missile tracking stations, etc. The report presents statistics that are summarized by kind-of-business classification based on the 1987 edition of the *Standard Industrial Classification Manual*. See text, Section 17, Business.

The Federal Communications Commission (FCC), established in 1934, regulates wire and radio communications. Only the largest carriers and holding companies file annual or monthly financial reports. The FCC has jurisdiction over interstate and foreign communication services but not over intrastate or local services. The gross operating revenues of the telephone carriers reporting annually to the FCC, however, are estimated to cover about 90 percent of the revenues of all U.S. telephone companies. Data are not comparable with Census Bureau *Annual Survey of Communication Services* because of coverage (ASCS includes all domestic long-distance telephone companies, all local exchange carriers, and all cellular telephone companies) and different accounting practices for those telephone companies which report to the FCC.

Reports filed by the broadcasting industry cover all radio and television stations operating in the United States. The private radio services represent the largest and most diverse group of licensees regulated by the FCC. These services provide voice, data communications, point-to-point, and point-to-multipoint radio communications for fixed and mobile communicators. Major users of these services are small businesses, the aviation industry, the maritime trades, the land transportation industry, manufacturing industry, state and local public safety and governmental authorities, emergency medical service providers, amateur radio operators, and personal radio operations (CB and the General Mobile Radio Service). The FCC also licenses entities as private and common carriers. Private and common carriers provide fixed and land mobile communications service on a for-profit basis. Principal sources of wire, radio, and television data are the FCC's *Annual Report* and its annual *Statistics of Communications Common Carriers*.

Statistics on the printed media are available from the Census Bureau, as well as from various private agencies. The censuses of manufactures (conducted by the Census Bureau every 5 years, for the years ending in "2" and "7") provide statistics on the number and circulation of newspapers and periodicals and on sales of books and pamphlets. Editor & Publisher Co., New York, NY, presents annual data on the

Communications and Information Technology 577

number and circulation of daily and Sunday newspapers in its *International Year Book*. Monthly data on new books and new editions appear in *Publishers Weekly*, issued by R. R. Bowker Company, New York. (See Table 938 for annual data.)

Advertising—Data on advertising expenditures are compiled primarily by McCann-Erickson, Inc., which compiles certain of the data shown (see Table 947). Monthly index figures of advertising in certain media are also published periodically by McCann-Erickson in *Advertising Age*.

The Broadcast Advertisers Reports distinguishes between spot and local advertising primarily on the basis of the type of advertiser to whom the time is sold, rather than how and by whom it is sold. In general, time purchased on behalf of retail or service establishments in the market is considered local, even though the establishments may be part of a national or regional chain. That is, spot advertising promotes a product, while local advertising promotes a given establishment. Network advertising, mutually exclusive of spot and local, is broadcast through the network system.

Postal Service—The Postal Service provides mail processing and delivery services within the United States. The Postal Reorganization Act of 1970 created the Postal Service, effective July 1971, as an independent establishment of the Federal Executive Branch.

Revenue and cost analysis describes the Postal Service's system of attributing revenues and costs to classes of mail and service. This system draws primarily upon probability sampling techniques to develop estimates of revenues, volumes, and weights, as well as costs by class of mail and special service. The costs attributed to classes of mail and special services are primarily incremental costs which vary in response to changes in volume; they account for roughly 60 percent of the total costs of the Postal Service. The balance represents "institutional costs." Statistics on revenues, volume of mail, and distribution of expenditures are presented in the Postal Service's annual report, *Cost and Revenue Analysis*, and its *Annual Report of the Postmaster General* and its annual *Comprehensive Statement on Postal Operations*.

Statistical reliability—For a discussion of statistical collection and estimation, sampling procedures, and measures of statistical reliability applicable to Census Bureau data, see Appendix III.

U.S. Census Bureau, Statistical Abstract of the United States: 1999

No. 917. Gross Domestic Income in Information Technologies (IT) Industries: 1990 to 1999

[In millions of dollars (330,076 represents $330,076,000,000), except as noted]

Industry	1987 SIC [1] code	1990	1995	1996	1997 est.	1998 est.	1999 est.
Total all IT industries	(X)	330,076	482,832	543,495	596,645	663,578	729,002
Percent share of the economy	(X)	5.8	6.6	7.1	7.3	7.8	8.2
Hardware	(X)	102,677	154,517	171,852	197,375	210,816	229,222
Computers and equipment	3571,2,5,7	24,660	28,369	30,188	34,475	36,819	40,390
Computers and equipment wholesale sales .	5045 (pt)	33,599	50,756	61,129	69,779	74,559	80,538
Computers and equipment retail sales .	5734 (pt)	1,857	2,841	2,777	3,167	3,383	3,661
Calculating and office machines, n.e.c. [2]	3578, 9	2,242	2,450	2,509	2,675	2,817	3,020
Electron tubes	3671	1,161	1,197	1,247	1,341	1,425	1,515
Printed circuit boards	3672	4,403	4,402	5,051	5,536	6,040	6,934
Semiconductors	3674	15,733	40,632	43,335	50,452	58,588	63,861
Passive electronic components	3675-9	11,543	15,280	15,055	14,574	15,317	16,619
Industrial instruments for measurement	3823	2,320	2,514	2,929	3,277	3,529	3,762
Instruments for measuring electricity	3825	3,299	3,957	4,878	5,200	5,480	5,864
Laboratory analytical instruments	3826	1,860	2,121	2,754	2,751	2,858	3,058
Software/services [3]	(X)	59,661	104,466	132,032	150,034	172,956	199,282
Computer programming services	7371	14,903	24,505	29,475	(NA)	(NA)	(NA)
Prepackaged software	7372	10,615	21,361	27,491	(NA)	(NA)	(NA)
Computer integrated systems design	7373	9,424	12,758	14,123	(NA)	(NA)	(NA)
Computer processing and data preparation . .	7374	10,256	20,493	28,687	(NA)	(NA)	(NA)
Information retrieval services	7375	2,435	3,668	4,835	(NA)	(NA)	(NA)
Computer services management	7376	1,369	1,961	2,035	(NA)	(NA)	(NA)
Computer rental leasing	7377	1,588	1,764	2,204	(NA)	(NA)	(NA)
Computer maintenance and repair	7378	4,274	6,520	8,417	(NA)	(NA)	(NA)
Computer related services, n.e.c. [2]	7379	3,006	8,730	11,538	(NA)	(NA)	(NA)
Communications hardware [3]	(X)	21,038	30,549	32,211	34,367	36,746	38,992
Telephone and telegraph equipment	3661	8,272	12,078	14,959	15,767	16,634	17,200
Radio and TV and communications equip . . .	3663	9,698	14,152	13,687	15,124	16,712	18,467
Communications services [3]	48	146,700	193,300	207,400	214,869	243,060	261,507
Telephone and telegraph communications . . .	481, 2, 9	119,100	145,200	157,000	158,600	182,253	193,894
Television broadcasting	4833	12,186	18,386	18,890	20,499	21,493	23,239
Cable and other pay TV services	4841	10,483	21,691	22,916	26,381	28,865	32,513

[2] NA Not available. X Not applicable. [1] 1987 Standard Industrial Classification code. See text, Section 17, Business. [2] N.e.c. means not elsewhere classified. [3] Includes other industries, not shown separately.

No. 918. Information Technologies (IT)—Employment and Wages: 1990 to 1997

[91,098 represents 91,098,000]

Industry	1987 SIC [1] code	Employment (1,000)			Annual wages and earnings (dol.)		
		1990	1995	1997	1990	1995	1997
Total private	(X)	91,098	97,885	103,120	23,209	27,164	29,787
Total IT-producing industries	(X)	4,018	4,240	4,846	36,774	46,405	52,920
Hardware	(X)	1,574	1,476	1,643	37,597	46,280	53,044
Electronic computers	3571	279	190	196	46,406	59,563	70,286
Computers and equipment wholesalers . .	5045 (pt)	295	286	329	46,314	54,305	63,436
Computers and equipment retailers	5734 (pt)	71	94	116	29,054	33,780	37,312
Computer storage devices & peripheral equipment	3572, 7	94	105	119	35,938	46,517	58,489
Computer terminals, office & accounting, machines, & office machines, n.e.c. [2] . . .	3575, 8, 9,	65	58	60	39,259	46,568	52,637
Electron tubes	3671	32	24	23	32,257	41,875	43,067
Semiconductors	3674	240	235	278	38,109	53,801	59,507
Printed circuit boards, electronic capacitors resistors, and coils [3]	3672, 5-8	169	187	206	24,209	28,294	31,453
Electronic components, n.e.c. [2]	3679	141	135	146	27,051	32,912	35,709
Industrial instruments for measurement . .	3823	67	64	66	31,697	38,427	43,464
Instruments for measuring electricity	3825	91	71	75	36,802	51,559	59,257
Analytical instruments	3826	30	28	30	34,453	44,193	52,204
Software/services [4]	(X)	790	1,109	1,433	38,763	50,718	58,688
Computer programming services	7371	151	245	322	41,857	52,731	60,028
Prepackaged software	7372	113	181	230	45,505	63,700	77,422
Computer integrated systems design	7373	98	130	163	43,795	54,711	61,430
Computer processing & data preparation . .	7374	197	223	249	30,452	39,749	43,660
Information retrieval services	7375	48	57	81	32,704	42,197	49,582
Computer services management, rental & leasing, & maintenance & repair	7376, 7, 9	127	205	309	41,185	51,827	60,365
Computer maintenance & repair	7378	40	49	57	34,296	37,819	40,559
Communications equipment [4]	(X)	345	337	347	34,283	43,220	49,983
Telephone and telegraph equipment	3661	126	112	120	37,197	49,902	57,440
Radio and TV communications equipment & communications equipment, n.e.c. [2] . . .	3663, 9	137	153	156	34,468	42,735	48,461
Communication services [4]	48	1,309	1,318	1,424	35,239	43,731	47,685
Telephone communications	481	913	900	975	37,230	46,774	50,683
Telephone & telegraph communications . .	482, 489	37	27	31	39,699	48,539	55,719
Television broadcasting	4833	115	123	128	41,726	47,180	51,421
Cable & other pay TV services	4841	126	156	175	25,994	34,553	37,654

X Not applicable.   [1] 1987 Standard Industrial Classification code. See text, Section 17, Business.   [2] N.e.c. means not elsewhere classified.   [3] Includes transformers and connectors.   [4] Includes other industries, not shown separately.

Source of Tables 917 and 918: U.S. Department of Commerce, Economics and Statistics Administration, *The Emerging Digital Economy II*, June 1999.

Communications and Information Technology 579

No. 919. Communications Industry—Finances: 1994 to 1997

[In millions of dollars (156,833 represents $156,833,000,000). Covers publicly reporting media and communications companies with revenues of over $1 million in 13 media and communication industry segments]

Industry	Revenue				Operating income			
	1994	1995	1996	1997	1994	1995	1996	1997
Total	156,833	175,088	202,629	227,506	23,004	23,481	24,924	28,671
Television broadcasting	21,882	23,006	26,627	30,083	4,277	3,814	4,482	5,448
Television network companies	16,613	17,091	19,812	21,948	3,001	2,290	2,702	3,322
Television station broadcasters	5,269	5,915	6,815	8,136	1,276	1,523	1,779	2,126
Radio broadcasting	1,688	1,928	2,543	3,392	236	284	366	538
Radio station broadcasters	1,546	1,776	2,364	3,144	233	269	348	513
Radio network companies	142	152	179	248	2	15	18	25
Subscription video services	19,663	24,098	29,190	34,358	3,414	3,442	3,252	3,929
Subscription video services operators	15,487	19,143	23,527	27,938	2,744	2,575	2,085	2,626
Cable and pay-per-view networks	4,176	4,954	5,663	6,421	670	867	1,167	1,303
Entertainment	33,328	36,142	43,646	48,396	4,008	4,434	3,906	3,931
Newspaper publishing	19,239	20,698	22,147	24,213	3,074	2,860	3,407	4,710
Consumer book publishing	4,287	4,249	4,435	3,708	512	531	437	281
Consumer magazine publishing	8,276	8,691	9,348	9,546	925	982	1,026	1,221
Consumer Online	625	1,187	2,574	3,793	72	-68	-138	-946
Business-to-business communications	1,994	2,235	2,337	2,563	211	254	278	398
Professional and educational publishing	10,793	12,389	13,153	14,314	1,226	1,377	1,456	1,211
Business information services	18,552	20,987	24,871	28,186	3,150	3,553	4,357	4,862
Financial information	11,369	12,497	14,277	15,300	2,304	2,647	2,920	2,957
Marketing information	3,516	4,156	4,689	5,468	468	379	638	775
Technology information	221	366	496	650	28	50	93	120
Health-care information	395	464	599	729	20	6	-32	18
Other business information companies	3,050	3,504	4,810	6,038	331	471	738	993
Advertising agencies	9,380	10,907	12,334	14,189	896	1,064	984	1,638
Specialty media	7,127	8,571	9,426	10,765	1,005	954	1,112	1,452

Source: Veronis, Suhler & Associates Inc., New York, NY, *Communications Industry Report,* annual (copyright).

No. 920. Media Usage and Consumer Spending: 1992 to 2002

[Estimates of time spent were derived using rating data for television and radio, survey research and consumer purchase data for recorded music, newspapers, magazines, books, home video, admissions for movies, and consumer on-line/Internet access services. Adults 18 and older except for recorded music, movies in theaters, and video games where estimates include persons 12 years old and older]

Item	1992	1993	1994	1995	1996	1997	1998, proj.	1999, proj.	2000, proj.	2001, proj.	2002, proj.
HOURS PER PERSON PER YEAR											
Total	3,324	3,295	3,393	3,391	3,393	3,368	3,368	3,371	3,380	3,391	3,398
Television	1,510	1,535	1,560	1,575	1,567	1,561	1,560	1,565	1,571	1,577	1,575
Broadcast TV	1,073	1,082	1,091	1,019	980	926	882	842	808	778	748
Network stations [1]	914	920	919	836	803	748	704	670	640	616	591
Independent stations	159	162	172	183	177	178	178	172	168	162	157
Subscription video services	437	453	469	556	587	635	678	723	763	799	827
Basic networks [2]	359	375	388	468	498	537	580	620	655	690	718
Premium channels	78	78	81	88	89	98	98	103	108	109	109
Radio	1,150	1,082	1,102	1,091	1,091	1,082	1,075	1,066	1,056	1,047	1,040
Recorded music	233	248	294	289	289	265	260	261	269	278	289
Daily newspapers	172	170	169	165	161	159	157	156	154	153	152
Consumer books	100	99	102	99	99	92	95	95	96	97	97
Consumer magazines	85	85	84	84	83	82	82	81	80	80	79
Home video [3]	42	43	45	45	45	49	52	53	55	56	58
Movies in theaters	11	12	12	12	12	13	13	13	13	13	13
Home video games	19	19	22	24	26	36	39	42	43	44	46
Consumer on-line Internet access	2	2	3	7	16	28	35	39	43	46	49
CONSUMER SPENDING PER PERSON PER YEAR (dol.)											
Total	395.75	420.22	443.42	466.03	496.87	523.69	559.94	593.12	631.91	670.89	707.55
Television	102.56	110.12	111.87	125.06	138.38	154.70	171.98	187.71	205.75	223.44	240.49
Broadcast TV											
Subscription video services	102.56	110.12	111.87	125.06	138.38	154.70	171.98	187.71	205.75	223.44	240.49
Radio											
Recorded music	43.05	47.42	56.35	56.92	57.34	55.42	55.82	57.72	61.64	65.54	68.89
Daily newspapers	48.54	48.25	49.12	50.08	50.90	50.90	51.74	52.62	53.75	54.66	55.65
Consumer books	68.95	72.75	77.62	79.23	80.95	78.03	81.99	84.91	87.84	91.26	94.94
Consumer magazines	34.26	35.27	36.36	36.10	36.80	37.61	38.42	39.51	40.61	41.71	42.81
Home video [3]	59.25	64.17	68.96	71.38	76.88	76.25	80.47	85.05	89.03	94.01	98.34
Movies in theaters	23.24	24.33	25.20	25.38	27.05	28.83	30.14	30.69	31.67	32.64	33.60
Home video games	11.51	12.56	11.75	10.54	11.45	16.42	17.19	17.67	18.71	19.49	20.04
Consumer on-line Internet access	4.39	5.35	6.20	11.33	17.13	25.52	32.18	37.25	42.92	48.15	52.79

- Represents zero.   [1] Includes affiliates of the Fox network and, beginning 1995, UPN and WB.   [2] Includes TBS.
[3] Playback of prerecorded tapes only.

Source: Veronis, Suhler & Associates Inc., New York, NY, *Communications Industry Report,* annual (copyright).

No. 921. Utilization of Selected Media: 1970 to 1997

[62.0 represents 62,000,000]

Item	Unit	1970	1980	1985	1990	1992	1993	1994	1995	1996	1997
Households with—											
Telephone service [1]	Percent	87.0	93.0	91.8	93.3	93.9	94.2	93.9	93.9	93.8	93.9
Radio [2]	Millions	62.0	78.6	87.1	94.4	96.6	97.3	98.0	98.0	98.0	98.0
Percent of total households	Percent	98.6	99.0	99.0	99.0	99.0	99.0	99.0	99.0	99.0	99.0
Average number of sets	Number	5.1	5.5	5.5	5.6	5.6	5.6	5.6	5.6	5.6	5.6
Television [3]	Millions	59	76	85	92	92	93	94	95	96	97
Percent of total households	Percent	95.3	97.9	98.1	98.2	98.3	98.3	98.3	98.3	98.3	98.4
Television sets in homes	Millions	81	128	155	193	192	201	211	217	223	229
Average number of sets per home	Number	1.4	1.7	1.8	2.1	2.1	2.2	2.2	2.3	2.3	2.4
Color sets	Millions	21	63	78	90	91	92	93	94	95	97
Cable television [4]	Millions	4	15	36	52	55	57	59	60	63	64
Percent of TV households	Percent	6.7	19.9	42.8	56.4	60.2	61.4	62.4	63.4	65.3	66.5
VCRs [4]	Millions	(NA)	1	18	63	69	72	74	77	79	82
Percent of TV households	Percent	(NA)	1.1	20.8	68.6	75.0	77.1	79.0	81.0	82.2	84.2
Commercial radio stations: [2]											
AM	Number	4,323	4,589	5,4,718	4,987	4,961	4,994	4,913	4,150	4,857	4,762
FM	Number	2,196	3,282	5,3,875	4,392	4,785	4,971	5,109	5,730	5,419	5,542
Television stations: [6] Total	Number	862	1,011	1,182	1,442	1,481	1,506	1,512	1,532	1,533	1,574
Commercial [3]	Number	677	734	883	1,092	1,118	1,137	1,145	1161	1,174	1,177
VHF	Number	501	516	520	547	551	552	561	562	554	588
UHF	Number	176	218	363	545	567	585	584	599	620	619
Cable television:											
Systems [6]	Number	2,490	4,225	6,844	9,575	11,075	11,217	11,214	11,218	11,119	10,950
Households served [7]	Millions	4.5	17.7	39.9	54.9	57.2	58.8	60.5	63.0	64.6	65.9
Daily newspaper circulation [8]	Millions	62	62	63	62	60	60	59	57	57	57

NA Not available. [1] For occupied housing units. 1970 and 1980 as of April 1; all other years as of March. Source: U.S. Census Bureau, 1970 and 1980 Census of Housing, Vol. 1; thereafter Federal Communications Commission, Trends in Telephone Service, July 1998. [2] As of December 31, except as noted. Source: Radio Advertising Bureau, New York, NY, through 1992, Radio Facts, annual, (copyright); beginning 1993, Radio Marketing Guide and Fact Book for Advertisers, annual, (copyright). Number of stations on the air compiled from Federal Communications Commission reports. [3] 1970, as of September of prior year; all other years as of January of year shown. Excludes Alaska and Hawaii. Source: Television Bureau of Advertising, Inc., Trends in Television, annual (copyright). [4] As of February. Excludes Alaska and Hawaii. Source: See footnote 3. [5] As of February 1986. [6] As of January 1. Source: Warren Publishing, Washington DC, Television and Cable Factbook (copyright). [7] Source: Nielsen Media Research, Nielsen Station Index, November diary estimates (copyright). [8] As of September 30. Source: Editor & Publisher, Co., New York, NY, Editor & Publisher International Year Book, annual (copyright).

Source: Compiled from sources mentioned in footnotes.

No. 922. Multimedia Audiences—Summary: 1998

[In percent, except total (197,462 represents 197,462,000). As of spring. For persons 18 years old and over. Represents the percent of persons participating during the prior week, except as indicated. Based on sample and subject to sampling error; see source for details]

Item	Total population (1,000)	Television viewing	Television prime time viewing	Cable viewing	Radio listening	Newspaper reading [1]	Accessed Internet [2]
Total	197,462	91.9	77.5	69.7	83.8	80.0	32.5
18 to 24 years old	24,807	89.8	71.6	65.4	91.4	74.4	42.6
25 to 34 years old	40,154	91.2	76.7	69.8	91.2	76.6	38.8
35 to 44 years old	44,393	91.1	77.1	71.3	90.1	82.0	40.8
45 to 54 years old	33,700	91.3	78.0	74.5	86.0	83.7	40.0
55 to 64 years old	22,149	92.7	79.8	71.3	77.1	81.7	20.2
65 years old and over	32,260	95.7	81.8	64.5	62.2	80.8	6.1
Male	94,827	92.3	77.5	71.0	85.5	80.5	34.8
Female	102,635	91.6	77.5	68.5	82.2	79.6	30.4
White	165,867	91.7	77.4	71.4	84.2	81.0	33.8
Black	23,257	95.8	81.2	63.4	83.4	75.5	20.1
Other	8,338	85.0	69.8	54.5	77.1	72.9	40.1
Spanish speaking	20,223	93.3	78.8	52.4	84.9	66.4	22.9
Not high school graduate	35,715	93.6	79.4	54.3	73.1	63.7	5.7
High school graduate	66,168	92.7	78.6	72.3	82.9	79.7	18.0
Attended college	52,173	91.4	76.2	72.7	88.7	83.8	44.0
College graduate	43,406	90.1	76.0	74.8	88.1	89.5	62.8
Employed:							
Full time	112,029	91.0	76.4	73.0	91.0	82.2	42.1
Part time	16,927	90.4	72.6	71.2	87.2	83.2	42.1
Not employed	68,506	93.8	80.6	64.0	71.2	75.6	14.4
Household income:							
Less than $10,000	15,015	92.9	78.0	47.2	70.2	61.3	11.5
$10,000 to $19,999	25,752	93.7	78.6	57.3	72.1	70.8	8.6
$20,000 to $29,999	26,135	93.0	79.6	63.1	79.3	75.2	15.0
$30,000 to $34,999	12,590	91.2	77.2	68.5	81.9	79.4	19.9
$35,000 to $39,999	12,034	92.8	79.8	67.9	84.1	82.0	25.1
$40,000 to $49,999	22,008	91.5	76.7	73.4	86.2	80.9	30.0
$50,000 or more	83,928	91.0	76.4	79.0	90.8	87.3	52.6

[1] In the past 4 weeks. [2] In the last 30 days.

Source: Mediamark Research Inc., New York, NY, Multimedia Audiences, spring 1999 (copyright).

Communications and Information Technology 581

No. 923. Internet Access and Usage and Online Service Usage: 1999

[For persons 18 years old and over (197,462 represents 197,462,000). As of spring. Based on sample and subject to sampling error; see source for details]

Item	Total adults	Any Online/ Internet usage	Have Internet access			Used the Internet in the last 30 days			Used any online service in the past 30 days
			Home or work	Home only	Work only	Home or work	Home only	Work only	
Total adults (1,000)	**197,462**	**67,228**	**83,677**	**53,719**	**38,930**	**64,144**	**44,913**	**31,101**	**53,052**
PERCENT DISTRIBUTION									
Age:									
18 to 34 years old	32.9	40.6	39.3	34.1	35.3	40.7	36.7	34.9	41.0
35 to 54 years old	39.5	49.2	47.9	52.4	56.1	49.2	52.3	57.4	49.2
55 years old and over	27.6	10.2	12.8	13.4	8.6	10.0	11.1	7.7	9.9
Sex:									
Male	48.0	51.0	49.3	50.5	53.1	51.4	52.5	55.4	50.7
Female	52.0	49.0	50.7	49.5	46.9	48.6	47.5	44.6	49.3
Household size:									
1 to 2 persons	46.4	36.7	37.4	34.8	40.1	36.8	35.6	40.3	36.1
3 to 4 persons	38.9	47.9	46.8	48.4	46.9	48.0	48.6	47.3	48.4
5 or more persons	14.7	15.4	15.8	16.8	13.0	15.2	15.8	12.4	15.5
Any child in household	42.3	49.1	48.7	50.5	49.3	48.8	49.3	49.3	49.6
Marital status:									
Single	23.3	27.5	26.6	21.6	22.1	27.5	23.4	21.5	28.1
Married	57.5	62.1	62.2	68.9	66.2	62.3	67.7	67.3	61.9
Other	19.2	10.3	11.3	9.6	11.6	10.1	8.9	11.2	10.1
Educational attainment:									
Graduated college plus	22.0	41.7	37.8	42.9	51.1	42.5	45.7	55.1	41.1
Attended college	26.4	35.6	34.6	33.2	30.5	35.8	33.8	30.0	35.5
Did not attend college	51.6	22.8	27.5	23.9	18.4	21.8	20.5	14.9	23.3
Household income:									
Less than $50,000	57.5	32.0	34.8	27.2	24.8	31.1	26.9	22.8	30.9
$50,000 to $74,000	20.7	27.5	27.4	27.3	28.9	27.8	27.1	28.3	26.6
$75,000 to $149,000	18.5	33.7	31.6	37.2	38.1	34.0	37.5	40.0	35.2
$150,000 or more	3.3	6.8	6.3	8.3	8.2	7.1	8.5	8.9	7.2

Source: Mediamark Research Inc., New York, NY, *CyberStats, spring 99* (copyright). Internet site <http://www.mediamark.com> (accessed 10 May 1999).

No. 924. Use of Home Computers: 1997

[In percent, except persons using computers (81,013 represents 81,013,000). As of October. Based on the Current Population Survey and subject to sampling error; see text, Section 1, Population, and Appendix III]

Characteristic	Persons using computers (1,000)	Percent of total	Frequency of use per week				Computer capabilities [1]			
			6 or 7 days	4 or 5 days	2 or 3 days	1 day or less	CD-ROM drive	Printer	Modem	Internet
Total [2]	**81,013**	**30.3**	**23.4**	**20.1**	**32.6**	**24.0**	**71.3**	**85.5**	**71.1**	**52.1**
Sex: Male	41,260	31.6	27.1	20.1	30.6	22.2	72.1	85.5	71.7	52.9
Female	39,753	29.1	19.6	20.0	34.6	25.8	70.6	85.6	70.5	51.2
Age: Under 5 years old	1,675	8.5	12.2	16.3	38.1	33.5	71.9	83.3	74.5	53.8
5 to 9 years old	7,599	37.1	11.8	17.6	44.2	26.4	74.7	83.8	71.5	50.5
10 to 14 years old	9,500	48.7	21.1	21.8	38.0	19.1	75.5	87.9	70.6	50.3
15 to 19 years old	8,395	43.1	24.7	22.4	32.4	20.5	73.7	88.0	69.9	52.3
20 to 24 years old	4,975	28.5	28.3	20.2	28.9	22.6	69.5	83.4	69.8	53.0
25 to 29 years old	5,963	31.7	26.1	22.3	30.0	21.7	70.1	80.4	75.8	58.4
30 to 39 years old	15,393	35.8	24.2	20.6	32.0	23.2	71.9	84.5	72.8	53.5
40 to 49 years old	15,346	38.3	24.3	18.8	30.3	26.6	73.9	87.4	73.0	54.4
50 to 59 years old	7,679	28.5	26.6	19.8	28.0	25.7	66.5	86.2	67.6	50.7
60 to 69 years old	3,162	16.2	29.7	17.5	24.1	28.6	61.0	86.8	63.5	42.3
70 years old and over	1,327	5.9	29.4	17.8	25.4	27.5	59.0	86.1	60.4	38.6
Race/ethnicity:										
White, non-Hispanic	68,026	35.5	23.5	20.2	32.1	24.3	72.4	87.1	72.8	53.7
Black, non-Hispanic	4,943	14.7	20.8	20.5	37.6	21.2	58.2	75.2	57.7	40.3
Hispanic	4,081	13.5	23.3	17.3	36.4	23.1	69.1	78.2	60.8	44.4
Family income: Less than $5,000 . .	1,517	13.3	31.1	16.7	26.8	25.3	63.2	81.9	66.2	44.6
$5,000 to $9,999	1,575	8.1	24.8	19.6	29.4	26.1	59.6	81.0	56.7	40.5
$10,000 to $14,999	2,197	9.7	26.2	17.7	31.4	24.8	55.9	74.5	54.7	38.7
$15,000 to $19,999	2,084	12.0	25.9	20.4	29.9	23.8	60.5	77.8	60.0	42.7
$20,000 to $24,999	3,645	17.1	25.1	18.9	31.4	24.5	59.9	80.9	58.1	38.8
$25,000 to $29,999	4,174	21.0	23.3	19.3	33.3	24.1	62.2	77.6	61.0	42.0
$30,000 to $34,999	5,003	25.7	22.5	20.5	32.9	24.1	66.4	82.6	64.1	43.7
$35,000 to $39,999	5,367	29.1	22.7	18.5	34.1	24.7	65.9	84.3	66.3	46.1
$40,000 to $49,999	9,627	35.4	22.2	19.5	33.3	25.1	68.2	86.0	67.6	46.4
$50,000 to $74,999	21,685	44.6	22.1	20.2	32.5	25.1	73.9	87.2	74.3	53.9
$75,000 and over	24,138	58.0	24.1	21.1	32.8	22.0	80.9	89.8	81.1	64.5

[1] For the most recently purchased computers for those with more than one.   [2] Includes other races, not shown separately.

Source: U.S. National Center for Education Statistics, *Digest of Education Statistics, 1999.*

No. 925. Telecommunications Industry—Carriers and Revenue: 1993 to 1997

[Revenue in millions of dollars (165,342 represents $165,342,000,000). Data based on carrier filings to the FCC. Because of reporting changes, data for 1997 are not strictly comparable with previous years; see source for details]

Category	Carriers					Telecommunications revenue				
	1993	1994	1995	1996	1997	1993	1994	1995	1996	1997
Total [1]	2,709	2,847	3,058	3,832	3,604	165,342	174,890	190,076	211,782	231,168
Local service providers	1,464	1,574	1,675	2,028	2,066	95,595	99,011	103,792	109,273	108,568
Incumbent local exchange carriers (ILECs)	1,281	1,347	1,347	1,376	1,410	95,228	98,431	102,820	107,905	105,154
Pay telephone providers	163	197	271	533	509	175	300	349	357	933
Competitors of ILECs	20	30	57	119	147	191	281	623	1,011	2,481
CAPs and CLECs [2]	20	30	57	94	129	191	281	623	1,011	1,919
Local resellers	(3)	(3)	(3)	8	11	(3)	(3)	(3)	(3)	206
Other local exchange carriers	(3)	(3)	(3)	13	3	(3)	(3)	(3)	(3)	157
Private carriers	(3)	(3)	(3)	(3)	2	(3)	(3)	(3)	(3)	112
Shared tenant service providers	(3)	(3)	(3)	4	2	(3)	(3)	(3)	(3)	87
Wireless service providers [4]	924	907	930	1,217	969	10,179	14,197	18,627	25,900	33,030
Telephony [5]	798	790	792	853	732	9,215	13,259	17,208	23,778	29,944
Paging service providers	126	117	138	200	137	(3)	(3)	(3)	(3)	2,861
Toll service providers	321	366	453	587	569	64,393	70,466	76,447	86,896	89,570
Interexchange carriers	83	97	130	149	151	61,118	66,381	70,938	79,057	79,080
Operator service providers	35	29	25	27	32	695	536	500	461	603
Prepaid service providers	(3)	(3)	8	16	18	(3)	(3)	16	238	519
Satellite service carriers	(3)	(3)	(3)	22	13	(3)	(3)	(3)	(3)	1,011
Toll resellers	171	206	260	345	340	1,869	2,840	4,220	6,564	8,010
Other toll carriers	32	34	30	28	15	711	709	773	577	348

[1] Revenue data include adjustments, not shown separately. Through 1996, revenue data include some non-telecommunications revenue, formerly reported as local exchange wireless revenue. [2] Competitive access providers and competitive local exchange carriers. [3] Data not available separately. [4] Includes specialized mobile radio services and other services, not shown separately. [5] Cellular service, personal communications service, and specialized mobile radio.

Source: U.S. Federal Communications Commission, *Trends in Telephone Service*, February 1999.

No. 926. Telephone Systems—Summary: 1985 to 1997

[112 represents 112,000,000. Covers principal carriers filing annual reports with Federal Communications Commission]

Item	Unit	1985	1990	1991	1992	1993	1994	1995	1996	1997
LOCAL EXCHANGE CARRIERS [1]										
Carriers [2]	Number	55	51	52	54	53	52	53	51	51
Access lines	Millions	112	130	137	140	149	157	166	178	194
Business access lines	Millions	31	36	38	39	41	42	46	49	53
Residential access lines	Millions	79	89	91	93	96	98	101	104	108
Other access lines (public, mobile, special)	Millions	2	6	7	8	13	17	19	25	33
Number of local calls (originating)	Billions	365	402	416	434	447	465	484	504	522
Number of toll calls (originating)	Billions	(NA)	63	67	72	78	83	94	95	101
Gross book cost of plant	Bil. dol.	191	240	246	254	264	272	284	296	309
Depreciation and amortization reserves	Bil. dol.	49	89	93	99	107	116	127	138	149
Net plant	Bil. dol.	142	151	153	155	156	157	157	158	160
Total assets	Bil. dol.	162	180	184	187	192	196	197	198	198
Total stockholders equity	Bil. dol.	63	74	76	77	73	72	72	74	72
Operating revenues	Bil. dol.	73	84	86	87	90	93	96	101	103
Local revenues	Bil. dol.	32	37	38	40	42	43	46	50	52
Operating expenses [3]	Bil. dol.	48	62	63	64	66	70	72	74	75
Net operating income [4]	Bil. dol.	13	14	14	14	14	13	14	16	16
Net income	Bil. dol.	9	11	10	9	5	9	11	13	12
Employees	(1,000)	(NA)	569	538	527	507	474	447	437	435
Compensation of employees	Bil. dol.	(NA)	23	22	22	23	22	21	23	22
Average monthly residential local telephone rate [5]	Dollars	(NA)	19.24	19.77	19.72	19.95	19.81	20.01	19.95	19.88
Average monthly single-line business telephone rate [5]	Dollars	(NA)	41.21	42.12	42.29	42.57	41.64	41.80	41.81	41.67
LONG DISTANCE CARRIERS										
Number of carriers with presubscribed lines	Number	(NA)	325	388	414	436	511	583	621	(NA)
Number of presubscribed lines	Millions	(NA)	132	135	139	143	148	153	159	(NA)
Total toll service revenues	Bil. dol.	43	52	54	58	62	67	74	82	89
Interstate switched access minutes	Bil. min.	167	307	328	350	371	401	432	468	497
INTERNATIONAL TELEPHONE SERVICE [6]										
Number of U.S. billed calls	Millions	411	984	1,371	1,643	1,926	2,313	2,821	3,485	4,229
Number of U.S. billed minutes	Millions	3,446	8,030	8,986	10,156	11,393	13,393	15,837	19,119	22,586
U.S. billed revenues	Mil. dol.	3,487	8,042	9,096	10,179	11,353	12,255	13,990	14,079	15,125
U.S. carrier revenue net of settlements with foreign carriers	Mil. dol.	2,358	5,280	5,798	6,835	7,649	7,966	9,053	8,433	9,689
Revenue from private-line service	Mil. dol.	172	201	303	313	356	440	506	649	840
Revenue from resale service	Mil. dol.	(NA)	167	440	511	593	1,120	1,687	3,457	4,088

NA Not available. [1] Gross operating revenues, gross plant, and total assets of reporting carriers estimated at more than 90 percent of total industry. New accounting rules became effective in 1990; prior years may not be directly comparable on a one-to-one basis. Includes Virgin Islands, and prior to 1991, Puerto Rico. [2] The reporting threshold for carriers is $100 million. [3] Excludes taxes. [4] After tax deductions. [5] Based on surveys conducted by FCC. [6] Beginning 1991, includes calls to and from Alaska, Hawaii, Puerto Rico, Canada, and Mexico.

Source: U.S. Federal Communications Commission, *Statistics of Communications Common Carriers*, annual.

Communications and Information Technology 583

No. 927. Telephone Communications—Operating Revenue and Expenses: 1990 to 1997

[Based on a sample of employer firms with one or more establishments that are primarily engaged in providing telephone, voice, and data communication services (160,482 represents $160,482,000,000). For SIC 481. Based on the 1987 Standard Industrial Classification code; see text, Section 17, Business]

Item	Total (mil. dol.)					Percent distribution		
	1990	1994	1995	1996	1997	1990	1995	1997
Operating revenue.	160,482	199,259	216,296	238,063	256,116	100.0	100.0	100.0
Local service	40,180	46,662	49,349	53,403	57,065	25.0	22.8	22.3
Long-distance service	67,698	81,037	86,834	94,039	98,528	42.2	40.1	38.5
Network access	30,044	32,988	34,131	36,101	37,447	18.7	15.8	14.6
Cellular and other radiotelephone.	6,002	16,848	22,837	28,520	33,453	3.7	10.6	13.1
Directory advertising	8,373	9,439	9,850	10,214	10,764	5.2	4.6	4.2
Other	8,185	12,285	13,295	15,786	18,859	5.1	6.1	7.4
Operating expenses	131,493	164,936	180,538	192,349	212,490	100.0	100.0	100.0
Annual payroll.	34,903	38,106	40,721	42,087	44,524	26.5	22.6	21.0
Employer contributions to social security and other supplemental benefits.	8,121	9,347	9,184	9,611	10,263	6.2	5.1	4.8
Access charges	23,214	30,047	33,748	36,018	39,781	17.7	18.7	18.7
Depreciation.	22,927	28,578	31,651	32,937	37,589	17.4	17.5	17.7
Lease and rental.	3,543	4,037	3,919	4,492	5,310	2.7	2.2	2.5
Purchased repairs.	2,977	4,413	4,907	5,243	6,533	2.3	2.7	3.1
Insurance	193	261	304	336	371	0.1	0.2	0.2
Tele. & other purchased comm. serv. . . .	504	1,321	1,858	2,030	2,373	0.4	1.0	1.1
Purchased utilities.	1,106	1,562	1,770	1,961	2,174	0.8	1.0	1.0
Purchased advertising	2,328	3,835	3,607	4,534	5,624	1.8	2.0	2.6
Taxes	5,086	6,603	7,539	7,978	9,021	3.9	4.2	4.2
Other	26,591	36,826	41,330	45,122	48,927	20.2	22.9	23.0

Source: U.S. Census Bureau, *Annual Survey of Communication Services.*

No. 928. Cellular Telephone Industry: 1990 to 1998

[Calendar year data, except as noted (5,283 represents 5,283,000). Based on a survey mailed to all cellular, personal communications services, and enhanced special mobile radio systems. For 1998 data, the universe was 3,073 systems and the response rate was 94 percent]

Item	Unit	1990	1992	1993	1994	1995	1996	1997	1998
Systems.	Number .	751	1,506	1,529	1,581	1,627	1,740	2,228	3,073
Subscribers.	1,000 . .	5,283	11,033	16,009	24,134	33,786	44,043	55,312	69,209
Cell sites [1]	Number .	5,616	10,307	12,805	17,920	22,663	30,045	51,600	65,887
Employees	Number .	21,382	34,348	39,775	53,902	68,165	84,161	109,387	134,754
Service revenue.	Mil. dol. .	4,548	7,822	10,891	14,229	19,081	23,635	27,486	33,133
Roamer revenue [2].	Mil. dol. .	456	974	1,360	1,830	2,542	2,781	2,974	3,501
Capital investment . [3].	Mil. dol. .	6,282	11,262	13,946	18,939	24,080	32,574	46,058	60,543
Average monthly bill [3]	Dollars. .	80.90	68.68	61.48	56.21	51.00	47.70	42.78	39.43
Average length of call [3]	Minutes .	2.20	2.58	2.41	2.24	2.15	2.32	2.31	2.39

[1] The basic geographic unit of a wireless PCS or cellular system. A city or county is divided into smaller "cells," each of which is equipped with a low-powered radio transmitter/receiver. The cells can vary in size depending upon terrain, capacity demands, etc. By controlling the transmission power, the radio frequencies assigned to one cell can be limited to the boundaries of that cell. When a wireless PCS or cellular phone moves from one cell toward another, a computer at the Switching Office monitors the movement and at the proper time, transfers or hands off the phone call to the new cell and another radio frequency. [2] Service revenue generated by subscribers' calls outside of their system areas. [3] As of December 31.
Source: Cellular Telecommunications Industry Association, Washington, DC, *Semi-annual Wireless Survey* (copyright).

No. 929. Radio and Television Broadcasting Services—Finances: 1990 to 1997

[In millions of dollars (28,017 represents $28,017,000,000). Based on a sample of taxable employer firms with one or more establishments primarily engaged in broadcasting to the public, except cable and other pay television services. Based on the 1987 Standard Industrial Classification Code; see text, Section 17, Business]

Item	Total (SIC 483)			Radio (SIC 4832)			Television (SIC 4833)		
	1990	1995	1997	1990	1995	1997	1990	1995	1997
Operating revenue	28,017	34,319	38,985	6,954	8,518	10,193	21,063	25,801	28,792
Station time sales	19,019	22,450	25,379	6,397	7,779	9,287	12,622	14,671	16,092
Network compensation	549	564	644	105	71	85	444	493	559
National/regional advertising.	7,226	8,166	8,891	1,522	1,765	2,002	5,704	6,401	6,889
Local advertising	11,244	13,720	15,844	4,770	5,943	7,200	6,474	7,777	8,644
Network time sales.	7,905	10,319	11,701	305	464	553	7,600	9,855	11,148
Other.	1,093	1,550	1,905	252	275	353	841	1,275	1,552
Operating expenses	24,145	28,038	30,648	6,317	6,997	8,154	17,828	21,041	22,494
Annual payroll.	6,333	7,933	8,848	2,428	2,864	3,304	3,905	5,069	5,544
Employer contributions to social security & other supplemental benefits.	998	1,303	1,397	326	361	416	672	942	981
Broadcast rights	7,642	8,260	8,801	264	304	303	7,378	7,956	8,498
Music license fees.	373	405	467	159	204	249	214	201	218
Depreciation.	1,345	1,324	1,548	477	403	491	868	921	1,057
Lease and rental	469	538	609	197	226	266	272	312	343
Purchased repairs	232	300	310	79	76	81	153	224	229
Insurance	143	168	164	64	69	76	79	99	88
Tele. & other purchased comm. serv. . .	240	278	300	115	123	140	125	155	160
Purchased utilities	246	281	280	99	104	110	147	177	170
Purchased advertising	947	1,115	1,353	368	409	454	579	706	899
Taxes	176	217	210	60	71	78	116	146	132
Other.	5,001	5,916	6,361	1,681	1,783	2,186	3,320	4,133	4,175

Source: U.S. Census Bureau, *Annual Survey of Communication Services.*

No. 930. Copyright Registration, by Subject Matter: 1990 to 1998

[In thousands (643.5 represents 643,500). For years ending **September 30.** Comprises claims to copyrights registered for both U.S. and foreign works]

Subject matter	1990	1995	1997	1998	Subject matter	1990	1995	1997	1998
Total	643.5	609.2	569.2	558.6	Sound recordings	37.5	34.0	35.7	31.6
Monographs [1]	179.7	196.0	176.4	189.3	Renewals.	51.8	30.6	28.6	25.4
Semiconductor chip products. . .	1.0	0.8	1.0	0.9	Musical works [2]	185.3	163.6	154.4	142.4
Serials.	111.5	88.7	83.3	72.6	Works of the visual arts [3]	76.7	95.5	89.6	96.0

[1] Includes computer software and machine readable works.   [2] Includes dramatic works, accompanying music, choreography, pantomimes motion pictures, and filmstrips.   [3] Two-dimensional works of fine and graphic art, including prints and art reproductions; sculptural works; technical drawings and models; photographs; commercial prints and labels; works of applied arts, cartographic works, and multimedia works.

Source: The Library of Congress, Copyright Office, *Annual Report.*

No. 931. Public Television Programming: 1984 to 1996

[**For October through September seasons.** General programming is directed at the general community. Instructional programming is directed at students in the classroom or otherwise in the general context of formal education]

Item	1984	1986	1988	1990	1992	1994	1996
Stations broadcasting	303	305	322	341	349	349	352
Number of broadcasters [1]	169	178	186	193	198	198	201
Average annual hours per broadcaster.	5,542	5,650	6,135	6,392	6,303	6,500	6,758
BROADCAST HOURS, PERCENT DISTRIBUTION							
Program content							
General.	100	100	100	100	100	100	100
News and public affairs [2]	88	86	85	86	90	92	92
Information and skills	14	16	16	18	17	19	19
Cultural	26	30	32	32	29	27	29
General children's and youth's	20	21	18	19	18	16	17
Sesame Street	8	7	6	6	15	20	20
Other	15	11	12	11	11	9	8
Instructional [3]	6	2	1	1	1	1	1
Children and youth	13	15	16	14	12	9	8
Adult	1	(NA)	(NA)	(NA)	9	6	5
Adult		(NA)	(NA)	(NA)	3	3	3
Producer	100	100	100	100	100	100	100
Local	6	5	5	5	4	5	5
Any public TV source.	44	38	27	32	31	33	36
U.S. Coproduction [4]	3	3	10	10	6	6	6
Children's TV Workshop.	16	[5]29	16	15	14	12	9
Independent producer	9	(5)	19	19	25	26	27
Foreign producer, international coproduction . .	13	15	14	12	11	10	10
Commercial producer.	3	6	4	4	5	5	4
Other	5	4	4	3	4	4	4
Distributor	100	100	100	100	100	100	100
Local distribution only	6	5	6	6	5	4	5
Public broadcasting service.	65	64	62	59	63	63	63
Regional public television network	13	14	18	24	23	23	25
Other	16	17	14	11	9	9	8

NA Not available.   [1] Beginning 1988, only broadcasters in the 50 U.S. States were surveyed. In prior years, the stations in the outlying areas were also included.   [2] Beginning 1986, this category includes "Business or Consumer."   [3] Some general audience programs with instructional applications were double counted if aired during school hours when school was in session. "The Electric Company" was one such program.   [4] Prior to 1986, "Consortium".   [5] Independent producer included with Children's TV Workshop for 1986.

Source: Corporation for Public Broadcasting, Washington, DC, *Programming Survey,* biennial.

No. 932. Public Broadcasting Systems—Income, by Source: 1980 to 1997

[**In millions of dollars (705 represents $705,000,000),** except number of stations and percents. Stations as of Dec. 31; fiscal year data for income. Includes nonbroadcast income]

Number of stations and income source	1980	1985	1990	1994	1995	1996	1997	Percent distribution		
								1980	1990	1997
CPB-qualified public radio stations [1] . .	217	288	318	403	407	408	694	(X)	(X)	(X)
Public television stations	290	317	341	351	351	352	352	(X)	(X)	(X)
Total income.	705	1,096	1,581	1,795	1,917	1,956	1,935	100	100	100
Federal government	193	179	267	330	338	339	322	27	17	17
State and local government [2]	272	358	474	510	560	518	537	39	30	28
Subscribers and auction/marathon. . . .	102	248	364	420	447	477	493	15	23	25
Business and industry.	72	171	262	301	294	291	280	10	17	14
Foundation	24	43	71	97	109	159	111	3	5	6
Other.	43	97	143	137	169	172	192	6	9	10

X Not applicable.   [1] Through 1996 includes CPB-supported developmental grantees/stations, and excludes repeater stations; beginning 1997 reflects a count of full-powered transmitters.   [2] Includes income received from state and other public colleges and universities.

Source: Corporation for Public Broadcasting (CPB), Washington, DC, *Public Broadcasting Income, Fiscal Year, 1997;* and unpublished data.

No. 933. Cable Television—Systems and Subscribers: 1970 to 1998

[Subscribers in thousands (4,500 represents 4,500,000), except percent. Estimated]

Year (As of Jan. 1)	Sys-tems	Sub-scribers	Year (As of Jan. 1)	Sys-tems	Sub-scribers	Subscriber size-group	Number of [1]— Sys-tems	Number of [1]— Sub-scribers	Percent of [1]— Sys-tems	Percent of [1]— Sub-scribers
1970	2,490	4,500	1989	9,050	47,500	1998, total [2]	10,719	64,463	100	100
1975	3,506	9,800	1990	9,575	50,000	50,000 and over.	273	32,519	3	50
1980	4,225	16,000	1991	10,704	51,000	20,000 to 49,999	449	13,582	4	21
1982	4,825	21,000	1992	11,075	53,000	10,000 to 19,999 . . .	483	6,867	5	11
1983	5,600	25,000	1993	11,100	55,000	5,000 to 9,999	641	4,494	6	7
1984	6,200	30,000	1994	11,200	57,000	3,500 to 4,999	385	1,619	4	3
1985	6,600	32,000	1995	11,126	58,000	1,000 to 3,499	1,868	3,550	17	6
1986	7,600	37,500	1996	11,119	60,280	500 to 999	1,370	987	13	2
1987	7,900	41,100	1997	10,950	64,050	250 to 499	1,352	485	13	1
1988	8,500	44,000	1998	10,845	64,170	Less than 250	3,054	360	28	1

[1] As of October 1.   [2] Total number of systems includes 844 not available by subscriber size-group.

Source: Warren Publishing, Inc., Washington, DC, *Television & Cable Factbook*, annual, (copyright).

No. 934. Cable and Pay TV—Summary: 1980 to 1998

[Cable TV for calendar year (17,500 represents 17,500,000). Pay TV as of Dec. 31 of year shown]

Year	Cable TV Avg. basic subscrib-ers (1,000)	Cable TV Avg. monthly basic rate (dol.)	Cable TV Revenue [1] (mil. dol.) Total	Cable TV Revenue [1] (mil. dol.) Basic	Pay TV Units [2] (1,000) Total [3]	Pay TV Units [2] (1,000) Pay cable	Pay TV Monthly rate (dol.) Total pay [3]	Pay TV Monthly rate (dol.) Pay cable	Pay TV Percent of homes passed by cable with pay TV	Pay TV Percent of homes with cable TV with pay TV
1980	17,500	7.69	2,609	1,615	8,581	7,336	8.91	8.62	26	47
1985	35,440	9.73	8,831	4,138	29,885	29,418	10.29	10.25	46	82
1990	50,520	16.78	17,582	10,174	39,902	39,751	10.35	10.30	46	77
1995	60,900	23.07	25,556	16,860	53,323	44,473	[4]8.54	8.54	50	74
1997	64,210	26.48	30,784	20,405	65,630	46,445	[4]8.29	8.00	51	74
1998, est. . .	65,400	27.43	33,656	21,509	70,100	47,300	[4]8.29	8.20	50	73

[1] Includes installation revenue, subscriber revenue, and nonsubscriber revenue; excludes telephony and high-speed access.   [2] Individual program services sold to subscribers.   [3] Includes multipoint distribution service (MDS), satellite TV (STV), multipoint multichannel distribution service (MMDS), satellite master antenna TV (SMATV), C-band satellite, and DBS satellite.   [4] Direct broadcast satellite average rate not included.

Source: Paul Kagan Associates Inc., Carmel, CA, *The Cable TV Financial Databook*, annual, 1998 (copyright); and *The Pay TV Newsletter*, March 31, 1996, and August 31, 1998.

No. 935. Cable and Pay TV—Revenue and Expenses: 1990 to 1997

[In millions of dollars (22,165 represents $22,165,000,000), except percent. Based on a sample of taxable employer firms with one or more establishments that are primarily engaged in the dissemination of visual and textual television programs on a subscription or fee basis. For SIC 4841. Based on the 1987 Standard Industrial Classification code; see text, Section 17, Business]

Item	Total 1990	Total 1994	Total 1995	Total 1996	Total 1997	Percent distribution 1990	Percent distribution 1995	Percent distribution 1997
Revenue	22,165	29,304	32,541	37,027	41,499	100.0	100.0	100.0
Advertising	1,882	3,597	4,466	5,007	5,627	8.5	13.7	13.6
Program revenue	3,816	4,714	4,843	5,438	6,313	17.2	14.9	15.2
Basic service.	10,933	14,547	16,310	18,621	21,134	49.3	50.1	50.9
Pay-per-view and other premium service	4,351	4,662	5,068	5,696	5,906	19.6	15.6	14.2
Installation fees	302	427	445	508	555	1.4	1.4	1.3
Other cable and pay TV revenue.	881	1,357	1,409	1,757	1,964	4.0	4.3	4.7
Operating expenses	19,354	23,492	26,428	30,471	35,060	100.0	100.0	100.0
Annual payroll	2,816	3,931	4,519	5,061	6,027	14.5	17.1	17.2
Employer contributions to Social Security and other supplemental benefits	588	915	1,000	1,150	1,293	3.0	3.8	3.7
Program and production costs [1]	5,926	8,333	9,442	11,239	12,839	30.6	35.7	36.6
Depreciation	3,611	3,934	4,433	4,990	6,117	18.7	16.8	17.4
Lease and rental payments	513	648	682	764	836	2.7	2.6	2.4
Purchased repairs	343	459	555	615	648	1.8	2.1	1.8
Insurance	110	162	175	190	213	0.6	0.7	0.6
Telephone, other purchased communications . .	133	225	283	321	350	0.7	1.1	1.0
Purchased utilities	188	210	215	241	265	1.0	0.8	0.8
Purchased advertising.	467	708	891	1,062	1,153	2.4	3.4	3.3
Taxes	310	424	429	436	470	1.6	1.6	1.3
Other operating expenses	4,349	3,543	3,804	4,402	4,849	22.5	14.4	13.8

[1] Includes costs from basic cable, pay-per-view, premium services, in-house programs, and other program and production costs.

Source: U.S. Census Bureau, *Annual Survey of Communication Services.*

No. 936. Recording Media—Manufacturers' Shipments and Value: 1982 to 1998

[577.4 represents 577,400,000. Domestic shipments based on reports of manufacturers representing more than 85 percent of the market. Domestic value data based on list prices of records and other media]

Medium	1982	1985	1990	1993	1994	1995	1996	1997	1998
UNIT SHIPMENTS [1] (mil.)									
Total [2]	577.4	653.0	865.7	955.6	1,122.7	1,112.7	1,137.2	1,063.4	1,124.3
CDs	(X)	22.6	286.5	495.4	662.1	722.9	778.9	753.1	847.0
CD singles	(X)	(X)	1.1	7.8	9.3	21.5	43.2	66.7	56.0
Cassettes	182.3	339.1	442.2	339.5	345.4	272.6	225.3	172.6	158.5
Cassette singles	(X)	(X)	87.4	85.6	81.1	70.7	59.9	42.2	26.4
Albums—LPs and EPs	243.9	167.0	11.7	1.2	1.9	2.2	2.9	2.7	3.4
Vinyl singles	137.2	120.7	27.6	15.1	11.7	10.2	10.1	7.5	5.4
Music video	(X)	(X)	9.2	11.0	11.2	12.6	16.9	18.6	27.2
VALUE (mil. dol.)									
Total [2]	3,641.6	4,378.8	7,541.1	10,046.6	12,068.0	12,320.3	12,533.8	12,236.8	13,723.5
CDs	(X)	389.5	3,451.6	6,511.4	8,464.5	9,377.4	9,934.7	9,915.1	11,416.0
CD singles	(X)	(X)	6.0	45.8	56.1	110.9	184.1	272.7	213.2
Cassettes	1,384.5	2,411.5	3,472.4	2,915.8	2,976.4	2,303.6	1,905.3	1,522.7	1,419.9
Cassette singles	(X)	(X)	257.9	298.5	274.9	236.3	189.3	133.5	94.4
Albums—LPs and EPs	1,925.1	1,280.5	86.5	10.6	17.8	25.1	36.8	33.3	34.0
Vinyl singles	283.0	281.0	94.4	51.2	47.2	46.7	47.5	35.6	25.7
Music video	(X)	(X)	172.3	213.3	231.1	220.3	236.1	323.9	508.0

X Not applicable. [1] Net units, after returns. [2] Includes discontinued media.
Source: Recording Industry Association of America, Washington, DC, Internet site <http://www.riaa.com> (accessed March 30 1999).

No. 937. Publishing Industry—Summary: 1987 to 1996

[In millions of dollars (9,025 represents $9,025,000,000), except as noted. Number in parentheses represents Standard Industrial Classification code; see text, Section 17, Business]

Item	Newspapers (SIC 2711)			Periodicals (SIC 2721)			Books (SIC 2731)		
	1987	1992	1996	1987	1992	1996	1987	1992	1996
Establishments	9,091	8,679	(NA)	4,020	4,699	(NA)	2,298	2,644	(NA)
With 20 or more employees	2,617	2,629	(NA)	876	991	(NA)	424	500	(NA)
Employees [1] (1,000)	435	417	403	110	116	121	70	80	85
Payroll	9,025	10,506	11,199	2,983	4,075	4,665	1,860	2,676	3,128
Value of receipts	31,849	34,124	39,171	17,329	22,034	24,930	12,620	16,731	21,363
Cost of materials	7,533	6,874	8,483	5,873	6,201	6,940	3,663	5,338	6,601
Value added [2]	24,311	27,247	30,692	11,452	15,833	17,982	9,111	11,494	14,792
New capital expends.	1,523	1,667	1,277	246	234	311	240	327	365
Fixed assets, gross assets	14,028	20,042	(NA)	2,528	2,769	(NA)	1,680	2,402	(NA)
Inventories, Dec. 31	857	767	894	902	1,067	1,216	2,091	2,944	3,320

NA Not available. [1] Represents the average number of production workers plus the number of other employees in mid-March. [2] By manufacture, derived by subtracting the cost of materials, supplies, containers, fuel, purchased electricity, and contract work from the value of shipments. This result is then adjusted by the addition of value added by merchandising operations, plus the net change in finished goods and work-in-process inventories between the beginning and the end of the year.
Source: U.S. Census Bureau, *1992 Census of Manufactures*, Industry Reports, series MC92-I-27A, and *Annual Survey of Manufactures*.

No. 938. New Books and Editions Published and Imports, by Subject: 1990 to 1997

[Covers listings in Bowker's American Book Publishing Record in year shown, plus titles issued in that year which were listed in following 6 months. Comprises new books (published for first time) and new editions (with changes in text or format). Excludes government publications; books sold only by subscription; dissertations; periodicals and quarterlies; and pamphlets under 49 pages]

Subject	New books and new editions					Imports				
	1990	1994	1995	1996	1997	1990	1994	1995	1996	1997
Total	46,738	51,663	62,039	68,175	64,711	6,414	8,172	8,539	9,271	8,369
Agriculture	514	532	673	675	871	86	87	97	72	119
Art	1,262	1,621	2,168	2,033	1,393	94	205	273	203	205
Biography	1,957	2,197	2,658	3,007	3,043	115	144	142	221	189
Business	1,191	1,616	1,843	1,788	1,642	134	276	268	238	188
Education	1,039	1,310	1,526	1,595	1,442	234	287	285	280	190
Fiction	5,764	5,415	7,605	8,573	8,329	166	247	251	280	273
General works	1,760	2,208	2,751	3,027	3,159	266	331	367	424	380
History	2,243	2,507	2,999	3,576	3,692	329	447	462	536	512
Home economics	758	1,004	1,395	1,447	1,545	19	31	41	22	22
Juvenile	5,172	5,321	5,678	5,353	3,439	103	45	63	47	54
Language	649	700	732	898	1,040	202	199	263	313	345
Law	896	1,168	1,230	1,357	1,383	138	261	215	264	296
Literature	2,049	2,356	2,525	3,082	2,697	242	326	308	428	331
Medicine	3,014	3,147	3,510	4,223	4,055	588	605	611	720	706
Music	289	364	479	461	428	52	49	73	67	46
Philosophy, psychology	1,683	1,741	2,068	2,333	2,209	284	379	346	393	380
Poetry and drama	874	1,065	1,407	1,566	1,537	119	226	206	231	196
Religion	2,285	2,730	3,324	3,803	3,820	176	225	235	310	278
Science	2,742	3,021	3,323	3,725	3,918	1,030	997	1,068	1,058	996
Sociology, economics	7,042	8,038	9,362	10,528	9,968	1,368	2,121	2,198	2,392	1,954
Sports, recreation	973	1,161	1,591	1,751	1,541	75	106	118	136	127
Technology	2,092	2,085	2,470	2,629	2,753	546	465	487	520	501
Travel	495	556	722	745	807	48	113	162	116	81

Source: R. R. Bowker Co., New Providence, NJ, *Publishers Weekly*. (Copyright by R.R. Bowker, A Unit of Cahners Business Information.)

Communications and Information Technology 587

No. 939. Books—Average Retail Prices: 1980 to 1997

[In dollars. Covers listings in Bowker's American Book Publishing Record in year shown, plus titles issued in that year which were listed in following 6 months. Comprises new books (published for first time) and new editions (with changes in text or format)]

Subject	1980	1985	1990	1992	1993	1994	1995	1996	1997
Hardcover [1]	24.64	31.46	42.12	45.05	34.98	44.65	47.15	50.00	50.27
Agriculture	27.55	36.77	54.24	53.76	41.84	58.10	49.00	45.00	47.54
Art................	27.70	35.15	42.18	44.59	39.99	39.97	41.23	53.40	46.00
Biography...........	19.77	22.20	29.58	30.41	28.37	30.43	30.01	31.67	33.19
Business	22.45	28.84	45.48	43.91	37.95	42.72	46.90	52.62	52.59
Education...........	17.01	27.28	38.72	48.77	38.60	47.98	43.00	47.09	45.37
Fiction	12.46	15.29	19.83	20.39	19.50	20.95	21.47	22.89	21.40
General works........	29.84	37.91	54.77	56.29	45.41	60.41	54.11	68.36	60.28
History.............	22.78	27.02	36.43	39.19	40.78	40.20	42.19	45.62	43.50
Home economics......	13.31	17.50	23.80	24.88	20.55	20.49	22.53	23.39	23.33
Juvenile	8.16	9.95	13.01	14.46	13.87	14.59	14.55	15.97	15.60
Language	22.16	28.68	42.98	49.68	34.02	52.09	54.89	58.81	57.94
Law................	33.25	41.70	60.78	76.21	53.94	72.32	73.09	88.51	89.14
Literature	18.70	24.53	35.80	39.23	35.30	37.77	38.49	43.28	44.88
Medicine...........	34.28	44.36	72.24	75.22	49.78	76.30	75.80	81.48	85.91
Music..............	21.79	28.79	41.86	47.37	41.44	39.27	43.27	39.21	43.67
Philosophy, psychology ..	21.70	28.11	40.58	46.85	39.44	44.71	45.26	48.40	48.05
Poetry and drama	17.85	22.14	32.19	36.76	31.06	31.56	34.96	34.15	36.75
Religion	17.61	19.13	31.31	35.31	29.16	30.73	34.27	36.62	40.52
Science	37.45	51.19	74.39	81.95	52.71	90.12	93.52	90.63	78.13
Sociology, economics ...	31.76	33.33	42.10	45.53	41.32	50.24	55.51	53.82	55.05
Sports, recreation......	15.92	23.43	30.52	34.62	32.28	33.39	32.14	34.71	32.34
Technology	33.64	50.37	76.80	82.18	56.31	81.03	88.28	91.59	89.96
Travel	16.80	24.66	30.41	33.28	26.22	32.13	38.30	33.91	33.58
Paperbacks:									
Mass market [2]	(NA)	3.63	4.57	5.22	5.82	5.70	6.53	6.57	6.34
Trade	8.60	13.98	17.45	18.81	20.56	20.56	21.71	21.41	22.56

NA Not available. [1] Excludes publications of the United States and other governmental units, books sold only by subscription, and dissertations. [2] "Pocket-sized" books sold primarily through magazine and news outlets, supermarkets, variety stores, etc.

Source: R. R. Bowker Co., New Providence, NJ, *The Bowker Annual: Library and Book Trade Almanac*. (Copyright by R.R. Bowker, A Unit of Cahners Business Information.)

No. 940. Periodicals—Average Retail Prices: 1994 to 1998

[In dollars]

Subject	1994	1995	1996	1997	1998
Agriculture	293.56	326.02	383.21	417.56	419.04
Anthropology	143.20	157.10	176.07	189.79	207.45
Art and architecture	87.17	92.24	97.99	101.06	102.30
Astronomy	746.36	840.93	993.03	1,071.36	1,087.53
Biology................................	556.93	620.18	731.84	824.81	891.40
Botany................................	422.25	475.10	556.14	607.42	644.47
Business and economics..................	194.94	227.43	271.13	307.21	339.55
Chemistry.............................	1,006.70	1,106.09	1,319.23	1,467.35	1,577.13
Education.............................	125.39	136.45	150.99	165.03	178.53
Engineering and technology...............	523.24	575.28	695.69	785.93	866.99
Food science...........................	272.22	308.20	352.20	385.11	440.44
General science.........................	369.40	416.28	487.86	548.10	607.80
General works..........................	63.09	66.73	76.04	80.66	80.53
Geography.............................	305.27	340.79	391.43	452.85	493.93
Geology...............................	469.41	516.08	628.26	703.95	740.14
Health sciences.........................	367.24	403.28	461.07	517.24	573.79
History................................	76.83	83.27	91.45	95.62	99.26
Language and literature..................	71.24	77.83	87.34	90.60	92.55
Law...................................	97.22	105.21	119.16	123.80	138.78
Library and information science............	136.23	153.58	172.45	181.35	202.30
Math and computer science	566.94	619.31	728.84	805.26	859.91
Military and naval science	133.50	153.75	168.00	184.13	209.50
Music.................................	52.75	57.50	60.89	65.27	67.93
Philosophy and religion	81.48	91.30	101.25	105.99	107.14
Physics	1,035.81	1,144.93	1,358.19	1,510.45	1,601.03
Political science.........................	105.37	119.91	138.24	151.75	166.05
Psychology	163.91	182.67	207.48	234.12	257.69
Recreation.............................	59.82	61.30	68.73	71.54	75.94
Sociology..............................	149.41	156.42	181.84	201.66	222.23
Technology	457.94	519.93	621.97	702.67	775.05
Zoology	421.74	471.55	539.72	594.28	641.06

Source: Library Journal, New York, NY, *Library Journal*, April 15, 1998. (Copyright by R.R. Bowker, A Unit of Cahners Business Information.)

No. 941. Newspapers and Periodicals—Number, by Type: 1980 to 1998

[Data refer to year of compilation of the Directory cited as the source, i.e., generally to year preceding year shown. Data for 1995 and prior years include Canada and Mexico]

Type	1980	1985	1990	1992	1993	1994	1995	1996	1997	1998
Newspapers [1]	9,620	9,134	11,471	11,339	12,597	12,513	12,246	10,466	10,042	10,508
Semiweekly	537	517	579	562	639	661	705	612	558	561
Weekly	7,159	6,811	8,420	8,293	9,177	9,067	9,011	7,655	7,191	7,236
Daily	1,744	1,701	1,788	1,755	1,850	1,831	1,710	1,537	1,582	1,527
Periodicals [1]	10,236	11,090	11,092	11,143	11,863	12,136	11,179	9,843	8,530	12,036
Weekly	1,716	1,367	553	466	485	487	513	442	350	364
Semimonthly [2]	645	801	435	371	199	209	216	307	139	156
Monthly	3,985	4,088	4,239	4,326	4,545	4,494	4,067	3,554	3,067	3,363
Bimonthly	1,114	1,361	2,087	2,143	2,359	2,475	2,568	2,216	1,943	2,168
Quarterly	1,444	1,759	2,758	3,024	3,199	3,370	3,621	3,280	2,893	3,309

[1] Includes other items not shown separately.   [2] Includes fortnightly (every 2 weeks).

Source: Gale Research Inc., Detroit, MI, *1999 Gale Directory of Publications and Broadcast Media,* 132nd edition; and earlier editions (copyright).

No. 942. Daily and Sunday Newspapers—Number and Circulation: 1970 to 1998

[Number of newspapers as of **February 1** the following year. Circulation figures as of **September 30 of year shown (62.1 represents 62,100,000).** For English language newspapers only]

Type	1970	1975	1980	1985	1990	1992	1993	1994	1995	1996	1997	1998
NUMBER												
Daily: Total [1]	1,748	1,756	1,745	1,676	1,611	1,570	1,556	1,548	1,533	1,520	1,509	1,489
Morning	334	339	387	482	559	596	623	635	656	686	705	721
Evening	1,429	1,436	1,388	1,220	1,084	954	935	935	891	846	816	781
Sunday	586	639	736	798	863	891	884	886	888	890	903	898
CIRCULATION (mil.)												
Daily: Total [1]	62.1	60.7	62.2	62.8	62.3	60.1	59.8	59.3	58.2	57.0	56.7	56.2
Morning	25.9	25.5	29.4	36.4	41.3	42.4	43.1	43.4	44.3	44.8	45.4	45.6
Evening	36.2	35.2	32.8	26.4	21.0	17.8	16.7	15.9	13.9	12.2	11.3	10.5
Sunday	49.2	51.1	54.7	58.8	62.6	62.2	62.6	62.3	61.5	60.8	60.5	60.1
PER CAPITA CIRCULATION [2]												
Daily: Total [1]	0.30	0.28	0.27	0.26	0.25	0.24	0.23	0.23	0.22	0.21	0.21	0.21
Morning	0.13	0.12	0.13	0.15	0.17	0.17	0.17	0.17	0.17	0.17	0.17	0.17
Evening	0.18	0.16	0.14	0.11	0.08	0.07	0.06	0.06	0.05	0.05	0.04	0.04
Sunday	0.24	0.24	0.24	0.25	0.25	0.24	0.24	0.24	0.23	0.23	0.23	0.23

[1] All-day newspapers are counted in both morning and evening columns but only once in total. Circulation is divided equally between morning and evening.   [2] Based on U.S. Census Bureau estimated resident population as of July 1.

Source: Editor & Publisher Co., New York, NY, *Editor & Publisher International Year Book,* annual (copyright).

No. 943. Daily Newspapers—Number and Circulation, by Size of City: 1980 to 1998

[Number of newspapers as of **February 1** the following year. Circulation as of **September 30 (29,413 represents 29,413,000).** For English language newspapers only. See Table 47 for number of cities by population size. All-day newspapers are counted in both morning and evening columns; circulation is divided equally between morning and evening]

Type of daily and population-size class	Number					Net paid circulation (1,000)				
	1980	1985	1990	1995	1998	1980	1985	1990	1995	1998
Morning dailies, total	387	482	559	656	721	29,413	36,361	41,311	44,310	45,643
In cities of—										
1,000,001 or more	20	22	18	25	27	8,795	9,367	6,508	10,173	10,697
500,001 to 1,000,000	27	24	22	22	26	5,705	6,897	4,804	5,587	6,127
100,001 to 500,000	99	121	138	153	154	8,996	12,197	20,051	17,214	16,733
50,001 to 100,000	75	87	100	138	159	2,973	3,653	4,373	5,602	5,831
25,001 to 50,000	64	83	102	115	128	1,701	2,145	3,209	3,150	3,356
Less than 25,000	102	145	179	203	227	1,243	2,099	2,365	2,584	2,900
Evening dailies, total	1,388	1,220	1,084	891	781	32,788	26,407	21,017	13,883	10,539
In cities of—										
1,000,001 or more	11	8	7	3	1	2,984	2,169	1,423	390	1
500,001 to 1,000,000	23	14	12	7	5	4,101	1,626	1,350	1,017	795
100,001 to 500,000	123	102	71	45	36	8,178	6,987	4,687	2,529	1,825
50,001 to 100,000	156	127	94	72	62	4,896	3,942	2,941	2,029	1,611
25,001 to 50,000	246	229	204	158	137	5,106	4,606	4,278	2,819	2,230
Less than 25,000	829	740	696	606	540	7,523	7,075	6,338	5,099	4,077

Source: Editor & Publisher Co., New York, NY, *Editor & Publisher International Year Book,* annual (copyright).

Communications and Information Technology   589

[Number of newspapers as of February 1 the following year. Circulation as of September 30 (**56,182 represents 56,182,000**). For English language newspapers only. New York, Massachusetts, and Virginia Sunday newspapers include national circulation]

State	Daily Number	Daily Circulation [1] Net paid (1,000)	Daily Circulation [1] Per capita [2]	Sunday Number	Sunday Net paid circulation [1] (1,000)	State	Daily Number	Daily Circulation [1] Net paid (1,000)	Daily Circulation [1] Per capita [2]	Sunday Number	Sunday Net paid circulation [1] (1,000)
U.S. ...	1,489	56,182	0.21	898	60,066	MO	43	1,001	0.18	23	1,269
AL	24	672	0.15	20	742	MT	11	192	0.22	7	194
AK	7	111	0.18	5	130	NE	17	447	0.27	6	424
AZ	16	779	0.17	11	899	NV	9	295	0.17	4	319
AR	30	473	0.19	16	523	NH	12	231	0.19	8	243
CA	93	6,074	0.19	59	6,166	NJ	19	1,409	0.17	16	1,703
CO	29	1,093	0.28	16	1,324	NM	18	296	0.17	13	296
CT	18	764	0.23	12	843	NY	59	6,406	0.35	36	5,478
DE	2	143	0.19	2	176	NC	47	1,365	0.18	37	1,501
DC	2	860	1.64	2	1,137	ND	10	172	0.27	7	178
FL	42	3,019	0.20	36	3,844	OH	84	2,502	0.22	38	2,741
GA	34	1,045	0.14	27	1,355	OK	44	665	0.20	38	808
HI	6	224	0.19	5	257	OR	19	693	0.21	11	732
ID	12	219	0.18	8	234	PA	85	2,838	0.24	40	3,243
IL	68	2,393	0.20	30	2,533	RI	6	232	0.23	3	269
IN	69	1,337	0.23	21	1,291	SC	15	635	0.17	14	748
IA	38	647	0.23	12	656	SD	11	159	0.22	4	135
KS	46	452	0.17	15	413	TN	25	871	0.16	16	1,049
KY	23	620	0.16	14	671	TX	88	2,947	0.15	85	3,953
LA	26	734	0.17	21	820	UT	6	316	0.15	6	359
ME	7	243	0.20	4	199	VT	8	126	0.21	3	102
MD	14	613	0.12	8	889	VA	28	2,690	0.40	17	1,185
MA	32	1,683	0.27	15	1,642	WA	24	1,166	0.20	16	1,257
MI	49	1,670	0.17	26	2,040	WV	22	372	0.21	12	382
MN	25	848	0.18	14	1,154	WI	35	962	0.18	17	1,092
MS	23	394	0.14	18	403	WY	9	87	0.18	4	65

[1] Circulation figures based on the principal community served by a newspaper which is not necessarily the same location as the publisher's office.   [2] Per capita based on estimated resident population as of July 1.

Source: Editor & Publisher Co., New York, NY, *Editor & Publisher International Year Book*, annual (copyright).

No. 945. U.S. Postal Service Rates for Letters and Post Cards: 1958 to 1999

[Domestic airmail letters discontinued in 1973 at 13 cents per ounce; superseded by express mail. Prior to February 3, 1991, international airmail rates were based on international zones which have been discontinued. Rates exclude Canada and Mexico]

Domestic mail date rate of change	Surface mail — Letters Each ounce	Surface mail — Letters First ounce	Surface mail — Letters Each added ounce	Surface mail Post cards	Surface mail Express mail [1]	International air mail date of rate change	Letters First 1/2 ounce	Letters Second 1/2 ounce	Letters Each added 1/2 ounce	Post cards	Aerogrammes
1958 (Aug. 1) ..	$0.04	(X)	(X)	$0.03	(X)	1961 (July 1) ..	(X)	(X)	(X)	$0.11	$0.11
1963 (Jan. 7) ...	$0.05	(X)	(X)	$0.04	(X)	1967 (May 1) ..	(X)	(X)	(X)	$0.13	$0.13
1968 (Jan. 7) ...	$0.06	(X)	(X)	$0.05	(X)	1971 (July 1) ..	(X)	(X)	(X)	$0.13	$0.13
1971 (May 16) ..	$0.08	(X)	(X)	$0.06	(X)	1974 (Mar. 2) ..	(X)	(X)	(X)	$0.18	$0.18
1974 (Mar. 2) ...	$0.10	(X)	(X)	$0.08	(X)	1976 (Jan. 3) ..	(X)	(X)	(X)	$0.21	$0.22
1975 (Sept. 14) .	(X)	$0.10	$0.09	$0.07	(X)	1981 (Jan. 1) ..	(X)	(X)	(X)	$0.28	$0.30
1975 (Dec. 31) ..	[2](X)	[2]$0.13	[2]$0.11	[2]$0.09	(X)	1985 (Feb. 17) ..	(X)	(X)	(X)	$0.33	$0.36
1978 (May 29) ..	(X)	$0.15	$0.13	$0.10	(X)	1988 (Apr. 17) .	(X)	(X)	(X)	$0.36	$0.39
1981 (Mar. 22) ..	(X)	$0.18	$0.17	$0.12	(X)	1991 (Feb. 3) ..	$0.50	$0.45	[3]$0.39	$0.40	$0.45
1981 (Nov. 1) ..	(X)	$0.20	$0.17	$0.13	$9.35	1995 (July 9) ..	$0.60	[3]$0.40	(X)	$0.40	$0.45
1985 (Feb.17) ...	(X)	$0.22	$0.17	$0.14	$10.75	1999 (Jan. 10) .	$0.60	[3]$0.40	(X)	$0.50	$0.50
1988 (Apr. 3) ...	(X)	$0.25	$0.20	$0.15	[4]$12.00						
1991 (Feb. 3) ...	(X)	$0.29	$0.23	$0.19	[4]$13.95						
1995 (Jan. 1) ...	(X)	$0.32	$0.23	$0.20	[4]$15.00						
1999 (Jan. 10) ..	(X)	$0.33	$0.22	$0.20	[4]$15.75						

X Not applicable.   [1] Post Office to addressee rates. Rates shown are for weights up to 2 pounds, all zones. Beginning Feb. 17, 1985, for weights between 2 and 5 lbs, $12.85 is charged. Prior to Nov. 1, 1981, rate varied by weight and distances. Over 5 pounds still varies by distance.   [2] As of October 11, 1975, surface mail service upgraded to level of airmail.   [3] Up to the limit of 64 ounces.   [4] Over 8 ounces and up to 2 pounds.

Source: U.S. Postal Service, "United States Domestic Postage Rate: Recent History," and unpublished data.

No. 946. U.S. Postal Service—Summary: 1980 to 1998

[For fiscal years; see text, Section 9, State and Local Government. **(106,311 represents 106,311,000,000).** Includes Puerto Rico and all outlying areas. See text, this section]

Item	1980	1990	1994	1995	1996	1997	1998
Offices, stations, and branches	**39,486**	**40,067**	**39,372**	**39,149**	**38,212**	**38,019**	**38,159**
Number of post offices	30,326	28,959	28,657	28,392	28,189	28,060	27,952
Number of stations and branches	9,160	11,108	10,715	10,757	10,023	9,959	10,207
Pieces of mail handled (mil.)	**106,311**	**166,301**	**178,039**	**180,734**	**183,440**	**190,888**	**197,943**
Domestic [1]	105,348	165,503	177,177	179,933	182,386	189,881	196,999
First class [2]	60,276	89,270	95,333	96,296	98,216	99,660	101,173
Express Mail	17	59	56	57	58	64	66
Priority Mail	248	518	770	869	937	1,068	1,164
Periodicals (formerly 2d class)	10,220	10,680	10,228	10,194	10,126	10,411	10,317
Standard A (formerly 3d class)	30,381	63,725	69,416	71,112	71,686	77,254	82,875
Standard B (formerly 4th class)	633	663	872	936	949	988	971
Mailgram	39	14	5	5	4	5	4
U.S. Postal Service	(NA)	538	449	412	360	377	377
Free for the blind	28	35	50	52	50	53	53
International surface	450	166	123	106	105	97	96
International air	513	632	740	696	949	910	848
Employees, total	**667**	**843**	**852**	**875**	**886**	**893**	**905**
Career	643	761	729	753	761	765	792
Headquarters	3	2	2	2	2	2	2
Headquarters support	(NA)	6	4	4	4	4	4
Inspection Service	5	4	4	4	4	4	4
Inspector General	(X)	(X)	(X)	(X)	(X)	(Z)	(Z)
Field Career	635	747	720	745	748	755	781
Postmasters	29	27	27	27	26	26	26
Supervisors/managers	36	43	35	35	35	36	37
Professional, administrative, and technical	5	10	11	11	11	11	12
Clerks	263	290	265	274	277	281	294
Mail handlers	37	51	55	57	58	59	62
City carriers	187	236	229	240	238	234	241
Motor vehicle operators	6	7	8	8	8	9	9
Rural carriers	33	42	45	46	48	50	52
Special delivery messengers	3	2	2	2	1	1	(X)
Building and equipment maintenance . .	27	33	37	38	39	40	41
Vehicle maintenance	5	5	5	5	5	6	6
Other [3]	4	1	1	2	2	2	2
Noncareer	25	83	123	122	125	128	113
Casuals	5	27	26	26	25	33	26
Transitional	(X)	(X)	38	32	33	27	17
Rural substitutes	20	43	47	50	54	55	56
Relief/Leave Replacements	(X)	12	13	13	13	13	13
Nonbargaining temporary	(X)	(Z)	1	1	1	1	1
Compensation and employee benefits (mil. dol.)	16,541	34,214	39,609	41,931	42,676	43,835	45,588
Avg. salary per employee (dol.) [4]	24,799	37,570	44,342	45,001	44,718	48,793	50,117
Pieces of mail per employee, (1,000)	159	197	209	207	207	214	219
Total revenue (mil. dol.) [5]	**19,253**	**40,074**	**49,576**	**54,509**	**56,544**	**58,331**	**60,116**
Operating postal revenue	17,143	39,201	49,252	54,176	56,309	58,133	60,005
Mail revenue [6]	16,377	37,892	47,739	52,490	54,538	56,267	58,039
First class mail	10,146	24,023	29,377	31,955	33,117	33,398	33,983
Priority mail [7]	612	1,555	2,653	3,075	3,322	3,857	4,150
Express mail [8]	184	630	671	711	737	825	855
Mailgram	15	8	2	2	2	2	2
Periodicals (formerly 2d class)	863	1,509	1,756	1,972	2,014	2,068	2,072
Standard mail A (formerly 3d class)	2,412	8,082	10,514	11,792	12,175	12,876	13,753
Standard mail B (formerly 4th class) . . .	805	919	1,353	1,525	1,524	1,628	1,626
International surface	154	222	205	205	199	192	184
International air	442	941	1,208	1,254	1,450	1,423	1,416
Service revenue	765	1,310	1,513	1,687	1,771	1,866	1,966
Registry [9]	157	174	120	118	113	95	89
Certified [9]	120	310	428	560	559	343	382
Insurance [9]	55	47	53	52	49	61	72
Collection-on-delivery	21	26	17	21	21	22	18
Special delivery [10]	73	6	5	3	4	1	(X)
Money orders	95	155	178	196	221	212	210
Other [9]	244	592	710	737	803	1,131	1,194
Operating expenses (mil. dol.) [11]	19,413	40,490	48,455	50,730	53,113	54,873	57,778

NA Not available.   X Not applicable.   Z Fewer than 500.   [1] Data for 1980 includes penalty and franked mail, not shown separately.   [2] Items mailed at 1st class rates and weighing 11 ounces or less.   [3] Includes discontinued operations, area offices, and nurses.   [4] For career bargaining unit employees. Includes fringe benefits.   [5] Net revenues after refunds of postage. Includes operating reimbursements, stamped envelope purchases, indemnity claims, and miscellaneous revenue and expenditure offsets. Shown in year which gave rise to the earnings.   [6] For 1980, includes penalty and franked mail, not shown separately. Later years have that mail distributed into the appropriate class.   [7] Provides 2 to 3 day delivery service.   [8] Overnight delivery of packages weighing up to 70 pounds.   [9] Beginning 1997, return receipt revenue broken out from registry, certified, and insurance and included in "other."   [10] Special delivery discontinued June 8, 1997.   [11] Shown in year in which obligation was incurred.

Source: U.S. Postal Service, *Annual Report of the Postmaster General* and *Comprehensive Statement on Postal Operations*, annual; and unpublished data.

Communications and Information Technology   591

No. 947. Advertising—Estimated Expenditures, by Medium: 1990 to 1998

[In millions of dollars (129,590 represents $129,590,000,000). See text, this section for definitions of types of advertising]

Medium	1990	1991	1992	1993	1994	1995	1996	1997	1998, est.
Total	129,590	127,470	132,650	139,540	151,680	162,930	175,230	187,529	200,320
National.	73,380	73,270	76,710	80,795	88,250	95,360	103,040	110,232	118,000
Local.	56,210	54,200	55,940	58,745	63,430	67,570	72,190	77,297	82,320
Newspapers	32,281	30,409	30,737	32,025	34,356	36,317	38,402	41,670	44,245
National	3,867	3,685	3,602	3,620	3,906	3,996	4,400	5,016	5,390
Local	28,414	26,724	27,135	28,405	30,450	32,321	34,002	36,654	38,855
Magazines	6,803	6,524	7,000	7,357	7,916	8,580	9,010	9,821	10,360
Weeklies.	2,864	2,670	2,739	2,850	3,140	3,347	3,581	3,850	4,040
Women's.	1,713	1,671	1,853	2,009	2,106	2,236	2,303	2,576	2,705
Monthlies	2,226	2,183	2,408	2,498	2,670	2,997	3,126	3,395	3,615
Farm publications.	215	215	231	243	262	283	297	325	340
Television	29,073	28,189	30,450	31,698	35,435	37,828	42,484	44,519	47,990
Four TV networks	9,863	9,533	10,249	10,209	10,942	11,600	13,081	13,020	13,735
Three TV networks	9,383	8,933	9,549	9,369	9,959	10,263	11,423	11,324	12,000
Cable TV networks	1,860	2,024	2,227	2,586	3,052	3,535	4,472	5,454	6,165
Syndication TV	1,109	1,253	1,370	1,576	1,734	2,016	2,218	2,438	2,620
Spot (national)	7,788	7,110	7,551	7,800	8,993	9,119	9,803	9,999	10,675
Spot (local)	7,856	7,565	8,079	8,435	9,464	9,985	10,944	11,436	12,295
Cable (non-network)	597	704	974	1,092	1,250	1,573	1,966	2,172	2,500
Radio.	8,726	8,476	8,654	9,457	10,529	11,338	12,269	13,491	14,455
Network	482	490	424	458	463	480	523	560	585
Spot	1,635	1,575	1,505	1,657	1,902	1,959	2,135	2,455	2,660
Local	6,609	6,411	6,725	7,342	8,164	8,899	9,611	10,476	11,210
Yellow Pages.	8,926	9,182	9,320	9,517	9,825	10,236	10,849	11,423	11,990
National	1,132	1,162	1,188	1,230	1,314	1,410	1,555	1,711	1,850
Local	7,794	8,020	8,132	8,287	8,511	8,826	9,294	9,712	10,140
Direct mail	23,370	24,460	25,391	27,266	29,638	32,866	34,509	36,890	39,470
Business papers	2,875	2,882	3,090	3,260	3,358	3,559	3,808	4,109	4,395
Outdoor	1,084	1,077	1,031	1,090	1,167	1,263	1,339	1,455	1,585
Miscellaneous	16,237	16,056	16,746	17,627	19,194	20,660	22,263	23,827	25,495

Source: McCann-Erickson, Inc., New York, NY. Compiled for Crain Communications, Inc. in *Advertising Age* (copyright).

No. 948. Magazine Advertising—Expenditures, by Product: 1985 to 1997

[In millions of dollars (4,961 represents $4,961,000,000). Space cost based on one-time rate; special rates used where applicable. Year-to-year data not strictly comparable, as a few minor publications are added or deleted]

Product	1985	1990	1991	1992	1993	1994	1995	1996	1997
Total.	4,961	6,753	6,608	7,186	7,667	9,029	10,212	11,282	12,755
Apparel, footwear, accessories	251	428	419	496	513	544	585	671	757
Automotive, accessories, equipment . .	549	900	941	1,035	1,064	1,223	1,328	1,447	1,777
Beer, wine, and liquor	240	277	279	247	204	199	220	226	270
Computers, office equipment and stationery	250	283	291	354	364	699	951	1,031	1,088
Business and consumer services	463	516	453	513	625	680	782	902	1,020
Drugs and remedies	135	163	167	299	368	438	479	641	816
Food and food products	342	444	437	459	470	512	677	665	684
Household equipment and supplies . . .	100	118	115	161	141	141	170	169	185
Household furnishings.	87	116	123	117	146	166	172	161	187
Jewelry, cameras, optical goods	101	157	157	158	168	183	231	270	297
Mail orders/direct response	* 328	531	574	617	725	904	962	988	1,099
Publishing and media	188	212	197	202	214	259	292	357	407
Retail.	121	255	201	190	219	248	256	321	410
Smoking materials	383	305	265	224	210	288	314	333	307
Toiletries and toilet goods	385	679	640	734	811	880	900	989	1,121
Travel, hotels, and resorts	245	380	346	350	378	449	469	518	571
Other.	793	989	1,005	1,030	1,047	1,216	1,425	1,593	1,757

Source: Publishers Information Bureau, Inc., New York, NY, as compiled by Competitive Media Reporting.

No. 949. Television—Expenditures for Network Advertising: 1995 to 1997

[In millions of dollars (12,402 represents $12,402,000,000). See text, this section, for a definition of network advertising. Beginning 1996, includes WB and UPN]

Product	1995	1996	1997	Product	1995	1996	1997
Total	12,402	14,740	15,225	Home electronics equipment	203	258	233
Apparel, footwear, accessories	340	412	370	Horticulture	37	31	35
Automotive	1,736	1,959	2,323	Household equipment,			
Beer and wine	367	391	402	supplies, and furnishings	382	424	400
Building material, equipment,				Insurance	143	255	189
fixture	62	53	60	Jewelry, cameras, optical goods	123	169	176
Computers, office equipment,				Laundry soaps, cleansers,			
and stat.	164	303	380	polishes	267	250	265
Confectionery, soft drinks	673	722	831	Movies	496	668	718
Consumer services	909	1,022	1,028	Pet products	95	110	126
Department, discount stores	393	463	517	Proprietary medicines	1,088	1,405	1,387
Financial planning services	85	153	177	Publishing and media	31	31	26
Food and food products	1,422	1,385	1,362	Restaurants and drive-ins	1,011	1,254	1,216
Freight, industrial development	69	137	103	Toiletries and toilet goods	1,163	1,265	1,376
Gas, lubricants, etc.	60	78	87	Toys and sporting goods	285	351	336
Home centers and hardware				Travel, hotels, and resorts	138	145	141
stores	73	82	75	Other	587	964	886

Source: Television Bureau of Advertising, Inc., New York, NY (copyright). Data compiled by Competitive Media Reporting, New York, NY.

No. 950. Television—Estimated Time Charges for Spot Advertising: 1995 to 1997

[In millions of dollars (6,586 represents $6,586,000,000). Data represent activity in the top 75 markets monitored by Competitive Media Reporting, currently covering approximately 382 stations. Data exclude National Syndicated activity. See text, this section, for definitions of types of advertising]

Product	1995	1996	1997	Product	1995	1996	1997
Total	6,586	7,038	7,219	Horticulture	42	46	43
Agriculture and farming	9	11	11	Household equipment, supplies,			
Apparel, footwear, accessories	59	79	66	and furnishings	156	153	142
Automotive	2,457	2,678	2,945	Insurance	208	234	270
Beer and wine	177	152	123	Jewelry, cameras, optical goods	41	44	35
Building material, equipment,				Laundry soaps, cleaners,			
fixtures	51	48	66	polishes	88	83	94
Computers, office equipment,				Pet products	35	44	45
and stationery	45	60	62	Political, unions, religious	53	172	31
Confectionery, soft drinks	285	292	290	Proprietary medicines	168	192	220
Consumer services	699	759	863	Publishing and media	83	85	73
Food and food products	883	830	894	Toiletries and toilet goods	241	246	243
Freight, industrial development	33	48	20	Toys and sporting goods	250	229	191
Gasoline, lubricants, etc.	123	124	118	Travel, hotels, and resorts	193	190	159
Home electronics equipment	151	163	125	Other	56	76	90

Source: Television Bureau of Advertising, Inc., New York, NY (copyright). Data compiled by Competitive Media Reporting, New York, NY, in the top 75 markets.

No. 951. Television—Expenditures for Retail/Local Advertising: 1995 to 1997

[In millions of dollars (6,608 represents $6,608,000,000). See headnote, Table 950]

Product	1995	1996	1997	Product	1995	1996	1997
Total	6,608	7,167	7,500	Hotels, resorts, U.S.	107	111	132
Amusements, entertainment	188	194	210	Insurance agencies	38	37	41
Appliance stores	309	332	295	Jewelry stores	33	38	40
Auto repair, service stations	103	107	99	Legal services	157	154	168
Auto supply, accessory stores	67	71	94	Leisure time stores and services	225	234	238
Auto, truck dealers	444	482	455	Loan, mortgage companies	75	98	168
Banks, S&L associations	141	172	169	Medical, dental services	181	214	243
Builders, home improvement	44	60	53	Movies	383	387	381
Carpet, floor covering stores	72	70	70	Newspapers	28	30	44
Clothing stores	168	173	178	Office equipment/supply stores	36	26	31
Department stores	226	202	257	Optical services, supplies	70	59	51
Discount department stores	152	171	211	Political	36	260	77
Drug stores	96	116	116	Radio, cable TV	240	220	239
Education services	121	136	158	Realtors, real estate developers	33	36	40
Financial planning services	28	43	58	Rental services (nonauto)	27	29	22
Food stores, supermarkets	291	309	336	Restaurants, drive-ins	1,116	1,138	1,252
Furniture stores	431	439	453	Shoe stores	29	39	50
Gas, electric, water companies	41	45	63	Shopping centers	38	41	40
Health clubs, reducing salons	115	120	118	Sport, hobby, toy stores	61	59	55
Home centers and hardware	180	189	195	Other	478	526	600

Source: Television Bureau of Advertising, Inc., New York, NY (copyright). Data compiled by Competitive Media Reporting, New York, NY, in the top 75 markets.

U.S. Census Bureau, Statistical Abstract of the United States: 1999

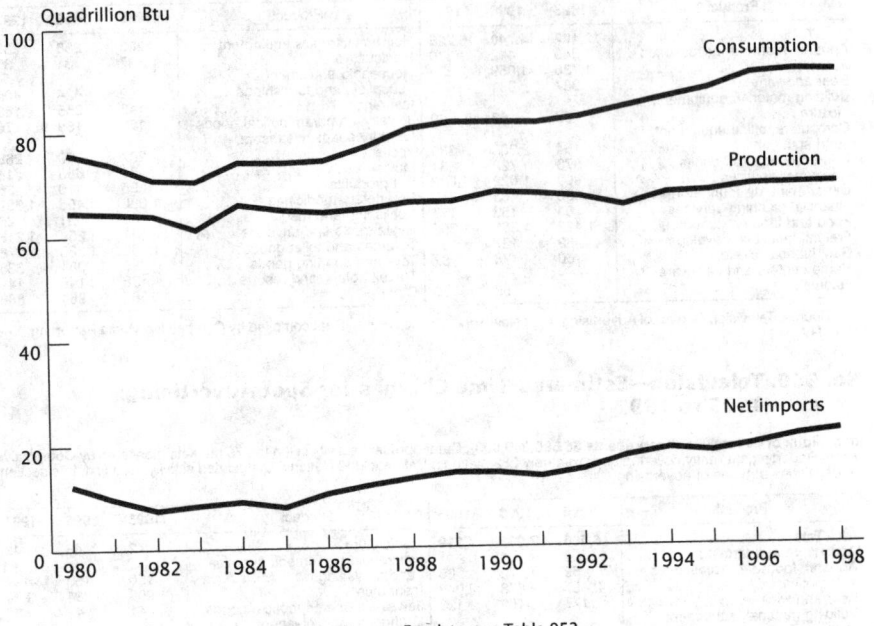

Figure 19.1
Energy Production, Trade, and Consumption: 1980 to 1998

Source: Chart prepared by U.S. Census Bureau. For data, see Table 952.

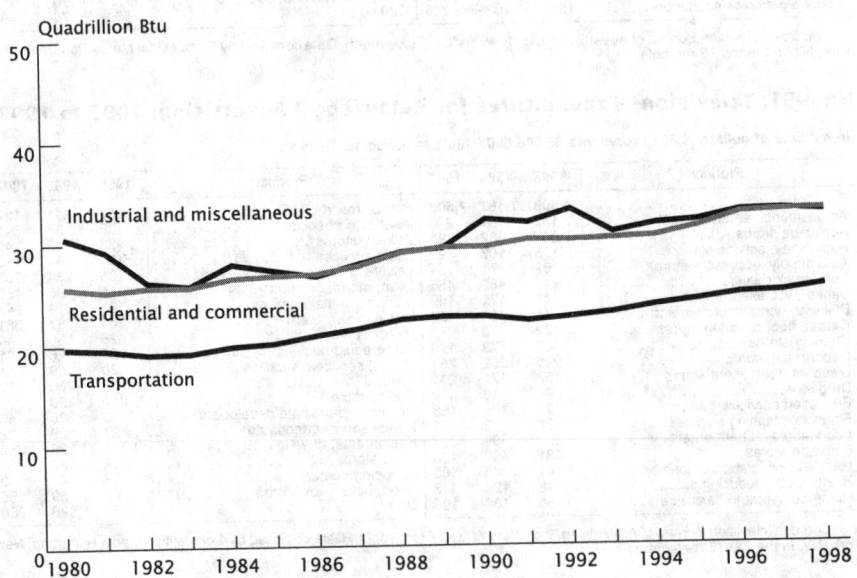

Figure 19.2
Energy Consumption, by End-Use Sector: 1980 to 1998

Source: Chart prepared by U.S. Census Bureau. For data, see Table 955.

U.S. Census Bureau, Statistical Abstract of the United States: 1999

Section 19
Energy

This section presents statistics on fuel resources, energy production and consumption, electric energy, hydroelectric power, nuclear power, solar energy, wood energy and the electric and gas utility industries. The principal sources are the U.S. Department of Energy's Energy Information Administration (EIA), the Edison Electric Institute, Washington, DC, and the American Gas Association, Arlington, VA. The Department of Energy was created in October 1977 and assumed and centralized the responsibilities of all or part of several agencies including the Federal Power Commission (FPC), the U.S. Bureau of Mines, the Federal Energy Administration, and the U.S. Energy Research and Development Administration. For additional data on transportation, see Section 21; on fuels, see Section 24; and on energy-related housing characteristics, see Section 25.

The EIA, in its *Annual Energy Review*, provides statistics and trend data on energy supply, demand, and prices. Information is included on petroleum and natural gas, coal, electricity, hydroelectric power, nuclear power, solar, wood, and geothermal energy. Among its annual reports are *Annual Energy Review, Electric Power Annual, Natural Gas Annual, Petroleum Supply Annual, State Energy Data Report, State Energy Price and Expenditure Report, Financial Statistics of Selected Electric Utilities, Performance Profiles of Major Energy Producers, Annual Energy Outlook*, and *International Energy Annual*. These various publications contain state, national, and international data on production of electricity, net summer capability of generating plants, fuels used in energy production, energy sales and consumption, and hydroelectric power. The EIA also issues the *Monthly Energy Review*, which presents current supply, disposition, and price data and monthly publications on petroleum, coal, natural gas, and electric power. Data on residential energy consumption,

expenditures, and conservation activities are available from EIA's Residential Energy Consumption Survey and are published triennially in *Residential Energy Consumption Survey: Consumption and Expenditures*, and *Residential Energy Consumption Survey: Housing Characteristics*, and other reports.

The Edison Electric Institute's monthly bulletin and annual *Statistical Year Book of the Electric Utility Industry for the Year* contain data on the distribution of electric energy by public utilities; information on the electric power supply, expansion of electric generating facilities, and the manufacture of heavy electric power equipment is presented in the annual *Year-End Summary of the Electric Power Situation in the United States*. The American Gas Association, in its monthly and quarterly bulletins and its yearbook, *Gas Facts*, presents data on gas utilities, financial and operating statistics.

Btu conversion factors—Various energy sources are converted from original units to the thermal equivalent using British thermal units (Btu). A Btu is the amount of energy required to raise the temperature of 1 pound of water 1 degree Fahrenheit (F) at or near 39.2 degrees F. Factors are calculated annually from the latest final annual data available; some are revised as a result. The following list provides conversion factors used in 1995 for production and consumption, in that order, for various fuels: Petroleum, 5.800 and 5.586 mil. Btu per barrel; total coal, 21.278 and 20.852 mil. Btu per short ton; and natural gas (dry), 1,028 Btu per cubic foot for both. The factors for the production of nuclear power and geothermal power were 10,676 and 20,914 Btu per kilowatt-hour, respectively. The fossil fuel steam-electric power plant generation factor of 10,272 Btu per kilowatt-hour was used for hydroelectric power generation and for wood and waste, wind, photovoltaic, and solar thermal energy consumed at electric utilities.

Energy   595

No. 952. Energy Supply and Disposition, by Type of Fuel: 1970 to 1998

[In quadrillion British thermal units (Btu). For Btu conversion factors, see text, this section]

Type of fuel	1970	1973	1975	1980	1985	1990	1994	1995	1996	1997	1998
Production	62.07	62.06	59.86	64.76	64.87	[1]67.87	67.46	67.76	68.92	69.04	69.16
Crude oil [2]	20.40	19.49	17.73	18.25	18.99	15.57	14.10	13.89	13.72	13.66	13.22
Natural gas liquids	2.51	2.57	2.37	2.25	2.24	2.18	2.39	2.44	2.53	2.50	2.41
Natural gas	21.67	22.19	19.64	19.91	16.98	18.36	19.35	19.10	19.30	19.39	19.47
Coal	14.61	13.99	14.99	18.60	19.33	22.46	22.07	21.98	22.65	23.16	23.58
Nuclear electric power	0.24	0.91	1.90	2.74	4.15	6.16	6.84	7.18	7.17	6.68	7.16
Hydroelectric power	2.63	2.86	3.16	2.90	2.97	[3]2.94	2.55	3.06	3.42	3.52	3.19
Geothermal	(Z)	0.04	0.07	0.11	0.20	[1]0.18	0.15	0.10	0.11	0.12	0.11
Biofuels [4]	(Z)	(Z)	(Z)	(Z)	(Z)	[1]2.63	2.84	2.85	2.94	2.72	(NA)
Net trade [5]	**-5.73**	**12.68**	**11.75**	**12.25**	**7.87**	**14.08**	**18.57**	**17.89**	**19.26**	**20.89**	**21.82**
Exports	2.66	2.05	2.36	3.72	4.23	4.91	4.13	4.58	4.71	4.63	4.32
Coal	1.94	1.43	1.76	2.42	2.44	2.77	1.88	2.32	2.37	(NA)	(NA)
Natural gas	0.07	0.08	0.07	0.05	0.06	0.09	0.16	0.16	0.16	(NA)	(NA)
Petroleum	0.55	0.49	0.44	1.16	1.66	1.82	1.99	1.99	2.06	(NA)	(NA)
Imports	8.39	14.73	14.11	15.97	12.10	18.99	22.70	22.47	23.96	25.53	26.15
Coal	(Z)	-1.42	-1.74	-2.39	-2.39	-2.71	-1.69	-2.14	-2.19	-2.01	-1.81
Natural gas [6]	0.82	0.98	0.90	0.96	0.90	1.46	2.52	2.75	2.85	2.90	3.04
Petroleum [6]	2.81	6.88	8.71	10.59	6.38	12.54	15.43	15.13	16.08	17.65	18.35
Consumption	**66.43**	**74.28**	**70.55**	**75.96**	**73.98**	**81.28**	**85.60**	**87.21**	**90.04**	**90.63**	**90.42**
Petroleum [7]	29.52	34.84	32.73	34.20	30.92	33.55	34.74	34.66	35.86	36.38	36.57
Natural gas [8]	21.79	22.51	19.95	20.39	17.83	19.30	21.29	22.16	22.56	22.54	21.84
Coal	12.26	12.97	12.66	15.42	17.48	19.10	19.54	19.61	20.51	21.02	21.20
Nuclear electric power	0.24	0.91	1.90	2.74	4.15	6.16	6.84	7.18	7.17	6.68	7.16
Renewable energy	2.67	3.06	3.29	3.23	3.61	6.17	6.28	6.85	7.39	(NA)	(NA)
Hydroelectric power [9]	2.65	2.98	3.19	3.09	3.37	2.93	2.97	3.41	3.78	3.82	3.45
Geothermal	0.01	0.04	0.07	0.11	0.20	0.18	0.15	0.10	0.11	0.12	0.11
Biofuels [4]	(Z)	-	-	0.01	0.02	0.02	0.02	0.02	0.02	0.02	0.02

- Represents or rounds to zero.   NA Not available.   Z Less than 50 trillion.   [1] There is a discontinuity in this time series between 1989 and 1990 due to the expanded coverage of nonelectric utility use of renewable energy beginning in 1990. [2] Includes lease condensate.   [3] There is a discontinuity in this time series between 1989 and 1990; beginning in 1990, pumped storage is removed and expanded coverage of industrial use of hydroelectric power is included.   [4] Includes wood, wood waste, peat, wood liquors, railroad ties, pitch, wood sludge, municipal solid waste, agricultural waste, straw, tires, landfill gases, fish oils, and/or other waste.   [5] Exports minus imports.   [6] Includes imports of crude oil for the Strategic Petroleum Reserve, which began in 1977. Includes imports of unfinished oils and natural gas plant liquids.   [7] Petroleum products supplied, including natural gas plant liquids and crude oil burned as fuel.   [8] Includes supplemental gaseous fuels.   [9] Includes net imports of electricity.

Source: U.S. Energy Information Administration, *Annual Energy Review* through 1989; thereafter, *Monthly Energy Review*, March 1999.

No. 953. Energy Supply and Disposition, by Type of Fuel—Estimates, 1995 to 1997, and Projections, 2005 to 2020

[Quadrillion Btu per year, except percent change. Projections are "reference" or mid-level forecasts. See report for methodology and assumptions used in generating projections]

Type of fuel	1995	1996	1997	2005	2010	2015	2020
Production, total	**72.31**	**73.66**	**73.22**	**76.89**	**79.16**	**81.28**	**82.85**
Crude oil and lease condensate	13.89	13.69	13.65	12.31	11.83	11.30	10.51
National gas liquids	2.37	2.60	2.57	2.80	3.06	3.32	3.47
Natural gas	19.12	19.32	19.47	22.17	24.44	26.84	28.12
Coal	21.98	22.75	23.33	25.20	25.91	26.95	28.12
Nuclear power	7.19	7.20	6.71	6.73	5.91	4.47	3.83
Imports, total	**22.38**	**23.85**	**25.34**	**32.65**	**36.66**	**39.33**	**42.15**
Crude oil [1]	15.70	16.31	17.86	21.53	23.91	24.96	26.03
Petroleum products [2]	3.19	3.98	3.89	6.45	7.35	8.50	9.92
Natural gas [3]	2.90	3.00	3.06	3.97	4.69	5.15	5.46
Other imports [3]	0.59	0.57	0.54	0.70	0.71	0.72	0.75
Exports, total	**4.50**	**4.57**	**4.44**	**4.47**	**4.62**	**4.59**	**4.68**
Petroleum [4]	2.02	2.04	2.09	2.05	2.11	2.02	2.00
Natural gas	0.16	0.16	0.16	0.21	0.24	0.27	0.32
Coal	2.32	2.37	2.19	2.21	2.27	2.31	2.36
Consumption, total [5]	**90.86**	**93.63**	**94.04**	**104.68**	**110.83**	**115.53**	**119.89**
Petroleum products [5]	34.74	36.03	36.49	41.25	44.22	46.20	48.08
Natural gas	22.18	22.59	22.59	25.89	28.79	31.64	33.17
Coal	19.96	20.60	21.09	23.31	24.06	25.05	26.26
Nuclear power	7.19	7.20	6.71	6.73	5.91	4.47	3.83
Renewable energy/other [6]	6.40	6.81	6.82	7.12	7.45	7.79	8.17

[1] Includes imports of crude oil for the Strategic Petroleum Reserve.   [2] Includes imports of finished petroleum products, imports of unfinished oils, alcohols, ethers, and blending components.   [3] Includes coal, coal coke (net), and electricity (net). [4] Includes crude oil and petroleum products.   [5] Includes natural gas plant liquids, crude oil consumed as a fuel, and nonpetroleum based liquids for blending, such as ethanol.   [6] Includes net electricity imports, methanol, and liquid hydrogen.

Source: U.S. Energy Information Administration, *Annual Energy Outlook 1999*.

No. 954. Selected Energy Indicators—Summary: 1970 to 1997

[Btu = British thermal unit. For Btu conversion factors, see text, this section. Minus sign (-) indicates decrease]

Item	1970	1973	1975	1980	1985	1990	1991	1992	1993	1994	1995	1996	1997
AVERAGE ANNUAL PERCENT CHANGE [1]													
Gross domestic product [2] ...	3.3	1.9	-0.2	-0.1	0.7	1.2	-0.9	2.7	2.3	3.4	2.0	2.7	3.7
Energy production, total [3][4] ..	4.6	-0.2	-1.8	0.3	-0.3	6.8	-0.5	-0.7	-2.4	3.4	0.5	1.8	-
Crude oil [5]	4.2	-0.9	-4.7	0.2	0.2	-3.4	0.8	-3.1	-4.9	-2.7	-1.5	-1.2	-1.1
Natural gas	6.4	-0.0	-6.1	-0.2	-1.2	2.8	-0.7	0.8	1.1	4.0	-1.3	1.0	0.9
Coal...............	2.2	-0.2	3.4	1.2	-0.4	5.1	-3.9	(Z)	-6.5	8.8	-0.4	3.0	2.3
Energy consumption, total [3][4] .	4.6	1.4	-2.6	-0.8	-0.0	3.3	-0.1	1.8	2.1	2.1	1.8	3.3	0.4
Petroleum products	4.8	1.9	-3.1	-1.6	-0.1	-1.9	-2.1	2.1	0.9	2.6	-0.2	3.4	1.2
Natural gas (dry)........	6.5	-0.3	-6.0	-0.3	-0.7	-0.5	1.6	2.6	3.4	2.2	4.0	1.8	0.1
Coal...............	1.1	2.4	-1.2	0.5	0.5	0.9	-1.7	2.4	3.2	1.0	0.3	4.5	2.0
PER CAPITA [6] (mil. Btu)													
Energy production	304	294	278	285	273	284	279	274	265	272	270	273	-
Energy consumption	327	351	327	335	310	338	333	336	339	343	346	354.0	352.0
Energy consumption per dollar of GDP [2] (1,000 Btu) .	19.6	19.0	18.2	16.5	13.9	13.7	13.8	13.7	13.7	13.5	13.5	13.6	13.1

- Represents zero. Z Less than .05 percent. [1] Represents percent change from immediate prior year; for example, 1970, change from 1965. Percent change derived from Btu values. [2] Gross domestic product in chained (1992) dollars. For definition of chained, see text, Section 14, Income. [3] Includes types of fuel or power, not shown separately. [4] Due to a lack of consistent historical data, some renewable energy sources are not included. [5] Includes lease condensate. [6] Based on resident population estimated as of July 1.

Source: U.S. Energy Information Administration, *Annual Energy Review*, and *Monthly Energy Review*.

No. 955. Energy Consumption, by End-Use Sector: 1970 to 1997

[There exits a discontinuity in the series between 1989 and 1990 due to the expanded coverage of nonelectric utility use of renewable energy beginning 1990. Btu = British thermal units. For Btu conversion factors, see text, this section]

Year	Total consumption (quad. Btu)	Residential and commercial (quad. Btu)	Industrial and miscellaneous (quad. Btu)	Transportation (quad. Btu)	Percent of total		
					Residential and commercial	Industrial and miscellaneous	Transportation
1970.......	66.43	21.71	28.63	16.09	32.7	43.1	24.2
1973.......	74.28	24.14	31.53	18.60	32.5	42.4	25.0
1975.......	70.55	23.90	28.40	18.25	33.9	40.3	25.9
1976.......	74.36	25.02	30.24	19.10	33.6	40.7	25.7
1977.......	76.29	25.39	31.08	19.82	33.3	40.7	26.0
1978.......	78.09	26.09	31.39	20.61	33.4	40.2	26.4
1979.......	78.90	25.81	32.61	20.47	32.7	41.3	25.9
1980.......	75.96	25.65	30.61	19.69	33.8	40.3	25.9
1981.......	73.99	25.24	29.24	19.51	34.1	39.5	26.4
1982.......	70.85	25.63	26.14	19.07	36.2	36.9	26.9
1983.......	70.52	25.63	25.75	19.13	36.3	36.5	27.1
1984.......	74.14	26.48	27.86	19.80	35.7	37.6	26.7
1985.......	73.98	26.70	27.22	20.07	36.1	36.8	27.1
1986.......	74.30	26.85	26.63	20.81	36.1	35.8	28.0
1987.......	76.89	27.62	27.83	21.45	35.9	36.2	27.9
1988.......	80.22	28.92	28.99	22.30	36.1	36.1	27.8
1989.......	81.35	29.42	29.36	22.56	36.2	36.1	27.7
1990.......	84.12	29.45	32.12	22.54	35.0	38.2	26.8
1991.......	84.03	30.12	31.78	22.12	35.8	37.8	26.3
1992.......	85.55	30.05	33.03	22.46	35.1	38.6	26.3
1993.......	87.37	31.17	33.31	22.88	35.7	38.1	26.2
1994.......	89.25	31.42	34.26	23.57	35.2	38.4	26.4
1995.......	90.86	32.30	34.48	24.07	35.5	37.9	26.5
1996.......	93.87	33.69	35.51	24.66	35.9	37.8	26.3
1997.......	94.21	33.72	35.67	24.81	35.8	37.9	26.3

Source: U.S. Energy Information Administration, *Annual Energy Review*.

Energy 597

No. 956. Energy Consumption—End-Use Sector and Selected Source, by State: 1996

[In trillions of Btu (93,398.5 represents 93,398,500,000,000,000), except as indicated. For Btu conversion factors, see text this section]

State	Total[1]	Per capita[2] (mil. Btu)	End-use sector				Source				
			Resi-dential	Com-mercial	Industrial	Trans-portation	Petro-leum	Natural gas (dry)	Coal	Hydro-electric power	Nuclear electric power
United States.....	**93,398.5**	**349.0**	**18,930.0**	**14,429.2**	**[3]35,420.3**	**24,619.0**	**35,866.2**	**22,598.1**	**20,519.6**	**3,881.3**	**7,167.6**
Alabama......	1,975.0	457.3	353.2	182.6	991.3	448.0	562.5	336.3	887.5	114.6	315.6
Alaska.......	696.8	1,143.6	49.5	66.7	419.2	161.4	224.0	443.6	11.2	13.1	-
Arizona......	1,114.8	244.7	251.6	238.2	226.8	398.3	427.4	121.7	343.2	98.0	306.4
Arkansas.....	1,012.9	401.5	195.3	119.4	430.2	268.0	309.7	277.7	260.2	28.9	141.9
California	7,697.1	238.5	1,340.4	1,193.5	2,289.7	2,873.5	3,341.9	1,865.1	53.9	487.6	362.2
Colorado......	1,133.5	291.2	255.0	240.2	302.4	335.9	412.2	314.7	340.3	17.6	-
Connecticut....	824.5	252.2	254.7	189.9	164.4	215.5	412.5	131.5	24.4	15.7	66.1
Delaware	273.2	373.4	57.3	42.8	106.0	67.1	139.0	55.9	50.8	0.0	-
Dist. of Columbia	177.4	335.4	38.3	110.0	3.2	25.9	35.4	34.2	0.6	0.0	-
Florida	3,579.4	244.3	1,002.7	761.1	582.0	1,233.6	1,629.6	510.7	694.5	2.2	270.6
Georgia	2,634.5	351.9	561.8	391.9	835.7	845.1	1,017.1	392.2	725.6	51.6	317.9
Hawaii	242.0	203.9	21.5	23.8	76.3	120.3	221.4	2.8	3.6	1.1	-
Idaho........	491.1	405.8	91.1	82.9	202.0	115.1	159.4	69.0	7.3	138.9	-
Illinois.......	3,897.4	327.6	986.5	722.4	1,356.5	832.0	1,272.8	1,140.6	906.9	1.1	741.2
Indiana.......	2,663.6	454.2	503.5	301.9	1,242.7	615.6	859.2	579.8	1,372.1	4.6	-
Iowa	1,090.7	382.4	240.5	156.3	417.5	276.4	371.3	274.3	380.5	9.7	41.7
Kansas.......	1,060.0	408.5	210.9	183.3	389.3	276.5	379.7	362.0	338.6	0.1	87.2
Kentucky	1,776.8	454.6	327.7	199.6	848.0	401.5	599.1	248.0	951.8	36.2	-
Louisiana	3,994.9	918.0	326.6	222.0	2,617.3	829.0	1,612.2	1,737.7	205.6	10.0	167.5
Maine........	538.4	433.5	102.1	57.8	271.9	106.6	253.2	5.8	5.9	76.3	53.8
Maryland	1,349.1	264.8	387.6	322.3	277.7	361.6	518.2	198.1	292.2	25.4	128.5
Massachusetts..	1,533.5	250.7	426.4	371.3	312.9	422.9	690.7	367.5	113.1	16.8	56.6
Michigan.....	3,249.2	332.4	795.9	577.8	1,099.5	776.0	998.4	1,026.7	789.3	26.2	285.0
Minnesota.....	1,688.9	360.4	377.8	227.5	635.6	448.0	638.6	375.1	345.5	92.9	128.5
Mississippi	1,098.4	402.3	205.3	117.5	432.4	343.2	424.0	277.4	128.1	0.0	98.0
Missouri	1,744.7	323.0	459.4	337.1	374.8	573.5	721.1	297.5	629.7	12.8	94.4
Montana......	395.1	449.6	70.4	55.6	167.6	101.5	175.3	63.2	135.7	143.0	-
Nebraska	604.4	364.8	140.5	123.2	160.1	180.6	235.6	133.8	179.0	16.6	100.5
Nevada	575.4	343.2	108.9	88.8	198.1	179.5	216.1	127.6	169.5	22.4	-
New Hampshire.	302.2	257.7	83.9	55.6	78.9	83.8	156.6	19.4	36.2	29.2	104.6
New Jersey....	2,574.9	319.8	565.3	520.4	655.0	834.1	1,228.0	624.6	62.4	[4]-1.0	117.1
New Mexico ...	595.2	344.1	87.5	101.8	217.5	188.4	209.4	228.2	279.2	2.2	-
New York	4,129.6	227.7	1,104.7	1,118.9	949.8	956.2	1,569.3	1,159.9	294.3	343.3	374.2
North Carolina..	2,416.5	325.4	583.1	414.1	773.3	646.0	885.1	220.8	687.0	66.2	358.2
North Dakota...	351.9	549.1	61.7	46.5	168.2	75.5	119.8	51.5	404.1	40.8	0.0
Ohio	4,115.7	367.9	930.8	649.2	1,640.5	895.2	1,236.6	972.0	1,448.8	4.1	147.9
Oklahoma.....	1,405.7	423.8	273.1	196.2	550.3	386.0	469.6	580.2	349.9	21.5	-
Oregon.......	1,108.1	341.6	234.9	180.0	386.3	306.9	363.9	175.3	20.3	491.3	-
Pennsylvania...	3,927.3	326.7	935.8	607.8	1,477.9	905.8	1,329.3	752.7	1,432.3	23.2	729.5
Rhode Island...	235.9	238.9	72.1	52.2	52.4	59.2	97.3	87.7	0.1	9.4	-
South Carolina..	1,426.8	379.4	291.5	191.0	614.1	330.2	445.1	154.1	352.5	23.6	462.9
South Dakota ..	244.7	331.6	61.8	41.1	61.5	80.4	116.7	37.4	33.2	82.5	-
Tennessee	2,067.9	385.2	475.3	139.4	905.1	548.0	690.7	289.3	648.6	111.6	243.5
Texas........	11,278.2	580.2	1,310.2	1,080.4	6,542.3	2,345.3	5,166.4	4,123.0	1,475.4	9.9	379.9
Utah	674.4	327.5	120.0	106.5	254.2	193.7	251.6	167.8	355.0	10.8	-
Vermont	162.4	275.7	46.1	27.3	36.7	52.4	85.2	7.4	-	41.0	40.4
Virginia.......	2,115.2	314.1	518.7	451.9	532.5	612.2	792.9	248.4	378.8	6.2	279.2
Washington....	2,135.2	380.6	435.5	321.2	757.8	620.8	842.1	247.5	90.9	1,045.5	59.4
West Virginia...	803.4	442.5	150.9	97.2	391.1	164.2	257.6	164.5	898.3	14.8	-
Wisconsin.....	1,791.4	346.5	403.6	278.9	708.8	400.3	550.0	408.0	452.8	29.3	107.5
Wyoming	423.2	882.1	41.0	44.5	235.3	102.3	145.5	107.6	473.0	12.7	-

- Represents zero. [1] Sources of energy includes geothermal, wood and waste, and net interstate sales of electricity, including losses, not shown separately. [2] Based on estimated resident population as of July 1. [3] Includes 27.2 trillion Btu of net imports of coal coke not allocated by State. [4] A negative number occurs when more electricity is expended than is created to provide electricity during peak demand periods.

Source: U.S. Energy Information Administration, State Energy Data Report, annual.

598 Energy

[In millions of dollars (515,800 represents $515,800,000,000), except as indicated. End-use sector and electric utilities exclude expenditures on energy sources such as hydropower, solar, wind, and geothermal. Also excludes expenditures for reported amounts of energy consumed by the energy industry for production, transportation, and processing operations]

State	Total [1]	End-use sector					Source		
		Residential	Commercial	Industrial	Transportation	Petroleum products	Natural gas	Coal	Electricity sales
U.S.	515,800	128,702	91,648	107,975	187,474	237,491	74,150	26,911	205,944
AL.........	9,172	2,107	1,051	2,455	3,560	4,121	1,033	1,313	3,686
AK.........	1,975	321	334	190	1,129	1,333	211	34	468
AZ.........	7,688	1,913	1,594	1,009	3,172	3,477	498	486	3,700
AR.........	5,218	1,280	658	1,194	2,087	2,385	732	384	2,103
CA.........	51,146	11,415	10,689	8,007	21,035	22,841	8,066	110	20,831
CO.........	6,312	1,429	1,204	909	2,770	3,160	980	356	2,142
CT.........	6,713	2,234	1,585	804	2,090	2,997	879	45	2,938
DE.........	1,546	431	253	317	545	762	205	83	658
DC.........	1,257	264	729	16	249	299	229	-	735
FL.........	22,956	7,107	4,503	2,074	9,272	10,847	1,517	1,169	11,745
GA	14,604	3,724	2,482	2,801	5,597	6,483	1,650	1,220	6,329
HI	2,165	365	376	425	998	1,318	39	5	1,018
ID	2,246	441	321	539	944	1,160	248	16	802
IL	23,343	6,493	4,472	5,295	7,084	9,123	4,397	1,325	9,657
IN	12,849	2,875	1,548	3,670	4,755	5,735	2,145	1,818	4,516
IA	6,092	1,512	813	1,640	2,127	2,933	1,009	389	2,069
KS.........	5,350	1,240	958	1,163	1,989	2,506	896	299	1,981
KY.........	8,239	1,642	922	2,319	3,357	4,260	796	1,083	3,004
LA.........	13,029	2,099	1,359	5,277	4,294	6,832	2,672	338	4,056
ME	2,836	831	415	624	965	1,642	31	16	1,097
MD	8,844	2,716	1,996	924	3,208	3,962	944	434	3,964
MA	11,845	3,600	2,830	1,588	3,827	5,265	2,109	177	4,705
MI	18,163	4,668	3,521	3,922	6,053	7,516	3,812	1,151	6,636
MN	8,826	2,113	1,071	2,041	3,601	4,526	1,242	410	2,983
MS	5,325	1,223	692	1,182	2,228	2,642	626	160	2,190
MO	10,094	2,691	1,756	1,486	4,161	4,982	1,193	594	3,892
MT	2,011	350	257	477	929	1,122	251	125	614
NE.........	3,372	739	591	615	1,427	1,730	506	139	1,128
NV.........	3,117	647	482	709	1,279	1,473	463	214	1,236
NH	2,314	738	475	312	789	1,153	110	57	1,056
NJ.........	17,498	4,689	4,065	2,765	5,980	7,708	2,938	98	6,944
NM	2,901	551	595	527	1,227	1,537	320	390	1,085
NY.........	31,573	10,258	9,447	3,599	8,269	11,225	6,401	431	14,435
NC	14,399	4,048	2,331	2,922	5,098	6,422	926	986	6,885
ND	1,660	313	217	526	606	836	114	482	448
OH	23,272	6,135	3,983	5,792	7,362	9,071	4,096	1,977	9,829
OK	6,338	1,542	946	1,256	2,594	3,008	1,333	355	2,295
OR	5,642	1,162	834	1,071	2,574	2,897	567	25	2,135
PA	24,172	7,079	4,150	5,332	7,611	9,835	3,765	2,006	9,937
RI	1,874	579	397	322	577	819	370	-	689
SC.........	7,585	1,956	1,095	1,953	2,581	3,132	621	487	3,703
SD.........	1,464	350	211	241	662	863	132	40	460
TN.........	10,379	2,315	730	3,063	4,271	4,968	1,017	796	4,224
TX.........	46,965	8,529	6,254	16,888	15,295	25,974	7,224	1,815	15,675
UT.........	3,160	601	484	576	1,499	1,693	439	410	968
VT.........	1,219	381	209	156	474	690	38	-	483
VA.........	12,412	3,520	2,328	1,674	4,890	5,810	1,140	520	5,312
WA	9,558	1,966	1,371	1,625	4,596	5,081	835	111	3,569
WV	4,036	903	524	1,143	1,466	1,978	538	1,113	1,375
WI	9,233	2,423	1,359	1,890	3,561	4,418	1,607	531	3,084
WY	1,708	199	183	566	761	945	244	388	473

- Represents zero. [1] Includes sources not shown separately. Total expenditures are the sum of purchases for each source (including electricity sales) less electric utility purchases of fuel.

Source: U.S. Energy Information Administration, *State Energy Price and Expenditure Report*, annual.

Energy 599

No. 958. Energy Expenditures and Average Fuel Prices, by Source and Sector: 1970 to 1995

[82,542 represents $82,542,000,000. For definition of Btu, see text, this section. End-use sector and electric utilities exclude expenditures and prices on energy sources such as hydropower, solar, wind, and geothermal. Also excludes expenditures for reported amounts of energy consumed by the energy industry for production, transportation, and processing operations]

Source and sector	1970	1973	1975	1980	1985	1990	1991	1992	1993	1994	1995
EXPENDITURES (mil. dol.)											
Total [1] [2]	82,542	111,591	171,680	373,868	436,619	472,583	470,287	475,155	492,663	505,878	515,800
Natural gas	10,891	13,933	20,061	51,061	72,938	64,102	64,697	68,400	75,941	77,716	74,150
Petroleum products [2] . . .	48,051	65,257	103,756	238,377	224,371	235,984	223,390	222,326	223,466	230,267	237,491
Motor gasoline	31,596	39,667	59,446	124,408	118,044	126,472	123,051	125,158	126,397	129,900	136,475
Coal.	4,594	6,251	13,047	22,648	29,719	28,381	27,866	27,417	27,857	27,251	26,911
Electricity sales	23,351	33,780	50,680	98,098	149,242	176,744	184,823	186,962	196,589	200,893	205,944
Residential sector.	20,083	27,078	36,844	68,825	98,307	110,147	115,666	116,118	125,270	127,186	128,702
Commercial sector	10,668	15,107	22,835	46,881	70,265	78,870	81,427	82,366	86,579	89,451	91,648
Industrial sector	16,421	23,502	41,067	94,489	106,886	103,017	101,764	103,956	106,082	109,298	107,975
Transportation sector [2] . .	35,370	45,904	70,934	163,674	161,161	180,550	171,431	172,714	174,762	179,944	187,474
Motor gasoline	30,525	38,598	57,992	121,809	115,201	123,775	120,557	122,700	124,546	127,945	134,470
Electric utilities.	4,316	7,817	16,396	37,435	42,558	38,441	36,500	35,764	36,651	35,955	34,671
AVERAGE FUEL PRICES (dol. per mil. Btu)											
All sectors	1.65	2.02	3.33	6.91	8.40	8.27	8.22	8.15	8.24	8.29	8.28
Residential sector.	2.12	2.73	3.83	7.55	11.14	11.44	11.62	11.52	11.89	12.22	12.13
Commercial sector	1.97	2.56	4.09	7.88	11.71	12.02	12.20	12.32	12.72	12.90	12.78
Industrial sector	0.83	1.09	2.20	4.71	6.05	5.28	5.21	5.17	5.16	5.16	5.01
Transportation sector . . .	2.31	2.57	4.02	8.61	8.26	8.27	7.98	7.91	7.87	7.88	8.04
Electric utilities.	0.32	0.46	0.96	1.75	1.85	1.46	1.37	1.34	1.35	1.30	1.23

[1] Includes electricity sales; excludes electricity generation.   [2] Includes sources or fuel types not shown separately.

Source: U.S. Energy Information Administration, *State Energy Price and Expenditure Report*, annual.

No. 959. Residential Energy Consumption, Expenditures, and Average Price, 1980 to 1993, and by Region, 1993

[For period April to March for 1980-1985; January to December for 1987 to 1993. Excludes Alaska and Hawaii in 1980. Covers occupied units only. Excludes household usage of gasoline for transportation and the use of wood or coal. Based on Residential Energy Consumption Survey; see source. For composition of regions, see inside front cover. Btu = British thermal unit; see text, this section]

Type of fuel	Unit	1980	1983	1985	1987	1990	1993 Total	North- east	Mid- west	South	West
CONSUMPTION											
Total	Quad. Btu . .	9.74	8.62	9.04	9.13	9.22	10.01	2.38	3.13	2.95	1.55
Avg. per household. . . .	Mil. Btu	126	103	105	101	98	103.6	122.4	134.3	87.9	76.0
Natural gas	Quad. Btu . .	5.31	4.77	4.98	4.83	4.86	5.27	1.11	2.07	1.18	0.91
Electricity	Quad. Btu . .	2.42	2.42	2.48	2.76	3.03	3.28	0.47	0.74	1.51	0.56
Fuel oil, kerosene	Quad. Btu . .	1.71	1.14	1.26	1.22	1.04	1.07	0.78	0.13	0.13	0.03
Liquid petroleum gas	Quad. Btu . .	0.31	0.29	0.31	0.32	0.28	0.38	0.03	0.19	0.13	0.04
EXPENDITURES											
Total	Bil. dol.	63.2	87.8	97.0	97.7	110.2	123.91	29.72	31.12	43.67	19.41
Avg. per household. . . .	Dollars.	815	1,048	1,123	1,080	1,172	1,282	1,526	1,336	1,304	953
Natural gas	Bil. dol.	17.8	27.1	29.8	26.1	27.3	32.04	8.60	11.13	7.24	5.07
Electricity	Bil. dol.	32.6	48.4	54.5	61.6	71.5	81.08	15.76	17.55	34.08	13.69
Fuel oil, kerosene	Bil. dol.	10.7	9.6	9.6	7.2	8.3	6.98	5.00	0.84	0.9	0.24
Liquid petroleum gas	Bil. dol.	2.1	2.7	3.1	2.8	3.1	3.81	0.35	1.59	1.46	0.41
AVERAGE PRICE											
Total	Dol./mil. Btu.	6.49	10.18	10.73	10.71	12.00	12.38	12.47	9.94	14.82	12.54
Natural gas	Dol./mil. Btu .	3.36	5.67	5.97	5.41	5.60	6.07	7.73	5.38	6.13	5.55
Electricity	Dol./mil. Btu.	13.46	19.98	21.94	22.34	23.60	24.69	33.55	23.69	22.61	24.23
Fuel oil, kerosene	Dol./mil. Btu .	6.29	8.42	7.64	5.89	7.90	6.52	6.41	6.46	6.92	8.00
Liquid petroleum gas	Dol./mil. Btu .	6.71	9.42	9.91	8.91	11.20	10.04	13.90	8.55	11.13	10.99

Source: U.S. Energy Information Administration, *Household Energy Consumption and Expenditures, 1993*, and prior reports. Survey not conducted in 1984, 1986, 1988, and 1989.

600   Energy

No. 960. Residential Energy Consumption and Expenditures, by Type of Fuel and Selected Household Characteristic: 1993

[For period January through December. Quad. = quadrillion. See headnote, Table 959]

Characteristic	Consumption (Btu)					Expenditures				
	Total [1] (quad.)	Avg. per house- hold[1] (mil.)	Natural gas (quad.)	Elec- tricity (quad.)	Fuel oil[2] (quad.)	Total[1] (bil. dol.)	Avg. per house- hold[1] (dol.)	Natural gas (bil. dol.)	Elec- tricity (bil. dol.)	Fuel oil[2] (bil. dol.)
Total households..	10.01	104	5.27	3.28	1.02	123.9	1,282	32.04	81.08	6.61
Single family detached....	7.21	121	3.77	2.34	0.78	87.0	1,462	22.23	56.44	5.20
Single family attached	0.70	96	0.41	0.24	0.05	9.3	1,266	2.65	6.22	0.34
Two-to-four unit building . . .	0.80	100	0.54	0.17	0.09	8.9	1,112	3.56	4.72	0.58
Five-or-more unit building . .	0.83	52	0.43	0.32	0.08	12.0	740	2.84	8.76	0.37
Mobile home	0.46	82	0.14	0.21	0.02	6.7	1,203	0.76	4.93	0.12
Year house built:										
1939 or earlier........	2.63	129	1.55	0.51	0.43	27.0	1,325	9.60	13.34	2.75
1940 to 1949	0.77	112	0.44	0.20	0.10	8.6	1,240	2.70	4.91	0.64
1950 to 1959	1.49	114	0.85	0.42	0.19	18.1	1,387	5.28	11.22	1.28
1960 to 1969	1.55	103	0.90	0.49	0.11	18.9	1,257	5.35	12.26	0.69
1970 to 1979	1.59	88	0.69	0.71	0.12	22.2	1,222	3.92	16.74	0.78
1980 to 1984	0.68	80	0.29	0.35	0.02	10.6	1,247	1.73	8.48	0.13
1985 to 1987	0.47	85	0.20	0.23	0.02	7.1	1,284	1.22	5.47	0.11
1988 to 1990	0.43	90	0.18	0.21	0.02	6.2	1,322	1.05	4.81	0.13
1991 to 1993	0.40	89	0.20	0.16	0.01	5.4	1,200	1.19	3.85	0.09
1993 family income:										
Less than $5,000......	0.32	80	0.18	0.10	0.03	4.0	991	1.14	2.52	0.18
$5,000 to $9,999	0.86	81	0.48	0.26	0.08	10.3	977	2.94	6.42	0.47
$10,000 to $14,999	1.00	90	0.58	0.29	0.09	11.7	1,051	3.51	7.17	0.58
$15,000 to $19,999	0.95	99	0.52	0.30	0.09	11.2	1,163	3.08	7.08	0.55
$20,000 to $24,999	0.84	97	0.43	0.28	0.08	10.3	1,182	2.62	6.75	0.51
$25,000 to $34,999	1.45	104	0.70	0.51	0.16	18.3	1,302	4.20	12.24	1.05
$35,000 to $49,999	1.90	109	0.96	0.65	0.21	24.1	1,379	5.87	16.18	1.36
$50,000 to $74,999	1.51	119	0.78	0.52	0.17	18.9	1,493	4.66	12.66	1.11
$75,000 or more	1.17	140	0.64	0.38	0.12	15.1	1,809	4.02	10.06	0.81

[1] Includes liquid petroleum gas not shown separately.   [2] Includes kerosene.

Source: U.S. Energy Information Administration, Household Energy Consumption and Expenditures, 1993.

No. 961. Manufacturing Primary Energy Consumption for all Purposes, by Type of Fuel and Major Industry Group: 1994

[In trillions of Btu (21,663 represents 21,663,000,000,000,000). Estimates represented in this table are for the primary consumption of energy for heat and power and as feedstocks or raw material inputs. Primary consumption is defined as the consumption of the energy that was originally produced offsite or was produced onsite from input materials not classified as energy. Examples of the latter are hydrogen produced from the electrolysis of brine; the output of captive (onsite) mines or wells; woodchips, bark, and woodwaste from wood purchased as a raw material input; and waste materials such as wastepaper and packing materials. Primary consumption excludes quantities of energy that are produced from other energy inputs and, therefore, avoids double counting. Based on the 1994 Manufacturing Energy Consumption Survey and subject to sampling variability]

Industry	SIC[1] code	Total	Net elec- tricity[2]	Resi- dual fuel oil	Distil- late fuel oil[3]	Natural gas[4]	LPG	Coal	Coke and breeze	Other[5]
All industries	(X)	21,663	2,656	490	158	6,835	1,631	2,105	449	7,926
Food and kindred products......	20	1,193	198	30	19	631	(D)	165	(D)	141
Tobacco products	21	(D)	3	1	(D)	(D)	(D)	(D)	-	(D)
Textile mill products...........	22	310	111	17	7	117	4	40	-	14
Apparel and other textile products .	23	(D)	26	(D)	1	25	(D)	(D)	-	(D)
Lumber and wood products	24	491	68	2	25	48	(D)	(D)	-	341
Furniture and fixtures	25	69	22	(Z)	1	24	1	3	-	18
Paper and allied products.......	26	2,665	223	173	9	575	5	307	-	1,373
Printing and publishing	27	112	59	(D)	2	48	(D)	-	-	2
Petroleum and coal products	2813	104	80	-	(D)	23	(D)	(Z)	1	1
Rubber and misc. plastic products .	30	287	149	10	4	110	3	5	-	6
Leather and leather products	31	(D)	3	2	(D)	(D)	(D)	-	-	(Z)
Stone, clay, and glass products . .	32	944	123	7	23	432	4	274	8	73
Primary metal industries........	33	2,462	493	43	13	811	5	922	424	85
Industrial machinery & equipment .	35	246	109	(D)	4	111	3	11	(D)	5
Electric and electronic equipment .	36	243	113	3	4	88	2	(D)	(D)	(S)
Transportation equipment.......	37	363	132	11	7	157	3	28	2	23
Instruments and related products. .	38	107	46	4	1	29	(D)	(D)	-	3
Misc. manufacturing industries ...	39	(D)	19	1	1	19	1	1	-	(D)

- Represents or rounds to zero. D Withheld to avoid disclosing data for individual establishments. S Withheld because Relative Standard Error is greater than 50 percent. X Not applicable. Z Less than 0.5 trillion Btu. [1] Standard Industrial Classification Code; see text, Section 17, Business. [2] Net electricity is obtained by aggregating purchases, transfers in, and generation from noncombustible renewable resources minus quantities sold and transferred out. Excludes electricity inputs from onsite cogeneration or generation from combustible fuels because that energy has already been included as generating fuel (for example, coal). [3] Includes Nos.1, 2, and 4 fuel oils and Nos. 1, 2, and 4 diesel fuels. [4] Includes natural gas obtained from utilities, transmission pipelines, and any other supplier such as brokers and producers. [5] Includes net steam, and other energy that respondents indicated was used to produce heat and power or as feedstock/raw material inputs.

Source: U.S. Energy Information Administration, Manufacturing Energy Consumption 1994.

Energy 601

No. 962. Commercial Buildings—Energy Consumption and Expenditures: 1995

[Covers buildings using one or more major fuel. Excludes industrial buildings, predominantly residential buildings, and buildings of less than 1,000 sq. ft. Based on a sample survey of building representatives and energy suppliers; therefore, subject to sampling variability. For characteristics of commercial buildings, see tables in Section 25, Construction and Housing. For composition of regions, see inside front cover]

Building characteristic	All buildings using any major fuel		Consumption (tril. Btu)			Expenditures (mil. dol.)		
	Number (1,000)	Square feet (mil.)	Major fuel, total [1]	Electricity	Natural gas	Major fuel, total [1]	Electricity	Natural gas
All buildings	**4,579**	**58,772**	**5,321**	**2,608**	**1,946**	**69,918**	**56,621**	**9,018**
Region:								
Northeast	725	11,883	1,035	436	297	16,479	13,059	1,739
Midwest	1,139	14,322	1,497	558	750	15,076	10,946	2,947
South	1,750	20,830	1,684	1,027	528	22,211	19,009	2,560
West	964	11,736	1,106	587	371	16,152	13,607	1,772
Year constructed:								
1919 or before	353	3,673	292	99	135	3,310	2,290	655
1920 to 1945	562	6,710	508	173	210	5,665	4,012	966
1946 to 1959	867	9,298	826	325	391	9,813	7,395	1,796
1960 to 1969	718	10,858	1,024	472	375	13,135	10,405	1,750
1970 to 1979	813	11,333	1,125	615	393	15,366	13,005	1,695
1980 to 1989	846	12,252	1,059	648	288	15,895	13,844	1,397
1990 to 1992	218	2,590	297	163	100	4,011	3,318	510
1993 to 1995	202	2,059	190	113	54	2,722	2,353	249
Principal activity within building:								
Assembly [2]	682	8,011	677	252	232	7,876	5,688	1,145
Education	309	7,740	614	221	245	7,129	5,168	1,117
Food sales	137	642	137	119	18	2,634	2,532	97
Food service	285	1,353	332	166	158	4,817	3,931	851
Health care	105	2,333	561	211	258	5,261	3,901	838
Lodging	158	3,618	461	187	213	5,114	3,838	966
Mercantile/services	1,289	12,728	973	508	395	14,025	11,655	1,979
Office	705	10,478	1,019	676	239	15,849	14,020	1,150
Warehouse and storage	580	8,481	325	176	106	4,709	3,934	559
Other	67	1,004	173	75	55	1,865	1,473	197
Vacant	261	2,384	51	18	26	638	481	119
Square footage:								
1,001 to 5,000	2,399	6,338	708	380	264	11,577	9,696	1,483
5,001 to 10,000	1,035	7,530	624	238	272	8,063	6,055	1,439
10,001 to 25,000	745	11,617	824	384	356	11,099	8,911	1,775
25,001 to 50,000	213	7,676	630	316	231	8,676	7,005	1,159
50,001 to 100,000	115	7,968	698	363	243	8,824	7,194	1,091
100,001 to 200,000	48	6,776	687	337	244	7,859	6,283	958
200,001 to 500,000	19	5,553	636	307	211	7,291	5,908	729
500,001 and over	6	5,313	514	282	125	6,530	5,568	385

[1] Includes fuel oil, propane, and purchased steam not shown separately.   [2] Includes public assembly, public order and safety, and religious worship.

Source: U.S. Energy Information Administration, *Commercial Buildings Energy Consumption and Expenditures, 1995.*

No. 963. Energy Prices: 1980 to 1997

Product	Unit	1980	1990	1991	1992	1993	1994	1995	1996	1997
Crude oil domestic first purchase price:										
Nominal	Dol./bbl	21.6	20.0	16.5	16.0	14.3	13.2	14.6	18.5	17.2
Real [1]	Dol./bbl	35.8	21.4	17.0	16.0	13.9	12.6	13.6	16.8	15.3
Motor gasoline	Cents/gal.	122.1	121.7	119.6	119.0	117.3	117.4	120.5	128.8	129.1
Leaded regular	Cents/gal.	119.1	114.9	(NA)	(NA)	(NA)	(NA)	(NA)	(NA)	(NA)
Unleaded regular	Cents/gal.	124.5	116.4	114.0	112.7	110.8	111.2	114.7	123.1	123.4
Premium	Cents/gal.	(NA)	134.9	132.1	131.6	130.2	130.5	133.6	141.3	141.6
Natural gas, residential	Dol./1,000 cu. ft.	3.7	5.8	5.8	5.9	6.2	6.4	6.1	6.3	6.9
Heating oil, residential	Cents/gal.	161.3	113.6	104.7	93.4	88.8	84.3	80.6	90.1	(NA)
Coal, all	Dol./short tons	28.8	30.5	30.0	29.4	28.6	28.0	27.0	26.5	26.2
Electricity, total	Cents/ kilowatthour	4.7	6.6	6.7	6.8	6.9	6.9	6.9	6.9	6.9
Uranium, domestic purchases	Dol./lb.	(NA)	15.7	13.7	13.5	13.1	10.3	11.1	13.8	12.9

NA Not available.   [1] In chained (1992) dollars, calculated by using gross domestic product implicit price deflators.

Source: U.S. Energy Information Administration, *Annual Energy Review.*

No. 964. Fossil Fuel Prices in Current and Constant (1992) Dollars: 1970 to 1997

[In cents per million British thermal units (Btu), except as indicated. All fuel prices taken as close to the point of production as possible. See text, this section, for explanation of Btu conversions from mineral fuels]

Fuel	1970	1973	1975	1980	1985	1990	1991	1992	1993	1994	1995	1996	1997
CURRENT DOLLARS													
Composite [1]	0.32	0.40	0.82	2.04	2.51	1.84	1.67	1.66	1.67	1.53	1.47	1.82	1.84
Crude oil	0.55	0.67	1.32	3.72	4.15	3.45	2.85	2.76	2.46	2.27	2.52	3.18	2.97
Natural gas	0.15	0.20	0.40	1.45	2.26	1.55	1.48	1.57	1.84	1.67	1.40	1.96	2.18
Bituminous coal [2]	0.26	0.36	0.84	1.09	1.15	1.00	0.99	0.97	0.93	0.91	0.88	0.87	0.85
Anthracite coal	0.49	0.62	1.50	1.86	2.04	1.75	1.61	1.52	1.46	1.60	1.76	1.63	1.51
CONSTANT (1992) DOLLARS													
Composite [1]	1.04	11.3	1.95	3.39	3.20	1.97	1.72	1.66	1.63	1.46	1.37	1.65	1.64
Crude oil	1.80	1.90	3.14	6.17	5.29	3.69	2.93	2.76	2.40	2.16	2.34	2.89	2.64
Natural gas	0.50	0.57	0.96	2.40	2.88	1.65	1.52	1.57	1.80	1.59	1.30	1.78	1.94
Bituminous coal [2]	0.86	1.03	1.99	1.81	1.46	1.06	1.02	0.97	0.90	0.86	0.82	0.79	0.76
Anthracite coal	1.60	1.75	3.55	3.08	2.60	1.86	1.66	1.52	1.42	1.52	1.64	1.48	1.34

[1] Weighted by relative importance of individual fuels in total fuels production. [2] Includes subbituminous and lignite.

Source: U.S. Energy Information Administration, *Annual Energy Review*.

No. 965. Energy Imports and Exports, by Type of Fuel: 1970 to 1997

[In quadrillion of Btu. For definition of Btu, see text, this section]

Type of fuel	1970	1973	1975	1980	1985	1990	1992	1993	1994	1995	1996	1997
Net imports:[1]												
Coal	-1.94	-1.45	-1.74	-2.39	-2.39	-2.70	-2.58	-1.78	-1.69	-2.14	-2.19	-2.00
Natural gas (dry)	0.77	0.98	0.91	0.96	0.89	1.46	1.94	2.25	2.52	2.74	2.85	2.88
Petroleum	6.92	12.98	12.51	13.50	8.95	15.30	14.96	16.40	17.26	16.87	18.21	19.12
Other [2]	-0.04	0.14	0.08	0.19	0.41	0.03	0.33	0.32	0.49	0.42	0.39	0.39
Imports:												
Coal	(Z)	(Z)	0.02	0.03	0.05	0.07	0.10	0.18	0.19	0.18	0.18	2.19
Natural gas (dry)	0.85	1.06	0.98	1.01	0.95	1.55	2.16	2.40	2.68	2.90	3.00	3.04
Petroleum	7.47	13.47	12.95	14.66	10.61	17.12	16.97	18.51	19.25	18.86	20.27	21.22
Other [2]	0.07	0.20	0.16	0.28	0.49	0.26	0.44	0.45	0.59	0.54	0.52	0.52
Exports:												
Coal	1.94	1.43	1.76	2.42	2.44	2.77	2.68	1.96	1.88	2.32	2.37	2.19
Natural gas (dry)	0.07	0.08	0.07	0.05	0.06	0.09	0.22	0.14	0.16	0.16	0.16	0.16
Petroleum	0.55	0.49	0.44	1.16	1.66	1.82	2.01	2.12	1.99	1.99	2.06	2.10
Other [2]	0.11	0.06	0.08	0.09	0.08	0.23	0.11	0.13	0.09	0.11	0.12	0.13

Z Less than .005 quadrillion Btu. [1] Net imports equals imports minus exports. Minus sign (-) denotes an excess of exports over imports. [2] Coal coke and small amounts of electricity transmitted across U.S. borders with Canada and Mexico.

Source: U.S. Energy Information Administration, *Annual Energy Review*.

No. 966. U.S. Foreign Trade in Selected Mineral Fuels: 1970 to 1997

[Minus sign (-) indicates an excess of imports over exports]

Mineral fuel	Unit	1970	1973	1975	1980	1985	1990	1994	1995	1996	1997
Natural gas:											
Imports	Bil. cu. ft.	821	1,033	953	985	950	1,532	2,624	2,841	2,937	2,990
Exports	Bil. cu. ft.	70	77	73	49	55	86	162	162	154	153
Net trade	Bil. cu. ft.	-751	-956	-880	-936	-894	-1446	-2462	-2687	-2,784	-2,833
Crude oil:											
Imports [1]	Mil. bbl.	483	1,184	1,498	1,926	1,168	2,151	2,578	2,639	2,740	3,002
Exports	Mil. bbl.	5	1	2	105	75	40	36	35	40	39
Net trade	Mil. bbl.	-478	-1,183	-1,496	-1,821	-1,093	-2,112	-2,542	-2,604	-2,700	-2,963
Petroleum products:											
Imports	Mil. bbl.	765	1,099	712	603	681	775	706	586	719	707
Exports	Mil. bbl.	89	84	74	94	211	273	308	312	318	327
Net trade	Mil. bbl.	-676	-1015	-638	-509	-470	-502	-398	-274	-402	-380
Coal:											
Imports	1,000 sh. tons	36	127	940	1,194	1,952	2,699	7,584	7,201	7,126	7,487
Exports	1,000 sh. tons	71,733	53,587	66,309	91,742	92,680	105,804	71,359	88,547	90,473	83,545
Net trade	1,000 sh. tons	71,697	53,460	65,369	90,548	90,728	103,105	63,775	81,346	83,347	76,058

[1] Beginning 1980, includes strategic petroleum reserve imports.

Source: U.S. Energy Information Administration, *Annual Energy Review*.

Energy 603

No. 967. Crude Oil Imports Into United States, by Country of Origin: 1970 to 1998

[In millions of barrels, (483 represents 483,000,000). Barrels contain 42 gallons]

Country of origin	1970	1973	1975	1980	1985	1990	1992	1993	1994	1995	1996	1997	1998
Total imports . . .	483	1,184	1,864	2,133	2,151	2,110	2,220	2,477	2,578	2,643	2,748	2,918	3,121
Total OPEC [1]	222	765	984	1,232	1,283	1,233	1,243	1,317	1,307	1,303	1,280	1,349	1,492
Persian Gulf [2], total	62	293	495	633	657	636	597	598	589	539	544	591	732
Iran	12	79	(Z)	-	-	12	-	-	-	-	(NA)	(NA)	(NA)
Iraq	-	1	125	161	188	-	-	-	-	-	-	32	122
Kuwait [3]	12	15	29	57	29	2	14	126	112	78	86	92	102
Qatar	-	3	-	1	1	-	-	-	-	-	-	-	1
Saudi Arabia [3]	15	169	333	407	436	622	585	468	473	460	457	467	506
United Arab Emirates. . .	23	26	8	8	3	1	-	4	4	1	1	-	1
Other OPEC [2], total	160	472	489	599	625	596	646	720	717	764	735	755	761
Algeria	2	44	21	22	23	16	9	9	8	10	3	2	(NA)
Ecuador [4]	-	17	12	29	14	19	23	44	[4]35	41	(NA)		
Gabon	-	-	5	18	23	31	45	55	71	84	67	80	(NA)
Indonesia	26	73	68	58	36	37	26	24	34	23	16	18	17
Libya	17	49	-	-	-	-	-	-	-	(NA)	(NA)	(NA)	
Nigeria	17	164	222	292	286	249	243	264	228	226	218	244	248
Venezuela	98	126	160	181	243	244	302	369	377	421	477	493	495
Non-OPEC [5], total . .	245	419	880	900	869	878	977	1,160	1,271	1,340	1,410	1,569	1,458
Canada	245	365	249	230	235	271	292	329	359	380	394	412	462
Malaysia.	(NA)	(NA)	(NA)	(NA)	(NA)	(NA)	(NA)	4	2	2	2	3	6
Mexico	-	(Z)	246	261	251	277	288	315	343	375	442	489	476
Norway.	-	-	23	46	35	27	43	50	69	95	107	104	79
Trinidad and Tobago	(Z)	22	26	27	28	26	26	20	23	23	21	20	19
United Kingdom	-	-	93	58	57	39	73	114	145	125	79	61	57

- Represents zero.   NA Not available.   Z Represents less than half the unit of measure.   [1] OPEC (Organization of Petroleum Exporting Countries) includes the Persian Gulf nations shown below, except Bahrain, which is not a member of OPEC, and also includes nations shown under "Other OPEC".   [2] Excludes petroleum imported into the United States indirectly from members of the OPEC countries.   [3] Imports from the Neutral Zone between Kuwait and Saudi Arabia are included in Saudi Arabia.   [4] Ecuador withdrew from OPEC on Dec. 31, 1992; therefore, it is included under OPEC for the period 1973 to 1992.   [5] Includes petroleum imported into the United States indirectly from member of OPEC, primarily from Caribbean and West European areas, as petroleum products that were refined from crude oil produced by OPEC.

Source: 1970, U.S. Bureau of Mines, *Minerals Yearbooks, Vol. I;* thereafter, U.S. Energy Information Administration, *Petroleum Supply Annual,* Vol. I.

No. 968. Crude Oil and Refined Products—Summary: 1973 to 1998

[Barrels of 42 gallons. Data are averages]

Year	Crude oil (1,000 bbl. per day)					Refined oil products (1,000 bbl. per day)			Total oil imports[2] (1,000 bbl. per day)	Crude oil stocks [3] (mil. bbl.)	
	Input to refineries	Domestic production	Imports Total [1]	Strategic reserve	Exports	Domestic demand	Imports	Exports		Total	Strategic reserve
1973	12,431	9,208	3,244	(X)	2	17,308	3,012	229	6,256	242	(X)
1974	12,133	8,774	3,477	(X)	3	16,653	2,635	218	6,112	265	(X)
1975	12,442	8,375	4,105	(X)	6	16,322	1,951	204	6,056	271	(X)
1976	13,416	8,132	5,287	(X)	8	17,461	2,026	215	7,313	285	(X)
1977	14,602	8,245	6,615	21	50	18,431	2,193	193	8,807	348	7
1978	14,739	8,707	6,356	161	158	18,847	2,008	204	8,363	376	67
1979	14,648	8,552	6,519	67	235	18,513	1,937	236	8,456	430	91
1980	13,481	8,597	5,263	44	287	17,056	1,646	258	6,909	466	108
1981	12,470	8,572	4,396	256	228	16,058	1,599	367	5,996	594	230
1982	11,774	8,649	3,488	165	236	15,296	1,625	579	5,113	644	294
1983	11,685	8,688	3,329	234	164	15,231	1,722	575	5,051	723	379
1984	12,044	8,879	3,426	197	181	15,726	2,011	541	5,437	796	451
1985	12,002	8,971	3,201	118	204	15,726	1,866	577	5,067	814	493
1986	12,716	8,680	4,178	48	154	16,281	2,045	631	6,224	843	512
1987	12,854	8,349	4,674	73	151	16,665	2,004	613	6,678	890	541
1988	13,246	8,140	5,107	51	155	17,283	2,295	661	7,402	890	560
1989	13,401	7,613	5,843	56	142	17,325	2,217	717	8,061	921	580
1990	13,409	7,355	5,894	27	109	16,988	2,123	748	8,018	908	586
1991	13,301	7,417	5,782	-	116	16,714	1,844	885	7,627	893	569
1992	13,411	7,171	6,083	10	89	17,033	1,805	861	7,888	893	575
1993	13,613	6,847	6,787	15	98	17,237	1,833	904	8,620	922	587
1994	13,866	6,662	7,063	12	99	17,718	1,933	843	8,996	929	592
1995	13,973	6,560	7,230	-	95	17,725	1,605	855	8,835	895	592
1996	14,195	6,465	7,508	-	110	18,309	1,971	871	9,478	850	566
1997	14,662	6,452	8,225	-	108	18,620	1,936	896	10,162	868	563
1998	14,837	6,243	8,550	-	110	18,684	1,832	821	10,382	894	571

- Represents zero.   X Not applicable.   [1] Includes Strategic Petroleum Reserve.   [2] Crude oil (including Strategic Petroleum Reserve imports) plus refined products.   [3] End of year.

Source: U.S. Energy Information Administration, *Monthly Energy Review.*

604   Energy

No. 969. Petroleum and Coal Products Corporations—Sales, Net Profit, and Profit Per Dollar of Sales: 1980 to 1998

[Represents SIC group 29. Profit rates are averages of quarterly figures at annual rates. Beginning 1988, excludes estimates for corporations with less than $250,000 in assets]

Item	Unit	1980	1985	1988	1989	1990	1992	1993	1994	1995	1996	1997	1998
Sales	Bil. dol. .	333.2	320.9	265.3	318.5	282.2	278.0	266.1	268.2	283.1	323.5	320.0	261.9
Net profit:													
Before income taxes.	Bil. dol. .	39.1	17.7	23.5	23.1	12.1	2.0	14.9	17.2	16.5	32.6	36.8	11.6
After income taxes	Bil. dol. .	25.5	12.7	19.4	17.8	10.8	3.1	13.0	14.9	13.9	26.6	29.4	10.5
Depreciation[1]	Bil. dol. .	11.6	22.1	18.5	18.7	18.0	18.3	17.4	17.1	16.7	15.9	15.6	15.1
Profits per dollar of sales:													
Before income taxes.	Cents . .	11.7	5.5	9.0	7.3	4.3	0.4	5.6	6.3	5.8	10.1	11.5	4.2
After income taxes	Cents . .	7.7	4.0	7.4	5.6	3.8	0.9	4.9	5.5	4.9	8.2	9.2	3.9
Profits on stockholders' equity:													
Before income taxes.	Percent .	30.7	11.7	17.7	16.4	8.6	1.6	11.8	13.2	12.6	23.2	23.5	7.1
After income taxes	Percent .	20.0	8.5	14.5	12.7	7.6	2.5	10.2	11.4	10.6	18.9	18.9	6.5

[1] Includes depletion and accelerated amortization of emergency facilities.
Source: 1980, U.S. Federal Trade Commission; thereafter, U.S. Census Bureau, *Quarterly Financial Report for Manufacturing, Mining and Trade Corporations.*

No. 970. Major Petroleum Companies—Financial Data Summary: 1973 to 1997

[Data represent a composite of approximately 42 major worldwide petroleum companies aggregated on a consolidated, total company basis]

Item	1973	1975	1980	1985	1990	1992	1993	1994	1995	1996	1997
FINANCIAL DATA (bil. dol.)											
Net income.	11.8	11.6	32.9	19.4	26.8	12.1	18.8	20.3	24.3	39.7	39.4
Depreciation, depletion, etc	10.5	11.3	32.5	53.0	38.7	43.3	39.0	38.9	43.1	44.4	47.6
Cash flow[1]	22.3	22.8	65.4	72.4	65.5	55.4	57.0	59.2	67.4	84.1	87.0
Dividends paid	4.0	4.7	9.3	12.0	15.9	16.5	15.5	16.4	17.6	18.9	19.8
Net internal funds available for investment or debt repayment[2]	18.3	18.1	56.1	60.4	49.6	38.9	41.5	42.8	49.8	65.2	67.2
Capital and exploratory expenditures.	16.3	26.9	62.1	58.3	59.6	53.6	51.8	51.5	57.3	71.1	81.5
Long-term capitalization	102.9	121.1	211.4	272.1	300.0	290.7	291.7	299.0	304.2	336.8	354.7
Long-term debt	22.5	28.9	49.8	93.5	90.4	94.0	91.6	89.1	85.4	80.8	86.1
Preferred stock	0.4	0.4	2.0	3.3	5.2	5.3	5.8	5.4	5.7	5.8	5.7
Common stock and retained earnings[3] . .	80.0	91.9	159.6	175.3	204.4	191.4	194.3	204.5	213.1	250.2	262.9
Excess of expenditures over cash income[4] .	-2.0	8.9	6.0	-2.1	10.0	14.7	10.3	8.7	7.5	-5.9	-14.3
RATIOS[5] (percent)											
Long-term debt to long-term capitalization . .	22.0	23.8	23.6	34.4	30.1	32.3	31.4	29.8	28.1	24.2	24.3
Net income to total average capital	12.0	10.0	17.0	7.0	9.1	4.1	6.5	6.8	7.8	12.3	11.4
Net income to average common equity	15.6	13.1	22.5	10.8	13.5	6.1	9.8	10.1	11.3	17.1	15.4

[1] Generally represents internally-generated funds from operations. Sum of net income and noncash charges such as depreciation, depletion, and amortization. [2] Cash flow minus dividends paid. [3] Includes common stock, capital surplus, and earned surplus accounts after adjustments. [4] Capital and exploratory expenditures plus dividends paid minus cash flow. [5] Represents approximate year-to-year comparisons because of changes in the makeup of the group due to mergers and other corporate changes.
Source: Carl H. Pforzheimer & Co., New York, NY, *Comparative Oil Company Statements, 1995-1996,* and earlier reports.

No. 971. Electric Utility Sales and Average Prices, by End-Use Sector: 1970 to 1997

[Prior to 1980, covers Class A and B privately-owned electric utilities; thereafter, Class A utilities whose electric operating revenues were $100 million or more during the previous year]

Year	Sales (bil. kWh)				Average price of electricity sold (cents per kWh)							
					Current dollars				Constant (1992) dollars [2]			
	Total [1]	Resi-dential	Com-mercial	Indus-trial	Total [1]	Resi-dential	Com-mercial	Indus-trial	Total [1]	Resi-dential	Com-mercial	Indus-trial
1970	1,392	466	307	571	1.7	2.2	2.1	1.0	5.6	7.2	6.9	3.3
1973	1,713	579	388	686	2.0	2.5	2.4	1.3	5.7	7.1	6.8	3.7
1975	1,747	588	403	688	2.9	3.5	3.5	2.1	6.9	8.3	8.3	5.0
1980	2,094	717	488	815	4.7	5.4	5.5	3.7	7.8	9.0	9.1	6.1
1981	2,147	722	514	826	5.5	6.2	6.3	4.3	8.3	9.4	9.5	6.5
1982	2,086	730	526	745	6.1	6.9	6.9	5.0	8.7	9.8	9.8	7.1
1983	2,151	751	544	776	6.3	7.2	7.0	5.0	8.6	9.8	9.6	6.8
1984	2,286	780	583	838	6.3	7.2	7.1	4.8	8.3	9.5	9.4	6.3
1985	2,324	794	606	837	6.4	7.4	7.3	5.0	8.2	9.4	9.3	6.4
1986	2,369	819	631	831	6.4	7.4	7.2	4.9	7.9	9.2	8.9	6.1
1987	2,457	850	660	858	6.4	7.4	7.1	4.8	7.7	8.9	8.5	5.8
1988	2,578	893	699	896	6.4	7.5	7.0	4.7	7.4	8.7	8.1	5.5
1989	2,647	906	726	926	6.5	7.6	7.2	4.7	7.2	8.5	8.0	5.2
1990	2,713	924	751	946	6.6	7.8	7.3	4.7	7.1	8.3	7.8	5.0
1991	2,762	955	766	947	6.7	8.0	7.5	4.8	6.9	8.2	7.7	4.9
1992	2,763	936	761	973	6.8	8.2	7.7	4.8	6.8	8.2	7.7	4.8
1993	2,861	995	795	977	6.9	8.3	7.7	4.8	6.7	8.1	7.5	4.7
1994	2,935	1,008	820	1,008	6.9	8.4	7.7	4.8	6.6	8.0	7.3	4.6
1995	3,013	1,043	863	1,013	6.9	8.4	7.7	4.7	6.4	7.8	7.1	4.4
1996	3,098	1,082	887	1,030	6.9	8.4	7.6	4.6	6.3	7.6	6.9	4.2
1997	3,120	1,072	913	1,036	6.9	8.5	7.6	4.6	6.1	7.6	6.8	4.1

[1] Includes other sectors not shown separately. [2] Based on the GDP implicit price deflator.
Source: U.S. Energy Information Administration, *Annual Energy Review.*

Energy 605

No. 972. Electric Utility Industry—Net Generation, Net Summer Capability, Generating Units, and Consumption of Fuels: 1980 to 1997

[Net generation for **calendar years;** other data as of **December 31**]

Item	Unit	1980	1990	1991	1992	1993	1994	1995	1996	1997
RETAIL SALES										
Retail sales, total...........	Bil. kWh ..	2,094	2,713	2,762	2,763	2,861	2,935	3,013	3,098	3,115
Net generation by electric utilities	Bil. kWh...	2,286	2,808	2,825	2,797	2,883	2,911	2,995	3,077	3,123
Purchases by utilities from nonutility purchasers	Bil. kWh...	1	116	139	166	189	209	222	229	(NA)
Imports	Bil. kWh...	25	23	31	37	39	52	47	47	(NA)
Exports	Bil. kWh...	4	21	9	9	11	8	9	9	(NA)
Losses and unaccounted for	Bil. kWh...	214	214	225	229	238	223	232	277	(NA)
NET GENERATION										
Total......................	Bil. kWh ..	2,286	2,808	2,825	2,797	2,883	2,911	2,995	3,077	3,123
Average annual change [1].........	Percent ...	3.5	0.9	0.6	-1.0	3.0	1.0	2.8	2.7	1.5
Net generation, kWh per kW of net summer capability [2]	Rate	3,951	4,067	4,076	4,024	4,119	4,147	4,248	4,333	(NA)
Source of energy:										
Coal [3]	Percent ...	50.8	55.6	54.9	56.3	56.9	56.2	55.2	57.0	57.3
Nuclear......................	Percent ...	11.0	20.5	21.7	22.1	21.2	22.0	22.5	22.0	20.1
Oil.........................	Percent ...	10.8	4.2	3.9	3.2	3.5	3.1	2.0	2.0	2.5
Gas	Percent ...	15.1	9.4	9.3	9.4	9.0	10.0	10.3	9.0	9.1
Hydro.......................	Percent ...	12.1	10.1	9.9	8.7	9.3	8.5	9.9	11.0	10.9
Type of prime mover: [4]										
Hydro.......................	Bil. kWh...	276	280	276	240	265	244	294	328	(NA)
Steam conventional [5]	Bil. kWh...	1,726	1,919	1,905	1,908	1,964	1,982	1,977	2,018	(NA)
Gas turbine and internal combustion .	Bil. kWh...	28	14	22	21	25	36	44	49	(NA)
Steam nuclear	Bil. kWh...	251	577	613	619	610	640	673	675	(NA)
Other	Bil. kWh...	6	11	10	10	10	9	6	7	(NA)
NET SUMMER CAPABILITY										
Total [6]	Mil. kW ...	579	691	693	695	700	702	705	710	(NA)
Average annual change [1]	Percent ...	3.3	0.8	0.4	0.3	0.7	0.3	0.4	0.7	(NA)
Hydro	Mil. kW ...	82	91	92	93	96	96	97	94	(NA)
Steam conventional [7]	Mil. kW ...	397	448	447	447	447	446	446	442	(NA)
Gas turbine	Mil. kW ...	43	46	48	50	52	55	57	53	(NA)
Steam nuclear.................	Mil. kW ...	52	100	100	99	99	99	99	101	(NA)
Internal combustion	Mil. kW ...	5	5	5	5	5	5	5	5	(NA)
Geothermal and other...........	Mil. kW ...	1	2	2	2	2	2	2	2	(NA)
Combined cycle...............	Mil. kW ...	(NA)	(NA)	(NA)	(NA)	(NA)	(NA)	(NA)	14	(NA)
NUMBER OF GENERATING UNITS										
Total [8]	Number ..	11,084	10,296	10,260	10,221	10,471	10,427	10,396	10,422	(NA)
Hydro	Number...	3,275	3,479	3,476	3,497	3,388	3,362	3,337	3,480	3,346
Steam conventional	Number...	2,862	2,354	2,284	2,307	2,221	2,170	2,157	2,153	(NA)
Gas turbine	Number...	1,447	1,460	1,485	1,501	1,411	1,446	1,486	1,542	(NA)
Steam nuclear.................	Number...	74	111	111	109	109	109	109	110	110
Internal combustion	Number...	3,410	2,847	2,803	2,807	2,976	2,953	2,920	2,884	(NA)
CONSUMPTION OF FOSSIL FUELS										
Net generation by fuel [9]	Quad. Btu .	18.56	20.32	20.07	19.99	20.58	20.92	20.92	21.44	(NA)
Coal	Quad. Btu .	12.12	16.19	16.03	16.21	16.79	16.90	16.99	17.91	(NA)
Percent of total	Percent ...	65.30	79.68	79.87	81.09	81.58	80.78	81.21	83.5	(NA)
Petroleum....................	Quad. Btu .	2.63	1.25	1.18	0.95	1.05	0.97	0.66	0.73	(NA)
Gas.........................	Quad. Btu .	3.81	2.88	2.86	2.83	2.74	3.05	3.28	2.81	(NA)
Fuel consumed:	Mil. sh.									
Coal........................	tons	569	774	772	780	814	817	829	875	900
Petroleum....................	Mil. bbl. ...	421	200	189	152	169	155	102	113	125
Gas.........................	Bil. cu. ft ...	3,682	2,787	2,789	2,766	2,682	2,987	3,197	2,732	2,968

NA Not available.   [1] Change from immediate prior year, except for 1980, change from 1975. For explanation of average annual percent change, see Guide to Tabular Presentation.   [2] Net summer capability is the steady hourly output that generating equipment is expected to supply to system load, exclusive of auxiliary power as demonstrated by test at the time of summer peak demand.   [3] Includes small percentage (.5 percent) from wood and waste, geothermal, and petroleum coke.   [4] A prime mover is the engine, turbine, water wheel, or similar machine which drives an electric generator.   [5] Fossil fuels only.   [6] Includes wind, solar thermal, and photovoltaic, not shown separately.   [7] Includes fossil steam, wood, and waste.   [8] Each prime mover type in combination plants counted separately. Includes geothermal, wind, and solar, not shown separately.   [9] Includes small amounts of wood, waste, wind, geothermal, solar thermal, and photovoltaic.

Source: U.S. Energy Information Administration, 1980, *Power Production, Fuel Consumption, and Installed Capacity Data—Annual,* and unpublished data; thereafter, *Electric Power Annual, Annual Energy Review,* and unpublished data.

606   Energy

No. 973. Electric Utility Industry—Capability, Peak Load, and Capacity Margin: 1980 to 1997

[Excludes Alaska and Hawaii. Capability represents the maximum kilowatt output with all power sources available and with hydraulic equipment under actual water conditions, allowing for maintenance, emergency outages, and system operating requirements. Capacity margin is the difference between capability and peak load]

Year	Capability at the time of— Summer peak load (1,000 kW) Amount	Change from prior year	Winter peak load (1,000 kW) Amount	Change from prior year	Noncoincident peak load Summer	Winter	Capacity margin Summer Amount (1,000 kW)	Percent of capability	Capacity margin Winter Amount (1,000 kW)	Percent of capability
1980	558,237	13,731	572,195	17,670	427,058	384,567	131,179	23.5	187,628	32.8
1981	572,219	13,982	586,569	14,374	429,349	397,800	142,870	25.0	188,769	32.2
1982	586,142	13,923	598,066	11,497	415,618	373,985	170,524	29.1	224,081	37.5
1983	596,449	10,307	612,453	14,387	447,526	410,779	148,923	25.0	201,674	32.9
1984	604,240	7,791	622,125	9,672	451,150	436,374	153,090	25.3	185,751	29.9
1985	621,597	17,357	636,475	14,350	460,503	423,660	161,094	25.9	212,815	33.4
1986	633,291	11,694	646,721	10,246	476,320	422,857	156,971	24.8	223,864	34.6
1987	648,118	14,827	662,977	16,256	496,185	448,277	151,933	23.4	214,700	32.4
1988	661,580	13,462	676,940	13,963	529,460	466,533	132,120	20.0	210,407	31.1
1989	673,316	11,736	685,249	8,309	523,432	496,378	149,884	22.3	188,871	27.6
1990	685,091	11,775	696,757	11,508	545,537	484,014	139,554	20.4	212,743	30.5
1991	690,915	5,824	703,212	6,455	551,320	485,435	139,595	20.2	217,777	31.0
1992	695,436	4,521	707,752	4,540	548,707	492,983	146,729	21.1	214,769	30.3
1993	694,250	1,186	711,957	4,205	575,356	521,733	118,894	17.1	190,224	26.7
1994	702,985	8,735	715,090	3,133	585,320	518,253	117,665	16.7	196,837	27.5
1995	714,222	11,237	727,679	12,589	620,249	544,684	93,973	13.2	182,995	25.1
1996	723,571	9,349	740,526	12,847	615,529	545,061	108,042	14.9	195,465	26.4
1997	729,079	5,508	743,774	3,248	631,355	560,228	97,724	13.4	183,546	24.7

Source: Edison Electric Institute, Washington, DC, *Statistical Yearbook of the Electric Utility Industry,* annual.

No. 974. Electric Energy Sales, by Class of Service, and by State: 1998

[In billions of kilowatt-hours (3,139.8 represents 3,139,800,000,000]

State	Total[1]	Residential	Commercial	Industrial	State	Total[1]	Residential	Commercial	Industrial
Total [2]	3,139.8	1,075.7	928.5	1,032.7					
					Missouri	65.6	26.5	22.8	15.3
Alabama	74.5	24.9	16.4	32.6	Montana	11.9	3.8	3.3	4.5
Alaska	4.8	1.7	2.2	0.8	Nebraska	22.6	8.0	6.5	6.6
Arizona	54.5	20.7	17.8	13.3	Nevada	24.2	7.8	5.5	10.0
Arkansas	36.9	13.0	7.6	15.6	New Hampshire	9.1	3.4	3.3	2.3
California	227.9	73.1	83.6	62.0	New Jersey . . . . . : . .	65.9	22.3	29.8	13.4
Colorado	38.1	12.3	14.6	10.3	New Mexico	17.5	4.5	5.4	6.2
Connecticut	28.4	10.9	11.3	5.9	New York	131.9	40.1	54.2	25.3
Delaware	10.1	3.3	3.1	3.7	North Carolina	109.1	40.6	31.4	35.1
Dist. of Columbia	10.1	1.6	7.9	0.3	North Dakota	8.3	3.4	2.3	2.1
Florida	175.0	87.8	63.3	18.3	Ohio	158.5	43.6	36.4	73.9
Georgia	102.3	36.8	30.2	34.0	Oklahoma	44.5	17.4	11.8	12.8
Hawaii	9.4	2.7	2.8	3.9	Oregon	47.6	17.2	14.0	15.9
Idaho	21.3	6.6	6.0	8.3	Pennsylvania	127.9	42.7	35.9	48.0
Illinois	126.5	37.2	38.1	42.4	Rhode Island	6.7	2.5	2.7	1.4
Indiana	89.1	26.5	18.5	43.5	South Carolina	68.5	21.6	14.8	31.3
Iowa	36.3	11.7	7.6	15.5	South Dakota	7.8	3.4	2.2	1.8
Kansas	32.3	10.9	11.4	9.4	Tennessee	87.0	33.4	24.8	27.8
Kentucky	76.8	21.0	12.2	40.6	Texas	291.1	100.8	73.0	104.3
Louisiana	71.5	24.8	15.3	28.7	Utah	20.4	5.7	6.5	7.4
Maine	12.0	3.7	3.3	5.0	Vermont	5.3	2.0	1.7	1.6
Maryland	56.3	21.9	23.4	10.1	Virginia	87.4	33.9	24.9	19.2
Massachusetts	47.7	16.3	20.8	9.9	Washington	88.3	31.8	21.6	31.4
Michigan	97.4	28.7	32.4	35.4	West Virginia	26.2	9.0	5.9	11.2
Minnesota	55.7	17.1	10.1	27.7	Wisconsin	60.1	18.5	15.7	25.1
Mississippi	40.1	14.8	10.0	14.6	Wyoming	11.8	2.0	2.4	7.2

[1] Includes other service not shown separately.   [2] Preliminary.

Source: U.S. Energy Information Administration, *Electric Power Annual.*

Energy   607

No. 975. Electric Energy—Net Generation and Net Summer Capability, by State: 1990 to 1997

[Capacity as of **Dec. 31. (2,808.2 represents 2,808,200,000,000).** Covers utilities for public use]

State	Net generation (bil. kWh)				Net summer capability (mil. kW)		State	Net generation (bil. kWh)				Net summer capability (mil. kW)	
			1997							1997			
	1990	1995	Total	Per-cent from coal	1995	1997		1990	1995	Total	Per-cent from coal	1995	1997
U.S....	2,808.2	2,994.5	3,122.5	57.3	706.1	712.0	MO	59.0	65.4	71.1	84.3	15.7	16.3
AL	76.2	99.6	113.7	63.0	20.5	20.7	MT	25.7	25.4	27.8	51.8	4.9	4.9
AK	4.5	4.8	5.1	4.6	1.7	1.7	NE	21.6	25.3	28.4	60.6	5.5	5.7
AZ	62.3	69.0	78.1	43.8	15.2	15.1	NV	19.3	20.0	22.9	66.7	5.6	5.6
AR	37.1	39.5	42.8	53.2	9.6	9.6	NH	10.8	13.9	14.3	28.5	2.5	2.5
CA	114.5	121.9	112.2	0.0	43.3	44.1	NJ	36.5	27.1	23.8	28.7	13.8	13.6
CO	31.3	32.7	34.4	93.1	6.6	6.8	NM	28.5	29.4	30.6	88.6	5.1	5.1
CT	32.2	26.9	13.2	19.3	6.7	6.3	NY	128.7	101.2	108.1	20.1	32.1	30.2
DE	7.1	8.3	6.6	59.7	2.2	2.2	NC	79.8	96.1	107.4	65.4	20.6	20.9
DC	0.4	0.2	0.7	0.0	0.8	0.8	ND	26.8	28.8	29.7	88.5	4.5	4.2
FL	123.6	147.2	148.0	44.6	35.9	37.1	OH	126.5	137.9	141.2	88.4	27.4	27.3
GA	97.6	102.0	101.8	65.0	22.3	22.8	OK	45.1	48.0	48.4	68.3	12.9	13.1
HI	8.0	6.2	6.2	0.0	1.6	1.6	OR	49.2	44.0	49.1	3.1	10.4	10.5
ID	8.6	10.1	13.5	0.0	2.6	2.6	PA	165.7	168.9	177.2	59.5	33.7	33.9
IL	127.0	145.2	131.1	58.0	33.1	33.5	RI	0.6	0.7	3.6	0.0	0.4	0.4
IN	97.7	105.2	110.5	98.6	20.7	20.7	SC	69.3	78.4	78.4	39.6	16.7	17.4
IA	29.0	33.5	34.1	84.3	8.2	8.2	SD	6.4	8.8	12.5	26.6	3.0	3.0
KS	33.9	38.2	34.1	80.0	9.7	9.7	TN	73.9	82.3	93.3	63.1	16.1	17.3
KY	73.8	86.2	91.6	96.0	15.4	15.7	TX	234.0	261.7	277.2	49.0	64.4	64.8
LA	58.2	65.6	61.1	34.3	17.0	17.2	VT	5.0	4.8	5.3	0.0	1.1	1.1
ME	9.1	2.7	3.2	0.0	2.4	2.4	VA	47.2	52.7	59.0	50.3	14.3	15.0
MD	31.5	44.7	44.6	61.5	11.0	11.0	WA	100.5	95.7	117.5	5.9	24.3	24.3
MA	36.5	27.0	33.9	36.8	9.3	9.4	WV	77.4	77.3	88.3	99.4	14.5	14.4
MI	89.1	92.5	89.6	73.2	22.0	22.0	WI	45.6	51.0	48.6	84.1	11.5	11.9
MN	41.6	42.5	40.3	67.2	8.9	9.2	WY	39.4	39.7	40.8	96.4	6.0	6.0
MS	22.9	26.4	31.2	40.0	7.2	7.2							

Source: U.S. Energy Information Administration, 1980, *Power Production, Fuel Consumption, and Installed Capacity Data,* annual; thereafter, *Electric Power Annual, Electric Power Monthly,* December issues, and *Inventory of Power Plants in the United States,* annual.

No. 976. Nuclear Power Plants—Number of Units, Net Generation, and Net Summer Capability, by State: 1997

State	Number of units	Net generation		Net summer capability		State	Number of units	Net generation		Net summer capability	
		Total (mil. kWh)	Percent of total[1]	Total (mil. kW)	Percent of total[1]			Total (mil. kWh)	Percent of total[1]	Total (mil. kW)	Percent of total[1]
U.S....	110	628,644	20.1	100.76	14.2	MN	3	10,819	26.8	1.57	17.1
						MS	1	10,813	34.6	1.18	16.4
AL	5	29,573	26.0	4.84	23.4	MO	1	8,955	12.6	1.14	7.0
AZ	3	29,314	37.6	3.75	24.8	NE	2	9,269	32.7	1.25	21.9
AR	2	14,208	33.2	1.69	17.6	NH	1	7,979	55.8	1.16	46.3
CA	5	30,512	27.2	4.75	10.8	NJ	4	13,908	58.5	3.86	28.3
CT	3	-125	-0.9	2.63	41.6	NY	6	29,570	27.4	4.85	16.0
FL	5	22,968	15.5	3.88	10.4	NC	5	32,453	30.2	4.64	22.2
GA	4	30,414	29.9	3.95	17.3	OH	2	15,331	10.9	2.04	7.5
IL	13	51,069	38.9	12.61	37.6	PA	9	67,655	38.2	8.96	26.4
IA	1	4,149	12.2	0.52	6.4	SC	7	44,916	57.3	6.42	36.9
KS	1	8,430	24.7	1.16	12.0	TN	3	24,648	26.4	3.35	19.4
LA	2	13,511	22.1	2.01	11.7	TX	4	37,358	13.5	4.93	7.6
ME	1	-	-	0.87	36.4	VT	1	4,267	80.2	0.50	45.2
MD	2	13,213	29.7	1.68	15.3	VA	4	27,084	45.9	3.39	22.6
MA	1	4,310	12.7	0.67	7.1	WA	1	6,244	5.3	1.11	4.6
MI	5	21,914	24.5	3.96	18.0	WI	3	3,916	8.1	1.45	12.2

- Represents zero. [1] For total capability and generation, see Table 975.

Source: U.S. Energy Information Administration, *Electric Power Annual* and *Electric Power Monthly,* December issues.

No. 977. Nuclear Power Plants—Number, Capacity, and Generation: 1980 to 1997

Item	1980	1985	1988	1989	1990	1991	1992	1993	1994	1995	1996	1997
Operable generating units [1]	71	96	109	111	112	111	109	110	109	109	109	107
Net summer capability [1][2] (mil. kW)	51.8	79.4	94.7	98.2	99.6	99.6	99.0	99.0	99.1	99.5	100.8	100.8
Net generation (bil. kWh)	251.1	383.7	527.0	529.4	576.9	612.6	618.8	610.3	640.4	673.4	674.7	629.4
Percent of total electric utility generation	11.0	15.5	19.5	19.0	20.5	21.7	22.1	21.2	22.0	22.5	21.9	20.1
Capacity factor [3]	56.3	58.0	63.5	62.2	66.0	70.2	70.9	70.5	73.8	77.4	76.3	70.8

[1] As of year-end. [2] Net summer capability is the peak steady hourly output that generating equipment is expected to supply to system load, exclusive of auxiliary and other power plant, as demonstrated by test at the time of summer peak demand. [3] Weighted average of monthly capacity factors. Monthly factors are derived by dividing actual monthly generation by the maximum possible generation for the month (hours in month times net maximum dependable capacity).

Source: U.S. Energy Information Administration, *Annual Energy Review* and *Monthly Energy Review* March 1996.

No. 978. Uranium Supply and Discharged Commercial Reactor Fuel: 1980 to 1997

[Years ending **Dec. 31,** except as noted. For additional data on uranium, see Section 24, Natural Resources on mining]

Item	Unit	1980	1985	1990	1972	1993	1994	1995	1996	1997
URANIUM CONCENTRATE										
Production	Mil. lb.	43.70	11.31	8.89	5.65	3.06	3.35	6.04	6.32	5.64
Exports	Mil. lb.	5.80	5.30	2.00	2.80	3.00	17.74	9.84	11.50	17.00
Imports	Mil. lb.	3.60	11.70	23.70	23.30	21.00	36.62	41.30	45.42	43.00
Utility purchases from domestic suppliers	Mil. lb.	(NA)	21.7	20.5	23.4	15.5	22.7	22.3	22.9	18.7
Loaded into U.S. Nuclear reactors [1]	Mil. lb.	(NA)	(NA)	(NA)	43.0	45.1	40.4	51.1	46.2	48.7
Inventories, total	Mil. lb.	(NA)	176.9	129.1	117.3	105.7	86.9	72.5	80.0	75.8
At domestic suppliers	Mil. lb.	(NA)	23.7	26.4	25.2	24.5	21.5	13.7	13.9	11.9
At electric utilities	Mil. lb.	(NA)	153.2	102.7	92.1	81.2	65.4	58.7	66.1	63.9
Average prices:										
Purchased imports	Dol. per lb	(NA)	20.08	12.55	11.34	10.53	8.95	10.20	13.15	11.81
Domestic purchases	Dol. per lb	(NA)	31.43	15.70	13.45	13.14	10.30	11.11	13.80	12.87
DISCHARGED COMMERCIAL REACTOR FUEL [2]										
Annual discharge [3]	Metric tons	1,193	1,330	2,084	2,192	2,102	1,809	2,292	2,174	(NA)
Inventory, year-end [3]	Metric tons	6,434	12,481	21,029	24,937	27,039	28,848	31,140	(NA)	(NA)

NA Not available. [1] Does not include any fuel rods removed from reactors and later reloaded into the reactor. [2] Uranium content. Source: Nuclear Assurance Corporation, Atlanta, GA. [3] Reprocessed fuel not included as inventory.

Source: Except as noted, U.S. Energy Information Administration, *Annual Energy Review, Uranium Industry Annual* and unpublished data.

No. 979. Electric Utilities—Generation, Sales, Revenue, and Customers: 1980 to 1997

[Sales and revenue are to and from ultimate customers]

Class	Unit	1980	1985	1990	1992	1993	1994	1995	1996	1997
Generation [1]	Bil. kWh.	2,286	2,470	2,808	2,797	2,883	2,911	2,995	3,077	3,123
Sales [2]	Bil. kWh.	2,126	2,306	2,684	2,735	2,850	2,935	3,013	3,098	3,140
Residential or domestic	Bil. kWh.	734	793	916	929	994	1,008	1,043	1,082	1,076
Percent of total	Percent	34.5	34.4	34.1	34.0	34.9	34.3	34.6	34.9	34.3
Commercial [3]	Bil. kWh.	524	606	739	756	803	820	863	887	928
Industrial [4]	Bil. kWh.	794	820	932	949	957	1,008	1,013	1,030	1,033
Revenue [2]	Bil. dol.	95.5	149.2	176.5	187.3	197.9	202.7	207.7	212.5	215.1
Residential or domestic	Bil. dol.	37.6	58.6	71.7	76.4	82.4	84.6	87.6	90.5	90.7
Percent of total	Percent	39.4	39.3	40.6	40.8	41.6	41.7	42.2	42.6	42.2
Commercial [3]	Bil. dol.	27.4	44.1	54.2	58.0	62.0	63.4	66.4	67.8	70.5
Industrial [4]	Bil. dol.	27.3	41.4	44.9	46.8	46.6	48.1	47.2	47.4	46.8
Ultimate customers, Dec. 31 [2]	Million	92.7	101.6	110.1	113.1	115.2	116.5	118.3	120.0	122.1
Residential or domestic	Million	82.2	89.8	97.0	99.6	101.3	102.3	103.9	105.3	107.0
Commercial [3]	Million	9.7	10.9	12.1	12.5	12.5	12.7	13.0	13.2	13.5
Industrial [4]	Million	0.5	0.5	0.5	0.5	0.5	0.6	0.6	0.6	0.6
Avg. kWh used per customer	1,000.	23.2	22.9	24.6	24.4	24.9	25.2	(NA)	25.8	25.7
Residential	1,000.	9.0	8.9	9.5	9.4	9.9	9.9	(NA)	10.3	10.1
Commercial [3]	1,000.	54.5	56.1	61.3	61.0	64.4	65.7	(NA)	78.0	68.7
Avg. annual bill per customer	Dollar	1,040	1,482	1,614	1,667	1,727	1,741	(NA)	1,769	1,761
Residential	Dollar	462	658	744	772	818	827	(NA)	859	849
Commercial [3]	Dollar	2,848	4,080	4,494	4,681	4,977	5,076	(NA)	5,140	5,209
Avg. revenue per kWh sold	Cents	4.49	6.47	6.57	6.85	6.94	6.91	6.89	6.86	6.85
Residential	Cents	5.12	7.39	7.83	8.22	8.29	8.38	8.40	8.36	8.43
Commercial [3]	Cents	5.22	7.27	7.33	7.67	7.73	7.73	7.69	7.64	7.59
Industrial [4]	Cents	3.44	5.04	4.81	4.93	4.87	4.77	4.66	4.60	4.53

NA Not available. [1] Source: U.S. Energy Information Administration, *Monthly Energy Review,* monthly. [2] Includes other types not shown separately. [3] Small light and power. [4] Large light and power.

Source: Except as noted, Edison Electric Institute, Washington, DC, *Statistical Yearbook of the Electric Utility Industry,* annual.

No. 980. Major Investor-Owned Electric Utilities—Balance Sheet and Income Account of Privately Owned Companies: 1993 to 1997

[In thousands of dollars (193,637,843 represents $193,637,843,000). As of Dec. 31. As of 1990, covers approximately 180 investor-owned electric utilities that during each of the last 3 years met any one or more of the following conditions — 1 mil. megawatthours of total sales; 100 megawatthours of sales for resale, 500 megawatthours of gross interchange out, and 500 megawatthours of wheeling for other]

Item	1993	1994	1995	1996	1997
COMPOSITE INCOME ACCOUNTS					
Operating revenue	193,637,843	196,281,500	199,966,979	207,459,078	214,322,732
Electric	176,354,365	179,307,260	183,655,263	188,900,781	195,202,204
Gas	16,686,912	16,221,506	15,580,382	17,869,394	18,598,414
Other utility	596,567	752,734	731,333	688,903	522,114
Operating expenses	161,908,147	164,207,153	165,321,023	173,920,492	181,758,787
Electric	146,118,013	148,662,734	150,598,710	156,937,816	164,465,582
Operation	91,328,230	93,107,998	91,880,940	97,206,642	103,353,465
Maintenance	12,446,914	12,021,790	11,767,040	12,049,844	12,329,419
Depreciation	18,098,736	18,679,022	19,885,482	21,193,742	23,012,231
Taxes other than income taxes	13,040,400	13,275,354	13,519,143	13,569,490	13,596,555
Regulatory debits (net)	429,481	706,108	1,142,138	683,185	641,813
Income taxes	8,296,900	9,625,569	11,479,763	11,194,656	11,840,864
Deferred income tax	2,993,143	1,831,593	1,473,977	1,616,998	-244,674
Investment tax credit (net)	-515,791	-584,701	-549,772	-576,741	-149,218
Gas	15,234,557	14,877,836	14,073,160	16,257,611	16,865,938
Income taxes	251,533	465,076	531,748	223,871	562,397
Other	14,983,024	14,412,760	13,541,412	16,033,740	8,844,711
Operating income	31,729,696	32,074,346	34,645,955	33,538,586	32,563,945
Electric	30,236,352	30,644,526	33,056,553	31,962,965	30,736,622
Gas	1,452,354	1,343,670	1,507,223	1,611,783	1,732,476
Other utility	40,990	86,150	82,180	-36,163	94,847
Total income before interest charges	33,076,094	33,883,899	36,457,369	35,152,873	35,051,433
Net interest charges	14,700,848	14,161,602	14,421,406	13,990,388	14,122,641
Interest expense	14,566,753	13,915,384	14,169,979	13,645,951	13,801,857
Less allow. for borrowed funds used during const'n	555,021	420,828	435,386	326,158	331,578
Other charges, net	688,756	667,046	686,814	670,597	237,721
Net income before extraordinary charges	18,375,606	19,722,298	22,035,963	21,162,485	20,928,793
Less extraordinary items after taxes	484,409	-165,288	-24,691	-65,696	2,537,855
Net income	17,891,198	19,887,586	22,060,655	21,228,180	18,390,938
Dividends declared - preferred stock	1,765,286	1,581,940	1,518,904	1,248,409	1,024,760
Earnings available for common stocks	16,125,912	18,305,646	20,541,751	19,979,771	17,366,178
Dividends declared - common stock	15,334,377	15,875,659	16,249,715	16,810,054	17,786,231
Additions total earnings	296,171	2,063,432	4,281,899	2,193,444	-755,318
COMPOSITE BALANCE SHEET					
Total assets and other debits	566,641,282	574,511,673	578,933,714	581,990,963	587,418,412
Utility plant, net	393,829,243	397,812,254	397,383,148	396,437,823	382,168,627
Electric utility plant, total	363,829,459	366,936,417	366,116,061	363,853,762	351,952,558
Electric utility plant	519,207,367	535,928,383	553,857,823	569,968,617	578,892,994
Construction work in progress	18,048,849	17,148,353	13,523,358	11,395,525	11,051,910
Less accumulated depreciation	173,426,756	186,140,318	201,265,120	217,510,379	237,992,346
Nuclear fuel, net	5,964,178	5,656,878	5,285,850	5,443,854	5,285,256
Other utility plant, net	24,035,606	25,218,959	25,981,238	27,140,206	28,423,520
Unaccounted for plant	(NA)	(NA)	(NA)	(NA)	-3,492,705
Other property and investments	20,063,695	23,479,360	27,987,677	33,119,898	42,463,011
Current and accrued assets	42,409,989	41,262,977	44,139,661	43,515,064	47,050,759
Deferred debits	110,338,355	111,957,082	109,423,227	108,918,179	111,606,444
CAPITALIZATION AND LIABILITIES					
Liabilities and other credits	566,641,282	574,511,673	578,933,714	581,990,963	587,418,412
Capitalization	360,455,273	364,724,736	365,774,716	365,782,779	370,755,230
Common stock	107,470,838	109,522,096	111,301,825	112,633,284	113,852,964
Retained earnings (adjusted)	52,826,059	54,960,728	59,195,307	61,692,140	61,598,944
Preferred stock	25,304,294	24,859,833	21,569,105	18,830,248	16,253,063
Long-term debt	174,854,082	175,382,079	173,708,479	172,627,107	179,050,259
Current liabilities and deferred credits	206,186,010	209,786,937	213,158,998	216,208,185	216,663,182
Other noncurrent liabilities	11,478,303	13,452,636	14,352,102	15,309,391	15,992,675
Current and accrued liabilities	48,878,976	48,035,058	49,929,403	49,341,620	51,112,314
Deferred credits	145,828,731	148,299,243	148,877,493	151,557,174	149,558,193
Accumulated deferred income taxes	104,964,188	107,054,667	108,615,175	110,537,249	107,426,447
Accumulated deferred investment tax credit	13,428,995	12,784,415	12,138,942	11,491,332	10,836,884
Other deferred credits (adjusted)	27,435,549	28,460,160	28,123,375	29,528,592	31,294,862
COMPOSITE FINANCIAL INDICATORS					
Activity:					
1. Electric fixed asset (net plant) turnover	0.48	0.49	0.50	0.52	0.55
2. Total asset turnover	0.34	0.34	0.35	0.36	0.36
Leverage:					
3. Current assets to current liabilities	0.87	0.86	0.88	0.88	0.92
4. Long term debt to capitalization	48.51	48.09	47.49	47.19	48.29
5. Preferred stock to capitalization	7.02	6.82	5.90	5.15	4.38
6. Common stock equity to capitalization	44.47	45.10	46.61	47.66	47.32
7. Total debts to total assets	32.48	32.35	31.89	31.57	32.23
8. Common stock equity to total assets	28.29	28.63	29.45	29.95	29.87
9. Interest coverage before taxes without AFUDC	2.78	3.10	3.37	3.36	3.39
Profitability:					
10. Profit margin	9.24	10.13	11.03	10.23	8.58
11. Return on average common stock equity	22.32	12.24	13.17	12.31	10.52
12. Return on investment	3.16	3.46	3.81	3.65	3.13

NA Not available.
Source: U.S. Energy Information Administration, *Electric Power Annual*.

610 Energy

No. 981. Nonutility Electric Power Producers—Summary, by Type of Fuel: 1989 to 1997

Type of fuel	1989	1990	1991	1992	1993	1994	1995	1996	1997
Installed capacity (megawatts)......	38,851	45,271	49,998	56,814	60,778	68,461	70,254	73,189	74,021
Coal [1]	6,422	6,937	7,351	8,503	9,772	10,372	10,877	11,370	11,236
Petroleum [2]	1,129	1,038	1,514	1,730	2,043	2,262	2,116	2,251	2,994
Natural gas	14,820	17,430	20,694	21,542	23,463	26,925	27,906	30,166	30,476
Other gas [3]	(4)	(4)	(4)	(4)	(4)	1,130	1,217	327	273
Petroleum/natural gas (combined) .	4,732	6,468	5,292	8,478	8,505	9,820	10,479	10,912	9,767
Hydroelectric	1,672	1,968	2,072	2,684	2,741	3,364	3,399	3,419	3,776
Geothermal	1,001	1,086	1,103	1,254	1,318	1,335	1,295	1,346	1,303
Solar.	200	360	360	360	360	354	354	354	354
Wind	1,339	1,405	1,652	1,822	1,813	1,737	1,723	1,670	1,607
Wood [5]	5,515	6,049	6,708	6,805	7,046	7,416	6,885	7,263	7,181
Waste [6]	1,825	2,323	2,741	3,006	3,131	3,150	3,430	3,463	3,715
Gross generation (mil. kilowatt hours).	189,896	220,058	251,747	296,001	325,226	354,925	375,901	382,423	384,707
Coal [1]	31,511	32,131	40,587	47,363	53,367	59,035	60,234	61,375	58,923
Petroleum [2]	5,742	7,330	7,814	10,963	13,364	15,069	15,049	14,959	15,620
Natural gas	99,632	116,969	131,820	158,798	174,282	179,735	196,633	198,555	206,411
Other gases [3]	(4)	(4)	(4)	(4)	(4)	12,480	13,984	14,750	13,342
Hydroelectric	7,124	8,153	8,180	9,446	11,511	13,227	14,774	16,555	17,905
Geothermal	5,416	7,235	8,014	8,578	9,749	10,122	9,912	10,198	9,110
Solar.	489	663	779	746	897	824	824	903	893
Wind	1,833	2,251	2,606	2,916	3,052	3,482	3,185	3,400	3,385
Wood [5]	27,835	30,812	33,785	36,255	37,421	38,595	37,283	37,525	35,218
Waste [6]	8,515	11,688	14,475	17,352	18,325	18,797	20,231	20,412	20,669

[1] Includes coal, anthracite, culm and coal waste.   [2] Includes petroleum, petroleum coke, diesel, kerosene, and petroleum sludge and tar.   [3] Includes butane, ethane, propane, and other gases. [4] Included in "Natural gas." [5] Includes wood, wood waste, peat, wood liquors, railroad ties, pitch and wood sludge.   [6] Includes municipal solid waste, agricultural waste, straw, tires, landfill gases and other waste.

Source: Energy Information Administration, *Annual Nonutility Power Producer Report.*

No. 982. Water Power—Developed and Undeveloped Capacity, by Division: 1980 to 1997

[In millions of kilowatts (64.4 represents 64,400,000. As of Dec. 31. Excludes all capacity of reversible equipment at pumped storage projects. Also excludes capacity precluded from development due to wild and scenic river legislation. For composition of divisions, see map inside front cover]

Division	Developed installed capacity							Estimated undeveloped capacity						
	1980	1990	1993	1994	1995	1996	1997	1980	1990	1993	1994	1995	1996	1997
United States......	64.4	73.0	74.0	74.1	74.2	74.8	73.5	129.9	73.9	73.6	73.5	71.0	70.0	64.1
New England..........	1.5	1.9	1.9	1.9	1.9	2.0	2.0	4.7	4.4	4.4	4.4	4.4	4.4	3.9
Middle Atlantic........	4.3	4.9	4.9	4.9	4.9	5.0	5.6	5.1	5.1	4.9	4.9	4.9	4.8	3.6
East North Central	0.9	1.1	1.2	1.2	1.2	1.2	1.2	2.0	1.7	1.7	1.7	1.7	1.6	1.5
West North Central	2.8	3.1	3.1	3.1	3.1	3.0	3.0	3.4	3.1	3.1	3.1	3.1	3.0	2.8
South Atlantic.........	5.9	6.7	6.7	6.7	6.7	6.8	6.8	9.6	7.0	7.2	7.2	7.2	7.3	6.8
East South Central	5.6	5.9	5.9	5.9	5.9	5.9	5.9	3.3	2.4	2.4	2.4	2.3	2.0	2.0
West South Central.....	2.3	2.7	2.7	2.7	2.7	2.7	2.8	4.7	4.6	4.6	4.6	4.6	4.6	4.0
Mountain.............	7.4	9.2	9.5	9.5	9.5	10.0	10.0	34.2	19.4	19.1	19.1	18.8	19.1	18.0
Pacific...............	33.7	37.5	38.1	38.2	38.3	38.3	36.2	62.9	26.2	26.2	26.1	24.0	22.9	21.5

Source: U.S. Federal Energy Regulatory Commission (formerly U.S. Federal Power Commission), *Hydroelectric Power Resources of the United States, Developed and Undeveloped*, January 1, 1988; and unpublished data.

No. 983. Solar Collector Shipments, by Type, End Use, and Market Sector: 1984 to 1997

[In thousands of square feet, except number of manufacturers. Solar collector is a device for intercepting sunlight, converting the light to heat, and carrying the heat to where it will be either used or stored. 1985 data are not available]

Year	Number of manufac- turers	Total ship- ments [1]	Collector type		End use			Market sector		
			Low tem- perature	Medium tempera- ture, spe- cial, other	Pool heating	Hot water	Space heating	Resi- dential	Com- mercial	Industrial
1984 [2]	225	17,191	4,479	11,939	4,427	8,930	2,370	13,980	2,091	289
1986 [2]	98	9,360	3,751	1,111	3,494	1,181	127	4,131	703	13
1987 [2]	59	7,269	3,157	957	3,111	964	23	3,775	305	11
1988 [2]	51	8,174	3,326	732	3,304	726	7	3,796	255	7
1989 [2]	44	11,482	4,283	1,989	4,688	1,374	205	5,804	424	42
1990	51	11,409	3,645	2,527	5,016	1,091	2	5,835	294	22
1991	48	6,574	5,585	989	5,535	989	24	6,322	225	13
1992	45	7,086	6,187	897	6,210	801	35	6,832	204	27
1993	41	6,968	6,025	931	6,040	880	15	6,694	215	31
1994	41	7,627	6,823	803	6,813	790	19	7,026	583	16
1995	36	7,666	6,813	840	6,763	755	132	6,966	604	82
1996	28	7,616	6,821	785	6,787	765	57	6,873	682	54
1997	29	8,138	7,524	606	7,528	595	10	7,360	768	7

[1] Includes high temperature collectors, end uses such process heating, and utility and other market sectors not shown separately.   [2] Declines between 1984 and 1989 are primarily due to the expiration of the Federal energy tax credit and industry consolidation.

Source: U.S. Energy Information Administration, *Solar Collector Manufacturing Activity*, annual.

Energy   611

No. 984. Renewable Energy Consumption Estimates, by Type: 1990 to 1997

[In quadrillion Btu. Renewable energy is obtained from sources that are essentially inexhaustible unlike fossil fuels of which there is a finite supply]

Source and sector	1990	1993	1994	1995	1996	1997
SOURCE						
Total	**6.16**	**6.43**	**6.31**	**6.83**	**7.32**	**7.09**
Consumption for electricity	3.94	4.15	4.00	4.43	(NA)	(NA)
Electric utilities	3.23	3.23	3.02	3.16	3.89	3.88
Hydroelectric power	2.93	2.77	2.55	3.04	3.42	3.53
Geothermal energy	0.18	0.16	0.15	0.10	0.11	0.12
Biofuels [1]	0.02	0.02	0.02	0.02	(NA)	(NA)
Wind energy [2]	(Z)	(Z)	(Z)	(Z)	(Z)	(Z)
Nonutility power generators	0.70	0.94	0.98	0.99	(NA)	(NA)
Hydroelectric power	0.08	0.12	0.14	0.15	0.17	0.19
Geothermal, solar, and wind energy	0.18	0.21	0.21	0.21	0.22	0.19
Biofuels [1]	0.44	0.57	0.59	0.59	(NA)	(NA)
Net imported electricity	0.10	0.27	0.31	0.28	0.33	0.22
Consumption for other uses [3]	2.22	2.25	2.30	(NA)	(NA)	(NA)
Biofuels [1]	2.63	2.78	2.85	(NA)	(NA)	(NA)
Solar and photovoltaic energy	0.07	0.07	0.07	(NA)	(NA)	(NA)
SECTOR						
Total	**6.16**	**6.43**	**6.31**	**6.76**	**7.32**	**7.09**
Residential and commercial	0.64	0.66	0.66	0.72	0.72	0.55
Industrial	2.21	2.45	2.53	2.49	2.63	2.56
Transportation	0.08	0.09	0.10	0.10	0.07	0.10
Electric utilities	3.23	3.23	3.02	3.45	3.89	3.88

NA Not available.   Z Less than 0.005 quadrillion Btu.   [1] Biofuels are fuelwood, wood byproducts, waste wood, municipal solid waste, manufacturing process waste, and alcohol fuels.   [2] Also includes photovoltaic and solar thermal energy.   [3] Included are nonutility thermal energy uses, such as space heating and industrial process heat production. Excluded are estimates for mechanical energy, such as shaft power from dams, wind machines, and solar-powered motors and activators.

Source: U.S. Energy Information Administration, *Annual Energy Review.*

No. 985. Privately Owned Gas Utility Industry—Balance Sheet and Income Account: 1980 to 1997

[In millions of dollars 75,851 represent $75,851,000,000. The gas utility industry consists of pipeline and distribution companies. Excludes operations of companies distributing gas in bottles or tanks]

Item	1980	1985	1990	1992	1993	1994	1995	1996	1997
COMPOSITE BALANCE SHEET									
Assets, total	75,851	104,478	121,686	129,400	135,813	137,911	141,965	121,328	134,715
Total utility plant	67,071	88,121	112,863	129,272	135,859	139,372	143,636	135,179	140,268
Depreciation and amortization	*26,162*	*36,377*	*49,483*	*53,005*	*60,152*	*61,140*	*62,723*	*58,815*	*62,554*
Utility plant (net)	40,909	51,744	63,380	76,267	75,707	78,232	80,912	76,364	77,714
Investment and fund accounts	15,530	23,871	23,872	21,883	23,342	22,658	26,489	13,207	22,812
Current and accrued assets	17,243	24,771	23,268	23,783	21,451	20,728	18,564	17,393	19,084
Deferred debits [1]	2,169	4,092	9,576	9,776	13,369	14,234	13,923	11,983	12,844
Liabilities, total	75,851	104,478	121,686	129,400	135,813	137,911	141,965	121,328	134,715
Capitalization, total	51,382	65,799	74,958	81,183	82,755	85,728	90,581	77,440	78,887
Capital stock	29,315	39,517	43,810	46,318	49,051	50,394	54,402	43,555	42,530
Long-term debts	22,067	26,282	31,148	34,865	33,693	35,296	35,548	33,644	35,971
Current and accrued liabilities	18,119	26,125	29,550	26,438	27,321	25,438	28,272	22,098	33,507
Deferred income taxes [2]	4,149	7,769	11,360	10,952	13,070	13,787	14,393	13,326	13,636
Other liabilities and credits	2,201	4,785	5,818	10,827	12,667	12,955	8,715	8,464	8,745
COMPOSITE INCOME ACCOUNTS									
Operating revenues, total	85,918	103,945	66,027	66,405	69,966	63,446	58,390	63,600	62,617
Operating expenses [3]	*81,789*	*98,320*	*60,137*	*60,042*	*62,977*	*56,789*	*50,760*	*56,695*	*59,375*
Operation and maintenance	74,508	88,572	51,627	48,054	50,468	43,879	37,966	43,742	46,070
Federal, state, and local taxes	4,847	6,590	4,957	6,031	6,185	6,613	6,182	6,362	7,182
Operating income	4,129	5,625	5,890	6,363	6,988	6,657	7,630	6,905	3,242
Utility operating income	4,471	6,030	6,077	6,572	7,177	6,851	7,848	7,013	3,337
Income before interest charges	6,929	7,636	8,081	7,223	8,754	8,200	9,484	8,030	4,193
Net income	4,194	3,785	4,410	3,750	5,589	5,011	5,139	4,797	48
Dividends	2,564	4,060	3,191	3,889	3,149	3,928	4,037	4,138	6,258

[1] Includes capital stock discount and expense and reacquired securities.   [2] Includes reserves for deferred income taxes.   [3] Includes expenses not shown separately.

Source: American Gas Association, Arlington, VA, *Gas Facts,* annual (copyright).

612   Energy

No. 986. Gas Utility Industry—Summary: 1980 to 1997

[Covers natural, manufactured, mixed, and liquid petroleum gas. Based on questionnaire mailed to all privately and municipally owned gas utilities in United States, except those with annual revenues less than $25,000]

Item	Unit	1980	1985	1990	1992	1993	1994	1995	1996	1997
End users [1]	1,000	47,223	49,971	54,261	56,132	57,028	57,960	58,728	59,820	59,802
Residential	1,000	43,489	45,929	49,802	51,525	52,358	53,243	53,955	54,968	54,998
Commercial	1,000	3,498	3,816	4,246	4,397	4,428	4,474	4,530	4,616	4,593
Industrial and other	1,000	187	179	166	165	181	181	181	183	173
Sales [2]	Tril. Btu	15,413	12,616	9,842	9,906	10,021	9,480	9,094	9,532	8,913
Residential	Tril. Btu	4,826	4,513	4,468	4,694	5,054	4,972	4,736	5,198	5,021
Percent of total	Percent	31.3	35.8	45.4	47.4	50.4	52.4	52.0	54.5	56.3
Commercial	Tril. Btu	2,453	2,338	2,192	2,209	2,397	2,351	2,204	2,395	2,244
Industrial	Tril. Btu	7,957	5,635	3,010	2,772	2,404	2,009	1,930	1,791	1,524
Other	Tril. Btu	177	130	171	231	167	148	224	148	124
Revenues [2]	Mil. dol	48,303	63,293	45,153	46,178	49,847	49,864	46,381	51,115	51,517
Residential	Mil. dol	17,432	26,864	25,000	26,702	29,787	30,563	28,741	32,022	33,068
Percent of total	Percent	36.1	42.4	55.4	57.8	59.8	61.3	61.9	62.6	64.2
Commercial	Mil. dol	8,183	12,722	10,604	10,865	12,076	12,254	11,410	12,726	12,666
Industrial	Mil. dol	22,215	23,086	8,996	7,913	7,351	6,475	5,652	5,821	5,284
Other	Mil. dol	473	621	553	698	632	572	579	546	498
Prices per mil. Btu [3]	Dollars	3.13	5.02	4.59	4.66	4.94	5.23	5.10	5.37	5.78
Residential	Dollars	3.61	5.95	5.60	5.69	5.89	6.14	6.06	6.17	6.59
Commercial	Dollars	3.34	5.44	4.84	4.92	5.04	5.21	5.18	5.31	5.64
Industrial	Dollars	2.79	4.10	2.99	2.85	3.02	3.17	3.00	3.32	3.53
Gas mains mileage	1,000	1,052	1,119	1,207	1,254	1,251	1,267	1,262	1,269	1,258
Field and gathering	1,000	84	94	90	86	73	72	62	58	46
Transmission	1,000	266	271	280	285	270	276	265	260	257
Distribution	1,000	702	754	837	883	908	919	935	952	955
Construction expenditures	Mil. dol	5,350	5,671	7,899	11,068	9,140	9,282	10,829	7,722	7,189
Transmission	Mil. dol	1,583	1,562	2,886	5,739	3,288	3,065	3,384	1,316	1,334
Distribution	Mil. dol	1,869	2,577	3,714	3,867	4,286	4,550	5,448	4,234	4,404
Production and storage	Mil. dol	1,150	790	309	349	253	230	366	651	347

[1] Annual average. [2] Excludes sales for resale. [3] For definition of Btu, see text, this section. [4] Includes general.

Source: American Gas Association, Arlington, VA, Gas Facts, annual (copyright).

No. 987. Gas Utility Industry—Customers, Sales, and Revenues, by State: 1997

[See headnote, Table 986. For definition of Btu, see text, this section]

State	Customers [1] (1,000) Total [2]	Resi-dential	Sales [3] (tril. Btu) Total [2]	Resi-dential	Revenues [3] (mil. dol.) Total [2]	Resi-dential	State	Customers [1] (1,000) Total [2]	Resi-dential	Sales [3] (tril. Btu) Total [2]	Resi-dential	Revenues [3] (mil. dol.) Total [2]	Resi-dential
U.S.	59,802	54,998	8,913	5,021	511,517	33,068	MS	442	396	78	27	370	166
							MO	1,408	1,274	199	129	1,199	822
							MT	238	210	36	22	172	107
AL	818	753	112	50	687	399	NE	502	442	84	47	428	263
AK	95	83	23	15	84	57	NV	454	426	45	26	244	158
AZ	683	641	58	26	355	209	NH	89	76	18	7	113	51
AR	611	542	91	43	487	283	NJ	2,389	2,172	476	226	2,800	1,720
CA	9,429	9,000	712	478	4,361	3,165							
CO	1,307	1,183	189	116	823	553	NM	480	441	60	37	303	212
CT	484	435	103	43	794	427	NY	4,379	4,049	634	392	5,011	3,495
DE	119	109	24	9	148	75	NC	835	728	150	54	967	466
DC	146	131	26	12	222	111	ND	113	99	26	12	110	56
FL	531	485	65	13	419	139	OH	3,224	2,976	515	372	3,077	2,645
GA	1,650	1,528	215	117	1,355	838	OK	946	856	130	73	696	438
HI	37	34	3	1	49	16	OR	516	455	75	34	364	212
ID	224	198	27	16	124	77	PA	2,537	2,340	410	265	2,919	2,060
IL	3,786	3,491	624	466	3,350	2,566	RI	226	204	33	18	272	170
IN	1,670	1,523	267	176	1,675	1,086	SC	484	430	97	25	542	211
IA	864	773	135	81	722	471	SD	148	130	25	13	127	76
KS	917	831	112	72	644	455	TN	913	812	164	63	919	419
KY	775	698	122	68	608	338	TX	3,849	3,519	565	244	2,728	1,479
LA	737	689	270	41	755	262	UT	610	569	92	61	408	295
ME	23	16	6	1	43	8	VT	32	27	8	3	42	18
MD	930	860	212	115	885	595	VA	889	805	137	70	992	598
MA	1,311	1,198	119	72	1,683	1,043	WA	754	676	134	63	605	341
MI	3,069	2,844	542	387	2,645	1,928	WV	371	339	66	37	378	247
MN	1,229	1,120	276	136	1,318	757	WI	1,398	1,271	267	134	1,430	824
							WY	135	120	24	13	92	55

[1] Averages for the year. [2] Includes other service, not shown separately. [3] Excludes sales for resale.

Source: American Gas Association, Arlington, VA, Gas Facts, annual (copyright).

Energy   613

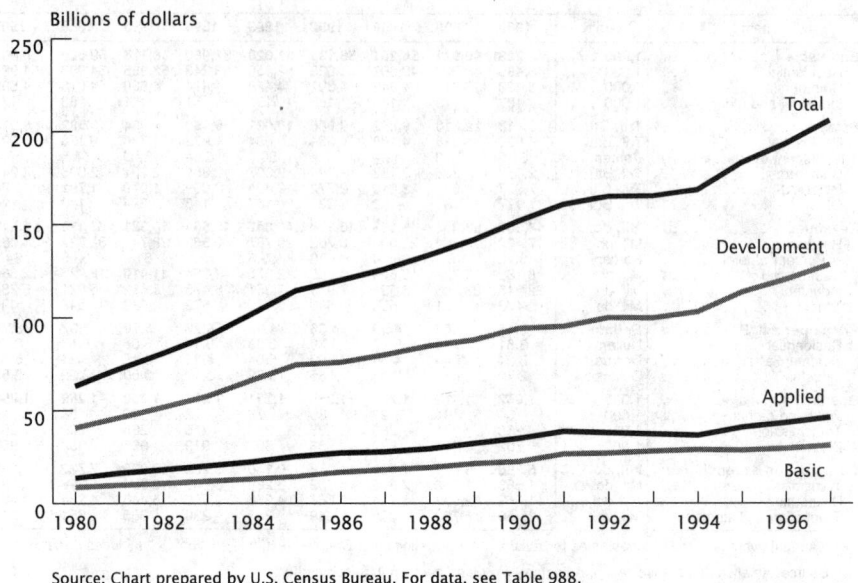

Figure 20.1
Research and Development Expenditures: 1980 to 1997

Billions of dollars

Source: Chart prepared by U.S. Census Bureau. For data, see Table 988.

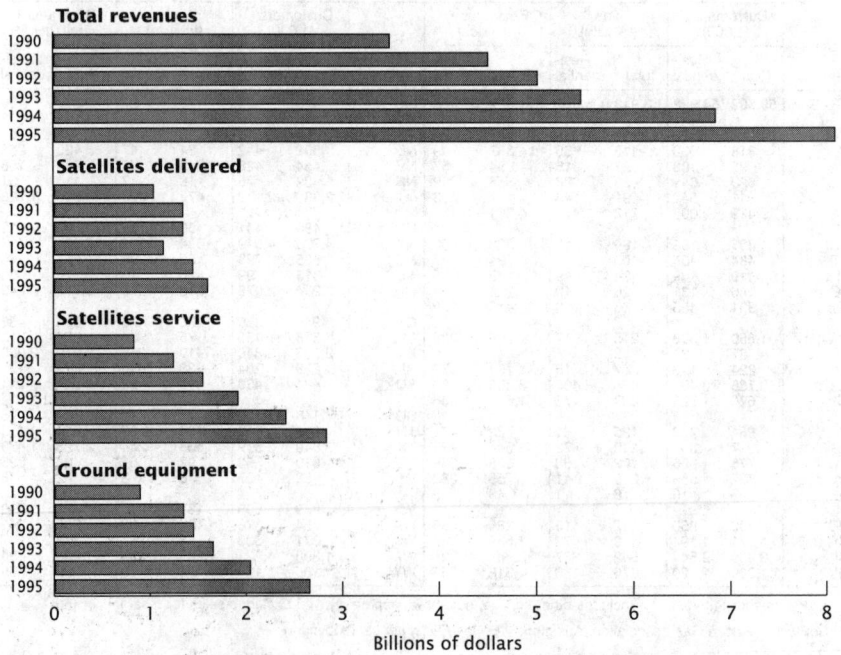

Figure 20.2
U.S. Commercial Space Revenues, by Type: 1990 to 1995

Billions of dollars

Source: Chart prepared by U.S. Census Bureau. For data, see Table 1007.

This section presents statistics on scientific, engineering, and technological resources, with emphasis on patterns of research and development (R&D) funding and on scientific, engineering, and technical personnel, education, and employment. Also included are statistics on space program outlays and accomplishments. Principal sources of these data are the National Science Foundation (NSF) and the National Aeronautics and Space Administration (NASA).

NSF gathers data chiefly through recurring surveys. Current NSF publications containing data on funds for research and development and on scientific and engineering personnel include the *Science Resources Studies Highlights* summaries series; *Detailed Statistical Tables*; and annual, biennial, triennial, and special reports. Titles or the areas of coverage of these reports include the following: *Science and Engineering Indicators; National Patterns of R&D Resources; Science and Engineering Personnel—A National Overview; Women and Minorities in Science and Engineering*; science and technology data presented in chart and tabular form in a pocket-size publication; *International Science and Technology Data Update*; profiles on human resources and funding in individual fields of science and engineering; *Federal Funds for Research and Development; Federal R&D Funding by Budget Function; Federal Support to Universities, Colleges, and Selected Nonprofit Institutions; Scientific and Engineering Facilities at Universities and Colleges; Geographic Distribution of Industrial R&D Expenditures; Research and Development in Industry*; R&D funds and graduate enrollment and support in academic science and engineering; characteristics of doctoral scientists and engineers and of recent graduates in the United States; *U.S. Scientists and Engineers*; and scientists,

engineers, and technicians in manufacturing, nonmanufacturing, and trade and regulated industries. Statistical surveys in these areas pose problems of concept and definition and the data should, therefore, be regarded as broad estimates rather than precise quantitative statements. See sources for details.

The National Science Board's biennial *Science and Engineering* Indicators contains data and analysis of international and domestic science and technology, including measures of inputs and outputs. The *Budget of the United States Government*, published by the U.S. Office of Management and Budget, contains summary financial data on Federal R&D programs.

Research and development outlays— NSF defines research as a "systematic and intensive study directed toward a fuller knowledge of the subject studied" and development as "the systematic use of scientific knowledge directed toward the production of useful materials, devices, systems, methods, or processes." National coverage of R&D expenditures is developed primarily from periodic surveys in four principal economic sectors: (1) *Government*, made up primarily of Federal executive agencies; (2) *industry*, consisting of manufacturing and nonmanufacturing firms and the federally funded research and development centers (FFRDCs) they administer; (3) *universities and colleges*, composed of universities, colleges, and their affiliated institutions, agricultural experiment stations, and associated schools of agriculture, and FFRDCs administered by educational institutions; and (4) *other nonprofit institutions*, consisting of such organizations as private philanthropic foundations, nonprofit research institutes, voluntary health agencies, and FFRDCs administered by nonprofit organizations. The R&D funds reported consist of current operating costs, including planning and administration costs, except as otherwise noted. They exclude funds for routine testing, mapping and surveying, collection of general-purpose data, dissemination of scientific information, and training of scientific personnel.

Scientists, engineers, and technicians—Scientists and engineers are defined as persons engaged in scientific

and engineering work at a level requiring a knowledge of sciences equivalent at least to that acquired through completion of a 4-year college course. Technicians are defined as persons engaged in technical work at a level requiring knowledge acquired through a technical institute, junior college, or other type of training less extensive than 4-year college training. Craftsmen and skilled workers are excluded.

Figure 20.3
Top 15 Universities—Federal Research and Development Obligations: 1995

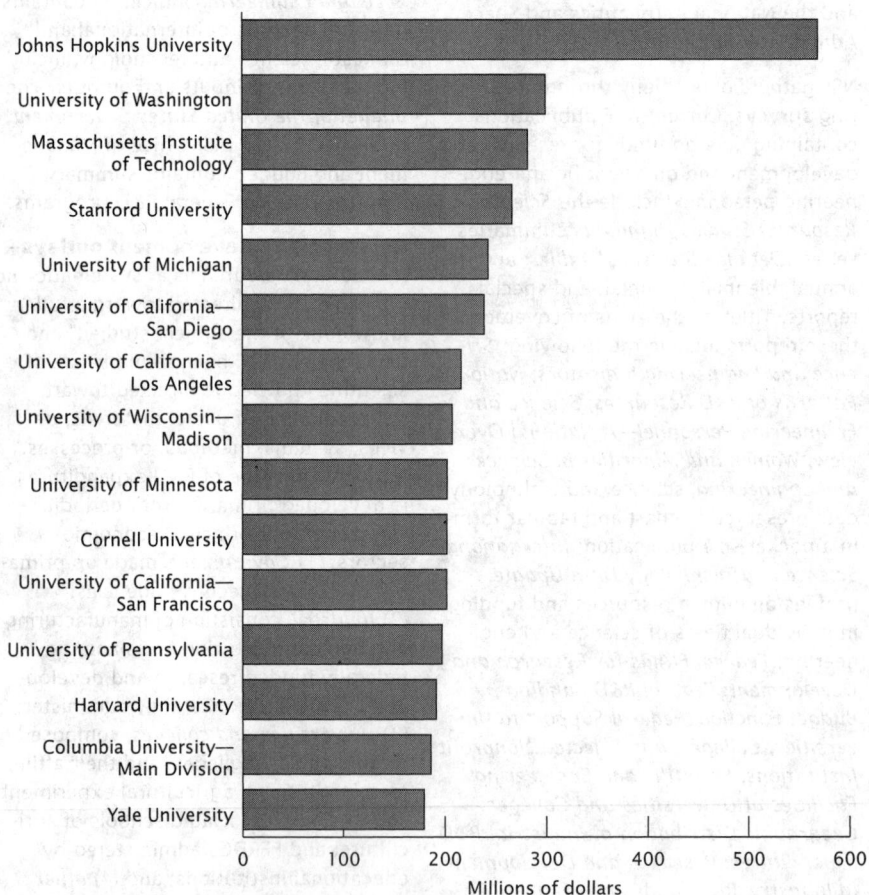

Source: Chart prepared by U.S. Census Bureau. For data, see Table 996.

616   Science and Technology

No. 988. R&D Expenditures: 1960 to 1998

[In millions of dollars, (13,669 represents $13,669,000,000) except as indicated. For calendar years]

Year	Total	Sources of funds					Objective (percent of total)			Character of work		
		Federal Govern-ment	Indus-try	Univer-sities/ col-leges	Non-profit	Non-Federal Govern-ment [1]	Defense related [2]	Space relat-ed [3]	Other	Basic research	Applied research	Devel-opment
1960....	13,669	8,879	4,516	66	122	88	53	3	44	1,256	3,059	9,355
1961....	14,514	9,441	4,757	72	146	98	50	6	44	1,476	3,115	9,924
1962....	15,577	10,086	5,123	82	177	109	49	7	44	1,780	3,688	10,110
1963....	17,446	11,582	5,456	93	195	122	42	14	45	2,060	3,855	11,531
1964....	19,053	12,726	5,887	108	198	135	37	19	44	2,358	4,189	12,507
1965....	20,192	13,147	6,548	130	221	146	33	21	46	2,618	4,361	13,214
1966....	22,010	14,117	7,330	156	249	158	32	20	48	2,886	4,638	14,486
1967....	23,279	14,511	8,144	190	267	166	35	14	50	3,113	4,838	15,328
1968....	24,646	14,956	9,006	219	286	178	35	14	52	3,361	5,141	16,144
1969....	25,965	15,213	10,010	228	311	203	35	11	54	3,471	5,448	17,046
1970....	26,235	14,970	10,446	251	340	228	33	10	56	3,567	5,742	16,926
1971....	26,910	15,183	10,823	282	364	259	33	10	58	3,698	5,817	17,395
1972....	28,661	15,976	11,713	308	389	276	33	8	59	3,829	6,098	18,734
1973....	30,905	16,563	13,296	331	417	298	32	7	61	4,051	6,662	20,193
1974....	33,238	17,193	14,882	380	470	314	29	7	64	4,439	7,312	21,488
1975....	35,565	18,437	15,823	424	542	340	28	7	65	4,827	8,048	22,691
1976....	39,314	20,179	17,698	463	608	367	27	8	65	5,291	8,964	25,059
1977....	43,233	21,988	19,637	541	683	384	27	7	66	5,925	9,653	27,655
1978....	48,582	24,279	22,456	651	768	429	26	6	68	6,841	10,695	31,047
1979....	55,269	27,100	26,092	760	841	477	25	6	70	7,736	12,073	35,460
1980....	63,076	29,857	30,926	877	911	505	24	5	70	8,651	13,724	40,701
1981....	72,190	33,666	35,956	1,031	974	564	24	5	70	9,741	16,389	46,060
1982....	80,633	37,113	40,705	1,159	1,037	619	26	5	69	10,658	18,261	51,714
1983....	89,742	41,362	45,274	1,329	1,135	642	28	4	68	11,859	20,323	57,560
1984....	101,940	46,319	52,225	1,463	1,228	706	29	3	68	13,176	22,481	66,284
1985....	114,344	52,493	58,013	1,680	1,365	793	30	3	67	14,510	25,389	74,444
1986....	119,907	54,475	61,079	1,944	1,466	942	32	3	65	16,885	27,225	75,796
1987....	125,841	58,254	62,669	2,215	1,658	1,044	32	3	65	18,213	27,819	79,809
1988....	133,463	59,930	68,076	2,441	1,880	1,135	30	3	66	19,381	29,466	84,614
1989....	141,550	60,301	75,091	2,774	2,136	1,248	28	4	68	21,477	32,304	87,767
1990....	151,655	61,456	83,374	3,096	2,367	1,361	25	4	70	22,556	34,981	94,118
1991....	160,521	60,564	92,484	3,411	2,585	1,477	23	5	73	26,630	38,699	95,193
1992....	164,933	60,694	96,404	3,558	2,770	1,507	22	4	74	27,044	37,996	99,894
1993....	165,188	60,351	96,702	3,654	2,928	1,554	22	4	74	28,115	37,325	99,749
1994....	168,586	60,700	99,324	3,904	3,081	1,576	20	4	76	28,917	36,643	103,024
1995....	183,045	63,102	110,985	4,112	3,154	1,692	19	5	77	28,756	40,973	113,316
1996....	196,011	63,215	123,520	4,322	3,225	1,730	18	5	78	31,545	43,057	121,410
1997, prel....	205,561	64,865	130,952	4,667	3,314	1,764	17	4	79	32,978	45,982	126,601
1998, prel....	220,617	66,636	143,714	4,974	3,449	1,845	16	4	80	34,426	49,753	136,438

[1] Non-Federal R&D expenditures to university and college performers. [2] R&D spending by the Department of Defense, including space activities, and a portion of the Department of Energy funds. [3] For the National Aeronautics and Space Administration only.
Source: U.S. National Science Foundation, *National Patterns of R&D Resources*, annual.

No. 989. Federal Obligations for R&D, by Agency: 1980 to 1999

[In millions of dollars, (29,830 represents $29,830,000,000). For fiscal years ending in year shown; see text, Section 9, State and Local Government. Includes those agencies with obligations of $1 billion or more in 1999]

Agency	1980	1985	1990	1994	1995	1996	1997	1998, prel.	1999, prel.
CURRENT DOLLARS									
Obligations, total [1].........	29,830	48,360	63,559	67,257	68,736	67,663	69,830	72,114	73,333
Dept. of Defense	13,981	29,792	37,268	34,575	34,346	34,495	34,788	34,833	34,350
Dept. of Health and Human Services .	3,780	5,451	8,406	11,022	11,455	11,953	12,788	13,718	14,821
National Aeronautics and Space Administration................	3,234	3,327	6,533	8,296	9,015	8,570	9,327	9,851	9,201
Dept. of Energy	4,754	4,966	5,681	6,048	6,145	5,345	5,604	5,833	6,541
National Science Foundation.......	882	1,346	1,690	2,040	2,149	2,188	2,249	2,357	2,655
Dept. of Agriculture	688	943	1,108	1,400	1,380	1,302	1,389	1,442	1,426
CONSTANT (1992) DOLLARS [2]									
Obligations, total [1].........	50,321	61,707	68,233	63,981	63,751	61,339	61,939	62,773	62,582
Dept. of Defense	23,585	38,014	40,009	32,891	31,855	31,271	30,857	30,321	29,314
Dept. of Health and Human Services .	6,377	6,955	9,024	10,485	10,624	10,836	11,343	11,941	12,648
National Aeronautics and Space Administration................	5,456	4,246	7,013	7,892	8,361	7,769	8,273	8,575	7,852
Dept. of Energy	8,019	6,337	6,045	5,753	5,699	4,845	4,970	5,078	5,582
National Science Foundation.......	1,488	1,717	1,814	1,941	1,993	1,984	1,994	2,052	2,266
Dept. of Agriculture	1,160	1,203	1,189	1,332	1,280	1,180	1,232	1,255	1,217

[1] Includes other agencies, not shown separately. [2] Based on gross domestic product implicit price deflator.
Source: U.S. National Science Foundation, *Federal Funds for Research and Development*, annual.

Science and Technology 617

No. 990. Performance Sector of R&D Expenditures 1993 to 1998

[In millions of dollars, (165,188 represents $165,188,000,000). For calendar years]

Year	Total	Federal Government	Industry — Total	Industry — Funded by Federal Government	Industry — Funded by Industry[2]	Industry — Funded by Industry FFRDCs[1]	Universities and colleges — Total	Universities and colleges — Federal Government	U&C Funded by — Non-Federal Government	U&C Funded by — Industry	U&C Funded by — Universities & colleges	U&C Funded by — Non-profits	U&C Funded by — Universities & colleges FFRDCs[3]	Other nonprofit institutions — Total	Other — Federal Government	Other Funded by — Industry	Other Funded by — Non-profits	Other Funded by — Nonprofit FFRDCs[1]
RESEARCH AND DEVELOPMENT TOTAL																		
1993	165,188	16,532	115,435	20,844	94,591	1,965	20,224	12,133	1,554	1,374	3,654	1,509	5,289	4,995	2,839	737	1,418	749
1994	168,586	16,432	117,393	20,261	97,131	2,202	21,340	12,840	1,576	1,431	3,904	1,589	5,305	5,155	2,900	762	1,493	759
1995	183,045	17,133	129,830	21,178	108,652	2,273	22,406	13,470	1,692	1,506	4,112	1,626	5,388	5,203	2,848	827	1,528	812
1996, prel	196,011	16,574	142,370	21,356	121,015	2,297	23,280	13,962	1,730	1,604	4,322	1,663	5,362	5,359	2,896	901	1,562	769
1997, prel	205,561	16,585	150,337	22,061	128,276	2,373	24,438	14,582	1,764	1,717	4,667	1,708	5,459	5,561	2,996	960	1,605	810
1998, prel	220,617	16,936	163,328	22,481	140,847	2,418	25,672	15,247	1,845	1,829	4,974	1,778	5,529	5,928	3,219	1,038	1,671	807
BASIC RESEARCH																		
1993	28,115	2,623	6,427	466	5,961	492	13,490	8,528	953	843	2,240	925	2,953	2,059	1,153	339	567	72
1994	28,917	2,553	6,514	436	6,078	503	14,266	9,057	966	877	2,393	974	2,934	2,073	1,126	351	597	74
1995	28,756	2,695	5,569	190	5,379	530	15,034	9,554	1,038	924	2,522	997	2,690	2,162	1,170	381	611	76
1996, prel	31,545	2,682	7,498	650	6,848	708	15,728	9,997	1,064	987	2,658	1,022	2,563	2,287	1,248	415	625	79
1997, prel	32,978	2,699	7,674	671	7,003	731	16,727	10,530	1,109	1,079	2,934	1,074	2,654	2,398	1,315	441	642	94
1998, prel	34,426	2,867	7,845	684	7,161	745	17,606	11,009	1,167	1,157	3,147	1,125	2,688	2,564	1,418	478	668	111
APPLIED RESEARCH																		
1993	37,325	4,838	24,251	4,295	19,956	435	5,075	2,508	493	436	1,159	479	962	1,661	900	251	511	103
1994	36,643	5,003	22,988	3,616	19,372	503	5,296	2,598	500	454	1,239	504	985	1,756	960	259	537	112
1995	40,973	5,007	26,919	3,164	23,755	535	5,555	2,721	537	478	1,304	516	1,060	1,766	935	281	550	131
1996, prel	43,057	4,815	29,010	3,640	25,370	231	5,783	2,841	546	506	1,364	525	1,275	1,821	952	306	562	122
1997, prel	45,982	4,830	31,653	3,760	27,893	239	5,868	2,868	537	522	1,420	520	1,385	1,884	980	326	578	123
1998, prel	49,753	5,135	34,580	3,832	30,748	243	6,164	3,024	556	551	1,498	535	1,562	1,966	1,012	353	602	104
DEVELOPMENT																		
1993	99,749	9,071	84,757	16,083	68,674	1,039	1,659	1,096	108	96	254	105	1,374	1,274	787	147	340	574
1994	103,024	8,876	87,890	16,209	71,681	1,196	1,778	1,185	110	100	272	111	1,386	1,325	815	152	358	573
1995	113,316	9,431	97,342	17,824	79,518	1,209	1,816	1,194	118	105	286	113	1,638	1,275	743	165	367	606
1996, prel	121,410	9,077	105,863	17,066	88,797	1,358	1,769	1,123	120	111	299	115	1,524	1,251	696	180	375	568
1997, prel	126,601	9,055	111,010	17,629	93,380	1,403	1,843	1,184	118	115	312	114	1,420	1,279	701	192	385	593
1998, prel	136,438	8,934	120,903	17,965	102,939	1,430	1,902	1,213	122	121	329	118	1,279	1,398	789	208	401	592

[1] For R&D funded by the Federal Government. FFRDCs are federally funded research and development centers. In 1994, 99 percent of total funds used were from Federal Government. [2] Includes all non-Federal sources. [3] Includes all R&D expenditures of FFRDCs administered by academic institutions and funded by the Federal Government.

Source: National Science Foundation, *National Patterns of R&D Resources*, annual series.

618 Science and Technology

[In millions of dollars, (183,013 represents $183,013,000,000). For the fiscal year]

State	Industry Total[1]	Industry Federal Government[2]	Industry Funded by— Total	Industry Funded by— Federal Government[3]	Industry Funded by— Industry[4]	Universities and colleges Total	Universities Funded by— Federal Government	Universities Funded by— Industry	Universities Funded by— Non-profits	Universities Funded by— Other[5]	Universities Non-profits[6]
United States ...	183,013	17,343	132,103	23,451	108,652	22,101	13,331	1,492	1,599	5,679	5,983
Alabama.........	1,681	642	686	273	413	335	190	29	22	94	18
Alaska.........	163	61	30	(D)	(D)	72	37	5	-	30	1
Arizona.........	1,995	178	1,356	620	736	380	210	23	12	134	6
Arkansas	330	58	181	(D)	(D)	88	33	8	3	44	3
California	36,133	1,844	28,710	6,925	21,785	2,594	1,797	120	198	480	607
Colorado........	2,603	168	1,865	274	1,591	394	260	24	35	74	51
Connecticut......	4,311	18	3,906	389	3,517	377	228	20	32	97	10
Delaware.......	1,149	15	1,077	12	1,065	53	27	4	5	17	3
District of Columbia .	3,128	2,106	672	17	656	181	133	13	15	21	169
Florida.........	5,223	554	4,101	1,634	2,467	559	317	36	29	176	8
Georgia	2,113	272	1,175	142	1,031	658	302	55	25	276	8
Hawaii	509	402	14	(D)	(D)	78	44	-	3	31	15
Idaho..........	914	28	827	(D)	(D)	59	20	7	2	30	1
Illinois	7,487	81	5,776	146	5,630	818	468	43	65	242	41
Indiana.........	3,163	62	2,721	382	2,339	376	197	35	20	123	4
Iowa	1,391	37	998	(D)	(D)	323	164	19	15	125	1
Kansas.........	764	12	569	(D)	(D)	181	70	11	8	92	1
Kentucky	594	6	452	4	448	135	60	17	5	54	1
Louisiana	423	45	61	(D)	(D)	315	136	21	19	138	2
Maine..........	345	4	286	(D)	(D)	32	16	4	1	11	23
Maryland	6,519	4,159	1,075	287	788	1,160	895	55	50	160	125
Massachusetts....	9,969	316	7,416	1,458	5,958	1,147	825	89	128	105	746
Michigan........	13,275	82	12,388	148	12,240	755	418	51	57	230	50
Minnesota.......	3,087	30	2,636	315	2,321	337	195	23	23	96	85
Mississippi	315	133	66	(D)	(D)	113	63	9	6	35	3
Missouri........	2,499	55	2,028	584	1,443	397	213	37	33	114	18
Montana........	119	34	17	(D)	(D)	67	27	6	1	33	2
Nebraska	336	23	150	(D)	(D)	157	55	11	3	88	6
Nevada	445	35	322	(D)	(D)	87	48	7	1	31	1
New Hampshire....	598	31	472	36	436	93	60	4	12	17	2
New Jersey......	9,128	344	8,200	197	8,002	443	209	26	33	176	15
New Mexico	3,295	481	1,461	1,380	81	230	157	11	7	56	13
New York	10,954	117	8,651	1,821	6,831	1,702	1,107	98	195	302	203
North Carolina.....	3,191	220	2,226	15	2,212	687	432	74	21	160	59
North Dakota......	98	25	12	(D)	(D)	60	28	3	2	27	1
Ohio	5,314	599	4,001	574	3,428	643	375	54	59	155	72
Oklahoma.......	529	45	288	38	249	186	60	11	17	99	9
Oregon.........	1,089	56	741	35	706	259	158	12	21	67	33
Pennsylvania.....	6,919	228	5,331	376	4,955	1,140	754	120	66	199	189
Rhode Island.....	896	254	520	(D)	(D)	106	72	2	2	29	17
South Carolina.....	996	34	739	(D)	(D)	220	109	19	19	72	3
South Dakota......	55	13	19	-	19	21	11	-	1	9	1
Tennessee	1,402	62	1,003	(D)	(D)	308	192	16	20	80	20
Texas..........	8,385	538	6,211	912	5,298	1,472	748	102	167	456	164
Utah..........	1,144	131	803	178	625	202	141	9	9	43	8
Vermont	308	5	248	(D)	(D)	54	33	5	4	12	1
Virginia.........	3,897	1,581	1,577	743	834	447	262	46	28	111	219
Washington......	5,241	160	4,294	(D)	(D)	486	340	39	15	91	301
West Virginia.....	475	140	243	(D)	(D)	53	30	3	4	15	6
Wisconsin.......	2,226	40	1,706	33	1,673	473	271	17	51	135	7
Wyoming	87	9	25	(D)	(D)	40	15	2	3	20	13
Other/unknown	5,805	771	1,772	3,502	8,875	548	320	30	30	167	2,620

- Represents or rounds to zero.   D Data withheld to avoiding disclosing information about individual companies.   [1]Includes university and college Federally Funded Research and Development Centers (FFRDCs), not shown separately.   [2]For R&D funded by the Federal Government.   [3]Includes performance at industry FFRDCs.   [4]Includes all non-Federal sources.   [5]Represents funding by state and local governments and universities and colleges.   [6]Data by state are for R&D funded by the Federal Government. United States total includes other support, not allocated by location.

Source: U.S. National Science Foundation, *National Patterns of R&D Resources*, 1998.

Science and Technology   619

No. 992. Federal Funding for R&D, by Selected Budget Functions: 1970 to 1999

[In millions of dollars, (15,339 represents $15,339,000,000). For fiscal years ending in year shown; see text, Section 9, State and Local Government. Excludes R&D plant. Represents budget authority. Functions shown are those for which $1 billion or more was authorized for 1999]

Function	1970	1980	1985	1990	1995	1996	1997	1998, prel.	1999, prel.
CURRENT DOLLARS									
Total [1]	15,339	29,739	49,887	63,781	68,791	69,049	71,653	73,639	75,229
Eight functions, percent of total ..	96.6	96.5	98.3	98.0	97.7	98.0	98.1	98.1	97.9
National defense.	7,981	14,946	33,698	39,925	37,204	37,801	39,591	39,871	39,699
Health.	1,084	3,694	5,418	8,308	11,407	11,867	12,670	13,557	14,622
Space research and technology [2] . . .	3,606	2,738	2,725	5,765	7,916	7,844	7,844	8,265	8,037
Energy [2]	574	3,603	2,389	2,715	2,844	2,521	2,372	1,143	1,470
General science	452	1,233	1,862	2,410	2,794	2,846	2,944	4,210	4,649
Natural resources and environment . .	340	999	1,059	1,386	1,988	1,802	1,886	2,015	2,013
Transportation	535	887	1,030	1,045	1,833	1,795	1,785	1,920	1,904
Agriculture.	238	585	836	950	1,194	1,176	1,203	1,243	1,272
CONSTANT (1992) DOLLARS [3]									
Total [1]	51,113	50,108	63,623	68,448	63,931	62,728	63,556	64,101	64,199
National defense.	26,594	25,183	42,977	42,847	34,575	34,341	35,117	34,707	33,879
Health.	3,612	6,224	6,910	8,916	10,601	10,781	11,239	11,801	12,478
Space research and technology [2] . . .	12,016	4,613	3,475	6,187	7,357	7,126	6,958	7,195	6,859
Energy [2]	1,913	6,071	3,047	2,925	2,643	2,290	2,104	995	1,254
General science	1,506	2,078	2,375	2,586	2,596	2,586	2,612	3,665	3,967
Natural resources and environment . .	1,133	1,683	1,351	1,487	1,848	1,637	1,673	1,754	1,718
Transportation	1,783	1,495	1,314	1,121	1,704	1,630	1,584	1,671	1,625
Agriculture.	793	986	1,066	1,020	1,109	1,068	1,067	1,082	1,085

[1] Includes other functions, not shown separately. [2] Beginning in FY 1998, a number of DOE programs were reclassified from energy (270). [3] Based on gross domestic product implicit price deflator.
Source: U.S. National Science Foundation, Federal R&D Funding by Budget Function, annual.

No. 993. National R&D Expenditures as a Percent of Gross Domestic Product, by Country: 1981 to 1997

Year	Total R&D					Nondefense R&D [1]				
	United States	Japan	Unified Germany	France	United Kingdom	Italy	United States	Japan	Unified Germany	France	United Kingdom	Italy

Year	United States	Japan	Unified Germany	France	United Kingdom	Italy	United States	Japan	Unified Germany	France	United Kingdom	Italy
1981 . .	2.32	2.13	2.43	1.97	2.37	0.88	1.75	(NA)	2.34	1.57	1.84	0.85
1985 . .	2.74	2.58	2.72	2.25	2.23	1.13	1.92	2.56	2.60	1.87	1.76	1.07
1990 . .	2.64	2.85	2.75	2.41	2.18	1.30	1.97	2.83	2.62	1.95	1.84	1.26
1993 . .	2.52	2.68	2.42	2.45	2.15	1.14	1.98	2.65	2.34	2.10	1.85	1.09
1994 . .	2.43	2.63	2.32	2.38	2.11	1.06	1.94	2.60	2.25	2.05	1.84	1.01
1995 . .	2.52	2.77	2.30	2.34	2.02	1.01	2.05	2.73	2.22	2.04	1.77	0.98
1996 . .	2.57	(NA)	2.28	2.32	1.94	1.03	2.11	(NA)	2.20	(NA)	1.71	(NA)
1997 . .	2.54	(NA)	2.26	(NA)	(NA)	1.06	2.10	(NA)	(NA)	(NA)	(NA)	(NA)

NA Not available. [1] Estimated.
Source: National Science Foundation, National Patterns of R&D Resources, annual; and Organization for Economic Co-operation and Development.

No. 994. R&D Expenditures in Science and Engineering at Universities and Colleges: 1981 to 1997

[In millions of dollars, (6,846 represents $6,846,000,000)]

Characteristic	1981	1990	1997	Characteristic	1981	1990	1997
CURRENT DOLLARS				CONSTANT (1992) DOLLARS [1]			
Total	6,846	16,285	24,348	Total	10,513	17,483	21,597
Basic research	4,593	10,641	16,678	Basic research	7,053	11,424	14,793
Applied R&D	2,253	5,644	7,670	Applied R&D	3,460	6,059	6,803
Source of funds:				Source of funds:			
All governments	5,115	10,960	16,379	All governments	7,855	11,766	14,528
Institutions' own funds . . .	1,004	3,006	4,544	Institutions' own funds . . .	1,542	3,227	4,031
Industry	292	1,128	1,713	Industry	448	1,211	1,519
Other	435	1,191	1,712	Other	668	1,279	1,519
Fields:				Fields:			
Physical sciences	765	1,807	2,364	Physical sciences	1,175	1,940	2,097
Environmental sciences . . .	550	1,068	1,539	Environmental sciences . .	845	1,147	1,365
Mathematical sciences . . .	87	222	293	Mathematical sciences . . .	134	238	260
Computer sciences	144	515	719	Computer sciences	221	553	638
Life sciences	3,695	8,726	13,608	Life sciences	5,674	9,368	12,070
Psychology	127	253	387	Psychology	195	272	343
Social sciences	366	703	1,117	Social sciences	562	755	991
Other sciences	145	336	504	Other sciences	223	361	447
Engineering	967	2,656	3,818	Engineering	1,485	2,851	3,387

[1] Based on gross domestic product implicit price deflator.
Source: U.S. National Science Foundation, Survey of Research and Development Expenditures at Universities and Colleges, annual.

No. 995. Federal Obligations to Universities and Colleges: 1970 to 1996

[In millions of dollars, (3,237 represents $3,237,000,000) except percent. For fiscal years ending in year shown; see text, Section 9, State and Local Government. Minus sign (-) indicates decrease]

Item	1970	1980	1985	1990	1993	1994	1995	1996
CURRENT DOLLARS								
Federal obligations, total	3,237	8,299	10,972	15,218	(NA)	(NA)	(NA)	(NA)
Annual percent change [1]	-6.5	9.1	9.3	-1.9	(NA)	(NA)	(NA)	(NA)
Academic science/engineering obligations	2,188	4,791	7,258	10,463	12,833	13,863	14,445	14,429
Percent of total	67.6	57.7	66.2	68.8	(NA)	(NA)	(NA)	(NA)
Research and development	1,447	4,161	6,246	9,009	11,024	11,894	12,165	12,323
Research and development plant	45	38	114	142	259	217	341	248
Other science/engineering activities	696	593	898	1,312	1,550	1,752	1,939	1,857
Nonscience/engineering activities	1,049	3,508	3,714	4,755	(NA)	(NA)	(NA)	(NA)
CONSTANT (1992) DOLLARS [2]								
Federal obligations, total	10,814	13,999	14,000	16,337	(NA)	(NA)	(NA)	(NA)
Annual percent change [1]	-11.2	0.2	5.6	-5.8	(NA)	(NA)	(NA)	(NA)
Academic science/engineering obligations	7,309	8,082	9,261	11,233	12,503	13,188	13,397	13,080
Percent of total	67.6	57.7	66.2	68.8	(NA)	(NA)	(NA)	(NA)
Research and development	4,833	7,018	7,970	9,672	10,740	11,315	11,282	11,171
Research and development plant	150	64	145	152	253	206	317	225
Other science/engineering activities	2,326	1,000	1,146	1,409	1,510	1,667	1,798	1,684
Nonscience/engineering activities	3,505	5,917	4,739	5,104	(NA)	(NA)	(NA)	(NA)

NA Not available. [1] Percent change from immediate prior year. [2] Based on gross domestic product implicit price deflator.

Source: U.S. National Science Foundation, *Survey of Federal S&E Support to Universities, Colleges, and Nonprofit Institutions*, annual.

No. 996. Federal R&D Obligations to Selected Universities and Colleges: 1981 to 1996

[In thousands of dollars, (4,410,931 represents $4,410,931,000). For fiscal years ending in year shown; see text, Section 9, State and Local Government. For the top 45 institutions receiving Federal R&D funds in 1996. Awards to the administrative offices of university systems are excluded from totals for individual institutions because that allocation of funds is unknown, but those awards are included in "total all institutions"]

Major institution ranked by total 1995 Federal R&D obligations	Obligations ($1,000)			Rank		
	1981	1985	1996	1981	1985	1996
Total, all institutions [1]	4,410,931	6,246,181	12,323,165	(X)	(X)	(X)
45 institutions, percent of total	62.1	60.8	59.1	(X)	(X)	(X)
Johns Hopkins University	363,429	297,374	611,683	1	1	1
University of Washington	99,965	146,179	309,853	4	4	2
Massachusetts Institute of Technology	146,035	189,558	229,174	2	2	5
Stanford University	106,073	174,961	294,859	3	3	3
University of Michigan	73,999	108,035	261,284	11	11	4
University of California—San Diego	91,403	103,633	226,260	6	13	6
University of California—Los Angeles	94,945	128,211	208,356	5	5	9
University of Wisconsin—Madison	86,918	124,604	208,300	8	7	10
University of Minnesota	72,001	103,272	192,556	14	14	13
Cornell University	72,671	119,966	178,194	13	8	16
University of California—San Francisco	64,814	98,536	218,935	15	16	7
University of Pennsylvania	76,136	103,119	216,699	10	15	8
Harvard University	87,830	109,414	205,360	7	9	11
Columbia University—Main Division	83,659	127,331	190,230	9	6	14
Yale University	73,526	109,227	197,042	12	10	12
University of Pittsburgh	38,512	58,620	154,120	29	28	22
Washington University	54,170	71,978	186,572	17	22	15
University of Colorado	46,146	71,424	168,953	22	23	17
University of North Carolina at Chapel Hill	38,447	63,105	164,603	30	27	19
Duke University	44,287	69,169	164,886	23	26	18
Pennsylvania State University	47,099	76,726	155,468	21	19	21
University Southern California	49,221	89,706	164,049	20	17	20
University of California—Berkeley	64,065	106,710	138,973	16	12	23
University of Arizona	36,308	49,740	120,770	33	37	26
Case Western Reserve University	33,744	47,994	136,514	38	40	24
University of Alabama—Birmingham	29,970	44,093	134,107	44	46	25
University of Texas at Austin	43,756	72,379	104,489	24	21	32
University of Illinois—Urbana Champaign	53,583	83,122	116,740	19	18	28
California Institute of Technology	32,959	55,083	112,221	40	32	29
University of Rochester	42,983	70,379	110,951	25	25	30
University of Chicago	53,992	71,194	118,110	18	24	27
Northwestern University	32,446	48,260	109,279	47	39	31
University of California—Davis	31,757	43,156	95,994	42	47	34
Ohio State University	42,899	56,065	90,923	26	30	39
Vanderbilt University	27,426	39,909	92,050	49	48	38
University of Iowa	35,300	55,117	93,542	34	31	35
University of Utah	38,163	50,938	88,622	31	36	41
University of Maryland—College Park	27,313	51,073	88,507	50	35	42
Indiana University	29,276	39,118	90,158	45	49	40
Georgetown University	10,327	18,194	73,604	103	91	50
Boston University	27,019	46,152	92,900	51	43	36
New York University	40,636	74,577	84,169	28	20	44
Baylor College of Medicine	35,062	45,837	92,211	35	45	37
University of Florida	30,845	47,716	81,495	43	41	46
University of Miami	28,956	33,709	76,826	46	59	48

X Not applicable. [1] Includes other institutions, not shown separately.

Source: U.S. National Science Foundation, *Federal S&E Support to Universities and Colleges and Nonprofit Institutions*, annual.

U.S. Census Bureau, Statistical Abstract of the United States: 1999

No. 997. Funds for Performance of Industrial R&D, by Source of Funds and Selected Industries: 1980 to 1997

[In millions of dollars, (44,505 represents $44,505,000,000). For calendar years. Covers basic research, applied research, and development]

Industry	1987 SIC [1] code	1980	1985	1990	1995	1996	1997
CURRENT DOLLARS							
Total funds	(X)	44,505	84,239	109,727	132,103	144,667	157,539
Chemicals and allied products	28	4,636	8,540	13,291	17,547	(D)	(D)
Petroleum refining and extraction	13,29	1,552	(D)	2,306	1,760	1,654	(D)
Machinery	35	5,901	12,216	14,446	(D)	13,455	18,499
Electrical equipment	36	9,175	14,432	13,400	18,751	22,498	24,585
Motor vehicles and motor vehicles equipment	371	4,955	6,984	(D)	(D)	(D)	(D)
Aircraft and missiles	372,376	9,198	22,231	20,635	16,951	16,224	16,296
Professional and scientific instruments	38	3,029	5,013	7,055	11,976	12,149	13,458
All other [2]	(X)	6,059	(D)	(D)	(D)	(D)	(D)
Company funds	(X)	30,476	57,043	81,602	108,652	121,015	133,611
Chemicals and allied products	28	4,264	8,310	13,168	17,337	17,520	18,628
Petroleum refining and extraction	13,29	1,401	2,194	2,289	1,754	1,630	1,612
Machinery	35	5,254	10,721	13,575	9,676	13,338	18,393
Electrical equipment	36	5,431	9,271	9,267	17,060	20,356	22,747
Motor vehicles and motor vehicles equipment	371	4,300	6,164	8,594	13,590	14,528	13,758
Aircraft and missiles	372,376	2,570	5,387	5,387	5,489	5,710	5,677
Professional and scientific instruments	38	2,456	4,622	6,318	8,516	8,207	8,958
All other [2]	(X)	4,800	10,112	23,004	35,230	39,726	43,838
CONSTANT (1992) DOLLARS [3]							
Total funds	(X)	73,769	107,270	117,230	122,590	131,277	140,159
Chemicals and allied products	28	7,684	10,875	14,200	16,283	(D)	(D)
Petroleum refining and extraction	13,29	2,573	(D)	2,464	1,633	1,501	(D)
Machinery	35	9,781	15,556	15,434	(D)	12,210	16,458
Electrical equipment	36	15,208	18,378	14,316	17,401	20,416	21,873
Motor vehicles and motor vehicles equipment	371	8,213	8,893	(D)	(D)	(D)	(D)
Aircraft and missiles	372,376	15,246	28,309	22,046	15,730	14,722	14,498
Professional and scientific instruments	38	5,021	6,384	7,537	11,114	11,025	11,973
All other [2]	(X)	10,043	(D)	(D)	(D)	(D)	(D)
Company funds	(X)	50,515	72,638	87,182	100,828	109,814	118,871
Chemicals and allied products	28	7,068	10,582	14,068	16,089	15,898	16,573
Petroleum refining and extraction	13,29	2,322	2,794	2,446	1,628	1,479	1,434
Machinery	35	8,709	13,652	14,503	8,979	12,103	16,364
Electrical equipment	36	9,002	11,806	9,901	15,831	18,472	20,238
Motor vehicles and motor vehicles equipment	371	7,127	7,849	9,182	12,611	13,183	12,240
Aircraft and missiles	372,376	4,260	7,193	5,755	5,094	5,181	5,051
Professional and scientific instruments	38	4,071	5,886	6,750	7,903	7,447	7,970
All other [2]	(X)	7,956	12,877	24,577	32,693	36,049	39,002

D Figure withheld to avoid disclosure of information pertaining to a specific organization or individual.   X Not applicable. [1] Prior to 1993, 1972 Standard Industrial Classification; beginning 1993, 1987 Standard Industrial Classification; see text, Section 17, Business.   [2] All other manufacturing and nonmanufacturing.   [3] Based on gross domestic product implicit price deflator.

Source: U.S. National Science Foundation, *Research and Development in Industry*, annual.

No. 998. R&D Funds in R&D-Performing Manufacturing Companies, by Industry: 1980 to 1997

Industry	1987 SIC [1] code	Total R&D funds as a percent of net sales					Company R&D funds as a percent of net sales				
		1980	1990	1995	1996	1997	1980	1990	1995	1996	1997
Total [2]	(X)	3.0	4.2	3.6	3.5	3.4	2.1	3.1	2.9	3.0	2.9
Food and kindred products [3]	20	0.4	(D)	0.5	0.4	0.5	(D)	0.5	0.5	0.4	0.5
Paper and allied products	26	1.0	1.0	(D)	(D)	(D)	1.0	1.0	1.0	1.2	1.1
Chemicals and allied products	28	3.6	5.3	4.7	(D)	(D)	3.3	5.3	4.7	5.3	5.3
Petroleum refining and extraction	13,29	0.6	0.9	0.7	0.7	(D)	0.5	0.9	0.7	0.7	0.6
Rubber products	30	2.2	(D)	(D)	(D)	(D)	(D)	2.1	1.6	1.8	1.4
Stone, clay, and glass products	32	1.4	(D)	1.5	1.3	1.8	1.3	1.7	1.5	1.2	1.8
Primary metals	33	0.7	0.8	0.5	(D)	0.7	0.5	0.8	0.5	0.6	0.6
Fabricated metal products	34	1.4	1.4	1.1	(D)	1.6	1.2	1.1	1.1	1.4	1.5
Machinery	35	5.0	7.7	(D)	5.2	5.6	4.5	7.2	3.6	5.1	5.6
Electrical equipment	36	6.6	6.5	6.0	6.7	6.2	3.9	4.5	5.4	6.1	5.7
Motor vehicles and motor vehicle equipment	371	4.9	(D)	(D)	(D)	(D)	4.2	3.7	3.6	4.2	3.8
Aircraft and missiles	372,376	13.7	11.8	12.9	12.9	11.2	3.8	3.1	4.2	4.5	3.9
Professional and scientific instruments	38	7.5	8.0	10.3	11.5	11.6	6.1	7.1	7.3	7.7	7.7

D Figure withheld to avoid disclosure of information pertaining to a specific organization or individual.   X Not applicable. [1] Prior to 1994, 1972 Standard Industrial Classification; beginning 1994, 1987 Standard Industrial Classification; see text, Section 17, Business.   [2] Includes all manufacturing industries.   [3] Includes tobacco products (SIC 21) beginning 1985.

Source: U.S. National Science Foundation, *Research and Development in Industry*, annual.

No. 999. Federal Obligations for Research, by Field of Science: 1980 to 1999

[In millions of dollars, (11,597 represents $11,597,000,000). **For fiscal years ending in year shown;** see text, Section 9, State and Local Government. Excludes R&D plant]

Field	1980	1985	1990	1994	1995	1996	1997	1998, prel.	1999, prel.
CURRENT DOLLARS									
Research, total	11,597	16,133	21,622	27,433	28,570	28,265	29,366	31,471	32,992
Basic	4,674	7,819	11,286	13,545	13,893	14,462	14,942	15,862	16,914
Applied	6,923	8,315	10,337	13,888	14,677	13,803	14,423	15,609	16,079
Life sciences	4,192	6,363	8,830	11,291	11,869	12,100	12,661	13,621	14,366
Psychology	199	327	449	550	621	513	545	578	612
Physical sciences	2,001	3,046	3,809	4,258	4,282	3,964	4,149	4,335	4,578
Environmental sciences	1,261	1,404	2,174	2,828	2,947	2,997	3,046	3,288	3,261
Mathematics and computer sciences ...	241	575	841	1,292	1,531	1,554	1,672	1,831	2,255
Engineering	2,830	3,618	4,227	5,509	5,740	5,680	5,690	6,090	6,023
Social sciences	524	460	630	647	679	674	696	824	883
Other sciences, n.e.c. [1]	350	342	664	1,058	902	783	906	904	994
CONSTANT (1992) DOLLARS [2]									
Research, total	19,564	20,586	23,212	26,097	26,498	25,623	26,047	27,394	28,155
Basic	7,885	9,977	12,116	12,885	12,885	13,111	13,254	13,807	14,434
Applied	11,679	10,610	11,097	13,211	13,613	12,513	12,794	13,587	13,721
Life sciences	7,072	8,119	9,479	10,741	11,008	10,969	11,231	11,857	12,260
Psychology	336	417	482	523	576	465	484	503	523
Physical sciences	3,375	3,887	4,089	4,051	3,971	3,594	3,680	3,774	3,907
Environmental sciences	2,127	1,791	2,334	2,690	2,734	2,717	2,701	2,862	2,783
Mathematics and computer sciences ...	406	734	903	1,229	1,420	1,409	1,483	1,594	1,924
Engineering	4,774	4,616	4,537	5,241	5,324	5,149	5,047	5,301	5,140
Social sciences	884	587	676	616	629	611	618	717	754
Other sciences, n.e.c. [1]	590	436	713	1,007	836	710	804	787	848

[1] N.e.c. = Not elsewhere classified.   [2] Based on gross domestic product implicit price deflator.

Source: U.S. National Science Foundation, *Federal Funds for Research and Development,* annual.

No. 1000. R&D Scientists and Engineers—Employment and Cost, by Industry: 1980 to 1997

[469.2 represents 469,200. Data are estimates; on average full-time-equivalent (FTE) basis]

Industry	1987 SIC [1] code	1980	1985	1990	1992	1993	1994	1995	1996	1997
EMPLOYED SCIENTISTS										
Average FTE of scientists and engineers (1,000) [2] [3]	(X)	469.2	646.8	758.5	772.0	766.6	766.6	757.3	789.5	859.3
Chemicals [4]	28	53.1	71.1	80.4	85.6	93.1	89.8	96.4	97.0	91.7
Machinery	35	65.7	81.7	113.3	99.3	97.4	83.9	69.5	78.0	88.0
Electrical equipment [5]	36	100.7	113.2	105.2	91.9	89.2	92.9	99.9	114.6	130.9
Motor vehicles	371	36.7	28.7	49.4	44.5	45.1	48.1	51.1	54.1	60.4
Aircraft and missiles.	372,376	90.6	130.2	115.3	92.9	97.9	85.4	68.2	79.5	95.1
CONSTANT (1992) DOLLARS [6]										
Cost per scientist or engineer ($1,000) [3] [7]	(X)	164.8	164.7	154.9	155.6	151.5	147.9	150.7	152.3	151.2
Chemicals [4]	28	152.5	148.6	174.5	91.8	(D)	(D)	84.0	82.1	(D)
Machinery	35	152.3	90.7	152.9	126.7	106.9	47.9	(D)	69.4	150.0
Electrical equipment [5]	36	154.5	156.4	154.9	147.4	144.5	141.5	146.7	152.2	147.6
Motor vehicles	371	234.2	142.0	(D)	(D)	(D)	(D)	(D)	(D)	(D)
Aircraft and missiles.	372,376	190.6	198.3	208.7	178.5	191.8	172.9	185.7	174.2	160.5

D Withheld to avoid disclosure.   X Not applicable.   [1] Prior to 1992, by 1972 Standard Industrial Classification; beginning 1992, 1987 Standard Industrial Classification; see text, Section 17, Business.   [2] The mean number of FTE R&D scientists and engineers employed in January of the year shown and the following January.   [3] Includes industries not shown separately.   [4] Includes allied products.   [5] Includes communication.   [6] Based on gross domestic product implicit price deflator.   [7] Represents the arithmetic mean of the numbers of R&D scientists and engineers reported in each industry for January in 2 consecutive years divided into total R&D expenditures in each industry.

Source: U.S. National Science Foundation, *Research and Development in Industry,* annual.

Science and Technology   623

No. 1001. Civilian Employment of Scientists, Engineers, and Technicians, by Occupation and Industry: 1996

[In thousands, (4,885.5 represents 4,885,500). Based on sample and subject to sampling error. For details, see source]

Occupation	Total [1]	Min- ing [2]	Con- struc- tion	Manu- facturing	Trans- por- tation [3]	Trade	Fire [4]	Serv- ices	Govern- ment	Self em- ployed
Scientists, engineers, and technicians.......	4,885.5	54.6	67.2	1,394.5	208.9	236.5	192.1	1,792.2	694.2	235.9
Scientists	665.7	11.4	0.4	79.9	5.4	3.8	11.8	258.9	197.9	92.5
Physical scientists	206.7	9.9	0.4	51.3	3.0	2.4	0.8	81.6	47.2	10.2
Life scientists...........	180.0	0.2	0.1	27.1	1.2	1.4	0.4	62.9	74.7	8.3
Mathematical scientists	15.6	(NA)	(NA)	1.5	0.4	(NA)	3.1	4.5	4.8	1.3
Social scientists	263.5	1.3	(NA)	(NA)	0.8	(NA)	7.6	109.9	71.2	72.7
Computer systems analysts, engineers and scientists	932.8	3.7	2.1	196.6	42.2	60.8	86.5	375.0	107.4	58.4
Engineers [5]	1,382.4	18.9	31.0	620.4	68.7	39.1	10.5	370.0	177.9	45.8
Civil engineers..........	196.1	0.6	10.9	7.5	5.3	0.5	0.4	86.6	71.3	13.0
Electrical/electronics	367.2	0.6	9.4	163.6	34.6	13.5	1.3	96.1	34.9	13.1
Mechanical engineers	227.9	1.6	5.1	131.2	4.2	7.2	(NA)	61.6	11.8	4.0
Engineering and science technicians..............	1,235.8	15.7	29.4	432.8	66.9	91.7	4.3	423.0	154.9	11.8
Electrical/electronics technicians............	297.4	1.0	7.9	104.3	21.4	69.5	1.4	70.0	20.3	1.7
Engineering technicians.....	400.2	4.9	4.2	150.9	25.5	11.4	0.3	105.9	92.9	3.2
Drafters	309.9	1.9	16.9	96.5	16.7	7.1	1.3	152.2	10.2	4.6
Science technicians	228.3	8.0	0.4	81.1	3.3	3.7	1.2	94.9	31.5	2.3
Surveyors..............	100.7	2.4	2.6	0.1	2.8	(NA)	0.7	62.5	22.0	7.5
Computer programmers	568.0	2.4	1.5	64.8	22.8	41.0	78.3	302.9	34.0	20.0

NA Not available.   [1] Includes agriculture, forestry, and fishing not shown separately.   [2] Includes oil and gas extraction.
[3] Includes communications and public utilities.   [4] Finance, insurance, and real estate.   [5] Includes kinds of engineers and technicians not shown separately.

Source: U.S. Bureau of Labor Statistics, *Monthly Labor Review*, November 1997; and unpublished data. (Data collected biennially.)

No. 1002. Graduate Science/Engineering Students in Doctorate-Granting Colleges: 1985 to 1997

[355.8 represents 355,800. As of fall. Includes outlying areas]

| Field of science or engineering | Total (1,000) | | | Percent— | | | | | | | |
| | | | | Female | | | Foreign | | Part-time | | |
	1985	1990	1997	1985	1990	1997	1990	1997	1985	1990	1997
Total, all surveyed fields	355.8	398.8	424.6	34.5	37.6	43.8	25.4	23.3	32.4	31.1	29.0
Science/engineering	317.2	351.7	359.5	29.5	32.4	38.2	27.7	26.3	30.7	28.9	27.1
Engineering, total	90.2	99.8	94.5	11.5	13.6	18.5	36.6	37.3	39.7	35.9	32.4
Sciences, total	226.9	251.9	265.0	36.6	39.8	45.2	24.1	22.3	27.2	26.1	25.2
Physical sciences	29.4	32.5	29.7	20.5	23.4	28.0	37.0	35.8	11.9	11.3	11.4
Environmental.........	14.1	12.9	13.0	25.3	29.1	36.2	20.1	18.9	23.8	23.6	23.5
Mathematical sciences ..	15.4	17.5	14.9	29.0	30.6	33.7	35.5	35.4	27.6	24.5	22.4
Computer sciences	24.2	28.1	30.1	25.2	23.2	26.7	32.7	37.8	48.6	47.2	45.2
Agricultural sciences ...	10.9	10.6	11.1	25.8	29.3	38.0	28.8	24.2	18.4	17.9	21.7
Biological sciences.....	42.2	46.4	52.9	42.5	45.5	49.5	24.2	20.7	16.1	14.8	14.8
Psychology..........	30.8	35.9	39.1	59.7	65.6	69.4	4.6	4.6	30.6	29.0	26.5
Social sciences	59.9	68.0	74.3	39.8	42.8	48.8	21.7	18.9	34.4	32.9	30.6
Health fields, total.	38.7	47.2	65.2	75.7	76.9	74.8	8.6	7.1	46.2	47.4	39.5

Source: U.S. National Science Foundation, *Survey of Graduate Science Engineering Students and Postdoctorates*, annual.

U.S. Census Bureau, Statistical Abstract of the United States: 1999

No. 1003. Science and Engineering Degree Recipients in 1995 and 1996:

[In thousands, (708.9 represents 708,900). Based on survey a and subject to sampling error; see source for details]

Degree and field	Graduates 1995 and 1996 (1,000)	1996 [1] Percent distribution				Median salary [4] ($1,000)
		In school [2]	Employed		Not employed or not FT students	
			In S&E [3]	In other		
Bachelor's recipients	**708.9**	**21**	**21**	**53**	**5**	**28.2**
All science fields	593.8	23	12	60	5	26.0
Computer and information sciences	41.0	6	57	34	3	37.7
Mathematical sciences	26.8	19	15	63	3	29.8
Life and related sciences	139.0	31	11	53	5	22.8
Physical and related sciences	36.6	38	26	33	3	27.3
Psychology	138.0	24	6	65	5	22.3
Social and related sciences	212.4	18	6	70	6	26.4
All engineering fields	115.1	13	65	18	3	37.7
Aerospace and related engineering	3.0	22	48	27	2	34.0
Chemical engineering	11.6	17	65	14	4	39.3
Civil and architectural engineering	20.7	14	63	20	3	34.4
Electrical, electronics, computer and communications engineering	32.9	10	70	16	4	40.5
Industrial engineering	5.8	8	66	24	2	37.6
Mechanical engineering	27.9	11	71	15	3	38.2
Other engineering	13.2	21	52	25	3	34.1
Master's recipients	**149.5**	**21**	**49**	**27**	**3**	**41.5**
All science fields	102.5	23	36	36	4	37.2
Computer and mathematical sciences	18.2	6	74	18	2	51.2
Mathematical sciences	7.9	27	37	32	3	39.7
Life and related sciences	15.3	32	37	27	4	32.4
Physical and related sciences	9.7	37	42	18	3	33.6
Social and related sciences	25.1	26	15	54	5	35.0
All engineering fields	47.0	15	75	9	2	49.9
Aerospace and related engineering	1.5	31	54	15	1	48.8
Chemical engineering	2.0	33	61	4	2	47.6
Civil and architectural engineering	6.5	11	76	11	1	41.9
Electrical, electronics, computer and communications engineering	16.2	15	77	7	1	55.0
Industrial engineering	3.2	13	70	16	1	49.9
Mechanical engineering	7.2	16	72	10	2	47.7
Other engineering	10.4	10	78	9	4	49.0

[1] As of April. [2] Full-time students. [3] In science and engineering. [4] For the principal job. Excludes full-time students, the self-employed, and persons whose principal job is less than 35 hours per week.
Source: National Science Foundation/SRS, *National Survey of Recent College Graduates: 1996.*

No. 1004. Doctorates Conferred, by Recipients' Characteristics: 1990 and 1997

[In percent, except as indicated]

Characteristic	1990, total	1997									
		All fields [1]	Engineering	Physical sciences [2]	Earth sciences	Mathematics	Computer sciences	Biological sciences [3]	Agricultural	Social sciences [4]	Psychology
Total conferred (number)	**36,068**	**42,705**	**6,052**	**3,711**	**862**	**1,112**	**889**	**5,717**	**966**	**4,049**	**3,489**
Male	63.7	59	87	78	76	77	83	57	74	61	33
Female	36.3	41	12	22	24	23	16	43	26	39	67
Median age [5]	33.9	34	31	30	33	31	32	31	34	35	33
CITIZENSHIP [6]											
Total conferred (number)	**34,697**	**39,058**	**5,677**	**3,488**	**799**	**1,032**	**820**	**5,415**	**893**	**3,726**	**3,103**
U.S. citizen	71.8	71	47	61	65	50	51	67	52	68	93
Foreign citizen	28.2	29	53	39	35	50	49	33	48	32	7
RACE/ETHNICITY [7]											
Total conferred (number)	**26,604**	**30,601**	**3,281**	**2,473**	**587**	**616**	**506**	**4,203**	**546**	**2,817**	**2,976**
White [8]	86.5	78	69	76	80	76	71	74	75	78	83
Black [8]	3.8	5	3	2	2	1	1	3	4	6	5
Asian/Pacific [8]	4.9	10	22	16	12	16	21	17	12	8	4
Indian/Alaskan [8]	0.4	1	-	-	-	-	-	-	1	1	1
Hispanic	3.1	4	3	3	3	3	3	3	5	3	6
Other/unknown	1.4	3	3	3	3	3	4	3	4	3	2

- Represents zero. [1] Includes other fields, not shown separately. [2] Astronomy, physics, and chemistry. [3] Biochemistry, botany, microbiology, physiology, zoology, and related fields. [4] Anthropology, sociology, political science, economics, international relations and related fields. [5] For definition of median, see Guide to Tabular Presentation. [6] For those with known citizenship. Includes those with temporary visas. [7] Excludes those with temporary visas. [8] Non-Hispanic.
Source: U.S. National Science Foundation, Division of Science Resources Studies, Survey of Earned Doctorates, *Selected Data on Science and Engineering Doctorate Awards*, annual.

U.S. Census Bureau, Statistical Abstract of the United States: 1999

No. 1005. Space Vehicle Systems—Net Sales and Backlog Orders: 1965 to 1998

[In millions of dollars, (2,449 represents $2,449,000,000). Backlog orders as of Dec. Based on data from major companies engaged in manufacture of aerospace products. Includes parts but excludes engines and propulsion units]

Year	Net sales			Backlog orders			Year	Net sales			Backlog orders		
	Total	Military	Non-military	Total	Military	Non-military		Total	Military	Non-military	Total	Military	Non-military
1965	2,449	602	1,847	2,203	503	1,700	1988	8,622	6,190	[1]2,432	10,838	7,880	[1]2,958
1970	1,956	1,025	931	1,184	786	398	1989	9,758	6,457	[1]3,301	13,356	9,192	[1]4,164
1975	2,119	1,096	1,023	1,304	1,019	285	1990	9,691	6,556	[1]3,135	12,462	8,130	[1]4,332
1980	3,483	1,461	2,022	1,814	951	863	1991	10,515	6,770	[1]3,745	11,664	6,221	[1]5,443
1981	3,856	1,736	2,120	3,174	2,164	1,010	1992	9,266	5,887	[1]3,379	12,809	7,622	[1]5,187
1982	4,749	2,606	2,143	4,337	2,403	1,934	1993	8,309	4,175	[1]4,133	15,203	8,332	[1]6,871
1983	4,940	2,420	2,520	4,865	2,733	2,132	1994	10,594	5,707	[1]4,887	12,888	6,732	[1]6,156
1984	5,225	3,019	2,206	4,624	3,099	1,525	1995	11,314	4,782	[1]6,532	15,650	5,872	[1]9,778
1985	6,300	4,241	2,059	6,707	4,941	1,766	1996	11,209	4,777	[1]6,432	18,262	5,864	[1]12,398
1986	6,304	4,579	[1]1,725	8,063	6,028	[1]2,035	1997	11,698	5,613	[1]6,085	23,004	9,125	[1]13,879
1987	8,051	5,248	[1]2,803	12,393	9,460	[1]2,933	1998	13,410	4,916	[1]8,494	23,357	8,790	[1]14,567

[1] Includes data for nonmilitary missile systems and parts.

Source: U.S. Census Bureau, Current Industrial Reports, MA-37D, Aerospace Industry (Orders, Sales, and Backlog) and, beginning 1994, Internet site <http://www.census.gov/cir/www>.

No. 1006. Federal Outlays for General Science, Space, and Other Technology: 1970 to 2004

[In billions of dollars, (4.5 represents $4,500,000,000). For fiscal years ending in year shown; see text, Section 9, State and Local Governments]

Year	Current dollars			Constant (1992) dollars		
	Total	General science/basic research	Space and other technologies	Total	General science/basic research	Space and other technologies
1970	4.5	0.9	3.6	16.0	3.4	12.6
1975	4.0	1.0	3.0	10.0	2.6	7.4
1980	5.8	1.4	4.5	10.0	2.4	7.6
1982	7.2	1.6	5.6	10.4	2.3	8.1
1983	7.9	1.6	6.3	10.9	2.3	8.6
1984	8.3	1.8	6.5	11.0	2.4	8.6
1985	8.6	2.0	6.6	11.1	2.6	8.5
1986	9.0	2.2	6.8	11.2	2.8	8.5
1987	9.2	2.2	7.0	11.2	2.7	8.4
1988	10.8	2.4	8.4	12.6	2.8	9.8
1989	12.8	2.6	10.2	14.4	2.9	11.4
1990	14.4	2.8	11.6	15.6	3.1	12.6
1991	16.1	3.1	13.0	16.5	3.2	13.3
1992	16.4	3.5	12.8	16.4	3.5	12.8
1993	17.0	3.9	13.1	16.4	3.8	12.6
1994	16.2	3.8	12.4	15.1	3.6	11.5
1995	16.7	4.1	12.6	15.2	3.7	11.5
1996	16.7	4.0	12.7	14.8	3.5	11.2
1997	17.1	4.1	13.1	15.0	3.6	11.4
1998	18.2	5.3	12.9	15.4	4.5	10.9
1999, est.	18.5	5.7	12.8	15.5	4.8	10.8
2000, est.	18.5	6.2	12.3	15.3	5.2	10.1
2001, est.	18.9	6.5	12.4	15.5	5.4	10.1
2002, est.	19.1	6.7	12.4	15.5	5.4	10.1
2003, est.	19.3	6.7	12.5	15.3	5.3	9.9
2004, est.	19.3	6.7	12.6	14.9	5.2	9.7

Source: U.S. Office of Management and Budget, Budget of the United States, Historical Tables, Fiscal Year 2000, annual.

No. 1007. U.S. Commercial Space Revenues, by Type: 1990 to 1995

[In millions of dollars (3,385 represents $3,385,000,000). For calendar years]

Industry	1990	1991	1992	1993	1994	1995 [1]
Total	3,385	4,370	4,860	5,295	6,640	7,768
Commercial satellites delivered	1,000	1,300	1,300	1,100	1,400	1,550
Satellite services	800	1,200	1,500	1,850	2,330	2,740
Fixed	735	1,115	1,275	1,600	1,980	2,340
Mobile	65	85	225	250	350	400
Satellite ground equipment	860	1,300	1,400	1,600	1,970	2,570
Mobile-equipment	145	280	350	420	480	510
Commercial launches	570	380	450	465	580	513
Remote sensing data and services	155	190	210	250	300	340
Commercial R&D infrastructure	-	-	-	30	60	55

- Represents zero. [1] Forecast.

Source: U.S. Department of Commerce, International Trade Administration, U.S. Industrial Outlook, annual; and unpublished data.

No. 1008. National Aeronautics and Space Administration—Budget Summary: 1998 to 2004

[In millions of dollars, (13,647.7 represents $13,647,700,000)]

Item	1998	1999	2000	2001	2002	2003	2004
Total	**13,647.7**	**13,665.0**	**13,578.4**	**13,752.4**	**13,757.4**	**13,750.4**	**13,750.4**
International space station	2,441.3	2,304.7	2,482.7	2,328.0	2,091.0	1,721.1	1,573.0
Space station	2,331.3	2,304.7	2,482.7	2,328.0	2,091.0	1,721.1	1,573.0
U.S. and Russian cooperative program	110.0	(X)	(X)	(X)	(X)	(X)	(X)
Launch vehicles and payload operations	3,118.2	3,175.3	3,155.3	3,216.0	3,198.5	3,203.7	3,209.2
Space shuttle	2,912.8	2,998.3	2,986.2	3,033.1	3,014.0	2,984.0	2,984.0
Payload utilization and operations	205.4	177.0	169.1	182.9	184.5	219.7	225.2
Science, aeronautics and technology	5,690.0	5,653.9	5,424.7	5,657.3	5,781.3	6,141.0	6,248.6
Space science	2,043.8	2,119.2	2,196.6	2,346.8	2,439.4	2,634.4	2,851.3
Life and microgravity sciences and applications	214.2	263.5	256.2	265.2	263.2	263.2	278.5
Earth science	1,417.3	1,413.8	1,459.1	1,462.8	1,420.5	1,373.0	1,424.4
Aerospace technology	1,483.9	1,338.9	1,006.5	950.4	981.6	1,013.6	998.6
Mission communication services	400.8	380.0	406.3	382.1	296.6	296.8	265.3
Academic programs	130.0	138.5	100.0	100.0	100.1	100.0	100.0
Future planning (space launch)	(NA)	(NA)	(NA)	150.0	280.0	460.0	330.0
Mission support	2,380.0	2,511.1	2,494.9	2,530.3	2,665.8	2,663.8	2,699.8
Safety, mission assurance, engineering and advanced concepts	37.8	35.6	43.0	45.0	49.0	49.0	49.0
Space communication services	194.2	185.8	89.7	109.3	174.2	89.5	35.9
Research and program management	2,025.6	2,121.2	2,181.2	2,195.0	2,261.6	2,344.3	2,432.9
Construction of facilities	122.4	168.5	181.0	181.0	181.0	181.0	181.0
Inspector General	18.2	20.0	20.8	20.8	20.8	20.8	20.8

NA Not available.   X Not applicable.

Source: U.S. National Aeronautics and Space Administration, Internet site <http://ifmp.nasa.gov/codeb/budget/2000HTML/MYB.htm>.

No. 1009. NASA Space Shuttle Operations Expenditures: 1996 to 1999

[In millions of dollars, (2,485.4 represents $2,485,400,000). Data are funding requirements fiscal years shown]

Operation	1996	1997	1998	1999
Total	**2,485.4**	**2,464.9**	**2,369.4**	**2,487.4**
Orbiter and integration	521.0	492.6	502.9	573.4
Orbiter	378.5	124.7	126.2	113.9
System integration	142.5	367.9	376.7	459.5
Propulsion	1,061.5	1,124.7	1,061.8	1,093.4
External tank	327.5	352.4	341.3	404.8
Space shuttle main engine	185.0	208.3	204.6	175.6
Reusable solid rocket motor	395.7	412.8	380.4	362.7
Solid rocket booster	153.3	151.2	135.5	150.3
Mission and launch operations	902.9	847.6	804.7	820.6
Launch and landing operations	544.0	801.4	710.1	728.4
Mission and crew operations	358.9	46.2	94.6	92.2

Source: U.S. National Aeronautics and Space Administration, *NASA Pocket Statistics*, annual.

No. 1010. Worldwide Successful Space Launches: 1957 to 1998

[Criterion of success is attainment of earth orbit or earth escape]

Country	Total, 1957-98	1957-64	1965-69	1970-74	1975-79	1980-84	1985-89	1990-94	1995	1996	1997	1998
Total	**3,969**	**289**	**586**	**555**	**607**	**605**	**550**	**466**	**75**	**73**	**86**	**77**
Soviet Union/CIS [1]	2,572	82	302	405	461	483	447	283	32	25	28	24
United States	1,158	207	279	139	126	93	61	122	27	33	37	34
Japan	54	-	-	5	10	12	11	9	2	1	2	2
ESA [2]	107	-	-	-	1	8	21	33	11	10	12	11
China	55	-	-	2	6	6	9	15	2	3	6	6
France	10	-	4	3	3	-	-	-	-	-	-	-
India	8	-	-	-	-	3	-	3	-	1	1	-
Israel	3	-	-	-	-	-	1	1	1	-	-	-
Australia	1	-	1	-	-	-	-	-	-	-	-	-
United Kingdom	1	-	-	1	-	-	-	-	-	-	-	-

- Represents zero.   [1] Commonwealth of Independent States.   [2] European Space Agency. Includes launches by Arianespace.

Source: Library of Congress, Congressional Research Service, Science Policy Research Division, *Space Activities of the United States, CIS, and Other Launching Countries/Organizations 1957-1994*, July 31, 1995; and forthcoming report.

Science and Technology   627

No. 1011. Space Shuttle Launches—Summary: 1981 to June 1999

Flight number	Mission date	Orbiter name	Crew size (up/down)	Days/hours duration	Flight number	Mission date	Orbiter name	Crew size (up/down)	Days/hours duration
1	4/12/81	Columbia	2	2	55	4/26/93	Columbia	7	10
2	11/12/81	Columbia	2	2	57	6/21/93	Endeavour	6	10
3	3/22/82	Columbia	2	8	51	9/12/93	Discovery	5	10
4	6/27/82	Columbia	2	7	58	10/18/93	Columbia	7	14
5	11/11/82	Columbia	4	5	61	12/2/93	Endeavour	7	11
6	4/4/83	Challenger	4	5	60	2/3/94	Discovery	6	8
7	6/18/83	Challenger	5	6	62	3/4/94	Columbia	5	14
8	8/30/83	Challenger	5	6	59	4/9/94	Endeavour	6	11
9	11/28/83	Columbia	6	10	65	7/8/94	Columbia	7	15
10	2/3/84	Challenger	5	8	64	9/9/94	Discovery	6	11
11	4/6/84	Challenger	5	7	68	9/30/94	Endeavour	6	11
12	8/30/84	Discovery	6	7	66	11/3/94	Atlantis	6	11
13	10/5/84	Challenger	7	8	63	2/3/95	Discovery	6	8
14	11/8/84	Discovery	5	8	67	3/2/95	Endeavour	7	17
15	1/24/85	Discovery	5	4	71	6/27/95	Atlantis	7/8	10
16	4/12/85	Discovery	7	7	70	7/13/95	Discovery	5	9
17	4/29/85	Challenger	7	7	69	9/7/95	Endeavour	5	11
18	6/17/85	Discovery	7	7	73	10/20/95	Columbia	7	16
19	7/29/85	Challenger	7	8	74	11/8/95	Atlantis	5	8
20	8/27/85	Discovery	5	7	72	1/11/96	Endeavour	6	9
21	10/3/85	Atlantis	5	4	75	2/22/96	Columbia	7	16
22	10/30/85	Challenger	8	7	76	3/22/96	Atlantis	6/5	9
23	11/26/85	Atlantis	7	7	77	5/19/96	Endeavour	6	10
24	1/12/86	Columbia	7	6	78	6/20/96	Columbia	7	17
25	1/28/86	Challenger	7	-	79	9/16/96	Atlantis	6	10
26	9/29/88	Discovery	5	4	80	11/20/96	Columbia	5	18
27	12/2/88	Atlantis	5	4	81	1/12/97	Atlantis	6	10/5
29	3/13/89	Discovery	5	5	82	2/11/97	Discovery	7	10/0
30	5/4/89	Atlantis	5	4	83	4/4/97	Columbia	7	3/23
28	8/8/89	Columbia	5	5	84	5/15/97	Atlantis	7/7	9/5
34	10/18/89	Atlantis	5	5	94	7/1/97	Columbia	7	15/7
33	11/22/89	Discovery	5	5	85	8/7/97	Discovery	5	11/20
32	1/9/90	Columbia	5	11	86	9/25/97	Atlantis	7/7	10/19
36	2/28/90	Atlantis	5	4	87	11/19/97	Columbia	6	15/17
31	4/24/90	Discovery	5	5	89	1/22/98	Endeavor	7/7	8/20
41	10/6/90	Discovery	5	4	90	4/17/98	Columbia	7	15/22
38	11/15/90	Atlantis	5	5	91	6/2/98	Discovery	6/7	9/19
35	12/2/90	Columbia	7	9	95	11/20/98	Discovery	7	8/22
37	4/5/91	Atlantis	5	6	88	12/04/98	Endeavor	6	11/19
39	4/28/91	Discovery	7	8	96	5/27/99	Discovery	6	9/19
40	6/5/91	Columbia	7	9					
43	8/2/91	Atlantis	5	9	Future missions in work				
48	9/12/91	Discovery	5	5					
44	11/24/91	Atlantis	6	7	93	7/20/99	Columbia	5	4/23
42	1/22/92	Discovery	7	8	99	9/16/99	Endeavor	6	11
45	3/24/92	Atlantis	7	9	103	10/14/99	Atlantis	7	10
49	5/7/92	Endeavour	7	9	101	12/2/99	Discovery	7	10/19
50	6/25/92	Columbia	7	14	92	2/24/2000	Discovery	7	9
46	7/31/92	Atlantis	7	8	97	3/23/2000	Endeavor	5	8
47	9/12/92	Endeavour	7	8	98	4/20/2000	Atlantis	5	9
52	10/22/92	Columbia	6	10	102	6/29/2000	Discovery	3	11
53	12/2/92	Discovery	5	7	100	7/27/2000	Atlantis	8	11
54	1/13/93	Endeavour	5	6					
56	4/8/93	Discovery	5	9					

- Represents zero.

Source: U.S. National Aeronautics and Space Administration, Internet site <http://www.ksc.nasa.gov/shuttle/missions/missions.html> (Accessed 28 June 1999).

No. 1012. Nobel Prize Laureates in Selected Sciences: 1901 to 1997

[Presented by location of award-winning research and by date of award]

Country	1901-1997				1901-1930	1931-1945	1946-1960	1961-1975	1976-1990	1991-1996	1997
	Total	Physics	Chemistry	Physiology/ Medicine							
Total	448	154	129	165	93	49	74	92	98	35	7
United States	190	67	44	79	6	14	38	41	63	24	4
United Kingdom	71	21	26	24	15	11	14	20	9	1	1
Germany [1]	61	17	29	15	27	11	4	8	7	3	-
France	25	11	7	7	13	2	-	5	2	2	1
Soviet Union	10	7	1	2	2	-	4	3	1	-	-
Japan	4	3	1	-	-	-	1	2	1	-	-
Other countries	87	28	21	38	30	11	13	13	15	5	1

- Represents zero. [1] Between 1946 and 1991, data are for the former West Germany only.

Source: U.S. National Science Foundation, unpublished data.

628 Science and Technology

Transportation—Land

This section presents statistics on revenues, passenger and freight traffic volume, and employment in various revenue-producing modes of the transportation industry, including motor vehicles, trains, and pipelines. Data are also presented on commuting travel, highway mileage and finances, motor vehicle travel, accidents, sales, and registrations; automobile operating costs; and characteristics of public transit, railroads, and pipelines.

The principal compiler of data on public roads and on operation of motor vehicles is the U.S. Department of Transportation's (DOT) Federal Highway Administration (FHWA). These data appear in FHWA's annual *Highway Statistics* and other publications. The U.S. Interstate Commerce Commission (ICC) presents data on interstate land transport in its publications, the *Annual Report to Congress* and the *Transport Statistics in the United States*, which contain data on railroads and motor carriers subject to ICC regulations.

The U.S. National Highway Traffic Safety Administration issues data on traffic accident deaths and death rates in two annual reports: the *Fact Book* and the *Fatal Accident Reporting System Annual Report*. DOT's Federal Railroad Administration presents data on accidents involving railroads in its annual *Accident/Incident Bulletin*, and the *Rail-Highway Crossing Accident/Incident and Inventory Bulletin*.

Various censuses and surveys conducted by the U.S. Census Bureau also provide data. Results of the censuses of transportation are presented in the *Truck Inventory and Use Survey*. The *Annual Survey of Manufactures* and reports of the censuses of manufactures, wholesale and retail trade, and service industries contain statistics on the motor vehicle and equipment industry and on retail, wholesale, and services aspects of this industry. Data on

persons commuting to work were collected as part of the 1980 census and are in various census reports.

Data are also presented in many nongovernment publications. Among them are the weekly and annual *Cars of Revenue Freight Loaded* and the annual *Yearbook of Railroad Facts*, both published by the Association of American Railroads, Washington, DC; *Transit Fact Book*, containing electric railway and motorbus statistics, published annually by the American Public Transit Association, Washington, DC.; *Accident Facts*, issued by the National Safety Council, Chicago, IL; and *Transportation in America*, issued by the Eno Foundation for Transportation, Westport, Connecticut.

Urban and rural highway mileage— Beginning in 1980, mileage is classified in urban and rural categories, rather than municipal and rural. Urban denotes the Federal-aid legislation definition of an area. Such areas include, as a minimum, a census place with a population of 5,000 to 49,999 or a designated urbanized area with a population of 50,000 or more. These Federal-aid urban areas may extend beyond corporate and census boundaries, and thus are not necessarily coextensive with municipal boundaries. Rural in 1980 refers to non-Federal-aid urban area mileage. Prior to 1980, municipal referred to roads within incorporated places, densely populated New England towns, and certain of the more populous unincorporated areas and rural to nonmunicipal roads.

Federal-aid highway systems—The Intermodal Surface Transportation Efficiency Act (ISTEA) of 1991 eliminated the historical Federal-Aid Highway Systems and created the National Highway System (NHS) and other Federal-aid highway categories. The final NHS was approved by Congress in December of 1995 under the National Highway System Designation Act.

Transportation—Land   629

Functional systems—Roads and streets are assigned to groups according to the character of service intended. The functional systems are (1) arterial highways that generally handle the long trips, (2) collector facilities that collect and disperse traffic between the arterials and the lower systems, and (3) local roads and streets that primarily serve direct access to residential areas, farms, and other local areas.

Regulatory bodies—The ICC, created by the U.S. Congress to regulate transportation in interstate commerce, has jurisdiction over railroads, trucking companies, bus lines, freight forwarders, water carriers, coal slurry pipelines, and transportation brokers. The Federal Energy Regulatory Commission is responsible for setting rates and charges for transportation and sale of natural gas and for establishing rates or charges for transportation.

Motor carriers—For 1960-73, Class I for-hire motor carriers of freight were classified by the ICC as those with $1 million or more of gross annual operating revenue; 1974-79, the class minimum was $3 million. Effective January 1, 1980, Class I carriers are those with $5 million or more in revenue. For 1960-68, Class I motor carriers of passengers were classified by the ICC as those with $200,000 or more of gross annual operating revenue; for 1969-76, as those with revenues of $1 million or more; and since 1977, as those with $3 million or more. Effective January 1, 1988, Class I motor carriers of passengers are those with $5 million or more in operating revenues; Class II less than $5 million in operating revenues.

Railroads—Railroad companies reporting to the ICC are divided into specific groups as follows: (1) Regular line-haul (interstate) railroads (and their nonoperating subsidiaries), (2) switching and terminal railroads, (3) private railroads prior to 1964 (identified by ICC as "circular" because they reported on brief circulars), and (4) unofficial railroads, so designated when their reports are received too late for tabulation. For the most part, the last three groups are not included in the statistics shown here.

For years prior to 1978, Class I railroads were those with annual revenues of $1 million or more for 1950-55; $3 million or more for 1956-64; $5 million or more for 1965-75; and $10 million or more for 1976-77. In 1978, the classification became Class I, those having more than $50 million gross annual operating revenue; Class II, from $10 million to $50 million+; and Class III, less than $10 million. Effective January 1, 1982, the ICC adopted a procedure to adjust the threshold for inflation by restating current revenues in constant 1978 dollars. In 1988, the criteria for Class I and Class II railroads were $92.0 million and $18.4 million, respectively. Also effective January 1, 1982, the ICC adopted a Carrier Classification Index Survey Form for carriers not filing annual report Form R-1 with the commission. Class II and Class III railroads are currently exempted from filing any financial report with the Commission. The form is used for reclassifying carriers.

Statistical reliability—For a discussion of statistical collection and estimation, sampling procedures, and measures of statistical reliability, see Appendix III.

No. 1013. Passenger and Freight Transportation Outlays, by Type of Transport: 1980 to 1997

[In billions of dollars ($338.1 represents $338,100,000,000). Freight data include outlays for mail and express. ICC=Interstate Commerce Commission]

Type of transport	1980	1985	1990	1992	1993	1994	1995	1996	1997
Total outlays [1]	**338.1**	**492.2**	**630.4**	**644.6**	**683.7**	**715.2**	**763.4**	**800.9**	**833.0**
Passenger:									
Private transportation	284.8	418.2	528.3	538.2	575.9	604.8	644.0	675.9	701.3
Automobiles [2]	276.7	410.3	518.0	529.3	566.5	594.4	633.5	664.2	687.6
New and used cars	73.3	139.3	165.5	152.9	165.0	184.4	181.8	185.7	189.2
Tires, tubes, accessories	22.2	29.6	25.4	32.8	34.8	31.7	40.2	42.8	43.1
Gasoline and oil	99.7	106.6	120.4	116.1	118.9	117.9	128.4	138.3	140.6
Insurance less claims	11.5	11.6	20.1	28.1	29.5	31.5	32.7	32.6	32.6
Interest on debt	17.5	26.7	35.5	25.7	28.1	34.5	40.7	41.8	38.2
Auto registration fees	2.9	4.8	6.1	7.1	7.4	7.4	7.0	7.1	7.2
Operators' permit fees	0.4	0.5	0.6	0.8	0.7	0.8	0.8	0.8	0.8
Repair, greasing, washing, parking, leasing, rentals [3]	38.0	58.1	91.8	103.8	112.2	116.4	128.7	143.6	154.9
Air	8.1	7.9	10.3	8.9	9.5	10.4	10.5	11.7	13.7
For-hire transportation	53.4	73.9	102.1	106.4	107.8	110.4	119.4	125.0	131.7
Local [4] . . . . ; .	19.8	27.3	34.2	36.0	37.4	38.9	43.2	44.3	46.4
Bus and transit [5]	9.3	13.5	16.7	17.9	18.7	20.0	21.6	21.9	22.8
School bus	3.8	5.9	7.6	8.1	7.6	7.8	9.1	10.4	10.8
Taxi	5.2	5.6	7.1	7.3	7.6	7.8	8.1	8.2	9.0
Railroad commutation	1.5	2.2	2.8	2.7	3.5	3.1	4.5	3.7	3.8
Intercity	28.3	39.5	53.0	53.1	52.8	53.8	57.7	62.4	65.7
Air	25.1	35.9	49.5	49.2	49.3	50.5	54.0	58.6	61.8
Rail [6]	1.5	1.6	1.7	1.9	1.8	1.8	2.2	2.2	2.2
Bus	1.7	2.0	1.8	1.9	1.7	1.4	1.5	1.5	1.6
International	5.3	7.1	14.9	17.3	17.6	17.7	18.4	18.4	19.6
Freight, total [4]	213.7	273.6	350.9	375.1	396.3	419.9	444.5	467.2	504.4
Highway	155.3	205.6	270.8	292.9	311.9	330.7	348.1	368.5	401.7
Truck, intercity	94.6	123.2	162.3	176.8	189.7	204.9	219.6	235.4	257.8
Truck, local	60.5	82.2	108.4	116.0	122.1	125.7	128.4	133.0	143.7
Rail	27.9	29.2	30.1	30.5	30.8	33.1	34.3	35.1	35.3
Water	15.5	18.4	20.1	19.9	20.8	21.2	24.9	25.0	25.3
Oil pipeline	7.5	8.9	8.5	8.5	8.4	8.3	9.1	8.6	8.7
Air carrier	4.0	6.8	13.7	15.0	15.8	17.2	18.7	20.1	22.7

[1] Total outlays less than sum of passenger and freight totals, as estimated freight costs included in costs of new cars, gasoline, oil, tires, and tubes have been excluded to prevent duplication. [2] Includes business-owned vehicles. [3] Includes storage. [4] Includes items not shown separately. [5] Includes Federal, state, and local government operating subsidies and capital grants. [6] Includes Federal operating subsidies and capital grants for Amtrak.

Source: Eno Transportation Foundation, Inc., Lansdowne, VA, *Transportation in America*, annual (copyright).

No. 1014. Volume of Domestic Intercity Freight and Passenger Traffic, by Type of Transport: 1980 to 1997

[Freight traffic in bil. ton-miles; passenger traffic in bil. passenger-miles. A ton-mile is the movement of 1 ton (2,000 pounds) of freight for the distance of 1 mile. A passenger-mile is the movement of one passenger for the distance of 1 mile. Comprises public and private traffic, both revenue and nonrevenue]

Type of transport	Traffic volume						Percent distribution					
	1980	1985	1990	1995	1996	1997	1980	1985	1990	1995	1996	1997
Freight traffic, total	**2,487**	**2,458**	**2,895**	**3,407**	**3,540**	**3,622**	**100.0**	**100.0**	**100.0**	**100.0**	**100.0**	**100.0**
Railroads	932	895	1,091	1,375	1,426	1,421	37.5	38.0	35.6	37.9	37.6	38.1
Truck:												
ICC truck	242	250	311	401	428	466	9.7	9.9	10.4	11.0	11.3	11.8
Non-ICC truck	313	360	424	520	549	585	12.6	11.8	14.9	15.1	15.6	16.0
Water:												
Rivers/canals	311	306	390	406	408	413	12.5	12.8	13.0	13.3	13.0	12.0
Great Lakes	96	76	85	91	90	95	3.9	4.0	2.7	2.5	2.5	2.7
Oil pipelines . . . . , . . .	588	564	584	601	631	628	23.6	23.2	23.1	19.9	19.5	19.1
Domestic airways [1] . . .	5	7	10	13	13	14	0.2	0.2	0.3	0.3	0.4	0.4
Passenger traffic, total . . .	**1,468**	**1,636**	**2,034**	**2,337**	**2,405**	**2,476**	**100.0**	**100.0**	**100.0**	**100.0**	**100.0**	**100.0**
Private automobiles . . .	1,210	1,310	1,639	1,881	1,917	1,968	82.5	82.7	79.4	81.3	81.3	81.3
Domestic airways [2] . . .	15	12	13	10	11	13	1.0	14.7	-	0.6	0.5	0.5
Air, public carrier	204	278	346	404	435	453	13.9	-	-	16.3	16.5	16.5
Bus [3]	27	24	23	28	29	30	1.9	1.8	1.4	1.1	1.1	1.1
Railroads [4]	11	11	13	14	13	14	0.7	0.7	0.7	0.7	0.7	0.6

- Represents zero. [1] Revenue service only for scheduled and nonscheduled carriers, with small section 418 all-cargo carriers included. Includes express mail, and excess baggage. [2] Includes general aviation (mostly private business) flying. [3] Excludes school and urban transit buses. [4] Includes intercity (Amtrak) and rail commuter service.

Source: Eno Transportation Foundation, Inc., Lansdowne VA, *Transportation in America*, annual (copyright).

U.S. Census Bureau, Statistical Abstract of the United States: 1999

No. 1015. Transportation Industry Summary: 1992

Kind of business	SIC code [1]	Establish-ments (number)	Revenue ($1,000)	Annual payroll ($1,000)	First-quarter payroll	Paid employees for pay period including March 12 (number)
Total transportation, except U.S. Post Office	(X)	(NA)	**327,623**	**92,211**	(NA)	**3,356,872**
Railroad transportation [2]	40	(NA)	28,349	8,753	(NA)	197,421
Passenger transportation	41	17,805	12,649	5,191	1,246	354,913
Local and suburban passenger transportation	411	8,275	5,968	2,624	613	153,278
Taxicabs	412	3,337	992	306	75	26,338
Other bus transport. and terminal service	413, 4, 5, 7	6,193	5,689	2,261	558	175,297
Intercity and rural bus service	413	607	1,092	483	116	20,404
Charter bus service	414	1,307	1,269	394	86	24,604
School buses	415	4,260	3,315	1,380	355	130,093
Bus terminal and service facilities	417	19	12	4	1	196
Motor freight transportation and warehousing	42	110,908	143,794	39,896	9,196	1,580,095
Trucking and courier services, except air.	421	101,169	135,437	37,760	8,691	1,484,655
Local trucking with storage	4214	4,512	4,191	1,346	303	64,417
Public warehousing and storage	422	9,718	8,330	2,127	504	95,145
Trucking terminal facilities.	423	21	27	8	2	295
Pipelines, except natural gas	46	844	7,063	821	203	16,779
Transportation services	47	46,593	23,890	7,850	1,854	329,202
Arrangement of passenger transportation	472	31,793	10,573	3,921	931	192,981
Freight shipping services	473	12,553	9,159	3,233	761	106,979
Other transportation services	474, 8	2,247	4,158	696	162	29,242
Rental of railroad cars	474	125	1,881	85	23	1,926
Misc. services incidental to transportation	478	2,122	2,277	612	140	27,316

NA Not available.   X Not applicable.   [1] 1987 Standard Industrial Classification, see Section 13, Labor Force.   [2] Includes Class I Freight railroads only. Source: Association of American Railroads, Washington, DC, *Railroad Facts*, annual.

Source: Except as noted, U.S. Census Bureau, *Census of Transportation, Communications and Utilities: 1992*.

No. 1016. Employment and Earnings in Transportation, by Industry: 1980 to 1998

[Annual averages of monthly figures. Based on Current Employment Statistics program; see Appendix III]

Industry	SIC code [1]	1980	1985	1990	1993	1994	1995	1996	1997	1998
NUMBER (1,000)										
Total transportation	(X)	2,960	3,761	3,511	3,598	3,761	3,904	4,019	4,106	4,208
Railroads	40	532	241	279	248	241	238	231	227	232
Class I railroads	4011	482	214	241	218	214	212	206	202	205
Local and interurban passengers .	41	265	404	338	379	404	419	437	451	462
Trucking and warehousing	42	(NA)	1,526	1,395	1,444	1,526	1,587	1,637	1,667	1,707
Water transportation	44	211	172	177	168	172	175	174	180	186
Air transportation	45	(NA)	1,023	968	988	1,023	1,068	1,107	1,128	1,157
Pipelines, exc. natural gas	46	21	17	19	18	17	15	15	14	14
Transportation services	47	(NA)	378	336	352	378	401	418	439	449
AVERAGE WEEKLY EARNINGS (dol.)										
Class I railroads	4011	427	786	727	782	786	811	850	892	845
Local and interurban passengers .	41	217	354	310	342	354	358	367	374	385
Trucking and warehousing	42	(NA)	499	450	484	499	501	515	532	545
Pipelines, exc. natural gas	46	441	872	711	817	872	888	909	902	918

NA Not available.   X Not applicable.   [1] 1987 Standard Industrial Classification, see text, Section 13, Labor Force.

Source: U.S. Bureau of Labor Statistics, Bulletins 2445 and 2481, Employment and Earnings, March and June issues.

U.S. Census Bureau, Statistical Abstract of the United States: 1999

No. 1017. Commodity Shipments—Value, Tons, and Ton-Miles: 1993 and 1997

Mode of transportation	Value		Tons		Ton-miles	
	1993	1997	1993	1997	1993	1997
All modes	**5,846,334**	**7,623,623**	**9,688,493**	**11,562,916**	**2,420,915**	**2,808,279**
Single modes	4,941,452	6,237,854	8,922,286	10,726,545	2,136,873	2,466,447
Truck [1]	4,403,494	5,518,716	6,385,915	7,992,437	869,536	1,094,924
For-hire truck	2,625,093	3,116,296	2,808,279	3,355,623	629,000	772,110
Private truck.	1,755,837	2,357,581	3,543,513	4,448,058	235,897	307,847
Rail	247,394	311,023	1,544,148	1,480,692	942,561	993,929
Water.	61,628	69,083	505,440	538,197	271,998	290,730
Shallow draft	40,707	51,430	362,454	402,759	164,371	207,179
Great Lakes.	(S)	1,048	33,041	36,630	12,395	13,618
Deep draft	19,749	16,605	109,945	98,807	95,232	69,933
Air (includes truck and air)	139,086	213,405	3,139	5,047	4,009	7,449
Pipeline [2]	89,849	125,626	483,645	710,172	(S)	(S)
Multiple modes	662,603	955,128	225,676	264,610	191,461	230,244
Parcel, U.S. Postal Service or courier .	563,277	865,661	18,892	24,677	13,151	18,512
Truck and rail	83,082	(S)	40,624	(S)	37,675	(S)
Truck and water.	9,392	9,366	67,995	66,944	40,610	46,439
Rail and water	3,636	2,053	79,222	78,955	70,219	74,518
Other multiple modes	3,216	5,849	18,943	36,188	(S)	34,187
Other and unknown modes	242,279	430,640	540,530	571,761	92,581	111,588

S Data do not meet publication standards due to high sampling variability or other reasons. [1] Excludes shipments of STCC 27, printed matter. [2] Excludes most shipments of crude oil.

Source: U.S. Bureau of Transportation Statistics, *National Transportation Statistics, 1996.* Data from U.S. Census Bureau, *1993 Commodity Flow Survey, U.S. Preliminary Report,* TC92-CF-52(P), July 1995.

No. 1018. Transportation Accidents, Deaths, and Injuries: 1990 to 1997

[For related data, see also Table 1047]

Year and casualty	Motor vehi-cle [1] (1,000)	Rail-road [2]	Air carriers				General aviation	Recre-ational boat-ing [6]	Gas pipe-lines [7]	Liquid pipe-lines [8]	Water-borne [9]	Rail Rapid Tran-sit [10]	Hazard-ous materi-als [11]
			Total	Air-lines [3]	Com-muter air car-riers [4]	On de-mand air car-riers [5]							
Accidents:													
1990 . . .	6,471	2,879	146	24	15	106	2,215	6,411	198	180	3,613	12,178	8,880
1995 . . .	6,699	2,459	123	36	12	75	2,053	8,019	161	188	4,196	14,327	14,743
1997 . . .	6,764	2,397	148	49	17	(NA)	1,858	8,044	182	179	3,704	15,151	13,853
Deaths:													
1990 . . .	44.6	599	97	39	7	50	767	865	6	3	85	117	8
1995 . . .	41.8	567	229	168	9	52	734	829	18	3	46	79	7
1997 . . .	42.0	602	93	8	46	(NA)	660	819	11	-	46	77	11
Injuries:													
1990 . . .	3,231	22,736	76	29	11	36	402	3,822	69	7	175	10,036	423
1995 . . .	3,465	12,546	64	25	25	14	395	4,141	53	11	145	11,238	399
1997 . . .	3,399	10,227	63	39	1	(NA)	365	4,555	88	5	109	12,285	226

- Represents or rounds to zero. NA Not available. [1] Data on deaths are from U.S. National Highway Traffic Safety Administration and are based on 30 day definition. Includes only police reported crashes. [2] Accidents which result in damages to railroad property. Grade crossing accidents are also included when classified as a train accident. Deaths exclude fatalities in railroad-highway grade crossing accidents. [3] Includes scheduled and nonscheduled (charter) air carriers. Represents serious injuries. [4] All scheduled service. Represents serious injuries. [5] All nonscheduled service. Represents serious injuries. [6] Accidents resulting in death; injury or requiring medical treatment beyond first aid; damages exceeding $500; or a person's disappearance. [7] Pipeline accidents/incidents are credited to year of occurrence; prior data are credited to the year filed. [8] Pipelines carrying hazardous materials, petroleum, and liquid petroleum products. [9] Covers accidents involving commercial vessels which must be reported to U.S. Coast Guard if there is property damage exceeding $25,000; material damage affecting the seaworthiness or efficiency of a vessel; stranding or grounding; loss of life; or injury causing a person's incapacity for more than 3 days. [10] Reporting criteria and source of data changed between 1989 and 1990; these data from 1990 to present are not comparable to earlier years. [11] Accidents, deaths, and injuries involving hazardous materials cover all types of transport.

Source: U.S. Bureau of Transportation Statistics, *National Transportation Statistics,* annual.

No. 1019. Highway Mileage—Functional Systems and Urban/Rural: 1997

[As of Dec. 31. For definition of urban, rural, see text, this section]

State	Functional systems					Urban	Rural
	Total	Interstate [1]	Other arterial	Collector	Local		
U.S	**3,944,597**	**46,048**	**378,451**	**793,120**	**2,718,166**	**836,109**	**3,108,488**
AL	93,356	905	8,746	20,306	63,379	20,126	73,230
AK	12,775	1,087	1,512	2,751	7,425	1,792	10,983
AZ	55,712	1,168	4,746	8,554	41,148	17,294	38,418
AR	94,366	546	6,833	20,110	66,769	9,874	84,492
CA	170,598	2,419	26,695	32,091	107,994	83,255	87,343
CO	85,069	953	8,150	16,610	59,126	13,859	71,210
CT	20,675	346	2,848	2,971	14,313	11,720	8,955
DE	5,722	41	617	943	4,110	1,982	3,740
DC	1,424	11	254	157	985	1,424	-
FL	114,572	1,472	11,997	14,446	86,253	48,321	66,251
GA	111,828	1,244	13,072	23,114	74,237	26,737	85,091
HI	4,165	54	754	789	2,534	1,867	2,298
ID	60,440	612	3,698	9,848	46,282	3,757	56,683
IL	137,785	2,165	13,884	21,495	100,166	35,802	101,983
IN	93,196	1,172	7,909	22,595	61,386	19,780	73,416
IA	112,804	782	9,446	31,501	71,075	9,421	103,383
KS	133,540	872	9,204	33,237	90,092	9,904	123,636
KY	73,031	762	5,452	17,621	49,105	11,024	62,007
LA	60,699	894	5,278	12,541	41,940	13,916	46,783
ME	22,643	367	2,312	5,925	14,021	2,628	20,015
MD	29,872	481	3,552	4,998	20,605	14,033	15,839
MA	35,024	566	5,644	5,480	23,130	22,906	12,118
MI	119,183	1,240	12,160	25,790	79,772	29,634	89,549
MN	130,815	913	12,617	29,520	87,623	15,532	115,283
MS	73,150	684	7,044	15,528	49,851	7,912	65,238
MO	122,766	1,178	9,304	25,071	86,925	16,388	106,378
MT	69,672	1,191	6,003	16,406	46,072	2,456	67,216
NE	92,813	482	7,883	20,773	63,658	5,133	87,680
NV	45,218	560	2,918	4,742	36,956	5,305	39,913
NH	15,119	224	1,548	2,706	10,601	2,921	12,198
NJ	35,920	420	5,407	4,587	25,194	24,234	11,686
NM	59,478	1,000	4,514	6,704	47,257	6,139	53,339
NY	112,480	1,499	13,639	20,532	75,984	40,747	71,733
NC	98,041	987	8,896	17,799	70,077	22,708	75,333
ND	86,719	572	5,873	11,434	68,840	1,829	84,890
OH	114,801	1,573	10,611	22,143	80,094	33,097	81,704
OK	112,593	930	7,838	25,386	78,305	13,078	99,515
OR	83,608	727	6,710	18,423	57,696	10,633	72,975
PA	119,129	1,750	13,156	19,763	83,976	33,727	85,402
RI	6,028	68	828	842	4,222	4,684	1,344
SC	64,773	828	6,805	13,395	43,677	10,583	54,190
SD	83,376	678	6,283	19,280	57,132	1,942	81,434
TN	86,026	1,074	8,606	18,036	58,197	17,321	68,705
TX	296,651	3,233	28,290	63,504	200,444	82,434	214,217
UT	42,970	940	3,326	7,818	30,878	6,920	36,050
VT	14,240	320	1,298	3,114	9,489	1,363	12,877
VA	69,632	1,106	8,150	14,217	45,939	18,656	50,976
WA	79,586	764	7,296	16,794	54,420	17,650	61,936
WV	35,271	549	3,237	8,794	22,682	3,177	32,094
WI	111,950	746	11,676	21,477	77,874	16,242	95,708
WY	33,293	913	3,662	10,459	18,256	2,242	31,051

- Represents zero. [1] Also includes freeways and expressways.

Source: U.S. Federal Highway Administration, *Highway Statistics*, annual.

U.S. Census Bureau, Statistical Abstract of the United States: 1999

No. 1020. Highway Mileage—Urban and Rural, by Type and Control, and Federal-Aid Highway System: 1980 to 1997

[In thousands, except percent (3,995 represents 3,995,000). As of Dec. 31. Data for urban and rural mileage are not comparable to years prior to 1980 because of classification changes; see text, this section]

Type and control	1980	1985	1990	1992	1993	1994	1995	1996	1997
Total mileage [1]	[2]3,955	3,862	3,880	3,902	3,905	3,906	3,912	3,934	3,959
Urban mileage	624	691	757	785	803	814	814	834	843
Under state control	79	111	96	104	106	110	(NA)	113	113
Under local control	543	578	661	680	696	702	(NA)	719	589
Rural mileage	[2]3,331	3,171	3,123	3,117	3,102	3,093	3,093	3,100	3,116
Percent surfaced [3]	77.5	88.1	88.6	88.9	88.7	91.3	(NA)	89	(NA)
Under state control	702	773	703	697	675	690	(NA)	693	677
Under local control	2,270	2,173	2,242	2,239	2,247	2,229	(NA)	2,238	2,140
Under Federal control	262	225	178	181	180	174	(NA)	169	(NA)

NA Not available.   [1] Beginning 1985, includes only public road mileage as defined 23 USC 402.   [2] Includes 98,000 miles of nonpublic road mileage previously contained in other rural categories.   [3] Covers soil-surfaced roads and roads with slag, gravel, stone, bituminous, or concrete surfaces.

Source: U.S. Federal Highway Administration, *Highway Statistics,* annual.

No. 1021. Highway Pavement Condition, by Type of Road System: 1996

Condition	Urban areas						Rural areas				
			Other						Other		
	Total	Inter-state	Freeways and express-ways	Prin-cipal arterial	Minor arterial	Collec-tor	Total	Inter-state	princi-pal arterial	Minor arterial	Major collector
Percent of road mileage rated—											
Above average	35	38	33	25	42	34	42	55	43	39	40
Average	42	53	55	49	37	39	42	41	49	51	38
Below average	23	9	12	26	21	27	17	4	7	11	22

Source: U.S. Federal Highway Administration, *Highway Statistics,* annual.

No. 1022. Funding for Highways: 1980 to 1997

[In millions of dollars (39,715 represents $39,715,000,000). Data compiled from reports of state and local authorities]

Type	1980	1985	1990	1993	1994	1995	1996	1997
Total receipts	39,715	61,506	75,294	88,380	88,296	95,313	101,497	106,446
Current income	37,604	54,957	69,730	80,610	80,514	87,694	92,179	97,274
Imposts on highway users [1]	22,559	35,599	44,264	54,401	54,476	59,562	(NA)	(NA)
Other taxes and fees	11,808	15,127	19,827	19,375	19,872	21,390	21,274	25,629
Investment income, other receipts	3,237	4,231	5,639	6,834	6,166	6,742	7,083	6,977
Bond issue proceeds [2]	2,111	6,549	5,564	7,770	7,782	7,619	9,318	9,172
Intergovernmental payments [3]	(X)	(X)	(X)	(X)	(X)	(X)	(X)	(X)
Funds from (+) or to (-) reserves [3]	2,080	-4,058	114	-1,955	962	-2,809	-3,339	-4,974
Total funds available	41,795	57,448	75,408	86,425	89,258	92,504	98,158	101,472
Total disbursements	41,795	57,448	75,408	86,425	89,258	92,504	98,158	101,472
Current disbursements	40,084	54,725	72,457	81,233	85,109	87,843	93,663	96,717
Capital outlay	20,337	27,138	35,151	39,528	41,780	43,097	46,519	48,939
Maintenance and traffic services	11,445	16,032	20,365	22,894	23,607	24,455	25,803	26,326
Administration and research	3,022	4,033	6,501	7,921	8,398	8,332	8,645	8,081
Law enforcement and safety	3,824	5,334	7,235	7,157	7,518	7,977	8,774	9,316
Interest on debt	1,456	2,188	3,205	3,733	3,806	3,982	3,922	4,055
Debt retirement [2]	1,711	2,723	2,951	5,192	4,149	4,661	4,495	4,755

NA Not available.   X Not applicable.   [1] Excludes amounts later allocated for nonhighway purposes.   [2] Excludes issue and redemption of short-term notes or refunding bonds.   [3] Plus sign (+) indicates net receipt of funds from other levels of government; minus sign (-) indicates net disbursement of funds to other levels.

Source: U.S. Federal Highway Administration, *Highway Statistics,* annual; and releases.

No. 1023. Public Highway Debt—State and Local Governments: 1980 to 1995

[In millions of dollars (2,357 represents $2,357,000,000). Long-term obligations. Data are for varying calendar and fiscal years. Excludes duplicated and interunit obligations]

Item	1980	1985	1988	1989	1990	1991	1992	1993	1994	1995
Total debt issued	2,357	8,194	4,594	5,900	5,838	9,516	12,988	14,178	10,833	11,306
State	1,135	5,397	2,702	3,775	3,277	6,252	9,460	10,035	5,739	4,718
Local	1,222	2,797	1,892	2,125	2,561	3,264	3,528	4,143	5,094	6,587
Total debt redeemed	1,982	4,606	2,774	3,729	5,158	6,138	7,665	10,823	6,103	5,635
State	1,109	3,835	1,547	2,813	2,041	4,352	5,388	8,082	3,622	2,940
Local	873	771	1,227	916	3,117	1,786	2,277	2,741	2,481	2,695
Total debt outstanding	27,519	33,379	41,663	43,834	44,514	47,892	53,539	58,373	63,062	68,733
Local	7,427	12,100	15,927	17,136	16,580	18,058	19,353	22,965	25,613	29,505

Source: U.S. Federal Highway Administration, *Highway Statistics,* annual.

Transportation—Land   635

No. 1024. Disbursement of State Highway Funds, by State: 1990 to 1997

[In millions of dollars ($53,580 represents $53,580,000,000). Comprises disbursements from current revenues. Includes transactions by state toll authorities. Excludes amounts allocated for collection expenses and nonhighway purposes, and bonds redeemed by refunding]

State	1990	1995	1997	State	1990	1995	1997	State	1990	1995	1997
U.S.	53,580	67,261	73,994	KS	697	1,019	1,087	ND	189	270	326
				KY	1,008	1,342	1,331	OH	2,271	2,637	2,940
AL	866	1,002	1,019	LA	923	1,195	1,189				
AK	336	438	435	ME	332	379	474	OK	827	828	867
AZ	1,525	1,199	1,359	MD	1,464	1,289	1,489	OR	765	888	992
AR	456	666	832	MA	1,055	2,501	3,287	PA	2,885	3,153	3,764
CA	4,294	5,966	6,219	MI	1,526	1,974	2,100	RI	214	290	225
CO	714	922	887	MN	1,228	1,210	1,450	SC	585	668	741
CT	1,204	1,153	1,173					SD	232	286	349
DE	315	441	449	MS	529	662	809	TN	1,174	1,230	1,351
DC	273	140	151	MO	937	1,313	1,492	TX	3,001	3,593	4,253
FL	1,677	3,402	3,734	MT	302	388	379	UT	355	431	802
GA	1,278	1,437	1,372	NE	449	578	611	VT	165	194	213
HI	297	307	387	NV	309	484	431	VA	1,874	2,107	2,358
				NH	299	328	360	WA	1,251	1,842	1,851
ID	300	350	403	NJ	1,831	2,102	2,247	WV	650	781	940
IL	2,645	2,985	2,992	NM	409	535	546	WI	979	1,252	1,354
IN	1,218	1,368	1,636	NY	2,874	4,515	4,778	WY	297	272	284
IA	869	1,078	1,173	NC	1,428	1,871	2,099				

Source: U.S. Federal Highway Administration, *Highway Statistics*, annual.

No. 1025. Federal Grants to State and Local Governments for Highway Trust Fund and Federal Transit Administration (FTA), by State: 1997

[Year ending Sept. 30. 20,467 represents $20,467,000,000]

State	Highway trust fund		FTA		State	Highway trust fund		FTA		State	Highway trust fund		FTA	
	Total (mil. dol.)	Per capita[1]	Total (mil. dol.)	Per capita[1]		Total (mil. dol.)	Per capita[1]	Total (mil. dol.)	Per capita[1]		Total (mil. dol.)	Per capita[1]	Total (mil. dol.)	Per capita[1]
U.S.	20,467	75.4	4,555	16.8	KS	186	71.7	5	2.1	ND	141	220.5	4	6.8
					KY	293	74.9	16	4.1	OH	763	68.2	94	8.4
AL	299	69.3	10	2.4	LA	256	58.8	48	11.1	OK	270	81.4	13	4.0
AK	240	394.0	2	2.9	ME	118	94.9	3	2.8	OR	340	104.7	164	50.6
AZ	334	73.2	35	7.7	MD	419	82.3	90	17.6	PA	934	77.7	256	21.3
AR	285	113.1	9	3.6	MA	1,025	167.5	225	36.8	RI	106	107.4	7	7.1
CA	2,097	65.0	675	20.9	MI	605	61.9	68	6.9	SC	252	67.0	10	2.8
CO	207	53.3	20	5.2	MN	302	64.5	13	2.7	SD	146	197.3	5	6.6
CT	368	112.7	72	21.9	MS	195	71.4	7	2.6	TN	378	70.5	40	7.4
DE	86	116.9	6	7.6	MO	444	82.2	62	11.5	TX	1,179	60.7	173	8.9
DC	94	178.0	117	220.6	MT	171	195.1	3	2.9	UT	153	74.4	43	20.9
FL	736	50.3	154	10.5	NE	167	101.0	6	3.3	VT	89	151.6	7	12.5
GA	473	63.2	119	15.8	NV	148	88.5	22	13.3	VA	442	65.6	37	5.5
HI	207	174.2	10	8.1	NH	105	89.3	3	2.9	WA	467	83.2	92	16.3
ID	161	133.0	4	3.2	NJ	644	80.0	352	43.7	WV	219	120.3	13	7.1
IL	704	59.1	281	23.6	NM	201	116.3	11	6.6	WI	329	63.7	40	7.7
IN	429	73.1	40	6.8	NY	1,201	66.2	752	41.4	WY	134	279.2	1	2.9
IA	229	80.3	20	6.9	NC	448	60.3	35	4.8					

[1] Based on U.S. Census Bureau resident population as of July 1; excluding population of the territories.
Source: U.S. Census Bureau, *Federal Expenditures by State for Fiscal Year*, annual.

No. 1026. State Gasoline Tax Rates, 1995 and 1997, and Motor Fuel Tax Receipts, 1997

State	Rate[1] (cents/gal.)		Receipts,[2] 1997 (mil. dol.)	State	Rate[1] (cents/gal.)		Receipts,[2] 1997 (mil. dol.)	State	Rate[1] (cents/gal.)		Receipts,[2] 1997 (mil. dol.)
	1995	1997			1995	1997			1995	1997	
AL	18.0	18.0	539	LA	20.0	20.0	499	OH	22.0	22.0	1,365
AK	8.0	8.0	17	ME	19.0	19.0	151	OK	17.0	17.0	382
AZ	18.0	18.0	486	MD	23.5	23.5	612	OR	24.0	24.0	378
AR	18.7	18.6	351	MA	21.0	21.0	590	PA	22.4	25.9	1,532
CO	22.0	22.0	442	MI	15.0	19.0	809	RI	29.0	29.0	125
CT	34.0	36.0	545	MN	20.0	20.0	527	SC	16.0	16.0	386
DE	23.0	23.0	97	MS	18.4	18.4	333	SD	18.0	21.0	101
DC	20.0	20.0	33	MO	15.0	17.0	630	TN	20.0	20.0	670
FL	12.3	12.8	1,392	MT	27.0	27.0	167	TX	20.0	20.0	2,365
GA	7.5	7.5	387	NE	25.4	24.5	280	UT	19.0	24.5	258
HI	16.0	16.0	68	NV	24.0	24.8	265	VT	16.0	20.0	65
ID	21.0	25.0	194	NH	18.7	18.7	121	VA	17.5	17.5	722
IL	19.0	19.0	1,123	NJ	10.5	10.5	493	WA	23.0	23.0	689
IN	15.0	15.0	695	NM	18.0	18.9	230	WV	25.4	25.4	271
IA	20.0	20.0	406	NY	21.9	22.8	1,377	WI	23.4	23.8	685
KS	18.0	18.0	315	NC	21.6	22.6	975	WY	9.0	9.0	53
KY	16.4	16.4	406	ND	18.0	20.0	94				

[1] In effect Dec. 31. [2] Represents net receipts.
Source: U.S. Federal Highway Administration, *Highway Statistics*, annual.

No. 1027. Motor Vehicle Registrations, 1980 to 1997, and Drivers Licenses, and Motorcycle Registrations 1997, by State

[In thousands (155,796 represents 155,796,000). Motor vehicle registrations cover publicly, privately, and commercially owned vehicles. For uniformity, data have been adjusted to a calendar-year basis as registration years in states differ; figures represent net numbers where possible, excluding re-registrations and nonresident registrations]

State	Automobiles, trucks, and buses [1]						1997		1997	
									Motor-cycle [1]	
								Auto-mobiles (incl. taxis)	registra-tion (incl. official)	Drivers licenses
	1980	1985	1990	1994	1995	1996	Total			
U.S	155,796	171,654	188,798	198,045	201,530	206,365	207,754	129,749	3,786	182,709
AL......	2,938	3,338	3,744	3,177	3,553	3,324	3,669	1,906	39	3,387
AK......	262	353	477	533	542	531	542	225	13	446
AZ......	1,917	2,235	2,825	2,813	2,873	2,983	3,143	1,853	74	3,120
AR......	1,574	1,384	1,448	1,567	1,613	1,633	1,634	857	14	1,879
CA......	16,873	18,899	21,926	22,339	22,432	25,214	24,945	15,706	441	20,385
CO	2,342	2,759	3,155	2,750	2,812	3,433	3,523	1,920	95	2,836
CT......	2,147	2,465	2,623	2,599	2,622	2,609	2,660	1,963	48	2,270
DE......	397	465	526	578	592	593	614	404	10	536
DC	268	326	262	249	243	237	234	196	1	356
FL......	7,614	9,865	10,950	10,252	10,369	10,889	10,874	7,375	204	11,749
GA	3,818	4,580	5,489	5,990	6,120	6,283	6,242	3,688	75	5,063
HI......	570	651	771	779	802	786	693	443	21	739
ID	834	854	1,054	1,035	1,043	1,061	1,081	494	35	844
IL.......	7,477	7,727	7,873	8,698	8,973	8,817	8,443	5,854	182	7,692
IN	3,826	4,024	4,366	4,889	5,072	5,216	5,346	3,248	98	3,924
IA	2,329	2,696	2,632	2,766	2,814	2,869	2,851	1,636	132	1,953
KS......	2,007	2,148	2,012	2,083	2,085	2,110	2,152	1,137	48	1,825
KY......	2,593	2,615	2,909	2,666	2,631	2,696	2,781	1,634	39	2,575
LA......	2,779	3,012	2,995	3,426	3,286	3,318	3,411	1,930	38	2,678
ME	724	840	977	946	967	959	1,059	637	28	901
MD	2,803	3,276	3,607	3,640	3,654	3,635	3,786	2,628	39	3,347
MA	3,749	3,738	3,726	4,027	4,502	4,702	5,070	3,832	89	4,393
MI......	6,488	6,727	7,209	7,574	7,674	8,010	8,024	5,111	154	6,751
MN	3,091	3,385	3,508	4,057	3,882	3,861	3,927	2,317	124	2,839
MS	1,577	1,746	1,875	2,063	2,144	2,182	2,234	1,263	31	1,723
MO	3,271	3,558	3,905	4,208	4,255	4,350	4,351	2,550	55	3,744
MT	680	652	783	950	968	973	980	455	21	662
NE......	1,254	1,257	1,384	1,458	1,467	1,479	1,507	812	18	1,179
NV......	655	709	853	985	1,047	1,096	1,146	659	23	1,186
NH	704	974	946	992	1,122	1,112	1,127	739	47	883
NJ......	4,761	4,909	5,652	5,839	5,906	5,822	5,817	4,269	94	5,576
NM	1,068	1,176	1,301	1,422	1,484	1,545	1,514	780	31	1,194
NY......	8,002	9,042	10,196	10,196	10,274	10,636	10,873	8,063	134	10,530
NC	4,532	4,450	5,162	5,443	5,682	5,759	5,786	3,480	70	5,399
ND	627	655	630	685	695	679	695	337	16	452
OH	7,771	8,102	8,410	9,664	9,810	9,770	10,108	6,700	219	8,186
OK	2,583	2,864	2,649	2,806	2,856	3,082	2,884	1,529	52	2,279
OR	2,081	2,204	2,445	2,753	2,785	2,851	2,891	1,578	62	2,277
PA......	6,926	7,209	7,971	8,482	8,481	8,640	8,825	6,050	182	8,318
RI	623	610	672	699	699	696	710	515	18	680
SC......	1,996	2,222	2,521	2,743	2,833	2,791	2,850	1,765	40	2,613
SD......	601	650	704	769	709	751	718	378	25	524
TN......	3,271	3,754	4,444	5,059	5,400	4,830	4,535	2,756	56	3,929
TX......	10,475	12,444	12,800	13,626	13,682	13,487	12,923	7,085	129	12,834
UT......	992	1,099	1,206	1,415	1,447	1,445	1,530	851	23	1,357
VT......	347	398	462	489	492	503	496	291	19	475
VA......	3,626	4,253	4,938	5,507	5,613	5,576	5,709	3,630	56	4,901
WA	3,225	3,526	4,257	4,465	4,503	4,603	4,702	2,691	104	4,010
WV	1,320	1,143	1,225	1,462	1,425	1,406	1,355	755	17	1,285
WI......	2,941	3,187	3,815	3,926	3,993	3,972	4,233	2,551	190	3,672
WY	467	500	528	508	601	562	553	222	15	353

[1] Excludes vehicles owned by military services.

Source: U.S. Federal Highway Administration, *Highway Statistics*, annual; and *Selected Highway Statistics and Charts*, annual.

No. 1028. Selected Motor Vehicle Indicators, by Model Year: 1992 to 1997

[In thousands of units (12,868 represents 12,868,000), except as indicated. A model year begins on Oct.1, and ends on Sept. 30. It covers the fourth quarter of one calendar year and the first three quarters of the next calendar year]

Sales and expenditures	1992	1993	1994	1995	1996	1997
New motor vehicle sales	12,868	13,913	15,179	15,233	15,460	15,380
New-car sales.	8,160	8,428	8,936	8,736	8,654	8,259
Domestic	6,195	6,595	7,173	7,167	7,361	6,924
U.S. nameplates.	5,048	5,348	5,707	5,518	5,428	4,964
Transplants	1,146	1,247	1,466	1,649	1,933	1,960
Import	1,966	1,833	1,763	1,570	1,293	1,335
New-truck sales	4,707	5,486	6,244	6,498	6,806	7,121
Light	4,446	5,167	5,869	6,070	6,389	6,707
Domestic.	4,026	4,789	5,499	5,666	5,976	6,155
Import.	421	378	370	404	413	552
Other.	261	320	375	427	417	414
Domestic-car production	5,643	5,827	6,548	6,466	6,194	5,879
Avg. expenditure per new car [1] (dollar).	16,893	17,526	18,431	18,849	19,397	20,305
Domestic (dollar).	16,281	16,595	17,406	17,695	18,064	18,580
Import (dollar).	18,861	20,998	22,598	24,111	26,972	29,296

[1] BEA estimate based on the manufacturer's suggested retail price.

Source: U.S. Bureau of Economic Analysis, *Survey of Current Business,* November 1997. Data from American Automobile Manufacturers Assoc., Inc., Washington, DC, and Ward's Automotive Reports; seasonally adjusted by BEA.

No. 1029. U.S. Truck Market—Import Penetration: 1975 to 1996

[Represents retail sales]

Year	Total U.S. sales	Domestic (lbs. GVWR) [1]			Imports		Percent of U.S. market	
		Total	14,000 lbs. & under	14,001- 33,000	Over 33,000	Total imports	From Japan	From Japan	Total imports
1975	2,478,219	2,248,904	1,973,853	191,903	83,148	229,315	228,097	9.2	9.3
1976	3,181,254	2,943,872	2,662,587	183,999	97,286	237,382	236,211	7.4	7.5
1977	3,675,439	3,352,255	3,011,667	199,945	140,643	323,184	321,364	8.7	8.8
1978	4,109,079	3,773,166	3,406,419	205,139	161,608	335,913	333,662	8.1	8.2
1979	3,479,794	3,009,867	2,635,604	200,969	173,294	469,701	465,701	13.4	13.5
1980	2,487,239	2,000,669	1,734,664	149,213	116,792	486,570	480,547	19.3	19.6
1981	2,260,318	1,809,188	1,587,093	122,395	99,700	451,130	443,504	19.6	20.0
1982	2,559,881	2,145,947	1,968,473	101,697	75,777	413,934	407,486	15.9	16.2
1983	3,129,476	2,658,269	2,477,238	99,384	81,647	471,207	463,515	14.8	15.1
1984	4,093,199	3,475,416	3,208,366	129,357	137,693	617,783	607,758	14.8	15.1
1985	4,681,698	3,902,417	3,629,080	139,756	133,581	779,281	768,625	16.4	16.6
1986	4,862,717	3,921,408	3,676,129	133,465	111,814	941,309	926,729	19.1	19.4
1987	4,912,374	4,054,738	3,790,606	133,872	130,260	857,636	840,297	17.1	17.5
1988	5,148,964	4,508,059	4,199,643	160,544	147,872	640,905	623,540	12.1	12.4
1989	4,941,220	4,403,299	4,113,467	145,104	144,728	537,921	514,532	10.4	10.9
1990	4,846,162	4,215,003	3,956,835	137,031	121,137	631,159	610,688	12.6	13.0
1991	4,364,672	3,813,173	3,605,779	108,751	98,643	551,499	539,556	12.4	12.6
1992	4,903,362	4,481,325	4,247,097	115,198	119,030	422,037	412,961	8.4	8.6
1993	5,680,994	5,287,379	5,000,430	129,063	157,886	393,615	381,433	6.7	6.9
1994	6,420,857	5,995,227	5,657,634	151,897	185,696	425,630	406,682	6.3	6.6
1995	6,481,357	6,064,154	5,690,903	171,948	201,303	417,203	393,573	6.1	6.4
1996	6,929,591	6,477,802	6,131,646	176,147	170,009	451,789	416,211	6.0	6.5

[1] GVWR = Gross vehicle gross weight rating in U.S. pounds.   [2] North American built.

Source: American Automobile Manufacturers Association, Washington, DC, *Motor Vehicle Facts and Figures,* annual (copyright).

No. 1030. Alternative Fueled Vehicles in Use, by Fuel Type: 1997 to 1999

Fuel	Alternative fueled vehicles			Fuel consumption (1,000) gasoline-equivalent gallons)		
	1997	1998	1999	1997	1998	1999
Fuels	369,807	395,625	418,128	311,692	334,541	351,539
Liquefied petroleum gases (LPG).	263,000	269,000	274,000	238,356	245,058	250,322
Compressed natural gas (CNG)	70,852	85,730	96,017	64,295	76,852	87,389
Liquefied natural gas (LNG)	813	1,358	1,517	3,714	6,338	6,888
M85 (Mixture: 85% methanol + 15% gasoline) . . .	21,040	21,578	21,829	1,554	1,395	1,301
Neat methanol (M100).	172	378	378	347	1,923	1,923
E85 (Mixture: 85% ethanol +15% gasoline)	9,130	11,743	17,892	1,280	1,615	2,243
E95 (Mixture: 95% ethanol + 5% gasoline)	347	14	14	1,136	59	59
Electricity	4,453	5,824	6,481	1,010	1,301	1,414

Source: Energy Information Administration, *Alternatives to Traditional Transportation Fuels: 1996.*

638   Transportation—Land

No. 1031. Motor Vehicle Production and Trade: 1980 to 1996

[8,010 represents 8,010,000]

Item	Unit	1980	1990	1991	1992	1993	1994		
United States	1,000...	8,010	9,784	8,811	9,702	10,898	12,263		
Passenger car production	1,000...	6,376	6,078	5,439	5,664	5,981	6,614		
Truck and bus production	1,000...	1,634	3,706	3,372	4,038	4,917	5,649		
Imports:									
Passenger cars (new) [1][2]	1,000...	3,116	3,945	3,736	3,575	3,808	4,097	4,114	4,064
Canada	1,000...	595	1,220	1,196	1,200	1,468	1,591	1,678	1,688
Germany, Federal Republic of	1,000...	339	245	172	206	184	188	207	234
Japan	1,000...	1,992	1,868	1,789	1,637	1,597	1,593	1,387	1,191
Trucks and buses (new) [2]	1,000...	747	766	716	777	722	708	662	688
Japan	1,000...	483	302	283	197	154	170	90	52
All-terrain vehicles	1,000...	(NA)	100	(NA)	(NA)	(NA)	(NA)	(NA)	(NA)
Motorcycles, total [3]	1,000...	1,120	169	(NA)	(NA)	(NA)	(NA)	(NA)	(NA)
Import value:									
Passenger cars (new) [1]	Mil. dol..	16,675	45,716	45,564	46,729	52,208	61,367	64,526	66,916
Trucks and buses, (new) [1]	Mil. dol..	1,985	8,155	8,221	10,000	10,104	10,909	11,792	12,381
Motorcycles [3][4]	Mil. dol..	1,142	361	(NA)	(NA)	(NA)	(NA)	(NA)	(NA)
Exports, number:									
Passenger cars (new) [1]	1,000...	617	794	755	851	864	1,019	989	974
Trucks and buses (new) exports	1,000...	186	159	208	161	181	274	254	316
Export value [1][5]	Mil. dol..	16,015	38,086	(NA)	(NA)	(NA)	(NA)	(NA)	(NA)
Passenger cars (new) [5]	Mil. dol..	3,932	9,708	9,886	11,893	12,476	14,591	14,251	14,392
Trucks and buses (new) [5]	Mil. dol..	2,977	2,845	3,388	3,073	3,399	5,238	5,209	6,246
Parts and accessories [6]	Mil. dol..	9,106	24,996	(NA)	(NA)	(NA)	(NA)	(NA)	(NA)
Factory sales:									
Passenger cars	1,000...	6,400	6,050	5,407	5,685	5,962	6,549	6,310	6,140
Trucks and buses	1,000...	1,667	3,725	3,387	4,062	4,895	5,640	5,713	5,776
Retail sales:									
Passenger cars (new) [1]	1,000...	8,979	9,300	8,175	8,213	8,518	8,991	8,635	8,527
Domestics [7]	1,000...	6,581	6,897	6,137	6,277	6,742	7,255	7,129	7,254
Imports [8]	1,000...	2,398	2,403	2,038	1,937	1,776	1,735	1,506	1,273
Trucks and buses [9]	1,000...	2,232	4,261	3,606	4,247	5,000	5,658	5,691	6,132
Light duty (up to 14,000 GVW) [10]	1,000...	1,964	3,984	3,621	4,264	5,015	5,673	5,703	(NA)
Med. duty (14,001-26,000 GVW) [10]	1,000...	92	71	50	57	64	69	80	(NA)
Heavy duty (over 26,000 GVW) [10]	1,000...	176	207	171	192	239	284	308	(NA)
Under 6,000 pounds	1,000...	985	2,866	2,719	3,212	3,754	4,132	4,031	4,398
Utility	1,000...	51	490	549	666	721	1,130	1,258	1,392
Van	1,000...	79	31	17	21	18	12	12	18
Minivan (cargo)	1,000...	(X)	83	66	63	70	82	73	64
Station wagon (truck chassis)	1,000...	(X)	112	110	201	321	-	-	-
Mini-passenger carrier	1,000...	(X)	750	706	840	1,002	1,132	1,113	1,098
6,000 to 10,000 pounds [11]	1,000...	975	1,097	876	1,021	1,232	1,506	1,631	1,690
Utility	1,000...	108	68	37	51	60	72	144	243
Van	1,000...	172	254	203	241	279	275	274	254
Pickup, conventional	1,000...	546	568	476	524	647	883	967	936
Station wagon (truck chassis)	1,000...	39	85	55	80	115	125	109	137
10,001 pounds and over	1,000...	271	298	242	275	330	388	428	(NA)

- Represents zero. NA Not available. X Not applicable. [1] Based on data from U.S. Dept. of Commerce. [2] Includes other countries, not shown separately. [3] Source: Motorcycle Industry Council, Inc., Irvine, CA. Data from U.S. Dept. of Commerce. Excludes mopeds/motorized bicycles and all-terrain vehicles. Excludes moped imports (motorcycle imports less than 51 cc's) from all countries (except Japan). [4] Represents c.i.f. value. [5] Covers assembled and unassembled vehicles. [6] Includes rubber tires and tubes and used vehicles. [7] Includes domestic models produced in Canada and Mexico. [8] Excludes domestic models produced in Canada. [9] Excludes motorcoaches and light-duty imports from foreign manufactures. Includes imports sold by franchised dealers of U.S. manufacturers. Starting in 1987, includes sales of trucks over 10,000 lbs. GVW by foreign manufacturers. [10] Gross vehicle weight (fully loaded vehicle). [11] Includes vehicles, not shown separately.

No. 1032. Motor Vehicles in Use, by Age of Vehicle: 1980 to 1995

[104.6 represents 104,600,000]

Item	Unit	1980	1985	1990	1991	1992	1993	1994	1995
Cars in use, total	Million	104.6	114.7	123.3	123.3	120.3	121.1	122.0	123.2
Under 5 years	Million	52.3	48.7	56.5	54.6	50.4	47.0	45.4	46.2
6-8 years	Million	25.2	27.8	22.6	25.5	27.5	28.7	27.7	26.9
9-11 years	Million	14.6	17.2	19.1	16.7	16.0	22.5	25.1	23.3
12 years and over	Million	12.5	21.0	25.1	26.6	26.4	31.1	31.4	26.8
Average age	Years	6.6	7.6	7.8	7.9	8.1	8.3	8.4	8.5
Cars retired from use [1]	1,000	8,405	7,729	8,897	8,565	11,194	7,366	7,824	7,414
Trucks in use, total	Million	35.2	42.4	56.0	58.2	61.2	82.5	71.4	70.2
Under 3 years	Million	8.8	9.0	12.8	12.0	11.3	12.1	13.7	15.4
3-5 years	Million	8.1	6.3	13.2	14.0	14.0	12.9	12.7	12.4
6-8 years	Million	7.4	10.2	8.0	9.9	11.9	14.0	13.6	13.1
9-11 years	Million	4.4	6.2	6.6	5.3	5.6	11.7	11.3	10.7
12 years and over	Million	6.5	10.7	15.5	17.0	18.3	23.2	20.1	18.6
Average age	Years	7.1	8.1	8.0	8.1	8.4	8.6	8.4	8.4
Trucks retired from use [1]	1,000	1,732	2,100	2,177	2,284	1,587	1,048	4,545	2,918

[1] For years ending June 30. Represents vehicles failing to re-register.

Source of Tables 1031 and 1032: Except as noted, American Automobile Manufacturers Association Inc., Detroit, MI, *Motor Vehicle Facts and Figures*, annual (copyright); and *World Motor Vehicle Data*, annual (copyright).

033. Motor Vehicle Registrations: 1980 to 1997

[In thousands (155,796 represents 155,796,000). Compiled principally from information obtained from state authorities, but it was necessary to draw on other sources and to make numerous estimates in order to complete series. Includes Alaska and Hawaii]

Item	1980	1990	1993	1994	1995	1996	1997
All motor vehicles	155,796	188,798	194,063	198,045	201,530	206,365	207,754
Private and commercial	153,265	185,541	190,643	194,532	197,941	202,714	204,079
Publicly owned...............	2,531	3,257	3,421	3,514	3,589	3,651	3,674
Automobiles [1]	121,601	133,700	127,327	127,883	128,387	129,728	129,749
Private and commercial	120,743	132,164	125,844	126,397	126,900	128,439	128,450
Publicly owned...............	857	1,536	1,484	1,486	1,487	1,289	1,299
Buses	529	627	654	670	686	697	698
Private and commercial	254	275	276	283	288	291	294
Publicly owned...............	275	351	378	388	398	406	403
Trucks [1]	33,667	54,470	66,082	69,491	72,458	75,940	77,307
Private and commercial	32,268	53,101	64,523	67,852	70,754	73,984	75,335
Publicly owned...............	1,399	1,369	1,559	1,639	1,704	1,956	1,972

[1] Trucks include pickups, panels and delivery vans. Beginning 1985, personal passenger vans, passenger minivans and utility-type vehicles are no longer included in automobiles but are included in trucks.

Source: U.S. Federal Highway Administration, *Highway Statistics*, annual.

No. 1034. Motor Vehicle Tires and Batteries: 1980 to 1995

[In millions]

Item	1980	1985	1990	1991	1992	1993	1994	1995
Tires, passenger car, total [1]	145.9	200.9	213.6	214.5	228.6	235.0	249.6	247.1
Radials	83.5	164.7	202.1	205.7	221.4	227.4	242.5	240.7
Replacement	106.9	141.5	152.3	155.4	165.8	165.1	170.0	166.8
Tires, truck and bus, total [1]	31.1	41.1	46.9	42.4	45.0	48.4	54.1	54.8
Radials	3.8	19.7	32.5	32.4	36.1	40.3	46.5	47.5
Replacement	24.4	32.1	36.6	32.9	33.7	35.7	36.8	36.7
Batteries, total [2]	61.7	74.4	79.7	79.8	(NA)	(NA)	(NA)	(NA)
Replacement automobile batteries ..	50.1	58.7	65.2	66.6	(NA)	(NA)	(NA)	(NA)

NA Not available. [1] Includes original equipment. Also includes exports, not shown separately. [2] Source: Battery Council International, Chicago, IL, and U.S. Census Bureau.

Source: Except as noted, The Rubber Manufacturers Association, Inc., Washington, DC, *RMA Monthly Tire Report*.

No. 1035. Automobile Output and Trade in National Income Accounts in Chained (1992) Dollars: 1990 to 1998

[In billions of dollars (125.8 represents $125,800,000,000). Vehicle output equals final dollar sales value of new vehicles, plus net dollar value of used vehicle sales adjusted for changes in inventories and net balance of vehicle exports and imports]

Item	1990	1992	1993	1994	1995	1996	1997	1998
Auto output, total	125.8	121.6	125.3	132.3	127.5	119.8	120.2	114.5
Final sales.....................	129.8	122.1	125.2	131.8	124.9	124.3	119.8	117.7
Personal consumption expenditures ..	133.3	117.6	121.6	123.7	122.3	121.5	123.7	129.7
Producers' durable equipment	33.0	35.3	38.8	47.8	42.7	44.7	44.2	43.1
Net exports	-38.7	-32.8	-36.6	-41.3	-42.2	-43.6	-49.8	-57.0
Government purchases	2.4	2.0	1.9	2.0	2.2	2.1	1.8	1.9
Change in business inventories.......	-3.9	-0.4	0.1	0.4	2.5	-4.7	0.4	-3.4
New	-3.6	0.1	1.0	0.9	2.5	-5.1	0.7	-0.4
Used	-0.3	-0.5	-0.8	-0.4	0.1	0.2	-0.2	-2.7

Source: U.S. Bureau of Economic Analysis, *The National Income and Product Accounts of the United States, 1929-94*, forthcoming; and *Survey of Current Business*, August 1998.

No. 1036. Recreational Vehicles—Number and Retail Value of Shipments: 1980 to 1997

[181.4 represents 181,400]

Item	1980	1985	1988	1989	1990	1991	1992	1993	1994	1995	1996	1997
NUMBER (1,000)												
Total	181.4	351.7	420.0	388.3	347.3	293.7	382.7	420.2	518.8	475.2	466.8	438.8
Motorized homes	99.9	233.5	277.1	261.6	226.5	172.6	226.3	243.8	306.7	281.0	274.6	239.3
Travel trailers	52.0	75.4	89.6	82.9	80.4	77.6	102.5	113.6	128.0	121.2	123.9	131.6
Folding camping trailers	24.5	35.9	42.3	33.9	30.7	33.9	43.3	51.9	61.7	61.1	57.3	57.6
Truck campers	5.0	6.9	11.0	9.9	9.7	9.6	10.6	10.9	11.4	11.9	11.0	10.3
RETAIL VALUE (mil. dol.)												
Total	1,952	6,904	9,061	9,019	8,101	6,623	8,774	9,518	12,196	12,104	12,365	11,928
Motorized homes	1,381	5,724	7,543	7,420	6,660	5,284	6,963	7,544	9,897	9,768	9,788	9,139
Travel trailers	485	997	1,254	1,252	1,220	1,107	1,523	1,644	1,912	1,927	2,171	2,356
Folding camping trailers	69	137	175	147	134	146	189	(NA)	276	290	284	309
Truck campers	17	46	88	81	86	87	99	(NA)	112	119	122	124

NA Not available.

Source: Recreation Vehicle Industry Association, Reston, VA, *RVIA Industry Profile 1997*. Data also in American Automobile Manufacturers Association of the United States, Inc., Washington, DC, *Motor Vehicle Facts and Figures*, annual (copyright).

No. 1037. Transportation to Work: 1990

[In thousands (84,215 represents 84,215,000), except as indicated. Based on workers 16 years old or older]

State	Means of transportation to work					Households with vehicles available		
	Car, truck, van		Percent using public transpor- tation	Worked at home	Average travel time to work [1] (minutes)	None	One vehicle	Two or more vehicles
	Drove alone	Car pooled						
United States	**84,215**	**15,378**	**5.3**	**3,406**	**22.4**	**10,602**	**31,039**	**50,306**
Alabama	1,374	267	0.8	31	21.2	156	466	885
Alaska	165	40	2.4	11	16.7	23	64	102
Arizona	1,178	239	2.1	48	21.6	107	532	730
Arkansas	765	153	0.5	28	19.0	88	303	501
California	9,982	2,036	4.9	453	24.6	923	3,452	6,006
Colorado	1,217	210	2.9	67	20.7	89	412	781
Connecticut	1,301	187	3.9	45	21.1	124	386	721
Delaware	258	43	2.4	8	20.0	20	80	147
District of Columbia	107	37	36.6	9	27.1	93	103	53
Florida	4,468	819	2.0	132	21.8	474	2,106	2,555
Georgia	2,379	468	2.8	65	22.7	244	730	1,393
Hawaii	344	116	7.4	19	23.8	35	129	193
Idaho	330	53	1.9	21	17.3	17	101	243
Illinois	3,742	653	10.1	144	25.1	588	1,476	2,138
Indiana	2,040	332	1.3	73	20.4	175	670	1,221
Iowa	971	157	1.2	89	16.2	75	332	657
Kansas	929	136	0.6	49	17.2	60	302	583
Kentucky	1,195	229	1.6	47	20.7	159	447	773
Louisiana	1,239	247	3.0	31	22.3	209	542	749
Maine	424	80	0.9	24	19.0	40	159	266
Maryland	1,733	376	8.1	65	27.0	216	554	979
Massachusetts	2,148	318	8.3	75	22.7	321	819	1,107
Michigan	3,328	429	1.6	100	21.2	344	1,133	1,943
Minnesota	1,593	247	3.6	116	19.1	142	517	988
Mississippi	777	184	0.8	19	20.6	111	307	494
Missouri	1,816	312	2.0	84	21.6	191	652	1,118
Montana	250	41	0.6	22	14.8	20	91	194
Nebraska	590	87	1.2	44	15.8	43	182	377
Nevada	444	94	2.7	12	19.8	36	174	256
New Hampshire	443	70	0.7	20	21.9	26	132	254
New Jersey	2,731	472	8.8	80	25.3	360	966	1,468
New Mexico	472	96	1.0	24	19.1	38	185	320
New York	4,461	861	24.8	213	28.6	1,994	2,153	2,492
North Carolina	2,528	530	1.0	71	19.8	242	786	1,489
North Dakota	210	31	0.6	24	13.0	16	73	152
Ohio	3,889	521	2.5	119	20.7	416	1,351	2,320
Oklahoma	1,079	191	0.6	41	19.3	91	414	701
Oregon	949	165	3.4	56	19.6	88	355	660
Pennsylvania	3,818	690	6.4	145	21.6	681	1,589	2,226
Rhode Island	376	58	2.5	10	19.2	40	132	206
South Carolina	1,235	277	1.1	31	20.5	137	402	720
South Dakota	233	33	0.3	31	13.8	17	76	166
Tennessee	1,763	324	1.3	52	21.5	181	593	1,079
Texas	5,821	1,134	2.2	185	22.2	489	2,190	3,392
Utah	541	111	2.3	26	18.9	29	153	355
Vermont	200	36	0.7	17	18.0	17	72	122
Virginia	2,281	500	4.0	103	24.0	205	717	1,370
Washington	1,701	282	4.5	86	22.0	141	582	1,149
West Virginia	493	107	1.1	16	21.0	94	247	347
Wisconsin	1,751	270	2.5	114	18.3	170	600	1,052
Wyoming	154	28	1.4	9	15.4	8	48	113

[1] Excludes persons who worked at home.

Source: U.S. Census Bureau, *Census of Population and Housing, 1990*.

Transportation—Land   641

No. 1038. Travel in the United States, by Selected Trip Characteristics: 1995

[656,462 represents 656,462,000. Trips of 100 miles or more, one way. U.S. destinations only. Data based on a sample and subject to sampling variability; see text. For definition of terms, see text, this section]

Trip characteristic	Household trips Number (1,000)	Per-cent	Person trips Number (1,000)	Per-cent	Person miles Number (1,000)	Per-cent	Personal use vehicle trips Number (1,000)	Per-cent	Personal use vehicle miles Number (1,000)	Per-cent
Total...............	656,462	100.0	1,001,319	100.0	826,804	100.0	505,154	100.0	280,127	100.0
Principal means of transportation:										
Personal use vehicles.........	505,154	77.0	813,858	81.3	451,590	54.6	505,154	100.0	280,127	100.0
Airplane.................	129,164	19.7	161,165	16.1	355,286	43.0	(X)	(X)	(X)	(X)
Commercial airplane........	124,884	19.0	155,936	15.6	347,934	42.1	(X)	(X)	(X)	(X)
Bus....................	17,340	2.6	20,445	2.0	13,309	1.6	(X)	(X)	(X)	(X)
Intercity bus...........	2,755	0.4	3,244	0.3	2,723	0.3	(X)	(X)	(X)	(X)
Charter or tour bus........	11,890	1.8	14,247	1.4	9,363	1.1	(X)	(X)	(X)	(X)
Train...................	4,200	0.6	4,994	0.5	4,356	0.5	(X)	(X)	(X)	(X)
Ship, boat, or ferry...........	391	0.1	614	0.1	1,834	0.2	(X)	(X)	(X)	(X)
Other..................	213	-	243	-	429	0.1	(X)	(X)	(X)	(X)
Round trip distance:										
Less than 300 miles..........	194,098	29.6	306,433	30.6	74,658	9.0	185,418	36.7	45,159	16.1
300 to 499 miles...........	174,389	26.6	274,045	27.4	106,007	12.8	159,743	31.6	61,779	22.1
500 5o 999 miles............	140,046	21.3	214,006	21.4	146,631	17.7	106,846	21.2	72,114	25.7
1,000 to 1,999 miles.........	76,110	11.6	108,331	10.8	153,316	18.5	36,722	7.3	49,953	17.8
2,000 miles or more..........	71,819	10.9	98,503	9.8	346,192	41.9	16,425	3.3	51,123	18.3
Mean (miles).............	872	(X)	827	(X)	(X)	(X)	555	(X)	(X)	(X)
Median (miles)...........	438	(X)	425	(X)	(X)	(X)	368	(X)	(X)	(X)
Calendar quarter:										
1st quarter.................	130,963	19.9	200,331	20.0	155,603	18.8	99,549	19.7	50,801	18.1
2d quarter	168,669	25.7	258,400	25.8	208,266	25.2	130,135	25.8	72,421	25.9
3d quarter	193,913	29.5	304,542	30.4	261,463	31.6	152,862	30.3	90,558	32.3
4th quarter	162,917	24.8	238,047	23.8	201,471	24.4	122,607	24.3	66,346	23.7
Main purpose of trip:										
Business	192,537	29.3	224,835	22.5	212,189	25.7	125,036	24.8	61,929	22.1
Pleasure	372,586	56.8	630,110	62.9	506,971	61.3	305,571	60.5	177,698	63.4
Visit friends or relatives	195,468	29.8	330,755	33.0	264,769	32.0	159,981	31.7	92,190	32.9
Leisure [1]	177,119	27.0	299,355	29.9	242,201	29.3	145,590	28.8	85,508	30.5
Rest or relaxation	65,017	9.9	115,154	11.5	100,838	12.2	53,780	10.6	33,598	12.0
Sightseeing	24,272	3.7	42,649	4.3	50,781	6.1	18,069	3.6	14,654	5.2
Outdoor recreation	39,899	6.1	65,418	6.5	41,620	5.0	35,987	7.1	19,407	6.9
Entertainment...........	37,456	5.7	58,757	5.9	42,929	5.2	27,920	5.5	14,531	5.2
Personal business	91,319	13.9	146,338	14.6	107,621	13.0	74,532	14.8	40,490	14.5
Other..................	19	-	36	-	23	-	16	-	9	-
Vacation or weekend trips:										
Vacation trip	301,197	45.9	515,383	51.5	484,144	58.6	236,055	46.7	154,167	55.0
Weekend trip..............	270,231	41.2	441,385	44.1	325,864	39.4	216,743	42.9	118,290	42.2
1 or 2 nights away from home. .	151,377	23.1	252,581	25.2	132,782	16.1	133,147	26.4	60,906	21.7
3 to 5 nights away from home. .	118,854	18.1	188,804	18.9	193,083	23.4	83,597	16.5	57,384	20.5
Travel party type and size:										
One adult, no children under 18 ..	386,479	58.9	386,510	38.6	352,350	42.6	275,034	54.4	144,795	51.7
Two or more adults, no children under 18.............	155,148	23.6	299,485	29.9	248,762	30.1	133,163	26.4	79,273	28.3
One adult, 1 or more children under 18.............	29,436	4.5	67,959	6.8	48,083	5.8	24,879	4.9	13,827	4.9
Two or more adults, 1 or more children under 18...........	66,086	10.1	225,875	22.6	158,334	19.2	60,497	12.0	34,758	12.4
No adult, 1 or more children under 18.............	19,313	2.9	21,489	2.1	19,275	2.3	11,581	2.3	7,472	2.7
Mean travel party size (household members)	1.6	(X)	2.2	(X)	(X)	(X)	1.7	(X)	(X)	(X)
Nights away from home:										
None..................	164,032	25.0	239,727	23.9	104,444	12.6	140,914	27.9	49,619	17.7
1 to 3 nights	321,227	48.9	502,465	50.2	331,504	40.1	259,354	51.3	131,559	47.0
4 to 7 nights	121,279	18.5	184,766	18.5	243,546	29.5	76,380	15.1	61,317	21.9
8 or more nights	49,924	7.6	74,361	7.4	147,309	17.8	28,506	5.6	37,631	13.4
Mean excluding none (nights)	4.5	(X)	4.3	(X)	(X)	(X)	4.0	(X)	(X)	(X)
Type of lodging at destination:										
One or more nights at destination .	486,305	100.0	751,958	100.0	709,097	100.0	359,745	100.0	226,001	100.0
Friend's or relative's home	211,832	43.6	345,506	45.9	290,428	41.0	170,271	47.3	103,180	45.7
Hotel, motel, or resort	201,264	41.4	282,929	37.6	318,323	44.9	126,160	35.1	82,447	36.5
Rented cabin, condo, or vacation home	17,607	3.6	30,648	4.1	31,161	4.4	14,631	4.1	10,809	4.8
Owned cabin, condo, or vacation home	20,205	4.2	38,572	5.1	26,269	3.7	18,103	5.0	9,819	4.3
Camper, trailer, recreational vehicle, tent..............	11,944	2.5	22,208	3.0	15,836	2.2	11,663	3.2	8,204	3.6
Other type of lodging........	23,452	4.8	32,095	4.3	27,080	3.8	18,917	5.3	11,542	5.1
Nights at destination:										
Mean nights at destination......	4.2	(X)	4.0	(X)	(X)	(X)	3.8	(X)	(X)	(X)
Friend's or relative's home	4.3	(X)	4.0	(X)	(X)	(X)	3.6	(X)	(X)	(X)
Hotel, motel, or resort	3.0	(X)	3.0	(X)	(X)	(X)	2.8	(X)	(X)	(X)

- Represents zero or a value too small to report.   X Not applicable.   [1]Includes other leisure activities not shown separately.

Source: U.S. Bureau of Transportation Statistics, *American Travel Survey*.

No. 1039. National Personal Transportation Survey (NPTS)— Summary of Travel Trends: 1969 to 1990

[62,504 represents 62,504,000. Data obtained by collecting information on all trips taken by the respondent on a specific day (known as travel day), combined with longer trips taken over a 2-week period (known as travel period). Contains data from previous NPTS surveys. For compatibility with previous survey data, all data are based only on trips taken during travel day. Be aware that terminology changes from survey to survey. See source for details]

Characteristics	Unit	1969	1977	1983	1990	Percent change, 1969-90	Annual percent change, 1969-90
Households, total	1,000	62,504	75,412	85,371	93,347	49.0	1.9
1 person.......................	1,000	10,980	16,214	19,354	22,999	109.0	3.6
2 persons.....................	1,000	18,448	22,925	27,169	30,114	63.0	2.4
3 persons.....................	1,000	10,746	13,046	14,756	16,128	50.0	2.0
4 persons or more	1,000	22,330	23,227	24,092	24,106	8.0	0.4
Persons, total	1,000	197,213	213,141	229,453	[1]239,416	21.0	0.9
Under 16 yrs. old.............	1,000	60,100	54,958	53,682	54,303	-10.0	-0.5
16-19 yrs. old	1,000	14,598	16,552	15,268	13,851	-5.0	-0.2
20-34 yrs. old	1,000	40,060	52,252	60,788	59,517	49.0	1.9
35-64 yrs. old	1,000	62,982	66,988	75,353	82,480	31.0	1.3
65 yrs. old and over	1,000	19,473	22,391	24,362	26,955	38.0	1.6
5 yrs. old and over	1,000	(NA)	198,434	212,932	222,101	12.0	0.9
Males.........................	1,000	94,465	102,521	111,514	114,441	21.0	0.8
16 yrs. old and over	1,000	66,652	74,542	83,645	86,432	30.0	1.1
Females.......................	1,000	102,748	110,620	117,939	124,975	22.0	0.8
16 yrs. old and over	1,000	73,526	83,721	92,080	96,371	31.0	1.1
Licensed drivers	1,000	102,986	127,552	147,015	163,025	58.0	2.2
Male	1,000	57,981	66,199	75,639	80,289	38.0	1.6
Female.......................	1,000	45,005	61,353	71,376	82,707	84.0	2.9
Workers	1,000	75,758	93,019	103,244	118,343	56.0	2.1
Male	1,000	48,487	55,625	58,849	63,996	32.0	1.3
Female.......................	1,000	27,271	37,394	44,395	54,334	99.0	3.3
Households with—							
No vehicle	1,000	12,876	11,538	11,548	8,573	-33.0	-1.9
One vehicle	1,000	30,252	26,092	28,780	30,654	1.0	0.1
Two vehicles	1,000	16,501	25,942	28,632	35,872	117.0	3.8
Three or more Vehicles	1,000	2,875	11,840	16,411	18,248	535.0	9.2
All vehicles available	1,000	72,500	120,098	143,714	165,221	128.0	4.0
Vehicle trips.................	Millions ..	87,284	108,826	126,874	158,927	82.0	2.9
Vehicle miles of travel (VMT)	Millions ..	775,940	907,603	1,002,139	1,409,600	82.0	2.9
Person trips..................	Millions ..	145,146	211,778	224,385	249,562	72.0	2.6
Person miles of travel	Millions ..	1,404,137	1,879,215	1,946,662	2,315,300	65.0	2.4
RATIOS							
Persons per household	Number...	[2]3.16	2.83	2.69	2.56	(NA)	(NA)
Vehicles per household	Number...	[2]1.16	1.59	1.68	1.77	(NA)	(NA)
Licensed drivers per household	Number...	[2]1.65	1.69	1.72	1.75	(NA)	(NA)
Vehicles per licensed driver	Number...	[2]0.70	0.94	0.98	1.01	(NA)	(NA)
Workers per household	Number...	[2]1.21	1.23	1.21	1.27	(NA)	(NA)
Vehicles per worker	Number...	[2]0.96	1.29	1.39	1.40	(NA)	(NA)
Daily vehicle trips per household.....	Number...	[2]3.83	3.95	4.07	4.66	(NA)	(NA)
Daily VMT per household..........	Number...	[2]34.01	32.97	32.16	41.37	(NA)	(NA)
Average vehicle trip length (miles)....	Number...	[2]8.89	8.34	7.90	8.87	(NA)	(NA)
Average annual VMT	Miles.....	12,423	12,036	11,739	15,100	22.0	(NA)
Home to work.................	Miles.....	4,183	3,815	3,538	4,853	16.0	(NA)
Shopping.....................	Miles.....	929	1,336	1,567	1,743	88.0	(NA)
Other family or personal business ..	Miles.....	1,270	1,444	1,816	3,014	137.0	(NA)
Social and recreational.	Miles.....	4,094	3,286	3,534	4,060	-1.0	(NA)
Average annual vehicle trips........	Number...	1,396	1,442	1,486	1,702	22.0	(NA)
Home to work.................	Number...	445	423	414	448	0.7	(NA)
Shopping.....................	Number...	213	268	297	345	62.0	(NA)
Other family or personal business ..	Number...	195	215	272	411	111.0	(NA)
Social and recreational.	Number...	312	320	335	349	12.0	(NA)
Average vehicle trip length.........	Miles.....	8.9	8.4	7.9	9.0	1.0	(NA)
Home to work.................	Miles.....	9.4	9.1	8.5	11.0	17.0	(NA)
Shopping.....................	Miles.....	4.4	5.0	5.3	5.1	16.0	(NA)
Other family or personal business ..	Miles.....	6.5	6.8	6.7	7.4	14.0	(NA)
Social and recreational.	Miles.....	13.1	10.3	10.5	11.8	-10.0	(NA)
Average vehicle occupancy [3]	Persons...	(NA)	1.9	1.7	1.6	[4]-1.3	(NA)
Home to work.................	Persons...	(NA)	1.3	1.3	1.1	[4]-1.3	(NA)
Shopping.....................	Persons...	(NA)	2.1	1.8	1.7	[4]-1.6	(NA)
Other family or personal business .	Persons...	(NA)	2.0	1.8	1.8	[4]-0.8	(NA)
Social and recreational.	Persons...	(NA)	2.4	2.1	2.1	[4]-1.0	(NA)
Journey-to-work trip mode	Percent ...	100.0	100.0	100.0	100.0	(NS)	(NS)
Auto	Percent...	82.7	80.5	77.6	91.4	(NS)	(NS)
Truck [5]	Percent...	8.1	12.5	14.8	(NA)	(NS)	(NS)
Public transit	Percent...	8.4	4.7	5.8	5.5	(NS)	(NS)
Other	Percent...	0.8	2.3	1.8	3.1	(NS)	(NS)

NA Not available.   NS Percent change irrelevant.   [1] Includes "don't know" and "refusals."   [2] Excludes pickups and other light-trucks as household vehicles.   [3] Includes other purposes not shown separately.   [4] Change from 1977.   [5] Household based trucks, primarily pickups.

Source: Federal Highway Administration, *National Personal Transportation Survey, Summary of Travel Trends, 1969, 1977, 1983*, and *1990*.

Transportation—Land   643

No. 1040. Roadway Congestion: 1996

[Various Federal, state, and local information sources were used to develop the data base with the primary source being the Federal Highway Administration's Highway Performance Monitoring System]

Urbanized area	Freeway daily vehicle miles of travel		Annual person hours of delay		Annual congestion cost		
	Total miles (1,000)	Per lane-mile of freeway	Total hours	Per 1,000 persons	Per driver (dol.)	Per capita (dol.)	Delay and fuel cost (mil. dol.)
Total, average	14,350	12,730	66,280	30	630	485	1,055
Albany-Schenectady-Troy NY	4,850	9,150	7,340	15	295	230	115
Albuquerque NM	3,600	12,415	19,055	34	700	535	300
Allentown-Bethlehem-Easton PA-NJ.	2,820	9,725	13,450	29	570	450	210
Atlanta GA	35,010	16,060	132,960	54	1,095	855	2,110
Austin TX	7,270	13,220	29,120	47	970	750	465
Bakersfield CA.	1,600	8,000	4,260	12	270	190	70
Baltimore MD	20,300	14,000	74,570	35	715	560	1,205
Beaumont TX	1,200	10,435	1,465	10	180	145	20
Boston MA	22,170	14,305	136,415	45	900	720	2,170
Boulder CO.	440	8,800	955	9	125	95	10
Brownsville TX.	280	9,335	995	7	165	110	15
Buffalo-Niagara Falls NY	5,750	9,350	14,845	14	285	225	240
Charlotte NC.	4,980	12,295	16,375	29	590	455	260
Chicago IL-Northwestern IN	45,200	17,155	250,840	32	670	510	4,005
Cincinnati OH-KY.	13,865	13,935	35,235	28	590	450	570
Cleveland OH	16,020	13,080	35,500	19	390	305	570
Colorado Springs CO	2,265	8,710	8,775	22	450	340	135
Columbus OH	10,980	12,765	24,995	25	505	395	400
Corpus Christi TX.	2,550	9,625	4,470	14	285	210	65
Dallas TX.	27,030	14,495	109,905	48	1,015	770	1,765
Denver CO	14,900	14,325	69,785	39	825	630	1,115
Detroit MI	29,690	15,960	200,000	53	1,095	840	3,165
El Paso TX-NM	3,970	10,445	7,815	13	290	205	125
Eugene-Springfield OR	1,165	10,590	2,340	11	220	165	35
Fort Worth TX	14,875	12,825	50,375	40	840	630	805
Fresno CA	2,000	8,335	8,320	16	350	245	130
Ft. Lauderdale-Hollywood-Pompano	10,250	13,310	45,560	31	625	490	730
Harrisburg PA	4,045	10,505	13,055	41	840	665	210
Hartford-Middletown CT.	7,300	11,495	19,045	30	640	505	320
Honolulu HI.	5,685	13,375	17,225	24	520	405	285
Houston TX.	35,150	14,555	150,240	49	1,055	785	2,405
Indianapolis IN.	10,800	12,345	25,160	25	505	400	400
Jacksonville FL	8,000	12,905	31,625	39	830	615	505
Kansas City MO-KS	16,930	10,105	39,175	29	610	470	630
Laredo TX.	415	7,545	1,525	10	200	135	20
Las Vegas NV	5,570	15,260	26,385	25	510	390	420
Los Angeles CA.	117,700	21,205	684,410	56	1,205	885	10,805
Louisville KY-IN	9,200	13,235	29,860	36	720	570	475
Memphis TN-AR-MS.	5,725	14,315	23,380	24	505	380	365
Miami-Hialeah FL.	11,500	16,665	92,585	45	905	710	1,460
Milwaukee WI	8,300	13,280	29,140	23	495	380	475
Minneapolis-St. Paul MN	22,900	14,495	62,720	28	575	455	1,020
Nashville TN	8,880	12,420	28,375	45	920	720	450
New Orleans LA.	5,450	12,825	27,320	25	500	385	430
New York NY-Northeastern NJ . . .	93,500	14,475	611,420	36	705	570	9,810
Norfolk VA	6,700	10,985	31,925	32	645	500	505
Oklahoma City OK	8,500	11,335	21,110	22	460	350	345
Omaha NE-IA	2,870	9,895	15,995	29	595	450	250
Orlando FL	7,640	10,685	33,730	32	660	505	535
Philadelphia PA-NJ.	21,385	12,255	116,580	22	445	345	1,825
Phoenix AZ.	13,200	15,085	67,640	29	590	455	1,070
Pittsburgh PA	10,310	8,700	48,440	25	485	390	755
Portland-Vancouver OR-WA	9,610	14,670	47,555	37	765	600	765
Providence-Pawtucket RI-MA	7,330	11,825	27,425	30	615	485	435
Rochester NY	5,300	10,930	11,590	19	405	305	190
Sacramento CA	10,750	13,030	42,150	34	730	545	670
Salem OR.	1,025	10,790	3,090	17	395	305	55
Salt Lake City UT.	6,950	12,635	16,830	19	430	300	270
San Antonio TX	13,275	12,705	34,470	28	605	450	550
San Bernardino-Riverside CA. . . .	16,280	16,530	61,950	46	1,030	735	990
San Diego CA	28,980	16,235	73,640	29	620	470	1,200
San Francisco-Oakland CA	43,300	17,390	202,985	52	1,055	835	3,250
San Jose CA.	17,320	13,910	83,145	52	1,070	825	1,315
Seattle-Everett WA.	22,100	16,870	110,090	56	1,155	915	1,780
Spokane WA	1,295	10,360	5,300	16	340	260	85
St. Louis MO-IL	23,700	13,165	81,245	40	825	635	1,280
Tacoma WA	4,805	16,015	14,670	25	535	405	240
Tampa FL.	5,010	12,845	25,220	31	610	480	395
Tucson AZ	1,650	10,315	13,530	21	420	330	210
Washington DC-MD-VA	33,370	18,185	231,080	67	1,290	1,055	3,655

Source: Texas Transportation Institute, College Station, Texas; *Roadway Congestion in Major Urban Areas,* annual (copyright).

No. 1041. Motor Vehicle Accidents—Number and Deaths: 1972 to 1997

[17.0 represents 17,000,000]

Item	Unit	1972 [1]	1980	1985	1990	1993	1994	1995	1996	1997
Motor vehicle accidents [2]	Million	17.0	17.9	19.3	11.5	11.9	11.2	10.7	11.2	13.8
Cars	Million	24.5	22.8	25.6	14.3	14.1	13.5	12.3	13.3	16.0
Trucks	Million	3.5	5.5	6.1	4.4	5.9	5.2	4.5	4.8	7.7
Motorcycles	1,000	343	560	480	180	187	178	152	135	138
Motor vehicle deaths within 1 yr. [3]	1,000	56.3	53.2	45.9	46.8	41.9	42.5	43.4	43.3	43.2
Noncollision accidents	1,000	15.8	14.7	12.6	4.9	4.2	4.4	4.4	4.5	4.2
Collision accidents:										
With other motor vehicles	1,000	23.9	23.0	19.9	19.9	18.3	18.9	19.0	19.5	21.3
With pedestrians	1,000	10.3	9.7	8.5	7.3	6.4	6.3	6.4	5.8	5.7
With fixed objects	1,000	3.9	3.7	3.2	13.1	11.5	11.5	12.1	12.3	10.8
Deaths within 30 days [4]	1,000	54.6	51.1	43.8	44.6	40.2	40.7	41.8	41.9	41.9
Vehicle occupants	1,000	41.4	36.8	31.5	33.9	31.1	32.0	33.1	33.4	33.6
Pedestrians	1,000	10.2	8.1	6.8	6.5	5.6	5.5	5.6	5.4	5.3
Motorcyclists [5]	1,000	3.0	5.1	4.6	3.2	2.4	2.3	2.2	2.2	2.1
Bicyclists	1,000	1.0	1.0	0.9	0.9	0.8	0.8	0.8	0.8	0.8
Traffic death rates: [4][6]										
Per 100,000 resident population	Rate	26.2	22.5	18.4	17.9	15.6	15.6	15.9	15.8	15.7
Per 100,000 registered vehicles	Rate	44.5	34.8	26.5	24.3	21.3	21.2	21.2	20.8	20.6
Per 100 million vehicle miles	Rate	4.3	3.3	2.5	2.1	1.7	1.7	1.7	1.7	1.6
Per 100,000 licensed drivers	Rate	46.1	35.2	27.9	26.7	23.2	23.2	23.6	23.3	23.0
Motor vehicle accidents [7]	Million	24.9	24.1	32.5	33.4	32.8	33.9	34.5	35.0	35.0
Injuries [7]	1,000	5,190	5,230	5,044	5,560	5,675	5,885	6,025	6,115	6,080
Economic loss [7][8]	Bil. dol.	28.7	57.1	76.0	95.9	104.1	110.5	115.6	120.8	123.7

[1] Represents peak year for deaths from motor vehicle accidents. [2] Covers only accidents occurring on the road. [3] Deaths that occur within 1 year of accident. Includes collision categories not shown separately. [4] Within 30 days of accident. Source: U.S. National Highway Traffic Safety Administration, unpublished data from Fatal Accident Reporting System. [5] Includes motor scooters and motorized bicycles (mopeds). [6] Based on 30-day definition of traffic deaths. [7] Source: Insurance Information Institute, New York, NY, *Insurance Facts.* Estimates based on official reports from a representative cross-section of states. Includes all motor vehicle accidents on and off the road and all injuries regardless of length of disability. [8] Wage loss; legal, medical, hospital, and funeral expenses; insurance administrative costs; and property damage.

Source: Except as noted, National Safety Council, Itasca, IL, *Accident Facts,* annual (copyright).

No. 1042. Motor Vehicle Deaths, by State: 1990 to 1997

[Includes both traffic and nontraffic motor vehicle deaths. See source for definitions]

State	1990	1995	1996	1997	Mileage rate [2] 1990	Mileage rate [2] 1997	State	1990	1995	1996	1997	Mileage rate [2] 1990	Mileage rate [2] 1997
U.S. [1]	46,814	43,363	43,300	43,200	2.2	1.7	MO	1,174	1,110	1,148	1,192	2.3	2.0
AL	1,234	1,111	1,142	1,181	2.9	2.3	MT	225	215	198	265	2.7	2.8
AK	102	86	80	77	2.6	1.8	NE	289	254	293	302	2.1	1.9
AZ	947	1,040	993	961	2.7	2.4	NV	405	312	348	347	4.0	2.4
AR	625	631	615	660	3.0	2.4	NH	154	118	134	125	1.6	1.2
CA	5,411	4,165	3,972	3,377	2.1	1.2	NJ	908	776	818	(NA)	1.5	(NA)
CO	583	645	434	516	2.1	1.4	NM	534	485	481	484	3.3	2.2
CT	395	318	310	337	1.5	1.2	NY	2,318	1,668	1,562	1,625	2.2	1.4
DE	151	123	120	147	2.3	1.9	NC	1,489	1,438	1,492	1,484	2.4	1.9
DC	91	(NA)	(NA)	(NA)	2.7	(NA)	ND	128	74	85	105	2.2	1.6
FL	3,049	2,812	2,813	2,847	2.8	2.2	OH	1,708	1,357	1,393	1,439	2.0	1.4
GA	1,659	1,494	1,578	1,584	2.3	1.8	OK	684	674	775	842	2.1	2.1
HI	186	127	145	131	2.3	1.6	OR	608	572	524	521	2.3	1.7
ID	259	263	258	259	2.6	2.1	PA	1,767	1,480	1,470	1,562	2.1	1.6
IL	1,650	1,589	1,475	1,404	2.0	1.5	RI	104	69	69	75	1.5	1.1
IN	1,097	960	981	(NA)	2.0	(NA)	SC	987	882	930	903	2.9	2.3
IA	481	527	465	468	2.1	1.8	SD	166	158	175	148	2.4	1.9
KS	453	438	491	483	2.0	1.9	TN	1,312	1,240	1,211	1,223	2.8	2.1
KY	850	856	844	865	2.5	2.1	TX	3,381	3,172	3,738	3,476	2.1	1.9
LA	1,023	880	809	840	2.7	2.1	UT	296	321	321	367	2.0	1.9
ME	215	189	168	192	1.8	1.5	VT	94	106	88	96	1.6	1.5
MD	741	682	614	609	1.8	1.3	VA	1,091	900	869	981	1.8	1.4
MA	655	448	417	443	1.4	0.9	WA	875	654	690	659	2.0	1.3
MI	1,633	1,537	1,505	1,446	2.0	1.7	WV	502	376	344	372	3.3	2.1
MN	644	597	576	598	1.7	1.3	WI	825	739	759	721	1.9	1.4
MS	863	868	811	861	3.5	2.9	WY	130	170	143	137	2.2	1.9

NA Not available. [1] Source: National Center for Health Statistics. [2] Deaths per 100 million vehicle miles.

Source: Except as noted, National Safety Council, Itasca, IL, *Accident Facts,* annual (copyright).

U.S. Census Bureau, Statistical Abstract of the United States: 1999

No. 1043. Fatal Motor Vehicle Accidents—National Summary: 1980 to 1997

[Based on data from the Fatal Accident Reporting System (FARS). FARS gathers data on accidents that result in loss of human life. FARS is operated and maintained by National Highway Traffic Safety Administration's (NHTSA) National Center for Statistics and Analysis (NCSA). FARS data are gathered on motor vehicle accidents that occurred on a roadway customarily open to the public, resulting in the death of a person within 30 days of the accident. Collection of these data depend on the use of police, hospital, medical examiner/coroner, and Emergency Medical Services reports; State vehicle registration, driver licensing, and highway department files; and vital statistics documents and death certificates. See source for further detail]

Item	1980	1985	1990	1993	1994	1995	1996	1997
Fatal accidents, total	45,284	39,196	39,836	35,780	36,254	37,241	37,351	37,280
One vehicle involved.	28,306	22,875	23,445	20,569	20,526	21,256	21,046	20,792
Two or more vehicles involved	16,978	16,321	16,391	15,211	15,728	15,985	16,305	16,488
Persons killed in fatal accidents . . .	51,091	43,825	44,599	40,150	40,716	41,817	41,907	41,967
Occupants [1]	41,927	36,043	37,134	33,574	34,318	35,291	35,579	35,693
Drivers	28,816	25,337	25,750	23,142	23,691	24,390	24,456	24,182
Passengers	12,972	10,619	11,276	10,361	10,518	10,784	11,021	10,773
Nonmotorists [1]	9,164	7,782	7,465	6,576	6,398	6,526	6,328	6,274
Pedestrians	8,070	6,808	6,482	5,649	5,489	5,584	5,412	5,307
Pedalcyclists	965	890	859	816	802	833	761	813
Occupant fatalities by type of vehicle, total	41,927	36,043	37,134	33,574	34,318	35,291	35,579	35,693
Passenger cars [1]	27,449	23,212	24,092	21,566	21,997	22,423	22,416	21,989
Mini-compact	3,141	3,571	3,556	2,635	2,339	2,207	2,011	1,745
Subcompact.	4,158	4,422	4,753	4,333	4,721	4,584	4,506	4,397
Compact	927	2,635	5,310	5,707	6,322	6,899	7,161	7,108
Intermediate.	3,878	4,391	4,849	4,483	4,407	4,666	4,626	4,736
Full size	4,831	2,974	2,386	2,067	2,074	2,116	2,111	2,222
Largest size	6,746	3,612	2,249	1,608	1,486	1,297	1,246	1,230
Motorcycles	4,961	4,417	3,129	2,336	2,190	2,114	2,045	2,018
Other motorized cycles	183	147	115	113	130	212	115	88
Multipurpose vehicles	895	855	1,214	1,521	1,757	1,935	2,138	2,378
Light trucks	6,591	5,834	7,387	6,990	7,147	7,633	7,763	7,846
Pickup	5,483	4,640	5,979	5,538	5,574	5,938	5,884	5,858
Van	1,000	791	1,154	1,365	1,508	1,639	1,829	1,921
Medium trucks.	285	157	134	90	109	96	89	120
Heavy trucks	977	820	571	515	561	552	532	597
Buses	46	57	32	18	18	33	21	17
Persons involved in fatal accident .	113,289	104,045	107,777	97,589	98,945	102,102	102,955	102,023
Occupants [1]	103,049	95,482	99,297	90,150	91,644	94,621	95,810	94,896
Drivers	62,957	57,883	58,893	53,401	54,549	56,164	56,793	56,602
Passengers	39,892	37,477	40,229	36,599	36,898	38,252	38,772	38,108
Nonoccupants [1]	10,240	8,563	8,480	7,439	7,301	7,478	7,138	7,127
Vehicle miles traveled (VMT) (100 million). .	15,273	17,742	21,444	22,967	23,576	24,227	24,822	25,604
Licensed drivers (1,000)	145,295	156,868	167,015	173,149	175,403	176,628	179,539	182,709
Registered vehicles (1,000)	161,490	177,098	192,915	198,041	201,802	197,065	201,626	203,568
Fatalities by road type [1]	(NA)	(NA)	44,599	40,150	40,716	41,817	41,907	41,967
Interstate	4,427	4,148	4,993	4,566	4,713	4,835	5,231	5,304
Federal-aid primary	(NA)	14,526	14,203	(NA)	(NA)	(NA)	(NA)	(NA)
Federal-aid secondary	(NA)	6,429	6,892	(NA)	(NA)	(NA)	(NA)	(NA)
Federal-aid urban	(NA)	8,116	8,432	(NA)	(NA)	(NA)	(NA)	(NA)
Non-Federal-aid	(NA)	10,408	10,039	(NA)	(NA)	(NA)	(NA)	(NA)
Fatal accidents by the highest blood alcohol concentration (BAC) in accident:								
0.00 percent	(NA)	48.5	50.6	56.5	59.3	58.7	59.2	61.5
0.01 to 0.09 percent	(NA)	10.3	9.7	8.5	8.5	8.6	8.7	8.2
0.10 percent and over	(NA)	41.2	39.7	35.0	32.2	32.6	32.2	30.4
Fatality rate by age group:								
Under 5 years old	6.9	5.2	4.9	4.5	4.8	4.3	4.6	4.1
5 years to 15 years old	8.7	7.4	6.4	5.8	6.0	5.9	5.7	5.6
16 years to 24 years old	46.0	37.1	35.2	30.2	30.8	31.1	30.5	29.2
25 years to 44 years old	24.6	19.6	19.7	16.9	16.3	17.2	16.9	16.5
45 years to 64 years old	17.2	14.5	14.9	13.0	13.3	13.4	13.7	14.1
65 years to 79 years old	19.6	18.0	18.8	17.9	18.7	18.5	18.6	19.0
80 years old and over	25.3	25.1	26.8	28.0	28.2	27.8	27.9	29.1
Fatalities per 100 million VMT.	3.3	2.5	2.1	1.7	1.7	1.7	1.7	1.6
Fatalities per 100,000 licensed drivers	35.2	27.9	26.7	23.2	23.2	23.7	23.3	23.0
Licensed driver per person.	0.6	0.7	0.7	0.7	0.7	0.7	0.7	(NA)
VMT per registered vehicle	9,458	10,018	11,107	12,189	11,683	11,793	11,807	12,101
Fatalities per 100,000 registered vehicles . .	31.6	24.8	23.1	21.3	20.2	21.2	20.8	20.6
Fatal crashes per 100 million VMT	2.9	2.2	1.9	1.6	1.5	1.5	1.5	1.5
Involved vehicles per fatal crash	1.4	1.5	1.5	1.5	1.5	1.5	1.5	1.5
Fatalities per fatal crash	1.2	1.1	1.1	1.1	1.1	1.1	1.1	1.1
Average occupants per fatal crash.	2.3	2.4	2.5	2.5	2.5	2.5	2.6	2.5
Fatalities per 100,000 population.	22.5	18.4	17.9	15.6	15.6	15.8	15.8	15.7

NA Not available. [1] Includes items not shown separately.

Source: National Highway Traffic Safety Administration, *Fatal Accident Reporting System*, annual.

No. 1044. Motor Vehicle Occupants and Nonoccupants Killed and Injured: 1985 to 1997

[Vehicle occupants accounted for almost 84 percent of traffic fatalities in 1995. The remaining 16 percent were pedestrians, pedalcyclists, and other nonoccupants]

Year	Occupants							Nonoccupants				
	Total	Total	Pas-senger cars	Light trucks	Large trucks	Motor-cycles	Buses	Other/unknown	Total	Pedes-trian	Pedal-cyclist	Other
KILLED												
1985.........	43,825	36,043	23,212	6,689	977	4,564	57	544	7,782	6,808	890	84
1986.........	46,087	38,234	24,944	7,317	926	4,566	39	442	7,853	6,779	941	133
1987.........	46,390	38,565	25,132	8,058	852	4,036	51	436	7,825	6,745	948	132
1988.........	47,087	39,170	25,808	8,306	911	3,662	54	429	7,917	6,870	911	136
1989.........	45,582	38,087	25,063	8,551	858	3,141	50	424	7,495	6,556	832	107
1990.........	44,599	37,134	24,092	8,601	705	3,244	32	460	7,465	6,482	859	124
1991.........	41,508	34,740	22,385	8,391	661	2,806	31	466	6,768	5,801	843	124
1992.........	39,250	32,880	21,387	8,098	585	2,395	28	387	6,370	5,549	723	98
1993.........	40,150	33,574	21,566	8,511	605	2,449	18	425	6,576	5,649	816	111
1994.........	40,716	34,318	21,997	8,904	670	2,320	18	409	6,398	5,489	802	107
1995.........	41,817	35,291	22,423	9,568	648	2,227	33	392	6,526	5,584	833	109
1996.........	41,907	35,581	22,416	9,901	621	2,160	21	462	6,326	5,412	761	153
1997.........	41,967	35,693	21,989	10,224	717	2,106	17	640	6,274	5,307	813	154
INJURED (1,000)												
1988.........	3,416	3,224	2,585	478	37	105	15	4	192	110	75	8
1989.........	3,284	3,088	2,431	511	43	83	15	5	196	112	73	11
1990.........	3,231	3,044	2,376	505	42	84	33	4	187	105	75	7
1991.........	3,097	2,931	2,235	563	28	80	21	4	166	88	67	11
1992.........	3,070	2,908	2,232	545	34	65	20	12	162	89	63	10
1993.........	3,125	2,958	2,257	590	32	58	17	4	166	93	65	9
1994.........	3,215	3,056	2,332	619	30	56	15	3	159	90	60	9
1995.........	3,386	3,232	2,416	709	30	55	18	4	154	84	61	9
1996.........	3,511	3,360	2,478	768	33	56	20	4	151	82	59	11
1997.........	3,399	3,253	2,378	768	31	54	17	5	146	77	58	11

Source: U.S. National Highway Traffic Safety Administration, *Traffic Safety Facts 1995, Overview,* annual.

No. 1045. Total Fatalities in Crashes Involving a Large Truck, by State: 1997

[Medium/heavy trucks represents trucks over 10,000 pounds GVW, including single unit trucks]

State	Total	Occupant fatalities med/heavy trucks	Occupant fatalities other vehicles	Non-occupant fatalities	State	Total	Occupant fatalities med/heavy trucks	Occupant fatalities other vehicles	Non-occupant fatalities
United States .	**5,355**	**717**	**4,189**	**449**	Missouri.......	158	13	138	7
Alabama	171	28	135	8	Montana	27	8	18	1
Alaska........	7	2	3	2	Nebraska......	53	5	45	3
Arizona	73	7	57	9	Nevada	31	3	23	5
Arkansas	135	23	105	7	New Hampshire..	12	2	8	2
California	409	69	273	67	New Jersey	89	4	77	8
Colorado	80	14	59	7	New Mexico	53	9	35	9
Connecticut	25	5	17	3	New York......	159	15	108	36
Delaware	16	3	12	1	North Carolina..	231	14	205	12
Dist. of Columbia.	4	-	2	2	North Dakota ...	12	3	9	-
Florida........	308	34	244	30	Ohio.........	220	24	179	17
Georgia	254	27	214	13	Oklahoma	104	19	75	10
Hawaii........	3	1	1	1	Oregon	79	13	60	6
Idaho.........	34	6	27	1	Pennsylvania ...	172	24	129	19
Illinois	166	21	120	25	Rhode Island ...	2	1	1	-
Indiana	157	21	131	5					
Iowa	89	12	74	3	South Carolina ..	90	11	73	6
Kansas	95	12	78	5	South Dakota ...	20	5	15	-
Kentucky	115	28	84	3	Tennessee	144	29	105	10
Louisiana	130	19	102	9	Texas	454	67	357	30
Maine	23	5	16	2	Utah	56	11	42	3
					Vermont.......	18	5	13	-
Maryland	84	14	62	8	Virginia.......	127	20	94	13
Massachusetts ..	39	4	28	7	Washington	89	13	73	3
Michigan	150	6	132	12	West Virginia ...	60	4	56	-
Minnesota	102	8	86	8	Wisconsin......	95	10	80	5
Mississippi	106	10	92	4	Wyoming	25	6	17	2

- Represents zero.

Source: U.S. National Highway Traffic Safety Administration, *Traffic Safety Facts,* annual.

No. 1046. Speeding-Related Traffic Fatalities and Costs, by Road Type and Speed Limit: 1997

[Includes fatalities that occurred on roads for which the speed limit was unknown. Includes costs for crashes that occurred on unknown road types. Totals may not equal sum of components due to independent rounding]

State	Traffic fatalities, total	Interstate Over 55 mph	Interstate 55 mph	Noninterstate 55 mph	50 mph	45 mph	40 mph	35 mph	Under 35 mph
United States.	41,967	1,304	413	4,040	505	1,532	787	1,367	1,415
Alabama.	1,189	48	1	118	9	133	24	40	25
Alaska	77	1	5	5	5	3	4	1	3
Arizona.	951	42	13	80	24	51	47	26	38
Arkansas	660	15	2	114	1	19	4	16	18
California	3,688	211	32	328	47	127	83	167	127
Colorado.	613	29	26	58	8	23	25	29	38
Connecticut.	338	-	25	5	25	1	4	4	6
Delaware	143	-	3	5	25	1	-	-	31
District of Columbia	60	-	-	-	-	1	-	-	31
Florida	2,782	73	24	97	28	113	55	85	91
Georgia	1,577	27	12	158	4	58	20	48	24
Hawaii	131	-	8	4	4	8	1	9	8
Idaho.	259	17	-	18	11	4	6	11	12
Illinois	1,395	41	33	206	1	28	12	56	75
Indiana.	935	18	9	69	18	28	31	28	31
Iowa	468	4	1	29	2	4	-	6	15
Kansas.	481	18	-	36	3	4	4	10	14
Kentucky	857	14	7	170	-	10	-	31	11
Louisiana	913	7	7	79	2	27	3	18	7
Maine.	192	6	-	3	10	24	6	11	5
Maryland	608	14	7	13	21	9	27	15	21
Massachusetts.	442	12	4	7	10	16	29	17	61
Michigan.	1,446	25	16	166	8	35	19	33	38
Minnesota.	600	3	8	83	4	7	1	2	15
Mississippi	861	35	2	74	28	34	5	18	15
Missouri	1,192	59	17	184	1	23	23	35	35
Montana.	265	6	1	42	1	4	-	10	4
Nebraska	302	7	-	8	24	4	2	4	6
Nevada	347	20	4	13	4	21	1	23	16
New Hampshire.	125	3	1	3	3	1	3	13	10
New Jersey.	774	-	3	4	11	9	14	10	22
New Mexico	484	32	2	27	4	17	5	17	21
New York	1,643	4	13	157	12	36	37	15	111
North Carolina.	1,483	15	12	303	5	104	-	66	5
North Dakota.	105	5	-	40	-	-	2	1	6
Ohio	1,441	30	4	186	2	20	14	35	31
Oklahoma.	838	53	3	85	8	64	17	22	10
Oregon.	523	7	5	94	5	12	4	11	13
Pennsylvania.	1,557	27	16	136	11	82	64	63	43
Rhode Island.	75	1	2	3	1	1	3	7	13
South Carolina.	903	32	12	159	12	95	17	64	24
South Dakota	148	9	-	26	-	4	4	1	3
Tennessee	1,223	18	9	80	16	58	38	50	51
Texas.	3,510	172	44	208	39	100	62	104	114
Utah	366	35	-	14	7	7	11	5	5
Vermont	96	7	-	-	14	3	3	7	1
Virginia.	984	32	14	132	-	40	8	33	18
Washington.	676	31	1	25	42	15	11	52	35
West Virginia.	379	10	2	44	5	11	11	9	5
Wisconsin.	725	7	3	134	2	14	6	12	23
Wyoming	137	22	-	9	-	2	1	1	3

- Represents or rounds to zero.

Source: U.S. National Highway Traffic Safety Administration, *Traffic Safety Facts 1995, Speeding. Traffic Safety Facts, Speeding,* annual.

648 Transportation—Land

No. 1047. Highway Mileage, Vehicle Miles of Travel, Accidents, and Fatalities, 1980 to 1997, and by Type of Highway System, 1997

[3,857 represents 3,857,000]

Year and type of system	Highway mileage (1,000)	Vehicle miles of travel (bil.)	Daily vehicle miles per mile	Fatal accidents Number	Fatal accidents Rate [1]	Nonfatal injury accidents Number (1,000)	Nonfatal injury accidents Rate [1]	Fatalities [2] Number	Fatalities [2] Rate [1]
1980	3,857	1,527	1,082	45,284	2.96	2,008	131	51,091	3.35
1985	3,862	1,774	1,259	39,168	2.21	2,219	125	43,825	2.47
1986	3,880	1,835	1,298	41,062	2.23	2,254	123	46,087	2.51
1987	3,874	1,921	1,361	41,434	2.15	2,294	119	46,390	2.41
1988	3,871	2,026	1,430	42,119	2.08	2,302	114	47,087	2.32
1989	3,877	2,096	1,489	40,718	1.93	2,384	113	45,582	2.16
1990	3,880	2,148	1,516	39,779	1.85	2,501	116	44,529	2.07
1991	3,889	2,172	1,530	36,895	1.70	2,210	102	41,462	(NA)
1992	3,902	2,240	1,568	34,928	1.56	2,216	99	39,235	1.75
1993	3,905	2,297	1,611	35,750	1.56	(NA)	(NA)	40,115	1.75
1994	3,907	2,360	1,655	36,223	1.53	(NA)	(NA)	40,676	1.72
1995	3,912	2,423	(NA)	37,221	1.54	2,335	96	41,798	1.73
1996	3,919	2,482	(NA)	37,351	1.50	2,411	97	41,907	1.69
1997	3,945	2,560	(NA)	37,280	1.46	2,400	94	41,967	1.64

NA Not available. [1] Rate per 100 million vehicle miles of travel. [2] Represents fatalities occurring within 30 days of accident. Excludes nontraffic accidents which, for example, occur outside the rights-of-way or other boundaries of roads that are open for public use.

Source: U.S. Federal Highway Administration, *Fatal and Injury Accident Rates on Public Roads in the United States*, annual.

No. 1048. Alcohol Involvement for Drivers in Fatal Crashes: 1985 and 1995

[BAC = blood alcohol concentration]

Drivers involved in fatal crashes	1985 Numbers of drivers	1985 Percentage with BAC of .10% or greater	1995 Numbers of drivers	1995 Percentage with BAC of .10% or greater	Change in percentage, 1985-95
Total drivers [1]	57,883	25.7	56,155	19.3	-25.0
Drivers by age group:					
16 to 20 years old.........	9,386	23.9	7,738	12.7	-47.0
21 to 24 years old.........	9,046	35.3	6,268	27.8	-21.0
25 to 34 years old.........	15,257	32.4	13,029	26.8	-17.0
35 to 44 years old.........	8,892	24.3	10,664	22.8	-6.0
45 to 64 years old.........	9,262	16.7	10,884	14.3	-14.0
65 years old and over	4,479	7.6	6,238	5.0	-34.0
Drivers by sex:					
Male..................	44,846	28.2	41,216	21.8	-23.0
Female................	12,142	15.5	14,179	11.2	-28.0
Drivers by vehicle type:					
Passenger cars	34,071	26.1	30,692	19.2	-27.0
Light trucks.............	12,372	28.7	17,420	22.4	-22.0
Large trucks.............	5,091	3.6	4,391	1.3	-62.0
Motorcycles.............	4,598	39.3	2,257	29.1	-26.0

[1] Does not add, due to unknown or other data not included.

Source: National Safety Council, Itasca, IL, *Accident Facts*, 1997 edition.

No. 1049. Age of Driver and Number in Accidents: 1996

Age group	Number	Percent	Fatal Number	Fatal Percent	All Number	All Percent	Per number of drivers Fatal [1]	Per number of drivers All [2]
Total	177,820,000	100.0	57,400	100.0	18,900,000	100.0	32	11
Under 16 years old.....	61,000	(Z)	500	0.9	90,000	0.5	([3])	([3])
16 years old	1,578,000	0.9	1,200	2.1	580,000	3.1	76	37
17 years old	2,195,000	1.2	1,600	2.8	670,000	3.5	73	31
18 years old	2,432,000	1.4	1,900	3.3	710,000	3.8	78	29
19 years old	2,653,000	1.5	1,800	3.1	670,000	3.5	68	25
19 years old and under ..	8,919,000	5.0	7,000	12.2	2,720,000	14.4	78	30
20 years old	2,828,000	1.6	1,800	3.1	600,000	3.2	64	21
21 years old	2,864,000	1.6	1,900	3.3	590,000	3.1	66	21
22 years old	2,880,000	1.6	1,800	3.1	560,000	3.0	63	19
23 years old	3,065,000	1.7	1,600	2.8	540,000	2.9	52	18
24 years old	3,625,000	2.0	1,600	2.8	540,000	2.9	44	15
20 to 24 years old	15,262,000	8.6	8,700	15.2	2,830,000	15.0	57	19
25 to 34 years old	37,781,000	21.2	13,000	22.6	4,600,000	24.3	34	12
35 to 44 years old	40,415,000	22.7	11,700	20.4	3,840,000	20.3	29	10
45 to 54 years old	30,928,000	17.4	7,100	12.4	2,360,000	12.5	23	8
55 to 64 years old	19,345,000	10.9	4,100	7.1	1,210,000	6.4	21	6
65 to 74 years old	15,648,000	8.8	3,000	5.2	810,000	4.3	19	5
75 years old and over...	9,522,000	5.4	2,800	4.9	530,000	2.8	29	6

Z Less than .05. [1] Per 100,000 licensed drivers. [2] Per 100 licensed drivers. [3] Rates for drivers under age 16 are substantially overstated due to the high proportion of unlicensed drivers involved.

Source: National Safety Council, Itasca, IL, *Accident Facts*, 1997 edition (copyright).

Transportation—Land   649

No. 1050. State Legislation—Alcohol and Road Safety Laws: Various Years

State	Alcohol legislation				Mandatory belt-use law				Speed limit changes, rural, 1995/96 [6]	
	Administrative license revocation since [1]	BAC limit [2]	Zero tolerance limit for minors [3]	Alcohol ignition interlock device [4]	Enforcement	Seating positions	Motorcycle helmet law [5]	Work zone speed law	Before	Currently
Alabama	1996	.08	.02	No	Secondary	Front	Yes [7]18	[8]No	65	70
Alaska	5/83	.10	.00	Yes	Secondary	All	18	No	(NA)	(NA)
Arizona	1992	.10	.00	No	Secondary	Front	18	No	55	75
Arkansas	3/95	.10	.02	Yes	Secondary	Front	21	[8]No	65	70
California	1989	.08	.01	[9]Yes	Standard	All	Yes	Yes	55	65
Colorado	1983	.10	.02	[9]Yes	Secondary	Front	No	Yes	65	75
Connecticut	1/90	.10	.02	No	Standard	[10]Front	18	[8]No	55	55
Delaware	Yes	.10	.02	[9]Yes	Secondary	Front	[11,12,13]19	Yes	(NA)	(NA)
District of Columbia	Yes	.10	.00	No	Standard	All	Yes	Yes	(NA)	(NA)
Florida	1990	.08	.02	Yes	Secondary	Front	Yes	Yes	65	70
Georgia	1995	.10	.02	[9]Yes	Standard	[10]Front	Yes	Yes	55	70
Hawaii	6/90	.08	.02	No	Standard	Front	[13]18	No	(NA)	(NA)
Idaho	7/94	.08	.02	No	Secondary	Front	18	Yes	65	75
Illinois	1/86	.08	.00	Yes	Secondary	Front	No	Yes	65	65
Indiana	Yes	.10	.02	Yes	Standard	Front	[11]18	Yes	65	65
Iowa	1963	.10	.02	Yes	Standard	Front	No	Yes	65	65
Kansas	1988	.08	.02	Yes	Secondary	All	18	Yes	65	70
Kentucky	No	.10	.02	No	Secondary	All	Yes	[8]No	65	65
Louisiana	1/84	.10	.02	Yes	Standard	[10]Front	Yes	[8]No	65	70
Maine	1984	.08	.00	[9]Yes	[14]Secondary	All	[11,15]15	Yes	65	65
Maryland	5/89	[16].10	.01	Yes	Standard	[10,17]Front	[13]Yes	[8]No	55	65
Massachusetts	No	.08	.02	No	Secondary	All	Yes	No	55	65
Michigan	No	.10	.02	No	Secondary	[10]Front	Yes	Yes	55	55
Minnesota	1976	.10	.01	No	Secondary	[10]Front	[11]18	Yes	65	70
Mississippi	1983	.10	.08	No	Secondary	Front	Yes	Yes	65	70
Missouri	1987	.10	.02	[9]Yes	Standard	[10]Front	Yes	Yes	70	60
Montana	No	.10	.02	Yes	Secondary	All	18	[8]No	65	[18]
Nebraska	1/93	.10	.02	Yes	Secondary	Front	18	Yes	65	75
Nevada	1983	.10	.02	[9]Yes	Secondary	All	Yes	Yes	55	75
New Hampshire	1/94	.08	.02	No	No	(NA)	18	Yes	65	65
New Jersey	No	.10	.01	No	Secondary	Front	[13]Yes	[8]No	(NA)	(NA)
New Mexico	1984	.08	.02	No	Standard	[10]Front	[13]18	No	55	75
New York	[19]11/94	[16].10	.02	[9]Yes	Standard	[10]Front	Yes	Yes	55	65
North Carolina	1983	.08	.00	Yes	Standard	Front	Yes	Yes	65	70
North Dakota	1983	.10	.02	No	Secondary	Front	[13]18	[8]No	65	70
Ohio	9/93	.10	.02	Yes	Standard	Front	[15]18	Yes	65	65
Oklahoma	1983	.10	.00	No	Standard	Front	18	[8]No	65	70
Oregon	1983	.08	.00	Yes	Standard	All	Yes	[8]No	65	65
Pennsylvania	No	.10	.02	No	Secondary	All	Yes	[8]No	55	65
Rhode Island	No	.10	.02	[9]Yes	Secondary	All	[20]()	[8]No	55	65
South Carolina	No	.10	No	No	Secondary	[21]Front	[13]21	Yes	65	65
South Dakota	No	.10	.00	No	Secondary	Front	18	Yes	65	75
Tennessee	No	.10	.02	Yes	Secondary	[10]Front	Yes	Yes	65	70
Texas	1995	.10	.00	[9]Yes	Standard	Front	Yes	[8]No	65	[22]70
Utah	1983	.08	.00	Yes	Secondary	Front	18	No	55	75
Vermont	[19]1969	.08	[23].02	No	Secondary	All	[13]Yes	No	65	65
Virginia	1/95	.08	.02	Yes	Secondary	Front	Yes	No	65	65
Washington	[24]6/94	.10	.02	Yes	Secondary	All	Yes	Yes	55	60
West Virginia	1981	.10	.02	Yes	Secondary	[10]Front	Yes	Yes	65	70
Wisconsin	1/88	[25].10	[26].00	[9]Yes	Secondary	[21]Front	[11]18	Yes	65	(NA)
Wyoming	1973	.10	No	No	Secondary	Front	18	Yes	65	75

NA Not available. [1]Year original law became effective, not when grandfather clauses expired. [2]Blood alcohol concentration that constitutes the threshold of legal intoxication. [3]Blood alcohol concentration that constitutes "zero tolerance" threshold for minors less than 21 years old unless noted. [4]Legislation for instruments designed to prevent drivers from starting their cars when breath alcohol content is at or above a set point. [5]Presence of law or age below which riders are required to wear helmet. [6]These are the maximum speed limits in each state. However, speed limits may be lower as individually posted. [7]Passengers. [8]No work zone speed law per se, but double fine for violation. [9]Primarily for repeat offenders but may also be applied to first time offenders under certain circumstances. [10]Required for certain ages at all seating positions. [11]Plus instruction permit holders. [12]Helmet possession required by all. [13]Reflectorization. [14]Secondary for 19 and older, standard for younger than 19. [15]Plus novice license holders. [16]BAC of .07 is prima facia evidence of DUI (MD); BAC of .05-.10 constitutes driving while ability impaired (NY). [17]Excluding front center seat. [18]No speed limit (reasonable and prudent). [19]Revocation by judicial action (NY) or Dept. of Motor Vehicles (VT). [20]Operators under 21 for first year; passengers. [21]Belt use required in rear seat if lap/shoulder belt is available. [22]Daytime. [23]Blood alcohol concentration that constitutes "zero tolerance" threshold for minors less than 18 years of age. [24]Applies only to second DUI offense. [25]Different legal limit for repeat offenders. [26]Blood alcohol concentration that constitutes "zero tolerance" threshold for minors less than 19 years of age.

Source: National Safety Council, Itasca, IL, Accident Facts (copyright).

No. 1051. Motor Vehicle Safety Defect Recalls, by Domestic and Foreign Manufacturers: 1980 to 1996

[Covers manufacturers reporting to U.S. National Highway Traffic Administration under Section 151 of National Traffic and Motor Vehicle Safety Act of 1966, as amended]

Manufacturer	Unit	1980	1985	1989	1990	1991	1992	1993	1994	1995	1996
Motor vehicles:											
Total recall campaigns [1]	Number ..	167	173	237	208	220	187	221	244	266	265
Domestic	Number...	129	137	182	159	168	142	178	178	190	197
Foreign	Number...	38	36	55	49	52	45	43	66	76	68
Total vehicles recalled	1,000	4,868	5,629	7,137	5,985	8,279	10,122	10,922	6,063	18,295	17,084
Domestic	1,000	3,943	4,995	6,173	4,070	6,646	6,545	7,655	4,280	9,041	15,104
Foreign	1,000	925	634	964	1,915	1,633	3,577	3,267	1,784	9,259	1,980
Motor vehicle tires:											
Recall campaigns [1]	Number...	24	19	11	13	12	7	5	5	3	1
Tires recalled	1,000	7,070	28	115	172	153	8	6	93	10	6

[1] A recall campaign is the notification to the Secretary of the U.S. Dept. of Transportation and to owners, purchasers, and dealers of motor vehicles and motor vehicle equipment.

Source: U.S. National Highway Traffic Safety Administration, *Motor Vehicles Recall Campaigns*, annual.

No. 1052. Cost of Owning and Operating an Automobile: 1980 to 1997

Item	Unit	1980	1990	1992	1993	1994	1995	1996	1997
Cost per mile [1]	Cents	27.95	40.96	45.77	45.14	46.65	48.91	51.43	53.08
Cost per 10,000 miles [1]	Dollars....	2,795	4,096	4,577	4,514	4,665	4,891	5,143	5,308
Variable cost	Cents/mile .	7.62	8.40	9.10	9.30	9.20	10.00	10.10	10.80
Gas and oil	Cents/mile .	5.86	5.40	6.00	6.00	5.60	6.00	5.90	6.60
Maintenance	Cents/mile .	1.12	2.10	2.20	2.40	2.50	2.60	2.80	2.80
Tires	Cents/mile .	0.64	0.90	0.90	0.90	1.10	1.40	1.40	1.40
Fixed cost	Dollars....	(NA)	(NA)	3,667	3,584	3,745	3,891	4,133	4,228
Insurance	Dollars....	490	675	747	724	697	716	782	809
License and registration	Dollars....	82	165	179	183	204	211	229	220
Depreciation	Dollars....	1,038	2,357	2,780	2,883	2,988	3,099	3,208	3,268
Finance charge	Dollars....	423	680	832	696	695	729	778	793

NA Not available. [1] Beginning 1990, not comparable to previous data.

Source: American Automobile Manufacturers Association Inc., Detroit, MI, *Motor Vehicle Facts and Figures*, annual (copyright).

No. 1053. Domestic Motor Fuel Consumption, by Type of Vehicle: 1970 to 1996

[Comprises all fuel types used for propulsion of vehicles under state motor fuels laws. Excludes Federal purchases for military use. Minus sign (-) indicates decrease]

Year	Fuel consumption				Avg. fuel consumption per vehicle (gal.)			Avg. miles per gallon		
	All vehicles (bil. gal.)	Avg. annual percent change [1]	Cars [2] (bil. gal.)	Buses [3] (bil. gal.)	Trucks [4] (bil. gal.)	Cars [2]	Buses [3]	Trucks [4]	Cars [2]	Buses [3]	Trucks [4]
1970 ..	92.3	5.4	67.7	0.8	11.3	688	2,172	2,467	13.5	5.5	5.5
1975 ..	109.0	2.5	74.1	1.1	14.6	619	2,279	2,722	14.0	5.8	5.6
1980 ..	115.0	-5.9	70.0	1.0	20.0	507	1,926	3,447	16.0	6.0	5.4
1981 ..	114.5	-0.4	69.1	1.1	20.3	496	1,938	3,565	16.4	5.9	5.3
1982 ..	113.4	-0.9	69.1	1.0	20.4	496	1,756	3,647	16.8	5.9	5.5
1983 ..	116.1	2.4	70.3	0.9	20.8	497	1,507	3,769	17.0	5.9	5.6
1984 ..	118.7	2.3	70.6	0.8	21.4	495	1,398	3,967	17.3	5.7	5.7
1985 ..	121.3	2.2	71.5	0.8	21.4	505	1,405	3,570	17.5	5.4	5.8
1986 ..	125.2	3.2	73.2	0.9	21.8	507	1,496	3,821	17.4	5.3	5.8
1987 ..	127.5	1.8	73.3	0.9	22.5	500	1,527	3,937	18.0	5.8	5.9
1988 ..	130.1	2.0	73.3	0.9	22.9	487	1,524	3,736	18.7	5.8	6.0
1989 ..	131.9	1.4	73.9	0.9	23.5	486	1,519	3,776	18.9	6.0	6.1
1990 ..	130.8	-0.8	69.6	0.9	24.5	461	1,428	3,953	20.2	6.4	6.0
1991 ..	128.6	-1.7	64.3	0.9	25.0	443	1,369	4,047	21.1	6.7	6.0
1992 ..	132.9	3.3	65.4	0.9	25.5	455	1,362	4,210	20.9	6.6	6.0
1993 ..	137.3	3.3	67.0	0.9	26.2	462	1,420	4,309	20.5	6.6	6.1
1994 ..	140.8	2.5	67.9	1.0	27.7	462	1,438	4,102	20.7	6.6	6.1
1995 ..	143.8	2.1	68.1	1.0	29.0	530	1,412	4,315	21.1	6.6	6.1
1996 ..	146.7	2.0	68.9	1.0	29.5	531	1,414	4,205	21.3	6.6	6.2

[1] From prior year, except 1970, change from 1965. [2] Includes taxicabs. The format used to report some vehicle types was changed. In previous years, some other two-axle four-tire vehicles were included in the passenger car category. Other two-axle four-tire vehicles are now separate from the truck category. [3] Includes school buses. [4] Includes combinations.

Source: U.S. Federal Highway Administration, *Highway Statistics Summary to 1985*, and *Highway Statistics*, annual.

No. 1054. Motor Vehicle Travel, by Type of Vehicle and by Speed: 1970 to 1997

[Travel in billions of vehicle-miles, except as indicated (1,110 represents 1,110,000,000,000). Travel estimates based on automatic traffic recorder data. Speed trend data for 1970 were collected by several state highway agencies, normally during summer months; beginning Oct. 1975, all states have monitored speeds at locations on several highway systems Monitoring Program]

Year	Vehicle-miles of travel (bil.)				Avg. miles per vehicle (1,000)			Motor vehicle speed on rural interstate				
					Passenger vehicles			Citations recorded (1,000) [2]	Avg. speed (miles per hour)	Percent of vehicles exceeding—		
	Total	Cars [1]	Buses	Trucks	Cars [1]	Buses	Trucks			55 mph	60 mph	65 mph
1970	1,110	917	4.5	186	10.3	12.0	9.9	200	63.8	87	69	44
1980	1,527	1,122	6.1	291	8.8	11.5	10.4	667	57.5	66	25	7
1985	1,775	1,256	4.5	391	9.4	7.5	10.5	8,449	59.5	75	44	17
1986	1,835	1,280	4.7	424	9.5	7.9	10.8	8,549	59.7	76	46	18
1987	1,921	1,325	5.3	457	9.7	8.9	11.1	7,992	59.7	74	46	19
1988	2,026	1,380	5.5	502	10.0	8.9	11.5	7,566	59.5	74	46	19
1989	2,096	1,412	5.7	536	10.2	9.1	11.7	7,488	60.1	77	49	22
1990	2,144	1,418	5.7	575	10.3	9.1	11.9	7,511	60.4	78	50	23
1991	2,172	1,367	5.8	649	10.3	9.1	12.2	7,594	59.9	76	48	21
1992	2,247	1,381	5.8	707	10.6	9.0	12.4	7,004	61.2	81	56	28
1993	2,296	1,385	6.1	746	10.5	9.4	12.4	6,433	60.8	78	51	24
1994	2,358	1,416	6.4	765	10.8	9.6	12.2	(NA)	(NA)	(NA)	(NA)	(NA)
1995	2,423	1,448	6.4	790	11.0	9.3	12.0	(NA)	(NA)	(NA)	(NA)	(NA)
1996	2,486	1,480	6.6	817	13.9	9.4	11.8	(NA)	(NA)	(NA)	(NA)	(NA)
1997	2,560	1,512	6.8	850	14.2	9.8	12.1	(NA)	(NA)	(NA)	(NA)	(NA)

NA Not available. [1] Includes motorcycles. [2] Citations issued for 55 mph violations.

Source: U.S. Federal Highway Administration, *Highway Statistics Summary,* annual.

No. 1055. Passenger Transit Industry—Summary: 1985 to 1997

[Includes Puerto Rico. Includes aggregate information for all transit systems in the United States. Excludes nontransit services such as taxicab, school bus, unregulated jitney, sightseeing bus, intercity bus, and special application mass transportation systems (e.g., amusement parks, airports, island, and urban park ferries) Includes active vehicles only]

Item	Unit	1985	1990	1994	1995	1996	1997
Operating systems	Number. . .	4,972	5,078	5,973	5,973	5,973	5,973
Motor bus systems	Number. . .	2,631	2,688	2,250	2,250	2,250	2,250
Passenger vehicles, active [1]	Number. . .	94,368	92,961	115,943	115,874	119,556	123,580
Motor bus	Number. . .	64,258	58,714	68,123	67,107	67,874	72,170
Trolley bus.	Number. . .	676	832	877	885	871	859
Heavy rail	Number. . .	9,326	10,419	10,138	10,157	10,201	10,242
Light rail	Number. . .	717	913	1,054	999	1,140	1,229
Commuter rail	Number. . .	4,035	4,415	4,517	4,565	4,665	4,943
Demand response	Number. . .	14,490	16,471	28,729	29,352	31,853	30,697
Operating funding, total	Mil. dol . . .	12,195	16,053	17,968	18,241	19,756	18,974
Passenger funding	Mil. dol . . .	4,575	5,891	6,756	6,801	7,417	7,599
Other operating funding [2]	Mil. dol . . .	702	895	2,271	2,812	3,068	2,962
Operating assistance	Mil. dol . . .	6,918	9,267	8,941	8,628	9,271	8,413
Federal	Mil. dol . . .	940	970	916	817	567	578
Local [3]	Mil. dol . . .	5,979	5,327	4,171	3,981	4,312	3,956
State [3]	Mil. dol . . .	([4])	2,970	3,854	3,830	4,392	3,879
Total expense	Mil. dol . . .	14,077	17,979	21,653	21,540	22,457	23,248
Operating expense	Mil. dol . . .	12,381	15,742	17,920	17,849	18,503	19,015
Reconciling expense	Mil. dol . . .	1,696	2,237	3,733	3,691	3,954	4,233
Capital expenditure, Federal.	Mil. dol . . .	2,510	2,380	3,577	5,481	4,125	4,049
Capital expenditures	Million	(NA)	2,873	2,623	3,422	3,593	4,121
Vehicle-miles operated [1]	Mil. dol . . .	2,791	3,242	3,467	3,550	3,663	3,841
Motor bus	Million	1,863	2,130	2,162	2,184	2,165	2,307
Trolley bus.	Million	16	14	14	14	14	14
Heavy rail	Million	451	537	532	537	543	558
Light rail	Million	17	24	34	35	38	41
Commuter rail	Million	183	213	231	238	242	251
Demand response	Million	247	306	464	507	617	623
Passengers carried [1]	Million	8,636	8,799	7,949	7,763	7,975	8,558
Motor bus	Million	5,675	5,677	4,871	4,848	4,912	5,199
Trolley bus.	Million	142	126	118	119	117	121
Heavy rail	Million	2,290	2,346	2,169	2,033	2,157	2,430
Light rail	Million	132	175	284	251	261	263
Commuter rail	Million	275	328	339	344	353	357
Demand response	Million	59	68	88	88	95	95
Avg. funding per passenger	Cents	53.0	66.9	85.0	87.6	87.6	88.8
Employees, number (avg.) [5]	1,000	270	273	304	311	306	340
Payroll, employee.	Mil. dol . . .	5,843	7,226	8,224	8,213	8,687	9,060
Fringe benefits, employee	Mil. dol . . .	2,868	3,986	4,452	4,484	4,563	4,677

NA Not available. [1] Includes other not shown separately. [2] Beginning 1994, includes taxes levied directly by transit agency and other dedicated funds, formerly included in Local. [3] Includes other operating revenue, nonoperating revenue, and auxiliary income. [4] For 1985, State and local combined. [5] Through 1992, represents employee equivalents of 2,080 hours = one employee; beginning 1993, equals actual employees.

Source: American Public Transit Association, Washington, DC, *Transit Fact Book,* annual. <http://www.apta.com/pubs/stats/index.htm>.

No. 1056. Class I Intercity Motor Carriers of Passengers: 1980 to 1997

[Carriers subject to ICC regulations. See text, this section. Minus sign (-) indicates deficit]

Item	Unit	1980	1985	1989	1990	1991	1992	1993	1994	1995	1996	1997
Carriers reporting [1]	Number.	48	43	20	21	21	21	21	20	20	17	17
Number of employees, average	1,000	31	24	(NA)	(NA)	(NA)	(NA)	(NA)	(NA)	(NA)	(NA)	(NA)
Compensation of employees	Mil. dol.	599	518	(NA)	(NA)	(NA)	(NA)	(NA)	(NA)	(NA)	(NA)	(NA)
Operating revenue	Mil. dol.	1,397	1,233	1,205	943	980	938	928	870	917	912	1,000
Passenger revenue [2]	Mil. dol.	947	836	890	738	793	755	751	721	770	772	835
Special bus revenue and other	Mil. dol.	215	184	165	90	187	183	177	149	147	140	165
Operating expenses	*Mil. dol.*	*1,318*	*1,168*	*1,133*	*1,015*	*967*	*874*	*880*	*919*	*899*	*878*	*948*
Net operating revenue	Mil. dol.	79	65	72	-72	13	64	48	-49	18	33	52
Ordinary income:												
Before income taxes	Mil. dol.	107	65	(NA)	(NA)	(NA)	(NA)	(NA)	(NA)	(NA)	(NA)	(NA)
After income taxes	Mil. dol.	90	53	12	-180	162	21	14	-67	-9	13	-2
Passenger vehicles in service [2]	1,000	8.6	8.4	(NA)	(NA)	(NA)	(NA)	(NA)	(NA)	(NA)	(NA)	(NA)
Vehicle-miles, passenger	Million.	781	567	(NA)	(NA)	(NA)	(NA)	(NA)	(NA)	(NA)	(NA)	(NA)
Revenue passengers carried	Million.	134	88	54	43	42	41	40	41	43	37	52
Expense per vehicle-mile	Dollar.	1.69	2.06	(NA)	(NA)	(NA)	(NA)	(NA)	(NA)	(NA)	(NA)	(NA)

NA Not available. [1] Excludes carriers preponderantly in local or suburban service and carriers engaged in transportation of both property and passengers. [2] Regular route intercity and local.

Source: Through 1993, U.S. Interstate Commerce Commission, *Transport Statistics in the United States*, Part 2, annual, thereafter, Bureau of Transportation Statistics, *Selected Earnings Data, Class I Motor Carriers of Passengers*.

No. 1057. Passenger Transportation Arrangement: 1995 to 1997

[In millions of dollars (12,574 represents $12,574,000,000). Represents SIC 4722]

Source of receipts	1995	1996	1997	Operating expenses	1995	1996	1997
Receipts, total [1]	**12,754**	**13,725**	**14,812**	**Expenses, total [1]**	**11,258**	**12,238**	**13,166**
Air carriers	7,174	7,689	8,332	Payroll, annual	4,745	5,114	5,460
Water carriers	679	653	649	Employer contributions [2]	718	791	802
Hotels and motels	951	1,045	1,151	Lease and rental payments	786	850	898
Motor coaches	342	421	466	Advertising and promotion	607	697	691
Railroads	122	147	156	Taxes and licenses	160	152	181
Rental cars	335	363	402	Utilities	505	544	553
Package tours	2,539	2,706	2,875	Depreciation	393	412	506
Other	612	701	781	Office Supplies	324	337	370
				Repair Services	151	161	195
				Other	2,869	3,180	3,510

[1] Receipts for firms primarily engaged in arranging passenger transportation. These estimates exclude receipts of transportation companies (airlines, railroads, etc.). [2] Includes contributions to social security and other supplemental benefits.

Source: U.S. Census Bureau, *Service Annual Survey*.

No. 1058. Motor Freight Transportation and Warehousing Services— Revenues, Expenses, and Payroll Expenses, and Payroll: 1995 and 1997

[In millions of dollars (172,727 represents $172,727,000,000)]

Kind of business	SIC [1] code	Operating revenue		Operating expenses		Annual payroll	
		1995	1997	1995	1997	1995	1997
Motor freight transport. and warehousing services [2]	42	172,727	195,979	160,321	181,332	49,373	55,835
Trucking and courier services, except by air [3]	421	161,806	183,153	151,628	170,998	46,478	52,438
Local trucking without storage	4212	43,830	49,972	38,695	43,871	9,885	11,624
Trucking, except local	4213	91,675	103,847	88,061	98,570	26,635	29,594
Local trucking with storage	4214	5,154	5,860	4,817	5,439	1,633	1,801
Courier services, except by air	4215	21,147	23,474	20,055	23,118	8,325	9,419
Public warehousing and storage	422	10,874	12,750	8,652	10,268	2,883	3,376
Farm product warehousing and storage	4221	749	710	595	576	182	179
Refrigerated warehousing and storage	4222	2,107	2,321	1,747	1,884	588	629
General warehousing and storage	4225	6,143	7,457	4,777	5,840	1,613	1,953
Special warehousing and storage [4]	4226	1,875	2,262	1,533	1,968	500	615

[1] Standard Industrial Classification. [2] Includes terminal and joint terminal maintenance facilities for motor carrier transportation (SIC 4231) not shown separately. [3] Excludes private motor carriers that operate as auxiliary establishments to nontransportation companies and independent owner-operators with no paid employees. [4] Includes household goods warehousing.

Source: U.S. Census Bureau, *Current Business Reports, 1996 Motor Freight Transportation and Warehousing Survey*.

U.S. Census Bureau, Statistical Abstract of the United States: 1999

No. 1059. Bus Profile: 1980 to 1997

Item	Unit	1980	1990	1995	1996	1997
FINANCIAL						
Expenditures, school bus..............	Mil. dol....	3,833	7,605	9,082	10,404	10,820
Operating revenues, intercity bus, Class I......	Mil. dol....	1,397	943	917	912	1,000
Operating expenses, intercity bus, Class I......	Mil. dol....	1,318	1,026	899	878	948
INVENTORY						
Operating companies, intercity bus, Class I.....	Number...	61	31	28	27	(NA)
Vehicles:						
Commercial & Federal bus	Number...	110,576	118,726	125,057	127,214	129,435
School & other bus	Number...	418,225	508,261	560,447	596,395	568,113
PERFORMANCE						
Vehicle-miles, all buses:						
Rural & urban highway................	Millions ...	6,059	5,726	6,383	6,563	6,836
Revenue:—						
Passenger miles, intercity bus............	Millions ...	(NA)	121,400	136,104	139,136	144,923
Passengers, intercity bus	1,000	370,000	334,000	366,500	347,900	350,600
Avg. miles traveled per vehicle, all buses	Miles....	11,458	9,133	9,312	9,446	9,799
Avg. annual fuel consumption, all buses.......	Gallon....	1,926	1,428	1,412	1,425	1,471
Avg. miles per gallon, all buses..............	Mpg	6.0	6.4	6.6	6.6	6.7
Average revenue per passenger mile.........	Cents	7.3	11.6	12.2	12.3	12.6
SAFETY						
Fatalities:						
School bus related	Number...	150	115	122	136	128
School bus occupants	Number...	9	11	13	10	10
Other vehicle occupants...............	Number...	88	64	72	101	95
Nonoccupants	Number...	53	40	37	25	23
Fatalities in vehicular accidents, all buses......	Number...	390	340	306	297	(NA)
Occupant fatality rate:						
Per 100 million vehicle-miles, all buses.......	Rate	0.8	0.5	0.5	0.4	0.2
Per 10,000 registered vehicles, all buses.....	Rate	0.9	0.5	0.5	0.4	0.2

NA Not available.

Source: U.S. Bureau of Transportation Statistics, *National Transportation Statistics,* annual.

No. 1060. Truck Profile: 1980 to 1997

Item	Unit	1980	1990	1995	1996	1997
FINANCIAL						
Revenues:						
Local intercity.....................	Mil. dol ...	(NA)	127,314	161,806	172,743	183,153
Class I intercity motor carriers of property:						
Operating revenue, total................	Mil. dol ...	1,290	46,710	(NA)	(NA)	(NA)
Operating expenses, total..............	Mil. dol ...	29,012	118,968	151,628	162,825	170,998
INVENTORY						
Truck registrations, total	1,000	5,791	6,196	6,719	7,013	7,083
PERFORMANCE						
Vehicle miles, total.................	Millions ...	108,491	146,242	178,156	182,971	191,345
Average miles traveled per vehicle:						
All trucks, total	Avg. miles .	18,736	23,603	26,514	26,092	27,013
Ton-miles, intercity..................	Millions ...	555,000	735,000	921,000	972,000	1,051,000
Average fuel consumption per vehicle	Gallons ...	3,447	3,953	4,315	4,221	4,217
Highway-user taxes, total	Mil. dol ...	9,888	19,356	25,116	(NA)	(NA)
SAFETY						
Occupant fatalities	Number...	8,748	9,306	10,216	10,522	10,941
Vehicle involvement, total (per 100 million vehicle-miles).....................	Rate	4.5	2.9	2.4	2.4	2.3

NA Not available.

Source: U.S. Bureau of Transportation Statistics, *National Transportation Statistics,* annual.

No. 1061. Trucking and Courier Services—Operating Revenue, Operating Expenses, and Equipment, by Type of Carrier: 1995 to 1997

[In millions of dollars, except as indicated (161,806 represents $161,806,000,000). Data cover SIC group 421. Excludes private motor carriers that operate as auxiliary establishments to nontransportation companies and independent owner-operators with no paid employees]

Item	All carriers			Specialty carriers			General carriers		
	1995	1996	1997	1995	1996	1997	1995	1996	1997
Operating revenues:									
Total [1]	161,806	172,743	183,153	49,139	52,464	55,411	112,667	120,279	127,742
Motor carrier	153,881	163,786	173,884	44,969	47,883	50,706	108,912	115,903	123,178
Local trucking	48,731	52,301	59,354	27,181	29,045	31,624	21,550	23,256	27,730
Long-distance trucking	105,150	111,485	114,530	17,788	18,838	19,082	87,362	92,647	95,448
Operating expenses:									
Total	151,628	162,825	170,998	44,556	47,685	49,560	107,072	115,140	121,438
Annual payroll	46,478	49,432	52,438	11,254	12,008	12,823	35,224	37,424	39,615
Employer contrib. to soc. sec. and other benefits	12,666	13,020	13,795	2,536	2,699	2,713	10,130	10,321	11,082
Purchased fuels	12,051	13,667	13,777	3,151	3,497	3,555	8,900	10,170	10,222
Purchased transportation	28,757	30,979	34,323	7,449	8,036	8,830	21,308	22,943	25,493
Lease and rental	2,794	2,970	3,148	738	767	875	2,056	2,203	2,273
Insurance	5,638	5,868	5,717	1,888	1,892	1,813	3,750	3,972	3,904
Maintenance and repair	8,876	9,281	9,465	2,894	3,107	3,237	5,982	6,174	6,228
Depreciation	8,702	9,186	9,289	2,882	3,028	3,069	5,820	6,158	6,220
Taxes and licenses	3,410	3,517	3,695	893	922	974	2,517	2,595	2,721
Drug and alcohol testing and rehabilitation programs	96	102	101	28	28	29	68	74	72
Other operating expenses	22,160	24,807	25,250	10,843	11,701	11,642	11,317	13,106	13,608
Equipment (1,000 units): [2]									
Trucks	311	332	346	121	130	134	190	202	212
Truck-tractors	736	755	784	165	175	178	571	580	606
Trailers (full and semi)	1,507	1,568	1,621	241	256	265	1,266	1,312	1,356

[1] Includes other revenue not shown separately. [2] Represents revenue generating equipment as of December 31, 1994. Includes owned and leased equipment.

Source: U.S. Census Bureau, *Current Business Reports, 1997 Transportation Annual Survey (formerly known as Motor Freight Transportation and Warehousing Survey)*.

No. 1062. Class I Intercity Motor Carriers of Property, by Carrier: 1980 to 1993

[Common carriers are carriers offering regular scheduled service. Contract carriers provide service at request of user. Minus sign (-) indicates loss]

Item	Unit	1980	1985	1989	1990	1991	1992	1993
Common carriers, gen. freight reporting	Number	298	237	192	191	201	208	220
Number of employees, average	1,000	413	376	461	465	474	490	511
Compensation of employees	Mil. dol.	9,803	10,217	12,854	13,556	14,032	14,967	15,987
Operating revenues	Mil. dol.	19,725	22,314	27,405	29,682	31,619	34,594	37,600
Operating expenses	Mil. dol.	18,870	21,037	26,242	28,340	30,269	32,977	35,729
Ordinary income before taxes	Mil. dol.	701	1,198	988	1,146	1,180	1,453	1,641
Net income	Mil. dol.	-72	658	659	746	749	878	985
Intercity vehicle-miles	Million	6,547	5,760	6,557	6,804	7,615	8,674	9,770
Intercity revenue freight carried	Mil. ton	178	136	145	157	169	196	225
Common carriers, other reporting [1]	Number	441	397	337	322	295	330	304
Number of employees, average	1,000	101	76	84	87	74	88	83
Compensation of employees	Mil. dol.	1,931	1,783	2,105	2,236	1,920	2,358	2,333
Operating revenues	Mil. dol.	8,792	7,962	8,321	9,042	7,761	9,367	9,315
Operating expenses	Mil. dol.	8,426	7,752	8,081	8,702	7,509	8,942	8,875
Ordinary income before taxes	Mil. dol.	230	123	117	198	122	309	354
Net income	Mil. dol.	14	94	88	153	85	221	250
Intercity vehicle-miles	Million	6,889	5,714	6,320	6,566	5,372	6,696	6,295
Intercity revenue freight carried	Mil. ton	324	303	278	302	253	298	296
Contract carrier, other [1]	Number	69	64	77	87	83	113	115
Number of employees, average	1,000	14	22	29	34	34	42	40
Compensation of employees	Mil. dol.	336	630	893	1,082	989	1,325	1,321
Operating revenues	Mil. dol.	1,272	1,942	2,946	3,486	3,644	4,501	4,581
Operating expenses	Mil. dol.	1,207	1,807	2,888	3,422	3,547	4,333	4,367
Ordinary income before taxes	Mil. dol.	48	103	15	3	53	127	181
Net income	Mil. dol.	28	69	3	-13	20	80	123
Intercity vehicle-miles	Million	934	1,227	1,826	2,044	2,339	2,933	2,913
Intercity revenue freight carried	Mil. ton	37	41	80	80	76	110	99
Carriers of household goods reporting	Number	28	40	36	36	36	32	31
Number of employees, average	1,000	10	11	12	13	12	12	10
Compensation of employees	Mil. dol.	157	240	276	296	298	291	252
Operating revenues	Mil. dol.	1,824	2,684	3,114	3,152	3,026	3,180	3,274
Intercity freight	Mil. dol.	1,676	2,388	2,703	2,702	2,318	2,787	2,834
Operating expenses	Mil. dol.	1,781	2,635	3,059	3,129	2,973	3,159	3,198
Ordinary income before taxes	Mil. dol.	74	79	41	12	27	-1	48
Net income	Mil. dol.	42	54	28	8	17	8	62
Power units, intercity service	1,000	25	35					
Intercity vehicle-miles	Million	969	1,171	1,229	1,366	1,086	1,136	949
Intercity revenue freight carried	Mil. ton	5	7	7	8	7	9	5

[1] Other than general freight.

Source: Through 1992, U.S. Interstate Commerce Commission, *Transport Statistics in the United States, Part 2*, annual; thereafter, Bureau of Transportation Statistics, *National Transportation Statistics*, annual.

Transportation—Land 655

No. 1063. Railroads, Class I—Summary: 1985 to 1997

[As of **Dec. 31**, or **calendar year** data, except as noted. Compiled from annual reports of class I railroads only except where noted. Financial data are not comparable with earlier years due to change in method of accounting for track and related structures. Minus sign (-) indicates deficit]

Item	Unit	1985	1990	1991	1992	1993	1994	1995	1996	1997
Class I line-hauling companies [1] . . .	Number.	23	14	14	13	13	13	11	10	9
Employees [2]	1,000 . .	302	216	206	197	193	190	188	182	178
Compensation	Mil. dol .	10,563	8,654	8,695	8,753	8,732	8,874	9,070	9,202	9,235
Average per hour	Dollars .	14.3	15.8	16.8	17.8	17.9	18.5	19.0	20.1	20.3
Average per year	Dollars .	34,991	39,987	42,131	44,336	45,354	46,714	48,188	50,611	51,889
Mileage:										
Railroad line owned [3]	1,000 . .	162	146	144	141	140	138	137	136	133
Railroad track owned [4]	1,000 . .	269	244	242	238	236	232	228	228	225
Equipment:										
Locomotives in service	Number.	22,548	18,835	18,344	18,004	18,161	18,505	18,812	19,269	19,684
Average horsepower	1,000 lb	2,469	2,665	2,714	2,750	2,777	2,832	2,927	2,985	3,060
Cars in service:										
Passenger train	Number.	2,502	(NA)	(NA)	(NA)	(NA)	(NA)	(NA)	(NA)	(NA)
Freight train [5]	1,000 . .	1,422	1,212	1,190	1,173	1,173	1,192	1,219	1,241	1,270
Freight cars [6]	1,000 . .	867	659	633	605	587	591	583	571	568
Income and expenses:										
Operating revenues	Mil. dol .	27,586	28,370	27,845	28,349	28,825	30,809	32,279	32,693	33,118
Operating expenses	Mil. dol .	25,225	24,652	28,061	25,325	24,517	25,511	27,897	26,331	27,291
Net revenue from operations . . .	*Mil. dol* .	*2,361*	*3,718*	*-216*	*3,024*	*4,308*	*5,298*	*4,383*	*6,361*	*5,827*
Income before fixed charges . . .	Mil. dol .	3,393	4,627	928	4,127	4,990	6,184	5,016	7,055	6,168
Provision for taxes [7]	Mil. dol .	660	1,088	-156	1,092	1,810	1,935	1,556	2,056	1,886
Ordinary income.	Mil. dol .	1,788	1,961	-91	2,055	2,258	3,315	2,439	3,885	3,156
Net income	Mil. dol .	1,882	1,977	-281	1,800	2,240	3,298	2,324	3,885	3,156
Net railway operating income . . .	Mil. dol .	1,746	2,648	-37	1,955	2,517	3,392	2,858	4,338	3,984
Total taxes [8]	Mil. dol .	3,169	3,780	2,649	3,732	4,343	4,512	4,075	4,669	4,514
Indus. return on net investment. .	Percent.	4.6	8.1	1.3	6.3	7.1	9.4	7.0	9.4	7.6
Gross capital expenditures	Mil. dol .	4,485	3,591	3,439	3,680	4,504	5,035	5,720	6,550	6,737
Balance sheet:										
Total property investment.	Mil. dol .	64,241	70,348	71,622	72,677	75,217	78,384	86,186	90,046	96,058
Accrued depreciation and										
amortization.	Mil. dol .	19,756	22,222	23,057	23,378	23,892	24,200	23,439	23,932	21,862
Net investment.	Mil. dol .	46,237	48,126	48,565	49,299	51,325	54,184	62,746	66,113	74,196
Shareholder's equity	Mil. dol .	27,605	23,662	22,603	23,115	24,658	27,389	31,419	32,255	34,996
Net working capital	Mil. dol .	1,084	-3,505	-3,988	-4,372	-3,295	-3,059	-2,634	-2,942	-3,434
Cash dividends	Mil. dol .	1,444	2,074	915	830	1,054	1,398	1,518	3,937	995
AMTRAK passenger traffic:										
Passenger revenue.	Mil. dol .	604.9	941.9	962.3	933.2	777.6	717.9	734.1	756.2	792.1
Revenue passengers carried . .	1,000 . .	20,945	22,382	21,693	21,678	21,511	21,239	20,349	19,700	20,200
Revenue passenger miles	Million. .	4,977	6,125	6,249	6,181	6,068	5,869	5,401	5,066	5,166
Averages:										
Revenue per passenger	Dollars	28.9	42.1	44.4	43.0	36.1	33.8	36.1	38.4	39.2
Revenue per passenger mile. .	Cents . .	12.2	15.4	15.4	15.1	12.8	12.2	13.6	14.9	15.3
Trip per passenger	Miles . .	237.6	273.7	288.0	285.1	277.7	(NA)	(NA)	(NA)	(NA)
Freight service:										
Freight revenue	Mil. dol .	26,688	24,471	26,949	27,508	27,991	29,931	31,356	31,889	32,322
Per ton-mile	Cents . .	3.0	2.7	2.6	2.6	2.5	2.5	2.4	2.4	2.4
Per ton originated	Dollar . .	20.2	19.3	19.5	19.7	20.0	20.4	20.2	19.8	20.4
Revenue-tons originated	Million. .	1,320	1,425	1,383	1,399	1,397	1,470	1,550	1,611	1,585
Revenue-tons carried	Million. .	1,985	2,024	1,987	2,022	2,047	2,185	2,322	2,229	2,114
Tons carried one mile	Billion . .	877	1,034	1,039	1,067	1,109	1,201	1,306	1,356	1,349
Average miles of road operated .	1,000 . .	161	133	130	126	124	123	125	127	122
Revenue ton-miles per mile of										
road.	1,000 . .	5,446	7,763	8,001	8,451	8,965	9,735	10,439	10,704	11,087
Revenue per ton-mile	Cents . .	3	3	3	3	3	2	2	2	2
Train miles	Million. .	347	380	375	390	405	441	458	469	475
Net ton-miles per train-mile [9] . .	Number.	2,574	2,755	2,796	2,759	2,759	2,746	2,870	2,912	2,861
Net ton-miles per loaded										
car-mile	Number.	62.7	69.1	71.6	70.9	71.6	72.2	73.6	75.0	74.0
Train-miles per train-hour.	Miles . .	21.9	23.7	23.7	23.7	23.1	22.4	21.8	22.0	19.2
Haul per ton, U.S. as a system . .	Miles . .	664	726	751	763	794	817	843	842	851
Accident: [10]										
All railroads.	Number.	35,340	26,440	24,662	22,553	20,400	18,038	15,586	13,108	(NA)
Persons killed.	Number.	1,036	1,297	1,194	1,170	1,279	1,226	1,146	1,023	(NA)
Persons injured	Number.	34,304	25,143	23,468	21,383	19,121	16,812	14,440	12,085	(NA)
Class I railroads.	Number.	29,388	20,450	18,728	17,055	15,058	12,428	10,565	8,000	(NA)
Persons killed.	Number.	955	1,166	1,069	1,047	1,124	1,080	994	818	(NA)
Persons injured	Number.	28,433	19,284	17,659	16,008	13,934	11,348	9,571	7,182	(NA)

NA Not available.   [1] See text, this section, for definition of Class I.   [2] Average mid-month count.   [3] Represents the aggregate length of roadway of all line-haul railroads. Excludes yard tracks, sidings, and parallel lines. (Includes estimate for class II and III railroads).   [4] Includes multiple main tracks, yard tracks, and sidings owned by both line-haul and switching and terminal. (Includes estimate for class II and III railroads).   [5] Includes cars owned by all railroads, private car companies, and shippers.   [6] Class I railroads only.   [7] Includes State income taxes.   [8] Includes payroll, income, and other taxes.   [9] Revenue and nonrevenue freight.   [10] Source: Federal Railroad Admin., *Accident Bulletin*, annual. Includes highway grade crossing casualties.

Source: Except as noted, Association of American Railroads, Washington, DC, *Railroad Facts, Statistics of Railroads of Class I,* annual, and *Analysis of Class I Railroads,* annual.

No. 1064. Railroads, Class I-Cars of Revenue Freight Loaded, 1970 to 1997, and by Commodity Group, 1996 and 1997

[In thousands (27,160 represents 27,160,000). Figures are 52-week totals. N.e.c.= Not elsewhere classified]

Year	Carloads Total	Piggy-back	Commodity group	Carloads 1996	1997	Commodity group	Carloads 1996	1997
1970....	27,160	1,450	Coal	6,694	6,709	Metals and products	579	600
1975....	23,217	1,308	Metallic ores	443	360	Stone, clay, and glass products	477	483
1980....	22,598	1,661	Chemicals, allied products....	1,524	1,578	Crushed stone, gravel, sand	679	687
1985....	19,574	2,863	Grain	1,235	1,200	Nonmetalic minerals, n.e.c	480	466
1990....	16,177	(NA)	Motor vehicles and equipment .	1,003	1,050	Waste and scrap materials	487	489
1993....	15,911	(NA)	Pulp, paper, allied products ...	527	525	Lumber, wood products, n.e.c. [1]	268	275
1994....	16,763	(NA)	Primary forest products	352	344	Coke	262	242
1995....	16,706	(NA)	Food and kindred prod., n.e.c. .	415	412	Petroleum product	276	291
1996....	16,521	(NA)	Grain mill products	490	505	All other carloads	328	346
1997, prel...	16,564	(NA)						

NA Not available. [1] Excludes furniture.

Source: Association of American Railroads, Washington, DC, *Weekly Railroad Traffic,* annual.

No. 1065. Railroads, Class I Line-Haul-Revenue Freight Originated, by Commodity Group: 1980 to 1996

[22,223 represents 22,223,000]

Commodity group	1980	1985	1990	1991	1992	1993	1994	1995	1996
Carloads (1,000) [1]	**22,223**	**19,501**	**21,401**	**20,868**	**21,205**	**21,683**	**23,179**	**23,726**	**24,159**
Coal	5,789	5,684	5,912	5,683	5,572	5,310	5,681	6,095	6,746
Farm products	1,866	1,494	1,689	1,605	1,646	1,636	1,459	1,692	1,530
Chemicals, allied products	1,322	1,296	1,531	1,556	1,568	1,606	1,695	1,642	1,639
Food and kindred products	1,767	1,224	1,307	1,316	1,352	1,380	1,381	1,377	1,302
Nonmetallic minerals [2]	1,474	1,196	1,202	1,075	1,029	1,044	1,138	1,159	1,176
Transportation equipment [3]	1,004	1,202	1,091	1,068	1,181	1,355	1,448	1,473	1,442
Lumber and wood products [3]	1,384	948	780	716	726	710	771	719	682
Pulp, paper, allied products	954	703	611	616	618	620	651	628	589
Petroleum and coal products	596	491	573	533	583	584	602	596	567
Stone, clay, and glass products	776	551	539	479	483	487	512	516	491
Metallic ores	1,258	511	508	499	489	443	440	463	443
Primary metal products	756	449	477	469	481	528	579	575	597
Waste and scrap materials	632	429	439	433	487	558	604	623	605
Machinery, exc. electrical [4]	77	35	39	39	39	37	40	41	40
Fabricated metal products [4]	72	31	31	34	32	37	37	32	29
Tons (mil.) [1]	**1,492**	**1,320**	**1,425**	**1,383**	**1,399**	**1,397**	**1,470**	**1,550**	**1,611**
Coal	522	538	579	560	554	534	574	627	705
Farm products	156	127	147	144	149	147	131	154	142
Chemicals, allied products	108	106	126	127	130	134	142	138	139
Nonmetallic minerals [2]	125	108	109	99	94	96	106	110	113
Food and kindred products	92	74	81	83	86	88	88	91	87
Lumber and wood products [3]	86	63	53	48	50	49	54	51	49
Metallic ores	105	47	47	45	45	41	40	44	42
Stone, clay, and glass products	54	44	44	39	40	40	42	43	42
Petroleum and coal products	38	33	40	37	41	41	43	43	42
Primary metal products	53	34	38	37	39	43	47	47	49
Pulp, paper, allied products	42	36	33	33	34	34	37	36	33
Waste and scrap materials	34	26	28	27	30	35	37	38	38
Transportation equipment	24	27	23	22	25	29	29	30	29
Machinery, exc. electrical [4]	2	1	1	1	1	1	1	1	1
Fabricated metal products [4]	2	1	1	1	1	1	1	1	1
Gross revenue (mil. dol.) [1]	**26,938**	**28,225**	**29,775**	**29,319**	**29,777**	**30,376**	**32,424**	**33,782**	**34,310**
Coal	4,956	6,556	6,954	6,903	6,717	6,481	7,021	7,356	7,706
Chemicals, allied products	2,946	3,342	3,933	4,043	4,123	4,277	4,520	4,553	4,660
Transportation equipment	1,917	3,110	3,100	2,633	2,753	3,021	3,257	3,269	3,390
Farm products	2,801	1,977	2,422	2,332	2,454	2,528	2,407	3,020	2,807
Food and kindred products	2,837	2,256	2,188	2,254	2,308	2,336	2,427	2,464	2,378
Pulp, paper, allied products [3]	1,652	1,641	1,486	1,502	1,508	1,511	1,510	1,543	1,485
Lumber and wood products [3]	1,543	1,525	1,390	1,282	1,342	1,324	1,421	1,385	1,409
Primary metal products	1,332	872	979	977	970	1,021	1,114	1,199	1,254
Stone, clay, and glass products	1,025	960	931	878	911	944	1,009	1,044	1,033
Petroleum and coal products	865	861	918	888	943	929	967	997	1,013
Nonmetallic minerals [2]	948	949	885	824	812	818	862	875	895
Waste and scrap materials	513	446	504	515	558	613	655	685	702
Metallic ores	597	403	408	400	409	385	378	394	382
Machinery, exc. electrical [4]	176	72	67	62	61	59	65	69	70
Fabricated metal products [4]	110	48	42	48	45	50	50	44	41

[1] Includes commodity groups and small packaged freight shipments, not shown separately. [2] Except fuels. [3] Except furniture. [4] Except ordnance, machinery, and transport.

Source: Association of American Railroads, Washington, DC, *Freight Commodity Statistics,* annual.

U.S. Census Bureau, Statistical Abstract of the United States: 1999

No. 1066. Railroad Freight—Producer Price Indexes: 1980 to 1998

[Dec. 1984=100. Reflects prices for shipping a fixed set of commodities under specified and unchanging conditions]

Commodity	1980	1985	1990	1992	1993	1994	1995	1996	1997	1998
Total railroad freight	**75.9**	**99.9**	**107.5**	**109.9**	**110.9**	**111.8**	**111.7**	**111.5**	**112.1**	**113.4**
Coal	75.8	100.0	104.2	105.9	106.6	107.5	107.3	106.7	107.0	109.0
Farm products	75.6	99.0	110.4	111.1	113.7	114.5	115.6	115.7	120.4	123.8
Food products	75.2	100.0	105.4	108.7	109.0	111.0	111.2	108.5	107.6	107.4
Metallic ores	74.5	100.2	106.5	106.6	106.7	104.6	101.9	103.5	103.4	104.2
Chemicals or allied products	75.6	100.1	111.7	115.6	116.2	117.6	120.0	119.2	119.6	120.2
Nonmetallic minerals	72.2	100.1	111.7	117.6	119.3	119.7	119.5	119.2	120.6	120.9
Wood or lumber products	72.7	100.0	107.5	108.8	109.7	110.0	110.0	112.8	111.0	110.3
Transportation equipment	81.7	100.0	107.5	110.8	113.1	115.3	112.8	114.0	113.2	113.4
Pulp, paper, or allied products	76.7	100.0	108.0	111.8	112.6	111.1	108.7	(NA)	111.2	113.8
Primary metal products	77.8	99.7	113.1	117.5	116.3	115.6	115.6	115.4	114.0	116.1
Clay, concrete, glass, or stone products .	74.2	100.0	114.1	116.5	117.9	120.1	121.4	121.1	119.8	121.8
Petroleum and coal products	76.1	99.7	109.2	109.5	110.6	114.8	114.3	114.1	120.5	122.3

NA Not available.

Source: U.S. Bureau of Labor Statistics, *Producer Price Indexes*, monthly and annual.

No. 1067. Petroleum Pipeline Companies—Characteristics: 1980 to 1997

[(173 represents 173,000). Covers pipeline companies operating in interstate commerce and subject to jurisdiction of Federal Energy Regulatory Commission]

Item	Unit	1980	1985	1990	1992	1993	1994	1995	1996	1997
Miles of pipeline, total	1,000	173	171	168	164	164	159	177	169	160
Gathering lines	1,000	36	35	32	29	29	30	35	32	31
Trunk lines	1,000	136	136	136	136	135	128	142	137	130
Total deliveries	Mil. bbl.	10,600	10,745	11,378	11,447	12,219	12,159	12,862	12,635	12,481
Crude oil	Mil. bbl.	6,405	6,239	6,563	6,541	6,708	6,785	6,952	6,975	6,795
Products	Mil. bbl.	4,195	4,506	4,816	4,906	5,511	5,373	5,910	5,660	5,686
Total trunk line traffic	Bil. bbl-miles .	3,405	3,342	3,500	3,428	3,051	3,566	3,619	3,734	3,683
Crude oil	Bil. bbl-miles .	1,948	1,842	1,891	1,853	1,382	1,823	1,899	1,912	1,901
Products	Bil. bbl-miles .	1,458	1,500	1,609	1,575	1,669	1,743	1,720	1,822	1,782
Carrier property value	Mil. dol.	19,752	21,605	25,828	27,106	31,625	26,363	27,460	28,043	30,655
Operating revenues	Mil. dol.	6,356	7,461	7,149	7,154	6,931	7,281	7,711	7,321	7,215
Net income	Mil. dol.	1,912	2,002	2,431	2,061	1,763	2,148	2,670	2,372	2,255

Source: PennWell Publishing Co., Houston, Texas, *Oil & Gas Journal*, annual (copyright).

No. 1068. Major Interstate Natural Gas Pipeline Companies—Summary: 1985 to 1991

[The classification of A and B interstate natural gas pipeline companies changed to major companies and nonmajor companies. Major natural gas pipleline companies are those whose combined sales for resale and natural gas transported or stored for a fee exceed 50 billion cubic feet. They account for more than 85 percent of all interstate natural gas]

Item	Unit	1985	1986	1987	1988	1989	1990	1991
Sales	Tril. cu. ft . .	11.3	7.8	6.5	6.4	5.6	4.5	3.9
Residential	Tril. cu. ft . .	0.3	0.2	0.2	0.3	0.1	0.2	0.2
Commercial, industrial	Tril. cu. ft . .	1.1	0.5	0.4	0.5	0.5	0.4	0.3
For resale	Tril. cu. ft . .	9.9	7.1	5.8	5.6	4.9	3.9	3.3
Operating revenues	Mil. dol . . .	49,106	33,859	27,565	27,501	25,695	22,574	21,420
From sales [1]	Mil. dol . . .	44,996	29,508	22,942	22,512	19,786	15,981	14,135
From transportation of gas of others	Mil. dol . . .	2,272	3,027	3,622	4,059	4,959	5,505	6,117
Other	Mil. dol . . .	1,838	1,325	1,002	929	950	1,088	1,167
Operation, maintenance expenses	Mil. dol . . .	42,528	27,460	21,794	22,742	20,829	17,446	17,335
Production	Mil. dol . . .	36,739	22,208	16,955	17,625	15,257	12,124	11,663
Storage	Mil. dol . . .	418	420	409	436	458	417	460
Transmission	Mil. dol . . .	3,409	2,984	2,598	2,589	2,589	2,720	2,880
Distribution	Mil. dol . . .	132	80	80	127	94	112	133
Administrative, general, and other	Mil. dol . . .	1,830	1,768	1,752	1,966	2,430	2,074	2,048
Pipeline mileage	1,000	230.2	217.3	249.5	246.9	253.2	230.2	249.5
Transmission lines	1,000	189.7	184.6	181.2	191.6	194.1	195.5	146.8
Field lines	1,000	69.6	64.5	62.9	55.5	55.1	54.0	50.7
Storage	1,000	4.8	4.6	4.3	4.8	4.8	5.0	4.7

[1] Includes other ultimate customers not shown separately.

Source: U.S. Energy Information Administration, *Statistics of Interstate Natural Gas Pipeline Companies*, annual.

Section 22
Transportation—Air and Water

This section presents data on civil air transportation, both passenger and cargo, and on water transportation, including inland waterways, oceanborne commerce, the merchant marine, cargo and vessel tonnages, and shipbuilding. Comparative data on various types of transportation carriers are presented in Section 21, Land Transportation.

Principal sources of these data are the annual *National Transportation Statistics*, issued by the U.S. Bureau of Transportation Statistics; the annual *Air Transport Facts and Figures* issued by the Air Transport Association of America, Washington, DC; and the annual *Waterborne Commerce of the United States* issued by the Corps of Engineers of the Department of the Army. In addition, the U.S. Census Bureau in its commodity transportation survey (part of the census of transportation, taken every 5 years, for years ending in "2" and "7") provides data on the type, weight, and value of commodities shipped by manufacturing establishments in the United States, by means of transportation, origin, and destination. See text, Section 17, Business, for a discussion of the 1997 Economic Census.

Additional sources of data on water transportation include *Merchant Fleets of the World,* issued periodically by the U.S. Maritime Administration; *The Bulletin,* issued monthly by the American Bureau of Shipping, New York, NY; and the annual *World Fleet Statistics* and the *Register Book,* published by Lloyd's Register of Shipping, London, England.

Civil aviation—Federal promotion and regulation of civil aviation have been carried out by the FAA and the Civil Aeronautics Board (CAB). The CAB promoted and regulated the civil air transportation industry within the United States and between the United States and foreign countries. The Board granted licenses to provide air transportation service, approved or disapproved proposed rates and fares, and approved or disapproved proposed agreements and corporate relationships involving air carriers. In December 1984, the CAB ceased to exist as an agency. Some of its functions were transferred to the Department of Transportation (DOT), as outlined below. The responsibility for investigation of aviation accidents resides with the National Transportation Safety Board.

The Office of the Secretary, DOT aviation activities include: negotiation of international air transportation rights, selection of U.S. air carriers to serve capacity controlled international markets, oversight of international rates and fares, maintenance of essential air service to small communities, and consumer affairs. DOT's Bureau of Transportation Statistics (BTS) handles aviation information functions formerly assigned to CAB. Prior to BTS, the Research and Special Programs Administration handled these functions.

The principal activities of the FAA include: the promotion of air safety; controlling the use of navigable airspace; prescribing regulations dealing with the competency of airmen, airworthiness of aircraft and air traffic control; operation of air route traffic control centers, airport traffic control towers, and flight service stations; the design, construction, maintenance, and inspection of navigation, traffic control, and communications equipment; and the development of general aviation.

The CAB published monthly and quarterly financial and traffic statistical data for the certificated route air carriers. BTS continues these publications, including both certificated and noncertificated (commuter) air carriers. The FAA publishes annually data on the use of airway facilities; data related to the location of airmen, aircraft, and airports; the volume of activity in the field of

Transportation—Air and Water 659

nonair carrier (general aviation) flying; and aircraft production and registration.

General aviation comprises all civil flying (including such commercial operations as small demand air taxis, agriculture application, powerline patrol, etc.) but excludes certificated route air carriers, supplemental operators, large-aircraft commercial operators, and commuter airlines.

Air carriers and service—The CAB previously issued "certificates of public convenience and necessity" under Section 401 of the Federal Aviation Act of 1958 for scheduled and nonscheduled (charter) passenger services and cargo services. It also issued certificates under Section 418 of the Act to cargo air carriers for domestic all-cargo service only. The DOT Office of the Secretary now issues the certificates under a "fit, willing, and able" test of air carrier operations. Carriers operating only a 60-seat-or-less aircraft are given exemption authority to carry passengers, cargo, and mail in scheduled and nonscheduled service under Part 298 of the DOT (formerly CAB) regulations. Exemption authority carriers who offer scheduled passenger service to an essential air service point must meet the "fit, willing, and able" test.

Vessel shipments, entrances, and clearances—Shipments by dry cargo vessels comprise shipments on all types of watercraft, except tanker vessels; shipments by tanker vessels comprise all types of cargo, liquid and dry, carried by tanker vessels.

A vessel is reported as entered only at the first port which it enters in the United States, whether or not cargo is unloaded at that port. A vessel is reported as cleared only at the last port at which clearance is made to a foreign port, whether or not it takes on cargo. Army and Navy vessels entering or clearing without commercial cargo are not included in the figures.

Units of measurement—Cargo (or freight) tonnage and shipping weight both represent the gross weight of the cargo including the weight of containers, wrappings, crates, etc. However, shipping weight excludes lift and cargo vans and similar substantial outer containers. Other tonnage figures generally refer to stowing capacity of vessels, 100 cubic feet being called 1 ton. Gross tonnage comprises the space within the frames and the ceiling of the hull, together with those closed-in spaces above deck available for cargo, stores, passengers, or crew, with certain minor exceptions. Net or registered tonnage is the gross tonnage less the spaces occupied by the propelling machinery, fuel, crew quarters, master's cabin, and navigation spaces. Substantially, it represents space available for cargo and passengers. The net tonnage capacity of a ship may bear little relation to weight of cargo. Deadweight tonnage is the weight in long tons required to depress a vessel from light water line (that is, with only the machinery and equipment on board) to load line. It is, therefore, the weight of the cargo, fuel, etc., which a vessel is designed to carry with safety.

U.S. Census Bureau, Statistical Abstract of the United States: 1999

No. 1069. Air and Water Transportation Industries—Summary: 1992 and 1997

[For establishments with payroll. **(10,409 represents $10,409,000,000).** See Tables 872 and 873 in Section 17, Business, for more 1997 economic census data]

Industry	1987 SIC [1] code	Establish- ments	Revenue (mil. dol.)	Annual payroll (mil. dol.)	Paid employees [2] (1,000)
1997 ECONOMIC CENSUS PRELIMINARY DATA					
Air transportation [3]:	45				
1997.		11,364	48,623	10,409	360
1992.		9,363	32,973	7,402	273
Water transportation:	44				
1997.		9,245	36,304	6,345	180
1992.		8,147	29,207	5,170	171
1992 ECONOMIC CENSUS DATA					
Air transportation [4]**. . . . .**	**45**	**(NA)**	**82,670**	**24,530**	**707**
Air transportation, including air					
courier services [4]	451,2	(NA)	76,503	22,734	627
Scheduled and air courier services [4].	451	(NA)	73,070	22,026	604
Scheduled [4]	4512	(NA)	62,057	19,090	505
Air courier services.	4513	2,639	11,013	2,935	99
Nonscheduled.	452	1,791	3,433	708	23
Airport terminal services.	458	3,252	6,168	1,796	80
Water transportation.	**44**	**8,147**	**29,207**	**5,170**	**171**
Water transportation of freight	441,2,3,4	836	14,704	1,523	37
Deep sea foreign and domestic freight	441, 2	615	11,948	1,148	27
Other water transportation of freight	443,4	221	2,756	375	10
Great Lakes-St. Lawrence Seaway freight	4432	26	559	81	1
Water transportation of freight, n.e.c. [5]	4449	195	2,197	293	9
Water transportation of passengers	448	1,033	4,133	508	23
Ferries.	4482	118	155	51	2
Water transportation of passengers, except by ferry	4481,9	915	3,978	457	22
Services incidental to water transportation	449	6,278	10,370	3,140	111
Marinas	4493	3,348	1,651	346	18
Other services incidental to water transportation . .	4491,2,9	2,930	8,719	2,794	93

NA Not available.   [1] 1987 Standard Industrial Classification code; see text, Section 17, Business.   [2] For the pay period including March 12.   [3] Excludes large certificated air passenger carriers which are out of scope for the 1997 Economic Census. [4] Revenue for scheduled air transportation includes revenues for large certificated passenger carriers that was reported to the Office of Airline Statistics, U.S. Dept. of Transportation, as published in *Air Carrier Financial Statistics Quarterly.*   [5] N.e.c. means not elsewhere classified.

Source: U.S. Census Bureau, *Census of Transportation, Communications, and Utilities: 1992,* UC92-A-1 and *1997 Economic Census, Core Business Statistics Series, Advance Report,* EC97X-CS1.

No. 1070. U. S. Scheduled Airline Industry—Summary: 1990 to 1997

[For calendar years or Dec. 31 **(465.6 represents 465,600,000).** For domestic and international operations. Covers carriers certificated under Section 401 of the Federal Aviation Act. Minus sign (-) indicates loss]

Item	Unit	1990	1991	1992	1993	1994	1995	1996	1997
SCHEDULED SERVICE									
Revenue passengers enplaned .	Mil.	465.6	452.3	475.1	488.5	528.8	547.8	581.2	598.9
Revenue passenger miles.	Bil.	457.9	448.0	478.6	489.7	519.4	540.7	578.7	605.4
Available seat miles.	Bil.	733.4	715.2	752.8	771.6	784.3	807.1	835.1	860.6
Revenue passenger load factor .	Percent .	62.4	62.6	63.6	63.5	66.2	67.0	69.3	70.4
Mean passenger trip length [1]. . .	Miles . . .	984	990	1,007	1,002	982	987	996	1,011
Freight and express ton miles . .	Mil. . . .	10,546	10,225	11,130	11,944	13,792	14,578	15,301	17,959
Aircraft departures.	1,000 . . .	6,924	6,783	7,051	7,245	7,531	8,062	8,230	8,157
FINANCES									
Total operating revenue [2]	Mil. dol. .	76,142	75,158	78,140	84,559	88,313	94,578	101,938	109,535
Passenger revenue	Mil. dol. .	58,453	57,092	59,828	63,945	65,422	69,594	75,286	79,469
Freight and express revenue . . .	Mil. dol. .	5,432	5,509	5,916	6,662	7,284	8,616	9,679	10,464
Mail revenue	Mil. dol. .	970	957	1,184	1,212	1,183	1,266	1,279	1,360
Charter revenue	Mil. dol. .	2,877	3,717	2,801	3,082	3,548	3,485	3,447	3,553
Total operating expense	Mil. dol. .	78,054	76,943	80,585	83,121	85,600	88,718	95,729	100,924
Operating profit.	Mil. dol. .	-1,912	-1,785	-2,444	1,438	2,713	5,860	6,209	8,611
Interest expense	Mil. dol. .	1,978	1,777	1,743	2,027	2,347	2,424	1,981	1,749
Net profit	Mil. dol. .	-3,921	-1,940	-4,791	-2,136	-344	2,314	2,804	5,195
Revenue per passenger mile . . .	Cents . . .	12.8	12.7	12.5	13.1	12.6	12.9	13.0	13.1
Rate of return on investment . . .	Percent .	-6.0	-0.5	-9.3	-0.4	5.2	11.9	11.5	14.9
Operating profit margin.	Percent .	-2.5	-2.4	-3.1	1.7	3.1	6.2	6.1	7.9
Net profit margin	Percent .	-5.1	-2.6	-6.1	-2.5	-0.4	2.4	2.8	4.7
EMPLOYEES [3]									
Total	1,000 . . .	545.8	533.6	540.4	537.1	539.8	547.0	564.4	586.5
Pilots and copilots	1,000 . . .	47.1	49.2	51.1	52.1	52.9	55.4	57.6	60.4
Other flight personnel.	1,000 . . .	8.9	8.0	8.2	8.1	7.7	8.6	8.9	10.7
Flight attendants	1,000 . . .	83.4	81.8	86.3	85.0	86.5	86.7	89.1	96.2
Mechanics	1,000 . . .	61.0	58.8	58.6	57.5	55.8	50.5	50.8	65.5
Aircraft and traffic servicing personnel.	1,000 . . .	251.2	237.3	243.1	242.8	247.2	251.1	266.5	269.6
All other.	1,000 . . .	94.2	98.4	93.2	91.7	89.7	94.8	91.6	84.1

[1] For definition of mean, see Guide to Tabular Presentation.   [2] Includes other types of revenues, not shown separately. [3] Average number of full time equivalents.

Source: Air Transport Association of America, Washington, DC, *Air Transport,* annual, and *Air Transport, Facts and Figures,* annual.

Transportation—Air and Water 661

No. 1071. Airline Cost Indexes: 1980 to 1998

[Covers U.S. major and national service carriers. Major carriers have operating revenues of $1 billion or more; nationals have operating revenues from $75 million to $1 billion. Minus sign (-) indicates decrease]

Index	Index (1982=100)								Percent distribution of cash operating expenses [1]			
	1980	1985	1990	1994	1995	1996	1997	1998	1980	1990	1995	1998
Composite index	86.8	102.8	122.6	129.9	131.3	136.6	136.6	134.1	100.0	100.0	100.0	100.0
Labor costs:												
Passenger carriers.	85.8	110.5	121.7	148.7	155.7	159.4	163.0	164.5	35.2	31.6	34.8	35.5
Cargo carriers.	78.3	116.0	148.8	145.4	151.7	159.6	156.0	157.2	27.3	30.0	31.0	30.5
Fuel	89.7	79.6	77.2	54.4	55.3	64.6	62.5	49.6	30.0	17.3	11.5	9.9
Aircraft fleet [2][3]	88.1	123.7	177.0	217.5	222.8	230.3	222.9	227.3	5.2	7.9	9.5	9.2
Interest [2][4]	88.1	98.0	96.0	87.6	93.5	86.9	72.1	66.5	3.2	2.6	3.0	1.8
Insurance	80.4	155.3	68.2	110.8	111.6	111.5	96.0	64.4	0.3	0.3	0.7	0.4
Maintenance material.	104.9	119.9	190.5	157.2	153.4	169.4	191.0	201.6	2.5	3.4	2.7	3.4
Landing fee	87.2	99.9	139.0	171.6	176.6	181.5	177.8	172.6	1.7	1.8	2.2	1.9
Traffic commissions [2].	75.4	112.9	169.2	163.3	139.4	130.7	117.2	106.1	4.9	9.4	8.5	6.5
Communication [2]	65.8	96.6	111.2	118.2	116.0	114.8	110.4	118.6	1.1	1.4	1.5	1.5
Advertising and promotion [2] . .	67.1	96.2	97.8	69.7	63.6	58.4	54.7	59.2	1.6	2.0	1.5	1.4
Passenger food [2]	90.6	98.9	128.4	120.6	110.9	104.0	102.8	105.1	2.9	3.5	3.3	3.2
All other	86.1	111.9	133.4	149.9	153.3	156.2	159.1	160.7	11.8	19.1	21.8	26.3

[1] Total operating expenses plus interest on long term debt, less depreciation and amortization.   [2] Passenger airlines only.   [3] Includes lease, aircraft and engine rentals, depreciation and amortization.   [4] Interest on debt.

Source: Air Transport Association of America, Washington, DC, *Air Transport,* annual; and unpublished data.

No. 1072. Top 40 Airports in 1997—Passengers Enplaned: 1987 and 1997

[In thousands (448,914 represents 448,914,000), except rank. For calendar year. Airports ranked by total passengers enplaned 1997]

Airport	1987 Total	rank	1997 Total	rank	Airport	1987 Total	rank	1997 Total	rank
All airports, total.	448,914	(X)	574,612	(X)	New York (La Guardia), NY	11,326	7	9,868	19
Top 40 airports	327,563	(X)	445,113	(X)	New York (John F. Kennedy), NY	10,140	10	9,731	20
Atlanta (Hartsfield Intl), GA . .	22,649	2	32,677	1	Philadelphia, PA	6,603	23	9,714	21
Chicago (O'Hare), IL	26,122	1	31,123	2	Salt Lake City, UT	4,729	28	9,427	22
Dallas/Ft. Worth, TX	19,905	3	27,256	3	Pittsburgh, PA.	8,156	16	9,224	23
Los Angeles, CA	18,970	4	22,596	4	Honolulu, HI	7,773	17	8,939	24
San Francisco, CA	13,117	6	16,858	5	Cincinnati, OH	3,265	35	7,638	25
Denver, CO	15,594	5	16,006	6	Washington (National), DC . .	7,113	18	7,010	26
Detroit (Wayne County), MI. .	9,254	13	14,773	7	San Diego, CA	4,901	27	6,719	27
Phoenix (Sky Harbor Intl), AZ	8,785	14	14,650	8	Baltimore, MD.	4,010	31	6,311	28
Las Vegas (McCarran Intl), NV	6,836	21	14,011	9	Portland, OR	2,834	39	6,233	29
St. Louis (Lambert-St Louis), MO	9,727	11	13,956	10	Tampa, FL.	4,682	29	5,901	30
Newark, NJ	11,289	8	13,783	11	Cleveland, OH	3,103	36	5,580	31
Minneapolis/St. Paul, MN . . .	8,310	15	13,775	12	Ft. Lauderdale, FL.	3,929	33	5,426	32
Houston (Intercontinental), TX	6,929	20	12,708	13	Kansas City, MO.	4,481	30	5,143	33
Miami, FL	9,342	12	12,073	14	Washington (Dulles Intl), DC	4,917	26	4,970	34
Seattle-Tacoma, WA	6,826	22	11,758	15	San Jose, CA	2,807	40	4,874	35
Orlando, FL	7,075	19	11,745	16	San Juan PR	2,995	37	4,721	36
Boston (Logan Intl), MA	10,255	9	10,453	17	Chicago (Midway), IL	2,541	41	4,392	37
Charlotte (Douglas Municipal), NC.	6,021	24	10,358	18	Oakland, CA.	1,918	54	4,378	38
					New Orleans, LA.	3,311	34	4,199	39
					Memphis, TN	5,023	25	4,156	40

X Not applicable.

Source: U.S. Bureau of Transportation Statistics, Office of Airline Information, *Airport Activity Statistics of Certificates Route Air Carriers, Calendar Year 1997* and the Federal Aviation Administration, *Airport Activity Statistics, 1987.*

No. 1073. Domestic Airline Markets: 1997

[For calendar year (3,725 represents 3,725,000). Data are for the 30 top markets and include and include all commercial airports in each metro area. Data do not include connecting passengers]

Market	Passengers	Market	Passengers
New York to—from Los Angeles	3,725	Chicago to—from Los Angeles	1,581
New York to—from Miami.	3,093	New York to—from West Palm Beach. . . .	1,530
New York to—from Chicago	2,980	Honolulu to—from Kona, Hawaii	1,493
New York to—from Boston	2,689	Los Angeles to—from Oakland	1,462
Honolulu to—from Kahului, Maui	2,620	Chicago to—from Detroit	1,433
New York to—from San Francisco	2,609	New York to—from Dallas/Ft. Worth	1,429
New York to—from Orlando	2,454	Los Angeles to—from Honolulu	1,423
New York to—from Washington	2,398	Chicago to—from Atlanta	1,359
Dallas/Ft. Worth to—from Houston.	2,219	Los Angeles to—from Phoenix	1,340
Los Angeles to—from Las Vegas.	2,111	Chicago to—from Minneapolis.	1,303
Los Angeles to—from San Francisco	2,021	Honolulu to—from Hilo, Hawaii	1,250
New York to—from Atlanta	2,016	Chicago to—from Dallas/Ft. Worth	1,206
New York to—from San Juan	1,834	Chicago to—from San Francisco	1,194
New York to—from Ft. Lauderdale	1,823	Boston to—from Washington.	1,182
Honolulu to—from Lihue, Kauai.	1,696	Chicago to—from Orlando	1,153

Source: Air Transport Association of America, Washington, DC, *Air Transport 1998.*

No. 1074. Worldwide Airline Fatalities: 1980 to 1998

[For scheduled air transport operations]

Year	Fatal accidents	Passenger deaths	Death rate [1]	Death rate [2]	Year	Fatal accidents	Passenger deaths	Death rate [1]	Death rate [2]
1980	22	814	0.14	0.09	1992	29	1,097	0.09	0.06
1985	22	1,066	0.14	0.09	1993	35	940	0.08	0.05
1987	26	901	0.09	0.06	1994	28	941	0.07	0.04
1988	29	737	0.07	0.04	1995	26	710	0.05	0.03
1989	27	817	0.07	0.05	1996	23	1,135	0.07	0.05
1990	25	495	0.04	0.03	1997	27	930	0.06	0.04
1991 [3]	30	653	0.06	0.04	1998	22	909	0.05	0.03

[1] Rate per 100 million passenger miles flown. [2] Rate per 100 million passenger kilometers flown. [3] Includes one ground collision counted as two accidents.

Source: International Civil Aviation Organization, Montreal, Canada, *Civil Aviation Statistics of the World*, annual.

No. 1075. Airline Passenger Screening Results: 1980 to 1997

[Calendar year data (585 represents 585,000,000)]

Item	1980	1985	1990	1994	1995	1996	1997
Persons screened (mil.)..............	585	993	1,145	1,261	1,263	1,497	1,660
WEAPONS DETECTED							
Firearms, total...................	2,022	2,987	2,853	2,994	2,390	2,155	2,067
Handguns....................	1,878	2,823	2,490	2,860	2,230	1,999	1,905
Long guns...................	36	90	59	134	160	156	162
Other guns..................	108	74	304	(X)	(X)	(NA)	(NA)
Other dangerous articles [1]	(X)	(X)	(X)	6,051	4,414	(NA)	(NA)
Explosive/incendiary devices	8	12	15	505	631	(NA)	(NA)
Persons arrested:							
Carrying firearms/explosives	1,031	1,310	1,337	1,433	1,194	999	924
Giving false information	32	42	18	35	68	131	72
Bomb threats received:							
Against airports..................	1,179	477	448	250	346	284	(NA)
Against aircraft..................	268	153	338	218	327	594	(NA)

NA Not available. X Not applicable. [1] For 1980-1990 data included firearms; beginning 1994 includes stunning devices, chemical agents, knives and other designated items.

Source: U.S. Bureau of Transportation Statistics, *National Transportation Statistics*, 1998, Internet site <http://www.bts.gov/btsprod/nts> (accessed 5 August 1998); and unpublished data.

No. 1076. Aircraft Accidents: 1982 to 1998

[For years ending December 31]

Item	Unit	1982	1985	1990	1995	1996	1997	1998
Air carrier accidents, all services [1].......	Number...	18	21	24	36	38	49	48
Fatal accidents..................	Number...	5	7	6	3	5	4	1
Fatalities...................	Number...	235	526	39	168	380	8	1
Aboard....................	Number...	223	525	12	162	350	6	-
Rates per 100,000 flight hours:								
Accidents...................	Rate.....	0.241	0.241	0.198	0.267	0.276	0.310	0.291
Fatal accidents	Rate.....	0.057	0.080	0.049	0.022	0.036	0.025	0.006
Commuter air carrier accidents [2]........	Number...	26	18	15	12	11	17	8
Fatal accidents..................	Number...	5	7	4	2	1	5	-
Fatalities...................	Number...	14	37	7	9	14	46	-
Aboard....................	Number...	14	36	5	9	12	46	-
Rates per 100,000 flight hours:								
Accidents...................	Rate.....	2.000	1.036	0.641	0.457	0.399	1.730	1.559
Fatal accidents	Rate.....	0.385	0.403	0.171	0.076	0.036	0.509	-
On-demand air taxi accidents [3]........	Number...	132	157	107	75	90	82	79
Fatal accidents..................	Number...	31	35	29	24	29	15	17
Fatalities...................	Number...	72	76	51	52	63	39	45
Aboard....................	Number...	72	75	49	52	63	39	41
Rates per 100,000 flight hours:								
Accidents...................	Rate.....	4.39	6.11	4.76	4.39	4.44	3.64	3.11
Fatal accidents	Rate.....	1.03	1.36	1.29	1.41	1.43	0.67	0.67
General aviation accidents [4]...........	Number...	3,233	2,739	2,215	2,053	1,907	1,858	1,907
Fatal accidents..................	Number...	591	498	443	412	360	356	361
Fatalities...................	Number...	1,187	956	767	734	632	660	621
Aboard....................	Number...	1,170	945	762	727	615	654	615
Rates per 100,000 flight hours:								
Accidents...................	Rate.....	10.90	9.66	7.77	8.23	7.66	7.29	7.12
Fatal accidents	Rate.....	1.99	1.75	1.55	1.64	1.45	1.40	1.35

- Represents zero. [1] U.S. air carriers operating under 14 CFR 121. Beginning 1997, includes aircraft with 10 or more seats, previously operating under 14 CFR 135. [2] All scheduled service of U.S. air carriers operating under 14 CFR 135. [3] All nonscheduled service of U.S. air carriers operating under 14 CFR 135. [4] U.S. civil registered aircraft not operated under 14 CFR 121 or 135.

Source: U.S. National Transportation Safety Board, Internet site <http://www.ntsb.gov/aviation/stats.htm> (Accessed 21 June 1999).

Transportation—Air and Water 663

No. 1077. On-Time Flight Arrivals and Departures at Major U.S. Airports: 1998

[In percent. Quarterly, based on gate arrival and departure times for domestic scheduled operations of U.S. major airlines. All U.S. airlines with 1 percent or more of total U.S. domestic scheduled airline passenger revenues are required to report on-time data. A flight is considered on time if it operated less than 15 minutes after the scheduled time shown in the carrier's computerized reservation system. Cancelled and diverted flights are considered late. See source for data on individual airlines]

Airport	On-time arrivals				On-time departures			
	1st. qtr.	2d. qtr.	3d. qtr.	4th. qtr.	1st. qtr.	2d. qtr.	3d. qtr.	4th. qtr.
Total, all airports	75.4	75.7	78.3	79.4	80.3	80.2	81.3	82.8
Total major airports	74.8	74.9	78.1	79.2	79.0	78.4	80.0	82.0
Atlanta, Hartsfield International	70.3	74.6	80.6	80.3	78.4	79.3	83.8	85.3
Baltimore/Washington International	78.8	76.2	82.0	83.9	85.0	80.0	85.5	85.8
Boston, Logan International	69.9	65.2	74.8	75.4	81.3	77.2	81.4	82.4
Charlotte Douglas.	84.4	81.3	84.7	80.8	84.8	79.7	82.9	80.4
Chicago, O'Hare	75.3	75.0	76.8	80.1	77.8	74.3	77.5	81.5
Cincinnati International	78.8	80.2	84.3	86.2	85.1	84.7	88.8	90.3
Dallas/Ft. Worth Regional	82.7	84.9	84.9	81.8	82.5	83.5	82.5	80.6
Denver International	80.9	77.7	80.6	79.4	81.4	80.5	81.9	82.0
Detroit, Metro Wayne	78.6	70.6	64.2	84.4	75.3	64.3	60.2	81.4
Houston George Bush.	77.8	81.1	82.5	81.4	82.8	84.8	85.5	84.2
Las Vegas, McCarran International	74.7	75.8	77.3	73.2	75.9	78.9	76.3	75.2
Los Angeles International.	71.4	70.5	79.1	74.6	75.5	79.4	82.1	80.5
Miami International	74.7	79.7	73.8	81.3	81.2	83.8	78.5	86.0
Minneapolis/St. Paul International	76.6	72.6	63.6	86.1	77.2	68.5	64.3	85.3
Newark International	66.4	65.0	76.6	80.3	76.9	72.9	80.0	83.7
New York, Kennedy International.	67.6	71.4	80.0	85.6	80.9	81.5	84.3	88.0
New York, LaGuardia	72.9	69.8	76.2	78.3	83.0	80.1	82.8	83.7
Orlando International	77.9	80.1	80.2	84.1	85.4	86.5	86.2	89.4
Philadelphia International.	71.5	71.5	77.4	78.0	77.6	75.3	78.8	77.2
Phoenix, Sky Harbor International	70.8	75.1	77.9	73.5	72.0	76.5	75.4	74.8
Pittsburgh, Greater International	84.3	78.7	83.1	81.1	86.1	79.7	83.0	80.9
Portland International	72.9	78.5	80.9	73.9	79.4	86.2	85.7	81.7
Ronald Reagan International	78.4	74.9	79.8	82.9	85.7	81.7	85.1	87.1
St. Louis, Lambert	72.2	74.3	81.1	82.5	74.6	74.2	81.6	83.6
Salt Lake City International	77.2	80.6	84.4	81.0	81.7	87.1	86.7	85.8
San Diego International, Lindbergh	73.2	72.0	79.3	74.0	77.6	80.6	83.1	80.4
San Francisco International	58.0	61.7	69.3	67.5	65.6	73.0	76.9	74.7
Seattle-Tacoma International	72.8	73.6	75.8	67.1	80.9	82.7	78.9	76.4
Tampa International	75.0	77.8	78.1	80.6	83.5	85.4	84.8	86.6

Source: U.S. Department of Transportation, Office of Consumer Affairs, *Air Travel Consumer Report*, monthly.

No. 1078. Consumer Complaints Against U.S. Airlines: 1990 to 1998

[Calendar year data. See source for data on individual airlines]

Complaint category	1990	1991	1992	1993	1994	1995	1996	1997	1998
Total	7,703	6,106	5,639	4,438	5,179	4,629	5,782	6,394	7,994
Flight problems [1]	3,034	1,877	1,624	1,211	1,586	1,133	1,628	1,699	2,277
Customer service [2]	758	714	695	599	805	667	999	1,418	1,715
Ticketing/boarding [3]	624	659	680	577	598	666	857	904	1,137
Baggage.	1,329	883	752	627	761	628	882	826	1,108
Refunds	701	783	721	482	393	576	521	531	602
Oversales [4]	399	301	265	257	301	263	353	414	388
Fares [5]	312	388	573	398	267	185	180	195	277
Advertising	96	96	54	51	94	66	61	57	40
Tours	29	23	12	16	127	18	16	13	23
Smoking.	74	30	25	30	20	15	13	5	4
Credit.	5	10	10	4	2	4	3	1	1
Other	342	342	228	186	225	408	269	331	422

[1] Cancellations, delays, etc. from schedule. [2] Unhelpful employees, inadequate meals or cabin service, treatment of delayed passengers. [3] Errors in reservations and ticketing; problems in making reservations and obtaining tickets. [4] All bumping problems, whether or not airline complied with DOT regulations. [5] Incorrect or incomplete information about fares, discount fare conditions, and availability, etc.

Source: U.S. Dept. of Transportation, Office of Consumer Affairs, *Air Travel Consumer Report*, monthly.

No. 1079. Commuter/Regional Airline Operations—Summary: 1980 to 1997

[Calendar year data (14.8 represents 14,800,000). Commuter/regional airlines operate primarily aircraft of predominately 75 passengers or less and 18,000 pounds of payload capacity serving short haul and small community markets. Represents operations within all North America by U.S. regional carriers. Averages are means. For definition of mean, see Guide to Tabular Presentation]

Item	Unit	1980	1985	1990	1993	1994	1995	1996	1997
Passenger carriers operating	Number.	214	179	150	130	125	124	109	104
Passengers enplaned	Millions .	14.8	[1]26.0	42.1	52.7	57.1	57.2	61.9	66.3
Average passengers enplaned per carrier. .	1,000 . .	69.2	152.4	277.5	405.2	457.0	461.4	568.3	637.5
Revenue passenger miles (RPM)	Billions .	1.92	[1]4.41	7.61	10.61	12.02	12.75	14.22	15.30
Average RPMs per carrier	Millions .	8.97	[1]24.64	50.75	81.59	96.15	102.80	130.49	147.09
Airports served	Number.	732	854	811	829	806	780	782	766
Average trip length	Miles. . .	129	173	183	201	210	223	230	231
Passenger aircraft operated	Number.	1,339	1,745	1,917	2,208	2,172	2,138	2,127	2,104
Average seating capacity (seats).	Number.	13.9	19.2	22.1	23.0	23.7	24.6	25.1	25.9
Fleet flying hours [2]	1,000 . .	1,740	2,854	3,447	4,490	4,565	4,659	4,568	4,695
Average annual utilization per aircraft.	Hours . .	1,299	1,635	1,798	2,033	2,102	2,179	2,148	2,231

[1] Adjusted to exclude a merger in 1986. [2] Prior to 1993, utilization results reflected airborne rather than block hours. Data inclusive of carriers which may have operated during only part of calendar year 1996.
Source: Regional Airline Association and AvStat Associates, Washington, DC, Annual Report of the Regional Airline Industry (copyright).

No. 1080. Civil Flying—Summary: 1970 to 1997

[As of Dec. 31 or for years ending Dec. 31, except as noted (50.5 represents $50,500,000)]

Item	Unit	1970	1980	1985	1990	1995	1996	1997
Airports in operation [1]	Number. . .	11,261	15,161	16,318	17,490	18,224	18,292	18,345
Heliports	Number. . .	790	2,336	3,120	4,085	4,559	4,596	4,626
Private	Number. . .	7,001	10,347	10,457	12,412	13,092	13,163	13,211
Airports with runway lights	Number. . .	3,554	4,738	4,941	4,822	4,838	4,847	4,832
Airports with paved runways.	Number. . .	3,805	5,833	6,721	7,694	8,195	8,218	8,248
Airport Improvement Program [2]	Mil. dol. . . .	50.5	639.0	842.1	1,244.7	1,418.1	1,379.9	1,475.9
Total civil aircraft.	1,000 . . .	154.5	259.4	274.9	275.9	(NA)	(NA)	(NA)
Active aircraft [3]	1,000 . . .	134.5	214.8	215.4	218.9	195.5	198.6	200.0
Air carriers, total [4]	1,000 . . .	2.8	3.8	4.7	6.7	7.4	7.5	7.6
General aviation aircraft [5]	1,000 . . .	131.7	211.0	210.7	212.2	188.1	191.1	192.4
Fixed-wing aircraft: Multi-engine . . .	1,000 . . .	18.4	31.7	33.6	32.7	24.6	25.6	26.2
Single-engine.	1,000 . . .	109.5	168.4	164.4	165.1	137.7	138.1	140.7
Rotorcraft [6]	1,000 . . .	2.2	6.0	6.4	7.4	5.8	6.6	6.8
Balloons, blimps, gliders, etc	1,000 . . .	1.6	5.0	6.3	7.0	4.7	4.2	4.1
Airman certificates held	1,000 . . .	1,002	1,195	1,105	1,195	1,290	1,157	1,157
Pilot [7]	1,000 . . .	733	827	710	703	639	622	616
Held by women	Percent . . .	4.0	6.4	6.1	5.8	6.0	5.9	5.8
Airline transport.	1,000 . . .	34	70	83	108	124	127	131
Commercial	1,000 . . .	187	183	152	149	134	129	125
Private.	1,000 . . .	304	357	311	299	261	254	248
Student	1,000 . . .	196	200	147	128	101	95	96
Nonpilot [8]	1,000 . . .	269	368	395	492	651	534	541
Ground technicians [9]	1,000 . . .	241	321	341	421	574	459	464
FAA employees: Total	Number. . .	53,125	55,340	47,245	51,269	48,324	48,618	49,531
Air traffic control specialists [10]	Number. . .	(NA)	27,190	23,580	24,339	23,208	22,823	22,985
Full performance [11]	Number. . .	(NA)	16,317	11,672	12,985	14,845	15,799	14,630
Developmental [11]	Number. . .	(NA)	4,387	4,304	5,042	2,272	1,999	2,312
Assistants [11]	Number. . .	(X)	1,465	1,153	355	335	319
Traffic management coordinators [12] . .	Number. . .	(X)	(X)	(X)	370	561	542	584
Electronic technicians/ATSS [13]	Number. . .	(NA)	8,871	6,856	6,458	6,749	6,927	7,021
Aviation safety inspectors	Number. . .	(NA)	2,038	1,897	2,984	2,991	3,265	3,577
Engineers	Number. . .	(NA)	2,436	2,457	2,745	2,810	2,860	2,860
Other	Number. . .	(NA)	14,805	12,455	14,743	12,566	12,743	13,088
General aviation: [5]								
Hours flown	Million . . .	26.0	41.0	34.1	34.8	26.6	26.9	27.7
Fuel consumed: [14] Gasoline	Mil. gal. . . .	362	520	420	353	287	289	292
Jet fuel [15].	Mil. gal. . . .	415	766	691	663	560	608	642

NA Not available. X Not applicable. [1] Existing airports, heliports, seaplane bases, etc. recorded with FAA. Includes military airports with joint civil and military use. Includes U.S. outlying areas. Airport-type definitions: Public—publicly owned and under control of a public agency; private—owned by a private individual or corporation. May or may not be open for public use. [2] Fiscal year data. Does not include System Planning Grants. Includes U.S. outlying areas. 1970-1980 data on obligated Federal funds for the Airport Development Aid Program. Thereafter, data are appropriated Federal funds under the Airport and Airway Improvement Act of 1982. [3] Registered aircraft that flew 1 or more hours during the year. [4] Includes helicopters. [5] See text, this section. Beginning 1995, excludes commuters and includes experimental aircraft, not shown separately. Prior to 1995, experimental aircraft were included in the appropriate type. Data beginning 1995 may not be comparable to data for earlier years due to revisions in survey procedures. [6] Includes autogyros; excludes air carrier helicopters. [7] Includes all active pilots. An active pilot is one with a pilot certificate and a valid medical certificate. Also includes pilots who hold a recreational certificate or only a helicopter, glider, or lighter than air certificate, not shown separately. [8] Includes dispatchers, flight navigators and engineers, and ground technicians—mechanics, parachute riggers, and ground and ground instructors. Data for 1996 on mechanics, repairmen, parachute riggers, ground instructors, and dispatchers are limited to those ages 70 years and less. [9] No medical examinations are required, therefore, data represent all certificates on record and include retired or otherwise inactive technicians. See footnote 8. [10] Includes all air traffic control specialists (staff positions, managers, supervisors, and for 1970-85 traffic management coordinators, not shown separately) and air traffic assistants. [11] Serving in-flight service stations, towers, and centers. [12] Prior to 1990, included in total air traffic control specialists. [13] Airway Transportation Systems Specialists [14] Source: 1970, U.S. Bureau of Mines; thereafter, FAA General Aviation Activity and Avionics Survey. Data for 1996 are estimated using new information on survey nonresponse and so are not strictly comparable to earlier years. [15] Includes kerosene-type and naphtha-type jet fuels.

Source: Except as noted, U.S. Federal Aviation Administration, FAA Statistical Handbook of Aviation, annual, last published in 1993. Internet site <http://api.hq.faa.gov/apohome.htm> and unpublished data.

Transportation—Air and Water   665

No. 1081. Net Orders for U.S. Civil Jet Transport Aircraft: 1985 to 1998

[1985 and 1990 are net new firm orders; beginning beginning 1993, net announced orders. Minus sign (-) indicates net cancellations. In 1997 Boeing acquired McDonnell Douglas]

Type of aircraft and customer	1985	1990	1993	1994	1995	1996	1997	1998
Total number [1]	468	670	31	79	421	595	501	601
U.S. customers	242	259	44	12	138	408	258	392
Foreign customers	226	411	-13	67	283	187	243	209
McDonnell Douglas MD-11, total . . .	-	52	-1	2	-6	9	11	12
U.S. customers	-	16	-	2	3	1	-	3
Foreign customers	-	36	-1	-	-9	8	11	9
McDonnell Douglas MD-80/90, total .	114	116	-1	1	51	29	-14	26
U.S. customers	37	91	6	-8	-	18	-11	24
Foreign customers	77	25	-7	9	51	11	-3	2
McDonnell Douglas MD-95, total . . .	-	-	-	-	50	-	-	65
U.S. customers	-	-	-	-	50	-	-	50
Foreign customers	-	-	-	-	-	-	-	15
Boeing 737, total	253	189	-34	49	189	349	280	350
U.S. customers	146	38	-29	9	85	284	120	207
Foreign customers	107	151	-5	40	104	65	160	143
Boeing 747, total	37	153	-25	-5	35	66	37	-4
U.S. customers	13	24	-25	-1	2	22	15	1
Foreign customers	24	129	-	-4	33	44	22	-5
Boeing 757, total	51	66	20	5	-7	44	45	47
U.S. customers	39	33	46	-1	-6	35	25	34
Foreign customers	12	33	-26	6	-1	9	20	13
Boeing 767, total	10	60	43	27	26	10	96	40
U.S. customers	4	23	41	11	4	11	85	31
Foreign customers	6	37	2	16	22	-1	11	9
Boeing 777, total	-	34	29	-	83	88	46	65
U.S. customers	-	34	5	-	-	37	24	42
Foreign customers	-	-	24	-	83	51	22	23

- Represents zero.   [1] Includes types of aircraft not shown separately.

Source: Aerospace Industries Association of America, Washington, DC, Research Center, Statistical Series 23, Internet site <http://www.aia-aerospace.org>.

No. 1082. U.S. Aircraft Shipments: 1980 to 1998

[Value in millions of dollars (18,929 represents $18,929,000,000)]

Year	Total		Civil						Military	
			Large transports		General aviation [1]		Helicopters			
	Units	Value	Units	Value	Units	Value	Units	Value	Units	Value
1980	14,677	18,929	387	9,895	11,877	2,486	1,366	656	1,047	5,892
1985	3,610	27,269	278	8,448	2,029	1,431	384	506	919	16,884
1990	3,321	38,585	521	22,215	1,144	2,007	603	254	1,053	14,109
1993	2,585	41,166	408	24,133	964	2,144	258	113	955	14,776
1994	2,309	36,568	309	18,124	928	2,357	308	185	764	15,902
1995	2,436	33,658	256	15,263	1,077	2,842	292	194	811	15,359
1996	2,232	36,247	269	17,564	1,130	3,127	278	193	555	15,363
1997, est.	2,814	45,315	374	25,810	1,569	4,674	346	231	525	14,600
1998, est.	3,400	56,150	530	37,000	2,030	5,300	340	240	500	13,610

[1] Excludes off-the-shelf military aircraft.

Source: U.S. Department of Commerce, International Trade Administration, Internet site <http://www.ita.doc.gov/industry/tai/green/trends.htm>.

No. 1083. Employment and Earnings in Aircraft Industries: 1985 to 1998

[Annual averages of monthly figures (794 represents 794,000). See headnote, Table 688]

Item	1987 SIC [1] code	Unit	1985	1990	1995	1996	1998
Employment: Total	(X)	1,000 . . .	794	898	549	591	612
Aircraft	3721	1,000 . . .	326	381	244	263	273
Aircraft engines and engine parts	3724	1,000 . . .	148	152	93	100	104
Aircraft equipment, n.e.c. [2]	3728	1,000 . . .	143	180	114	137	146
Guided missiles, space vehicles, and parts . .	376	1,000 . . .	177	185	98	91	89
Average weekly earnings: [3]	(X)						
Aircraft engines and parts₂	3724	Dollars . .	542	637	770	838	840
Aircraft equipment, n.e.c. [2]	3728	Dollars . .	506	570	677	752	741
Guided missiles, space vehicles, and parts . .	376	Dollars . .	515	612	765	842	841
Average hourly earnings: [3]	(X)						
Aircraft, excluding lump sum benefits	3721	Dollars . .	13.18	15.66	19.97	20.76	21.08
Aircraft with lump sum benefits	3721	Dollars . .	13.40	16.32	20.02	21.09	21.14
Aircraft engines and parts₂	3724	Dollars . .	12.85	14.84	17.34	18.58	18.93
Aircraft equipment, n.e.c. [2]	3728	Dollars . .	11.66	13.37	15.93	16.67	16.80
Guided missiles, space vehicles, and parts . .	376	Dollars . .	12.14	14.39	17.74	19.54	19.98

X Not applicable.   [1] 1987 Standard Industrial Classification; see text, Section 17, Business.   [2] N.e.c. means not elsewhere classified.   [3] For production workers.

Source: U.S. Bureau of Labor Statistics, *Employment and Earnings,* monthly, June issues and Internet site <http://stats.bls.gov/ceshome.htm>.

No. 1084. Aerospace—Sales, New Orders, and Backlog: 1990 to 1997

[In billions of dollars (136.6 represents $136,600,000,000), except as indicated. Reported by establishments in which the principal business is the development and/or production of aerospace products]

Item	1990	1992	1993	1994	1995	1996	1997
Net sales.	136.6	118.7	109.9	104.3	102.8	103.1	114.2
Percent U.S. Government	53.8	50.0	49.9	54.8	49.5	49.8	43.1
Complete aircraft and parts [1]	49.9	54.0	48.9	43.3	42.5	41.8	54.5
Aircraft engines and parts	16.4	13.7	12.2	11.3	12.5	15.7	12.4
Missiles and space vehicles, parts . . .	22.0	21.3	18.1	18.4	18.4	16.5	17.4
Other products, services	48.3	29.7	30.7	31.3	29.4	29.1	29.9
Net, new orders	146.0	100.3	79.7	88.7	109.1	126.3	119.9
Backlog, Dec. 31	250.1	236.1	211.8	192.6	202.6	229.9	234.5

[1] Except engines sold separately.

Source: U.S. Census Bureau, *Current Industrial Reports*, Series MA-37D, Internet site <http://www.census.gov/econ/www/manumenu.htm>.

No. 1085. Aerospace Industry Sales, by Product Group and Customer: 1985 to 1999

[In billions of dollars (96.6 represents $96,600,000,000). Due to reporting practices and tabulating methods, figures may differ from those in Table 1084]

Item	Current dollars					Constant (1987) dollars [3]				
	1985	1990	1995	1998 [1]	1999 [2]	1985	1990	1995	1998 [1]	1999 [2]
Total sales.	96.6	134.4	107.8	140.5	145.0	97.8	121.6	85.7	107.7	109.0
PRODUCT GROUP										
Aircraft, total	50.5	71.4	55.0	77.8	80.9	51.1	64.6	43.8	59.6	60.8
Civil [4]	13.7	31.3	24.0	47.2	49.4	13.9	28.3	19.1	36.2	37.1
Military	36.8	40.1	31.1	30.6	31.5	37.2	36.3	24.7	23.4	23.7
Missiles	11.4	14.2	7.4	7.5	7.9	11.6	12.8	5.9	5.8	5.9
Space	18.6	26.4	27.4	31.8	32.0	18.8	23.9	21.8	24.4	24.1
Related products and services [5] . .	16.1	22.4	18.0	23.4	24.2	16.3	20.3	14.3	17.9	18.2
CUSTOMER GROUP										
Aerospace, total	80.5	112.0	89.8	117.1	120.9	81.5	101.3	71.5	89.7	90.8
DOD [6]	53.2	60.5	42.4	40.2	41.5	53.9	54.8	33.7	30.8	31.2
NASA [7] and other agencies . . .	6.3	11.1	11.4	10.8	10.9	6.3	10.0	9.1	8.3	8.2
Other customers [8]	21.0	40.4	36.0	66.1	68.5	21.3	36.5	28.6	50.6	51.5
Related products and services [5] . .	16.1	22.4	18.0	23.4	24.2	16.3	20.3	14.3	17.9	18.2

[1] Preliminary. [2] Estimate. [3] Based on AIAs aerospace composite price deflator. [4] All civil sales of aircraft (domestic and export sales of jet transports, commuters, business, and personal aircraft and helicopters). [5] Electronics, software, and ground support equipment, plus sales of non-aerospace products which are produced by aerospace-manufacturing use technology, processes, and materials derived from aerospace products. [6] Department of Defense. [7] National Aeronautics and Space Administration. [8] Includes civil aircraft sales (see footnote 4), commercial space sales, all exports of military aircraft and missiles and related propulsion and parts.

Source: Aerospace Industries Association of America, Inc., Washington, DC, *1998 Year-End Review and Forecast*, Internet site <http://www.aia-aerospace.org> (accessed 13 April 1999).

No. 1086. Aerospace Industry—Net Profits After Taxes: 1980 to 1998

[For calendar year (2,588 represents $2,588,000,000). Minus sign (-) indicates loss]

Year	Aerospace industry profits				All manufacturing corporations profits as a percent of—		
	Total (mil. dol.)	As percent of—					
		Sales	Assets	Equity	Sales	Assets	Equity
1980	2,588	4.3	5.2	16.0	4.8	6.9	13.9
1983	2,829	3.5	4.1	12.1	4.1	5.1	10.5
1984	3,639	4.1	4.7	14.1	4.6	6.0	12.5
1985	3,274	3.1	3.6	11.1	3.8	4.6	10.1
1986	3,093	2.8	3.1	9.4	3.7	4.2	9.5
1987	4,582	4.1	4.4	14.6	4.9	5.6	12.8
1988	4,883	4.3	4.4	14.9	6.0	6.9	16.2
1989	3,866	3.3	3.3	10.7	5.0	5.6	13.7
1990	4,487	3.4	3.4	11.5	4.0	4.3	10.7
1991	[1]2,484	1.8	1.9	6.1	2.5	2.6	6.4
1992	[1]-1,836	-1.4	-1.2	-5.2	1.0	1.0	2.6
1993	4,621	3.6	3.5	13.2	2.8	2.9	8.1
1994	5,655	4.7	4.3	14.8	5.4	5.8	15.6
1995	4,633	3.8	3.5	11.1	5.7	6.2	16.2
1996	7,150	5.6	5.1	17.1	6.0	6.5	16.8
1997	7,221	5.2	4.8	17.3	6.2	6.6	16.6
1998	7,442	5.0	4.7	17.5	6.9	6.9	17.8

[1] Reflects unusually large nonoperating expenses totalling $3.4 billion in 1991 and $8.7 billion in 1992 due to the initial implementation of a change in accounting for future retirement benefit costs and defense-downsizing restructuring charges. Many large aerospace corporations chose to write off against first quarter earnings amounts required to comply with FASB 106.

Source: Aerospace Industries Association of America, Washington, DC, *1998 Year-end Review and Forecast*.

Transportation—Air and Water   667

No. 1087. United States Total and Aerospace Foreign Trade: 1970 to 1998

[In millions of dollars (3,225 represents $3,225,000,000), except percent. Data are reported as exports of domestic merchandise, including Department of Defense shipments and undocumented exports to Canada, f.a.s. (free alongside ship) basis, and imports for consumption, customs value basis. Minus sign (-) indicates deficit]

Year	Merchandise trade			Aerospace trade							
				Exports							
								Civil			
	Trade balance	Imports	Exports	Trade balance	Imports	Total	Percent of U.S. exports	Total	Transports	Military	
1970	3,225	39,952	43,176	3,097	308	3,405	7.9	2,516	1,283	889	
1971	-1,476	45,563	44,087	3,830	373	4,203	9.5	3,080	1,567	1,123	
1972	-5,729	55,583	49,854	3,230	565	3,795	7.6	2,954	1,119	841	
1973	2,390	69,476	71,865	4,360	782	5,142	7.2	3,788	1,664	1,354	
1974	-3,884	103,321	99,437	6,350	745	7,095	7.1	5,273	2,655	1,822	
1975	9,551	99,305	108,856	7,045	747	7,792	7.2	5,324	2,397	2,468	
1976	-7,820	124,614	116,794	7,267	576	7,843	6.7	5,677	2,468	2,166	
1977	-28,353	151,534	123,182	6,850	731	7,581	6.2	5,049	1,936	2,532	
1978	-30,205	176,052	145,847	9,058	943	10,001	6.9	6,018	2,558	3,983	
1979	-23,922	210,285	186,363	10,123	1,624	11,747	6.3	9,772	4,998	1,975	
1980	-19,696	245,262	225,566	11,952	3,554	15,506	6.9	13,248	6,727	2,258	
1981	-22,267	260,982	238,715	13,134	4,500	17,634	7.4	13,312	7,180	4,322	
1982	-27,510	243,952	216,442	11,035	4,568	15,603	7.2	9,608	3,834	5,995	
1983	-52,409	258,048	205,639	12,619	3,446	16,065	7.8	10,595	4,683	5,470	
1984	-106,703	330,678	223,976	10,082	4,926	15,008	6.7	9,659	3,195	5,350	
1985	-117,712	336,526	218,815	12,593	6,132	18,725	8.6	12,942	5,518	5,783	
1986	-138,279	365,438	227,159	11,826	7,902	19,728	8.7	14,851	6,276	4,875	
1987	-152,119	406,241	254,122	14,575	7,905	22,480	8.8	15,768	6,377	6,714	
1988	-118,526	440,952	322,426	17,860	9,087	26,947	8.4	20,298	8,766	6,651	
1989	-109,399	473,211	363,812	22,083	10,028	32,111	8.8	25,619	12,313	6,492	
1990	-101,718	495,311	393,592	27,282	11,801	39,083	9.9	31,517	16,691	7,566	
1991	-66,723	488,453	421,730	30,785	13,003	43,788	10.4	35,548	20,881	8,239	
1992	-84,501	532,665	448,164	31,356	13,662	45,018	11.0	36,906	22,379	8,111	
1993	-115,568	580,659	465,091	27,235	12,183	39,418	8.5	31,823	18,146	7,596	
1994	-150,630	663,256	512,626	25,010	12,363	37,373	7.3	30,050	15,931	7,322	
1995	-158,801	743,543	584,742	21,561	11,509	33,071	5.7	25,079	10,606	7,991	
1996	-170,214	795,289	625,075	26,602	13,668	40,270	6.4	29,477	13,624	10,792	
1997	-181,488	870,671	689,182	32,239	18,134	50,374	7.3	40,075	21,028	10,299	
1998	-231,100	913,597	682,497	40,960	23,110	64,071	9.4	51,999	31,427	12,072	

Source: Air Transport Association of America, Washington, DC, *Air Transport, Facts and Figures*, annual.

No. 1088. International Transportation Transactions of the United States: 1985 to 1998

[In millions of dollars (19,085 represents $19,085,000,000). Data are international transportation transactions recorded for balance of payment purposes (see Table 1307). Receipts include freight on exports carried by U.S.-operated carriers and foreign carrier expenditures in U.S. ports. Payments include freight on imports carried by foreign carriers and U.S. carrier port expenditures abroad. Freight on exports carried by foreign carriers is excluded since such payments are directly or indirectly for foreign account. Similarly, freight on U.S. imports carried by U.S. carriers is a domestic rather than an international transaction. Minus sign (-) indicates excess of payments over receipts]

Item	1985	1990	1992	1993	1994	1995	1996	1997	1998
Total receipts	19,085	37,339	38,147	38,486	40,751	44,990	46,487	47,795	45,516
Ocean passenger fares	60	154	176	237	287	285	329	217	306
Other ocean transportation	8,846	12,141	11,328	11,533	12,404	13,581	12,502	12,230	10,860
Freight	3,440	4,326	4,136	4,056	4,506	5,282	4,703	4,571	3,786
Port expenditures	5,274	7,815	7,192	7,477	7,898	8,299	7,799	7,659	7,074
Charter hire	132	-	-	-	-	-	-	-	-
Air passenger fares [1]	4,351	15,144	16,442	16,291	16,710	18,624	20,084	20,572	19,690
Other air transportation	5,347	8,174	8,374	8,567	9,311	10,016	10,928	12,013	11,864
Freight	706	2,432	2,589	2,814	3,175	3,654	3,958	4,610	4,757
Port expenditures	4,641	5,742	5,785	5,753	6,136	6,362	6,970	7,403	7,107
Miscellaneous receipts	481	1,726	1,827	1,858	2,039	2,484	2,644	2,763	2,796
Total payments	22,087	35,497	34,372	35,933	39,081	41,698	43,222	47,100	50,256
Ocean passenger fares	154	248	301	341	353	353	453	358	399
Other ocean transportation	10,698	13,078	11,781	12,473	13,694	14,068	13,492	14,095	15,677
Import freight	8,114	10,904	9,752	10,462	11,369	11,514	11,259	11,908	13,652
Port expenditures	2,048	2,174	2,029	2,011	2,325	2,554	2,233	2,187	2,025
Charter hire	536	-	-	-	-	-	-	-	-
Air passenger fares [1]	6,290	10,283	10,302	11,069	12,709	14,310	15,365	17,780	19,398
Other air transportation	4,719	9,881	10,468	10,497	10,525	11,061	11,751	12,575	12,559
Import freight	1,666	2,207	2,376	2,580	2,914	3,113	3,201	3,541	3,624
Port expenditures	3,053	7,674	8,092	7,917	7,611	7,948	8,550	9,034	8,935
Miscellaneous payments	226	2,007	1,520	1,553	1,800	1,906	2,161	2,292	2,223
Balance	-3,002	1,842	3,775	2,553	1,670	3,292	3,265	695	-4,750

- Represents zero. [1] Beginning 1990, includes interairline settlements.

Source: U.S. Bureau of Economic Analysis, *Survey of Current Business*, July 1999; and unpublished data.

No. 1089. Federal Expenditures for Civil Functions of the Corps of Engineers, United States Army: 1970 to 1997

[In millions of dollars (1,128 represents $1,128,000,000). For fiscal years ending in year shown, see text, Section 9, State and Local Government. These expenditures represent the work of the Corps of Engineers to plan, design, construct, operate, and maintain civil works projects and activities, particularly in the management and improvement of rivers, harbors, and waterways for navigation, flood control, and multiple purposes. The amounts listed below do not include the expenditure of funds contributed, advanced, or reimbursed by other government agencies or local interests. Includes Puerto Rico and outlying areas]

Fiscal year	Total program [1]	Navigation	Flood control	Multiple purpose	Fiscal year	Total program [1]	Navigation	Flood control	Multiple purpose
1970	1,128	398	379	331	1990	3,297	1,391	1,397	375
1980	3,061	1,225	1,228	551	1991	3,511	1,473	1,447	443
1984	3,085	1,383	1,154	445	1992	3,675	1,562	1,469	469
1985	2,956	1,234	1,187	419	1993	3,335	1,461	1,243	464
1986	3,163	1,345	1,300	402	1994	3,727	1,607	1,436	521
1987	2,937	1,135	1,272	411	1995	3,796	1,620	1,399	598
1988	3,086	1,271	1,271	423	1996	3,627	1,566	1,349	557
1989	3,252	1,395	1,253	462	1997	3,745	1,620	1,430	545

[1] Includes expenditures which are not associated with a specific purpose (e.g., headquarters staff supervision, management, and administration activities, and some research and development activities).

Source: U.S. Army Corps of Engineers, *Report of Civil Works Expenditures by State and Fiscal Year*, annual.

No. 1090. Freight Carried on Major U.S. Waterways: 1975 to 1997

[In millions of tons (3.2 represents 3,200,000)]

Item	1975	1980	1985	1990	1993	1994	1995	1996	1997
Atlantic intracoastal waterway	3.2	4.0	3.1	4.2	3.8	3.7	3.5	4.3	3.6
Great Lakes.	193.8	183.5	148.1	167.1	159.6	175.3	177.7	181.8	188.6
Gulf intracoastal waterway	97.0	94.5	102.5	115.5	114.9	117.6	117.9	118.0	118.1
Mississippi River system [1]	453.4	584.2	527.8	659.6	660.4	693.3	710.1	701.8	707.1
Mississippi River mainstream.	311.2	441.5	384.0	475.6	475.1	496.8	520.2	505.6	504.7
Ohio River system [2].	171.4	179.3	203.9	260.0	257.2	270.5	267.6	270.9	274.9
Columbia River.	38.1	49.2	42.4	51.4	51.2	50.9	57.1	51.2	52.7
Snake River.	2.0	5.1	3.5	4.8	5.3	5.9	6.8	5.7	6.1

[1] Main channels and all tributaries of the Mississippi, Illinois, Missouri and Ohio Rivers. [2] Main channels and all navigable tributaries and embayments of the Ohio, Tennessee, and Cumberland Rivers.

Source: U.S. Army Corps of Engineers, *Waterborne Commerce of the United States*, annual.

No. 1091. Waterborne Commerce, by Type of Commodity: 1990 to 1997

[In millions of short tons (2,163.9 represents 2,163,900,000). Domestic trade includes all commercial movements between United States ports and on inland rivers, Great Lakes, canals, and connecting channels of the United States, Puerto Rico, and Virgin Islands]

Commodity	1990	1995	1996	1997 Total	1997 Domestic	1997 Foreign imports	1997 Foreign exports
Total [1].	**2,163.9**	**2,240.4**	**2,284.1**	**2,333.1**	**1,112.5**	**788.3**	**432.3**
Coal.	339.9	324.5	328.7	326.0	232.3	10.3	83.4
Petroleum and petroleum products	923.2	907.1	954.4	988.2	396.7	533.5	58.0
Crude petroleum.	485.7	504.6	531.8	553.3	120.4	429.3	3.6
Petroleum products [1].	437.5	402.5	422.7	434.9	276.3	104.2	54.4
Gasoline	116.9	114.4	119.1	114.7	89.5	19.4	5.8
Distillate fuel oil.	77.4	76.7	84.5	88.2	65.7	16.6	5.9
Residual fuel oil.	145.2	111.9	112.3	114.4	76.7	29.2	8.5
Chemicals and related products	123.8	153.7	152.3	156.7	81.1	25.1	50.5
Crude material, inedible [1].	374.7	381.7	388.7	400.9	246.5	93.2	61.2
Forest products, wood and chips	55.7	47.2	45.4	44.0	19.7	3.8	20.5
Pulp and waste paper	11.8	14.9	12.6	11.9	0.2	1.1	10.6
Soil, sand, gravel, rock, and stone	144.2	152.5	159.2	167.8	135.4	26.7	5.7
Primary manufactured goods [1]	76.0	106.3	108.9	117.0	37.2	63.9	15.9
Papers products	10.7	13.1	13.7	14.3	1.4	3.8	9.1
Lime, cement and glass	28.3	33.9	33.7	38.4	15.7	20.6	2.1
Primary iron and steel products	25.1	44.1	45.7	48.0	14.4	31.9	1.7
Food and farm products [1]	267.5	303.2	284.9	271.7	93.7	29.0	149.0
Fish	3.2	3.6	2.0	2.1	0.1	1.1	0.9
Grain [1]	157.3	167.9	152.4	131.0	49.1	1.7	80.2
Corn	96.1	105.0	94.0	77.1	33.1	0.1	43.9
Wheat	44.5	48.5	46.6	40.6	12.4	0.3	27.9
Oilseeds	36.0	46.1	50.1	53.4	25.8	0.5	27.1
Soybeans.	32.2	42.0	46.2	48.4	21.5	0.2	26.7
Vegetables products	6.7	9.0	7.5	8.9	1.6	2.7	4.6
Processed grain and animal feed.	28.2	33.0	28.2	30.8	8.7	1.0	21.1

[1] Includes categories not shown separately.

Source: U.S. Army Corps of Engineers, *Waterborne Commerce of the United States*, annual.

Transportation—Air and Water   669

No. 1092. Flag Merchant Vessels—Private Shipyards: 1998

[As of October 1 (16,853 represents 16,853,000). Covers ocean going vessels of 1,000 gross tons and over engaged in foreign and domestic trade, and inactive vessels. Excludes vessels operating exclusively on Great Lakes, inland waterways, and those owned by the United States Army and Navy, and special types such as cable ships, tugs, etc.]

Vessel type	Number						Deadweight tons (1,000)					
	Total	Tank-er [1]	Dry bulk [2]	Con-tainer-ship	Cruise/Pas-sen-ger [3]	Other [4]	Total	Tank-er [1]	Dry bulk [2]	Con-tainer-ship	Cruise/Pas-sen-ger [3]	Other [4]
Total	**473**	**156**	**15**	**91**	**12**	**199**	**16,853**	**9,415**	**579**	**3,096**	**116**	**3,647**
Active vessels	265	113	11	84	4	53	12,094	7,414	497	2,964	37	1,182
Privately owned	255	112	11	83	1	48	11,978	7,397	497	2,948	7	1,129
U.S. foreign trade . .	81	5	5	55	-	16	3,082	185	279	2,243	-	375
Foreign-to-foreign . .	14	13	1	-	-	-	1,123	1,059	64	-	-	-
Domestic trade	124	86	4	25	1	8	6,826	5,922	113	639	7	145
Coastal	64	57	4	1	-	2	2,585	2,390	113	39	-	43
Noncontiguous. . .	60	29	-	24	1	6	4,241	3,532	-	600	7	102
Military Sea Lift Command	36	8	1	3	-	24	947	231	41	66	-	609
Government owned. . .	10	1	-	1	3	5	116	17	-	16	30	53
Ready reserve force.	2	-	-	-	1	1	24	-	-	-	9	15
Other custody	4	1	-	1	-	2	55	17	-	16	-	22
Other reserve	4	-	-	-	2	2	37	-	-	-	21	16
Inactive vessels	208	43	4	7	8	146	4,759	2,001	82	132	79	2,465
Privately owned	28	16	4	4	-	4	1,336	1,132	82	78	-	44
Laid-up (Not trading) [5]	27	15	4	4	-	4	1,302	1,098	82	78	-	44
Laid-up (Marad Custody)	1	1	-	-	-	-	34	34	-	-	-	-
Government owned: National Defense reserve fleet	180	27	-	3	8	142	3,423	869	-	54	79	2,421
Ready reserve fleet .	89	10	-	2	1	76	1,882	304	-	34	17	1,527
Other reserve	46	9	-	1	-	36	907	342	-	20	-	545
Non-retention [6]	45	8	-	-	7	30	634	223	-	-	62	349

- Represents zero. [1] Includes liquified natural gas and intergrated tug barge vessels. [2] Includes bulk/oil, ore/oil, ore/bulk/oil carriers and intergrated tug barges. [3] Includes combination passenger and cargo vessels. [4] Breakbulk ships, partial containerships, refrigerated cargo ships, barge, specialized cargo, and roll-on roll-off ships. [5] Vessels idle 30 days or more. [6] Vessels not actively maintained.

Source: Maritime Administration, Office of Statistical and Economic Analysis.

No. 1093. Private Shipyards—Summary: 1980 to 1999

[For calendar year, unless noted. (178.0 represents 178,000)]

Item	Unit	1980	1985	1990	1994	1995	1996	1997	1998	1999 [1]
Employment [2]	1,000. . .	178.0	138.3	130.8	107.2	105.0	100.4	98.6	99.6	99.9
Production workers	1,000. . .	138.8	101.2	93.6	79.7	77.8	73.5	70.8	71.6	70.3
Building activity: Merchant vessels: [3]										
Under construction [4] . . .	Number .	69	10	-	1	3	10	14	12	5
Ordered.	Number .	7	-	3	3	8	5	6	1	2
Delivered	Number .	23	3	-	1	1	1	4	5	1
Cancelled.	Number .	4	-	-	-	-	-	4	3	-
Under contract [5]	Number .	49	7	3	3	10	14	12	5	6
Naval vessels: [3]										
Under construction [4] . . .	Number .	99	100	95	60	57	46	46	42	46
Ordered.	Number .	11	11	7	12	6	11	4	17	-
Delivered	Number .	19	26	15	15	17	11	8	13	4
Under contract [5]	Number .	91	85	87	57	46	46	42	46	42
Unfinished work: [4]										
Commercial ships	Mil. dol.	2,070	450	-	58.3	93.4	365.4	572.1	746.5	596.6
Naval ships	Mil. dol. .	7,107	12,091	24,495	19,679	20,768	17,734	20,116	19,097	18,079

- Represents zero. [1] As of June 1. [2] Annual average of monthly data. [3] Vessels of 1,000 tons or larger. [4] As of Jan. 1. [5] As of Dec. 31.

Source: 1980 and 1985, Shipbuilders Council of America, Arlington, VA., unpublished data; beginning 1990, U.S. Maritime Administration, unpublished data.

No. 1094. Employees in Government and Private Shipyards: 1960 to 1998

[In thousands (208 represents 208,000). Annual average employment in establishments primarily engaged in building and repairing of ships, barges, and lighters, whether self-propelled or towed by other craft. Includes all full- and part-time employees]

Year	Total	Private yards	Federal yards	Year	Total	Private yards	Federal yards	Year	Total	Private yards	Federal yards
1960	208	112	96	1989	196	126	71	1994	148	107	41
1970	216	134	83	1990	198	130	68	1995	139	106	33
1975	220	154	66	1991	193	131	62	1996	127	103	24
1980	250	178	72	1992	183	125	58	1997	122	100	22
1985	219	138	80	1993	163	113	50	1998	122	100	22

Source: U.S. Bureau of Labor Statistics, *Employment and Earnings*, monthly, March and June issues; and Internet site <http://stats.bls.gov/ceshome.htm>.

No. 1095. Employment on U.S. Flag Merchant Vessels and Basic Monthly Wage Scale for Able-Bodied Seamen: 1975 to 1997

[Employment in thousands (20.5 represents 20,500)]

Year	Employment [1]	Year	Employment [1]	Year	East coast wage rate [2]	West coast wage rate [2]	Year	East coast wage rate [2]	West coast wage rate [2]
1975	20.5	1992	9.2	1975	612	900	1992	1,655	2,438
1980	19.6	1993	9.3	1980	967	1,414	1993	1,721	2,438
1985	13.1	1994	9.1	1985	1,419	2,029	1994	1,790	2,536
1989	9.9	1995	7.9	1989	1,448	2,218	1995	1,918	2,637
1990	11.1	1996	7.5	1990	1,505	2,218	1996	2,014	2,769
1991	11.7	1997	8.6	1991	1,518	2,329	1997	2,094	2,879

[1] As of June 30, except beginning 1980, as of Sept. 30. Estimates of personnel employed on merchant ships, 1,000 gross tons and over. Excludes vessels on inland waterways, Great Lakes, and those owned by, or operated for, U.S. Army and Navy, and special types such as cable ships, tugs, etc.   [2] As of January. Basic monthly wage, over and above subsistence (board and room); excludes overtime and fringe pay benefits. West coast incorporates extra pay for Saturdays and Sundays at sea into base wages but east coast does not.

Source: U.S. Maritime Administration, *U.S. Merchant Marine Data Sheet*, monthly; and unpublished data.

No. 1096. Worldwide Tanker Casualties: 1975 to 1998

[(188 represents 188,000). Data for 1975 and 1980 covers tankers, ore/oil carriers and bulk/oil vessels of 6,000 deadweight tons and over; beginning 1985, 10,000 deadweight tons and over; excludes liquid gas carriers. Incident is counted in the year it is reported. Based on data from "Lloyd's List" published by Lloyd's of London. "Casualties" include weather damage, strandings, collisions and other contact, fires and explosions, machinery damage, and other mishaps]

Item	Unit	1975	1980	1985	1990	1993	1994	1995	1996	1997	1998
Casualties	Number	906	(NA)	340	541	314	270	280	241	270	201
Total losses [1]	Number	22	15	12	10	9	11	6	2	9	2
Deaths	Number	90	132	53	119	26	88	8	15	(NA)	(NA)
Oil spills	Number	45	32	9	31	24	29	18	24	22	22
Amount	1,000 tons	188	136	80	61	120	110	4	72	50	9
Amount	Mil. gallons	58	42	25	19	37	33	1	22	15	3

NA Not available.   [1] Excludes losses due to hostilities.

Source: Tanker Advisory Center, Inc., New York, NY, "Worldwide Tanker Casualty Returns," quarterly.

No. 1097. Merchant Vessels—World and United States: 1970 to 1996

[(20,980 represents 20,980,000). Through 1992, as of mid-year; thereafter for year-end. For propelled sea-going merchant ships of not less than 100 gross tonnage]

Year	World completed Number	World completed Gross tonnage (1,000)	World owned Number	World owned Gross tonnage (1,000)	U.S. completed Number	U.S. completed Gross tonnage (1,000)	U.S. registered Number	U.S. registered Gross tonnage (1,000)
1970	2,814	20,980	52,444	227,490	156	375	2,983	18,463
1980	2,412	13,101	73,832	419,911	205	555	5,579	18,464
1985	1,964	18,157	76,395	416,269	66	180	6,447	19,518
1990	1,672	15,885	78,336	423,627	16	15	6,348	21,328
1992	1,506	18,633	79,845	444,305	27	54	5,737	18,228
1993	1,505	20,025	80,655	457,915	30	14	5,646	14,087
1994	1,789	19,612	80,676	475,859	28	29	5,270	13,655
1995	1,856	22,565	82,890	490,662	30	14	5,292	12,760
1996	1,745	25,881	84,264	507,873	29	24	5,289	12,024

Source: Through 1992, Lloyd's Register of Shipping, London, England, *Statistical Tables*, annual; and *Annual Summary of Merchant Ships Completed in the World*; thereafter, *World Fleet Statistics*, annual.

Transportation—Air and Water   671

No. 1098. Merchant Vessels—Ships and Tonnage Lost Worldwide: 1980 to 1996

[For merchant vessels of 100 gross tonnage and above (1,791 represents 1,791,000). Excludes ships which have been declared constructive losses but have undergone repair during the year. Loss counted in the year the casualty occurred, providing that information was available at time of relevant publication]

Type of ship	Ships lost					Gross tonnage lost (1,000)				
	1980	1990	1994	1995	1996	1980	1990	1994	1995	1996
Total............	363	160	171	190	151	1,791	1,047	1,532	1,055	836
Tankers	24	8	16	12	12	707	138	638	172	179
Ore/bulk carriers [1]	21	15	19	19	18	458	687	590	447	303
General cargo	211	87	76	88	77	478	202	237	218	240
Container ships	2	-	-	-	6	6	-	-	-	94
Passenger [2]	9	-	2	1	-	112	-	26	185	-
Fishing.............	96	50	58	70	38	30	20	41	33	20

- Represents zero.   [1] Includes ore/bulk/oil carriers.   [2] Includes passenger cargo/ships.

Source: Lloyd's Register of Shipping, London, England, *Casualty Return,* annual.

No. 1099. Merchant Fleets of the World: 1998

[Vessels of 1,000 gross tons and over. As of Oct. 1. Specified countries have 100 or more ships]

Country of registry	Total	Tanker	Dry bulk [1]	Container-ship	Roll-on/roll-off	Cruise/passenger	Other [2]
World total	27,730	6,739	5,744	2,341	864	449	11,593
United States	473	156	15	91	58	12	141
Privately-owned	283	128	15	87	26	1	26
Government-owned...	190	28	-	4	32	11	115
Foreign total	27,257	6,583	5,729	2,250	806	437	11,452
Panama	4,456	971	1,293	469	68	51	1,604
Liberia	1,632	691	456	170	12	40	263
Russia	1,472	273	113	25	11	7	1,043
China	1,465	244	332	96	14	34	745
Cyprus	1,436	173	488	121	20	15	619
Malta	1,305	349	371	45	39	7	494
Bahamas..........	1,029	241	151	53	37	60	487
Singapore	877	386	129	162	5	1	194
Saint Vincent	782	96	135	30	38	5	478
Greece	741	257	318	44	16	19	87
Japan	708	284	177	32	49	15	151
Norway (NIS) [3]	652	288	105	4	40	12	203
Philippines	533	68	211	11	18	8	217
Turkey	521	74	169	12	15	8	243
Netherlands........	504	71	6	46	15	9	357
Germany	499	20	-	278	10	6	185
Indonesia	484	121	24	12	11	8	308
Korea (South)	435	107	112	45	1	3	167
Antigua & Barbuda ...	405	11	17	85	16	-	276
Malaysia	372	110	58	50	8	2	144
Belize............	367	51	20	5	3	-	288
Italy	345	192	30	14	41	21	47
Denmark (DIS) [3]	305	66	13	59	9	-	158
India............	292	96	128	6	-	2	60
Thailand	289	89	39	12	-	1	148
Ukraine..........	267	21	10	3	12	9	212
Honduras	232	27	13	4	5	3	180
Romania	197	8	39	2	9	-	139
Hong Kong	190	10	107	41	-	-	32
Taiwan	183	17	52	75	1	-	38
Sweden	173	64	8	-	41	5	55
Brazil............	172	79	45	6	9	1	32
Isle of Man	149	71	22	21	11	1	23
United Kingdom	142	63	4	23	5	21	26
Marshall Islands	130	43	59	20	2	-	6
Cambodia	128	-	12	3	3	-	110
Syria............	124	-	3	-	1	-	120
Norway..........	124	41	6	-	7	2	68
Iran	120	25	45	3	2	-	45
Spain	119	36	9	19	32	-	23
Vietnam	113	12	9	-	1	-	91
Portugal	112	28	13	4	3	-	64
Egypt	112	16	22	-	9	-	64
All other	2,564	693	356	140	157	60	1,158

- Represents zero.   [1] Includes bulk/oil, ore/oil, and ore/bulk/oil carriers.   [2] Breakbulk ships, partial containerships, refrigerated cargo ships, barge and specialized cargo ships.   [3] International Shipping Registry which is an open registry under which the ship flies the flag of the specified nation but is exempt from certain taxation and other regulations.

Source: U.S. Maritime Administration, *Merchant Fleets of the World,* summary report, annual; and unpublished data.

U.S. Census Bureau, Statistical Abstract of the United States: 1999

Section 23
Agriculture

This section presents statistics on farms and farm operators; land use; farm income, expenditures, and debt; farm output, productivity, and marketings; foreign trade in agricultural products; specific crops; and livestock, poultry, and their products.

The principal sources are the reports issued by the National Agricultural Statistics Service (NASS) and the Economic Research Service (ERS) of the U.S. Department of Agriculture. The information from the 1997 Census of Agriculture is available in printed form in the Volume 1, Geographic Area Series; in electronic format on CD-ROM; and on the Internet (http://www.nass.usda.gov/census/). The Department of Agriculture publishes annually *Agricultural Statistics*, a general reference book on agricultural production, supplies, consumption, facilities, costs, and returns. The Economic Research Service publishes data on farm assets, debt, and income in the annual *Farm Business Economic Report*. Sources of current data on agricultural exports and imports include *Foreign Agricultural Trade of the United States*, published by the ERS, and the reports of the U.S. Census Bureau, particularly *U.S. Imports of Merchandise on CD-ROM*, and *U.S. Exports of Merchandise on CD-ROM*.

The 45 field offices of the NASS collect data on crops, livestock and products, agricultural prices, farm employment, and other related subjects mainly through sample surveys. Information is obtained on some 75 crops and 50 livestock items as well as scores of items pertaining to agricultural production and marketing. State estimates and supporting information are sent to the Agricultural Statistics Board of NASS which reviews the estimates and issues reports containing state and national data. Among these reports are annual summaries such as *Crop Production, Crop Values, Agricultural Prices*, and *Livestock*

Production, Disposition and Income. For more information about concepts and methods underlying USDA's statistical series, see *Major Statistical Series of the U.S. Department of Agriculture* (Agricultural Handbook No. 671), a 12-volume set of publications.

Farms and farmland—The definitions of a farm have varied through time. Since 1850, when minimum criteria defining a farm for census purposes first were established, the farm definition has been changed nine times. The current definition, first used for the 1974 census, is any place from which $1,000 or more of agricultural products were produced and sold, or normally would have been sold, during the census year.

Acreage designated as "land in farms" consists primarily of agricultural land used for crops, pasture, or grazing. It also includes woodland and wasteland not actually under cultivation or used for pasture or grazing, provided it was part of the farm operator's total operation. Land in farms includes acres set aside under annual commodity acreage programs as well as acres in the Conservation Reserve and Wetlands Reserve Programs for places meeting the farm definition. Land in farms is an operating unit concept and includes land owned and operated as well as land rented from others. All grazing land, except land used under government permits on a per-head basis, was included as "land in farms" provided it was part of a farm or ranch.

Since 1945, an evaluation of census coverage has been conducted for each census of agriculture to provide estimates of the completeness of census farm counts. According to coverage evaluation results, the past five censuses of agriculture included an average of 92 percent of U.S. farms and 98 percent of agriculture production. The

Agriculture   673

1997 coverage evaluation program was designed to measure four components of error in the census farm counts. These components include undercount due to farms not on the mail list; overcount due to farms duplicated or enumerated more than once; undercount due to farms incorrectly classified as nonfarms; and overcount due to nonfarms incorrectly classified as farms. The first component, mail list undercount, is by far the largest component of coverage error. The percentage of farms missed in the census varies considerably by state. In general, farms not on the mail list tended to be small in acreage, production, and sales of agricultural products. For more explanation about mail list compilation and census coverage, see Appendixes A and C, *1997 Census of Agriculture*, Volume 1, reports.

Farm income—The final agricultural sector output comprises cash receipts from farm marketings of crops and livestock, Federal government payments made directly to farmers for farm-related activities, rental value of farm homes, value of farm products consumed in farm homes, and other farm-related income such as machine hire and custom work. Farm marketings represent quantities of agricultural products sold by farmers multiplied by prices received per unit of production at the local market. Information on prices received for farm products is generally obtained by the NASS Agricultural Statistics Board from surveys of firms (such as grain elevators, packers, and processors) purchasing agricultural commodities directly from producers. In some cases, the price information is obtained directly from the producers.

Crops—Estimates of crop acreage and production by the NASS are based on current sample survey data obtained from

individual producers and objective yield counts, reports of carlot shipments, market records, personal field observations by field statisticians, and reports from other sources. Prices received by farmers are marketing year averages. These averages are based on U.S. monthly prices weighted by monthly marketings during specific periods. U.S. monthly prices are state average prices weighted by marketings during the month. Marketing year average prices do not include allowances for outstanding loans, government purchases, deficiency payments or disaster payments.

All state prices are based on individual state marketing years, while U.S. marketing year averages are based on standard marketing years for each crop. For a listing of the crop marketing years and the participating states in the monthly program, see *Crop Values*. Value of production is computed by multiplying state prices by each state's production. The U.S. value of production is the sum of state values for all states. Value of production figures shown in Tables 1128-1131, 1135, and 1136 should not be confused with cash receipts from farm marketings which relate to sales during a calendar year, irrespective of the year of production.

Livestock—Annual inventory numbers of livestock and estimates of livestock, dairy, and poultry production prepared by the Department of Agriculture are based on information from farmers and ranchers obtained by probability survey sampling methods.

Statistical reliability—For a discussion of statistical collection and estimation, sampling procedures, and measures of statistical reliability pertaining to Department of Agriculture data, see Appendix III.

No. 1100. Farms—Number and Acreage, by Size of Farm: 1987 to 1997

[2,088 represents 2,088,000]

Size of farm	Number of farms (1,000)			Land in farms (mil. acres)			Cropland harvested (mil. acres)			Percent distribution, 1997		
	1987	1992	1997	1987	1992	1997	1987	1992	1997	Number of farms	All land in farms	Cropland harvested
Total	2,088	1,925	1,912	964.5	945.5	931.8	282.2	295.9	309.4	100.0	100.0	100.0
Under 10 acres.	183	166	154	0.7	0.7	0.6	0.2	0.2	0.2	8.1	0.1	0.1
10 to 49 acres	412	388	411	11.1	10.3	11.0	3.9	3.5	3.6	21.5	1.2	1.2
50 to 99 acres	311	283	295	22.5	20.4	21.2	7.9	7.2	7.0	15.4	2.3	2.3
100 to 179 acres. . . .	334	301	298	45.3	40.7	40.2	17.1	15.4	14.3	15.6	4.3	4.6
180 to 259 acres.	192	172	165	41.5	37.2	35.5	17.2	15.5	14.0	8.6	3.8	4.5
260 to 499 acres.	286	255	238	103.0	91.7	85.4	47.3	43.6	39.3	12.4	9.2	12.7
500 to 999 acres.	200	186	176	138.5	129.3	122.1	67.4	68.6	65.4	9.2	13.1	21.1
1,000 to 1,999 acres . .	102	102	101	138.8	139.0	138.8	61.1	69.3	73.8	5.3	14.9	23.9
2,000 acres and over. .	67	71	75	463.2	476.3	476.9	60.2	72.5	91.8	3.9	51.2	29.7

No. 1101. Farms—Number and Acreage, by Tenure of Operator: 1987 to 1997

[2,088 represents 2,088,000. *Full owners* own all the land they operate. *Part owners* own a part and rent from others the rest of the land they operate]

Item and year	Unit	Total	Full owner	Part owner	Tenant	Percent distribution			
						Total	Full owner	Part owner	Tenant
NUMBER OF FARMS									
1987	1,000. . . .	2,088	1,239	609	240	100.0	59.3	29.2	11.5
1992	1,000. . . .	1,925	1,112	597	217	100.0	57.7	31.0	11.3
1997	1,000. . . .	1,912	1,147	574	191	100.0	60.0	30.0	10.0
Under 50 acres	1,000. . . .	564	460	57	48	100.0	81.6	10.1	8.5
50 to 179 acres	1,000. . . .	593	409	131	53	100.0	69.0	22.1	8.9
180 to 499 acres	1,000. . . .	403	189	169	45	100.0	46.9	41.9	11.2
500 to 999 acres	1,000. . . .	176	50	103	23	100.0	28.4	58.5	13.0
1,000 acres or more	1,000. . . .	176	40	114	22	100.0	22.7	64.8	12.5
LAND IN FARMS									
1987	Mil. acres.	964	318	520	127	100.0	32.9	53.9	13.2
1992	Mil. acres.	946	296	527	123	100.0	31.3	55.7	13.0
1997	Mil. acres.	932	316	508	108	100.0	33.9	54.5	11.6

No. 1102. Farm Operators—Tenure and Characteristics: 1992 and 1997

[In thousands, except as indicated (1,925 represents 1,925,000)]

Characteristic	All farms		Farms with sales of $10,000 and over		Characteristic	All farms		Farms with sales of $10,000 and over	
	1992	1997	1992	1997		1992	1997	1992	1997
Total operators	1,925	1,912	1,019	949	Full owner	1,112	1,147	422	404
					Part owner.	597	574	448	419
White	1,882	1,865	1,003	932	Tenant.	217	191	148	126
Black	19	18	5	4	Principal occupation:				
American Indian, Eskimo, and Aleut	8	10	3	4	Farming	1,053	962	754	675
Asian or Pacific Islander. . .	8	9	5	5	Other.	872	950	265	274
Other	8	10	3	3	Place of residence: [2]				
					On farm operated	1,379	1,362	736	681
Operators of Hispanic origin [1]	21	28	8	11	Not on farm operated . . .	409	413	215	201
					Years on present farm: [2]				
Female	145	165	50	52	2 years or less	95	93	41	35
					3 to 4 years	133	127	58	46
Under 25 years old	28	21	17	12	5 to 9 years	259	264	121	109
25 to 34 years old	179	128	112	72	10 years or more	1,113	1,114	648	616
35 to 44 years old	382	371	217	200	Days worked off farm: [2]				
45 to 54 years old	429	467	223	232	None.	802	755	536	476
55 to 64 years old	430	427	229	212	Less than 100 days	165	165	104	98
65 years old and over	478	497	220	222	100 to 199 days	162	168	76	76
Average age (years)	53.3	54.3	51.9	53.2	200 days or more	666	709	226	229

[1] Operators of Hispanic origin may be of any race. [2] Excludes not reported.

Source of Tables 1100-1102: U.S. Dept. of Agriculture, National Agricultural Statistics Service, *Census of Agriculture: 1992*, Vol. 1; and *1997*, Vol. 1.

U.S. Census Bureau, Statistical Abstract of the United States: 1999

No. 1103. Farms—Number, Acreage, and Value, by Type of Organization: 1992 and 1997

[1,925 represents 1,925,000]

Item	Unit	Total [1]	Individual or family	Partner-ship	Corpo-ration	Total [1]	Individual or family	Partner-ship	Corpora-tion
						Percent distribution			
ALL FARMS									
Number of farms:									
1992	1,000 ...	1,925	1,653	187	73	100.0	85.9	9.7	3.8
1997	1,000 ...	1,912	1,643	169	84	100.0	85.9	8.8	4.4
Land in farms:									
1992	Mil. acres.	946	604	153	123	100.0	63.9	16.2	13.0
1997	Mil. acres.	932	585	149	131	100.0	62.8	16.0	14.1
Value of land and buildings: [2]									
1992	Bil. dol. ..	687	474	109	85	100.0	69.0	15.8	12.4
1997	Bil. dol. ..	860	593	133	114	100.0	69.0	15.5	13.3
Value of farm products sold:									
1992	Bil. dol. ..	163	88	29	44	100.0	54.1	18.0	27.2
1997	Bil. dol. ..	197	103	36	57	100.0	52.6	18.4	29.1
FARMS WITH SALES OF $10,000 AND OVER									
Number of farms:									
1992	1,000 ...	1,019	820	131	61	100.0	80.5	12.8	6.0
1997	1,000 ...	949	758	114	70	100.0	79.9	12.0	7.4
Land in farms:									
1992	Mil. acres.	822	512	143	119	100.0	62.2	17.4	14.4
1997	Mil. acres.	802	485	138	126	100.0	60.5	17.2	15.7

[1] Includes other types, not shown separately. [2] Based on a sample of farms.

No. 1104. Corporate Farms—Characteristics, by Type: 1997

[131.5 represents 131,500,000]

Item	Unit	All corpo-rations	Total	Family held corporations 1-10 stock-holders	11 or more stock-holders	Total	Other corporations 1-10 stock-holders	11 or more stock-holders
Farms	Number...	84,002	76,103	74,308	1,795	7,899	6,870	1,029
Percent distribution	Percent...	100.0	90.6	88.5	2.1	9.4	8.2	1.2
Land in farms	Mil. acres..	131.5	119.6	109.6	10.0	11.9	8.8	3.1
Average per farm	Acres	1,565	1,571	1,474	5,571	1,507	1,284	2,994
Value of—								
Land and buildings [1]	Bil. dol.	113.7	99.3	91.6	7.7	14.4	9.3	5.1
Average per farm.	$1,000	1,380	1,338	1,264	4,429	1,769	1,288	5,450
Farm products sold	Bil. dol.	56.9	45.9	40.8	5.1	11.0	7.3	3.8
Average per farm.	$1,000 ...	677	603	548	2,862	1,395	1,057	3,649

[1] Based on a sample of farms.

No. 1105. Farms—Number, Acreage, and Value of Sales, by Size of Sales: 1997

[1,912 represents 1,912,000]

Value of products sold	Farms (1,000)	Acreage Total (mil.)	Acreage Average per farm	Value of sales Total (mil. dol.)	Value of sales Average per farm (dol.)	Percent distribution Farms	Percent distribution Acreage	Percent distribution Value of sales
Total	1,912	931.8	487	196,865	102,970	100.0	100.0	100.0
Less than $10,000	963	129.5	134	2,937	3,050	50.4	13.9	1.5
Less than $2,500	497	63.8	128	424	854	26.0	6.8	0.2
$2,500-$4,999	228	26.3	115	820	3,591	12.0	2.8	0.4
$5,000-$9,999	238	39.4	166	1,693	7,113	12.4	4.2	0.9
$10,000 or more	949	802.3	846	193,928	204,373	49.6	86.1	98.5
$10,000-$24,999	274	75.3	275	4,372	15,955	14.3	8.1	2.2
$25,000-$49,999	171	82.0	481	6,084	35,642	8.9	8.8	3.1
$50,000-$99,999	158	118.0	746	11,347	71,741	8.3	12.7	5.8
$100,000-$249,999	189	207.5	1,095	30,143	159,137	9.9	22.3	15.3
$250,000-$499,999	88	138.4	1,577	30,505	347,531	4.6	14.9	15.5
$500,000-$999,999	43	91.3	2,129	29,365	685,140	2.2	9.8	14.9
$1,000,000 or more	26	89.8	3,464	82,110	3,166,152	1.4	9.6	41.7

Source of Tables 1103-1105: U.S. Dept. of Agriculture, National Agricultural Statistics Service. *1997 Census of Agriculture*, Vol. 1.

676 Agriculture

No. 1106. Farms—Number, Acreage, and Value, by State: 1992 and 1997

[1,925 represents 1,925,000]

State	All farms								Farms with sales of $10,000 or more, 1997		
	Number of farms (1,000)		Land in farms (mil. acres)		Average size of farm (acres)		Total value [1] (mil. dol.)		Number of farms (1,000)	Land in farms (mil. acres)	Average size of farm (acres)
	1992	1997	1992	1997	1992	1997	1992	1997			
United States. .	1,925	1,912	945.5	931.8	491	487	687,432	859,839	949	802.3	846
Alabama	38	41	8.5	8.7	223	210	8,350	12,340	13	5.2	406
Alaska	1	1	0.9	0.9	1,803	1,608	249	267	(Z)	0.7	3,088
Arizona	7	6	35.0	26.9	5,173	4,379	10,984	10,360	3	25.5	8,681
Arkansas	44	45	14.1	14.4	322	318	12,407	16,255	20	11.4	556
California	78	74	29.0	27.7	373	374	63,689	69,768	42	25.2	605
Colorado	27	28	34.0	32.6	1,252	1,154	14,568	19,993	15	28.9	1,943
Connecticut	3	4	0.4	0.4	105	97	2,138	2,104	1	0.2	159
Delaware.	3	2	0.6	0.6	224	236	1,351	1,499	2	0.5	319
Florida	35	35	10.8	10.5	306	300	21,801	23,048	15	8.8	596
Georgia	41	40	10.0	10.7	246	265	11,437	15,842	16	7.5	468
Hawaii	5	5	1.6	1.4	298	263	3,854	3,460	2	1.3	572
Idaho	22	22	13.5	11.8	609	530	9,077	11,983	12	10.3	866
Illinois	78	73	27.3	27.2	351	372	41,844	56,475	50	25.6	515
Indiana	63	58	15.6	15.1	249	261	21,732	30,853	33	13.5	415
Iowa	97	91	31.3	31.2	325	343	38,063	51,438	67	29.2	435
Kansas	63	62	46.7	46.1	738	748	21,725	26,517	39	42.6	1,099
Kentucky	90	82	13.7	13.3	151	162	14,775	18,943	36	9.7	268
Louisiana	26	24	7.8	7.9	306	331	7,474	9,077	10	6.3	661
Maine	6	6	1.3	1.2	218	209	1,396	1,456	2	0.8	337
Maryland	13	12	2.2	2.2	171	178	6,570	6,825	6	1.8	295
Massachusetts . . .	5	6	0.5	0.5	100	93	2,421	2,535	3	0.3	130
Michigan	47	46	10.1	9.9	217	215	11,517	16,490	23	8.1	359
Minnesota	75	73	25.7	26.0	342	354	23,319	29,927	47	23.0	486
Mississippi	32	31	10.2	10.1	318	323	7,952	10,555	10	6.9	658
Missouri	98	99	28.5	28.8	291	292	22,070	30,589	44	22.2	505
Montana	23	24	59.6	58.6	2,613	2,414	13,578	16,970	15	52.3	3,499
Nebraska	53	51	44.4	45.5	839	885	22,713	29,200	40	43.6	1,092
Nevada	3	3	9.3	6.4	3,205	2,266	2,347	2,474	1	6.2	4,209
New Hampshire . .	2	3	0.4	0.4	158	141	836	945	1	0.2	222
New Jersey	9	9	0.8	0.8	93	91	5,590	5,403	4	0.6	179
New Mexico	14	14	46.8	45.8	3,281	3,249	9,220	8,801	5	41.6	7,593
New York	32	32	7.5	7.3	231	228	9,130	9,117	17	5.7	334
North Carolina . . .	52	49	8.9	9.1	172	185	13,950	18,566	23	7.2	314
North Dakota	31	31	39.4	39.4	1,267	1,290	13,163	15,635	23	36.4	1,590
Ohio	71	69	14.2	14.1	201	206	20,626	28,450	36	11.8	328
Oklahoma	67	74	32.1	33.2	480	448	15,754	20,188	30	26.7	899
Oregon	32	34	17.6	17.4	552	513	11,824	16,316	13	15.5	1,193
Pennsylvania	45	45	7.2	7.2	160	158	14,752	16,891	25	5.4	221
Rhode Island	1	1	0.1	0.1	76	75	313	325	(Z)	(Z)	107
South Carolina . . .	20	20	4.5	4.6	221	228	5,093	6,558	6	2.9	470
South Dakota	34	31	44.8	44.4	1,316	1,418	12,264	15,237	24	40.2	1,669
Tennessee	75	77	11.2	11.1	149	145	13,977	20,066	21	6.7	315
Texas	181	194	130.9	131.3	725	676	65,060	77,351	65	108.0	1,662
Utah	14	14	9.6	12.0	712	848	4,704	6,894	6	11.0	1,776
Vermont	5	6	1.3	1.3	235	217	1,730	1,876	3	1.0	321
Virginia	42	41	8.3	8.2	197	200	13,534	15,813	16	5.9	364
Washington	30	29	15.7	15.2	520	523	14,178	18,410	14	12.8	913
West Virginia	17	18	3.3	3.5	192	194	2,810	3,790	4	1.5	401
Wisconsin	68	66	15.5	14.9	228	227	14,285	18,504	40	12.4	309
Wyoming	9	9	32.9	34.1	3,772	3,692	5,242	7,460	6	30.9	5,349

Z Less than 500 farms or 50,000 acres.   [1] Value of land and buildings. Based on reports for a sample of farms.

Source: U.S. Dept. of Agriculture, National Agricultural Statistics Service, *1997 Census of Agriculture*, Vol. 1.

Agriculture   677

No. 1107. Farms—Number and Acreage: 1980 to 1998

[As of **June 1 (2,440 represents 2,440,000)**. Based on 1974 census definition; for definition of farms and farmland, see text of this section. Data for census years (indicated by italics) have been adjusted for underenumeration and are used as reference points along with data from acreage and livestock surveys in estimating data for other years. Minus sign (-) indicates decrease]

Year	Farms Number (1,000)	Farms Annual change [1] (1,000)	Land in farms Total (mil. acres)	Land in farms Average per farm (acres)	Year	Farms Number (1,000)	Farms Annual change [1] (1,000)	Land in farms Total (mil. acres)	Land in farms Average per farm (acres)
1980	2,440	3	1,039	426	*1992*	*2,108*	*-9*	*979*	*464*
1985	2,293	-41	1,012	441	1993	2,202	94	969	440
1986	2,250	-43	1,005	447	1994	2,198	-4	966	440
1987	*2,213*	*-37*	*999*	*451*	1995	2,196	-2	963	438
1988	2,201	-12	994	452	1996	2,191	-5	959	438
1989	2,175	-26	991	456	1997	2,191	-	956	436
1990	2,146	-29	987	460	1998	2,192	1	954	435
1991	2,117	-29	982	464					

- Represents zero.   [1] Annual change from immediate preceding year.

Source: U.S. Dept. of Agriculture, National Agricultural Statistics Service, *Farm Numbers, 1975-80; Farms and Land in Farms, Final Estimates by States, 1979-1987; Farms and Land in Farms, Final Estimates, 1988-1992; Farms and Land in Farms, Final Estimates, 1993-1997*; and *Farms and Land In Farms,* July releases.

No. 1108. Farms—Number and Acreage, by State: 1990 and 1998

[**2,146 represents 2,146,000**. See headnote, Table 1107]

State	Farms (1,000) 1990	Farms (1,000) 1998	Acreage (mil.) 1990	Acreage (mil.) 1998	Acreage per farm 1990	Acreage per farm 1998	State	Farms (1,000) 1990	Farms (1,000) 1998	Acreage (mil.) 1990	Acreage (mil.) 1998	Acreage per farm 1990	Acreage per farm 1998
U.S.	2,146	2,192	987	954	460	435	Missouri	108	110	30	30	281	274
							Montana	25	28	61	58	2,449	2,091
Alabama	47	49	10	10	215	194	Nebraska	57	55	47	46	826	844
Alaska	1	1	1	1	1,707	1,625	Nevada	3	3	9	7	3,560	2,300
Arizona	8	8	36	28	4,641	3,582	New Hampshire	3	3	(Z)	(Z)	163	135
Arkansas	47	50	16	15	330	298	New Jersey	8	10	1	1	107	86
California	85	89	31	29	362	320	New Mexico	14	16	45	45	3,296	2,831
Colorado	27	30	33	32	1,249	1,092	New York	39	38	8	8	218	205
Connecticut	4	4	(Z)	(Z)	108	93	North Carolina	62	58	10	9	156	162
Delaware	3	3	1	1	207	215	North Dakota	34	31	41	40	1,209	1,274
Florida	41	45	11	11	266	236	Ohio	83	80	16	15	188	186
Georgia	48	50	13	11	260	226	Oklahoma	70	83	33	34	471	410
Hawaii	5	6	2	1	357	262	Oregon	37	40	18	17	488	435
Idaho	22	25	14	12	628	490	Pennsylvania	53	60	8	8	153	128
Illinois	83	79	28	28	342	352	Rhode Island	1	1	(Z)	(Z)	95	87
Indiana	68	66	16	16	240	236	South Carolina	25	25	5	5	208	196
Iowa	104	97	34	33	322	340	South Dakota	35	33	44	44	1,266	1,354
Kansas	69	65	48	48	694	731	Tennessee	87	91	12	12	139	131
Kentucky	93	90	14	14	152	154	Texas	196	226	132	132	673	582
Louisiana	32	30	9	8	278	273	Utah	13	15	11	12	856	773
Maine	7	7	1	1	201	186	Vermont	7	7	1	1	222	200
Maryland	15	13	2	2	148	168	Virginia	46	49	9	9	193	180
Massachusetts	6	6	1	1	100	95	Washington	37	40	16	16	432	393
Michigan	54	52	11	10	200	200	West Virginia	21	21	4	4	180	176
Minnesota	89	80	30	29	337	361	Wisconsin	80	78	18	16	220	210
Mississippi	40	42	13	12	325	276	Wyoming	9	9	35	35	3,899	3,761

Z Less than 500,000 acres.

Source: U.S. Dept. of Agriculture, National Agricultural Statistics Service, *Farms and Land in Farms, Final Estimates, 1988-1992*; and *Farms and Land In Farms,* July releases.

No. 1109. Gross Farm Product—Summary: 1980 to 1997

[In billions of dollars (142.9 represents $142,900,000,000). For definition of gross product, see text, Section 14, Income. Minus sign (-) indicates decrease]

Item	1980	1985	1989	1990	1991	1992	1993	1994	1995	1996	1997
CURRENT DOLLARS											
Farm output, total...............	142.9	152.7	177.2	185.6	180.3	187.7	186.5	202.9	196.7	222.1	225.3
Cash receipts from farm marketings......	140.3	136.3	166.7	172.3	170.4	172.2	181.7	180.9	194.1	201.7	207.2
Farm housing...................	5.1	5.0	5.0	5.1	5.2	5.3	5.5	5.8	5.9	6.1	6.3
Farm products consumed on farms	1.2	0.9	0.7	0.7	0.6	0.6	0.5	0.5	0.5	0.4	0.5
Other farm income	2.4	4.6	4.9	4.8	5.1	4.6	4.9	4.9	5.5	6.3	7.1
Change in farm inventories..........	-6.1	5.8	-	2.6	-1.1	5.0	-6.2	10.8	-9.3	7.6	4.3
Less: Intermediate goods and services purchased [1]...................	86.8	85.6	101.0	106.0	107.3	107.1	113.5	119.4	124.4	130.5	135.1
Equals: **Gross farm product**...........	56.1	67.1	76.2	79.6	72.9	80.6	73.0	83.5	72.3	91.6	90.2
Less: Consumption of fixed capital	18.7	20.7	21.1	21.8	22.4	23.2	23.4	23.7	24.8	25.8	26.6
Indirect business tax [2]..........	3.0	3.3	3.9	4.4	4.4	4.5	4.4	4.8	5.1	5.1	5.5
Plus: Subsidies to operators............	1.0	6.3	9.3	7.5	6.8	7.7	11.3	6.6	6.1	6.1	6.2
Equals: **Farm national income**	35.5	49.4	60.5	61.0	52.9	60.5	56.5	61.5	48.4	66.9	64.4
CHAINED (1992) DOLLARS [3]											
Farm output, total................	144.5	163.6	169.7	177.0	178.7	187.7	182.4	199.4	190.7	195.7	208.3
Cash receipts from farm marketings	146.3	149.3	159.7	164.0	168.9	172.2	177.9	178.2	188.8	177.3	191.0
Farm housing..................	7.4	6.2	5.6	5.6	5.5	5.3	5.2	5.2	5.2	5.1	5.0
Farm products consumed on farms	1.4	1.1	0.7	0.6	0.6	0.6	0.5	0.5	0.5	0.4	0.4
Other farm income	2.4	4.7	4.5	4.7	5.0	4.6	4.8	4.8	5.0	5.3	6.2
Change in farm inventories..........	-7.0	6.9	-	2.5	-1.7	5.0	-7.3	11.7	-11.0	7.1	4.3
Less: Intermediate goods and services purchased [1]...................	102.0	96.6	104.1	106.2	107.1	107.1	111.4	114.7	118.5	116.9	118.2
Equals: **Gross farm product**...........	46.7	66.9	65.9	70.8	71.6	80.6	71.0	85.0	72.0	78.6	90.3

- Represents zero.   [1] Includes rent paid to nonoperator landlords.   [2] Includes nontax liability.   [3] See text, Section 14, Income.

Source: U.S. Bureau of Economic Analysis, *National Income and Product Accounts of the United States 1929-94*, Vol. 2; and *Survey of Current Business*, August 1998.

No. 1110. Value Added to Economy by Agricultural Sector: 1980 to 1997

[In billions of dollars (148.0 represents $148,000,000,000). Data are consistent with the net farm income accounts and include income and expenses related to the farm operator dwellings. The concept presented is consistent with that employed by the Organization for Economic Co-operation and Development]

Item	1980	1985	1989	1990	1991	1992	1993	1994	1995	1996	1997
Final agricultural sector output .	148.0	153.5	181.0	188.7	183.7	191.3	190.7	207.9	202.8	228.5	230.8
Final crop output (sales) [1]........	64.4	74.1	81.5	83.3	81.0	89.0	82.4	100.3	95.8	115.6	112.5
Final animal output (sales) [1].......	70.3	68.7	83.8	90.2	87.3	87.1	91.7	89.7	87.6	92.2	96.2
Services and forestry	13.3	10.7	15.8	15.3	15.4	15.2	16.6	17.9	19.4	20.7	22.1
Machine hire and customwork.....	0.7	1.5	1.7	1.8	1.8	1.8	1.9	2.1	1.9	2.2	2.6
Forest products sold	1.0	1.4	2.0	1.8	1.8	2.2	2.6	2.7	2.9	2.8	2.8
Other farm income	0.6	3.2	4.9	4.5	4.7	4.2	4.6	4.4	5.2	5.9	6.3
Gross imputed rental value of farm dwellings	11.0	4.7	7.2	7.2	7.2	7.0	7.6	8.7	9.3	9.8	10.3
Less: Intermediate consumption outlays	77.0	73.5	88.7	92.9	94.6	93.5	100.6	104.9	109.0	112.9	118.6
Farm origin [2]...............	34.9	29.3	38.1	39.5	38.6	38.6	41.2	41.3	41.6	42.7	45.7
Feed purchased	21.0	16.9	20.7	20.4	19.3	20.1	21.4	22.6	23.8	25.2	25.2
Livestock and poultry purchased .	10.7	9.2	12.9	14.6	14.1	13.6	14.6	13.3	12.3	11.2	13.8
Manufactured inputs [2].........	22.4	20.2	20.6	22.0	23.2	22.7	23.1	24.4	26.2	28.6	29.0
Fertilizers and lime...........	9.5	7.5	8.2	8.2	8.7	8.3	8.4	9.2	10.0	10.9	10.9
Pesticides	3.5	4.3	5.0	5.4	6.3	6.5	6.7	7.2	7.7	8.5	8.8
Other intermediate expenses [2]	19.7	24.1	30.0	31.4	32.8	32.2	36.2	39.2	41.2	41.5	43.9
Repair and maintenance of capital items	7.1	6.4	8.4	8.6	8.6	8.5	9.2	9.1	9.5	10.3	10.4
Plus: Net government transactions [3] ..	-2.8	2.9	5.1	3.1	2.1	2.7	6.9	1.0	0.1	0.1	0.1
Direct Government payments	1.3	7.7	10.9	9.3	8.2	9.2	13.4	7.9	7.3	7.3	7.5
Property taxes	3.9	4.5	5.5	5.9	5.8	6.1	6.2	6.5	6.7	6.8	7.0
Equals: **Gross value added**........	68.2	82.9	97.4	98.9	91.2	100.5	97.0	104.0	93.9	115.7	112.3
Less: Capital consumption	21.5	19.4	18.1	18.1	18.2	18.3	18.4	18.7	19.1	19.4	19.5
Equals: Net value added	46.7	63.5	79.3	80.7	73.0	82.1	78.6	85.3	74.8	96.3	92.8
Less: Employee compensation	8.3	8.5	10.7	12.5	12.3	12.3	13.2	13.5	14.3	15.4	16.0
Less: Net rent received by nonoperator landlords	6.1	7.7	9.4	10.0	9.9	11.2	11.0	11.8	11.8	14.3	13.2
Less: Real estate and nonreal estate interest	16.3	18.6	13.9	13.4	12.1	11.1	10.8	11.7	12.7	13.2	13.7
Equals: **Net farm income**	16.1	28.6	45.3	44.7	38.6	47.5	43.6	48.3	36.0	53.4	49.8

[1] Includes home consumption and value of inventory adjustment.   [2] Includes other outlays not shown separately.   [3] Direct Government payments minus motor vehicle registration and licensing fees and property taxes.

Source: U.S. Dept. of Agriculture, Economic Research Service, *Farm Business Economic Report, 1997* (ECI-1998).

Agriculture   679

No. 1111. Farm Income—Cash Receipts From Farm Marketings: 1990 to 1997

[In millions of dollars (169,517 represents $169,517,000,000). Represents gross receipts from commercial market sales as well as net Commodity Credit Corporation loans. The source estimates and publishes individual cash receipt values only for major commodities and major producing states. The U.S. receipts for individual commodities, computed as the sum of the reported states, may understate the value of sales for some commodities. The degree of underestimation in some of the minor commodities can be substantial]

Commodity	1990	1995	1996	1997	Commodity	1990	1995	1996	1997
Total	169,517	188,108	199,580	208,665	Sunflower	217	470	379	471
Livestock and products [1]	89,220	87,018	93,005	96,568	Vegetables [1]	11,464	14,913	14,561	15,086
Cattle and calves	39,302	34,004	31,103	36,094	Beans, dry	687	567	715	558
Hogs	11,525	10,264	12,698	13,197	Potatoes	2,502	2,494	2,585	2,259
Sheep and lambs	414	559	613	634	Broccoli	268	443	415	501
Dairy products	20,153	19,894	22,820	20,989	Carrots	281	440	398	478
Broilers	8,365	11,762	13,905	14,152	Corn, sweet	476	640	642	650
Chicken eggs	4,010	3,880	4,762	4,531	Lettuce	844	1,990	1,384	1,608
Turkeys	2,393	2,822	3,075	2,880	Onions	486	738	704	710
Horses/mules	490	559	636	710	Peppers, green	150	453	475	503
Aquaculture [2]	541	822	845	857	Tomatoes	1,627	1,605	1,678	1,852
Crops [1]	80,297	101,090	106,575	112,097	Fruits/nuts [1]	9,416	11,119	11,933	12,790
Rice	1,052	1,282	1,566	1,657	Oranges	1,719	1,749	1,844	1,717
Wheat	6,412	9,115	9,156	8,926	Apples	1,078	1,579	1,846	1,527
Barley	823	825	975	799	Grapes	1,677	2,046	2,367	3,053
Corn	13,348	18,952	20,734	20,456	Strawberries	590	813	771	908
Hay	3,271	3,292	3,883	4,633	Almonds	598	881	1,018	1,127
Sorghum grain	1,002	1,379	1,518	1,619	Sugarbeets	1,182	1,071	1,211	1,349
Cotton	5,488	6,851	6,983	6,515	Cane for sugar	820	893	864	842
Tobacco	2,733	2,548	2,796	2,886	Christmas trees	110	444	451	463
Peanuts	1,258	1,014	1,030	932	Greenhouse/nursery . .	8,677	10,456	10,905	11,431
Soybeans	10,756	13,872	14,814	18,321	Mushrooms	667	758	762	768

[1] Includes other commodities not shown separately.   [2] See also Table 1162.

No. 1112. Cash Receipts for Selected Commodities—Leading States: 1997

[36,094 represents $36,094,000,000. See headnote, Table 1111]

State	Value of receipts (mil. dol.)	Percent of total receipts	Rank	State	Value of receipts (mil. dol.)	Percent of total receipts	Rank
Cattle and calves . . .	36,094	100.0	(X)	Corn	20,456	100.0	(X)
Texas	5,849	16.2	1	Iowa	3,777	18.4	1
Nebraska	4,385	12.1	2	Illinois	3,524	17.2	2
Kansas	4,354	12.0	3	Nebraska	2,643	12.9	3
Colorado	2,286	6.3	4	Indiana	1,600	7.8	4
Oklahoma	2,009	5.5	5	Minnesota	1,325	6.4	5
Dairy products	20,989	100.0	(X)	Soybean	18,321	100.0	(X)
California	3,618	17.2	1	Illinois	3,293	17.9	1
Wisconsin	2,948	14.0	2	Iowa	3,107	16.9	2
New York	1,528	7.2	3	Indiana	1,550	8.4	3
Pennsylvania	1,526	7.2	4	Minnesota	1,511	8.2	4
Minnesota	1,200	5.7	5	Ohio	1,360	7.4	5

X Not applicable.

No. 1113. Balance Sheet of the Farming Sector: 1980 to 1997

[In billions of dollars, except as indicated (983 represents $983,000,000,000). As of December 31]

Item	1980	1985	1989	1990	1991	1992	1993	1994	1995	1996	1997
Assets	983	773	814	842	845	870	906	938	982	1,034	1,089
Real estate	783	586	601	620	626	643	674	707	756	799	849
Livestock and poultry [1] . . .	61	46	66	71	68	71	73	68	58	60	67
Machinery, motor vehicles [2]	80	83	84	86	86	85	86	88	89	89	88
Crops [3]	33	23	24	23	22	24	23	23	27	32	30
Purchased inputs	(NA)	1	3	3	3	4	4	5	3	4	5
Financial assets	27	33	37	38	41	43	46	48	49	49	50
Claims	983	773	814	842	845	870	906	938	982	1,034	1,089
Debt	167	178	138	138	139	139	142	147	151	156	165
Real estate debt	90	100	76	75	75	75	76	78	79	82	85
Nonreal estate debt [4]	77	78	62	63	64	64	66	69	71	74	80
Equity	816	595	677	704	706	731	764	791	831	878	923
Farm debt/equity ratio (percent)	20.4	29.8	20.4	19.6	19.7	19.0	18.6	18.5	18.1	17.8	17.9
Farm debt/asset ratio (percent)	17.0	23.0	16.9	16.4	16.5	16.0	15.7	15.6	15.4	15.1	15.2

NA Not available.   [1] Excludes horses, mules, and broilers.   [2] Include only farm share value for trucks and autos.   [3] All non-CCC crops held on farms plus the value above loan rate for crops held under Commodity Credit Corporation.   [4] Excludes debt for nonfarm purposes.

Source of Tables 1111-1113: U.S. Dept. of Agriculture, Economic Research Service, *Farm Business Economic Report, 1997* (ECI-1998).

No. 1114. Farm Assets, Debt, and Income, by State: 1996 and 1997

[**Assets and debt**, as of **December 31 (1,033,858 represents $1,033,858,000,000).** Farm income data are after inventory adjustment and include income and expenses related to the farm operator's dwelling]

State	Assets (mil. dol.)		Debt (mil. dol.)		Debt/asset ratio (percent)		Final agricultural sector output (mil. dol.)		Net farm income (mil. dol.)	
	1996	1997	1996	1997	1996	1997	1996	1997	1996	1997
United States..	1,033,858	1,088,842	156,074	165,413	15.1	15.2	228,452	230,771	53,352	49,824
Alabama	14,651	15,613	1,626	1,745	11.1	11.2	3,845	3,936	1,096	1,284
Alaska.........	612	643	15	19	2.5	3.0	36	39	11	14
Arizona	15,283	16,103	1,257	1,347	8.2	8.4	2,298	2,359	701	610
Arkansas.......	18,350	18,639	3,676	4,003	20.0	21.5	6,571	6,384	2,066	1,857
California......	79,212	82,251	14,602	15,558	18.4	18.9	25,263	26,793	5,892	5,791
Colorado	21,657	22,778	3,396	3,555	15.7	15.6	4,759	4,847	838	788
Connecticut	2,627	2,709	204	242	7.8	9.0	521	556	153	151
Delaware.......	1,851	1,938	321	357	17.4	18.4	851	841	115	96
Florida.........	25,991	26,332	4,128	4,376	15.9	16.6	6,528	6,499	1,830	1,839
Georgia........	18,352	19,243	3,164	3,363	17.2	17.5	6,513	6,679	2,297	2,512
Hawaii.........	4,716	4,944	234	251	5.0	5.1	524	523	19	19
Idaho	14,920	16,002	2,743	2,903	18.4	18.1	3,771	3,612	825	524
Illinois	68,579	73,050	8,352	8,848	12.2	12.1	10,394	9,806	2,272	2,185
Indiana	34,108	36,812	4,985	5,319	14.6	14.5	6,166	6,238	1,204	1,366
Iowa..........	64,181	71,642	11,506	12,080	17.9	16.9	14,080	13,584	3,931	3,674
Kansas	33,994	34,700	6,318	6,695	18.6	19.3	9,081	9,622	1,882	1,789
Kentucky.......	21,792	23,107	3,009	3,206	13.8	13.9	4,015	4,477	1,109	1,501
Louisiana.......	8,381	8,698	1,572	1,629	18.8	18.7	2,582	2,386	747	583
Maine	2,071	2,092	353	366	17.0	17.5	551	531	86	22
Maryland	8,356	8,526	994	1,042	11.9	12.2	1,820	1,789	362	275
Massachusetts ...	3,428	3,542	297	333	8.7	9.4	552	604	162	187
Michigan	18,895	19,669	2,886	3,070	15.3	15.6	3,862	4,164	397	474
Minnesota	39,975	41,444	8,011	8,664	20.0	20.9	9,697	9,122	2,276	1,318
Mississippi	13,625	14,140	2,503	2,584	18.4	18.3	3,990	3,983	946	873
Missouri........	34,525	36,942	5,305	5,662	15.4	15.3	5,981	6,139	1,190	1,404
Montana	21,138	22,274	2,585	2,692	12.2	12.1	2,192	2,295	349	323
Nebraska.......	40,976	43,664	8,016	8,459	19.6	19.4	11,219	10,509	3,378	2,085
Nevada........	3,157	3,287	233	244	7.4	7.4	360	363	57	54
New Hampshire ..	1,050	1,077	80	87	7.6	8.1	190	190	51	44
New Jersey	6,653	6,721	572	587	8.6	8.7	936	899	261	173
New Mexico.....	13,211	13,758	1,264	1,280	9.6	9.3	1,831	2,023	355	382
New York.......	13,108	12,967	2,238	2,352	17.1	18.1	3,313	3,205	471	233
North Carolina ...	20,723	21,178	3,345	3,514	16.1	16.6	9,300	9,657	3,370	3,513
North Dakota	22,489	22,617	3,754	3,970	16.7	17.6	4,163	3,191	1,053	105
Ohio..........	33,873	36,311	3,643	3,916	10.8	10.8	5,716	6,342	1,344	1,928
Oklahoma	22,630	24,125	4,102	4,291	18.1	17.8	4,088	4,986	579	1,133
Oregon	18,005	18,483	2,222	2,373	12.3	12.8	3,768	3,828	537	443
Pennsylvania	21,932	22,606	2,548	2,658	11.6	11.8	4,670	4,559	944	594
Rhode Island	456	472	37	37	8.0	7.7	93	94	45	43
South Carolina ...	7,654	7,881	896	937	11.7	11.9	1,831	1,906	502	581
South Dakota	20,173	21,361	3,765	3,937	18.7	18.4	4,494	4,217	1,460	1,046
Tennessee	20,516	21,656	2,147	2,337	10.5	10.8	2,663	2,794	417	535
Texas	85,767	93,007	10,471	11,140	12.2	12.0	14,489	15,901	2,698	3,574
Utah	8,488	8,837	710	767	8.4	8.7	1,045	1,091	204	209
Vermont	2,502	2,482	363	377	14.5	15.2	574	575	136	116
Virginia	18,441	18,849	1,841	1,943	10.0	10.3	2,787	2,668	597	466
Washington	20,774	21,658	3,098	3,284	14.9	15.2	6,542	5,968	1,471	761
West Virginia	3,774	3,895	390	400	10.3	10.3	475	487	17	17
Wisconsin	27,566	28,908	5,361	5,629	19.5	19.5	6,594	6,487	579	200
Wyoming.......	8,667	9,204	936	984	10.8	10.7	866	1,021	69	133

Source: U.S. Dept. of Agriculture, Economic Research Service, *Farm Business Economic Report, 1997* (ECI-1998).

Agriculture 681

No. 1115. Farm Income—Farm Marketings, 1996 and 1997, and Principal Commodities, 1997, by State

[In millions of dollars (199,580 represents $199,580,000,000). Cattle include calves and greenhouse includes nursery]

State	1996 Total	1996 Crops	1996 Live-stock and products	1997 Total	1997 Crops	1997 Live-stock and products	State rank for total farm marketings and four principal commodities in order of marketing receipts
U.S. ...	199,580	106,575	93,005	208,665	112,097	96,568	Cattle, dairy products, corn, soybeans
AL	3,170	808	2,362	3,227	796	2,431	26-Broilers, cattle, cotton, chicken eggs
AK	29	23	6	32	26	6	50-Greenhouse, dairy products, hay, potatoes
AZ	2,145	1,306	840	2,145	1,257	888	31-Cattle, dairy products, lettuce, cotton
AR	5,844	2,470	3,374	5,862	2,446	3,416	11-Broilers, soybeans, rice, cotton
CA	23,497	17,285	6,212	25,289	18,995	6,294	1-Dairy products, grapes, greenhouse, cattle
CO	4,125	1,362	2,763	4,399	1,388	3,012	17-Cattle, corn, wheat, dairy products
CT	489	253	236	496	279	218	43-Greenhouse, dairy products, aquaculture, chicken eggs
DE	753	180	573	748	174	573	40-Broilers, soybeans, greenhouse, corn
FL	6,244	5,038	1,206	6,243	4,978	1,265	9-Greenhouse, oranges, tomatoes, sugar
GA	5,731	2,452	3,279	5,887	2,445	3,442	10-Broilers, cotton, peanuts, chicken eggs
HI	487	420	66	483	415	68	45-Pineapples, sugar, greenhouse, macadamia nuts
ID	3,372	2,043	1,330	3,315	1,926	1,389	24-Cattle, dairy products, potatoes, wheat
IL	8,516	6,453	2,063	9,276	7,339	1,937	5-Corn, soybeans, hogs, cattle
IN	5,533	3,620	1,913	5,506	3,610	1,896	14-Corn, soybeans, hogs, chicken eggs
IA	12,148	6,698	5,451	12,841	7,311	5,530	3-Corn, soybeans, hogs, cattle
KS	7,519	2,978	4,541	9,001	3,985	5,017	6-Cattle, wheat, corn, sorghum grain
KY	3,569	1,842	1,727	3,633	1,655	1,978	21-Tobacco, horses/mules, cattle, soybeans
LA	2,328	1,641	688	2,140	1,481	659	32-Cotton, sugar, rice, soybeans
ME	482	220	262	486	228	258	44-Potatoes, dairy products, chicken eggs, aquaculture
MD	1,540	639	901	1,538	623	915	36-Broilers, greenhouse, dairy products, soybeans
MA	502	392	110	532	430	102	41-Cranberries, greenhouse, dairy products, apples
MI	3,604	2,154	1,450	3,588	2,236	1,352	22-Dairy products, corn, greenhouse, soybeans
MN	8,800	4,654	4,147	8,155	4,101	4,054	8-Soybeans, corn, dairy products, hogs
MS	3,438	1,504	1,934	3,476	1,470	2,006	23-Broilers, cotton, soybeans, aquaculture
MO	4,872	2,409	2,463	5,564	2,768	2,795	13-Soybeans, cattle, corn, hogs
MT	1,999	1,203	797	2,063	1,072	991	33-Cattle, wheat, barley, hay
NE	9,211	3,933	5,277	10,092	4,550	5,542	4-Cattle, corn, soybeans, hogs
NV	287	132	154	310	130	180	47-Cattle, hay, dairy products, onions
NH	169	97	72	166	97	69	48-Dairy products, greenhouse, apples, cattle
NJ	803	607	196	776	596	180	39-Greenhouse, dairy prod., cranberries, green pepper
NM	1,704	506	1,198	1,915	562	1,354	34-Cattle, dairy products, hay, chili pepper
NY	3,031	981	2,050	2,896	1,037	1,859	28-Dairy products, greenhouse, apples, cattle
NC	7,897	3,466	4,431	8,302	3,608	4,694	7-Hogs, broilers, tobacco, greenhouse
ND	3,429	2,891	539	3,313	2,702	611	25-Wheat, cattle, sunflower, soybeans
OH	4,796	2,853	1,943	5,345	3,476	1,869	16-Soybeans, corn, dairy products, greenhouse
OK	3,519	1,105	2,414	4,369	1,308	3,061	18-Cattle, wheat, hogs, broilers
OR	2,904	2,246	658	3,113	2,373	740	27-Greenhouse, cattle, hay, wheat
PA	4,148	1,283	2,865	4,128	1,339	2,789	20-Dairy products, greenhouse, cattle, chicken eggs
RI	84	73	11	83	74	9	49-Greenhouse, dairy products, sweet corn, potatoes
SC	1,616	869	748	1,695	898	797	35-Broilers, tobacco, greenhouse, cotton
SD	3,509	1,875	1,634	4,237	2,417	1,820	19-Cattle, corn, soybeans, wheat
TN	2,405	1,406	999	2,292	1,287	1,005	30-Cattle, soybeans, broilers, tobacco
TX	12,960	5,139	7,821	13,461	5,277	8,184	2-Cattle, cotton, greenhouse, dairy products
UT	872	228	644	953	238	715	37-Cattle, dairy products, hay, hogs
VT	532	99	433	513	97	416	42-Dairy products, cattle, greenhouse, hay
VA	2,384	907	1,477	2,401	863	1,538	29-Broilers, cattle, dairy products, tobacco
WA	5,497	3,833	1,665	5,382	3,778	1,604	15-Apples, dairy products, wheat, cattle
WV	388	79	309	394	71	324	46-Broilers, cattle, dairy products, turkeys
WI	6,030	1,732	4,299	5,756	1,686	4,070	12-Dairy products, cattle, corn, soybeans
WY	667	189	478	845	199	646	38-Cattle, sugar beets, hay, sheep/lambs

Source: U.S. Dept. of Agriculture, Economic Research Service, *Farm Business Economic Report, 1997* (ECI-1998).

682   Agriculture

[1990-92=100, except as noted]

Item	1990	1995	1997	1998	Item	1990	1995	1997	1998
Prices received, all products	104	102	107	101	**Prices paid, total** [3]	99	109	117	115
Crops [1]	103	112	116	107	Production	99	108	117	112
Food grains	100	134	128	103	Feed	103	103	123	105
Feed grains and hay	105	112	117	100	Livestock & poultry	102	82	94	88
Cotton	107	127	112	107	Seed	102	110	119	122
Tobacco	97	103	104	104	Fertilizer	97	121	121	112
Oil-bearing crops	105	104	131	107	Agricultural chemicals	95	116	120	122
Fruits	97	100	108	114	Fuels	100	89	108	87
Commercial vegetables [2]	102	120	122	120	Supplies & repairs	96	112	118	119
Potatoes & dry beans	133	107	90	98	Autos and trucks	97	115	119	119
Livestock and products	105	92	98	96	Farm machinery	96	120	129	132
Meat animals	105	85	92	79	Building materials	99	114	118	118
Dairy products	105	98	102	118	Farm services	96	115	117	116
Poultry and eggs	105	107	113	117	Interest	107	101	107	108
					Taxes	95	109	115	119
					Wage rates	96	114	123	129
					Parity ratio (1910-14=100) [4]	51	45	44	42

[1] Includes other items not shown separately. [2] Excludes potatoes and dry beans. [3] Includes production items, interest, taxes, wage rates, and a family living component. The family living component is the Consumer Price Index for all urban consumers from the Bureau of Labor Statistics. See text, Section 15, Prices, and Table 776. [4] Ratio of prices received by farmers to prices paid.

Source: U.S. Dept. of Agriculture, National Agricultural Statistics Service, *Agricultural Prices: Annual Summary*.

No. 1117. Value of Selected Commodities Produced Under Contracts: 1997

[59,826 represents $59,826,000,000. Marketing contracts refer to verbal or written agreements between a buyer and a grower that set a price and determine an outlet for a specified quantity of a commodity before harvest or before the farmer markets the commodity. Production contracts involve paying the farmer a fee for providing management, labor, facilities, and equipment, while assigning ownership of the product to the contractor. Excludes Alaska and Hawaii. Based on Agricultural Resource Management Study, for details see source]

Commodity	Value of production under contract (mil. dol.)	Percent of total production [1]	Commodity	Value of production under contract (mil. dol.)	Percent of total production [1]
Total	59,826	[2]31	Sugar beets	973	82
Marketing contracts [3]	41,610	[2]22	Vegetables	3,374	24
Cattle	2,735	9	**Production contracts** [3]	18,215	[2]10
Corn	1,720	8	Broilers	6,664	99
Cotton	1,923	33	Cattle	4,280	14
Fruits	7,199	59	Hogs	3,097	33
Soybeans	1,672	9	Vegetables	1,145	8

[1] Represents percent of production under contract as percent of total commodity production, except as noted. [2] Percent of total value of agricultural production. [3] Includes other commodities not shown separately.

Source: U.S. Dept. of Agriculture, Economic Research Service, *"Managing Risk in Farming: Concepts, Research, and Analysis"*, Agricultural Economic Report No. 774, March 1999.

No. 1118. Civilian Consumer Expenditures for Farm Foods: 1980 to 1997

[In billions of dollars, except percent (264.4 represents $264,400,000,000). Excludes imported and nonfarm foods, such as coffee and seafood, as well as food consumed by the military, or exported]

Item	1980	1985	1989	1990	1991	1992	1993	1994	1995	1996	1997
Consumer expenditures, total	264.4	345.4	419.4	449.8	465.1	474.5	489.2	512.2	529.5	546.7	561.1
Farm value, total	81.7	86.4	103.8	106.2	101.6	105.1	109.6	109.6	113.8	122.2	120.0
Marketing bill, total [1]	182.7	259.0	315.6	343.6	363.5	369.4	379.6	402.6	415.7	424.5	441.1
Percent of total consumer expenditures	69.1	75.0	75.3	76.4	78.2	77.9	77.6	78.6	78.5	77.6	78.6
At-home expenditures [2]	180.1	220.8	255.5	276.2	286.1	289.6	294.9	308.7	316.9	328.0	334.7
Farm value	65.9	66.6	77.9	80.2	76.7	76.9	76.4	75.3	76.1	81.6	78.0
Marketing bill [1]	114.2	154.2	177.6	196.0	209.4	212.7	218.5	233.4	240.8	246.4	256.7
Away-from-home expenditures	84.3	124.6	163.9	173.6	179.0	184.9	194.3	203.5	214.8	218.7	226.4
Farm value	15.8	19.8	25.9	26.0	24.9	28.2	33.2	34.3	37.7	40.6	42.0
Marketing bill [1]	68.5	104.8	138.0	147.6	154.1	156.7	161.1	169.2	174.9	178.1	184.4
Marketing bill cost components:											
Labor cost	81.5	115.6	145.1	154.0	160.9	168.4	178.0	186.1	196.6	204.6	216.2
Packaging materials	21.0	26.9	35.2	36.5	38.1	40.1	40.9	43.3	48.2	47.7	48.7
Rail and truck transport	13.0	16.5	18.6	19.8	20.4	20.6	21.2	21.8	22.3	22.9	23.6
Corporate profits before taxes	9.9	10.4	12.9	13.2	15.2	15.7	17.2	17.9	19.5	19.2	18.4
Fuels and electricity	9.0	13.1	14.8	15.2	16.3	16.7	18.4	20.5	18.6	19.6	18.4
Advertising	7.3	12.5	15.7	17.1	17.5	18.0	18.6	19.3	19.8	20.6	20.0
Depreciation	7.8	15.4	16.4	16.3	15.8	16.2	17.2	18.1	18.9	19.6	20.1
Net interest	3.4	6.1	12.3	13.5	12.2	10.9	10.1	11.0	11.6	12.1	13.0
Net rent	6.8	9.3	12.7	13.9	15.9	17.2	17.9	18.9	19.8	20.4	21.0
Repairs	3.6	4.8	5.7	6.2	6.4	6.6	7.2	7.8	7.9	8.2	8.4
Taxes	8.3	11.7	14.6	15.7	16.5	17.5	18.2	18.7	19.1	19.7	20.2
Other	11.0	16.7	11.5	22.2	28.3	21.5	14.7	19.2	13.4	9.9	10.5

[1] The difference between expenditures for domestic farm-originated food products and the farm value or payment farmers received for the equivalent farm products. [2] Food primarily purchased from retail food stores for use at home.

Source: U.S. Dept. of Agriculture, Economic Research Service, *Food Cost Review*, annual; *Food Review*, periodic; and *Agricultural Statistics*, annual.

No. 1119. Indexes of Farm Production, Input Use, and Productivity: 1980 to 1996

[1992=100]

Item	1980	1985	1988	1989	1990	1991	1992	1993	1994	1995	1996
Farm output [1]	79	89	82	89	94	94	100	94	107	101	106
Livestock and products [2]	85	89	94	94	95	98	100	101	107	110	109
Meat animals	98	94	97	97	96	99	100	100	103	104	100
Dairy products	85	94	96	95	98	98	100	99	114	115	115
Poultry and eggs	64	71	83	86	92	96	100	104	109	114	119
Crops [2]	75	89	75	86	92	92	100	89	106	96	103
Feed crops	76	100	62	85	88	86	100	76	102	83	98
Food grains	94	95	76	83	107	82	100	96	97	90	93
Oil crops	81	96	72	88	87	94	100	85	115	99	107
Cotton and cottonseed	68	82	96	75	96	109	100	100	122	110	117
Tobacco	102	87	78	80	94	96	100	94	85	93	80
Vegetables and melons	70	82	81	85	93	97	100	97	113	108	112
Fruits and nuts	90	86	102	98	97	96	100	107	111	102	102
Other crops	57	69	86	89	94	97	100	99	105	110	110
Farm input [3]	119	106	100	100	101	102	100	101	104	105	102
Farm labor	123	108	103	104	102	106	100	96	96	92	100
Farm real estate	113	107	99	101	100	100	100	98	100	99	101
Durable equipment	166	139	113	108	105	103	100	97	94	92	89
Energy	121	98	102	101	100	101	100	100	103	109	104
Agricultural chemicals [4]	119	97	91	94	95	100	100	105	106	90	97
Other purchased inputs [5]	117	99	99	103	103	104	100	110	117	121	116
Farm output per unit of input	66	84	83	90	93	92	100	94	103	97	104

[1] Annual production available for eventual human use. [2] Includes items not shown separately. [3] Based on physical quantities of resources used in production. [4] Includes fertilizer, lime, and pesticides. [5] Includes purchased services and miscellaneous inputs.

Source: U.S. Dept. of Agriculture, Economic Research Service, *Agricultural Outlook*, monthly. Also published in the U.S. Council of Economic Advisors, *Economic Report of the President*, annual.

No. 1120. Agricultural Exports and Imports—Volume, by Principal Commodities: 1990 to 1998

[In thousands of metric tons (2,737 represents 2,737,000)]

Exports	1990	1995	1997	1998	Imports	1990	1995	1997	1998
Animal products [1]	2,737	5,606	5,723	6,153	Fruits, nuts, vegetables	4,573	6,214	7,470	8,171
Wheat and products [2]	28,282	33,458	25,851	27,546	Bananas	3,094	3,664	3,773	3,913
Feed grains and products	61,397	67,403	49,091	47,278	Green coffee	1,174	953	1,131	1,140
Rice	2,509	3,275	2,508	3,722	Cocoa and products	765	620	767	863
Feeds and fodders	10,979	13,338	12,352	11,775	Meat and products [5]	1,165	1,045	1,154	1,293
Protein meal	5,138	6,404	7,311	8,225					
Oilseeds and products [3]	15,778	23,596	26,764	21,479	Vegetable oils	1,183	1,561	1,880	1,949
Vegetable oils	1,204	2,510	2,590	3,074	Rubber, crude natural	840	1,044	1,068	1,200
Fruits, nuts, vegetables [4]	5,552	6,905	7,239	7,142	Sugar	1,856	1,599	2,975	2,047
Cotton and linters	1,733	2,118	1,652	1,663	Spices	129	155	184	223
Tobacco, unmanufactured	223	209	222	212	Tobacco, unmanufactured	187	190	294	224

[1] Includes meat and products, poultry meats, dairy products, and fats, oils and greases. Excludes live animals, hides, skins, and eggs. [2] Includes flour and bulgur. [3] Includes soybeans, sunflowerseeds, peanuts, cottonseed, safflowerseed, flaxseed, and nondefatted soybean flour. [4] Excludes fruit juices. [5] Excludes poultry.

Source: U.S. Dept. of Agriculture, Economic Research Service, *U.S. Agricultural Trade Update*, February 26, 1999; and *Foreign Agricultural Trade of the United States*, calendar year supplements.

No. 1121. Agricultural Exports and Imports—Value: 1980 to 1998

[In billions of dollars, except percent (23.9 represents $23,900,000,000). Includes Puerto Rico. Excludes forest products and distilled liquors; includes crude rubber and similar gums (now mainly plantation products). Includes shipments under foreign aid programs]

Year	Trade balance	Exports, domestic products	Percent of all exports	Imports for consumption	Percent of all imports	Year	Trade balance	Exports, domestic products	Percent of all exports	Imports for consumption	Percent of all imports
1980	23.9	41.2	18	17.4	7	1993	17.7	42.9	10	25.2	4
1985	9.1	29.0	13	20.0	6	1994	19.2	46.2	10	27.1	4
1989	18.2	40.1	12	21.9	5	1995	26.0	56.3	10	30.3	4
1990	16.6	39.5	11	22.9	5	1996	26.8	60.4	10	33.7	4
1991	16.5	39.4	10	22.9	5	1997	21.0	57.2	9	36.3	4
1992	18.3	43.1	10	24.8	5	1998	14.8	51.8	8	37.1	4

Source: U.S. Dept. of Agriculture, Economic Research Service, *U.S. Agricultural Trade Update*, February 26, 1999; and *Foreign Agricultural Trade of the United States*, calendar year supplements. Also in *Agricultural Statistics*, annual.

No. 1122. Agricultural Imports—Value, by Selected Commodity, 1980 to 1998, and by Leading Countries of Origin, 1997

[In millions of dollars (17,366 represents $17,366,000,000)]

Commodity	1980	1990	1995	1996	1997	1998	Leading countries of origin, 1997
Total	**17,366**	**22,910**	**30,336**	**33,655**	**36,300**	**37,073**	**Canada, Mexico, Indonesia**
Competitive products.	10,374	17,336	21,873	25,448	26,948	28,055	Canada, Mexico, Italy
Cattle, live	237	978	1,413	1,121	1,124	1,144	Canada, Mexico, Japan
Beef and veal	1,780	1,872	1,447	1,341	1,609	1,842	Canada, Australia, New Zealand
Pork	486	938	686	728	754	682	Canada, Denmark, Poland
Dairy products	488	891	1,118	1,274	1,225	1,465	New Zealand, Ireland, Italy
Fruits and preparations. .	564	2,218	2,249	2,834	2,847	2,852	Mexico, Chile, Argentina
Vegetables and preparations	864	2,317	3,189	3,526	3,707	4,375	Mexico, Canada, Spain
Wine	692	917	1,153	1,430	1,711	1,876	France, Italy, Chile
Malt beverages	367	923	1,166	1,316	1,495	1,712	Netherlands, Mexico, Canada
Grains and feeds.	371	1,188	2,312	2,657	2,963	2,878	Canada, Thailand, Italy
Sugar and related products.	2,205	1,213	1,335	1,889	1,852	1,682	Canada, Dominican Republic, Brazil
Oilseeds and products . .	599	947	1,800	2,147	2,242	2,211	Canada, Italy, Philippines
Noncompetitive products . .	6,992	5,574	8,464	8,207	9,353	9,018	Indonesia, Colombia, Mexico
Coffee and products. . .	4,186	1,915	3,263	2,788	3,886	3,431	Colombia, Mexico, Brazil
Rubber, crude natural. . .	817	707	1,629	1,468	1,229	977	Indonesia, Thailand, Malaysia
Cocoa and products. . . .	920	1,072	1,106	1,400	1,471	1,666	Canada, Indonesia, Cote d'Ivoire
Bananas and plantains . .	430	939	1,140	1,184	1,220	1,202	Costa Rica, Ecuador, Colombia

Source: U.S. Dept. of Agriculture, Economic Research Service, *U.S. Agricultural Trade Update*, February 26, 1999; and *Foreign Agricultural Trade of the United States*, calendar year supplements.

No. 1123. Imports Share of Food Consumption, by Commodity: 1990 to 1997

[In percent. Import share is the total quantity imported divided by the quantity available for domestic human food consumption. Calculated from supply and utilization balance sheets. A portion of the imports of some commodities is exported; therefore, the ratios presented here may overstate the importance of imports in domestic consumption for some commodity groups. Similarly, a portion of the imports of some commodities is diverted to such nonfood uses as feed, seed, alcohol and fuel production, and industrial uses. This too can overstate the importance of imports]

Commodity	1990	1995	1996	1997	Commodity	1990	1995	1996	1997
Red meat.	8.1	6.5	6.4	7.1	Grapes.	37.6	38.8	42.2	41.2
Beef	9.8	8.3	8.0	9.2	Fruit juice.	47.6	25.0	30.5	27.7
Pork	5.6	3.8	3.7	3.8	Orange.	46.3	14.0	18.8	17.6
Fish and shellfish	56.3	55.3	58.5	62.1	Apple	63.9	53.7	63.4	59.4
Dairy products [1]	1.9	1.9	1.9	1.9	Fresh vegetables.	7.5	9.5	11.0	10.3
Cheese [2]	4.8	4.7	4.5	4.1	Cucumbers	33.7	38.1	42.9	39.5
Salad and cooking oils [3]	5.9	12.1	12.3	12.4	Peppers	19.7	19.1	19.5	20.4
Fresh fruits.	30.6	33.5	34.1	34.0	Tomatoes	20.5	30.2	34.0	32.2
Citrus.	3.4	7.1	6.7	7.0	Wheat [4]	4.6	7.7	10.4	10.4
Apples	4.7	7.7	7.4	7.2	Rice [5]	7.9	10.2	10.6	13.5
Bananas	99.8	99.8	99.8	99.8	Cane and beet sugar [6]	24.9	19.1	30.9	27.9

[1] Milk equivalent of all dairy products calculated on a milkfat basis. [2] Natural equivalent of cheese and cheese products. Includes all types of cheese except full-skim American and cottage, pot, and baker's cheeses. [3] Olive and canola oil imports. [4] Flour and other wheat products included. Grain equivalent. [5] Rough equivalent. Includes milled rice converted to rough basis at annual extraction rate. [6] Import share is the quantity of imports for domestic consumption (net of re-exports) divided by domestic food consumption.

Source: U.S. Dept. of Agriculture, Economic Research Service, *Food Consumption, Prices, and Expenditures*, annual.

No. 1124. Selected Farm Products—United States and World Production and Exports: 1995 to 1998

[In metric tons, except as indicated (59 represents 59,000,000). Metric ton=1.102 short tons or .984 long tons]

Commodity	Unit	Amount						United States as percent of world		
		United States			World					
		1995	1997	1998	1995	1997	1998	1995	1997	1998
PRODUCTION [1]										
Wheat	Million.	59	68	69	538	610	586	11.0	11.2	11.8
Corn for grain	Million.	187	234	248	515	574	597	36.3	40.8	41.5
Soybeans	Million.	59	73	75	125	156	156	47.4	46.8	48.1
Rice, milled	Million.	5.6	6.0	6.1	371	384	378	1.5	1.6	1.6
Cotton [2]	Million bales [3].	19.7	18.9	18.8	85.9	89.6	91.6	23.0	21.0	20.5
EXPORTS [4]										
Wheat [5]	Million.	33.1	28.1	28.5	98.8	100.3	95.8	33.5	28.0	29.7
Corn	Million.	52.7	37.7	44.0	64.9	63.4	63.2	33.5	59.5	69.6
Soybeans	Million.	23.2	23.7	22.0	32.0	40.3	38.8	72.5	58.7	56.8
Rice, milled basis	Million.	3.1	2.3	3.1	21.0	19.0	27.3	14.8	12.1	11.4
Cotton [2]	Million bales [3].	9.4	6.9	7.5	28.4	26.8	26.6	33.0	25.7	28.2

[1] Production years vary by commodity. In most cases, includes harvests from July 1 of the year shown through June 30 of the following year. [2] For production and trade years ending in year shown. [3] Bales of 480 lb. net weight. [4] Trade years may vary by commodity. [5] Includes wheat flour on a grain equivalent.

Source: U.S. Department of Agriculture, Foreign Agricultural Service, *Foreign Agricultural Commodity Circular Series*, periodic.

Agriculture **685**

No. 1125. Agricultural Exports—Value, by Principal Commodities: 1980 to 1998

[In millions of dollars, except percent (41,234 represents $41,234,000,000). See headnote, Table 1121]

Commodity	Value (mil. dol.) 1980	1985	1990	1995	1996	1997	1998	Percent 1980	1990	1998
Total agricultural exports [1]	41,234	29,041	39,517	56,348	60,445	57,245	51,829	100.0	100.0	100.0
Grains and feeds [1]	19,126	11,882	14,409	18,644	20,863	15,368	14,008	46.4	36.5	27.0
Feed grains and products.......	9,852	6,112	7,150	8,341	9,575	6,219	5,210	23.9	18.1	10.1
Corn.....................	8,492	5,206	6,026	7,304	8,404	5,180	4,382	20.6	15.2	8.5
Wheat and products	6,660	3,898	4,035	5,734	6,466	4,302	3,905	16.2	10.2	7.5
Rice......................	1,289	665	801	996	1,029	932	1,208	3.2	2.0	2.3
Oilseeds and products [1]	9,394	5,794	5,705	8,921	10,792	12,057	9,462	22.8	14.4	18.3
Soybeans	5,880	3,732	3,548	5,400	7,324	7,379	4,835	14.3	9.0	9.3
Soybean oilcake and meal	1,666	870	979	986	1,430	1,865	1,604	4.1	2.5	3.1
Vegetable oils and waxes.......	1,216	870	810	1,820	1,375	1,766	2,239	3.0	2.1	4.3
Animals and animal products [1]	3,768	4,150	6,696	11,018	11,254	11,468	10,674	9.2	16.9	20.6
Hides and skins, incl. furskins	1,046	1,295	1,751	1,748	1,675	1,651	1,259	2.6	4.4	2.4
Cattle hides	637	1,007	1,369	1,465	1,327	1,337	993	1.6	3.5	1.9
Meats and meat products.......	890	905	2,558	4,522	4,590	4,597	4,371	2.2	6.5	8.4
Beef and veal	249	467	1,580	2,647	2,429	2,497	2,326	0.6	4.0	4.5
Fats, oils, and greases..........	769	619	424	827	614	562	664	1.9	1.1	1.3
Poultry and poultry products	603	384	906	2,345	2,828	2,779	2,530	1.5	2.3	4.9
Cotton, excluding linters	2,864	1,633	2,783	3,681	2,715	2,682	2,545	7.0	7.0	4.9
Tobacco, unmanufactured	1,334	1,521	1,441	1,400	1,390	1,553	1,459	3.3	3.6	2.8
Fruits and preparations	1,335	1,186	2,379	3,300	3,291	3,451	3,200	3.3	6.0	6.2
Fresh fruits	739	743	1,486	1,973	1,971	2,100	1,838	1.8	3.8	3.5
Vegetables and preparations	1,188	930	2,225	3,637	3,822	4,144	4,222	2.9	5.6	8.1
Nuts and preparations...........	757	683	976	1,410	1,626	1,446	1,360	1.9	2.5	2.6
Other......................	1,468	1,262	2,903	4,337	4,692	5,075	4,899	3.6	7.3	9.5

[1] Includes commodities not shown separately.

Source: U.S. Dept. of Agriculture, Economic Research Service, U.S. Agricultural Trade Update, February 26, 1999; and Foreign Agricultural Trade of the United States, calendar year supplements. Also in Agricultural Statistics, annual.

No. 1126. Agricultural Exports—Value, by Selected Countries of Destination: 1980 to 1998

[41,234 represents $41,234,000,000. See headnote, Table 1121. Totals include transshipments through Canada, but transshipments are not distributed by country prior to 1982 and beginning 1996]

Country	Value (mil. dol.) 1980	1985	1990	1994	1995	1996	1997	1998	Percent 1980	1990	1998
Total agricultural exports [1] ..	41,234	29,041	39,517	46,244	56,348	60,445	57,245	51,829	100.0	100.0	100.0
Asia [1]	15,046	11,191	17,640	20,621	28,173	28,468	25,705	20,871	36.5	44.8	40.3
Japan......................	6,133	5,409	8,104	9,457	11,169	11,696	10,536	9,091	14.9	20.6	17.5
Korea, South...............	1,797	1,413	2,644	2,339	3,759	3,853	2,863	2,227	4.4	6.7	4.3
Taiwan [2]..................	1,095	1,231	1,661	2,149	2,601	2,965	2,616	1,797	2.7	4.2	3.5
China [2]....................	2,277	157	814	1,084	2,635	2,081	1,613	1,336	5.6	2.1	2.6
Iraq......................	256	326	329	-	-	3	82	96	0.7	0.8	0.2
Hong Kong	437	389	701	1,244	1,503	1,490	1,712	1,492	1.1	1.8	2.9
Pakistan..................	158	266	338	245	451	352	442	194	0.4	0.9	0.4
Western Europe [1][3].........	12,917	7,002	7,353	7,346	8,811	9,397	9,728	8,172	31.4	18.7	15.8
European Union [4]...........	12,177	6,542	6,851	7,028	8,465	9,019	9,105	7,866	29.6	17.4	15.2
Netherlands..............	3,476	1,869	1,581	1,703	2,073	2,051	2,040	1,553	8.5	4.0	3.0
Germany.................	2,373	1,009	1,158	1,056	1,223	1,464	1,355	1,217	5.8	2.9	2.3
Spain [5].................	1,488	837	937	846	1,169	1,064	1,157	1,030	3.6	2.4	2.0
United Kingdom	996	604	829	946	1,058	1,216	1,312	1,255	2.5	2.1	2.4
Italy....................	1,203	669	710	547	699	788	763	681	3.0	1.8	1.3
France	765	403	528	453	533	524	567	491	1.9	1.3	0.9
Latin America [1]	6,154	4,224	5,092	8,170	8,039	10,436	10,417	11,389	15.0	13.0	22.0
Mexico..................	2,469	1,439	2,553	4,593	3,540	5,447	5,184	6,163	6.0	6.5	11.9
Venezuela................	703	638	351	398	478	474	572	511	1.7	0.9	1.0
Canada.....................	1,908	1,622	4,197	5,567	5,812	6,143	6,795	7,016	4.7	10.7	13.5
Soviet Union (former) [6]........	1,138	1,923	2,271	1,009	1,333	1,746	1,204	835	2.8	5.8	1.6
Eastern Europe.............	1,644	414	537	311	290	417	284	272	4.0	1.4	0.5
Africa [1]	2,237	2,488	1,935	2,421	2,818	2,723	2,282	2,090	5.5	4.9	4.0
Algeria..................	195	227	513	370	388	292	315	256	0.5	1.3	0.5
Egypt...................	774	891	693	850	1,309	1,256	964	904	1.9	1.8	1.7

- Represents or rounds to zero. [1] Includes areas not shown separately. [2] See text, Section 30, International Statistics. [3] Includes Canary Islands and Madeira Islands. [4] Includes Belgium, Luxembourg, Denmark, Greece, Ireland, and Portugal. Beginning 1995, also includes Austria, Finland, and Sweden. As of Jan. 1, 1981, Greece became a member of the European Union. As of Jan. 1, 1986, Spain and Portugal became members of the European Union. For consistency, data for all years are shown on same basis. [5] As of Jan. 1, 1984, includes Canary Islands and Spanish Africa, not elsewhere classified. [6] Beginning 1997, covers Russia only.

Source: U.S. Dept. of Agriculture, Economic Research Service, Foreign Agricultural Trade of the United States, calendar year supplements. Also in Agricultural Statistics, annual.

No. 1127. Cropland Used for Crops and Acreages of Crops Harvested: 1980 to 1998

[In millions of acres, except as indicated (382 represents 382,000,000)]

Item	1980	1985	1990	1992	1993	1994	1995	1996	1997	1998
Cropland used for crops.....	382	372	341	337	330	339	332	346	349	344
Index (1977=100).........	101	98	90	89	87	90	88	92	92	91
Cropland harvested [1].........	342	334	310	305	297	310	302	314	321	314
Crop failure	10	7	6	8	11	7	8	10	7	10
Cultivated summer fallow	30	31	25	24	22	22	22	22	21	20
Acres of crops harvested [2] ...	352	342	322	317	308	321	314	326	332	325

[1] Land supporting one or more harvested crops.   [2] Area in principal crops harvested as reported by Crop Reporting Board plus acreages in fruits, vegetables for sale, tree nuts, and other minor crops.

Source: U.S. Dept. of Agriculture, Economic Research Service, *Economic Indicators of the Farm Sector: Production and Efficiency Statistics*, annual. Also in *Agricultural Statistics*, annual. Beginning 1992 *Agricultural Resources and Environmental Indicators*, periodical, and *AREI Updates: Cropland Use*, No. 12, annual.

No. 1128. Principal Crops—Production, Supply, and Disappearance: 1990 to 1998

[74.2 represents 74,200,000. Marketing year beginning May 1 for hay, June 1 for wheat, August 1 for cotton and rice, September 1 for soybeans and corn. Acreage, production, and yield of all crops periodically revised on basis of census data]

Crop and year	Acreage (mil.)— Planted	Acreage (mil.)— Harvested	Yield per acre	Production	Farm price [1]	Farm value (mil. dol.)	Total supply [2]	Disappearance Total [3]	Disappearance Exports	Ending stocks
Corn for grain:			Bu.	Mil. bu.	$/bu.			Mil. bu.		
1990.........	74.2	67.0	119	7,934	2.28	18,192	9,282	7,761	1,725	1,521
1995.........	71.5	65.2	114	7,400	3.24	24,118	8,974	8,548	2,228	426
1996.........	79.2	72.6	127	9,233	2.71	25,149	9,672	8,789	1,795	883
1997.........	79.5	72.7	127	9,207	2.43	22,352	10,099	8,791	1,504	1,308
1998.........	80.2	72.6	134	9,761	1.95	19,093	11,081	9,295	1,725	1,786
Soybeans:			Bu.	Mil. bu.	$/bu.			Mil. bu.		
1990.........	57.8	56.5	34.1	1,926	5.74	11,042	2,169	1,840	557	329
1995.........	62.5	61.5	35.3	2,174	6.72	14,617	2,516	2,333	851	183
1996.........	64.2	63.3	37.6	2,380	7.35	17,440	2,575	2,444	882	131
1997.........	70.0	69.1	38.9	2,689	6.47	17,373	2,839	2,639	870	200
1998.........	72.4	70.8	38.9	2,757	5.35	14,660	2,975	2,580	830	395
Hay:			Sh. tons	Mil. sh. tons	$/ton			Mil. sh. tons		
1990.........	(NA)	61.0	2.40	146	[4][5]80.60	10,462	173	146	(NA)	27
1995.........	(NA)	59.6	2.59	154	[4][5]82.20	11,042	175	154	(NA)	21
1996.........	(NA)	61.2	2.45	150	[4][5]95.80	12,723	171	153	(NA)	17
1997.........	(NA)	61.1	2.50	153	[4][5]100.00	13,250	170	148	(NA)	22
1998.........	(NA)	60.0	2.52	151	[4][5]87.00	11,720	173	(NA)	(NA)	(NA)
Wheat:			Bu.	Mil. bu.	$/bu.			Mil. bu.		
1990.........	77.0	69.1	39.5	2,730	2.61	7,184	3,303	2,435	1,069	868
1995.........	69.0	61.0	35.8	2,183	4.55	9,787	2,757	2,381	1,241	376
1996.........	75.1	62.8	36.3	2,277	4.30	9,782	2,746	2,302	1,001	444
1997.........	70.4	62.8	39.5	2,481	3.38	8,287	3,020	2,297	1,040	722
1998.........	65.9	59.0	43.2	2,550	2.70	6,932	3,368	2,388	1,025	980
Cotton:			Lb.	Mil. bales [6]	cents/lb.			Mil. bales [6]		
1990.........	12.3	11.7	634	[7]15.5	68.2	5,076	18.5	16.5	7.8	[8]2.3
1995.........	16.9	16.0	537	[7]17.9	76.5	6,575	21.0	18.3	7.7	[8]2.6
1996.........	14.7	12.9	705	[7]18.9	70.5	6,408	21.4	22.0	7.0	[8]3.9
1997.........	13.9	13.4	673	[7]18.8	66.2	5,976	22.2	22.8	7.5	[8]3.9
1998.........	13.4	10.7	618	[7]13.8	65.3	4,322	16.9	18.0	4.2	[8]3.4
Tobacco: [9]			Lb.	Mil. lb.	$/lb.			Mil. lb.		
1990.........	(NA)	0.7	2,218	1,626	[5]1.74	2,827	3,969	1,796	631	2,149
1995.........	(NA)	0.7	1,914	1,270	[5]1.82	2,305	3,742	1,516	534	2,226
1996.........	(NA)	0.7	2,072	1,519	[5]1.88	2,854	3,728	1,697	628	2,031
1997.........	(NA)	0.8	2,137	1,787	[5]1.80	3,217	3,762	1,511	530	(NA)
1998.........	(NA)	0.7	2,104	1,530	[5]1.84	2,809	(NA)	(NA)	(NA)	(NA)
Rice, rough:			Lb.	Mil. cwt.	$/cwt.			Mil. cwt.		
1990.........	2.9	2.8	5,529	156	6.68	1,047	187	163	71	25
1995.........	3.1	3.1	5,621	174	9.15	1,587	213	188	83	25
1996.........	2.8	2.8	6,120	172	9.96	1,690	207	179	78	24
1997.........	3.1	3.1	5,897	183	9.70	1,756	219	192	85	28
1998.........	3.3	3.3	5,669	188	8.50	1,618	225	195	86	30

NA Not available.   [1] Except as noted, marketing year average price. U.S. prices are computed by weighting U.S. monthly prices by estimated monthly marketings and do not include an allowance for outstanding loans and government purchases and payments.   [2] Comprises production, imports, and beginning stocks.   [3] Includes feed, residual, and other domestic uses not shown separately.   [4] Prices are for hay sold baled.   [5] Season average prices received by farmers. U.S. prices are computed by weighting state prices by estimated sales and include an allowance for outstanding loans and government purchases, if any, for crops under government programs.   [6] Bales of 480 pounds, net weight.   [7] State production figures, which conform with annual ginning enumeration with allowance for cross-state ginnings, rounded to thousands and added for U.S. totals.   [8] Stock estimates based on Census Bureau data which results in an unaccounted difference between supply and use estimates and changes in ending stocks.   [9] Flue-cured and cigar wrapper, crop year July-June; all other types October-September. Farm-sales-weight basis.

Source: Production—U.S. Dept. of Agriculture, National Agricultural Statistics Service. In *Crop Production*, annual; and *Crop Values*, annual. Supply and disappearance—U.S. Dept. of Agriculture, Economic Research Service, *Feed Situation*, quarterly; *Fats and Oils Situation*, quarterly; *Wheat Situation*, quarterly; *Tobacco Situation*, quarterly; *Cotton and Wool Outlook Statistics*, periodic; and *Agricultural Supply and Demand Estimates*, periodic. Data are also in *Agricultural Statistics*, annual; and *Agricultural Outlook*, monthly.

Agriculture   687

No. 1129. Corn—Acreage, Production, and Value, by Leading States: 1996 to 1998

[72,644 represents 72,644,000. One bushel of corn=56 pounds]

State	Acreage harvested (1,000 acres)			Yield per acre (bu.)			Production (mil. bu.)			Price ($/bu.)			Farm value (mil. dol.)		
	1996	1997	1998	1996	1997	1998	1996	1997	1998	1996	1997	1998	1996	1997	1998
U.S. [1]	72,644	72,671	72,604	127	127	134	9,233	9,207	9,761	2.71	2.43	1.95	25,149	22,352	19,093
IA	12,400	11,900	12,200	138	138	145	1,711	1,642	1,769	2.60	2.33	1.90	4,449	3,826	3,361
IL	10,800	11,050	10,450	136	129	141	1,469	1,425	1,473	2.79	2.53	2.05	4,098	3,606	3,021
NE	8,250	8,600	8,550	143	132	145	1,180	1,135	1,240	2.64	2.32	1.95	3,115	2,634	2,418
MN	6,950	6,450	6,750	125	132	153	869	851	1,033	2.47	2.15	1.75	2,146	1,831	1,807
IN	5,450	5,750	5,550	123	122	137	670	702	760	2.78	2.53	2.05	1,864	1,775	1,559
OH	2,800	3,550	3,340	111	134	141	311	476	471	2.75	2.48	2.00	855	1,180	942
SD	3,650	3,400	3,550	100	96	121	365	326	430	2.31	2.15	1.60	843	702	687
KS	2,350	2,600	2,850	152	143	147	357	372	419	2.83	2.47	1.95	1,011	918	817
WI	3,000	3,050	2,950	111	132	137	333	403	404	2.62	2.34	1.90	872	942	768
MO	2,540	2,600	2,500	134	115	114	340	299	285	2.77	2.45	1.90	943	733	542
MI	2,250	2,180	2,050	94	117	111	212	255	228	2.66	2.40	1.90	563	612	432
TX	1,770	1,750	1,850	112	138	100	198	242	185	3.19	2.74	2.35	632	662	435
CO	890	980	1,070	142	146	145	126	143	155	2.76	2.59	2.10	349	371	326
KY	1,200	1,150	1,180	124	103	115	149	118	136	3.00	2.62	2.10	446	310	285
PA	1,070	1,010	1,050	119	98	111	127	99	117	2.99	2.92	2.45	381	289	286
ND	600	590	825	91	99	107	55	58	88	2.43	2.12	1.65	133	124	146
NY	630	600	580	103	110	114	65	66	66	2.98	2.62	2.15	193	173	142
TN	650	620	620	116	102	96	75	63	60	2.90	2.65	2.05	219	168	122
NC	900	830	770	95	89	70	86	77	54	3.43	2.83	2.25	293	219	121
LA	523	417	540	125	117	81	65	49	44	3.50	2.70	2.05	229	132	90
MD	465	410	400	139	90	109	65	37	44	3.05	2.98	2.35	197	110	102

[1] Includes other states, not shown separately.

Source: U.S. Dept. of Agriculture, National Agricultural Statistics Service, *Crop Production*, annual; and *Crop Values*, annual.

No. 1130. Soybeans—Acreage, Production, and Value, by Leading States: 1996 to 1998

[63,349 represents 63,349,000. One bushel of soybeans=60 pounds]

State	Acreage harvested (1,000 acres)			Yield per acre (bu.)			Production (mil. bu.)			Price ($/bu.)			Farm value (mil. dol.)		
	1996	1997	1998	1996	1997	1998	1996	1997	1998	1996	1997	1998	1996	1997	1998
U.S. [1]	63,349	69,110	70,811	38	39	39	2,380	2,689	2,757	7.35	6.47	5.35	17,440	17,373	14,660
IA	9,450	10,400	10,450	44	46	48	416	478	502	7.36	6.33	5.30	3,060	3,028	2,658
IL	9,850	9,950	10,650	41	43	44	399	428	469	7.55	6.56	5.45	3,012	2,807	2,554
MN	5,900	6,550	6,800	38	39	42	224	255	286	7.26	6.20	5.10	1,628	1,584	1,457
IN	5,360	5,300	5,600	38	44	42	204	231	235	7.34	6.59	5.35	1,495	1,519	1,258
OH	4,490	4,340	4,390	35	44	44	157	191	193	7.42	6.49	5.30	1,166	1,239	1,024
MO	4,050	4,850	5,000	37	36	34	150	175	170	7.29	6.39	5.30	1,092	1,116	901
NE	3,010	3,550	3,750	45	41	44	135	144	165	7.19	6.28	5.15	974	903	850
SD	2,670	3,250	3,420	34	35	39	91	114	133	7.08	6.11	4.90	643	695	654
AR	3,500	3,600	3,400	32	31	25	112	110	85	7.36	6.88	5.70	824	755	485
KS	2,000	2,350	2,500	37	37	30	74	87	75	7.17	6.42	5.35	531	558	401
MI	1,640	1,860	1,890	29	39	39	47	72	74	7.15	6.47	5.25	334	463	387
WI	870	1,000	1,100	37	44	47	32	44	52	7.24	6.38	5.30	233	281	274
ND	845	1,140	1,525	29	29	27	25	34	49	7.05	6.10	5.00	173	205	244
MS	1,750	2,070	2,000	31	31	24	54	64	48	7.34	6.90	6.05	398	443	290

[1] Includes other states, not shown separately.

Source: U.S. Dept. of Agriculture, National Agricultural Statistics Service, *Crop Production*, annual; and *Crop Values*, annual.

No. 1131. Wheat—Acreage, Production, and Value, by Leading States: 1996 to 1998

[62,819 represents 62,819,000. One bushel of wheat= 60 pounds]

State	Acreage harvested (1,000 acres)			Yield per acre (bu.)			Production (mil. bu.)			Price ($/bu.)			Farm value (mil. dol.)		
	1996	1997	1998	1996	1997	1998	1996	1997	1998	1996	1997	1998	1996	1997	1998
U.S. [1]	62,819	62,840	59,002	36.3	39.5	43.2	2,277	2,481	2,550	4.30	3.38	2.70	9,782	8,287	6,932
KS	8,800	10,900	10,100	29.0	46.0	49.0	255	501	495	4.63	3.16	2.55	1,182	1,584	1,262
ND	12,515	11,095	9,610	31.6	24.3	32.3	395	269	311	4.19	3.82	3.20	1,638	1,019	983
OK	4,900	5,300	5,100	19.0	32.0	39.0	93	170	199	4.73	3.21	2.60	440	544	517
MT	6,360	5,840	5,280	27.5	31.1	32.0	175	182	169	4.24	3.62	3.35	743	652	554
WA	2,745	2,580	2,565	66.5	64.0	61.4	183	165	157	4.14	3.39	2.60	756	561	402
TX	2,900	4,100	3,900	26.0	29.0	35.0	75	119	137	4.98	3.25	2.70	375	386	369
SD	3,854	3,419	3,294	36.1	28.7	36.7	139	98	121	4.07	3.41	2.85	567	335	335
CO	2,268	2,750	2,610	33.3	32.8	39.7	76	90	104	4.26	3.17	2.60	321	286	269

[1] Includes other states, not shown separately.

Source: U.S. Dept. of Agriculture, National Agricultural Statistics Service, *Crop Production*, annual; and *Crop Values*, annual.

688 Agriculture

No. 1132. Greenhouse and Nursery Crops—Summary, by Type of Product: 1990 to 1997

[In millions of dollars, except per capita (8,677 represents $8,677,000,000). Based on a survey of 36 commercial floriculture states and estimates by source]

Item	Total	Cut flowers	Potted flowering plants	Foliage plants	Bedding plants	Cut cultivated greens	Other [1]
Domestic production: [2]							
1990.	8,677	529	701	693	1,032	121	5,601
1995.	10,434	479	868	728	1,689	128	6,542
1996.	10,876	467	872	743	1,777	134	6,883
1997.	11,393	494	893	761	1,953	119	7,173
Imports:							
1990.	526	326	18	25	(NA)	14	143
1995.	855	512	30	53	(NA)	24	236
1996.	950	573	38	54	(NA)	28	257
1997.	1,002	595	22	89	(NA)	47	249
RETAIL CONSUMER EXPENDITURES [3]							
Total:							
1990.	29,273	4,826	2,707	2,510	1,548	679	17,003
1995.	35,346	5,758	3,386	2,805	2,533	773	20,091
1996.	37,015	6,067	3,395	2,905	2,666	823	21,159
1997.	38,666	6,354	3,395	3,144	2,929	877	21,967
Per capita (dol.): [4]							
1990.	117	19	11	10	6	3	68
1995.	134	22	13	10	10	3	76
1997.	144	24	12	12	11	3	82

NA Not available. [1] Includes turfgrass (sod), bulbs, nursery stock, groundcovers, and other greenhouse and nursery products except the following: seeds, cut Christmas trees, and food crops grown under cover. [2] Equivalent wholesale values. [3] Excludes services such as landscaping, installation, and maintenance. [4] Based on U.S. Census Bureau estimated resident population as of July 1.

Source: U.S. Dept. of Agriculture, Economic Research Service, unpublished data.

No. 1133. Fresh Fruits and Vegetables—Supply and Use: 1990 to 1998

[In millions of pounds, except per capita in pounds (7,327 represents 7,327,000,000)]

Year	Utilized production [1]	Imports [2]	Supply, [1] total	Consumption Total	Consumption Per capita	Exports [2]
FRUITS						
Citrus:						
1990.	7,327	184	7,510	5,331	21.4	2,179
1995.	8,635	449	9,084	6,333	24.1	2,751
1997.	9,389	499	9,888	7,169	26.8	2,719
1998.	9,763	601	10,364	7,777	28.8	2,586
Noncitrus: [3]						
1990.	12,122	7,852	19,974	17,978	70.4	1,995
1995.	12,983	9,388	22,371	19,521	74.3	2,850
1997.	13,611	10,087	23,699	20,525	76.7	3,174
VEGETABLES & MELONS						
1990.	34,629	3,265	38,774	34,577	138.4	2,685
1995.	38,105	4,698	43,884	38,627	146.8	3,525
1997.	42,583	5,858	49,459	43,917	163.9	3,698
1998.	40,816	6,478	48,388	42,758	158.2	3,710
POTATOES						
1990.	11,335	684	12,019	11,691	46.8	327
1995.	12,910	685	13,595	13,011	49.5	584
1997.	12,897	765	13,662	12,992	48.5	670
1998.	13,325	1,061	14,386	13,735	50.8	650

[1] Crop-year basis for fruits. [2] Fiscal year for fruits; calendar year for vegetables and potatoes. [3] Includes bananas.

No. 1134. Nuts—Supply and Use: 1990 to 1997

[In millions of pounds (shelled) (326.2 represents 326,200,000)]

Year	Beginning stocks	Marketable production [1]	Imports	Supply, total	Consumption	Exports	Ending stocks
1990.	326.2	961.5	198.4	1,486.1	609.6	522.6	354.0
1995.	334.1	770.3	204.0	1,308.4	512.8	543.8	251.8
1996.	251.8	821.9	212.8	1,286.5	524.2	605.9	156.4
1997.	156.4	1,221.0	242.2	1,609.6	589.8	692.9	326.9

[1] Utilized production minus inedibles and noncommercial usage.

Source of Tables 1133 and 1134: U.S. Dept. of Agriculture, Economic Research Service, *Fruit and Tree Nuts Situation and Outlook Yearbook* and *Vegetables and Specialties Situation and Outlook Yearbook.*

Agriculture   689

No. 1135. Commercial Vegetable and Other Specified Crops—Area, Production, and Value, 1996 to 1998, and Leading Producing States, 1998

[290 represents 290,000. Except as noted, relates to commercial production for fresh market and processing combined. Includes market garden areas but excludes minor producing acreage in minor producing states. Excludes production for home use in farm and nonfarm gardens. Value is for season or crop year and should not be confused with calendar-year income]

Crop	Area [1] (1,000 acres)			Production [2] (1,000 short tons)			Value [3] (mil. dol.)			Leading states in order of production, 1998
	1996	1997	1998	1996	1997	1998	1996	1997	1998	
Beans, snap.....	290	290	279	983	919	950	307	282	354	WI, OR, MI [4]
Beans, dry edible..	1,751	1,759	1,914	1,396	1,469	1,541	652	577	605	ND, MI, NE
Broccoli.......	134	131	133	785	844	920	416	481	554	CA, AZ
Cabbage.......	79	80	83	1,287	1,447	1,379	235	281	320	CA, NY, TX [5]
Cantaloups.....	101	103	105	1,079	1,042	1,131	393	374	420	CA, AZ, TX
Carrots.......	140	133	137	2,252	2,498	2,426	484	535	499	CA, MI, CO [5]
Cauliflower......	48	44	46	368	344	358	237	218	246	CA, AZ
Celery........	28	27	27	951	906	921	200	266	224	CA, MI, TX
Corn, sweet.....	702	702	703	4,452	4,524	4,491	650	669	676	(NA)
Fresh market...	228	236	236	1,156	1,182	1,240	391	419	437	FL, CA, GA
Processed.....	474	466	467	3,296	3,342	3,251	259	250	239	MN, WA, WI
Cucumbers......	162	160	160	1,056	1,199	1,189	327	350	364	MI, NC, TX [4]
Lettuce, head	221	205	205	3,134	3,775	3,276	913	1,324	994	CA, AZ, CO
Lettuce, leaf	41	49	50	459	519	554	247	299	323	CA, AZ, OH
Lettuce, Romaine [6] ...	33	34	40	428	493	575	162	191	254	CA, AZ, FL
Mushrooms [6] ...	135	136	145	389	388	404	758	766	800	(NA)
Onions........	166	166	164	3,205	3,438	3,257	605	729	831	CA, WA, OR
Peppers, green ...	66	56	57	832	748	715	466	480	483	CA, FL, NJ
Potatoes	1,426	1,354	1,394	24,963	23,355	23,888	2,425	2,622	2,493	ID, WA, WI
Strawberries.....	48	44	45	813	814	844	769	903	1,028	CA, FL, OR
Sweet potatoes ...	84	82	84	661	666	594	191	211	187	NC, LA, CA
Tomatoes.......	460	398	415	13,089	11,612	10,958	1,658	1,645	1,638	(NA)
Fresh market...	121	115	115	1,682	1,639	1,563	647	1,040	1,095	FL, CA, VA
Processed.....	339	283	300	11,407	9,973	9,395	711	605	543	CA, OH, IN
Watermelons.....	199	179	173	2,136	1,996	1,844	270	305	285	FL, CA, TX

NA not available. [1] Area of crops for harvest for fresh market, including any partially harvested or not harvested because of low prices or other factors, plus area harvested for processing. [2] Excludes some quantities not marketed. [3] Fresh market vegetables valued at f.o.b. shipping point. Processing vegetables are equivalent returns at packinghouse door. [4] Processed only. [5] Fresh market only. [6] Area is shown in million square feet. All data are for marketing year ending June 30.

Source: U.S. Dept. of Agriculture, National Agricultural Statistics Service, *Vegetables*, annual summary. Also in *Agricultural Statistics*, annual.

No. 1136. Fruits and Nuts—Utilized Production and Value, 1996 to 1998, and Leading Producing States, 1998

[10,330 represents 10,330,000,000]

Fruit or nut	Unit	Utilized production [1]			Farm value (mil. dol.)			Leading states in order of production, 1998
		1996	1997	1998	1996	1997	1998	
Apples (36 states) [2]	Mil. lb	10,330	10,254	10,597	1,641	1,575	1,226	WA, NY, MI
Apricots	1,000 tons ..	79	130	108	35	43	35	CA, WA, UT
Avocados	1,000 tons ..	191	178	(NA)	273	278	(NA)	CA, FL
Cherries, sweet	1,000 tons ..	152	223	207	223	279	226	WA, OR, MI
Cherries, tart	Mil. lb	260	283	306	42	45	(NA)	MI, UT, NY
Cranberries...............	1,000 bbl. [3]	4,671	5,497	5,387	308	350	(NA)	WI, MA, NJ
Dates (CA)	1,000 tons ..	23	21	22	25	23	25	CA
Grapefruit (4 states)	Mil. boxes [4] .	66	70	64	289	283	234	FL, CA, TX
Grapes (13 states)	1,000 tons ..	5,537	7,287	5,592	2,376	3,122	2,492	CA, WA, NY
Lemons (2 states)...........	Mil. boxes [5] .	26	25	22	261	302	243	CA, AZ
Nectarines (CA)	1,000 tons ..	247	264	230	117	99	109	CA
Olives (CA)	1,000 tons ..	166	104	90	102	67	40	CA
Oranges and tangerines (4 states)..	Mil. boxes [6] .	266	295	323	1,932	1,953	2,096	FL, CA, AZ
Papayas	Mil. lb	42	39	39	17	19	12	HI
Peaches (31 states)	Mil. lb	2,044	2,508	2,351	390	444	443	CA, SC, GA
Pears...................	1,000 tons ..	820	1,042	924	308	288	277	WA, CA, OR
Pineapples	1,000 tons ..	347	324	332	96	92	93	HI
Plums and prunes (fresh)........	1,000 tons [7] .	932	892	517	282	245	(NA)	CA
Tangelos (FL).............	Mil. boxes [7] .	2	4	3	15	19	11	FL
Temples (FL)	Mil. boxes [7] .	2	2	2	14	13	11	FL
Almonds (shelled basis) (CA)	Mil. lb	510	759	520	1,018	1,161	898	CA
Hazelnuts (in the shell)	1,000 tons ..	19	47	16	16	42	15	OR, WA
Macadamia nuts............	Mil. lb	57	58	53	44	44	36	HI
Pecans (in the shell) (11 states) ...	Mil. lb	210	335	155	134	259	191	GA, TX, NM
Pistachios	Mil. lb	105	180	188	122	203	186	CA
Walnuts, English (in the shell)	1,000 tons ..	208	269	220	329	385	(NA)	CA

NA Not available. [1] Excludes quantities not harvested or not marketed. [2] Production in commercial orchards with 100 or more bearing age trees. [3] Barrels of 100 pounds. [4] Approximate average, net weight, is 67 lb. in AZ and CA; 85 in FL; and 80 in TX. [5] About 76 lb. net. [6] Net contents of box varies. In CA and AZ approximate average for oranges and tangerines is 75 lb.; FL oranges, 90 lb.; TX oranges, 85 lb.; and FL tangerines, 95 lb. [7] Approximate net weight is 90 lb.

Source: U.S. Dept. of Agriculture, National Agricultural Statistics Service, *Noncitrus Fruits and Nuts*, annual; and *Citrus Fruits*, annual.

No. 1137. Meat Supply and Use: 1980 to 1998

[In millions of pounds (carcass weight equivalent) (53,151 represents 53,151,000,000). Carcass weight equivalent is the weight of the animal minus entrails, head, hide, and internal organs; includes fat and bone. Covers Federal and state inspected, and farm slaughter]

Year and type of meat	Production	Imports	Supply,[1] total	Consumption[2]	Exports	Ending stocks
RED MEAT AND POULTRY						
1980	53,151	2,668	57,036	54,695	1,124	1,217
1985	56,271	3,255	60,631	58,651	926	1,054
1990	62,255	3,295	66,673	62,937	2,472	1,263
1995	74,070	2,837	78,637	69,912	6,956	1,769
1997	76,322	3,065	81,120	70,364	8,831	1,924
1998	78,642	3,463	84,030	73,065	8,949	2,017
ALL RED MEATS						
1980	38,978	2,668	42,481	41,170	429	882
1985	39,409	3,255	43,505	42,311	461	733
1990	38,787	3,295	42,742	40,784	1,250	707
1995	43,677	2,831	47,512	43,968	2,614	930
1997	43,358	3,059	47,176	43,096	3,185	895
1998	45,284	3,458	49,637	45,235	3,406	996
Beef:						
1980.	21,643	2,064	24,166	23,560	173	432
1985.	23,728	2,071	26,271	25,523	328	420
1990.	22,743	2,356	25,434	24,031	1,006	397
1995.	25,222	2,103	27,873	25,533	1,821	519
1997.	25,490	2,343	28,210	25,609	2,136	465
1998.	25,760	2,642	28,867	26,303	2,171	393
Pork:						
1980.	16,617	550	17,521	16,838	252	431
1985.	14,807	1,128	16,283	15,865	128	289
1990.	15,354	898	16,565	16,031	238	296
1995.	17,849	664	18,951	17,768	787	396
1997.	17,274	633	18,273	16,821	1,044	408
1998.	19,011	704	20,123	18,308	1,229	586
Veal:						
1980.	400	21	432	420	2	9
1985.	515	20	549	533	4	11
1990.	327	(NA)	331	325	(NA)	6
1995.	319	(NA)	326	319	(NA)	7
1997.	334	(NA)	341	333	(NA)	8
1998.	262	(NA)	270	265	(NA)	5
Lamb and mutton:						
1980.	318	33	362	351	1	9
1985.	359	36	403	389	1	13
1990.	363	41	412	397	6	8
1995.	287	64	362	348	6	8
1997.	260	83	352	333	5	14
1998.	251	112	377	359	6	12
POULTRY, TOTAL						
1980	14,173	-	14,555	13,525	695	334
1985	16,862	-	17,126	16,340	465	321
1990	23,468	-	23,931	22,153	1,222	556
1995	30,393	6	31,125	25,944	4,342	839
1997	32,964	6	33,944	27,269	5,646	1,029
1998	33,358	5	34,393	27,829	5,543	1,021
Broilers:						
1980.	11,252	-	11,364	10,682	567	115
1985.	13,520	-	13,646	13,072	417	158
1990.	18,430	-	18,651	17,266	1,143	242
1995.	24,827	1	25,287	20,832	3,894	560
1997.	27,041	5	27,687	22,416	4,664	607
1998.	27,618	5	28,230	22,847	4,672	711
Mature chicken:						
1980.	551	-	581	507	53	21
1985.	525	-	537	503	21	13
1990.	523	-	530	496	25	9
1995.	496	3	513	406	99	7
1997.	510	-	516	125	384	7
1998.	524	-	532	100	426	6
Turkeys:						
1980.	2,370	-	2,610	2,337	75	198
1985.	2,817	-	2,943	2,765	27	150
1990.	4,514	-	4,750	4,390	54	306
1995.	5,069	2	5,326	4,706	348	271
1997.	5,412	1	5,741	4,727	598	415
1998.	5,216	-	5,631	4,882	445	304

- Represents zero.   NA Not available.   [1] Total supply equals production plus imports plus ending stocks of previous year.
[2] Includes shipments to territories.

Source: U.S. Department of Agriculture, Economic Research Service, *Food Consumption, Prices, and Expenditures, 1970-1997*; and *Agricultural Outlook*, monthly.

Agriculture   691

No. 1138. Livestock Inventory and Production: 1980 to 1999

[Production in live weight (111.2 represents 111,200,000); includes animals for slaughter market, younger animals shipped to other states for feeding or breeding purposes, farm slaughter and custom slaughter consumed on farms where produced, minus livestock shipped into states for feeding or breeding with an adjustment for changes in inventory]

Type of livestock	Unit	1980	1985	1990	1993	1994	1995	1996	1997	1998	1999
ALL CATTLE [1]											
Inventory: [2] Number on farms	Mil	111.2	109.6	95.8	99.2	101.0	102.8	103.5	101.7	99.7	98.5
Total value.	Bil. dol. .	55.8	44.0	59.0	64.4	66.5	63.2	52.1	53.4	60.2	58.6
Value per head.	Dol . . .	502	402	616	649	659	615	503	525	603	594
Production: Quantity	Bil. lb . .	40.3	40.1	39.2	41.1	41.6	42.5	40.9	40.9	41.6	(NA)
Beef, price per 100 lb . .	Dol . . .	62.40	53.70	74.60	72.60	66.70	61.80	58.70	63.10	59.60	(NA)
Calves, price per 100 lb .	Dol . . .	76.80	62.10	95.60	91.20	87.20	73.10	58.40	78.90	78.80	(NA)
Value of production	Bil. dol. .	25.5	21.2	29.3	28.8	26.5	24.7	22.1	24.8	24.1	(NA)
HOGS AND PIGS											
Inventory: [3] Number on farms	Mil	67.3	54.1	53.8	58.2	57.9	59.7	58.2	56.1	61.2	62.2
Total value.	Bil. dol. .	3.8	4.1	4.3	4.1	4.3	3.2	4.1	5.3	5.0	2.8
Value per head.	Dol . . .	56.00	75.00	79.10	71.20	74.90	53.20	70.70	94.00	82.00	46.00
Production: Quantity	Bil. lb . .	23.4	20.2	21.3	23.8	24.4	24.4	23.1	24.0	25.8	(NA)
Price per 100 lb	Dol . . .	38.00	44.00	53.70	45.20	39.90	40.50	51.90	52.90	34.40	(NA)
Value of production	Bil. dol. .	8.9	8.9	11.3	10.7	9.7	9.8	11.9	12.6	8.6	(NA)
SHEEP AND LAMBS											
Inventory: [2] Number on farms	Mil	12.7	10.7	11.4	10.2	9.8	9.0	8.5	8.0	7.8	7.2
Total value.	Mil. dol	993	654	901	714	681	663	732	762	798	640
Value per head.	Dol . . .	78.20	61.10	79.30	70.60	69.90	74.70	86.50	96.00	102.0	88.00
Production: Quantity	Mil. lb . .	746	704	781	734	637	602	572	603	556	(NA)
Sheep, price per 100 lb .	Dol . . .	21.30	23.90	23.20	28.60	30.90	28.00	29.90	37.90	30.60	(NA)
Lambs, price per 100 lb .	Dol . . .	63.60	67.70	55.50	64.40	65.60	78.20	88.20	90.30	72.30	(NA)
Value of production	Mil. dol	403	434	374	422	366	414	441	490	356	(NA)

NA Not available. [1] Includes milk cows. [2] As of Jan. 1. [3] As of Dec. 1 of preceding year.
Source: U.S. Dept. of Agriculture, National Agricultural Statistics Service, *Meat Animals—Production, Disposition, and Income*, annual; and annual livestock summaries. Also in *Agricultural Statistics*, annual.

No. 1139. Livestock Operations, by Size of Herd: 1995 to 1997

[In thousands (1,191 represents 1,191,000). An operation is any place having one or more head on hand at any time during the year]

Size of herd	1995	1996	1997	Size of herd	1995	1996	1997
CATTLE [1]				MILK COWS [2]			
Total operations	1,191	1,177	1,148	Total operations	140	131	124
1 to 49 head.	746	734	715	1 to 49 head.	79	72	66
50 to 99 head.	208	205	201	50 to 99 head	39	38	36
100 to 499 head	210	211	205	100 or more head	21	21	21
500 to 999 head	18	18	18				
1,000 head or more	9	9	9	HOGS AND PIGS			
				Total operations	168	142	122
BEEF COWS [2]				1 to 99 head.	97	82	69
Total operations	898	886	873	100 to 499 head	44	36	28
1 to 49 head.	716	704	692	500 to 999 head	15	13	12
50 to 99 head	105	106	104	1,000 to 1,999 head.	7	7	7
100 to 499 head	70	70	71	2,000 to 4,999 head.	4	3	4
500 head or more	6	5	6	5,000 head or more	1	2	2

[1] Includes calves. [2] Included in operations with cattle.
Source: U.S. Dept. of Agriculture, National Agricultural Statistics Service, *Cattle Final Estimates, 1994-1998*, January 1999; *Milk Cows and Production Final Estimates 1993-1997*, January 1999; and *Hogs and Pigs Final Estimates 1993-1997*, December 1998.

No. 1140. Hogs and Pigs—Number, Production, and Value, by State: 1996 to 1998

[56,124 represents 56,124,000. See headnote, Table 1138]

State	Number on farms [1] (1,000)			Quantity produced (mil. lb.)			Value of production (mil. dol.)			Commercial slaughter [2] (mil. lb.)	
	1996	1997	1998	1996	1997	1998	1996	1997	1998	1997	1998
U.S. [3]	56,124	61,158	62,156	23,080	23,979	25,756	11,902	12,552	8,637	23,534	25,898
IL	4,400	4,700	4,850	1,953	1,820	1,895	981	929	625	2,203	2,409
IN	3,750	3,950	4,050	1,568	1,533	1,697	780	775	540	1,231	1,580
IA	12,400	14,600	15,300	5,123	5,420	6,301	2,635	2,801	1,998	6,309	7,481
MN	4,850	5,700	5,700	1,954	2,081	2,400	1,027	1,112	836	1,762	2,027
MO	3,450	3,550	3,300	1,333	1,411	1,405	666	713	448	897	999
NE	3,550	3,500	3,400	1,514	1,425	1,451	812	785	535	1,471	1,606
NC	9,300	9,600	9,700	3,426	3,828	3,751	1,822	2,072	1,319	2,301	2,383

[1] As of December 1. [2] Includes slaughter in federally inspected and other slaughter plants; excludes animals slaughtered on farms. [3] Includes other states not shown separately.
Source: U.S. Dept. of Agriculture, National Agricultural Statistics Service, *Meat Animals-Production, Disposition and Income*, annual.

692 Agriculture

No. 1141. Cattle and Calves—Number, Production, and Value, by State: 1996 to 1999

[101,656 represents 101,656,000. Includes milk cows. See headnote, Table 1138]

State	Number on farms [1] (1,000)			Quantity produced (mil. lb.)			Value of production (mil. dol.)			Commercial slaughter [2] (mil. lb.)	
	1997	1998	1999	1996	1997	1998	1996	1997	1998	1997	1998
U.S. [3]	101,656	99,744	98,522	40,941	40,892	41,565	22,070	24,804	24,100	42,605	42,672
CA	4,900	4,900	5,000	1,736	1,937	1,928	674	896	871	1,279	1,268
CO	3,250	3,250	3,150	1,956	1,871	1,982	1,191	1,189	1,172	3,090	2,941
IA	3,900	3,700	3,650	1,793	1,888	1,753	1,043	1,090	951	1,259	1,125
KS	6,600	6,550	6,550	3,599	3,695	3,764	2,082	2,257	2,188	8,547	8,950
MN	2,650	2,500	2,500	1,189	1,135	1,070	668	672	602	1,407	901
MO	4,550	4,350	4,400	1,208	1,165	1,129	611	826	779	121	91
MT	2,700	2,600	2,600	1,082	1,045	1,052	587	689	668	20	25
NE	6,650	6,750	6,650	3,928	4,030	4,213	2,592	2,429	2,316	8,925	9,052
OK	5,400	5,400	5,200	1,859	1,960	1,834	991	1,354	1,222	43	33
SD	3,850	3,700	3,850	1,401	1,296	1,422	794	863	903	318	327
TX	14,300	14,500	14,000	7,028	7,005	7,502	4,087	4,370	4,437	7,352	7,731

[1] As of January 1.   [2] Data cover cattle only. Includes slaughter in federally inspected and other slaughter plants; excludes animals slaughtered on farms.   [3] Includes other states not shown separately.

Source: U.S. Dept. of Agriculture, National Agricultural Statistics Service, *Meat Animals-Production, Disposition and Income*, annual.

No. 1142. Milk Cows—Number, Production, and Value, by State: 1996 to 1998

[9,372 represents 9,372,000]

State	Number on farms [1] (1,000)			Milk produced on farms (mil. lb.)			Value of production [2] (mil. dol.)		
	1996	1997	1998	1996	1997	1998	1996	1997	1998
United States [3]	9,372	9,252	9,158	154,006	156,091	157,441	23,003	21,126	24,520
California	1,349	1,391	1,420	25,848	27,582	27,607	3,720	3,633	4,294
Idaho	256	272	292	4,735	5,193	5,765	658	639	836
Michigan	320	306	300	5,430	5,410	5,391	816	738	828
Minnesota	583	569	551	9,440	9,210	9,275	1,378	1,215	1,442
New York	702	699	701	11,510	11,530	11,740	1,717	1,547	1,810
Pennsylvania	634	629	623	10,484	10,662	10,847	1,653	1,527	1,744
Texas	397	378	352	6,120	5,768	5,605	924	790	880
Washington	257	253	248	5,279	5,305	5,326	792	732	848
Wisconsin	1,449	1,393	1,369	22,376	22,368	22,842	3,300	2,982	3,541

[1] Average number during year. Represents cows and heifers that have calved, kept for milk; excluding heifers not yet fresh.   [2] Valued at average returns per 100 pounds of milk in combined marketings of milk and cream. Includes value of milk fed to calves.   [3] Includes other states not shown separately.

Source: U.S. Dept. of Agriculture, National Agricultural Statistics Service, *Dairy Products*, annual; and *Milk: Production, Disposition, and Income*, annual.

No. 1143. Milk Production and Manufactured Dairy Products: 1980 to 1998

[334 represents 334,000]

Item	Unit	1980	1985	1990	1993	1994	1995	1996	1997	1998
Number of farms with milk cows	1,000	334	269	193	157	148	140	131	124	116
Cows and heifers that have calved, kept for milk	Mil. head . .	10.8	11.0	10.0	9.6	9.5	9.5	9.4	9.3	9.2
Milk produced on farms	Bil. lb . . .	128	143	148	151	154	155	154	156	157
Production per cow	1,000 lb. . . .	11.9	13.0	14.8	15.7	16.2	16.4	16.4	16.9	17.2
Whole milk sold from farms [1]	Bil. lb . . .	126	141	146	149	152	154	153	155	156
Value of milk produced	Bil. dol. . . .	16.9	18.4	20.4	19.5	20.2	20.1	23.0	21.1	24.5
Gross farm income, dairy products	Bil. dol. . . .	16.7	18.1	20.2	19.3	20.0	19.9	22.8	21.0	24.3
Cash receipts from marketing of milk and cream [1]	Bil. dol. . . .	16.6	18.1	20.1	19.3	20.0	19.9	22.8	20.9	24.3
Number of dairy manufacturing plants	Number	2,257	2,061	1,723	1,534	1,532	1,495	1,422	1,384	1,340
Manufactured dairy products:										
Butter (incl. whey butter)	Mil. lb	1,145	1,248	1,302	1,315	1,296	1,264	1,174	1,151	1,082
Cheese, total [2]	Mil. lb	3,984	5,081	6,059	6,528	6,735	6,917	7,218	7,330	7,502
American (excl. full-skim American). . .	Mil. lb	2,376	2,855	2,894	2,957	2,974	3,131	3,281	3,286	3,326
Cream and Neufchatel	Mil. lb	229	294	431	540	573	544	575	615	624
All Italian varieties	Mil. lb	983	1,491	2,207	2,495	2,626	2,674	2,812	2,881	3,001
Cottage cheese: Creamed [3]	Mil. lb	825	716	832	748	731	711	690	706	729
Condensed bulk milk	Mil. lb	952	1,232	1,426	1,605	1,593	1,372	1,270	1,275	1,265
Nonfat dry milk [4]	Mil. lb	1,168	1,398	902	964	1,242	1,243	1,068	1,223	1,140
Dry whey [5]	Mil. lb	690	987	1,143	1,196	1,212	1,147	1,117	1,137	1,180
Yogurt, plain and fruit flavored.	Mil. lb	(NA)	(NA)	(NA)	(NA)	1,393	1,646	1,588	1,574	1,616
Ice cream, regular	Mil. gal . . .	830	901	824	866	876	862	879	914	937
Ice cream, lowfat [6]	Mil. gal . . .	293	301	352	325	325	359	357	366	409

NA Not available.   [1] Comprises sales to plants and dealers, and retail sales by farmers direct to consumers.   [2] Includes varieties not shown separately.   [3] Includes partially creamed (low fat).   [4] Includes dry skim milk for animal feed.   [5] Includes animal but excludes modified whey production.   [6] Includes freezer-made milkshake in most states.

Source: U.S. Dept. of Agriculture, National Agricultural Statistics Service, *Dairy Products*, annual; and *Milk: Production, Disposition, and Income*, annual.

Agriculture   693

No. 1144. Milk Production and Commercial Use: 1980 to 1998

[In billions of pounds milkfat basis (128.4 represents 128,400,000,000)]

Year	Production	Farm use	Commercial Farm marketings	Beginning stock	Imports	Commercial supply total	CCC net removals[1]	Ending stock	Commercial Disappearance	Milk price per 100 lb.[2] (dol.)
1980	128.4	2.3	126.1	5.3	2.1	133.5	8.8	5.6	119.0	13.1
1985	143.0	2.5	140.6	4.8	2.8	148.2	13.2	4.5	130.5	12.8
1990	147.7	2.0	145.7	4.1	2.7	152.5	8.5	5.1	138.8	13.7
1995	155.3	1.6	153.7	4.3	2.9	160.9	2.1	4.1	154.7	12.8
1997	156.1	1.4	154.7	4.7	2.7	162.1	1.1	4.9	156.1	13.4
1998	157.4	1.4	156.1	4.9	4.6	165.6	0.4	5.3	159.9	15.4

[1] Removals from commercial supply by Commodity Credit Corporation. [2] Wholesale price received by farmers for all milk delivered to plants and dealers.

Source: U.S. Dept. of Agriculture, Economic Research Service, *Agricultural Outlook*, monthly.

No. 1145. Broiler, Turkey, and Egg Production: 1980 to 1998

[For year ending November 30 (392 represents 392,000,000)]

Item	Unit	1980	1985	1990	1992	1993	1994	1995	1996	1997	1998
Chickens:[1]											
Number[2]	Million	392	370	352	371	380	386	388	393	410	424
Value per head[2]	Dollars	1.88	1.90	2.29	2.26	2.37	2.34	2.41	2.65	2.72	2.69
Value, total[2]	Mil. dol.	737	704	805	838	898	902	935	1,039	1,113	1,140
Number sold[3]	Million	238	220	208	207	197	201	179	174	191	194
Price per lb.[3]	Cents	11.0	14.8	9.3	8.6	10.0	7.6	6.5	6.7	7.7	8.0
Value of sales[3]	Mil. dol.	129	152	94	89	96	73	60	59	71	76
PRODUCTION											
Broilers:[4]											
Number	Million	3,963	4,470	5,864	6,402	6,694	7,018	7,326	7,598	7,764	7,934
Weight	Bil. lb.	15.5	18.9	25.6	28.8	30.6	32.5	34.2	36.5	37.5	38.6
Price per lb	Cents	27.7	30.1	32.6	31.8	34.0	35.0	34.4	38.1	37.7	39.3
Production value	Mil. dol.	4,303	5,668	8,366	9,174	10,417	11,372	11,762	13,903	14,159	15,145
Turkeys:											
Number	Million	165	185	282	289	288	287	293	303	301	284
Weight	Bil. lb.	3.1	3.7	6.0	6.3	6.4	6.5	6.8	7.2	7.2	7.0
Price per lb	Cents	41.3	49.1	39.4	37.7	39.0	40.4	41.0	43.3	39.9	38.0
Production value	Mil. dol.	1,272	1,820	2,393	2,396	2,509	2,643	2,769	3,124	2,884	2,662
Eggs:											
Number	Billion	69.7	68.4	67.9	70.5	71.9	73.9	74.8	76.4	77.5	79.7
Price per dozen	Cents	56.3	57.2	70.9	57.6	63.4	61.4	62.4	74.9	70.3	65.5
Production value	Mil. dol.	3,268	3,262	4,021	3,397	3,800	3,790	3,893	4,776	4,540	4,350

[1] Excludes commercial broilers. [2] As of December 1. [3] Data for 1980 represent number produced and production value. [4] Young chickens of the heavy breeds and other meat-type birds, to be marketed at 2-5 lbs. live weight and from which no pullets are kept for egg production.

Source: U.S. Dept. of Agriculture, National Agricultural Statistics Service, *Poultry—Production and Value*, annual; *Turkeys*, annual; and *Layers and Egg Production*, annual.

No. 1146. Broiler and Turkey Production, by State: 1996 to 1998

[In millions of pounds, liveweight production (36,483 represents 36,483,000,000)]

State	Broilers 1996	1997	1998	Turkeys 1996	1997	1998	State	Broilers 1996	1997	1998	Turkeys 1996	1997	1998
U.S.[1]	36,483	37,541	38,554	7,233	7,225	7,003	MO	1,059	1,075	1,097	579	563	598
AL	4,192	4,350	4,517	(NA)	(NA)	(NA)	NC	3,542	3,658	3,592	1,458	1,354	1,270
AR	5,660	5,590	5,619	526	525	496	OH	240	229	235	227	218	179
CA	1,171	1,210	(NA)	493	481	443	OK	877	869	994	(NA)	(NA)	(NA)
CO	(NA)	(NA)	(NA)	179	147	(NA)	OR	107	109	(NA)	(NA)	(NA)	(NA)
DE	1,417	1,413	1,429	(NA)	(NA)	(NA)	PA	654	690	691	246	235	233
FL	591	596	632	(NA)	(NA)	(NA)	SC	786	830	848	281	368	356
GA	5,655	5,914	5,892	17	6	(NA)	SD	(NA)	(NA)	(NA)	99	115	123
IN	(NA)	(NA)	(NA)	351	360	352	TN	603	624	716	(NA)	(NA)	(NA)
IA	77	(NA)	(NA)	222	188	(NA)	TX	1,886	2,094	2,160	(NA)	(NA)	(NA)
KY	331	498	843	(NA)	(NA)	(NA)	VA	1,244	1,219	1,264	485	504	533
MD	1,386	1,417	1,367	7	13	15	WA	196	194	(NA)	(NA)	(NA)	(NA)
MN	252	241	207	948	1,015	1,028	WV	395	381	358	87	87	88
MS	3,109	3,313	3,468	(NA)	(NA)	(NA)	WI	152	158	164	(NA)	(NA)	(NA)

NA Not available. [1] Includes other states not shown separately.

Source: U.S. Dept. of Agriculture, National Agricultural Statistics Service, *Poultry—Production and Value*, annual; and *Turkeys*, annual.

This section presents data on the area, ownership, production, trade, reserves, and disposition of natural resources. Natural resources is defined here as including forestry, fisheries, and mining and mineral products.

Forestry—Presents data on the area, ownership, and timber resource of commercial timberland; forestry statistics covering the National Forests and Forest Service cooperative programs; product data for lumber, pulpwood, woodpulp, paper and paperboard, and similar data.

The principal sources of data relating to forests and forest products are *An Analysis of the Timber Situation in the United States, 1989-2040, 1990; Forest Resources of the United States, 1992; U.S. Timber Production, Trade, Consumption, and Price Statistics; Land Areas of the National Forest System*, issued annually by the Forest Service of the Department of Agriculture; *Agricultural Statistics* issued by the Department of Agriculture; and reports of the census of manufactures (taken every 5 years) and the annual *Current Industrial Reports*, issued by the Census Bureau issued on the Internet, and in print in the annual *Manufacturing Profiles*. Additional information is published in the monthly *Survey of Current Business* of the Bureau of Economic Analysis; and the annual *Wood Pulp and Fiber Statistics* and *The Statistics of Paper, Paperboard, and Wood Pulp* of the American Forest and Paper Association, Washington, DC.

The completeness and reliability of statistics on forests and forest products vary considerably. The data for forest land area and stand volumes are much more reliable for areas which have been recently surveyed than for those for which only estimates are available. In general,

more data are available for lumber and other manufactured products such as particle board and softwood panels, etc., than for the primary forest products such as poles and piling and fuelwood.

Fisheries—The principal source of data relating to fisheries is *Fisheries of the United States*, issued annually by the National Marine Fisheries Service (NMFS), National Oceanic and Atmospheric Administration (NOAA). The NMFS collects and disseminates data on commercial landings of fish and shellfish. Annual reports include quantity and value of commercial landings of fish and shellfish disposition of landings, and number and kinds of fishing vessels and fishing gear. Reports for the fish-processing industry include annual output for the wholesaling and fish processing establishments, annual and seasonal employment. The principal source for these data is the annual *Fisheries of the United States*.

Mining and mineral products—Presents data relating to mineral industries and their products, general summary measures of production and employment, and more detailed data on production, prices, imports and exports, consumption, and distribution for specific industries and products. Data on mining and mineral products may also be found in Sections 26 and 30 of this Abstract; data on mining employment may be found in Section 13.

Mining comprises the extraction of minerals occurring naturally (coal, ores, crude petroleum, natural gas) and quarrying, well operation, milling, refining and processing, and other preparation customarily done at the mine or well site or as a part of extraction activity. (Mineral preparation plants are usually operated together with mines or quarries.) Exploration for minerals is included as is the development of mineral properties.

The principal governmental sources of these data are the *Minerals Yearbook* and *Mineral Commodity Summaries*, published by the U.S. Geological Survey, Department of the Interior, and various monthly and annual publications of the Energy Information Administration, Department of Energy. See text, Section 19, for a list of Department of Energy publications. In addition, the Census Bureau conducts a census of mineral industries every 5 years (1997 results are in the process of being released). Nongovernment sources include the *Annual Statistical Report* of the American Iron and Steel Institute, Washington, DC; *Metals Week* and the monthly *Engineering and Mining Journal*, issued by the McGraw-Hill Publishing Co., New York, NY; *The Iron Age*, issued weekly by the Chilton Co., Philadelphia, PA; and the *Joint Association Survey of the U.S. Oil and Gas Industry*, conducted jointly by the American Petroleum Institute, Independent Petroleum Association of America, and Mid-Continent Oil and Gas Association.

Mineral statistics, with principal emphasis on commodity detail, have been collected by the U.S. Geological Survey and the former Bureau of Mines since 1880. Current data in U.S. Geological Survey publications include quantity and value of nonfuel minerals produced, sold or used by producers, or shipped; quantity of minerals stocked; crude materials treated and prepared minerals recovered; and consumption of mineral raw materials.

Censuses of mineral industries have been conducted by the Census Bureau at various intervals since 1840. Beginning with the 1967 census, legislation provides for a census to be conducted every 5 years for years ending in "2" and "7." The censuses provide, for the various types of mineral establishments, information on operating costs, capital expenditures, labor, equipment, and energy requirements in relation to their value of shipments and other receipts. Commodity statistics on many manufactured mineral products are also collected by the Census Bureau at monthly, quarterly, or annual intervals and issued in its *Current Industrial Reports* series.

In general, figures shown in the individual commodity tables include data for outlying areas and may therefore not agree with summary tables. Except for crude petroleum and refined products, the export and import figures include foreign trade passing through the customs districts of United States and Puerto Rico but exclude shipments between U.S. territories and the customs districts.

No. 1147. Gross Domestic Product of Agriculture, Forestry, Fishing, Mining, and Timber-Related Industries in Current and Real (1992) Dollars, by Industry: 1990 to 1997

[In billions of dollars (5,743.8 represents $5,743,800,000,000), except as indicated. Industry classifications based on the 1987 Standard Industrial Classification (SIC). Data include nonfactor charges (capital consumption allowances, indirect business taxes, etc.) as well as factor charges against gross product; corporate profits and capital consumption allowances have been shifted from a company to an establishment basis]

Industry	Current dollars				Chained (1992) dollars			
	1990	1995	1996	1997	1990	1995	1996	1997
All industries, total [1]	5,743.8	7,269.6	7,661.6	8,110.9	6,136.3	6,761.7	6,994.8	7,269.8
Industries covered	298.1	308.0	339.9	350.0	277.3	289.7	295.0	319.5
Percent of all industries	5.19	4.24	4.44	4.32	4.52	4.28	4.22	4.39
Agriculture, forestry, and fishing.	108.7	109.5	130.4	131.7	99.3	106.2	114.2	127.6
Farms	79.5	72.3	91.6	90.2	70.7	72.0	78.6	90.3
Agricultural services	29.1	37.2	38.8	41.5	28.6	34.7	36.2	38.0
Mining [1]	112.3	98.7	113.8	120.5	96.9	107.4	103.0	109.9
Metal mining	4.8	6.7	6.1	5.8	3.7	5.5	5.7	6.2
Coal mining	13.2	12.0	12.9	13.2	12.0	15.4	17.2	18.1
Oil and gas extraction	86.4	70.5	84.3	90.1	73.5	77.4	70.6	75.4
Nonmetallic minerals, except fuels . . .	7.8	9.4	10.4	11.4	7.7	9.3	10.2	10.8
Timber-related manufacturing	77.1	99.8	95.7	97.8	81.1	76.1	77.8	82.0
Lumber and wood products	31.8	40.9	39.1	42.8	37.0	31.7	31.4	33.1
Paper and allied products	45.3	58.9	56.6	55.0	44.1	44.4	46.4	48.9

[1] For additional industries, see Table 722.

Source: U.S. Bureau of Economic Analysis, *Survey of Current Business,* November 1998.

No. 1148. National Forest System—Summary: 1980 to 1997

[For fiscal years ending in year shown; see text, Section 9, State and Local Government. Includes Alaska and Puerto Rico, except as noted]

Item	Unit	1980	1990	1991	1992	1993	1994	1995	1996	1997
Timber cut, total value	Mil. dol . . .	737	1,191	1,012	938	918	786	616	544	498
Commercial and cost sales: [1]										
Volume	Mil. bd. ft . .	9,178	10,500	8,475	7,290	5,917	4,815	3,866	3,725	3,285
Value	Mil. dol . . .	730	1,188	1,009	935	915	783	616	544	498
Free use:										
Volume	Mil. bd. ft . .	2,070	151	121	80	80	80	80	80	80
Value [2]	Mil. dol . . .	5.7	1	1	1	1	1	1	1	1
Misc. forest products:										
Value	Mil. dol . . .	1.1	3	3	3	3	3	3	3	3
Livestock grazing: [3]										
Cattle and horses [4]	1,000	1,521	1,236	1,265	1,408	1,318	1,224	1,311	1,167	1,225
Sheep and goats	1,000	1,328	958	1,029	1,183	1,111	925	1,068	859	932
Roads and trails:										
Road construction [5]	Miles.	925	857	910	853	816	487	424	418	359
Trail construction [5][6]	Miles.	2,419	1,635	1,921	1,976	1,976	2,113	2,139	1,696	(NA)
Receipts, total	Mil. dol . . .	703	971	772	614	504	515	387	273	285
Timber use	Mil. dol . . .	625	849	667	520	425	432	303	195	197
Grazing use	Mil. dol . . .	16	10	11	11	11	11	9	7	7
Special land use, etc	Mil. dol . . .	62	112	93	84	68	72	75	71	81
Payments to local govt. [7]	Mil. dol . . .	240	368	335	322	323	309	273	256	234

NA Not available. [1] Includes land exchanges. [2] Includes some free use timber not reducible to board feet. [3] Covers number actually grazed. Excludes Puerto Rico. [4] Excludes animals under 6 months of age. [5] Includes reconstruction. [6] Includes work accomplished by Human Resource Programs and volunteers. [7] Payments made in following year.

Source: U.S. Forest Service, *Timber Demand and Technology Assessment,* RWU-4861. Also in *Agricultural Statistics,* annual.

Natural Resources 697

No. 1149. National Forest System Land—States and Other Areas: 1997

[In thousands of acres (231,864 represents 231,864,000). As of Sept. 30]

State and other area	Gross area within unit boundaries [1]	National Forest System Land [2]	Other lands within unit boundaries	State and other area	Gross area within unit boundaries [1]	National Forest System Land [2]	Other lands within unit boundaries
Total	231,864	191,813	40,051	Montana	19,116	16,877	2,239
				Nebraska	442	352	90
United States. . .	231,808	191,785	40,023	Nevada.	6,285	5,824	461
Alabama	1,290	665	625	New Hampshire . . .	827	725	102
Alaska	24,271	21,969	2,302	New Jersey	-	-	-
Arizona.	11,889	11,252	637	New Mexico.	10,367	9,327	1,040
Arkansas.	3,530	2,577	953	New York	-	-	-
California.	24,424	20,647	3,777	North Carolina	3,169	1,244	1,925
Colorado.	16,058	14,508	1,550	North Dakota	1,106	1,106	-
Connecticut	-	-	-	Ohio.	841	227	614
Delaware.	-	-	-	Oklahoma	555	392	163
Florida	1,418	1,147	271	Oregon.	17,503	15,656	1,847
Georgia	1,847	865	982	Pennsylvania	743	513	230
Hawaii	-	-	-	Rhode Island	-	-	-
Idaho	21,688	20,461	1,227	South Carolina	1,376	612	764
Illinois.	846	278	568	South Dakota.	2,272	2,013	259
Indiana	647	196	451	Tennessee.	1,215	634	581
Iowa.	-	-	-	Texas	1,994	755	1,239
Kansas	116	108	8	Utah.	9,203	8,113	1,090
Kentucky.	2,110	693	1,417	Vermont	827	366	461
Louisiana	1,025	604	421	Virginia	3,230	1,657	1,573
Maine	93	53	40	Washington	10,074	9,177	897
Maryland.	-	-	-	West Virginia	1,870	1,033	837
Massachusetts	-	-	-	Wisconsin	2,025	1,521	504
Michigan	4,898	2,857	2,041	Wyoming.	9,693	9,248	445
Minnesota	5,477	2,837	2,640				
Mississippi.	2,312	1,158	1,154	Puerto Rico	56	28	28
Missouri	3,064	1,494	1,570	Virgin Islands.	-	-	-

- Represents zero or rounds to zero.   [1] Comprises all publicly and privately owned land within authorized boundaries of national forests, purchase units, national grasslands, Land utilization projects, research and experimental areas, and other areas.   [2] Federally owned land within the "gross area within unit boundaries."

Source: U.S. Forest Service, *Land Areas of the National Forest System,* annual.

No. 1150. Forest and Timberland Area, Sawtimber and Stock: 1970 to 1992

[As of Jan. 1. 754 acres represents 754,000,000 acres]

Year and region	Total forest land (mil. acres)	Timberland, ownership [1]				Sawtimber, net volume [3]		Growing stock, net volume [4]	
		All owner- ships (mil. acres)	Federally owned or man- aged [2] (mil. acres)	State, county, and municipal (mil. acres)	Private (mil. acres)	Total (bil. bd. ft.)	Soft- wood (bil. bd. ft.)	Total (bil. cu. ft.)	Soft- wood (bil. cu. ft.)
United States, 1970 . .	754	504	116	29	360	2,587	2,035	694	458
North	(NA)	154	11	18	126	295	81	146	39
South	(NA)	203	15	3	185	569	302	191	87
Rocky Mountains	(NA)	65	42	2	20	398	384	101	95
Pacific Coast.	(NA)	82	47	5	29	1,325	1,268	257	238
United States, 1987 . .	731	485	97	34	354	2,853	2,040	766	453
North	165	154	11	19	124	459	126	190	48
South	203	197	16	4	177	781	388	245	106
Rocky Mountains	142	61	39	3	20	411	394	108	100
Pacific Coast.	220	72	31	8	32	1,202	1,132	223	199
United States, 1992 . .	737	490	97	35	358	2,992	2,047	786	450
North	168	158	11	19	127	540	137	207	51
South	212	199	16	4	179	842	389	251	103
Rocky Mountains	140	63	40	3	20	415	397	110	101
Pacific Coast.	217	70	30	8	32	1,196	1,124	218	195

NA Not available.   [1] Timberland is forest land that is producing or is capable of crops of industrial wood and not withdrawn from timber utilization by statute or administrative regulation. Areas qualifying as timberland have the capability of producing in excess of 20 cubic feet per acre per year of industrial wood in natural stands. Currently inaccessible and inoperable areas are included.   [2] Includes Indian lands.   [3] Sawtimber is timber suitable for sawing into lumber. Live trees of commercial species containing at least one 12-foot sawlog or two noncontiguous 8-foot logs, and meeting regional specifications for freedom from defect. Softwood trees must be at least 9.0-inches diameter, and hardwood trees must be at least 11.0-inches diameter at 4 1/2 feet above ground. International 1/4-inch rule.   [4] Live trees of commercial species meeting specified standards of quality or vigor. Cull trees are excluded. Includes only trees 5.0-inches diameter or larger at 4 1/2 feet above ground.

Source: U.S. Forest Service, *Forest Resources of the United States, 1992.*

698   Natural Resources

No. 1151. Timber-Based Industries—Summary of Manufactures: 1992 and 1996

[221.7 represents 221,700. Data based on *1987 Standard Industrial Classification Manual*, published by the Office of Management and Budget, see text, Section 26, Manufactures. N.e.c. = Not elsewhere classified]

Industry	SIC [1] code	1992 All employees Number (1,000)	1992 Payroll (mil. dol.)	1992 Value of shipments (bil. dol.)	1996 All employees Number (1,000)	1996 Payroll (mil. dol.)	1996 Value of shipments (bil. dol.)
Logging and sawmills	241/242	221.7	4,739	31.3	254.5	5,984	45.1
Logging............................	2411	83.6	1,693	13.8	83.0	1,856	15.4
Sawmills/planing mills, general	2421	138.1	3,046	21.1	138.0	3,465	26.7
Hardwood dimension and flooring mills	2426	28.5	502	2.0	31.7	631	2.8
Special product sawmills, n.e.c.............	2429	1.8	31	0.1	1.8	32	0.2
Millwork and veneer [2]	243	224.8	5,029	24.8	257.3	6,233	31.8
Millwork...........................	2431	86.3	1,984	9.6	95.3	2,364	11.8
Wood kitchen cabinets...................	2434	62.8	1,308	4.9	71.7	1,607	6.6
Hardwood veneer and plywood	2435	20.1	395	2.2	21.3	456	2.6
Softwood veneer and plywood.............	2436	31.3	827	5.4	31.9	931	6.0
Structural wood members, n.e.c.	2439	24.3	515	2.5	37.1	876	4.7
Wood containers	244	39.9	640	2.9	50.9	893	4.1
Wood buildings, mobile homes	245	56.1	1,227	6.6	81.8	2,077	11.9
Miscellaneous wood products...............	249	84.6	1,737	10.4	94.2	2,125	13.7
Pulp mills	261	15.9	689	5.5	15.0	701	5.5
Paper mills	262	130.6	5,421	32.8	116.4	5,599	39.6
Paperboard mills	263	51.5	2,136	16.1	54.8	2,599	20.3
Paperboard containers and boxes	265	198.8	5,706	32.6	212.0	6,727	40.4
Setup paperboard boxes	2652	6.6	129	0.4	(S)	(S)	(S)
Corrugated and solid fiber boxes	2653	111.7	3,264	19.8	127.4	4,060	25.9
Fiber cans, tubes, drums, and similar products..	2655	12.4	337	1.9	11.9	356	2.1
Sanitary food containers, except folding	2656	15.4	386	2.5	13.6	389	2.7
Folding paperboard boxes, including sanitary....	2657	52.7	1,590	7.9	53.2	1,777	9.0
Converted paper and paperboard products [3]	267	229.1	6,525	46.1	232.4	7,321	54.9

S Does not meet publication standards.   [1] Standard Industrial Classification code; see text, Section 17, Business.
[2] Includes plywood and structural members.   [3] Except containers and boxes.

Source: U.S. Census Bureau, *Census of Manufactures, 1992 Final Industry Series*, and *Annual Survey of Manufactures*.

No. 1152. Timber Products—Production, Foreign Trade, and Consumption, by Type of Product: 1980 to 1997

[In millions of cubic feet (12,123 represents 12,123,000,000, roundwood equivalent]

Item	Unit	1980	1990	1991	1992	1993	1994	1995	1996	1997
Industrial roundwood:										
Domestic production........	Mil. cu. ft..	12,123	14,674	14,051	14,455	14,184	14,515	14,501	14,664	15,361
Imports	Mil. cu. ft..	2,570	3,121	2,841	3,122	3,516	3,701	3,988	4,045	4,154
Exports	Mil. cu. ft..	1,857	2,207	2,287	2,226	2,044	2,042	2,214	2,182	2,314
Consumption.............	Mil. cu. ft..	12,836	15,587	14,605	15,351	15,656	16,174	16,275	16,527	17,201
Lumber:										
Domestic production........	Mil. cu. ft..	5,305	7,404	6,858	7,058	6,870	7,082	6,826	7,072	7,120
Imports	Mil. cu. ft..	1,545	1,893	1,698	1,947	2,227	2,384	2,515	2,615	2,620
Exports	Mil. cu. ft..	395	573	604	548	519	501	481	471	602
Consumption.............	Mil. cu. ft..	6,455	8,725	7,953	8,457	8,577	8,965	8,861	9,215	9,139
Plywood and veneer:										
Domestic production........	Mil. cu. ft..	1,175	1,422	1,271	1,299	1,300	1,327	1,314	1,297	1,211
Imports	Mil. cu. ft..	120	97	83	100	100	94	107	97	114
Exports	Mil. cu. ft..	45	109	95	106	100	86	89	87	103
Consumption.............	Mil. cu. ft..	1,250	1,410	1,259	1,293	1,300	1,334	1,333	1,307	1,222
Pulp products:										
Domestic production........	Mil. cu. ft..	4,390	5,285	5,370	5,488	5,393	5,531	5,847	5,795	5,794
Imports	Mil. cu. ft..	880	1,083	1,017	1,036	1,128	1,181	1,304	1,262	1,352
Exports	Mil. cu. ft..	579	673	773	823	753	795	943	925	858
Consumption.............	Mil. cu. ft..	4,691	5,696	5,614	5,702	5,768	5,917	6,208	6,132	6,288
Logs:										
Imports	Mil. cu. ft..	25	4	2	7	15	18	13	18	20
Pulpwood chips, exports........	Mil. cu. ft..	278	178	214	225	211	230	250	278	422
Fuelwood consumption........	Mil. cu. ft..	3,105	3,177	3,187	3,202	3,244	3,297	3,360	3,420	2,542

Source: U.S. Forest Service, *Timber Demand and Technology Assessment*, RWU-4861.

Natural Resources   699

No. 1153. Selected Timber Products—Imports and Exports: 1980 to 1997

Product	Unit	1980	1990	1991	1992	1993	1994	1995	1996	1997
IMPORTS [1]										
Lumber, total [2]	Mil. bd. ft . .	9,866	13,063	11,708	13,427	15,369	16,534	17,524	18,363	18,237
From Canada	Percent . . .	97.5	91.2	98.4	98.4	98.2	97.4	97.0	97.1	96.2
Logs, total	Mil. bd. ft.[3] .	128	28	15	45	95	112	80	115	128
From Canada	Percent . . .	97.4	70.7	63.4	91.5	93.6	75.9	40.9	57.3	82.9
Paper and board [4]	1,000 tons .	8,780	13,148	12,167	12,543	13,971	14,918	15,654	14,418	14,721
Woodpulp	1,000 tons .	4,051	4,893	4,997	5,029	5,413	5,650	5,969	5,692	6,287
Plywood	Mil. sq. ft.[5] .	1,235	1,687	1,457	1,776	1,786	1,692	1,951	1,772	2,111
EXPORTS										
Lumber, total [2]	Mil. bd. ft . .	2,494	4,566	3,880	3,498	3,255	3,082	2,929	2,878	2,871
To: Canada	Percent . . .	25.3	14.4	14.6	16.3	17.4	19.8	22.2	23.1	24.8
Japan	Percent . . .	26.0	27.8	31.3	31.8	36.3	34.3	33.4	33.4	25.6
Europe	Percent . . .	23.8	15.0	19.4	21.0	16.8	17.6	17.5	16.9	20.6
Logs, total	Mil. bd. ft.[3] .	3,261	4,213	3,761	3,279	2,876	2,684	2,820	2,640	2,398
To: Canada	Percent . . .	9.7	9.4	11.3	12.7	13.6	16.2	25.4	19.7	29.7
Japan	Percent . . .	78.0	62.3	56.5	62.3	65.4	67.9	61.3	68.7	56.2
China: Mainland	Percent . . .	2.7	8.6	9.9	7.2	4.6	2.8	0.7	0.6	0.8
Paper and board [4]	1,000 tons .	5,214	6,796	8,331	8,971	9,126	10,097	10,944	12,122	10,306
Woodpulp	1,000 tons .	3,806	5,905	6,338	7,222	6,499	6,728	8,261	7,170	6,422
Plywood	Mil. sq. ft.[5] .	413	1,766	1,553	1,760	1,677	1,455	1,517	1,500	1,802

[1] Customs value of imports; see text, Section 28, Foreign Commerce. [2] Includes railroad ties. [3] Log scale. [4] Includes paper and board products. Excludes hardboard. [5] 3/8 inch basis.

Source: U.S. Forest Service, *Timber Demand and Technology Assessment*, RWU-4851. Also in *Agricultural Statistics*, annual.

No. 1154. Lumber Consumption, by Species Group and End Use: 1993 to 1997

[In million board feet (56.9 represents 56,900,000), except per capita in board feet]. Per capita consumption based on estimated resident population as of July 1]

Item	1993	1994	1995	1996	1997	End-use	1993	1994	1995	1996	1997
Total	56.9	59.8	59.3	62.2	63.0	New housing	16.3	16.1	15.9	19.0	(NA)
						Residential upkeep and					
Per capita	220	229	225	234	235	improvements	12.0	12.3	12.4	17.7	(NA)
						New nonresidential					
						residential construction [1]	5.6	5.7	5.8	4.6	(NA)
Species group:											
Softwoods	45.7	48.2	47.6	50.2	50.9	Manufacturing	5.5	5.5	5.5	7.6	(NA)
Hardwoods	11.2	11.6	11.7	12.0	12.1	Shipping	8.4	8.5	8.5	6.3	(NA)
						Other [2]	8.8	8.9	8.8	6.8	(NA)

NA Not available. [1] In addition to new construction, includes railroad ties laid as replacements in existing track and lumber used by railroads for railcar repair. [2] Includes upkeep and improvement of nonresidential buildings and structures; made-at-home projects, such as furniture, boats, and picnic tables; made-on-the-job items such as advertising and display structures; and miscellaneous products and uses.

Source: U.S. Forest Service, *Timber Demand and Technology Assessment*, RWU-4851. Also in *Agricultural Statistics*, annual.

No. 1155. Selected Timber Products—Producer Price Indexes: 1990 to 1998

[1982=100]

Product	1990	1991	1992	1993	1994	1995	1996	1997	1998
Lumber and wood products	129.7	132.1	146.6	174.0	180.0	178.1	176.1	183.8	179.1
Lumber	124.6	124.9	144.7	183.4	188.4	173.4	179.8	194.5	179.3
Softwood lumber	123.8	125.7	148.6	193.0	198.1	178.5	189.5	206.5	182.4
Hardwood lumber	131.0	128.5	140.7	163.3	168.3	167.0	163.9	174.1	178.7
Millwork	130.4	135.5	143.3	156.6	162.4	163.8	166.6	170.9	171.1
General millwork	132.0	138.1	146.3	158.5	163.6	165.4	167.9	171.1	172.4
Prefabricated structural members	122.3	122.4	132.7	159.7	169.3	163.5	167.5	177.8	170.1
Plywood	114.2	114.3	133.3	152.8	158.6	165.3	156.4	159.3	157.6
Softwood plywood	119.6	120.8	147.2	169.7	176.8	188.1	173.7	175.5	175.5
Hardwood plywood and related products . . .	102.7	102.8	106.9	115.4	122.3	122.2	124.9	127.1	126.9
Other wood products	114.7	118.6	124.5	135.3	137.7	143.7	127.5	128.4	135.4
Boxes	119.1	123.6	127.5	138.2	141.3	145.0	147.1	149.2	150.7
Pulp, paper, and allied products	141.2	142.9	145.2	147.3	152.5	172.2	168.7	167.9	171.7
Pulp, paper, and prod, ex bldg paper	132.9	129.8	129.2	127.6	133.1	163.4	149.7	144.7	147.2
Woodpulp	151.3	119.2	118.9	104.2	115.9	183.2	133.1	128.6	122.0
Wastepaper	138.9	121.4	117.5	117.4	209.5	187.1	141.6	163.3	146.0
Paper	128.8	126.9	123.2	123.8	126.0	159.0	149.4	143.9	146.0
Writing and printing papers	129.1	124.8	120.2	120.5	121.7	158.4	144.6	140.0	140.9
Newsprint	119.6	120.9	109.8	112.1	116.7	161.8	159.5	133.9	143.2
Paperboard	135.7	130.2	134.3	130.0	140.5	183.1	155.1	144.4	151.7
Converted paper & paperboard products	135.2	134.8	134.8	133.7	136.7	157.0	153.4	148.4	152.2
Office supplies and accessories	121.4	119.5	116.4	115.3	116.9	134.9	132.9	131.0	131.1
Building paper & building board mill prods . .	112.2	111.8	119.6	132.7	144.1	144.9	137.2	129.6	132.8

Source: U.S. Bureau of Labor Statistics, *Producer Price Indexes*, monthly.

Selected Species—Stumpage Prices In Current and Constant (1992) Dollars: 1990 to 1997

[In dollars per 1,000 board feet. Stumpage prices are based on sales of sawtimber from National Forests]

Species	Current dollars					Constant (1992) dollars [1]				
	1990	1994	1995	1996	1997	1990	1994	1995	1996	1997
Softwoods:										
Douglas fir [2]	466	652	454	436	331	470	635	426	400	305
Southern pine [3]	127	266	248	241	307	128	259	233	221	282
Sugar pine [4]	285	625	397	318	234	287	609	373	292	215
Ponderosa pine [4][5]	218	291	150	274	270	220	283	141	251	248
Western hemlock [6]	203	335	297	248	211	205	326	279	227	194
Hardwoods:										
All eastern hardwoods [7]	146	352	309	259	287	293	707	620	520	576
Oak, white, red, and black [7]	188	317	297	237	265	378	637	596	475	531
Maple, sugar [8]	135	313	286	238	357	271	629	574	478	717

[1] Deflated by the producer price index, all commodities. [2] Western Washington and western Oregon. [3] Southern region. [4] Pacific Southwest region (formerly California region). [5] Includes Jeffrey pine. [6] Pacific Northwest region. [7] Eastern and Southern regions. [8] Eastern region.

Source: U.S. Forest Service, *Timber Demand and Technology Assessment*, RWU-4851. Also in *Agricultural Statistics*, annual.

No. 1157. Paper and Paperboard—Production and New Supply: 1980 to 1997

[In thousands of short tons (63,600 represents 63,600,000)]

Item	1980	1990	1991	1992	1993	1994	1995	1996	1997
Production, total	63,600	80,445	81,234	84,701	86,693	90,897	91,352	92,195	96,828
Paper, total	30,116	39,361	39,084	40,973	41,745	43,356	42,894	42,477	44,679
Paperboard, total	30,926	39,318	40,343	41,895	43,113	45,724	46,640	47,901	50,332
Unbleached kraft	15,295	20,357	20,960	21,658	21,447	22,469	22,697	22,178	23,222
Semichemical	4,724	5,640	5,552	5,762	5,672	5,943	5,662	5,619	6,047
Bleached kraft	3,836	4,399	4,572	4,503	4,583	5,029	5,304	5,236	5,548
Recycled	7,071	8,921	9,259	9,973	11,410	12,283	12,977	14,868	15,514
Wet machine board E	138	96	96	93	95	96	96	96	96
Building paper E	1,369	723	782	795	797	787	787	787	787
Insulating board E	1,051	946	929	945	943	934	934	934	934
New supply, all grades, excluding products	67,783	87,683	86,014	89,631	93,146	97,448	98,196	96,247	101,157
Paper, total	37,126	49,485	47,380	49,232	51,246	53,077	52,762	50,642	54,120
Newsprint	11,377	13,412	12,462	12,658	12,750	12,889	12,762	11,768	12,612
Printing/writing papers	16,124	25,456	24,651	26,013	27,846	29,444	29,543	28,291	30,753
Packaging and ind. conv. papers	5,243	4,718	4,596	4,783	4,628	4,640	4,241	4,288	4,234
Tissue	4,382	5,899	5,672	5,778	6,022	6,105	6,215	6,294	6,521
Paperboard, total	27,689	36,301	36,753	38,453	39,950	42,435	43,448	43,611	45,061
Construction and other	2,968	1,897	1,881	1,946	1,949	1,935	1,947	1,994	1,991

Source: American Forest and Paper Association, Washington, DC, *Monthly Statistical Summary of Paper, Paperboard and Woodpulp*.

No. 1158. Newsprint—Production, Stocks, Consumption, and Price Index: 1980 to 1997

[In thousands of metric tons (8,625 represents 8,625,000), except price index]

Country and item	1980	1990	1991	1992	1993	1994	1995	1996	1997
Canada:									
Production	8,625	9,068	8,855	8,755	9,130	9,299	9,226	9,015	(NA)
Capacity	(NA)	10,100	10,175	9,841	9,604	9,695	9,575	9,769	(NA)
Stocks at mills, end of year	165	315	565	351	362	225	208	428	(NA)
United States:									
Capacity	(NA)	6,162	6,400	6,625	6,617	6,604	6,580	6,526	(NA)
Consumption, estimate	10,088	12,241	12,126	12,126	11,268	11,505	11,535	11,826	11,256
Production	4,239	5,997	6,206	6,424	6,412	6,336	6,352	6,304	(NA)
Stocks at mill, end of year	21	46	98	59	81	60	76	94	(NA)
Producer price index (1982=100)	[1]88.5	119.6	120.9	109.8	112.1	116.7	161.8	159.5	133.9

NA Not available. [1] Average for 11 months.

Source: 1980-1993, U.S. Bureau of Economic Analysis, *Survey of Current Business*, monthly; beginning 1994, American Forest and Paper Association, Washington, DC, and Canadian Pulp & Paper Association.

Natural Resources 701

No. 1159. Fishery Products—Domestic Catch, Imports, and Disposition: 1980 to 1997

[Live weight, in millions of pounds (11,357 represents 11,357,000,000). For data on commercial catch for selected countries, see Table 1394, Section 30, Comparative International Statistics]

Item	1980	1990	1991	1992	1993	1994	1995	1996	1997
Total	11,357	16,349	16,364	16,106	20,334	19,309	16,484	16,474	17,131
For human food	8,006	12,662	13,020	13,242	13,821	13,714	13,584	13,625	13,739
For industrial use	3,351	3,687	3,344	2,864	6,513	5,595	2,900	2,848	3,392
Domestic catch	6,482	9,404	9,484	9,637	10,467	10,461	9,788	9,565	9,845
For human food	3,654	7,041	7,031	7,618	8,214	7,936	7,667	7,476	7,248
For industrial use	2,828	2,363	2,453	2,019	2,253	2,525	2,121	2,090	2,597
Imports [1]	4,875	6,945	6,879	6,469	9,867	8,848	6,696	6,909	7,286
For human food	4,352	5,621	5,989	5,624	5,607	5,778	5,917	6,150	6,491
For industrial use [2]	523	1,324	890	845	4,260	3,070	779	759	795
Disposition of domestic catch	6,482	9,404	9,484	9,637	10,467	10,461	9,788	9,565	9,846
Fresh and frozen	2,621	6,501	6,541	7,288	7,744	7,475	7,099	7,054	6,877
Canned	1,161	751	674	543	649	622	769	678	648
Cured	96	126	119	100	115	95	90	93	108
Reduced to meal, oil, etc.	2,604	2,026	2,150	1,696	1,959	2,269	1,830	1,740	2,213

[1] Excludes imports of edible fishery products consumed in Puerto Rico; includes landings of tuna caught by foreign vessels in American Samoa.   [2] Fish meal and sea herring.

No. 1160. Fisheries—Quantity and Value of Domestic Catch: 1980 to 1997

Year	Quantity (mil. lb. [1])			Value (mil. dol.)	Average price per lb. (cents)	Year	Quantity (mil. lb. [1])			Value (mil. dol.)	Average price per lb. (cents)
	Total	For human food	For industrial products [2]				Total	For human food	For industrial products [2]		
1980	6,482	3,654	2,828	2,237	34.5	1989	8,463	6,204	2,259	3,238	38.3
1981	5,977	3,547	2,430	2,388	40.0	1990	9,404	7,041	2,363	3,522	37.5
1982	6,367	3,285	3,082	2,390	37.5	1991	9,484	7,031	2,453	3,308	34.9
1983	6,439	3,238	3,201	2,355	36.6	1992	9,637	7,618	2,019	3,678	38.2
1984	6,438	3,320	3,118	2,350	36.5	1993	[3]10,467	8,214	2,253	3,471	33.2
1985	6,258	3,294	2,964	2,326	37.2	1994	10,461	7,936	2,525	3,807	36.8
1986	6,031	3,393	2,638	2,763	45.8	1995	9,788	7,667	2,121	3,770	38.5
1987	6,896	3,946	2,950	3,115	45.2	1996	9,565	7,474	2,091	3,487	36.5
1988	7,192	4,588	2,604	3,520	48.9	1997	9,846	7,248	2,598	3,467	35.2

[1] Live weight.   [2] Meal, oil, fish solubles, homogenized condensed fish, shell products, bait, and animal food.   [3] Represents record year.

No. 1161. Domestic Fish and Shellfish Catch and Value, by Species: 1990 to 1997

Species	Quantity (1,000 lb.)				Value ($1,000)			
	1990	1995	1996	1997	1990	1995	1996	1997
Total	9,403,571	9,787,554	9,564,888	9,845,784	3,521,995	3,735,615	3,486,713	3,466,605
Fish, total [1]	8,091,068	8,520,086	8,272,709	8,397,286	1,900,097	1,915,642	1,790,966	1,722,205
Cod:								
Atlantic	95,881	29,631	31,422	28,619	61,329	28,184	26,634	24,464
Pacific	526,396	591,399	605,314	661,314	91,384	109,680	111,978	142,429
Flounder	254,519	423,443	459,527	566,353	112,921	150,239	154,049	130,769
Halibut	70,454	44,796	49,092	69,864	96,700	66,781	83,468	117,362
Menhaden	1,962,160	1,846,959	1,755,471	2,027,802	93,896	99,131	94,150	112,050
Pollock, Alaska	3,108,031	2,852,618	2,623,131	2,512,455	268,344	259,614	238,129	242,589
Sablefish	89,802	65,904	59,949	52,925	58,865	123,694	109,009	108,776
Salmon	733,146	1,020,765	877,056	567,658	612,367	486,107	368,729	270,370
Tuna	62,393	63,864	85,439	82,855	105,040	102,638	110,256	109,794
Shellfish, total [1]	1,312,503	1,267,468	1,292,179	1,448,498	1,621,898	1,819,973	1,695,747	1,744,400
Clams	139,198	134,224	123,239	114,184	130,194	140,414	127,779	129,686
Crabs	499,416	363,639	391,797	429,963	483,837	511,987	426,705	429,547
Lobsters:								
American	61,017	66,406	71,641	83,921	154,677	214,838	241,796	267,216
Oysters	29,193	40,380	38,007	39,652	93,718	101,574	114,839	111,185
Scallops:								
Calico	(NA)	957	(NA)	1,613	(NA)	1,219	(NA)	3,601
Sea	39,917	18,316	18,162	13,789	153,696	92,826	101,823	90,291
Shrimp	346,494	306,869	316,879	290,255	491,433	570,034	509,203	544,056

NA Not available.   [1] Includes other types of fish and shellfish, not shown separately.

Source of Tables 1159-1161: U.S. National Oceanic and Atmospheric Administration, National Marine Fisheries Service, *Fisheries of the United States*, annual.

702   Natural Resources

No. 1162. U.S. Private Aquaculture—Trout and Catfish Production and Value: 1990 to 1998

Item	Unit	1990	1992	1993	1994	1995	1996	1997	1998
TROUT FOODSIZE									
Number sold	Millions .	67.8	64.5	60.9	58.3	60.2	56.5	59.3	57.1
Total weight	Mil. lb . .	56.8	55.2	54.6	52.1	55.6	53.6	56.9	55.1
Total value of sales	Mil. dol. .	64.6	51.0	54.3	52.7	60.8	57.0	60.7	59.7
Average price received	Dol./lb . .	1.14	0.92	0.99	1.01	1.09	1.06	1.07	1.08
Percent sold to processors	Percent .	58	71	63	68	68	67	63	59
CATFISH FOODSIZE									
Number sold	Millions .	272.9	373.2	379.1	347.6	321.8	375.4	391.8	407.8
Total weight	Mil. lb . .	392.4	497.3	495.8	479.4	481.5	526.3	569.6	598.5
Total value of sales	Mil. dol. .	305.1	302.4	352.9	373.6	378.1	403.3	406.8	440.7
Average price received	Dol./lb . .	0.78	0.61	0.71	0.78	0.79	0.77	0.71	0.74
Fish sold to processors	Mil. lb . .	360.4	457.4	459.0	439.3	446.9	472.1	524.9	564.4
Avg. price paid by processors	Cents/lb .	75.8	59.8	70.9	78.4	78.6	77.3	71.2	74.3
Processor sales	Mil. lb . .	183.1	231.3	233.5	216.5	227.0	237.2	261.8	281.4
Avg. price received by processors	Cents/lb .	224.1	200.5	218.6	238.5	240.3	236.9	226.0	229.0
Inventory (Jan. 1)	Mil. lb . .	9.4	11.6	9.5	11.6	10.9	11.9	11.9	10.8

Source: U.S. Dept. of Agriculture, National Agricultural Statistics Service, *Trout Production* released September; *Catfish Production* released February; and *Catfish Processing* released February. Also in *Agricultural Statistics,* annual.

No. 1163. Supply of Selected Fishery Items: 1980 to 1997

[In millions of pounds (425 represents 425,000,000). Totals available for U.S. consumption are supply minus exports plus imports. Round weight is the complete or full weight as caught]

Item	Unit	1980	1985	1990	1991	1992	1993	1994	1995	1996	1997
Shrimp	Heads-off weight. .	425	633	734	744	820	808	847	832	842	923
Tuna, canned	Canned weight. . .	666	759	856	933	922	835	850	875	859	829
Clams	Meat weight.	102	164	152	144	155	156	144	144	134	124
American lobster	Round weight. . . .	69	108	95	107	95	92	101	94	97	112
Snow crab	Round weight. . . .	54	45	37	60	88	66	40	42	46	110
Salmon, canned	Canned weight. . .	126	113	148	131	73	114	117	147	104	82
Spiny lobster	Round weight. . . .	127	154	89	85	81	76	76	89	81	76
Scallops	Meat weight.	51	72	74	62	69	66	76	62	71	66
Oysters	Meat weight.	71	90	56	47	50	48	50	63	58	58
Sardines, canned	Canned weight. . .	69	76	61	52	41	41	48	44	46	49
King crab	Round weight. . . .	133	11	19	20	15	8	12	21	30	45
Crab meat, canned	Canned weight. . .	9	8	9	11	9	9	9	12	13	15

Source: U.S. National Oceanic and Atmospheric Administration, National Marine Fisheries Service, *Fisheries of the United States,* annual.

No. 1164. Canned, Fresh, and Frozen Fishery Products: 1980 to 1997

[Fresh fishery products exclude Alaska and Hawaii. Canned fishery products data are for natural pack only]

Product	Production (mil. lb.)						Value (mil. dol.)					
	1980	1990	1994	1995	1996	1997	1980	1990	1994	1995	1996	1997
Canned, [1]	1,516	1,178	1,768	1,927	1,877	1,565	1,928	1,562	1,796	1,887	1,800	1,593
Tuna	602	581	610	667	676	627	1,144	902	963	939	957	919
Salmon	200	196	207	244	197	162	376	366	329	419	284	253
Clam products	77	110	122	129	129	125	66	76	106	110	117	115
Mackerel [2]	38	23	(NA)	(NA)	(NA)	(NA)	12	11	(NA)	(NA)	(NA)	(NA)
Sardines, Maine	20	13	16	14	18	16	32	17	28	24	30	29
Shrimp	16	1	(Z)	1	1	1	80	3	4	7	6	5
Crabs [3]	5	1	(Z)	(Z)	(Z)	(Z)	19	4	(Z)	(Z)	(Z)	(Z)
Oysters [3]	(Z)	1	(Z)	(Z)	(Z)	(Z)	(Z)	1	(Z)	(Z)	(Z)	(Z)
Fish fillets and steaks. .	202	441	425	385	423	398	261	843	836	841	904	909
Cod	31	65	58	65	67	79	43	132	135	152	158	179
Flounder	49	54	35	35	29	26	87	154	89	86	80	75
Haddock	17	7	3	3	4	7	29	24	12	11	14	24
Ocean perch, Atlantic	7	1	(Z)	(Z)	(Z)	1	9	1	1	1	1	2
Rockfish	14	33	23	25	20	15	13	53	33	38	42	30
Pollock, Atlantic	9	12	7	4	2	1	9	21	16	10	5	2
Pollock, Alaska	(NA)	164	141	135	136	112	(NA)	174	144	184	158	129
Other	74	105	158	118	165	157	71	284	406	359	446	468

NA Not available. Z Less than 500,000 pounds or $500,000. [1] Includes other products, not shown separately. [2] Includes Jack and a small amount of Pacific mackerel. [3] Includes oyster specialties. [4] Fresh and frozen.

Source: U.S. National Oceanic and Atmospheric Administration, National Marine Fisheries Service, *Fisheries of the United States,* annual.

U.S. Census Bureau, Statistical Abstract of the United States: 1999

No. 1165. Summary of Mineral Operations: 1967 to 1997

[Represents mineral operations only. Beginning 1967, excludes single unit establishments without paid employees]

Item	Unit	1967	1972	1977	1982	1987	1992	1997
Establishments	Number. . .	28,579	25,269	31,359	42,241	33,617	30,787	26,100
With 20 or more employees	Number. . .	5,682	5,312	6,632	(NA)	6,299	5,600	(NA)
Including all operations in manufactures .	Number. . .	29,688	26,178	31,967	42,585	34,041	31,261	(NA)
Excluding oil and gas extraction.	Number. . .	12,221	10,771	12,912	12,267	10,707	9,896	9,414
Employees, total	1,000 . . .	567	595	799	1,114	698	638	550
Production workers [1]	1,000 . . .	433	443	593	762	451	415	(NA)
All other	1,000 . . .	134	152	206	352	247	223	(NA)
Worker-hours, production workers [1]	Million	892	909	1,183	1,578	942	876	(NA)
Worker-hours per production workers . . .	1,000 . . .	2.1	2.1	2.0	2.1	2.1	2.1	(NA)
Payroll, total	Mil. dol . .	4,187	6,226	13,167	28,637	21,739	24,199	22,145
Wages, production workers [1]	Mil. dol . .	2,888	4,250	9,082	18,030	12,443	13,833	(NA)
Salaries, all other employees	Mil. dol . .	1,299	1,976	4,085	10,607	9,296	10,366	(NA)
Cost of supplies, etc. [2]	Mil. dol . . .	10,576	14,884	46,079	109,697	62,423	65,653	(NA)
Value added in mining.	Mil. dol . . .	19,330	26,471	68,013	188,055	110,959	113,621	(NA)
Metal mining	Mil. dol . . .	1,557	2,382	3,504	3,215	4,610	6,724	(NA)
Coal mining.	Mil. dol . . .	2,091	3,754	11,266	18,631	17,068	17,252	(NA)
Oil and gas extraction	Mil. dol . . .	13,394	17,612	48,587	159,937	80,049	80,016	(NA)
Nonmetallic minerals mining	Mil. dol . . .	2,288	2,723	4,656	6,273	9,233	9,629	(NA)
Value of shipments and receipts	Mil. dol . . .	22,784	36,319	96,375	250,000	157,964	162,095	158,482
Capital expenditures	Mil. dol . . .	4,058	5,036	17,718	47,753	15,418	17,179	(NA)

NA Not available. [1] Represents employees up through the working foreman level in manual work. Includes development and exploration workers. [2] Includes purchased machinery installed.

Source: U.S. Census Bureau, *Census of Mineral Industries, 1972, 1977, 1982, 1987,* and *1992;* and *1997 Economic Census, Core Business Statistics Series,* Series EC97X-CS1.

No. 1166. Mining and Primary Metal Production Indexes: 1980 to 1998

[Index 1992=100]

Industry group	1980	1990	1991	1992	1993	1994	1995	1996	1997	1998
Mining	111.5	104.8	102.6	100.0	99.9	102.4	102.0	103.7	105.8	104.1
Coal	83.4	103.7	100.1	100.0	93.7	102.5	101.9	105.0	107.8	109.7
Oil and gas extraction.	124.4	106.4	104.7	100.0	101.1	101.7	100.5	101.8	103.1	99.9
Crude oil and natural gas. . . .	115.1	101.6	101.9	100.0	98.0	98.1	96.5	95.9	95.7	95.0
Oil and gas drilling	236.8	151.1	128.6	100.0	122.6	127.0	126.4	138.0	149.3	135.0
Metal mining	65.2	93.1	93.3	100.0	98.8	100.5	101.5	104.0	110.0	110.2
Iron ore	128.5	104.1	101.7	100.0	100.0	104.3	112.3	111.3	113.5	112.8
Nonferrous ores	52.8	91.9	92.1	100.0	98.6	99.9	100.1	103.0	109.6	110.0
Copper ore	65.6	89.4	92.4	100.0	102.0	104.7	104.8	108.7	109.9	106.7
Primary metals, manufacturing . .	108.0	104.0	96.7	100.0	105.7	113.4	116.8	119.8	125.3	123.8
Nonferrous metals	92.4	100.9	97.7	100.0	104.0	113.0	115.8	120.6	126.7	127.5
Copper.	75.9	81.6	88.3	100.0	116.7	111.7	122.0	103.6	110.5	107.2
Aluminum	115.1	100.4	102.2	100.0	91.7	81.8	83.7	88.5	89.4	92.1
Iron and steel	119.0	106.4	96.0	100.0	107.1	113.7	117.7	119.2	124.2	120.7

Source: Board of Governors of the Federal Reserve System, *Federal Reserve Bulletin,* monthly; and *Industrial Production and Capacity Utilization,* Statistical Release G.17, monthly.

No. 1167. Mineral Industries—Employment, Hours, and Earnings: 1990 to 1998

Item	Unit	1990	1995	1998	Item	Unit	1990	1995	1998
All mining:					Avg. weekly hours	Number .	43.9	44.2	42.7
All employees	1,000 . . .	709	581	575	Avg. weekly earnings . .	Dollars . .	568	642	719
Production workers	1,000 . . .	509	424	436	Metal mining:				
Avg. weekly hours . . .	Number . .	44.1	44.7	43.9	All employees	1,000 . . .	58	51	51
Avg. weekly earnings . .	Dollars . .	603	684	744	Production workers	1,000 . . .	46	41	39
Coal mining:					Avg. weekly hours	Number .	42.8	43.8	44.5
All employees	1,000 . . .	147	104	91	Avg. weekly earnings . .	Dollars . .	601	735	812
Production workers	1,000 . . .	119	84	75	Nonmetallic minerals,				
Avg. weekly hours . . .	Number . .	44.0	44.9	44.8	except fuels:				
Avg. weekly earnings . .	Dollars . .	735	828	858	All employees	1,000 . . .	110	105	108
Oil and gas extraction:					Production workers	1,000 . . .	83	80	82
All employees	1,000 . . .	395	320	326	Avg. weekly hours	Number .	45.3	46.6	46.4
Production workers	1,000 . . .	261	218	242	Avg. weekly earnings . .	Dollars . .	525	624	683

Source: U.S. Bureau of Labor Statistics, *Bulletin 2370* and *Employment and Earnings,* March and June issues.

No. 1168. Mineral Production: 1990 to 1998

[Data represent production as measured by mine shipments, mine sales, or marketable production]

Mineral	Unit	1990	1995	1997	1998
FUEL MINERALS					
Coal, total	Mil. sh. tons	1,029.1	1,033.0	1,089.9	1,118.7
Bituminous	Mil. sh. tons	693.2	613.8	653.8	665.1
Subbituminous	Mil. sh. tons	244.3	328.0	345.1	363.6
Lignite	Mil. sh. tons	88.1	86.5	86.3	84.8
Anthracite	Mil. sh. tons	3.5	4.7	4.7	5.2
Natural gas (marketed production)	Tril. cu. ft.	18.59	19.51	19.87	19.94
Petroleum (crude).	Mil. bbl. [1]	2,686	2,394	2354.98	2,279
Uranium (recoverable content)	Mil. lb.	8.9	6.0	5.64	4.71
NONFUEL MINERALS					
Asbestos (sales).	1,000 metric tons . .	(D)	9.3	6.9	6.0
Barite, primary, sold/used by producers. .	1,000 metric tons . .	430	543	692	660
Boron minerals, sold or used by producers	1,000 metric tons . .	1,090	1,190	1,190	(NA)
Bromine, sold or used by producers	1,000 metric tons . .	177	218	247	234
Cement:					
Portland.	Mil. metric tons	67.0	73.3	78.9	(NA)
Masonry	Mil. metric tons	2.9	3.6	(NA)	(NA)
Clays	1,000 metric tons . .	42,900	43,100	42,000	43,000
Diatomite.	1,000 metric tons . .	631	722	773	767
Feldspar [2]	1,000 metric tons . .	630	880	900	800
Fluorspar, finished shipments	1,000 metric tons . .	64	51	-	-
Garnet (abrasive)	1,000 metric tons . .	47.0	46.3	64.9	57
Gypsum, crude.	Mil. metric tons	14.9	16.6	18.6	19.0
Helium [3]	Mil. cu. meters	84.8	99	(NA)	(NA)
Lime, sold or used by producers	Mil. metric tons	15.8	18.5	19.7	20.4
Mica, scrap & flake, sold/used by producers	1,000 metric tons . .	109	108	114	81
Peat, sales by producers	1,000 metric tons . .	721	660	753	(NA)
Perlite, processed, sold or used.	1,000 metric tons . .	576	700	706	688
Phosphate rock (marketable)	Mil. metric tons . . .	46.3	43.5	43.3	44.6
Potash (K_2O equivalent) sales.	1,000 metric tons . .	1,710	1,480	1,400	1,300
Pumice & pumicite, producer sales	1,000 metric tons . .	443	529	577	616
Salt, common, sold/used by producers . .	Mil. metric tons . .	36.9	40.8	40.6	42.1
Sand & gravel, sold/used by producer . .	Mil. metric tons	855	935	981	1,049
Construction.	Mil. metric tons	829	907	952	1,020
Industrial	Mil. metric tons	26	28.2	28.5	29.0
Silica [4]	Metric tons.	3,710	979	(NA)	(NA)
Sodium carbonate (natural) (soda ash) . .	1,000 metric tons . .	9,100	10,100	10,700	10,300
Sodium sulfate (natural)	1,000 metric tons . .	349	327	318	290
Stone [5]	Mil. metric tons	1,110	2,420	2,600	2,580
Crushed and broken	Mil. metric tons	1,110	1,260	1,420	1,500
Dimension	1,000 metric tons . .	1,120	1,160	1,180	1,080
Sulfur: Frasch mines (shipments).	1,000 metric tons . .	3,680	(D)	(D)	(D)
Talc, and pyrophyllite, crude	1,000 metric tons . .	1,270	1,060	1,050	958
Tripoli	1,000 metric tons . .	81	80	(NA)	(NA)
Vermiculite concentrate	1,000 metric tons . .	209	171	(D)	(D)
METALS					
Antimony ore and concentrate.	Metric tons.	(D)	262	356	500
Aluminum	1,000 metric tons . .	4,048	3,375	3,603	3,700
Bauxite (dried)	1,000 metric tons . .	(D)	(D)	(NA)	(NA)
Copper (recoverable content)	1,000 metric tons . .	1,590	1,850	1,940	1,850
Gold (recoverable content)	Metric tons.	294	317	360	350
Iron ore (gross weight) [6]	Mil. metric tons	57.0	61.1	62.8	62.0
Lead (recoverable content)	1,000 metric tons . .	484	386	448	449
Magnesium metal	1,000 metric tons . .	139	142	125	117
Manganiferous ore (gross weight) [7] . . .	1,000 metric ton . . .	(D)	(D)	(D)	(D)
Mercury [8]	Metric tons.	562	(D)	(D)	(D)
Molybdenum (concentrate)	1,000 metric tons . .	61.6	60.9	60.9	53.5
Nickel	1,000 metric tons . .	0.3	1.6	-	-
Palladium metal	Kilograms	5,930	5,260	8,400	10,500
Platinum metal	Kilograms	1,810	1,590	2,610	3,500
Silver (recoverable content)	Metric tons.	2,120	1,560	2,150	2,100
Titanium concentrate: Ilmenite (gross weight)	1,000 metric tons . .	(D)	(D)	(D)	(D)
Tungsten ore and concentrate [9]	Metric tons.	(D)	(D)	(D)	(D)
Zinc (recoverable content)	1,000 metric tons . .	515	614	605	655

- Represents zero.   D Withheld to avoid disclosing individual company data.   NA Not available.   [1] 42 gal. bbl.   [2] Includes aplite, 1992-97.   [3] Refined only.   [4] Includes grindstones, oilstones, whetstones, and deburring media. Excludes grinding pebbles, and tubemill liners.   [5] Excludes abrasive stone, bituminous limestone and sandstone, and ground soapstone, all included elsewhere in table; 1993 excludes dimension stone. Includes calcareous marl and slate.   [6] Represents shipments; includes byproduct ores.   [7] 5 to 35 percent manganiferous ore.   [8] Mercury produced as a byproduct of gold ores only.   [9] Content of ore and concentrate.

Source: Nonfuels, through 1994, U.S. Bureau of Mines, thereafter, U.S. Geological Survey, *Minerals Yearbook* and *Mineral Commodities Summaries*, annual; fuels, U.S. Energy Information Administration, *Annual Energy Review*.

No. 1169. Mineral Production Value: 1990 to 1998

[In millions of dollars (141,608 represents $141,608,000,000). Value derived by multiplying production times price at source of production]

Mineral	1990	1995	1996	1997	1998, est.
Mineral production, total............	**141,608**	**123,486**	**145,206**	**147,204**	**(NA)**
Mineral fuels, total.................	**108,144**	**84,783**	**106,197**	**106,524**	**83,601**
Coal, total [1].............................	22,415	19,469	19,691	19,777	19,668
Bituminous	19,014	15,688	15,875	16,110	16,036
Anthracite	138	187	177	165	174
Natural gas (wellhead)	31,789	30,241	42,858	46,098	39,082
Petroleum (crude)........................	53,801	35,006	43,561	40,576	24,792
Uranium U_3O_8.........................	140	67	87	73	58
Industrial minerals, total	**21,022**	**24,679**	**25,994**	**27,606**	**(NA)**
Asbestos (sales)	[4]	[4]	[4]	[4]	[4]
Asphalt, related bitumens (native) [3]	3,480	(NA)	(NA)	(NA)	(NA)
Barite, primary, sold/used by producers	16	10	15	16	15
Boron minerals, sold/used by producers	436	560	519	580	(NA)
Bromine, sold/used by producers	173	186	150	198	227
Calcium chloride (natural)	[4]	(NA)	(NA)	(NA)	(NA)
Cement:					
Portland	3,683	4,920	5,310	5,710	(NA)
Masonry	225	307	321	339	(NA)
Clays	1,620	1,730	1,710	1,670	(NA)
Diatomite	138	171	176	184	182
Feldspar [5]	28	37	39	43	40
Fluorspar, finished shipments	[4]	[4]	[4]	[4]	[4]
Garnet (abrasive)	7	4	6	6	(NA)
Gemstones (estimate)..................	53	49	43	25	23
Gypsum, crude	100	121	124	132	137
Helium [6]	113	196	193	206	(NA)
Lime, sold/used by producers...........	902	1,100	1,170	1,200	(NA)
Mica, scrap and flake, sold/used by producers.......	6	6	8	9	9
Peat (sales by producers)	19	17.0	18.5	17.5	(NA)
Perlite, processed, sold/used by producers	17	22	21	23	(NA)
Phosphate rock (marketable)	1,075	947	1,060	1,076	1,131
Potash (K_2O equivalent)................	303	284	299	320	(NA)
Pumice and pumicite (sales by producers)	11	13.2	14.8	16.1	15
Salt (common), sold/used by producers	827	1,000	1,060	993	(NA)
Sand and gravel, sold/used by producers ...	3,686	4,400	4,500	4,778	(NA)
Silica, special [2]	[8]	1	1	(NA)	(NA)
Sodium carbonate (natural) (soda ash).....	836	829	926	915	(NA)
Sodium sulfate (natural).................	34	28	27	35	(NA)
Stone [7].............................	5,822	6,970	7,410	8,295	(NA)
Crushed and broken	5,591	6,740	7,180	8,070	(NA)
Dimension...........................	231	233	234	225	205
Sulfur: Frasch mines (shipments)	335	[4]	[4]	[4]	(NA)
Talc and pyrophyllite, crude [8]	31	32	31	(NA)	(NA)
Tripoli................................	3	11	18	16	(NA)
Vermiculite concentrate	19	[4]	[4]	[4]	(NA)
Industrial minerals, undistributed	504	725	820	803	(NA)
Metals, total .... [9]	**12,442**	**14,024**	**13,015**	**13,074**	**(NA)**
Antimony ore and concentrate [9]	[10]	[12]	[12]	[12]	(NA)
Bauxite (dried equivalent)	[10]	[12]	[12]	[12]	(NA)
Copper (recoverable content)	4,311	5,640	4,610	4,580	(NA)
Gold (recoverable content)...............	3,650	3,950	4,090	3,850	(NA)
Iron ore (gross weight) [11]...............	1,741	1,730	1,770	1,890	(NA)
Lead (recoverable content)	491	359	459	460	(NA)
Magnesium metal [12]	433	476	455	400	(NA)
Manganiferous ore (gross weight) [13] ...	[10]	[12]	[12]	[12]	(NA)
Mercury [14]	[10]	[12]	[12]	[12]	(NA)
Molybdenum (concentrate)...............	348	651	456	(D)	(NA)
Palladium metal.......................	22	22	26	50	(NA)
Platinum metal........................	27	21	24	33	(NA)
Silver (recoverable content)	329	259	262	338	(NA)
Titanium concentrate: Ilmenite (gross weight)	[10]	[12]	[12]	[12]	(NA)
Tungsten ore and concentrate	[10]	[12]	[12]	[12]	(NA)
Vanadium (recoverable content)	[10]	[12]	[12]	[12]	(NA)
Zinc mine production (recoverable content)........	847	756	674	860	(NA)
Metals, undistributed	242	161	190	614	(NA)

NA Not available.   [1] Includes subbituminous and lignite.   [2] Includes grindstones, oilstones, whetstones, and deburring media.   [3] 1990-92, excluded from industrial minerals.   [4] Included in "Industrial minerals, undistributed."   [5] 1992-93, includes aplite.   [6] Refined only.   [7] Ex- cludes abrasive stone, bituminous limestone and sandstone, and ground soapstone; 1993 excludes dimension stone. State ranks based on publishable data. Includes calcareous marl and slate.   [8] 1990-92, talc only.   [9] Antimony content.   [10] Included with "metals, undistributed."   [11] Represents shipments; includes byproduct orders.   [12] Canvass for magnesium chloride for magnesium metal discontinued in 1986.   [13] 5 to 35 percent manganiferous ore.   [14] Mercury produced as a byproduct of gold ores only.

Source: Nonfuels, through 1994, U.S. Bureau of Mines, thereafter, U.S. Geological Survey, *Minerals Yearbook* and *Mineral Commodities Summaries*, annual; fuels, U.S. Energy Information Administration, *Annual Energy Review.*

No. 1170. Nonfuel Mineral Commodities—Summary: 1997

Mineral	Unit	Mineral disposition		Net import reliance [1] (percent)	Consumption, apparent	Average price per unit (dollars)	Employment (number)
		Production	Exports				
Aluminum	1,000 metric tons	5,300	1,600	23	6,900	[2]0.75	18,000
Antimony (contained)	Metric tons	[3]31,000	4,500	(NA)	(NA)	[2]1.10	100
Asbestos	1,000 metric tons	9	13	38	21	(D)	30
Barite	1,000 metric tons	700	35	71	2,435	[4]25.00	380
Bauxite and alumina	1,000 metric tons	(NA)	1,300	100	4,300	[4]27.00	(NA)
Beryllium (contained)	Metric tons	210	45	[5]	205	[2][6]327	425
Bismuth (contained)	Metric tons	(D)	200	(D)	(D)	[2]3.50	30
Boron (B_2O_3 content)	1,000 metric tons	622	(NA)	[5]	(NA)	[4][7]340	900
Bromine (contained)	1,000 metric tons	250	14	-	341	[8][9]0.988	1,700
Cadmium (contained)	Metric tons	[3]1,750	100	33	2,600	[2][10]1.00	150
Cement	1,000 metric tons	80,900	850	14	93,602	[4]74.50	17,900
Chromium	1,000 metric tons	[11]124	33	76	513	[4][12]150	(NA)
Clays	1,000 metric tons	43,900	4,970	[5]	39,000	(NA)	13,900
Cobalt (contained)	Metric tons	[11]2,000	1,700	78	9,200	[2]23.00	(NA)
Copper (Mine, contained)	1,000 metric tons	1,920	670	12	2,830	[2]1.08	13,300
Diamond (industrial)	Million carats	135	139	(NA)	244	[13]0.44	(NA)
Diatomite	1,000 metric tons	705	144	[5]	561	[4]252	1,000
Feldspar	1,000 metric tons	930	8	-	931	[4]45.09	400
Fluorspar	1,000 metric tons	121	60	100	609	(NA)	-
Garnet (industrial)	Metric tons	71,000	13,000	[5]	59,000	[4]50-2,000	250
Gemstones	Million dollars	67	2,700	99	5,370	(NA)	800
Germanium (contained)	Kilograms	20,000	(NA)	(NA)	30,000	[8][14]1,475	115
Gold (contained)	Metric tons	325	550	[5]	(NA)	[15]325	14,000
Graphite (crude)	1,000 metric tons	-	27	100	28	[4][16]716	(NA)
Gypsum (crude)	1,000 short tons	17,000	200	30	26,300	[4]7.10	6,000
Iodine	Metric tons	1,330	2,400	65	3,700	[8]14.60	40
Iron ore (usable)	Million metric tons	62	5	15	73.7	[4][17]30.41	7,500
Iron and steel scrap (metal)	Million metric tons	78	9	[5]	70	[4]124.00	38,000
Iron and steel slag (metal)	1,000 metric tons	21,000	3	1	21,400	[4]7.00	2,500
Lead (contained)	1,000 metric tons	450	30	14	1,660	[2]0.470	1,200
Lime	1,000 metric tons	19,300	58	1	19,500	[4]55.40	5,700
Magnesium compounds	1,000 metric tons	400	55	33	595	(NA)	600
Magnesium metal	1,000 metric tons	190	40	10	166	[2][18]1.65	1,400
Manganese (gross weight)	1,000 metric tons	-	63	100	715	[4]2.44	(NA)
Mercury	Metric tons	[11]400	60	(D)	(D)	200.00	(NA)
Mica, scrap and flake	1,000 metric tons	91	7	3	100	[4]91.00	(NA)
Molybdenum (contained)	Metric tons	55,500	50,000	[5]	11,700	[8]8.50	700
Nickel (contained)	Metric tons	16,100	17,300	54	150,000	[6]6,931	4
Nitrogen (fixed)-ammonia	1,000 metric tons	13,000	500	14	15,100	[4]192	2,500
Peat	1,000 metric tons	500	20	58	1,200	[4]26.00	800
Perlite	1,000 metric tons	703	38	11	790	[4]31.82	140
Phosphate rock	1,000 metric tons	46,300	600	[5]	42,500	[4]23.70	5,000
Platinum-group metals	Kilograms	10,800	60,100	(NA)	(NA)	[2][19]394.83	550
Potash (K_2O equivalent)	1,000 metric tons	1,430	450	76	5,890	[4][20]140	1,650
Pumice and pumicite	1,000 metric tons	538	13	21	680	[4]26.29	70
Salt	1,000 metric tons	41,700	675	14	48,700	[4][21]20.00	4,150
Silicon (contained)	1,000 metric tons	424	41	34	637	[2][22]0.55	(NA)
Silver (contained)	Metric tons	1,600	3,000	(NA)	(NA)	4.62	1,400
Sodium carbonate (soda ash)	1,000 metric tons	10,400	4,000	[5]	6,480	[23]105	2,800
Sodium sulfate	1,000 metric tons	320	80	12	659	[24]114	240
Stone (crushed)	Million metric tons	1,390	4	-	1,397	[4]5.55	78,000
Sulfur (all forms)	1,000 metric tons	11,900	730	11	13,500	[4][25]38.00	3,100
Talc	1,000 metric tons	1,060	197	[5]	955	[4]122	750
Tin (contained)	Metric tons	[11]11,000	4,500	85	49,000	[2]2.65	(NA)
Titanium dioxide	Metric tons	1,330	368	[5]	1,150	[2][26]0.93	4,600
Tungsten (contained)	Metric tons	(D)	20	85	11,400	[27]6.60	60
Vermiculite	1,000 metric tons	(D)	8	(D)	(D)	(D)	230
Zinc (contained)	1,000 metric tons	607	427	35	1,500	[2]0.810	2,700
Zirconium (ZrO2) content	Metric tons	(D)	26,590	(D)	(D)	[4][28]400	(NA)

- Represents or rounds to zero. D Withheld to avoid disclosure. NA Not available. [1] Calculated as a percent of apparent consumption. [2] Price per pound. [3] Refinery production. [4] Price per metric ton. [5] Net exporter. [6] Metal, vacuum-cast ingot. [7] Granulated pentahydrate borax in bulk, f.o.b mine. [8] Dollars per kilogram. [9] Cents per kilogram, bulk, purified bromine. [10] 1- to 5-short ton lots. [11] Secondary production. [12] Turkish, chromite price. [13] Value of imports per carat. [14] Zone refined, first reduction quality. [15] Price per troy ounce. [16] Price of flake imports. [17] Delivered, No. 1 Heavy Melting composite price. [18] Year-end price. [19] Dealer price of platinum. [20] Price of K_2O, muriate. [21] Vacuum and open pan, bulk, pellets and packaged, f.o.b. mine and plant. [22] Ferrosilicon, 50% Si. [23] Quoted year-end price, dense, bulk, f.o.b. Green river, WY, dollars per short ton. [24] Quoted price, bulk, f.o.b. works, East, dollars per short ton. [25] Rutile, list, year-end. [26] Dollars per unit W03 (7.93 kilograms of contained tungsten per unit). [27] All forms. [28] Price for imported zircon, f.o.b. U.S. east coast.

Source: U.S. Geological Survey, *Mineral Commodity Summaries,* annual.

No. 1171. Selected Mineral Products—Average Prices: 1980 to 1998

[Excludes Alaska and Hawaii, except as noted]

Year	Nonfuels								Fuels		
	Copper, electro-lytic [1] (cents per lb.)	Plati-num [2] (dol./ troy oz.)	Gold (dol./ fine oz.)	Silver (dol./ fine oz.)	Lead [3] (cents per lb.)	Tin (New York) [4] (cents per lb.)	Zinc [5] (cents per lb.)	Sulfur, crude [6] (dol./ metric ton)	Bitumi-nous coal [7] (dol./ short ton)	Crude petro-leum [7] (dol./ bbl.)	Natural gas [7] (dol./ 1,000 cu. ft.)
1980	101	677	613	20.63	43	846	37	89.06	24.52	21.59	1.59
1981	84	446	460	10.52	37	733	45	111.48	26.29	31.77	1.98
1982	73	327	376	7.95	26	654	39	108.27	27.14	28.52	2.46
1983	77	424	424	11.44	22	655	41	87.24	25.85	26.19	2.59
1984	67	357	361	8.14	26	624	49	94.31	25.51	25.88	2.66
1985	67	291	318	6.14	19	596	40	106.46	25.10	24.09	2.51
1986	66	461	368	5.47	22	383	38	105.22	23.70	12.51	1.94
1987	83	553	478	7.01	36	419	42	89.78	23.00	15.40	1.67
1988	121	523	438	6.53	37	441	60	85.95	22.00	12.58	1.69
1989	131	507	383	5.50	39	520	82	86.62	21.76	15.86	1.69
1990	123	467	385	4.82	46	386	75	80.14	21.71	20.03	1.71
1991	109	371	363	4.04	34	363	53	71.45	21.45	16.54	1.64
1992	107	360	345	3.94	35	402	58	48.14	20.99	15.99	1.74
1993	92	374	361	4.30	32	350	46	31.86	19.79	14.25	2.04
1994	111	411	385	5.29	37	369	49	28.60	19.34	13.19	1.85
1995	138	425	386	5.15	42	416	56	43.74	18.74	14.62	1.55
1996	109	398	390	5.19	49	412	51	34.48	18.42	18.46	2.17
1997	107	397	333	4.9	47	381	65	38.00	18.11	17.23	2.32
1998	80	406	300	5.1	45	377	52	(NA)	17.51	10.88	196.00

NA Not available. [1] Domestic market prices for wirebar, 1970, 1975-77; prices for cathode thereafter. [2] Average annual dealer prices. [3] 1970, New York prices; beginning 1975, nationwide delivered basis. [4] Straits tin through 1975; thereafter, composite price. [5] Prime western. Beginning 1975, delivered price. [6] F.o.b. works. [7] Average value at the point of production or domestic first purchase price. [8] Includes lignite.

Source: Nonfuels, through 1994, U.S. Bureau of Mines, thereafter, U.S. Geological Survey, *Minerals Yearbook* and *Mineral Commodities Summaries*, annual; fuels, U.S. Energy Information Administration, *Annual Energy Review* and *Monthly Energy Review.*

No. 1172. Value of Domestic Nonfuel Mineral Production, by State: 1990 to 1998

[In millions of dollars (33,445 represents $33,445,000,000). Data may not add due to rounding]

State	1990	1995	1997	1998	State	1990	1995	1997	1998
United States ..	33,445	38,506	40,471	40,034	Missouri	1,105	1,140	1,310	1,360
					Montana	573	574	498	500
Alabama	559	706	881	947	Nebraska	90	146	165	174
Alaska	577	538	958	911	Nevada	2,621	3,060	3,270	3,100
Arizona	3,085	4,190	3,540	2,820	New Hampshire.....	36	50	[1]49	[1]53
Arkansas	381	492	487	598	New Jersey	229	243	267	[1]301
California	2,771	2,760	3,040	2,970					
					New Mexico	1,103	1,130	1,040	860
Colorado	377	570	524	604	New York	773	886	955	939
Connecticut	122	93	[1]80	[1]105	North Carolina......	586	735	741	785
Delaware [2]	10	[2]9	[2]12	[2]11	North Dakota	25	31	34	35
Florida	1,574	1,540	1,830	1,960	Ohio	733	891	1,040	1,150
Georgia	1,504	1,690	1,680	2,140					
					Oklahoma	259	357	386	408
Hawaii	106	114	[1]94	86	Oregon	205	239	285	272
Idaho...........	375	510	469	444	Pennsylvania	1,031	1,080	1,200	1,280
Illinois	667	828	829	862	Rhode Island	18	31	[1]27	[1]28
Indiana	428	589	670	698	South Carolina	450	447	567	589
Iowa	310	456	486	524					
					South Dakota	319	332	328	269
Kansas	349	498	539	535	Tennessee	663	665	707	709
Kentucky	359	432	498	489	Texas	1,459	1,680	1,790	1,920
Louisiana	368	434	402	379	Utah	1,335	1,850	1,680	1,300
Maine	55	68	70	76	Vermont..........	87	60	[1]84	[1]96
Maryland	368	324	371	358					
					Virginia	507	515	642	679
Massachusetts	128	190	193	192	Washington	483	582	555	583
Michigan	1,440	1,520	1,660	1,660	West Virginia	133	181	205	204
Minnesota	1,482	1,530	1,680	1,560	Wisconsin........	215	416	358	261
Mississippi	111	131	175	190	Wyoming	911	973	1,120	1,060

[1] Partial data only. [2] Includes District of Columbia.

Source: 1990, U.S. Bureau of Mines, *Minerals Yearbook,* annual, and *Mineral Commodities Summaries,* annual; thereafter, U.S. Geological Survey.

No. 1173. Principal Fuels, Nonmetals, and Metals—World Production and the U.S. Share: 1980 to 1998

Mineral	Unit	World production				Percent U.S. of world			
		1980	1990	1995	1998, prel.	1980	1990	1995	1998, prel.
Fuels: [1]									
Coal	Mil. sh. ton	4,193	5,353	5,134	[2]5,218	19.8	19.2	20.1	[2]20.9
Petroleum (crude)	Bil. bbl	21.8	22.1	22.8	24.4	14.4	12.1	10.5	9.4
Natural gas (dry, marketable)	Tril. cu. ft	53.5	73.6	77.9	[2]81.7	36.3	24.2	23.9	[2]23.1
Natural gas plant liquids	Bil. bbl	1.3	1.7	2.0	[2]2.1	45.7	33.7	32.1	[2]31.6
Nonmetals:									
Asbestos	1,000 metric tons	4,699	4,003	2,420	1,950	2	(D)	(Z)	(Z)
Barite	1,000 metric tons	7,495	5,633	4,300	6,200	27	8	13	11
Feldspar	1,000 metric tons	3,202	5,456	6,780	8,100	20	12	13	10
Fluorspar	1,000 metric tons	5,006	5,131	4,050	4,540	2	1	1	-
Gypsum	Mil. metric tons	78	100	97	105	14	15	17	18
Mica (incl. scrap)	1,000 metric tons	228	215	253	281	46	51	43	29
Nitrogen, (fixed) - ammonia	Mil. metric tons	74	97	96	101	20	13	14	13
Phosphate rock, gross wt.	Mil. metric tons	144	162	130	141	38	29	33	32
Potash (K_2O equivalent)	Mil. metric tons	28	28	25	25	8	6	6	5
Sulfur, elemental	Mil. metric tons	55	58	53	54	22	20	22	21
Metals, mine basis:									
Bauxite	Mil. metric tons	89	109	107	125	2	(D)	(D)	(D)
Columbian concentrates (Nb content)	1,000 metric tons	15	15	18	20	-	-	-	-
Copper	1,000 metric tons	7,405	9,017	10,100	11,900	16	18	18	17
Gold	Metric tons	1,219	2,133	2,220	2,400	2	14	14	15
Iron ore	Mil. metric tons	891	982	1,027	1,020	8	6	6	6
Lead [2]	1,000 metric tons	3,470	3,353	2,780	3,080	17	15	14	16
Mercury	Metric tons	6,806	4,523	3,160	2,600	16	12	(D)	(D)
Molybdenum	1,000 metric tons	111	128	141	136	62	48	43	39
Nickel [2]	1,000 metric tons	779	965	1,030	1,170	2	(Z)	(Z)	(Z)
Silver	1,000 metric tons	11	16	15	16	9	13	10	-
Tantalum concentrates	Metric tons	544	400	362	412	-	-	-	-
Titanium concentrates:									
Ilmenite	1,000 metric tons	3,726	4,072	3,970	4,000	14	(D)	(D)	(D)
Rutile	1,000 metric tons	436	481	416	414	(D)	(D)	(D)	(D)
Tungsten [2]	1,000 metric tons	52	43	39	34	5	14	(D)	(D)
Vanadium [2]	1,000 metric tons	37	31	35	35	12	(D)	(D)	(D)
Zinc [2]	1,000 metric tons	5,954	7,184	7,240	7,800	6	8	9	-
Metals, smelter basis:									
Aluminum	1,000 metric tons	15,383	19,292	19,900	22,200	30	21	17	17
Cadmium	1,000 metric tons	18	20	19	20	9	8	7	10
Copper	1,000 metric tons	7,649	9,472	10,200	11,900	14	15	16	16
Iron, pig	Mil. metric tons	514	532	533	544	12	9	10	9
Lead [3]	1,000 metric tons	5,430	5,763	5,590	3,080	23	23	25	24
Magnesium [4]	1,000 metric tons	316	354	389	389	49	39	37	30
Raw Steel	Mil. metric tons	717	771	755	783	14	12	13	13
Tin [5]	1,000 metric tons	251	223	201	216	1	-	-	-
Zinc	1,000 metric tons	6,049	7,060	7,550	7,800	6	5	5	9

- Represents or rounds to zero.   D Withheld to avoid disclosing company data.   Z Less than half the unit of measure. [1] Source: Energy Information Administration, *International Energy Annual*.   [2] Content of ore and concentrate.   [3] Refinery production.   [4] Primary production; no smelter processing necessary.   [5] Production from primary sources only.

Source: Nonfuels, through 1994, U.S. Bureau of Mines, thereafter, U.S. Geological Survey, *Minerals Yearbook*, annual, and *Mineral Commodities Summaries*, annual; fuels, U.S. Energy Information Administration, *Annual Energy Review. International Energy Annual 1997*, and *Monthly Energy Review*.

No. 1174. Federal Strategic and Critical Materials Inventory: 1990 to 1997

[As of **Dec. 31.** Covers strategic and critical materials essential to military and industrial requirements in time of national emergency]

Mineral	Unit	Quantity [1]				Value (mil. dol.) [2]			
		1990	1995	1996	1997	1990	1995	1996	1997
Tin	1,000 metric ton	169	130	116	104	962	908	712	651
Silver	1,000 troy oz	92,151	46,667	46,667	39,152	374	158	158	96
Cobalt	Mil. lb	53	44	40	38	443	1,121	872	900
Bauxite [3]	1,000 lg. ton	18,033	16,032	15,380	14,006	888	203	207	111
Manganese [4]	1,000 sh. ton	4,017	2,817	2,683	2,691	962	464	464	330
Tungsten [5]	Mil. lb	82	82	82	82	253	253	323	283
Zinc	1,000 sh. ton	379	301	286	244	483	281	272	256
Titanium	1,000 sh. ton	37	37	37	37	402	221	249	249
Platinum	1,000 troy oz	453	453	432	440	186	154	134	162
Chromium [6]	1,000 sh. ton	1,074	1,192	1,145	1,128	917	839	980	1,125
Diamonds:									
Stones	Carat 1,000	7,777	5,135	4,655	3,751	267	52	78	99
Industrial, bort	Carat 1,000	17,353	1,967	816	62	16	9	4	4

[1] Consists of stockpile and nonstockpile grades and reflects uncommitted balances.   [2] Market values are estimated trade values of similar materials and not necessarily amounts that would be realized at time of sale.   [3] Consists of abrasive grade, metallic grade Jamaica, metallic grade Suriname, and refractory.   [4] Consists of chemical grade, dioxide battery natural, dioxide battery synthetic, electrolytic, ferro-high carbon, ferro-med. carbon, ferro-silicon, and metal.   [5] Consists of carbide powder, ferro, metal powder, and ores and concentrates.   [6] Consists of ferro-high carbon, ferro-low carbon, ferro-silicon, and metal.

Source: U.S. Defense Logistics Agency, *Statistical Supplement, Stockpile Report to the Congress* (AP-3).

U.S. Census Bureau, *Statistical Abstract of the United States: 1999*

No. 1175. Net U.S. Imports of Selected Minerals and Metals as Percent of Apparent Consumption: 1980 to 1998

[In percent. Based on net imports which equal the difference between imports and exports plus or minus Government stockpile and industry stock changes]

Mineral	1980	1990	1992	1993	1994	1995	1996	1997	1998
Bauxite [1]	94	98	100	100	99	99	100	100	100
Columbium	100	100	100	100	100	100	100	100	100
Manganese	98	100	100	100	100	100	100	100	100
Mica (sheet) . . .	100	100	100	100	100	100	100	100	100
Strontium	100	100	100	100	100	100	100	100	100
Tin.	79	71	80	84	83	84	83	86	85
Barite.	44	71	52	72	64	65	70	76	80
Cobalt	93	86	85	85	80	80	80	80	80
Potash	65	68	68	72	76	75	77	80	80
Tantalum	90	71	73	81	75	80	79	75	79
Tungsten	53	81	86	81	95	90	89	84	78
Chromium.	91	84	76	79	81	81	78	77	77
Nickel.	76	64	59	63	64	60	59	54	65
Titanium	32	(3)	(D)	(D)	(D)	64	50	63	49
Zinc [2].	60	41	33	36	35	35	33	35	35
Aluminum	(3)	36	31	31	31	29	27	27	26
Cadmium	55	(3)	1	19	30	23	22	23	25
Gypsum	35	46	50	64	3	21	32	16	21
Copper.	16	15	20	12	12	21	13	13	18
Iron and steel . .	13	13	13	15	22	21	20	20	18
Sulfur.	14	21	12	14	18	14	14	14	17
Iron ore	25	3	2	7	13	7	14	13	16
Silver.	7	(NA)	(NA)	(NA)	(NA)	(NA)	(NA)	(3)	(3)
Platinum group .	87	88	(NA)	(NA)	(NA)	(NA)	(NA)	(NA)	(NA)
Mercury	27	(D)	(D)	(D)	(D)	(D)	(D)	(D)	(D)
Selenium	59	46	48	39	31	31	38	(D)	(D)
Vanadium	35	(D)	(D)	(D)	(D)	(D)	(D)	(D)	(D)

D Withheld to avoid disclosure.   NA Not available.   [1] Includes alumina.   [2] Beginning 1990, effect of sharp rise in exports of concentrates. If calculated on a refined zinc-only basis, reliance would be about the same as pre-1990 level; 1990, 64%; 1991, 61%; 1992, 61%; 1993, 67%; 1994,70%; 1995, 71%; and 1996 and 1997, 70%.   [3] Net exports.

Source: Through 1994, U.S. Bureau of Mines; thereafter, U.S. Geological Survey, *Mineral Commodity Summaries;* import and export data from U.S. Census Bureau.

No. 1176. Federal Offshore Leasing, Exploration, Production, and Revenue: 1990 to 1998

[See source for explanation of terms and for reliability statement]

Item	Unit	1990	1992	1993	1994	1995	1996	1997	1998
Tracts offered	Number. .	10,459	9,618	10,164	10,861	10,995	12,230	9,870	(NA)
Tracts leased	Number. .	825	204	336	560	835	1,537	1,780	(NA)
Acres offered	1,000 . .	56,789	52,380	55,070	58,895	59,700	69,994	53,397	(NA)
Acres leased.	1,000 . .	4,263	1,021	1,714	2,775	4,342	8,249	9,637	(NA)
Bonus paid for leased tracts . .	Bil. dol. . .	0.6	0.1	0.1	0.3	0.4	0.9	(NA)	(NA)
New wells being drilled:									
Active.	Number. .	120	104	129	120	124	835	186	(NA)
Suspended	Number. .	266	180	193	222	247	1,323	244	(NA)
Wells completed	Number. .	13,167	13,209	13,181	13,342	13,475	1,527	12,912	(NA)
Wells plugged and abandoned .	Number. .	14,677	16,348	16,709	17,427	18,008	18,268	18,728	19,374
Revenue, total [1]	Bil. dol. . .	3.4	2.6	2.9	2.6	2.6	3.9	4.8	3.5
Bonuses.	Bil. dol. . .	0.6	0.1	0.1	0.3	0.4	0.6	1.2	0.3
Oil and gas royalties [1].	Bil. dol. . .	2.6	2.3	2.5	2.3	2.1	3.0	3.5	3.0
Rentals.	Bil. dol. . .	0.1	0.1	(Z)	(Z)	0.9	0.1	0.1	0.2
Sales value [2]	Bil. dol. . .	17.0	15.1	16.4	15.0	13.8	27.6	31.1	26.5
Crude oil.	Bil. dol. . .	5.9	5.3	4.9	4.4	5.4	6.4	7.5	6.0
Condensate.	Bil. dol. . .	1.1	1.0	0.9	0.7	0.9	1.3	1.4	1.2
Natural gas	Bil. dol. . .	9.5	8.2	9.9	9.8	7.5	11.8	13.3	12.1
Sales volume:									
Crude oil.	Mil. bbls. .	274	302	307	319	357	373	404	423
Condensate.	Mil. bbls. .	51	52	55	51	50	52	65	81
Natural gas	Bil. cu. ft .	5,093	4,686	4,533	4,700	4,692	5,024	5,077	4,959

NA Not available.   Z Less than $50 million.   [1] Includes condensate royalties.   [2] Production value is value at time of production, not current value.

Source: U.S. Dept. of the Interior, Minerals Management Service, *Federal Offshore Statistics,* annual.

No. 1177. Petroleum Industry—Summary: 1980 to 1998

[Includes all costs incurred for drilling and equipping wells to point of completion as productive wells or abandonment after drilling becomes unproductive. Based on sample of operators of different size drilling establishments]

Item	Unit	1980	1990	1992	1993	1994	1995	1996	1997	1998
Crude oil producing wells (Dec. 31).	1,000...	548	602	594	584	582	574	574	573	554
Daily output per well.........	Bbl.....	15.9	12.2	12.1	11.7	11.4	11.4	11.3	11.3	11.4
Completed wells drilled, total.....	1,000...	57.5	24.9	18.5	20.1	17.1	16.7	18.14	20.9	(NA)
Crude oil................	1,000...	30.8	10.9	7.8	7.4	5.8	6.7	7.18	8.1	(NA)
Gas.................	1,000...	15.2	9.5	7.3	9.1	8.6	7.3	8.00	9.7	(NA)
Dry................	1,000...	11.6	4.5	3.5	3.6	2.8	2.8	3.0	3.2	(NA)
Average depth per well [1]........	Feet ...	4,174	4,614	5,173	5,410	5,787	5,432	5,374	5,485	(NA)
Average cost per well [1].........	$1,000..	368	384	383	427	483	513	496.1	(NA)	(NA)
Average cost per foot [1]......	Dollars..	77.02	76.07	70.27	75.30	79.49	87	88.92	(NA)	(NA)
Crude oil production, total.......	Mil. bbl..	3,138	2,685	2,617	2,499	2,432	2,406	2,366	2,355	2,282
Value at wells...........	Bil. dol..	67.7	53.8	41.8	35.6	32.1	35.0	43.6	40.6	24.8
Average price per barrel.....	Dollars..	21.59	20.03	15.99	14.25	13.19	14.62	18.46	17.23	10.88
Lower 48 states............	Mil. bbl..	2,548	2,037	1,992	1,921	1,863	1,853	1,851	1,882	1,853
Alaska.................	Mil. bbl..	590	647	626	577	569	542	508	473	429
Onshore................	Mil. bbl..	2,760	2,290	2,173	2,046	1,931	1,838	1,789	1,753	1,672
Offshore...............	Mil. bbl..	377	395	445	453	500	557	570	602	607
Imports: Crude oil...........	Mil. bbl..	1,921	2,151	2,220	2,477	2,578	2,639	2,740	2,919	3,178
Refined petroleum products....	Mil. bbl..	601	775	659	669	706	719	707	731	
Exports: Crude oil...........	Mil. bbl..	104.8	39.8	32.5	35.8	36.1	34.7	40.2	39.4	40.1
Proved reserves.............	Bil. bbl..	29.8	26.3	23.7	23.0	22.5	22.40	22.02	22.55	(NA)
Operable refineries..........	Number	319	205	199	187	179	175	170	164	163
Capacity (Jan. 1)..........	Mil. bbl..	6,566	5,683	5,731	5,519	5,486	5,632	5,595	5,639	5,734
Refinery input, total.........	Mil. bbl..	5,117	5,325	5,340	5,482	5,482	5,555	5,654	5,807	5,869
Crude oil............	Mil. bbl..	4,920	4,895	4,895	4,968	5,063	5,099	5,179	5,351	5,417
Natural gas plant liquids.....	Mil. bbl..	168	172	172	179	172	172	164	153	150
Other liquids..........	Mil. bbl..	29	259	274	336	252	285	307	303	303
Refinery output, total.........	Mil. bbl..	5,336	5,574	5,621	5,763	5,763	5,836	5,957	6,117	6,190
Motor gasoline..........	Mil. bbl..	2,369	2,540	2,577	2,665	2,621	2,723	2,759	2,825	2,865
Jet fuel.............	Mil. bbl..	365	544	511	518	529	518	555	566	555
Distillate fuel oil..........	Mil. bbl..	971	1,066	1,084	1,142	1,168	1,153	1,212	1,237	1,248
Residual fuel oil..........	Mil. bbl..	577	347	325	307	303	288	266	259	277
Liquefied petroleum gases ...	Mil. bbl..	120	183	223	215	223	237	1,212	1,237	1,248
Utilization rate.............	Percent .	75.4	87.1	87.9	91.5	92.6	92.0	94.1	95.2	95.4

NA Not available. [1] Source: American Petroleum Institute, *Joint Association Survey on Drilling Costs*, annual.

Source: Except as noted, U.S. Energy Information Administration, *Annual Energy Review, Petroleum Supply Annual; U.S. Crude Oil, Natural Gas, and Natural Gas Liquids Reserves*; and *Monthly Energy Review*.

No. 1178. U.S. Petroleum Balance: 1980 to 1998

[In millions of barrels (6,242 represents 6,242,000,000)]

Item	1980	1990	1993	1994	1995	1996	1997	1998
Petroleum products supplied for domestic use	**6,242**	**6,201**	**6,291**	**6,467**	**7,087**	**6,701**	**6,796**	**6,905**
Production of products	5,765	5,934	6,182	6,244	6,940	6,511	6,671	6,733
Crude input to refineries	4,934	4,894	4,969	5,061	5,718	5,195	5,351	5,434
Oil, field production..............	3,138	2,685	2,499	2,431	2,406	2,366	2,355	2,282
Alaska................	592	647	577	569	542	510	473	429
Lower 48 States	2,555	2,037	1,922	1,863	1,853	1,856	1,882	1,853
Net imports	1,821	2,112	2,441	2,542	2,604	2,708	2,963	3,137
Imports (gross excluding SPR) [1]	1,910	2,142	2,472	2,574	2,639	2,748	3,002	3,178
SPR [1] imports	16	10	5	4	-	-	-	-
Exports	-105	40	36	36	35	40	39	40
Other sources	33	98	28	88	102	122	34	15
Natural gas liquids (NGL), supply	577	574	664	694	708	716	721	717
Other liquids	253	465	550	489	514	599	599	582
Net imports of refined products	484	326	134	217	101	181	154	225
Imports	578	598	461	518	407	491	469	508
Exports	94	272	327	302	307	310	315	283
Stock withdrawal, refined products	-7	-59	-24	6	46	9	-29	-53
TYPE OF PRODUCT SUPPLIED								
Total products supplied for domestic use	**6,242**	**6,201**	**6,291**	**6,467**	**6,469**	**6,701**	**6,796**	**6,905**
Finished motor gasoline	2,407	2,641	2,729	2,774	2,843	2,888	2,926	3,012
Distillate fuel oil................	1,049	1,103	1,110	1,154	1,170	1,232	1,254	1,263
Residual fuel oil	918	449	394	373	311	311	291	324
Liquified petroleum gases [2]...........	414	568	633	686	693	736	744	713
Other	1,454	1,440	1,425	1,480	1,452	1,535	1,582	1,593
ENDING STOCKS								
Ending stocks, all oils	**1,392**	**1,621**	**1,647**	**1,653**	**1,563**	**1,052**	**1,560**	**1,647**
Crude oil and lease condensate.......	358	323	335	337	303	284	305	324
Strategic Petroleum Reserve (SPR) [1]	108	586	587	592	592	566	563	571
Other	926	712	725	724	668	202	692	752

- Represents zero. [1] SPR=Strategic petroleum reserve. For more information, see Table 968. [2] Includes ethane.

Source: U.S. Energy Information Administration, *Petroleum Supply Annual*.

Natural Resources **711**

No. 1179. Crude Petroleum and Natural Gas—Production and Value, by Major Producing States: 1990 to 1997

[2,685 mil. bbl. represents 2,685,000,000 bbl. or 18,594 bil. cu. ft. represents 18,594,000,000,000 cu. ft.]

State	Crude petroleum						Natural gas marketed production [1]					
	Quantity (mil. bbl.)			Value (mil. dol.)			Quantity (bil. cu. ft.)			Value (mil. dol.)		
	1990	1995	1997	1990	1995	1997	1990	1995	1997	1990	1995	1997
Total [2] ...	2,685	2,406	2,355	53,772	35,004	40,574	18,594	19,506	19,865	31,658	30,286	46,131
AL......	18	19	15	387	306	276	135	520	583	373	948	1,557
AK......	658	542	473	10,086	6,088	7,050	403	470	468	554	771	850
AR......	10	9	8	222	132	148	175	187	209	360	565	841
CA......	322	279	285	5,732	3,906	4,500	363	280	286	857	483	687
CO......	31	29	26	722	466	487	243	523	637	377	497	1,418
FL......	6	6	6	(NA)	(NA)	(NA)	6	6	6	15	8	(NA)
IL.......	20	16	16	467	274	308	1	-	-	1	(Z)	(NA)
IN.......	3	3	2	73	47	46	(Z)	-	1	1	-	1
KS......	59	44	40	1,359	709	742	574	721	687	893	985	1,406
KY......	5	3	3	124	57	54	75	75	80	169	123	212
LA......	148	131	134	3,409	2,096	2,578	5,242	5,108	5,230	9,587	8,048	12,352
MI......	20	11	10	458	189	188	140	238	306	420	399	670
MS......	30	20	21	630	294	356	95	96	107	167	118	186
MT......	20	17	16	429	247	264	50	50	52	90	68	84
NE......	5	4	3	119	58	60	1	2	2	2	3	3
NM......	66	65	70	1,472	1,080	1,328	965	1,626	1,559	1,629	2,056	2,750
NY......	(Z)	-	-	9	-	5	25	18	16	55	42	41
ND......	39	29	36	849	457	632	52	49	52	93	(NA)	113
OH......	8	8	9	196	138	153	155	126	116	393	294	314
OK......	117	88	83	2,690	1,459	1,588	2,258	1,812	1,704	3,548	2,616	3,960
PA......	2	2	1	54	33	25	178	111	80	417	315	(NA)
TX......	674	560	537	15,060	9,167	10,013	6,343	6,330	6,454	9,939	10,208	15,976
UT......	23	20	19	524	354	359	146	241	257	249	277	478
WV......	2	2	2	43	32	26	178	186	172	568	414	(NA)
WY......	103	79	70	2,169	1,223	1,222	736	674	738	856	1,198	1,790

- Represents zero.   NA Not available.   Z Less than 500 million cubic feet or less than $500,000.   [1] Excludes nonhydrocarbon gases.   [2] Includes other states not shown separately. State production does not include state offshore production.

Source: U.S. Energy Information Administration, *Petroleum Supply Annual*, and *Petroleum Marketing Annual; and Natural Gas Annual*, and *Natural Gas Monthly*.

No. 1180. Crude Oil, Natural Gas, and Natural Gas Liquids—Reserves by State: 1990 and 1997

[As of **December 31.** Proved reserves are estimated quantities of the mineral, which geological and engineering data demonstrate with reasonable certainty, to be recoverable in future years from known reservoirs under existing economic and operating conditions. Indicated reserves of crude oil are quantities other than proved reserves, which may become economically recoverable from existing productive reservoirs through the application of improved recovery techniques using current technology. Based on a sample of operators of oil and gas wells]

Area	1990				1997			
	Crude oil		Natural gas (bil. cu. ft.)	Natural gas liquids (mil. bbl.)	Crude oil		Natural gas (bil. cu. ft.)	Natural gas liquids (mil. bbl.)
	Proved (mil. bbl.)	Indicated (mil. bbl.)			Proved (mil. bbl.)	Indicated (mil. bbl.)		
United States	26,254	3,483	169,346	7,586	22,546	3,207	167,223	7,973
Lower 48 States	19,730	2,514	160,046	7,246	17,385	2,375	156,661	7,342
Alabama............	44	(Z)	[4]4,125	170	47	-	4,968	93
Alaska	6,524	969	9,300	340	5,161	832	10,562	631
Arkansas	60	1	1,731	9	45	-	1,475	7
California	[2]4,658	[2]1,425	[2]3,185	[2]105	[2]3,750	1,264	2,273	95
Colorado...........	305	8	4,555	169	198	22	6,828	264
Florida	(NA)	(NA)	(NA)	(NA)	91	-	96	17
Illinois	131	-	(NA)	(NA)	92	-	(NA)	(NA)
Indiana.............	(NA)	-	(NA)	(NA)	10	-	(NA)	(NA)
Kansas.............	(NA)	(NA)	(NA)	(NA)	238	-	6,989	271
Kentucky	321	(Z)	9,614	313	20	-	1,364	48
Louisiana	33	-	1,016	25	714	313	9,673	437
Michigan...........	(NA)	(NA)	(NA)	(NA)	68	2	2,195	50
Mississippi	(NA)	(NA)	(NA)	(NA)	183	-	582	6
Montana...........	(NA)	(NA)	(NA)	(NA)	159	1	762	5
Nebraska	221	-	899	15	21	-	(NA)	(NA)
New Mexico	(NA)	(NA)	(NA)	(NA)	735	146	15,514	869
New York	687	256	17,260	990	(NA)	(NA)	224	(NA)
North Dakota.......	285	-	586	60	279	6	479	47
Ohio	65	-	1,214	(NA)	43	-	985	(NA)
Oklahoma..........	734	37	16,151	657	605	20	13,439	685
Pennsylvania	22	-	1,720	(NA)	17	-	1,852	(NA)
Texas..............	[2]7,106	618	[2]38,192	[2]2,575	[2]5,687	479	37,761	2,687
Utah	249	44	1,510	[3]	234	70	1,839	[3]
Virginia............	(NA)	(NA)	138	(NA)	(NA)	(NA)	2,446	(NA)
West Virginia........	31	-	2,207	86	26	-	2,846	71
Wyoming	794	42	9,944	[4]812	627	11	13,562	761
Federal offshore.......	2,805	49	31,433	619	3,477	41	28,466	920

- Represents or rounds to zero.   NA Not available.   Z Less than 500,000 barrels.   [1] Includes state offshore.   [2] Excludes Federal offshore.   [3] Included with Wyoming.   [4] Includes Utah.

Source: Energy Information Administration, *U.S. Crude Oil, Natural Gas, and Natural Gas Liquids Reserves, Annual Report 1997*, December 1998.

712 Natural Resources

No. 1181. World Crude Oil Production, by Major Producing Country: 1980 to 1997

[In thousands of barrels per day (59,600 barrels represents 59,600,000 barrels)]

Country	1980	1990	1991	1992	1993	1994	1995	1996	1997
World, total [1]	59,600	60,566	60,207	60,213	60,236	60,991	62,335	63,711	66,420
Saudi Arabia	9,900	6,410	8,115	8,332	8,198	8,120	8,231	8,218	8,562
United States	8,597	7,355	7,417	7,171	6,847	6,662	6,560	6,465	6,452
Russia	(X)	(X)	(X)	7,632	6,730	6,135	5,995	5,850	5,920
Iran	1,662	3,088	3,312	3,429	3,540	3,618	3,643	3,686	3,664
Venezuela.	2,168	2,137	2,375	2,371	2,450	2,588	2,750	2,938	3,315
China.	2,114	2,774	2,835	2,845	2,890	2,939	2,990	3,131	3,200
Norway.	528	1,704	1,890	2,229	2,350	2,521	2,768	3,104	3,143
Mexico	1,936	2,553	2,680	2,669	2,673	2,685	2,618	2,855	3,023
United Kingdom	1,622	1,820	1,797	1,825	1,915	2,375	2,489	2,568	2,518
Nigeria	2,055	1,810	1,892	1,943	1,960	1,931	1,993	2,001	2,332
United Arab Emirates	1,709	2,117	2,386	2,266	2,159	2,193	2,233	2,278	2,316
Kuwait	1,656	1,175	190	1,058	1,852	2,025	2,057	2,062	2,083
Canada	1,435	1,553	1,548	1,605	1,679	1,746	1,805	1,837	1,922
Indonesia	1,577	1,462	1,592	1,504	1,511	1,510	1,503	1,547	1,520
Libya	1,787	1,375	1,483	1,433	1,361	1,378	1,390	1,401	1,446
Algeria	1,106	1,175	1,230	1,214	1,162	1,180	1,202	1,242	1,277
Iraq	2,514	2,040	305	425	512	553	560	579	1,155
Oman	282	685	700	740	776	810	851	883	904
Egypt.	595	873	874	881	890	896	920	922	856
Brazil	182	631	630	626	643	671	695	795	841
Argentina	491	483	485	553	594	650	715	756	834
Malaysia.	283	619	646	653	640	645	682	695	746
Angola	150	475	500	526	509	536	646	709	714
India	182	660	615	561	534	590	703	651	675
Colombia	126	440	419	433	456	450	585	623	652
Qatar.	472	406	395	423	413	415	442	510	649
Australia	380	575	545	535	503	536	562	570	588
Syria	164	388	492	481	554	560	575	582	561

X Not applicable. [1] Includes countries not shown separately.

Source: U. S. Energy Information Administration, *International Energy Annual, 1997.*

No. 1182. Liquefied Petroleum Gases—Summary: 1980 to 1998

[In millions of 42-gallon barrels (561 barrels represents 561,000,000 barrels). Includes ethane]

Item	1980	1990	1992	1993	1994	1995	1996	1997	1998
Production.	561	638	720	850	734	760	789	799	775
At natural gas plants	441	456	500	634	511	521	547	547	529
At refineries	121	182	222	216	223	234	242	252	246
Imports	79	68	57	70	67	53	61	62	71
Refinery input.	85	107	172	179	108	105	102	96	92
Exports	9	14	18	16	14	21	19	18	15
Stocks, Dec. 31	116	98	98	117	99	93	86	89	115

Source: U.S. Energy Information Administration, *Petroleum Supply Annual.*

No. 1183. Natural Gas Plant Liquids—Production and Value: 1980 to 1998

[Barrels of 42 gallons (576 barrels represents 576,000,000 barrels)]

Item	Unit	1980	1990	1992	1993	1994	1995	1996	1997	1998
Field production [1]	Mil. bbl . . .	576	566	621	634	630	643	670	663	642
Pentanes plus	Mil. bbl . . .	126	112	121	122	119	122	123	116	113
Liquefied petroleum gases .	Mil. bbl . . .	441	454	500	512	511	521	547	547	529
Natural gas processed	Tril. cu. ft. .	15	15	16	16	16	17	17	17	(NA)

NA Not available. [1] Includes other finished petroleum products, not shown separately.

Source: U.S. Energy Information Administration, *Energy Data Reports, Petroleum Statement Annual, Petroleum Supply Annual,* and *Natural Gas Annual.*

Natural Resources 713

No. 1184. Natural Gas—Supply, Consumption, Reserves, and Marketed Production: 1980 to 1998

[182 represents 182,000 wells]

Item	Unit	1980	1990	1991	1992	1993	1994	1995	1996	1997	1998, prel.
Producing wells (year-end)	1,000	182	269	276	276	282	292	299	302	304	330
Production value at wells	Bil. dol	32.1	31.8	30.3	32.6	38.7	36.5	30.2	42.9	46.1	39.1
Avg. per 1,000 cu. ft	Dollars	1.59	1.71	1.64	1.74	2.04	1.85	1.55	2.17	2.32	1.96
Proved reserves [1]	Tril. cu. ft	199	169	167	165	162	164	165	166	167	(NA)
Marketed production [2],[3]	**Tril. cu. ft**	**20.2**	**18.6**	**18.5**	**18.7**	**19.0**	**19.7**	**19.5**	**19.8**	**19.9**	**19.9**
Minus: Extraction losses [3]	Tril. cu. ft	0.8	0.8	0.8	0.9	0.9	0.9	0.9	1.0	1.0	1.0
Equals: Dry production	Tril. cu. ft	19.4	17.8	17.7	17.8	18.1	18.8	18.6	18.8	18.9	19.0
Plus: Withdrawals from storage	Tril. cu. ft	2.0	2.0	2.8	2.8	2.7	2.5	3.0	2.9	2.8	(NA)
Plus: Imports [4]	Tril. cu. ft	1.0	1.5	1.8	2.1	2.4	2.6	2.8	2.9	3.0	(NA)
Plus: Balancing item	Tril. cu. ft	-0.6	-0.2	-0.5	-0.5	-0.1	-0.4	-0.2	0.3	0.1	(NA)
Equals: Total supply	Tril. cu. ft	21.9	21.3	21.8	22.8	23.6	24.2	24.8	25.6	25.5	(NA)
Minus: Exports	Tril. cu. ft	0.5	0.9	0.1	0.2	0.1	0.2	0.2	0.2	0.2	(NA)
Minus: Additions to storage [5]	Tril. cu. ft	1.9	2.5	2.7	2.6	2.8	2.9	2.6	3.0	2.9	(NA)
Equals: Consumption, total	**Tril. cu. ft**	**19.9**	**18.7**	**19.0**	**19.5**	**20.3**	**20.7**	**21.6**	**22.0**	**22.0**	**21.3**
Lease and plant fuel	Tril. cu. ft	1.0	1.2	1.1	1.2	1.2	1.1	1.2	1.3	1.2	(NA)
Pipeline fuel	Tril. cu. ft	0.6	0.7	0.6	0.6	0.6	0.7	0.7	0.7	0.8	(NA)
Residential	Tril. cu. ft	4.8	4.4	4.6	4.7	5.0	4.8	4.9	5.2	5.0	(NA)
Commercial [6]	Tril. cu. ft	2.6	2.6	2.7	2.8	2.9	2.9	3.0	3.2	3.2	(NA)
Industrial	Tril. cu. ft	7.2	7.0	7.2	7.5	8.0	8.2	8.6	8.9	8.8	(NA)
Vehicle fuel	Tril. cu. ft	(NA)	(Z)	(Z)	(Z)	1.0	1.7	2.7	2.9	4.4	(NA)
Electric utilities	Tril. cu. ft	3.7	3.8	2.8	2.8	2.7	3.0	3.2	2.7	3.0	(NA)
World production (dry)	Tril. cu. ft	53.5	73.6	74.8	74.9	76.3	76.8	77.9	81.7	81.7	(NA)
U.S. production (dry)	Tril. cu. ft	19.4	17.8	17.7	17.8	18.1	18.8	18.6	18.8	18.9	(NA)
Percent U.S. of world	Percent	36.3	24.2	23.7	23.8	23.7	24.5	23.9	23.0	23.1	(NA)

NA Not available.   Z Less than .05 trillion cubic feet.   [1] Estimated, end of year. Source: U.S. Energy Information Administration, *U.S. Crude Oil, Natural Gas, and Natural Gas Liquids Reserves, annual.* [2] Marketed production includes gross withdrawals from reservoirs less quantities used for reservoir repressuring and quantities vented or flared. For 1980 and thereafter, it excludes the nonhydrocarbon gases subsequently removed. [3] Volumetric reduction in natural gas resulting from the extraction of natural gas constituents at natural gas processing plants. [4] Includes imports of liquefied natural gas. [5] Includes liquefied natural gas (LNG) storage in above ground tanks. [6] Includes deliveries to municipalities and public authorities for institutional heating and other purposes.

Source: Except as noted, U.S. Energy Information Administration, *Annual Energy Review, International Energy Annual, Natural Gas Annual,* Volumes I and II and *Monthly Energy Review.*

No. 1185. World Natural Gas Production, by Major Producing Country: 1980 to 1997

[In trillion cubic feet (53.45 represents 53,450,000,000,000)]

Country	1980	1990	1991	1992	1993	1994	1995	1996	1997
World, total [1]	**53.45**	**73.61**	**74.81**	**74.87**	**76.30**	**76.80**	**77.92**	**81.66**	**81.71**
Russia	(X)	(X)	(X)	22.62	21.81	21.45	21.01	21.23	20.17
United States	**19.40**	**17.81**	**17.70**	**17.84**	**18.10**	**18.82**	**18.60**	**18.79**	**18.90**
Canada	2.76	3.85	4.06	4.52	4.91	5.26	5.64	5.78	5.85
United Kingdom	1.32	1.75	2.01	1.93	2.31	2.47	2.67	3.18	3.24
Netherlands	3.40	2.69	3.04	3.06	3.11	2.95	2.97	3.37	2.99
Algeria	0.41	1.79	1.93	1.97	1.90	1.81	2.05	2.19	2.47
Indonesia	0.63	1.53	1.72	1.79	1.97	2.21	2.24	2.35	2.37
Uzbekistan	(X)	(X)	(X)	1.51	1.59	1.67	1.70	1.70	1.74
Iran	0.25	0.84	0.92	0.88	0.96	1.12	1.25	1.42	1.60
Norway	0.92	0.98	0.97	1.04	0.97	1.04	1.08	1.45	1.60
Saudi Arabia	0.33	1.08	1.13	1.20	1.27	1.33	1.34	1.46	1.53
Malaysia	0.06	0.65	0.75	0.80	0.88	0.92	1.02	1.23	1.36
United Arab Emirates	0.20	0.78	0.92	1.02	0.94	0.91	1.11	1.19	1.27
Mexico	1.01	0.94	0.94	0.92	0.90	0.91	0.94	1.10	1.19
Australia	0.33	0.72	0.75	0.82	0.86	0.92	1.03	1.05	1.04
Venezuela	0.52	0.76	0.79	0.76	0.82	0.88	0.89	0.96	1.00
Argentina	0.28	0.63	0.70	0.71	0.76	0.79	0.88	0.94	0.97
Turkmenistan	(X)	(X)	(X)	2.02	2.29	1.26	1.14	1.31	0.90
India	0.05	0.40	0.45	0.48	0.53	0.59	0.63	0.70	0.83
Germany	0.93	0.72	0.67	0.68	0.68	0.67	0.71	0.79	0.78
China	0.51	0.51	0.53	0.53	0.56	0.59	0.60	0.67	0.75
Pakistan	0.29	0.48	0.53	0.55	0.58	0.63	0.65	0.70	0.70
Italy	0.44	0.61	0.61	0.64	0.69	0.73	0.72	0.71	0.68
Qatar	0.18	0.28	0.33	0.40	0.48	0.48	0.48	0.48	0.63
Ukraine	(X)	(X)	(X)	0.74	0.68	0.64	0.62	0.64	0.62
Romania	1.20	1.00	0.88	0.78	0.75	0.69	0.68	0.63	0.54
Thailand	-	0.21	0.24	0.25	0.31	0.34	0.37	0.43	0.52
Egypt	0.03	0.29	0.32	0.35	0.40	0.42	0.44	0.47	0.48

- Represents zero.   X Not applicable.   [1] Includes countries not shown separately.

Source: U. S. Energy Information Administration, *International Energy Annual, 1997.*

No. 1186. Coal and Coke—Summary: 1980 to 1998

[(830 short tons represents 830,000,000 short tons). Includes coal consumed at mines. Demonstrated coal reserve base for United States on Jan. 1, 1997, was an estimated 508 billion tons. Recoverability varies between 40 and 90 percent for individual deposits; 50 percent or more of overall U.S. coal reserve base is believed to be recoverable]

Item	Unit	1980	1990	1993	1994	1995	1996	1997	1998, prel.
COAL									
Coal production, total [1]	Mil. sh. tons.	830	1,029	945	1,034	1,033	1,064	1,090	1,119
Value	Mil. dol.	20,453	22,404	18,624	20,076	19,460	19,608	19,800	(NA)
Anthracite production	Mil. sh. tons	6.1	3.5	4.3	4.6	4.7	4.8	(NA)	(NA)
Bituminous coal and lignite:									
Production	Mil. sh. tons	824	1,026	945	1,034	1,033	1,064	1,090	(NA)
Underground	Mil. sh. tons	337	425	351	399	396	410	421	(NA)
Surface	Mil. sh. tons	487	605	594	634	637	654	669	(NA)
Exports	Mil. sh. tons	92	106	75	71	89	90	84	77
Imports	Mil. sh. tons	1.2	2.7	7.3	7.6	7.2	7.1	7.5	8.7
Consumption [2]	Mil. sh. tons	703	896	926	930	941	983	(NA)	(NA)
Electric power utilities	Mil. sh. tons	569	774	814	817	829	875	900	(NA)
Industrial	Mil. sh. tons	126	115	106	107	106	103	(NA)	(NA)
Number of mines	Number	5,598	3,243	2,475	2,354	2,104	1,903	1,828	(NA)
Daily employment	1,000	225	131	101	98	90	83	82	(NA)
Production, by state:									
Alabama	Mil. sh. tons	26	29	25	23	25	25	24	23
Illinois	Mil. sh. tons	63	60	41	53	48	47	41	40
Indiana	Mil. sh. tons	31	36	29	31	26	30	35	37
Kentucky	Mil. sh. tons	150	173	156	162	154	152	156	150
Montana	Mil. sh. tons	30	38	36	42	39	38	41	43
Ohio	Mil. sh. tons	39	35	29	30	26	29	29	28
Pennsylvania	Mil. sh. tons	93	71	60	62	62	68	76	81
Virginia	Mil. sh. tons	41	47	39	37	34	36	36	34
West Virginia	Mil. sh. tons	122	169	131	162	163	170	174	171
Wyoming	Mil. sh. tons	95	184	210	237	264	278	282	314
Other states	Mil. sh. tons	140	187	189	195	192	192	195	198
World production	Mil. sh. tons	4,193	5,353	4,906	5,018	5,134	5,208	5,218	(NA)
COKE									
Coke production [3]	Mil. sh. tons	46.13	27.62	23.18	22.69	23.75	23.08	22.12	(NA)
Imports	Mil. sh. tons	0.66	0.77	1.53	1.61	1.82	1.11	1.57	(NA)
Exports	Mil. sh. tons	2.07	0.57	0.84	0.66	0.75	1.12	0.83	(NA)
Consumption	Mil. sh. tons	41.28	27.82	24.29	24.00	24.45	23.04	22.85	(NA)

NA Not available. [1] Includes bituminous coal, lignite, and anthracite. [2] Includes some categories not shown separately. [3] Includes beehive coke.

Source: U.S. Energy Information Administration, Coal Industry, annual; Annual Energy Review, and Quarterly Coal Report, and unpublished data.

No. 1187. World Coal Production, by Major Producing Country: 1980 to 1997

[In millions of short tons (4,193 represents 4,193,000,000)]

Country	1980	1990	1991	1992	1993	1994	1995	1996	1997
World, total	4,193	5,353	5,029	5,026	4,906	5,018	5,134	5,208	5,218
China	684	1,190	1,199	1,229	1,304	1,404	1,537	1,540	1,553
United States	830	1,029	996	998	945	1,034	1,033	1,064	1,090
India	126	233	253	270	281	291	301	340	329
Australia	116	226	236	249	248	248	267	272	293
Russia	(X)	(X)	(X)	406	364	320	310	304	288
Germany	532	514	388	346	315	292	273	265	252
South Africa	132	193	196	203	207	216	227	227	243
Poland	254	237	231	219	218	220	220	221	220
Canada	40	75	78	72	76	80	83	84	87
Ukraine	(X)	(X)	(X)	147	128	105	93	82	87
Kazakhstan	(X)	(X)	(X)	139	123	120	91	84	80
Czech Republic	(X)	(X)	(X)	(X)	77	82	79	77	72
Korea, North	51	71	73	74	78	78	78	79	68
Greece	26	57	58	61	60	63	64	66	66
Turkey	20	52	51	57	54	60	61	62	62
Indonesia	1	9	14	24	30	34	46	55	60
United Kingdom	144	104	105	94	75	54	52	55	54
Romania	39	43	36	42	43	45	44	51	41
Serbia and Montenegro	(X)	(X)	(X)	47	41	40	44	42	40
Colombia	5	23	26	26	23	25	28	33	36
Spain	41	40	37	37	35	33	31	30	29
Bulgaria	33	35	31	33	32	32	31	32	29
Thailand	2	14	16	17	17	19	20	24	24
Hungary	28	19	19	17	16	16	15	17	17
Vietnam	6	5	5	5	7	6	9	11	11
Mexico	4	9	8	7	8	10	10	10	10

X Not applicable.

Source: U.S. Energy Information Administration, International Energy Annual.

Natural Resources 715

No. 1188. Demonstrated Coal Reserves, by Type of Coal and Major Producing State: 1997

[In millions of short tons (507,740 represents 507,740,000,000). As of January 1. The demonstrated reserve base represents the sum of coal in both measured and indicated resource categories of reliability. Measured resources of coal are estimates that have a high degree of geologic assurance from sample analyses and measurements from closely spaced and geological well known sample sites. Indicated resources are estimates based partly from sample and analyses and measurements and partly from reasonable geologic projections. For more information on the classification of coal resources and related terminology, see report cited below]

State	Total reserves	Type of coal				Method of mining	
		Anthracite	Bituminous	Sub-bituminous	Lignite	Underground	Surface
United States	**507,740**	**7,477**	**270,910**	**185,118**	**44,235**	**341,775**	**165,965**
Alabama	4,547	-	3,464	-	1,083	1,290	3,256
Alaska	6,126	-	698	5,414	14	5,423	703
Colorado	16,756	26	8,711	3,830	4,190	11,979	4,777
Illinois	105,069	-	105,069	-	-	88,461	16,608
Indiana	9,917	-	9,917	-	-	8,860	1,057
Iowa	2,190	-	2,190	-	-	1,733	457
Kentucky	32,041	-	32,041	-	-	18,508	13,533
Kentucky, Eastern	12,086	-	12,086	-	-	2,247	9,839
Kentucky, Western	19,954	-	19,954	-	-	16,261	3,694
Missouri	5,994	-	5,994	-	-	1,479	4,515
Montana	119,677	-	1,385	102,531	15,760	70,958	48,718
New Mexico	12,483	2	3,706	8,774	-	6,204	6,279
North Dakota	9,395	-	-	-	9,395	-	9,395
Ohio	23,664	-	23,664	-	-	17,789	5,875
Oklahoma	1,575	-	1,575	-	-	1,237	338
Pennsylvania	28,646	7,220	21,427	-	-	24,232	4,414
Anthracite	7,220	7,220	-	-	-	3,850	3,370
Bituminous	21,427	-	21,427	-	-	20,382	1,044
Texas	12,931	-	-	-	12,931	-	12,931
Utah	5,850	-	5,849	1	-	5,583	268
Virginia	2,202	126	2,077	-	-	1,528	674
Washington	1,390	-	304	1,078	8	1,332	57
West Virginia	35,397	-	35,397	-	-	30,968	4,429
Wyoming	67,815	-	4,343	63,472	-	42,516	25,299
East of the MS River	243,156	7,345	234,728	-	1,083	192,939	50,217
West of the MS River	264,584	132	36,182	185,118	43,152	148,836	115,747

- Represents or rounds to zero.

Source: U.S. Energy Information Administration, *U.S. Coal Reserves: 1997 Update*, February 1999.

No. 1189. Uranium Concentrate (U₃O₈) Industry—Summary: 1990 to 1998

[See also Table 978]

Item	Unit	1990	1991	1992	1993	1994	1995	1996	1997	1998
Exploration and development, surface drilling	Mil. ft.	1.7	1.8	1.1	1.1	0.7	1.3	3.0	4.9	4.6
Expenditures	Mil. dol.	17.1	17.8	14.5	11.3	3.7	6.0	10.1	30.4	21.7
Number of mines operated	Number	39	15	17	12	12	12	13	14	15
Underground	Number	27	6	4	-	-	-	1	1	4
Openpit	Number	2	2	1	-	-	-	-	-	-
In situ leaching	Number	7	6	4	5	5	5	6	7	6
Other sources	Number	3	1	8	7	7	7	6	6	5
Mine production	1,000 pounds	5,876	5,182	986	2,050	2,526	3,528	4,705	4,710	4,782
Underground	1,000 pounds	(D)	(D)	(D)	-	-	-	(D)	(D)	(D)
Openpit	1,000 pounds	1,881	2,528	(D)	-	-	-	-	-	-
In situ leaching	1,000 pounds	(D)	(D)	(D)	(D)	2,448	3,372	4,379	4,084	3,721
Other sources	1,000 pounds	3,995	2,654	986	2,050	78	156	326	626	1,062
Uranium concentrate production	1,000 pounds	8,886	7,952	5,645	3,063	3,352	6,043	6,321	5,643	4,705
Concentrate shipments from mills and plants	1,000 pounds	12,957	8,437	6,853	3,374	6,319	5,500	5,982	5,817	4,863
Employment	Person-years	1,335	1,016	682	871	980	1,107	1,118	1,097	1,120

- Represents zero or rounds to zero.   D Data withheld to avoid disclosing figures for individual companies.

Source: U.S. Department of Energy, *Uranium Industry,* annual.

Construction and Housing

This section presents data on the construction industry and on various indicators of its activity and costs; on housing units and their characteristics and occupants; and on the characteristics and vacancy rates for commercial buildings. This edition contains data from the newly released 1997 American Housing Survey.

The principal source of these data is the U.S. Census Bureau, which issues a variety of current publications. Construction statistics compiled by the Census Bureau appear in its monthly *Current Construction Reports* series with various quarterly or annual supplements; *Housing Starts* and *Housing Completions* present data by type of structure and by four major census regions; *New One-Family Houses Sold and For Sale* also provides statistics annually on physical and financial characteristics for all new housing by the four major census regions; *Price Index of New One-Family Houses Sold* presents quarterly figures and annual regional data; and *Housing Units Authorized by Building Permits* covers approximately 19,000 permit-issuing jurisdictions in the United States (prior to 1995, 17,000 places). Statistics on expenditures by owners of residential properties are issued quarterly and annually in *Expenditures for Residential Upkeep and Improvements*. *Value of New Construction Put in Place* presents data on all types of construction and includes monthly composite cost indexes. Reports of the censuses of construction industries (see below) are also issued on various topics.

Other Census Bureau publications include the *Current Housing Reports* series, which comprises the quarterly *Housing Vacancies*, the quarterly *Market Absorption of Apartments*, the biennial *American Housing Survey* (formerly *Annual Housing Survey*), and reports of the censuses of housing and of construction industries.

Construction Review, published quarterly by the International Trade Administration, U.S. Department of Commerce, contains many of the census series and other construction statistics series from the Federal Government and private agencies.

Other sources include the monthly *Dodge Construction Potentials* of F. W. Dodge Division, McGraw-Hill Information Systems Company, New York, NY, which presents national and state data on construction contracts; the National Association of Home Builders with state-level data on housing starts; the National Association of REALTORS, which presents data on existing home sales; the Society of Industrial and Office Realtors and Oncor International on commercial office and industrial space; the Bureau of Economic Analysis, which presents data on residential capital and gross housing product; and the U.S. Energy Information Administration , which provides data on commercial buildings through its periodic sample surveys.

Censuses and surveys—Censuses of the construction industry were first conducted by the Census Bureau for 1929, 1935, and 1939; beginning in 1967, a census has been taken every 5 years (for years ending in "2" and "7"). The latest complete reports are for 1992. The 1997 census results, part of the 1997 Economic Census, are being released on a flow basis. See Tables 1190 and 1191 for some preliminary data.

The census of construction industries, covers all employer establishments primarily engaged in (1) building construction by general contractors or operative builders; (2) heavy (nonbuilding) construction by general contractors; and (3) construction by special trade contractors. The 1997 census was conducted in accordance with the 1997 *North American Industry Classification System* (NAICS); the 1992 census was conducted in accordance with the

Construction and Housing 717

1987 *Standard Industrial Classification* (SIC). This sector now includes construction management and land subdividers and developers, not included previously. See text, Section 17, Business, for general information on the SIC and NAICS.

From 1850 through 1930, the Census Bureau collected some housing data as part of its censuses of population and agriculture. Beginning in 1940, separate censuses of housing have been taken at 10-year intervals. For the 1970 and 1980 censuses, data on year-round housing units were collected and issued on occupancy and structural characteristics, plumbing facilities, value, and rent; for 1990 such characteristics were presented for all housing units.

The American Housing Survey (*Current Housing Reports* Series H-150 and H-170), which began in 1973, provided an annual and ongoing series of data on selected housing and demographic characteristics until 1983. In 1984, the name of the survey was changed from the Annual Housing Survey. Currently, national data are collected every other year, and data for selected metropolitan areas are collected on a rotating basis. All samples represent a cross section of the housing stock in their respective areas. Estimates are subject to both sampling and nonsampling errors; caution should therefore be used in making comparisons between years.

Data on residential mortgages were collected continuously from 1890 to 1970, except 1930, as part of the decennial census by the Census Bureau. Since 1973, mortgage status data, limited to single family homes on less than 10 acres with no business on the property, have been presented in the American Housing Survey. Data on mortgage activity are covered in Section 16, Banking.

Housing units—In general, a housing unit is a group of rooms or a single room occupied or intended for occupancy as separate living quarters; that is, the occupants do not live and eat with any other persons in the structure, and there is direct access from the outside or through a common hall. Transient accommodations, barracks for workers, and institutional-type quarters are not counted as housing units.

Statistical reliability—For a discussion of statistical collection and estimation, sampling procedures, and measures of statistical reliability applicable to Census Bureau data, see Appendix III.

U.S. Census Bureau, Statistical Abstract of the United States: 1999

No. 1190. Construction—Summary (SIC Basis): 1992 and 1997

[Preliminary. For establishments with payroll (539,085 represents $539,085,000,000). See Tables 872 and 873 in Section 17, Business, for more 1997 Economic Census data]

Industry	1987 SIC code [1]	Establishments		Value of business done (mil. dol.)		Annual payroll (mil. dol.)		Paid employees [2] (1,000)	
		1992	1997	1992	1997	1992	1997	1992	1997
Construction, total	C	572,851	631,595	539,085	832,489	117,730	170,283	4,668	5,617
Building construction—general contractors and operative builders . .	15	168,407	182,315	220,231	362,381	27,078	39,154	1,097	1,266
Heavy construction contractors [2]	16	37,180	38,983	98,528	128,362	23,728	29,258	799	858
Special trade contractors	17	367,263	410,297	220,325	341,747	66,924	101,871	2,772	3,492

[1] 1987 Standard Industrial Classification code; see text, Section 17, Business. [2] Average of the pay periods including March, May, August, and November 12.

Source: U.S. Census Bureau, *1997 Economic Census, Core Business Statistics Series, Advance,* EC97X-CS1.

No. 1191. Construction Industries—Summary (NAICS Basis): 1997

[Preliminary. For establishments with payroll (865,314 represents $865,314,000,000). See Tables 872 and 873 in Section 17, Business, for more 1997 Economic Census data]

Industry	1997 NAICS code [1]	Establishments	Revenue (mil. dol.)	Annual payroll (mil. dol.)	Paid employees [2] (1,000)
Construction	23	649,601	865,314	174,679	5,733
Building, developing, and general contracting . .	233	198,124	391,088	42,592	1,358
Heavy construction	234	42,010	133,905	30,723	900
Special trade contractors	235	409,467	340,321	101,364	3,475

[1] 1997 North American Industrial Classification System code; see text, Section 17, Business. [2] Average of the pay periods including March, May, August, and November 12.

Source: U.S. Census Bureau, *1997 Economic Census, Core Business Statistics Series, Advance Report,* EC97X-CS1.

No. 1192. Construction Materials—Producer Price Indexes: 1990 to 1998

[1982=100, except as noted. For discussion of producer price index, see text, Section 15, Prices. This index, more formally known as the special commodity grouping index for construction materials, covers materials incorporated as integral part of a building or normally installed during construction and not readily removable. Excludes consumer durables such as kitchen ranges, refrigerators, etc. This index is not the same as the stage-of-processing index of intermediate materials and components for construction]

Commodity	1990	1991	1992	1993	1994	1995	1996	1997	1998 [1]
Construction materials	119.6	120.4	122.5	128.6	133.8	138.8	139.6	142.1	141.4
Interior solvent based paint	133.0	140.2	141.7	142.9	148.1	164.5	175.6	180.5	185.7
Plastic construction products	117.2	115.1	112.7	116.6	122.9	133.8	130.9	128.2	126.2
Douglas fir, dressed	138.4	139.6	169.5	237.6	236.2	198.8	227.1	221.3	185.8
Southern pine, dressed	111.2	111.0	130.6	168.8	182.6	166.9	177.9	201.2	176.7
Millwork	130.4	135.5	143.3	156.6	162.4	163.8	166.6	170.9	171.1
Softwood plywood	119.6	120.8	147.2	169.7	176.8	188.1	173.7	175.5	175.5
Hardwood plywood and related products	102.7	102.8	106.9	115.4	122.3	122.2	124.9	127.1	126.9
Softwood plywood veneer, ex. reinforced/backed . . .	142.3	138.5	168.3	216.0	207.8	203.5	189.3	201.7	180.2
Building paper and building board mill products	112.2	111.8	119.6	132.7	144.1	144.9	137.2	129.6	132.8
Steel pipe and tubes [2]	102.6	100.8	94.1	92.8	96.9	104.4	103.2	106.9	109.5
Builders hardware	133.0	138.1	141.4	144.9	148.0	153.2	156.5	158.4	160.8
Plumbing fixtures and brass fittings	144.3	149.7	153.1	155.9	159.6	166.0	171.1	174.5	175.1
Heating equipment	131.6	134.1	137.3	140.4	142.5	147.5	151.2	152.4	153.2
Metal doors, sash, and trim	131.4	134.6	135.0	136.6	142.0	156.5	159.3	161.0	161.3
Siding, aluminum [3]	(NA)	(NA)	116.7	117.2	119.4	132.4	125.5	132.1	134.4
Outdoor lighting equipment [4]	113.0	114.7	115.3	115.5	115.4	120.8	122.9	123.2	123.1
Commercial fluorescent fixtures [5]	113.0	116.5	117.6	117.4	116.2	121.0	123.4	122.8	118.9
Architectural and ornamental metalwork [6]	118.7	119.2	117.7	119.5	123.4	128.0	131.3	133.5	135.4
Fabricated ferrous wire products [2]	114.6	115.9	117.5	119.3	122.6	125.7	126.8	128.0	130.1
Elevators, escalators, and other lifts.	110.1	108.7	109.4	110.7	112.4	113.0	113.7	114.8	116.0
Stamped metal outlet box	158.0	160.8	166.5	172.9	179.1	183.5	186.3	189.0	191.5
Concrete ingredients and related products	115.3	118.4	119.4	123.4	128.7	134.7	138.8	142.5	147.6
Concrete products	113.5	116.6	117.2	120.2	124.6	129.4	133.2	136.0	140.1
Clay construction products exc. refractories.	129.9	130.2	132.0	135.1	138.3	141.3	142.3	143.5	144.9
Prep. asphalt and tar roofing and siding products. . .	95.8	96.2	94.3	94.9	92.9	97.8	97.4	96.5	95.8
Gypsum products	105.2	99.3	99.9	108.3	136.1	154.5	154.0	170.8	177.2
Insulation materials.	108.4	110.8	102.3	105.8	111.9	118.8	118.9	117.7	119.7
Paving mixtures and blocks	101.2	103.2	100.2	102.0	103.2	105.8	107.6	113.2	112.5

NA Not available. [1] Preliminary. [2] June 1982=100. [3] December 1982=100. [4] June 1985=100. [5] Recessed nonair. [6] December 1983=100.

Source: U.S. Bureau of Labor Statistics, *Producer Price Indexes,* monthly and annual.

No. 1193. Price and Cost Indexes for Construction: 1980 to 1998

[1992=100. Excludes Alaska and Hawaii. Indexes of certain of these sources are published on bases different from those shown here]

Name of index	1980	1985	1990	1993	1994	1995	1996	1997	1998
U.S. Census Bureau:									
Composite fixed-weighted [1]	68.6	82.9	98.5	103.7	108.0	112.5	115.0	118.7	122.0
Implicit price deflator [2]	67.8	81.8	97.8	103.8	108.1	112.6	115.2	118.9	122.2
U.S. Census Bureau houses under construction: [3]									
Fixed-weighted	67.6	81.4	98.6	104.9	109.7	114.4	116.4	119.9	123.3
Price deflator	66.4	79.6	97.2	104.8	109.5	114.3	116.5	119.9	123.0
Federal Highway Administration, composite [4]	92.5	97.1	103.2	103.0	109.5	115.9	116.1	124.7	122.2
Bureau of Reclamation composite [5]	70	84	96	103	106	110	112	116	118
Turner Construction Co.: Building construction [6]	61	83	98	102	105	109	112	117	122
E. H. Boeckh, building cost index: [7]									
Residences	(NA)	82.4	94.2	103.9	107.4	111.0	112.9	115.8	118.1
Apartments, hotels, and office buildings	(NA)	83.8	94.9	102.8	105.6	109.0	111.1	113.9	116.2
Commercial and factory buildings	(NA)	82.3	94.4	102.6	105.7	108.3	110.7	114.7	116.6
Engineering News-Record: [8]									
Buildings	68.5	85.7	95.4	105.7	109.8	109.8	113.0	118.7	119.7
Construction	64.9	84.2	94.9	104.5	108.5	109.8	112.8	116.9	118.8
Handy-Whitman public utility: [9]									
Buildings [10]	78	90	101	105	112	115	118	122	123
Electric	68	83	97	103	107	111	112	115	117
Gas [11]	67	85	96	103	109	111	112	115	117
Water	73	88	98	104	109	112	115	118	120
C. A. Turner Telephone Plant [12]	90	89	99	102	103	110	115	117	117

NA Not available. [1] Weighted average of the various indexes used to deflate the Construction Put in Place series. In calculating the index, the weights (i.e., the composition of current dollar estimates in 1992 by category) are held constant. [2] Derived ratio of total current to constant dollar Construction Put in Place (multiplied by 100). [3] Excludes value of site. [4] Based on average contract unit bid prices for composite mile (involving specific average amounts of excavation, paving, reinforcing steel, structural steel, and structural concrete). [5] Derived from the four quarterly indexes which are weighted averages of costs of labor, materials, and equipment for the construction of dams and reclamation projects. [6] Based on firm's cost experience with respect to labor rates, materials prices, competitive conditions, efficiency of plant and management, and productivity. [7] Average of 20 cities for types shown. Weights based on surveys of building costs. Wage rates used for both common and skilled labor. [8] Building construction index computed on the basis of a hypothetical unit of construction requiring 6 bbl. of portland cement, 1,088 M bd. ft. of 2" x 4" lumber, 2,500 lb. of structural steel, and 68.38 hours of skilled labor. General construction index based on same materials components combined with 200 hours of common labor. [9] Based on data covering public utility construction costs in six geographic regions. Covers skilled and common labor. [10] As derived by U.S. Census Bureau. Covers steam generation plants only. [11] As derived by U.S. Census Bureau. Reflects costs for structures and improvements at water pumping and treatment plants. [12] Computed by the Census Bureau by averaging the weighted component indexes published for six geographic regions.

Source: U.S. Census Bureau. In U.S. Department of Commerce, International Trade Administration, *Construction Review*, quarterly.

No. 1194. Value of New Construction Put in Place: 1964 to 1998

[In millions of dollars (75,097 represents $75,097,000,000). Represents value of construction put in place during year; differs from building permit and construction contract data in timing and coverage. Includes installed cost of normal building service equipment and selected types of industrial production equipment (largely site fabricated). Excludes cost of shipbuilding, land, and most types of machinery and equipment. For methodology, see Appendix III]

Year	Current dollars					Constant (1992) dollars				
		Private					Private			
	Total	Total [1]	Resi-dential buildings	Nonresi-dential buildings	Public	Total	Total [1]	Resi-dential buildings	Nonresi-dential buildings	Public
1964	75,097	54,893	30,526	17,385	20,203	351,300	259,680	145,486	84,232	91,620
1970	105,890	77,982	35,863	28,171	27,908	372,274	279,212	133,133	100,780	93,062
1975	152,635	109,342	51,581	35,409	43,293	351,973	259,048	128,254	84,282	92,925
1977	200,501	157,418	92,004	38,245	43,083	408,528	324,777	193,479	81,170	83,751
1978	239,867	189,721	109,838	48,824	50,146	439,075	350,182	203,568	93,436	88,893
1979	272,873	216,228	116,444	64,765	56,646	446,503	357,949	192,873	111,235	88,554
1980	273,936	210,290	100,381	72,480	63,646	403,900	315,821	150,943	112,874	88,079
1981	289,070	224,378	99,241	85,569	64,691	396,267	313,358	139,656	122,748	82,910
1982	279,332	216,268	84,676	92,690	63,064	369,135	290,057	115,525	126,705	79,077
1983	311,576	248,126	125,521	87,069	63,450	403,929	324,785	166,981	114,716	79,144
1984	369,025	298,787	153,849	107,680	70,238	463,057	377,445	197,126	135,650	85,612
1985	401,370	323,555	158,474	127,466	77,815	490,943	399,530	199,105	156,349	91,413
1986	429,924	345,342	187,148	120,917	84,582	507,275	411,174	224,557	143,070	96,101
1987	441,647	350,999	194,656	123,247	90,648	502,468	401,642	223,516	140,110	100,826
1988	455,618	360,883	198,101	130,854	94,735	499,621	397,693	218,972	143,467	101,928
1989	469,797	371,623	196,551	139,953	98,174	495,387	393,262	208,748	147,825	102,124
1990	468,532	361,054	182,856	143,506	107,478	479,016	370,102	188,045	146,661	108,914
1991	424,176	314,067	157,835	116,570	110,109	429,592	319,248	160,989	118,266	110,345
1992	452,086	336,239	187,819	105,646	115,847	451,998	336,126	187,687	105,615	115,872
1993	478,648	362,688	210,455	110,635	115,960	461,078	347,851	200,502	106,729	113,227
1994	519,539	399,346	238,874	120,285	120,193	480,620	367,247	218,005	111,416	113,373
1995	537,409	407,477	230,688	135,022	129,933	477,386	360,040	201,677	120,627	117,346
1996	583,445	448,969	256,640	150,350	134,476	506,485	388,324	220,017	131,188	118,161
1997	618,225	475,123	265,863	167,610	143,102	520,123	398,699	221,756	141,129	121,424
1998	665,446	520,073	294,326	181,915	145,373	544,729	424,345	239,201	148,017	120,384

[1] Includes other types of private construction, not shown separately.

Source: U.S. Census Bureau, *Current Construction Reports*, Series C30, *Value of Construction*, monthly.

720   Construction and Housing

NOTE: Index citations refer to **table** numbers, not page numbers.

U.S. Census Bureau, Statistical Abstract of the United States: 1999

NOTE: Index citations refer to **table** numbers, not page numbers.

NOTE: Index citations refer to **table** numbers, not page numbers.

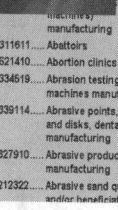

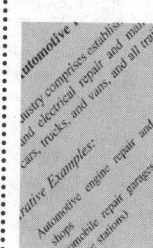

No. 1195. Value of New Construction Put in Place, by Type: 1990 to 1998

[In millions of dollars (468,532 represents $468,532,000,000). Represents value of construction put in place during year; differs from building permit and construction contract data in timing and coverage. Includes installed cost of normal building service equipment and selected types of industrial production equipment (largely site fabricated). Excludes cost of shipbuilding, land, and most types of machinery and equipment. For methodology, see Appendix III]

Type of construction	Current dollars					Constant (1992) dollars				
	1990	1995	1996	1997	1998	1990	1995	1996	1997	1998
Total new construction .	**468,532**	**537,409**	**583,445**	**618,225**	**665,446**	**479,016**	**477,386**	**506,485**	**520,123**	**544,729**
Private construction	**361,054**	**407,477**	**448,969**	**475,123**	**520,073**	**370,102**	**360,040**	**388,324**	**398,699**	**424,345**
Residential buildings	182,856	230,688	256,460	265,863	294,326	188,045	201,677	220,017	221,756	239,201
New housing units	127,987	162,898	179,448	187,328	213,909	131,632	142,413	153,966	156,248	173,828
1 unit	108,737	145,009	159,124	164,444	189,453	111,832	126,773	136,516	137,156	153,937
2 or more units	19,250	17,889	20,324	22,883	24,457	19,800	15,640	17,450	19,092	19,891
Improvements	54,869	67,790	77,012	78,535	80,417	56,414	59,264	66,052	65,509	65,372
Nonresidential buildings . . .	143,506	135,022	150,350	167,610	181,915	146,661	120,627	131,188	141,129	148,017
Industrial	33,636	32,505	32,657	31,359	32,270	34,373	29,043	28,503	26,405	26,269
Office	35,055	25,613	27,886	34,305	41,541	35,838	22,891	24,329	28,876	33,803
Hotels, motels	10,679	7,112	10,912	12,898	14,904	10,917	6,351	9,521	10,864	12,121
Other commercial	40,047	42,654	48,188	51,809	53,783	40,922	38,098	42,042	43,628	43,749
Religious	3,566	4,326	4,534	5,777	6,729	3,642	3,864	3,955	4,861	5,472
Educational	4,616	5,493	6,742	8,693	9,629	4,715	4,908	5,880	7,316	7,840
Hospital and institutional .	10,868	11,248	11,780	13,546	13,663	11,103	10,051	10,280	11,413	11,121
Miscellaneous [1]	5,040	6,071	7,650	9,223	9,395	5,151	5,421	6,677	7,767	7,643
Farm nonresidential	2,801	3,014	3,658	3,815	3,891	2,862	2,692	3,192	3,210	3,165
Public utilities	28,933	35,859	36,070	35,544	37,267	29,537	32,401	31,771	30,644	31,705
Telecommunications	9,803	11,093	11,772	11,698	12,441	9,891	10,073	10,245	9,985	10,612
Other public utilities	19,130	24,766	24,298	23,846	24,826	19,646	22,328	21,525	20,659	21,093
Railroads	2,600	3,509	4,398	4,922	5,320	2,633	3,201	3,894	4,204	4,489
Electric light and power .	11,299	14,049	11,211	11,260	11,574	11,572	12,656	9,914	9,783	9,827
Gas	4,820	6,279	7,674	6,695	6,667	5,013	5,637	6,814	5,828	5,697
Petroleum pipelines . . .	411	929	1,015	969	1,265	428	834	903	843	1,080
All other private [2]	2,957	2,893	2,431	2,292	2,674	2,997	2,643	2,156	1,960	2,256
Public construction	**107,478**	**129,933**	**134,476**	**143,102**	**145,373**	**108,914**	**117,346**	**118,161**	**121,424**	**120,384**
Buildings	43,615	57,754	60,047	63,489	66,137	44,583	51,506	52,348	53,424	53,810
Housing and redevelopment	3,808	4,698	4,113	3,795	4,047	3,914	4,108	3,532	3,165	3,291
Industrial	1,434	1,508	1,389	999	1,012	1,465	1,348	1,214	843	824
Educational	16,055	25,783	27,148	28,915	29,916	16,398	23,027	23,693	24,340	24,336
Hospital	2,860	4,236	4,472	4,934	3,978	2,924	3,785	3,905	4,157	3,239
Other [3]	19,458	21,528	22,924	24,846	27,183	19,882	19,238	20,004	20,919	22,119
Highways and streets	32,105	37,616	39,860	44,292	44,792	31,777	34,501	35,258	37,833	37,525
Military facilities	2,665	3,011	2,591	2,556	2,578	2,683	2,728	2,280	2,169	2,131
Conservation and development	4,686	6,308	5,910	5,612	5,511	4,870	5,724	5,245	4,801	4,681
Sewer systems	10,276	8,420	9,142	9,166	8,707	10,670	7,640	8,110	7,842	7,398
Water supply facilities	4,909	4,709	5,234	5,662	5,871	4,987	4,186	4,550	4,817	4,903
Miscellaneous public [4]	9,223	12,116	11,691	12,325	11,777	9,344	11,060	10,370	10,537	9,936

[1] Includes amusement and recreational buildings, bus and airline terminals, animal hospitals and shelters, etc.   [2] Includes privately owned streets and bridges, parking areas, sewer and water facilities, parks and playgrounds, golf courses, airfields, etc.   [3] Includes general administrative buildings, prisons, police and fire stations, courthouses, civic centers, passenger terminals, space facilities, postal facilities, etc.   [4] Includes open amusement and recreational facilities, power generating facilities, transit systems, airfields, open parking facilities, etc.

Source: U.S. Census Bureau, *Current Construction Reports*, Series C30, *Value of Construction*, monthly.

Construction and Housing   721

No. 1196. Construction Contracts—Value of Construction and Floor Space of Buildings, by Class of Construction: 1980 to 1998

[(151.8 represents $151,800,000,000) Building construction includes new structures and additions; nonbuilding construction includes major alterations to existing structures which affect only valuation, since no additional floor area is created by "alteration"]

Year	Total	Resi-dential build-ings	Nonresidential buildings									Non-building con-struction
			Total	Com-mer-cial [1]	Manu-fac-turing	Educa-tional [2]	Health	Public build-ings	Reli-gious	Social and recrea-tional	Mis-cella-neous	
VALUE (bil. dol.)												
1980	151.8	60.4	56.9	27.7	9.2	7.4	5.4	1.6	1.2	2.7	1.7	34.5
1985	235.6	102.1	92.1	54.6	8.1	10.0	7.8	3.1	2.0	4.0	2.5	41.4
1988	262.2	116.2	97.9	51.6	9.5	14.1	8.2	4.4	2.2	4.7	3.2	48.1
1989	271.3	116.2	106.1	53.6	12.7	15.9	8.8	5.2	2.0	5.0	2.9	49.0
1990	246.0	100.9	95.4	44.8	8.4	16.6	9.2	5.7	2.2	5.3	3.1	49.7
1991	230.8	94.4	86.2	32.7	8.3	19.0	9.6	6.2	2.4	5.1	3.0	50.2
1992	252.2	110.6	87.0	32.8	8.9	17.6	10.9	5.8	2.5	5.5	3.1	54.6
1993	271.5	123.9	88.8	34.2	9.0	19.3	10.5	3.9	2.4	6.8	2.6	58.9
1994	296.7	133.6	101.5	40.8	11.2	21.0	10.5	6.1	2.5	6.5	3.0	61.6
1995	306.5	127.8	114.2	46.6	13.8	22.9	10.8	6.3	2.8	7.1	3.8	64.4
1996	331.8	146.4	120.3	51.8	13.1	22.9	11.1	6.3	2.9	8.1	4.0	65.1
1997	358.4	152.6	136.5	58.6	14.1	27.8	11.5	6.9	3.7	9.8	4.0	69.4
1998	375.3	173.0	134.0	63.9	10.1	26.9	10.8	6.0	3.8	9.3	3.1	68.2
FLOOR SPACE (mil. sq. ft.)												
1980	3,102	1,839	1,263	738	220	103	55	18	28	49	52	(X)
1985	3,853	2,324	1,529	1,039	165	111	73	28	32	44	38	(X)
1988	3,594	2,181	1,413	883	162	142	71	38	32	49	37	(X)
1989	3,516	2,115	1,400	867	158	151	72	41	27	48	35	(X)
1990	3,020	1,817	1,203	694	128	152	69	47	29	51	32	(X)
1991	2,634	1,653	981	476	100	177	72	50	29	45	33	(X)
1992	2,799	1,864	936	462	95	156	77	41	30	42	32	(X)
1993	3,062	2,091	971	481	110	165	75	30	30	51	29	(X)
1994	3,411	2,267	1,144	600	143	172	72	45	30	51	31	(X)
1995	3,453	2,172	1,281	700	163	186	70	40	33	56	33	(X)
1996	3,773	2,478	1,295	721	155	177	77	41	32	60	32	(X)
1997	4,076	2,566	1,510	838	188	199	86	47	41	76	34	(X)
1998	4,483	2,902	1,581	974	149	194	81	38	42	74	29	(X)

X Not applicable.   [1] Includes nonindustrial warehouses.   [2] Includes science.

Source: F.W. Dodge, a Division of the McGraw-Hill Companies, New York, NY (copyright).

No. 1197. Construction Contracts—Value, by State: 1990 to 1998

[In millions of dollars (246,022 represents $246,022,000,000). Represents value of construction in states in which work was actually done. See headnote, Table 1196]

State	1990	1995	1998			State	1990	1995	1998		
			Total [1]	Resi-dential	Non-residen-tial				Total [1]	Resi-dential	Non-residen-tial
U.S.	246,022	306,503	375,263	173,008	134,038	MO	3,833	6,438	6,048	2,741	2,164
AL	2,939	4,308	5,976	2,241	2,243	MT	332	865	935	345	275
AK	1,919	1,660	1,239	379	411	NE	1,318	1,694	1,980	795	633
AZ	4,553	8,784	11,673	6,748	3,338	NV	3,334	5,555	6,398	3,044	2,308
AR	1,438	2,903	2,531	1,302	827	NH	1,021	1,039	1,606	717	520
CA	37,318	29,045	39,560	18,179	14,131	NJ	6,141	6,454	7,865	3,270	3,373
CO	3,235	6,476	9,416	5,486	2,553	NM	1,124	2,108	1,999	817	671
CT	3,058	3,124	3,417	1,563	1,409	NY	14,137	13,380	13,185	3,896	5,746
DE	787	871	892	460	297	NC	6,614	10,599	14,329	8,279	4,388
DC	795	656	725	82	520	ND	506	791	1,103	286	469
FL	16,975	21,453	28,200	15,192	9,411	OH	9,885	12,430	15,127	6,192	6,149
GA	7,120	12,156	16,065	8,394	5,507	OK	2,164	2,968	3,501	1,578	1,175
HI	2,831	2,273	1,653	522	711	OR	3,101	5,451	5,046	2,697	1,608
ID	986	1,864	2,015	1,216	479	PA	10,117	9,348	11,398	4,117	4,844
IL	10,796	11,744	14,120	5,723	5,526	RI	594	465	648	337	194
IN	6,350	7,896	9,494	4,603	3,451	SC	3,664	4,580	7,067	3,225	2,003
IA	2,034	2,883	3,249	1,214	1,007	SD	468	706	791	297	243
KS	2,193	3,264	3,978	1,685	1,362	TN	4,388	7,167	9,155	4,188	3,343
KY	3,174	4,464	5,687	2,571	1,859	TX	13,197	22,999	32,415	15,168	11,988
LA	3,191	4,354	4,371	1,544	1,685	UT	1,884	4,218	3,858	1,972	1,411
ME	897	1,076	1,594	587	389	VT	515	484	551	262	175
MD	6,056	6,299	6,255	3,111	2,423	VA	7,180	8,794	11,081	5,225	4,077
MA	5,135	7,411	8,841	3,422	3,745	WA	6,185	7,334	8,431	4,047	3,061
MI	7,646	9,946	11,593	5,491	3,736	WV	1,253	1,215	1,157	241	343
MN	4,953	5,607	7,297	3,275	2,851	WI	4,654	5,652	5,867	2,947	1,656
MS	1,569	2,718	3,291	1,101	1,245	WY	462	532	587	236	104

[1] Includes nonbuilding construction, not shown separately.

Source: F.W. Dodge, a Division of the McGraw-Hill Companies, New York, NY (copyright).

722   Construction and Housing

No. 1198. New Privately-Owned Housing Units Authorized, by State: 1997 and 1998

[1,441.1 represents 1,441,100. Based on about 19,000 places in United States having building permit systems]

State	Housing units (1,000) 1997	Total 1998	1 unit 1998	Valuation (mil. dol.) 1997	Total 1998	1 unit 1998
U.S.	1,441.1	1,612.3	1,187.6	141,004	165,266	142,241
AL	17.7	20.5	14.7	1,537	1,791	1,501
AK	2.6	2.9	2.0	334	385	303
AZ	57.8	63.9	50.5	5,776	6,766	6,085
AR	11.0	10.0	7.2	761	798	703
CA	109.6	124.0	93.4	15,396	18,230	15,862
CO	43.1	51.2	36.1	4,659	5,777	4,858
CT	9.3	11.9	9.1	1,101	1,394	1,263
DE	4.7	5.3	4.6	381	499	465
DC	(Z)	0.4	0.3	1	35	27
FL	134.0	148.6	97.9	12,205	14,123	10,864
GA	75.1	85.4	67.9	6,460	7,859	7,093
HI	3.7	3.3	2.9	507	484	447
ID	10.3	11.7	10.3	1,042	1,251	1,173
IL	46.3	48.0	36.2	5,087	5,618	4,936
IN	35.2	40.7	31.6	3,706	4,333	3,885
IA	10.7	13.1	8.9	1,012	1,292	1,059
KS	13.6	15.3	10.9	1,350	1,516	1,309
KY	18.1	20.6	15.4	1,484	1,731	1,517
LA	15.1	16.5	13.9	1,332	1,541	1,434
ME	4.7	6.3	5.7	451	642	602
MD	26.0	30.9	23.8	2,357	2,903	2,567
MA	17.2	19.3	16.3	2,172	2,519	2,278
MI	49.2	54.5	44.2	5,102	5,880	5,293
MN	24.9	30.4	25.0	2,758	3,485	3,101
MS	10.1	12.9	8.7	716	890	722
MO	25.2	25.7	20.0	2,265	2,425	2,145
MT	2.5	2.6	1.5	204	217	157
NE	9.9	9.6	6.0	711	787	637
NV	34.8	37.0	24.4	2,788	2,807	2,258
NH	5.4	5.8	5.3	572	658	632
NJ	28.0	31.3	25.5	2,533	2,936	2,662
NM	10.3	10.3	9.2	887	979	934
NY	32.9	38.4	22.8	3,064	3,826	2,943
NC	73.0	80.5	62.4	6,723	8,062	7,223
ND	3.2	3.0	1.7	222	245	183
OH	46.5	48.0	36.6	4,795	5,410	4,852
OK	11.2	14.4	9.7	1,014	1,286	1,071
OR	27.0	25.9	16.9	2,838	2,827	2,278
PA	39.9	41.6	35.1	3,802	4,219	3,883
RI	2.7	2.6	2.5	250	284	277
SC	30.1	33.6	24.5	2,651	3,087	2,641
SD	3.2	3.5	2.6	256	297	257
TN	34.1	34.1	28.3	3,104	3,428	3,165
TX	126.0	156.7	99.8	10,725	13,682	11,269
UT	19.3	20.9	16.3	1,880	2,210	1,910
VT	1.8	2.2	1.8	192	234	206
VA	45.5	50.2	40.0	4,119	4,744	4,280
WA	41.1	45.7	28.6	4,225	4,745	3,599
WV	4.1	3.8	3.1	309	323	289
WI	31.9	35.4	24.0	2,998	3,556	2,905
WY	1.7	1.9	1.6	190	251	236

Z Less than 50 units.

Source: U.S. Census Bureau, Construction Reports, Series C40, Building Permits, monthly.

No. 1199. New Privately-Owned Housing Units Started—Selected Characteristics: 1970 to 1998

[In thousands (1,434 represents 1,434,000). For composition of regions, see map inside front cover]

Year	Total units	Structures with— One unit	2 to 4 units	5 or more units	Region North-east	Mid-west	South	West	Condominium units [1] Total	Single-family	Multi-family
1970	1,434	813	85	536	218	294	612	311	(NA)	(NA)	(NA)
1973	2,045	1,132	118	795	277	440	899	429	241	69	172
1974	1,338	888	68	382	183	317	553	285	175	46	130
1975	1,160	892	64	204	149	294	442	275	65	20	45
1976	1,538	1,162	86	289	169	400	569	400	95	30	64
1977	1,987	1,451	122	414	202	465	783	538	118	41	77
1978	2,020	1,433	125	462	200	451	824	545	156	42	114
1979	1,745	1,194	122	429	178	349	748	470	198	43	156
1980	1,292	852	110	331	125	218	643	306	186	35	150
1981	1,084	705	91	288	117	165	562	240	181	36	145
1982	1,062	663	80	320	117	149	591	205	170	40	130
1983	1,703	1,068	113	522	168	218	935	382	276	77	199
1984	1,750	1,084	121	544	204	243	866	436	291	96	194
1985	1,742	1,072	93	576	252	240	782	468	225	79	146
1986	1,805	1,179	84	542	294	296	733	483	214	80	134
1987	1,621	1,146	65	409	269	298	634	420	196	73	123
1988	1,488	1,081	59	348	235	274	575	404	148	53	95
1989	1,376	1,003	55	318	179	266	536	396	118	37	82
1990	1,193	895	37	260	131	253	479	329	75	22	53
1991	1,014	840	36	138	113	233	414	254	60	21	39
1992	1,200	1,030	31	139	127	288	497	288	74	35	40
1993	1,288	1,126	29	133	126	298	562	302	86	45	41
1994	1,457	1,198	35	224	138	329	639	351	96	48	48
1995	1,354	1,076	34	244	118	290	615	331	93	47	47
1996	1,477	1,161	45	271	132	322	662	361	107	53	54
1997	1,474	1,134	44	296	137	304	670	363	110	56	54
1998	1,617	1,271	43	303	148	330	743	395	113	59	54

NA Not available. [1] Type of ownership under which the owners of the individual housing units are also joint owners of the common areas of the building or community. Includes a small number of cooperatively-owned units.

Source: U.S. Census Bureau, Current Construction Reports, Series C20, Housing Starts, monthly.

Housing and Construction 723

No. 1200. New Privately-Owned Housing Units Started, by State: 1996 to 1999

[In thousands of units (1,469.0 represents 1,469,000)]

State	1996	1997	1998	1999 Total units	1999 Single-family units	State	1996	1997	1998	1999 Total units	1999 Single-family units
U.S.	1,469.0	1,476.0	1,623.0	1,631.0	1,286.0	MO	28.5	28.0	31.2	31.3	26.5
AL......	23.6	21.8	23.9	23.1	18.1	MT......	2.8	2.5	2.2	2.3	1.5
AK......	2.6	2.5	2.7	2.7	2.0	NE......	10.0	9.8	9.3	9.4	6.6
AZ......	56.0	58.2	66.5	65.6	53.0	NV......	38.5	35.6	37.1	36.9	26.1
AR......	13.9	12.9	12.8	12.9	9.8	NH......	4.8	5.3	5.6	5.9	5.3
CA......	95.0	109.2	125.6	132.7	103.4	NJ......	23.6	26.8	33.0	33.7	29.3
CO......	43.7	43.7	49.7	48.8	36.7	NM......	10.8	10.4	10.0	9.8	8.6
CT......	8.5	9.1	12.5	12.6	10.7	NY......	31.2	30.5	32.2	33.7	22.4
DE......	4.7	4.9	5.7	5.7	5.2	NC......	68.6	74.0	81.4	79.9	64.9
DC......	-	-	0.4	0.3	0.2	ND......	2.5	3.3	3.2	3.2	2.0
FL......	129.1	135.0	149.8	152.6	110.0	OH......	47.8	44.6	48.8	49.0	39.9
GA......	79.1	78.8	88.2	85.9	71.9	OK......	13.5	13.2	15.5	15.4	11.5
HI......	4.2	3.8	3.4	3.6	3.1	OR......	28.8	26.6	26.1	23.6	15.8
ID	11.4	10.5	9.9	10.0	8.9	PA......	37.4	38.7	35.6	36.9	31.8
IL.......	50.1	46.6	51.7	52.1	42.9	RI......	2.4	2.6	3.1	3.1	3.0
IN	37.9	36.0	43.1	42.1	35.6	SC......	30.0	31.2	33.4	33.2	26.2
IA	12.6	11.2	11.0	11.2	8.4	SD......	3.9	3.4	3.7	3.8	3.0
KS......	15.1	13.6	14.5	14.7	11.7	TN......	42.2	38.1	37.5	36.7	30.5
KY......	21.5	20.6	22.5	22.5	18.0	TX......	125.0	133.8	155.9	155.3	107.9
LA......	19.3	16.8	14.1	14.3	12.3	UT......	24.3	19.8	18.2	18.2	14.1
ME......	4.9	4.6	5.7	5.8	5.3	VT......	2.2	1.8	2.0	2.2	1.9
MD......	26.7	26.4	32.2	32.3	26.9	VA	47.0	46.9	51.9	52.7	44.3
MA......	17.0	16.9	19.5	20.2	18.1	WA	40.6	40.6	43.9	41.2	28.6
MI	52.7	49.0	55.9	55.6	47.7	WV	4.9	5.1	4.8	4.9	4.0
MN......	27.5	25.2	29.9	30.2	26.3	WI	32.5	30.7	29.9	30.2	22.3
MS......	13.1	12.2	14.9	14.5	11.0	WY	2.5	1.9	2.0	2.0	1.7

- Represents or rounds to zero.

Source: National Association of Home Builders, Economics Division, Washington, DC. Data provided by the Econometric Forecasting Service.

No. 1201. Characteristics of New Privately Owned One-Family Houses Completed: 1970 to 1998

[Percent distribution, except as indicated (793 represents 793,000). Data beginning 1980 show percent distribution of characteristics for all houses completed (includes new houses completed, houses built for sale completed, contractor-built and owner-built houses completed, and houses completed for rent). Data for 1970 cover contractor-built, owner-built, and houses for rent for year construction started and houses sold for year of sale. Percents exclude houses for which characteristics specified were not reported]

Characteristic	1970	1980	1990	1995	1998	Characteristic	1970	1980	1990	1995	1998
Total houses (1,000)....	793	957	966	1,066	1,160	Bedrooms	100	100	100	100	100
						2 or less...........	13	17	15	13	12
Financing............	100	100	100	100	100	3................	63	63	57	57	55
Mortgage	84	82	82	88	91	4 or more	24	20	29	30	33
FHA-insured	30	16	14	8	8	Bathrooms	100	100	100	100	100
VA-guaranteed.....	7	8	4	5	4	1 1/2 or less	52	27	13	11	8
Conventional	47	55	62	74	78	2................	32	48	42	41	41
Rural Housing Service [1]	(2)	3	2	1	1	2 1/2 or more	16	25	45	48	52
Cash or equivalent....	16	18	18	12	9	Heating fuel	100	100	100	100	100
						Electricity	28	50	33	28	26
Floor area	100	100	100	100	100	Gas..............	62	41	59	67	70
Under 1,200 sq. ft ...	36	21	11	10	7	Oil...............	8	3	5	3	3
1,200 to 1,599 sq. ft...	28	29	22	22	20	Other.............	1	5	3	1	1
1,600 to 1,999 sq. ft...	16	22	22	23	22	Heating system.......	100	100	100	100	100
2,000 to 2,399 sq. ft...	21	13	17	17	18	Warm air furnace.....	71	57	65	67	72
2,400 sq. ft. and over ..	(3)	15	29	28	32	Electric heat pump....	(NA)	24	23	25	21
Average (sq. ft.).....	1,500	1,740	2,080	2,095	2,190	Other.............	29	19	12	9	7
Median (sq. ft.)	1,385	1,595	1,905	1,920	2,000	Central air-conditioning. ..	100	100	100	100	100
						With	34	63	76	80	83
Number of stories	100	100	100	100	100	Without	66	37	24	20	17
1...............	74	60	46	49	48	Fireplaces	100	100	100	100	100
2 or more..........	17	31	49	48	50	No fireplace	65	43	34	37	39
Split level	10	8	4	3	2	1 or more..........	35	56	66	63	61
Foundation..........	100	100	100	100	100	Parking facilities	100	100	100	100	100
Full or partial basement.	37	36	38	39	37	Garage	58	69	82	84	86
Slab	36	45	40	42	45	Carport	17	7	2	2	1
Crawl space	27	19	21	19	18	No garage or carport ..	25	24	16	14	12

NA Not available. [1] Prior to 1998, Farmers Home Administration. [2] Included with "Conventional" financing. [3] Included with floor area of 2,000 to 2,399 square feet.

Source: U.S. Census Bureau and U.S. Dept. of Housing and Urban Development, Current Construction Reports, Series C25, New One-Family Houses Sold, monthly, and Characteristics of New Housing, annual.

No. 1202. New Privately Owned One-Family Houses Sold, by Region and Type of Financing, 1980 to 1998, and by Sales-Price Group, 1998

[In thousands (545 represents 545,000). Based on a national probability sample of monthly interviews with builders or owners of one-family houses for which building permits have been issued or, for nonpermit areas, on which construction has started. For details, see source. For composition of regions, see map inside front cover]

Year and sales-price group	Total sales	Region				Financing type			
		North-east	Midwest	South	West	Conven-tional [1]	FHA and VA	Rural Housing Service [2]	Cash
1980	545	50	81	267	145	302	196	14	32
1985	688	112	82	323	170	403	208	11	64
1988	676	101	97	276	202	437	171	6	62
1989	650	86	102	260	202	416	162	14	58
1990	534	71	89	225	149	337	138	10	50
1991	509	57	93	215	144	329	128	9	43
1992	610	65	116	259	170	428	134	7	41
1993	666	60	123	295	188	476	147	6	37
1994	670	61	123	295	191	490	130	9	41
1995	667	55	125	300	187	490	129	9	39
1996	757	74	137	337	209	570	140	9	38
1997	804	78	140	363	223	616	137	6	46
1998	**886**	**81**	**164**	**398**	**243**	**693**	**136**	**9**	**48**
Under $70,000	19	(B)	(B)	16	(B)	11	6	(B)	(B)
$70,000 to $79,999	22	(B)	3	17	(B)	11	8	(B)	(B)
$80,000 to $99,999	91	3	16	57	15	48	34	4	5
$100,000 to $119,999	112	5	20	61	25	73	32	(B)	5
$120,000 to $149,999	183	12	33	82	56	136	35	(B)	11
$150,000 to $199,999	208	19	42	80	67	178	18	(B)	12
$200,000 to $249,999	104	13	22	40	29	97	(B)	(B)	5
$250,000 to $299,999	59	11	11	20	17	57	(B)	(B)	(B)
$300,000 and over	88	17	15	25	31	84	(B)	(B)	5

B Withheld because estimate did not meet publication standards on the basis of sample size.   [1] Includes all other types of financing.   [2] Prior to 1996, the Farmers Home Administration.

Source: U.S. Census Bureau and U.S. Dept. of Housing and Urban Development, *Current Construction Reports*, Series C25, *Characteristics of New Housing*, annual; and *New One-Family Houses Sold*, monthly.

No. 1203. Median Sales Price of New Privately Owned One-Family Houses Sold, by Region: 1980 to 1998

[In dollars. For definition of median, see Guide to Tabular Presentation. For composition of regions, see map inside front cover]

Year	U.S.	North-east	Midwest	South	West	Year	U.S.	North-east	Midwest	South	West
1980	64,600	69,500	63,400	59,600	72,300	1991	120,000	155,900	110,000	100,000	141,100
1984	79,900	88,600	85,400	72,000	87,300	1992	121,500	169,000	115,600	105,500	130,400
1985	84,300	103,300	80,300	75,000	92,600	1993	126,500	162,600	125,000	115,000	135,000
1986	92,000	125,000	88,300	80,200	95,700	1994	130,000	169,000	132,900	116,900	140,400
1987	104,500	140,000	95,000	88,000	111,000	1995	133,900	180,000	134,000	124,500	141,400
1988	112,500	149,000	101,600	92,000	126,500	1996	140,000	186,000	138,000	126,200	153,900
1989	120,000	159,600	108,800	96,400	139,000	1997	146,000	190,000	149,900	129,600	160,000
1990	122,900	159,000	107,900	99,000	147,500	1998	152,500	200,000	157,500	135,800	163,500

Source: U.S. Census Bureau and U.S. Dept. of Housing and Urban Development, *Current Construction Reports*, Series C25, *Characteristics of New Housing*, annual; and *New One-Family Houses Sold*, monthly.

No. 1204. New Mobile Homes Placed for Residential Use and Average Sales Price, by Region: 1980 to 1998

[233.7 represents 233,700. A mobile home is a moveable dwelling, 10 feet or more wide and 35 feet or more long, designed to be towed on its own chassis and without need of permanent foundation. Excluded are travel trailers, motor homes, and modular housing. Data are based on a probability sample and subject to sampling variability; see source. For composition of region, see map inside front cover]

Year	Units placed (1,000)					Average sales price (dol.)				
	Total	North-east	Midwest	South	West	U.S.	North-east	Midwest	South	West
1980	233.7	12.3	32.3	140.3	48.7	19,800	18,500	18,600	18,200	25,400
1985	283.4	20.2	38.6	187.6	36.9	21,800	22,700	21,500	20,400	28,700
1988	224.3	22.7	39.1	130.7	31.8	25,100	27,000	24,600	22,700	33,900
1989	202.8	20.2	39.1	112.8	30.6	27,200	30,200	26,700	24,100	37,800
1990	195.4	18.8	37.7	108.4	30.6	27,800	30,000	27,000	24,500	39,300
1991	174.1	14.3	35.4	97.6	27.0	27,700	30,400	27,600	24,500	38,600
1992	212.0	15.0	42.2	124.4	30.4	28,400	30,900	28,800	25,400	39,000
1993	242.5	15.4	44.5	146.7	35.9	30,500	32,000	31,400	27,700	40,500
1994	286.1	16.2	53.0	174.4	42.5	33,500	33,900	34,600	30,500	44,600
1995	310.7	14.6	56.0	198.3	41.8	36,300	37,600	36,600	34,000	46,800
1996	319.7	15.4	56.6	205.1	42.6	38,400	40,200	39,600	36,100	47,700
1997	296.5	13.7	50.9	188.8	43.1	41,100	43,900	41,600	38,700	50,900
1998	331.0	13.4	53.9	216.5	47.1	43,800	45,900	44,100	41,600	53,700

Source: U.S. Census Bureau, *Current Construction Reports*, Series C20, *Housing Starts*, monthly.

U.S. Census Bureau, Statistical Abstract of the United States: 1999

No. 1205. Existing One-Family Houses Sold and Price, by Region: 1970 to 1998

[1,612 represents 1,612,000. Based on data (adjusted and aggregated to regional and national totals) reported by participating real estate multiple listing services. For definition of median, see Guide to Tabular Presentation. For composition of regions, see map inside front cover]

Year	Houses sold (1,000)					Median sales price (dol.)				
	Total	North-east	Midwest	South	West	Total	North-east	Midwest	South	West
1970	1,612	251	501	568	292	23,000	25,700	20,100	22,200	24,300
1972	2,252	361	630	788	473	26,700	29,800	23,900	26,400	28,400
1973	2,334	367	674	847	446	28,900	32,800	25,300	29,000	31,000
1974	2,272	354	645	839	434	32,000	35,800	27,700	32,200	34,800
1975	2,476	370	701	862	543	35,300	39,300	30,100	34,800	39,600
1976	3,064	439	881	1,033	712	38,100	41,800	32,900	36,500	46,100
1977	3,650	515	1,101	1,231	803	42,900	44,400	36,700	39,800	57,300
1978	3,986	516	1,144	1,416	911	48,700	47,900	42,200	45,100	66,700
1979	3,827	526	1,061	1,353	887	55,700	53,600	47,800	51,300	77,400
1980	2,973	403	806	1,092	672	62,200	60,800	51,900	58,300	89,300
1981	2,419	353	632	917	516	66,400	63,700	54,300	64,400	96,200
1982	1,990	354	490	780	366	67,800	63,500	55,100	67,100	98,900
1983	2,697	477	692	1,004	524	70,300	72,200	56,600	69,200	94,900
1984	2,829	478	720	1,006	624	72,400	78,700	57,100	71,300	95,800
1985	3,134	561	806	1,063	704	75,500	88,900	58,900	75,200	95,400
1986	3,474	635	922	1,145	773	80,300	104,800	63,500	78,200	100,900
1987	3,436	618	892	1,163	763	85,600	133,300	66,000	80,400	113,200
1988	3,513	606	865	1,224	817	89,300	143,000	68,400	82,200	124,900
1989 [1]	3,325	490	832	1,185	818	89,500	127,700	71,800	84,400	127,100
1990	3,219	458	809	1,193	759	92,000	126,400	75,300	85,100	129,600
1991	3,186	463	812	1,173	737	97,100	129,100	79,500	88,500	135,300
1992	3,479	521	913	1,242	802	99,700	128,900	83,000	91,500	131,500
1993	3,786	550	967	1,386	882	103,100	129,100	86,000	94,300	132,500
1994	3,916	552	965	1,436	962	107,200	129,100	89,300	95,700	139,400
1995	3,888	547	945	1,433	964	110,500	126,700	94,800	97,700	141,000
1996	4,196	584	986	1,511	1,116	115,800	127,800	101,000	103,400	147,100
1997	4,381	606	1,005	1,596	1,174	121,800	131,800	107,000	109,600	155,200
1998	4,970	662	1,130	1,868	1,309	128,400	135,900	114,300	116,200	164,800

[1] Beginning 1989 data not comparable to earlier years due to rebenchmarking.

Source: NATIONAL ASSOCIATION OF REALTORS, Washington, DC, prior to 1990, *Home Sales*, monthly, and *Home Sales Yearbook: 1990*; (copyright); thereafter, *Real Estate Outlook; Market Trends & Insights*, monthly (copyright).

No. 1206. Median Sales Price of Existing One-Family Homes, by Selected Metropolitan Area: 1996 to 1998

[In thousands of dollars (115.8 represents $115,800). For the top 60 areas in sales price in 1998. Areas are metropolitan statistical areas defined by source as of 1992]

Metropolitan area	1996	1997	1998	Metropolitan area	1996	1997	1998
U.S., all areas	115.8	121.8	128.4	Minneapolis-St. Paul, MN-WI	113.9	118.4	128.0
Albuquerque, NM	122.3	126.7	128.2	Nashville, TN	112.7	115.2	116.7
Atlanta, GA	100.7	108.4	115.4	New Haven-Meriden, CT	133.3	134.1	137.8
Atlantic City, NJ	108.0	109.7	112.8	New York-N. New Jersey-			
Aurora-Elgin, IL	137.0	141.8	146.2	Long Island, NY-NJ-CT	174.5	177.9	188.1
Baltimore, MD	113.0	118.2	120.6	NY: Bergen-Passaic, NJ	199.4	205.4	213.5
Birmingham, AL	114.1	118.9	122.7	NY: Middlesex-Somerset-			
Boston, MA	189.3	196.2	212.6	Hunterdon, NJ	175.9	176.7	184.2
Charleston, SC	94.9	103.6	120.0	NY: Monmouth-Ocean, NJ	144.7	147.7	152.6
Charlotte-Gastonia-Rock Hill,				NY: Nassau-Suffolk, NY	159.8	164.0	175.4
NC-SC	116.8	124.2	134.0	NY: Newark, NJ	(NA)	193.0	199.2
Chicago, IL	153.2	158.9	166.8	Orange Cnty.(Anaheim-			
Cincinnati, OH-KY-IN	104.8	110.5	116.3	Santa Ana) CA	213.4	229.8	261.7
Cleveland, OH	111.9	116.8	121.8	Phoenix, AZ	105.3	113.7	120.2
Colorado Springs, CO	126.6	130.5	138.5	Portland, OR	141.5	152.4	158.1
Columbus, OH	108.2	117.6	121.7	Providence, RI	118.1	119.6	124.4
Dallas, TX	103.5	112.0	120.4	Raleigh-Durham, NC	145.4	152.8	159.8
Denver, CO	133.4	140.6	152.2	Reno, NV	140.0	143.4	147.2
Detroit, MI	111.4	119.6	132.6	Richmond-Petersburg, VA	108.7	114.2	122.0
Eugene-Springfield, OR	116.2	119.4	124.4	Riverside-San Bernardino, CA	115.2	114.6	121.2
Ft. Lauderdale-Hollywood-				Sacramento, CA	115.3	116.3	125.6
Pompano Beach, FL	112.3	123.7	128.6	Salt Lake City-Ogden, UT	122.7	128.6	133.5
Greensboro-Winston-Salem-				San Diego, CA	174.5	185.2	207.1
High Point, NC	112.7	117.3	123.5	San Francisco Bay Area, CA	266.7	286.2	321.7
Greenville-Spartanburg, SC	105.5	112.8	113.1	Sarasota, FL	107.7	114.1	123.1
Hartford, CT	139.2	138.1	142.8	Seattle, WA	164.6	171.3	175.3
Kansas City, MO-KS	98.8	106.8	114.0	Springfield, MA	106.0	106.5	110.5
Lake County, IL	144.7	153.5	159.4	Tallahassee, FL	109.8	111.7	114.6
Las Vegas, NV	118.5	123.2	128.2	Trenton, NJ	136.4	137.7	139.5
Los Angeles Area, CA	172.9	176.5	192.6	Tucson, AZ	105.5	106.8	112.6
Madison, WI	122.2	126.8	131.8	Washington, DC-MD-VA	160.7	166.3	172.1
Memphis, TN-AR-MS	96.1	103.7	109.8	Worcester, MA	131.2	135.8	138.7
Miami-Hialeah, FL	113.2	117.7	121.5	W. Palm Beach-Boca Raton-			
Milwaukee, WI	119.4	125.3	132.9	Delray Beach, FL	126.6	133.4	126.6

NA Not available.
Source: NATIONAL ASSOCIATION OF REALTORS, Washington, DC, *Real Estate Outlook: Market Trends & Insights*, monthly (copyright).

726 Construction and Housing

No. 1207. Existing Home Sales, by State: 1990 to 1998

[In thousands (3,599 represents 3,599,000)]

State	1990	1995	1997	1998	State	1990	1995	1997	1998
United States ..	3,599	4,350	4,915	5,589	Missouri............	77.1	100.8	107.0	116.0
Alabama..........	52.0	69.0	78.0	84.0	Montana	13.5	14.8	16.8	18.3
Alaska...........	12.3	10.2	13.5	17.1	Nebraska.........	23.6	25.0	27.5	33.3
Arizona..........	71.8	120.3	133.1	155.1	Nevada	26.9	31.0	31.4	38.4
Arkansas	33.7	45.0	46.3	54.9	New Hampshire.....	13.5	26.2	35.8	40.5
California........	413.1	426.7	596.2	665.4	New Jersey	85.7	102.4	115.7	129.9
Colorado	77.7	102.5	117.2	130.6	New Mexico	24.7	27.6	24.9	27.1
Connecticut	37.4	43.3	43.8	49.9	New York	135.9	149.7	161.0	183.1
Delaware	7.9	9.5	8.6	8.6	North Carolina......	98.9	157.7	183.8	211.6
District of Columbia ..	7.2	7.0	8.7	13.0	North Dakota	8.5	8.5	9.4	11.4
Florida...........	281.1	379.6	408.4	454.4	Ohio.............	146.9	173.1	176.2	191.4
Georgia	91.2	101.0	102.6	117.5	Oklahoma	62.2	74.5	84.0	95.5
Hawaii	19.0	10.3	11.5	14.7	Oregon	56.6	58.7	60.8	63.1
Idaho............	22.3	27.1	28.0	29.7	Pennsylvania	143.2	163.2	167.6	175.4
Illinois	163.3	183.4	200.1	235.3	Rhode Island	9.6	13.6	15.8	19.0
Indiana	83.6	102.6	112.7	125.9	South Carolina	54.3	70.7	84.6	98.7
Iowa	42.8	43.2	48.0	56.5	South Dakota	10.8	11.9	13.5	14.3
Kansas	36.8	50.5	57.0	66.8	Tennessee	66.2	106.6	121.8	136.2
Kentucky	47.9	61.5	64.3	71.8	Texas	311.8	367.9	424.0	512.1
Louisiana	57.1	77.3	82.4	91.7	Utah	29.4	43.5	42.7	44.9
Maine	17.0	25.5	28.9	32.9	Vermont..........	7.2	7.9	6.4	6.8
Maryland	67.0	63.5	73.3	92.4	Virginia	89.3	94.8	103.6	133.4
Massachusetts	47.9	69.4	90.6	100.0	Washington	85.9	110.9	140.5	159.2
Michigan	137.6	142.2	143.6	161.9	West Virginia	22.6	26.1	27.2	29.3
Minnesota	68.1	81.6	93.9	108.5	Wisconsin.........	62.1	78.2	87.5	101.1
Mississippi	28.2	41.3	43.5	48.2	Wyoming	8.5	11.4	11.3	12.0

Source: NATIONAL ASSOCIATION OF REALTORS, Washington, DC, *Real Estate Outlook: Market Trends & Insights*, monthly (copyright).

No. 1208. New Apartments Completed and Rented in 3 Months, by Region: 1980 to 1997

[196.1 **represents 196,100**. Structures with five or more units, privately financed, nonsubsidized, unfurnished rental apartments. Based on sample and subject to sampling variability; see source for details. For composition of regions, see inside front cover]

Year and rent	Number (1,000)					Percent rented in 3 months				
	U.S.	North-east	Mid-west	South	West	U.S.	North-east	Mid-west	South	West
1980	196.1	14.2	43.8	91.5	46.6	75	77	77	74	75
1981	135.3	4.9	36.9	68.4	25.1	80	85	86	78	75
1982	117.0	4.6	21.9	66.8	23.7	72	74	79	70	72
1983	191.5	3.5	41.1	115.1	31.8	69	73	86	63	69
1984	313.2	3.8	41.2	194.4	73.9	67	64	79	63	70
1985	365.2	8.1	54.0	166.1	137.0	65	69	72	59	68
1986	407.6	16.9	64.5	171.7	154.5	66	70	70	62	67
1987	345.6	11.3	66.0	124.5	143.9	63	73	65	59	64
1988	284.5	8.7	60.4	91.7	123.8	66	52	73	58	69
1989	247.8	13.4	45.8	86.3	102.3	70	74	74	68	69
1990 [1]	214.3	12.7	44.3	77.2	80.0	67	66	75	64	65
1991	165.3	6.8	37.9	63.6	57.0	70	83	78	65	68
1992	110.2	10.9	34.0	37.4	28.0	74	75	80	72	70
1993	77.2	3.7	25.3	27.7	20.5	75	37	81	76	73
1994	104.0	3.7	32.2	44.5	23.6	80	96	78	78	85
1995	155.0	7.1	31.7	78.5	37.7	73	74	75	72	73
1996	191.3	6.1	37.2	96.9	51.1	72	61	77	69	75
1997	189.2	7.7	34.1	96.1	51.3	73	55	81	72	72
Less than $450	14.7	0.2	3.1	9.1	2.4	81	63	74	85	77
$450 to $649........	52.0	0.3	16.3	25.1	10.4	73	69	78	72	71
$450 to $549	22.1	0.1	7.4	11.1	3.6	75	51	83	72	71
$550 to $649	29.9	0.2	8.9	14.0	6.8	72	77	74	72	70
$650 to $849........	63.7	2.4	8.2	31.8	21.5	73	49	87	72	74
$650 to $749	37.3	1.9	5.6	17.9	12.0	74	39	85	75	74
$750 to $849	26.4	0.5	2.6	13.9	9.5	72	94	91	67	74
$850 or more........	58.7	4.8	6.6	30.1	17.2	71	56	85	71	71
Median monthly asking rent ..	$724	([2])	$624	$727	$760	(X)	(X)	(X)	(X)	(X)

X Not applicable.   [1] Due to revised estimation procedures, data beginning 1990 not strictly comparable with prior years. [2] Over $850.

Source: U.S. Census Bureau, *Current Housing Reports*, Series H130, *Market Absorption of Apartments,* and unpublished data.

Construction and Housing   727

No. 1209. Recent Home Buyers—General Characteristics: 1976 to 1998

[As of **October.** Based on a sample survey; subject to sampling variability]

Item	Unit	1976	1980	1985	1990	1994	1995	1996	1997	1998
Median purchase price....	Dollars ..	43,340	68,714	90,400	131,200	145,400	147,700	153,200	159,700	167,900
First-time buyers	Dollars ..	37,670	61,450	75,100	106,000	125,000	128,300	130,100	135,400	142,200
Repeat buyers [1]	Dollars ..	50,090	75,750	106,200	149,400	163,500	164,300	170,700	178,700	189,800
Average monthly										
mortgage payment......	Dollars ..	329	599	896	1,127	1,028	1,062	1,087	1,114	1,212
Percent of income	Percent..	24.0	32.4	30.0	33.8	31.4	32.6	32.6	32.8	32.3
Percent buying—										
New houses.........	Percent..	15.1	22.4	23.8	21.2	22.0	21.5	22.7	20.9	21.2
Existing houses.......	Percent..	84.9	77.6	76.2	78.8	78.0	78.5	77.3	79.1	78.8
Single-family houses....	Percent..	88.8	82.4	87.0	83.8	83.9	83.1	82.6	81.6	82.3
Other houses [2]	Percent..	11.2	17.6	13.0	16.2	16.1	16.9	17.4	18.4	17.7
For the first time	Percent..	44.8	32.9	36.6	41.9	47.1	46.2	44.7	46.8	46.2
Average age:										
First-time buyers	Years ...	28.1	28.3	28.4	30.5	31.6	32.1	32.4	32.1	32.2
Repeat buyers [1]	Years ...	35.9	36.4	38.4	39.1	41.7	40.7	41.1	41.1	41.1
Downpayment/sales price ..	Percent..	25.2	28.0	24.8	23.3	20.2	20.4	19.5	20.3	19.3
First-time buyers	Percent..	18.0	20.5	11.4	15.7	13.7	13.3	12.4	13.7	12.8
Repeat buyers [1]	Percent..	30.8	32.7	32.7	28.9	26.1	26.8	25.3	26.1	24.9

[1] Buyers who previously owned a home.   [2] Includes multifamily, condominiums and co-ops.
Source: Chicago Title Corporation, Chicago, IL, *Who's Buying Homes in America* (copyright).

No. 1210. Total Housing Inventory for the United States: 1970 to 1998

[In thousands (69,778 represents 69,778,000), except percent. Based on the Current Population Survey and the Housing Vacancy Survey and subject to sampling error; see source for details]

Item	1970	1975	1980	1985	1990	1993	1994	1995	1996	1997	1998
All housing units	69,778	78,821	87,739	97,333	106,283	109,611	110,952	112,655	114,139	115,621	117,282
Vacant	6,137	6,896	8,101	9,446	12,059	11,894	12,257	12,669	13,155	13,419	13,748
Year-round vacant.......	4,391	5,202	5,995	7,400	9,128	8,937	9,229	9,570	9,945	10,114	10,516
For rent	1,299	1,647	1,575	2,221	2,662	2,809	2,858	2,946	3,008	2,978	3,046
For sale only.........	427	591	734	1,006	1,064	894	953	1,022	1,082	1,133	1,205
Rented or sold	427	536	623	664	660	625	772	810	834	867	927
Held off market	2,238	2,429	3,064	3,510	4,742	4,609	4,646	4,793	5,022	5,136	5,338
Occasional use	615	649	814	977	1,485	1,508	1,612	1,667	1,709	1,818	1,792
Usual residence else-											
where...........	429	470	568	659	1,068	994	815	801	852	885	910
Other.............	1,195	1,309	1,683	1,875	2,189	2,108	2,219	2,325	2,461	2,433	2,636
Seasonal [1].............	1,746	1,694	2,106	2,046	2,931	2,957	3,028	3,099	3,209	3,305	3,232
Total occupied	63,640	71,925	79,638	87,887	94,224	97,717	98,695	99,985	100,984	102,202	103,534
Owner	40,834	46,463	52,223	56,152	60,248	62,533	63,136	64,739	66,041	67,143	68,638
Renter	22,806	25,462	27,415	31,736	33,976	35,184	35,558	35,246	34,943	35,059	34,896
PERCENT DISTRIBUTION											
All housing units	100.0	100.0	100.0	100.0	100.0	100.0	100.0	100.0	100.0	100.0	100.0
Vacant	8.8	8.7	9.2	9.7	11.3	10.9	11.0	11.2	11.5	11.6	11.7
Total occupied	91.2	91.3	90.8	90.3	88.7	89.1	89.0	88.8	88.5	88.4	88.3
Owner	58.5	58.9	59.5	57.7	56.7	57.0	56.9	57.5	57.9	58.1	58.5
Renter	32.7	32.3	31.2	32.6	32.0	32.1	32.0	31.3	30.6	30.3	29.8

[1] Beginning 1990 includes vacant seasonal mobile homes. For years shown, seasonal vacant housing units were underreported prior to 1990.
Source: U.S. Census Bureau, Internet site <http://www.census.gov/hhes/www/housing/hvs/historic/index.html> (accessed 26 March 1999).

No. 1211. Vacancy Rates for Housing Units—Characteristics: 1990 to 1998

[In percent. Rate is relationship between vacant housing for rent or for sale and the total rental and homeowner supply, which comprises occupied units, units rented or sold and awaiting occupancy, and vacant units available for rent or sale. For composition of regions, see map inside front cover. Based on the Current Population Survey/Housing Vacancy Survey; see source for details]

Characteristic	Rental units					Homeowner units				
	1990	1995 [1]	1996	1997	1998	1990	1995 [1]	1996	1997	1998
Total units....	7.2	7.6	7.8	7.7	7.9	1.7	1.5	1.6	1.6	1.7
Inside MSAs	7.1	7.6	7.7	7.5	7.7	1.7	1.5	1.6	1.6	1.6
Outside MSAs	7.6	7.9	8.7	8.8	9.2	1.8	1.6	1.7	1.9	2.0
Northeast	6.1	7.2	7.4	6.7	6.7	1.6	1.5	1.6	1.6	1.5
Midwest	6.4	7.2	7.9	8.0	7.9	1.3	1.3	1.3	1.2	1.4
South	8.8	8.3	8.6	9.1	9.6	2.1	1.7	1.8	1.9	2.0
West	6.6	7.5	7.2	6.6	6.7	1.8	1.7	1.7	1.8	1.7
Units in structure:										
1 unit	4.0	5.4	5.5	5.8	6.3	1.4	1.4	1.4	1.5	1.6
2 units or more...	9.0	9.0	9.2	9.0	9.0	7.1	4.8	5.1	4.4	4.4
5 units or more...	9.6	9.5	9.6	9.1	9.4	8.4	5.1	6.0	4.6	4.5
Units with—										
3 rooms or less ..	10.3	11.4	11.3	11.1	10.8	10.2	9.2	10.0	9.6	9.7
4 rooms	8.0	8.2	8.9	8.6	8.9	3.2	2.8	3.2	3.3	3.5
5 rooms	5.7	5.8	5.8	6.0	6.5	2.0	1.8	1.9	1.9	1.9
6 rooms or more .	3.0	3.8	3.7	3.9	4.3	1.1	1.1	1.1	1.1	1.2

[1] Beginning 1995, based on 1990 population census controls.
Source: U.S. Census Bureau, Internet site <http://www.census.gov/hhes/www/housing/hvs/annual98/ann98ind.html> (accessed 6 July 1999).

728   Construction and Housing

No. 1212. Housing Units—Characteristics, by Tenure and Region: 1997

[In thousands of units (112,357 represents 112,357,000), except as indicated. As of Oct. 1. Based on the American Housing Survey; see Appendix III. For composition of regions, see map inside front cover]

Characteristic	Total housing units	Sea-sonal	Total	Owner	Renter	North-east	Mid-west	South	West	Vacant
			Year-round units							
			Occupied							
Total units................	**112,357**	**3,166**	**99,487**	**65,487**	**34,000**	**19,484**	**23,951**	**34,808**	**21,245**	**9,704**
Percent distribution........	100.0	2.8	88.5	58.3	30.3	17.3	21.3	31.0	18.9	8.6
Units in structure:										
Single family detached.........	68,109	1,831	62,111	53,756	8,355	10,238	16,416	22,726	12,731	4,167
Single family attached..........	6,778	157	5,840	3,030	2,810	1,586	1,061	1,944	1,249	781
2 to 4 units.................	10,363	129	8,973	1,756	7,216	3,014	2,131	1,945	1,884	1,261
5 to 9 units.................	5,657	78	4,852	491	4,361	939	1,071	1,572	1,270	727
10 to 19 units...............	5,025	59	4,264	319	3,945	757	831	1,595	1,081	702
20 to 49 units...............	3,877	75	3,292	355	2,936	925	609	820	938	509
50 or more units.............	4,247	108	3,611	524	3,087	1,431	676	730	774	528
Mobile home or trailer.........	8,301	729	6,544	5,255	1,289	593	1,156	3,476	1,319	1,028
Stories in structure: [1]										
One story.................	3,709	58	3,173	312	2,861	254	480	1,359	1,080	478
2 stories.................	12,210	125	10,582	1,355	9,227	1,916	1,984	3,344	3,339	1,503
3 stories.................	7,317	105	6,229	944	5,284	2,036	1,997	1,228	967	983
4 to 6 stories...............	3,742	93	3,176	496	2,681	1,907	543	361	365	473
7 or more stories............	2,190	68	1,831	338	1,493	953	315	369	195	290
Foundation: [2]										
Full or partial basement.........	31,922	325	30,087	26,865	3,223	9,893	13,053	4,654	2,488	1,508
Crawlspace.................	19,806	684	17,518	14,059	3,459	703	2,563	9,195	5,058	1,604
Concrete slab...............	21,238	552	19,073	14,931	4,141	1,067	1,631	10,189	6,186	1,614
Other..................	1,921	426	1,273	931	341	161	230	633	248	222
Year structure built:										
1939 and earlier..............	22,342	458	19,441	11,254	8,186	7,256	6,339	3,543	2,301	2,444
1940 to 1949...............	8,389	234	7,321	4,602	2,720	1,665	1,760	2,345	1,551	833
1950 to 1959...............	13,852	439	12,476	8,878	3,598	2,596	3,300	3,877	2,704	936
1960 to 1969...............	15,949	465	14,313	9,453	4,860	2,452	3,285	5,191	3,385	1,171
1970 to 1979...............	23,300	832	20,571	13,138	7,433	2,593	4,476	8,356	5,145	1,896
1980 or later...............	28,527	737	25,367	18,163	7,202	2,921	4,791	11,495	6,158	2,422
Median year................	1967	1970	1967	1968	1965	1953	1962	1973	1971	1965
Main heating equipment:										
Warm-air furnace.............	66,699	1,972	58,603	41,977	16,626	7,719	18,810	19,046	13,029	6,124
Electric heat pump............	12,745	450	11,101	7,750	3,351	350	662	8,579	1,510	1,194
Steam or hot water system......	14,008	79	12,929	7,143	5,786	9,236	2,304	692	697	999
Floor, wall, or pipeless furnace	6,105	74	5,588	2,533	3,055	510	588	1,519	2,970	442
Built-in electric units...........	5,089	183	4,531	2,093	2,438	1,140	1,022	866	1,503	375
Room heaters with flue.........	1,768	56	1,584	859	725	153	182	925	324	128
Room heaters without flue.......	2,020	40	1,754	1,031	723	36	62	1,588	67	226
Stoves..................	1,386	170	1,142	944	198	173	177	471	321	74
Fireplaces.................	281	40	225	176	48	13	24	90	97	18
Cooking stoves..............	138	12	123	45	78	52	17	47	7	3
None...................	617	-	617	232	384	4	5	170	437	-
Portable electric heaters.........	847	67	708	377	331	15	12	520	162	72
Other...................	656	24	582	326	256	82	86	294	121	49
Kitchen equipment:										
Lacking complete facilities.......	5,629	416	2,289	515	1,774	515	456	629	690	2,924
With complete facilities..........	106,728	2,750	97,198	64,972	32,226	18,969	23,496	34,179	20,555	6,780
Kitchen sink................	111,191	3,044	98,878	65,316	33,563	19,375	23,818	34,650	21,036	9,269
Refrigerator................	109,357	2,922	99,017	65,310	33,707	19,391	23,862	34,672	21,092	7,417
Burners and oven.............	108,779	2,860	98,318	65,023	33,295	19,306	23,727	34,372	20,913	7,601
Burners only...............	267	5	247	165	82	28	37	85	98	14
Oven only................	514	16	454	177	277	60	101	202	91	45
Dishwasher................	57,642	990	53,116	41,162	11,954	9,267	11,312	19,462	13,076	3,535
Washing machine............	80,133	1,258	75,901	60,708	15,193	13,744	18,757	27,978	15,422	2,974
Clothes dryer...............	76,470	1,334	71,669	58,231	13,438	12,565	18,373	26,096	14,635	3,467
Disposal in kitchen sink.........	45,843	740	41,984	28,888	13,096	4,169	10,136	13,786	13,894	3,118
Air conditioning: Central.........	57,168	974	52,303	38,789	13,514	4,416	13,119	26,728	8,038	3,891
Percent of total units........	50.9	30.8	52.6	59.2	39.7	22.7	54.8	76.8	37.8	40.1
One or more room units........	28,715	562	26,133	15,561	10,573	8,653	6,582	7,760	3,139	2,019
Source of water:										
Public system or private company ..	98,654	2,025	88,008	55,547	32,462	16,885	20,471	30,607	20,046	8,621
Percent of total units........	87.8	64.0	88.5	84.8	95.5	86.7	85.5	87.9	94.4	88.8
Well serving 1 to 5 units.........	12,891	917	11,055	9,608	1,447	2,511	3,392	3,995	1,157	919
Other...................	812	224	424	332	92	88	89	206	41	164
Means of sewage disposal:										
Public sewer...............	85,775	1,272	76,906	45,920	30,986	15,087	18,860	24,549	18,410	7,598
Percent of total units........	76.3	40.2	77.3	70.1	91.1	77.4	78.7	70.5	86.7	78.3
Septic tank, cesspool, chemical toilet..................	26,161	1,662	22,479	19,507	2,973	4,396	5,060	10,204	2,820	2,019
Other...................	421	233	102	61	41	1	31	55	15	86

- Represents or rounds to zero.   [1] Limited to multiunit structures.   [2] Limited to single-family units.

Source: U.S. Census Bureau, *Current Housing Reports*, Series H150/97, *American Housing Survey in the United States.*

Construction and Housing   729

No. 1213. Housing Units—Size of Units and Lot: 1997

[In thousands (112,357 represents 112,357,000), except as indicated. As of Oct. 1. Based on the American Housing Survey; see Appendix III. For composition of regions, see map inside front cover]

Item	Total hous- ing units	Sea- sonal	Year-round units							Vacant
			Occupied							
			Total	Owner	Renter	North- east	Mid- west	South	West	
Total units	**112,357**	**3,166**	**99,487**	**65,487**	**34,000**	**19,484**	**23,951**	**34,808**	**21,245**	**9,704**
Rooms:										
1 room	471	18	328	5	323	95	67	51	114	125
2 rooms	1,470	112	951	100	851	333	123	218	278	406
3 rooms	11,715	627	9,399	1,037	8,361	2,403	2,039	2,556	2,400	1,690
4 rooms	23,468	1,286	19,038	6,996	12,042	3,324	4,290	6,881	4,542	3,145
5 rooms	24,476	552	21,760	14,828	6,932	3,558	5,078	8,683	4,441	2,165
6 rooms	21,327	295	19,885	16,415	3,470	3,639	4,878	7,318	4,050	1,147
7 rooms	13,782	154	13,113	11,900	1,213	2,656	3,352	4,461	2,644	516
8 rooms or more	15,647	122	15,014	14,207	807	3,475	4,122	4,640	2,776	510
Median number of rooms	5.3	4.1	5.4	6.1	4.1	5.5	5.6	5.4	5.2	4.3
Complete bathrooms:										
No bathrooms	1,673	412	750	319	432	220	192	182	157	510
1 bathroom	51,729	1,668	44,223	19,801	24,421	10,795	11,659	13,509	8,259	5,838
1 and one-half bathrooms	16,162	232	14,987	11,628	3,360	3,360	4,778	4,142	2,707	943
2 or more bathrooms	42,794	854	39,527	33,739	5,787	5,109	7,322	16,975	10,121	2,413
Square footage of unit:										
Single detached and mobile homes [1]	76,410	2,560	68,655	59,011	9,644	10,831	17,572	26,202	14,050	5,195
Less than 500	1,402	369	778	491	287	82	132	356	207	254
500 to 749	3,188	381	2,286	1,369	917	227	535	1,127	398	521
750 to 999	6,576	364	5,586	4,121	1,465	531	1,329	2,647	1,079	627
1,000 to 1,499	17,030	468	15,432	12,886	2,546	1,443	3,386	7,045	3,558	1,130
1,500 to 1,999	15,007	196	14,071	12,598	1,473	1,828	3,387	5,367	3,488	741
2,000 to 2,499	10,680	113	10,194	9,526	663	1,992	2,949	3,281	1,973	373
2,500 to 2,999	5,944	45	5,660	5,315	345	1,303	1,758	1,633	967	238
3,000 to 3,999	5,469	45	5,212	4,966	245	1,244	1,651	1,501	815	212
4,000 or more	3,229	49	3,023	2,825	198	801	890	903	429	157
Other [2]	7,885	529	6,414	4,915	1,499	1,380	1,556	2,342	1,137	941
Median square footage	1,702	932	1,750	1,825	1,276	2,154	1,888	1,570	1,674	1,321
Lot size:										
Single detached and attached units and mobile homes	83,188	2,717	74,495	62,041	12,454	12,417	18,633	28,146	15,299	5,976
Less than one-eighth acre	12,087	640	10,175	7,515	2,659	1,761	2,691	2,745	2,977	1,273
One-eighth to one-quarter acre	22,045	586	19,915	16,284	3,632	2,625	5,309	6,547	5,434	1,544
One-quarter to one-half acre	15,414	319	14,235	12,381	1,854	2,217	3,578	5,542	2,899	860
One-half up to one acre	9,841	269	8,977	7,858	1,120	1,915	1,961	4,103	999	595
1 to 5 acres	14,185	346	13,067	11,345	1,723	2,580	2,765	6,166	1,557	771
5 to 10 acres	2,143	58	1,990	1,791	199	300	578	797	315	96
10 acres or more	4,293	260	3,687	3,238	450	562	1,252	1,422	451	346
Other [2]	3,180	239	2,449	1,629	817	457	499	824	667	491
Median acreage	0.35	0.26	0.35	0.38	0.23	0.43	0.32	0.45	0.23	0.24

[1] Does not include selected vacant units.   [2] Represents units not reported or size unknown.
Source: U.S. Census Bureau, *Current Housing Reports*, Series H150/97, *American Housing Survey in the United States.*

No. 1214. Occupied Housing Units—Tenure, by Race of Householder: 1991 to 1997

[In thousands (93,147 represents 93,147,000), except percent. As of fall. Based on the American Housing Survey; see Appendix III]

Race of householder and tenure	1991	1993	1995	1997
ALL RACES [1]				
Occupied units, total	93,147	94,724	97,693	99,487
Owner occupied	59,796	61,252	63,544	65,487
Percent of occupied	64.2	64.7	65.0	65.8
Renter occupied	33,351	33,472	34,150	34,000
WHITE				
Occupied units, total	79,140	80,029	81,611	82,154
Owner occupied	53,749	54,878	56,507	57,781
Percent of occupied	67.9	68.6	69.2	70.3
Renter occupied	25,391	25,151	25,104	24,372
BLACK				
Occupied units, total	10,832	11,128	11,773	12,085
Owner occupied	4,635	4,788	5,137	5,457
Percent of occupied	42.8	43.0	43.6	45.2
Renter occupied	6,197	6,340	6,637	6,628
HISPANIC ORIGIN [2]				
Occupied units, total	6,239	6,614	7,757	8,513
Owner occupied	2,423	2,788	3,245	3,646
Percent of occupied	38.8	42.2	41.8	42.8
Renter occupied	3,816	3,826	4,512	4,867

[1] Includes other races, not shown separately.   [2] Persons of Hispanic origin may be of any race.
Source: U.S. Census Bureau, *Current Housing Reports*, Series H150/91, H150/93, H150/95RV, and H150/97, *American Housing Survey in the United States.*

No. 1215. Homeownership Rates, by Age of Householder and Family Status: 1985 to 1998

[In percent. Represents the proportion of owner households to the total number of occupied households. Based on the Current Population Survey/Housing Vacancy Survey; see source for details]

Age of householder and family status	1985	1990	1991	1992	1993 [1]	1994	1995	1996	1997	1998
United States	63.9	63.9	64.1	64.1	64.0	64.0	64.7	65.4	65.7	66.3
AGE OF HOUSEHOLDER										
Less than 25 years old.	17.2	15.7	15.3	14.9	14.8	14.9	15.9	18.0	17.7	18.2
25 to 29 years old.	37.7	35.2	33.8	33.6	33.6	34.1	34.4	34.7	35.0	36.2
30 to 34 years old.	54.0	51.8	51.2	50.5	50.8	50.6	53.1	53.0	52.6	53.6
35 to 39 years old.	65.4	63.0	62.2	61.4	61.8	61.2	62.1	62.1	62.6	63.7
40 to 44 years old.	71.4	69.8	69.5	69.1	68.6	68.2	68.6	69.0	69.7	70.0
45 to 49 years old.	74.3	73.9	73.7	74.2	73.7	73.8	73.7	74.4	74.2	73.9
50 to 54 years old.	77.5	76.8	76.1	76.2	77.2	76.8	77.0	77.2	77.7	77.8
55 to 59 years old.	79.2	78.8	79.5	79.3	78.9	78.4	78.8	79.4	79.7	79.8
60 to 64 years old.	79.9	79.8	80.5	81.2	80.9	80.1	80.3	80.7	80.5	82.1
65 to 69 years old.	79.5	80.0	81.4	80.8	80.7	80.6	81.0	82.4	81.9	81.9
70 to 74 years old.	76.8	78.4	78.8	79.0	79.9	80.1	80.9	81.4	82.0	82.2
75 years old and over	69.8	72.3	73.1	73.3	73.4	73.5	74.6	75.3	75.8	76.2
Less than 35 years old.	39.9	38.5	37.8	37.6	37.3	37.3	38.6	39.1	38.7	39.3
35 to 44 years old.	68.1	66.3	65.8	65.1	65.1	64.5	65.2	65.5	66.1	66.9
45 to 54 years old.	75.9	75.2	74.8	75.1	75.3	75.2	75.2	75.6	75.8	75.7
55 to 64 years old.	79.5	79.3	80.0	80.2	79.9	79.3	79.5	80.0	80.1	80.9
65 years and over.	74.8	76.3	77.2	77.1	77.3	77.4	78.1	78.9	79.1	79.3
FAMILY STATUS										
Family households:										
Married-couple families	78.2	78.1	78.5	78.7	78.7	78.8	79.6	80.2	80.8	81.5
Male householder, no spouse present.	57.8	55.2	54.3	53.6	53.7	52.8	55.3	55.5	54.0	55.7
Female householder, no spouse present.	45.8	44.0	43.9	43.6	43.9	44.2	45.1	46.1	46.1	47.0
Nonfamily households:										
One-person	45.8	49.0	49.4	49.8	49.8	49.8	50.5	51.4	51.8	52.1
Male householder.	38.8	42.4	43.1	43.5	42.8	43.1	43.8	44.9	45.2	45.7
Female householder	51.3	53.6	53.8	54.1	54.6	54.5	55.4	56.0	56.7	56.9
Other										
Male householder.	30.1	31.7	31.8	32.4	32.6	33.6	34.2	35.5	35.9	36.7
Female householder	30.6	32.5	33.8	34.0	35.0	34.3	33.0	35.9	39.5	40.3

[1] Based on 1990 census controls.

Source: U.S. Census Bureau, <http://www.census.gov/hhes/www/hvs.html> (accessed 26 March 1999).

No. 1216. Homeownership Rates, by State: 1985 to 1998

[In percent. See headnote, Table 1215]

State	1985	1990	1995	1996	1997	1998	State	1985	1990	1995	1996	1997	1998
United States . .	63.9	63.9	64.7	65.4	65.7	66.3	Missouri.	69.2	64.0	69.4	70.2	70.5	70.7
Alabama	70.4	68.4	70.1	71.0	71.3	72.9	Montana	66.5	69.1	68.7	68.6	67.5	68.6
Alaska	61.2	58.4	60.9	62.9	67.2	66.3	Nebraska	68.5	67.3	67.1	66.8	66.7	69.9
Arizona	64.7	64.5	62.9	62.0	63.0	64.3	Nevada	57.0	55.8	58.6	61.1	61.2	61.4
Arkansas	66.6	67.8	67.2	66.6	66.7	66.7	New Hampshire	65.5	65.0	66.0	65.0	66.8	69.6
California	54.2	53.8	55.4	55.0	55.7	56.0	New Jersey	62.3	65.0	64.9	64.6	63.1	63.1
Colorado	63.6	59.0	64.6	64.5	64.1	65.2	New Mexico	68.2	68.6	67.0	67.1	69.6	71.3
Connecticut	69.0	67.9	68.2	69.0	68.1	69.3	New York	50.3	53.3	52.7	52.7	52.6	52.8
Delaware	70.3	67.7	71.7	71.5	69.2	71.0	North Carolina.	68.0	69.0	70.1	70.4	70.2	71.3
Dist of Columbia	37.4	36.4	39.2	40.4	42.5	40.3	North Dakota	69.9	67.2	67.3	68.2	68.1	68.0
Florida	67.2	65.1	66.6	67.1	66.9	66.9	Ohio	67.9	68.7	67.9	69.2	69.0	70.7
Georgia	62.7	64.3	66.6	69.3	70.9	71.2	Oklahoma	70.5	70.3	69.8	68.4	68.5	69.7
Hawaii	51.0	55.5	50.2	50.6	50.2	52.8	Oregon	61.5	64.4	63.2	63.1	61.0	63.4
Idaho.	71.0	69.4	72.0	71.4	72.3	72.6	Pennsylvania	71.6	73.8	71.5	71.7	73.3	73.9
Illinois	60.6	63.0	66.4	68.2	68.1	68.0	Rhode Island	61.4	58.5	57.9	56.6	58.7	59.8
Indiana	67.6	67.0	71.0	74.2	74.1	72.6	South Carolina	72.0	71.4	71.3	72.9	74.1	76.6
Iowa	69.9	70.7	71.4	72.8	72.7	72.1	South Dakota	67.6	66.2	67.5	67.8	67.6	67.3
Kansas	68.3	69.0	67.5	67.5	66.5	66.7	Tennessee	67.6	68.3	67.0	68.8	70.2	71.3
Kentucky	68.5	65.8	71.2	73.2	75.0	75.1	Texas	60.5	59.7	61.4	61.8	61.5	62.5
Louisiana	70.2	67.8	65.3	64.9	66.4	66.6	Utah	71.5	70.1	71.5	72.7	72.5	73.7
Maine	73.7	74.2	76.7	76.5	74.9	74.6	Vermont.	69.5	72.6	70.4	70.3	69.1	69.1
Maryland	65.6	64.9	65.8	66.9	70.5	68.7	Virginia	68.5	69.8	68.1	68.5	68.4	69.4
Massachusetts	60.5	58.6	60.2	61.7	62.3	61.3	Washington	66.8	61.8	61.6	63.1	62.9	64.9
Michigan	70.7	72.3	72.2	73.3	73.3	74.4	West Virginia	75.9	72.0	73.1	74.3	74.6	74.8
Minnesota	70.0	68.0	73.3	75.4	75.4	75.4	Wisconsin.	63.8	68.3	67.5	68.2	68.3	70.1
Mississippi	69.6	69.4	71.1	73.0	73.7	75.1	Wyoming	73.2	68.9	69.0	68.0	67.6	70.0

Source: U.S. Census Bureau, <http://www.census.gov/hhes/www/hvs.html> (accessed 26 March 1999).

U.S. Census Bureau, Statistical Abstract of the United States: 1999

No. 1217. Occupied Housing Units—Costs, by Region: 1997

[As of fall. (65,487 represents 65,487,000). Specified owner-occupied units are limited to one-unit structures on less than 10 acres and no business on property. Specified renter-occupied units exclude one-unit structures on 10 acres or more. See headnote Table 1218 for an explanation of housing costs. For composition of regions, see map inside front cover. Based on the American Housing Survey; see Appendix III]

Category	Number (1,000)					Percent distribution				
	Total units	North-east	Mid-west	South	West	Total units	North-east	Mid-west	South	West
OWNER OCCUPIED UNITS										
Total	65,487	12,241	16,902	23,650	12,694	100.0	100.0	100.0	100.0	100.0
Monthly housing costs:										
Less than $300	18,886	1,923	4,912	8,910	3,142	28.8	15.7	29.1	37.7	24.8
$300 to $399	6,936	1,493	2,186	2,185	1,073	10.6	12.2	12.9	9.2	8.5
$400 to $499	5,368	1,339	1,430	1,769	830	8.2	10.9	8.5	7.5	6.5
$500 to $599	4,612	967	1,379	1,625	641	7.0	7.9	8.2	6.9	5.0
$600 to $699	4,251	849	1,241	1,531	629	6.5	6.9	7.3	6.5	5.0
$700 to $799	3,792	765	1,078	1,355	595	5.8	6.2	6.4	5.7	4.7
$800 to $999	6,402	1,204	1,752	2,124	1,322	9.8	9.8	10.4	9.0	10.4
$1,000 to $1,249	5,249	1,168	1,252	1,562	1,267	8.0	9.5	7.4	6.6	10.0
$1,250 to $1,499	3,602	922	744	891	1,046	5.5	7.5	4.4	3.8	8.2
$1,500 or more	6,386	1,613	928	1,700	2,146	9.8	13.2	5.5	7.2	16.9
Median (dol.) [1]	534	647	494	439	705	(X)	(X)	(X)	(X)	(X)
RENTER OCCUPIED UNITS										
Total	34,000	7,242	7,050	11,157	8,551	100.0	100.0	100.0	100.0	100.0
Monthly housing costs:										
Less than $300	4,544	998	1,199	1,596	751	13.4	13.8	17.0	14.3	8.8
$300 to $399	3,808	606	1,128	1,427	648	11.2	8.4	16.0	12.8	7.6
$400 to $499	4,945	803	1,351	1,786	1,007	14.5	11.1	19.2	16.0	11.8
$500 to $599	5,327	1,087	1,115	1,775	1,349	15.7	15.0	15.8	15.9	15.8
$600 to $699	4,365	1,122	736	1,255	1,252	12.8	15.5	10.4	11.2	14.6
$700 to $799	3,162	727	493	940	1,002	9.3	10.0	7.0	8.4	11.7
$800 to $999	3,133	841	355	881	1,056	9.2	11.6	5.0	7.9	12.3
$1,000 to $1,249	1,395	326	136	314	619	4.1	4.5	1.9	2.8	7.2
$1,250 to $1,499	556	165	45	106	239	1.6	2.3	0.6	1.0	2.8
$1,500 or more	589	186	59	129	215	1.7	2.6	0.8	1.2	2.5
No cash rent.	2,171	380	432	947	412	6.4	5.2	6.1	8.5	4.8
Median (dol.) [1]	549	594	473	517	625	(X)	(X)	(X)	(X)	(X)

X Not applicable. [1] For explanation of median, see Guide to Tabular Presentation.

No. 1218. Occupied Housing Units—Financial Summary, by Selected Characteristics of the Householder: 1997

[In thousands of units (99,487 represents 99,487,000), except as indicated. As of fall. Housing costs include real estate taxes, property insurance, utilities, fuel, water, garbage collection, and mortgage. Based on the American Housing Survey; see Appendix III]

Characteristic	Total occupied units	Tenure		Black		Hispanic origin [1]		Elderly [2]		Households below poverty level	
		Owner	Renter	Owner	Renter	Owner	Renter	Owner	Renter	Owner	Renter
Total units [3]	99,487	65,487	34,000	5,457	6,628	3,646	4,867	16,493	4,413	6,619	9,108
Monthly housing costs:											
Less than $300	23,430	18,886	4,544	1,845	1,399	1,016	616	8,785	1,205	3,494	2,531
$300-$399.	10,744	6,936	3,808	572	864	263	531	2,679	470	805	1,248
$400-$499.	10,312	5,368	4,945	455	1,055	247	751	1,534	536	563	1,311
$500-$599.	9,939	4,612	5,327	530	982	242	869	912	515	418	1,089
$600-$699.	8,615	4,251	4,365	377	721	277	705	677	438	304	797
$700-$799.	6,955	3,792	3,162	325	469	216	495	403	268	219	469
$800-$999.	9,535	6,402	3,133	490	449	396	455	468	231	238	452
$1,000 or more	17,777	15,237	2,540	863	262	987	219	1,034	297	575	347
Median amount (dol.) [4]	542	534	549	464	480	620	549	287	453	285	426
Monthly housing costs as per-cent of income: [5]											
Less than 5 percent	4,790	4,433	357	340	56	192	48	760	44	23	14
5 to 9 percent	12,648	11,438	1,210	767	196	496	148	2,768	79	96	61
10 to 14 percent.	14,146	11,246	2,900	786	486	477	282	3,023	157	235	89
15 to 19 percent.	14,371	10,232	4,139	735	681	499	477	2,224	238	321	199
20 to 24 percent.	11,650	7,556	4,095	577	792	379	516	1,582	337	328	328
25 to 29 percent.	8,663	5,198	3,465	514	657	389	507	1,155	492	365	534
30 to 34 percent.	6,232	3,486	2,746	344	523	236	492	918	349	383	488
35 to 39 percent.	4,110	2,109	2,001	241	403	145	330	612	300	351	368
40 percent or more	18,527	8,652	9,876	993	2,156	766	1,712	2,993	1,833	3,434	5,229
Median amount (percent). . . .	20.7	17.5	28.9	16.1	25.4	21.7	32.8	18.3	38.7	54.6	65.5
Median monthly costs (dol.): [4]											
Electricity	63	70	46	73	49	67	45	61	39	63	45
Piped gas.	42	46	31	49	34	33	23	46	28	42	30
Fuel oil	63	66	49	67	44	79	24	64	52	60	44

[1] Persons of Hispanic origin may be of any race. [2] Householders 65 years old and over. [3] Includes units with mortgage payment not reported and no cash rent not shown separately. [4] For explanation of median, see Guide to Tabular Presentation. [5] Money income before taxes.

Source of Tables 1217 and 1218: U.S. Census Bureau, Current Housing Reports, Series H-150/97, American Housing Survey in the United States.

No. 1219. Mortgage Characteristics—Owner Occupied Units: 1997

[In thousands (65,487 represents 65,487,000). As of fall. Based on the American Housing Survey; see Appendix III]

Mortgage characteristic	Total occupied units	Housing unit characteristics		Household characteristics				
		New construc-tion [1]	Mobile homes	Black	Hispanic	Elderly [2]	Moved in past year	Below poverty level
ALL OWNERS								
Total [3]	65,487	4,894	5,255	5,457	3,646	16,493	5,093	6,619
Mortgages currently on property:								
None, owned free and clear	25,453	1,018	2,936	2,047	1,217	12,649	1,056	4,177
Reverse mortgage	29	-	-	-	-	29	-	5
Regular and home equity mortgages	5,757	352	95	357	163	293	199	198
Regular mortgage only	27,670	3,128	1,847	2,478	1,962	2,050	3,470	1,578
Home equity mortgage only	2,708	130	101	141	69	527	102	138
Regular mortgage, home equity not reported	2,427	147	163	268	139	558	172	314
No regular mortgage, home equity not reported	1,443	119	113	165	96	388	94	209
Number of regular and home equity mortgages:								
1 mortgage	29,210	3,174	1,914	2,473	1,947	2,508	3,465	1,677
2 mortgages	6,345	398	106	452	232	326	272	227
3 mortgages or more	444	19	15	39	12	23	16	16
Type of home equity mortgage: Units with 1 or more home equity mortgages	8,465	482	196	499	232	819	301	336
Lump sum only	3,354	220	108	259	109	298	109	126
Credit line only	4,765	233	64	209	119	498	160	184
Both	40	2	2	-	-	2	5	2
OWNERS WITH ONE OR MORE REGULAR MORTGAGES								
Total [3]	35,855	3,627	2,105	3,104	2,264	2,901	3,842	2,090
Type of primary mortgage:								
FHA	5,065	396	95	799	510	224	611	298
VA	1,936	160	20	263	147	104	165	77
Farmers Home Administration	364	37	14	57	29	52	24	26
Other types	25,579	2,873	1,769	1,626	1,433	1,859	2,841	1,323
Mortgage origination:								
Placed new mortgage(s)	34,766	3,613	2,030	2,995	2,181	2,801	3,747	2,000
Assumed	957	14	74	93	72	95	87	80
Wrap-around	26	-	-	3	-	-	3	6
Combination of the above	106	-	-	13	10	5	5	5
Payment plan of primary mortgage:								
Fixed payment, self amortizing	27,590	2,825	1,643	2,380	1,812	1,869	2,959	1,401
Adjustable rate mortgage	2,955	343	160	157	171	205	343	140
Adjustable term mortgage	256	41	39	34	12	35	58	43
Graduated payment mortgage	376	45	9	25	14	12	65	9
Balloon	328	56	9	7	18	16	61	19
Combination of the above	360	48	11	28	27	13	54	16

- Represents or rounds to zero. [1] Constructed in the past 4 years. [2] 65 years old and over. [3] Includes types not known and not reported.

Source: U.S. Census Bureau, Current Housing Reports, Series H150/97, American Housing Survey in the United States.

No. 1220. Debt Status of Homeowners, by Selected Characteristic: 1997

[In percent. See headnote, Table 821]

Homeowner characteristic	All home-owners	No mort-gage debt	First mort-gage only [1]	Home equity line of credit	Traditional home equity loan	Either type of home equity loan
All homeowners	100	100	100	100	100	100
Age of head:						
18 to 34 years old	16	7	24	6	23	12
35 to 44 years old	23	9	31	28	32	30
45 to 54 years old	20	12	24	34	27	31
55 to 64 years old	16	18	13	20	11	17
65 years old and over	26	55	8	12	6	10
Family income:						
Less than $15,000	10	20	4	2	2	2
$15,000 to $24,999	16	26	11	3	6	4
$25,000 to $49,999	34	32	38	25	32	27
$50,000 to $74,999	23	12	26	38	42	39
$75,000 to $99,999	10	5	13	16	8	14
$100,000 or more	8	5	8	16	11	14
Home equity [2]:						
Less than $50,000	41	24	55	21	69	38
$50,000 to $99,999	33	38	29	40	21	34
$100,000 or more	26	37	16	39	10	28

[1] Excludes those who have only a home equity line of credit. [2] Home equity consists of the market value of the home less all debts secured by the home, including balances outstanding on equity lines of credit and traditional home equity loans.

Source: Board of Governors of the Federal Reserve System, Federal Reserve Bulletin, April 1998.

Construction and Housing 733

No. 1221. Heating Equipment and Fuels for Occupied Units: 1991 to 1997

[As of fall. (93,147 represents 93,147,000). Based on American Housing Survey. See Appendix III]

Type of equipment or fuel	Number (1,000)				Percent distribution	
	1991	1993	1995	1997	1991	1997
Occupied units, total	**93,147**	**94,724**	**97,692**	**99,487**	**100.0**	**100.0**
Heating equipment:						
Warm air furnace.	49,423	51,248	53,165	58,603	53.1	58.9
Heat pumps.	7,638	8,422	9,406	11,101	8.2	11.2
Steam or hot water	13,929	13,657	13,669	12,929	15.0	13.0
Floor, wall, or pipeless furnace.	4,291	4,746	4,963	5,588	4.6	5.6
Built-in electric units.	6,755	6,722	7,035	4,531	7.3	4.6
Room heaters with flue.	2,549	1,766	1,620	1,584	2.7	1.6
Room heaters without flue	2,111	1,597	1,642	1,754	2.3	1.8
Fireplaces, stoves, portable heaters or other . .	5,590	5,654	5,150	2,780	6.0	2.8
None.	861	911	1,044	620	0.9	0.6
House main heating fuel:						
Utility gas.	47,018	47,669	49,203	51,052	50.5	51.3
Fuel oil, kerosene, etc..	12,462	12,189	12,029	10,855	13.4	10.9
Electricity.	23,714	25,107	26,771	29,202	25.5	29.4
Bottled, tank, or LP gas	3,882	3,922	4,251	5,398	4.2	5.4
Coal or coke.	319	297	210	183	0.3	0.2
Wood and other fuel	4,890	4,630	4,186	2,177	5.2	2.2
None.	862	910	1,043	620	0.9	0.6
Cooking fuel:						
Electricity.	54,232	55,887	57,621	58,818	58.2	59.1
Gas [1]	38,119	37,996	39,218	40,083	40.9	40.3
Other fuel	424	479	566	474	0.5	0.5
None.	372	362	287	113	0.4	0.1

[1] Includes utility, bottled, tank, and LP gas.

Source: U.S. Census Bureau, *Current Housing Reports*, Series H150/91, H150/93, H150/95RV, and H150/97, *American Housing Survey in the United States*.

No. 1222. Occupied Housing Units—Housing Indicators, by Selected Characteristics of the Householder: 1997

[In thousands of units (99,487 represents 99,487,000). As of fall. Based on the American Housing Survey; see Appendix III]

Characteristic	Total occu-pied units	Tenure		Black		Hispanic origin [1]		Elderly [2]		Households below poverty level	
		Owner	Renter	Owner	Renter	Owner	Renter	Owner	Renter	Owner	Renter
Total units	**99,487**	**65,487**	**34,000**	**5,457**	**6,628**	**3,646**	**4,867**	**16,493**	**4,413**	**6,619**	**9,108**
Amenities:											
Porch, deck, balcony or patio .	75,986	55,374	20,612	4,217	3,689	2,835	2,477	13,737	2,371	5,156	4,791
Usable fireplace	31,825	27,702	4,123	1,554	460	1,106	354	5,575	280	1,721	526
Separate dining room	39,077	31,411	7,666	2,805	1,635	1,555	917	7,269	749	2,696	1,690
With 2 or more living rooms or recreation rooms	34,515	31,582	2,932	2,493	479	1,263	191	7,181	312	2,226	499
Garage or carport with home .	58,027	47,488	10,539	2,903	1,173	2,566	1,543	12,208	1,210	3,754	1,969
Cars and trucks available:											
No cars, trucks, or vans	9,447	2,480	6,967	480	2,438	132	1,174	1,713	2,028	944	3,636
Other households without cars	7,494	5,165	2,329	178	175	373	391	704	123	560	475
1 car with or without trucks or vans	47,902	30,544	17,357	2,541	3,019	1,673	2,313	9,808	1,961	3,509	3,991
2 cars.	27,573	21,185	6,389	1,803	904	1,117	845	3,688	270	1,381	883
3 or more cars	7,071	6,112	958	455	92	352	143	579	31	226	123
With cars, no trucks or vans . .	51,617	32,456	19,161	3,241	3,501	1,654	2,590	9,667	1,881	3,308	4,096
1 truck or van with or without cars	28,096	22,171	5,925	1,346	474	1,346	829	3,952	308	1,742	971
2 or more trucks or vans	10,327	8,380	1,948	390	215	514	273	1,160	195	626	405
Internal deficiencies:											
Signs of rats in last 3 months .	920	425	495	78	154	68	180	79	42	92	211
Holes in floors	1,168	487	680	81	209	54	184	99	48	126	288
Open cracks or holes	5,748	2,719	3,029	387	778	229	493	420	212	342	1,010
Broken plaster or peeling paint (interior of unit)	2,938	1,239	1,699	189	461	94	378	256	130	177	635
No electrical wiring	40	33	7	3	-	-	5	5	3	17	5
Exposed wiring	788	457	331	58	84	35	74	106	43	68	123
Rooms without electric outlet .	2,122	1,160	962	119	238	88	181	281	106	190	323
Water leakage [3]	9,667	5,177	4,490	558	1,054	338	594	817	311	476	1,126

- Represents zero. [1] Persons of Hispanic origin may be of any race. [2] Householders 65 years old and over. [3] During the 12 months prior to the survey.

Source: U.S. Census Bureau, *Current Housing Reports*, Series H150/97, *American Housing Survey in the United States*.

No. 1223. Appliances and Office Equipment Used by Households, by Region and Family Income: 1997

[Preliminary (101.5 represents 101,500,000). Represents appliances possessed and generally used by the household. Based on Residential Energy Consumption Survey; see source. For composition of regions, see map inside front cover]

Type of appliance	House-holds using appliance	Region				Family income in 1997			
		North-east	Mid-west	South	West	Under $10,000	$10,000-$24,999	$25,000-$49,999	$50,000 and over
Total households (mil.)	101.5	19.7	24.1	35.9	21.8	13.3	29.1	31.1	27.9
PERCENT WITH—									
Air conditioner:									
Central system	47.1	22.3	51.4	69.7	27.6	27.7	37.7	50.7	62.2
Room	26.1	41.4	27.4	24.3	13.9	33.9	29.8	25.4	19.2
Clothes washer	77.4	76.0	78.9	81.9	69.6	52.7	69.0	81.5	93.4
Clothes dryer [1]	71.1	66.7	75.7	74.2	65.1	36.2	61.0	77.1	91.8
Electric	55.0	48.2	50.1	66.3	48.2	31.0	49.0	59.9	67.5
Natural gas	15.3	17.9	23.9	7.4	16.6	4.8	11.1	16.4	23.6
Dishwasher	50.2	48.5	46.9	51.5	53.1	15.7	35.5	53.6	78.2
Ceiling fan	60.1	51.3	63.6	71.2	46.0	39.3	55.2	64.4	70.3
Freezer	33.2	25.7	41.8	36.9	24.2	25.7	30.0	35.1	37.9
One	30.2	24.2	38.4	33.1	22.0	23.6	27.5	32.2	34.1
Two or more	2.9	1.5	3.4	3.8	2.2	2.0	2.5	2.9	3.8
Microwave oven	83.0	78.7	86.9	82.4	83.3	60.3	81.1	86.7	91.5
Oven	98.8	99.3	99.1	98.6	98.2	96.4	98.7	99.4	99.3
Electric	61.5	49.7	56.6	72.0	60.1	49.2	58.7	63.9	67.5
Natural gas	33.2	44.8	38.1	22.1	35.7	41.8	34.8	31.5	29.5
Self cleaning oven	44.0	48.5	45.0	41.8	42.7	18.1	31.1	47.0	66.6
Range	99.2	99.6	99.4	99.0	98.8	96.8	99.1	99.8	99.6
Electric	60.3	48.8	55.6	70.9	58.4	49.2	58.4	62.9	64.6
Natural gas	34.6	45.5	39.4	23.5	37.7	42.0	35.5	32.8	32.1
Refrigerator	99.9	99.9	99.9	99.9	99.7	99.3	99.9	99.9	100.0
Frost free	86.8	85.2	85.1	90.0	84.7	73.0	83.1	88.5	95.2
Water heater [1]	100.0	100.0	100.0	100.0	100.0	100.0	100.0	100.0	100.0
Electric	39.5	26.5	27.6	58.3	33.3	41.9	43.9	39.9	33.1
Natural gas	51.7	46.8	66.4	37.4	63.2	46.3	48.0	51.7	58.0
Stereo equipment	68.8	66.7	67.0	67.8	74.4	45.2	60.1	73.7	83.7
Color TV	98.7	98.8	99.0	98.7	98.2	96.1	98.4	99.2	99.6
One	31.9	31.8	32.1	29.1	36.1	55.6	40.5	27.3	16.6
Two	37.4	36.1	36.2	38.9	37.2	30.9	37.7	41.6	35.4
Three	19.1	20.8	20.4	18.4	17.3	7.5	15.5	20.4	26.8
Four	7.6	7.5	7.8	8.9	5.5	1.7	3.6	8.2	14.0
Five or more	2.8	2.6	2.5	3.4	2.2	(S)	1.1	1.7	6.8
VCR	87.6	86.1	89.7	86.0	89.0	66.8	84.0	91.6	96.6
Personal computers	35.0	31.9	38.0	31.0	41.3	9.7	16.5	36.9	64.5
One	29.2	27.2	32.4	25.9	32.8	7.9	14.5	32.8	50.6
Two or more	5.9	4.7	5.6	5.1	8.5	(S)	2.0	4.1	13.8
With modem	20.4	17.8	21.7	18.2	24.9	5.2	8.6	19.7	40.7
With laser printer	12.4	11.3	12.9	11.7	14.2	2.5	4.4	12.8	25.1
Used 15 hrs. per week or less . .	25.2	21.5	27.7	23.0	29.2	6.3	12.2	28.2	44.4
Used 16 hrs. per week or more .	9.9	10.4	10.2	8.0	12.1	3.4	4.2	8.7	20.0
Personal use only	4.7	4.5	5.2	4.2	5.3	2.3	2.3	4.1	9.1
Business use only	2.1	2.3	2.5	1.1	3.1	(S)	(S)	1.4	5.0
Both	3.1	3.6	2.6	2.7	3.7	(S)	1.2	3.3	6.0
Cordless phone	61.4	59.6	63.8	61.4	60.2	35.3	51.5	66.9	77.9
Facsimile machine	6.2	6.5	5.3	5.6	8.1	(S)	2.5	5.3	13.3
Photocopier	3.7	3.8	3.9	3.5	3.9	(S)	1.5	3.9	7.3
Answering machine	58.4	62.2	61.0	54.2	59.1	30.2	49.1	62.3	77.2

S Figure does not meet publication standards.   [1] Includes other types, not shown separately.
Source: U.S. Energy Information Administration, Internet site <http://www.eia.doe/emeu/consumption> (accessed 20 May 1998).

No. 1224. Net Stock of Residential Capital: 1985 to 1997

[In billions of dollars (4,683.3 represents $4,683,300,000,000). End of year estimates]

Item	1985	1988	1989	1990	1991	1992	1993	1994	1995	1996	1997
Total residential capital [1]	**4,683.3**	**5,737.1**	**6,054.7**	**6,295.7**	**6,407.8**	**6,749.5**	**7,152.5**	**7,643.5**	**7,964.4**	**8,378.2**	**8,791.1**
By type of owner and legal form of organization:											
Private	4,578.2	5,602.7	5,911.1	6,147.3	6,258.5	6,591.4	6,983.1	7,465.8	7,779.0	8,185.5	8,590.9
Corporate	55.6	65.3	67.1	68.6	69.4	72.3	74.0	76.1	78.3	81.5	84.3
Noncorporate	4,522.6	5,537.4	5,844.0	6,078.7	6,189.1	6,519.1	6,909.2	7,389.6	7,700.7	8,104.0	8,506.6
Government	105.1	134.4	143.6	148.4	149.3	158.2	169.4	177.7	185.4	192.7	200.2
Federal	32.0	46.2	50.3	51.4	50.1	52.9	56.1	58.7	61.1	63.2	65.3
State and local	73.1	88.3	93.3	97.0	99.2	105.3	113.3	119.1	124.3	129.5	134.9
By tenure group:											
Owner-occupied	3,254.0	4,043.9	4,298.3	4,494.3	4,597.9	4,870.7	5,211.9	5,629.7	5,899.7	6,241.1	6,587.8
Farm	128.6	142.5	146.9	151.2	152.0	156.8	162.2	170.7	175.1	180.0	184.7
Nonfarm	3,125.3	3,901.4	4,151.4	4,343.1	4,445.9	4,713.9	5,049.6	5,459.0	5,724.7	6,061.1	6,403.1
Tenant-occupied	1,302.3	1,534.0	1,587.1	1,626.7	1,634.7	1,694.1	1,743.4	1,807.1	1,849.9	1,914.4	1,972.3
Farm	5.6	6.3	6.4	6.7	6.7	6.9	7.3	7.8	8.1	8.4	8.6
Nonfarm	1,296.7	1,527.7	1,580.7	1,620.1	1,628.0	1,687.2	1,736.2	1,799.3	1,841.8	1,906.0	1,963.7

[1] Includes stocks of other nonfarm residential capital, which consists of dormitories, fraternity and sorority houses, and nurses' homes.
Source: U.S. Bureau of Economic Analysis, Survey of Current Business, monthly, September 1998 issue.

Construction and Housing   735

No. 1225. Expenditures by Residential Property Owners for Improvements and Maintenance and Repairs, by Type of Property and Activity: 1980 to 1997

[In millions of dollars (46,338 represents $46,338,000,000)]

Year and type of expenditure	Total	One-unit properties with owner occupant	Other properties	Additions and alterations Total	To structures Additions	To structures Alterations	To property outside of structures	Major replacements	Maintenance and repairs
1980	46,338	31,481	14,857	21,336	4,183	11,193	5,960	9,816	15,187
1982	45,291	29,779	15,512	18,774	2,641	10,711	5,423	9,707	16,810
1983	49,295	32,524	16,771	20,271	4,739	11,673	3,859	10,895	18,128
1984	69,784	43,781	26,003	27,822	6,007	14,486	7,329	13,067	28,894
1985	80,267	47,742	32,525	28,775	3,966	17,599	7,211	16,134	35,358
1986	91,274	54,298	36,976	38,608	7,377	21,192	10,040	16,695	35,971
1987	94,082	54,791	39,291	39,978	9,557	21,641	8,779	15,875	38,229
1988	101,117	60,822	40,295	43,339	11,333	22,703	9,303	16,893	40,885
1989	100,891	59,858	41,033	39,786	6,828	23,129	9,828	18,415	42,689
1990	106,773	59,683	47,090	37,253	8,561	21,920	6,771	18,215	51,305
1991	97,528	58,083	39,445	30,944	7,914	16,076	6,954	16,744	49,840
1992	103,734	67,316	36,418	40,186	6,783	22,700	10,704	18,393	45,154
1993	108,305	70,746	37,559	45,797	12,757	24,781	8,259	20,809	41,699
1994	115,030	77,270	37,760	48,828	9,647	28,672	10,509	23,248	42,953
1995	111,683	75,362	36,321	44,726	7,936	26,893	9,897	24,910	42,047
1996, total [1]	**114,919**	**76,094**	**38,825**	**53,456**	**12,035**	**30,064**	**11,357**	**24,465**	**36,997**
Heating and air conditioning [2]	10,315	7,028	3,287	2,637	(NA)	2,637	(NA)	4,741	2,937
Plumbing	7,884	4,398	3,486	1,892	(NA)	1,892	(NA)	2,239	3,753
Roofing	9,964	6,435	3,529	(NA)	(NA)	(NA)	(NA)	6,809	3,155
Painting	12,126	6,658	5,474	(NA)	(NA)	(NA)	(NA)	(NA)	12,126
1997, total [1]	**118,569**	**82,216**	**36,353**	**55,530**	**11,042**	**33,046**	**11,442**	**24,463**	**38,576**
Heating and air conditioning [2]	10,904	7,648	3,256	3,041	(NA)	3,041	(NA)	5,917	1,945
Plumbing	10,434	5,788	4,646	3,668	(NA)	3,668	(NA)	2,765	4,000
Roofing	11,493	7,885	3,608	(NA)	(NA)	(NA)	(NA)	6,662	4,832
Painting	11,348	7,443	3,905	(NA)	(NA)	(NA)	(NA)	(NA)	11,348

NA Not available.   [1] Includes types of expenditures not separately specified.   [2] Central air-conditioning.

Source: U.S. Census Bureau, Current Construction Reports, Series C50, Expenditures for Residential Improvement, quarterly.

No. 1226. Rental Units, by Type of Owner: 1995

[In thousands (8,773 represents 8,773,000). For privately owned rental properties. Based on the Property Owners and Managers Survey and subject to sampling error; see source for details]

Characteristic	Single family properties Total	Single family properties Detached	Multifamily properties Total	2 units	3 to 4 units	5 to 9 units	10 to 19 units	20 to 49 units	50 units or more
All properties [1]	**8,773**	**6,438**	**20,585**	**3,085**	**2,471**	**1,894**	**1,468**	**2,224**	**9,443**
With individual or partnership owners [2]	7,746	5,752	16,915	2,953	2,347	1,713	1,236	1,858	6,808
Under 25 years old	-	-	14	5	3	-	3	-	3
25 to 34 years old	218	118	490	155	130	68	24	44	69
35 to 44 years old	1,146	823	1,514	475	281	232	114	122	289
45 to 54 years old	1,663	1,237	2,808	670	496	372	184	341	744
55 to 64 years old	1,747	1,336	2,698	561	494	337	218	373	716
65 to 74 years old	1,425	1,093	1,995	428	349	232	167	201	618
75 years or older	891	713	958	270	220	94	109	65	221
Male	5,130	3,814	9,584	1,866	1,540	1,103	768	1,181	3,125
Female	2,316	1,744	2,261	838	545	347	150	174	206
White	6,307	4,654	10,400	2,264	1,731	1,270	825	1,234	3,077
Black	595	499	599	241	197	79	17	14	51
American Indian or Alaskan Native	41	30	22	4	8	3	-	-	7
Asian or Pacific Islander	254	192	442	90	79	53	50	63	107
Other	174	127	217	56	49	32	7	30	43
Hispanic	436	322	479	135	126	80	27	59	52
Non-Hispanic	6,719	5,017	11,104	2,492	1,925	1,334	864	1,276	3,213
Percent of rental income spent on maintenance:									
None	1,261	1,020	283	185	27	27	7	-	36
1 to 4 percent	1,426	1,022	1,530	407	280	141	105	122	475
5 to 9 percent	1,429	1,057	2,844	513	385	275	230	338	1,103
10 to 19 percent	1,741	1,303	4,446	784	658	400	380	431	1,793
20 to 29 percent	764	516	2,287	317	283	256	145	263	1,023
30 to 39 percent	316	211	1,270	158	118	103	58	162	671
40 to 49 percent	182	114	751	78	35	95	83	89	370
50 to 74 percent	231	174	935	73	128	73	65	130	466
75 percent or more	300	219	639	132	123	78	26	91	190

- Represents zero.   [1] Includes properties with other owners not shown separately.   [2] Includes properties with owners not reporting.

Source: U.S. Census Bureau, Internet site <http://www.census.gov/hhes/www/poms.html> (accessed 23 April 1997).

No. 1227. Commercial Office Space—Overview for Selected Market Areas: 1998

[As of **mid-October. (3,491,274 represents 3,491,274,000).** For the 76 market areas with the highest vacancy rates in 1998. Data based on responses from individuals knowledgeable in the local markets]

Market area	Inventory (1,000 sq. ft.)	Vacant space (1,000 sq. ft.)	Vacancy rate (percent)	Construction (1,000 sq. ft.)	Net absorption [1] (1,000 sq. ft.)
United States, all market areas [2] . . .	3,491,274	305,624	8.8	119,764	111,526
Albuquerque, NM	10,801	1,072	9.9	525	733
Allentown, PA	7,581	1,067	14.1	233	1,057
Annapolis, MD	2,428	201	8.3	44	-172
Atlanta, GA	71,423	6,505	9.1	4,220	(NA)
Baltimore, MD	39,001	4,559	11.7	450	245
Bridgeport/Stratford, CT.	7,619	844	11.1	351	437
Bristol, VA.	710	65	9.2	22	(NA)
Buffalo, NY	8,286	961	11.6	278	638
Charleston, SC	3,728	314	8.4	250	193
Chicago, IL	148,604	17,517	11.8	2,814	3,848
Cincinnati, OH	32,284	2,832	8.8	520	4,542
Cleveland, OH.	36,144	4,396	12.2	650	1,491
Columbia, SC	9,955	839	8.4	305	360
Corpus Christi, CA	2,789	534	19.2	(NA)	-5
Dallas, TX.	134,864	17,629	13.1	12,171	7,007
Dayton, OH.	12,103	1,940	16.0	18	147
Denver, CO.	63,708	6,476	10.2	2,200	5,213
Des Moines, IA	9,228	884	9.6	88	168
El Paso, TX.	6,850	864	12.6	120	175
Fort Lauderdale, FL	15,293	1,596	10.4	1,258	1,219
Fort Worth, TX.	18,433	2,195	11.9	365	41
Fresno, CA	13,168	1,437	10.9	156	353
Grand Rapids, MI.	10,190	959	9.4	415	447
Greensboro, NC.	14,181	1,859	13.1	423	369
Greenville, SC	5,014	585	11.7	325	474
Hartford, CT	20,689	4,261	20.6	-	(NA)
Indianapolis, IN	19,759	2,318	11.7	791	600
Jacksonville, FL.	22,669	2,291	10.1	1,760	1,695
Knoxville, TN.	9,715	870	9.0	170	80
Las Vegas, NV	13,936	1,625	11.7	950	1,777
Little Rock, AR.	10,380	918	8.8	240	238
Los Angeles-Central, CA	27,836	5,120	18.4	(NA)	-380
Los Angeles-East, CA	2,740	247	9.0	40	117
Los Angeles-Inland Empire, CA.	6,241	1,131	18.1	117	90
Los Angeles-Orange County, CA	53,810	4,611	8.6	1,201	3,167
Los Angeles-San Fernando Valley, CA . . .	31,601	3,792	12.0	600	494
Los Angeles-San Gabriel, CA	12,267	1,840	15.0	(NA)	1,195
Los Angeles-South Bay, CA	29,707	5,494	18.5	377	997
Los Angeles-West, CA	46,829	3,893	8.3	951	1,753
Louisville, KY.	14,196	1,841	13.0	450	424
Melbourne, FL.	4,211	592	14.1	44	89
Miami, FL.	28,729	2,758	9.6	1,296	973
Milwaukee, WI	25,577	2,555	10.0	165	451
Mobile, AL.	3,363	450	13.4	46	180
Nashua, NH	1,891	229	12.1	106	-58
New Haven, CT.	12,500	2,060	16.5	290	300
New Jersey-Central	62,469	6,924	11.1	4,301	3,193
New Jersey-Northern	63,887	11,466	17.9	2,086	3,691
New Jersey-Southern	15,606	1,618	10.4	571	1,817
New Orleans, LA	17,822	2,814	15.8	(NA)	140
New York-Long Island, NY	37,355	3,298	8.8	720	1,213
Oakland, CA	15,190	3,209	21.1	275	(NA)
Oklahoma City, OK.	14,025	2,324	16.6	(NA)	-43
Philadelphia, PA.	85,517	7,542	8.8	1,112	1,892
Pittsburgh, PA.	33,602	4,107	12.2	241	-634
Providence, RI.	9,140	946	10.4	45	656
Richmond, VA.	19,349	1,645	8.5	242	398
Roanoke, VA.	2,797	333	11.9	39	51
Rochester, NY.	13,443	1,490	11.1	477	301
Sacramento, CA.	26,877	2,220	8.3	2,701	719
Saint Louis, MO.	35,913	3,392	9.4	1,356	1,656
San Antonio, TX.	16,833	1,956	11.6	446	47
Shreveport, LA	3,621	879	24.3	(NA)	27
Sioux Falls, SD	1,838	206	11.2	21	100
Sonoma County, CA	4,736	509	10.7	91	254
South Bend, IN	2,916	252	8.6	140	237
Syracuse, NY	9,211	1,427	15.5	-	249
Tampa, FL	22,161	2,048	9.2	1,078	810
Toledo, OH	6,674	1,265	18.9	107	131
Tucson, AZ	6,350	614	9.7	197	-108
Tulsa, OK.	14,929	1,283	8.6	-	954
Ventura/Oxnard, CA	9,375	1,225	13.1	200	260
West Palm Beach, FL.	8,946	1,020	11.4	340	859
Wichita, KS.	6,001	997	16.6	(NA)	24
Wilmington, DE	11,002	1,103	10.0	113	407
Youngstown, OH	2,500	315	12.6	25	-5

- Represents zero.   NA Not available.   [1] Net change in occupied stock.   [2] Includes other market areas, not shown separately.

Source: Society of Industrial and Office REALTORS, Washington DC, *1999 Comparative Statistics of Industrial and Office Real Estate Markets* (copyright).

No. 1228. Commercial Buildings—Selected Characteristics, by Square Footage of Floorspace: 1995

[Excludes buildings 1,000 square feet or smaller (4,579 represents 4,579,000). Building type based on predominant activity in which the occupants were engaged. Based on a sample survey of building representatives conducted between August and December 1995; therefore, subject to sampling variability. For composition of regions, see map inside front cover]

Characteristic	Number of buildings (1,000)	Floorspace (mil. sq. ft.)							Mean sq. ft. per building (1,000)	Median sq. ft. per building (1,000)
		Total	Within buildings having square footage of—							
			5,000 or less	5,001 to 10,000	10,001 to 25,000	25,001 to 50,000	50,001 to 100,000	100,001 and over		
All buildings	4,579	58,772	6,338	7,530	11,617	7,676	7,968	17,643	12.8	5.0
Region:										
Northeast	725	11,883	995	1,223	2,118	1,380	1,371	4,795	16.4	5.0
Midwest	1,139	14,322	1,772	1,678	2,701	1,726	1,920	4,526	12.6	4.5
South	1,750	20,830	2,428	2,786	4,481	2,664	2,980	5,491	11.9	4.8
West	964	11,736	1,144	1,842	2,317	1,905	1,697	2,831	12.2	5.5
Year constructed:										
1919 or before	353	3,673	442	756	957	407	386	[3]340	10.4	5.5
1920 to 1945	562	6,710	855	981	1,241	595	750	2,288	11.9	4.8
1946 to 1959	867	9,298	1,180	1,710	1,942	1,260	1,293	1,913	10.7	4.3
1960 to 1969	718	10,858	889	1,132	2,163	1,650	1,453	3,572	15.1	5.5
1970 to 1979	813	11,333	1,245	1,186	2,071	1,337	1,453	4,040	13.9	5.0
1980 to 1989	846	12,252	1,087	1,102	2,809	1,701	1,816	3,737	14.5	5.0
1990 to 1992	218	2,590	316	368	251	378	410	867	11.9	3.5
1993 to 1995	202	2,059	324	296	184	349	407	[4]264	10.2	3.5
Principal activity within building:										
Education	309	7,740	250	404	1,045	1,825	1,752	[1]2,216	25.1	8.5
Food sales	137	642	234	(S)	(S)	(S)	(S)	(NA)	4.7	2.5
Food service	285	1,353	550	390	(S)	(S)	(S)	(NA)	4.8	3.0
Health care	105	2,333	152	(S)	243	175	(S)	1,483	22.2	4.5
Lodging	158	3,618	150	269	748	512	613	[1]1,105	22.8	9.0
Mercantile/services	1,289	12,728	1,841	2,202	2,939	1,180	1,274	3,292	9.9	4.0
Office	705	10,478	1,084	915	1,580	1,293	1,542	4,064	14.9	4.0
Public assembly	326	3,948	312	786	940	485	499	[1]655	12.1	6.0
Public order and safety	87	1,271	(S)	(S)	368	(S)	(S)	(NA)	14.6	5.0
Religious worship	269	2,792	301	662	1,120	392	(S)	(NA)	10.4	8.0
Warehouse	580	8,481	807	991	1,530	1,165	1,147	2,841	14.6	5.5
Other	67	1,004	(S)	(S)	(S)	(S)	(S)	(NA)	14.9	5.0
Vacant	261	2,384	399	497	503	148	225	(NA)	9.1	4.0
Government owned	553	12,076	630	924	1,546	2,023	2,211	4,741	21.8	7.0
Nongovernment owned	4,025	46,696	5,709	6,606	10,071	5,653	5,757	9,209	11.6	4.8
Fuels used alone or in combination:										
Electricity	4,358	57,275	6,008	7,064	11,310	7,641	7,925	17,326	13.1	5.0
Natural gas	2,522	38,838	3,020	4,542	7,654	5,309	5,658	12,655	15.4	5.5
Fuel oil	634	14,670	987	713	1,445	1,164	1,992	8,368	23.1	4.8
Propane	589	5,344	997	881	1,342	562	637	[1]772	9.1	4.0
District heat	115	5,941	(S)	(S)	407	673	792	3,848	51.6	12.5
District chilled water	53	2,521	(S)	(S)	239	275	348	1,576	47.7	12.5
Any other	213	2,336	278	414	413	223	419	[2]252	16.2	4.0
Workers:										
Fewer than 5	2,505	13,885	4,184	3,636	3,806	770	518	[3]415	5.5	3.0
5 to 9	798	6,291	1,202	1,608	2,090	529	567	(NA)	7.9	4.8
10 to 19	625	7,102	695	1,637	2,399	1,099	557	[3]480	11.4	7.5
20 to 49	400	9,132	225	615	2,513	2,620	2,087	[1]940	22.8	16.3
50 to 99	138	6,931	(S)	(S)	567	1,644	2,108	[1]2,325	50.3	37.5
100 to 249	71	5,988	(S)	(S)	155	913	1,472	3,431	84.4	55.0
250 or more	43	9,443	(S)	(S)	(S)	(S)	658	8,598	220.1	120.0
Weekly operating hours:										
39 or less	899	6,143	1,544	1,619	1,354	576	426	(NA)	6.8	4.0
40 to 48	1,257	13,233	1,701	2,033	3,382	1,981	1,776	[1]2,144	10.5	4.8
49 to 60	969	12,242	1,264	1,707	2,562	2,103	1,897	2,709	12.6	5.5
61 to 84	567	10,052	653	1,020	1,873	1,182	1,354	3,970	17.7	6.0
85 to 167	420	6,202	618	503	1,024	749	988	2,319	14.8	4.3
168 (open continuously)	466	10,908	559	647	1,422	1,085	1,527	5,670	23.4	6.0

NA Not available.   S Figure does not meet publication standards.   [1] 100,001 to 500,000 square feet.   [2] 200,001 to 500,000 square feet.   [3] 100,001 to 200,000 square feet.   [4] 200,001 square feet and over.

Source: U.S. Energy Information Administration, *Commercial Buildings Energy Consumption Survey, 1995*, Internet site <http://www.eia.doe.gov/emeu/cbecs/contents.html> (accessed 26 August 1998).

No. 1229. Commercial Buildings—Number and Size, by Principal Activity: 1995

[See headnote, Table 1228. **(4,579 represents 4,579,000)** For composition of regions, see map inside front cover]

Building characteristics	All build-ings [1]	Educa-tion	Food sales	Food service	Health care	Lodging	Mercan-tile/ services	Offices	Public assem-bly	Reli-gious worship	Ware-house
NUMBER (1,000)											
All buildings	**4,579**	**309**	**137**	**285**	**105**	**158**	**1,289**	**705**	**326**	**269**	**580**
Region: Northeast	725	39	(S)	41	14	10	241	112	46	41	88
Midwest	1,139	42	(S)	69	19	38	390	157	89	57	163
South	1,750	111	73	109	51	51	457	298	134	97	223
West	964	117	32	66	21	59	201	138	57	74	105
Year constructed:											
1919 or before	353	18	(S)	(S)	(S)	(S)	112	57	37	20	31
1920 to 1945	562	42	(S)	(S)	(S)	7	154	74	72	(S)	59
1946 to 1959	867	72	(S)	(S)	19	33	278	128	38	65	79
1960 to 1969	718	66	(S)	25	7	53	229	75	63	50	68
1970 to 1979	813	45	42	66	34	24	207	158	60	53	73
1980 to 1986	846	36	(S)	74	(S)	25	212	151	33	58	161
1990 to 1992	218	17	(S)	(S)	(S)	(S)	47	38	20	(S)	38
1993 to 1995	202	13	(S)	(S)	(S)	(S)	49	23	(S)	(S)	71
FLOORSPACE (mil. sq. ft.)											
All buildings	**58,772**	**7,740**	**642**	**1,353**	**2,333**	**3,618**	**12,728**	**10,478**	**3,948**	**2,792**	**8,481**
Region: Northeast	11,883	1,930	(S)	166	408	350	2,838	2,154	694	442	1,480
Midwest	14,322	1,997	(S)	474	466	909	3,203	2,338	957	633	2,044
South	20,830	2,315	287	443	916	1,313	4,864	3,483	1,367	1,006	3,436
West	11,736	1,498	209	271	543	1,047	1,822	2,503	930	711	1,522
Year constructed:											
1919 or before	3,673	521	(S)	(S)	(S)	(S)	816	599	381	266	192
1920 to 1945	6,710	1,080	(S)	(S)	(S)	170	1,118	1,155	706	(S)	1,076
1946 to 1959	9,298	1,921	(S)	(S)	356	607	1,895	1,262	498	637	1,236
1960 to 1969	10,858	1,841	(S)	192	428	972	2,342	1,206	821	535	1,530
1970 to 1979	11,333	1,232	165	285	748	576	2,749	2,095	736	510	1,616
1980 to 1986	12,252	614	(S)	305	425	829	2,727	3,377	399	598	2,104
1990 to 1992	2,590	238	(S)	(S)	(S)	(S)	632	568	221	(S)	318
1993 to 1995	2,059	293	(S)	(S)	(S)	(S)	449	217	(S)	(S)	409

S Figure does not meet publication standards. [1] Includes other commercial buildings, not shown separately.
Source: U.S. Energy Information Administration, *Commercial Buildings Energy Consumption Survey, 1995*, Internet site <http://www.eia.doe.gov/emeu/cbecs/contents.html> (accessed 28 August 1998).

No. 1230. Office Buildings—Vacancy Rates for Major Markets: 1980 to 1998

[As of end of year. Excludes government owned and occupied, owner-occupied, and medical office buildings]

Market	1980	1985	1990	1991	1992	1993	1994	1995	1996	1997	1998
Total [1]	**4.6**	**16.9**	**20.0**	**20.2**	**20.5**	**19.4**	**16.2**	**14.3**	**12.4**	**10.1**	**9.7**
Atlanta, GA	10.0	21.0	19.1	19.5	19.4	16.8	13.0	10.4	9.2	10.5	11.2
Baltimore, MD	7.2	11.5	20.0	21.0	20.6	17.3	15.5	17.0	14.3	11.6	10.0
Boston, MA	3.8	13.1	19.6	19.1	17.5	17.7	13.3	10.4	6.2	4.4	7.1
Charlotte, NC	(NA)	16.7	16.5	19.4	(NA)	(NA)	10.0	8.9	8.2	7.1	7.2
Chicago, IL	7.0	16.5	18.6	20.0	22.1	21.4	18.7	15.5	15.5	(NA)	14.4
Cincinnati, OH	(NA)	(NA)	(NA)	(NA)	19.4	(NA)	15.3	(NA)	13.1	11.5	9.9
Colorado Springs, CO	(NA)	(NA)	(NA)	(NA)	(NA)	(NA)	(NA)	(NA)	(NA)	(NA)	8.1
Dallas, TX	8.6	23.0	25.8	26.0	31.3	29.5	21.7	18.7	16.2	14.7	15.0
Denver, CO	6.6	24.7	24.8	23.0	21.5	15.9	12.8	12.1	10.8	9.3	7.6
Detroit, MI	(NA)	(NA)	(NA)	(NA)	(NA)	21.4	19.7	16.9	11.1	8.5	6.9
Fort Lauderdale, FL	(NA)	(NA)	23.0	24.9	22.9	(NA)	10.8	(NA)	10.5	10.4	10.0
Houston, TX	4.0	27.6	24.9	27.3	27.0	25.1	24.7	21.9	17.5	12.1	10.7
Indianapolis, IN	0.9	15.3	16.8	20.2	22.4	18.8	18.4	14.3	(NA)	14.2	11.2
Los Angeles, CA	(NA)	(NA)	21.2	21.4	21.2	21.0	19.6	23.2	22.1	13.8	14.2
Memphis, TN	(NA)	(NA)	(NA)	(NA)	(NA)	(NA)	(NA)	(NA)	13.6	12.0	12.5
Miami, FL	2.4	20.9	23.4	22.6	18.5	19.0	15.4	13.8	12.4	11.2	11.4
Minneapolis, MN	(NA)	(NA)	(NA)	18.9	19.9	(NA)	8.2	(NA)	6.5	6.2	7.0
Nashville, TN	(NA)	(NA)	25.1	18.4	(NA)	(NA)	7.5	(NA)	6.9	6.0	7.5
New Jersey (Central)	(NA)	(NA)	(NA)	(NA)	(NA)	(NA)	20.7	(NA)	16.0	11.2	9.9
New Jersey (North)	(NA)	(NA)	(NA)	(NA)	(NA)	(NA)	16.5	(NA)	14.5	11.9	10.0
New York, NY [2]	3.1	7.9	16.0	18.8	18.3	17.9	16.3	17.0	16.0	(NA)	8.6
Orlando, FL	6.3	14.5	18.2	17.3	19.0	17.8	16.3	16.2	13.7	10.9	12.4
Philadelphia, PA	(NA)	(NA)	(NA)	(NA)	(NA)	(NA)	12.1	(NA)	6.5	6.4	7.1
Phoenix, AZ	(NA)	(NA)	27.6	24.8	24.4	(NA)	11.8	(NA)	11.5	9.3	8.9
Pittsburgh, PA	1.2	16.1	16.3	14.2	(NA)	17.0	15.8	14.5	(NA)	15.4	14.0
Raleigh, NC	(NA)	(NA)	(NA)	(NA)	(NA)	(NA)	(NA)	(NA)	(NA)	15.4	14.0
Richmond, VA	(NA)	(NA)	(NA)	(NA)	(NA)	(NA)	11.9	(NA)	9.7	(NA)	6.0
Sacramento, CA	(NA)	(NA)	(NA)	(NA)	(NA)	(NA)	14.1	(NA)	9.7	9.7	10.7
St. Louis, MO	(NA)	(NA)	21.0	20.5	21.8	19.1	18.1	12.7	12.4	12.3	11.8
St. Paul, MN	(NA)	(NA)	(NA)	19.7	18.5	(NA)	15.2	(NA)	13.4	12.3	9.6
San Diego, CA	(NA)	24.7	19.5	23.7	23.8	22.1	18.8	17.4	12.5	9.9	7.2
Silicon Valley, CA	(NA)	(NA)	(NA)	(NA)	(NA)	(NA)	12.7	(NA)	14.1	10.1	9.1
Tampa/St. Petersburg	(NA)	(NA)	(NA)	(NA)	(NA)	(NA)	(NA)	(NA)	8.7	5.8	8.3
Washington, DC	2.5	9.0	19.0	17.6	15.4	14.1	13.4	10.8	13.0	9.1	8.8
West Palm Beach, CA	(NA)	(NA)	(NA)	(NA)	(NA)	(NA)	16.8	(NA)	9.3	8.0	5.8
Wilmington, DE	(NA)	(NA)	20.3	21.0	19.8	(NA)	16.2	(NA)	12.0	12.3	13.5
Winston-Salem/Greensboro	(NA)	(NA)	(NA)	(NA)	(NA)	(NA)	16.7	(NA)	9.5	9.7	8.7
								13.2	(NA)	14.1	14.5

NA Not available. [1] Includes other North American markets not shown separately. In 1998, 45 markets were covered.
[2] Refers to Manhattan.
Source: ONCOR International, Houston, TX, 1980 and 1985, *National Office Market Report*, semi-annual; 1989-1990, *International Office Market Report*, semi-annual; thereafter, *Year-End (year) Market Data Book*, annual (copyright).

Construction and Housing 739

Figure 26.1
Gross Domestic Product in Manufacturing: 1990 to 1997

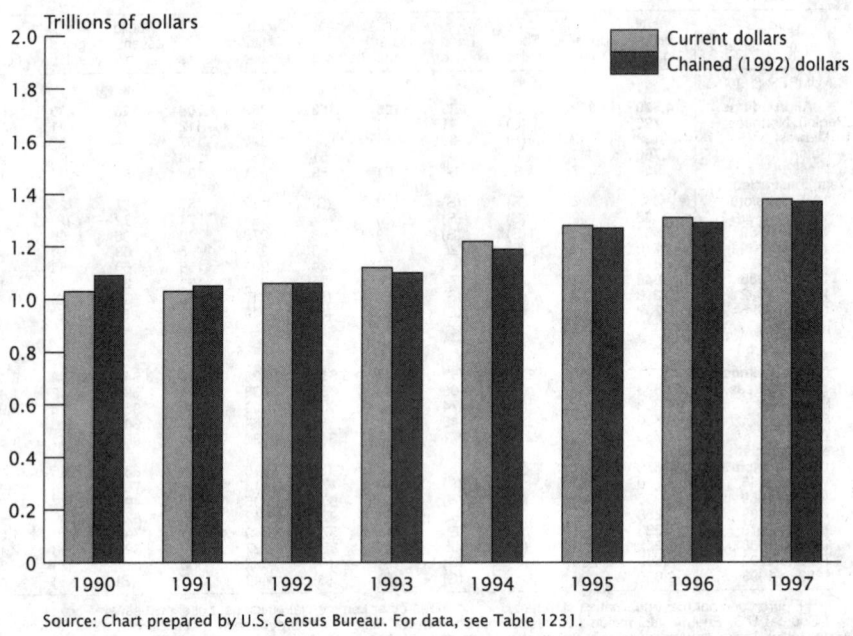

Source: Chart prepared by U.S. Census Bureau. For data, see Table 1231.

Figure 26.2
Manufacturers Shipments, and New Orders: 1990 to 1997

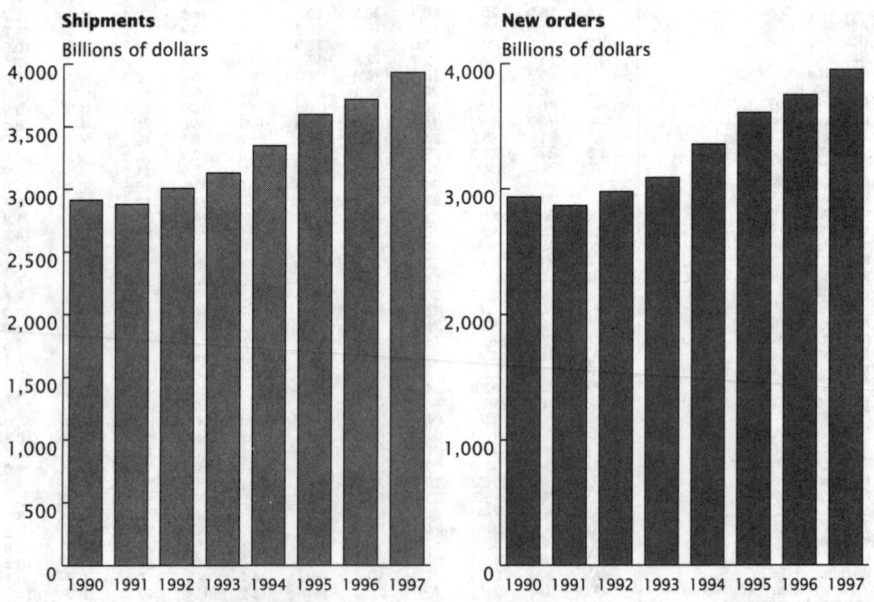

Source: Chart prepared by U.S. Census Bureau. For data, see Table 1237.

740 Manufactures

Section 26

Manufactures

This section presents summary data for manufacturing as a whole and more detailed information for major industry groups and selected products. The types of measures shown at the different levels include data for establishments, employment and wages, plant and equipment expenditures, value and quantity of production and shipments, value added by manufacture, inventories, and various indicators of financial status.

The principal sources of these data are U.S. Census Bureau reports of the censuses of manufactures conducted every 5 years, the *Annual Survey of Manufactures*, and *Manufacturing Profiles*, an annual compilation of the formerly printed series of *Current Industrial Reports*. Indexes of industrial production are presented monthly in the Federal Reserve Board's *Federal Reserve Bulletin*. These numbers were recently changed to a new index base year (1992 = 100) as of early 1997. Reports on current activities of industries or current movements of individual commodities are compiled by such government agencies as the Bureau of Labor Statistics; the Economic research Service of the Department of Agriculture; the International Trade Administration; and by private research or trade associations such as The Conference Board, Inc., the American Iron and Steel Institute, the Electronic Industries Association, and several others.

Data on financial aspects of manufacturing industries are collected by the Bureau of Economic Analysis (BEA) and the Census Bureau. Industry aggregates in the form of balance sheets, profit and loss statements, analyses of sales and expenses, lists of subsidiaries, and types and amounts of security issues are published for leading manufacturing corporations registered with the Securities and Exchange Commission. The BEA issues

data on capital in manufacturing industries and capacity utilization rates in manufacturing. See also Section 17, Business Enterprise.

Censuses and annual surveys—The first census of manufactures covered the year 1809. Between 1809 and 1963, a census was conducted at periodic intervals. Since 1967, it has been taken every 5 years (for years ending in "2" and "7"). Results from the 1997 census are expected in 1999 and 2000. Census data, either direct reports or estimates from administrative records, are obtained for every manufacturing plant with one paid employee or more. The *Annual Survey of Manufactures (ASM)*, conducted for the first time in 1949, collects data for the years between censuses for the more general measure of manufacturing activity covered in detail by the censuses. The annual survey data are estimates derived from a scientifically selected sample of establishments. The 1996 annual survey is based on a sample of about 58,000 establishments of an approximate total of 230,000. These establishments represent all manufacturing establishments of multiunit companies and all single-establishment manufacturing companies mailed schedules in the 1992 Census of Manufactures. For the current panel of the ASM sample, all establishments of companies with 1992 shipments in manufacturing in excess of $500 million were included in the survey with certainty. For the remaining portion of the mail survey, the establishment was defined as the sampling unit. For this portion, all establishments with 250 employees or more and establishments with a very large value of shipments also were included. Therefore, of the 58,000 establishments included in the ASM panel, approximately 33,000 are selected with certainty. These establishments account for approximately 80 percent of total

Manufactures 741

value of shipments in the 1992 census. Smaller establishments in the remaining portion of the mail survey were selected by sample.

Establishments and classification— The censuses of manufactures for 1947 through 1992 cover operating manufacturing establishments as defined in the *Standard Industrial Classification Manual* (SIC), issued by the U.S. Office of Management and Budget (see text, Section 13). The Manual is also used for classifying establishments in the annual surveys. The comparability of manufactures data over time is affected by changes in the official definitions of industries as presented in the Manual. It is important to note, therefore, that the 1987 edition of the Manual was used for the 1987 and 1992 censuses; and the 1972 edition of the Manual and the 1977 Supplement were used for the 1972 through 1982 censuses. This Manual defines an industry as a number of establishments producing a single product or a closely related group of products. In the main, an establishment is classified in a particular industry if its production of a product or product group exceeds in value added its production of any other product group. While some establishments produce only the products of the industry in which they are classified, few within an industry specialize to that extent. The statistics on employment, payrolls, value added, inventories, and expenditures, therefore, reflect both the primary and secondary activities of the establishments in that industry. For this reason, care should be exercised in relating such statistics to the total shipments figures of products primary to the industry. Beginning with 1997 census, the Manual will be replaced with a new way of organizing economic statistics called the North American Industry Classification System (NAICS) (see Table 1245 as an example and the new *North American Industry Classification System (NAICS) - United States, 1997.*

Establishment—Establishment signifies a single physical plant site or factory. It is not necessarily identical to the business unit or company, which may consist of one or more establishments. A company operating establishments at more than one location is required to submit a separate report for each location. An establishment engaged in distinctly different lines of activity and maintaining separate payroll and inventory records is also required to submit separate reports.

Durable goods—Items with a normal life expectancy of 3 years or more. Automobiles, furniture, household appliances, and mobile homes are common examples.

Nondurable goods—Items which generally last for only a short time (3 years or less). Food, beverages, clothing, shoes, and gasoline are common examples.

Statistical reliability—For a discussion of statistical collection and estimation, sampling procedures, and measures of statistical reliability applicable to Census Bureau data, see Appendix III.

No. 1231. Gross Domestic Product in Manufacturing in Current and Real (1992) Dollars, by Industry: 1990 to 1997

[In billions of dollars (5,743.8 represents $5,743,837,000,000). Data are based on the 1987 Standard Industrial Classification (SIC). Data include nonfactor charges (capital consumption allowances, indirect business taxes, etc.) as well as factor charges against gross product; corporate profits and capital consumption allowances have been shifted from a company to an establishment basis]

Industry	1990	1991	1992	1993	1994	1995	1996	1997
CURRENT DOLLARS								
Gross domestic product	**5,743.8**	**5,916.7**	**6,244.4**	**6,558.1**	**6,947.0**	**7,269.6**	**7,661.6**	**8,110.9**
Manufacturing	1,031.4	1,028.1	1,063.6	1,116.5	1,216.1	1,282.2	1,309.1	1,378.9
Durable goods	572.8	558.3	573.4	615.7	679.2	716.8	737.3	784.0
Lumber and wood products	31.8	30.0	32.0	34.6	38.4	40.9	39.1	42.8
Furniture and fixtures	15.4	15.1	16.2	17.7	18.5	19.4	20.5	22.1
Stone, clay, and glass products	24.8	22.9	25.1	25.1	28.8	30.2	31.3	33.7
Primary metal industries	42.6	39.6	39.0	42.0	46.3	51.7	51.5	53.2
Fabricated metal products	69.4	67.6	70.1	73.7	84.2	87.6	93.1	99.3
Industrial machinery	114.8	105.7	108.6	110.9	122.3	141.5	148.8	158.9
Electronic & other electric equipment	94.9	98.2	98.6	114.6	132.9	136.7	141.6	157.3
Motor vehicles and equipment	46.1	42.3	52.8	71.5	87.4	85.2	82.4	85.4
Other transportation equipment	60.5	62.0	56.5	53.5	49.5	46.1	49.0	50.7
Instruments and related products	52.2	54.6	54.2	50.9	48.7	49.1	55.5	55.9
Misc. manufacturing industries	20.2	20.3	20.1	21.1	22.2	23.3	24.6	24.8
Nondurable goods	458.6	469.8	490.3	500.8	536.9	570.5	571.8	594.9
Food and kindred products	94.2	99.2	102.1	103.2	109.6	123.2	116.0	118.5
Tobacco manufactures	16.4	17.8	18.4	15.2	16.3	17.3	17.0	18.4
Textile mill products	21.7	22.3	25.4	25.5	25.4	24.5	24.7	25.5
Apparel and other textile products	25.2	25.9	27.2	27.4	28.2	27.4	26.7	28.4
Paper and allied products	45.3	44.8	45.8	47.7	51.3	58.9	56.6	55.0
Printing and publishing	73.9	75.9	79.7	80.0	86.0	84.7	92.4	98.4
Chemicals and allied products	110.3	114.1	120.5	124.6	140.6	156.1	155.8	158.8
Petroleum and coal products	33.0	29.7	28.2	31.3	30.4	28.3	29.6	35.2
Rubber and misc. plastic products	34.0	35.7	38.1	41.3	44.4	44.9	48.6	52.0
Leather and leather products	4.6	4.4	4.8	4.5	4.7	5.2	4.4	4.8
CHAINED (1992) DOLLARS								
Gross domestic product, total [1]	**6,136.3**	**6,079.4**	**6,244.4**	**6,389.6**	**6,610.7**	**6,761.7**	**6,994.8**	**7,269.8**
Manufacturing	1,090.0	1,050.2	1,063.6	1,100.8	1,193.2	1,271.6	1,293.8	1,369.9
Percent of all industries								
Durable goods	600.4	568.0	573.4	608.3	671.3	727.0	769.0	838.6
Lumber and wood products	37.0	34.1	32.0	28.5	29.8	31.7	31.4	33.1
Furniture and fixtures	15.8	14.9	16.2	17.9	18.0	18.7	18.6	19.7
Stone, clay, and glass products	25.5	22.9	25.1	24.5	27.0	27.2	27.6	29.3
Primary metal industries	39.0	38.6	39.0	43.2	45.0	44.1	46.9	48.0
Fabricated metal products	72.6	68.2	70.1	73.4	84.5	87.8	88.6	93.0
Industrial machinery	113.2	103.6	108.6	115.1	131.5	162.9	183.2	215.2
Electronic & other electric equipment	92.5	95.9	98.6	118.3	145.8	178.7	213.2	261.2
Motor vehicles and equipment	56.8	46.8	52.8	66.7	78.0	77.7	73.2	77.8
Other transportation equipment	69.1	64.0	56.5	52.3	47.6	43.3	43.9	44.1
Instruments and related products	58.7	58.0	54.2	48.7	45.1	42.0	40.2	36.3
Misc. manufacturing industries	22.2	21.1	20.1	20.5	21.5	22.8	23.3	23.1
Nondurable goods	489.4	482.2	490.3	492.5	522.0	545.1	527.8	537.6
Food and kindred products	103.2	102.3	102.1	103.8	106.5	125.8	105.7	106.7
Tobacco manufactures	24.9	21.5	18.4	16.1	22.3	23.8	22.5	21.3
Textile mill products	22.6	23.1	25.4	26.0	27.3	26.4	25.6	25.7
Apparel and other textile products	26.5	26.4	27.2	27.2	28.3	28.6	27.0	28.2
Paper and allied products	44.1	44.6	45.8	50.2	52.1	44.4	46.4	48.9
Printing and publishing	84.5	80.8	79.7	75.3	78.0	77.1	76.1	76.7
Chemicals and allied products	117.3	115.8	120.5	120.6	131.2	139.6	140.3	141.2
Petroleum and coal products	28.4	28.3	28.2	27.8	27.6	30.4	32.3	32.4
Rubber and misc. plastic products	34.4	35.3	38.1	41.3	45.4	47.1	49.5	53.7
Leather and leather products	4.8	4.5	4.8	4.5	4.5	4.7	4.1	4.3

[1] For additional industry detail, see Table 722.

Source: U.S. Bureau of Economic Analysis, *National Income and Product Accounts, 1929-94*, and *Survey of Current Business*, November 1998.

Manufactures 743

No. 1232. Manufactures—Summary: 1982 to 1996

[For establishment coverage, see text, this section]

Item	Unit	1982	1987	1992	1994 [1]	1995 [1]	1996 [1]
ALL ESTABLISHMENTS							
Number of establishments [2]	1,000 ...	358	369	382	(NA)	(NA)	(NA)
With 20 or more employees	1,000 ...	123	126	125	(NA)	(NA)	(NA)
Employee size-class:							
Establishments [3]	1,000 ...	348	359	371	(NA)	(NA)	(NA)
Under 20	1,000 ...	230	238	252	(NA)	(NA)	(NA)
20 to 99	1,000 ...	84	86	85	(NA)	(NA)	(NA)
100 to 249	1,000 ...	21	22	22	(NA)	(NA)	(NA)
250 to 999	1,000 ...	11	11	11	(NA)	(NA)	(NA)
1,000 and over	1,000 ...	2	2	2	(NA)	(NA)	(NA)
Form of organization:							
Corporate	1,000 ...	283.2	287.4	304.0	(NA)	(NA)	(NA)
Noncorporate [4]	1,000 ...	74.0	81.5	77.7	(NA)	(NA)	(NA)
Individual proprietorship	1,000 ...	45.6	35.4	40.9	(NA)	(NA)	(NA)
Partnership	1,000 ...	15.0	13.2	10.3	(NA)	(NA)	(NA)
All employees: [5]							
Annual average [6]	Million...	19.094	18.952	18.205	18.327	18.730	18.667
Payroll	Bil. dol...	379.6	475.7	559.1	593.6	624.4	645.1
Payroll per employee	$1,000 ..	19.9	25.2	30.7	32.4	33.3	34.5
Production workers:							
Annual average	Million...	12.401	12.280	11.641	11.947	12.253	12.169
Percent of all employees	Percent..	64.9	64.8	63.9	65.2	65.4	65.2
Hours	Billion ...	23.5	24.3	23.6	24.6	25.1	25.0
Hours per worker	1,000 ...	1.898	1.979	2.024	2.056	2.046	2.055
Wages	Bil. dol...	204.787	251.450	281.538	304.663	317.768	324.496
Percent of payroll for all employees	Percent..	53.9	52.9	50.4	51.3	50.9	50.3
Wages per worker	$1,000 ...	16.514	20.476	24.185	25.501	25.934	26.666
Wages per worker hour	Dollar ...	8.72	10.35	11.95	12.40	12.68	12.98
Value added by manufacture [7]	Bil. dol...	824.1	1,165.7	1,425.2	1,598.0	1,711.4	1,749.7
Per production worker	$1,000 ...	66.458	94.927	122.431	133.756	139.674	143.782
Per production worker hour	Dollar ...	35.06	47.97	60.56	65.39	68.26	69.96
Per dollar of workers' wages	Dollar ...	4.02	4.64	5.07	5.27	5.39	5.39
Cost of materials [8]	Bil. dol...	1,130	1,320	1,573	1,752	1,897	1,975
Value of shipments [8]	Bil. dol...	1,960	2,476	3,005	3,340	3,594	3,715
Per production worker	$1,000 ...	158.1	203.0	258.0	280.2	293.3	305.4
End-of-year inventories	Bil. dol...	307	333	374	397	421	427
New capital expenditures [9]	Bil. dol...	74.6	78.6	103.2	112.0	128.4	139.3
Gross book value of depreciable assets	Bil. dol...	692	868	1,128	(NA)	(NA)	(NA)
Machinery and equipment	Bil. dol...	527	671	896	(NA)	(NA)	(NA)
Assets per employee	$1,000 ..	36.2	48.6	66.6	(NA)	(NA)	(NA)
Operation ratios:							
Value added to shipments	Ratio ...	42.0	47.1	47.9	48.0	47.7	47.1
Inventories to shipments	Ratio ...	15.7	13.4	12.5	11.9	11.7	11.5
Payroll to value added	Ratio ...	46.1	40.8	34.7	37.2	36.5	36.9
MULTIUNIT COMPANIES							
Establishments	1,000 ...	81.7	80.9	81.0	(NA)	(NA)	(NA)
Employees	Million...	14.3	13.8	13.1	(NA)	(NA)	(NA)
Production workers	Million...	8.8	8.5	8.0	(NA)	(NA)	(NA)
Payroll	Bil. dol...	307.5	377.3	436.0	(NA)	(NA)	(NA)
Wages, production workers	Bil. dol...	159.1	191.8	211.2	(NA)	(NA)	(NA)
Value added by manufacture	Bil. dol...	678.4	953.6	1,160	(NA)	(NA)	(NA)
New capital expenditures	Bil. dol...	65.2	66.5	87.8	(NA)	(NA)	(NA)
SINGLE UNIT COMPANIES							
Establishments	1,000 ...	276.3	288.0	300.7	(NA)	(NA)	(NA)
Employees	Million...	4.8	5.1	5.1	(NA)	(NA)	(NA)
Payroll	Bil. dol...	72.1	98.3	123.1	(NA)	(NA)	(NA)
Value added by manufacture	Bil. dol...	145.7	212.1	265.0	(NA)	(NA)	(NA)

NA Not available. [1] Estimated data based on *Annual Survey of Manufactures;* see text, Manufactures section. [2] Includes administrative and auxiliary units. [3] Excludes administrative offices and auxiliary units. [4] Includes forms of organization not shown separately. [5] Includes data for employees of manufacturing establishments engaged in distribution and construction work. [6] Data are based on pay periods ending nearest 15th of March, May, August, and November. [7] Adjusted value added; takes into account (a) value added by merchandising operations (that is, difference between the sales value and cost of merchandise sold without further manufacture, processing, or assembly), plus (b) net change in finished goods and work-in-process inventories between beginning and end of year. [8] Includes extensive and unmeasurable duplication from shipments between establishments in the same industry classification. [9] Includes plants under construction and not yet in operation.

Note: Reports for manufacturing industries for 1997 from the *1997 Economic Census* are being issued on a flow basis beginning in the summer of 1999.

Source: Except as noted, U.S. Census Bureau, *Census of Manufactures, 1982, 1987,* and *1992;* and *Annual Survey of Manufactures.*

No. 1233. Manufactures—Summary, by Industry: 1992 and 1996

[16,949 represents 16,949,000. Data based on various editions of the *Standard Industrial Classification (SIC) Manual*, published by the Office of Management and Budget; see text, Section 26, Manufactures. N.e.c. = Not elsewhere classified]

Industry	SIC code	1992 All employees Number (1,000)	1992 All employees Payroll (mil. dol.)	1992 Production workers (1,000)	1992 Value added by manufacture (mil. dol.)	1992 Value of shipments (mil. dol.)	1996 All employees Number (1,000)	1996 All employees Payroll Total (mil. dol.)	1996 All employees Payroll Per employee (dol.)	1996 Production workers (1,000)	1996 Value added by manufacture Total (mil. dol.)	1996 Value added by manufacture Per production worker (dol.)	1996 Value of shipments (mil. dol.)
All manufacturing establishments. . . .	D	16,949	494,109	11,641	1,424,700	3,004,723	18,665.6	645,032	34,557	12,168.0	1,749,662	143,792	3,715,428
Food and kindred products.	20	1,503	36,772	1,100	157,260	406,963	1,516.6	40,380	26,625	1,112.6	178,783	160,689	461,324
Meat products	201	400	7,564	343	19,141	94,072	433.4	8,921	20,584	370.2	23,518	63,528	102,103
Dairy products	202	135	3,720	85	15,258	52,720	130.9	4,018	30,695	82.8	15,724	189,903	58,123
Preserved fruits and vegetables . .	203	216	4,825	179	23,644	47,806	204.4	5,131	25,103	169.4	24,506	144,664	51,708
Grain mill products	204	107	3,375	74	21,000	49,957	100.3	3,425	34,148	70.1	21,667	309,087	58,473
Bakery products	205	215	5,599	133	17,905	28,494	219.9	6,158	28,004	136.6	20,712	151,625	32,741
Sugar and confectionery products . .	206	91	2,402	71	10,950	22,710	88.6	2,603	29,379	68.7	12,640	183,988	26,265
Fats and oils	207	28	778	19	3,770	18,724	25.8	813	31,512	17.8	4,258	239,213	23,388
Beverages	208	144	4,786	74	29,260	57,957	142.8	5,103	35,735	71.5	35,210	492,448	68,387
Miscellaneous foods and kindred products .	209	166	3,723	121	16,333	34,523	170.9	4,209	24,628	125.5	20,548	163,729	40,136
Tobacco products	21	38	1,524	27	27,207	35,198	31.4	1,522	48,471	22.7	25,860	1,139,207	34,482
Cigarettes	211	25	1,205	19	24,802	29,746	20.5	1,236	60,293	14.7	23,442	1,594,694	28,987
Cigars	212	3	53	2	190	287	2.9	66	22,759	2.2	287	130,455	450
Chewing and smoking tobacco . . .	213	3	92	2	1,213	1,608	2.4	76	31,667	1.8	1,508	837,778	1,818
Tobacco stemming and redrying . . .	214	7	174	5	1,002	3,557	5.5	144	26,182	4.0	624	156,000	3,228
Textile mill products	22	616	12,398	529	30,060	70,753	576.4	13,215	22,927	489.0	32,555	66,575	80,242
Broadwoven fabric mills, cotton . . .	221	56	1,147	50	2,504	5,811	51.9	1,216	23,430	46.7	2,471	52,912	6,699
Broadwoven fabric mills, manmade. . .	222	87	1,850	77	4,008	8,767	73.9	1,816	24,574	63.0	4,307	68,365	9,750
Broadwoven fabric mills, wool	223	14	279	12	691	1,612	13.4	298	22,239	11.7	673	57,521	1,756
Narrow fabric mills.	224	17	323	14	706	1,274	16.7	370	22,156	13.4	817	60,970	1,524
Knitting mills.	225	195	3,400	170	8,052	16,985	169.3	3,405	20,112	147.1	8,986	61,088	19,517
Textile finishing, except wool	226	51	1,143	41	2,786	7,089	51.0	1,307	25,627	41.1	3,145	76,521	7,271
Carpets and rugs	227	49	1,088	39	3,480	9,828	55.0	1,368	24,873	43.8	4,076	93,059	11,184
Yarn and thread mills	228	92	1,744	84	4,059	11,274	83.9	1,805	21,514	75.7	3,806	50,277	12,823
Miscellaneous textile goods.	229	55	1,423	42	3,775	8,113	61.3	1,630	26,591	46.6	4,276	91,760	9,720
Apparel and other textile products. . . .	23	985	15,325	824	36,423	71,658	864.9	14,920	17,251	726.5	38,366	52,809	77,628
Men's and boys' suits and coats . . .	231	44	723	37	1,375	2,430	27.1	516	19,041	22.2	1,239	55,811	1,968
Men's and boys' furnishings	232	261	3,649	228	9,864	17,867	199.7	3,094	15,493	177.6	9,423	53,057	18,507
Women's and misses' outerwear . . .	233	306	4,597	256	10,836	21,631	294.1	4,606	15,661	249.5	11,045	44,269	22,282
Women's and children's undergarments . .	234	54	798	46	2,193	3,943	38.1	645	16,929	32.0	1,916	59,875	4,244

See footnotes at end of table.

U.S. Census Bureau, Statistical Abstract of the United States: 1999

No. 1233. Manufactures—Summary, by Industry: 1992 and 1996—Continued

[See headnote, page 745]

Industry	SIC code	1992 All employees — Number (1,000)	1992 All employees — Payroll (mil. dol.)	1992 Production workers (1,000)	1992 Value added by manufacture (mil. dol.)	1992 Value of shipments (mil. dol.)	1996 All employees — Number (1,000)	1996 Payroll — Total (mil. dol.)	1996 Payroll — Per employee (dol.)	1996 Production workers (1,000)	1996 Value added by manufacture — Total (mil. dol.)	1996 Value added by manufacture — Per production worker (dol.)	1996 Value of shipments (mil. dol.)
Apparel, other textile products—Con.													
Hats, caps, and millinery	235	19	280	16	572	976	17	307	17,953	14	599	41,888	977
Girls' and children's outerwear	236	53	775	44	1,667	3,145	34	542	16,179	28	2,063	75,018	3,874
Fur goods	237	1	21	1	68	172	1	14	17,500	1	68	68,000	104
Miscellaneous apparel and accessories	238	37	566	30	1,260	2,378	31	554	18,105	25	1,445	58,980	2,738
Miscellaneous fabricated textile products	239	211	3,918	169	8,586	19,118	224	4,641	20,737	179	10,603	59,401	22,934
Lumber and wood products	24	656	13,882	540	33,154	81,565	739	17,314	23,438	613	41,486	67,699	106,518
Logging	241	83	1,689	69	5,017	13,592	83	1,856	22,361	68	5,775	84,553	15,411
Sawmills and planing mills	242	168	3,585	144	8,848	23,294	172	4,129	24,076	147	10,404	70,583	29,697
Millwork, plywood, and structural members	243	224	5,005	181	10,844	24,744	257	6,233	24,225	209	13,274	63,451	31,798
Wood containers	244	40	645	33	1,321	2,942	51	893	17,544	43	1,909	44,707	4,059
Wood buildings and mobile homes	245	56	1,234	44	2,531	6,645	82	2,077	25,391	68	4,606	68,237	11,889
Miscellaneous Wood Products	249	84	1,725	69	4,593	10,348	94	2,125	22,558	78	5,518	70,925	13,664
Furniture and fixtures [2]	25	471	10,227	372	22,840	43,826	515	12,414	24,128	414	27,200	65,669	55,697
Household furniture	251	253	4,804	213	10,942	20,508	273	5,674	20,769	233	12,464	53,609	25,426
Office Furniture	252	68	1,868	51	4,626	7,979	70	2,172	31,252	53	5,447	102,195	9,444
Public building and related furniture	253	30	732	23	1,736	4,483	37	1,031	27,567	29	2,290	78,694	7,366
Partitions and fixtures	254	75	1,818	55	3,633	6,580	81	2,246	27,728	61	4,182	68,896	7,951
Miscellaneous furniture and fixtures	259	45	1,005	31	2,353	4,276	54	1,290	24,112	39	2,818	72,817	5,510
Paper and allied products	26	626	20,492	479	60,174	133,201	631	22,947	36,389	488	72,290	148,287	160,661
Pulp mills	261	16	689	12	2,554	5,466	15	701	46,733	11	2,201	198,288	5,508
Paper mills	262	131	5,421	100	14,848	32,786	116	5,599	48,101	90	18,848	208,726	39,566
Paperboard mills	263	52	2,136	39	8,195	16,140	55	2,599	47,427	42	9,655	231,535	20,271
Paperboard containers and boxes	265	199	5,722	151	12,406	32,655	212	6,727	31,731	163	15,668	96,300	40,389
Miscellaneous converted paper products	267	229	6,524	176	22,171	46,154	232	7,321	31,502	182	25,918	142,720	54,927
Printing and publishing	27	1,492	41,136	785	112,446	166,153	1,515	46,175	30,479	801	130,946	163,539	195,435
Newspapers	271	414	10,437	134	26,920	33,782	403	11,199	27,768	136	30,692	226,342	39,171
Periodicals	272	115	4,077	20	15,880	22,104	121	4,665	38,714	16	17,982	1,096,463	24,930
Books	273	130	4,037	57	14,325	21,378	136	4,675	34,451	57	17,857	313,281	26,696
Miscellaneous publishing	274	65	1,720	24	8,473	10,908	69	2,049	29,782	25	9,699	381,850	12,511
Commercial printing	275	567	15,337	408	31,898	56,229	604	18,015	29,806	437	38,407	87,828	67,842
Manifold business forms	276	48	1,341	34	3,922	7,429	41	1,263	30,507	28	3,878	138,996	7,724
Greeting cards	277	23	584	12	3,389	4,190	21	1,636	29,720	12	3,989	335,210	5,011
Blankbooks and bookbinding	278	66	1,461	51	3,640	5,049	65	1,598	24,775	50	4,388	87,936	6,428
Printing trade services	279	65	2,142	46	3,999	5,086	55	2,074	37,778	39	4,055	103,444	5,123

See footnotes at end of table.

U.S. Census Bureau, Statistical Abstract of the United States: 1999

No. 1233. Manufactures—Summary, by Industry: 1992 and 1996—Continued

[See headnote, page 745]

Industry	SIC code	1992 — All employees		Production workers (1,000)	Value added by manufacture (mil. dol.)	Value of shipments (mil. dol.)	1996 — All employees	Payroll		Production workers (1,000)	Value added by manufacture		Value of shipments (mil. dol.)
		Number[1] (1,000)	Payroll (mil. dol.)				Number[1] (1,000)	Total (mil. dol.)	Per employee (dol.)		Total (mil. dol.)	Per production worker (dol.)	
Chemicals and allied products	28	**849**	**32,502**	**479**	**164,346**	**305,420**	**824**	**36,331**	**44,086**	**477**	**194,412**	**407,743**	**367,442**
Industrial inorganic chemicals	281	103	4,214	55	16,724	27,331	80	3,749	46,804	45	16,567	366,527	27,741
Plastics materials and synthetics	282	129	5,137	86	20,979	48,698	115	5,086	44,188	79	25,025	315,574	59,567
Drugs	283	194	7,840	93	48,602	67,792	213	9,891	46,393	106	59,813	562,152	86,533
Soap, cleaners, and toilet goods	284	123	3,927	75	26,182	42,875	126	4,389	37,965	75	31,801	425,716	51,809
Paints and allied products	285	51	1,710	26	7,154	14,973	51	1,940	34,778	28	8,497	304,552	18,257
Industrial organic chemicals	286	125	5,495	72	26,132	64,397	126	6,765	53,733	75	28,886	386,693	75,672
Agricultural chemicals	287	40	1,451	25	8,659	18,841	37	1,593	43,406	24	12,277	520,212	23,356
Miscellaneous chemical products	289	84	2,727	48	9,915	20,512	76	2,919	38,408	45	11,547	256,031	24,508
Petroleum and coal products	29	**114**	**4,967**	**74**	**23,408**	**150,227**	**106**	**5,238**	**49,415**	**69**	**31,656**	**458,119**	**174,285**
Petroleum refining	291	75	3,640	48	18,607	136,551	67	3,738	55,625	43	26,006	599,217	158,068
Asphalt paving and roofing materials	295	26	846	18	3,006	7,749	25	988	39,206	18	3,464	191,381	9,611
Miscellaneous petroleum and coal products	299	14	481	7	1,796	5,927	14	512	37,647	8	2,187	287,763	6,605
Rubber and misc. plastic products	30	**907**	**23,156**	**698**	**58,652**	**113,593**	**1,018**	**28,436**	**27,936**	**800**	**74,945**	**93,716**	**150,468**
Tires and inner tubes	301	65	2,499	53	6,504	11,814	65	2,701	41,682	54	7,079	131,093	14,209
Rubber and plastics footwear	302	14	216	11	464	868	8	165	20,122	7	442	65,970	936
Hose and belting and plastics and packing	305	52	1,411	38	3,290	3,290	61	1,859	30,626	46	4,528	98,649	8,232
Fabricated rubber products, n.e.c	306	105	2,617	79	6,024	11,474	122	3,137	25,819	95	7,275	76,418	14,468
Miscellaneous plastics products, n.e.c.	308	671	16,413	516	42,370	83,487	763	20,574	26,975	598	55,621	93,027	112,623
Leather and leather products	31	**101**	**1,806**	**83**	**4,527**	**9,694**	**77**	**1,600**	**20,725**	**65**	**4,742**	**73,406**	**9,309**
Leather tanning and finishing	311	17	420	13	891	2,905	15	393	26,554	12	1,313	105,887	3,134
Footwear cut stock	313	4	63	3	149	317	3	58	21,481	2	162	77,143	326
Footwear, except rubber	314	49	762	41	2,060	3,898	37	704	19,183	31	1,907	61,516	3,605
Leather gloves and mittens	315	3	35	2	69	140	2	45	19,565	2	53	26,500	145
Luggage	316	10	191	8	509	968	6	151	26,034	4	747	173,721	1,115
Handbags and personal leather goods	317	11	202	9	470	861	8	139	16,951	7	328	49,697	580
Leather goods, n.e.c	319	8	133	6	304	575	7	110	16,176	6	233	37,581	404

See footnotes at end of table.

Manufactures 747

No. 1233. Manufactures—Summary, by Industry: 1992 and 1996—Continued

[See headnote, page 745]

Industry	SIC code	1992					1996						
		All employees		Production workers (1,000)	Value added by manufacture (mil. dol.)	Value of shipments (mil. dol.)	All employees			Production workers (1,000)	Value added by manufacture		Value of shipments (mil. dol.)
		Number [1] (1,000)	Payroll (mil. dol.)				Number [1] (1,000)	Payroll			Total (mil. dol.)	Per production worker (dol.)	
								Total (mil. dol.)	Per employee (dol.)				
Stone, clay, and glass products	32	469	13,113	357	34,641	62,521	520	15,857	30,471	402	46,055	114,479	82,441
Flat glass	321	12	451	10	1,311	2,073	12	524	45,565	9	1,717	184,624	2,671
Glass and glassware, pressed or blown	322	66	2,075	56	5,900	9,033	60	2,029	34,101	51	6,532	127,082	10,057
Products of purchased glass	323	55	1,369	42	3,757	6,904	64	1,771	27,890	50	4,850	97,782	9,060
Cement, hydraulic	324	17	595	13	2,149	4,051	17	693	41,006	13	3,509	280,720	5,818
Structural clay products	325	31	734	24	1,695	2,857	31	845	27,083	25	2,176	86,693	3,566
Pottery and related products	326	37	863	29	1,995	2,817	45	1,149	25,647	36	2,696	74,066	3,830
Concrete, gypsum, and plaster products	327	174	4,741	126	11,008	23,024	205	6,083	29,746	152	15,739	103,410	32,691
Cut stone and stone products	328	12	282	9	604	1,007	17	412	24,094	13	999	76,846	1,512
Miscellaneous nonmetallic mineral products	329	66	2,004	49	6,222	10,756	72	2,350	32,867	53	7,838	148,166	13,237
Primary metal industries [2]	33	662	22,202	508	52,027	138,287	687	25,644	37,306	543	69,539	128,088	178,298
Blast furnace and basic steel products	331	239	9,179	182	22,173	58,449	221	9,950	45,023	174	29,180	167,701	74,552
Iron and steel foundries	332	122	3,739	99	6,873	11,860	128	4,373	34,111	106	9,061	85,240	15,937
Primary nonferrous metals	333	35	1,334	27	3,391	13,905	35	1,408	40,344	26	4,200	159,091	15,424
Secondary nonferrous metals	334	13	407	9	1,233	6,131	15	500	33,333	11	1,410	125,893	7,127
Nonferrous rolling and drawing	335	147	4,635	109	12,335	37,101	162	5,627	34,670	123	16,670	135,971	48,820
Nonferrous foundries (castings)	336	75	1,942	59	3,927	7,002	94	2,662	28,349	79	5,856	73,939	10,519
Miscellaneous primary metal products	339	31	966	22	2,097	3,837	32	1,125	35,047	23	3,164	137,565	5,919
Fabricated metal products	34	1,362	38,962	994	83,761	166,532	1,483	46,130	31,106	1,114	107,990	96,904	214,006
Metal cans and shipping containers	341	40	1,465	33	3,736	13,263	33	1,369	41,485	27	3,999	148,111	13,454
Cutlery, handtools, and hardware	342	134	3,648	99	9,044	15,448	140	4,220	30,164	107	11,750	109,506	20,197
Plumbing and heating, except electric	343	42	1,152	29	3,105	5,825	45	1,246	27,566	32	4,412	139,620	7,836
Fabricated structural metal products	344	389	10,362	275	21,256	44,876	432	12,555	29,042	315	27,974	88,863	59,388
Screw machine products, bolts, etc.	345	91	2,624	68	6,269	9,026	104	3,265	31,515	81	6,936	85,524	11,797
Metal forgings and stampings	346	234	7,749	185	14,913	30,621	259	9,696	37,407	211	19,880	94,352	41,282
Metal services, n.e.c.	347	108	2,652	83	5,679	9,953	129	3,454	26,754	99	7,793	78,638	14,003
Ordnance and accessories, n.e.c.	348	62	2,124	35	4,536	6,855	40	1,466	36,377	24	3,528	146,390	5,222
Miscellaneous fabricated metal products	349	263	7,185	186	16,224	30,667	300	8,858	29,497	219	21,718	99,350	40,828
Industrial machinery and equipment	35	1,739	57,231	1,086	132,923	258,661	1,981	70,730	35,713	1,287	187,218	145,469	381,794
Engines and turbines	351	83	3,135	52	7,738	17,549	79	3,186	40,534	55	10,513	192,899	23,554
Farm and garden machinery	352	86	2,354	63	7,318	14,784	94	2,918	31,209	70	9,545	136,357	21,292
Construction and related machinery	353	176	5,664	108	12,489	27,193	205	7,157	34,929	133	18,178	136,677	41,509
Metalworking machinery	354	255	8,571	178	16,542	26,474	295	10,985	37,263	211	22,673	107,252	36,841
Special industry machinery	355	162	5,515	91	11,667	21,522	192	7,311	38,019	110	19,221	174,895	35,751
General industrial machinery	356	244	7,742	154	17,817	31,443	265	9,130	34,466	172	23,110	134,439	41,458
Computer and office equipment	357	251	10,143	89	29,229	66,709	259	11,211	43,286	96	41,135	428,044	103,270
Refrigeration and service machinery	358	179	5,264	125	13,597	27,544	201	6,493	32,384	147	17,521	119,029	39,197
Industrial machinery, n.e.c.	359	304	8,843	227	16,527	25,443	392	12,340	31,496	293	25,322	86,423	38,922

See footnotes at end of table.

No. 1233. Manufactures—Summary, by Industry: 1992 and 1996—Continued

[See headnote, page 745]

		1992					1996						
		All employees		Production workers (1,000)	Value added by manufacture (mil. dol.)	Value of shipments (mil. dol.)	All employees			Production workers (1,000)	Value added by manufacture		Value of shipments (mil. dol.)
SIC code	Industry	Number[1] (1,000)	Payroll (mil. dol.)				Number[1] (1,000)	Payroll Total (mil. dol.)	Per employee (dol.)		Total (mil. dol.)	Per production worker (dol.)	
36	Electronics; other electric equipment	1,439	44,197	911	121,158	216,764	1,557	54,311	34,893	1,006	184,013	182,861	320,615
361	Electric distribution equipment	68	1,946	48	5,437	9,797	74	2,499	33,954	51	6,700	130,350	12,331
362	Electrical industrial apparatus	157	4,387	106	10,850	19,266	171	5,373	31,366	120	14,278	119,182	26,926
363	Household appliances	103	2,571	83	7,964	18,633	108	3,072	28,418	87	9,466	108,680	22,157
364	Electric lighting and wiring equipment	148	3,974	107	11,307	19,844	157	4,617	29,370	117	13,428	114,769	24,562
365	Household audio and video equipment	47	1,123	35	3,486	10,614	49	1,333	27,428	37	3,459	93,235	11,266
366	Communications equipment	239	9,111	114	26,522	42,955	258	11,522	44,590	120	38,705	323,891	68,232
367	Electronic components and accessories	530	16,752	317	44,305	73,642	588	20,830	35,431	368	84,059	228,359	127,996
369	Misc. electrical equipment and supplies	147	4,332	100	11,287	22,013	151	5,067	33,490	106	13,920	130,827	27,146
37	Transportation equipment	1,647	62,735	1,080	158,326	399,269	1,467	63,532	43,310	1,032	176,598	171,089	465,172
371	Motor vehicles and equipment	703	26,213	565	80,935	238,384	772	32,867	42,574	634	105,889	167,139	329,155
372	Aircraft and parts	548	22,647	281	47,661	104,858	377	18,733	49,729	190	45,220	237,500	83,394
373	Ship and boat building and repairing	163	4,634	122	8,560	15,249	141	4,353	30,807	108	7,903	72,906	15,634
374	Railroad equipment	28	900	21	2,015	4,714	31	1,141	37,288	23	2,590	114,097	7,067
375	Motorcycles, bicycles, and parts	13	343	10	891	2,134	18	565	30,707	14	1,435	103,986	3,094
376	Guided missiles, space vehicles, parts	146	6,780	50	15,246	26,508	81	4,632	57,185	29	9,986	346,736	17,928
379	Miscellaneous transportation equipment	46	1,218	33	3,018	7,423	47	1,241	26,461	35	3,564	103,304	8,900
38	Instruments and related products	907	33,067	460	89,394	134,940	821	33,783	41,164	423	97,987	171,593	151,016
381	Search and navigation equipment	253	10,962	103	24,299	35,039	186	9,540	51,208	68	21,071	310,782	30,371
382	Measuring and controlling devices	276	9,632	138	21,775	34,730	272	10,562	38,817	141	29,028	205,435	46,741
384	Medical instruments and supplies	264	8,522	154	26,082	39,535	268	9,957	37,098	157	31,051	197,777	47,406
385	Ophthalmic goods	29	714	20	1,938	2,675	27	757	28,037	17	2,390	140,588	3,417
386	Photographic equipment and supplies	77	3,061	39	14,862	22,119	61	2,798	46,096	36	14,032	393,053	22,297
387	Watches, clocks, watchcases and parts	8	177	6	438	843	6	169	26,825	4	415	96,512	785
39	Misc. manufacturing industries	366	8,417	255	21,975	39,498	397	10,042	25,276	283	27,021	95,346	48,597
391	Jewelry, silverware, and plated ware	46	1,068	32	2,501	5,731	43	1,070	24,711	30	2,761	92,651	6,360
393	Musical instruments	12	273	9	589	982	13	328	25,426	10	685	66,505	1,173
394	Toys and sporting goods	98	2,133	71	6,816	12,123	103	2,489	24,189	76	8,327	109,422	14,748
395	Pens, pencils, office, and art supplies	30	684	21	2,030	3,515	35	838	24,220	26	2,643	102,442	4,351
396	Costume jewelry and notions	27	557	19	1,366	2,316	24	560	23,045	19	1,406	75,187	2,389
399	Miscellaneous manufactures	153	3,702	103	8,674	14,832	179	4,757	26,531	123	11,199	91,271	19,575

[1] Represents the average of production workers plus all other employees for the payroll period ended nearest the 15th of March.   [2] Includes other industries not shown separately.

Note: Reports for manufacturing industries for 1997 from the 1997 Economic Census are being issued on a flow basis beginning in the summer of 1999.

Source: U.S. Census Bureau, 1992 Census of Manufactures and Annual Survey of Manufactures.

Manufactures   749

No. 1234. Manufactures Summary: 1996

[18,667 represents 18,667,000. Sum of state totals may not add to U.S. total because U.S. and state figures were independently derived]

State	All employees [1]			Production workers [1]		Value added by manufactures [2]		
		Payroll					Per production worker (dol.)	Value of shipments [3] (mil. dol.)
	Number (1,000)	Total (mil. dol.)	Per employee (dol.)	Total (1,000)	Wages (mil. dol.)	Total (mil. dol.)		
United States ...	18,667	645,140	34,561	12,169	324,612	1,750,493	143,847	3,719,743
Alabama.........	383	10,587	27,679	285	6,675	27,451	96,422	66,257
Alaska..........	16	488	30,873	12	339	1,470	124,568	3,939
Arizona..........	208	7,191	34,554	120	2,857	22,850	189,782	36,961
Arkansas	239	5,829	24,410	188	4,036	18,512	98,414	44,310
California	1,938	71,164	36,724	1,162	29,028	188,805	162,427	368,329
Colorado.........	196	6,792	34,686	118	3,122	19,215	162,704	39,191
Connecticut......	299	12,785	42,802	153	4,699	24,772	161,484	44,369
Delaware	60	2,840	47,178	27	784	5,791	212,890	13,601
District of Columbia .	13	630	49,180	3	97	1,512	504,133	1,975
Florida..........	486	14,853	30,554	297	6,553	38,621	130,170	76,387
Georgia	585	17,593	30,100	411	9,634	51,753	125,797	115,898
Hawaii..........	17	509	29,789	10	251	1,609	159,257	3,146
Idaho...........	74	2,383	32,152	53	1,312	7,977	149,944	18,315
Illinois..........	996	36,986	37,124	625	17,625	92,011	147,171	196,845
Indiana..........	660	22,976	34,812	477	14,290	61,896	129,678	133,787
Iowa	250	7,839	31,307	177	4,725	27,021	153,092	61,981
Kansas..........	209	6,902	32,994	145	4,006	18,820	129,970	46,152
Kentucky........	296	9,162	30,933	216	5,752	35,040	162,524	82,531
Louisiana	175	6,037	34,439	123	3,706	25,125	203,606	75,961
Maine...........	89	2,674	30,175	66	1,760	6,675	100,988	14,445
Maryland	192	6,968	36,309	112	3,226	17,455	155,707	35,700
Massachusetts....	475	19,026	40,071	264	7,723	44,047	166,655	79,254
Michigan.........	967	41,782	43,230	629	22,643	85,688	136,186	205,744
Minnesota........	432	15,590	36,071	256	6,886	34,716	135,399	73,273
Mississippi	239	5,654	23,666	190	3,838	17,295	91,024	39,564
Missouri	415	13,572	32,712	263	6,743	40,208	152,650	85,222
Montana.........	22	588	26,584	15	376	1,707	111,582	4,930
Nebraska	110	3,086	28,033	80	1,916	9,218	115,229	25,023
Nevada	41	1,195	29,299	27	627	3,275	120,408	6,194
New Hampshire....	107	3,576	33,293	71	1,848	10,815	152,969	19,348
New Jersey......	540	22,919	42,419	279	7,905	49,995	179,257	96,001
New Mexico	43	1,304	30,053	28	651	11,745	427,087	16,364
New York	950	35,641	37,533	555	14,541	90,665	163,448	163,697
North Carolina.....	856	23,796	27,815	628	13,879	76,475	121,814	155,911
North Dakota......	22	570	25,796	15	340	1,808	117,390	4,794
Ohio...........	1,074	39,790	37,065	720	22,618	105,497	146,462	232,721
Oklahoma.........	167	4,859	29,098	119	2,963	15,875	133,856	35,220
Oregon..........	232	7,869	33,859	157	4,317	21,838	138,917	45,022
Pennsylvania......	918	31,978	34,849	590	16,026	82,922	140,594	165,889
Rhode Island......	83	2,565	30,870	55	1,261	5,407	97,779	9,959
South Carolina.....	366	10,658	29,112	272	6,557	30,769	113,162	66,794
South Dakota	46	1,220	26,746	32	651	3,974	125,753	10,488
Tennessee	533	15,394	28,877	397	9,449	42,288	106,411	95,851
Texas..........	1,055	36,008	34,131	665	17,032	116,631	175,464	284,151
Utah	119	3,511	29,576	79	1,924	11,239	141,731	22,010
Vermont	48	1,483	30,969	33	788	3,986	122,652	8,554
Virginia..........	399	12,555	31,474	284	7,100	42,519	149,926	80,795
Washington.......	342	13,197	38,610	207	6,429	31,929	154,169	71,874
West Virginia......	76	2,521	33,083	55	1,607	8,965	163,885	17,679
Wisconsin........	601	19,779	32,910	416	11,324	53,619	128,984	114,464
Wyoming	10	268	27,608	7	175	999	140,746	2,874

[1] Includes employment and payroll at administrative offices and auxiliary units. All employees represents the average of production workers plus all other employees for the payroll period ended nearest the 12th of March. Production workers represents the average of the employment for the payroll periods ended nearest the 12th of March, May, August, and November. [2] Adjusted value added; takes into account (a) value added by merchandising operations (that is, difference between the sales value and cost of merchandise sold without further manufacture, processing, or assembly), plus (b) net change in finished goods and work-in-process inventories between beginning and end of year. [3] Includes extensive and unmeasurable duplication from shipments between establishments in the same industry classification.

Note: Reports for manufacturing by state for 1997 from the *1997 Economic Census* are being issued on a flow basis beginning in the summer of 1999.

Source: U.S. Census Bureau, *Annual Survey of Manufactures, Geographic Area Statistics*, Series M96(AS)-3.

No. 1235. Average Hourly Earnings of Production Workers in Manufacturing Industries, by State: 1980 to 1998

[In dollars]

State	1980	1990	1995	1997	1998	State	1980	1990	1995	1997	1998
United States ..	7.27	10.83	12.37	13.17	13.49	Missouri..........	7.26	10.74	12.17	12.98	13.35
Alabama	6.49	9.39	11.14	11.86	12.11	Montana	8.78	11.51	12.94	13.29	13.77
Alaska...........	10.22	12.46	11.00	11.78	11.09	Nebraska.........	7.38	9.66	11.19	12.10	12.32
Arizona	7.29	10.21	11.16	11.67	12.18	Nevada	7.72	11.05	12.62	14.17	14.42
Arkansas	5.71	8.51	10.05	10.78	11.11	New Hampshire.....	5.87	10.83	11.94	12.55	12.77
California	7.70	11.48	12.55	13.24	13.67	New Jersey	7.31	11.76	13.56	14.24	14.58
Colorado	7.63	10.94	12.51	13.31	13.73	New Mexico	5.79	9.04	10.68	11.74	12.51
Connecticut	7.08	11.53	13.71	14.46	14.83	New York	7.18	11.11	12.50	13.19	13.53
Delaware	7.58	12.39	14.20	14.81	15.33	North Carolina.....	5.37	8.79	10.56	11.41	11.84
District of Columbia [1] .	8.46	12.51	13.66	14.05	(NA)	North Dakota	6.56	9.27	10.75	11.29	11.45
Florida..........	5.98	8.98	10.18	10.95	11.43	Ohio	8.57	12.64	14.42	15.30	15.78
Georgia	5.77	9.17	10.71	11.64	12.04	Oklahoma	7.36	10.73	11.52	12.36	12.62
Hawaii...........	6.83	10.99	12.82	13.11	13.14	Oregon	8.65	11.15	12.75	13.39	14.06
Idaho...........	7.55	10.60	11.46	12.46	12.78	Pennsylvania	7.59	11.04	12.81	13.78	14.07
Illinois	8.02	11.44	12.64	13.35	13.74	Rhode Island	5.59	9.45	10.62	11.31	11.59
Indiana	8.49	12.03	13.91	14.79	14.96	South Carolina	5.59	8.84	10.16	10.35	10.54
Iowa	8.67	11.27	12.73	13.57	13.92	South Dakota	6.50	8.48	9.36	9.96	10.22
Kansas	7.37	10.94	12.39	13.45	13.85	Tennessee	6.08	9.55	10.78	11.71	12.06
Kentucky	7.34	10.70	12.22	13.17	13.80	Texas	7.15	10.47	11.47	12.03	12.15
Louisiana	7.74	11.61	13.43	14.14	14.64	Utah	7.02	10.32	11.62	12.85	13.10
Maine	6.00	10.59	12.39	13.12	13.50	Vermont..........	6.14	10.52	12.21	12.70	13.03
Maryland	7.61	11.57	13.49	14.14	14.31	Virginia	6.22	10.07	11.72	12.51	12.91
Massachusetts	6.51	11.39	12.79	13.42	13.79	Washington	(NA)	12.61	14.73	15.16	15.75
Michigan	9.52	13.86	16.31	17.18	17.57	West Virginia	8.08	11.53	12.64	13.17	13.71
Minnesota	7.61	11.23	12.79	13.63	13.91	Wisconsin.........	8.03	11.11	12.76	13.66	14.04
Mississippi	5.44	8.37	9.76	10.41	10.72	Wyoming	7.01	10.83	11.96	14.54	14.88

NA Not available.   [1] Washington PMSA (Primary Metropolitan Statistical Area).

Source: U.S. Bureau of Labor Statistics, *Employment and Earnings*, May 1999 issue and earlier issues.

No. 1236. Manufactures' Shipments, Inventories, and New Orders: 1970 to 1997

[In billions of dollars, except ratio. 634 represents $634,000,000,000]

Year	Shipments	Inventories (Dec, 31)[1]	Ratio of inventories to shipments[2]	New orders	Unfilled orders (Dec. 31)	Year	Shipments	Inventories (Dec, 31)[1]	Ratio of inventories to shipments[2]	New orders	Unfilled orders (Dec. 31)
1970	634	101	1.91	625	106	1984	2,288	334	1.75	2,315	370
1971	671	102	1.76	672	107	1985	2,334	330	1.72	2,348	384
1972	756	108	1.58	770	120	1986	2,336	318	1.63	2,342	390
1973	875	124	1.63	913	158	1987	2,476	333	1.58	2,513	427
1974	1,018	158	1.86	1,047	187	1988	2,695	363	1.56	2,739	471
						1989	2,840	385	1.65	2,875	505
1975	1,039	160	1.77	1,023	171						
1976	1,186	175	1.66	1,194	180	1990	2,912	398	1.70	2,934	527
1977	1,358	188	1.58	1,381	202	1991	2,878	384	1.65	2,866	515
1978	1,523	209	1.55	1,580	259	1992	3,005	375	1.47	2,979	489
1979	1,727	239	1.61	1,771	303	1993	3,128	376	1.44	3,092	453
						1994	3,348	396	1.38	3,357	462
1980	1,853	262	1.61	1,876	326						
1981	2,018	280	1.74	2,015	323	1995	3,595	421	1.42	3,608	475
1982	1,960	307	1.97	1,946	309	1996	3,715	427	1.39	3,749	509
1983	2,071	308	1.67	2,105	343	1997	3,929	446	1.36	3,952	532

[1] Beginning in 1982, inventories are stated at current cost and are not comparable to the book value estimates for prior years.   [2] Ratio based on December seasonally adjusted data.

Source: U.S. Census Bureau, Current Industrial Reports, *Manufacturers' Shipments, Inventories, and Orders: 1987-1997*, Series M3-1(97); and earlier reports.

Manufactures   751

U.S. Census Bureau, Statistical Abstract of the United States: 1999

No. 1237. Value of Manufactures' Shipments, Inventories, and New Orders, by Industry: 1993 to 1997

[In millions of dollars (3,127,625 represents $3,127,625,000,000). Based on 1987 Standard Industrial Classification (SIC). Based on a sample survey of most manufacturing companies with $500 million or more in annual shipments]

Industry	SIC code	Shipments 1993	1994	1995	1996	1997	Inventories (Dec. 31) 1993	1994	1995	1996	1997	New orders 1993	1994	1995	1996	1997
All manufacturing industries	D	3,127,625	3,348,019	3,594,663	3,715,460	3,929,419	375,982	395,974	421,285	427,130	446,131	3,092,381	3,356,797	3,607,586	3,749,299	3,952,025
Durable goods	(X)	1,630,635	1,789,576	1,927,029	2,004,159	2,158,699	233,306	247,001	261,138	266,547	278,766	1,596,974	1,794,508	1,941,378	2,036,536	2,180,708
Stone, clay, and glass products	32	65,610	71,230	75,932	82,442	90,221	7,443	7,688	8,359	8,679	8,832	65,945	71,562	76,085	82,142	89,893
Primary metals	33	142,685	161,188	180,314	178,297	188,916	20,093	22,555	24,052	24,385	24,785	144,018	167,685	178,702	180,362	193,987
Fabricated metal products	34	175,118	190,544	204,384	214,007	226,120	23,402	25,127	25,507	27,384	29,046	172,121	191,099	205,388	215,791	228,567
Industrial machinery and equipment	35	278,063	313,047	353,338	381,795	408,860	47,092	51,189	57,108	55,912	58,164	277,416	325,788	358,910	383,749	409,215
Computer and office equipment	357	69,249	78,230	91,343	91,270	111,334	10,473	10,640	12,630	10,277	9,869	68,497	81,595	91,045	103,689	108,986
Electronic and other	36	233,622	266,405	301,447	320,616	351,554	30,765	34,571	37,991	37,953	39,102	233,991	266,386	307,634	319,157	356,557
Electronic components	367	81,236	97,131	120,129	127,996	143,750	10,311	11,391	12,720	13,145	13,778	79,822	97,910	125,680	126,130	145,674
Transportation equipment [1]	37	414,694	450,809	461,806	465,173	502,301	59,140	59,364	57,663	62,347	66,877	386,643	440,817	465,839	495,239	507,667
Motor vehicles and parts	371	267,365	314,637	327,908	329,155	346,606	13,865	15,341	15,838	15,852	15,568	268,545	316,146	328,390	328,914	346,901
Aircraft, missiles, and parts	372, 6	116,345	103,316	100,063	101,322	121,393	9,536	9,403	9,573	9,995	11,255	88,070	90,217	106,062	129,688	124,151
Instruments and related products	38	137,387	138,400	144,719	151,017	162,981	22,492	22,273	24,233	24,517	25,143	133,249	133,232	144,175	149,344	165,453
All other durable goods	(X)	183,456	197,953	205,089	210,812	227,746	22,879	24,234	25,225	25,370	26,817	183,591	197,939	204,645	210,752	229,369
Nondurable goods [1]	(X)	1,496,990	1,558,443	1,667,634	1,711,301	1,770,720	142,676	148,973	160,147	160,583	167,365	1,495,407	1,562,289	1,666,208	1,712,763	1,771,317
Food and kindred products [1]	20	422,220	430,963	446,961	461,297	470,447	31,529	32,652	34,827	35,973	37,301	(NA)	(NA)	(NA)	(NA)	(NA)
Beverages	208	58,562	61,347	64,398	68,387	70,768	5,721	5,902	6,489	7,199	7,871	(NA)	(NA)	(NA)	(NA)	(NA)
Tobacco products	21	28,383	30,021	32,984	34,482	38,693	6,575	6,063	6,100	6,256	6,149	(NA)	(NA)	(NA)	(NA)	(NA)
Textile mill products	22	73,955	78,027	79,874	80,243	83,871	8,821	9,346	9,841	9,479	9,743	(NA)	(NA)	(NA)	(NA)	(NA)
Paper and allied products	26	133,263	143,649	173,716	160,661	161,992	13,795	14,290	17,173	15,887	16,108	(NA)	(NA)	(NA)	(NA)	(NA)
Chemicals and allied products [1]	28	314,907	333,905	361,391	367,674	389,189	35,505	36,737	39,604	40,794	43,880	(NA)	(NA)	(NA)	(NA)	(NA)
Industrial chemicals	281,2,6,8,9	158,771	169,909	186,970	184,018	193,265	17,142	17,710	19,157	19,603	20,335	(NA)	(NA)	(NA)	(NA)	(NA)
Drugs, soaps, toiletries	283-4	117,888	122,352	130,932	138,573	150,016	13,964	14,425	15,596	16,099	18,195	(NA)	(NA)	(NA)	(NA)	(NA)
Petroleum and coal products	29	144,834	143,328	151,439	138,573	177,314	9,865	10,661	10,829	12,046	11,806	(NA)	(NA)	(NA)	(NA)	(NA)
Rubber and plastics products	30	122,777	135,145	145,739	150,467	156,599	12,770	14,145	15,093	15,584	16,300	(NA)	(NA)	(NA)	(NA)	(NA)

NA Not available. X Not applicable. [1] Includes industries not shown separately.

Source: U.S. Census Bureau, Current Industrial Reports, Series M3-1(97), *Manufactures' Shipments, Inventories, and Orders: 1987-1997.*

U.S. Census Bureau, Statistical Abstract of the United States: 1999

No. 1238. Value of Manufacturers' Shipments, Inventories, and New Orders, by Market Grouping: 1993 to 1997

[In millions of dollars (3,127,625,000,000). Based on 1987 Standard Industrial Classification (SIC). For definition of individual market groupings, see publication cited below. Based on a sample survey of most manufacturing companies with $500 million or more in annual shipments]

Market grouping	Shipments					Inventories (Dec. 31)					New orders				
	1993	1994	1995	1996	1997	1993	1994	1995	1996	1997	1993	1994	1995	1996	1997
All manufacturing industries	**3,127,625**	**3,348,019**	**3,594,663**	**3,715,460**	**3,929,419**	**375,982**	**395,974**	**421,285**	**427,130**	**446,131**	**3,092,381**	**3,356,797**	**3,607,586**	**3,749,299**	**3,952,025**
Market categories:															
Automotive equipment	134,229	155,406	160,793	162,253	169,145	6,776	7,284	7,537	7,697	7,755	134,526	155,702	160,887	162,310	169,310
Home goods and apparel	195,574	205,985	210,653	210,324	220,994	27,423	29,409	30,359	28,056	29,226	194,976	205,505	211,040	209,912	222,405
Consumer staples	691,292	706,036	742,164	780,340	809,598	59,946	61,776	65,704	67,944	71,473	691,346	706,182	742,360	780,545	809,563
Machinery and equipment	524,479	569,333	613,526	652,978	711,993	86,613	92,596	99,957	104,241	111,413	505,542	567,922	624,687	672,605	729,607
Business supplies	248,468	258,551	276,451	289,085	302,490	21,886	23,155	25,052	25,326	26,644	248,203	258,913	276,675	289,251	302,437
Construction materials and supplies	199,227	217,556	228,247	238,116	252,549	23,488	24,939	26,381	26,721	27,689	198,463	219,305	228,242	239,060	253,766
Defense products	86,034	80,793	78,031	75,896	79,523	21,858	19,230	17,146	16,067	16,442	73,530	76,283	76,598	81,145	72,066
Other material, supplies and intermediate products	1,048,322	1,154,359	1,284,798	1,306,468	1,383,127	127,992	137,585	149,149	151,078	155,489	1,045,795	1,166,985	1,287,097	1,314,471	1,392,871
Durable goods industries:															
Nondefense capital goods	400,882	429,272	475,387	512,068	563,933	80,561	86,884	94,498	98,027	104,787	380,329	428,364	486,134	535,575	577,978
Excluding aircraft and parts	330,245	368,193	413,760	448,495	483,149	55,908	60,949	68,579	66,453	69,237	331,278	380,160	418,414	450,084	490,101
Defense capital goods	84,085	77,096	73,415	71,947	75,194	22,557	19,665	17,305	16,178	16,693	71,904	71,683	70,903	77,283	67,706
Durables excluding capital goods	1,145,668	1,283,208	1,378,227	1,420,144	1,519,572	130,188	140,452	149,335	152,342	157,286	1,144,741	1,294,461	1,384,341	1,423,678	1,535,024
Miscellaneous series:															
Producers' durable equipment	1,032,475	1,143,391	1,225,170	1,285,908	1,383,145	144,239	155,298	165,868	171,014	179,571	1,016,530	1,151,557	1,240,694	1,304,326	1,405,864
Household durable goods	88,522	95,167	98,645	98,437	106,074	12,499	13,834	14,676	14,160	14,549	88,914	95,500	98,500	97,963	107,403
Information technology industries	179,581	199,492	223,048	247,295	270,844	28,506	29,923	34,170	31,765	32,528	178,434	202,336	223,687	246,156	272,605
Health care equipment and products	106,335	108,896	114,691	122,805	132,540	14,233	14,422	15,621	16,505	17,853	105,737	107,266	114,183	122,984	133,451

Source: U.S. Census Bureau, Current Industrial Reports, Series M3-1(97), *Manufacturers' Shipments, Inventories, and Orders: 1987-1997*.

U.S. Census Bureau, Statistical Abstract of the United States: 1999

No. 1239. Ratios of Manufacturers' Inventories to Shipments and Unfilled Orders to Shipments, by Industry Group: 1993 to 1997

[Based on seasonally adjusted data]

Industry	Inventory/shipments ratio					Unfilled orders/shipments ratio				
	1993	1994	1995	1996	1997	1993	1994	1995	1996	1997
All manufacturing industries............	1.44	1.38	1.42	1.39	1.36	3.14	2.92	2.81	2.93	2.80
Durable goods industries	1.67	1.61	1.64	1.62	1.54	3.80	3.50	3.38	3.40	3.33
Stone, clay, and glass products .	1.32	1.25	1.31	1.31	1.18	1.23	1.17	1.14	1.05	0.87
Primary metals	1.62	1.46	1.62	1.59	1.57	1.85	1.92	1.89	1.97	2.24
Fabricated metal products	1.55	1.56	1.56	1.56	1.53	1.45	1.40	1.38	1.44	1.47
Industrial machinery and equipment..............	1.95	1.92	1.91	1.77	1.69	2.26	2.53	2.43	2.36	2.18
Electronic and other electrical equipment.............	1.57	1.55	1.50	1.44	1.33	2.21	1.94	1.96	1.82	1.81
Transportation equipment	1.68	1.55	1.54	1.67	1.59	11.47	10.61	10.43	11.66	10.87
Instruments and related products..............	2.00	1.94	2.00	1.97	1.84	4.10	4.18	3.91	3.69	3.54
Nondurable goods industries.....	1.17	1.10	1.16	1.13	1.13	0.71	0.75	0.68	0.72	0.69
Food and kindred products	0.88	0.85	0.90	0.93	0.92	(NA)	(NA)	(NA)	(NA)	(NA)
Tobacco products..........	2.57	2.25	2.09	1.95	1.78	(NA)	(NA)	(NA)	(NA)	(NA)
Textile mill products	1.50	1.44	1.58	1.44	1.45	(NA)	(NA)	(NA)	(NA)	(NA)
Paper and allied products	1.25	1.10	1.23	1.22	1.13	(NA)	(NA)	(NA)	(NA)	(NA)
Chemicals and allied products ..	1.36	1.25	1.33	1.32	1.34	(NA)	(NA)	(NA)	(NA)	(NA)
Petroleum and coal products ...	0.95	0.89	0.89	0.81	0.88	(NA)	(NA)	(NA)	(NA)	(NA)
Rubber and plastics products...	1.21	1.17	1.25	1.26	1.22	(NA)	(NA)	(NA)	(NA)	(NA)

NA Not available.

Source: U.S. Census Bureau, Current Industrial Reports, *Manufacturers' Shipments, Inventories, and Orders: 1987-1997*, Series M3-1(97).

No. 1240. Industrial Production Indexes, by Industry: 1980 to 1998

[1992=100. Beginning 1990, data based on 1987 Standard Industrial Classification (SIC), earlier years based on 1977 SIC; see text, Section 26, Manufactures]

Industry	SIC code	1980	1990	1991	1992	1993	1994	1995	1996	1997	1998
Total index	(X)	79.7	98.9	97.0	100.0	103.5	109.1	114.4	119.5	126.8	131.4
Manufacturing.................	(X)	75.5	98.5	96.2	100.0	103.7	109.9	115.9	121.4	129.7	135.1
Durable goods................	(X)	73.4	99.0	95.5	100.0	105.4	114.2	124.0	134.1	147.1	157.5
Lumber and products	24	80.4	101.6	94.5	100.0	100.8	105.9	107.9	110.4	114.2	116.9
Furniture and fixtures	25	79.1	100.9	94.8	100.0	104.9	108.1	111.4	113.2	117.7	121.5
Stone, clay, and glass products....	32	96.5	105.0	97.2	100.0	102.1	107.8	110.9	118.3	122.3	125.9
Primary metals..............	33	108.0	104.0	96.7	100.0	105.7	113.4	116.8	119.8	125.3	123.8
Iron and steel	331,2	119.0	106.4	96.0	100.0	107.1	113.7	113.7	119.2	124.2	120.7
Fabricated metal products	34	94.4	101.2	96.2	100.0	104.4	112.2	116.4	120.2	124.7	127.2
Industrial, commercial machinery [1]..	35	70.5	100.1	95.4	100.0	109.9	124.9	143.9	159.8	179.4	203.7
Computer and office equipment ..	357	13.9	81.4	82.3	100.0	120.5	149.3	211.3	298.8	423.7	650.4
Electrical machinery	36	48.6	87.7	89.6	100.0	109.6	131.4	166.3	206.0	253.4	291.5
Transportation equipment.......	37	70.3	102.3	96.5	100.0	103.6	107.4	106.4	107.9	117.1	123.1
Motor vehicles and parts	371	65.8	95.3	88.5	100.0	113.2	130.4	132.7	132.6	139.9	141.2
Autos and light trucks	371pt	58.1	99.3	91.0	100.0	111.5	125.2	121.7	122.5	127.8	128.5
Aerospace and miscellaneous ...	372-6,9	74.3	109.8	105.0	100.0	93.9	85.0	80.7	83.8	94.7	105.0
Instruments	38	73.6	98.4	99.8	100.0	100.8	99.8	103.6	107.7	110.3	113.1
Nondurable goods	(X)	78.3	97.9	97.0	100.0	101.8	105.2	107.1	107.9	111.3	112.0
Foods.....................	20	79.7	97.0	98.4	100.0	102.0	103.7	105.8	105.4	108.0	109.5
Tobacco products	21	108.5	105.4	98.9	100.0	84.1	104.4	111.8	113.5	110.9	106.0
Textile mill products..........	22	89.0	93.2	92.7	100.0	105.3	110.6	110.2	108.9	112.2	112.7
Paper and products	26	75.2	96.0	96.8	100.0	104.0	108.4	109.6	108.8	114.4	115.2
Printing and publishing	27	72.4	103.1	99.1	100.0	100.7	100.7	101.4	101.6	105.2	105.2
Chemicals and products	28	75.9	97.3	96.4	100.0	101.5	104.7	107.3	110.0	114.9	115.5
Petroleum products...........	29	95.9	100.3	99.1	100.0	102.9	102.7	104.5	106.8	109.8	112.2
Rubber and plastics products ...	30	53.3	92.2	90.7	100.0	106.9	116.5	119.7	123.3	128.2	132.6
Leather and products	31	181.6	107.8	98.4	100.0	101.0	93.6	86.9	87.3	81.9	75.3
Mining	C	111.5	104.8	102.6	100.0	99.9	102.4	102.0	103.7	105.8	104.1
Utilities.......................	(X)	87.3	98.3	100.4	100.0	103.9	105.3	109.0	112.6	112.8	114.6

X Not applicable.   [1] Includes computer equipment.

Source: Board of Governors of the Federal Reserve System, *Federal Reserve Bulletin*, monthly; and *Industrial Production and Capacity Utilization*, Statistical Release G.17, monthly.

No. 1241. Index of Manufacturing Capacity: 1980 to 1998

[1992 output=100. Annual figures are averages of quarterly data. Capacity represents estimated quantity of output relative to output in 1992 which the *current* stock of plant and equipment in manufacturing industries was capable of producing. Primary processing industries comprise textiles, lumber, paper and pulp, petroleum, rubber, stone, clay, glass, primary metals, fabricated metals, and a portion of chemicals. Advanced processing industries comprise chemical products, food, beverages, tobacco, apparel, furniture, printing and publishing, leather, machinery, transportation equipment, instruments, ordnance, and miscellaneous industry groups]

Year	Index of capacity	Relation of output to capacity (percent)			Year	Index of capacity	Relation of output to capacity (percent)		
		All manu-facturing	Primary processing	Advanced processing			All manu-facturing	Primary processing	Advanced processing
1980	95	79	77	81	1990	121	81	84	80
1981	98	78	77	79	1991	123	78	80	77
1982	100	72	69	73	1992	126	79	82	78
1983	102	74	74	74	1993	129	80	84	79
1984	105	80	80	80	1994	133	83	87	81
1985	109	79	79	79	1995	140	83	86	81
1986	112	79	80	78	1996	149	81	85	80
1987	114	81	84	80	1997	158	82	85	81
1988	116	84	87	82	1998	167	81	84	80
1989	118	84	86	82					

Source: Board of Governors of the Federal Reserve System, *Capacity Utilization In Manufacturing, Mining, Utilities, and Industrial Materials*, G.3., monthly.

No. 1242. Finances and Profits of Manufacturing Corporations: 1980 to 1998

[In billions of dollars (1,897 represents $1,897,000,000,000). Beginning 1990, data exclude estimates for corporations with less than $250,000 in assets at time of sample selection. Prior years include estimates for corporations in this size category. See Table 911 for individual industry data]

Item	1980	1990	1991	1992	1993	1994	1995	1996	1997	1998
Net sales................	1,913	2,811	2,761	2,890	3,014	3,256	3,528	3,758	3,920	3,934
Net operating profit	129	173	133	151	180	242	268	277	298	296
Net profit:										
Before taxes.............	146	158	99	31	118	244	274	307	331	318
After taxes..............	93	110	66	22	83	175	198	225	245	238
Cash dividends.............	36	62	60	63	67	70	81	96	108	119
Net income retained in business ..	58	48	6	-41	16	105	117	129	136	119

Source: 1980, U.S. Federal Trade Commission; thereafter, U.S. Census Bureau, *Quarterly Financial Report for Manufacturing, Mining, and Trade Corporations.*

No. 1243. U.S. Exports of Manufactures, Origin of World Exports of Manufacture: 1981 to 1996

[In billions of dollars (148 represents $148,000,000,000), except percents]

Item	1981-85, average	1986-90, average	1992	1993	1994	1995	1996
U.S. manufactures export value	148	227	350	365	409	464	498
Machinery & transport equipment	92	141	215	225	252	283	307
Chemicals............................	21	32	45	46	52	62	63
Other................................	34	54	90	94	104	119	128
Origin of world exports of manufactures (percent):							
United States [1]	13.0	11.5	12.6	13.1	12.7	12.4	12.9
Machinery & transport equipment	17.1	14.6	15.8	16.4	15.7	14.9	15.5
Chemicals	15.1	13.2	13.4	13.9	13.5	13.2	13.3
Other	8.0	7.0	8.3	8.7	8.5	8.8	9.2
Germany [2]...........................	13.4	14.6	13.9	12.0	11.8	12.4	11.9
Japan	13.4	12.4	11.8	12.6	11.8	11.4	10.2
Other G-7 countries [3]	21.7	21.5	21.0	20.1	19.7	20.4	21.0
East Asian NICs [4]..................	6.4	7.8	8.1	8.8	8.9	9.4	9.3

[1] U.S. exports are domestic exports only. [2] Prior to 1991, data are for former West Germany only. [3] Other Group of Seven (G-7) Countries: Canada, France, Italy, United Kingdom. [4] East Asian newly industrialized countries (NICs): Hong Kong, S. Korea, Singapore, Taiwan.

Source: U.S. Dept. of Commerce, International Trade Administration, Office of Trade and Economic Analysis. Based on United Nations Commodity Trade Statistics, *Statistical Yearbook of the Republic of China (Taiwan)*, and unpublished data.

U.S. Census Bureau, Statistical Abstract of the United States: 1999

No. 1244. Alcoholic Beverages—Summary: 1980 to 1996

[193 mil. bbl. represents 193,000,000. For 1980-1985, stocks on hand for years ending June 30; later data for years ending September 30. All other items for fiscal years ending in year shown; see text, Section 9, State and Local Government. Includes Puerto Rico. Excludes imports]

Item	Unit	1980	1985	1990	1992	1993	1994	1995	1996, prel.
Beer:									
Breweries operated	Number [2]	86	103	286	392	480	619	879	1,504
Production [1] . . . . [3]	Mil. bbl. [2]	193	194	202	202	202	203	200	199
Value of shipments [3]	Mil. dol. [2]	9,362	12,216	15,186	17,302	16,629	16,714	17,108	18,196
Tax-paid withdrawals	Mil. bbl. [2]	172	175	182	182	180	180	177	177
Stocks on hand	Mil. bbl. [2]	15	14	14	13.4	13.7	13.4	13.5	13.3
Distilled spirits:									
Production facilities operated . .	Number . . . [5] . .	143	117	143	143	132	150	153	(NA)
Production [1] [4]	Mil. tax gal. [5] . .	236	117	122	110	111	99	104	(NA)
Tax-paid withdrawals [6]	Mil. tax gal. [5] . .	330	306	251	246	240	229	235	(NA)
Stocks on hand [4]	Mil. tax gal. [5] . .	696	588	451	365	420	410	452	(NA)
Whiskey:									
Production [1]	Mil. tax gal. [5] . .	87	65	77	62	59	59	69	(NA)
Stocks on hand	Mil. tax gal. [5] . .	566	467	365	309	361	354	358	(NA)
Still wines:									
Production [1] . . . . [8] . . .	Mil. wine gal. [7] .	982	622	577	484	417	438	412	577
Tax-paid withdrawals [8]	Mil. wine gal. [7] .	340	414	468	387	354	356	366	382
Stocks on hand [9]	Mil. wine gal. [7] .	486	602	562	525	520	477	398	473

NA Not available.   [1] Production represents total amount removed from fermenters, including distilling material, and includes increase after fermentation (by amelioration, sweetening, and addition of wine spirits).   [2] Barrels of 31 wine gallons.   [3] Source: U.S. Census Bureau, *Census of Manufactures*, and *Annual Survey of Manufactures*.   [4] Excludes alcohol produced for industrial use. Also excludes vodka and gin production.   [5] For spirits of 100 proof or over, a tax gallon is equivalent to the proof gallon; for spirits of less than 100 proof, the tax gallon is equivalent to the wine gallon. A proof gallon is the alcoholic equivalent of a U.S. gallon at 60 degrees F, containing 50 percent of ethyl alcohol by volume.   [6] Includes ethyl alcohol.   [7] A wine gallon is the U.S. gallon equivalent to the volume of 231 cubic inches.   [8] Includes special natural wines.   [9] Excludes distilling materials.

Source: Except as noted, U.S. Bureau of Alcohol, Tobacco, and Firearms, *Alcohol and Tobacco Summary Statistics*, annual; beginning 1985, *Monthly Statistical Release, Distilled Spirits*, Report Symbol 76; and *Wines*, Report Symbol, ATF A:I 5120-3.

No. 1245. Manufacturing (1997 NAICS Basis)—Summary: 1997

[Data are preliminary and are subject to change; they will be superceded by data released in later reports. Includes only establishments with payroll]

Description	NAICS code	Establishments	Shipments (bil. dol.)	Annual payroll (bil. dol.)	Paid employees (1,000)
Manufacturing, total		**364,377**	**3,855.5**	**574.1**	**16,999.6**
Food manufacturing	311	26,970	425.3	38.9	1,489.6
Beverage & tobacco product	312	2,774	96.6	6.8	177.3
Textile mills	313	4,714	60.1	10.3	400.7
Textile product mills	314	7,226	31.9	4.8	220.9
Apparel	315	17,831	67.7	13.1	744.1
Leather & allied product.	316	1,824	10.7	1.9	89.7
Wood product	321	17,101	88.7	14.4	572.1
Paper manufacturing.	322	5,925	150.7	22.3	573.5
Printing & related support activities	323	43,054	98.7	26.4	846.7
Petroleum & coal products.	324	2,143	178.9	5.6	110.0
Chemical	325	13,482	417.7	40.8	903.3
Plastics & rubber products	326	16,686	159.0	29.8	1,024.4
Nonmetallic mineral product	327	16,404	88.1	16.5	508.9
Primary metal	331	5,298	173.9	24.1	609.3
Fabricated metal product	332	62,684	245.9	57.3	1,780.0
Machinery.	333	30,580	271.5	53.4	1,435.0
Computer & electronic product	334	17,240	431.4	71.4	1,689.8
Electrical equipment, appliance, & components .	335	7,108	112.4	19.0	595.2
Transportation equipment	336	13,206	577.9	80.2	1,886.6
Furniture & related product.	337	20,694	65.4	15.1	606.7
Miscellaneous	339	31,433	102.9	22.1	735.8

Source: U.S. Census Bureau, *1997 Economic Census, Core Business Statistics Series*, Series EC97X-CS1.

No. 1246. Tobacco Products—Summary: 1980 to 1997

[Production data are for calendar years. Excludes cigars produced in customs bonded manufacturing warehouses]

Item	Unit	1980	1990	1991	1992	1993	1994	1995	1996	1997
PRODUCTION										
Cigarettes	Billions . . .	714	710	695	719	661	726	747	758	720
Cigars	Billions . . .	3.5	1.9	1.7	1.7	1.8	1.9	2.1	2.4	2.4
Tobacco [1]	Mil. lb.	163	142	142	141	133	132	131	131	134
Consumption per person [2]	Lb. [3]	7.9	5.5	5.4	5.4	5.0	5.0	5.0	4.7	4.5
Cigarettes	1,000	4	3	3	3	3	3	3	3	2
Cigars [4]	Number . . .	24	13	12	12	11	12	15	18	19
Consumer expenditures . .	Bil. dol. . . .	21.0	43.8	47.4	48.4	49.0	47.7	48.6	51.9	53.7
Cigarettes	Bil. dol. . . .	19.4	41.6	45.2	45.8	46.2	44.5	45.1	48.7	50.4
Cigars	Bil. dol. . . .	0.7	0.7	0.7	0.6	0.7	0.9	1.0	0.9	1.1
Other	Bil. dol. . . .	0.9	1.5	1.8	2.0	2.1	2.3	2.5	2.2	2.2

[1] Smoking and chewing tobaccos and snuff output.   [2] Based on estimated population 18 years old and over, as of July 1, including Armed Forces abroad.   [3] Unstemmed processing weight equivalent.   [4] Weighing over 3 pounds per 1,000.
Source: U.S. Dept. of Agriculture, Economic Research Service, *Tobacco Situation and Outlook*, quarterly.

No. 1247. Cotton, Wool, and Manmade Fibers—Consumption, by End-Use: 1997

[Represents products manufactured by U.S. mills. Excludes glass fiber]

Year	Cotton		Wool		Manufactured fibers					
							Artificial [1]		Synthetic [2]	
	Total (mil. lb.)	Total (mil. lb.)	Percent of end-use	Total (mil. lb.)	Percent of end-use	Total (mil. lb.)	Percent of end-use	Total (mil. lb.)	Percent of end-use	Total (mil. lb.)	Percent of end-use
Total	**17,622**	**5,395**	**30.6**	**196**	**1.1**	**12,031**	**68.3**	**444**	**2.5**	**11,587**	**65.8**
Apparel	7,030	3,441	48.9	142	2.0	3,448	49.0	248	3.5	3,200	45.5
Home textiles	2,733	1,564	57.2	13	0.5	1,156	42.3	78	2.9	1,078	39.5
Floor coverings	4,063	31	0.8	26	0.6	4,006	98.6	-	0.0	4,006	98.6
Industrial [3]	3,797	360	9.5	15	0.4	3,421	90.1	119	3.1	3,303	87.0

- Represents or rounds to zero.   [1] Rayon and acetate.   [2] Nylon, polyester, acrylic, and olefin.   [3] Includes consumer-type products.

Source: Fiber Economics Bureau, Inc., Washington, DC, *Textile Organon*, monthly (copyright).

No. 1248. Broadwoven and Knit Fabrics—Shipments, Foreign Trade, and Apparent Consumption: 1997

[4,246,048 represents 4,246,048,000. Fabric blends as shown in the CIR report, MQ22T are reported based on the chief weight of the fiber; whereas, fabrics blends as shown for imports are based on the chief value of the fiber. Apparent consumption represents new domestic supply and is derived by subtracting exports for the total manufacturers' shipments plus imports]

Product description	Manufacturers' shipments (quantity)	Imports for consumption		Percent imports to manufacturers' shipments	Exports of domestic merchandise		Percent exports to manufacturers' shipments	Apparent consumption (quantity)
		Quantity	Value [1] ($1,000)		Quantity	Value ($1,000)		
BROADWOVEN FABRICS (quantity 1,000 sq. meters)								
Cotton fabrics [2]	4,246,048	1,591,422	1,800,985	37.5	300,772	690,927	7.1	5,536,698
Manmade fiber fabrics	9,794,370	1,026,708	1,406,822	10.8	442,025	988,050	4.7	10,074,779
Silk fabrics	808	31,708	320,284	3,925.8	2,710	20,931	335.5	29,806
Wool fabrics	146,510	31,460	310,213	21.5	13,340	68,933	9.1	164,630
KNIT FABRICS (quantity in 1,000 kilograms)								
Total	**909,027**	**74,210**	**713,407**	**8.2**	**72,080**	**614,871**	**7.9**	**906,897**
Pile fabrics	80,561	34,237	367,861	42.5	18,855	188,431	23.4	65,179
Elastic fabric	37,983	336	5,034	0.9	11,354	113,680	29.9	49,001
Other warp knit fabrics	93,998	9,312	92,640	9.9	5,631	61,992	6.0	90,317
Other narrow knit fabrics	5,397	847	9,618	15.7	4,698	39,466	87.0	9,248
Other knit fabrics	691,088	29,478	238,254	4.3	31,542	211,302	4.6	693,152

[1] Dollar value represents the c.i.f. (cost, insurance, and freight) at the first port of entry in the United States plus calculated import duty.   [2] Includes all cotton and chiefly cotton mixed with manmade fiber. products, however; export data is available on a total basis.

Source: U.S. Census Bureau, *Manufacturing Profiles*, Series MP.

No. 1249. Selected Apparel—Shipments, Foreign Trade, and Apparent Consumption: 1997

[Quantity in thousands of units (11,887 represents 11,887,000), value in millions of dollars (188.7 represents $188,700,000)]

Product description	Manufactures' shipments		Exports of domestic merchandise		Imports for consumption		Apparent consumption	
	Quantity	Value	Quantity	Value	Quantity	Value	Quantity	Value
Men's and boys' apparel:								
Sweaters	11,887	188.7	52,452	168.7	45,576	571.7	5,011	591.7
Tops, except sweaters	(D)	(D)	525,192	1,261.7	1,620,516	7,710.3	(D)	(D)
Bottoms	602,289	7,793.4	300,120	1,172.7	715,920	4,703.3	1,018,089	11,324.0
Coats:								
Suit type, dress and sport .	11,784	731.3	5,976	61.2	14,160	494.3	19,968	1,164.4
Other coats	57,643	1,664.3	17,112	94.0	144,684	2,312.0	185,215	3,882.3
Suits	9,296	792.5	3,768	41.8	83,940	582.9	89,468	1,333.6
Swimwear.	1,940	32.3	876	4.2	43,608	151.1	44,672	179.2
Women's and girls' apparel:								
Sweaters	56,153	743.8	2,808	15.1	193,344	2,056.6	246,689	2,785.3
Dresses	178,702	4,341.3	28,896	147.7	200,736	1,980.3	350,542	6,173.9
Tops, except sweaters	(D)	(D)	220,632	469.8	1,194,240	6,437.9	(D)	(D)
Skirts.	76,131	1,119.7	11,496	53.3	125,004	978.2	189,639	2,044.6
Coats and jackets	52,117	1,921.4	19,224	155.3	152,628	2,696.6	185,521	4,462.7
Bottoms, except skirts.	526,438	5,569.5	159,960	543.9	590,628	4,082.9	957,106	9,108.5
Suits	(D)	(D)	7,008	60.7	111,192	347.8	(D)	(D)
Swimwear.	55,846	938.3	12,264	56.5	41,448	237.1	85,030	1,118.9
Infants' apparel.	159,018	719.6	135,828	163.3	501,336	1,231.5	524,526	1,787.8

D Data withheld to avoid disclosing figures or individual companies.
Source: U.S. Census Bureau, *Manufacturing Profiles*, Series MP/96. and <http://www.census.gov/ftp/pub/industry/1/mq23a975.pdf> (issued 19 August 1998).

Manufactures 757

No. 1250. Footwear—Production, Foreign Trade, and Apparent Consumption: 1997

[Quantity in thousands of pairs (188,304 represents 188,304,000 pairs), value in thousands of dollars (412,057 represents $412,057,000)]

Product description	Manufac-turers' ship-ments (quantity)	Exports of domestic merchandise		Percent exports to domestic produc-tion	Imports for consumption		Apparent consump-tion (quantity)	Percent imports to apparent consump-tion
		Quantity	Value		Quantity	Value		
Total	188,434	27,731	412,057	14.7	1,459,736	15,137,411	1,620,439	90.1
Rubber or plastic uppers and rubber or plastic soles.	21,338	4,307	44,492	20.2	517,924	3,095,025	534,955	96.8
Waterproof	12,299	384	5,219	3.1	3,389	26,046	15,304	22.1
Not waterproof	9,039	3,923	39,273	43.4	514,535	3,068,979	519,651	99.0
Leather uppers	66,296	11,287	274,734	17.0	628,766	9,845,954	683,775	92.0
Athletic.	5,061	7,080	156,680	139.9	434,992	5,961,894	432,973	100.5
Leather soles.	21,767	2,816	77,819	12.9	52,213	1,282,976	71,164	73.4
Made with steel safety toes	1,724	173	9,588	10.0	8,584	193,321	10,135	84.7
Boots, ex. with steel safety toes.	6,824	488	14,265	7.2	4,682	112,721	11,018	42.5
Shoes, ex. with steel safety toes	13,219	2,155	53,966	16.3	38,947	976,934	50,011	77.9
Other soles	39,468	1,391	40,235	3.5	141,561	2,601,084	179,638	78.8
Made with steel safety toes	1,965	-	-	(NA)	-	-	1,965	0.0
Boots, ex. with steel safety toes.	7,952	1,391	40,235	17.5	141,561	2,601,084	148,122	95.6
Shoes, ex. with steel safety toes	29,551	-	-	(NA)	-	-	29,551	0.0
Fabric uppers	85,884	9,624	92,831	11.2	313,046	2,196,432	389,306	80.4
Rubber or plastic soles	57,752	7,111	73,625	12.3	255,355	1,780,502	305,996	83.5
Athletic	14,538	5,931	62,929	(D)	82,986	1,105,174	(D)	(D)
All other	43,214	1,180	10,696	(D)	172,369	675,328	(D)	(D)
With all other soles	28,132	2,513	19,206	8.9	57,691	415,930	72,677	79.4

- Represents zero.   D Data withheld to avoid disclosure.   NA Not available.

Source: U.S. Census Bureau, *Manufacturing Profiles,* Series MP/97, annual; and <http://ftp.census.gov/pub/industry/1/ma31a97.pdf> (released 13 August 1998).

No. 1251. Inorganic Fertilizers, Chemicals, and Pharmaceutical Preparations—Value of Shipments: 1990 to 1997

[In millions of dollars (1,072 represents $1,072,000,000)]

Product	Product code	Unit	1990	1994	1995	1996	1997
INORGANIC FERTILIZERS							
Ammonia, synthetic anhydrous	28731 31	Mil. dol . . .	1,072	1,509	1,662	1,690	1,578
Ammonium sulfate	28731 57	Mil. dol . . .	130	165	1,953	214	181
Urea (100%)	28732	Mil. dol . . .	640	657	848	912	772
Nitric acid (100%).	28731 11	Mil. dol . . .	81	118	168	197	216
Phosphoric acid (100% P2O5)	28741 81,85	Mil. dol . . .	1,226	1,085	1,220	1,227	1,405
Sulfuric acid, gross (100%)	28193	Mil. dol . . .	589	488	539	578	528
Superphosphates and other fertilizer materials. .	28742	Mil. dol . . .	2,711	2,830	3,594	3,928	3,675
INORGANIC CHEMICAL SHIPMENTS							
Alkalies and chlorine.	2812	Mil. dol . . .	3,187	2,275	3,169	3,212	3,070
Inorganic color pigments	2816	Mil. dol . . .	2,261	2,471	2,284	2,487	2,659
Inorganic chemicals n.e.c.	2819	Mil. dol . . .	13,612	12,676	14,179	14,526	14,512
Household bleaching compounds	28422 00	Mil. dol . . .	724	955	923	891	920
PHARMACEUTICAL PREP. SHIPMENTS							
Pharmaceutical preparations, except biologicals		**Mil. dol . . .**	**33,954**	**48,209**	**48,864**	**51,844**	**62,593**
Affecting neoplasms, endocrine systems, and metabolic disease.	28341	Mil. dol . . .	2,743	4,120	4,076	4,788	6,873
Acting on the central nervous system and sense organs.	28342	Mil. dol . . .	7,219	8,990	9,228	10,123	12,280
Acting on the cardiovascular system	28343	Mil. dol . . .	4,815	5,674	5,988	6,912	8,262
Acting on the respiratory system	28344	Mil. dol . . .	3,724	5,566	5,196	4,994	5,486
Acting on the digestive system	28345	Mil. dol . . .	4,840	8,479	8,593	8,494	10,100
Acting on the skin.	28346	Mil. dol . . .	1,558	2,090	2,171	2,185	1,982
Vitamin, nutrient, and hematinic preps.	28347	Mil. dol . . .	2,588	4,402	4,812	5,281	7,109
Affecting parasitic and infective disease	28348	Mil. dol . . .	5,411	7,257	7,196	7,304	8,690
Pharmaceutical preps. for veterinary use	28349	Mil. dol . . .	1,057	1,631	1,605	1,763	1,813

Source: U.S. Census Bureau, through 1992, *Current Industrial Reports,* MA28A, and MA28G, annual; thereafter, *Manufacturing Profiles,* Series MP, annual.

No. 1252. Fiber, Rugs, Carpeting, and Sheets—Shipments: 1990 to 1997

Product	Unit	1990	1992	1993	1994	1995	1996	1997
All fibers [1]	Mil. lbs . . .	812	926	1,008	1,036	953	912	905
Raw wool [2][3]	Mil. lbs . . .	133	151	157	153	142	142	144
Noils, and fiber [4]	Mil. lbs . . .	20	21	23	19	20	23	20
Other fibers	Mil. lbs . . .	659	754	829	864	792	748	740
Knit fabric production	Mil. lbs . . .	1,901	2,179	2,188	2,211	2,131	1,919	1,974
Rugs, carpet and carpeting	Mil. dol . . .	8,527	8,749	9,283	9,531	9,770	10,148	10,262
Sheets	1,000 doz. .	14,716	15,300	16,331	16,190	15,282	16,108	16,480
Pillow cases	1,000 doz. .	12,443	12,945	14,464	14,622	14,232	14,234	15,305
Terry towels	1,000 doz. .	41,855	46,885	47,161	48,348	47,939	46,991	44,940

[1] Includes man-made fiber top converted from tow without combing. A number of companies were added for 1990 based on information in the 1987 Census of Manufactures. Data were received from these companies for 1990; therefore, the information shown for years prior to 1990 may not be directly comparable. These changes represent approximately 20 percent of the total fibers consumed on the woolen system and worsted combing.   [2] Data are shown on a scoured basis for greasy wool.
[3] Shorn and pulled wool of sheep excludes raw wool consumed in cotton system spinning to avoid disclosing figures for individual companies.   [4] Includes reprocessed and reused wool, mohair, alpaca, vicuna, and other specialty fibers as well as tops and noils consumed in woolen spinning and mohair consumed in worsted combing. Does not include wool tops consumed in cotton system spinning.

Source: U.S. Census Bureau, 1990 and 1992, *Current Industrial Reports*, MA22K, MA22Q, and MQ23X, annual; thereafter, *Manufacturing Profiles*, Series MP, annual.

No. 1253. Glass Containers, Clay Construction Products, and Refractories—Shipments: 1990 to 1997

[In millions of dollars (285 represents 285,000,000)]

Product	1990	1992	1993	1994	1995	1996	1997
Glass container shipments	285	283	290	285	269	257	254
Brick shipments [1]	1,014	920	990	1,102	1,092	1,235	1,340
Clay tile shipments [2]	687	646	687	756	728	779	874
Clay pipe and fittings shipments	60	38	33	33	35	45	44
Refractory shipments	2,003	1,956	1,930	2,047	2,222	2,341	2,404
Clay	771	786	773	906	941	930	968
Nonclay	1,232	1,170	1,157	1,141	1,282	1,411	1,436

[1] Building or common and face bricks.   [2] Floor and wall tile including quarry tile.

Source: U.S. Census Bureau, 1990 and 1992, *Current Industrial Reports*, M32G, MQ32D, and MA32C, annual; thereafter, *Manufacturing Profiles*, Series MP, annual.

No. 1254. Aluminum Mill Products—Shipments, by Product: 1997 and 1998

[Quantity in thousands of pounds (16,311,489 represents 16,311,489,000), receipts in thousands of dollars (1,321,202 represents $1,321,202,000)]

Product description	1997			1998		
	Gross shipments	Total receipts	Net shipments [1]	Gross shipments	Total receipts	Net shipments [1]
Aluminum mill products, total .	16,311,489	1,321,202	14,990,287	16,545,857	1,367,202	15,178,655
Sheet, plate, and foil	11,165,874	775,043	10,390,831	11,278,670	834,265	10,444,405
Sheet	9,624,301	775,043	8,849,258	9,717,288	834,265	8,883,023
Plate	402,487	-	402,487	408,596	-	408,596
Foil	1,139,086	-	1,139,086	1,152,786	-	1,152,786
Rod, wire, and cable	1,140,801	446,287	694,514	1,192,477	456,286	736,191
Rod and bare wire	504,370	446,287	58,083	545,514	456,286	89,228
Cable and insulated wire	636,431	-	636,431	646,963	-	646,963
Rod, bar, pipe, tube and shapes	3,646,886	99,872	3,547,014	3,714,040	76,651	3,637,389
Rod and bar (rolled and extruded) . . .	471,565	99,872	371,693	468,805	76,651	392,154
Pipe and tube (extruded and drawn) . .	341,442	(D)	341,442	359,250	(D)	359,250
Extruded shapes	2,833,879	-	2,833,879	2,885,985	-	2,885,985
All other	357,928	-	357,928	360,670	-	360,670

- Represents zero.   D Withheld to avoid disclosure of individual companies.   [1] Net shipments are derived by subtracting domestic receipts from gross shipments.

Source: U.S. Census Bureau, *Manufacturing Profiles, 1996,* Series MP/96; and <http://www.census.gov/ftp/pub/industry/1/m33d9813.pdf> (issued 30 June 1999).

Manufactures   759

No. 1255. Iron and Steel Industry—Summary: 1990 to 1998

[For financial data, the universe in 1992 consists of the companies that produced 68 percent of the total reported raw steel production. The financial data represent the operations of the steel segment of the companies. Minus sign (-) indicates net loss]

Item	Unit	1990	1992	1993	1994	1995	1996	1997	1998
Steel mill products, apparent supply . . .	Mil. tons [1] . .	97.8	95.0	104.6	121.3	114.8	125.0	131.0	(NA)
Net shipments	Mil. tons [1] . .	85.0	82.2	89.0	95.1	97.5	100.9	105.9	102.1
Exports	Mil. tons [1] . .	4.3	4.3	4.0	3.8	7.1	5.0	6.0	5.5
Imports	Mil. tons [1] . .	17.2	17.1	19.5	30.1	24.4	29.2	31.2	41.5
Scrap consumed	Mil. tons [1] . .	50.1	51.9	58.5	60.0	62.0	62.0	64.0	(NA)
Scrap inventory	Mil. tons [1] . .	3.6	3.3	3.6	4.0	4.1	5.3	5.0	(NA)
Iron and steel products: Exports	Mil. tons [1] . .	5.3	5.3	4.7	4.9	8.2	6.2	7.4	(NA)
Imports	Mil. tons [1] . .	21.9	21.9	21.8	32.7	27.3	32.1	34.4	(NA)
Capacity by steelmaking process	Mil. net tons	116.7	113.1	109.9	108.2	112.4	116.1	121.4	(NA)
Revenue	Bil. dol.	30.9	26.9	29.5	34.1	35.1	35.0	35.9	(NA)
Net income	Bil. dol.	0.1	-4.1	1.9	1.3	1.5	0.4	1.1	(NA)
Stockholders' equity	Bil. dol.	2.1	2.8	-0.6	3.7	7.4	10.2	10.9	(NA)
Total assets	Bil. dol.	28.3	28.8	30.6	34.3	35.1	35.8	37.0	(NA)
Capital expenditures	Bil. dol.	2.6	1.8	1.5	2.2	2.5	2.3	2.6	(NA)
Working capital ratio [2]	Ratio	1.8	1.4	1.5	1.5	1.6	1.7	1.6	(NA)
Inventories	Bil. dol.	4.7	4.5	4.6	5.0	5.1	5.4	5.6	(NA)
Average employment	1,000	164	140	127	126	123	119	112	(NA)
Hours worked	Million	350	293	274	273	269	259	247	(NA)
Index of output, all employees [3]	1987=100 . .	109.6	117.1	133.5	142.4	142.7	153.6	(NA)	(NA)
Producer price indexes: [4]									
Iron and steel, total	1982=100 . .	117.2	111.5	116.0	122.0	128.8	125.8	126.5	122.6
Steel mill products	1982=100 . .	112.1	106.4	108.2	113.4	120.1	115.6	116.4	113.9
Electrometallurgical products	1982=100 . .	120.1	115.5	115.7	117.0	126.0	157.7	163.0	158.9
Iron ore	1982=100 . .	83.3	83.7	82.7	82.7	91.8	96.7	96.3	95.5
Scrap, iron and steel	1982=100 . .	166.0	139.2	172.5	192.9	202.7	191.1	188.9	164.9
Foundry and forge shop products . . .	1982=100 . .	117.2	120.1	121.3	123.9	129.3	132.6	134.1	135.0

NA Not available. [1] In millions of short tons. [2] Current assets to current liabilities. [3] Output per hour. Source: U.S. Bureau of Labor Statistics, Internet site <http://stats.bls.gov/iprhome.htm>. [4] Source: U.S. Bureau of Labor Statistics, *Producer Price Indexes*, monthly and annual.

Source: American Iron and Steel Institute, Washington, DC, *Annual Statistical Report* (copyright).

No. 1256. Raw Steel, Pig Iron, and Ferroalloys Production: 1990 to 1998

[In millions (849.4 represents 849,400,000), except percent]

Item	1990	1992	1993	1994	1995	1996	1997	1998, prel.
Raw steel (net tons):								
World production	849.4	797.0	802.0	799.6	829.4	826.9	874.9	(NA)
U.S. production	98.9	92.9	97.9	100.6	104.9	105.3	108.6	107.6
Percent of world	11.6	11.8	12.2	12.6	12.6	12.7	12.4	(NA)
Furnace:								
Basic oxygen process . .	58.5	57.6	59.3	61.0	62.5	60.4	61.1	59.7
Electric	36.9	35.3	38.5	39.6	42.4	44.9	47.5	48.0
Open hearth	3.5	-	-	-	-	-	-	-
Grade:								
Carbon	86.6	82.5	86.9	89.5	92.7	93.6	95.9	(NA)
Alloy and stainless	12.3	10.4	11.0	11.1	12.3	11.7	12.6	(NA)
Pig iron and ferroalloys production (sh. tons)	54.8	52.2	53.1	54.4	56.1	54.5	54.7	53.2

- Represents or rounds to zero. NA Not available.

Source: American Iron and Steel Institute, Washington, DC, *Annual Statistical Report* (copyright).

No. 1257. Steel Products—Net Shipments, by Market Classes: 1990 to 1998

[In thousands of short tons (84,981 represents 84,981,000). Comprises carbon, alloy, and stainless steel]

Market class	1990	1992	1993	1994	1995	1996	1997	1998, prel.
Total [1]	84,981	82,241	89,022	95,084	97,494	100,878	105,858	102,143
Automotive	11,100	11,092	12,719	14,753	14,622	14,665	15,251	(NA)
Steel service centers, distributors	21,111	21,328	23,714	24,153	23,751	27,124	27,800	(NA)
Construction, incl. maintenance [2]	9,245	9,536	13,429	10,935	14,892	15,561	15,885	(NA)
Containers, packaging, shipping	4,474	3,974	4,355	4,495	4,139	4,101	4,163	(NA)
Machinery, industrial equipment, tools . .	2,388	1,951	2,191	2,427	2,310	2,410	2,355	(NA)
Steel for converting and processing . . .	9,441	9,226	9,451	10,502	10,440	10,245	11,263	(NA)
Rail transportation	1,080	1,052	1,223	1,248	1,373	1,400	1,410	(NA)
Contractors' products	2,870	2,694	2,913	3,348	(2)	(2)	(2)	(2)
Oil and gas industries	1,892	1,454	1,526	1,703	2,643	3,254	3,811	(NA)
Electrical equipment	2,453	2,136	2,213	2,299	2,397	2,401	2,434	(NA)
Appliances, utensils, and cutlery	1,540	1,503	1,592	1,736	1,589	1,713	1,635	(NA)

[1] Includes nonclassified shipments and other classes not shown separately. [2] Beginning 1994, contractors' products included with construction.

Source: American Iron and Steel Institute, Washington, DC, *Annual Statistical Report* (copyright).

760 Manufactures

No. 1258. U.S. Machine Tool Consumption—Gross New Orders and Exports: 1997 and 1998

[Value in millions of dollars (6,021 represents $6,021,000,000)]

Item	1997				1998			
	Total	Metal cutting machines	Metal forming machines	Other manufac- turing technol- ogy	Total	Metal cutting machines	Metal forming machines	Other manufac- turing technology
New order units, total . . .	43,358	35,440	3,014	4,904	37,053	30,898	3,745	2,411
Northeast [1]	7,500	6,195	455	850	6,228	5,083	736	408
South [2]	6,145	4,840	508	797	5,520	4,493	639	388
Midwest [3]	15,232	12,262	901	2,069	13,307	11,218	1,267	822
Central [4]	8,536	7,055	737	744	7,636	6,402	723	511
West [5]	5,945	5,088	413	444	4,363	3,702	379	282
New order value, total . . .	6,021	4,944	612	466	5,306	4,374	538	395
Northeast [1]	887	789	61	37	731	622	78	30
South [2]	768	632	78	58	725	592	86	47
Midwest [3]	2,539	1,960	300	279	2,326	1,882	222	222
Central [4]	1,082	908	107	67	937	774	95	68
West [5]	745	655	65	25	587	504	56	27
Export order units [6]	3,177	2,448	182	547	2,414	1,894	265	255
Export order value [6]	644	546	43	55	457	339	77	41

[1] Covers Maine, New Hampshire, Vermont, New York, Massachusettes, Connecticut, Rhode Island, New Jersey, and Pennsylvania.   [2] Covers Delaware, Maryland, Virginia, West Virginia, Kentucky, North Carolina, South Carolina, Tennessee, Mississippi, Alabama, Georgia, and Florida.   [3] Covers Wisconsin, Michigan, Ohio, Illinois, and Indiana.   [4] Covers Minnesota, North Dakota, South Dakota, Montana, Wyoming, Idaho, Iowa, Nebraska, Kansas, Missouri, Oklahoma, Arkansas, Louisiana, Texas, New Mexico, Colorado, and Utah.   [5] Covers Washington, Oregon, California, Nevada, and Arizona.   [6] Represents orders placed with U.S. builders.

Source: The Association for Manufacturing Technology, Mclean, VA, and American Machine Tool Distributors Association, Rockville, MD, *U.S. Machine Tool Consumption Report*, monthly.

No. 1259. Metalworking Machinery—Shipments: 1990 to 1997

[In millions of dollars (3,426.1 represents $3,426,100,000)]

Product	Product code	1990	1992	1993	1994	1995	1996	1997
Metalworking machinery	(X)	3,426.1	3,073.9	3,222.5	3,780.1	4,547.1	4,607.8	5,010.3
Metal cutting type [1]	(X)	2,371.3	1,999.7	2,084.9	2,463.0	3,036.6	3,141.1	3,583.3
Boring machines [2]	3541D	([2])	98.0	84.7	129.8	172.4	88.9	80.2
Drilling machines [2]	3541D	184.1	37.5	37.1	52.0	78.9	99.5	89.2
Gear cutting machines	35413	102.7	79.6	87.7	100.6	137.1	164.3	213.5
Grinding and polishing machines	35414	433.6	335.1	360.9	443.3	549.6	541.3	595.0
Lathes [3]	35415	355.6	258.9	305.5	390.8	478.0	451.1	480.7
Milling machines [4]	35416	214.3	210.4	180.2	138.9	194.8	199.7	280.2
Machining centers [5]	3541A	437.0	377.9	485.4	552.4	698.8	779.4	931.6
Station type machines . . . . [6]	3541B	502.1	434.7	374.8	455.1	477.0	498.6	551.9
Other metal cutting machine tools [6] . . .	3541C	141.9	166.5	166.2	200.1	246.2	316.0	358.3
Metal forming type.	(X)	1,080.2	1,074.0	1,139.6	1,317.1	1,510.5	1,466.6	1,427.0
Punching and shearing machines	35421 pt.	200.1	172.9	213.4	294.4	326.3	331.4	319.2
Bending and forming machines	35421 pt.	222.9	270.0	255.3	253.2	256.9	283.0	258.5
Presses, except forging.	35422	308.3	288.2	345.7	376.4	379.2	402.0	422.4
Forging machines [7]	35423 pt.	73.9	(D)	(D)	(D)	(D)	(D)	(D)
Other metal forming [7]	35423 pt.	275.0	342.8	325.2	393.0	548.1	450.2	426.9

D Data withheld to avoid disclosure.   X Not applicable.   [1] Data for "All lathes (turning machines)" and "All milling machines," valued at under $3,025 each are included in total "Metal cutting type" for 199   [2] For 1990, data for "Boring machines" were combined with "Drilling machines" to avoid disclosing individual company data.   [3] For 1993 through 1997 product code 35415, "Lathes," excludes the value for product code 35415 09, All Lathes valued under $3,025 each.   [4] For 1993 through 1997 product code 35416, "Milling machines," excludes the value for product code 35416 09, "All milling machines valued under $3,025 each."   [5] Multi-function numerically controlled machines.   [6] Excludes those designed primarily for home workshops, labs, etc.   [7] For 1991 through 1997, and 1988 data for "Forging machines" have been combined with "Other metal forming machines" to avoid disclosing individual company.

Source: U.S. Census Bureau, *Manufacturing Profiles*, Series MP, annual; and release date: July 14, 1998, <http://www.census.gov/ftp/pub/industrymq35w97a.txt>.

U.S. Census Bureau, Statistical Abstract of the United States: 1999

No. 1260. Selected Types of Construction Machinery—Value of Shipments: 1990 to 1997

[In millions of dollars (2,235.9 represents $2,235,900,000)]

Product description	Product code	1990	1993	1994	1995	1996	1997
Tractor shovel loaders	3531C	2,235.9	2,354.4	2,632.6	3,041.8	3,340.1	3,911.6
Power cranes, draglines, and shovels	3531E	1,511.8	1,719.4	2,252.5	2,561.4	2,740.3	2,928.8
Mixers, pavers, and related equipment	3531F	609.6	877.1	1,079.8	1,168.8	1,145.8	1,276.3
Off-highway trucks, truck-type tractor, chassis trailers, coal haulers, or wagons	3531G pt.	1,453.1	(D)	(D)	1,597.4	1,697.2	1,720.3
Motor graders and light maintainers	3531G pt	408.0	(D)	445.2	479.9	588.4	(D)
Rough terrain forklifts	3531G pt	209.3	201.9	270.9	355.4	412.3	499.9
Equipment for mounting on tractors	3531N	258.6	249.8	286.6	(X)	(X)	(X)
Self-propelled continuous ditchers and trenchers	3531J	129.7	143.6	174.0	193.5	209.1	238.7
Construction machinery for mounting on trucks, tractors, and other prime movers . . .	3531Q	(NA)	(NA)	(NA)	(NA)	214.5	254.7
Aerial work platforms	3531P 90	814.9	637.4	844.9	1,131.1	(D)	(D)

D Data withheld to avoid disclosing figures for individual companies.   X Not applicable.

Source: U.S. Census Bureau, through 1992, *Current Industrial Reports,* Series MA35D; thereafter, *Manufacturing Profiles,* Series MP, annual.

No. 1261. Mining and Mineral Processing Equipment—Shipments: 1996 and 1997

Product	Product code	Number of companies 1997	Quantity (units)		Value (mil. dol.)	
			1996	1997	1996	1997
Mining and mineral processing equipment .	(X)	(X)	(X)	(X)	1,791	2,128
Portable crushing, screening, washing, and combination plants	3531K	17	676	976	97	130
Underground mining machinery [1]	35325	28	6,849	16,741	443	671
Crushing/pulverizing/screening machinery [2]	35327	40	4,030	4,153	345	434
Drills and other mining machinery, n.e.c. [1][3] . .	35328	25	16,739,738	16,453,351	462	459
Portable drilling rigs and parts	3533A	31	2,267,781	3,416,465	444	434

X Not applicable.   [1] Excludes parts.   [2] Excludes portables and parts.   [3] n.e.c. = Not elsewhere classified.

Source: U.S. Census Bureau, *Manufacturing Profiles,* Series MP, annual; and <http://www.census.gov/ftp/pub/industry/1/ma35f97.pdf> (issued 21 July 1998).

No. 1262. Engines, Refrigeration and Heating Equipment, and Pumps and Compressors—Shipments: 1994 to 1997

[(24,178 represents 24,178,000)]

Product	Product code	Unit	1994	1995	1996	1997
Internal combustion engines produced	(X)	1,000	24,178	23,274	23,353	23,874
Gasoline (except outboard, aircraft, and auto) . . .	35191	1,000	23,287	22,287	22,659	22,788
Nonautomotive diesel (except aircraft)	35193	1,000	220	246	270	314
Automotive diesel	35194	1,000	661	732	685	763
Natural gas and LPG	35196	1,000	9	9	9	9
Air-conditioning, heating equipment shipments:						
Heat transfer equipment	35851	Mil. dol . .	(NA)	(NA)	4,280	4,267
Room air-conditioners and dehumidifiers	35856	Mil. dol . . .	(NA)	(NA)	1,020	1,496
Motor vehicle mechanical air-conditioning systems	35857	Mil. dol . . .	(NA)	(NA)	2,208	1,819
Compressors and compressor units	3585A	Mil. dol . . .	(NA)	(NA)	3,092	3,585
Automotive air-conditioning compressors	3585B	Mil. dol . . .	(NA)	(NA)	1,652	1,492
Nonelectric warm air furnaces and dehumidifiers .	3585C	Mil. dol . . .	(NA)	(NA)	1,562	1,679
Unitary air conditioners	3585E	Mil. dol . . .	(NA)	(NA)	4,625	4,671
Air source heat pumps	3585F	Mil. dol . . .	(NA)	(NA)	1,046	1,114
Pumps and compressors [1]	(X)	**Mil. dol . . .**	**7,291**	**7,373**	**8,327**	**8,665**
Industrial pumps	35612	Mil. dol . . .	2,638	2,700	3,093	3,072
Domestic water systems	35613	Mil. dol . . .	325	329	361	357
Air and gas compressors	35633	Mil. dol . . .	(NA)	2,466	2,665	2,831

NA Not available.   X Not applicable.   [1] Includes products not shown separately.

Source: U.S. Census Bureau, *Manufacturing Profiles,* Series MP, annual.

762   Manufactures

No. 1263. Computers and Office and Accounting Machines—Value of Shipments: 1990 to 1997

[In millions of dollars (25,630.1 represents 25,630,100,000)]

Selected products	Product class	1990	1992	1993	1994	1995	1996	1997
Electronic computers	3571	25,630.1	28,571.2	29,659.1	38,260.7	49,038.1	50,681.5	49,605.5
Host computers (multi-users)	35711 00	(NA)	(NA)	(NA)	(NA)	(NA)	(NA)	15,328.2
Single user computers	35712 00	(NA)	(NA)	(NA)	(NA)	(NA)	(NA)	33,307.9
Other computers	35719 00	(NA)	(NA)	(NA)	(NA)	(NA)	(NA)	969.5
Large-scale processing equipment [1]	35713	(NA)	5,267.1	4,104.4	4,458.5	5,288.8	5,962.3	(NA)
Medium-scale & small-scale processing equipment.	35714	(NA)	3,347.3	2,442.3	2,815.5	2,278.6	2,401.6	(NA)
Personal computers and workstations [1] . . .	35715	(NA)	17,059.6	18,888.8	24,298.0	34,349.3	35,767.9	(NA)
Portable computers [1]	35716	(NA)	1,644.2	2,575.6	5,028.3	5,774.3	5,290.8	(NA)
Loaded computer processor boards and board subassemblies [2]	36798	2,247.2	13,745.8	15,087.1	17,514.8	24,447.7	24,937.3	25,283.4
Computer storage devices & equipment	35721	7,488.2	6,282.4	5,730.7	5,555.6	7,903.0	8,909.2	8,617.2
Parts for computer storage devices & subassemblies	35722	955.2	1,357.1	1,496.4	1,951.9	2,235.6	1,719.9	2,142.5
Computer terminals	35751	2,066.7	1,707.9	1,531.3	1,243.5	1,086.0	1,103.9	791.7
Computer peripheral equipment, n.e.c.	35771	7,696.6	8,505.6	9,810.2	11,943.6	12,331.0	12,462.8	13,686.2
Parts for input/output equipment	35772	3,705.5	3,053.2	2,554.3	2,498.7	2,391.0	5,504.8	2,487.5
Calculating and accounting machines [3]	35784	(D)	967.5	1,454.2	1,261.5	1,278.9	1,485.0	1,621.4
Magnetic and optical recording media	36950	3,695.4	4,336.8	4,483.3	4,777.1	5,106.2	5,739.1	5,242.8

D Withheld to avoid disclosing data for individual companies.   NA Not available.   [1] Prior to 1992, product class separation for computers is not available.   [2] These data are collected on two Current Industrial Report forms, MA35R, "Computers and Office and Accounting Machines (Shipments) and MA36Q, Semiconductors, Printed Circuit Boards, And Other Electronic Components. [3] Product classes 35781 and 35782 were combined to product class 35784 beginning 1991.
Source: U.S. Census Bureau, *Manufacturing Profiles*, Series MP, annual.

No. 1264. Computers and Office and Accounting Machines—Shipments: 1996 and 1997

[Quantity (19,939 represents 19,939,000, value (50,682 represents $50,682,000,000)]

Product	Product code	Number of companies, 1997	Quantity (1,000)		Value (mil. dol.)	
			1996	1997	1996	1997
Electronic computers (automatic data processors) . .	3571	172	19,939	20,124	50,682	49,606
Host computers (multi-users):						
Large scale systems and unix servers	35711 10	16	(NA)	377	(NA)	6,065
Medium-scale systems and unix servers	35711 20	29	(NA)	2,414	(NA)	8,328
PC servers	35711 30	16	(NA)	161	(NA)	644
Other host computers	35711 90	6	(NA)	33	(NA)	291
Single user computers:						
Personal computers	35712 10	44	(NA)	13,473	(NA)	21,931
Workstations	35712 20	23	(NA)	476	(NA)	5,137
Laptops (AC/DC)	35712 30	10	(NA)	503	(NA)	1,257
Notebooks, subnotebooks (battery operated)	35712 40	12	(NA)	1,899	(NA)	4,755
Personal digital assistants	35712 50	1	(NA)	(D)	(NA)	(D)
Other portable computers	35712 60	4	(NA)	128	(NA)	123
Other single user computers	35712 90	4	(NA)	175	(NA)	105
Other computers	35719	45	(NA)	485	(NA)	969
Computer storage devices and equipment	35721	86	(X)	(X)	8,909	8,617
Parts for computer storage devices and subassemblies. .	35722	16	(X)	(X)	1,720	2,143
Computer terminals	35751	51	(X)	(X)	1,104	792
Parts for computer terminals.	35752	9	(X)	(X)	199	(D)
Computer peripheral equipment, n.e.c. [1]	35771	253	(X)	(X)	11,463	13,686
Calculating and accounting machines	35784	41	(X)	(X)	1,485	1,621
Automatic typing and word processing machines	35792	3	(D)	(D)	(D)	(D)
Mailing, letter handling, addressing machines	35795	31	(X)	(X)	1,231	1,398
Other office machines, n.e.c. [1]	35799	44	(X)	(X)	580	603
Printed circuit assemblies	36798	694	(X)	(X)	24,937	25,283
Magnetic and optical recording media	36950	57	(X)	(X)	5,739	5,243

D Withheld to avoid disclosure of individual companies.   NA Not applicable.   X Not available.   [1] N.e.c. = Not elsewhere classified.
Source: U.S. Census Bureau, *Manufacturing Profiles*, Series MP, annual.

No. 1265. Computers and Industrial Electronics—Factory Shipments: 1990 to 1996

[In millions of dollars (50,793 represents $50,793,000,000)]

Item	1990	1991	1992	1993	1994	1995	1996
Computer and peripheral equipment, total	50,793	50,121	51,932	54,821	59,254	73,555	78,673
Computers	25,973	26,691	29,036	30,002	38,261	49,038	50,682
Peripheral equipment	24,820	23,430	22,896	24,819	20,993	24,517	27,992
Industrial electronics, total.	26,183	26,126	26,778	27,250	29,927	33,732	35,300
Controlling, processing equipment	12,728	12,653	12,881	13,961	15,014	16,450	16,986
Testing, measuring equipment	6,859	7,492	7,484	7,332	8,416	10,109	10,874
Nuclear electronic equipment	567	571	533	519	477	501	503
Robots, accessories, and components	275	294	(NA)	(NA)	(NA)	(NA)	(NA)
Other electronic equipment	5,754	5,137	5,880	5,438	6,020	6,672	6,937

NA Not available.
Source: Electronic Industries Association, Washington, DC, *Electronic Market Data Book*, annual (copyright).

Manufactures   763

No. 1266. Consumer Electronics and Electronic Components— Factory Sales, by Product Category: 1990 to 1998

[In millions of dollars (43,033 represents 43,033,000,000). Factory sales include imports]

Product category	1990	1993	1994	1995	1996	1997	1998, prel.
Total	**43,033**	**52,469**	**58,230**	**62,541**	**68,264**	**72,365**	**76,028**
Video products:							
Direct-view color TV	6,197	7,316	7,225	6,798	6,492	6,026	6,298
LCD color TV	50	45	42	44	39	38	37
Projection TV	626	841	1,117	1,417	1,426	1,361	1,629
TV/VCR combinations	178	599	710	723	697	684	782
Monochrome TV	99	40	38	34	29	27	22
LCD Monochrome TV	33	33	32	31	32	30	25
Other video:							
VCR decks	2,439	2,851	2,869	2,767	2,815	2,618	2,273
Camcorders	2,260	1,958	1,985	2,135	2,084	1,894	1,919
Laser disc players	72	123	122	108	66	25	11
Home satellite earth stations	421	408	900	1,265	1,493	1,254	1,084
Videocassette players	65	61	64	59	43	39	20
Home and portable products:							
Compact audio systems	1,270	1,464	1,703	1,677	1,157	1,419	1,606
Separate audio components	1,935	1,635	1,686	1,911	1,808	1,609	1,555
Home radios	360	307	306	284	291	300	330
Portable audio equipment	1,645	2,187	2,495	2,506	2,149	2,033	2,259
Mobile electronics:							
After market auto sound equipment	1,192	1,604	1,898	1,931	1,814	1,811	1,815
Factory installed auto sound	3,100	3,199	3,225	3,100	2,512	2,710	2,540
Cellular telephones	1,133	1,257	1,275	1,431	1,656	(NA)	(NA)
Pagers	118	198	230	300	370	460	550
Vehicle security	190	294	401	464	255	325	330
Home office products:							
Cordless telephones	842	1,046	1,106	1,141	1,176	1,679	1,756
Corded telephones	638	617	610	557	553	528	473
Telephone answering devices	827	1,026	1,153	1,077	1,004	1,020	1,095
Home computers	4,187	8,190	10,088	12,600	15,040	15,950	16,640
Computer peripherals	1,980	2,450	3,100	3,850	975	1,212	1,440
Computer software (incl. CD-ROM)	971	1,600	2,050	2,500	3,000	3,450	3,930
Personal Wordprocessors	656	558	504	451	404	347	312
Home fax machines	920	888	964	919	839	1,139	626
Home security systems	1,440	940	1,110	1,130	1,350	1,400	1,520
Electronic gaming:							
Electronic gaming hardware	975	1,650	1,575	1,500	1,600	1,650	1,980
Electronic gaming software	2,400	2,625	2,925	3,000	3,500	3,900	4,480
Blank media:							
Blank audio cassettes	376	362	353	334	314	281	249
Blank videocassettes	948	779	730	708	725	695	674
Blank floppy diskettes	314	345	353	373	300	250	232
Accessories and batteries:							
Electronic accessories	793	759	874	816	982	982	1,115
Total primary batteries	1,383	2,215	2,412	2,600	2,676	2,869	3,140

Source: Electronic Industries Association, Washington, DC, *Electronic Market Data Book*, annual (copyright).

No. 1267. Communication Equipment—Value of Shipments: 1990 to 1997

[In millions of dollars (36,990.3 represents $36,990,300,000)]

Product description	Product class	1990	1991	1992	1993	1994	1995	1996	1997
Communication equipment . .		**36,990.3**	**37,821.0**	**39,501.9**	**42,113.8**	**49,598.1**	**56,362.0**	**65,608.6**	**74,482.8**
Telephone switching and switchboard equipment	36611	7,537.1	6,956.6	7,291.3	7,240.9	8,067.6	8,178.4	9,617.7	10,618.1
Carrier line equipment and modems	36613	5,013.8	4,298.4	4,810.6	4,993.3	5,114.0	5,868.6	7,544.6	7,686.8
Other telephone and telegraph equipment and components	36614	3,180.5	4,909.5	5,507.3	7,026.4	8,479.5	10,510.0	14,030.9	17,846.9
Communication systems and equipment (except broadcast)	36631	14,768.0	14,987.9	15,162.8	16,196.7	19,977.5	23,031.9	25,332.5	28,550.9
Broadcast, studio, and related electronic equipment	36632	1,856.4	1,836.3	1,948.2	2,077.5	2,469.5	2,844.7	3,000.2	3,350.5
Intercommunications systems, including inductive paging systems (selective calling)	36693	346.1	303.8	288.5	241.7	283.7	296.0	277.8	252.7
Alarm systems [1]	36691	1,027.2	1,145.0	1,370.4	1,532.4	1,550.5	1,662.1	1,802.8	1,921.1
Vehicular and pedestrian traffic control equipment and electrical railway signals and attachments . .	36692	470.6	491.1	597.3	573.4	669.9	710.7	762.0	805.5
Electronic teaching machines, teaching aids, trainers and simulators . .	36991	1,208.8	1,411.0	1,310.8	847.7	838.5	913.3	865.7	809.9
Laser sources [1]	36992	(NA)	(NA)	(NA)	(NA)	726.4	787.5	843.8	1,020.9
Ultrasonic equipment	36995	108.8	113.7	119.2	127.3	137.5	172.3	184.3	187.8
Other electronic systems and equipment, n.e.c. [2]	36999	1,473.0	720.8	1,095.5	1,256.5	1,283.5	1,386.5	1,346.3	1,431.8

NA Not available. [1] Beginning in 1994, data for laser equipment, instrumentation, and components have been eliminated from this survey. Only laser sources are being collected. [2] Product class 36997 changed to product class 36999 for 1992. Product classes 36998, 39992, and 39447 are no longer collected on this survey.

Source: U.S. Census Bureau, *Manufacturing Profiles*, Series MP, annual; and <http://www.census.gov/ftp/pub/industry/ 1/ma36p97.pdf> (released 06 October 1998).

No. 1268. Semiconductors, Printed Circuit Boards, and Other Electronic Components—Value of Shipments, by Class of Product: 1990 to 1997

[In millions of dollars (1,096.5 represents $1,096,500,000). N.e.c. = Not elsewhere classified]

Class of product	Product code	1990	1993	1994	1995	1996	1997
Transmittal, industrial, and special-purpose electron tubes (except x-ray)	36713	1,096.5	677.6	1,120.5	854.9	611.9	699.1
Electron tubes, receiving type	36714	24.2	27.1	(1)	(1)	(1)	(1)
Cathode ray picture tubes, including rebuilt	36714	1,344.1	2,231.5	¹2,627.1	¹2,907.0	¹3,272.0	¹3,433.6
Electron tube parts	36715	142.6	160.1	114.9	120.2	153.1	161.0
Printed circuit boards	36720	7,174.5	6,273.0	6,812.3	8,367.3	8,216.8	8,784.6
Integrated microcircuits (semiconductor networks)	36741	16,623.3	23,636.1	36,020.4	48,437.9	52,639.3	56,866.1
Transistors	36742	682.3	704.5	834.6	942.3	945.9	801.2
Diodes and rectifiers	36743	668.2	640.7	829.5	1,066.7	861.4	786.5
Other semiconductor devices	36749	5,741.0	6,908.2	9,915.4	12,639.4	10,976.1	10,271.5
Capacitors for electronic applications	36750	1,391.5	1,294.3	1,512.3	1,785.3	1,653.4	2,006.6
Resistors	36760	799.8	716.5	869.5	953.2	911.9	992.8
Coils, transformers, reactors, and chokes for electronic applications	36770	975.6	1,121.4	1,250.7	1,411.8	1,435.6	1,450.8
Coaxial connectors	36781	420.0	419.0	642.4	731.6	656.9	624.5
Cylindrical connectors	36782	513.6	482.8	511.3	552.9	642.5	586.2
Rack and panel connectors	36783	500.0	427.6	545.6	540.5	530.7	673.3
Printed circuit connectors	36784	804.9	859.4	923.4	1,026.4	1,095.3	1,276.2
Other connectors including parts	36785	1,085.0	1,152.8	1,377.2	1,401.9	1,617.1	1,795.5
Filters (except microwave) and piezoelectric devices	36791	457.4	534.3	674.1	729.2	719.3	692.6
Microwave components and devices	36793	1,368.7	1,136.3	1,227.2	1,233.4	1,251.4	1,238.5
Transducers, electrical/electronic input or output	36795	741.1	832.5	970.5	1,111.3	1,104.8	1,209.2
Switches, mechanical types for electronic circuitry	36796	579.4	572.6	621.5	666.3	738.0	828.3
Printed circuit assemblies	36798	8,269.3	15,087.1	17,514.8	24,447.7	24,937.3	25,283.4
All other electronic components n.e.c	36799	4,898.3	5,257.6	6,149.7	6,978.1	7,199.1	7,637.6

[1] Product codes combined to avoid disclosing figures for individual companies.

Source: U.S. Census Bureau, *Manufacturing Profiles*, Series MP, annual; and <http://www.census.gov/industry/ ma36q97.txt> (Released August 1998).

No. 1269. Selected Instruments and Related Products—Shipments: 1990 to 1997

[In millions of dollars (1,418 represents 1,418,000,000]

Product	Product code	1990	1993	1994	1995	1996	1997
Automatic regulating and control valves	34918	1,418	1,648	1,807	1,860	1,893	2,057
Solenoid-operated valves (except nuclear and fluid power transfer)	34919	346	406	452	464	522	536
Aeronautical, nautical, and navigational instruments	38121	2,518	2,121	1,859	2,125	2,274	2,536
Search & detection, navigation & guidance systems and equipment	38122	32,420	28,604	25,567	24,697	26,094	26,644
Laboratory apparatus and laboratory furniture [1]	38210	1,675	1,598	1,811	1,837	1,799	1,881
Controls for monitoring residential and commercial environments and appliance	38220	1,982	2,310	2,521	2,533	2,648	2,679
Process control instruments	38230	5,224	5,935	6,240	6,439	6,745	6,788
Integrating and totalizing meters for gas and liquids	38242	725	777	859	915	963	1,079
Counting devices	38243	210	285	354	364	367	428
Motor vehicle instruments [2]	38244	1,457	1,768	2,092	2,193	2,219	2,245
Integrating instruments, electrical	38251	396	461	440	445	458	457
Test equipment for testing electrical, radio and communication circuits, and motors	38252	6,156	6,572	7,582	9,255	10,390	10,979
Instruments to measure electricity	38253	586	526	554	555	500	504
Analytical, scientific instruments (except optical)	38260	4,412	4,766	5,534	5,737	5,478	5,902
Sighting, tracking, and fire-control equipment, optical type	38271	581	769	652	655	613	575
Optical instruments and lenses [3]	38274	1,252	1,456	1,597	1,579	1,749	1,999
Aircraft engine instruments (except flight)	38291	579	552	430	430	530	554
Physical properties and kinematic testing equip	38292	1,012	1,175	1,199	1,374	1,369	1,490
Nuclear radiation detection and monitoring instruments	38294	567	519	489	501	497	478
Commercial, geophysical, meteorological, and general purpose instruments	38295	1,140	1,271	1,344	1,373	1,452	1,614
Surveying and drafting instruments	38296	274	301	324	356	365	366

[1] Includes laboratory furniture. Prior to 1990, laboratory furniture was included in product class 38296. [2] Includes some data previously classified in product class 37149, "Other motor vehicle parts and accessories, new, n.e.c." [3] Beginning 1992, product classes 38272, "Binoculars and astronomical instruments," and 38273, "Other optical instruments and lenses" were combined into product class 38274; prior years have been restated to reflect revision.

Source: U.S. Census Bureau, 1990, *Current Industrial Reports*, MA38B; thereafter *Manufacturing Profiles*, Series MP, annual.

Manufactures 765

No. 1270. Switchgear, Switchboard Apparatus, Relays, and Industrial Controls—Shipments: 1990 to 1997

[In millions of dollars (388 represents 388,000,000), except as indicated]

Product	Product code	Companies, 1997 (number)	1990	1993	1994	1995	1996	1997
Power circuit breakers............	36132	33	388	521	551	443	413	456
Low volt panelboards & dist. boards ..	36133	125	1,722	1,687	1,751	2,025	2,093	2,187
Fuses and fuse equipment.........	36134	24	419	320	382	500	522	557
Molded case circuit breakers, 1,000 volts and under	36135	33	959	1,010	1,133	1,173	1,218	1,284
Duct, 1,000 volts and under	36136	22	194	200	228	239	255	278
Switchgear, except ducts	36139	129	1,324	1,581	1,664	1,758	1,868	1,912
General purpose and other relays	36251	116	805	751	804	808	787	851
Specific purpose industrial controls ...	36252	250	2,020	2,322	2,748	3,312	3,455	3,523
General purpose industrial controls ...	36253	262	2,912	3,326	3,840	4,189	4,324	4,354
Motor controller accessories & parts for industrial controls	36254	132	452	476	512	503	516	554

Source: U.S. Census Bureau, 1990, *Current Industrial Reports*, MA36A, annual; thereafter, *Manufacturing Profiles*, Series MP, annual.

No. 1271. Selected Industrial Air Pollution Control Equipment—Shipments: 1997

[Quantity in number of units, value in millions of dollars (651,953 represents $651,953,000,000)]

Product	Product code	Number of companies	New orders Quantity	New orders Value	Shipments Quantity	Shipments Value	Backlog (Dec. 31) Quantity	Backlog (Dec. 31) Value
Selected industrial air pollution control equipment................	35646	108	91,460	651,953	88,677	722,485	12,583	342,075
Particulate emissions collectors...	(X)	88	79,000	498,953	76,199	497,447	11,982	181,807
Electrostatic precipitators	35646 51	16	(D)	91,295	(D)	110,978	(D)	58,784
Fabric filters............	35646 54	52	60,704	282,797	57,662	266,870	10,333	70,145
Mechanical collectors........	35646 55	36	(D)	77,127	(D)	62,014	(D)	35,378
Wet scrubbers	35646 58	27	1,244	47,734	1,249	57,585	221	17,500
Gaseous emissions control devices.................	(X)	41	993	121,947	978	194,020	297	152,347
Catalytic oxidation systems...	35646 70	12	(D)	(D)	185	34,373	(D)	(D)
Thermal and direct oxidation systems...............	35646 72	17	250	47,968	235	40,890	63	18,894
Scrubbers (gas absorber).....	35646 73	14	503	26,082	470	23,140	139	9,269
Gas absorbers	35646 76	7	20	5,167	35	9,900	(D)	(D)
Other.................	35646 79	15	11,467	31,053	11,500	31,018	304	7,921

D Data withheld to avoid disclosure of company data.   X Not applicable.

Source: U.S. Census Bureau, *Manufacturing Profiles*, Series MP, annual.

No. 1272. Toy Industry—Shipments and Quantity, by Type of Product: 1996 to 1998

[(7,078 represents $17,078,000,000]

Products	Shipments (mil. dol.) 1996	Shipments (mil. dol.) 1997	Shipments (mil. dol.) 1998	Quantity (mil.) 1996	Quantity (mil.) 1997	Quantity (mil.) 1998
Total................	17,078	19,508	20,321	3,068	3,433	3,533
Video games...............	2,940	4,253	5,106	69	112	159
Other industry	14,138	15,255	15,215	2,999	3,321	3,374
Infant/preschool	1,384	1,403	1,379	211	218	214
Dolls..................	2,089	2,154	2,085	258	252	252
Plush	984	1,353	1,614	147	259	303
Action figure toys	832	1,046	907	158	186	154
Vehicles	1,386	1,544	1,633	280	349	411
Ride-ons	770	743	728	35	34	33
Games/puzzles............	1,428	1,479	1,506	254	248	245
Activity toys	2,077	2,087	2,097	608	680	682
All other toys	3,188	3,446	3,266	1,048	1,095	1,080

Source: Toy Manufactures of America, Inc., New York, NY, *Toy Industry Fact Book*, annual (copyright).

Domestic Trade
and Services

This section presents statistics relating to the distributive trades and service industries. Data shown for the trades, classified by kind of business, and for the various categories of services (e.g., personal, business, repair, hotel) cover sales or receipts, establishments, employees, payrolls, and other items. The principal sources of these data are census reports and survey reports of the U.S. Census Bureau. Data on gross product in trade and service industries usually appear in the *Survey of Current Business*, issued by the U.S. Bureau of Economic Analysis. Financial data for firms engaged in retail, wholesale, or service activities appear in the annual *Statistics of Income*, published by the Internal Revenue Service.

Censuses—Censuses of retail trade and wholesale trade have been taken at various intervals since 1929. Limited coverage of the service industries started in 1933. Beginning with the 1967 census, legislation provides for a census of each area to be conducted every 5 years (for years ending in "2" and "7"). The industries covered in the censuses and surveys of business are those classified in three divisions defined in the *Standard Industrial Classification Manual* (see text, Section 13). *Retail trade* refers to places of business primarily engaged in selling merchandise for personal or household consumption; *wholesale trade*, to establishments primarily engaged in selling goods to dealers and distributors for resale or to purchasers who buy for business and farm uses; and *services*, to establishments primarily engaged in providing a wide range of services for individuals and for businesses.

Beginning with the 1954 Censuses of Retail Trade and Service industries, data for nonemployer establishments are included

and published separately. The census of wholesale trade excludes establishments with no paid employees. Beginning in 1977, sales taxes and finance charges are excluded from sales (or receipt) figures of the three censuses. In 1982 and prior censuses, the count of establishments represented the number in business at the end of the year. Beginning 1987, the count of establishments represents those in business at any time during the year.

For the 1987 and 1992 Censuses of Service Industries, hospitals operated by governmental organizations are included. Government-operated facilities in other service kind-of-business classifications are excluded from the census. In 1987 and 1992, data were not collected for elementary and secondary schools, colleges and universities, labor unions and similar organizations, and political organizations.

The census of retail trade beginning in 1977, excludes nonemployer direct sellers. Beginning 1982, the census treated each leased department in a store as a separate establishment and classified it according to the kind of business it conducted. In prior years, data for leased departments were consolidated with the data for stores in which they were located.

Current surveys—Current sample surveys conducted by the Census Bureau cover various aspects of the retail and wholesale trade and selected service industries. Its *Monthly Retail Trade Report* contains monthly estimates of sales, inventories, and inventory/sales ratios, purchases, and accounts receivable for the United States, by kind of business. Annual figures on sales, year-end inventories, and sales/inventory ratios,

Domestic Trade and Services   767

by kind of business, appear in the *Annual Benchmark Report for Retail Trade.*

Statistics from the Bureau's monthly wholesale trade survey include national estimates of merchant wholesalers' sales, inventories, and stock-sales ratios by major summary groups—durable and nondurable—and selected kinds of business. Merchant wholesalers are those wholesalers who take title to the goods they sell (e.g., jobbers, exporters, importers, major distributors). These data, based on reports submitted by a sample of firms, appear in the *Monthly Wholesale Trade Report.* Annual figures on sales, sales-inventory ratios, year-end inventories, and purchases appear in the *Annual Benchmark Report for Wholesale Trade.*

The *Service Annual Survey* provides annual estimates of nationwide receipts for selected personal, business, leasing and repair, amusement and entertainment, social and health, and other professional service industries in the United States. For selected accommodation, social, health, and other professional service industries, separate estimates are developed for receipts of taxable firms and revenue and expenses for firms and organizations exempt from Federal income taxes. The estimates for tax exempt firms in these industries are derived from a sample of employer firms only. All other estimates represent the combined total for employer and nonemployer firms.

The *Transportation Annual Survey* provides annual, nationwide estimates of detailed revenue and expenses for firms engaged in providing commercial motor freight transportation or public warehousing services. This includes firms furnishing local or long distance trucking or transfer services or in storage of farm products, furniture or household goods, or commercial goods of any nature. The survey excludes private trucking and owner-operators with no paid employees.

The *Annual Survey of Communication Services* provides detailed nationwide estimates of detailed revenue and expenses for employer firms primarily engaged in providing telephone, radio and television broadcasting, cable television, or other communication services.

For the current sample survey programs, retail trade coverage is the same as for the census; wholesale trade coverage is limited to merchant wholesalers, and selected services coverage is less inclusive than the census.

Estimates obtained from annual and monthly surveys are based on sample data and are not expected to agree exactly with results that would be obtained from a complete census of all establishments. Data include estimates for sampling units not reporting.

Statistical reliability—For a discussion of statistical collection and estimation, sampling procedures, and measures of statistical reliability applicable to Census Bureau data, see Appendix III.

U.S. Census Bureau, Statistical Abstract of the United States: 1999

No. 1273. Gross Domestic Product in Domestic Trade and Service Industries in Current and Real (1992) Dollars: 1990 to 1996

[In billions of dollars (870.7 represents $870,700,000,000), except percent. For definition of gross domestic product, see text, Section 14, Based on 1987 Standard Industrial Classification]

Industry	Current dollars				Chained (1992) dollars [1]			
	1990	1994	1995	1996	1990	1994	1995	1996
Wholesale and retail trade	870.7	1,083.3	1,122.0	1,184.7	906.9	1,049.7	1,080.0	1,141.9
Percent of gross domestic product	15.2	15.6	15.4	15.5	14.8	15.9	16.0	16.5
Wholesale trade.	367.2	468.0	484.4	516.8	360.5	448.6	457.5	493.3
Retail trade.	503.5	615.3	637.6	667.9	546.4	601.2	622.5	648.5
Services.	1,059.4	1,350.4	1,440.3	1,539.5	1,181.7	1,256.5	1,298.8	1,342.9
Percent of gross domestic product	18.4	19.4	19.8	20.2	19.3	19.0	19.3	19.4
Hotels and other lodging places	46.1	57.4	60.6	63.7	49.2	54.4	55.4	55.8
Personal services.	38.2	45.8	46.6	49.1	41.7	42.6	42.4	43.3
Business services.	199.0	256.0	283.3	318.5	216.5	247.1	271.3	295.7
Auto repair, services, and garages	48.9	59.3	61.1	65.0	54.0	53.3	53.3	55.3
Miscellaneous repair services	17.7	19.2	20.7	22.5	21.5	16.7	17.0	15.9
Motion pictures	20.4	23.0	25.9	29.9	22.1	21.8	23.9	26.2
Amusement and recreation services	39.1	51.4	56.2	60.8	42.8	47.5	49.7	51.6
Health services	307.9	410.2	428.9	447.0	356.9	369.7	371.6	376.6
Legal services	80.7	93.8	96.5	100.0	91.5	86.0	85.5	85.1
Educational services.	39.8	52.3	55.1	58.2	44.3	48.9	49.6	50.7
Social services.	29.6	43.2	46.7	49.3	32.5	41.6	43.7	44.9
Membership organizations	35.0	45.1	47.0	48.9	38.3	42.1	42.5	43.1
Other services	147.8	182.6	199.9	215.2	160.4	175.4	184.6	192.9
Private households.	9.4	11.0	11.8	11.5	10.2	10.4	10.8	10.1

[1] See text, Section 14, Income.

Source: U.S. Bureau of Economic Analysis, *Survey of Current Business*, August 1997.

No. 1274. Retail Trade—Summary: 1972 to 1992

[1,665 represents 1,665,000. 1972 through 1982 based on 1972 Standard Industrial Classification (SIC) code; beginning 1987 based on 1987 SIC code. Comparability of data over time is affected by changes in the SIC code]

Item	Unit	1972	1977	1982	1987	1992
Firms, total [1]	1,000	1,665	1,567	1,573	1,992	2,212
Multiunit establishments [1] [2]	1,000	301	343	415	498	528
Establishments, total [1]	1,000	1,780	1,855	1,923	2,420	2,672
With payroll	1,000	1,265	1,304	1,324	1,504	1,526
With sales of $1,000,000 or more [3]	1,000	74	119	193	259	326
Consumer Price Index: [4]						
All items	1982-84=100 . .	41.8	60.6	96.5	113.6	140.3
All commodities.	1982-84=100 . .	44.5	64.2	97.0	107.7	129.1
Sales	Bil. dol.	457	723	1,066	1,540	1,949
By establishments with payroll	Bil. dol.	440	700	1,039	1,493	1,895
By multiunit establishments [2]	Bil. dol.	202	341	567	844	1,137
Percent of total sales	Percent	44.0	47.1	53.2	54.8	58.3
Percent of multiunit sales by 100-or-more establishment multiunits [5]	Percent	55.8	55.8	54.5	54.6	57.0
In 1987 dollars [6]	Bil. dol.	1,042	1,170	1,175	1,540	1,669
Percent of sales by corporations [3]	Percent	76.4	79.8	84.6	88.9	89.9
Per capita sales: [7]						
Current dollars	Dollars	2,186	3,291	4,601	6,357	7,643
Constant (1987) dollars [6]	Dollars	4,978	5,325	5,073	6,357	6,544
Sales as percent of personal income	Percent	46.6	45.2	39.6	40.5	37.9
Payroll, entire year	Bil. dol.	55.4	85.9	123.6	177.5	222.9
Percent of sales [8]	Percent	12.6	12.3	11.9	11.9	11.8
Paid employees, March 12 pay period	1,000	11,211	13,040	14,468	17,780	18,407

[1] Through 1982, represents the number of establishments and firms in business at the end of year. Beginning 1987, represents the number of establishments and firms in business at any time during year. [2] Establishments of firms that operate at two or more locations. [3] Through 1982, represents establishments with and without payroll. Beginning 1987, represents only establishments with payroll. [4] Source: U.S. Bureau of Labor Statistics, *Monthly Labor Review*. Beginning 1982, CPI-U annual averages, see text, Section 15, Prices. [5] Prior to 1982, data provided for percent of multiunit sales by 101-or-more establishment units. [6] Based on implicit price deflators for retail sales supplied by U.S. Bureau of Economic Analysis. [7] Based on estimated resident population as of July 1. [8] Covers only establishments with payroll.

Source: Except as noted, U.S. Census Bureau, *Census of Retail Trade, 1972*, RC72-S-1; *1977*, RC77-52; *1982*, RC82-A-52 and RC82-I-1; *1987*, RC87-A-52, RC87-N-1, and RC87-S-1; and *1992*, RC92-A-52, RC92-N-1, and RC92-S-1.

U.S. Census Bureau, Statistical Abstract of the United States: 1999

No. 1275. Retail Trade—Establishments, Employees, and Payroll: 1990 and 1996

[(1,529.7 represents 1,529,700) except as indicated. Covers establishments with payroll. Employees are for the week including March 12. Most government employees are excluded. For statement on methodology, see Appendix III]

Kind of business	1987 SIC code [1]	Establishments (1,000)		Employees (1,000)		Payroll (bil. dol.)	
		1990	1996	1990	1996	1990	1996
Retail trade, total	(G)	1,529.7	1,579.3	19,815	21,487	241.7	317.7
Building materials and garden supplies [2] . . .	52	71.9	64.7	703	768	11.9	15.4
Lumber and other building materials	521	27.5	24.3	403	475	7.5	10.1
Paint, glass, and wallpaper stores	523	10.2	9.8	54	49	0.9	1.0
Hardware stores	525	19.0	14.3	143	124	1.9	1.8
Retail nurseries and garden stores	526	10.1	11.3	76	81	1.0	1.3
Mobile home dealers	527	4.2	4.8	23	37	0.4	1.1
General merchandise stores [2]	53	36.6	36.9	2,135	2,261	22.9	28.6
Department stores	531	10.1	10.8	1,710	1,850	18.3	23.0
Variety stores	533	10.0	10.8	109	93	1.0	0.9
Misc. general merchandise stores.	539	15.0	14.8	310	316	3.6	4.7
Food stores [2]	54	186.1	179.3	3,124	3,300	35.8	44.1
Grocery stores	541	132.5	129.2	2,757	2,981	32.4	40.5
Meat and fish markets	542	9.3	7.9	54	46	0.6	0.6
Fruit and vegetable markets	543	2.9	3.3	19	19	0.2	0.3
Candy, nut, confectionery stores.	544	5.4	4.7	29	28	0.2	0.3
Retail bakeries	546	19.9	20.2	176	148	1.5	1.5
Automotive dealers and service stations [2] . . .	55	207.3	202.0	2,104	2,267	40.0	55.5
New and used car dealers	551	26.1	24.6	917	1,015	23.9	35.1
Used car dealers.	552	14.3	22.0	56	86	1.0	1.9
Auto and home supply stores	553	43.4	43.8	305	346	5.1	6.8
Gasoline service stations	554	104.8	96.2	701	713	7.5	9.0
Boat dealers.	555	4.6	5.1	34	33	0.6	0.8
Recreational vehicle dealers	556	2.7	3.0	24	28	0.5	0.8
Motorcycle dealers.	557	3.4	3.8	22	29	0.4	0.7
Apparel and accessory stores [2]	56	150.2	132.7	1,193	1,087	12.2	13.2
Men's and boys' clothing stores	561	14.7	13.8	108	92	1.5	1.4
Women's clothing stores.	562	50.2	40.6	439	327	4.0	3.5
Women's accessory and specialty stores . .	563	7.7	8.6	46	50	0.5	0.6
Children's and infants' wear stores	564	5.6	5.2	36	45	0.3	0.4
Family clothing stores.	565	17.8	19.6	283	329	3.0	4.1
Shoe stores	566	37.4	31.7	206	181	2.2	2.3
Misc. apparel and accessory stores	569	9.1	10.2	47	53	0.5	0.7
Furniture and homefurnishings stores [2] . .	57	108.1	115.7	749	878	12.3	16.7
Furniture and homefurnishings stores [2] . . .	571	61.1	66.0	430	476	7.2	9.3
Furniture stores	5712	30.8	31.4	245	258	4.3	5.4
Floor covering stores	5713	13.2	14.7	77	81	1.5	1.9
Drapery and upholstery stores	5714	3.4	2.8	16	11	0.2	0.2
Misc. homefurnishings stores	5719	13.3	16.6	92	125	1.1	1.8
Household appliance stores	572	10.0	10.0	63	64	1.1	1.3
Radio, television, music and computer stores [2]	573	34.2	39.1	245	336	3.9	6.2
Radio, TV, and electronic stores	5731	16.5	15.9	120	165	2.1	3.1
Computer and software stores	5734	5.1	9.6	33	69	0.8	1.7
Record and prerecorded tape stores . . .	5735	7.1	8.9	60	73	0.6	0.8
Eating and drinking places [2]	58	402.6	466.4	6,461	7,417	49.6	69.1
Eating places	5812	286.8	368.5	5,700	6,716	43.8	62.7
Drinking places	5813	43.8	53.9	267	326	2.0	2.8
Miscellaneous retail [2]	59	349.0	365.4	2,487	2,640	33.2	43.2
Drug stores and proprietary stores	591	50.0	43.2	593	588	8.3	10.6
Liquor stores [3]	592	30.8	28.8	141	129	1.6	1.7
Used merchandise stores	593	15.0	23.5	79	117	0.9	1.6
Sporting goods and bicycle shops	5941	21.4	25.2	139	189	1.6	2.5
Book stores	5942	11.7	13.1	86	117	0.8	1.4
Stationery stores.	5943	4.8	4.0	34	23	0.4	0.4
Jewelry stores.	5944	26.6	27.7	161	137	2.3	2.7
Hobby, toy, and game shops	5945	9.4	10.8	83	109	0.8	1.3
Camera, photo supply stores	5946	3.6	3.0	22	18	0.4	0.3
Gift, novelty, and souvenir shops	5947	29.5	36.1	164	194	1.4	2.0
Sewing, needlework, and piece goods. . . .	5949	8.2	6.9	68	51	0.5	0.5
Catalog and mail-order houses	5961	7.2	8.2	141	180	2.6	4.5
Merchandising machine operators	5962	5.1	6.7	76	73	1.3	1.4
Direct selling establishments	5963	8.8	14.9	107	119	1.7	2.3
Fuel dealers.	598	12.0	11.3	100	95	2.2	2.4
Florists	5992	25.8	26.7	131	126	1.2	1.4
Optical goods stores	5995	13.2	14.7	66	73	1.1	1.4
Administrative and auxiliary	(X)	18.0	16.2	860	869	23.7	31.7

X Not applicable.   [1] Based on 1987 Standard Industrial Classification; see text, Section 17, Business.   [2] Includes kinds of business not shown separately.   [3] Includes government employees.

Source: U.S. Census Bureau, *County Business Patterns*, annual.

No. 1276. Retail and Wholesale Trade—Establishments, Sales, Payroll, and Employees, by Kind of Business (NAICS Basis): 1997

[Includes only establishments with payroll]

Kind of business	1997 NAICS code [1]	Establish-ments	Sales, revenue, receipts, and shipments ($1,000)	Annual payroll ($1,000)	Paid employees [2]
Retail trade, total	**44-45**	**1,120,249**	**2,456,574,247**	**238,792,423**	**14,115,559**
Motor vehicle and parts dealers	441	122,970	647,535,234	50,600,918	1,742,969
Furniture & home furnishings stores	442	64,498	71,797,971	9,934,532	483,310
Electronics & appliance stores	443	43,480	70,343,099	7,277,757	350,278
Building material & garden equipment and supplies dealers	444	93,115	230,279,924	25,806,984	1,124,433
Food & beverage stores	445	149,919	400,970,661	40,799,563	2,909,537
Health & personal care stores	446	83,194	117,671,505	15,347,098	904,494
Gasoline stations	447	126,059	197,751,207	11,463,080	917,933
Clothing & clothing accessories stores	448	156,752	138,656,713	16,761,476	1,335,663
Sporting goods, hobby, book, & music stores	451	68,963	62,796,899	7,254,653	566,671
General merchandise stores	452	36,636	330,163,770	30,816,980	2,505,892
Miscellaneous store retailers	453	130,081	79,534,863	10,248,405	757,943
Nonstore retailers	454	44,582	109,072,401	12,480,977	516,436
Wholesale trade, total	**42**	**453,184**	**4,055,023,223**	**215,741,330**	**5,820,391**
Wholesale trade, durable goods	421	290,260	2,189,603,850	133,719,852	3,409,803
Wholesale trade, nondurable goods	422	162,924	1,865,419,373	82,021,478	2,410,588
Merchant wholesalers, total		**375,155**	**2,337,228,314**	**159,109,949**	**4,607,866**
Wholesale trade, durable goods	421	240,621	1,214,386,597	100,153,535	2,764,848
Wholesale trade, nondurable goods	422	134,534	1,122,841,717	58,956,414	1,843,018

[1] Based on 1997 North American Industry Classification System; see text, Section 17, Business.   [2] Definition of paid employees varies among sectors.

Source: U.S. Census Bureau, *1997 Economic Census*, EC97X-CS1.

No. 1277. Comparative Statistics in Retail Trade, by Kind of Business: 1992 and 1997

[Covers establishments with payroll. Based on 1987 Standard Industrial Classification (SIC) code; see text, Section 17, Business]

Kind of business	1987 SIC code	Establish-ments (1,000) 1992	1997	Sales, receipts, revenue/shipments (mil. dol.) 1992	1997	Annual payroll (mil. dol.) 1992	1997	Paid employees [1] (1,000) 1992	1997
Retail trade, total	**(G)**	**1,526**	**1,566**	**1,894,880**	**2,562,094**	**222,868**	**293,578**	**18,407**	**21,349**
Building materials & garden supplies	52	69	69	98,832	153,831	11,790	17,529	666	855
General merchandise stores	53	35	35	245,330	328,636	24,503	30,637	2,079	2,495
Food stores	54	181	174	369,199	419,840	37,228	43,354	2,969	3,147
Automotive dealers	55	202	201	529,853	785,314	39,376	55,659	1,943	2,291
Apparel and accessory stores	56	145	126	101,714	118,604	12,039	13,729	1,145	1,122
Furniture and homefurnishings stores	57	110	115	93,206	137,996	11,869	16,429	702	868
Eating and drinking places	58	434	(S)	195,317	(S)	52,570	(S)	6,548	(S)
Miscellaneous retail stores	59	351	(S)	261,429	(S)	33,494	(S)	2,357	(S)

S Figure does not meet publication standards.   [1] Definition of paid employees varies among sectors.

Source: U.S. Census Bureau, *1997 Economic Census*, EC97X-CS1.

U.S. Census Bureau, *Statistical Abstract of the United States: 1999*

No. 1278. Retail Trade Sales—Summary: 1980 to 1998

[In billions of dollars (957 represents $957,000,000,000) except as indicated. Sales and inventories for leased departments and concessions are tabulated in the kind-of-business category of the leased department or concession. Based on Current Business Survey, see Appendix III]

Year	Sales					Nondurable goods (bil. dol.)			
	Total (bil. dol.)	Annual percent change [1]	Per capita [2] (dol.)	Index of sales (1982= 100)	Durable goods (bil. dol.)	Total	Dept. stores [3]	Inventories at cost [4] (bil. dol.)	Inventory/ sales ratios [4][5]
1980	957	6.7	4,213	89.5	299	658	85	121	(NA)
1985	1,375	6.9	5,779	128.6	498	877	126	182	1.55
1988	1,656	7.5	6,774	154.9	629	1,027	152	219	1.53
1989	1,759	6.2	7,127	164.5	657	1,102	161	237	1.59
1990	1,845	4.9	7,395	172.5	669	1,176	166	240	1.56
1991	1,856	0.6	7,361	173.6	650	1,206	173	243	1.57
1992	1,952	5.2	7,653	182.5	704	1,248	186	252	1.50
1993	2,074	6.3	8,046	193.9	780	1,294	200	268	1.50
1994	2,230	7.5	8,567	208.5	882	1,348	217	292	1.53
1995	2,329	4.5	8,865	217.8	940	1,390	231	307	1.54
1996	2,461	5.7	9,281	230.2	1,009	1,453	244	316	1.52
1997	2,566	4.3	9,588	240.0	1,058	1,508	261	324	1.49
1998	2,696	5.1	9,984	252.2	1,132	1,563	279	334	1.44

NA Not available. [1] Change from immediate prior year. [2] Based on U.S. Census Bureau estimates of resident population as of July 1. [3] Excludes leased departments. [4] As of Dec. 31. Includes warehouses. Adjusted for seasonal variations. [5] Sales data also adjusted for holiday and trading-day differences.
Source: U.S. Census Bureau, Current Business Reports, Annual Benchmark Report for Retail Trade, January 1988 Through December 1997, (BR/97-RV) and prior issues; and unpublished data.

No. 1279. Retail Trade—Sales, by Kind of Business: 1980 to 1998

[In billions of dollars (957.4 represents $957,400,000,000). See headnote, Table 1278. Based on Current Business Survey, see Appendix III]

Kind of business	1987 SIC code [1]	1980	1985	1990	1994	1995	1996	1997	1998
Retail trade, total.		957.4	1,375.0	1,844.6	2,229.9	2,329.3	2,461.2	2,566.2	2,695.9
Durable goods [2]		299.2	498.1	668.8	882.1	939.7	1,008.5	1,058.2	1,132.5
Building materials and garden supplies [2]	52	50.8	71.2	94.6	124.9	130.1	140.3	150.5	166.1
Building materials, supply stores	521,3	35.0	50.8	70.3	94.6	98.2	106.2	116.1	127.0
Hardware stores	525	8.3	10.5	12.5	14.0	14.1	14.4	14.6	15.3
Automotive dealers	55 exc. 554	164.1	303.2	387.6	521.8	556.7	599.7	625.7	661.4
Motor vehicle, misc. automotive dealers. . .	551,2,5,6,7,9	146.2	278.0	356.8	487.6	520.8	561.3	587.7	622.5
Motor vehicle dealers	551,2	137.7	263.1	338.7	463.7	493.7	531.9	553.2	583.1
New and used car dealers	551	130.5	251.6	316.0	430.6	456.2	490.0	507.5	533.5
Auto and home supply stores	553	18.0	25.2	30.8	34.1	40.0	38.4	38.0	38.9
Furniture and homefurnishings stores [2]	57	44.2	68.3	91.5	120.3	130.3	137.9	146.7	159.3
Furniture, homefurnishings stores [2]	71	26.3	38.3	50.5	59.9	62.3	66.0	71.6	76.2
Furniture stores	5712	(NA)	23.9	30.8	35.4	36.7	39.0	42.8	45.3
Floor covering stores	5713	(NA)	7.9	10.7	11.7	12.0	12.1	13.1	14.5
Household appliance, radio, TV, and computer stores	5722,31,34	14.0	25.1	33.0	50.1	57.2	60.7	64.0	71.6
Household appliance stores	5722	(NA)	8.4	8.8	8.8	9.6	9.7	10.3	10.7
Radio, TV, and computer stores	5731,34	(NA)	16.7	24.3	41.3	47.6	51.1	53.8	60.9
Sporting goods and bicycle shops	5941	(NA)	8.7	15.0	19.0	20.2	21.2	22.1	23.4
Book stores	5942	(NA)	4.5	7.4	10.3	11.5	12.4	12.7	13.0
Jewelry stores	5944	(NA)	11.2	15.2	18.0	19.1	20.2	19.5	22.3
Nondurable goods [2]		658.1	876.9	1,175.8	1,347.8	1,389.6	1,452.7	1,508.0	1,563.4
General merchandise stores	53	109.0	158.6	215.5	282.3	298.0	313.2	331.5	353.5
Department stores [3]	531	85.5	126.4	165.8	217.4	231.1	244.5	261.2	278.6
Variety stores	533	7.8	8.5	8.3	9.5	9.9	10.6	11.5	11.9
Misc. general merchandise stores.	539	15.7	23.8	41.4	55.4	57.0	58.1	58.8	62.9
Food stores	54	220.2	285.1	368.3	397.4	407.4	421.0	429.8	443.0
Grocery stores	541	205.6	269.5	348.2	376.5	385.0	397.0	403.0	414.6
Gasoline service stations . . . . [2]	554	94.1	113.3	138.5	143.9	149.6	157.6	158.7	149.6
Apparel and accessory stores [2]	56	49.3	70.2	95.8	110.0	110.9	114.6	117.8	124.0
Men's and boys' clothing stores	561	7.7	8.5	10.5	10.1	9.4	9.6	10.6	11.5
Women's clothing specialty stores	562,3	17.6	26.1	32.8	34.0	32.2	31.8	31.5	31.6
Women's clothing stores	562	15.9	23.6	29.8	29.9	27.8	27.0	26.2	25.5
Family clothing stores.	565	10.8	17.8	28.4	38.5	40.6	43.0	45.1	48.7
Shoe stores	566	10.5	13.1	18.0	19.1	19.3	20.0	20.4	20.9
Eating and drinking places	58	90.1	127.9	190.1	217.1	222.1	228.2	236.2	247.0
Eating places [2]	5812	80.4	117.6	178.7	204.9	209.0	214.4	222.0	231.6
Restaurants, lunchrooms, cafeterias . . .	5812 pt	(NA)	68.2	99.9	111.6	111.7	114.9	119.5	126.5
Refreshment places	5812 pt	(NA)	48.1	75.7	90.4	93.9	95.7	98.5	99.9
Drinking places	5813	(NA)	10.3	11.5	12.2	13.0	13.7	14.1	15.5
Drug stores and proprietary stores	591	31.0	47.0	70.6	81.3	84.7	90.5	98.2	105.7
Liquor stores	592	16.9	19.5	21.7	21.9	21.7	22.7	24.0	25.0
Nonstore retailers	596	22.8	28.3	45.6	62.5	62.8	68.8	74.9	79.4
Catalog and mail-order houses	5961	(NA)	15.8	26.6	39.9	40.0	43.8	48.7	54.9
Fuel dealers	598	(NA)	16.8	15.6	16.0	16.9	19.0	17.7	14.9

NA Not available. [1] Based on 1987 Standard Industrial Classification code; see text, Section 17, Business. [2] Includes kinds of business, not shown separately. [3] Excludes leased departments.
Source: U.S. Census Bureau, Current Business Reports, Annual Benchmark Report for Retail Trade, January 1989 Through December 1997, (BR/97-RV) and prior issues; and unpublished data.

No. 1280. Retail Trade—Merchandise Inventories and Inventory/Sales Ratio, by Kind of Business: 1990 to 1998

[239.8 represents $239,800,000,000. As of **Dec. 31**. Includes warehouses. Adjusted for seasonal variations. Sales data also adjusted for holiday and trading-day differences. See headnote, Table 1278]

Kind of business	1987 SIC code [1]	Inventories at cost [2] (bil. dol.)				Inventory/sales ratios			
		1990	1996	1997	1998	1990	1996	1997	1998
Total		**239.8**	**316.5**	**323.6**	**333.7**	**1.56**	**1.52**	**1.49**	**1.44**
Excluding automotive group		*176.7*	*226.7*	*232.1*	*240.7*	*1.44*	*1.43*	*1.42*	*1.38*
Durable goods stores [3]		121.2	168.9	174.4	178.8	2.26	1.99	1.92	1.81
Building materials group stores	52	17.0	23.5	25.2	27.2	2.28	1.96	1.97	1.87
Automotive dealers	55 exc. 554	63.1	89.8	91.5	92.9	2.04	1.78	1.70	1.60
Furniture group stores	57	17.4	25.1	24.6	25.9	2.36	2.17	1.93	1.89
Nondurable goods stores [3]		118.6	147.6	149.2	154.8	1.19	1.19	1.18	1.16
General merchandise stores	53	42.4	59.2	58.9	59.9	2.33	2.20	2.10	1.98
Department stores	531	33.4	47.8	48.6	48.8	2.40	2.26	2.19	2.05
Food stores	54	25.0	29.0	28.3	29.7	0.81	0.81	0.80	0.79
Apparel and accessory stores	56	19.7	22.7	24.2	25.2	2.49	2.38	2.45	2.42

[1] Based on 1987 Standard Industrial Classification code; see text, Section 17, Business.   [2] Excludes supplies and equipment used in store and warehouse operations that are not for resale.   [3] Includes kinds of business not shown separately.
Source: U.S. Census Bureau, *Current Business Reports, Annual Benchmark Report for Retail Trade, January 1988 Through December 1997* (BR/97-RV); and unpublished data.

No. 1281. Retail Trade—Purchases and Gross Margin, by Kind of Business: 1990 to 1996

[1,259 represents $1,259,000,000,000. Estimated. As of **Dec. 31**. Includes warehouses. Adjusted for seasonal variations. Sales data also adjusted for holiday and trading-day differences. See headnote, Table 1278]

Kind of business	1987 SIC code [1]	Purchases (bil. dol.)			Gross margin (bil. dol.)			Gross margin as percent of sales		
		1990	1995	1996	1990	1995	1996	1990	1995	1996
Total		**1,259**	**1,599**	**1,693**	**589**	**745**	**778**	**31.9**	**32.0**	**31.6**
Excluding automotive group		*942*	*1,142*	*1,199*	*519*	*638*	*668*	*35.6*	*36.0*	*35.9*
Durable goods stores [2]		492	701	753	177	250	261	26.5	26.6	25.9
Building materials group stores	52	65	91	98	30	40	44	31.2	31.1	31.0
Automotive dealers	55 exc. 554	317	457	493	70	107	110	18.0	19.2	18.3
Furniture group stores	57	57	85	90	35	47	49	38.1	36.1	35.3
Nondurable goods stores [2]		767	898	940	412	495	517	35.0	35.6	35.6
General merchandise stores	53	149	213	223	66	88	91	30.6	29.6	29.2
Department stores	531	111	158	167	55	76	79	33.2	32.8	32.4
Food stores	54	277	300	310	93	109	112	25.3	26.7	26.7
Apparel and accessory stores	56	55	65	67	41	45	48	43.2	40.7	41.6

[1] Based on 1987 Standard Industrial Classification code; see text, Section 17, Business.   [2] Includes kinds of business not shown separately.
Source: U.S. Census Bureau, *Current Business Reports, Annual Benchmark Report for Retail Trade, January 1988 Through December 1997* (BR/97-RV).

No. 1282. Franchised New Car Dealerships—Summary: 1980 to 1998

[130.5 represents $130,500,000,000]

Item	Unit	1980	1985	1990	1992	1993	1994	1995	1996	1997	1998
Dealerships [1]	Number .	27,900	24,725	24,825	23,500	22,950	22,850	22,800	22,750	22,700	22,600
Sales	Bil. dol . .	130.5	251.6	316.0	333.8	377.3	430.6	456.2	490.0	507.5	533.5
New cars sold [2]	1,000 . .	8,979	10,983	9,296	8,211	8,519	8,991	8,635	8,526	8,272	8,142
Used vehicles sold	1,000 . .	9,717	13,300	14,180	15,140	16,300	17,760	18,480	19,170	19,190	19,390
Employment	1,000 . .	745	857	925	875	908	963	996	1,032	1,051	1,063
Annual payroll	Bil. dol . .	11.0	20.1	24.1	25.1	26.7	29.8	31.8	34.0	37.4	(NA)
Advertising expenses	Bil. dol . .	1.2	2.8	3.7	3.8	4.1	4.3	4.6	5.0	5.1	5.3
Dealer pretax profits as a percentage of sales	Percent .	0.6	2.2	1.0	1.4	1.6	1.8	1.4	1.5	1.4	1.7

NA Not available.   [1] At beginning of year.   [2] Data provided by Ward's Automotive Reports.
Source: National Automobile Dealers Association, McLean, VA, *NADA Data*, annual.

No. 1283. Motor Vehicle Retail Sales: 1980 to 1997

[In thousands (11,466 represents $11,466,000)]

Type	1980	1985	1989	1990	1991	1992	1993	1994	1995	1996	1997
Retail sales, total	**11,466**	**15,724**	**14,713**	**14,146**	**12,539**	**13,116**	**14,199**	**15,411**	**15,116**	**15,456**	**15,500**
Passenger cars (new), total	8,979	11,042	9,772	9,300	8,175	8,213	8,517	8,990	8,634	8,527	8,272
Domestic [1]	6,581	8,205	7,073	6,897	6,137	6,277	6,741	7,255	7,128	7,254	6,917
Imports	2,398	2,838	2,699	2,403	2,038	1,936	1,776	1,735	1,506	1,273	1,355
Trucks (new), total	2,487	4,682	4,941	4,846	4,365	4,903	5,681	6,421	6,481	6,930	7,228
Domestic [1]	2,001	3,902	4,403	4,215	3,813	4,481	5,287	5,995	6,064	6,478	6,633
Imports	486	780	538	631	551	422	394	426	417	452	595

[1] North American built.
Source: American Automobile Manufacturers Association, Detroit, MI, *Motor Vehicle Facts and Figures*, annual (copyright).

U.S. Census Bureau, Statistical Abstract of the United States: 1999

No. 1284. Retail Foodstores—Number and Sales, by Type: 1990 to 1997

[(254.4 represents 254,400) except as indicated]

Type of foodstore	Number [1] (1,000)					Sales [2] (bil. dol.)					Percent distribution			
											Number		Sales	
	1990	1994	1995	1996	1997	1990	1994	1995	1996	1997	1990	1997	1990	1997
Total.	254.4	248.3	247.3	246.3	245.3	368.3	399.3	410.5	421.0	429.8	100.0	100.0	100.0	100.0
Grocery stores [3]	172.9	165.6	164.3	163.0	161.7	348.2	378.6	385.0	397.0	403.0	67.7	65.9	94.5	93.8
Supermarkets [3]	25.0	24.6	24.1	23.8	24.1	260.1	289.0	293.2	302.5	307.5	9.9	9.8	70.6	71.5
Conventional	13.7	12.0	11.1	10.8	11.1	90.7	81.5	68.9	69.2	59.2	5.7	4.5	24.6	13.8
Superstore [4]	5.8	6.5	6.8	7.1	7.3	87.6	107.6	116.7	127.0	132.9	2.2	3.0	23.8	30.9
Warehouse [5]	3.4	2.9	2.7	2.4	2.2	33.1	27.7	26.0	24.3	22.2	1.3	0.9	9.0	5.2
Combination food and drug [6]	1.6	2.4	2.7	2.4	2.8	34.8	51.7	59.3	61.3	64.7	0.5	1.1	9.4	15.1
Superwarehouse [7] . .	0.3	0.5	0.6	0.5	0.5	12.6	16.2	17.8	15.3	11.9	0.2	0.2	3.4	2.8
Hypermarket [8] . . .	0.1	0.2	0.2	0.2	0.2	1.3	4.3	4.5	5.4	16.6	(Z)	0.1	0.4	3.9
Convenience stores [9] . .	59.2	61.5	62.1	62.7	62.1	37.0	40.3	37.4	38.8	42.0	19.1	25.3	10.0	9.8
Superette [10]	88.7	79.6	78.1	76.5	75.5	51.1	49.2	54.4	55.7	53.5	38.6	30.8	13.9	12.4
Specialized food stores [11] .	81.5	82.7	83.0	83.3	83.6	20.1	20.7	22.4	24.0	26.8	32.3	34.1	5.5	6.2

Z Less than 0.05 percent. [1] Estimated. [2] Includes nonfood items. [3] A grocery store, primarily self-service in operation, providing a full range of departments, and having at least $2.5 million in annual sales in 1985 dollars. [4] Contains greater variety of products than conventional supermarkets, including specialty and service departments, and considerable nonfood (general merchandise) products. [5] Contains limited product variety and fewer services provided, incorporating case lot stocking and shelving practices. [6] Contains a pharmacy, a nonprescription drug department, and a greater variety of health and beauty aids than that carried by conventional supermarkets. [7] A larger warehouse store that offers expanded product variety and often service meat, deli, or seafood departments. [8] A very large store offering a greater variety of general merchandise—like clothes, hardware, and seasonal goods—and personal care products than other grocery stores. [9] A small grocery store selling a limited variety of food and nonfood products, typically open extended hours. [10] A grocery store, primarily self-service in operation, selling a wide variety of food and nonfood products with annual sales below $2.5 million (1985 dollars). [11] Primarily engaged in the retail sale of a single food category such as meat and seafood stores and retail bakeries.

Source: U.S. Dept. of Agriculture, Economic Research Service, Food Marketing Review, annual.

No. 1285. Percent of Supermarkets Offering Selected Services and Product Lines: 1990 to 1998

[In percent. Based on a sample survey of chain and independent supermarkets and subject to sampling variability; for details, see source]

Service or product line offered	1990	1997	1998	Service or product line offered	1990	1997	1998
Service delicatessen.	73	81	81	Salad bar	18	24	24
Service bakery	60	69	69	Automated teller machines (ATMs) .	20	62	62
Service meat.	42	60	59	Banking in store	(NA)	22	21
Service fish.	33	43	43	Pharmacy.	15	26	32
Separate cheese department	33	30	31	Warehouse aisle	(NA)	16	17

NA Not available.

Source: Progressive Grocer, New York, NY, Progressive Grocer 66th Annual Report (copyright). Used by permission of Progressive Grocer magazine.

No. 1286. Food and Alcoholic Beverage Sales, by Sales Outlet: 1985 to 1997

[In billions of dollars (397.5 represents $397,500,000,000)]

Sales outlet	1985	1989	1990	1991	1992	1993	1994	1995	1996	1997
Food sales, total [1].	397.5	510.4	552.1	574.9	584.2	603.8	631.6	655.9	681.2	707.4
Off-premise use	228.7	278.9	303.9	319.3	319.3	325.3	341.9	357.6	372.9	387.2
Food stores	204.9	241.9	262.1	271.2	270.1	272.6	285.9	293.2	302.9	309.6
Other stores	16.4	26.3	30.2	33.7	36.0	38.7	40.6	48.0	52.4	58.9
Home-delivered, mail order	2.8	4.6	5.3	5.8	6.4	7.1	8.4	8.8	9.8	10.4
Farmers, manufacturers, wholesalers [2].	4.6	6.1	6.3	6.6	6.7	7.0	7.1	7.6	7.8	8.4
Food service [2]	168.8	231.5	248.2	255.6	264.9	278.5	289.7	298.3	308.2	320.3
Alcoholic beverage sales, total.	64.0	75.6	81.1	82.5	82.5	82.9	85.1	87.2	90.9	94.5
Packaged alcoholic beverages. . . .	38.2	43.1	46.4	47.3	46.3	46.0	47.6	48.2	50.1	51.9
Liquor stores.	17.1	17.3	18.6	19.1	18.4	18.2	18.6	18.4	19.2	20.3
Food stores	17.0	19.8	21.2	21.2	20.9	20.7	21.8	22.3	23.1	23.6
All other	4.2	6.0	6.7	7.0	7.0	7.2	7.2	7.6	7.8	8.1
Alcoholic drinks.	25.8	32.5	34.6	35.2	36.2	36.9	37.5	39.0	40.8	42.6
Eating and drinking places [3] . . .	20.7	25.0	26.8	27.3	27.8	28.3	28.6	29.5	30.7	31.8
Hotels and motels [3]	3.4	3.8	3.8	3.7	3.8	3.8	4.0	4.2	4.5	4.9
All other.	1.8	3.7	4.0	4.2	4.6	4.8	5.0	5.4	5.6	6.0

[1] Includes taxes and tips. Excludes home food production. [2] Includes food furnished and donations. [3] Includes tips.

Source: U.S. Dept. of Agriculture, Economic Research Service, Food Consumption, Prices, and Expenditures, 1970-97. <http://www.econ.ag.gov>.

774 Domestic Trade and Services

No. 1287. Commercial and Noncommercial Groups—Food and Drink Sales: 1980 to 1999

[In millions of dollars (238,149 represents $238,149,000,000) except as indicated. Excludes military. Data refer to sales to consumers of food and alcoholic beverages. Sales are estimated. For details, see source]

Type of group	Number, 1996	Sales (mil. dol.)							
		1980	1985	1990	1995	1996	1997	1998	1999 [1]
Total	814,207	119,004	172,787	238,149	294,631	307,086	320,146	337,272	352,781
Commercial restaurant services [2][3]	636,805	101,529	151,762	211,606	265,910	277,381	290,131	306,591	321,355
Eating places [2]	395,071	72,276	111,657	155,552	198,293	206,211	215,246	227,391	238,109
Full-service restaurants. . . .	183,253	39,307	57,939	77,811	96,396	100,830	105,064	111,801	117,279
Limited-service restaurants [4] .	185,891	28,699	47,477	69,798	92,901	96,106	100,575	105,553	110,409
Bars and taverns [5]	36,435	7,785	8,338	9,533	9,948	10,276	10,543	11,061	11,459
Managed services [2]	19,117	6,818	9,460	14,149	18,186	19,410	20,516	21,779	22,959
Manufacturing and industrial plants	(NA)	2,121	2,721	3,856	4,814	5,066	5,384	5,745	6,023
Colleges and universities . . .	(NA)	1,140	1,738	2,788	3,989	4,317	4,631	5,008	5,378
Lodging places [2]	27,619	6,768	10,557	13,568	15,561	16,193	16,879	17,852	18,673
Hotel restaurants.	17,993	4,964	8,986	12,355	14,516	15,154	15,852	16,807	17,629
Motel restaurants.	7,883	1,151	975	483	618	613	605	616	615
Retail hosts [2][6]	137,288	3,264	5,254	9,513	12,589	13,443	14,280	15,464	16,585
Department store restaurants . . . . [6]	4,721	857	865	876	1,038	1,079	(NA)	(NA)	(NA)
Grocery store restaurants [6] . .	60,522	830	2,074	5,432	6,624	7,041	(NA)	(NA)	(NA)
Gasoline service stations . . .	43,149	492	1,052	1,718	2,520	2,729	(NA)	(NA)	(NA)
Recreation and sports	14,970	1,452	1,972	2,871	3,866	4,041	4,382	4,411	4,603
Noncommercial restaurant services [2]	177,402	17,475	21,025	26,543	28,722	29,705	30,015	30,681	31,426
Employee restaurant services . .	5,525	1,635	1,971	1,864	1,364	1,274	1,238	1,119	1,067
Industrial, commercial organizations	2,306	1,377	1,682	1,603	1,129	1,031	(NA)	(NA)	(NA)
Educational restaurant services.	96,986	4,610	5,978	7,671	9,059	9,328	9,479	9,711	9,968
Elementary and secondary schools	94,044	2,312	2,919	3,700	4,533	4,728	4,901	4,981	5,093
Hospitals	6,175	6,668	7,104	8,968	9,219	9,577	9,415	9,505	9,614
Miscellaneous [2]	32,576	1,521	2,077	2,892	3,673	3,842	4,064	4,244	4,433
Clubs	10,514	1,056	1,537	1,993	2,278	2,381	(NA)	(NA)	(NA)

NA Not available.   [1] Projection.   [2] Includes other types of groups, not shown separately.   [3] Data for establishments with payroll.   [4] Fast-food restaurants.   [5] For establishments serving food.   [6] Beginning 1990, a portion of delicatessen sales in grocery stores are considered food service.

Source: National Restaurant Association, Washington, DC, *Restaurant Numbers: A Statistical Digest for the Restaurant Industry*, 1998; *Restaurant Industry in Review*, annual; and *National Restaurant Association Restaurant Industry Forecast*, December 1998 (copyright).

No. 1288. U.S. Mail Order Sales, by Kind of Business: 1990 to 1995

[In millions of dollars (151,640 represents $151,640,000,000). Mail order sales represent orders placed by mail, phone, or electronically without the person ordering coming to the point of sale to place the order, or the seller coming to the office or home of the orderer to take the order or using an agent to collect the order. Excludes orders placed at catalog desks or elsewhere in stores even in response to a catalog but does include products or services delivered in the store as long as the order was placed by mail, phone, or electronically. Statistics are generated independently each year and are not adjusted for any discontinuities of available data]

Kind of business	1990	1991	1992	1993	1994	1995
Total mail order sales	**151,640**	**162,050**	**168,050**	**186,700**	**200,760**	**219,900**
Consumer, total	98,190	107,970	110,740	118,970	129,740	141,810
Products	57,500	64,940	65,210	71,960	78,460	86,350
Specialty [1]	44,520	50,010	50,560	57,720	64,810	70,920
Apparel.	4,250	4,410	4,820	5,230	6,160	6,800
Books.	2,760	2,770	3,120	3,100	3,200	3,950
Collectibles	1,690	1,810	2,000	2,360	2,200	2,140
Computer software & hardware	1,000	1,330	2,160	3,350	4,430	3,250
Health products	2,480	2,770	2,940	4,010	5,080	5,840
Magazines.	6,020	6,580	6,340	6,280	6,600	6,900
Multi-products	7,410	8,440	6,860	10,190	10,760	11,340
Newspapers	3,020	3,020	3,020	3,020	3,080	3,080
Sporting goods	3,460	3,910	3,650	4,030	4,610	4,580
General merchandise	12,980	14,930	14,650	14,240	13,650	15,430
Services	40,690	43,030	45,530	47,010	51,280	55,460
Nonfinancial	21,660	25,740	26,620	26,980	28,400	29,530
Financial	19,030	17,290	18,910	20,030	22,880	25,930
Business products and services	53,450	54,080	57,310	67,730	71,020	78,090
Business supplies [1]	7,160	9,180	10,060	14,080	16,420	21,940
Data processing-oriented supplies.	1,520	2,060	2,320	1,840	770	710
Computer hardware	700	1,800	2,400	6,000	8,000	11,300
Business services [1]	8,900	8,940	10,410	13,300	12,640	13,310
Communications	4,240	4,140	5,580	8,050	7,900	7,900
Information	2,500	2,500	2,500	2,850	2,310	2,710
Industrial	5,390	5,560	6,440	8,150	8,160	8,040
Generalized mail order marketers [2]	32,000	30,400	30,400	32,200	33,800	34,800

[1] Includes other kinds of business not shown separately.   [2] Mail order as part of the overall selling channel mix of multichannel industrial marketers not specializing in mail order selling.

Source: Fishman, Arnold L., data are extracted from *Annual Guides to Mail Order Sales, 1990-1996*, Marketing Logistics, Inc., Highland Park, IL, 60035 (copyright). For 1990-92, *Portable Mail Order Industry Statistics, 1993 Edition*, Richard D. Irwin, Inc., Burr Ridge, IL, 1994 (copyright).

Domestic Trade and Services   775

No. 1289. Catalog Sales—Method Used and Characteristic of Purchaser: 1996

[In thousands (191,986 represents 191,986,000), except percent. Based on population 18 and over as of July 1. Data are estimates]

Characteristic	Adult population 18 yrs. old and over	Bought from catalog							
		Total	Percent	By fax	By mail	By phone	At catalog store	Via commercial online service	Via the Internet
Total adults......	**191,986**	**109,834**	**57.2**	**3,113**	**66,907**	**75,737**	**9,167**	**1,267**	**590**
18-24 years old......	25,055	12,447	49.7	187	8,065	7,914	970	103	43
25-34 years old......	41,660	24,482	58.8	737	14,317	17,611	2,039	523	286
35-44 years old......	42,571	26,406	62.0	1,132	15,454	19,757	2,342	278	197
45-54 years old......	30,886	19,119	61.9	737	11,544	14,443	1,412	263	33
55-64 years old......	20,722	11,702	56.5	179	7,093	7,694	971	57	25
65 years old or older....	31,091	15,678	50.4	142	10,435	8,319	1,434	43	6
Sex:									
Males............	92,172	47,994	52.1	1,510	29,092	32,363	3,551	752	391
Females.........	99,814	61,840	62.0	1,603	37,815	43,374	5,616	515	199
Race:									
White............	162,046	95,408	58.9	2,821	57,963	67,155	7,337	1,051	558
Black............	22,336	10,734	48.1	159	6,702	6,156	1,620	101	7

No. 1290. Merchandise or Services Ordered by Mail or Phone in Last 12 Months, by Characteristic of Purchaser: 1996

[In thousands (191,986 represents 191,986,000), except percent. Based on population 18 and over as of July 1. Data are estimates]

Characteristic	Adult population 18 yrs. old and over	Persons ordering merchandise or services by mail or phone			
		By mail		By phone	
		Persons ordering	Percent	Persons ordering	Percent
Total adults........	**191,986**	**106,086**	**55.3**	**100,793**	**52.5**
18-24 years old.......	25,055	12,562	50.1	10,846	43.3
25-34 years old.........	41,660	23,545	56.5	23,121	55.5
35-44 years old.........	42,571	23,792	55.9	25,313	59.5
45-54 years old.........	30,886	18,010	58.3	18,326	59.3
55-64 years old.........	20,722	11,463	55.3	10,840	52.3
65 years old or older......	31,091	16,713	53.8	12,347	39.7
Sex:					
Males..............	92,172	46,575	50.5	46,088	50.0
Females.............	99,814	59,511	59.6	54,704	54.8
Race:					
White..............	162,046	92,065	56.8	88,750	54.8
Black..............	22,336	10,086	45.2	8,650	38.7

No. 1291. Population Ordering by Catalog, by Type of Product, and Characteristic of Purchaser: 1996

[In thousands (191,986 represents 191,986,000). Survey conducted fall of 1996. Purchases ordered within 12 months prior to survey. Based on population 18 and over as of July 1. Data are estimates]

Characteristic	Adult population 18 yrs. old and over	Specific items ordered									
		Clothing	Electronic equipment	Food	Gardening	Hardware	Home furnishing (bed & bath)	Housewares	Nonfood gifts	Sporting goods	Toys/games
Total adults	**191,986**	**63,741**	**16,551**	**6,684**	**8,045**	**6,210**	**23,264**	**16,095**	**9,817**	**12,510**	**14,386**
18-24 years old......	25,055	7,035	1,754	403	322	559	1,855	1,437	694	1,510	1,130
25-34 years old......	41,660	13,134	4,279	931	1,334	930	5,358	3,555	2,106	2,723	4,379
35-44 years old......	42,571	15,568	4,692	1,889	2,445	1,448	6,787	4,137	2,599	3,747	4,094
45-54 years old......	30,886	11,529	3,282	1,220	1,632	1,102	4,412	2,892	2,244	2,458	2,263
55-64 years old......	20,722	6,639	1,364	897	1,069	1,101	2,636	1,815	1,098	1,129	1,288
65 or older.........	31,091	9,836	1,181	1,345	1,243	1,071	2,216	2,258	1,075	944	1,231
Sex:											
Male..........	92,172	22,571	10,878	2,434	3,283	4,427	5,875	4,956	2,763	8,667	5,113
Female	99,814	41,170	5,674	4,250	4,761	1,783	17,389	11,139	7,054	3,843	9,273
Race:											
White..........	162,046	55,642	14,071	5,826	7,254	5,446	20,271	14,198	9,091	11,462	12,334
Black..........	22,336	6,397	1,664	652	431	682	2,371	1,452	448	638	1,621

Source of Tables 1289-1991: Simmons Market Research Bureau, New York, NY, *Study of Media and Markets* (copyright).

U.S. Census Bureau, Statistical Abstract of the United States: 1999

No. 1292. Shopping Centers—Number, Gross Leasable Area, and Retail Sales, by Gross Leasable Area: 1990 to 1998

[As of **December 31**. A shopping center is a group of architecturally unified commercial establishments built on a site that is planned, developed, owned, and managed as an operating unit related in its location, size, and type of shops to the trade area that the unit serves. The unit provides on-site parking in definite relationship to the types and total size of the stores. The data base attempts to include all centers with three or more stores. Estimates are based on a sample of data available on shopping center properties; for details, contact source]

Year	Total	Gross leasable area (sq. ft.)					
		Less than 100,001	100,001-200,000	200,001-400,000	400,001-800,000	800,001-1,000,000	More than 1 million
NUMBER							
1990	36,515	23,231	8,756	2,781	1,102	288	357
1995	41,235	26,001	9,974	3,345	1,234	301	380
1996	42,130	26,497	10,186	3,477	1,276	309	385
1997	42,953	26,928	10,400	3,595	1,324	316	390
1998	43,661	27,317	10,581	3,696	1,354	319	395
Percent distribution	100.0	62.6	24.2	8.5	3.1	0.7	0.9
Percent change, 1997-98	1.6	1.4	1.7	2.8	2.3	0.9	1.3
GROSS LEASABLE AREA							
1990 (mil. sq. ft.)	4,390	1,125	1,197	734	618	259	457
1995 (mil. sq. ft.)	4,967	1,267	1,368	886	689	271	486
1996 (mil. sq. ft.)	5,101	1,293	1,399	926	711	278	493
1997 (mil. sq. ft.)	5,229	1,318	1,431	960	736	285	500
1998 (mil. sq. ft.)	5,333	1,340	1,458	988	752	287	507
Percent distribution	100.0	25.1	27.3	18.5	14.1	5.4	9.5
Percent change, 1997-98	2.0	1.7	1.9	3.0	2.1	0.9	1.4
RETAIL SALES							
1990 (bil. dol.)	706.4	205.1	179.5	108.0	91.7	45.1	77.0
1995 (bil. dol.)	893.8	259.6	227.1	136.4	115.8	57.0	97.8
1996 (bil. dol.)	933.9	271.2	237.3	142.6	121.0	60.0	102.2
1997 (bil. dol.)	980.0	284.6	249.0	149.7	126.9	62.5	107.4
1998 (bil. dol.)	1,032.4	299.7	262.2	157.7	133.7	65.8	113.2
Percent distribution	100.0	29.0	25.4	15.3	12.9	11.0	10.9
Percent change, 1997-98	5.3	5.3	5.3	5.4	5.3	5.3	5.4

No. 1293. Shopping Centers—Number, Gross Leasable Area, and Retail Sales, by State: 1998

[See headnote, Table 1292. Minus sign (-) indicates decrease]

State	Number	Gross leasable area (mil. sq. ft.)	Retail sales (bil. dol.)	Percent change, 1997-98 Number	Gross leasable area	Retail sales	State	Number	Gross leasable area (mil. sq. ft.)	Retail sales (bil. dol.)	Percent change, 1997-98 Number	Gross leasable area	Retail sales
U.S.	**43,661**	**5,333**	**1,032.4**	**1.6**	**2.0**	**5.3**							
							MO	887	111	22.7	0.9	0.7	4.3
AL	630	74	15.5	0.8	1.2	3.3	MT	94	10	2.0	-	-	5.3
AK	68	8	2.0	-	-	6.7	NE	264	34	5.7	2.9	3.3	1.6
AZ	1,019	121	24.5	0.5	0.7	4.7	NV	353	44	6.7	6.6	8.7	-2.6
AR	370	36	5.5	1.1	1.1	3.1	NH	220	23	4.3	0.8	0.9	6.8
CA	5,887	680	124.2	2.0	2.5	2.7							
							NJ	1,219	166	28.2	1.8	1.9	4.1
CO	741	98	22.9	1.9	2.4	3.5	NM	303	29	6.4	1.1	1.7	3.0
CT	785	95	18.6	1.5	1.3	5.1	NY	1,732	243	44.6	1.8	3.3	1.8
DE	139	22	4.3	0.9	1.7	4.6	NC	1,584	169	29.0	1.9	2.3	2.7
DC	87	9	1.7	2.6	1.3	3.9	ND	87	9	2.1	-	-	5.3
FL	3,278	415	93.2	1.9	1.9	4.0							
							OH	1,704	246	41.6	1.2	1.2	3.7
GA	1,576	170	31.5	1.9	2.1	2.9	OK	568	60	13.2	0.2	0.8	3.2
HI	182	19	4.2	-	-	7.9	OR	502	57	9.3	4.1	4.5	1.2
ID	161	19	3.3	2.8	2.2	2.3	PA	1,638	235	40.2	1.4	1.9	3.5
IL	2,096	254	41.8	1.8	1.6	4.0	RI	200	18	3.8	-	-	5.4
IN	905	120	21.4	1.4	1.8	3.0							
							SC	804	79	15.6	2.0	2.8	2.0
IA	308	41	7.5	2.2	3.9	1.0	SD	58	7	3.1	3.1	3.9	1.1
KS	481	57	11.6	1.1	2.6	2.3	TN	1,200	133	23.0	0.8	1.2	4.0
KY	616	67	13.9	0.6	0.8	4.0	TX	2,976	359	87.3	1.4	1.5	3.5
LA	700	84	18.7	1.0	1.1	3.8	UT	236	34	6.5	1.9	4.7	-0.2
ME	200	17	4.1	-	-	6.8							
							VT	113	8	1.8	-	-	6.5
MD	904	125	24.9	2.9	2.5	2.8	VA	1,269	167	31.6	2.1	2.7	2.9
MA	992	113	23.3	1.3	1.6	4.2	WA	763	99	17.7	2.3	1.0	4.6
MI	1,018	135	25.3	2.5	2.9	2.2	WV	162	22	3.8	2.2	1.8	2.2
MN	471	67	13.9	0.7	0.8	4.5	WI	625	77	14.6	1.8	1.9	3.5
MS	430	41	8.2	0.3	0.9	2.9	WY	53	6	1.4	-	-	4.6

- Represents zero.

Source of Tables 1292 and 1293: National Research Bureau, Chicago Data for 1990 published by Monitor Publishing, Clearwater, FL, in *Monitor Magazine*, November/December 1991 (copyright). Data for 1995-98 published by International Council of Shopping Centers in *Shopping Centers Today*, April issues (copyright—Interactive Mark Systems, Inc.).

No. 1294. Retail Sales, by Type of Store and State: 1996 and 1997

[In millions of dollars, (2,465,147 represents $2,465,147,000,000) except as indicated. Kind-of-business classification based on 1987 Standard Industrial Classification (SIC) code; see text, Section 17, Business. Data are estimates]

State	All stores [1]				Food stores				General merchandise stores			
		1997			Total (SIC 54)		Grocery stores (SIC 541)		Total (SIC 53)		Department stores (SIC 531)	
	1996, total	Total	Sales per household [2] Amount (dol.)	Percent change, 1996-97	1996	1997	1996	1997	1996	1997	1996	1997
U.S...	2,465,147	2,546,287	25,437	1.8	424,091	428,842	401,246	403,855	309,404	322,463	240,828	253,197
AL	36,729	38,063	23,122	2.1	6,485	6,600	6,203	6,281	5,487	5,964	4,387	4,799
AK	6,816	6,991	32,852	1.4	1,424	1,434	1,385	1,390	946	978	657	681
AZ	42,748	44,995	25,678	1.1	8,276	8,807	8,017	8,491	5,409	5,290	4,079	4,041
AR	22,053	22,872	23,563	2.7	3,613	3,605	3,508	3,482	3,585	3,768	2,892	3,060
CA	268,442	275,289	24,345	0.5	48,393	47,304	45,194	43,956	32,989	34,185	22,541	23,700
CO	39,777	41,783	27,002	2.3	7,083	7,085	6,863	6,832	4,816	5,230	3,723	4,069
CT	34,037	34,661	28,193	2.1	6,278	6,408	5,872	5,964	3,416	3,579	2,691	2,851
DE	7,902	8,186	29,616	2.5	1,289	1,313	1,203	1,220	1,179	1,092	927	866
DC	3,760	3,670	16,627	-0.1	620	645	546	566	218	166	190	145
FL.....	158,978	166,211	28,015	1.9	25,542	26,312	24,253	24,862	18,540	19,552	13,793	14,723
GA	70,003	73,999	26,639	3.2	11,932	12,539	11,405	11,923	9,153	9,753	7,376	7,943
HI.....	13,322	13,359	34,141	-0.5	2,266	2,264	2,103	2,090	2,197	2,256	957	1,012
ID.....	11,661	12,307	27,694	3.0	2,252	2,436	2,198	2,366	1,296	1,406	966	1,061
IL.....	105,802	107,901	24,547	1.1	15,454	15,172	14,460	14,133	12,628	13,047	10,466	10,859
IN.....	54,930	56,603	25,421	2.1	7,913	7,855	7,531	7,438	7,397	7,883	6,031	6,459
IA.....	28,189	29,108	26,290	2.9	5,363	5,468	5,110	5,186	3,669	3,912	3,034	3,249
KS	23,538	23,975	24,057	0.8	4,175	4,224	4,057	4,084	3,304	3,453	2,550	2,685
KY	33,815	35,048	23,557	2.3	6,095	6,177	5,900	5,949	5,153	5,577	4,324	4,720
LA	37,956	39,122	24,866	2.2	7,347	7,289	7,030	6,945	5,703	5,971	4,510	4,740
ME	12,355	12,481	26,023	0.4	2,610	2,640	2,492	2,509	1,201	1,191	744	747
MD	46,228	47,058	25,048	1.0	8,645	8,633	8,118	8,118	5,388	5,662	4,109	4,368
MA	57,583	59,263	25,680	2.4	10,722	11,193	9,809	10,187	5,578	5,498	4,006	4,013
MI.....	94,787	98,234	26,891	1.2	12,478	12,828	11,586	11,857	14,960	15,593	13,146	13,753
MN	45,256	46,788	26,303	2.5	7,208	7,074	6,780	6,621	5,541	5,908	4,535	4,864
MS	19,021	19,635	19,888	1.6	3,813	3,918	3,592	3,678	3,259	3,367	2,501	2,592
MO	52,460	54,169	25,916	1.9	8,920	8,800	8,616	8,464	7,434	8,005	6,424	6,934
MT	8,296	8,565	24,942	2.3	1,542	1,531	1,493	1,475	929	974	676	717
NE	15,599	16,354	25,709	4.6	2,698	3,266	2,564	3,099	1,942	1,985	1,547	1,574
NV	18,443	20,020	28,313	-0.7	3,474	3,728	3,360	3,588	2,282	2,369	1,844	1,925
NH	14,175	14,577	33,016	1.5	2,861	2,825	2,735	2,688	1,796	1,914	1,219	1,311
NJ.....	76,932	78,291	26,918	0.8	13,630	13,791	12,628	12,714	7,550	7,409	5,974	5,909
NM	15,786	16,435	26,138	2.2	2,829	2,945	2,736	2,835	1,989	2,198	1,606	1,780
NY	140,700	142,486	21,347	1.0	25,031	24,553	22,514	21,966	13,646	13,467	10,766	10,750
NC	72,058	76,018	26,411	3.6	12,982	13,546	12,429	12,910	8,452	8,891	6,789	7,188
ND	6,619	6,841	27,560	3.3	1,028	1,060	992	1,018	985	1,006	804	826
OH	110,692	114,815	26,912	3.0	17,734	18,140	16,783	17,088	14,621	14,896	12,044	12,348
OK	26,793	27,841	21,816	2.9	4,457	4,308	4,259	4,090	3,904	4,176	3,156	3,412
OR	33,367	35,062	27,513	3.6	5,300	5,426	5,090	5,187	5,241	5,871	3,664	4,179
PA	113,492	116,304	25,309	2.4	19,216	19,112	17,981	17,789	12,320	12,479	10,290	10,485
RI.....	7,801	7,853	21,094	0.3	1,542	1,475	1,400	1,331	782	779	577	583
SC	33,343	34,544	24,713	1.2	6,355	6,538	6,177	6,324	3,963	4,239	3,244	3,494
SD	7,651	7,972	28,854	3.1	1,257	1,289	1,221	1,246	948	976	746	781
TN	51,706	53,796	25,903	2.3	8,363	8,385	8,115	8,099	7,623	8,149	6,079	6,560
TX	170,864	176,772	25,302	1.0	29,494	30,153	28,293	28,782	23,601	24,528	18,572	19,499
UT	16,871	17,922	27,529	3.3	3,395	3,671	3,306	3,556	2,136	2,231	1,629	1,719
VT	5,652	5,754	25,504	1.4	1,244	1,238	1,197	1,185	368	372	271	275
VA	67,433	69,713	27,565	2.3	12,675	12,819	12,158	12,233	8,095	8,665	5,855	6,319
WA	51,953	53,397	24,488	0.7	9,271	9,464	8,914	9,055	6,708	7,135	4,830	5,185
WV	14,177	14,484	20,363	2.2	2,937	2,905	2,866	2,821	2,036	2,134	1,608	1,689
WI.....	51,825	53,860	27,443	2.6	7,749	7,816	7,339	7,369	6,443	6,738	5,049	5,318
WY	4,769	4,840	26,537	1.4	830	834	815	815	594	600	432	438

See footnotes at end of table.

U.S. Census Bureau, Statistical Abstract of the United States: 1999

No. 1294. Retail Sales, by Type of Store and State: 1996 and 1997—Continued

[See headnote, page 778]

State	Automotive dealers (SIC 55 exc. 554) 1996	1997	Eating and drinking places (SIC 58) 1996	1997	Gasoline service stations (SIC 554) 1996	1997	Building materials and garden supplies (SIC 52) 1996	1997	Apparel and accessory stores (SIC 56) 1996	1997	Furniture and homefurnishings stores (SIC 57) 1996	1997
U.S. . . .	605,128	631,625	243,843	245,314	160,271	156,291	128,045	144,681	113,103	112,579	134,370	141,851
AL.	9,613	9,833	3,140	3,138	2,763	2,742	2,061	2,357	1,594	1,615	1,554	1,617
AK.	1,249	1,274	732	717	408	476	462	512	307	289	259	272
AZ.	10,013	10,998	5,486	5,601	2,658	2,512	2,108	2,456	1,503	1,521	2,354	2,602
AR.	6,334	6,512	1,733	1,744	1,820	1,942	1,291	1,475	712	717	757	819
CA.	59,854	63,505	25,916	26,278	17,754	16,903	14,929	16,541	13,923	14,017	17,652	18,365
CO	8,998	9,517	5,255	5,462	2,290	2,289	2,207	2,609	1,348	1,367	2,573	2,759
CT.	7,072	7,431	2,575	2,555	2,418	2,162	1,896	2,131	1,846	1,785	1,629	1,752
DE.	1,673	1,735	777	808	439	430	480	563	326	354	505	578
DC	155	146	1,093	1,065	185	168	53	66	337	329	276	252
FL.	44,202	45,848	16,230	16,474	8,272	7,972	7,403	8,722	7,583	7,689	9,428	10,212
GA	17,038	17,837	7,539	7,708	4,600	4,687	3,906	4,671	3,217	3,371	3,948	4,211
HI	2,073	1,989	1,892	1,849	680	633	472	544	1,058	1,117	619	617
ID	3,108	3,330	1,252	1,276	824	672	891	1,007	355	343	649	709
IL	26,900	27,714	11,413	11,494	6,254	5,959	4,464	5,105	5,017	4,931	7,076	7,554
IN	13,943	14,541	5,683	5,687	4,091	3,967	2,778	3,107	1,714	1,666	2,918	3,032
IA	7,421	7,643	2,538	2,518	2,407	2,423	1,563	1,742	856	860	1,252	1,366
KS.	6,347	6,514	2,250	2,153	1,730	1,557	1,034	1,155	757	783	1,186	1,302
KY.	7,804	8,016	3,290	3,300	2,942	2,905	2,046	2,367	1,115	1,092	1,354	1,381
LA.	9,659	9,993	3,645	3,747	2,725	2,703	1,809	2,088	1,542	1,543	1,508	1,566
ME	2,460	2,504	871	865	823	811	848	929	603	566	401	418
MD	10,455	10,714	4,889	4,831	2,705	2,528	2,214	2,395	2,438	2,343	2,839	3,021
MA	11,769	12,479	5,635	5,603	3,753	3,524	2,794	3,010	3,576	3,744	2,728	2,771
MI	26,146	27,106	9,260	9,232	6,122	6,025	4,678	5,173	3,830	3,676	5,598	6,059
MN	11,205	11,784	4,172	4,190	3,531	3,556	2,610	3,018	1,619	1,614	2,287	2,434
MS	4,720	4,746	1,493	1,517	1,335	1,342	1,022	1,239	653	627	690	729
MO	13,982	14,589	5,355	5,375	4,342	4,285	2,419	2,738	1,749	1,665	2,381	2,555
MT	1,962	2,036	1,122	1,124	588	598	618	705	242	230	442	471
NE.	3,857	3,844	1,542	1,481	1,223	1,098	667	775	540	515	902	913
NV.	3,904	4,385	2,362	2,452	1,026	1,019	1,044	1,187	708	729	1,050	1,168
NH	3,035	3,310	950	963	786	704	925	1,033	666	647	669	653
NJ.	19,859	20,386	5,966	5,891	4,238	4,002	3,432	3,661	5,119	4,963	4,641	4,816
NM	3,481	3,528	2,094	2,111	1,209	1,180	877	1,059	540	507	835	873
NY.	28,702	29,654	13,367	13,259	6,974	6,575	6,890	7,509	10,096	9,967	8,093	8,382
NC	17,447	18,794	7,372	7,526	4,473	4,572	5,085	5,833	3,099	3,099	4,118	4,299
ND	1,865	1,947	587	582	581	598	367	414	196	190	251	261
OH	28,007	29,531	12,015	12,165	7,522	7,308	5,071	5,829	3,762	3,699	6,163	6,453
OK	7,984	8,298	2,613	2,644	1,923	2,063	1,102	1,226	1,025	1,032	1,058	1,129
OR	8,302	8,935	2,873	2,932	2,128	2,066	2,300	2,538	1,365	1,371	1,753	1,835
PA.	29,267	30,505	9,216	9,290	6,486	6,758	5,657	6,243	5,217	5,284	5,030	5,098
RI	1,466	1,519	765	772	618	586	359	375	367	350	327	338
SC.	7,797	7,908	3,583	3,587	2,338	2,230	2,255	2,685	1,615	1,657	1,744	1,836
SD.	2,099	2,207	704	710	705	744	392	441	244	246	331	336
TN.	14,143	15,110	4,967	4,894	3,839	3,685	2,823	3,275	2,037	2,040	2,273	2,378
TX.	47,877	49,451	16,945	17,095	11,262	10,939	6,879	8,034	7,927	7,684	7,808	8,623
UT.	4,033	4,340	1,909	1,978	1,130	1,113	983	1,131	643	668	1,124	1,227
VT.	1,223	1,275	440	424	420	410	455	478	234	231	193	201
VA.	15,093	15,622	6,636	6,601	4,199	4,114	3,474	3,931	3,388	3,350	4,397	4,750
WA	11,826	12,063	4,733	4,700	3,433	3,366	3,718	4,037	2,300	2,311	2,965	2,991
WV	3,344	3,435	1,234	1,226	1,032	1,024	957	1,070	460	458	590	602
WI	13,294	14,135	5,119	5,126	3,703	3,809	3,050	3,240	1,591	1,588	3,014	3,076
WY	1,068	1,112	613	592	562	554	225	253	142	137	178	195

[1] Includes other types of stores, not shown separately.   [2] Based on number of households as of July 1 as estimated by source. Minus sign (-) indicates decrease.

Source: Market Statistics, a division of Claritas Inc., Arlington VA, *The Survey of Buying Power Data Service*, annual (copyright).

Domestic Trade and Services   779

U.S. Census Bureau, Statistical Abstract of the United States: 1999

No. 1295. Retail Trade—Summary of Establishments, by State: 1996

[(1,579.3 represents 1,579,300) except as indicated. Covers establishments with payroll. Employees are for the week including March 12. Most government employees are excluded. Kind-of-business classification based on 1987 Standard Industrial Classification (SIC) code; see text, Section 17, Business. For statement on methodology, see Appendix III]

State	Establishments (1,000) Total [1]	Food stores (SIC 54)	Automotive dealers and service stations (SIC 55)	Eating and drinking places (SIC 58)	Paid employees (1,000) Total [1]	Food stores (SIC 54)	Automotive dealers and service stations (SIC 55)	Eating and drinking places (SIC 58)	Annual payroll (mil. dol.) Total [1]	Food stores (SIC 54)	Automotive dealers and service stations (SIC 55)	Eating and drinking places (SIC 58)
U.S. ...	1,579.3	179.3	202.0	466.4	21,487	3,300	2,267	7,417	317,660	44,093	55,536	69,146
AL	25.7	3.2	4.5	5.9	337	58	40	109	4,181	564	846	847
AK	4.0	0.4	0.4	1.3	45	9	5	15	895	191	143	226
AZ	23.5	2.2	2.7	7.6	364	51	43	138	5,474	836	1,143	1,218
AR	16.2	1.9	2.8	3.8	196	28	24	61	2,637	302	467	466
CA	160.8	17.6	16.9	53.0	2,235	291	216	834	37,159	5,537	6,000	8,301
CO	26.0	1.9	3.0	8.1	362	46	36	143	5,470	852	954	1,350
CT	21.1	2.2	2.5	6.2	264	47	27	78	4,631	699	777	839
DE	5.0	0.5	0.6	1.4	67	10	7	23	981	144	183	229
DC	3.7	0.4	0.2	1.6	50	5	1	26	1,004	97	30	386
FL	91.3	9.8	11.6	24.3	1,276	210	132	441	18,727	2,586	3,517	4,160
GA	44.1	5.0	6.3	11.7	669	120	70	228	9,370	1,145	1,730	2,122
HI.....	8.0	0.9	0.6	2.7	113	14	8	47	1,850	245	213	583
ID.....	8.0	0.7	1.2	2.4	95	14	13	33	1,338	201	294	253
IL.....	66.1	6.6	7.7	21.6	956	129	94	329	14,557	1,707	2,382	3,160
IN.....	34.9	2.9	5.3	10.5	531	74	59	196	6,825	886	1,292	1,602
IA.....	19.8	1.8	3.1	6.0	254	43	32	84	3,106	483	626	620
KS	16.9	1.5	2.5	4.9	225	32	25	79	3,012	390	552	624
KY	22.9	2.8	3.8	5.7	318	48	38	113	4,064	524	741	940
LA	23.6	3.6	3.2	6.1	334	58	39	115	4,230	612	837	983
ME....	9.6	1.4	1.3	2.6	103	19	12	31	1,507	234	250	314
MD....	28.1	3.1	3.0	8.0	408	60	44	134	6,456	1,021	1,148	1,327
MA....	39.5	4.4	4.3	12.7	530	92	45	176	8,808	1,203	1,165	1,940
MI	56.0	6.9	7.4	16.6	812	141	85	281	11,642	1,739	2,301	2,397
MN	28.6	2.6	4.0	8.1	442	55	50	142	6,310	682	1,047	1,252
MS....	15.8	2.4	2.7	3.2	187	35	24	57	2,315	347	486	437
MO....	33.3	3.2	5.2	9.5	460	59	55	166	6,466	750	1,283	1,460
MT	7.5	0.7	1.0	2.5	76	10	10	30	931	136	195	233
NE	11.5	1.2	1.8	3.5	149	24	17	51	1,810	247	351	391
NV	8.9	0.9	0.9	2.9	134	18	15	50	2,238	341	434	522
NH	8.9	1.1	1.1	2.3	114	21	12	33	1,730	252	334	330
NJ	50.6	6.4	5.5	15.0	588	101	57	163	10,748	1,664	1,646	1,886
NM	10.2	0.9	1.4	3.0	137	17	17	52	1,881	278	374	445
NY	110.9	16.5	9.6	34.3	1,183	201	92	375	19,482	2,774	2,368	4,411
NC	46.7	5.2	7.2	12.0	625	93	69	217	8,828	1,092	1,691	1,908
ND	5.0	0.5	0.8	1.5	58	8	8	21	675	82	166	149
OH....	64.5	7.1	8.6	20.3	1,008	158	102	355	14,001	1,915	2,336	2,935
OK....	20.0	2.5	3.0	5.6	251	35	30	93	3,197	406	641	751
OR....	21.0	2.3	2.4	6.8	279	45	33	103	4,363	703	838	949
PA	72.0	7.9	8.8	21.9	957	162	101	299	13,494	1,936	2,312	2,659
RI.....	6.7	0.8	0.8	2.3	74	13	7	27	1,074	169	156	276
SC	24.4	2.8	3.6	6.4	315	50	35	114	4,131	565	777	972
SD	5.8	0.6	0.9	1.7	66	10	9	23	784	107	177	166
TN	32.6	4.0	4.9	8.0	466	74	50	158	6,548	737	1,259	1,433
TX	104.1	13.2	14.6	29.6	1,525	231	164	536	22,339	2,772	4,185	5,051
UT	10.5	0.9	1.5	3.0	168	25	20	57	2,351	346	430	460
VT	5.3	0.8	0.7	1.3	52	10	6	17	719	118	130	156
VA	39.1	4.9	5.2	10.3	558	83	63	183	8,157	1,145	1,544	1,706
WA....	33.4	3.6	3.9	11.1	443	72	46	163	7,130	1,250	1,218	1,605
WV....	10.9	1.5	1.8	2.8	127	22	17	40	1,567	252	311	326
WI	32.4	2.7	4.5	11.3	456	64	55	160	5,918	749	1,127	1,248
WY....	4.1	0.3	0.7	1.2	43	5	7	17	547	77	129	140

[1] Includes other kinds of business not shown separately.

Source: U.S. Census Bureau, County Business Patterns, annual.

U.S. Census Bureau, Statistical Abstract of the United States: 1999

No. 1296. Merchant Wholesalers—Summary: 1990 to 1998

[In billions of dollars (1,793.8 represents $1,793,800,000,000) except ratios. Inventories and stock/sales ratios, as of December, seasonally adjusted. Data reflect latest revision. Based on Current Business Survey; see Appendix III]

Kind of business	1987 SIC code [1]	1990	1993	1994	1995	1996	1997	1998
SALES (bil. dol.)								
Merchant wholesalers		1,793.8	1,940.2	2,075.7	2,265.7	2,420.7	2,500.1	2,561.4
Durable goods	50	881.2	986.9	1,082.3	1,179.2	1,245.8	1,311.3	1,357.5
Motor vehicles, parts, and supplies	501	173.9	179.3	197.2	202.6	211.1	216.6	228.0
Furniture and homefurnishings	502	33.9	34.9	36.7	40.9	43.6	40.9	41.1
Lumber and construction materials	503	63.6	71.5	78.1	77.1	85.8	90.2	91.5
Professional and commercial equipment.	504	114.3	159.2	165.7	194.6	231.4	237.0	255.1
Metals and minerals, except petroleum.	505	77.8	80.2	92.4	100.5	98.4	107.9	104.4
Electrical goods	506	116.5	131.9	150.2	169.8	173.8	201.2	206.0
Hardware, plumbing and heating equipment . . .	507	52.7	55.5	63.7	67.6	70.5	76.0	79.4
Machinery, equipment and supplies	508	157.0	160.6	169.8	182.7	187.3	206.4	222.0
Miscellaneous durable goods	509	91.4	113.8	128.3	143.3	143.9	135.2	130.0
Nondurable goods.	51	912.6	953.3	993.4	1,086.5	1,174.9	1,188.8	1,204.0
Paper and paper products	511	51.6	59.2	67.6	82.0	82.7	84.8	91.6
Drugs, proprietaries, and sundries	512	51.5	72.2	83.2	95.0	102.9	113.6	133.2
Apparel, piece goods, and notions	513	64.9	70.4	72.5	70.6	75.5	82.8	83.4
Groceries and related products	514	272.5	285.3	288.6	304.7	315.4	327.5	343.5
Farm-product raw materials	515	107.6	96.0	95.4	113.7	130.2	125.3	108.2
Chemicals and allied products	516	35.7	39.1	41.8	47.8	53.5	55.7	55.0
Petroleum and petroleum products	517	148.5	139.3	143.0	150.6	177.8	166.5	145.6
Beer, wine, and distilled beverages	518	49.3	51.3	53.0	54.1	56.4	55.0	58.0
Miscellaneous nondurable goods	519	131.0	140.4	148.2	168.2	180.7	177.6	185.4
INVENTORIES (bil. dol.)								
Merchant wholesalers		195.6	215.9	234.9	253.1	256.2	273.0	287.0
Durable goods	50	126.2	135.6	149.0	160.3	161.7	177.8	187.5
Motor vehicles, parts, and supplies	501	23.5	24.4	25.5	27.0	26.6	29.0	29.5
Furniture and homefurnishings	502	4.6	4.8	4.9	5.1	5.3	5.5	5.6
Lumber and construction materials	503	6.0	6.7	7.4	7.4	7.7	7.8	7.5
Professional and commercial equipment.	504	15.8	17.9	20.5	22.8	22.3	25.9	24.4
Metals and minerals, except petroleum.	505	10.7	11.1	12.8	12.8	12.7	13.9	14.7
Electrical goods	506	15.9	17.5	20.2	23.5	23.0	25.8	27.8
Hardware, plumbing and heating equipment . . .	507	8.5	9.3	10.8	11.0	12.1	12.4	13.6
Machinery, equipment and supplies	508	31.5	29.2	31.6	34.7	35.9	41.8	47.7
Miscellaneous durable goods	509	9.8	14.6	15.2	15.8	16.0	15.8	16.7
Nondurable goods.	51	69.4	80.2	85.9	92.8	94.5	95.2	99.4
Paper and paper products	511	4.9	6.3	7.0	8.3	8.6	9.0	9.3
Drugs, proprietaries, and sundries	512	6.5	10.4	11.6	12.0	13.7	13.5	15.7
Apparel, piece goods, and notions	513	9.8	11.4	12.2	11.9	11.8	12.2	12.2
Groceries and related products	514	14.7	15.7	16.1	16.7	17.8	15.8	16.1
Farm-product raw materials	515	8.8	10.0	10.4	12.3	9.6	12.1	12.4
Chemicals and allied products	516	3.1	3.7	4.1	4.6	4.7	4.9	5.2
Petroleum and petroleum products	517	4.4	4.0	4.9	4.9	5.7	4.8	4.0
Beer, wine, and distilled beverages	518	4.4	4.5	4.6	4.8	5.0	5.1	5.5
Miscellaneous nondurable goods	519	12.7	14.2	14.9	17.3	17.7	17.9	19.0
STOCK/SALES RATIO								
Merchant wholesalers		1.31	1.33	1.28	1.28	1.25	1.30	1.32
Durable goods	50	1.75	1.61	1.55	1.56	1.54	1.61	1.65
Motor vehicles, parts, and supplies	501	1.66	1.63	1.50	1.54	1.47	1.70	1.51
Furniture and homefurnishings	502	1.71	1.69	1.45	1.48	1.44	1.59	1.69
Lumber and construction materials	503	1.33	1.01	1.03	1.13	1.07	1.05	0.94
Professional and commercial equipment.	504	1.58	1.35	1.37	1.29	1.13	1.23	1.13
Metals and minerals, except petroleum.	505	1.60	1.62	1.54	1.54	1.52	1.51	1.76
Electrical goods	506	1.71	1.50	1.51	1.58	1.68	1.52	1.61
Hardware, plumbing and heating equipment . . .	507	1.90	1.94	1.90	1.89	2.04	1.95	2.03
Machinery, equipment and supplies	508	2.49	2.16	2.11	2.10	2.29	2.37	2.59
Miscellaneous durable goods	509	1.27	1.52	1.35	1.31	1.31	1.43	1.57
Nondurable goods.	51	0.90	1.03	0.99	0.99	0.94	0.96	0.96
Paper and paper products	511	1.16	1.21	1.11	1.20	1.21	1.24	1.17
Drugs, proprietaries, and sundries	512	1.49	1.65	1.59	1.44	1.52	1.33	1.28
Apparel, piece goods, and notions	513	1.77	2.12	2.07	2.00	1.73	1.72	1.77
Groceries and related products	514	0.66	0.67	0.64	0.63	0.69	0.57	0.56
Farm-product raw materials	515	1.04	1.20	1.19	1.25	0.89	1.18	1.36
Chemicals and allied products	516	0.97	1.14	1.09	1.08	1.05	1.05	1.14
Petroleum and petroleum products	517	0.33	0.39	0.40	0.37	0.35	0.37	0.36
Beer, wine, and distilled beverages	518	0.95	1.06	1.02	1.03	1.08	1.04	1.09
Miscellaneous nondurable goods	519	1.17	1.22	1.13	1.18	1.17	1.20	1.09

[1] Based on 1987 Standard Industrial Classification code; see text, Section 17, Business.

Source: U.S. Census Bureau, *Current Business Reports, Annual Benchmark Report for Wholesale Trade, January 1988 Through February 1998*, (BW/97-RV), and unpublished data.

U.S. Census Bureau, Statistical Abstract of the United States: 1999

No. 1297. Comparative Statistics in Wholesale Trade, by Kind of Business: 1992 and 1997

[495.5 establishments represents 495,500 establishments. Covers establishments with payroll. Based on 1987 Standard Industrial Classification (SIC) code; see text, Section 17, Business]

Kind of business	1987 SIC code	Establishments (1,000)		Sales, receipts, revenue/shipments (mil. dol.)		Annual payroll (mil. dol.)		Paid employees [1] (1,000)	
		1992	1997	1992	1997	1992	1997	1992	1997
Wholesale trade		495.5	518.2	3,238,520	4,212,312	173,272	234,445	5,791	6,507
Durable goods	50	313.5	335.3	1,593,874	2,293,821	105,155	147,502	3,349	3,880
Nondurable goods	51	182.0	182.9	1,644,647	1,918,491	68,117	86,942	2,442	2,627
Merchant whole-salers		414.8	440.2	1,847,274	2,498,395	127,987	177,877	4,588	5,295
Durable goods	50	264.6	285.7	902,789	1,322,482	78,264	113,999	2,714	3,236
Nondurable goods	51	150.2	154.5	944,485	1,175,913	49,723	63,877	1,874	2,060

[1] Definition of paid employees varies among sectors.

Source: U.S. Census Bureau, 1997 Economic Census, EC97X-CS1.

No. 1298. Selected Service Industries—Summary: 1987 and 1992

[For establishments with payroll]

Kind of business	1987 SIC code [1]	Establishments [2] (1,000)		Receipts or expenses [3] (mil. dol.)		Paid employees [4] (1,000)	
		1987	1992	1987	1992	1987	1992
Firms subject to Federal income tax [5]	(X)	1,626	1,825	772,194	1,202,613	16,055	19,290
Hotels and other lodging places [6]	70 ex. 704	47	49	51,865	69,204	1,411	1,489
Personal services	72	185	197	31,491	43,280	1,105	1,218
Business services	73	252	307	166,322	274,892	4,414	5,542
Automotive repair, services, and parking	75	151	172	51,423	70,033	785	864
Miscellaneous repair services	76	66	72	20,838	30,732	346	428
Amusement and recreation services and museums [7]	78, 79, 84	99	115	57,638	92,915	1,094	1,382
Health services	80	407	442	182,289	299,067	3,592	4,453
Legal services	81	138	152	66,998	101,114	808	924
Social services	83	43	59	7,330	13,349	357	505
Engineering and management services [8]	87 ex. 8733	205	233	127,344	192,819	1,969	2,271
Firms exempt from Federal income tax [5]	(X)	176	209	253,284	423,900	6,737	8,109
Selected health services	8011 pt; 8021 pt; 805, 6, 8, 9	19	24	184,920	312,050	4,648	5,565
Social services	83	63	82	26,884	47,170	1,110	1,407
Selected membership organizations . . .	861, 2, 4, 9	68	72	22,028	33,795	539	603

X Not applicable.   [1] Based on 1987 Standard Industrial Classification; see text, Section 17, Business.   [2] Number of establishments in business at any time during the year.   [3] Receipts refer to establishments subject to Federal income tax. Expenses refer to establishments exempt from Federal income tax.   [4] For pay period including March 12.   [5] Includes other kinds of business, not shown separately.   [6] Excludes membership lodging.   [7] Includes motion pictures.   [8] Except non-commercial research organizations.

Source: U.S. Census Bureau, 1992 Census of Service Industries, Geographic Area Series, SC92-A-52.

No. 1299. National Nonprofit Associations—Number, by Type: 1980 to 1997

[Data compiled during last few months of year previous to year shown and the beginning months of year shown]

Type	1980	1990	1995	1997	Type	1980	1990	1995	1997
Total	14,726	22,289	22,663	22,901	Fraternal, foreign inter-est, nationality, ethnic .	435	573	552	541
Trade, business, commercial	3,118	3,918	3,757	3,755	Religious	797	1,172	1,230	1,230
Agriculture	677	940	1,122	1,124	Veteran, hereditary, patriotic	208	462	686	745
Legal, governmental, public admin., military .	529	792	776	780	Hobby, avocational . . .	910	1,475	1,549	1,548
Scientific, engineering, tech	1,039	1,417	1,355	1,381	Athletic sports	504	840	838	836
					Labor unions	235	253	245	245
Educational	[1]2,376	1,291	1,290	1,310	Chambers of Com-				
Cultural	([1])	1,886	1,918	1,918	merce [2]	105	168	168	162
Social welfare	994	1,705	1,885	1,934	Greek and non-Greek				
Health, medical	1,413	2,227	2,348	2,453	letter societies	318	340	336	335
Public affairs	1,068	2,249	2,148	2,113	Fan clubs	(NA)	581	460	491

NA Not available.   [1] Data for cultural associations included with educational associations.   [2] National and binational.

Source: Gale Research Inc., Detroit, MI. Compiled from Encyclopedia of Associations, annual (copyright).

No. 1300. Service Industries—Summary of Taxable Firms: 1992

[8,593.5 establishments represents 8,593,500 establishments]

Kind of business	1987 SIC code [1]	All establishments		Establishments with payroll			
		Establishments [2] (1,000)	Receipts (mil. dol.)	Establishments [2] (1,000)	Receipts (mil. dol.)	Annual payroll (mil. dol.)	Paid employees [3] (1,000)
Firms subject to Federal income tax [4] ..	(X)	8,593.5	1,345,146	1,825.4	1,202,613	452,697	19,290
Hotels and other lodging places [4][5]	70 ex. 704	92.9	71,038	48.6	69,204	19,633	1,489
Hotels and motels..................	701	69.1	68,508	41.7	67,193	19,187	1,456
Personal services [4]..................	72	1,320.9	59,598	197.1	43,280	14,379	1,218
Laundry, cleaning, and garment services....	721	124.4	18,805	55.8	17,140	5,588	426
Photographic studios, portrait	722	64.3	4,280	11.4	3,191	853	67
Beauty and barber shops	723, 4	471.6	15,951	87.7	10,347	4,428	402
Funeral service and crematories	726	25.2	7,588	15.6	7,145	1,856	88
Business services [4]	73	2,056.2	309,439	306.6	274,892	109,299	5,542
Advertising [4]	731	91.6	22,673	19.0	19,456	7,223	196
Advertising agencies	7311	(NA)	(NA)	13.9	13,608	5,649	132
Credit reporting and collection.........	732	14.6	6,377	7.5	6,151	2,163	98
Mailing, reproduction, stenographic [4]	733	154.5	20,990	32.1	18,339	5,522	235
Direct mail advertising services	7331	(NA)	(NA)	3.9	6,434	1,777	79
Services to dwellings and other buildings ...	734	460.5	23,586	57.6	19,003	9,164	818
Miscellaneous equipment rental and leasing .	735	52.4	22,782	24.8	21,778	4,905	200
Personnel supply services [4]	736	54.1	38,709	31.2	38,163	26,436	1,975
Help supply services	7363	(NA)	(NA)	19.0	33,587	24,075	1,842
Computer and data processing services [4] ...	737	223.6	104,650	59.1	101,073	35,598	886
Computer programming services	7371	(NA)	(NA)	23.3	23,548	10,890	243
Prepackaged software	7372	(NA)	(NA)	7.1	20,802	6,614	131
Computer integrated systems design.....	7373	(NA)	(NA)	5.0	14,805	4,151	98
Data processing and preparation	7374	(NA)	(NA)	7.3	20,200	6,796	230
Information retrieval services	7375	(NA)	(NA)	1.1	3,900	1,098	32
Computer maintenance and repair	7378	(NA)	(NA)	5.0	7,353	2,300	63
Detective and armored car services	7381	(NA)	(NA)	11.6	9,193	5,794	482
Photofinishing laboratories	7384	(NA)	(NA)	7.8	4,415	1,200	69
Auto repair, services, and parking [4]........	75	454.3	78,512	172.0	70,033	15,550	864
Automotive rentals, no drivers [4].........	751	22.2	20,906	10.6	20,574	2,757	132
Truck rental and leasing, no drivers	7513	(NA)	(NA)	4.3	7,445	1,029	42
Passenger car rental	7514	(NA)	(NA)	4.9	10,280	1,475	81
Automotive repair shops [4]	753	334.5	46,200	128.7	39,746	10,337	520
Top and body repair and paint shops	7532	(NA)	(NA)	35.0	12,262	3,445	166
General automotive repair shops	7538	(NA)	(NA)	64.8	17,773	4,406	230
Automotive services, except repair........	754	85.8	7,661	22.5	6,047	1,776	160
Miscellaneous repair services [4]...........	76	269.8	35,237	71.6	30,732	9,695	428
Electrical repair shops...........	762	71.6	11,875	21.2	10,667	3,707	162
Amusement and recreation services [4][6]......	78, 79, 84	691.7	103,556	114.8	92,915	25,357	1,382
Motion picture prod., distribution, services ...	781, 2	54.1	34,289	13.0	33,062	8,084	249
Motion picture theaters	783	8.1	5,879	6.9	5,817	788	105
Video tape rental	784	33.7	5,495	22.0	5,075	944	124
Producers, orchestras, entertainers [7]	792	288.6	13,054	10.1	8,625	2,895	69
Commercial sports	794	71.6	9,010	3.8	7,594	4,022	90
Physical fitness facilities..............	7991	29.6	4,135	9.2	3,824	1,043	130
Health services [4]	80	1,005.5	321,650	441.7	299,067	129,093	4,453
Offices and clinics of doctors of medicine ...	801	328.9	151,824	197.7	141,429	68,732	1,357
Offices and clinics of dentists	802	138.5	36,939	108.8	35,523	13,039	555
Offices, clinics of doctors of osteopathy....	803	14.2	4,008	8.7	3,638	1,650	47
Offices, clinics of other health practitioners [4] .	804	243.0	23,892	74.7	18,926	6,150	283
Offices and clinics of chiropractors	8041	41.4	6,555	27.3	5,918	1,652	85
Offices and clinics of optometrists......	8042	26.0	5,333	17.1	4,940	1,301	69
Nursing and personal care facilities	805	51.8	34,742	15.0	33,990	15,954	1,135
Hospitals [4].......................	806	(NA)	(NA)	1.4	31,083	10,556	428
General medical and surgical hospitals ...	8062	(NA)	(NA)	0.7	24,162	8,013	323
Medical and dental laboratories [4]........	807	29.4	15,172	16.0	14,460	4,804	178
Medical laboratories................	8071	(NA)	(NA)	8.4	12,511	3,980	139
Home health care services	808	(NA)	(NA)	8.0	10,414	4,853	342
Legal services	81	326.9	108,443	151.7	101,114	39,328	924
Selected educational services............	823, 4, 9	240.7	9,158	14.7	7,242	2,457	133
Social services [4]	83	617.4	18,201	59.1	13,349	5,466	505
Child day care services	835	524.4	8,708	35.3	5,270	2,388	283
Engineering and architectural services [4].....	871	225.4	83,033	68.1	78,770	32,745	825
Engineering services	8711	131.3	67,716	41.8	65,245	27,247	658
Architectural services..............	8712	71.6	12,682	17.9	11,244	4,408	122
Accounting, auditing, and bookkeeping......	872	325.5	37,191	79.1	34,038	14,001	521
Research and testing services [8]	873 ex. 8733	30.4	22,910	13.5	22,690	9,227	282
Management and public relations [4]........	874	735.8	72,490	72.1	57,321	23,371	644
Management services	8741	111.0	23,774	19.7	21,728	8,516	278
Management consulting services	8742	(NA)	(NA)	33.8	22,629	9,620	212

NA Not available. X Not applicable. [1] Based on 1987 Standard Industrial Classification; see text, Section 17, Business. [2] Represents the number of establishments in business at any time during year. [3] For pay period including March 12. [4] Includes other kinds of business, not shown separately. [5] Excludes membership lodging. [6] Includes motion pictures and museums. [7] Excludes motion picture producers. [8] Excludes noncommercial research organizations.

Source: U.S. Census Bureau, *1992 Census of Service Industries*, SC92-A-52 and SC92-N-1.

U.S. Census Bureau, Statistical Abstract of the United States: 1999

No. 1301. Service Industries—Annual Receipts of Taxable Firms: 1985 to 1997

[In billions of dollars (45.4 represents $45,400,000,000). Covers employer and nonemployer firms except as noted. Estimated]

Kind of business	1987 SIC code [1]	1985	1990	1993	1994	1995	1996	1997
Hotels and other lodging places [2]	70 ex. 704	45.4	64.2	74.1	79.6	84.1	88.9	94.0
Hotels and motels	701	43.5	62.0	71.5	76.7	81.1	85.8	90.7
Personal services [3]	72	36.7	54.7	62.6	66.1	70.6	73.9	76.9
Laundry, cleaning, and garment services	721	12.8	17.3	19.1	19.7	20.7	21.5	22.9
Beauty shops	7231	9.0	12.8	14.6	15.2	16.4	17.0	18.3
Barber shops	7241	1.2	1.4	1.5	1.6	1.6	1.6	1.8
Funeral service and crematories	726	5.2	6.8	8.2	8.6	9.4	10.0	10.6
Business services [3]	73	155.9	280.7	337.4	375.1	425.1	484.2	552.5
Advertising	731	14.9	22.0	23.4	24.2	27.1	30.6	34.2
Advertising agencies	7311	11.1	16.1	16.7	17.3	19.3	21.4	23.7
Credit reporting and collection	732	3.7	5.8	7.0	7.1	7.7	8.6	9.2
Mailing, reproduction, stenographic [3]	733	14.5	20.8	21.9	22.3	24.4	25.9	28.2
Direct mail advertising services	7331	3.8	7.0	7.3	7.3	7.5	8.2	9.3
Commercial art and graphic design	7336	(NA)	6.1	6.0	6.3	6.8	7.3	8.3
Services to dwellings and other buildings	734	13.3	22.3	23.5	25.7	27.5	30.6	33.9
Miscellaneous equipment rental and leasing	735	(NA)	23.1	24.6	26.4	29.5	30.9	32.7
Personnel supply services	736	14.7	32.5	42.1	48.0	59.4	68.6	80.1
Employment agencies	7361	3.7	6.2	5.6	6.5	7.7	9.0	11.8
Help supply services	7363	(NA)	26.4	36.5	41.4	51.6	59.6	68.2
Computer and data processing services [3]	737	45.1	88.1	117.9	135.6	156.4	184.4	215.5
Computer programming services	7371	(NA)	21.3	27.4	31.1	35.1	42.1	50.3
Prepackaged software	7372	(NA)	16.5	25.2	28.9	33.2	39.3	43.2
Computer integrated systems design	7373	(NA)	12.9	16.2	17.0	17.5	20.2	26.1
Data processing and preparation	7374	(NA)	17.8	23.7	29.2	35.6	41.0	43.4
Information retrieval services	7375	(NA)	3.5	4.3	4.6	5.3	6.9	9.1
Computer maintenance and repair	7378	(NA)	7.0	8.3	9.3	10.7	12.1	13.5
Miscellaneous business services [3]	738	(NA)	65.8	77.0	85.7	93.1	104.6	118.6
Detective and armored car services	7381	(NA)	9.0	10.3	10.8	11.9	13.5	14.5
Photofinishing laboratories	7384	4.3	5.6	6.4	6.6	6.8	7.3	7.7
Automotive repair, services, and parking [3]	75	51.7	73.7	84.3	91.9	99.2	106.7	111.8
Automotive rentals, no drivers [3]	751	14.6	20.8	22.7	24.4	26.6	29.4	30.1
Truck rental and leasing, without drivers	7513	5.5	8.5	8.1	9.0	10.1	11.2	11.0
Passenger car rental	7514	(NA)	9.0	11.4	12.2	12.9	14.5	15.2
Automotive repair shops [3]	753	30.5	43.5	49.7	54.6	58.6	62.0	65.3
Top & body repair & paint shops	7532	(NA)	13.5	15.0	16.4	17.8	18.7	19.8
General automotive repair shops	7538	(NA)	19.6	22.7	25.2	27.3	28.8	30.3
Automotive services, except repair	754	(NA)	6.5	8.3	9.3	10.4	11.5	12.2
Miscellaneous repair services	76	20.7	32.8	36.8	40.7	44.9	46.1	48.1
Electrical repair shops	762	(NA)	11.3	12.4	13.1	14.5	14.6	15.6
Motion pictures	78	21.5	40.0	49.8	53.5	57.2	60.3	63.0
Motion picture produc., distribution, allied services	781, 2	15.0	28.9	37.7	40.3	43.3	46.3	48.2
Motion picture theaters	783	3.8	6.1	6.0	6.2	6.5	7.0	7.6
Video tape rental	784	(NA)	6.0	6.2	7.0	7.4	7.0	7.2
Amusement and recreation services [3]	79	31.2	50.1	63.7	68.5	77.5	85.7	93.8
Producers, orchestras, entertainers	792	6.4	10.7	15.4	16.1	17.5	19.7	21.7
Commercial sports	794	5.0	8.6	9.9	11.1	13.1	14.6	16.7
Sports clubs, managers, & promoters	7941	(NA)	3.7	5.1	6.1	7.7	8.9	10.0
Amusement parks	7996	2.6	4.9	5.6	5.9	6.3	6.8	7.3
Membership sports and recreation clubs	7997	3.5	4.8	6.0	6.4	6.8	7.4	7.7
Health services [3]	80	147.4	271.2	335.1	351.4	376.3	398.4	421.3
Offices and clinics of doctors of medicine	801	72.1	128.9	154.2	159.6	168.0	172.9	179.9
Offices and clinics of dentists	802	20.6	31.5	38.9	41.7	44.9	47.4	51.0
Offices of other health practitioners	804	7.9	20.1	25.4	25.9	27.4	28.4	29.9
Offices and clinics of chiropractors	8041	2.7	5.5	6.9	6.8	6.7	7.0	7.3
Nursing and personal care facilities	805	17.5	30.2	36.2	37.3	41.1	44.3	46.9
Hospitals [4]	806	15.7	26.5	33.3	35.1	38.4	44.7	50.2
Medical and dental laboratories	807	5.4	12.0	15.1	15.4	15.5	16.1	16.5
Medical laboratories	8071	3.9	10.0	12.7	13.0	12.9	13.3	13.7
Home health care services	808	(NA)	7.6	13.2	15.4	18.0	19.6	19.2
Legal services	81	52.8	97.6	112.1	114.6	116.0	124.7	132.8
Social services	83	(NA)	15.5	20.1	22.5	24.9	27.7	30.5
Child day care services	8351	2.6	7.1	9.4	10.1	10.9	11.4	12.8
Residential care	8361	(NA)	4.6	5.4	5.9	6.4	7.2	7.7
Museums, botanical, zoological gardens	84	(NA)	0.1	0.2	0.2	0.2	0.3	0.3
Engineering and management services [3]	87	(NA)	198.4	222.9	235.4	263.8	292.3	322.2
Engineering services	8711	(NA)	64.8	67.1	68.1	73.9	80.3	88.5
Architectural services	8712	(NA)	13.0	13.5	14.8	16.5	18.4	19.0
Accounting, auditing, & bookkeeping	8721	21.2	32.6	39.8	42.6	48.8	54.4	59.3
Research and testing services [5]	873, ex. 87	(NA)	20.4	24.6	25.6	26.8	30.8	35.0
Management services	8741	(NA)	20.6	23.4	24.3	27.6	27.8	30.3
Management consulting services	8742	(NA)	28.9	34.5	38.5	46.4	53.4	61.7
Arrangement of passenger transportation	472	6.3	12.3	12.4	13.1	14.2	15.4	16.6
Real estate agents and managers	653	31.3	63.0	79.2	80.9	82.7	90.2	99.2

NA Not available.   [1] Standard Industrial Classification; see text, Section 17, Business.   [2] Excludes those on membership basis.   [3] Includes other kinds of businesses, not shown separately.   [4] Covers employer firms only.   [5] Excludes noncommercial research organizations.

Source: U.S. Census Bureau, *Current Business Reports, Service Annual Survey: 1997* (BS/97); and unpublished data.

No. 1302. Lodging Industry Summary: 1990 to 1996

Year	Average occupancy rate (percent)	Average room rate (dol.)	Room size of property	1996 Establishments	1996 Rooms (mil.)	Item	1996 Business traveler	1996 Leisure traveler
1990	63.3	57.96	Total	47,000	3.6	Typical night:		
1991	60.9	58.08				Made reservations .	91%	81%
1992	61.7	58.91	Percent:			Amount paid	$73.00	$67.60
1993	63.6	60.53	Under 75 rooms...	66.6	25.6			
1994	65.2	62.86	75-149 rooms	21.9	31.0	Length of stay:		
1995	65.5	65.81	150-299 rooms ...	8.5	22.3	One night	37%	46%
1996	65.2	69.66	300 or more	3.0	21.1	Two nights	23%	26%
						Three or more	39%	29%

Source: American Hotel & Motel Association, Washington, DC, *Lodging Industry Profile* (copyright).

No. 1303. Service Industries—Summary of Tax-Exempt Firms: 1992

[208.9 represents 208,900]. Covers establishments with payroll]

Kind of business	1987 SIC code [1]	Establishments [2] (1,000)	Revenues (mil. dol.)	Annual payroll (mil. dol.)	Paid employees [3] (1,000)
Firms exempt from Federal income tax [4] ..	(X)	208.9	446,256	186,672	8,109
Nursing and personal care facilities	805	5.9	15,220	7,591	498
Hospitals	806	5.7	279,735	126,202	4,566
Hospitals, excluding government.	806	3.6	203,360	87,062	3,252
Social services [4]	83	81.7	53,672	19,331	1,407
Individual and family social services	832	28.9	16,046	6,381	434
Residential care.	836	15.0	10,615	4,830	319
Business associations	861	14.3	11,068	3,157	102
Civic, social, and fraternal associations	864	41.8	13,176	3,657	355
Research and testing services	873	3.8	12,535	4,511	126

X Not applicable.   [1] Based on 1987 Standard Industrial Classification; see text, Section 17, Business.   [2] Represents the number of establishments in business at any time during year.   [3] For pay period including March 12.   [4] Includes other kinds of business, not shown separately.

Source: U.S. Census Bureau, *1992 Census of Service Industries*, SC92-A-52 and SC92-N-1.

No. 1304. Selected Service Industries—Revenue and Expenses for Tax-Exempt Firms: 1990 to 1997

[In billions of dollars (7.9 represents $7,900,000,000). Estimated from a sample of employer firms only. N.e.c. = Not elsewhere classified]

Kind of business	1987 SIC code [1]	Revenue 1990	Revenue 1996	Revenue 1997	Expenses 1990	Expenses 1996	Expenses 1997
Selected amusement and recreation services [2]	792, 7991, 7997, 7999	7.9	13.3	14.6	(NA)	12.5	13.3
Offices and clinics of doctors of medicine	801	12.9	26.2	28.4	12.5	25.5	28.4
Nursing and personal care facilities	805	12.1	18.5	19.7	(NA)	18.2	19.0
Hospitals	806	233.6	337.8	347.8	225.6	327.8	332.2
Home health care services.	808	3.9	8.0	8.1	3.6	7.9	7.9
Health and allied services, n.e.c.	809	5.3	10.4	10.8	5.2	9.9	10.1
Social services.	83	45.3	75.2	83.2	39.4	67.9	74.9
Individual and family social services	8322	13.0	22.3	24.1	12.6	20.9	23.7
Job training and related services	8331	4.9	6.8	7.4	4.5	6.7	6.9
Child day care services	8351	2.9	5.6	5.9	3.0	5.3	5.8
Residential care	8361	8.8	15.4	17.7	8.6	14.8	16.3
Selected membership organizations [3]	86 (pt)	31.5	48.9	51.1	28.6	45.4	47.4
Research and testing services	873	11.0	14.9	16.8	10.0	14.7	15.8

NA Not available.   [1] Standard Industrial Classification; see text, Section 17, Business.   [2] Covers theatrical producers, bands, orchestras, and entertainers (SIC 792); physical fitness facilities (SIC 7991); membership sports and recreation clubs (SIC 7997); and amusement and recreation services, not elsewhere classified (SIC 7999).   [3] Includes business associations (SIC 861); professional membership organizations (SIC 862); civic, social, and fraternal organizations (SIC 864); and other membership organizations, except labor unions and political and religious organizations (SIC 869).

Source: U.S. Census Bureau, *Current Business Reports, Service Annual Survey: 1997* (BS/97).

Domestic Trade and Services   785

No. 1305. Services—Establishments, Sales, Payroll, and Employees (NAICS Basis): 1997

[289,871 represents 289,871,000. Includes only establishments with payroll]

Kind of business	1997 NAICS code [1]	Establishments	Sales, revenue, receipts, and shipments ($1,000)	Annual payroll ($1,000)	Paid employees [2]
Real estate, rental & leasing, total............	53	289,871	249,518,839	43,559,512	1,761,179
Real estate..........................	531	222,540	162,824,225	29,702,597	1,170,943
Rental and leasing services	532	65,099	79,156,509	12,853,738	569,445
Lessors of intangible assets except copyrighted works...........................	533	2,232	7,538,105	1,003,177	20,791
Professional, scientific & technical............	54	621,605	608,627,386	233,322,967	5,416,055
Professional, scientific, & technical services.....	541	621,605	608,627,386	233,322,967	5,416,055
Management of companies & enterprises, total	55	(S)	(S)	(S)	(S)
Management of companies & enterprises	551	(S)	(S)	(S)	(S)
Administrative & support & waste:					
Management & remediation services, total......	56	276,588	302,757,446	137,703,968	7,439,208
Administrative & support services........	561	260,252	262,463,279	128,798,748	7,159,402
Waste management & remediation services ...	562	16,336	40,294,167	8,905,220	279,806
Educational services, total..................	61	40,996	20,934,202	6,628,868	332,490
Educational services	611	40,996	20,934,202	6,628,868	332,490
Health care & social assistance, total..........	62	645,841	889,598,804	379,307,741	13,616,915
Ambulatory health care services	621	454,853	347,752,717	155,174,906	4,405,829
Hospitals...........................	622	6,892	391,786,805	157,286,260	4,979,441
Nursing & residential care facilities..........	623	57,359	92,833,001	42,161,596	2,477,373
Social assistance	624	126,737	57,226,281	24,684,979	1,754,272
Arts, entertainment, & recreation, total	71	99,690	103,114,150	32,329,384	1,571,886
Performing arts, spectator sports, and related industries.........................	711	31,201	37,734,267	14,366,928	325,724
Museums, historical sites, & similar institutions...	712	5,564	6,541,300	1,822,095	91,061
Amusement, gambling, & recreation industries ...	713	62,925	58,838,583	16,140,361	1,155,101
Accomodation & foodservices, total	72	(S)	(S)	(S)	(S)
Accommodation	721	(S)	(S)	(S)	(S)
Foodservices & drinking places	722	(S)	(S)	(S)	(S)
Other services (except public administration), total ..	81	521,292	270,413,461	67,096,281	3,317,947
Repair & maintenance..................	811	236,139	108,634,315	30,490,634	1,300,417
Personal & laundry services	812	186,028	58,813,352	18,838,610	1,229,430
Religious, grantmaking, civic, professional and similar org........................	813	99,125	102,965,794	17,767,037	788,100

S Figure does not meet publication standards.   [1] Based on 1997 North American Industry Classification System, see text, Section 17, Business.   [2] Definition of paid employees varies among sectors.

Source: U.S. Census Bureau, *1997 Economic Census*, EC97X-CS1.

No. 1306. Comparative Statistics In Service Industries by Kind of Business: 1992 and 1997

[2,034 represents 2,034,000. Includes only establishments with payroll. N.e.c. = not elsewhere classified]

Kind of business	1987 SIC code [1]	Establishments (1,000)		Sales, receipts, revenue/shipments (bil. dol.)		Annual payroll (bil. dol.)		Paid employees [2] (1,000)	
		1992	1997	1992	1997	1992	1997	1992	1997
Service industries, total ...	(G)	2,034	2,307	1,649	2,453	639	922	27,399	34,224
Hotels, rooming houses, camps, and other lodging places	70	52	(S)	70	(S)	20	(S)	1,507	(S)
Personal services............	72	197	205	43	53	14	18	1,218	1,311
Business services............	73	307	398	275	550	109	215	5,542	8,750
Automotive repair services, and parking....................	75	172	192	70	101	16	23	864	1,110
Miscellaneous repair services....	76	72	67	31	38	10	12	428	427
Motion pictures	78	42	46	44	64	10	14	478	569
Amusement & recreation services .	79	84	97	58	95	19	30	1,120	1,529
Health services	80	465	499	623	815	275	347	10,017	11,370
Legal services	81	153	168	102	124	40	48	945	978
Educational services..........	82	21	27	10	17	3	6	196	256
Social services.............	83	141	162	67	94	25	34	1,912	2,273
Museums, art galleries, & botanical & zoological gardens ..	84	4	5	3	6	1	2	70	89
Membership organizations	86	72	66	36	47	10	13	603	597
Eng. acctg, research, mgt, & rel. serv. (exc. noncomm research org.)........................	87	238	297	208	331	85	129	2,419	3,139
Services, n.e.c.	89	15	(S)	8	(S)	3	(S)	81	(S)

S Figure does not meet publication standards.   [1] See footnote 1 in Table 1300.   [2] Definition of paid employees varies among sectors.

Source: U.S. Census Bureau, *1997 Economic Census*, EC97X-CS1.

Section 28
Foreign Commerce and Aid

This section presents data on the flow of goods, services, and capital between the United States and other countries; changes in official reserve assets of the United States; international investments; and foreign assistance programs.

The Bureau of Economic Analysis publishes current figures on U.S. international transactions and the U.S. international investment position in its monthly *Survey of Current Business*. Statistics for the foreign aid programs are presented by the Agency for International Development (AID) in its annual *U.S. Overseas Loans and Grants and Assistance from International Organizations* and by the Department of Agriculture in its *Foreign Agricultural Trade of the United States*.

The principal source of merchandise import and export data is the U.S. Census Bureau. Current data are presented monthly in *U.S. International Trade in Goods and Services* report Series FT 900. Census Bureau *Catalog & Guide* and the *Guide to Foreign Trade Statistics* lists the Bureau's monthly and annual products and services in this field. In addition, the International Trade Administration and the Bureau of Economic Analysis present summary as well as selected commodity and country data for U.S. foreign trade in the *U.S. Foreign Trade Highlights* and the *Survey of Current Business*, respectively. The merchandise trade data in the latter source include balance of payments adjustments to the Census Bureau data. The Treasury Department's *Monthly Treasury Statement of Receipts and Outlays of the United States Government* contains information on import duties.

International accounts—The international transactions tables (Nos. 1307 to 1309) show, for given time periods, the transfer of goods, services, grants, and financial assets and liabilities between the

United States and the rest of the world. The international investment position table (No. 1310) presents, for specific dates, the value of U.S. investments abroad and of foreign investments in the United States. The movement of foreign and U.S. capital as presented in the balance of payments is not the only factor affecting the total value of foreign investments. Among the other factors are changes in the valuation of assets or liabilities, including changes in prices of securities, defaults, expropriations, and write-offs.

Direct investment abroad means the ownership or control, directly or indirectly, by one person of 10 percent or more of the voting securities of an incorporated business enterprise or an equivalent interest in an unincorporated business enterprise. Direct investment position is the value of U.S. parents' claims on the equity of and receivables due from foreign affiliates, less foreign affiliates' receivables due from their U.S. parents. Income consists of parents' shares in the earnings of their affiliates plus net interest received by parents on intercompany accounts, less withholding taxes on dividends and interest.

Foreign aid—Foreign assistance is divided into three major categories—grants (military supplies and services and other grants), credits, and other assistance (through net accumulation of foreign currency claims from the sale of agricultural commodities). *Grants* are transfers for which no payment is expected (other than a limited percentage of the foreign currency "counterpart" funds generated by the grant), or which at most involve an obligation on the part of the receiver to extend aid to the United States or other countries to achieve a common objective. *Credits* are loan disbursements or transfers under other agreements which give rise to specific obligations to repay, over a period of years, usually with interest. All known returns to the U.S. Government stemming from grants and credits (reverse grants, returns of grants, and payments of principal) are taken into account in net grants and net credits, but no allowance is made for interest or commissions. *Other assistance* represents the transfer of U.S. farm products in exchange for foreign currencies (plus, since enactment of Public Law 87-128, currency claims from principal and interest collected on credits extended under the farm products program), less the Government's disbursements of the currencies as grants, credits, or for purchases. The net acquisition of currencies represents net transfers of resources to foreign countries under the agricultural programs, in addition to those classified as grants or credits.

The basic instrument for extending military aid to friendly nations has been the Mutual Defense Assistance Program authorized by the Congress in 1949. Prior to 1952, economic and technical aid was authorized in the Foreign Assistance Act of 1948, the 1950 Act for International Development, and other legislation which set up programs for specific countries. In 1952, these economic, technical, and military aid programs were combine under the Mutual Security Act, which in turn was followed by the Foreign Assistance Act passed in 1961. Appropriations to provide military assistance were also made in the Department of Defense Appropriation Act (rather than the Foreign Assistance Appropriation Act) beginning in 1966 for certain countries in Southeast Asia and in other legislation concerning program for specific countries (such as Israel). Figures on activity under the Foreign Assistance Act as reported in the *Foreign Grants and Credits* series differ from data published by AID or its immediate predecessors, due largely to differences in reporting, timing, and treatment of particular items.

Exports—The Census Bureau compiles export data primarily from Shipper's Export Declarations required to be filed with customs officials for shipments leaving the United States. They include U.S. exports

under mutual security programs and exclude shipments to U.S. Armed Forces for their own use.

The value reported in the export statistics is generally equivalent to a free alongside ship (f.a.s.) value at the U.S. port of export, based on the transaction price, including inland freight, insurance, and other charges incurred in placing the merchandise alongside the carrier at the U.S. port of exportation. This value, as defined, excludes the cost of loading merchandise aboard the exporting carrier and also excludes freight, insurance, and any other charges or transportation and other costs beyond the U.S. port of exportation. The country of destination is defined as the country of ultimate destination or country where the merchandise is to be consumed, further processed, or manufactured, as known to the shipper at the time of exportation. When ultimate destination is not known, the shipment is statistically credited to the last country to which the shipper knows the merchandise will be shipped in the same form as exported.

For certain "low-valued" shipments, the export statistics include estimates based upon selected samples of such shipments. The dollar value of the "low-valued" shipments have varied. For instance, effective January 1987 through September 1989, data are estimated for shipments valued under $1,501; from October 1989 through December 1989, data are estimated for shipments valued under $2,501 to all countries.

Effective January 1990, the United States began substituting Canadian import statistics for U.S. exports to Canada. As a result of the data exchange between the United States and Canada, the United States has adopted the Canadian import exemption level for its export statistics based on shipments to Canada.

Data are estimated for shipments valued under $2,501 to all countries, except Canada, using factors based on the ratios of low-valued shipments to individual country totals. These shipments represent slightly less than 2.5 percent of the

788   Foreign Commerce and Aid

monthly value of U.S. exports to those countries. Data are estimated for shipments reported on Canadian import documents which total less than $900 (Canadian). Such shipments represent 2 percent of the monthly value of U.S. exports to Canada.

Prior to 1989, exports were based on Schedule B, Statistical Classification of Domestic and Foreign Commodities Exported from the United States. These statistics were retabulated and published using Schedule E, Standard International Trade Classification, Revision 2. Beginning in 1989, Schedule B classifications were based on the Harmonized System and made to coincide with the Standard International Trade Classification, Revision 3. This revision will affect the comparability of most export series beginning with the 1989 data for commodities.

Imports—The Census Bureau compiles import data from various customs forms required to be filed with customs officials. Data on import values are presented on two bases in this section: The c.i.f. (cost, insurance, and freight) and the customs import value (as appraised by the U.S. Customs Service in accordance with legal requirements of the Tariff Act of 1930, as amended). This latter valuation, primarily used for collection of import duties, frequently does not reflect the actual transaction value. Country of origin is defined as country where the merchandise was grown, mined, or manufactured. If country of origin is unknown, country of shipment is reported.

Imports are classified either as "General imports" or "Imports for consumption." *General imports* are a combination of entries for immediate consumption, entries into customs bonded warehouses, and entries into U.S. Foreign Trade Zones, thus generally reflecting total arrivals of merchandise. *Imports for consumption* are a combination of entries for immediate consumption, withdrawals from warehouses for consumption, and entries of merchandise into U.S. customs territory from U.S. Foreign Trade Zones, thus generally reflecting the total of the commodities entered into U.S. consumption channels.

Since July 1953, the import statistics include estimates, not classified by commodity, for certain low-valued shipments. For instance, from January 1985 through September 1989, import statistics include estimates for shipments valued under $1,001. Effective October 1989, import statistics are fully compiled on shipments valued over $1,250 or, under certain textile programs, for any article which must be reported on a formal entry. Value data for shipments valued under $1,251 and not required to be reported on formal entries are estimated for individual countries using factors based on the ratios of low-valued shipments to individual country totals for past periods. The estimated low-valued shipments generally amount to slightly less than 4 percent of the import total.

Prior to 1989, imports were based on the Tariff Schedule of the United States Annotated. The statistics were retabulated and published using Schedule A, Standard International Trade Classification, Revision 2. Beginning in 1989, the statistics are based on the Harmonized Tariff Schedule of the United States, which coincides with the Standard International Trade Classification, Revision 3. This revision will affect the comparability of most import series beginning with the 1989 data.

Area coverage—Except as noted, the geographic area covered by the export and import trade statistics is the United States Customs area (includes the 50 states, the District of Columbia, and Puerto Rico), the U.S. Virgin Islands (effective January 1981), and U.S. Foreign Trade Zones (effective July 1982). Data for selected tables and total values for 1980 have been revised to reflect the U.S. Virgin Islands' trade with foreign countries, where possible.

Statistical reliability—For a discussion of statistical collection and estimation, sampling procedures, and measures of statistical reliability applicable to Census Bureau data, see Appendix III.

U.S. Census Bureau, Statistical Abstract of the United States: 1999

No. 1307. U.S. International Transactions, by Type of Transaction: 1980 to 1998

[In millions of dollars (344,440 represents $344,400,000). Minus sign (-) indicates debits]

Type of transaction	1980	1985	1990	1991	1992	1993	1994	1995	1996	1997	1998
Exports of goods and services and income receipts	**344,440**	**387,806**	**708,135**	**729,513**	**748,431**	**776,404**	**868,041**	**1,005,715**	**1,074,425**	**1,197,206**	**1,192,231**
Exports of goods and services	271,834	289,070	536,058	579,956	615,909	641,783	702,073	793,482	849,806	938,543	933,907
Goods, balance of payments basis	224,250	215,915	389,307	416,913	440,352	456,832	502,398	575,845	612,057	678,715	670,246
Services	47,584	73,155	146,751	163,043	175,557	184,951	199,675	217,637	237,749	258,828	263,661
Transfers under U.S. military agency sales contracts	9,029	8,718	9,932	11,135	12,387	13,471	12,787	13,395	15,736	17,561	17,155
Travel	10,588	17,762	43,007	48,385	54,742	57,875	58,417	63,395	69,751	73,301	71,250
Passenger fares	2,591	4,411	15,298	15,854	16,618	16,528	16,997	18,909	20,413	20,789	19,996
Other transportation	11,618	14,674	22,042	22,631	21,531	21,958	23,754	26,081	26,074	27,006	25,518
Royalties and license fees	7,085	6,678	16,634	17,819	20,841	21,695	26,712	30,289	32,470	33,781	36,808
Other private services	6,276	20,035	39,170	46,531	48,597	52,541	60,121	63,502	72,412	85,566	92,116
U.S. Government miscellaneous services	398	878	668	690	841	883	887	818	893	824	818
Income receipts	72,606	98,736	172,078	149,558	132,523	134,621	165,968	212,233	224,619	258,663	258,324
Income receipts on U.S.-owned assets abroad	72,606	98,736	170,906	148,268	131,098	133,187	164,425	210,472	222,863	256,861	256,467
Direct investment receipts	37,146	35,604	66,309	59,062	58,005	67,708	77,874	95,991	103,314	115,795	102,846
Other private receipts	32,898	57,633	94,072	81,186	65,977	60,353	82,423	109,768	114,958	137,507	150,001
U.S. Government receipts	2,562	5,499	10,525	8,019	7,115	5,126	4,128	4,713	4,591	3,559	3,620
Compensation of employees	(NA)	(NA)	1,172	1,290	1,425	1,434	1,543	1,761	1,756	1,802	1,857
Imports of goods and services and income payments	**-333,774**	**-484,106**	**-759,646**	**-735,048**	**-763,187**	**-823,167**	**-950,529**	**-1,083,844**	**-1,161,533**	**-1,298,705**	**-1,368,718**
Imports of goods and services	-291,241	-410,950	-615,996	-609,440	-652,934	-711,722	-800,468	-891,021	-954,124	-1,043,273	-1,098,189
Goods, balance of payments basis	-249,750	-338,088	-498,337	-490,981	-536,458	-589,441	-668,590	-749,574	-803,327	-876,366	-917,178
Services	-41,491	-72,862	-117,659	-118,459	-116,476	-122,281	-131,878	-141,447	-150,797	-166,907	-181,011
Direct defense expenditures	-10,851	-13,108	-17,531	-16,409	-13,835	-12,086	-10,217	-10,043	-11,029	-11,698	-12,841
Travel	-10,397	-24,558	-37,349	-35,322	-38,552	-40,713	-43,782	-44,916	-48,048	-52,051	-56,105
Passenger fares	-3,607	-6,444	-10,531	-10,012	-10,603	-11,410	-13,062	-14,663	-15,818	-18,138	-19,797
Other transportation	-11,790	-15,643	-24,966	-24,975	-23,767	-24,524	-26,019	-27,034	-27,403	-28,959	-30,457
Royalties and license fees	-724	-1,170	-3,135	-4,035	-5,161	-5,032	-5,852	-6,919	-7,837	-9,390	-11,292
Other private services	-2,909	-10,203	-22,229	-25,590	-22,296	-26,261	-30,386	-35,249	-37,975	-43,909	-47,670
U.S. Government miscellaneous services	-1,214	-1,735	-1,919	-2,116	-2,263	-2,255	-2,560	-2,623	-2,687	-2,762	-2,849
Income payments	-42,532	-73,156	-143,649	-121,608	-110,253	-111,445	-150,061	-192,823	-207,409	-255,432	-270,529
Income payments on foreign-owned assets in the U.S.	-42,532	-73,156	-140,185	-121,582	-105,501	-106,313	-144,109	-186,560	-201,109	-248,676	-263,423
Direct investment payments	-8,635	-7,282	-3,907	1,742	-3,341	-9,133	-23,467	-32,186	-35,568	-46,575	-43,441
Other private payments	-21,214	-42,745	-95,508	-82,452	-63,079	-57,804	-76,450	-97,004	-97,901	-114,051	-128,863
U.S. Government payments	-12,684	-23,129	-40,770	-40,872	-39,081	-39,376	-44,192	-57,370	-67,640	-88,050	-91,119
Compensation of employees	(NA)	(NA)	-3,464	-4,026	-4,752	-5,132	-5,952	-6,263	-6,300	-6,756	-7,106
Unilateral current transfers, net	**-8,349**	**-22,762**	**-27,821**	**9,819**	**-35,873**	**-38,522**	**-39,192**	**-35,437**	**-42,187**	**-41,966**	**-44,075**
U.S. Government grants	-5,486	-11,268	-10,359	29,193	-16,320	-17,036	-14,978	-11,190	-15,337	-12,386	-13,057
U.S. Government pensions and other transfers	-1,818	-2,138	-3,224	-3,775	-4,043	-4,104	-4,556	-3,451	-4,466	-4,239	-4,350
Private remittances and other transfers	-1,044	-9,357	-14,238	-15,599	-15,510	-17,383	-19,658	-20,796	-22,384	-25,341	-26,668

U.S. Census Bureau, Statistical Abstract of the United States: 1999

Type of transaction	1980	1985	1990	1991	1992	1993	1994	1995	1996	1997	1998
Capital account transactions, net	(NA)	315	-6,579	-4,479	612	-88	-469	372	672	292	617
U.S. assets abroad, net (increase/financial outflow (-))	-85,815	-44,946	-81,570	-64,732	-74,877	-201,014	-176,586	-330,675	-380,762	-465,296	-292,818
U.S. official reserve assets, net	-7,003	-3,858	-2,158	5,763	3,901	-1,379	5,346	-9,742	6,668	-1,010	-6,784
Gold	(NA)	(NA)	(NA)	(NA)	(NA)	(NA)	(NA)	(NA)	(NA)	(NA)	(NA)
Special drawing rights	1,136	-897	-192	-177	2,316	-537	-441	-808	370	-350	-149
Reserve position in the International Monetary Fund	-1,667	908	731	-367	-2,692	-44	494	-2,466	-1,280	-3,575	-5,118
Foreign currencies	-6,472	-3,869	-2,697	6,307	4,277	-797	5,293	-6,468	7,578	2,915	-1,517
U.S. Govt. assets, other than official reserve assets, net	-5,162	-2,821	2,317	2,924	-1,667	-351	-390	-984	-989	68	-429
U.S. credits and other long-term assets	-9,860	-7,657	-8,410	-12,879	-7,408	-6,311	-5,383	-4,859	-5,025	-5,417	-4,676
Repayments on U.S. credits and other long-term assets	4,456	4,719	10,856	16,776	5,807	6,270	5,088	4,125	3,930	5,438	4,102
U.S. foreign currency holdings and U.S. short-term assets, net	242	117	-130	-974	-66	-310	-95	-250	106	47	145
U.S. private assets, net	-73,651	-38,268	-81,729	-73,419	-77,111	-199,284	-181,542	-319,949	-386,441	-464,354	-285,605
Direct investments abroad	-19,222	-19,121	-37,519	-38,233	-48,733	-84,412	-80,697	-99,481	-92,694	-109,955	-132,829
Foreign securities	-3,568	-7,481	-28,765	-45,673	-49,166	-146,253	-60,309	-100,074	-115,859	-89,174	-102,817
U.S. claims on unaffiliated foreigners reported by U.S. nonbanking concerns	-4,023	-10,342	-27,824	11,097	-387	766	-36,336	-45,286	-86,333	-120,403	-25,041
U.S. claims reported by U.S. banks, n.i.e. [1]	-46,838	-1,323	12,379	-610	21,175	30,615	-4,200	-75,108	-91,555	-144,822	-24,918
Foreign assets in the U.S., net (increase/financial inflow (+))	62,612	146,452	142,028	111,332	171,815	283,230	307,306	467,552	574,847	751,661	502,637
Foreign official assets in the U.S., net	15,497	-1,119	33,910	17,389	40,477	71,753	39,583	109,880	127,390	18,119	-21,684
U.S. Government securities	11,895	-1,139	30,243	16,147	22,403	53,014	36,827	72,712	120,679	-2,161	-3,625
U.S. Treasury securities	9,708	-838	29,576	14,846	18,454	48,952	30,750	68,977	115,671	-6,690	-9,957
Other	2,187	-301	667	1,301	3,949	4,062	6,077	3,735	5,008	4,529	6,332
Other U.S. Government liabilities	615	844	1,868	1,367	2,191	1,313	1,564	-105	-316	-1,798	-3,113
U.S. liabilities reported by U.S. banks, n.i.e. [1]	-159	645	3,385	1,484	16,571	14,841	3,665	34,008	5,704	22,286	-11,469
Other foreign official assets	3,145	-1,469	-1,586	1,359	-688	2,585	-2,473	3,265	1,323	-208	-3,477
Other foreign assets in the U.S., net	47,115	147,570	108,118	93,944	131,338	211,477	267,723	357,672	447,457	733,542	524,321
Direct investments in U.S.	16,918	20,079	48,951	23,695	20,975	52,552	47,438	59,644	88,977	109,264	193,375
U.S. Treasury securities	2,645	20,433	-2,534	18,826	37,131	24,381	34,274	99,548	154,996	146,433	46,155
U.S. securities other than U.S. Treasury securities	5,457	50,962	1,592	35,144	30,043	80,092	56,971	96,367	130,240	196,258	218,026
U.S. currency flows	4,500	5,200	18,800	15,400	13,400	18,900	23,400	12,300	17,362	24,782	16,622
U.S. liabilities to unaffiliated foreigners reported by U.S. nonbanking concerns	6,852	9,851	45,133	-3,115	13,573	10,489	1,302	59,637	39,404	107,779	9,412
U.S. liabilities reported by U.S. banks, n.i.e. [1]	10,743	41,045	-3,824	3,994	16,216	25,063	104,338	30,176	16,478	149,026	40,731
Statistical discrepancy (sum of above items with sign reversed)	20,886	17,242	25,454	-46,405	-46,921	3,157	-8,571	-23,683	-65,462	-143,192	10,126
Balance on goods	-25,500	-122,173	-109,030	-74,068	-96,106	-132,609	-166,192	-173,729	-191,270	-196,651	-246,932
Balance on services	6,093	294	29,091	44,584	59,081	62,669	67,797	76,190	86,952	91,921	82,650
Balance on income	30,073	25,580	28,429	23,950	22,269	23,176	15,907	19,410	17,210	3,231	-12,205
Balance on current account	2,317	-119,062	-79,332	4,284	-50,629	-85,286	-121,680	-113,566	-129,295	-143,465	-220,562

NA Not available. [1] Not included elsewhere.

Source: U.S. Bureau of Economic Analysis, *Survey of Current Business*, July 1999.

No. 1308. U.S. Balances on International Transactions, by Area and Selected Country: 1997 and 1998

[In millions of dollars (-196,651 represents -$196,651,000,000). Minus sign (-) indicates debits]

Area or country	1997, balance on—				1998, balance on—			
	Goods [1]	Services	Income	Current account	Goods [1]	Services	Income	Current account
All areas	-196,651	91,921	3,231	-143,465	-246,932	82,650	-12,205	-220,562
Western Europe.............	-22,806	22,007	-14,551	-15,785	-34,909	21,401	-17,504	-31,336
European Economic	-21,292	19,821	-14,417	-15,253	-30,155	20,348	-19,564	-28,679
Belgium-Luxembourg	3,046	1,066	-682	3,346	5,496	1,048	-213	6,263
France................	-4,802	3,006	-125	-2,083	-6,483	2,276	-336	-4,748
Germany	-18,813	2,147	-640	-16,489	-23,339	2,382	-900	-21,049
Italy	-10,456	769	1,724	-8,276	-12,031	886	2,342	-9,104
Netherlands	12,070	3,910	6,950	22,871	11,271	3,404	6,679	21,298
United Kingdom	3,415	2,557	-26,653	-19,404	3,483	4,107	-30,798	-21,809
Eastern Europe	-733	1,306	112	-2,258	-3,534	1,009	72	-5,811
Canada	-17,989	6,846	12,758	1,079	-18,996	4,372	10,961	-4,276
Latin America, other Western Hemisphere..............	-5,800	12,842	9,384	4,895	-4,131	14,970	7,511	5,858
Mexico	-15,569	739	-489	-19,921	-17,066	1,577	-1,418	-21,697
Venezuela	-6,894	2,048	47	-4,887	-2,718	2,425	-297	-678
Japan [2]	-57,059	19,544	-25,214	-62,886	-65,255	16,540	-26,443	-75,354
Other Asia and Africa	-99,294	24,472	-110	-90,719	-126,510	20,573	-6,242	-128,923
Australia	7,030	2,560	5,400	14,857	6,403	1,846	3,141	11,253
South Africa............	478	254	538	1,043	562	235	722	1,292
International and unallocated	(NA)	2,344	15,452	7,352	(NA)	1,939	16,299	8,027

NA Not available. [1] Adjusted to balance of payments basis; excludes exports under U.S. military sales contracts and imports under direct defense expenditures. [2] Includes Ryukyu Islands.
Source: U.S. Bureau of Economic Analysis, *Survey of Current Business*, July 1999 issue.

No. 1309. Private Services Transaction, by Type of Service and Country: 1990 to 1997

[In millions of dollars (137,322 represents $137,322,000,000)]

Type of service and country	Exports				Imports			
	1990	1995	1996	1997	1990	1995	1996	1997
Total private services	137,322	204,229	224,213	239,215	100,571	133,355	142,261	156,236
Travel.........................	43,007	63,395	69,751	73,268	37,349	44,916	48,048	51,220
Overseas.....................	30,806	54,331	59,905	63,014	28,929	35,281	37,406	39,876
Canada	7,093	6,207	6,842	6,824	3,541	4,319	4,670	4,901
Mexico.......................	5,108	2,857	3,004	3,430	4,879	5,316	5,972	6,443
Passenger fares	15,298	18,909	20,413	20,895	10,531	14,663	15,818	18,235
Other transportation..............	22,042	26,081	26,074	26,911	24,966	27,034	27,403	28,949
Freight......................	8,379	11,273	11,146	11,773	15,046	16,455	16,539	17,644
Port services.................	13,662	14,809	14,929	15,137	9,920	10,579	10,864	11,305
Royalties and license fees	16,634	30,289	32,823	33,676	3,135	6,919	7,854	9,411
Other private services	40,341	65,555	75,152	84,465	24,590	39,823	43,138	48,421
Affiliated services.............	13,622	20,791	23,779	26,336	9,118	14,215	16,668	18,324
Unaffilated services...........	26,719	44,764	51,374	58,128	15,472	25,607	26,469	30,098
Education	5,126	7,515	7,888	8,278	658	1,125	1,247	1,347
Financial services...........	4,417	7,029	8,382	11,064	2,475	2,472	2,995	3,906
Insurance, net	230	1,296	1,971	2,391	1,910	5,360	3,773	5,208
Telecommunications	2,735	3,228	3,270	3,771	5,583	7,305	8,304	8,113
Business, professional, and technical services	7,752	16,064	19,678	21,304	2,093	4,822	5,550	6,571
Advertising...............	130	425	551	581	243	833	976	863
Computer and data processing services.................	1,031	1,340	1,634	1,616	44	126	139	270
Management, consulting, and public relations services	354	1,489	1,680	2,139	135	465	593	782
Legal services	451	1,667	1,973	2,085	111	469	580	568
Construction, engineering, architectural, & mining services .	867	2,550	3,560	4,084	170	345	489	346
Canada.......................	15,753	18,032	19,938	20,501	9,307	11,467	12,794	14,063
Europe........................	48,608	73,637	82,348	85,986	40,030	53,247	54,280	61,847
France......................	5,590	8,022	8,965	9,438	4,192	6,012	5,977	6,883
Germany	7,431	12,793	13,579	13,488	6,851	7,662	7,812	8,015
Italy........................	3,305	4,557	4,913	5,015	3,481	3,769	3,549	3,720
Netherlands	3,279	6,143	7,165	7,650	1,945	3,220	3,263	3,549
Switzerland..................	(NA)	3,859	4,337	4,238	(NA)	2,311	2,627	2,761
United Kingdom..............	13,064	18,748	20,433	23,630	11,626	16,224	16,424	21,246
Latin America and other Western Hemisphere	21,815	32,240	35,129	42,154	20,299	27,189	30,001	32,509
Brazil.......................	(NA)	5,066	5,258	6,401	(NA)	1,180	1,446	1,781
Mexico......................	7,967	7,392	8,138	9,334	8,279	10,780	11,769	13,120
Venezuela	1,283	2,512	2,417	2,760	662	708	777	733
Other countries................	45,822	75,204	80,889	84,713	28,224	39,170	42,225	45,248
Australia....................	3,303	4,327	4,690	5,001	2,300	2,161	2,605	2,635
Japan	21,230	33,346	33,657	34,002	10,564	13,599	13,009	14,253
Korea, Republic of	(NA)	5,727	7,374	6,885	(NA)	3,618	4,163	4,541
Taiwan......................	(NA)	4,440	4,053	4,625	(NA)	2,888	2,738	3,380
Int'l organizations and unallocated	5,324	5,116	5,909	5,866	2,711	2,286	2,956	2,574

NA Not available.
Source: U.S. Bureau of Economic Analysis, *Survey of Current Business*, October 1998.

792 Foreign Commerce and Aid

No. 1310. International Investment Position: 1990 to 1998

[In millions of dollars (-240,553 represents -240,553,000,000). Estimates for end of year; subject to considerable error due to nature of basic data]

Type of investment	1990	1992	1993	1994	1995	1996	1997	1998
U.S. net international investment position:								
Current cost	-240,553	-421,096	-295,261	-300,480	-500,170	-578,705	-968,208	-1,239,168
Market value	-166,846	-454,605	-180,373	-174,290	-422,617	-547,493	-1,066,262	-1,537,466
U.S.-owned assets abroad:								
Current cost	2,149,982	2,298,640	2,718,424	2,956,788	3,405,761	3,958,502	4,508,626	4,930,896
Market value	2,291,734	2,464,196	3,055,316	3,276,086	3,869,663	4,544,502	5,288,892	5,947,983
U.S. official reserve assets	174,664	147,435	164,945	163,394	176,061	160,739	134,836	146,006
Gold	102,406	87,168	102,556	100,110	101,279	96,698	75,929	75,291
Special drawing rights	10,989	8,503	9,039	10,039	11,037	10,312	10,027	10,603
Reserve position in IMF	9,076	11,759	11,818	12,030	14,649	15,435	18,071	24,111
Foreign currencies	52,193	40,005	41,532	41,215	49,096	38,294	30,809	36,001
U.S. Government assets, other	81,993	80,722	81,029	80,123	81,095	82,046	81,960	82,382
U.S. loans and other long-term assets	81,365	79,087	79,106	77,814	78,548	79,637	79,607	80,179
Repayable in dollars	80,040	77,987	78,100	77,336	78,120	79,261	79,273	79,874
Other	1,325	1,100	1,006	478	428	376	334	305
U.S. foreign currency holdings and short-term assets	628	1,635	1,923	2,309	2,547	2,409	2,353	2,203
U.S. private assets:								
Current cost	1,893,325	2,070,483	2,472,450	2,713,271	3,148,605	3,715,717	4,291,830	4,702,508
Market value	2,035,077	2,236,039	2,809,342	3,032,569	3,612,507	4,301,717	5,072,096	5,719,595
Direct investments abroad:								
Current cost	590,010	633,074	690,655	748,505	843,253	940,243	1,004,228	1,123,441
Market value	731,762	798,630	1,027,547	1,067,803	1,307,155	1,526,243	1,784,494	2,140,528
Foreign securities	342,313	515,083	853,528	948,668	1,169,636	1,467,985	1,739,400	1,968,956
Bonds	144,717	200,817	309,666	321,208	392,827	465,057	538,400	561,826
Corporate stocks	197,596	314,266	543,862	627,460	776,809	1,002,928	1,201,000	1,407,130
U.S. claims on unaffiliated foreigners [1]	265,315	254,303	242,022	322,980	367,567	449,978	562,396	596,222
U.S. claims reported by U.S. banks [2]	695,687	668,023	686,245	693,118	768,149	857,511	985,806	1,013,889
Foreign-owned assets in the United States:								
Current cost	2,390,535	2,719,736	3,013,685	3,257,268	3,905,931	4,537,207	5,476,834	6,170,064
Market value	2,458,580	2,918,801	3,235,689	3,450,376	4,292,280	5,091,995	6,355,154	7,485,449
Foreign official assets in the U.S.	373,293	437,263	509,422	535,217	671,710	799,033	835,709	836,053
U.S. Government securities	291,228	329,317	381,687	407,152	497,776	610,469	614,530	620,249
U.S. Treasury securities	285,911	322,600	373,050	396,887	482,773	590,704	589,792	588,987
Other	5,317	6,717	8,637	10,265	15,003	19,765	24,738	31,262
Other U.S. Government liabilities	17,243	20,801	22,113	23,678	23,573	23,257	21,459	18,346
U.S. liabilities reported by U.S. banks [2]	39,880	54,967	69,721	73,386	107,394	113,098	135,384	123,915
Other foreign official assets	24,942	32,178	35,901	31,001	42,967	52,209	64,336	73,543
Other foreign assets in the U.S:								
Current cost	2,017,242	2,282,473	2,504,263	2,722,051	3,234,221	3,738,174	4,641,125	5,334,011
Market value	2,085,287	2,481,538	2,726,267	2,915,159	3,620,570	4,292,962	5,519,445	6,649,396
Direct investments:								
Current cost	471,556	497,112	546,394	564,745	619,377	674,330	764,045	878,717
Market value	539,601	696,177	768,398	757,853	1,005,726	1,229,118	1,642,365	2,194,102
U.S. Treasury securities	152,452	197,739	221,501	235,684	358,537	502,562	662,228	727,344
U.S. currency	85,933	114,804	133,734	157,185	169,484	186,846	211,628	228,250
U.S. securities other than U.S. Treasury securities	460,644	599,447	696,449	739,695	971,356	1,199,461	1,578,694	2,021,820
Corporate and other bonds	238,903	299,287	355,822	368,077	481,214	588,044	715,196	900,749
Corporate stocks	221,741	300,160	340,627	371,618	490,142	611,417	863,498	1,121,071
U.S. liabilities to unaffiliated foreigners [1]	213,406	220,666	229,038	239,817	300,424	346,727	453,555	460,787
U.S. liabilities reported by U.S. banks [2]	633,251	652,705	677,147	784,925	815,043	828,248	970,975	1,017,093

[1] Reported by U.S. nonbanking concerns.   [2] Not included elsewhere.

Source: U.S. Bureau of Economic Analysis, *Survey of Current Business*, July 1999.

No. 1311. U.S. Reserve Assets: 1990 to 1998

[In billions of dollars ($83.3 represents $83,300,000,000). As of end of year, except as indicated]

Type	1990	1991	1992	1993	1994	1995	1996	1997	1998
Total	83.3	77.7	71.3	73.4	74.3	85.8	75.1	70.0	81.8
Gold stock [1]	11.1	11.1	11.1	11.1	11.1	11.1	11.0	11.1	11.0
Special drawing rights	11.0	11.2	8.5	9.0	10.0	11.0	10.3	10.0	10.6
Foreign currencies	52.2	45.9	40.0	41.5	41.2	49.1	38.3	30.8	36.0
Reserve position in IMF [2]	9.1	9.5	11.8	11.8	12.0	14.6	15.4	18.1	24.1

[1] Includes gold in Exchange Stabilization Fund; excludes gold held under earmark at Federal Reserve banks for foreign and international accounts. Beginning 1975, gold assets were valued at $42.22 pursuant to the amending of Section 2 of the Par Value Modification Act, PL-93-110, approved September 21, 1973.   [2] International Monetary Fund.

Source: Board of Governors of the Federal Reserve System, *Federal Reserve Bulletin*, monthly; and Department of the Treasury, *Treasury Bulletin*, monthly.

Foreign Commerce and Aid   793

No. 1312. Foreign Direct Investment Position in the United States on a Historical-Cost Basis, by Industry and Selected Countries: 1997 and 1998

[In millions of dollars ($681,651 represents $681,651,000,000)]

Country	1997 Total [1]	Petro-leum	Manufac-turing, total	Whole-sale	1998 Total [1]	Petro-leum	Manufac-turing, total	Whole-sale
All countries..............	693,207	42,085	273,122	87,630	811,756	53,254	329,346	96,261
Canada......................	69,866	3,177	27,811	4,190	74,840	2,633	26,152	5,098
Europe	432,622	29,750	197,819	39,015	539,906	42,771	252,893	43,554
Austria......................	1,829	(D)	298	282	4,872	(D)	365	485
Belgium.....................	6,438	1,221	3,529	840	9,577	(D)	4,232	1,018
Denmark....................	2,929	5	708	1,782	3,229	4	711	2,010
Finland......................	3,557	(D)	1,615	(D)	4,321	(D)	2,224	1,012
France......................	49,503	(D)	29,099	1,911	62,167	(D)	37,820	1,972
Germany....................	71,289	(D)	34,522	12,250	95,045	312	51,018	12,405
Ireland......................	10,493	639	2,748	823	13,227	739	4,874	1,980
Italy........................	3,089	294	627	468	3,830	(D)	907	423
Luxembourg................	5,363	-	2,941	1,420	20,214	-	(D)	1,311
Netherlands................	89,570	12,949	31,565	6,303	96,904	11,505	35,109	5,606
Norway	3,045	(D)	1,380	(D)	3,616	(D)	1,595	269
Spain........................	2,266	4	587	120	2,292	-3	714	154
Sweden.....................	12,842	(D)	8,576	1,171	14,564	(D)	9,065	2,028
Switzerland................	38,281	194	21,187	1,801	54,011	252	26,310	2,579
United Kingdom...........	131,315	11,680	58,342	8,170	151,335	26,277	64,022	10,099
Latin America and other Western Hemisphere	33,546	3,427	3,930	2,179	32,210	4,072	4,329	1,858
South and Central America	10,212	-783	273	425	11,916	-457	1,067	270
Mexico	3,315	-8	631	459	4,029	-9	887	495
Panama	6,023	-56	-7	-48	7,025	(D)	482	-108
Other Western Hemisphere	23,333	4,211	3,657	1,754	20,294	4,529	3,262	1,588
Bahamas..................	1,905	(D)	127	354	2,141	(D)	131	440
Netherlands Antilles	5,722	2,689	1,217	165	4,727	(D)	795	(D)
United Kingdom Islands, Caribbean .	12,022	(D)	1,867	687	10,395	1,578	1,792	608
Africa	1,465	(D)	-14	1	884	-4	-90	21
Middle East	6,593	(D)	944	91	7,831	1,061	966	131
Israel.......................	1,955	-	923	91	2,459	-3	601	129
Kuwait......................	2,935	4	7	2	(D)	(D)	9	3
Saudi Arabia...............	1,565	(D)	1	(Z)	(D)	(D)	3	-1
Asia and Pacific	149,115	4,215	42,632	42,153	156,085	2,720	45,096	45,598
Australia....................	14,703	4,522	2,414	-64	14,755	3,202	2,982	-55
Hong Kong.................	1,797	-16	316	648	2,097	(D)	358	599
Japan.......................	125,131	212	37,356	40,628	132,569	234	39,918	43,114
Singapore...................	3,271	20	1,047	196	1,813	2	244	267
Taiwan......................	2,749	-1	1,253	476	3,120	-2	1,505	558

- Represents or rounds to zero.   D Suppressed to avoid disclosure of data of individual companies.   Z Less than $50 million.
Source: U.S. Bureau of Economic Analysis, *Survey of Current Business*, July 1999.

No. 1313. U.S. Affiliates of Foreign Companies—Assets, Sales, Employment, Land, Exports, and Imports: 1997

[(3,034,404 represents $3,034,404,000,000). A U.S. affiliate is a U.S. business enterprise in which one foreign owner (individual, branch, partnership, association, trust, corporation, or government) has a direct or indirect voting interest of 10 percent or more. Estimates cover the universe of nonbank affiliates]

Industry	Total assets (mil. dol.)	Sales (mil. dol.) [1]	Employ-ment (1,000) [2]	Employee compen-sation (mil. dol.)	Gross book value (mil. dol.) Plant and equip-ment [3]	Land	Merchan-dise exports [4] (mil. dol.)	Merchan-dise imports [4] (mil. dol.)
Total	3,034,404	1,717,240	5,164.3	230,337	866,197	54,312	140,924	261,482
Petroleum.................	123,753	157,770	105.0	6,730	118,095	2,022	7,797	19,547
Manufacturing	648,564	623,313	2,271.0	112,578	317,297	11,462	67,719	88,085
Chemicals and allied products..	191,541	143,236	393.1	25,277	94,052	2,280	15,492	16,346
Wholesale trade [5].........	266,063	449,847	522.5	25,829	95,565	3,222	59,050	148,214
Motor vehicles and auto parts and supplies.	91,878	117,028	88.1	4,765	50,604	807	4,708	49,479
Farm-product raw materials ...	10,679	34,067	21.2	736	2,434	112	13,866	2,831
Retail trade................	54,723	102,531	839.2	17,281	34,558	3,365	1,952	3,679
Finance, except banking	847,626	74,409	60.3	10,317	7,923	514	(D)	(D)
Insurance	704,133	102,180	165.0	11,065	30,248	973	-	-
Real estate	104,334	16,857	24.7	1,141	88,473	16,559	(D)	2
Services...................	113,797	66,435	682.9	22,610	56,367	7,974	622	(D)
Other.....................	171,411	123,898	493.7	22,786	117,671	8,220	3,702	934

- Represents zero.   D Suppressed to avoid disclosure of data of individual companies.   [1] Excludes returns, discounts, allowances, and sales and excise taxes.   [2] Average number of full-time and part-time employees.   [3] Includes mineral rights and minor amounts of property other than land.   [4] F.a.s. value at port of exportation.   [5] Includes industries not shown separately.
Source: U.S. Bureau of Economic Analysis, *Survey of Current Business*, June 1999; and *Foreign Direct Investment in the United States, Operations of U.S. Affiliates of Foreign Companies*, Revised 1996 Estimates and Preliminary 1997 Estimates.

794   Foreign Commerce and Aid

No. 1314. Foreign Direct Investment in the United States—Gross Book Value and Employment of U.S. Affiliates of Foreign Companies, by State: 1990 to 1997

[578,355 represents 578,355,000,000. A U.S. affiliate is a U.S. business enterprise in which one foreign owner (individual, branch, partnership, association, trust corporation, or government) has a direct or indirect voting interest of 10 percent or more. Estimates cover the universe of nonbank U.S. affiliates]

State and other area	Gross book value of property, plant, and equipment (mil. dol.)				Total employment				
								1997	
	1990	1995	1996	1997	1990 (1,000)	1995 (1,000)	1996 (1,000)	Total (1,000)	Percent of all busi- nesses
Total	578,355	769,491	825,695	866,197	4,734.5	4,941.8	5,105.0	5,164.3	(X)
United States	552,902	733,089	784,972	839,573	4,704.4	4,898.9	5,068.1	5,134.7	4.8
Alabama.	7,300	10,598	11,981	13,006	55.7	60.6	61.7	65.0	4.1
Alaska	19,435	25,558	26,234	25,922	13.2	9.8	10.2	8.7	4.3
Arizona.	7,234	6,699	9,604	9,797	57.1	51.9	57.8	59.4	3.4
Arkansas	2,344	3,666	3,829	3,934	29.2	32.1	37.6	35.2	3.7
California	75,768	96,576	102,703	91,788	555.9	548.6	557.5	569.4	4.9
Colorado.	6,544	8,602	9,368	9,833	56.3	72.2	72.7	80.3	4.7
Connecticut.	5,357	8,466	8,902	8,703	75.9	73.3	85.1	83.8	5.8
Delaware	5,818	2,919	3,105	3,323	43.1	15.8	16.3	19.1	5.6
District of Columbia	3,869	4,983	4,864	4,339	11.4	13.4	12.8	11.2	2.8
Florida	18,659	24,865	30,251	29,598	205.7	210.0	239.8	240.9	4.2
Georgia	16,729	22,432	23,799	25,403	161.0	180.1	195	188.9	6.0
Hawaii	11,830	15,972	15,324	15,157	53.0	48.9	47.5	50.1	11.4
Idaho	776	1,026	1,270	1,407	11.7	11.3	12.3	12.4	2.9
Illinois	23,420	34,305	34,687	37,649	245.8	237.0	236.1	224.5	4.4
Indiana.	13,426	18,782	16,711	18,367	126.9	136.9	127.2	128.3	5.1
Iowa	2,712	4,527	5,304	5,444	32.8	35.8	37.7	37.8	3.1
Kansas.	5,134	3,233	4,741	5,696	29.6	34.0	42.7	45.4	4.2
Kentucky	9,229	15,136	15,610	16,909	65.7	83.4	86.5	89.5	6.1
Louisiana	17,432	20,543	23,226	25,151	61.4	51.0	55.7	58.0	3.8
Maine.	2,080	3,885	4,092	3,960	26.6	29.1	30.4	31.6	6.7
Maryland	5,713	9,197	9,984	10,578	79.6	95.0	93.8	92.0	4.8
Massachusetts.	8,890	12,707	14,345	15,473	131.2	141.5	162.3	159.5	5.7
Michigan.	12,012	21,370	18,733	20,914	139.6	170.3	162.8	171.4	4.4
Minnesota.	11,972	8,688	9,858	9,972	89.8	79.8	89.8	96.6	4.4
Mississippi	2,989	3,055	2,570	2,967	23.6	22.6	20.6	21.7	2.4
Missouri	5,757	8,327	10,310	10,945	73.7	79.3	84.1	84.0	3.7
Montana	2,181	1,938	1,935	2,041	5.1	4.4	4.5	4.4	1.5
Nebraska	776	1,320	1,791	2,027	14.9	15.7	19.1	20.8	2.9
Nevada	5,450	8,242	8,589	8,784	22.7	25.0	25.5	25.5	3.1
New Hampshire	1,446	2,212	2,284	2,546	25.9	30.0	30.8	31.6	6.2
New Jersey.	18,608	26,175	27,706	30,488	227.0	205.2	209.4	212.4	6.6
New Mexico	4,312	4,363	4,447	4,945	17.4	16.2	15.4	17.4	3.1
New York	36,424	52,992	53,374	53,711	347.5	343.8	349.9	351.5	5.1
North Carolina	15,234	21,475	23,965	24,019	181.0	225.3	231.6	225.0	7.1
North Dakota.	1,251	915	1,125	1,166	3.1	3.2	4.7	3.5	1.4
Ohio	20,549	29,932	33,572	35,095	219.1	222.1	226.7	234.1	4.9
Oklahoma.	6,049	5,448	5,538	5,723	43.6	34.2	36.7	34.4	3.0
Oregon.	3,427	5,807	6,146	7,269	39.1	49.7	49.2	52.0	4.0
Pennsylvania.	16,587	24,432	25,344	25,671	221.6	231.6	238.3	225.0	4.6
Rhode Island.	1,120	2,240	2,604	2,628	13.3	16.2	19.2	18.5	4.6
South Carolina.	10,067	13,438	15,509	16,847	104.7	111.6	117.2	116.9	7.9
South Dakota	553	665	792	986	4.5	4.6	5.6	10.4	3.5
Tennessee	10,280	14,227	15,603	17,123	116.9	136.3	136.4	149.4	6.6
Texas.	57,079	68,142	75,728	77,906	299.5	326.4	330.2	350.6	4.8
Utah	3,918	5,612	6,451	7,719	21.0	28.6	32.7	36.7	4.3
Vermont	631	1,037	1,056	1,031	7.7	10.4	9.9	9.8	4.0
Virginia.	10,702	15,129	17,479	20,158	113.3	141.4	146.2	143.3	5.3
Washington.	7,985	11,462	11,920	12,275	77.5	83.0	86.6	86.6	4.0
West Virginia.	7,975	7,809	7,507	6,714	34.9	31.9	26.1	27.2	4.8
Wisconsin	5,088	7,415	8,100	8,003	81.4	71.5	73.6	76.5	3.3
Wyoming	2,782	4,544	5,001	4,956	5.8	6.9	6.5	6.9	4.0
Puerto Rico.	1,499	2,174	1,848	1,686	16.1	27.4	20	17.1	(NA)
Other territories and offshore .	18,484	17,798	20,156	22,952	9.0	13.1	10.9	10.3	(NA)
Foreign.	5,470	16,430	18,719	1,986	5.0	2.4	6	2.2	(NA)
Unspecified [1]	(NA)	(NA)	(NA)	33,505	(NA)	(NA)	(NA)	(NA)	(NA)

NA Not available.   X Not applicable.   [1] Covers property, plant, and equipment not located in a particular state, including aircraft, railroad rolling stock, satellites, undersea cable, and trucks engaged in interstate transportation.

Source: U.S. Bureau of Economic Analysis, *Survey of Current Business*, June 1999, and *Foreign Direct Investment in the United States, Operations of U.S. Affiliates of Foreign Companies*, annual.

Foreign Commerce and Aid   795

No. 1315. U.S. Businesses Acquired or Established by Foreign Direct Investors— Investment Outlays, by Industry of U.S. Business Enterprise and Country of Ultimate Beneficial Owner: 1990 to 1998

[In millions of dollars (65,932 represents $65,932,000,000). Foreign direct investment is the ownership or control directly or indirectly, by one foreign individual branch, partnership, association, trust, corporation, or government of 10 percent or more of the voting securities of a U.S. business enterprise or an equivalent interest in an unincorporated one. Data represent number and full cost of acquisitions of existing U.S. business enterprises, including business segments or operating units of existing U.S. business enterprises and establishments of new enterprises. Investments may be made by the foreign direct investor itself, or indirectly by an existing U.S. affiliate of the foreign direct investor. Covers investments in U.S. business enterprises with assets of over $1 million, or ownership of 200 acres of U.S. land]

Industry and country	1990	1992	1993	1994	1995	1996	1997	1998, prel.
Total...............	65,932	15,333	26,229	45,626	57,195	79,929	69,708	201,027
INDUSTRY								
Petroleum..............	1,141	463	882	469	1,520	1,059	762	72,136
Manufacturing...........	23,898	6,014	11,090	21,218	26,643	27,835	19,603	89,679
Wholesale trade..........	1,676	698	837	2,156	1,168	4,746	2,612	907
Retail trade.............	1,250	256	1,495	1,542	2,838	2,988	435	1,963
Depository institutions [1]......	897	529	958	2,026	2,301	1,944	3,547	1,104
Finance, except depository institutions [1]......	2,121	797	1,599	2,195	7,837	8,676	7,019	6,195
Insurance..............	2,093	291	1,105	450	654	4,688	8,526	4,325
Real estate.............	7,771	2,161	1,883	2,647	2,996	4,175	4,119	5,272
Services...............	19,369	2,023	4,162	7,163	5,881	15,292	12,187	9,951
Other [2]................	5,716	2,101	2,218	5,760	5,359	8,528	10,898	9,496
COUNTRY								
Canada...............	3,430	1,351	3,797	4,128	8,029	9,700	11,755	21,480
Europe...............	36,011	8,344	16,845	31,920	38,195	49,427	44,014	160,612
France...............	10,217	406	1,249	1,404	1,129	6,021	2,578	14,129
Germany [3]............	2,363	1,964	2,841	3,328	13,117	12,858	6,464	39,949
Netherlands..........	2,247	1,331	2,074	1,537	1,061	6,476	10,244	19,446
Switzerland..........	3,905	1,259	804	5,044	7,533	4,910	6,745	3,637
United Kingdom.......	13,096	2,255	8,238	17,261	9,094	14,757	11,834	76,881
Other Europe.........	4,183	1,129	1,639	3,346	6,261	4,405	6,149	6,570
Latin America and other Western Hemisphere........	796	1,438	874	1,352	1,550	1,790	924	10,457
South and Central America...	399	1,152	527	(D)	1,283	(D)	166	813
Other Western Hemisphere....	397	286	347	(D)	267	(D)	758	9,644
Africa................	(D)	(D)	(D)	(D)	(D)	(D)	(D)	145
Middle East.............	472	238	1,308	(D)	447	(D)	847	2,968
Asia and Pacific..........	23,170	3,716	3,004	5,263	8,688	12,751	11,786	5,207
Australia.............	1,412	164	129	1,522	2,270	2,222	7,600	1,726
Japan................	19,933	2,921	2,065	2,715	3,602	8,813	2,326	2,872
Other Asia and Pacific......	1,825	631	810	1,026	2,816	1,716	1,860	609

D Suppressed to avoid disclosure of data of individual companies. [1] Prior to 1992, "depository institutions" excludes, and "finance, depository institutions" includes, savings institutions and credit unions. Beginning with 1992, savings institutions and credit unions have been reclassified from "finance, except depository institutions" to "depository institutions". [2] For investments in which more than one investor participated, each investor and each investor's outlays are classified by country of each ultimate beneficial owner. [3] Prior to 1990, this line includes data only for the Federal Republic of Germany. Beginning in 1990, this line also includes the former German Democratic Republic (GDR). This change has no effect on the data because, prior to 1991, there were no U.S. affiliates of the former GDR.

Source: U.S. Bureau of Economic Analysis, *Survey of Current Business*, June 1999, and previous June issues.

No. 1316. U.S. Direct Investment Position Abroad, Capital Outflows, and Income, by Industry of Foreign Affiliates: 1995 to 1997

[In millions of dollars (699,015 represents $699,015,000,000)]

Industry	Direct investment position on a historical-cost basis			Capital outflows (inflows (-))			Income		
	1995	1996	1997	1995	1996	1997	1995	1996	1997
All industries, total.......	699,015	777,203	860,723	92,074	74,833	114,537	87,346	92,105	100,703
Petroleum..............	68,639	74,499	85,726	675	5,058	11,455	9,036	11,692	12,114
Manufacturing...........	243,954	272,244	288,290	44,472	25,149	32,280	34,325	34,365	37,532
Food and kindred products..	28,896	32,998	38,380	3,718	2,700	6,325	4,480	4,826	5,116
Chemicals and allied products..	61,374	72,209	73,487	16,924	5,657	8,026	8,614	9,525	9,415
Primary and fabricated metals..	11,555	14,178	14,732	1,570	5,283	1,054	1,380	1,353	1,535
Industrial machinery and equipment.................	29,626	31,597	33,563	4,408	2,565	4,529	4,251	4,555	5,083
Electronic and other electric equipment.............	27,514	31,623	33,833	7,060	3,883	3,930	4,466	4,217	4,861
Transportation equipment.....	34,076	33,839	36,439	5,888	561	3,846	3,709	3,182	4,842
Other manufacturing.......	50,913	55,801	57,855	4,903	4,500	4,570	7,425	6,707	6,679
Wholesale trade...........	68,102	69,638	69,080	8,880	5,701	3,403	9,118	8,488	9,041
Depository institutions........	29,181	33,673	34,359	1,032	1,488	2,935	3,242	3,083	2,953
Finance [1], insurance, and real estate.................	218,313	240,972	280,920	22,001	23,035	45,410	24,589	27,817	29,815
Services...............	29,721	35,793	40,874	4,014	3,343	5,464	4,136	3,588	5,258
Other industries...........	41,105	50,384	61,475	11,000	11,061	13,591	2,902	3,072	3,991

[1] Excludes depository institutions.

Source: U.S. Bureau of Economic Analysis, *Survey of Current Business*, April 1999.

No. 1317. U.S. Direct Investment Position Abroad on a Historical-Cost Basis, by Country: 1990 to 1998

[In millions of dollars (430,521 represents $430,521,000,000). U.S. investment abroad is the ownership or control by one U.S. person of 10 percent or more of the voting securities of an incorporated foreign business enterprise or an equivalent interest in a unincorporated foreign business enterprise. Negative position can occur when a U.S. parent company's liabilities to the foreign affiliate are greater than its equity in, and loans to the foreign affiliate]

Country	1990	1992	1993	1994	1995	1996	1997	1998
All countries	430,521	502,063	564,283	612,893	699,015	795,195	865,531	980,565
Canada	69,508	68,690	69,922	74,221	83,498	89,592	96,031	103,908
Europe.	214,739	248,744	285,735	297,133	344,596	389,378	420,108	489,539
Austria	1,113	1,371	1,312	2,197	2,829	2,854	2,638	3,838
Belgium.	9,464	11,381	11,697	14,714	18,706	18,740	17,430	18,920
Denmark.	1,726	1,676	1,735	2,030	2,161	2,554	2,173	2,628
Finland	544	343	414	761	965	1,070	1,312	1,700
France	19,164	25,157	24,312	27,322	33,358	35,200	35,800	39,188
Germany.	27,609	33,003	36,811	38,878	44,242	41,281	38,490	42,853
Greece	282	372	410	482	533	566	634	660
Ireland	5,894	7,607	9,019	7,239	7,996	10,133	12,862	15,936
Italy	14,063	13,015	12,748	14,808	17,096	16,193	14,809	14,638
Luxembourg.	1,697	2,031	5,611	6,310	5,929	7,753	10,109	14,930
Netherlands.	19,120	20,700	20,911	29,889	42,113	54,118	64,361	79,386
Norway.	4,209	3,825	3,757	5,026	4,741	5,483	6,934	7,609
Portugal	897	1,290	1,264	1,181	1,413	1,423	1,425	1,474
Spain	7,868	8,757	6,689	9,572	10,856	12,252	11,232	12,807
Sweden	1,787	1,881	2,374	1,905	6,816	5,248	5,463	6,053
Switzerland	25,099	28,698	33,056	27,908	31,125	30,744	31,420	37,616
Turkey	522	732	995	874	973	1,059	1,041	1,069
United Kingdom	72,707	85,176	109,208	100,817	106,332	134,559	153,108	178,648
Other	974	1,729	3,411	5,219	6,412	8,148	8,868	9,588
Latin America	43,348	54,339	59,302	116,478	131,377	155,925	178,505	196,655
South America	22,933	28,760	31,210	37,673	49,170	57,372	68,372	73,290
Argentina.	2,531	3,327	4,442	5,692	7,660	7,893	10,004	11,489
Brazil.	14,384	16,313	16,772	17,885	25,002	29,105	35,091	37,802
Chile.	1,896	2,544	2,749	5,062	6,216	8,156	8,975	9,132
Colombia	1,677	3,053	2,930	3,463	3,506	3,531	4,436	4,317
Ecuador.	280	295	555	784	889	922	838	952
Peru	599	620	622	971	1,335	2,281	2,467	2,587
Venezuela	1,087	1,972	2,362	3,087	3,634	4,474	5,381	5,697
Other	479	636	778	728	928	1,010	1,181	1,315
Central America	20,415	25,579	28,092	30,083	33,493	37,667	47,735	56,387
Costa Rica	251	274	298	607	921	1,223	1,544	2,126
Guatemala	130	115	139	200	233	331	357	429
Honduras	262	239	159	140	68	129	183	186
Mexico	10,313	13,730	15,221	16,968	16,873	19,351	24,181	25,877
Panama.	9,289	11,038	12,043	11,905	15,123	16,335	21,056	26,957
Other	169	182	233	262	273	298	413	812
Other Western Hemisphere. . . .	28,065	36,969	41,180	48,722	48,714	60,886	62,397	66,978
Bahamas	4,004	4,167	3,138	2,808	1,768	1,876	1,599	287
Barbados	252	340	471	391	698	848	791	1,077
Bermuda	20,169	26,736	28,666	28,355	28,374	37,091	37,660	41,076
Dominican Republic	529	779	1,039	266	330	400	476	535
Jamaica.	625	892	1,049	1,167	1,287	1,583	1,948	2,105
Netherlands Antilles	-4,501	-1,989	-62	6,739	6,835	7,597	4,423	4,472
Trinidad and Tobago	485	565	691	529	673	786	651	1,054
U.K. Islands, Caribbean	5,929	5,401	5,544	7,858	8,358	10,121	14,051	15,713
Other	574	75	645	608	392	583	797	658
Africa.	3,650	4,469	5,469	5,760	6,017	8,162	11,157	13,491
Egypt	1,231	1,334	1,510	1,090	1,093	1,366	1,612	1,955
Nigeria	-401	301	478	605	629	1,020	1,387	1,925
South Africa	775	879	900	1,132	1,422	1,495	2,451	2,363
Other	2,045	1,955	2,581	2,933	2,873	4,281	5,706	7,247
Middle East.	3,959	5,759	6,571	6,367	7,198	8,294	8,803	10,599
Israel	746	1,335	1,604	1,483	1,831	2,045	2,028	3,067
Saudi Arabia	1,899	2,351	2,587	2,100	2,741	3,476	3,826	4,209
United Arab Emirates.	409	429	524	357	500	598	567	710
Other	905	1,644	1,856	2,427	2,126	2,174	2,382	2,613
Asia and Pacific.	254,887	304,681	92,671	108,528	122,711	139,548	146,610	161,797
Australia	15,110	16,928	19,047	20,196	24,328	30,006	29,910	33,676
China	354	563	916	2,557	2,765	3,848	5,071	6,348
Hong Kong	6,055	8,693	10,063	11,092	11,768	14,391	19,267	20,802
India	372	484	599	1,030	1,105	1,344	1,563	1,480
Indonesia	3,207	4,384	4,864	6,355	6,777	8,322	6,664	6,932
Japan	22,599	26,591	31,095	34,117	37,309	34,578	33,725	38,153
Korea, South	2,695	2,912	3,427	4,334	5,557	6,508	6,430	7,365
Malaysia	1,466	1,596	1,975	3,148	4,237	5,663	6,522	6,193
New Zealand	3,156	3,314	3,064	3,893	4,601	5,940	6,523	6,136
Philippines.	1,355	1,666	1,953	2,484	2,719	3,543	3,295	3,192
Singapore	3,975	6,715	8,875	10,940	12,140	14,912	17,864	19,783
Taiwan	2,226	2,827	3,113	3,775	4,293	4,476	4,668	4,937
Thailand	1,790	2,594	2,943	3,585	4,283	5,000	3,946	5,721
Other	356	696	737	1,022	830	1,019	1,161	1,080
International	2,535	3,131	3,433	4,406	3,618	4,295	4,317	4,578
Addenda:								
Eastern Europe	(D)	731	2,356	4,029	5,136	6,651	7,743	8,143
European Communities(12). . . .	180,491	210,164	240,414	253,242	301,345	337,184	368,997	433,658
OPEC [1]	7,145	10,692	11,737	13,794	15,546	17,641	20,554	23,252

D Figure withheld to avoid disclosure.   [1] OPEC=Organization of Petroleum Exporting Countries. Includes Algeria, Ecuador, Gabon, Indonesia, Iran, Iraq, Kuwait, Libya, Nigeria, Qatar, Saudi Arabia, United Arab Emirates, and Venezuela. Prior to 1993, Ecuador was also a member and was included in this line.
Source: U.S. Bureau of Economic Analysis, *Survey of Current Business,* July 1999, and earlier issues.

Foreign Commerce and Aid   797

No. 1318. U.S. Government Foreign Grants and Credits, by Type and Country: 1966 to 1998

[In millions of dollars (70,381 represents $70,381,000,000). See text, this section. Negative figures (-) occur when the total of grant returns, principal repayments, and/or foreign currencies disbursed by the U.S. government exceeds new grants and new credits utilized and/or acquisitions of foreign currencies through new sales of farm products]

Country	1966-75, total	1976-85, total	1986-95, total	1993	1994	1995	1996	1997	1998
Total, net	70,381	104,191	90,669	18,002	16,426	12,668	16,645	12,749	13,820
Investment in financial institutions	2,719	10,432	13,504	1,143	1,430	1,517	1,833	1,588	1,580
Western Europe	1,004	1,618	-5,411	349	174	177	270	319	258
Austria	-19	34	-72	-1	-1	-1	-1	-1	(Z)
Belgium and Luxembourg	17	-46	-48	-	-	-	-	-	-
Denmark	64	-58	-13	-	-	-	-	-	-
Finland	-19	21	-72	-26	-1	-1	-1	-1	(Z)
France	-93	-222	-93	-2	-1	1	-	(Z)	-
Germany	-117	-117	-6,459	-1	-	(Z)	(Z)	-	-
Iceland	-8	-12	-8	-	-	-	-	-	-
Ireland	-51	7	5	-8	36	-	11	39	8
Italy	85	133	-233	(Z)	-	(Z)	-	-	-
Netherlands	116	-180	-2	-	-	-	-	-	-
Norway	379	-257	-33	4	-	-	-	-	-
Portugal	34	1,003	796	112	115	-16	-3	-12	-15
Spain	607	965	-867	31	-55	-59	-48	-37	-37
Sweden	17	-1	-15	-	-	-	-	-	-
United Kingdom	-546	-964	-1,465	-118	-120	-118	-125	-127	-130
Yugoslavia	84	174	-149	(X)	(X)	(X)	(X)	(X)	(X)
Former Yugoslavia [2]:									
Bosnia and Hercegovina	(X)	(X)	227	51	84	92	235	252	220
Croatia	(X)	(X)	124	63	52	9	-10	-7	-12
Macedonia	(X)	(X)	5	1	3	1	3	18	6
Slovenia	(X)	(X)	-48	-6	-17	-24	-27	-16	-16
Former Yugoslavia - Regional [3]	(X)	(X)	1	9	-1	(Z)	(Z)	-8	6
Other [1] and unspecified [3]	455	1,139	3,010	241	81	293	236	220	228
Eastern Europe	226	1,029	12,352	3,372	2,910	1,963	1,953	1,413	1,785
Albania	-	-	173	48	16	15	58	11	16
Bulgaria	-	-	93	22	8	6	13	14	13
Czechoslovakia	-	-5	17	15	1	-2	3	-11	-
Czech Republic	(X)	(X)	7	2	2	3	9	5	4
Estonia	(X)	(X)	31	1	(Z)	2	7	4	5
Hungary	-5	6	41	3	4	35	15	-16	12
Latvia	(X)	(X)	35	1	3	2	10	4	8
Lithuania	(X)	(X)	96	24	15	28	17	23	14
Poland	-75	1,017	3,490	33	8	5	49	28	36
Romania	92	55	43	15	18	8	29	3	26
Slovakia	-	-	4	1	1	2	12	11	6
Soviet Union	214	-44	-267	(X)	(X)	(X)	(X)	(X)	(X)
Newly independent states:									
Armenia	(X)	(X)	352	96	127	102	80	26	38
Azerbaijan	(X)	(X)	42	-	24	19	14	4	5
Belarus	(X)	(X)	236	120	37	49	31	19	4
Georgia	(X)	(X)	285	103	86	89	79	38	27
Kazakhstan	(X)	(X)	70	14	17	16	59	52	67
Kyrgyzstan	(X)	(X)	175	105	36	33	38	26	30
Moldova	(X)	(X)	85	35	22	19	15	8	5
Russia	(X)	(X)	3,989	2,164	1,184	455	421	356	435
Tajikistan	(X)	(X)	94	19	30	34	32	27	27
Turkmenistan	(X)	(X)	73	34	13	16	19	1	3
Ukraine	(X)	(X)	352	70	105	170	232	95	140
Uzbekistan	(X)	(X)	8	1	6	1	4	2	6
Former Soviet Union - Regional [3]	(X)	(X)	1,711	240	735	617	584	595	659
Other [2] and unspecified [3]	(X)	(X)	1,119	207	413	241	124	85	200
Near East and South Asia	17,195	50,777	29,164	8,019	7,042	3,022	7,552	4,723	4,979
Afghanistan	185	56	403	51	9	10	14	17	-0
Bangladesh	701	1,670	1,590	123	202	87	48	42	27
Cyprus	20	138	151	14	16	6	11	10	14
Egypt	271	13,600	26,592	2,766	2,258	1,637	1,620	1,377	2,014
Greece	905	362	2,774	313	262	261	12	-211	-240
India	3,810	1,021	767	92	45	48	55	237	160
Iran	914	-847	-42	-	-	-	-21	-	-
Iraq [4]	-5	5	892	116	135	128	119	4	(Z)
Israel	3,760	25,417	25,116	3,295	3,106	420	5,294	2,896	2,840
Jordan	618	1,320	754	125	98	129	168	232	160
Kuwait	-	-	-16,058	-	-	-	-	-	-
Lebanon	90	233	22	7	5	5	11	3	1
Nepal	105	177	193	21	20	19	21	24	20
Oman	(Z)	79	42	20	1	4	12	25	20
Pakistan	2,048	1,971	1,222	-35	-158	-187	-164	-62	-82
Saudi Arabia	23	-20	-16,855	-	-	-	-	-	-
Sri Lanka	153	512	596	88	41	26	6	7	7
Syria	15	262	3	3	-	-	-	-	-
Turkey	2,703	3,760	2,956	813	224	147	-61	-19	-162
United Arab Emirates	-	-	-4,070	-	-	-	-	-	-
Yemen (Sanaa)	3	(Z)	-	-	-	-	-	-	-
Yemen	24	216	263	22	1	3	5	12	4
UNRWA [5]	296	596	622	140	7	103	72	59	78
West Bank-Gaza	11	13	162	19	64	58	33	53	80
Other and unspecified [3]	546	236	1,071	27	705	118	298	20	44

See footnotes at end of table.

U.S. Census Bureau, Statistical Abstract of the United States: 1999

No. 1318. U.S. Government Foreign Grants and Credits, by Type and Country: 1966 to 1998—Continued

[See headnote, p. 798]

Country	1966-75, total	1976-85, total	1986-95, total	1993	1994	1995	1996	1997	1998
Africa	**3,610**	**11,067**	**16,231**	**1,989**	**2,031**	**2,213**	**1,945**	**1,339**	**1,277**
Algeria	263	345	413	-11	28	755	644	93	45
Angola	6	115	120	16	58	37	42	41	35
Benin	12	44	101	13	17	14	13	23	14
Botswana	35	169	168	15	15	18	9	9	4
Burkina	40	287	221	26	14	23	11	15	17
Burundi	5	62	171	19	55	39	2	4	6
Cameroon	50	150	247	23	13	4	4	(Z)	9
Cape Verde	1	68	77	7	7	11	10	11	7
Chad	20	145	240	22	10	14	8	6	3
Congo, Democratic Republic of the (former Zaire)	342	939	766	9	1	1	(Z)	(Z)	1
Cote d'Ivoire	57	57	240	23	38	16	22	16	8
Eritrea	-	-	41	4	28	8	18	17	16
Ethiopia	297	310	969	179	168	127	104	77	116
Ghana	203	152	370	60	65	63	34	55	40
Guinea	68	74	239	41	38	28	29	28	18
Kenya	76	549	682	99	54	35	6	27	36
Lesotho	27	197	166	9	8	13	4	5	3
Liberia	86	459	438	46	66	67	58	28	16
Madagascar	13	86	240	28	23	33	42	35	44
Malawi	30	56	404	50	37	64	36	30	22
Mali	58	199	367	39	30	31	12	11	36
Mauritania	20	161	94	10	2	2	2	5	4
Morocco	413	948	662	12	27	-48	-4	-42	-49
Mozambique	1	175	813	94	82	114	53	78	74
Niger	64	223	342	30	16	31	15	11	13
Nigeria	284	267	506	18	52	1	-4	-10	-4
Rwanda	13	91	513	39	220	138	93	87	28
Senegal	48	361	458	58	33	24	38	36	18
Sierra Leone	36	85	111	13	10	11	28	18	13
Somalia	47	582	1,313	522	34	26	10	9	3
South Africa	-11	2	376	66	71	112	99	111	89
Sudan	52	1,358	936	53	60	11	16	24	23
Swaziland	8	58	124	15	10	13	21	12	14
Tanzania	123	259	261	28	24	19	16	18	26
Togo	18	60	109	9	8	3	1	1	2
Tunisia	376	563	-56	-4	2	-5	-24	-9	-22
Uganda	33	40	357	65	57	56	41	56	17
Zambia	35	331	497	52	21	27	21	47	14
Zimbabwe	(Z)	271	269	29	34	29	22	20	46
Other and unspecified [3]	361	769	1,866	164	492	245	393	336	473
Far East and Pacific	**34,767**	**9,651**	**-8,396**	**25**	**751**	**749**	**780**	**130**	**735**
Australia	276	-12	-273	-2	-1	-	-	-	-
Burma	43	31	18	-2	-2	-2	-2	-2	-2
Cambodia	1,760	87	125	29	16	39	36	27	33
China	-	49	396	14	6	136	113	227	249
Hong Kong	41	11	30	1	1	73	133	44	17
Indonesia	1,390	1,660	171	-64	24	25	44	-48	19
Japan and Ryukyu Islands	-345	-210	-10,458	-2	-1	(Z)	(Z)	-	-
Korea, Republic of	5,426	3,518	-3,569	-431	-55	-50	-62	-52	-52
Laos	1,868	8	8	1	2	3	4	3	3
Malaysia	86	39	-74	(Z)	1	(Z)	1	1	1
Mongolia	-	-	95	47	18	11	7	14	19
New Zealand	95	-68	-28	-	-	-	-	-	-
Pacific Islands, Trust Territory of the [6]	488	1,260	2,104	152	317	209	215	140	175
Philippines	729	1,466	3,177	131	-52	55	64	-46	296
Singapore	78	110	-183	(Z)	(Z)	1	(Z)	-	-
Taiwan	1,523	648	-1,291	-9	-8	-5	-3	-1	-1
Thailand	996	733	678	85	247	203	196	-288	-68
Vietnam	19,720	18	7	1	(Z)	(Z)	-	48	-10
Other and unspecified [3]	595	302	671	73	238	51	34	64	57
Western Hemisphere	**6,841**	**9,849**	**15,415**	**807**	**1,005**	**476**	**491**	**592**	**987**
Argentina	34	21	457	86	33	-27	-52	-84	-88
Bolivia	270	413	1,370	151	156	101	100	122	96
Brazil	1,518	399	39	-187	-59	-204	-191	-33	88
Canada	272	317	-589	-41	-120	-	-	-	-
Chile	724	-565	-177	-36	-33	-25	-3	-6	-8
Colombia	846	298	-267	-220	20	4	27	25	42
Costa Rica	103	687	721	14	-5	-30	-44	-30	-28
Dominican Republic	360	550	614	161	(Z)	-15	-19	-29	-14
Ecuador	144	153	351	15	18	5	6	6	2
El Salvador	93	1,681	2,929	217	92	119	79	92	44

See footnotes at end of table.

U.S. Census Bureau, Statistical Abstract of the United States: 1999

No. 1318. U.S. Government Foreign Grants and Credits, by Type and Country: 1966 to 1998—Continued

[See headnote, p. 798]

Country	1966-75, total	1976-85, total	1986-95, total	1993	1994	1995	1996	1997	1998
Western Hemisphere—Continued									
Guatemala	160	270	1,013	76	57	39	4	37	35
Guyana	71	36	116	9	11	10	11	12	12
Haiti	67	370	835	67	125	156	82	92	87
Honduras	113	801	1,546	101	54	77	31	29	47
Jamaica	120	643	914	37	99	30	-13	-30	-22
Mexico	305	1,162	-44	-147	-229	-199	-127	-91	-126
Nicaragua	150	197	843	43	46	41	37	43	70
Panama	210	205	568	49	8	8	-4	-15	-20
Paraguay	86	22	7	1	3	1	2	3	2
Peru	274	757	1,673	145	157	150	75	133	88
Trinidad and Tobago	21	151	-95	-11	-9	-14	-15	5	204
Uruguay	116	-9	7	2	2	1	3	2	1
Venezuela	115	-34	-151	2	2	-3	1	1	4
Other [7] and unspecified [3]	671	1,325	2,733	274	579	250	502	309	473
Other international organizations and unspecified areas [3]	4,018	9,768	17,809	2,299	1,084	2,551	1,821	2,646	2,218

- Represents zero or rounds to zero.   X Not applicable.   Z Less than $500,000.   [1] Includes European Atomic Energy Community, European Coal and Steel Community, European Payments Union, European Productivity Agency, North Atlantic Treaty Organization, and Organization for European Economic Cooperation.   [2] In 1992, some successor countries assumed portions of outstanding credits of the former Yugoslavia (assignment of the remaining portions is pending). Subsequent negative totals reflect payments to the United States on these assumed credits which were greater than the extension of new credits and grants to these countries.   [3] In recent years, significant amounts of foreign assistance has been reported on a regional, inter-regional, and worldwide basis. Country totals in this table may understate actual assistance to many countries.   [4] Foreign assistance to Iraq in 1991-96 was direct humanitarian assistance to ethnic minorities of Northern Iraq after the conflict in the Persian Gulf.   [5] United Nations Relief and Works Agency for Palestine refugees.   [6] Excludes transactions with Commonwealth of the Northern Mariana Islands after October 1986; includes transactions with Federated States of Micronesia, Republic of the Marshall Islands, and Republic of Palau.   [7] Includes Andean Development Corporation, Caribbean Development Bank, Central American Bank for Economic Integration, Eastern Caribbean Central Bank, Inter-American Institute of Agricultural Science, Organizations of American States, and Pan American Health Organization.

Source: U.S. Bureau of Economic Analysis, press releases, and unpublished data.

No. 1319. U.S. Foreign Economic and Military Aid Programs: 1980 to 1997

[In millions of dollars (9,695 represents 9,695,000,000). For years ending September 30. Economic aid shown here represents U.S. economic aid—not just aid under the Foreign Assistance Act. Major components in recent years include AID, Food for Peace, Peace Corps, and paid-in subscriptions to international financial institutions, such as IBRD, and IDB. Annual figures are gross unadjusted program figures]

Year and region	Total economic and military aid	Economic aid			Military aid		
		Total	Loans	Grants	Total	Loans	Grants
1980	9,695	7,573	1,993	5,580	2,122	1,450	672
1981	10,550	7,305	1,460	5,845	3,245	2,546	699
1982	12,324	8,129	1,454	6,675	4,195	3,084	1,111
1983	14,202	8,603	1,619	6,984	5,599	3,932	1,667
1984	15,524	9,038	1,621	7,417	6,486	4,401	2,085
1985	18,128	12,327	1,579	10,748	5,801	2,365	3,436
1986	16,739	10,900	1,330	9,570	5,839	1,980	3,859
1987	14,488	9,386	1,138	8,248	5,102	953	4,149
1988	13,792	8,961	852	8,109	4,831	763	4,068
1989	14,688	9,860	694	9,166	4,828	410	4,418
1990	15,727	10,834	756	10,078	4,893	404	4,489
1991	16,663	11,904	354	11,550	4,760	428	4,332
1992	15,589	11,242	494	10,748	4,347	345	4,002
1993	28,196	24,054	462	23,593	4,143	855	3,288
1994	15,870	11,940	887	11,053	3,931	770	3,161
1995	15,108	11,295	190	11,105	3,813	558	3,255
1996	13,559	9,589	329	9,260	3,970	544	3,426
1997, total	**13,035**	**9,170**	**218**	**8,952**	**3,864**	**298**	**3,566**
Near East	5,414	2,279	30	2,249	3,135	-	3,135
Sub Saharan Africa	1,172	1,156	42	1,114	16	-	16
Latin America	752	741	40	701	11	-	11
Asia	606	599	81	518	7	-	7
Europe	884	508	10	498	376	298	78
New Independent States . .	563	559	15	544	4	-	4
Oceania and other.	21	20	-	20	1	-	1
Nonregional	3,622	3,307	-	3,307	315	-	315

- Represents zero or rounds to zero.

Source: U.S. Agency for International Development, *U.S. Overseas Loans and Grants and Assistance From International Organizations*, annual.

No. 1320. U.S. Foreign Military Aid, by Region and Selected Countries, 1995 to 1997

[In thousands of dollars (3,812,746 represents $3,812,746,000). For years ending Sept. 30. Military aid data include Milit. Assistance Program (MAP) grants, foreign military credit sales, International Military Education and Training, and excess defense articles. N.I.S.=New Independent States]

Region and country	1995	1996	1997	Region and country	1995	1996	1997
Total	3,812,746	3,970,233	3,864,437	Panama.	425	-	-
				Asia [1]	3,804	6,508	6,781
Near East [1]	3,111,501	3,204,683	3,135,275	Cambodia	273	1,403	1,463
Egypt	1,301,000	1,301,009	1,301,000	Malaysia	504	613	631
Israel	1,800,000	1,800,000	1,800,000	Philippines	-	1,210	1,295
Jordan.	8,303	101,202	31,700	Thailand	96	1,445	1,600
Morocco	724	830	812	Europe [1]	566,928	606,598	376,085
Tunisia	800	816	837	Bulgaria.	400	708	903
Sub-Saharan Africa [1]. . .	4,955	11,046	16,343	Czech Republic. . . .	500	795	737
Ghana.	222	257	243	Greece	229,683	224,054	122,528
Kenya.	283	297	304	Hungary	796	1,034	1,014
Senegal. . ,.	598	637	697	Latvia	903	388	535
Latin America [1].	21,881	10,717	11,052	Poland	1,747	1,021	1,000
Bolivia.	3,597	547	509	Portugal.	500	769	551
Colombia	10,588	95	-	Slovakia	473	473	621
Dominican Rep	213	507	622	Turkey.	329,152	321,095	176,454
Ecuador.	293	547	425	N.I.S.	1,722	4,508	3,904
El Salvador	404	535	455	Russia.	413	760	842
Honduras.	325	500	425	Ukraine	707	1,019	1,015
Jamaica.	174	469	487	Oceania and other	376	420	461
Mexico	400	992	1,008	Nonregional	101,579	125,753	314,536

- Represents zero.   [1] Includes countries not shown separately.

Source: U.S. Agency for International Development, *U.S. Overseas Loans and Grants and Assistance From International Organizations*, annual.

No. 1321. U.S. Foreign Aid—Economic Assistance, by Region and Selected Countries: 1995 to 1997

[In thousands of dollars (11,294,639 represents $11,294,639,000). For years ending Sept. 30. N.I.S.=New Independent States]

Region and country	1995	1996	1997	Region and country	1995	1996	1997
Total	11,294,639	9,589,560	9,170,285	El Salvador	63,214	78,436	31,168
				Guatemala.	39,199	37,333	61,379
Near East [1]	2,310,372	2,146,415	2,278,914	Haiti.	157,592	99,325	101,460
Egypt	975,825	824,262	810,743	Honduras.	29,685	25,800	28,543
Israel	1,200,000	1,200,000	1,200,000	Jamaica.	23,967	32,097	23,614
Jordan.	13,506	32,466	152,683	Mexico	9,931	25,276	10,583
Lebanon	13,380	1,026	11,031	Nicaragua	31,373	27,254	26,795
Morocco	15,035	15,821	18,888	Peru [1]	131,576	103,366	126,169
West Bank/Gaza	80,909	63,448	67,012	Asia [1]	571,818	462,682	599,572
Sub-Saharan Africa [1]. . .	1,306,081	1,106,508	1,155,994	Bangladesh	146,774	55,142	77,847
Angola	44,760	83,470	49,187	India	164,429	157,175	125,552
Benin	20,337	16,389	16,983	Indonesia.	61,564	33,459	34,798
Botswana.	31,905	1,776	965	Cambodia	42,115	27,500	35,000
Burkina Faso	15,912	13,394	13,055	Korea, South	-	6,287	50,155
Cote D'Ivoire	1,800	21,587	14,221	Nepal	100	15,667	19,376
Eritrea	10,452	13,550	24,621	Pakistan	16,993	16,493	42,317
Ethiopia	119,494	110,810	79,189	Philippines	17,121	57,042	40,356
Ghana.	39,172	43,501	47,303	Vietnam	5,112	-	48,303
Guinea	19,671	15,671	31,604	Europe [1]	686,098	562,140	507,946
Kenya	26,450	16,122	28,899	Bosnia Hercegovina. .	71,900	245,325	183,616
Liberia.	51,643	57,912	37,339	Bulgaria.	38,525	32,633	11,488
Madagascar	30,015	19,684	18,724	Croatia	12,345	15,630	2,217
Malawi.	67,820	31,354	37,089	Cyprus	-	9,376	4,000
Mali	34,758	30,912	38,350	Hungary	26,012	19,564	1,704
Mozambique.	66,709	59,273	54,953	Lithuania	22,252	17,989	11,977
Namibia.	16,815	6,766	10,329	Macedonia.	13,512	9,655	1,174
Niger.	18,895	4,846	7,963	Ireland, Republic of . .	39,200	-	39,200
Rwanda.	166,021	120,527	86,854	N.I.S [1]	842,503	628,663	559,142
Senegal	24,386	19,776	20,976	Armenia.	52,526	70,724	16,751
Somalia.	14,778	9,399	5,918	Belarus	11,067	25,041	-
South Africa	100,120	116,709	79,476	Georgia	39,273	20,023	1,729
Sudan	30,067	23,521	27,234	Kazakhstan	40,191	29,725	9,730
Tanzania	31,469	11,788	12,190	Kyrgyz Republic	25,104	17,034	5,256
Uganda	57,826	39,519	64,924	Moldova	21,723	31,769	4,578
Zambia	29,555	10,978	16,160	Russia.	353,196	178,060	64,978
Zimbabwe	21,584	19,497	11,227	Tajikistan	8,401	3,368	10,640
Latin America [1]	717,121	680,509	740,895	Turkemenistan	5,343	28,952	3,024
Bolivia.	65,570	90,062	131,214	Ukraine	178,779	120,771	49,722
Colombia.	17,306	16,766	35,111	Uzberistan	11,515	10,874	4,397
Costa Rica	6,244	2,139	110	Oceania and other	6,765	21,769	20,693
Dominican Rep	15,692	13,831	14,499				
Ecuador.	14,286	13,559	15,086	Nonregional	4,853,881	3,980,874	3,307,129

- Represents zero.   [1] Includes countries and regional organizations not shown separately.

Source: U.S. Agency for International Development, *U.S. Overseas Loans and Grants and Assistance From International Organizations*, annual.

50,775 represents $850,775,000,000). Data presented on a balance of payments basis and will not agree andise trade Tables 1323 to 1331]

	Exports			Imports			Trade balance		
	1996	1997	1998	1996	1997	1998	1996	1997	1998
. . . . . .	850,775	937,593	931,315	959,349	1,047,799	1,099,902	-108,574	-110,207	-168,587
. . . .	611,983	679,325	671,055	803,320	877,279	919,040	-191,337	-197,955	-247,985
Servic	238,792	258,268	260,260	156,029	170,520	180,862	82,763	87,748	79,398
Travel	69,751	73,268	70,854	48,048	51,220	53,292	21,703	22,048	17,562
Passenger fares	20,413	20,895	19,986	15,818	18,235	18,693	4,595	2,660	1,293
Other transportation	26,074	26,911	25,818	27,403	28,949	29,999	-1,329	-2,038	-4,181
Royalties and license fees.	32,823	33,676	34,827	7,854	9,411	10,960	24,969	24,265	23,867
Other private services. . .	73,073	84,465	91,024	43,138	48,421	52,783	29,935	36,044	38,241
Other [1]	15,765	18,269	16,968	11,081	11,488	12,312	4,684	6,781	4,656
U.S. government miscel. services	893	784	783	2,687	2,796	2,823	-1,794	-2,012	-2,040

[1] Represents transfers under U.S. military sales contracts for exports and direct defense expenditures for imports.

Source: U.S. Census Bureau, U.S. International Trade in Goods and Services, Series FT-900(98).

No. 1323. U.S. Exports and General Imports in Goods: 1970 to 1998

[In billions of dollars (43.8 represents $43,800,000,000). Domestic and foreign exports, are f.a.s. (free alongside ship) value basis; general imports are on customs value basis]

Year	Total goods [1]			Manufactured goods [2][3]			Agricultural products [4]			Mineral fuels [3][5]		
	Exports	Imports	Balance	Exports	Imports	Balance	Exports	Imports	Balance	Exports	Imports	Balance
1970 . .	43.8	40.4	3.4	31.7	27.3	4.4	7.3	5.8	1.6	1.6	3.1	-1.5
1971 . .	44.7	46.2	-1.5	32.9	32.1	0.8	7.8	5.8	2.0	1.5	3.7	-2.2
1972 . .	50.5	56.4	-5.9	36.5	39.7	-3.2	9.5	6.5	3.0	1.6	4.8	-3.2
1973 . .	72.5	70.5	2.0	48.5	47.1	1.3	17.9	8.5	9.4	1.7	8.2	-6.5
1974 . .	100.0	102.6	-2.5	68.5	57.8	10.7	22.3	10.4	11.9	3.4	25.5	-22.0
1975 . .	109.3	98.5	10.8	76.9	54.0	22.9	22.1	9.5	12.6	4.5	26.5	-22.0
1976 . .	117.0	123.5	-6.5	83.1	67.6	15.5	23.3	11.2	12.1	4.2	34.0	-29.8
1977 . .	123.2	151.0	-27.8	88.9	80.5	8.4	24.2	13.6	10.6	4.2	47.2	-43.0
1978 . .	145.9	174.8	-28.8	103.6	104.3	-0.7	29.8	15.0	14.8	3.9	42.0	-38.1
1979 . .	186.5	209.5	-22.9	132.7	117.1	15.6	35.2	16.9	18.3	5.7	59.9	-54.2
1980 . .	225.7	245.3	-19.5	160.7	133.0	27.7	41.8	17.4	24.3	8.2	78.9	-70.7
1981 . .	238.7	261.0	-22.3	171.7	149.8	22.0	43.8	17.2	26.6	10.3	81.2	-70.9
1982 . .	216.4	244.0	-27.5	155.3	151.7	3.6	37.0	15.7	21.3	12.8	65.3	-52.5
1983 . .	205.6	258.0	-52.4	148.5	171.2	-22.7	36.5	16.5	19.9	9.8	57.8	-48.0
1983 . .	205.6	258.0	-52.4	148.7	170.9	-22.2	36.1	16.0	20.2	9.8	57.8	-48.0
1984 . .	224.0	330.7	-106.7	164.1	230.9	-66.8	37.9	19.3	18.6	9.7	60.8	-51.1
1985 . .	218.8	336.5	-117.7	168.0	257.5	-89.5	29.3	19.5	9.8	10.3	53.7	-43.4
1986 . .	227.2	365.4	-138.3	179.8	296.7	-116.8	26.3	20.9	5.4	8.4	37.2	-28.8
1987 . .	254.1	406.2	-152.1	199.9	324.4	-124.6	28.7	20.3	8.4	8.0	44.1	-36.1
1988 . .	322.4	441.0	-118.5	255.6	361.4	-105.7	37.1	20.7	16.4	8.5	41.0	-32.5
1989 . .	363.8	473.2	-109.4	287.0	379.4	-92.4	41.6	21.1	20.5	9.9	52.6	-42.7
1990 . .	393.6	495.3	-101.7	315.4	388.8	-73.5	39.6	22.3	17.2	12.4	64.7	-52.3
1991 . .	421.7	488.5	-66.7	345.1	392.4	-47.3	39.4	22.1	17.2	12.3	54.1	-41.8
1992 . .	448.2	532.7	-84.5	368.5	434.3	-65.9	43.1	23.4	19.8	11.3	55.3	-43.9
1993 . .	465.1	580.7	-115.6	388.7	479.9	-91.2	42.8	23.6	19.2	9.9	55.9	-46.0
1994 . .	512.6	663.3	-150.6	431.1	557.3	-126.3	45.9	26.0	20.0	9.0	56.4	-47.4
1995 . .	584.7	743.4	-158.7	486.7	629.7	-143.0	56.0	29.3	26.8	10.5	59.1	-48.6
1996 . .	625.1	795.3	-170.2	524.7	658.8	-134.1	60.6	32.6	28.1	12.4	78.1	-65.7
1997 . .	689.2	870.7	-181.5	592.5	728.9	-136.4	57.1	35.2	21.9	13.0	78.3	-65.3
1998 . .	682.1	911.9	-229.8	596.6	790.8	-194.2	52.0	35.7	16.3	10.4	57.3	-47.0

[1] Includes nonmonetary gold, military grant aid, special category shipments, trade between the U.S. Virgin Islands and foreign countries and undocumented exports to Canada. Adjustments were also made for carryover. Import values are based on transaction prices whenever possible ("f.a.s." for 1974-1979 and Customs value thereafter). Import data before 1974 do not exist on a transaction price valuation basis. [2]Manufactured goods include commodity sections 5-9 under Schedules A and E for 1970-1982 and SITC Rev. 3 for 1983-forward. Manufactures include undocumented exports to Canada, nonmonetary gold (excluding gold ore, scrap, and base bullion), and special category shipments. [3]Data for 1970-1980 exclude trade between the U.S. Virgin Islands and foreign countries. Census data concordances link the 1980-92 trade figures into time series that are as consistent as possible. Data for 1970-79 are not linked and are from published sources. Import values are "f.a.s." for 1974-1979 and Customs value thereafter; these values are based on transaction prices while maintaining a data series as consistent as possible over time. Import data before 1974 do not exist on a transaction price valuation basis. 1991 Imports include revisions for passenger cars, trucks, petroleum and petroleum products not included elsewhere; see footnote 7 on page 18 for more details. [4]Agricultural products for 1983-forward utilize the latest census definition that excludes manufactured goods that were previously classified as manufactured agricultural products. [5]Mineral fuels include commodity section 3 under SITC Rev. 1 for 1970-1976, SITC Rev. 2 for 1977-1982 and SITC Rev. 3 for 1983-forward.

Source: U.S. International Trade Administration, through 1996, U.S. Foreign Trade Highlights, annual; and thereafter, <http://www.ita.doc.gov/industry/otea/usfth/aggregate/H198t03.txt> (release 22 June 22 1999).

No. 1324. U.S. Exports and Imports for Consumption of Merchandise, by Major Customs District: 1990 to 1998

[In billions of dollars ($393.0 represents $393,000,000,000). Exports are f.a.s. (free alongside ship) value all years; imports are on customs value basis]

Customs district	Exports					Imports for consumption				
	1990	1995	1996	1997	1998	1990	1995	1996	1997	1998
Total [1]	393.0	584.7	625.1	689.2	682.1	490.6	738.6	789.9	861.7	905.7
Anchorage, AK	3.7	5.9	6.1	7.6	7.7	0.7	5.7	6.9	7.2	7.3
Baltimore, MD	6.7	9.0	8.3	7.6	6.6	11.2	14.4	14.0	14.7	16.3
Boston	5.6	4.6	5.0	5.7	6.0	12.2	13.4	13.7	14.7	14.7
Buffalo, NY	15.8	30.5	32.3	39.2	38.8	19.2	29.1	29.3	30.4	35.4
Charleston, SC [2]	6.7	10.1	10.8	12.3	11.9	6.8	10.4	11.6	12.3	14.0
Chicago, IL	10.2	18.4	18.7	19.6	19.2	18.3	31.3	33.5	37.1	38.5
Cleveland, OH	4.0	7.8	10.2	14.0	15.1	11.3	21.7	23.6	26.2	27.4
Dallas/Fort Worth, TX	3.4	4.4	3.8	5.3	5.9	4.8	8.8	9.8	11.4	12.7
Detroit, MI	35.6	56.8	60.8	66.7	69.8	37.8	64.7	69.4	75.7	76.4
Duluth, MN	0.8	1.4	1.5	1.4	1.5	3.9	6.0	6.5	6.5	5.0
El Paso, TX	3.9	7.9	9.6	10.2	11.4	5.0	12.9	13.6	14.9	17.4
Great Falls, MT	2.4	3.0	3.2	4.3	4.3	4.7	6.9	8.0	8.9	8.7
Honolulu, HI	0.5	1.1	1.3	1.6	1.0	2.1	2.7	2.7	2.7	2.2
Houston/Galveston, TX	17.6	27.4	27.1	28.5	27.9	21.6	23.4	28.2	28.9	26.5
Laredo, TX	15.2	24.3	29.7	39.1	41.9	10.0	24.7	31.9	38.1	41.9
Los Angeles, CA	42.1	67.0	69.0	74.2	63.7	64.1	96.3	99.9	110.3	115.9
Miami, FL	11.2	22.7	24.5	29.5	30.2	7.1	11.9	13.5	16.2	18.5
Milwaukee, WI	0.1	0.1	0.1	0.2	0.2	1.1	1.5	1.4	1.5	1.7
Minneapolis, MN	0.9	1.3	1.4	1.6	1.1	2.0	2.8	3.3	3.7	4.1
Mobile, AL [2]	1.9	3.4	3.4	3.8	4.0	3.4	3.9	4.9	4.8	4.9
New Orleans, LA	18.0	28.4	31.0	30.4	27.8	24.1	34.4	35.4	35.4	36.3
New York, NY	50.9	61.4	61.9	67.1	67.7	68.0	87.6	93.4	103.1	112.2
Nogales, AZ	2.1	4.0	4.2	4.9	6.5	4.2	7.7	7.2	8.6	10.5
Norfolk, VA [2]	11.7	14.4	15.2	16.1	15.1	7.4	8.6	9.4	9.9	10.9
Ogdensburg, NY	7.9	9.2	9.9	10.6	10.6	9.8	14.4	15.9	17.4	18.3
Pembina, ND	3.4	5.5	5.9	7.1	7.4	4.1	7.2	7.4	7.7	8.1
Philadelphia, PA	4.0	6.7	9.2	7.7	7.5	18.3	18.3	19.0	19.0	19.3
Port Arthur, TX	0.9	1.3	1.0	1.3	1.0	3.2	4.8	6.0	6.4	4.6
Portland, ME	1.7	2.1	2.1	2.1	2.1	4.3	4.4	5.2	5.3	5.2
Portland, OR	5.8	10.2	10.0	8.5	7.1	5.6	7.9	7.5	9.6	9.7
Providence, RI	(Z)	0.1	0.0	0.1	0.0	1.3	0.9	1.3	1.3	1.0
San Diego, CA	3.4	6.1	7.5	9.0	9.8	4.3	8.9	11.0	14.0	16.4
San Francisco, CA	23.1	43.7	47.8	48.1	42.7	28.0	58.8	57.7	58.7	55.5
San Juan, PR	2.5	2.6	2.5	2.8	3.4	5.4	6.8	7.2	8.0	8.4
Savannah, GA	7.4	10.9	10.9	13.4	13.5	9.8	14.7	16.1	18.0	19.6
Seattle, WA	32.6	31.4	37.1	44.8	47.2	20.9	24.1	25.1	30.1	32.3
St. Albans, VT	4.0	4.4	4.1	3.0	3.3	5.2	7.4	7.9	8.1	8.3
St. Louis, MO	0.3	0.3	1.6	1.3	2.0	3.0	4.4	4.8	5.7	6.3
Tampa, FL	4.3	6.7	6.9	7.4	7.4	7.0	9.2	9.2	9.4	11.6
Virgin Islands of the U.S.	0.2	0.2	0.2	0.2	0.2	2.1	2.1	2.8	3.3	2.3
Washington, DC	1.1	2.3	2.1	2.2	2.3	0.8	1.2	1.3	1.6	1.8
Wilmington, NC	3.0	4.4	4.2	4.0	3.9	3.3	7.4	7.6	8.9	8.8

Z Less than $50 million. [1] Totals shown for exports reflect the value of estimated parcel post and Special Category shipments, and beginning 1990, adjustments for undocumented exports to Canada which are not distributed by customs district. Beginning 1990, the value of bituminous coal exported through Norfolk, VA; Charleston, SC; and Mobile, AL is reflected in the total but not distributed by district. [2] Beginning 1990, excludes exports of bituminous coal.

Source: U.S. Census Bureau, 1980, Highlights of U.S. Export and Import Trade, FT 990; 1990, U.S. Merchandise Trade: Selected Highlights, series FT 920, monthly; and beginning 1995, U.S. Export History and U.S. Import History on compact disc.

No. 1325. Export and Import Unit Value Indexes—Selected Countries: 1994 to 1998

[Indexes in U.S. dollars, 1995=100. A unit value is an implicit price derived from value and quantity data]

Country	Export unit value					Import unit value				
	1994	1995	1996	1997	1998	1994	1995	1996	1997	1998
United States	95.2	100.0	100.6	99.0	95.9	95.7	100.0	101.0	98.5	92.6
Australia	91.9	100.0	101.2	97.7	86.7	95.2	100.0	99.9	94.6	86.8
Canada	93.0	100.0	101.3	99.3	93.4	96.9	100.0	100.3	99.4	97.2
Denmark	88.1	100.0	98.6	88.4	(NA)	86.1	100.0	97.4	88.7	(NA)
France	88.5	100.0	97.4	86.5	86.3	88.5	100.0	98.1	87.3	86.4
Germany	86.4	100.0	(NA)	(NA)	(NA)	86.0	100.0	(NA)	(NA)	(NA)
Italy	92.4	100.0	110.1	99.4	(NA)	85.2	(NA)	100.1	90.7	(NA)
Japan	92.6	100.0	92.5	86.5	(NA)	92.3	100.0	100.7	95.1	(NA)
Netherlands	86.6	100.0	95.5	(NA)	(NA)	87.8	100.0	96.1	(NA)	(NA)
Norway	87.1	100.0	106.1	98.7	82.7	88.9	100.0	97.8	88.3	84.0
Sweden	88.8	100.0	93.6	87.2	82.7	90.9	100.0	95.6	89.2	83.6
United Kingdom	94.2	100.0	99.9	99.2	(NA)	91.5	100.0	98.9	97.3	(NA)

NA Not available.

Source: International Monetary Fund, Washington, DC, International Financial Statistics, monthly (copyright).

Foreign Commerce and Aid 803

No. 1326. U.S. Exports, by State of Origin: 1990 to 1998

[In millions of dollars ($394,045 represents $394,045,000,000). Exports are on a f.a.s. value basis. Exports are based on origin of movement]

State and other area	1990	1997	1998 Total	Rank	State and other area	1990	1997	1998 Total	Rank
Total	394,045	688,896	682,977	(X)	Montana	229	530	420.6	49
United States ..	315,065	615,788	612,390	(X)	Nebraska	693	1,971	1,995.1	38
					Nevada	394	1,075	687.5	46
Alabama	2,834	5,932	6,371.9	25	New Hampshire.....	973	1,597	1,727.9	42
Alaska	2,850	2,721	1,953.9	39	New Jersey	7,633	15,167	15,371.0	13
Arizona	3,729	13,820	11,414.5	17					
Arkansas	920	2,305	2,285.8	34	New Mexico	249	1,776	1,854.7	40
California	44,520	99,161	95,768.0	1	New York	22,072	37,979	37,383.5	4
					North Carolina......	8,010	16,402	15,705.5	12
Colorado	2,274	5,120	5,266.1	27	North Dakota	360	778	749.7	45
Connecticut	4,356	7,058	7,297.1	24	Ohio	13,378	24,903	24,851.7	7
Delaware	1,344	2,067	2,232.1	36					
District of Columbia ..	320	485	348.4	(X)	Oklahoma	1,646	2,728	2,785.3	33
Florida...........	11,634	23,234	24,452.0	8	Oregon	4,065	9,151	9,031.3	21
					Pennsylvania	8,491	16,069	15,974.2	10
Georgia	5,763	12,949	13,475.9	14	Rhode Island	595	1,088	1,101.9	44
Hawaii	179	334	276.4	50	South Carolina	3,116	7,517	7,749.0	23
Idaho............	898	1,664	1,509.9	43					
Illinois	12,965	26,455	28,914.2	6	South Dakota	205	517	446.2	48
Indiana	5,273	12,029	12,318.1	16	Tennessee	3,746	9,233	9,551.7	19
					Texas	32,931	76,184	78,875.3	2
Iowa	2,189	5,118	4,901.3	28	Utah	1,596	3,239	2,980.7	32
Kansas	2,113	4,292	4,039.3	30	Vermont...........	1,154	3,811	3,668.4	31
Kentucky	3,175	7,953	8,099.5	22					
Louisiana	14,199	18,732	16,836.1	9	Virginia	9,333	12,755	12,513.9	15
Maine	870	1,723	1,825.0	41	Washington	24,432	32,752	38,249.1	3
					West Virginia	1,550	2,276	2,105.9	37
Maryland	2,592	5,214	4,721.6	29	Wisconsin.........	5,158	10,125	9,751.9	18
Massachusetts	9,501	16,526	15,878.2	11	Wyoming	264	560	500.0	47
Michigan	18,474	32,254	28,977.4	5					
Minnesota	5,091	9,447	9,147.3	20	Puerto Rico	3,600	5,601	6,273.8	(X)
Mississippi	1,605	2,290	2,285.8	35	Virgin Islands	51	233	89.6	(X)
Missouri.........	3,130	6,724	5,762.2	26	Other [1]	75,328	67,275	64,223.4	(X)

X Not applicable.   [1] Includes unreported, not specified, special category, estimated shipments, foreign trade zone, re-exports, and any timing adjustments.

Source: U.S. Census Bureau, *U.S. Merchandise Trade,* Series FT 900, December issues.

No. 1327. U.S. Agriculture Exports, by State: 1996 and 1997

[In millions of dollars (59,891 represents $59,891,000,000)]

State	1996	1997 Total	Soybeans and products	Feed grains and products	Live animals and meat	State	1996	1997 Total	Soybeans and products	Feed grains and products	Live animals and meat
U.S......	59,891	57,365	9,254	8,448	4,893	MT.	896	327	-	36	16
						NE.	3,510	3,308	526	1,121	737
AL........	494	535	42	-	23	NV.	5	6	-	-	1
AK........	-	-	-	-	-	NH.	1	1	-	-	-
AZ........	409	370	-	-	44	NJ.	149	168	17	-	2
AR........	1,686	1,918	435	39	4						
CA........	7,208	7,694	-	-	159	NM.	75	70	-	19	15
CO........	1,100	872	-	135	250	NY.	400	396	-	60	20
CT........	43	80	-	-	-	NC.	1,400	1,515	135	-	117
DE........	133	147	30	-	-	ND.	1,734	1,083	95	152	20
FL.........	1,230	1,212	4	-	33	OH.	1,602	1,361	610	270	32
GA........	1,224	1,273	39	-	42						
						OK.	517	385	29	46	19
HI	115	126	-	-	-	OR.	749	729	-	-	4
ID	935	841	-	40	71	PA.	544	542	44	-	145
IL.........	3,974	3,748	1,550	1,300	213	RI	1	1	-	-	-
IN	2,049	1,853	791	587	61	SC.	340	354	52	-	7
IA	4,640	4,146	1,615	1,504	482						
						SD.	1,163	1,163	353	337	113
KS........	3,112	2,650	287	608	628	TN.	500	540	156	-	23
KY........	1,046	1,110	174	133	189	TX.	3,477	3,054	27	330	655
LA........	662	704	138	-	1	UT.	145	125	-	-	50
ME........	40	39	-	-	-	VT.	8	11	-	-	-
MD........	247	271	69	58	-						
						VA.	486	520	63	-	78
MA........	29	48	-	-	-	WA.	1,941	1,857	-	37	93
MI	1,186	886	182	191	95	WV.	34	31	-	-	-
MN........	3,031	2,611	871	784	203	WI.	1,371	1,219	125	297	151
MS........	777	821	211	-	24	WY.	52	40	-	12	13
MO	1,314	1,543	582	354	64	Unallocated ...	2,107	3,062	-	-	-

- Represents or rounds to zero.

Source: U.S. Dept. of Agriculture, Economic Research Service, *Foreign Agricultural Trade of the United States (FATUS),* annual.

No. 1328. U. S. Exports, Imports, and Merchandise Trade Balance, by Country: 1994 to 1998

[In millions of dollars (512,626.5 represents 512,626,500,000). Includes silver ore and bullion. Country totals include exports of special category commodities, if any. Data include nonmonetary gold and includes trade of Virgin Islands with foreign countries. Minus sign (-) denotes an excess of imports over exports]

Country	Exports, domestic, and foreign					General imports					Merchandise trade balance				
	1994	1995	1996	1997	1998	1994	1995	1996	1997	1998	1994	1995	1996	1997	1998
Total	512,626.5	584,742.0	625,075.0	689,182.4	682,976.7	663,255.7	743,542.8	795,289.3	870,670.7	913,828.2	-150,629.2	-158,800.8	-170,214.3	-181,488.2	-230,851.5
Afghanistan	5.4	4.1	16.9	11.5	7.0	6.1	5.4	16.4	10.0	16.7	-0.6	-1.3	0.5	1.5	-9.7
Albania	16.0	13.5	12.1	3.1	14.9	6.1	9.5	10.3	11.7	12.4	9.9	4.0	1.7	-8.6	2.5
Algeria	1,191.5	774.0	635.2	691.6	650.2	1,526.9	1,749.5	2,125.7	2,439.5	1,631.3	-335.4	-975.5	-1,490.5	-1,747.9	-981.1
Andorra	4.8	16.4	24.5	21.7	23.0	0.1	0.2	2.5	0.3	0.1	4.7	16.2	22.0	21.4	22.9
Angola	197.3	259.6	268.3	280.6	354.3	2,061.3	2,232.3	2,901.5	2,779.1	2,251.5	-1,864.0	-1,972.6	-2,633.2	-2,498.6	-1,897.2
Anguilla	12.8	14.6	12.8	18.1	16.7	0.3	0.1	0.8	0.7	2.1	12.5	14.5	12.0	17.4	14.6
Antigua	64.8	97.1	82.4	84.5	95.8	5.3	3.1	8.9	4.8	1.9	59.5	94.1	73.5	79.6	93.9
Argentina	4,461.6	4,189.2	4,516.8	5,810.0	5,885.3	1,725.4	1,760.9	2,279.2	2,228.2	2,252.1	2,736.2	2,428.3	2,237.6	3,581.8	3,633.2
Armenia	73.9	70.4	57.4	62.1	51.4	5.3	16.2	1.5	6.0	16.7	73.0	54.2	56.0	56.1	34.7
Aruba	273.6	247.4	234.6	238.4	351.2	461.2	420.6	558.1	610.2	471.0	-187.5	-173.2	-323.5	-371.8	-119.8
Australia	9,780.5	10,789.1	12,008.4	12,062.9	11,929.3	3,202.0	3,322.9	3,868.9	4,602.3	5,381.9	6,578.5	7,466.2	8,139.6	7,460.6	6,547.4
Austria	1,371.7	2,017.2	2,009.8	2,074.7	2,506.1	1,749.7	1,963.1	2,200.3	2,368.4	2,558.0	-378.0	53.9	-190.5	-293.7	-51.9
Azerbaijan	27.4	35.6	54.0	62.3	122.8	0.3	0.8	4.5	5.7	4.9	27.1	34.8	49.5	56.6	117.9
Bahamas, The	684.9	661.3	726.0	809.5	815.1	202.8	156.5	164.0	154.9	142.5	482.0	504.8	561.1	654.6	672.6
Bahrain	443.9	254.9	244.2	406.1	294.9	147.5	134.2	116.3	116.4	155.5	296.4	120.8	127.9	289.8	139.4
Bangladesh	232.1	325.1	210.1	259.0	317.7	1,080.1	1,257.2	1,343.0	1,679.4	1,845.7	-848.0	-932.2	-1,132.9	-1,420.4	-1,528.0
Barbados	161.1	185.7	222.5	280.9	281.1	34.5	37.7	41.2	42.1	35.3	126.6	148.0	181.3	238.7	245.8
Byelarus	46.4	48.0	53.1	40.6	30.4	53.5	44.9	52.2	66.0	105.4	-7.1	3.1	0.9	-25.4	-75.0
Belgium	10,939.3	12,465.5	12,532.2	13,420.3	13,918.1	6,354.3	6,053.9	6,775.7	7,911.9	8,421.9	4,585.0	6,411.6	5,756.6	5,508.4	5,496.2
Belize	115.2	99.8	106.6	114.8	119.9	50.8	52.2	68.2	77.3	66.0	64.4	47.6	38.5	37.5	53.9
Benin	25.9	34.1	27.4	51.6	43.6	10.1	9.8	13.6	7.7	3.6	15.8	24.3	13.8	43.9	40.0
Bermuda	299.9	298.5	281.9	338.1	400.3	9.1	10.3	11.5	29.8	11.5	290.8	288.2	270.4	308.2	388.8
Bolivia	184.9	213.5	269.5	295.1	402.9	260.3	262.5	275.2	223.3	223.6	-75.4	-49.0	-5.7	71.9	179.3
Bosnia and Hercegovina	39.0	28.4	58.8	102.5	40.0	4.5	3.3	10.1	8.3	7.4	34.5	25.1	48.6	94.2	32.6
Botswana	22.7	35.8	28.9	43.1	35.6	13.6	21.2	27.0	24.6	19.7	9.1	14.5	1.9	18.5	15.9
Brazil	8,101.6	11,439.4	12,717.5	15,914.7	15,157.0	8,682.6	8,832.9	8,773.4	9,625.5	10,122.5	-581.0	2,606.6	3,944.2	6,289.2	5,034.5
British Virgin Islands	47.1	49.3	53.9	64.6	62.7	14.6	11.4	6.6	13.1	7.5	32.5	37.9	47.3	51.5	55.2
Brunei	375.8	189.9	374.7	178.1	122.9	45.6	38.3	48.3	55.8	210.8	330.3	151.6	326.4	122.3	-87.9
Bulgaria	110.0	131.8	137.5	109.6	115.1	215.5	188.5	126.5	171.4	219.1	-105.5	-56.7	11.0	-61.8	-104.0
Burkina Faso	7.3	14.6	10.4	18.3	16.1	0.4	0.4	3.9	1.0	0.6	6.8	14.2	6.5	17.3	15.5
Cameroon	53.7	45.5	71.3	121.4	75.2	55.0	57.3	64.5	57.2	53.3	-1.3	-11.7	6.8	64.3	21.9
Canada	114,438.5	127,226.1	134,210.3	151,766.7	156,307.6	128,405.9	144,369.8	155,892.6	168,200.9	174,843.8	-13,967.4	-17,143.7	-21,682.3	-16,434.2	-18,536.2
Cayman Islands	202.2	180.3	208.0	270.3	421.7	52.5	18.3	16.9	19.6	18.1	149.6	162.0	191.2	250.7	403.6
Chad	7.5	10.8	3.4	3.1	3.5	1.8	3.2	3.2	2.9	7.3	5.7	7.6	0.2	0.2	-3.8
Chile	2,773.8	3,614.9	4,139.5	4,368.4	3,985.2	1,820.5	1,930.8	2,262.2	2,293.1	2,452.9	953.3	1,684.1	1,877.3	2,075.3	1,532.3
China	9,281.8	11,753.6	11,992.6	12,862.3	14,258.0	38,786.7	45,543.2	51,512.6	62,557.6	71,155.9	-29,504.9	-33,789.6	-39,520.0	-49,695.3	-56,897.9
Colombia	4,064.3	4,624.4	4,714.3	5,197.0	4,816.1	3,171.0	3,791.1	4,423.8	4,737.3	4,651.5	893.3	833.3	290.5	459.7	165.2
Congo (Brazzaville)	38.0	54.7	62.9	74.7	92.0	403.4	206.9	315.3	471.5	315.4	-365.5	-152.2	-252.4	-396.8	-223.4
Congo (Kinshawa)	39.5	77.1	73.3	37.8	34.0	179.6	266.9	258.7	281.8	171.6	-140.1	-189.9	-185.3	-244.0	-137.6
Costa Rica	1,870.0	1,736.5	1,816.4	2,024.4	2,299.3	1,647.1	1,843.1	1,974.2	2,323.2	2,745.5	222.9	-106.6	-157.9	-298.8	-446.2
Croatia	146.8	139.9	106.0	138.7	96.8	114.7	93.7	71.2	82.8	72.5	32.0	46.2	34.8	55.9	24.3
Cyprus	208.8	257.8	256.9	244.5	162.6	17.9	13.0	17.4	16.4	31.8	190.9	244.8	239.6	228.1	130.8
Czech Republic	296.8	362.7	412.2	589.8	568.3	315.8	363.4	482.3	609.8	671.9	-19.0	-0.7	-70.1	-20.0	-103.6
Denmark	1,214.8	1,517.7	1,731.0	1,756.9	1,874.3	2,121.6	1,945.0	2,141.5	2,137.7	2,381.7	-906.8	-427.3	-410.5	-380.8	-507.4

See footnotes at end of table.

U.S. Census Bureau, Statistical Abstract of the United States: 1999

No. 1328. U.S. Exports, Imports, and Merchandise Trade Balance, by Country: 1994 to 1998—Continued

[See headnote, page 805]

Country	Exports, domestic, and foreign					General imports					Merchandise trade balance				
	1994	1995	1996	1997	1998	1994	1995	1996	1997	1998	1994	1995	1996	1997	1998
Djibouti	6.7	8.5	8.3	7.3	20.1	0.1	0.1	0.0	0.0	0.5	6.7	8.4	8.3	7.3	19.6
Dominica	25.6	26.5	34.2	37.4	52.1	6.9	6.6	7.7	9.1	6.4	18.6	19.9	26.5	28.3	45.7
Dominican Republic	2,798.8	3,014.9	3,190.5	3,924.0	3,977.4	3,090.6	3,399.0	3,574.8	4,326.8	4,443.1	-291.8	-384.0	-384.3	-402.8	-465.7
Ecuador	1,194.6	1,538.3	1,258.5	1,525.9	1,686.6	1,726.2	1,939.9	1,958.1	2,054.8	1,755.2	-531.6	-401.6	-699.6	-528.9	-68.6
Egypt	2,854.8	2,985.1	3,153.3	3,835.4	3,059.8	548.7	606.4	680.5	657.5	660.3	2,306.0	2,378.7	2,472.9	3,177.9	2,399.5
El Salvador	931.2	1,110.6	1,074.5	1,400.1	1,515.0	609.2	812.2	975.4	1,346.2	1,438.2	322.0	298.4	99.1	53.8	76.8
Estonia	33.3	138.9	83.6	47.4	87.3	29.3	62.3	55.1	76.8	125.4	4.0	76.6	28.5	-29.3	-38.1
Ethiopia	143.8	147.5	148.1	121.2	88.4	-	-	-	-	52.3	143.8	147.5	148.1	121.2	36.1
Federated States of Micronesia	24.6	23.3	24.7	29.0	31.0	13.2	13.0	11.3	11.9	12.6	11.3	10.2	13.5	17.2	18.4
Fiji	118.2	31.6	27.5	32.8	74.2	97.1	78.0	74.7	84.6	101.1	21.1	-46.4	-47.2	-51.8	-26.9
Finland	1,068.3	1,249.7	2,438.6	1,741.1	1,915.1	1,800.7	2,270.0	2,388.8	2,391.5	2,594.8	-732.4	-1,020.3	49.8	-650.4	-679.7
France	13,618.7	14,245.2	14,455.5	15,964.9	17,728.0	16,699.0	17,209.4	18,645.8	20,636.4	24,077.3	-3,080.2	-2,964.3	-4,190.3	-4,671.5	-6,349.3
French Guiana	195.6	441.7	300.7	493.7	246.5	3.2	5.3	4.7	2.4	3.2	192.5	436.4	296.0	491.4	243.3
French Polynesia	72.0	82.3	88.7	105.2	99.8	14.3	14.1	17.2	35.4	33.8	57.7	68.2	71.5	69.9	66.0
Gabon	40.2	54.4	56.1	84.5	62.4	1,134.3	1,464.0	1,983.7	2,202.3	1,268.3	-1,094.1	-1,409.6	-1,927.6	-2,117.7	-1,205.9
Gambia	3.9	6.2	8.5	9.7	9.3	2.4	2.3	2.0	2.9	2.0	1.5	3.9	6.5	6.8	7.3
Georgia	78.2	95.2	82.5	140.6	136.5	1.3	10.6	7.6	7.0	14.2	76.9	84.6	74.9	133.6	122.3
Germany	19,229.0	22,394.3	23,495.0	24,458.3	26,641.9	31,744.3	36,844.0	38,945.1	43,121.5	49,823.9	-12,515.3	-14,449.8	-15,450.1	-18,663.2	-23,182.0
Ghana	124.5	167.2	295.7	315.0	223.4	198.5	196.1	171.4	155.3	144.4	-74.0	-28.9	124.3	159.8	79.0
Gibraltar	23.1	18.4	11.7	8.8	8.8	4.0	4.9	6.5	2.8	6.0	19.1	13.5	5.2	6.0	2.8
Greece	829.0	1,518.8	824.5	949.3	1,355.1	455.3	397.3	506.0	453.2	467.1	373.7	1,121.5	318.5	496.2	888.0
Greenland	3.3	2.4	4.1	4.9	6.1	9.5	7.4	6.4	7.9	7.3	-6.2	-5.0	-2.2	-3.0	-1.2
Grenada	23.5	26.8	35.7	40.6	56.5	7.2	5.3	3.6	6.5	12.1	16.2	21.5	32.1	34.1	44.4
Guadeloupe	51.2	69.3	66.0	57.6	61.1	1.9	1.3	1.4	3.5	2.3	49.3	68.0	64.6	54.1	58.8
Guatemala	1,352.2	1,646.6	1,566.1	1,729.6	1,940.9	1,282.7	1,526.7	1,678.5	1,990.2	2,072.0	69.5	119.9	-112.4	-260.6	-131.1
Guinea	49.8	66.7	87.1	82.8	65.4	92.1	99.0	116.5	127.7	115.6	-42.3	-32.3	-29.4	-44.9	-50.2
Guyana	109.8	141.2	136.9	142.5	145.5	98.0	107.4	109.5	112.8	135.3	11.7	33.8	27.4	29.7	10.2
Haiti	204.5	550.2	474.8	499.1	547.8	58.7	129.8	143.6	188.2	271.8	145.8	420.4	331.3	310.9	276.0
Honduras	1,011.8	1,278.9	1,642.6	2,018.9	2,322.8	1,097.6	1,441.3	1,795.4	2,322.3	2,544.9	-85.8	-162.4	-152.8	-303.4	-222.1
Hong Kong	11,441.0	14,231.4	13,966.3	15,117.1	12,923.5	9,695.6	10,291.2	9,864.5	10,287.8	10,538.4	1,745.4	3,940.2	4,101.8	4,829.3	2,385.1
Hungary	309.0	295.3	330.7	485.5	482.5	470.3	547.0	676.2	1,078.9	1,567.4	-161.3	-251.7	-345.5	-593.5	-1,084.9
Iceland	111.8	170.6	257.1	179.2	236.5	248.7	232.7	236.0	230.8	268.0	-136.9	-62.2	21.2	-51.6	-31.5
India	2,294.0	3,295.8	3,328.3	3,607.6	3,544.7	5,309.5	5,726.3	6,169.5	7,322.4	8,224.6	-3,015.5	-2,430.5	-2,841.2	-3,714.8	-4,679.9
Indonesia	2,808.8	3,359.6	3,976.8	4,522.3	2,290.9	6,546.9	7,435.3	8,249.9	9,188.4	9,337.6	-3,738.2	-4,075.7	-4,273.1	-4,666.1	-7,046.7
Iran	328.9	277.3	2.8	1.1	0.9	(X)	(X)	(X)	(X)	(X)	(X)	(X)	(X)	(X)	(X)
Iraq	0.8	0.2	2.8	82.0	106.5	(X)	(X)	(X)	311.9	1,199.4	(X)	(X)	(X)	-229.9	-1,092.9
Ireland	3,418.6	4,108.8	3,668.7	4,642.2	5,653.0	2,893.5	4,078.7	4,803.9	5,866.6	8,384.9	525.2	30.1	-1,135.2	-1,224.4	-2,731.9
Israel	4,995.8	5,621.1	6,011.9	5,994.7	6,977.5	5,229.4	5,708.7	6,433.6	7,326.0	8,628.0	-233.6	-87.6	-421.7	-1,331.3	-1,650.5
Italy	7,182.7	8,861.6	8,797.1	8,994.7	9,027.0	14,802.2	16,348.3	18,324.8	19,407.5	21,012.8	-7,619.4	-7,486.7	-9,527.8	-10,412.8	-11,985.8
Ivory Coast	111.2	173.2	141.1	150.9	151.6	185.4	214.1	397.4	289.0	417.6	-74.2	-40.9	-256.3	-138.1	-266.0
Jamaica	1,065.5	1,420.4	1,491.0	1,416.5	1,303.7	746.6	847.0	838.2	738.0	753.3	318.9	573.4	652.9	678.4	550.4
Japan	53,487.7	64,342.6	67,606.8	65,548.5	57,880.9	119,155.7	123,479.1	115,187.0	121,663.2	121,981.6	-65,668.0	-59,136.5	-47,580.2	-56,114.8	-64,093.7
Jordan	287.3	335.3	345.2	402.5	353.1	29.0	28.8	25.2	25.3	16.4	258.3	306.5	320.1	377.1	336.7
Kazakhstan	130.2	80.9	138.3	346.3	103.1	62.3	122.9	121.2	128.9	168.7	67.9	-42.1	17.2	217.4	-65.6
Kenya	169.6	114.0	104.6	225.3	199.0	108.8	101.5	106.5	114.0	98.5	60.8	12.5	-2.0	111.4	100.5
Kiribati	23.4	2.3	4.2	2.7	2.6	0.9	1.2	1.2	1.7	1.1	22.4	1.1	3.0	1.0	1.5

See footnotes at end of table.

U.S. Census Bureau, Statistical Abstract of the United States: 1999

Country	Exports, domestic and foreign					General imports					Merchandise trade balance				
	1994	1995	1996	1997	1998	1994	1995	1996	1997	1998	1994	1995	1996	1997	1998
Kuwait	1,175.9	1,437.3	1,983.6	1,390.0	1,479.4	1,457.5	1,335.5	1,651.2	1,816.4	1,272.2	-281.5	101.8	332.4	-426.4	207.2
Kyrgyzstan	6.0	24.7	46.9	28.4	20.6	7.7	8.3	5.0	2.4	0.3	-1.8	16.3	41.9	25.9	20.3
Latvia	101.1	89.5	166.6	217.8	186.8	41.4	81.9	102.9	145.1	114.8	59.7	7.6	63.7	72.7	72.0
Lebanon	442.0	592.3	627.0	551.9	514.1	25.4	35.1	41.5	77.8	82.4	416.6	557.2	585.6	474.2	431.7
Lesotho	3.4	2.7	2.6	2.4	1.4	63.0	62.1	65.4	86.5	100.1	-59.6	-59.4	-62.7	-84.2	-98.7
Liberia	46.4	41.7	49.8	42.9	50.0	3.5	9.8	26.9	4.8	25.1	42.9	31.9	22.9	38.1	24.9
Liechtenstein	13.9	14.9	8.9	12.5	7.3	98.3	126.2	91.1	116.5	242.9	-84.4	-111.3	-82.3	-104.0	-235.6
Lithuania	41.2	52.0	62.9	87.4	62.2	15.3	26.4	34.4	79.8	81.2	25.9	25.6	28.6	7.6	-19.0
Luxembourg	228.4	374.4	242.2	712.1	606.1	287.5	234.0	203.8	238.8	373.9	-59.1	140.4	38.3	473.2	232.2
Macau	21.2	29.9	29.8	65.0	40.8	791.3	895.3	857.6	1,021.0	1,108.6	-770.1	-865.5	-827.9	-956.0	-1,067.8
Macedonia	14.0	21.3	14.4	33.8	14.9	82.1	88.8	124.8	147.1	175.4	-68.1	-67.6	-110.5	-113.3	-160.5
Madagascar	47.9	10.0	11.5	11.5	14.6	57.1	57.3	45.5	62.6	71.4	-9.2	-47.3	-34.0	-51.0	-56.8
Malawi	18.7	17.8	13.3	17.6	14.5	56.5	40.9	72.5	82.8	60.5	-37.8	-23.1	-59.2	-65.3	-46.0
Malaysia	6,969.0	8,816.1	8,546.2	10,780.0	8,952.9	13,981.7	17,454.7	17,828.8	18,026.7	19,001.4	-7,012.6	-8,638.6	-9,282.6	-7,246.7	-10,048.5
Mali	19.0	23.2	18.4	120.9	25.4	6.1	3.6	4.9	3.8	3.4	13.0	19.6	13.5	22.3	22.0
Malta	87.6	106.7	125.2	26.2	268.3	95.7	132.4	208.6	223.6	340.5	-8.0	-25.8	-83.5	-102.7	-72.2
Marshall Islands	33.1	31.7	29.4	23.6	24.8	8.0	11.0	3.9	7.3	5.8	25.2	20.6	25.5	16.3	19.0
Martinique	31.1	38.4	35.3	33.9	26.4	3.5	2.1	1.0	2.4	1.0	27.5	36.3	34.3	31.4	25.4
Mauritania	14.0	43.1	15.1	20.9	19.5	3.5	5.5	5.3	0.2	0.4	10.5	37.6	9.8	20.6	19.1
Mauritius	23.7	24.7	25.2	31.4	23.3	216.6	229.7	217.0	238.4	271.6	-192.9	-204.9	-191.8	-207.0	-248.3
Mexico	50,843.5	46,292.1	56,791.5	71,388.4	79,010.1	49,493.8	62,100.6	74,297.3	85,937.5	94,708.7	1,349.7	-15,808.6	-17,505.8	-14,549.1	-15,698.6
Moldova	23.4	10.2	21.6	19.7	20.6	3.0	24.8	29.7	53.7	111.6	20.4	-14.6	-8.1	-34.0	-91.0
Monaco	5.6	9.5	3.1	6.9	6.4	17.5	12.2	15.9	19.6	25.6	-11.9	-2.7	-12.8	-12.7	-19.2
Morocco	408.7	517.4	476.3	434.7	552.3	192.0	239.3	247.1	295.9	343.2	216.7	278.1	229.2	138.9	209.1
Mozambique	39.4	49.3	23.0	45.6	45.7	15.3	27.6	26.6	30.5	25.8	24.1	21.7	-3.5	15.1	19.9
Namibia	16.4	26.5	22.7	25.0	51.2	27.8	11.5	27.1	63.0	51.8	-11.4	15.0	-4.5	-38.1	-0.6
Netherlands	13,581.6	16,557.7	16,662.6	19,826.7	19,003.8	6,006.8	6,405.0	6,583.1	7,292.8	7,591.0	7,574.8	10,152.7	10,079.4	12,533.8	11,412.8
Netherlands Antilles	521.0	504.0	529.6	475.2	742.1	425.3	289.9	684.8	579.8	307.6	95.7	214.1	-155.2	-104.6	434.5
New Caledonia	27.3	22.4	28.7	34.4	19.3	22.7	40.2	54.8	51.9	17.7	4.7	-17.8	-26.1	-17.5	1.6
New Zealand	1,507.8	1,691.4	1,728.5	1,962.1	1,884.6	1,421.1	1,451.8	1,463.2	1,579.2	1,645.0	86.6	239.6	265.4	382.9	239.6
Nicaragua	185.7	249.7	262.3	289.8	336.6	167.2	238.7	350.4	439.3	453.3	18.5	11.0	-88.1	-149.5	-116.7
Niger	12.0	39.5	27.2	24.8	18.2	2.4	1.6	0.7	29.8	26.5	9.6	38.0	26.5	-5.0	16.5
Nigeria	509.1	602.8	818.4	813.1	819.6	4,429.9	4,930.4	5,978.3	6,349.4	4,194.6	-3,920.9	-4,327.7	-5,159.9	-5,536.4	-3,375.0
Norway	1,267.3	1,293.0	1,559.0	1,721.3	1,709.1	2,353.4	3,086.1	3,992.5	3,752.0	2,873.6	-1,086.1	-1,793.7	-2,433.5	-2,030.7	-1,164.5
Oman	219.1	222.0	216.8	340.8	302.7	458.3	294.9	414.4	242.4	216.7	-239.2	-72.9	-197.7	98.4	86.0
Pakistan	718.3	941.2	1,271.4	1,240.1	726.2	1,011.6	1,197.1	1,265.7	1,442.2	1,691.4	-293.3	-255.8	5.7	-202.2	-965.2
Panama	1,277.0	1,389.6	1,380.5	1,536.1	1,752.8	322.4	307.1	346.1	367.2	312.5	954.6	1,082.5	1,034.4	1,168.9	1,440.3
Papua New Guinea	65.7	50.8	69.2	116.6	65.4	114.8	50.1	85.6	64.5	129.6	-49.1	0.7	-16.4	52.1	-64.2
Paraguay	787.6	992.4	897.5	913.4	785.9	80.1	55.0	42.3	40.7	33.5	707.5	937.4	855.2	872.8	752.4
Peru	1,407.5	1,775.3	1,773.8	1,953.3	2,056.2	841.1	1,034.5	1,260.9	1,772.3	1,977.3	566.4	740.8	512.9	181.0	78.9
Philippines	3,886.0	5,294.8	6,142.4	7,417.3	6,736.2	5,719.1	7,006.5	8,161.4	10,445.0	11,948.9	-1,833.0	-1,711.7	-2,019.0	-3,027.6	-5,212.7
Poland	625.2	776.1	968.3	1,169.9	881.6	651.2	663.9	627.9	695.6	782.6	-26.0	112.2	340.4	474.4	99.0
Portugal	1,054.3	898.1	960.7	954.2	887.7	898.5	1,056.6	1,016.5	1,138.0	1,265.8	155.8	-158.5	-55.8	-183.8	-378.1
Qatar	161.9	225.9	207.7	379.0	354.1	80.9	90.9	157.1	157.4	220.4	81.0	135.0	50.6	221.7	133.7
Romania	339.7	253.1	265.6	258.0	339.5	194.7	222.4	248.5	399.8	393.3	145.0	30.7	17.1	-141.8	-53.8

See footnotes at end of table.

U.S. Census Bureau, Statistical Abstract of the United States: 1999

No. 1328. U.S. Exports, Imports, and Merchandise Trade Balance, by Country: 1994 to 1998—Continued

[See headnote, page 805]

Country	Exports, domestic, and foreign					General imports					Merchandise trade balance				
	1994	1995	1996	1997	1998	1994	1995	1996	1997	1998	1994	1995	1996	1997	1998
Russia	2,578.1	2,823.3	3,345.8	3,364.9	3,584.7	3,245.0	4,030.0	3,576.8	4,319.0	5,733.7	-666.9	-1,206.6	-231.0	-954.0	-2,149.0
Saudi Arabia	6,013.4	6,154.9	7,311.3	8,437.8	10,524.9	7,688.0	8,376.7	10,467.2	9,364.8	6,338.9	-1,674.6	-2,221.8	-3,155.9	-927.0	4,186.0
Senegal	42.4	67.9	55.8	51.8	59.2	11.3	5.0	5.5	6.8	5.2	31.2	62.9	50.3	44.9	54.0
Singapore	13,019.9	15,333.2	16,720.0	17,696.2	15,673.5	15,357.7	18,560.5	20,343.1	20,074.6	18,357.4	-2,337.8	-3,227.3	-3,623.1	-2,378.4	-2,683.9
Slovakia	42.8	61.0	62.6	82.0	110.7	130.7	129.5	124.6	165.6	165.7	-87.9	-68.5	-62.0	-83.6	-55.0
Somalia	29.9	8.1	4.2	2.8	2.7	0.1	0.1	0.2	0.3	0.6	29.7	7.9	4.1	2.4	2.1
South Africa	2,172.3	2,750.6	3,111.9	2,997.2	3,626.1	2,030.5	2,208.0	2,323.3	2,510.1	3,055.5	141.8	542.6	788.5	487.2	570.6
South Korea	18,025.4	25,379.9	26,621.1	25,046.1	16,538.3	19,629.3	24,183.9	22,655.1	23,173.1	23,936.5	-1,603.9	1,195.9	3,966.0	1,873.0	-7,398.2
Spain	4,802.5	5,526.0	5,499.6	5,154.7	5,464.6	3,735.1	3,879.5	4,279.8	4,605.5	4,784.3	1,067.4	1,646.5	1,219.8	933.3	680.3
Sri Lanka	197.7	279.1	211.1	154.7	190.1	1,093.0	1,259.7	1,393.0	1,620.0	1,765.9	-895.2	-980.5	-1,181.9	-1,465.3	-1,575.8
St. Lucia	80.5	80.9	84.5	89.3	92.4	26.5	35.2	22.3	34.2	22.4	54.0	45.7	62.2	55.1	70.0
St. Vincent	38.2	43.2	45.0	54.4	274.2	5.4	7.8	6.8	4.3	4.8	32.7	34.4	38.2	50.0	269.4
Sudan	54.5	43.4	51.3	36.4	6.8	35.1	22.7	18.7	12.1	3.1	19.4	20.7	32.6	24.3	3.7
Suriname	121.8	189.7	222.7	183.0	187.2	43.3	100.2	96.6	91.5	106.1	78.5	89.5	126.0	91.5	81.1
Sweden	2,518.4	3,079.8	3,440.5	3,314.1	3,819.4	5,040.9	6,256.4	7,152.7	7,298.9	7,836.7	-2,522.5	-3,176.6	-3,722.2	-3,984.8	-4,017.3
Switzerland	5,624.0	6,227.5	8,373.4	8,306.9	7,251.3	6,373.1	7,593.8	7,792.6	8,405.1	8,675.9	-749.1	-1,366.4	580.8	-98.2	-1,424.6
Syria	197.9	223.4	226.3	180.4	161.4	64.3	61.2	15.2	27.9	45.8	133.6	162.1	211.1	152.6	115.6
Taiwan	17,108.8	19,289.6	18,460.2	20,365.7	18,157.1	26,705.8	28,971.8	29,907.3	32,628.5	33,122.9	-9,597.0	-9,682.2	-11,447.1	-12,262.8	-14,965.8
Tajikistan	15.2	17.7	17.2	18.6	12.2	59.6	40.9	32.8	8.5	32.6	-44.5	-23.2	-15.6	10.0	-20.4
Tanzania	48.9	66.3	50.2	64.9	66.9	14.9	22.4	18.9	26.6	31.6	34.0	43.9	31.3	38.3	35.3
Thailand	4,865.1	6,665.0	7,197.5	7,349.4	5,233.4	10,305.8	11,348.1	11,336.1	12,601.5	13,434.3	-5,440.7	-4,683.1	-4,138.6	-5,252.1	-8,200.9
Togo	12.4	18.5	20.0	25.6	25.5	4.1	3.5	4.2	9.4	2.2	8.4	15.1	15.8	16.2	23.3
Trinidad and Tobago	540.5	689.2	665.5	1,105.9	982.8	1,113.2	1,086.2	1,313.2	1,134.3	970.9	-572.7	-397.1	-647.7	-28.3	11.9
Tunisia	327.2	215.0	189.2	252.3	196.8	53.9	70.4	75.8	63.1	61.5	273.3	144.6	113.4	189.2	135.3
Turkey	2,752.4	2,768.1	2,846.6	3,539.5	3,512.5	1,574.9	1,797.9	1,778.2	2,121.1	2,545.6	1,177.5	970.3	1,068.4	1,418.5	966.9
Turkmenistan	137.4	34.2	43.5	117.7	28.0	1.7	1.2	0.5	2.1	2.8	135.7	33.0	43.0	115.6	25.2
Turks and Caicos Islands	27.7	33.5	17.2	58.6	63.8	3.0	5.0	5.1	5.3	4.7	24.7	28.6	12.1	53.3	59.1
Uganda	27.7	22.1	17.2	35.2	29.8	34.9	13.2	15.9	37.8	15.2	-7.1	8.9	1.3	-2.5	14.6
Ukraine	180.3	223.4	395.1	402.9	367.5	323.4	405.6	506.9	410.0	530.7	-143.1	-182.2	-111.9	-7.1	-163.2
United Arab Emirates	1,598.7	2,006.5	2,533.2	2,607.1	2,369.6	448.6	459.2	498.8	920.1	660.8	1,150.1	1,547.2	2,034.4	1,687.0	1,708.8
United Kingdom	26,899.5	28,856.5	30,962.5	36,425.3	39,070.2	25,057.5	26,929.5	28,978.8	32,659.3	34,792.5	1,842.1	1,927.0	1,983.7	3,766.0	4,277.7
Uruguay	310.7	395.9	482.9	547.6	591.4	167.7	167.2	260.5	228.9	255.8	143.0	228.7	222.4	318.7	335.6
Uzbekistan	89.6	63.4	351.8	234.1	147.3	2.9	18.7	159.0	39.1	34.1	86.7	44.7	192.8	195.1	113.2
Venezuela	4,039.3	4,640.4	4,749.4	6,601.6	6,519.8	8,371.3	9,764.0	13,173.1	13,477.2	9,282.4	-4,332.0	-5,123.6	-8,423.7	-6,875.6	-2,762.6
Vietnam	172.7	252.5	616.4	286.6	274.2	50.6	198.9	331.8	388.5	553.4	122.2	53.6	284.7	-101.9	-279.2
Western Samoa	7.3	7.6	11.9	11.1	10.4	0.3	0.5	1.0	2.5	6.8	7.0	7.1	10.9	8.6	3.6
Yemen, Republic of	178.0	185.2	255.9	153.4	177.4	182.7	41.6	31.2	16.0	37.6	-4.7	143.6	224.7	137.4	139.8
Yugoslavia, Fed. Rep. of	0.5	2.2	46.0	49.1	73.9	-	32.9	8.2	10.4	12.6	0.5	-30.9	37.8	38.7	61.3
Zambia	32.6	48.9	46.0	29.3	21.6	63.5	32.9	64.2	55.9	47.3	-30.9	16.0	-18.3	-26.6	-25.7
Zimbabwe	92.8	122.0	90.7	81.9	93.1	102.4	97.7	133.0	139.5	127.0	-9.6	24.3	-42.3	-57.5	-33.9

- Represents zero or rounds to zero.   X Not applicable.

Source: U.S. Census Bureau, *U.S. International Trade in Goods and Services*, Series FT 900, December issues.

No. 1329. U.S. Exports and General Imports, by Selected SITC Commodity Groups: 1995 to 1998

[In millions of dollars (584,742 represents $584,742,000,000). SITC=Standard International Trade Classification. N.e.s.=Not elsewhere specified]

Commodity group	Exports [1]				General imports [2]			
	1995	1996	1997	1998	1995	1996	1997	1998
Total	584,742	624,767	689,182	682,977	743,445	791,364	870,671	913,828
Agricultural commodities	54,850	59,311	55,639	50,608	29,258	32,565	35,164	35,741
Animal feeds	3,667	4,183	4,621	4,050	472	633	648	606
Cereal flour	1,163	1,170	1,241	1,272	1,082	1,213	1,328	1,460
Coffee	15	4	7	10	2,985	2,491	3,575	3,063
Corn	7,521	8,623	5,426	4,617	66	116	103	142
Cotton, raw and linters	3,711	2,740	2,716	2,563	29	300	20	19
Hides and skins	1,621	1,515	1,503	1,126	140	133	130	110
Live animals	521	533	685	678	1,729	1,595	1,655	1,718
Meat and preparations	6,450	6,958	6,885	6,411	2,317	2,317	2,656	2,847
Oils/fats, vegetable	1,293	1,024	1,398	1,825	1,157	1,416	1,381	1,324
Rice	994	1,029	933	1,208	121	157	217	182
Soybeans	5,422	7,447	7,479	4,878	32	31	86	54
Sugar	5	5	3	3	682	1,001	956	709
Tobacco, unmanufactured	1,397	1,390	1,548	1,459	555	1,053	1,129	780
Vegetables and fruits	7,098	7,313	7,472	7,321	6,581	7,514	7,752	8,372
Wheat	5,464	6,302	4,196	3,712	238	247	359	284
Other agricultural	8,508	9,075	9,526	9,475	11,072	12,348	13,169	14,071
Manufactured goods	451,828	483,874	550,529	551,368	629,685	659,867	728,928	792,422
ADP equipment, office machinery . .	36,410	39,666	43,698	40,745	62,703	66,499	74,993	76,846
Airplane parts	10,349	11,723	13,266	15,046	2,616	3,464	4,917	5,905
Airplanes	13,836	18,962	25,552	35,328	3,651	3,943	4,557	6,933
Alcoholic bev, distilled	390	385	385	385	1,844	2,048	2,186	2,295
Aluminum	3,775	3,485	3,768	3,599	5,819	4,828	5,558	5,962
Artwork/antiques	1,071	887	1,120	1,149	2,666	2,791	3,587	3,977
Basketware, etc	1,996	2,239	2,494	2,583	2,942	3,014	3,364	3,835
Chemicals, cosmetics	3,835	4,323	4,873	4,749	2,307	2,443	2,677	2,893
Chemicals, dyeing	2,585	2,716	3,294	3,467	2,079	2,165	2,485	2,470
Chemicals, fertilizers	3,219	3,070	3,123	3,274	1,391	1,400	1,374	1,568
Chemicals, inorganic	4,541	4,657	5,264	4,744	4,658	4,954	5,132	5,118
Chemicals, medicinal	6,434	7,160	8,087	9,457	5,543	7,076	8,748	10,885
Chemicals, n.e.s	9,131	9,651	11,160	10,830	3,925	4,568	4,821	4,822
Chemicals, organic	16,106	14,744	16,408	14,903	13,334	14,820	16,874	18,300
Chemicals, plastics	14,958	15,467	17,274	16,616	7,155	7,443	8,237	8,565
Cigarettes	4,770	4,736	4,417	4,166	64	69	75	103
Clothing	6,482	7,285	8,396	8,508	39,523	41,559	48,408	53,743
Copper	1,728	1,553	1,441	1,276	2,983	2,953	3,254	3,063
Cork, wood, lumber	5,637	5,501	5,146	4,093	6,149	7,532	8,179	7,625
Crude fertilizers	1,525	1,526	1,621	1,599	1,164	1,176	1,334	1,298
Electrical machinery	53,139	56,637	65,816	65,412	75,051	75,525	80,370	79,366
Fish and preparations	3,177	2,930	2,624	2,170	6,739	6,657	7,687	8,105
Footwear	671	761	800	720	12,098	12,749	14,026	13,879
Furniture and parts	3,125	3,323	3,942	4,408	8,338	9,431	11,144	13,338
Gem diamonds	171	151	108	124	5,951	6,588	7,595	8,489
General industrial machinery	24,394	26,599	30,603	30,044	24,125	25,286	26,321	28,802
Glassware	630	680	813	714	1,333	1,413	1,553	1,607
Glass	1,644	1,814	2,125	1,998	1,468	1,679	1,750	1,774
Gold, nonmonetary	5,055	6,641	5,673	5,393	2,155	2,737	3,035	3,571
Iron and steel mill products	5,349	4,795	5,637	5,475	12,279	13,368	14,285	17,161
Lighting, plumbing	1,293	1,358	1,535	1,406	2,284	2,579	2,944	3,391
Metal manufactures, n.e.s	8,060	9,234	10,309	10,657	10,010	10,843	12,242	13,505
Metal ores; scrap	5,564	4,278	4,662	3,592	4,004	4,048	4,156	4,101
Metalworking machinery	4,626	5,241	5,702	5,272	5,926	6,789	7,325	7,928
Nickel	284	307	347	365	1,197	1,137	1,144	894
Optical goods	1,113	1,378	1,697	1,907	2,148	2,327	2,493	2,727
Paper and paperboard	9,572	9,837	10,283	9,914	12,470	11,637	11,697	12,796
Photographic equipment	3,351	3,743	3,865	3,477	5,145	5,271	5,759	5,656
Plastic articles, n.e.s	3,847	4,439	5,092	5,548	5,101	5,306	5,676	6,140
Platinum	318	248	437	392	1,694	1,716	1,973	3,057
Pottery	99	95	101	103	1,667	1,569	1,683	1,719
Power generating machinery	21,856	22,292	27,221	28,566	20,493	22,499	24,601	28,132
Printed materials	4,325	4,346	4,605	4,667	2,584	2,700	2,871	3,072
Pulp and waste paper	6,206	4,034	3,868	3,435	3,827	2,648	2,639	2,443
Records/magnetic media	6,263	6,555	6,815	6,053	3,896	4,078	4,137	4,387
Rubber articles, n.e.s	888	972	1,256	1,290	1,415	1,465	1,553	1,645
Rubber tires and tubes	1,858	1,959	2,394	2,549	3,144	3,074	3,417	4,095

See footnotes at end of table.

U.S. Census Bureau, Statistical Abstract of the United States: 1999

No. 1329. U.S. Exports and General Imports, by Selected SITC Commodity Groups: 1995 to 1998—Continued

[In millions of dollars (18,616 represents $18,616,000,000)]

Commodity group	Exports [1]				General imports [2]			
	1995	1996	1997	1998	1995	1996	1997	1998
Manufactured goods—Continued								
Scientific instruments	18,616	20,599	24,039	24,143	11,581	12,385	13,969	15,505
Ships, boats	1,178	1,064	1,366	1,716	816	1,029	875	1,134
Silver and bullion	663	638	641	624	580	569	472	662
Spacecraft	655	636	994	1,102	169	232	239	142
Specialized industrial machinery . . .	23,311	25,659	29,162	27,317	18,972	18,509	21,182	22,970
Television, VCR, etc.	(NA)	(NA)	24,093	23,401	(NA)	(NA)	36,771	42,462
Textile yarn, fabric	7,192	7,814	8,975	8,973	9,980	10,248	11,951	12,890
Toys/games/sporting goods	3,560	3,693	3,827	3,342	13,074	14,734	17,374	18,691
Travel goods	253	306	330	304	3,408	3,581	3,841	3,944
Watches/clocks/parts	248	277	310	311	2,785	2,805	2,838	3,207
Wood manufactures	1,633	1,685	1,958	1,692	3,687	4,037	4,668	5,634
Mineral fuel	10,358	12,057	12,682	9,957	59,109	73,028	78,277	57,646
Coal	3,714	3,849	3,586	3,191	703	606	655	726
Crude oil	6	460	1,040	670	42,814	50,582	54,226	37,534
Petroleum preparations	3,244	3,948	3,899	2,855	9,096	13,858	13,904	10,945
Liquified propane/butane	316	302	298	204	852	1,263	1,158	931
Natural gas	266	261	275	243	3,182	4,002	5,477	5,338
Other mineral	2,812	3,237	3,584	2,794	2,462	2,717	2,857	2,172
Reexports	36,581	40,690	44,153	45,769	(X)	(X)	(X)	(X)
Agricultural commodities	1,174	1,252	1,439	1,396	(X)	(X)	(X)	(X)
Manufactured goods	34,848	38,798	41,958	43,851	(X)	(X)	(X)	(X)
Mineral fuels	120	168	284	113	(X)	(X)	(X)	(X)
Other, reexports	439	472	472	409	(X)	(X)	(X)	(X)

NA Not available.   X Not applicable.   [1] F.a.s. or "free alongside ship basis."   [2] Customs value basis.

Source: U.S. Census Bureau, *U.S. International Trade in Goods and Services*, Series FT-900(98); and previous annual revision releases.

No. 1330. U.S. Exporting Companies Profile, by Company Type and Employment-Size Class: 1987 and 1992

Company type and employment-size class	Number of exporters		Known export value [1] (mil. dol.)		Percent of—			
					Number of exporters		Known export value	
	1987	1992	1987	1992	1987	1992	1987	1992
All companies, total	69,354	112,854	159,913	348,960	100.0	100.0	100.0	100.0
No employees	8,351	15,534	8,293	9,178	12.0	13.8	5.2	2.6
1 to 19 employees	30,818	51,186	11,911	29,397	44.4	45.4	7.4	8.4
20 to 49 employees	11,619	18,501	5,058	17,005	16.8	16.4	3.2	4.9
50 to 99 employees	6,911	10,505	5,235	13,840	10.0	9.3	3.3	4.0
100 to 249 employees . . .	5,703	8,679	6,100	18,371	8.2	7.7	3.8	5.3
250 to 499 employees . .	2,469	3,621	5,616	15,055	3.6	3.2	3.5	4.3
500 or more employees .	3,483	4,828	117,700	246,114	5.0	4.3	73.6	70.5
Manufacturers	29,127	42,763	115,740	241,522	42.0	37.9	72.4	69.2
No employees	1,561	1,949	1,565	1,971	2.3	1.7	1.0	0.6
1 to 19 employees	7,998	12,342	810	2,534	11.5	10.9	0.5	0.7
20 to 49 employees	6,301	9,949	1,115	4,217	9.1	8.8	0.7	1.2
50 to 99 employees	4,523	6,781	1,639	4,897	6.5	6.0	1.0	1.4
100 to 249 employees . . .	4,182	5,999	3,376	9,809	6.0	5.3	2.1	2.8
250 to 499 employees . . .	1,881	2,594	3,130	8,990	2.7	2.3	2.0	2.6
500 or more employees . . .	2,681	3,149	104,105	209,104	3.9	2.8	65.1	59.9
Wholesalers	23,114	39,713	25,471	50,989	33.3	35.2	15.9	14.6
No employees	1,859	4,503	1,166	1,882	2.7	4.0	0.7	0.5
1 to 19 employees	14,697	25,296	7,358	16,730	21.2	22.4	4.6	4.8
20 to 49 employees	3,583	5,673	3,100	7,128	5.2	5.0	1.9	2.0
50 to 99 employees	1,546	2,182	3,064	5,419	2.2	1.9	1.9	1.6
100 to 249 employees . . .	869	1,338	2,042	4,820	1.3	1.2	1.3	1.4
250 to 499 employees . . .	305	406	1,543	1,942	0.4	0.4	1.0	0.6
500 or more employees . . .	255	315	7,197	13,068	0.4	0.3	4.5	3.7
Other companies	15,907	26,910	15,267	53,158	22.9	23.8	9.5	15.2
No employees	3,972	6,030	2,221	2,754	5.7	5.3	1.4	0.8
1 to 19 employees	7,975	13,364	3,714	9,934	11.5	11.8	2.3	2.8
20 to 49 employees	1,706	2,826	835	5,625	2.5	2.5	0.5	1.6
50 to 99 employees	825	1,488	524	3,380	1.2	1.3	0.3	1.0
100 to 249 employees . . .	622	1,271	666	3,547	0.9	1.1	0.4	1.0
250 to 499 employees . . .	270	586	924	3,998	0.4	0.5	0.6	1.1
500 or more employees . . .	537	1,345	6,384	23,921	0.8	1.2	4.0	6.9
Unclassified companies	1,206	3,468	3,436	3,291	1.7	3.1	2.1	0.9

[1] Known value is defined as the value of exports by known exporters, i.e., those export transactions that could be matched to specific companies. Export values are on f.a.s. or "free alongside ship basis." Total export value was $251 billion in 1987 and $448 billion in 1992.

Source: U.S. Census Bureau, *A Profile of U.S. Exporting Companies, 1992*, CB-97-135 press release.

810 Foreign Commerce and Aid

No. 1331. Domestic Exports and Imports for Consumption of Merchandise, by Selected SIC-Based Product Category: 1990 to 1997

[In millions of dollars ($374,537 represents $374,537,000,000). Includes nonmonetary gold]

SIC-based product category	SIC[1] code	1990	1992	1993	1994	1995	1996	1997
Domestic exports, total [2]	(X)	374,537	425,377	439,282	482,141	547,300	583,221	688,896
Agricultural, forestry and fishery products	(X)	26,225	26,785	25,324	26,102	33,418	36,234	31,224
Agricultural products	01	22,597	22,633	21,615	22,189	29,391	32,380	27,460
Livestock and livestock products	02	829	871	836	973	920	989	1,132
Forestry products	08	281	324	276	263	272	271	279
Fish, fresh or chilled; and other marine products [3]	09	2,518	2,959	2,596	2,677	2,836	2,594	2,352
Mineral commodities	(X)	7,335	7,210	5,584	5,650	7,159	7,284	7,598
Metallic ores and concentrates	10	1,137	1,084	799	1,018	1,562	1,091	1,250
Bituminous, lignite and anthracite coal	11,12	4,513	4,241	3,090	2,858	3,572	3,694	3,406
Crude petroleum and natural gas	13	638	737	588	576	729	1,197	1,566
Nonmetallic minerals, exc. fuels	14	1,047	1,148	1,107	1,199	1,296	1,302	1,375
Manufactured commodities	(X)	330,403	383,082	400,721	441,501	496,421	530,484	596,539
Food and kindred products	20	16,160	19,761	20,509	23,094	26,021	27,041	28,488
Tobacco manufactures	21	5,040	4,509	4,253	5,367	5,222	5,238	4,956
Textile mill products	22	3,635	4,473	4,687	5,151	5,696	6,177	7,081
Apparel and related products	23	2,848	4,599	5,433	6,145	7,190	8,104	9,279
Lumber and related products	24	6,523	6,802	7,361	7,252	7,424	7,401	7,312
Furniture and fixtures	25	1,589	2,518	2,818	3,030	2,953	3,101	3,643
Paper and allied products	26	8,631	9,969	9,457	11,000	14,943	14,002	14,512
Printing and publishing	27	3,150	3,808	4,057	4,070	4,471	4,534	4,791
Chemicals and allied products	28	37,806	41,953	42,742	48,950	57,897	58,503	65,080
Petroleum and coal products	29	6,794	6,403	6,163	5,510	6,014	7,158	7,331
Rubber and misc. plastics products	30	6,398	7,872	8,554	9,942	11,025	12,093	14,187
Leather and leather products	31	1,388	1,541	1,536	1,539	1,565	1,725	1,907
Stone, clay, and glass products	32	3,295	3,855	3,844	4,215	4,796	5,097	5,847
Primary metal products	33	13,116	15,105	18,669	16,327	20,191	21,279	22,694
Fabricated metal products	34	11,138	13,265	13,497	13,395	15,161	16,612	17,921
Machinery, except electrical	35	61,229	68,554	72,279	82,120	95,909	104,055	117,531
Electric and electronic machinery	36	39,807	45,992	52,947	63,839	76,235	79,533	93,767
Transportation equipment	37	68,113	82,862	80,196	85,068	82,699	92,887	108,465
Instruments and related products	38	19,524	22,815	24,699	26,560	29,581	32,842	36,978
Misc. manufactured commodities	39	4,296	5,446	5,288	5,813	7,383	6,763	7,279
Imports for consumption, total [2]	(X)	490,554	525,091	574,863	657,884	739,661	790,470	862,426
Agricultural, forestry and fishery products	(X)	12,750	14,216	15,866	17,427	19,799	20,661	22,817
Agricultural products	01	5,925	6,716	7,839	8,657	9,803	10,950	12,231
Livestock and livestock products	02	1,453	1,873	2,161	2,047	2,450	2,377	2,483
Forestry products	08	1,015	1,088	1,068	1,208	1,932	1,810	1,625
Fish, fresh or chilled; and other marine products [3]	09	4,357	4,540	4,798	5,515	5,614	5,525	6,478
Mineral commodities	(X)	51,391	44,823	45,965	47,300	51,050	57,144	53,313
Metallic ores and concentrates	10	1,500	1,167	1,108	1,283	1,413	1,407	1,406
Bituminous, lignite and anthracite coal	11,12	93	127	218	229	248	238	257
Crude petroleum and natural gas	13	48,917	42,796	43,871	44,949	48,495	54,463	50,030
Nonmetallic minerals, exc. fuels	14	881	734	767	839	894	1,035	1,619
Manufactured commodities	(X)	407,043	445,127	490,289	567,052	639,729	680,609	750,206
Food and kindred products	20	16,564	17,445	16,090	17,342	18,326	20,948	22,600
Tobacco manufactures	21	94	285	467	163	169	245	463
Textile mill products	22	6,807	7,808	6,161	6,534	6,965	7,169	8,370
Apparel and related products	23	24,644	30,533	35,475	38,561	41,208	43,075	50,191
Lumber and related products	24	5,446	6,700	8,901	10,528	10,406	12,194	13,531
Furniture and fixtures	25	5,235	5,601	6,242	7,522	8,303	9,320	11,008
Paper and allied products	26	11,669	10,382	10,891	11,772	16,757	14,784	14,839
Printing and publishing	27	1,849	2,046	2,211	2,422	2,902	2,996	3,210
Chemicals and allied products	28	21,611	25,849	27,259	31,697	38,079	42,826	48,382
Petroleum and coal products	29	14,472	10,410	9,906	9,504	8,971	18,768	22,149
Rubber and misc. plastics products	30	9,731	11,287	13,053	14,393	15,973	16,891	18,320
Leather and leather products	31	10,944	11,342	11,692	12,977	13,628	14,187	15,459
Stone, clay, and glass products	32	5,845	5,951	6,431	7,594	8,498	9,088	10,178
Primary metal products	33	23,232	22,891	22,772	30,106	33,519	34,583	37,727
Fabricated metal products	34	11,608	12,436	12,941	14,664	16,213	17,492	19,317
Machinery, except electrical	35	55,021	62,274	73,370	89,705	106,391	112,907	125,777
Electric and electronic machinery	36	55,736	65,596	76,869	94,332	114,912	114,066	120,879
Transportation equipment	37	89,599	92,930	102,259	115,998	122,344	129,235	140,684
Instruments and related products	38	16,846	20,338	22,080	24,410	27,473	28,747	31,545
Misc. manufactured commodities	39	20,090	23,025	25,219	26,830	28,694	31,088	25,579

X Not applicable.   [1] Standard Industrial Classification.   [2] Includes scrap and waste, used or secondhand merchandise, manufactured commodities not identified by kind, and timing adjustments.   [3] Includes frozen and packaged fish.

Source: U.S. Census Bureau, *U.S. International Trade in Goods and Services,* Series FT 900, December issues.

U.S. Census Bureau, Statistical Abstract of the United States: 1999

Figure 29.1
Selected Outlying Areas of the United States

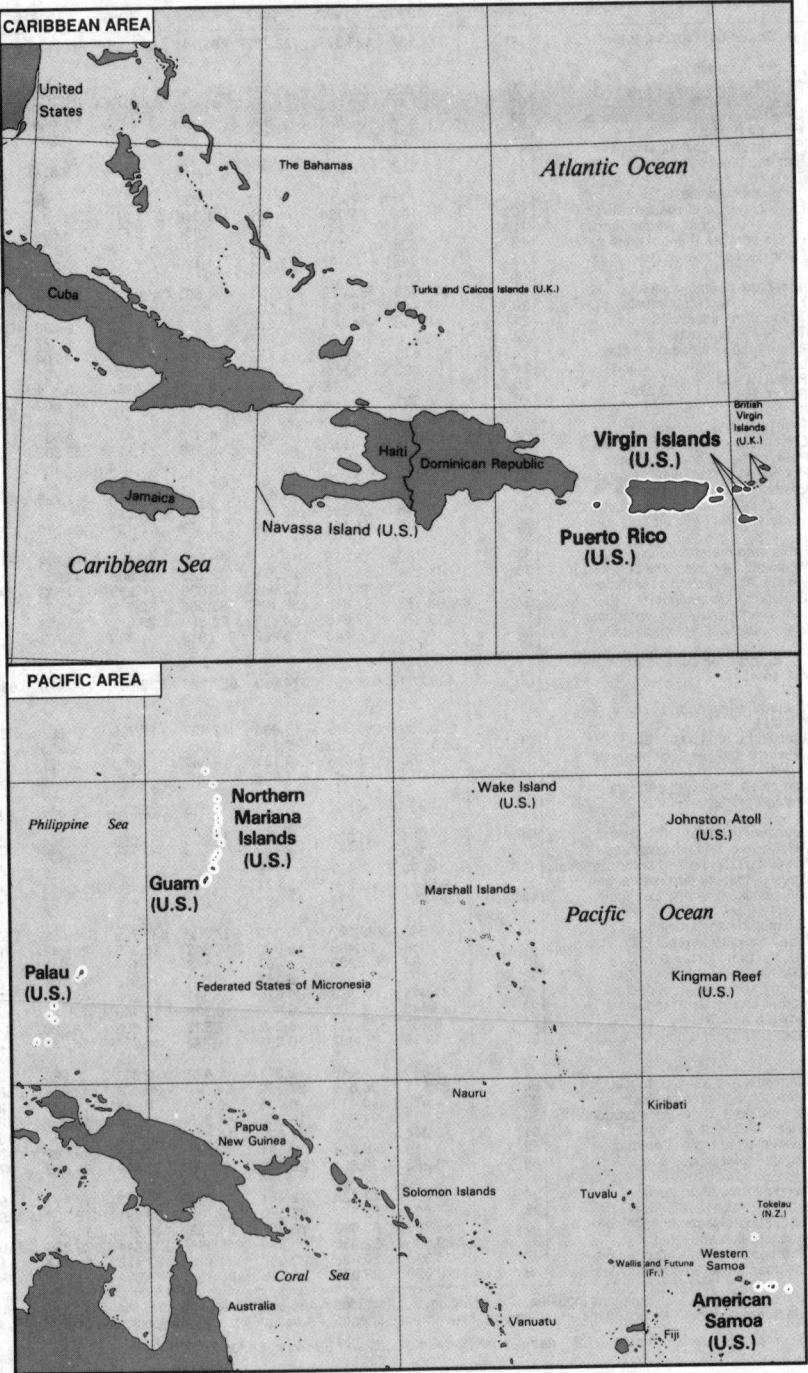

U.S. Census Bureau, Statistical Abstract of the United States: 1999

Section 29

Outlying Areas

This section presents summary economic and social statistics for Puerto Rico, Virgin Islands, Guam, American Samoa, and the Northern Mariana Islands. Primary sources are the decennial censuses of population and housing and the censuses of agriculture, business, manufactures, and construction (taken every 5 years) conducted by the U.S. Census Bureau; the annual *Vital Statistics of the United States* , issued by the National Center for Health Statistics; and the annual *Income and Product* of the Puerto Rico Planning Board, San Juan.

Jurisdiction—The United States gained jurisdiction over these areas as follows: The islands of *Puerto Rico* and *Guam*, surrendered by Spain to the United States in October 1898, were ceded to the United States by the Treaty of Paris, ratified in 1899. Puerto Rico became a commonwealth on July 25, 1952, thereby achieving a high degree of local autonomy under its own constitution. The *Virgin Islands*, comprising 50 islands and cays, was purchased by the United States from Denmark in 1917. *American Samoa*, a group of seven islands, was acquired by the United States in accordance with a convention among the United States, Great Britain, and Germany, ratified in 1900 (Swains Island was annexed in 1925). By an agreement approved by the Security Council and the United States, the Northern Mariana Islands, previously under Japanese mandate, was administered by the United States between 1947 and 1986 under the United Nations trusteeship system. The Northern Mariana Islands became a commonwealth in 1986.

Censuses—Because characteristics of the outlying areas differ, the presentation of census data for them is not uniform. The

1960 Census of Population covered all of the places listed above except the Northern Mariana Islands (their census was conducted in April 1958 by the Office of the High Commissioner), while the 1960 Census of Housing also excluded American Samoa. The 1970, 1980, and 1990 Censuses of Population and Housing covered all five areas. The 1959, 1969, and 1978 Censuses of Agriculture covered Puerto Rico, American Samoa, Guam, and the Virgin Islands; the 1964, 1974, and 1982 censuses covered the same areas except American Samoa; and the 1969, 1978, 1987, and 1992 censuses included the Northern Mariana Islands. Beginning in 1967, Congress authorized the economic censuses, to be taken at 5-year intervals, for years ending in "2" and "7." Prior economic censuses were conducted in Puerto Rico for 1949, 1954, 1958, and 1963 and in Guam and the Virgin Islands for 1958 and 1963. In 1967, the census of construction industries was added for the first time in Puerto Rico; in 1972, Virgin Islands and Guam were covered. For 1982, 1987, and 1992 the economic censuses covered the Northern Mariana Islands.

Information in other sections—In addition to the statistics presented in this section, other data are included as integral parts of many tables showing distribution by states in various sections of the *Abstract.* See "Outlying areas of the United States" in the Index. For definition and explanation of terms used, see Section 1, Population; Section 4, Education; Section 23, Agriculture; Section 25, Construction and Housing; Section 26, Manufactures; and Section 27, Domestic Trade and Services.

U.S. Census Bureau, Statistical Abstract of the United States: 1999

No. 1332. Estimated Resident Population With Projections: 1970 to 2020

[In thousands (2,722 represents 2,722,000). Population data generally are de facto figures for the present territory. Population estimates were derived from information available as of early 1999. See text, Section 30, Comparative International Statistics, for general comments regarding the data. For details of methodology, coverage, and reliability, see source]

Area	1970	1980	1990	1995	1997	1998	1999	2000, proj.	2010, proj.	2020, proj.
Puerto Rico	2,722	3,210	3,537	3,731	3,827	3,860	3,888	3,910	4,051	4,104
American Samoa	27	32	47	57	60	62	64	65	81	96
Guam	86	107	134	144	146	149	152	154	183	211
Virgin Islands	63	98	104	114	117	118	120	121	133	143
Northern Mariana Islands	12	17	44	58	64	67	69	72	99	124

Source: U.S. Census Bureau, International Data Base.

No. 1333. Vital Statistics—Specified Areas: 1960 to 1997

[Births, deaths, and infant deaths by place of residence. Rates for 1960, 1970, 1980, and 1990 based on population enumerated as of **April 1;** for other years, on population estimated as of **July 1**]

Area and year	Births Number	Births Rate [1]	Deaths Number	Deaths Rate [1]	Infant deaths Number	Infant deaths Rate [2]
Puerto Rico:						
1960	76,314	32.5	15,791	6.7	3,307	43.3
1970	67,628	24.8	18,080	6.7	1,930	28.5
1980	72,986	22.8	20,413	6.4	1,351	18.5
1990	66,417	18.8	25,957	7.3	888	13.4
1995	63,425	17.0	30,032	8.1	804	12.7
1996	63,141	16.7	29,731	7.9	561	8.9
1997	63,668	16.6	26,484	6.9	(NA)	(NA)
Guam:						
1965	2,523	32.8	336	4.4	82	32.5
1970	2,842	28.8	355	5.8	62	21.6
1980	2,945	27.8	393	3.7	43	14.6
1990	3,839	28.6	520	3.9	31	8.1
1995	4,180	29.0	592	4.1	38	9.4
1996	4,259	29.4	599	4.1	(NA)	(NA)
1997	4,307	29.5	632	4.3	(NA)	(NA)
Virgin Islands:						
1960	1,180	36.8	332	10.3	42	35.6
1970	2,898	46.8	469	7.9	72	24.8
1980	2,504	25.9	504	5.2	61	24.4
1990	2,267	21.8	480	4.6	33	14.6
1995	2,063	18.1	664	5.8	34	16.6
1996	1,905	16.8	575	5.1	(NA)	(NA)
1997	2,005	17.5	623	4.8	(NA)	(NA)

NA Not available. [1] Per 1,000 population. [2] Per 1,000 live births.
Source: U.S. National Center for Health Statistics, *Vital Statistics of the United States,* annual.

No. 1334. Land Area and Population Characteristics, by Area: 1990

[As of **April 1.** For definition of median, see Guide to Tabular Presentation]

Item	United States	Puerto Rico	Virgin Islands	Guam	American Samoa	Northern Mariana Islands
Land area (sq. miles)	3,536,338	3,427	134	210	77	179
Total resident population	**248,709,873**	**3,522,037**	**101,809**	**133,152**	**46,773**	**43,345**
Per square mile	70.3	1,027.9	760.9	634.1	607.4	242.2
Percent increase, 1980-90	9.8	10.2	5.4	25.6	44.8	158.3
Urban	187,053,487	2,508,346	37,885	50,801	15,599	12,151
Rural	61,656,386	1,013,691	63,924	82,351	31,174	31,194
Male	121,239,418	1,705,642	49,210	70,945	24,023	22,802
Female	127,470,455	1,816,395	52,599	62,207	22,750	20,543
Males per 100 females	95.1	93.9	93.6	114.0	105.6	111.0
Median age (years)	32.9	28.4	28.2	25.0	20.9	27.4
Male (years)	31.7	27.2	27.1	25.2	20.6	29.9
Female (years)	34.1	29.6	29.2	24.9	21.2	24.9
Marital status, persons 15 years and over	195,142,002	2,563,818	72,365	93,200	28,952	33,030
Never married	52,559,853	711,470	27,539	30,759	11,412	13,810
Married [1]	111,498,578	1,499,449	35,199	54,717	15,958	17,869
Widowed or divorced	31,083,571	352,899	9,627	7,724	1,582	1,351
Households and families:						
Households	91,947,410	1,054,924	32,020	31,373	6,607	6,873
Persons in households	242,012,129	3,487,667	100,488	124,596	46,267	31,856
Persons per household	2.63	3.31	3.14	3.97	7.00	4.63
Families	64,517,947	886,339	23,012	27,313	6,301	5,312
Husband-wife families	50,708,322	634,872	13,197	21,342	5,153	3,947
Children ever born per 1,000 females 15 to 44 years	1,223	1,512	1,662	1,523	1,757	1,226

[1] For Puerto Rico, includes consensually married couples and for all areas, includes separated couples.
Source: U.S. Census Bureau, *1990 Census of Population,* CP-1 and CP-2 parts 1, (United States), 53 (Puerto Rico), 55 (Virgin Islands); *1990 Census of Population and Housing,* CPH-1, parts 53A and 55; CPH-6, parts G (Guam), AS (American Samoa), and CNMI (Commonwealth of the Northern Mariana Islands); and Summary Tape File, parts 3C, (United States), 3A (Puerto Rico), and 3 (Virgin Islands).

No. 1335. Selected Social and Economic Characteristics, by Area: 1990

[As of **April 1**]

Characteristic	United States	Puerto Rico	Virgin Islands	Guam	American Samoa	Northern Mariana Islands
EDUCATIONAL ATTAINMENT						
Persons 25 years and over.........	158,868,436	1,952,297	55,639	66,700	19,570	24,633
Less than 9th grade	16,502,211	691,835	12,908	9,238	3,664	4,285
9th to 12th grade, no diploma.........	22,841,507	290,173	11,278	8,602	5,239	4,016
High school graduate	47,642,763	410,559	14,021	22,220	6,253	8,659
Some college or associate degree.......	39,571,702	281,248	9,011	14,984	3,062	3,818
Bachelor's degree or higher..........	32,310,253	278,482	8,421	11,656	1,352	3,855
EMPLOYMENT STATUS						
Total persons, 16 years old and over ...	191,829,271	2,497,078	70,323	90,990	27,991	32,522
In labor force..................	125,182,378	1,180,162	47,553	66,138	14,198	26,589
Percent of total	65.3	47.3	67.6	72.7	50.7	81.8
Armed forces..................	1,708,928	5,486	110	11,952	11	8
Civilian labor force	123,473,450	1,174,676	47,443	54,186	14,187	26,581
Employed..................	115,681,202	934,736	44,267	52,144	13,461	25,965
Unemployed.................	7,792,248	239,940	3,176	2,042	726	616
Percent of civilian labor force	6.3	20.4	6.7	3.8	5.1	2.3
Not in labor force...............	66,646,893	1,316,916	22,770	24,852	13,793	5,933
FAMILY INCOME IN 1989						
Families, census year	65,049,428	889,998	23,012	27,313	6,301	5,312
Percent distribution by income class	100.0	100.0	100.0	100.0	100.0	100.0
Less than $5,000	4.0	25.1	8.8	4.0	11.0	8.2
$5,000 to $9,999	5.6	24.9	9.5	4.7	19.2	13.9
$10,000 to $14,999.............	7.2	16.5	12.8	8.3	17.0	13.1
$15,000 to $24,999.............	16.4	17.5	20.6	21.1	23.6	21.6
$25,000 or more................	66.9	16.0	48.3	61.9	29.1	43.2
Median income (dollars)	35,225	9,988	24,036	31,178	15,979	21,275
RESIDENCE IN 1985						
Persons 5 years and over	230,445,777	3,219,765	92,579	118,055	39,821	39,206
Same house...................	122,796,970	2,190,479	56,098	54,665	30,759	11,479
Different house in this area	102,540,097	879,691	25,003	24,763	2,763	6,870
Outside area..................	5,108,710	149,595	11,478	38,627	6,299	20,857
LANGUAGE SPOKEN AT HOME						
Persons 5 years and over	230,445,777	3,219,765	92,579	118,055	39,821	39,206
Speak only English at home..........	198,600,798	(NA)	70,442	44,048	1,203	1,878

NA Not available.

Source: U.S. Census Bureau, *1990 Census of Population and Housing,* Summary Tape File, parts 3C, (United States), 3A, and unpublished data, (Puerto Rico), and 3 (Virgin Islands); *1990 Census of Population,* CP-2 parts 1,(United States), 53 (Puerto Rico), 55 (Virgin Islands); CPH-L-98, *The Foreign Born Population in the United States: 1990; 1990 Census of Population and Housing,* CPH-6, parts G (Guam), AS (American Samoa), and CNMI (Commonwealth of the Northern Mariana Islands).

No. 1336. Federal Direct Payments for Individuals: 1990 and 1998

[In thousands of dollars (3,582,246 represents $3,582,246,000). For fiscal years ending **September 30**]

Selected program payments	1990					1998				
	Puerto Rico	Guam	Virgin Islands	American Samoa	Northern Mariana Islands	Puerto Rico	Guam	Virgin Islands	American Samoa	Northern Mariana Islands
Total............	3,582,246	87,338	100,428	13,837	5,084	6,028,575	208,137	173,581	34,929	19,315
Pell Grants............	240,545	1,260	432	113	298	211,331	1,387	1,137	351	622
Medicare: Hospital Insurance [1].........	186,950	2,273	4,977	-	-	501,790	715	12,579	-	-
Supplemental medical [1] insurance	209,525	2,227	3,722	-	-	609,284	373	6,694	-	-
Social Security:										
Disability insurance....	560,910	1,907	5,692	2,410	-	1,016,167	6,914	10,943	6,680	730
Retirement insurance ..	1,077,133	11,372	31,601	4,330	-	1,701,136	39,078	56,730	6,932	2,743
Survivors insurance ...	461,999	6,430	11,056	3,873	-	722,433	23,118	19,259	7,381	3,516
Federal workers compensation	7,342	734	50	85	-	13,434	758	122	62	-
Veterans:										
Pension and disability ..	280,801	3,578	1,797	1,354	133	352,591	6,318	1,771	2,780	392
Education assistance ..	3,086	178	28	36	1	4,666	451	89	257	25
Federal retirement and disability [2]	161,315	34,150	8,326	1,605	477	227,308	78,497	14,636	5,073	707
Federal payments for unemployment compensation	129,298	(²)	4,659	-	-	281,781	(²)	4,653	-	-
Food Stamps	(²)	14,362	18,403	-	2,775	(²)	34,413	21,851	5,300	5,100
Housing assistance	218,396	8,182	8,262	-	1,400	342,886	15,849	18,330	-	2,445
Other..............	44,945	685	1,424	31	-	43,769	266	4,787	114	3,035

- Represents zero.   [1] Includes retirement and disability payments to former U.S. Postal Service employees.   [2] Food stamp program in Puerto Rico was replaced by the Nutrition Assistance Grant Program in 1982.

Source: U.S. Census Bureau, *Consolidated Federal Funds Report,* annual. <http://www.census.gov/govs/www/cffr.html>; (accessed 17 June, 1999).

Outlying Areas 815

No. 1337. Public Elementary and Secondary Schools, by Areas: 1997

[For school year ending in year shown, unless otherwise indicated]

Item	Puerto Rico	Guam	Virgin Islands	American Samoa	Item	Puerto Rico	Guam	Virgin Islands	American Samoa
PUBLIC EL/SEC					School staff	48,359	2,176	2,212	923
Enrollment, fall	618,861	33,393	22,385	14,766	Teachers	39,743	1,552	1,580	734
Elementary (kindergarten-grade 8)	454,132	25,217	15,703	11,346	Other support services staff	21,751	797	728	448
Secondary (grades 9-12 and post graduates)	164,729	8,176	6,682	3,420	Current expenditures [1] ($1,000)	1,800,000	145,623	127,754	36,498
Staff, fall	71,333	3,263	3,185	1,470	HIGHER EDUCATION				
School district staff	1,223	290	245	99	Enrollment, fall	168,933	5,335	2,898	1,239

[1] Public elementary and secondary day schools.

Source: U.S. National Center for Education Statistics, unpublished data.

No. 1338. Puerto Rico—Summary: 1970 to 1998

[2,722 represents 2,722,000]

Item	Unit	1970	1980	1985	1990	1995	1996	1997	1998
POPULATION									
Total [1]	1,000	2,722	3,184	3,378	3,527	3,719	3,733	3,805	3,833
Persons per family	Number	4.6	4.3	3.9	3.7	3.5	3.5	3.5	3.5
EDUCATION [2]									
Enrollment, total	1,000	922.6	1,090.9	1,107.9	(NA)	(NA)	(NA)	(NA)	(NA)
Public day school	1,000	672.3	716.1	692.9	651.2	621.4	627.6	618.9	(NA)
Other public	1,000	103.9	149.5	152.0	(NA)	(NA)	(NA)	(NA)	(NA)
Private schools	1,000	89.1	95.2	102.7	145.8	145.9	148.0	(NA)	(NA)
College and university	1,000	57.3	130.1	155.5	156.0	165.4	168.7	159.3	(NA)
Expenses	Mil. dol.	288.8	825.0	1,171.8	1,686.4	2,555.8	2,787.7	2,846.8	(NA)
As percent of GNP	Percent	6.2	7.5	7.8	7.8	9.0	9.1	8.9	(NA)
P.R. Dept. of Education	Mil. dol.	254.6	612.2	810.2	1,054.2	1,689.4	1,903.0	1,910.9	(NA)
Personal consumption	Mil. dol.	34.2	212.8	361.6	644.2	866.4	884.7	935.9	(NA)
LABOR FORCE [3]									
Total [4]	1,000	765	907	985	1,124	1,219	1,268	1,298	1,317
Employed [5]	1,000	686	753	774	963	1,051	1,092	1,128	1,317
Agriculture [6]	1,000	68	38	39	36	34	32	31	31
Manufacturing	1,000	132	143	141	168	172	167	162	161
Trade	1,000	128	138	150	185	211	218	228	236
Government	1,000	106	184	183	222	232	246	261	244
Unemployed [7]	1,000	79	154	211	161	168	175	170	179
Unemployment rate [7]	Rate	10	17	21	14	14	14	13	13.6
Compensation of employees	Mil. dol.	2,800	7,200	9,442	13,639	17,773	18,990	19,920	21,006
Avg. compensation	Dollar	4,082	9,563	12,456	14,854	16,911	17,390	17,660	18,475
Salary and wages	Mil. dol.	2,555	6,290	8,137	11,681	15,300	16,350	17,156	18,127
INCOME [8]									
Personal income:									
Current dollars	Mil. dol.	3,753	11,002	14,588	21,105	27,378	30,122	32,076	33,678
Constant (1954) dollars	Mil. dol.	2,654	3,985	4,274	5,551	6,547	7,119	7,454	7,654
Disposable personal income:									
Current dollars	Mil. dol.	3,565	10,403	13,760	19,914	25,591	28,184	30,020	31,403
Constant (1954) dollars	Mil. dol.	2,521	3,768	4,032	5,238	6,119	6,661	6,977	7,137
Average family income:									
Current dollars	Dollar	6,366	14,858	16,914	22,234	25,881	28,293	29,783	30,860
Constant (1954) dollars	Dollar	4,503	5,381	4,957	5,848	6,177	6,646	6,921	7,013
BANKING [9]									
Assets	Mil. dol.	3,322	10,223	21,209	27,902	39,859	39,671	42,380	46,088.1
TOURISM [8]									
Number of visitors	1,000	1,225.0	2,140.0	2,061.6	3,425.8	4,086.6	4,110.2	4,349.7	4,670.8
Visitor expenditures	Mil. dol.	235.4	618.7	757.7	1,366.4	1,827.6	1,898.3	2,046.3	2,232.9
Average per visitor	Dollar	192	289	368	399	447	462	470	478.0
Net income from tourism	Mil. dol.	89.8	202.2	223.1	383.3	498.7	526.8	553.5	597.9

NA Not available. [1] 1970, 1980, and 1990 enumerated as of April 1; all other years estimated as of July 1. [2] Enrollment for the first school month. Expenses for school year ending in year shown. Since 1990, does not include all public schools or enrollment. [3] Annual average of monthly figures. For fiscal years. [4] Beginning 1980, for population 16 years old and over; 1970, for population 14 years and over. [5] Includes other employment not shown separately. [6] Includes forestry and fisheries. [7] Percent unemployed of the labor force. [8] For fiscal years. [9] As of June 30. Does not include Federal savings banks and international banking entities.

Source: Puerto Rico Planning Board, San Juan, PR, *Income and Product*, annual; and *Socioeconomics Statistics*, annual.

No. 1339. Puerto Rico—Gross Product and Net Income: 1980 to 1998

[In millions of dollars (11,065 represents $11,065,000,000). For fiscal years ending June 30. Data for 1998 are preliminary]

Item	1980	1985	1990	1994	1995	1996	1997	1998
Gross domestic product	11,065	15,002	21,619	26,641	28,452	30,331	32,096	34,817
Agriculture	380	357	434	369	318	375	368	402
Manufacturing	5,306	7,909	12,126	16,748	17,867	19,040	19,797	23,016
Contract construction and mining [1]	369	334	720	928	1,006	1,095	1,217	1,323
Transportation & other public services [2]	1,279	1,709	2,468	3,134	3,276	3,557	3,726	4,069
Trade	2,273	3,160	4,728	5,635	5,989	6,290	6,495	6,990
Finance, insurance, real estate	1,486	2,547	3,896	5,246	5,730	5,084	6,522	6,898
Services	1,279	1,837	3,015	4,332	4,724	5,075	5,348	5,758
Government	1,897	2,346	3,337	3,987	4,440	4,841	5,220	5,246
Commonwealth	1,574	1,996	2,884	3,395	3,793	4,122	4,457	4,457
Municipalities	323	350	453	592	647	719	763	789
Rest of the world	-3,372	-5,287	-8,985	-13,050	-14,195	-15,925	-16,754	19,784
Statistical discrepancy	166	91	-121	-689	-703	-846	-591	123
Domestic net income	9,007	12,182	17,941	22,041	23,653	25,266	26,534	27,937
Agriculture	435	410	486	420	442	474	514	535
Manufacturing	4,756	7,117	11,277	15,688	16,685	17,796	18,473	21,333
Mining	9	10	26	28	30	33	37	39
Contract construction	337	309	679	830	903	985	1,097	1,190
Transportation and other public services [2]	1,022	1,248	1,778	2,193	2,360	2,521	2,620	2,882
Trade	1,609	2,285	3,420	3,875	4,108	4,352	4,546	4,872
Finance, insurance, and real estate	1,200	2,141	3,280	4,294	4,735	5,015	5,346	5,835
Services	1,114	1,606	2,643	3,775	4,146	4,431	4,682	5,014
Commonwealth government [3]	1,897	2,346	3,337	3,987	4,440	4,841	5,220	5,246
Rest of the world	-3,372	-5,287	-8,985	-13,050	-14,195	-15,181	-16,001	19,008

[1] Mining includes only quarries. [2] Includes other public utilities, and radio and television broadcasting. [3] Includes public enterprises not elsewhere classified.

No. 1340. Puerto Rico—Transfer Payments: 1985 to 1998

[In millions of dollars (3,531 represents $3,531,000,000). Data represent transfer payments between Federal and state governments and other nonresidents. See headnote, Table 1339]

Item	1985	1990	1994	1995	1996	1997	1998
Total receipts	3,531	4,871	5,957	6,236	7,033	7,660	7,983
Federal government	3,348	4,649	5,630	5,912	6,748	7,337	7,589
Transfers to individuals [1]	3,283	4,577	5,532	5,838	6,675	7,255	7,474
Veterans benefits	317	349	414	440	472	484	496
Medicare	220	368	570	661	1,061	1,299	1,226
Old age, disability, survivors (social security)	1,581	2,055	2,722	2,912	3,101	3,282	3,472
Nutritional assistance	780	880	995	1,063	1,071	1,087	1,109
Industry subsidies	65	72	98	74	73	82	115
U.S. state governments	17	18	23	18	17	17	18
Other nonresidents	166	205	304	307	268	306	376
Total payments	1,180	1,801	2,211	2,301	2,348	2,387	2,476
Federal government	1,145	1,756	2,055	2,132	2,268	2,349	2,420
Transfers from individuals	508	817	1,003	1,052	1,127	1,156	1,187
Contribution to medicare	44	97	142	162	167	165	168
Employee contribution for social security	463	720	859	888	958	988	1,017
Transfers from industries	13	16	32	49	37	47	44
Unemployment insurance	189	247	211	184	191	203	217
Employer contribution for social security	435	675	810	847	914	944	972
Other nonresidents [2]	35	45	155	169	78	39	55
Net balance	2,351	3,070	3,746	3,935	4,685	5,272	5,508
Federal government	2,203	2,893	3,575	3,780	4,479	4,988	5,169
U.S. state governments	14	16	16	13	12	13	14
Other nonresidents	134	162	155	143	193	271	325

[1] Includes other receipts and payments not shown separately. [2] Includes U.S. state governments.

Source of Tables 1339 and 1340: Puerto Rico Planning Board, San Juan, PR, *Economic Report of the Governor, 1997-98.*

No. 1341. Puerto Rico—Merchandise Imports and Exports: 1980 to 1998

[In millions of dollars (9,018 represents $9,018,000,000). Imports are imports for consumption; see text, Section 28, Foreign Commerce and Aid]

Item	1980	1985	1989	1990	1991	1992	1993	1994	1995	1996	1997	1998
Imports	9,018	10,162	15,010	16,200	15,079	16,476	16,124	17,152	18,969	19,422	21,928	21,706
From U.S.	5,345	6,130	10,193	10,792	10,306	11,463	11,179	11,455	12,213	12,220	13,904	13,318
From other	3,673	4,032	4,817	5,408	4,773	5,013	4,945	5,697	6,756	7,202	8,024	8,388
Exports	6,576	11,087	17,455	20,402	21,128	20,445	20,351	22,711	23,573	22,379	26,653	28,109
To U.S.	5,643	9,873	15,334	17,915	18,729	17,990	17,613	20,098	20,986	19,907	25,045	25,610
To other	933	1,214	2,121	2,487	2,399	2,465	2,738	2,613	2,587	2,472	1,608	2,499

Source: U.S. Census Bureau, *Foreign Commerce and Navigation of the United States,* annual; *U.S. Trade with Puerto Rico and U.S. Possessions, FT 895;* and, through 1988, *Highlights of U.S. Export and Import Trade, FT990;* thereafter, *FT920* supplement.

No. 1342. Puerto Rico—Economic Summary, by Industry: 1996

[Covers establishments with payroll. Employees are for the week including **March 12**. Most government employees are excluded. For statement on methodology, see Appendix III]

Industry	1987 SIC code [1]	Total establish-ments	Employment-size class					Employees [2]	Annual payroll (mil. dol.)
			1 to 4	5 to 9	10 to 19	20 to 49	50 or more		
Total [2]	(X)	**40,514**	**24,286**	**6,597**	**4,216**	**3,215**	**2,200**	**650,241**	**10,464.8**
Agricultural services, forestry, and fishing	A	156	112	30	5	8	1	777	7.0
Mining	B	42	17	4	7	10	4	954	14.1
Nonmetallic minerals, except fuels	14	31	11	3	5	9	3	760	10.3
Construction [2]	C	1,971	931	311	237	262	230	48,677	629.1
General contractors and operative builders	15	829	369	129	92	126	113	23,031	280.5
Special trade contractors	17	973	513	154	121	111	74	16,638	219.8
Manufacturing [2]	D	2,165	682	254	334	371	524	159,117	3,218.4
Food and kindred products	20	314	100	42	57	59	56	18,753	342.2
Textile mill products	22	19	2	3	4	3	7	3,194	34.5
Apparel and other textile products	23	232	59	20	30	34	89	23,090	240.5
Furniture and fixtures	25	153	69	19	31	24	10	2,377	26.4
Paper and allied products	26	44	4	3	8	13	16	2,170	42.9
Printing and publishing	27	227	112	43	36	19	17	5,028	113.8
Chemicals and allied products	28	188	27	14	21	28	98	34,032	1,070.7
Petroleum and coal products	29	27	6	2	8	4	7	1,537	50.8
Rubber and misc. plastic products	30	80	13	8	11	27	21	4,681	92.0
Leather and leather products	31	23	4	2	2	1	14	6,233	73.6
Stone, clay, and glass products	32	166	52	21	29	49	15	4,395	88.8
Fabricated metal products	34	192	67	21	40	40	25	4,889	80.5
Industrial machinery and equip	35	82	41	9	11	8	13	7,085	162.8
Electronic and other electronic equip	36	104	10	5	14	13	62	21,317	382.6
Instruments and related products	38	66	8	5	3	9	41	11,984	253.5
Transportation and public utilities [2]	E	1,503	924	222	149	123	85	33,075	761.7
Trucking and warehousing	42	557	367	79	57	43	11	5,118	104.4
Water transportation	44	83	31	12	12	11	17	6,308	102.1
Air transportation	45	81	28	13	13	12	15	3,400	60.4
Transportation services	47	454	347	59	24	15	9	2,616	42.0
Communication	48	154	50	30	25	30	19	13,175	410.5
Electric, gas, and sanitary services	49	41	14	4	8	4	11	1,538	30.3
Wholesale trade [2]	F	2,678	1,247	544	428	301	158	37,408	806.0
Durable goods	50	1,409	640	316	229	168	56	16,332	349.8
Nondurable goods	51	1,250	605	222	198	128	97	20,464	433.6
Retail trade [2]	G	13,744	7,864	2,622	1,587	1,182	489	144,416	1,540.7
Building materials, garden supplies	52	925	580	184	82	64	15	7,172	81.7
General merchandise stores	53	436	145	66	80	78	67	19,181	201.9
Food stores	54	1,924	1,191	282	157	128	166	26,460	252.1
Automotive dealers and service stations	55	2,256	1,503	447	150	102	54	15,429	215.0
Apparel and accessory stores	56	1,895	769	562	405	142	17	15,746	145.1
Furniture and home furnishings	57	948	507	240	142	51	8	6,657	87.8
Eating and drinking places	58	2,770	1,557	352	324	427	110	33,397	271.5
Finance, insurance, and real estate [2]	H	2,460	1,317	500	328	190	125	41,908	976.1
Depository institutions	60	376	98	79	128	48	23	13,995	352.1
Nondepository institutions	61	403	112	141	70	55	25	7,627	177.0
Insurance carriers	63	103	43	17	8	20	15	4,253	112.7
Insurance agents, brokers, and service	64	295	170	52	33	21	19	4,152	119.0
Real estate	65	1,180	830	198	81	38	33	10,194	146.2
Services [2]	I	13,704	9,373	1,948	1,060	739	584	179,228	2,457.5
Personal services	72	889	654	144	58	30	3	4,056	43.9
Business services	73	1,586	796	280	180	134	196	52,193	605.3
Auto repair, services, and parking	75	1,057	792	145	76	32	12	5,543	71.8
Motion pictures	78	154	75	16	32	24	7	1,864	19.0
Amusement and recreation services	79	347	219	47	33	34	14	3,445	35.1
Health services	80	4,449	3,529	543	178	110	89	39,959	582.3
Legal services	81	1,230	1,053	98	54	19	6	4,086	86.0
Education services	82	575	163	81	80	136	115	23,483	336.9
Social services	83	603	329	116	77	42	39	10,423	99.9
Membership organizations	86	802	550	115	67	42	28	7,370	81.5
Engineering and management services	87	1,224	774	215	134	66	35	10,817	220.1

[1] 1987 Standard Industrial Classification (SIC) code; see text, Section 17, Business Enterprise. [2] Includes other establishments not shown separately.

Source: U.S. Census Bureau, *County Business Patterns*, annual.

No. 1343. Highway Statistics (Most Current Year) for Puerto Rico and the Territories

Item	Puerto Rico, 1994	Virgin Islands, 1996	Guam, 1996	American Samoa, 1993	Northern Mariana Islands, 1995
Motor-vehicle registrations:					
Total..................................	1,661,000	57,135	112,893	5,117	15,133
Automobiles........................	1,432,000	43,754	79,080	4,628	14,559
Buses..............................	4,000	1,121	858	203	200
Trucks.............................	225,000	12,260	32,955	286	374
Trailers.............................	17,000	158	3,621	52	36
Motorcycles........................	22,000	226	617	29	57
Driver licenses in force [1].........	1,529,000	(NA)	47,928	4,111	11,481
Learner permits issued............	81,000	4,550	6,008	36	3,530
Operator licenses issued...........	314,000	22,728	36,008	3,644	7,951
Chauffeur licenses issued..........	87,000	(NA)	5,692	398	-
Motorcycle licenses issued.........	-	(NA)	220	-	-
Motor vehicle tax receipts ($1,000)......	71,216	1,613	6,277	250	1,028
Registration fees..................	61,305	1,314	5,789	219	849
Driver licenses....................	4,823	299	488	27	179
Motor carriers.....................	332	(NA)	(NA)	2	-
Other.............................	4,755	(NA)	(NA)	2	-
Motor-fuel consumption: [2]					
Territorial tax rate (cents/gal.) on Dec. 31:					
Gasoline..........................	16	14	11	12	10
Diesel and LPG....................	8	14	10	12	10
Net gallons taxed (1,000)...........	1,200,751	38,746	90,866	3,150	65,932
At prevailing rates................	1,198,377	(NA)	(NA)	3,150	65,932
At other rates.....................	2,374	(NA)	(NA)	-	-
Motor-fuel tax receipts: [2] ($1,000)					
Gross gallonage receipts...........	170,988	5,425	3,132	61	6,593
Less:					
Refunds paid.....................	799	(NA)	(NA)	116	-
Dedicated gallonage tax...........	119	(NA)	(NA)	-	-
Other receipts.....................	852	(NA)	(NA)	-	-
Net total receipts..................	170,922	5,425	5,363	(55)	6,593
Highway receipts ($1,000)..........	650,455	31,422	486	19,497	5,448
Highway-user revenue..............	290,753	772	(NA)	195	-
General funds.....................	299,974	5,038	(NA)	277	899
FHWA funds.......................	54,204	14,504	54	18,908	3,749
Other federal funds................	-	11,108	432	117	800
Highway disbursements ($1,000)......	650,455	20,558	17,081	622	5,448
Capital outlay......................	484,860	14,100	9,631	19	3,749
Maintenance......................	42,468	952	4,337	422	587
Administration....................	103,282	6,353	2,627	181	172
Highway law enforcement..........	19,845	105	486	-	940

- Represents or rounds to zero.   NA Not available.   [1] For American Samoa, data are licenses in force instead of license issued.   [2] 1996 data for Puerto Rico.

Source: U.S. Federal Highway Administration, *Highway Statistics*, annual.

No. 1344. Guam, Virgin Islands, and Northern Mariana Islands— Economic Summary: 1992

[Sales and payroll in millions of dollars (3,018 represents $3,018,000,000)]

Item	Guam	Virgin Islands	Northern Mariana Islands	Item	Guam	Virgin Islands	Northern Mariana Islands
Total: Establishments.......	1,955	2,932	1,266	Wholesale trade:			
Sales.................	3,018	2,281	1,132	Establishments..........	154	114	60
Annual payroll...........	567	338	161	Sales.................	428	414	132
Paid employees [1].....	33,057	20,968	20,105	Annual payroll..........	32	21	6
Unpaid family workers [2]...	337	330	268	Paid employees [1].....	1,715	1,030	534
Construction: Establishments..	240	147	103	Unpaid family workers [2]...	4	1	3
Sales.................	709	169	88	Retail trade:			
Annual payroll...........	178	44	18	Establishments..........	886	1,339	616
Paid employees [1].....	9,131	2,224	3,036	Sales.................	1,114	881	384
Unpaid family workers [2]...	17	3	20	Annual payroll..........	141	120	38
Manufacturing:				Paid employees [1].....	9,565	8,859	4,715
Establishments.........	48	78	73	Unpaid family workers [2]...	237	239	157
Sales.................	110	134	264	Services: Establishments....	627	1,254	414
Annual payroll...........	23	23	49	Sales.................	656	682	264
Paid employees [1].....	1,130	1,196	6,267	Annual payroll..........	193	130	51
Unpaid family workers [2]...	8	3	4	Paid employees [1].....	11,516	7,659	5,553
				Unpaid family workers [2]...	71	84	84

[1] For pay period including March 12.   [2] Includes those who worked 15 hours or more during the week including March 12.

Source: U.S. Census Bureau, *1992 Economic Census of Outlying Areas*, OA92-E-5 to OA92-E-7.

Outlying Areas   819

No. 1345. Population Estimates and Vital Statistics in the Largest Puerto Rico Municipios: 1990 and 1997

Municipios ranked by 1997 population	1990	1997	Demographic components of population change				
			Percent change	Births	Deaths	Natural change	Residual change
Puerto Rico	**3,522,037**	**3,827,038**	**8.7**	**464,075**	**203,724**	**260,351**	**44,650**
San Juan	437,745	436,334	-0.3	53,357	33,011	20,346	-21,757
Bayamon	220,262	233,784	6.1	27,449	11,879	15,570	-2,048
Ponce	187,749	189,900	1.1	26,016	11,601	14,415	-12,264
Carolina	177,806	189,853	6.8	21,351	9,135	12,216	-169
Caguas	133,447	141,871	6.3	17,888	7,750	10,138	-1,714
Guaynabo	92,886	104,901	12.9	11,919	4,850	7,069	4,946
Arecibo	93,385	102,773	10.1	11,643	6,261	5,382	4,006
Mayagez	100,371	100,001	-0.4	11,331	6,304	5,027	-5,397
Toa Baja	89,454	92,947	3.9	11,065	4,139	6,926	-3,433
Trujillo Alto	61,120	75,658	23.8	8,124	2,767	5,357	9,181
Aquadilla	59,335	67,010	12.9	7,145	3,674	3,471	4,204
Vega Baja	55,997	61,906	10.6	8,191	3,166	5,025	884
Toa Alta	44,101	61,113	38.6	6,737	1,764	4,973	12,039
Humacao	55,203	58,918	6.7	7,486	3,097	4,389	-674
Juana Diaz	45,198	50,848	12.5	6,725	2,388	4,337	1,313
Rio Grande	45,648	50,825	11.3	6,281	2,362	3,919	1,258
Canovanas	36,816	50,786	37.9	6,229	2,087	4,142	9,828
Cayey	46,553	50,600	8.7	6,088	2,771	3,317	730
Cidra	35,601	49,440	38.9	4,611	1,587	3,024	10,815
Cabo Rojo	38,521	47,105	22.3	4,505	2,473	2,032	6,552
Yauco	42,058	44,176	5.0	5,448	2,291	3,157	-1,039
San Sebastian	38,799	43,989	13.4	4,506	2,300	2,206	2,984
Guayama	41,588	43,216	3.9	5,929	2,471	3,458	-1,830
Juncos	30,612	42,753	39.7	4,038	1,803	2,235	9,906
Yabucoa	36,483	41,848	14.7	4,689	1,937	2,752	2,613
Isabela	39,147	41,728	6.6	4,842	2,442	2,400	181
Manati	38,692	40,190	3.9	5,784	2,468	3,316	-1,818
Hatillo	32,703	39,621	21.2	4,074	1,884	2,190	4,728
Aguada	35,911	38,791	8.0	4,646	1,663	2,983	-103
Fajardo	36,882	38,218	3.6	5,317	2,468	2,849	-1,513
Moca	32,926	37,544	14.0	4,313	1,484	2,829	1,789
San German	34,962	36,984	5.8	4,232	2,144	2,088	-66
Corozal	33,095	36,957	11.7	4,802	1,607	3,195	667
Coamo	33,837	36,856	8.9	4,797	1,901	2,896	123
San Lorenzo	35,163	36,314	3.3	4,524	2,005	2,519	-1,368
Vega Alta	34,559	36,064	4.4	4,531	1,679	2,852	-1,347
Utuado	34,980	35,012	0.1	4,262	1,967	2,295	-2,263
Morovis	25,288	33,380	32.0	4,029	1,105	2,924	5,168
Gurabo	28,737	33,053	15.0	3,987	1,579	2,408	1,908
Dorado	30,759	32,985	7.2	3,967	1,489	2,478	-252
Catano	34,587	32,414	-6.3	4,623	1,959	2,664	-4,837
Lares	29,015	32,381	11.6	3,971	1,664	2,307	1,059
Camuy	28,917	32,135	11.1	4,030	1,643	2,387	831
Las Piedras	27,896	31,252	12.0	3,838	1,423	2,415	941
Aguas Buenas	25,424	30,193	18.8	3,332	1,242	2,090	2,679
Salinas	28,335	29,755	5.0	4,299	1,707	2,592	-1,172
Naranjito	27,914	29,457	5.5	4,052	1,273	2,779	-1,236
Barranquitas	25,605	28,587	11.6	4,362	1,220	3,142	-160
Loiza	29,307	28,372	-3.2	3,917	1,305	2,612	-3,547
Aibonito	24,971	28,178	12.8	3,456	1,310	2,146	1,061
Guayanilla	21,581	27,830	29.0	2,784	1,175	1,609	4,640
Anasco	25,234	27,463	8.8	3,228	1,471	1,757	472
Penuelas	22,515	26,858	19.3	3,393	1,125	2,268	2,075
Lajas	23,271	26,663	14.6	2,790	1,423	1,367	2,025
Barceloneta	20,947	26,644	27.2	2,929	1,265	1,664	4,033
Quebradillas	21,425	26,109	21.9	2,889	1,185	1,704	2,980
Naguabo	22,620	25,943	14.7	2,882	1,456	1,426	1,897
Orocovis	21,158	24,690	16.7	3,455	1,052	2,403	1,129
Sabana Grande	22,843	24,644	7.9	2,990	1,467	1,523	278
Villalba	23,559	23,213	-1.5	3,961	1,045	2,916	-3,262
Guanica	19,984	21,847	9.3	2,569	1,313	1,256	607
Patillas	19,633	21,725	10.7	2,638	1,105	1,533	559
Comerio	20,265	20,965	3.5	2,721	982	1,739	-1,039
Adjuntas	19,451	20,525	5.5	2,656	1,048	1,608	-534
Arroyo	18,910	19,905	5.3	2,589	1,054	1,535	-540
Ciales	18,084	19,568	8.2	2,634	903	1,731	-247
Santa Isabel	19,318	19,454	0.7	3,173	1,217	1,956	-1,820
Luquillo	18,100	19,025	5.1	2,577	1,093	1,484	-559
Ceiba	17,145	18,571	8.3	2,494	801	1,693	-267
Jayuya	15,527	16,612	7.0	2,378	855	1,523	-438
Hormigueros	15,212	16,052	5.5	1,509	855	654	186
Rincon	12,213	13,760	12.7	1,670	738	932	615
Maunabo	12,347	13,605	10.2	1,644	694	950	308
Las Marias	9,306	9,929	6.7	1,165	452	713	-90
Vieques	8,602	9,311	8.2	1,239	642	597	112
Florida	8,689	9,052	4.2	1,402	551	851	-488
Maricao	6,206	6,361	2.5	860	305	555	-400
Culebra	1,542	1,738	12.7	243	80	163	33

Source: U.S. Census Bureau, <http://www.census.gov/population/www/estimates/puerto-rico.html>.

820 Outlying Areas

Section 30
Comparative International Statistics

This section presents statistics for the world as a whole and for many countries on a comparative basis with the United States. Data are shown for population, births and deaths, social and industrial indicators, finances, agriculture, communication, and military affairs.

Statistics of the individual nations may be found primarily in official national publications, generally in the form of yearbooks, issued by most of the nations at various intervals in their own national languages and expressed in their own or customary units of measure. (For a listing of selected publications, see Guide to Sources.) For handier reference, especially for international comparisons, the Statistical Office of the United Nations compiles data as submitted by member countries and issues a number of international summary publications, generally in English and French. Among these are the *Statistical Yearbook*; the *Demographic Yearbook*; the *Yearbook of International Trade Statistics*; the *Yearbook of National Accounts Statistics: Vol. II, International Tables*; *Population and Vital Statistics Reports* (quarterly); the *Monthly Bulletin of Statistics*; and the *Energy Statistics Yearbook*. Specialized agencies of the United Nations also issue international summary publications on agricultural, labor, health, and education statistics. Among these are the *Production Yearbook* and *Trade Yearbook* issued by the Food and Agriculture Organization, the *Yearbook of Labour Statistics* issued by the International Labour Office, *World Health Statistics* issued by the World Health Organization, and the *Statistical Yearbook* issued by the Educational, Scientific, and Cultural Organization.

The U.S. Census Bureau presents estimates and projections of basic demographic measures for countries and regions of the world in the *World Population Reports* (WP) series. The *International Population Reports* (Series P95), and *International Briefs* (series IB) also present population figures for many foreign countries. Detailed population statistics are also available from the Census Bureau's International Data Base.

The International Monetary Fund (IMF) and the Organization for Economic Cooperation and Development (OECD) also compile data on international statistics. The IMF publishes a series of reports relating to financial data. These include *International Financial Statistics, Direction of Trade*, and *Balance of Payments Yearbook*, published in English, French, and Spanish. The OECD publishes a vast number of statistical publications in various fields such as economics, health, and education. Among these are *OECD in Figures, Main Economic Indicators, Economic Outlook, National Accounts, Labour Force Statistics, OECD Health Data*, and *Education at a Glance*.

Statistical coverage, country names, and classifications—Problems of space and availability of data limit the number of countries and the extent of statistical coverage shown. The list of countries included and the spelling of country names are based almost entirely on the list of sovereign nations, dependencies, and areas of special sovereignty provided by the U.S. Department of State.

In recent years, several important changes took place in the status of the world's nations. In 1990, a unified Germany was formed from the Federal Republic of Germany (West) and the German Democratic Republic (East). The Republic of Yemen was formed by union of the Yemen Arab Republic and the People's Democratic Republic of Yemen. Also in 1990, Namibia, once a

Comparative International Statistics 821

United Nations mandate, realized its independence from South Africa.

In 1991, the Soviet Union broke up into 15 independent countries: Armenia, Azerbaijan, Belarus, Estonia, Georgia, Kazakhstan, Kyrgyzstan, Latvia, Lithuania, Moldova, Russia, Tajikistan, Turkmenistan, Ukraine, and Uzbekistan.

In 1992, the Socialist Federal Republic of Yugoslavia dissolved; none of the successor states has been recognized as its continuation. The United States recognizes Bosnia and Herzegovina, Croatia, Slovenia, and The Former Yugoslav Republic of Macedonia as independent countries. Serbia and Montenegro have asserted the formation of a joint independent state, but this entity has not been formally recognized as a state by the United States.

On January 1, 1993, Czechoslovakia was succeeded by two independent countries: the Czech Republic and Slovakia. Eritrea announced its independence from Ethiopia in April 1993 and was subsequently recognized as an independent nation by the United States.

The population estimates and projections used in Tables 1349, 1350, and 1352 were prepared by the Census Bureau. For each country, the data on population, by age and sex, fertility, mortality, and international migration were evaluated and, where necessary, adjusted for inconsistencies and errors in the data. In most instances, comprehensive projections were made by the component method, resulting in distributions of the population by age and sex and requiring an assessment of probable future trends of fertility, mortality, and international migration.

Economic associations—The Organization for European Economic Co-operation (OEEC), a regional grouping of Western European countries established in 1948 for the purpose of harmonizing national economic policies and conditions, was succeeded on September 30, 1961, by the Organization for Economic Cooperation and Development (OECD). The member nations of the OECD are Australia, Austria, Belgium,

Canada, Czech Republic, Denmark, Finland, France, Germany, Greece, Hungary, Iceland, Ireland, Italy, Japan, Luxembourg, Mexico, the Netherlands, New Zealand, Norway, Poland, Portugal, South Korea, Spain, Sweden, Switzerland, Turkey, the United Kingdom, and the United States.

Quality and comparability of the data—The quality and comparability of the data presented here are affected by a number of factors:

1) The year for which data are presented may not be the same for all subjects for a particular country or for a given subject for different countries, though the data shown are the most recent available. All such variations have been noted. The data shown are for calendar years except as otherwise specified.

(2) The bases, methods of estimating, methods of data collection, extent of coverage, precision of definition, scope of territory, and margins of error may vary for different items within a particular country, and for like items for different countries. Footnotes and headnotes to the tables give a few of the major time-periods and coverage qualifications attached to the figures; considerably more detail is presented in the source publications. Many of the measures shown are, at best, merely rough indicators of magnitude.

(3) Figures shown in this section for the United States may not always agree with figures shown in the preceding sections. Disagreements may be attributable to the use of differing original sources, a difference in the definition of geographic limits (the 50 states, conterminous United States only, or the United States including certain outlying areas and possessions), or to possible adjustments made in the United States figures by the United Nations or other sources in order to make them more comparable with figures from other countries.

International comparisons of national accounts data—In order to compare national accounts data for different countries, it is necessary to convert each country's data into a common unit of currency, usually the U.S. dollar. The market exchange rates which are often used in converting national currencies do not necessarily reflect the relative purchasing power in the various countries. It is necessary that the goods and services produced in different countries be valued consistently if the differences observed are meant to reflect real differences in the volumes of goods and services produced. The use of purchasing power parities (see Table 1363) instead of exchange rates is intended to achieve this objective.

The method used to present the data shown in Table 1363 is to construct volume measures directly by revaluing the goods and services sold in different countries at a common set of international prices. By dividing the ratio of the gross domestic products of two countries expressed in their own national currencies by the corresponding ratio calculated at constant international prices, it is possible to derive the implied purchasing power parity (PPP) between the two currencies concerned. PPPs show how many units of currency are needed in one country to buy the same amount of goods and services which one unit of currency will buy in the other country. For further information, see *National Accounts, Main Aggregates, Volume I,* issued annually by the Organization for Economic Cooperation and Development, Paris, France.

International Standard Industrial Classification—The original version of the International Standard Industrial Classification of All Economic Activities (ISIC) was adopted in 1948. Wide use has been made both nationally and internationally in classifying data according to kind of economic

activity in the fields of production, employment, national income, and other economic statistics. A number of countries have utilized the ISIC as the basis for devising their industrial classification scheme.

Substantial comparability has been attained between the industrial classifications of many other countries, including the United States and the ISIC by ensuring, as far as practicable, that the categories at detailed levels of classification in national schemes fitted into only one category of the ISIC. For more detail, see the Census Bureau's, *The International Standard Industrial Classification and the U.S. Standard Industrial Classification,* Technical Paper No. 14, and the text of Section 27, Manufactures. The United Nations, the International Labour Organization, the Food and Agriculture Organization, and other international bodies have utilized the ISIC in publishing and analyzing statistical data. Revisions of the ISIC were issued in 1958, 1968, and 1989.

International maps—A series of regional world maps is provided on pages 824-830. References are included in Table 1349 for easy location of individual countries on the maps. The Robinson map projection is used for this series of maps. A map projection is used to portray all or part of the round Earth on a flat surface, but this cannot be done without some distortion. For the Robinson projection, distortion is very low along the Equator and within 45 degrees of the center but is greatest near the poles. For additional information on map projections and maps, please contact the Earth Science Information Center, U.S. Geological Survey, 507 National Center, Reston, VA 22092.

U.S. Census Bureau, Statistical Abstract of the United States: 1999

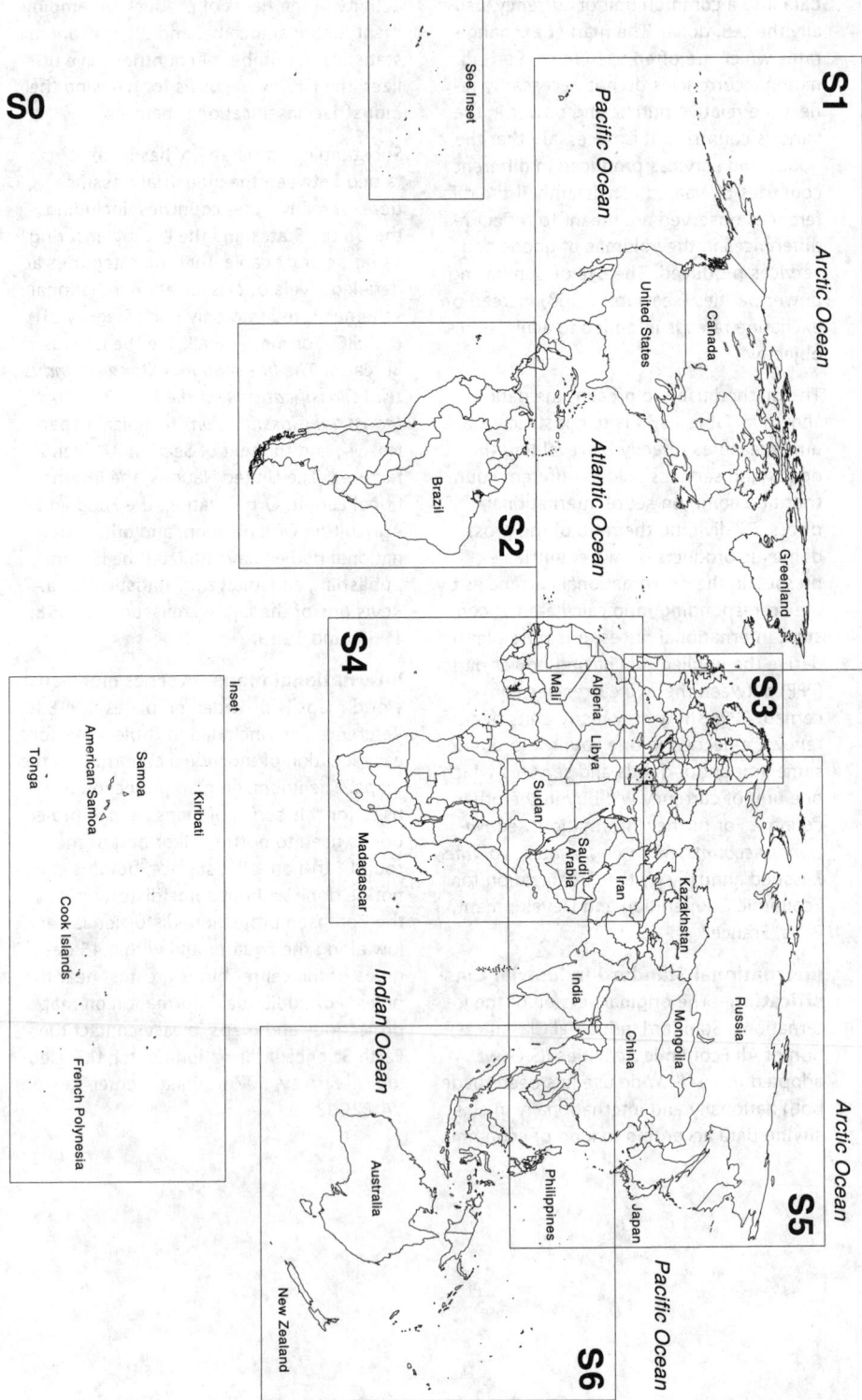

S0

S1

Arctic Ocean

Pacific Ocean

United States

Canada

Greenland

Atlantic Ocean

See Inset

S2

Brazil

S4

Algeria

Mali

Libya

Sudan

Saudi Arabia

Iran

Madagascar

S3

Kazakhstan

Russia

Mongolia

China

India

Japan

Philippines

Arctic Ocean

S5

Pacific Ocean

Indian Ocean

Australia

New Zealand

S6

Inset

Tonga

Samoa

American Samoa

Kiribati

Cook Islands

French Polynesia

U.S. Census Bureau, Statistical Abstract of the United States: 1999

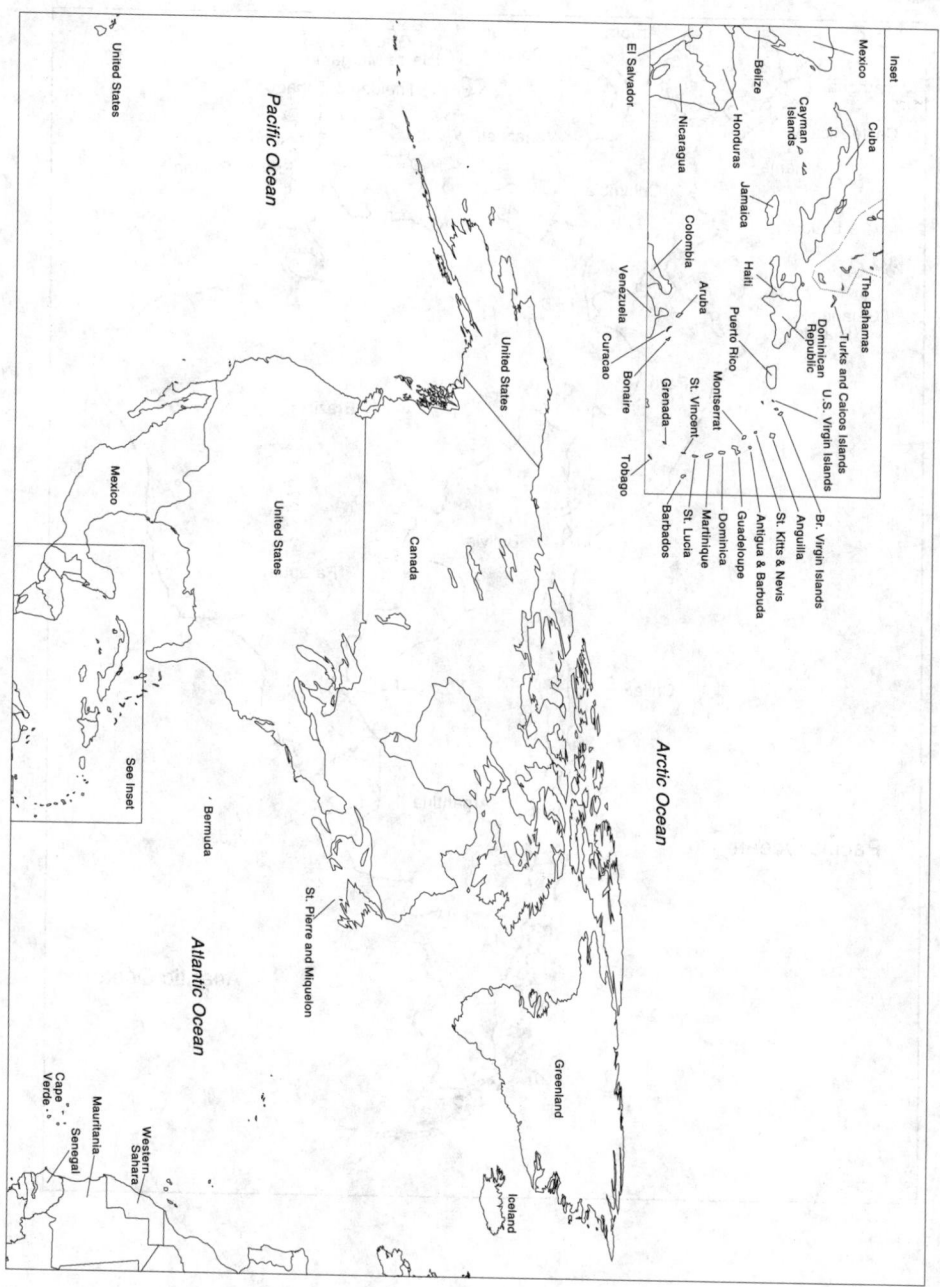

U.S. Census Bureau, Statistical Abstract of the United States: 1999

Nicaragua

Aruba

Curacao

Bonaire

Barbados

Grenada

Isla de Margarita

Trinidad & Tobago

Costa Rica

Panama

Venezuela

Guyana

Suriname

French Guiana

Colombia

Ecuador

Galapagos
Islands

Peru

Brazil

Bolivia

Paraguay

Chile

Pacific Ocean

Argentina

Uruguay

Atlantic Ocean

U.S. Census Bureau, Statistical Abstract of the United States: 1999

S3

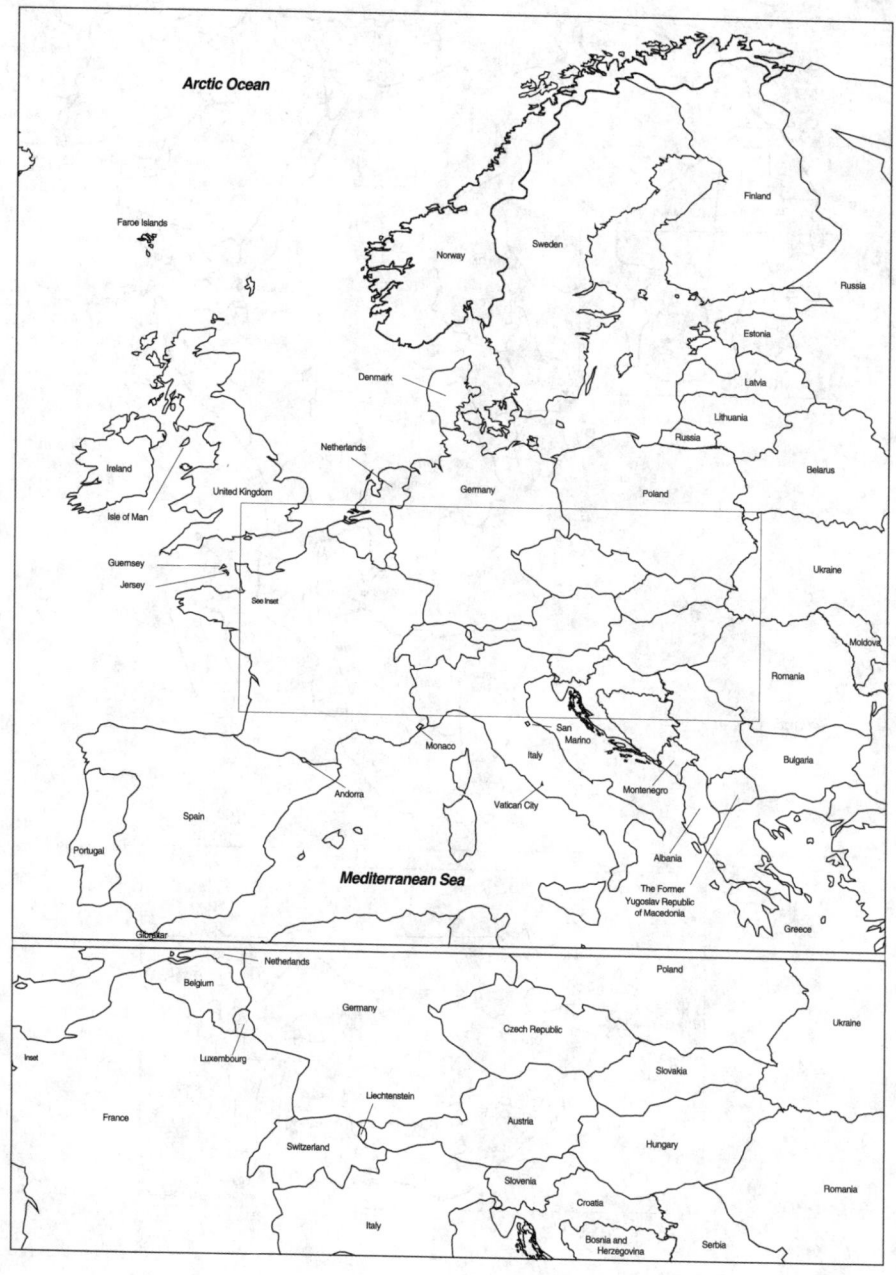

Arctic Ocean

Faroe Islands

Norway

Sweden

Finland

Russia

Estonia

Latvia

Lithuania

Russia

Belarus

Ireland

United Kingdom

Isle of Man

Denmark

Netherlands

Germany

Poland

Ukraine

Guernsey

Jersey

See Inset

Moldova

Romania

Monaco

San Marino

Italy

Bulgaria

Andorra

Vatican City

Montenegro

Spain

Albania

Portugal

The Former Yugoslav Republic of Macedonia

Greece

Gibraltar

Mediterranean Sea

Netherlands

Poland

Belgium

Germany

Czech Republic

Ukraine

Inset

Luxembourg

Slovakia

Liechtenstein

France

Austria

Hungary

Switzerland

Slovenia

Romania

Italy

Croatia

Bosnia and Herzegovina

Serbia

U.S. Census Bureau, Statistical Abstract of the United States: 1999

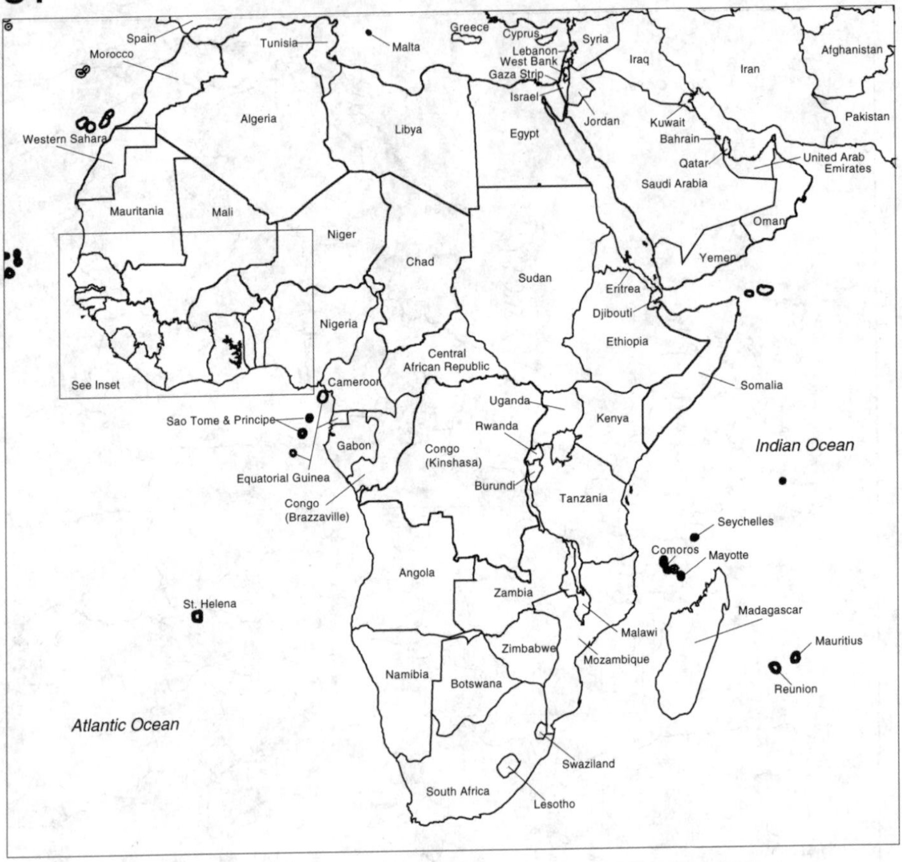

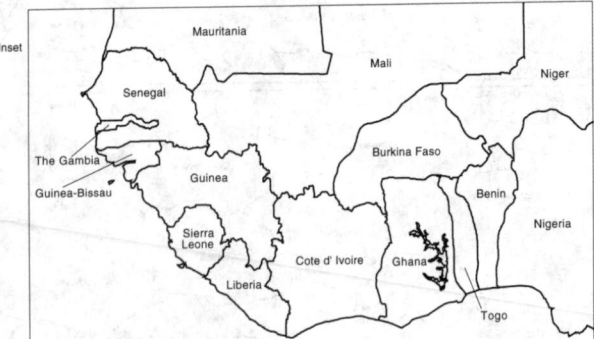

Spain
Morocco
Tunisia
Malta
Greece
Cyprus
Lebanon
West Bank
Gaza Strip
Syria
Iraq
Iran
Afghanistan
Western Sahara
Algeria
Libya
Israel
Egypt
Jordan
Kuwait
Bahrain
Qatar
Saudi Arabia
Pakistan
United Arab Emirates
Mauritania
Mali
Niger
Chad
Sudan
Eritrea
Djibouti
Ethiopia
Oman
Yemen
Somalia
Nigeria
Central African Republic
See Inset
Cameroon
Sao Tome & Principe
Uganda
Rwanda
Kenya
Indian Ocean
Gabon
Congo (Kinshasa)
Equatorial Guinea
Burundi
Tanzania
Congo (Brazzaville)
Seychelles
Comoros
Mayotte
Angola
Zambia
Madagascar
Mauritius
St. Helena
Malawi
Zimbabwe
Mozambique
Reunion
Namibia
Botswana
Atlantic Ocean
Swaziland
South Africa
Lesotho

Inset
Mauritania
Mali
Niger
Senegal
Burkina Faso
The Gambia
Guinea
Benin
Nigeria
Guinea-Bissau
Sierra Leone
Cote d' Ivoire
Ghana
Liberia
Togo

U.S. Census Bureau, Statistical Abstract of the United States: 1999

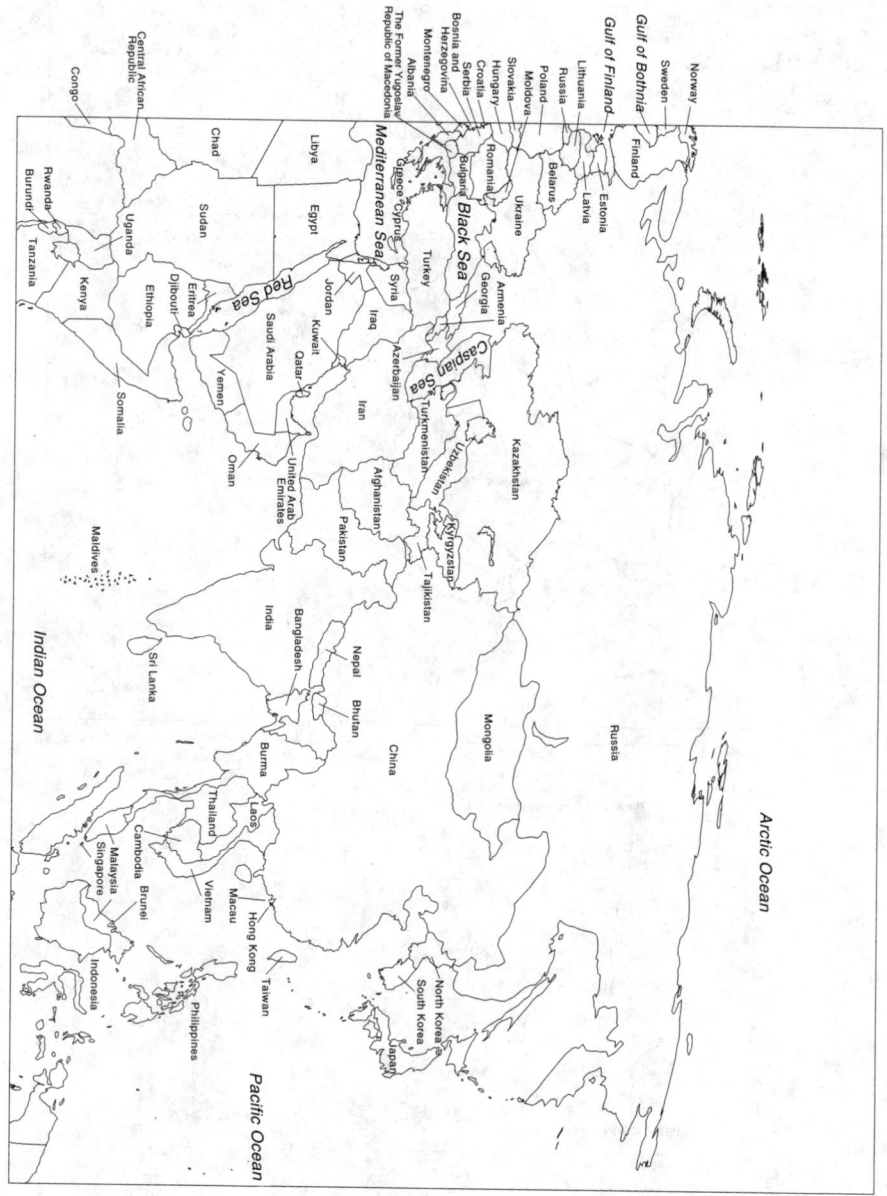

U.S. Census Bureau, Statistical Abstract of the United States: 1999

S6

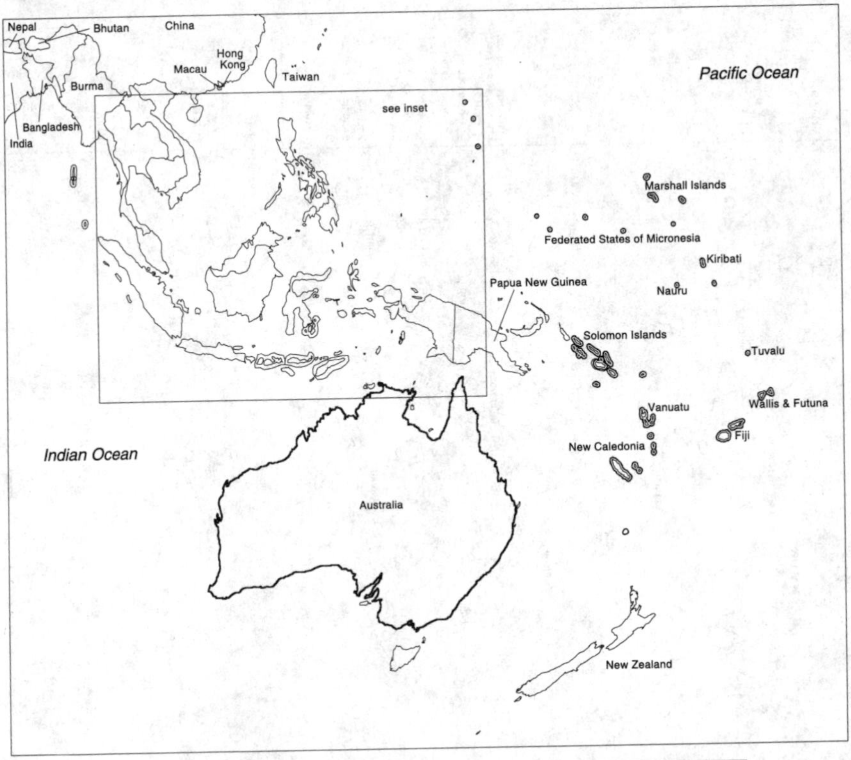

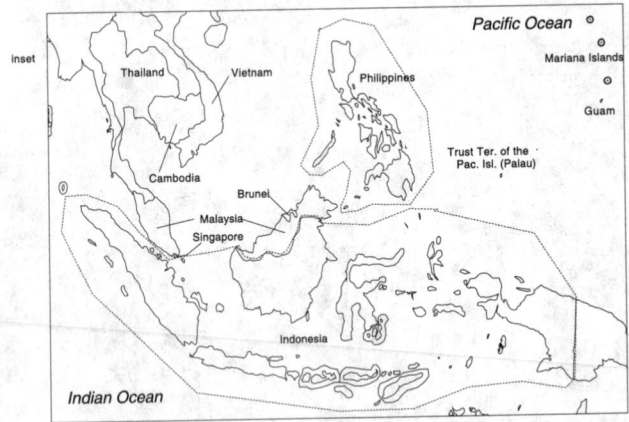

Nepal Bhutan China
Burma
Macau Hong Kong Taiwan
Bangladesh
India
see inset

Pacific Ocean

Marshall Islands

Federated States of Micronesia

Kiribati

Papua New Guinea Nauru

Solomon Islands Tuvalu

Indian Ocean Vanuatu Wallis & Futuna

New Caledonia Fiji

Australia

New Zealand

inset Thailand Vietnam Philippines

Pacific Ocean

Mariana Islands

Guam

Cambodia Brunei Trust Ter. of the Pac. Isl. (Palau)

Malaysia
Singapore

Indonesia

Indian Ocean

830 Comparative International Statistics

No. 1346. Total World Population: 1980 to 2050

[As of midyear (**4,454** represents 4,454,000,000)]

Year	Popula-tion (mil.)	Average annual [1] Growth rate (per-cent)	Average annual [1] Popula-tion change (mil.)	Year	Popula-tion (mil.)	Average annual [1] Growth rate (per-cent)	Average annual [1] Popula-tion change (mil.)	Year	Popula-tion (mil.)	Average annual [1] Growth rate (per-cent)	Average annual [1] Popula-tion change (mil.)
1980	4,454	1.69	76.1	1999	5,996	1.27	76.9	2020	7,562	0.90	68.2
1985	4,851	1.68	82.4	2000	6,073	1.25	76.3	2030	8,215	0.76	62.4
1990	5,277	1.55	82.5	2005	6,453	1.16	75.5	2040	8,810	0.62	54.5
1995	5,682	1.37	78.6	2010	6,832	1.11	76.0	2050	9,298	(NA)	(NA)

NA Not available. [1] Represents change from year shown to immediate succeeding year.

Source: U.S. Census Bureau, "Total Midyear Population for the World: 1950-2050," published 28 December 1998; <http://www.census.gov/ipc/www/worldpop.html>.

No. 1347. World Summary: 1980 to 1997

[**4.8** represents 4,800,000. See text of this section for general comments concerning quality of the data]

Item	Unit	1980	1985	1990	1992	1993	1994	1995	1996	1997
Agriculture, forestry, fishing:										
Coffee	Mil. metric tons .	4.8	5.8	6.1	5.9	5.6	5.8	5.5	6.2	6.0
Cotton (lint)	Mil. metric tons .	13.9	17.3	18.4	18.1	16.9	18.7	20.3	19.7	19.9
Tobacco	Mil. metric tons .	5.3	7.1	7.1	8.4	8.3	6.4	6.3	7.4	8.6
Roundwood	Mil. cubic meters.	2,920	3,167	3,448	3,279	3,277	3,301	3,411	3,448	3,358
Fish catches	Mil. metric tons .	72.3	87.2	99.0	101.7	105.2	113.5	117.3	121.0	(NA)
Industrial production:										
Wine	Mil. metric tons .	35.2	29.5	28.7	29.4	25.9	25.6	25.5	27.4	26.9
Sugar	Mil. metric tons .	84.5	98.5	111.5	117.0	109.8	109.5	118.7	127.1	124.9
Wheat flour	Mil. metric tons .	229.7	267.9	295.1	312.3	312.3	312.5	320.2	327.9	324.5
Electricity	Bil. kWh	8,247	9,747	11,788	12,142	12,395	12,713	13,147	13,620	(NA)
Pig iron and ferroalloys	Mil. metric tons .	542	507	531	507	506	516	534	525	(NA)
Sawnwood	Mil. cubic meters.	451	468	505	437	431	434	427	(NA)	434
Woodpulp	Mil. metric tons .	125.8	141.8	155.1	152.0	151.2	161.9	161.9	(NA)	(NA)
Newsprint	Mil. metric tons .	25.4	28.3	32.5	32.3	32.5	33.9	34.8	36.3	(NA)
Merchant vessels, launched . .	Mil. gross tons . .	13.9	17.3	14.7	20.5	18.7	16.3	(NA)	15.5	22.2
External trade:										
Imports, c.i.f	Bil. U.S. dollars .	2,047	2,028	3,557	3,795	3,735	4,262	5,046	5,314	5,479
Exports, f.o.b	Bil. U.S. dollars .	1,998	1,927	3,425	3,661	3,661	4,169	4,969	5,171	5,340
Civil aviation, kilometers flown [1] .	Millions	9,362	10,565	14,350	15,310	17,118	18,249	19,470	20,601	(NA)

NA Not available. [1] Scheduled services of members of International Civil Aviation Organization.

Source: Statistical Division of the United Nations, New York, NY, *Monthly Bulletin of Statistics,* (copyright).

No. 1348. Religious Population of the World: 1998

[In thousands, except percent (**5,929,839** represents 5,929,839,000). Refers to adherents of all religions as defined and enumerated for each of the world's countries in *World Encyclopedia (1982),* projected to mid-1998, adjusted for recent data]

Religion	Total	Percent distribution	Africa	Asia	Latin America	Northern America	Europe [1]	Oceania
Total population. . .	**5,929,839**	**100.0**	**778,484**	**3,588,877**	**499,534**	**304,078**	**729,406**	**29,460**
Christians	1,943,038	32.8	356,277	283,734	462,965	256,882	558,729	24,451
Affiliated Christians . . .	1,835,352	31.0	323,782	275,836	456,919	222,678	536,092	20,045
Roman Catholics . . .	1,026,501	17.3	114,316	106,399	442,808	69,536	286,124	7,318
Protestants	316,445	5.3	74,436	43,998	45,295	69,437	76,776	6,503
Orthodox	213,743	3.6	33,660	15,232	549	4,852	158,775	675
Anglicans	63,748	1.1	27,957	856	853	3,260	25,632	5,190
Other Christians . . .	373,832	6.3	74,853	143,080	44,331	83,519	25,551	2,498
Unaffiliated Christians .	107,686	1.8	32,495	7,898	6,046	34,204	22,637	4,406
Atheists	149,913	2.5	420	121,451	2,673	1,569	23,444	356
Baha'is	6,764	0.1	1,695	3,260	825	753	126	105
Buddhists	353,794	6.0	138	348,806	622	2,445	1,517	266
Chinese folk-religionists [2].	379,162	6.4	33	377,795	184	839	250	61
Confucians	6,241	0.1	-	6,207	-	-	11	23
Ethnic religionists	248,565	4.2	97,200	148,189	1,231	424	1,262	259
Hindus	761,689	12.8	2,411	755,500	785	1,266	1,382	345
Jains	3,922	0.1	65	3,850	-	7	-	-
Jews	14,111	0.2	230	4,139	1,121	5,996	2,530	95
Mandeans	38	-	-	38	-	-	-	-
Muslims . . . . . [3]	1,164,622	19.6	315,000	812,000	1,624	4,349	31,401	248
New-religionists [3]	100,144	1.7	27	98,548	604	759	155	51
Nonreligious [4]	759,655	12.8	4,863	600,822	15,300	27,500	108,000	3,170
Other religionists	1,001	0.0	68	11	95	585	233	9
Shintoists	2,789	0.0	-	2,727	-	55	-	-
Sikhs	22,332	0.4	53	21,531	-	498	236	14
Spiritists	11,785	0.2	3	-	11,498	148	129	7
Zoroastrians	274	-	1	269	-	3	1	-

- Represents or rounds to zero. [1] Includes Russia. [2] Persons professing no religion, nonbelievers, agnostics, freethinkers, and dereligionized secularists indifferent to all religion. [3] Followers of traditional Chinese religion. [4] Followers of Asiatic 20th-century New Religions, New Religious movements, radical new crisis religions, and non-Christian syncretistic mass religions.

Source: Encyclopaedia Britannica, Inc., Chicago, IL, *Britannica Book of the Year.* Reprinted with permission from *Britannica Book of the Year,* 1999 © 1999 Encyclopaedia Britannica, Inc.

Comparative International Statistics 831

No. 1349. Population, by Country: 1980 to 2000

[**4,453,778 represents 4,453,778,000.** Population data generally are de facto figures for the present territory. Population estimates were derived from information available as of early 1999. See text of this section for general comments concerning the data. For details of methodology, coverage, and reliability, see source. Minus sign (-) indicates decrease]

Country or area	Map refer-ence	Midyear population (1,000)				Popu-lation rank, 1999	Annual rate of growth,[1] 1990-2000 (percent)	Popula-tion per sq. mile, 1999	Area (sq. mile)
		1980	1990	1999	2000, proj.				
World	S0	4,453,778	5,276,992	5,996,215	6,073,099	(X)	1.4	118	50,627,993
Afghanistan	S5	14,985	14,767	25,825	26,668	39	5.9	103	250,000
Albania	S3	2,699	3,273	3,365	3,401	129	0.4	318	10,579
Algeria	S4	18,862	25,352	31,133	31,788	34	2.3	34	919,591
Andorra	S3	34	53	66	68	202	2.5	379	174
Angola	S4	6,794	8,430	11,178	11,487	66	3.1	23	481,351
Antigua and Barbuda	S1	69	63	64	64	206	0.3	378	170
Argentina	S2	28,237	32,634	36,738	37,215	31	1.3	35	1,056,637
Armenia	S5	3,115	3,366	3,409	3,396	128	0.1	296	11,506
Australia	S6	14,616	17,033	18,784	18,950	53	1.1	6	2,941,285
Austria	S3	7,549	7,718	8,139	8,148	85	0.5	255	31,942
Azerbaijan	S5	6,173	7,200	7,908	7,956	88	1.0	237	33,436
Bahamas, The	S1	210	251	284	288	176	1.3	73	3,888
Bahrain	S4	348	502	629	642	162	2.5	2,632	239
Bangladesh	S5	88,077	109,897	127,118	129,147	8	1.6	2,459	51,703
Barbados	S1	252	255	259	259	178	0.2	1,561	166
Belarus	S3	9,644	10,215	10,402	10,391	72	0.2	130	80,154
Belgium	S3	9,847	9,962	10,182	10,186	75	0.2	872	11,672
Belize	S1	144	190	236	242	181	2.4	27	8,803
Benin	S4	3,444	4,676	6,306	6,517	95	3.3	148	42,710
Bhutan	S5	1,281	1,585	1,952	1,996	144	2.3	108	18,147
Bolivia	S2	5,439	6,620	7,983	8,139	87	2.1	19	418,683
Bosnia and Herzegovina	S3	4,092	4,360	3,482	3,592	126	-1.9	176	19,741
Botswana	S4	903	1,304	1,464	1,479	147	1.3	6	226,012
Brazil	S2	122,936	151,040	171,853	173,791	5	1.4	53	3,265,061
Brunei	S6	185	254	323	331	174	2.6	159	2,035
Bulgaria	S3	8,844	8,966	8,195	8,156	83	-0.9	192	42,683
Burkina Faso	S4	6,939	9,024	11,576	11,892	65	2.8	110	105,714
Burma	S5	33,766	41,068	48,081	48,852	25	1.7	189	253,954
Burundi	S4	4,138	5,285	5,736	5,931	100	1.2	579	9,903
Cambodia	S5	6,499	8,717	11,627	11,919	64	3.1	171	68,154
Cameroon	S4	8,761	11,894	15,456	15,892	59	2.9	85	181,251
Canada	S1	24,593	27,791	31,006	31,330	35	1.2	9	3,560,219
Cape Verde	S1	296	349	406	411	172	1.6	261	1,556
Central African Republic	S4	2,244	2,798	3,445	3,516	127	2.3	14	240,533
Chad	S4	4,507	5,889	7,557	7,760	89	2.8	16	486,178
Chile	S2	11,094	13,128	14,974	15,155	60	1.4	52	289,112
China [2]	S5	984,736	1,138,895	1,246,872	1,256,168	1	1.0	346	3,600,930
Colombia	S2	26,583	32,985	39,309	40,037	28	1.9	98	401,042
Comoros	S4	334	429	563	581	163	3.0	672	838
Congo (Brazzaville) [3]	S4	1,620	2,206	2,717	2,776	133	2.3	21	131,853
Congo (Kinshasa) [3]	S4	28,129	37,978	50,481	51,988	23	3.1	58	875,521
Costa Rica	S2	2,307	3,022	3,674	3,744	120	2.1	188	19,560
Cote d'Ivoire	S4	8,261	11,904	15,818	16,190	57	3.1	129	122,780
Croatia	S3	4,593	4,754	4,677	4,681	112	-0.2	214	21,829
Cuba	S1	9,653	10,545	11,096	11,139	68	0.5	259	42,803
Cyprus	S5	611	681	754	759	157	1.1	211	3,568
Czech Republic	S3	10,289	10,310	10,281	10,284	73	-	212	48,440
Denmark	S3	5,123	5,141	5,357	5,375	104	0.4	327	16,359
Djibouti	S4	279	370	447	454	166	2.0	53	8,486
Dominica	S1	75	72	65	64	205	-1.2	224	290
Dominican Republic	S1	5,697	6,997	8,130	8,262	86	1.7	435	18,680
Ecuador	S2	8,123	10,308	12,562	12,782	62	2.2	118	106,888
Egypt	S4	42,441	56,106	67,274	68,495	15	2.0	175	384,344
El Salvador	S1	4,527	5,041	5,839	5,925	98	1.6	730	8,000
Equatorial Guinea	S4	256	369	466	478	164	2.6	43	10,830
Eritrea	S4	2,555	2,945	3,985	4,142	118	3.4	85	46,842
Estonia	S3	1,482	1,573	1,409	1,398	148	-1.2	81	17,413
Ethiopia	S4	36,413	48,015	59,680	60,967	19	2.4	138	432,310
Fiji	S6	635	738	813	823	156	1.1	115	7,054
Finland	S3	4,780	4,986	5,158	5,165	106	0.4	44	117,942
France	S3	53,870	56,735	58,978	59,128	21	0.4	280	210,668
Gabon	S4	808	1,078	1,226	1,244	151	1.4	12	99,486
Gambia, The	S4	676	964	1,336	1,381	149	3.6	346	3,861
Georgia	S5	5,048	5,457	5,066	5,034	108	-0.8	188	26,911
Germany	S3	78,298	79,357	82,087	82,081	12	0.3	607	135,236
Ghana	S4	10,880	15,190	18,888	19,272	52	2.4	213	88,811
Greece	S3	9,643	10,123	10,707	10,751	69	0.6	212	50,502
Grenada	S2	90	94	97	98	195	0.4	741	131
Guatemala	S1	7,232	9,631	12,336	12,670	63	2.7	295	41,865
Guinea	S4	4,320	5,936	7,539	7,611	90	2.5	79	94,927
Guinea-Bissau	S4	789	998	1,235	1,263	150	2.4	114	10,811
Guyana	S2	759	748	705	703	160	-0.6	9	76,004
Haiti	S1	5,056	6,048	6,884	6,992	93	1.4	647	10,641
Honduras	S1	3,625	4,740	5,997	6,130	97	2.6	139	43,201
Hungary	S3	10,711	10,352	10,186	10,167	74	-0.2	286	35,653
Iceland	S1	228	255	273	274	177	0.7	7	38,707
India	S5	690,462	850,558	1,000,849	1,017,645	2	1.8	872	1,147,950
Indonesia	S6	154,936	187,728	216,108	219,267	4	1.6	306	705,189
Iran	S5	39,274	55,717	65,180	65,865	17	1.7	103	631,660

See footnotes at end of table.

832 Comparative International Statistics

No. 1349. Population, by Country: 1980 to 2000—Continued

[See headnote, page 832]

Country or area	Map refer- ence	Midyear population (1,000) 1980	1990	1999	2000, proj.	Popu- lation rank, 1999	Annual rate of growth, 1990- 2000 (percent)	Popula- tion per sq. mile, 1999	Area (sq. mile)
Iraq	S5	13,233	18,135	22,427	23,151	44	2.4	134	167,556
Ireland	S3	3,401	3,508	3,633	3,647	122	0.4	137	26,598
Israel	S4	3,737	4,512	5,750	5,852	99	2.6	733	7,849
Italy	S3	56,451	56,761	56,735	56,687	22	-	500	113,521
Jamaica	S1	2,229	2,466	2,652	2,669	134	0.8	634	4,181
Japan	S5	116,807	123,537	126,182	126,434	9	0.2	828	152,411
Jordan	S4	2,168	3,277	4,561	4,701	113	3.6	129	35,344
Kazakhstan	S5	14,994	16,708	16,825	16,816	56	0.1	16	1,049,150
Kenya	S4	16,685	23,674	28,809	29,251	37	2.1	131	219,788
Kiribati	S6	58	72	86	87	197	1.9	309	277
Korea, North	S5	17,114	20,019	21,386	21,688	48	0.8	460	46,490
Korea, South	S5	38,124	42,869	46,885	47,351	26	1.0	1,237	37,911
Kuwait	S5	1,370	2,131	1,991	2,068	142	-0.3	289	6,880
Kyrgyzstan	S5	3,623	4,390	4,546	4,584	114	0.4	59	76,641
Laos	S5	3,293	4,191	5,407	5,557	102	2.8	61	89,112
Latvia	S3	2,525	2,672	2,354	2,327	138	-1.4	95	24,903
Lebanon	S4	3,075	3,130	3,563	3,620	124	1.5	902	3,950
Lesotho	S4	1,346	1,744	2,129	2,167	140	2.2	182	11,718
Liberia	S4	1,900	2,265	2,924	3,090	131	3.1	79	37,189
Libya	S4	3,065	4,140	4,993	5,114	109	2.1	7	679,359
Liechtenstein	S3	25	29	32	32	214	1.2	516	62
Lithuania	S5	3,436	3,702	3,585	3,572	123	-0.4	142	25,174
Luxembourg	S3	364	382	429	433	169	1.2	430	998
Macedonia, The Former Yugoslav Republic of	S3	1,893	2,031	2,023	2,035	141	-	204	9,928
Madagascar	S4	8,678	11,525	14,873	15,295	61	2.8	66	224,533
Malawi	S4	6,129	9,139	10,000	10,154	77	1.1	275	36,324
Malaysia	S6	13,764	17,507	21,376	21,820	49	2.2	169	126,853
Maldives	S5	154	218	300	310	175	3.5	2,592	116
Mali	S4	6,731	8,231	10,429	10,751	71	2.7	22	471,042
Malta	S4	364	354	382	383	173	0.8	3,079	124
Marshall Islands	S6	31	46	66	68	203	3.9	937	70
Mauritania	S4	1,550	1,979	2,582	2,660	136	3.0	6	397,838
Mauritius	S4	964	1,074	1,182	1,196	152	1.1	1,656	714
Mexico	S1	68,686	84,748	100,294	102,027	11	1.9	135	742,486
Micronesia, Federated States of.	S6	77	109	132	133	191	2.0	485	271
Moldova	S5	3,996	4,398	4,461	4,467	115	0.2	343	13,012
Monaco	S3	27	30	32	32	213	0.7	41,633	1
Mongolia	S5	1,662	2,216	2,617	2,655	135	1.8	4	604,247
Montenegro [4]	S3	579	616	680	681	161	1.0	128	5,333
Morocco	S4	19,487	24,685	29,662	30,205	36	2.0	172	172,317
Mozambique	S4	12,103	14,056	19,124	19,614	51	3.3	63	302,737
Namibia	S4	975	1,409	1,648	1,674	145	1.7	5	317,873
Nauru	S6	8	9	11	11	224	1.3	1,308	8
Nepal	S5	15,016	19,333	24,303	24,920	40	2.5	460	52,819
Netherlands	S3	14,144	14,952	15,808	15,878	58	0.6	1,206	13,104
New Zealand	S6	3,113	3,299	3,662	3,698	121	1.1	35	103,734
Nicaragua	S2	2,776	3,591	4,717	4,851	110	3.0	102	46,430
Niger	S4	5,629	7,644	9,962	10,260	78	2.9	20	489,073
Nigeria	S4	65,699	86,530	113,829	117,171	10	3.0	324	351,649
Norway	S3	4,086	4,242	4,439	4,456	116	0.5	37	118,865
Oman	S5	1,175	1,773	2,447	2,533	137	3.6	30	82,031
Pakistan	S5	85,219	113,914	138,123	141,145	7	2.1	459	300,664
Palau	S6	13	15	18	19	219	2.1	104	177
Panama	S2	1,956	2,388	2,779	2,821	132	1.7	95	29,340
Papua New Guinea	S6	2,991	3,823	4,705	4,812	111	2.3	27	174,405
Paraguay	S2	3,193	4,236	5,434	5,580	101	2.8	35	153,398
Peru	S2	17,295	21,989	26,625	27,136	38	2.1	54	494,208
Philippines	S6	51,092	65,037	79,346	80,961	13	2.2	689	115,124
Poland	S3	35,578	38,109	38,609	38,644	30	0.1	328	117,571
Portugal	S3	9,778	9,871	9,918	9,902	79	-	280	35,382
Qatar	S5	231	482	724	750	158	4.4	170	4,247
Romania	S5	22,109	22,775	22,334	22,291	45	-0.2	251	88,934
Russia	S5	139,045	148,088	146,394	145,905	6	-0.1	22	6,592,817
Rwanda	S4	5,170	7,161	8,155	8,337	84	1.5	847	9,633
Saint Kitts and Nevis	S1	44	40	43	43	210	0.8	308	139
Saint Lucia	S1	122	140	154	156	188	1.1	653	236
Saint Vincent and the Grenadines	S1	98	113	121	121	192	0.7	921	131
Samoa	S0	155	186	230	235	182	2.3	209	1,100
San Marino	S3	21	23	25	25	216	0.9	1,082	23
Sao Tome and Principe	S4	94	119	155	160	187	2.9	418	371
Saudi Arabia	S4	9,949	15,871	21,505	22,246	47	3.4	26	829,996
Senegal	S4	5,640	7,408	10,052	10,390	76	3.4	136	74,131
Serbia [4]	S3	9,262	9,705	10,526	10,530	70	0.8	309	34,116
Seychelles	S4	66	73	79	80	198	0.8	450	176
Sierra Leone	S4	3,333	4,283	5,297	5,509	105	2.5	192	27,653
Singapore	S6	2,414	3,039	3,532	3,572	125	1.6	14,658	241
Slovakia	S3	4,966	5,263	5,396	5,401	103	0.3	111	48,440
Slovenia	S3	1,885	1,969	1,971	1,970	143	-	252	7,819
Solomon Islands	S6	233	336	455	470	165	3.4	43	10,633

See footnotes at end of table.

Comparative International Statistics 833

U.S. Census Bureau, Statistical Abstract of the United States: 1999

Country or area	Map refer- ence	Midyear population (1,000) 1980	1990	1999	2000, proj.	Popu- lation rank, 1999	Annual rate of growth,[1] 1990- 2000 (percent)	Popula- tion per sq. mile, 1999	Area (sq. mile)
Somalia	S4	5,791	6,675	7,141	7,434	92	1.1	29	242,216
South Africa	S4	29,252	37,191	43,426	43,982	27	1.7	92	471,444
Spain	S3	37,488	38,793	39,168	39,208	29	0.1	203	192,819
Sri Lanka	S5	14,900	17,193	19,145	19,355	50	1.2	766	24,996
Sudan	S4	19,064	26,628	34,476	35,530	32	2.9	38	917,375
Suriname	S2	355	396	431	434	168	0.9	7	62,344
Swaziland	S4	607	840	985	1,004	155	1.8	148	6,641
Sweden	S3	8,310	8,559	8,911	8,939	82	0.4	56	158,927
Switzerland	S3	6,385	6,844	7,275	7,289	91	0.6	474	15,355
Syria	S4	8,774	12,620	17,214	17,759	54	3.4	242	71,062
Taiwan [2]	S5	17,848	20,279	22,113	22,319	46	1.0	1,775	12,456
Tajikistan	S5	3,969	5,332	6,103	6,194	96	1.5	110	55,251
Tanzania	S4	18,690	24,886	31,271	31,963	33	2.5	91	342,100
Thailand	S5	47,026	55,052	60,609	61,164	18	1.1	307	197,595
Togo	S4	2,596	3,680	5,081	5,263	107	3.6	242	21,000
Tonga	S0	93	101	109	110	194	0.8	394	277
Trinidad and Tobago	S2	1,091	1,198	1,102	1,087	154	-1.0	556	1,981
Tunisia	S4	6,443	8,207	9,514	9,645	81	1.6	159	59,985
Turkey	S5	45,121	56,125	65,599	66,620	16	1.7	220	297,591
Turkmenistan	S5	2,875	3,668	4,366	4,436	117	1.9	23	188,456
Tuvalu	S6	7	9	11	11	225	1.6	1,055	10
Uganda	S4	12,298	17,227	22,805	23,452	43	3.1	296	77,108
Ukraine	S5	50,047	51,600	49,811	49,507	24	-0.4	214	233,089
United Arab Emirates	S5	1,000	1,952	2,344	2,386	139	2.0	73	32,278
United Kingdom	S3	56,314	57,507	59,113	59,247	20	0.3	634	93,278
United States	S1	227,726	249,949	272,640	274,943	3	1.0	77	3,539,227
Uruguay	S2	2,920	3,106	3,309	3,333	130	0.7	49	67,035
Uzbekistan	S5	16,000	20,624	24,102	24,423	41	1.7	140	172,741
Vanuatu	S6	117	154	189	193	185	2.2	33	5,699
Venezuela	S2	14,768	19,325	23,203	23,596	42	2.0	68	340,560
Vietnam	S5	53,661	66,314	77,311	78,350	14	1.7	615	125,622
Yemen	S5	8,527	12,023	16,942	17,521	55	3.8	83	203,849
Zambia	S4	5,638	7,957	9,664	9,872	80	2.2	34	285,992
Zimbabwe	S4	7,298	9,958	11,163	11,272	67	1.2	75	149,293
AREAS OF SPECIAL SOVER- EIGNTY AND DEPENDENCIES									
American Samoa	S0	32	47	64	65	207	3.3	830	77
Anguilla	S1	7	8	12	12	223	3.5	328	35
Aruba	S1	60	67	69	69	201	0.4	922	75
Bermuda	S1	55	58	62	63	208	0.9	3,302	19
Cayman Islands	S1	17	27	39	41	212	4.3	392	100
Cook Islands	S0	18	18	20	20	217	1.1	217	93
Faroe Islands	S3	43	47	41	40	211	-1.7	76	541
French Guiana	S2	68	116	168	173	186	4.0	5	34,421
French Polynesia	S0	151	201	242	246	179	2.0	171	1,413
Gaza Strip [5]	S4	453	635	1,113	1,163	153	6.0	7,564	147
Gibraltar	S3	29	31	29	29	215	-0.6	12,590	2
Greenland	S1	50	56	60	60	209	0.8	(Z)	131,931
Guadeloupe	S1	337	378	421	425	170	1.2	619	680
Guam	S6	107	134	152	154	189	1.4	726	209
Guernsey	S3	53	61	65	66	204	0.8	873	75
Hong Kong	S5	5,063	5,688	6,847	6,967	94	2.0	17,931	382
Jersey	S3	76	84	90	90	196	0.8	1,986	45
Macau	S6	256	352	437	445	167	2.4	70,790	6
Man, Isle of	S3	64	69	76	76	199	1.0	333	227
Martinique	S1	339	374	412	416	171	1.1	1,007	409
Mayotte	S4	52	90	149	157	190	5.6	1,029	145
Montserrat	S1	12	13	13	13	222	0.3	333	39
Netherlands Antilles	S2	173	189	208	210	183	1.1	560	371
New Caledonia	S6	139	168	197	200	184	1.7	27	7,243
Northern Mariana Islands	S6	17	44	69	72	200	4.9	377	184
Puerto Rico	S1	3,210	3,537	3,888	3,910	119	1.0	1,124	3,459
Reunion	S4	507	600	718	730	159	2.0	744	965
Saint Helena	S4	6	7	7	7	226	0.8	45	158
Saint Pierre and Miquelon	S1	6	6	7	7	227	0.8	75	93
Turks and Caicos Islands	S1	7	12	17	17	220	4.2	102	166
Virgin Islands	S1	100	104	120	121	193	1.5	887	135
Virgin Islands, British	S1	11	16	19	20	218	2.2	331	58
Wallis and Futuna	S6	11	14	15	15	221	1.1	143	106
West Bank [5]	S4	833	1,080	1,611	1,662	146	4.3	740	2,178
Western Sahara	S4	126	191	239	245	180	2.5	2	102,703

- Represents or rounds to zero. X Not applicable. Z Less than one person per square mile. [1] Computed by the exponential method. For explanation of average annual percent change, see Guide to Tabular Presentation. [2] With the establishment of diplomatic relations with China on January 1, 1979, the U.S. Government recognized the People's Republic of China as the sole legal government of China and acknowledged the Chinese position that there is only one China and that Taiwan is part of China. [3] "Congo" is the official short-form name for both the Republic of Congo and the Democratic Republic of the Congo. To distinguish one from the other the U.S. Dept. of State adds the capital in parentheses. This practice is unofficial and provisional. [4] The U.S. view is that the Socialist Federal Republic of Yugoslavia has dissolved and no successor state represents its continuation. Serbia and Montenegro have asserted the formation of a joint independent state, but this entity has not been recognized by the United States. [5] The Gaza Strip and West Bank are Israeli occupied with interim status subject to Israeli/Palestinian negotiations. The final status is to be determined.

Source: U.S. Census Bureau, "International Data Base" (as of 28 December 1998); <http://www.census.gov/ipc/www/idbnew.html>.

No. 1350. Age Distribution, by Country: 1999 and 2000

[**In percent.** Covers countries with 10 million or more population in 1999]

Country or area	1999 Under 15 years old	1999 65 years old and over	2000, proj. Under 15 years old	2000, proj. 65 years old and over	Country or area	1999 Under 15 years old	1999 65 years old and over	2000, proj. Under 15 years old	2000, proj. 65 years old and over
World, total. . . .	30.3	6.8	30.0	6.9	Korea, North	25.6	6.2	25.6	6.5
Afghanistan	42.8	2.8	42.7	2.8	Korea, South	22.1	6.7	21.9	6.9
Algeria.	37.3	3.9	36.4	3.9	Madagascar	44.6	3.3	44.5	3.3
Angola.	44.9	2.8	44.9	2.8	Malawi.	45.1	2.7	44.7	2.7
Argentina	27.4	10.2	27.3	10.3	Malaysia	35.4	4.0	35.0	4.1
Australia.	21.0	12.5	20.8	12.6	Mali.	47.4	3.2	47.4	3.1
Bangladesh	37.7	3.3	36.3	3.3	Mexico.	35.2	4.2	34.8	4.3
Belarus	19.4	13.5	18.8	13.6	Morocco.	35.8	4.5	35.2	4.6
Belgium	17.2	16.9	17.0	17.1	Mozambique	44.8	2.3	44.7	2.3
Brazil.	29.8	5.2	29.4	5.3	Nepal	41.4	3.4	41.1	3.4
Burkina Faso	48.0	3.0	47.9	2.9	Netherlands	18.3	13.6	18.2	13.7
Burma	36.2	4.2	36.0	4.2	Nigeria.	44.8	2.9	44.8	3.0
Cambodia.	45.2	3.0	45.0	3.0	Pakistan.	41.4	4.1	40.9	4.1
Cameroon	45.9	3.3	45.8	3.3	Peru	35.4	4.6	35.1	4.7
Canada	19.6	12.5	19.3	12.6	Philippines	37.3	3.6	37.0	3.6
Chile	27.9	7.1	27.6	7.2	Poland.	19.8	12.0	19.2	12.2
China [1]	25.5	6.8	25.1	7.0	Romania	18.6	13.3	18.1	13.5
Colombia	33.0	4.6	32.7	4.6	Russia.	19.1	12.5	18.4	12.6
Congo (Kinshasa) [2] . .	48.2	2.6	48.2	2.6	Saudi Arabia.	43.0	2.5	42.9	2.6
Cote d'Ivoire	46.6	2.2	46.4	2.2	Senegal	48.0	2.8	47.8	2.7
Cuba	21.7	9.6	21.4	9.7	Serbia [3]	20.2	13.1	19.9	13.5
Czech Republic	16.9	13.8	16.6	13.8	South Africa	34.4	4.6	34.1	4.6
Ecuador.	35.2	4.5	34.5	4.5	Spain	14.9	16.6	14.8	16.8
Egypt	35.6	3.7	35.2	3.7	Sri Lanka	27.1	6.4	26.6	6.5
Ethiopia	46.1	2.8	46.3	2.8	Sudan	45.1	2.2	44.8	2.3
France.	18.7	16.0	18.5	16.1	Syria	45.7	2.9	45.3	2.9
Germany	15.4	16.1	15.2	16.5	Taiwan [1].	22.0	8.4	21.6	8.6
Ghana	42.4	3.2	41.7	3.2	Tanzania	44.4	2.9	44.3	2.9
Greece	15.8	16.8	15.6	17.2	Thailand.	23.9	6.2	23.5	6.5
Guatemala	42.7	3.6	42.5	3.6	Turkey	30.4	5.9	29.8	6.0
Hungary	17.4	14.5	17.3	14.6	Uganda	51.2	2.2	51.2	2.2
India	34.1	4.6	33.7	4.7	Ukraine	18.4	13.9	17.9	13.9
Indonesia	30.4	4.1	30.1	4.3	United Kingdom.	19.2	15.7	19.1	15.7
Iran	35.9	4.5	34.6	4.6	United States	21.6	12.6	21.4	12.6
Iraq.	43.7	3.1	43.4	3.1	Uzbekistan	37.2	4.7	36.3	4.7
Italy.	14.3	17.9	14.2	18.2	Venezuela	33.3	4.6	32.8	4.6
Japan	15.0	16.5	14.9	17.0	Vietnam	33.6	5.3	32.7	5.4
Kazakhstan	28.5	7.0	27.8	7.0	Yemen.	47.8	3.2	47.5	3.1
Kenya	42.9	2.7	42.1	2.8	Zimbabwe	43.2	2.6	42.6	2.7

[1] See footnote 2, Table 1349. [2] See footnote 3, Table 1349. [3] See footnote 4, Table 1349.

Source: U.S. Census Bureau, "International Data Base" (as of 28 December 1998); <http://www.census.gov/ipc/www/idbnew.html>.

No. 1351. Foreign Population in Selected OECD Countries: 1985 to 1995

[In Australia, Canada, and the United States, the data refer to people present in the country who are foreign born. In the European countries and Japan, they generally refer to foreigners and represent the nationalities of residents; as a result, persons born in these countries may be counted among the foreign population, whereas others, who are foreign born, may have acquired the host-country nationality. Except as noted, data are from population registers]

Country	Number (1,000) 1985	Number (1,000) 1990	Number (1,000) 1995	Percent of total population 1985	Percent of total population 1990	Percent of total population 1995
United States [1].	(NA)	19,767	(NA)	(NA)	7.9	(NA)
Australia [2].	(NA)	(NA)	[3]4,125	(NA)	(NA)	[3]22.7
Austria	304	456	724	4.0	5.9	9.0
Belgium	847	905	910	8.6	9.1	9.0
Canada [1]	(NA)	[4]4,343	(NA)	(NA)	[4]15.6	(NA)
Denmark.	117	161	223	2.3	3.1	4.2
Finland	17	26	69	0.3	0.5	1.3
France [1]	(NA)	3,597	(NA)	(NA)	6.3	(NA)
Germany [5]	4,379	5,343	7,174	7.2	8.4	8.8
Italy	423	781	991	0.7	1.4	1.7
Japan [6]	851	1,075	1,362	0.7	0.9	1.1
Luxembourg	98	113	138	26.7	29.4	33.4
Netherlands	553	692	728	3.8	4.6	5.0
Norway.	102	143	161	2.4	3.4	3.7
Spain	242	279	500	0.6	0.7	1.2
Sweden	389	484	532	4.6	5.6	5.2
Switzerland	940	1,100	1,331	14.5	16.3	18.9
United Kingdom [2].	1,731	1,723	2,060	3.1	3.2	3.4

NA Not available. [1] Census data. [2] Labor force survey. [3] 1994 data. [4] 1991 data. [5] Western Germany only for 1985 and 1990. [6] Includes foreigners staying for more than 90 days.

Source: Organization for Economic Cooperation and Development, Paris, France, The OECD Observer, No. 192, February/March 1995, (copyright) and Trends in International Migration, Annual Report 1996 (copyright).

Comparative International Statistics 835

No. 1352. Vital Statistics, by Country: 1999 and 2000

[Covers countries with 10 million or more population in 1999]

Country or area	Crude birth rate [1] 1999	Crude birth rate [1] 2000, proj.	Crude death rate [2] 1999	Crude death rate [2] 2000, proj.	Expectation of life at birth (years) 1999	Expectation of life at birth (years) 2000, proj.	Infant mortality rate [3] 1999	Infant mortality rate [3] 2000, proj.	Total fertility rate [4] 1999	Total fertility rate [4] 2000, proj.
United States	14.3	14.2	8.8	8.8	76.2	76.3	6.3	6.7	2.07	2.07
Afghanistan	41.9	41.6	17.0	16.6	47.3	47.8	140.6	137.5	5.94	5.87
Algeria	27.0	26.5	5.5	5.4	69.2	69.6	43.8	42.2	3.27	3.16
Angola	43.1	42.6	16.4	15.9	48.4	48.9	129.2	125.9	6.12	6.05
Argentina	19.9	19.9	7.6	7.6	74.8	75.0	18.4	17.8	2.66	2.64
Australia	13.2	13.0	6.9	6.9	80.1	80.4	5.1	5.0	1.81	1.80
Bangladesh	25.2	24.8	8.5	8.3	60.6	61.1	69.7	67.1	2.86	2.77
Belarus	9.7	9.7	13.7	13.9	68.1	68.0	14.4	14.6	1.32	1.31
Belgium	10.0	9.7	10.4	10.5	77.5	77.7	6.2	6.1	1.49	1.48
Brazil	20.4	19.9	8.8	9.1	64.1	63.8	35.4	33.8	2.28	2.23
Burkina Faso	45.8	45.5	17.6	17.5	45.9	45.7	107.2	105.2	6.56	6.48
Burma	28.5	28.0	12.4	12.3	54.7	55.0	76.3	74.2	3.63	3.57
Cambodia	41.1	40.8	16.2	15.9	48.2	48.5	105.1	103.4	5.81	5.81
Cameroon	41.8	41.6	14.0	13.9	51.3	51.2	75.7	74.5	5.80	5.73
Canada	11.9	11.6	7.3	7.3	79.4	79.6	5.5	5.4	1.65	1.64
Chile	17.8	17.4	5.5	5.5	75.5	75.8	10.0	9.6	2.25	2.21
China [5]	15.1	14.6	7.0	7.0	69.9	70.3	43.3	41.1	1.80	1.79
Colombia . . . . . . [6]	24.5	24.0	5.6	5.5	70.5	70.9	24.3	23.2	2.87	2.85
Congo (Kinshasa) [6] .	46.4	46.0	15.0	14.8	49.4	49.6	99.5	97.3	6.45	6.39
Cote d'Ivoire	41.8	41.4	16.2	16.2	46.1	45.9	94.2	92.4	5.89	5.80
Cuba	12.9	12.7	7.4	7.4	75.8	75.9	7.8	7.7	1.58	1.60
Czech Republic	9.8	10.7	10.9	10.8	74.4	74.6	6.7	6.6	1.28	1.39
Ecuador	22.3	21.4	5.1	5.0	72.2	72.5	30.7	29.3	2.63	2.51
Egypt	26.8	26.3	8.3	8.1	62.4	62.7	67.5	65.7	3.33	3.24
Ethiopia	44.3	44.0	21.4	21.6	40.5	40.1	124.6	123.5	6.81	6.75
France	11.4	11.1	9.2	9.2	78.6	78.8	5.6	5.6	1.61	1.58
Germany	8.7	8.5	10.8	10.8	77.2	77.3	5.1	5.1	1.26	1.27
Ghana	31.8	30.8	10.4	10.2	57.1	57.5	76.2	74.8	4.11	3.95
Greece	9.5	9.4	9.4	9.5	78.4	78.6	7.1	7.0	1.30	1.29
Guatemala	35.6	35.1	6.8	6.6	66.5	66.9	46.2	44.6	4.74	4.66
Hungary	10.8	10.9	13.3	13.1	71.2	71.5	9.5	9.2	1.45	1.45
India	25.4	24.9	8.5	8.3	63.4	63.9	60.8	58.5	3.18	3.11
Indonesia	22.8	22.4	8.1	8.1	62.9	63.4	57.3	55.4	2.57	2.53
Iran	20.7	20.1	5.4	5.3	69.8	70.2	29.7	28.1	2.45	2.30
Iraq	38.4	38.2	6.6	6.6	66.5	66.5	62.4	62.4	5.12	5.01
Italy	9.3	9.4	10.3	10.4	78.5	78.6	6.3	6.2	1.22	1.25
Japan	10.5	10.6	8.1	8.3	80.1	80.2	4.1	4.1	1.48	1.50
Kazakhstan	17.2	17.1	10.3	10.5	63.4	63.2	58.8	59.4	2.09	2.07
Kenya	30.8	29.9	14.6	15.0	47.0	46.5	59.1	58.8	3.88	3.69
Korea, North	21.4	20.4	6.9	6.9	70.1	70.7	25.5	24.3	2.30	2.30
Korea, South	16.0	15.8	5.7	5.7	74.3	74.7	7.6	7.4	1.79	1.80
Madagascar	41.5	41.2	13.6	13.3	53.2	53.6	89.1	87.6	5.70	5.64
Malawi	39.5	38.9	23.8	24.0	36.3	36.0	132.1	130.5	5.48	5.33
Malaysia	26.1	25.6	5.3	5.2	70.7	71.0	21.7	20.9	3.35	3.32
Mali	49.5	49.1	18.6	18.1	47.5	48.0	119.4	117.2	6.96	6.89
Mexico	25.0	24.5	4.8	4.8	72.0	72.4	24.6	23.4	2.85	2.79
Morocco	25.8	25.2	6.1	6.0	68.9	69.2	51.0	48.9	3.24	3.13
Mozambique	42.8	42.0	17.3	16.8	45.9	46.4	117.6	114.9	5.88	5.76
Nepal	35.3	35.0	10.2	9.9	58.4	59.0	73.6	71.2	4.78	4.68
Netherlands	11.4	11.1	8.7	8.7	78.2	78.3	5.1	5.1	1.49	1.48
Nigeria	41.8	41.4	13.0	13.0	53.3	53.1	69.5	68.2	6.02	5.95
Pakistan	33.5	32.6	10.5	10.2	59.4	59.7	91.9	90.3	4.73	4.56
Peru	26.1	25.5	5.7	5.6	70.4	70.8	39.0	37.1	3.23	3.14
Philippines	27.9	27.3	6.5	6.4	66.6	66.8	33.9	33.2	3.46	3.38
Poland	10.6	11.5	9.7	9.7	73.1	73.3	12.8	12.4	1.45	1.54
Romania	10.1	10.9	11.6	11.5	70.8	71.2	18.1	17.5	1.27	1.36
Russia	9.6	9.7	15.0	15.0	65.1	65.3	23.0	22.7	1.34	1.33
Saudi Arabia	37.4	37.2	4.9	4.7	70.6	71.1	38.8	36.3	6.34	6.30
Senegal	43.9	43.4	10.7	10.4	57.8	58.3	59.8	58.4	6.11	6.04
Serbia [7]	12.5	12.5	9.7	9.7	73.5	73.7	16.5	15.9	1.74	1.73
South Africa	25.9	25.5	12.8	13.3	54.8	53.9	52.0	52.0	3.09	3.02
Spain	10.0	10.2	9.7	9.8	77.7	77.9	6.4	6.3	1.24	1.27
Sri Lanka	18.2	17.9	6.0	6.1	72.7	72.8	16.1	15.9	2.10	2.08
Sudan	39.3	38.8	10.6	10.3	56.4	56.8	70.9	69.2	5.58	5.47
Syria	37.0	36.1	5.4	5.3	68.1	68.4	36.4	35.2	5.37	5.19
Taiwan [5]	14.6	14.5	5.3	5.2	77.5	78.2	6.0	5.7	1.77	1.77
Tanzania	40.4	40.0	16.8	16.8	46.2	46.0	95.3	93.6	5.40	5.31
Thailand	16.5	16.2	7.2	7.2	69.2	69.4	29.5	28.3	1.82	1.80
Turkey	20.9	20.4	5.3	5.2	73.3	73.8	35.8	33.3	2.41	2.35
Uganda	48.5	48.0	18.4	17.9	43.1	43.5	90.7	88.5	7.03	6.96
Ukraine	9.5	9.6	16.4	16.4	65.9	66.0	21.7	21.7	1.34	1.32
United Kingdom	11.9	11.8	10.6	10.6	77.4	77.5	5.8	5.7	1.71	1.72
Uzbekistan	23.4	23.2	7.8	7.9	63.9	63.7	71.6	72.1	2.82	2.77
Venezuela	22.3	21.5	4.9	4.9	73.0	73.3	26.5	25.5	2.61	2.53
Vietnam	20.8	20.0	6.6	6.5	68.1	68.5	34.8	33.7	2.41	2.31
Yemen	43.3	43.3	9.9	9.5	60.0	60.5	69.8	67.4	7.06	6.99
Zimbabwe	30.6	30.0	20.4	20.8	38.9	38.6	61.2	60.7	3.71	3.56

[1] Number of births during 1 year per 1,000 persons (based on midyear population).   [2] Number of deaths during 1 year per 1,000 persons (based on midyear population).   [3] Number of deaths of children under 1 year of age per 1,000 live births in a calendar year.   [4] Average number of children that would be born if all women lived to the end of their childbearing years and, at each year of age, they experienced the birth rates occurring in the specified year.   [5] See footnote 2, Table 1349.   [6] See footnote 3, Table 1349.   [7] Serbia and Montenegro have asserted the formation of a joint independent state, but this entity has not been recognized by the United States. Data in this table are for Serbia alone.

Source: U.S. Census Bureau, "International Data Base" (as of 28 December 1998); <http://www.census.gov/ipc/www/idbnew.html>.

836   Comparative International Statistics

No. 1353. Death Rates, by Cause and Country

[Age-standardized death rate per 100,000 population. For explanation of age-adjustment, see text, Section 2, Vital Statistics. The standard population for this table is the old European standard; see source for details. Deaths classified to ninth revision of International Classification of Diseases; see text, Section 2, Vital Statistics]

Country	Year	Ischemic heart disease	Cerebro-vascular disease	Cancer of — Lung, trachea, bronchus	Stomach	Female breast	Bronchitis,[1] emphysema, asthma	Chronic liver disease and cirrhosis	Motor vehicle traffic accidents	Suicide and self-inflicted injury
United States	1994	157.6	48.0	56.7	4.8	29.7	9.1	10.2	15.6	11.8
Australia	1994	161.0	66.2	38.4	7.1	29.2	11.3	6.5	10.5	12.6
Austria	1995	150.3	81.4	33.2	14.9	31.4	11.7	24.3	13.0	20.2
Bulgaria	1994	231.4	230.3	33.5	19.6	22.0	9.9	20.1	13.3	15.9
Canada	1995	134.9	45.6	50.8	6.8	30.3	6.0	7.9	10.1	13.0
Czech Republic	1993	276.6	168.0	53.1	17.4	31.2	19.6	16.5	13.6	18.1
Denmark	1992	190.3	72.0	51.1	7.8	40.6	36.5	13.5	10.2	20.4
Finland	1995	207.4	90.9	31.3	10.6	25.1	15.6	10.0	7.5	26.1
France	1994	54.3	46.0	34.8	7.5	28.2	8.5	15.0	13.5	19.3
Germany	1995	151.2	78.3	36.2	13.6	31.7	16.6	20.7	10.7	13.9
Hungary	1995	253.5	161.7	66.1	21.5	33.2	37.9	80.2	16.3	30.9
Italy	1993	90.0	85.5	42.2	16.7	29.5	20.9	20.7	13.3	7.2
Japan	1994	36.4	75.8	28.0	31.2	9.6	10.1	11.2	9.9	15.1
Netherlands	1995	110.5	61.9	50.6	10.3	36.6	13.0	4.8	7.3	9.2
New Zealand	1993	195.1	76.1	40.7	8.2	34.0	11.3	4.1	16.6	12.6
Norway	1994	150.8	72.4	31.6	10.7	28.7	10.6	4.7	6.2	12.1
Poland	1995	107.1	78.8	53.1	17.9	22.9	17.5	13.6	18.5	14.6
Portugal	1995	74.5	187.4	22.3	23.7	24.9	8.9	21.1	23.2	7.5
Romania	1995	248.4	243.4	34.4	17.1	22.2	13.4	50.6	(NA)	12.6
Russia	1995	378.9	288.8	43.1	33.3	22.1	36.0	(NA)	21.8	41.2
Spain	1994	70.3	75.4	34.8	13.8	24.6	6.9	16.2	13.3	7.4
Sweden	1995	158.1	61.0	24.6	7.2	24.8	9.0	5.7	5.3	14.2
Switzerland	1994	100.4	48.8	33.7	8.6	33.1	17.7	8.4	8.4	19.6
United Kingdom:										
England and Wales	1995	176.5	71.5	47.0	9.8	35.9	8.8	6.5	5.6	6.6
Scotland	1995	217.6	103.9	66.0	11.4	36.4	7.4	11.5	7.6	11.9

NA Not available. [1] Chronic and unspecified.

Source: World Health Organization, Geneva, Switzerland, *World Health Statistics Annual*.

No. 1354. Death Rates From Injuries, by Mechanism and Country

[Average annual injury deaths per 100,000 population for time period indicated]

Country	Time period	Total	Motor vehicle traffic	Firearm	Poisoning	Fall	Suffocation	Drowning	Unspecified	All other injury
United States	1995	56.3	16.2	13.7	6.2	4.3	3.9	1.9	3.0	7.1
Australia	1993-95	39.7	11.0	2.9	6.8	2.9	4.4	2.2	3.5	6.0
Canada	1994-95	44.7	10.5	3.9	6.7	5.0	6.1	2.1	4.9	5.5
Denmark	1994-95	69.9	10.5	2.1	13.4	25.7	7.8	3.0	0.6	6.8
England and Wales	1993-95	30.5	6.2	0.4	6.4	4.4	3.8	1.1	4.9	3.3
France	1992-94	74.7	14.9	6.3	4.6	7.1	14.1	4.2	18.6	4.9
Israel	1993-95	32.9	10.3	2.8	0.7	2.6	3.1	1.2	8.7	3.5
Netherlands	1995	33.2	7.7	0.5	2.4	4.2	4.9	1.6	9.2	2.7
New Zealand	1984-93	55.8	21.3	3.1	5.9	7.0	5.6	3.7	1.4	7.8
Norway	1990-94	57.4	7.2	4.3	6.1	6.4	5.3	4.7	16.4	7.0
Scotland	1986-95	49.9	9.8	0.6	7.9	11.8	5.0	3.2	3.9	7.7

Source: U.S. National Center for Health Statistics, *Advance Data*, No. 303, October 7, 1998.

U.S. Census Bureau, Statistical Abstract of the United States: 1999

[In percent. G.D.P.=gross domestic product; for explanation, see text, Section 14, Income]

Country	Total health expenditures					Public health expenditures				
	1980	1990	1995	1997	1998	1980	1990	1995	1997	1998
United States	9.1	12.6	14.1	13.9	14.0	3.9	5.1	6.5	6.5	6.5
Australia	7.3	8.3	8.4	8.4	(NA)	4.6	5.6	5.6	5.6	(NA)
Austria	7.7	7.2	8.0	8.3	(NA)	5.3	5.3	5.8	6.0	(NA)
Belgium	6.5	7.5	7.9	7.6	(NA)	5.4	6.7	6.9	6.7	(NA)
Canada	7.3	9.2	9.7	9.2	9.3	5.5	6.9	6.9	6.4	6.5
Czech Republic	3.8	5.4	7.5	7.2	7.2	3.7	5.2	6.9	6.6	6.6
Denmark.	8.7	8.2	8.0	8.0	8.0	7.7	7.1	6.8	6.7	6.7
Finland.	6.5	8.0	7.6	7.4	(NA)	5.1	6.5	5.7	5.7	(NA)
France	7.6	8.9	9.9	9.6	9.6	6.0	6.6	8.0	7.1	7.1
Germany [1]	8.8	8.7	10.4	10.7	10.6	7.0	6.7	8.1	8.3	8.1
Greece	3.6	4.2	5.8	8.6	(NA)	2.9	3.5	4.4	5.0	(NA)
Hungary	(NA)	6.1	7.1	6.5	(NA)	(NA)	(NA)	4.9	4.5	(NA)
Iceland	6.2	7.9	8.2	7.9	8.3	5.5	6.9	6.9	6.7	7.0
Ireland	8.7	6.7	7.0	6.3	6.1	7.1	4.9	5.2	4.9	4.8
Italy	7.0	8.1	7.7	7.6	(NA)	5.6	6.3	5.4	5.3	(NA)
Japan	6.4	6.0	7.2	7.2	7.4	4.5	4.6	5.6	5.7	5.8
Korea, South	2.9	3.9	3.9	6.0	(NA)	0.8	1.7	1.9	2.7	(NA)
Luxembourg	6.2	6.6	6.7	7.0	(NA)	5.7	6.1	6.2	6.4	(NA)
Mexico	(NA)	3.6	4.9	4.7	(NA)	(NA)	2.1	2.8	2.8	(NA)
Netherlands	7.9	8.3	8.8	8.5	(NA)	5.9	6.1	6.7	6.2	(NA)
New Zealand.	6.0	7.0	7.3	7.6	8.0	5.3	5.8	5.6	5.9	6.2
Norway.	7.0	7.8	8.0	7.5	(NA)	5.9	6.5	6.6	6.2	(NA)
Poland	(NA)	4.4	4.5	5.2	(NA)	(NA)	(NA)	4.2	4.7	(NA)
Portugal	5.8	6.5	8.2	7.9	(NA)	3.7	4.3	5.0	4.7	(NA)
Spain.	5.6	6.9	7.3	7.4	(NA)	4.5	5.4	5.7	5.6	(NA)
Sweden	9.4	8.8	8.5	8.6	(NA)	8.7	7.9	7.1	7.2	(NA)
Switzerland	6.9	8.3	9.6	10.0	(NA)	4.6	5.7	6.9	7.0	(NA)
Turkey	3.3	3.6	3.3	4.0	(NA)	0.9	2.2	2.4	2.9	(NA)
United Kingdom	5.6	6.0	6.9	6.8	6.9	5.0	5.1	5.8	5.8	5.8

NA Not available. [1] Data prior to 1991 are for former West Germany.

Source: Organization for Economic Cooperation and Development, Paris, France, OECD Health Data 98; and OECD in Figures, 1998 Edition (copyright).

No. 1356. Average Temperatures and Precipitation—Selected International Cities

[In degrees Fahrenheit, except as noted. Data are generally based on a standard 30-year period; for details, see source. For data on U.S. cities, see Tables 420-423]

City	January					July				
	Average high	Average low	Warmest	Coldest	Average precipitation (inches)	Average high	Average low	Warmest	Coldest	Average precipitation (inches)
Athens, Greece	55	44	70	28	1.9	89	73	108	61	0.2
Baghdad, Iraq	58	38	75	25	1.1	110	78	122	61	-
Bangkok, Thailand	89	71	95	54	0.4	90	78	99	72	6.2
Beijing, China	34	17	54	1	0.2	86	72	104	63	8.8
Berlin, Germany.	35	26	58	-11	(NA)	73	56	95	41	(NA)
Bogota, Colombia.	66	43	84	27	1.9	64	47	82	32	1.8
Brasilia, Brazil	81	64	95	54	(NA)	79	52	97	37	(NA)
Buenos Aires, Argentina .	85	64	104	44	4.2	58	41	88	23	2.3
Cairo, Egypt	65	49	86	32	0.2	93	72	108	63	-
Calcutta, India	77	57	91	48	0.3	89	80	100	72	13.1
Hong Kong, China	67	58	79	43	1.1	89	81	97	70	14.3
Istanbul, Turkey	46	37	64	16	3.7	82	66	100	50	0.7
Jakarta, Indonesia	83	75	92	72	(NA)	88	74	92	67	(NA)
Karachi, Pakistan	76	55	93	39	0.3	89	83	109	68	3.5
Lagos, Nigeria	82	79	93	64	(NA)	79	76	88	70	(NA)
London, England	45	36	61	15	2.4	72	56	93	45	1.8
Madrid, Spain	51	32	68	14	1.8	90	61	104	46	0.4
Manila, Philippines	86	71	95	61	0.8	88	76	99	70	15.9
Mexico City, Mexico . . .	70	45	86	26	0.3	74	56	86	37	5.1
Montreal, Canada.	21	7	52	-31	2.8	79	61	93	43	3.4
Moscow, Russia.	21	11	46	-33	1.4	71	55	95	41	3.2
Nairobi, Kenya.	77	58	88	45	1.8	71	54	85	43	0.5
New Delhi, India.	68	48	85	32	0.9	93	81	111	70	7.9
Paris, France.	43	34	59	1	(NA)	75	58	95	41	(NA)
Rio De Janeiro, Brazil . . .	91	74	109	64	5.3	81	64	102	52	1.8
Rome, Italy	55	39	64	19	3.2	83	66	100	55	0.6
Seoul, Korea	33	21	55	-1	(NA)	82	71	97	55	(NA)
Sydney, Australia	79	65	109	49	4.0	62	44	80	32	2.5
Tokyo, Japan	48	35	66	25	2.0	82	71	95	55	5.3
Toronto, Canada	28	15	59	-24	1.9	79	60	99	45	2.8

- Represents zero.   NA Not available.

Source: U.S. National Oceanic and Atmospheric Administration, Climates of the World.

No. 1357. Selected Environmental Data—OECD Countries

[Figures are for the latest available year. Varying definitions and survey methods can limit the comparability across countries]

Country	Air pollutant emissions per capita			Waste generated			
					Nuclear [3], 1995		
	Sulfur oxides (kilograms)	Nitrogen oxides (kilograms)	Carbon dioxide [1] (tons)	Municipal [2] (kilograms per capita)	Amount (tons)	Per unit of energy (tons per Mtoe [4])	Per 1,000 persons (kilograms)
Australia............	119	120	17	690	-	-	-
Austria.............	8	22	8	510	-	-	-
Belgium............	24	33	12	480	121	2.2	11.9
Canada............	89	67	16	630	1,690	7.2	57.1
Czech Republic......	68	40	12	310	46	1.1	4.5
Denmark...........	34	55	12	540	-	-	-
Finland............	20	51	12	410	68	2.2	13.3
France............	17	29	6	590	1,200	5.0	20.6
Germany...........	23	23	11	[5]400	470	1.3	5.8
Greece............	52	36	8	340	-	-	-
Hungary...........	67	19	6	500	52	2.2	5.1
Iceland............	32	110	9	570	-	-	-
Ireland............	46	32	10	430	-	-	-
Italy..............	25	37	7	470	-	-	-
Japan.............	7	11	9	400	914	1.7	7.3
Korea, South........	33	28	9	400	216	1.5	4.8
Luxembourg	19	48	20	460	-	-	-
Mexico............	23	16	4	300	20	0.3	0.2
Netherlands	9	32	12	570	14	0.2	0.9
New Zealand........	11	46	9	[6]350	-	-	-
Norway............	8	51	8	590	-	-	-
Poland............	61	30	9	320	(NA)	(NA)	(NA)
Portugal...........	36	37	5	350	-	-	-
Spain.............	53	31	6	370	168	1.6	4.3
Sweden............	11	40	6	440	213	4.5	24.1
Switzerland.........	5	18	6	600	77	2.5	10.9
Turkey............	31	13	3	590	-	-	-
United Kingdom......	34	35	9	480	1,713	3.3	29.2
United States.......	63	75	21	720	2,100	1.1	8.0

- Represents zero.   NA Not available.   [1] Carbon dioxide from energy use only. Excludes international marine bunkers.
[2] Municipal waste is that which is collected and treated by or for municipalities: household waste and bulky waste as well as comparable waste from small communities or industrial enterprises; and market and garden residue.   [3] Wastes from spent fuel measured in terms of heavy metal.   [4] Mtoe=million tons of oil equivalent (primary energy supply).   [5] Excludes separate collection by private sector.   [6] Household waste only.

Source: Organization for Economic Cooperation and Development, Paris, France, Toward Sustainable Development: Environmental Indicators, July 1998 and OECD in Figures, annual.

No. 1358. Carbon Dioxide Emissions From Consumption of Fossil Fuels, by Country, 1990 to 1997, and Projections, 2000 and 2010

[In million metric tons of carbon (5,887 represents 5,887,000,000). Includes carbon dioxide emissions from the consumption of petroleum, natural gas, and coal, and the flaring of natural gas]

Country	1990	1993	1994	1995	1996	1997, prel.	2000	2010
World, total	5,887	5,893	5,932	5,993	6,159	6,232	6,430	8,018
Australia	74	78	78	81	81	89	(NA)	(NA)
Brazil	58	64	69	72	74	77	73	121
Canada........................	128	131	136	137	140	143	151	162
China	620	712	767	782	801	822	930	1,391
France	103	98	95	97	103	102	103	109
Germany.......................	(X)	241	236	235	234	234	244	265
India..........................	156	186	195	226	235	237	273	386
Indonesia......................	40	54	56	59	66	67	(NA)	(NA)
Iran	56	65	68	71	71	73	(NA)	(NA)
Italy	113	108	106	116	116	116	122	138
Japan.........................	274	279	295	292	304	297	273	322
Korea, South	61	84	93	101	109	116	112	168
Mexico	81	84	88	86	91	94	97	127
Netherlands	60	59	59	60	62	64	62	67
Poland	91	91	86	81	93	95	(NA)	(NA)
Russia.........................	(X)	537	480	443	438	422	(NA)	(NA)
Saudi Arabia	57	65	67	68	71	74	(NA)	(NA)
South Africa....................	81	90	94	96	96	99	(NA)	(NA)
Spain	62	62	64	65	65	68	(NA)	(NA)
Taiwan	32	43	44	49	53	61	(NA)	(NA)
Thailand.......................	23	32	35	43	46	47	(NA)	(NA)
Turkey.........................	35	39	38	41	42	45	46	65
Ukraine	(X)	142	118	120	106	106	(NA)	(NA)
United Kingdom	167	157	155	152	154	157	156	170
United States	1,352	1,388	1,406	1,421	1,470	1,488	1,585	1,790

NA Not available.   X Not applicable.

Source: U.S. Energy Information Administration, International Energy Annual, 1997, and International Energy Outlook, 1999.

U.S. Census Bureau, Statistical Abstract of the United States: 1999

No. 1359. Educational Attainment, by Country: 1996

[Percent distribution. Persons 25 to 64 years old]

Country	Total	Early childhood, primary and lower secondary education only	Upper secondary education only	Nonuniversity tertiary education only	University education only
Australia	100	43	32	10	15
Austria	100	29	63	2	6
Belgium	100	47	30	13	11
Canada	100	24	29	31	17
Czech Republic	100	16	74	([1])	[1]10
Denmark	100	34	44	7	15
Finland	100	33	46	9	12
France	100	40	41	9	10
Germany	100	19	60	9	13
Greece	100	56	25	7	12
Hungary	100	37	50	([1])	[1]13
Ireland	100	50	28	12	11
Italy	100	62	30	([1])	[1]8
Korea, South	100	39	42	([1])	[1]19
Luxembourg	100	71	18	([1])	[1]11
Netherlands	100	37	40	([1])	[1]23
New Zealand	100	40	35	14	11
Norway	100	18	55	11	16
Poland	100	26	61	3	10
Portugal	100	80	9	3	7
Spain	100	70	13	5	13
Sweden	100	26	47	14	13
Switzerland	100	20	58	12	10
Turkey	100	83	11	([1])	[1]6
United Kingdom	100	24	55	9	13
United States	100	14	52	8	26

[1] Nonuniversity tertiary education included in university education only.

Source: Organization for Economic Cooperation and Development, Paris, France, *Education at a Glance*, annual, (copyright).

No. 1360. Participation in Job-Related Continuing Education and Training, by Country: 1994-1995

[Percentage of the employed population 25 to 64 years old. Data refer to all job-related education and training organized, financed, or sponsored by authorities, provided by employers, or self-financed. Job-related continuing education and training refers to all organized, systematic education and training activities in which people take part in order to obtain knowledge and/or learn new skills for a current or a future job, to increase earnings, improve job and/or career opportunities in current or other fields, and generally to improve their opportunities for advancement and promotion]

Country	Total	Male	Female	Country	Total	Male	Female
United States	46	45	47	New Zealand	47	46	47
Australia	38	38	38	Poland	17	17	17
Canada	38	38	37	Switzerland	32	33	30
Ireland	24	21	29	United Kingdom	52	51	53
Netherlands	33	35	29				

Source: Organization for Economic Cooperation and Development, Paris, France, *Education at a Glance*, annual (copyright).

No. 1361. Number of Foreign Students in Selected OECD Countries: 1995

[Covers students enrolled in a program at the university level or its equivalent]

Country of origin	Total [1]	Country of destination						
		United States	Belgium	Canada	France	Germany	Japan	United Kingdom
Total [1]	1,313,064	452,599	34,966	54,712	165,350	154,536	53,511	156,977
United States	23,276	(X)	213	3,742	2,945	4,512	1,164	6,243
Canada	27,250	22,747	98	(X)	1,035	463	131	1,713
Mexico	12,075	9,003	36	783	605	277	98	598
Japan	56,668	45,276	55	4,530	1,219	1,599	(X)	2,673
Korea, South	61,382	33,599	36	1,360	1,601	4,799	17,788	784
France	32,433	5,843	5,137	(NA)	(X)	5,872	131	8,936
Germany	41,220	8,592	655	722	5,332	(X)	270	9,518
Greece	36,638	3,699	928	198	2,806	8,231	14	10,374
Ireland	12,407	909	67	99	547	541	15	9,799
Italy	29,742	2,704	4,421	148	3,372	5,890	57	3,107
Netherlands	11,945	1,847	2,949	153	841	2,564	39	2,009
Spain	21,142	5,126	1,542	142	3,263	4,241	44	4,983
United Kingdom	24,161	7,786	321	1,938	4,217	3,535	218	(X)
Turkey	35,305	6,716	870	151	1,734	22,747	37	1,183
Russia	10,116	4,832	65	-	891	2,727	122	302

- Represents zero.   NA Not available.   X Not applicable.   [1] Includes other countries, not shown separately.

Source: Organization for Economic Cooperation and Development, Paris, France, *Education at a Glance*, annual (copyright).

840   Comparative International Statistics

No. 1362. Gross National Product, by Country: 1997

[**44 represents $44,000,000,000.** Gross national product calculated using the World Bank Atlas method; for details, see source. Some economies had missing data but were included in the ranking process at their approximate level, so that the relative order of other economies remains consistent. In 1997, Luxembourg and Liechtenstein were judged to have the highest values of GNP per capita but exact values were not available. Minus sign (-) indicates decrease]

Country	Gross national product Total (bil. dol.)	Rank	Average annual growth, 1990-97 (percent)	Gross national product per capita Amount (dol.)	Rank	Average annual growth, 1990-97 (percent)	GNP on purchasing power parity basis Per capita Total (bil. dol.)	Amount (dol.)	Rank
Algeria	44	54	1.7	1,500	122	-0.5	124	4,250	106
Argentina	319	17	8.1	8,950	57	6.7	360	10,100	64
Australia	383	14	0.6	20,650	23	-0.6	362	19,510	24
Austria	225	22	0.8	27,920	12	0.7	178	22,010	16
Bangladesh	44	53	6.3	360	179	4.6	135	1,090	189
Belarus	22	63	11.1	2,150	105	11.4	49	4,820	98
Belgium	272	20	2.4	26,730	14	2.1	235	23,090	13
Bolivia	8	97	3.7	970	141	1.4	22	2,810	139
Brazil	784	8	3.3	4,790	73	1.9	1,039	6,350	90
Bulgaria	10	85	-6.5	1,170	132	-6.0	32	3,870	115
Canada	595	9	4.0	19,640	25	2.9	659	21,750	17
Chile	71	43	7.2	4,820	72	5.7	179	12,240	55
China	1,055	7	8.5	860	145	7.4	3,770	3,070	135
Colombia	87	40	3.2	2,180	104	1.2	263	6,570	83
Congo (Kinshasa)	5	107	-5.7	110	209	-8.6	36	760	201
Costa Rica	9	87	3.0	2,680	95	1.7	23	6,510	85
Croatia	19	70	3.7	4,060	78	3.8	23	4,930	97
Czech Republic	54	48	1.0	5,240	70	1.2	107	10,380	63
Denmark	184	25	4.1	34,890	7	3.6	124	23,450	12
Egypt	72	42	6.4	1,200	129	4.5	186	3,080	134
Ethiopia	7	103	5.7	110	209	3.0	30	500	209
Finland	127	32	6.2	24,790	20	5.9	101	19,660	23
France	1,542	4	3.6	26,300	15	3.2	1,301	22,210	15
Germany	2,321	3	1.9	28,280	11	1.7	1,737	21,170	19
Ghana	7	99	4.3	390	173	1.7	29	1,610	165
Greece	122	33	1.1	11,640	49	0.7	132	12,540	54
Guatemala	17	75	4.6	1,580	116	1.8	43	4,060	110
Honduras	4	118	6.4	740	152	3.5	14	2,260	150
Hong Kong	[1]164	27	5.2	[1]25,200	19	2.1	158	24,350	9
Hungary	46	52	4.7	4,510	75	5.1	71	6,970	80
India	357	15	6.1	370	177	4.3	1,599	1,660	163
Indonesia	222	23	4.3	1,110	135	2.6	679	3,390	125
Iran	109	35	3.2	1,780	112	1.5	347	5,690	92
Ireland	65	44	8.2	17,790	28	7.3	64	17,420	31
Israel	94	38	1.9	16,180	32	-0.6	103	17,680	30
Italy	1,160	6	1.6	20,170	24	1.4	1,156	20,100	22
Jamaica	4	123	-2.3	1,550	119	-2.9	9	3,330	129
Japan	4,812	2	1.8	38,160	4	1.5	3,076	24,400	8
Kazakhstan	21	64	1.7	1,350	125	2.4	56	3,530	124
Kenya	10	86	2.9	340	180	0.4	33	1,160	184
Korea South	485	11	4.9	10,550	53	3.9	618	13,430	52
Lebanon	14	79	(NA)	3,350	87	(NA)	25	6,090	91
Malaysia	98	37	7.5	4,530	74	4.8	168	7,730	77
Mexico	349	16	8.2	3,700	81	6.3	765	8,110	73
Morocco	34	56	-2.2	1,260	128	-3.9	88	3,210	131
Netherlands	403	12	3.4	25,830	18	2.8	332	21,300	18
New Zealand	60	47	0.9	15,830	35	-0.4	59	15,780	38
Nigeria	33	57	5.1	280	191	2.1	102	860	198
Norway	159	28	3.4	36,100	5	2.8	107	24,260	10
Pakistan	65	45	-	500	164	-2.4	202	1,580	168
Peru	64	46	7.3	2,610	98	5.4	112	4,580	103
Philippines	88	39	5.3	1,200	129	3.0	270	3,670	119
Poland	139	30	6.8	3,590	83	6.7	251	6,510	85
Portugal	110	34	4.5	11,010	52	4.3	141	14,180	47
Romania	32	60	-6.7	1,410	124	-6.5	96	4,270	105
Russia	395	13	0.3	2,680	95	0.6	631	4,280	104
Saudi Arabia	143	29	1.9	7,150	64	-1.4	211	10,540	61
Singapore	102	36	8.8	32,810	8	6.7	91	29,230	3
South Africa	130	31	1.3	3,210	89	-0.4	292	7,190	79
Spain	570	10	3.0	14,490	38	2.8	617	15,690	39
Sri Lanka	15	77	7.3	800	148	5.9	46	2,460	146
Sudan	8	94	6.4	290	189	4.2	38	1,370	177
Sweden	232	21	1.4	26,210	16	1.3	168	19,010	25
Switzerland	305	18	2.7	43,060	3	2.5	188	26,580	7
Syria	17	74	3.6	1,120	134	0.9	45	3,000	136
Tanzania	[2]7	101	3.9	[2]210	202	1.2	19	620	207
Thailand	166	26	-1.1	2,740	94	-2.1	393	6,490	87
Turkey	199	24	8.6	3,130	91	6.8	412	6,470	88
Uganda	7	102	6.0	330	183	3.0	24	1,160	184
Ukraine	53	50	-3.2	1,040	139	-2.4	110	2,170	154
United Kingdom	1,231	5	4.0	20,870	22	3.7	1,222	20,710	20
United States	7,783	1	3.8	29,080	10	2.8	7,783	29,080	4
Uruguay	20	65	5.0	6,130	69	4.2	30	9,110	70
Venezuela	79	41	7.4	3,480	85	5.2	197	8,660	71
Vietnam	24	62	5.6	310	186	3.8	122	1,590	167

- Represents or rounds to zero.   NA Not available.   [1] Data refer to gross domestic product.   [2] Data refer to mainland Tanzania only.

Source: The World Bank, Washington, DC, *World Development Indicators CD-ROM*, annual.

Comparative International Statistics 841

No. 1363. Gross Domestic Product, by Country: 1980 to 1998

[7,329 represents $7,329,000,000,000]

Country	Purchasing power parity basis [1] Amount (bil. dol.) 1980	1985	1990	1995	1996	1997	Per capita (dollars) 1980	1985	1990	1995	1996	1997	Constant (1990) price levels and exchange rates [2] Amount (bil. dol.) 1980	1985	1990	1995	1996	1997	1998	Annual growth rate [3] (percent) 1997	1998
OECD, total [4][5]	7,329	10,851	15,186	19,330	20,226	21,246	8,480	12,070	16,220	19,804	20,576	21,487	12,939	14,460	16,941	18,420	18,985	19,627	20,074	3.4	2.3
OECD Europe [4]	3,032	4,363	6,118	7,719	8,022	8,408	7,386	10,381	14,160	17,329	17,924	18,698	5,731	6,210	7,243	7,759	7,902	8,120	8,345	2.8	2.8
European Union [6]	2,819	4,027	5,631	7,086	7,350	7,687	7,932	11,222	15,447	19,042	19,699	20,546	5,358	5,784	6,742	7,210	7,333	7,527	7,739	2.7	2.8
Australia	126	195	273	369	389	407	8,569	12,364	16,000	20,437	21,223	21,949	216	253	296	342	354	364	383	2.8	5.1
Austria	65	92	129	169	178	186	8,593	12,171	16,712	21,041	22,129	23,077	127	136	159	176	179	183	189	2.5	3.3
Belgium	87	120	166	219	226	237	8,844	12,100	16,679	21,577	22,205	23,242	163	169	196	209	212	218	225	3.0	2.9
Canada	245	373	513	663	681	720	9,977	14,361	18,452	22,400	22,735	23,761	434	498	573	617	624	647	667	3.7	3.0
Czech Republic	(X)	(X)	111	124	131	135	(NA)	(NA)	10,660	12,037	12,709	13,087	(X)	(X)	133	125	131	135	131	1.0	-2.8
Denmark	46	69	88	120	128	135	8,897	13,450	17,094	22,946	24,345	25,514	99	114	135	131	136	144	151	3.3	2.9
Finland	38	57	81	93	98	105	7,841	11,646	16,193	18,293	19,030	20,488	97	111	135	128	136	144	151	6.0	4.7
France	500	708	984	1,181	1,198	1,248	9,281	12,811	17,347	20,321	20,520	21,293	963	1,030	1,195	1,261	1,278	1,307	1,349	2.3	3.2
Germany	645	919	1,269	1,701	1,738	1,809	8,235	11,826	15,991	20,834	21,221	22,049	1,321	1,421	1,640	1,771	1,794	1,833	1,884	2.2	2.7
Greece	50	71	93	132	139	146	5,207	7,153	9,187	12,613	13,253	13,912	83	76	83	88	90	93	97	3.2	3.6
Hungary	(NA)	(NA)	87	92	94	100	(NA)	(NA)	8,359	8,951	9,236	9,875	(NA)	(NA)	36	32	32	34	35	4.6	4.9
Iceland	2	3	4	6	6	7	9,311	13,077	17,294	22,203	23,533	24,836	5	5	6	7	7	7	8	4.4	5.6
Ireland	18	27	40	64	67	75	5,182	7,476	11,375	17,854	18,484	20,634	32	36	46	61	66	73	81	10.6	10.5
Italy	467	666	945	1,139	1,183	1,223	8,268	11,746	16,257	19,872	20,616	21,265	877	945	1,094	1,157	1,164	1,182	1,199	1.5	1.4
Japan	939	1,467	2,202	2,863	3,018	3,100	8,036	12,150	17,824	22,797	23,980	24,574	2,007	2,369	2,970	3,191	3,316	3,344	3,250	0.8	-2.8
Korea, South	89	173	334	570	620	666	2,322	4,238	7,787	12,648	13,602	14,477	118	173	254	364	390	411	387	5.5	-5.8
Luxembourg	4	5	9	13	13	14	9,766	14,520	22,809	31,858	31,807	33,119	7	8	10	14	14	14	15	3.7	5.5
Mexico	254	370	482	619	661	720	3,805	4,957	5,834	6,843	7,181	7,697	220	242	263	283	298	319	334	7.0	4.8
Netherlands	121	171	239	314	327	346	8,572	11,805	15,962	20,327	21,089	22,142	229	243	284	315	325	337	349	3.7	3.8
New Zealand	24	37	45	62	64	67	7,584	11,198	13,352	17,000	17,345	17,846	36	42	43	50	51	53	52	2.4	-0.8
Norway	37	57	72	101	112	118	9,047	13,751	17,512	23,209	25,547	26,771	91	106	115	138	146	151	154	3.4	2.1
Poland	(NA)	(NA)	186	253	266	289	(NA)	(NA)	4,876	6,554	6,884	7,487	(NA)	(NA)	59	75	78	81	84	6.9	4.7
Portugal	44	61	95	132	137	145	4,494	6,068	9,600	13,344	14,521	14,562	51	53	69	75	78	81	84	3.7	3.9
Spain	217	307	458	569	596	629	5,781	7,993	11,787	14,521	15,183	15,990	369	395	492	526	539	558	579	3.5	3.8
Sweden	75	109	146	169	174	181	9,061	13,016	17,004	19,139	19,730	20,439	186	205	230	235	238	242	249	1.8	2.9
Switzerland	74	106	144	180	178	184	11,642	16,153	21,242	25,428	25,015	25,902	186	200	228	228	228	232	236	1.7	2.1
Turkey	100	168	264	347	376	412	2,252	3,340	4,691	5,620	5,999	6,463	91	115	151	177	189	203	209	7.6	2.8
United Kingdom	444	647	912	1,069	1,148	1,209	7,875	11,413	15,847	18,233	19,521	20,483	752	828	976	1,041	1,065	1,101	1,123	3.4	2.1
United States	**2,709**	**4,048**	**5,554**	**7,034**	**7,391**	**7,824**	**11,896**	**16,976**	**22,224**	**26,727**	**27,831**	**29,326**	**4,295**	**4,846**	**5,554**	**6,179**	**6,440**	**6,781**	**7,044**	**5.3**	**3.9**

NA Not applicable.   X Not available.   [1] The goods and services produced in different countries should be valued consistently if the differences observed are meant to reflect real differences in the volumes of goods and services produced. The use of purchasing power parities (PPP) instead of exchange rates is intended to achieve this objective. PPPs show how many units of currency are needed in one country to buy the same amount of goods and services which one unit of currency will buy in the other country. See text of this section.   [2] Based on constant (1990) price data, converted to U.S. dollars using 1990 exchange rates.   [3] Percent change from immediate prior year. Minus sign (-) indicates decrease.   [4] Excludes Czech Republic, Hungary, and Poland.   [5] Excludes South Korea.   [6] For countries, see text of this section.

Source: Organization for Economic Cooperation and Development, Paris, France, National Accounts, Main Aggregates, Vol. I, annual; and "OECD Statistics GDP," published July 1999; <http://www.oecd.org/std/gdp.htm> (copyright).

No. 1364. International Economic Composite Indexes, by Country: 1980 to 1998

[Average annual percent change from previous year; derived from indexes with base 1990=100. The coincident index changes are for calendar years and the leading index changes are for years ending June 30 because they lead the coincident indexes by about 6 months, on average. The G-7 countries are United States, Canada, France, Germany, Italy, United Kingdom, and Japan. Minus sign (-) indicates decrease]

Country	1980	1985	1989	1990	1991	1992	1993	1994	1995	1996	1997	1998
LEADING INDEX												
Total, 13 countries	2.3	2.2	4.5	2.0	-1.5	-0.7	-0.5	3.6	5.2	2.5	3.1	1.6
12 countries, excluding U.S.. . . .	6.7	4.5	6.0	3.5	-1.3	-2.4	-2.5	3.1	5.6	3.4	3.2	0.8
G-7 countries	2.3	2.0	4.3	1.8	-1.6	-1.1	-0.9	3.2	5.0	2.4	3.1	1.6
North America	-2.9	-0.8	1.8	-0.7	-2.1	2.0	3.0	4.7	4.8	1.1	3.1	2.9
United States	-3.3	-1.1	1.9	-0.5	-1.8	2.2	2.9	4.4	4.6	1.1	3.0	2.9
Canada	2.0	3.5	0.5	-2.9	-5.6	-1.4	5.4	9.1	7.0	1.2	4.1	3.2
Four European countries	3.0	2.6	3.8	1.8	0.9	1.0	-0.5	3.5	3.8	0.5	2.9	4.3
France	3.2	1.1	3.8	-0.7	1.4	3.3	0.5	3.5	2.8	-1.1	3.7	2.5
Germany	2.2	2.3	4.5	4.1	3.5	-0.3	-3.1	2.2	3.9	-0.2	3.9	4.8
Italy	5.6	5.1	2.9	2.7	-2.1	0.9	-0.2	5.5	4.7	2.0	1.3	7.6
United Kingdom	2.2	3.2	3.3	0.3	-1.6	0.7	2.5	3.7	4.1	2.3	1.6	2.6
Seven Pacific region countries	12.5	7.0	8.9	5.8	-3.0	-5.8	-5.3	2.1	7.4	6.8	3.5	-3.0
Australia	5.6	7.5	3.2	-	-4.5	4.7	5.7	7.0	3.7	2.0	2.3	7.0
Taiwan	4.0	5.8	11.1	6.0	0.8	7.4	4.8	7.2	7.3	3.9	7.9	7.4
Thailand	1.9	5.1	11.5	12.7	4.5	5.5	7.3	10.2	9.8	5.6	0.3	-2.9
Japan	15.0	7.4	9.2	6.1	-4.0	-8.8	-8.5	-0.4	7.4	8.0	3.6	-4.9
Korea, South	-2.1	5.3	11.4	5.6	4.5	5.4	4.6	12.5	11.2	5.1	2.5	-2.3
Malaysia	4.0	-1.5	2.6	1.4	2.3	-1.6	0.2	6.6	3.4	0.2	2.2	-4.3
New Zealand	2.3	5.8	1.6	1.8	-2.2	3.4	4.3	2.7	1.7	1.3	1.9	2.0
COINCIDENT INDEX												
Total, 13 countries	0.1	3.4	4.5	3.4	0.3	0.7	-0.1	2.7	3.0	2.7	3.0	2.0
12 countries, excluding U.S.. . . .	1.7	3.1	5.6	5.3	2.4	0.2	-1.6	1.8	2.6	2.1	1.8	0.2
G-7 countries	-0.1	3.3	4.3	3.3	0.1	0.4	-0.5	2.4	2.5	2.5	2.9	2.5
North America	-2.4	3.8	2.8	0.1	-3.7	1.2	2.7	4.7	3.5	3.5	4.7	4.9
United States	-2.7	3.7	2.8	0.1	-3.7	1.3	2.8	4.7	3.5	3.7	4.8	5.0
Canada	2.2	5.7	2.7	0.1	-4.3	0.1	2.2	4.6	3.1	1.5	4.0	3.9
Four European countries	0.4	2.2	4.8	4.7	1.0	-0.8	-4.1	1.5	2.9	1.7	2.5	4.2
France	-1.9	-0.7	8.5	5.1	-0.5	-1.3	-6.0	1.5	3.4	0.4	3.0	7.2
Germany	1.6	2.5	3.7	6.0	4.0	-0.4	-3.3	1.1	2.0	0.5	0.4	3.1
Italy	6.0	3.9	3.2	5.6	3.4	0.4	-7.3	-0.3	2.1	2.8	2.2	3.1
United Kingdom	-2.7	3.9	3.8	1.0	-4.5	-2.1	0.2	4.0	4.4	4.4	5.6	3.5
Seven Pacific region countries	3.1	3.8	6.7	6.5	4.3	1.2	0.3	1.8	2.3	2.5	1.0	-3.7
Australia	4.0	6.8	9.4	0.6	-8.0	-1.9	1.3	9.0	8.5	2.9	2.6	5.1
Taiwan	8.5	5.1	8.6	4.1	7.2	7.5	6.5	7.1	4.7	2.9	7.5	7.0
Thailand	2.4	1.4	12.3	12.0	3.3	5.5	10.7	8.9	9.4	5.9	-3.3	-8.5
Japan	3.4	3.6	6.3	6.8	4.8	0.6	-0.9	-	0.6	1.9	0.5	-3.7
Korea, South	-3.5	6.2	6.9	9.4	8.5	5.0	4.6	9.5	9.7	6.6	2.2	-13.9
Malaysia	-0.1	-5.8	3.9	2.4	5.3	1.2	2.4	3.1	2.5	0.4	-1.4	-7.6
New Zealand	1.4	1.3	-1.0	0.6	-1.3	0.8	3.3	5.5	4.6	4.3	2.5	0.8

- Represents or rounds to zero.

Source: Center for International Business Cycle Research, Columbia University, New York, NY, *International Economic Indicators*, monthly.

No. 1365. Selected International Economic Indicators, by Country: 1980 to 1998

[Data cover gross domestic product (GDP) at market prices. Gross fixed capital formation covers private and government sectors except military. Savings data are calculated by deducting outlays—such as personal consumption expenditures, interest paid, and transfer payments to foreigners—from disposable personal income]

Year	United States	France	Ger-many	Italy	Nether-lands	United Kingdom	Japan	Canada
Ratio of gross fixed capital formation to GDP (current prices):								
1980	19.6	23.4	22.6	24.5	21.4	18.8	31.6	23.1
1985	18.8	20.1	19.5	20.7	19.7	18.2	27.5	19.8
1990	16.2	22.6	20.9	20.3	20.9	20.6	31.7	20.8
1995	16.3	18.8	21.4	18.3	19.1	16.3	28.5	16.9
1997	17.1	18.1	19.9	18.0	20.0	16.7	28.4	18.7
1998	(NA)	18.4	19.4	18.1	20.0	17.4	26.2	19.0
Ratio of savings to disposable personal income:								
1980	8.5	17.6	14.2	21.6	11.0	11.7	17.9	14.3
1985	7.2	14.0	12.8	19.4	11.1	9.1	15.6	14.0
1990	5.3	12.5	14.7	17.0	15.5	7.4	12.1	11.1
1995	3.4	16.0	12.4	14.5	11.6	10.3	13.7	7.4
1997	2.1	16.3	12.1	12.4	11.3	9.5	12.6	2.1
1998	0.5	15.5	11.8	11.5	(NA)	7.0	13.6	1.2

NA Not available.

Source: U.S. Dept. of Commerce, International Trade Administration, Office of Trade and Economic Analysis, based on official statistics of listed countries.

Comparative International Statistics   843

No. 1366. Annual Percent Change in Consumer Prices, by Country: 1994 to 1998

[Change from previous year. See text of this section for general comments concerning the data. For additional qualifications of the data for individual countries, see source. Minus sign (-) indicates decrease]

Country	1994	1995	1996	1997	1998	Country	1994	1995	1996	1997	1998
United States	2.6	2.8	2.9	2.3	1.6	Kenya.	29.0	0.8	8.8	12.0	5.8
Argentina	4.2	3.4	0.2	0.5	0.9	Korea, South	6.2	4.5	4.9	4.4	7.5
Australia	1.9	4.6	2.6	0.3	0.9	Malaysia	3.7	5.3	3.5	2.7	5.3
Bangladesh	3.6	5.8	2.7	5.6	(NA)	Mexico	7.0	35.0	34.4	20.6	15.9
Belgium	2.4	1.5	2.1	1.6	1.0	Netherlands	1.8	1.9	2.1	2.2	2.0
Brazil	2,076	66.0	15.8	6.9	3.2	Nigeria	57.0	72.8	29.3	8.2	10.3
Canada.	0.2	2.2	1.6	1.6	1.0	Norway	1.4	2.5	1.3	2.6	2.3
Chile	11.4	8.2	7.4	6.1	5.1	Pakistan	12.4	12.3	10.4	11.4	6.2
Colombia.	23.8	21.0	20.2	18.5	20.7	Philippines.	9.1	8.0	9.0	5.9	9.7
Egypt.	8.2	15.7	7.2	4.6	4.2	Portugal	4.9	4.1	3.1	2.2	2.8
France	1.7	1.8	2.0	1.2	0.7	Russia	307.4	197.4	47.6	14.6	27.8
Germany.	2.7	1.8	1.5	1.8	1.0	South Africa.	9.0	8.6	7.4	8.6	6.9
Greece	10.9	8.9	8.2	5.5	4.8	Spain	4.7	4.7	3.6	2.0	1.8
India.	10.2	10.2	9.0	7.2	13.2	Sweden	2.2	2.5	0.5	0.5	-0.1
Indonesia	9.6	9.4	8.0	6.7	57.6	Switzerland	0.8	1.8	0.8	0.5	0.1
Iran	31.5	49.6	28.9	17.2	19.4	Thailand	5.0	5.8	5.8	5.6	8.1
Israel	12.3	10.0	11.3	9.0	5.4	Turkey	106.3	88.1	80.3	85.7	84.6
Italy	4.0	5.2	4.0	2.0	2.0	United Kingdom . . .	2.5	3.4	2.4	3.1	3.4
Japan	0.7	-0.1	0.1	1.7	0.6	Venezuela.	60.8	59.9	99.9	50.0	35.8

NA Not available.

Source: International Monetary Fund, Washington, DC, *International Financial Statistics*, monthly (copyright).

No. 1367. Comparative Price Levels—Selected OECD Countries: 1999

[As of April. Example of data: An item that costs $1.00 in the United States would cost $1.51 (U.S. dollars) in Japan]

Country	United States (U.S. dollar)	Canada (Canadian dollar)	Mexico (new peso)	Japan (yen)	France (franc)	Germany (Deutsche mark)	Italy (lire)	United Kingdom (pound)
United States	100	124	148	66	88	90	109	87
Australia.	85	105	126	57	75	76	93	74
Austria	108	134	160	72	95	97	118	94
Belgium	103	127	153	68	91	92	112	89
Canada	81	100	120	54	71	72	88	70
Czech Republic	42	52	63	28	37	38	46	37
Denmark.	131	162	195	87	116	118	143	114
Finland.	118	146	176	78	104	106	129	103
France	113	140	168	75	100	101	124	99
Germany	112	138	166	74	99	100	122	97
Greece.	86	106	127	57	75	77	93	74
Hungary	45	55	66	30	39	40	49	39
Iceland	122	151	181	81	108	109	133	106
Ireland	98	121	146	65	87	88	107	86
Italy	92	113	136	61	81	82	100	80
Japan	151	186	224	100	133	135	165	131
Korea, South.	58	72	87	39	52	52	64	51
Luxembourg	101	124	149	67	89	90	110	88
Mexico.	67	83	100	45	59	60	74	59
Netherlands	106	131	157	70	93	95	116	92
New Zealand.	83	102	123	55	73	74	91	72
Norway.	132	163	196	87	116	118	144	115
Poland	52	64	77	34	45	46	56	45
Portugal	77	95	114	51	68	69	84	67
Spain	84	104	125	56	74	75	92	73
Sweden	119	147	177	79	105	107	130	104
Switzerland.	136	169	203	90	120	122	149	119
Turkey	54	67	81	36	48	49	60	47
United Kingdom	115	142	171	76	101	103	126	100

Source: Organization for Economic Cooperation and Development, Paris, France, *Main Economic Indicators*, July 1999 (copyright).

No. 1368. At-Home Food and Beverage Expenditures, by Country: 1994

[Percent of total personal consumption expenditures. Expenditures spent on food and alcoholic beverages that were consumed at home]

Country	Food [1]	Alcoholic beverages	Country	Food [1]	Alcoholic beverages
United States	7.4	1.0	Korea, South	[3]29.1	(NA)
Australia	14.9	4.4	Mexico	24.5	2.5
Canada.............	10.3	2.4	Netherlands.........	11.4	1.4
France	14.8	1.9	Philippines..........	[2]55.6	(NA)
Germany............	[2]17.3	(NA)	Singapore	13.8	1.6
Greece	31.7	2.9	South Africa.........	27.5	6.5
Hungary	27.5	6.3	Sweden	14.6	2.7
India...............	51.3	0.5	Switzerland	[3]24.4	(NA)
Israel	20.5	0.9	Thailand	23.3	3.8
Italy	17.2	1.0	United Kingdom	11.2	6.1
Japan..............	[3]17.6	(NA)	Venezuela..........	[2]38.2	(NA)

NA Not available. [1] Food expenditures include nonalcoholic beverages. [2] Food includes nonalcoholic and alcoholic beverages. [3] Food expenditures include all beverages and tobacco.

Source: U.S. Dept. of Agriculture, Economic Research Service, *Food Consumption, Prices, and Expenditures, 1970-97.*

No. 1369. Per Capita Consumption of Meat and Poultry: 1998

[Preliminary. In kilograms per capita. Beef, veal, and pork quantities are as of September and in carcass-weight equivalents; poultry quantities are as of July and are on ready-to-cook basis]

Country	Pork Quantity	Pork Rank	Country	Poultry Quantity	Poultry Rank	Country	Beef and veal Quantity	Beef and veal Rank
Denmark.........	71.1	1	Hong Kong	60.5	1	Argentina	63.3	1
Czech Republic	63.2	2	United States	47.1	2	Uruguay	59.7	2
Spain...........	58.5	3	Israel	43.9	3	United States	44.6	3
Hong Kong	56.5	4	Saudi Arabia	36.7	4	Australia	40.8	4
Germany	56.4	5	Taiwan	35.8	5	Romania	40.8	5
Austria	55.1	6	Canada..........	33.3	6	New Zealand	38.6	6
Netherlands	44.2	7	Australia	30.9	7	Brazil	34.7	7
Belgium-			Singapore	29.9	8	Bulgaria.........	33.5	8
Luxembourg	43.4	8	Ireland	28.0	9	Canada.........	32.8	9
Taiwan	42.5	9	Hungary	27.4	10	Czech Republic....	32.0	10
Ireland	40.1	10						
United States	30.7	19						

Source: U.S. Department of Agriculture, Foreign Agricultural Service, *Livestock and Poultry: World Markets and Trade,* annual.

No. 1370. Motor Vehicle Transportation Indicators for Selected Countries: 1996

[129,728 represents 129,728,000]

Item	United States	Canada	Chile	France	Ger- many	Japan	Mexico	Sweden	United Kingdom
NUMBER (1,000)									
Automobiles.	129,728	13,183	971	25,500	40,988	47,000	8,607	3,662	21,092
Motorcycles [1]	3,871	320	32	2,990	2,470	15,120	270	119	578
Buses.	697	64	29	82	90	244	139	15	107
Trucks	75,940	6,933	110	5,173	4,173	22,118	4,287	311	2,631
Per 1,000 persons:									
Automobiles	484.1	457.4	67.3	437.3	490.7	374.7	89.9	411.4	360.6
Motorcycles	14.4	11.1	2.2	51.3	29.6	120.5	2.8	13.4	9.9
Buses	2.6	2.2	2.0	1.4	1.1	1.9	1.5	1.7	1.8
Trucks	283.4	240.5	7.6	88.7	50.0	176.3	44.8	34.9	45.0
ROADS									
Total kilometers (1,000)	6,308	[2]912	79	893	633	1,160	252	138	372
Kilometers per 1,000 persons	23.54	[2]31.65	5.48	15.30	7.58	9.25	2.63	15.50	6.36
Kilometers per square kilometer	0.69	[2]0.10	0.11	1.64	1.81	3.10	0.13	0.34	1.54
VEHICLE KILOMETERS OF TRAVEL									
Automobiles (bil.)	2,363	(NA)	(NA)	364	500	421	(NA)	58	362
Motorcycles (bil.) [1]	16	(NA)	(NA)	6	12	(NA)	(NA)	1	4
Buses (bil.)	11	(NA)	(NA)	2	4	7	(NA)	2	5
Trucks (bil.)	[3]1,607	(NA)	(NA)	101	60	262	(NA)	5	70
AVERAGE VEHICLE KILOMETERS PER VEHICLE									
Automobiles.	18,215	(NA)	(NA)	14,275	12,199	8,957	(NA)	15,838	17,163
Motorcycles [1]	4,120	(NA)	(NA)	2,007	4,776	(NA)	(NA)	5,294	6,990
Buses.	15,103	(NA)	(NA)	28,049	38,909	27,869	(NA)	140,067	44,579
Trucks	[3]21,160	(NA)	(NA)	20,297	26,259	11,909	(NA)	17,235	31,783

NA Not available. [1] Includes mopeds. Data for France are for 1993. [2] Data are for 1995. [3] Includes two-axle four-tire vehicles that are not cars. These are vans, sport-utility vehicles and pickup trucks.

Source: U.S. Federal Highway Administration, *Highway Statistics, 1997.*

U.S. Census Bureau, Statistical Abstract of the United States: 1999

No. 1371. Newspapers, Radio, Television, Telephones, and Computers, by Country

[Rates per 1,000 persons except as noted. See text of this section for general comments about the data. For data qualifications for countries, see source]

Country	Daily newspaper circulation,[1] 1996	Radio receivers,[2] 1996	Television receivers,[3] 1996	Telephone main lines per 100 persons,[4] 1997	Mobile telephones,[4] 1997	Personal computers,[5] 1997
Algeria	38	239	104	5	1	4
Argentina	123	677	221	19	56	39
Australia	297	1,385	554	50	264	362
Austria	294	740	518	49	144	211
Belgium	160	792	463	47	95	235
Brazil	40	435	223	10	28	26
Bulgaria	253	531	390	32	8	30
Canada	159	1,078	714	61	139	271
Chile	(NA)	354	215	18	28	54
China	(NA)	195	319	6	10	6
Colombia	49	565	123	15	35	33
Cuba	119	351	236	3	-	(NA)
Czech Republic	256	806	534	32	51	83
Denmark	311	1,146	592	63	273	360
Dominican Republic	48	177	94	9	16	(NA)
Ecuador	70	342	128	8	13	13
Egypt	38	316	119	6	-	7
Finland	455	1,385	605	56	417	311
France	218	943	591	58	99	174
Germany	311	946	564	55	99	256
Ghana	14	238	93	-	1	2
Greece	(NA)	477	238	52	89	45
Guatemala	31	73	57	4	6	3
Honduras	55	409	95	4	2	-
Hungary	189	697	438	26	69	49
India	(NA)	105	61	2	1	2
Indonesia	23	155	67	2	5	8
Iran	24	237	64	11	4	33
Iraq	20	228	82	3	-	(NA)
Ireland	153	703	411	41	146	241
Israel	291	530	291	45	283	186
Italy	104	874	524	45	204	113
Jamaica	64	482	181	14	22	5
Japan	580	957	684	48	304	202
Korea, South	(NA)	1,037	337	44	150	151
Kuwait	376	688	510	23	116	83
Lebanon	141	892	373	15	135	32
Malaysia	163	432	170	19	113	46
Mexico	97	324	270	10	18	37
Morocco	26	241	111	5	3	3
Netherlands	305	963	514	56	110	280
New Zealand	223	1,027	521	49	149	264
Norway	593	920	460	53	381	361
Pakistan	(NA)	92	21	2	1	5
Panama	62	299	187	12	6	(NA)
Peru	85	271	125	7	18	12
Philippines	82	159	51	3	18	14
Poland	113	518	337	19	22	36
Portugal	75	306	336	38	152	74
Puerto Rico	127	715	270	34	45	(NA)
Romania	(NA)	317	231	14	9	9
Russia	105	344	405	18	3	32
Saudi Arabia	59	319	260	12	17	44
Singapore	324	739	384	45	273	400
South Africa	30	316	118	11	37	42
Spain	99	328	406	40	110	122
Sweden	446	907	499	68	358	350
Switzerland	330	969	443	66	147	395
Syria	20	274	69	9	-	2
Taiwan	[6]158	(NA)	[6]317	50	69	(NA)
Thailand	65	204	189	8	33	20
Turkey	111	178	333	24	26	21
United Kingdom	332	1,445	516	52	151	242
United States	**212**	**2,115**	**805**	**64**	**206**	**407**
Uruguay	296	610	242	23	46	22
Venezuela	206	471	179	12	46	37

- Represents or rounds to zero.   NA Not available. [1] Publications containing general news and appearing at least 4 times a week; may range in size from a single sheet to 50 or more pages. Circulation data refer to average circulation per issue or number of printed copies per issue and include copies sold outside the country.   [2] Data cover estimated number of receivers in use and apply to all types of receivers for radio broadcasts to the public, including receivers connected to a radio "redistribution system" but excluding television sets.   [3] Estimated number of sets in use.   [4] As of December 31.   [5] In many countries mainframe computers are used extensively, and thousands of users can be connected to a single mainframe computer; thus the number of PCs understates the total use of computers.   [6] Source: U.S. Census Bureau. Data from Republic of China publications. Television data for 1995.

Source: Newspapers, radio, and television—United Nations Educational, Scientific, and Cultural Organization, Paris, France, *Statistical Yearbook,* (copyright); telephones— International Telecommunications Union, Geneva, Switzerland, *World Telecommunication Indicators,* (copyright); and mobile phones and personal computers— The World Bank, Washington, DC, *1999 World Development Indicators* (copyright).

U.S. Census Bureau, Statistical Abstract of the United States: 1999

No. 1372. Gross Public Debt, Expenditures, and Taxes, by Country: 1980 to 1998

[Percent of gross domestic product. Expenditures cover current outlays plus net capital outlays. Taxes cover current receipts but exclude capital receipts]

Country	Gross debt			Expenditures			Taxes		
	1980	1990	1998	1980	1990	1998	1980	1990	1998
United States	37.0	55.3	56.7	31.4	35.2	32.8	30.0	32.5	34.4
Australia	(NA)	22.7	33.6	31.4	32.1	32.9	27.7	32.5	33.4
Austria	37.7	57.9	63.1	48.1	48.6	49.4	44.5	46.2	47.3
Belgium	78.2	125.7	115.9	57.8	53.5	51.0	47.4	48.1	49.7
Canada	44.0	71.5	89.8	38.8	46.7	42.1	30.3	42.1	43.4
Czech Republic	(X)	(X)	(NA)	(X)	(X)	41.4	(X)	(X)	38.9
Denmark.	44.7	65.8	59.5	56.2	56.0	55.1	48.1	55.0	56.1
Finland.	14.1	14.4	49.8	38.1	44.5	49.1	38.4	49.9	50.6
France	30.9	40.2	66.5	46.1	49.8	54.3	43.6	48.3	50.9
Germany	31.1	43.2	63.1	47.9	45.1	46.9	43.9	43.0	44.8
Greece.	22.9	90.1	106.3	30.4	48.2	41.8	25.1	32.1	39.4
Hungary	(NA)	(NA)	(NA)	(NA)	(NA)	44.3	(NA)	(NA)	39.7
Iceland.	25.2	36.9	45.6	32.5	39.3	36.2	31.8	36.0	36.5
Ireland	72.7	97.2	56.6	48.2	39.0	33.1	33.1	36.7	35.5
Italy	[1]58.1	105.4	119.9	42.1	54.0	49.1	32.4	42.8	46.4
Japan	51.2	61.4	97.3	32.0	31.3	36.9	25.6	34.2	30.8
Korea, South.	16.0	8.2	11.0	19.3	18.1	25.6	18.7	21.8	25.4
Netherlands	46.9	78.8	67.4	55.8	54.1	47.2	45.9	49.0	46.5
New Zealand.	(NA)	(NA)	(NA)	(NA)	48.8	39.8	(NA)	44.0	40.7
Norway.	47.6	32.4	33.4	43.8	49.7	46.9	45.8	52.3	50.8
Poland	(NA)	(NA)	(NA)	(NA)	(NA)	45.7	(NA)	(NA)	41.9
Portugal	32.8	65.3	57.7	23.6	40.6	43.6	27.9	35.5	41.3
Spain	18.3	50.6	73.3	32.2	42.5	41.8	29.1	38.2	40.0
Sweden	44.3	44.3	75.5	60.1	59.1	60.8	50.6	63.3	63.0
United Kingdom	54.0	39.1	56.6	(NA)	41.8	40.2	(NA)	40.3	40.6

NA Not available.   X Not applicable.   [1] Data for 1980 not comparable with later years.

Source: Organization for Economic Cooperation and Development, Paris, *OECD Economic Outlook*, June 1999 (copyright).

No. 1373. Percent Distribution of Tax Receipts, by Country: 1980 to 1996

Country	Income and profits taxes [2]				Social security contributions			Taxes on goods and services [5]		
	Total [1]	Total [3]	Individual	Corporate	Total [4]	Employees	Employers	Total [3]	General consumption taxes [6]	Taxes on specific goods, services [7]
United States:										
1980	100.0	49.8	39.1	10.8	21.9	9.2	11.9	17.6	7.0	8.3
1990	100.0	45.4	37.7	7.7	25.8	11.0	13.4	17.3	8.0	7.1
1996	100.0	47.2	37.6	9.6	24.7	10.6	12.9	17.2	7.9	7.1
Canada:										
1980	100.0	46.6	34.1	11.6	10.5	3.7	6.6	32.6	11.5	13.0
1990	100.0	48.6	41.0	7.0	14.3	4.4	9.7	25.9	14.4	9.5
1996	100.0	47.3	37.7	8.9	16.3	5.3	10.7	24.9	14.3	8.3
France:										
1980	100.0	18.1	12.9	5.1	42.7	11.1	28.4	30.4	21.1	8.4
1990	100.0	17.2	11.8	5.3	44.1	13.2	27.2	28.4	18.8	8.7
1996	100.0	18.0	14.1	3.8	43.1	13.0	26.6	27.3	17.7	8.8
Germany [8]										
1980	100.0	35.1	29.6	5.5	34.3	15.3	18.4	27.1	16.6	9.3
1990	100.0	32.4	27.6	4.8	37.5	16.2	19.1	26.7	16.6	9.2
1996	100.0	28.4	24.7	3.8	40.6	17.6	20.5	27.9	17.6	9.3
Italy:										
1980	100.0	31.1	23.1	7.8	38.0	6.9	28.4	26.5	15.6	9.7
1990	100.0	36.5	26.3	10.0	32.9	6.3	23.6	28.0	14.7	10.6
1996	100.0	34.4	25.1	9.2	34.2	6.8	23.7	25.9	13.0	9.8
Japan:										
1980	100.0	46.1	24.3	21.8	29.1	10.2	14.8	16.3	-	14.1
1990	100.0	48.5	26.8	21.6	29.0	11.0	15.0	13.2	4.3	7.3
1996	100.0	36.6	20.2	16.4	36.5	14.2	18.6	15.4	5.3	8.0
Netherlands:										
1980	100.0	32.8	26.3	6.6	38.1	15.7	17.8	25.2	15.8	7.3
1990	100.0	32.2	24.7	7.5	37.4	23.1	7.5	26.4	16.5	7.5
1996	100.0	27.0	17.5	9.5	39.6	25.0	6.8	28.6	16.1	9.5
Sweden:										
1980	100.0	43.5	41.0	2.5	28.8	0.1	27.6	24.0	13.4	9.2
1990	100.0	41.6	38.5	3.1	27.2	0.1	26.0	25.0	14.9	9.2
1996	100.0	41.0	35.3	5.6	29.8	4.5	24.9	22.8	13.5	8.6
United Kingdom:										
1980	100.0	38.2	30.7	8.2	16.6	6.4	10.1	29.2	14.8	13.3
1990	100.0	39.3	28.6	11.1	17.1	6.5	10.0	30.8	16.9	12.6
1996	100.0	36.8	25.9	10.5	17.3	7.2	9.6	35.2	19.4	14.0

- Represents zero.   [1] Includes property taxes, employer payroll taxes other than Social Security contributions, and miscellaneous taxes, not shown separately.   [2] Includes taxes on capital gains.   [3] Includes other taxes not shown separately.   [4] Includes contributions of self-employed not shown separately.   [5] Taxes on the production, sales, transfer, leasing, and delivery of goods and services and rendering of services.   [6] Primary value-added and sales taxes.   [7] For example, excise taxes on alcohol, tobacco, and gasoline.   [8] Data are for former West Germany.

Source: Organization for Economic Cooperation and Development, Paris, France, *Revenue Statistics of OECD Member Countries*, annual (copyright).

Comparative International Statistics   847

No. 1374. Civilian Labor Force, Employment, and Unemployment, by Country: 1980 to 1998

[106.9 represents 106,900,000. Data based on U.S. labor force definitions (see source) except that minimum age for population base varies as follows: United States, France, Sweden, and United Kingdom, 16 years; Australia, Canada, Japan, Netherlands, Germany, and Italy (beginning 1995), 15 years; and Italy (1980 and 1990) 14 years]

Year	United States	Australia	Canada	France	Germany[1]	Italy	Japan	Netherlands	Sweden	United Kingdom
Civilian labor force (mil.):										
1980	106.9	6.7	12.0	22.9	27.3	21.1	55.7	5.9	4.3	26.5
1990	[2]125.8	8.4	14.3	24.3	29.4	[2]22.7	63.1	[2]6.6	[2]4.6	28.7
1995	[2]132.3	9.0	14.9	[2]24.8	[3]29.6	[2]22.7	66.0	7.3	4.5	28.5
1996	133.9	9.1	15.1	25.1	[3]29.5	22.8	66.5	7.4	4.5	28.6
1997	[2]136.3	9.2	15.4	25.2	[3]29.4	22.9	67.2	7.5	4.4	28.8
1998	[2]137.7	9.3	15.6	25.3	[3]29.4	23.0	[3]67.2	(NA)	4.4	[3]28.8
Labor force participation rate:[4]										
1980	63.8	62.1	64.6	57.5	54.7	48.2	62.6	55.4	66.9	62.5
1990	[2]66.5	64.6	67.3	56.0	55.3	[2]47.2	62.6	[2]56.1	[2]67.4	64.1
1995	[2]66.6	64.6	64.8	[2]55.2	[3]53.0	[2]47.5	62.9	59.3	64.1	62.7
1996	66.8	64.6	64.9	55.4	[3]52.5	47.7	63.0	59.7	64.0	62.7
1997	[2]67.1	64.3	64.8	55.2	[3]52.2	47.7	63.2	60.5	[3]63.4	[3]62.8
1998	[2]67.1	64.4	65.1	(NA)	(NA)	47.8	[3]62.8	(NA)	[3]63.1	(NA)
Civilian employment (mil.):										
1980	99.3	6.3	11.1	21.4	26.5	20.2	54.6	5.5	4.2	24.7
1990	[2]118.8	7.9	13.2	22.1	28.0	[2]21.1	61.7	[2]6.2	[2]4.5	26.7
1995	[2]124.9	8.2	13.5	21.9	[3]27.7	[2]20.0	63.9	6.8	4.1	26.0
1996	126.7	8.3	13.7	22.0	[3]27.4	20.1	64.2	6.9	4.0	26.3
1997	[2]129.6	8.4	13.9	22.0	[3]27.1	20.1	64.9	7.1	4.0	26.7
1998	[2]131.5	8.6	14.3	22.3	[3]27.2	20.2	[3]64.4	(NA)	4.0	[3]26.9
Employment-population ratio:[5]										
1980	59.2	58.3	59.7	53.8	53.1	46.1	61.3	52.1	65.6	58.1
1990	[2]62.8	60.1	61.9	50.9	52.6	[2]43.9	61.3	[2]52.6	[2]66.1	59.6
1995	[2]62.9	59.1	58.6	48.7	[3]49.6	[2]41.8	60.9	55.1	58.3	57.2
1996	63.2	59.1	58.6	48.5	[3]48.7	41.9	60.9	55.9	57.6	57.6
1997	[2]63.8	58.8	58.9	48.3	[3]48.1	41.8	61.0	57.4	[3]57.0	[3]58.3
1998	[2]64.1	59.2	59.7	(NA)	(NA)	41.9	[3]60.2	(NA)	[3]57.8	(NA)
Unemployment rate:										
1980	7.1	6.1	7.5	6.5	2.8	4.4	2.0	6.0	2.0	7.0
1990	[2]5.6	6.9	8.1	9.1	5.0	[2]7.0	2.1	[2]6.2	[2]1.8	6.9
1995	[2]5.6	8.5	9.5	11.8	[3]6.5	[2]12.0	3.2	7.0	9.1	8.7
1996	5.4	8.6	9.7	12.5	[3]7.2	12.1	3.4	6.4	9.9	8.2
1997	[2]4.9	8.6	9.2	12.4	[3]7.8	12.3	3.4	5.2	10.1	7.0
1998	[2]4.5	8.0	8.3	11.8	[3]7.5	12.3	[3]4.1	(NA)	8.4	[3]6.3
Under 25 years old	10.4	15.2	15.2	(NA)	(NA)	33.6	(NA)	(NA)	17.2	[6]12.3
Teenagers [7]	14.6	20.0	20.0	(NA)	(NA)	37.0	(NA)	(NA)	21.2	(NA)
20 to 24 years old	7.9	11.9	12.3	(NA)	(NA)	32.5	(NA)	(NA)	15.9	(NA)
25 years old and over	3.4	6.2	7.0	(NA)	(NA)	9.1	(NA)	(NA)	7.3	[6]5.0

NA Not available. [1] Former West Germany. [2] Break in series. Data not comparable with prior years. [3] Preliminary. [4] Civilian labor force as a percent of the civilian working age population. Germany and Japan include the institutionalized population as part of the working age population. [5] Civilian employment as a percent of the civilian working age population. Germany and Japan include the institutionalized population as part of the working age population. [6] Data are for spring quarter. [7] 16 to 19 years old in the United States, and Sweden; 15 to 19 years old in Canada, Australia, and Italy.

Source: U.S. Bureau of Labor Statistics, *Comparative Civilian Labor Force Statistics, Ten Countries, 1959-1998*, April 1999, and *Monthly Labor Review*.

No. 1375. Unemployment Rates, by Country: 1995 to 1998

[Annual averages. The standardized unemployment rates shown here are calculated as the number of unemployed persons as a percentage of the civilian labor force. The unemployed are persons of working age who, in the reference period, are without work, available for work and have taken specific steps to find work]

Country	1995	1997	1998	Country	1995	1997	1998
OECD, total	7.5	7.4	7.1	Ireland	12.3	9.9	7.8
European Union	10.7	10.7	10.0	Italy	11.9	12.1	12.3
				Japan	3.1	3.4	4.1
United States	5.6	4.9	4.5	Luxembourg	2.9	2.8	2.8
Australia	8.6	8.5	8.0	Netherlands	6.9	5.2	4.0
Austria	3.9	4.5	4.7	New Zealand	6.3	6.6	7.5
Belgium	9.9	9.4	9.5	Norway	5.0	4.1	3.3
Canada	9.5	9.2	8.4	Poland	(NA)	11.2	10.6
Czech Republic	(NA)	4.8	6.5	Portugal	7.3	6.8	5.1
Denmark	7.2	5.6	5.1	Spain	22.9	20.8	18.8
Finland	16.2	12.7	11.4	Sweden	8.8	9.9	8.3
France	11.7	12.3	11.7	Switzerland	3.5	4.2	(NA)
Germany	8.2	9.9	9.4	United Kingdom	8.7	7.0	6.3
Hungary	(NA)	8.9	8.0				

NA Not available.

Source: Organization for Economic Cooperation and Development, Paris, France, *OECD News Release, Standardized Unemployment Rates*, 9 July 1999.

848 Comparative International Statistics

No. 1376. Civilian Employment-Population Ratio and Females as Percent of Total Civilian Employment, by Country: 1980 to 1998

[See headnote, Table 1374]

| Country | Civilian employment-population ratio [1] | | | | | | | | Civilian employment, percent female | | | |
| | Women | | | | Men | | | | | | | |
	1980	1990	1995	1998	1980	1990	1995	1998	1980	1990	1995	1998
United States ..	47.7	[2]54.3	[2]55.6	[2]57.1	72.0	[2]72.0	[2]70.8	[2]71.6	42.4	[2]45.2	[2]46.1	[2]46.2
Australia	41.9	49.3	50.3	50.8	75.1	71.2	68.1	67.8	36.4	41.5	43.1	43.4
Canada	46.7	54.0	52.1	53.4	73.1	70.1	65.5	66.2	39.6	44.4	45.2	45.5
France	40.3	41.6	41.1	(NA)	68.9	61.3	57.1	(NA)	39.5	43.0	44.4	(NA)
Germany [3]	38.9	[2]40.9	[4]39.6	(NA)	69.6	[2]65.6	[4]60.4	(NA)	39.2	[2]41.0	[4]41.6	(NA)
Italy	27.9	[2]29.2	[2]28.3	29.3	66.0	[2]60.0	[2]56.5	55.6	31.7	[2]34.7	[2]35.3	36.4
Japan	45.7	48.0	[4]47.4	[4]47.4	77.9	75.4	75.0	[4]73.9	38.4	40.3	40.3	[4]40.5
Sweden	58.0	[2]61.8	54.7	[4]53.6	73.6	[2]70.6	62.1	[4]62.2	45.2	[2]47.8	48.1	[4]47.4
United Kingdom .	44.8	49.8	49.6	(NA)	72.8	70.3	65.5	(NA)	40.4	43.4	44.9	(NA)

NA Not available. [1] Civilian employment as a percent of the civilian working age population. [2] Break in series. Data not comparable with prior years. [3] Former West Germany. [4] Preliminary.
Source: U.S. Bureau of Labor Statistics, *Comparative Civilian Labor Force Statistics, Ten Countries, 1959-1998*, April 1999, and *Monthly Labor Review*.

No. 1377. Female Labor Force Participation Rates, by Country: 1980 to 1997

[In percent. Female labor force of all ages divided by female population 15-64 years old]

Country	1980	1990	1995	1997	Country	1980	1990	1995	1997
Australia	52.7	62.9	64.8	64.7	Korea, South	(NA)	51.3	53.2	54.8
Austria	48.7	55.4	62.3	61.9	Luxembourg	39.9	50.7	58.0	60.9
Belgium	47.0	52.4	56.1	(NA)	Mexico	33.7	23.6	40.1	42.8
Canada	57.8	67.8	67.6	67.8	Netherlands	35.5	[1]53.1	[1]59.0	62.2
Czech Republic	(NA)	69.1	[1]65.4	64.4	New Zealand	44.6	[1]62.9	63.3	64.9
Denmark	(NA)	78.5	73.6	75.1	Norway	62.3	71.2	72.4	75.8
Finland	70.1	72.9	70.3	71.3	Poland	(NA)	(NA)	61.1	60.0
France	54.4	57.6	59.4	59.8	Portugal	54.3	62.9	62.4	65.1
Germany [2]	52.8	57.4	61.7	61.8	Spain	32.2	41.2	45.1	47.1
Greece	33.0	43.6	45.9	(NA)	Sweden	74.1	[1]80.1	76.1	74.5
Hungary	(NA)	(NA)	50.5	49.4	Switzerland	54.1	59.6	[1]67.8	69.4
Iceland	(NA)	(NA)	82.4	(NA)	Turkey	(NA)	36.7	34.2	30.2
Ireland	36.3	38.9	47.8	50.4	United Kingdom	58.3	65.5	66.0	67.5
Italy	39.6	45.9	[1]43.3	44.1	**United States**	59.7	[1]68.9	70.7	71.3
Japan	54.8	60.3	62.1	63.7					

NA Not available. [1] Break in series. Data not comparable with prior years. [2] Prior to 1991 data are for former West Germany.
Source: Organization for Economic Cooperation and Development, Paris, France, *Labour Force Statistics*, annual (copyright).

No. 1378. Civilian Employment, by Industry and Country: 1990 and 1998

[118,793 represents 118,793,000. Data based on U.S. labor force definitions except that minimum age for population base varies as follows: United States, France, Sweden, and United Kingdom, 16 years; Australia, Canada, Germany, Italy (1998), Japan, 15 years; and Italy (1990), 14 years. For the United States, France, and Italy the data are not comparable between 1990 and 1998. Industries based on International Standard Industrial Classification; see text of this section]

Industry	United States	Aus-tralia	Canada	France	Ger-many	Italy	Japan	Sweden	United Kingdom
TOTAL EMPLOYMENT (1,000)									
1990, total	118,793	7,859	13,165	22,098	27,952	21,080	61,710	4,501	26,818
Agriculture, forestry, fishing	3,394	440	551	1,248	965	1,879	4,270	178	573
Industry [1]	29,834	1,865	3,117	6,425	10,875	[2]6,842	20,890	1,268	8,128
Manufacturing	21,346	1,170	2,105	4,708	8,839	4,755	15,010	943	[3]5,971
Services	85,565	5,554	9,497	14,425	16,112	12,355	36,550	3,056	18,117
1998, total	131,463	8,597	14,326	[4]22,350	(NA)	20,167	[4]64,550	4,023	(NA)
Agriculture, forestry, fishing	3,509	428	551	[4]976	(NA)	1,332	[4]3,330	119	(NA)
Industry [1]	29,871	1,814	3,189	[4]5,421	(NA)	[2]6,464	[4]20,430	1,005	(NA)
Manufacturing	20,733	1,104	2,254	(NA)	(NA)	4,908	[4]13,790	774	(NA)
Services	98,083	6,354	10,587	[4]15,954	(NA)	12,373	[4]40,800	2,899	(NA)
PERCENT DISTRIBUTION									
1990, total	100	100	100	100	100	100	100	100	100
Agriculture, forestry, fishing	3	6	4	6	3	9	7	4	2
Industry [1]	25	24	24	29	39	[2]32	34	28	30
Manufacturing	18	15	16	21	32	23	24	21	[3]22
Services	72	71	72	65	58	59	59	68	68
1998, total	100	100	100	[4]100	100	100	[4]100	100	100
Agriculture, forestry, fishing	3	5	4	[4]4	(NA)	7	[4]5	3	(NA)
Industry [1]	23	21	22	[4]24	(NA)	[2]32	[4]32	25	(NA)
Manufacturing	16	13	16	(NA)	(NA)	24	[4]21	19	(NA)
Services	75	74	74	[4]71	(NA)	61	[4]63	72	(NA)

NA Not available. [1] Includes mining and construction. [2] Public utilities included in industry. [3] Includes mining.
[4] Preliminary.
Source: U.S. Bureau of Labor Statistics, *Comparative Civilian Labor Force Statistics, Ten Countries, 1959-1998*, April 1999 and unpublished data.

Comparative International Statistics 849

[Industrial production index measures output in the manufacturing, mining, and electric and gas utilities industries. Minus sign (-) indicates decrease]

Country	Index (1990=100)								Annual percent change				
	1980	1985	1992	1993	1994	1995	1996	1997	1992-93	1993-94	1994-95	1995-96	1996-97
OECD, total.....	79.5	86.3	99.2	98.5	103.1	106.8	109.4	114.6	-0.6	4.6	3.6	2.5	4.7
Australia........	76.6	84.9	98.2	101.1	107.0	107.6	110.5	112.4	3.0	5.9	0.5	2.7	1.7
Austria..........	76.0	82.9	100.7	99.2	103.2	108.3	109.1	115.3	-1.5	4.0	4.9	0.8	5.6
Belgium.........	82.2	85.6	98.0	92.9	94.6	100.7	101.6	106.1	-5.2	1.9	6.5	0.8	4.4
Canada [1].......	81.2	93.9	97.2	101.6	108.2	113.2	114.7	120.7	4.5	6.4	4.7	1.3	5.2
Czech Republic....	(X)	(X)	71.9	68.1	69.5	69.0	70.4	73.5	-5.3	2.1	-0.7	2.0	4.5
Finland..........	76.6	88.1	92.4	97.5	108.5	116.0	119.7	131.7	5.6	11.3	6.8	3.2	10.0
France..........	89.2	89.2	97.6	93.9	97.6	99.6	99.9	103.6	-3.9	4.0	2.1	0.2	3.8
Germany [2]......	82.9	85.6	100.1	92.4	95.7	96.9	97.3	100.6	-7.6	3.6	1.2	0.4	3.4
Greece..........	90.9	97.4	98.0	95.2	96.4	98.2	99.3	100.6	-2.9	1.3	1.8	1.2	1.3
Hungary.........	102.6	112.6	73.7	76.6	84.0	87.9	90.8	100.9	3.9	9.6	4.7	3.3	11.1
Ireland..........	54.2	69.5	112.7	119.0	133.2	158.3	170.9	197.1	5.6	11.9	18.9	8.0	15.3
Italy............	87.9	84.7	97.8	95.7	101.7	107.9	104.8	107.7	-2.1	6.2	6.1	-2.9	2.7
Japan	67.7	80.3	96.0	91.8	93.0	96.0	98.3	101.7	-4.4	1.3	3.3	2.3	3.5
Korea, South....	33.1	54.5	116.0	121.1	134.5	150.5	161.6	172.6	4.4	11.0	11.9	7.3	6.8
Luxembourg.....	73.1	82.2	99.5	95.3	100.9	102.3	100.4	107.6	-4.3	5.9	1.4	-1.9	7.2
Mexico [3].......	84.0	88.8	107.9	108.2	103.4	104.5	115.2	125.9	0.3	4.8	-7.8	10.2	9.3
Netherlands	90.8	91.6	101.5	100.4	105.3	108.3	111.3	113.4	-1.1	4.9	2.9	2.7	1.9
Norway..........	64.5	78.1	108.5	112.6	120.4	127.5	134.1	138.8	3.8	6.9	5.9	5.2	3.5
Poland..........	(NA)	122.4	86.7	91.2	103.3	114.1	124.4	138.8	5.1	13.3	10.5	9.0	11.6
Portugal.........	64.1	73.9	97.7	92.6	92.4	96.7	98.0	100.4	-5.2	-0.2	4.7	1.3	2.5
Spain...........	83.0	85.7	96.3	91.8	98.8	103.6	102.3	109.4	-4.7	7.6	4.8	-1.3	6.9
Sweden [4].......	81.4	90.2	94.8	94.6	105.2	118.5	122.1	131.5	-0.2	11.2	12.6	3.1	7.7
Switzerland......	80.4	83.0	99.5	97.7	101.8	103.9	103.8	109.4	-1.8	4.3	2.0	-0.1	5.4
United Kingdom....	81.5	88.0	97.0	99.1	104.4	106.2	107.4	108.2	2.2	5.4	1.7	1.1	0.8
United States	80.5	89.0	101.1	104.6	110.2	115.7	120.8	128.1	3.5	5.4	4.9	4.5	6.0

NA Not available. X Not applicable. [1] Gross domestic product in industry at factor cost and 1986 prices. [2] 1980-90 former West Germany; later data use 1990 annual average data for West Germany as base year. [3] Includes construction. [4] Mining and manufacturing.

Source: Organization for Economic Cooperation and Development, Paris, France, *Main Economic Indicators, Historical Statistics, 1969-1988,* 1990; and *Main Economic Indicators,* monthly (copyright).

No. 1380. Patents, by Country: 1997

[Includes only U.S. patents granted to residents of areas outside of the United States and its territories]

Country	Total [1]	Inventions	Designs	Country	Total [1]	Inventions	Designs
Total............	54,211	50,276	3,667	Switzerland	1,179	1,090	89
				Sweden	970	867	100
Japan...........	24,184	23,179	948	Netherlands........	894	808	55
Germany.........	7,291	7,008	239	Australia..........	577	534	43
France..........	3,202	2,958	212	Israel	568	478	76
United Kingdom.....	2,904	2,678	196	Belgium	559	515	40
Canada..........	2,816	2,379	418	Finland	468	452	15
Taiwan..........	2,597	2,057	539	Austria	432	333	89
Korea, South	1,965	1,891	73	Denmark...........	393	376	17
Italy	1,417	1,239	165	Other countries	1,795	1,434	353

[1] Includes patents for botanical plants and reissues, not shown separately.

Source: U.S. Patent and Trademark Office, Technology Assessment and Forecast Data Base.

No. 1381. Measures of Value Added in Manufacturing in Selected OECD Countries: 1985 and 1996

[United States=100. For details on methodology, see source]

Country	1985		1996 [1]		Country	1985		1996 [1]	
	Per person engaged	Per hour worked	Per person engaged	Per hour worked		Per person engaged	Per hour worked	Per person engaged	Per hour worked
United States	100	100	100	100	France	72	86	69	84
Canada..........	82	84	67	68	Germany [2]......	76	86	63	82
Mexico..........	34	31	33	(NA)	Netherlands.......	86	107	75	97
Japan...........	78	69	76	74	Sweden	68	87	74	90
Australia........	54	56	50	51	United Kingdom ...	55	60	58	67

NA Not available. [1] 1990 for Mexico; 1994 for Australia; and 1995 for Netherlands. [2] Data are for former West Germany.

Source: Organization for Economic Cooperation and Development, Paris, France, *Science, Technology and Industry Outlook 1998,* 1998 (copyright).

[1992=100. Data relate to employees (wage and salary earners) in Belgium, Italy, the Netherlands, and the United Kingdom, and to all employed persons (employees and self-employed workers) in the other countries. Minus sign (-) indicates decrease. For explanation of average annual percent change, see Guide to Tabular Presentation]

Index	United States	Can-ada	Japan	Bel-gium	France	Ger-many [1]	Italy	Nether-lands	Nor-way	Swe-den	United King-dom
Output per hour:											
1980	71.9	75.2	63.9	64.5	70.5	77.3	64.0	69.8	76.7	74.0	54.4
1985	87.8	89.7	77.3	86.6	83.8	88.9	81.5	89.7	90.2	87.1	71.1
1990	97.8	95.2	95.4	96.9	99.1	99.0	92.8	98.6	96.6	95.0	89.2
1995	114.9	108.4	109.3	108.9	114.3	111.2	113.9	119.9	102.0	122.4	107.4
1996	117.3	106.6	111.9	110.0	117.9	115.1	114.4	124.4	102.6	125.4	106.1
1997	122.3	109.6	117.4	116.7	125.9	121.8	117.4	130.2	103.2	133.6	106.6
Average annual percent change:											
1979-85	3.3	2.3	3.5	6.1	3.0	2.0	4.9	4.4	2.4	3.0	4.4
1985-90	2.2	1.2	4.3	2.3	3.4	2.2	2.6	1.9	1.4	1.8	4.6
1990-97	3.2	2.0	3.0	2.7	3.5	3.0	3.4	4.1	0.9	5.0	2.6
Compensation per hour, national currency basis: [2]											
1980	55.8	47.7	58.6	52.7	41.3	53.9	27.9	64.7	39.0	37.4	33.1
1985	75.3	69.9	72.5	74.5	73.7	70.2	60.1	81.9	63.4	58.4	53.6
1990	91.0	89.5	90.7	89.9	91.8	89.4	84.0	90.8	92.3	87.6	82.2
1995	108.3	103.7	109.5	111.6	107.7	117.7	112.3	110.6	109.2	106.2	110.9
1996	110.7	106.0	110.5	114.1	109.4	123.7	119.4	113.9	114.4	113.4	112.2
1997	115.3	108.8	114.0	116.5	112.6	126.6	125.2	117.0	119.6	118.3	116.8
Average annual percent change:											
1979-85	7.1	8.3	4.7	7.8	12.8	5.9	16.7	4.9	10.0	9.6	11.8
1985-90	3.9	5.1	4.6	3.8	4.5	5.0	6.9	2.1	7.8	8.5	8.9
1990-97	3.4	2.8	3.3	3.8	3.0	5.1	5.9	3.7	3.8	4.4	5.1
Real hourly compensation: [2] [3]											
1980	95.0	92.1	75.4	87.0	80.6	74.8	78.8	87.8	86.0	87.5	68.8
1985	98.2	94.0	81.4	87.5	90.8	80.7	88.9	90.6	90.8	87.2	78.5
1990	97.7	95.9	95.3	95.1	97.3	96.4	94.3	96.5	97.7	97.4	90.3
1995	99.7	99.5	107.4	104.6	102.0	108.5	98.4	103.1	102.7	96.8	103.1
1996	99.0	100.1	108.4	104.7	101.6	112.6	100.9	104.2	106.3	102.7	101.8
1997	100.8	101.1	109.8	105.3	103.3	113.0	103.8	104.8	108.3	105.8	102.6
Average annual percent change:											
1979-85	0.3	0.4	1.1	0.8	2.3	1.8	1.5	0.3	0.6	-0.5	2.6
1985-90	-0.1	0.4	3.2	1.7	1.4	3.6	1.2	1.3	1.5	2.2	2.8
1990-97	0.4	0.8	2.0	1.5	0.9	2.3	1.4	1.2	1.5	1.2	1.9
Unit labor costs, national currency:											
1980	77.6	63.4	91.7	81.7	58.6	69.6	43.7	92.7	50.8	50.6	60.9
1985	85.8	77.9	93.8	86.1	88.0	78.9	73.8	91.3	70.2	67.1	75.4
1990	93.1	94.0	95.0	92.7	92.6	90.3	90.5	92.1	95.6	92.3	92.1
1995	94.3	95.7	100.1	102.5	94.2	105.9	98.6	92.3	107.1	86.8	103.3
1996	94.3	99.4	98.8	103.7	92.8	107.5	104.4	91.5	111.5	90.4	105.8
1997	94.3	99.3	97.1	99.8	89.4	103.9	106.6	89.9	115.9	88.5	109.5
Average annual percent change:											
1979-85	3.7	5.9	1.2	1.5	9.5	3.8	11.2	0.5	7.4	6.4	7.1
1985-90	1.6	3.8	0.3	1.5	1.0	2.7	4.2	0.2	6.4	6.6	4.1
1990-97	0.2	0.8	0.3	1.1	-0.5	2.0	2.4	-0.3	2.8	-0.6	2.5
Unit labor costs, U.S. dollar basis: [4]											
1980	77.6	65.6	51.5	90.0	73.5	59.9	62.9	82.1	63.9	69.6	80.1
1985	85.8	68.9	49.9	46.6	51.9	41.9	47.6	48.4	50.8	45.4	55.4
1990	93.1	97.3	83.1	89.2	90.0	87.3	93.0	88.9	95.0	90.8	93.0
1995	94.3	84.2	135.1	111.8	100.0	115.5	74.6	101.2	105.0	70.8	92.3
1996	94.3	88.1	115.1	107.6	96.1	111.6	83.4	95.4	107.3	78.5	93.4
1997	94.3	86.7	101.7	89.6	81.1	93.5	77.1	81.0	101.6	67.5	101.5
Average annual percent change:											
1979-85	3.7	3.2	-0.3	-9.7	-3.3	-4.1	-3.2	-7.6	-1.7	-5.2	-1.3
1985-90	1.6	7.1	10.8	13.8	11.7	15.8	14.3	12.9	13.3	14.8	10.9
1990-97	0.2	-1.6	2.9	0.1	-1.5	1.0	-2.6	-1.3	1.0	-4.2	1.3
Employment:											
1980	111.6	115.5	87.4	120.9	124.7	102.2	126.4	107.5	134.5	130.9	159.0
1985	106.0	109.5	91.9	104.6	110.0	94.9	105.4	94.9	120.7	122.0	123.3
1990	105.4	111.5	95.8	102.5	105.1	100.3	106.8	101.1	105.4	117.2	116.2
1995	102.5	107.5	93.5	95.5	92.6	87.3	93.6	89.7	107.2	98.8	99.4
1996	102.2	110.2	92.9	94.2	91.5	84.6	92.8	88.7	109.4	98.1	100.7
1997	103.1	113.7	92.7	92.7	90.3	82.6	92.1	89.0	112.4	97.1	101.2
Average annual percent change:											
1979-85	-1.4	-0.8	1.2	-2.7	-2.3	-1.1	-2.9	-2.3	-1.8	-1.2	-4.9
1985-90	-0.1	0.4	0.8	-0.4	-0.9	1.1	0.3	1.3	-2.7	-0.8	-1.2
1990-97	-0.3	0.3	-0.5	-1.4	-2.1	-2.7	-2.1	-1.8	0.9	-2.7	-2.0
Aggregate hours:											
1980	107.5	113.6	93.8	121.3	131.5	110.3	123.0	111.4	135.0	124.0	160.5
1985	104.6	108.7	98.4	103.0	108.9	99.3	101.4	96.1	120.2	119.4	125.2
1990	104.8	112.0	100.9	104.2	104.5	100.1	108.2	101.6	103.7	116.4	118.1
1995	104.0	109.1	92.0	95.6	92.0	84.3	94.4	90.0	106.9	106.3	100.4
1996	103.7	112.1	92.2	94.7	91.2	80.4	92.8	88.9	108.6	106.0	102.0
1997	105.3	115.8	91.4	93.3	89.7	78.6	92.5	89.2	111.3	105.0	102.5
Average annual percent change:											
1979-85	-1.2	-0.8	1.1	-3.3	-3.3	-1.8	-3.1	-2.5	-1.8	-0.8	-5.3
1985-90	-	0.6	0.5	0.2	-0.8	0.2	1.3	1.1	-2.9	-0.5	-1.2
1990-97	0.1	0.5	-1.4	-1.6	-2.2	-3.4	-2.2	-1.8	1.0	-1.5	-2.0

- Represents or rounds to zero.   [1] Former West Germany.   [2] Compensation includes, but real hourly compensation excludes, adjustments for payroll and employment taxes that are not compensation to employees, but are labor costs to employers.   [3] Index of hourly compensation divided by the index of consumer prices to adjust for changes in purchasing power.   [4] Indexes in national currency adjusted for changes in prevailing exchange rates.

Source: Bureau of Labor Statistics, *International Comparisons of Manufacturing Productivity and Unit Labor Cost Trends, 1997 Revised Data*, March 16, 1999.

Comparative International Statistics   851

No. 1383. Indexes of Hourly Compensation Costs for Production Workers in Manufacturing, by Country: 1980 to 1997

[United States=100. Compensation costs include all pay made directly to the worker—pay for time worked and not worked (eg. leave, except sick leave), other direct pay, employer expenditures for legally required insurance programs and contractual and private benefit plans, and for some countries, other labor taxes. Data adjusted for exchange rates. Area averages are trade-weighted to account for difference in countries' relative importance to U.S. trade in manufactured goods. The trade weights used are the sum of U.S. imports of manufactured products for consumption (customs value) and U.S. domestic exports of manufactured products (f.a.s. value) in 1992; see source for detail]

Area or country	1980	1985	1990	1995	1996	1997	Area or country	1980	1985	1990	1995	1996	1997
United States	100	100	100	100	100	100	Austria [6]	90	58	119	147	139	120
Total [1]	67	52	83	95	91	84	Belgium	133	69	129	155	146	125
OECD [2]	74	57	90	103	98	90	Denmark	110	62	121	140	136	121
Europe	100	61	116	129	125	112	Finland [7]	83	63	141	140	133	118
Asian newly industrializing economies [3]	12	13	25	37	39	36	France	91	58	104	116	113	99
Canada	88	84	106	93	94	91	Germany [6][8]	124	73	147	187	180	155
Mexico	22	12	11	9	9	10	Greece	38	28	45	53	54	(NA)
Australia [4]	86	63	88	88	93	88	Ireland	60	46	78	79	78	74
Hong Kong [5]	15	13	21	28	29	30	Italy	83	59	117	94	100	92
Israel	38	31	57	61	62	66	Luxembourg	122	60	112	136	127	(NA)
Japan	56	49	86	139	118	106	Netherlands	122	67	121	140	130	113
Korea, South	10	9	25	42	46	40	Norway	117	80	144	142	142	130
New Zealand	54	34	56	59	62	60	Portugal	21	12	25	31	32	29
Singapore	15	19	25	43	47	45	Spain	60	36	76	75	76	67
Sri Lanka	2	2	2	3	3	(NA)	Sweden	127	74	140	125	138	122
Taiwan	10	12	26	34	34	32	Switzerland	112	74	140	170	160	133
							United Kingdom	77	48	85	80	80	85

NA Not available. [1] The 28 foreign economies shown below. [2] Organization for Economic Cooperation and Development; see text of this section. [3] Hong Kong, South Korea, Singapore, and Taiwan. [4] Includes nonproduction workers, except in managerial, executive, professional, and higher supervisory positions. [5] Average of selected manufacturing industries. [6] Excludes workers in establishments considered handicraft manufactures (including all printing and publishing and miscellaneous manufacturing in Austria). [7] Includes workers in mining and electrical power plants. [8] Former West Germany.

Source: U.S. Bureau of Labor Statistics, News Release USDL 98-376, September 16, 1998.

No. 1384. Income Tax and Social Security Contributions as Percent of Labor Costs: 1996

[Data are for single individual at the income level of the average production worker]

Country	Labor costs [1] (dol.)	Percent of labor costs			
		Total	Income tax	Social security contributions	
				Employee	Employer
Belgium	38,455	56	19	10	26
Germany	33,936	51	18	17	17
Switzerland	32,146	30	10	10	10
Italy	32,064	51	12	7	32
Luxembourg	30,386	35	12	11	12
Netherlands	29,683	44	5	31	8
United States	29,584	31	17	7	7
Canada	29,019	32	21	5	6
Denmark	28,993	45	36	9	-
Finland	28,992	50	23	6	20
Sweden	27,658	50	22	4	25
Norway	27,184	38	19	7	11
France	26,447	50	6	13	30
Australia	26,323	24	23	2	-
Japan	26,168	19	6	7	7
Austria	26,125	42	7	15	20
United Kingdom	26,062	33	16	8	9
Ireland	24,658	36	20	5	11
Spain	22,548	39	10	5	24
Korea South	22,518	6	2	-	2
New Zealand	22,243	22	22	-	-
Iceland	20,212	24	21	-	4
Greece	16,301	36	1	12	22
Turkey	14,107	36	20	7	9
Czech Republic	13,692	43	7	9	26
Portugal	13,084	34	6	9	19
Poland	11,710	45	12	-	33
Hungary	9,852	52	12	8	32
Mexico	8,562	25	4	4	17

- Represents or rounds to zero. [1] Adjusted for purchasing power parities, see text of this section.

Source: Organization for Economic Cooperation and Development, Paris, France, The OECD Observer, No. 214, October/November 1998 (copyright).

No. 1385. World Primary Energy Production, by Region and Type: 1980 to 1997

[In quadrillion Btu (286.4 represents 286,400,000,000,000,000). Btu=British thermal units. For Btu conversion factors, see source]

Region and type	1980	1985	1990	1991	1992	1993	1994	1995	1996	1997
World total [1]	286.4	304.2	351.2	348.1	350.0	351.4	356.8	365.0	374.9	381.3
North America	80.9	84.6	91.9	92.4	92.5	91.7	95.0	95.9	98.3	98.9
United States	64.8	64.9	70.8	70.5	70.0	68.3	70.7	71.0	72.3	72.3
Central and South America	12.1	13.6	16.7	17.7	18.0	18.9	19.9	21.4	22.6	24.3
Western Europe	30.7	37.3	38.5	38.4	38.7	39.3	40.2	41.3	43.8	43.6
Eastern Europe and former U.S.S.R.	66.7	75.0	81.9	75.5	71.4	67.1	62.4	60.5	60.9	59.2
Middle East	42.2	25.8	41.0	40.3	43.6	45.8	46.9	48.0	49.0	52.0
Africa	18.1	19.3	21.6	22.6	23.0	22.8	23.0	24.2	24.7	26.5
Far East and Oceania . . .	35.8	48.7	59.6	61.2	62.8	65.8	69.3	73.8	75.6	76.9
Crude oil	128.1	115.4	129.5	128.8	129.1	128.9	130.5	133.3	136.6	142.1
Natural gas	52.7	61.4	76.1	76.7	76.9	78.4	79.1	80.3	84.1	84.3
Natural gas liquids	5.1	5.8	6.9	7.1	7.4	7.7	7.8	8.1	8.3	8.5
Coal	74.5	85.8	92.3	87.7	88.4	86.3	88.5	90.1	91.5	92.2
Hydroelectric power	18.1	20.6	22.6	23.0	23.0	24.4	24.5	25.9	26.1	26.4
Nuclear electric power. . .	7.6	15.4	20.4	21.3	21.4	22.1	22.5	23.4	24.2	24.0
Geothermal, solar and wind	0.4	0.6	1.3	1.4	1.5	1.6	1.6	1.6	1.7	1.8

[1] Includes biomass, geothermal energy, and solar energy produced in the United States and not used for generating electricity, not shown separately by type.

Source: U.S. Energy Information Administration, *International Energy Annual*.

No. 1386. World Primary Energy Consumption, by Region and Type: 1980 to 1997

[In quadrillion Btu (282.6 represents 282,600,000,000,000,000). Btu=British thermal units. For Btu conversion factors, see source]

Region and type	1980	1985	1990	1991	1992	1993	1994	1995	1996	1997
World total [1]	282.6	307.5	346.8	347.3	349.0	353.4	357.6	365.5	375.6	379.5
North America	89.3	88.3	100.0	99.9	101.8	103.8	106.1	107.9	111.5	112.2
United States	76.0	74.0	84.1	84.0	85.6	87.4	89.2	90.9	93.9	94.2
Central and South America	11.4	12.3	14.1	14.8	15.1	15.7	16.5	17.3	18.3	18.9
Western Europe	58.6	59.9	64.1	65.0	64.1	64.5	64.4	66.1	67.5	68.5
Eastern Europe and former U.S.S.R.	61.4	70.7	74.2	69.5	65.6	61.0	55.5	53.2	52.8	51.6
Middle East	5.9	8.6	11.1	11.2	12.0	12.7	13.3	13.9	14.5	15.2
Africa	6.8	8.5	9.3	9.7	10.0	10.2	10.5	10.8	11.1	11.4
Far East and Oceania . . .	49.2	59.3	74.0	77.2	80.5	85.4	91.2	96.2	99.8	101.9
Petroleum	130.9	123.1	134.9	136.1	136.6	136.6	139.1	142.4	145.4	148.7
Natural gas	54.2	63.7	75.1	76.2	76.3	78.5	78.3	80.2	84.1	83.9
Coal	71.6	84.2	90.5	87.2	88.1	88.2	89.3	89.8	91.8	92.8
Hydroelectric power	18.3	21.0	22.7	23.2	23.2	24.6	24.8	26.1	26.4	26.6
Nuclear electric power. . .	7.6	15.4	20.4	21.3	21.4	22.1	22.5	23.4	24.2	24.0
Geothermal, solar and wind	0.3	0.5	1.3	1.4	1.5	1.6	1.6	1.6	1.7	1.8

[1] See footnote 1, Table 1385.

Source: U.S. Energy Information Administration, *International Energy Annual*.

No. 1387. World Energy Consumption, by Region and Energy Source, 1990 and 1996, and Projections, 2000 to 2020

[In quadrillion Btu (343.8 represents 343,800,000,000,000,000). Btu=British thermal units. For Btu conversion factors, see source]

Region and energy source	1990	1996	Projections				
			2000	2005	2010	2015	2020
World total	343.8	375.5	402.7	454.3	504.2	555.1	611.8
North America	99.7	111.6	119.3	126.9	134.9	141.3	147.5
United States	83.9	93.3	99.2	104.7	110.8	115.5	119.9
Central and South America	13.7	17.7	21.0	26.3	32.6	39.4	47.7
Western Europe	60.0	64.0	67.6	71.3	74.6	77.9	81.5
Eastern Europe and former Soviet Union . . .	73.6	52.4	52.0	56.9	61.0	65.3	69.8
Middle East	13.1	17.3	20.1	23.5	27.0	30.6	34.7
Africa	9.2	11.1	12.0	13.8	15.5	17.1	18.9
Far East and Oceania	74.4	101.4	110.8	135.7	158.5	183.4	211.8
Oil	134.9	145.7	157.7	172.7	190.4	207.5	224.6
Natural gas	72.0	82.2	90.1	111.3	130.8	153.6	177.5
Coal	90.6	92.8	97.7	107.1	116.0	124.8	138.3
Nuclear	20.4	24.1	24.5	24.9	25.2	23.6	21.7
Other	25.9	30.7	32.7	38.3	41.9	45.6	49.7

Source: U.S. Energy Information Administration, 1990 and 1996, *International Energy Annual 1996*; projections, *International Energy Outlook 1999*.

Comparative International Statistics   853

No. 1388. Energy Consumption and Production, by Country: 1990 and 1997

[346.9 represents 346,900,000,000,000,000. See text of this section for general comments about the data. For data qualifications for countries, see source]

Country	Primary energy consumed Total (quad. Btu) 1990	Primary energy consumed Total (quad. Btu) 1997, prel.	Primary energy consumed Per capita (mil. Btu) 1990	Primary energy consumed Per capita (mil. Btu) 1997, prel.	Dry natural gas production (tril. cu. ft.) 1990	Dry natural gas production (tril. cu. ft.) 1997	Crude petroleum production (1,000 barrels per day) 1990	Crude petroleum production (1,000 barrels per day) 1997	Coal production (mil. short tons) 1990	Coal production (mil. short tons) 1997
World	**346.8**	**379.5**	**66**	**65**	**73.6**	**81.7**	**60,566**	**66,420**	**5,353**	**5,218**
United States	**84.1**	**94.2**	**337**	**352**	**17.8**	**18.9**	**7,355**	**6,452**	**1,029**	**1,090**
Algeria	1.2	1.3	49	45	1.8	2.5	1,175	1,277	(Z)	(Z)
Argentina	1.9	2.5	59	71	0.6	1.0	483	834	(Z)	(Z)
Australia	3.7	4.5	217	241	0.7	1.0	575	588	226	293
Austria	1.2	1.3	150	160	0.1	0.1	22	19	3	1
Bahrain	0.3	0.3	520	452	0.2	0.2	42	40	(NA)	(NA)
Bangladesh	0.3	0.4	2	3	0.2	0.3	1	2	(NA)	(NA)
Belarus	(X)	1.1	(X)	106	(X)	(Z)	(NA)	36	(X)	(NA)
Belgium	2.2	2.6	217	253	(Z)	-	(NA)	(NA)	3	(Z)
Brazil	5.7	7.6	39	48	0.1	0.2	631	841	5	5
Bulgaria	1.3	0.9	141	113	-	(Z)	4	1	35	29
Burma	(NA)	(NA)	(NA)	(NA)	(Z)	0.1	13	10	(Z)	(Z)
Canada	10.9	12.2	392	402	3.9	5.9	1,553	1,922	75	87
Chile	0.6	0.9	43	61	0.1	0.1	20	7	2	1
China	27.0	36.6	23	29	0.5	0.8	2,774	3,200	1,190	1,553
Colombia	0.9	1.2	28	33	0.2	0.2	440	652	23	36
Congo (Kinshasa) [1]	(NA)	(NA)	(NA)	(NA)	-	-	29	28	(Z)	(Z)
Cuba	0.5	0.4	46	40	(Z)	(Z)	14	30	-	(Z)
Czech Republic	(X)	1.9	(X)	182	(X)	(Z)	(X)	3	(X)	72
Denmark	0.8	1.0	158	184	0.1	0.3	121	230	(NA)	(NA)
Ecuador	(NA)	(NA)	(NA)	(NA)	(Z)	(Z)	285	388	(NA)	(NA)
Egypt	1.4	1.8	27	29	0.3	0.5	873	856	-	(Z)
Finland	1.1	1.2	228	232	(NA)	(NA)	(NA)	(NA)	(NA)	(NA)
France	8.8	9.7	156	166	0.1	0.1	61	36	15	8
Germany	(X)	14.2	(X)	173	(X)	0.8	(X)	56	(X)	252
Greece	1.1	1.2	103	112	(Z)	(Z)	15	9	57	66
Hong Kong	0.5	0.6	84	94	(NA)	(NA)	(NA)	(NA)	(NA)	(NA)
Hungary	1.3	1.1	124	108	0.2	0.2	40	35	19	17
India	7.8	11.8	9	12	0.4	0.8	660	675	233	329
Indonesia	2.2	3.7	12	18	1.5	2.4	1,462	1,520	9	60
Iran	3.1	4.2	57	68	0.8	1.6	3,088	3,664	1	1
Iraq	0.9	1.2	51	56	0.2	0.1	2,040	1,155	(NA)	(NA)
Ireland	0.4	0.5	105	133	0.1	0.1	(NA)	(NA)	(Z)	(Z)
Israel	0.5	0.7	97	118	(Z)	(Z)	(Z)	(Z)	(NA)	(Z)
Italy	7.0	7.7	122	131	0.6	0.7	87	112	11	5
Japan	18.1	21.3	147	169	0.1	0.1	11	10	11	5
Korea, North	2.1	1.9	103	81	(NA)	(NA)	(NA)	(NA)	71	68
Korea, South	3.7	7.5	86	162	(NA)	(NA)	(NA)	(NA)	19	5
Kuwait	0.5	0.7	210	359	0.2	0.3	1,175	2,083	(NA)	(NA)
Libya	0.5	0.6	123	102	0.2	0.2	1,375	1,446	(NA)	(NA)
Malaysia	1.0	1.7	55	78	0.7	1.4	619	746	(Z)	(Z)
Mexico	5.0	5.8	58	59	0.9	1.2	2,553	3,023	9	10
Morocco	0.3	0.4	13	13	(Z)	(Z)	(Z)	(Z)	1	1
Netherlands	3.4	3.9	225	249	2.7	3.0	70	53	(NA)	(NA)
New Zealand	0.7	0.8	217	210	0.2	0.2	40	58	3	3
Nigeria	0.7	0.9	7	7	0.1	0.2	1,810	2,332	(Z)	(Z)
Norway	1.6	1.8	373	404	1.0	1.6	1,704	3,143	(Z)	(Z)
Pakistan	1.2	1.7	10	13	0.5	0.7	62	57	3	4
Peru	(NA)	(NA)	(NA)	(NA)	(Z)	(Z)	129	118	(Z)	(Z)
Philippines	0.7	1.0	12	13	-	(Z)	5	1	1	1
Poland	4.0	4.2	104	109	0.1	0.2	2	6	237	220
Portugal	0.7	0.9	75	92	(NA)	(NA)	(NA)	(NA)	(Z)	-
Romania	2.9	1.9	125	85	1.0	0.5	163	134	43	41
Russia	(X)	26.6	(X)	181	(X)	20.2	(X)	5,920	(X)	288
Saudi Arabia	3.2	4.2	212	215	1.1	1.5	6,410	8,562	(NA)	(NA)
Serbia	(X)	0.7	(X)	69	(X)	(Z)	(X)	20	(X)	40
South Africa	3.4	4.3	91	99	-	0.1	(NA)	(NA)	193	243
Spain	3.9	4.5	101	114	0.1	(Z)	16	8	40	29
Sweden	2.2	2.2	251	244	(Z)	(Z)	(Z)	(Z)	(Z)	-
Switzerland	1.2	1.2	174	171	(Z)	-	(NA)	(NA)	(NA)	(NA)
Syria	0.6	0.7	49	47	0.1	0.1	388	561	(NA)	(NA)
Taiwan	2.0	3.4	100	156	0.1	(Z)	3	1	1	(Z)
Tajikistan	(X)	(NA)	(X)	(NA)	(X)	(Z)	(X)	1	(X)	(Z)
Thailand	1.3	2.5	22	42	0.2	0.5	44	72	14	24
Trinidad and Tobago	(NA)	(NA)	(NA)	(NA)	0.2	0.3	150	124	(NA)	(NA)
Tunisia	(NA)	(NA)	(NA)	(NA)	(Z)	0.1	93	90	(NA)	(NA)
Turkey	2.0	2.8	35	43	(Z)	(Z)	73	68	52	62
Ukraine	(X)	6.6	(X)	130	(X)	0.6	(X)	58	(X)	87
United Arab Emirates	1.2	1.8	641	678	0.8	1.3	2,117	2,316	(NA)	(NA)
United Kingdom	9.4	10.1	164	171	1.8	3.2	1,820	2,518	104	54
Venezuela	2.1	2.7	108	115	0.8	1.0	2,137	3,315	2	6
Vietnam	0.3	0.6	4	8	(Z)	(Z)	50	191	5	11

- Represents zero.   NA Not available.   X Not applicable.   Z Less than .05 trillion cubic feet, 500 barrels per day, or 500,000 short tons.   [1] See footnote 3, Table 1349.

Source: U.S. Energy Information Administration, *International Energy Annual*.

No. 1389. Net Electricity Generation by Type and Country: 1996

[12,962.5 represents 12,962,500,000,000]

Country	Total [1] (bil. kWh)	Thermal [2]	Hydro	Nuclear
World, total	12,962.5	62.0	19.4	17.6
Argentina	65.8	46.0	43.5	10.5
Australia	167.1	90.9	9.1	-
Austria	52.0	34.8	65.2	-
Belgium	71.1	41.8	0.3	57.9
Brazil	287.1	4.6	91.7	0.8
Bulgaria	40.6	50.3	5.9	43.8
Canada	555.0	20.6	63.5	15.9
China [3]	1,000.2	80.5	18.1	1.4
Colombia.	43.7	21.5	78.5	-
Czech Republic . . .	59.9	76.4	3.3	20.4
Denmark	50.4	97.7	(Z)	-
Egypt	48.2	77.1	22.9	-
Finland	66.0	54.2	17.8	28.0
France	484.8	8.7	13.3	77.9
Germany	520.3	66.2	4.2	29.2
Greece	40.0	89.1	10.8	-
Hungary	33.1	58.7	0.6	40.7
India.	405.6	81.3	16.9	1.8
Indonesia	69.9	80.7	15.7	-
Iran	78.0	90.4	9.6	-
Italy	227.2	80.0	18.3	-
Japan	950.1	61.0	8.4	30.2
Kazakhstan	55.6	86.8	13.1	0.2
Korea, North	34.0	34.5	65.5	-
Korea, South	194.2	61.2	2.7	36.2
Malaysia	50.1	89.8	10.2	-
Mexico	154.5	71.5	20.1	4.8
Netherlands.	80.0	94.2	0.1	4.9
New Zealand	35.3	22.1	72.2	-
Norway.	103.4	0.8	99.2	-
Pakistan	54.6	57.3	42.1	0.6
Paraguay	47.6	0.1	99.9	-
Poland	134.9	97.1	2.9	-
Romania	58.1	71.6	26.9	1.6
Russia	805.4	68.2	19.0	12.8
Saudi Arabia	97.8	100.0	-	-
Serbia and Montenegro [4]	36.4	68.7	31.3	-
South Africa.	186.9	93.0	0.7	6.3
Spain	165.5	43.6	23.8	32.3
Sweden	134.5	10.3	37.9	51.7
Switzerland	54.0	3.6	52.1	44.3
Taiwan [3]	129.5	65.1	6.9	28.1
Thailand	86.3	91.6	8.4	-
Turkey	91.2	56.0	43.9	-
Ukraine.	175.1	50.1	6.5	43.4
United Kingdom . . .	322.5	72.2	1.0	26.6
United States	3,447.1	68.1	10.0	19.6
Uzbekistan	43.0	85.0	15.0	-
Venezuela	71.0	25.4	74.6	-

- Represents zero.   Z Less than .05 percent.   [1] Includes geothermal, wind, photovoltaic, and solar thermal generation, not shown separately. [2] Electricity generated from coal, oil, and gas.   [3] See footnote 2, Table 1349.   [4] See footnote 4, Table 1349.

Source: U.S. Energy Information Administration, *International Energy Annual 1997.*

No. 1390. Commercial Nuclear Power Generation, by Country: 1990 to 1998

[Generation for **calendar years;** other data as of **December (1,743.9 represents 1,743,900,000,000)**]

Country	Reactors				Gross electricity generated (bil. kWh)				Gross capacity (1,000 kW)			
	1990	1995	1997	1998	1990	1995	1997	1998	1990	1995	1997	1998
Total.	368	423	433	436	1,743.9	2,271.7	2,351.1	2,424.2	301,745	358,414	368,471	371,544
United States . .	112	109	109	107	606.4	705.7	655.1	705.6	105,998	105,810	106,541	106,005
Argentina	2	2	2	2	7.0	7.0	7.9	7.5	1,005	1,005	1,005	1,005
Armenia	(NA)	1	1	1	(NA)	0.3	1.3	1.6	(NA)	408	408	408
Belgium	7	7	7	7	42.7	41.3	47.4	46.1	5,740	5,911	5,995	5,995
Brazil	1	1	1	1	2.0	2.5	3.1	3.3	657	657	657	657
Bulgaria	(NA)	6	6	6	(NA)	17.1	17.0	17.1	(NA)	3,760	3,760	3,760
Canada	19	22	21	21	74.0	100.2	84.4	72.8	13,855	16,699	15,795	15,795
China [1].	(NA)	(NA)	2	2	(NA)	(NA)	12.4	13.0	(NA)	(NA)	1,968	1,968
Czech Republic .	(NA)	(NA)	(NA)	4	(NA)	(NA)	(NA)	13.2	(NA)	(NA)	(NA)	1,760
Finland.	4	4	4	4	18.9	18.9	20.8	21.8	2,400	2,400	2,605	2,760
France	58	56	56	56	314.1	377.2	386.1	385.9	58,862	60,674	60,674	60,674
Germany	22	21	20	20	147.2	154.1	170.3	161.7	23,973	24,035	23,496	23,496
Great Britain . . .	42	34	35	35	68.8	82.7	97.6	99.5	15,274	14,022	15,272	15,272
Hungary	4	4	4	4	13.6	14.0	13.9	13.9	1,760	1,840	1,840	1,840
India	6	10	10	10	6.0	7.6	9.3	11.4	1,330	2,270	2,270	2,270
Italy	2	(NA)	(NA)	(NA)	(NA)	(NA)	5.4	5.3	1,132	(NA)	(NA)	(NA)
Japan	40	50	53	53	191.9	286.0	317.8	326.9	31,645	41,356	45,248	45,248
Lithuania	(NA)	2	2	2	(NA)	9.6	12.2	13.5	(NA)	3,000	3,000	3,000
Mexico	1	2	2	2	2.1	7.9	9.5	9.5	675	1,350	1,350	1,350
Netherlands . . .	2	2	2	1	3.4	4.0	2.4	3.8	540	540	540	480
Pakistan	1	1	1	1	0.4	0.5	0.4	0.4	137	137	137	137
Romania.	(NA)	(NA)	1	1	(NA)	(NA)	4.6	5.3	(NA)	(NA)	706	706
Russia	(NA)	29	29	29	(NA)	98.7	108.0	103.7	(NA)	21,266	21,266	21,266
Slovakia	(NA)	(NA)	4	4	(NA)	(NA)	10.8	10.3	(NA)	(NA)	1,760	1,760
Slovenia	1	1	1	1	4.6	4.7	5.0	5.0	664	664	664	664
South Africa . . .	2	2	2	2	8.9	11.9	13.2	14.3	1,930	1,930	1,930	1,930
South Korea . . .	9	10	12	14	52.8	63.9	76.5	87.3	7,616	8,615	10,315	12,015
Spain.	10	9	9	9	54.3	55.4	55.3	59.1	7,984	7,400	7,572	7,625
Sweden	12	12	12	12	68.2	69.9	67.5	73.5	10,344	10,442	10,445	10,445
Switzerland	5	5	5	5	23.6	24.8	25.2	25.7	3,079	3,200	3,229	3,229
Taiwan [1]	6	6	6	6	32.9	35.3	36.2	36.9	5,146	5,144	5,144	5,144
Ukraine	(NA)	15	14	14	(NA)	70.5	79.1	74.2	(NA)	13,880	12,880	12,880

- Represents zero.   NA Not available.   [1] See footnote 2, Table 1349.

Source: McGraw-Hill, Inc., New York, NY, *Nucleonics Week,* March issues (copyright).

Comparative International Statistics   855

No. 1391. World Production of Major Mineral Commodities: 1990 to 1998

[5,353 represents 5,353,000,000]

Country	Unit	1990	1995	1997	1998 est.	Leading producers, 1997
MINERAL FUELS						
Coal.	Mil. short tons. .	5,353	5,134	5,218	(NA)	China, United States, India
Dry natural gas	Tril. cu. ft. . . .	73.6	77.9	81.7	(NA)	Russia, United States, Canada
Natural gas plant liquids [1] . . .	Mil. barrels [2]. . .	1,691	2,002	2,099	(NA)	United States, Saudi Arabia, Canada
Petroleum, crude	Mil. barrels [2]. . .	22,107	22,752	24,243	(NA)	Saudi Arabia, United States, Russia
NONMETALLIC MINERALS						
Cement, hydraulic	Mil. metric tons .	1,160	1,444	1,512	1,500	China, Japan, United States
Diamond, gem and industrial .	Mil. carats	111	113	118	(NA)	Australia, Russia, Congo (Kinshasa)
Nitrogen in ammonia.	Mil. metric tons .	97.5	96.1	101.0	101.0	China, United States, India
Phosphate rock	Mil. metric tons .	162	130	138	141	United States, Morocco, China
Potash, marketable.	Mil. metric tons .	27.5	24.7	25.7	24.9	Canada, Germany, Russia
Salt	Mil. metric tons .	183	192	201	200	United States, China, Germany
Sulfur, elemental basis	Mil. metric tons .	57.8	53.2	53.6	54.0	United States, Canada, China
METALS						
Aluminum [3]	Mil. metric tons .	19.3	19.9	21.4	22.2	United States, Russia, Canada
Bauxite, gross weight	Mil. metric tons .	113.0	107.0	123.0	125.0	Australia, Guinea, Brazil
Chromite, gross weight [1]	1,000 metric tons	13,200	14,300	12,500	12,600	South Africa, Turkey, India
Copper, metal content [4].	1,000 metric tons	8,950	10,100	11,400	11,900	Chile, United States, Canada
Gold, metal content [5].	Metric tons	2,180	2,220	2,410	2,400	South Africa, United States, Australia
Iron ore, gross weight [5]	Mil. metric tons .	983	1,030	1,040	1,020	China, Brazil, Australia
Lead, metal content [4]	1,000 metric tons	3,370	2,780	3,010	3,080	China, Australia, United States
Manganese ore, gross weight.	Mil. metric tons .	26.1	23.0	(NA)	(NA)	China, South Africa, Ukraine
Nickel, metal content [4]	1,000 metric tons	974	1,030	1,120	1,170	Russia, Canada, New Caledonia
Steel, crude	Mil. metric tons .	771	755	795	783	European Union, China, Japan
Tin, metal content [4]	1,000 metric tons	221	195	211	216	China, Indonesia, Peru
Zinc, metal content [4].	1,000 metric tons	7,150	7,240	7,460	7,800	China, Canada, Australia

NA Not available.   [1] Excludes China.   [2] 42-gallon barrels.   [3] Unalloyed ingot metal.   [4] Mine output.   [5] Includes iron ore concentrates and iron ore agglomerates.

Source: Mineral fuels, Energy Information Administration, *International Energy Annual*; nonmetallic minerals and metals, 1990, U.S. Bureau of Mines, thereafter, U.S. Geological Survey, *Minerals Yearbook; Annual Reports;* and *Mineral Commodity Summaries, 1998.*

No. 1392. Forest Area, Deforestation, and Production of Forest Products

[32,712 represents 32,712,000. Forest area is land under natural or planted stands of trees whether productive or not. Average annual deforestation refers to the permanent conversion of natural forest area to other uses, including shifting cultivation, permanent agriculture, ranching, settlements, and infrastructure development. Deforested areas do not include areas logged but intended for regeneration or areas degraded by fuelwood gathering, acid precipitation, or forest fires. Minus sign (-) indicates an increase in forest area]

Country	Forest area, 1995 (1,000 sq. km)	Average annual deforestation, 1990-95			Production, 1996 (mil. cubic meters)	
		Total (sq. km)	Percent change		Fuelwood, charcoal	Industrial roundwood
World, total.	32,712	101,724	0.3		1,865	1,490
Angola	222	2,370	1.0		6	1
Argentina	339	894	0.3		4	6
Australia	409	-170	-		3	20
Bolivia	483	5,814	1.2		1	1
Brazil	5,511	25,544	0.5		136	85
Burma	272	3,874	1.4		21	3
Canada	2,446	-1,764	-0.1		5	183
Central African Republic	299	1,282	0.4		3	1
China	1,333	866	0.1		204	109
Colombia	530	2,622	0.5		18	3
Congo (Kinshasa).	(NA)	(NA)	(NA)		45	3
Finland	200	166	0.1		4	43
India	650	-72	-		279	25
Indonesia	1,098	10,844	1.0		154	47
Japan	251	132	0.1		-	23
Mexico	554	5,080	0.9		17	6
Papua New Guinea	369	1,332	0.4		6	3
Peru	676	2,168	0.3		7	2
Russia	7,635	-			29	67
Sudan	416	3,526	0.8		15	2
Sweden	244	24	-		4	53
Tanzania.	325	3,226	1.0		36	2
United States . . . . [1]	2,125	-5,886	-0.3		89	407
Venezuela.	440	5,034	1.1		1	1
Zambia.	314	2,644	0.8		13	1

- Represents or rounds to zero.   NA Not available.

Source: Food and Agriculture Organization of the United Nations, Rome, Italy, *State of the World's Forests, 1999* (copyright).

No. 1393. Unmanufactured Tobacco and Cigarettes—Selected Countries: 1995 to 1998

[5,546 represents 5,546,000. Tobacco is on dry weight basis]

Country	Unmanufactured tobacco (1,000 metric tons)			Country	Cigarettes (bil. pieces)		
	1995	1997	1998		1995	1997	1998
PRODUCTION				**PRODUCTION**			
World, total	5,546	7,143	6,155	World, total	5,599	5,643	5,609
China	2,083	3,051	2,272	China	1,735	1,684	1,675
United States	513	729	627	United States	746	720	716
India	528	561	572	Japan	263	255	250
Brazil	324	485	371	Indonesia	186	225	214
Turkey	170	245	221	Russia	141	175	179
				Germany	221	182	178
EXPORTS				Brazil	174	183	178
World, total	1,767	2,042	1,927	United Kingdom	156	170	160
Brazil	256	319	280	Netherlands	101	116	116
United States	209	222	210				
Zimbabwe	174	160	178	**EXPORTS**			
Turkey	136	161	151	World, total	987	1,009	1,023
Malawi	99	111	111	United States	231	217	215
				United Kingdom	85	108	101
IMPORTS				Brazil	54	73	79
World, total	1,781	1,980	1,929	Singapore	50	70	67
United States	199	307	275	Germany	85	70	65
Germany	210	222	230	Hong Kong	74	46	46
Russia	148	185	178	China	63	40	45
United Kingdom	141	158	132				
Netherlands	89	105	108	**IMPORTS**			
				World, total	668	661	650
CONSUMPTION				Japan	72	73	73
World, total	6,305	6,210	6,107	Russia	78	59	56
China	2,209	2,126	2,101	Singapore	38	58	56
United States	699	674	665	France	51	53	54
India	464	477	478	Italy	39	42	42
Russia	142	175	179	Hong Kong	59	31	32
Japan	197	184	178	United Kingdom	20	26	28

Source: U.S. Dept. of Agriculture, Foreign Agricultural Service, *Tobacco: World Markets and Trade*, June 1999.

No. 1394. World Food Production, by Commodity: 1990 to 1998

[In millions of metric tons (1,768.8 represents 1,768,800,000)]

Commodity	1990	1992	1993	1994	1995	1996	1997	1998, prel.
Grains, total	1,768.8	1,790.0	1,714.0	1,760.8	1,712.6	1,870.1	1,876.8	1,843.2
Wheat	588.0	562.4	559.0	524.8	538.6	582.8	610.0	586.6
Coarse grains	828.7	872.0	799.7	871.6	802.7	907.1	880.9	878.7
Corn	482.3	538.5	476.1	560.2	516.6	591.2	574.0	593.7
Rice, milled	352.0	355.6	355.4	364.5	371.3	380.3	386.0	378.0
Oils	58.1	61.4	63.5	70.0	72.8	75.3	77.7	80.2
Soybeans	104.2	117.4	117.8	137.7	124.9	132.2	157.0	158.1
Rapeseed	25.1	25.3	26.8	30.4	34.5	31.6	33.3	36.9
Pulses [1]	58.4	51.0	55.7	56.3	54.8	54.4	55.8	56.8
Vegetables and melons [1]	461.4	478.6	509.5	532.1	559.6	589.9	596.3	599.4
Fruits [1]	352.2	379.0	384.7	391.0	406.4	425.5	432.9	431.2
Nuts [1]	4.6	5.0	5.3	5.3	5.0	5.0	5.6	5.4
Red meat	117.2	119.1	117.7	119.9	124.2	128.3	130.3	133.3
Poultry	37.4	41.8	43.6	46.8	50.6	53.6	55.1	55.8
Milk	441.3	423.7	393.5	383.7	380.8	379.7	381.4	383.8

[1] Data from Food and Agriculture Organization of the United Nations.

Source: U.S. Department of Agriculture, Economic Research Service, *Agricultural Outlook*, monthly.

No. 1395. Fisheries—Commercial Catch, by Country: 1990 to 1996

[In thousands of metric tons, live weight (97,854 represents 97,854,000). Catch of fish, crustaceans, mollusks (including weight of shells). Does not include marine mammals and aquatic plants]

Country	1990	1994	1995	1996	Country	1990	1994	1995	1996
World [1]	97,854	113,458	117,278	121,010	Korea, South	1,745	2,701	2,688	2,772
Canada	1,626	1,076	933	971	Mexico	1,401	1,267	1,359	1,499
Chile	5,195	7,839	7,591	6,911	Norway	1,745	2,551	2,803	2,963
China	12,095	23,834	28,418	31,937	Peru	6,875	12,005	8,943	9,522
Denmark	1,518	1,916	2,044	1,723	Philippines	2,210	2,233	2,221	2,133
Iceland	1,508	1,560	1,616	2,064	Russia	7,808	3,781	4,374	4,729
India	3,794	4,738	4,906	5,260	Spain	1,380	1,310	1,370	1,289
Indonesia	3,044	3,917	4,145	4,402	Thailand	2,786	3,522	3,756	3,648
Japan	10,354	7,398	6,787	6,793	**United States**	5,868	5,926	5,638	5,394
Korea, North (est.)	1,753	1,802	1,850	1,800	Vietnam	960	1,150	1,100	1,000

[1] Includes other countries, not shown separately.

Source: U.S. National Oceanic and Atmospheric Administration, National Marine Fisheries Service, *Fisheries of the United States*, annual. Data from Food and Agriculture Organization of the United Nations, Rome, Italy.

Comparative International Statistics 857

No. 1396. Meat Production, by Country: 1990 to 1998

[In thousands of metric tons, carcass weight (178,830 represents 178,830,000). Covers beef and veal (incl. buffalo meat), pork (incl. bacon and ham), mutton and lamb (incl. goat meat), horsemeat, and poultry. Refers to meat from animals slaughtered within the national boundaries irrespective of origin of animals, and relates to commercial and farm slaughter. Excludes lard, tallow, and edible offals. See text of this section for general comments concerning the data]

Country	1990	1995	1997	1998	Country	1990	1995	1997	1998
World [1]	178,830	202,551	211,641	215,537	Italy	3,948	3,983	4,069	4,069
Argentina	3,290	3,415	3,234	3,142	Japan	3,503	3,201	3,058	2,987
Brazil	7,709	10,082	11,403	11,700	Mexico	2,801	3,799	3,902	4,080
China	28,584	47,853	53,229	55,141	Russia	(X)	5,805	4,800	4,427
France	5,744	6,306	6,518	6,512	Spain	3,467	3,975	4,277	4,373
Germany	7,259	5,976	5,935	5,805	United Kingdom	3,319	3,823	3,646	3,798
India	3,830	4,392	4,553	4,569	United States	28,610	33,863	34,888	35,738

X Not applicable.   [1] Includes other countries, not shown separately.

Source: Food and Agriculture Organization of the United Nations, Rome, Italy, FAO AGRISTAT database.

No. 1397. Wheat, Rice, and Corn Production, by Country: 1995 to 1998

[In thousands of metric tons (582,774 represents 582,774,000). Rice data cover paddy. Data for each country pertain to the calendar year in which all or most of the crop was harvested. See text of this section for general comments concerning quality of the data]

Country	Wheat			Rice			Corn		
	1995	1997	1998	1995	1997	1998	1995	1997	1998
World	582,774	609,988	586,585	551,036	570,969	559,863	516,637	573,990	593,732
Argentina	8,600	14,800	10,750	877	1,011	1,354	11,100	19,360	14,500
Australia	16,504	19,417	21,000	951	1,336	1,350	317	340	310
Bangladesh	1,245	1,454	1,800	26,533	28,296	26,703	-	-	-
Brazil	1,526	2,400	2,200	10,026	8,529	10,956	32,480	30,860	32,500
Burma	150	150	150	17,000	15,346	16,034	270	250	250
Canada	25,037	24,280	24,400	-	-	-	7,271	7,180	8,900
China	102,215	123,300	110,000	185,214	200,700	190,000	112,000	104,300	124,000
Egypt	5,700	5,850	6,000	4,399	5,285	4,500	5,353	6,010	6,300
France	30,862	33,764	40,100	124	113	122	12,394	16,754	14,800
Germany	17,763	19,827	20,127	-	-	-	2,395	3,188	2,782
India	65,470	69,275	66,047	119,442	123,191	121,512	9,530	11,088	9,800
Indonesia	-	-	-	51,100	48,462	50,769	6,000	5,700	6,300
Italy	7,653	6,601	8,135	1,311	1,412	1,308	8,454	10,137	8,600
Mexico	3,468	3,500	3,300	349	469	480	17,780	17,000	17,500
Pakistan	17,002	16,650	18,700	5,951	6,500	6,976	1,283	1,251	1,300
Russia	30,100	44,200	26,900	462	331	331	1,700	2,700	800
Thailand	-	-	-	21,800	22,803	21,667	3,700	3,700	4,300
Turkey	15,500	16,000	18,000	346	346	354	1,800	2,100	2,200
Ukraine	16,273	18,400	14,900	80	65	77	3,392	5,300	2,000
United States	59,404	67,534	69,410	7,887	8,300	8,529	187,970	233,864	247,943

- Represents or rounds to zero.

No. 1398. Wheat, Rice, and Corn—Exports and Imports of Leading Countries: 1996 to 1998

[In thousands of metric tons (38,258 represents 38,258,000). Wheat data are for trade year beginning in July of year shown; rice data are for calendar year; corn data are for trade year beginning in October of year shown. Countries listed are the six leading exporters or importers in 1998]

Leading exporters	Exports			Leading importers	Imports		
	1996	1997	1998		1996	1997	1998
WHEAT				WHEAT			
European Union	38,258	36,033	34,105	European Union	22,904	25,781	20,810
United States	27,257	28,315	28,576	Egypt	6,897	7,156	7,200
Canada	19,501	20,134	14,500	Japan	6,264	6,200	6,200
Australia	19,225	15,343	14,000	Brazil	5,573	6,194	5,800
Argentina	10,198	10,666	6,500	Korea, South	3,465	3,917	4,400
Turkey	967	1,306	3,000	Algeria	3,628	5,191	4,000
RICE				RICE			
Thailand	5,256	6,367	5,500	Bangladesh	46	1,100	2,650
Vietnam	3,268	3,776	3,500	Indonesia	808	6,081	2,500
India	2,105	3,300	2,850	Philippines	682	1,288	1,850
United States	2,495	2,784	2,743	European Union	1,570	1,552	1,490
Pakistan	1,834	2,299	2,000	Brazil	849	1,400	850
China	938	3,732	1,500	Nigeria	350	731	800
CORN				CORN			
United States	45,597	38,214	45,722	Japan	15,963	16,422	16,000
Argentina	10,828	12,500	9,000	European Union	10,172	10,223	10,630
European Union	8,055	8,912	8,614	Korea, South	8,336	7,528	7,000
China	3,892	6,173	4,000	Mexico	3,141	4,376	4,750
Hungary	828	1,235	1,200	Taiwan	5,741	4,472	4,500
Former Yugoslavia	750	500	500	Egypt	3,179	3,141	3,250

Source of Tables 1397 and 1398: U.S. Department of Agriculture, Economic Research Service, unpublished data from the PS&D (Production, supply and distribution) database.

No. 1399. United States and Foreign Stock Markets—Market Capitalization and Value of Shares Traded: 1990 to 1998

[In billions of U.S. dollars (3,059.4 represents $3,059,400,000,000). Market capitalization is the market value of all domestic listed companies at the end of the year. The market value of a company is the share price times the number of shares outstanding. Value of shares traded is the annual total turnover of listed company shares]

Country	Market capitalization				Value of shares traded			
	1990	1995	1997	1998	1990	1995	1997	1998
United States	3,059.4	6,857.6	11,308.8	(NA)	1,751.3	5,108.6	10,216.1	(NA)
Argentina	3.3	37.8	59.3	45.3	0.9	4.6	25.7	15.1
Australia	107.6	245.2	696.7	(NA)	39.3	98.7	310.9	(NA)
Austria	11.5	32.5	35.7	(NA)	18.6	25.8	24.6	(NA)
Belgium	65.4	105.0	137.0	(NA)	6.4	15.2	29.7	(NA)
Brazil	16.4	147.6	255.5	160.9	5.6	79.2	203.3	146.7
Canada	241.9	366.3	567.6	(NA)	71.3	183.7	355.6	(NA)
Chile	13.6	73.9	72.0	51.9	0.8	11.1	7.4	4.4
China	(NA)	42.1	206.4	231.3	(NA)	49.8	369.6	284.8
Denmark	39.1	56.2	93.8	(NA)	11.1	25.9	46.9	(NA)
Finland	22.7	44.1	73.3	(NA)	3.9	19.0	36.4	(NA)
France	314.4	522.1	674.4	(NA)	116.9	364.6	405.5	(NA)
Germany	355.1	577.4	825.2	(NA)	501.8	573.5	1,029.2	(NA)
Greece	15.2	17.1	34.2	80.0	3.9	6.1	21.1	46.8
Hong Kong	83.4	303.7	413.3	(NA)	34.6	106.9	489.4	(NA)
India	38.6	127.2	128.5	105.2	21.9	13.7	54.0	64.3
Indonesia	8.1	66.6	29.1	21.2	4.0	14.4	41.7	10.6
Ireland	(NA)	25.8	24.1	(NA)	(NA)	13.2	15.2	(NA)
Israel	3.3	36.4	45.3	39.6	5.5	9.2	10.7	11.3
Italy	148.8	209.5	344.7	(NA)	42.6	86.9	198.2	(NA)
Japan	2,917.7	3,667.3	2,216.7	(NA)	1,602.4	1,231.6	1,251.8	(NA)
Korea, South	110.6	182.0	41.9	114.6	75.9	185.2	170.2	144.4
Kuwait	(NA)	14.4	25.9	(NA)	(NA)	6.4	34.6	(NA)
Luxembourg	10.5	30.4	33.9	(NA)	0.1	0.2	0.6	(NA)
Malaysia	48.6	222.7	93.6	107.1	10.9	76.8	147.0	29.6
Mexico	32.7	90.7	156.6	91.7	12.2	34.4	52.6	34.2
Netherlands	119.8	356.5	468.7	(NA)	40.2	248.6	284.9	(NA)
New Zealand	8.8	32.0	90.5	(NA)	1.9	8.4	24.6	(NA)
Norway	26.1	44.6	66.5	(NA)	14.0	24.4	46.4	(NA)
Philippines	5.9	58.9	31.4	35.3	1.2	14.7	19.8	10.1
Portugal	9.2	18.4	39.0	63.0	1.7	4.2	20.9	47.5
Russia	(NA)	15.9	128.2	20.6	(NA)	0.5	16.4	10.5
Saudi Arabia	(NA)	40.9	59.4	42.6	(NA)	6.2	16.5	13.7
Singapore	34.3	148.0	106.3	(NA)	20.3	60.5	64.0	(NA)
South Africa	137.5	280.5	232.1	170.3	8.2	17.0	44.9	58.3
Spain	111.4	197.8	290.4	(NA)	41.0	59.8	453.0	(NA)
Sweden	97.9	178.0	272.7	(NA)	17.6	93.2	176.2	(NA)
Switzerland	160.0	433.6	575.3	(NA)	(NA)	310.9	494.9	(NA)
Taiwan	100.7	187.2	287.8	260.0	715.0	383.1	1,297.5	890.5
Turkey	19.1	20.8	61.1	33.6	5.8	51.4	59.1	68.5
United Kingdom	848.9	1,407.7	1,996.2	(NA)	278.7	510.1	829.1	(NA)

NA Not available.

Source: International Finance Corporation, Washington, DC, *Emerging Stock Markets Factbook*, annual, (copyright).

No. 1400. Dow Jones World Stock Index, by Country and Industry: 1995 to 1998

[Index figures shown are as of **December 31. Indexes based on June 30, 1982=100 for United States; December 31, 1991=100 for World**. Based on share prices denominated in U.S. dollars. Stocks in countries that impose significant restrictions on foreign ownership are included in the world index in the same proportion that shares are available to foreign investors]

Industry	1995	1996	1997	1998	Industry	1995	1996	1997	1998
World, total	133.46	147.57	166.63	202.79	Asia/Pacific	119.80	108.93	77.93	81.03
Americas	143.61	173.40	227.09	283.79	Australia	127.90	148.78	156.23	175.03
United States	581.43	700.56	922.35	1,169.34	Hong Kong	223.67	299.50	223.42	203.23
Canada	108.25	135.41	190.22	194.30	Indonesia	172.48	187.42	145.78	158.89
Mexico	77.96	94.31	375.72	287.32	Japan	114.08	95.63	73.63	67.70
Europe	136.54	162.41	191.64	234.99	Malaysia	223.08	265.49	114.64	109.14
Austria	101.29	110.00	126.68	115.72	New Zealand	176.17	203.35	155.58	132.41
Belgium	142.56	158.64	210.25	317.82	Singapore	195.91	199.84	127.74	111.33
Denmark	112.42	137.26	213.02	204.94	Thailand	196.76	126.66	59.94	61.45
Finland	202.88	280.72	411.28	743.15					
France	120.03	142.38	182.44	239.58	Basic materials	130.91	136.62	119.65	112.04
Germany	138.24	161.41	232.98	273.36	Conglomerate	146.57	171.32	169.13	195.49
Ireland	152.83	196.04	274.91	377.12	Consumer, cyclical	135.13	148.64	160.15	200.47
Italy	103.51	113.62	223.02	313.21	Consumer, noncyclical . .	130.19	152.04	188.21	242.92
Netherlands	167.30	207.58	316.06	381.19	Energy	132.32	163.27	188.61	181.99
Norway	129.21	159.87	209.76	147.04	Financial services	134.62	142.64	168.20	186.70
Spain	114.31	149.44	286.63	393.72	Industrial	118.38	122.31	117.79	128.77
Sweden	163.14	213.88	341.28	371.21	Technology . . . :	168.07	197.94	242.59	370.31
Switzerland	232.62	236.03	352.50	401.54	Utilities	118.44	123.90	152.77	212.87
United Kingdom	124.49	152.02	198.16	223.11					

Source: Dow Jones & Company, Inc., New York, NY, *Wall Street Journal*, selected issues (copyright).

Comparative International Statistics 859

No. 1401. Foreign Stock Market Activity—Morgan Stanley Capital International Indexes: 1995 to 1998

[Index figures shown are as of **December 31. January 1, 1970=100, except as noted**. Based on share prices denominated in U.S. dollars. EMG=Emerging Markets Global. GDP=Gross Domestic Product]

Index and country	Index			Percent change [1]		Index and country	Index			Percent change [1]	
	1995	1997	1998	1997	1998		1995	1997	1998	1997	1998
DEVELOPED MARKETS						Switzerland	1,569	2,274	2,788	43.2	22.6
						United Kingdom	716	1,052	1,208	19.1	14.8
World index [2]	734	937	1,150	14.2	22.8	Hong Kong	4,818	4,609	4,259	-25.8	-7.6
EAFE index [3]	1,136	1,188	1,405	0.2	18.2	Japan	3,348	2,133	2,224	-24.2	4.3
Europe index.	733	1,057	1,337	21.6	26.5	Singapore	2,735	1,733	1,480	-31.1	-14.6
Pacific index	2,362	1,576	1,595	-26.3	1.2						
Far East index.	3,384	2,188	2,215	-27.4	1.2	EMERGING MARKETS					
						EMG Far East index .	263.7	135.5	128.4	-50.4	-5.3
GDP-weighted indexes:						India [5]	98.8	104.2	80.4	9.6	-22.9
World index	874	1,104	1,387	13.4	25.6	Indonesia	508.2	163.0	110.2	-72.4	-32.4
EAFE index [3]	1,205	1,334	1,669	4.4	25.1	Korea, South.	173.8	35.1	(NA)	-67.3	(NA)
						Malaysia	347.0	135.0	93.1	-68.8	-31.0
United States	581	929	1,196	31.7	28.8	Pakistan [5]	91.5	91.6	36.1	24.2	-60.6
Canada	403.9	567.5	525.3	11.2	-7.4	Philippines	442.5	199.8	229.6	-60.8	14.9
						Sri Lanka [5]	105.6	98.6	71.7	11.5	-27.3
Australia	304.2	301.7	313.2	-12.6	3.8	Taiwan	227.9	294.8	231.5	-6.9	-21.5
New Zealand [4].	114.2	107.9	80.7	-16.7	-25.2	Thailand	523.3	72.9	86.6	-77.5	18.7
Austria	890	922	914	0.3	-0.9						
Belgium	897	1,081	1,782	10.8	64.8	EMG Latin America . .	782	1,192	737	28.4	-38.2
Denmark.	1,124	1,794	1,934	33.0	7.8	Argentina	1,239	1,764	1,282	21.9	-27.3
Finland [4].	128.8	196.8	431.1	16.0	119.1	Brazil	578	984	551	23.4	-44.1
France	672	887	1,242	10.6	40.0	Chile	903	770	534	2.0	-30.7
Germany	818	1,131	1,449	23.3	28.2	Colombia [5]	110.2	162.0	88.6	37.8	-45.3
Ireland [4]	215.7	314.8	418.6	13.3	33.0	Mexico	744	1,304	846	50.9	-35.1
Italy	208.6	309.0	466.5	33.6	51.0	Peru [5]	221.3	253.3	146.6	17.7	-42.1
Netherlands	1,192	1,805	2,187	21.6	21.1	Venezuela.	75.4	218.8	103.5	27.4	-52.7
Norway.	1,023	1,358	934	4.8	-31.2						
Portugal [4]	68.4	130.2	163.2	43.9	25.4	Greece [4].	238.2	320.5	560.9	32.7	75.0
Spain	162.3	272.6	403.1	23.1	47.9	Jordan	96.1	83.7	71.7	-1.8	-14.3
Sweden	1,796	2,713	3,056	11.6	12.6	Turkey	103.1	287.5	133.6	111.4	-53.5

NA Not available.   [1] Percent change during calendar year (e.g. December 31, 1996, through December 31, 1997). Adjusted for foreign exchange fluctuations relative to U.S. dollar.   [2] Includes South African gold mines quoted in London.   [3] Europe, Australian, Far East Index. Comprises all European and Far East countries listed under developed markets plus Australia, Malaysia, and New Zealand.   [4] January 1, 1988=100.   [5] December 1992=100.

Source: Morgan Stanley Capital International, New York, NY, unpublished data (copyright). This information may not be reproduced or redisseminated in any form without prior written permission from Morgan Stanley Capital International. This information is provided on an "as is" basis. Neither Morgan Stanley or any other party makes any representation or warranty of any kind either express or implied, with respect to this information (or the results to be obtained by the use thereof) and Morgan Stanley expressly disclaims any and all warranties of originality, accuracy, completeness, merchantability, and fitness for any particular purpose. The user of this information assumes the entire risk of any use made of the information. In no event shall Morgan Stanley or any other part be liable to the user for any direct or indirect damages, including without limitation, any lost profits, lost savings, or other incidental or consequential damages arising out of use of this information.

No. 1402. Foreign Stock Market Indices: 1980 to 1998

[**As of year end**. The DAX index is a total return index which includes dividends, whereas the other foreign indices are price indices which exclude dividends]

Year	London FTSE 100	Tokyo Nikkei 225	Hong Kong Hang Seng	Germany DAX-30	Paris CAC-40
1980	647	7,116	1,477	481	(X)
1985	1,413	13,113	1,752	1,366	(X)
1990	2,144	23,849	3,025	1,398	1,518
1992	2,847	16,925	5,512	1,545	1,858
1993	3,418	17,417	11,888	2,267	2,268
1994	3,066	19,723	8,191	2,107	1,881
1995	3,689	19,868	10,073	2,254	1,872
1996	4,119	19,361	13,452	2,889	2,316
1997	5,136	15,259	10,723	4,250	2,999
1998	5,883	13,842	9,507	5,002	3,943

X Not applicable.

Source: Global Financial Data, Alhambra, CA (http://www.globalfindata.com), unpublished data. (Copyright.)

No. 1403. Foreign Exchange Rates: 1998

[Foreign currency units per U.S. dollar; end-of-year values were used if annual averages were unavailable. Rates shown include market, official, principal, and secondary rates, as published by the International Monetary Fund in *International Financial Statistics*]

Country	Currency	1998	Country	Currency	1998
Afghanistan	Afghanis	3,000	Laos	Kip	3,298
Albania	Leks	150.6	Latvia	Lats	0.590
Algeria	Algerian Dinar	58.74	Lebanon	Lebanese Pounds	1,516
Antigua and Barbuda	E.Caribbean Dollar	2.700	Lesotho	Loti	5.528
Argentina	Pesos	1.000	Liberia	Liberian Dollar	1.000
Armenia	Dram	504.9	Libya [1]	Libyan Dinars	0.389
Aruba	Aruban Florins	1.790	Lithuania	Litai	4.000
Australia	Australian Dollar	1.592	Luxembourg	Francs	36.30
Austria	Schillings	12.38	Macedonia, The Former		
Bahamas, The	Bahamian Dollar	1.000	Yugoslav Republic of	Denar	54.46
Bahrain	Dinars	0.376	Madagascar	Malagasy Francs	5,441
Bangladesh	Taka	46.91	Malaysia	Ringgit	3.924
Barbados	Barbados Dollar	2.000	Maldives	Rufiyaa	11.77
Belarus [1]	Rubel	46,069	Mali	Cfa Francs	591.2
Belgium	Francs	36.30	Malta	Maltese Liri	0.389
Belize	Belize Dollar	2.000	Mauritania [1]	Ouguiyas	174.0
Benin	Cfa Francs	590.0	Mauritius	Rupees	22.80
Bhutan	Ngultrum	41.26	Mexico	New Pesos	9.136
Botswana	Pula	4.226	Moldova	Lei	5.371
Brazil	Reais	1.161	Mongolia	Tugriks	840.8
Bulgaria	Leva	1,760	Morocco	Dirhams	9.604
Burkina Faso	Cfa Francs	590.0	Mozambique	Meticais	11,875
Burma	Kyats	6.343	Namibia	Namibia Dollar	5.528
Cambodia	Riels	3,744	Nepal	Rupees	65.98
Cameroon	Cfa Francs	590.0	Netherlands	Guilders	1.984
Canada	Canadian Dollar	1.484	Netherlands Antilles	Guilders	1.790
Cape Verde	Escudos	98.16	New Zealand	New Zealand Dollar	1.868
Central African Republic	Cfa Francs	590.0	Nicaragua	Cordobas	10.58
Chad	Cfa Francs	590.0	Niger	Cfa Francs	590.0
Chile	Pesos	460.3	Norway	Kroner	7.545
China	Yuan	8.279	Oman	Rials Omani	0.385
Comoros	Comorian Francs	442.5	Pakistan	Rupees	45.01
Congo (Brazzaville)	Cfa Francs	590.0	Panama	Balboas	1.000
Costa Rica	Colones	257.2	Papua New Guinea	Kina	2.074
Cote d'Ivoire	Cfa Francs	590.0	Paraguay	Guaranies	2,756
Croatia	Kuna	6.362	Philippines	Pesos	40.89
Cyprus	Cyprus Pounds	0.518	Poland	Zlotys	3.475
Czech Republic	Koruny	32.29	Portugal	Escudos	180.1
Denmark	Kroner	6.701	Qatar	Riyals	3.640
Djibouti	Djibouti Francs	177.7	Russia	Rubles	9.705
Dominica	E.Caribbean Dollar	2.700	Rwanda	Rwanda Francs	312.3
Dominican Republic	Pesos	15.27	Saint Kitts and Nevis	E.Caribbean Dollar	2.700
Ecuador	Sucres	5,447	Saint Lucia	E.Caribbean Dollar	2.700
Egypt	Egyptian Pounds	3.388	Saint Vincent and the		
El Salvador	Colones	8.755	Grenadines	E.Caribbean Dollar	2.700
Equatorial Guinea	Cfa Francs	590.0	Saudi Arabia	Riyals	3.745
Estonia	Krooni	14.07	Senegal	Cfa Francs	590.0
Ethiopia	Birr	7.116	Seychelles	Rupees	5.262
Fiji	Fiji Dollar	1.987	Sierra Leone	Leones	1,564
Finland	Markkaa	5.344	Singapore	Singapore Dollar	1.674
France	Francs	5.900	Slovakia	Koruny	35.23
Gabon	Cfa Francs	590.0	Slovenia	Tolars	166.1
Georgia	Lari	1.390	Solomon Islands	Solomon Isl Dollar	4.816
Germany	Deutsche Mark	1.760	South Africa	Rand	5.528
Greece	Drachmas	295.5	Spain	Pesetas	149.4
Grenada	E.Caribbean Dollar	2.700	Sri Lanka	Rupees	64.59
Guatemala	Quetzales	6.395	Suriname	Guilders	401.0
Guyana	Guyana Dollar	150.5	Swaziland	Langeni	5.528
Haiti	Gourdes	16.77	Sweden	Kronor	7.950
Honduras	Lempiras	13.39	Switzerland	Swiss Francs	1.450
Hong Kong	Hong Kong Dollar	7.745	Syria [1]	Syrian Pounds	11.23
Hungary	Forint	214.4	Tanzania	Tanzania Shilling	664.7
Iceland	Kronur	70.96	Thailand	Baht	41.36
India	Rupees	41.26	Togo	Cfa Francs	590.0
Indonesia	Rupiah	10,014	Tonga	Pa'Anga	1.492
Iran	Rials	1,752	Trinidad and Tobago	Tt Dollars	6.298
Iraq	Dinars	0.311	Tunisia	Dinars	1.139
Ireland	Irish Pounds	0.702	Turkey	Liras	260,724
Israel	New Sheqalim	3.800	Uganda	Uganda Shilling	1,240
Italy	Lire	1,736	Ukraine	Hryvnias	2.450
Jamaica	Jamaica Dollars	36.55	United Arab Emirates	Dirhams	3.673
Japan	Yen	130.9	United Kingdom	Pounds Sterling	0.604
Jordan	Dinars	0.709	Uruguay	Pesos	10.47
Kazakhstan	Tenge	78.30	Vanuatu	Vatu	127.5
Kenya	Kenya Shillings	60.37	Venezuela	Venezuela	547.6
Korea, South	Won	1,401	Yemen	Rials	135.9
Kuwait	Dinars	0.305	Zambia	Kwacha	1,862
Kyrgyzstan	Soms	20.84	Zimbabwe	Zimbabwe Dollar	23.68

[1] Based on two or three quarters of data.

Source: U.S. Dept. of Commerce, International Trade Administration, "Foreign Exchange Rates, 1992-98"; published 18 August 1999; <http://www.ita.doc.gov/industry/otea/usfth/aggregate/HI98t37.txt>.

Comparative International Statistics   861

No. 1404. Reserve Assets and International Transaction Balances, by Country: 1995 to 1998

[In millions of U.S. dollars (74,780 represents $74,780,000,000). Assets include holdings of convertible foreign currencies, special drawing rights, and reserve position in International Monetary Fund and exclude gold holdings. Minus sign (-) indicates debits]

Country	Total reserve assets				Current account balance			Merchandise trade balance		
			1998							
	1995	1997	Total	Currency holdings[1]	1995	1997	1998	1995	1997	1998
United States	74,780	58,910	70,710	36,000	-115,220	-155,380	-233,760	-171,880	-196,010	-246,030
Algeria	2,005	8,047	6,846	6,844	(NA)	(NA)	(NA)	(NA)	(NA)	(NA)
Argentina	14,288	22,320	24,752	24,488	-2,768	-9,429	(NA)	2,358	-2,287	(NA)
Australia	11,896	16,845	15,407	14,133	-19,654	-12,591	-17,932	-4,223	1,849	-5,429
Austria	18,730	19,736	22,432	20,918	-5,448	-4,996	(NA)	-6,656	-4,274	(NA)
Bangladesh.......	2,340	1,582	1,905	1,892	-824	-327	(NA)	-2,324	-1,748	(NA)
Belgium	16,177	16,190	18,272	15,763	14,248	13,939	12,111	9,555	7,800	7,561
Brazil	49,708	50,827	42,580	42,578	-18,136	-33,840	(NA)	-3,157	-8,364	(NA)
Burma	561	250	315	315	(NA)	(NA)	(NA)	(NA)	(NA)	(NA)
Cameroon........	4	1	1	1	90	(NA)	(NA)	627	(NA)	(NA)
Canada	15,049	17,823	23,308	19,911	-4,328	-10,304	-11,213	25,855	17,135	12,625
Chile	14,140	17,306	15,663	15,049	-1,398	-4,057	-4,552	1,369	-1,295	-2,494
China...........	75,377	142,762	149,188	144,959	1,618	29,718	(NA)	18,050	46,222	(NA)
Colombia	8,102	9,507	8,294	7,523	-4,365	-5,682	(NA)	-2,699	-2,728	(NA)
Congo (Kinshasa)[2] .	59	60	1	(Z)	-650	-252	(NA)	516	941	(NA)
Cote d'Ivoire	529	618	856	855	-493	35	(NA)	1,376	1,806	(NA)
Denmark........	11,016	19,124	15,264	13,753	1,855	883	(NA)	6,528	5,553	(NA)
Ecuador	1,628	2,093	1,620	1,595	-735	-743	(NA)	354	598	(NA)
Egypt..........	16,181	18,665	18,124	17,888	-254	-711	(NA)	-7,597	-8,632	(NA)
Finland.........	10,038	8,417	9,695	8,508	5,202	6,664	7,324	12,346	11,460	12,304
France	26,853	30,927	44,312	38,753	10,840	39,470	40,160	11,000	28,070	26,170
Germany	85,005	77,587	74,024	64,133	-22,560	-2,770	-5,870	65,110	71,750	83,180
Ghana	698	(NA)	377	293	-145	-541	(NA)	-257	-638	(NA)
Greece	14,780	12,595	17,458	17,188	-2,864	-4,860	(NA)	-2,433	-1,732	(NA)
Hungary	11,974	8,408	9,319	9,239	-2,535	-982	-2,304	-2,123		-2,123
India	17,922	24,688	27,341	26,598	-5,563	-3,532	-7,147	-6,719	-10,349	-10,973
Indonesia	13,708	16,587	22,713	22,401	-6,431	-4,890	1,503	6,533	10,074	(NA)
Ireland	8,630	6,526	9,397	8,622	1,721	1,984	1,503	13,557	18,646	24,142
Israel..........	8,119	20,332	22,674	22,674	-6,205	-5,014	(NA)	-7,597	-5,848	(NA)
Italy...........	34,905	55,739	29,888	25,447	25,076	32,403	19,998	38,729	39,878	35,631
Japan	183,250	219,648	215,471	203,215	111,040	94,350	120,700	131,790	101,600	122,390
Kenya	353	788	783	765	-480	-454	(NA)	-738	-883	(NA)
Korea, South......	32,678	20,368	51,975	51,963	-8,507	-8,167	(NA)	-4,444	-3,179	(NA)
Kuwait	3,561	3,452	3,947	3,486	5,016	7,935	2,940	5,579	6,534	2,254
Malaysia........	23,774	20,788	25,559	24,728	-8,469	-4,792	(NA)	-103	3,876	(NA)
Mexico.........	16,847	28,797	31,799	31,461	-1,576	-7,454	-15,786	7,089	623	-7,743
Morocco.........	3,601	3,993	4,435	4,389	-1,186	-87	(NA)	-2,482	-1,864	(NA)
Nepal..........	586	626	756	748	-356	-418	(NA)	-961	-1,308	(NA)
Netherlands	33,714	24,865	21,418	17,536	23,983	21,985	(NA)	22,102	17,883	(NA)
Nigeria	1,443	(NA)	(NA)	(NA)	-2,578	552	(NA)	3,513	5,706	(NA)
Norway.........	22,518	23,400	18,607	16,927	4,854	8,017	-2,161	8,571	11,152	1,566
Pakistan........	1,733	1,195	1,028	1,027	-3,338	-1,754	(NA)	-2,882	-2,392	(NA)
Peru	8,222	10,982	9,566	9,563	-4,314	-3,407	(NA)	-2,168	-1,739	(NA)
Philippines	6,372	7,266	9,226	9,101	-1,980	-4,351	1,287	-8,944	-11,127	-28
Poland	14,774	20,407	26,432	26,317	854	-5,744	(NA)	-1,646	-9,822	(NA)
Portugal........	15,850	15,660	15,825	15,067	-144	-1,877	(NA)	-8,910	-9,551	(NA)
Romania........	1,579	3,803	2,867	2,866	-1,780	-2,348	(NA)	-1,577	-1,980	(NA)
Saudi Arabia	8,622	7,353	7,520	6,014	-5,325	257	(NA)	24,390	34,362	(NA)
Singapore.......	68,695	71,289	74,928	74,418	14,361	14,803	(NA)	977	1,145	(NA)
South Africa	2,820	4,799	4,357	4,171	-2,756	-1,931	(NA)	1,715	1,992	(NA)
Spain..........	34,485	68,398	55,258	52,490	513	2,486	-1,606	-18,244	-13,347	-18,707
Sri Lanka	2,088	2,024	1,980	1,950	-770	-388	(NA)	-985	-629	(NA)
Sudan	163	82	91	91	-500	-828	-957	-510	-828	-1,137
Sweden	24,051	10,824	14,098	12,420	4,940	7,301	4,783	15,978	17,921	17,976
Switzerland	36,413	39,028	41,191	38,346	21,779	23,714	(NA)	3,223	2,414	(NA)
Syria	(NA)	(NA)	(NA)	(NA)	367	564	(NA)	-143	454	(NA)
Thailand........	35,982	26,179	28,825	28,434	-13,554	-3,024	14,230	-7,968	1,551	16,234
Trinidad and Tobago .	358	706	783	783	294	(NA)	(NA)	588	(NA)	(NA)
Turkey	12,442	18,658	19,489	19,442	-2,338	-2,679	(NA)	-13,212	-15,398	(NA)
United Kingdom....	42,020	32,320	32,210	27,360	-5,970	10,030	2,480	-18,530	-19,490	-34,120
Venezuela.......	6,283	14,378	11,920	11,612	2,014	4,684	(NA)	7,013	10,773	(NA)

NA Not available.   Z Less than $500,000.   [1] Holdings of convertible foreign currencies.   [2] See footnote 3, Table 1349.

Source: International Monetary Fund, Washington, DC, *International Financial Statistics,* monthly, (copyright).

U.S. Census Bureau, Statistical Abstract of the United States: 1999

No. 1405. Foreign Trade—Destination of Exports and Source of Imports for Selected Countries

[In billions of dollars (166.7 represents $166,700,000,000), except as indicated. All exports are f.o.b. (free on board) and all imports are c.i.f. (cost, insurance, freight)]

Country	Year	World¹	Canada	France	Germany	Hong Kong	Italy	Japan	Netherlands	United Kingdom	United States
EXPORTS											
Belgium-Luxembourg	1997	166.7	0.5	26.9	30.9	1.4	8.5	1.7	20.2	16.5	8.1
Canada	1997	202.8	(X)	1.2	1.9	1.2	1.1	8.0	1.2	2.6	165.5
China	1997	182.8	1.9	2.3	6.5	43.8	2.2	31.8	4.4	3.8	32.7
France	1997	283.7	2.4	(X)	45.0	2.9	26.3	4.9	13.3	28.7	18.5
Germany	1997	502.4	3.8	52.1	(X)	4.4	36.4	11.1	33.1	41.6	42.4
Hong Kong	1997	188.2	2.8	3.0	7.3	(X)	1.9	11.4	3.2	6.4	40.9
Italy	1997	238.0	1.9	29.0	38.9	4.0	(X)	4.7	6.8	16.9	18.9
Japan	1997	421.0	6.1	5.6	18.0	27.3	3.8	(X)	9.8	13.7	117.1
Korea, South	1996	124.5	1.2	1.2	4.7	11.1	0.9	15.8	1.7	3.2	16.6
Netherlands	1996	161.5	0.5	17.4	46.0	1.0	9.2	1.8	(X)	15.0	5.7
Spain	1996	102.6	0.4	20.6	15.0	0.6	9.0	1.2	3.5	8.5	4.3
Taiwan	1996	117.3	1.4	1.3	3.7	27.2	1.1	13.8	3.9	2.8	27.2
United Kingdom	1997	268.4	3.2	22.8	29.7	4.8	11.3	6.7	20.7	(X)	32.0
United States	1996	582.1	119.1	13.5	22.2	12.3	8.3	63.6	15.5	28.7	(X)
PERCENT DISTRIBUTION											
Belgium-Luxembourg	1997	100.0	0.3	16.2	18.6	0.8	5.1	1.0	12.1	9.9	4.9
Canada	1997	100.0	(X)	0.6	0.9	0.6	0.5	3.9	0.6	1.3	81.6
China	1997	100.0	1.0	1.3	3.6	24.0	1.2	17.4	2.4	2.1	17.9
France	1997	100.0	0.8	(X)	15.9	1.0	9.3	1.7	4.7	10.1	6.5
Germany	1997	100.0	0.7	10.4	(X)	0.9	7.2	2.2	6.6	8.3	8.4
Hong Kong	1997	100.0	1.5	1.6	3.9	(X)	1.0	6.1	1.7	3.4	21.7
Italy	1997	100.0	0.8	12.2	16.4	1.7	(X)	2.0	2.8	7.1	7.9
Japan	1997	100.0	1.4	1.3	4.3	6.5	0.9	(X)	2.3	3.3	27.8
Korea, South	1996	100.0	1.0	1.0	3.8	8.9	0.7	12.7	1.4	2.6	13.3
Netherlands	1996	100.0	0.3	10.8	28.5	0.6	5.7	1.1	(X)	9.3	3.5
Spain	1996	100.0	0.4	20.1	14.6	0.6	8.7	1.2	3.4	8.3	4.2
Taiwan	1996	100.0	1.2	1.1	3.1	23.2	0.9	11.8	3.3	2.4	23.2
United Kingdom	1997	100.0	1.2	8.5	11.1	1.8	4.2	2.5	7.7	(X)	11.9
United States	1996	100.0	20.5	2.3	3.8	2.1	1.4	10.9	2.7	4.9	(X)
IMPORTS											
Belgium-Luxembourg	1997	153.2	0.9	21.5	28.5	0.4	6.0	3.6	27.3	13.9	11.6
Canada	1997	193.2	(X)	3.7	3.9	0.9	2.2	9.0	0.8	4.7	132.8
China	1997	142.4	2.0	3.2	6.2	7.0	2.5	29.0	1.1	2.0	16.3
France	1997	270.5	1.8	(X)	45.3	0.7	26.7	9.2	13.7	22.8	24.0
Germany	1997	428.4	2.8	44.7	(X)	2.1	32.9	19.9	33.3	29.5	32.3
Hong Kong	1997	213.3	1.6	2.9	5.0	(X)	4.0	28.7	1.9	5.6	16.4
Italy	1997	208.1	1.7	27.4	37.4	0.2	(X)	4.2	12.8	13.9	10.4
Japan	1997	338.8	9.8	5.8	12.4	2.3	5.9	(X)	2.0	7.2	75.7
Korea, South	1996	144.1	2.7	2.2	7.2	1.1	3.1	31.4	1.2	3.0	30.9
Netherlands	1996	158.1	0.9	11.1	33.3	2.1	5.5	6.0	(X)	15.2	13.4
Spain	1996	121.6	0.5	21.7	18.1	0.2	11.7	3.4	4.8	10.1	7.7
Taiwan	1996	103.0	1.4	4.1	5.0	1.8	1.6	27.6	1.5	1.8	20.1
United Kingdom	1997	290.3	3.5	25.5	37.2	2.4	13.9	14.8	17.9	(X)	35.4
United States	1996	817.6	159.7	19.2	40.0	10.3	19.0	118.0	7.0	29.7	(X)
PERCENT DISTRIBUTION											
Belgium-Luxembourg	1997	100.0	0.6	14.1	18.6	0.3	3.9	2.4	17.8	9.1	7.5
Canada	1997	100.0	(X)	1.9	2.0	0.5	1.1	4.7	0.4	2.4	68.7
China	1997	100.0	1.4	2.3	4.3	4.9	1.7	20.4	0.8	1.4	11.4
France	1997	100.0	0.6	(X)	16.7	0.3	9.9	3.4	5.1	8.4	8.9
Germany	1997	100.0	0.7	10.4	(X)	0.5	7.7	4.7	7.8	6.9	7.5
Hong Kong	1997	100.0	0.7	1.3	2.3	(X)	1.9	13.5	0.9	2.6	7.7
Italy	1997	100.0	0.8	13.2	18.0	0.1	(X)	2.0	6.2	6.7	5.0
Japan	1997	100.0	2.9	1.7	3.7	0.7	1.7	(X)	0.6	2.1	22.3
Korea, South	1996	100.0	1.9	1.5	5.0	0.8	2.1	21.8	0.8	2.1	21.4
Netherlands	1996	100.0	0.6	7.0	21.1	1.4	3.5	3.8	(X)	9.6	8.5
Spain	1996	100.0	0.5	17.8	14.9	0.1	9.6	2.8	4.0	8.3	6.3
Taiwan	1996	100.0	1.3	4.0	4.9	1.8	1.5	26.8	1.4	1.8	19.6
United Kingdom	1997	100.0	1.2	8.8	12.8	0.8	4.8	5.1	6.2	(X)	12.2
United States	1996	100.0	19.5	2.3	4.9	1.3	2.3	14.4	0.9	3.6	(X)

X Not applicable.   ¹ Includes other countries not shown separately.

Source: Organization for Economic Cooperation and Development, Paris, France, *International Trade by Commodities Statistics CD-ROM, SITC/CTCI-Rev.3, 1988-1997, 1998, Vol. 3.*

No. 1406. International Tourism Receipts—Leading Countries: 1990 to 1998

[In millions of dollars, except as indicated (268,928 represents $268,928,000,000). Excludes international transport receipts. Minus sign (-) indicates decrease]

Country	Total receipts					Percent change, 1997-98	Percent of world total	
	1990	1995	1996	1997	1998		1990	1998
World, total [1]	268,928	405,110	436,594	435,981	444,741	2.0	100.0	100.0
United States	43,007	63,395	69,751	73,268	74,240	1.3	16.0	16.7
Italy	20,016	28,729	30,017	29,714	30,427	2.4	7.4	6.8
France	20,184	27,527	28,357	28,009	29,700	6.0	7.5	6.7
Spain	18,593	25,388	26,690	26,651	29,585	11.0	6.9	6.7
United Kingdom	14,940	19,073	19,173	20,039	21,295	6.3	5.6	4.8
Germany	14,288	17,908	17,546	16,509	16,840	2.0	5.3	3.8
China	2,218	8,733	10,200	12,074	12,500	3.5	0.8	2.8
Austria	13,417	14,593	13,990	12,393	12,164	-1.8	5.0	2.7
Canada	6,339	7,874	8,623	8,770	9,133	4.1	2.4	2.1
Australia	4,088	7,857	9,113	9,026	8,575	-5.0	1.5	1.9
Poland	358	6,614	8,444	8,679	8,400	-3.2	0.1	1.9
Turkey	3,225	4,957	5,962	8,088	8,300	2.6	1.2	1.9
Switzerland	7,411	9,365	8,826	7,902	8,208	3.9	2.8	1.8
Mexico	5,467	6,178	6,934	7,594	7,850	3.4	2.0	1.8
Hong Kong	5,032	9,604	10,836	9,242	7,114	-23.0	1.9	1.6
Russia	(NA)	4,312	6,868	6,900	7,107	3.0	(NA)	1.6
Singapore	4,904	8,337	7,958	6,843	6,501	-5.0	1.8	1.5
Thailand	4,326	7,664	8,664	7,048	6,392	-9.3	1.6	1.4
Netherlands	4,155	6,575	6,544	6,219	5,749	-7.6	1.5	1.3
Korea, South	3,559	5,587	5,430	5,116	5,700	11.4	1.3	1.3

NA Not available.   [1] Includes other countries not shown separately.
Source: World Tourism Organization, Madrid, Spain, unpublished data (copyright).

No. 1407. Net Flow of Financial Resources to Developing Countries: 1980 to 1997

[In billions of U.S. dollars (75.4 represents $75,400,000,000). Net flow covers loans, grants, and grant-like flows minus amortization on loans. Military flows are excluded. Developing countries cover countries designated by Development Assistance Committee (DAC) as developing. Official development assistance covers all flows to developing countries and multilateral institutions provided by official agencies, including state and local governments, or by their executive agencies, which are administered with the promotion of economic development and welfare of developing countries as their main objective and whose financial terms are intended to be concessional in character with grant element of at least 25 percent. Other official flows cover export credits and portfolio investment from the official sector]

Origin and type of resource	1980	1985	1990	1992	1993	1994	1995	1996	1997
Net flows to DAC Part I developing countries [1][2]	75.4	45.2	76.4	115.8	135.4	165.9	164.6	195.5	187.6
Official development assistance	27.3	29.4	53.0	60.9	56.5	59.2	58.9	55.4	48.3
Other official flows	5.3	3.4	8.6	8.9	7.9	10.5	9.9	5.6	6.1
Private flows at market terms	40.4	9.4	9.8	40.1	65.3	90.2	89.8	128.9	128.5
Private voluntary agencies	2.4	2.9	5.1	6.0	5.7	6.0	6.0	5.6	4.6
United States	13.9	1.8	11.1	33.5	58.2	59.7	47.0	55.7	75.0
Official development assistance	7.1	9.4	11.4	11.7	10.1	9.9	7.4	9.4	6.9
Other official flows	1.1	0.2	-0.4	1.3	0.1	0.9	1.5	1.1	0.3
Private flows at market terms	4.3	-9.3	-2.4	17.7	45.4	46.3	35.6	42.7	65.3
Private voluntary agencies	1.3	1.5	2.5	2.8	2.6	2.6	2.5	2.5	2.5
Australia	0.9	1.2	1.5	4.2	2.1	2.1	2.5	1.4	1.3
Austria	0.3	0.2	0.6	0.8	0.7	1.0	0.9	1.9	1.7
Belgium	2.9	1.3	0.1	2.2	0.7	2.2	-0.2	5.6	-11.5
Canada	3.2	1.7	3.5	4.2	5.3	5.6	5.1	6.7	10.0
Denmark	0.8	0.4	1.1	1.6	1.4	1.3	1.8	1.9	1.9
Finland	0.2	0.3	1.0	0.8	0.3	0.6	0.6	1.1	0.4
France	11.6	8.9	5.7	10.8	10.9	12.7	12.5	17.5	14.0
Germany	10.6	5.8	13.6	8.9	15.4	23.9	21.2	20.8	19.7
Ireland	(Z)	0.1	0.2	0.2	0.1	0.2	0.2	0.4	0.3
Italy	4.0	2.2	3.2	6.2	2.4	3.4	2.8	4.7	8.1
Japan	6.8	11.6	17.2	16.2	15.9	28.5	42.3	38.1	29.5
Luxembourg	(NA)	(NA)	(NA)	5.9	0.1	0.1	0.1	0.1	0.1
Netherlands	2.4	2.6	4.0	3.4	5.6	4.7	6.8	9.5	8.1
New Zealand	0.1	0.1	0.1	0.1	0.1	0.1	0.2	0.1	0.2
Norway	0.9	0.6	1.2	1.4	1.2	1.5	1.7	1.7	1.6
Portugal	(NA)	(NA)	0.3	0.4	0.2	0.3	0.4	0.9	1.3
Spain	(NA)	(NA)	1.0	1.6	1.4	3.5	2.0	4.3	7.4
Sweden	1.9	1.4	2.8	3.0	2.5	2.4	2.2	2.0	2.1
Switzerland	2.7	2.5	3.4	3.1	3.6	0.1	1.1	-1.5	-3.5
United Kingdom	12.2	2.5	6.5	9.3	7.3	12.0	13.4	22.5	19.7
Net flows to DAC Part II countries in transition [1]	(NA)	(NA)	(NA)	25.0	21.5	11.2	19.4	31.1	78.0
Official aid [3]	(NA)	(NA)	(NA)	6.9	7.1	7.5	9.2	5.7	5.1
Other official flows	(NA)	(NA)	(NA)	2.3	5.3	4.5	6.7	1.8	0.9
Private flows at market terms	(NA)	(NA)	(NA)	15.5	8.8	-1.1	3.1	23.3	70.9
Private voluntary agencies	(NA)	(NA)	(NA)	0.2	0.4	0.4	0.4	0.4	1.2

NA Not available.   Z Less than $50 million.   [1] Known as the "List of Developing Countries and Territories," the DAC List of Aid Recipients was split into two parts in 1993 in recognition of the new aid requirements for transition economies of eastern Europe and of the rapid progress of some developing countries with reduced aid needs. Part I countries are the "traditional" developing countries to which aid can be counted as official development assistance. Part II countries are the "more advanced" developing countries of Central and Eastern Europe (Bulgaria, Czech Republic, Estonia, Hungary, Latvia, Lithuania, Poland, Romania, and Slovakia) and of the Newly Independent States of the former Soviet Union (Belarus, Russia, and Ukraine). In 1996, the Bahamas, Brunei, Kuwait, Qatar, Singapore, and the United Arab Emirates were reclassified from Part I to Part II more advanced developing status. In 1997, Bermuda, Cayman Islands, Cyprus, Falkland Islands, Hong Kong, Israel, and Taiwan were reclassified from Part I to Part II status, and Moldova shifted from Part II to Part I status.   [2] Country totals may not sum to DAC totals because debt forgiveness of nonofficial development assistance claims is not included in DAC totals.   [3] Official flows to Part II countries that have the same concessional and qualitative features as official development assistance are designated official aid. Only flows to Part I countries are eligible to be recorded as official development assistance.
Source: Organization for Economic Cooperation and Development, Paris, France, Annual Reports of the Development Assistance Committee.

864   Comparative International Statistics

[46,902 represents $46,902,000,000. External public debt is defined as debt repayable to external creditors in foreign currency, goods, or services, with an original or extended maturity of more than 1 year, which is a direct obligation of, or has repayment guaranteed by, a public body in the borrowing country. Excludes undisbursed debt (amounts not yet drawn by recipient) and unguaranteed private debt, which for some countries is substantial. Debt contracted for the purchase of military equipment is not usually reported. **Debt service payments** represent the sum of interest payments and repayments of principal on external public debt]

Country	Total external public debt (mil. dol.)							Debt service ratio [3] (percent)		
			1996							
	1990	1995	Total [1]	Bilateral official	Banks	Multilateral organizations	Bonds [2]	1990	1995	1996
Argentina	46,902	55,967	62,389	10,027	1,049	9,891	41,159	37	34	44
Bangladesh	11,973	15,469	15,401	5,323	25	9,859	-	29	15	12
Brazil	87,669	97,180	94,584	16,803	8,784	9,426	56,076	22	37	41
China	45,512	94,671	102,257	21,737	24,437	17,695	11,105	12	10	9
Colombia	14,667	13,946	14,811	1,738	4,054	4,765	3,409	41	29	35
Congo (Kinshasa) [4]	9,004	9,618	9,258	6,081	517	2,319	4	15	2	2
Cote d'Ivoire	10,663	11,899	11,364	5,122	2,525	3,664	-	35	23	26
Ecuador	9,864	12,062	12,432	2,198	1,055	2,909	6,013	33	26	23
Egypt	27,347	30,584	28,915	23,370	445	4,192	-	27	13	12
Ethiopia	8,479	9,772	9,480	6,643	26	2,485	-	35	19	42
Hungary	18,002	23,782	18,420	678	1,545	2,761	13,263	34	39	41
India [5]	71,058	80,369	74,403	23,915	14,182	29,331	1,088	31	28	24
Indonesia	48,042	65,305	60,105	28,911	6,003	17,248	1,141	33	31	37
Malaysia	11,589	16,023	15,697	2,815	3,084	1,403	7,788	13	7	8
Mexico	75,970	94,384	93,435	10,936	7,154	17,756	53,595	21	28	35
Morocco	22,307	22,110	20,771	8,840	3,294	6,527	286	22	33	28
Pakistan	16,504	23,804	23,692	10,261	309	12,194	300	23	27	27
Peru	13,625	18,922	20,412	11,344	122	3,594	4,773	11	16	35
Philippines	24,037	29,905	27,934	12,084	589	7,938	5,707	27	16	14
Poland	39,259	41,071	39,215	28,335	323	2,175	8,270	5	11	6
Sudan	9,153	9,778	9,368	5,692	1,589	2,083	-	6	9	5
Syria	14,915	16,755	16,696	14,523	-	1,029	-	23	5	4
Thailand	12,452	16,951	17,037	7,623	3,319	2,984	1,905	17	12	12
Tunisia	6,659	8,721	8,687	3,154	1,090	3,631	474	25	17	17
Turkey	38,869	50,313	48,168	7,494	15,324	7,707	14,174	29	28	22
Venezuela	24,506	28,491	28,450	1,269	1,985	2,787	20,659	23	22	17

- Represents or rounds to zero.   [1] Includes other types of creditors not shown separately.   [2] Covers publicly issued and privately placed bonds.   [3] Debt service payments as percent of exports.   [4] See footnote 3, Table 1349.   [5] Fiscal year basis.

Source: The World Bank, Washington, DC, *World Debt Tables*, periodic.

No. 1409. Foreign Direct Investment Flows in OECD Countries: 1995 to 1997

[In millions of dollars (232,068 represents $232,068,000,000). 1997 data, preliminary. Data are converted to U.S. dollars using the yearly average exchange rate]

Country	Inflows			Outflows		
	1995	1996	1997	1995	1996	1997
OECD, total	232,068	215,815	258,051	307,366	288,573	382,022
Australia	13,202	5,456	9,346	3,728	6,306	6,219
Austria	636	3,842	1,739	1,043	1,405	1,450
Belgium-Luxembourg	10,558	14,117	12,525	11,786	8,365	6,709
Canada	10,780	6,416	8,217	11,165	8,524	12,896
Czech Republic	2,562	972	1,252	37	25	25
Denmark	4,179	776	2,970	3,018	2,484	4,045
Finland	1,063	1,109	1,542	1,498	3,598	4,405
France	23,681	21,960	23,178	15,760	30,419	35,591
Germany	13,449	-2,720	-188	38,791	29,546	33,166
Greece	4,272	5,928	3,585	(NA)	(NA)	(NA)
Hungary	4,453	1,983	2,085	43	-3	431
Iceland	14	61	126	24	65	26
Ireland	2,019	2,756	3,153	(NA)	(NA)	(NA)
Italy	4,817	3,535	3,779	5,732	6,465	12,164
Japan	41	228	3,224	22,629	23,420	25,992
Korea, South	1,176	2,325	2,341	3,552	4,670	4,287
Mexico	9,526	9,185	12,478	(NA)	(NA)	(NA)
Netherlands	11,611	7,766	8,678	19,629	23,214	20,157
New Zealand [1]	2,690	3,687	1,339	1,747	-1,257	-756
Norway	1,644	3,437	3,692	2,844	5,341	4,114
Poland [2]	3,659	4,498	3,077	42	53	36
Portugal	695	708	1,728	689	785	1,856
Spain	6,217	6,468	5,540	3,608	5,222	10,142
Sweden	14,455	5,074	9,665	11,221	4,662	11,382
Switzerland	2,224	2,797	4,408	12,214	15,981	14,516
Turkey	935	913	852	163	325	319
United Kingdom	22,738	26,084	36,972	44,329	34,125	58,313
United States	58,772	76,453	90,748	92,074	74,833	114,537

NA Not available.   [1] For fiscal year ending March 31.   [2] Data are on a transaction basis. 1997 flows, preliminary data on a cash basis only (equity capital and loans received).

Source: Organization for Economic Cooperation and Development, Paris, France, *International Direct Investment Statistics Yearbook, 1998,* 1999.

Comparative International Statistics   865

No. 1410. Military Expenditures and Armed Forces Personnel, by Country: 1990 and 1995

[Military expenditures in millions of dollars, except as indicated (306,200 represents $306,200,000,000). Personnel data as of July. See also Table 583. For most countries, data for expenditures and for gross national product (GNP) were based on local currencies which were deflated to constant 1995 local currency values before conversion to U.S. dollar equivalents. In general, the rates used for conversion are the 1995 average par/market exchange rates as supplied by the International Bank for Reconstruction and Development. Armed Forces refer to active-duty military personnel, including paramilitary forces where those forces resemble regular units in their organization, equipment, training, or mission. Reserve forces are not included]

Country	Military expenditures						Armed Forces personnel			
	Current dollars		Constant (1995) dollars				Number (1,000)		Per 1,000 population	
					1995					
	1990	1995	1990	Total	Percent of GNP	Per capita (dollars)	1990	1995	1990	1995
United States......	306,200	277,800	351,900	277,800	3.8	1,056	2,181	1,620	8.7	6.2
Algeria [1].........	697	1,238	801	1,238	3.2	43	126	120	5.0	4.2
Angola [1]........	(NA)	225	(NA)	225	3.0	22	115	82	13.6	8.1
Argentina........	3,436	4,684	3,949	4,684	1.7	137	85	65	2.6	1.9
Australia.........	5,866	8,401	6,741	8,401	2.5	465	68	58	4.0	3.2
Bangladesh	317	502	365	502	1.7	4	103	115	0.9	1.0
Belgium	5,356	4,449	6,155	4,449	1.7	439	106	47	10.6	4.6
Brazil..........	8,555	10,900	9,832	10,900	1.7	68	295	285	2.0	1.8
Bulgaria [1].......	3,887	1,073	4,467	1,073	2.8	125	129	86	14.4	10.0
Burma	1,093	1,833	1,256	1,833	3.9	41	230	322	5.6	7.1
Canada.........	9,187	9,077	10,560	9,077	1.7	318	87	70	3.3	2.5
Chile [2].........	1,154	2,243	1,327	2,243	3.8	158	95	102	7.2	7.2
China [1].........	48,440	63,510	55,660	63,510	2.3	53	3,500	2,930	3.1	2.4
Colombia........	1,225	2,000	1,408	2,000	2.6	55	110	146	3.3	4.0
Congo (Kinshasa) [3]..	(NA)	17	(NA)	17	0.3	-	55	49	1.5	1.1
Croatia	(X)	2,114	(X)	2,114	10.5	425	(X)	60	(X)	12.1
Cuba...........	1,400	350	1,609	350	1.6	32	297	70	28.1	6.4
Czech Republic [1]....	(X)	2,368	(X)	2,368	2.3	229	434	68	(X)	6.6
Egypt [1].........	1,468	2,653	1,687	2,653	5.7	43	434	430	7.7	6.9
France.........	44,800	47,770	51,480	47,770	3.1	826	550	504	9.7	8.7
Germany	48,540	41,160	55,790	41,160	1.9	496	545	352	6.9	4.2
Greece	4,182	5,056	4,806	5,056	5.5	482	201	213	19.9	20.3
Hungary [1].......	1,277	961	1,468	961	1.5	95	94	71	9.1	7.0
India [2]........	6,635	7,831	7,626	7,831	2.4	8	1,262	1,265	1.5	1.4
Indonesia [2].......	1,699	3,398	1,952	3,398	1.8	17	283	280	1.5	1.4
Iran [1].........	8,098	4,191	9,307	4,191	2.6	65	1,390	390	7.7	6.8
Iraq [1].........	14,110	(NA)	16,210	(NA)	(NA)	(NA)	1,390	390	75.4	18.9
Israel...........	7,168	8,734	8,237	8,734	9.6	1,646	190	185	42.1	34.9
Italy...........	19,150	19,380	22,010	19,380	1.8	338	493	435	8.5	7.6
Japan..........	40,740	50,240	46,820	50,240	1.0	401	250	240	2.0	1.9
Jordan.........	397	481	456	481	7.7	117	100	112	30.5	27.3
Kazakhstan [1].....	(X)	426	(X)	426	0.9	25	(X)	28	(X)	1.7
Kenya [1]........	173	173	198	173	2.3	6	20	22	0.8	0.8
Korea, North [1].....	5,940	6,000	6,827	6,000	28.6	255	1,200	1,040	56.0	44.3
Korea, South	10,780	14,410	12,390	14,410	3.4	320	650	655	15.2	14.5
Kuwait..........	13,170	3,488	15,130	3,488	11.6	1,919	7	20	3.3	11.0
Libya [2].........	(NA)	1,999	(NA)	1,999	6.0	381	86	76	19.7	14.5
Malaysia	1,271	2,444	1,461	2,444	3.0	125	130	122	7.4	6.2
Mexico..........	1,058	2,321	1,215	2,321	1.0	25	175	175	2.1	1.9
Netherlands	8,129	8,012	9,343	8,012	2.1	518	104	67	7.0	4.3
New Zealand	897	740	1,030	740	1.3	211	11	10	3.3	2.9
Nigeria [2]	674	(NA)	775	(NA)	(NA)	(NA)	94	89	1.1	0.9
Pakistan.........	3,120	3,740	3,586	3,740	6.1	30	550	587	4.8	4.6
Peru	683	989	784	989	1.7	41	125	115	5.7	4.8
Philippines	1,232	1,151	1,416	1,151	1.5	16	109	110	1.7	1.5
Poland [1].........	8,752	4,887	10,060	4,887	2.3	127	313	278	8.2	7.2
Romania [1]	3,869	2,520	4,446	2,520	2.5	115	126	209	5.5	9.5
Russia [1]	(X)	76,000	(X)	76,000	11.4	513	(X)	1,400	(X)	9.4
Saudi Arabia......	23,160	17,210	26,620	17,210	13.5	919	146	175	9.2	9.3
Singapore	2,106	3,970	2,421	3,970	4.7	1,191	56	60	18.4	18.0
Slovakia [1]	(X)	577	(X)	577	3.0	108	(X)	52	(X)	9.7
Slovenia [1]	(X)	344	(X)	344	1.5	176	(X)	10	(X)	5.1
South Africa......	4,545	2,895	5,223	2,895	2.2	71	263	210	6.8	5.4
Spain	8,382	8,652	9,633	8,652	1.6	221	263	210	1.3	6.0
Sri Lanka	411	585	472	585	4.6	32	22	110	1.3	6.0
Sweden.........	5,138	6,042	5,905	6,042	2.8	683	65	51	7.6	5.8
Syria [1][2].......	4,391	3,563	5,046	3,563	7.2	236	408	320	32.3	21.2
Taiwan..........	8,938	13,140	10,270	13,140	5.0	618	370	425	18.2	20.0
Tanzania........	98	69	112	69	1.8	2	40	35	1.6	1.2
Thailand.........	2,372	4,014	2,726	4,014	2.5	69	283	288	5.1	4.9
Turkey..........	4,323	6,606	4,968	6,606	4.0	108	769	805	13.7	13.1
Ukraine [1]........	(X)	3,588	(X)	3,588	2.9	70	(X)	476	(X)	9.3
United Kingdom.....	37,090	33,400	42,630	33,400	3.0	572	308	233	5.4	4.0
Vietnam [1].......	723	544	831	544	2.6	7	1,052	550	15.9	7.6

- Represents or rounds to zero.   NA Not available.   X Not applicable.   [1] Military expenditures estimated.   [2] Data probably omit a major share of total military expenditures, probably including most arms acquisitions.   [3] See footnote 3, Table 1349.

Source: U.S. Arms Control and Disarmament Agency, *World Military Expenditures and Arms Transfers*, annual.

Section 31

20ᵗʰ Century Statistics

This new section presents summary statistics that cover the social, economic, and political organization of the United States. The main objective is to present some of the important historical trends for this century in statistical form. Population growth, the arrival of many different immigrant groups, the changing marital status, types of households, and age structure are some of the demographic trends covered. Increased life expectancy, school enrollment, and educational attainment along with the growth in household income are covered as well as the fall in the incidence of some diseases. Relatedly, changes in the workplace are covered with greater female participation and fewer agricultural workers. The Nation's economy is covered by trends in the Gross Domestic Product, labor force, and basic economic measures such as housing starts, retail sales, industrial production, and foreign trade. Special sectors in the economy, such as agriculture, transportation with the automobile and airlines, and communications with radio, television, and cable TV are also portrayed. The growth of the Federal Government, social welfare and health programs, and rise and fall in national defense between wars and peacetime are also covered. Presidential elections and changes in the composition of congress are presented in this reflective look at this century in statistics.

Statistics in this section start in 1900 where possible or the earliest year available (i.e., 1912 for data on diseases, 1913 for consumer prices, 1929 for Gross Domestic Product and unemployment, and 1940 for housing). Space considerations prevented showing every year available in most tables. However, the compact disc version of the *Statistical Abstract* will present all years that are available.

U.S. Census Bureau, Statistical Abstract of the United States: 1999

No. 1411. Population: 1900 to 1998

[In thousands, except percent. Estimates as of July 1. Prior to 1940, excludes Alaska and Hawaii. Total population includes Armed Forces abroad; civilian population excludes Armed Forces. For basis of estimates, see text, Section 1, Population]

Year	Total			Resident			Civilian		
	Popula-tion	Net change [1]	Percent change [1]	Popula-tion	Net change [1]	Percent change [1]	Popula-tion	Net change [1]	Percent change [1]
1900	(NA)	(NA)	(NA)	76,094	6,514	9.36	(NA)	(NA)	(NA)
1905	(NA)	(NA)	(NA)	83,822	7,728	10.16	(NA)	(NA)	(NA)
1910	(NA)	(NA)	(NA)	92,407	8,585	10.24	(NA)	(NA)	(NA)
1915	(NA)	(NA)	(NA)	100,546	8,139	8.81	(NA)	(NA)	(NA)
1920	(NA)	(NA)	(NA)	106,461	5,915	5.88	(NA)	(NA)	(NA)
1925	(NA)	(NA)	(NA)	115,829	9,368	8.80	(NA)	(NA)	(NA)
1930	123,188	(NA)	(NA)	123,077	7,248	6.26	122,923	(NA)	(NA)
1935	127,362	4,174	3.39	127,250	4,173	3.39	127,099	4,176	3.40
1940	132,122	4,760	3.74	131,954	4,704	3.70	131,658	4,559	3.59
1945	139,928	7,806	5.91	132,481	527	0.40	127,573	-4,085	-3.10
1950	152,271	12,343	8.82	151,868	19,387	14.63	150,790	23,217	18.20
1955	165,931	13,660	8.97	165,069	13,201	8.69	162,967	12,177	8.08
1960	180,671	14,740	8.88	179,979	14,910	9.03	178,140	15,173	9.31
1965	194,303	13,632	7.55	193,526	13,547	7.53	191,605	13,465	7.56
1970	205,052	10,749	5.53	203,984	10,458	5.40	201,895	10,290	5.37
1975	215,973	10,921	5.33	215,465	11,481	5.63	213,789	11,894	5.89
1980	227,726	11,753	5.44	227,225	11,760	5.46	225,621	11,832	5.53
1985	238,466	10,740	4.72	237,924	10,699	4.71	236,219	10,598	4.70
1990	249,948	11,482	4.81	249,439	11,515	4.84	247,798	11,579	4.90
1995	263,044	13,096	5.24	262,765	13,326	5.34	261,414	13,616	5.49
1998	270,561	7,517	2.86	270,299	7,534	2.87	269,078	7,664	2.93

NA Not available.   [1] Net or percent change from prior year shown; 1900 from 1895.
Source: U.S. Census Bureau, *Current Population Reports*, P25-311, P25-802, and P25-1095; and "Monthly estimates of the United States population: April 1, 1980, to November 1, 1998"; release date: December 28, 1998; <http://www.census.gov/population/estimates/nation/intfile1-1.txt>.

No. 1412. Population Characteristics: 1900 to 1998

Year	Sex			Race				Urban	Rural
					Black and other races				
	Total	Male	Female	White	Total	Black	Other	Urban	Rural
NUMBER (1,000)									
Census: [1]									
1900	75,995	38,816	37,178	66,809	9,185	8,834	351	30,215	45,997
1910	91,972	47,332	44,640	81,732	10,241	9,828	413	42,064	50,164
1920	105,711	53,900	51,810	94,821	10,890	10,463	427	54,253	51,768
1930	122,775	62,137	60,638	110,287	12,488	11,891	597	69,161	54,042
1940	131,669	66,062	65,608	118,215	13,455	12,866	589	74,705	57,459
1950	150,697	74,833	75,864	134,942	15,755	15,042	713	96,847	54,479
1960	179,323	88,331	90,992	158,832	20,492	18,872	1,620	125,269	54,054
1970 [2]	203,302	98,926	104,309	178,098	25,138	22,581	2,557	149,647	53,565
1980 [3]	226,542	110,053	116,493	194,713	31,833	26,683	5,150	167,051	59,495
1990 [3]	248,718	121,271	127,494	208,727	40,038	30,511	9,527	187,053	61,656
Estimates:									
1990	249,948	121,613	127,825	209,182	40,257	30,623	9,634	(NA)	(NA)
1991	252,639	122,943	129,184	210,961	41,166	31,131	10,035	(NA)	(NA)
1992	255,374	124,404	130,590	212,860	42,134	31,667	10,467	(NA)	(NA)
1993	258,083	125,767	131,979	214,677	43,069	32,179	10,890	(NA)	(NA)
1994	260,599	127,028	133,261	216,365	43,925	32,654	11,271	(NA)	(NA)
1995	263,044	128,272	134,493	218,010	44,755	33,098	11,657	(NA)	(NA)
1996	265,463	129,483	135,707	219,623	45,568	33,518	12,050	(NA)	(NA)
1997	268,008	130,760	136,984	221,317	46,427	33,973	12,454	(NA)	(NA)
1998	270,561	132,046	138,252	223,001	47,298	34,431	12,867	(NA)	(NA)
PERCENT DISTRIBUTION									
Census: [1]									
1900	100.0	51.1	48.9	87.9	12.1	11.6	0.5	39.6	60.4
1910	100.0	51.5	48.5	88.9	11.1	10.7	0.4	45.6	54.4
1920	100.0	51.0	49.0	89.7	10.3	9.9	0.4	51.2	48.8
1930	100.0	50.6	49.4	89.8	10.2	9.7	0.5	56.1	43.9
1940	100.0	50.2	49.8	89.8	10.2	9.8	0.4	56.5	43.5
1950	100.0	49.7	50.3	89.5	10.5	10.0	0.5	64.0	36.0
1960	100.0	49.3	50.7	88.6	11.4	10.5	0.9	69.9	30.1
1970 [2]	100.0	48.7	51.3	87.6	12.4	11.1	1.3	73.6	26.4
1980 [3]	100.0	48.6	51.4	85.9	14.1	11.8	2.3	73.7	26.3
1990 [3]	100.0	48.8	51.3	83.9	16.1	12.3	3.8	75.2	24.8
Estimates:									
1990	100.0	48.7	51.1	83.7	16.1	12.3	3.9	(NA)	(NA)
1995	100.0	48.8	51.1	82.9	17.0	12.6	4.4	(NA)	(NA)
1998	100.0	48.8	51.1	82.4	17.5	12.7	4.8	(NA)	(NA)

NA Not available.   [1] Beginning 1960, includes Alaska and Hawaii.   [2] The revised 1970 resident population count is 203,302,031; which incorporates changes due to errors found after tabulations were completed.   [3] Total population count has been revised since the 1980 and 1990 census publications to 226,542,199 and 248,718,301, respectively.
Source: U.S. Census Bureau, *U.S. Census of Population: 1940*, Vol. II, Part 1, and Vol. IV, Part 1; *1950*, Vol. II, Part 1; *1960*, Vol. I, Part 1; *1970*, Vol. I, Part B; *Current Population Reports*, P25-1095 and P25-1130; and "Resident Population of the United States: Estimates, by Sex, Race, and Hispanic Origin, with Median Age"; release date: December 28, 1998; <http://www.census.gov/population/estimates/nation/intfile3-1.txt>.

No. 1413. Resident Population, by Age: 1900 to 1997

[In thousands (75,995 represents 75,995,000), except as indicated. 1900-30, resident population; 1940-70, total population, including Armed Forces overseas. 1970-97, resident population]

Year	Total, all years	Under 5 yrs. old	5-14 yrs. old	15-24 yrs. old	25-34 yrs. old	35-44 yrs. old	45-54 yrs. old	55-64 yrs. old	65 yrs. old and over
NUMBER (1,000)									
Census									
1900	[1]75,995	9,171	16,954	14,891	12,085	9,212	6,397	4,003	3,080
1910	[1]91,972	10,631	18,868	18,121	15,152	11,658	8,370	5,054	3,950
1920	[1]105,711	11,573	22,039	18,708	17,158	14,121	10,498	6,532	4,933
1930	[1]122,775	11,444	24,612	22,422	18,954	17,199	13,018	8,397	6,634
1940	131,669	10,542	22,431	23,921	21,339	18,333	15,512	10,572	9,019
1950 [2]	150,697	16,164	24,319	22,098	23,759	21,450	17,343	13,295	12,270
1960 [2]	179,323	20,321	35,465	24,020	22,818	24,081	20,485	15,572	16,560
1970	203,212	17,154	40,746	35,441	24,907	23,088	23,220	18,590	20,066
1980	226,546	16,298	34,940	42,472	37,181	25,638	22,732	21,786	25,498
1990	248,765	18,763	35,105	37,029	43,170	37,441	25,060	21,115	31,081
Estimates (July 1)									
1991	252,124	19,187	35,879	36,385	42,865	39,288	25,746	21,001	31,778
1992	255,002	19,489	36,288	36,220	42,371	39,901	27,411	20,920	32,285
1993	257,753	19,670	36,944	36,154	41,798	40,809	28,657	20,912	32,812
1994	260,292	19,694	37,462	36,125	41,231	41,689	29,871	21,007	33,208
1995	262,761	19,526	37,941	36,178	40,720	42,550	31,097	21,131	33,618
1996	265,179	19,324	38,435	36,208	40,236	43,358	32,355	21,352	33,955
1997	267,636	19,150	38,840	36,623	39,544	44,005	33,622	21,817	34,198
PERCENT DISTRIBUTION									
Census									
1900	[1]100.0	12.1	22.3	19.6	15.9	12.1	8.4	5.3	4.1
1910	[1]100.0	11.6	20.5	19.7	16.5	12.7	9.1	5.5	4.3
1920	[1]100.0	10.9	20.8	17.7	16.2	13.4	9.9	6.2	4.7
1930	[1]100.0	9.3	20.0	18.3	15.4	14.0	10.6	6.8	5.4
1940	100.0	8.0	17.0	18.2	16.2	13.9	11.8	8.0	6.8
1950 [2]	100.0	10.7	16.1	14.7	15.8	14.2	11.5	8.8	8.1
1960 [2]	100.0	11.3	19.8	13.4	12.7	13.4	11.4	8.7	9.2
1970	100.0	8.4	20.1	17.4	12.3	11.4	11.4	9.1	9.9
1980	100.0	7.2	15.4	18.7	16.4	11.3	10.0	9.6	11.3
1990	100.0	7.5	14.1	14.9	17.4	15.1	10.1	8.5	12.5
Estimates (July 1)									
1995	100.0	7.4	14.4	13.8	15.5	16.2	11.8	8.0	12.8
1997	100.0	7.2	14.5	13.7	14.8	16.4	12.6	8.2	12.8
NET CHANGE (1,000)									
Census									
1900-1910	15,978	1,461	1,913	3,229	3,067	2,446	1,973	1,052	869
1910-1920	13,738	942	3,171	587	2,005	2,463	2,129	1,478	984
1920-1930	17,064	-129	2,573	3,715	1,796	3,078	2,520	1,865	1,701
1930-1940	8,894	-903	-2,182	1,499	2,385	1,134	2,494	2,175	2,386
1940-1950 [2]	19,028	5,622	1,888	-1,823	2,420	3,117	1,831	2,722	3,250
1950-1960 [2]	28,626	4,157	11,146	1,922	-941	2,631	3,143	2,278	4,290
1960-1970	23,889	-3,167	5,280	11,421	2,089	-994	2,735	3,017	3,506
1970-1980	23,334	-856	-5,806	7,031	12,274	2,550	-488	3,196	5,433
1980-1990	22,219	2,465	165	-5,443	5,989	11,803	2,328	-671	5,583
Estimates (July 1)									
1990-1997	18,871	387	3,735	-406	-3,626	6,564	8,562	702	3,117
1989-1990	1,946	260	391	-362	-266	1,026	427	-126	399
1900-1991	3,359	424	774	-644	-305	1,847	686	-114	697
1991-1992	2,878	302	409	-165	-494	613	1,665	-81	507
1992-1993	2,751	181	656	-66	-573	908	1,246	-8	527
1993-1994	2,539	24	518	-29	-567	880	1,214	95	396
1994-1995	2,469	-168	479	53	-511	861	1,226	124	410
1995-1996	2,418	-202	494	30	-484	808	1,258	221	337
1996-1997	2,457	-174	405	415	-692	647	1,267	465	243

[1] Includes age not stated, not shown separately.　　[2] Denotes first year for which figures include Alaska and Hawaii.

Sources: U.S. Census Bureau, census, 1900-50, *U.S. Census of Population: 1950*, Vol. IV, Part 3, Chapter A; 1960, *U.S. Census of Population: 1960*, Vol. I, Part 1; 1970, *U.S. Census of Population: 1970*, Vol. I, Part 1; 1980, *1980 Census of Population*, Vol. 1, Part B; 1990, *1990 Census of Population*, CP-1-1; estimates, 1991-98, Internet release 1.

U.S. Census Bureau, Statistical Abstract of the United States, 1999

No. 1414. Resident Population, by State: 1900 to 1998

[In thousands. As of July 1, except as indicated]

State	1900	1910	1920	1930	1940	1950	1960	1970	1980 (April)	1990	1998
United States..	76,094	92,407	106,466	123,077	131,954	151,868	179,975	203,302	226,546	249,439	270,299
Alabama........	1,830	2,150	2,359	2,647	2,845	3,058	3,274	3,444	3,894	4,048	4,352
Alaska.........	(NA)	(NA)	(NA)	(NA)	(NA)	135	229	303	402	553	614
Arizona........	124	206	340	434	499	756	1,321	1,775	2,718	3,679	4,669
Arkansas	1,314	1,583	1,756	1,859	1,955	1,908	1,789	1,923	2,286	2,354	2,538
California	1,490	2,406	3,554	5,711	6,950	10,677	15,870	19,971	23,668	29,926	32,667
Colorado........	543	804	937	1,040	1,130	1,325	1,769	2,210	2,890	3,304	3,971
Connecticut......	910	1,122	1,391	1,613	1,708	2,016	2,544	3,032	3,108	3,289	3,274
Delaware	185	203	219	239	269	321	449	548	594	669	744
District of Columbia .	278	334	440	488	690	806	765	757	638	604	523
Florida	530	756	962	1,471	1,915	2,810	5,004	6,791	9,746	13,019	14,916
Georgia	2,220	2,618	2,926	2,910	3,119	3,458	3,956	4,588	5,463	6,506	7,642
Hawaii	(NA)	(NA)	(NA)	(NA)	(NA)	498	642	770	965	1,113	1,193
Idaho..........	163	329	433	447	522	590	671	713	944	1,012	1,229
Illinois	4,828	5,668	6,663	7,644	7,905	8,738	10,086	11,110	11,427	11,447	12,045
Indiana.........	2,518	2,713	2,947	3,242	3,433	3,967	4,674	5,195	5,490	5,555	5,899
Iowa	2,231	2,228	2,400	2,475	2,537	2,625	2,756	2,825	2,914	2,780	2,862
Kansas.........	1,473	1,692	1,769	1,883	1,788	1,916	2,183	2,249	2,364	2,481	2,629
Kentucky	2,148	2,299	2,421	2,623	2,859	2,936	3,041	3,221	3,661	3,693	3,936
Louisiana	1,384	1,667	1,813	2,105	2,370	2,697	3,260	3,645	4,206	4,219	4,369
Maine..........	695	745	771	800	849	917	975	994	1,125	1,231	1,244
Maryland	1,189	1,302	1,464	1,636	1,839	2,355	3,113	3,924	4,217	4,797	5,135
Massachusetts.....	2,788	3,365	3,882	4,250	4,318	4,686	5,160	5,689	5,737	6,018	6,147
Michigan........	2,423	2,832	3,723	4,834	5,315	6,407	7,834	8,882	9,262	9,311	9,817
Minnesota.......	1,754	2,086	2,403	2,576	2,790	2,997	3,425	3,806	4,076	4,387	4,725
Mississippi	1,553	1,802	1,800	2,006	2,176	2,176	2,182	2,217	2,521	2,577	2,752
Missouri	3,108	3,301	3,404	3,646	3,786	3,964	4,326	4,678	4,917	5,126	5,439
Montana........	245	380	543	539	558	593	679	694	787	800	880
Nebraska.......	1,067	1,198	1,300	1,380	1,316	1,327	1,417	1,485	1,570	1,581	1,663
Nevada	43	82	78	92	113	162	291	489	800	1,219	1,747
New Hampshire....	412	431	444	466	492	532	609	738	921	1,112	1,185
New Jersey......	1,884	2,550	3,198	4,068	4,175	4,872	6,103	7,171	7,365	7,758	8,115
New Mexico	196	329	363	427	531	689	954	1,017	1,303	1,520	1,737
New York	7,283	9,137	10,282	12,647	13,456	14,865	16,838	18,241	17,558	18,002	18,175
North Carolina....	1,897	2,221	2,588	3,167	3,574	4,068	4,573	5,084	5,882	6,657	7,546
North Dakota.....	321	580	646	682	640	619	634	618	653	637	638
Ohio	4,161	4,786	5,799	6,662	6,929	7,980	9,734	10,657	10,798	10,862	11,209
Oklahoma........	800	1,671	2,055	2,401	2,325	2,229	2,336	2,559	3,025	3,147	3,347
Oregon.........	415	677	788	956	1,086	1,532	1,772	2,092	2,633	2,859	3,282
Pennsylvania......	6,313	7,706	8,740	9,649	9,896	10,507	11,329	11,801	11,864	11,896	12,001
Rhode Island......	430	545	613	686	719	786	855	950	947	1,005	988
South Carolina.....	1,342	1,523	1,685	1,745	1,902	2,113	2,392	2,591	3,122	3,499	3,836
South Dakota	403	590	640	693	641	655	683	666	691	697	738
Tennessee	2,023	2,191	2,329	2,619	2,935	3,315	3,575	3,926	4,591	4,891	5,431
Texas..........	3,055	3,922	4,723	5,844	6,425	7,776	9,624	11,199	14,229	17,045	19,760
Utah...........	277	377	453	509	552	696	900	1,059	1,461	1,730	2,100
Vermont	344	357	353	360	363	379	389	445	511	564	591
Virginia.........	1,858	2,071	2,347	2,427	2,720	3,315	3,986	4,651	5,347	6,214	6,791
Washington......	523	1,148	1,373	1,568	1,740	2,387	2,855	3,413	4,132	4,901	5,689
West Virginia	959	1,231	1,470	1,733	1,907	2,006	1,853	1,744	1,950	1,792	1,811
Wisconsin........	2,072	2,345	2,679	2,950	3,143	3,438	3,962	4,418	4,706	4,902	5,224
Wyoming........	93	147	197	226	250	290	331	332	470	453	481

NA Not available.

Source: U.S. Census Bureau, 1900-1940, *Current Population Reports*, Series P25-139; 1950, *Current Population Reports*, Series P25-304; 1960, *Current Population Reports*, Series P25-460; 1970, *Current Population Reports*, Series P25-957; 1980, *Current Population Reports*, Series, P25-1106; 1990 and 1998, estimates were released to the public with Press Release CB98-242, December 1998.

No. 1415. Population of the Largest 75 Cities: 1900 to 1996

Rank	1900 Place	Population	1930 Place	Population	1960 Place	Population	1996 Place	Population
1	New York City, NY	3,437,202	New York City, NY	6,930,446	New York City, NY	7,781,984	New York, NY	7,380,906
2	Chicago, IL	1,698,575	Chicago, IL	3,376,438	Chicago, IL	3,550,404	Los Angeles, CA.	3,553,638
3	Philadelphia, PA	1,293,697	Philadelphia, PA	1,950,961	Los Angeles, CA.	2,479,015	Chicago, IL	2,721,547
4	St. Louis, MO.	575,238	Detroit, MI	1,568,662	Philadelphia, PA.	2,002,512	Houston, TX	1,744,058
5	Boston, MA	560,892	Los Angeles, CA.	1,238,048	Detroit, MI	1,670,144	Philadelphia, PA.	1,478,002
6	Baltimore, MD	508,957	Cleveland, OH	900,429	Baltimore, MD	939,024	San Diego, CA.	1,171,121
7	Cleveland, OH	381,768	St. Louis, MO.	821,960	Houston, TX	938,219	Phoenix, AZ.	1,159,014
8	Buffalo, NY	352,387	Baltimore, MD	804,874	Cleveland, OH.	876,050	San Antonio, TX.	1,067,816
9	San Francisco, CA	342,782	Boston, MA	781,188	Washington, DC.	763,956	Dallas, TX.	1,053,292
10	Cincinnati, OH	325,902	Pittsburgh, PA	669,817	St. Louis, MO.	750,026	Detroit, MI	1,000,272
11	Pittsburgh, PA	321,616	San Francisco, CA	634,394	Milwaukee, WI	741,324	San Jose, CA.	838,744
12	New Orleans, LA	287,104	Milwaukee, WI.	578,249	San Francisco, CA	740,316	Indianapolis, IN [1]	746,737
13	Detroit, MI.	285,704	Buffalo, NY	573,076	Boston, MA	697,197	San Francisco, CA	735,315
14	Milwaukee, WI.	285,315	Washington, DC.	486,869	Dallas, TX.	679,684	Jacksonville, FL [1]	679,792
15	Washington, DC.	278,718	Minneapolis, MN.	464,356	New Orleans, LA	627,525	Baltimore, MD.	675,401
16	Newark, NJ.	246,070	New Orleans, LA	458,762	Pittsburgh, PA.	604,332	Columbus, OH.	657,053
17	Jersey City, NJ.	206,433	Cincinnati, OH	451,160	San Antonio, TX.	587,718	El Paso, TX.	599,865
18	Louisville, KY.	204,731	Newark, NJ.	442,337	San Diego, CA.	573,224	Memphis, TN.	596,725
19	Minneapolis, MN.	202,718	Kansas City, MO.	399,746	Seattle, WA.	557,087	Milwaukee, WI.	590,503
20	Providence, RI.	175,597	Seattle, WA.	365,583	Buffalo, NY	532,759	Boston, MA	558,394
21	Indianapolis, IN.	169,164	Indianapolis, IN.	364,161	Cincinnati, OH.	502,550	Washington, DC.	543,213
22	Kansas City, MO.	163,752	Rochester, NY.	328,132	Memphis, TN.	497,524	Austin, TX.	541,278
23	St. Paul, MN.	163,065	Jersey City, NJ.	316,715	Denver, CO.	493,887	Seattle, WA.	524,704
24	Rochester, NY.	162,608	Louisville, KY.	307,745	Atlanta, GA.	487,455	Nashville-Davidson, TN [1]	511,263
25	Denver, CO.	133,859	Portland, OR.	301,815	Minneapolis, MN.	482,872	Cleveland, OH.	498,246
26	Toledo, OH	131,822	Houston, TX	292,352	Indianapolis, IN.	476,258	Denver, CO.	497,840
27	Allegheny, PA.	129,896	Toledo, OH	290,718	Kansas City, MO.	475,539	Portland, OR.	480,824
28	Columbus, OH.	125,560	Columbus, OH.	290,564	Columbus, OH.	471,316	Fort Worth, TX.	479,716
29	Worcester, MA.	118,421	Denver, CO.	287,861	Phoenix, AZ.	439,170	New Orleans, LA	476,625
30	Syracuse, NY.	108,374	Oakland, CA.	284,063	Newark, NJ.	405,220	Oklahoma City, OK	469,852
31	New Haven, CT.	108,027	St. Paul, MN.	271,606	Louisville, KY.	390,639	Tucson, AZ.	449,002
32	Paterson, NJ.	105,171	Atlanta, GA.	270,366	Portland, OR.	372,676	Charlotte, NC.	441,297
33	Fall River, MA.	104,863	Dallas, TX.	260,475	Oakland, CA.	367,548	Kansas City, MO.	441,259
34	St. Joseph, MO.	102,979	Birmingham, AL.	259,678	Fort Worth, TX.	356,268	Virginia Beach, VA	430,385
35	Omaha, NE.	102,555	Akron, OH.	255,040	Long Beach, CA.	344,168	Honolulu, HI [2]	423,475
36	Los Angeles, CA.	102,479	Memphis, TN.	253,143	Birmingham, AL.	340,887	Long Beach, CA.	421,904
37	Memphis, TN.	102,320	Providence, RI.	252,981	Oklahoma City, OK	324,253	Albuquerque, NM	419,681
38	Scranton, PA.	102,026	San Antonio, TX.	231,542	Rochester, NY.	318,611	Atlanta, GA.	401,907
39	Lowell, MA.	94,969	Omaha, NE.	214,006	Toledo, OH.	318,003	Fresno, CA.	396,011
40	Albany, NY	94,151	Syracuse, NY.	209,326	St. Paul, MN.	313,411	Tulsa, OK.	378,491
41	Cambridge, MA.	91,886	Dayton, OH.	200,982	Norfolk, VA.	305,872	Las Vegas, NV.	376,906
42	Portland, OR.	90,426	Worcester, MA.	195,311	Omaha, NE.	301,598	Sacramento, CA.	376,243
43	Atlanta, GA.	89,872	Oklahoma City, OK	185,389	Honolulu, HI.	294,194	Oakland, CA.	367,230
44	Grand Rapids, MI	87,565	Richmond, VA.	182,929	Miami, FL.	291,688	Miami, FL.	365,127
45	Dayton, OH.	85,333	Youngstown, OH.	170,002	Akron, OH.	290,351	Omaha, NE.	364,253
46	Richmond, VA.	85,050	Grand Rapids, MI	168,592	El Paso, TX.	276,687	Minneapolis, MN.	358,785
47	Nashville, TN.	80,865	Hartford, CT.	164,072	Jersey City, NJ.	276,101	St. Louis, MO.	351,565
48	Seattle, WA.	80,671	Fort Worth, TX.	163,447	Tampa, FL.	274,970	Pittsburgh, PA.	350,363
49	Hartford, CT.	79,850	New Haven, CT.	162,655	Dayton, OH.	262,332	Cincinnati, OH.	345,818
50	Reading, PA.	78,961	Flint, MI	156,492	Tulsa, OK.	261,685	Colorado Springs, CO.	345,127
51	Wilmington, DE.	76,508	Nashville, TN.	153,866	Wichita, KS.	254,698	Mesa, AZ.	344,764
52	Camden, NJ.	75,935	Springfield, MA.	149,900	Richmond, VA.	219,958	Wichita, KS.	320,395
53	Trenton, NJ.	73,307	San Diego, CA.	147,995	Syracuse, NY.	216,038	Toledo, OH.	317,606
54	Bridgeport, CT.	70,996	Bridgeport, CT.	146,716	Tucson, AZ.	212,892	Buffalo, NY.	310,548
55	Lynn, MA.	68,513	Scranton, PA.	143,433	Des Moines, IA.	208,982	Santa Ana, CA.	302,419
56	Oakland, CA.	66,960	Des Moines, IA.	142,559	Providence, RI.	207,498	Arlington, TX.	294,816
57	Lawrence, MA.	62,559	Long Beach, CA.	142,032	San Jose, CA.	204,196	Anaheim, CA.	288,945
58	New Bedford, MA	62,442	Tulsa, OK.	141,258	Mobile, AL.	202,779	Tampa, FL.	285,206
59	Des Moines, IA.	62,139	Salt Lake City, UT	140,267	Charlotte, NC.	201,564	Corpus Christi, TX	280,260
60	Springfield, MA.	62,059	Paterson, NJ.	138,513	Albuquerque, NM	201,189	Newark, NJ.	268,510
61	Somerville, MA.	61,643	Yonkers, NY.	134,646	Jacksonville, FL.	201,030	Louisville, KY.	260,689
62	Troy, NY.	60,651	Norfolk, VA.	129,710	Flint, MI	196,940	St. Paul, MN.	259,606
63	Hoboken, NJ.	59,364	Jacksonville, FL.	129,549	Sacramento, CA.	191,667	Birmingham, AL.	258,543
64	Evansville, IN.	59,007	Albany, NY	127,412	Yonkers, NY.	190,634	Riverside, CA.	255,069
65	Manchester, NH.	56,987	Trenton, NJ.	123,356	Salt Lake City, UT	189,454	Aurora, CO.	252,341
66	Utica, NY.	56,383	Kansas City, KS.	121,857	Worcester, MA.	186,587	Anchorage, AK.	250,505
67	Peoria, IL.	56,100	Chattanooga, TN	119,798	Austin, TX.	186,545	Raleigh, NC.	243,835
68	Charleston, SC.	55,807	Camden, NJ.	118,700	Spokane, WA.	181,608	Lexington-Fayette, KY	239,942
69	Savannah, GA.	54,244	Erie, PA.	115,967	St. Petersburg, FL	181,298	St. Petersburg, FL	235,988
70	Salt Lake City, UT	53,531	Spokane, WA.	115,514	Gary, IN	178,320	Norfolk, VA.	233,430
71	San Antonio, TX.	53,321	Fall River, MA.	115,274	Grand Rapids, MI	177,313	Stockton, CA.	232,660
72	Duluth, MN.	52,969	Fort Wayne, IN.	114,946	Springfield, MA.	174,463	Jersey City, NJ.	229,039
73	Erie, PA.	52,733	Elizabeth, NJ.	114,589	Nashville, TN.	170,874	Rochester, NY.	221,594
74	Elizabeth, NJ.	52,130	Cambridge, MA.	113,643	Corpus Christi, TX	167,690	Akron, OH.	216,882
75	Wilkes-Barre, PA	51,721	New Bedford, MA	112,597	Youngstown, OH.	166,689	Baton Rouge, LA	215,882

[1] Represents the portion of a consolidated city that is not within one or more separately incorporated places. [2] The population shown in this table is for the CDP; the 1990 census population for the city and county of Honolulu is 836,231.

Source: U.S. Census Bureau, 1900-1990, *Population of the 100 Largest Cities and Other Urban Places in the United States: 1790 to 1990*, Working Paper No. 27; 1996, "Estimates of the Population of Cities with Populations of 100,000 and Greater"; <http://www.census.gov/population/stimates/metro-city/SC100K96.txt>; published November 1997.

No. 1416. Immigration, by Leading Country or Region of Last Residence: 1901 to 1997

[In thousands (8,795.4 represents 8,795,400). Data for years prior to 1906 relate to country where alien came; data from 1906-1979 and 1984-1997 are for country of last permanent residence; and data for 1980-1983 refer to country of birth. Because of changes in boundaries, changes in lists of countries, and lack of data for specified countries, data are not comparable for all years. For 1938-45, Austria included with Germany]

Region and country of last residence	1901-1910	1911-1920	1921-1930	1931-1940	1941-1950	1951-1960	1961-1970	1971-1980	1981-1990	1991-1997
All countries	8,795.4	5,735.8	4,107.2	528.4	1,035.0	2,515.5	3,321.7	4,493.3	7,338.1	6,944.6
Europe	8,056.0	4,321.9	2,463.2	347.6	621.1	1,325.7	1,123.5	800.4	761.6	1,036.6
Austria-Hungary	2,145.3	896.3	63.5	11.4	28.3	103.7	26.0	16.0	24.9	17.9
Austria	668.2	453.6	32.9	3.6	24.9	67.1	20.6	9.5	18.3	12.1
Hungary	808.5	442.7	30.7	7.9	3.5	36.6	5.4	6.6	6.5	5.8
Germany	341.5	143.9	412.2	114.1	226.6	477.8	190.8	74.4	92.0	58.9
Ireland	339.1	146.2	211.2	11.0	19.8	48.4	33.0	11.5	32.0	53.0
Italy	2,045.9	1,109.5	455.3	68.0	57.7	185.5	214.1	129.4	67.3	54.2
Norway-Sweden	440.0	161.5	165.8	8.7	20.8	44.6	32.6	10.5	15.2	11.8
Norway	190.5	66.4	68.5	4.7	10.1	22.9	15.5	3.9	4.2	3.6
Sweden	249.5	95.1	97.2	4.0	10.7	21.7	17.1	6.5	11.0	8.2
Soviet Union	1,597.3	921.2	61.7	1.4	0.6	0.7	2.5	39.0	57.7	377.7
Italy	2,045.9	1,109.5	455.3	68.0	57.7	185.5	214.1	129.4	67.3	54.2
United Kingdom	526.0	341.4	339.6	31.6	139.3	202.8	213.8	137.4	14.7	117.2
Asia	323.5	247.2	112.1	16.6	37.0	153.2	427.6	1,588.2	2,738.2	2,141.2
China	20.6	21.3	29.9	4.9	9.7	9.7	34.8	124.3	346.7	303.4
Philippines	[1]	[1]	[1]	0.5	4.7	19.3	98.4	355.0	548.8	401.9
Vietnam	[2]	[2]	[2]	[2]	[2]	0.3	4.3	172.8	280.8	226.5
America	361.9	1,143.7	1,516.7	160.0	354.8	996.9	1,716.4	1,982.7	3,615.2	3,427.0
Canada & Newfoundland	179.2	742.2	924.5	108.5	171.7	378.0	413.3	169.9	156.9	139.1
Mexico	49.6	219.0	459.3	60.6	60.6	299.8	453.9	640.3	1,655.8	1,800.8
Caribbean	107.5	123.4	74.9	49.7	49.7	123.1	470.2	741.1	872.1	753.8
Cuba	[2]	[2]	15.9	26.3	26.3	78.9	208.5	264.9	144.6	125.0
Central America	8.2	17.2	15.8	5.9	21.7	44.8	101.3	134.6	468.1	387.6
South America	17.3	41.9	42.2	7.8	21.8	91.6	257.9	295.7	461.8	398.5
Africa	7.4	8.4	6.3	1.8	7.4	14.1	29.0	80.8	176.9	245.9
Oceania	13.0	13.4	8.7	2.5	14.6	13.0	25.1	41.2	45.2	36.3
Not specified	33.5	1.1	0.2	-	0.1	12.5	0.1	-	1.0	0.2

- Represents or rounds to zero.   [1] Prior to 1934, Philippine immigrants were recorded as insular travel.   [2] Data not reported separately.

Source: U.S. Immigration and Naturalization Service, *Statistical Yearbook*, annual.

No. 1417. Native and Foreign-Born Population, by Place of Birth: 1900 to 1997

[1900-1990, data are based on a sample from the census; 1995 and 1997, based on the Current Population Survey; for details, see text, Section 1, Population. See source for sampling variability]

Year	Total population	Native population — Total	Born in the U.S total	Born abroad — total	Born in outlying areas[1]	Born abroad or at sea of American parents	Foreign born — Number	From— Europe	Asia	Latin America
NUMBER (1,000) Census										
1900	75,995	65,653	65,583	70	3	67	10,341	8,882	120	137
1910	91,972	78,456	78,381	75	7	68	13,516	11,810	191	280
1920	105,711	91,790	91,659	131	38	93	13,921	11,916	238	589
1930	122,775	108,571	108,304	267	136	131	14,204	11,748	276	792
1940	131,669	120,074	119,795	279	157	122	11,595	(NA)	(NA)	(NA)
1950	150,216	139,869	139,442	426	330	96	10,347	(NA)	(NA)	(NA)
1960	179,326	169,588	168,526	1,062	660	402	9,738	7,256	491	908
1970	203,210	193,591	191,329	2,261	891	1,370	9,619	5,741	825	1,804
1980	226,546	212,466	210,323	2,143	1,088	1,055	14,080	5,150	2,540	4,372
1990	248,710	228,943	225,696	3,247	1,382	1,864	19,767	4,350	4,979	8,408
Current Population Survey										
1995	262,105	239,115	(NA)	(NA)	(NA)	(NA)	22,990	(NA)	(NA)	(NA)
1997	266,792	241,014	(NA)	(NA)	(NA)	(NA)	25,778	(NA)	(NA)	(NA)
PERCENT DISTRIBUTION Census										
1900	100.0	85.3	71.3	0.1	-	0.1	14.7	12.8	0.2	0.3
1920	100.0	86.8	74.1	0.1	-	0.1	13.2	11.3	0.2	0.6
1930	100.0	88.4	74.7	0.2	0.1	0.1	11.6	9.6	0.2	0.6
1940	100.0	91.2	82.3	0.2	0.1	0.1	8.8	(NA)	(NA)	(NA)
1950	100.0	93.1	92.8	0.3	0.2	0.1	6.9	(NA)	(NA)	(NA)
1960	100.0	94.6	93.9	0.6	0.4	0.2	5.4	4.1	0.3	0.5
1970	100.0	95.2	94.4	1.1	0.4	0.7	4.8	2.8	0.4	0.9
1980	100.0	93.8	92.8	0.9	0.5	0.5	6.2	2.3	1.1	1.9
1990	100.0	92.1	90.7	1.3	0.6	0.7	7.9	1.7	2.0	3.4
Current Population Survey										
1995	100.0	91.2	(NA)	(NA)	(NA)	(NA)	8.8	(NA)	(NA)	(NA)
1997	100.0	90.3	(NA)	(NA)	(NA)	(NA)	9.7	(NA)	(NA)	(NA)

- Represents or round to zero.   NA Not available.   [1] Includes Puerto Rico for all years and prior to 1960 includes Alaska and Hawaii.

U.S. Census Bureau, *Historical Census Statistics on the Foreign-Born Population of the United States: 1850 to 1990*, Working Paper No. 29, February 1999; and <http://www.census.gov/population/socdemo/foreign/95/95tab-1.txt> (released 8 April 1997); and <http://www.census.gov/population/socdemo/foreign/97/ppltab1.txt> (released 9 April 1998).

No. 1418. Marital Status of the Population, by Sex: 1900 to 1998

[In thousands (25,493 represents 25,493,000), except percent. Persons 15 years old and over, except as indicated]

Year	Males Total	Never married	Married	Widowed	Divorced	Females Total	Never married	Married	Widowed	Divorced
NUMBER (1,000)										
Census										
1900...............	25,493	10,262	13,919	1,173	84	24,176	7,549	13,781	2,706	114
1910...............	32,311	12,521	18,065	1,467	156	29,993	8,918	17,664	3,167	185
1920...............	36,828	12,940	21,820	1,754	234	35,122	9,601	21,295	3,909	273
1930...............	43,829	14,938	26,311	2,023	489	42,795	11,294	26,156	4,728	572
1940...............	49,336	16,377	30,191	2,144	624	49,362	12,752	30,087	5,700	823
1950...............	53,511	13,319	36,859	2,262	1,070	56,055	10,379	37,570	6,734	1,373
1960...............	59,913	13,919	42,623	2,072	1,299	63,616	10,990	42,891	7,880	1,855
1970...............	69,349	18,315	46,981	2,128	1,925	75,861	15,604	47,644	9,610	3,002
1980...............	83,836	25,132	52,009	2,156	4,539	91,420	21,027	52,497	11,318	6,577
1990...............	93,817	28,805	55,678	2,378	6,957	101,325	23,755	55,821	12,122	9,627
Current Population Survey										
1950 [1]............	54,601	14,400	36,866	2,264	1,071	57,102	11,418	37,577	6,734	1,373
1960 [1]............	60,273	15,274	41,781	2,112	1,106	64,607	12,252	42,583	8,064	1,708
1970...............	70,559	19,832	47,109	2,051	1,567	77,766	17,167	48,148	9,734	2,717
1980...............	81,947	24,227	51,813	1,977	3,930	89,914	20,226	52,965	10,758	5,966
1990...............	91,955	27,505	55,833	2,333	6,283	99,838	22,718	56,797	11,477	8,845
1995...............	97,704	30,286	57,570	2,284	7,383	105,028	24,693	58,984	11,082	10,270
1998...............	101,123	31,591	58,633	2,569	8,331	108,168	26,713	59,333	11,029	11,093
PERCENT DISTRIBUTION										
Census										
1900...............	100.0	40.3	54.6	4.6	0.3	100.0	31.2	57.0	11.2	0.5
1940...............	100.0	33.2	61.2	4.3	1.3	100.0	25.8	61.0	11.5	1.7
1950...............	100.0	24.9	68.9	4.2	2.0	100.0	18.5	67.0	12.0	2.4
1960...............	100.0	23.2	71.1	3.5	2.2	100.0	17.3	67.4	12.4	2.9
1970...............	100.0	26.4	67.7	3.1	2.8	100.0	20.6	62.8	12.7	4.0
1980...............	100.0	30.0	62.0	2.6	5.4	100.0	23.0	57.4	12.4	7.2
1990...............	100.0	30.7	59.3	2.5	7.4	100.0	23.4	55.1	12.0	9.5
Current Population Survey										
1950 [1]............	100.0	26.4	67.5	4.1	2.0	100.0	20.0	65.8	11.8	2.4
1960* [1]...........	100.0	25.3	69.3	3.5	1.8	100.0	19.0	65.9	12.5	2.6
1970...............	100.0	28.1	66.8	2.9	2.2	100.0	22.1	61.9	12.5	3.5
1980...............	100.0	29.6	63.2	2.4	4.8	100.0	22.5	58.9	12.0	6.6
1990...............	100.0	29.9	60.7	2.5	6.8	100.0	22.8	56.9	11.5	8.9
1995...............	100.0	31.0	58.9	2.3	7.6	100.0	23.5	56.2	10.6	9.8
1998...............	100.0	31.2	58.0	2.5	8.2	100.0	24.7	54.9	10.2	10.3

[1] Persons 14 years old and over.
Source: U.S. Census Bureau,1900-1950, *U.S. Census of Population: 1950*, Vol. II, Part 1; 1960, *Census of Population: 1960*, Vol. I; 1970, *U.S. Census of Population: 1970*, Vol. I, Part 1; 1980, *Census of Population: 1980*, Vol. I, Part 1; 1990, *Census of Population: 1990, General Population Characteristics, (CP-1-1)*; and Current Population Reports, Series P20-514, "Marital Status and Living Arrangements: March 1998 (Update)", and earlier reports.

No. 1419. Households, by Type and Size: 1900 to 1998

[In thousands (15,964 represents 15,964,000), except percent. 1900-1940, as of April; beginning 1947, as of March]

Year	Total households	Family households Total	Married couples	Male household	Female household	Nonfamily households Total	Male household	Female household	Average size household
NUMBER (1,000)									
Census									
1900...............	15,964	(NA)	(NA)	(NA)	(NA)	(NA)	(NA)	(NA)	4.76
1910...............	20,256	(NA)	(NA)	(NA)	(NA)	(NA)	(NA)	(NA)	4.54
1920...............	24,352	(NA)	(NA)	(NA)	(NA)	(NA)	(NA)	(NA)	4.34
1930...............	29,905	(NA)	(NA)	(NA)	(NA)	(NA)	(NA)	(NA)	4.11
1940...............	34,949	31,491	26,571	1,510	3,410	3,458	1,599	1,859	3.67
Current Population Survey									
1947...............	39,107	34,964	30,612	1,129	3,223	4,143	1,388	2,755	3.56
1950...............	43,554	38,838	34,075	1,169	3,594	4,716	1,668	3,048	3.37
1960...............	52,799	44,905	39,254	1,228	4,422	7,895	2,716	5,179	3.33
1970...............	63,401	51,456	44,728	1,228	5,500	11,945	4,063	7,882	3.14
1980 [1]...........	80,776	59,550	49,112	1,733	8,705	21,226	8,807	12,419	2.76
1990...............	93,347	66,090	52,317	2,884	10,890	27,257	11,606	15,651	2.63
1995...............	98,990	69,305	53,858	3,226	12,220	29,686	13,190	16,496	2.65
1998...............	102,528	70,880	54,317	3,911	12,652	31,648	14,133	17,516	2.62
PERCENT DISTRIBUTION									
1940...............	100.0	90.1	76.0	4.3	9.8	9.9	4.6	5.3	(X)
1947...............	100.0	89.4	78.3	2.9	8.2	10.6	3.5	7.0	(X)
1950...............	100.0	89.2	78.2	2.7	8.3	10.8	3.8	7.0	(X)
1960...............	100.0	85.0	74.3	2.3	8.4	15.0	5.1	9.8	(X)
1970...............	100.0	81.2	70.5	1.9	8.7	18.8	6.4	12.4	(X)
1980 [1]...........	100.0	73.7	60.8	2.1	10.8	26.3	10.9	15.4	(X)
1990...............	100.0	70.8	56.0	3.1	11.7	29.2	12.4	16.8	(X)
1998...............	100.0	69.1	53.0	3.8	12.3	30.9	13.8	17.1	(X)

NA Not available.   X Not applicable.   [1] Revised using population controls based on the 1980 census.
Source: U.S. Census Bureau, 1890-1930, *U.S. Census of Population: 1950*, Vol. IV, Special Reports, General Characteristics of Families; 1940-1998, *Current Population Reports*, Series P-20, Nos. 176 and 251; and *Current Population Reports*, Series P20-515.

20th Century Statistics   873

No. 1420. Live Births, Deaths, Infant Deaths, and Maternal Deaths: 1900 to 1997

[Prior to 1960, excludes Alaska and Hawaii. Beginning 1970, excludes births to, and deaths of nonresidents of the United States. See Appendix III. 1900-1930, deaths for death registration states only]

Year	Number (1,000)			Rate per 1,000 population				Death rates per 100,000 population				
		Deaths			Deaths			Tuberculosis, all forms	Malignant neoplasms[3]	Major cardiovascular/renal diseases	Influenza and pneumonia[4]	Motor vehicle accidents[5]
	Births	Total	Infant[1]	Births	Total	Infant[1]	Maternal[2]					
1900....	(NA)	(NA)	(NA)	(NA)	17.2	(NA)	(NA)	194.4	64.0	345.2	202.2	(NA)
1905....	(NA)	(NA)	(NA)	(NA)	15.9	(NA)	(NA)	179.9	73.4	384.0	169.3	(NA)
1910....	2,777	697	(NA)	30.1	14.7	(NA)	(NA)	153.8	76.2	371.9	155.9	1.8
1915....	2,965	816	78	29.5	13.2	99.9	60.8	140.1	80.7	383.5	145.9	5.8
1920....	2,950	1,118	130	27.7	13.0	85.8	79.9	113.1	83.4	364.9	207.3	10.3
1925....	2,909	1,192	135	25.1	11.7	71.7	64.7	84.8	92.0	391.5	121.7	16.8
1930....	2,618	1,327	142	21.3	11.3	64.6	67.3	71.1	97.4	414.4	102.5	26.7
1935....	2,377	1,393	120	18.7	10.9	55.7	58.2	55.1	108.2	431.2	104.2	28.6
1940....	2,559	1,417	111	19.4	10.8	47.0	37.6	45.9	120.3	485.7	70.3	26.2
1945....	2,858	1,402	105	20.4	10.6	38.3	20.7	39.9	134.0	508.2	51.6	21.2
1950....	3,632	1,452	104	24.1	9.6	29.2	8.3	22.5	139.8	510.8	31.3	23.1
1955....	4,104	1,529	107	25.0	9.3	26.4	4.7	9.1	146.5	506.0	27.1	23.4
1957....	4,308	1,633	112	25.3	9.6	26.3	4.1	7.8	148.6	523.4	35.8	22.7
1960....	4,258	1,712	111	23.7	9.5	26.0	3.7	6.1	149.2	521.8	37.3	21.3
1965....	3,760	1,828	93	19.4	9.4	24.7	3.2	4.1	153.5	516.4	31.9	25.4
1970....	3,731	1,921	75	18.4	9.5	20.0	2.2	2.6	162.8	496.0	30.9	26.9
1975....	3,144	1,893	51	14.6	9.1	16.1	1.5	1.6	171.7	455.8	26.1	21.5
1980....	3,612	1,990	46	15.9	8.5	12.6	1.0	0.9	183.9	436.4	24.1	23.5
1985....	3,761	2,086	40	15.8	8.6	10.6	0.8	0.7	203.2	411.0	28.4	19.3
1990....	4,158	2,148	38	16.7	8.6	9.2	0.8	0.7	194.0	368.3	32.0	18.8
1995....	3,900	2,312	30	14.8	8.8	7.6	0.8	0.5	204.9	362.1	31.6	16.5
1997....	3,895	2,315	28	14.6	8.6	7.1	0.8	0.4	200.8	352.2	33.0	15.8

NA Not available. [1] Infants under 1 year, excluding fetal deaths; rates per 1,000 registered live births. [2] Per 10,000 live births from deliveries and complications of pregnancy, childbirth, and the puerperium. Beginning 1979, deaths are classified according to the ninth revision of the International Classification of Diseases; earlier years classified according to the revision in use at the time; see text, Section 2, Vital Statistics. [3] Includes neoplasms of lymphatic and hematopoietic tissues. [4] All years, excludes pneumonia of newborn; 1900-1920, excludes capillary bronchitis. [5] 1910-1925, excludes automobile collisions with trains and streetcars and motorcycle accidents.

Source: 1900-1970, U.S. Public Health Service, Vital Statistics of the United States, annual, Vol. I and Vol. II; 1971-1997, U.S. National Center for Health Statistics, Vital Statistics of the United States, annual; National Vital Statistics Report (NVSR) (formerly Monthly Vital Statistics Report); and unpublished data.

No. 1421. Expectation of Life at Birth, by Race and Sex: 1900 to 1997

[In years. Beginning 1970, excludes deaths of nonresidents of the United States]

Year	All races			White			Black and other			Black		
	Total	Male	Female	Total	Male	Female	Total	Male	Female	Total	Male	Female
DEATH-REGISTRATION STATES												
1900	47.3	46.3	48.3	47.6	46.6	48.7	33.0	32.5	33.5	(NA)	(NA)	(NA)
1905	48.7	47.3	50.2	49.1	47.6	50.6	31.3	29.6	33.1	(NA)	(NA)	(NA)
1910	50.0	48.4	51.8	50.3	48.6	52.0	35.6	33.8	37.5	(NA)	(NA)	(NA)
1915	54.5	52.5	56.8	55.1	53.1	57.5	38.9	37.5	40.5	(NA)	(NA)	(NA)
1920	54.1	53.6	54.6	54.9	54.4	55.6	45.3	45.5	45.2	(NA)	(NA)	(NA)
1925	59.0	57.6	60.6	60.7	59.3	62.4	45.7	44.9	46.7	(NA)	(NA)	(NA)
UNITED STATES[1]												
1930	59.7	58.1	61.6	61.4	59.7	63.5	48.1	47.3	49.2	(NA)	(NA)	(NA)
1935	61.7	59.9	63.9	62.9	61.0	65.0	53.1	51.3	55.2	(NA)	(NA)	(NA)
1940	62.9	60.8	65.2	64.2	62.1	66.6	53.1	51.5	54.9	(NA)	(NA)	(NA)
1945	65.9	63.6	67.9	66.8	64.4	69.5	57.7	56.1	59.6	(NA)	(NA)	(NA)
1950	68.2	65.6	71.1	69.1	66.5	72.2	60.8	59.1	62.9	(NA)	(NA)	(NA)
1955	69.6	66.7	72.8	70.5	67.4	73.7	63.7	61.4	66.1	(NA)	(NA)	(NA)
1960	69.7	66.6	73.1	70.6	67.4	74.1	63.6	61.1	66.3	(NA)	(NA)	(NA)
1965	70.2	66.8	73.8	71.1	67.6	74.8	64.3	61.2	67.6	(NA)	(NA)	(NA)
1970	70.8	67.1	74.7	71.7	68.0	75.6	65.3	61.3	69.4	64.1	60.0	68.3
1975	72.6	68.8	76.6	73.4	69.5	77.3	68.0	63.7	72.4	66.8	62.4	71.3
1980	73.7	70.0	77.4	74.4	70.7	78.1	69.5	65.3	73.6	68.1	63.8	72.5
1985	74.7	71.1	78.2	75.3	71.8	78.7	71.0	67.0	74.8	69.3	65.0	73.4
1990	75.4	71.8	78.8	76.1	72.7	79.4	71.2	67.0	75.2	69.1	64.5	73.6
1995	75.8	72.5	78.9	76.5	73.4	79.6	71.9	67.9	75.7	69.6	65.2	73.9
1997	76.5	73.6	79.2	77.1	74.3	79.4	(NA)	(NA)	(NA)	71.2	67.3	74.7

NA Not available. [1] Alaska included in 1959 and Hawaii in 1960.

Source: Except as noted, U.S. National Center for Health Statistics, Vital Statistics of the United States, annual, and National Vital Statistics Reports (NVSR) (formerly Monthly Vital Statistics Reports).

No. 1422. Social Welfare Expenditures Under Public Programs and National Health Care Expenditures: 1929 to 1997

Year	Social welfare expenditures under Public Programs [1]					National health care expenditures [3]		
		Percent of—		Percent for—			Percent	
	Total (bil. dol.)	Total GDP [2]	Total govt. outlays	Social insurance	Public aid	Total (bil. dol.)	Of total GDP [2]	Government health expenditures
1929	4	3.9	36.3	8.7	1.5	3.6	3.5	13.6
1935	7	9.5	48.6	6.2	45.8	2.9	4.0	19.2
1940	9	9.2	49.0	14.5	40.9	4.0	3.9	20.3
1945	9	4.4	8.4	15.3	11.2	(NA)	(NA)	(NA)
1950	24	8.9	37.6	21.0	10.6	12.7	4.3	27.2
1955	33	8.6	32.7	30.1	9.2	17.7	4.3	25.7
1960	52	10.3	38.4	36.9	7.8	26.9	5.1	24.5
1970	146	14.8	46.5	37.6	11.3	73.2	4.5	37.8
1975	289	19.1	56.6	42.5	14.3	130.7	4.7	42.1
1980	493	18.6	57.2	46.6	14.8	247.3	7.9	42.4
1985	732	18.4	54.4	50.5	13.4	428.7	10.3	40.6
1990	1,049	18.5	58.2	49.0	14.0	699.4	12.2	40.5
1991	1,160	19.8	60.3	48.4	15.6	766.8	13.0	41.5
1992	1,267	20.6	63.7	48.9	16.4	836.5	13.4	42.2
1993	1,367	21.1	66.6	48.2	16.2	898.5	13.7	42.9
1994	1,436	21.0	64.5	47.6	16.6	947.7	13.6	44.6
1995	1,505	20.9	67.5	46.8	16.9	993.7	13.7	45.8
1996	(NA)	(NA)	(NA)	(NA)	(NA)	1,042.5	13.6	46.2
1997	(NA)	(NA)	(NA)	(NA)	(NA)	1,092.4	13.5	46.4

NA Not available.   [1] For additional detail on social welfare expenditures, see Tables 607-609.   [2] Gross domestic product. Source: Bureau of Economic Analysis.   [3] For additional detail on national health expenditures, see Tables 163-165.

Source: Except as noted, Social welfare expenditures, U.S. Social Security Administration, *Social Welfare Expenditures Under Public Programs in the United States, 1929-1966*, Research Report Number 25; and *Social Security Bulletin*, Vol. 60, No. 3, 1997; and unpublished data; and health expenditures for 1929-1955, U.S. Social Security Administration, *Compendium of National Health Expenditures Data*, DHEW Pub. No. (SSA)73-11903, and *National Health Expenditures, Calendar Years 1929-1971*, Research and Statistics Note, No. 3, DHEW Pub. No. (SSA) 73-11701; thereafter, U.S. Health Care Financing Administration, *Health Care Financing Review*, fall 1998.

No. 1423. Specified Reportable Diseases: 1912 to 1997

[Rate per 100,000 population enumerated as of April 1 for 1940, 1950, 1960, 1970, 1980, and 1990 and estimated as of July 1 for all other years]

Year	Tuberculosis, all forms [1]	Syphillis and its sequelae	Gonorrhea	Malaria	Typhoid and paratyphoid fever [2]	Diphtheria	Pertussis (Whooping cough)	Measles	Acute poliomyelitis	Acquired immunodeficiency [3]
1912	(NA)	(NA)	(NA)	(NA)	81.8	139.0	(NA)	310.0	5.5	(X)
1920	(NA)	145.3	175.4	173.0	33.8	139.0	80.0	480.5	2.2	(X)
1925	(NA)	181.2	149.3	86.8	40.0	82.1	131.2	194.3	5.3	(X)
1930	101.5	185.4	135.5	80.0	22.1	54.1	135.6	340.8	7.5	(X)
1935	87.9	205.6	130.8	108.1	14.4	30.8	141.9	584.6	8.5	(X)
1940	78.0	359.7	133.8	59.2	7.4	11.8	139.6	220.7	7.4	(X)
1945	86.8	282.3	225.8	47.4	3.7	14.1	101.0	110.2	10.3	(X)
1950	80.4	154.2	204.0	1.4	1.6	3.8	80.1	210.1	22.1	(X)
1955	46.9	76.0	149.2	0.3	1.0	1.2	38.2	337.9	17.6	(X)
1960	30.8	68.0	139.6	(Z)	0.5	0.5	8.3	245.4	1.8	(X)
1965	25.3	59.7	163.8	0.1	0.2	0.1	3.5	135.1	(Z)	(X)
1970	18.3	44.8	294.2	1.5	0.2	0.2	2.1	23.2	(Z)	(X)
1975	15.9	37.3	464.1	0.2	0.2	0.1	0.8	11.3	(Z)	(X)
1980	12.3	30.3	441.9	0.9	0.2	(Z)	0.8	5.9	(Z)	(X)
1985	9.3	28.4	383.1	0.4	0.2	(Z)	1.5	1.2	-	3.5
1990	10.3	53.8	276.6	0.5	0.2	-	1.8	11.2	-	16.7
1991	10.4	51.7	249.5	0.5	0.2	-	1.1	3.8	-	17.3
1992	10.5	45.3	201.6	0.4	0.2	-	1.6	0.9	-	17.8
1993	9.8	39.7	172.4	0.6	0.2	(NA)	2.6	0.1	-	40.2
1994	9.4	32.0	168.4	0.5	0.2	-	1.8	0.4	-	30.1
1995	8.7	26.2	149.5	0.6	0.1	(NA)	2.0	0.1	-	27.2
1996	8.0	20.0	122.8	0.7	0.2	(Z)	2.9	0.2	(Z)	25.2
1997	7.4	17.4	121.4	0.8	0.1	(Z)	2.5	0.1	(Z)	21.9

- Represents zero.   NA Not available.   X Not applicable.   Z Less than .05 cases per 100,000.   [1] New reported active cases. New diagnostic standards introduced in 1980.   [2] Beginning 1950, excludes paratyphoid fever.   [3] AIDS became a notifiable disease in 1984.

Source: 1912, U.S. Public Health Service, *Public Health Reports*, various issues; 1920-1950, U.S. National Office of Vital Statistics, *Vital Statistics, Special Reports*, Vol. 37, No. 9; 1951-1970, U.S. Center for Disease Control, *Morbidity and Mortality Weekly Report, Annual Supplement*; 1971-1997, U.S. Centers for Disease Control and Prevention, Atlanta, GA, *Summary of Notifiable Diseases, United States, 1997, Morbidity and Mortality Weekly Report*, Vol. 46, No. 54, November 20, 1998.

U.S. Census Bureau, Statistical Abstract of the United States: 1999

No. 1424. Food Consumption Per Capita and Food Expenditures: 1929 to 1997

[In pounds, retail weight, except as indicated. Consumption represents the residual after exports, nonfood use and ending stocks are subtracted from the sum of beginning stocks, domestic production, and imports. Based on U.S. Census Bureau estimated population]

Year	Consumption								Food expenditures	
	Red meat, total [1]	Poultry, total	Fish and shellfish, total	Fruits, total	Veg-etables, total	Milk, total (gallons)	Carbon-ated soft drinks, total (gallons)	Alcoholic, total (gallons) [2]	Percent of dispos-able personal income	Percent spent away from home
1929	(NA)	(NA)	(NA)	(NA)	(NA)	(NA)	(NA)	(NA)	23.9	13.4
1935	(NA)	(NA)	(NA)	(NA)	(NA)	(NA)	(NA)	(NA)	24.0	12.9
1940	(NA)	(NA)	(NA)	(NA)	(NA)	(NA)	(NA)	(NA)	21.1	15.2
1945	(NA)	(NA)	(NA)	(NA)	(NA)	(NA)	(NA)	(NA)	19.5	19.6
1950	(NA)	(NA)	(NA)	(NA)	(NA)	(NA)	(NA)	(NA)	20.6	17.8
1955	(NA)	(NA)	(NA)	(NA)	(NA)	(NA)	(NA)	(NA)	18.8	18.6
1960	(NA)	(NA)	(NA)	(NA)	(NA)	(NA)	(NA)	(NA)	17.4	19.9
1965	(NA)	(NA)	(NA)	(NA)	(NA)	(NA)	(NA)	(NA)	15.0	22.8
1970	131.7	33.8	11.7	237.7	335.4	31.3	24.3	35.7	13.8	26.3
1975	125.8	32.9	12.1	252.1	337.0	29.5	28.2	39.7	13.9	28.5
1980	126.4	40.8	12.4	262.4	336.4	27.6	35.1	42.8	13.4	32.2
1985	124.9	45.5	15.0	269.4	358.1	26.7	35.7	40.7	12.0	35.8
1990	112.3	56.3	15.0	273.5	382.8	25.7	46.3	39.9	11.6	36.7
1995	115.1	62.9	14.9	285.4	405.0	24.3	51.6	38.0	10.9	38.2
1996	112.8	64.4	14.7	289.8	416.2	24.3	52.0	38.6	10.8	38.0
1997	111.0	64.8	14.5	294.7	416.0	24.0	53.0	38.9	10.7	38.0

NA Not available.   [1] Boneless, trimmed weight.   [2] Adult population.

Source: U.S. Dept. of Agriculture, Economic Research Service, *Food Consumption, Prices, and Expenditures*, annual; and unpublished data. *Agricultural Outlook*, monthly.

No. 1425. Education Summary—Enrollment, Graduates, and Degrees: 1900 to 1998, and Projections 1999 and 2000

[For school year beginning in year shown. (17,072 represents 17,072,000)]

Year	Elementary and secondary school enrollment						High school graduate		Higher education		
	Total (1,000)		Public (1,000)			Grades 9-12 enroll-ment as per-cent 14-17 year olds	Total (1,000)	As per-cent of 17 yr. old popu-lation	Enroll-ment (1,000)	BA degrees conferred [1] (1,000)	
	Number	K-8	9-12	Number	K-8	9-12					Total (1,000)	As per-cent high school gradu-ates 4 years earlier
1900	17,072	16,422	650	15,703	15,161	542	10.6	[2]95	[2]6.4	[2]238	28.7	36
1905	18,056	17,231	824	16,642	15,919	723	12.4	(NA)	(NA)	(NA)	32.0	32
1910	19,636	18,349	1,288	18,035	16,878	1,157	17.8	[3]156	[3]8.8	354	37.5	30
1915	22,172	20,306	1,866	20,352	18,641	1,711	24.5	(NA)	(NA)	441	45.3	25
1920	24,049	21,292	2,757	22,409	19,872	2,537	35.0	[4]311	[4]16.8	(NA)	(NA)	(NA)
1925	27,180	23,127	4,053	24,741	20,984	3,757	45.9	(NA)	(NA)	941	97.3	27
1930	28,695	23,553	5,142	25,977	21,207	4,770	54.9	747	32.1	(NA)	(NA)	(NA)
1935	29,006	22,644	6,362	26,367	20,393	5,975	65.9	1,015	42.7	1,208	143.1	17
1940	27,910	20,726	7,184	25,296	18,582	6,714	73.0	1,080	47.4	1,677	136.2	11
1945	26,124	19,937	6,187	23,300	17,678	5,622	67.7	(NA)	(NA)	2,281	382.5	35
1950	29,301	22,831	6,470	25,706	19,900	5,806	76.6	1,415	63.1	2,653	309.5	26
1955	35,872	28,177	7,696	31,163	24,290	6,873	83.5	1,964	67.9	(NA)	365.2	25
1960	43,070	33,191	9,879	37,260	28,439	8,821	89.0	2,665	76.4	5,921	520.1	27
1965	48,368	35,366	13,002	42,068	30,466	11,602	91.9	2,937	75.9	8,581	839.7	31
1970	51,257	36,610	14,647	45,894	32,558	13,336	92.0	3,148	73.7	11,185	925.7	31
1975	49,819	34,215	15,604	44,819	30,515	14,304	91.1	3,020	71.8	12,097	935.1	30
1980	46,208	31,639	14,570	40,877	27,647	13,231	90.3	2,643	73.0	12,247	987.8	33
1985	44,979	31,229	13,750	39,422	27,034	12,388	92.4	2,503	73.2	13,819	1,094.5	41
1990	46,448	33,973	12,475	41,216	29,878	11,338	93.7	2,482	73.2	14,359	1,136.6	41
1991	47,246	34,580	12,666	42,047	30,506	11,541	94.4	2,490	72.2	14,487	1,165.2	43
1992	48,198	35,300	12,898	42,823	31,088	11,735	94.5	2,479	71.7	14,305	1,169.3	45
1993	48,936	35,784	13,152	43,465	31,504	11,961	94.4	2,538	70.7	14,279	1,160.1	46
1994	49,707	36,258	13,449	44,111	31,898	12,213	93.2	2,548	70.0	14,261	1,164.8	47
1995	50,541	36,772	13,769	44,841	32,341	12,500	93.3	2,623	69.6	14,300	1,166.0	47
1996	51,376	37,245	14,131	45,593	32,759	12,834	93.3	2,708	69.0	14,351	1,172.0	47
1997	51,821	37,496	14,325	45,954	32,951	13,003	92.8	(NA)	(NA)	14,589	1,166.0	46
1998	52,719	38,110	14,609	46,792	33,522	13,270	(NA)	(NA)	(NA)	14,758	1,161.0	46
1999, proj.	53,112	38,338	14,774	47,142	33,722	13,420	(NA)	(NA)	(NA)	14,889	1,173.0	45
2000, proj. .	53,446	38,543	14,903	47,440	33,903	13,537	(NA)	(NA)	(NA)			

NA Not available.   [1] Prior to 1906, includes first professional degrees.   [2] 1899 data.   [3] 1909 data.   [4] 1919 data.

Source: U.S. National Center for Education Statistics, 1900-1985, *120 Years of Education, A Statistical Portrait*; beginning 1990, *Digest of Education Statistics*, annual.

No. 1426. Educational Attainment, by Sex: 1910 to 1998

[As of **March,** except as indicated. Noninstitutional population, except 1940, 1950, 1960 based on resident population]

Year	Total Less than 5 years of elementary school	Total High school completion or higher[1]	Total 4 or more years of college[2]	Male Less than 5 years of elementary school	Male High school completion or higher[1]	Male 4 or more years of college[2]	Female Less than 5 years of elementary school	Female High school completion or higher[1]	Female 4 or more years of college[2]
1910[3]	23.8	13.5	2.7	(NA)	(NA)	(NA)	(NA)	(NA)	(NA)
1920[3]	22.0	16.4	3.3	(NA)	(NA)	(NA)	(NA)	(NA)	(NA)
1930[3]	17.5	19.1	3.9	(NA)	(NA)	(NA)	(NA)	(NA)	(NA)
1940, April	13.5	24.1	4.6	14.8	22.3	5.4	12.2	25.9	3.7
1947	10.4	32.6	5.4	11.4	30.8	6.1	9.5	34.3	4.6
1950, April	10.8	33.3	6.0	11.9	31.5	7.1	9.8	35.1	5.0
1960, April	8.3	41.0	7.7	9.4	39.4	9.6	7.3	42.5	5.8
1965	6.8	49.0	9.4	7.7	48.0	12.0	5.9	49.9	7.1
1970	5.3	55.2	11.0	5.9	55.0	14.1	4.7	55.4	8.2
1975	4.2	62.5	13.9	4.7	63.1	17.6	3.8	62.1	10.6
1980	3.4	68.6	17.0	3.6	69.2	20.9	3.2	68.1	13.6
1985	2.7	73.9	19.4	2.9	74.4	23.1	2.5	73.5	16.0
1990	2.4	77.6	21.3	2.7	77.7	24.4	2.2	77.5	18.4
1991	2.4	78.4	21.4	2.7	78.5	24.3	2.1	78.3	18.8
1992	2.1	79.4	21.4	2.3	79.7	24.3	2.0	79.2	18.6
1993	2.1	80.2	21.9	2.2	80.5	24.8	2.0	80.0	19.2
1994	1.9	80.9	22.2	2.1	81.0	25.1	2.0	80.7	19.6
1995	1.8	81.7	23.0	2.0	81.7	26.0	1.7	81.6	20.2
1996	1.8	81.7	23.6	1.9	81.9	26.0	1.7	81.6	21.4
1997	1.7	82.1	23.9	1.8	82.0	26.2	1.7	81.6	21.7
1998	1.6	82.8	24.4	1.7	82.8	26.5	1.6	82.9	22.4

NA Not available. [1] 1910 to 1992, includes all persons with at least 4 years of high school; thereafter, represents persons that are high school graduates only. [2] Beginning 1993, persons with a bachelor's degree or higher. [3] Estimates based on Census Bureau retrojection of 1940 Census data on education; see 1960 Census Monograph, "Education of the American Population," by John K. Folger and Charles B. Nam.

Source: Except as indicated, U.S. Census Bureau, Current Population Reports, P20-513; and <http://148.129.31:80/population/socdemo/education/tablea-01.txt> (released 10 December 1998).

No. 1427. Money Income of Families—Median Income in Current and Constant (1997) Dollars, by Race and Type of Family: 1947 to 1997

[Constant dollars based on CPI-U-X1 deflator. Based on Current Population Survey; see text, Sections 1 and 14, and Appendix III. For definition of median, see Guide to Tabular Presentation]

Year	Current dollars All families[1]	Current dollars White	Current dollars Black[2]	Current dollars Married-couple families Total	Current dollars Married-couple families Wife in paid labor force	Current dollars Female householder, no husband present	Constant (1997) dollars All families[1]	Constant (1997) dollars White	Constant (1997) dollars Black[2]	Constant (1997) dollars Married-couple families Total	Constant (1997) dollars Married-couple families Wife in paid labor force	Constant (1997) dollars Female householder, no husband present
1947	3,031	3,157	1,614	3,109	(NA)	2,172	20,102	20,938	10,704	20,620	(NA)	14,405
1950	3,319	3,445	1,869	3,446	4,003	1,922	20,332	21,104	11,449	21,110	24,522	11,774
1955	4,418	4,613	2,544	4,599	5,622	2,471	24,367	25,443	14,031	25,366	31,008	13,629
1960	5,620	5,835	3,230	5,873	6,900	2,968	28,013	29,084	16,100	29,274	34,393	14,794
1965	6,957	7,251	3,993	7,265	8,597	3,532	32,649	34,029	18,739	34,095	40,346	16,576
1970	9,867	10,236	6,279	10,516	12,276	5,093	38,345	39,779	24,401	40,867	47,707	19,792
1975	13,719	14,268	8,779	14,867	17,237	6,844	39,180	40,748	25,072	42,458	49,227	19,546
1980	21,023	21,904	12,674	23,141	26,879	10,408	40,999	42,717	24,717	45,129	52,419	20,297
1985	27,735	29,152	16,786	31,100	36,431	13,660	41,371	43,484	25,039	46,390	54,342	20,376
1990	35,353	36,915	21,423	39,895	46,777	16,932	43,414	45,332	26,308	48,991	57,442	20,793
1991	35,939	37,783	21,548	40,995	48,169	16,692	42,351	44,524	25,392	48,309	56,763	19,670
1992	36,573	38,670	21,103	41,890	49,775	17,025	41,839	44,238	24,141	47,921	56,941	19,476
1993	36,959	39,300	21,542	43,005	51,204	17,443	41,051	43,652	23,927	47,767	56,874	19,374
1994	38,782	40,884	24,698	44,959	53,309	18,236	42,001	44,277	26,748	48,690	57,733	19,750
1995	40,611	42,646	25,970	47,062	55,823	19,691	42,769	44,913	27,350	49,563	58,790	20,738
1996	42,300	44,756	26,522	49,707	58,381	19,911	43,271	45,783	27,131	50,848	59,721	20,368
1997	44,568	46,754	28,602	51,591	60,669	21,023	44,568	46,754	28,602	51,591	60,669	21,023

NA Not available. [1] Includes other races not shown separately. [2] 1947-1966, Black and other races.

Source: U.S. Census Bureau, Current Population Reports, P60-200 and P60-203; and <http://www.census.gov/hhes/income/histinc/f05.html> and <http://www.census.gov/hhes/income/histinc/f07.html> (accessed 15 June 1999).

U.S. Census Bureau, Statistical Abstract of the United States: 1999

No. 1428. Housing Units—Historical Trends for Selected Characteristics: 1940 to 1997

[1940 to 1990, as of **April 1** and based on the Census of Population and and Housing, which represents historical trends for housing. Data for 1997 based on American Housing Survey and represent current trends. The two sources are not directly comparable due to several differences in methodology; see sources for details]

Characteristic	1940	1950	1960	1970	1980	1990	1997
TENURE							
Occupied units, total	34,855	42,826	53,024	63,445	80,390	91,947	99,487
Owner occupied.	15,196	23,560	32,797	39,886	51,795	59,025	65,487
Percent of occupied	43.6	55.0	61.9	62.9	64.4	64.2	65.8
Renter occupied.	19,659	19,266	20,227	23,560	28,595	32,923	34,000
UNITS IN STRUCTURE							
All housing units [1]	37,325	45,983	58,315	67,699	86,759	102,264	112,357
1, detached	23,731	29,116	40,103	44,801	53,596	60,383	68,109
1, attached	[2]2,835	[3]2,799	3,655	1,990	3,587	5,378	6,778
2	3,464	5,302	4,464	5,444	5,309	4,948	[4]
3 or 4	2,259	3,374	3,088	3,563	4,373	4,928	10,363
5 or more	3,928	5,078	6,238	9,829	15,478	18,105	18,806
5 to 9	(NA)	2,138	(NA)	(NA)	3,835	4,936	5,657
10 to 49	(NA)	2,268	(NA)	(NA)	7,083	8,774	8,902
50 or more	(NA)	671	(NA)	(NA)	4,560	4,395	4,247
Mobile home or trailer	(NA)	315	767	2,073	4,416	7,400	8,301
Other	[5]1,108	(NA)	(NA)	(NA)	(NA)	1,121	(NA)
PLUMBING FACILITIES							
All housing units	35,026	44,502	58,315	67,657	86,693	102,264	112,357
Complete plumbing facilities	19,174	28,729	48,537	62,984	84,359	101,162	110,149
Lacking complete plumbing facilities	15,852	15,773	9,778	4,672	2,334	1,102	2,208
VEHICLES AVAILABLE [6]							
Occupied housing units	33,884	41,829	53,022	63,445	80,390	91,947	99,487
None	(NA)	(NA)	11,417	11,081	10,390	10,602	9,447
1	(NA)	(NA)	30,189	30,268	28,565	31,039	31,658
2	(NA)	(NA)	10,074	18,600	27,347	34,361	38,445
3 or more	(NA)	(NA)	1,342	3,495	14,088	15,945	19,938
TELEPHONE IN HOUSING UNIT [7]							
Occupied housing units	33,884	41,829	53,024	63,450	80,390	91,947	99,487
With telephone	(NA)	(NA)	41,618	55,177	74,720	87,130	93,377
No telephone	(NA)	(NA)	11,406	8,273	5,670	4,817	6,110

NA Not available. [1] Data for 1970 and 1980 are "Year-round housing units," which exclude seasonal and migratory vacant units. [2] Includes 1,656,858 units classified as "2-family side-by-side." [3] Includes 1,588,902 units classified as "1 and 2 dwelling unit." [4] Structures with "2 units" included with units of "3 or 4." [5] Covers 166,975 units classified as "Other dwelling place" and 940,726 units classified as "1- to 4-family with business." [6] For 1960 and 1970, vehicles available was restricted to only automobiles; beginning 1980, includes trucks and vans of 1-ton capacity or less. [7] Beginning 1980, data are not completely comparable with earlier years due to change in question asked.

Source: U.S. Census Bureau, 1940 to 1990, *1990 Census of Housing*, Series CH-1, and earlier Census reports; also *Current Housing Reports*, Series H-121-94-1, "Tracking the American Dream—50 Years of Housing History From the Census Bureau: 1940-1990." 1997, *Current Housing Reports*, Series H150-97, American Housing Survey in the United States.

No. 1429. National Air Pollutant Emissions: 1900 to 1997

[In thousands of tons, except as indicated. PM-10=Particulate matter of less than 10 microns. Methodologies to estimate data for 1970 to 1984 period and 1985 to present emissions differ. Beginning with 1985, the estimates are based on a modified National Acid Precipitation Assessment Program inventory]

Year	Emissions							Resident population (1,000)	Real gross domestic product [2] (bil. dol.)
	PM-10	PM-10, fugitive dust [1]	Sulfur dioxide	Nitrogen dioxides	Volatile organic compounds	Carbon monoxide	Lead (ton)		
1900	(NA)	(NA)	9,988	2,611	8,503	(NA)	(NA)	76,094	(NA)
1905	(NA)	(NA)	13,959	3,314	8,850	(NA)	(NA)	83,822	(NA)
1910	(NA)	(NA)	17,275	4,102	9,117	(NA)	(NA)	92,407	(NA)
1915	(NA)	(NA)	20,290	4,672	9,769	(NA)	(NA)	100,546	(NA)
1920	(NA)	(NA)	21,144	5,159	10,004	(NA)	(NA)	106,461	(NA)
1925	(NA)	(NA)	23,264	7,302	14,257	(NA)	(NA)	115,829	(NA)
1930	(NA)	(NA)	21,106	8,018	19,451	(NA)	(NA)	123,077	719.7
1935	(NA)	(NA)	16,978	6,639	17,208	(NA)	(NA)	127,250	698.4
1940	15,956	(NA)	19,953	7,374	17,161	93,615	(NA)	132,457	941.2
1945	16,545	(NA)	26,373	9,332	18,140	98,112	(NA)	133,434	1,626.7
1950	17,133	(NA)	22,358	10,093	20,936	102,609	(NA)	151,868	1,611.3
1955	16,346	(NA)	21,453	11,667	23,249	106,177	(NA)	165,069	2,001.1
1960	15,558	(NA)	22,227	14,140	24,459	109,745	(NA)	179,979	2,262.9
1965	14,198	(NA)	26,380	17,424	30,247	118,912	(NA)	193,526	2,881.1
1970	13,190	(NA)	31,161	21,639	30,817	128,761	220,869	203,984	3,397.6
1975	7,803	(NA)	28,011	23,151	25,895	115,968	159,659	215,465	3,873.9
1980	7,287	(NA)	25,905	24,875	26,167	116,702	74,153	227,225	4,615.0
1985	4,695	40,889	23,230	23,488	24,227	115,644	22,890	237,924	5,323.5
1990	5,425	24,419	23,678	23,436	20,935	95,794	4,975	249,440	6,136.3
1995	4,306	22,454	19,189	23,768	20,558	89,151	3,924	262,761	6,761.7
1997	8,428	25,153	20,369	23,582	19,214	87,451	3,915	267,636	7,269.8

NA Not available. [1] Sources such as agricultural tilling, construction, mining and quarrying, paved roads, unpaved roads, and wind erosion. [2] Gross domestic product in chained (1992) dollars; see Table 1434 and text, Section 14, Income.

Source: U.S. Environmental Protection Agency, *National Air Pollutant Emission Trends, 1900-1997*, EPA 454/C-98-007.

No. 1430. Employment Status of the Civilian Population: 1929 to 1998

[In thousands (49,180 represents 49,180,000), except as indicated. Annual averages of monthly figures. For the civilian noninstitutional population 16 years old and over, except as indicated. 1947-98, based on Current Population Survey; see text, Section 13, Labor Force]

Year	Civilian noninstitutional population	Civilian labor force		Employment/ population ratio [1]	Employed		Unemployed		Not in labor force, number
		Total	Employed		Agriculture	Nonagricultural industries	Number	Percent of labor force	
14 AND OVER									
1929	(NA)	49,180	47,630	(NA)	10,450	37,180	1,550	3.2	(NA)
1930	(NA)	49,820	45,480	(NA)	10,340	35,140	4,340	8.7	(NA)
1933	(NA)	51,590	38,760	(NA)	10,090	28,670	12,830	24.9	(NA)
1935	(NA)	52,870	42,260	(NA)	10,110	32,150	10,610	20.1	(NA)
1940	99,840	55,640	47,520	47.6	9,540	37,980	8,120	14.6	44,200
1945	94,090	53,860	52,820	56.1	8,580	44,240	1,040	1.9	40,230
1947	106,018	60,168	57,812	54.5	8,256	49,557	2,356	3.9	45,850
16 AND OVER									
1947	101,827	59,350	57,038	56.0	7,890	49,148	2,311	3.9	42,477
1950	104,995	62,208	58,918	56.1	7,160	51,758	3,288	5.3	42,787
1955	109,683	65,023	62,170	56.7	6,450	55,722	2,852	4.4	44,660
1960	117,245	69,628	65,778	56.1	5,458	60,318	3,852	5.5	47,617
1965	126,513	74,455	71,088	56.2	4,361	66,726	3,366	4.5	52,058
1970	137,085	82,771	78,678	57.4	3,463	75,215	4,093	4.9	54,315
1971	140,216	84,382	79,367	56.6	3,394	75,972	5,016	5.9	55,834
1972	144,126	87,034	82,153	57.0	3,484	78,669	4,882	5.6	57,091
1973	147,096	89,429	85,064	57.8	3,470	81,594	4,365	4.9	57,667
1974	150,120	91,949	86,794	57.8	3,515	83,279	5,156	5.6	58,171
1975	153,153	93,775	85,846	56.1	3,408	82,438	7,929	8.5	59,377
1976	156,150	96,158	88,752	56.8	3,331	85,421	7,406	7.7	59,991
1977	159,033	99,009	92,017	57.9	3,283	88,734	6,991	7.1	60,025
1978	161,910	102,251	96,048	59.3	3,387	92,661	6,202	6.1	59,659
1979	164,863	104,962	98,824	59.9	3,347	95,477	6,137	5.8	59,900
1980	167,745	106,940	99,303	59.2	3,364	95,938	7,637	7.1	60,806
1981	170,130	108,670	100,397	59.0	3,368	97,030	8,273	7.6	61,460
1982	172,271	110,204	99,526	57.8	3,401	96,125	10,678	9.7	62,067
1983	174,215	111,550	100,834	57.9	3,383	97,450	10,717	9.6	62,665
1984	176,383	113,544	105,005	59.5	3,321	101,685	8,539	7.5	62,839
1985	178,206	115,461	107,150	60.1	3,179	103,971	8,312	7.2	62,744
1986	180,587	117,834	109,597	60.7	3,163	106,434	8,237	7.0	62,752
1987	182,753	119,865	112,440	61.5	3,208	109,232	7,425	6.2	62,888
1988	184,613	121,669	114,968	62.3	3,169	111,800	6,701	5.5	62,944
1989	186,393	123,869	117,342	63.0	3,199	114,142	6,528	5.3	62,523
1990	189,164	125,840	118,793	62.8	3,223	115,570	7,047	5.6	63,324
1991	190,925	126,346	117,718	61.7	3,269	114,449	8,628	6.8	64,578
1992	192,805	128,105	118,492	61.5	3,247	115,245	9,613	7.5	64,700
1993	194,838	129,200	120,259	61.7	3,115	117,144	8,940	6.9	65,638
1994	196,814	131,056	123,060	62.5	3,409	119,651	7,996	6.1	65,758
1995	198,584	132,304	124,900	62.9	3,440	121,460	7,404	5.6	66,280
1996	200,591	133,943	126,708	63.2	3,443	123,264	7,236	5.4	66,647
1997	203,133	136,297	129,558	63.8	3,399	126,159	6,739	4.9	66,837
1998	205,220	137,673	131,463	64.1	3,378	128,085	6,210	4.5	67,547

NA Not available. [1] Civilian employed as a percent of the civilian noninstitutional population.
Source: U.S. Bureau of Labor Statistics, Bulletin 2307; and *Employment and Earnings*, monthly.

No. 1431. Marital Status of Women in the Civilian Labor Force: 1900 to 1998

[Persons 16 years old and over, except as indicated. **1900-60, as of month indicated; 1955-98, annual averages of monthly figures.** For civilian noninstitutional population. Based on the Current Population Survey; see text, Section 1, Population, and Appendix III]

Year	Female labor force (1,000)				Female participation rate [3]			
	Total	Single	Married [1]	Other [2]	Total	Single	Married [1]	Other [2]
1900 (June) [4]	4,997	3,307	769	920	(NA)	(NA)	(NA)	(NA)
1910 (April) [4]	7,640	4,602	1,891	1,147	(NA)	(NA)	(NA)	(NA)
1920 (Jan.) [4]	8,347	[5]6,427	1,920	([5])	(NA)	(NA)	(NA)	(NA)
1930 (April) [4]	10,632	5,735	3,071	1,826	(NA)	(NA)	(NA)	(NA)
1940 (April) [4]	13,007	6,377	4,675	1,955	(NA)	(NA)	(NA)	(NA)
1950 (April) [4]	16,553	5,274	8,635	2,644	(NA)	(NA)	(NA)	(NA)
1960 (April) [4]	22,410	5,282	13,610	3,518	(NA)	(NA)	(NA)	(NA)
1955	20,548	5,281	10,809	4,458	35.7	61.1	28.5	40.7
1960	23,240	5,410	12,893	4,937	37.7	58.6	31.9	41.6
1965	26,200	5,976	14,829	5,396	39.3	54.5	34.9	40.7
1970	31,543	7,265	18,475	5,804	43.3	56.8	40.5	40.3
1975	37,475	9,125	21,484	6,866	46.3	59.8	44.3	40.1
1980	45,487	11,865	24,980	8,643	51.5	64.4	49.9	43.6
1985	51,050	13,163	27,894	9,993	54.5	66.6	53.8	45.1
1990	56,829	14,612	30,901	11,315	57.5	66.7	58.4	47.2
1995	60,944	15,467	33,359	12,118	58.9	66.8	61.0	47.4
1998	63,714	17,087	33,857	12,771	59.8	68.5	61.2	48.8

NA Not available. [1] Husband present. [2] Widowed, divorced, or separated. [3] Percent of civilian noninstitutional population of each specified group in the civilian labor force. [4] 1900-1930, persons 15 years old and over and 1940-1960, persons 14 years old and over. [5] Widowed or divorced included with "Single."
Source: U.S. Census Bureau, 1900-30, *U.S. Census of Population: 1930*, Vol. IV.; 1940-60, *U.S. Census of Population: 1970*, Vol. I; and 1955-98, U.S. Bureau of Labor Statistics, *Bulletin 2307*; and unpublished data.

U.S. Census Bureau, Statistical Abstract of the United States: 1999

No. 1432. Nonfarm Establishments, by Industry: 1919 to 1998

[27,078 represents 27,078,000. Based on data from establishment reports. See headnote, Table 688 in Section 13, Labor Force]

Item and year	Total	Goods-producing Total	Mining	Construction	Manufacturing	Service-producing Total	T & PU [1]	Wholesale trade	Retail trade	FIRE [2]	Services	Government
EMPLOYEES (1,000)												
1919	27,078	12,828	1,133	1,036	10,659	14,250	3,711	(NA)	(NA)	(NA)	(NA)	2,676
1925	28,766	12,489	1,089	1,461	9,939	16,277	3,826	(NA)	(NA)	(NA)	(NA)	2,800
1930	29,409	11,958	1,009	1,387	9,562	17,451	3,685	(NA)	(NA)	(NA)	(NA)	3,148
1935	27,039	10,893	897	927	9,069	16,146	2,786	(NA)	(NA)	(NA)	(NA)	3,481
1940	32,361	13,221	925	1,311	10,985	19,140	3,038	1,841	4,909	1,485	3,665	4,202
1945	40,374	17,507	836	1,147	15,524	22,867	3,906	1,955	5,359	1,481	4,222	5,944
1950	45,197	18,506	901	2,364	15,241	26,691	4,034	2,643	6,743	1,888	5,356	6,026
1955	50,641	20,513	792	2,839	16,882	30,128	4,141	2,934	7,601	2,298	6,240	6,914
1960	54,189	20,434	712	2,926	16,796	33,755	4,004	3,153	8,238	2,628	7,378	8,353
1965	60,765	21,926	632	3,232	18,062	38,839	4,036	3,477	9,239	2,977	9,036	10,074
1970	70,880	23,578	623	3,588	19,367	47,302	4,515	4,006	11,034	3,645	11,548	12,554
1975	76,945	22,600	752	3,525	18,323	54,345	4,542	4,430	12,630	4,165	13,892	14,686
1980	90,406	25,658	1,027	4,346	20,285	64,748	5,146	5,292	15,018	5,160	17,890	16,241
1985	97,387	24,842	927	4,668	19,248	72,544	5,233	5,727	17,315	5,948	21,927	16,394
1990	109,403	24,905	709	5,120	19,076	84,497	5,777	6,173	19,601	6,709	27,934	18,304
1995	117,191	24,265	581	5,160	18,524	92,925	6,132	6,378	21,187	6,806	33,117	19,305
1998	125,832	25,256	575	5,965	18,716	100,576	6,549	6,825	22,475	7,341	37,525	19,862
PERCENT DISTRIBUTION												
1919	100.0	47.4	4.2	3.8	39.4	52.6	13.7	-	-	-	-	9.9
1930	100.0	40.7	3.4	4.7	32.5	59.3	12.5	-	-	-	-	10.7
1940	100.0	40.9	2.9	4.1	33.9	59.1	9.4	5.7	15.2	4.6	11.3	13.0
1950	100.0	40.9	2.0	5.2	33.7	59.1	8.9	5.8	14.9	4.2	11.9	13.3
1960	100.0	37.7	1.3	5.4	31.0	62.3	7.4	5.8	15.2	4.8	13.6	15.4
1970	100.0	33.3	0.9	5.1	27.3	66.7	6.4	5.7	15.6	5.1	16.3	17.7
1980	100.0	28.4	1.1	4.8	22.4	71.6	5.7	5.9	16.6	5.7	19.8	18.0
1990	100.0	22.8	0.6	4.7	17.4	77.2	5.3	5.6	17.9	6.1	25.5	16.7
1998	100.0	20.1	0.5	4.7	14.9	79.9	5.2	5.4	17.9	5.8	29.8	15.8
WEEKLY EARNINGS [3]												
1950	53	(NA)	67	70	58	(NA)	(NA)	55	40	48	(NA)	(NA)
1960	81	(NA)	105	113	90	(NA)	(NA)	91	58	75	(NA)	(NA)
1970	120	(NA)	164	196	133	(NA)	156	137	82	113	97	(NA)
1980	235	(NA)	397	368	289	(NA)	351	267	147	210	191	(NA)
1990	345	(NA)	603	526	442	(NA)	496	411	194	357	319	(NA)
1998	442	(NA)	744	643	563	(NA)	606	538	255	512	420	(NA)

- Represents zero.   NA Not available.   [1] Transportation and public utilities.   [2] Finance, insurance, and real estate.
[3] Average hours and earnings. Private production and related workers in mining, manufacturing, and construction; nonsupervisory employees in other industries.
Source: U.S. Bureau of Labor Statistics, *Employment and Earnings*, monthly, June issues and Internet site <http://stats.bls.gov/ceshome.htm>.

No. 1433. Personal Consumption Expenditures, by Type: 1929 to 1997

Year	Total [1]	Food and tobacco	Clothing [2]	Personal care	Housing	Household operation	Medical care	Personal business	Transportation	Recreation
1929	77.5	21.2	11.2	1.1	11.7	10.7	3.1	3.9	7.7	4.4
1933	45.9	12.8	5.4	0.7	8.1	6.4	2.1	2.5	4.0	2.2
1935	55.9	17.6	7.0	0.8	7.9	7.7	2.4	2.8	5.4	2.6
1940	71.2	22.0	8.9	1.0	9.7	10.4	3.2	3.2	7.2	3.8
1945	119.9	43.5	19.6	2.0	12.8	15.5	5.2	4.2	6.8	6.2
1950	192.7	58.1	23.7	2.4	21.7	29.1	9.4	6.6	25.4	11.2
1955	259.1	73.6	28.4	3.7	34.4	37.3	14.2	10.1	34.9	14.6
1960	332.2	89.2	32.7	5.6	48.2	46.7	22.1	14.6	42.9	18.5
1965	444.3	108.8	41.4	8.1	65.4	62.1	34.1	20.9	59.1	26.8
1970	648.1	154.6	57.6	11.8	94.0	84.8	60.0	32.0	81.1	43.1
1975	1,029.1	238.2	85.6	16.7	147.0	135.4	107.9	53.0	130.2	70.5
1980	1,760.4	376.2	132.3	26.6	255.2	232.6	206.4	101.2	238.4	116.3
1985	2,704.8	497.3	188.3	39.1	407.1	342.0	366.7	182.6	372.8	185.9
1990	3,839.3	672.5	262.7	57.3	586.3	436.2	615.6	290.1	463.3	281.6
1995	4,953.9	780.4	321.8	71.8	750.4	559.4	875.0	388.8	574.1	404.2
1997	5,493.7	832.3	353.3	79.4	829.8	620.7	957.3	459.1	636.4	462.9
PERCENT DISTRIBUTION										
1929	100.0	27.4	14.5	1.4	15.1	13.8	4.0	5.0	9.9	5.7
1950	100.0	30.2	12.3	1.2	11.3	15.1	4.9	3.4	13.2	5.8
1970	100.0	23.9	8.9	1.8	14.5	13.1	9.3	4.9	12.5	6.7
1990	100.0	17.5	6.8	1.5	15.3	11.4	16.0	7.6	12.1	7.3
1997	100.0	15.2	6.4	1.4	15.1	11.3	17.4	8.4	11.6	8.4

[1] Includes other categories, not shown separately.   [2] Includes accessories, and jewelry.

Source: U.S. Bureau of Economic Analysis, *National Income and Product Accounts of the United States, 1929-94: Vol. 1*; and *Survey of Current Business*, August 1998.

No. 1434. Gross Domestic Product in Current and Real (1992) Dollars: 1929 to 1998

[In billions of dollars (103.8 represents $103,800,000,000). For definition of gross domestic product and chained dollars, see text, Section 14, Income]

Year	Current dollars					Chained (1992) dollars				
	Gross domestic product	Personal consumption expenditures	Gross private domestic investment	Net exports of goods and services	Government consumption expenditures and gross investment	Gross domestic product	Personal consumption expenditures	Gross private domestic investment	Net exports of goods and services	Government consumption expenditures and gross investment
1929	103.8	77.5	16.7	0.4	9.3	790.9	593.9	92.4	(NA)	105.4
1930	91.1	70.2	10.6	0.3	9.9	719.7	562.1	59.8	(NA)	116.2
1931	76.4	60.7	5.9	-	9.8	674.0	544.9	37.6	(NA)	121.2
1932	58.6	48.7	1.1	-	8.7	584.3	496.1	9.9	(NA)	117.1
1933	56.2	45.9	1.7	0.1	8.6	577.3	484.8	16.4	(NA)	112.8
1934	65.9	51.4	3.7	0.3	10.4	641.1	519.0	31.5	(NA)	127.3
1935	73.1	55.9	6.7	-0.2	10.8	698.4	550.9	58.0	(NA)	131.3
1936	83.6	62.2	8.7	-0.2	13.0	790.0	606.9	75.5	(NA)	152.5
1937	91.8	66.8	12.2	-	12.7	831.5	629.7	94.0	(NA)	147.0
1938	85.9	64.2	7.1	0.9	13.7	801.2	619.5	61.3	(NA)	157.8
1939	91.9	67.2	9.3	0.8	14.6	866.5	654.0	79.5	(NA)	171.6
1940	101.2	71.2	13.6	1.4	15.0	941.2	688.0	111.3	(NA)	174.2
1941	126.7	81.0	18.2	1.0	26.5	1,101.8	737.1	137.3	(NA)	288.0
1942	161.6	88.9	10.5	-0.3	62.7	1,308.9	719.7	72.1	(NA)	692.0
1943	198.3	99.7	6.1	-2.4	94.9	1,523.0	739.5	41.9	(NA)	1,032.2
1944	219.7	108.5	7.8	-2.2	105.6	1,644.7	761.0	52.2	(NA)	1,158.5
1945	223.2	119.9	10.9	-0.9	93.3	1,626.7	808.4	68.8	(NA)	1,012.0
1946	222.6	144.3	31.3	7.1	39.9	1,447.7	907.9	176.8	(NA)	349.0
1947	244.6	162.3	35.0	10.8	36.5	1,430.7	926.2	169.9	(NA)	290.3
1948	269.7	175.4	48.1	5.4	40.8	1,491.0	946.4	216.0	(NA)	310.3
1949	267.8	178.9	36.7	5.2	47.0	1,479.8	972.2	163.2	(NA)	345.8
1950	294.6	192.7	54.2	0.7	47.1	1,611.3	1,034.1	234.1	(NA)	344.6
1951	339.7	208.7	60.3	2.4	68.3	1,734.0	1,049.2	235.2	(NA)	468.6
1952	358.6	219.7	54.0	1.0	83.8	1,798.7	1,082.4	210.6	(NA)	566.2
1953	379.7	233.5	56.3	-0.8	90.7	1,881.4	1,135.0	220.4	(NA)	605.2
1954	381.3	240.7	53.8	0.3	86.4	1,868.2	1,158.9	209.9	(NA)	562.6
1955	415.1	259.1	69.0	0.4	86.7	2,001.1	1,242.6	261.9	(NA)	541.3
1956	438.0	271.9	72.2	2.3	91.6	2,040.2	1,278.2	257.9	(NA)	542.8
1957	461.0	286.7	70.6	4.0	99.8	2,078.5	1,308.2	246.1	(NA)	566.8
1958	467.3	296.3	64.5	0.4	106.1	2,057.5	1,318.8	224.5	(NA)	585.3
1959	507.2	318.1	78.8	-1.7	112.0	2,210.2	1,394.6	271.7	(NA)	618.5
1960	526.6	332.2	78.8	2.4	113.2	2,262.9	1,432.6	270.5	(NA)	617.2
1961	544.8	342.6	77.9	3.4	120.9	2,314.3	1,461.5	267.6	(NA)	647.2
1962	585.2	363.4	87.9	2.4	131.4	2,454.8	1,533.8	302.1	(NA)	686.0
1963	617.4	383.0	93.4	3.3	137.7	2,559.4	1,596.6	321.6	(NA)	701.9
1964	663.0	411.4	101.7	5.5	144.4	2,708.4	1,692.3	348.3	(NA)	715.9
1965	719.1	444.3	118.0	3.9	153.0	2,881.1	1,799.1	397.2	(NA)	737.6
1966	787.8	481.9	130.4	1.9	173.6	3,069.2	1,902.0	430.6	(NA)	804.6
1967	833.6	509.5	128.0	1.4	194.6	3,147.2	1,958.6	411.8	(NA)	865.6
1968	910.6	559.8	139.9	-1.3	212.1	3,293.9	2,070.2	433.3	(NA)	892.4
1969	982.2	604.7	155.0	-1.2	223.8	3,393.6	2,147.5	458.3	(NA)	887.5
1970	1,035.6	648.1	150.2	1.2	236.1	3,397.6	2,197.8	426.1	(NA)	866.8
1971	1,125.4	702.5	176.0	-3.0	249.9	3,510.0	2,279.5	474.9	(NA)	851.0
1972	1,237.3	770.7	205.6	-8.0	268.9	3,702.3	2,415.9	531.8	(NA)	854.1
1973	1,382.6	851.6	242.9	0.6	287.6	3,916.3	2,532.6	595.5	(NA)	848.4
1974	1,496.9	931.2	245.6	-3.1	323.2	3,891.2	2,514.7	546.5	(NA)	862.9
1975	1,630.6	1,029.1	225.4	13.6	362.6	3,873.9	2,570.0	446.6	(NA)	876.3
1976	1,819.0	1,148.8	286.6	-2.3	385.9	4,082.9	2,714.3	537.4	(NA)	876.8
1977	2,026.9	1,277.1	356.6	-23.7	416.9	4,273.6	2,829.8	622.1	(NA)	884.7
1978	2,291.4	1,428.8	430.8	-26.1	457.9	4,503.0	2,951.6	693.4	(NA)	910.6
1979	2,557.5	1,593.5	480.9	-24.0	507.1	4,630.6	3,020.2	709.7	(NA)	924.9
1980	2,784.2	1,760.4	465.9	-14.9	572.8	4,615.0	3,009.7	628.3	(NA)	941.4
1981	3,115.9	1,941.3	556.2	-15.0	633.4	4,720.7	3,046.4	686.0	(NA)	947.7
1982	3,242.1	2,076.8	501.1	-20.5	684.8	4,620.3	3,081.5	587.2	-14.1	960.1
1983	3,514.5	2,283.4	547.1	-51.7	735.7	4,803.7	3,240.6	642.1	-63.3	987.3
1984	3,902.4	2,492.3	715.6	-102.0	796.6	5,140.1	3,407.6	833.4	-127.3	1,018.4
1985	4,180.7	2,704.8	715.1	-114.2	875.0	5,323.5	3,566.5	823.8	-147.9	1,080.1
1986	4,422.2	2,892.7	722.5	-131.5	938.5	5,487.7	3,708.7	811.8	-163.9	1,135.0
1987	4,692.3	3,094.5	747.2	-142.1	992.8	5,649.5	3,822.3	821.5	-156.2	1,165.9
1988	5,049.6	3,349.7	773.9	-106.1	1,032.0	5,865.2	3,972.7	828.2	-114.4	1,180.9
1989	5,438.7	3,594.8	829.2	-80.4	1,095.1	6,062.0	4,064.6	863.5	-82.7	1,213.9
1990	5,743.8	3,839.3	799.7	-71.3	1,176.1	6,136.3	4,132.2	815.0	-61.9	1,250.4
1991	5,916.7	3,975.1	736.2	-20.5	1,225.9	6,079.4	4,105.8	738.1	-22.3	1,258.0
1992	6,244.4	4,219.8	790.4	-29.5	1,263.8	6,244.4	4,219.8	790.4	-29.5	1,263.8
1993	6,558.1	4,459.2	876.2	-60.7	1,283.4	6,389.6	4,343.6	863.6	-70.2	1,252.1
1994	6,947.0	4,717.0	1,007.9	-90.9	1,313.0	6,610.7	4,486.0	975.7	-104.6	1,252.3
1995	7,269.6	4,953.9	1,043.2	-83.9	1,356.4	6,761.7	4,605.6	996.1	-96.5	1,254.5
1996	7,661.6	5,215.7	1,131.9	-91.2	1,405.2	6,994.8	4,752.4	1,084.1	-111.2	1,268.2
1997	8,110.9	5,493.7	1,256.0	-93.4	1,454.6	7,269.8	4,913.5	1,206.4	-136.1	1,285.0
1998	8,511.0	5,807.9	1,367.1	-151.2	1,487.1	7,551.9	5,153.3	1,330.1	-238.2	1,296.9

- Represents zero. NA Not available.

Source: U.S. Bureau of Economic Analysis, *National Income and Product Accounts of the United States, 1929-94, Vol.1* and *Vol. 2;* and *Survey of Current Business,* May 1999.

No. 1435. Consumer and Gross Domestic Price Indexes: 1913 to 1998

Year	Purchasing power of the dollar [1]		Consumer price index [2] (1982-84=100)				Chained-type price indexes [3] (1992=100)		Annual percent change from prior year [4]	
	Producer prices	Consumer prices	All items	Food	Shelter	Medical care	Gross domestic product	Personal consumption expenditures	Consumer price index	Personal consumption expenditures
1913	(NA)	10.077	9.9	10.0	(NA)	(NA)	(NA)	(NA)	(NA)	(NA)
1915	(NA)	9.843	10.1	10.0	(NA)	(NA)	(NA)	(NA)	1.0	(NA)
1920	(NA)	4.989	20.0	21.0	(NA)	(NA)	(NA)	(NA)	15.6	(NA)
1925	(NA)	5.701	17.5	16.5	(NA)	(NA)	(NA)	(NA)	2.3	(NA)
1929	(NA)	5.833	17.1	16.5	(NA)	(NA)	13.1	13.1	-	(NA)
1930	(NA)	5.986	16.7	15.6	(NA)	(NA)	12.6	12.5	-2.3	-4.3
1931	(NA)	6.563	15.2	12.9	(NA)	(NA)	11.3	11.1	-9.0	-10.8
1932	(NA)	7.317	13.7	10.7	(NA)	(NA)	10.1	9.8	-9.9	-11.8
1933	(NA)	7.712	13.0	10.4	(NA)	(NA)	9.8	9.5	-5.1	-3.6
1934	(NA)	7.464	13.4	11.6	(NA)	(NA)	10.3	9.9	3.1	4.6
1935	(NA)	7.281	13.7	12.4	(NA)	10.2	10.5	10.2	2.2	2.4
1936	(NA)	7.213	13.9	12.6	(NA)	10.2	10.6	10.2	1.5	0.9
1937	(NA)	6.961	14.4	13.1	(NA)	10.3	11.0	10.6	3.6	3.6
1938	(NA)	7.093	14.1	12.1	(NA)	10.3	10.8	10.4	-2.1	-2.3
1939	(NA)	7.195	13.9	11.8	(NA)	10.3	10.6	10.3	0.7	-1.0
1940	(NA)	7.126	14.0	12.0	(NA)	10.4	10.7	10.4	5.0	0.8
1941	(NA)	6.788	14.7	13.1	(NA)	10.4	11.4	11.0	10.9	6.2
1942	(NA)	6.132	16.3	15.4	(NA)	10.7	12.3	12.4	6.1	12.4
1943	(NA)	5.779	17.3	17.1	(NA)	11.2	13.0	13.5	1.7	9.1
1944	(NA)	5.680	17.6	16.9	(NA)	11.6	13.4	14.3	2.3	5.8
1945	(NA)	5.552	18.0	17.3	(NA)	11.9	13.7	14.8	8.3	4.0
1946	(NA)	5.115	19.5	19.8	(NA)	12.5	15.4	15.9	14.4	7.1
1947	(NA)	4.474	22.3	24.1	(NA)	13.5	17.1	17.5	8.1	10.3
1948	(NA)	4.151	24.1	26.1	(NA)	14.4	18.1	18.5	-1.2	5.8
1949	(NA)	4.193	23.8	25.0	(NA)	14.8	18.1	18.4	1.3	-0.8
1950	3.546	4.151	24.1	25.4	(NA)	15.1	18.3	18.6	7.9	1.3
1951	3.247	3.846	26.0	28.2	(NA)	15.9	19.5	19.9	1.9	6.8
1952	3.268	3.765	26.5	28.7	(NA)	16.7	19.9	20.3	0.8	2.1
1953	3.300	3.735	26.7	28.3	22.0	17.3	20.2	20.6	0.7	1.3
1954	3.289	3.717	26.9	28.2	22.5	17.8	20.4	20.8	-0.4	1.0
1955	3.279	3.732	26.8	27.8	22.7	18.2	20.7	20.9	1.5	0.4
1956	3.195	3.678	27.2	28.0	23.1	18.9	21.4	21.3	3.3	2.1
1957	3.077	3.549	28.1	28.9	24.0	19.7	22.2	21.9	2.8	3.0
1958	3.012	3.457	28.9	30.2	24.5	20.6	22.7	22.5	0.7	2.5
1959	3.021	3.427	29.1	29.7	24.7	21.5	23.0	22.8	1.7	1.5
1960	2.994	3.373	29.6	30.0	25.2	22.3	23.3	23.2	1.0	1.7
1961	2.994	3.340	29.9	30.4	25.4	22.9	23.5	23.4	1.0	1.1
1962	2.985	3.304	30.2	30.6	25.8	23.5	23.8	23.7	1.3	1.1
1963	2.994	3.265	30.6	31.1	26.1	24.1	24.1	24.0	1.3	1.3
1964	2.985	3.220	31.0	31.5	26.5	24.6	24.5	24.3	1.6	1.3
1965	2.933	3.166	31.5	32.2	27.0	25.2	25.0	24.7	2.9	1.6
1966	2.841	3.080	32.4	33.8	27.8	26.3	25.7	25.3	3.1	2.6
1967	2.809	2.993	33.4	34.1	28.8	28.2	26.5	26.0	4.2	2.6
1968	2.732	2.873	34.8	35.3	30.1	29.9	27.6	27.0	5.5	4.0
1969	2.632	2.726	36.7	37.1	32.6	31.9	28.9	28.2	5.7	4.1
1970	2.545	2.574	38.8	39.2	35.5	34.0	30.5	29.5	4.4	4.7
1971	2.469	2.466	40.5	40.4	37.0	36.1	32.1	30.8	3.2	4.5
1972	2.392	2.391	41.8	42.1	38.7	37.3	33.4	31.9	6.2	3.5
1973	2.193	2.251	44.4	48.2	40.5	38.8	35.3	33.6	11.0	5.4
1974	1.901	2.029	49.3	55.1	44.4	42.4	38.5	37.0	9.1	10.1
1975	1.718	1.859	53.8	59.8	48.8	47.5	42.1	40.0	5.8	8.1
1976	1.645	1.757	56.9	61.6	51.5	52.0	44.6	42.3	6.5	5.7
1977	1.546	1.649	60.6	65.5	54.9	57.0	47.4	45.1	7.6	6.6
1978	1.433	1.532	65.2	72.0	60.5	61.8	50.9	48.4	11.3	7.3
1979	1.289	1.380	72.6	79.9	68.9	67.5	55.2	52.8	13.5	9.0
1980	1.136	1.215	82.4	86.8	81.0	74.9	60.3	58.5	10.3	10.9
1981	1.041	1.098	90.9	93.6	90.5	82.9	66.0	63.7	6.2	9.0
1982	1.000	1.035	96.5	97.4	96.9	92.5	70.2	67.4	3.2	5.8
1983	0.984	1.003	99.6	99.4	99.1	100.6	73.2	70.5	4.3	4.5
1984	0.964	0.961	103.9	103.2	104.0	106.8	75.9	73.1	3.6	3.8
1985	0.955	0.928	107.6	105.6	109.8	113.5	78.5	75.8	1.9	3.7
1986	0.969	0.913	109.6	109.0	115.8	122.0	80.6	78.0	3.6	2.8
1987	0.949	0.880	113.6	113.5	121.3	130.1	83.1	81.0	4.1	3.8
1988	0.926	0.846	118.3	118.2	127.1	138.6	86.1	84.3	4.8	4.2
1989	0.880	0.807	124.0	125.1	132.8	149.3	89.7	88.4	5.4	4.9
1990	0.839	0.766	130.7	132.4	140.0	162.8	93.6	92.9	4.2	5.1
1991	0.822	0.734	136.2	136.3	146.3	177.0	97.3	96.8	3.0	4.2
1992	0.812	0.713	140.3	137.9	151.2	190.1	100.0	100.0	3.0	3.3
1993	0.802	0.692	144.5	140.9	155.7	201.4	102.6	102.7	2.6	2.7
1994	0.797	0.675	148.2	144.3	160.5	211.0	105.1	105.2	2.8	2.4
1995	0.782	0.656	152.4	148.4	165.7	220.5	107.5	107.6	3.0	2.3
1996	0.762	0.638	156.9	153.3	171.0	228.2	109.5	109.8	2.3	2.0
1997	0.759	0.623	160.5	157.3	176.3	234.6	111.6	111.8	1.6	1.9
1998	0.766	0.600	163.0	160.7	182.1	242.1	112.7	112.7	1.6	0.8

- Represents zero.   NA Not available.   [1] Producer prices, 1982 = $1.00; consumer prices 1982-84 = $1.00.   [2] Represents annual averages of monthly figures.   [3] For definition of chained dollars, see text, Section 14, Income.   [4] Change from prior year. For 1915, change from 1914; for 1920, from 1919; for 1925, from 1924; and 1929, from 1928.

Source: purchasing power and consumer prices, U.S. Bureau of Labor Statistics, *Monthly Labor Review* and *CPI Detailed Report*, January issues; and chain-type prices, U.S. Bureau of Economic Analysis, *The National Income and Product Accounts of the United States*, 1929-94, Vol. 2; and *Survey of Current Business*, May 1999.

No. 1436. Stock Prices and Yields: 1900 to 1998

Year	Stand-ard and Poor's 500 com-posite (1941-43=10)[1,2]	NYSE com-posite (Dec. 31, 1965=50)[3]	NASDAQ com-posite (Feb. 5, 1971=100)[3]	Com-posite[3] (65 stocks)	Year-end close	Yearly high	Yearly low	Trans-porta-tion[3] (20 stocks)	Utility[3] (15 stocks)	Divi-dend price ratio[4]	Earn-ings price ratio[5]	New York Stock Exchange volume of trading (mil. shares)
		Stock prices			Dow-Jones & Co., Inc.	Industrial (30 stocks)					Common stock yields Standard & Poor's (percent)[1]		
1900 ..	6.2	(NA)	(NA)	(NA)	(NA)	(NA)	(NA)	(NA)	(NA)	(NA)	(NA)	139
1910 ..	9.4	(NA)	(NA)	(NA)	(NA)	(NA)	(NA)	(NA)	(NA)	(NA)	(NA)	164
1920 ..	8.0	(NA)	(NA)	(NA)	72.0	109.9	66.8	(NA)	(NA)	(NA)	(NA)	227
1929 ..	26.0	(NA)	(NA)	(NA)	248.5	386.1	195.4	(NA)	(NA)	3.47	7.51	1,125
1933 ..	9.0	(NA)	(NA)	(NA)	99.9	110.5	49.7	(NA)	(NA)	4.21	4.36	655
1935 ..	10.6	(NA)	(NA)	(NA)	144.1	149.4	96.0	(NA)	(NA)	3.82	7.23	382
1940 ..	11.0	(NA)	(NA)	(NA)	131.1	153.3	110.4	(NA)	(NA)	5.59	9.80	208
1945 ..	15.2	(NA)	(NA)	(NA)	192.9	196.6	150.5	(NA)	(NA)	4.17	6.39	378
1950 ..	18.4	(NA)	(NA)	(NA)	235.4	236.6	193.9	(NA)	(NA)	6.57	15.20	525
1955 ..	40.5	(NA)	(NA)	(NA)	488.4	490.8	385.7	(NA)	(NA)	4.08	8.72	650
1960 ..	55.9	30.9	34.5	205.9	615.9	688.2	564.2	130.9	100.0	3.47	5.88	767
1965 ..	88.2	50.0	67.0	340.9	969.3	976.6	832.7	247.5	152.6	3.00	5.87	1,556
1970 ..	83.2	50.2	89.6	272.8	838.9	848.2	627.5	171.5	121.8	3.83	6.45	2,937
1975 ..	86.2	47.6	77.6	261.7	852.4	888.9	619.1	172.7	83.7	4.31	9.15	4,693
1980 ..	118.8	77.9	202.3	373.4	964.0	1,005.2	730.0	398.1	114.4	5.26	12.66	11,352
1985 ..	186.8	121.6	324.4	616.5	1,546.5	1,570.9	1,178.7	708.2	174.8	4.25	8.12	27,511
1990 ..	334.6	180.5	373.8	920.6	2,633.7	3,024.3	2,344.1	910.2	209.7	3.61	6.47	39,665
1991 ..	376.2	229.4	586.3	1,156.8	3,168.8	3,204.6	2,447.0	1,358.0	226.2	3.24	4.79	45,266
1992 ..	415.7	240.2	677.0	1,204.6	3,301.1	3,435.2	3,087.4	1,449.2	221.0	2.99	4.22	51,376
1993 ..	451.4	259.1	776.8	1,381.0	3,754.1	3,818.9	3,219.3	1,762.3	229.3	2.78	4.46	66,923
1994 ..	460.4	250.9	752.0	1,274.4	3,834.4	4,002.8	3,520.8	1,455.0	181.5	2.82	5.83	73,420
1995 ..	541.7	329.5	1,052.1	1,693.2	5,117.1	5,266.7	3,794.4	1,981.0	225.4	2.56	6.09	87,218
1996 ..	670.5	392.3	1,291.0	2,025.8	6,448.3	6,624.0	5,000.1	2,255.7	232.5	2.19	5.24	104,636
1997 ..	873.4	511.2	1,570.4	2,607.4	7,908.3	8,340.1	6,315.8	3,256.5	273.1	1.77	4.57	133,312
1998 ..	1,085.5	596.1	2,192.7	2,870.8	9,181.4	9,457.9	7,379.7	3,149.3	312.3	1.49	3.46	169,745

NA Not available. [1] Source: U.S. Council of Economic Advisors, *Economic Report of the President*, annual. [2] Annual average of daily closing prices. The S&P 500 composite index includes 400 industrial stocks, 20 transportation, 40 public utility, and 40 financial stocks. [3] As of end of December. [4] Aggregate cash dividends (based on latest known annual rate) divided by aggregate market value based on Wednesday closing prices. Averages of monthly figures. [5] Averages of quarterly ratios which are ratio of earnings (after taxes) for 4 quarters ending with particular quarter to price index for last day of that quarter.

Source: Except as noted, Global Financial Data, Alhambra, CA, "US Stock Market Capitalization Indices"; <http://www.globalfindata.com/tbcap.htm>; and "Global Financial Data Dow Jones Industrial Average"; <http://www.globalfindata.com/tbdjia.htm>; (accessed 19 April 1999) and unpublished data. (Copyright).

No. 1437. Bond Yields and Interest Rates: 1900 to 1998

Year	U.S. Treasury securities 3 month bills (new issues)	Corporate bonds (Moody's) Aaa	Corporate bonds (Moody's) Baa	High grade municipal bonds (Standard & Poors)	New home mortgage yields	Commer-cial paper, 6 months	Prime rate charged by banks	Discount rate Federal Reserve Bank of New York	Federal funds rate
1900....	(NA)	(NA)	(NA)	3.12	(NA)	5.71	(NA)	(NA)	(NA)
1910....	(NA)	(NA)	(NA)	3.97	(NA)	5.72	(NA)	(NA)	(NA)
1920....	(NA)	6.12	(NA)	4.98	(NA)	7.50	(NA)	(NA)	(NA)
1929....	(NA)	4.73	5.90	4.27	(NA)	5.85	5.50-6.00	5.16	(NA)
1933....	0.52	4.49	7.76	4.71	(NA)	1.73	1.50-4.00	2.56	(NA)
1935....	0.14	3.60	(NA)	3.40	(NA)	0.75	1.50	(NA)	(NA)
1940....	0.01	2.84	4.75	2.50	(NA)	0.56	1.50	1.00	(NA)
1945....	0.38	2.62	3.29	1.67	(NA)	0.75	1.50	1.00	(NA)
1950....	1.22	2.62	3.24	1.98	(NA)	1.45	2.07	1.59	(NA)
1955....	1.75	3.06	3.53	2.53	(NA)	2.18	3.16	1.89	1.78
1960....	2.93	4.41	5.19	3.73	(NA)	3.85	4.82	3.53	3.22
1965....	3.95	4.49	4.87	3.27	5.81	4.38	4.54	4.04	4.07
1970....	6.46	8.04	9.11	6.51	8.45	7.71	7.91	5.95	7.18
1975....	5.84	8.83	10.61	6.89	9.00	6.32	7.86	6.25	5.82
1980....	11.51	11.94	13.67	8.51	12.66	12.29	15.27	11.77	13.36
1985....	7.48	11.37	12.72	9.18	11.55	8.01	9.93	7.69	8.10
1990....	7.51	9.32	10.36	7.25	10.05	7.95	10.01	6.98	8.10
1991....	5.42	8.77	9.80	6.89	9.32	5.85	8.46	5.45	5.69
1992....	3.45	8.14	8.98	6.41	8.24	3.80	6.25	3.25	3.52
1993....	3.02	7.22	7.93	5.63	7.20	3.30	6.00	3.00	3.02
1994....	4.29	7.96	8.62	6.19	7.49	4.93	7.15	3.60	4.21
1995....	5.51	7.59	8.20	5.95	7.87	5.93	8.83	5.21	5.83
1996....	5.02	7.37	8.05	5.75	7.80	5.42	8.27	5.02	5.30
1997....	5.07	7.26	7.86	5.55	7.71	5.62	8.44	5.00	5.46
1998....	4.81	6.53	7.22	5.12	7.07	(NA)	8.35	4.92	5.35

NA Not available.

Source: Board of Governors of the Federal Reserve System. 1900-1940, *Banking and Monetary Statistics;* 1945-1960, *Supplement to Banking & Monetary Statistics;* and 1965-1998, *Federal Reserve Bulletin,* monthly issues.

U.S. Census Bureau, Statistical Abstract of the United States: 1999

No. 1438. Economic Indicators for Construction, Real Estate, Manufacturing, Retail, and Foreign Trade Sectors: 1929 to 1998

Year	Contracts awarded [1] Value (bil. dol.)	Contracts awarded [1] Floor space [2] (mil. sq. ft.)	New housing units started [3] (1,000)	New one-family houses sold [4] (1,000)	Existing one-family houses sold [5] (1,000)	Manufacturing shipments [6] (bil. dol.)	Index of manufacturing production [7]	Retail sales total [8] (bil. dol.)	Sales of cars and trucks [9] (1,000)	Exports [10] (bil. dol.)	General imports [10] (bil. dol.)
1929	5.8	791	509	(NA)	(NA)	(NA)	(NA)	48.5	(NA)	5.2	4.4
1930	4.5	510	330	(NA)	(NA)	(NA)	(NA)	(NA)	(NA)	3.8	3.1
1931	3.1	366	254	(NA)	(NA)	(NA)	(NA)	(NA)	2,231	2.4	2.1
1932	1.4	156	134	(NA)	(NA)	(NA)	(NA)	(NA)	(NA)	1.6	1.3
1933	1.3	147	93	(NA)	(NA)	(NA)	(NA)	24.5	1,787	1.7	1.5
1934	1.5	152	126	(NA)	(NA)	(NA)	(NA)	(NA)	(NA)	2.1	1.7
1935	1.8	252	221	(NA)	(NA)	(NA)	(NA)	32.8	3,419	2.3	2.0
1936	2.7	410	319	(NA)	(NA)	(NA)	(NA)	38.3	(NA)	2.5	2.4
1937	2.9	446	336	(NA)	(NA)	(NA)	(NA)	42.2	4,153	3.3	3.1
1938	3.2	429	406	(NA)	(NA)	(NA)	(NA)	38.1	(NA)	3.1	2.0
1939	3.6	513	515	(NA)	(NA)	(NA)	(NA)	42.0	3,245	3.2	2.3
1940	4.0	690	603	(NA)	(NA)	(NA)	(NA)	46.4	(NA)	4.0	2.6
1941	6.0	941	706	(NA)	(NA)	(NA)	(NA)	55.3	4,665	5.1	3.3
1942	8.3	1,296	356	(NA)	(NA)	(NA)	(NA)	57.2	(NA)	8.1	2.8
1943	3.3	448	191	(NA)	(NA)	(NA)	(NA)	63.2	(NA)	13.0	3.4
1944	2.0	229	142	(NA)	(NA)	(NA)	(NA)	70.2	(NA)	14.3	3.9
1945	3.3	397	326	(NA)	(NA)	(NA)	(NA)	78.0	(NA)	9.8	4.2
1946	7.5	946	1,023	(NA)	(NA)	(NA)	(NA)	[11]104.8	(NA)	9.7	4.9
1947	9.2	1,060	1,268	(NA)	(NA)	186	20.6	122.4	(NA)	14.4	5.8
1948	11.1	1,060	1,362	(NA)	(NA)	217	21.3	133.6	(NA)	12.7	7.1
1949	11.8	1,038	1,466	(NA)	(NA)	193	20.2	133.8	(NA)	12.1	6.6
1950	16.6	1,475	1,952	(NA)	(NA)	224	23.5	147.2	(NA)	10.3	8.9
1951	17.2	1,279	1,491	(NA)	(NA)	261	25.4	156.5	6,275	15.0	11.0
1952	18.1	1,288	1,504	(NA)	(NA)	270	26.4	162.4	(NA)	15.2	10.7
1953	18.8	1,306	1,438	(NA)	(NA)	298	28.8	169.1	6,773	15.8	10.9
1954	20.6	1,486	1,551	(NA)	(NA)	280	26.9	169.1	(NA)	15.1	10.2
1955	24.6	1,695	1,646	(NA)	(NA)	318	30.3	183.9	8,481	15.5	11.4
1956	31.6	2,017	1,349	(NA)	(NA)	333	31.6	189.7	(NA)	19.1	12.6
1957	32.2	2,003	1,224	(NA)	(NA)	345	31.9	200.0	6,927	20.9	13.0
1958	35.1	2,101	1,382	(NA)	(NA)	327	29.7	200.4	(NA)	17.9	12.8
1959	36.3	2,337	1,554	(NA)	(NA)	363	33.5	215.4	7,065	17.6	15.2
1960	36.3	2,154	1,252	(NA)	(NA)	371	34.1	219.5	(NA)	20.6	14.7
1961	37.1	2,203	1,313	(NA)	(NA)	371	34.2	[11]219.0	6,872	21.0	14.7
1962	41.3	2,414	1,463	(NA)	(NA)	400	37.3	235.6	8,192	21.7	16.4
1963	45.5	2,711	1,610	(NA)	(NA)	421	39.5	246.7	8,990	23.3	17.1
1964	47.3	2,738	1,529	(NA)	(NA)	448	42.2	261.9	9,494	26.5	18.7
1965	49.3	2,843	1,473	(NA)	(NA)	492	46.8	284.1	10,885	27.5	21.4
1966	50.2	2,643	1,165	(NA)	(NA)	538	51.0	304.0	10,664	30.3	25.5
1967	54.5	2,820	1,292	(NA)	(NA)	558	52.0	313.8	9,882	31.5	26.8
1968	61.7	3,129	1,508	(NA)	1,569	603	54.9	339.3	11,487	34.6	33.2
1969	68.3	3,249	1,467	(NA)	1,594	642	57.4	362.9	11,552	38.0	36.0
1970	68.3	2,938	1,434	485	1,612	634	54.8	375.2	10,211	43.8	40.4
1971	(NA)	(NA)	2,052	656	2,018	671	55.6	414.2	12,338	44.7	46.2
1972	(NA)	(NA)	2,357	718	2,252	756	61.5	458.5	13,569	50.5	56.4
1973	(NA)	(NA)	2,045	634	2,334	875	66.9	511.9	14,572	72.5	70.5
1974	(NA)	(NA)	1,338	519	2,272	1,018	65.9	542.0	11,541	100.0	102.6
1975	(NA)	(NA)	1,160	549	2,476	1,039	59.3	588.1	11,103	109.3	98.5
1976	110.0	2,810	1,538	646	3,064	1,186	65.4	656.4	13,291	117.0	123.5
1977	141.0	3,542	1,987	819	3,650	1,358	71.2	722.0	14,859	123.2	151.0
1978	160.6	4,114	2,020	817	3,986	1,523	75.8	804.2	15,423	145.9	174.8
1979	170.9	3,919	1,745	709	3,827	1,727	78.5	896.8	14,153	186.5	209.5
1980	151.8	3,102	1,292	545	2,973	1,853	75.5	957.4	11,466	225.7	245.3
1981	157.3	2,805	1,084	436	2,419	2,018	76.7	1,038.0	10,796	238.7	261.0
1982	157.1	2,455	1,062	412	1,990	1,960	72.1	1,069.4	10,542	216.4	244.0
1983	194.1	3,387	1,703	623	2,697	2,071	76.3	1,170.2	12,312	205.6	258.0
1984	214.3	3,661	1,750	639	2,829	2,288	83.8	1,286.9	14,484	224.0	330.7
1985	235.6	3,853	1,742	688	3,134	2,334	85.7	1,375.0	15,724	218.8	336.5
1986	249.3	3,935	1,805	750	3,474	2,336	88.1	1,449.6	16,322	227.2	365.4
1987	259.0	3,756	1,621	671	3,436	2,476	92.8	1,541.3	15,189	254.1	406.2
1988	262.2	3,594	1,488	676	3,513	2,695	97.1	1,656.2	15,679	322.4	441.0
1989	271.3	3,516	1,376	650	3,325	2,840	99.0	1,759.0	14,713	363.8	473.2
1990	246.0	3,020	1,193	534	3,219	2,912	98.5	1,844.6	14,146	393.6	495.3
1991	230.8	2,634	1,014	509	3,186	2,878	96.2	1,855.9	12,539	421.7	488.5
1992	252.2	2,799	1,200	610	3,479	3,005	100.0	1,951.6	13,116	448.2	532.7
1993	271.5	3,062	1,288	666	3,786	3,128	103.7	2,073.8	14,199	465.1	580.7
1994	296.7	3,411	1,457	670	3,916	3,348	109.9	2,229.9	15,411	512.6	663.3
1995	306.5	3,453	1,354	667	3,888	3,595	115.9	2,329.3	15,116	584.7	743.4
1996	331.8	3,773	1,477	757	4,196	3,715	121.4	2,461.2	15,456	625.1	795.3
1997	358.4	4,076	1,474	804	4,381	3,929	129.7	2,566.2	(NA)	689.2	870.7
1998	375.3	4,483	1,617	886	4,970	(NA)	135.1	2,696.0	(NA)	682.1	911.9

NA Not available. [1] Source: F. W. Dodge Division, McGraw-Hill Information Systems Company, New York, NY (copyright). [2] For 1929-1955, for 37 states; 1956-1969, for 48 states; thereafter, for 50 states. [3] Prior to 1959, excludes farm housing. Source: U.S. Census Bureau, *Current Construction Reports*, Series C20, monthly. [4] Source: U.S. Census Bureau and U.S. Dept. of Housing and Urban Development, *Current Construction Reports*, Series C25, annual reports. [5] Source: See Table 1205. [6] U.S. Census Bureau, *Current Industrial Reports*, Series M3-1(97); and earlier reports. [7] Board of Governors of the Federal Reserve System, *Industrial Production and Capacity Utilization*, Statistical Release G.17, monthly. [8] Source: U.S. Census Bureau, *Current Business Reports, Annual Benchmark Report for Retail Trade, January 1988 Through December 1998*, (BR/98-RV) and prior issues. [9] Source: American Automobile Manufacturers Association, *Motor Vehicle Facts and Figures*, annual (copyright). [10] Source: U.S. International Trade Administration, *U.S. Foreign Trade Highlights*, annual. [11] Break in series. Not entirely comparable with earlier years.

Source: Compiled from sources listed in footnotes.

U.S. Census Bureau, Statistical Abstract of the United States: 1999

No. 1439. Transportation Indicators for Motor Vehicles and Airlines: 1900 to 1998

Year	Motor vehicles, total (1,000)	Passenger cars — Number (1,000)	Passenger cars — Rate per 1,000 persons	Motor vehicles, total (mil.)	Average travel per vehicle (miles)	Number[1]	Rate per 100 million VMT	Public road miles (1,000)	Passengers carried (mil.)	Fatal accidents per 100,000 departures	Revenue per passenger mile[2]
1900....	8	8	0.1	100	12,500	36	36.00	2,320	(NA)	(NA)	(NA)
1905....	79	77	0.9	970	12,310	252	25.98	2,360	(NA)	(NA)	(NA)
1910....	469	458	5.0	3,580	7,641	1,599	44.66	2,430	(NA)	(NA)	(NA)
1915....	2,491	2,332	23.2	19,530	7,840	6,779	34.71	2,745	(NA)	(NA)	(NA)
1920....	9,239	8,132	76.4	47,600	5,152	12,155	25.54	3,105	(NA)	(NA)	(NA)
1925....	20,069	17,481	150.9	122,346	6,096	20,771	16.98	3,246	(NA)	(NA)	(NA)
1930....	26,750	23,035	187.2	206,320	7,713	31,204	15.12	3,259	(NA)	(NA)	(NA)
1935....	26,546	22,568	177.4	228,568	8,610	34,494	15.09	3,310	(NA)	(NA)	(NA)
1940....	32,453	27,466	208.1	302,188	9,311	32,914	10.89	3,287	3.2	(NA)	(NA)
1945....	31,035	25,797	194.7	250,173	8,061	26,785	10.71	3,319	7.2	(NA)	(NA)
1950....	49,162	40,339	265.6	458,246	9,321	33,186	7.24	3,313	19.1	0.242	27.62
1955....	62,689	52,145	315.9	605,646	9,661	36,688	6.06	3,418	41.4	0.275	23.86
1960....	73,858	61,671	342.7	718,762	9,732	36,399	5.06	3,546	57.9	0.311	21.40
1965....	90,358	75,258	388.9	887,812	9,826	47,089	5.30	3,690	94.7	0.167	17.95
1970....	108,418	89,244	437.5	1,109,724	10,236	53,816	4.85	3,730	171.7	0.039	14.39
1975....	132,949	106,706	495.2	1,327,664	9,986	45,500	3.43	3,838	205.1	0.043	13.61
1980....	155,796	121,601	535.2	1,527,295	9,803	51,091	3.35	3,860	296.9	0.000	12.89
1985....	171,689	127,885	537.5	1,774,826	10,337	43,825	2.47	3,864	382.0	0.069	10.46
1990....	188,798	133,700	536.0	2,144,362	11,358	44,599	2.08	3,867	465.6	0.087	9.42
1991....	188,136	128,300	508.9	2,172,050	11,545	41,508	1.91	3,884	452.3	0.059	9.03
1992....	190,362	126,581	496.4	2,247,151	11,805	39,250	1.75	3,901	475.1	0.057	8.60
1993....	194,063	127,327	494.0	2,296,378	11,833	40,150	1.75	3,905	488.5	0.014	8.72
1994....	198,045	127,883	491.3	2,357,588	11,904	40,716	1.73	3,907	528.8	0.053	8.20
1995....	201,530	128,387	488.6	2,422,696	12,022	41,817	1.73	3,912	547.8	0.025	8.15
1996....	206,365	129,728	489.2	2,485,848	12,046	41,907	1.69	3,919	581.2	0.036	8.00
1997....	207,754	129,749	484.6	2,560,373	12,324	41,967	1.64	3,945	599.1	0.037	7.89
1998....	(NA)	(NA)	(NA)	(NA)	(NA)	(NA)	(NA)	(NA)	614.2	0.012	7.74

NA Not available. [1] Beginning 1980, covers only persons injured in highway vehicular crash that died within 30 days. [2] In constant (1982) dollars. Also known as constant dollar yield.
Source: U.S. Federal highway Administration, Highway Statistics Summary to 1995, and Highway Statistics, annual; and Air Transport Association, <http://www.air-transport.org/public/industry/28.asp> and <http:www.air-transport.org/public/industry/27.asp> (accessed 17 August 1999).

No. 1440. Selected Communications Media: 1920 to 1998

Year	Telephone service[1]	Radio[2]	Television[3]	Cable TV[4]	VCRs[4]	VHF[3]	UHF[3]	Systems (number)[5]	Households served[6] (mil.)	Number[7]	Circulation[7] (mil.)
1920	35	(NA)	(NA)	(NA)	(NA)	(NA)	(NA)	(NA)	(NA)	2,042	27.8
1925	39	(NA)	(NA)	(NA)	(NA)	(NA)	(NA)	(NA)	(NA)	2,008	33.7
1930	41	39	(NA)	(NA)	(NA)	(NA)	(NA)	(NA)	(NA)	1,942	39.6
1935	32	(NA)	(NA)	(NA)	(NA)	(NA)	(NA)	(NA)	(NA)	1,950	38.2
1940	37	73	(NA)	(NA)	(NA)	(NA)	(NA)	(NA)	(NA)	1,878	41.1
1945	46	(NA)	(NA)	(NA)	(NA)	(NA)	(NA)	(NA)	(NA)	1,749	48.4
1950	62	91	9	(NA)	(NA)	98	-	(NA)	(NA)	1,772	53.8
1955	72	94	63	(NA)	(NA)	297	114	400	0.2	1,760	56.1
1960	78	94	85	(NA)	(NA)	440	75	640	0.7	1,763	58.9
1965	85	95	90	2.3	(NA)	481	88	1,325	1.3	1,751	60.4
1970	91	99	95	6.7	(NA)	501	176	2,490	4.5	1,748	62.1
1975	95	99	97	12.6	(NA)	514	192	3,506	9.8	1,756	60.7
1980	93	99	98	19.9	1.1	516	218	4,225	17.7	1,745	62.2
1985	92	99	98	42.8	20.9	520	363	6,600	39.9	1,676	62.8
1990	93	99	98	56.4	68.6	547	545	9,575	54.9	1,611	62.3
1991	94	99	98	58.9	71.9	547	551	10,704	55.8	1,586	60.7
1992	94	99	98	60.2	75.0	551	567	11,035	56.4	1,570	60.2
1993	94	99	98	61.4	77.1	552	585	11,108	57.2	1,556	59.8
1994	94	99	98	62.4	79.0	561	584	11,214	60.5	1,548	59.3
1995	94	99	98	63.4	81.0	562	599	11,218	63.0	1,533	58.2
1996	94	99	98	65.3	82.2	554	620	11,119	64.6	1,520	57.0
1997	94	99	98	66.5	84.2	558	619	10,950	65.9	1,509	56.7
1998	(NA)	(NA)	98	67.2	84.6	562	642	10,845	(NA)	1,489	56.2

- Represents zero. NA Not available. [1] For occupied housing units. Census years as of April 1; all other years as of March. Source: U.S. Census Bureau, 1970 and 1980 Census of Housing, Vol. 1; thereafter Federal Communications Commission, Trends in Telephone Service, July 1998. [2] As of December 31, except as noted. Source: Radio Advertising Bureau, New York, NY, through 1992, Radio Facts, annual, (copyright); beginning 1993, Radio Marketing Guide and Fact Book for Advertisers, annual, (copyright). Number of stations on the air compiled from Federal Communications Commission reports. [3] Through 1970, as of September of prior year; all other years as of January of year shown. Excludes Alaska and Hawaii. Source: Television Bureau of Advertising, Inc., Trends in Television, annual (copyright). [4] As of February. Excludes Alaska and Hawaii. Source: See footnote 3. [5] As of January 1. Source: Warren Publishing, Washington DC, Television and Cable Factbook (copyright). [6] Source: Nielsen Media Research, Nielsen Station Index, November diary estimates (copyright). [7] As of September 30. Source: Editor & Publisher, Co., New York, NY, Editor & Publisher International Year Book, annual (copyright). Source: Compiled from sources mentioned in footnotes.

U.S. Census Bureau, Statistical Abstract of the United States: 1999

No. 1441. Agriculture—Farms, Acreage, Income, and Foreign Trade: 1900 to 1998

[Farms and land as of **June 1. (5,740 represents 5,740,000).** Based on various definitions of farms; 1975-1998, based on 1974 census definition; for definition of farms and farmland, see text, Section 23, Agriculture. Data for farms and land in census years (indicated by italics) have been adjusted for underenumeration and are used as reference points along with data from acreage and livestock surveys in estimating data for other years]

Year	Land in farms			Value added to U.S. economy by agricultural sector [1]				Agricultural [2]			
	Farms (1,000)	Total (mil. acres)	Average per farm (acres)	Final agricultural sector output (mil. dol.)	Crop output (mil. dol.)	Animal output (mil. dol.)	Net farm income (mil. dol.)	Index of prices received by farmers (1990- 92=100)	Acreage of harvested crops (mil. acres)	Exports, domestic products (bil. dol.)	Imports for consumption (bil. dol.)
1900....	5,740	841	147	(NA)	(NA)	(NA)	(NA)	(NA)	(NA)	[3]0.9	[3]0.4
1910....	6,366	881	139	7,707	3,599	3,663	4,176	(NA)	(NA)	0.9	0.8
1920....	6,454	959	149	16,632	8,352	7,445	7,794	(NA)	(NA)	3.9	3.4
1930....	6,295	990	157	11,201	4,036	6,302	4,257	(NA)	(NA)	1.5	1.9
1935....	6,812	1,055	155	9,821	4,143	4,995	5,277	(NA)	(NA)	0.7	0.9
1940....	6,102	1,065	175	10,617	4,005	5,868	4,481	(NA)	(NA)	0.7	1.2
1945....	5,859	1,142	195	24,632	10,523	13,057	12,313	(NA)	(NA)	2.2	1.7
1950....	5,388	1,161	216	32,820	13,192	18,144	13,648	(NA)	345	3.0	3.2
1955....	4,654	1,202	258	33,247	14,255	17,128	11,305	(NA)	340	3.1	3.8
1960....	3,962	1,177	297	37,886	15,672	19,872	11,212	(NA)	324	4.5	4.0
1965....	3,356	1,140	340	44,086	19,024	22,194	12,899	(NA)	298	6.1	4.0
1970....	2,954	1,103	373	55,101	20,523	30,768	14,366	(NA)	293	7.0	5.7
1975....	2,521	1,059	420	99,783	50,441	42,988	25,547	73	336	21.8	9.4
1980....	2,440	1,039	426	147,994	64,358	70,318	16,141	98	352	40.5	17.3
1985....	2,293	1,012	441	153,519	74,105	68,690	28,648	91	342	31.2	19.7
1987....	2,213	999	451	151,673	64,478	75,743	37,427	89	302	27.9	20.7
1990....	2,146	987	460	188,742	83,275	90,198	44,938	104	322	40.4	22.7
1991....	2,117	982	464	183,704	80,985	87,291	38,639	100	318	37.8	22.7
1992....	2,108	979	464	191,309	89,036	87,089	47,538	98	317	42.6	24.5
1993....	2,202	969	440	190,671	82,383	91,701	43,567	101	308	42.9	24.6
1994....	2,198	966	440	207,891	100,314	89,691	48,266	100	321	44.0	26.6
1995....	2,196	963	438	202,824	95,805	87,632	35,984	102	314	54.7	29.9
1996....	2,191	959	438	228,452	115,591	92,190	53,352	112	326	59.9	32.6
1997....	2,191	956	436	230,771	112,498	96,200	49,824	107	332	57.4	35.8
1998....	2,192	954	435	(NA)	(NA)	(NA)	(NA)	101	325	53.7	37.0

NA Not available. [1] Final sector output is the gross value of the commodities and services produced within a year. Net farm income is the farm operators' share of income from the sector's production activities. [2] 1900-1965, for year ending June 30; beginning 1970 for year ending Sept. 30. [3] 1901 data.
Source: U.S. Dept. of Agriculture, National Agricultural Statistics Service, *Farms and Land in Farms*, various Statistical Bulletins; U.S. Dept. of Agriculture, *Farm Business Economic Report*, annual; *Agricultural Prices: Annual Summary*; and *Foreign Agricultural Trade of the United States*, Jan-Feb. issues. Also in *Agricultural Statistics*, annual.

No. 1442. Production Indicators for Agricultural, Fishery, Mineral, and Manufactured Products: 1900 to 1998

Year	Agricultural products [1]				Mineral products [2]			Manufactured products			Electric energy net generation [2] (mil. kWh)
	Corn for grain (mil. bu.)	Wheat (mil. bu.)	Cotton (1,000 bales)	Tobacco (mil. lbs.)	Crude petroleum (mil. bbls.)	Natural gas marketed (bil. cu. ft.)	Coal (1,000 sh. tons)	Fishery landed catch [3] (mil. lb.)	Raw steel [4] (mil. tons)	Pas- senger cars [5] (1,000)	
1900 ...	(NA)	599	10,124	852	64	128	269,684	(NA)	11.2	4	(NA)
1910 ...	(NA)	625	11,609	1,142	210	509	501,596	(NA)	28.3	181	(NA)
1920 ...	2,695	843	13,429	1,509	443	812	658,265	(NA)	46.2	1,906	39,405
1930 ...	1,757	887	13,932	1,648	898	1,979	536,911	3,224	44.6	2,787	91,112
1935 ...	2,001	628	10,638	1,302	997	1,969	424,532	4,135	38.2	3,274	95,287
1940 ...	2,207	815	12,566	1,460	1,353	2,734	512,256	4,060	67.0	3,717	141,837
1945 ...	2,577	1,108	9,015	1,991	1,714	4,042	632,551	4,598	79.7	70	222,486
1950 ...	2,764	1,019	10,014	2,030	1,974	6,282	560,388	4,901	96.8	6,666	329,141
1955 ...	2,873	937	14,721	2,193	2,484	9,405	490,838	4,809	117.0	7,920	547,038
1960 ...	3,907	1,355	14,272	1,944	2,575	12,771	434,329	4,942	99.3	6,675	755,374
1965 ...	4,103	1,316	14,938	1,855	2,849	16,040	526,954	4,777	131.5	9,306	1,055,252
1970 ...	4,152	1,352	10,192	1,906	3,517	21,921	612,659	4,917	131.5	6,547	1,531,609
1975 ...	5,841	2,127	8,302	2,182	3,057	20,109	654,641	4,877	116.6	6,713	1,917,649
1980 ...	6,639	2,381	11,122	1,786	3,138	20,180	829,700	6,482	111.8	6,400	2,286,439
1985 ...	8,875	2,424	13,432	1,512	3,274	17,270	883,638	6,258	88.3	8,002	2,469,841
1990 ...	7,934	2,730	15,505	1,626	2,685	18,594	1,029,076	9,404	98.9	6,050	2,808,151
1991 ...	7,475	1,980	17,614	1,664	2,707	18,532	995,984	9,484	87.9	5,407	2,825,023
1992 ...	9,477	2,467	16,219	1,722	2,617	18,712	997,545	9,637	92.9	5,685	2,797,219
1993 ...	6,338	2,396	16,134	1,613	2,499	18,982	945,425	10,467	97.9	5,962	2,882,525
1994 ...	10,051	2,321	19,662	1,583	2,432	19,710	1,033,504	10,461	100.6	6,549	2,910,712
1995 ...	7,400	2,183	17,900	1,270	2,394	19,506	1,032,974	9,788	104.9	6,310	2,994,529
1996 ...	9,233	2,277	18,942	1,519	2,360	19,751	1,063,856	9,565	105.3	6,140	3,077,442
1997 ...	9,207	2,481	18,793	1,787	2,355	19,866	1,089,932	9,846	108.6	(NA)	3,122,523
1998 ...	9,761	2,550	13,796	1,530	2,279	19,945	1,118,673	(NA)	107.6	(NA)	3,212,171

NA Not available. [1] Source: U.S. Department of Agriculture, National Agricultural Statistics Service, *Agricultural Statistics*, annual. [2] Source: 1900-1945, U.S. Bureau of Mines, *Minerals Yearbook*; 1950-1998, U.S. Energy Information Administration, *Annual Energy Review*. [3] Source: U.S. national Oceanic and Atmospheric Administration, National Marine Fisheries Service, *Fisheries in the United States*, annual. [4] Source: American Iron and Steel Institute, Washington, DC, *Annual Statistical Report* (copyright). [5] Amerian Automobile Manufacturers Association, *Motor Vehicle Facts and Figures*, annual.
Source: Compiled from sources indicated above.

No. 1443. Federal Government—Receipts, Outlays, Debt, and Employment: 1900 to 1999

[In millions of dollars, except as indicated. Budget figures prior to 1933 are based on the "Administrative Budget" concepts rather than the "Unified Budget" concepts. Employment figures are as end of fiscal year. 1998 and 1999 estimated]

Year				Source of receipts					Executive branch civilian employment [1]		
	Total receipts	Outlays	Surplus or deficit (-)	Individual income taxes	Corporation income taxes	Social insurance & retirement receipts [2]	National defense outlays	Gross Federal debt, total	Executive branch, total	Department of Defense	Civilian agencies
1900 ..	567	521	46	(NA)	(NA)	(NA)	(NA)	(NA)	[3]231	[3]45	[3]187
1905 ..	544	567	-23	(NA)	(NA)	(NA)	(NA)	(NA)	(NA)	(NA)	(NA)
1910 ..	676	694	-18	(NA)	(NA)	(NA)	(NA)	(NA)	380	58	322
1915 ..	683	746	-63	(NA)	(NA)	(NA)	(NA)	(NA)	387	58	329
1920 ..	6,649	6,358	291	(NA)	(NA)	(NA)	(NA)	(NA)	645	237	408
1925 ..	3,641	2,924	717	(NA)	(NA)	(NA)	(NA)	(NA)	542	95	447
1929 ..	3,862	3,127	734	(NA)	(NA)	(NA)	(NA)	(NA)	568	103	465
1930 ..	4,058	3,320	738	(NA)	(NA)	(NA)	(NA)	(NA)	589	103	485
1933 ..	1,997	4,598	-2,602	(NA)	(NA)	(NA)	(NA)	(NA)	604	101	502
1935 ..	3,609	6,412	-2,803	527	529	31	(NA)	(NA)	766	147	619
1940 ..	6,548	9,468	-2,920	892	1,197	1,785	1,660	50,696	699	256	443
1941 ..	8,712	13,653	-4,941	1,314	2,124	1,940	6,435	57,531	1,081	556	525
1942 ..	14,634	35,137	-20,503	3,263	4,719	2,452	25,658	79,200	1,934	1,291	643
1943 ..	24,001	78,555	-54,554	6,505	9,557	3,044	66,699	142,648	2,935	2,200	735
1944 ..	43,747	91,304	-47,557	19,705	14,838	3,473	79,143	204,079	2,930	2,246	683
1945 ..	45,159	92,712	-47,553	18,372	15,988	3,451	82,965	260,123	3,370	2,635	736
1946 ..	39,296	55,232	-15,936	16,098	11,883	3,115	42,681	270,991	2,212	1,416	795
1947 ..	38,514	34,496	4,018	17,935	8,615	3,422	12,808	257,149	1,637	859	777
1948 ..	41,560	29,764	11,796	19,315	9,678	3,751	9,105	252,031	1,569	871	698
1949 ..	39,415	38,835	580	15,552	11,192	3,781	13,150	252,610	1,573	880	694
1950 ..	39,443	42,562	-3,119	15,755	10,449	4,338	13,724	256,853	1,439	753	686
1951 ..	51,616	45,514	6,102	21,616	14,101	5,674	23,566	255,288	1,974	1,235	738
1952 ..	66,167	67,686	-1,519	27,934	21,226	6,445	46,089	259,097	2,066	1,337	729
1953 ..	69,608	76,101	-6,493	29,816	21,238	6,820	52,802	265,963	2,026	1,332	694
1954 ..	69,701	70,855	-1,154	29,542	21,101	7,208	49,266	270,812	1,875	1,209	666
1955 ..	65,451	68,444	-2,993	28,747	17,861	7,862	42,729	274,366	1,860	1,187	673
1956 ..	74,587	70,640	3,947	32,188	20,880	9,320	42,523	272,693	1,864	1,180	684
1957 ..	79,990	76,578	3,412	35,620	21,167	9,997	45,430	272,252	1,869	1,161	708
1958 ..	79,636	82,405	-2,769	34,724	20,074	11,239	46,815	279,666	1,817	1,097	720
1959 ..	79,249	92,098	-12,849	36,719	17,309	11,722	49,015	287,465	1,805	1,078	727
1960 ..	92,492	92,191	301	40,715	21,494	14,683	48,130	290,525	1,808	1,047	761
1961 ..	94,388	97,723	-3,335	41,338	20,954	16,439	49,601	292,648	1,825	1,042	782
1962 ..	99,676	106,821	-7,146	45,571	20,523	17,046	52,345	302,928	1,896	1,070	827
1963 ..	106,560	111,316	-4,756	47,588	21,579	19,804	53,400	310,324	1,911	1,050	861
1964 ..	112,613	118,528	-5,915	48,697	23,493	21,963	54,757	316,059	1,884	1,030	855
1965 ..	116,817	118,228	-1,411	48,792	25,461	22,242	50,620	322,318	1,901	1,034	867
1966 ..	130,835	134,532	-3,698	55,446	30,073	25,546	58,111	328,498	2,051	1,138	913
1967 ..	148,822	157,464	-8,643	61,526	33,971	32,619	71,417	340,445	2,251	1,303	949
1968 ..	152,973	178,134	-25,161	68,726	28,665	33,923	81,926	368,685	2,289	1,317	972
1969 ..	186,882	183,640	3,242	87,249	36,678	39,015	82,497	365,769	2,301	1,342	960
1970 ..	192,807	195,649	-2,842	90,412	32,829	44,362	81,692	380,921	2,203	1,219	983
1971 ..	187,139	210,172	-23,033	86,230	26,785	47,325	78,872	408,176	2,144	1,154	989
1972 ..	207,309	230,681	-23,373	94,737	32,166	52,574	79,174	435,936	2,117	1,108	1,009
1973 ..	230,799	245,707	-14,908	103,246	36,153	63,115	76,681	466,291	2,083	1,053	1,030
1974 ..	263,224	269,359	-6,135	118,952	38,620	75,071	79,347	483,893	2,140	1,070	1,070
1975 ..	279,090	332,332	-53,242	122,386	40,621	84,534	86,509	541,925	2,149	1,042	1,107
1976 ..	298,060	371,792	-73,732	131,603	41,409	90,769	89,619	628,970	2,157	1,010	1,147
1977 ..	355,559	409,218	-53,659	157,626	54,892	106,485	97,241	706,398	2,182	1,009	1,173
1978 ..	399,561	458,746	-59,186	180,988	59,952	120,967	104,495	776,602	2,224	1,000	1,225
1979 ..	463,302	504,032	-40,729	217,841	65,677	138,939	116,342	829,470	2,161	960	1,201
1980 ..	517,112	590,947	-73,835	244,069	64,600	157,803	133,995	909,050	2,161	960	1,201
1981 ..	599,272	678,249	-78,976	285,917	61,137	182,720	157,513	994,845	2,143	984	1,159
1982 ..	617,766	745,755	-127,989	297,744	49,207	201,498	185,309	1,137,345	2,110	990	1,121
1983 ..	600,562	808,380	-207,818	288,938	37,022	208,994	209,903	1,371,710	2,157	1,026	1,131
1984 ..	666,486	851,874	-185,388	298,415	56,893	239,376	227,413	1,564,657	2,171	1,044	1,127
1985 ..	734,088	946,423	-212,334	334,531	61,331	265,163	252,748	1,817,521	2,252	1,107	1,145
1986 ..	769,215	990,460	-221,245	348,959	63,143	283,901	273,375	2,120,629	2,175	1,068	1,108
1987 ..	854,353	1,004,122	-149,769	392,557	83,926	303,318	281,999	2,346,125	2,232	1,090	1,142
1988 ..	909,303	1,064,489	-155,187	401,181	94,508	334,335	290,361	2,601,307	2,222	1,050	1,172
1989 ..	991,190	1,143,671	-152,481	445,690	103,291	359,416	303,559	2,868,039	2,238	1,075	1,162
1990 ..	1,031,969	1,253,163	-221,194	466,884	93,507	380,047	299,331	3,206,564	2,250	1,034	1,216
1991 ..	1,055,041	1,324,400	-269,359	467,827	98,086	396,016	273,292	3,598,498	2,243	1,013	1,230
1992 ..	1,091,279	1,381,681	-290,402	475,964	100,270	413,689	298,350	4,002,136	2,225	952	1,274
1993 ..	1,154,401	1,409,414	-255,013	509,680	117,520	428,300	291,086	4,351,416	2,157	891	1,266
1994 ..	1,258,627	1,461,731	-203,104	543,055	140,385	461,475	281,642	4,643,705	2,085	850	1,235
1995 ..	1,351,830	1,515,729	-163,899	590,244	157,004	484,473	272,066	4,921,018	2,012	802	1,210
1996 ..	1,453,062	1,560,512	-107,450	656,417	171,824	509,414	265,748	5,181,934	1,934	768	1,166
1997 ..	1,579,292	1,601,235	-21,943	737,466	182,293	539,371	270,473	5,369,707	1,872	723	1,149
1998 ..	1,657,858	1,667,815	-9,957	767,768	190,842	571,374	264,112	5,543,589	(NA)	(NA)	(NA)
1999 ..	1,742,736	1,733,217	9,519	791,454	197,965	595,886	265,489	5,738,119	(NA)	(NA)	(NA)

NA Not available. [1] End of fiscal year counts. Excludes Postal Service. 1940 to 1953 are estimates. [2] Includes some off-budget amounts; most of the off-budget amounts are direct payments for individuals (social security benefits). [3] 1901 data.

Source: 1940-1999, Office of Management and Budget, *Historical Tables, Budget of the United States Government, Fiscal Year 2000;* and 1900-39 for employment, U.S. Civil Service Commission (currently Office of Personnel Management, Federal Civilian Manpower Statistics; and 1900-39 for finances, U.S. Department of the Treasury, *Statistical Appendix to Annual Report of the Secretary of the Treasury, 1970.*

No. 1444. National Defense and Veterans—Summary: 1900 to 1998

[For fiscal year ending in year shown]

Year	National defense and veterans outlays (bil. dol.) Total outlays	Defense outlays [1]	Veterans outlays [2]	Defense outlays, percent of— Federal outlays	GDP [3]	Active duty military personnel (1,000) Total	Army	Navy	Marine Corps	Air Force	Veterans (1,000)
1900	0.3	0.2	0.1	36.6	(NA)	125.9	101.7	18.8	5.4	(X)	1,224
1915	0.5	0.3	0.2	46.1	(NA)	174.1	106.8	57.1	10.3	(X)	773
1918	6.4	6.1	0.3	48.5	(NA)	2,897.2	2,395.7	448.6	52.8	(X)	(NA)
1919	11.5	11.0	0.5	59.5	(NA)	1,172.6	851.6	272.1	48.8	(X)	(NA)
1920	2.9	2.4	0.5	37.1	(NA)	343.3	204.3	121.8	17.2	(X)	5,146
1930	1.5	0.8	0.6	25.3	(NA)	255.6	139.4	96.9	19.4	(X)	4,680
1940	2.2	1.7	0.6	17.5	1.7	458.4	269.0	161.0	28.3	(X)	4,286
1941	7.0	6.4	0.6	47.1	5.6	1,801.1	1,462.3	284.4	54.4	(X)	4,337
1942	26.2	25.7	0.5	73.0	17.8	3,858.8	3,075.6	640.6	142.6	(X)	4,485
1943	67.0	66.7	0.3	84.9	37.1	9,044.7	6,994.5	1,741.8	308.5	(X)	5,002
1944	79.0	79.1	-0.1	86.7	37.9	11,451.7	7,994.8	2,981.4	475.6	(X)	5,689
1945	83.1	83.0	0.1	89.5	37.5	12,055.9	8,266.4	3,319.6	469.9	(X)	6,498
1950	22.6	13.7	8.8	32.2	5.0	1,459.5	593.2	380.7	74.3	411.3	19,077
1951	29.1	23.6	5.5	51.8	7.3	3,249.4	1,531.8	736.6	192.6	788.4	18,919
1952	51.4	46.1	5.3	68.1	13.2	3,635.9	1,596.4	824.3	232.0	983.3	19,338
1953	57.3	52.8	4.5	69.4	14.2	3,555.1	1,533.8	794.4	249.2	977.6	20,196
1954	53.9	49.3	4.6	69.5	13.0	3,302.1	1,404.6	725.7	223.9	947.9	20,951
1955	47.4	42.7	4.7	62.4	10.8	2,935.1	1,109.3	660.7	205.2	959.9	21,861
1960	53.6	48.1	5.4	52.2	9.3	2,475.4	873.1	617.0	170.6	814.8	22,534
1965	56.3	50.6	5.7	42.8	7.4	2,653.9	969.1	670.0	190.2	824.7	21,834
1966	64.0	58.1	5.9	43.2	7.7	3,092.2	1,199.8	743.3	261.3	887.4	25,534
1967	78.2	71.4	6.7	45.4	8.8	3,375.5	1,442.5	750.2	285.3	897.5	25,805
1968	89.0	81.9	7.0	46.0	9.4	3,546.1	1,570.3	763.6	307.3	904.9	26,273
1969	90.1	82.5	7.6	44.9	8.7	3,458.1	1,512.2	773.8	309.8	862.4	26,925
1970	90.4	81.7	8.7	41.8	8.1	3,064.8	1,322.5	691.1	259.7	791.3	26,976
1971	88.6	78.9	9.8	37.5	7.3	2,713.0	1,123.8	621.6	212.4	755.3	27,523
1972	89.9	79.2	10.7	34.3	6.7	2,322.0	811.0	586.9	198.2	725.8	27,956
1973	88.7	76.7	12.0	31.2	5.9	2,251.9	801.0	563.7	196.1	691.2	28,125
1974	92.7	79.3	13.4	29.5	5.5	2,162.0	783.3	545.9	188.8	644.0	28,218
1975	103.1	86.5	16.6	26.0	5.6	2,128.1	784.3	535.1	196.0	612.8	28,281
1980	155.2	134.0	21.2	22.7	4.9	2,050.6	777.0	527.2	188.5	558.0	28,640
1990	328.4	299.3	29.1	23.9	5.3	2,043.7	732.4	579.4	196.7	535.2	27,320
1995	310.0	272.1	37.9	17.9	3.8	1,518.2	508.6	434.6	174.6	400.4	26,198
1997	309.8	270.5	39.3	16.9	3.4	1,438.6	491.7	395.6	173.9	377.4	25,551
1998	307.2	264.1	43.1	16.2	3.2	(NA)	(NA)	(NA)	(NA)	(NA)	25,188

NA Not available. X Not applicable. [1] Source: 1900-39, U.S. Bureau of the Budget, unpublished data. Data represent outlays of Department of the Army and Department of the Navy. [2] Source: 1900-39, Veterans Administration, Annual Report of Administrator of Veterans Affairs. [3] Represents fiscal year Gross Domestic Product (GDP).

Source: Except as noted, budget data, U.S. Office of Management and Budget, *Historical Tables, Budget of the United States Government, Fiscal Year 2000*; personnel, U.S. Department of Defense, *Selected Manpower Statistics*, annual; and veterans, U.S. Department of Veterans affairs, *Annual Report of the Secretary of Veterans Affairs*.

No. 1445. Vote Cast for President, by Major Political Party: 1900 to 1996

[Prior to 1960, excludes Alaska and Hawaii; prior to 1964, excludes DC]

Year	Candidates for President Democratic	Republican	Vote cast for President Total popular vote [1] (1,000)	Democratic Popular vote Number (1,000)	Percent	Electoral vote	Republican Popular vote Number (1,000)	Percent	Electoral vote
1900	McKinley	Bryan	13,962	6,357	45.5	155	7,218	51.7	292
1904	Parker	Roosevelt	13,522	5,084	37.6	140	7,628	56.4	336
1908	Bryan	Taft	14,888	6,412	43.1	162	7,675	51.6	321
1912	Wilson	Taft	15,037	6,297	41.9	435	3,487	23.2	8
1916	Wilson	Hughes	18,480	9,128	49.4	277	8,534	46.2	254
1920	Cox...........	Harding	26,769	9,133	34.1	127	16,153	60.3	404
1924	Davis.........	Coolidge	29,095	8,387	28.8	136	15,720	54.0	382
1928	Smith.........	Hoover........	36,806	15,008	40.8	87	21,437	58.2	444
1932	F. D. Roosevelt .	Hoover........	39,759	22,830	57.4	472	15,761	39.6	59
1936	F. D. Roosevelt ..	Landon	45,655	27,757	60.8	523	16,684	36.5	8
1940	F. D. Roosevelt ..	Willkie	49,900	27,313	54.7	449	22,348	44.8	82
1944	F. D. Roosevelt ..	Dewey........	47,977	25,613	53.4	432	22,018	45.9	99
1948	Truman	Dewey........	48,794	24,179	49.6	303	21,991	45.1	189
1952	Stevenson	Eisenhower.....	61,551	27,315	44.4	89	33,936	55.1	442
1956	Stevenson	Eisenhower.....	62,027	26,023	42.0	73	35,590	57.4	457
1960	Kennedy	Nixon.........	68,838	34,227	49.7	303	34,108	49.5	219
1964	Johnson.......	Goldwater.....	70,645	43,130	61.1	486	27,178	38.5	52
1968	Humphrey	Nixon.........	73,212	31,275	42.7	191	31,785	43.4	301
1972	McGovern	Nixon.........	77,719	29,170	37.5	17	47,170	60.7	520
1976	Carter	Ford	81,556	40,831	50.1	297	39,148	48.0	240
1980	Carter	Reagan	86,515	35,484	41.0	49	43,904	50.7	489
1984	Mondale.......	Reagan	92,653	37,577	40.6	13	54,455	58.8	525
1988	Dukakis	Bush	91,595	41,809	45.6	111	48,886	53.4	426
1992	Clinton........	Bush	104,425	44,909	43.0	370	39,104	37.4	168
1996	Clinton........	Dole	96,278	47,402	49.2	379	39,199	40.7	159

[1] Include votes for minor party candidates, independents, unpledged electors, and scattered write-in votes.
Source: 1900-32, U.S. Census Bureau, *Historical Statistics of the United States, Colonial Times to 1970*; 1936-96: Congressional Quarterly, Inc., Washington, DC. *America at the Polls 2*, 1965, and *America Votes*, biennial, (copyright).

No. 1446. Political Party Affiliations in Congress and the Presidency: 1939 to 1997

[D=Democrat, R=Republican. Figures are for beginning of the first session of each Congress, except as indicated. Excludes vacancies at beginning of session]

Year	Congress	House Majority party	House Principal minority party	House Other (except vacancies)	Senate Majority party	Senate Principal minority party	Senate Other (except vacancies)	President
1939-1940 . . .	76th	D-261	R-164	4	D-69	R-23	4	D (F. Roosevelt)
1941-1942 . . .	77th	D-268	R-162	5	D-66	R-28	2	D (F. Roosevelt)
1943-1944 . . .	78th	D-218	R-208	4	D-58	R-37	1	D (F. Roosevelt)
1945-1946 . . .	79th	D-242	R-190	2	D-56	R-38	1	D (Truman)
1947-1948 . . .	80th	R-245	D-188	1	R-51	D-45	-	D (Truman)
1949-1950 . . .	81st	D-263	R-171	1	D-54	R-42	-	D (Truman)
1951-1952 . . .	82d	D-234	R-199	1	D-49	R-47	-	D (Truman)
1953-1954 . . .	83d	R-221	D-211	1	R-48	D-47	1	R (Eisenhower)
1955-1956 . . .	84th	D-232	R-203	-	D-48	R-47	1	R (Eisenhower)
1957-1958 . . .	85th	D-233	R-200	-	D-49	R-47	-	R (Eisenhower)
1959-1960 . . .	86th	D-283	R-153	-	D-64	R-34	-	R (Eisenhower)
1961-1962 . . .	87th	D-263	R-174	-	D-65	R-35	-	D (Kennedy)
1963-1964 . . .	88th	D-258	R-177	-	D-67	R-33	-	D (L. Johnson)
								D (Kennedy)
1965-1966 . . .	89th	D-295	R-140	-	D-68	R-32	-	D (L. Johnson)
1967-1968 . . .	90th	D-246	R-187	-	D-64	R-36	-	D (L. Johnson)
1969-1970 . . .	91st	D-245	R-189	-	D-57	R-43	-	R (Nixon)
1961-1962 . . .	87th	D-263	R-174	-	D-65	R-35	-	D (Kennedy)
1963-1964 . . .	88th	D-258	R-177	-	D-67	R-33	-	D (Kennedy)
1965-1966 . . .	89th	D-295	R-140	-	D-68	R-32	-	D (Johnson)
1967-1968 . . .	90th	D-247	R-187	-	D-64	R-36	-	D (Johnson)
1969-1970 . . .	91st	D-243	R-192	-	D-57	R-43	-	R (Nixon)
1971-1972 [1][2] .	92d	D-254	R-180	-	D-54	R-44	2	R (Nixon)
1973-1974 [3] . .	93d	D-239	R-192	1	D-56	R-42	2	R (Nixon)
1975-1976 [3] . .	94th	D-291	R-144	-	D-60	R-37	2	R (Ford)
1977-1978 [4] . .	95th	D-292	R-143	-	D-61	R-38	1	D (Carter)
1979-1980 [4] . .	96th	D-276	R-157	-	D-58	R-41	1	D (Carter)
1981-1982 [4] . .	97th	D-243	R-192	-	R-53	D-46	1	R (Reagan)
1983-1984 . . .	98th	D-269	R-165	-	R-54	D-46	-	R (Reagan)
1985-1986 . . .	99th	D-252	R-182	-	R-53	D-47	-	R (Reagan)
1987-1988 . . .	100th	D-258	R-177	-	D-55	R-45	-	R (Reagan)
1989-1990 [5] . .	101st	D-259	R-174	-	D-55	R-45	-	R (Bush)
1991-1992 [5] . .	102d	D-267	R-167	1	D-56	R-44	-	R (Bush)
1993-1994 [5] . .	103d	D-258	R-176	1	D-57	R-43	-	D (Clinton)
1995-1996 [5] . .	104th	R-230	D-204	1	R-52	D-48	-	D (Clinton)
1996 [5]	104th	R-236	D-197	1	R-53	D-46	-	D (Clinton)
1997 [5][6]	105th	R-226	D-207	2	R-55	D-45	-	D (Clinton)

- Represents zero.   [1] Senate had one Independent and one Conservative-Republican.   [2] House had one Independent-Democrat.   [3] Senate had one Independent, one Conservative-Republican, and one undecided (New Hampshire).   [4] Senate had one Independent.   [5] House had one Independent-Socialist.   [6] As of beginning of second session.

Source: U.S. Congress, Joint Committee on Printing, *Congressional Directory*, annual; beginning 1977, biennial.

No. 1447. World Population, by Region: 1950 to 1998

[In millions (2,556.0 represents 2,556,000,000), except as indicated]

Year	World, total [1]	Africa, total	Near East	Asia, excluding Near East	Latin America and the Caribbean	Europe Total	Europe Western Europe	Northern America Total	Northern America United States
NUMBER									
1950	2,556.0	228.3	43.7	1,367.7	165.8	571.7	304.4	166.3	152.3
1955	2,780.3	253.4	49.7	1,488.1	189.5	603.5	314.0	182.1	165.9
1960	3,039.5	282.9	57.4	1,627.5	217.9	639.0	325.7	199.0	180.7
1965	3,345.4	317.7	65.7	1,804.9	250.4	674.9	340.3	214.5	194.3
1970	3,706.6	359.5	74.7	2,037.7	286.0	702.5	351.6	226.9	205.1
1975	4,086.3	408.0	86.6	2,279.2	323.5	728.6	361.1	239.3	216.0
1980	4,453.8	468.3	100.6	2,497.6	362.0	750.3	366.8	252.4	227.7
1985	4,850.6	540.3	117.3	2,732.6	401.9	769.3	370.5	264.5	238.5
1990	5,277.0	620.8	134.9	2,985.9	443.0	788.0	376.5	277.9	249.9
1995	5,682.4	705.6	152.7	3,220.7	483.6	798.5	384.4	292.8	263.0
1998	5,918.6	760.0	165.0	3,356.0	507.6	799.4	386.6	301.1	270.3
PERCENT DISTRIBUTION									
1950	100.0	8.9	1.7	53.5	6.5	22.4	11.9	6.5	6.0
1960	100.0	9.3	1.9	53.5	7.2	21.0	10.7	6.5	5.9
1970	100.0	9.7	2.0	55.0	7.7	19.0	9.5	6.1	5.5
1980	100.0	10.5	2.3	56.1	8.1	16.8	8.2	5.7	5.1
1990	100.0	11.8	2.6	56.6	8.4	14.9	7.1	5.3	4.7
1998	100.0	12.8	2.8	56.7	8.6	13.5	6.5	5.1	4.6

[1] Includes Oceania.

Source: U.S. Census Bureau, International Data Base.

U.S. Census Bureau, Statistical Abstract of the United States: 1999

Appendix I
Guide to Sources of Statistics, State Statistical Abstracts, and Foreign Statistical Abstracts

Alphabetically arranged, this guide contains references to the important primary sources of statistical information for the United States published since 1990. Secondary sources have been included if the information contained in them is presented in a particularly convenient form or if primary sources are not readily available. Nonrecurrent publications presenting compilations or estimates for years later than 1990 or types of data not available in regular series are also included.

Much valuable information may also be found in state reports, foreign statistical abstracts, which are included at the end of this appendix and in reports for particular commodities, industries, or similar segments of our economic and social structures, many of which are not included here.

Publications listed under each subject are divided into two main groups: "U.S. Government" and "Nongovernment." The location of the publisher of each report is given except for Federal agencies located in Washington, DC. Most Federal publications may be purchased from the Superintendent of Documents, U.S. Government Printing Office, Washington, DC 20402, tel. 202-512-1800, (website <http://www.access.gpo.gov>or from Government Printing Office bookstores in certain major cities. In some cases, Federal publications may be obtained from the issuing agency.

U.S. GOVERNMENT

Administration for Children and Families
Quarterly Public Assistance Statistics. Annual.

Administrative Office of the United States Courts
Calendar Year Reports on Authorized Wiretaps. (State and Federal.)

Federal Court Management Statistics. Annual.

Federal Judicial Caseload Statistics. Annual.

Judicial Business of the United States Courts.

Statistical Tables for the Federal Judiciary. Semiannual.

Agency for International Development
U.S. Overseas Loans and Grants and Assistance From International Organizations. Annual.

Army, Corps of Engineers
Waterborne Commerce of the United States (in five parts). Annual.

Board of Governors of the Federal Reserve System
Annual Statistical Digest.

Federal Reserve Banks. Monthly review published by each Bank with special reference to its own Federal Reserve District.

Federal Reserve Bulletin. Monthly. (Also monthly releases on industrial production indexes.)

Domestic Offices, Commercial Bank Assets and Liabilities Consolidated Report of Condition. Quarterly.

Flow of Funds Accounts: Seasonally Adjusted and Unadjusted. Z.1(780). Quarterly.

Industrial Production and Capacity Utilization G.17. Monthly.

Money Stock, Liquid Assets, and Debt Measures. H.6. Weekly.

Bureau of Alcohol, Tobacco, and Firearms
Alcohol and Tobacco Summary Statistics. Annual.

Bureau of Economic Analysis
National Income and Product Accounts of the United States, 1929-1994: Statistical Tables, 1998.

Bureau of Economic Analysis —Con.

Survey of Current Business. Monthly. (March, June, September, and December issues contain data on U.S. international transactions. Articles on foreign direct investment in the United States, U.S. direct investment abroad, and other topics appear periodically in other issues.)

U.S. Direct Investment Abroad: 1994 Benchmark Survey, 1997.

U.S. Direct Investment Abroad: Operations of U.S. Parent Companies and their Foreign Affiliates. Preliminary, 1995. Estimates, 1997.

Bureau of Justice Statistics

Age patterns of victims of serious violent crimes. September 1997.

Alcohol and crime: An analysis of national data on the prevalence of alcohol involvement in crime. April 1998.

Campus law enforcement agencies, 1995. December 1996.

Capital punishment. Annual. 1996. December 1997.

Carjacking in U.S., 1992-96. March 1996.

Census of state and local law enforcement agencies, 1996. June 1998.

Changes in criminal victimization, 1994-95. April 1997.

Characteristics of adults on probation, 1995, December 1997.

Child victimizers: Violent offenders and their victims. March 1996.

Civil Justice Survey of State Courts, 1992, CD-ROM. July 1996.

Comparing case processing statistics. September 1996.

Contract cases in large counties: Civil Justice Survey of State Courts, 1992. February 1996.

Correctional populations in the United States annual.

Criminal Victimization in the United States Annual.

Expenditure and Employment Data for the Criminal Justice System. Annual.

Federal criminal case processing, 1997. June 1998.

Federal law enforcement officers, 1996. January 1998.

Federal tort trials and verdicts, 1994-95. January 1998.

Felony defendants in large urban counties: Biennial.

Felony sentences in state courts. Biennial.

Felony sentences in the United States. Biennial.

Female victims of violent crime. December 1996.

Firearm injury from crime: Firearms, crime, and criminal justice. April 1996.

HIV in prisons and jails 1995. August 1997.

Households Touched by Crime. Annual.

Indigent defense. February 1996.

Bureau of Justice Statistics —Con.

Justice expenditure and employment in the United States, 1990. May 1998.

Juvenile delinquents in the Federal criminal justice system. February 1997.

Juveniles prosecuted in state criminal courts, 1994: National Survey of Prosecutors. March 1997.

Lifetime likelihood of going to state or Federal prison. March 1997.

Local police departments, 1993: A LEMAS report. April 1996.

Motor Vehicle Theft

National Corrections Reporting Program. Annual.

Noncitizens in the Federal criminal justice system: Federal Justice Statistics Program. August 1996.

Parole in the United States Annual.

Presale firearm checks: A national estimate. February 1997.

Prison and jail inmates 1995. August 1996.

Prison and jail inmates at midyear, 1997. January 1998.

Prisoner petitions in the Federal courts, 1980-96

Prisoners in State and Federal Institutions. Annual.

Probation and parole populations, 1996. August 1997.

Profile of jail inmates, 1996. April 1998.

Prosecutors in state courts. Biennial.

Sex differences in violent victimization, 1994. September 1997.

Sex offenses and offenders. January 1997.

Sheriffs' departments 1993. June 1996.

Sourcebook of criminal justice statistics, 1994-95 editions, CDROM. October 1997.

State court sentencing of convicted felons. Biennial.

Students' reports of school crime: 1989 and 1995. April 1998.

Substance abuse and treatment of adults on probation, 1995. March 1998.

Survey of state criminal history information systems, 1995. May 1997.

Violence by intimates: Analysis of data on crimes by current or former spouses, boyfriends, and girlfriends. March 1998.

Violence-related injuries treated in hospital emergency departments. August 1997.

Bureau of Labor Statistics

Comparative Labor Force Statistics, Ten Countries. Annual.

Compensation and Working Conditions. Quarterly.

Consumer Expenditure Survey, Integrated Diary and Interview Survey data.

Consumer Prices: Energy and Food. Monthly.

CPI Detailed Report. Monthly.

Employee Benefits in Medium and Large Firms. Biennial.

U.S. Census Bureau, Statistical Abstract of the United States: 1999

Bureau of Labor Statistics —Con.

Employee Benefits in Small Private Establishments. Biennial.

Employee Benefits in State and Local Governments. Biennial.

Employer Costs for Employee Compensation. Annual.

Employment and Earnings. Monthly.

Employment and Wages. Annual.

Employment Cost Index. Quarterly.

Employment Cost Indexes and Levels. Annual.

Employment, Hours, and Earnings, United States, 1988-96. 1996. (Bulletin 2481.)

Employment Outlook: 1994-2005. (Bulletin 2472.)

The Employment Situation. Monthly.

Geographic Profile of Employment and Unemployment. Annual.

International Comparisons of Hourly Compensation Costs for Production Workers in Manufacturing. Annual.

International Comparisons of Manufacturing Productivity and Unit Labor Cost Trends. Annual.

Monthly Labor Review.

Occupational Injuries and Illnesses in the United States by Industry. Annual.

Occupational Projections and Training Data. Biennial.

Producer Price Indexes. Detailed report. Monthly, with annual supplement.

Productivity Measures for Selected Industries and Government Services. Annual.

Real Earnings. Monthly.

Relative Importance of Components in the Consumer Price Indexes. Annual.

State and Metropolitan Area Employment and Unemployment. Monthly.

U.S. Import and Export Price Indexes. Monthly.

Usual Weekly Earnings of Wage and Salary Workers. Quarterly.

Work Experience of the Population. Annual.

Bureau of Land Management

Public Land Statistics. Annual.

Bureau of Mines

Minerals Yearbook. Annual.

Bureau of the Mint

Annual Report of the Director.

Bureau of Reclamation

Summary Statistics:

Vol. I, Water, Land, and Related Data.

Census Bureau

Major reports, such as the Census of Population, which consist of many volumes, are listed by their general, all-inclusive titles. In most cases, separate reports of the most recent censuses are available for each state, subject, industry, etc.

Census Bureau —Con.

Annual Benchmark Report for Retail Trade.

Annual Benchmark Report for Wholesale Trade.

Annual Survey of Communication Services.

Annual Survey of Manufactures. (1996, most recent.)

Census of Construction Industries. Quinquennial. (1997, most recent.)

Census of Finance, Insurance, and Real Estate Industries. Quinquennial. (1997, most recent.)

Census of Governments. Government Organization (GC 97)

Census of Governments. Quinquennial.

Census of Housing. Decennial. (1990, most recent.)

Census of Manufactures. Quinquennial. (1997, most recent.)

Census of Mineral Industries. Quinquennial.(1997, most recent.)

Census of Population. Decennial. (1990, most recent.)

Census of Retail Trade. Quinquennial. (1997, most recent.)

Census of Service Industries. Quinquennial. (1997, most recent.)

Census of Transportation. Communications, and Utilities. Quinquennial. (1997, most recent.)

Census of Wholesale Trade. Quinquennial. (1997, most recent.)

City Employment. Annual. (GE90 No. 2.)

Congressional District Data:

1990 Census of Population and Housing, 1990 CPH-4, Congressional Districts of the 103rd Congress.

CFFR Consolidated Federal Funds Report. Annual.

Volume I County Areas

Volume II Subcounty Areas

County Business Patterns. Annual.

Current Construction Reports: Housing Starts, C20 (monthly); New Residential Construction in Selected Metropolitan Statistical Areas, C21 (quarterly); Housing Completions, C22 (monthly); New One-Family Houses Sold and for Sale, C25 (monthly with annual report, Characteristics of New Housing); Price Index of New One-Family Houses Sold, C27 (quarterly); Value of Construction Put in Place, C30 (monthly with occasional historical supplement); Housing Units Authorized by Building Permits, C40 (monthly and annual); Residential Improvements and Repairs, C50 (quarterly and annual).

Current Governments Reports: Public Employment, GE No. 1 (annual); City Employment, GE No. 2 (annual); Local Government Employment in Selected Metropolitan Areas and Large Counties, GE No. 3 (annual); County Government Employment, GE No. 4 (annual).

Census Bureau —Con.

Current Housing Reports: Housing Vacancies, H-111 (quarterly and annual); Market Absorption of Apartments, H-130 (quarterly and annual); Characteristics of Apartments Completed, H-131 (annual); Annual Housing Survey, H-150 (series of six biennial reports); Annual Housing Survey—Housing Characteristics for Selected Metropolitan Areas, H-170.

Current Industrial Report, Survey of Pollution Abatement Costs and Expenditures, series MA-200.

Current Population Reports. (Series P20.)

Estimates and Projections, P25, Consumer Income and Poverty, P60 and Household Economic Studies, P70.

Economic Census of Outlying Area. Quinquennial.

Federal Aid to States for Fiscal Year. Annual.

FES Federal Expenditures by State for Fiscal Year. Annual.

International Briefs. (Series IB.)

International Population Reports. (Series IPC.)

Manufacturing Profiles. (series MP-1.) Annual.

Manufacturers' Shipments, Inventories, and Orders. Monthly.

Manufacturers' Shipments, Inventories, and Orders: 1987-96. Annual summary. (Current Industrial Reports M3-1(95).)

Manufacturers' Shipments to Federal Government Agencies. (Current Industrial Reports MA-175.) Conducted for economic census years ending in 2 and 7.)

Merchant Wholesalers Measures of Value Produced, Capital Expenditures, Depreciable Assets, and Operating Expenses. (1997, most recent.)

Minority-Owned Businesses. Quinquennial. (1997, Most recent.)

Monthly Retail Trade Report. Sales and Inventories.

Monthly Wholesale Trade Report. Sales and Inventories.

Population Profile of the United States. (Biennial Series P23.)

Quarterly Financial Report for Manufacturing, Mining, and Trade Corporations.

Selected Characteristics of Retail Trade-Measures of Value Produced, Capital Expenditures, Depreciable Assets, and Operating Expenses. (1992, most recent.)

Selected Characteristics of Selected Service Industries—Capital Expenditures, Depreciable Assets, and Operating Expenses. (1992, most recent.)

Service Annual Survey Report.

Special Studies Reports. (Series on Special Studies, P23.)

Summary of U.S. International Trade in Goods and Services: includes cumulative data. (FT 900.)

Census Bureau —Con.

Survey of the Origin of Exports of Manufacturing Establishments. Triennial. (Current Industrial Reports M76 (AS)-8.)

Survey of Plant Capacity Utilization. (Current Industrial Reports MQ-C1.)

Transportation Annual Survey.

Truck Inventory and Use Survey. Quinquennial. (1997, most recent.)

U.S. Commodity Exports and Imports as Related to Output. (Series ES2.)

U.S. Trade with Puerto Rico and U.S. Possessions. Monthly and Annual. (FT 895.)

World Population Profile: 1998 (Series WP.)

Centers for Disease Control and Prevention, Atlanta, GA

Morbidity and Mortality Weekly Report. Annual.

Coast Guard

Annual Report of the Secretary of Transportation.

Marine Casualty Statistics. Annual.

Polluting Incidents in and Around U.S. Waters. Annual.

Comptroller of the Currency

Quarterly Journal.

Congressional Clerk of the House

Statistics of the Presidential and Congressional Election Years. Biennial.

Council of Economic Advisers

Economic Indicators. Monthly.

Economic Report of the President. Annual.

Council on Environmental Quality

Environmental Quality. Annual.

Department of Agriculture

Agricultural Chemical Usage. Field crops, vegetables (fruits and vegetables alternate years), restricted use pesticides. Chemical application rates and acres treated, selected states and U.S. Annual.

Agricultural Income and Finance. Situation and Outlook Report. Quarterly.

Agricultural Outlook. 11 issues per year.

Agricultural Price Reports. Reports on prices received for farm commodities, prices paid for farm supplies, indexes and parity ratios. Monthly and annual.

Agriculture and Trade Reports (five per year).

  Western Europe

  China

  Developing Economies

  Pacific Rim

  USSR

CATFISH. 12 issues of Catfish processing, plus 4 issues of catfish production and annual issue of Trout Production.

Census of Agriculture. Quinquennial. (1997, most recent.)

U.S. Census Bureau, Statistical Abstract of the United States: 1999

Department of Agriculture —Con.

Geographic Area Series (Internet, CD-ROM, Print), Volume 1

Cheddar Cheese Prices. U.S., regional prices for 40 and 640 LB blocks and 500 LB barrels; sales volumes. Weekly.

Cotton ginnings and winter wheat and rye seedings.

Crop Production Reports. Acreage, yield, and production of various commodities. Monthly and annual.

Crop Values Report. Price and value of various commodities. Annual.

Economic Indicators of the Farm Sector. A series of five annual issues.

Farm Labor. Quarterly.

Farmline. 11 issues per year.

Farm Numbers, Value. Farm numbers and land in farms, agricultural cash rents, agricultural land values, foreign ownership of U.S. Agricultural Land (ERS). Annual.

Financial Characteristics of U.S. (Agriculture Information Bulletin. No. 569.) Annual.

Food Consumption, Prices, and Expenditures, 1996. (Statistical Bulletin No. 928.) Revised annually.

Food Marketing Review, (Agricultural Economic Report No. 743). Revised annually.

Food Review. Quarterly.

Food Spending in American Households. (Statistical Bulletin No. 824.) Annual.

Foreign Agricultural Trade of the United States (FATUS). Bimonthly with annual supplements on calendar year and fiscal year trade statistics.

Fruit and Vegetable Reports. Acreage, yield, production, value, and utilization of various fruits and vegetables. Periodic.

Journal of Agricultural Economics Research. Quarterly.

Livestock and Meat Statistics, 1970-92. (Statistical Bulletin No. 874.) Annual.

Livestock Reports. Cattle, Cattle on Feed, Hogs and Pigs. Sheep, Goats, Wool, and Mohair. Monthly, Quarterly, and Annual.

Milk and Dairy Products Reports. Milk cows, milk production, and dairy products. Monthly and Annual.

Other Reports. Reports on varied items including cold storage, catfish, cherries, cranberries, trout, farm employment and wages, farm production expenditures, mink, mushrooms, and floriculture crops. Monthly and annual.

Poultry and Egg Reports. Reports covering eggs, chickens, turkeys, hatcheries, egg products, and poultry slaughter. Weekly, monthly, annual.

Rural Conditions and Trends. Quarterly.

Rural Development Perspectives. Three issues per year.

Situation and Outlook Reports. Issued for agricultural exports, cotton and wool, dairy, feed, fruit and tree nuts,

Department of Agriculture —Con.

agricultural resources, livestock and poultry, oil crops, rice, aquaculture, sugar and sweeteners, tobacco, vegetables, wheat, and world agriculture. Periodic.

Stock Reports. Stocks of grain, hops, peanuts, potatoes, rice, and soybeans. Quarterly, annual, periodic.

U.S. Egg and Poultry Statistical Series, 1960-92. (Statistical Bulletin No. 872.) Periodic.

Usual planting and harvesting dates. Dates for major field crops. Periodic.

Weekly Weather and Crop Bulletin. Report summarizing weather and its effect on crops the previous week. Weekly.

Department of Agriculture, Food and Nutrition Service

Annual Historical Review:

Food and Consumer Service Programs.

Department of Defense

Foreign Military Sales and Military Assistance Facts. Annual.

Department of Education

Annual Report.

Department of Health and Human Services

Annual Report.

Department of Housing and Urban Development

Survey of Mortgage Lending Activity. Monthly and quarterly press releases.

Department of Labor

Annual Report of the Secretary.

Department of State

United States Contribution to International Organizations. Issued in the House Documents series. Annual.

Department of State, Bureau of Consular Affairs

Report of the Visa Office. Annual. (Dept. of State Pub. 8810.)

Summary of Passport Statistics. Annual.

Department of Transportation

Airport Activity Statistics of Certified Route Air Carriers. Annual.

National Transportation Statistics, 1998.

Report of Passenger Travel Between the United States and Foreign Countries. Annual, semiannual, quarterly. Monthly.

Transportation Safety Information Report. Quarterly.

U.S. International Air Travel Statistics. Annual.

Department of the Treasury

Active Foreign Credits of the United States Government. Quarterly.

Consolidated Financial Statements of the United States Government. (Prototype.)

Daily Treasury Statement.

Monthly Statement of the Public Debt of the United States.

Monthly Treasury Statement of Receipts and Outlays of the United States Government.

Statement of United States Currency and Coin. Monthly.

Treasury Bulletin. Quarterly.

United States Government Annual Report and Appendix.

Department of Veterans Affairs

Annual Report of The Secretary of Veterans Affairs.

Disability Compensation, Pension, and Death Pension Data. Annual.

Government Life Insurance Programs for Veterans and Members of the Service. Annual.

Loan Guaranty Highlights. Quarterly.

Projections of The Veteran Population by State and County to the Year 2010.

Selected Compensation and Pension Data by State of Residence. Annual.

State and County Veteran Population Estimates. Annual.

Summary of Medical Programs. Annual.

Drug Enforcement Administration

Drug Abuse and Law Enforcement Statistics. Irregular.

Employment and Training Administration

Employment and Training Report of the President. Annual.

Unemployment Insurance Claims. Weekly.

Energy Information Administration

Annual Energy Outlook.

Annual Energy Review.

Coal Industry Annual.

Cost and Quality of Fuels for Electric Utility Plants. Annual.

Electric Power Annual.

Electric Power Monthly.

Electric Sales and Revenue. Annual.

Financial Statistics of Selected Electric Utilities. Annual.

International Energy Annual.

International Energy Outlook.

Inventory of Power Plants in the United States. Annual.

Monthly Energy Review.

Natural Gas Annual.

Natural Gas Monthly.

Performance Profiles of Major Energy Producers. Annual.

Energy Information Administration —Con.

Petroleum Marketing Monthly.

Petroleum Supply Annual.

Petroleum Supply Monthly.

Quarterly Coal Report.

Renewable Energy Annual.

Residential Energy Consumption Survey: Housing Characteristics. Triennial.

Residential Transportation Energy Consumption Survey. Triennial.

Short-Term Energy Outlook. Quarterly.

State Energy Data Report. Annual.

State Energy Price and Expenditure Report. Annual.

Uranium Industry Annual.

Weekly Coal Production.

U.S. Crude Oil, Natural Gas, and Natural Gas Liquids Reserves. Annual.

Energy Research and Development Administration

The Nuclear Industry. Annual.

Environmental Protection Agency

Air Quality Data. Annual.

Cost of Clean Water. Annual.

Federal Certification Test Results for Motor Vehicles. Annual.

Municipal Water Facilities Inventory. Quinquennial.

National Air Pollutant Emission Trends, 1900-96.

National Air Quality and Emissions Trends Report. 1996.

Needs Survey, Conveyance and Treatment of Municipal Wastewater Summaries of Technical Data. Biennial.

Pesticides Monitoring Journal. Quarterly.

Radiation Data and Reports. Monthly.

Sewage Facility Construction. Annual.

Summary of Water Enforcement Actions Pursued by EPA since December 3, 1970. (Updated continuously.)

Export-Import Bank of the United States

Annual Report.

Report to the U.S. Congress on Export Credit Competition and the Export-Import Bank of the United States. Annual.

Farm Credit Administration

Annual Report on the Work of the Cooperative Farm Credit System.

Loans and Discounts of Farm Credit Banks and Associations. Annual.

Production Credit Association: Summary of Operations. Annual.

Report to the Federal Land Bank Associations. Annual.

Federal Bureau of Investigation
Bomb Summary. Annual.
Crime in the United States. Annual.
Hate Crime Statistics. Annual.
Law Enforcement Officers Killed and Assaulted. Annual.

Federal Communications Commission
Annual Report.
Statistics of Communications Common Carriers. Annual.

Federal Deposit Insurance Corporation
Annual Report.
Data Book-Operating Banks and Branches. Annual.
Quarterly Banking Profile.
Statistics on Banking. Annual, and Historical 1934-1996, Volume I.
Trust Assets of Insured Commercial Banks. Annual.
Quarterly Banking Review.

Federal Highway Administration
Highway Statistics. Annual.

Federal Railroad Administration
Accident/Incident Bulletin. Summary, statistics, and analysis of accidents on railroads in the United States. Annual.
Rail-Highway Crossing Accident/Incident and Inventory Bulletin. Annual.

Forest Service
An Analysis of the Timber Situation in the United States: 1989-2040.
Land Areas of the National Forest System. Annual.
The 1993 RPA Timber Assessment Update. Forthcoming.
U.S. Timber Production, Trade, Consumption, and Price Statistics. Annual.

Fish and Wildlife Service
Federal Aid in Fish and Wildlife Restoration. Annual.
1996 National Survey of Fishing, Hunting, and Wildlife Associated Recreation.

General Services Administration
Inventory Report on Real Property Leased to the United States Throughout the World. Annual.

Geological Survey
A Statistical Summary of Data from the U.S. Geological Survey's National Water Quality Networks. (Open-File Report 83-533.)
Mineral Commodity Summaries. Annual.
Mineral Industry Surveys. (Monthly, quarterly, or annual report.)
Minerals Yearbook. (Monthly, quarterly, or annual report.)

Health Care Financing Administration
Health Care Financing Review. Medicare and Medicaid Statistical Supplement. Annual.
Health Care Financing Research Reports. Occasional.
Health Care Financing Review. Quarterly.

Immigration and Naturalization Service
I&N Reporter. Quarterly.
Statistical Yearbook of the Immigration and Naturalization Service. Annual.
Wage Statistics of Class I Railroads in the United States. Annual. (Statement No. 300.)

International Trade Administration
Business America. Monthly. (Issues in March, June, September, and December contain quarterly data on key International comparisons.)
Construction Review. Quarterly.
Electric Current Abroad. Irregular. (1998, most recent.)
U.S. Foreign Trade Highlights. Annual.
U.S. Global Trade Outlook. Irregular.
U.S. Industry and Trade Outlook. Annual. (1998, most recent.)

International Trade Commission
Synthetic Organic Chemicals, U.S. Production and Sales. Annual.

Internal Revenue Service
Corporation Income Tax Returns. Annual.
IRS Data Book.
Statistics of Income Bulletin. Quarterly.
Statistics of Income Division. (Annual report on Corporation Income Tax Returns.
Periodic compendiums on Studies of International Income and Taxes.)

Interstate Commerce Commission
Class I Freight Railroads Selected Earnings Data. Quarterly.
Monthly Report of Class I Railroad Employees, by Group. (Statement No. 350.)
Quarterly Report.
Transport Statistics in the United States. Issued annually in two separate parts:
Part 1: Railroads
Part 2: Motor Carriers

Library of Congress
Annual Report.

Maritime Administration
Annual Report.
Employment Report of United States Flag Merchant Fleet Ocean-going Vessels 1,000 Gross Tons and Over. Quarterly.
Seafaring Wage Rates. Biennial.

896   Appendix I

Mine Safety and Health Administration

Informational Reports by Mining Industry: Coal; Metallic Minerals; Nonmetallic Minerals (except stone and coal); Stone, Sand, and Gravel. Annual.

Mine Injuries and Worktime. (Some preliminary data.) Quarterly.

National Advisory Council on International Monetary and Financial Policies

Annual Report to the President and to the Congress.

National Aeronautics and Space Administration

Annual Procurement Report.

The Civil Service Work Force.

Pocket Statistics. Annual.

The National Agricultural Library
(for technical agricultural publications)

Annual Report

National Center for Education Statistics

College and University Library Survey.

The Condition of Education. Annual.

Digest of Education Statistics. Annual.

Earned Degrees Conferred. Annual.

Faculty Salaries, Tenure, and Benefits. Annual.

Fall Enrollment in Colleges and Universities. Annual.

Financial Statistics of Higher Education.

National Assessment of Educational Progress.

National Education Longitudinal Study. Reports issued on 8th graders from 1988 and their transition to higher education and the labor force.

Projections of Education Statistics. Annual.

Revenues and Expenditures for Public Elementary and Secondary Education. Annual.

Statistics of Public Elementary and Secondary School Systems. Fall. Annual.

National Center for Health Statistics

Ambulatory Care Visits to Physician Offices, Hospital Outpatient Departments and Emergency Departments. Annual.

Health: United States. Annual. (DHHS Pub. No. PHS year-1232.)

National Hospital Discharge Survey: Annual Summary. Annual.

National Vital Statistics Reports (NVRS.) Monthly.

Vital and Health Statistics. (A series of statistical reports covering health-related topics.)

Series 10: Health Interview Survey Statistics. Irregular.

Current Estimates from the Health Interview Survey. Annual.

National Center for Health Statistics —Con.

Series 11: Health and Nutrition Examination Survey Statistics. Irregular. .

Series 13: Health Resources Utilization Statistics. Irregular.

Series 14: Health Resources: Manpower and Facilities Statistics. Irregular.

Series 20: Mortality Data. Irregular.

Series 21: Natality, Marriage, and Divorce Data. Irregular.

Series 23: National Survey of Family Growth Statistics. Irregular.

Vital Statistics of the United States. Annual.

Volume I, Natality

Volume II, Mortality

Volume III, Marriage and Divorce

Internet address:
http://www.cdc.gov/nchswww/

National Credit Union Administration

Annual Report.

Midyear Statistics.

Yearend Statistics.

National Guard Bureau

Annual Review of the Chief.

The National Library of Medicine
(for clinical medical reports)

Annual Report.

National Oceanic and Atmospheric Administration

Climatological Data. Issued in sections for states and outlying areas. Monthly with annual summary.

Climatography of the United States, No. 20, Supplement No. 1, Freeze/Frost Data.

General Summary of Tornadoes. Annual.

Hourly Precipitation Data. Monthly with annual summary; for each state.

Local Climatological Data. Monthly with annual summary; for major cities.

Storm Data. Monthly.

Weekly Weather and Crop Bulletin. National summary.

National Park Service

Federal Recreation Fee Report. Annual.

National Park Statistical Abstract. Annual.

National Science Foundation

Academic Research and Development Expenditures. Detailed Statistical Tables. Annual

Academic Science and Engineering: Graduate Enrollment and Support: Detailed Statistical Tables. Annual

Characteristics of Doctoral Scientists and Engineers in the United States. Detailed Statistical Tables. Biennial.

Characteristics of Recent Science/Engineering Graduates. Detailed Statistical Tables. Biennial.

Appendix I   897

National Science Foundation —Con.

Federal Funds for Research and Development. Detailed Statistical Tables. Annual.

Federal R&D Funding by Budget Function. Report. Annual.

Federal Science and Engineering Support to Universities, Colleges, and Nonprofit Institutions. Detailed Statistical Tables. Annual.

Federal Support to Universities, Colleges, and Nonprofit Institutions. Detailed Statistical Tables. Annual.

Graduate Students and Post-doctorates in Science and Engineering. Annual.

Immigrant Scientists, Engineers and Technicians. Detailed Statistical Tables. Annual.

International Science and Technology Data Update. Report. Annual.

National Patterns of R&D Resources. Report. Annual.

Planned R&D Expenditures of Major U.S. Firms. Special Report. (NSF 91-306.)

Research and Development in Industry. Detailed Statistical Tables. Annual.

Science and Engineering Degrees, by Race/Ethnicity of Recipients. Detailed Statistical Tables. Annual.

Science and Engineering Doctorates Awards. Detailed Statistical Tables. Annual.

Science and Engineering Indicators. Report. Biennial.

Science and Engineering Personnel: A National Overview. Report. Biennial.

Science and Engineering Profiles. Annual.

Science and Technology Pocket Data Book. Report. Annual.

Science Resources Studies. Data Brief. Frequent.

Scientific and Engineering Research Facilities at Universities and Colleges. Report. Biennial.

Scientists, Engineers, and Technicians in Manufacturing Industries. Detailed Statistical Tables. Triennial.

Scientists, Engineers, and Technicians in Nonmanufacturing Industries. Detailed Statistical Tables. Triennial.

Scientists, Engineers, and Technicians in Trade and Regulated Industries. Detailed Statistical Tables. Triennial.

Survey of Direct U.S. Private Capital Investment in Research and Development Facilities in Japan. Report. (NSH 91-312.)

U.S. Scientists and Engineers. Detailed Statistical Tables. Biennial.

Women, Minorities, and Persons with Disabilities. Report. Biennial

Woman, Minorities in Science and Engineering. Report. Biennial.

National Transportation Safety Board

Accidents; Air Carriers. Annual.

Accidents; General Aviation. Annual.

Office of Civil Defense

Annual Statistical Report.

Office of Management and Budget

The Budget of the United States Government. Annual.

Office of Personnel Management

Civil Service Retirement and Disability Fund. Report. Annual.

Demographic Profile of the Federal Workforce. Biennial. (Even years.)

Employment and Trends. Bimonthly. (Odd months.)

Employment by Geographic Area. Biennial. (Even years.)

Occupations of Federal White-Collar and Blue-Collar Workers. Biennial. (Odd years.)

Pay Structure of the Federal Civil Service. Annual.

Statistical Abstract for the Federal Employee Benefit Programs. Annual.

Work Years and Personnel Costs. Annual.

Office of Thrift Supervision

Annual Report.

Patent and Trademark Office

Commissioner of Patents and Trademarks Annual Report.

Technology Assessment and Forecast Reports

"All Technologies." Annual.

"State Country." Annual.

"Patenting Trends in the United States." Annual.

Railroad Retirement Board, Chicago, IL

Annual Report.

Monthly Benefit Statistics.

Statistical Supplement to the Annual Report.

Rehabilitation Services Administration.

Annual Report.

Caseload Statistics of State Vocational Rehabilitation Agencies in Fiscal Year. Annual.

Rural Electrification Administration

Annual Statistical Report—Rural Telephone Borrowers.

Securities and Exchange Comission

Annual Report.

Small Business Administration

Annual Report.

Handbook of Small Business Data.

The State of Small Business.

U.S. Census Bureau, Statistical Abstract of the United States: 1999

Securities and Exchange Commission

Annual Report.

Social Security Administration

Income of the Population 55 and over, 1994. 1996.

Public Social Welfare Expenditures, Fiscal Year 1994. Social Security Bulletin, No. 3, 1997.

Social Security Beneficiaries by State and County Data. Annual.

Social Security Administration —Con.

Social Security Bulletin. Quarterly with annual statistical supplement. (Data on Social Security Benefits, OASDI, Supplemental Security Income, Aid to Families with Dependent Children, Medicare, Medicaid, Low Income Home Energy Assistance, Food Stamps, Black Lung benefits, and other programs.)

Social Security Programs in the United States, 1997.

State Assistance Programs for SSI Recipients. Annual.

Supplemental Security Income, State and County Data. Annual.

NONGOVERNMENT

AAFRC Trust For Philanthropy, New York, NY

Giving USA. Annual.

Advisory Commission on Intergovernmental Relations, Washington, DC

Characteristics of Federal Grant-in-Aid Programs to State and Local Governments: Grants Funded FY 93. (Every 3 years.)

Changing Public Attitudes on Governments and Taxes. Annual.

Significant Features of Fiscal Federalism. Annual.

Aerospace Industries, New York, NY

Aerospace Facts and Figures. Annual.

Aerospace Industry Year-End Review and Forecast. Annual.

Commercial Helicopter Shipments. Quarterly.

Employment in the Aerospace Industry. Monthly.

Exports of Aerospace Products. Quarterly.

Imports of Aerospace Products. Quarterly.

Manufacturing Production, Capacity, and Utilization in Aerospace and Aircraft and parts. Quarterly.

Orders, Shipments, Backlog and inventories for Aircraft, Missiles, & Parts. Quarterly.

Survey of Aerospace Employment. Annual.

Air Transport Association of America, Washington, DC

Air Transport Association Annual Report.

The Alan Guttmacher Institute, New York, NY

Family Planning Perspectives. Bimonthly.

American Automobile Manufacturers Association, Detroit MI.

Motor Vehicle Facts and Figures. Annual

World Motor Vehicle Data. Annual.

American Bureau of Metal Statistics, Inc., Secaucus, NJ

Non-Ferrous Metal Data.

American Bureau of Shipping, Paramus, NJ

The Record. Annual with one supplement.

American Council on Education, Washington, DC

A Fact Book on Higher Education. Quarterly.

National Norms for Entering College Freshmen. Annual.

American Council of Life Insurance, Washington, DC

Life Insurance Fact Book. Biennial. (Odd years)

American Dental Association, Chicago, IL

Dental Statistics Handbook. Triennial.

Dental Students' Register. Annual.

Distribution of Dentists in the United States by Region and State. Triennial.

Survey of Dental Practice. Annual.

American Financial Services Association, Washington, DC

AFSA Annual Research Report and Second Mortgage Lending Report on Finance Companies. Annual.

AFSA Annual Research Report and Second Mortgage Lending Report Supplements. Annual.

American Forest & Paper Association, Washington, DC

Statistical Roundup.

Statistics of Paper, Paperboard, and Wood Pulp. Annual.

Wood Pulp and Fiber Statistics. Annual.

American Frozen Food Institute, Burlingame, CA

Frozen Food Pack Statistics. Annual.

American Gas Association, Arlington, VA

Gas Facts. Annual.

American Iron and Steel Institute, Washington, DC
Annual Statistical Report.

American Jewish Committee, New York, NY
American Jewish Year Book.

American Medical Association, Chicago, IL
Physician Characteristics and Distribution in the U.S. Annual.
Physician Marketplace Statistics. Annual.
Socioeconomic Characteristics of Medical Practice. 1995.
U.S. Medical Licensure Statistics, and License Requirements. Annual.

American Metal Market, New York, NY
Daily Newspapers.
Metal Statistics. Annual.

American Osteopathic Association, Chicago, IL
Yearbook and Directory of Osteopathic Physicians. Annual.

American Petroleum Institute, Washington, DC
American Petroleum Institute, Independent Petroleum Association of America, and Mid-Continent Oil and Gas Association
Petroleum Industry Environmental Report. Annual.
Quarterly Well Completion Report.
The Basic Petroleum Data Book. Annual.

American Public Transit Association, Washington, DC
Transit Fact Book. Annual.
Internet address: http://www.apta.com

Association of American Railroads, Washington, DC
Analysis of Class I Railroads. Annual.
Cars of Revenue Freight Loaded. Weekly with annual summary.
Freight Commodity Statistics, Class I Railroads in the United States. Annual.
Yearbook of Railroad Facts.

Association of Racing Commissioners International, Inc., Lexington, KY
Statistical Reports on Greyhound Racing in the United States. Annual.
Statistical Reports on Horse Racing in the United States. Annual.
Statistical Reports on Jai Alai in the United States. Annual.

Book Industry Study Group, Inc., New York, NY
Consumer Research Study on Book Purchasing. Annual.

Bowker (R.R.) Company, New Providence, NJ
American Library Directory. Annual.
Bowker Annual Library and Book Trade Almanac.
Library Journal. Semimonthly.
Publishers Weekly.
School Library Journal. Monthly.

Boy Scouts of America, Irving, TX
Annual Report.

Bridge Commodity Research Bureau, a Bridge Information Systems Inc., Chicago, IL.
Bridge News Summaries. Daily
Commodity Year Book Update Disk. (Three editions annually.)
CRB Commodity Index Report. Weekly.
CRB Commodity Year Book. Annual.
CRB Futures Perspective. Weekly.
CRB Infotech. CD
Electronic Futures Trend Analyzer. Daily.
Final Markets. End of day.
Futures Market Service. Weekly.
Futures Market Service Fundamental & Technical Commentary. Daily and weekly.
Price Service. Daily
The Blue Line. Daily

The Bureau of National Affairs, Inc., Washington, DC
Basic Patterns in Union Contracts. Annual.
BNA's Employment Outlook. Quarterly.
BNA's Job Absence and Turnover. Quarterly.
Briefing Sessions on Employee Relations Workbook. Annual.
Calendar of Negotiations. Annual.
Directory of U.S. Labor Organizations. Annual.
National Labor Relations Board Election Statistics. Annual.
NLRB Representation and Decertification Elections Statistics. Quarterly.
PPF Survey (Personnel Policies Forum.) Three times a year.

Carl H. Pforzheimer & Co., New York, NY
Comparative Oil Company Statistics, 1997-1998. Annual.

Chronicle of Higher Education, Inc., Washington, DC
Almanac. Annual.

College Entrance Examination Board, New York, NY
National Report on College-Bound Seniors. Annual.

The Conference Board, New York, NY
The Conference Board Economic Times. Monthly.

900   Appendix I

Congressional Quarterly Inc., Washington, DC

America Votes. A handbook of contemporary American election statistics, compiled and edited by Richard M. Scammon, Alice V. McGillivray and Rhodes Cook. Biennial.

Corporation for Public Broadcasting, Washington, DC

Average Revenue Profiles for Public Broadcasting Grantees. Annual.

Frequently asked Questions About Public Broadcasting Periodic.

Public Broadcasting Stations' Income from State Governments and State Colleges & Universities Ranked State-By-State. Annual.

Public Radio and Television Programming Content by Category. Biennial.

The Council of State Governments, Lexington, KY

The Book of the States. Biennial.

State Administrative Officials Classified by Function. Biennial.

State Elective Officials and the Legislatures. Biennial.

State Legislative Leadership, Committees, and Staff. Biennial.

Credit Union National Association, Inc., Madison, WI

The Credit Union Report. Annual.

Credit Union Services Profile. Annual.

Operating Ratios and Spreads. Semiannual.

Dataquest Inc., San Jose, CA

Consolidated Data Base.

Dealerscope Merchandising, Philadelphia, PA

Merchandising. Annual.

Decker Communications, Inc., New York, NY

Marketing Communications. (Advertising.) Monthly.

Dodge, F.W., National Information Services Division, McGraw-Hill Information Systems Co., New York, NY

Dodge Construction Potentials. Monthly.

Dow Jones & Co., New York, NY.

Wall Street Journal.

Daily except Saturdays, Sundays, and holidays.

The Dun & Bradstreet Corporation, Murray Hill, NJ.

The Business Failure Record. Annual.

The Business Starts Record. Annual.

Monthly Business Failure Report.

Monthly Business Starts Report.

Monthly New Business Incorporations Report.

Edison Electric Institute, Washington, DC

Statistical Yearbook of the Electric Utility Industry. Annual.

Editor & Publisher Co., New York, NY

Editor & Publisher. Weekly.

Free Paper Publisher. Monthly.

International Year Book. Annual.

Market Guide. Annual.

Electronic Industries Alliance, Arlington, VA

Electronic Market Data Book. Annual.

Electronic Market Trends. Monthly.

Electronics Foreign Trade. Monthly.

ENO Transportation Foundation, Leesburg, VA

Transportation in America. mid-year, annually with periodic supplements.

Euromonitor, London, England

Consumer Asia. Annual.

Consumer Canada 1996.

Consumer China. Annual.

Consumer Eastern Europe. Annual.

Consumer Europe. Annual.

Consumer International. Annual.

Consumer Latin America. Annual.

Consumer Mexico 1996.

Consumer USA 1996

European Marketing Data and Statistics. Annual.

International Marketing Data and Statistics. Annual.

World Economic Factbook. Annual.

Federal National Mortgage Association, Washington, DC

Annual Report.

Food and Agriculture Organization of the United Nations, Rome, Italy

Production Yearbook.

Trade Yearbook.

Yearbook of Fishery Statistics.

Yearbook of Forest Products.

Fortune (Time Warner), New York, NY

The Fortune Directory of the 500 Largest Industrial Corporations.

The Fortune Directory of the 500 Global Industrial Corporations.

The Foundation Center, New York, NY

The Foundation Grants Index, 1998. Edition 26. 1997.

Guide to U.S. Foundations, Their Trustees, Officers, and Donors, Vol. 1, 1997 Edition.

Gale Research Inc., Detroit, MI

Gale Directory of Publications and Broadcast Media. 1999.

General Aviation Manufacturers Association, Washington, DC
Shipment Report. Quarterly and Annual.
Statistical Databook. Annual.

Girl Scouts of the U.S.A., New York, NY
Annual Report.

Health Insurance Association of America, Washington, DC
Source Book of Health Insurance Data. Annual.

Independent Petroleum Association of America, Washington, DC
IPAA Weekly Oil Trends.
IPAA Wholesale Oil Prices. Monthly.
The Oil & Natural Gas Producing Industry in Your State. Annual.
U.S. Petroleum Statistics. Semiannual.

Institute for Criminal Justice Ethics, New York, NY
Criminal Justice Ethics. Semiannual.

Insurance Information Institute, New York, NY
Insurance Facts. Annual.
Internet address: http://www.iii.org

Inter-American Development Bank, Washington, DC
Annual Report.
Economic and Social Progress in Latin America. Annual Survey.

International City Management Association, Washington, DC
Baseline Data Reports. Bimonthly.
Compensation: An Annual Report on Local Government Executive Salaries and Fringe Benefits.
Municipal Year Book. Annual.
Special Data Issues. Periodical.

International Labour Office, Geneva, Switzerland
Yearbook of Labour Statistics.

International Monetary Fund, Washington, DC
Annual Report.
Balance of Payments Statistics. Monthly with annual yearbook.
Direction of Trade Statistics. Monthly with annual yearbook.
Government Finance Statistics Yearbook.
International Financial Statistics. Monthly with annual yearbook.

Investment Company Institute, Washington, DC
Mutual Fund Fact Book. Annual.

Jane's Information Group, Coulsdon, UK and Alexandria, VA
Jane's Air-Launched Weapons. (Binder-4 monthly update.)

Jane's Information Group, Coulsdon, UK and Alexandria, VA —Con.
Jane's All the World's Aircraft. Annual.
Jane's Armour and Artillery. Annual.
Jane's Avionics. Annual.
Jane's Fighting Ships. Annual.
Jane's Infantry Weapons. Annual.
Jane's Merchant Ships. Annual.
Jane's Military Communications. Annual.
Jane's Military Logistics. Annual.
Jane's Military Training Systems. Annual.
Jane's NATO Handbook. Annual.
Jane's Spaceflight Directory. Annual.

John Blair & Company, New York, NY
Statistical Trends in Broadcasting. Annual.

Joint Center for Political and Economic Studies, Washington, DC
Black Elected Officials: A National Roster. Annual.

Laventhol & Horwath, Philadelphia, PA
The Executive Conference Center: A Statistical and Financial Profile. Annual.
Gaming Industry Study. Annual.
Lifecare Industry. Annual. (Analysis of facilities by size and section of the country for selected financial data, resident census information, and medical costs.)
National Trends of Business in the Lodging Industry. Monthly. (Analysis of nationwide trends in sales, occupancy, and room rates of hotels, motor hotels, and economy lodging facilities.)
Separate reports on the segments of lodging industries. Annuals. (Reports covering economy, all-suite, and resort.)
U.S. Lodging Industry. Annual. (Report on hotel and motor hotel operations.)
Worldwide Lodging Industry. Annual. (Report on international hotel operations.)

Lebhar-Friedman, Inc., New York, NY
Accounting Today. Biweekly.
Apparel Merchandising. Monthly.

Lloyd's Register of Shipping, London, England
Casualty Return. (Annual statistical summary of all merchant ships totally lost or reported broken up during year.)
Merchant Shipbuilding Returns. (Quarterly Statistical summary of world shipbuilding.)
World Fleet Statistics. (An end-year analysis of world merchant fleet.)

Market Statistics, New York, NY
The Survey of Buying Power Data Service. Annual.

McGraw-Hill Informations Service Co., Washington, DC

Electrical world Directory of Electric Utilities. Annual.

Engineering and Mining Journal. Monthly.

Keystone Coal Industry Manual. Annual.

Metropolitan Life Insurance Company, New York, NY

Health and Safety Education.

Moody's Investors Service, New York, NY

Moody's Manuals. (Volumes on Industrials, OTC, Banks and Finance, International, Municipals and Governments, Transportation, and Public Utilities.) Annual with weekly supplements.

National Academy of Sciences, Washington, DC

Science, Engineering, and Humanities Doctorates in the United States. Biennial.

Summary Report. Doctorate Recipients from United States Universities. Annual.

National Air Carrier Association, Washington, DC

Annual Report.

National Association of Hosiery Manufacturers, Charlotte, NC

Hosiery Statistics. Annual.

National Association of Latino Elected and Appointed Officials, Washington, DC

National Roster of Hispanic Elected Officials. Annual.

NATIONAL ASSOCIATION OF REALTORS, Washington, DC

Real Estate Outlook: Market Trends & Insights. Monthly.

National Association of State Budget Officers, Washington, DC

"State Expenditure Report". Annual.

Fiscal Survey of the States. Semi-annual.

National Association of State Park Directors, Tuscon, AZ

Annual Information Exchange.

National Catholic Educational Association, Washington, DC

Catholic Schools in America. Annual.

United States Catholic Elementary and Secondary Schools. Staffing and Enrollment. Annual.

U.S. Catholic Elementary Schools and their Finances. Biennial.

U.S. Catholic Secondary Schools and their Finances. Biennial.

National Center for State Courts, Williamsburg, VA

State Court Caseload Statistics. Annual.

National Coal Association, Washington, DC

Steam-Electric Plant Factors. Annual.

Coal Data. Annual.

National Council of the Churches of Christ in the U.S.A., New York, NY

Yearbook of American and Canadian Churches. Annual.

National Council of Savings Institutions, Washington, DC

Fact Book of National Council of Savings Institutions. Annual.

National Education Association, Washington, DC

Estimates of School Statistics. Annual.

Rankings of the States. Annual.

Status of the American Public School Teacher, 1995-96. Quinquennial.

National Fire Protection Association, Quincy, MA

NFPA Journal. Bimonthly.

National Food Processors Association, Washington, DC

Canned Fruit and Vegetable Pack and Stock Situation Reports. Quarterly.

National Golf Foundation, Jupiter, FL

Americans' Attitudes on Golf (in their communities).

Commercial Golf Range Participation and Supply in the U.S.

Commercial Golf Ranges in the U.S.

Directory of Executive and Par-3 Golf Courses in U.S.

Directory of Golf: The People and Businesses in Golf. Annual.

Directory of U.S. Golf Courses.

Directory of U.S. Golf Practice Ranges and Learning Centers.

Directory of Golf Retailers: Off-Course Golf Retail Stores in U.S.

Golf Consumer Potential.

Golf Consumer Spending in the U.S.

Golf Facilities in Canada.

Golf Facilities in the U.S. - 1998.

Golf Facility Employee Compensation Study.

Golf Participation in Canada.

Golf Participation in U.S. - 1998.

Golf Travel Market Report for the U.S.

High-Interest Women Golfers—Target Marketing for Success.

Hot Spots for Golf Course Construction Activity in the USA.

NGF's*Infosearch: Accessing the World's Largest Golf Business Library.*

Operating and Financial Performance Profiles of Golf Facilities in the U.S.

Operational Profile of Canadian Golf Facilities.

Senior Golfer Profile.

National Golf Foundation, Jupiter, FL —Con.
Trends in the Golf Industry. Biennially
Women in Golf—1991-1996

National Governors' Association, Washington, DC
Directory of Governors of the American States, Commonwealths & Territories. Annual.
Governors' Staff Directory. Biannual.

National Governors' Association and National Association of State Budget Officers, Washington, DC
The Fiscal Survey of States. Biannual.

National Marine Manufacturers Association, Chicago, IL.
Boating. (A Statistical Report on America's Top Family Sport.) Annual.
State Boat Registration. Annual.

National Restaurant Association, Washington, DC
Limited-Service Restaurant Trends. Annual.
Restaurant Economic Trends. Monthly.
Restaurant Industry Employee Profile. 1998.
Restaurant Industry Forecast. Annual.
Restaurant Industry in Review. Annual.
Restaurant Industry Operations Report. Annual.
Restaurant Industry Pocket Factbook. Annual.
Restaurant Numbers: A Statistical Digest for the Restaurant Industry. 1998.
Restaurant Spending. Annual.
Restaurants USA. Monthly.
Survey of Benefits for Hourly Restaurant Employees. 1998.
Survey of Wage Rates for Hourly Restaurant Employees. Biennial.
Tableservice Restaurant Trends. Annual.
Internet address:
http://www.restaurant.org

National Sporting Goods Association, Mt. Prospect, IL
The Sporting Goods Market in 1999. Annual.
Sports Participation in 1998. Annual.

New York Stock Exchange, Inc., New York, NY
Fact Book. Annual.

Organization for Economic Cooperation and Development, Paris, France
Annual Oil Market Report.
Coal Information. Annual.
Energy Balances of OECD Countries. Annual.
Energy Prices and Taxes. Quarterly.
Energy Statistics. Annual.
Financial Market Trends. Triennial.

Organization for Economic Cooperation and Development, Paris, France —Con.
Food Consumption Statistics. Irregular.
Geographical Distribution of Financial Flows to Developing Countries.
Historical Statistics of Foreign Trade Series A. Annual.
Indicators of Industrial Activity. Quarterly.
Industrial Structure Statistics. Annual.
The Iron and Steel Industry. Annual.
Labour Force Statistics. Annual.
Latest Information on National Accounts of Developing Countries. Annual.
Main Economic Indicators. Monthly.
Main Science and Technology Indicators. Biennial.
Maritime Transport. Annual.
Meat Balances in OECD Countries. Annual.
Milk and Milk Products Balances in OECD Countries. Annual.
National Accounts of OECD Countries. Annual.

Vol. I: Main Aggregates.
Vol. II: Detailed Tables.

OECD Economic Outlook. Bi-annual. Historical Statistics. Annual.
OECD Economic Studies. Annual for member countries.
OECD Employment Outlook. Annual.
OECD Financial Statistics. Annual (three vols.) and monthly supplements.
OECD Health Data (Diskette)
OECD Health Systems: Facts and Trends.
OECD Microtables on Foreign Trade by Commodities covering Series B (individual reporting countries) and Series C (total reporting countries). Annual from 1977.
Oil and Gas Information. Annual.
The Pulp and Paper Industry. Annual.
Quarterly Labor Force Statistics.
Quarterly National Accounts.
Quarterly Oil Statistics and Energy Balances.
Revenue Statistics of OECD Member Countries. Annual.
Review of Fisheries in OECD Member Countries. Annual.
Statistical Trends in Transport (ECMT.)
Statistics of Area Production and Field of Crop Products in OECD Member Countries.

Statistics of Foreign Trade:

Monthly Statistics of Foreign Trade. (Series A.)
Foreign Trade by Commodities. (Series C.) Annual.

Tourism Policy and International Tourism in OECD Member Countries. Annual.
Uranium Resources Production and Demand. Biennial.
World Energy Statistics and Balances.

Pan American Health Organization, Washington, DC
Health Conditions in the Americas. Quadrennial.

Pannell Kerr Forster, Houston, TX
Clubs in Town and Country. Annual.
Trends in the Hotel Industry, International Edition. Annual.
Trends in the Hotel Industry, U.S.A. Edition. Annual.

PennWell Publishing Co.,Tulsa, OK
Offshore. Monthly.
Oil and Gas Journal. Weekly.

Population Association of America, Washington, DC
Demography. Quarterly.
Population Index. (Princeton University, Princeton, NJ, Woodrow Wilson School of Public and International Affairs for the Population Association of America, Inc.) Quarterly.

Puerto Rico Planning Board, San Juan, PR
Balance of Payments—Puerto Rico. Annual.
Economic Activity Index. Monthly.
Economic Indicators. Monthly.
Economic Projections. Annual.
Economic Report to the Governor. Annual.
External Trade Statistics-Puerto Rico. Annual.
Income and Product. Annual.
Input-Output—Puerto Rico. Every 5 years.
Statistical Appendix to the Economic Report to the Government. Annual.

Radio Advertising Bureau, New York, NY
Radio Facts. Annual.

Reed Elsevier, Inc., Newton, MA
Broadcasting & Cable Yearbook.

Regional Airline Association, Washington, DC
Annual Report.
Broadcasting Magazine. Weekly.

Research Associates of Washington, Arlington, VA
Inflation Measures for Schools, Colleges, and Libraries. Annual.
State Profiles: Financing Public Higher Education Rankings. Annual.
Wages and Cost of Living: 508 County Indexes. (1995, most recent.)

Securities Industry Association, New York, NY
Foreign Activity Report. Quarterly.
Securities Industry Trends. Periodic.
SIA Securities Industry Fact Book. Annual.

Shipbuilders Council of America, Arlington, VA
Annual Report.

Simmons Market Research Bureau, Chicago, IL
Study of Media Markets. Annual.

Soil Conservation Service
National Resources Inventory. Periodic.

Standard and Poor's Corporation, New York, NY
Analyst's Handbook. Annual with monthly cumulative supplements.
Corporation Records. Six basic volumes; News Supplements, daily; Dividend Record, daily, and cumulative monthly and annual.
Daily Stock Price Records. Quarterly.
Security Owner's Stock Guide. Monthly.
Statistical Service. (Security Price Index Record; business and financial basic statistics with monthly supplement.)

Tanker Advisory Center, Inc., New York, NY
Worldwide Tanker Casualty Returns. Annual.

United Nations Educational, Scientific and Cultural Organization, Paris, France
Statistical Yearbook.

United Nations Statistics Division, New York, NY
Compendium of Human Settlements Statistics. (Series N.)
Demographic Yearbook. (Series R.)
Energy Balances and Electricity Profiles. (Series W.)
Energy Statistics Yearbook. (Series J.)
Industrial Statistics Yearbook: (Series P.)
  Commodity Production Statistics.
International Trade Statistics Yearbook. (Series G.)
Monthly Bulletin of Statistics. (Series Q.)
National Accounts Statistics: (Series X, Annually.)
  Main Aggregates and Detailed Tables.
  Analysis of Main Aggregates.
Population and Vital Statistics Report. (Series A, Quarterly.)
Social Statistics and Indicators: (Series K, Occasional.)
  The World's Women: Trends and Statistics.
  Women's Indicators and Statistics Database (CD and diskette only.)
Statistical Yearbook. (Series; also available in CD-ROM, Series S/CD)
World Statistics Pocketbook. (Series V, Annually.)

U.S. Census Bureau, Statistical Abstract of the United States: 1999

United States Council for Energy Awareness, Washington, DC

U.S. Public Opinion on Nuclear Energy. (Polling reports updated periodically.)

United States League of Savings Institutions, Chicago, IL

Savings Institutions Sourcebook. Annual.

United States Telephone Association, Washington, DC

Statistics of the Local Exchange Carriers. Annual.

United Way of America, Alexandria, VA

Annual Directory.

University of Michigan, Center for Political Studies, Institute for Social Research, Ann Arbor, MI

National Election Studies Cumulative Datafile. Biennial.

Warren Publishing, Inc., Washington, DC

Cable Action Update. Weekly.

Cable and Station Coverage Atlas. Annual.

Television Action Update. Weekly.

Television and Cable Factbook. Annual.

TV Station & Cable Ownership Directory. Semi-annual.

William B. Dana Co., New York, NY

Commercial and Financial Chronicle. Semi-weekly.

World Almanac/Pharos Books, New York, NY

The World Almanac and Book of Facts. Annual.

World Health Organization, Geneva, Switzerland

Epidemiological and Vital Statistics Report. Monthly.

World Health Statistics. Quarterly and annual.

Guide to State Statistical Abstracts

This bibliography includes the most recent statistical abstracts for states published since 1987 plus those that will be issued in late 1999. For some states, a near equivalent has been listed in substitution for or in addition to a statistical abstract. All sources contain statistical tables on a variety of subjects for the state as a whole, its component parts, or both. The page counts given for publications are approximate. Internet sites also contain statistical data.

Alabama

University of Alabama, Center for Business and Economic Research, Box 870221, Tuscaloosa 35487-0221. 205-348-6191. Internet site <http://www.cba.ua.edu/cber/>

Economic Abstract of Alabama. 1997. 488 pp.

Alaska

Department of Commerce and Economic Development, Division of Trade & Development, P.O. Box 110804, Juneau 99811-0804. 907-465-2017. Internet site <http://www.commerce.state.ak.us/trade/>

The Alaska Economy Performance Report. 1996

Arizona

University of Arizona, Economic and Business Research, College of Business and Public Administration, McClelland Hall 401 Tucson Arizona 85721-0001. 520-621-2155. Fax 520-621-2150. Internet site <http://www.bpa.arizona.edu/newpage>

Arizona Statistical Abstract: A 1997 Data Handbook. 616 pp.

Arizona Economic Indicators. 52 pp. Biennial.

Arizona's Economy. 16 pp. (Quarterly newsletter and data.)

Arkansas

University of Arkansas at Little Rock, Institute for Economic Advancement, Economic Research, 2801 South University, Little Rock 72204. 501-569-8551.

Arkansas State and County Economic Data. 1998 16 pp. (Revised annually.)

University of Arkansas at Little Rock, Institute for Economic Advancement, Census State Data Center, Little Rock 72204. 501-569-8530.

Arkansas Statistical Abstract, 1998. 700 pp. (Revised biennially.)

California

Department of Finance, 915 L Street, 8th Floor, Sacramento 95814, 916-322-4651. Internet site <http://www.dof.ca.gov/>

California Statistical Abstract, 1998.

Colorado

University of Colorado, Business Research Division, Campus Box 420, Boulder 80309-0420. 303-492-8227. Internet site <http://www.colorado.edu/libraries/govpubs/online/htm>

Statistical Abstract of Colorado, 1987. 600 pp. (Latest and last edition).

Connecticut

Connecticut Department of Economic & Community Development, 505 Hudson St., Hartford 06106. 1-860-270-8165. Internet site <http://www.state.ct.us/ecd/>

Connecticut Market Data. Fall/winter 1999. (Diskette also available.)

Connecticut Town Profiles, 1998-99. 340 pp.

Delaware

Delaware Economic Development Office, 99 Kings Highway, Dover 19901. 302-739-4271. Internet site <http://www.state.de.us/govern/agencies/dedo/index.htm>

Delaware Statistical Overview, 1998.

District of Columbia

Office of Planning, Data Management Division, 801 North Capitol St., N.E. Washington 20002. 202-442-7603.

1990 Census, Population and Housing for the District of Columbia 72 pp.

1990 Census: Social, Economic and Housing. (44 pp. for each of nine volumes).

Socio-Economic Indicators by Census Tract. 221 pp.

Socio-Economic Indicators of Change by Census Tract, 1980-1990. 146 pp.

Office of Policy and Evaluation, Executive Office of the Mayor, 1 Judiciary Square, Suite 920, 441 4th St., N.W., Washington 20001. 202-727-6979.

Indices—A Statistical Index to DC Services, Dec. 1994-96. 331 pp.

U.S. Census Bureau, Statistical Abstract of the United States: 1999

Florida

University of Florida, Bureau of Economic and Business Research, 221 Matherly Hall, Gainesville 32611-7145.   352-392-0171. Internet site <http://www.cba.ufl.edu/bebr/>

Florida Statistical Abstract, 1998. 32nd ed. 800 pp. Also available on diskette.

Florida County Perspectives, 1998. One profile for each county. Annual.

Florida County Rankings, 1998.

Florida and the Nation, 1999.

Georgia

University of Georgia, Selig Center for Economic Growth, Terry College of Business, Athens 30602-6269.   706-542-4085. Internet site <http://www.selig.uga.edu/>

Georgia Statistical Abstract, 1998-99. 500 pp.

University of Georgia, College of Agricultural and Environmental Sciences, Athens 30602-4356.   706-542-8938. Fax 706-542-8934. Internet site <http://www.uga.edu/caes/>

The Georgia County Guide. 1998. 17th ed. Annual. 200 pp.

Hawaii

Hawaii State Department of Business, and Economic Development & Tourism, Research and Economic Analysis Division, Statistics Branch P.O. Box 2359, Honolulu 96804. Inquiries 808-586-2481; Copies 808-586-2423. Internet site <http://www.hawaii.gov/dbedt>

The State of Hawaii Data Book 1997: A Statistical Abstract. 30th ed. 679 pp.

Idaho

Department of Commerce, 700 West State St., Boise 83720-0093.   208-334-2470. Internet site <http://www.idoc.state.id.us>

County Profiles of Idaho, 1998.

Idaho Facts, 1998.

Idaho Facts Data Book, 1995.

Profile of Rural Idaho 1999.

University of Idaho, Center for Business Development and Research, Moscow 83844-3227.   208-885-6611. Internet site <http://www.daho.edu/cbdr/puec>

Idaho Statistical Abstract, 4th ed. 1996.

Illinois

University of Illinois, Bureau of Economic and Business Research, 428 Commerce West, 1206 South 6th Street, Champaign 61820.   217-333-2332. Internet site <http://www.¢ba.uiuc.edu/research>

Illinois Statistical Abstract. 1998. 855 pages

Indiana

Indiana University, Indiana Business Research Center, School of Business, 801 W. Michigan St. Indianapolis 46202-5151. 317-274-2979. Internet site <http://www.iupui.edu/it/ibrc/>

Indiana Factbook, 1998-99. 393 pages.

Iowa

Public Interest Institute, 600 N. Jackson Street, Mount Pleasant, IA 52641. 319-385-3462. Internet site <http://www.limitedgovernment.org>

1996 Statistical Profile of Iowa.

Kansas

University of Kansas, Institute for Public Policy and Business Research, 607 Blake Hall, Lawrence 66045-2960. 785-864-3701. Internet site <http://www.ukans.edu/cwis/units/IPPBR/>

Kansas Statistical Abstract, 1997. 32nd ed. 1998.

Kentucky

Kentucky Cabinet for Economic Development, Division of Research, 500 Mero Street, Capital Plaza Tower, Frankfort 40601.   502-564-4886. Internet site <http://www.edc.state.ky.us>

Kentucky Deskbook of Economic Statistics. 34th ed. 1998.

Louisiana

University of New Orleans, Division of Business and Economic Research, New Orleans 70148.   504-280-6240. Internet site <http://leap.nlu.edu/STAAB.HTM>

Statistical Abstract of Louisiana. 10th ed. 1997.

Maine

Maine Department of Economic and Community Development, State House Station 59, Augusta 04333.   207-287-2656. Internet site <http://www.econdeumaine.com>

Maine: A Statistical Summary. (Updated periodically.)

Maryland

RESI, 800 York Road Towson University, Towson 21252-0001.   410-830-7374. Internet site <http://www.resiusa.org>

Maryland Statistical Abstract. 1997. 356 pp.

Massachusetts

Massachusetts Institute for Social and Economic Research, Box 37515, University of Massachusetts at Amherst 01003-7515. 413-545-3460. Fax 413-545-3686. Internet site <http://www.umass.edu/miser/>

Population Estimates for Massachusetts Cities and Towns. 1995.

Projection of the Population, Mass., Cities and Towns, Years 1990-2010.

Journey to work in Mass., 1990.

Minnesota

Department of Trade and Economic Development, Business and Community Development Division, 121 East 7th Place 500 Metro Square Building, St. Paul 55101-2146. 651-297-1291.

Compare Minnesota: An Economic and Statistical Factbook, 1998-99.

*Economic Report to the Governor: State of Minnesota, 1998.*140 pp.

Office of State Demographer, Minnesota Planning, 300 Centennial Bldg., St. Paul 55155. 651-296-2557. Internet site <http://www.mnplan.state.mn.us/demography/>

Minnesota Population and Household Estimates, 1997. Available diskette in Lotus, dBase or ASCII formats.

Minnesota Population Projections, 2025.

Mississippi

Mississippi State University, College of Business and Industry, Division of Research, P.O. Box 5288 Mississippi State 39762. 601-325-3817. Internet site <http://www.msu.msstate.edu/>

Mississippi Statistical Abstract. 1998. 520 pp.

Missouri

University of Missouri, Business and Public Administration Research Center, Columbia 65211. 573-882-4805. Internet site <http://tiger.bpa.missouri.edu/bparc/>

Statistical Abstract for Missouri, 1997 Biennial. 256 pp.

Montana

Montana Department of Commerce, Census and Economic Information Center, 1424 9th Ave., Helena 59620. 406-444-2896. Internet site <http://commerce.state.mt.us/ceic/>

Statistical Reports from the Montana County Database. (Separate county and State reports; available by subject section as well as complete reports by county and state, updated periodically.)

Nebraska

Department of Economic Development, Division of Research, Box 94666, Lincoln 68509. 402-471-3111. Fax 402-471-3778. Internet site <http://www.ded.state.ne.us/>

Nebraska Statistical Handbook. 1998-1999. 300 pp. (Available only on internet).

Nevada

Department of Administration, Budget and Planning Division, 209 East Musser Street, Suite 200, Carson City 89710. 775-684-0222. Internet site <http://www.state.nv.us/budget/>

Nevada Statistical Abstract. 1996. Biennial. 225 pp.

New Hampshire

Office of State Planning, 2 1/2 Beacon St., Concord 03301-4497. 603-271-2155. Fax 603-271-1728. Internet site <http://www.state.nh.us/osp/nhresnet/>

Current Estimates and Trends in New Hampshire's Housing Supply. Update: 1997. 32 pp.

1997 Population Estimates for New Hampshire Cities and Towns

Statistical Profile of New Hampshire, 1970-1990. 12pp.

New Hampshire (State Seal) A Brief Look, Jul. 1997. 21 pp. (Contact source for other statistical series).

New Jersey

New Jersey State Data Center, NJ Department of Labor, P.O. Box 388, Trenton 08625-0388. 609-984-2595. Internet site <http://www.state.nj.us/labor/lra/njsdc.html>

New Jersey Source Book, 1993. 156 pp.

New Mexico

University of New Mexico, Bureau of Business and Economic Research, 1920 Lomas N.E. Albuquerque 87131-6021. 505-277-6626. Fax 505-277-2773. Internet site <http://www.unm.edu/bber/>

County Profiles. 1997. 72 pp.

Community Profiles for Selected New Mexico cities.

Population Projections for the State of New Mexico, 1997.

U.S. Census Bureau, Statistical Abstract of the United States: 1999

New York

Nelson A. Rockefeller Institute of Government, 411 State Street, Albany 12203-1003.   518-443-5522. Internet site <http://www.rockinst.org/>

New York State Statistical Yearbook, 1998. 23rd ed. 600 pp.

North Carolina

Office of Governor Office of State Planning, 116 West Jones Street, Raleigh 27603-8003.   919-733-4131. Fax 919-715-3562. Internet site <http://www.ospl.state. nc.us/#Demographer>

Statistical Abstract of North Carolina Counties, 1991. 6th edition. (No longer being published.)

North Dakota

University of North Dakota, Box 8369, Bureau of Business and Economic Research, Grand Forks 58202. 701-777-2637.

The Statistical Abstract of North Dakota. 1988. 700 pp.

North Dakota Department of Economic Development & Finance, 1833 E. Bismark Expressway, Bismark 58504-6708. 701-328-5300. Internet site <http://www.und.nodal.edu>

State of North Dakota Economic, Demographic, Public Services, and Fiscal Condition. May 1998. 155 pp.

Ohio

Department of Development, Office of Strategic Research, P.O. Box 1001, Columbus 43216-1001.   614-466-2115. Internet site <http://www.odod.ohio.gov/>

Research products and services. (Updated continuously.)

The Ohio State University, School of Public Policy and Management, 1775 College Road, Columbus 43210-1399. 614-292-8696. Internet site <http://ppm. ohio-state.edu/ppm/>

Benchmark Ohio, 1993. Biennial. 300 pp.

Oklahoma

University of Oklahoma, Center for Economic and Management Research, 307 West Brooks Street, Room 4, Norman 73019.   405-325-2931. Fax 405-325-7688. Internet site <http://origins. ou.edu/>

Statistical Abstract of Oklahoma, 1998. Annual. 409 pp.

Oregon

Secretary of State, Business Services Division, Publication Services Bldg., 255 Capital Street, NE, Suite 180, Salem 97310.   503-986-2234. Internet site <http://www.sos.state.or.us/>

Oregon Blue Book. 1999-2000. Biennial. 431 pp.

Pennsylvania

Pennsylvania State Data Center, Institute of State and Regional Affairs, Penn State Harrisburg, 777 West Harrisburg Pike, Middletown Pennsylvania 17057-4898. 717-948-6336. Internet site <http://www. psdc.hbg.tsu.edu>

Pennsylvania Statistical Abstract, 1998. 301 pp.

Rhode Island

Rhode Island Economic Development Corporation, 1 West Exchange Street, Providence 02903.   401-222-2601. Fax 401-222-2102. Internet site <http:// www.riedc.com/>

Rhode Island 1990 Census of Population and Housing Summary. May 1994.

The Rhode Island Economy. Mar 1999.

South Carolina

Budget and Control Board, Office of Research and Statistical Services, R. C. Dennis Building, Room 425, Columbia 29201.   803-734-3781. Internet site <http://www.orss. state.sc.us/specproj.html/>

South Carolina Statistical Abstract: 1998. 440 pp.

South Dakota

University of South Dakota, State Data Center, Business Research Bureau, Vermillion 57069-2390.   605-677-5287. Internet site <http://www.usd.edu/brbinfo/>

1998 South Dakota Community Abstracts. 404 pp.

Tennessee

University of Tennessee at Knoxville, Center for Business and Economic Research, College of Business Administration 100 Glocker, Knoxville 37996-4170. 423-974-5441. Internet site <http://cber. bus.utk.edu/>

Tennessee Statistical Abstract, 1996-97. 16th ed. 807 pp. Biennial.

Texas

Dallas Morning News, Communications Center, P.O. Box 655237, Dallas 75265-5237.   214-977-8261.

Texas Almanac, 1998-99. 672 pp.

Utah

University of Utah, Bureau of Economic and Business Research, David Eccles School of Business 1645 East Campus Center Drive, Salt Lake City 84112-9302.   801-581-6333. Internet site <http://www.business. utah.edu/BEBR/>

Statistical Abstract of Utah. 1996. (Centennial.)

Utah Foundation, 10 West 100 South, Suite 323, Salt Lake City 84101-1544. 801-364-1837.

Statistical Review of Government in Utah. 1998.

U.S. Census Bureau, Statistical Abstract of the United States: 1999

Vermont

Labor Market Information, Department of Employment and Training, 5 Green Mountain Drive, P.O. Box 488, Montpelier 05601-0488. 802-828-4202. Internet site <http://www.det.state.vt.us/>

Demographic and Economic Profiles. Annual. Regional county reports also available.

Virginia

University of Virginia, Weldon Cooper Center for Public Service, 918 Emmet Street, North Suite 300, Charlottesville 22903-4832. 804-982-5585. Internet site <http://www.virginia.edu/coopercenter/>

Virginia Statistical Abstract, 1996-97. Biennial. 950 pp.

Washington

Washington State Office of Financial Management, Forecasting Division P.O. Box 43113 Olympia 98504-3113. 360-902-0599. Fax 360-664-8941. Internet site <http://www.wa.gov/ofm/>

Washington State Data Book, 1997. 300 pp.

Population Trends for Washington State. Annual. 48 pages.

West Virginia

West Virginia University, College of Business and Economics, Bureau of Business and Economic Research, P.O. Box 6025, Morgantown 26506-6026. 304-293-7831. Internet site <http://www.be.wvu.edu/index.htm>

West Virginia —Con.

West Virginia Statistical Abstract, 1995-1996 Biennial. 480 pp.

County Data Profiles, 1998-99. Annual. 50 pp.

Census Data Profiles. Decennial. 30 pp.

West Virginia Economic Outlook. Annual. 50 pp.

West Virginia Research League, Inc., P.O. Box 11176, Charleston 25339. 304-766-9495.

Economic Indicators. 1995. 215 pp.

The 1998 Statistical Handbook. 94 pp.

Wisconsin

Wisconsin Legislative Reference Bureau, P.O. Box 2037, Madison 53701-2037. 608-266-7098. Internet site <http://www.legis.state.wi.us/lrb/bb/97bb.html/>

1997-1998 Wisconsin Blue Book. 950 pp. Biennial.

Wyoming

Department of Administration and Information, Division of Economic Analysis, 2001 Capitol Avenue, 327 E. Emerson Building, Cheyenne 82002-0060. 307-777-7504. Internet site <http://www.state.wy.us/ai/ai.html>

The Equality State Almanac 1998. 6th ed. 120 pp.

U.S. Census Bureau, Statistical Abstract of the United States: 1999

Guide to Foreign Statistical Abstracts

This bibliography presents recent statistical abstracts for Mexico, Russia, and member nations of the Organization for Economic Cooperation and Development. All sources contain statistical tables on a variety of subjects for the individual countries. Many of the following publications provide text in English as well as in the national language(s). For further information on these publications, contact the named statistical agency which is responsible for editing the publication.

Austria
Osterreichisches Statistisches Zentralamt, P.O. Box 9000, A-1033 Vienna

Statistisches Jahrbuch for die Republik Osterreich. Annual. 1997 554 pp. (In German.)

Australia
Australian Bureau of Statistics, Canberra

Yearbook Australia. Annual. 1998 809 pp. (In English.)

Belgium
Institut National de Statistique, 44 rue de Louvain, 1000 Brussels

Annuaire statistique de la Belgique. Annual. 1994 822 pp. (In French and Dutch.)

Canada
Statistics Canada, Ottawa, Ontario, KIA OT6

Canada Yearbook: A review of economic, social and political developments in Canada. 1997 515 pp. Irregular. (In English and French.)

Croatia
Republika Hrvatska, Republicki Zavod Za Statistiku

Statisticki Ijetopis 1995 644 pp. (In English and Serbo-Croatian.)

Czech Republic
Czech Statistical Office, Sokolovska 142, 186 04 Praha 8

Statisticka Rocenka Ceske Rpubliky 1997 711 pp. (In English and Czech.)

Denmark
Danmarks Statistik, Postboks 2550 Sejrogade 11, DK 2100, Copenhagen

Statistical Yearbook. 1997. Annual. 559 pp. (In Danish with English translations of table headings.)

Finland
Central Statistical Office of Finland, Box 504 SF-00101 Helsinki

Statistical Yearbook of Finland. Annual. 1997 663 pp. (In English, Finnish, and Swedish.)

France
Institut National de la Statistique et des Etudes Economiques, Paris 18, Bld. Adolphe Pinard, 75675 Paris (Cedex 14)

Annuaire Statistique de la France. Annual. 1998 981 pp. (In French.)

Greece
National Statistical Office, 14-16 Lycourgou St., 101-66 Athens

Concise Statistical Yearbook 1995 254 pp. (In English.)

Statistical Yearbook of Greece. Annual. 1996 532 pp. (plus 7 pages of diagrams). (In English and Greek.)

Iceland
Hagstofa Islands/Statistical Bureau, Hverfisgata 8-10, Reykjavik.

Statistical Abstract of Iceland. 1994. Irregular. 303 pp. (In English and Icelandic.)

Ireland
Central Statistics Office, Earlsfort Terrace, Dublin 2

Statistical Abstract. Annual. 1997 411 pp. (In English.)

Italy
ISTAT (Istituto Centrale di Statistica), Via Cesare Balbo 16, 00100 Rome

Annuario Statistico Italiano. Annual. 1997 791 pp. (In Italian.)

Japan
Statistics Bureau, Management & Coordination Agency, 19-1 Wakamatsucho, Shinjuku Tokyo 162

Japan Statistical Yearbook. Annual. 1998 918 pp. (In English and Japanese.)

Luxembourg
STATEC (Service Central de la Statistique et des Etudes), P.O. Box 304, L-2013, Luxembourg

Annuaire Statistique. Annual. 1997. (In French.)

Mexico
Instituto Nacional de Estadistica Geografia e Informatica, Avda. Insurgentes Sur No. 795-PH Col. Napoles, Del. Benito Juarez 03810 Mexico, D.F.

Anuario estadistico de los Estados Unidos Mexicanos. Annual. 1996 646 pp. Also on disc. (In Spanish.) *Agenda Estadistica* 1994 186 pp.

Netherlands
Centraal Bureau voor de Statistiek. 428 Prinses Beatrixlaan P.O. Box 959, 2270 AZ Voorburg

Statistisch Yearbook 1998. 585 pp. (In English.)

New Zealand

Department of Statistics, Wellington

New Zealand Official Yearbook. Annual. 1998 606 pp. (In English.)

Norway

Central Bureau of Statistics, Skippergate 15, P.B. 8131 Dep. N-Oslo 1

Statistical Yearbook. Annual. 1997 475 pp. (In English and Norwegian.)

Portugal

INE (Instituto Nacional de Estatistica), Avenida Antonio Jose de Almeida, P-1078 Lisbon Codex

Anuario Estatistico: de Portugal. 1995 339 pp. (In Portugese.)

Russia

State Committee of Statistics of Russia, Moscow

Russian Federation in the Year 1993. Statistical Yearbook. 1997 746 pp. (In Russian.)

Slovakia

Statistical Office of the Slovak Republic, Mileticova 3, 824 67 Bratislava

Statisticka Rocenka Slovensak 1997. 727 pp. (In English and Slovak)

Slovenia

Statistical Office of the Republic of Slovenia, Vozarski Pot 12, 61000 Ljubljana

Statisticni Letopis Republike Slovenije 1997. 657 pp. (In Slovenian.)

Spain

INE (Instituto Nacional de Estadistica), Paseo de la Castellana, 183, Madrid 16

Anuario Estadistico de Espana. Annual. 1996 848 pp. (In Spanish.)

Anuario Estadistico. 1988. (Edicion Manual.) 976 pp.

Sweden

Statistics Sweden, S-11581 Stockholm

Statistical Yearbook of Sweden. Annual. 1998 559 pp. (In English and Swedish.)

Switzerland

Bundesamt fur Statistik, Hallwylstrasse 15, CH-3003, Bern

Statistisches Jahrbuch der Schweiz. Annual. 1998 549 pp. (In French and German.)

Turkey

State Institute of Statistics, Prime Ministry, 114 Necatibey Caddesi, Bakanliklar, Yenisehir, Ankara

Statistical Yearbook of Turkey. 1996 690 pp. (In English and Turkish.)

Turkey in Statistics 1994 150 pp. (In English and Turkish.)

United Kingdom

Central Statistical Office, Great George Street, London SW1P 3AQ

Annual Abstract of Statistics. Annual. 1991 349 pp. (In English.)

West Germany

Statistische Bundesamt, Postfach 5528, 6200 Wiesbaden

Statistisches Jahrbuch fur die Bundesrepublic Deutschland. Annual. 1997 755 pp. (In German.)

Statistisches Jahrbuch fur das Ausland. 1997. 398 pp.

Appendix II
Metropolitan Areas: Concepts, Components, and Population

Statistics for metropolitan areas (MAs) shown in the Statistical Abstract represent areas defined by the U.S. Office of Management and Budget (OMB) according to published standards that are applied to Census Bureau data. The general concept of an MA is that of a core area containing a large population nucleus, together with adjacent communities having a high degree of economic and social integration with that core. Currently defined MAs are based on application of 1990 standards (which appeared in the Federal Register on March 30, 1990) to 1990 decennial census data and to subsequent Census Bureau population estimates and special census data. Current MA definitions were announced by OMB effective June 30, 1999. MAs include metropolitan statistical areas (MSAs), consolidated metropolitan statistical areas (CMSAs), and primary metropolitan statistical areas (PMSAs).

In this appendix, Table E presents geographic components and 1998 population estimates for each MSA, CMSA, and PMSA outside of New England. Table D presents definitions and data for New England county metropolitan areas (NECMAs), the county-based alternative metropolitan areas for the city- and town-based MSAs and CMSAs of the six New England states.

Standard definitions of metropolitan areas were first issued in 1949 by the then Bureau of the Budget (predecessor of OMB), under the designation "standard metropolitan area" (SMA). The term was changed to "standard metropolitan statistical area" (SMSA) in 1959 and to "metropolitan statistical area" (MSA) in 1983. The collective term "metropolitan area" (MA) became effective in 1990.

OMB has been responsible for the official metropolitan areas since they were first defined, except for the period 1977 to 1981, when they were the responsibility of the Office of Federal Statistical Policy and Standards, Department of Commerce. The standards for defining metropolitan areas were modified in 1958, 1971, 1975, 1980, and 1990.

Defining MSAs, CMSAs, and PMSA— The current standards provide that each newly qualifying MSA must include at least: one city with 50,000 or more inhabitants, or a Census Bureau-defined urbanized area (of at least 50,000 inhabitants) and a total metropolitan population of at least 100,000 (75,000 in New England). Under the standards, the county (or counties) that contains the largest city becomes the "central county" (counties), along with any adjacent counties that have at least 50 percent of their population in the urbanized area surrounding the largest city. Additional "outlying counties" are included in the MSA if they meet specified requirements of commuting to the central counties and other selected requirements of metropolitan character (such as population density and percent urban). In New England, the MSAs are defined in terms of cities and towns rather than counties. An area that meets these requirements for recognition as an MSA and also has a population of 1 million or more may be recognized as a CMSA if separate component areas can be identified within the entire area by meeting statistical criteria specified in the standards, and local opinion indicates there is support for the component areas. If recognized, the component areas are designated PMSAs, and the entire area becomes a CMSA. PMSAs, like the CMSAs that contain them, are composed of entire counties, except in New England where they are composed of cities and towns. If no PMSAs are recognized, the entire area is designated as an MSA. As of the June 30, 1999, OMB announcement, there were 258 MSAs, and 18 CMSAs comprising 73 PMSAs in the United States. In addition, there were three MSAs, one CMSA, and three PMSAs in Puerto Rico.

U.S. Census Bureau, Statistical Abstract of the United States: 1999

Central cities and MA titles—The largest city in each MSA/CMSA is designated a "central city." Additional cities qualify if specified requirements are met concerning population size and commuting patterns. The title of each MSA consists of the names of up to three of its central cities and the name of each state into which the MSA extends. However, a central city with less than 250,000 population and less than one-third the population of the area's largest city is not included in an MSA title unless local opinion supports its inclusion. Titles of PMSAs also typically are based on central city names but in certain cases consist of county names. Generally, titles of CMSAs are based on the titles of their component PMSAs.

Defining New England County Metropolitan Areas NECMAs—The OMB defines NECMAs as a county-based alternative to the city- and town-based New England MSAs and CMSAs. The NECMA for an MSA or CMSA includes: the county containing the first-named city in that MSA/CMSA title (this county may include the first-named cities of other MSAs/CMSAs as well), and each additional county having at least half its population in the MSAs/CMSAs whose first-named cities are in the previously identified county. NECMAs are not identified for individual PMSAs. There are 12 NECMAs, including 1 for the Boston-Worcester-Lawrence, MA-NH-ME-CT CMSA and 1 for the Connecticut portion of the New York-Northern New Jersey-Long Island, NY-NJ-CT-PA CMSA. Central cities of a NECMA are those cities in the NECMA that qualify as central cities of an MSA or a CMSA. NECMA titles derive from names of central cities.

Changes in MA definitions over time—Changes in the definitions of MAs since the 1950 census have consisted chiefly of the recognition of new areas as they reached the minimum required city or area population, and the addition of counties (or cities and towns in New England) to existing areas as new decennial census data showed them to qualify. In some instances, formerly separate MAs have been merged, components of an MA have been transferred from one MA to another, or components have been dropped from an MA. The large majority of changes have taken place on the basis of decennial census data. However, Census Bureau population estimates and special censuses serve as the basis for intercensal updates.

Because of these historical changes in geographic definitions, users must be cautious in comparing MA data from different dates. For some purposes, comparisons of data for MAs as defined at given dates may be appropriate; for other purposes, it may be preferable to maintain consistent MA definitions.

In Tables A, B, and C below, data are given for MAs as defined for specific dates, thereby indicating the extent of change in population and land area resulting from revisions in definitions.

U.S. Census Bureau, Statistical Abstract of the United States: 1999

Table A. Number, Population, and Land Area of MAs as Defined at Specified Dates From 1960 to 1998

[The differences in population shown here for each year within each column of the table result entirely from net expansion of metropolitan territory through changes in the MA definitions. The differences in population over time shown for each MA definition (on the successive lines of the table) result entirely from population changes within that territory, unaffected by changes in MA definitions. The changes in 1990 land area result entirely from net change in MA territory. All data include Alaska and Hawaii and exclude Puerto Rico. Subtraction of any line of the table from the line below will show the net effect of change in population and land area undergone by the MAs as the result of changes in definitions between the specified dates. Such changes may have occurred throughout the period, not on any single date, and may have included reductions in, as well as additions to, MA territory. Census population data through 1980 include corrections made since publication. The area data for the 1960, 1970, and 1980 census definitions of MAs differ from the data published in those censuses because of subsequent remeasurement of land areas and changes in inland water area occurring for the 1990 census]

MA definition as of—	Num-ber of MAs	Population					Land area, 1990 (sq. mi.)
		1960 (April 1)	1970 (April 1)	1980 (April 1)	1990 (April 1)	1996 (July 1)	
1960 census (Nov. 1960)	212	[1]112,885,139	130,982,661	140,793,427	155,088,626	163,749,752	308,742
1970 census (Feb. 28, 1971). . .	243	[2]119,593,498	[3]139,479,806	151,662,221	167,896,646	178,120,036	386,241
1980 census (June 30, 1981) [4] .	318	131,318,714	153,693,767	169,430,623	188,759,597	201,283,896	565,288
1985 (June 30)	[5]280	132,887,134	155,700,823	172,169,456	192,135,964	(NA)	569,816
1987 (June 30) [6]	[5]281	133,003,445	155,832,688	172,334,547	192,345,395	205,287,889	572,284
1988 (June 30) [7]	[5]282	133,088,400	155,937,275	172,454,948	192,476,951	(NA)	573,560
1989 (June 30) [7]	[5]283	133,233,777	156,084,580	172,601,873	192,618,846	(NA)	574,622
1990 census (June 30, 1990) [7] .	[5]284	133,275,412	156,137,337	172,679,870	192,725,741	205,693,810	580,136
1992 (Dec. 31) [7]	[5]268	136,171,803	159,324,950	176,664,738	197,466,567	210,995,329	669,927
1993 (June 30) [7] [8]	[5]268	136,336,055	159,508,927	176,894,619	197,724,892	211,287,210	673,057
1994 (June 30) [7]	[5]269	136,402,452	159,581,985	176,984,458	197,823,630	211,395,107	674,021
1995 (June 30) [7]	[5]271	136,497,691	159,687,106	177,145,020	198,018,535	211,621,489	699,960
1996 (June 30) [7]	[5]273	136,603,905	159,801,301	177,286,407	198,166,336	211,785,351	701,784
1998 (June 30) [7]	[5]274	136,648,568	159,859,564	177,362,423	198,245,023	211,873,874	704,383

NA Not available. [1] Corresponds to total MA population for 1960 published in 1960 census (112,885,178), corrected by subtracting population (39) erroneously included in Franklin County, Ohio (Columbus metropolitan area). [2] Corresponds to total 1960 population for 1970 MAs published in 1970 census (119,594,754), corrected by subtracting 1,256 population from Lawrence-Haverhill metropolitan area; this represented an addition to the 1960 population of Andover town made subsequent to the original census tabulations, and therefore not reflected in state or national totals. [3] Corresponds to total MA population for 1970 published in 1970 census (139,418,811), plus net corrections made subsequent to publication. [4] MAs as defined for the 1982 economic censuses. [5] MSAs and CMSAs. [6] MAs as defined for the 1987 economic censuses. [7] Data exclude the portion of Sullivan City in Crawford County, MO (1990 population 1,116) added to the St. Louis, MO-IL MSA by congressional action effective Dec. 22, 1987. [8] MAs as defined for the 1992 economic censuses.

Table B. Nonmetropolitan Population and Land Area as Defined at Specified Dates From 1960 to 1998

[See headnote for Table A. Nonmetropolitan population and land area are equivalent to that portion of the total national population and land area not included within MAs at the dates specified]

Metropolitan area definition as of—	Population					Land area, 1990 (sq. mi.)
	1960 (April 1)	1970 (April 1)	1980 (April 1)	1990 (April 1)	1996 (July 1)	
1960 census (Nov. 1960)	66,438,036	72,319,370	85,752,378	93,621,247	101,534,031	3,231,027
1970 census (Feb. 28, 1971)	59,729,677	63,822,225	74,883,584	80,813,227	87,163,747	3,153,527
1980 census (June 30, 1981)	48,004,461	49,608,264	57,115,182	59,950,276	63,999,887	2,974,481
1985 (June 30).	46,436,041	47,601,208	54,376,349	56,573,909	(NA)	2,969,952
1987 (June 30).	46,319,730	47,469,343	54,211,258	56,364,478	59,995,894	2,967,484
1988 (June 30).	46,234,775	47,364,756	54,090,857	56,232,922	(NA)	2,966,208
1989 (June 30).	46,089,398	47,217,451	53,943,932	56,091,027	(NA)	2,965,146
1990 census (June 30, 1990)	46,047,763	47,164,694	53,865,935	55,984,132	59,589,973	2,959,632
1992 (Dec. 31).	43,151,372	43,977,081	49,883,008	51,243,306	54,288,454	2,866,411
1993 (June 30)	42,987,120	43,793,104	49,649,464	50,984,981	53,996,573	2,863,281
1994 (June 30)	42,920,723	43,720,046	49,557,741	50,886,243	53,888,676	2,862,317
1995 (June 30)	42,825,484	43,614,925	49,397,179	50,691,338	53,662,294	2,836,378
1996 (June 30)	42,719,270	43,500,730	49,255,792	50,543,537	53,498,432	2,834,554
1998 (June 30)	42,674,607	43,442,467	49,179,776	50,464,850	53,409,909	2,831,956

NA Not available.

Source of Tables A and B: U.S. Census Bureau, 1960-70, *U.S. Census of Population*, Vol. 1; *1980 Census of Population*, Vol. 1, Chapters A and B and *Supplementary Report, Metropolitan Statistical Areas* (PC80-S1-18); *1990 Census of Population and Housing Data Paper Listing* (CPH-L-10 and CPH-L-118); *1990 Census of Population and Housing, Supplementary Reports, Metropolitan Areas as Defined by the Office of Management and Budget, June 30, 1993*, (1990 CPH-S-1-1); and *Population Paper Listing* (PPL-60 and PPL-83).

Table C. Percent of Total U.S. Population and Percent of Land Area Inside MAs as Defined at Specified Dates From 1960 to 1998

[See headnote for Table A]

Metropolitan area definition as of—	Percent of population					Percent of land area, 1990
	1960 (April 1)	1970 (April 1)	1980 (April 1)	1990 (April 1)	1996 (July 1)	
1960 census (Nov. 1960).........	63.0	64.4	62.1	62.4	61.7	8.7
1970 census (Feb. 28, 1971)....	66.7	68.6	66.9	67.5	67.1	10.9
1980 census (June 30, 1981)....	73.2	75.6	74.8	75.9	75.9	16.0
1985 (June 30)	74.1	76.6	76.0	77.3	(NA)	16.1
1987 (June 30)	74.2	76.7	76.1	77.3	77.4	16.2
1988 (June 30)	74.2	76.7	76.1	77.4	(NA)	16.2
1989 (June 30)	74.3	76.8	76.2	77.4	(NA)	16.2
1990 census (June 30, 1990)....	74.3	76.8	76.2	77.5	77.5	16.4
1992 (Dec. 31).............	75.9	78.4	78.0	79.4	79.5	18.9
1993 (June 30)	76.0	78.5	78.1	79.5	79.6	19.0
1994 (June 30)	76.1	78.5	78.1	79.5	79.7	19.1
1995 (June 30)	76.1	78.5	78.2	79.6	79.8	19.8
1996 (June 30)	76.2	78.6	78.3	79.7	79.8	19.8
1998 (June 30)	76.2	78.6	78.3	79.7	79.9	19.9

NA Not available.

Source: U.S. Census Bureau, 1960-70, *U.S. Census of Population*, Vol. 1; *1980 Census of Population*, Vol. 1, Chapters A and B and *Supplementary Report, Metropolitan Statistical Areas* (PC80-S1-18); *1990 Census of Population and Housing Data Paper Listing* (CPH-L-10 and CPH-L-118); *1990 Census of Population and Housing, Supplementary Reports, Metropolitan Areas as Defined by the Office of Management and Budget, June 30, 1993*, (1990 CPH-S-1-1); and *Population Paper Listing* (PPL-60 and PPL-83).

Table D. New England County Metropolitan Areas (NECMAs)

[In thousands. As of July 1]

NECMA	Population, 1998	NECMA	Population, 1998	NECMA	Population, 1998
Bangor, ME	142	Burlington, VT	193	New London-Norwich, CT ...	246
Penobscot County........	142	Chittenden County	143	New London County	246
Barnstable-Yarmouth, MA ...	208	Franklin County	44	Pittsfield, MA	133
Barnstable County........	208	Grand Isle County........	6	Berkshire County	133
Boston-Worcester-Lawrence-		Hartford, CT	1,110	Portland, ME	254
Lowell-Brockton, MA-NH ...	5,867	Hartford County	828	Cumberland County.......	254
Bristol County, MA	518	Middlesex County	150	Providence-Warwick-	
Essex County, MA........	699	Tolland County	132	Pawtucket, RI	906
Middlesex County, MA	1,424	Lewiston-Auburn, ME	101	Bristol County...........	49
Norfolk County, MA.......	643	Androscoggin County......	101	Kent County............	162
Plymouth County, MA	468	New Haven-Bridgeport-		Providence County	574
Suffolk County, MA	642	Stamford-Waterbury-		Washington County.......	121
Worcester County, MA.....	732	Danbury, CT............	1,632	Springfield, MA...........	589
Hillsborough County, NH ...	363	Fairfield County	838	Hampden County	440
Rockingham County, NH ...	271	New Haven County	794	Hampshire County	149
Strafford County, NH	109				

Source: U.S. Census Bureau, "County Population Estimates and Demographic Components of Population Change: July 1, 1990 to July 1, 1998"; published 12 March 1999; <http://www.census.gov/population/estimates/county/co-98-8/98C800.txt>.

U.S. Census Bureau, Statistical Abstract of the United States: 1999

Table E. Metropolitan Areas Outside of New England and Their Components as of June 30, 1999

[Population estimated as of July 1, 1998. All metropolitan areas are arranged alphabetically. PMSAs are included under their respective CMSAs, see CMSA entry. This table presents data for MAs outside New England only]

Area	Population, 1998 (1,000)
Abilene, TX MSA	122
Taylor County	122
Albany, GA MSA	118
Dougherty County	95
Lee County	23
Albany-Schenectady-Troy, NY MSA	872
Albany County	293
Montgomery County	51
Rensselaer County	153
Saratoga County	198
Schenectady County	146
Schoharie County	32
Albuquerque, NM MSA	679
Bernalillo County	526
Sandoval County	88
Valencia County	65
Alexandria, LA MSA	127
Rapides Parish	127
Allentown-Bethlehem-Easton, PA MSA	617
Carbon County	59
Lehigh County	299
Northampton County	259
Altoona, PA MSA	131
Blair County	131
Amarillo, TX MSA	209
Potter County	109
Randall County	100
Anchorage, AK MSA	255
Anchorage Borough	255
Anniston, AL MSA	117
Calhoun County	117
Appleton-Oshkosh-Neenah, WI MSA	344
Calumet County	38
Outagamie County	156
Winnebago County	150
Asheville, NC MSA	214
Buncombe County	195
Madison County	19
Athens, GA MSA	139
Clarke County	91
Madison County	24
Oconee County	24
Atlanta, GA MSA	3,746
Barrow County	40
Bartow County	72
Carroll County	83
Cherokee County	134
Clayton County	209
Cobb County	566
Coweta County	85
DeKalb County	594
Douglas County	90
Fayette County	89
Forsyth County	86
Fulton County	739
Gwinnett County	522
Henry County	105
Newton County	58
Paulding County	74
Pickens County	20
Rockdale County	68
Spalding County	58
Walton County	54
Auburn-Opelika, AL MSA	100
Lee County	100
Augusta-Aiken, GA-SC MSA	458
Columbia County, GA	91
McDuffie County, GA	22
Richmond County, GA	191
Aiken County, SC	134
Edgefield County, SC	20
Austin-San Marcos, TX MSA	1,106
Bastrop County	50
Caldwell County	32
Hays County	89
Travis County	711
Williamson County	224
Bakersfield, CA MSA	631
Kern County	631
Baton Rouge, LA MSA	575
Ascension Parish	72
East Baton Rouge Parish	395
Livingston Parish	88
West Baton Rouge Parish	21
Beaumont-Port Arthur, TX MSA	376
Hardin County	49
Jefferson County	242
Orange County	85
Bellingham, WA MSA	157
Whatcom County	157
Benton Harbor, MI MSA	160
Berrien County	160
Billings, MT MSA	126
Yellowstone County	126
Biloxi-Gulfport-Pascagoula, MS MSA	349
Hancock County	40
Harrison County	178
Jackson County	131
Binghamton, NY MSA	249
Broome County	197
Tioga County	52
Birmingham, AL MSA	909
Blount County	46
Jefferson County	660
St. Clair County	62
Shelby County	141
Bismarck, ND MSA	91
Burleigh County	67
Morton County	25
Bloomington, IN MSA	115
Monroe County	115
Bloomington-Normal, IL MSA	143
McLean County	143
Boise City, ID MSA	396
Ada County	276
Canyon County	120
Brownsville-Harlingen, TX MSA	326
Cameron County	326
Bryan-College Station, TX MSA	133
Brazos County	133
Buffalo-Niagara Falls, NY MSA	1,153
Erie County	934
Niagara County	218
Canton-Massillon, OH MSA	402
Carroll County	29
Stark County	373
Casper, WY MSA	63
Natrona County	63
Cedar Rapids, IA MSA	183
Linn County	183
Champaign-Urbana, IL MSA	168
Champaign County	168
Charleston-North Charleston, SC MSA	541
Berkeley County	137
Charleston County	316
Dorchester County	88
Charleston, WV MSA	253
Kanawha County	202
Putnam County	51
Charlotte-Gastonia-Rock Hill, NC-SC MSA	1,383
Cabarrus County, NC	120
Gaston County, NC	184
Lincoln County, NC	58
Mecklenburg County, NC	631
Rowan County, NC	126
Union County, NC	110
York County, SC	154
Charlottesville, VA MSA	149
Albemarle County	78
Fluvanna County	19
Greene County	14
Charlottesville city	38
Chattanooga, TN-GA MSA	450
Hamilton County, TN	295
Marion County, TN	27
Catoosa County, GA	51
Dade County, GA	15
Walker County, GA	63
Cheyenne, WY MSA	79
Laramie County	79
Chicago-Gary-Kenosha, IL-IN-WI CMSA	8,810
Chicago, IL PMSA	7,939
Cook County, IL	5,190
DeKalb County, IL	84
DuPage County, IL	880
Grundy County, IL	37
Kane County, IL	391
Kendall County, IL	52
Lake County, IL	605
McHenry County, IL	241
Will County, IL	459
Gary, IN PMSA	624
Lake County, IN	478
Porter County, IN	146
Kankakee, IL PMSA	102
Kankakee County, IL	102
Kenosha, WI PMSA	144
Kenosha County, WI	144

U.S. Census Bureau, Statistical Abstract of the United States: 1999

	Popu-lation, 1998 (1,000)		Popu-lation, 1998 (1,000)		Popu-lation, 1998 (1,000)
Chico-Paradise, CA MSA	**195**	Hunt County	71	**Eau Claire, WI MSA**	**144**
Butte County	195	Kaufman County	66	Chippewa County	55
		Rockwall County	37	Eau Claire County	89
Cincinnati-Hamilton, OH-KY-IN CMSA	**1,948**	**Fort Worth-Arlington, TX PMSA**	**1,593**	**El Paso, TX MSA**	**703**
Cincinnati, OH-KY-IN PMSA	**1,618**	Hood County	37	El Paso County	703
Brown County, OH	41	Johnson County	118	**Elkhart-Goshen, IN MSA**	**172**
Clermont County, OH	176	Parker County	82	Elkhart County	172
Hamilton County, OH	847	Tarrant County	1,355		
Warren County, OH	146			**Elmira, NY MSA**	**92**
Boone County, KY	80	**Danville, VA MSA**	**108**	Chemung County	92
Campbell County, KY	87	Pittsylvania County	57		
Gallatin County, KY	7	Danville city	51	**Enid, OK MSA**	**57**
Grant County, KY	20			Garfield County	57
Kenton County, KY	147	**Davenport-Moline-Rock Island, IA-IL MSA**	**358**		
Pendleton County, KY	14	Scott County, IA	159	**Erie, PA MSA**	**276**
Dearborn County, IN	47	Henry County, IL	52	Erie County	276
Ohio County, IN	5	Rock Island County, IL	148		
Hamilton-Middletown, OH PMSA	**330**			**Eugene-Springfield, OR MSA**	**314**
Butler County, OH	330	**Dayton-Springfield, OH MSA**	**949**	Lane County	314
		Clark County	145		
Clarksville-Hopkinsville, TN-KY MSA	**200**	Greene County	147	**Evansville-Henderson, IN-KY MSA**	**291**
Montgomery County, TN	127	Miami County	98	Posey County, IN	27
Christian County, KY	72	Montgomery County	558	Vanderburgh County, IN	168
				Warrick County, IN	52
Cleveland-Akron, OH CMSA	**2,912**	**Daytona Beach, FL MSA**	**471**	Henderson County, KY	44
Akron, OH PMSA	**689**	Flagler County	47		
Portage County	151	Volusia County	423	**Fargo-Moorhead, ND-MN MSA**	**168**
Summit County	538			Cass County, ND	117
Cleveland-Lorain-Elyria, OH PMSA	**2,223**	**Decatur, AL MSA**	**143**	Clay County, MN	52
Ashtabula County	103	Lawrence County	33		
Cuyahoga County	1,381	Morgan County	109	**Fayetteville, NC MSA**	**285**
Geauga County	89			Cumberland County	285
Lake County	224	**Decatur, IL MSA**	**114**		
Lorain County	282	Macon County	114	**Fayetteville-Springdale-Rogers, AR MSA**	**273**
Medina County	144			Benton County	134
		Denver-Boulder-Greeley, CO CMSA	**2,365**	Washington County	138
Colorado Springs, CO MSA	**490**	**Boulder-Longmont, CO PMSA**	**267**		
El Paso County	490	Boulder County	267	**Flagstaff, AZ-UT MSA**	**120**
		Denver, CO PMSA	**1,939**	Coconino County, AZ	114
Columbia, MO MSA	**129**	Adams County	324	Kane County, UT	6
Boone County	129	Arapahoe County	473		
		Denver County	499	**Florence, AL MSA**	**137**
Columbia, SC MSA	**512**	Douglas County	141	Colbert County	53
Lexington County	205	Jefferson County	502	Lauderdale County	84
Richland County	307	**Greeley, CO PMSA**	**159**		
		Weld County	159	**Florence, SC MSA**	**125**
Columbus, GA-AL MSA	**272**			Florence County	125
Chattahoochee County, GA	17	**Des Moines, IA MSA**	**437**		
Harris County, GA	22	Dallas County	37	**Fort Collins-Loveland, CO MSA**	**231**
Muscogee County, GA	183	Polk County	360	Larimer County	231
Russell County, AL	50	Warren County	40		
				Fort Myers-Cape Coral, FL MSA	**393**
Columbus, OH MSA	**1,470**	**Detroit-Ann Arbor-Flint, MI CMSA**	**5,458**	Lee County	393
Delaware County	92	**Ann Arbor, MI PMSA**	**548**		
Fairfield County	124	Lenawee County	98	**Fort Pierce-Port St. Lucie, FL MSA**	**295**
Franklin County	1,021	Livingston County	146	Martin County	116
Licking County	137	Washtenaw County	303	St. Lucie County	179
Madison County	42	**Detroit, MI PMSA**	**4,474**		
Pickaway County	54	Lapeer County	88	**Fort Smith, AR-OK MSA**	**194**
		Macomb County	788	Crawford County, AR	50
Corpus Christi, TX MSA	**388**	Monroe County	143	Sebastian County, AR	106
Nueces County	316	Oakland County	1,176	Sequoyah County, OK	38
San Patricio County	71	St. Clair County	160		
		Wayne County	2,118	**Fort Walton Beach, FL MSA**	**169**
Corvallis, OR MSA	**78**	**Flint, MI PMSA**	**436**	Okaloosa County	169
Benton County	78	Genesee County	436		
				Fort Wayne, IN MSA	**481**
Cumberland, MD-WV MSA	**98**	**Dothan, AL MSA**	**135**	Adams County	33
Allegany County, MD	71	Dale County	49	Allen County	314
Mineral County, WV	27	Houston County	86	De Kalb County	39
				Huntington County	37
Dallas-Fort Worth, TX CMSA	**4,802**	**Dover, DE MSA**	**124**	Wells County	27
Dallas, TX PMSA	**3,210**	Kent County	124	Whitley County	30
Collin County	429				
Dallas County	2,051	**Dubuque, IA MSA**	**88**	**Fresno, CA MSA**	**870**
Denton County	384	Dubuque County	88	Fresno County	756
Ellis County	104			Madera County	115
Henderson County	69	**Duluth, MN-WI MSA**	**236**		
		St. Louis County, MN	193		
		Douglas County, WI	43		

Appendix II 919

	Popu-lation, 1998 (1,000)		Popu-lation, 1998 (1,000)		Popu-lation, 1998 (1,000)
Gadsden, AL MSA	104	Galveston-Texas City, TX		Kalamazoo-Battle Creek,	
Etowah County	104	PMSA	246	MI MSA	446
		Galveston County	246	Calhoun County	141
Gainesville, FL MSA	199	Houston, TX PMSA	3,932	Kalamazoo County	230
Alachua County	199	Chambers County	24	Van Buren County	76
		Fort Bend County	338		
Glens Falls, NY MSA	122	Harris County	3,206	Kansas City, MO-KS MSA	1,737
Warren County	61	Liberty County	65	Cass County, MO	81
Washington County	60	Montgomery County	272	Clay County, MO	176
		Waller County	27	Clinton County, MO	19
Goldsboro, NC MSA	112			Jackson County, MO	655
Wayne County	112	Huntington-Ashland,		Lafayette County, MO	33
		WV-KY-OH MSA	314	Platte County, MO	70
Grand Forks, ND-MN MSA	98	Cabell County, WV	94	Ray County, MO	24
Grand Forks County, ND	67	Wayne County, WV	42	Johnson County, KS	430
Polk County, MN	31	Boyd County, KY	50	Leavenworth County, KS	71
		Carter County, KY	27	Miami County, KS	27
Grand Junction, CO MSA	113	Greenup County, KY	37	Wyandotte County, KS	152
Mesa County	113	Lawrence County, OH	64		
				Killeen-Temple, TX MSA	301
Grand Rapids-Muskegon-Holland, MI MSA	1,038	Huntsville, AL MSA	340	Bell County	223
Allegan County	102	Limestone County	62	Coryell County	78
Kent County	545	Madison County	278		
Muskegon County	167			Knoxville, TN MSA	659
Ottawa County	224	Indianapolis, IN MSA	1,519	Anderson County	71
		Boone County	44	Blount County	101
Great Falls, MT MSA	79	Hamilton County	163	Knox County	367
Cascade County	79	Hancock County	55	Loudon County	39
		Hendricks County	95	Sevier County	65
Green Bay, WI MSA	215	Johnson County	109	Union County	16
Brown County	215	Madison County	131		
		Marion County	813	Kokomo, IN MSA	100
Greensboro-Winston-Salem-High Point, NC		Morgan County	66	Howard County	83
		Shelby County	43	Tipton County	17
MSA	1,168				
Alamance County	119	Iowa City, IA MSA	103	La Crosse, WI-MN MSA	122
Davidson County	141	Johnson County	103	La Crosse County, WI	103
Davie County	32			Houston County, MN	19
Forsyth County	288	Jackson, MI MSA	156		
Guilford County	388	Jackson County	156	Lafayette, LA MSA	376
Randolph County	121			Acadia Parish	58
Stokes County	43	Jackson, MS MSA	430	Lafayette Parish	187
Yadkin County	35	Hinds County	247	St. Landry Parish	84
		Madison County	73	St. Martin Parish	48
Greenville, NC MSA	127	Rankin County	110		
Pitt County	127			Lafayette, IN MSA	172
		Jackson, TN MSA	101	Clinton County	33
Greenville-Spartanburg-Anderson, SC MSA	918	Chester County	15	Tippecanoe County	139
Anderson County	161	Madison County	86		
Cherokee County	49			Lake Charles, LA MSA	180
Greenville County	354	Jacksonville, FL MSA	1,045	Calcasieu Parish	180
Pickens County	107	Clay County	137		
Spartanburg County	247	Duval County	736	Lakeland-Winter Haven, FL	
		Nassau County	55	MSA	453
Harrisburg-Lebanon-Carlisle, PA MSA	616	St. Johns County	116	Polk County	453
Cumberland County	209				
Dauphin County	246	Jacksonville, NC MSA	142	Lancaster, PA MSA	456
Lebanon County	117	Onslow County	142	Lancaster County	456
Perry County	44				
		Jamestown, NY MSA	138	Lansing-East Lansing, MI	
Hattiesburg, MS MSA	111	Chautauqua County	138	MSA	450
Forrest County	74			Clinton County	63
Lamar County	37	Janesville-Beloit, WI MSA	151	Eaton County	101
		Rock County	151	Ingham County	285
Hickory-Morganton, NC					
MSA	323	Johnson City-Kingsport-Bristol, TN-VA MSA	462	Laredo, TX MSA	188
Alexander County	31	Carter County, TN	53	Webb County	188
Burke County	83	Hawkins County, TN	50		
Caldwell County	76	Sullivan County, TN	151	Las Cruces, NM MSA	169
Catawba County	133	Unicoi County, TN	17	Dona Ana County	169
		Washington County, TN	102		
Honolulu, HI MSA	872	Scott County, VA	23	Las Vegas, NV-AZ MSA	1,322
Honolulu County	872	Washington County, VA	49	Clark County, NV	1,162
		Bristol city, VA	17	Nye County, NV	29
Houma, LA MSA	194			Mohave County, AZ	131
Lafourche Parish	89	Johnstown, PA MSA	236		
Terrebonne Parish	105	Cambria County	156	Lawrence, KS MSA	93
		Somerset County	80	Douglas County	93
Houston-Galveston-Brazoria, TX CMSA	4,408				
		Jonesboro, AR MSA	78	Lawton, OK MSA	114
Brazoria, TX PMSA	230	Craighead County	78	Comanche County	114
Brazoria County	230				
		Joplin, MO MSA	149	Lexington, KY MSA	450
		Jasper County	100	Bourbon County	19
		Newton County	49	Clark County	32
				Fayette County	242

920   Appendix II

U.S. Census Bureau, Statistical Abstract of the United States: 1999

	Population, 1998 (1,000)
Jessamine County	37
Madison County	67
Scott County	31
Woodford County	23
Lima, OH MSA	**154**
Allen County	107
Auglaize County	47
Lincoln, NE MSA	**236**
Lancaster County	236
Little Rock-North Little Rock, AR MSA	**556**
Faulkner County	78
Lonoke County	50
Pulaski County	350
Saline County	77
Longview-Marshall, TX MSA	**209**
Gregg County	113
Harrison County	60
Upshur County	36
Los Angeles-Riverside-Orange County, CA CMSA	**15,781**
Los Angeles-Long Beach, CA PMSA	**9,214**
Los Angeles County	9,214
Orange County, CA PMSA	**2,722**
Orange County	2,722
Riverside-San Bernardino, CA PMSA	**3,114**
Riverside County	1,479
San Bernardino County	1,635
Ventura, CA PMSA	**732**
Ventura County	732
Louisville, KY-IN MSA	**999**
Bullitt County, KY	59
Jefferson County, KY	672
Oldham County, KY	44
Clark County, IN	94
Floyd County, IN	72
Harrison County, IN	35
Scott County, IN	23
Lubbock, TX MSA	**229**
Lubbock County	229
Lynchburg, VA MSA	**208**
Amherst County	30
Bedford County	56
Campbell County	50
Bedford city	6
Lynchburg city	65
Macon, GA MSA	**320**
Bibb County	156
Houston County	106
Jones County	23
Peach County	24
Twiggs County	10
Madison, WI MSA	**425**
Dane County	425
Mansfield, OH MSA	**175**
Crawford County	47
Richland County	127
McAllen-Edinburg-Mission, TX MSA	**522**
Hidalgo County	522
Medford-Ashland, OR MSA	**173**
Jackson County	173
Melbourne-Titusville-Palm Bay, FL MSA	**466**
Brevard County	466
Memphis, TN-AR-MS MSA	**1,093**
Fayette County, TN	30
Shelby County, TN	869

	Population, 1998 (1,000)
Tipton County, TN	47
Crittenden County, AR	50
DeSoto County, MS	97
Merced, CA MSA	**198**
Merced County	198
Miami-Fort Lauderdale, FL CMSA	**3,656**
Fort Lauderdale, FL PMSA	**1,503**
Broward County	1,503
Miami, FL PMSA	**2,152**
Miami-Dade County	2,152
Milwaukee-Racine, WI CMSA	**1,646**
Milwaukee-Waukesha, WI PMSA	**1,460**
Milwaukee County	912
Ozaukee County	81
Washington County	114
Waukesha County	353
Racine, WI PMSA	**186**
Racine County	186
Minneapolis-St. Paul, MN-WI MSA	**2,831**
Anoka County, MN	292
Carver County, MN	65
Chisago County, MN	41
Dakota County, MN	343
Hennepin County, MN	1,060
Isanti County, MN	30
Ramsey County, MN	486
Scott County, MN	79
Sherburne County, MN	60
Washington County, MN	196
Wright County, MN	85
Pierce County, WI	36
St. Croix County, WI	59
Missoula, MT MSA	**89**
Missoula County	89
Mobile, AL MSA	**532**
Baldwin County	133
Mobile County	399
Modesto, CA MSA	**426**
Stanislaus County	426
Monroe, LA MSA	**147**
Ouachita Parish	147
Montgomery, AL MSA	**322**
Autauga County	42
Elmore County	62
Montgomery County	218
Muncie, IN MSA	**117**
Delaware County	117
Myrtle Beach, SC MSA	**175**
Horry County	175
Naples, FL MSA	**199**
Collier County	199
Nashville, TN MSA	**1,156**
Cheatham County	35
Davidson County	534
Dickson County	42
Robertson County	53
Rutherford County	166
Sumner County	124
Williamson County	118
Wilson County	84
New Orleans, LA MSA	**1,309**
Jefferson Parish	451
Orleans Parish	466
Plaquemines Parish	26
St. Bernard Parish	66
St. Charles Parish	48
St. James Parish	21

	Population, 1998 (1,000)
St. John the Baptist Parish	42
St. Tammany Parish	189
New York-Northern New Jersey-Long Island, NY-NJ-CT-PA CMSA (pt.) [1]	**18,401**
Bergen-Passaic, NJ PMSA	**1,344**
Bergen County, NJ	859
Passaic County, NJ	486
Dutchess County, NY PMSA	**265**
Dutchess County, NY	265
Jersey City, NJ PMSA	**557**
Hudson County, NJ	557
Middlesex-Somerset-Hunterdon, NJ PMSA	**1,122**
Hunterdon County, NJ	122
Middlesex County, NJ	716
Somerset County, NJ	283
Monmouth-Ocean, NJ PMSA	**1,093**
Monmouth County, NJ	603
Ocean County, NJ	490
Nassau-Suffolk, NY PMSA	**2,673**
Nassau County, NY	1,302
Suffolk County, NY	1,371
New York, NY PMSA	**8,693**
Bronx County, NY	1,196
Kings County, NY	2,268
New York County, NY	1,551
Putnam County, NY	93
Queens County, NY	1,999
Richmond County, NY	407
Rockland County, NY	281
Westchester County, NY	898
Newark, NJ PMSA	**1,952**
Essex County, NJ	750
Morris County, NJ	460
Sussex County, NJ	143
Union County, NJ	501
Warren County, NJ	99
Newburgh, NY-PA PMSA	**369**
Orange County, NY	329
Pike County, PA	40
Trenton, NJ PMSA	**332**
Mercer County, NJ	332
Norfolk-Virginia Beach-Newport News, VA-NC MSA	**1,542**
Gloucester County, VA	35
Isle of Wight County, VA	29
James City County, VA	44
Mathews County, VA	9
York County, VA	59
Chesapeake city, VA	200
Hampton city, VA	137
Newport News city, VA	179
Norfolk city, VA	215
Poquoson city, VA	11
Portsmouth city, VA	99
Suffolk city, VA	63
Virginia Beach city, VA	432
Williamsburg city, VA	12
Currituck County, NC	18
Ocala, FL MSA	**242**
Marion County	242
Odessa-Midland, TX MSA	**245**
Ector County	126
Midland County	120
Oklahoma City, OK MSA	**1,039**
Canadian County	85
Cleveland County	201
Logan County	31
McClain County	26
Oklahoma County	633
Pottawatomie County	62
Omaha, NE-IA MSA	**694**
Cass County, NE	24
Douglas County, NE	444
Sarpy County, NE	121

	Popu-lation, 1998 (1,000)		Popu-lation, 1998 (1,000)		Popu-lation, 1998 (1,000)
Washington County, NE...	19	**Provo-Orem, UT MSA**	336	**Saginaw-Bay City-Midland,**	
Pottawattamie County, IA..	86	Utah County...........	336	**MI MSA**...............	402
				Bay County	110
Orlando, FL MSA	1,505	**Pueblo, CO MSA**.........	135	Midland County.........	82
Lake County...........	202	Pueblo County	135	Saginaw County	210
Orange County	806				
Osceola County	146	**Punta Gorda, FL MSA**.....	135	**St. Cloud, MN MSA**	162
Seminole County	351	Charlotte County........	135	Benton County	34
				Stearns County.........	128
Owensboro, KY MSA.....	91	**Raleigh-Durham-Chapel**			
Daviess County	91	**Hill, NC MSA**............	1,080	**St. Joseph, MO MSA**......	97
		Chatham County........	45	Andrew County.........	16
Panama City, FL MSA	147	Durham County	202	Buchanan County	82
Bay County	147	Franklin County	45		
		Johnston County........	107	**St. Louis, MO-IL MSA**	2,564
Parkersburg-Marietta,		Orange County	110	Franklin County, MO	92
WV-OH MSA...........	150	Wake County	571	Jefferson County, MO ...	196
Wood County, WV.......	87			Lincoln County, MO.....	37
Washington County, OH...	63	**Rapid City, SD MSA**	88	St. Charles County, MO...	272
		Pennington County	88	St. Louis County, MO	999
Pensacola, FL MSA.......	400			Warren County, MO.....	25
Escambia County	282	**Reading, PA MSA**	356	St. Louis city, MO	339
Santa Rosa County.....	117	Berks County	356	Clinton County, IL	36
				Jersey County, IL	21
Peoria-Pekin, IL MSA	345	**Redding, CA MSA**	164	Madison County, IL......	259
Peoria County	182	Shasta County	164	Monroe County, IL......	27
Tazewell County	128			St. Clair County, IL	262
Woodford County	35	**Reno, NV MSA**	314		
		Washoe County	314	**Salinas, CA MSA**.........	366
Philadelphia-Wilmington-				Monterey County	366
Atlantic City, PA-NJ- DE-		**Richland-Kennewick-Pasco,**			
MD CMSA............	5,988	**WA MSA**..............	183	**Salt Lake City-Ogden, UT**	
Atlantic-Cape May, NJ		Benton County	136	**MSA**.................	1,268
PMSA	336	Franklin County	46	Davis County	233
Atlantic County, NJ	238			Salt Lake County	851
Cape May County, NJ	98	**Richmond-Petersburg, VA**		Weber County	184
Philadelphia, PA-NJ		**MSA**................	957		
PMSA...............	4,947	Charles City County	7	**San Angelo, TX MSA**......	103
Bucks County, PA	588	Chesterfield County.....	246	Tom Green County	103
Chester County, PA.....	422	Dinwiddie County	25		
Delaware County, PA....	543	Goochland County	18	**San Antonio, TX MSA**	1,538
Montgomery County, PA ..	720	Hanover County	82	Bexar County	1,353
Philadelphia County, PA..	1,436	Henrico County........	246	Comal County	73
Burlington County, NJ	420	New Kent County	13	Guadalupe County	80
Camden County, NJ	505	Powhatan County	22	Wilson County	31
Gloucester County, NJ....	248	Prince George County ...	30		
Salem County, NJ.......	65	Colonial Heights city ...	17	**San Diego, CA MSA**......	2,781
Vineland-Millville-		Hopewell city	23	San Diego County.......	2,781
Bridgeton, NJ PMSA	140	Petersburg city	35		
Cumberland County, NJ...	140	Richmond city.........	194	**San Francisco-Oakland-**	
Wilmington-Newark,				**San Jose, CA CMSA**	6,816
DE-MD PMSA	565	**Roanoke, VA MSA**........	228	**Oakland, CA PMSA**	2,319
New Castle County, DE ...	483	Botetourt County.......	29	Alameda County.......	1,400
Cecil County, MD	83	Roanoke County.......	81	Contra Costa County....	918
		Roanoke city	94	**San Francisco, CA PMSA** .	1,683
Phoenix-Mesa, AZ MSA....	2,931	Salem city	25	Marin County	237
Maricopa County........	2,784			San Francisco County....	746
Pinal County............	147	**Rochester, MN MSA**	117	San Mateo County	701
		Olmsted County	117	**San Jose, CA PMSA**	1,641
Pine Bluff, AR MSA.......	82			Santa Clara County......	1,641
Jefferson County........	82	**Rochester, NY MSA**.......	1,082	**Santa Cruz-Watsonville,**	
		Genesee County	61	**CA PMSA**	243
Pittsburgh, PA MSA	2,346	Livingston County	66	Santa Cruz County	243
Allegheny County	1,268	Monroe County........	716	**Santa Rosa, CA PMSA**....	433
Beaver County	184	Ontario County	100	Sonoma County	433
Butler County.........	171	Orleans County	45	**Vallejo-Fairfield-Napa,**	
Fayette County	145	Wayne County	95	**CA PMSA**	497
Washington County.....	206			Napa County	119
Westmoreland County....	372	**Rockford, IL MSA**	357	Solano County	377
		Boone County	39		
Pocatello, ID MSA........	75	Ogle County..........	51	**San Luis Obispo-**	
Bannock County	75	Winnebago County	268	**Atascadero-Paso Robles,**	
				CA MSA	234
Portland-Salem, OR-WA		**Rocky Mount, NC MSA**	146	San Luis Obispo County ..	234
CMSA................	2,149	Edgecombe County......	55		
Portland-Vancouver,		Nash County..........	91	**Santa Barbara-Santa Maria-**	
OR-WA PMSA	1,819			**Lompoc, CA MSA**	390
Clackamas County, OR ..	335	**Sacramento-Yolo, CA**		Santa Barbara County....	390
Columbia County, OR ...	44	**CMSA**................	1,686		
Multnomah County, OR ..	631	**Sacramento, CA PMSA**	1,532	**Santa Fe, NM MSA**	142
Washington County, OR..	400	El Dorado County.......	159	Los Alamos County......	18
Yamhill County, OR	82	Placer County.........	229	Santa Fe County........	123
Clark County, WA	327	Sacramento County.....	1,144		
Salem, OR PMSA	330	**Yolo, CA PMSA**	154	**Sarasota-Bradenton, FL**	
Marion County, OR	269	Yolo County	154	**MSA**.................	543
Polk County, OR........	62			Manatee County........	240
				Sarasota County........	303

U.S. Census Bureau, Statistical Abstract of the United States: 1999

	Popu- lation, 1998 (1,000)
Savannah, GA MSA	286
Bryan County	23
Chatham County	226
Effingham County	36
Scranton-Wilkes-Barre- **Hazleton, PA MSA**	615
Columbia County	64
Lackawanna County	208
Luzerne County	314
Wyoming County	29
Seattle-Tacoma-Bremerton, **WA CMSA**	3,424
Bremerton, WA PMSA	233
Kitsap County	233
Olympia, WA PMSA	202
Thurston County	202
Seattle-Bellevue-Everett, **WA PMSA**	2,313
Island County	70
King County	1,655
Snohomish County	588
Tacoma, WA PMSA	677
Pierce County	677
Sharon, PA MSA	122
Mercer County	122
Sheboygan, WI MSA	110
Sheboygan County	110
Sherman-Denison, TX **MSA**	103
Grayson County	103
Shreveport-Bossier City, LA **MSA**	379
Bossier Parish	93
Caddo Parish	242
Webster Parish	43
Sioux City, IA-NE MSA	120
Woodbury County, IA	102
Dakota County, NE	19
Sioux Falls, SD MSA	163
Lincoln County	20
Minnehaha County	143
South Bend, IN MSA	258
St. Joseph County	258
Spokane, WA MSA	409
Spokane County	409
Springfield, IL MSA	204
Menard County	12
Sangamon County	191
Springfield, MO MSA	305
Christian County	49
Greene County	227
Webster County	29
State College, PA MSA	133
Centre County	133
Steubenville-Weirton, **OH-WV MSA**	135
Jefferson County, OH	75
Brooke County, WV	26
Hancock County, WV	34
Stockton-Lodi, CA MSA	550
San Joaquin County	550
Sumter, SC MSA	107
Sumter County	107

	Popu- lation, 1998 (1,000)
Syracuse, NY MSA	735
Cayuga County	81
Madison County	71
Onondaga County	458
Oswego County	124
Tallahassee, FL MSA	261
Gadsden County	44
Leon County	217
Tampa-St. Petersburg- **Clearwater, FL MSA**	2,257
Hernando County	127
Hillsborough County	925
Pasco County	326
Pinellas County	878
Terre Haute, IN MSA	149
Clay County	27
Vermillion County	17
Vigo County	105
Texarkana, TX-Texarkana, **AR MSA**	123
Bowie County, TX	84
Miller County, AR	40
Toledo, OH MSA	610
Fulton County	42
Lucas County	449
Wood County	119
Topeka, KS MSA	165
Shawnee County	165
Tucson, AZ MSA	791
Pima County	791
Tulsa, OK MSA	777
Creek County	67
Osage County	43
Rogers County	68
Tulsa County	544
Wagoner County	55
Tuscaloosa, AL MSA	161
Tuscaloosa County	161
Tyler, TX MSA	169
Smith County	169
Utica-Rome, NY MSA	295
Herkimer County	64
Oneida County	231
Victoria, TX MSA	83
Victoria County	83
Visalia-Tulare-Porterville, **CA MSA**	355
Tulare County	355
Waco, TX MSA	203
McLennan County	203
Washington-Baltimore, **DC-MD-VA-WV CMSA**	7,285
Baltimore, MD PMSA	2,484
Anne Arundel County, MD	476
Baltimore County, MD	722
Carroll County, MD	150
Harford County, MD	215
Howard County, MD	236
Queen Anne's County, MD	40
Baltimore city, MD	646
Hagerstown, MD PMSA	127
Washington County, MD	127
Washington, DC-MD-VA- **WV PMSA**	4,674

	Popu- lation, 1998 (1,000)
District of Columbia, DC	523
Calvert County, MD	72
Charles County, MD	118
Frederick County, MD	187
Montgomery County, MD	841
Prince George's County, MD	778
Arlington County, VA	177
Clarke County, VA	13
Culpeper County, VA	33
Fairfax County, VA	929
Fauquier County, VA	54
King George County, VA	17
Loudoun County, VA	144
Prince William County, VA	260
Spotsylvania County, VA	84
Stafford County, VA	87
Warren County, VA	30
Alexandria city, VA	118
Fairfax city, VA	21
Falls Church city, VA	10
Fredericksburg city, VA	22
Manassas city, VA	35
Manassas Park city, VA	9
Berkeley County, WV	71
Jefferson County, WV	41
Waterloo-Cedar Falls, IA **MSA**	121
Black Hawk County	121
Wausau, WI MSA	123
Marathon County	123
West Palm Beach-Boca **Raton, FL MSA**	1,033
Palm Beach County	1,033
Wheeling, WV-OH MSA	153
Marshall County, WV	35
Ohio County, WV	48
Belmont County, OH	69
Wichita, KS MSA	544
Butler County	62
Harvey County	34
Sedgwick County	448
Wichita Falls, TX MSA	137
Archer County	8
Wichita County	129
Williamsport, PA MSA	117
Lycoming County	117
Wilmington, NC MSA	218
Brunswick County	68
New Hanover County	150
Yakima, WA MSA	218
Yakima County	218
York, PA MSA	373
York County	373
Youngstown-Warren, OH **MSA**	592
Columbiana County	112
Mahoning County	255
Trumbull County	225
Yuba City, CA MSA	137
Sutter County	77
Yuba County	60
Yuma, AZ MSA	132
Yuma County	132

[1] Five PMSAs of the New York-Northern New Jersey-Long Island, NY-NJ-CTPA CMSA are in Connecticut and therefore do not appear in this table; also, the CMSA's population shown here reflects the absence of those PMSAs.

Source: U.S. Census Bureau, "County Population Estimates and Demographic Components of Population Change: July 1, 1990 to July 1, 1998;" published 12 March 1999; <http://www.census.gov/population/estimates/county/co-98-8/98C800.txt>.

Appendix III
Limitations of the Data

Introduction—The data presented in this *Statistical Abstract* came from many sources. The sources include not only Federal statistical bureaus and other organizations that collect and issue statistics as their principal activity, but also governmental administrative and regulatory agencies, private research bodies, trade associations, insurance companies, health associations, and private organizations such as the National Education Association and philanthropic foundations. Consequently, the data vary considerably as to reference periods, definitions of terms and, for ongoing series, the number and frequency of time periods for which data are available.

The statistics presented were obtained and tabulated by various means. Some statistics are based on complete enumerations or censuses while others are based on samples. Some information is extracted from records kept for administrative or regulatory purposes (school enrollment, hospital records, securities registration, financial accounts, social security records, income tax returns, etc.), while other information is obtained explicitly for statistical purposes through interviews or by mail. The estimation procedures used vary from highly sophisticated scientific techniques to crude "informed guesses."

Each set of data relates to a group of individuals or units of interest referred to as the *target universe* or *target population* or simply as the *universe* or *population*. Prior to data collection, the target universe should be clearly defined. For example, if data are to be collected for the universe of households in the United States, it is necessary to define a "household." The target universe may not be completely tractable. Cost and other considerations may restrict data collection to a *survey universe* based on some available list; such list may be it of date. This list is called a *survey frame* or *sampling frame*.

The data in many tables are based on data obtained for all population units, *a census*, or on data obtained for only a portion, a *sample*, of the population units. When the data presented are based on a sample, the sample is usually a scientifically selected *probability sample*. This is a sample selected from a list or sampling frame in such a way that every possible sample has a known chance of selection and usually each unit selected can be assigned a number, greater than zero and less than or equal to one, representing its likelihood or probability of selection.

For large-scale sample surveys, the probability sample of units is often selected as a multistage sample. The first stage of a multistage sample is the selection of a probability sample of large groups of population members, referred to as primary sampling units (PSUs). For example, in a national multistage household sample, PSUs are often counties or groups of counties. The second stage of a multistage sample is the selection, within each PSU selected at the first stage, of smaller groups of population units, referred to as secondary sampling units. In subsequent stages of selection, smaller and smaller nested groups are chosen until the ultimate sample of population units is obtained. To qualify a multistage sample as a probability sample, all stages of sampling must be carried out using probability sampling methods.

Prior to selection at each stage of a multistage (or a single stage) sample, a list of the sampling units or sampling frame for that stage must be obtained. For example, for the first stage of selection of a national household sample, a list of the counties and county groups that form the PSUs must be obtained. For the final stage of selection, lists of households, and sometimes persons within the households, have to be compiled in the field. For surveys of economic entities and for the economic censuses, the Census

U.S. Census Bureau, Statistical Abstract of the United States: 1999

Bureau generally uses a frame constructed from the Bureau's Standard Statistical Establishment List (SSEL). The SSEL contains all establishments with payroll in the United States including small single establishment firms as well as large multiestablishment firms.

Wherever the quantities in a table refer to an entire universe, but are constructed from data collected in a sample survey, the table quantities are referred to as *sample estimates*. In constructing a sample estimate, an attempt is made to come as close as is feasible to the corresponding universe quantity that would be obtained from a complete census of the universe. Estimates based on a sample will, however, generally differ from the hypothetical census figures. Two classifications of errors are associated with estimates based on sample surveys: (1) *sampling error*—the error arising from the use of a sample, rather than a census, to estimate population quantities and (2) *nonsampling error*—those errors arising from nonsampling sources. As discussed below, the magnitude of the sampling error for an estimate can usually be estimated from the sample data. However, the magnitude of the nonsampling error for an estimate can rarely be estimated. Consequently, actual error in an estimate exceeds the error that can be estimated.

The particular sample used in a survey is only one of a large number of possible samples of the same size which could have been selected using the same sampling procedure. Estimates derived from the different samples would, in general, differ from each other. The *standard error* (SE) is a measure of the variation among the estimates derived from all possible samples. The standard error is the most commonly used measure of the sampling error of an estimate. Valid estimates of the standard errors of survey estimates can usually be calculated from the data collected in a probability sample. For convenience, the standard error is sometimes expressed as a percent of the estimate and is called the relative standard error or *coefficient of variation* (CV). For example, an estimate of 200 units with an estimated standard error of 10 units has an estimated CV of 5 percent.

A sample estimate and an estimate of its standard error or CV can be used to construct interval estimates that have a prescribed confidence that the interval includes the average of the estimates derived from all possible samples with a known probability. To illustrate, if all possible samples were selected under essentially the same general conditions and using the same sample design and if an estimate and its estimated standard error were calculated from each sample, then: 1) Approximately 68 percent of the intervals from one standard error below the estimate to one standard error above the estimate would include the average estimate derived from all possible samples; 2) approximately 90 percent of the intervals from 1.6 standard errors below the estimate to 1.6 standard errors above the estimate would include the average estimate derived from all possible samples; and 3) approximately 95 percent of the intervals from two standard errors below the estimate to two standard errors above the estimate would include the average estimate derived from all possible samples.

Thus, for a particular sample, one can say with the appropriate level of confidence (e.g., 90% or 95%) that the average of all possible samples is included in the constructed interval. Example of a confidence interval: An estimate is 200 units with a standard error of 10 units. An approximately 90 percent confidence interval (plus or minus 1.6 standard errors) is from 184 to 216.

All surveys and censuses are subject to nonsampling errors. Nonsampling errors are of two kinds—*random* and *nonrandom*. Random nonsampling errors arise because of the varying interpretation of questions (by respondents or interviewers) and varying actions of coders, keyers, and other processors. Some randomness is also introduced when respondents must estimate values. these same errors usually have a nonrandom component. Nonrandom nonsampling errors result from total nonresponse (no usable data obtained for a sampled unit), partial or item nonresponse (only a portion of a response may be usable), inability or unwillingness on the part of respondents to provide correct information, difficulty

U.S. Census Bureau, Statistical Abstract of the United States: 1999

interpreting questions, mistakes in recording or keying data, errors of collection or processing, and coverage problems (overcoverage and undercoverage of the target universe). Random nonresponse errors usually, but not always, result in an understatement of sampling errors and thus an overstatement of the precision of survey estimates. Estimating the magnitude of nonsampling errors would require special experiments or access to independent data and, consequently, the magnitudes are seldom available.

Nearly all types of nonsampling errors that affect surveys also occur in complete censuses. Since surveys can be conducted on a smaller scale than censuses, nonsampling errors can presumably be controlled more tightly. Relatively more funds and effort can perhaps be expended toward eliciting responses, detecting and correcting response error, and reducing processing errors. As a result, survey results can sometimes be more accurate than census results.

To compensate for suspected nonrandom errors, adjustments of the sample estimates are often made. For example, adjustments are frequently made for nonresponse, both total and partial. Adjustments made for either type of nonresponse are often referred to as *imputations*. Imputation for total nonresponse is usually made by substituting for the questionnaire responses of the nonrespondents the "average" questionnaire responses of the respondents. These imputations usually are made separately within various groups of sample members, formed by attempting to place respondents and nonrespondents together that have "similar" design or ancillary characteristics. Imputation for item nonresponse is usually made by substituting for a missing item the response to that item of a respondent having characteristics that are "similar" to those of the nonrespondent.

For an estimate calculated from a sample survey, the *total error* in the estimate is composed of the sampling error, which can usually be estimated from the sample, and the nonsampling error, which usually cannot be estimated from the sample. The total error present in a population quantity obtained from a complete census is composed of only nonsampling errors. Ideally, estimates of the total error associated with data given in the *Statistical Abstract* tables should be given. However, due to the unavailability of estimates of nonsampling errors, only estimates of the levels of sampling errors, in terms of estimated standard errors or coefficients of variation, are available. To obtain estimates of the estimated standard errors from the sample of interest, obtain a copy of the referenced report which appears at the end of each table.

Principal data bases—Beginning below are brief descriptions of 36 of the sample surveys and censuses that provide a substantial portion of the data contained in this *Abstract*.

SECTION 1. POPULATION

Source and Title: U.S. Census Bureau, *Census of Population*

Tables: See tables citing *Census of Population* in Section 1 and also in Sections 2, 4, 6, 8, 13, 14, 21, and 29.

Universe, Frequency, and Types of Data: Complete count of U.S. population conducted every 10 years since 1790. Data obtained on number and characteristics of people in the United States.

Type of Data Collection Operation: In 1970, 1980, and 1990 complete census for some items—age, sex, race, marital status, and relationship to householder. In 1970, other items collected from a 5% and a 15% probability (systematic) sample of the population. In 1980, approximately 19% of the housing units were included in the sample; in 1990, approximately 17%.

Data Collection and Imputation Procedures: In 1970, extensive use of mail questionnaires in urban areas; personal interviews in most rural areas. In 1980 and 1990, mail questionnaires were used in even more areas than in 1970, with personal interviews in the remainder. Extensive telephone and personal followup for nonrespondents was done in the censuses. Imputations were made for missing characteristics.

Estimates of Sampling Error: Sampling errors for data are estimated for all items collected by sample and vary by

926   Appendix III

characteristic and geographic area. The CVs for national and state estimates are generally very small.

Other (Nonsampling) Errors: Since 1950, evaluation programs have been conducted to provide information on the magnitude of some sources of nonsampling errors such as response bias and undercoverage in each census. Results from the evaluation program for the 1990 census indicate that the net under coverage amounted to about 1.5% to 2% of the total resident population.

Sources of Additional Material: U.S. Census Bureau, *The Coverage of Population in the 1980 Census*, PHC80-E4; *Content Reinterview Study: Accuracy of Data for Selected Population and Housing Characteristics as Measured by Reinterview*, PHC80-E2; *1980 Census of Population*, Vol. 1., (PC80-1), Appendixes B, C, and D.

Source and Title: U.S. Census Bureau, *Current Population Survey (CPS)*.

Tables: See tables citing *Current Population Reports* primarily in Section 1, but also in Sections 2, 3, 4, 8, 12, 13, 14, 18, 23, and 29. Many Bureau of Labor Statistics' (BLS) tables in Section 13 are CPS based.

Universe, Frequency, and Types of Data: Nationwide monthly sample survey of civilian noninstitutional population, 15 years old or over, to obtain data on employment, unemployment, and a number of other characteristics.

Type of Data Collection Operation: Multistage probability sample of about 50,000 households in 754 PSUs in 1996. Over-sampling in some states and the largest MSAs to improve reliability for those areas of employment data on annual average basis. A continual sample rotation system is used. Households are in sample 4 months, out for 8 months, and in for 4 more. Month-to-month overlap is 75%; year-to-year overlap is 50%.

Data Collection and Imputation Procedures: For first and fifth months that a household is in sample, personal interviews; other months, approximately, 85% of the data collected by phone. Imputation is done for both item and total nonresponse. Adjustment for total nonresponse is done by a predefined cluster of units, by MSA size and residence; for item nonresponse imputation varies by subject matter.

Estimates of Sampling Error: Estimated CVs on national annual averages for labor force, total employment, and nonagricultural employment, 0.2%; for total unemployment and agricultural employment, 1.0% to 2.5%. The estimated CVs for family income and poverty rate for all persons in 1986 are 0.5% and 1.5%, respectively. CVs for subnational areas, such as states, would be larger and would vary by area.

Other (Nonsampling) Errors: Estimates of response bias on unemployment are not available, but estimates of unemployment are usually 5% to 9% lower than estimates from reinterviews. Four to 5.0% of sample households unavailable for interviews.

Sources of Additional Material: U.S. Census Bureau and Bureau of Labor Statistics, *Concepts and Methods Used in Labor Force Statistics from Current Population Survey* (Census Series P-23, No. 62; BLS Report No. 463) and U.S. Census Bureau, *Current Population Survey* (Tech. Paper 40) and Bureau of Labor Statistics, *Employment and Earnings*, monthly, Explanatory Notes and Estimates of Error, Tables 1-A through 1-H and *BLS Handbook of Methods*, Chapter 1 (Bulletin 2490.)

SECTION 2. VITAL STATISTICS

Source and Title: U.S. National Center for Health Statistics (NCHS), *National Vital Statistics System.*

Tables: See tables citing *Vital Statistics of the United States;* 348 in Section 5; and 1333 in Section 29.

Universe, Frequency, and Types of Data: Annual data on births and deaths in the United States.

Type of Data Collection Operation: Mortality data based on complete file of death records, except 1972, based on 50% sample. Natality statistics 1951-71, based on 50% sample of birth certificates, except a 20% to 50% in 1967, received by NCHS. Beginning 1972, data from some states received through Vital Statistics Cooperative Program (VSCP) and complete file used; data from other states based on 50% sample. Beginning 1986, all reporting areas participated in the VSCP.

Data Collection and Imputation Procedures: Reports based on records from registration offices of all states, District of Columbia, New York City, Puerto Rico, Virgin Islands, and Guam.

Estimates of Sampling Error: For recent years, CVs for births are small due to large portion of total file in sample (except for very small estimated totals).

Other (Nonsampling) Errors: Data on births and deaths believed to be at least 99% complete.

Sources of Additional Material: U.S. National Center for Health Statistics, *Vital Statistics of the United States*, Vol. I and Vol. II, annual, and *National Vital Statistics Report*.

(See Section 1 above for information pertaining to Tables 106-109.)

SECTION 3. HEALTH AND NUTRITION

Source and Title: U.S. National Center for Health Statistics, *National Health Interview Survey (NHIS)*.

Tables: 198, 202, 222, 223, 230-233, and 239.

Universe, Frequency, and Types of Data: Continuous data collection covering the civilian noninstitutional population to obtain information on personal and demographic characteristics, illnesses, injuries, impairments, and other health topics.

Type of Data Collection Operation: Multistage probability sample of 49,000 households (in 198 PSUs) from 1985 to 1994; 43,000 households (358 design PSUs) from 1995 on, selected in groups of about four adjacent households.

Data Collection and Imputation Procedures: Some missing data items (e.g., age) are imputed using an average value. Unit nonresponse is compensated for by an adjustment to the survey weights

Estimates of Sampling Error: Estimated CVs: For physician visits by males, 1.5%; for workdays lost by males, 3.5%; for persons injured at home, 4.7%.

Other (Nonsampling) Errors: Response rate was 93.8% in 1996 for the NHIS.

Sources of Additional Material: U.S. National Center for Health Statistics, "Current Estimates from the National Health Interview Survey, U.S., 1996," Vital and Health Statistics, Series 10 #200.

(See Section 13 for information pertaining to Table 193, Section 15 for Table 183, and Section 27 for Table 192.)

SECTION 4. EDUCATION

Source and Title: U.S. Department of Education, National Center for Education Statistics, *Higher Education General Information Survey (HEGIS), Fall Enrollment in Institutions of Higher Education;* beginning 1986, *Integrated Postsecondary Education Data Survey (IPEDS), Fall Enrollment*

Tables: 308, 309, 312, and 313.

Universe, Frequency, and Types of Data: Annual survey of all institutions and branches listed in the *Directory* to obtain data on total enrollment by sex, level of enrollment, type of program, racial/ethnic characteristics (every other year prior to 1990, then annually) and attendance status of student, and on first-time students.

Type of Data Collection Operation: Complete census.

Data Collection and Imputation Procedures: Survey package is usually mailed in the spring with surveys due at varying dates in the summer and fall; mail and phone followup procedures for nonrespondents. Missing data are imputed by using data of similar institutions.

Estimates of Sampling Error: Not applicable.

Other (Nonsampling) Errors: For degree-granting institutions approximately 92% response rate in fall 1996.

Sources of Additional Material: U.S. Department of Education, National Center for Education Statistics, *Fall Enrollment in Higher Education*, annual.

Source and Title: U.S. Department of Education, National Center for Education Statistics, *Higher Education General Information Survey (HEGIS), Financial Statistics of Institutions of Higher Education;* beginning 1986, *Integrated Postsecondary Education Data Survey (IPEDS), Finance*.

Tables: 254, 257, 312, and 315.

Universe, Frequency, and Types of Data: Annual survey of all institutions and branches listed in the *Education Directory, Colleges and Universities*, to obtain data on financial status and operations, including current funds revenues, current funds expenditures, and physical plant assets.

Type of Data Collection Operation: Complete census.

Data Collection and Imputation Procedures: Survey package is usually mailed in the spring with surveys due at varying dates in the summer and fall; mail and phone followup procedures for nonrespondents. Missing data are imputed by using data of similar institutions.

Estimates of Sampling Error: Not applicable.

Other (Nonsampling) Errors: For 1996, a 96% response rate for institutions of higher education; 83% for degree-granting institutions.

Sources of Additional Material: U.S. Department of Education, National Center for Education Statistics, *Financial Statistics*.

Source and Title: U.S. Department of Education, National Center for Education Statistics, *Higher Education General Information Survey (HEGIS), Degrees and Other Formal Awards Conferred.* Beginning 1986, *Integrated Postsecondary Education Data Survey (IPEDS), Completions.*

Tables: 329-334.

Universe, Frequency, and Types of Data: Annual survey of all institutions and branches listed in the *Education Directory, Colleges and Universities* to obtain data on earned degrees and other formal awards, conferred by field of study, level of degree, sex, and by racial/ethnic characteristics (every other year prior to 1990, then annually).

Type of Data Collection Operation: Complete census.

Data Collection and Imputation Procedures: Survey package is usually mailed in the spring with surveys due at varying dates in the summer and fall; mail and phone followup procedures for nonrespondents. Missing data are imputed by using data of similar institutions.

Estimates of Sampling Error: Not applicable.

Other (Nonsampling) Errors: For 1995-96, approximately 98% response rate for degree-granting institutions.

Sources of Additional Material: U.S. Department of Education, National Center for Education Statistics, *Completions*, annual.

(See Sections 1 and 9 for information pertaining to the U.S. Census Bureau and Section 5 for information pertaining to Table 268.)

SECTION 5. LAW ENFORCEMENT, COURTS, AND PRISONS

Source and Title: U.S. Federal Bureau of Investigation, *Uniform Crime Reporting (UCR) Program*

Tables: 342-347, 349-352, 357, 358, and 360.

Universe, Frequency, and Types of Data: Monthly reports on the number of criminal offenses that become known to law enforcement agencies. Data are collected on crimes cleared by arrest, by age, sex, and race of offender and on assaults on law enforcement officers.

Type of Data Collection Operation: Crime statistics are based on reports of crime data submitted either directly to the FBI by contributing law enforcement agencies or through cooperating state UCR programs.

Data Collection and Imputation Procedures: States with UCR programs collect data directly from individual law enforcement agencies and forward reports, prepared in accordance with UCR standards, to FBI. Accuracy and consistency edits are performed by FBI.

Estimates of Sampling Error: Not applicable.

Other (Nonsampling) Errors: Coverage of 95% of the population (92.9% in MSAs, 77.4% in "other cities," and 77.1% in rural areas) by UCR program, though varying number of agencies report. Some error may be present through incorrect reporting.

Sources of Additional Material: U.S. Federal Bureau of Investigation, *Crime in the United States, Hate Crime Statistics,* annual, *Law Enforcement Officers Killed & Assaulted,* annual.

Source and Title: U.S. Bureau of Justice Statistics (BJS), *National Crime Victimization Survey.*

U.S. Census Bureau, Statistical Abstract of the United States: 1999

Tables: 353-356, Table 268 in Section 4, and Table 715 in Section 13.

Universe, Frequency, and Types of Data: Monthly survey of individuals and households in the United States to obtain data on criminal victimization of those units for compilation of annual estimates.

Type of Data Collection Operation: National probability sample survey of about 50,000 interviewed households in 376 PSUs selected from a list of addresses from the 1980 census, supplemented by new construction permits and an area sample where permits are not required.

Data Collection and Imputation Procedures: Interviews are conducted every 6 months for 3 years for each household in the sample; 8,000 households are interviewed monthly. Personal interviews are used in the first and fifth interviews; the intervening interviews are conducted by telephone whenever possible.

Estimates of Sampling Error: CVs in 1994: 2.7% for crimes of violence; 8.5% for estimate of rape/sexual assault counts; 5.5% for robbery counts; 2.8% for assault counts; 8.0% for personal theft counts; 1.9% for property crimes; 3.0% for burglary counts; 2.0% for theft; and 4.4% for motor vehicle theft counts.

Other (Nonsampling) Errors: Respondent recall errors which may include reporting incidents for other than the reference period; interviewer coding and processing errors; and possible mistaken reporting or classifying of events. Adjustment is made for a household noninterview rate of about 4% and for a within-household noninterview rate of 7%.

Sources of Additional Material: U.S. Bureau of Justice Statistics, *Criminal Victimization in the United States*, annual.

(See Section 2 for details on Table 348.)

SECTION 7. PARKS AND RECREATION

(See Section 27 for details on Tables 432 and 456.)

SECTION 8. ELECTIONS

(See Section 1 above for information pertaining to Tables 487 and 488 and Section 9 for information pertaining to Table 481.)

SECTION 9. STATE AND LOCAL GOVERNMENT FINANCES AND EMPLOYMENT

Source and Title: U.S. Census Bureau, *Census of Governments.*

Tables: See tables in Section 9 citing *Census of Governments* and Table 481 in Section 8.

Universe, Frequency, and Types of Data: Survey of all governmental units in the United States conducted every 5 years to obtain data on government revenue, expenditures, debt, assets, employment and employee retirement systems, property values, public school systems, and number, size, and structure of governments.

Type of Data Collection Operation: Complete census. List of units derived through classification of government units recently authorized in each state and identification, counting, and classification of existing local governments and public school systems.

Data Collection and Imputation Procedures: Data collected through field and office compilation of financial data from official records and reports for states and large local governments; mail canvass of selected data items, like state tax revenue and employee retirement systems; and collection of local government statistics through central collection arrangements with state governments.

Estimates of Sampling Error: Not applicable.

Other (Nonsampling) Errors: Some nonsampling errors may arise due to possible inaccuracies in classification, response, and processing.

Sources of Additional Material: U.S. Census Bureau, *Census of Governments, 1987*, various reports, and *State Government Finances in 1990*, GF 90, No. 3.

Source and Title: U.S. Census Bureau, *Annual Surveys of State and Local Government.*

Tables: See tables citing *Public Employment* and *Government Finances* in Section 9 and Table 285 in Section 4; and Table 620 in Section 12.

930 Appendix III

Universe, Frequency, and Types of Data: Sample survey conducted annually to obtain data on revenue, expenditure, debt, and employment of state and local governments. Universe is all governmental units in the United States (about 87,000).

Type of Data Collection Operation: Sample of about 22,000 units includes all state governments, county governments with 50,000+ population, municipalities and townships with 25,000+ population, all school districts with 10,000+ enrollment in October 1986, and other governments meeting certain criteria; probability sample for remaining units.

Data Collection and Imputation Procedures: Field and office compilation of data from official records and reports for states and large local governments; central collection of local governmental financial data through cooperative agreements with a number of state governments; mail canvass of other units with mail and telephone followups of nonrespondents. Data for nonresponses are imputed from previous year data or obtained from secondary sources, if available.

Estimates of Sampling Error: CVs for estimates of major employment and financial items are generally less than 2% for most states and less than 1.2% for the majority of states.

Other (Nonsampling) Errors: Nonresponse rate is less than 15% for number of units. Other possible errors may result from undetected inaccuracies in classification, response, and processing.

Sources of Additional Material: U.S. Census Bureau, *Public Employment in 1990*, GE 90, No. 1, *Governmental Finances in 1989-90*, GF 90, No. 5, and *Census of Governments, 1987*, various reports.

SECTION 10. FEDERAL GOVERNMENT

Source and Title: U.S. Internal Revenue Service, *Statistics of Income, Individual Income Tax Returns.*

Tables: 558-562.

Universe, Frequency, and Types of Data: Annual study of unaudited individual income tax returns, Forms 1040, 1040A, and 1040EZ, filed by U.S. citizens and residents. Data provided on various financial characteristics by size of adjusted gross income, marital status, and by taxable and nontaxable returns. Data by state, based on 100% file, also include returns from 1040NR, filed by nonresident aliens plus certain self-employment tax returns.

Type of Data Collection Operation: Annual stratified probability sample of approximately 125,000 returns broken into sample strata based on the larger of total income or total loss amounts as well as the size of business plus farm receipts. Sampling rates for sample strata varied from .025% to 100%.

Data Collection and Imputation Procedures: Computer selection of sample of tax return records. Data adjusted during editing for incorrect, missing, or inconsistent entries to ensure consistency with other entries on return.

Estimates of Sampling Error: Estimated CVs for tax year 1987: Adjusted gross income less deficit .13%; salaries and wages .20%; and tax-exempt interest received 4.51%. (State data not subject to sampling error.)

Other (Nonsampling) Errors: Processing errors and errors arising from the use of tolerance checks for the data.

Sources of Additional Material: U.S. Internal Revenue Service, *Statistics of Income, Individual Income Tax Returns*, annual.

SECTION 12. SOCIAL INSURANCE AND HUMAN SERVICES

Source and Title: U.S. Social Security Administration, *Benefit Data.*

Tables: 616 and 617.

Universe, Frequency, and Types of Data: All persons receiving monthly benefits under Title II of Social Security Act. Data on number and amount of benefits paid by type and state.

Type of Data Collection Operation: Data based on administrative records. Data based on 100% files, as well as 10% and 1% sample files.

Data Collection and Imputation Procedures: Records used consist of actions pursuant to applications dated by subsequent post-entitlement actions.

Estimates of Sampling Error: Varies by size of estimate and sample file size.

Other (Nonsampling) Errors: Processing errors, which are believed to be small.

Sources of Additional Material: U.S. Social Security Administration, *Annual Statistical Supplement to the Social Security Bulletin.*

Source and Title: U.S. Social Security Administration, *Supplemental Security Income (SSI) Program.*

Tables: 631 and 632.

Universe, Frequency, and Types of Data: All eligible aged, blind, or disabled persons receiving SSI benefit payments under SSI program. Data include number of persons receiving federally administered SSI, amounts paid, and state administered supplementation.

Type of Data Collection Operation: Data based on administrative records.

Data Collection and Imputation Procedures: Data adjusted to reflect returned checks and overpayment refunds. For federally administered payments, actual adjusted amounts are used.

Estimates of Sampling Error: Not applicable.

Other (Nonsampling) Errors: Processing errors, which are believed to be small.

Sources of Additional Material: U.S. Social Security Administration, *Annual Statistical Supplement to the Social Security Bulletin.*

(See Section 1 above for information pertaining to the Current Population Survey and Section 9 for information pertaining to Annual Surveys of State and Local Government.)

SECTION 13. LABOR FORCE, EMPLOYMENT, AND EARNINGS

Source and Title: U.S. Bureau of Labor Statistics (BLS), *Current Employment Statistics (CES) Program.*

Tables: 688-690, 698; in Section 3, Table 193; in Section 21, Table 1016; and in Section 22, Table 1083.

Universe, Frequency, and Types of Data: Monthly survey covering about 6 million nonagricultural establishments to obtain data on employment, hours, and earnings, by industry.

Type of Data Collection Operation: Sample survey of about 390,000 establishments in June 1998.

Data Collection and Imputation Procedures: Cooperating state agencies mail questionnaires to sample establishments to develop state and local estimates; information is forwarded to BLS where national estimates are prepared.

Estimates of Sampling Error: Estimated CVs for employment, 0.1%, for average weekly hours paid, 0.1% and for average hourly earnings, 0.2%.

Other (Nonsampling) Errors: Estimates of employment adjusted annually to reflect complete universe. Average adjustment is 0.3%.

Sources of Additional Material: U.S. Bureau of Labor Statistics, *Employment and Earnings*, monthly, Explanatory Notes and Estimates of Error, Tables 2-A through 2-G.

(See Section 1 above for information pertaining to the Current Population Survey and Section 5 for information pertaining to Table 715.)

SECTION 14. INCOME, EXPENDITURES, AND WEALTH

Source and Title: Board of Governors of the Federal Reserve System, *Survey of Consumer Finances.*

Tables: 771 and 772, and in Section 16, 801, 803-805, and 826.

Universe, Frequency, and Types of Data: Periodic sample survey of families. In this survey a given household is divided into a primary economic unit and other economic units. The primary economic unity, which may be a single individual, is generally chosen as the unit that contains the person who either holds the title to the home or is the first person listed on the lease. The primary unit is used as the reference family. The survey collects detailed data on the composition of family balance sheets, the terms of loans, and relationships with financial institutions. It also gathered information on the employment history and pension rights of the survey respondent and the spouse or partner of the respondent.

Type of Data Collection Operation: The survey employs a two-part strategy for sampling families. Some families were selected by standard multistage area-probability sampling methods from the 48 contiguous states. The remaining families in the survey were selected using tax data under the strict rules governing confidentiality and the rights of potential respondents to refuse participation.

Data Collection and Imputation Procedures: The Survey Research Center at the University of Michigan collected the 1989 survey data between August 1989 and March 1990. Adjustments for nonresponse errors are made through systematic imputation of unanswered questions and through weighting adjustments based on data used in the sample design for families that refused participation.

Estimates of Sampling Error: Because of the complex design of the survey, the estimation of potential sampling errors is not straightforward.

Other (Nonsampling) Errors: The achieved sample of 3,143 families represents a response rate of about 69 percent in the area-probability sample and a rate of about 34% in the tax-data sample. Proper training of interviewers and careful design of questionnaires were used to control inaccurate survey responses.

Sources of Additional Material: Board of Governors of the Federal Reserve System, "Changes in Family Finances from 1983 to 1989: Evidence from the Survey of Consumer Finances," *Federal Reserve Bulletin,* January 1992.

(See Section 1 above for information pertaining to the U.S. Census Bureau.)

SECTION 15. PRICES

Source and Title: U.S. Bureau of Labor Statistics (BLS), *Consumer Price Index (CPI)*

Tables: 775-778, 790, and in Section 3, Table 183.

Universe, Frequency, and Types of Data: Monthly survey of price changes of all types of consumer goods and services purchased by urban wage earners and clerical workers prior to 1978 and urban consumers thereafter. Both indexes continue to be published.

Type of Data Collection Operation: Prior to 1978, sample of various consumer items in 56 urban areas; thereafter, in 85 PSUs, except from January 1987 through March 1988, when 91 areas were sampled.

Data Collection and Imputation Procedures: Prices of consumer items are obtained from about 57,000 housing units and 19,000 other reporters in 85 areas. Prices of food, fuel, and a few other items are obtained monthly; prices of most other commodities and services are collected every month in the five largest geographic areas and every other month in others.

Estimates of Sampling Error: Estimates of standard errors are not available at present.

Other (Nonsampling) Errors: Errors result from inaccurate reporting, difficulties in defining concepts and their operational implementation, and introduction of product quality changes and new products.

Sources of Additional Material: U.S. Bureau of Labor Statistics, *The Consumer Price Index:* 1987 Revision, Report 736, and *BLS Handbook of Methods,* Chapter 19, Bulletin 2414.

Source and Title: U.S. Bureau of Labor Statistics, *Producer Price Index (PPI)*

Tables: 775, 781-783, and in Section 21, Table 1066; in Section 24, Table 1155; and in Section 25, Table 1192.

Universe, Frequency, and Types of Data: Monthly survey of producing companies to determine price changes of all commodities produced in the United States for sale in commercial transactions. Data on agriculture, forestry, fishing, manufacturing, mining, gas, electricity, public utilities, and a few services.

Type of Data Collection Operation: Probability sample of approximately 3,100 about 75,000 quotations per month.

Data Collection and Imputation Procedures: Data are collected by mail. If transaction prices are not supplied, list prices are used. Some prices are obtained from trade publications, organized exchanges, and government agencies. To calculate index, price changes are multiplied by their relative weights based on total net selling value of all commodities in 1982.

Estimates of Sampling Error: Not applicable.

Other (Nonsampling) Errors: Not available at present.

Sources of Additional Material: U.S. Bureau of Labor Statistics, *BLS Handbook of Methods*, Chapter 16, Bulletin 2414.

SECTION 16. BANKING, FINANCE AND INSURANCE

(See Section 14 for information pertaining to Tables 801, 803-805, and 826 and Section 17 for information pertaining to Table 796.)

SECTION 17. BUSINESS ENTERPRISE

Source and Title: U.S. Census Bureau, *County Business Patterns.*

Tables: 874-876, 881, and in Section 16, Table 796; in Section 27, Tables 1275 and 1305; and in Section 29, Table 1342.

Universe, Frequency, and Types of Data: Annual tabulation of basic data items extracted from the Standard Statistical Establishment List, a file of all known single and multiestablishment companies maintained and updated by the U.S. Census Bureau. Data include number of establishments, number of employees, first-quarter and annual payrolls, and number of establishments by employment size class. Data are excluded for self-employed persons, domestic service workers, railroad employees, agricultural production workers, and most government employees.

Type of Data Collection Operation: The annual Company Organization Survey provides individual establishment data for multiestablishment companies. Data for single establishment companies are obtained from various Census Bureau programs, such as the Annual Survey of Manufactures and Current Business Surveys, as well as from administrative records of the Internal Revenue Service and the Social Security Administration.

Estimates of Sampling Error: Not Applicable.

Other (Nonsampling) Error: Response rates of greater than 90% for the 1993 Company Organization Survey.

Sources of Additional Materials: U.S. Census Bureau, *General Explanation of County Business Patterns.*

Source and Title: U.S. Internal Revenue Service, *Statistics of Income, Sole Proprietorship Returns* and *Statistics of Income Bulletin.*

Tables: 861-864.

Universe, Frequency, and Types of Data: Annual study of unaudited income tax returns of nonfarm sole proprietorships, Form 1040 with business schedules. Data provided on various financial characteristics by industry.

Type of Data Collection Operation: Stratified probability sample of approximately 31,000 sole proprietorships for tax year 1990. The sample is classified based on presence or absence of certain business schedules; the larger of total income or loss; and size of business plus farm receipts. Sampling rates vary from .043% to 100%.

Data Collection and Imputation Procedures: Computer selection of sample of tax return records. Data adjusted during editing for incorrect, missing, or inconsistent entries to ensure consistency with other entries on return.

Estimates of Sampling Error: Estimated CVs for tax year 1990 are not available; for 1987 (the latest available): For sole proprietorships, business receipts, 1.66%; net income, (less loss), 1.33%; depreciation 2.17%; interest expense 2.80%; and employee benefit programs 7.55%.

Other (Nonsampling) Errors: Processing errors and errors arising from the use of tolerance checks for the data.

Sources of Additional Material: U.S. Internal Revenue Service, *Statistics of Income, Sole Proprietorship Returns* (for years through 1980) and *Statistics of Income Bulletin*, Vol. 10, No. 1 (summer 1990).

Source and Title: U.S. Internal Revenue Service, *Statistics of Income, Partnership Returns* and *Statistics of Income Bulletin.*

Tables: 861-863, 865, and 866.

Universe, Frequency, and Types of Data: Annual study of unaudited income tax returns of partnerships, Form 1065. Data provided on various financial characteristics by industry.

Type of Data Collection Operation: Stratified probability sample of approximately 28,000 partnership returns from a population of 1,660,000 filed during calendar year 1990. The sample is classified based on combinations of gross receipts, net income or loss, and total assets, and on industry. Sampling rates vary from .04% to 100%.

Data Collection and Imputation Procedures: Computer selection of sample of tax return records. Data are adjusted during editing for incorrect, missing, or inconsistent entries to ensure consistency with other entries on return. Data not available due to regulations are not imputed.

Estimates of Sampling Error: Estimated CVs for tax year 1988 (latest available): For number of partnerships, .51%; business receipts, .78%; net income, 3.03%; net loss, 2.21%; and total assets, 1.22%.

Other (Nonsampling) Errors: Processing errors and errors arising from the use of tolerance checks for the data.

Sources of Additional Material: U.S. Internal Revenue Service, *Statistics of Income, Partnership Returns* and *Statistics of Income Bulletin,* Vol. 10, No. 1 (summer 1990).

Source and Title: U.S. Internal Revenue Service, *Corporation Income Tax Returns*

Tables: 861-863 and 869-871.

Universe, Frequency, and Types of Data: Annual study of unaudited corporation income tax returns, Forms 1120 and 1120 (A, F, L, PC, REIT, RIC, and S), filed by corporations or businesses legally defined as corporations. Data provided on various financial characteristics by industry and size of total assets, and business receipts.

Type of Data Collection Operation: Stratified probability sample of approximately 85,000 returns for 1987, distributed by sample classes generally based on type of return, size of total assets, size of net income or deficit, and selected business activity. Sampling rates for sample strata varied from .25% to 100%.

Data Collection and Imputation Procedures: Computer selection of sample of tax return records. Data adjusted during editing for incorrect, missing, or inconsistent entries to ensure consistency with other entries on return and to achieve statistical definitions.

Estimates of Sampling Error: Estimated CVs for 1988: Number of returns in subgroups ranged from 1.4% with assets under $100,000, to 0% with assets over $100 mil.; for amount of net income and amount of income tax, .18%.

Other (Nonsampling) Errors: Processing errors and errors arising from the use of tolerance checks for the data.

Sources of Additional Material: U.S. Internal Revenue Service, *Statistics of Income, Corporation Income Tax Returns,* annual.

SECTION 18. COMMUNICATIONS

(See Section 1 for information pertaining to Table 924 and Section 26 for information pertaining to Table 937.)

SECTION 19. ENERGY

Source and Title: U.S. Energy Information Administration, *Residential Energy Consumption Survey.*

Tables: 959, 960 and Table 1223 in Section 25.

Universe, Frequency, and Types of Data: Triennial survey of households and fuel suppliers. Data are obtained on energy-related household characteristics, housing unit characteristics, use of fuels, and energy consumption and expenditures by fuel type.

Type of Data Collection Operation: Probability sample of 7,183 eligible units in 129 PSUs. For responding units, fuel consumption and expenditure data obtained from fuel suppliers to those households.

Data Collection and Imputation Procedures: Personal interviews. Extensive followup of nonrespondents including mail questionnaires for some households. Adjustments for nonrespondents were made in weighting for respondents. Most item nonresponses were imputed.

Estimates of Sampling Error: Estimated CVs for household averages: For consumption, 1.3%; for expenditures, 1.0%; for various fuels, values ranged from 1.4% for electricity to 5.9% for LPG.

Other (Nonsampling) Errors: Household response rate of 86.7%. Nonconsumption data were mostly imputed for mail respondents (5.2% of eligible units). Usable responses from fuel suppliers for various fuels ranged from 82.8% for electricity to 55.7% for fuel oil.

Appendix III   935

Sources of Additional Material: U.S. Energy Information Administration, *Household Energy Consumption and Expenditures, 1993* and *Housing Characteristics, 1993.*

SECTION 21. TRANSPORTATION—LAND

(See Section 1 for information pertaining to Table 1037, Section 13 for Table 1016, Section 15 for Table 1066, and Section 27 for Table 1057.)

SECTION 22. TRANSPORTATION—AIR AND WATER

(See Section 13 for information pertaining to Table 1083.)

SECTION 23. AGRICULTURE

Source and Title: U.S. Department of Agriculture, National Agriculture Statistics Service (NASS), *Census of Agriculture.*

Tables: 1100-1106.

Universe, Frequency, and Types of Data: Complete count of U.S. farms and ranches conducted once every 5 years with data at the national, state, and county level. Data published on farm numbers and related items/characteristics.

Type of Data Collection Operation: Complete census for number of farms; land in farms; estimated market value of land and buildings, machinery and equipment, and agriculture products sold; total cropland; irrigated land; total farm production expenses; farm operator characteristics; livestock and poultry inventory and sales; and selected crops harvested.

Data Collection and Imputation Procedures: Data collection is by mailing questionnaires to all farmers and ranchers. Nonrespondents are conducted by telephone and correspondence followups. Imputations were made for all nonresponse item/characteristics.

Estimates of Sampling Error: Variability in the estimates is due to the sample selection and estimation for items collected by sample and census nonresponse estimation procedures. The CVs for national and state estimates are generally very small. Approximately 85% response rate.

Other (Nonsampling) Errors: Nonsampling errors are due to incompleteness of the census mailing list, duplications on the list, respondent reporting errors, errors in editing reported data, and in imputation for missing data. Evaluation studies are conducted to measure certain nonsampling errors such as list coverage and classification error. Results from the evaluation program for the 1987 census indicate the net under coverage amounted to about 7.2% of the Nation's total farms.

Sources of Additional Material: U.S. Department of Agriculture (NASS), *1997 Census of Agriculture,* Volume 2, Subject Series—Part 1, *Agriculture Atlas of the U.S.,* Part 2, *Coverage Evaluation,* Part 3, *Rankings of States and Counties,* Part 4, *History,* Part 5, *ZIP Code Tabulation of Selected Items;* and Volume 4, *Farm and Ranch Irrigation Survey.*

Source and Title: U.S. Department of Agriculture, National Agricultural Statistics Service (NASS), *Basic Area Frame Sample.*

Tables: See tables citing NASS in source notes in Section 23, which pertain to this or the following two surveys.

Universe, Frequency, and Types of Data: Two annual area sample surveys of U.S. farm operators: June agricultural survey collects data on planted acreage and livestock inventories; and a February Farm Costs and Returns survey that collects data on total farm production, expenses, and specific commodity costs of production.

Type of Data Collection Operation: Stratified probability sample of about 16,000 land area units of about 1 sq. mile (range from 0.1 sq. mile in cities to several sq. miles in open grazing areas). Sample includes 60,000 parcels of agricultural land. About 20% of the sample replaced annually.

Data Collection and Imputation Procedures: Data collection is by personal enumeration. Imputation is based on enumerator observation or data reported by respondents having similar agricultural characteristics.

Estimates of Sampling Error: Estimated CVs range from 1% to 2% for regional estimates to 3% to 6% for state estimates of livestock inventories.

Other (Nonsampling) Errors: Minimized through rigid quality controls on the collection process and careful review of all reported data.

Sources of Additional Material: U.S. Department of Agriculture, SRS, *Scope and Methods of the Statistical Reporting Service,* (name changed to National Agricultural Statistics Service), Miscellaneous Publication No. 1308, September 1983 (revised).

Source and Title: U.S. Department of Agriculture National Agricultural Statistics Service (NASS), *Multiple Frame Surveys*

Tables: See tables citing NASS in source notes in Section 23, which pertain to this or the following survey.

Universe, Frequency, and Types of Data: Surveys of U.S. farm operators to obtain data on major livestock inventories, selected crop acreages and production, grain stocks, and farm labor characteristics; and to obtain farm economic data for price indexing.

Type of Data Collection Operation: Primary frame is obtained from general or special purpose lists, supplemented by a probability sample of land areas used to estimate for list incompleteness.

Data Collection and Imputation Procedures: Mail, telephone, or personal interviews used for initial data collection. Mail nonrespondent followup by phone and personal interviews. Imputation based on average of respondents.

Estimates of Sampling Error: Estimated CVs for number of hired farm workers is about 3%. Estimated CVs range from 1% to 2% for regional estimates to 3% to 6% for state estimates of livestock inventories.

Other (Nonsampling) Errors: In addition to above, replicated sampling procedures used to monitor effects of changes in survey procedures.

Sources of Additional Material: U.S. Department of Agriculture, SRS, *Scope and Methods of the Statistical Reporting Service,* (name changed to National Agricultural Statistics Service), Miscellaneous Publication No. 1308, September 1983 (revised).

Source and Title: U.S. Department of Agriculture, National Agricultural Statistics Service (NASS), *Objective Yield Surveys.*

Tables: See tables citing NASS in source notes in Section 23, which pertain to this or the preceding survey.

Universe, Frequency, and Types of Data: Surveys for data on corn, cotton, potatoes, soybeans, wheat, and rice to forecast and estimate yields.

Type of Data Collection Operation: Random location of plots in probability sample s selected in June from Basic Area Frame Sample (see above).

Data Collection and Imputation Procedures: Enumerators count and measure plant characteristics in sample fields. Production measured from plots at harvest. Harvest loss measured from post harvest gleanings.

Estimates of Sampling Error: CVs for national estimates of production are about 2% to 3%.

Other (Nonsampling) Errors: In addition to above, replicated sampling procedures used to monitor effects of changes in survey procedures.

Sources of Additional Material: U.S. Department of Agriculture, SRS, *Scope and Methods of the Statistical Reporting Service,* (name changed to National Agricultural Statistics Service), Miscellaneous Publication No. 1308, September 1983 (revised).

(See Section 1 above for information pertaining to the Census of Population and Current Population Survey.)

SECTION 24. NATURAL RESOURCES

(See Section 15 for Table 1155.)

SECTION 25. CONSTRUCTION AND HOUSING

Source and Title: U.S. Census Bureau, *Monthly Survey of Construction.*

Tables: 1199 and 1201-1204.

Universe, Frequency, and Types of Data: Survey conducted monthly of newly constructed housing units (excluding mobile homes). Data are collected on the start, completion, and sale of housing. (Annual figures are aggregates of monthly estimates.)

Type of Data Collection Operation: Probability sample of housing units obtained from building permits selected from 17,000 places. For nonpermit places, multistage probability sample of new housing units selected in 169 PSUs. In those areas, all roads are canvassed in selected enumeration districts.

U.S. Census Bureau, Statistical Abstract of the United States: 1999

Data Collection and Imputation Procedures: Data are obtained by telephone inquiry and field visit.

Estimates of Sampling Error: Estimated CVs of 3% to 4% for estimates of national totals but are as high as 20% for estimated totals of more detailed characteristics, such as housing units in multiunit structures.

Other (Nonsampling) Errors: Response rate is over 90% for most items. Nonsampling errors are attributed to definitional problems, differences in interpretation of questions, incorrect reporting, inability to obtain information about all cases in the sample, and processing errors.

Sources of Additional Material: U.S. Census Bureau, *Construction Reports, Series C20, Housing Starts; C22, Housing Completions;* and C25, *New One-Family Houses Sold and For Sale.*

Source and Title: U.S. Census Bureau, *Value of Construction Put in Place.*

Tables: 1194 and 1195.

Universe, Frequency, and Types of Data: Survey conducted monthly on total value of all construction put in place in the current month, both public and private projects. Construction values include costs of materials and labor, contractors' profits, overhead costs, cost of architectural and engineering work, and miscellaneous project costs. (Annual figures are aggregates of monthly estimates.)

Type of Data Collection Operation: Varies by type of activity. Total cost of private one-family houses started each month is distributed into value put in place using fixed patterns of monthly construction progress; using a multi-stage probability sample, data for private multifamily housing are obtained by mail from owners of multiunit projects. Data for residential additions and alterations are obtained in a quarterly survey measuring expenditures; monthly estimates are interpolated from quarterly data. Estimates of value of private nonresidential construction, and state and local government construction are obtained by mail from owners (or agents) for a probability sample of projects. Estimates of farm nonresidential construction expenditures are based on U.S. Department of Agriculture annual estimates of construction; public utility estimates are obtained from reports submitted to Federal regulatory agencies and from private utility companies; estimates of Federal construction are based on monthly data supplied by Federal agencies.

Data Collection and Imputation Procedures: See "Type of Data Collection Operation." Imputation accounts for approximately 20% of estimated value of construction each month.

Estimates of Sampling Error: CV estimates for private nonresidential construction range from 3% for estimated value of industrial buildings to 9% for religious buildings. CV is approximately 2% for total new private nonresidential buildings.

Other (Nonsampling) Errors: For directly measured data series based on samples, some nonsampling errors may arise from processing errors, imputations, and misunderstanding of questions. Indirect data series are dependent on the validity of the underlying assumptions and procedures.

Sources of Additional Material: U.S. Census Bureau, *Construction Reports, Series C30, Value of Construction Put in Place.*

Source and Title: U.S. Census Bureau, *American Housing Survey.*

Tables: See tables citing *American Housing Survey* in source notes.

Universe, Frequency, and Types of Data: Conducted nationally in the fall in odd numbered years to obtain data on the approximately 112 million occupied or vacant housing units in the United States (group quarters are excluded). Data include characteristics of occupied housing units, vacant units, new housing and mobile home units, financial characteristics, recent mover households, housing and neighborhood quality indicators, and energy characteristics.

Type of Data Collection Operation: The national sample was a multistage probability sample with about 53,000 units eligible for interview in 1997. Sample units, selected within 394 PSUs, were surveyed over a 5-month period.

Data Collection and Imputation Procedures: For 1997, the survey was conducted by personal interviews. The

938 Appendix III

interviewers obtained the information from the occupants or, if the unit was vacant, from informed persons such as landlords, rental agents, or knowledgeable neighbors.

Estimates of Sampling Error: For the national sample, illustrations of the SE of the estimates are provided in the Appendix D of the 1997 report. As an example, the estimated CV is about 0.2% for the estimated percentage of owner occupied units with two persons.

Other (Nonsampling) Errors: Response rate was about 97%. Nonsampling errors may result from incorrect or incomplete responses, errors in coding and recording, and processing errors. For the 1997 national sample, approximately 1.7% of the total housing inventory was not adequately represented by the AHS sample.

Sources of Additional Material: U.S. Census Bureau, *Current Housing Reports,* Series H-150 and H-170, *American Housing Survey.*

(See Section 1 above for information pertaining to the Census of Population, Section 15 pertaining to Table 1192 and Section 19 for Table 1223.)

SECTION 26. MANUFACTURES

Source and Title: U.S. Census Bureau, *Census of Manufactures.*

Tables: See tables citing *Census of Manufactures* or the *1997 Economic Census* in source notes in Section 26 and also Table 937 in Section 18 and Table 1344 in Section 29.

Universe, Frequency, and Types of Data: Conducted every 5 years to obtain information on labor, materials, capital input and output characteristics, plant location, and legal form of organization for all plants in the United States with one or more paid employees. Universe was 350,000 manufacturing establishments in 1987.

Type of Data Collection Operation: Complete enumeration of data items obtained from 200,000 firms. Administrative records from Internal Revenue Service and Social Security Administration are used for 150,000 smaller single-location firms, which were determined by various cutoffs based on size and industry.

Data Collection and Imputation Procedures: Five mail and telephone followups for larger nonrespondents. Data for small single-location firms (generally those with fewer than 10 employees) not mailed census questionnaires were estimated from administrative records of IRS and SSA. Data for nonrespondents were imputed from related responses or administrative records from IRS and SSA. Approximately 8% of total value of shipments was represented by fully imputed records in 1987.

Estimates of Sampling Error: Not applicable.

Other (Nonsampling) Errors: Based on evaluation studies, estimates of nonsampling errors for 1972 were about 1.3% for estimated total payroll; 2% for total employment; and 1% for value of shipments. Estimates for later years are not available.

Sources of Additional Material: U.S. Census Bureau, *1987 Census of Manufactures, Industry Series, Geographic Area Series, and Subject Series.*

Source and Title: U.S. Census Bureau, *Annual Survey of Manufactures.*

Tables: See tables citing *Annual Survey of Manufactures* in source notes.

Universe, Frequency, and Types of Data: Conducted annually to provide basic measures of manufacturing activity for intercensal years for all manufacturing establishments having one or more paid employees.

Type of Data Collection Operation: Sampling frame is 350,000 establishments in the 1987 Census of Manufactures (see above), supplemented by Social Security Administration lists of new manufacturers and new manufacturing establishments of multi-establishment companies identified annually by the Census Bureau's Company Organization Survey. A probability sample of about 55,000 establishments is selected. All establishments of companies with more than $500 million of manufacturing shipments in 1987 are included with certainty. All establishments with 250+ employees are also included with certainty along with a probability sample of smaller establishments.

U.S. Census Bureau, Statistical Abstract of the United States: 1999

Data Collection and Imputation Procedures: Survey is conducted by mail with phone and mail followups of nonrespondents. Imputation (for all nonresponse items) is based on previous year reports, or for new establishments in survey, on industry averages.

Estimates of Sampling Error: Estimated standard errors for number of employees, new expenditure, and for value added totals are given in annual publications. For U.S. level industry statistics, most estimated standard errors are 2% or less but vary considerably for detailed characteristics.

Other (Nonsampling) Errors: Response rate is about 85%. Nonsampling errors include those due to collection, reporting, and transcription errors, many of which are corrected through computer and clerical checks.

Sources of Additional Material: U.S. Census Bureau, *Annual Survey of Manufactures*, and Technical Paper 24.

SECTION 27. DOMESTIC TRADE AND SERVICES

Source and Title: U.S. Census Bureau, *Census of Wholesale Trade, Census of Retail Trade,* and *Census of Service Industries.*

Tables: See tables citing the above censuses or the *1997 Economic Census* in source notes in Section 27 and Table 1344 in Section 29.

Universe, Frequency, and Types of Data: Conducted every 5 years to obtain data on number of establishments, number of employees, total payroll size, total sales, and other industry-specific statistics. In 1987, the universe was all employer establishments primarily engaged in wholesale trade and employer and nonemployer establishments in retail trade or service industries.

Type of Data Collection Operation: All wholesale firms with paid employees surveyed; all retail and service large employer firms surveyed (i.e. all employer firms above the payroll size cutoff established to separate large from small employers) plus a 10-percent sample of smaller employer firms. Firms with no employees were not required to file a census return.

Data Collection and Imputation Procedures: Mail questionnaire is utilized with both mail and telephone followups for nonrespondents. Data for nonrespondents and all employer firms in retail trade and service industries are obtained from administrative records of IRS and the Social Security Administration.

Estimates of Sampling Error: Not applicable.

Other (Nonsampling) Errors: Response rate in 1987 of 80% for single establishment firms; 83% for multi-establishment firms. Item response ranged from 60% to 90% with higher rates for less detailed questions.

Sources of Additional Material: U.S. Census Bureau, Appendix A of *Census of Retail Trade; Census of Service Industries; Census of Wholesale Trade;* and *History of the 1987 Economic Censuses,* April 1992.

Source and Title: U.S. Census Bureau, *Current Business Surveys.*

Tables: 1278-1280, 1296, 1301, 1304, and Table 192 in Section 3, Tables 432 and 456 in Section 7, and Table 1057 in Section 21.

Universe, Frequency, and Types of Data: Provides monthly estimates of retail sales by kind of business and geographic area, and end-of-month inventories of retail stores; wholesale sales and end-of-month inventories; and annual receipts of selected service industries.

Type of Data Collection Operation: Probability sample of all firms from a list frame and, additionally, for retail and service an area frame. The list frame is the Bureau's Standard Statistical Establishment List (SSEL) updated quarterly for recent birth Employer Identification (EI) Numbers issued by the Internal Revenue Service and assigned a kind-of-business code by the Social Security Administration. The largest firms are included monthly; a sample of others is included every 3 months on a rotating basis. The area frame covers businesses not subjected to sampling on the list frame.

Data Collection and Imputation Procedures: Data are collected by mail questionnaire with telephone followups for nonrespondents. Imputation made for each nonresponse item and each item failing edit checks.

Estimates of Sampling Error: For the 1989 monthly surveys, CVs are about 0.6% for estimated total retail sales, 1.7% for wholesale sales, and 1.3% for wholesale inventories. For dollar volume of receipts, CVs from the *Service Annual Survey* vary by kind of business and range between 1.5% to 15.0%. Sampling errors are shown in monthly publications.

Other (Nonsampling) Errors: Imputation rates are about 18% to 23% for monthly retail sales, 20% to 25% for wholesale sales, about 25% to 30% for monthly wholesale inventories, and 14% for the *Service Annual Survey.*

Sources of Additional Material: U.S. Census Bureau, *Current Business Reports, Monthly Retail Trade, Monthly Wholesale Trade,* and *Service Annual Survey.*

(See Section 17 for information pertaining to Tables 1275 and 1305.)

SECTION 28. FOREIGN COMMERCE AND AID

Source and Title: U.S. Census Bureau, *Foreign Trade—Export Statistics.*

Tables: See U.S. Census Bureau citations for export statistics in source notes in Section and 28 and also Table 1341 in Section 29.

Universe, Frequency, and Types of Data: The export declarations collected by Customs are processed each month to obtain data on the movement of U.S. merchandise exports to foreign countries. Data obtained include value, quantity, and shipping weight of exports by commodity, country of destination, Customs district of exportation, and mode of transportation.

Type of Data Collection Operation: Shipper's Export Declarations are required to be filed for the exportation of merchandise valued over $1,500. Customs officials collect and transmit the documents to the U.S. Census Bureau on a flow basis for data compilation. Value data for shipments valued under $1,501 are estimated, based on established percentages of individual country totals.

Data Collection and Imputation Procedures: Statistical copies of Shipper's Export Declarations are received on a daily basis from Customs ports throughout the country and subjected to a monthly processing cycle. They are fully processed to the extent they reflect items valued over $1,500. Estimates for shipments valued at $1,500 or less are made, based on established percentages of individual country totals.

Estimates of Sampling Error: Not applicable.

Other (Nonsampling) Errors: Clerical and complex computer checks intercept most processing errors and minimize otherwise significant reporting errors; other nonsampling errors are caused by undercounting of exports to Canada due to the nonreceipt of some Shipper's Export Declarations.

Sources of Additional Material: U.S. Census Bureau, *U.S. Merchandise Trade: Exports, General Imports, and Imports for Consumption, SITC, Commodity by Country,* FT 925 (discontinued after 1996).

Source and Title: U.S. Census Bureau, *Foreign Trade—Import Statistics.*

Tables: See U.S. Census Bureau citations for import statistics in source notes in Section 28 and also Table 1341 in Section 29.

Universe, Frequency, and Types of Data: The import entry documents collected are processed each month to obtain data on the movement of merchandise imported into the United States. Data obtained include value, quantity, and shipping weight by commodity, country of origin, Customs district of entry, and mode of transportation.

Type of Data Collection Operation: Import entry documents are required to be filed for the importation of goods into the United States valued over $1,000 or for articles which must be reported on formal entries. Customs officials collect and transmit statistical copies of the documents to the U.S. Census Bureau on a flow basis for data compilation. Estimates for shipments valued under $1,001 and not reported on formal entries are based on established percentages of individual country totals.

Data Collection and Imputation Procedures: Statistical copies of import entry documents, received on a daily basis from Customs ports of entry throughout the country, are subjected to a monthly processing cycle. They are fully processed to the extent they reflect items valued at $1,001 and over or items which must be reported on formal entries.

Estimates of Sampling Error: Not applicable.

Other (Nonsampling) Errors: Verification of statistical data reporting by Customs officials prior to transmittal and a subsequent program of clerical and computer checks are utilized to hold nonsampling errors arising from reporting and/or processing errors to a minimum.

Sources of Additional Material: U.S. Census Bureau, *U.S. Merchandise Trade: Exports, General Imports and Imports for Consumption, SITC, Commodity by Country*, FT 925 (discontinued after 1996).

SECTION 29. OUTLYING AREAS

(See Section 1 for information pertaining to Tables 1334 and 1335, Section 2 for Table 1333, Section 17 for Table 1342, Section 28 for Table 1341, and Sections 26 and 27 for Table 1344.)

U.S. Census Bureau, Statistical Abstract of the United States: 1999

Appendix IV
Weights and Measures

[For assistance on metric usage, call or write the Office of Metric Programs, U.S. Department of Commerce, Washington, DC 20230 (301-975-3690) Internet site <http://www.nist.gov/metric>]

Symbol	When you know conventional	Multiply by	To find metric	Symbol
in	inch	2.54	centimeter	cm
ft	foot	30.48	centimeter	cm
yd	yard	0.91	meter	m
mi	mile	1.61	kilometer	km
in^2	square inch	6.45	square centimeter	cm^2
ft^2	square foot	0.09	square meter	m^2
yd^2	square yard	0.84	square meter	m^2
mi^2	square mile	2.59	square kilometer	km^2
	acre	0.41	hectare	ha
oz	ounce [1]	28.35	gram	g
lb	pound [1]	.45	kilograms	kg
oz (troy)	ounce [2]	31.10	gram	g
	short ton (2,000 lb)	0.91	metric ton	t
	long ton (2,240 lb)	1.02	metric ton	t
fl oz	fluid ounce	29.57	milliliter	mL
c	cup	0.24	liter	L
pt	pint	0.47	liter	L
qt	quart	0.95	liter	L
gal	gallon	3.78	liter	L
ft^3	cubic foot	0.03	cubic meter	m^3
yd^3	cubic yard	0.76	cubic meter	m^3
F	degrees Fahrenheit (subtract 32)	0.55	degrees Celsius	C

Symbol	When you know metric	Multiply by	To find conventional	Symbol
cm	centimeter	0.39	inch	in
cm	centimeter	0.33	foot	ft
m	meter	1.09	yard	yd
km	kilometer	0.62	mile	mi
cm^2	square centimeter	0.15	square inch	in^2
m^2	square meter	10.76	square foot	ft^2
m^2	square meter	1.20	square yard	yd^2
km^2	square kilometer	0.39	square mile	mi^2
ha	hectare	2.47	acre	
g	gram	.035	ounce [1]	oz
kg	kilogram	2.21	pounds [1]	lb
g	gram	.032	ounce [2]	oz (troy)
t	metric ton	1.10	short ton (2,000 lb)	
t	metric ton	0.98	long ton (2,240 lb)	
mL	milliliter	0.03	fluid ounce	fl oz
L	liter	4.24	cup	c
L	liter	2.13	pint (liquid)	pt
L	liter	1.05	quart (liquid)	qt
L	liter	0.26	gallon	gal
m^3	cubic meter	35.32	cubic foot	ft^3
m^3	cubic meter	1.32	cubic yard	yd^3
C	degrees Celsius (after multiplying, add 32)	1.80	degrees Fahrenheit	F

[1] For weighing ordinary commodities. [2] For weighing precious metals, jewels, etc.

Tables Deleted From the
1998 Edition of the Statistical Abstract

U.S. Census Bureau, Statistical Abstract of the United States: 1999

U.S. Census Bureau, Statistical Abstract of the United States: 1999

Appendix VI

New Tables

U.S. Census Bureau, Statistical Abstract of the United States: 1999

U.S. Census Bureau, Statistical Abstract of the United States: 1999

U.S. Census Bureau, Statistical Abstract of the United States: 1999

Index

Table	Table

NOTE: Index citations refer to **table** numbers, not page numbers.

NOTE: Index citations refer to **table** numbers, not page numbers.

NOTE: Index citations refer to **table** numbers, not page numbers.

NOTE: Index citations refer to **table** numbers, not page numbers.

U.S. Census Bureau, Statistical Abstract of the United States: 1999

NOTE: Index citations refer to **table** numbers, not page numbers.

NOTE: Index citations refer to **table** numbers, not page numbers.

U.S. Census Bureau, Statistical Abstract of the United States: 1999

NOTE: Index citations refer to **table** numbers, not page numbers.

NOTE: Index citations refer to **table** numbers, not page numbers.

U.S. Census Bureau, Statistical Abstract of the United States: 1999

NOTE: Index citations refer to **table** numbers, not page numbers.

U.S. Census Bureau, Statistical Abstract of the United States: 1999

NOTE: Index citations refer to **table** numbers, not page numbers.

U.S. Census Bureau, Statistical Abstract of the United States: 1999

NOTE: Index citations refer to **table** numbers, not page numbers.

NOTE: Index citations refer to **table** numbers, not page numbers.

U.S. Census Bureau, Statistical Abstract of the United States: 1999

NOTE: Index citations refer to **table** numbers, not page numbers.

NOTE: Index citations refer to **table** numbers, not page numbers.

NOTE: Index citations refer to **table** numbers, not page numbers.

NOTE: Index citations refer to **table** numbers, not page numbers.

NOTE: Index citations refer to **table** numbers, not page numbers.

968   Index

U.S. Census Bureau, Statistical Abstract of the United States: 1999

NOTE: Index citations refer to **table** numbers, not page numbers.

U.S. Census Bureau, Statistical Abstract of the United States: 1999

NOTE: Index citations refer to **table** numbers, not page numbers.

NOTE: Index citations refer to **table** numbers, not page numbers.

U.S. Census Bureau, Statistical Abstract of the United States: 1999

NOTE: Index citations refer to **table** numbers, not page numbers.

NOTE: Index citations refer to **table** numbers, not page numbers.

NOTE: Index citations refer to **table** numbers, not page numbers.

NOTE: Index citations refer to **table** numbers, not page numbers.

NOTE: Index citations refer to **table** numbers, not page numbers.

NOTE: Index citations refer to **table** numbers, not page numbers.

U.S. Census Bureau, Statistical Abstract of the United States: 1999

NOTE: Index citations refer to **table** numbers, not page numbers.

NOTE: Index citations refer to **table** numbers, not page numbers.

U.S. Census Bureau, Statistical Abstract of the United States: 1999

NOTE: Index citations refer to **table** numbers, not page numbers.

NOTE: Index citations refer to **table** numbers, not page numbers.

U.S. Census Bureau, Statistical Abstract of the United States: 1999

NOTE: Index citations refer to **table** numbers, not page numbers.

NOTE: Index citations refer to **table** numbers, not page numbers.

NOTE: Index citations refer to **table** numbers, not page numbers.

NOTE: Index citations refer to **table** numbers, not page numbers.

U.S. Census Bureau, Statistical Abstract of the United States: 1999

NOTE: Index citations refer to **table** numbers, not page numbers.

U.S. Census Bureau, Statistical Abstract of the United States: 1999

NOTE: Index citations refer to **table** numbers, not page numbers.

U.S. Census Bureau, Statistical Abstract of the United States: 1999

NOTE: Index citations refer to **table** numbers, not page numbers.

U.S. Census Bureau, Statistical Abstract of the United States: 1999

NOTE: Index citations refer to **table** numbers, not page numbers.

U.S. Census Bureau, Statistical Abstract of the United States: 1999

NOTE: Index citations refer to **table** numbers, not page numbers.

NOTE: Index citations refer to **table** numbers, not page numbers.

U.S. Census Bureau, Statistical Abstract of the United States: 1999

NOTE: Index citations refer to **table** numbers, not page numbers.

NOTE: Index citations refer to **table** numbers, not page numbers.

U.S. Census Bureau, Statistical Abstract of the United States: 1999

NOTE: Index citations refer to **table** numbers, not page numbers.

NOTE: Index citations refer to **table** numbers, not page numbers.

U.S. Census Bureau, Statistical Abstract of the United States: 1999

NOTE: Index citations refer to **table** numbers, not page numbers.

NOTE: Index citations refer to **table** numbers, not page numbers.

U.S. Census Bureau, Statistical Abstract of the United States: 1999

NOTE: Index citations refer to **table** numbers, not page numbers.

U.S. Census Bureau, Statistical Abstract of the United States: 1999

NOTE: Index citations refer to **table** numbers, not page numbers.

U.S. Census Bureau, Statistical Abstract of the United States: 1999

NOTE: Index citations refer to **table** numbers, not page numbers.

NOTE: Index citations refer to **table** numbers, not page numbers.

U.S. Census Bureau, Statistical Abstract of the United States: 1999

NOTE: Index citations refer to **table** numbers, not page numbers.